STUDENT
BIBLE

STUDENT
BIBLE

ENGLISH STANDARD VERSION

CONTENTS

THE BOOKS OF THE BIBLE
IN ALPHABETICAL ORDER

INTRODUCTION
TO THE STUDENT BIBLE

PURPOSE

The *ESV Student Bible* is designed for younger teenagers transitioning to their first study Bible. With content adapted from the award-winning *ESV Student Study Bible*, the portable *Student Bible* will help young people as they learn to study God's Word on their own and apply it to all of life. The *Student Bible* provides a more compact and streamlined edition for students to use in their journey with Christ, while retaining many of the key features of the *Student Study Bible*.

The purpose of the *ESV Student Bible*, then, is to provide for students a full-text ESV Bible that they can carry with them anywhere—in school, at church, and in personal reading and reflection. Book introductions, articles, and other added content help young men and women to know and understand the Word of God. The doctrinal perspective is that of classic evangelical orthodoxy, in the historic stream of the Reformation, lifting high the gospel of grace. Throughout the *Student Bible*, as in every ESV Bible that Crossway publishes, the goal is to communicate the value and sufficiency of God's Word for all of life.

May the Lord bless your reading and study of his Word.

FEATURES OF THE ESV STUDENT BIBLE

- Helpful articles explaining how the events and teaching of the entire Bible, as well as the Old Testament and New Testament individually, fit together.
- Timelines of the Old and New Testaments as well as "snapshot timelines" for each Bible book.
- Brief introductions and basic outlines for each Bible book.
- Interesting "Getting the Message" facts and observations about life in Bible times.
- Profiles of key people in the story of the Bible.
- Articles on important topics like salvation, the church, and doctrine, written for readers of all ages.
- A glossary of more than 300 words and phrases created specifically for the Student Study Bible.
- 8 full-color maps—created with the latest satellite imagery, digital technology, and cartographic techniques.

ABOUT THE ESV BIBLE

The English Standard Version® (ESV®) Bible is a great choice—for personal reading and study, for private devotions and family prayers, and for teaching, preaching, and worship. An essentially literal translation, the ESV Bible combines word-for-word accuracy with readability, literary excellence, and depth of meaning. More than 100 of the world's leading Bible scholars and teachers were involved in creating the ESV Bible. Trusted worldwide, the ESV is a treasure for life.

PREFACE

THE BIBLE

The Bible is God's personal Word to us. In the Bible, God tells us how he made the world and why we are here. He tells us that his eternal Son, Jesus Christ, died on the cross for our sins and was raised from the dead, and that, because of this, we can live forever in heaven with him. Because God is always good and truthful, his written Word, the Bible, is worthy of our complete confidence and trust.

ENGLISH TRANSLATIONS OF THE BIBLE

God's message to us was recorded in the Bible between 2,000 and 3,500 years ago. The Bible was not originally written in English, but in Hebrew, Aramaic, and Greek. Since most of us today do not know these languages, God has enabled people around the world to translate his written Word into thousands of different languages. In 1526, William Tyndale became the first person to translate the New Testament from the original Greek into English. The most famous English translation of the Bible, the King James Version, was published in England in 1611. For many years, it was the Bible that most English-speaking people read. Millions of people still read it today.

But as time has passed, the English language has changed. Various words and phrases in the King James Version have become harder to understand. So through the years several new translations have been made. These include the English Revised Version (1885), the American Standard Version (1901), and the Revised Standard Version (1952; 1971). The English Standard Version (ESV) Bible is a part of this historic tradition of Bible translation.

Translating from one language to another is never easy. Bible translators must know Hebrew, Aramaic, and Greek. They need good English writing skills. They must be able to choose words that people of all ages will understand. They must be humble enough to let other translators correct their work. No one is able to do this work perfectly. Translators can only try their best to be faithful to God's Word and helpful to readers. There are two main ways most of them do this.

Some Bible translators use a "thought-for-thought" method of translation. They read the Hebrew, Aramaic, or Greek and decide how to put the basic thoughts into English words. They are generally not concerned with keeping the original order of the sentence. They also may leave out words they don't think are needed for understanding a thought. Sometimes they try to make long sentences easier to understand by dividing them into several shorter sentences.

Other translators use a "word-for-word" translation method. They translate the Bible in a way that reflects every single word in the original Hebrew, Aramaic, and Greek texts as transparently as possible. They also translate sentences in a way that pays greater attention to the order in which they were originally written. Until recent times, this was the way most English Bible translations were done. The ESV is this kind of translation—a "word-for-word" translation—which we believe is the best way to show *what* the Bible says and *how* it says it.

Sometimes this may mean you will read words that you'll see only in the Bible or hear in church—words like "justification" and "sanctification." Or you will read words that mean something different in the Bible than in current English. The word "unclean" is an example of this. Although such words may be unfamiliar, they are important words that are worth learning.

Bible translators also want readers to come to know and love the Bible as much as they do, so while trying to be as accurate as possible in their work, they also try to use English words that are as interesting and beautiful as the Bible's original Hebrew, Aramaic, and Greek words.

There are a couple of words, in particular, that you should know about as a Bible reader. You will often find the Old and New Testament authors using the word "Behold!" This is a helpful word because it means something like "Pay careful attention to the words that come next!" It helps us read more carefully.

Another word you should know about is one of the Bible's names for God. The Old Testament authors used three different Hebrew words to describe God. These are translated as "God," "Lord" (spelled the way we usually spell it), or "Lord" (spelled with small capital letters). The last one translates God's personal name. He revealed this name to Moses in Exodus 3:14.

SPECIAL NOTES IN THE ESV BIBLE

As you read the ESV Bible, you will often see a number following a word, which will call your attention to a note at the bottom of the page. For instance, at Genesis 1:26, when you read, "Let us make man[1] . . .", the number 1 invites you to read note 1 at the bottom of the page. These notes will help you in various ways.

For example, some things you read may make you think that the Bible doesn't say very much about women. You will read that God made "man" in his image (Gen. 1:26). In Psalm 1:1, you will read about God making promises to "the man" who serves him. In the New Testament you will often read about someone addressing a group of people as "brothers" without saying anything about "sisters." Or you will read about promises to "sons" (Rom. 8:14). The notes on these verses will help you see that the Bible is not ignoring girls or women. The note on Genesis 1:26 will tell you that the Hebrew word translated "man" includes both men and women. Notes in the New Testament will show you where the Greek word translated "brothers" includes both "brothers and sisters." The note on Romans 8:14 shows you that "sons" also includes "daughters."

Second, you may be troubled when you see words like "slave," "servant," and "bondservant." You will likely wonder if the Bible approves of the sort of slavery that existed in the United States and other nations in past times and that still exists in some nations today. The Bible condemns such slavery many times, and it often explains how people in these situations should be treated.

As the ESV notes will tell you, the Old Testament uses the Hebrew word *ebed* to describe all sorts of servants. A servant could be someone who agreed to work for someone else for pay, or to repay a debt. In some cases, he might have agreed to work for someone for the rest of his life. A servant could also be someone captured in war and made to serve someone else, or someone sold into slavery. Readers have to pay attention to each situation. In the Old Testament the ESV uses the word "slave" when people were owned by someone else and had little chance of freedom. Otherwise it normally uses the word "servant."

The New Testament uses the Greek word *doulos* (or *sundoulos*) to describe people in the same types of situations. The ESV translates the word as "slave" when someone had little hope of becoming free. It translates the word as "bondservant" when someone could gain freedom by paying a set price or by serving for a set length of time. It translates the word "servant" when a person simply worked for someone else. As with "man" and "brothers and sisters," the ESV includes notes to help you know which kind of situation you are reading about.

Third, the Bible often uses names that have a special meaning. The names may be those of people or places. The ESV provides notes when the text cannot really be understood unless you know what the name means.

Fourth, the Bible describes several kinds of skin diseases with a word that the ESV translates as "leprosy." The notes let you know that the word does not refer to Hansen's Disease, the type of leprosy most familiar to modern readers.

Fifth, sometimes the ESV translators had to choose between two English words that mean nearly the same thing. Knowing both words may help you understand the verse better. These notes begin with the word "Or" and then give the second possible meaning.

Finally, you will find brackets and special notes at Psalm 145:13, Mark 16:8, and John 7:52. Translators use the oldest and best Hebrew, Aramaic, and Greek copies available. Some of these manuscripts include the words in brackets in Psalm 145:13. Most of them leave out Mark 16:9–20 and John 7:53–8:11 or place them somewhere else.

The ESV translators made other decisions about the best manuscripts to use, to translate the Bible from Hebrew, Aramaic, and Greek into English. You can read about these translation choices in the *ESV Study Bible* or in the more detailed preface to the standard edition of the ESV. This standard edition of the ESV also includes a fuller set of textual notes. It is available for free online access at esvbible.org.

THE PURPOSE OF THE ESV BIBLE

Many people made the ESV Bible translation possible. We hope this Bible will help you know God by trusting in Christ through the power of the Holy Spirit. Our prayer is, "The grace of the Lord Jesus Christ and the love of God and the fellowship of the Holy Spirit be with you all" (2 Cor. 13:14).

Soli Deo Gloria!—To God alone be the glory!
*The Translation Oversight Committee**

*A complete list of the Translation Oversight Committee, the Translation Review Scholars, and the Advisory Council is available upon request from Crossway.

AN OVERVIEW OF THE BIBLE

How does the Bible as a whole fit together? The events recorded in the Bible took place over a span of thousands of years and in several different cultural settings. What is their unifying thread?

One unifying thread in the Bible is its divine authorship. *Every book of the Bible is God's word.* The events recorded in the Bible are there because God wanted them to be recorded, and he had them recorded with his people and their instruction in mind: "For whatever was written in former days was written for our instruction, that through endurance and through the encouragement of the Scriptures we might have hope" (Rom. 15:4).

GOD'S PLAN FOR HISTORY

God also has *a unified plan for history* (Eph. 1:10, 12). The work of Christ on earth, especially his crucifixion and resurrection, is the climax of history. It is the great turning point. The present era looks *back* on Christ's completed work but also *forward* to the consummation of his work when he will come again in the new heavens and earth.

GOD'S PROMISES AND PREDICTIONS

The Old Testament directly points forward to Christ through promises of God's salvation. God gave some *specific* promises in the Old Testament relating to the coming of Christ as the Messiah, the Savior in the line of David. But God often gives more *general* promises concerning a future great day of salvation, without spelling out all the details of how he will accomplish it. Sometimes the promises take *explicit* form (e.g., the coming of the Messiah), and sometimes they take *symbolic* form (e.g., the animal sacrifices). All of the OT promises find their "yes" in Jesus (2 Cor. 1:20).

GOD'S WARNINGS AND CURSES

God's relation to people also includes warnings, threatenings, and cursings, which anticipate and point forward to Christ in two distinct ways. First, *Christ is the Lamb of God* who bore the curse of sin on the cross (John 1:29; 2 Cor. 5:21; Gal. 3:13; 1 Pet. 2:24). Every instance of the wrath of God against sin, and his punishment of sin, looks forward to the wrath that was poured out on Christ on the cross. Second, *Christ will*

wage war against sin and exterminate it at his second coming. All earlier judgments against sin anticipate the final judgment.

GOD'S COVENANT COMMITMENT AND INSTRUCTION

The promises of God in the Old Testament come in the context not only of God's *commitment* to his people but also of *instruction* about the people's commitment and obligations to God. When God makes a covenant with man, God is the sovereign, so he specifies the obligations on both sides. "I will be their God" is the fundamental obligation on God's side, while "they shall be my people" is the fundamental obligation on the human side.

For example, in the first call of Abram (Gen. 12:1-2) God's commitment takes the form of promises, blessings, and curses. The *promises and blessings* point forward to Christ, who is the fulfillment of the promises and the source of final blessings. The *curses* point forward to Christ both in his bearing the curse and in his execution of judgment and curse against sin, especially at the second coming.

Christ fulfilled the *obligations* of God's covenants through perfect obedience (Heb. 5:8), receiving the reward of obedience in his resurrection and ascension (Phil. 2:9-10). By dealing with God's wrath against sin, Christ reconciled believers to God, bringing about the intimacy with God that all of the OT covenants anticipated.

CHRIST IS THE OFFSPRING OF ABRAHAM AND THE LAST ADAM

God's promises to Abraham were the foundation for the nation of Israel. Abraham was obligated to walk blamelessly before God (Gen. 17:1). But only Christ is without sin (Heb. 4:15), making him the ultimate offspring to whom the other offspring all point (Gal. 3:16). Through Christ, believers are united to him and thereby themselves become "Abraham's offspring" (Gal. 3:29). Believers, Jews and Gentiles alike, become heirs to the promises of God made to Abraham and his offspring (Gal. 3:28-29).

Christ is not only the offspring of Abraham, but—reaching back farther in time to an earlier promise of God—the offspring of the woman: "I will put enmity between you [the serpent] and the woman, and between your offspring and her offspring; he shall bruise your head, and you shall bruise his heel" (Gen. 3:15). The conquest over the serpent, and therefore the conquest of evil and the reversal of its effects, is to take place through the offspring of the woman. One can trace this offspring down from Eve through Seth and his godly descendants, through Noah, and down to Abraham, where God's promise takes the specific form of offspring for Abraham. Thus Christ is not only the offspring of Abraham but the last Adam (1 Cor. 15:45–49). Like Adam, he represents all who belong to him. And he reverses the effects of Adam's fall.

SHADOWS, PREFIGURES, AND "TYPES" OF CHRIST

The Old Testament anticipates Christ the Savior by "shadows" and "types"—examples, symbols, pictures—of the things that were to come (see 1 Cor. 10:6, 11; Heb. 8:5). *Animal sacrifices* in the Old Testament prefigure the final sacrifice of Christ. The *temple*, as a dwelling place for God, prefigured Christ, who is the final "dwelling place" of God, and through whom God is with his people (Matt. 1:23; John 2:21). The OT *priests* were types of Christ, the final high priest (Heb. 7:11–8:7).

The fulfillment of all these OT shadows and types takes place preeminently in Christ (2 Cor. 1:20; Eph. 1:10). But in the New Testament those people who are "in Christ," who place their trust in him and experience fellowship with his person and his blessings, receive the benefits of what he has accomplished. Therefore one can also find anticipations or "types" in the Old Testament that point forward to the NT church,

the people in the New Testament who belong to Christ.

Some OT symbols also may point forward especially to the consummation of salvation that takes place in the new heaven and the new earth yet to come (2 Pet. 3:13; Rev. 21:1–22:5). Old Testament Jerusalem prefigured the new Jerusalem that will come "down out of heaven from God" (Rev. 21:2).

CHRIST IS THE MEDIATOR

Sinful man needs a *mediator* who will approach God on his behalf. Jesus Christ, who is both God and man, and who is innocent of sin, is the only one who can mediate (1 Tim. 2:5–6) and the only one who can save (Acts 4:12).

All the instances of salvation and mediation in the Old Testament prefigure Christ. *Prophets* bring God's word to his people. Godly *kings* bring God's rule to bear on the people. *Priests* represent the people in coming before God's presence. Christ is the prophet, king, and priest who fulfills all three functions in a final way (Heb. 1:1–3).

We can also look at *wise men*, who bring God's wisdom to others; *warriors*, who bring God's deliverance from enemies; and *singers*, who bring praise to God on behalf of the people and speak of God to the people. *Covenants* bring God's word to the people. The *temple* brings God's presence to the people. *Animal sacrifices* bring God's forgiveness to the people. In reading the Bible, we should look for ways in which God brings his word and his presence to people through the *means* he establishes. All these means perform a mediatorial role, and because there is only one mediator, clearly they all point to Christ.

THE
OLD TESTAMENT

THE THEOLOGY AND DATES
OF THE OLD TESTAMENT

THE ESSENTIAL COMPONENTS OF THE OLD TESTAMENT STORY

The Old Testament can be understood as an unfolding story with a number of basic components:

1. *Monotheism.* There is only one true God, who made and rules heaven and earth and all mankind. The Old Testament invites Israel to commit themselves to him in exclusive loyalty and love (Deut. 6:4–9).

2. *Creation and fall.* The one Creator God made Adam and Eve with dignity and purpose, calling them to live faithfully to God and to spread the blessings of Eden throughout the earth. Because they betrayed God's purpose, all people since the fall are beset with sins and weaknesses that only God's grace can redeem and heal.

3. *Election and covenant.* The one true God chose a people for himself and bound himself to them by his covenant (Ex. 19:4–6; Deut. 7:6–11). This covenant expressed God's intention to save the people, and through them to bring light to the rest of the world, in order to restore all things to their proper functioning in the world God made. The land of Israel was to be a kind of reconstituted Eden, which would flourish as the people's faithfulness flourished (or languish if the people were unfaithful). God's covenants generally involve one person who represents the whole people (e.g., Adam, Noah, Abraham, David); the rest of the people experience the covenant by virtue of their inclusion in the community represented. The covenant representative was required to embody the ideal of covenant faithfulness as a model for those on whose behalf he had acted.

4. *Covenant membership.* In his covenant, God offers his grace to his people: the forgiveness of their sins, the shaping of their lives in this world to reflect his own glory, and a part to play in bringing light to the Gentiles. The faithful are those covenant members who lay hold of this grace from the heart, enjoying the full benefits of God's love. Judgments upon the whole people often come because too many of them have been unfaithful; these judgments do not bring the story of God's people to an end but serve rather to purify and chasten that people (often by removing unbelieving members).

5. *Eschatology.* The story of God's people is headed toward a glorious future in which all kinds of people will come to know the Lord and join his people. The promise of a lasting dynasty for David (2 Sam. 7:16) becomes the expectation that a final heir of his line will one day arise, take his Davidic throne, and lead his people in the great task of bringing light to the Gentiles.

THE PARTS OF THE OLD TESTAMENT IN RELATION TO THE STORY

The Old Testament is thus the story of the one true Creator God, who called the family of Abraham to be his remedy for the defilement that came into the world through the sin of Adam and Eve. God rescued Israel from slavery in Egypt in fulfillment of this plan, and established them as a theocracy for the sake of displaying his existence and character to the rest of the world. God sent his blessings and curses upon Israel in order to pursue that purpose. God never abandoned that purpose, even in the face of the most grievous unfaithfulness in Israel.

This overarching story serves as a grand narrative or worldview story for Israel: each member of the people was to see himself or herself as an heir of this story, with all its glory and shame; as a steward of the story, responsible to pass it on to the next generation; and as a participant, whose faithfulness could play a role, by God's mysterious wisdom, in the story's progress.

Some would say that we should read the entire Old Testament as a story. This does not help the reader, for the very obvious reason that not everything in the Old Testament is narrative or "story." For example, there are laws (in the Pentateuch), whose purpose was to maintain order by guiding judges in what penalties to impose and by specifying the minimum standard of behavior necessary to preserve the theocracy; there is wisdom (in the books of Job, Proverbs, and Ecclesiastes, as well as in the Psalms), which helps God's people live well daily; there are songs (especially the Psalms) that the people of God should sing in corporate worship; there are poems (especially the Song of Solomon; compare Prov. 5:15–20) celebrating such wonders as romantic love; and lots more. Therefore it is better to speak of reading the parts of the Old Testament in relation to its overarching story. That is, we can see the parts in relation to the "Big Story" that unifies the whole. The Proverbs help people to live their little stories in such a way as to contribute to the Big Story. The Psalms—many of which explicitly recount parts of the Big Story—help people live as faithful members of the worshiping people of God. The Prophets keep recalling the Big Story, calling their audiences to live faithfully in its light. The Big Story tells us that God's purpose is to restore our humanity to its proper function, and thus it reminds each person of the human nature he shares with every other human being, and of the duty and benefit of seeking the good of others. For example, enjoying the love of a faithful spouse is a way of experiencing renewed humanity—a way that displays God's goodness to the rest of the world (as in the Song of Solomon).

All of these factors explain why it is possible for the NT authors both to say that the Sinai covenant is done away with and at the same time to affirm that this covenant includes principles that cannot pass away, because they are part of the larger story of which the Sinai covenant is one chapter.

THE OLD TESTAMENT AS CHRISTIAN SCRIPTURE

The Old Testament presents itself, then, as a story that is headed toward fulfillment. The Old Testament closes with both anxiety and hope under Persian rule (see Malachi). The NT authors, most of whom were Jewish Christians, saw themselves as heirs of the OT story, and as authorized to describe its proper completion in the death and resurrection of Jesus and the messianic era that this ushered in. These authors viewed and used the Old Testament as Christian Scripture, and they urged their audiences (many of whom were Gentile Christians) to do the same. They saw the Old Testament as constituting the earlier chapters of the story in which Christians are now participating.

By understanding that there are earlier and later chapters in the story of God's work for his people, we can see how the OT era and the Christian era exhibit both continuity and discontinuity. The Old Testament had looked forward to an internationalized people of God, without explaining exactly how that would connect to the theocracy of Israel. The theocracy defined the people of God as predominantly coming from a particular ethnic group in a particular land; Gentile converts ("sojourners") were protected (Ex. 12:49; 20:10; 22:21; Lev. 19:10) but could not be full-status members of the theocratic community. The New Testament abolishes the distinction (Eph. 2:19), because the theocracy as such is no longer in existence and many of its provisions are done away with (see Acts 10:34–35; Heb. 9:11–14). At the same time, the character of the one Creator God, and his interest in restoring the image of God in human beings, transcends the specific arrangements of the theocracy: hence the moral commands of God apply to Christians as they did to the faithful in Israel (see Rom. 13:8–10).

OLD TESTAMENT TIMELINE: AN OVERVIEW

The following page provides a concise OT timeline and overview. The dates (all B.C.) are either the exact year or a close approximation thereof, determined by correlating dates in the Bible with ancient Near Eastern sources (such as Assyrian accession lists, Babylonian king-lists, and Egyptian historical sources). Often dates can be further confirmed by ancient Assyrian and Babylonian documents which give narrative accounts of the same historical events, as recorded by those two countries. All of this adds great confidence and credibility to the truth and historicity of the Bible text itself.

Patriarchs to Judges (c. 2166–1030)

	1446 Date for Exodus	1260 Date for Exodus
Abraham	2166–1991	2000–1825
Isaac	2066–1886	1900–1720
Jacob	2006–1859	1840–1693
Joseph	1915–1805	1749–1639
Moses' birth	1526	1340
Exodus	1446	1260
Desert wanderings	1446–1406	1260–1220
Entrance into Canaan	1406	1220
Period of the judges	1375 to 1050–1030	1210 to 1050–1030

United Monarchy (c. 1050–931)

	Dates	Notes
Saul's reign	1050–1030 to 1010	
David's reign	1010–971	
Solomon's reign	971–931	

Divided Monarchy to Exile (931–586)

Kingdom divided	931	
Syro-Ephraimite war	740–732	Pekah (Israel) and Rezin (Syria) pressure Jotham and Ahaz (Judah) to join their opposition to Tiglath-pileser III (Assyria)
Fall of Samaria (Israel)	722	Shalmaneser V (727–722) and Sargon II (722–705) of Assyria
Josiah's reforms	628	
Battle of Carchemish	605	Daniel and three friends exiled to Babylon
Jerusalem attacked	597	Nebuchadnezzar II takes exiles to Babylon including Jehoiachin and Ezekiel
Fall of Jerusalem (Judah)	586	Nebuchadnezzar II takes more exiles to Babylon

Return from Exile (539–445)

Fall of Babylon	539	Cyrus of Persia (539–530)
1st return of exiles to Jerusalem	538	
Temple building begins	536	
Temple completed	516	Darius I (522–486)
Esther in palace of Xerxes	478	Xerxes I/Ahasuerus (485–464)
2nd return of exiles to Jerusalem under Ezra	458	Artaxerxes I (464–423)
3rd return of exiles to Jerusalem under Nehemiah	445	

THE HEBREW CALENDAR COMPARED TO THE GREGORIAN (MODERN) CALENDAR

The Hebrew calendar was composed of 12 lunar months, each of which began when the thin crescent moon was first visible at sunset. They were composed of approximately 29/30 days and were built around the agricultural seasons. Apparently some of the names of the months were changed after the time of Israel's exile in Babylon (e.g., the first month of Abib changed to Nisan; for dates of the exile, see p. xvii).

Hebrew Month	Gregorian (Modern) Month	Biblical References
First Month: Abib (Preexile) Nisan (Postexile) Festivals: 14th/15th: Passover (Ex. 12:18; Lev. 23:5) 15th–21st: Unleavened Bread (Ex. 12:14–20; Lev. 23:6) 16th: First Fruits (Lev. 23:9–11)	March–April	Ex. 13:4; 23:15; 34:18; Deut. 16:1; Neh. 2:1; Est. 3:7 (compare Gen. 8:13; Ex. 12:2, 18; 40:2, 17; Lev. 23:5; Num. 9:1; 20:1; 28:16; 33:3; Josh. 4:19; 1 Chron. 12:15; 27:2, 3; 2 Chron. 29:3, 17; 35:1; Ezra 6:19; 7:9; 8:31; 10:17; Est. 3:7, 12; Ezek. 29:17; 30:20; 45:18, 21; Dan. 10:4)
Second Month: Ziv (Preexile) Iyyar (Postexile) Festival: 14th: Later Passover (Num. 9:10–11)	April–May	1 Kings 6:1, 37 (compare Gen. 7:11; 8:14; Ex. 16:1; Num. 1:1, 18; 9:11; 10:11; 1 Chron. 27:4; 2 Chron. 3:2; 30:2, 13, 15; Ezra 3:8)
Third Month: Sivan Festivals: 4th: Pentecost [Feast of Weeks] (Lev. 23:15–16)	May–June	Est. 8:9 (compare Ex. 19:1; 1 Chron. 27:5; 2 Chron. 15:10; 31:7; Ezek. 31:1)
Fourth Month: Tammuz	June–July	Ezek. 8:14 (compare 2 Kings 25:3; 1 Chron. 27:7; Jer. 39:2; 52:6; Ezek. 1:1; Zech. 8:19)
Fifth Month: Ab	July–August	Not mentioned by name in the Bible (compare Num. 33:38; 2 Kings 25:8; 1 Chron. 27:8; Ezra 7:8, 9; Jer. 1:3; 28:1; 52:12; Ezek. 20:1; Zech. 7:3, 5; 8:19)
Sixth Month: Elul	August–September	Neh. 6:15 (compare 1 Chron. 27:9; Ezek. 8:1; Hag. 1:1, 15)
Seventh Month: Ethanim (Preexile) Tishri (Postexile) Festivals: 1st: Trumpets (Lev. 23:24; Num. 29:1) 10th: Day of Atonement (Lev. 16:29–34; 23:27–32) 15th–21st: Booths (Lev. 23:34–40) 22nd: Solemn assembly (Lev. 23:36)	September–October	1 Kings 8:2 (compare Gen. 8:4; Lev. 16:29; 23:24, 27, 34, 39, 41; 25:9; Num. 29:1, 7, 12; 2 Kings 25:25; 1 Chron. 27:10; 2 Chron. 5:3; 7:10; 31:7; Ezra 3:1, 6; Neh. 7:73; 8:2, 14; Jer. 28:17; 41:1; Ezek. 45:25; Hag. 2:1; Zech. 7:5; 8:19)
Eighth Month: Bul (Preexile) Marchesvan (Postexile)	October–November	1 Kings 6:38 (compare 1 Kings 12:32, 33; 1 Chron. 27:11; Zech. 1:1)
Ninth Month: Chislev (Kislev) Festival: 25th: Dedication (John 10:22)	November–December	Neh. 1:1; Zech. 7:1 (compare 1 Chron. 27:12; Ezra 10:9; Jer. 36:9, 22; Hag. 2:10, 18)
Tenth Month: Tebeth	December–January	Est. 2:16 (compare Gen. 8:5; 2 Kings 25:1; 1 Chron. 27:13; Ezra 10:16; Jer. 39:1; 52:4; Ezek. 24:1; 29:1; 33:21; Zech. 8:19)
Eleventh Month: Shebat	January–February	Zech. 1:7 (compare Deut. 1:3; 1 Chron. 27:14)
Twelfth Month: Adar*	February–March	Ezra 6:15; Est. 3:7, 13; 8:12; 9:1, 15, 17, 19, 21 (compare 2 Kings 25:27; 1 Chron. 27:15; Jer. 52:31; Ezek. 32:1; 32:17)

*Periodically, a 13th month was added so that the lunar calendar would account for the entire solar year.

INTRODUCTION TO GENESIS

Creation	c. 2091 B.C. Call of Abraham	1876 B.C. Israel goes to Egypt	1446 B.C. Exodus from Egypt

AUTHOR, DATE, AND RECIPIENTS

Traditionally, Moses is considered to have been the author of Genesis and the rest of the Pentateuch (see Num. 33:2; Deut. 31:24; John 5:46). Of course, Moses lived much later than the events of Genesis. Presumably, stories were passed down about those earlier events, and Moses brought them all together.

The first audience would have been the Israelites Moses led through the wilderness. For readers today, Genesis is an essential introduction to the rest of the Bible. It is rightly called the book of beginnings.

THEME

The theme of Genesis is creation, sin, and re-creation. God made the world very good, but first cursed it and then destroyed it in the flood because of man's disobedience. The new world after the flood was also spoiled by human sin (ch. 11). God chose Abraham for a special purpose. Through his family, all nations would be blessed (12:1–3). God's purpose will eventually be fulfilled through Abraham's descendants (ch. 49).

KEY THEMES

1. The Lord God commissions human beings to be his representatives on earth. They are to take care of the earth and govern the other creatures (1:1–2:25).

2. Instead of acting as God's representatives on earth, the first man and woman—Adam and Eve—listen to the serpent and follow his advice. Their disobedience has devastating results for all mankind and for the entire created world (3:1–24; 6:5–6).

3. God graciously announces that Eve's offspring will free humanity from the serpent's control (3:15). Genesis then begins tracing the history of one family that will become the people of Israel. This family has a special relationship with God and will become a source of blessing to fallen humanity (12:1–3).

4. As a result of Adam's disobedience, his unique relationship with the ground degenerates, resulting in hard work and later in flood and famine. But the special family descending from Adam also brings relief from the difficulties (3:17–19; 5:29; 50:19–21).

5. While Eve's punishment centers on pain in bearing children (3:16), women play an essential role in continuing the unique family line. With God's help, even barrenness is overcome (11:30; 21:1–7; 25:21; 38:1–30).

6. The corruption of human nature causes families to be torn apart (4:1–16; 13:5–8; 25:22–23; 27:41–45; 37:2–35). Although Genesis shows the reality of family conflicts, individual members of the chosen family can also help resolve those conflicts (13:8–11; 33:1–11; 45:1–28; 50:15–21).

7. The wicked are exiled from Eden and scattered throughout the earth (3:22–24; 4:12–16; 11:9), but God is kind to his chosen people and promises them a land of their own (12:1–2, 7; 15:7–21; 28:13–14; 50:24).

8. God is prepared to destroy almost the entire human race because of its corruption (6:7, 11–12; 18:17–33), but he still wants his world to be populated by righteous people (1:28; 9:1; 15:1–5; 35:11).

OUTLINE

GENESIS

The Creation of the World

1 In the beginning, God created the heavens and the earth. ² The earth was without form and void, and darkness was over the face of the deep. And the Spirit of God was hovering over the face of the waters.

³ And God said, "Let there be light," and there was light. ⁴ And God saw that the light was good. And God separated the light from the darkness. ⁵ God called the light Day, and the darkness he called Night. And there was evening and there was morning, the first day.

⁶ And God said, "Let there be an expanse in the midst of the waters, and let it separate the waters from the waters." ⁷ And God made the expanse and separated the waters that were under the expanse from the waters that were above the expanse. And it was so. ⁸ And God called the expanse Heaven. And there was evening and there was morning, the second day.

⁹ And God said, "Let the waters under the heavens be gathered together into one place, and let the dry land appear." And it was so. ¹⁰ God called the dry land Earth, and the waters that were gathered together he called Seas. And God saw that it was good.

¹¹ And God said, "Let the earth sprout vegetation, plants yielding seed, and fruit trees bearing fruit in which is their seed, each according to its kind, on the earth." And it was so. ¹² The earth brought forth vegetation, plants yielding seed according to their own kinds, and trees bearing fruit in which is their seed, each according to its kind. And God saw that it was good. ¹³ And there was evening and there was morning, the third day.

¹⁴ And God said, "Let there be lights in the expanse of the heavens to separate the day from the night. And let them be for signs and for seasons, and for days and years, ¹⁵ and let them be lights in the expanse of the heavens to give light upon the earth." And it was so. ¹⁶ And God made the two great lights—the greater light to rule the day and the lesser light to rule the night—and the stars. ¹⁷ And God set them in the expanse of the heavens to give light on the earth, ¹⁸ to rule over the day and over the night, and to separate the light from the darkness. And God saw that it was good. ¹⁹ And there was evening and there was morning, the fourth day.

²⁰ And God said, "Let the waters swarm with swarms of living creatures, and let birds fly above the earth across the expanse of the heavens." ²¹ So God created the great sea creatures and every living creature that moves, with which the waters swarm,

according to their kinds, and every winged bird according to its kind. And God saw that it was good. ²² And God blessed them, saying, "Be fruitful and multiply and fill the waters in the seas, and let birds multiply on the earth." ²³ And there was evening and there was morning, the fifth day.

²⁴ And God said, "Let the earth bring forth living creatures according to their kinds—livestock and creeping things and beasts of the earth according to their kinds." And it was so. ²⁵ And God made the beasts of the earth according to their kinds and the livestock according to their kinds, and everything that creeps on the ground according to its kind. And God saw that it was good.

²⁶ Then God said, "Let us make man[1] in our image, after our likeness. And let them have dominion over the fish of the sea and over the birds of the heavens and over the livestock and over all the earth and over

---

[1] The Hebrew word used here for *man* includes both men and women (see 1:27) and refers to the entire human race (see Preface)

every creeping thing that creeps on the earth."

27 So God created man in his own image,
   in the image of God he created him;
   male and female he created them.

28 And God blessed them. And God said to them, "Be fruitful and multiply and fill the earth and subdue it, and have dominion over the fish of the sea and over the birds of the heavens and over every living thing that moves on the earth." **29** And God said,

PROFILE

ADAM

Adam, whose name means "man," was the first human being. Created out of dust, he was made in the image of God. Adam was given dominion over the rest of creation and was placed in the garden of Eden to care for it. God created Eve as a helper for Adam, and together they enjoyed perfect fellowship with their Creator. But Adam and Eve chose to disobey God, which brought sin and death into the world. Because of their sin, all humans are now born sinners and will someday die. The Bible tells the story of how God redeems his creation from the curse of Adam's sin. "For as in Adam all die, so also in Christ shall all be made alive" (1 Cor. 15:22).

KEY REFERENCE: GENESIS 2:7

"Behold, I have given you every plant yielding seed that is on the face of all the earth, and every tree with seed in its fruit. You shall have them for food. **30** And to every beast of the earth and to every bird of the heavens and to everything that creeps on the earth, everything that has the breath of life, I have given every green plant for food." And it was so. **31** And God saw everything that he had made, and behold, it was very good. And there was evening and there was morning, the sixth day.

The Seventh Day, God Rests

2 Thus the heavens and the earth were finished, and all the host of them. **2** And on the seventh day God finished his work that he had done, and he rested on the seventh day from all his work that he had done. **3** So God blessed the seventh day and made it holy, because on it God rested from all his work that he had done in creation.

The Creation of Man and Woman

4 These are the generations
   of the heavens and the earth when
      they were created,
   in the day that the LORD[1] God made
      the earth and the heavens.

5 When no bush of the field was yet in the land and no small plant of the field had yet sprung up—for the LORD God had not caused it to rain on the land, and there was

GETTING THE MESSAGE

Father, Son, and Holy Spirit. God said, "Let *us* make man" (1:26). This phrase could be the Bible's earliest indication that God exists as three persons in one: Father, Son, and Holy Spirit. Christians refer to this as the doctrine of the Trinity.

no man to work the ground, **6** and a mist was going up from the land and was watering the whole face of the ground— **7** then the LORD God formed the man of dust from the ground and breathed into his nostrils the breath of life, and the man became a living creature. **8** And the LORD God planted a garden in Eden, in the east, and there he put the man whom he had formed. **9** And out of the ground the LORD God made to spring up every tree that is pleasant to the sight and good for food. The tree of life was in the midst of the garden, and the tree of the knowledge of good and evil.

10 A river flowed out of Eden to water the garden, and there it divided and became four rivers. **11** The name of the first is the Pishon. It is the one that flowed around the whole land of Havilah, where there is gold. **12** And the gold of that land is good;

[1] The word LORD, when spelled with small capital letters, translates the Hebrew word for God's personal name, *Yahweh* (see Preface)

bdellium and onyx stone are there. ¹³ The name of the second river is the Gihon. It is the one that flowed around the whole land of Cush. ¹⁴ And the name of the third river is the Tigris, which flows east of Assyria. And the fourth river is the Euphrates.

¹⁵ The LORD God took the man and put him in the garden of Eden to work it and keep it. ¹⁶ And the LORD God commanded the man, saying, "You may surely eat of every tree of the garden, ¹⁷ but of the tree of the knowledge of good and evil you shall not eat, for in the day that you eat of it you shall surely die."

¹⁸ Then the LORD God said, "It is not good that the man should be alone; I will make him a helper fit for him." ¹⁹ Now out of the ground the LORD God had formed every beast of the field and every bird of the heavens and brought them to the man to see

> ### GETTING THE MESSAGE
>
> **The Euphrates** (2:14) is the longest and most important river in southwest Asia. Early settlers depended on the river for commerce and agriculture. The Euphrates and Tigris rivers form what is today the Shatt-al-Arab, a waterway that flows into the Persian Gulf.

what he would call them. And whatever the man called every living creature, that was its name. ²⁰ The man gave names to all livestock and to the birds of the heavens and to every beast of the field. But for Adam there was not found a helper fit for him. ²¹ So the LORD God caused a deep sleep to fall upon the man, and while he slept took one of his ribs and closed up its place with flesh. ²² And the rib that the LORD God had taken from the man he made into a woman and brought her to the man. ²³ Then the man said,

> "This at last is bone of my bones
>   and flesh of my flesh;
> she shall be called Woman,
>   because she was taken out of Man."¹

²⁴ Therefore a man shall leave his father and his mother and hold fast to his wife, and they shall become one flesh. ²⁵ And the man

and his wife were both naked and were not ashamed.

The Fall

3 Now the serpent was more crafty than any other beast of the field that the LORD God had made.

He said to the woman, "Did God actually say, 'You shall not eat of any tree in the garden'?" ² And the woman said to the serpent, "We may eat of the fruit of the trees in the garden, ³ but God said, 'You shall not eat of the fruit of the tree that is in the midst of the garden, neither shall you touch it, lest you

> ## PROFILE
> # EVE
>
> God created Eve, whose name means "life," as a helper for Adam. Fashioned from one of Adam's ribs, Eve became the mother (that is, the female ancestor) of all human beings. Though enjoying perfect fellowship with God, Eve was deceived by the serpent and disobeyed God by eating from the tree of the knowledge of good and evil. Because of their sin, Adam and Eve were driven from the paradise of Eden and began to experience great hardship. For Eve, that included pain in childbearing. Yet, as promised in Genesis 3:15, one of her offspring would defeat the serpent and bring salvation and eternal life to all who put their trust in him.
>
> **KEY REFERENCE:** GENESIS 2:23

die.'" ⁴ But the serpent said to the woman, "You will not surely die. ⁵ For God knows that when you eat of it your eyes will be opened, and you will be like God, knowing good and evil." ⁶ So when the woman saw that the tree was good for food, and that it was a delight to the eyes, and that the tree was to be desired to make one wise, she took of its fruit and ate, and she also gave some to her husband who was with her, and he ate. ⁷ Then the eyes of both were opened, and they knew that they were naked. And

---

¹ The Hebrew words for *woman* (*ishshah*) and *man* (*ish*) sound alike

they sewed fig leaves together and made themselves loincloths.

⁸ And they heard the sound of the LORD God walking in the garden in the cool of the day, and the man and his wife hid themselves from the presence of the LORD God among the trees of the garden. ⁹ But the LORD God called to the man and said to him, "Where are you?" ¹⁰ And he said, "I heard the sound of you in the garden, and I was afraid, because I was naked, and I hid myself." ¹¹ He said, "Who told you that you were naked? Have you eaten of the tree of which I commanded you not to eat?" ¹² The man said, "The woman whom you gave to be with me, she gave me fruit of the tree, and I ate." ¹³ Then the LORD God said to the woman, "What is this that you have done?" The woman said, "The serpent deceived me, and I ate."

¹⁴ The LORD God said to the serpent,

"Because you have done this,
    cursed are you above all livestock
    and above all beasts of the field;
on your belly you shall go,
    and dust you shall eat
    all the days of your life.
¹⁵ I will put enmity between you and the
        woman,
    and between your offspring and her
        offspring;
he shall bruise your head,
    and you shall bruise his heel."

¹⁶ To the woman he said,

"I will surely multiply your pain in
        childbearing;
    in pain you shall bring forth chil-
        dren.
Your desire shall be for your hus-
        band,
    and he shall rule over you."

¹⁷ And to Adam he said,

"Because you have listened to the voice
        of your wife
    and have eaten of the tree
of which I commanded you,
    'You shall not eat of it,'
cursed is the ground because of you;
    in pain you shall eat of it all the
        days of your life;

¹⁸ thorns and thistles it shall bring forth
        for you;
    and you shall eat the plants of the
        field.
¹⁹ By the sweat of your face
    you shall eat bread,
till you return to the ground,
    for out of it you were taken;
for you are dust,
    and to dust you shall return."

²⁰ The man called his wife's name Eve, because she was the mother of all living.¹ ²¹ And the LORD God made for Adam and for his wife garments of skins and clothed them.

²² Then the LORD God said, "Behold, the man has become like one of us in knowing good and evil. Now, lest he reach out his hand and take also of the tree of life and eat, and live forever—" ²³ therefore the LORD God sent him out from the garden of Eden to work the ground from which he was taken.

Cherubim (3:24) are angels who guard holy places. They appear in various places in the Bible. "Cherubim" is the Hebrew plural form of "cherub."

²⁴ He drove out the man, and at the east of the garden of Eden he placed the cherubim and a flaming sword that turned every way to guard the way to the tree of life.

Cain and Abel

4 Now Adam knew Eve his wife, and she conceived and bore Cain, saying, "I have gotten² a man with the help of the LORD." ² And again, she bore his brother Abel. Now Abel was a keeper of sheep, and Cain a worker of the ground. ³ In the course of time Cain brought to the LORD an offering of the fruit of the ground, ⁴ and Abel also brought of the firstborn of his flock and of their fat portions. And the LORD had regard for Abel and his offering, ⁵ but for Cain and his offering he had no regard. So Cain was very angry, and his face fell. ⁶ The LORD said to Cain, "Why are you angry, and why has your face fallen? ⁷ If you do well, will you not be accepted? And if you do not do well,

¹ *Eve* sounds like the Hebrew for *life-giver* ² *Cain* sounds like the Hebrew for *gotten*

sin is crouching at the door. Its desire is for you, but you must rule over it."

⁸ Cain spoke to Abel his brother. And when they were in the field, Cain rose up against his brother Abel and killed him. ⁹ Then the LORD said to Cain, "Where is Abel your brother?" He said, "I do not know; am I my brother's keeper?" ¹⁰ And the LORD said, "What have you done? The voice of your brother's blood is crying to me from the ground. ¹¹ And now you are cursed from the ground, which has opened its mouth to receive your brother's blood from your hand. ¹² When you work the ground, it shall no longer yield to you its strength. You shall be a fugitive and a wanderer on the earth." ¹³ Cain said to the LORD, "My punishment is greater than I can bear. ¹⁴ Behold, you have driven me today away from the ground, and from your face I shall be hidden. I shall be a fugitive and a wanderer on the earth, and whoever finds me will kill me." ¹⁵ Then the LORD said to him, "Not so! If anyone kills Cain, vengeance shall be taken on him sevenfold." And the LORD put a mark on Cain, lest any who found him should attack him. ¹⁶ Then Cain went away from the presence of the LORD and settled in the land of Nod,¹ east of Eden.

¹⁷ Cain knew his wife, and she conceived and bore Enoch. When he built a city, he called the name of the city after the name of his son, Enoch. ¹⁸ To Enoch was born Irad, and Irad fathered Mehujael, and Mehujael fathered Methushael, and Methushael fathered Lamech. ¹⁹ And Lamech took two wives. The name of the one was Adah, and the name of the other Zillah. ²⁰ Adah bore Jabal; he was the father of those who dwell in tents and have livestock. ²¹ His brother's name was Jubal; he was the father of all those who play the lyre and pipe. ²² Zillah also bore Tubal-cain; he was the forger of all instruments of bronze and iron. The sister of Tubal-cain was Naamah.

²³ Lamech said to his wives:

"Adah and Zillah, hear my voice;
    you wives of Lamech, listen to what
    I say:
I have killed a man for wounding
    me,
    a young man for striking me.

²⁴ If Cain's revenge is sevenfold,
    then Lamech's is seventy-sevenfold."

²⁵ And Adam knew his wife again, and she bore a son and called his name Seth, for she said, "God has appointed² for me another offspring instead of Abel, for Cain killed him." ²⁶ To Seth also a son was born, and he called his name Enosh. At that time people began to call upon the name of the LORD.

Adam's Descendants to Noah

5 This is the book of the generations of Adam. When God created man, he made him in the likeness of God. ² Male and female he created them, and he blessed them and named them Man when they were created. ³ When Adam had lived 130 years, he fathered a son in his own likeness, after his image, and named him Seth. ⁴ The days of Adam after he fathered Seth were 800 years; and he had other sons and daughters.

> ### GETTING THE MESSAGE
>
> **Two men who never died.** Enoch and Elijah are the only people in the Bible who did not die a natural death. Instead, they were taken by God (5:24; 2 Kings 2:11).

⁵ Thus all the days that Adam lived were 930 years, and he died.

⁶ When Seth had lived 105 years, he fathered Enosh. ⁷ Seth lived after he fathered Enosh 807 years and had other sons and daughters. ⁸ Thus all the days of Seth were 912 years, and he died.

⁹ When Enosh had lived 90 years, he fathered Kenan. ¹⁰ Enosh lived after he fathered Kenan 815 years and had other sons and daughters. ¹¹ Thus all the days of Enosh were 905 years, and he died.

¹² When Kenan had lived 70 years, he fathered Mahalalel. ¹³ Kenan lived after he fathered Mahalalel 840 years and had other sons and daughters. ¹⁴ Thus all the days of Kenan were 910 years, and he died.

¹⁵ When Mahalalel had lived 65 years, he fathered Jared. ¹⁶ Mahalalel lived after he fathered Jared 830 years and had other sons and daughters. ¹⁷ Thus all the days of Mahalalel were 895 years, and he died.

---

¹ Nod means wandering ² Seth sounds like the Hebrew for he appointed

[18] When Jared had lived 162 years he fathered Enoch. [19] Jared lived after he fathered Enoch 800 years and had other sons and daughters. [20] Thus all the days of Jared were 962 years, and he died.

[21] When Enoch had lived 65 years, he fathered Methuselah. [22] Enoch walked with God after he fathered Methuselah 300 years and had other sons and daughters. [23] Thus all the days of Enoch were 365 years. [24] Enoch walked with God, and he was not, for God took him.

PROFILE
NOAH

Noah was a righteous man who faithfully walked with God despite the wickedness of his generation. When God chose to destroy the earth because of its hopeless corruption, Noah alone found favor in his eyes. God instructed Noah to build an ark that would keep him and his family safe during the coming flood. Noah also took representative pairs of each kind of animal with him into the ark, to replenish the earth after the flood. God made a covenant with Noah, promising that he would never again destroy the earth with a flood. The New Testament calls Noah a "herald of righteousness" (2 Pet. 2:5).

KEY REFERENCE: GENESIS 6:7-8

[25] When Methuselah had lived 187 years, he fathered Lamech. [26] Methuselah lived after he fathered Lamech 782 years and had other sons and daughters. [27] Thus all the days of Methuselah were 969 years, and he died.

[28] When Lamech had lived 182 years, he fathered a son [29] and called his name Noah, saying, "Out of the ground that the LORD has cursed, this one shall bring us relief[1] from our work and from the painful toil of our hands." [30] Lamech lived after he fathered Noah 595 years and had other sons and daughters. [31] Thus all the days of Lamech were 777 years, and he died.

[32] After Noah was 500 years old, Noah fathered Shem, Ham, and Japheth.

Increasing Corruption on Earth

6 When man began to multiply on the face of the land and daughters were born to them, [2] the sons of God saw that the daughters of man were attractive. And they took as their wives any they chose. [3] Then the LORD said, "My Spirit shall not abide in man forever, for he is flesh: his days shall be 120 years." [4] The Nephilim[2] were on the earth in those days, and also afterward, when the sons of God came in to the daughters of man and they bore children to them. These were the mighty men who were of old, the men of renown.

[5] The LORD saw that the wickedness of man was great in the earth, and that every intention of the thoughts of his heart was only evil continually. [6] And the LORD

GETTING THE MESSAGE

Favor in the eyes of the Lord. "Favor" (6:8) is another word for God's grace. Of all the people living at the time of the flood, only Noah and his family found favor in God's sight.

regretted that he had made man on the earth, and it grieved him to his heart. [7] So the LORD said, "I will blot out man whom I have created from the face of the land, man and animals and creeping things and birds of the heavens, for I am sorry that I have made them." [8] But Noah found favor in the eyes of the LORD.

Noah and the Flood

[9] These are the generations of Noah. Noah was a righteous man, blameless in his generation. Noah walked with God. [10] And Noah had three sons, Shem, Ham, and Japheth. [11] Now the earth was corrupt in God's sight, and the earth was filled with violence. [12] And God saw the earth, and behold, it was corrupt, for all flesh had corrupted their way on the earth. [13] And God said to Noah, "I have determined to make an end of all flesh, for the earth is filled with violence through them. Behold, I will destroy them with the earth. [14] Make yourself an ark of gopher

[1] Noah sounds like the Hebrew for relief [2] Or giants

wood. Make rooms in the ark, and cover it inside and out with pitch. ¹⁵This is how you are to make it: the length of the ark 300 cubits, its breadth 50 cubits, and its height 30 cubits. ¹⁶Make a roof for the ark, and finish it to a cubit above, and set the door of the ark in its side. Make it with lower, second, and third decks. ¹⁷For behold, I will bring a flood of waters upon the earth to destroy all flesh in which is the breath of life under heaven. Everything that is on the earth shall die. ¹⁸But I will establish my covenant with you, and you shall come into the ark, you, your sons, your wife, and your sons' wives with you. ¹⁹And of every living thing of all flesh, you shall bring two of every sort into the ark to keep them alive with you. They shall be male and female. ²⁰Of the birds according to their kinds, and of the animals according to their kinds, of every creeping thing of the ground, according to its kind, two of every sort shall come in to you to keep them alive. ²¹Also take with you every sort of food that is eaten, and store it up. It shall serve as food for you and for them." ²²Noah did this; he did all that God commanded him.

7 Then the Lord said to Noah, "Go into the ark, you and all your household, for I have seen that you are righteous before me in this generation. ²Take with you seven pairs of all clean animals, the male and his mate, and a pair of the animals that are not clean, the male and his mate, ³and seven pairs of the birds of the heavens also, male and female, to keep their offspring alive on the face of all the earth. ⁴For in seven days I will send rain on the earth forty days and forty nights, and every living thing that I have made I will blot out from the face of the ground." ⁵And Noah did all that the Lord had commanded him.

⁶Noah was six hundred years old when the flood of waters came upon the earth. ⁷And Noah and his sons and his wife and his sons' wives with him went into the ark to escape the waters of the flood. ⁸Of clean animals, and of animals that are not clean, and of birds, and of everything that creeps on the ground, ⁹two and two, male and female, went into the ark with Noah, as God had commanded Noah. ¹⁰And after seven days the waters of the flood came upon the earth.

¹¹In the six hundredth year of Noah's life, in the second month, on the seventeenth day of the month, on that day all the fountains of the great deep burst forth, and the windows of the heavens were opened. ¹²And rain fell upon the earth forty days and forty nights. ¹³On the very same day Noah and his sons, Shem and Ham and Japheth, and Noah's wife and the three wives of his sons with them entered the ark, ¹⁴they and every beast, according to its kind, and all the livestock according to their kinds, and every creeping thing that creeps on the earth, according to its kind, and every bird, according to its kind, every winged creature. ¹⁵They went into the ark with Noah, two and two of all flesh in which there was the breath of life. ¹⁶And those that entered, male and female of all flesh, went in as God had commanded him. And the Lord shut him in.

> ### GETTING THE MESSAGE
>
> **Why did Noah take seven pairs of each clean animal but only one pair of each unclean animal?** After the flood, some clean animals were needed for making sacrifices and for food. To ensure their survival, it was necessary to have more than one pair of each kind in the ark.

¹⁷The flood continued forty days on the earth. The waters increased and bore up the ark, and it rose high above the earth. ¹⁸The waters prevailed and increased greatly on the earth, and the ark floated on the face of the waters. ¹⁹And the waters prevailed so mightily on the earth that all the high mountains under the whole heaven were covered. ²⁰The waters prevailed above the mountains, covering them fifteen cubits deep. ²¹And all flesh died that moved on the earth, birds, livestock, beasts, all swarming creatures that swarm on the earth, and all mankind. ²²Everything on the dry land in whose nostrils was the breath of life died. ²³He blotted out every living thing that was on the face of the ground, man and animals and creeping things and birds of the heavens. They were blotted out from the earth. Only Noah was left, and those who were with him in the ark. ²⁴And the waters prevailed on the earth 150 days.

The Flood Subsides

8 But God remembered Noah and all the beasts and all the livestock that were with him in the ark. And God made a wind blow over the earth, and the waters subsided. ² The fountains of the deep and the windows of the heavens were closed, the rain from the heavens was restrained, ³ and the waters receded from the earth continually. At the end of 150 days the waters had abated, ⁴ and in the seventh month, on the seventeenth day of the month, the ark came to rest on the mountains of Ararat. ⁵ And the waters continued to abate until the tenth month; in the tenth month, on the first day of the month, the tops of the mountains were seen.

⁶ At the end of forty days Noah opened the window of the ark that he had made ⁷ and sent forth a raven. It went to and fro until the waters were dried up from the earth. ⁸ Then he sent forth a dove from him, to see

GETTING THE MESSAGE

Extending an olive branch. The universal symbol for peace—a dove with an olive branch—is based on the Bible story of the flood (8:11).

if the waters had subsided from the face of the ground. ⁹ But the dove found no place to set her foot, and she returned to him to the ark, for the waters were still on the face of the whole earth. So he put out his hand and took her and brought her into the ark with him. ¹⁰ He waited another seven days, and again he sent forth the dove out of the ark. ¹¹ And the dove came back to him in the evening, and behold, in her mouth was a freshly plucked olive leaf. So Noah knew that the waters had subsided from the earth. ¹² Then he waited another seven days and sent forth the dove, and she did not return to him anymore.

¹³ In the six hundred and first year, in the first month, the first day of the month, the waters were dried from off the earth. And Noah removed the covering of the ark and looked, and behold, the face of the ground was dry. ¹⁴ In the second month, on the twenty-seventh day of the month, the earth had dried out. ¹⁵ Then God said to Noah, ¹⁶ "Go out from the ark, you and your wife, and your sons and your sons' wives with you. ¹⁷ Bring out with you every living thing that is with you of all flesh—birds and animals and every creeping thing that creeps on the earth—that they may swarm on the earth, and be fruitful and multiply on the earth." ¹⁸ So Noah went out, and his sons and his wife and his sons' wives with him. ¹⁹ Every beast, every creeping thing, and every bird, everything that moves on the earth, went out by families from the ark.

God's Covenant with Noah

²⁰ Then Noah built an altar to the LORD and took some of every clean animal and some of every clean bird and offered burnt offerings on the altar. ²¹ And when the LORD smelled the pleasing aroma, the LORD said in his heart, "I will never again curse the ground because of man, for the intention of man's heart is evil from his youth. Neither will I ever again strike down every living creature as I have done. ²² While the earth remains, seedtime and harvest, cold and heat, summer and winter, day and night, shall not cease."

9 And God blessed Noah and his sons and said to them, "Be fruitful and multiply and fill the earth. ² The fear of you and the dread of you shall be upon every beast of the earth and upon every bird of the heavens, upon everything that creeps on the ground and all the fish of the sea. Into your hand they are delivered. ³ Every moving thing that lives shall be food for you. And as I gave you the green plants, I give you everything. ⁴ But you shall not eat flesh with its life, that is, its blood. ⁵ And for your lifeblood I will require a reckoning: from every beast I will require it and from man. From his fellow man I will require a reckoning for the life of man.

⁶ "Whoever sheds the blood of man,
   by man shall his blood be shed,
   for God made man in his own image.

⁷ And you, be fruitful and multiply, increase greatly on the earth and multiply in it."

⁸ Then God said to Noah and to his sons with him, ⁹ "Behold, I establish my covenant with you and your offspring after you, ¹⁰ and with every living creature that is with you, the birds, the livestock, and every beast of the earth with you, as many as came out of the ark; it is for every beast

of the earth. [11] I establish my covenant with you, that never again shall all flesh be cut off by the waters of the flood, and never again shall there be a flood to destroy the earth." [12] And God said, "This is the sign of the covenant that I make between me and you and every living creature that is with you, for all future generations: [13] I have set my bow in the cloud, and it shall be a sign of the covenant between me and the earth. [14] When I bring clouds over the earth and the bow is seen in the clouds, [15] I will remember my covenant that is between me and you and every living creature of all flesh. And the waters shall never again become a flood to destroy all flesh. [16] When the bow is in the clouds, I will see it and remember the everlasting covenant between God and every living creature of all flesh that is on the earth." [17] God said to Noah, "This is the sign of the covenant that I have established between me and all flesh that is on the earth."

Noah's Descendants

[18] The sons of Noah who went forth from the ark were Shem, Ham, and Japheth. (Ham was the father of Canaan.) [19] These three were the sons of Noah, and from these the people of the whole earth were dispersed.

[20] Noah began to be a man of the soil, and he planted a vineyard. [21] He drank of the wine and became drunk and lay uncovered in his tent. [22] And Ham, the father of Canaan, saw the nakedness of his father and told his two brothers outside. [23] Then Shem and Japheth took a garment, laid it on both their shoulders, and walked backward and covered the nakedness of their father. Their faces were turned backward, and they did not see their father's nakedness. [24] When Noah awoke from his wine and knew what his youngest son had done to him, [25] he said,

"Cursed be Canaan;
    a servant of servants shall he be to
      his brothers."

[26] He also said,

"Blessed be the LORD, the God of Shem;
    and let Canaan be his servant.
[27]   May God enlarge Japheth,[1]
    and let him dwell in the tents of
      Shem,
    and let Canaan be his servant."

[1] Japheth sounds like the Hebrew for enlarge

[28] After the flood Noah lived 350 years. [29] All the days of Noah were 950 years, and he died.

Nations Descended from Noah

10 These are the generations of the sons of Noah, Shem, Ham, and Japheth. Sons were born to them after the flood.

[2] The sons of Japheth: Gomer, Magog, Madai, Javan, Tubal, Meshech, and Tiras. [3] The sons of Gomer: Ashkenaz, Riphath, and Togarmah. [4] The sons of Javan: Elishah, Tarshish, Kittim, and Dodanim. [5] From these the coastland peoples spread in their lands, each with his own language, by their clans, in their nations.

[6] The sons of Ham: Cush, Egypt, Put, and Canaan. [7] The sons of Cush: Seba, Havilah, Sabtah, Raamah, and Sabteca. The sons of Raamah: Sheba and Dedan. [8] Cush fathered

> ### GETTING THE MESSAGE
>
> **What did the Tower of Babel look like?**
> The Tower of Babel (11:1–9) probably resembled the ziggurats of ancient Mesopotamia. The most famous of these is the Great Ziggurat of Ur. Its remains can be seen today in southeastern Iraq.

Nimrod; he was the first on earth to be a mighty man. [9] He was a mighty hunter before the LORD. Therefore it is said, "Like Nimrod a mighty hunter before the LORD." [10] The beginning of his kingdom was Babel, Erech, Accad, and Calneh, in the land of Shinar. [11] From that land he went into Assyria and built Nineveh, Rehoboth-Ir, Calah, and [12] Resen between Nineveh and Calah; that is the great city. [13] Egypt fathered Ludim, Anamim, Lehabim, Naphtuhim, [14] Pathrusim, Casluhim (from whom the Philistines came), and Caphtorim.

[15] Canaan fathered Sidon his firstborn and Heth, [16] and the Jebusites, the Amorites, the Girgashites, [17] the Hivites, the Arkites, the Sinites, [18] the Arvadites, the Zemarites, and the Hamathites. Afterward the clans of the Canaanites dispersed. [19] And the territory of the Canaanites extended from Sidon in the direction of Gerar as far as Gaza, and in the direction of Sodom, Gomorrah, Admah, and Zeboiim, as far as Lasha. [20] These are the

11 GENESIS 11:28

sons of Ham, by their clans, their languages, their lands, and their nations.

²¹ To Shem also, the father of all the children of Eber, the elder brother of Japheth, children were born. ²² The sons of Shem: Elam, Asshur, Arpachshad, Lud, and Aram. ²³ The sons of Aram: Uz, Hul, Gether, and Mash. ²⁴ Arpachshad fathered Shelah; and Shelah fathered Eber. ²⁵ To Eber were born two sons: the name of the one was Peleg,¹ for in his days the earth was divided, and his brother's name was Joktan. ²⁶ Joktan fathered Almodad, Sheleph, Hazarmaveth, Jerah, ²⁷ Hadoram, Uzal, Diklah, ²⁸ Obal, Abimael, Sheba, ²⁹ Ophir, Havilah, and Jobab; all these were the sons of Joktan. ³⁰ The territory in which they lived extended from Mesha in the direction of Sephar to the hill country of the east. ³¹ These are the sons of Shem, by their clans, their languages, their lands, and their nations.

GETTING THE MESSAGE

Sinful pride and rebellion against God brought negative consequences to the Tower of Babel builders—a warning to us today (11:7–9).

³² These are the clans of the sons of Noah, according to their genealogies, in their nations, and from these the nations spread abroad on the earth after the flood.

The Tower of Babel

11 Now the whole earth had one language and the same words. ² And as people migrated from the east, they found a plain in the land of Shinar and settled there. ³ And they said to one another, "Come, let us make bricks, and burn them thoroughly." And they had brick for stone, and bitumen for mortar. ⁴ Then they said, "Come, let us build ourselves a city and a tower with its top in the heavens, and let us make a name for ourselves, lest we be dispersed over the face of the whole earth." ⁵ And the LORD came down to see the city and the tower, which the children of man had built. ⁶ And the LORD said, "Behold, they are one people, and they have all one language, and this is only the beginning of what they will do. And

nothing that they propose to do will now be impossible for them. ⁷ Come, let us go down and there confuse their language, so that they may not understand one another's speech." ⁸ So the LORD dispersed them from there over the face of all the earth, and they left off building the city. ⁹ Therefore its name was called Babel, because there the LORD confused² the language of all the earth. And from there the LORD dispersed them over the face of all the earth.

Shem's Descendants

¹⁰ These are the generations of Shem. When Shem was 100 years old, he fathered Arpachshad two years after the flood. ¹¹ And Shem lived after he fathered Arpachshad 500 years and had other sons and daughters.

¹² When Arpachshad had lived 35 years, he fathered Shelah. ¹³ And Arpachshad lived after he fathered Shelah 403 years and had other sons and daughters.

¹⁴ When Shelah had lived 30 years, he fathered Eber. ¹⁵ And Shelah lived after he fathered Eber 403 years and had other sons and daughters.

¹⁶ When Eber had lived 34 years, he fathered Peleg. ¹⁷ And Eber lived after he fathered Peleg 430 years and had other sons and daughters.

¹⁸ When Peleg had lived 30 years, he fathered Reu. ¹⁹ And Peleg lived after he fathered Reu 209 years and had other sons and daughters.

²⁰ When Reu had lived 32 years, he fathered Serug. ²¹ And Reu lived after he fathered Serug 207 years and had other sons and daughters.

²² When Serug had lived 30 years, he fathered Nahor. ²³ And Serug lived after he fathered Nahor 200 years and had other sons and daughters.

²⁴ When Nahor had lived 29 years, he fathered Terah. ²⁵ And Nahor lived after he fathered Terah 119 years and had other sons and daughters.

²⁶ When Terah had lived 70 years, he fathered Abram, Nahor, and Haran.

Terah's Descendants

²⁷ Now these are the generations of Terah. Terah fathered Abram, Nahor, and Haran; and Haran fathered Lot. ²⁸ Haran died in the presence of his father Terah in the land of

¹ Peleg means division ² Babel sounds like the Hebrew for confused

his kindred, in Ur of the Chaldeans. ²⁹ And Abram and Nahor took wives. The name of Abram's wife was Sarai, and the name of Nahor's wife, Milcah, the daughter of Haran the father of Milcah and Iscah. ³⁰ Now Sarai was barren; she had no child.

³¹ Terah took Abram his son and Lot the son of Haran, his grandson, and Sarai his daughter-in-law, his son Abram's wife, and they went forth together from Ur of the Chaldeans to go into the land of Canaan, but when they came to Haran, they settled there. ³² The days of Terah were 205 years, and Terah died in Haran.

The Call of Abram

12 Now the LORD said to Abram, "Go from your country and your kindred and your father's house to the land that I will show you. ² And I will make of you a great nation, and I will bless you and make your name great, so that you will be a blessing. ³ I will bless those who bless you, and him who dishonors you I will curse, and in you all the families of the earth shall be blessed."

⁴ So Abram went, as the LORD had told him, and Lot went with him. Abram was seventy-five years old when he departed from Haran. ⁵ And Abram took Sarai his wife, and Lot his brother's son, and all their possessions that they had gathered, and the people that they had acquired in Haran, and they set out to go to the land of Canaan. When they came to the land of Canaan, ⁶ Abram passed through the land to the place at Shechem, to the oak of Moreh. At that time the Canaanites were in the land. ⁷ Then the LORD appeared to Abram and said, "To your offspring I will give this land." So he built there an altar to the LORD, who had appeared to him. ⁸ From there he moved to the hill country on the east of Bethel and pitched his tent, with Bethel on the west and Ai on the east. And there he built an altar to the LORD and called upon the name of the LORD. ⁹ And Abram journeyed on, still going toward the Negeb.

Abram and Sarai in Egypt

¹⁰ Now there was a famine in the land. So Abram went down to Egypt to sojourn there, for the famine was severe in the land. ¹¹ When he was about to enter Egypt, he said to Sarai his wife, "I know that you are a woman beautiful in appearance, ¹² and when the Egyptians see you, they will say, 'This is his wife.' Then they will kill me, but they will let you live. ¹³ Say you are my sister, that it may go well with me because of you, and that my life may be spared for your sake." ¹⁴ When Abram entered Egypt, the Egyptians saw that the woman was very beautiful. ¹⁵ And when the princes of Pharaoh saw her, they praised her to Pharaoh. And the woman was taken into Pharaoh's house. ¹⁶ And for her sake he dealt well with Abram; and he had sheep, oxen, male donkeys, male servants, female servants, female donkeys, and camels.

PROFILE
ABRAHAM

God called Abraham to leave his native country for a land that he would show him. When Abraham arrived in Canaan, God promised to give the land to him and his descendants, who would become the nation of Israel. The Lord promised that the whole world would be blessed through Abraham and his descendants. Abraham faced the ultimate test of faith when God commanded him to sacrifice his son Isaac. Because Abraham was willing to do so, God once again promised to bless him and to multiply his offspring. God spared Isaac from death by providing a substitute sacrifice, foreshadowing the substitutionary death of Christ on the cross.

KEY REFERENCE: GENESIS 15:5–6

¹⁷ But the LORD afflicted Pharaoh and his house with great plagues because of Sarai, Abram's wife. ¹⁸ So Pharaoh called Abram and said, "What is this you have done to me? Why did you not tell me that she was your wife? ¹⁹ Why did you say, 'She is my sister,' so that I took her for my wife? Now then, here is your wife; take her, and go." ²⁰ And Pharaoh gave men orders concerning him, and they sent him away with his wife and all that he had.

Abram and Lot Separate

13 So Abram went up from Egypt, he and his wife and all that he had, and Lot with him, into the Negeb.

2 Now Abram was very rich in livestock, in silver, and in gold. 3 And he journeyed on from the Negeb as far as Bethel to the place where his tent had been at the beginning, between Bethel and Ai, 4 to the place where he had made an altar at the first. And there Abram called upon the name of the LORD. 5 And Lot, who went with Abram, also had flocks and herds and tents, 6 so that the land could not support both of them dwelling together; for their possessions were so great that they could not dwell together, 7 and there was strife between the herdsmen of Abram's livestock and the herdsmen of Lot's livestock. At that time the Canaanites and the Perizzites were dwelling in the land.

8 Then Abram said to Lot, "Let there be no strife between you and me, and between your herdsmen and my herdsmen, for we are kinsmen. 9 Is not the whole land before

GETTING THE MESSAGE

Altars were tables or platforms used for presenting sacrifices to God. They could be built of stone, mud-brick, or dirt mounds. The first altar mentioned in the Bible is the one Noah built after the flood (8:20; see also 12:8).

you? Separate yourself from me. If you take the left hand, then I will go to the right, or if you take the right hand, then I will go to the left." 10 And Lot lifted up his eyes and saw that the Jordan Valley was well watered everywhere like the garden of the LORD, like the land of Egypt, in the direction of Zoar. (This was before the LORD destroyed Sodom and Gomorrah.) 11 So Lot chose for himself all the Jordan Valley, and Lot journeyed east. Thus they separated from each other. 12 Abram settled in the land of Canaan, while Lot settled among the cities of the valley and moved his tent as far as Sodom. 13 Now the men of Sodom were wicked, great sinners against the LORD.

14 The LORD said to Abram, after Lot had separated from him, "Lift up your eyes and look from the place where you are, northward and southward and eastward and westward, 15 for all the land that you see I will give to you and to your offspring forever. 16 I will

make your offspring as the dust of the earth, so that if one can count the dust of the earth, your offspring also can be counted. 17 Arise, walk through the length and the breadth of the land, for I will give it to you." 18 So Abram moved his tent and came and settled by the oaks of Mamre, which are at Hebron, and there he built an altar to the LORD.

Abram Rescues Lot

14 In the days of Amraphel king of Shinar, Arioch king of Ellasar, Chedorlaomer king of Elam, and Tidal king of Goiim, 2 these kings made war with Bera king of Sodom, Birsha king of Gomorrah, Shinab king of Admah, Shemeber king of Zeboiim, and the king of Bela (that is, Zoar). 3 And all these joined forces in the Valley of Siddim (that is, the Salt Sea). 4 Twelve years they had served Chedorlaomer, but in the thirteenth year they rebelled. 5 In the fourteenth year Chedorlaomer and the kings who were with him came and defeated the Rephaim in Ashteroth-karnaim, the Zuzim in Ham, the Emim in Shaveh-kiriathaim, 6 and the Horites in their hill country of Seir as far as El-paran on the border of the wilderness. 7 Then they turned back and came to En-mishpat (that is, Kadesh) and defeated all the country of the Amalekites, and also the Amorites who were dwelling in Hazazon-tamar.

8 Then the king of Sodom, the king of Gomorrah, the king of Admah, the king of Zeboiim, and the king of Bela (that is, Zoar) went out, and they joined battle in the Valley of Siddim 9 with Chedorlaomer king of Elam, Tidal king of Goiim, Amraphel king of Shinar, and Arioch king of Ellasar, four kings against five. 10 Now the Valley of Siddim was full of bitumen pits, and as the kings of Sodom and Gomorrah fled, some fell into them, and the rest fled to the hill country. 11 So the enemy took all the possessions of Sodom and Gomorrah, and all their provisions, and went their way. 12 They also took Lot, the son of Abram's brother, who was dwelling in Sodom, and his possessions, and went their way.

13 Then one who had escaped came and told Abram the Hebrew, who was living by the oaks of Mamre the Amorite, brother of Eshcol and of Aner. These were allies of Abram. 14 When Abram heard that his kinsman had been taken captive, he led

forth his trained men, born in his house, 318 of them, and went in pursuit as far as Dan. ¹⁵ And he divided his forces against them by night, he and his servants, and defeated them and pursued them to Hobah, north of Damascus. ¹⁶ Then he brought back all the possessions, and also brought back his kinsman Lot with his possessions, and the women and the people.

Abram Blessed by Melchizedek

¹⁷ After his return from the defeat of Chedorlaomer and the kings who were with him, the king of Sodom went out to meet him at the Valley of Shaveh (that is, the King's Valley). ¹⁸ And Melchizedek king of Salem brought out bread and wine. (He was priest of God Most High.) ¹⁹ And he blessed him and said,

"Blessed be Abram by God Most High,
    Possessor of heaven and earth;

> **GETTING THE MESSAGE**
>
> **Non-Levite priests?** Melchizedek (14:17–21) and Jesus Christ are the only approved priests in the Bible who were not Levites. The New Testament book of Hebrews explains why this is important.

²⁰   and blessed be God Most High,
        who has delivered your enemies
            into your hand!"

And Abram gave him a tenth of everything. ²¹ And the king of Sodom said to Abram, "Give me the persons, but take the goods for yourself." ²² But Abram said to the king of Sodom, "I have lifted my hand to the Lord, God Most High, Possessor of heaven and earth, ²³ that I would not take a thread or a sandal strap or anything that is yours, lest you should say, 'I have made Abram rich.' ²⁴ I will take nothing but what the young men have eaten, and the share of the men who went with me. Let Aner, Eshcol, and Mamre take their share."

God's Covenant with Abram

15 After these things the word of the Lord came to Abram in a vision: "Fear not, Abram, I am your shield; your reward shall be very great." ² But Abram said, "O Lord God, what will you give me, for I continue childless, and the heir of my house is Eliezer of Damascus?" ³ And Abram said, "Behold, you have given me no offspring, and a member of my household will be my heir." ⁴ And behold, the word of the Lord came to him: "This man shall not be your heir; your very own son shall be your heir." ⁵ And he brought him outside and said, "Look toward heaven, and number the stars, if you are able to number them." Then he

PROFILE

MELCHIZEDEK

Melchizedek is among the most mysterious figures in Scripture. King of Salem, a city identified with Jerusalem, and "priest of God Most High," Melchizedek's name means "king of righteousness." Following Abraham's defeat of Chedorlaomer and his rescue of Lot, Melchizedek provided a meal of bread and wine for Abraham and his men. He then blessed Abraham, attributing Abraham's victory over his enemies to God Most High. In response to Melchizedek's blessing, Abraham gave the priest-king a tenth of everything he had. David mentions Melchizedek in the messianic Psalm 110, and the writer of Hebrews presents Melchizedek as a foreshadowing of Jesus Christ, who is both priest and king.

KEY REFERENCE: GENESIS 14:18-20

said to him, "So shall your offspring be." ⁶ And he believed the Lord, and he counted it to him as righteousness.

⁷ And he said to him, "I am the Lord who brought you out from Ur of the Chaldeans to give you this land to possess." ⁸ But he said, "O Lord God, how am I to know that I shall possess it?" ⁹ He said to him, "Bring me a heifer three years old, a female goat three years old, a ram three years old, a turtledove, and a young pigeon." ¹⁰ And he brought him all these, cut them in half, and laid each half over against the other. But he did not cut the birds in half. ¹¹ And when

birds of prey came down on the carcasses, Abram drove them away.

¹² As the sun was going down, a deep sleep fell on Abram. And behold, dreadful and great darkness fell upon him. ¹³ Then the LORD said to Abram, "Know for certain that your offspring will be sojourners in a land that is not theirs and will be servants there, and they will be afflicted for four hundred years. ¹⁴ But I will bring judgment on the nation that they serve, and afterward they shall come out with great possessions. ¹⁵ As for you, you shall go to your fathers in peace; you shall be buried in a good old age. ¹⁶ And they shall come back here in the fourth generation, for the iniquity of the Amorites is not yet complete."

¹⁷ When the sun had gone down and it was dark, behold, a smoking fire pot and a flaming torch passed between these pieces. ¹⁸ On that day the LORD made a covenant with Abram, saying, "To your offspring I give

> ### GETTING THE MESSAGE
>
> Abram **believed the LORD** (15:6), and that was the basis for God counting him as righteous. Such faith remains the basis for God's justification of Christians in the New Testament (Gal. 2:16).

this land, from the river of Egypt to the great river, the river Euphrates, ¹⁹ the land of the Kenites, the Kenizzites, the Kadmonites, ²⁰ the Hittites, the Perizzites, the Rephaim, ²¹ the Amorites, the Canaanites, the Girgashites and the Jebusites."

Sarai and Hagar

16 Now Sarai, Abram's wife, had borne him no children. She had a female Egyptian servant whose name was Hagar. ² And Sarai said to Abram, "Behold now, the LORD has prevented me from bearing children. Go in to my servant; it may be that I shall obtain children by her." And Abram listened to the voice of Sarai. ³ So, after Abram had lived ten years in the land of Canaan, Sarai, Abram's wife, took Hagar the Egyptian, her servant, and gave her to Abram her husband as a wife. ⁴ And he went in to Hagar, and she conceived. And when she saw that she had conceived, she looked with

contempt on her mistress. ⁵ And Sarai said to Abram, "May the wrong done to me be on you! I gave my servant to your embrace, and when she saw that she had conceived, she looked on me with contempt. May the LORD judge between you and me!" ⁶ But Abram said to Sarai, "Behold, your servant is in your power; do to her as you please." Then Sarai dealt harshly with her, and she fled from her.

⁷ The angel of the LORD found her by a spring of water in the wilderness, the spring on the way to Shur. ⁸ And he said, "Hagar, servant of Sarai, where have you come from and where are you going?" She said, "I am fleeing from my mistress Sarai." ⁹ The angel of the LORD said to her, "Return to your mistress and submit to her." ¹⁰ The angel of the LORD also said to her, "I will surely multiply your offspring so that they cannot be numbered for multitude." ¹¹ And the angel of the LORD said to her,

> "Behold, you are pregnant
>   and shall bear a son.
> You shall call his name Ishmael,[1]
>   because the LORD has listened to
>   your affliction.
> ¹² He shall be a wild donkey of a man,
>   his hand against everyone
> and everyone's hand against him,
> and he shall dwell over against all his
>   kinsmen."

¹³ So she called the name of the LORD who spoke to her, "You are a God of seeing," for she said, "Truly here I have seen him who looks after me." ¹⁴ Therefore the well was called Beer-lahai-roi;[2] it lies between Kadesh and Bered.

¹⁵ And Hagar bore Abram a son, and Abram called the name of his son, whom Hagar bore, Ishmael. ¹⁶ Abram was eighty-six years old when Hagar bore Ishmael to Abram.

Abraham and the Covenant of Circumcision

17 When Abram was ninety-nine years old the LORD appeared to Abram and said to him, "I am God Almighty; walk before me, and be blameless, ² that I may make my covenant between me and you, and may multiply you greatly." ³ Then Abram fell on his face. And God said to him, ⁴ "Behold, my covenant is with you, and you shall be the

---

[1] *Ishmael* means *God hears* [2] *Beer-lahai-roi* means *the well of the Living One who sees me*

father of a multitude of nations. ⁵ No longer shall your name be called Abram,¹ but your name shall be Abraham,² for I have made you the father of a multitude of nations. ⁶ I will make you exceedingly fruitful, and I will make you into nations, and kings shall come from you. ⁷ And I will establish my covenant between me and you and your offspring after you throughout their generations for an everlasting covenant, to be God to you and to your offspring after you. ⁸ And I will give to you and to your offspring after you the land of your sojournings, all the land of Canaan, for an everlasting possession, and I will be their God."

⁹ And God said to Abraham, "As for you, you shall keep my covenant, you and your offspring after you throughout their generations. ¹⁰ This is my covenant, which you shall keep, between me and you and your offspring after you: Every male among you

Taking servants as wives. It was common in ancient cultures for a married man to take a servant as a wife (16:3). But this was contrary to God's original design for marriage (2:24).

shall be circumcised. ¹¹ You shall be circumcised in the flesh of your foreskins, and it shall be a sign of the covenant between me and you. ¹² He who is eight days old among you shall be circumcised. Every male throughout your generations, whether born in your house or bought with your money from any foreigner who is not of your offspring, ¹³ both he who is born in your house and he who is bought with your money, shall surely be circumcised. So shall my covenant be in your flesh an everlasting covenant. ¹⁴ Any uncircumcised male who is not circumcised in the flesh of his foreskin shall be cut off from his people; he has broken my covenant."

Isaac's Birth Promised

¹⁵ And God said to Abraham, "As for Sarai your wife, you shall not call her name Sarai, but Sarah³ shall be her name. ¹⁶ I will bless her, and moreover, I will give you a son by her. I will bless her, and she shall become

nations; kings of peoples shall come from her." ¹⁷ Then Abraham fell on his face and laughed and said to himself, "Shall a child be born to a man who is a hundred years old? Shall Sarah, who is ninety years old, bear a child?" ¹⁸ And Abraham said to God, "Oh that Ishmael might live before you!" ¹⁹ God said, "No, but Sarah your wife shall bear you a son, and you shall call his name Isaac.⁴ I will establish my covenant with him as an everlasting covenant for his offspring after him. ²⁰ As for Ishmael, I have heard you; behold, I have blessed him and will make him fruitful and multiply him greatly. He

PROFILE
ISHMAEL

Ishmael was Abraham's eldest son. His mother was Hagar, the maidservant of Abraham's wife Sarah. Ishmael was around 16 years old when his half-brother, Isaac, was born. Sarah overheard Ishmael mocking his younger brother, so she angrily expelled Hagar and Ishmael from her household and sent them to wander in the desert. God protected them, however, and promised that Ishmael would become a great nation. Ishmael grew to be strongly independent and, as the Lord had prophesied, he lived a life of hostility toward others. Ishmael settled in the wilderness of Paran, where he became an expert archer. Because Ishmael was Abraham's son, God blessed him. He had 12 sons, who became princes of 12 tribes.

KEY REFERENCE: GENESIS 16:11-12

shall father twelve princes, and I will make him into a great nation. ²¹ But I will establish my covenant with Isaac, whom Sarah shall bear to you at this time next year." ²² When he had finished talking with him, God went up from Abraham. ²³ Then Abraham took Ishmael his son and all those born in his house or bought with his money, every male among the men of Abraham's house, and he circumcised the flesh of their foreskins that very day, as God had said to

¹ Abram means exalted father ² Abraham means father of a multitude ³ Sarai and Sarah mean princess ⁴ Isaac means he laughs

him. ²⁴ Abraham was ninety-nine years old when he was circumcised in the flesh of his foreskin. ²⁵ And Ishmael his son was thirteen years old when he was circumcised in the flesh of his foreskin. ²⁶ That very day Abraham and his son Ishmael were circumcised. ²⁷ And all the men of his house, those born in the house and those bought with money from a foreigner, were circumcised with him.

18 And the LORD appeared to him by the oaks of Mamre, as he sat at the door of his tent in the heat of the day. ² He lifted up his eyes and looked, and behold,

PROFILE
SARAH

Sarah was Abraham's wife and was also his half-sister. On two occasions, to save himself from possible danger, Abraham said that Sarah was his "sister," failing to mention that she was also his wife. After many years of not being able to bear children, Sarah encouraged Abraham to start a family with her maidservant, Hagar. This plan backfired when, upon conceiving, Hagar became condescending toward Sarah. Later, God promised Abraham that he would give him a son through Sarah. Since she was 90 years old at the time, and Abraham himself was 100, Sarah's initial response to the promise was laughter. However, one year later, Sarah gave birth to Isaac, the child of promise. She thus became an ancestor of Christ.

KEY REFERENCE: GENESIS 17:15–16

three men were standing in front of him. When he saw them, he ran from the tent door to meet them and bowed himself to the earth ³ and said, "O Lord, if I have found favor in your sight, do not pass by your servant. ⁴ Let a little water be brought, and wash your feet, and rest yourselves under the tree, ⁵ while I bring a morsel of bread, that you may refresh yourselves, and after that you may pass on—since you have come to your servant." So they said, "Do as you have said." ⁶ And Abraham went quickly into

the tent to Sarah and said, "Quick! Three seahs of fine flour! Knead it, and make cakes." ⁷ And Abraham ran to the herd and took a calf, tender and good, and gave it to a young man, who prepared it quickly. ⁸ Then he took curds and milk and the calf that he had prepared, and set it before them. And he stood by them under the tree while they ate.

⁹ They said to him, "Where is Sarah your wife?" And he said, "She is in the tent." ¹⁰ The LORD said, "I will surely return to you about this time next year, and Sarah your wife shall have a son." And Sarah was listening at the tent door behind him. ¹¹ Now Abraham and Sarah were old, advanced in years. The way of women had ceased to be with Sarah. ¹² So Sarah laughed to herself, saying, "After I am worn out, and my lord is old, shall I have pleasure?" ¹³ The LORD said to Abraham, "Why did Sarah laugh and say,

GETTING THE MESSAGE

Isaac means "he laughs." When Abraham and Sarah heard that they were going to have a son in their old age, they both laughed (17:17; 18:12). When Isaac was born, however, they and all their friends laughed with joy (21:6)!

'Shall I indeed bear a child, now that I am old?' ¹⁴ Is anything too hard for the LORD? At the appointed time I will return to you, about this time next year, and Sarah shall have a son." ¹⁵ But Sarah denied it, saying, "I did not laugh," for she was afraid. He said, "No, but you did laugh."

¹⁶ Then the men set out from there, and they looked down toward Sodom. And Abraham went with them to set them on their way. ¹⁷ The LORD said, "Shall I hide from Abraham what I am about to do, ¹⁸ seeing that Abraham shall surely become a great and mighty nation, and all the nations of the earth shall be blessed in him? ¹⁹ For I have chosen him, that he may command his children and his household after him to keep the way of the LORD by doing righteousness and justice, so that the LORD may bring to Abraham what he has promised him." ²⁰ Then the LORD said, "Because the outcry against Sodom and Gomorrah is great and their sin is very grave, ²¹ I will go down

to see whether they have done altogether according to the outcry that has come to me. And if not, I will know."

Abraham Intercedes for Sodom

²² So the men turned from there and went toward Sodom, but Abraham still stood before the LORD. ²³ Then Abraham drew near and said, "Will you indeed sweep away the righteous with the wicked? ²⁴ Suppose there are fifty righteous within the city. Will you then sweep away the place and not spare it for the fifty righteous who are in it? ²⁵ Far be it from you to do such a thing, to put the righteous to death with the wicked, so that the righteous fare as the wicked! Far be that from you! Shall not the Judge of all the earth do what is just?" ²⁶ And the LORD said, "If I find at Sodom fifty righteous in the city, I will spare the whole place for their sake."

²⁷ Abraham answered and said, "Behold, I have undertaken to speak to the Lord, I who am but dust and ashes. ²⁸ Suppose five of the fifty righteous are lacking. Will you destroy the whole city for lack of five?" And he said, "I will not destroy it if I find forty-five there." ²⁹ Again he spoke to him and said, "Suppose forty are found there." He answered, "For the sake of forty I will not do it." ³⁰ Then he said, "Oh let not the Lord be angry, and I will speak. Suppose thirty are found there." He answered, "I will not do it, if I find thirty there." ³¹ He said, "Behold, I have undertaken to speak to the Lord. Suppose twenty are found there." He answered, "For the sake of twenty I will not destroy it." ³² Then he said, "Oh let not the Lord be angry, and I will speak again but this once. Suppose ten are found there." He answered, "For the sake of ten I will not destroy it." ³³ And the LORD went his way, when he had finished speaking to Abraham, and Abraham returned to his place.

God Rescues Lot

19 The two angels came to Sodom in the evening, and Lot was sitting in the gate of Sodom. When Lot saw them, he rose to meet them and bowed himself with his face to the earth ² and said, "My lords, please turn aside to your servant's house and spend the night and wash your feet. Then you may rise up early and go on your way." They said, "No; we will spend the night in the town square." ³ But he pressed them strongly; so they turned aside to him and entered his house. And he made them a feast and baked unleavened bread, and they ate.

⁴ But before they lay down, the men of the city, the men of Sodom, both young and old, all the people to the last man, surrounded the house. ⁵ And they called to Lot, "Where are the men who came to you tonight? Bring them out to us, that we may know them." ⁶ Lot went out to the men at the entrance, shut the door after him, ⁷ and said, "I beg you, my brothers, do not act so wickedly. ⁸ Behold, I have two daughters who have not known any man. Let me bring them out to you, and do to them as you please. Only do nothing to these men, for they have come under the shelter of my roof." ⁹ But they said, "Stand back!" And they said, "This fellow came to sojourn, and he has become the judge! Now we will deal worse with you than with them." Then they pressed hard against

---

GETTING THE MESSAGE

The city gate was a place where leaders made key decisions (Prov. 31:23; Lam. 5:14). Lot's presence at the city gate (Gen. 19:1) shows that he had a position of importance in Sodom.

---

the man Lot, and drew near to break the door down. ¹⁰ But the men reached out their hands and brought Lot into the house with them and shut the door. ¹¹ And they struck with blindness the men who were at the entrance of the house, both small and great, so that they wore themselves out groping for the door.

¹² Then the men said to Lot, "Have you anyone else here? Sons-in-law, sons, daughters, or anyone you have in the city, bring them out of the place. ¹³ For we are about to destroy this place, because the outcry against its people has become great before the LORD, and the LORD has sent us to destroy it." ¹⁴ So Lot went out and said to his sons-in-law, who were to marry his daughters, "Up! Get out of this place, for the LORD is about to destroy the city." But he seemed to his sons-in-law to be jesting.

¹⁵ As morning dawned, the angels urged Lot, saying, "Up! Take your wife and your

two daughters who are here, lest you be swept away in the punishment of the city." ¹⁶ But he lingered. So the men seized him and his wife and his two daughters by the hand, the Lord being merciful to him, and they brought him out and set him outside the city. ¹⁷ And as they brought them out, one said, "Escape for your life. Do not look back or stop anywhere in the valley. Escape to the hills, lest you be swept away." ¹⁸ And Lot said to them, "Oh, no, my lords. ¹⁹ Behold, your servant has found favor in your sight, and you have shown me great kindness in saving

PROFILE
LOT

Abraham's nephew Lot traveled with him to the promised land of Canaan. When the combined wealth of Abraham and Lot proved too much for one place, Abraham generously offered his nephew first choice of the land. Lot chose the fertile Jordan Valley, settling in Sodom. Later, Abraham rescued Lot when he was taken captive by invaders. When the wicked city of Sodom was destroyed, God allowed Lot's family to escape. Lot's wife disobeyed by looking back, however, and was turned into a pillar of salt. Filled with fear, Lot and his daughters hid in a cave. Both daughters, desperate to have children, tricked Lot into fathering a son with them. Despite his shortcomings, Lot is described in 2 Pet. 2:7–10 as a righteous man.

KEY REFERENCE: GENESIS 19:15–16

my life. But I cannot escape to the hills, lest the disaster overtake me and I die. ²⁰ Behold, this city is near enough to flee to, and it is a little one. Let me escape there—is it not a little one?—and my life will be saved!" ²¹ He said to him, "Behold, I grant you this favor also, that I will not overthrow the city of which you have spoken. ²² Escape there quickly, for I can do nothing till you arrive there." Therefore the name of the city was called Zoar.¹

God Destroys Sodom

²³ The sun had risen on the earth when Lot came to Zoar. ²⁴ Then the Lord rained on Sodom and Gomorrah sulfur and fire from the Lord out of heaven. ²⁵ And he overthrew those cities, and all the valley, and all the inhabitants of the cities, and what grew on the ground. ²⁶ But Lot's wife, behind him, looked back, and she became a pillar of salt.

²⁷ And Abraham went early in the morning to the place where he had stood before the Lord. ²⁸ And he looked down toward Sodom and Gomorrah and toward all the land of the valley, and he looked and, behold, the smoke of the land went up like the smoke of a furnace.

²⁹ So it was that, when God destroyed the cities of the valley, God remembered Abraham and sent Lot out of the midst of the overthrow when he overthrew the cities in which Lot had lived.

Lot and His Daughters

³⁰ Now Lot went up out of Zoar and lived in the hills with his two daughters, for he was afraid to live in Zoar. So he lived in a cave with his two daughters. ³¹ And the first-born said to the younger, "Our father is old, and there is not a man on earth to come in to us after the manner of all the earth. ³² Come, let us make our father drink wine, and we will lie with him, that we may preserve offspring from our father." ³³ So they made their father drink wine that night. And the firstborn went in and lay with her father. He did not know when she lay down or when she arose.

³⁴ The next day, the firstborn said to the younger, "Behold, I lay last night with my father. Let us make him drink wine tonight also. Then you go in and lie with him, that we may preserve offspring from our father." ³⁵ So they made their father drink wine that night also. And the younger arose and lay with him, and he did not know when she lay down or when she arose. ³⁶ Thus both the daughters of Lot became pregnant by their father. ³⁷ The firstborn bore a son and called his name Moab.² He is the father of the Moabites to this day. ³⁸ The younger also bore a son and called his name Ben-ammi.³ He is the father of the Ammonites to this day.

¹ Zoar means little ² Moab sounds like the Hebrew for from father ³ Ben-ammi means son of my people

Abraham and Abimelech

20 From there Abraham journeyed toward the territory of the Negeb and lived between Kadesh and Shur; and he sojourned in Gerar. ² And Abraham said of Sarah his wife, "She is my sister." And Abimelech king of Gerar sent and took Sarah. ³ But God came to Abimelech in a dream by night and said to him, "Behold, you are a dead man because of the woman whom you have taken, for she is a man's wife." ⁴ Now Abimelech had not approached her. So he said, "Lord, will you kill an innocent people? ⁵ Did he not himself say to me, 'She is my sister'? And she herself said, 'He is my brother.' In the integrity of my heart and the innocence of my hands I have done this." ⁶ Then God said to him in the dream, "Yes, I know that you have done this in the integrity of your heart, and it was I who kept you from sinning against me. Therefore I did not let you touch her. ⁷ Now then, return the man's wife, for he is a prophet, so that he will pray for you, and you shall live. But if you do not return her, know that you shall surely die, you and all who are yours."

⁸ So Abimelech rose early in the morning and called all his servants and told them all these things. And the men were very much afraid. ⁹ Then Abimelech called Abraham and said to him, "What have you done to us? And how have I sinned against you, that you have brought on me and my kingdom a great sin? You have done to me things that ought not to be done." ¹⁰ And Abimelech said to Abraham, "What did you see, that you did this thing?" ¹¹ Abraham said, "I did it because I thought, 'There is no fear of God at all in this place, and they will kill me because of my wife.' ¹² Besides, she is indeed my sister, the daughter of my father though not the daughter of my mother, and she became my wife. ¹³ And when God caused me to wander from my father's house, I said to her, 'This is the kindness you must do me: at every place to which we come, say of me, "He is my brother."'"

¹⁴ Then Abimelech took sheep and oxen, and male servants and female servants, and gave them to Abraham, and returned Sarah his wife to him. ¹⁵ And Abimelech said, "Behold, my land is before you; dwell where it pleases you." ¹⁶ To Sarah he said, "Behold, I have given your brother a thousand pieces of silver. It is a sign of your innocence in the eyes of all who are with you, and before everyone you are vindicated." ¹⁷ Then Abraham prayed to God, and God healed Abimelech, and also healed his wife and female slaves so that they bore children. ¹⁸ For the LORD had closed all the wombs of the house of Abimelech because of Sarah, Abraham's wife.

The Birth of Isaac

21 The LORD visited Sarah as he had said, and the LORD did to Sarah as he had promised. ² And Sarah conceived and bore Abraham a son in his old age at the time of which God had spoken to him. ³ Abraham called the name of his son who was born to him, whom Sarah bore him, Isaac.[1] ⁴ And Abraham circumcised his son Isaac when he was eight days old, as God had commanded

---

GETTING THE MESSAGE

What is the Negeb? The Negeb (20:1) is a dry area of rolling hills in southern Israel. Abraham, Isaac, and Jacob lived there. Hagar sought refuge in the Negeb. Later, it provided refuge for Israelites fleeing from invading armies.

---

him. ⁵ Abraham was a hundred years old when his son Isaac was born to him. ⁶ And Sarah said, "God has made laughter for me; everyone who hears will laugh over me." ⁷ And she said, "Who would have said to Abraham that Sarah would nurse children? Yet I have borne him a son in his old age."

God Protects Hagar and Ishmael

⁸ And the child grew and was weaned. And Abraham made a great feast on the day that Isaac was weaned. ⁹ But Sarah saw the son of Hagar the Egyptian, whom she had borne to Abraham, laughing. ¹⁰ So she said to Abraham, "Cast out this slave woman with her son, for the son of this slave woman shall not be heir with my son Isaac." ¹¹ And the thing was very displeasing to Abraham on account of his son. ¹² But God said to Abraham, "Be not displeased because of the boy and because of your slave woman. Whatever Sarah says to you, do as she tells

---

[1] *Isaac* means *he laughs*

you, for through Isaac shall your offspring be named. ¹³ And I will make a nation of the son of the slave woman also, because he is your offspring." ¹⁴ So Abraham rose early in the morning and took bread and a skin of water and gave it to Hagar, putting it on her shoulder, along with the child, and sent her away. And she departed and wandered in the wilderness of Beersheba.

¹⁵ When the water in the skin was gone, she put the child under one of the bushes. ¹⁶ Then she went and sat down opposite him

PROFILE
ISAAC

God had promised Abraham that the world would be blessed through his descendants. When Isaac was born to Abraham and Sarah, it was the initial fulfillment of that promise. At God's command, Isaac was almost sacrificed by his father, but his life was spared when God provided a ram to be sacrificed in his place. This prefigured the sacrifice of God's own Son in the place of all who would believe in him. Isaac settled in Gerar, a Philistine city, where he became prosperous. He married Rebekah, who bore him twin sons, Jacob and Esau. Although Esau was his favorite son, Isaac was tricked by Jacob into giving him the blessing intended for his older brother.

KEY REFERENCE: GENESIS 21:1–3

a good way off, about the distance of a bow-shot, for she said, "Let me not look on the death of the child." And as she sat opposite him, she lifted up her voice and wept. ¹⁷ And God heard the voice of the boy, and the angel of God called to Hagar from heaven and said to her, "What troubles you, Hagar? Fear not, for God has heard the voice of the boy where he is. ¹⁸ Up! Lift up the boy, and hold him fast with your hand, for I will make him into a great nation." ¹⁹ Then God opened her eyes, and she saw a well of water. And she went and filled the skin with water and gave the

boy a drink. ²⁰ And God was with the boy, and he grew up. He lived in the wilderness and became an expert with the bow. ²¹ He lived in the wilderness of Paran, and his mother took a wife for him from the land of Egypt.

A Treaty with Abimelech

²² At that time Abimelech and Phicol the commander of his army said to Abraham, "God is with you in all that you do. ²³ Now therefore swear to me here by God that you will not deal falsely with me or with my descendants or with my posterity, but as I have dealt kindly with you, so you will deal with me and with the land where you have sojourned." ²⁴ And Abraham said, "I will swear."

²⁵ When Abraham reproved Abimelech about a well of water that Abimelech's servants had seized, ²⁶ Abimelech said, "I do

GETTING THE MESSAGE

Why fight over a well? Wells were of great importance in the hot, dry climate of Israel. Lack of water was a constant threat. Both military generals and civilian travelers would often plan their routes according to the location of wells. (See 21:25–31.)

not know who has done this thing; you did not tell me, and I have not heard of it until today." ²⁷ So Abraham took sheep and oxen and gave them to Abimelech, and the two men made a covenant. ²⁸ Abraham set seven ewe lambs of the flock apart. ²⁹ And Abimelech said to Abraham, "What is the meaning of these seven ewe lambs that you have set apart?" ³⁰ He said, "These seven ewe lambs you will take from my hand, that this may be a witness for me that I dug this well." ³¹ Therefore that place was called Beersheba,¹ because there both of them swore an oath. ³² So they made a covenant at Beersheba. Then Abimelech and Phicol the commander of his army rose up and returned to the land of the Philistines. ³³ Abraham planted a tamarisk tree in Beersheba and called there on the name of the Lord, the Everlasting God. ³⁴ And Abraham sojourned many days in the land of the Philistines.

¹ *Beersheba* means *well of seven* or *well of the oath*

The Sacrifice of Isaac

22 After these things God tested Abraham and said to him, "Abraham!" And he said, "Here I am." ² He said, "Take your son, your only son Isaac, whom you love, and go to the land of Moriah, and offer him there as a burnt offering on one of the mountains of which I shall tell you." ³ So Abraham rose early in the morning, saddled his donkey, and took two of his young men with him, and his son Isaac. And he cut the wood for the burnt offering and arose and went to the place of which God had told him. ⁴ On the third day Abraham lifted up his eyes and saw the place from afar. ⁵ Then Abraham said to his young men, "Stay here with the donkey; I and the boy will go over there and worship and come again to you." ⁶ And Abraham took the wood of the burnt offering and laid it on Isaac his son. And he took in his hand the fire and the knife. So they went both of them together. ⁷ And Isaac said to his father Abraham, "My father!" And he said, "Here I am, my son." He said, "Behold, the fire and the wood, but where is the lamb for a burnt offering?" ⁸ Abraham said, "God will provide for himself the lamb for a burnt offering, my son." So they went both of them together.

⁹ When they came to the place of which God had told him, Abraham built the altar there and laid the wood in order and bound Isaac his son and laid him on the altar, on top of the wood. ¹⁰ Then Abraham reached out his hand and took the knife to slaughter his son. ¹¹ But the angel of the LORD called to him from heaven and said, "Abraham, Abraham!" And he said, "Here I am." ¹² He said, "Do not lay your hand on the boy or do anything to him, for now I know that you fear God, seeing you have not withheld your son, your only son, from me." ¹³ And Abraham lifted up his eyes and looked, and behold, behind him was a ram, caught in a thicket by his horns. And Abraham went and took the ram and offered it up as a burnt offering instead of his son. ¹⁴ So Abraham called the name of that place, "The LORD will provide"; as it is said to this day, "On the mount of the LORD it shall be provided."

¹⁵ And the angel of the LORD called to Abraham a second time from heaven ¹⁶ and said, "By myself I have sworn, declares the LORD, because you have done this and have not withheld your son, your only son, ¹⁷ I will surely bless you, and I will surely multiply your offspring as the stars of heaven and as the sand that is on the seashore. And your offspring shall possess the gate of his enemies, ¹⁸ and in your offspring shall all the nations of the earth be blessed, because you have obeyed my voice." ¹⁹ So Abraham returned to his young men, and they arose and went together to Beersheba. And Abraham lived at Beersheba.

²⁰ Now after these things it was told to Abraham, "Behold, Milcah also has borne children to your brother Nahor: ²¹ Uz his firstborn, Buz his brother, Kemuel the father of Aram, ²² Chesed, Hazo, Pildash, Jidlaph, and Bethuel." ²³ (Bethuel fathered Rebekah.) These eight Milcah bore to Nahor, Abraham's brother. ²⁴ Moreover, his concubine, whose name was Reumah, bore Tebah, Gaham, Tahash, and Maacah.

Sarah's Death and Burial

23 Sarah lived 127 years; these were the years of the life of Sarah. ² And Sarah died at Kiriath-arba (that is, Hebron) in the land of Canaan, and Abraham went in to mourn for Sarah and to weep for her. ³ And Abraham rose up from before his dead and said to the Hittites, ⁴ "I am a sojourner and foreigner among you; give me property among you for a burying place, that I may bury my dead out of my sight." ⁵ The Hittites answered Abraham, ⁶ "Hear us, my lord; you are a prince of God among us. Bury your dead in the choicest of our tombs. None of us will withhold from you his tomb to hinder you from burying your dead." ⁷ Abraham rose and bowed to the Hittites, the people of the land. ⁸ And he said to them, "If you are willing that I should bury my dead out of my sight, hear me and entreat for me Ephron the son of Zohar, ⁹ that he may give me the cave of Machpelah, which he owns; it is at the end of his field. For the full price let him give it to me in your presence as property for a burying place."

¹⁰ Now Ephron was sitting among the Hittites, and Ephron the Hittite answered Abraham in the hearing of the Hittites, of all who went in at the gate of his city, ¹¹ "No, my lord, hear me: I give you the field, and I give you the cave that is in it. In the sight of the sons of my people I give it to you. Bury your dead." ¹² Then Abraham bowed down

before the people of the land. ¹³ And he said to Ephron in the hearing of the people of the land, "But if you will, hear me: I give the price of the field. Accept it from me, that I may bury my dead there." ¹⁴ Ephron answered Abraham, ¹⁵ "My lord, listen to me: a piece of land worth four hundred shekels of silver, what is that between you and me? Bury your dead." ¹⁶ Abraham listened to Ephron, and Abraham weighed out for Ephron the silver that he had named in the hearing of the Hittites, four hundred shekels of silver, according to the weights current among the merchants.

¹⁷ So the field of Ephron in Machpelah, which was to the east of Mamre, the field with the cave that was in it and all the trees that were in the field, throughout its whole area, was made over ¹⁸ to Abraham as a possession in the presence of the Hittites, before all who went in at the gate of his city.

GETTING THE MESSAGE

Two biblical firsts. The burial of Sarah (23:19) is the first biblical record of a burial. Abraham's purchase of the burial plot is also the first biblical record of a business transaction.

¹⁹ After this, Abraham buried Sarah his wife in the cave of the field of Machpelah east of Mamre (that is, Hebron) in the land of Canaan. ²⁰ The field and the cave that is in it were made over to Abraham as property for a burying place by the Hittites.

Isaac and Rebekah

24 Now Abraham was old, well advanced in years. And the LORD had blessed Abraham in all things. ² And Abraham said to his servant, the oldest of his household, who had charge of all that he had, "Put your hand under my thigh, ³ that I may make you swear by the LORD, the God of heaven and God of the earth, that you will not take a wife for my son from the daughters of the Canaanites, among whom I dwell, ⁴ but will go to my country and to my kindred, and take a wife for my son Isaac." ⁵ The servant said to him, "Perhaps the woman may not be willing to follow me to this land. Must I then take your son back to the land from which

you came?" ⁶ Abraham said to him, "See to it that you do not take my son back there. ⁷ The LORD, the God of heaven, who took me from my father's house and from the land of my kindred, and who spoke to me and swore to me, 'To your offspring I will give this land,' he will send his angel before you, and you shall take a wife for my son from there. ⁸ But if the woman is not willing to follow you, then you will be free from this oath of mine; only you must not take my son back there." ⁹ So the servant put his hand under the thigh of Abraham his master and swore to him concerning this matter.

¹⁰ Then the servant took ten of his master's camels and departed, taking all sorts of choice gifts from his master; and he arose and went to Mesopotamia to the city of Nahor. ¹¹ And he made the camels kneel down outside the city by the well of water at the time of evening, the time when women go out to draw water. ¹² And he said, "O LORD, God of my master Abraham, please grant me success today and show steadfast love to my master Abraham. ¹³ Behold, I am standing by the spring of water, and the daughters of the men of the city are coming out to draw water. ¹⁴ Let the young woman to whom I shall say, 'Please let down your jar that I may drink,' and who shall say, 'Drink, and I will water your camels'—let her be the one whom you have appointed for your servant Isaac. By this I shall know that you have shown steadfast love to my master."

¹⁵ Before he had finished speaking, behold, Rebekah, who was born to Bethuel the son of Milcah, the wife of Nahor, Abraham's brother, came out with her water jar on her shoulder. ¹⁶ The young woman was very attractive in appearance, a maiden whom no man had known. She went down to the spring and filled her jar and came up. ¹⁷ Then the servant ran to meet her and said, "Please give me a little water to drink from your jar." ¹⁸ She said, "Drink, my lord." And she quickly let down her jar upon her hand and gave him a drink. ¹⁹ When she had finished giving him a drink, she said, "I will draw water for your camels also, until they have finished drinking." ²⁰ So she quickly emptied her jar into the trough and ran again to the well to draw water, and she drew for all his camels. ²¹ The man gazed at her in silence to learn whether the LORD had prospered his journey or not.

22 When the camels had finished drinking, the man took a gold ring weighing a half shekel, and two bracelets for her arms weighing ten gold shekels, **23** and said, "Please tell me whose daughter you are. Is there room in your father's house for us to spend the night?" **24** She said to him, "I am the daughter of Bethuel the son of Milcah, whom she bore to Nahor." **25** She added, "We have plenty of both straw and fodder, and room to spend the night." **26** The man bowed his head and worshiped the LORD **27** and said, "Blessed be the LORD, the God of my master Abraham, who has not forsaken his steadfast love and his faithfulness toward my master. As for me, the LORD has led me in the way to the house of my master's kinsmen." **28** Then the young woman ran and told her mother's household about these things.

29 Rebekah had a brother whose name was Laban. Laban ran out toward the man, to the spring. **30** As soon as he saw the ring and the bracelets on his sister's arms, and heard the words of Rebekah his sister, "Thus the man spoke to me," he went to the man. And behold, he was standing by the camels at the spring. **31** He said, "Come in, O blessed of the LORD. Why do you stand outside? For I have prepared the house and a place for the camels." **32** So the man came to the house and unharnessed the camels, and gave straw and fodder to the camels, and there was water to wash his feet and the feet of the men who were with him. **33** Then food was set before him to eat. But he said, "I will not eat until I have said what I have to say." He said, "Speak on."

34 So he said, "I am Abraham's servant. **35** The LORD has greatly blessed my master, and he has become great. He has given him flocks and herds, silver and gold, male servants and female servants, camels and donkeys. **36** And Sarah my master's wife bore a son to my master when she was old, and to him he has given all that he has. **37** My master made me swear, saying, 'You shall not take a wife for my son from the daughters of the Canaanites, in whose land I dwell, **38** but you shall go to my father's house and to my clan and take a wife for my son.' **39** I said to my master, 'Perhaps the woman will not follow me.' **40** But he said to me, 'The LORD, before whom I have walked, will send his

angel with you and prosper your way. You shall take a wife for my son from my clan and from my father's house. **41** Then you will be free from my oath, when you come to my clan. And if they will not give her to you, you will be free from my oath.'

42 "I came today to the spring and said, 'O LORD, the God of my master Abraham, if now you are prospering the way that I go, **43** behold, I am standing by the spring of water. Let the virgin who comes out to draw water, to whom I shall say, "Please give me a little water from your jar to drink," **44** and who will say to me, "Drink, and I will draw for your camels also," let her be the woman whom the LORD has appointed for my master's son.'

45 "Before I had finished speaking in my heart, behold, Rebekah came out with her water jar on her shoulder, and she went down to the spring and drew water. I said

> ### GETTING THE MESSAGE
>
> **Family ties.** Laban took responsibility for his sister Rebekah (24:29–51). Apparently their father, who was still alive, was unable to do so.

to her, 'Please let me drink.' **46** She quickly let down her jar from her shoulder and said, 'Drink, and I will give your camels drink also.' So I drank, and she gave the camels drink also. **47** Then I asked her, 'Whose daughter are you?' She said, 'The daughter of Bethuel, Nahor's son, whom Milcah bore to him.' So I put the ring on her nose and the bracelets on her arms. **48** Then I bowed my head and worshiped the LORD and blessed the LORD, the God of my master Abraham, who had led me by the right way to take the daughter of my master's kinsman for his son. **49** Now then, if you are going to show steadfast love and faithfulness to my master, tell me; and if not, tell me, that I may turn to the right hand or to the left."

50 Then Laban and Bethuel answered and said, "The thing has come from the LORD; we cannot speak to you bad or good. **51** Behold, Rebekah is before you; take her and go, and let her be the wife of your master's son, as the LORD has spoken."

⁵² When Abraham's servant heard their words, he bowed himself to the earth before the LORD. ⁵³ And the servant brought out jewelry of silver and of gold, and garments, and gave them to Rebekah. He also gave to her brother and to her mother costly ornaments. ⁵⁴ And he and the men who were with him ate and drank, and they spent the night there. When they arose in the morning, he said, "Send me away to my master." ⁵⁵ Her brother and her mother said, "Let the young woman remain with us a while, at least ten days; after that she may go." ⁵⁶ But he said to

PROFILE

REBEKAH

Because he did not want Isaac to marry a Canaanite, Abraham sent his servant to Mesopotamia to find a wife for his son. The servant prayed for a sign to help him recognize the woman God had appointed for this purpose. Rebekah's actions were the precise answer to the servant's prayer. She was beautiful and hospitable, and in an act of faith she left her country and her family so that she could journey to Canaan and marry Isaac. Like Sarah, Rebekah was barren. Isaac prayed on her behalf, and God heard his prayer. Rebekah gave birth to Jacob and Esau. Favoring Jacob above his brother, Rebekah instructed him to trick his father into giving him the blessing intended for Esau.

KEY REFERENCE: GENESIS 25:23

them, "Do not delay me, since the LORD has prospered my way. Send me away that I may go to my master." ⁵⁷ They said, "Let us call the young woman and ask her." ⁵⁸ And they called Rebekah and said to her, "Will you go with this man?" She said, "I will go." ⁵⁹ So they sent away Rebekah their sister and her nurse, and Abraham's servant and his men. ⁶⁰ And they blessed Rebekah and said to her,

"Our sister, may you become
    thousands of ten thousands,
and may your offspring possess
    the gate of those who hate him!"

⁶¹ Then Rebekah and her young women arose and rode on the camels and followed the man. Thus the servant took Rebekah and went his way.

⁶² Now Isaac had returned from Beer-lahai-roi and was dwelling in the Negeb. ⁶³ And Isaac went out to meditate in the field toward evening. And he lifted up his eyes and saw, and behold, there were camels coming. ⁶⁴ And Rebekah lifted up her eyes, and when she saw Isaac, she dismounted from the camel ⁶⁵ and said to the servant, "Who is that man, walking in the field to meet us?" The servant said, "It is my master." So she took her veil and covered herself. ⁶⁶ And the servant told Isaac all the things that he had done. ⁶⁷ Then Isaac brought her into the tent of Sarah his mother and took Rebekah, and she became his wife, and he loved her. So Isaac was comforted after his mother's death.

Abraham's Death and His Descendants

25 Abraham took another wife, whose name was Keturah. ² She bore him Zimran, Jokshan, Medan, Midian, Ishbak, and Shuah. ³ Jokshan fathered Sheba and Dedan. The sons of Dedan were Asshurim, Letushim, and Leummim. ⁴ The sons of Midian were Ephah, Epher, Hanoch, Abida, and Eldaah. All these were the children of Keturah. ⁵ Abraham gave all he had to Isaac. ⁶ But to the sons of his concubines Abraham gave gifts, and while he was still living he sent them away from his son Isaac, eastward to the east country.

⁷ These are the days of the years of Abraham's life, 175 years. ⁸ Abraham breathed his last and died in a good old age, an old man and full of years, and was gathered to his people. ⁹ Isaac and Ishmael his sons buried him in the cave of Machpelah, in the field of Ephron the son of Zohar the Hittite, east of Mamre, ¹⁰ the field that Abraham purchased from the Hittites. There Abraham was buried, with Sarah his wife. ¹¹ After the death of Abraham, God blessed Isaac his son. And Isaac settled at Beer-lahai-roi.

¹² These are the generations of Ishmael, Abraham's son, whom Hagar the Egyptian, Sarah's servant, bore to Abraham. ¹³ These are the names of the sons of Ishmael, named in the order of their birth: Nebaioth, the firstborn of Ishmael; and Kedar, Adbeel, Mibsam, ¹⁴ Mishma, Dumah, Massa, ¹⁵ Hadad, Tema,

Jetur, Naphish, and Kedemah. **16** These are the sons of Ishmael and these are their names, by their villages and by their encampments, twelve princes according to their tribes. **17** (These are the years of the life of Ishmael: 137 years. He breathed his last and died, and was gathered to his people.) **18** They settled from Havilah to Shur, which is opposite Egypt in the direction of Assyria. He settled over against all his kinsmen.

The Birth of Esau and Jacob

19 These are the generations of Isaac, Abraham's son: Abraham fathered Isaac, **20** and Isaac was forty years old when he took Rebekah, the daughter of Bethuel the Aramean of Paddan-aram, the sister of Laban the Aramean, to be his wife. **21** And Isaac prayed to the LORD for his wife, because she was barren. And the LORD granted his prayer, and Rebekah his wife conceived. **22** The children struggled together within her, and she said, "If it is thus, why is this happening to me?" So she went to inquire of the LORD. **23** And the LORD said to her,

> "Two nations are in your womb,
>   and two peoples from within you
>   shall be divided;
>   the one shall be stronger than the
>   other,
>   the older shall serve the younger."

24 When her days to give birth were completed, behold, there were twins in her womb. **25** The first came out red, all his body like a hairy cloak, so they called his name Esau. **26** Afterward his brother came out with his hand holding Esau's heel, so his name was called Jacob.[1] Isaac was sixty years old when she bore them.

27 When the boys grew up, Esau was a skillful hunter, a man of the field, while Jacob was a quiet man, dwelling in tents. **28** Isaac loved Esau because he ate of his game, but Rebekah loved Jacob.

Esau Sells His Birthright

29 Once when Jacob was cooking stew, Esau came in from the field, and he was exhausted. **30** And Esau said to Jacob, "Let me eat some of that red stew, for I am exhausted!" (Therefore his name was called Edom.[2]) **31** Jacob said, "Sell me your birthright now." **32** Esau said, "I am about to die; of

what use is a birthright to me?" **33** Jacob said, "Swear to me now." So he swore to him and sold his birthright to Jacob. **34** Then Jacob gave Esau bread and lentil stew, and he ate and drank and rose and went his way. Thus Esau despised his birthright.

God's Promise to Isaac

26 Now there was a famine in the land, besides the former famine that was in the days of Abraham. And Isaac went to Gerar to Abimelech king of the Philistines. **2** And the LORD appeared to him and said, "Do not go down to Egypt; dwell in the land of which I shall tell you. **3** Sojourn in this land, and I will be with you and will bless you, for to you and to your offspring I will give all these lands, and I will establish the oath that I swore to Abraham your father. **4** I will multiply your offspring as the stars

GETTING THE MESSAGE

Tents (25:27) were temporary shelters made of cloth and were often woven from black goat's hair. The tent was held up by ropes and poles. Most tents were rectangular in shape. Because nomadic families moved often, they had little furniture. Tents still provide housing for nomadic peoples living in the Middle East today.

of heaven and will give to your offspring all these lands, and in your offspring all the nations of the earth shall be blessed, **5** because Abraham obeyed my voice and kept my charge, my commandments, my statutes, and my laws."

Isaac and Abimelech

6 So Isaac settled in Gerar. **7** When the men of the place asked him about his wife, he said, "She is my sister," for he feared to say, "My wife," thinking, "lest the men of the place should kill me because of Rebekah," because she was attractive in appearance. **8** When he had been there a long time, Abimelech king of the Philistines looked out of a window and saw Isaac laughing with Rebekah his wife. **9** So Abimelech called Isaac and said, "Behold, she is your wife. How then could you say, 'She is my sister'?"

---

[1] *Jacob* means *He takes by the heel,* or *He cheats* [2] *Edom* sounds like the Hebrew for *red*

Isaac said to him, "Because I thought, 'Lest I die because of her.'" [10] Abimelech said, "What is this you have done to us? One of the people might easily have lain with your wife, and you would have brought guilt upon us." [11] So Abimelech warned all the people, saying, "Whoever touches this man or his wife shall surely be put to death."

[12] And Isaac sowed in that land and reaped in the same year a hundredfold. The LORD blessed him, [13] and the man became rich, and gained more and more until he became very wealthy. [14] He had possessions of flocks and herds and many servants, so that the Philistines envied him. [15] (Now the Philistines had stopped and filled with earth all the wells that his father's servants had dug in the days of Abraham his father.) [16] And Abimelech said to Isaac, "Go away from us, for you are much mightier than we."

> ### GETTING THE MESSAGE
>
> **A father's blessing** (ch. 27) was not just a symbolic gesture. It established the identity of the heir, granting him all the privileges of that position. The father's blessing was even seen as in some way shaping his future.

[17] So Isaac departed from there and encamped in the Valley of Gerar and settled there. [18] And Isaac dug again the wells of water that had been dug in the days of Abraham his father, which the Philistines had stopped after the death of Abraham. And he gave them the names that his father had given them. [19] But when Isaac's servants dug in the valley and found there a well of spring water, [20] the herdsmen of Gerar quarreled with Isaac's herdsmen, saying, "The water is ours." So he called the name of the well Esek,[1] because they contended with him. [21] Then they dug another well, and they quarreled over that also, so he called its name Sitnah.[2] [22] And he moved from there and dug another well, and they did not quarrel over it. So he called its name Rehoboth,[3] saying, "For now the LORD has made room for us, and we shall be fruitful in the land."

[23] From there he went up to Beersheba. [24] And the LORD appeared to him the same night and said, "I am the God of Abraham your father. Fear not, for I am with you and will bless you and multiply your offspring for my servant Abraham's sake." [25] So he built an altar there and called upon the name of the LORD and pitched his tent there. And there Isaac's servants dug a well.

[26] When Abimelech went to him from Gerar with Ahuzzath his adviser and Phicol the commander of his army, [27] Isaac said to them, "Why have you come to me, seeing that you hate me and have sent me away from you?" [28] They said, "We see plainly that the LORD has been with you. So we said, let there be a sworn pact between us, between you and us, and let us make a covenant with you, [29] that you will do us no harm, just as we have not touched you and have done to you nothing but good and have sent you away in peace. You are now the blessed of the LORD." [30] So he made them a feast, and they ate and drank. [31] In the morning they rose early and exchanged oaths. And Isaac sent them on their way, and they departed from him in peace. [32] That same day Isaac's servants came and told him about the well that they had dug and said to him, "We have found water." [33] He called it Shibah;[4] therefore the name of the city is Beersheba to this day.

[34] When Esau was forty years old, he took Judith the daughter of Beeri the Hittite to be his wife, and Basemath the daughter of Elon the Hittite, [35] and they made life bitter for Isaac and Rebekah.

Isaac Blesses Jacob

27 When Isaac was old and his eyes were dim so that he could not see, he called Esau his older son and said to him, "My son"; and he answered, "Here I am." [2] He said, "Behold, I am old; I do not know the day of my death. [3] Now then, take your weapons, your quiver and your bow, and go out to the field and hunt game for me, [4] and prepare for me delicious food, such as I love, and bring it to me so that I may eat, that my soul may bless you before I die."

[5] Now Rebekah was listening when Isaac spoke to his son Esau. So when Esau went to the field to hunt for game and bring it, [6] Rebekah said to her son Jacob, "I heard your father speak to your brother Esau, [7] 'Bring me game and prepare for me delicious food, that I may eat it and bless you before the

---

[1] *Esek* means *contention* [2] *Sitnah* means *enmity* [3] *Rehoboth* means *broad places*, or *room* [4] *Shibah* sounds like the Hebrew for *oath*

LORD before I die.' **8** Now therefore, my son, obey my voice as I command you. **9** Go to the flock and bring me two good young goats, so that I may prepare from them delicious food for your father, such as he loves. **10** And you shall bring it to your father to eat, so that he may bless you before he dies." **11** But Jacob said to Rebekah his mother, "Behold, my brother Esau is a hairy man, and I am a smooth man. **12** Perhaps my father will feel me, and I shall seem to be mocking him and bring a curse upon myself and not a blessing." **13** His mother said to him, "Let your curse be on me, my son; only obey my voice, and go, bring them to me."

14 So he went and took them and brought them to his mother, and his mother prepared delicious food, such as his father loved. **15** Then Rebekah took the best garments of Esau her older son, which were with her in the house, and put them on Jacob her younger son. **16** And the skins of the young goats she put on his hands and on the smooth part of his neck. **17** And she put the delicious food and the bread, which she had prepared, into the hand of her son Jacob.

18 So he went in to his father and said, "My father." And he said, "Here I am. Who are you, my son?" **19** Jacob said to his father, "I am Esau your firstborn. I have done as you told me; now sit up and eat of my game, that your soul may bless me." **20** But Isaac said to his son, "How is it that you have found it so quickly, my son?" He answered, "Because the LORD your God granted me success." **21** Then Isaac said to Jacob, "Please come near, that I may feel you, my son, to know whether you are really my son Esau or not." **22** So Jacob went near to Isaac his father, who felt him and said, "The voice is Jacob's voice, but the hands are the hands of Esau." **23** And he did not recognize him, because his hands were hairy like his brother Esau's hands. So he blessed him. **24** He said, "Are you really my son Esau?" He answered, "I am." **25** Then he said, "Bring it near to me, that I may eat of my son's game and bless you." So he brought it near to him, and he ate; and he brought him wine, and he drank. **26** Then his father Isaac said to him, "Come near and kiss me, my son." **27** So he came near and kissed him. And Isaac smelled the smell of his garments and blessed him and said,

"See, the smell of my son
   is as the smell of a field that the
      LORD has blessed!
28 May God give you of the dew of heaven
   and of the fatness of the earth
   and plenty of grain and wine.
29 Let peoples serve you,
   and nations bow down to you.
Be lord over your brothers,
   and may your mother's sons bow
      down to you.
Cursed be everyone who curses you,
   and blessed be everyone who
      blesses you!"

PROFILE
ESAU

Esau, whose name means "hairy," was the son of Isaac and Rebekah and the elder twin brother of Jacob. Esau was a skillful hunter and his father's favorite son, but he brought misery upon his parents by marrying two Hittite women. Esau carelessly sold his birthright to Jacob for a bowl of stew. Jacob then tricked Isaac into giving him the blessing intended for his brother. In response, Esau tried to kill Jacob. Years later, however, Jacob and Esau were reconciled. Esau founded the nation of Edom, which became an enemy of Israel. Jacob the chosen one and Esau the one not chosen typify the age-long struggle between the people of God and their adversaries.

KEY REFERENCE: GENESIS 27:36

30 As soon as Isaac had finished blessing Jacob, when Jacob had scarcely gone out from the presence of Isaac his father, Esau his brother came in from his hunting. **31** He also prepared delicious food and brought it to his father. And he said to his father, "Let my father arise and eat of his son's game, that you may bless me." **32** His father Isaac said to him, "Who are you?" He answered, "I am your son, your firstborn, Esau." **33** Then Isaac trembled very violently and said, "Who was it then that hunted game and brought it to me, and I ate it all before you came, and I have blessed him? Yes, and he shall be blessed." **34** As soon as Esau heard the words of his father, he cried out with an exceedingly great and bitter cry and said to his father, "Bless me, even me also, O my father!" **35** But he said, "Your brother came deceitfully, and he has taken away your blessing." **36** Esau said, "Is he not rightly named Jacob?[1] For he has cheated me these two times. He took away my birthright, and behold, now he has taken away my blessing." Then he said, "Have you not reserved a blessing for me?" **37** Isaac answered and said to Esau, "Behold, I have made him lord over you, and all his brothers I have given to him for servants, and with grain and wine I have sustained him. What then can I do for you, my son?" **38** Esau said to his father, "Have you but one blessing, my father? Bless me, even me also, O my father." And Esau lifted up his voice and wept.

39 Then Isaac his father answered and said to him:

> "Behold, away from the fatness of the
>   earth shall your dwelling be,
>   and away from the dew of heaven
>   on high.
> **40** By your sword you shall live,
>   and you shall serve your brother;
>   but when you grow restless
>   you shall break his yoke from your
>   neck."

41 Now Esau hated Jacob because of the blessing with which his father had blessed him, and Esau said to himself, "The days of mourning for my father are approaching; then I will kill my brother Jacob." **42** But the words of Esau her older son were told to Rebekah. So she sent and called Jacob her younger son and said to him, "Behold, your brother Esau comforts himself about you by planning to kill you. **43** Now therefore, my son, obey my voice. Arise, flee to Laban my brother in Haran **44** and stay with him a while, until your brother's fury turns away— **45** until your brother's anger turns away from you, and he forgets what you have done to him. Then I will send and bring you from there. Why should I be bereft of you both in one day?"

46 Then Rebekah said to Isaac, "I loathe my life because of the Hittite women. If Jacob marries one of the Hittite women like these, one of the women of the land, what good will my life be to me?"

Jacob Sent to Laban

28 Then Isaac called Jacob and blessed him and directed him, "You must not take a wife from the Canaanite women. **2** Arise, go to Paddan-aram to the house of Bethuel your mother's father, and take as your wife from there one of the daughters of Laban your mother's brother. **3** God Almighty bless you and make you fruitful and multiply you, that you may become a company of peoples. **4** May he give the blessing of Abraham to you and to your offspring with you, that you may take possession of the land of your sojournings that God gave to Abraham!" **5** Thus Isaac sent Jacob away. And he went to Paddan-aram, to Laban, the son of Bethuel the Aramean, the brother of Rebekah, Jacob's and Esau's mother.

Esau Marries an Ishmaelite

6 Now Esau saw that Isaac had blessed Jacob and sent him away to Paddan-aram to take a wife from there, and that as he blessed him he directed him, "You must not take a wife from the Canaanite women," **7** and that Jacob had obeyed his father and his mother and gone to Paddan-aram. **8** So when Esau saw that the Canaanite women did not please Isaac his father, **9** Esau went to Ishmael and took as his wife, besides the wives he had, Mahalath the daughter of Ishmael, Abraham's son, the sister of Nebaioth.

Jacob's Dream

10 Jacob left Beersheba and went toward Haran. **11** And he came to a certain place and stayed there that night, because the sun had set. Taking one of the stones of the place, he put it under his head and lay down in that place to sleep. **12** And he dreamed, and behold, there was a ladder set up on the earth, and the top of it reached to heaven. And behold, the angels of God were ascending and descending on it! **13** And behold, the LORD stood above it and said, "I am the LORD, the God of Abraham your father and the God of Isaac. The land on which you lie I will give to you and to your offspring. **14** Your offspring shall be like the dust of the earth, and you shall spread abroad to the west and

[1] *Jacob* means *He takes by the heel*, or *He cheats*

to the east and to the north and to the south, and in you and your offspring shall all the families of the earth be blessed. ¹⁵ Behold, I am with you and will keep you wherever you go, and will bring you back to this land. For I will not leave you until I have done what I have promised you." ¹⁶ Then Jacob awoke from his sleep and said, "Surely the LORD is in this place, and I did not know it." ¹⁷ And he was afraid and said, "How awesome is this place! This is none other than the house of God, and this is the gate of heaven."

¹⁸ So early in the morning Jacob took the stone that he had put under his head and set it up for a pillar and poured oil on the top of it. ¹⁹ He called the name of that place Bethel,¹ but the name of the city was Luz at the first. ²⁰ Then Jacob made a vow, saying, "If God will be with me and will keep me in this way that I go, and will give me bread to eat and clothing to wear, ²¹ so that I come again to my father's house in peace, then the LORD shall be my God, ²² and this stone, which I have set up for a pillar, shall be God's house. And of all that you give me I will give a full tenth to you."

Jacob Marries Leah and Rachel

29 Then Jacob went on his journey and came to the land of the people of the east. ² As he looked, he saw a well in the field, and behold, three flocks of sheep lying beside it, for out of that well the flocks were watered. The stone on the well's mouth was large, ³ and when all the flocks were gathered there, the shepherds would roll the stone from the mouth of the well and water the sheep, and put the stone back in its place over the mouth of the well.

⁴ Jacob said to them, "My brothers, where do you come from?" They said, "We are from Haran." ⁵ He said to them, "Do you know Laban the son of Nahor?" They said, "We know him." ⁶ He said to them, "Is it well with him?" They said, "It is well; and see, Rachel his daughter is coming with the sheep!" ⁷ He said, "Behold, it is still high day; it is not time for the livestock to be gathered together. Water the sheep and go, pasture them." ⁸ But they said, "We cannot until all the flocks are gathered together and the stone is rolled from the mouth of the well; then we water the sheep."

⁹ While he was still speaking with them, Rachel came with her father's sheep, for she was a shepherdess. ¹⁰ Now as soon as Jacob saw Rachel the daughter of Laban his mother's brother, and the sheep of Laban his mother's brother, Jacob came near and rolled the stone from the well's mouth and watered the flock of Laban his mother's brother. ¹¹ Then Jacob kissed Rachel and wept aloud. ¹² And Jacob told Rachel that he was her father's kinsman, and that he

PROFILE
RACHEL

Rachel was the daughter of Laban, uncle of Jacob. She became Jacob's wife. Since she was a shepherdess, it is fitting that Rachel's name means "ewe." Rachel was a beautiful woman, and the Bible says that Jacob loved her immediately. So deep was his love for her that after being deceived into marrying her older sister Leah, Jacob promised to work an additional seven years for Laban so that he could marry Rachel as well. There was constant strife between the sisters because Jacob favored Rachel, and because Rachel was envious of Leah's ability to have children. After many years of waiting, however, Rachel gave birth to Joseph and Benjamin. Ruth 4:11 says that Rachel and Leah "together built up the house of Israel."

KEY REFERENCE: GENESIS 29:18, 20

was Rebekah's son, and she ran and told her father.

¹³ As soon as Laban heard the news about Jacob, his sister's son, he ran to meet him and embraced him and kissed him and brought him to his house. Jacob told Laban all these things, ¹⁴ and Laban said to him, "Surely you are my bone and my flesh!" And he stayed with him a month.

¹⁵ Then Laban said to Jacob, "Because you are my kinsman, should you therefore serve me for nothing? Tell me, what shall your wages be?" ¹⁶ Now Laban had two daughters. The name of the older was Leah, and the

¹ Bethel means the house of God

name of the younger was Rachel. [17] Leah's eyes were weak, but Rachel was beautiful in form and appearance. [18] Jacob loved Rachel. And he said, "I will serve you seven years for your younger daughter Rachel." [19] Laban said, "It is better that I give her to you than that I should give her to any other man; stay with me." [20] So Jacob served seven years for Rachel, and they seemed to him but a few days because of the love he had for her.

[21] Then Jacob said to Laban, "Give me my wife that I may go in to her, for my time is completed." [22] So Laban gathered together all the people of the place and made a feast. [23] But in the evening he took his daughter Leah and brought her to Jacob, and he went in to her. [24] (Laban gave his female servant Zilpah to his daughter Leah to be her servant.) [25] And in the morning, behold,

> ▶ **GETTING THE MESSAGE**
>
> **Giving servants** as gifts to the bride (29:24) was very common in Old Testament times. Doing so provided the newly married woman the help she would need in running a household. Having servants also gave the wife a position of status within her community.

it was Leah! And Jacob said to Laban, "What is this you have done to me? Did I not serve with you for Rachel? Why then have you deceived me?" [26] Laban said, "It is not so done in our country, to give the younger before the firstborn. [27] Complete the week of this one, and we will give you the other also in return for serving me another seven years." [28] Jacob did so, and completed her week. Then Laban gave him his daughter Rachel to be his wife. [29] (Laban gave his female servant Bilhah to his daughter Rachel to be her servant.) [30] So Jacob went in to Rachel also, and he loved Rachel more than Leah, and served Laban for another seven years.

Jacob's Children

[31] When the LORD saw that Leah was hated, he opened her womb, but Rachel was barren. [32] And Leah conceived and bore a

son, and she called his name Reuben,[1] for she said, "Because the LORD has looked upon my affliction; for now my husband will love me." [33] She conceived again and bore a son, and said, "Because the LORD has heard that I am hated, he has given me this son also." And she called his name Simeon.[2] [34] Again she conceived and bore a son, and said, "Now this time my husband will be attached to me, because I have borne him three sons." Therefore his name was called Levi.[3] [35] And she conceived again and bore a son, and said, "This time I will praise the LORD." Therefore she called his name Judah.[4] Then she ceased bearing.

30 When Rachel saw that she bore Jacob no children, she envied her sister. She said to Jacob, "Give me children, or I shall die!" [2] Jacob's anger was kindled against Rachel, and he said, "Am I in the place of God, who has withheld from you the fruit of the womb?" [3] Then she said, "Here is my servant Bilhah; go in to her, so that she may give birth on my behalf, that even I may have children through her." [4] So she gave him her servant Bilhah as a wife, and Jacob went in to her. [5] And Bilhah conceived and bore Jacob a son. [6] Then Rachel said, "God has judged me, and has also heard my voice and given me a son." Therefore she called his name Dan.[5] [7] Rachel's servant Bilhah conceived again and bore Jacob a second son. [8] Then Rachel said, "With mighty wrestlings I have wrestled with my sister and have prevailed." So she called his name Naphtali.[6]

[9] When Leah saw that she had ceased bearing children, she took her servant Zilpah and gave her to Jacob as a wife. [10] Then Leah's servant Zilpah bore Jacob a son. [11] And Leah said, "Good fortune has come!" so she called his name Gad.[7] [12] Leah's servant Zilpah bore Jacob a second son. [13] And Leah said, "Happy am I! For women have called me happy." So she called his name Asher.[8]

[14] In the days of wheat harvest Reuben went and found mandrakes in the field and brought them to his mother Leah. Then Rachel said to Leah, "Please give me some of your son's mandrakes." [15] But she said to her, "Is it a small matter that you have taken away my husband? Would you take away my

---

[1] *Reuben* means *See, a son* [2] *Simeon* sounds like the Hebrew for *heard* [3] *Levi* sounds like the Hebrew for *attached* [4] *Judah* sounds like the Hebrew for *praise* [5] *Dan* sounds like the Hebrew for *judged* [6] *Naphtali* sounds like the Hebrew for *wrestling* [7] *Gad* sounds like the Hebrew for *good fortune* [8] *Asher* sounds like the Hebrew for *happy*

son's mandrakes also?" Rachel said, "Then he may lie with you tonight in exchange for your son's mandrakes." **16** When Jacob came from the field in the evening, Leah went out to meet him and said, "You must come in to me, for I have hired you with my son's mandrakes." So he lay with her that night. **17** And God listened to Leah, and she conceived and bore Jacob a fifth son. **18** Leah said, "God has given me my wages because I gave my servant to my husband." So she called his name Issachar.[1]

19 And Leah conceived again, and she bore Jacob a sixth son. **20** Then Leah said, "God has endowed me with a good endowment; now my husband will honor me, because I have borne him six sons." So she called his name Zebulun.[2] **21** Afterward she bore a daughter and called her name Dinah.

22 Then God remembered Rachel, and God listened to her and opened her womb. **23** She conceived and bore a son and said, "God has taken away my reproach." **24** And she called his name Joseph,[3] saying, "May the LORD add to me another son!"

Jacob's Prosperity

25 As soon as Rachel had borne Joseph, Jacob said to Laban, "Send me away, that I may go to my own home and country. **26** Give me my wives and my children for whom I have served you, that I may go, for you know the service that I have given you." **27** But Laban said to him, "If I have found favor in your sight, I have learned by divination that the LORD has blessed me because of you. **28** Name your wages, and I will give it." **29** Jacob said to him, "You yourself know how I have served you, and how your livestock has fared with me. **30** For you had little before I came, and it has increased abundantly, and the LORD has blessed you wherever I turned. But now when shall I provide for my own household also?" **31** He said, "What shall I give you?" Jacob said, "You shall not give me anything. If you will do this for me, I will again pasture your flock and keep it: **32** let me pass through all your flock today, removing from it every speckled and spotted sheep and every black lamb, and the spotted and speckled among the goats, and they shall be my wages. **33** So my honesty will answer for me later, when you come

to look into my wages with you. Every one that is not speckled and spotted among the goats and black among the lambs, if found with me, shall be counted stolen." **34** Laban said, "Good! Let it be as you have said." **35** But that day Laban removed the male goats that were striped and spotted, and all the female goats that were speckled and spotted, every one that had white on it, and every lamb that was black, and put them in the charge of his sons. **36** And he set a distance of three days' journey between himself and Jacob, and Jacob pastured the rest of Laban's flock.

37 Then Jacob took fresh sticks of poplar and almond and plane trees, and peeled white streaks in them, exposing the white of the sticks. **38** He set the sticks that he had peeled in front of the flocks in the troughs, that is, the watering places, where the flocks came to drink. And since they bred when they came to drink, **39** the flocks bred in front of the sticks and so the flocks brought forth striped, speckled, and spotted. **40** And Jacob separated the lambs and set the faces of the flocks toward the striped and all the black in the flock of Laban. He put his own droves apart and did not put them with Laban's flock. **41** Whenever the stronger of the flock were breeding, Jacob would lay the sticks in the troughs before the eyes of the flock, that they might breed among the sticks, **42** but for the feebler of the flock he would not lay them there. So the feebler would be Laban's, and the stronger Jacob's. **43** Thus the man increased greatly and had large flocks, female servants and male servants, and camels and donkeys.

Jacob Flees from Laban

31 Now Jacob heard that the sons of Laban were saying, "Jacob has taken all that was our father's, and from what was our father's he has gained all this wealth." **2** And Jacob saw that Laban did not regard him with favor as before. **3** Then the LORD said to Jacob, "Return to the land of your fathers and to your kindred, and I will be with you."

4 So Jacob sent and called Rachel and Leah into the field where his flock was **5** and said to them, "I see that your father does not regard me with favor as he did before. But the God of my father has been with me. **6** You

[1] *Issachar* sounds like the Hebrew for *wages*, or *hire* [2] *Zebulun* sounds like the Hebrew for *honor* [3] *Joseph* means *May he add*, and sounds like the Hebrew for *taken away*

know that I have served your father with all my strength, **7** yet your father has cheated me and changed my wages ten times. But God did not permit him to harm me. **8** If he said, 'The spotted shall be your wages,' then all the flock bore spotted; and if he said, 'The striped shall be your wages,' then all the flock bore striped. **9** Thus God has taken away the livestock of your father and given them to me. **10** In the breeding season of the flock I lifted up my eyes and saw in a dream that the goats that mated with the flock were striped, spotted, and mottled. **11** Then the angel of God said to me in the dream, 'Jacob,' and I said, 'Here I am!' **12** And he said, 'Lift up your eyes and see, all the goats that mate with the flock are striped, spotted, and mottled, for I have seen all that Laban is doing to you. **13** I am the God of Bethel, where you

> ### GETTING THE MESSAGE
>
> **Why was Laban so upset when his household gods were stolen?** Household gods (31:30) had a more practical use than just idol worship. They served as titles of ownership to one's property and inheritance.

anointed a pillar and made a vow to me. Now arise, go out from this land and return to the land of your kindred.'" **14** Then Rachel and Leah answered and said to him, "Is there any portion or inheritance left to us in our father's house? **15** Are we not regarded by him as foreigners? For he has sold us, and he has indeed devoured our money. **16** All the wealth that God has taken away from our father belongs to us and to our children. Now then, whatever God has said to you, do."

17 So Jacob arose and set his sons and his wives on camels. **18** He drove away all his livestock, all his property that he had gained, the livestock in his possession that he had acquired in Paddan-aram, to go to the land of Canaan to his father Isaac. **19** Laban had gone to shear his sheep, and Rachel stole her father's household gods. **20** And Jacob tricked Laban the Aramean, by not telling him that he intended to flee. **21** He fled with all that he had and arose and crossed

the Euphrates, and set his face toward the hill country of Gilead.

22 When it was told Laban on the third day that Jacob had fled, **23** he took his kinsmen with him and pursued him for seven days and followed close after him into the hill country of Gilead. **24** But God came to Laban the Aramean in a dream by night and said to him, "Be careful not to say anything to Jacob, either good or bad."

25 And Laban overtook Jacob. Now Jacob had pitched his tent in the hill country, and Laban with his kinsmen pitched tents in the hill country of Gilead. **26** And Laban said to Jacob, "What have you done, that you have tricked me and driven away my daughters like captives of the sword? **27** Why did you flee secretly and trick me, and did not tell me, so that I might have sent you away with mirth and songs, with tambourine and lyre? **28** And why did you not permit me to kiss my sons and my daughters farewell? Now you have done foolishly. **29** It is in my power to do you harm. But the God of your father spoke to me last night, saying, 'Be careful not to say anything to Jacob, either good or bad.' **30** And now you have gone away because you longed greatly for your father's house, but why did you steal my gods?" **31** Jacob answered and said to Laban, "Because I was afraid, for I thought that you would take your daughters from me by force. **32** Anyone with whom you find your gods shall not live. In the presence of our kinsmen point out what I have that is yours, and take it." Now Jacob did not know that Rachel had stolen them.

33 So Laban went into Jacob's tent and into Leah's tent and into the tent of the two female servants, but he did not find them. And he went out of Leah's tent and entered Rachel's. **34** Now Rachel had taken the household gods and put them in the camel's saddle and sat on them. Laban felt all about the tent, but did not find them. **35** And she said to her father, "Let not my lord be angry that I cannot rise before you, for the way of women is upon me." So he searched but did not find the household gods.

36 Then Jacob became angry and berated Laban. Jacob said to Laban, "What is my offense? What is my sin, that you have hotly pursued me? **37** For you have felt through all my goods; what have you found of a'' your household goods? Set it here before my kinsmen and your kinsmen, that they may decide between us two. **38** These twenty years I have been with you. Your ewes and your female goats have not miscarried, and I have not eaten the rams of your flocks. **39** What was torn by wild beasts I did not bring to you. I bore the loss of it myself. From my hand you required it, whether stolen by day or stolen by night. **40** There I was: by day the heat consumed me, and the cold by night, and my sleep fled from my eyes. **41** These twenty years I have been in your house. I served you fourteen years for your two daughters, and six years for your flock, and you have changed my wages ten times. **42** If the God of my father, the God of Abraham and the Fear of Isaac, had not been on my side, surely now you would have sent me away empty-handed. God saw my affliction and the labor of my hands and rebuked you last night."

43 Then Laban answered and said to Jacob, "The daughters are my daughters, the children are my children, the flocks are my flocks, and all that you see is mine. But what can I do this day for these my daughters or for their children whom they have borne? **44** Come now, let us make a covenant, you and I. And let it be a witness between you and me." **45** So Jacob took a stone and set it up as a pillar. **46** And Jacob said to his kinsmen, "Gather stones." And they took stones and made a heap, and they ate there by the heap. **47** Laban called it Jegar-sahadutha, but Jacob called it Galeed. **48** Laban said, "This heap is a witness between you and me today." Therefore he named it Galeed, **49** and Mizpah,[1] for he said, "The LORD watch between you and me, when we are out of one another's sight. **50** If you oppress my daughters, or if you take wives besides my daughters, although no one is with us, see, God is witness between you and me."

51 Then Laban said to Jacob, "See this heap and the pillar, which I have set between you and me. **52** This heap is a witness, and the pillar is a witness, that I will not pass over this heap to you, and you will not pass over this heap and this pillar to me, to do harm. **53** The God of Abraham and the God of Nahor, the God of their father, judge between us." So Jacob swore by the Fear of his father Isaac,

54 and Jacob offered a sacrifice in the hill country and called his kinsmen to eat bread. They ate bread and spent the night in the hill country. **55** Early in the morning Laban arose and kissed his grandchildren and his daughters and blessed them. Then Laban departed and returned home.

Jacob Fears Esau

32 Jacob went on his way, and the angels of God met him. **2** And when Jacob saw them he said, "This is God's camp!" So he called the name of that place Mahanaim.[2]

PROFILE

JACOB

Jacob was the son of Isaac and Rebekah. His name means "he grasps the heel" or "he cheats." Jacob used deception to receive the blessing intended for his brother Esau. He then fled to the home of his uncle Laban. When Jacob asked permission to marry Laban's daughter Rachel, Laban agreed but then tricked him into marrying her older sister Leah instead. However, Jacob was allowed to marry Rachel as well, and he eventually became the father of 12 sons and a daughter. As he was returning to Canaan, Jacob wrestled with an angel of the Lord. During this struggle he was given a new name, Israel, which means "struggles with God." Jacob's 12 sons became the 12 tribes of Israel.

KEY REFERENCE: GENESIS 32:27–28

---

3 And Jacob sent messengers before him to Esau his brother in the land of Seir, the country of Edom, **4** instructing them, "Thus you shall say to my lord Esau: Thus says your servant Jacob, 'I have sojourned with Laban and stayed until now. **5** I have oxen, donkeys, flocks, male servants, and female servants. I have sent to tell my lord, in order that I may find favor in your sight.'"

6 And the messengers returned to Jacob, saying, "We came to your brother Esau,

---

[1] *Mizpah* means *watchpost* [2] *Mahanaim* means *two camps*

and he is coming to meet you, and there are four hundred men with him." **7** Then Jacob was greatly afraid and distressed. He divided the people who were with him, and the flocks and herds and camels, into two camps, **8** thinking, "If Esau comes to the one camp and attacks it, then the camp that is left will escape."

9 And Jacob said, "O God of my father Abraham and God of my father Isaac, O LORD who said to me, 'Return to your country and to your kindred, that I may do you good,' **10** I am not worthy of the least of all the deeds of steadfast love and all the faithfulness that you have shown to your servant, for with only my staff I crossed this Jordan, and now I have become two camps. **11** Please deliver me from the hand of my brother, from the hand of Esau, for I fear him, that he may come and attack me, the mothers with the children. **12** But you said, 'I will surely do you

GETTING THE MESSAGE

The Jabbok River. The Hebrew word for "wrestle" is *abbaq*. This has led many scholars to believe that the Jabbok River (32:22) was named after Jacob's famous wrestling match with God.

good, and make your offspring as the sand of the sea, which cannot be numbered for multitude.'"

13 So he stayed there that night, and from what he had with him he took a present for his brother Esau, **14** two hundred female goats and twenty male goats, two hundred ewes and twenty rams, **15** thirty milking camels and their calves, forty cows and ten bulls, twenty female donkeys and ten male donkeys. **16** These he handed over to his servants, every drove by itself, and said to his servants, "Pass on ahead of me and put a space between drove and drove." **17** He instructed the first, "When Esau my brother meets you and asks you, 'To whom do you belong? Where are you going? And whose are these ahead of you?' **18** then you shall say, 'They belong to your servant Jacob. They are a present sent to my lord Esau. And moreover, he is behind us.'" **19** He likewise instructed the second and the third

and all who followed the droves, "You shall say the same thing to Esau when you find him, **20** and you shall say, 'Moreover, your servant Jacob is behind us.'" For he thought, "I may appease him with the present that goes ahead of me, and afterward I shall see his face. Perhaps he will accept me." **21** So the present passed on ahead of him, and he himself stayed that night in the camp.

Jacob Wrestles with God

22 The same night he arose and took his two wives, his two female servants, and his eleven children, and crossed the ford of the Jabbok. **23** He took them and sent them across the stream, and everything else that he had. **24** And Jacob was left alone. And a man wrestled with him until the breaking of the day. **25** When the man saw that he did not prevail against Jacob, he touched his hip socket, and Jacob's hip was put out of joint as he wrestled with him. **26** Then he said, "Let me go, for the day has broken." But Jacob said, "I will not let you go unless you bless me." **27** And he said to him, "What is your name?" And he said, "Jacob." **28** Then he said, "Your name shall no longer be called Jacob, but Israel,[1] for you have striven with God and with men, and have prevailed." **29** Then Jacob asked him, "Please tell me your name." But he said, "Why is it that you ask my name?" And there he blessed him. **30** So Jacob called the name of the place Peniel,[2] saying, "For I have seen God face to face, and yet my life has been delivered." **31** The sun rose upon him as he passed Penuel, limping because of his hip. **32** Therefore to this day the people of Israel do not eat the sinew of the thigh that is on the hip socket, because he touched the socket of Jacob's hip on the sinew of the thigh.

Jacob Meets Esau

33 And Jacob lifted up his eyes and looked, and behold, Esau was coming, and four hundred men with him. So he divided the children among Leah and Rachel and the two female servants. **2** And he put the servants with their children in front, then Leah with her children, and Rachel and Joseph last of all. **3** He himself went on before them, bowing himself to the ground seven times, until he came near to his brother.

---

[1] *Israel* means *He strives with God*, or *God strives* [2] *Peniel* means *the face of God*

⁴ But Esau ran to meet him and embraced him and fell on his neck and kissed him, and they wept. ⁵ And when Esau lifted up his eyes and saw the women and children, he said, "Who are these with you?" Jacob said, "The children whom God has graciously given your servant." ⁶ Then the servants drew near, they and their children, and bowed down. ⁷ Leah likewise and her children drew near and bowed down. And last Joseph and Rachel drew near, and they bowed down. ⁸ Esau said, "What do you mean by all this company that I met?" Jacob answered, "To find favor in the sight of my lord." ⁹ But Esau said, "I have enough, my brother; keep what you have for yourself." ¹⁰ Jacob said, "No, please, if I have found favor in your sight, then accept my present from my hand. For I have seen your face, which is like seeing the face of God, and you have accepted me. ¹¹ Please accept my blessing that is brought to you, because God has dealt graciously with me, and because I have enough." Thus he urged him, and he took it.

¹² Then Esau said, "Let us journey on our way, and I will go ahead of you." ¹³ But Jacob said to him, "My lord knows that the children are frail, and that the nursing flocks and herds are a care to me. If they are driven hard for one day, all the flocks will die. ¹⁴ Let my lord pass on ahead of his servant, and I will lead on slowly, at the pace of the livestock that are ahead of me and at the pace of the children, until I come to my lord in Seir." ¹⁵ So Esau said, "Let me leave with you some of the people who are with me." But he said, "What need is there? Let me find favor in the sight of my lord." ¹⁶ So Esau returned that day on his way to Seir. ¹⁷ But Jacob journeyed to Succoth, and built himself a house and made booths for his livestock. Therefore the name of the place is called Succoth.[1]

¹⁸ And Jacob came safely to the city of Shechem, which is in the land of Canaan, on his way from Paddan-aram, and he camped before the city. ¹⁹ And from the sons of Hamor, Shechem's father, he bought for a hundred pieces of money the piece of land on which he had pitched his tent. ²⁰ There he erected an altar and called it El-Elohe-Israel.[2]

The Defiling of Dinah

34 Now Dinah the daughter of Leah, whom she had borne to Jacob, went out to see the women of the land. ² And when Shechem the son of Hamor the Hivite, the prince of the land, saw her, he seized her and lay with her and humiliated her. ³ And his soul was drawn to Dinah the daughter of Jacob. He loved the young woman and spoke tenderly to her. ⁴ So Shechem spoke to his father Hamor, saying, "Get me this girl for my wife."

⁵ Now Jacob heard that he had defiled his daughter Dinah. But his sons were with his livestock in the field, so Jacob held his peace until they came. ⁶ And Hamor the father of Shechem went out to Jacob to speak with him. ⁷ The sons of Jacob had come in from the field as soon as they heard of it, and the

GETTING THE MESSAGE

The name **Succoth** (33:17) means "booths." A booth was a temporary dwelling resembling a tent or a hut. Most of the people around Succoth were nomads, and they probably lived in tents or booths.

men were indignant and very angry, because he had done an outrageous thing in Israel by lying with Jacob's daughter, for such a thing must not be done.

⁸ But Hamor spoke with them, saying, "The soul of my son Shechem longs for your daughter. Please give her to him to be his wife. ⁹ Make marriages with us. Give your daughters to us, and take our daughters for yourselves. ¹⁰ You shall dwell with us, and the land shall be open to you. Dwell and trade in it, and get property in it." ¹¹ Shechem also said to her father and to her brothers, "Let me find favor in your eyes, and whatever you say to me I will give. ¹² Ask me for as great a bride price[3] and gift as you will, and I will give whatever you say to me. Only give me the young woman to be my wife."

¹³ The sons of Jacob answered Shechem and his father Hamor deceitfully, because he had defiled their sister Dinah. ¹⁴ They said to them, "We cannot do this thing, to give our sister to one who is uncircumcised, for

---

[1] *Succoth* means *booths* [2] *El-Elohe-Israel* means *God, the God of Israel* [3] That is, money paid by the groom to the bride's family

that would be a disgrace to us. [15] Only on this condition will we agree with you—that you will become as we are by every male among you being circumcised. [16] Then we will give our daughters to you, and we will take your daughters to ourselves, and we will dwell with you and become one people. [17] But if you will not listen to us and be circumcised, then we will take our daughter, and we will be gone."

[18] Their words pleased Hamor and Hamor's son Shechem. [19] And the young man did not delay to do the thing, because he delighted in Jacob's daughter. Now he was the most honored of all his father's house. [20] So Hamor and his son Shechem came to the gate of their city and spoke to the men of their city, saying, [21] "These men are at peace

GETTING THE MESSAGE

Terebinths are huge, spreading trees that grow to a height of 20–26 feet (6–8 m). They have reddish-green leaves and red berries that grow in clusters. A perfumed, oily resin flows out of the bark when it is cut. Terebinths grow in hot, dry places, and were thus a source of welcome shade to the people of the Bible (35:4; Hos. 4:13).

with us; let them dwell in the land and trade in it, for behold, the land is large enough for them. Let us take their daughters as wives, and let us give them our daughters. [22] Only on this condition will the men agree to dwell with us to become one people—when every male among us is circumcised as they are circumcised. [23] Will not their livestock, their property and all their beasts be ours? Only let us agree with them, and they will dwell with us." [24] And all who went out of the gate of his city listened to Hamor and his son Shechem, and every male was circumcised, all who went out of the gate of his city.

[25] On the third day, when they were sore, two of the sons of Jacob, Simeon and Levi, Dinah's brothers, took their swords and came against the city while it felt secure and killed all the males. [26] They killed Hamor and his son Shechem with the sword and took Dinah out of Shechem's

house and went away. [27] The sons of Jacob came upon the slain and plundered the city, because they had defiled their sister. [28] They took their flocks and their herds, their donkeys, and whatever was in the city and in the field. [29] All their wealth, all their little ones and their wives, all that was in the houses, they captured and plundered.

[30] Then Jacob said to Simeon and Levi, "You have brought trouble on me by making me stink to the inhabitants of the land, the Canaanites and the Perizzites. My numbers are few, and if they gather themselves against me and attack me, I shall be destroyed, both I and my household." [31] But they said, "Should he treat our sister like a prostitute?"

God Blesses and Renames Jacob

35 God said to Jacob, "Arise, go up to Bethel and dwell there. Make an altar there to the God who appeared to you when you fled from your brother Esau. [2] So Jacob said to his household and to all who were with him, "Put away the foreign gods that are among you and purify yourselves and change your garments. [3] Then let us arise and go up to Bethel, so that I may make there an altar to the God who answers me in the day of my distress and has been with me wherever I have gone." [4] So they gave to Jacob all the foreign gods that they had, and the rings that were in their ears. Jacob hid them under the terebinth tree that was near Shechem.

[5] And as they journeyed, a terror from God fell upon the cities that were around them, so that they did not pursue the sons of Jacob. [6] And Jacob came to Luz (that is, Bethel), which is in the land of Canaan, he and all the people who were with him, [7] and there he built an altar and called the place El-bethel,[1] because there God had revealed himself to him when he fled from his brother. [8] And Deborah, Rebekah's nurse, died, and she was buried under an oak below Bethel. So he called its name Allon-bacuth.[2]

[9] God appeared to Jacob again, when he came from Paddan-aram, and blessed him. [10] And God said to him, "Your name is Jacob; no longer shall your name be called Jacob, but Israel shall be your name." So he called his name Israel. [11] And God said to him, "I am God Almighty: be fruitful and multiply. A nation and a company of nations shall come from you, and kings shall come

---

[1] El-bethel means God of Bethel [2] Allon-bacuth means oak of weeping

from your own body. [12] The land that I gave to Abraham and Isaac I will give to you, and I will give the land to your offspring after you." [13] Then God went up from him in the place where he had spoken with him. [14] And Jacob set up a pillar in the place where he had spoken with him, a pillar of stone. He poured out a drink offering on it and poured oil on it. [15] So Jacob called the name of the place where God had spoken with him Bethel.

The Deaths of Rachel and Isaac

[16] Then they journeyed from Bethel. When they were still some distance from Ephrath, Rachel went into labor, and she had hard labor. [17] And when her labor was at its hardest, the midwife said to her, "Do not fear, for you have another son." [18] And as her soul was departing (for she was dying), she called his name Ben-oni;[1] but his father called him Benjamin.[2] [19] So Rachel died, and she was buried on the way to Ephrath (that is, Bethlehem), [20] and Jacob set up a pillar over her tomb. It is the pillar of Rachel's tomb, which is there to this day. [21] Israel journeyed on and pitched his tent beyond the tower of Eder.

[22] While Israel lived in that land, Reuben went and lay with Bilhah his father's concubine. And Israel heard of it.

Now the sons of Jacob were twelve. [23] The sons of Leah: Reuben (Jacob's firstborn), Simeon, Levi, Judah, Issachar, and Zebulun. [24] The sons of Rachel: Joseph and Benjamin. [25] The sons of Bilhah, Rachel's servant: Dan and Naphtali. [26] The sons of Zilpah, Leah's servant: Gad and Asher. These were the sons of Jacob who were born to him in Paddan-aram.

[27] And Jacob came to his father Isaac at Mamre, or Kiriath-arba (that is, Hebron), where Abraham and Isaac had sojourned. [28] Now the days of Isaac were 180 years. [29] And Isaac breathed his last, and he died and was gathered to his people, old and full of days. And his sons Esau and Jacob buried him.

Esau's Descendants

36 These are the generations of Esau (that is, Edom). [2] Esau took his wives from the Canaanites: Adah the daughter of Elon the Hittite, Oholibamah the daughter of Anah the daughter of Zibeon the Hivite, [3] and Basemath, Ishmael's daughter, the sister of Nebaioth. [4] And Adah bore to Esau, Eliphaz; Basemath bore Reuel; [5] and Oholibamah bore Jeush, Jalam, and Korah. These are the sons of Esau who were born to him in the land of Canaan.

[6] Then Esau took his wives, his sons, his daughters, and all the members of his household, his livestock, all his beasts, and all his property that he had acquired in the land of Canaan. He went into a land away from his brother Jacob. [7] For their possessions were too great for them to dwell together. The land of their sojournings could not support them because of their livestock. [8] So Esau settled in the hill country of Seir. (Esau is Edom.)

[9] These are the generations of Esau the father of the Edomites in the hill country of Seir. [10] These are the names of Esau's sons: Eliphaz the son of Adah the wife of Esau, Reuel the son of Basemath the wife of Esau. [11] The sons of Eliphaz were Teman, Omar, Zepho, Gatam, and Kenaz. [12] (Timna was a concubine of Eliphaz, Esau's son; she bore Amalek to Eliphaz.) These are the sons of Adah, Esau's wife. [13] These are the sons of Reuel: Nahath, Zerah, Shammah, and Mizzah. These are the sons of Basemath, Esau's wife. [14] These are the sons of Oholibamah the daughter of Anah the daughter of Zibeon, Esau's wife: she bore to Esau Jeush, Jalam, and Korah.

[15] These are the chiefs of the sons of Esau. The sons of Eliphaz the firstborn of Esau: the chiefs Teman, Omar, Zepho, Kenaz, [16] Korah, Gatam, and Amalek; these are the chiefs of Eliphaz in the land of Edom; these are the sons of Adah. [17] These are the sons of Reuel, Esau's son: the chiefs Nahath, Zerah, Shammah, and Mizzah; these are the chiefs of Reuel in the land of Edom; these are the sons of Basemath, Esau's wife. [18] These are the sons of Oholibamah, Esau's wife: the chiefs Jeush, Jalam, and Korah; these are the chiefs born of Oholibamah the daughter of Anah, Esau's wife. [19] These are the sons of Esau (that is, Edom), and these are their chiefs.

[20] These are the sons of Seir the Horite, the inhabitants of the land: Lotan, Shobal, Zibeon, Anah, [21] Dishon, Ezer, and Dishan; these are the chiefs of the Horites, the sons of Seir in the land of Edom. [22] The sons of

---

[1] Ben-oni could mean son of my sorrow, or son of my strength [2] Benjamin means son of the right hand

Lotan were Hori and Hemam; and Lotan's sister was Timna. 23 These are the sons of Shobal: Alvan, Manahath, Ebal, Shepho, and Onam. 24 These are the sons of Zibeon: Aiah and Anah; he is the Anah who found the hot springs in the wilderness, as he pastured the donkeys of Zibeon his father. 25 These are the children of Anah: Dishon and Oholibamah the daughter of Anah. 26 These are the sons of Dishon: Hemdan, Eshban, Ithran, and Cheran. 27 These are the sons of Ezer: Bilhan, Zaavan, and Akan. 28 These are the sons of Dishan: Uz and Aran. 29 These are the chiefs of the Horites: the chiefs Lotan, Shobal, Zibeon, Anah, 30 Dishon, Ezer, and Dishan; these are the chiefs of the Horites, chief by chief in the land of Seir.

31 These are the kings who reigned in the land of Edom, before any king reigned over the Israelites. 32 Bela the son of Beor

GETTING THE MESSAGE

A long walk! Jacob sent Joseph to see how his brothers were doing, as they tended their sheep (37:14). Joseph headed northward, probably walking, and didn't find his brothers until he came to Dothan (v. 17). The journey would have been more than 50 miles (80 km)!

reigned in Edom, the name of his city being Dinhabah. 33 Bela died, and Jobab the son of Zerah of Bozrah reigned in his place. 34 Jobab died, and Husham of the land of the Temanites reigned in his place. 35 Husham died, and Hadad the son of Bedad, who defeated Midian in the country of Moab, reigned in his place, the name of his city being Avith. 36 Hadad died, and Samlah of Masrekah reigned in his place. 37 Samlah died, and Shaul of Rehoboth on the Euphrates reigned in his place. 38 Shaul died, and Baal-hanan the son of Achbor reigned in his place. 39 Baal-hanan the son of Achbor died, and Hadar reigned in his place, the name of his city being Pau; his wife's name was Mehetabel, the daughter of Matred, daughter of Mezahab.

40 These are the names of the chiefs of Esau, according to their clans and their dwelling places, by their names: the chiefs Timna, Alvah, Jetheth, 41 Oholibamah, Elah, Pinon, 42 Kenaz, Teman, Mibzar, 43 Magdiel, and Iram; these are the chiefs of Edom (that is, Esau, the father of Edom), according to their dwelling places in the land of their possession.

Joseph's Dreams

37 Jacob lived in the land of his father's sojournings, in the land of Canaan. 2 These are the generations of Jacob.

Joseph, being seventeen years old, was pasturing the flock with his brothers. He was a boy with the sons of Bilhah and Zilpah, his father's wives. And Joseph brought a bad report of them to their father. 3 Now Israel loved Joseph more than any other of his sons, because he was the son of his old age. And he made him a robe of many colors. 4 But when his brothers saw that their father loved him more than all his brothers, they hated him and could not speak peacefully to him.

5 Now Joseph had a dream, and when he told it to his brothers they hated him even more. 6 He said to them, "Hear this dream that I have dreamed: 7 Behold, we were binding sheaves in the field, and behold, my sheaf arose and stood upright. And behold, your sheaves gathered around it and bowed down to my sheaf." 8 His brothers said to him, "Are you indeed to reign over us? Or are you indeed to rule over us?" So they hated him even more for his dreams and for his words.

9 Then he dreamed another dream and told it to his brothers and said, "Behold, I have dreamed another dream. Behold, the sun, the moon, and eleven stars were bowing down to me." 10 But when he told it to his father and to his brothers, his father rebuked him and said to him, "What is this dream that you have dreamed? Shall I and your mother and your brothers indeed come to bow ourselves to the ground before you?" 11 And his brothers were jealous of him, but his father kept the saying in mind.

Joseph Sold by His Brothers

12 Now his brothers went to pasture their father's flock near Shechem. 13 And Israel said to Joseph, "Are not your brothers pasturing the flock at Shechem? Come, I will send you to them." And he said to him, "Here I am." 14 So he said to him, "Go now, see if it is well with your brothers and with the flock, and bring me word." So he sent

him from the Valley of Hebron, and he came to Shechem. ¹⁵ And a man found him wandering in the fields. And the man asked him, "What are you seeking?" ¹⁶ "I am seeking my brothers," he said. "Tell me, please, where they are pasturing the flock." ¹⁷ And the man said, "They have gone away, for I heard them say, 'Let us go to Dothan.'" So Joseph went after his brothers and found them at Dothan.

¹⁸ They saw him from afar, and before he came near to them they conspired against him to kill him. ¹⁹ They said to one another, "Here comes this dreamer. ²⁰ Come now, let us kill him and throw him into one of the pits. Then we will say that a fierce animal has devoured him, and we will see what will become of his dreams." ²¹ But when Reuben heard it, he rescued him out of their hands, saying, "Let us not take his life." ²² And Reuben said to them, "Shed no blood; throw him into this pit here in the wilderness, but do not lay a hand on him"—that he might rescue him out of their hand to restore him to his father. ²³ So when Joseph came to his brothers, they stripped him of his robe, the robe of many colors that he wore. ²⁴ And they took him and threw him into a pit. The pit was empty; there was no water in it.

²⁵ Then they sat down to eat. And looking up they saw a caravan of Ishmaelites coming from Gilead, with their camels bearing gum, balm, and myrrh, on their way to carry it down to Egypt. ²⁶ Then Judah said to his brothers, "What profit is it if we kill our brother and conceal his blood? ²⁷ Come, let us sell him to the Ishmaelites, and let not our hand be upon him, for he is our brother, our own flesh." And his brothers listened to him. ²⁸ Then Midianite traders passed by. And they drew Joseph up and lifted him out of the pit, and sold him to the Ishmaelites for twenty shekels of silver. They took Joseph to Egypt.

²⁹ When Reuben returned to the pit and saw that Joseph was not in the pit, he tore his clothes ³⁰ and returned to his brothers and said, "The boy is gone, and I, where shall I go?" ³¹ Then they took Joseph's robe and slaughtered a goat and dipped the robe in the blood. ³² And they sent the robe of many colors and brought it to their father and said, "This we have found; please identify whether it is your son's robe or not." ³³ And

he identified it and said, "It is my son's robe. A fierce animal has devoured him. Joseph is without doubt torn to pieces." ³⁴ Then Jacob tore his garments and put sackcloth on his loins and mourned for his son many days. ³⁵ All his sons and all his daughters rose up to comfort him, but he refused to be comforted and said, "No, I shall go down to Sheol to my son, mourning." Thus his father wept for him. ³⁶ Meanwhile the Midianites had sold him in Egypt to Potiphar, an officer of Pharaoh, the captain of the guard.

Judah and Tamar

38 It happened at that time that Judah went down from his brothers and turned aside to a certain Adullamite, whose name was Hirah. ² There Judah saw the daughter of a certain Canaanite whose name was Shua. He took her and went in to her,

GETTING THE MESSAGE

A costly demonstration of grief.
The Hebrew custom of tearing one's garments (37:29, 34) was an expression of grief, often after learning of the death of a loved one. It would surely have had great significance in a day when most people owned very few items of clothing.

³ and she conceived and bore a son, and he called his name Er. ⁴ She conceived again and bore a son, and she called his name Onan. ⁵ Yet again she bore a son, and she called his name Shelah. Judah was in Chezib when she bore him.

⁶ And Judah took a wife for Er his firstborn, and her name was Tamar. ⁷ But Er, Judah's firstborn, was wicked in the sight of the LORD, and the LORD put him to death. ⁸ Then Judah said to Onan, "Go in to your brother's wife and perform the duty of a brother-in-law to her, and raise up offspring for your brother." ⁹ But Onan knew that the offspring would not be his. So whenever he went in to his brother's wife he would waste the semen on the ground, so as not to give offspring to his brother. ¹⁰ And what he did was wicked in the sight of the LORD, and he put him to death also. ¹¹ Then Judah said to Tamar his daughter-in-law, "Remain a widow in your father's house, till Shelah

my son grows up"—for he feared that he would die, like his brothers. So Tamar went and remained in her father's house.

¹² In the course of time the wife of Judah, Shua's daughter, died. When Judah was comforted, he went up to Timnah to his sheepshearers, he and his friend Hirah the Adullamite. ¹³ And when Tamar was told, "Your father-in-law is going up to Timnah to shear his sheep," ¹⁴ she took off her widow's garments and covered herself with a veil, wrapping herself up, and sat at the entrance to Enaim, which is on the road to Timnah. For she saw that Shelah was grown up, and she had not been given to him in marriage. ¹⁵ When Judah saw her, he thought she was a prostitute, for she had covered her face. ¹⁶ He turned to her at the roadside and said, "Come, let me come in to you," for he did not know that she was

GETTING THE MESSAGE

Levirate marriage is the practice of a man marrying the widow of his deceased brother, if she had no children (38:8). A child of this second marriage would provide security for the widow and would carry on the name of the deceased brother.

his daughter-in-law. She said, "What will you give me, that you may come in to me?" ¹⁷ He answered, "I will send you a young goat from the flock." And she said, "If you give me a pledge, until you send it—" ¹⁸ He said, "What pledge shall I give you?" She replied, "Your signet and your cord and your staff that is in your hand." So he gave them to her and went in to her, and she conceived by him. ¹⁹ Then she arose and went away, and taking off her veil she put on the garments of her widowhood.

²⁰ When Judah sent the young goat by his friend the Adullamite to take back the pledge from the woman's hand, he did not find her. ²¹ And he asked the men of the place, "Where is the cult prostitute who was at Enaim at the roadside?" And they said, "No cult prostitute has been here." ²² So he returned to Judah and said, "I have not found her. Also, the men of the place said, 'No cult prostitute

has been here.'" ²³ And Judah replied, "Let her keep the things as her own, or we shall be laughed at. You see, I sent this young goat, and you did not find her."

²⁴ About three months later Judah was told, "Tamar your daughter-in-law has been immoral. Moreover, she is pregnant by immorality." And Judah said, "Bring her out, and let her be burned." ²⁵ As she was being brought out, she sent word to her father-in-law, "By the man to whom these belong, I am pregnant." And she said, "Please identify whose these are, the signet and the cord and the staff." ²⁶ Then Judah identified them and said, "She is more righteous than I, since I did not give her to my son Shelah." And he did not know her again.

²⁷ When the time of her labor came, there were twins in her womb. ²⁸ And when she was in labor, one put out a hand, and the midwife took and tied a scarlet thread on his hand, saying, "This one came out first." ²⁹ But as he drew back his hand, behold, his brother came out. And she said, "What a breach you have made for yourself!" Therefore his name was called Perez.[1] ³⁰ Afterward his brother came out with the scarlet thread on his hand, and his name was called Zerah.

Joseph and Potiphar's Wife

39 Now Joseph had been brought down to Egypt, and Potiphar, an officer of Pharaoh, the captain of the guard, an Egyptian, had bought him from the Ishmaelites who had brought him down there. ² The LORD was with Joseph, and he became a successful man, and he was in the house of his Egyptian master. ³ His master saw that the LORD was with him and that the LORD caused all that he did to succeed in his hands. ⁴ So Joseph found favor in his sight and attended him, and he made him overseer of his house and put him in charge of all that he had. ⁵ From the time that he made him overseer in his house and over all that he had, the LORD blessed the Egyptian's house for Joseph's sake; the blessing of the LORD was on all that he had, in house and field. ⁶ So he left all that he had in Joseph's charge, and because of him he had no concern about anything but the food he ate.

Now Joseph was handsome in form and appearance. ⁷ And after a time his master's

¹ Perez means a breach

wife cast her eyes on Joseph and said, "Lie with me." **8** But he refused and said to his master's wife, "Behold, because of me my master has no concern about anything in the house, and he has put everything that he has in my charge. **9** He is not greater in this house than I am, nor has he kept back anything from me except you, because you are his wife. How then can I do this great wickedness and sin against God?" **10** And as she spoke to Joseph day after day, he would not listen to her, to lie beside her or to be with her.

11 But one day, when he went into the house to do his work and none of the men of the house was there in the house, **12** she caught him by his garment, saying, "Lie with me." But he left his garment in her hand and fled and got out of the house. **13** And as soon as she saw that he had left his garment in her hand and had fled out of the house, **14** she called to the men of her household and said to them, "See, he has brought among us a Hebrew to laugh at us. He came in to me to lie with me, and I cried out with a loud voice. **15** And as soon as he heard that I lifted up my voice and cried out, he left his garment beside me and fled and got out of the house." **16** Then she laid up his garment by her until his master came home, **17** and she told him the same story, saying, "The Hebrew servant, whom you have brought among us, came in to me to laugh at me. **18** But as soon as I lifted up my voice and cried, he left his garment beside me and fled out of the house."

19 As soon as his master heard the words that his wife spoke to him, "This is the way your servant treated me," his anger was kindled. **20** And Joseph's master took him and put him into the prison, the place where the king's prisoners were confined, and he was there in prison. **21** But the LORD was with Joseph and showed him steadfast love and gave him favor in the sight of the keeper of the prison. **22** And the keeper of the prison put Joseph in charge of all the prisoners who were in the prison. Whatever was done there, he was the one who did it. **23** The keeper of the prison paid no attention to anything that was in Joseph's charge, because the LORD was with him. And whatever he did, the LORD made it succeed.

Joseph Interprets Two Prisoners' Dreams

40 Some time after this, the cupbearer of the king of Egypt and his baker committed an offense against their lord the king of Egypt. **2** And Pharaoh was angry with his two officers, the chief cupbearer and the chief baker, **3** and he put them in custody in the house of the captain of the guard, in the prison where Joseph was confined. **4** The captain of the guard appointed Joseph to be with them, and he attended them. They continued for some time in custody.

5 And one night they both dreamed—the cupbearer and the baker of the king of Egypt, who were confined in the prison—each his own dream, and each dream with its own interpretation. **6** When Joseph came to them in the morning, he saw that they were troubled. **7** So he asked Pharaoh's officers who were with him in custody in his

GETTING THE MESSAGE

Cupbearers (40:1) were high-ranking officials who served the kings of the ancient Near East. Their job was dangerous: before bringing any drink to the king, they tasted it to make sure that it had not been poisoned.

master's house, "Why are your faces downcast today?" **8** They said to him, "We have had dreams, and there is no one to interpret them." And Joseph said to them, "Do not interpretations belong to God? Please tell them to me."

9 So the chief cupbearer told his dream to Joseph and said to him, "In my dream there was a vine before me, **10** and on the vine there were three branches. As soon as it budded, its blossoms shot forth, and the clusters ripened into grapes. **11** Pharaoh's cup was in my hand, and I took the grapes and pressed them into Pharaoh's cup and placed the cup in Pharaoh's hand." **12** Then Joseph said to him, "This is its interpretation: the three branches are three days. **13** In three days Pharaoh will lift up your head and restore you to your office, and you shall place Pharaoh's cup in his hand as formerly, when you were his cupbearer. **14** Only remember me, when it is well with you, and please do me the kindness to mention me to Pharaoh, and so get me out of this house. ¹⁵ For I was indeed stolen out of the land of the Hebrews, and here also I have done nothing that they should put me into the pit."

¹⁶ When the chief baker saw that the interpretation was favorable, he said to Joseph, "I also had a dream: there were three cake baskets on my head, ¹⁷ and in the uppermost

PROFILE
JOSEPH

Joseph, whom the Bible describes as a "just man" (Matt. 1:19), was a descendant of David and a carpenter by trade. Betrothed to Mary when she was found to be with child, Joseph sought to show compassion and divorce her quietly, even though it looked like Mary had committed adultery. An angel of the Lord appeared to Joseph in a dream, however, assuring him that Mary's child was from the Holy Spirit (Matt. 1:20-21). Joseph trusted God and took Mary as his wife. He traveled with Mary to his ancestral home of Bethlehem, where she gave birth to Jesus. When Herod the Great sought to kill Jesus, Joseph took Mary and the child and escaped to Egypt (Matt. 2:13-18). Following Herod's death, they returned to Palestine and settled in Nazareth. Joseph later fathered at least four other sons and at least two daughters. Since he is not mentioned in the incident related in Matt. 12:46, it is likely that Joseph died before Jesus began his ministry.

KEY REFERENCE: MATTHEW 1:19-21

basket there were all sorts of baked food for Pharaoh, but the birds were eating it out of the basket on my head." ¹⁸ And Joseph answered and said, "This is its interpretation: the three baskets are three days. ¹⁹ In three days Pharaoh will lift up your head—from you!—and hang you on a tree. And the birds will eat the flesh from you."

²⁰ On the third day, which was Pharaoh's birthday, he made a feast for all his servants and lifted up the head of the chief cupbearer

and the head of the chief baker among his servants. ²¹ He restored the chief cupbearer to his position, and he placed the cup in Pharaoh's hand. ²² But he hanged the chief baker, as Joseph had interpreted to them. ²³ Yet the chief cupbearer did not remember Joseph, but forgot him.

Joseph Interprets Pharaoh's Dreams

41 After two whole years, Pharaoh dreamed that he was standing by the Nile, ² and behold, there came up out of the Nile seven cows attractive and plump, and they fed in the reed grass. ³ And behold, seven other cows, ugly and thin, came up out of the Nile after them, and stood by the other cows on the bank of the Nile. ⁴ And the ugly, thin cows ate up the seven attractive, plump cows. And Pharaoh awoke. ⁵ And he fell asleep and dreamed a second time. And behold, seven ears of grain, plump and good, were growing on one stalk. ⁶ And behold, after them sprouted seven ears, thin and blighted by the east wind. ⁷ And the thin ears swallowed up the seven plump, full ears. And Pharaoh awoke, and behold, it was a dream. ⁸ So in the morning his spirit was troubled, and he sent and called for all the magicians of Egypt and all its wise men. Pharaoh told them his dreams, but there was none who could interpret them to Pharaoh.

⁹ Then the chief cupbearer said to Pharaoh, "I remember my offenses today. ¹⁰ When Pharaoh was angry with his servants and put me and the chief baker in custody in the house of the captain of the guard, ¹¹ we dreamed on the same night, he and I, each having a dream with its own interpretation. ¹² A young Hebrew was there with us, a servant of the captain of the guard. When we told him, he interpreted our dreams to us, giving an interpretation to each man according to his dream. ¹³ And as he interpreted to us, so it came about. I was restored to my office, and the baker was hanged."

¹⁴ Then Pharaoh sent and called Joseph, and they quickly brought him out of the pit. And when he had shaved himself and changed his clothes, he came in before Pharaoh. ¹⁵ And Pharaoh said to Joseph, "I have had a dream, and there is no one who can interpret it. I have heard it said of you that when you hear a dream you can interpret it." ¹⁶ Joseph answered Pharaoh, "It is not in me; God will give Pharaoh a favorable

answer." **17** Then Pharaoh said to Joseph, "Behold, in my dream I was standing on the banks of the Nile. **18** Seven cows, plump and attractive, came up out of the Nile and fed in the reed grass. **19** Seven other cows came up after them, poor and very ugly and thin, such as I had never seen in all the land of Egypt. **20** And the thin, ugly cows ate up the first seven plump cows, **21** but when they had eaten them no one would have known that they had eaten them, for they were still as ugly as at the beginning. Then I awoke. **22** I also saw in my dream seven ears growing on one stalk, full and good. **23** Seven ears, withered, thin, and blighted by the east wind, sprouted after them, **24** and the thin ears swallowed up the seven good ears. And I told it to the magicians, but there was no one who could explain it to me."

25 Then Joseph said to Pharaoh, "The dreams of Pharaoh are one; God has revealed to Pharaoh what he is about to do. **26** The seven good cows are seven years, and the seven good ears are seven years; the dreams are one. **27** The seven lean and ugly cows that came up after them are seven years, and the seven empty ears blighted by the east wind are also seven years of famine. **28** It is as I told Pharaoh; God has shown to Pharaoh what he is about to do. **29** There will come seven years of great plenty throughout all the land of Egypt, **30** but after them there will arise seven years of famine, and all the plenty will be forgotten in the land of Egypt. The famine will consume the land, **31** and the plenty will be unknown in the land by reason of the famine that will follow, for it will be very severe. **32** And the doubling of Pharaoh's dream means that the thing is fixed by God, and God will shortly bring it about. **33** Now therefore let Pharaoh select a discerning and wise man, and set him over the land of Egypt. **34** Let Pharaoh proceed to appoint overseers over the land and take one-fifth of the produce of the land of Egypt during the seven plentiful years. **35** And let them gather all the food of these good years that are coming and store up grain under the authority of Pharaoh for food in the cities, and let them keep it. **36** That food shall be a reserve for the land against the seven years of famine that are to occur in the land of Egypt, so that the land may not perish through the famine."

Joseph Rises to Power

37 This proposal pleased Pharaoh and all his servants. **38** And Pharaoh said to his servants, "Can we find a man like this, in whom is the Spirit of God?" **39** Then Pharaoh said to Joseph, "Since God has shown you all this, there is none so discerning and wise as you are. **40** You shall be over my house, and all my people shall order themselves as you command. Only as regards the throne will I be greater than you." **41** And Pharaoh said to Joseph, "See, I have set you over all the land of Egypt." **42** Then Pharaoh took his signet ring from his hand and put it on Joseph's hand, and clothed him in garments of fine linen and put a gold chain about his neck. **43** And he made him ride in his second chariot. And they called out before him, "Bow the knee!" Thus he set him over all the land of Egypt. **44** Moreover, Pharaoh said to

GETTING THE MESSAGE

Signets were seals that bore a unique mark representing their owner. Some signets were worn around the neck; others were worn as rings (41:42). The signet was pressed into soft clay to leave an impression of its mark. Signet impressions were used to certify important documents.

Joseph, "I am Pharaoh, and without your consent no one shall lift up hand or foot in all the land of Egypt." **45** And Pharaoh called Joseph's name Zaphenath-paneah. And he gave him in marriage Asenath, the daughter of Potiphera priest of On. So Joseph went out over the land of Egypt.

46 Joseph was thirty years old when he entered the service of Pharaoh king of Egypt. And Joseph went out from the presence of Pharaoh and went through all the land of Egypt. **47** During the seven plentiful years the earth produced abundantly, **48** and he gathered up all the food of these seven years, which occurred in the land of Egypt, and put the food in the cities. He put in every city the food from the fields around it. **49** And Joseph stored up grain in great abundance, like the sand of the sea, until he ceased to measure it, for it could not be measured.

⁵⁰ Before the year of famine came, two sons were born to Joseph. Asenath, the daughter of Potiphera priest of On, bore them to him. ⁵¹ Joseph called the name of the firstborn Manasseh. "For," he said, "God has made me forget all my hardship and all my father's house."¹ ⁵² The name of the second he called Ephraim, "For God has made me fruitful in the land of my affliction."²

⁵³ The seven years of plenty that occurred in the land of Egypt came to an end, ⁵⁴ and the seven years of famine began to come, as Joseph had said. There was famine in all lands, but in all the land of Egypt there was bread. ⁵⁵ When all the land of Egypt was famished, the people cried to Pharaoh for bread. Pharaoh said to all the Egyptians, "Go to Joseph. What he says to you, do."

⁵⁶ So when the famine had spread over all the land, Joseph opened all the storehouses and sold to the Egyptians, for the famine was severe in the land of Egypt. ⁵⁷ Moreover, all the earth came to Egypt to Joseph to buy grain, because the famine was severe over all the earth.

Joseph's Brothers Go to Egypt

42 When Jacob learned that there was grain for sale in Egypt, he said to his sons, "Why do you look at one another?" ² And he said, "Behold, I have heard that there is grain for sale in Egypt. Go down and buy grain for us there, that we may live and not die." ³ So ten of Joseph's brothers went down to buy grain in Egypt. ⁴ But Jacob did not send Benjamin, Joseph's brother, with his brothers, for he feared that harm might happen to him. ⁵ Thus the sons of Israel came to buy among the others who came, for the famine was in the land of Canaan.

⁶ Now Joseph was governor over the land. He was the one who sold to all the people of the land. And Joseph's brothers came and bowed themselves before him with their faces to the ground. ⁷ Joseph saw his brothers and recognized them, but he treated them like strangers and spoke roughly to them. "Where do you come from?" he said. They said, "From the land of Canaan, to buy food." ⁸ And Joseph recognized his brothers, but they did not recognize him. ⁹ And Joseph remembered the dreams that he had dreamed of them. And he said to them, "You are spies; you have come to see the naked-ness of the land." ¹⁰ They said to him, "No, my lord, your servants have come to buy food. ¹¹ We are all sons of one man. We are honest men. Your servants have never been spies."

¹² He said to them, "No, it is the nakedness of the land that you have come to see." ¹³ And they said, "We, your servants, are twelve brothers, the sons of one man in the land of Canaan, and behold, the youngest is this day with our father, and one is no more." ¹⁴ But Joseph said to them, "It is as I said to you. You are spies. ¹⁵ By this you shall be tested: by the life of Pharaoh, you shall not go from this place unless your young-est brother comes here. ¹⁶ Send one of you, and let him bring your brother, while you remain confined, that your words may be tested, whether there is truth in you. Or else, by the life of Pharaoh, surely you are spies." ¹⁷ And he put them all together in custody for three days.

¹⁸ On the third day Joseph said to them, "Do this and you will live, for I fear God: ¹⁹ if you are honest men, let one of your brothers remain confined where you are in custody, and let the rest go and carry grain for the famine of your households, ²⁰ and bring your youngest brother to me. So your words will be verified, and you shall not die." And they did so. ²¹ Then they said to one another, "In truth we are guilty concerning our brother, in that we saw the distress of his soul, when he begged us and we did not listen. That is why this distress has come upon us." ²² And Reuben answered them, "Did I not tell you not to sin against the boy? But you did not listen. So now there comes a reckoning for his blood." ²³ They did not know that Joseph understood them, for there was an interpreter between them. ²⁴ Then he turned away from them and wept. And he returned to them and spoke to them. And he took Simeon from them and bound him before their eyes. ²⁵ And Joseph gave orders to fill their bags with grain, and to replace every man's money in his sack, and to give them provisions for the journey. This was done for them.

²⁶ Then they loaded their donkeys with their grain and departed. ²⁷ And as one of them opened his sack to give his donkey fodder at the lodging place, he saw his money in the mouth of his sack. ²⁸ He said

¹ *Manasseh* sounds like the Hebrew for *making to forget* ² *Ephraim* sounds like the Hebrew for *making fruitful*

to his brothers, "My money has been put back; here it is in the mouth of my sack!" At this their hearts failed them, and they turned trembling to one another, saying, "What is this that God has done to us?"

²⁹ When they came to Jacob their father in the land of Canaan, they told him all that had happened to them, saying, ³⁰ "The man, the lord of the land, spoke roughly to us and took us to be spies of the land. ³¹ But we said to him, 'We are honest men; we have never been spies. ³² We are twelve brothers, sons of our father. One is no more, and the youngest is this day with our father in the land of Canaan.' ³³ Then the man, the lord of the land, said to us, 'By this I shall know that you are honest men: leave one of your brothers with me, and take grain for the famine of your households, and go your way. ³⁴ Bring your youngest brother to me. Then I shall know that you are not spies but honest men, and I will deliver your brother to you, and you shall trade in the land.'"

³⁵ As they emptied their sacks, behold, every man's bundle of money was in his sack. And when they and their father saw their bundles of money, they were afraid. ³⁶ And Jacob their father said to them, "You have bereaved me of my children: Joseph is no more, and Simeon is no more, and now you would take Benjamin. All this has come against me." ³⁷ Then Reuben said to his father, "Kill my two sons if I do not bring him back to you. Put him in my hands, and I will bring him back to you." ³⁸ But he said, "My son shall not go down with you, for his brother is dead, and he is the only one left. If harm should happen to him on the journey that you are to make, you would bring down my gray hairs with sorrow to Sheol."

Joseph's Brothers Return to Egypt

43 Now the famine was severe in the land. ² And when they had eaten the grain that they had brought from Egypt, their father said to them, "Go again, buy us a little food." ³ But Judah said to him, "The man solemnly warned us, saying, 'You shall not see my face unless your brother is with you.' ⁴ If you will send our brother with us, we will go down and buy you food. ⁵ But if you will not send him, we will not go down, for the man said to us, 'You shall not see my face, unless your brother is with you.'" ⁶ Israel said, "Why did you treat me

so badly as to tell the man that you had another brother?" ⁷ They replied, "The man questioned us carefully about ourselves and our kindred, saying, 'Is your father still alive? Do you have another brother?' What we told him was in answer to these questions. Could we in any way know that he would say, 'Bring your brother down'?" ⁸ And Judah said to Israel his father, "Send the boy with me, and we will arise and go, that we may live and not die, both we and you and also our little ones. ⁹ I will be a pledge of his safety. From my hand you shall require him. If I do not bring him back to you and set him before you, then let me bear the blame forever. ¹⁰ If we had not delayed, we would now have returned twice."

¹¹ Then their father Israel said to them, "If it must be so, then do this: take some of the choice fruits of the land in your bags, and carry a present down to the man, a little

GETTING THE MESSAGE

Money in the form of coins did not come into use until around the sixth century B.C. In Joseph's time, in the nineteenth century B.C., items such as spices, gems, or precious metals were used as money.

balm and a little honey, gum, myrrh, pistachio nuts, and almonds. ¹² Take double the money with you. Carry back with you the money that was returned in the mouth of your sacks. Perhaps it was an oversight. ¹³ Take also your brother, and arise, go again to the man. ¹⁴ May God Almighty grant you mercy before the man, and may he send back your other brother and Benjamin. And as for me, if I am bereaved of my children, I am bereaved."

¹⁵ So the men took this present, and they took double the money with them, and Benjamin. They arose and went down to Egypt and stood before Joseph.

¹⁶ When Joseph saw Benjamin with them, he said to the steward of his house, "Bring the men into the house, and slaughter an animal and make ready, for the men are to dine with me at noon." ¹⁷ The man did as Joseph told him and brought the men to Joseph's house. ¹⁸ And the men were afraid because they were brought to Joseph's

house, and they said, "It is because of the money, which was replaced in our sacks the first time, that we are brought in, so that he may assault us and fall upon us to make us servants and seize our donkeys." **19** So they went up to the steward of Joseph's house and spoke with him at the door of the house, **20** and said, "Oh, my lord, we came down the first time to buy food. **21** And when we came to the lodging place we opened our sacks, and there was each man's money in the mouth of his sack, our money in full weight. So we have brought it again with us, **22** and we have brought other money down with us to buy food. We do not know who put our money in our sacks." **23** He replied, "Peace to you, do not be afraid. Your God and the God of your father has put treasure in your sacks for you. I received your money." Then he brought Simeon out to them. **24** And when the man had brought the men into Joseph's house and given them water, and they had washed their feet, and when he had given their donkeys fodder, **25** they prepared the present for Joseph's coming at noon, for they heard that they should eat bread there.

26 When Joseph came home, they brought into the house to him the present that they had with them and bowed down to him to the ground. **27** And he inquired about their welfare and said, "Is your father well, the old man of whom you spoke? Is he still alive?" **28** They said, "Your servant our father is well; he is still alive." And they bowed their heads and prostrated themselves. **29** And he lifted up his eyes and saw his brother Benjamin, his mother's son, and said, "Is this your youngest brother, of whom you spoke to me? God be gracious to you, my son!" **30** Then Joseph hurried out, for his compassion grew warm for his brother, and he sought a place to weep. And he entered his chamber and wept there. **31** Then he washed his face and came out. And controlling himself he said, "Serve the food." **32** They served him by himself, and them by themselves, and the Egyptians who ate with him by themselves, because the Egyptians could not eat with the Hebrews, for that is an abomination to the Egyptians. **33** And they sat before him, the firstborn according to his birthright and the youngest according to his youth. And the men looked at one another in amazement. **34** Portions were

taken to them from Joseph's table, but Benjamin's portion was five times as much as any of theirs. And they drank and were merry with him.

Joseph Tests His Brothers

44 Then he commanded the steward of his house, "Fill the men's sacks with food, as much as they can carry, and put each man's money in the mouth of his sack, **2** and put my cup, the silver cup, in the mouth of the sack of the youngest, with his money for the grain." And he did as Joseph told him.

3 As soon as the morning was light, the men were sent away with their donkeys. **4** They had gone only a short distance from the city. Now Joseph said to his steward, "Up, follow after the men, and when you overtake them, say to them, 'Why have you repaid evil for good? **5** Is it not from this that my lord drinks, and by this that he practices divination? You have done evil in doing this.'"

6 When he overtook them, he spoke to them these words. **7** They said to him, "Why does my lord speak such words as these? Far be it from your servants to do such a thing! **8** Behold, the money that we found in the mouths of our sacks we brought back to you from the land of Canaan. How then could we steal silver or gold from your lord's house? **9** Whichever of your servants is found with it shall die, and we also will be my lord's servants." **10** He said, "Let it be as you say: he who is found with it shall be my servant, and the rest of you shall be innocent." **11** Then each man quickly lowered his sack to the ground, and each man opened his sack. **12** And he searched, beginning with the eldest and ending with the youngest. And the cup was found in Benjamin's sack. **13** Then they tore their clothes, and every man loaded his donkey, and they returned to the city.

14 When Judah and his brothers came to Joseph's house, he was still there. They fell before him to the ground. **15** Joseph said to them, "What deed is this that you have done? Do you not know that a man like me can indeed practice divination?" **16** And Judah said, "What shall we say to my lord? What shall we speak? Or how can we clear ourselves? God has found out the guilt of your servants; behold, we are my lord's servants, both we and he also in whose hand the cup has been found." ¹⁷ But he said, "Far be it from me that I should do so! Only the man in whose hand the cup was found shall be my servant. But as for you, go up in peace to your father."

¹⁸ Then Judah went up to him and said, "Oh, my lord, please let your servant speak a word in my lord's ears, and let not your anger burn against your servant, for you are like Pharaoh himself. ¹⁹ My lord asked his servants, saying, 'Have you a father, or a brother?' ²⁰ And we said to my lord, 'We have a father, an old man, and a young brother, the child of his old age. His brother is dead, and he alone is left of his mother's children, and his father loves him.' ²¹ Then you said to your servants, 'Bring him down to me, that I may set my eyes on him.' ²² We said to my lord, 'The boy cannot leave his father, for if he should leave his father, his father would die.' ²³ Then you said to your servants, 'Unless your youngest brother comes down with you, you shall not see my face again.'

²⁴ "When we went back to your servant my father, we told him the words of my lord. ²⁵ And when our father said, 'Go again, buy us a little food,' ²⁶ we said, 'We cannot go down. If our youngest brother goes with us, then we will go down. For we cannot see the man's face unless our youngest brother is with us.' ²⁷ Then your servant my father said to us, 'You know that my wife bore me two sons. ²⁸ One left me, and I said, "Surely he has been torn to pieces," and I have never seen him since. ²⁹ If you take this one also from me, and harm happens to him, you will bring down my gray hairs in evil to Sheol.'

³⁰ "Now therefore, as soon as I come to your servant my father, and the boy is not with us, then, as his life is bound up in the boy's life, ³¹ as soon as he sees that the boy is not with us, he will die, and your servants will bring down the gray hairs of your servant our father with sorrow to Sheol. ³² For your servant became a pledge of safety for the boy to my father, saying, 'If I do not bring him back to you, then I shall bear the blame before my father all my life.' ³³ Now therefore, please let your servant remain instead of the boy as a servant to my lord, and let the boy go back with his brothers. ³⁴ For how can I go back to my father if the boy is not

with me? I fear to see the evil that would find my father."

Joseph Provides for His Brothers and Family

45 Then Joseph could not control himself before all those who stood by him. He cried, "Make everyone go out from me." So no one stayed with him when Joseph made himself known to his brothers. ² And he wept aloud, so that the Egyptians heard it, and the household of Pharaoh heard it. ³ And Joseph said to his brothers, "I am Joseph! Is my father still alive?" But his brothers could not answer him, for they were dismayed at his presence.

⁴ So Joseph said to his brothers, "Come near to me, please." And they came near. And he said, "I am your brother, Joseph, whom you sold into Egypt. ⁵ And now do not be distressed or angry with yourselves because you sold me here, for God sent me

---

GETTING THE MESSAGE

Joseph's words **"God sent me"** reveal his faith in the providence of God who used his brothers' evil act for great good— the preservation of Joseph and all his family (45:7).

---

before you to preserve life. ⁶ For the famine has been in the land these two years, and there are yet five years in which there will be neither plowing nor harvest. ⁷ And God sent me before you to preserve for you a remnant on earth, and to keep alive for you many survivors. ⁸ So it was not you who sent me here, but God. He has made me a father to Pharaoh, and lord of all his house and ruler over all the land of Egypt. ⁹ Hurry and go up to my father and say to him, 'Thus says your son Joseph, God has made me lord of all Egypt. Come down to me; do not tarry. ¹⁰ You shall dwell in the land of Goshen, and you shall be near me, you and your children and your children's children, and your flocks, your herds, and all that you have. ¹¹ There I will provide for you, for there are yet five years of famine to come, so that you and your household, and all that you have, do not come to poverty.' ¹² And now your eyes see, and the eyes of my brother Benjamin see, that it is my mouth that speaks to you.

¹³ You must tell my father of all my honor in Egypt, and of all that you have seen. Hurry and bring my father down here." ¹⁴ Then he fell upon his brother Benjamin's neck and wept, and Benjamin wept upon his neck. ¹⁵ And he kissed all his brothers and wept upon them. After that his brothers talked with him.

¹⁶ When the report was heard in Pharaoh's house, "Joseph's brothers have come," it pleased Pharaoh and his servants. ¹⁷ And Pharaoh said to Joseph, "Say to your brothers, 'Do this: load your beasts and go back to the land of Canaan, ¹⁸ and take your father and your households, and come to me, and I will give you the best of the land of Egypt, and you shall eat the fat of the land.' ¹⁹ And you, Joseph, are commanded to say, 'Do this: take wagons from the land of Egypt for your little ones and for your wives, and bring your father, and come. ²⁰ Have no concern for your goods, for the best of all the land of Egypt is yours.'"

²¹ The sons of Israel did so: and Joseph gave them wagons, according to the command of Pharaoh, and gave them provisions for the journey. ²² To each and all of them he gave a change of clothes, but to Benjamin he gave three hundred shekels of silver and five changes of clothes. ²³ To his father he sent as follows: ten donkeys loaded with the good things of Egypt, and ten female donkeys loaded with grain, bread, and provision for his father on the journey. ²⁴ Then he sent his brothers away, and as they departed, he said to them, "Do not quarrel on the way."

²⁵ So they went up out of Egypt and came to the land of Canaan to their father Jacob. ²⁶ And they told him, "Joseph is still alive, and he is ruler over all the land of Egypt." And his heart became numb, for he did not believe them. ²⁷ But when they told him all the words of Joseph, which he had said to them, and when he saw the wagons that Joseph had sent to carry him, the spirit of their father Jacob revived. ²⁸ And Israel said, "It is enough; Joseph my son is still alive. I will go and see him before I die."

Joseph Brings His Family to Egypt

46 So Israel took his journey with all that he had and came to Beersheba, and offered sacrifices to the God of his father Isaac. ² And God spoke to Israel in visions of the night and said, "Jacob, Jacob." And he said, "Here I am." ³ Then he said, "I am God, the God of your father. Do not be afraid to go down to Egypt, for there I will make you into a great nation. ⁴ I myself will go down with you to Egypt, and I will also bring you up again, and Joseph's hand shall close your eyes."

⁵ Then Jacob set out from Beersheba. The sons of Israel carried Jacob their father, their little ones, and their wives, in the wagons that Pharaoh had sent to carry him. ⁶ They also took their livestock and their goods, which they had gained in the land of Canaan, and came into Egypt, Jacob and all his offspring with him, ⁷ his sons, and his sons' sons with him, his daughters, and his sons' daughters. All his offspring he brought with him into Egypt.

⁸ Now these are the names of the descendants of Israel, who came into Egypt, Jacob and his sons. Reuben, Jacob's firstborn, ⁹ and the sons of Reuben: Hanoch, Pallu, Hezron, and Carmi. ¹⁰ The sons of Simeon: Jemuel, Jamin, Ohad, Jachin, Zohar, and Shaul, the son of a Canaanite woman. ¹¹ The sons of Levi: Gershon, Kohath, and Merari. ¹² The sons of Judah: Er, Onan, Shelah, Perez, and Zerah (but Er and Onan died in the land of Canaan); and the sons of Perez were Hezron and Hamul. ¹³ The sons of Issachar: Tola, Puvah, Yob, and Shimron. ¹⁴ The sons of Zebulun: Sered, Elon, and Jahleel. ¹⁵ These are the sons of Leah, whom she bore to Jacob in Paddan-aram, together with his daughter Dinah; altogether his sons and his daughters numbered thirty-three.

¹⁶ The sons of Gad: Ziphion, Haggi, Shuni, Ezbon, Eri, Arodi, and Areli. ¹⁷ The sons of Asher: Imnah, Ishvah, Ishvi, Beriah, with Serah their sister. And the sons of Beriah: Heber and Malchiel. ¹⁸ These are the sons of Zilpah, whom Laban gave to Leah his daughter; and these she bore to Jacob—sixteen persons.

¹⁹ The sons of Rachel, Jacob's wife: Joseph and Benjamin. ²⁰ And to Joseph in the land of Egypt were born Manasseh and Ephraim, whom Asenath, the daughter of Potiphera the priest of On, bore to him. ²¹ And the sons of Benjamin: Bela, Becher, Ashbel, Gera, Naaman, Ehi, Rosh, Muppim, Huppim, and Ard. ²² These are the sons of Rachel, who were born to Jacob—fourteen persons in all.

²³ The son of Dan: Hushim. ²⁴ The sons of Naphtali: Jahzeel, Guni, Jezer, and Shillem. ²⁵ These are the sons of Bilhah, whom Laban gave to Rachel his daughter, and these she bore to Jacob—seven persons in all.

²⁶ All the persons belonging to Jacob who came into Egypt, who were his own descendants, not including Jacob's sons' wives, were sixty-six persons in all. ²⁷ And the sons of Joseph, who were born to him in Egypt, were two. All the persons of the house of Jacob who came into Egypt were seventy.

Jacob and Joseph Reunited

²⁸ He had sent Judah ahead of him to Joseph to show the way before him in Goshen, and they came into the land of Goshen. ²⁹ Then Joseph prepared his chariot and went up to meet Israel his father in Goshen. He presented himself to him and fell on his neck and wept on his neck a good while. ³⁰ Israel said to Joseph, "Now let me die, since I have seen your face and know that you are still alive." ³¹ Joseph said to his brothers and to his father's household, "I will go up and tell Pharaoh and will say to him, 'My brothers and my father's household, who were in the land of Canaan, have come to me. ³² And the men are shepherds, for they have been keepers of livestock, and they have brought their flocks and their herds and all that they have.' ³³ When Pharaoh calls you and says, 'What is your occupation?' ³⁴ you shall say, 'Your servants have been keepers of livestock from our youth even until now, both we and our fathers,' in order that you may dwell in the land of Goshen, for every shepherd is an abomination to the Egyptians."

Jacob's Family Settles in Goshen

47 So Joseph went in and told Pharaoh, "My father and my brothers, with their flocks and herds and all that they possess, have come from the land of Canaan. They are now in the land of Goshen." ² And from among his brothers he took five men and presented them to Pharaoh. ³ Pharaoh said to his brothers, "What is your occupation?" And they said to Pharaoh, "Your servants are shepherds, as our fathers were." ⁴ They said to Pharaoh, "We have come to sojourn in the land, for there is no pasture for your servants' flocks, for the famine is severe in the land of Canaan. And now,

please let your servants dwell in the land of Goshen." ⁵ Then Pharaoh said to Joseph, "Your father and your brothers have come to you. ⁶ The land of Egypt is before you. Settle your father and your brothers in the best of the land. Let them settle in the land of Goshen, and if you know any able men among them, put them in charge of my livestock."

⁷ Then Joseph brought in Jacob his father and stood him before Pharaoh, and Jacob blessed Pharaoh. ⁸ And Pharaoh said to Jacob, "How many are the days of the years of your life?" ⁹ And Jacob said to Pharaoh, "The days of the years of my sojourning are 130 years. Few and evil have been the days of the years of my life, and they have not attained to the days of the years of the life of my fathers in the days of their sojourning." ¹⁰ And Jacob blessed Pharaoh and went out from the presence of Pharaoh. ¹¹ Then Joseph settled his father and his brothers and gave

> ### GETTING THE MESSAGE
>
> **The Land of Goshen** probably covered a small area. But it was very fertile and was a good place to raise sheep and cattle (46:28–34).

them a possession in the land of Egypt, in the best of the land, in the land of Rameses, as Pharaoh had commanded. ¹² And Joseph provided his father, his brothers, and all his father's household with food, according to the number of their dependents.

Joseph and the Famine

¹³ Now there was no food in all the land, for the famine was very severe, so that the land of Egypt and the land of Canaan languished by reason of the famine. ¹⁴ And Joseph gathered up all the money that was found in the land of Egypt and in the land of Canaan, in exchange for the grain that they bought. And Joseph brought the money into Pharaoh's house. ¹⁵ And when the money was all spent in the land of Egypt and in the land of Canaan, all the Egyptians came to Joseph and said, "Give us food. Why should we die before your eyes? For our money is gone." ¹⁶ And Joseph answered, "Give your livestock, and I will give you food in exchange for your livestock, if your money is gone." ¹⁷ So they

brought their livestock to Joseph, and Joseph gave them food in exchange for the horses, the flocks, the herds, and the donkeys. He supplied them with food in exchange for all their livestock that year. ¹⁸ And when that year was ended, they came to him the following year and said to him, "We will not hide from my lord that our money is all spent. The herds of livestock are my lord's. There is nothing left in the sight of my lord but our bodies and our land. ¹⁹ Why should we die before your eyes, both we and our land? Buy us and our land for food, and we with our land will be servants to Pharaoh. And give us seed that we may live and not die, and that the land may not be desolate."

²⁰ So Joseph bought all the land of Egypt for Pharaoh, for all the Egyptians sold their fields, because the famine was severe on them. The land became Pharaoh's. ²¹ As for the people, he made servants of them from

GETTING THE MESSAGE

"Do not bury me in Egypt." Once a family burial plot had been established, it was customary for future generations to be buried there as well (47:29–30). This helped to tie the family closer together and also to secure their property rights.

one end of Egypt to the other. ²² Only the land of the priests he did not buy, for the priests had a fixed allowance from Pharaoh and lived on the allowance that Pharaoh gave them; therefore they did not sell their land.

²³ Then Joseph said to the people, "Behold, I have this day bought you and your land for Pharaoh. Now here is seed for you, and you shall sow the land. ²⁴ And at the harvests you shall give a fifth to Pharaoh, and four fifths shall be your own, as seed for the field and as food for yourselves and your households, and as food for your little ones." ²⁵ And they said, "You have saved our lives; may it please my lord, we will be servants to Pharaoh." ²⁶ So Joseph made it a statute concerning the land of Egypt, and it stands to this day, that Pharaoh should have the fifth; the land of the priests alone did not become Pharaoh's.

²⁷ Thus Israel settled in the land of Egypt, in the land of Goshen. And they gained pos-

sessions in it, and were fruitful and multiplied greatly. ²⁸ And Jacob lived in the land of Egypt seventeen years. So the days of Jacob, the years of his life, were 147 years.

²⁹ And when the time drew near that Israel must die, he called his son Joseph and said to him, "If now I have found favor in your sight, put your hand under my thigh and promise to deal kindly and truly with me. Do not bury me in Egypt, ³⁰ but let me lie with my fathers. Carry me out of Egypt and bury me in their burying place." He answered, "I will do as you have said." ³¹ And he said, "Swear to me"; and he swore to him. Then Israel bowed himself upon the head of his bed.

Jacob Blesses Ephraim and Manasseh

48 After this, Joseph was told, "Behold, your father is ill." So he took with him his two sons, Manasseh and Ephraim. ² And it was told to Jacob, "Your son Joseph has come to you." Then Israel summoned his strength and sat up in bed. ³ And Jacob said to Joseph, "God Almighty appeared to me at Luz in the land of Canaan and blessed me, ⁴ and said to me, 'Behold, I will make you fruitful and multiply you, and I will make of you a company of peoples and will give this land to your offspring after you for an everlasting possession.' ⁵ And now your two sons, who were born to you in the land of Egypt before I came to you in Egypt, are mine; Ephraim and Manasseh shall be mine, as Reuben and Simeon are. ⁶ And the children that you fathered after them shall be yours. They shall be called by the name of their brothers in their inheritance. ⁷ As for me, when I came from Paddan, to my sorrow Rachel died in the land of Canaan on the way, when there was still some distance to go to Ephrath, and I buried her there on the way to Ephrath (that is, Bethlehem)."

⁸ When Israel saw Joseph's sons, he said, "Who are these?" ⁹ Joseph said to his father, "They are my sons, whom God has given me here." And he said, "Bring them to me, please, that I may bless them." ¹⁰ Now the eyes of Israel were dim with age, so that he could not see. So Joseph brought them near him, and he kissed them and embraced them. ¹¹ And Israel said to Joseph, "I never expected to see your face; and behold, God has let me see your offspring also." ¹² Then Joseph removed them from his knees, and he bowed himself with his face to the earth.

¹³ And Joseph took them both, Ephraim in his right hand toward Israel's left hand, and Manasseh in his left hand toward Israel's right hand, and brought them near him. ¹⁴ And Israel stretched out his right hand and laid it on the head of Ephraim, who was the younger, and his left hand on the head of Manasseh, crossing his hands (for Manasseh was the firstborn). ¹⁵ And he blessed Joseph and said,

> "The God before whom my fathers
>   Abraham and Isaac walked,
>   the God who has been my shepherd
>   all my life long to this day,
> ¹⁶   the angel who has redeemed me from
>   all evil, bless the boys;
>   and in them let my name be carried
>   on, and the name of my fathers
>   Abraham and Isaac;
>   and let them grow into a multitude
>   in the midst of the earth."

¹⁷ When Joseph saw that his father laid his right hand on the head of Ephraim, it displeased him, and he took his father's hand to move it from Ephraim's head to Manasseh's head. ¹⁸ And Joseph said to his father, "Not this way, my father; since this one is the firstborn, put your right hand on his head." ¹⁹ But his father refused and said, "I know, my son, I know. He also shall become a people, and he also shall be great. Nevertheless, his younger brother shall be greater than he, and his offspring shall become a multitude of nations." ²⁰ So he blessed them that day, saying,

> "By you Israel will pronounce blessings,
>   saying,
>   'God make you as Ephraim and as
>   Manasseh.'"

Thus he put Ephraim before Manasseh. ²¹ Then Israel said to Joseph, "Behold, I am about to die, but God will be with you and will bring you again to the land of your fathers. ²² Moreover, I have given to you rather than to your brothers one mountain slope that I took from the hand of the Amorites with my sword and with my bow."

Jacob Blesses His Sons

49 Then Jacob called his sons and said, "Gather yourselves together, that I may tell you what shall happen to you in days to come.

² "Assemble and listen, O sons of Jacob,
    listen to Israel your father.

³ "Reuben, you are my firstborn,
    my might, and the firstfruits of my
      strength,
    preeminent in dignity and preemi-
      nent in power.
⁴ Unstable as water, you shall not have
      preeminence,
    because you went up to your
      father's bed;
    then you defiled it—he went up to
      my couch!

⁵ "Simeon and Levi are brothers;
    weapons of violence are their
      swords.
⁶ Let my soul come not into their coun-
      cil;
    O my glory, be not joined to their
      company.
  For in their anger they killed men,
    and in their willfulness they ham-
      strung oxen.
⁷ Cursed be their anger, for it is fierce,
    and their wrath, for it is cruel!
  I will divide them in Jacob
    and scatter them in Israel.

⁸ "Judah, your brothers shall praise you;
    your hand shall be on the neck of
      your enemies;
    your father's sons shall bow down
      before you.
⁹ Judah is a lion's cub;
    from the prey, my son, you have
      gone up.
  He stooped down; he crouched as a
      lion
    and as a lioness; who dares rouse
      him?
¹⁰ The scepter shall not depart from
      Judah,
    nor the ruler's staff from between
      his feet,
  until tribute comes to him;
    and to him shall be the obedience
      of the peoples.
¹¹ Binding his foal to the vine
    and his donkey's colt to the choice
      vine,
  he has washed his garments in wine
    and his vesture in the blood of
      grapes.

12 His eyes are darker than wine,
    and his teeth whiter than milk.

13 "Zebulun shall dwell at the shore of the
    sea;
        he shall become a haven for ships,
    and his border shall be at Sidon.

14 "Issachar is a strong donkey,
    crouching between the sheepfolds.

15 He saw that a resting place was good,
    and that the land was pleasant,
        so he bowed his shoulder to bear,
    and became a servant at forced labor.

16 "Dan shall judge his people
    as one of the tribes of Israel.

17 Dan shall be a serpent in the way,
    a viper by the path,
        that bites the horse's heels
    so that his rider falls backward.

18 I wait for your salvation, O LORD.

19 "Raiders shall raid Gad,[1]
    but he shall raid at their heels.

20 "Asher's food shall be rich,
    and he shall yield royal delicacies.

21 "Naphtali is a doe let loose
    that bears beautiful fawns.

22 "Joseph is a fruitful bough,
    a fruitful bough by a spring;
        his branches run over the wall.

23 The archers bitterly attacked him,
    shot at him, and harassed him
        severely,

24 yet his bow remained unmoved;
    his arms were made agile
        by the hands of the Mighty One of
        Jacob
        (from there is the Shepherd, the
        Stone of Israel),

25 by the God of your father who will
    help you,
        by the Almighty who will bless you
    with blessings of heaven above,
    blessings of the deep that crouches
        beneath,
    blessings of the breasts and of the
        womb.

26 The blessings of your father
    are mighty beyond the blessings of
        my parents,
        up to the bounties of the everlasting
    hills.

May they be on the head of Joseph,
    and on the brow of him who was set
        apart from his brothers.

27 "Benjamin is a ravenous wolf,
    in the morning devouring the prey
    and at evening dividing the spoil."

Jacob's Death and Burial

28 All these are the twelve tribes of Israel. This is what their father said to them as he blessed them, blessing each with the blessing suitable to him. 29 Then he commanded them and said to them, "I am to be gathered to my people; bury me with my fathers in the cave that is in the field of Ephron the Hittite, 30 in the cave that is in the field at Machpelah, to the east of Mamre, in the land of Canaan, which Abraham bought with the field from Ephron the Hittite to possess as a burying place. 31 There they buried Abraham and Sarah his wife. There they buried Isaac and Rebekah his wife, and there I buried Leah— 32 the field and the cave that is in it were bought from the Hittites." 33 When Jacob finished commanding his sons, he drew up his feet into the bed and breathed his last and was gathered to his people.

50 Then Joseph fell on his father's face and wept over him and kissed him. 2 And Joseph commanded his servants the physicians to embalm his father. So the physicians embalmed Israel. 3 Forty days were required for it, for that is how many are required for embalming. And the Egyptians wept for him seventy days.

4 And when the days of weeping for him were past, Joseph spoke to the household of Pharaoh, saying, "If now I have found favor in your eyes, please speak in the ears of Pharaoh, saying, 5 'My father made me swear, saying, "I am about to die: in my tomb that I hewed out for myself in the land of Canaan, there shall you bury me." Now therefore, let me please go up and bury my father. Then I will return.'" 6 And Pharaoh answered, "Go up, and bury your father, as he made you swear." 7 So Joseph went up to bury his father. With him went up all the servants of Pharaoh, the elders of his household, and all the elders of the land of Egypt, 8 as well as all the household of Joseph, his brothers, and his father's household. Only

---

[1] *Gad* sounds like the Hebrew for *raiders* and *raid*

their children, their flocks, and their herds were left in the land of Goshen. ⁹ And there went up with him both chariots and horsemen. It was a very great company. ¹⁰ When they came to the threshing floor of Atad, which is beyond the Jordan, they lamented there with a very great and grievous lamentation, and he made a mourning for his father seven days. ¹¹ When the inhabitants of the land, the Canaanites, saw the mourning on the threshing floor of Atad, they said, "This is a grievous mourning by the Egyptians." Therefore the place was named Abel-mizraim;¹ it is beyond the Jordan. ¹² Thus his sons did for him as he had commanded them, ¹³ for his sons carried him to the land of Canaan and buried him in the cave of the field at Machpelah, to the east of Mamre, which Abraham bought with the field from Ephron the Hittite to possess as a burying place. ¹⁴ After he had buried his father, Joseph returned to Egypt with his brothers and all who had gone up with him to bury his father.

God's Good Purposes

¹⁵ When Joseph's brothers saw that their father was dead, they said, "It may be that Joseph will hate us and pay us back for all the evil that we did to him." ¹⁶ So they sent a message to Joseph, saying, "Your father gave this command before he died: ¹⁷ 'Say to Joseph, "Please forgive the transgression of your brothers and their sin, because they did evil to you."' And now, please forgive the transgression of the servants of the God of your father." Joseph wept when they spoke to him. ¹⁸ His brothers also came and fell down before him and said, "Behold, we are

your servants." ¹⁹ But Joseph said to them, "Do not fear, for am I in the place of God? ²⁰ As for you, you meant evil against me, but God meant it for good, to bring it about that many people should be kept alive, as they are today. ²¹ So do not fear; I will provide for you and your little ones." Thus he comforted them and spoke kindly to them.

The Death of Joseph

²² So Joseph remained in Egypt, he and his father's house. Joseph lived 110 years. ²³ And Joseph saw Ephraim's children of the third generation. The children also of

> ### GETTING THE MESSAGE
>
> **God's providence.** When Joseph's brothers sold him into slavery, the outcome could have been tragic. But God in his providence brought good out of their evil actions (50:20). This was a foreshadowing of God's bringing the ultimate good—eternal salvation—out of the wicked actions of the men who crucified Jesus (Acts 2:22–24).

Machir the son of Manasseh were counted as Joseph's own. ²⁴ And Joseph said to his brothers, "I am about to die, but God will visit you and bring you up out of this land to the land that he swore to Abraham, to Isaac, and to Jacob." ²⁵ Then Joseph made the sons of Israel swear, saying, "God will surely visit you, and you shall carry up my bones from here." ²⁶ So Joseph died, being 110 years old. They embalmed him, and he was put in a coffin in Egypt.

¹ Abel-mizraim means mourning of Egypt

INTRODUCTION TO EXODUS

1876 B.C.	1526 B.C.	1446 B.C.
Israel goes to Egypt	Moses born	Exodus from Egypt

AUTHOR AND DATE

Exodus (meaning exit) is best understood to have been written primarily by Moses, like the rest of the Pentateuch, though some details (such as the narrative of his death in Deuteronomy 34) were clearly added at a later time. It also appears that some language and references were updated for later readers. There is no consensus among scholars as to the date when the events of the exodus took place. A common view is that the exodus occurred in c. 1446 B.C. This is based on the calculation of 480 years from Israel's departure from Egypt to the fourth year of Solomon's reign (c. 966 B.C.; see 1 Kings 6:1). However, because Exodus 1:11 depicts Israel working on a city called Raamses, some scholars believe that this would mean that the exodus occurred during the reign of Raamses II in Egypt (c. 1279–1213 B.C.), possibly around 1260 B.C.

THEME

The overarching theme of Exodus is the fulfillment of God's promises to the patriarchs. The success of the exodus must be credited to the power and purpose of God, who remembers his promises, punishes sin, and forgives the repentant. The book highlights Moses' faithfulness and prayerfulness.

KEY THEMES

1. *Covenant promises.* The events and instructions in Exodus are described as the Lord remembering his covenant promises to Abraham (2:24; 3:6, 14–17; 6:2–8). The promises extend to both Abraham's descendants and all the nations of the world (Gen. 12:1–3). They include land (which Israel will inhabit), numerous offspring (which will secure their ongoing identity), and blessing (God cares for them and other nations). The fulfillment of these promises is rooted in Israel's covenant relationship with the Lord (Gen. 17:7–8).

2. *Covenant mediator.* Moses mediates between the Lord and his people. Through Moses the Lord reveals his purposes to Israel and sustains the covenant relationship.

3. *Covenant presence.* God's presence with his people is highlighted throughout the book of Exodus.

OUTLINE

EXODUS

Israel Increases Greatly in Egypt

1 These are the names of the sons of Israel who came to Egypt with Jacob, each with his household: ² Reuben, Simeon, Levi, and Judah, ³ Issachar, Zebulun, and Benjamin, ⁴ Dan and Naphtali, Gad and Asher. ⁵ All the descendants of Jacob were seventy persons; Joseph was already in Egypt. ⁶ Then Joseph died, and all his brothers and all that generation. ⁷ But the people of Israel were fruitful and increased greatly; they multiplied and grew exceedingly strong, so that the land was filled with them.

Pharaoh Oppresses Israel

⁸ Now there arose a new king over Egypt, who did not know Joseph. ⁹ And he said to his people, "Behold, the people of Israel are too many and too mighty for us. ¹⁰ Come, let us deal shrewdly with them, lest they multiply, and, if war breaks out, they join our enemies and fight against us and escape from the land." ¹¹ Therefore they set taskmasters over them to afflict them with heavy burdens. They built for Pharaoh store cities, Pithom and Raamses. ¹² But the more they were oppressed, the more they multiplied and the more they spread abroad. And the Egyptians were in dread of the people of Israel. ¹³ So they ruthlessly made the people of Israel work as slaves ¹⁴ and made their lives bitter with hard service, in mortar and brick, and in all kinds of work in the field. In all their work they ruthlessly made them work as slaves.

¹⁵ Then the king of Egypt said to the Hebrew midwives, one of whom was named Shiphrah and the other Puah, ¹⁶ "When you serve as midwife to the Hebrew women and see them on the birthstool, if it is a son, you shall kill him, but if it is a daughter, she shall live." ¹⁷ But the midwives feared God and did not do as the king of Egypt commanded them, but let the male children live. ¹⁸ So the king of Egypt called the midwives and said to them, "Why have you done this, and let the male children live?" ¹⁹ The midwives said to Pharaoh,

"Because the Hebrew women are not like the Egyptian women, for they are vigorous and give birth before the midwife comes to them." ²⁰ So God dealt well with the midwives. And the people multiplied and grew very strong. ²¹ And because the midwives feared God, he gave them families. ²² Then Pharaoh commanded all his people, "Every son that is born to the Hebrews you shall cast into the Nile, but you shall let every daughter live."

The Birth of Moses

2 Now a man from the house of Levi went and took as his wife a Levite woman. ² The woman conceived and bore a son, and

when she saw that he was a fine child, she hid him three months. ³ When she could hide him no longer, she took for him a basket made of bulrushes and daubed it with bitumen and pitch. She put the child in it and placed it among the reeds by the river bank. ⁴ And his sister stood at a distance to know what would be done to him. ⁵ Now the daughter of Pharaoh came down to bathe at the river, while her young women walked beside the river. She saw the basket among the reeds and sent her servant woman, and she took it. ⁶ When she opened it, she saw the child, and behold, the baby was crying. She took pity on him and said, "This is one of the Hebrews' children." ⁷ Then his sister said to Pharaoh's daughter, "Shall I go and call you a nurse from the Hebrew women to nurse the child for you?" ⁸ And Pharaoh's daughter said to her, "Go." So the girl went and called the child's mother. **9** And Pharaoh's daughter said to her, "Take this child away and nurse him for me, and I will give you your wages." So the woman took the child and nursed him. **10** When the child grew older, she brought him to Pharaoh's daughter, and he became her son. She named him Moses, "Because," she said, "I drew him out of the water."[1]

MOSES

Moses' life was spared when his mother hid him in a reed basket and set him adrift on the Nile. Rescued by Pharaoh's daughter and raised as a prince, Moses nonetheless recognized the Hebrews as his people. After killing an Egyptian who was beating a Hebrew slave, Moses fled to Midian, where he married Zipporah. God spoke to him through a burning bush, instructing him to return to Egypt and rescue the Hebrews from slavery to the Egyptians. After performing powerful signs before Pharaoh, Moses led the Hebrews out of Egypt and brought them to Mount Sinai, where he received the Law and the Ten Commandments. He led the people of Israel for 40 years as they wandered in the wilderness. Through Moses God redeemed his people from slavery in Egypt, prefiguring Christ's eternal redemption of his people from slavery to sin.

KEY REFERENCE: EXODUS 33:17

Moses Flees to Midian

11 One day, when Moses had grown up, he went out to his people and looked on their burdens, and he saw an Egyptian beating a Hebrew, one of his people. **12** He looked this way and that, and seeing no one, he struck down the Egyptian and hid him in the sand. **13** When he went out the next day, behold, two Hebrews were struggling together. And he said to the man in the wrong, "Why do you strike your companion?" **14** He answered, "Who made you a prince and a

judge over us? Do you mean to kill me as you killed the Egyptian?" Then Moses was afraid, and thought, "Surely the thing is known." **15** When Pharaoh heard of it, he sought to kill Moses. But Moses fled from Pharaoh and stayed in the land of Midian. And he sat down by a well.

16 Now the priest of Midian had seven daughters, and they came and drew water and filled the troughs to water their father's flock. **17** The shepherds came and drove them away, but Moses stood up and saved them, and watered their flock. **18** When they came home to their father Reuel, he said, "How is it that you have come home so soon today?" **19** They said, "An Egyptian delivered us out of the hand of the shepherds and even drew water for us and watered the flock." **20** He said to his daughters, "Then where is he? Why have you left the man? Call him, that he may eat bread." **21** And Moses was content to dwell with the man, and he gave Moses

his daughter Zipporah. **22** She gave birth to a son, and he called his name Gershom, for he said, "I have been a sojourner[2] in a foreign land."

God Hears Israel's Groaning

23 During those many days the king of Egypt died, and the people of Israel groaned because of their slavery and cried out for help. Their cry for rescue from slavery came up to God. **24** And God heard their groaning, and God remembered his covenant with Abraham, with Isaac, and with Jacob. **25** God saw the people of Israel—and God knew.

The Burning Bush

3 Now Moses was keeping the flock of his father-in-law, Jethro, the priest of Midian, and he led his flock to the west side of the wilderness and came to Horeb, the mountain of God. **2** And the angel of the LORD appeared to him in a flame of fire out of the midst of a bush. He looked, and

[1] *Moses* sounds like the Hebrew for *draw out* [2] *Gershom* sounds like the Hebrew for *sojourner*

behold, the bush was burning, yet it was not consumed. ³ And Moses said, "I will turn aside to see this great sight, why the bush is not burned." ⁴ When the LORD saw that he turned aside to see, God called to him out of the bush, "Moses, Moses!" And he said, "Here I am." ⁵ Then he said, "Do not come near; take your sandals off your feet, for the place on which you are standing is holy ground." ⁶ And he said, "I am the God of your father, the God of Abraham, the God of Isaac, and the God of Jacob." And Moses hid his face, for he was afraid to look at God.

⁷ Then the LORD said, "I have surely seen the affliction of my people who are in Egypt and have heard their cry because of their taskmasters. I know their sufferings, ⁸ and I have come down to deliver them out of the hand of the Egyptians and to bring them up out of that land to a good and broad land, a land flowing with milk and honey, to the place of the Canaanites, the Hittites, the Amorites, the Perizzites, the Hivites, and the Jebusites. ⁹ And now, behold, the cry of the people of Israel has come to me, and I have also seen the oppression with which the Egyptians oppress them. ¹⁰ Come, I will send you to Pharaoh that you may bring my people, the children of Israel, out of Egypt." ¹¹ But Moses said to God, "Who am I that I should go to Pharaoh and bring the children of Israel out of Egypt?" ¹² He said, "But I will be with you, and this shall be the sign for you, that I have sent you: when you have brought the people out of Egypt, you shall serve God on this mountain."

¹³ Then Moses said to God, "If I come to the people of Israel and say to them, 'The God of your fathers has sent me to you,' and they ask me, 'What is his name?' what shall I say to them?" ¹⁴ God said to Moses, "I AM WHO I AM." And he said, "Say this to the people of Israel, 'I AM has sent me to you.'" ¹⁵ God also said to Moses, "Say this to the people of Israel, 'The LORD,[1] the God of your fathers, the God of Abraham, the God of Isaac, and the God of Jacob, has sent me to you.' This is my name forever, and thus I am to be remembered throughout all generations. ¹⁶ Go and gather the elders of Israel together and say to them, 'The LORD, the God of your fathers, the God of Abraham, of Isaac, and of Jacob, has appeared to me,

saying, "I have observed you and what has been done to you in Egypt, ¹⁷ and I promise that I will bring you up out of the affliction of Egypt to the land of the Canaanites, the Hittites, the Amorites, the Perizzites, the Hivites, and the Jebusites, a land flowing with milk and honey."' ¹⁸ And they will listen to your voice, and you and the elders of Israel shall go to the king of Egypt and say to him, 'The LORD, the God of the Hebrews, has met with us; and now, please let us go a three days' journey into the wilderness, that we may sacrifice to the LORD our God.' ¹⁹ But I know that the king of Egypt will not let you go unless compelled by a mighty hand. ²⁰ So I will stretch out my hand and strike Egypt with all the wonders that I will do in it; after that he will let you go. ²¹ And I will give this people favor in the sight of the Egyptians; and when you go, you shall not go empty, ²² but each woman shall ask of her

> ### GETTING THE MESSAGE
>
> **Holy** means "set apart for God's special purpose." It is a condition of purity and freedom from sin. When the Bible speaks of God's holiness it means his utter separateness from everything else that exists, especially from all forms of evil (3:5).

neighbor, and any woman who lives in her house, for silver and gold jewelry, and for clothing. You shall put them on your sons and on your daughters. So you shall plunder the Egyptians."

Moses Given Powerful Signs

4 Then Moses answered, "But behold, they will not believe me or listen to my voice, for they will say, 'The LORD did not appear to you.'" ² The LORD said to him, "What is that in your hand?" He said, "A staff." ³ And he said, "Throw it on the ground." So he threw it on the ground, and it became a serpent, and Moses ran from it. ⁴ But the LORD said to Moses, "Put out your hand and catch it by the tail"—so he put out his hand and caught it, and it became a staff in his hand— ⁵ "that they may believe that the LORD, the God of their fathers, the God of Abraham, the God of Isaac, and the God of Jacob, has appeared to you." ⁶ Again,

---

[1] *Yahweh*, God's personal name, sounds like the Hebrew for *I AM* (see Preface and note at Genesis 2:4)

the LORD said to him, "Put your hand inside your cloak." And he put his hand inside his cloak, and when he took it out, behold, his hand was leprous[1] like snow. [7] Then God said, "Put your hand back inside your cloak." So he put his hand back inside his cloak, and when he took it out, behold, it was restored like the rest of his flesh. [8] "If they will not believe you," God said, "or listen to the first sign, they may believe the latter sign. [9] If they will not believe even these two signs or listen to your voice, you shall take some water from the Nile and pour it on the dry ground, and the water that you shall take from the Nile will become blood on the dry ground."

[10] But Moses said to the LORD, "Oh, my Lord, I am not eloquent, either in the past or since you have spoken to your servant, but

I am slow of speech and of tongue." [11] Then the LORD said to him, "Who has made man's mouth? Who makes him mute, or deaf, or seeing, or blind? Is it not I, the LORD? [12] Now therefore go, and I will be with your mouth and teach you what you shall speak." [13] But he said, "Oh, my Lord, please send someone else." [14] Then the anger of the LORD was kindled against Moses and he said, "Is there not Aaron, your brother, the Levite? I know that he can speak well. Behold, he is coming out to meet you, and when he sees you, he will be glad in his heart. [15] You shall speak to him and put the words in his mouth, and I will be with your mouth and with his mouth and will teach you both what to do. [16] He shall speak for you to the people, and he shall be your mouth, and you shall be as God to him. [17] And take in your hand this staff, with which you shall do the signs."

Moses Returns to Egypt

[18] Moses went back to Jethro his father-in-law and said to him, "Please let me go back to my brothers in Egypt to see whether they are still alive." And Jethro said to Moses, "Go in peace." [19] And the LORD said to Moses in Midian, "Go back to Egypt, for all the men who were seeking your life are dead." [20] So Moses took his wife and his sons and had them ride on a donkey, and went back to the land of Egypt. And Moses took the staff of God in his hand.

[21] And the LORD said to Moses, "When you go back to Egypt, see that you do before Pharaoh all the miracles that I have put in your power. But I will harden his heart, so that he will not let the people go. [22] Then you shall say to Pharaoh, 'Thus says the LORD, Israel is my firstborn son, [23] and I say to you, "Let my son go that he may serve me." If you refuse to let him go, behold, I will kill your firstborn son.'"

[24] At a lodging place on the way the LORD met him and sought to put him to death. [25] Then Zipporah took a flint and cut off her son's foreskin and touched Moses' feet with it and said, "Surely you are a bridegroom of blood to me!" [26] So he let him alone. It was then that she said, "A bridegroom of blood," because of the circumcision.

[27] The LORD said to Aaron, "Go into the wilderness to meet Moses." So he went and met him at the mountain of God and kissed him. [28] And Moses told Aaron all the words of the LORD with which he had sent him to speak, and all the signs that he had commanded him to do. [29] Then Moses and Aaron went and gathered together all the elders of the people of Israel. [30] Aaron spoke all the words that the LORD had spoken to Moses and did the signs in the sight of the people. [31] And the people believed; and when they heard that the LORD had visited the people of Israel and that he had seen their affliction, they bowed their heads and worshiped.

Making Bricks Without Straw

5 Afterward Moses and Aaron went and said to Pharaoh, "Thus says the LORD, the God of Israel, 'Let my people go, that they may hold a feast to me in the wilderness.'" [2] But Pharaoh said, "Who is the LORD, that I should obey his voice and let Israel go? I do not know the LORD, and moreover, I will

[1] *Leprosy* was a term for several skin diseases (see Leviticus 13)

not let Israel go." ³ Then they said, "The God of the Hebrews has met with us. Please let us go a three days' journey into the wilderness that we may sacrifice to the LORD our God, lest he fall upon us with pestilence or with the sword." ⁴ But the king of Egypt said to them, "Moses and Aaron, why do you take the people away from their work? Get back to your burdens." ⁵ And Pharaoh said, "Behold, the people of the land are now many, and you make them rest from their burdens!" ⁶ The same day Pharaoh commanded the taskmasters of the people and their foremen, ⁷ "You shall no longer give the people straw to make bricks, as in the past; let them go and gather straw for themselves. ⁸ But the number of bricks that they made in the past you shall impose on them, you shall by no means reduce it, for they are idle. Therefore they cry, 'Let us go and offer sacrifice to our God.' ⁹ Let heavier work be laid on the men that they may labor at it and pay no regard to lying words."

¹⁰ So the taskmasters and the foremen of the people went out and said to the people, "Thus says Pharaoh, 'I will not give you straw. ¹¹ Go and get your straw yourselves wherever you can find it, but your work will not be reduced in the least.'" ¹² So the people were scattered throughout all the land of Egypt to gather stubble for straw. ¹³ The taskmasters were urgent, saying, "Complete your work, your daily task each day, as when there was straw." ¹⁴ And the foremen of the people of Israel, whom Pharaoh's taskmasters had set over them, were beaten and were asked, "Why have you not done all your task of making bricks today and yesterday, as in the past?"

¹⁵ Then the foremen of the people of Israel came and cried to Pharaoh, "Why do you treat your servants like this? ¹⁶ No straw is given to your servants, yet they say to us, 'Make bricks!' And behold, your servants are beaten; but the fault is in your own people." ¹⁷ But he said, "You are idle, you are idle; that is why you say, 'Let us go and sacrifice to the LORD.' ¹⁸ Go now and work. No straw will be given you, but you must still deliver the same number of bricks." ¹⁹ The foremen of the people of Israel saw that they were in trouble when they said, "You shall by no means reduce your number of bricks, your daily task each day." ²⁰ They met Moses and Aaron, who were waiting for them, as they came out from Pharaoh; ²¹ and they said to them, "The LORD look on you and judge, because you have made us stink in the sight of Pharaoh and his servants, and have put a sword in their hand to kill us."

²² Then Moses turned to the LORD and said, "O Lord, why have you done evil to this people? Why did you ever send me? ²³ For since I came to Pharaoh to speak in your name, he has done evil to this people, and you have not delivered your people at all."

God Promises Deliverance

6 But the LORD said to Moses, "Now you shall see what I will do to Pharaoh; for with a strong hand he will send them out, and with a strong hand he will drive them out of his land."

² God spoke to Moses and said to him, "I am the LORD. ³ I appeared to Abraham,

GETTING THE MESSAGE

Why was straw needed for making bricks? To withstand the harsh weather in Egypt, buildings needed especially strong bricks. Mixing straw with the clay allowed the clay to bind together and helped the bricks to dry evenly (5:10).

to Isaac, and to Jacob, as God Almighty, but by my name the LORD I did not make myself known to them. ⁴ I also established my covenant with them to give them the land of Canaan, the land in which they lived as sojourners. ⁵ Moreover, I have heard the groaning of the people of Israel whom the Egyptians hold as slaves, and I have remembered my covenant. ⁶ Say therefore to the people of Israel, 'I am the LORD, and I will bring you out from under the burdens of the Egyptians, and I will deliver you from slavery to them, and I will redeem you with an outstretched arm and with great acts of judgment. ⁷ I will take you to be my people, and I will be your God, and you shall know that I am the LORD your God, who has brought you out from under the burdens of the Egyptians. ⁸ I will bring you into the land that I swore to give to Abraham, to Isaac, and to Jacob. I will give it to you for a possession. I am the LORD.'" ⁹ Moses spoke thus to the people of Israel, but they did not listen to

Moses, because of their broken spirit and harsh slavery. [10] So the LORD said to Moses, [11] "Go in, tell Pharaoh king of Egypt to let the people of Israel go out of his land." [12] But Moses said to the LORD, "Behold, the people of Israel have not listened to me. How then shall Pharaoh listen to me, for I am of uncircumcised lips?" [13] But the LORD spoke to Moses and Aaron and gave them a charge about the people of Israel and about Pharaoh king of Egypt: to bring the people of Israel out of the land of Egypt.

The Genealogy of Moses and Aaron

[14] These are the heads of their fathers' houses: the sons of Reuben, the firstborn of Israel: Hanoch, Pallu, Hezron, and Carmi; these are the clans of Reuben. [15] The sons of Simeon: Jemuel, Jamin, Ohad, Jachin, Zohar, and Shaul, the son of a Canaanite woman; these are the clans of Simeon. [16] These are the names of the sons of Levi according to their generations: Gershon, Kohath, and Merari, the years of the life of Levi being 137 years. [17] The sons of Gershon: Libni and Shimei, by their clans. [18] The sons of Kohath: Amram, Izhar, Hebron, and Uzziel, the years of the life of Kohath being 133 years. [19] The sons of Merari: Mahli and Mushi. These are the clans of the Levites according to their generations. [20] Amram took as his wife Jochebed his father's sister, and she bore him Aaron and Moses, the years of the life of Amram being 137 years. [21] The sons of Izhar: Korah, Nepheg, and Zichri. [22] The sons of Uzziel: Mishael, Elzaphan, and Sithri. [23] Aaron took as his wife Elisheba, the daughter of Amminadab and the sister of Nahshon, and she bore him Nadab, Abihu, Eleazar, and Ithamar. [24] The sons of Korah: Assir, Elkanah, and Abiasaph; these are the clans of the Korahites. [25] Eleazar, Aaron's son, took as his wife one of the daughters of Putiel, and she bore him Phinehas. These are the heads of the fathers' houses of the Levites by their clans.

[26] These are the Aaron and Moses to whom the LORD said: "Bring out the people of Israel from the land of Egypt by their hosts." [27] It was they who spoke to Pharaoh king of Egypt about bringing out the people of Israel from Egypt, this Moses and this Aaron.

[28] On the day when the LORD spoke to Moses in the land of Egypt, [29] the LORD said to Moses, "I am the LORD; tell Pharaoh king of Egypt all that I say to you." [30] But Moses said to the LORD, "Behold, I am of uncircumcised lips. How will Pharaoh listen to me?"

Moses and Aaron Before Pharaoh

7 And the LORD said to Moses, "See, I have made you like God to Pharaoh, and your brother Aaron shall be your prophet. [2] You shall speak all that I command you, and your brother Aaron shall tell Pharaoh to let the people of Israel go out of his land. [3] But I will harden Pharaoh's heart, and though I multiply my signs and wonders in the land of Egypt, [4] Pharaoh will not listen to you. Then I will lay my hand on Egypt and bring my hosts, my people the children of Israel, out of the land of Egypt by great acts of judgment. [5] The Egyptians shall know that I am the LORD, when I stretch out my hand against Egypt and bring out the people of Israel from among them." [6] Moses and Aaron did so; they did just as the LORD commanded them. [7] Now Moses was eighty years old, and Aaron eighty-three years old, when they spoke to Pharaoh.

[8] Then the LORD said to Moses and Aaron, [9] "When Pharaoh says to you, 'Prove yourselves by working a miracle,' then you shall say to Aaron, 'Take your staff and cast it down before Pharaoh, that it may become a serpent.'" [10] So Moses and Aaron went to Pharaoh and did just as the LORD commanded. Aaron cast down his staff before Pharaoh and his servants, and it became a serpent. [11] Then Pharaoh summoned the wise men and the sorcerers, and they, the magicians of Egypt, also did the same by their secret arts. [12] For each man cast down his staff, and they became serpents. But Aaron's staff swallowed up their staffs. [13] Still Pharaoh's heart was hardened, and he would not listen to them, as the LORD had said.

The First Plague: Water Turned to Blood

14 Then the LORD said to Moses, "Pharaoh's heart is hardened; he refuses to let the people go. **15** Go to Pharaoh in the morning, as he is going out to the water. Stand on the bank of the Nile to meet him, and take in your hand the staff that turned into a serpent. **16** And you shall say to him, 'The LORD, the God of the Hebrews, sent me to you, saying, "Let my people go, that they may serve me in the wilderness." But so far, you have not obeyed. **17** Thus says the LORD, "By this you shall know that I am the LORD: behold, with the staff that is in my hand I will strike the water that is in the Nile, and it shall turn into blood. **18** The fish in the Nile shall die, and the Nile will stink, and the Egyptians will grow weary of drinking water from the Nile." ' " **19** And the LORD said to Moses, "Say to Aaron, 'Take your staff and stretch out your hand over the waters of Egypt, over their rivers, their canals, and their ponds, and all their pools of water, so that they may become blood, and there shall be blood throughout all the land of Egypt, even in vessels of wood and in vessels of stone.' "

20 Moses and Aaron did as the LORD commanded. In the sight of Pharaoh and in the sight of his servants he lifted up the staff and struck the water in the Nile, and all the water in the Nile turned into blood. **21** And the fish in the Nile died, and the Nile stank, so that the Egyptians could not drink water from the Nile. There was blood throughout all the land of Egypt. **22** But the magicians of Egypt did the same by their secret arts. So Pharaoh's heart remained hardened, and he would not listen to them, as the LORD had said. **23** Pharaoh turned and went into his house, and he did not take even this to heart. **24** And all the Egyptians dug along the Nile for water to drink, for they could not drink the water of the Nile. **25** Seven full days passed after the LORD had struck the Nile.

The Second Plague: Frogs

8 Then the LORD said to Moses, "Go in to Pharaoh and say to him, 'Thus says the LORD, "Let my people go, that they may serve me. **2** But if you refuse to let them go, behold, I will plague all your country with frogs. **3** The Nile shall swarm with frogs that shall come up into your house and into your bedroom and on your bed and into the houses of your servants and your people, and into your ovens and your kneading bowls. **4** The frogs shall come up on you and on your people and on all your servants." ' " **5** And the LORD said to Moses, "Say to Aaron, 'Stretch out your hand with your staff over the rivers, over the canals and over the pools, and make frogs come up on the land of Egypt!' " **6** So Aaron stretched out his hand over the waters of Egypt, and the frogs came up and covered the land of Egypt. **7** But the magicians did the same by their secret arts and made frogs come up on the land of Egypt.

8 Then Pharaoh called Moses and Aaron and said, "Plead with the LORD to take away the frogs from me and from my people, and I will let the people go to sacrifice to the LORD." **9** Moses said to Pharaoh, "Be pleased to command me when I am to plead for you and for your servants and for your people,

GETTING THE MESSAGE

River turned to blood. Egypt's most important gods were associated with the Nile River. Turning the Nile to blood proved that the God of Israel had supreme control of the rivers.

that the frogs be cut off from you and your houses and be left only in the Nile." **10** And he said, "Tomorrow." Moses said, "Be it as you say, so that you may know that there is no one like the LORD our God. **11** The frogs shall go away from you and your houses and your servants and your people. They shall be left only in the Nile." **12** So Moses and Aaron went out from Pharaoh, and Moses cried to the LORD about the frogs, as he had agreed with Pharaoh. **13** And the LORD did according to the word of Moses. The frogs died out in the houses, the courtyards, and the fields. **14** And they gathered them together in heaps, and the land stank. **15** But when Pharaoh saw that there was a respite, he hardened his heart and would not listen to them, as the LORD had said.

The Third Plague: Gnats

16 Then the LORD said to Moses, "Say to Aaron, 'Stretch out your staff and strike the dust of the earth, so that it may become gnats in all the land of Egypt.' " **17** And they did so. Aaron stretched out his hand with his staff and struck the dust of the earth, and there were gnats on man and beast. All the dust of the earth became gnats in all the land of Egypt. [18] The magicians tried by their secret arts to produce gnats, but they could not. So there were gnats on man and beast. [19] Then the magicians said to Pharaoh, "This is the finger of God." But Pharaoh's heart was hardened, and he would not listen to them, as the LORD had said.

The Fourth Plague: Flies

[20] Then the LORD said to Moses, "Rise up early in the morning and present yourself to Pharaoh, as he goes out to the water, and say to him, 'Thus says the LORD, "Let my people go, that they may serve me. [21] Or else, if you will not let my people go, behold, I will send swarms of flies on you and your servants and your people, and into your houses. And the houses of the Egyptians shall be filled with swarms of flies, and also the ground

GETTING THE MESSAGE

Frogs. The Egyptians worshiped the god Hekt, who was portrayed as having the head of a frog.

on which they stand. [22] But on that day I will set apart the land of Goshen, where my people dwell, so that no swarms of flies shall be there, that you may know that I am the LORD in the midst of the earth. [23] Thus I will put a division between my people and your people. Tomorrow this sign shall happen."'" [24] And the LORD did so. There came great swarms of flies into the house of Pharaoh and into his servants' houses. Throughout all the land of Egypt the land was ruined by the swarms of flies.

[25] Then Pharaoh called Moses and Aaron and said, "Go, sacrifice to your God within the land." [26] But Moses said, "It would not be right to do so, for the offerings we shall sacrifice to the LORD our God are an abomination to the Egyptians. If we sacrifice offerings abominable to the Egyptians before their eyes, will they not stone us? [27] We must go three days' journey into the wilderness and sacrifice to the LORD our God as he tells us." [28] So Pharaoh said, "I will let you go to sacrifice to the LORD your God

in the wilderness; only you must not go very far away. Plead for me." [29] Then Moses said, "Behold, I am going out from you and I will plead with the LORD that the swarms of flies may depart from Pharaoh, from his servants, and from his people, tomorrow. Only let not Pharaoh cheat again by not letting the people go to sacrifice to the LORD." [30] So Moses went out from Pharaoh and prayed to the LORD. [31] And the LORD did as Moses asked, and removed the swarms of flies from Pharaoh, from his servants, and from his people; not one remained. [32] But Pharaoh hardened his heart this time also, and did not let the people go.

The Fifth Plague: Egyptian Livestock Die

9 Then the LORD said to Moses, "Go in to Pharaoh and say to him, 'Thus says the LORD, the God of the Hebrews, "Let my people go, that they may serve me. [2] For if you refuse to let them go and still hold them, [3] behold, the hand of the LORD will fall with a very severe plague upon your livestock that are in the field, the horses, the donkeys, the camels, the herds, and the flocks. [4] But the LORD will make a distinction between the livestock of Israel and the livestock of Egypt, so that nothing of all that belongs to the people of Israel shall die."'" [5] And the LORD set a time, saying, "Tomorrow the LORD will do this thing in the land." [6] And the next day the LORD did this thing. All the livestock of the Egyptians died, but not one of the livestock of the people of Israel died. [7] And Pharaoh sent, and behold, not one of the livestock of Israel was dead. But the heart of Pharaoh was hardened, and he did not let the people go.

The Sixth Plague: Boils

[8] And the LORD said to Moses and Aaron, "Take handfuls of soot from the kiln, and let Moses throw them in the air in the sight of Pharaoh. [9] It shall become fine dust over all the land of Egypt, and become boils breaking out in sores on man and beast throughout all the land of Egypt." [10] So they took soot from the kiln and stood before Pharaoh. And Moses threw it in the air, and it became boils breaking out in sores on man and beast. [11] And the magicians could not stand before Moses because of the boils, for the boils came upon the magicians and upon all the Egyptians. [12] But the LORD hardened

the heart of Pharaoh, and he did not listen to them, as the LORD had spoken to Moses.

The Seventh Plague: Hail

¹³ Then the LORD said to Moses, "Rise up early in the morning and present yourself before Pharaoh and say to him, 'Thus says the LORD, the God of the Hebrews, "Let my people go, that they may serve me. ¹⁴ For this time I will send all my plagues on you yourself, and on your servants and your people, so that you may know that there is none like me in all the earth. ¹⁵ For by now I could have put out my hand and struck you and your people with pestilence, and you would have been cut off from the earth. ¹⁶ But for this purpose I have raised you up, to show you my power, so that my name may be proclaimed in all the earth. ¹⁷ You are still exalting yourself against my people and will not let them go. ¹⁸ Behold, about this time tomorrow I will cause very heavy hail to fall, such as never has been in Egypt from the day it was founded until now. ¹⁹ Now therefore send, get your livestock and all that you have in the field into safe shelter, for every man and beast that is in the field and is not brought home will die when the hail falls on them."'" ²⁰ Then whoever feared the word of the LORD among the servants of Pharaoh hurried his slaves and his livestock into the houses, ²¹ but whoever did not pay attention to the word of the LORD left his slaves and his livestock in the field.

²² Then the LORD said to Moses, "Stretch out your hand toward heaven, so that there may be hail in all the land of Egypt, on man and beast and every plant of the field, in the land of Egypt." ²³ Then Moses stretched out his staff toward heaven, and the LORD sent thunder and hail, and fire ran down to the earth. And the LORD rained hail upon the land of Egypt. ²⁴ There was hail and fire flashing continually in the midst of the hail, very heavy hail, such as had never been in all the land of Egypt since it became a nation. ²⁵ The hail struck down everything that was in the field in all the land of Egypt, both man and beast. And the hail struck down every plant of the field and broke every tree of the field. ²⁶ Only in the land of Goshen, where the people of Israel were, was there no hail.

²⁷ Then Pharaoh sent and called Moses and Aaron and said to them, "This time I have sinned; the LORD is in the right, and

I and my people are in the wrong. ²⁸ Plead with the LORD, for there has been enough of God's thunder and hail. I will let you go, and you shall stay no longer." ²⁹ Moses said to him, "As soon as I have gone out of the city, I will stretch out my hands to the LORD. The thunder will cease, and there will be no more hail, so that you may know that the earth is the LORD's. ³⁰ But as for you and your servants, I know that you do not yet fear the LORD God." ³¹ (The flax and the barley were struck down, for the barley was in the ear and the flax was in bud. ³² But the wheat and the emmer were not struck down, for they are late in coming up.) ³³ So Moses went out of the city from Pharaoh and stretched out his hands to the LORD, and the thunder and the hail ceased, and the rain no longer poured upon the earth. ³⁴ But when Pharaoh saw that the rain and the hail and the thunder had ceased, he sinned yet again

GETTING THE MESSAGE

Death of livestock (9:1). A number of the Egyptian gods were portrayed as having the head of an animal: Apis and Mnevis (bulls) and Khnum (a ram). Isis was depicted with cow horns on her head.

and hardened his heart, he and his servants. ³⁵ So the heart of Pharaoh was hardened, and he did not let the people of Israel go, just as the LORD had spoken through Moses.

The Eighth Plague: Locusts

10 Then the LORD said to Moses, "Go in to Pharaoh, for I have hardened his heart and the heart of his servants, that I may show these signs of mine among them, ² and that you may tell in the hearing of your son and of your grandson how I have dealt harshly with the Egyptians and what signs I have done among them, that you may know that I am the LORD."

³ So Moses and Aaron went in to Pharaoh and said to him, "Thus says the LORD, the God of the Hebrews, 'How long will you refuse to humble yourself before me? Let my people go, that they may serve me. ⁴ For if you refuse to let my people go, behold, tomorrow I will bring locusts into your country, ⁵ and they shall cover the face of the land, so that no one can see the land.

And they shall eat what is left to you after the hail, and they shall eat every tree of yours that grows in the field, ⁶ and they shall fill your houses and the houses of all your servants and of all the Egyptians, as neither your fathers nor your grandfathers have seen, from the day they came on earth to this day.'" Then he turned and went out from Pharaoh.

⁷ Then Pharaoh's servants said to him, "How long shall this man be a snare to us? Let the men go, that they may serve the LORD their God. Do you not yet understand that Egypt is ruined?" ⁸ So Moses and Aaron were brought back to Pharaoh. And he said to them, "Go, serve the LORD your God. But which ones are to go?" ⁹ Moses said, "We will go with our young and our old. We will go with our sons and daughters and with our flocks and herds, for we must hold a feast to the LORD." ¹⁰ But he said to them,

GETTING THE MESSAGE

Was Pharaoh considered a god?
According to some ancient Egyptian sources, each morning the pharaoh would conduct "the Rite of the House of the Morning," a ritual believed to awaken the sun god, causing the sun to rise.

"The LORD be with you, if ever I let you and your little ones go! Look, you have some evil purpose in mind. ¹¹ No! Go, the men among you, and serve the LORD, for that is what you are asking." And they were driven out from Pharaoh's presence.

¹² Then the LORD said to Moses, "Stretch out your hand over the land of Egypt for the locusts, so that they may come upon the land of Egypt and eat every plant in the land, all that the hail has left." ¹³ So Moses stretched out his staff over the land of Egypt, and the LORD brought an east wind upon the land all that day and all that night. When it was morning, the east wind had brought the locusts. ¹⁴ The locusts came up over all the land of Egypt and settled on the whole country of Egypt, such a dense swarm of locusts as had never been before, nor ever will be again. ¹⁵ They covered the face of the whole land, so that the land was darkened, and they ate all the plants in the land and

all the fruit of the trees that the hail had left. Not a green thing remained, neither tree nor plant of the field, through all the land of Egypt. ¹⁶ Then Pharaoh hastily called Moses and Aaron and said, "I have sinned against the LORD your God, and against you. ¹⁷ Now therefore, forgive my sin, please, only this once, and plead with the LORD your God only to remove this death from me." ¹⁸ So he went out from Pharaoh and pleaded with the LORD. ¹⁹ And the LORD turned the wind into a very strong west wind, which lifted the locusts and drove them into the Red Sea. Not a single locust was left in all the country of Egypt. ²⁰ But the LORD hardened Pharaoh's heart, and he did not let the people of Israel go.

The Ninth Plague: Darkness

²¹ Then the LORD said to Moses, "Stretch out your hand toward heaven, that there may be darkness over the land of Egypt, a darkness to be felt." ²² So Moses stretched out his hand toward heaven, and there was pitch darkness in all the land of Egypt three days. ²³ They did not see one another, nor did anyone rise from his place for three days, but all the people of Israel had light where they lived. ²⁴ Then Pharaoh called Moses and said, "Go, serve the LORD; your little ones also may go with you; only let your flocks and your herds remain behind." ²⁵ But Moses said, "You must also let us have sacrifices and burnt offerings, that we may sacrifice to the LORD our God. ²⁶ Our livestock also must go with us; not a hoof shall be left behind, for we must take of them to serve the LORD our God, and we do not know with what we must serve the LORD until we arrive there." ²⁷ But the LORD hardened Pharaoh's heart, and he would not let them go. ²⁸ Then Pharaoh said to him, "Get away from me; take care never to see my face again, for on the day you see my face you shall die." ²⁹ Moses said, "As you say! I will not see your face again."

A Final Plague Threatened

11 The LORD said to Moses, "Yet one plague more I will bring upon Pharaoh and upon Egypt. Afterward he will let you go from here. When he lets you go, he will drive you away completely. ² Speak now in the hearing of the people, that they ask, every man of his neighbor and every woman of

her neighbor, for silver and gold jewelry." ³ And the LORD gave the people favor in the sight of the Egyptians. Moreover, the man Moses was very great in the land of Egypt, in the sight of Pharaoh's servants and in the sight of the people.

⁴ So Moses said, "Thus says the LORD: 'About midnight I will go out in the midst of Egypt, ⁵ and every firstborn in the land of Egypt shall die, from the firstborn of Pharaoh who sits on his throne, even to the firstborn of the slave girl who is behind the handmill, and all the firstborn of the cattle. ⁶ There shall be a great cry throughout all the land of Egypt, such as there has never been, nor ever will be again. ⁷ But not a dog shall growl against any of the people of Israel, either man or beast, that you may know that the LORD makes a distinction between Egypt and Israel.' ⁸ And all these your servants shall come down to me and bow down to me, saying, 'Get out, you and all the people who follow you.' And after that I will go out." And he went out from Pharaoh in hot anger. ⁹ Then the LORD said to Moses, "Pharaoh will not listen to you, that my wonders may be multiplied in the land of Egypt."

¹⁰ Moses and Aaron did all these wonders before Pharaoh, and the LORD hardened Pharaoh's heart, and he did not let the people of Israel go out of his land.

The Passover

12 The LORD said to Moses and Aaron in the land of Egypt, ² "This month shall be for you the beginning of months. It shall be the first month of the year for you. ³ Tell all the congregation of Israel that on the tenth day of this month every man shall take a lamb according to their fathers' houses, a lamb for a household. ⁴ And if the household is too small for a lamb, then he and his nearest neighbor shall take according to the number of persons; according to what each can eat you shall make your count for the lamb. ⁵ Your lamb shall be without blemish, a male a year old. You may take it from the sheep or from the goats, ⁶ and you shall keep it until the fourteenth day of this month, when the whole assembly of the congregation of Israel shall kill their lambs at twilight.

⁷ "Then they shall take some of the blood and put it on the two doorposts and the lin-

tel of the houses in which they eat it. ⁸ They shall eat the flesh that night, roasted on the fire; with unleavened bread and bitter herbs they shall eat it. ⁹ Do not eat any of it raw or boiled in water, but roasted, its head with its legs and its inner parts. ¹⁰ And you shall let none of it remain until the morning; anything that remains until the morning you shall burn. ¹¹ In this manner you shall eat it: with your belt fastened, your sandals on your feet, and your staff in your hand. And you shall eat it in haste. It is the LORD's Passover. ¹² For I will pass through the land of Egypt that night, and I will strike all the firstborn in the land of Egypt, both man and beast; and on all the gods of Egypt I will execute judgments: I am the LORD. ¹³ The blood shall be a sign for you, on the houses where you are. And when I see the blood, I will pass

over you, and no plague will befall you to destroy you, when I strike the land of Egypt.

¹⁴ "This day shall be for you a memorial day, and you shall keep it as a feast to the LORD; throughout your generations, as a statute forever, you shall keep it as a feast. ¹⁵ Seven days you shall eat unleavened bread. On the first day you shall remove leaven out of your houses, for if anyone eats what is leavened, from the first day until the seventh day, that person shall be cut off from Israel. ¹⁶ On the first day you shall hold a holy assembly, and on the seventh day a holy assembly. No work shall be done on those days. But what everyone needs to eat, that alone may be prepared by you. ¹⁷ And you shall observe the Feast of Unleavened Bread, for on this very day I brought your hosts out of the land of Egypt. Therefore you shall observe this day, throughout your

generations, as a statute forever. [18] In the first month, from the fourteenth day of the month at evening, you shall eat unleavened bread until the twenty-first day of the month at evening. [19] For seven days no leaven is to be found in your houses. If anyone eats what is leavened, that person will be cut off from the congregation of Israel, whether he is a sojourner or a native of the land. [20] You shall eat nothing leavened; in all your dwelling places you shall eat unleavened bread."

[21] Then Moses called all the elders of Israel and said to them, "Go and select lambs for yourselves according to your clans, and kill the Passover lamb. [22] Take a bunch of hyssop and dip it in the blood that is in the basin, and touch the lintel and the two doorposts with the blood that is in the basin. None of you shall go out of the door of his house until the morning. [23] For the LORD will pass through to strike the Egyptians, and when he sees the blood on the lintel and on the two doorposts, the LORD will pass over the door and will not allow the destroyer to enter your houses to strike you. [24] You shall observe this rite as a statute for you and for your sons forever. [25] And when you come to the land that the LORD will give you, as he has promised, you shall keep this service. [26] And when your children say to you, 'What do you mean by this service?' [27] you shall say, 'It is the sacrifice of the LORD's Passover, for he passed over the houses of the people of Israel in Egypt, when he struck the Egyptians but spared our houses.'" And the people bowed their heads and worshiped. [28] Then the people of Israel went and did so; as the LORD had commanded Moses and Aaron, so they did.

The Tenth Plague: Death of the Firstborn

[29] At midnight the LORD struck down all the firstborn in the land of Egypt, from the firstborn of Pharaoh who sat on his throne to the firstborn of the captive who was in the dungeon, and all the firstborn of the livestock. [30] And Pharaoh rose up in the night, he and all his servants and all the Egyptians. And there was a great cry in Egypt, for there was not a house where someone was not dead. [31] Then he summoned Moses and Aaron by night and said, "Up, go out from among my people, both you and the people of Israel; and go, serve the LORD, as you have said. [32] Take your flocks and your herds, as you have said, and be gone, and bless me also!"

The Exodus

[33] The Egyptians were urgent with the people to send them out of the land in haste. For they said, "We shall all be dead." [34] So the people took their dough before it was leavened, their kneading bowls being bound up in their cloaks on their shoulders. [35] The people of Israel had also done as Moses told them, for they had asked the Egyptians for silver and gold jewelry and for clothing. [36] And the LORD had given the people favor in the sight of the Egyptians, so that they let them have what they asked. Thus they plundered the Egyptians.

[37] And the people of Israel journeyed from Rameses to Succoth, about six hundred thousand men on foot, besides women and children. [38] A mixed multitude also went up with them, and very much livestock, both flocks and herds. [39] And they baked unleavened cakes of the dough that they had brought out of Egypt, for it was not leavened, because they were thrust out of Egypt and could not wait, nor had they prepared any provisions for themselves.

[40] The time that the people of Israel lived in Egypt was 430 years. [41] At the end of 430 years, on that very day, all the hosts of the LORD went out from the land of Egypt. [42] It was a night of watching by the LORD, to bring them out of the land of Egypt; so this same night is a night of watching kept to the LORD by all the people of Israel throughout their generations.

Institution of the Passover

[43] And the LORD said to Moses and Aaron, "This is the statute of the Passover: no foreigner shall eat of it, [44] but every slave[1] that is bought for money may eat of it after you have circumcised him. [45] No foreigner or hired worker may eat of it. [46] It shall be eaten in one house; you shall not take any of the flesh outside the house, and you shall not break any of its bones. [47] All the congregation of Israel shall keep it. [48] If a stranger shall sojourn with you and would keep the Passover to the LORD, let all his males be circumcised. Then he may come near and keep it; he shall be as a native of the land.

[1] Or servant; the Hebrew word (ebed) can mean either voluntary service or forced service (see Preface)

But no uncircumcised person shall eat of it. [49] There shall be one law for the native and for the stranger who sojourns among you."

[50] All the people of Israel did just as the LORD commanded Moses and Aaron. [51] And on that very day the LORD brought the people of Israel out of the land of Egypt by their hosts.

Consecration of the Firstborn

13 The LORD said to Moses, [2] "Consecrate to me all the firstborn. Whatever is the first to open the womb among the people of Israel, both of man and of beast, is mine."

The Feast of Unleavened Bread

[3] Then Moses said to the people, "Remember this day in which you came out from Egypt, out of the house of slavery, for by a strong hand the LORD brought you out from this place. No leavened bread shall be eaten. [4] Today, in the month of Abib, you are going out. [5] And when the LORD brings you into the land of the Canaanites, the Hittites, the Amorites, the Hivites, and the Jebusites, which he swore to your fathers to give you, a land flowing with milk and honey, you shall keep this service in this month. [6] Seven days you shall eat unleavened bread, and on the seventh day there shall be a feast to the LORD. [7] Unleavened bread shall be eaten for seven days; no leavened bread shall be seen with you, and no leaven shall be seen with you in all your territory. [8] You shall tell your son on that day, 'It is because of what the LORD did for me when I came out of Egypt.' [9] And it shall be to you as a sign on your hand and as a memorial between your eyes, that the law of the LORD may be in your mouth. For with a strong hand the LORD has brought you out of Egypt. [10] You shall therefore keep this statute at its appointed time from year to year.

[11] "When the LORD brings you into the land of the Canaanites, as he swore to you and your fathers, and shall give it to you, [12] you shall set apart to the LORD all that first opens the womb. All the firstborn of your animals that are males shall be the LORD's. [13] Every firstborn of a donkey you shall redeem with a lamb, or if you will not redeem it you shall break its neck. Every firstborn of man among your sons you shall redeem. [14] And when in time to come your son asks you, 'What does this mean?' you shall say

to him, 'By a strong hand the LORD brought us out of Egypt, from the house of slavery. [15] For when Pharaoh stubbornly refused to let us go, the LORD killed all the firstborn in the land of Egypt, both the firstborn of man and the firstborn of animals. Therefore I sacrifice to the LORD all the males that first open the womb, but all the firstborn of my sons I redeem.' [16] It shall be as a mark on your hand or frontlets between your eyes, for by a strong hand the LORD brought us out of Egypt."

Pillars of Cloud and Fire

[17] When Pharaoh let the people go, God did not lead them by way of the land of the Philistines, although that was near. For God said, "Lest the people change their minds when they see war and return to Egypt." [18] But God led the people around by the way

GETTING THE MESSAGE

The word **redeem** (13:13) means to free someone or something from harm by paying a price. Jesus is the supreme example of redemption in the Bible. He paid the ultimate price—his very life—to bring freedom from sin and eternal life to all who would put their trust in him.

of the wilderness toward the Red Sea. And the people of Israel went up out of the land of Egypt equipped for battle. [19] Moses took the bones of Joseph with him, for Joseph had made the sons of Israel solemnly swear, saying, "God will surely visit you, and you shall carry up my bones with you from here." [20] And they moved on from Succoth and encamped at Etham, on the edge of the wilderness. [21] And the LORD went before them by day in a pillar of cloud to lead them along the way, and by night in a pillar of fire to give them light, that they might travel by day and by night. [22] The pillar of cloud by day and the pillar of fire by night did not depart from before the people.

Crossing the Red Sea

14 Then the LORD said to Moses, [2] "Tell the people of Israel to turn back and encamp in front of Pi-hahiroth, between Migdol and the sea, in front of Baal-zephon; you shall encamp facing it, by the sea. [3] For

Pharaoh will say of the people of Israel, 'They are wandering in the land; the wilderness has shut them in.' ⁴ And I will harden Pharaoh's heart, and he will pursue them, and I will get glory over Pharaoh and all his host, and the Egyptians shall know that I am the LORD." And they did so.

⁵ When the king of Egypt was told that the people had fled, the mind of Pharaoh and his servants was changed toward the people, and they said, "What is this we have done, that we have let Israel go from serving us?" ⁶ So he made ready his chariot and took his army with him, ⁷ and took six hundred chosen chariots and all the other chariots of Egypt with officers over all of them. ⁸ And the LORD hardened the heart of Pharaoh king of Egypt, and he pursued the people of Israel while the people of Israel were going

GETTING THE MESSAGE

Chariots (14:23) were two-wheeled vehicles pulled by horses. They were made of wood and leather. Mainly intended for battle, chariots often had two riders: a driver and a warrior. Chariots were also used for hunting and for transportation. They were symbols of wealth and power. Egyptian pharaohs were sometimes buried with a chariot.

out defiantly. ⁹ The Egyptians pursued them, all Pharaoh's horses and chariots and his horsemen and his army, and overtook them encamped at the sea, by Pi-hahiroth, in front of Baal-zephon.

¹⁰ When Pharaoh drew near, the people of Israel lifted up their eyes, and behold, the Egyptians were marching after them, and they feared greatly. And the people of Israel cried out to the LORD. ¹¹ They said to Moses, "Is it because there are no graves in Egypt that you have taken us away to die in the wilderness? What have you done to us in bringing us out of Egypt? ¹² Is not this what we said to you in Egypt: 'Leave us alone that we may serve the Egyptians'? For it would have been better for us to serve the Egyptians than to die in the wilderness." ¹³ And Moses said to the people, "Fear not, stand firm, and see the salvation of the LORD, which he will work for you today. For the Egyptians whom

you see today, you shall never see again. ¹⁴ The LORD will fight for you, and you have only to be silent."

¹⁵ The LORD said to Moses, "Why do you cry to me? Tell the people of Israel to go forward. ¹⁶ Lift up your staff, and stretch out your hand over the sea and divide it, that the people of Israel may go through the sea on dry ground. ¹⁷ And I will harden the hearts of the Egyptians so that they shall go in after them, and I will get glory over Pharaoh and all his host, his chariots, and his horsemen. ¹⁸ And the Egyptians shall know that I am the LORD, when I have gotten glory over Pharaoh, his chariots, and his horsemen."

¹⁹ Then the angel of God who was going before the host of Israel moved and went behind them, and the pillar of cloud moved from before them and stood behind them, ²⁰ coming between the host of Egypt and the host of Israel. And there was the cloud and the darkness. And it lit up the night without one coming near the other all night.

²¹ Then Moses stretched out his hand over the sea, and the LORD drove the sea back by a strong east wind all night and made the sea dry land, and the waters were divided. ²² And the people of Israel went into the midst of the sea on dry ground, the waters being a wall to them on their right hand and on their left. ²³ The Egyptians pursued and went in after them into the midst of the sea, all Pharaoh's horses, his chariots, and his horsemen. ²⁴ And in the morning watch the LORD in the pillar of fire and of cloud looked down on the Egyptian forces and threw the Egyptian forces into a panic, ²⁵ clogging their chariot wheels so that they drove heavily. And the Egyptians said, "Let us flee from before Israel, for the LORD fights for them against the Egyptians."

²⁶ Then the LORD said to Moses, "Stretch out your hand over the sea, that the water may come back upon the Egyptians, upon their chariots, and upon their horsemen." ²⁷ So Moses stretched out his hand over the sea, and the sea returned to its normal course when the morning appeared. And as the Egyptians fled into it, the LORD threw the Egyptians into the midst of the sea. ²⁸ The waters returned and covered the chariots and the horsemen; of all the host of Pharaoh that had followed them into the sea, not one of them remained. ²⁹ But

the people of Israel walked on dry ground through the sea, the waters being a wall to them on their right hand and on their left. ³⁰ Thus the LORD saved Israel that day from the hand of the Egyptians, and Israel saw the Egyptians dead on the seashore. ³¹ Israel saw the great power that the LORD used against the Egyptians, so the people feared the LORD, and they believed in the LORD and in his servant Moses.

The Song of Moses

15 Then Moses and the people of Israel sang this song to the LORD, saying,

"I will sing to the LORD, for he has
     triumphed gloriously;
     the horse and his rider he has
         thrown into the sea.
² The LORD is my strength and my song,
     and he has become my salvation;
     this is my God, and I will praise him,
     my father's God, and I will exalt him.
³ The LORD is a man of war;
     the LORD is his name.

⁴ "Pharaoh's chariots and his host he
     cast into the sea,
     and his chosen officers were sunk
         in the Red Sea.
⁵ The floods covered them;
     they went down into the depths like
         a stone.
⁶ Your right hand, O LORD, glorious in
     power,
     your right hand, O LORD, shatters
         the enemy.
⁷ In the greatness of your majesty you
     overthrow your adversaries;
     you send out your fury; it consumes
         them like stubble.
⁸ At the blast of your nostrils the waters
     piled up;
     the floods stood up in a heap;
     the deeps congealed in the heart of
         the sea.
⁹ The enemy said, 'I will pursue, I will
     overtake,
     I will divide the spoil, my desire
         shall have its fill of them.
     I will draw my sword; my hand
         shall destroy them.'
¹⁰ You blew with your wind; the sea
     covered them;
     they sank like lead in the mighty
         waters.

¹¹ "Who is like you, O LORD, among the
     gods?
     Who is like you, majestic in holiness,
     awesome in glorious deeds, doing
         wonders?
¹² You stretched out your right hand;
     the earth swallowed them.

¹³ "You have led in your steadfast love
     the people whom you have
         redeemed;
     you have guided them by your
         strength to your holy abode.
¹⁴ The peoples have heard; they tremble;
     pangs have seized the inhabitants
         of Philistia.
¹⁵ Now are the chiefs of Edom dismayed;
     trembling seizes the leaders of Moab;
     all the inhabitants of Canaan have
         melted away.
¹⁶ Terror and dread fall upon them;
     because of the greatness of your
         arm, they are still as a stone,
     till your people, O LORD, pass by,
     till the people pass by whom you
         have purchased.
¹⁷ You will bring them in and plant them
     on your own mountain,
     the place, O LORD, which you have
         made for your abode,
     the sanctuary, O Lord, which your
         hands have established.
¹⁸ The LORD will reign forever and ever."

¹⁹ For when the horses of Pharaoh with his chariots and his horsemen went into the sea, the LORD brought back the waters of the sea upon them, but the people of Israel walked on dry ground in the midst of the sea. ²⁰ Then Miriam the prophetess, the sister of Aaron, took a tambourine in her hand, and all the women went out after her with tambourines and dancing. ²¹ And Miriam sang to them:

"Sing to the LORD, for he has tri-
     umphed gloriously;
     the horse and his rider he has thrown
         into the sea."

Bitter Water Made Sweet

²² Then Moses made Israel set out from the Red Sea, and they went into the wilderness of Shur. They went three days in the wilderness and found no water. ²³ When they came to Marah, they could not drink

the water of Marah because it was bitter; therefore it was named Marah.[1] **24** And the people grumbled against Moses, saying, "What shall we drink?" **25** And he cried to the LORD, and the LORD showed him a log, and he threw it into the water, and the water became sweet.

There the LORD made for them a statute and a rule, and there he tested them, **26** saying, "If you will diligently listen to the voice of the LORD your God, and do that which is right in his eyes, and give ear to his commandments and keep all his statutes, I will put none of the diseases on you that I put on the Egyptians, for I am the LORD, your healer."

27 Then they came to Elim, where there were twelve springs of water and seventy palm trees, and they encamped there by the water.

▶ GETTING THE MESSAGE

Manna for Christians today? The manna that appeared each morning with the dew foreshadowed Jesus Christ, who is the true Bread from heaven (John 6:30–58).

Bread from Heaven

16 They set out from Elim, and all the congregation of the people of Israel came to the wilderness of Sin, which is between Elim and Sinai, on the fifteenth day of the second month after they had departed from the land of Egypt. **2** And the whole congregation of the people of Israel grumbled against Moses and Aaron in the wilderness, **3** and the people of Israel said to them, "Would that we had died by the hand of the LORD in the land of Egypt, when we sat by the meat pots and ate bread to the full, for you have brought us out into this wilderness to kill this whole assembly with hunger."

4 Then the LORD said to Moses, "Behold, I am about to rain bread from heaven for you, and the people shall go out and gather a day's portion every day, that I may test them, whether they will walk in my law or not. **5** On the sixth day, when they prepare what they bring in, it will be twice as much as they gather daily." **6** So Moses and Aaron

said to all the people of Israel, "At evening you shall know that it was the LORD who brought you out of the land of Egypt, **7** and in the morning you shall see the glory of the LORD, because he has heard your grumbling against the LORD. For what are we, that you grumble against us?" **8** And Moses said, "When the LORD gives you in the evening meat to eat and in the morning bread to the full, because the LORD has heard your grumbling that you grumble against him—what are we? Your grumbling is not against us but against the LORD."

9 Then Moses said to Aaron, "Say to the whole congregation of the people of Israel, 'Come near before the LORD, for he has heard your grumbling.'" **10** And as soon as Aaron spoke to the whole congregation of the people of Israel, they looked toward the wilderness, and behold, the glory of the LORD appeared in the cloud. **11** And the LORD said to Moses, **12** "I have heard the grumbling of the people of Israel. Say to them, 'At twilight you shall eat meat, and in the morning you shall be filled with bread. Then you shall know that I am the LORD your God.'"

13 In the evening quail came up and covered the camp, and in the morning dew lay around the camp. **14** And when the dew had gone up, there was on the face of the wilderness a fine, flake-like thing, fine as frost on the ground. **15** When the people of Israel saw it, they said to one another, "What is it?" For they did not know what it was. And Moses said to them, "It is the bread that the LORD has given you to eat. **16** This is what the LORD has commanded: 'Gather of it, each one of you, as much as he can eat. You shall each take an omer, according to the number of the persons that each of you has in his tent.'" **17** And the people of Israel did so. They gathered, some more, some less. **18** But when they measured it with an omer, whoever gathered much had nothing left over, and whoever gathered little had no lack. Each of them gathered as much as he could eat. **19** And Moses said to them, "Let no one leave any of it over till the morning." **20** But they did not listen to Moses. Some left part of it till the morning, and it bred worms and stank. And Moses was angry with them. **21** Morning by morning they gathered it, each

---

[1] *Marah* means *bitterness*

as much as he could eat; but when the sun grew hot, it melted.

²² On the sixth day they gathered twice as much bread, two omers each. And when all the leaders of the congregation came and told Moses, ²³ he said to them, "This is what the LORD has commanded: 'Tomorrow is a day of solemn rest, a holy Sabbath to the LORD; bake what you will bake and boil what you will boil, and all that is left over lay aside to be kept till the morning.'" ²⁴ So they laid it aside till the morning, as Moses commanded them, and it did not stink, and there were no worms in it. ²⁵ Moses said, "Eat it today, for today is a Sabbath to the LORD; today you will not find it in the field. ²⁶ Six days you shall gather it, but on the seventh day, which is a Sabbath, there will be none."

²⁷ On the seventh day some of the people went out to gather, but they found none. ²⁸ And the LORD said to Moses, "How long will you refuse to keep my commandments and my laws? ²⁹ See! The LORD has given you the Sabbath; therefore on the sixth day he gives you bread for two days. Remain each of you in his place; let no one go out of his place on the seventh day." ³⁰ So the people rested on the seventh day.

³¹ Now the house of Israel called its name manna. It was like coriander seed, white, and the taste of it was like wafers made with honey. ³² Moses said, "This is what the LORD has commanded: 'Let an omer of it be kept throughout your generations, so that they may see the bread with which I fed you in the wilderness, when I brought you out of the land of Egypt.'" ³³ And Moses said to Aaron, "Take a jar, and put an omer of manna in it, and place it before the LORD to be kept throughout your generations." ³⁴ As the LORD commanded Moses, so Aaron placed it before the testimony to be kept. ³⁵ The people of Israel ate the manna forty years, till they came to a habitable land. They ate the manna till they came to the border of the land of Canaan. ³⁶ (An omer is the tenth part of an ephah.)

Water from the Rock

17 All the congregation of the people of Israel moved on from the wilderness of Sin by stages, according to the commandment of the LORD, and camped at Rephidim, but there was no water for the people to drink. ² Therefore the people quarreled with Moses and said, "Give us water to drink." And Moses said to them, "Why do you quarrel with me? Why do you test the LORD?" ³ But the people thirsted there for water, and the people grumbled against Moses and said, "Why did you bring us up out of Egypt, to kill us and our children and our livestock with thirst?" ⁴ So Moses cried to the LORD, "What shall I do with this people? They are almost ready to stone me." ⁵ And the LORD said to Moses, "Pass on before the people, taking with you some of the elders of Israel, and take in your hand the staff with which you struck the Nile, and go. ⁶ Behold, I will stand before you there on the rock at Horeb, and you shall strike the rock, and water shall come out of it, and the people will drink." And Moses did so, in the sight of the elders

GETTING THE MESSAGE

Who were the Amalekites?
The Amalekites were nomads living in the northern Sinai peninsula. They were the first to attack the Israelites after the exodus. They remained a threat to Israel for hundreds of years.

of Israel. ⁷ And he called the name of the place Massah[1] and Meribah,[2] because of the quarreling of the people of Israel, and because they tested the LORD by saying, "Is the LORD among us or not?"

Israel Defeats Amalek

⁸ Then Amalek came and fought with Israel at Rephidim. ⁹ So Moses said to Joshua, "Choose for us men, and go out and fight with Amalek. Tomorrow I will stand on the top of the hill with the staff of God in my hand." ¹⁰ So Joshua did as Moses told him, and fought with Amalek, while Moses, Aaron, and Hur went up to the top of the hill. ¹¹ Whenever Moses held up his hand, Israel prevailed, and whenever he lowered his hand, Amalek prevailed. ¹² But Moses' hands grew weary, so they took a stone and put it under him, and he sat on it, while Aaron and Hur held up his hands, one on one side, and the other on the other side. So

[1] *Massah* means *testing* [2] *Meribah* means *quarreling*

his hands were steady until the going down of the sun. 13 And Joshua overwhelmed Amalek and his people with the sword.

14 Then the LORD said to Moses, "Write this as a memorial in a book and recite it in the ears of Joshua, that I will utterly blot out the memory of Amalek from under heaven." 15 And Moses built an altar and called the name of it, The LORD Is My Banner, 16 saying, "A hand upon the throne of the LORD! The LORD will have war with Amalek from generation to generation."

Jethro's Advice

18 Jethro, the priest of Midian, Moses' father-in-law, heard of all that God had done for Moses and for Israel his people, how the LORD had brought Israel out of Egypt. 2 Now Jethro, Moses' father-in-law, had taken Zipporah, Moses' wife, after he had sent her home, 3 along with her two sons. The name of the one was Gershom (for he said, "I have been a sojourner[1] in a foreign land"), 4 and the name of the other, Eliezer[2] (for he said, "The God of my father was my help, and delivered me from the sword of Pharaoh"). 5 Jethro, Moses' father-in-law, came with his sons and his wife to Moses in the wilderness where he was encamped at the mountain of God. 6 And when he sent word to Moses, "I, your father-in-law Jethro, am coming to you with your wife and her two sons with her," 7 Moses went out to meet his father-in-law and bowed down and kissed him. And they asked each other of their welfare and went into the tent. 8 Then Moses told his father-in-law all that the LORD had done to Pharaoh and to the Egyptians for Israel's sake, all the hardship that had come upon them in the way, and how the LORD had delivered them. 9 And Jethro rejoiced for all the good that the LORD had done to Israel, in that he had delivered them out of the hand of the Egyptians.

10 Jethro said, "Blessed be the LORD, who has delivered you out of the hand of the Egyptians and out of the hand of Pharaoh and has delivered the people from under the hand of the Egyptians. 11 Now I know that the LORD is greater than all gods, because in this affair they dealt arrogantly with the people." 12 And Jethro, Moses' father-in-law, brought a burnt offering and sacrifices to God; and

Aaron came with all the elders of Israel to eat bread with Moses' father-in-law before God.

13 The next day Moses sat to judge the people, and the people stood around Moses from morning till evening. 14 When Moses' father-in-law saw all that he was doing for the people, he said, "What is this that you are doing for the people? Why do you sit alone, and all the people stand around you from morning till evening?" 15 And Moses said to his father-in-law, "Because the people come to me to inquire of God; 16 when they have a dispute, they come to me and I decide between one person and another, and I make them know the statutes of God and his laws." 17 Moses' father-in-law said to him, "What you are doing is not good. 18 You and the people with you will certainly wear yourselves out, for the thing is too heavy for you. You are not able to do it alone. 19 Now obey my voice; I will give you advice, and God be with you! You shall represent the people before God and bring their cases to God, 20 and you shall warn them about the statutes and the laws, and make them know the way in which they must walk and what they must do. 21 Moreover, look for able men from all the people, men who fear God, who are trustworthy and hate a bribe, and place such men over the people as chiefs of thousands, of hundreds, of fifties, and of tens. 22 And let them judge the people at all times. Every great matter they shall bring to you, but any small matter they shall decide themselves. So it will be easier for you, and they will bear the burden with you. 23 If you do this, God will direct you, you will be able to endure, and all this people also will go to their place in peace."

24 So Moses listened to the voice of his father-in-law and did all that he had said. 25 Moses chose able men out of all Israel and made them heads over the people, chiefs of thousands, of hundreds, of fifties, and of tens. 26 And they judged the people at all times. Any hard case they brought to Moses, but any small matter they decided themselves. 27 Then Moses let his father-in-law depart, and he went away to his own country.

Israel at Mount Sinai

19 On the third new moon after the people of Israel had gone out of the land of Egypt, on that day they came into

---

[1] Gershom sounds like the Hebrew for sojourner [2] Eliezer means My God is help

the wilderness of Sinai. ²They set out from Rephidim and came into the wilderness of Sinai, and they encamped in the wilderness. There Israel encamped before the mountain, ³while Moses went up to God. The LORD called to him out of the mountain, saying, "Thus you shall say to the house of Jacob, and tell the people of Israel: ⁴You yourselves have seen what I did to the Egyptians, and how I bore you on eagles' wings and brought you to myself. ⁵Now therefore, if you will indeed obey my voice and keep my covenant, you shall be my treasured possession among all peoples, for all the earth is mine; ⁶and you shall be to me a kingdom of priests and a holy nation. These are the words that you shall speak to the people of Israel."

⁷So Moses came and called the elders of the people and set before them all these words that the LORD had commanded him. ⁸All the people answered together and said, "All that the LORD has spoken we will do." And Moses reported the words of the people to the LORD. ⁹And the LORD said to Moses, "Behold, I am coming to you in a thick cloud, that the people may hear when I speak with you, and may also believe you forever."

When Moses told the words of the people to the LORD, ¹⁰the LORD said to Moses, "Go to the people and consecrate them today and tomorrow, and let them wash their garments ¹¹and be ready for the third day. For on the third day the LORD will come down on Mount Sinai in the sight of all the people. ¹²And you shall set limits for the people all around, saying, 'Take care not to go up into the mountain or touch the edge of it. Whoever touches the mountain shall be put to death. ¹³No hand shall touch him, but he shall be stoned or shot; whether beast or man, he shall not live.' When the trumpet sounds a long blast, they shall come up to the mountain." ¹⁴So Moses went down from the mountain to the people and consecrated the people; and they washed their garments. ¹⁵And he said to the people, "Be ready for the third day; do not go near a woman."

¹⁶On the morning of the third day there were thunders and lightnings and a thick cloud on the mountain and a very loud trumpet blast, so that all the people in the camp trembled. ¹⁷Then Moses brought the people out of the camp to meet God, and they took their stand at the foot of the mountain. ¹⁸Now Mount Sinai was wrapped in smoke because the LORD had descended on it in fire. The smoke of it went up like the smoke of a kiln, and the whole mountain trembled greatly. ¹⁹And as the sound of the trumpet grew louder and louder, Moses spoke, and God answered him in thunder. ²⁰The LORD came down on Mount Sinai, to the top of the mountain. And the LORD called Moses to the top of the mountain, and Moses went up.

²¹And the LORD said to Moses, "Go down and warn the people, lest they break through to the LORD to look and many of them perish. ²²Also let the priests who come near to the LORD consecrate themselves, lest the LORD break out against them." ²³And Moses said to the LORD, "The people cannot come up to Mount Sinai, for you yourself warned us, saying, 'Set limits around the mountain and consecrate it.'" ²⁴And the LORD said

> ### GETTING THE MESSAGE
>
> **On eagles' wings.** The kind of eagle that the author of Exodus probably had in mind had a wingspan of 8 to 10 feet (2–3 m), making it a fitting symbol of the Lord's ability to rescue his people from their life of slavery in Egypt (19:4).

to him, "Go down, and come up bringing Aaron with you. But do not let the priests and the people break through to come up to the LORD, lest he break out against them." ²⁵So Moses went down to the people and told them.

The Ten Commandments

20 And God spoke all these words, saying,

²"I am the LORD your God, who brought you out of the land of Egypt, out of the house of slavery.

³"You shall have no other gods before me.

⁴"You shall not make for yourself a carved image, or any likeness of anything that is in heaven above, or that is in the earth beneath, or that is in the water under the earth. ⁵You shall not bow down to them or serve them, for I the LORD your God am a jealous God, visiting the iniquity of the fathers on the children to the third and the fourth generation of those who hate me, ⁶but showing

steadfast love to thousands of those who love me and keep my commandments.

7 "You shall not take the name of the LORD your God in vain, for the LORD will not hold him guiltless who takes his name in vain.

8 "Remember the Sabbath day, to keep it holy. 9 Six days you shall labor, and do all your work, 10 but the seventh day is a Sabbath to the LORD your God. On it you shall not do any work, you, or your son, or your daughter, your male servant, or your female servant, or your livestock, or the sojourner who is within your gates. 11 For in six days the LORD made heaven and earth, the sea, and all that is in them, and rested on the seventh day. Therefore the LORD blessed the Sabbath day and made it holy.

GETTING THE MESSAGE

How did people end up as slaves?
The word translated "slave" can refer to several types of persons. Debt was the most common reason that people became slaves. The security provided by a good employer led some slaves to choose to remain in that status permanently. In ancient times, people could generally not be bought and sold at will, unlike much of the more horrific slavery in recent centuries around the world. Slavery has continued even to the present day, as vulnerable men, women, and even children are often forced into various kinds of unjust slavery.

12 "Honor your father and your mother, that your days may be long in the land that the LORD your God is giving you.

13 "You shall not murder.

14 "You shall not commit adultery.

15 "You shall not steal.

16 "You shall not bear false witness against your neighbor.

17 "You shall not covet your neighbor's house; you shall not covet your neighbor's wife, or his male servant, or his female servant, or his ox, or his donkey, or anything that is your neighbor's."

18 Now when all the people saw the thunder and the flashes of lightning and the sound of the trumpet and the mountain smoking, the people were afraid and trembled, and they stood far off 19 and said to Moses, "You speak to us, and we will listen; but do not let God speak to us, lest we die." 20 Moses said to the people, "Do not fear, for God has come to test you, that the fear of him may be before you, that you may not sin." 21 The people stood far off, while Moses drew near to the thick darkness where God was.

Laws About Altars

22 And the LORD said to Moses, "Thus you shall say to the people of Israel: 'You have seen for yourselves that I have talked with you from heaven. 23 You shall not make gods of silver to be with me, nor shall you make for yourselves gods of gold. 24 An altar of earth you shall make for me and sacrifice on it your burnt offerings and your peace offerings, your sheep and your oxen. In every place where I cause my name to be remembered I will come to you and bless you. 25 If you make me an altar of stone, you shall not build it of hewn stones, for if you wield your tool on it you profane it. 26 And you shall not go up by steps to my altar, that your nakedness be not exposed on it.'

Laws About Slaves

21 "Now these are the rules that you shall set before them. 2 When you buy a Hebrew slave,[1] he shall serve six years, and in the seventh he shall go out free, for nothing. 3 If he comes in single, he shall go out single; if he comes in married, then his wife shall go out with him. 4 If his master gives him a wife and she bears him sons or daughters, the wife and her children shall be her master's, and he shall go out alone. 5 But if the slave plainly says, 'I love my master, my wife, and my children; I will not go out free,' 6 then his master shall bring him to God, and he shall bring him to the door or the doorpost. And his master shall bore his ear through with an awl, and he shall be his slave forever.

7 "When a man sells his daughter as a slave, she shall not go out as the male slaves do. 8 If she does not please her master, who has designated her for himself, then he shall let her be redeemed. He shall have no right to sell her to a foreign people, since he has broken faith with her. 9 If he designates her for his son, he shall deal with her as with a daughter. 10 If he takes another wife

---

1 Or *servant*; the Hebrew word (*ebed*) can mean either voluntary service or forced service (see Preface); also 21:5, 6, 7

to himself, he shall not diminish her food, her clothing, or her marital rights. **11** And if he does not do these three things for her, she shall go out for nothing, without payment of money.

12 "Whoever strikes a man so that he dies shall be put to death. **13** But if he did not lie in wait for him, but God let him fall into his hand, then I will appoint for you a place to which he may flee. **14** But if a man willfully attacks another to kill him by cunning, you shall take him from my altar, that he may die.

15 "Whoever strikes his father or his mother shall be put to death.

16 "Whoever steals a man and sells him, and anyone found in possession of him, shall be put to death.

17 "Whoever curses his father or his mother shall be put to death.

18 "When men quarrel and one strikes the other with a stone or with his fist and the man does not die but takes to his bed, **19** then if the man rises again and walks outdoors with his staff, he who struck him shall be clear; only he shall pay for the loss of his time, and shall have him thoroughly healed.

20 "When a man strikes his slave,[1] male or female, with a rod and the slave dies under his hand, he shall be avenged. **21** But if the slave survives a day or two, he is not to be avenged, for the slave is his money.

22 "When men strive together and hit a pregnant woman, so that her children come out, but there is no harm, the one who hit her shall surely be fined, as the woman's husband shall impose on him, and he shall pay as the judges determine. **23** But if there is harm, then you shall pay life for life, **24** eye for eye, tooth for tooth, hand for hand, foot for foot, **25** burn for burn, wound for wound, stripe for stripe.

26 "When a man strikes the eye of his slave, male or female, and destroys it, he shall let the slave go free because of his eye. **27** If he knocks out the tooth of his slave, male or female, he shall let the slave go free because of his tooth.

28 "When an ox gores a man or a woman to death, the ox shall be stoned, and its flesh shall not be eaten, but the owner of the ox shall not be liable. **29** But if the ox has been accustomed to gore in the past, and its owner has been warned but has not kept it

in, and it kills a man or a woman, the ox shall be stoned, and its owner also shall be put to death. **30** If a ransom is imposed on him, then he shall give for the redemption of his life whatever is imposed on him. **31** If it gores a man's son or daughter, he shall be dealt with according to this same rule. **32** If the ox gores a slave, male or female, the owner shall give to their master thirty shekels of silver, and the ox shall be stoned.

Laws About Restitution

33 "When a man opens a pit, or when a man digs a pit and does not cover it, and an ox or a donkey falls into it, **34** the owner of the pit shall make restoration. He shall give money to its owner, and the dead beast shall be his.

35 "When one man's ox butts another's, so that it dies, then they shall sell the live

---

GETTING THE MESSAGE

Restitution. The Mosaic law decreed that those who caused others to lose property, through either theft or carelessness, had to make full restitution for the loss. By contrast, many other societies in both ancient and modern times have decreed prison time and even death for crimes against property.

---

ox and share its price, and the dead beast also they shall share. **36** Or if it is known that the ox has been accustomed to gore in the past, and its owner has not kept it in, he shall repay ox for ox, and the dead beast shall be his.

22 "If a man steals an ox or a sheep, and kills it or sells it, he shall repay five oxen for an ox, and four sheep for a sheep. **2** If a thief is found breaking in and is struck so that he dies, there shall be no bloodguilt for him, **3** but if the sun has risen on him, there shall be bloodguilt for him. He shall surely pay. If he has nothing, then he shall be sold for his theft. **4** If the stolen beast is found alive in his possession, whether it is an ox or a donkey or a sheep, he shall pay double.

5 "If a man causes a field or vineyard to be grazed over, or lets his beast loose and it

---

[1] Or *servant*; the Hebrew word (*ebed*) can mean either voluntary service or forced service (see Preface); also 21:26, 27, 32

feeds in another man's field, he shall make restitution from the best in his own field and in his own vineyard.

⁶ "If fire breaks out and catches in thorns so that the stacked grain or the standing grain or the field is consumed, he who started the fire shall make full restitution.

⁷ "If a man gives to his neighbor money or goods to keep safe, and it is stolen from the man's house, then, if the thief is found, he shall pay double. ⁸ If the thief is not found, the owner of the house shall come near to God to show whether or not he has put his hand to his neighbor's property. ⁹ For every breach of trust, whether it is for an ox, for a donkey, for a sheep, for a cloak, or for any kind of lost thing, of which one says, 'This is it,' the case of both parties shall come before God. The one whom God condemns shall pay double to his neighbor.

¹⁰ "If a man gives to his neighbor a donkey or an ox or a sheep or any beast to keep safe, and it dies or is injured or is driven away, without anyone seeing it, ¹¹ an oath by the Lord shall be between them both to see whether or not he has put his hand to his neighbor's property. The owner shall accept the oath, and he shall not make restitution. ¹² But if it is stolen from him, he shall make restitution to its owner. ¹³ If it is torn by beasts, let him bring it as evidence. He shall not make restitution for what has been torn.

¹⁴ "If a man borrows anything of his neighbor, and it is injured or dies, the owner not being with it, he shall make full restitution. ¹⁵ If the owner was with it, he shall not make restitution; if it was hired, it came for its hiring fee.

Laws About Social Justice

¹⁶ "If a man seduces a virgin who is not betrothed and lies with her, he shall give the bride-price[1] for her and make her his wife. ¹⁷ If her father utterly refuses to give her to him, he shall pay money equal to the bride-price for virgins.

¹⁸ "You shall not permit a sorceress to live.

¹⁹ "Whoever lies with an animal shall be put to death.

²⁰ "Whoever sacrifices to any god, other than the Lord alone, shall be devoted to destruction.[2]

²¹ "You shall not wrong a sojourner or oppress him, for you were sojourners in the land of Egypt. ²² You shall not mistreat any widow or fatherless child. ²³ If you do mistreat them, and they cry out to me, I will surely hear their cry, ²⁴ and my wrath will burn, and I will kill you with the sword, and your wives shall become widows and your children fatherless.

²⁵ "If you lend money to any of my people with you who is poor, you shall not be like a moneylender to him, and you shall not exact interest from him. ²⁶ If ever you take your neighbor's cloak in pledge, you shall return it to him before the sun goes down, ²⁷ for that is his only covering, and it is his cloak for his body; in what else shall he sleep? And if he cries to me, I will hear, for I am compassionate.

²⁸ "You shall not revile God, nor curse a ruler of your people.

²⁹ "You shall not delay to offer from the fullness of your harvest and from the outflow of your presses. The firstborn of your sons you shall give to me. ³⁰ You shall do the same with your oxen and with your sheep: seven days it shall be with its mother; on the eighth day you shall give it to me.

³¹ "You shall be consecrated to me. Therefore you shall not eat any flesh that is torn by beasts in the field; you shall throw it to the dogs.

23 "You shall not spread a false report. You shall not join hands with a wicked man to be a malicious witness. ² You shall not fall in with the many to do evil, nor shall you bear witness in a lawsuit, siding with the many, so as to pervert justice, ³ nor shall you be partial to a poor man in his lawsuit.

⁴ "If you meet your enemy's ox or his donkey going astray, you shall bring it back to him. ⁵ If you see the donkey of one who hates you lying down under its burden, you shall refrain from leaving him with it; you shall rescue it with him.

⁶ "You shall not pervert the justice due to your poor in his lawsuit. ⁷ Keep far from a false charge, and do not kill the innocent and righteous, for I will not acquit the wicked. ⁸ And you shall take no bribe, for a bribe blinds the clear-sighted and subverts the cause of those who are in the right.

[1] That is, money paid by the groom to the bride's family; also 22:17 [2] That is, destroyed or made an offering because of sin, at God's command

⁹ "You shall not oppress a sojourner. You know the heart of a sojourner, for you were sojourners in the land of Egypt.

Laws About the Sabbath and Festivals

¹⁰ "For six years you shall sow your land and gather in its yield, ¹¹ but the seventh year you shall let it rest and lie fallow, that the poor of your people may eat; and what they leave the beasts of the field may eat. You shall do likewise with your vineyard, and with your olive orchard.

¹² "Six days you shall do your work, but on the seventh day you shall rest; that your ox and your donkey may have rest, and the son of your servant woman, and the alien, may be refreshed.

¹³ "Pay attention to all that I have said to you, and make no mention of the names of other gods, nor let it be heard on your lips.

¹⁴ "Three times in the year you shall keep a feast to me. ¹⁵ You shall keep the Feast of Unleavened Bread. As I commanded you, you shall eat unleavened bread for seven days at the appointed time in the month of Abib, for in it you came out of Egypt. None shall appear before me empty-handed. ¹⁶ You shall keep the Feast of Harvest, of the firstfruits of your labor, of what you sow in the field. You shall keep the Feast of Ingathering at the end of the year, when you gather in from the field the fruit of your labor. ¹⁷ Three times in the year shall all your males appear before the Lord GOD.

¹⁸ "You shall not offer the blood of my sacrifice with anything leavened, or let the fat of my feast remain until the morning.

¹⁹ "The best of the firstfruits of your ground you shall bring into the house of the LORD your God.

"You shall not boil a young goat in its mother's milk.

Conquest of Canaan Promised

²⁰ "Behold, I send an angel before you to guard you on the way and to bring you to the place that I have prepared. ²¹ Pay careful attention to him and obey his voice; do not rebel against him, for he will not pardon your transgression, for my name is in him.

²² "But if you carefully obey his voice and do all that I say, then I will be an enemy to your enemies and an adversary to your adversaries.

²³ "When my angel goes before you and brings you to the Amorites and the Hittites and the Perizzites and the Canaanites, the Hivites and the Jebusites, and I blot them out, ²⁴ you shall not bow down to their gods nor serve them, nor do as they do, but you shall utterly overthrow them and break their pillars in pieces. ²⁵ You shall serve the LORD your God, and he will bless your bread and your water, and I will take sickness away from among you. ²⁶ None shall miscarry or be barren in your land; I will fulfill the number of your days. ²⁷ I will send my terror before you and will throw into confusion all the people against whom you shall come, and I will make all your enemies turn their backs to you. ²⁸ And I

> ### GETTING THE MESSAGE

What was the purpose of the Mosaic covenant? Israel was already God's chosen people because of the promises God made to Abraham. The covenant with Moses established the nation as a holy kingdom of priests, dedicated to serving God and teaching other nations about him (19:5–6). Israel was a theocracy, a nation ruled directly by God. The Mosaic covenant established the political, social, and religious aspects of Israel's life.

---

will send hornets before you, which shall drive out the Hivites, the Canaanites, and the Hittites from before you. ²⁹ I will not drive them out from before you in one year, lest the land become desolate and the wild beasts multiply against you. ³⁰ Little by little I will drive them out from before you, until you have increased and possess the land. ³¹ And I will set your border from the Red Sea to the Sea of the Philistines, and from the wilderness to the Euphrates, for I will give the inhabitants of the land into your hand, and you shall drive them out before you. ³² You shall make no covenant with them and their gods. ³³ They shall not dwell in your land, lest they make you sin against me; for if you serve their gods, it will surely be a snare to you."

The Covenant Confirmed

24 Then he said to Moses, "Come up to the LORD, you and Aaron, Nadab, and Abihu, and seventy of the elders of Israel, and worship from afar. ² Moses alone shall come near to the LORD, but the others shall not come near, and the people shall not come up with him."

³ Moses came and told the people all the words of the LORD and all the rules. And all the people answered with one voice and said, "All the words that the LORD has spoken we will do." ⁴ And Moses wrote down all the words of the LORD. He rose early in the morning and built an altar at the foot of the mountain, and twelve pillars, according to the twelve tribes of Israel. ⁵ And he sent young men of the people of Israel, who offered burnt offerings and sacrificed peace offerings of oxen to the LORD. ⁶ And Moses took half of the blood and put it in basins, and half of the blood he threw against the altar. ⁷ Then he took the Book of the Covenant and read it in the hearing of the people. And they said, "All that the LORD has spoken we will do, and we will be obedient." ⁸ And Moses took the blood and threw it on the people and said, "Behold the blood of the covenant that the LORD has made with you in accordance with all these words."

⁹ Then Moses and Aaron, Nadab, and Abihu, and seventy of the elders of Israel went up, ¹⁰ and they saw the God of Israel. There was under his feet as it were a pavement of sapphire stone, like the very heaven for clearness. ¹¹ And he did not lay his hand on the chief men of the people of Israel; they beheld God, and ate and drank.

¹² The LORD said to Moses, "Come up to me on the mountain and wait there, that I may give you the tablets of stone, with the law and the commandment, which I have written for their instruction." ¹³ So Moses rose with his assistant Joshua, and Moses went up into the mountain of God. ¹⁴ And he said to the elders, "Wait here for us until we return to you. And behold, Aaron and Hur are with you. Whoever has a dispute, let him go to them."

¹⁵ Then Moses went up on the mountain, and the cloud covered the mountain. ¹⁶ The glory of the LORD dwelt on Mount Sinai, and the cloud covered it six days. And on the seventh day he called to Moses out of the midst of the cloud. ¹⁷ Now the appearance of the glory of the LORD was like a devouring fire on the top of the mountain in the sight of the people of Israel. ¹⁸ Moses entered the cloud and went up on the mountain. And Moses was on the mountain forty days and forty nights.

Contributions for the Sanctuary

25 The LORD said to Moses, ² "Speak to the people of Israel, that they take for me a contribution. From every man whose heart moves him you shall receive the contribution for me. ³ And this is the contribution that you shall receive from them: gold, silver, and bronze, ⁴ blue and purple and scarlet yarns and fine twined linen, goats' hair, ⁵ tanned rams' skins, goatskins, acacia wood, ⁶ oil for the lamps, spices for the anointing oil and for the fragrant incense, ⁷ onyx stones, and stones for setting, for the ephod and for the breastpiece. ⁸ And let them make me a sanctuary, that I may dwell in their midst. ⁹ Exactly as I show you concerning the pattern of the tabernacle, and of all its furniture, so you shall make it.

The Ark of the Covenant

¹⁰ "They shall make an ark of acacia wood. Two cubits and a half shall be its length, a cubit and a half its breadth, and a cubit and a half its height. ¹¹ You shall overlay it with pure gold, inside and outside shall you overlay it, and you shall make on it a molding of gold around it. ¹² You shall cast four rings of gold for it and put them on its four feet, two rings on the one side of it, and two rings on the other side of it. ¹³ You shall make poles of acacia wood and overlay them with gold. ¹⁴ And you shall put the poles into the rings on the sides of the ark to carry the ark by them. ¹⁵ The poles shall remain in the rings of the ark; they shall not be taken from it. ¹⁶ And you shall put into the ark the testimony that I shall give you.

¹⁷ "You shall make a mercy seat of pure gold. Two cubits and a half shall be its length, and a cubit and a half its breadth. ¹⁸ And you shall make two cherubim of gold; of hammered work shall you make them, on the two ends of the mercy seat. ¹⁹ Make one cherub on the one end, and one cherub on the other end. Of one piece with the mercy seat shall you make the cherubim on its two

ends. ²⁰The cherubim shall spread out their wings above, overshadowing the mercy seat with their wings, their faces one to another; toward the mercy seat shall the faces of the cherubim be. ²¹And you shall put the mercy seat on the top of the ark, and in the ark you shall put the testimony that I shall give you. ²²There I will meet with you, and from above the mercy seat, from between the two cherubim that are on the ark of the testimony, I will speak with you about all that I will give you in commandment for the people of Israel.

The Table for Bread

²³ "You shall make a table of acacia wood. Two cubits shall be its length, a cubit its breadth, and a cubit and a half its height. ²⁴ You shall overlay it with pure gold and make a molding of gold around it. ²⁵And you shall make a rim around it a handbreadth wide, and a molding of gold around the rim. ²⁶ And you shall make for it four rings of gold, and fasten the rings to the four corners at its four legs. ²⁷Close to the frame the rings shall lie, as holders for the poles to carry the table. ²⁸You shall make the poles of acacia wood, and overlay them with gold, and the table shall be carried with these. ²⁹And you shall make its plates and dishes for incense, and its flagons and bowls with which to pour drink offerings; you shall make them of pure gold. ³⁰ And you shall set the bread of the Presence on the table before me regularly.

The Golden Lampstand

³¹ "You shall make a lampstand of pure gold. The lampstand shall be made of hammered work: its base, its stem, its cups, its calyxes, and its flowers shall be of one piece with it. ³² And there shall be six branches going out of its sides, three branches of the lampstand out of one side of it and three branches of the lampstand out of the other side of it; ³³ three cups made like almond blossoms, each with calyx and flower, on one branch, and three cups made like almond blossoms, each with calyx and flower, on the other branch—so for the six branches going out of the lampstand. ³⁴ And on the lampstand itself there shall be four cups made like almond blossoms, with their calyxes and flowers, ³⁵ and a calyx of one piece with it under each pair of the

six branches going out from the lampstand. ³⁶ Their calyxes and their branches shall be of one piece with it, the whole of it a single piece of hammered work of pure gold. ³⁷ You shall make seven lamps for it. And the lamps shall be set up so as to give light on the space in front of it. ³⁸ Its tongs and their trays shall be of pure gold. ³⁹ It shall be made, with all these utensils, out of a talent of pure gold. ⁴⁰ And see that you make them after the pattern for them, which is being shown you on the mountain.

The Tabernacle

26

"Moreover, you shall make the tabernacle with ten curtains of fine twined linen and blue and purple and scarlet yarns; you shall make them with cherubim skillfully worked into them. ² The length of each curtain shall be twenty-eight cubits, and the breadth of each curtain four cubits; all the curtains shall be the same

size. ³ Five curtains shall be coupled to one another, and the other five curtains shall be coupled to one another. ⁴ And you shall make loops of blue on the edge of the outermost curtain in the first set. Likewise you shall make loops on the edge of the outermost curtain in the second set. ⁵ Fifty loops you shall make on the one curtain, and fifty loops you shall make on the edge of the curtain that is in the second set; the loops shall be opposite one another. ⁶ And you shall make fifty clasps of gold, and couple the curtains one to the other with the clasps, so that the tabernacle may be a single whole. ⁷ "You shall also make curtains of goats' hair for a tent over the tabernacle; eleven curtains shall you make. ⁸ The length of each curtain shall be thirty cubits, and the breadth of each curtain four cubits. The eleven curtains shall be the same size. ⁹ You shall couple five curtains by themselves, and six curtains by themselves, and the sixth curtain you shall double over at the front of the tent. ¹⁰ You shall make fifty loops on the edge of the curtain that is outermost in one set, and fifty loops on the edge of the curtain that is outermost in the second set. ¹¹ "You shall make fifty clasps of bronze, and put the clasps into the loops, and couple the tent together that it may be a single whole. ¹² And the part that remains of the curtains of the tent, the half curtain that remains, shall hang over the back of the tabernacle. ¹³ And the extra that remains in the length of the curtains, the cubit on the one side, and the cubit on the other side, shall hang over the sides of the tabernacle, on this side and that side, to cover it. ¹⁴ And you shall make for the tent a covering of tanned rams' skins and a covering of goatskins on top.

¹⁵ "You shall make upright frames for the tabernacle of acacia wood. ¹⁶ Ten cubits shall be the length of a frame, and a cubit and a half the breadth of each frame. ¹⁷ There shall be two tenons in each frame, for fitting together. So shall you do for all the frames of the tabernacle. ¹⁸ You shall make the frames for the tabernacle: twenty frames for the south side; ¹⁹ and forty bases of silver you shall make under the twenty frames, two bases under one frame for its two tenons, and two bases under the next frame for its two tenons; ²⁰ and for the second side of the tabernacle, on the north side twenty frames, ²¹ and their forty bases of silver, two bases under one frame, and two bases under the next frame. ²² And for the rear of the tabernacle westward you shall make six frames. ²³ And you shall make two frames for corners of the tabernacle in the rear;

²⁴ they shall be separate beneath, but joined at the top, at the first ring. Thus shall it be with both of them; they shall form the two corners. ²⁵ And there shall be eight frames, with their bases of silver, sixteen bases; two bases under one frame, and two bases under another frame.

²⁶ "You shall make bars of acacia wood, five for the frames of the one side of the tabernacle, ²⁷ and five bars for the frames of the other side of the tabernacle, and five bars for the frames of the side of the tabernacle at the rear westward. ²⁸ The middle bar, halfway up the frames, shall run from end to end. ²⁹ You shall overlay the frames with gold and shall make their rings of gold for holders for the bars, and you shall overlay the bars with gold. ³⁰ Then you shall erect the tabernacle according to the plan for it that you were shown on the mountain.

³¹ "And you shall make a veil of blue and purple and scarlet yarns and fine twined linen. It shall be made with cherubim skillfully worked into it. ³² And you shall hang it on four pillars of acacia overlaid with gold, with hooks of gold, on four bases of silver. ³³ And you shall hang the veil from the clasps, and bring the ark of the testimony in there within the veil. And the veil shall separate for you the Holy Place from the Most Holy. ³⁴ You shall put the mercy seat on the ark of the testimony in the Most Holy Place. ³⁵ And you shall set the table outside the veil, and the lampstand on the south side of the tabernacle opposite the table, and you shall put the table on the north side.

³⁶ "You shall make a screen for the entrance of the tent, of blue and purple and scarlet yarns and fine twined linen, embroidered with needlework. ³⁷ And you shall make for the screen five pillars of acacia, and overlay them with gold. Their hooks shall be of gold, and you shall cast five bases of bronze for them.

The Bronze Altar

27 "You shall make the altar of acacia wood, five cubits long and five cubits broad. The altar shall be square, and its height shall be three cubits. ² And you shall make horns for it on its four corners; its horns shall be of one piece with it, and you shall overlay it with bronze. ³ You shall make pots for it to receive its ashes, and shovels and basins and forks and fire pans.

You shall make all its utensils of bronze. ⁴ You shall also make for it a grating, a network of bronze, and on the net you shall make four bronze rings at its four corners. ⁵ And you shall set it under the ledge of the altar so that the net extends halfway down the altar. ⁶ And you shall make poles for the altar, poles of acacia wood, and overlay them with bronze. ⁷ And the poles shall be put through the rings, so that the poles are on the two sides of the altar when it is carried. ⁸ You shall make it hollow, with boards. As it has been shown you on the mountain, so shall it be made.

The Court of the Tabernacle

⁹ "You shall make the court of the tabernacle. On the south side the court shall have hangings of fine twined linen a hundred cubits long for one side. ¹⁰ Its twenty pillars and their twenty bases shall be of bronze, but the hooks of the pillars and their fillets shall be of silver. ¹¹ And likewise for its length on the north side there shall be hangings a hundred cubits long, its pillars twenty and their bases twenty, of bronze, but the hooks of the pillars and their fillets shall be of silver. ¹² And for the breadth of the court on the west side there shall be hangings for fifty cubits, with ten pillars and ten bases. ¹³ The breadth of the court on the front to the east shall be fifty cubits. ¹⁴ The hangings for the one side of the gate shall be fifteen cubits, with their three pillars and three bases. ¹⁵ On the other side the hangings shall be fifteen cubits, with their three pillars and three bases. ¹⁶ For the gate of the court there shall be a screen twenty cubits long, of blue and purple and scarlet yarns and fine twined linen, embroidered with needlework. It shall have four pillars and with them four bases. ¹⁷ All the pillars around the court shall be filleted with silver. Their hooks shall be of silver, and their bases of bronze. ¹⁸ The length of the court shall be a hundred cubits, the breadth fifty, and the height five cubits, with hangings of fine twined linen and bases of bronze. ¹⁹ All the utensils of the tabernacle for every use, and all its pegs and all the pegs of the court, shall be of bronze.

Oil for the Lamp

²⁰ "You shall command the people of Israel that they bring to you pure beaten olive oil for the light, that a lamp may regularly be set up to burn. ²¹ In the tent of meeting, outside the veil that is before the testimony, Aaron and his sons shall tend it from evening to morning before the LORD. It shall be a statute forever to be observed throughout their generations by the people of Israel.

The Priests' Garments

28 "Then bring near to you Aaron your brother, and his sons with him, from among the people of Israel, to serve me as priests—Aaron and Aaron's sons, Nadab and Abihu, Eleazar and Ithamar. ² And you shall make holy garments for Aaron your brother, for glory and for beauty. ³ You shall speak to all the skillful, whom I have filled with a spirit of skill, that they make Aaron's garments to consecrate him for my priesthood. ⁴ These are the garments that they shall make: a breastpiece, an ephod, a robe, a coat of checker work, a turban, and a sash. They shall make holy garments for Aaron your brother and his sons to serve me as priests. ⁵ They shall receive gold, blue and purple and scarlet yarns, and fine twined linen.

⁶ "And they shall make the ephod of gold, of blue and purple and scarlet yarns, and of fine twined linen, skillfully worked. ⁷ It shall have two shoulder pieces attached to its two edges, so that it may be joined together. ⁸ And the skillfully woven band on it shall be made like it and be of one piece with it, of gold, blue and purple and scarlet yarns, and fine twined linen. ⁹ You shall take two onyx stones, and engrave on them the names of the sons of Israel, ¹⁰ six of their names on the one stone, and the names of the remaining six on the other stone, in the order of their birth. ¹¹ As a jeweler engraves signets, so shall you engrave the two stones with the names of the sons of Israel. You shall enclose them in settings of gold filigree. ¹² And you shall set the two stones on the shoulder pieces of the ephod, as stones of remembrance for the sons of Israel. And Aaron shall bear their names before the LORD on his two shoulders for remembrance. ¹³ You shall make settings of gold filigree, ¹⁴ and two chains of pure gold, twisted like cords; and you shall attach the corded chains to the settings.

¹⁵ "You shall make a breastpiece of judgment, in skilled work. In the style of the ephod you shall make it — of gold, blue and purple and scarlet yarns, and fine twined linen shall you make it. ¹⁶ It shall be square and doubled, a span its length and a span its breadth. ¹⁷ You shall set in it four rows of stones. A row of sardius, topaz, and carbuncle shall be the first row; ¹⁸ and the second row an emerald, a sapphire, and a diamond; ¹⁹ and the third row a jacinth, an agate, and an amethyst; ²⁰ and the fourth row a beryl, an onyx, and a jasper. They shall be set in gold filigree. ²¹ There shall be twelve stones with their names according to the names of the sons of Israel. They shall be like signets, each engraved with its name, for the twelve tribes. ²² You shall make for the breastpiece twisted chains like cords, of pure gold. ²³ And you shall make for the breastpiece two rings of gold, and

GETTING THE MESSAGE

The **gold bells** along the hems of the high priest's garment (28:33) served two purposes. They alerted people that the high priest was present, and they reminded the priest himself to be reverent and careful in carrying out his sacred duties.

put the two rings on the two edges of the breastpiece. ²⁴ And you shall put the two cords of gold in the two rings at the edges of the breastpiece. ²⁵ The two ends of the two cords you shall attach to the two settings of filigree, and so attach it in front to the shoulder pieces of the ephod. ²⁶ You shall make two rings of gold, and put them at the two ends of the breastpiece, on its inside edge next to the ephod. ²⁷ And you shall make two rings of gold, and attach them in front to the lower part of the two shoulder pieces of the ephod, at its seam above the skillfully woven band of the ephod. ²⁸ And they shall bind the breastpiece by its rings to the rings of the ephod with a lace of blue, so that it may lie on the skillfully woven band of the ephod, so that the breastpiece shall not come loose from the ephod. ²⁹ So Aaron shall bear the names of the sons of Israel in the breastpiece of judgment on his heart,

when he goes into the Holy Place, to bring them to regular remembrance before the LORD. ³⁰ And in the breastpiece of judgment you shall put the Urim and the Thummim, and they shall be on Aaron's heart, when he goes in before the LORD. Thus Aaron shall bear the judgment of the people of Israel on his heart before the LORD regularly.

³¹ "You shall make the robe of the ephod all of blue. ³² It shall have an opening for the head in the middle of it, with a woven binding around the opening, like the opening in a garment, so that it may not tear. ³³ On its hem you shall make pomegranates of blue and purple and scarlet yarns, around its hem, with bells of gold between them, ³⁴ a golden bell and a pomegranate, a golden bell and a pomegranate, around the hem of the robe. ³⁵ And it shall be on Aaron when he ministers, and its sound shall be heard when he goes into the Holy Place before the LORD, and when he comes out, so that he does not die.

³⁶ "You shall make a plate of pure gold and engrave on it, like the engraving of a signet, 'Holy to the LORD.' ³⁷ And you shall fasten it on the turban by a cord of blue. It shall be on the front of the turban. ³⁸ It shall be on Aaron's forehead, and Aaron shall bear any guilt from the holy things that the people of Israel consecrate as their holy gifts. It shall regularly be on his forehead, that they may be accepted before the LORD.

³⁹ "You shall weave the coat in checker work of fine linen, and you shall make a turban of fine linen, and you shall make a sash embroidered with needlework.

⁴⁰ "For Aaron's sons you shall make coats and sashes and caps. You shall make them for glory and beauty. ⁴¹ And you shall put them on Aaron your brother, and on his sons with him, and shall anoint them and ordain them and consecrate them, that they may serve me as priests. ⁴² You shall make for them linen undergarments to cover their naked flesh. They shall reach from the hips to the thighs; ⁴³ and they shall be on Aaron and on his sons when they go into the tent of meeting or when they come near the altar to minister in the Holy Place, lest they bear guilt and die. This shall be a statute forever for him and for his offspring after him.

Consecration of the Priests

29 "Now this is what you shall do to them to consecrate them, that they may serve me as priests. Take one bull of the herd and two rams without blemish, ² and unleavened bread, unleavened cakes mixed with oil, and unleavened wafers smeared with oil. You shall make them of fine wheat flour. ³ You shall put them in one basket and bring them in the basket, and bring the bull and the two rams. ⁴ You shall bring Aaron and his sons to the entrance of the tent of meeting and wash them with water. ⁵ Then you shall take the garments, and put on Aaron the coat and the robe of the ephod, and the ephod, and the breastpiece, and gird him with the skillfully woven band of the ephod. ⁶ And you shall set the turban on his head and put the holy crown on the turban. ⁷ You shall take the anointing oil and pour it on his head and anoint him. ⁸ Then you shall bring his sons and put coats on them, ⁹ and you shall gird Aaron and his sons with sashes and bind caps on them. And the priesthood shall be theirs by a statute forever. Thus you shall ordain Aaron and his sons.

¹⁰ "Then you shall bring the bull before the tent of meeting. Aaron and his sons shall lay their hands on the head of the bull. ¹¹ Then you shall kill the bull before the Lord at the entrance of the tent of meeting, ¹² and shall take part of the blood of the bull and put it on the horns of the altar with your finger, and the rest of the blood you shall pour out at the base of the altar. ¹³ And you shall take all the fat that covers the entrails, and the long lobe of the liver, and the two kidneys with the fat that is on them, and burn them on the altar. ¹⁴ But the flesh of the bull and its skin and its dung you shall burn with fire outside the camp; it is a sin offering.

¹⁵ "Then you shall take one of the rams, and Aaron and his sons shall lay their hands on the head of the ram, ¹⁶ and you shall kill the ram and shall take its blood and throw it against the sides of the altar. ¹⁷ Then you shall cut the ram into pieces, and wash its entrails and its legs, and put them with its pieces and its head, ¹⁸ and burn the whole ram on the altar. It is a burnt offering to the Lord. It is a pleasing aroma, a food offering to the Lord.

¹⁹ "You shall take the other ram, and Aaron and his sons shall lay their hands on the head of the ram, ²⁰ and you shall kill the ram and take part of its blood and put it on the tip of the right ear of Aaron and on the tips of the right ears of his sons, and on the thumbs of their right hands and on the great toes of their right feet, and throw the rest of the blood against the sides of the altar. ²¹ Then you shall take part of the blood that is on the altar, and of the anointing oil, and sprinkle it on Aaron and his garments, and on his sons and his sons' garments with him. He and his garments shall be holy, and his sons and his sons' garments with him.

²² "You shall also take the fat from the ram and the fat tail and the fat that covers the entrails, and the long lobe of the liver and the two kidneys with the fat that is on them, and the right thigh (for it is a ram of ordination), ²³ and one loaf of bread and one cake of bread made with oil, and one wafer out of the basket of unleavened bread that is before the Lord. ²⁴ You shall put all these on the palms of Aaron and on the palms of his sons, and wave them for a wave offering before the Lord. ²⁵ Then you shall take them from their hands and burn them on the altar on top of the burnt offering, as a pleasing aroma before the Lord. It is a food offering to the Lord.

²⁶ "You shall take the breast of the ram of Aaron's ordination and wave it for a wave offering before the Lord, and it shall be your portion. ²⁷ And you shall consecrate

the breast of the wave offering that is waved and the thigh of the priests' portion that is contributed from the ram of ordination, from what was Aaron's and his sons'. ²⁸ It shall be for Aaron and his sons as a perpetual due from the people of Israel, for it is a contribution. It shall be a contribution from the people of Israel from their peace offerings, their contribution to the LORD.

²⁹ "The holy garments of Aaron shall be for his sons after him; they shall be anointed in them and ordained in them. ³⁰ The son who succeeds him as priest, who comes into the tent of meeting to minister in the Holy Place, shall wear them seven days.

³¹ "You shall take the ram of ordination and boil its flesh in a holy place. ³² And Aaron and his sons shall eat the flesh of the ram and the bread that is in the basket in the entrance of the tent of meeting.

GETTING THE MESSAGE

Altar of incense. Incense was burned to purify the altars after animals had been slaughtered there. Incense also symbolized Israel's constant prayer to God.

³³ They shall eat those things with which atonement was made at their ordination and consecration, but an outsider shall not eat of them, because they are holy. ³⁴ And if any of the flesh for the ordination or of the bread remain until the morning, then you shall burn the remainder with fire. It shall not be eaten, because it is holy.

³⁵ "Thus you shall do to Aaron and to his sons, according to all that I have commanded you. Through seven days shall you ordain them, ³⁶ and every day you shall offer a bull as a sin offering for atonement. Also you shall purify the altar, when you make atonement for it, and shall anoint it to consecrate it. ³⁷ Seven days you shall make atonement for the altar and consecrate it, and the altar shall be most holy. Whatever touches the altar shall become holy.

³⁸ "Now this is what you shall offer on the altar: two lambs a year old day by day regularly. ³⁹ One lamb you shall offer in the morning, and the other lamb you shall offer

at twilight. ⁴⁰ And with the first lamb a tenth measure of fine flour mingled with a fourth of a hin of beaten oil, and a fourth of a hin of wine for a drink offering. ⁴¹ The other lamb you shall offer at twilight, and shall offer with it a grain offering and its drink offering, as in the morning, for a pleasing aroma, a food offering to the LORD. ⁴² It shall be a regular burnt offering throughout your generations at the entrance of the tent of meeting before the LORD, where I will meet with you, to speak to you there. ⁴³ There I will meet with the people of Israel, and it shall be sanctified by my glory. ⁴⁴ I will consecrate the tent of meeting and the altar. Aaron also and his sons I will consecrate to serve me as priests. ⁴⁵ I will dwell among the people of Israel and will be their God. ⁴⁶ And they shall know that I am the LORD their God, who brought them out of the land of Egypt that I might dwell among them. I am the LORD their God.

The Altar of Incense

30 "You shall make an altar on which to burn incense; you shall make it of acacia wood. ² A cubit shall be its length, and a cubit its breadth. It shall be square, and two cubits shall be its height. Its horns shall be of one piece with it. ³ You shall overlay it with pure gold, its top and around its sides and its horns. And you shall make a molding of gold around it. ⁴ And you shall make two golden rings for it. Under its molding on two opposite sides of it you shall make them, and they shall be holders for poles with which to carry it. ⁵ You shall make the poles of acacia wood and overlay them with gold. ⁶ And you shall put it in front of the veil that is above the ark of the testimony, in front of the mercy seat that is above the testimony, where I will meet with you. ⁷ And Aaron shall burn fragrant incense on it. Every morning when he dresses the lamps he shall burn it, ⁸ and when Aaron sets up the lamps at twilight, he shall burn it, a regular incense offering before the LORD throughout your generations. ⁹ You shall not offer unauthorized incense on it, or a burnt offering, or a grain offering, and you shall not pour a drink offering on it. ¹⁰ Aaron shall make atonement on its horns once a year. With the blood of the sin offering of atonement he shall make atonement for it once in the year throughout your generations. It is most holy to the LORD."

The Census Tax

¹¹ The LORD said to Moses, ¹² "When you take the census of the people of Israel, then each shall give a ransom for his life to the LORD when you number them, that there be no plague among them when you number them. ¹³ Each one who is numbered in the census shall give this: half a shekel according to the shekel of the sanctuary (the shekel is twenty gerahs), half a shekel as an offering to the LORD. ¹⁴ Everyone who is numbered in the census, from twenty years old and upward, shall give the LORD's offering. ¹⁵ The rich shall not give more, and the poor shall not give less, than the half shekel, when you give the LORD's offering to make atonement for your lives. ¹⁶ You shall take the atonement money from the people of Israel and shall give it for the service of the tent of meeting, that it may bring the people of Israel to remembrance before the LORD, so as to make atonement for your lives."

The Bronze Basin

¹⁷ The LORD said to Moses, ¹⁸ "You shall also make a basin of bronze, with its stand of bronze, for washing. You shall put it between the tent of meeting and the altar, and you shall put water in it, ¹⁹ with which Aaron and his sons shall wash their hands and their feet. ²⁰ When they go into the tent of meeting, or when they come near the altar to minister, to burn a food offering to the LORD, they shall wash with water, so that they may not die. ²¹ They shall wash their hands and their feet, so that they may not die. It shall be a statute forever to them, even to him and to his offspring throughout their generations."

The Anointing Oil and Incense

²² The LORD said to Moses, ²³ "Take the finest spices: of liquid myrrh 500 shekels, and of sweet-smelling cinnamon half as much, that is, 250, and 250 of aromatic cane, ²⁴ and 500 of cassia, according to the shekel of the sanctuary, and a hin of olive oil. ²⁵ And you shall make of these a sacred anointing oil blended as by the perfumer; it shall be a holy anointing oil. ²⁶ With it you shall anoint the tent of meeting and the ark of the testimony, ²⁷ and the table and all its utensils, and the lampstand and its utensils, and the altar of incense, ²⁸ and the altar of burnt offering with all its utensils and the basin and its stand. ²⁹ You shall consecrate them, that they may be most holy. Whatever touches them will become holy. ³⁰ You shall anoint Aaron and his sons, and consecrate them, that they may serve me as priests. ³¹ And you shall say to the people of Israel, 'This shall be my holy anointing oil throughout your generations. ³² It shall not be poured on the body of an ordinary person, and you shall make no other like it in composition. It is holy, and it shall be holy to you. ³³ Whoever compounds any like it or whoever puts any of it on an outsider shall be cut off from his people.'"

³⁴ The LORD said to Moses, "Take sweet spices, stacte, and onycha, and galbanum, sweet spices with pure frankincense (of each shall there be an equal part), ³⁵ and make an incense blended as by the perfumer, seasoned with salt, pure and holy. ³⁶ You shall

> ### GETTING THE MESSAGE
>
> The level of detail given in God's **instructions for the tabernacle** in ch. 30 emphasizes that Israel is to worship the Lord in their midst according to his word and plan.

beat some of it very small, and put part of it before the testimony in the tent of meeting where I shall meet with you. It shall be most holy for you. ³⁷ And the incense that you shall make according to its composition, you shall not make for yourselves. It shall be for you holy to the LORD. ³⁸ Whoever makes any like it to use as perfume shall be cut off from his people."

Oholiab and Bezalel

31 The LORD said to Moses, ² "See, I have called by name Bezalel the son of Uri, son of Hur, of the tribe of Judah, ³ and I have filled him with the Spirit of God, with ability and intelligence, with knowledge and all craftsmanship, ⁴ to devise artistic designs, to work in gold, silver, and bronze, ⁵ in cutting stones for setting, and in carving wood, to work in every craft. ⁶ And behold, I have appointed with him Oholiab, the son of Ahisamach, of the tribe of Dan. And I have given to all able men ability, that they may

make all that I have commanded you: [7] the tent of meeting, and the ark of the testimony, and the mercy seat that is on it, and all the furnishings of the tent, [8] the table and its utensils, and the pure lampstand with all its utensils, and the altar of incense, [9] and the altar of burnt offering with all its utensils, and the basin and its stand, [10] and the finely worked garments, the holy garments for Aaron the priest and the garments of his sons, for their service as priests, [11] and the anointing oil and the fragrant incense for

the Holy Place. According to all that I have commanded you, they shall do."

The Sabbath

[12] And the LORD said to Moses, [13] "You are to speak to the people of Israel and say, 'Above all you shall keep my Sabbaths, for this is a sign between me and you throughout your generations, that you may know that I, the LORD, sanctify you. [14] You shall keep the Sabbath, because it is holy for you. Everyone who profanes it shall be put to death. Whoever does any work on it, that soul shall be cut off from among his people. [15] Six days shall work be done, but the

seventh day is a Sabbath of solemn rest, holy to the LORD. Whoever does any work on the Sabbath day shall be put to death. [16] Therefore the people of Israel shall keep the Sabbath, observing the Sabbath throughout their generations, as a covenant forever. [17] It is a sign forever between me and the people of Israel that in six days the LORD made heaven and earth, and on the seventh day he rested and was refreshed.'"

[18] And he gave to Moses, when he had finished speaking with him on Mount Sinai, the two tablets of the testimony, tablets of stone, written with the finger of God.

The Golden Calf

32 When the people saw that Moses delayed to come down from the mountain, the people gathered themselves together to Aaron and said to him, "Up, make us gods who shall go before us. As for this Moses, the man who brought us up out of the land of Egypt, we do not know what has become of him." [2] So Aaron said to them, "Take off the rings of gold that are in the ears of your wives, your sons, and your daughters, and bring them to me." [3] So all the people took off the rings of gold that were in their ears and brought them to Aaron. [4] And he received the gold from their hand and fashioned it with a graving tool and made a golden calf. And they said, "These are your gods, O Israel, who brought you up out of the land of Egypt!" [5] When Aaron saw this, he built an altar before it. And Aaron made a proclamation and said, "Tomorrow shall be a feast to the LORD." [6] And they rose up early the next day and offered burnt offerings and brought peace offerings. And the people sat down to eat and drink and rose up to play.

[7] And the LORD said to Moses, "Go down, for your people, whom you brought up out of the land of Egypt, have corrupted themselves. [8] They have turned aside quickly out of the way that I commanded them. They have made for themselves a golden calf and have worshiped it and sacrificed to it and said, 'These are your gods, O Israel, who brought you up out of the land of Egypt!'" [9] And the LORD said to Moses, "I have seen this people, and behold, it is a stiff-necked people. [10] Now therefore let me alone, that my wrath may burn hot against them and I may consume them, in order that I may make a great nation of you."

PROFILE

AARON

Aaron was Moses' brother and his spokesperson before Israel and Pharaoh. When Pharaoh refused to release the Hebrews, Aaron stretched out his rod to bring plagues upon the Egyptians. He helped Moses lead the Israelites out of Egypt and through the wilderness. At Sinai, however, Aaron gave in to the Israelites' sinful demand and designed a golden calf for them to worship. On another occasion, when the Lord miraculously provided water in the wilderness, both Moses and Aaron failed to give proper honor to the Lord, and as a result they were forbidden entry into the Promised Land. As a descendant of Levi, Aaron became Israel's first high priest, and all future priests were his descendants.

KEY REFERENCE: EXODUS 4:15

[11] But Moses implored the LORD his God and said, "O LORD, why does your wrath burn hot against your people, whom you have brought out of the land of Egypt with great power and with a mighty hand? [12] Why should the Egyptians say, 'With evil intent did he bring them out, to kill them in the mountains and to consume them from the face of the earth'? Turn from your burning anger and relent from this disaster against your people. [13] Remember Abraham, Isaac, and Israel, your servants, to whom you swore by your own self, and said to them, 'I will multiply your offspring as the stars of heaven, and all this land that I have promised I will give to your offspring, and they shall inherit it forever.'" [14] And the LORD relented from the disaster that he had spoken of bringing on his people.

[15] Then Moses turned and went down from the mountain with the two tablets of the testimony in his hand, tablets that were written on both sides; on the front and on the back they were written. [16] The tablets were the work of God, and the writing was the writing of God, engraved on the tablets. [17] When Joshua heard the noise of the people as they shouted, he said to Moses, "There is a noise of war in the camp." [18] But he said, "It is not the sound of shouting for victory, or the sound of the cry of defeat, but the sound of singing that I hear." [19] And as soon as he came near the camp and saw the calf and the dancing, Moses' anger burned hot, and he threw the tablets out of his hands and broke them at the foot of the mountain. [20] He took the calf that they had made and burned it with fire and ground it to powder and scattered it on the water and made the people of Israel drink it.

[21] And Moses said to Aaron, "What did this people do to you that you have brought such a great sin upon them?" [22] And Aaron said, "Let not the anger of my lord burn hot. You know the people, that they are set on evil. [23] For they said to me, 'Make us gods who shall go before us. As for this Moses, the man who brought us up out of the land of Egypt, we do not know what has become of him.' [24] So I said to them, 'Let any who have gold take it off.' So they gave it to me, and I threw it into the fire, and out came this calf."

[25] And when Moses saw that the people had broken loose (for Aaron had let them break loose, to the derision of their enemies), [26] then Moses stood in the gate of the camp and said, "Who is on the LORD's side? Come to me." And all the sons of Levi gathered around him. [27] And he said to them, "Thus says the LORD God of Israel, 'Put your sword on your side each of you, and go to and fro from gate to gate throughout the camp, and each of you kill his brother and his companion and his neighbor.'" [28] And the sons of Levi did according to the word of Moses. And that day about three thousand men of the people fell. [29] And Moses said, "Today you have been ordained for the service of the LORD, each one at the cost of his son and of his brother, so that he might bestow a blessing upon you this day."

[30] The next day Moses said to the people, "You have sinned a great sin. And now I will go up to the LORD; perhaps I can make atonement for your sin." [31] So Moses returned to the LORD and said, "Alas, this people has sinned a great sin. They have made for themselves gods of gold. [32] But now, if you will forgive their sin—but if not, please blot me out of your book that you have written." [33] But the LORD said to Moses, "Whoever has sinned against me, I will blot out of my book. [34] But now go, lead the people to the place about which I have spoken to you; behold, my angel shall go before you. Nevertheless, in the day when I visit, I will visit their sin upon them."

[35] Then the LORD sent a plague on the people, because they made the calf, the one that Aaron made.

The Command to Leave Sinai

33 The LORD said to Moses, "Depart; go up from here, you and the people whom you have brought up out of the land of Egypt, to the land of which I swore to Abraham, Isaac, and Jacob, saying, 'To your offspring I will give it.' [2] I will send an angel before you, and I will drive out the Canaanites, the Amorites, the Hittites, the Perizzites, the Hivites, and the Jebusites. [3] Go up to a land flowing with milk and honey; but I will not go up among you, lest I consume you on the way, for you are a stiff-necked people."

[4] When the people heard this disastrous word, they mourned, and no one put on his ornaments. [5] For the LORD had said to Moses, "Say to the people of Israel, 'You are

a stiff-necked people; if for a single moment I should go up among you, I would consume you. So now take off your ornaments, that I may know what to do with you.' " 6 Therefore the people of Israel stripped themselves of their ornaments, from Mount Horeb onward.

The Tent of Meeting

7 Now Moses used to take the tent and pitch it outside the camp, far off from the camp, and he called it the tent of meeting. And everyone who sought the Lord would go out to the tent of meeting, which was outside the camp. 8 Whenever Moses went out to the tent, all the people would rise up, and each would stand at his tent door, and watch Moses until he had gone into the tent. 9 When Moses entered the tent, the pillar of cloud would descend and stand at the entrance of the tent, and the Lord would speak with Moses. 10 And when all the people saw the pillar of cloud standing at the entrance of the tent, all the people would rise up and worship, each at his tent door. 11 Thus the Lord used to speak to Moses face to face, as a man speaks to his friend. When Moses turned again into the camp, his assistant Joshua the son of Nun, a young man, would not depart from the tent.

Moses' Intercession

12 Moses said to the Lord, "See, you say to me, 'Bring up this people,' but you have not let me know whom you will send with me. Yet you have said, 'I know you by name, and you have also found favor in my sight.' 13 Now therefore, if I have found favor in your sight, please show me now your ways, that I may know you in order to find favor in your sight. Consider too that this nation is your people." 14 And he said, "My presence will go with you, and I will give you rest." 15 And he said to him, "If your presence will not go with me, do not bring us up from here. 16 For how shall it be known that I have found favor in your sight, I and your people? Is it not in your going with us, so that we are distinct, I and your people, from every other people on the face of the earth?"

17 And the Lord said to Moses, "This very thing that you have spoken I will do, for you have found favor in my sight, and I know you by name." 18 Moses said, "Please show me your glory." 19 And he said, "I will make all my goodness pass before you and will

proclaim before you my name 'The Lord.' And I will be gracious to whom I will be gracious, and will show mercy on whom I will show mercy. 20 But," he said, "you cannot see my face, for man shall not see me and live." 21 And the Lord said, "Behold, there is a place by me where you shall stand on the rock, 22 and while my glory passes by I will put you in a cleft of the rock, and I will cover you with my hand until I have passed by. 23 Then I will take away my hand, and you shall see my back, but my face shall not be seen."

Moses Makes New Tablets

34 The Lord said to Moses, "Cut for yourself two tablets of stone like the first, and I will write on the tablets the words that were on the first tablets, which you broke. 2 Be ready by the morning, and come up in the morning to Mount Sinai, and present yourself there to me on the top of the mountain. 3 No one shall come up with you, and let no one be seen throughout all the mountain. Let no flocks or herds graze opposite that mountain." 4 So Moses cut two tablets of stone like the first. And he rose early in the morning and went up on Mount Sinai, as the Lord had commanded him, and took in his hand two tablets of stone. 5 The Lord descended in the cloud and stood with him there, and proclaimed the name of the Lord. 6 The Lord passed before him and proclaimed, "The Lord, the Lord, a God merciful and gracious, slow to anger, and abounding in steadfast love and faithfulness, 7 keeping steadfast love for thousands, forgiving iniquity and transgression and sin, but who will by no means clear the guilty, visiting the iniquity of the fathers on the children and the children's children, to the third and the fourth generation." 8 And Moses quickly bowed his head toward the earth and worshiped. 9 And he said, "If now I have found favor in your sight, O Lord, please let the Lord go in the midst of us, for it is a stiff-necked people, and pardon our iniquity and our sin, and take us for your inheritance."

The Covenant Renewed

10 And he said, "Behold, I am making a covenant. Before all your people I will do marvels, such as have not been created in all the earth or in any nation. And all the

people among whom you are shall see the work of the LORD, for it is an awesome thing that I will do with you.

11 "Observe what I command you this day. Behold, I will drive out before you the Amorites, the Canaanites, the Hittites, the Perizzites, the Hivites, and the Jebusites. **12** Take care, lest you make a covenant with the inhabitants of the land to which you go, lest it become a snare in your midst. **13** You shall tear down their altars and break their pillars and cut down their Asherim **14** (for you shall worship no other god, for the LORD, whose name is Jealous, is a jealous God), **15** lest you make a covenant with the inhabitants of the land, and when they whore after their gods and sacrifice to their gods and you are invited, you eat of his sacrifice, **16** and you take of their daughters for your sons, and their daughters whore after their gods and make your sons whore after their gods.

17 "You shall not make for yourself any gods of cast metal.

18 "You shall keep the Feast of Unleavened Bread. Seven days you shall eat unleavened bread, as I commanded you, at the time appointed in the month Abib, for in the month Abib you came out from Egypt. **19** All that open the womb are mine, all your male livestock, the firstborn of cow and sheep. **20** The firstborn of a donkey you shall redeem with a lamb, or if you will not redeem it you shall break its neck. All the firstborn of your sons you shall redeem. And none shall appear before me empty-handed.

21 "Six days you shall work, but on the seventh day you shall rest. In plowing time and in harvest you shall rest. **22** You shall observe the Feast of Weeks, the firstfruits of wheat harvest, and the Feast of Ingathering at the year's end. **23** Three times in the year shall all your males appear before the LORD God, the God of Israel. **24** For I will cast out nations before you and enlarge your borders; no one shall covet your land, when you go up to appear before the LORD your God three times in the year.

25 "You shall not offer the blood of my sacrifice with anything leavened, or let the sacrifice of the Feast of the Passover remain until the morning. **26** The best of the firstfruits of your ground you shall bring to the house of the LORD your God. You shall not boil a young goat in its mother's milk."

27 And the LORD said to Moses, "Write these words, for in accordance with these words I have made a covenant with you and with Israel." **28** So he was there with the LORD forty days and forty nights. He neither ate bread nor drank water. And he wrote on the tablets the words of the covenant, the Ten Commandments.

The Shining Face of Moses

29 When Moses came down from Mount Sinai, with the two tablets of the testimony in his hand as he came down from the mountain, Moses did not know that the skin of his face shone because he had been talking with God. **30** Aaron and all the people of Israel saw Moses, and behold, the skin of his face shone, and they were afraid to come near him. **31** But Moses called to them, and Aaron and all the leaders of the congregation returned to him, and Moses talked

> **GETTING THE MESSAGE**
>
> **The Jewish year** was based on the annual rotation of the sun, moon, and stars, and on the cycle for planting and harvesting crops. The Old Testament refers to days, months, years, and seasons, but no passages specify a complete calendar.

with them. **32** Afterward all the people of Israel came near, and he commanded them all that the LORD had spoken with him in Mount Sinai. **33** And when Moses had finished speaking with them, he put a veil over his face.

34 Whenever Moses went in before the LORD to speak with him, he would remove the veil, until he came out. And when he came out and told the people of Israel what he was commanded, **35** the people of Israel would see the face of Moses, that the skin of Moses' face was shining. And Moses would put the veil over his face again, until he went in to speak with him.

Sabbath Regulations

35 Moses assembled all the congregation of the people of Israel and said to them, "These are the things that the LORD has commanded you to do. **2** Six days work shall be done, but on the seventh day you shall have a Sabbath of solemn rest, holy to the LORD. Whoever does any work on it shall be put to death. ³ You shall kindle no fire in all your dwelling places on the Sabbath day."

Contributions for the Tabernacle

⁴ Moses said to all the congregation of the people of Israel, "This is the thing that the LORD has commanded. ⁵ Take from among you a contribution to the LORD. Whoever is of a generous heart, let him bring the LORD's contribution: gold, silver, and bronze; ⁶ blue and purple and scarlet yarns and fine twined linen; goats' hair, ⁷ tanned rams' skins, and goatskins; acacia wood, ⁸ oil for the light, spices for the anointing oil and for the fragrant incense, ⁹ and onyx stones and stones for setting, for the ephod and for the breastpiece.

¹⁰ "Let every skillful craftsman among you come and make all that the LORD has commanded: ¹¹ the tabernacle, its tent and its covering, its hooks and its frames, its bars, its pillars, and its bases; ¹² the ark with its poles, the mercy seat, and the veil of the screen; ¹³ the table with its poles and all its utensils, and the bread of the Presence; ¹⁴ the lampstand also for the light, with its utensils and its lamps, and the oil for the light; ¹⁵ and the altar of incense, with its poles, and the anointing oil and the fragrant incense, and the screen for the door, at the door of the tabernacle; ¹⁶ the altar of burnt offering, with its grating of bronze, its poles, and all its utensils, the basin and its stand; ¹⁷ the hangings of the court, its pillars and its bases, and the screen for the gate of the court; ¹⁸ the pegs of the tabernacle and the pegs of the court, and their cords; ¹⁹ the finely worked garments for ministering in the Holy Place, the holy garments for Aaron the priest, and the garments of his sons, for their service as priests."

²⁰ Then all the congregation of the people of Israel departed from the presence of Moses. ²¹ And they came, everyone whose heart stirred him, and everyone whose spirit moved him, and brought the LORD's contribution to be used for the tent of meeting, and for all its service, and for the holy garments. ²² So they came, both men and women. All who were of a willing heart brought brooches and earrings and signet rings and armlets, all sorts of gold objects, every man dedicating an offering of gold to the LORD. ²³ And every one who possessed blue or purple or scarlet yarns or fine linen or goats' hair or tanned rams' skins or goatskins brought them. ²⁴ Everyone who could make a contribution of silver or bronze brought it as the LORD's contribution. And every one who possessed acacia wood of any use in the work brought it. ²⁵ And every skillful woman spun with her hands, and they all brought what they had spun in blue and purple and scarlet yarns and fine twined linen. ²⁶ All the women whose hearts stirred them to use their skill spun the goats' hair. ²⁷ And the leaders brought onyx stones and stones to be set, for the ephod and for the breastpiece, ²⁸ and spices and oil for the light, and for the anointing oil, and for the fragrant incense. ²⁹ All the men and women, the people of Israel, whose heart moved them to bring anything for the work that the LORD had commanded by Moses to be done brought it as a freewill offering to the LORD.

Construction of the Tabernacle

³⁰ Then Moses said to the people of Israel, "See, the LORD has called by name Bezalel the son of Uri, son of Hur, of the tribe of Judah; ³¹ and he has filled him with the Spirit of God, with skill, with intelligence, with knowledge, and with all craftsmanship, ³² to devise artistic designs, to work in gold and silver and bronze, ³³ in cutting stones for setting, and in carving wood, for work in every skilled craft. ³⁴ And he has inspired him to teach, both him and Oholiab the son of Ahisamach of the tribe of Dan. ³⁵ He has filled them with skill to do every sort of work done by an engraver or by a designer or by an embroiderer in blue and purple and scarlet yarns and fine twined linen, or by a weaver—by any sort of workman or skilled designer.

36 "Bezalel and Oholiab and every craftsman in whom the LORD has put skill and intelligence to know how to do any work in the construction of the sanctuary shall work in accordance with all that the LORD has commanded."

² And Moses called Bezalel and Oholiab and every craftsman in whose mind the LORD had put skill, everyone whose heart stirred him up to come to do the work. ³ And they received from Moses all the contribution that the people of Israel had brought

for doing the work on the sanctuary. They still kept bringing him freewill offerings every morning, ⁴ so that all the craftsmen who were doing every sort of task on the sanctuary came, each from the task that he was doing, ⁵ and said to Moses, "The people bring much more than enough for doing the work that the LORD has commanded us to do." ⁶ So Moses gave command, and word was proclaimed throughout the camp, "Let no man or woman do anything more for the contribution for the sanctuary." So the people were restrained from bringing, ⁷ for the material they had was sufficient to do all the work, and more.

⁸ And all the craftsmen among the workmen made the tabernacle with ten curtains. They were made of fine twined linen and blue and purple and scarlet yarns, with cherubim skillfully worked. ⁹ The length of each curtain was twenty-eight cubits, and the breadth of each curtain four cubits. All the curtains were the same size.

¹⁰ He coupled five curtains to one another, and the other five curtains he coupled to one another. ¹¹ He made loops of blue on the edge of the outermost curtain of the first set. Likewise he made them on the edge of the outermost curtain of the second set. ¹² He made fifty loops on the one curtain, and he made fifty loops on the edge of the curtain that was in the second set. The loops were opposite one another. ¹³ And he made fifty clasps of gold, and coupled the curtains one to the other with clasps. So the tabernacle was a single whole.

¹⁴ He also made curtains of goats' hair for a tent over the tabernacle. He made eleven curtains. ¹⁵ The length of each curtain was thirty cubits, and the breadth of each curtain four cubits. The eleven curtains were the same size. ¹⁶ He coupled five curtains by themselves, and six curtains by themselves. ¹⁷ And he made fifty loops on the edge of the outermost curtain of the one set, and fifty loops on the edge of the other connecting curtain. ¹⁸ And he made fifty clasps of bronze to couple the tent together that it might be a single whole. ¹⁹ And he made for the tent a covering of tanned rams' skins and goatskins.

²⁰ Then he made the upright frames for the tabernacle of acacia wood. ²¹ Ten cubits was the length of a frame, and a cubit and a half the breadth of each frame. ²² Each frame had two tenons for fitting together. He did this for all the frames of the tabernacle. ²³ The frames for the tabernacle he made thus: twenty frames for the south side. ²⁴ And he made forty bases of silver under the twenty frames, two bases under one frame for its two tenons, and two bases under the next frame for its two tenons. ²⁵ For the second side of the tabernacle, on the north side, he made twenty frames ²⁶ and their forty bases of silver, two bases under one frame and two bases under the next frame. ²⁷ For the rear of the tabernacle westward he made six frames. ²⁸ He made two frames for corners of the tabernacle in the rear. ²⁹ And they were separate beneath but joined at the top, at the first ring. He

GETTING THE MESSAGE

Acacia wood was highly valued for its beauty and durability. Around the Mediterranean, some acacias are like shrubs, while others grow up to 50 feet (15 m) tall. They are one of the few large trees hardy enough to withstand the harsh desert climate. They are also resistant to insects, which find the taste of the wood unpleasant.

made two of them this way for the two corners. ³⁰ There were eight frames with their bases of silver: sixteen bases, under every frame two bases.

³¹ He made bars of acacia wood, five for the frames of the one side of the tabernacle, ³² and five bars for the frames of the other side of the tabernacle, and five bars for the frames of the tabernacle at the rear westward. ³³ And he made the middle bar to run from end to end halfway up the frames. ³⁴ And he overlaid the frames with gold, and made their rings of gold for holders for the bars, and overlaid the bars with gold.

³⁵ He made the veil of blue and purple and scarlet yarns and fine twined linen; with cherubim skillfully worked into it he made it. ³⁶ And for it he made four pillars of acacia and overlaid them with gold. Their hooks were of gold, and he cast for them four bases of silver. ³⁷ He also made a screen for the entrance of the tent, of blue and purple and

scarlet yarns and fine twined linen, embroidered with needlework, 38 and its five pillars with their hooks. He overlaid their capitals, and their fillets were of gold, but their five bases were of bronze.

Making the Ark

37 Bezalel made the ark of acacia wood. Two cubits and a half was its length, a cubit and a half its breadth, and a cubit and a half its height. 2 And he overlaid it with pure gold inside and outside, and made a molding of gold around it. 3 And he cast for it four rings of gold for its four feet, two rings on its one side and two rings on its other side. 4 And he made poles of acacia wood and overlaid them with gold 5 and put the poles into the rings on the sides of the ark to carry the ark. 6 And he made a mercy seat of pure gold. Two cubits and a half was

its length, and a cubit and a half its breadth. 7 And he made two cherubim of gold. He made them of hammered work on the two ends of the mercy seat, 8 one cherub on the one end, and one cherub on the other end. Of one piece with the mercy seat he made the cherubim on its two ends. 9 The cherubim spread out their wings above, overshadowing the mercy seat with their wings, with their faces one to another; toward the mercy seat were the faces of the cherubim.

Making the Table

10 He also made the table of acacia wood. Two cubits was its length, a cubit its breadth, and a cubit and a half its height. 11 And he overlaid it with pure gold, and made a molding of gold around it. 12 And he made a rim around it a handbreadth wide, and made a molding of gold around the rim. 13 He cast for it four rings of gold and fastened the rings to the four corners at its four legs. 14 Close to the frame were the

rings, as holders for the poles to carry the table. 15 He made the poles of acacia wood to carry the table, and overlaid them with gold. 16 And he made the vessels of pure gold that were to be on the table, its plates and dishes for incense, and its bowls and flagons with which to pour drink offerings.

Making the Lampstand

17 He also made the lampstand of pure gold. He made the lampstand of hammered work. Its base, its stem, its cups, its calyxes, and its flowers were of one piece with it. 18 And there were six branches going out of its sides, three branches of the lampstand out of one side of it and three branches of the lampstand out of the other side of it; 19 three cups made like almond blossoms, each with calyx and flower, on one branch, and three cups made like almond blossoms, each with calyx and flower, on the other branch—so for the six branches going out of the lampstand. 20 And on the lampstand itself were four cups made like almond blossoms, with their calyxes and flowers, 21 and a calyx of one piece with it under each pair of the six branches going out of it. 22 Their calyxes and their branches were of one piece with it. The whole of it was a single piece of hammered work of pure gold. 23 And he made its seven lamps and its tongs and its trays of pure gold. 24 He made it and all its utensils out of a talent of pure gold.

Making the Altar of Incense

25 He made the altar of incense of acacia wood. Its length was a cubit, and its breadth was a cubit. It was square, and two cubits was its height. Its horns were of one piece with it. 26 He overlaid it with pure gold, its top and around its sides and its horns. And he made a molding of gold around it, 27 and made two rings of gold on it under its molding, on two opposite sides of it, as holders for the poles with which to carry it. 28 And he made the poles of acacia wood and overlaid them with gold.

29 He made the holy anointing oil also, and the pure fragrant incense, blended as by the perfumer.

Making the Altar of Burnt Offering

38 He made the altar of burnt offering of acacia wood. Five cubits was its length, and five cubits its breadth. It was square, and three cubits was its height.

² He made horns for it on its four corners. Its horns were of one piece with it, and he overlaid it with bronze. ³ And he made all the utensils of the altar, the pots, the shovels, the basins, the forks, and the fire pans. He made all its utensils of bronze. ⁴ And he made for the altar a grating, a network of bronze, under its ledge, extending halfway down. ⁵ He cast four rings on the four corners of the bronze grating as holders for the poles. ⁶ He made the poles of acacia wood and overlaid them with bronze. ⁷ And he put the poles through the rings on the sides of the altar to carry it with them. He made it hollow, with boards.

Making the Bronze Basin

⁸ He made the basin of bronze and its stand of bronze, from the mirrors of the ministering women who ministered in the entrance of the tent of meeting.

Making the Court

⁹ And he made the court. For the south side the hangings of the court were of fine twined linen, a hundred cubits; ¹⁰ their twenty pillars and their twenty bases were of bronze, but the hooks of the pillars and their fillets were of silver. ¹¹ And for the north side there were hangings of a hundred cubits, their twenty pillars, their twenty bases were of bronze, but the hooks of the pillars and their fillets were of silver. ¹² And for the west side were hangings of fifty cubits, their ten pillars, and their ten bases; the hooks of the pillars and their fillets were of silver. ¹³ And for the front to the east, fifty cubits. ¹⁴ The hangings for one side of the gate were fifteen cubits, with their three pillars and three bases. ¹⁵ And so for the other side. On both sides of the gate of the court were hangings of fifteen cubits, with their three pillars and their three bases. ¹⁶ All the hangings around the court were of fine twined linen. ¹⁷ And the bases for the pillars were of bronze, but the hooks of the pillars and their fillets were of silver. The overlaying of their capitals was also of silver, and all the pillars of the court were filleted with silver. ¹⁸ And the screen for the gate of the court was embroidered with needlework in blue and purple and scarlet yarns and fine twined linen. It was twenty cubits long and five cubits high in its breadth, corresponding to the hangings of the court. ¹⁹ And their pillars were four in number. Their four bases were of bronze, their hooks of silver, and the overlaying of their capitals and their fillets of silver. ²⁰ And all the pegs for the tabernacle and for the court all around were of bronze.

Materials for the Tabernacle

²¹ These are the records of the tabernacle, the tabernacle of the testimony, as they were recorded at the commandment of Moses, the responsibility of the Levites under the direction of Ithamar the son of Aaron the priest. ²² Bezalel the son of Uri, son of Hur, of the tribe of Judah, made all that the LORD commanded Moses; ²³ and with him was Oholiab the son of Ahisamach, of the tribe of Dan, an engraver and designer and embroiderer in blue and purple and scarlet yarns and fine twined linen.

²⁴ All the gold that was used for the work, in all the construction of the sanctuary, the gold from the offering, was twenty-nine

> ### GETTING THE MESSAGE
>
> **Cubits** were a basic unit of measurement in Israel. One cubit equaled the distance from the elbow to the fingertips—about 18 inches (46 cm).

talents and 730 shekels, by the shekel of the sanctuary. ²⁵ The silver from those of the congregation who were recorded was a hundred talents and 1,775 shekels, by the shekel of the sanctuary: ²⁶ a beka a head (that is, half a shekel, by the shekel of the sanctuary), for everyone who was listed in the records, from twenty years old and upward, for 603,550 men. ²⁷ The hundred talents of silver were for casting the bases of the sanctuary and the bases of the veil; a hundred bases for the hundred talents, a talent a base. ²⁸ And of the 1,775 shekels he made hooks for the pillars and overlaid their capitals and made fillets for them. ²⁹ The bronze that was offered was seventy talents and 2,400 shekels; ³⁰ with it he made the bases for the entrance of the tent of meeting, the bronze altar and the bronze grating for it and all the utensils of the altar, ³¹ the bases around the court, and the bases of the gate of the court, all the pegs of the tabernacle, and all the pegs around the court.

Making the Priestly Garments

39 From the blue and purple and scarlet yarns they made finely woven garments, for ministering in the Holy Place. They made the holy garments for Aaron, as the LORD had commanded Moses.

² He made the ephod of gold, blue and purple and scarlet yarns, and fine twined linen. ³ And they hammered out gold leaf, and he cut it into threads to work into the blue and purple and the scarlet yarns, and into the fine twined linen, in skilled design. ⁴ They made for the ephod attaching shoulder pieces, joined to it at its two edges. ⁵ And the skillfully woven band on it was of one piece with it and made like it, of gold, blue and purple and scarlet yarns, and fine twined linen, as the LORD had commanded Moses.

> ### GETTING THE MESSAGE
>
> **Linen** was made from the flax plant. The plants were pulled up by their roots and dried before undergoing a process known as "retting," which loosened the fibers. The fibers were then beaten and combed so that they could be spun into thread. The result was a fabric that was light, durable, and easy to bleach. It was ideal for the hot, dry climate of ancient Israel.

⁶ They made the onyx stones, enclosed in settings of gold filigree, and engraved like the engravings of a signet, according to the names of the sons of Israel. ⁷ And he set them on the shoulder pieces of the ephod to be stones of remembrance for the sons of Israel, as the LORD had commanded Moses.
⁸ He made the breastpiece, in skilled work, in the style of the ephod, of gold, blue and purple and scarlet yarns, and fine twined linen. ⁹ It was square. They made the breastpiece doubled, a span its length and a span its breadth when doubled. ¹⁰ And they set in it four rows of stones. A row of sardius, topaz, and carbuncle was the first row; ¹¹ and the second row, an emerald, a sapphire, and a diamond; ¹² and the third row, a jacinth, an agate, and an amethyst; ¹³ and the fourth row, a beryl, an onyx, and a jasper. They were enclosed in settings of gold filigree. ¹⁴ There were twelve stones with their names according to the names of the sons of Israel. They were like signets, each engraved with its name, for the twelve tribes. ¹⁵ And they made on the breastpiece twisted chains like cords, of pure gold. ¹⁶ And they made two settings of gold filigree and two gold rings, and put the two rings on the two edges of the breastpiece. ¹⁷ And they put the two cords of gold in the two rings at the edges of the breastpiece. ¹⁸ They attached the two ends of the two cords to the two settings of filigree. Thus they attached it in front to the shoulder pieces of the ephod. ¹⁹ Then they made two rings of gold, and put them at the two ends of the breastpiece, on its inside edge next to the ephod. ²⁰ And they made two rings of gold, and attached them in front to the lower part of the two shoulder pieces of the ephod, at its seam above the skillfully woven band of the ephod. ²¹ And they bound the breastpiece by its rings to the rings of the ephod with a lace of blue, so that it should lie on the skillfully woven band of the ephod, and that the breastpiece should not come loose from the ephod, as the LORD had commanded Moses.

²² He also made the robe of the ephod woven all of blue, ²³ and the opening of the robe in it was like the opening in a garment, with a binding around the opening, so that it might not tear. ²⁴ On the hem of the robe they made pomegranates of blue and purple and scarlet yarns and fine twined linen. ²⁵ They also made bells of pure gold, and put the bells between the pomegranates all around the hem of the robe, between the pomegranates— ²⁶ a bell and a pomegranate, a bell and a pomegranate around the hem of the robe for ministering, as the LORD had commanded Moses.

²⁷ They also made the coats, woven of fine linen, for Aaron and his sons, ²⁸ and the turban of fine linen, and the caps of fine linen, and the linen undergarments of fine twined linen, ²⁹ and the sash of fine twined linen and of blue and purple and scarlet yarns, embroidered with needlework, as the LORD had commanded Moses.

³⁰ They made the plate of the holy crown of pure gold, and wrote on it an inscription, like the engraving of a signet, "Holy to the LORD." ³¹ And they tied to it a cord of blue to fasten it on the turban above, as the LORD had commanded Moses.

³² Thus all the work of the tabernacle of the tent of meeting was finished, and the people of Israel did according to all that the LORD had commanded Moses; so they did. ³³ Then they brought the tabernacle to Moses, the tent and all its utensils, its hooks, its frames, its bars, its pillars, and its bases; ³⁴ the covering of tanned rams' skins and goatskins, and the veil of the screen; ³⁵ the ark of the testimony with its poles and the mercy seat; ³⁶ the table with all its utensils, and the bread of the Presence; ³⁷ the lampstand of pure gold and its lamps with the lamps set and all its utensils, and the oil for the light; ³⁸ the golden altar, the anointing oil and the fragrant incense, and the screen for the entrance of the tent; ³⁹ the bronze altar, and its grating of bronze, its poles, and all its utensils; the basin and its stand; ⁴⁰ the hangings of the court, its pillars, and its bases, and the screen for the gate of the court, its cords, and its pegs; and all the utensils for the service of the tabernacle, for the tent of meeting; ⁴¹ the finely worked garments for ministering in the Holy Place, the holy garments for Aaron the priest, and the garments of his sons for their service as priests. ⁴² According to all that the LORD had commanded Moses, so the people of Israel had done all the work. ⁴³ And Moses saw all the work, and behold, they had done it; as the LORD had commanded, so had they done it. Then Moses blessed them.

The Tabernacle Erected

40 The LORD spoke to Moses, saying, ² "On the first day of the first month you shall erect the tabernacle of the tent of meeting. ³ And you shall put in it the ark of the testimony, and you shall screen the ark with the veil. ⁴ And you shall bring in the table and arrange it, and you shall bring in the lampstand and set up its lamps. ⁵ And you shall put the golden altar for incense before the ark of the testimony, and set up the screen for the door of the tabernacle. ⁶ You shall set the altar of burnt offering before the door of the tabernacle of the tent of meeting, ⁷ and place the basin between the tent of meeting and the altar, and put water in it. ⁸ And you shall set up the court all around, and hang up the screen for the gate of the court.

⁹ "Then you shall take the anointing oil and anoint the tabernacle and all that is in

it, and consecrate it and all its furniture, so that it may become holy. ¹⁰ You shall also anoint the altar of burnt offering and all its utensils, and consecrate the altar, so that the altar may become most holy. ¹¹ You shall also anoint the basin and its stand, and consecrate it. ¹² Then you shall bring Aaron and his sons to the entrance of the tent of meeting and shall wash them with water ¹³ and put on Aaron the holy garments. And you shall anoint him and consecrate him, that he may serve me as priest. ¹⁴ You shall bring his sons also and put coats on them, ¹⁵ and anoint them, as you anointed their father, that they may serve me as priests. And their anointing shall admit them to a perpetual priesthood throughout their generations."

¹⁶ This Moses did; according to all that the LORD commanded him, so he did. ¹⁷ In the first month in the second year, on the

> ### GETTING THE MESSAGE
>
> Israel has witnessed some incredible events, such as the 10 plagues and the parting of the Sea. Now, at the end of Exodus, **God's glory fills the tabernacle** and he will lead them to the Promised Land.

first day of the month, the tabernacle was erected. ¹⁸ Moses erected the tabernacle. He laid its bases, and set up its frames, and put in its poles, and raised up its pillars. ¹⁹ And he spread the tent over the tabernacle and put the covering of the tent over it, as the LORD had commanded Moses. ²⁰ He took the testimony and put it into the ark, and put the poles on the ark and set the mercy seat above on the ark. ²¹ And he brought the ark into the tabernacle and set up the veil of the screen, and screened the ark of the testimony, as the LORD had commanded Moses. ²² He put the table in the tent of meeting, on the north side of the tabernacle, outside the veil, ²³ and arranged the bread on it before the LORD, as the LORD had commanded Moses. ²⁴ He put the lampstand in the tent of meeting, opposite the table on the south side of the tabernacle, ²⁵ and set up the lamps before the LORD, as the LORD had commanded Moses. ²⁶ He put the golden altar in the tent of meeting before the veil, ²⁷ and burned fragrant incense on it, as the Lord had commanded Moses. ²⁸ He put in place the screen for the door of the tabernacle. ²⁹ And he set the altar of burnt offering at the entrance of the tabernacle of the tent of meeting, and offered on it the burnt offering and the grain offering, as the Lord had commanded Moses. ³⁰ He set the basin between the tent of meeting and the altar, and put water in it for washing, ³¹ with which Moses and Aaron and his sons washed their hands and their feet. ³² When they went into the tent of meeting, and when they approached the altar, they washed, as the Lord commanded Moses. ³³ And he erected the court around the tabernacle and the altar, and set up the screen of the gate of the court. So Moses finished the work.

The Glory of the Lord

³⁴ Then the cloud covered the tent of meeting, and the glory of the Lord filled the tabernacle. ³⁵ And Moses was not able to enter the tent of meeting because the cloud settled on it, and the glory of the Lord filled the tabernacle. ³⁶ Throughout all their journeys, whenever the cloud was taken up from over the tabernacle, the people of Israel would set out. ³⁷ But if the cloud was not taken up, then they did not set out till the day that it was taken up. ³⁸ For the cloud of the Lord was on the tabernacle by day, and fire was in it by night, in the sight of all the house of Israel throughout all their journeys.

INTRODUCTION TO LEVITICUS

1876 B.C.	1526 B.C.	1446 B.C.
Israel goes to Egypt	Moses born	Exodus/events of Leviticus

AUTHOR

As with the other books of the Pentateuch, it is best to see Moses as the source and primary author of Leviticus. In Leviticus, Moses continues the story of Exodus.

THEME AND PURPOSE

The book of Leviticus goes into deeper detail about the divine-human relationship put in place on Mount Sinai (Exodus 19–40). Leviticus assumes that Israel is sinful and impure, and it describes how to deal with sin and impurity so that the holy Lord can dwell among his people.

PROBLEMS IN UNDERSTANDING LEVITICUS

Readers may find Leviticus difficult to understand because they lack firsthand experience of the practices it describes.

Ritual vs. ethical commands. Chapters 1–16 describe various "ritual" regulations, while chs. 17–27 focus on ethical commands. Because the rituals of chs. 1–16 are unfamiliar, they are often seen as being disconnected from the ethical emphasis of the later chapters. It is more accurate, however, to see the entire book as being concerned with Israel's being holy to the Lord.

Unclean, clean, holy. Leviticus often uses these terms differently than today. Modern readers might think of "clean" vs. "unclean" as being the same as healthy vs. unhealthy. In Leviticus, however, these words do not refer to hygiene. Rather, they describe the types of actions a person may or may not engage in, or the places he may or may not go. For example, those who are unclean may not partake of a peace offering (7:20). A modern analogy might be registering to vote: a person who is "registered" may vote, whereas a person who is not registered may not vote. The ritually "clean" person is not necessarily more righteous than one who is ritually unclean, just as a person who is registered to vote is not necessarily more righteous than a person who is not.

Even though ritual states and moral states are different, however, the ritual states in Leviticus also seem to symbolize grades of moral purity. By constantly calling the Israelites to *ritual* purity, the Lord was reminding them of their need for also seeking *moral* purity (20:24–26).

NT relevance of commands in Leviticus. What does Leviticus have to do with the church today? The sacrificial system of Leviticus has ceased for the people of God; it has been fulfilled in the coming of Christ (see Heb. 9:1–14, 24–28; 10:1–14). However, studying these laws is important because the sacrifices point to different aspects of the meaning of Christ's sacrifice of himself.

Second, the Holiness Code (chs. 17–27) deals with sanctification, that is, how one lives in the covenant community. The NT applies to Christians the same principle stated in Leviticus 11:44, "be holy, for I am holy" (see 1 Pet. 1:16). On the other hand, several details of the Holiness Code concern more symbolic aspects of holiness that are no longer followed in the Christian era (such as laws prohibiting garments with two kinds of cloth, Lev. 19:19, or prohibiting the shaving of the edges of a beard, 21:5). Further, the NT envisions a people of God transcending national boundaries. Therefore, current civil governments need not follow the OT civil laws (such as capital punishment for adultery; 20:10), although of course all governments must pursue justice, and Leviticus may certainly help in this regard.

KEY THEMES

1. The holy Lord is present among his people (Ex. 40:34; Lev. 1:1). They must therefore admit their sin and impurity and strive for personal holiness.

2. In order to approach God, worshipers must be wholehearted in their devotion (1:1–6:7; 22:17–30).

3. Those called to be spiritual leaders, such as priests, bear a heavier responsibility than the laypeople (chs. 4; 21). In addition to the outward holiness that the priests receive when they are ordained, they must maintain inward holiness (chs. 8; 9; 10; 21).

4. As is seen in the Day of Atonement ritual (ch. 16), the total cleansing of sins and uncleanness happens only when the innermost part of the tabernacle is purified. Humans, by themselves, can never achieve complete purification from sin.

5. Atonement is a gracious act of the Lord (17:11).

OUTLINE

LEVITICUS

Laws for Burnt Offerings

1 The LORD called Moses and spoke to him from the tent of meeting, saying, ² "Speak to the people of Israel and say to them, When any one of you brings an offering to the LORD, you shall bring your offering of livestock from the herd or from the flock.

³ "If his offering is a burnt offering from the herd, he shall offer a male without blemish. He shall bring it to the entrance of the tent of meeting, that he may be accepted before the LORD. ⁴ He shall lay his hand on the head of the burnt offering, and it shall be accepted for him to make atonement for him. ⁵ Then he shall kill the bull before the

---

GETTING THE MESSAGE

Burnt offerings were the most costly type of sacrifice. Unlike other offerings, none of the remains could be used for other purposes.

LORD, and Aaron's sons the priests shall bring the blood and throw the blood against the sides of the altar that is at the entrance of the tent of meeting. ⁶ Then he shall flay the burnt offering and cut it into pieces, ⁷ and the sons of Aaron the priest shall put fire on the altar and arrange wood on the fire. ⁸ And Aaron's sons the priests shall arrange the pieces, the head, and the fat, on the wood that is on the fire on the altar; ⁹ but its entrails and its legs he shall wash with water. And the priest shall burn all of it on the altar, as a burnt offering, a food offering with a pleasing aroma to the LORD.

¹⁰ "If his gift for a burnt offering is from the flock, from the sheep or goats, he shall bring a male without blemish, ¹¹ and he shall kill it on the north side of the altar before the LORD, and Aaron's sons the priests shall throw its blood against the sides of the altar. ¹² And he shall cut it into pieces, with its head and its fat, and the priest shall arrange them on the wood that is on the fire on the

altar, ¹³ but the entrails and the legs he shall wash with water. And the priest shall offer all of it and burn it on the altar; it is a burnt offering, a food offering with a pleasing aroma to the LORD.

¹⁴ "If his offering to the LORD is a burnt offering of birds, then he shall bring his offering of turtledoves or pigeons. ¹⁵ And the priest shall bring it to the altar and wring off its head and burn it on the altar. Its blood shall be drained out on the side of the altar. ¹⁶ He shall remove its crop with its contents and cast it beside the altar on the east side, in the place for ashes. ¹⁷ He shall tear it open by its wings, but shall not sever it completely. And the priest shall burn it on the altar, on the wood that is on the fire. It is a burnt offering, a food offering with a pleasing aroma to the LORD.

Laws for Grain Offerings

2 "When anyone brings a grain offering as an offering to the LORD, his offering shall be of fine flour. He shall pour oil on it and put frankincense on it ² and bring it to Aaron's sons the priests. And he shall take from it a handful of the fine flour and oil, with all of its frankincense, and the priest shall burn this as its memorial portion on the altar, a food offering with a pleasing aroma to the LORD. ³ But the rest of the grain offering shall be for Aaron and his sons; it is a most holy part of the LORD's food offerings.

⁴ "When you bring a grain offering baked in the oven as an offering, it shall be unleavened loaves of fine flour mixed with oil or unleavened wafers smeared with oil. ⁵ And if your offering is a grain offering baked on a griddle, it shall be of fine flour unleavened, mixed with oil. ⁶ You shall break it in pieces and pour oil on it; it is a grain offering. ⁷ And if your offering is a grain offering cooked in a pan, it shall be made of fine flour with oil. ⁸ And you shall bring the grain offering that is made of these things to the LORD, and when it is presented to the priest, he shall bring it to the altar. ⁹ And the priest shall

take from the grain offering its memorial portion and burn this on the altar, a food offering with a pleasing aroma to the Lord. ¹⁰ But the rest of the grain offering shall be for Aaron and his sons; it is a most holy part of the Lord's food offerings.

¹¹ "No grain offering that you bring to the Lord shall be made with leaven, for you shall burn no leaven nor any honey as a food offering to the Lord. ¹² As an offering of firstfruits you may bring them to the Lord, but they shall not be offered on the altar for a pleasing aroma. ¹³ You shall season all your grain offerings with salt. You shall not let the salt of the covenant with your God be missing from your grain offering; with all your offerings you shall offer salt.

¹⁴ "If you offer a grain offering of first-fruits to the Lord, you shall offer for the grain offering of your firstfruits fresh ears, roasted with fire, crushed new grain. ¹⁵ And you shall put oil on it and lay frankincense on it; it is a grain offering. ¹⁶ And the priest shall burn as its memorial portion some of the crushed grain and some of the oil with all of its frankincense; it is a food offering to the Lord.

Laws for Peace Offerings

3 "If his offering is a sacrifice of peace offering, if he offers an animal from the herd, male or female, he shall offer it without blemish before the Lord. ² And he shall lay his hand on the head of his offering and kill it at the entrance of the tent of meeting, and Aaron's sons the priests shall throw the blood against the sides of the altar. ³ And from the sacrifice of the peace offering, as a food offering to the Lord, he shall offer the fat covering the entrails and all the fat that is on the entrails, ⁴ and the two kidneys with the fat that is on them at the loins, and the long lobe of the liver that he shall remove with the kidneys. ⁵ Then Aaron's sons shall burn it on the altar on top of the burnt offering, which is on the wood on the fire; it is a food offering with a pleasing aroma to the Lord.

⁶ "If his offering for a sacrifice of peace offering to the Lord is an animal from the flock, male or female, he shall offer it without blemish. ⁷ If he offers a lamb for his offering, then he shall offer it before the Lord, ⁸ lay his hand on the head of his offering, and kill it in front of the tent of meeting; and Aaron's sons shall throw its blood against the sides of the altar. ⁹ Then from the sacrifice of the peace offering he shall offer as a food offering to the Lord its fat; he shall remove the whole fat tail, cut off close to the backbone, and the fat that covers the entrails and all the fat that is on the entrails ¹⁰ and the two kidneys with the fat that is on them at the loins and the long lobe of the liver that he shall remove with the kidneys. ¹¹ And the priest shall burn it on the altar as a food offering to the Lord.

¹² "If his offering is a goat, then he shall offer it before the Lord ¹³ and lay his hand on its head and kill it in front of the tent of meeting, and the sons of Aaron shall throw its blood against the sides of the altar. ¹⁴ Then he shall offer from it, as his offering for a food offering to the Lord, the fat covering the entrails and all the fat that is on the entrails ¹⁵ and the two kidneys with the fat that is on them at the

GETTING THE MESSAGE

Grain offerings. Grain was highly valued by nomads such as the Israelites, since it could not be grown in the desert. Grain offerings were thus an act of worship and thanksgiving.

loins and the long lobe of the liver that he shall remove with the kidneys. ¹⁶ And the priest shall burn them on the altar as a food offering with a pleasing aroma. All fat is the Lord's. ¹⁷ It shall be a statute forever throughout your generations, in all your dwelling places, that you eat neither fat nor blood."

Laws for Sin Offerings

4 And the Lord spoke to Moses, saying, ² "Speak to the people of Israel, saying, If anyone sins unintentionally in any of the Lord's commandments about things not to be done, and does any one of them, ³ if it is the anointed priest who sins, thus bringing guilt on the people, then he shall offer for the sin that he has committed a bull from the herd without blemish to the Lord for a sin offering. ⁴ He shall bring the bull to the entrance of the tent of meeting before the Lord and lay his hand on the head of the bull and kill the bull before the Lord. ⁵ And

the anointed priest shall take some of the blood of the bull and bring it into the tent of meeting, [6] and the priest shall dip his finger in the blood and sprinkle part of the blood seven times before the LORD in front of the veil of the sanctuary. [7] And the priest shall put some of the blood on the horns of the altar of fragrant incense before the LORD that is in the tent of meeting, and all the rest of the blood of the bull he shall pour out at the base of the altar of burnt offering that is at the entrance of the tent of meeting. [8] And all the fat of the bull of the sin offering he shall remove from it, the fat that covers the entrails and all the fat that is on the entrails [9] and the two kidneys with the fat that is on them at the loins and the long lobe of the liver that he shall remove with the kidneys [10] (just as these are taken from the ox of the sacrifice of the peace offerings); and the priest shall burn them on the altar of burnt offering. [11] But the skin of the bull

> ### GETTING THE MESSAGE
>
> **Peace offerings** were also called fellowship offerings. They expressed peace and fellowship between the person making the offering and the Lord.

and all its flesh, with its head, its legs, its entrails, and its dung— [12] all the rest of the bull—he shall carry outside the camp to a clean place, to the ash heap, and shall burn it up on a fire of wood. On the ash heap it shall be burned up.

[13] "If the whole congregation of Israel sins unintentionally and the thing is hidden from the eyes of the assembly, and they do any one of the things that by the LORD's commandments ought not to be done, and they realize their guilt, [14] when the sin which they have committed becomes known, the assembly shall offer a bull from the herd for a sin offering and bring it in front of the tent of meeting. [15] And the elders of the congregation shall lay their hands on the head of the bull before the LORD, and the bull shall be killed before the LORD. [16] Then the anointed priest shall bring some of the blood of the bull into the tent of meeting, [17] and the priest shall dip his finger in the blood and sprinkle it seven times before

the LORD in front of the veil. [18] And he shall put some of the blood on the horns of the altar that is in the tent of meeting before the LORD, and the rest of the blood he shall pour out at the base of the altar of burnt offering that is at the entrance of the tent of meeting. [19] And all its fat he shall take from it and burn on the altar. [20] Thus shall he do with the bull. As he did with the bull of the sin offering, so shall he do with this. And the priest shall make atonement for them, and they shall be forgiven. [21] And he shall carry the bull outside the camp and burn it up as he burned the first bull; it is the sin offering for the assembly.

[22] "When a leader sins, doing unintentionally any one of all the things that by the commandments of the LORD his God ought not to be done, and realizes his guilt, [23] or the sin which he has committed is made known to him, he shall bring as his offering a goat, a male without blemish, [24] and shall lay his hand on the head of the goat and kill it in the place where they kill the burnt offering before the LORD; it is a sin offering. [25] Then the priest shall take some of the blood of the sin offering with his finger and put it on the horns of the altar of burnt offering and pour out the rest of its blood at the base of the altar of burnt offering. [26] And all its fat he shall burn on the altar, like the fat of the sacrifice of peace offerings. So the priest shall make atonement for him for his sin, and he shall be forgiven.

[27] "If anyone of the common people sins unintentionally in doing any one of the things that by the LORD's commandments ought not to be done, and realizes his guilt, [28] or the sin which he has committed is made known to him, he shall bring for his offering a goat, a female without blemish, for his sin which he has committed. [29] And he shall lay his hand on the head of the sin offering and kill the sin offering in the place of burnt offering. [30] And the priest shall take some of its blood with his finger and put it on the horns of the altar of burnt offering and pour out all the rest of its blood at the base of the altar. [31] And all its fat he shall remove, as the fat is removed from the peace offerings, and the priest shall burn it on the altar for a pleasing aroma to the LORD. And the priest shall make atonement for him, and he shall be forgiven.

32 "If he brings a lamb as his offering for a sin offering, he shall bring a female without blemish 33 and lay his hand on the head of the sin offering and kill it for a sin offering in the place where they kill the burnt offering. 34 Then the priest shall take some of the blood of the sin offering with his finger and put it on the horns of the altar of burnt offering and pour out all the rest of its blood at the base of the altar. 35 And all its fat he shall remove as the fat of the lamb is removed from the sacrifice of peace offerings, and the priest shall burn it on the altar, on top of the LORD's food offerings. And the priest shall make atonement for him for the sin which he has committed, and he shall be forgiven.

5 "If anyone sins in that he hears a public adjuration to testify, and though he is a witness, whether he has seen or come to know the matter, yet does not speak, he shall bear his iniquity; 2 or if anyone touches an unclean thing, whether a carcass of an unclean wild animal or a carcass of unclean livestock or a carcass of unclean swarming things, and it is hidden from him and he has become unclean, and he realizes his guilt; 3 or if he touches human uncleanness, of whatever sort the uncleanness may be with which one becomes unclean, and it is hidden from him, when he comes to know it, and realizes his guilt; 4 or if anyone utters with his lips a rash oath to do evil or to do good, any sort of rash oath that people swear, and it is hidden from him, when he comes to know it, and he realizes his guilt in any of these; 5 when he realizes his guilt in any of these and confesses the sin he has committed, 6 he shall bring to the LORD as his compensation for the sin that he has committed, a female from the flock, a lamb or a goat, for a sin offering. And the priest shall make atonement for him for his sin.

7 "But if he cannot afford a lamb, then he shall bring to the LORD as his compensation for the sin that he has committed two turtledoves or two pigeons, one for a sin offering and the other for a burnt offering. 8 He shall bring them to the priest, who shall offer first the one for the sin offering. He shall wring its head from its neck but shall not sever it completely, 9 and he shall sprinkle some of the blood of the sin offering on the side of the altar, while the rest of the blood shall be drained out at the base of the altar; it is a sin offering. 10 Then he shall offer the second for a burnt offering according to the rule. And the priest shall make atonement for him for the sin that he has committed, and he shall be forgiven.

11 "But if he cannot afford two turtledoves or two pigeons, then he shall bring as his offering for the sin that he has committed a tenth of an ephah of fine flour to a sin offering. He shall put no oil on it and shall put no frankincense on it, for it is a sin offering. 12 And he shall bring it to the priest, and the priest shall take a handful of it as its memorial portion and burn this on the altar, on the LORD's food offerings; it is a sin offering. 13 Thus the priest shall make atonement for him for the sin which he has committed in any one of these things, and he shall be forgiven. And the remainder shall be for the priest, as in the grain offering."

> ### GETTING THE MESSAGE

Sin offerings atoned for unintentional sins (4:1–35) and for sins of omission (5:1–13). The sacrificial animal was burned "outside the camp" (4:12), rather than at the base of the altar. This foreshadowed the sacrificial death of Jesus Christ, who was crucified "outside the camp" (Heb. 13:13).

Laws for Guilt Offerings

14 The LORD spoke to Moses, saying, 15 "If anyone commits a breach of faith and sins unintentionally in any of the holy things of the LORD, he shall bring to the LORD as his compensation, a ram without blemish out of the flock, valued in silver shekels, according to the shekel of the sanctuary, for a guilt offering. 16 He shall also make restitution for what he has done amiss in the holy thing and shall add a fifth to it and give it to the priest. And the priest shall make atonement for him with the ram of the guilt offering, and he shall be forgiven.

17 "If anyone sins, doing any of the things that by the LORD's commandments ought not to be done, though he did not know it, then realizes his guilt, he shall bear his iniquity. 18 He shall bring to the priest a ram without blemish out of the flock, or its equivalent for a guilt offering, and the priest

shall make atonement for him for the mistake that he made unintentionally, and he shall be forgiven. ¹⁹ It is a guilt offering; he has indeed incurred guilt before the LORD."

6 The LORD spoke to Moses, saying, ² "If anyone sins and commits a breach of faith against the LORD by deceiving his neighbor in a matter of deposit or security, or through robbery, or if he has oppressed his neighbor ³ or has found something lost and lied about it, swearing falsely — in any of all the things that people do and sin thereby — ⁴ if he has sinned and has realized his guilt and will restore what he took by robbery or what he got by oppression or the deposit that was committed to him or the lost thing that he found ⁵ or anything about which he has sworn falsely, he shall restore it in full and shall add a fifth to it, and give it to him to whom it belongs on the day he realizes his guilt. ⁶ And he shall bring to the priest as his compensation to the LORD a ram without blemish out of the flock, or its equivalent for a guilt offering. ⁷ And the priest shall make atonement for him before the LORD, and he shall be forgiven for any of the things that one may do and thereby become guilty."

The Priests and the Offerings

⁸ The LORD spoke to Moses, saying, ⁹ "Command Aaron and his sons, saying, This is the law of the burnt offering. The burnt offering shall be on the hearth on the altar all night until the morning, and the fire of the altar shall be kept burning on it. ¹⁰ And the priest shall put on his linen garment and put his linen undergarment on his body, and he shall take up the ashes to which the fire has reduced the burnt offering on the altar and put them beside the altar. ¹¹ Then he shall take off his garments and put on other garments and carry the ashes outside the camp to a clean place. ¹² The fire on the altar shall be kept burning on it; it shall not go out. The priest shall burn wood on it every morning, and he shall arrange the burnt offering on it and shall burn on it the fat of the peace offerings. ¹³ Fire shall be kept burning on the altar continually; it shall not go out.

¹⁴ "And this is the law of the grain offering. The sons of Aaron shall offer it before the LORD in front of the altar. ¹⁵ And one shall take from it a handful of the fine flour of the grain offering and its oil and all the frankincense that is on the grain offering and burn this as its memorial portion on the altar, a pleasing aroma to the LORD. ¹⁶ And the rest of it Aaron and his sons shall eat. It shall be eaten unleavened in a holy place. In the court of the tent of meeting they shall eat it. ¹⁷ It shall not be baked with leaven. I have given it as their portion of my food offerings. It is a thing most holy, like the sin offering and the guilt offering. ¹⁸ Every male among the children of Aaron may eat of it, as decreed forever throughout your generations, from the LORD's food offerings. Whatever touches them shall become holy."

¹⁹ The LORD spoke to Moses, saying, ²⁰ "This is the offering that Aaron and his sons shall offer to the LORD on the day when he is anointed: a tenth of an ephah of fine flour as a regular grain offering, half of it in the morning and half in the evening. ²¹ It shall be made with oil on a griddle. You shall bring it well mixed, in baked pieces like a grain offering, and offer it for a pleasing aroma to the LORD. ²² The priest from among Aaron's sons, who is anointed to succeed him, shall offer it to the LORD as decreed forever. The whole of it shall be burned. ²³ Every grain offering of a priest shall be wholly burned. It shall not be eaten."

²⁴ The LORD spoke to Moses, saying, ²⁵ "Speak to Aaron and his sons, saying, This is the law of the sin offering. In the place where the burnt offering is killed shall the sin offering be killed before the LORD; it is most holy. ²⁶ The priest who offers it for sin shall eat it. In a holy place it shall be eaten, in the court of the tent of meeting. ²⁷ Whatever touches its flesh shall be holy, and when any of its blood is splashed on a garment, you shall wash that on which it was splashed in a holy place. ²⁸ And the earthenware vessel in which it is boiled shall be broken. But if it is boiled in a bronze vessel, that shall be scoured and rinsed in water. ²⁹ Every male among the priests may eat of it; it is most holy. ³⁰ But no sin offering shall be eaten from which any blood is brought into the tent of meeting to make atonement in the Holy Place; it shall be burned up with fire.

7 "This is the law of the guilt offering. It is most holy. ² In the place where they kill the burnt offering they shall kill the guilt offering, and its blood shall be thrown

against the sides of the altar. ³ And all its fat shall be offered, the fat tail, the fat that covers the entrails, ⁴ the two kidneys with the fat that is on them at the loins, and the long lobe of the liver that he shall remove with the kidneys. ⁵ The priest shall burn them on the altar as a food offering to the LORD; it is a guilt offering. ⁶ Every male among the priests may eat of it. It shall be eaten in a holy place. It is most holy. ⁷ The guilt offering is just like the sin offering; there is one law for them. The priest who makes atonement with it shall have it. ⁸ And the priest who offers any man's burnt offering shall have for himself the skin of the burnt offering that he has offered. ⁹ And every grain offering baked in the oven and all that is prepared on a pan or a griddle shall belong to the priest who offers it. ¹⁰ And every grain offering, mixed with oil or dry, shall be shared equally among all the sons of Aaron.

¹¹ "And this is the law of the sacrifice of peace offerings that one may offer to the LORD. ¹² If he offers it for a thanksgiving, then he shall offer with the thanksgiving sacrifice unleavened loaves mixed with oil, unleavened wafers smeared with oil, and loaves of fine flour well mixed with oil. ¹³ With the sacrifice of his peace offerings for thanksgiving he shall bring his offering with loaves of leavened bread. ¹⁴ And from it he shall offer one loaf from each offering, as a gift to the LORD. It shall belong to the priest who throws the blood of the peace offerings. ¹⁵ And the flesh of the sacrifice of his peace offerings for thanksgiving shall be eaten on the day of his offering. He shall not leave any of it until the morning. ¹⁶ But if the sacrifice of his offering is a vow offering or a freewill offering, it shall be eaten on the day that he offers his sacrifice, and on the next day what remains of it shall be eaten. ¹⁷ But what remains of the flesh of the sacrifice on the third day shall be burned up with fire. ¹⁸ If any of the flesh of the sacrifice of his peace offering is eaten on the third day, he who offers it shall not be accepted, neither shall it be credited to him. It is tainted, and he who eats of it shall bear his iniquity.

¹⁹ "Flesh that touches any unclean thing shall not be eaten. It shall be burned up with fire. All who are clean may eat flesh, ²⁰ but the person who eats of the flesh of the sac-

rifice of the LORD's peace offerings while an uncleanness is on him, that person shall be cut off from his people. ²¹ And if anyone touches an unclean thing, whether human uncleanness or an unclean beast or any unclean detestable creature, and then eats some flesh from the sacrifice of the LORD's peace offerings, that person shall be cut off from his people."

²² The LORD spoke to Moses, saying, ²³ "Speak to the people of Israel, saying, You shall eat no fat, of ox or sheep or goat. ²⁴ The fat of an animal that dies of itself and the fat of one that is torn by beasts may be put to any other use, but on no account shall you eat it. ²⁵ For every person who eats of the fat of an animal of which a food offering may be made to the LORD shall be cut off from his people. ²⁶ Moreover, you shall eat no blood whatever, whether of fowl or of animal, in

> ### GETTING THE MESSAGE
>
> The account of the **ordination of Aaron and his sons** as priests (8:1–36) is divided into seven parts by the phrase "as the LORD commanded." The number seven often symbolizes completion in the Old Testament.

any of your dwelling places. ²⁷ Whoever eats any blood, that person shall be cut off from his people."

²⁸ The LORD spoke to Moses, saying, ²⁹ "Speak to the people of Israel, saying, Whoever offers the sacrifice of his peace offerings to the LORD shall bring his offering to the LORD from the sacrifice of his peace offerings. ³⁰ His own hands shall bring the LORD's food offerings. He shall bring the fat with the breast, that the breast may be waved as a wave offering before the LORD. ³¹ The priest shall burn the fat on the altar, but the breast shall be for Aaron and his sons. ³² And the right thigh you shall give to the priest as a contribution from the sacrifice of your peace offerings. ³³ Whoever among the sons of Aaron offers the blood of the peace offerings and the fat shall have the right thigh for a portion. ³⁴ For the breast that is waved and the thigh that is contributed I have taken from the people of Israel, out of the sacrifices of their peace offerings,

and have given them to Aaron the priest and to his sons, as a perpetual due from the people of Israel. ³⁵ This is the portion of Aaron and of his sons from the LORD's food offerings, from the day they were presented to serve as priests of the LORD. ³⁶ The LORD commanded this to be given them by the people of Israel, from the day that he anointed them. It is a perpetual due throughout their generations."

³⁷ This is the law of the burnt offering, of the grain offering, of the sin offering, of the guilt offering, of the ordination offering, and of the peace offering, ³⁸ which the LORD commanded Moses on Mount Sinai, on the day that he commanded the people of Israel to bring their offerings to the LORD, in the wilderness of Sinai.

GETTING THE MESSAGE

What were the Urim and the Thummim?
Mentioned in 8:8 and in various other Old Testament passages, the Urim and the Thummim remain a mystery to modern readers. All that is known is that they were worn on the garment of the high priest, and were used in seeking the Lord's will on particular matters.

Consecration of Aaron and His Sons

8 The LORD spoke to Moses, saying, ² "Take Aaron and his sons with him, and the garments and the anointing oil and the bull of the sin offering and the two rams and the basket of unleavened bread. ³ And assemble all the congregation at the entrance of the tent of meeting." ⁴ And Moses did as the LORD commanded him, and the congregation was assembled at the entrance of the tent of meeting.

⁵ And Moses said to the congregation, "This is the thing that the LORD has commanded to be done." ⁶ And Moses brought Aaron and his sons and washed them with water. ⁷ And he put the coat on him and tied the sash around his waist and clothed him with the robe and put the ephod on him and tied the skillfully woven band of the ephod around him, binding it to him with the band. ⁸ And he placed the breastpiece on him, and in the breastpiece he put the Urim and the Thummim. ⁹ And he set the turban

on his head, and on the turban, in front, he set the golden plate, the holy crown, as the LORD commanded Moses.

¹⁰ Then Moses took the anointing oil and anointed the tabernacle and all that was in it, and consecrated them. ¹¹ And he sprinkled some of it on the altar seven times, and anointed the altar and all its utensils and the basin and its stand, to consecrate them. ¹² And he poured some of the anointing oil on Aaron's head and anointed him to consecrate him. ¹³ And Moses brought Aaron's sons and clothed them with coats and tied sashes around their waists and bound caps on them, as the LORD commanded Moses.

¹⁴ Then he brought the bull of the sin offering, and Aaron and his sons laid their hands on the head of the bull of the sin offering. ¹⁵ And he killed it, and Moses took the blood, and with his finger put it on the horns of the altar around it and purified the altar and poured out the blood at the base of the altar and consecrated it to make atonement for it. ¹⁶ And he took all the fat that was on the entrails and the long lobe of the liver and the two kidneys with their fat, and Moses burned them on the altar. ¹⁷ But the bull and its skin and its flesh and its dung he burned up with fire outside the camp, as the LORD commanded Moses.

¹⁸ Then he presented the ram of the burnt offering, and Aaron and his sons laid their hands on the head of the ram. ¹⁹ And he killed it, and Moses threw the blood against the sides of the altar. ²⁰ He cut the ram into pieces, and Moses burned the head and the pieces and the fat. ²¹ He washed the entrails and the legs with water, and Moses burned the whole ram on the altar. It was a burnt offering with a pleasing aroma, a food offering for the LORD, as the LORD commanded Moses.

²² Then he presented the other ram, the ram of ordination, and Aaron and his sons laid their hands on the head of the ram. ²³ And he killed it, and Moses took some of its blood and put it on the lobe of Aaron's right ear and on the thumb of his right hand and on the big toe of his right foot. ²⁴ Then he presented Aaron's sons, and Moses put some of the blood on the lobes of their right ears and on the thumbs of their right hands and on the big toes of their right feet. And Moses threw the blood against the sides of

the altar. ²⁵ Then he took the fat and the fat tail and all the fat that was on the entrails and the long lobe of the liver and the two kidneys with their fat and the right thigh, ²⁶ and out of the basket of unleavened bread that was before the LORD he took one unleavened loaf and one loaf of bread with oil and one wafer and placed them on the pieces of fat and on the right thigh. ²⁷ And he put all these in the hands of Aaron and in the hands of his sons and waved them as a wave offering before the LORD. ²⁸ Then Moses took them from their hands and burned them on the altar with the burnt offering. This was an ordination offering with a pleasing aroma, a food offering to the LORD. ²⁹ And Moses took the breast and waved it for a wave offering before the LORD. It was Moses' portion of the ram of ordination, as the LORD commanded Moses.

³⁰ Then Moses took some of the anointing oil and of the blood that was on the altar and sprinkled it on Aaron and his garments, and also on his sons and his sons' garments. So he consecrated Aaron and his garments, and his sons and his sons' garments with him.

³¹ And Moses said to Aaron and his sons, "Boil the flesh at the entrance of the tent of meeting, and there eat it and the bread that is in the basket of ordination offerings, as I commanded, saying, 'Aaron and his sons shall eat it.' ³² And what remains of the flesh and the bread you shall burn up with fire. ³³ And you shall not go outside the entrance of the tent of meeting for seven days, until the days of your ordination are completed, for it will take seven days to ordain you. ³⁴ As has been done today, the LORD has commanded to be done to make atonement for you. ³⁵ At the entrance of the tent of meeting you shall remain day and night for seven days, performing what the LORD has charged, so that you do not die, for so I have been commanded." ³⁶ And Aaron and his sons did all the things that the LORD commanded by Moses.

The Lord Accepts Aaron's Offering

9 On the eighth day Moses called Aaron and his sons and the elders of Israel, ² and he said to Aaron, "Take for yourself a bull calf for a sin offering and a ram for a burnt offering, both without blemish, and offer them before the LORD. ³ And say to the people of Israel, 'Take a male goat for a sin offering, and a calf and a lamb, both a year old without blemish, for a burnt offering, ⁴ and an ox and a ram for peace offerings, to sacrifice before the LORD, and a grain offering mixed with oil, for today the LORD will appear to you.'" ⁵ And they brought what Moses commanded in front of the tent of meeting, and all the congregation drew near and stood before the LORD. ⁶ And Moses said, "This is the thing that the LORD commanded you to do, that the glory of the LORD may appear to you." ⁷ Then Moses said to Aaron, "Draw near to the altar and offer your sin offering and your burnt offering and make atonement for yourself and for the people, and bring the offering of the people and make atonement for them, as the LORD has commanded."

⁸ So Aaron drew near to the altar and killed the calf of the sin offering, which was for himself. ⁹ And the sons of Aaron presented the blood to him, and he dipped his finger in the blood and put it on the horns of the altar and poured out the blood at the base of the altar. ¹⁰ But the fat and the kidneys and the long lobe of the liver from the sin offering he burned on the altar, as the LORD commanded Moses. ¹¹ The flesh and the skin he burned up with fire outside the camp.

¹² Then he killed the burnt offering, and Aaron's sons handed him the blood, and he threw it against the sides of the altar. ¹³ And they handed the burnt offering to him, piece by piece, and the head, and he burned them on the altar. ¹⁴ And he washed the entrails and the legs and burned them with the burnt offering on the altar.

¹⁵ Then he presented the people's offering and took the goat of the sin offering that was for the people and killed it and offered it as a sin offering, like the first one. ¹⁶ And he presented the burnt offering and offered it according to the rule. ¹⁷ And he presented the grain offering, took a handful of it, and burned it on the altar, besides the burnt offering of the morning.

¹⁸ Then he killed the ox and the ram, the sacrifice of peace offerings for the people. And Aaron's sons handed him the blood, and he threw it against the sides of the altar. ¹⁹ But the fat pieces of the ox and of the ram, the fat tail and that which covers the entrails and the kidneys and the long lobe of the liver— ²⁰ they put the fat pieces on the

breasts, and he burned the fat pieces on the altar, **21** but the breasts and the right thigh Aaron waved for a wave offering before the LORD, as Moses commanded.

22 Then Aaron lifted up his hands toward the people and blessed them, and he came down from offering the sin offering and the burnt offering and the peace offerings. **23** And Moses and Aaron went into the tent of meeting, and when they came out they blessed the people, and the glory of the LORD appeared to all the people. **24** And fire came out from before the LORD and consumed the burnt offering and the pieces of fat on the altar, and when all the people saw it, they shouted and fell on their faces.

The Death of Nadab and Abihu

10 Now Nadab and Abihu, the sons of Aaron, each took his censer and put fire in it and laid incense on it and offered unauthorized fire before the LORD, which he had not commanded them. **2** And fire came out from before the LORD and consumed them, and they died before the LORD. **3** Then Moses said to Aaron, "This is what the LORD has said: 'Among those who are near me I will be sanctified, and before all the people I will be glorified.'" And Aaron held his peace.

4 And Moses called Mishael and Elzaphan, the sons of Uzziel the uncle of Aaron, and said to them, "Come near; carry your brothers away from the front of the sanctuary and out of the camp." **5** So they came near and carried them in their coats out of the camp, as Moses had said. **6** And Moses said to Aaron and to Eleazar and Ithamar his sons, "Do not let the hair of your heads hang loose, and do not tear your clothes, lest you die, and wrath come upon all the congregation; but let your brothers, the whole house of Israel, bewail the burning that the LORD has kindled. **7** And do not go outside the entrance of the tent of meeting, lest you die, for the anointing oil of the LORD is upon you." And they did according to the word of Moses.

8 And the LORD spoke to Aaron, saying, **9** "Drink no wine or strong drink, you or your sons with you, when you go into the tent of meeting, lest you die. It shall be a statute forever throughout your generations. **10** You are to distinguish between the holy and the common, and between the unclean and the clean, **11** and you are to teach the people of Israel all the statutes that the LORD has spoken to them by Moses."

12 Moses spoke to Aaron and to Eleazar and Ithamar, his surviving sons: "Take the grain offering that is left of the LORD's food offerings, and eat it unleavened beside the altar, for it is most holy. **13** You shall eat it in a holy place, because it is your due and your sons' due, from the LORD's food offerings, for so I am commanded. **14** But the breast that is waved and the thigh that is contributed you shall eat in a clean place, you and your sons and your daughters with you, for they are given as your due and your sons' due from the sacrifices of the peace offerings of the people of Israel. **15** The thigh that is contributed and the breast that is waved they shall bring with the food offerings of the fat pieces to wave for a wave offering before the LORD, and it shall be yours and your sons' with you as a due forever, as the LORD has commanded."

16 Now Moses diligently inquired about the goat of the sin offering, and behold, it was burned up! And he was angry with Eleazar and Ithamar, the surviving sons of Aaron, saying, **17** "Why have you not eaten the sin offering in the place of the sanctuary, since it is a thing most holy and has been given to you that you may bear the iniquity of the congregation, to make atonement for them before the LORD? **18** Behold, its blood was not brought into the inner part of the sanctuary. You certainly ought to have eaten it in the sanctuary, as I commanded." **19** And Aaron said to Moses, "Behold, today they have offered their sin offering and their burnt offering before the LORD, and yet such things as these have happened to me! If I had eaten the sin offering today, would the LORD have approved?" **20** And when Moses heard that, he approved.

Clean and Unclean Animals

11 And the LORD spoke to Moses and Aaron, saying to them, **2** "Speak to the people of Israel, saying, These are the living things that you may eat among all the animals that are on the earth. **3** Whatever parts the hoof and is cloven-footed and chews the cud, among the animals, you may eat. **4** Nevertheless, among those that chew the cud or part the hoof, you shall not eat these: The camel, because it chews the cud but does not part the hoof, is unclean to you.

5 And the rock badger, because it chews the cud but does not part the hoof, is unclean to you. 6 And the hare, because it chews the cud but does not part the hoof, is unclean to you. 7 And the pig, because it parts the hoof and is cloven-footed but does not chew the cud, is unclean to you. 8 You shall not eat any of their flesh, and you shall not touch their carcasses; they are unclean to you.

9 "These you may eat, of all that are in the waters. Everything in the waters that has fins and scales, whether in the seas or in the rivers, you may eat. 10 But anything in the seas or the rivers that does not have fins and scales, of the swarming creatures in the waters and of the living creatures that are in the waters, is detestable to you. 11 You shall regard them as detestable; you shall not eat any of their flesh, and you shall detest their carcasses. 12 Everything in the waters that does not have fins and scales is detestable to you.

13 "And these you shall detest among the birds; they shall not be eaten; they are detestable: the eagle, the bearded vulture, the black vulture, 14 the kite, the falcon of any kind, 15 every raven of any kind, 16 the ostrich, the nighthawk, the sea gull, the hawk of any kind, 17 the little owl, the cormorant, the short-eared owl, 18 the barn owl, the tawny owl, the carrion vulture, 19 the stork, the heron of any kind, the hoopoe, and the bat.

20 "All winged insects that go on all fours are detestable to you. 21 Yet among the winged insects that go on all fours you may eat those that have jointed legs above their feet, with which to hop on the ground. 22 Of them you may eat: the locust of any kind, the bald locust of any kind, the cricket of any kind, and the grasshopper of any kind. 23 But all other winged insects that have four feet are detestable to you.

24 "And by these you shall become unclean. Whoever touches their carcass shall be unclean until the evening, 25 and whoever carries any part of their carcass shall wash his clothes and be unclean until the evening. 26 Every animal that parts the hoof but is not cloven-footed or does not chew the cud is unclean to you. Everyone who touches them shall be unclean. 27 And all that walk on their paws, among the animals that go on all fours, are unclean to you. Whoever touches their carcass shall be unclean until the evening, 28 and he who carries their carcass shall wash his clothes and be unclean until the evening; they are unclean to you.

29 "And these are unclean to you among the swarming things that swarm on the ground: the mole rat, the mouse, the great lizard of any kind, 30 the gecko, the monitor lizard, the lizard, the sand lizard, and the chameleon. 31 These are unclean to you among all that swarm. Whoever touches them when they are dead shall be unclean until the evening. 32 And anything on which any of them falls when they are dead shall be unclean, whether it is an article of wood or a garment or a skin or a sack, any article that is used for any purpose. It must be put into water, and it shall be unclean until

GETTING THE MESSAGE

The word **unclean** occurs more than 130 times in the Old Testament, with half of those occurrences in Leviticus. It is not a statement about a person's hygiene. Rather, it relates to holiness in worship and in personal conduct.

the evening; then it shall be clean. 33 And if any of them falls into any earthenware vessel, all that is in it shall be unclean, and you shall break it. 34 Any food in it that could be eaten, on which water comes, shall be unclean. And all drink that could be drunk from every such vessel shall be unclean. 35 And everything on which any part of their carcass falls shall be unclean. Whether oven or stove, it shall be broken in pieces. They are unclean and shall remain unclean for you. 36 Nevertheless, a spring or a cistern holding water shall be clean, but whoever touches a carcass in them shall be unclean. 37 And if any part of their carcass falls upon any seed grain that is to be sown, it is clean, 38 but if water is put on the seed and any part of their carcass falls on it, it is unclean to you.

39 "And if any animal which you may eat dies, whoever touches its carcass shall be unclean until the evening, 40 and whoever eats of its carcass shall wash his clothes and

be unclean until the evening. And whoever carries the carcass shall wash his clothes and be unclean until the evening.

⁴¹ "Every swarming thing that swarms on the ground is detestable; it shall not be eaten. ⁴² Whatever goes on its belly, and whatever goes on all fours, or whatever has many feet, any swarming thing that swarms on the ground, you shall not eat, for they are detestable. ⁴³ You shall not make yourselves detestable with any swarming thing that swarms, and you shall not defile yourselves with them, and become unclean through them. ⁴⁴ For I am the LORD your God. Consecrate yourselves therefore, and be holy, for I am holy. You shall not defile yourselves with any swarming thing that crawls on the ground. ⁴⁵ For I am the LORD who brought you up out of the land of Egypt

GETTING THE MESSAGE

Leprosy. The "leprosy" mentioned in the Bible was not what is commonly called leprosy today (Hansen's disease). Rather, it may have been a form of psoriasis or a fungal infection. Nonetheless it was highly contagious, so those who had leprosy had to follow strict rules of hygiene.

to be your God. You shall therefore be holy, for I am holy."

⁴⁶ This is the law about beast and bird and every living creature that moves through the waters and every creature that swarms on the ground, ⁴⁷ to make a distinction between the unclean and the clean and between the living creature that may be eaten and the living creature that may not be eaten.

Purification After Childbirth

12 The LORD spoke to Moses, saying, ² "Speak to the people of Israel, saying, If a woman conceives and bears a male child, then she shall be unclean seven days. As at the time of her menstruation, she shall be unclean. ³ And on the eighth day the flesh of his foreskin shall be circumcised. ⁴ Then she shall continue for thirty-three days in the blood of her purifying. She shall not touch anything holy, nor come into the sanctuary, until the days of her purifying are

completed. ⁵ But if she bears a female child, then she shall be unclean two weeks, as in her menstruation. And she shall continue in the blood of her purifying for sixty-six days.

⁶ "And when the days of her purifying are completed, whether for a son or for a daughter, she shall bring to the priest at the entrance of the tent of meeting a lamb a year old for a burnt offering, and a pigeon or a turtledove for a sin offering, ⁷ and he shall offer it before the LORD and make atonement for her. Then she shall be clean from the flow of her blood. This is the law for her who bears a child, either male or female. ⁸ And if she cannot afford a lamb, then she shall take two turtledoves or two pigeons, one for a burnt offering and the other for a sin offering. And the priest shall make atonement for her, and she shall be clean."

Laws About Leprosy

13 The LORD spoke to Moses and Aaron, saying, ² "When a person has on the skin of his body a swelling or an eruption or a spot, and it turns into a case of leprous[1] disease on the skin of his body, then he shall be brought to Aaron the priest or to one of his sons the priests, ³ and the priest shall examine the diseased area on the skin of his body. And if the hair in the diseased area has turned white and the disease appears to be deeper than the skin of his body, it is a case of leprous disease. When the priest has examined him, he shall pronounce him unclean. ⁴ But if the spot is white in the skin of his body and appears no deeper than the skin, and the hair in it has not turned white, the priest shall shut up the diseased person for seven days. ⁵ And the priest shall examine him on the seventh day, and if in his eyes the disease is checked and the disease has not spread in the skin, then the priest shall shut him up for another seven days. ⁶ And the priest shall examine him again on the seventh day, and if the diseased area has faded and the disease has not spread in the skin, then the priest shall pronounce him clean; it is only an eruption. And he shall wash his clothes and be clean. ⁷ But if the eruption spreads in the skin, after he has shown himself to the priest for his cleansing, he shall appear again before the priest. ⁸ And the priest shall look, and if the

_____
[1] *Leprosy* was a term for several skin diseases

eruption has spread in the skin, then the priest shall pronounce him unclean; it is a leprous disease.

⁹ "When a man is afflicted with a leprous disease, he shall be brought to the priest, ¹⁰ and the priest shall look. And if there is a white swelling in the skin that has turned the hair white, and there is raw flesh in the swelling, ¹¹ it is a chronic leprous disease in the skin of his body, and the priest shall pronounce him unclean. He shall not shut him up, for he is unclean. ¹² And if the leprous disease breaks out in the skin, so that the leprous disease covers all the skin of the diseased person from head to foot, so far as the priest can see, ¹³ then the priest shall look, and if the leprous disease has covered all his body, he shall pronounce him clean of the disease; it has all turned white, and he is clean. ¹⁴ But when raw flesh appears on him, he shall be unclean. ¹⁵ And the priest shall examine the raw flesh and pronounce him unclean. Raw flesh is unclean, for it is a leprous disease. ¹⁶ But if the raw flesh recovers and turns white again, then he shall come to the priest, ¹⁷ and the priest shall examine him, and if the disease has turned white, then the priest shall pronounce the diseased person clean; he is clean.

¹⁸ "If there is in the skin of one's body a boil and it heals, ¹⁹ and in the place of the boil there comes a white swelling or a reddish-white spot, then it shall be shown to the priest. ²⁰ And the priest shall look, and if it appears deeper than the skin and its hair has turned white, then the priest shall pronounce him unclean. It is a case of leprous disease that has broken out in the boil. ²¹ But if the priest examines it and there is no white hair in it and it is not deeper than the skin, but has faded, then the priest shall shut him up seven days. ²² And if it spreads in the skin, then the priest shall pronounce him unclean; it is a disease. ²³ But if the spot remains in one place and does not spread, it is the scar of the boil, and the priest shall pronounce him clean.

²⁴ "Or, when the body has a burn on its skin and the raw flesh of the burn becomes a spot, reddish-white or white, ²⁵ the priest shall examine it, and if the hair in the spot has turned white and it appears deeper than the skin, then it is a leprous disease. It has broken out in the burn, and the priest shall

pronounce him unclean; it is a case of leprous disease. ²⁶ But if the priest examines it and there is no white hair in the spot and it is no deeper than the skin, but has faded, the priest shall shut him up seven days, ²⁷ and the priest shall examine him the seventh day. If it is spreading in the skin, then the priest shall pronounce him unclean; it is a case of leprous disease. ²⁸ But if the spot remains in one place and does not spread in the skin, but has faded, it is a swelling from the burn, and the priest shall pronounce him clean, for it is the scar of the burn.

²⁹ "When a man or woman has a disease on the head or the beard, ³⁰ the priest shall examine the disease. And if it appears deeper than the skin, and the hair in it is yellow and thin, then the priest shall pronounce him unclean. It is an itch, a leprous disease of the head or the beard. ³¹ And if the priest examines the itching disease and it appears no deeper than the skin and there is no black hair in it, then the priest shall shut up the person with the itching disease for seven days, ³² and on the seventh day the priest shall examine the disease. If the itch has not spread, and there is in it no yellow hair, and the itch appears to be no deeper than the skin, ³³ then he shall shave himself, but the itch he shall not shave; and the priest shall shut up the person with the itching disease for another seven days. ³⁴ And on the seventh day the priest shall examine the itch, and if the itch has not spread in the skin and it appears to be no deeper than the skin, then the priest shall pronounce him clean. And he shall wash his clothes and be clean. ³⁵ But if the itch spreads in the skin after his cleansing, ³⁶ then the priest shall examine him, and if the itch has spread in the skin, the priest need not seek for the yellow hair; he is unclean. ³⁷ But if in his eyes the itch is unchanged and black hair has grown in it, the itch is healed and he is clean, and the priest shall pronounce him clean.

³⁸ "When a man or a woman has spots on the skin of the body, white spots, ³⁹ the priest shall look, and if the spots on the skin of the body are of a dull white, it is leukoderma that has broken out in the skin; he is clean.

⁴⁰ "If a man's hair falls out from his head, he is bald; he is clean. ⁴¹ And if a man's hair falls out from his forehead, he has baldness

of the forehead; he is clean. ⁴²But if there is on the bald head or the bald forehead a reddish-white diseased area, it is a leprous disease breaking out on his bald head or his bald forehead. ⁴³Then the priest shall examine him, and if the diseased swelling is reddish-white on his bald head or on his bald forehead, like the appearance of leprous disease in the skin of the body, ⁴⁴he is a leprous man, he is unclean. The priest must pronounce him unclean; his disease is on his head.

⁴⁵"The leprous person who has the disease shall wear torn clothes and let the hair of his head hang loose, and he shall cover his upper lip and cry out, 'Unclean, unclean.' ⁴⁶He shall remain unclean as long as he has the disease. He is unclean. He shall live alone. His dwelling shall be outside the camp.

GETTING THE MESSAGE

In the Old Testament, **lepers** tore their garments and veiled their faces (13:45) as signs of mourning, and to show that they were separated from public worship and community life. In the New Testament, Jesus had a special concern for lepers and other social outcasts (Luke 7:22).

⁴⁷"When there is a case of leprous disease in a garment, whether a woolen or a linen garment, ⁴⁸in warp or woof of linen or wool, or in a skin or in anything made of skin, ⁴⁹if the disease is greenish or reddish in the garment, or in the skin or in the warp or the woof or in any article made of skin, it is a case of leprous disease, and it shall be shown to the priest. ⁵⁰And the priest shall examine the disease and shut up that which has the disease for seven days. ⁵¹Then he shall examine the disease on the seventh day. If the disease has spread in the garment, in the warp or the woof, or in the skin, whatever be the use of the skin, the disease is a persistent leprous disease; it is unclean. ⁵²And he shall burn the garment, or the warp or the woof, the wool or the linen, or any article made of skin that is diseased, for it is a persistent leprous disease. It shall be burned in the fire.

⁵³"And if the priest examines, and if the disease has not spread in the garment, in the warp or the woof or in any article made of skin, ⁵⁴then the priest shall command that they wash the thing in which is the disease, and he shall shut it up for another seven days. ⁵⁵And the priest shall examine the diseased thing after it has been washed. And if the appearance of the diseased area has not changed, though the disease has not spread, it is unclean. You shall burn it in the fire, whether the rot is on the back or on the front.

⁵⁶"But if the priest examines, and if the diseased area has faded after it has been washed, he shall tear it out of the garment or the skin or the warp or the woof. ⁵⁷Then if it appears again in the garment, in the warp or the woof, or in any article made of skin, it is spreading. You shall burn with fire whatever has the disease. ⁵⁸But the garment, or the warp or the woof, or any article made of skin from which the disease departs when you have washed it, shall then be washed a second time, and be clean."

⁵⁹This is the law for a case of leprous disease in a garment of wool or linen, either in the warp or the woof, or in any article made of skin, to determine whether it is clean or unclean.

Laws for Cleansing Lepers

14 The LORD spoke to Moses, saying, ²"This shall be the law of the leprous person for the day of his cleansing. He shall be brought to the priest, ³and the priest shall go out of the camp, and the priest shall look. Then, if the case of leprous disease is healed in the leprous person, ⁴the priest shall command them to take for him who is to be cleansed two live clean birds and cedarwood and scarlet yarn and hyssop. ⁵And the priest shall command them to kill one of the birds in an earthenware vessel over fresh water. ⁶He shall take the live bird with the cedarwood and the scarlet yarn and the hyssop, and dip them and the live bird in the blood of the bird that was killed over the fresh water. ⁷And he shall sprinkle it seven times on him who is to be cleansed of the leprous disease. Then he shall pronounce him clean and shall let the living bird go into the open field. ⁸And he who is to be cleansed shall wash his clothes and shave off all his hair and bathe himself in water,

and he shall be clean. And after that he may come into the camp, but live outside his tent seven days. ⁹ And on the seventh day he shall shave off all his hair from his head, his beard, and his eyebrows. He shall shave off all his hair, and then he shall wash his clothes and bathe his body in water, and he shall be clean.

¹⁰ "And on the eighth day he shall take two male lambs without blemish, and one ewe lamb a year old without blemish, and a grain offering of three tenths of an ephah of fine flour mixed with oil, and one log of oil. ¹¹ And the priest who cleanses him shall set the man who is to be cleansed and these things before the LORD, at the entrance of the tent of meeting. ¹² And the priest shall take one of the male lambs and offer it for a guilt offering, along with the log of oil, and wave them for a wave offering before the LORD. ¹³ And he shall kill the lamb in the place where they kill the sin offering and the burnt offering, in the place of the sanctuary. For the guilt offering, like the sin offering, belongs to the priest; it is most holy. ¹⁴ The priest shall take some of the blood of the guilt offering, and the priest shall put it on the lobe of the right ear of him who is to be cleansed and on the thumb of his right hand and on the big toe of his right foot. ¹⁵ Then the priest shall take some of the log of oil and pour it into the palm of his own left hand ¹⁶ and dip his right finger in the oil that is in his left hand and sprinkle some oil with his finger seven times before the LORD. ¹⁷ And some of the oil that remains in his hand the priest shall put on the lobe of the right ear of him who is to be cleansed and on the thumb of his right hand and on the big toe of his right foot, on top of the blood of the guilt offering. ¹⁸ And the rest of the oil that is in the priest's hand he shall put on the head of him who is to be cleansed. Then the priest shall make atonement for him before the LORD. ¹⁹ The priest shall offer the sin offering, to make atonement for him who is to be cleansed from his uncleanness. And afterward he shall kill the burnt offering. ²⁰ And the priest shall offer the burnt offering and the grain offering on the altar. Thus the priest shall make atonement for him, and he shall be clean.

²¹ "But if he is poor and cannot afford so much, then he shall take one male lamb for a guilt offering to be waved, to make atonement for him, and a tenth of an ephah of fine flour mixed with oil for a grain offering, and a log of oil; ²² also two turtledoves or two pigeons, whichever he can afford. The one shall be a sin offering and the other a burnt offering. ²³ And on the eighth day he shall bring them for his cleansing to the priest, to the entrance of the tent of meeting, before the LORD. ²⁴ And the priest shall take the lamb of the guilt offering and the log of oil, and the priest shall wave them for a wave offering before the LORD. ²⁵ And he shall kill the lamb of the guilt offering. And the priest shall take some of the blood of the guilt offering and put it on the lobe of the right ear of him who is to be cleansed, and on the thumb of his right hand and on the big toe of his right foot. ²⁶ And the priest shall pour some of the oil into the palm of his own left hand, ²⁷ and shall sprinkle with his right finger some of the oil that is in his left hand seven times before the LORD. ²⁸ And the priest shall put some of the oil that is in his hand on the lobe of the right ear of him who is to be cleansed and on the thumb of his right hand and on the big toe of his right foot, in the place where the blood of the guilt offering was put. ²⁹ And the rest of the oil that is in the priest's hand he shall put on the head of him who is to be cleansed, to make atonement for him before the LORD. ³⁰ And he shall offer, of the turtledoves or pigeons, whichever he can afford, ³¹ one for a sin offering and the other for a burnt offering, along with a grain offering. And the priest shall make atonement before the LORD for him who is being cleansed. ³² This is the law for him in whom is a case of leprous disease, who cannot afford the offerings for his cleansing."

Laws for Cleansing Houses

³³ The LORD spoke to Moses and Aaron, saying, ³⁴ "When you come into the land of Canaan, which I give you for a possession, and I put a case of leprous disease in a house in the land of your possession, ³⁵ then he who owns the house shall come and tell the priest, 'There seems to me to be some case of disease in my house.' ³⁶ Then the priest shall command that they empty the house before the priest goes to examine the disease, lest all that is in the house be declared unclean. And afterward the priest

shall go in to see the house. 37 And he shall examine the disease. And if the disease is in the walls of the house with greenish or reddish spots, and if it appears to be deeper than the surface, 38 then the priest shall go out of the house to the door of the house and shut up the house seven days. 39 And the priest shall come again on the seventh day, and look. If the disease has spread in the walls of the house, 40 then the priest shall command that they take out the stones in which is the disease and throw them into an unclean place outside the city. 41 And he shall have the inside of the house scraped all around, and the plaster that they scrape off they shall pour out in an unclean place outside the city. 42 Then they shall take other stones and put them in the place of those stones, and he shall take other plaster and plaster the house.

GETTING THE MESSAGE

Could a house have leprosy?
The Israelites were told what to do if a house had a "leprous disease" (14:34). This most likely referred to things like mold, mildew, or fungus.

43 "If the disease breaks out again in the house, after he has taken out the stones and scraped the house and plastered it, 44 then the priest shall go and look. And if the disease has spread in the house, it is a persistent leprous disease in the house; it is unclean. 45 And he shall break down the house, its stones and timber and all the plaster of the house, and he shall carry them out of the city to an unclean place. 46 Moreover, whoever enters the house while it is shut up shall be unclean until the evening, 47 and whoever sleeps in the house shall wash his clothes, and whoever eats in the house shall wash his clothes.

48 "But if the priest comes and looks, and if the disease has not spread in the house after the house was plastered, then the priest shall pronounce the house clean, for the disease is healed. 49 And for the cleansing of the house he shall take two small birds, with cedarwood and scarlet yarn and hyssop, 50 and shall kill one of the birds in an earthenware vessel over fresh water 51 and

shall take the cedarwood and the hyssop and the scarlet yarn, along with the live bird, and dip them in the blood of the bird that was killed and in the fresh water and sprinkle the house seven times. 52 Thus he shall cleanse the house with the blood of the bird and with the fresh water and with the live bird and with the cedarwood and hyssop and scarlet yarn. 53 And he shall let the live bird go out of the city into the open country. So he shall make atonement for the house, and it shall be clean."

54 This is the law for any case of leprous disease: for an itch, 55 for leprous disease in a garment or in a house, 56 and for a swelling or an eruption or a spot, 57 to show when it is unclean and when it is clean. This is the law for leprous disease.

Laws About Bodily Discharges

15 The LORD spoke to Moses and Aaron, saying, 2 "Speak to the people of Israel and say to them, When any man has a discharge from his body, his discharge is unclean. 3 And this is the law of his uncleanness for a discharge: whether his body runs with his discharge, or his body is blocked up by his discharge, it is his uncleanness. 4 Every bed on which the one with the discharge lies shall be unclean, and everything on which he sits shall be unclean. 5 And anyone who touches his bed shall wash his clothes and bathe himself in water and be unclean until the evening. 6 And whoever sits on anything on which the one with the discharge has sat shall wash his clothes and bathe himself in water and be unclean until the evening. 7 And whoever touches the body of the one with the discharge shall wash his clothes and bathe himself in water and be unclean until the evening. 8 And if the one with the discharge spits on someone who is clean, then he shall wash his clothes and bathe himself in water and be unclean until the evening. 9 And any saddle on which the one with the discharge rides shall be unclean. 10 And whoever touches anything that was under him shall be unclean until the evening. And whoever carries such things shall wash his clothes and bathe himself in water and be unclean until the evening. 11 Anyone whom the one with the discharge touches without having rinsed his hands in water shall wash his clothes and bathe himself in water and be unclean until

the evening. [12] And an earthenware vessel that the one with the discharge touches shall be broken, and every vessel of wood shall be rinsed in water.

[13] "And when the one with a discharge is cleansed of his discharge, then he shall count for himself seven days for his cleansing, and wash his clothes. And he shall bathe his body in fresh water and shall be clean. [14] And on the eighth day he shall take two turtledoves or two pigeons and come before the LORD to the entrance of the tent of meeting and give them to the priest. [15] And the priest shall use them, one for a sin offering and the other for a burnt offering. And the priest shall make atonement for him before the LORD for his discharge.

[16] "If a man has an emission of semen, he shall bathe his whole body in water and be unclean until the evening. [17] And every garment and every skin on which the semen comes shall be washed with water and be unclean until the evening. [18] If a man lies with a woman and has an emission of semen, both of them shall bathe themselves in water and be unclean until the evening.

[19] "When a woman has a discharge, and the discharge in her body is blood, she shall be in her menstrual impurity for seven days, and whoever touches her shall be unclean until the evening. [20] And everything on which she lies during her menstrual impurity shall be unclean. Everything also on which she sits shall be unclean. [21] And whoever touches her bed shall wash his clothes and bathe himself in water and be unclean until the evening. [22] And whoever touches anything on which she sits shall wash his clothes and bathe himself in water and be unclean until the evening. [23] Whether it is the bed or anything on which she sits, when he touches it he shall be unclean until the evening. [24] And if any man lies with her and her menstrual impurity comes upon him, he shall be unclean seven days, and every bed on which he lies shall be unclean.

[25] "If a woman has a discharge of blood for many days, not at the time of her menstrual impurity, or if she has a discharge beyond the time of her impurity, all the days of the discharge she shall continue in uncleanness. As in the days of her impurity, she shall be unclean. [26] Every bed on which she lies, all the days of her discharge, shall be to

her as the bed of her impurity. And everything on which she sits shall be unclean, as in the uncleanness of her menstrual impurity. [27] And whoever touches these things shall be unclean, and shall wash his clothes and bathe himself in water and be unclean until the evening. [28] But if she is cleansed of her discharge, she shall count for herself seven days, and after that she shall be clean. [29] And on the eighth day she shall take two turtledoves or two pigeons and bring them to the priest, to the entrance of the tent of meeting. [30] And the priest shall use one for a sin offering and the other for a burnt offering. And the priest shall make atonement for her before the LORD for her unclean discharge.

[31] "Thus you shall keep the people of Israel separate from their uncleanness, lest they die in their uncleanness by defiling my tabernacle that is in their midst."

[32] This is the law for him who has a discharge and for him who has an emission of semen, becoming unclean thereby; [33] also for her who is unwell with her menstrual impurity, that is, for anyone, male or female, who has a discharge, and for the man who lies with a woman who is unclean.

The Day of Atonement

16 The LORD spoke to Moses after the death of the two sons of Aaron, when they drew near before the LORD and died, [2] and the LORD said to Moses, "Tell Aaron your brother not to come at any time into the Holy Place inside the veil, before the mercy seat that is on the ark, so that he may not die. For I will appear in the cloud over the mercy seat. [3] But in this way Aaron shall come into the Holy Place: with a bull from the herd for a sin offering and a ram for a burnt offering. [4] He shall put on the holy linen coat and shall have the linen undergarment on his body, and he shall tie the linen sash around his waist, and wear the linen turban; these are the holy garments. He shall bathe his body in water and then put them on. [5] And he shall take from the congregation of the people of Israel two male goats for a sin offering, and one ram for a burnt offering.

[6] "Aaron shall offer the bull as a sin offering for himself and shall make atonement for himself and for his house. [7] Then he shall take the two goats and set them before the

LORD at the entrance of the tent of meeting. ⁸ And Aaron shall cast lots over the two goats, one lot for the LORD and the other lot for Azazel. ⁹ And Aaron shall present the goat on which the lot fell for the LORD and use it as a sin offering, ¹⁰ but the goat on which the lot fell for Azazel shall be presented alive before the LORD to make atonement over it, that it may be sent away into the wilderness to Azazel.

¹¹ "Aaron shall present the bull as a sin offering for himself, and shall make atonement for himself and for his house. He shall kill the bull as a sin offering for himself. ¹² And he shall take a censer full of coals of fire from the altar before the LORD, and two handfuls of sweet incense beaten small, and he shall bring it inside the veil ¹³ and put the incense on the fire before the LORD, that the cloud of the incense may cover the mercy

> ## GETTING THE MESSAGE
>
> **The Day of Atonement** was the most solemn of all Hebrew festivals, focusing on personal remorse for sin. Today it is called Yom Kippur.

seat that is over the testimony, so that he does not die. ¹⁴ And he shall take some of the blood of the bull and sprinkle it with his finger on the front of the mercy seat on the east side, and in front of the mercy seat he shall sprinkle some of the blood with his finger seven times.

¹⁵ "Then he shall kill the goat of the sin offering that is for the people and bring its blood inside the veil and do with its blood as he did with the blood of the bull, sprinkling it over the mercy seat and in front of the mercy seat. ¹⁶ Thus he shall make atonement for the Holy Place, because of the uncleannesses of the people of Israel and because of their transgressions, all their sins. And so he shall do for the tent of meeting, which dwells with them in the midst of their uncleannesses. ¹⁷ No one may be in the tent of meeting from the time he enters to make atonement in the Holy Place until he comes out and has made atonement for himself and for his house and for all the assembly of Israel. ¹⁸ Then

he shall go out to the altar that is before the LORD and make atonement for it, and shall take some of the blood of the bull and some of the blood of the goat, and put it on the horns of the altar all around. ¹⁹ And he shall sprinkle some of the blood on it with his finger seven times, and cleanse it and consecrate it from the uncleannesses of the people of Israel.

²⁰ "And when he has made an end of atoning for the Holy Place and the tent of meeting and the altar, he shall present the live goat. ²¹ And Aaron shall lay both his hands on the head of the live goat, and confess over it all the iniquities of the people of Israel, and all their transgressions, all their sins. And he shall put them on the head of the goat and send it away into the wilderness by the hand of a man who is in readiness. ²² The goat shall bear all their iniquities on itself to a remote area, and he shall let the goat go free in the wilderness.

²³ "Then Aaron shall come into the tent of meeting and shall take off the linen garments that he put on when he went into the Holy Place and shall leave them there. ²⁴ And he shall bathe his body in water in a holy place and put on his garments and come out and offer his burnt offering and the burnt offering of the people and make atonement for himself and for the people. ²⁵ And the fat of the sin offering he shall burn on the altar. ²⁶ And he who lets the goat go to Azazel shall wash his clothes and bathe his body in water, and afterward he may come into the camp. ²⁷ And the bull for the sin offering and the goat for the sin offering, whose blood was brought in to make atonement in the Holy Place, shall be carried outside the camp. Their skin and their flesh and their dung shall be burned up with fire. ²⁸ And he who burns them shall wash his clothes and bathe his body in water, and afterward he may come into the camp.

²⁹ "And it shall be a statute to you forever that in the seventh month, on the tenth day of the month, you shall afflict yourselves and shall do no work, either the native or the stranger who sojourns among you. ³⁰ For on this day shall atonement be made for you to cleanse you. You shall be clean before the LORD from all your sins. ³¹ It is a Sabbath of solemn rest to you, and you shall afflict yourselves; it is a statute forever.

³² And the priest who is anointed and consecrated as priest in his father's place shall make atonement, wearing the holy linen garments. ³³ He shall make atonement for the holy sanctuary, and he shall make atonement for the tent of meeting and for the altar, and he shall make atonement for the priests and for all the people of the assembly. ³⁴ And this shall be a statute forever for you, that atonement may be made for the people of Israel once in the year because of all their sins." And Aaron did as the LORD commanded Moses.

The Place of Sacrifice

17 And the LORD spoke to Moses, saying, ² "Speak to Aaron and his sons and to all the people of Israel and say to them, This is the thing that the LORD has commanded. ³ If any one of the house of Israel kills an ox or a lamb or a goat in the camp, or kills it outside the camp, ⁴ and does not bring it to the entrance of the tent of meeting to offer it as a gift to the LORD in front of the tabernacle of the LORD, bloodguilt shall be imputed to that man. He has shed blood, and that man shall be cut off from among his people. ⁵ This is to the end that the people of Israel may bring their sacrifices that they sacrifice in the open field, that they may bring them to the LORD, to the priest at the entrance of the tent of meeting, and sacrifice them as sacrifices of peace offerings to the LORD. ⁶ And the priest shall throw the blood on the altar of the LORD at the entrance of the tent of meeting and burn the fat for a pleasing aroma to the LORD. ⁷ So they shall no more sacrifice their sacrifices to goat demons, after whom they whore. This shall be a statute forever for them throughout their generations.

⁸ "And you shall say to them, Any one of the house of Israel, or of the strangers who sojourn among them, who offers a burnt offering or sacrifice ⁹ and does not bring it to the entrance of the tent of meeting to offer it to the LORD, that man shall be cut off from his people.

Laws Against Eating Blood

¹⁰ "If any one of the house of Israel or of the strangers who sojourn among them eats any blood, I will set my face against that person who eats blood and will cut him off from among his people. ¹¹ For the life of the flesh is in the blood, and I have given it for you on the altar to make atonement for your souls, for it is the blood that makes atonement by the life. ¹² Therefore I have said to the people of Israel, No person among you shall eat blood, neither shall any stranger who sojourns among you eat blood.

¹³ "Any one also of the people of Israel, or of the strangers who sojourn among them, who takes in hunting any beast or bird that may be eaten shall pour out its blood and cover it with earth. ¹⁴ For the life of every creature is its blood: its blood is its life. Therefore I have said to the people of Israel, You shall not eat the blood of any creature, for the life of every creature is its blood. Whoever eats it shall be cut off. ¹⁵ And every person who eats what dies of itself or what is torn by beasts, whether he is a native or a sojourner, shall wash his clothes and bathe himself in water and be unclean until the

---

GETTING THE MESSAGE

Were the Israelites vegetarians? During their wilderness journey, the Israelites seldom ate the meat of large animals. It was eaten only on special occasions.

---

evening; then he shall be clean. ¹⁶ But if he does not wash them or bathe his flesh, he shall bear his iniquity."

Unlawful Sexual Relations

18 And the LORD spoke to Moses, saying, ² "Speak to the people of Israel and say to them, I am the LORD your God. ³ You shall not do as they do in the land of Egypt, where you lived, and you shall not do as they do in the land of Canaan, to which I am bringing you. You shall not walk in their statutes. ⁴ You shall follow my rules and keep my statutes and walk in them. I am the LORD your God. ⁵ You shall therefore keep my statutes and my rules; if a person does them, he shall live by them: I am the LORD.

⁶ "None of you shall approach any one of his close relatives to uncover nakedness. I am the LORD. ⁷ You shall not uncover the nakedness of your father, which is the nakedness of your mother; she is your mother, you shall not uncover her nakedness. ⁸ You shall not uncover the nakedness of your father's wife; it is your father's naked-

ness. **9** You shall not uncover the nakedness of your sister, your father's daughter or your mother's daughter, whether brought up in the family or in another home. **10** You shall not uncover the nakedness of your son's daughter or of your daughter's daughter, for their nakedness is your own nakedness. **11** You shall not uncover the nakedness of your father's wife's daughter, brought up in your father's family, since she is your sister. **12** You shall not uncover the nakedness of your father's sister; she is your father's relative. **13** You shall not uncover the nakedness of your mother's sister, for she is your mother's relative. **14** You shall not uncover the nakedness of your father's brother, that is, you shall not approach his wife; she is your aunt. **15** You shall not uncover the nakedness of your daughter-in-law; she is your son's wife, you shall not uncover her nakedness.

> ### GETTING THE MESSAGE
>
> **Abomination** describes a behavior or action that is utterly repulsive and detestable to God. The offenses listed in 18:24–30 defile not only the person who committed the act but the entire land.

16 You shall not uncover the nakedness of your brother's wife; it is your brother's nakedness. **17** You shall not uncover the nakedness of a woman and of her daughter, and you shall not take her son's daughter or her daughter's daughter to uncover her nakedness; they are relatives; it is depravity. **18** And you shall not take a woman as a rival wife to her sister, uncovering her nakedness while her sister is still alive.

19 "You shall not approach a woman to uncover her nakedness while she is in her menstrual uncleanness. **20** And you shall not lie sexually with your neighbor's wife and so make yourself unclean with her. **21** You shall not give any of your children to offer them to Molech, and so profane the name of your God: I am the LORD. **22** You shall not lie with a male as with a woman; it is an abomination. **23** And you shall not lie with any animal and so make yourself unclean with it, neither shall any woman give herself to an animal to lie with it: it is perversion.

24 "Do not make yourselves unclean by any of these things, for by all these the nations I am driving out before you have become unclean, **25** and the land became unclean, so that I punished its iniquity, and the land vomited out its inhabitants. **26** But you shall keep my statutes and my rules and do none of these abominations, either the native or the stranger who sojourns among you **27** (for the people of the land, who were before you, did all of these abominations, so that the land became unclean), **28** lest the land vomit you out when you make it unclean, as it vomited out the nation that was before you. **29** For everyone who does any of these abominations, the persons who do them shall be cut off from among their people. **30** So keep my charge never to practice any of these abominable customs that were practiced before you, and never to make yourselves unclean by them: I am the LORD your God."

The LORD Is Holy

19 And the LORD spoke to Moses, saying, **2** "Speak to all the congregation of the people of Israel and say to them, You shall be holy, for I the LORD your God am holy. **3** Every one of you shall revere his mother and his father, and you shall keep my Sabbaths: I am the LORD your God. **4** Do not turn to idols or make for yourselves any gods of cast metal: I am the LORD your God.

5 "When you offer a sacrifice of peace offerings to the LORD, you shall offer it so that you may be accepted. **6** It shall be eaten the same day you offer it or on the day after, and anything left over until the third day shall be burned up with fire. **7** If it is eaten at all on the third day, it is tainted; it will not be accepted, **8** and everyone who eats it shall bear his iniquity, because he has profaned what is holy to the LORD, and that person shall be cut off from his people.

Love Your Neighbor as Yourself

9 "When you reap the harvest of your land, you shall not reap your field right up to its edge, neither shall you gather the gleanings after your harvest. **10** And you shall not strip your vineyard bare, neither shall you gather the fallen grapes of your vineyard. You shall leave them for the poor and for the sojourner: I am the LORD your God.

¹¹ "You shall not steal; you shall not deal falsely; you shall not lie to one another. ¹² You shall not swear by my name falsely, and so profane the name of your God: I am the LORD.

¹³ "You shall not oppress your neighbor or rob him. The wages of a hired worker shall not remain with you all night until the morning. ¹⁴ You shall not curse the deaf or put a stumbling block before the blind, but you shall fear your God: I am the LORD.

¹⁵ "You shall do no injustice in court. You shall not be partial to the poor or defer to the great, but in righteousness shall you judge your neighbor. ¹⁶ You shall not go around as a slanderer among your people, and you shall not stand up against the life of your neighbor: I am the LORD.

¹⁷ "You shall not hate your brother in your heart, but you shall reason frankly with your neighbor, lest you incur sin because of him. ¹⁸ You shall not take vengeance or bear a grudge against the sons of your own people, but you shall love your neighbor as yourself: I am the LORD.

You Shall Keep My Statutes

¹⁹ "You shall keep my statutes. You shall not let your cattle breed with a different kind. You shall not sow your field with two kinds of seed, nor shall you wear a garment of cloth made of two kinds of material.

²⁰ "If a man lies sexually with a woman who is a slave, assigned to another man and not yet ransomed or given her freedom, a distinction shall be made. They shall not be put to death, because she was not free; ²¹ but he shall bring his compensation to the LORD, to the entrance of the tent of meeting, a ram for a guilt offering. ²² And the priest shall make atonement for him with the ram of the guilt offering before the LORD for his sin that he has committed, and he shall be forgiven for the sin that he has committed.

²³ "When you come into the land and plant any kind of tree for food, then you shall regard its fruit as forbidden. Three years it shall be forbidden to you; it must not be eaten. ²⁴ And in the fourth year all its fruit shall be holy, an offering of praise to the LORD. ²⁵ But in the fifth year you may eat of its fruit, to increase its yield for you: I am the LORD your God.

²⁶ "You shall not eat any flesh with the blood in it. You shall not interpret omens or tell fortunes. ²⁷ You shall not round off the hair on your temples or mar the edges of your beard. ²⁸ You shall not make any cuts on your body for the dead or tattoo yourselves: I am the LORD.

²⁹ "Do not profane your daughter by making her a prostitute, lest the land fall into prostitution and the land become full of depravity. ³⁰ You shall keep my Sabbaths and reverence my sanctuary: I am the LORD.

³¹ "Do not turn to mediums or necromancers; do not seek them out, and so make yourselves unclean by them: I am the LORD your God.

³² "You shall stand up before the gray head and honor the face of an old man, and you shall fear your God: I am the LORD.

³³ "When a stranger sojourns with you in your land, you shall not do him wrong.

GETTING THE MESSAGE

Beards. Art from Bible times often shows Israelite men with full, rounded beards. This set them apart from the Egyptians and Romans, who were generally clean-shaven. Other peoples living in Palestine would cut or clip their beards. The Israelites were forbidden to do so, perhaps to show their commitment to God in a pagan culture (19:27).

³⁴ You shall treat the stranger who sojourns with you as the native among you, and you shall love him as yourself, for you were strangers in the land of Egypt: I am the LORD your God.

³⁵ "You shall do no wrong in judgment, in measures of length or weight or quantity. ³⁶ You shall have just balances, just weights, a just ephah, and a just hin: I am the LORD your God, who brought you out of the land of Egypt. ³⁷ And you shall observe all my statutes and all my rules, and do them: I am the LORD."

Punishment for Child Sacrifice

20 The LORD spoke to Moses, saying, ² "Say to the people of Israel, Any one of the people of Israel or of the strangers who sojourn in Israel who gives any of his children to Molech shall surely be put to death. The people of the land shall stone

him with stones. ³ I myself will set my face against that man and will cut him off from among his people, because he has given one of his children to Molech, to make my sanctuary unclean and to profane my holy name. ⁴ And if the people of the land do at all close their eyes to that man when he gives one of his children to Molech, and do not put him to death, ⁵ then I will set my face against that man and against his clan and will cut them off from among their people, him and all who follow him in whoring after Molech.

⁶ "If a person turns to mediums and necromancers, whoring after them, I will set my face against that person and will cut him off from among his people. ⁷ Consecrate yourselves, therefore, and be holy, for I am the Lord your God. ⁸ Keep my statutes and do them; I am the Lord who sanctifies you.

GETTING THE MESSAGE

Private sin, public action. Though sexual immorality is often considered a private matter, it was not dealt with privately in ancient Israel. The Israelites understood that people's religious and moral behavior affected the lives and well-being of their families and neighbors. Therefore, the community as a whole was responsible for carrying out the punishment for sexual sin.

⁹ For anyone who curses his father or his mother shall surely be put to death; he has cursed his father or his mother; his blood is upon him.

Punishments for Sexual Immorality

¹⁰ "If a man commits adultery with the wife of his neighbor, both the adulterer and the adulteress shall surely be put to death. ¹¹ If a man lies with his father's wife, he has uncovered his father's nakedness; both of them shall surely be put to death; their blood is upon them. ¹² If a man lies with his daughter-in-law, both of them shall surely be put to death; they have committed perversion; their blood is upon them. ¹³ If a man lies with a male as with a woman, both of them have committed an abomination; they shall surely be put to death; their blood is upon them. ¹⁴ If a man takes a woman and her mother also, it is depravity; he and they

shall be burned with fire, that there may be no depravity among you. ¹⁵ If a man lies with an animal, he shall surely be put to death, and you shall kill the animal. ¹⁶ If a woman approaches any animal and lies with it, you shall kill the woman and the animal; they shall surely be put to death; their blood is upon them.

¹⁷ "If a man takes his sister, a daughter of his father or a daughter of his mother, and sees her nakedness, and she sees his nakedness, it is a disgrace, and they shall be cut off in the sight of the children of their people. He has uncovered his sister's nakedness, and he shall bear his iniquity. ¹⁸ If a man lies with a woman during her menstrual period and uncovers her nakedness, he has made naked her fountain, and she has uncovered the fountain of her blood. Both of them shall be cut off from among their people. ¹⁹ You shall not uncover the nakedness of your mother's sister or of your father's sister, for that is to make naked one's relative; they shall bear their iniquity. ²⁰ If a man lies with his uncle's wife, he has uncovered his uncle's nakedness; they shall bear their sin; they shall die childless. ²¹ If a man takes his brother's wife, it is impurity. He has uncovered his brother's nakedness; they shall be childless.

You Shall Be Holy

²² "You shall therefore keep all my statutes and all my rules and do them, that the land where I am bringing you to live may not vomit you out. ²³ And you shall not walk in the customs of the nation that I am driving out before you, for they did all these things, and therefore I detested them. ²⁴ But I have said to you, 'You shall inherit their land, and I will give it to you to possess, a land flowing with milk and honey.' I am the Lord your God, who has separated you from the peoples. ²⁵ You shall therefore separate the clean beast from the unclean, and the unclean bird from the clean. You shall not make yourselves detestable by beast or by bird or by anything with which the ground crawls, which I have set apart for you to hold unclean. ²⁶ You shall be holy to me, for I the Lord am holy and have separated you from the peoples, that you should be mine.

²⁷ "A man or a woman who is a medium or a necromancer shall surely be put to death. They shall be stoned with stones; their blood shall be upon them."

Holiness and the Priests

21 And the LORD said to Moses, "Speak to the priests, the sons of Aaron, and say to them, No one shall make himself unclean for the dead among his people, ² except for his closest relatives, his mother, his father, his son, his daughter, his brother, ³ or his virgin sister (who is near to him because she has had no husband; for her he may make himself unclean). ⁴ He shall not make himself unclean as a husband among his people and so profane himself. ⁵ They shall not make bald patches on their heads, nor shave off the edges of their beards, nor make any cuts on their body. ⁶ They shall be holy to their God and not profane the name of their God. For they offer the LORD's food offerings, the bread of their God; therefore they shall be holy. ⁷ They shall not marry a prostitute or a woman who has been defiled, neither shall they marry a woman divorced from her husband, for the priest is holy to his God. ⁸ You shall sanctify him, for he offers the bread of your God. He shall be holy to you, for I, the LORD, who sanctify you, am holy. ⁹ And the daughter of any priest, if she profanes herself by whoring, profanes her father; she shall be burned with fire.

¹⁰ "The priest who is chief among his brothers, on whose head the anointing oil is poured and who has been consecrated to wear the garments, shall not let the hair of his head hang loose nor tear his clothes. ¹¹ He shall not go in to any dead bodies nor make himself unclean, even for his father or for his mother. ¹² He shall not go out of the sanctuary, lest he profane the sanctuary of his God, for the consecration of the anointing oil of his God is on him: I am the LORD. ¹³ And he shall take a wife in her virginity. ¹⁴ A widow, or a divorced woman, or a woman who has been defiled, or a prostitute, these he shall not marry. But he shall take as his wife a virgin of his own people, ¹⁵ that he may not profane his offspring among his people, for I am the LORD who sanctifies him."

¹⁶ And the LORD spoke to Moses, saying, ¹⁷ "Speak to Aaron, saying, None of your offspring throughout their generations who has a blemish may approach to offer the bread of his God. ¹⁸ For no one who has a blemish shall draw near, a man blind or lame, or one who has a mutilated face or a limb too long, ¹⁹ or a man who has an injured foot or an injured hand, ²⁰ or a hunchback or a dwarf or a man with a defect in his sight or an itching disease or scabs or crushed testicles. ²¹ No man of the offspring of Aaron the priest who has a blemish shall come near to offer the LORD's food offerings; since he has a blemish, he shall not come near to offer the bread of his God. ²² He may eat the bread of his God, both of the most holy and of the holy things, ²³ but he shall not go through the veil or approach the altar, because he has a blemish, that he may not profane my sanctuaries, for I am the LORD who sanctifies them." ²⁴ So Moses spoke to Aaron and to his sons and to all the people of Israel.

22 And the LORD spoke to Moses, saying, ² "Speak to Aaron and his sons so that they abstain from the holy things of the people of Israel, which they dedicate to me, so that they do not profane my holy

GETTING THE MESSAGE

The eating of holy things. Only priests and their families were allowed to eat the meat from sacrifices. Servants who were members of the household could also partake of the offerings, but hired laborers could not do so.

name: I am the LORD. ³ Say to them, 'If any one of all your offspring throughout your generations approaches the holy things that the people of Israel dedicate to the LORD, while he has an uncleanness, that person shall be cut off from my presence: I am the LORD. ⁴ None of the offspring of Aaron who has a leprous disease or a discharge may eat of the holy things until he is clean. Whoever touches anything that is unclean through contact with the dead or a man who has had an emission of semen, ⁵ and whoever touches a swarming thing by which he may be made unclean or a person from whom he may take uncleanness, whatever his uncleanness may be— ⁶ the person who touches such a thing shall be unclean until the evening and shall not eat of the holy things unless he has bathed his body in water. ⁷ When the sun goes down he shall be clean, and afterward he may eat of the holy things, because they are his food. ⁸ He shall not eat what dies of itself or is torn by beasts, and so make himself unclean by it: I am the LORD.' ⁹ They shall therefore keep my charge, lest they bear sin for it and die thereby when they profane it: I am the LORD who sanctifies them.

¹⁰ "A lay person shall not eat of a holy thing; no foreign guest of the priest or hired worker shall eat of a holy thing, ¹¹ but if a priest buys a slave as his property for money, the slave may eat of it, and anyone born in his house may eat of his food. ¹² If a priest's daughter marries a layman, she shall not eat of the contribution of the holy things. ¹³ But if a priest's daughter is widowed or divorced and has no child and returns to her father's house, as in her youth, she may eat of her father's food; yet no lay person shall eat of it. ¹⁴ And if anyone eats of a holy thing unintentionally, he shall add the fifth of its value to it and give the holy thing to the priest. ¹⁵ They shall not profane the holy things of the people of Israel, which they contribute to the LORD, ¹⁶ and so cause them to bear iniquity and guilt, by eating their holy things: for I am the LORD who sanctifies them."

Acceptable Offerings

¹⁷ And the LORD spoke to Moses, saying, ¹⁸ "Speak to Aaron and his sons and all the people of Israel and say to them, When any one of the house of Israel or of the sojourners in Israel presents a burnt offering as his offering, for any of their vows or freewill offerings that they offer to the LORD, ¹⁹ if it is to be accepted for you it shall be a male without blemish, of the bulls or the sheep or the goats. ²⁰ You shall not offer anything that has a blemish, for it will not be acceptable for you. ²¹ And when anyone offers a sacrifice of peace offerings to the LORD to fulfill a vow or as a freewill offering from the herd or from the flock, to be accepted it must be perfect; there shall be no blemish in it. ²² Animals blind or disabled or mutilated or having a discharge or an itch or scabs you shall not offer to the LORD or give them to the LORD as a food offering on the altar. ²³ You may present a bull or a lamb that has a part too long or too short for a freewill offering, but for a vow offering it cannot be accepted. ²⁴ Any animal that has its testicles bruised or crushed or torn or cut you shall not offer to the LORD; you shall not do it

within your land, ²⁵ neither shall you offer as the bread of your God any such animals gotten from a foreigner. Since there is a blemish in them, because of their mutilation, they will not be accepted for you."

²⁶ And the LORD spoke to Moses, saying, ²⁷ "When an ox or sheep or goat is born, it shall remain seven days with its mother, and from the eighth day on it shall be acceptable as a food offering to the LORD. ²⁸ But you shall not kill an ox or a sheep and her young in one day. ²⁹ And when you sacrifice a sacrifice of thanksgiving to the LORD, you shall sacrifice it so that you may be accepted. ³⁰ It shall be eaten on the same day; you shall leave none of it until morning: I am the LORD.

³¹ "So you shall keep my commandments and do them: I am the LORD. ³² And you shall not profane my holy name, that I may be sanctified among the people of Israel. I am the LORD who sanctifies you, ³³ who brought you out of the land of Egypt to be your God: I am the LORD."

Feasts of the LORD

23 The LORD spoke to Moses, saying, ² "Speak to the people of Israel and say to them, These are the appointed feasts of the LORD that you shall proclaim as holy convocations; they are my appointed feasts.

The Sabbath

³ "Six days shall work be done, but on the seventh day is a Sabbath of solemn rest, a holy convocation. You shall do no work. It is a Sabbath to the LORD in all your dwelling places.

The Passover

⁴ "These are the appointed feasts of the LORD, the holy convocations, which you shall proclaim at the time appointed for them. ⁵ In the first month, on the fourteenth day of the month at twilight, is the LORD's Passover. ⁶ And on the fifteenth day of the same month is the Feast of Unleavened Bread to the LORD; for seven days you shall eat unleavened bread. ⁷ On the first day you shall have a holy convocation; you shall not do any ordinary work. ⁸ But you shall present a food offering to the LORD for seven days. On the seventh day is a holy convocation; you shall not do any ordinary work."

The Feast of Firstfruits

9 And the LORD spoke to Moses, saying, 10 "Speak to the people of Israel and say to them, When you come into the land that I give you and reap its harvest, you shall bring the sheaf of the firstfruits of your harvest to the priest, 11 and he shall wave the sheaf before the LORD, so that you may be accepted. On the day after the Sabbath the priest shall wave it. 12 And on the day when you wave the sheaf, you shall offer a male lamb a year old without blemish as a burnt offering to the LORD. 13 And the grain offering with it shall be two tenths of an ephah of fine flour mixed with oil, a food offering to the LORD with a pleasing aroma, and the drink offering with it shall be of wine, a fourth of a hin. 14 And you shall eat neither bread nor grain parched or fresh until this same day, until you have brought the offering of your God: it is a statute forever throughout your generations in all your dwellings.

The Feast of Weeks

15 "You shall count seven full weeks from the day after the Sabbath, from the day that you brought the sheaf of the wave offering. 16 You shall count fifty days to the day after the seventh Sabbath. Then you shall present a grain offering of new grain to the LORD. 17 You shall bring from your dwelling places two loaves of bread to be waved, made of two tenths of an ephah. They shall be of fine flour, and they shall be baked with leaven, as firstfruits to the LORD. 18 And you shall present with the bread seven lambs a year old without blemish, and one bull from the herd and two rams. They shall be a burnt offering to the LORD, with their grain offering and their drink offerings, a food offering with a pleasing aroma to the LORD. 19 And you shall offer one male goat for a sin offering, and two male lambs a year old as a sacrifice of peace offerings. 20 And the priest shall wave them with the bread of the firstfruits as a wave offering before the LORD, with the two lambs. They shall be holy to the LORD for the priest. 21 And you shall make a proclamation on the same day. You shall hold a holy convocation. You shall not do any ordinary work. It is a statute forever in all your dwelling places throughout your generations.

22 "And when you reap the harvest of your land, you shall not reap your field right up to its edge, nor shall you gather the gleanings after your harvest. You shall leave them for the poor and for the sojourner: I am the LORD your God."

The Feast of Trumpets

23 And the LORD spoke to Moses, saying, 24 "Speak to the people of Israel, saying, In the seventh month, on the first day of the month, you shall observe a day of solemn rest, a memorial proclaimed with blast of trumpets, a holy convocation. 25 You shall not do any ordinary work, and you shall present a food offering to the LORD."

The Day of Atonement

26 And the LORD spoke to Moses, saying, 27 "Now on the tenth day of this seventh month is the Day of Atonement. It shall be for you a time of holy convocation, and you shall afflict yourselves and present a food offering to the LORD. 28 And you shall not do any work on that very day, for it is a

The Feast of Weeks is known in the New Testament as Pentecost (Acts 2:1). It was a celebration honoring the Lord as provider of all crops and as the One who deserved the firstfruits of those crops.

Day of Atonement, to make atonement for you before the LORD your God. 29 For whoever is not afflicted on that very day shall be cut off from his people. 30 And whoever does any work on that very day, that person I will destroy from among his people. 31 You shall not do any work. It is a statute forever throughout your generations in all your dwelling places. 32 It shall be to you a Sabbath of solemn rest, and you shall afflict yourselves. On the ninth day of the month beginning at evening, from evening to evening shall you keep your Sabbath."

The Feast of Booths

33 And the LORD spoke to Moses, saying, 34 "Speak to the people of Israel, saying, On the fifteenth day of this seventh month and for seven days is the Feast of Booths to the LORD. 35 On the first day shall be a holy convocation; you shall not do any ordinary work. 36 For seven days you shall present food offerings to the LORD. On the eighth

day you shall hold a holy convocation and present a food offering to the LORD. It is a solemn assembly; you shall not do any ordinary work.

37 "These are the appointed feasts of the LORD, which you shall proclaim as times of holy convocation, for presenting to the LORD food offerings, burnt offerings and grain offerings, sacrifices and drink offerings, each on its proper day, 38 besides the LORD's Sabbaths and besides your gifts and besides all your vow offerings and besides all your freewill offerings, which you give to the LORD.

39 "On the fifteenth day of the seventh month, when you have gathered in the produce of the land, you shall celebrate the feast of the LORD seven days. On the first day shall be a solemn rest, and on the eighth day shall be a solemn rest. 40 And you shall

take on the first day the fruit of splendid trees, branches of palm trees and boughs of leafy trees and willows of the brook, and you shall rejoice before the LORD your God seven days. 41 You shall celebrate it as a feast to the LORD for seven days in the year. It is a statute forever throughout your generations; you shall celebrate it in the seventh month. 42 You shall dwell in booths for seven days. All native Israelites shall dwell in booths, 43 that your generations may know that I made the people of Israel dwell in booths when I brought them out of the land of Egypt: I am the LORD your God."

44 Thus Moses declared to the people of Israel the appointed feasts of the LORD.

The Lamps

24 The LORD spoke to Moses, saying, 2 "Command the people of Israel to bring you pure oil from beaten olives for the lamp, that a light may be kept burning regularly. 3 Outside the veil of the testi-

mony, in the tent of meeting, Aaron shall arrange it from evening to morning before the LORD regularly. It shall be a statute forever throughout your generations. 4 He shall arrange the lamps on the lampstand of pure gold before the LORD regularly.

Bread for the Tabernacle

5 "You shall take fine flour and bake twelve loaves from it; two tenths of an ephah shall be in each loaf. 6 And you shall set them in two piles, six in a pile, on the table of pure gold before the LORD. 7 And you shall put pure frankincense on each pile, that it may go with the bread as a memorial portion as a food offering to the LORD. 8 Every Sabbath day Aaron shall arrange it before the LORD regularly; it is from the people of Israel as a covenant forever. 9 And it shall be for Aaron and his sons, and they shall eat it in a holy place, since it is for him a most holy portion out of the LORD's food offerings, a perpetual due."

Punishment for Blasphemy

10 Now an Israelite woman's son, whose father was an Egyptian, went out among the people of Israel. And the Israelite woman's son and a man of Israel fought in the camp, 11 and the Israelite woman's son blasphemed the Name, and cursed. Then they brought him to Moses. His mother's name was Shelomith, the daughter of Dibri, of the tribe of Dan. 12 And they put him in custody, till the will of the LORD should be clear to them.

13 Then the LORD spoke to Moses, saying, 14 "Bring out of the camp the one who cursed, and let all who heard him lay their hands on his head, and let all the congregation stone him. 15 And speak to the people of Israel, saying, Whoever curses his God shall bear his sin. 16 Whoever blasphemes the name of the LORD shall surely be put to death. All the congregation shall stone him. The sojourner as well as the native, when he blasphemes the Name, shall be put to death.

An Eye for an Eye

17 "Whoever takes a human life shall surely be put to death. 18 Whoever takes an animal's life shall make it good, life for life. 19 If anyone injures his neighbor, as he has done it shall be done to him, 20 fracture for fracture, eye for eye, tooth for tooth; whatever injury he has given a person shall be given to him. 21 Whoever kills an animal

shall make it good, and whoever kills a person shall be put to death. ²² You shall have the same rule for the sojourner and for the native, for I am the LORD your God." ²³ So Moses spoke to the people of Israel, and they brought out of the camp the one who had cursed and stoned him with stones. Thus the people of Israel did as the LORD commanded Moses.

The Sabbath Year

25 The LORD spoke to Moses on Mount Sinai, saying, ² "Speak to the people of Israel and say to them, When you come into the land that I give you, the land shall keep a Sabbath to the LORD. ³ For six years you shall sow your field, and for six years you shall prune your vineyard and gather in its fruits, ⁴ but in the seventh year there shall be a Sabbath of solemn rest for the land, a Sabbath to the LORD. You shall not sow your field or prune your vineyard. ⁵ You shall not reap what grows of itself in your harvest, or gather the grapes of your undressed vine. It shall be a year of solemn rest for the land. ⁶ The Sabbath of the land shall provide food for you, for yourself and for your male and female slaves¹ and for your hired worker and the sojourner who lives with you, ⁷ and for your cattle and for the wild animals that are in your land: all its yield shall be for food.

The Year of Jubilee

⁸ "You shall count seven weeks of years, seven times seven years, so that the time of the seven weeks of years shall give you forty-nine years. ⁹ Then you shall sound the loud trumpet on the tenth day of the seventh month. On the Day of Atonement you shall sound the trumpet throughout all your land. ¹⁰ And you shall consecrate the fiftieth year, and proclaim liberty throughout the land to all its inhabitants. It shall be a jubilee for you, when each of you shall return to his property and each of you shall return to his clan. ¹¹ That fiftieth year shall be a jubilee for you; in it you shall neither sow nor reap what grows of itself nor gather the grapes from the undressed vines. ¹² For it is a jubilee. It shall be holy to you. You may eat the produce of the field.

¹³ "In this year of jubilee each of you shall return to his property. ¹⁴ And if you make a sale to your neighbor or buy from your neighbor, you shall not wrong one another. ¹⁵ You shall pay your neighbor according to the number of years after the jubilee, and he shall sell to you according to the number of years for crops. ¹⁶ If the years are many, you shall increase the price, and if the years are few, you shall reduce the price, for it is the number of the crops that he is selling to you. ¹⁷ You shall not wrong one another, but you shall fear your God, for I am the LORD your God.

¹⁸ "Therefore you shall do my statutes and keep my rules and perform them, and then you will dwell in the land securely. ¹⁹ The land will yield its fruit, and you will eat your fill and dwell in it securely. ²⁰ And if you say, 'What shall we eat in the seventh year, if we may not sow or gather in our crop?'

²¹ I will command my blessing on you in the sixth year, so that it will produce a crop sufficient for three years. ²² When you sow in the eighth year, you will be eating some of the old crop; you shall eat the old until the ninth year, when its crop arrives.

Redemption of Property

²³ "The land shall not be sold in perpetuity, for the land is mine. For you are strangers and sojourners with me. ²⁴ And in all the country you possess, you shall allow a redemption of the land.

²⁵ "If your brother becomes poor and sells part of his property, then his nearest redeemer shall come and redeem what his brother has sold. ²⁶ If a man has no one to redeem it and then himself becomes prosperous and finds sufficient means to redeem it, ²⁷ let him calculate the years since he sold it and pay back the balance to the

¹ Or *servants*; the Hebrew word (*ebed*) can mean either voluntary service or forced service (see Preface)

man to whom he sold it, and then return to his property. **28** But if he does not have sufficient means to recover it, then what he sold shall remain in the hand of the buyer until the year of jubilee. In the jubilee it shall be released, and he shall return to his property.

29 "If a man sells a dwelling house in a walled city, he may redeem it within a year of its sale. For a full year he shall have the right of redemption. **30** If it is not redeemed within a full year, then the house in the walled city shall belong in perpetuity to the buyer, throughout his generations; it shall not be released in the jubilee. **31** But the houses of the villages that have no wall around them shall be classified with the fields of the land. They may be redeemed, and they shall be released in the jubilee. **32** As for the cities of the Levites, the Levites may redeem at any time the houses in the cities they possess. **33** And if one of the Levites exercises his right of redemption, then the house that was sold in a city they possess shall be released in the jubilee. For the houses in the cities of the Levites are their possession among the people of Israel. **34** But the fields of pastureland belonging to their cities may not be sold, for that is their possession forever.

Kindness for Poor Brothers

35 "If your brother becomes poor and cannot maintain himself with you, you shall support him as though he were a stranger and a sojourner, and he shall live with you. **36** Take no interest from him or profit, but fear your God, that your brother may live beside you. **37** You shall not lend him your money at interest, nor give him your food for profit. **38** I am the LORD your God, who brought you out of the land of Egypt to give you the land of Canaan, and to be your God.

39 "If your brother becomes poor beside you and sells himself to you, you shall not make him serve as a slave: **40** he shall be with you as a hired worker and as a sojourner. He shall serve with you until the year of the jubilee. **41** Then he shall go out from you, he and his children with him, and go back to his own clan and return to the possession of his fathers. **42** For they are my servants, whom I brought out of the land of Egypt; they shall not be sold as slaves. **43** You shall not rule over him ruthlessly but shall fear your God. **44** As for your male and female

slaves whom you may have: you may buy male and female slaves from among the nations that are around you. **45** You may also buy from among the strangers who sojourn with you and their clans that are with you, who have been born in your land, and they may be your property. **46** You may bequeath them to your sons after you to inherit as a possession forever. You may make slaves of them, but over your brothers the people of Israel you shall not rule, one over another ruthlessly.

Redeeming a Poor Man

47 "If a stranger or sojourner with you becomes rich, and your brother beside him becomes poor and sells himself to the stranger or sojourner with you or to a member of the stranger's clan, **48** then after he is sold he may be redeemed. One of his brothers may redeem him, **49** or his uncle or his cousin may redeem him, or a close relative from his clan may redeem him. Or if he grows rich he may redeem himself. **50** He shall calculate with his buyer from the year when he sold himself to him until the year of jubilee, and the price of his sale shall vary with the number of years. The time he was with his owner shall be rated as the time of a hired worker. **51** If there are still many years left, he shall pay proportionately for his redemption some of his sale price. **52** If there remain but a few years until the year of jubilee, he shall calculate and pay for his redemption in proportion to his years of service. **53** He shall treat him as a worker hired year by year. He shall not rule ruthlessly over him in your sight. **54** And if he is not redeemed by these means, then he and his children with him shall be released in the year of jubilee. **55** For it is to me that the people of Israel are servants. They are my servants whom I brought out of the land of Egypt: I am the LORD your God.

Blessings for Obedience

26 "You shall not make idols for yourselves or erect an image or pillar, and you shall not set up a figured stone in your land to bow down to it, for I am the LORD your God. **2** You shall keep my Sabbaths and reverence my sanctuary: I am the LORD.

3 "If you walk in my statutes and observe my commandments and do them, **4** then I will give you your rains in their season, and the land shall yield its increase, and the trees of the field shall yield their fruit. **5** Your threshing shall last to the time of the grape harvest, and the grape harvest shall last to the time for sowing. And you shall eat your bread to the full and dwell in your land securely. **6** I will give peace in the land, and you shall lie down, and none shall make you afraid. And I will remove harmful beasts from the land, and the sword shall not go through your land. **7** You shall chase your enemies, and they shall fall before you by the sword. **8** Five of you shall chase a hundred, and a hundred of you shall chase ten thousand, and your enemies shall fall before you by the sword. **9** I will turn to you and make you fruitful and multiply you and will confirm my covenant with you. **10** You shall eat old store long kept, and you shall clear out the old to make way for the new. **11** I will make my dwelling among you, and my soul shall not abhor you. **12** And I will walk among you and will be your God, and you shall be my people. **13** I am the LORD your God, who brought you out of the land of Egypt, that you should not be their slaves. And I have broken the bars of your yoke and made you walk erect.

Punishment for Disobedience

14 "But if you will not listen to me and will not do all these commandments, **15** if you spurn my statutes, and if your soul abhors my rules, so that you will not do all my commandments, but break my covenant, **16** then I will do this to you: I will visit you with panic, with wasting disease and fever that consume the eyes and make the heart ache. And you shall sow your seed in vain, for your enemies shall eat it. **17** I will set my face against you, and you shall be struck down before your enemies. Those who hate you shall rule over you, and you shall flee when none pursues you. **18** And if in spite of this you will not listen to me, then I will discipline you again sevenfold for your sins, **19** and I will break the pride of your power, and I will make your heavens like iron and your earth like bronze. **20** And your strength shall be spent in vain, for your land shall not yield its increase, and the trees of the land shall not yield their fruit.

21 "Then if you walk contrary to me and will not listen to me, I will continue striking you, sevenfold for your sins. **22** And I

will let loose the wild beasts against you, which shall bereave you of your children and destroy your livestock and make you few in number, so that your roads shall be deserted.

23 "And if by this discipline you are not turned to me but walk contrary to me, **24** then I also will walk contrary to you, and I myself will strike you sevenfold for your sins. **25** And I will bring a sword upon you, that shall execute vengeance for the covenant. And if you gather within your cities, I will send pestilence among you, and you shall be delivered into the hand of the enemy. **26** When I break your supply of bread, ten women shall bake your bread in a single oven and shall dole out your bread again by weight, and you shall eat and not be satisfied.

27 "But if in spite of this you will not listen to me, but walk contrary to me, **28** then I will walk contrary to you in fury, and I myself

> ### GETTING THE MESSAGE
>
> **"Certain terms and conditions apply."**
> Like any modern-day agreement between two parties, God's covenant with Israel involved certain conditions. There were blessings for those who kept the covenant (26:1-13) and punishment for those who broke it (26:14-46).

will discipline you sevenfold for your sins. **29** You shall eat the flesh of your sons, and you shall eat the flesh of your daughters. **30** And I will destroy your high places and cut down your incense altars and cast your dead bodies upon the dead bodies of your idols, and my soul will abhor you. **31** And I will lay your cities waste and will make your sanctuaries desolate, and I will not smell your pleasing aromas. **32** And I myself will devastate the land, so that your enemies who settle in it shall be appalled at it. **33** And I will scatter you among the nations, and I will unsheathe the sword after you, and your land shall be a desolation, and your cities shall be a waste.

34 "Then the land shall enjoy its Sabbaths as long as it lies desolate, while you are in your enemies' land; then the land shall rest, and enjoy its Sabbaths. **35** As long as it lies desolate it shall have rest, the rest that it did not have on your Sabbaths when you were dwelling in it. **36** And as for those of you who are left, I will send faintness into their hearts in the lands of their enemies. The sound of a driven leaf shall put them to flight, and they shall flee as one flees from the sword, and they shall fall when none pursues. **37** They shall stumble over one another, as if to escape a sword, though none pursues. And you shall have no power to stand before your enemies. **38** And you shall perish among the nations, and the land of your enemies shall eat you up. **39** And those of you who are left shall rot away in your enemies' lands because of their iniquity, and also because of the iniquities of their fathers they shall rot away like them.

40 "But if they confess their iniquity and the iniquity of their fathers in their treachery that they committed against me, and also in walking contrary to me, **41** so that I walked contrary to them and brought them into the land of their enemies—if then their uncircumcised heart is humbled and they make amends for their iniquity, **42** then I will remember my covenant with Jacob, and I will remember my covenant with Isaac and my covenant with Abraham, and I will remember the land. **43** But the land shall be abandoned by them and enjoy its Sabbaths while it lies desolate without them, and they shall make amends for their iniquity, because they spurned my rules and their soul abhorred my statutes. **44** Yet for all that, when they are in the land of their enemies, I will not spurn them, neither will I abhor them so as to destroy them utterly and break my covenant with them, for I am the Lord their God. **45** But I will for their sake remember the covenant with their forefathers, whom I brought out of the land of Egypt in the sight of the nations, that I might be their God: I am the Lord."

46 These are the statutes and rules and laws that the Lord made between himself and the people of Israel through Moses on Mount Sinai.

Laws About Vows

27 The Lord spoke to Moses, saying, **2** "Speak to the people of Israel and say to them, If anyone makes a special vow to the Lord involving the valuation of persons, **3** then the valuation of a male from twenty years old up to sixty years old shall be fifty shekels of silver, according to the shekel of the sanctuary. **4** If the person is a female, the valuation shall be thirty shekels. **5** If the person is from five years old up to twenty years old, the valuation shall be for a male twenty shekels, and for a female ten shekels. **6** If the person is from a month old up to five years old, the valuation shall be for a male five shekels of silver, and for a female the valuation shall be three shekels of silver. **7** And if the person is sixty years old or over, then the valuation for a male shall be fifteen shekels, and for a female ten shekels. **8** And if someone is too poor to pay the valuation, then he shall be made to stand before the priest, and the priest shall value him; the priest shall value him according to what the vower can afford.

9 "If the vow is an animal that may be offered as an offering to the Lord, all of it that he gives to the Lord is holy. **10** He shall not exchange it or make a substitute for it, good for bad, or bad for good; and if he does in fact substitute one animal for another, then both it and the substitute shall be holy. **11** And if it is any unclean animal that may not be offered as an offering to the Lord, then he shall stand the animal before the priest, **12** and the priest shall value it as either good or bad; as the priest values it, so it shall be. **13** But if he wishes to redeem it, he shall add a fifth to the valuation.

14 "When a man dedicates his house as a holy gift to the Lord, the priest shall value it as either good or bad; as the priest values it, so it shall stand. **15** And if the donor wishes to redeem his house, he shall add a fifth to the valuation price, and it shall be his.

16 "If a man dedicates to the Lord part of the land that is his possession, then the valuation shall be in proportion to its seed. A homer of barley seed shall be valued at fifty shekels of silver. **17** If he dedicates his field from the year of jubilee, the valuation shall stand, **18** but if he dedicates his field after the jubilee, then the priest shall calculate the price according to the years that remain until the year of jubilee, and a deduction shall be made from the valuation. **19** And if he who dedicates the field wishes to redeem it, then he shall add a fifth to its valuation price, and it shall remain his. **20** But if he does not wish to redeem the field, or if he has sold the field to another man, it shall not be redeemed anymore. [21] But the field, when it is released in the jubilee, shall be a holy gift to the LORD, like a field that has been devoted. The priest shall be in possession of it. [22] If he dedicates to the LORD a field that he has bought, which is not a part of his possession, [23] then the priest shall calculate the amount of the valuation for it up to the year of jubilee, and the man shall give the valuation on that day as a holy gift to the LORD. [24] In the year of jubilee the field shall return to him from whom it was bought, to whom the land belongs as a possession. [25] Every valuation shall be according to the shekel of the sanctuary: twenty gerahs shall make a shekel.

[26] "But a firstborn of animals, which as a firstborn belongs to the LORD, no man may dedicate; whether ox or sheep, it is the LORD's. [27] And if it is an unclean animal, then he shall buy it back at the valuation, and add a fifth to it; or, if it is not redeemed, it shall be sold at the valuation.

[28] "But no devoted thing that a man devotes to the LORD, of anything that he has, whether man or beast, or of his inherited field, shall be sold or redeemed; every devoted thing is most holy to the LORD. [29] No one devoted, who is to be devoted for destruction[1] from mankind, shall be ransomed; he shall surely be put to death.

[30] "Every tithe of the land, whether of the seed of the land or of the fruit of the trees, is the LORD's; it is holy to the LORD. [31] If a man wishes to redeem some of his tithe, he shall add a fifth to it. [32] And every tithe of herds and flocks, every tenth animal of all that pass under the herdsman's staff, shall be holy to the LORD. [33] One shall not differentiate between good or bad, neither shall he make a substitute for it; and if he does substitute for it, then both it and the substitute shall be holy; it shall not be redeemed."

[34] These are the commandments that the LORD commanded Moses for the people of Israel on Mount Sinai.

---

[1] That is, destroyed or made an offering because of sin, at God's command

INTRODUCTION TO NUMBERS

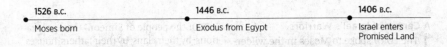

1526 B.C.
Moses born

1446 B.C.
Exodus from Egypt

1406 B.C.
Israel enters
Promised Land

AUTHOR AND DATE

Moses is the source and primary author of the book of Numbers, which is the fourth volume in the Pentateuch. Its English name comes from the censuses in chs. 1–4 and 26.

Numbers tells of Israel's journey from Mount Sinai to the borders of the Promised Land, summarizing some 40 years of the nation's history. With Israel having been freed from slavery in Egypt and then receiving the law (Exodus and Leviticus), the book of Numbers begins with the people's final preparations to leave Sinai. It then records their triumphal setting out, before a series of events in which the people grumbled about the difficulty of the journey and the impossibility of conquering Canaan. This response leads God to delay their entry to Canaan by 40 years. The closing chapters of the book tell how the people at last set out again and reach the banks of the Jordan, ready to cross into the land promised to their forefathers.

THEME AND PURPOSE

The theme of Numbers is the gradual fulfillment of the promises to Abraham that his descendants would be the people of God and would occupy the land of Canaan. The book shows the reality of God's presence with Israel in the pillar of cloud and fire over the tabernacle. It also shows how Israel's unbelief delays the entry into Canaan and costs many lives. Nevertheless, by the end of the book, Israel is ready to enter the land.

KEY THEMES

There were four elements to God's promise to Abraham in Genesis 12:1–3, and they all play a role in Numbers:

1. *The land.* Numbers describes Israel's journey toward the Promised Land.

2. *Descendants.* Abraham had been promised that his descendants would be as many as the stars of heaven (Gen. 15:5). Jacob's family consisted of just 70 persons when he entered Egypt (Gen. 46:27). Now they had increased immensely. The first census (Num. 1:1–46) showed that the fighting men numbered 603,550. That did not include women and children. Surveying their camp from a hilltop, Balaam declared, "Who can count the dust of Jacob or number the fourth part of Israel?" (23:10). Balaam went on to predict that Israel would become a powerful kingdom in its own right: "a star shall come out of Jacob, and a scepter shall rise out of Israel" (24:17).

3. *Covenant relationship with God.* The essence of the covenant was, "You shall be my people, and I will be your God." The Lord's presence with Israel is constantly highlighted throughout the book of Numbers.

4. *Blessing to the nations.* This is the aspect of the promises to Abraham that is least apparent in Numbers. To a greater or lesser degree, the nations that Israel encounters are all hostile. Nevertheless Balaam recalls the phrasing of Genesis 12:3 when he says, "Blessed are those who bless you, and cursed are those who curse you" (Num. 24:9). Nations who treat Israel generously by blessing her will themselves be blessed.

OUTLINE

Numbers consists of three major blocks of material describing the events and laws associated with three centers where Israel encamped for a significant time. These centers are Sinai (chs. 1–10), Kadesh (chs. 13–19), and the plains of Moab (chs. 22–36). They are linked by two short travelogues recording what occurred as Israel journeyed from one camp to the next.

I. Israel Prepares to Enter the Land (1:1–10:10)

II. Marching from Sinai to Kadesh (10:11–12:16)

III. Forty Years near Kadesh (13:1–19:22)

IV. Marching from Kadesh to the Plains of Moab (20:1–21:35)

V. Israel in the Plains of Moab (22:1–36:13)

NUMBERS

A Census of Israel's Warriors

1 The LORD spoke to Moses in the wilderness of Sinai, in the tent of meeting, on the first day of the second month, in the second year after they had come out of the land of Egypt, saying, ² "Take a census of all the congregation of the people of Israel, by clans, by fathers' houses, according to the number of names, every male, head by head. ³ From twenty years old and upward, all in Israel who are able to go to war, you and Aaron shall list them, company by company. ⁴ And there shall be with you a man from each tribe, each man being the head of the house of his fathers. ⁵ And these are the names of the men who shall assist you. From Reuben, Elizur the son of Shedeur; ⁶ from Simeon, Shelumiel the son of Zurishaddai; ⁷ from Judah, Nahshon the son of Amminadab; ⁸ from Issachar, Nethanel the son of Zuar; ⁹ from Zebulun, Eliab the son of Helon; ¹⁰ from the sons of Joseph, from Ephraim, Elishama the son of Ammihud, and from Manasseh, Gamaliel the son of Pedahzur; ¹¹ from Benjamin, Abidan the son of Gideoni; ¹² from Dan, Ahiezer the son of Ammishaddai; ¹³ from Asher, Pagiel the son of Ochran; ¹⁴ from Gad, Eliasaph the son of Deuel; ¹⁵ from Naphtali, Ahira the son of Enan." ¹⁶ These were the ones chosen from the congregation, the chiefs of their ancestral tribes, the heads of the clans of Israel.

¹⁷ Moses and Aaron took these men who had been named, ¹⁸ and on the first day of the second month, they assembled the whole congregation together, who registered themselves by clans, by fathers' houses, according to the number of names from twenty years old and upward, head by head, ¹⁹ as the LORD commanded Moses. So he listed them in the wilderness of Sinai.

²⁰ The people of Reuben, Israel's firstborn, their generations, by their clans, by their fathers' houses, according to the number of names, head by head, every male from twenty years old and upward, all who were able to go to war: ²¹ those listed of the tribe of Reuben were 46,500.

²² Of the people of Simeon, their generations, by their clans, by their fathers' houses, those of them who were listed, according to the number of names, head by head, every male from twenty years old and upward, all who were able to go to war: ²³ those listed of the tribe of Simeon were 59,300.

²⁴ Of the people of Gad, their generations, by their clans, by their fathers' houses, according to the number of the names, from twenty years old and upward, all who were able to go to war: ²⁵ those listed of the tribe of Gad were 45,650.

GETTING THE MESSAGE

Where do the events in Numbers take place? Chapters 1–9 take place near Mount Sinai. In chs. 10–12 the people travel to Kadesh, where they will spend the next 40 years (chs. 13–19). Next they journey toward Canaan (chs. 20–21), and in the final chapters of Numbers (22–36) they camp in the plains of Moab, across the Jordan River from the Promised Land.

²⁶ Of the people of Judah, their generations, by their clans, by their fathers' houses, according to the number of names, from twenty years old and upward, every man able to go to war: ²⁷ those listed of the tribe of Judah were 74,600.

²⁸ Of the people of Issachar, their generations, by their clans, by their fathers' houses, according to the number of names, from twenty years old and upward, every man able to go to war: ²⁹ those listed of the tribe of Issachar were 54,400.

³⁰ Of the people of Zebulun, their generations, by their clans, by their fathers' houses, according to the number of names, from twenty years old and upward, every man able to go to war: ³¹ those listed of the tribe of Zebulun were 57,400.

³² Of the people of Joseph, namely, of the people of Ephraim, their generations, by their clans, by their fathers' houses, accord-

ing to the number of names, from twenty years old and upward, every man able to go to war: [33] those listed of the tribe of Ephraim were 40,500.

[34] Of the people of Manasseh, their generations, by their clans, by their fathers' houses, according to the number of names, from twenty years old and upward, every man able to go to war: [35] those listed of the tribe of Manasseh were 32,200.

[36] Of the people of Benjamin, their generations, by their clans, by their fathers' houses, according to the number of names, from twenty years old and upward, every man able to go to war: [37] those listed of the tribe of Benjamin were 35,400.

[38] Of the people of Dan, their generations, by their clans, by their fathers' houses, according to the number of names, from

twenty years old and upward, every man able to go to war: [39] those listed of the tribe of Dan were 62,700.

[40] Of the people of Asher, their generations, by their clans, by their fathers' houses, according to the number of names, from twenty years old and upward, every man able to go to war: [41] those listed of the tribe of Asher were 41,500.

[42] Of the people of Naphtali, their generations, by their clans, by their fathers' houses, according to the number of names, from twenty years old and upward, every man able to go to war: [43] those listed of the tribe of Naphtali were 53,400.

[44] These are those who were listed, whom Moses and Aaron listed with the help of the chiefs of Israel, twelve men, each representing his fathers' house. [45] So all those listed of

the people of Israel, by their fathers' houses, from twenty years old and upward, every man able to go to war in Israel— [46] all those listed were 603,550.

Levites Exempted

[47] But the Levites were not listed along with them by their ancestral tribe. [48] For the LORD spoke to Moses, saying, [49] "Only the tribe of Levi you shall not list, and you shall not take a census of them among the people of Israel. [50] But appoint the Levites over the tabernacle of the testimony, and over all its furnishings, and over all that belongs to it. They are to carry the tabernacle and all its furnishings, and they shall take care of it and shall camp around the tabernacle. [51] When the tabernacle is to set out, the Levites shall take it down, and when the tabernacle is to be pitched, the Levites shall set it up. And if any outsider comes near, he shall be put to death. [52] The people of Israel shall pitch their tents by their companies, each man in his own camp and each man by his own standard. [53] But the Levites shall camp around the tabernacle of the testimony, so that there may be no wrath on the congregation of the people of Israel. And the Levites shall keep guard over the tabernacle of the testimony." [54] Thus did the people of Israel; they did according to all that the LORD commanded Moses.

Arrangement of the Camp

2 The LORD spoke to Moses and Aaron, saying, [2] "The people of Israel shall camp each by his own standard, with the banners of their fathers' houses. They shall camp facing the tent of meeting on every side. [3] Those to camp on the east side toward the sunrise shall be of the standard of the camp of Judah by their companies, the chief of the people of Judah being Nahshon the son of Amminadab, [4] his company as listed being 74,600. [5] Those to camp next to him shall be the tribe of Issachar, the chief of the people of Issachar being Nethanel the son of Zuar, [6] his company as listed being 54,400. [7] Then the tribe of Zebulun, the chief of the people of Zebulun being Eliab the son of Helon, [8] his company as listed being 57,400. [9] All those listed of the camp of Judah, by their companies, were 186,400. They shall set out first on the march.

[10] "On the south side shall be the standard of the camp of Reuben by their companies, the chief of the people of Reuben being Elizur the son of Shedeur, [11] his company as listed being 46,500. [12] And those to camp next to him shall be the tribe of Simeon, the chief of the people of Simeon being Shelumiel the son of Zurishaddai, [13] his company as listed being 59,300. [14] Then the tribe of Gad, the chief of the people of Gad being Eliasaph the son of Reuel, [15] his company as listed being 45,650. [16] All those listed of the camp of Reuben, by their companies, were 151,450. They shall set out second.

[17] "Then the tent of meeting shall set out, with the camp of the Levites in the midst of the camps; as they camp, so shall they set out, each in position, standard by standard.

[18] "On the west side shall be the standard of the camp of Ephraim by their companies, the chief of the people of Ephraim being Elishama the son of Ammihud, [19] his company as listed being 40,500. [20] And next to him shall be the tribe of Manasseh, the chief of the people of Manasseh being Gamaliel the son of Pedahzur, [21] his company as listed being 32,200. [22] Then the tribe of Benjamin, the chief of the people of Benjamin being Abidan the son of Gideoni, [23] his company as listed being 35,400. [24] All those listed of the camp of Ephraim, by their companies, were 108,100. They shall set out third on the march.

[25] "On the north side shall be the standard of the camp of Dan by their companies, the chief of the people of Dan being Ahiezer the son of Ammishaddai, [26] his company as listed being 62,700. [27] And those to camp next to him shall be the tribe of Asher, the chief of the people of Asher being Pagiel the son of Ochran, [28] his company as listed being 41,500. [29] Then the tribe of Naphtali, the chief of the people of Naphtali being Ahira the son of Enan, [30] his company as listed being 53,400. [31] All those listed of the camp of Dan were 157,600. They shall set out last, standard by standard."

[32] These are the people of Israel as listed by their fathers' houses. All those listed in the camps by their companies were 603,550. [33] But the Levites were not listed among the people of Israel, as the LORD commanded Moses.

[34] Thus did the people of Israel. According to all that the LORD commanded Moses, so they camped by their standards, and so they set out, each one in his clan, according to his fathers' house.

The Sons of Aaron

3 These are the generations of Aaron and Moses at the time when the LORD spoke with Moses on Mount Sinai. [2] These are the names of the sons of Aaron: Nadab the firstborn, and Abihu, Eleazar, and Ithamar. [3] These are the names of the sons of Aaron, the anointed priests, whom he ordained to serve as priests. [4] But Nadab and Abihu died before the LORD when they offered unauthorized fire before the LORD in the wilderness of Sinai, and they had no children. So Eleazar and Ithamar served as priests in the lifetime of Aaron their father.

> ### GETTING THE MESSAGE
>
> **Guard duty.** It was the Levites' job to put to death anyone other than Aaron and his sons who attempted to enter the holy ground of the tabernacle. This included Israelites and not just outsiders. Only those whom God had chosen could be appointed to serve as priests.

Duties of the Levites

[5] And the LORD spoke to Moses, saying, [6] "Bring the tribe of Levi near, and set them before Aaron the priest, that they may minister to him. [7] They shall keep guard over him and over the whole congregation before the tent of meeting, as they minister at the tabernacle. [8] They shall guard all the furnishings of the tent of meeting, and keep guard over the people of Israel as they minister at the tabernacle. [9] And you shall give the Levites to Aaron and his sons; they are wholly given to him from among the people of Israel. [10] And you shall appoint Aaron and his sons, and they shall guard their priesthood. But if any outsider comes near, he shall be put to death."

[11] And the LORD spoke to Moses, saying, [12] "Behold, I have taken the Levites from among the people of Israel instead of every firstborn who opens the womb among the people of Israel. The Levites shall be mine,

[13] for all the firstborn are mine. On the day that I struck down all the firstborn in the land of Egypt, I consecrated for my own all the firstborn in Israel, both of man and of beast. They shall be mine: I am the LORD."

[14] And the LORD spoke to Moses in the wilderness of Sinai, saying, [15] "List the sons of Levi, by fathers' houses and by clans; every male from a month old and upward you shall list." [16] So Moses listed them according to the word of the LORD, as he was commanded. [17] And these were the sons of Levi by their names: Gershon and Kohath and Merari. [18] And these are the names of the sons of Gershon by their clans: Libni and Shimei. [19] And the sons of Kohath by their clans: Amram, Izhar, Hebron, and Uzziel. [20] And the sons of Merari by their clans: Mahli and Mushi. These are the clans of the Levites, by their fathers' houses.

[21] To Gershon belonged the clan of the Libnites and the clan of the Shimeites; these were the clans of the Gershonites. [22] Their listing according to the number of all the males from a month old and upward was 7,500. [23] The clans of the Gershonites were to camp behind the tabernacle on the west, [24] with Eliasaph, the son of Lael as chief of the fathers' house of the Gershonites. [25] And the guard duty of the sons of Gershon in the tent of meeting involved the tabernacle, the tent with its covering, the screen for the entrance of the tent of meeting, [26] the hangings of the court, the screen for the door of the court that is around the tabernacle and the altar, and its cords—all the service connected with these.

[27] To Kohath belonged the clan of the Amramites and the clan of the Izharites and the clan of the Hebronites and the clan of the Uzzielites; these are the clans of the Kohathites. [28] According to the number of all the males, from a month old and upward, there were 8,600, keeping guard over the sanctuary. [29] The clans of the sons of Kohath were to camp on the south side of the tabernacle, [30] with Elizaphan the son of Uzziel as chief of the fathers' house of the clans of the Kohathites. [31] And their guard duty involved the ark, the table, the lampstand, the altars, the vessels of the sanctuary with which the priests minister, and the screen; all the service connected with these. [32] And Eleazar the son of Aaron the priest was to be chief over the chiefs of the Levites, and to have oversight of those who kept guard over the sanctuary.

[33] To Merari belonged the clan of the Mahlites and the clan of the Mushites: these are the clans of Merari. [34] Their listing according to the number of all the males from a month old and upward was 6,200. [35] And the chief of the fathers' house of the clans of Merari was Zuriel the son of Abihail. They were to camp on the north side of the tabernacle. [36] And the appointed guard duty of the sons of Merari involved the frames of the tabernacle, the bars, the pillars, the bases, and all their accessories; all the service connected with these; [37] also the pillars around the court, with their bases and pegs and cords.

[38] Those who were to camp before the tabernacle on the east, before the tent of meeting toward the sunrise, were Moses and Aaron and his sons, guarding the sanctuary itself, to protect the people of Israel. And any outsider who came near was to be put to death. [39] All those listed among the Levites, whom Moses and Aaron listed at the commandment of the LORD, by clans, all the males from a month old and upward, were 22,000.

Redemption of the Firstborn

[40] And the LORD said to Moses, "List all the firstborn males of the people of Israel, from a month old and upward, taking the number of their names. [41] And you shall take the Levites for me—I am the LORD—instead of all the firstborn among the people of Israel, and the cattle of the Levites instead of all the firstborn among the cattle of the people of Israel." [42] So Moses listed all the firstborn among the people of Israel, as the LORD commanded him. [43] And all the firstborn males, according to the number of names, from a month old and upward as listed were 22,273.

[44] And the LORD spoke to Moses, saying, [45] "Take the Levites instead of all the firstborn among the people of Israel, and the cattle of the Levites instead of their cattle. The Levites shall be mine: I am the LORD. [46] And as the redemption price for the 273 of the firstborn of the people of Israel, over and above the number of the male Levites, [47] you shall take five shekels per head; you shall take them according to the shekel of

the sanctuary (the shekel of twenty gerahs), ⁴⁸ and give the money to Aaron and his sons as the redemption price for those who are over." ⁴⁹ So Moses took the redemption money from those who were over and above those redeemed by the Levites. ⁵⁰ From the firstborn of the people of Israel he took the money, 1,365 shekels, by the shekel of the sanctuary. ⁵¹ And Moses gave the redemption money to Aaron and his sons, according to the word of the LORD, as the LORD commanded Moses.

Duties of the Kohathites

4 The LORD spoke to Moses and Aaron, saying, ² "Take a census of the sons of Kohath from among the sons of Levi, by their clans and their fathers' houses, ³ from thirty years old up to fifty years old, all who can come on duty, to do the work in the tent of meeting. ⁴ This is the service of the sons of Kohath in the tent of meeting: the most holy things. ⁵ When the camp is to set out, Aaron and his sons shall go in and take down the veil of the screen and cover the ark of the testimony with it. ⁶ Then they shall put on it a covering of goatskin and spread on top of that a cloth all of blue, and shall put in its poles. ⁷ And over the table of the bread of the Presence they shall spread a cloth of blue and put on it the plates, the dishes for incense, the bowls, and the flagons for the drink offering; the regular showbread also shall be on it. ⁸ Then they shall spread over them a cloth of scarlet and cover the same with a covering of goatskin, and shall put in its poles. ⁹ And they shall take a cloth of blue and cover the lampstand for the light, with its lamps, its tongs, its trays, and all the vessels for oil with which it is supplied. ¹⁰ And they shall put it with all its utensils in a covering of goatskin and put it on the carrying frame. ¹¹ And over the golden altar they shall spread a cloth of blue and cover it with a covering of goatskin, and shall put in its poles. ¹² And they shall take all the vessels of the service that are used in the sanctuary and put them in a cloth of blue and cover them with a covering of goatskin and put them on the carrying frame. ¹³ And they shall take away the ashes from the altar and spread a purple cloth over it. ¹⁴ And they shall put on it all the utensils of the altar, which are used for the service there, the fire pans, the forks, the shovels, and the basins, all the utensils of the altar; and they shall spread on it a covering of goatskin, and shall put in its poles. ¹⁵ And when Aaron and his sons have finished covering the sanctuary and all the furnishings of the sanctuary, as the camp sets out, after that the sons of Kohath shall come to carry these, but they must not touch the holy things, lest they die. These are the things of the tent of meeting that the sons of Kohath are to carry.

¹⁶ "And Eleazar the son of Aaron the priest shall have charge of the oil for the light, the fragrant incense, the regular grain offering, and the anointing oil, with the oversight of the whole tabernacle and all that is in it, of the sanctuary and its vessels."

¹⁷ The LORD spoke to Moses and Aaron, saying, ¹⁸ "Let not the tribe of the clans of the Kohathites be destroyed from among the Levites, ¹⁹ but deal thus with them, that they

---

> ### GETTING THE MESSAGE
>
> **Symbols of holiness** are found all throughout Numbers. The tabernacle objects that were farther from the presence of God in the Most Holy Place could be made of ordinary materials like bronze. Within the Most Holy Place, everything was overlaid with pure gold.

---

may live and not die when they come near to the most holy things: Aaron and his sons shall go in and appoint them each to his task and to his burden, ²⁰ but they shall not go in to look on the holy things even for a moment, lest they die."

²¹ The LORD spoke to Moses, saying, ²² "Take a census of the sons of Gershon also, by their fathers' houses and by their clans. ²³ From thirty years old up to fifty years old, you shall list them, all who can come to do duty, to do service in the tent of meeting. ²⁴ This is the service of the clans of the Gershonites, in serving and bearing burdens: ²⁵ they shall carry the curtains of the tabernacle and the tent of meeting with its covering and the covering of goatskin that is on top of it and the screen for the entrance of the tent of meeting ²⁶ and the hangings of the court and the screen for the entrance of the gate of the court that

is around the tabernacle and the altar, and their cords and all the equipment for their service. And they shall do all that needs to be done with regard to them. 27 All the service of the sons of the Gershonites shall be at the command of Aaron and his sons, in all that they are to carry and in all that they have to do. And you shall assign to their charge all that they are to carry. 28 This is the service of the clans of the sons of the Gershonites in the tent of meeting, and their guard duty is to be under the direction of Ithamar the son of Aaron the priest.

29 "As for the sons of Merari, you shall list them by their clans and their fathers' houses. 30 From thirty years old up to fifty years old, you shall list them, everyone who can come on duty, to do the service of the tent of meeting. 31 And this is what they are charged to carry, as the whole of their service in the tent of meeting: the frames of the tabernacle, with its bars, pillars, and bases, 32 and the pillars around the court with their bases, pegs, and cords, with all their equipment and all their accessories. And you shall list by name the objects that they are required to carry. 33 This is the service of the clans of the sons of Merari, the whole of their service in the tent of meeting, under the direction of Ithamar the son of Aaron the priest."

34 And Moses and Aaron and the chiefs of the congregation listed the sons of the Kohathites, by their clans and their fathers' houses, 35 from thirty years old up to fifty years old, everyone who could come on duty, for service in the tent of meeting; 36 and those listed by clans were 2,750. 37 This was the list of the clans of the Kohathites, all who served in the tent of meeting, whom Moses and Aaron listed according to the commandment of the LORD by Moses.

38 Those listed of the sons of Gershon, by their clans and their fathers' houses, 39 from thirty years old up to fifty years old, everyone who could come on duty for service in the tent of meeting— 40 those listed by their clans and their fathers' houses were 2,630. 41 This was the list of the clans of the sons of Gershon, all who served in the tent of meeting, whom Moses and Aaron listed according to the commandment of the LORD.

42 Those listed of the clans of the sons of Merari, by their clans and their fathers' houses, 43 from thirty years old up to fifty years old, everyone who could come on duty, for service in the tent of meeting— 44 those listed by clans were 3,200. 45 This was the list of the clans of the sons of Merari, whom Moses and Aaron listed according to the commandment of the LORD by Moses.

46 All those who were listed of the Levites, whom Moses and Aaron and the chiefs of Israel listed, by their clans and their fathers' houses, 47 from thirty years old up to fifty years old, everyone who could come to do the service of ministry and the service of bearing burdens in the tent of meeting, 48 those listed were 8,580. 49 According to the commandment of the LORD through Moses they were listed, each one with his task of serving or carrying. Thus they were listed by him, as the LORD commanded Moses.

Unclean People

5 The LORD spoke to Moses, saying, 2 "Command the people of Israel that they put out of the camp everyone who is leprous[1] or has a discharge and everyone who is unclean through contact with the dead. 3 You shall put out both male and female, putting them outside the camp, that they may not defile their camp, in the midst of which I dwell." 4 And the people of Israel did so, and put them outside the camp; as the LORD said to Moses, so the people of Israel did.

Confession and Restitution

5 And the LORD spoke to Moses, saying, 6 "Speak to the people of Israel, When a man or woman commits any of the sins that people commit by breaking faith with the LORD, and that person realizes his guilt, 7 he shall confess his sin that he has committed. And he shall make full restitution for his wrong, adding a fifth to it and giving it to him to whom he did the wrong. 8 But if the man has no next of kin to whom restitution may be made for the wrong, the restitution for wrong shall go to the LORD for the priest, in addition to the ram of atonement with which atonement is made for him. 9 And every contribution, all the holy donations of the people of Israel, which they bring to the priest, shall be his. 10 Each one shall keep

[1] Leprosy was a term for several skin diseases (see Leviticus 13)

his holy donations: whatever anyone gives to the priest shall be his.'"

A Test for Adultery

¹¹ And the LORD spoke to Moses, saying, ¹² "Speak to the people of Israel, If any man's wife goes astray and breaks faith with him, ¹³ if a man lies with her sexually, and it is hidden from the eyes of her husband, and she is undetected though she has defiled herself, and there is no witness against her, since she was not taken in the act, ¹⁴ and if the spirit of jealousy comes over him and he is jealous of his wife who has defiled herself, or if the spirit of jealousy comes over him and he is jealous of his wife, though she has not defiled herself, ¹⁵ then the man shall bring his wife to the priest and bring the offering required of her, a tenth of an ephah of barley flour. He shall pour no oil on it and put no frankincense on it, for it is a grain offering of jealousy, a grain offering of remembrance, bringing iniquity to remembrance.

¹⁶ "And the priest shall bring her near and set her before the LORD. ¹⁷ And the priest shall take holy water in an earthenware vessel and take some of the dust that is on the floor of the tabernacle and put it into the water. ¹⁸ And the priest shall set the woman before the LORD and unbind the hair of the woman's head and place in her hands the grain offering of remembrance, which is the grain offering of jealousy. And in his hand the priest shall have the water of bitterness that brings the curse. ¹⁹ Then the priest shall make her take an oath, saying, 'If no man has lain with you, and if you have not turned aside to uncleanness while you were under your husband's authority, be free from this water of bitterness that brings the curse. ²⁰ But if you have gone astray, though you are under your husband's authority, and if you have defiled yourself, and some man other than your husband has lain with you, ²¹ then' (let the priest make the woman take the oath of the curse, and say to the woman) 'the LORD make you a curse and an oath among your people, when the LORD makes your thigh fall away and your body swell. ²² May this water that brings the curse pass into your bowels and make your womb swell and your thigh fall away.' And the woman shall say, 'Amen, Amen.'

²³ "Then the priest shall write these curses in a book and wash them off into the water of bitterness. ²⁴ And he shall make the woman drink the water of bitterness that brings the curse, and the water that brings the curse shall enter into her and cause bitter pain. ²⁵ And the priest shall take the grain offering of jealousy out of the woman's hand and shall wave the grain offering before the LORD and bring it to the altar. ²⁶ And the priest shall take a handful of the grain offering, as its memorial portion, and burn it on the altar, and afterward shall make the woman drink the water. ²⁷ And when he has made her drink the water, then, if she has defiled herself and has broken faith with her husband, the water that brings the curse shall enter into her and cause bitter pain, and her womb shall swell, and her thigh shall fall away, and the woman shall become a curse among her people. ²⁸ But if

---

GETTING THE MESSAGE

What is a "grain offering of jealousy"?
This was part of a ritual to determine the guilt or innocence of a woman accused of adultery (5:11–31). Oil and frankincense were not poured over this offering, as they were with other grain offerings. The lack of these elements showed that this was not a joyful occasion.

---

the woman has not defiled herself and is clean, then she shall be free and shall conceive children.

²⁹ "This is the law in cases of jealousy, when a wife, though under her husband's authority, goes astray and defiles herself, ³⁰ or when the spirit of jealousy comes over a man and he is jealous of his wife. Then he shall set the woman before the LORD, and the priest shall carry out for her all this law. ³¹ The man shall be free from iniquity, but the woman shall bear her iniquity."

The Nazirite Vow

6 And the LORD spoke to Moses, saying, ² "Speak to the people of Israel and say to them, When either a man or a woman makes a special vow, the vow of a Nazirite, to separate himself to the LORD, ³ he shall separate himself from wine and strong drink. He shall drink no vinegar made from wine or strong drink and shall not drink any juice of

grapes or eat grapes, fresh or dried. ⁴ All the days of his separation he shall eat nothing that is produced by the grapevine, not even the seeds or the skins.

⁵ "All the days of his vow of separation, no razor shall touch his head. Until the time is completed for which he separates himself to the LORD, he shall be holy. He shall let the locks of hair of his head grow long.

⁶ "All the days that he separates himself to the LORD he shall not go near a dead body. ⁷ Not even for his father or for his mother, for brother or sister, if they die, shall he make himself unclean, because his separation to God is on his head. ⁸ All the days of his separation he is holy to the LORD.

⁹ "And if any man dies very suddenly beside him and he defiles his consecrated head, then he shall shave his head on the day of his cleansing; on the seventh day he shall shave it. ¹⁰ On the eighth day he shall bring two turtledoves or two pigeons to the

GETTING THE MESSAGE

Nazirites were dedicated laypersons. Samson, Samuel, and John the Baptist were lifelong Nazirites.

priest to the entrance of the tent of meeting, ¹¹ and the priest shall offer one for a sin offering and the other for a burnt offering, and make atonement for him, because he sinned by reason of the dead body. And he shall consecrate his head that same day ¹² and separate himself to the LORD for the days of his separation and bring a male lamb a year old for a guilt offering. But the previous period shall be void, because his separation was defiled.

¹³ "And this is the law for the Nazirite, when the time of his separation has been completed: he shall be brought to the entrance of the tent of meeting, ¹⁴ and he shall bring his gift to the LORD, one male lamb a year old without blemish for a burnt offering, and one ewe lamb a year old without blemish as a sin offering, and one ram without blemish as a peace offering, ¹⁵ and a basket of unleavened bread, loaves of fine flour mixed with oil, and unleavened wafers smeared with oil, and their grain offering

and their drink offerings. ¹⁶ And the priest shall bring them before the LORD and offer his sin offering and his burnt offering, ¹⁷ and he shall offer the ram as a sacrifice of peace offering to the LORD, with the basket of unleavened bread. The priest shall offer also its grain offering and its drink offering. ¹⁸ And the Nazirite shall shave his consecrated head at the entrance of the tent of meeting and shall take the hair from his consecrated head and put it on the fire that is under the sacrifice of the peace offering. ¹⁹ And the priest shall take the shoulder of the ram, when it is boiled, and one unleavened loaf out of the basket and one unleavened wafer, and shall put them on the hands of the Nazirite, after he has shaved the hair of his consecration, ²⁰ and the priest shall wave them for a wave offering before the LORD. They are a holy portion for the priest, together with the breast that is waved and the thigh that is contributed. And after that the Nazirite may drink wine.

²¹ "This is the law of the Nazirite. But if he vows an offering to the LORD above his Nazirite vow, as he can afford, in exact accordance with the vow that he takes, then he shall do in addition to the law of the Nazirite."

Aaron's Blessing

²² The LORD spoke to Moses, saying, ²³ "Speak to Aaron and his sons, saying, Thus you shall bless the people of Israel: you shall say to them,

²⁴   The LORD bless you and keep you;
²⁵   the LORD make his face to shine upon
           you and be gracious to you;
²⁶   the LORD lift up his countenance
           upon you and give you peace.

²⁷ "So shall they put my name upon the people of Israel, and I will bless them."

Offerings at the Tabernacle's Consecration

7 On the day when Moses had finished setting up the tabernacle and had anointed and consecrated it with all its furnishings and had anointed and consecrated the altar with all its utensils, ² the chiefs of Israel, heads of their fathers' houses, who were the chiefs of the tribes, who were over those who were listed, approached ³ and brought their offerings before the LORD, six wagons

and twelve oxen, a wagon for every two of the chiefs, and for each one an ox. They brought them before the tabernacle. ⁴Then the LORD said to Moses, ⁵"Accept these from them, that they may be used in the service of the tent of meeting, and give them to the Levites, to each man according to his service." ⁶So Moses took the wagons and the oxen and gave them to the Levites. ⁷Two wagons and four oxen he gave to the sons of Gershon, according to their service. ⁸And four wagons and eight oxen he gave to the sons of Merari, according to their service, under the direction of Ithamar the son of Aaron the priest. ⁹But to the sons of Kohath he gave none, because they were charged with the service of the holy things that had to be carried on the shoulder. ¹⁰And the chiefs offered offerings for the dedication of the altar on the day it was anointed; and the chiefs offered their offering before the altar. ¹¹And the LORD said to Moses, "They shall offer their offerings, one chief each day, for the dedication of the altar."

¹²He who offered his offering the first day was Nahshon the son of Amminadab, of the tribe of Judah. ¹³And his offering was one silver plate whose weight was 130 shekels, one silver basin of 70 shekels, according to the shekel of the sanctuary, both of them full of fine flour mixed with oil for a grain offering; ¹⁴one golden dish of 10 shekels, full of incense; ¹⁵one bull from the herd, one ram, one male lamb a year old, for a burnt offering; ¹⁶one male goat for a sin offering; ¹⁷and for the sacrifice of peace offerings, two oxen, five rams, five male goats, and five male lambs a year old. This was the offering of Nahshon the son of Amminadab.

¹⁸On the second day Nethanel the son of Zuar, the chief of Issachar, made an offering. ¹⁹He offered for his offering one silver plate whose weight was 130 shekels, one silver basin of 70 shekels, according to the shekel of the sanctuary, both of them full of fine flour mixed with oil for a grain offering; ²⁰one golden dish of 10 shekels, full of incense; ²¹one bull from the herd, one ram, one male lamb a year old, for a burnt offering; ²²one male goat for a sin offering; ²³and for the sacrifice of peace offerings, two oxen, five rams, five male goats, and five male lambs a year old. This was the offering of Nethanel the son of Zuar.

²⁴On the third day Eliab the son of Helon, the chief of the people of Zebulun: ²⁵his offering was one silver plate whose weight was 130 shekels, one silver basin of 70 shekels, according to the shekel of the sanctuary, both of them full of fine flour mixed with oil for a grain offering; ²⁶one golden dish of 10 shekels, full of incense; ²⁷one bull from the herd, one ram, one male lamb a year old, for a burnt offering; ²⁸one male goat for a sin offering; ²⁹and for the sacrifice of peace offerings, two oxen, five rams, five male goats, and five male lambs a year old. This was the offering of Eliab the son of Helon.

³⁰On the fourth day Elizur the son of Shedeur, the chief of the people of Reuben: ³¹his offering was one silver plate whose weight was 130 shekels, one silver basin of 70 shekels, according to the shekel of the sanctuary, both of them full of fine flour mixed with oil for a grain offering; ³²one golden dish of 10 shekels, full of incense; ³³one bull from the herd, one ram, one male lamb a year old, for a burnt offering; ³⁴one male goat for a sin offering; ³⁵and for the sacrifice of peace offerings, two oxen, five rams, five male goats, and five male lambs a year old. This was the offering of Elizur the son of Shedeur.

³⁶On the fifth day Shelumiel the son of Zurishaddai, the chief of the people of Simeon: ³⁷his offering was one silver plate whose weight was 130 shekels, one silver basin of 70 shekels, according to the shekel of the sanctuary, both of them full of fine flour mixed with oil for a grain offering; ³⁸one golden dish of 10 shekels, full of incense; ³⁹one bull from the herd, one ram, one male lamb a year old, for a burnt offering; ⁴⁰one male goat for a sin offering; ⁴¹and for the sacrifice of peace offerings, two oxen, five rams, five male goats, and five male lambs a year old. This was the offering of Shelumiel the son of Zurishaddai.

⁴²On the sixth day Eliasaph the son of Deuel, the chief of the people of Gad: ⁴³his offering was one silver plate whose weight was 130 shekels, one silver basin of 70 shekels, according to the shekel of the sanctuary, both of them full of fine flour mixed with oil for a grain offering; ⁴⁴one golden dish of 10 shekels, full of incense; ⁴⁵one bull from the herd, one ram, one male lamb a year old, for a burnt offering; ⁴⁶one male goat

for a sin offering; ⁴⁷ and for the sacrifice of peace offerings, two oxen, five rams, five male goats, and five male lambs a year old. This was the offering of Eliasaph the son of Deuel.

⁴⁸ On the seventh day Elishama the son of Ammihud, the chief of the people of Ephraim: ⁴⁹ his offering was one silver plate whose weight was 130 shekels, one silver basin of 70 shekels, according to the shekel of the sanctuary, both of them full of fine flour mixed with oil for a grain offering; ⁵⁰ one golden dish of 10 shekels, full of incense; ⁵¹ one bull from the herd, one ram, one male lamb a year old, for a burnt offering; ⁵² one male goat for a sin offering; ⁵³ and for the sacrifice of peace offerings, two oxen, five rams, five male goats, and five male lambs a year old. This was the offering of Elishama the son of Ammihud.

⁵⁴ On the eighth day Gamaliel the son of Pedahzur, the chief of the people of Manasseh: ⁵⁵ his offering was one silver plate whose weight was 130 shekels, one silver basin of 70 shekels, according to the shekel of the sanctuary, both of them full of fine flour mixed with oil for a grain offering; ⁵⁶ one golden dish of 10 shekels, full of incense; ⁵⁷ one bull from the herd, one ram, one male lamb a year old, for a burnt offering; ⁵⁸ one male goat for a sin offering; ⁵⁹ and for the sacrifice of peace offerings, two oxen, five rams, five male goats, and five male lambs a year old. This was the offering of Gamaliel the son of Pedahzur.

⁶⁰ On the ninth day Abidan the son of Gideoni, the chief of the people of Benjamin: ⁶¹ his offering was one silver plate whose weight was 130 shekels, one silver basin of 70 shekels, according to the shekel of the sanctuary, both of them full of fine flour mixed with oil for a grain offering; ⁶² one golden dish of 10 shekels, full of incense; ⁶³ one bull from the herd, one ram, one male lamb a year old, for a burnt offering; ⁶⁴ one male goat for a sin offering; ⁶⁵ and for the sacrifice of peace offerings, two oxen, five rams, five male goats, and five male lambs a year old. This was the offering of Abidan the son of Gideoni.

⁶⁶ On the tenth day Ahiezer the son of Ammishaddai, the chief of the people of Dan: ⁶⁷ his offering was one silver plate whose weight was 130 shekels, one silver basin of 70 shekels, according to the shekel of the sanctuary, both of them full of fine flour mixed with oil for a grain offering; ⁶⁸ one golden dish of 10 shekels, full of incense; ⁶⁹ one bull from the herd, one ram, one male lamb a year old, for a burnt offering; ⁷⁰ one male goat for a sin offering; ⁷¹ and for the sacrifice of peace offerings, two oxen, five rams, five male goats, and five male lambs a year old. This was the offering of Ahiezer the son of Ammishaddai.

⁷² On the eleventh day Pagiel the son of Ochran, the chief of the people of Asher: ⁷³ his offering was one silver plate whose weight was 130 shekels, one silver basin of 70 shekels, according to the shekel of the sanctuary, both of them full of fine flour mixed with oil for a grain offering; ⁷⁴ one golden dish of 10 shekels, full of incense; ⁷⁵ one bull from the herd, one ram, one male lamb a year old, for a burnt offering; ⁷⁶ one male goat for a sin offering; ⁷⁷ and for the sacrifice of peace offerings, two oxen, five rams, five male goats, and five male lambs a year old. This was the offering of Pagiel the son of Ochran.

⁷⁸ On the twelfth day Ahira the son of Enan, the chief of the people of Naphtali: ⁷⁹ his offering was one silver plate whose weight was 130 shekels, one silver basin of 70 shekels, according to the shekel of the sanctuary, both of them full of fine flour mixed with oil for a grain offering; ⁸⁰ one golden dish of 10 shekels, full of incense; ⁸¹ one bull from the herd, one ram, one male lamb a year old, for a burnt offering; ⁸² one male goat for a sin offering; ⁸³ and for the sacrifice of peace offerings, two oxen, five rams, five male goats, and five male lambs a year old. This was the offering of Ahira the son of Enan.

⁸⁴ This was the dedication offering for the altar on the day when it was anointed, from the chiefs of Israel: twelve silver plates, twelve silver basins, twelve golden dishes, ⁸⁵ each silver plate weighing 130 shekels and each basin 70, all the silver of the vessels 2,400 shekels according to the shekel of the sanctuary, ⁸⁶ the twelve golden dishes, full of incense, weighing 10 shekels apiece according to the shekel of the sanctuary, all the gold of the dishes being 120 shekels; ⁸⁷ all the cattle for the burnt offering twelve bulls, twelve rams, twelve male lambs a year old,

with their grain offering; and twelve male goats for a sin offering; ⁸⁸ and all the cattle for the sacrifice of peace offerings twenty-four bulls, the rams sixty, the male goats sixty, the male lambs a year old sixty. This was the dedication offering for the altar after it was anointed.

⁸⁹ And when Moses went into the tent of meeting to speak with the LORD, he heard the voice speaking to him from above the mercy seat that was on the ark of the testimony, from between the two cherubim; and it spoke to him.

The Seven Lamps

8 Now the LORD spoke to Moses, saying, ² "Speak to Aaron and say to him, When you set up the lamps, the seven lamps shall give light in front of the lampstand." ³ And Aaron did so: he set up its lamps in front of the lampstand, as the LORD commanded Moses. ⁴ And this was the workmanship of the lampstand, hammered work of gold. From its base to its flowers, it was hammered work; according to the pattern that the LORD had shown Moses, so he made the lampstand.

Cleansing of the Levites

⁵ And the LORD spoke to Moses, saying, ⁶ "Take the Levites from among the people of Israel and cleanse them. ⁷ Thus you shall do to them to cleanse them: sprinkle the water of purification upon them, and let them go with a razor over all their body, and wash their clothes and cleanse themselves. ⁸ Then let them take a bull from the herd and its grain offering of fine flour mixed with oil, and you shall take another bull from the herd for a sin offering. ⁹ And you shall bring the Levites before the tent of meeting and assemble the whole congregation of the people of Israel. ¹⁰ When you bring the Levites before the LORD, the people of Israel shall lay their hands on the Levites, ¹¹ and Aaron shall offer the Levites before the LORD as a wave offering from the people of Israel, that they may do the service of the LORD. ¹² Then the Levites shall lay their hands on the heads of the bulls, and you shall offer the one for a sin offering and the other for a burnt offering to the LORD to make atonement for the Levites. ¹³ And you shall set the Levites before Aaron and his sons, and shall offer them as a wave offering to the LORD.

¹⁴ "Thus you shall separate the Levites from among the people of Israel, and the Levites shall be mine. ¹⁵ And after that the Levites shall go in to serve at the tent of meeting, when you have cleansed them and offered them as a wave offering. ¹⁶ For they are wholly given to me from among the people of Israel. Instead of all who open the womb, the firstborn of all the people of Israel, I have taken them for myself. ¹⁷ For all the firstborn among the people of Israel are mine, both of man and of beast. On the day that I struck down all the firstborn in the land of Egypt I consecrated them for myself, ¹⁸ and I have taken the Levites instead of all the firstborn among the people of Israel. ¹⁹ And I have given the Levites as a gift to Aaron and his sons from among the people of Israel, to do the service for the people of Israel at the tent of meeting and to make

GETTING THE MESSAGE

Laying on of hands in the Old Testament was used primarily in dealing with sacrificial offerings, usually animals. This act identified the animal as belonging to a particular person. The animal was seen to be taking that person's place as a sacrifice (8:12).

atonement for the people of Israel, that there may be no plague among the people of Israel when the people of Israel come near the sanctuary."

²⁰ Thus did Moses and Aaron and all the congregation of the people of Israel to the Levites. According to all that the LORD commanded Moses concerning the Levites, the people of Israel did to them. ²¹ And the Levites purified themselves from sin and washed their clothes, and Aaron offered them as a wave offering before the LORD, and Aaron made atonement for them to cleanse them. ²² And after that the Levites went in to do their service in the tent of meeting before Aaron and his sons; as the LORD had commanded Moses concerning the Levites, so they did to them.

Retirement of the Levites

²³ And the LORD spoke to Moses, saying, ²⁴ "This applies to the Levites: from twenty-five years old and upward they shall come

to do duty in the service of the tent of meeting. **25** And from the age of fifty years they shall withdraw from the duty of the service and serve no more. **26** They minister to their brothers in the tent of meeting by keeping guard, but they shall do no service. Thus shall you do to the Levites in assigning their duties."

The Passover Celebrated

9 And the LORD spoke to Moses in the wilderness of Sinai, in the first month of the second year after they had come out of the land of Egypt, saying, **2** "Let the people of Israel keep the Passover at its appointed time. **3** On the fourteenth day of this month, at twilight, you shall keep it at its appointed time; according to all its statutes and all its rules you shall keep it." **4** So Moses told the people of Israel that they should keep the

Passover. **5** And they kept the Passover in the first month, on the fourteenth day of the month, at twilight, in the wilderness of Sinai; according to all that the LORD commanded Moses, so the people of Israel did. **6** And there were certain men who were unclean through touching a dead body, so that they could not keep the Passover on that day, and they came before Moses and Aaron on that day. **7** And those men said to him, "We are unclean through touching a dead body. Why are we kept from bringing the LORD's offering at its appointed time among the people of Israel?" **8** And Moses said to them, "Wait, that I may hear what the LORD will command concerning you."

9 The LORD spoke to Moses, saying, **10** "Speak to the people of Israel, saying, If any one of you or of your descendants is unclean through touching a dead body, or is on a long journey, he shall still keep the Passover to the LORD. **11** In the second month

on the fourteenth day at twilight they shall keep it. They shall eat it with unleavened bread and bitter herbs. **12** They shall leave none of it until the morning, nor break any of its bones; according to all the statute for the Passover they shall keep it. **13** But if anyone who is clean and is not on a journey fails to keep the Passover, that person shall be cut off from his people because he did not bring the LORD's offering at its appointed time; that man shall bear his sin. **14** And if a stranger sojourns among you and would keep the Passover to the LORD, according to the statute of the Passover and according to its rule, so shall he do. You shall have one statute, both for the sojourner and for the native."

The Cloud Covering the Tabernacle

15 On the day that the tabernacle was set up, the cloud covered the tabernacle, the tent of the testimony. And at evening it was over the tabernacle like the appearance of fire until morning. **16** So it was always: the cloud covered it by day and the appearance of fire by night. **17** And whenever the cloud lifted from over the tent, after that the people of Israel set out, and in the place where the cloud settled down, there the people of Israel camped. **18** At the command of the LORD the people of Israel set out, and at the command of the LORD they camped. As long as the cloud rested over the tabernacle, they remained in camp. **19** Even when the cloud continued over the tabernacle many days, the people of Israel kept the charge of the LORD and did not set out. **20** Sometimes the cloud was a few days over the tabernacle, and according to the command of the LORD they remained in camp; then according to the command of the LORD they set out. **21** And sometimes the cloud remained from evening until morning. And when the cloud lifted in the morning, they set out, or if it continued for a day and a night, when the cloud lifted they set out. **22** Whether it was two days, or a month, or a longer time, that the cloud continued over the tabernacle, abiding there, the people of Israel remained in camp and did not set out, but when it lifted they set out. **23** At the command of the LORD they camped, and at the command of the LORD they set out. They kept the charge of the LORD, at the command of the LORD by Moses.

The Silver Trumpets

10 The LORD spoke to Moses, saying, 2 "Make two silver trumpets. Of hammered work you shall make them, and you shall use them for summoning the congregation and for breaking camp. 3 And when both are blown, all the congregation shall gather themselves to you at the entrance of the tent of meeting. 4 But if they blow only one, then the chiefs, the heads of the tribes of Israel, shall gather themselves to you. 5 When you blow an alarm, the camps that are on the east side shall set out. 6 And when you blow an alarm the second time, the camps that are on the south side shall set out. An alarm is to be blown whenever they are to set out. 7 But when the assembly is to be gathered together, you shall blow a long blast, but you shall not sound an alarm. 8 And the sons of Aaron, the priests, shall blow the trumpets. The trumpets shall be to you for a perpetual statute throughout your generations. 9 And when you go to war in your land against the adversary who oppresses you, then you shall sound an alarm with the trumpets, that you may be remembered before the LORD your God, and you shall be saved from your enemies. 10 On the day of your gladness also, and at your appointed feasts and at the beginnings of your months, you shall blow the trumpets over your burnt offerings and over the sacrifices of your peace offerings. They shall be a reminder of you before your God: I am the LORD your God."

Israel Leaves Sinai

11 In the second year, in the second month, on the twentieth day of the month, the cloud lifted from over the tabernacle of the testimony, 12 and the people of Israel set out by stages from the wilderness of Sinai. And the cloud settled down in the wilderness of Paran. 13 They set out for the first time at the command of the LORD by Moses. 14 The standard of the camp of the people of Judah set out first by their companies, and over their company was Nahshon the son of Amminadab. 15 And over the company of the tribe of the people of Issachar was Nethanel the son of Zuar. 16 And over the company of the tribe of the people of Zebulun was Eliab the son of Helon.

17 And when the tabernacle was taken down, the sons of Gershon and the sons of Merari, who carried the tabernacle, set out. 18 And the standard of the camp of Reuben set out by their companies, and over their company was Elizur the son of Shedeur. 19 And over the company of the tribe of the people of Simeon was Shelumiel the son of Zurishaddai. 20 And over the company of the tribe of the people of Gad was Eliasaph the son of Deuel.

21 Then the Kohathites set out, carrying the holy things, and the tabernacle was set up before their arrival. 22 And the standard of the camp of the people of Ephraim set out by their companies, and over their company was Elishama the son of Ammihud. 23 And over the company of the tribe of the people of Manasseh was Gamaliel the son of Pedahzur. 24 And over the company of the tribe of the people of Benjamin was Abidan the son of Gideoni.

GETTING THE MESSAGE

The **ark of the covenant** traveled in front of the Israelites as they marched to Kadesh (10:33); like the cloud (11:25), it symbolized God's presence and his guidance of the people.

25 Then the standard of the camp of the people of Dan, acting as the rear guard of all the camps, set out by their companies, and over their company was Ahiezer the son of Ammishaddai. 26 And over the company of the tribe of the people of Asher was Pagiel the son of Ochran. 27 And over the company of the tribe of the people of Naphtali was Ahira the son of Enan. 28 This was the order of march of the people of Israel by their companies, when they set out.

29 And Moses said to Hobab the son of Reuel the Midianite, Moses' father-in-law, "We are setting out for the place of which the LORD said, 'I will give it to you.' Come with us, and we will do good to you, for the LORD has promised good to Israel." 30 But he said to him, "I will not go. I will depart to my own land and to my kindred." 31 And he said, "Please do not leave us, for you know where we should camp in the wilderness, and you will serve as eyes for us. 32 And if you do go with us, whatever good the LORD will do to us, the same will we do to you."

[33] So they set out from the mount of the LORD three days' journey. And the ark of the covenant of the LORD went before them three days' journey, to seek out a resting place for them. [34] And the cloud of the LORD was over them by day, whenever they set out from the camp.

[35] And whenever the ark set out, Moses said, "Arise, O LORD, and let your enemies be scattered, and let those who hate you flee before you." [36] And when it rested, he said, "Return, O LORD, to the ten thousand thousands of Israel."

The People Complain

11 And the people complained in the hearing of the LORD about their misfortunes, and when the LORD heard it, his anger was kindled, and the fire of the LORD burned among them and consumed some outlying parts of the camp. [2] Then the people

---

GETTING THE MESSAGE

Bdellium (11:7) has been described as a precious stone similar to a pearl. It has also been described as a pale, yellow tree resin. Ancient history books tell of its being used to make perfumes, which means it was probably a resin.

---

cried out to Moses, and Moses prayed to the LORD, and the fire died down. [3] So the name of that place was called Taberah,[1] because the fire of the LORD burned among them.

[4] Now the rabble that was among them had a strong craving. And the people of Israel also wept again and said, "Oh that we had meat to eat! [5] We remember the fish we ate in Egypt that cost nothing, the cucumbers, the melons, the leeks, the onions, and the garlic. [6] But now our strength is dried up, and there is nothing at all but this manna to look at."

[7] Now the manna was like coriander seed, and its appearance like that of bdellium. [8] The people went about and gathered it and ground it in handmills or beat it in mortars and boiled it in pots and made cakes of it. And the taste of it was like the taste of cakes baked with oil. [9] When the dew fell upon the camp in the night, the manna fell with it.

[10] Moses heard the people weeping throughout their clans, everyone at the door of his tent. And the anger of the LORD blazed hotly, and Moses was displeased. [11] Moses said to the LORD, "Why have you dealt ill with your servant? And why have I not found favor in your sight, that you lay the burden of all this people on me? [12] Did I conceive all this people? Did I give them birth, that you should say to me, 'Carry them in your bosom, as a nurse carries a nursing child,' to the land that you swore to give their fathers? [13] Where am I to get meat to give to all this people? For they weep before me and say, 'Give us meat, that we may eat.' [14] I am not able to carry all this people alone; the burden is too heavy for me. [15] If you will treat me like this, kill me at once, if I find favor in your sight, that I may not see my wretchedness."

Elders Appointed to Aid Moses

[16] Then the LORD said to Moses, "Gather for me seventy men of the elders of Israel, whom you know to be the elders of the people and officers over them, and bring them to the tent of meeting, and let them take their stand there with you. [17] And I will come down and talk with you there. And I will take some of the Spirit that is on you and put it on them, and they shall bear the burden of the people with you, so that you may not bear it yourself alone. [18] And say to the people, 'Consecrate yourselves for tomorrow, and you shall eat meat, for you have wept in the hearing of the LORD, saying, "Who will give us meat to eat? For it was better for us in Egypt." Therefore the LORD will give you meat, and you shall eat. [19] You shall not eat just one day, or two days, or five days, or ten days, or twenty days, [20] but a whole month, until it comes out at your nostrils and becomes loathsome to you, because you have rejected the LORD who is among you and have wept before him, saying, "Why did we come out of Egypt?"'" [21] But Moses said, "The people among whom I am number six hundred thousand on foot, and you have said, 'I will give them meat, that they may eat a whole month!' [22] Shall flocks and herds be slaughtered for them, and be enough for them? Or shall all the fish of the sea be gathered together for them, and be enough for them?" [23] And the LORD said to Moses, "Is the LORD's hand shortened?

---

[1] Taberah means burning

Now you shall see whether my word will come true for you or not."

24 So Moses went out and told the people the words of the LORD. And he gathered seventy men of the elders of the people and placed them around the tent. 25 Then the LORD came down in the cloud and spoke to him, and took some of the Spirit that was on him and put it on the seventy elders. And as soon as the Spirit rested on them, they prophesied. But they did not continue doing it.

26 Now two men remained in the camp, one named Eldad, and the other named Medad, and the Spirit rested on them. They were among those registered, but they had not gone out to the tent, and so they prophesied in the camp. 27 And a young man ran and told Moses, "Eldad and Medad are prophesying in the camp." 28 And Joshua the son of Nun, the assistant of Moses from his youth, said, "My lord Moses, stop them." 29 But Moses said to him, "Are you jealous for my sake? Would that all the LORD's people were prophets, that the LORD would put his Spirit on them!" 30 And Moses and the elders of Israel returned to the camp.

Quail and a Plague

31 Then a wind from the LORD sprang up, and it brought quail from the sea and let them fall beside the camp, about a day's journey on this side and a day's journey on the other side, around the camp, and about two cubits above the ground. 32 And the people rose all that day and all night and all the next day, and gathered the quail. Those who gathered least gathered ten homers. And they spread them out for themselves all around the camp. 33 While the meat was yet between their teeth, before it was consumed, the anger of the LORD was kindled against the people, and the LORD struck down the people with a very great plague. 34 Therefore the name of that place was called Kibroth-hattaavah,[1] because there they buried the people who had the craving. 35 From Kibroth-hattaavah the people journeyed to Hazeroth, and they remained at Hazeroth.

Miriam and Aaron Oppose Moses

12 Miriam and Aaron spoke against Moses because of the Cushite woman whom he had married, for he had married a Cushite woman. 2 And they said, "Has the LORD indeed spoken only through Moses? Has he not spoken through us also?" And the LORD heard it. 3 Now the man Moses was very meek, more than all people who were on the face of the earth. 4 And suddenly the LORD said to Moses and to Aaron and Miriam, "Come out, you three, to the tent of meeting." And the three of them came out. 5 And the LORD came down in a pillar of cloud and stood at the entrance of the tent and called Aaron and Miriam, and they both came forward. 6 And he said, "Hear my words: If there is a prophet among you, I the LORD make myself known to him in a vision; I speak with him in a dream. 7 Not so with my servant Moses. He is faithful in all my house. 8 With him

> ### GETTING THE MESSAGE
>
> **Did Moses have a second wife?**
> The "Cushite woman" mentioned in 12:1 was probably Moses' second wife. "Cush" can refer to Ethiopia or to a much larger portion of Africa, depending on the era in biblical history. The controversy about her may have been due to ethnic prejudice. If so, God's response indicates that the Lord's people must reject such prejudice.

I speak mouth to mouth, clearly, and not in riddles, and he beholds the form of the LORD. Why then were you not afraid to speak against my servant Moses?" 9 And the anger of the LORD was kindled against them, and he departed.

10 When the cloud removed from over the tent, behold, Miriam was leprous,[2] like snow. And Aaron turned toward Miriam, and behold, she was leprous. 11 And Aaron said to Moses, "Oh, my lord, do not punish us because we have done foolishly and have sinned. 12 Let her not be as one dead, whose flesh is half eaten away when he comes out of his mother's womb." 13 And Moses cried to the LORD, "O God, please heal her—please." 14 But the LORD said to Moses, "If her father had but spit in her face, should she not be shamed seven days? Let her be shut outside the camp seven days, and after that she may

[1] *Kibroth-hattaavah* means *graves of craving* [2] *Leprosy* was a term for several skin diseases (see Leviticus 13)

be brought in again." ¹⁵ So Miriam was shut outside the camp seven days, and the people did not set out on the march till Miriam was brought in again. ¹⁶ After that the people set out from Hazeroth, and camped in the wilderness of Paran.

Spies Sent into Canaan

13 The LORD spoke to Moses, saying, ² "Send men to spy out the land of Canaan, which I am giving to the people of Israel. From each tribe of their fathers you shall send a man, every one a chief

---

PROFILE

MIRIAM

Miriam was the sister of Moses and Aaron. It was probably Miriam who saw Pharaoh's daughter rescue Moses from the water, and offered to call a Hebrew woman to nurse the child. As a result, Moses was nursed by his own mother, who was paid wages to care for him. Miriam was a prophetess. Following the exodus she led the women of Israel in song and dance to celebrate God's deliverance. Along with Aaron, she criticized Moses for marrying a Cushite woman, thus challenging his authority. God punished Miriam by inflicting her with leprosy, though she was healed after Moses prayed for her. Micah 6:4 lists Miriam alongside her brothers as one whom God appointed to lead Israel.

KEY REFERENCE: EXODUS 15:20–21

---

among them." ³ So Moses sent them from the wilderness of Paran, according to the command of the LORD, all of them men who were heads of the people of Israel. ⁴ And these were their names: From the tribe of Reuben, Shammua the son of Zaccur; ⁵ from the tribe of Simeon, Shaphat the son of Hori; ⁶ from the tribe of Judah, Caleb the son of Jephunneh; ⁷ from the tribe of Issachar, Igal the son of Joseph; ⁸ from the tribe of Ephraim, Hoshea the son of Nun; ⁹ from the tribe of Benjamin, Palti the son of Raphu; ¹⁰ from the tribe of Zebulun, Gaddiel

the son of Sodi; ¹¹ from the tribe of Joseph (that is, from the tribe of Manasseh), Gaddi the son of Susi; ¹² from the tribe of Dan, Ammiel the son of Gemalli; ¹³ from the tribe of Asher, Sethur the son of Michael; ¹⁴ from the tribe of Naphtali, Nahbi the son of Vophsi; ¹⁵ from the tribe of Gad, Geuel the son of Machi. ¹⁶ These were the names of the men whom Moses sent to spy out the land. And Moses called Hoshea the son of Nun Joshua.

¹⁷ Moses sent them to spy out the land of Canaan and said to them, "Go up into the Negeb and go up into the hill country, ¹⁸ and see what the land is, and whether the people who dwell in it are strong or weak, whether they are few or many, ¹⁹ and whether the land that they dwell in is good or bad, and whether the cities that they dwell in are camps or strongholds, ²⁰ and whether the land is rich or poor, and whether there are trees in it or not. Be of good courage and bring some of the fruit of the land." Now the time was the season of the first ripe grapes.

²¹ So they went up and spied out the land from the wilderness of Zin to Rehob, near Lebo-hamath. ²² They went up into the Negeb and came to Hebron. Ahiman, Sheshai, and Talmai, the descendants of Anak, were there. (Hebron was built seven years before Zoan in Egypt.) ²³ And they came to the Valley of Eshcol and cut down from there a branch with a single cluster of grapes, and they carried it on a pole between two of them; they also brought some pomegranates and figs. ²⁴ That place was called the Valley of Eshcol,¹ because of the cluster that the people of Israel cut down from there.

Report of the Spies

²⁵ At the end of forty days they returned from spying out the land. ²⁶ And they came to Moses and Aaron and to all the congregation of the people of Israel in the wilderness of Paran, at Kadesh. They brought back word to them and to all the congregation, and showed them the fruit of the land. ²⁷ And they told him, "We came to the land to which you sent us. It flows with milk and honey, and this is its fruit. ²⁸ However, the people who dwell in the land are strong, and the cities are fortified and very large. And besides, we saw the descendants of Anak

¹ *Eshcol* means *cluster*

there. ²⁹ The Amalekites dwell in the land of the Negeb. The Hittites, the Jebusites, and the Amorites dwell in the hill country. And the Canaanites dwell by the sea, and along the Jordan."

³⁰ But Caleb quieted the people before Moses and said, "Let us go up at once and occupy it, for we are well able to overcome it." ³¹ Then the men who had gone up with him said, "We are not able to go up against the people, for they are stronger than we are." ³² So they brought to the people of Israel a bad report of the land that they had spied out, saying, "The land, through which we have gone to spy it out, is a land that devours its inhabitants, and all the people that we saw in it are of great height. ³³ And there we saw the Nephilim (the sons of Anak, who come from the Nephilim), and we seemed to ourselves like grasshoppers, and so we seemed to them."

GETTING THE MESSAGE

Exaggerated claims? The spies' reports about the size of the people of Canaan were exaggerations calculated to scare the people (13:25–33). However, their report about the size of the cities was true. Canaanite cities of that time were large and heavily defended. The city walls were often built of stone, and some were as thick as 24 feet (7.3 m).

The People Rebel

14 Then all the congregation raised a loud cry, and the people wept that night. ² And all the people of Israel grumbled against Moses and Aaron. The whole congregation said to them, "Would that we had died in the land of Egypt! Or would that we had died in this wilderness! ³ Why is the LORD bringing us into this land, to fall by the sword? Our wives and our little ones will become a prey. Would it not be better for us to go back to Egypt?" ⁴ And they said to one another, "Let us choose a leader and go back to Egypt."

⁵ Then Moses and Aaron fell on their faces before all the assembly of the congregation of the people of Israel. ⁶ And Joshua the son of Nun and Caleb the son of Jephunneh, who were among those who had spied out

the land, tore their clothes ⁷ and said to all the congregation of the people of Israel, "The land, which we passed through to spy it out, is an exceedingly good land. ⁸ If the LORD delights in us, he will bring us into this land and give it to us, a land that flows with milk and honey. ⁹ Only do not rebel against the LORD. And do not fear the people of the land, for they are bread for us. Their protection is removed from them, and the LORD is with us; do not fear them." ¹⁰ Then

all the congregation said to stone them with stones. But the glory of the LORD appeared at the tent of meeting to all the people of Israel. ¹¹ And the LORD said to Moses, "How long will this people despise me? And how long will they not believe in me, in spite of all the signs that I have done among them? ¹² I will strike them with the pestilence and disinherit them, and I will make of you a nation greater and mightier than they."

Moses Intercedes for the People

¹³ But Moses said to the LORD, "Then the Egyptians will hear of it, for you brought

up this people in your might from among them, [14] and they will tell the inhabitants of this land. They have heard that you, O LORD, are in the midst of this people. For you, O LORD, are seen face to face, and your cloud stands over them and you go before them, in a pillar of cloud by day and in a pillar of fire by night. [15] Now if you kill this people as one man, then the nations who have heard your fame will say, [16] 'It is because the LORD was not able to bring this people into the land that he swore to give to them that he has killed them in the wilderness.' [17] And now, please let the power of the Lord be great as you have promised, saying, [18] 'The LORD is slow to anger and abounding in steadfast love, forgiving iniquity and transgression, but he will by no means clear the guilty, visiting the iniquity of the fathers on the children, to the third and the fourth generation.' [19] Please pardon the iniquity of this people, according to the greatness of your steadfast love, just as you have forgiven this people, from Egypt until now."

GETTING THE MESSAGE

God's **glory** (14:21) refers to his measureless power and splendor.

God Promises Judgment

[20] Then the LORD said, "I have pardoned, according to your word. [21] But truly, as I live, and as all the earth shall be filled with the glory of the LORD, [22] none of the men who have seen my glory and my signs that I did in Egypt and in the wilderness, and yet have put me to the test these ten times and have not obeyed my voice, [23] shall see the land that I swore to give to their fathers. And none of those who despised me shall see it. [24] But my servant Caleb, because he has a different spirit and has followed me fully, I will bring into the land into which he went, and his descendants shall possess it. [25] Now, since the Amalekites and the Canaanites dwell in the valleys, turn tomorrow and set out for the wilderness by the way to the Red Sea."

[26] And the LORD spoke to Moses and to Aaron, saying, [27] "How long shall this wicked congregation grumble against me? I have heard the grumblings of the people of Israel, which they grumble against me. [28] Say

to them, 'As I live, declares the LORD, what you have said in my hearing I will do to you: [29] your dead bodies shall fall in this wilderness, and of all your number, listed in the census from twenty years old and upward, who have grumbled against me, [30] not one shall come into the land where I swore that I would make you dwell, except Caleb the son of Jephunneh and Joshua the son of Nun. [31] But your little ones, who you said would become a prey, I will bring in, and they shall know the land that you have rejected. [32] But as for you, your dead bodies shall fall in this wilderness. [33] And your children shall be shepherds in the wilderness forty years and shall suffer for your faithlessness, until the last of your dead bodies lies in the wilderness. [34] According to the number of the days in which you spied out the land, forty days, a year for each day, you shall bear your iniquity forty years, and you shall know my displeasure.' [35] I, the LORD, have spoken. Surely this will I do to all this wicked congregation who are gathered together against me: in this wilderness they shall come to a full end, and there they shall die."

[36] And the men whom Moses sent to spy out the land, who returned and made all the congregation grumble against him by bringing up a bad report about the land— [37] the men who brought up a bad report of the land—died by plague before the LORD. [38] Of those men who went to spy out the land, only Joshua the son of Nun and Caleb the son of Jephunneh remained alive.

Israel Defeated in Battle

[39] When Moses told these words to all the people of Israel, the people mourned greatly. [40] And they rose early in the morning and went up to the heights of the hill country, saying, "Here we are. We will go up to the place that the LORD has promised, for we have sinned." [41] But Moses said, "Why now are you transgressing the command of the LORD, when that will not succeed? [42] Do not go up, for the Lord is not among you, lest you be struck down before your enemies. [43] For there the Amalekites and the Canaanites are facing you, and you shall fall by the sword. Because you have turned back from following the LORD, the LORD will not be with you." [44] But they presumed to go up to the heights of the hill country, although neither the ark of the covenant of the LORD nor

Moses departed out of the camp. ⁴⁵ Then the Amalekites and the Canaanites who lived in that hill country came down and defeated them and pursued them, even to Hormah.

Laws About Sacrifices

15 The LORD spoke to Moses, saying, ² "Speak to the people of Israel and say to them, When you come into the land you are to inhabit, which I am giving you, ³ and you offer to the LORD from the herd or from the flock a food offering or a burnt offering or a sacrifice, to fulfill a vow or as a freewill offering or at your appointed feasts, to make a pleasing aroma to the LORD, ⁴ then he who brings his offering shall offer to the LORD a grain offering of a tenth of an ephah of fine flour, mixed with a quarter of a hin of oil; ⁵ and you shall offer with the burnt offering, or for the sacrifice, a quarter of a hin of wine for the drink offering for each lamb. ⁶ Or for a ram, you shall offer for a grain offering two tenths of an ephah of fine flour mixed with a third of a hin of oil. ⁷ And for the drink offering you shall offer a third of a hin of wine, a pleasing aroma to the LORD. ⁸ And when you offer a bull as a burnt offering or sacrifice, to fulfill a vow or for peace offerings to the LORD, ⁹ then one shall offer with the bull a grain offering of three tenths of an ephah of fine flour, mixed with half a hin of oil. ¹⁰ And you shall offer for the drink offering half a hin of wine, as a food offering, a pleasing aroma to the LORD.

¹¹ "Thus it shall be done for each bull or ram, or for each lamb or young goat. ¹² As many as you offer, so shall you do with each one, as many as there are. ¹³ Every native Israelite shall do these things in this way, in offering a food offering, with a pleasing aroma to the LORD. ¹⁴ And if a stranger is sojourning with you, or anyone is living permanently among you, and he wishes to offer a food offering, with a pleasing aroma to the LORD, he shall do as you do. ¹⁵ For the assembly, there shall be one statute for you and for the stranger who sojourns with you, a statute forever throughout your generations. You and the sojourner shall be alike before the LORD. ¹⁶ One law and one rule shall be for you and for the stranger who sojourns with you."

¹⁷ The LORD spoke to Moses, saying, ¹⁸ "Speak to the people of Israel and say to them, When you come into the land to which I bring you ¹⁹ and when you eat of the bread of the land, you shall present a contribution to the LORD. ²⁰ Of the first of your dough you shall present a loaf as a contribution; like a contribution from the threshing floor, so shall you present it. ²¹ Some of the first of your dough you shall give to the LORD as a contribution throughout your generations.

Laws About Unintentional Sins

²² "But if you sin unintentionally, and do not observe all these commandments that the LORD has spoken to Moses, ²³ all that the LORD has commanded you by Moses, from the day that the LORD gave commandment, and onward throughout your generations, ²⁴ then if it was done unintentionally without the knowledge of the congregation, all the congregation shall offer one bull from the herd for a burnt offering, a pleasing aroma to the LORD, with its grain offering and its drink offering, according to the rule, and one male goat for a sin offering. ²⁵ And the priest shall make atonement for all the congregation of the people of Israel, and they shall be forgiven, because it was a mistake, and they have brought their offering, a food offering to the LORD, and their sin offering before the LORD for their mistake. ²⁶ And all the congregation of the people of Israel shall be forgiven, and the stranger who sojourns among them, because the whole population was involved in the mistake.

²⁷ "If one person sins unintentionally, he shall offer a female goat a year old for a sin offering. ²⁸ And the priest shall make atonement before the LORD for the person who makes a mistake, when he sins unintentionally, to make atonement for him, and he shall be forgiven. ²⁹ You shall have one law for him who does anything unintentionally, for him who is native among the people of Israel and for the stranger who sojourns among them. ³⁰ But the person who does anything with a high hand, whether he is native or a sojourner, reviles the LORD, and that person shall be cut off from among his people. ³¹ Because he has despised the word of the LORD and has broken his commandment, that person shall be utterly cut off; his iniquity shall be on him."

A Sabbathbreaker Executed

³² While the people of Israel were in the wilderness, they found a man gathering sticks on the Sabbath day. ³³ And those who found him gathering sticks brought him to Moses and Aaron and to all the congregation. ³⁴ They put him in custody, because it had not been made clear what should be done to him. ³⁵ And the LORD said to Moses, "The man shall be put to death; all the congregation shall stone him with stones outside the camp." ³⁶ And all the congregation

PROFILE
KORAH

Korah, who was from the tribe of Levi, led a rebellion against Moses and Aaron. Dathan, Abiram, and 250 well-known chiefs of the congregation joined with him. Korah and his men accused Moses and Aaron of exalting themselves above the people of Israel. They failed to recognize, however, that it is God who gives authority to whomever he chooses. As punishment for their rebellion, Korah, Dathan, and Abiram, together with their households and possessions, were swallowed up by the earth in front of the people of Israel. God sent fire to consume the 250 chiefs. The people of Israel grumbled against Moses and Aaron and remained sympathetic to the punished rebels, so God sent a plague as further punishment.

KEY REFERENCE: NUMBERS 16:31-35

brought him outside the camp and stoned him to death with stones, as the LORD commanded Moses.

Tassels on Garments

³⁷ The LORD said to Moses, ³⁸ "Speak to the people of Israel, and tell them to make tassels on the corners of their garments throughout their generations, and to put a cord of blue on the tassel of each corner. ³⁹ And it shall be a tassel for you to look at and remember all the commandments of the LORD, to do them, not to follow after your own heart and your own eyes, which you are inclined to whore after. ⁴⁰ So you shall remember and do all my commandments, and be holy to your God. ⁴¹ I am the LORD your God, who brought you out of the land of Egypt to be your God: I am the LORD your God."

Korah's Rebellion

16 Now Korah the son of Izhar, son of Kohath, son of Levi, and Dathan and Abiram the sons of Eliab, and On the son of Peleth, sons of Reuben, took men. ² And they rose up before Moses, with a number of the people of Israel, 250 chiefs of the congregation, chosen from the assembly, well-known men. ³ They assembled themselves together against Moses and against Aaron and said to them, "You have gone too far! For all in the congregation are holy, every one of them, and the LORD is among them. Why then do you exalt yourselves above the assembly of the LORD?" ⁴ When Moses heard it, he fell on his face, ⁵ and he said to Korah and all his company, "In the morning the LORD will show who is his, and who is holy, and will bring him near to him. The one whom he chooses he will bring near to him. ⁶ Do this: take censers, Korah and all his company; ⁷ put fire in them and put incense on them before the LORD tomorrow, and the man whom the LORD chooses shall be the holy one. You have gone too far, sons of Levi!" ⁸ And Moses said to Korah, "Hear now, you sons of Levi: ⁹ is it too small a thing for you that the God of Israel has separated you from the congregation of Israel, to bring you near to himself, to do service in the tabernacle of the LORD and to stand before the congregation to minister to them, ¹⁰ and that he has brought you near him, and all your brothers the sons of Levi with you? And would you seek the priesthood also? ¹¹ Therefore it is against the LORD that you and all your company have gathered together. What is Aaron that you grumble against him?"

¹² And Moses sent to call Dathan and Abiram the sons of Eliab, and they said, "We will not come up. ¹³ Is it a small thing that you have brought us up out of a land flowing with milk and honey, to kill us in the wilderness, that you must also make yourself a prince over us? ¹⁴ Moreover, you have not brought us into a land flowing with milk and honey, nor given us inheritance of fields and vineyards. Will you put out the eyes of these men? We will not come up."

¹⁵ And Moses was very angry and said to the LORD, "Do not respect their offering. I have not taken one donkey from them, and I have not harmed one of them."

¹⁶ And Moses said to Korah, "Be present, you and all your company, before the LORD, you and they, and Aaron, tomorrow. ¹⁷ And let every one of you take his censer and put incense on it, and every one of you bring before the LORD his censer, 250 censers; you also, and Aaron, each his censer." ¹⁸ So every man took his censer and put fire in them and laid incense on them and stood at the entrance of the tent of meeting with Moses and Aaron. ¹⁹ Then Korah assembled all the congregation against them at the entrance of the tent of meeting. And the glory of the LORD appeared to all the congregation.

²⁰ And the LORD spoke to Moses and to Aaron, saying, ²¹ "Separate yourselves from among this congregation, that I may consume them in a moment." ²² And they fell on their faces and said, "O God, the God of the spirits of all flesh, shall one man sin, and will you be angry with all the congregation?" ²³ And the LORD spoke to Moses, saying, ²⁴ "Say to the congregation, Get away from the dwelling of Korah, Dathan, and Abiram."

²⁵ Then Moses rose and went to Dathan and Abiram, and the elders of Israel followed him. ²⁶ And he spoke to the congregation, saying, "Depart, please, from the tents of these wicked men, and touch nothing of theirs, lest you be swept away with all their sins." ²⁷ So they got away from the dwelling of Korah, Dathan, and Abiram. And Dathan and Abiram came out and stood at the door of their tents, together with their wives, their sons, and their little ones. ²⁸ And Moses said, "Hereby you shall know that the LORD has sent me to do all these works, and that it has not been of my own accord. ²⁹ If these men die as all men die, or if they are visited by the fate of all mankind, then the LORD has not sent me. ³⁰ But if the LORD creates something new, and the ground opens its mouth and swallows them up with all that belongs to them, and they go down alive into Sheol, then you shall know that these men have despised the LORD."

³¹ And as soon as he had finished speaking all these words, the ground under them split apart. ³² And the earth opened its mouth and swallowed them up, with their households and all the people who belonged to Korah and all their goods. ³³ So they and all that belonged to them went down alive into Sheol, and the earth closed over them, and they perished from the midst of the assembly. ³⁴ And all Israel who were around them fled at their cry, for they said, "Lest the earth swallow us up!" ³⁵ And fire came out from the LORD and consumed the 250 men offering the incense.

³⁶ Then the LORD spoke to Moses, saying, ³⁷ "Tell Eleazar the son of Aaron the priest to take up the censers out of the blaze. Then scatter the fire far and wide, for they have become holy. ³⁸ As for the censers of these men who have sinned at the cost of their lives, let them be made into hammered plates as a covering for the altar, for they offered them before the LORD, and they became holy. Thus they shall be a sign to the

GETTING THE MESSAGE

What is a censer? A censer (16:17) was a vessel used for burning incense before the Lord. Censers were usually made of stone, but portable ones could be made of bronze. They held live coals for burning the incense.

people of Israel." ³⁹ So Eleazar the priest took the bronze censers, which those who were burned had offered, and they were hammered out as a covering for the altar, ⁴⁰ to be a reminder to the people of Israel, so that no outsider, who is not of the descendants of Aaron, should draw near to burn incense before the LORD, lest he become like Korah and his company—as the LORD said to him through Moses.

⁴¹ But on the next day all the congregation of the people of Israel grumbled against Moses and against Aaron, saying, "You have killed the people of the LORD." ⁴² And when the congregation had assembled against Moses and against Aaron, they turned toward the tent of meeting. And behold, the cloud covered it, and the glory of the LORD appeared. ⁴³ And Moses and Aaron came to the front of the tent of meeting, ⁴⁴ and the LORD spoke to Moses, saying, ⁴⁵ "Get away from the midst of this congregation, that

I may consume them in a moment." And they fell on their faces. ⁴⁶ And Moses said to Aaron, "Take your censer, and put fire on it from off the altar and lay incense on it and carry it quickly to the congregation and make atonement for them, for wrath has gone out from the LORD; the plague has begun." ⁴⁷ So Aaron took it as Moses said and ran into the midst of the assembly. And behold, the plague had already begun among the people. And he put on the incense and made atonement for the people. ⁴⁸ And he stood between the dead and the living, and the plague was stopped. ⁴⁹ Now those who died in the plague were 14,700, besides those who died in the affair of Korah. ⁵⁰ And Aaron returned to Moses at the entrance of the tent of meeting, when the plague was stopped.

Aaron's Staff Buds

17 The LORD spoke to Moses, saying, ² "Speak to the people of Israel, and get from them staffs, one for each fathers' house, from all their chiefs according to their fathers' houses, twelve staffs. Write each man's name on his staff, ³ and write Aaron's name on the staff of Levi. For there shall be one staff for the head of each fathers' house. ⁴ Then you shall deposit them in the tent of meeting before the testimony, where I meet with you. ⁵ And the staff of the man whom I choose shall sprout. Thus I will make to cease from me the grumblings of the people of Israel, which they grumble against you." ⁶ Moses spoke to the people of Israel. And all their chiefs gave him staffs, one for each chief, according to their fathers' houses, twelve staffs. And the staff of Aaron was among their staffs. ⁷ And Moses deposited the staffs before the LORD in the tent of the testimony.

⁸ On the next day Moses went into the tent of the testimony, and behold, the staff of Aaron for the house of Levi had sprouted and put forth buds and produced blossoms, and it bore ripe almonds. ⁹ Then Moses brought out all the staffs from before the LORD to all the people of Israel. And they looked, and each man took his staff. ¹⁰ And the LORD said to Moses, "Put back the staff of Aaron before the testimony, to be kept as a sign for the rebels, that you may make an end of their grumblings against me, lest

they die." ¹¹ Thus did Moses; as the LORD commanded him, so he did.

¹² And the people of Israel said to Moses, "Behold, we perish, we are undone, we are all undone. ¹³ Everyone who comes near, who comes near to the tabernacle of the LORD, shall die. Are we all to perish?"

Duties of Priests and Levites

18 So the LORD said to Aaron, "You and your sons and your father's house with you shall bear iniquity connected with the sanctuary, and you and your sons with you shall bear iniquity connected with your priesthood. ² And with you bring your brothers also, the tribe of Levi, the tribe of your father, that they may join you and minister to you while you and your sons with you are before the tent of the testimony. ³ They shall keep guard over you and over the whole tent, but shall not come near to the vessels of the sanctuary or to the altar lest they, and you, die. ⁴ They shall join you and keep guard over the tent of meeting for all the service of the tent, and no outsider shall come near you. ⁵ And you shall keep guard over the sanctuary and over the altar, that there may never again be wrath on the people of Israel. ⁶ And behold, I have taken your brothers the Levites from among the people of Israel. They are a gift to you, given to the LORD, to do the service of the tent of meeting. ⁷ And you and your sons with you shall guard your priesthood for all that concerns the altar and that is within the veil; and you shall serve. I give your priesthood as a gift, and any outsider who comes near shall be put to death."

⁸ Then the LORD spoke to Aaron, "Behold, I have given you charge of the contributions made to me, all the consecrated things of the people of Israel. I have given them to you as a portion and to your sons as a perpetual due. ⁹ This shall be yours of the most holy things, reserved from the fire: every offering of theirs, every grain offering of theirs and every sin offering of theirs and every guilt offering of theirs, which they render to me, shall be most holy to you and to your sons. ¹⁰ In a most holy place shall you eat it. Every male may eat it; it is holy to you. ¹¹ This also is yours: the contribution of their gift, all the wave offerings of the people of Israel. I have given them to you, and to your sons and daughters with you, as a perpetual

due. Everyone who is clean in your house may eat it. ¹²All the best of the oil and all the best of the wine and of the grain, the firstfruits of what they give to the LORD, I give to you. ¹³The first ripe fruits of all that is in their land, which they bring to the LORD, shall be yours. Everyone who is clean in your house may eat it. ¹⁴Every devoted thing in Israel shall be yours. ¹⁵Everything that opens the womb of all flesh, whether man or beast, which they offer to the LORD, shall be yours. Nevertheless, the firstborn of man you shall redeem, and the firstborn of unclean animals you shall redeem. ¹⁶And their redemption price (at a month old you shall redeem them) you shall fix at five shekels in silver, according to the shekel of the sanctuary, which is twenty gerahs. ¹⁷But the firstborn of a cow, or the firstborn of a sheep, or the firstborn of a goat, you shall not redeem; they are holy. You shall sprinkle their blood on the altar and shall burn their fat as a food offering, with a pleasing aroma to the LORD. ¹⁸But their flesh shall be yours, as the breast that is waved and as the right thigh are yours. ¹⁹All the holy contributions that the people of Israel present to the LORD I give to you, and to your sons and daughters with you, as a perpetual due. It is a covenant of salt forever before the LORD for you and for your offspring with you." ²⁰And the LORD said to Aaron, "You shall have no inheritance in their land, neither shall you have any portion among them. I am your portion and your inheritance among the people of Israel.

²¹"To the Levites I have given every tithe in Israel for an inheritance, in return for their service that they do, their service in the tent of meeting, ²²so that the people of Israel do not come near the tent of meeting, lest they bear sin and die. ²³But the Levites shall do the service of the tent of meeting, and they shall bear their iniquity. It shall be a perpetual statute throughout your generations, and among the people of Israel they shall have no inheritance. ²⁴For the tithe of the people of Israel, which they present as a contribution to the LORD, I have given to the Levites for an inheritance. Therefore I have said of them that they shall have no inheritance among the people of Israel."

²⁵And the LORD spoke to Moses, saying, ²⁶"Moreover, you shall speak and say to the Levites, 'When you take from the people of Israel the tithe that I have given you from them for your inheritance, then you shall present a contribution from it to the LORD, a tithe of the tithe. ²⁷And your contribution shall be counted to you as though it were the grain of the threshing floor, and as the fullness of the winepress. ²⁸So you shall also present a contribution to the LORD from all your tithes, which you receive from the people of Israel. And from it you shall give the LORD's contribution to Aaron the priest. ²⁹Out of all the gifts to you, you shall present every contribution due to the LORD; from each its best part is to be dedicated.' ³⁰Therefore you shall say to them, 'When you have offered from it the best of it, then the rest shall be counted to the Levites as produce of the threshing floor, and as produce of the winepress. ³¹And you may eat it

in any place, you and your households, for it is your reward in return for your service in the tent of meeting. ³²And you shall bear no sin by reason of it, when you have contributed the best of it. But you shall not profane the holy things of the people of Israel, lest you die.'"

Laws for Purification

19 Now the LORD spoke to Moses and to Aaron, saying, ²"This is the statute of the law that the LORD has commanded: Tell the people of Israel to bring you a red heifer without defect, in which there is no blemish, and on which a yoke has never come. ³And you shall give it to Eleazar the priest, and it shall be taken outside the camp and slaughtered before him. ⁴And Eleazar the priest shall take some of its blood with his finger, and sprinkle some of its blood toward the front of the tent of meeting seven times. ⁵And the heifer shall be burned in his sight. Its skin, its flesh, and its blood, with

its dung, shall be burned. ⁶ And the priest shall take cedarwood and hyssop and scarlet yarn, and throw them into the fire burning the heifer. ⁷ Then the priest shall wash his clothes and bathe his body in water, and afterward he may come into the camp. But the priest shall be unclean until evening. ⁸ The one who burns the heifer shall wash his clothes in water and bathe his body in water and shall be unclean until evening. ⁹ And a man who is clean shall gather up the ashes of the heifer and deposit them outside the camp in a clean place. And they shall be kept for the water for impurity for the congregation of the people of Israel; it is a sin offering. ¹⁰ And the one who gathers the ashes of the heifer shall wash his clothes and be unclean until evening. And this shall be a perpetual statute for the people of Israel, and for the stranger who sojourns among them.

¹¹ "Whoever touches the dead body of any person shall be unclean seven days. ¹² He shall cleanse himself with the water on the third day and on the seventh day, and so be clean. But if he does not cleanse himself on the third day and on the seventh day, he will not become clean. ¹³ Whoever touches a dead person, the body of anyone who has died, and does not cleanse himself, defiles the tabernacle of the LORD, and that person shall be cut off from Israel; because the water for impurity was not thrown on him, he shall be unclean. His uncleanness is still on him.

¹⁴ "This is the law when someone dies in a tent: everyone who comes into the tent and everyone who is in the tent shall be unclean seven days. ¹⁵ And every open vessel that has no cover fastened on it is unclean. ¹⁶ Whoever in the open field touches someone who was killed with a sword or who died naturally, or touches a human bone or a grave, shall be unclean seven days. ¹⁷ For the unclean they shall take some ashes of the burnt sin offering, and fresh water shall be added in a vessel. ¹⁸ Then a clean person shall take hyssop and dip it in the water and sprinkle it on the tent and on all the furnishings and on the persons who were there and on whoever touched the bone, or the slain or the dead or the grave. ¹⁹ And the clean person shall sprinkle it on the unclean on the third day and on the seventh day. Thus

on the seventh day he shall cleanse him, and he shall wash his clothes and bathe himself in water, and at evening he shall be clean. ²⁰ "If the man who is unclean does not cleanse himself, that person shall be cut off from the midst of the assembly, since he has defiled the sanctuary of the LORD. Because the water for impurity has not been thrown on him, he is unclean. ²¹ And it shall be a statute forever for them. The one who sprinkles the water for impurity shall wash his clothes, and the one who touches the water for impurity shall be unclean until evening. ²² And whatever the unclean person touches shall be unclean, and anyone who touches it shall be unclean until evening."

The Death of Miriam

20 And the people of Israel, the whole congregation, came into the wilderness of Zin in the first month, and the people stayed in Kadesh. And Miriam died there and was buried there.

The Waters of Meribah

² Now there was no water for the congregation. And they assembled themselves together against Moses and against Aaron. ³ And the people quarreled with Moses and said, "Would that we had perished when our brothers perished before the LORD! ⁴ Why have you brought the assembly of the LORD into this wilderness, that we should die here, both we and our cattle? ⁵ And why have you made us come up out of Egypt to bring us to this evil place? It is no place for grain or figs or vines or pomegranates, and there is no water to drink." ⁶ Then Moses and Aaron went from the presence of the assembly to the entrance of the tent of meeting and fell on their faces. And the glory of the LORD appeared to them, ⁷ and the LORD spoke to Moses, saying, ⁸ "Take the staff, and assemble the congregation, you and Aaron your brother, and tell the rock before their eyes to yield its water. So you shall bring water out of the rock for them and give drink to the congregation and their cattle." ⁹ And Moses took the staff from before the LORD, as he commanded him.

Moses Strikes the Rock

¹⁰ Then Moses and Aaron gathered the assembly together before the rock, and he said to them, "Hear now, you rebels: shall we bring water for you out of this rock?"

¹¹ And Moses lifted up his hand and struck the rock with his staff twice, and water came out abundantly, and the congregation drank, and their livestock. ¹² And the LORD said to Moses and Aaron, "Because you did not believe in me, to uphold me as holy in the eyes of the people of Israel, therefore you shall not bring this assembly into the land that I have given them." ¹³ These are the waters of Meribah, where the people of Israel quarreled with the LORD, and through them he showed himself holy.

Edom Refuses Passage

¹⁴ Moses sent messengers from Kadesh to the king of Edom: "Thus says your brother Israel: You know all the hardship that we have met: ¹⁵ how our fathers went down to Egypt, and we lived in Egypt a long time. And the Egyptians dealt harshly with us and our fathers. ¹⁶ And when we cried to the LORD, he heard our voice and sent an angel and brought us out of Egypt. And here we are in Kadesh, a city on the edge of your territory. ¹⁷ Please let us pass through your land. We will not pass through field or vineyard, or drink water from a well. We will go along the King's Highway. We will not turn aside to the right hand or to the left until we have passed through your territory." ¹⁸ But Edom said to him, "You shall not pass through, lest I come out with the sword against you." ¹⁹ And the people of Israel said to him, "We will go up by the highway, and if we drink of your water, I and my livestock, then I will pay for it. Let me only pass through on foot, nothing more." ²⁰ But he said, "You shall not pass through." And Edom came out against them with a large army and with a strong force. ²¹ Thus Edom refused to give Israel passage through his territory, so Israel turned away from him.

The Death of Aaron

²² And they journeyed from Kadesh, and the people of Israel, the whole congregation, came to Mount Hor. ²³ And the LORD said to Moses and Aaron at Mount Hor, on the border of the land of Edom, ²⁴ "Let Aaron be gathered to his people, for he shall not enter the land that I have given to the people of Israel, because you rebelled against my command at the waters of Meribah. ²⁵ Take Aaron and Eleazar his son and bring them up to Mount Hor. ²⁶ And strip Aaron of his garments and put them on Eleazar his son. And Aaron shall be gathered to his people and shall die there." ²⁷ Moses did as the LORD commanded. And they went up Mount Hor in the sight of all the congregation. ²⁸ And Moses stripped Aaron of his garments and put them on Eleazar his son. And Aaron died there on the top of the mountain. Then Moses and Eleazar came down from the mountain. ²⁹ And when all the congregation saw that Aaron had perished, all the house of Israel wept for Aaron thirty days.

Arad Destroyed

21 When the Canaanite, the king of Arad, who lived in the Negeb, heard that Israel was coming by the way of Atharim, he fought against Israel, and took some of them captive. ² And Israel vowed a vow

---

> **GETTING THE MESSAGE**
>
> **The King's Highway** (20:17) is the main trade route from Damascus to Arabia. It runs north to south, east of the Jordan River and Dead Sea. The King's Highway has been in continuous use for more than 3,000 years.

---

to the LORD and said, "If you will indeed give this people into my hand, then I will devote their cities to destruction."[1] ³ And the LORD heeded the voice of Israel and gave over the Canaanites, and they devoted them and their cities to destruction. So the name of the place was called Hormah.[2]

The Bronze Serpent

⁴ From Mount Hor they set out by the way to the Red Sea, to go around the land of Edom. And the people became impatient on the way. ⁵ And the people spoke against God and against Moses, "Why have you brought us up out of Egypt to die in the wilderness? For there is no food and no water, and we loathe this worthless food." ⁶ Then the LORD sent fiery serpents among the people, and they bit the people, so that many people of Israel died. ⁷ And the people came to Moses and said, "We have sinned, for we have spoken against the LORD and against you. Pray to the LORD,

---

[1] That is, destroy or make an offering because of sin, at God's command; also 21:3 [2] *Hormah* means *destruction*

that he take away the serpents from us." So Moses prayed for the people. ⁸ And the LORD said to Moses, "Make a fiery serpent and set it on a pole, and everyone who is bitten, when he sees it, shall live." ⁹ So Moses made a bronze serpent and set it on a pole. And if a serpent bit anyone, he would look at the bronze serpent and live.

The Song of the Well

¹⁰ And the people of Israel set out and camped in Oboth. ¹¹ And they set out from Oboth and camped at Iye-abarim, in the wilderness that is opposite Moab, toward the sunrise. ¹² From there they set out and camped in the Valley of Zered. ¹³ From there they set out and camped on the other side of the Arnon, which is in the wilderness that extends from the border of the Amorites, for the Arnon is the border of Moab, between

> ### GETTING THE MESSAGE
>
> **The bronze serpent.** When the people of Israel looked upon the serpent in order to live (21:9), it was a prophetic picture of the day when believers would look to the crucified Christ for salvation (John 3:14–15).

Moab and the Amorites. ¹⁴ Therefore it is said in the Book of the Wars of the LORD,

> "Waheb in Suphah, and the valleys of the Arnon,
> ¹⁵ and the slope of the valleys
> that extends to the seat of Ar,
> and leans to the border of Moab."

¹⁶ And from there they continued to Beer; that is the well of which the LORD said to Moses, "Gather the people together, so that I may give them water." ¹⁷ Then Israel sang this song:

> "Spring up, O well!—Sing to it!—
> ¹⁸ the well that the princes made,
> that the nobles of the people dug,
> with the scepter and with their staffs."

And from the wilderness they went on to Mattanah, ¹⁹ and from Mattanah to Nahaliel, and from Nahaliel to Bamoth, ²⁰ and from Bamoth to the valley lying in the region of Moab by the top of Pisgah that looks down on the desert.

King Sihon Defeated

²¹ Then Israel sent messengers to Sihon king of the Amorites, saying, ²² "Let me pass through your land. We will not turn aside into field or vineyard. We will not drink the water of a well. We will go by the King's Highway until we have passed through your territory." ²³ But Sihon would not allow Israel to pass through his territory. He gathered all his people together and went out against Israel to the wilderness and came to Jahaz and fought against Israel. ²⁴ And Israel defeated him with the edge of the sword and took possession of his land from the Arnon to the Jabbok, as far as to the Ammonites, for the border of the Ammonites was strong. ²⁵ And Israel took all these cities, and Israel settled in all the cities of the Amorites, in Heshbon, and in all its villages. ²⁶ For Heshbon was the city of Sihon the king of the Amorites, who had fought against the former king of Moab and taken all his land out of his hand, as far as the Arnon. ²⁷ Therefore the ballad singers say,

> "Come to Heshbon, let it be built;
>   let the city of Sihon be established.
> ²⁸ For fire came out from Heshbon,
>   flame from the city of Sihon.
> It devoured Ar of Moab,
>   and swallowed the heights of the Arnon.
> ²⁹ Woe to you, O Moab!
>   You are undone, O people of Chemosh!
> He has made his sons fugitives,
>   and his daughters captives,
>   to an Amorite king, Sihon.
> ³⁰ So we overthrew them;
>   Heshbon, as far as Dibon, perished;
>   and we laid waste as far as Nophah;
>   fire spread as far as Medeba."

King Og Defeated

³¹ Thus Israel lived in the land of the Amorites. ³² And Moses sent to spy out Jazer, and they captured its villages and dispossessed the Amorites who were there. ³³ Then they turned and went up by the way to Bashan. And Og the king of Bashan came out against them, he and all his people, to battle at Edrei. ³⁴ But the LORD said to Moses, "Do not fear him, for I have given him into your hand, and all his people, and his land. And you shall do to him as you did to Sihon

king of the Amorites, who lived at Heshbon." ³⁵ So they defeated him and his sons and all his people, until he had no survivor left. And they possessed his land.

Balak Summons Balaam

22 Then the people of Israel set out and camped in the plains of Moab beyond the Jordan at Jericho. ² And Balak the son of Zippor saw all that Israel had done to the Amorites. ³ And Moab was in great dread of the people, because they were many. Moab was overcome with fear of the people of Israel. ⁴ And Moab said to the elders of Midian, "This horde will now lick up all that is around us, as the ox licks up the grass of the field." So Balak the son of Zippor, who was king of Moab at that time, ⁵ sent messengers to Balaam the son of Beor at Pethor, which is near the River in the land of the people of Amaw, to call him, saying,

> ## GETTING THE MESSAGE
>
> **Balaam remembered.** Evidence for Balaam's existence can be seen on an eighth-century B.C. inscription found in Jordan. It begins with, "Inscription of Balaam the son of Beor, the man who was seer of the gods."

"Behold, a people has come out of Egypt. They cover the face of the earth, and they are dwelling opposite me. ⁶ Come now, curse this people for me, since they are too mighty for me. Perhaps I shall be able to defeat them and drive them from the land, for I know that he whom you bless is blessed, and he whom you curse is cursed."

⁷ So the elders of Moab and the elders of Midian departed with the fees for divination in their hand. And they came to Balaam and gave him Balak's message. ⁸ And he said to them, "Lodge here tonight, and I will bring back word to you, as the LORD speaks to me." So the princes of Moab stayed with Balaam. ⁹ And God came to Balaam and said, "Who are these men with you?" ¹⁰ And Balaam said to God, "Balak the son of Zippor, king of Moab, has sent to me, saying, ¹¹ 'Behold, a people has come out of Egypt, and it covers the face of the earth. Now come, curse them for me. Perhaps I shall be able to fight

against them and drive them out.'" ¹² God said to Balaam, "You shall not go with them. You shall not curse the people, for they are blessed." ¹³ So Balaam rose in the morning and said to the princes of Balak, "Go to your own land, for the LORD has refused to let me go with you." ¹⁴ So the princes of Moab rose and went to Balak and said, "Balaam refuses to come with us."

¹⁵ Once again Balak sent princes, more in number and more honorable than these. ¹⁶ And they came to Balaam and said to

BALAAM

Balaam was a well-known non-Israelite prophet. Balak, the king of Moab, was terrified of the Israelites, and so he summoned Balaam to place a curse on them. God spoke to Balaam, however, and forbade him to curse Israel. He permitted Balaam to go to Balak on the condition that he speak only as the Lord instructed. God reinforced this condition in a grimly humorous episode involving a talking donkey. Balak tried many times to persuade Balaam to curse Israel, but his plan backfired. Balaam instead pronounced four blessings on the nation. Although Balaam was unable to curse the Israelites, he later advised Balak to send women to seduce Israel away from God and into idolatry (31:6).

KEY REFERENCE: NUMBERS 22:22–35

him, "Thus says Balak the son of Zippor: 'Let nothing hinder you from coming to me, ¹⁷ for I will surely do you great honor, and whatever you say to me I will do. Come, curse this people for me.'" ¹⁸ But Balaam answered and said to the servants of Balak, "Though Balak were to give me his house full of silver and gold, I could not go beyond the command of the LORD my God to do less or more. ¹⁹ So you, too, please stay here tonight, that I may know what more the LORD will say to me." ²⁰ And God came to Balaam at night and said to him, "If the men have come to call you, rise, go with them; but only do what I tell you." **21** So Balaam rose in the morning and saddled his donkey and went with the princes of Moab.

Balaam's Donkey and the Angel

22 But God's anger was kindled because he went, and the angel of the LORD took his stand in the way as his adversary. Now he was riding on the donkey, and his two servants were with him. **23** And the donkey saw the angel of the LORD standing in the road, with a drawn sword in his hand. And the donkey turned aside out of the road and went into the field. And Balaam struck the donkey, to turn her into the road. **24** Then the angel of the LORD stood in a narrow path between the vineyards, with a wall on either side. **25** And when the donkey saw the angel of the LORD, she pushed against the wall

> ### GETTING THE MESSAGE
>
> **Aram.** The pagan prophet Balaam described himself as being from Aram (23:7). Aram was a confederation of small towns in present-day Syria. It was named for Aram, the son of Shem and grandson of Noah. It was in this region that the Aramaic language developed.

and pressed Balaam's foot against the wall. So he struck her again. **26** Then the angel of the LORD went ahead and stood in a narrow place, where there was no way to turn either to the right or to the left. **27** When the donkey saw the angel of the LORD, she lay down under Balaam. And Balaam's anger was kindled, and he struck the donkey with his staff. **28** Then the LORD opened the mouth of the donkey, and she said to Balaam, "What have I done to you, that you have struck me these three times?" **29** And Balaam said to the donkey, "Because you have made a fool of me. I wish I had a sword in my hand, for then I would kill you." **30** And the donkey said to Balaam, "Am I not your donkey, on which you have ridden all your life long to this day? Is it my habit to treat you this way?" And he said, "No."

31 Then the LORD opened the eyes of Balaam, and he saw the angel of the LORD standing in the way, with his drawn sword

in his hand. And he bowed down and fell on his face. **32** And the angel of the LORD said to him, "Why have you struck your donkey these three times? Behold, I have come out to oppose you because your way is perverse before me. **33** The donkey saw me and turned aside before me these three times. If she had not turned aside from me, surely just now I would have killed you and let her live." **34** Then Balaam said to the angel of the LORD, "I have sinned, for I did not know that you stood in the road against me. Now therefore, if it is evil in your sight, I will turn back." **35** And the angel of the LORD said to Balaam, "Go with the men, but speak only the word that I tell you." So Balaam went on with the princes of Balak.

36 When Balak heard that Balaam had come, he went out to meet him at the city of Moab, on the border formed by the Arnon, at the extremity of the border. **37** And Balak said to Balaam, "Did I not send to you to call you? Why did you not come to me? Am I not able to honor you?" **38** Balaam said to Balak, "Behold, I have come to you! Have I now any power of my own to speak anything? The word that God puts in my mouth, that must I speak." **39** Then Balaam went with Balak, and they came to Kiriath-huzoth. **40** And Balak sacrificed oxen and sheep, and sent for Balaam and for the princes who were with him.

41 And in the morning Balak took Balaam and brought him up to Bamoth-baal, and from there he saw a fraction of the people.

Balaam's First Oracle

23 And Balaam said to Balak, "Build for me here seven altars, and prepare for me here seven bulls and seven rams." **2** Balak did as Balaam had said. And Balak and Balaam offered on each altar a bull and a ram. **3** And Balaam said to Balak, "Stand beside your burnt offering, and I will go. Perhaps the LORD will come to meet me, and whatever he shows me I will tell you." And he went to a bare height, **4** and God met Balaam. And Balaam said to him, "I have arranged the seven altars and I have offered on each altar a bull and a ram." **5** And the LORD put a word in Balaam's mouth and said, "Return to Balak, and thus you shall speak." **6** And he returned to him, and behold, he and all the princes of Moab were standing beside his burnt offering. **7** And Balaam took up his discourse and said,

> "From Aram Balak has brought me,
>> the king of Moab from the eastern mountains:
> 'Come, curse Jacob for me,
>> and come, denounce Israel!'
> **8** How can I curse whom God has not cursed?
>> How can I denounce whom the Lord has not denounced?
> **9** For from the top of the crags I see him,
>> from the hills I behold him;
> behold, a people dwelling alone,
>> and not counting itself among the nations!
> **10** Who can count the dust of Jacob
>> or number the fourth part of Israel?
> Let me die the death of the upright,
>> and let my end be like his!"

11 And Balak said to Balaam, "What have you done to me? I took you to curse my enemies, and behold, you have done nothing but bless them." **12** And he answered and said, "Must I not take care to speak what the Lord puts in my mouth?"

Balaam's Second Oracle

13 And Balak said to him, "Please come with me to another place, from which you may see them. You shall see only a fraction of them and shall not see them all. Then curse them for me from there." **14** And he took him to the field of Zophim, to the top of Pisgah, and built seven altars and offered a bull and a ram on each altar. **15** Balaam said to Balak, "Stand here beside your burnt offering, while I meet the Lord over there." **16** And the Lord met Balaam and put a word in his mouth and said, "Return to Balak, and thus shall you speak." **17** And he came to him, and behold, he was standing beside his burnt offering, and the princes of Moab with him. And Balak said to him, "What has the Lord spoken?" **18** And Balaam took up his discourse and said,

> "Rise, Balak, and hear;
>> give ear to me, O son of Zippor:
> **19** God is not man, that he should lie,
>> or a son of man, that he should change his mind.
> Has he said, and will he not do it?
>> Or has he spoken, and will he not fulfill it?
> **20** Behold, I received a command to bless:
>> he has blessed, and I cannot revoke it.
> **21** He has not beheld misfortune in Jacob,
>> nor has he seen trouble in Israel.
> The Lord their God is with them,
>> and the shout of a king is among them.
> **22** God brings them out of Egypt
>> and is for them like the horns of the wild ox.
> **23** For there is no enchantment against Jacob,
>> no divination against Israel;
> now it shall be said of Jacob and Israel,
>> 'What has God wrought!'
> **24** Behold, a people! As a lioness it rises up
>> and as a lion it lifts itself;
> it does not lie down until it has devoured the prey
>> and drunk the blood of the slain."

25 And Balak said to Balaam, "Do not curse them at all, and do not bless them at all." **26** But Balaam answered Balak, "Did I not tell you, 'All that the Lord says, that I must do'?" **27** And Balak said to Balaam, "Come now, I will take you to another place. Perhaps it will please God that you may curse them for me from there." **28** So Balak took Balaam to the top of Peor, which overlooks the desert. **29** And Balaam said to Balak, "Build for me here seven altars and prepare for me here seven bulls and seven rams." **30** And Balak did as Balaam had said, and offered a bull and a ram on each altar.

Balaam's Third Oracle

24 When Balaam saw that it pleased the Lord to bless Israel, he did not go, as at other times, to look for omens, but set his face toward the wilderness. **2** And Balaam lifted up his eyes and saw Israel camping tribe by tribe. And the Spirit of God came upon him, **3** and he took up his discourse and said,

> "The oracle of Balaam the son of Beor,
>> the oracle of the man whose eye is opened,

4 the oracle of him who hears the words
      of God,
      who sees the vision of the Almighty,
      falling down with his eyes uncov-
         ered:
5 How lovely are your tents, O Jacob,
      your encampments, O Israel!
6 Like palm groves that stretch afar,
      like gardens beside a river,
   like aloes that the LORD has planted,
      like cedar trees beside the waters.
7 Water shall flow from his buckets,
      and his seed shall be in many
         waters;
   his king shall be higher than Agag,
      and his kingdom shall be exalted.
8 God brings him out of Egypt
      and is for him like the horns of the
         wild ox;
   he shall eat up the nations, his adver-
      saries,

> ### GETTING THE MESSAGE
>
> **Wild oxen** (24:8) are believed to be the
> ancestors of domestic cattle. In the Old
> Testament, the wild ox was a symbol of
> strength.

   and shall break their bones in pieces
      and pierce them through with his
         arrows.
9 He crouched, he lay down like a lion
      and like a lioness; who will rouse
         him up?
   Blessed are those who bless you,
      and cursed are those who curse you."

10 And Balak's anger was kindled against
Balaam, and he struck his hands together.
And Balak said to Balaam, "I called you to
curse my enemies, and behold, you have
blessed them these three times. 11 Therefore
now flee to your own place. I said, 'I will
certainly honor you,' but the LORD has held
you back from honor." 12 And Balaam said
to Balak, "Did I not tell your messengers
whom you sent to me, 13 'If Balak should
give me his house full of silver and gold,
I would not be able to go beyond the word
of the LORD, to do either good or bad of my
own will. What the LORD speaks, that will
I speak'? 14 And now, behold, I am going to
my people. Come, I will let you know what

this people will do to your people in the
latter days."

Balaam's Final Oracle

15 And he took up his discourse and said,

   "The oracle of Balaam the son of Beor,
      the oracle of the man whose eye is
         opened,
16   the oracle of him who hears the words
         of God,
      and knows the knowledge of the
         Most High,
   who sees the vision of the Almighty,
      falling down with his eyes uncov-
         ered:
17 I see him, but not now;
      I behold him, but not near:
   a star shall come out of Jacob,
      and a scepter shall rise out of Israel;
   it shall crush the forehead of Moab
      and break down all the sons of
         Sheth.
18 Edom shall be dispossessed;
      Seir also, his enemies, shall be
         dispossessed.
      Israel is doing valiantly.
19 And one from Jacob shall exercise
         dominion
      and destroy the survivors of cities!"

20 Then he looked on Amalek and took up
his discourse and said,

   "Amalek was the first among the
         nations,
      but its end is utter destruction."

21 And he looked on the Kenite, and took
up his discourse and said,

   "Enduring is your dwelling place,
      and your nest is set in the rock.
22 Nevertheless, Kain shall be burned
      when Asshur takes you away cap-
         tive."

23 And he took up his discourse and said,

   "Alas, who shall live when God does
         this?
24   But ships shall come from Kittim
      and shall afflict Asshur and Eber;
      and he too shall come to utter
         destruction."

25 Then Balaam rose and went back to his
place. And Balak also went his way.

Baal Worship at Peor

25 While Israel lived in Shittim, the people began to whore with the daughters of Moab. ² These invited the people to the sacrifices of their gods, and the people ate and bowed down to their gods. ³ So Israel yoked himself to Baal of Peor. And the anger of the LORD was kindled against Israel. ⁴ And the LORD said to Moses, "Take all the chiefs of the people and hang them in the sun before the LORD, that the fierce anger of the LORD may turn away from Israel." ⁵ And Moses said to the judges of Israel, "Each of you kill those of his men who have yoked themselves to Baal of Peor."

⁶ And behold, one of the people of Israel came and brought a Midianite woman to his family, in the sight of Moses and in the sight of the whole congregation of the people of Israel, while they were weeping in the entrance of the tent of meeting. ⁷ When Phinehas the son of Eleazar, son of Aaron the priest, saw it, he rose and left the congregation and took a spear in his hand ⁸ and went after the man of Israel into the chamber and pierced both of them, the man of Israel and the woman through her belly. Thus the plague on the people of Israel was stopped. ⁹ Nevertheless, those who died by the plague were twenty-four thousand.

The Zeal of Phinehas

¹⁰ And the LORD said to Moses, ¹¹ "Phinehas the son of Eleazar, son of Aaron the priest, has turned back my wrath from the people of Israel, in that he was jealous with my jealousy among them, so that I did not consume the people of Israel in my jealousy. ¹² Therefore say, 'Behold, I give to him my covenant of peace, ¹³ and it shall be to him and to his descendants after him the covenant of a perpetual priesthood, because he was jealous for his God and made atonement for the people of Israel.'"

¹⁴ The name of the slain man of Israel, who was killed with the Midianite woman, was Zimri the son of Salu, chief of a father's house belonging to the Simeonites. ¹⁵ And the name of the Midianite woman who was killed was Cozbi the daughter of Zur, who was the tribal head of a father's house in Midian.

¹⁶ And the LORD spoke to Moses, saying, ¹⁷ "Harass the Midianites and strike them down, ¹⁸ for they have harassed you with their wiles, with which they beguiled you in the matter of Peor, and in the matter of Cozbi, the daughter of the chief of Midian, their sister, who was killed on the day of the plague on account of Peor."

Census of the New Generation

26 After the plague, the LORD said to Moses and to Eleazar the son of Aaron, the priest, ² "Take a census of all the congregation of the people of Israel, from twenty years old and upward, by their fathers' houses, all in Israel who are able to go to war." ³ And Moses and Eleazar the priest spoke with them in the plains of Moab by the Jordan at Jericho, saying, ⁴ "Take a census of the people, from twenty years old and upward," as the LORD commanded Moses. The people of Israel who came out of the land of Egypt were:

⁵ Reuben, the firstborn of Israel; the sons of Reuben: of Hanoch, the clan of the Hanochites; of Pallu, the clan of the Palluites; ⁶ of Hezron, the clan of the Hezronites; of Carmi, the clan of the Carmites. ⁷ These are the clans of the Reubenites, and those listed were 43,730. ⁸ And the sons of Pallu: Eliab. ⁹ The sons of Eliab: Nemuel, Dathan, and Abiram. These are the Dathan and Abiram, chosen from the congregation, who contended against Moses and Aaron in the company of Korah, when they contended against the LORD ¹⁰ and the earth opened its mouth and swallowed them up together with Korah, when that company died, when the fire devoured 250 men, and they became a warning. ¹¹ But the sons of Korah did not die.

¹² The sons of Simeon according to their clans: of Nemuel, the clan of the Nemuelites; of Jamin, the clan of the Jaminites; of Jachin, the clan of the Jachinites; ¹³ of Zerah, the clan of the Zerahites; of Shaul, the clan of the Shaulites. ¹⁴ These are the clans of the Simeonites, 22,200.

¹⁵ The sons of Gad according to their clans: of Zephon, the clan of the Zephonites; of Haggi, the clan of the Haggites; of Shuni, the clan of the Shunites; ¹⁶ of Ozni, the clan of the Oznites; of Eri, the clan of the Erites; ¹⁷ of Arod, the clan of the Arodites; of Areli, the clan of the Arelites. ¹⁸ These are the clans of the sons of Gad as they were listed, 40,500.

¹⁹ The sons of Judah were Er and Onan; and Er and Onan died in the land of Canaan. ²⁰ And the sons of Judah according

to their clans were: of Shelah, the clan of the Shelanites; of Perez, the clan of the Perezites; of Zerah, the clan of the Zerahites. ²¹ And the sons of Perez were: of Hezron, the clan of the Hezronites; of Hamul, the clan of the Hamulites. ²² These are the clans of Judah as they were listed, 76,500.

²³ The sons of Issachar according to their clans: of Tola, the clan of the Tolaites; of Puvah, the clan of the Punites; ²⁴ of Jashub, the clan of the Jashubites; of Shimron, the clan of the Shimronites. ²⁵ These are the clans of Issachar as they were listed, 64,300.

²⁶ The sons of Zebulun, according to their clans: of Sered, the clan of the Seredites; of Elon, the clan of the Elonites; of Jahleel, the clan of the Jahleelites. ²⁷ These are the clans of the Zebulunites as they were listed, 60,500.

²⁸ The sons of Joseph according to their clans: Manasseh and Ephraim. ²⁹ The sons of Manasseh: of Machir, the clan of the Machirites; and Machir was the father of Gilead; of Gilead, the clan of the Gileadites. ³⁰ These are the sons of Gilead: of Iezer, the clan of the Iezerites; of Helek, the clan of the Helekites; ³¹ and of Asriel, the clan of the Asrielites; and of Shechem, the clan of the Shechemites; ³² and of Shemida, the clan of the Shemidaites; and of Hepher, the clan of the Hepherites. ³³ Now Zelophehad the son of Hepher had no sons, but daughters. And the names of the daughters of Zelophehad were Mahlah, Noah, Hoglah, Milcah, and Tirzah. ³⁴ These are the clans of Manasseh, and those listed were 52,700.

³⁵ These are the sons of Ephraim according to their clans: of Shuthelah, the clan of the Shuthelahites; of Becher, the clan of the Becherites; of Tahan, the clan of the Tahanites. ³⁶ And these are the sons of Shuthelah: of Eran, the clan of the Eranites. ³⁷ These are the clans of the sons of Ephraim as they were listed, 32,500. These are the sons of Joseph according to their clans.

³⁸ The sons of Benjamin according to their clans: of Bela, the clan of the Belaites; of Ashbel, the clan of the Ashbelites; of Ahiram, the clan of the Ahiramites; ³⁹ of Shephupham, the clan of the Shuphamites; of Hupham, the clan of the Huphamites. ⁴⁰ And the sons of Bela were Ard and Naaman: of Ard, the clan of the Ardites; of Naaman, the clan of the Naamites. ⁴¹ These

are the sons of Benjamin according to their clans, and those listed were 45,600.

⁴² These are the sons of Dan according to their clans: of Shuham, the clan of the Shuhamites. These are the clans of Dan according to their clans. ⁴³ All the clans of the Shuhamites, as they were listed, were 64,400.

⁴⁴ The sons of Asher according to their clans: of Imnah, the clan of the Imnites; of Ishvi, the clan of the Ishvites; of Beriah, the clan of the Beriites. ⁴⁵ Of the sons of Beriah: of Heber, the clan of the Heberites; of Malchiel, the clan of the Malchielites. ⁴⁶ And the name of the daughter of Asher was Serah. ⁴⁷ These are the clans of the sons of Asher as they were listed, 53,400.

⁴⁸ The sons of Naphtali according to their clans: of Jahzeel, the clan of the Jahzeelites; of Guni, the clan of the Gunites; ⁴⁹ of Jezer, the clan of the Jezerites; of Shillem, the clan of the Shillemites. ⁵⁰ These are the clans of Naphtali according to their clans, and those listed were 45,400.

⁵¹ This was the list of the people of Israel, 601,730.

⁵² The LORD spoke to Moses, saying, ⁵³ "Among these the land shall be divided for inheritance according to the number of names. ⁵⁴ To a large tribe you shall give a large inheritance, and to a small tribe you shall give a small inheritance; every tribe shall be given its inheritance in proportion to its list. ⁵⁵ But the land shall be divided by lot. According to the names of the tribes of their fathers they shall inherit. ⁵⁶ Their inheritance shall be divided according to lot between the larger and the smaller."

⁵⁷ This was the list of the Levites according to their clans: of Gershon, the clan of the Gershonites; of Kohath, the clan of the Kohathites; of Merari, the clan of the Merarites. ⁵⁸ These are the clans of Levi: the clan of the Libnites, the clan of the Hebronites, the clan of the Mahlites, the clan of the Mushites, the clan of the Korahites. And Kohath was the father of Amram. ⁵⁹ The name of Amram's wife was Jochebed the daughter of Levi, who was born to Levi in Egypt. And she bore to Amram Aaron and Moses and Miriam their sister. ⁶⁰ And to Aaron were born Nadab, Abihu, Eleazar, and Ithamar. ⁶¹ But Nadab and Abihu died when they offered unauthorized fire before

the LORD. ⁶² And those listed were 23,000, every male from a month old and upward. For they were not listed among the people of Israel, because there was no inheritance given to them among the people of Israel.

⁶³ These were those listed by Moses and Eleazar the priest, who listed the people of Israel in the plains of Moab by the Jordan at Jericho. ⁶⁴ But among these there was not one of those listed by Moses and Aaron the priest, who had listed the people of Israel in the wilderness of Sinai. ⁶⁵ For the LORD had said of them, "They shall die in the wilderness." Not one of them was left, except Caleb the son of Jephunneh and Joshua the son of Nun.

The Daughters of Zelophehad

27 Then drew near the daughters of Zelophehad the son of Hepher, son of Gilead, son of Machir, son of Manasseh, from the clans of Manasseh the son of Joseph. The names of his daughters were: Mahlah, Noah, Hoglah, Milcah, and Tirzah. ² And they stood before Moses and before Eleazar the priest and before the chiefs and all the congregation, at the entrance of the tent of meeting, saying, ³ "Our father died in the wilderness. He was not among the company of those who gathered themselves together against the LORD in the company of Korah, but died for his own sin. And he had no sons. ⁴ Why should the name of our father be taken away from his clan because he had no son? Give to us a possession among our father's brothers."

⁵ Moses brought their case before the LORD. ⁶ And the LORD said to Moses, ⁷ "The daughters of Zelophehad are right. You shall give them possession of an inheritance among their father's brothers and transfer the inheritance of their father to them. ⁸ And you shall speak to the people of Israel, saying, 'If a man dies and has no son, then you shall transfer his inheritance to his daughter. ⁹ And if he has no daughter, then you shall give his inheritance to his brothers. ¹⁰ And if he has no brothers, then you shall give his inheritance to his father's brothers. ¹¹ And if his father has no brothers, then you shall give his inheritance to the nearest kinsman of his clan, and he shall possess it. And it shall be for the people of Israel a statute and rule, as the LORD commanded Moses.'"

Joshua to Succeed Moses

¹² The LORD said to Moses, "Go up into this mountain of Abarim and see the land that I have given to the people of Israel. ¹³ When you have seen it, you also shall be gathered to your people, as your brother Aaron was, ¹⁴ because you rebelled against my word in the wilderness of Zin when the congregation quarreled, failing to uphold me as holy at the waters before their eyes." (These are the waters of Meribah of Kadesh in the wilderness of Zin.) ¹⁵ Moses spoke to the LORD,

PROFILE

ELEAZAR

Eleazar was the third son of Aaron. His older brothers, Nadab and Abihu, died after offering unauthorized fire before the Lord. Following their death, Eleazar and his younger brother, Ithamar, were placed in charge of the tent of meeting. Eleazar supervised those who guarded the sanctuary. After Aaron's death, he became high priest of Israel. He assisted Moses in taking a census of Israel. This was to establish the size of the tribes so that each could be given an appropriate inheritance. Moses commissioned Joshua as his successor in the presence of Eleazar, who later helped Joshua divide the Promised Land among the tribes of Israel. Eleazar died soon after the death of Aaron. He had one son, Phinehas, and was an ancestor of Ezra the scribe.

KEY REFERENCE: NUMBERS 20:25-28

saying, ¹⁶ "Let the LORD, the God of the spirits of all flesh, appoint a man over the congregation ¹⁷ who shall go out before them and come in before them, who shall lead them out and bring them in, that the congregation of the LORD may not be as sheep that have no shepherd." ¹⁸ So the LORD said to Moses, "Take Joshua the son of Nun, a man in whom is the Spirit, and lay your hand on him. ¹⁹ Make him stand before Eleazar the priest and all the congregation, and you shall commission him in their sight. ²⁰ You shall invest him with some of your authority, that all the congregation of the people of Israel may obey. [21] And he shall stand before Eleazar the priest, who shall inquire for him by the judgment of the Urim before the LORD. At his word they shall go out, and at his word they shall come in, both he and all the people of Israel with him, the whole congregation." [22] And Moses did as the LORD commanded him. He took Joshua and made him stand before Eleazar the priest and the whole congregation, [23] and he laid his hands on him and commissioned him as the LORD directed through Moses.

Daily Offerings

28 The LORD spoke to Moses, saying, [2] "Command the people of Israel and say to them, 'My offering, my food for my food offerings, my pleasing aroma, you shall

---

GETTING THE MESSAGE

How wealthy would the Israelites become? The sacrifices described in chs. 28–29 called for a total of 113 bulls, 1,086 lambs, more than a ton of flour, and 1,000 bottles of oil and wine. Israel would have had to become a successful agricultural society after reaching the Promised Land in order to meet the requirements for these sacrifices.

---

be careful to offer to me at its appointed time.' [3] And you shall say to them, This is the food offering that you shall offer to the LORD: two male lambs a year old without blemish, day by day, as a regular offering. [4] The one lamb you shall offer in the morning, and the other lamb you shall offer at twilight; [5] also a tenth of an ephah of fine flour for a grain offering, mixed with a quarter of a hin of beaten oil. [6] It is a regular burnt offering, which was ordained at Mount Sinai for a pleasing aroma, a food offering to the LORD. [7] Its drink offering shall be a quarter of a hin for each lamb. In the Holy Place you shall pour out a drink offering of strong drink to the LORD. [8] The other lamb you shall offer at twilight. Like the grain offering of the morning, and like its drink offering, you shall offer it as a food offering, with a pleasing aroma to the LORD.

Sabbath Offerings

[9] "On the Sabbath day, two male lambs a year old without blemish, and two tenths of an ephah of fine flour for a grain offering, mixed with oil, and its drink offering: [10] this is the burnt offering of every Sabbath, besides the regular burnt offering and its drink offering.

Monthly Offerings

[11] "At the beginnings of your months, you shall offer a burnt offering to the LORD: two bulls from the herd, one ram, seven male lambs a year old without blemish; [12] also three tenths of an ephah of fine flour for a grain offering, mixed with oil, for each bull, and two tenths of fine flour for a grain offering, mixed with oil, for the one ram; [13] and a tenth of fine flour mixed with oil as a grain offering for every lamb; for a burnt offering with a pleasing aroma, a food offering to the LORD. [14] Their drink offerings shall be half a hin of wine for a bull, a third of a hin for a ram, and a quarter of a hin for a lamb. This is the burnt offering of each month throughout the months of the year. [15] Also one male goat for a sin offering to the LORD; it shall be offered besides the regular burnt offering and its drink offering.

Passover Offerings

[16] "On the fourteenth day of the first month is the LORD's Passover, [17] and on the fifteenth day of this month is a feast. Seven days shall unleavened bread be eaten. [18] On the first day there shall be a holy convocation. You shall not do any ordinary work, [19] but offer a food offering, a burnt offering to the LORD: two bulls from the herd, one ram, and seven male lambs a year old; see that they are without blemish; [20] also their grain offering of fine flour mixed with oil; three tenths of an ephah shall you offer for a bull, and two tenths for a ram; [21] a tenth shall you offer for each of the seven lambs; [22] also one male goat for a sin offering, to make atonement for you. [23] You shall offer these besides the burnt offering of the morning, which is for a regular burnt offering. [24] In the same way you shall offer daily, for seven days, the food of a food offering, with a pleasing aroma to the LORD. It shall be offered besides the regular burnt offering and its drink offering. [25] And on the seventh

day you shall have a holy convocation. You shall not do any ordinary work.

Offerings for the Feast of Weeks

26 "On the day of the firstfruits, when you offer a grain offering of new grain to the LORD at your Feast of Weeks, you shall have a holy convocation. You shall not do any ordinary work, 27 but offer a burnt offering, with a pleasing aroma to the LORD: two bulls from the herd, one ram, seven male lambs a year old; 28 also their grain offering of fine flour mixed with oil, three tenths of an ephah for each bull, two tenths for one ram, 29 a tenth for each of the seven lambs; 30 with one male goat, to make atonement for you. 31 Besides the regular burnt offering and its grain offering, you shall offer them and their drink offering. See that they are without blemish.

Offerings for the Feast of Trumpets

29 "On the first day of the seventh month you shall have a holy convocation. You shall not do any ordinary work. It is a day for you to blow the trumpets, 2 and you shall offer a burnt offering, for a pleasing aroma to the LORD: one bull from the herd, one ram, seven male lambs a year old without blemish; 3 also their grain offering of fine flour mixed with oil, three tenths of an ephah for the bull, two tenths for the ram, 4 and one tenth for each of the seven lambs; 5 with one male goat for a sin offering, to make atonement for you; 6 besides the burnt offering of the new moon, and its grain offering, and the regular burnt offering and its grain offering, and their drink offering, according to the rule for them, for a pleasing aroma, a food offering to the LORD.

Offerings for the Day of Atonement

7 "On the tenth day of this seventh month you shall have a holy convocation and afflict yourselves. You shall do no work, 8 but you shall offer a burnt offering to the LORD, a pleasing aroma: one bull from the herd, one ram, seven male lambs a year old: see that they are without blemish. 9 And their grain offering shall be of fine flour mixed with oil, three tenths of an ephah for the bull, two tenths for the one ram, 10 a tenth for each of the seven lambs: 11 also one male goat for a sin offering, besides the sin offering of atone-

ment, and the regular burnt offering and its grain offering, and their drink offerings.

Offerings for the Feast of Booths

12 "On the fifteenth day of the seventh month you shall have a holy convocation. You shall not do any ordinary work, and you shall keep a feast to the LORD seven days. 13 And you shall offer a burnt offering, a food offering, with a pleasing aroma to the LORD, thirteen bulls from the herd, two rams, fourteen male lambs a year old; they shall be without blemish; 14 and their grain offering of fine flour mixed with oil, three tenths of an ephah for each of the thirteen bulls, two tenths for each of the two rams, 15 and a tenth for each of the fourteen lambs; 16 also one male goat for a sin offering, besides the regular burnt offering, its grain offering and its drink offering.

> ### GETTING THE MESSAGE
>
> During the **Feast of Booths**, the Israelites were to live in temporary dwellings ("booths") as a reminder of their life in the wilderness. The large number of sacrifices offered during the eight days shows the importance of this feast. The Feast of Booths was celebrated in October, at the end of the agricultural year. It was also a time to pray for plenty of rain in the next year. In Israel, rain is expected only between October and April.

17 "On the second day twelve bulls from the herd, two rams, fourteen male lambs a year old without blemish, 18 with the grain offering and the drink offerings for the bulls, for the rams, and for the lambs, in the prescribed quantities; 19 also one male goat for a sin offering, besides the regular burnt offering and its grain offering, and their drink offerings.

20 "On the third day eleven bulls, two rams, fourteen male lambs a year old without blemish, 21 with the grain offering and the drink offerings for the bulls, for the rams, and for the lambs, in the prescribed quantities; 22 also one male goat for a sin offering, besides the regular burnt offering and its grain offering and its drink offering.

²³ "On the fourth day ten bulls, two rams, fourteen male lambs a year old without blemish, ²⁴ with the grain offering and the drink offerings for the bulls, for the rams, and for the lambs, in the prescribed quantities; ²⁵ also one male goat for a sin offering, besides the regular burnt offering, its grain offering and its drink offering.

²⁶ "On the fifth day nine bulls, two rams, fourteen male lambs a year old without blemish, ²⁷ with the grain offering and the drink offerings for the bulls, for the rams, and for the lambs, in the prescribed quantities; ²⁸ also one male goat for a sin offering; besides the regular burnt offering and its grain offering and its drink offering.

²⁹ "On the sixth day eight bulls, two rams, fourteen male lambs a year old without blemish, ³⁰ with the grain offering and the drink offerings for the bulls, for the rams, and for the lambs, in the prescribed quantities; ³¹ also one male goat for a sin offering; besides the regular burnt offering, its grain offering, and its drink offerings.

³² "On the seventh day seven bulls, two rams, fourteen male lambs a year old without blemish, ³³ with the grain offering and the drink offerings for the bulls, for the rams, and for the lambs, in the prescribed quantities; ³⁴ also one male goat for a sin offering; besides the regular burnt offering, its grain offering, and its drink offering.

³⁵ "On the eighth day you shall have a solemn assembly. You shall not do any ordinary work, ³⁶ but you shall offer a burnt offering, a food offering, with a pleasing aroma to the LORD: one bull, one ram, seven male lambs a year old without blemish, ³⁷ and the grain offering and the drink offerings for the bull, for the ram, and for the lambs, in the prescribed quantities; ³⁸ also one male goat for a sin offering; besides the regular burnt offering and its grain offering and its drink offering.

³⁹ "These you shall offer to the LORD at your appointed feasts, in addition to your vow offerings and your freewill offerings, for your burnt offerings, and for your grain offerings, and for your drink offerings, and for your peace offerings."

⁴⁰ So Moses told the people of Israel everything just as the LORD had commanded Moses.

Men and Vows

30 Moses spoke to the heads of the tribes of the people of Israel, saying, "This is what the LORD has commanded. ² If a man vows a vow to the LORD, or swears an oath to bind himself by a pledge, he shall not break his word. He shall do according to all that proceeds out of his mouth.

Women and Vows

³ "If a woman vows a vow to the LORD and binds herself by a pledge, while within her father's house in her youth, ⁴ and her father hears of her vow and of her pledge by which she has bound herself and says nothing to her, then all her vows shall stand, and every pledge by which she has bound herself shall stand. ⁵ But if her father opposes her on the day that he hears of it, no vow of hers, no pledge by which she has bound herself shall stand. And the LORD will forgive her, because her father opposed her.

⁶ "If she marries a husband, while under her vows or any thoughtless utterance of her lips by which she has bound herself, ⁷ and her husband hears of it and says nothing to her on the day that he hears, then her vows shall stand, and her pledges by which she has bound herself shall stand. ⁸ But if, on the day that her husband comes to hear of it, he opposes her, then he makes void her vow that was on her, and the thoughtless utterance of her lips by which she bound herself. And the LORD will forgive her. ⁹ (But any vow of a widow or of a divorced woman, anything by which she has bound herself, shall stand against her.) ¹⁰ And if she vowed in her husband's house or bound herself by a pledge with an oath, ¹¹ and her husband heard of it and said nothing to her and did not oppose her, then all her vows shall stand, and every pledge by which she bound herself shall stand. ¹² But if her husband makes them null and void on the day that he hears them, then whatever proceeds out of her lips concerning her vows or concerning her pledge of herself shall not stand. Her husband has made them void, and the LORD will forgive her. ¹³ Any vow and any binding oath to afflict herself, her husband may establish, or her husband may make void. ¹⁴ But if her husband says nothing to her from day to day, then he establishes all her vows or all her pledges that are upon her. He has established them, because he said

nothing to her on the day that he heard of them. **15** But if he makes them null and void after he has heard of them, then he shall bear her iniquity."

16 These are the statutes that the LORD commanded Moses about a man and his wife and about a father and his daughter while she is in her youth within her father's house.

Vengeance on Midian

31 The LORD spoke to Moses, saying, **2** "Avenge the people of Israel on the Midianites. Afterward you shall be gathered to your people." **3** So Moses spoke to the people, saying, "Arm men from among you for the war, that they may go against Midian to execute the LORD's vengeance on Midian. **4** You shall send a thousand from each of the tribes of Israel to the war." **5** So there were provided, out of the thousands of Israel, a thousand from each tribe, twelve thousand armed for war. **6** And Moses sent them to the war, a thousand from each tribe, together with Phinehas the son of Eleazar the priest, with the vessels of the sanctuary and the trumpets for the alarm in his hand. **7** They warred against Midian, as the LORD commanded Moses, and killed every male. **8** They killed the kings of Midian with the rest of their slain, Evi, Rekem, Zur, Hur, and Reba, the five kings of Midian. And they also killed Balaam the son of Beor with the sword. **9** And the people of Israel took captive the women of Midian and their little ones, and they took as plunder all their cattle, their flocks, and all their goods. **10** All their cities in the places where they lived, and all their encampments, they burned with fire, **11** and took all the spoil and all the plunder, both of man and of beast. **12** Then they brought the captives and the plunder and the spoil to Moses, and to Eleazar the priest, and to the congregation of the people of Israel, at the camp on the plains of Moab by the Jordan at Jericho.

13 Moses and Eleazar the priest and all the chiefs of the congregation went to meet them outside the camp. **14** And Moses was angry with the officers of the army, the commanders of thousands and the commanders of hundreds, who had come from service in the war. **15** Moses said to them, "Have you let all the women live? **16** Behold, these, on Balaam's advice, caused the people of Israel

to act treacherously against the LORD in the incident of Peor, and so the plague came among the congregation of the LORD. **17** Now therefore, kill every male among the little ones, and kill every woman who has known man by lying with him. **18** But all the young girls who have not known man by lying with him keep alive for yourselves. **19** Encamp outside the camp seven days. Whoever of you has killed any person and whoever has touched any slain, purify yourselves and your captives on the third day and on the seventh day. **20** You shall purify every garment, every article of skin, all work of goats' hair, and every article of wood."

21 Then Eleazar the priest said to the men in the army who had gone to battle: "This is the statute of the law that the LORD has commanded Moses: **22** only the gold, the silver,

the bronze, the iron, the tin, and the lead, **23** everything that can stand the fire, you shall pass through the fire, and it shall be clean. Nevertheless, it shall also be purified with the water for impurity. And whatever cannot stand the fire, you shall pass through the water. **24** You must wash your clothes on the seventh day, and you shall be clean. And afterward you may come into the camp."

25 The LORD said to Moses, **26** "Take the count of the plunder that was taken, both of man and of beast, you and Eleazar the priest and the heads of the fathers' houses of the congregation, **27** and divide the plunder into two parts between the warriors who went out to battle and all the congregation. **28** And levy for the LORD a tribute from the men of war who went out to battle, one out of five hundred, of the people and of the oxen and of the donkeys and of the flocks. **29** Take it from their half and give it to Eleazar the priest as a contribution to the LORD. **30** And from the people of Israel's half you shall take one drawn out of every fifty, of the people, of the oxen, of the donkeys, and of the flocks, of all the cattle, and give them to the Levites who keep guard over the tabernacle of the LORD." ³¹ And Moses and Eleazar the priest did as the LORD commanded Moses.

³² Now the plunder remaining of the spoil that the army took was 675,000 sheep, ³³ 72,000 cattle, ³⁴ 61,000 donkeys, ³⁵ and 32,000 persons in all, women who had not known man by lying with him. ³⁶ And the half, the portion of those who had gone out in the army, numbered 337,500 sheep, ³⁷ and the LORD's tribute of sheep was 675. ³⁸ The cattle were 36,000, of which the LORD's tribute was 72. ³⁹ The donkeys were 30,500, of which the LORD's tribute was 61. ⁴⁰ The persons were 16,000, of which the LORD's tribute was 32 persons. ⁴¹ And Moses gave the tribute, which was the contribution for the LORD, to Eleazar the priest, as the LORD commanded Moses.

⁴² From the people of Israel's half, which Moses separated from that of the men who had served in the army— ⁴³ now the congregation's half was 337,500 sheep, ⁴⁴ 36,000 cattle, ⁴⁵ and 30,500 donkeys, ⁴⁶ and 16,000 persons— ⁴⁷ from the people of Israel's half Moses took one of every 50, both of persons and of beasts, and gave them to the Levites who kept guard over the tabernacle of the LORD, as the LORD commanded Moses.

⁴⁸ Then the officers who were over the thousands of the army, the commanders of thousands and the commanders of hundreds, came near to Moses ⁴⁹ and said to Moses, "Your servants have counted the men of war who are under our command, and there is not a man missing from us. ⁵⁰ And we have brought the LORD's offering, what each man found, articles of gold, armlets and bracelets, signet rings, earrings, and beads, to make atonement for ourselves before the LORD." ⁵¹ And Moses and Eleazar the priest received from them the gold, all crafted articles. ⁵² And all the gold of the contribution that they presented to the LORD, from the commanders of thousands and the commanders of hundreds, was 16,750 shekels. ⁵³ (The men in the army had each taken plunder for himself.) ⁵⁴ And Moses and Eleazar the priest received the gold from the commanders of thousands and of hundreds, and brought it into the tent of meeting, as a memorial for the people of Israel before the LORD.

Reuben and Gad Settle in Gilead

32 Now the people of Reuben and the people of Gad had a very great number of livestock. And they saw the land of Jazer and the land of Gilead, and behold, the place was a place for livestock. ² So the people of Gad and the people of Reuben came and said to Moses and to Eleazar the priest and to the chiefs of the congregation, ³ "Ataroth, Dibon, Jazer, Nimrah, Heshbon, Elealeh, Sebam, Nebo, and Beon, ⁴ the land that the LORD struck down before the congregation of Israel, is a land for livestock, and your servants have livestock." ⁵ And they said, "If we have found favor in your sight, let this land be given to your servants for a possession. Do not take us across the Jordan."

⁶ But Moses said to the people of Gad and to the people of Reuben, "Shall your brothers go to the war while you sit here? ⁷ Why will you discourage the heart of the people of Israel from going over into the land that the LORD has given them? ⁸ Your fathers did this, when I sent them from Kadesh-barnea to see the land. ⁹ For when they went up to the Valley of Eshcol and saw the land, they discouraged the heart of the people of Israel from going into the land that the LORD had given them. ¹⁰ And the LORD's anger was kindled on that day, and he swore, saying, ¹¹ 'Surely none of the men who came up out of Egypt, from twenty years old and upward, shall see the land that I swore to give to Abraham, to Isaac, and to Jacob, because they have not wholly followed me, ¹² none except Caleb the son of Jephunneh the Kenizzite and Joshua the son of Nun, for they have wholly followed the LORD.' ¹³ And the LORD's anger was kindled against Israel, and he made them wander in the wilderness forty years, until all the generation that had done evil in the sight of the LORD was gone. ¹⁴ And behold, you have risen in your fathers' place, a brood of sinful men, to increase still more the fierce anger of the LORD against Israel! ¹⁵ For if you turn away from following him, he will again abandon them in the wilderness, and you will destroy all this people."

¹⁶ Then they came near to him and said, "We will build sheepfolds here for our

livestock, and cities for our little ones, [17] but we will take up arms, ready to go before the people of Israel, until we have brought them to their place. And our little ones shall live in the fortified cities because of the inhabitants of the land. [18] We will not return to our homes until each of the people of Israel has gained his inheritance. [19] For we will not inherit with them on the other side of the Jordan and beyond, because our inheritance has come to us on this side of the Jordan to the east." [20] So Moses said to them, "If you will do this, if you will take up arms to go before the LORD for the war, [21] and every armed man of you will pass over the Jordan before the LORD, until he has driven out his enemies from before him [22] and the land is subdued before the LORD; then after that you shall return and be free of obligation to the LORD and to Israel, and this land shall be your possession before the LORD. [23] But if you will not do so, behold, you have sinned against the LORD, and be sure your sin will find you out. [24] Build cities for your little ones and folds for your sheep, and do what you have promised." [25] And the people of Gad and the people of Reuben said to Moses, "Your servants will do as my lord commands. [26] Our little ones, our wives, our livestock, and all our cattle shall remain there in the cities of Gilead, [27] but your servants will pass over, every man who is armed for war, before the LORD to battle, as my lord orders."

[28] So Moses gave command concerning them to Eleazar the priest and to Joshua the son of Nun and to the heads of the fathers' houses of the tribes of the people of Israel. [29] And Moses said to them, "If the people of Gad and the people of Reuben, every man who is armed to battle before the LORD, will pass with you over the Jordan and the land shall be subdued before you, then you shall give them the land of Gilead for a possession. [30] However, if they will not pass over with you armed, they shall have possessions among you in the land of Canaan." [31] And the people of Gad and the people of Reuben answered, "What the LORD has said to your servants, we will do. [32] We will pass over armed before the LORD into the land of Canaan, and the possession of our inheritance shall remain with us beyond the Jordan."

[33] And Moses gave to them, to the people of Gad and to the people of Reuben and to the half-tribe of Manasseh the son of Joseph, the kingdom of Sihon king of the Amorites and the kingdom of Og king of Bashan, the land and its cities with their territories, the cities of the land throughout the country. [34] And the people of Gad built Dibon, Ataroth, Aroer, [35] Atroth-shophan, Jazer, Jogbehah, [36] Beth-nimrah and Beth-haran, fortified cities, and folds for sheep. [37] And the people of Reuben built Heshbon, Elealeh, Kiriathaim, [38] Nebo, and Baal-meon (their names were changed), and Sibmah. And they gave other names to the cities that they built. [39] And the sons of Machir the son of Manasseh went to Gilead and captured it, and dispossessed the Amorites who were in

> ### GETTING THE MESSAGE
>
> **Amorites.** The Amorites inhabited the land west of the Euphrates River, which included Canaan. In fact, the name "Amorite" means "westerner." They spoke a dialect similar to both the Canaanites and the Hebrews and were often considered to be a Canaanite tribe. However, many of the Canaanites considered the Amorites to be barbaric and uncivilized. Eventually Israel would conquer the Amorites and absorb them into Hebrew culture as servants.

it. [40] And Moses gave Gilead to Machir the son of Manasseh, and he settled in it. [41] And Jair the son of Manasseh went and captured their villages, and called them Havvoth-jair.[1] [42] And Nobah went and captured Kenath and its villages, and called it Nobah, after his own name.

Recounting Israel's Journey

33 These are the stages of the people of Israel, when they went out of the land of Egypt by their companies under the leadership of Moses and Aaron. [2] Moses wrote down their starting places, stage by stage, by command of the LORD, and these are their stages according to their starting places. [3] They set out from Rameses in the first month, on the fifteenth day of the first month. On the day after the Passover, the

---

[1] *Havvoth-jair* means *the villages of Jair*

people of Israel went out triumphantly in the sight of all the Egyptians, 4 while the Egyptians were burying all their firstborn, whom the LORD had struck down among them. On their gods also the LORD executed judgments.

5 So the people of Israel set out from Rameses and camped at Succoth. 6 And they set out from Succoth and camped at Etham, which is on the edge of the wilderness. 7 And they set out from Etham and turned back to Pi-hahiroth, which is east of Baal-zephon, and they camped before Migdol. 8 And they set out from before Hahiroth and passed through the midst of the sea into the wilderness, and they went a three days' journey in the wilderness of Etham and camped at Marah. 9 And they set out from Marah and came to Elim; at Elim there were twelve springs of water and seventy palm trees, and they camped there. 10 And

GETTING THE MESSAGE

Chronicling a journey, as seen in ch. 33, was a form of record keeping employed widely in ancient times. These detailed records were a valuable resource for later historians. The detailed records in the Bible, in particular, help to confirm its historical accuracy.

they set out from Elim and camped by the Red Sea. 11 And they set out from the Red Sea and camped in the wilderness of Sin. 12 And they set out from the wilderness of Sin and camped at Dophkah. 13 And they set out from Dophkah and camped at Alush. 14 And they set out from Alush and camped at Rephidim, where there was no water for the people to drink. 15 And they set out from Rephidim and camped in the wilderness of Sinai. 16 And they set out from the wilderness of Sinai and camped at Kibroth-hattaavah. 17 And they set out from Kibroth-hattaavah and camped at Hazeroth. 18 And they set out from Hazeroth and camped at Rithmah. 19 And they set out from Rithmah and camped at Rimmon-perez. 20 And they set out from Rimmon-perez and camped at Libnah. 21 And they set out from Libnah and camped at Rissah. 22 And they set out from Rissah and camped at Kehelathah.

23 And they set out from Kehelathah and camped at Mount Shepher. 24 And they set out from Mount Shepher and camped at Haradah. 25 And they set out from Haradah and camped at Makheloth. 26 And they set out from Makheloth and camped at Tahath. 27 And they set out from Tahath and camped at Terah. 28 And they set out from Terah and camped at Mithkah. 29 And they set out from Mithkah and camped at Hashmonah. 30 And they set out from Hashmonah and camped at Moseroth. 31 And they set out from Moseroth and camped at Bene-jaakan. 32 And they set out from Bene-jaakan and camped at Hor-haggidgad. 33 And they set out from Hor-haggidgad and camped at Jotbathah. 34 And they set out from Jotbathah and camped at Abronah. 35 And they set out from Abronah and camped at Ezion-geber. 36 And they set out from Ezion-geber and camped in the wilderness of Zin (that is, Kadesh). 37 And they set out from Kadesh and camped at Mount Hor, on the edge of the land of Edom.

38 And Aaron the priest went up Mount Hor at the command of the LORD and died there, in the fortieth year after the people of Israel had come out of the land of Egypt, on the first day of the fifth month. 39 And Aaron was 123 years old when he died on Mount Hor.

40 And the Canaanite, the king of Arad, who lived in the Negeb in the land of Canaan, heard of the coming of the people of Israel.

41 And they set out from Mount Hor and camped at Zalmonah. 42 And they set out from Zalmonah and camped at Punon. 43 And they set out from Punon and camped at Oboth. 44 And they set out from Oboth and camped at Iye-abarim, in the territory of Moab. 45 And they set out from Iyim and camped at Dibon-gad. 46 And they set out from Dibon-gad and camped at Almon-diblathaim. 47 And they set out from Almon-diblathaim and camped in the mountains of Abarim, before Nebo. 48 And they set out from the mountains of Abarim and camped in the plains of Moab by the Jordan at Jericho; 49 they camped by the Jordan from Beth-jeshimoth as far as Abel-shittim in the plains of Moab.

Drive Out the Inhabitants

50 And the LORD spoke to Moses in the plains of Moab by the Jordan at Jericho,

saying, **51** "Speak to the people of Israel and say to them, When you pass over the Jordan into the land of Canaan, **52** then you shall drive out all the inhabitants of the land from before you and destroy all their figured stones and destroy all their metal images and demolish all their high places. **53** And you shall take possession of the land and settle in it, for I have given the land to you to possess it. **54** You shall inherit the land by lot according to your clans. To a large tribe you shall give a large inheritance, and to a small tribe you shall give a small inheritance. Wherever the lot falls for anyone, that shall be his. According to the tribes of your fathers you shall inherit. **55** But if you do not drive out the inhabitants of the land from before you, then those of them whom you let remain shall be as barbs in your eyes and thorns in your sides, and they shall trouble you in the land where you dwell. **56** And I will do to you as I thought to do to them."

Boundaries of the Land

34 The LORD spoke to Moses, saying, **2** "Command the people of Israel, and say to them, When you enter the land of Canaan (this is the land that shall fall to you for an inheritance, the land of Canaan as defined by its borders), **3** your south side shall be from the wilderness of Zin alongside Edom, and your southern border shall run from the end of the Salt Sea on the east. **4** And your border shall turn south of the ascent of Akrabbim, and cross to Zin, and its limit shall be south of Kadesh-barnea. Then it shall go on to Hazar-addar, and pass along to Azmon. **5** And the border shall turn from Azmon to the Brook of Egypt, and its limit shall be at the sea.

6 "For the western border, you shall have the Great Sea and its coast. This shall be your western border.

7 "This shall be your northern border: from the Great Sea you shall draw a line to Mount Hor. **8** From Mount Hor you shall draw a line to Lebo-hamath, and the limit of the border shall be at Zedad. **9** Then the border shall extend to Ziphron, and its limit shall be at Hazar-enan. This shall be your northern border.

10 "You shall draw a line for your eastern border from Hazar-enan to Shepham. **11** And the border shall go down from Shepham to Riblah on the east side of Ain. And the border shall go down and reach to the shoulder of the Sea of Chinnereth on the east. **12** And the border shall go down to the Jordan, and its limit shall be at the Salt Sea. This shall be your land as defined by its borders all around."

13 Moses commanded the people of Israel, saying, "This is the land that you shall inherit by lot, which the LORD has commanded to give to the nine tribes and to the half-tribe. **14** For the tribe of the people of Reuben by fathers' houses and the tribe of the people of Gad by their fathers' houses have received their inheritance, and also the half-tribe of Manasseh. **15** The two tribes and the half-tribe have received their inheritance beyond the Jordan east of Jericho, toward the sunrise."

List of Tribal Chiefs

16 The LORD spoke to Moses, saying, **17** "These are the names of the men who shall divide the land to you for inheritance: Eleazar the priest and Joshua the son of Nun. **18** You shall take one chief from every tribe to divide the land for inheritance. **19** These are the names of the men: Of the tribe of Judah, Caleb the son of Jephunneh. **20** Of the tribe of the people of Simeon, Shemuel the son of Ammihud. **21** Of the tribe of Benjamin, Elidad the son of Chislon. **22** Of the tribe of the people of Dan a chief, Bukki the son of Jogli. **23** Of the people of Joseph: of the tribe of the people of Manasseh a chief, Hanniel the son of Ephod. **24** And of the tribe of the people of Ephraim a chief, Kemuel the son of Shiphtan. **25** Of the tribe of the people of Zebulun a chief, Elizaphan the son of Parnach. **26** Of the tribe of the people of Issachar a chief, Paltiel the son of Azzan. **27** And of the tribe of the people of Asher a chief, Ahihud the son of Shelomi. **28** Of the tribe of the people of Naphtali a chief, Pedahel the son of Ammihud. **29** These are the men whom the LORD commanded to divide the inheritance for the people of Israel in the land of Canaan."

Cities for the Levites

35 The LORD spoke to Moses in the plains of Moab by the Jordan at Jericho, saying, **2** "Command the people of Israel to give to the Levites some of the inheritance of their possession as cities for them to dwell in. And you shall give to the Levites pasturelands around the cities. ³ The cities shall be theirs to dwell in, and their pasturelands shall be for their cattle and for their livestock and for all their beasts. ⁴ The pasturelands of the cities, which you shall give to the Levites, shall reach from the wall of the city outward a thousand cubits all around. ⁵ And you shall measure, outside the city, on the east side two thousand cubits, and on the south side two thousand cubits, and on the west side two thousand cubits, and on the north side two thousand cubits, the city being in the middle. This shall belong to them as pastureland for their cities.

⁶ "The cities that you give to the Levites shall be the six cities of refuge, where you shall permit the manslayer to flee, and in addition to them you shall give forty-two cities. ⁷ All the cities that you give to the Levites shall be forty-eight, with their pasturelands. ⁸ And as for the cities that you shall give from the possession of the people of Israel, from the larger tribes you shall take many, and from the smaller tribes you shall take few; each, in proportion to the inheritance that it inherits, shall give of its cities to the Levites."

Cities of Refuge

⁹ And the LORD spoke to Moses, saying, ¹⁰ "Speak to the people of Israel and say to them, When you cross the Jordan into the land of Canaan, ¹¹ then you shall select cities to be cities of refuge for you, that the manslayer who kills any person without intent may flee there. ¹² The cities shall be for you a refuge from the avenger, that the manslayer may not die until he stands before the congregation for judgment. ¹³ And the cities that you give shall be your six cities of refuge. ¹⁴ You shall give three cities beyond the Jordan, and three cities in the land of Canaan, to be cities of refuge. ¹⁵ These six cities shall be for refuge for the people of Israel, and for the stranger and for the sojourner among them, that anyone who kills any person without intent may flee there.

¹⁶ "But if he struck him down with an iron object, so that he died, he is a murderer. The murderer shall be put to death. ¹⁷ And if he struck him down with a stone tool that could cause death, and he died, he is a murderer. The murderer shall be put to death. ¹⁸ Or if he struck him down with a wooden tool that could cause death, and he died, he is a murderer. The murderer shall be put to death. ¹⁹ The avenger of blood shall himself put the murderer to death; when he meets him, he shall put him to death. ²⁰ And if he pushed him out of hatred or hurled something at him, lying in wait, so that he died, ²¹ or in enmity struck him down with his hand, so that he died, then he who struck the blow shall be put to death. He is a murderer. The avenger of blood shall put the murderer to death when he meets him.

²² "But if he pushed him suddenly without enmity, or hurled anything on him without lying in wait ²³ or used a stone that could cause death, and without seeing him dropped it on him, so that he died, though he was not his enemy and did not seek his harm, ²⁴ then the congregation shall judge between the manslayer and the avenger of blood, in accordance with these rules. ²⁵ And the congregation shall rescue the manslayer from the hand of the avenger of blood, and the congregation shall restore him to his city of refuge to which he had fled, and he shall live in it until the death of the high priest who was anointed with the holy oil. ²⁶ But if the manslayer shall at any time go beyond the boundaries of his city of refuge to which he fled, ²⁷ and the avenger of blood finds him outside the boundaries of his city of refuge, and the avenger of blood kills the manslayer, he shall not be guilty of blood. ²⁸ For he must remain in his city of refuge until the death of the high priest, but after the death of the high priest the manslayer may return to the land of his possession. ²⁹ And these things shall be for a statute and rule for you throughout your generations in all your dwelling places.

³⁰ "If anyone kills a person, the murderer shall be put to death on the evidence of witnesses. But no person shall be put to death on the testimony of one witness. ³¹ Moreover, you shall accept no ransom for the life of a murderer, who is guilty of death, but he shall be put to death. ³² And you shall accept no ransom for him who has fled to his city of refuge, that he may return to dwell in the land before the death of the high priest. ³³ You shall not pollute the land in which you live, for blood pollutes the land, and no atonement can be made for the land for the blood that is shed in it,

except by the blood of the one who shed it. [34] You shall not defile the land in which you live, in the midst of which I dwell, for I the LORD dwell in the midst of the people of Israel."

Marriage of Female Heirs

36 The heads of the fathers' houses of the clan of the people of Gilead the son of Machir, son of Manasseh, from the clans of the people of Joseph, came near and spoke before Moses and before the chiefs, the heads of the fathers' houses of the people of Israel. [2] They said, "The LORD commanded my lord to give the land for inheritance by lot to the people of Israel, and my lord was commanded by the LORD to give the inheritance of Zelophehad our brother to his daughters. [3] But if they are married to any of the sons of the other tribes of the people of Israel, then their inheritance will be taken from the inheritance of our fathers and added to the inheritance of the tribe into which they marry. So it will be taken away from the lot of our inheritance. [4] And when the jubilee of the people of Israel comes, then their inheritance will be added to the inheritance of the tribe into which they marry, and their inheritance will be taken from the inheritance of the tribe of our fathers."

[5] And Moses commanded the people of Israel according to the word of the LORD, saying, "The tribe of the people of Joseph is right. [6] This is what the LORD commands concerning the daughters of Zelophehad: 'Let them marry whom they think best, only they shall marry within the clan of the tribe of their father. [7] The inheritance of the people of Israel shall not be transferred from one tribe to another, for every one of the people of Israel shall hold on to the inheritance of the tribe of his fathers. [8] And every daughter who possesses an inheritance in any tribe of the people of Israel shall be wife to one of the clan of the tribe of her father, so that every one of the people of Israel may possess the inheritance of his fathers. [9] So no inheritance shall be transferred from one tribe to another, for each of the tribes of the people of Israel shall hold on to its own inheritance.'"

[10] The daughters of Zelophehad did as the LORD commanded Moses, [11] for Mahlah, Tirzah, Hoglah, Milcah, and Noah, the daughters of Zelophehad, were married to sons of their father's brothers. [12] They were married into the clans of the people of Manasseh the son of Joseph, and their inheritance remained in the tribe of their father's clan.

[13] These are the commandments and the rules that the LORD commanded through Moses to the people of Israel in the plains of Moab by the Jordan at Jericho.

INTRODUCTION TO DEUTERONOMY

1446 B.C.	1408 B.C.	1406 B.C.
Exodus from Egypt	Moses addresses Israel in Moab	Israel enters Promised Land

THEME

Deuteronomy, the final book in the Pentateuch, contains Moses' last three sermons and two prophetic poems about Israel's future. Reflecting on the nation's past mistakes, Moses urges the people not to repeat those errors when they enter the Promised Land. Possessing Canaan will fulfill the promises made to the patriarchs, but if the people fall into idolatry or fail to keep the law, they will be exiled.

PURPOSE AND BACKGROUND

Deuteronomy is largely a sermon, or set of sermons, preached by Moses to all of Israel shortly before his death. It is a motivational sermon, urging Israel's faithful obedience to the covenant laws given 40 years previously at Sinai (Exodus 19–40).

The sermon is especially important because of Israel's earlier failure to conquer the land (see Deut. 1:19–46). Now that they are back at the eastern border of the Promised Land, Moses wants to ensure that the people will be obedient this time. The sermon encourages obedience by constantly reassuring them of God's faithfulness and his power to keep his promises. God is still faithful, despite Israel's persistent sin (e.g., 1:19–46; 9:1–29). He is merciful to his sinful people, for the sake of his promises to Abraham.

In Deuteronomy, Moses urges Israel to trust and obey, and to conquer the land. He highlights God's uniqueness (e.g., ch. 4), his power over other nations and armies (e.g., 2:1–23), and his grace and faithfulness. He reminds the people that God promised the land, that God's gift of the land is undeserved (9:4–6), and that the land is full of good things (e.g., 6:10–12).

Moses emphasizes the importance of God's law, given at Sinai (e.g., see 5:1–3). The large central section of Deuteronomy (12:1–26:19) recites the law and urges Israel to keep it. The law is wide-ranging, incorporating all areas

of life (economics, family and sexual relationships, religious observance, leadership, justice, guidance, food, property, and warfare). The details of the laws expand upon the great command of 6:5, that Israel is to love the Lord with all its heart, soul, and strength. Chapters 12–16 show what such total love of God will look like and provide examples of what the Ten Commandments (ch. 5) mean in practice.

KEY THEMES

1. God's uniqueness (4:1–40).

2. Israel's election (4:5–9; 7:6; 10:14–15; 14:1–2, 21).

3. The land's goodness (1:25; 6:10–11; 8:7–13; 11:8–15).

4. God's faithful promise-keeping (1:8, 19–46; 7:1–26; 8:1–20; 9:1–10:11).

5. God's power to defeat the enemies in the land (2:1–3:11; 4:1–40; 7:1–26).

6. Exhortations to Israel to love, serve, fear, and obey God (6:5; 10:12–13; 13:4).

7. Warnings against idolatry and instruction for proper worship of God (4:9–31; 5:6–10; 7:1–5; 8:19–20; 12:1–32; 13:1–18).

8. The impact of God's laws (12:1–27:26).

9. Moses' imminent death (1:37; 3:26; 4:21; 32:51; 34:1–12).

OUTLINE

DEUTERONOMY

The Command to Leave Horeb

1 These are the words that Moses spoke to all Israel beyond the Jordan in the wilderness, in the Arabah opposite Suph, between Paran and Tophel, Laban, Hazeroth, and Dizahab. ² It is eleven days' journey from Horeb by the way of Mount Seir to Kadesh-barnea. ³ In the fortieth year, on the first day of the eleventh month, Moses spoke to the people of Israel according to all that the LORD had given him in commandment to them, ⁴ after he had defeated Sihon the king of the Amorites, who lived in Heshbon, and Og the king of Bashan, who lived in Ashtaroth and in Edrei. ⁵ Beyond the Jordan, in the land of Moab, Moses undertook to explain this law, saying, ⁶ "The LORD our God said to us in Horeb, 'You have stayed long enough at this mountain. ⁷ Turn and take your journey, and go to the hill country of the Amorites and to all their neighbors in the Arabah, in the hill country and in the lowland and in the Negeb and by the seacoast, the land of the Canaanites, and Lebanon, as far as the great river, the river Euphrates. ⁸ See, I have set the land before you. Go in and take possession of the land that the LORD swore to your fathers, to Abraham, to Isaac, and to Jacob, to give to them and to their offspring after them.'

Leaders Appointed

⁹ "At that time I said to you, 'I am not able to bear you by myself. ¹⁰ The LORD your God has multiplied you, and behold, you are today as numerous as the stars of heaven. ¹¹ May the LORD, the God of your fathers, make you a thousand times as many as you are and bless you, as he has promised you! ¹² How can I bear by myself the weight and burden of you and your strife? ¹³ Choose for your tribes wise, understanding, and experienced men, and I will appoint them as your heads.' ¹⁴ And you answered me, 'The thing that you have spoken is good for us to do.' ¹⁵ So I took the heads of your tribes, wise and experienced men, and set them as heads over you, commanders of thousands, commanders of hundreds, commanders of fifties, commanders of tens, and officers, throughout your tribes. ¹⁶ And I charged your judges at that time, 'Hear the cases between your brothers, and judge righteously between a man and his brother or the alien who is with him. ¹⁷ You shall not be partial in judgment. You shall hear the small and the great alike. You shall not be intimidated by anyone, for the judgment is God's. And the case that is too hard for you, you shall bring to me, and I will hear it.' ¹⁸ And I commanded you at that time all the things that you should do.

GETTING THE MESSAGE

The Arabah (1:7) refers to the rugged and extremely dry region surrounding and south of the Dead Sea. The Israelites' travels took them through this area.

Israel's Refusal to Enter the Land

¹⁹ "Then we set out from Horeb and went through all that great and terrifying wilderness that you saw, on the way to the hill country of the Amorites, as the LORD our God commanded us. And we came to Kadesh-barnea. ²⁰ And I said to you, 'You have come to the hill country of the Amorites, which the LORD our God is giving us. ²¹ See, the LORD your God has set the land before you. Go up, take possession, as the LORD, the God of your fathers, has told you. Do not fear or be dismayed.' ²² Then all of you came near me and said, 'Let us send men before us, that they may explore the land for us and bring us word again of the way by which we must go up and the cities into which we shall come.' ²³ The thing seemed good to me, and I took twelve men from you, one man from each tribe. ²⁴ And they turned and went up into the hill country, and came to the Valley of Eshcol and spied it out. ²⁵ And they took in their hands

some of the fruit of the land and brought it down to us, and brought us word again and said, 'It is a good land that the LORD our God is giving us.'

²⁶ "Yet you would not go up, but rebelled against the command of the LORD your God. ²⁷ And you murmured in your tents and said, 'Because the LORD hated us he has brought us out of the land of Egypt, to give us into the hand of the Amorites, to destroy us. ²⁸ Where are we going up? Our brothers have made our hearts melt, saying, "The people are greater and taller than we. The cities are great and fortified up to heaven. And besides, we have seen the sons of the Anakim there."' ²⁹ Then I said to you, 'Do not be in dread or afraid of them. ³⁰ The LORD

GETTING THE MESSAGE

Was Deuteronomy a treaty? There are many similarities between the book of Deuteronomy and various ancient Near Eastern treaties that date from the time of Moses. When a nation made a treaty with a less powerful nation, the document began with the past relationship between the countries. Next, the treaty stated the laws that would govern the relationship from that point on. Finally, the treaty concluded with a list of blessings and punishments for obedience or disobedience.

your God who goes before you will himself fight for you, just as he did for you in Egypt before your eyes, ³¹ and in the wilderness, where you have seen how the LORD your God carried you, as a man carries his son, all the way that you went until you came to this place.' ³² Yet in spite of this word you did not believe the LORD your God, ³³ who went before you in the way to seek you out a place to pitch your tents, in fire by night and in the cloud by day, to show you by what way you should go.

The Penalty for Israel's Rebellion

³⁴ "And the LORD heard your words and was angered, and he swore, ³⁵ 'Not one of these men of this evil generation shall see the good land that I swore to give to your fathers, ³⁶ except Caleb the son of

Jephunneh. He shall see it, and to him and to his children I will give the land on which he has trodden, because he has wholly followed the LORD!' ³⁷ Even with me the LORD was angry on your account and said, 'You also shall not go in there. ³⁸ Joshua the son of Nun, who stands before you, he shall enter. Encourage him, for he shall cause Israel to inherit it. ³⁹ And as for your little ones, who you said would become a prey, and your children, who today have no knowledge of good or evil, they shall go in there. And to them I will give it, and they shall possess it. ⁴⁰ But as for you, turn, and journey into the wilderness in the direction of the Red Sea.'

⁴¹ "Then you answered me, 'We have sinned against the LORD. We ourselves will go up and fight, just as the LORD our God commanded us.' And every one of you fastened on his weapons of war and thought it easy to go up into the hill country. ⁴² And the LORD said to me, 'Say to them, Do not go up or fight, for I am not in your midst, lest you be defeated before your enemies.' ⁴³ So I spoke to you, and you would not listen; but you rebelled against the command of the LORD and presumptuously went up into the hill country. ⁴⁴ Then the Amorites who lived in that hill country came out against you and chased you as bees do and beat you down in Seir as far as Hormah. ⁴⁵ And you returned and wept before the LORD, but the LORD did not listen to your voice or give ear to you. ⁴⁶ So you remained at Kadesh many days, the days that you remained there.

The Wilderness Years

2 "Then we turned and journeyed into the wilderness in the direction of the Red Sea, as the LORD told me. And for many days we traveled around Mount Seir. ² Then the LORD said to me, ³ 'You have been traveling around this mountain country long enough. Turn northward ⁴ and command the people, "You are about to pass through the territory of your brothers, the people of Esau, who live in Seir; and they will be afraid of you. So be very careful. ⁵ Do not contend with them, for I will not give you any of their land, no, not so much as for the sole of the foot to tread on, because I have given Mount Seir to Esau as a possession. ⁶ You shall purchase food from them with money, that you may eat, and you shall also buy water from them with money, that you may drink. ⁷ For the

LORD your God has blessed you in all the work of your hands. He knows your going through this great wilderness. These forty years the LORD your God has been with you. You have lacked nothing." ' 8 So we went on, away from our brothers, the people of Esau, who live in Seir, away from the Arabah road from Elath and Ezion-geber.

"And we turned and went in the direction of the wilderness of Moab. 9 And the LORD said to me, 'Do not harass Moab or contend with them in battle, for I will not give you any of their land for a possession, because I have given Ar to the people of Lot for a possession.' 10 (The Emim formerly lived there, a people great and many, and tall as the Anakim. 11 Like the Anakim they are also counted as Rephaim, but the Moabites call them Emim. 12 The Horites also lived in Seir formerly, but the people of Esau dispossessed them and destroyed them from before them and settled in their place, as Israel did to the land of their possession, which the LORD gave to them.) 13 'Now rise up and go over the brook Zered.' So we went over the brook Zered. 14 And the time from our leaving Kadesh-barnea until we crossed the brook Zered was thirty-eight years, until the entire generation, that is, the men of war, had perished from the camp, as the LORD had sworn to them. 15 For indeed the hand of the LORD was against them, to destroy them from the camp, until they had perished.

16 "So as soon as all the men of war had perished and were dead from among the people, 17 the LORD said to me, 18 'Today you are to cross the border of Moab at Ar. 19 And when you approach the territory of the people of Ammon, do not harass them or contend with them, for I will not give you any of the land of the people of Ammon as a possession, because I have given it to the sons of Lot for a possession.' 20 (It is also counted as a land of Rephaim. Rephaim formerly lived there—but the Ammonites call them Zamzummim— 21 a people great and many, and tall as the Anakim; but the LORD destroyed them before the Ammonites, and they dispossessed them and settled in their place, 22 as he did for the people of Esau, who live in Seir, when he destroyed the Horites before them and they dispossessed them and settled in their place even to this day.

23 As for the Avvim, who lived in villages as far as Gaza, the Caphtorim, who came from Caphtor, destroyed them and settled in their place.) 24 'Rise up, set out on your journey and go over the Valley of the Arnon. Behold, I have given into your hand Sihon the Amorite, king of Heshbon, and his land. Begin to take possession, and contend with him in battle. 25 This day I will begin to put the dread and fear of you on the peoples who are under the whole heaven, who shall hear the report of you and shall tremble and be in anguish because of you.'

The Defeat of King Sihon

26 "So I sent messengers from the wilderness of Kedemoth to Sihon the king of Heshbon, with words of peace, saying, 27 'Let me pass through your land. I will go only by the road; I will turn aside neither

GETTING THE MESSAGE

Nations fought for control of **Gilead** (2:36) because an international trade route, known as the King's Highway, passed through it. The region was also an important area for agriculture. It was especially famous for the "balm of Gilead," a resin used as medicine (Jer. 8:22).

to the right nor to the left. 28 You shall sell me food for money, that I may eat, and give me water for money, that I may drink. Only let me pass through on foot, 29 as the sons of Esau who live in Seir and the Moabites who live in Ar did for me, until I go over the Jordan into the land that the LORD our God is giving to us.' 30 But Sihon the king of Heshbon would not let us pass by him, for the LORD your God hardened his spirit and made his heart obstinate, that he might give him into your hand, as he is this day. 31 And the LORD said to me, 'Behold, I have begun to give Sihon and his land over to you. Begin to take possession, that you may occupy his land.' 32 Then Sihon came out against us, he and all his people, to battle at Jahaz. 33 And the LORD our God gave him over to us, and we defeated him and his sons and all his people. 34 And we captured all his cities at that time and devoted to destruction[1] every

---

[1] That is, destroyed or made an offering because of sin, at God's command; also 3:6; 7:2, 26; 13:15; 20:17

city, men, women, and children. We left no survivors. **35** Only the livestock we took as spoil for ourselves, with the plunder of the cities that we captured. **36** From Aroer, which is on the edge of the Valley of the Arnon, and from the city that is in the valley, as far as Gilead, there was not a city too high for us. The LORD our God gave all into our hands. **37** Only to the land of the sons of Ammon you did not draw near, that is, to all the banks of the river Jabbok and the cities of the hill country, whatever the LORD our God had forbidden us.

The Defeat of King Og

3 "Then we turned and went up the way to Bashan. And Og the king of Bashan came out against us, he and all his people, to battle at Edrei. **2** But the LORD said to me, 'Do not fear him, for I have given him and all his people and his land into your hand. And you shall do to him as you did to

The Jordan River begins in the foothills of Mount Hermon and empties into the Dead Sea. The Jordan is more than 200 miles (322 km) long—the longest river in Palestine.

Sihon the king of the Amorites, who lived at Heshbon.' **3** So the LORD our God gave into our hand Og also, the king of Bashan, and all his people, and we struck him down until he had no survivor left. **4** And we took all his cities at that time—there was not a city that we did not take from them—sixty cities, the whole region of Argob, the kingdom of Og in Bashan. **5** All these were cities fortified with high walls, gates, and bars, besides very many unwalled villages. **6** And we devoted them to destruction, as we did to Sihon the king of Heshbon, devoting to destruction every city, men, women, and children. **7** But all the livestock and the spoil of the cities we took as our plunder. **8** So we took the land at that time out of the hand of the two kings of the Amorites who were beyond the Jordan, from the Valley of the Arnon to Mount Hermon **9** (the Sidonians call Hermon Sirion, while the Amorites call it Senir), **10** all the cities of the tableland and all Gilead and all Bashan, as far as Salecah

and Edrei, cities of the kingdom of Og in Bashan. **11** (For only Og the king of Bashan was left of the remnant of the Rephaim. Behold, his bed was a bed of iron. Is it not in Rabbah of the Ammonites? Nine cubits was its length, and four cubits its breadth, according to the common cubit.)

12 "When we took possession of this land at that time, I gave to the Reubenites and the Gadites the territory beginning at Aroer, which is on the edge of the Valley of the Arnon, and half the hill country of Gilead with its cities. **13** The rest of Gilead, and all Bashan, the kingdom of Og, that is, all the region of Argob, I gave to the half-tribe of Manasseh. (All that portion of Bashan is called the land of Rephaim. **14** Jair the Manassite took all the region of Argob, that is, Bashan, as far as the border of the Geshurites and the Maacathites, and called the villages after his own name, Havvoth-jair, as it is to this day.) **15** To Machir I gave Gilead, **16** and to the Reubenites and the Gadites I gave the territory from Gilead as far as the Valley of the Arnon, with the middle of the valley as a border, as far over as the river Jabbok, the border of the Ammonites; **17** the Arabah also, with the Jordan as the border, from Chinnereth as far as the Sea of the Arabah, the Salt Sea, under the slopes of Pisgah on the east.

18 "And I commanded you at that time, saying, 'The LORD your God has given you this land to possess. All your men of valor shall cross over armed before your brothers, the people of Israel. **19** Only your wives, your little ones, and your livestock (I know that you have much livestock) shall remain in the cities that I have given you, **20** until the LORD gives rest to your brothers, as to you, and they also occupy the land that the LORD your God gives them beyond the Jordan. Then each of you may return to his possession which I have given you.' **21** And I commanded Joshua at that time, 'Your eyes have seen all that the LORD your God has done to these two kings. So will the LORD do to all the kingdoms into which you are crossing. **22** You shall not fear them, for it is the LORD your God who fights for you.'

Moses Forbidden to Enter the Land

23 "And I pleaded with the LORD at that time, saying, **24** 'O Lord GOD, you have only begun to show your servant your greatness and your mighty hand. For what god is there in heaven or on earth who can do such works and mighty acts as yours? ²⁵ Please let me go over and see the good land beyond the Jordan, that good hill country and Lebanon.' ²⁶ But the LORD was angry with me because of you and would not listen to me. And the LORD said to me, 'Enough from you; do not speak to me of this matter again. ²⁷ Go up to the top of Pisgah and lift up your eyes westward and northward and southward and eastward, and look at it with your eyes, for you shall not go over this Jordan. ²⁸ But charge Joshua, and encourage and strengthen him, for he shall go over at the head of this people, and he shall put them in possession of the land that you shall see.' ²⁹ So we remained in the valley opposite Beth-peor.

Moses Commands Obedience

4 "And now, O Israel, listen to the statutes and the rules that I am teaching you, and do them, that you may live, and go in and take possession of the land that the LORD, the God of your fathers, is giving you. ² You shall not add to the word that I command you, nor take from it, that you may keep the commandments of the LORD your God that I command you. ³ Your eyes have seen what the LORD did at Baal-peor, for the LORD your God destroyed from among you all the men who followed the Baal of Peor. ⁴ But you who held fast to the LORD your God are all alive today. ⁵ See, I have taught you statutes and rules, as the LORD my God commanded me, that you should do them in the land that you are entering to take possession of it. ⁶ Keep them and do them, for that will be your wisdom and your understanding in the sight of the peoples, who, when they hear all these statutes, will say, 'Surely this great nation is a wise and understanding people.' ⁷ For what great nation is there that has a god so near to it as the LORD our God is to us, whenever we call upon him? ⁸ And what great nation is there, that has statutes and rules so righteous as all this law that I set before you today?

⁹ "Only take care, and keep your soul diligently, lest you forget the things that your eyes have seen, and lest they depart from your heart all the days of your life. Make them known to your children and your children's children — ¹⁰ how on the day that you

stood before the LORD your God at Horeb, the LORD said to me, 'Gather the people to me, that I may let them hear my words, so that they may learn to fear me all the days that they live on the earth, and that they may teach their children so.' ¹¹ And you came near and stood at the foot of the mountain, while the mountain burned with fire to the heart of heaven, wrapped in darkness, cloud, and gloom. ¹² Then the LORD spoke to you out of the midst of the fire. You heard the sound of words, but saw no form; there was only a voice. ¹³ And he declared to you his covenant, which he commanded you to perform, that is, the Ten Commandments, and he wrote them on two tablets of stone. ¹⁴ And the LORD commanded me at that time to teach you statutes and rules, that you might do them in the land that you are going over to possess.

Idolatry Forbidden

¹⁵ "Therefore watch yourselves very carefully. Since you saw no form on the day that the LORD spoke to you at Horeb out of the midst of the fire, ¹⁶ beware lest you act corruptly by making a carved image for yourselves, in the form of any figure, the likeness of male or female, ¹⁷ the likeness of any animal that is on the earth, the likeness of any winged bird that flies in the air, ¹⁸ the likeness of anything that creeps on the ground, the likeness of any fish that is in the water under the earth. ¹⁹ And beware lest you raise your eyes to heaven, and when you see the sun and the moon and the stars, all the host of heaven, you be drawn away and bow down to them and serve them, things that the LORD your God has allotted to all the peoples under the whole heaven. ²⁰ But the LORD has taken you and brought you out of the iron furnace, out of Egypt, to be a people of his own inheritance, as you are this day. ²¹ Furthermore, the LORD was angry with me because of you, and he swore that I should not cross the Jordan, and that I should not enter the good land that the LORD your God is giving you for an inheritance. ²² For I must die in this land; I must not go over the Jordan. But you shall go over and take possession of that good land. ²³ Take care, lest you forget the covenant of the LORD your God, which he made with you, and make a carved image, the form of anything that the LORD your God has forbidden you.

²⁴ For the LORD your God is a consuming fire, a jealous God.

²⁵ "When you father children and children's children, and have grown old in the land, if you act corruptly by making a carved image in the form of anything, and by doing what is evil in the sight of the LORD your God, so as to provoke him to anger, ²⁶ I call heaven and earth to witness against you today, that you will soon utterly perish from the land that you are going over the Jordan to possess. You will not live long in it, but will be utterly destroyed. ²⁷ And the LORD will scatter you among the peoples, and you will be left few in number among the nations where the LORD will drive you. ²⁸ And there you will serve gods of wood and stone, the work of human hands, that neither see, nor hear, nor eat, nor smell. ²⁹ But from there you will seek the LORD your God and you will find him, if you search after

---

GETTING THE MESSAGE

A book of sermons? Deuteronomy consists of at least three addresses or sermons from Moses to Israel. Moses encourages Israel to obey all the commandments of God.

---

him with all your heart and with all your soul. ³⁰ When you are in tribulation, and all these things come upon you in the latter days, you will return to the LORD your God and obey his voice. ³¹ For the LORD your God is a merciful God. He will not leave you or destroy you or forget the covenant with your fathers that he swore to them.

The LORD Alone Is God

³² "For ask now of the days that are past, which were before you, since the day that God created man on the earth, and ask from one end of heaven to the other, whether such a great thing as this has ever happened or was ever heard of. ³³ Did any people ever hear the voice of a god speaking out of the midst of the fire, as you have heard, and still live? ³⁴ Or has any god ever attempted to go and take a nation for himself from the midst of another nation, by trials, by signs, by wonders, and by war, by a mighty hand and an outstretched arm, and by great deeds

of terror, all of which the LORD your God did for you in Egypt before your eyes? ³⁵ To you it was shown, that you might know that the LORD is God; there is no other besides him. ³⁶ Out of heaven he let you hear his voice, that he might discipline you. And on earth he let you see his great fire, and you heard his words out of the midst of the fire. ³⁷ And because he loved your fathers and chose their offspring after them and brought you out of Egypt with his own presence, by his great power, ³⁸ driving out before you nations greater and mightier than you, to bring you in, to give you their land for an inheritance, as it is this day, ³⁹ know therefore today, and lay it to your heart, that the LORD is God in heaven above and on the earth beneath; there is no other. ⁴⁰ Therefore you shall keep his statutes and his commandments, which I command you today, that it may go well with you and with your children after you, and that you may prolong your days in the land that the LORD your God is giving you for all time."

Cities of Refuge

⁴¹ Then Moses set apart three cities in the east beyond the Jordan, ⁴² that the manslayer might flee there, anyone who kills his neighbor unintentionally, without being at enmity with him in time past; he may flee to one of these cities and save his life: ⁴³ Bezer in the wilderness on the tableland for the Reubenites, Ramoth in Gilead for the Gadites, and Golan in Bashan for the Manassites.

Introduction to the Law

⁴⁴ This is the law that Moses set before the people of Israel. ⁴⁵ These are the testimonies, the statutes, and the rules, which Moses spoke to the people of Israel when they came out of Egypt, ⁴⁶ beyond the Jordan in the valley opposite Beth-peor, in the land of Sihon the king of the Amorites, who lived at Heshbon, whom Moses and the people of Israel defeated when they came out of Egypt. ⁴⁷ And they took possession of his land and the land of Og, the king of Bashan, the two kings of the Amorites, who lived to the east beyond the Jordan; ⁴⁸ from Aroer, which is on the edge of the Valley of the Arnon, as far as Mount Sirion (that is, Hermon), ⁴⁹ together with all the Arabah on the east side of the Jordan as far as the Sea of the Arabah, under the slopes of Pisgah.

The Ten Commandments

5 And Moses summoned all Israel and said to them, "Hear, O Israel, the statutes and the rules that I speak in your hearing today, and you shall learn them and be careful to do them. ² The LORD our God made a covenant with us in Horeb. ³ Not with our fathers did the LORD make this covenant, but with us, who are all of us here alive today. ⁴ The LORD spoke with you face to face at the mountain, out of the midst of the fire, ⁵ while I stood between the LORD and you at that time, to declare to you the word of the LORD. For you were afraid because of the fire, and you did not go up into the mountain. He said:

⁶ "'I am the LORD your God, who brought you out of the land of Egypt, out of the house of slavery.

⁷ "'You shall have no other gods before me.

⁸ "'You shall not make for yourself a carved image, or any likeness of anything that is in heaven above, or that is on the earth beneath, or that is in the water under the earth. ⁹ You shall not bow down to them or serve them; for I the LORD your God am a jealous God, visiting the iniquity of the fathers on the children to the third and fourth generation of those who hate me, ¹⁰ but showing steadfast love to thousands of those who love me and keep my commandments.

¹¹ "'You shall not take the name of the LORD your God in vain, for the LORD will not hold him guiltless who takes his name in vain.

¹² "'Observe the Sabbath day, to keep it holy, as the LORD your God commanded you. ¹³ Six days you shall labor and do all your work, ¹⁴ but the seventh day is a Sabbath to the LORD your God. On it you shall not do any work, you or your son or your daughter or your male servant or your female servant, or your ox or your donkey or any of your livestock, or the sojourner who is within your gates, that your male servant and your female servant may rest as well as you. ¹⁵ You shall remember that you were a slave in the land of Egypt, and the LORD your God brought you out from there with a mighty hand and an outstretched arm. Therefore the LORD your God commanded you to keep the Sabbath day.

¹⁶ "'Honor your father and your mother, as the LORD your God commanded you, that your days may be long, and that it may go well with you in the land that the LORD your God is giving you.

¹⁷ "'You shall not murder.

¹⁸ "'And you shall not commit adultery.

¹⁹ "'And you shall not steal.

²⁰ "'And you shall not bear false witness against your neighbor.

²¹ "'And you shall not covet your neighbor's wife. And you shall not desire your neighbor's house, his field, or his male servant, or his female servant, his ox, or his donkey, or anything that is your neighbor's.'

²² "These words the LORD spoke to all your assembly at the mountain out of the midst of the fire, the cloud, and the thick darkness, with a loud voice; and he added no more. And he wrote them on two tablets of stone and gave them to me. ²³ And as soon as you heard the voice out of the midst of the darkness, while the mountain was burning with fire, you came near to me, all the heads of your tribes, and your elders. ²⁴ And you said, 'Behold, the LORD our God has shown us his glory and greatness, and we have heard his voice out of the midst of the fire. This day we have seen God speak with man, and man still live. ²⁵ Now therefore why should we die? For this great fire will consume us. If we hear the voice of the LORD our God any more, we shall die. ²⁶ For who is there of all flesh, that has heard the voice of the living God speaking out of the midst of fire as we have, and has still lived? ²⁷ Go near and hear all that the LORD our God will say, and speak to us all that the LORD our God will speak to you, and we will hear and do it.'

²⁸ "And the LORD heard your words, when you spoke to me. And the LORD said to me, 'I have heard the words of this people, which they have spoken to you. They are right in all that they have spoken. ²⁹ Oh that they had such a heart as this always, to fear me and to keep all my commandments, that it might go well with them and with their descendants forever! ³⁰ Go and say to them, "Return to your tents." ³¹ But you, stand here by me, and I will tell you the whole commandment and the statutes and the rules that you shall teach them, that they may do them in the land that I am giving them to possess.' ³² You shall be careful therefore to do as the LORD your God has commanded you. You shall not turn aside to the right hand or to the

left. [33] You shall walk in all the way that the LORD your God has commanded you, that you may live, and that it may go well with you, and that you may live long in the land that you shall possess.

The Greatest Commandment

6 "Now this is the commandment—the statutes and the rules—that the LORD your God commanded me to teach you, that you may do them in the land to which you are going over, to possess it, [2] that you may fear the LORD your God, you and your son and your son's son, by keeping all his statutes and his commandments, which I command you, all the days of your life, and that your days may be long. [3] Hear therefore, O Israel, and be careful to do them, that it may go well with you, and that you may multiply greatly, as the LORD, the God of

your fathers, has promised you, in a land flowing with milk and honey.

[4] "Hear, O Israel: The LORD our God, the LORD is one. [5] You shall love the LORD your God with all your heart and with all your soul and with all your might. [6] And these words that I command you today shall be on your heart. [7] You shall teach them diligently to your children, and shall talk of them when you sit in your house, and when you walk by the way, and when you lie down, and when you rise. [8] You shall bind them as a sign on your hand, and they shall be as frontlets between your eyes. [9] You shall write them on the doorposts of your house and on your gates.

[10] "And when the LORD your God brings you into the land that he swore to your fathers, to Abraham, to Isaac, and to Jacob, to give you—with great and good cities that you did not build, [11] and houses full of all

good things that you did not fill, and cisterns that you did not dig, and vineyards and olive trees that you did not plant—and when you eat and are full, [12] then take care lest you forget the LORD, who brought you out of the land of Egypt, out of the house of slavery. [13] It is the LORD your God you shall fear. Him you shall serve and by his name you shall swear. [14] You shall not go after other gods, the gods of the peoples who are around you—[15] for the LORD your God in your midst is a jealous God—lest the anger of the LORD your God be kindled against you, and he destroy you from off the face of the earth.

[16] "You shall not put the LORD your God to the test, as you tested him at Massah. [17] You shall diligently keep the commandments of the LORD your God, and his testimonies and his statutes, which he has commanded you. [18] And you shall do what is right and good in the sight of the LORD, that it may go well with you, and that you may go in and take possession of the good land that the LORD swore to give to your fathers [19] by thrusting out all your enemies from before you, as the LORD has promised.

[20] "When your son asks you in time to come, 'What is the meaning of the testimonies and the statutes and the rules that the LORD our God has commanded you?' [21] then you shall say to your son, 'We were Pharaoh's slaves in Egypt. And the LORD brought us out of Egypt with a mighty hand. [22] And the LORD showed signs and wonders, great and grievous, against Egypt and against Pharaoh and all his household, before our eyes. [23] And he brought us out from there, that he might bring us in and give us the land that he swore to give to our fathers. [24] And the LORD commanded us to do all these statutes, to fear the LORD our God, for our good always, that he might preserve us alive, as we are this day. [25] And it will be righteousness for us, if we are careful to do all this commandment before the LORD our God, as he has commanded us.'

A Chosen People

7 "When the LORD your God brings you into the land that you are entering to take possession of it, and clears away many nations before you, the Hittites, the Girgashites, the Amorites, the Canaanites, the Perizzites, the Hivites, and the Jebusites,

seven nations more numerous and mightier than you, ² and when the Lord your God gives them over to you, and you defeat them, then you must devote them to complete destruction. You shall make no covenant with them and show no mercy to them. ³ You shall not intermarry with them, giving your daughters to their sons or taking their daughters for your sons, ⁴ for they would turn away your sons from following me, to serve other gods. Then the anger of the Lord would be kindled against you, and he would destroy you quickly. ⁵ But thus shall you deal with them: you shall break down their altars and dash in pieces their pillars and chop down their Asherim and burn their carved images with fire.

⁶ "For you are a people holy to the Lord your God. The Lord your God has chosen you to be a people for his treasured possession, out of all the peoples who are on the face of the earth. ⁷ It was not because you were more in number than any other people that the Lord set his love on you and chose you, for you were the fewest of all peoples, ⁸ but it is because the Lord loves you and is keeping the oath that he swore to your fathers, that the Lord has brought you out with a mighty hand and redeemed you from the house of slavery, from the hand of Pharaoh king of Egypt. ⁹ Know therefore that the Lord your God is God, the faithful God who keeps covenant and steadfast love with those who love him and keep his commandments, to a thousand generations, ¹⁰ and repays to their face those who hate him, by destroying them. He will not be slack with one who hates him. He will repay him to his face. ¹¹ You shall therefore be careful to do the commandment and the statutes and the rules that I command you today.

¹² "And because you listen to these rules and keep and do them, the Lord your God will keep with you the covenant and the steadfast love that he swore to your fathers. ¹³ He will love you, bless you, and multiply you. He will also bless the fruit of your womb and the fruit of your ground, your grain and your wine and your oil, the increase of your herds and the young of your flock, in the land that he swore to your fathers to give you. ¹⁴ You shall be blessed above all peoples. There shall not be male or female barren among you or among your livestock. ¹⁵ And the Lord will take away from you all sickness, and none of the evil diseases of Egypt, which you knew, will he inflict on you, but he will lay them on all who hate you. ¹⁶ And you shall consume all the peoples that the Lord your God will give over to you. Your eye shall not pity them, neither shall you serve their gods, for that would be a snare to you.

¹⁷ "If you say in your heart, 'These nations are greater than I. How can I dispossess them?' ¹⁸ you shall not be afraid of them but you shall remember what the Lord your God did to Pharaoh and to all Egypt, ¹⁹ the great trials that your eyes saw, the signs, the wonders, the mighty hand, and the outstretched arm, by which the Lord your God brought you out. So will the Lord your God do to all the peoples of whom you are afraid. ²⁰ Moreover, the Lord your God will send hornets among them, until those who are left and hide themselves from you are destroyed. ²¹ You shall not be in dread of them, for the Lord your God is in your midst, a great and awesome God. ²² The Lord your God will clear away these nations before you little by little. You may not make an end of them at once, lest the wild beasts grow too numerous for you. ²³ But the Lord your God will give them over to you and throw them into great confusion, until they are destroyed. ²⁴ And he will give their kings into your hand, and you shall make their name perish from under heaven. No one shall be able to stand against you until you have destroyed them. ²⁵ The carved images of their gods you shall burn with fire. You shall not covet the silver or the gold that is on them or take it for yourselves, lest you be ensnared by it, for it is an abomination to the Lord your God. ²⁶ And you shall not bring an abominable thing into your house and become devoted to destruction like it. You shall utterly detest and abhor it, for it is devoted to destruction.

Remember the Lord Your God

8 "The whole commandment that I command you today you shall be careful to do, that you may live and multiply, and go in and possess the land that the Lord swore to give to your fathers. ² And you shall remember the whole way that the Lord your God has led you these forty years in the wilderness, that he might humble you, testing you to know what was in your heart, whether you would keep his commandments or not. ³ And he humbled you and let you hunger and fed you with manna, which you did not know, nor did your fathers know, that he might make you know that man does not live by bread alone, but man lives by every word that comes from the mouth of the LORD. ⁴ Your clothing did not wear out on you and your foot did not swell these forty years. ⁵ Know then in your heart that, as a man disciplines his son, the LORD your God disciplines you. ⁶ So you shall keep the commandments of the LORD your God by walking in his ways and by fearing him. ⁷ For the LORD your God is bringing you into a good land, a land of brooks of water, of fountains and springs, flowing out in the valleys and hills, ⁸ a land of wheat and barley, of

GETTING THE MESSAGE

Jesus quoted from the book of Deuteronomy more than any other Old Testament book. He quoted 8:3 when tempted by Satan (Matt. 4:4).

vines and fig trees and pomegranates, a land of olive trees and honey, ⁹ a land in which you will eat bread without scarcity, in which you will lack nothing, a land whose stones are iron, and out of whose hills you can dig copper. ¹⁰ And you shall eat and be full, and you shall bless the LORD your God for the good land he has given you.

¹¹ "Take care lest you forget the LORD your God by not keeping his commandments and his rules and his statutes, which I command you today, ¹² lest, when you have eaten and are full and have built good houses and live in them, ¹³ and when your herds and flocks multiply and your silver and gold is multiplied and all that you have is multiplied, ¹⁴ then your heart be lifted up, and you forget the LORD your God, who brought you out of the land of Egypt, out of the house of slavery, ¹⁵ who led you through the great and terrifying wilderness, with its fiery serpents and scorpions and thirsty ground where there was no water, who brought you water out of the flinty rock, ¹⁶ who fed you in the wilderness with manna that your fathers

did not know, that he might humble you and test you, to do you good in the end. ¹⁷ Beware lest you say in your heart, 'My power and the might of my hand have gotten me this wealth.' ¹⁸ You shall remember the LORD your God, for it is he who gives you power to get wealth, that he may confirm his covenant that he swore to your fathers, as it is this day. ¹⁹ And if you forget the LORD your God and go after other gods and serve them and worship them, I solemnly warn you today that you shall surely perish. ²⁰ Like the nations that the LORD makes to perish before you, so shall you perish, because you would not obey the voice of the LORD your God.

Not Because of Righteousness

9 "Hear, O Israel: you are to cross over the Jordan today, to go in to dispossess nations greater and mightier than you, cities great and fortified up to heaven, ² a people great and tall, the sons of the Anakim, whom you know, and of whom you have heard it said, 'Who can stand before the sons of Anak?' ³ Know therefore today that he who goes over before you as a consuming fire is the LORD your God. He will destroy them and subdue them before you. So you shall drive them out and make them perish quickly, as the LORD has promised you.

⁴ "Do not say in your heart, after the LORD your God has thrust them out before you, 'It is because of my righteousness that the LORD has brought me in to possess this land,' whereas it is because of the wickedness of these nations that the LORD is driving them out before you. ⁵ Not because of your righteousness or the uprightness of your heart are you going in to possess their land, but because of the wickedness of these nations the LORD your God is driving them out from before you, and that he may confirm the word that the LORD swore to your fathers, to Abraham, to Isaac, and to Jacob.

⁶ "Know, therefore, that the LORD your God is not giving you this good land to possess because of your righteousness, for you are a stubborn people. ⁷ Remember and do not forget how you provoked the LORD your God to wrath in the wilderness. From the day you came out of the land of Egypt until you came to this place, you have been rebellious against the LORD. ⁸ Even at Horeb you provoked the LORD to wrath, and the LORD was so angry with you that he was

ready to destroy you. 9 When I went up the mountain to receive the tablets of stone, the tablets of the covenant that the LORD made with you, I remained on the mountain forty days and forty nights. I neither ate bread nor drank water. 10 And the LORD gave me the two tablets of stone written with the finger of God, and on them were all the words that the LORD had spoken with you on the mountain out of the midst of the fire on the day of the assembly. 11 And at the end of forty days and forty nights the LORD gave me the two tablets of stone, the tablets of the covenant. 12 Then the LORD said to me, 'Arise, go down quickly from here, for your people whom you have brought from Egypt have acted corruptly. They have turned aside quickly out of the way that I commanded them; they have made themselves a metal image.'

The Golden Calf

13 "Furthermore, the LORD said to me, 'I have seen this people, and behold, it is a stubborn people. 14 Let me alone, that I may destroy them and blot out their name from under heaven. And I will make of you a nation mightier and greater than they.' 15 So I turned and came down from the mountain, and the mountain was burning with fire. And the two tablets of the covenant were in my two hands. 16 And I looked, and behold, you had sinned against the LORD your God. You had made yourselves a golden calf. You had turned aside quickly from the way that the LORD had commanded you. 17 So I took hold of the two tablets and threw them out of my two hands and broke them before your eyes. 18 Then I lay prostrate before the LORD as before, forty days and forty nights. I neither ate bread nor drank water, because of all the sin that you had committed, in doing what was evil in the sight of the LORD to provoke him to anger. 19 For I was afraid of the anger and hot displeasure that the LORD bore against you, so that he was ready to destroy you. But the LORD listened to me that time also. 20 And the LORD was so angry with Aaron that he was ready to destroy him. And I prayed for Aaron also at the same time. 21 Then I took the sinful thing, the calf that you had made, and burned it with fire and crushed it, grinding it very small, until it was as fine as dust. And I threw the dust of it into the brook that ran down from the mountain.

22 "At Taberah also, and at Massah and at Kibroth-hattaavah you provoked the LORD to wrath. 23 And when the LORD sent you from Kadesh-barnea, saying, 'Go up and take possession of the land that I have given you,' then you rebelled against the commandment of the LORD your God and did not believe him or obey his voice. 24 You have been rebellious against the LORD from the day that I knew you.

25 "So I lay prostrate before the LORD for these forty days and forty nights, because the LORD had said he would destroy you. 26 And I prayed to the LORD, 'O Lord GOD, do not destroy your people and your heritage, whom you have redeemed through your greatness, whom you have brought out of Egypt with a mighty hand. 27 Remember your servants, Abraham, Isaac, and Jacob. Do not regard the stubbornness of this people, or their wickedness or their sin, 28 lest

A **sojourner** was a person from another country who was living and working in Israel. The Israelites were taught to love and respect the sojourners living among them, for they themselves had been sojourners in Egypt (10:19).

the land from which you brought us say, "Because the LORD was not able to bring them into the land that he promised them, and because he hated them, he has brought them out to put them to death in the wilderness." 29 For they are your people and your heritage, whom you brought out by your great power and by your outstretched arm.'

New Tablets of Stone

10 "At that time the LORD said to me, 'Cut for yourself two tablets of stone like the first, and come up to me on the mountain and make an ark of wood. 2 And I will write on the tablets the words that were on the first tablets that you broke, and you shall put them in the ark.' 3 So I made an ark of acacia wood, and cut two tablets of stone like the first, and went up the mountain with the two tablets in my hand. 4 And he wrote on the tablets, in the same writing as before, the Ten Commandments that the

LORD had spoken to you on the mountain out of the midst of the fire on the day of the assembly. And the LORD gave them to me. ⁵ Then I turned and came down from the mountain and put the tablets in the ark that I had made. And there they are, as the LORD commanded me."

⁶ (The people of Israel journeyed from Beeroth Bene-jaakan to Moserah. There Aaron died, and there he was buried. And his son Eleazar ministered as priest in his place. ⁷ From there they journeyed to Gudgodah, and from Gudgodah to Jotbathah, a land with brooks of water. ⁸ At that time the LORD set apart the tribe of Levi to carry the ark of the covenant of the LORD to stand before the LORD to minister to him and to bless in his name, to this day. ⁹ Therefore Levi has no portion or inheritance with his brothers. The LORD is his inheritance, as the LORD your God said to him.)

GETTING THE MESSAGE

God promised his people that they would **live long in the land** of Israel, if they would love, obey, and serve him (11:9, 21). They failed to do this and were eventually defeated and taken into exile (2 Kings 17; 25).

¹⁰ "I myself stayed on the mountain, as at the first time, forty days and forty nights, and the LORD listened to me that time also. The LORD was unwilling to destroy you. ¹¹ And the LORD said to me, 'Arise, go on your journey at the head of the people, so that they may go in and possess the land, which I swore to their fathers to give them.'

Circumcise Your Heart

¹² "And now, Israel, what does the LORD your God require of you, but to fear the LORD your God, to walk in all his ways, to love him, to serve the LORD your God with all your heart and with all your soul, ¹³ and to keep the commandments and statutes of the LORD, which I am commanding you today for your good? ¹⁴ Behold, to the LORD your God belong heaven and the heaven of heavens, the earth with all that is in it. ¹⁵ Yet the LORD set his heart in love on your fathers and chose their offspring after them,

you above all peoples, as you are this day. ¹⁶ Circumcise therefore the foreskin of your heart, and be no longer stubborn. ¹⁷ For the LORD your God is God of gods and Lord of lords, the great, the mighty, and the awesome God, who is not partial and takes no bribe. ¹⁸ He executes justice for the fatherless and the widow, and loves the sojourner, giving him food and clothing. ¹⁹ Love the sojourner, therefore, for you were sojourners in the land of Egypt. ²⁰ You shall fear the LORD your God. You shall serve him and hold fast to him, and by his name you shall swear. ²¹ He is your praise. He is your God, who has done for you these great and terrifying things that your eyes have seen. ²² Your fathers went down to Egypt seventy persons, and now the LORD your God has made you as numerous as the stars of heaven.

Love and Serve the LORD

11 "You shall therefore love the LORD your God and keep his charge, his statutes, his rules, and his commandments always. ² And consider today (since I am not speaking to your children who have not known or seen it), consider the discipline of the LORD your God, his greatness, his mighty hand and his outstretched arm, ³ his signs and his deeds that he did in Egypt to Pharaoh the king of Egypt and to all his land, ⁴ and what he did to the army of Egypt, to their horses and to their chariots, how he made the water of the Red Sea flow over them as they pursued after you, and how the LORD has destroyed them to this day, ⁵ and what he did to you in the wilderness, until you came to this place, ⁶ and what he did to Dathan and Abiram the sons of Eliab, son of Reuben, how the earth opened its mouth and swallowed them up, with their households, their tents, and every living thing that followed them, in the midst of all Israel. ⁷ For your eyes have seen all the great work of the LORD that he did.

⁸ "You shall therefore keep the whole commandment that I command you today, that you may be strong, and go in and take possession of the land that you are going over to possess, ⁹ and that you may live long in the land that the LORD swore to your fathers to give to them and to their offspring, a land flowing with milk and honey. ¹⁰ For the land that you are entering to take possession of it is not like the land of Egypt, from which you

have come, where you sowed your seed and irrigated it, like a garden of vegetables. ¹¹ But the land that you are going over to possess is a land of hills and valleys, which drinks water by the rain from heaven, ¹² a land that the LORD your God cares for. The eyes of the LORD your God are always upon it, from the beginning of the year to the end of the year.

¹³ "And if you will indeed obey my commandments that I command you today, to love the LORD your God, and to serve him with all your heart and with all your soul, ¹⁴ he will give the rain for your land in its season, the early rain and the later rain, that you may gather in your grain and your wine and your oil. ¹⁵ And he will give grass in your fields for your livestock, and you shall eat and be full. ¹⁶ Take care lest your heart be deceived, and you turn aside and serve other gods and worship them; ¹⁷ then the anger of the LORD will be kindled against you, and he will shut up the heavens, so that there will be no rain, and the land will yield no fruit, and you will perish quickly off the good land that the LORD is giving you.

¹⁸ "You shall therefore lay up these words of mine in your heart and in your soul, and you shall bind them as a sign on your hand, and they shall be as frontlets between your eyes. ¹⁹ You shall teach them to your children, talking of them when you are sitting in your house, and when you are walking by the way, and when you lie down, and when you rise. ²⁰ You shall write them on the doorposts of your house and on your gates, ²¹ that your days and the days of your children may be multiplied in the land that the LORD swore to your fathers to give them, as long as the heavens are above the earth. ²² For if you will be careful to do all this commandment that I command you to do, loving the LORD your God, walking in all his ways, and holding fast to him, ²³ then the LORD will drive out all these nations before you, and you will dispossess nations greater and mightier than you. ²⁴ Every place on which the sole of your foot treads shall be yours. Your territory shall be from the wilderness to the Lebanon and from the River, the river Euphrates, to the western sea. ²⁵ No one shall be able to stand against you. The LORD your God will lay the fear of you and the dread of you on all the land that you shall tread, as he promised you.

²⁶ "See, I am setting before you today a blessing and a curse: ²⁷ the blessing, if you obey the commandments of the LORD your God, which I command you today, ²⁸ and the curse, if you do not obey the commandments of the LORD your God, but turn aside from the way that I am commanding you today, to go after other gods that you have not known. ²⁹ And when the LORD your God brings you into the land that you are entering to take possession of it, you shall set the blessing on Mount Gerizim and the curse on Mount Ebal. ³⁰ Are they not beyond the Jordan, west of the road, toward the going down of the sun, in the land of the Canaanites who live in the Arabah, opposite Gilgal, beside the oak of Moreh? ³¹ For you are to cross over the Jordan to go in to take possession of the land that the LORD your God is giving you. And when you possess it and live in it, ³² you shall be careful to do all the statutes and the rules that I am setting before you today.

The LORD's Chosen Place of Worship

12 "These are the statutes and rules that you shall be careful to do in the land that the LORD, the God of your fathers, has given you to possess, all the days that you live on the earth. ² You shall surely destroy all the places where the nations whom you shall dispossess served their gods, on the high mountains and on the hills and under every green tree. ³ You shall tear down their altars and dash in pieces their pillars and burn their Asherim with fire. You shall chop down the carved images of their gods and destroy their name out of that place. ⁴ You shall not worship the LORD your God in that way. ⁵ But you shall seek the place that the LORD your God will choose out of all your tribes to put his name and make his habitation there. There you shall go, ⁶ and there you shall bring your burnt offerings and your sacrifices, your tithes and the contribution that you present, your vow offerings, your freewill offerings, and the firstborn of your herd and of your flock. ⁷ And there you shall eat before the LORD your God, and you shall rejoice, you and your households, in all that you undertake, in which the LORD your God has blessed you.

⁸ "You shall not do according to all that we are doing here today, everyone doing whatever is right in his own eyes, ⁹ for you

have not as yet come to the rest and to the inheritance that the LORD your God is giving you. ¹⁰ But when you go over the Jordan and live in the land that the LORD your God is giving you to inherit, and when he gives you rest from all your enemies around, so that you live in safety, ¹¹ then to the place that the LORD your God will choose, to make his name dwell there, there you shall bring all that I command you: your burnt offerings and your sacrifices, your tithes and the contribution that you present, and all your finest vow offerings that you vow to the LORD. ¹² And you shall rejoice before the LORD your God, you and your sons and your daughters, your male servants and your female servants, and the Levite that is within your towns, since he has no portion or inheritance with you. ¹³ Take care that you do not offer your burnt offerings at any place that you see, ¹⁴ but at the place that the LORD will choose in one of your tribes, there you shall offer your burnt offerings, and there you shall do all that I am commanding you.

¹⁵ "However, you may slaughter and eat meat within any of your towns, as much as you desire, according to the blessing of the LORD your God that he has given you. The unclean and the clean may eat of it, as of the gazelle and as of the deer. ¹⁶ Only you shall not eat the blood; you shall pour it out on the earth like water. ¹⁷ You may not eat within your towns the tithe of your grain or of your wine or of your oil, or the firstborn of your herd or of your flock, or any of your vow offerings that you vow, or your freewill offerings or the contribution that you present, ¹⁸ but you shall eat them before the LORD your God in the place that the LORD your God will choose, you and your son and your daughter, your male servant and your female servant, and the Levite who is within your towns. And you shall rejoice before the LORD your God in all that you undertake. ¹⁹ Take care that you do not neglect the Levite as long as you live in your land.

²⁰ "When the LORD your God enlarges your territory, as he has promised you, and you say, 'I will eat meat,' because you crave meat, you may eat meat whenever you desire. ²¹ If the place that the LORD your God will choose to put his name there is too far from you, then you may kill any of your herd or your flock, which the LORD has given you,

as I have commanded you, and you may eat within your towns whenever you desire. ²² Just as the gazelle or the deer is eaten, so you may eat of it. The unclean and the clean alike may eat of it. ²³ Only be sure that you do not eat the blood, for the blood is the life, and you shall not eat the life with the flesh. ²⁴ You shall not eat it; you shall pour it out on the earth like water. ²⁵ You shall not eat it, that all may go well with you and with your children after you, when you do what is right in the sight of the LORD. ²⁶ But the holy things that are due from you, and your vow offerings, you shall take, and you shall go to the place that the LORD will choose, ²⁷ and offer your burnt offerings, the flesh and the blood, on the altar of the LORD your God. The blood of your sacrifices shall be poured out on the altar of the LORD your God, but the flesh you may eat. ²⁸ Be careful to obey all these words that I command you, that it may go well with you and with your children after you forever, when you do what is good and right in the sight of the LORD your God.

Warning Against Idolatry

²⁹ "When the LORD your God cuts off before you the nations whom you go in to dispossess, and you dispossess them and dwell in their land, ³⁰ take care that you be not ensnared to follow them, after they have been destroyed before you, and that you do not inquire about their gods, saying, 'How did these nations serve their gods?—that I also may do the same.' ³¹ You shall not worship the LORD your God in that way, for every abominable thing that the LORD hates they have done for their gods, for they even burn their sons and their daughters in the fire to their gods.

³² "Everything that I command you, you shall be careful to do. You shall not add to it or take from it.

13 "If a prophet or a dreamer of dreams arises among you and gives you a sign or a wonder, ² and the sign or wonder that he tells you comes to pass, and if he says, 'Let us go after other gods,' which you have not known, 'and let us serve them,' ³ you shall not listen to the words of that prophet or that dreamer of dreams. For the LORD your God is testing you, to know whether you love the LORD your God with all your heart and with all your soul. ⁴ You shall walk after the LORD your God and fear him and keep his commandments and obey his voice, and you shall serve him and hold fast to him. ⁵ But that prophet or that dreamer of dreams shall be put to death, because he has taught rebellion against the LORD your God, who brought you out of the land of Egypt and redeemed you out of the house of slavery, to make you leave the way in which the LORD your God commanded you to walk. So you shall purge the evil from your midst.

⁶ "If your brother, the son of your mother, or your son or your daughter or the wife you embrace or your friend who is as your own soul entices you secretly, saying, 'Let us go and serve other gods,' which neither you nor your fathers have known, ⁷ some of the gods of the peoples who are around you, whether near you or far off from you, from the one end of the earth to the other, ⁸ you shall not yield to him or listen to him, nor shall your eye pity him, nor shall you spare him, nor shall you conceal him. ⁹ But you shall kill him. Your hand shall be first against him to put him to death, and afterward the hand of all the people. ¹⁰ You shall stone him to death with stones, because he sought to draw you away from the LORD your God, who brought you out of the land of Egypt, out of the house of slavery. ¹¹ And all Israel shall hear and fear and never again do any such wickedness as this among you.

¹² "If you hear in one of your cities, which the LORD your God is giving you to dwell there, ¹³ that certain worthless fellows have gone out among you and have drawn away the inhabitants of their city, saying, 'Let us go and serve other gods,' which you have not known, ¹⁴ then you shall inquire and make search and ask diligently. And behold, if it be true and certain that such an abomination has been done among you, ¹⁵ you shall surely put the inhabitants of that city to the sword, devoting it to destruction, all who are in it and its cattle, with the edge of the sword. ¹⁶ You shall gather all its spoil into the midst of its open square and burn the city and all its spoil with fire, as a whole burnt offering to the LORD your God. It shall be a heap forever. It shall not be built again. ¹⁷ None of the devoted things shall stick to your hand, that the LORD may turn from the fierceness of his anger and show you mercy and have compassion on you and multiply you, as he swore to your fathers, ¹⁸ if you obey the voice of the LORD your God, keeping all his commandments that I am commanding you today, and doing what is right in the sight of the LORD your God.

Clean and Unclean Food

14 "You are the sons of the LORD your God. You shall not cut yourselves or make any baldness on your foreheads for the dead. ² For you are a people holy to the LORD your God, and the LORD has chosen you to be a people for his treasured possession, out of all the peoples who are on the face of the earth.

³ "You shall not eat any abomination. ⁴ These are the animals you may eat: the ox, the sheep, the goat, ⁵ the deer, the gazelle, the roebuck, the wild goat, the ibex, the antelope, and the mountain sheep. ⁶ Every animal that parts the hoof and has the hoof cloven in two and chews the cud, among

GETTING THE MESSAGE

Death penalty for apostasy? Anyone who urged a fellow Israelite to "go and serve other gods" was to be put to death (13:6–11). While the New Testament does not prescribe death for such an offense, it gives serious warning to anyone who leads another person into sin (Matt. 18:6).

the animals, you may eat. ⁷ Yet of those that chew the cud or have the hoof cloven you shall not eat these: the camel, the hare, and the rock badger, because they chew the cud but do not part the hoof, are unclean for you. ⁸ And the pig, because it parts the hoof but does not chew the cud, is unclean for you. Their flesh you shall not eat, and their carcasses you shall not touch.

⁹ "Of all that are in the waters you may eat these: whatever has fins and scales you may eat. ¹⁰ And whatever does not have fins and scales you shall not eat; it is unclean for you.

¹¹ "You may eat all clean birds. ¹² But these are the ones that you shall not eat: the eagle, the bearded vulture, the black vulture, ¹³ the kite, the falcon of any kind; ¹⁴ every raven of any kind; ¹⁵ the ostrich, the nighthawk, the sea gull, the hawk of any kind; ¹⁶ the little owl and the short-eared owl, the barn owl ¹⁷ and the tawny owl, the carrion vulture and the cormorant, ¹⁸ the stork, the heron

of any kind; the hoopoe and the bat. ¹⁹ And all winged insects are unclean for you; they shall not be eaten. ²⁰ All clean winged things you may eat.

²¹ "You shall not eat anything that has died naturally. You may give it to the sojourner who is within your towns, that he may eat it, or you may sell it to a foreigner. For you are a people holy to the LORD your God.

"You shall not boil a young goat in its mother's milk.

Tithes

²² "You shall tithe all the yield of your seed that comes from the field year by year. ²³ And before the LORD your God, in the place that he will choose, to make his name dwell there, you shall eat the tithe of your grain, of your wine, and of your oil, and the firstborn of your herd and flock, that you may learn to fear the LORD your God always. ²⁴ And if the way is too long for you, so that you are not able to carry the tithe, when the LORD your God blesses you, because the place is too far from you, which the LORD your God chooses, to set his name there, ²⁵ then you shall turn it into money and bind up the money in your hand and go to the place that the LORD your God chooses ²⁶ and spend the money for whatever you desire—oxen or sheep or wine or strong drink, whatever your appetite craves. And you shall eat there before the LORD your God and rejoice, you and your household. ²⁷ And you shall not neglect the Levite who is within your towns, for he has no portion or inheritance with you.

²⁸ "At the end of every three years you shall bring out all the tithe of your produce in the same year and lay it up within your towns. ²⁹ And the Levite, because he has no portion or inheritance with you, and the sojourner, the fatherless, and the widow, who are within your towns, shall come and eat and be filled, that the LORD your God may bless you in all the work of your hands that you do.

The Sabbatical Year

15 "At the end of every seven years you shall grant a release. ² And this is the manner of the release: every creditor shall release what he has lent to his neighbor. He shall not exact it of his neighbor, his brother, because the LORD's release has been proclaimed. ³ Of a foreigner you may exact it, but whatever of yours is with your brother your hand shall release. ⁴ But there will be no poor among you; for the LORD will bless you in the land that the LORD your God is giving you for an inheritance to possess— ⁵ if only you will strictly obey the voice of the LORD your God, being careful to do all this commandment that I command you today. ⁶ For the LORD your God will bless you, as he promised you, and you shall lend to many nations, but you shall not borrow, and you shall rule over many nations, but they shall not rule over you.

⁷ "If among you, one of your brothers should become poor, in any of your towns within your land that the LORD your God is giving you, you shall not harden your heart or shut your hand against your poor brother, ⁸ but you shall open your hand to him and lend him sufficient for his need, whatever it may be. ⁹ Take care lest there be an unworthy thought in your heart and you say, 'The seventh year, the year of release is near,' and your eye look grudgingly on your poor brother, and you give him nothing, and he cry to the LORD against you, and you be guilty of sin. ¹⁰ You shall give to him freely, and your heart shall not be grudging when you give to him, because for this the LORD your God will bless you in all your work and in all that you undertake. ¹¹ For there will never cease to be poor in the land. Therefore I command you, 'You shall open wide your hand to your brother, to the needy and to the poor, in your land.'

¹² "If your brother, a Hebrew man or a Hebrew woman, is sold¹ to you, he shall serve you six years, and in the seventh year you shall let him go free from you. ¹³ And when you let him go free from you, you shall not let him go empty-handed. ¹⁴ You shall furnish him liberally out of your flock, out of your threshing floor, and out of your winepress. As the LORD your God has blessed you, you shall give to him. ¹⁵ You shall remember that you were a slave in the land of Egypt, and the LORD your God redeemed you; therefore I command you this today. ¹⁶ But if he says to you, 'I will not go out from you,' because he loves you and your household, since he is well-off with

¹ Or *sells himself*

you, [17] then you shall take an awl, and put it through his ear into the door, and he shall be your slave[1] forever. And to your female slave you shall do the same. [18] It shall not seem hard to you when you let him go free from you, for at half the cost of a hired worker he has served you six years. So the LORD your God will bless you in all that you do.

[19] "All the firstborn males that are born of your herd and flock you shall dedicate to the LORD your God. You shall do no work with the firstborn of your herd, nor shear the firstborn of your flock. [20] You shall eat it, you and your household, before the LORD your God year by year at the place that the LORD will choose. [21] But if it has any blemish, if it is lame or blind or has any serious blemish whatever, you shall not sacrifice it to the LORD your God. [22] You shall eat it within your towns. The unclean and the clean alike may eat it, as though it were a gazelle or a deer. [23] Only you shall not eat its blood; you shall pour it out on the ground like water.

Passover

16 "Observe the month of Abib and keep the Passover to the LORD your God, for in the month of Abib the LORD your God brought you out of Egypt by night. [2] And you shall offer the Passover sacrifice to the LORD your God, from the flock or the herd, at the place that the LORD will choose, to make his name dwell there. [3] You shall eat no leavened bread with it. Seven days you shall eat it with unleavened bread, the bread of affliction—for you came out of the land of Egypt in haste—that all the days of your life you may remember the day when you came out of the land of Egypt. [4] No leaven shall be seen with you in all your territory for seven days, nor shall any of the flesh that you sacrifice on the evening of the first day remain all night until morning. [5] You may not offer the Passover sacrifice within any of your towns that the LORD your God is giving you, [6] but at the place that the LORD your God will choose, to make his name dwell in it, there you shall offer the Passover sacrifice, in the evening at sunset, at the time you came out of Egypt. [7] And you shall cook it and eat it at the place that the LORD your God will choose. And in the morning you shall turn and go to your tents. [8] For six days you shall eat unleavened bread, and

on the seventh day there shall be a solemn assembly to the LORD your God. You shall do no work on it.

The Feast of Weeks

[9] "You shall count seven weeks. Begin to count the seven weeks from the time the sickle is first put to the standing grain. [10] Then you shall keep the Feast of Weeks to the LORD your God with the tribute of a freewill offering from your hand, which you shall give as the LORD your God blesses you. [11] And you shall rejoice before the LORD your God, you and your son and your daughter, your male servant and your female servant, the Levite who is within your towns, the sojourner, the fatherless, and the widow who are among you, at the place that the LORD your God will choose, to make his name dwell there. [12] You shall remember

GETTING THE MESSAGE

What is unleavened bread? Leaven is another name for yeast. Because bread made without yeast does not rise, unleavened bread is flat. During the exodus, the Israelites left Egypt so quickly that there was no time for their bread to rise. Unleavened bread was therefore used in Passover celebrations.

that you were a slave in Egypt; and you shall be careful to observe these statutes.

The Feast of Booths

[13] "You shall keep the Feast of Booths seven days, when you have gathered in the produce from your threshing floor and your winepress. [14] You shall rejoice in your feast, you and your son and your daughter, your male servant and your female servant, the Levite, the sojourner, the fatherless, and the widow who are within your towns. [15] For seven days you shall keep the feast to the LORD your God at the place that the LORD will choose, because the LORD your God will bless you in all your produce and in all the work of your hands, so that you will be altogether joyful.

[16] "Three times a year all your males shall appear before the LORD your God at

---

[1] Or servant; the Hebrew word (ebed) can mean either voluntary service or forced service (see Preface)

the place that he will choose: at the Feast of Unleavened Bread, at the Feast of Weeks, and at the Feast of Booths. They shall not appear before the LORD empty-handed. ¹⁷ Every man shall give as he is able, according to the blessing of the LORD your God that he has given you.

Justice

¹⁸ "You shall appoint judges and officers in all your towns that the LORD your God is giving you, according to your tribes, and they shall judge the people with righteous judgment. ¹⁹ You shall not pervert justice. You shall not show partiality, and you shall not accept a bribe, for a bribe blinds the eyes of the wise and subverts the cause of the righteous. ²⁰ Justice, and only justice, you shall follow, that you may live and inherit the land that the LORD your God is giving you.

GETTING THE MESSAGE

Threshing is the process of separating kernels of grain (such as barley and wheat) from their stalks. This was done by beating the stalks or by using an ox or a donkey to pull a weighted sled over the harvest. Often large, flat rocks were used as threshing floors (16:13).

Forbidden Forms of Worship

²¹ "You shall not plant any tree as an Asherah beside the altar of the LORD your God that you shall make. ²² And you shall not set up a pillar, which the LORD your God hates.

17 "You shall not sacrifice to the LORD your God an ox or a sheep in which is a blemish, any defect whatever, for that is an abomination to the LORD your God.

² "If there is found among you, within any of your towns that the LORD your God is giving you, a man or woman who does what is evil in the sight of the LORD your God, in transgressing his covenant, ³ and has gone and served other gods and worshiped them, or the sun or the moon or any of the host of heaven, which I have forbidden, ⁴ and it is told you and you hear of it, then you shall inquire diligently, and if it is true and certain that such an abomination has been done in Israel, ⁵ then you shall bring out

to your gates that man or woman who has done this evil thing, and you shall stone that man or woman to death with stones. ⁶ On the evidence of two witnesses or of three witnesses the one who is to die shall be put to death; a person shall not be put to death on the evidence of one witness. ⁷ The hand of the witnesses shall be first against him to put him to death, and afterward the hand of all the people. So you shall purge the evil from your midst.

Legal Decisions by Priests and Judges

⁸ "If any case arises requiring decision between one kind of homicide and another, one kind of legal right and another, or one kind of assault and another, any case within your towns that is too difficult for you, then you shall arise and go up to the place that the LORD your God will choose. ⁹ And you shall come to the Levitical priests and to the judge who is in office in those days, and you shall consult them, and they shall declare to you the decision. ¹⁰ Then you shall do according to what they declare to you from that place that the LORD will choose. And you shall be careful to do according to all that they direct you. ¹¹ According to the instructions that they give you, and according to the decision which they pronounce to you, you shall do. You shall not turn aside from the verdict that they declare to you, either to the right hand or to the left. ¹² The man who acts presumptuously by not obeying the priest who stands to minister there before the LORD your God, or the judge, that man shall die. So you shall purge the evil from Israel. ¹³ And all the people shall hear and fear and not act presumptuously again.

Laws Concerning Israel's Kings

¹⁴ "When you come to the land that the LORD your God is giving you, and you possess it and dwell in it and then say, 'I will set a king over me, like all the nations that are around me,' ¹⁵ you may indeed set a king over you whom the LORD your God will choose. One from among your brothers you shall set as king over you. You may not put a foreigner over you, who is not your brother. ¹⁶ Only he must not acquire many horses for himself or cause the people to return to Egypt in order to acquire many horses, since the LORD has said to you, 'You shall never return that way again.' ¹⁷ And he shall

not acquire many wives for himself, lest his heart turn away, nor shall he acquire for himself excessive silver and gold.

¹⁸ "And when he sits on the throne of his kingdom, he shall write for himself in a book a copy of this law, approved by the Levitical priests. ¹⁹ And it shall be with him, and he shall read in it all the days of his life, that he may learn to fear the LORD his God by keeping all the words of this law and these statutes, and doing them, ²⁰ that his heart may not be lifted up above his brothers, and that he may not turn aside from the commandment, either to the right hand or to the left, so that he may continue long in his kingdom, he and his children, in Israel.

Provision for Priests and Levites

18 "The Levitical priests, all the tribe of Levi, shall have no portion or inheritance with Israel. They shall eat the LORD's food offerings as their inheritance. ² They shall have no inheritance among their brothers; the LORD is their inheritance, as he promised them. ³ And this shall be the priests' due from the people, from those offering a sacrifice, whether an ox or a sheep: they shall give to the priest the shoulder and the two cheeks and the stomach. ⁴ The firstfruits of your grain, of your wine and of your oil, and the first fleece of your sheep, you shall give him. ⁵ For the LORD your God has chosen him out of all your tribes to stand and minister in the name of the LORD, him and his sons for all time.

⁶ "And if a Levite comes from any of your towns out of all Israel, where he lives — and he may come when he desires — to the place that the LORD will choose, ⁷ and ministers in the name of the LORD his God, like all his fellow Levites who stand to minister there before the LORD, ⁸ then he may have equal portions to eat, besides what he receives from the sale of his patrimony.

Abominable Practices

⁹ "When you come into the land that the LORD your God is giving you, you shall not learn to follow the abominable practices of those nations. ¹⁰ There shall not be found among you anyone who burns his son or his daughter as an offering, anyone who practices divination or tells fortunes or interprets omens, or a sorcerer ¹¹ or a charmer or a medium or a necromancer or one who inquires of the dead, ¹² for whoever does these things is an abomination to the LORD. And because of these abominations the LORD your God is driving them out before you. ¹³ You shall be blameless before the LORD your God, ¹⁴ for these nations, which you are about to dispossess, listen to fortune-tellers and to diviners. But as for you, the LORD your God has not allowed you to do this.

A New Prophet like Moses

¹⁵ "The LORD your God will raise up for you a prophet like me from among you, from your brothers — it is to him you shall listen — ¹⁶ just as you desired of the LORD your God at Horeb on the day of the assembly, when you said, 'Let me not hear again the voice of the LORD my God or see this great fire any more, lest I die.' ¹⁷ And the LORD said to me, 'They are right in what they have spoken. ¹⁸ I will raise up for them a prophet

like you from among their brothers. And I will put my words in his mouth, and he shall speak to them all that I command him. ¹⁹ And whoever will not listen to my words that he shall speak in my name, I myself will require it of him. ²⁰ But the prophet who presumes to speak a word in my name that I have not commanded him to speak, or who speaks in the name of other gods, that same prophet shall die.' ²¹ And if you say in your heart, 'How may we know the word that the LORD has not spoken?' — ²² when a prophet speaks in the name of the LORD, if the word does not come to pass or come true, that is a word that the LORD has not spoken; the prophet has spoken it presumptuously. You need not be afraid of him.

Laws Concerning Cities of Refuge

19 "When the LORD your God cuts off the nations whose land the LORD your God is giving you, and you dispossess them and dwell in their cities and in their houses, ² you shall set apart three cities for

yourselves in the land that the LORD your God is giving you to possess. ³ You shall measure the distances and divide into three parts the area of the land that the LORD your God gives you as a possession, so that any manslayer can flee to them.

⁴ "This is the provision for the manslayer, who by fleeing there may save his life. If anyone kills his neighbor unintentionally without having hated him in the past — ⁵ as when someone goes into the forest with his neighbor to cut wood, and his hand swings the axe to cut down a tree, and the head slips from the handle and strikes his neighbor so that he dies — he may flee to one of these cities and live, ⁶ lest the avenger of blood in hot anger pursue the manslayer and overtake him, because the way is long, and strike him fatally, though the man did not deserve to die, since he had not hated his neighbor in the past. ⁷ Therefore I command you, You shall set apart three cities. ⁸ And if the LORD your God enlarges your territory, as he has sworn to your fathers, and gives you all the land that he promised to give to your fathers — ⁹ provided you are careful to keep all this commandment, which I command you today, by loving the LORD your God and by walking ever in his ways — then you shall add three other cities to these three, ¹⁰ lest innocent blood be shed in your land that the LORD your God is giving you for an inheritance, and so the guilt of bloodshed be upon you.

¹¹ "But if anyone hates his neighbor and lies in wait for him and attacks him and strikes him fatally so that he dies, and he flees into one of these cities, ¹² then the elders of his city shall send and take him from there, and hand him over to the avenger of blood, so that he may die. ¹³ Your eye shall not pity him, but you shall purge the guilt of innocent blood from Israel, so that it may be well with you.

Property Boundaries

¹⁴ "You shall not move your neighbor's landmark, which the men of old have set, in the inheritance that you will hold in the land that the LORD your God is giving you to possess.

Laws Concerning Witnesses

¹⁵ "A single witness shall not suffice against a person for any crime or for any wrong in connection with any offense that he has committed. Only on the evidence of two witnesses or of three witnesses shall a charge be established. ¹⁶ If a malicious witness arises to accuse a person of wrongdoing, ¹⁷ then both parties to the dispute shall appear before the LORD, before the priests and the judges who are in office in those days. ¹⁸ The judges shall inquire diligently, and if the witness is a false witness and has accused his brother falsely, ¹⁹ then you shall do to him as he had meant to do to his brother. So you shall purge the evil from your midst. ²⁰ And the rest shall hear and fear, and shall never again commit any such evil among you. ²¹ Your eye shall not pity. It shall be life for life, eye for eye, tooth for tooth, hand for hand, foot for foot.

Laws Concerning Warfare

20 "When you go out to war against your enemies, and see horses and chariots and an army larger than your own, you shall not be afraid of them, for the LORD your God is with you, who brought you up out of the land of Egypt. ² And when you draw near to the battle, the priest shall come forward and speak to the people ³ and shall say to them, 'Hear, O Israel, today you are drawing near for battle against your enemies: let not your heart faint. Do not fear or panic or be in dread of them, ⁴ for the LORD your God is he who goes with you to fight for you against your enemies, to give you the victory.' ⁵ Then the officers shall speak to the people, saying, 'Is there any man who has built a new house and has not dedicated it? Let him go back to his house, lest he die in the battle and another man dedicate it. ⁶ And is there any man who has planted a vineyard and has not enjoyed its fruit? Let him go back to his house, lest he die in the battle and another man enjoy its fruit. ⁷ And is there any man who has betrothed a wife and has not taken her? Let him go back to his house, lest he die in the battle and another man take her.' ⁸ And the officers shall speak further to the people, and say, 'Is there any man who is fearful and fainthearted? Let him go back to his house, lest he make the heart of his fellows melt like his own.' ⁹ And when the officers have finished speaking to the people, then commanders shall be appointed at the head of the people.

[10] "When you draw near to a city to fight against it, offer terms of peace to it. [11] And if it responds to you peaceably and it opens to you, then all the people who are found in it shall do forced labor for you and shall serve you. [12] But if it makes no peace with you, but makes war against you, then you shall besiege it. [13] And when the LORD your God gives it into your hand, you shall put all its males to the sword, [14] but the women and the little ones, the livestock, and everything else in the city, all its spoil, you shall take as plunder for yourselves. And you shall enjoy the spoil of your enemies, which the LORD your God has given you. [15] Thus you shall do to all the cities that are very far from you, which are not cities of the nations here. [16] But in the cities of these peoples that the LORD your God is giving you for an inheritance, you shall save alive nothing that breathes, [17] but you shall devote them to complete destruction, the Hittites and the Amorites, the Canaanites and the Perizzites, the Hivites and the Jebusites, as the LORD your God has commanded, [18] that they may not teach you to do according to all their abominable practices that they have done for their gods, and so you sin against the LORD your God.

[19] "When you besiege a city for a long time, making war against it in order to take it, you shall not destroy its trees by wielding an axe against them. You may eat from them, but you shall not cut them down. Are the trees in the field human, that they should be besieged by you? [20] Only the trees that you know are not trees for food you may destroy and cut down, that you may build siegeworks against the city that makes war with you, until it falls.

Atonement for Unsolved Murders

21 "If in the land that the LORD your God is giving you to possess someone is found slain, lying in the open country, and it is not known who killed him, [2] then your elders and your judges shall come out, and they shall measure the distance to the surrounding cities. [3] And the elders of the city that is nearest to the slain man shall take a heifer that has never been worked and that has not pulled in a yoke. [4] And the elders of that city shall bring the heifer down to a valley with running water, which is neither plowed nor sown, and shall break the heifer's neck there in the valley. [5] Then the priests, the sons of Levi, shall come forward, for the LORD your God has chosen them to minister to him and to bless in the name of the LORD, and by their word every dispute and every assault shall be settled. [6] And all the elders of that city nearest to the slain man shall wash their hands over the heifer whose neck was broken in the valley, [7] and they shall testify, 'Our hands did not shed this blood, nor did our eyes see it shed. [8] Accept atonement, O LORD, for your people Israel, whom you have redeemed, and do not set the guilt of innocent blood in the midst of your people Israel, so that their blood guilt be atoned for.' [9] So you shall purge the guilt of innocent blood from your midst, when you do what is right in the sight of the LORD.

GETTING THE MESSAGE

Inheritance rights. In Israel, the firstborn son received a double share of the inheritance. The firstborn also had more responsibility for the family than other children. The law protected the special rights of the firstborn (21:15–17).

Marrying Female Captives

[10] "When you go out to war against your enemies, and the LORD your God gives them into your hand and you take them captive, [11] and you see among the captives a beautiful woman, and you desire to take her to be your wife, [12] and you bring her home to your house, she shall shave her head and pare her nails. [13] And she shall take off the clothes in which she was captured and shall remain in your house and lament her father and her mother a full month. After that you may go in to her and be her husband, and she shall be your wife. [14] But if you no longer delight in her, you shall let her go where she wants. But you shall not sell her for money, nor shall you treat her as a slave, since you have humiliated her.

Inheritance Rights of the Firstborn

[15] "If a man has two wives, the one loved and the other unloved, and both the loved and the unloved have borne him children, and if the firstborn son belongs to the

unloved, [16] then on the day when he assigns his possessions as an inheritance to his sons, he may not treat the son of the loved as the firstborn in preference to the son of the unloved, who is the firstborn, [17] but he shall acknowledge the firstborn, the son of the unloved, by giving him a double portion of all that he has, for he is the firstfruits of his strength. The right of the firstborn is his.

A Rebellious Son

[18] "If a man has a stubborn and rebellious son who will not obey the voice of his father or the voice of his mother, and, though they discipline him, will not listen to them, [19] then his father and his mother shall take hold of him and bring him out to the elders of his city at the gate of the place where he lives, [20] and they shall say to the

> ### GETTING THE MESSAGE
>
> **Why did the Israelites sew tassels on their garments?** In the ancient world, tassels were worn by nobles and other high-class people. In Israel they were worn by *everyone* as a mark of their special status and responsibilities as God's chosen people (22:12; Num. 15:37–41).

elders of his city, 'This our son is stubborn and rebellious; he will not obey our voice; he is a glutton and a drunkard.' [21] Then all the men of the city shall stone him to death with stones. So you shall purge the evil from your midst, and all Israel shall hear, and fear.

A Man Hanged on a Tree Is Cursed

[22] "And if a man has committed a crime punishable by death and he is put to death, and you hang him on a tree, [23] his body shall not remain all night on the tree, but you shall bury him the same day, for a hanged man is cursed by God. You shall not defile your land that the LORD your God is giving you for an inheritance.

Various Laws

22 "You shall not see your brother's ox or his sheep going astray and ignore them. You shall take them back to your brother. [2] And if he does not live near you and you do not know who he is, you shall bring it home to your house, and it shall stay with you until your brother seeks it. Then you shall restore it to him. [3] And you shall do the same with his donkey or with his garment, or with any lost thing of your brother's, which he loses and you find; you may not ignore it. [4] You shall not see your brother's donkey or his ox fallen down by the way and ignore them. You shall help him to lift them up again.

[5] "A woman shall not wear a man's garment, nor shall a man put on a woman's cloak, for whoever does these things is an abomination to the LORD your God.

[6] "If you come across a bird's nest in any tree or on the ground, with young ones or eggs and the mother sitting on the young or on the eggs, you shall not take the mother with the young. [7] You shall let the mother go, but the young you may take for yourself, that it may go well with you, and that you may live long.

[8] "When you build a new house, you shall make a parapet for your roof, that you may not bring the guilt of blood upon your house, if anyone should fall from it.

[9] "You shall not sow your vineyard with two kinds of seed, lest the whole yield be forfeited, the crop that you have sown and the yield of the vineyard. [10] You shall not plow with an ox and a donkey together. [11] You shall not wear cloth of wool and linen mixed together.

[12] "You shall make yourself tassels on the four corners of the garment with which you cover yourself.

Laws Concerning Sexual Immorality

[13] "If any man takes a wife and goes in to her and then hates her [14] and accuses her of misconduct and brings a bad name upon her, saying, 'I took this woman, and when I came near her, I did not find in her evidence of virginity,' [15] then the father of the young woman and her mother shall take and bring out the evidence of her virginity to the elders of the city in the gate. [16] And the father of the young woman shall say to the elders, 'I gave my daughter to this man to marry, and he hates her; [17] and behold, he has accused her of misconduct, saying, "I did not find in your daughter evidence of virginity." And yet this is the evidence of my daughter's virginity.' And they shall spread the cloak before the elders of the city. [18] Then the elders of that city shall take the

man and whip him, [19] and they shall fine him a hundred shekels of silver and give them to the father of the young woman, because he has brought a bad name upon a virgin of Israel. And she shall be his wife. He may not divorce her all his days. [20] But if the thing is true, that evidence of virginity was not found in the young woman, [21] then they shall bring out the young woman to the door of her father's house, and the men of her city shall stone her to death with stones, because she has done an outrageous thing in Israel by whoring in her father's house. So you shall purge the evil from your midst.

[22] "If a man is found lying with the wife of another man, both of them shall die, the man who lay with the woman, and the woman. So you shall purge the evil from Israel.

[23] "If there is a betrothed virgin, and a man meets her in the city and lies with her, [24] then you shall bring them both out to the gate of that city, and you shall stone them to death with stones, the young woman because she did not cry for help though she was in the city, and the man because he violated his neighbor's wife. So you shall purge the evil from your midst.

[25] "But if in the open country a man meets a young woman who is betrothed, and the man seizes her and lies with her, then only the man who lay with her shall die. [26] But you shall do nothing to the young woman; she has committed no offense punishable by death. For this case is like that of a man attacking and murdering his neighbor, [27] because he met her in the open country, and though the betrothed young woman cried for help there was no one to rescue her.

[28] "If a man meets a virgin who is not betrothed, and seizes her and lies with her, and they are found, [29] then the man who lay with her shall give to the father of the young woman fifty shekels of silver, and she shall be his wife, because he has violated her. He may not divorce her all his days.

[30] "A man shall not take his father's wife, so that he does not uncover his father's nakedness.

Those Excluded from the Assembly

23 "No one whose testicles are crushed or whose male organ is cut off shall enter the assembly of the LORD.

[2] "No one born of a forbidden union may enter the assembly of the LORD. Even to the tenth generation, none of his descendants may enter the assembly of the LORD.

[3] "No Ammonite or Moabite may enter the assembly of the LORD. Even to the tenth generation, none of them may enter the assembly of the LORD forever, [4] because they did not meet you with bread and with water on the way, when you came out of Egypt, and because they hired against you Balaam the son of Beor from Pethor of Mesopotamia, to curse you. [5] But the LORD your God would not listen to Balaam; instead the LORD your God turned the curse into a blessing for you, because the LORD your God loved you. [6] You shall not seek their peace or their prosperity all your days forever.

[7] "You shall not abhor an Edomite, for he is your brother. You shall not abhor an Egyptian, because you were a sojourner in his land. [8] Children born to them in the third generation may enter the assembly of the LORD.

Uncleanness in the Camp

[9] "When you are encamped against your enemies, then you shall keep yourself from every evil thing.

[10] "If any man among you becomes unclean because of a nocturnal emission, then he shall go outside the camp. He shall not come inside the camp, [11] but when evening comes, he shall bathe himself in water, and as the sun sets, he may come inside the camp.

[12] "You shall have a place outside the camp, and you shall go out to it. [13] And you shall have a trowel with your tools, and when you sit down outside, you shall dig a hole with it and turn back and cover up your excrement. [14] Because the LORD your God walks in the midst of your camp, to deliver you and to give up your enemies before you, therefore your camp must be holy, so that he may not see anything indecent among you and turn away from you.

Miscellaneous Laws

[15] "You shall not give up to his master a slave[1] who has escaped from his master to you. [16] He shall dwell with you, in your midst, in the place that he shall choose

---

[1] Or *servant*; the Hebrew word (*ebed*) can mean either voluntary service or forced service (see Preface)

within one of your towns, wherever it suits him. You shall not wrong him.

¹⁷ "None of the daughters of Israel shall be a cult prostitute, and none of the sons of Israel shall be a cult prostitute. ¹⁸ You shall not bring the fee of a prostitute or the wages of a dog[1] into the house of the LORD your God in payment for any vow, for both of these are an abomination to the LORD your God.

¹⁹ "You shall not charge interest on loans to your brother, interest on money, interest on food, interest on anything that is lent for interest. ²⁰ You may charge a foreigner interest, but you may not charge your brother interest, that the LORD your God may bless you in all that you undertake in the land that you are entering to take possession of it.

²¹ "If you make a vow to the LORD your God, you shall not delay fulfilling it, for the

> **GETTING THE MESSAGE**

What was an upper millstone? Israelite women ground their grain in mills made of two circular stones. The grain was placed on the flat lower stone and then crushed as the upper millstone rolled over it. To deprive the miller of either stone would make her work impossible (24:6).

LORD your God will surely require it of you, and you will be guilty of sin. ²² But if you refrain from vowing, you will not be guilty of sin. ²³ You shall be careful to do what has passed your lips, for you have voluntarily vowed to the LORD your God what you have promised with your mouth.

²⁴ "If you go into your neighbor's vineyard, you may eat your fill of grapes, as many as you wish, but you shall not put any in your bag. ²⁵ If you go into your neighbor's standing grain, you may pluck the ears with your hand, but you shall not put a sickle to your neighbor's standing grain.

Laws Concerning Divorce

24 "When a man takes a wife and marries her, if then she finds no favor in his eyes because he has found some indecency in her, and he writes her a certificate of divorce and puts it in her hand and sends

her out of his house, and she departs out of his house, ² and if she goes and becomes another man's wife, ³ and the latter man hates her and writes her a certificate of divorce and puts it in her hand and sends her out of his house, or if the latter man dies, who took her to be his wife, ⁴ then her former husband, who sent her away, may not take her again to be his wife, after she has been defiled, for that is an abomination before the LORD. And you shall not bring sin upon the land that the LORD your God is giving you for an inheritance.

Miscellaneous Laws

⁵ "When a man is newly married, he shall not go out with the army or be liable for any other public duty. He shall be free at home one year to be happy with his wife whom he has taken.

⁶ "No one shall take a mill or an upper millstone in pledge, for that would be taking a life in pledge.

⁷ "If a man is found stealing one of his brothers of the people of Israel, and if he treats him as a slave or sells him, then that thief shall die. So you shall purge the evil from your midst.

⁸ "Take care, in a case of leprous[2] disease, to be very careful to do according to all that the Levitical priests shall direct you. As I commanded them, so you shall be careful to do. ⁹ Remember what the LORD your God did to Miriam on the way as you came out of Egypt.

¹⁰ "When you make your neighbor a loan of any sort, you shall not go into his house to collect his pledge. ¹¹ You shall stand outside, and the man to whom you make the loan shall bring the pledge out to you. ¹² And if he is a poor man, you shall not sleep in his pledge. ¹³ You shall restore to him the pledge as the sun sets, that he may sleep in his cloak and bless you. And it shall be righteousness for you before the LORD your God.

¹⁴ "You shall not oppress a hired worker who is poor and needy, whether he is one of your brothers or one of the sojourners who are in your land within your towns. ¹⁵ You shall give him his wages on the same day, before the sun sets (for he is poor and counts on it), lest he cry against you to the LORD, and you be guilty of sin.

[1] Or *male prostitute* [2] *Leprosy* was a term for several skin diseases (see Leviticus 13)

16 "Fathers shall not be put to death because of their children, nor shall children be put to death because of their fathers. Each one shall be put to death for his own sin.

17 "You shall not pervert the justice due to the sojourner or to the fatherless, or take a widow's garment in pledge, 18 but you shall remember that you were a slave in Egypt and the LORD your God redeemed you from there; therefore I command you to do this.

19 "When you reap your harvest in your field and forget a sheaf in the field, you shall not go back to get it. It shall be for the sojourner, the fatherless, and the widow, that the LORD your God may bless you in all the work of your hands. 20 When you beat your olive trees, you shall not go over them again. It shall be for the sojourner, the fatherless, and the widow. 21 When you gather the grapes of your vineyard, you shall not strip it afterward. It shall be for the sojourner, the fatherless, and the widow. 22 You shall remember that you were a slave in the land of Egypt; therefore I command you to do this.

25 "If there is a dispute between men and they come into court and the judges decide between them, acquitting the innocent and condemning the guilty, 2 then if the guilty man deserves to be beaten, the judge shall cause him to lie down and be beaten in his presence with a number of stripes in proportion to his offense. 3 Forty stripes may be given him, but not more, lest, if one should go on to beat him with more stripes than these, your brother be degraded in your sight.

4 "You shall not muzzle an ox when it is treading out the grain.

Laws Concerning Levirate Marriage

5 "If brothers dwell together, and one of them dies and has no son, the wife of the dead man shall not be married outside the family to a stranger. Her husband's brother shall go in to her and take her as his wife and perform the duty of a husband's brother to her. 6 And the first son whom she bears shall succeed to the name of his dead brother, that his name may not be blotted out of Israel. 7 And if the man does not wish to take his brother's wife, then his brother's wife shall go up to the gate to the elders and say, 'My husband's brother refuses to perpetuate his brother's name in Israel; he

will not perform the duty of a husband's brother to me.' 8 Then the elders of his city shall call him and speak to him, and if he persists, saying, 'I do not wish to take her,' 9 then his brother's wife shall go up to him in the presence of the elders and pull his sandal off his foot and spit in his face. And she shall answer and say, 'So shall it be done to the man who does not build up his brother's house.' 10 And the name of his house shall be called in Israel, 'The house of him who had his sandal pulled off.'

Miscellaneous Laws

11 "When men fight with one another and the wife of the one draws near to rescue her husband from the hand of him who is beating him and puts out her hand and seizes him by the private parts, 12 then you shall cut off her hand. Your eye shall have no pity.

GETTING THE MESSAGE

Shoes and sandals were considered the most humble articles of clothing. They were removed at the doorway before entering a home. People also removed their shoes during periods of mourning. Going barefoot was a sign of poverty and shame (25:9–10).

13 "You shall not have in your bag two kinds of weights, a large and a small. 14 You shall not have in your house two kinds of measures, a large and a small. 15 A full and fair weight you shall have, a full and fair measure you shall have, that your days may be long in the land that the LORD your God is giving you. 16 For all who do such things, all who act dishonestly, are an abomination to the LORD your God.

17 "Remember what Amalek did to you on the way as you came out of Egypt, 18 how he attacked you on the way when you were faint and weary, and cut off your tail, those who were lagging behind you, and he did not fear God. 19 Therefore when the LORD your God has given you rest from all your enemies around you, in the land that the LORD your God is giving you for an inheritance to possess, you shall blot out the memory of Amalek from under heaven; you shall not forget.

Offerings of Firstfruits and Tithes

26 "When you come into the land that the LORD your God is giving you for an inheritance and have taken possession of it and live in it, ² you shall take some of the first of all the fruit of the ground, which you harvest from your land that the LORD your God is giving you, and you shall put it in a basket, and you shall go to the place that the LORD your God will choose, to make his name to dwell there. ³ And you shall go to the priest who is in office at that time and say to him, 'I declare today to the LORD your God that I have come into the land that the LORD swore to our fathers to give us.' ⁴ Then the priest shall take the basket from your hand and set it down before the altar of the LORD your God.

⁵ "And you shall make response before the LORD your God, 'A wandering Aramean was my father. And he went down into Egypt and sojourned there, few in number, and

there he became a nation, great, mighty, and populous. ⁶ And the Egyptians treated us harshly and humiliated us and laid on us hard labor. ⁷ Then we cried to the LORD, the God of our fathers, and the LORD heard our voice and saw our affliction, our toil, and our oppression. ⁸ And the LORD brought us out of Egypt with a mighty hand and an outstretched arm, with great deeds of terror, with signs and wonders. ⁹ And he brought us into this place and gave us this land, a land flowing with milk and honey. ¹⁰ And behold, now I bring the first of the fruit of the ground, which you, O LORD, have given me.' And you shall set it down before the LORD your God and worship before the LORD your God. ¹¹ And you shall rejoice in all the good that the LORD your God has given to you and to your house, you, and the Levite, and the sojourner who is among you.

¹² "When you have finished paying all the tithe of your produce in the third year, which is the year of tithing, giving it to the Levite, the sojourner, the fatherless, and the widow, so that they may eat within your towns and be filled, ¹³ then you shall say before the LORD your God, 'I have removed the sacred portion out of my house, and moreover, I have given it to the Levite, the sojourner, the fatherless, and the widow, according to all your commandment that you have commanded me. I have not transgressed any of your commandments, nor have I forgotten them. ¹⁴ I have not eaten of the tithe while I was mourning, or removed any of it while I was unclean, or offered any of it to the dead. I have obeyed the voice of the LORD my God. I have done according to all that you have commanded me. ¹⁵ Look down from your holy habitation, from heaven, and bless your people Israel and the ground that you have given us, as you swore to our fathers, a land flowing with milk and honey.'

¹⁶ "This day the LORD your God commands you to do these statutes and rules. You shall therefore be careful to do them with all your heart and with all your soul. ¹⁷ You have declared today that the LORD is your God, and that you will walk in his ways, and keep his statutes and his commandments and his rules, and will obey his voice. ¹⁸ And the LORD has declared today that you are a people for his treasured possession, as he has promised you, and that you are to keep all his commandments, ¹⁹ and that he will set you in praise and in fame and in honor high above all nations that he has made, and that you shall be a people holy to the LORD your God, as he promised."

The Altar on Mount Ebal

27 Now Moses and the elders of Israel commanded the people, saying, "Keep the whole commandment that I command you today. ² And on the day you cross over the Jordan to the land that the LORD your God is giving you, you shall set up large stones and plaster them with plaster. ³ And you shall write on them all the words of this law, when you cross over to enter the land that the LORD your God is giving you, a land flowing with milk and honey, as the LORD, the God of your fathers, has promised you. ⁴ And when you have crossed over the Jordan, you shall set up these stones, concerning which I command you today, on Mount Ebal, and you shall plaster them with plaster. ⁵ And there you shall build an altar to the LORD your God, an altar of stones. You shall wield no iron tool on them; **6** you shall build an altar to the LORD your God of uncut stones. And you shall offer burnt offerings on it to the LORD your God, **7** and you shall sacrifice peace offerings and shall eat there, and you shall rejoice before the LORD your God. **8** And you shall write on the stones all the words of this law very plainly."

Curses from Mount Ebal

9 Then Moses and the Levitical priests said to all Israel, "Keep silence and hear, O Israel: this day you have become the people of the LORD your God. **10** You shall therefore obey the voice of the LORD your God, keeping his commandments and his statutes, which I command you today."

11 That day Moses charged the people, saying, **12** "When you have crossed over the Jordan, these shall stand on Mount Gerizim to bless the people: Simeon, Levi, Judah, Issachar, Joseph, and Benjamin. **13** And these shall stand on Mount Ebal for the curse: Reuben, Gad, Asher, Zebulun, Dan, and Naphtali. **14** And the Levites shall declare to all the men of Israel in a loud voice:

15 "'Cursed be the man who makes a carved or cast metal image, an abomination to the LORD, a thing made by the hands of a craftsman, and sets it up in secret.' And all the people shall answer and say, 'Amen.'

16 "'Cursed be anyone who dishonors his father or his mother.' And all the people shall say, 'Amen.'

17 "'Cursed be anyone who moves his neighbor's landmark.' And all the people shall say, 'Amen.'

18 "'Cursed be anyone who misleads a blind man on the road.' And all the people shall say, 'Amen.'

19 "'Cursed be anyone who perverts the justice due to the sojourner, the fatherless, and the widow.' And all the people shall say, 'Amen.'

20 "'Cursed be anyone who lies with his father's wife, because he has uncovered his father's nakedness.' And all the people shall say, 'Amen.'

21 "'Cursed be anyone who lies with any kind of animal.' And all the people shall say, 'Amen.'

22 "'Cursed be anyone who lies with his sister, whether the daughter of his father or the daughter of his mother.' And all the people shall say, 'Amen.'

23 "'Cursed be anyone who lies with his mother-in-law.' And all the people shall say, 'Amen.'

24 "'Cursed be anyone who strikes down his neighbor in secret.' And all the people shall say, 'Amen.'

25 "'Cursed be anyone who takes a bribe to shed innocent blood.' And all the people shall say, 'Amen.'

26 "'Cursed be anyone who does not confirm the words of this law by doing them.' And all the people shall say, 'Amen.'

Blessings for Obedience

28 "And if you faithfully obey the voice of the LORD your God, being careful to do all his commandments that I command you today, the LORD your God will set you high above all the nations of the earth. **2** And all these blessings shall come upon you and overtake you, if you obey the voice of the LORD your God. **3** Blessed shall you be in the city, and blessed shall you be in the field. **4** Blessed shall be the fruit of your womb and the fruit of your ground and the fruit of your cattle, the increase of your herds and the young of your flock. **5** Blessed shall be your basket and your kneading bowl. **6** Blessed shall you be when you come in, and blessed shall you be when you go out.

7 "The LORD will cause your enemies who rise against you to be defeated before you. They shall come out against you one way and flee before you seven ways. **8** The LORD will command the blessing on you in your barns and in all that you undertake. And he will bless you in the land that the LORD your God is giving you. **9** The LORD will establish you as a people holy to himself, as he has sworn to you, if you keep the commandments of the LORD your God and walk in his ways. **10** And all the peoples of the earth shall see that you are called by the name of the LORD, and they shall be afraid of you. **11** And the LORD will make you abound in prosperity, in the fruit of your womb and in the fruit of your livestock and in the fruit of your ground, within the land that the LORD swore to your fathers to give you. **12** The LORD will open to you his good treasury, the heavens, to give the rain to your land in its season and to bless all the work of your hands.

And you shall lend to many nations, but you shall not borrow. ¹³ And the LORD will make you the head and not the tail, and you shall only go up and not down, if you obey the commandments of the LORD your God, which I command you today, being careful to do them, ¹⁴ and if you do not turn aside from any of the words that I command you today, to the right hand or to the left, to go after other gods to serve them.

Curses for Disobedience

¹⁵ "But if you will not obey the voice of the LORD your God or be careful to do all his commandments and his statutes that I command you today, then all these curses shall come upon you and overtake you. ¹⁶ Cursed shall you be in the city, and cursed shall you be in the field. ¹⁷ Cursed shall be your basket and your kneading bowl. ¹⁸ Cursed shall be the fruit of your womb and the fruit of your ground, the increase of your herds and the young of your flock. ¹⁹ Cursed shall you be when you come in, and cursed shall you be when you go out.

²⁰ "The LORD will send on you curses, confusion, and frustration in all that you undertake to do, until you are destroyed and perish quickly on account of the evil of your deeds, because you have forsaken me. ²¹ The LORD will make the pestilence stick to you until he has consumed you off the land that you are entering to take possession of it. ²² The LORD will strike you with wasting disease and with fever, inflammation and fiery heat, and with drought and with blight and with mildew. They shall pursue you until you perish. ²³ And the heavens over your head shall be bronze, and the earth under you shall be iron. ²⁴ The LORD will make the rain of your land powder. From heaven dust shall come down on you until you are destroyed.

²⁵ "The LORD will cause you to be defeated before your enemies. You shall go out one way against them and flee seven ways before them. And you shall be a horror to all the kingdoms of the earth. ²⁶ And your dead body shall be food for all birds of the air and for the beasts of the earth, and there shall be no one to frighten them away. ²⁷ The LORD will strike you with the boils of Egypt, and with tumors and scabs and itch, of which you cannot be healed. ²⁸ The LORD will strike you with madness and blindness and confusion of mind, ²⁹ and you

shall grope at noonday, as the blind grope in darkness, and you shall not prosper in your ways. And you shall be only oppressed and robbed continually, and there shall be no one to help you. ³⁰ You shall betroth a wife, but another man shall ravish her. You shall build a house, but you shall not dwell in it. You shall plant a vineyard, but you shall not enjoy its fruit. ³¹ Your ox shall be slaughtered before your eyes, but you shall not eat any of it. Your donkey shall be seized before your face, but shall not be restored to you. Your sheep shall be given to your enemies, but there shall be no one to help you. ³² Your sons and your daughters shall be given to another people, while your eyes look on and fail with longing for them all day long, but you shall be helpless. ³³ A nation that you have not known shall eat up the fruit of your ground and of all your labors, and you shall be only oppressed and crushed continually, ³⁴ so that you are driven mad by the sights that your eyes see. ³⁵ The LORD will strike you on the knees and on the legs with grievous boils of which you cannot be healed, from the sole of your foot to the crown of your head.

³⁶ "The LORD will bring you and your king whom you set over you to a nation that neither you nor your fathers have known. And there you shall serve other gods of wood and stone. ³⁷ And you shall become a horror, a proverb, and a byword among all the peoples where the LORD will lead you away. ³⁸ You shall carry much seed into the field and shall gather in little, for the locust shall consume it. ³⁹ You shall plant vineyards and dress them, but you shall neither drink of the wine nor gather the grapes, for the worm shall eat them. ⁴⁰ You shall have olive trees throughout all your territory, but you shall not anoint yourself with the oil, for your olives shall drop off. ⁴¹ You shall father sons and daughters, but they shall not be yours, for they shall go into captivity. ⁴² The cricket shall possess all your trees and the fruit of your ground. ⁴³ The sojourner who is among you shall rise higher and higher above you, and you shall come down lower and lower. ⁴⁴ He shall lend to you, and you shall not lend to him. He shall be the head, and you shall be the tail.

⁴⁵ "All these curses shall come upon you and pursue you and overtake you till you

are destroyed, because you did not obey the voice of the LORD your God, to keep his commandments and his statutes that he commanded you. **46** They shall be a sign and a wonder against you and your offspring forever. **47** Because you did not serve the LORD your God with joyfulness and gladness of heart, because of the abundance of all things, **48** therefore you shall serve your enemies whom the LORD will send against you, in hunger and thirst, in nakedness, and lacking everything. And he will put a yoke of iron on your neck until he has destroyed you. **49** The LORD will bring a nation against you from far away, from the end of the earth, swooping down like the eagle, a nation whose language you do not understand, **50** a hard-faced nation who shall not respect the old or show mercy to the young. **51** It shall eat the offspring of your cattle and the fruit of your ground, until you are destroyed; it also shall not leave you grain, wine, or oil, the increase of your herds or the young of your flock, until they have caused you to perish.

52 "They shall besiege you in all your towns, until your high and fortified walls, in which you trusted, come down throughout all your land. And they shall besiege you in all your towns throughout all your land, which the LORD your God has given you. **53** And you shall eat the fruit of your womb, the flesh of your sons and daughters, whom the LORD your God has given you, in the siege and in the distress with which your enemies shall distress you. **54** The man who is the most tender and refined among you will begrudge food to his brother, to the wife he embraces, and to the last of the children whom he has left, **55** so that he will not give to any of them any of the flesh of his children whom he is eating, because he has nothing else left, in the siege and in the distress with which your enemy shall distress you in all your towns. **56** The most tender and refined woman among you, who would not venture to set the sole of her foot on the ground because she is so delicate and tender, will begrudge to the husband she embraces, to her son and to her daughter, **57** her afterbirth that comes out from between her feet and her children whom she bears, because lacking everything she will eat them secretly, in the siege and in

the distress with which your enemy shall distress you in your towns.

58 "If you are not careful to do all the words of this law that are written in this book, that you may fear this glorious and awesome name, the LORD your God, **59** then the LORD will bring on you and your offspring extraordinary afflictions, afflictions severe and lasting, and sicknesses grievous and lasting. **60** And he will bring upon you again all the diseases of Egypt, of which you were afraid, and they shall cling to you. **61** Every sickness also and every affliction that is not recorded in the book of this law, the LORD will bring upon you, until you are destroyed. **62** Whereas you were as numerous as the stars of heaven, you shall be left few in number, because you did not obey the voice of the LORD your God. **63** And as the LORD took delight in doing you good and multiplying you, so the LORD will take delight in bringing ruin upon you and destroying you. And you shall be plucked off the land that you are entering to take possession of it.

64 "And the LORD will scatter you among all peoples, from one end of the earth to the other, and there you shall serve other gods of wood and stone, which neither you nor your fathers have known. **65** And among these nations you shall find no respite, and there shall be no resting place for the sole of your foot, but the LORD will give you there a trembling heart and failing eyes and a languishing soul. **66** Your life shall hang in doubt before you. Night and day you shall be in dread and have no assurance of your life. **67** In the morning you shall say, 'If only it were evening!' and at evening you shall say, 'If only it were morning!' because of the dread that your heart shall feel, and the sights that your eyes shall see. **68** And the LORD will bring you back in ships to Egypt, a journey that I promised that you should never make again; and there you shall offer yourselves for sale to your enemies as male and female slaves, but there will be no buyer."

The Covenant Renewed in Moab

29 These are the words of the covenant that the LORD commanded Moses to make with the people of Israel in the land of Moab, besides the covenant that he had made with them at Horeb.

2 And Moses summoned all Israel and said to them: "You have seen all that the LORD did before your eyes in the land of Egypt, to Pharaoh and to all his servants and to all his land, 3 the great trials that your eyes saw, the signs, and those great wonders. 4 But to this day the LORD has not given you a heart to understand or eyes to see or ears to hear. 5 I have led you forty years in the wilderness. Your clothes have not worn out on you, and your sandals have not worn off your feet. 6 You have not eaten bread, and you have not drunk wine or strong drink, that you may know that I am the LORD your God. 7 And when you came to this place, Sihon the king of Heshbon and Og the king of Bashan came out against us to battle, but we defeated them. 8 We took their land and gave it for an inheritance to

---

GETTING THE MESSAGE

Brimstone most likely refers to sulfur. It is a bright yellow, highly combustible mineral that puts out a terrible odor when it burns. Brimstone is abundant in the area around the Dead Sea. During earthquakes hot gases are released from inside the earth, which can cause the brimstone deposits to burst into flame (29:23).

---

the Reubenites, the Gadites, and the half-tribe of the Manassites. 9 Therefore keep the words of this covenant and do them, that you may prosper in all that you do.

10 "You are standing today all of you before the LORD your God: the heads of your tribes, your elders, and your officers, all the men of Israel, 11 your little ones, your wives, and the sojourner who is in your camp, from the one who chops your wood to the one who draws your water, 12 so that you may enter into the sworn covenant of the LORD your God, which the LORD your God is making with you today, 13 that he may establish you today as his people, and that he may be your God, as he promised you, and as he swore to your fathers, to Abraham, to Isaac, and to Jacob. 14 It is not with you alone that I am making this sworn covenant, 15 but with whoever is standing here with us today

before the LORD our God, and with whoever is not here with us today.

16 "You know how we lived in the land of Egypt, and how we came through the midst of the nations through which you passed. 17 And you have seen their detestable things, their idols of wood and stone, of silver and gold, which were among them. 18 Beware lest there be among you a man or woman or clan or tribe whose heart is turning away today from the LORD our God to go and serve the gods of those nations. Beware lest there be among you a root bearing poisonous and bitter fruit, 19 one who, when he hears the words of this sworn covenant, blesses himself in his heart, saying, 'I shall be safe, though I walk in the stubbornness of my heart.' This will lead to the sweeping away of moist and dry alike. 20 The LORD will not be willing to forgive him, but rather the anger of the LORD and his jealousy will smoke against that man, and the curses written in this book will settle upon him, and the LORD will blot out his name from under heaven. 21 And the LORD will single him out from all the tribes of Israel for calamity, in accordance with all the curses of the covenant written in this Book of the Law. 22 And the next generation, your children who rise up after you, and the foreigner who comes from a far land, will say, when they see the afflictions of that land and the sicknesses with which the LORD has made it sick— 23 the whole land burned out with brimstone and salt, nothing sown and nothing growing, where no plant can sprout, an overthrow like that of Sodom and Gomorrah, Admah, and Zeboiim, which the LORD overthrew in his anger and wrath — 24 all the nations will say, 'Why has the LORD done thus to this land? What caused the heat of this great anger?' 25 Then people will say, 'It is because they abandoned the covenant of the LORD, the God of their fathers, which he made with them when he brought them out of the land of Egypt, 26 and went and served other gods and worshiped them, gods whom they had not known and whom he had not allotted to them. 27 Therefore the anger of the LORD was kindled against this land, bringing upon it all the curses written in this book, 28 and the LORD uprooted them from their land in anger and fury and great

wrath, and cast them into another land, as they are this day.'

²⁹ "The secret things belong to the LORD our God, but the things that are revealed belong to us and to our children forever, that we may do all the words of this law.

Repentance and Forgiveness

30 "And when all these things come upon you, the blessing and the curse, which I have set before you, and you call them to mind among all the nations where the LORD your God has driven you, ² and return to the LORD your God, you and your children, and obey his voice in all that I command you today, with all your heart and with all your soul, ³ then the LORD your God will restore your fortunes and have mercy on you, and he will gather you again from all the peoples where the LORD your God has scattered you. ⁴ If your outcasts are in the uttermost parts of heaven, from there the LORD your God will gather you, and from there he will take you. ⁵ And the LORD your God will bring you into the land that your fathers possessed, that you may possess it. And he will make you more prosperous and numerous than your fathers. ⁶ And the LORD your God will circumcise your heart and the heart of your offspring, so that you will love the LORD your God with all your heart and with all your soul, that you may live. ⁷ And the LORD your God will put all these curses on your foes and enemies who persecuted you. ⁸ And you shall again obey the voice of the LORD and keep all his commandments that I command you today. ⁹ The LORD your God will make you abundantly prosperous in all the work of your hand, in the fruit of your womb and in the fruit of your cattle and in the fruit of your ground. For the LORD will again take delight in prospering you, as he took delight in your fathers, ¹⁰ when you obey the voice of the LORD your God, to keep his commandments and his statutes that are written in this Book of the Law, when you turn to the LORD your God with all your heart and with all your soul.

The Choice of Life and Death

¹¹ "For this commandment that I command you today is not too hard for you, neither is it far off. ¹² It is not in heaven, that you should say, 'Who will ascend to heaven for us and bring it to us, that we may hear it and do it?' ¹³ Neither is it beyond the sea, that you should say, 'Who will go over the sea for us and bring it to us, that we may hear it and do it?' ¹⁴ But the word is very near you. It is in your mouth and in your heart, so that you can do it.

¹⁵ "See, I have set before you today life and good, death and evil. ¹⁶ If you obey the commandments of the LORD your God that I command you today, by loving the LORD your God, by walking in his ways, and by keeping his commandments and his statutes and his rules, then you shall live and multiply, and the LORD your God will bless you in the land that you are entering to take possession of it. ¹⁷ But if your heart turns away, and you will not hear, but are drawn away to worship other gods and serve them, ¹⁸ I declare to you today, that you shall surely perish. You shall not live long in the land that you are going over the Jordan to enter and possess. ¹⁹ I call heaven and earth to

> ### GETTING THE MESSAGE
>
> **Walk this way!** The Bible often describes godly living as "walking" with the Lord (30:16; Ps. 23:4; Eph. 4:1).

witness against you today, that I have set before you life and death, blessing and curse. Therefore choose life, that you and your offspring may live, ²⁰ loving the LORD your God, obeying his voice and holding fast to him, for he is your life and length of days, that you may dwell in the land that the LORD swore to your fathers, to Abraham, to Isaac, and to Jacob, to give them."

Joshua to Succeed Moses

31 So Moses continued to speak these words to all Israel. ² And he said to them, "I am 120 years old today. I am no longer able to go out and come in. The LORD has said to me, 'You shall not go over this Jordan.' ³ The LORD your God himself will go over before you. He will destroy these nations before you, so that you shall dispossess them, and Joshua will go over at your head, as the LORD has spoken. ⁴ And the LORD will do to them as he did to Sihon and Og, the kings of the Amorites, and to their land, when he destroyed them. ⁵ And the LORD will give them over to you, and you shall do to them according to the whole commandment that I have commanded you. **6** Be strong and courageous. Do not fear or be in dread of them, for it is the LORD your God who goes with you. He will not leave you or forsake you."

7 Then Moses summoned Joshua and said to him in the sight of all Israel, "Be strong and courageous, for you shall go with this people into the land that the LORD has sworn to their fathers to give them, and you shall put them in possession of it. **8** It is the LORD who goes before you. He will be with you; he will not leave you or forsake you. Do not fear or be dismayed."

The Reading of the Law

9 Then Moses wrote this law and gave it to the priests, the sons of Levi, who carried the ark of the covenant of the LORD, and to all the elders of Israel. **10** And Moses commanded them, "At the end of every seven years, at the set time in the year of release, at the Feast of Booths, **11** when all Israel comes to appear before the LORD your God at the place that he will choose, you shall read this law before all Israel in their hearing. **12** Assemble the people, men, women, and little ones, and the sojourner within your towns, that they may hear and learn to fear the LORD your God, and be careful to do all the words of this law, **13** and that their children, who have not known it, may hear and learn to fear the LORD your God, as long as you live in the land that you are going over the Jordan to possess."

Joshua Commissioned to Lead Israel

14 And the LORD said to Moses, "Behold, the days approach when you must die. Call Joshua and present yourselves in the tent of meeting, that I may commission him." And Moses and Joshua went and presented themselves in the tent of meeting. **15** And the LORD appeared in the tent in a pillar of cloud. And the pillar of cloud stood over the entrance of the tent.

16 And the LORD said to Moses, "Behold, you are about to lie down with your fathers. Then this people will rise and whore after the foreign gods among them in the land that they are entering, and they will forsake me and break my covenant that I have made with them. **17** Then my anger will be kindled against them in that day, and I will forsake them and hide my face from them, and they will be devoured. And many evils and troubles will come upon them, so that they will say in that day, 'Have not these evils come upon us because our God is not among us?' **18** And I will surely hide my face in that day because of all the evil that they have done, because they have turned to other gods.

19 "Now therefore write this song and teach it to the people of Israel. Put it in their mouths, that this song may be a witness for me against the people of Israel. **20** For when I have brought them into the land flowing with milk and honey, which I swore to give to their fathers, and they have eaten and are full and grown fat, they will turn to other gods and serve them, and despise me and break my covenant. **21** And when many evils and troubles have come upon them, this song shall confront them as a witness (for it will live unforgotten in the mouths of their offspring). For I know what they are inclined to do even today, before I have brought them into the land that I swore to give." **22** So Moses wrote this song the same day and taught it to the people of Israel.

23 And the LORD commissioned Joshua the son of Nun and said, "Be strong and courageous, for you shall bring the people of Israel into the land that I swore to give them. I will be with you."

24 When Moses had finished writing the words of this law in a book to the very end, **25** Moses commanded the Levites who carried the ark of the covenant of the LORD, **26** "Take this Book of the Law and put it by the side of the ark of the covenant of the LORD your God, that it may be there for a witness against you. **27** For I know how rebellious and stubborn you are. Behold, even today while I am yet alive with you, you have been rebellious against the LORD. How much more after my death! **28** Assemble to me all the elders of your tribes and your officers, that I may speak these words in their ears and call heaven and earth to witness against them. **29** For I know that after my death you will surely act corruptly and turn aside from the way that I have commanded you. And in the days to come evil will befall you, because you will do what is evil in the sight of the LORD, provoking him to anger through the work of your hands."

The Song of Moses

³⁰ Then Moses spoke the words of this song until they were finished, in the ears of all the assembly of Israel:

32 "Give ear, O heavens, and I will speak,
　　and let the earth hear the words of my mouth.
² May my teaching drop as the rain,
　　my speech distill as the dew,
　like gentle rain upon the tender grass,
　　and like showers upon the herb.
³ For I will proclaim the name of the LORD;
　　ascribe greatness to our God!

⁴ "The Rock, his work is perfect,
　　for all his ways are justice.
　A God of faithfulness and without iniquity,
　　just and upright is he.
⁵ They have dealt corruptly with him;
　　they are no longer his children
　　　because they are blemished;
　they are a crooked and twisted generation.
⁶ Do you thus repay the LORD,
　　you foolish and senseless people?
　Is not he your father, who created you,
　　who made you and established you?
⁷ Remember the days of old;
　　consider the years of many generations;
　ask your father, and he will show you,
　　your elders, and they will tell you.
⁸ When the Most High gave to the nations their inheritance,
　　when he divided mankind,
　he fixed the borders of the peoples
　　according to the number of the sons of God.
⁹ But the LORD's portion is his people,
　　Jacob his allotted heritage.

¹⁰ "He found him in a desert land,
　　and in the howling waste of the wilderness;
　he encircled him, he cared for him,
　　he kept him as the apple of his eye.
¹¹ Like an eagle that stirs up its nest,
　　that flutters over its young,
　spreading out its wings, catching them,
　　bearing them on its pinions,
¹² the LORD alone guided him,
　　no foreign god was with him.

¹³ He made him ride on the high places of the land,
　　and he ate the produce of the field,
　and he suckled him with honey out of the rock,
　　and oil out of the flinty rock.
¹⁴ Curds from the herd, and milk from the flock,
　　with fat of lambs,
　rams of Bashan and goats,
　　with the very finest of the wheat—
　and you drank foaming wine made from the blood of the grape.

¹⁵ "But Jeshurun grew fat, and kicked;
　　you grew fat, stout, and sleek;
　then he forsook God who made him
　　and scoffed at the Rock of his salvation.
¹⁶ They stirred him to jealousy with strange gods;
　　with abominations they provoked him to anger.

> **GETTING THE MESSAGE**
>
> Idols represent gods that don't actually exist, but the **demons** behind idol worship are real (32:17).

¹⁷ They sacrificed to demons that were no gods,
　　to gods they had never known,
　to new gods that had come recently,
　　whom your fathers had never dreaded.
¹⁸ You were unmindful of the Rock that bore you,
　　and you forgot the God who gave you birth.

¹⁹ "The LORD saw it and spurned them,
　　because of the provocation of his sons and his daughters.
²⁰ And he said, 'I will hide my face from them;
　　I will see what their end will be,
　for they are a perverse generation,
　　children in whom is no faithfulness.
²¹ They have made me jealous with what is no god;
　　they have provoked me to anger with their idols.

So I will make them jealous with
  those who are no people;
I will provoke them to anger with a
  foolish nation.
22 For a fire is kindled by my anger,
  and it burns to the depths of Sheol,
devours the earth and its increase,
  and sets on fire the foundations of
    the mountains.

23 "'And I will heap disasters upon them;
  I will spend my arrows on them;
24 they shall be wasted with hunger,
  and devoured by plague
  and poisonous pestilence;
I will send the teeth of beasts against
    them,
  with the venom of things that crawl
    in the dust.
25 Outdoors the sword shall bereave,
  and indoors terror,
for young man and woman alike,
  the nursing child with the man of
    gray hairs.
26 I would have said, "I will cut them to
    pieces;
  I will wipe them from human mem-
    ory,"
27 had I not feared provocation by the
    enemy,
  lest their adversaries should misun-
    derstand,
lest they should say, "Our hand is
    triumphant,
  it was not the LORD who did all this."'

28 "For they are a nation void of counsel,
  and there is no understanding in
    them.
29 If they were wise, they would under-
    stand this;
  they would discern their latter end!
30 How could one have chased a thou-
    sand,
  and two have put ten thousand to
    flight,
unless their Rock had sold them,
  and the LORD had given them up?
31 For their rock is not as our Rock;
  our enemies are by themselves.
32 For their vine comes from the vine of
    Sodom
  and from the fields of Gomorrah;
their grapes are grapes of poison;
  their clusters are bitter;

33 their wine is the poison of serpents
  and the cruel venom of asps.

34 "'Is not this laid up in store with me,
  sealed up in my treasuries?
35 Vengeance is mine, and recompense,
  for the time when their foot shall
    slip;
for the day of their calamity is at hand,
  and their doom comes swiftly.'
36 For the LORD will vindicate his people
  and have compassion on his ser-
    vants,
when he sees that their power is gone
  and there is none remaining, bond
    or free.
37 Then he will say, 'Where are their gods,
  the rock in which they took refuge,
38 who ate the fat of their sacrifices
  and drank the wine of their drink
    offering?
Let them rise up and help you;
  let them be your protection!

39 "'See now that I, even I, am he,
  and there is no god beside me;
I kill and I make alive;
  I wound and I heal;
  and there is none that can deliver
    out of my hand.
40 For I lift up my hand to heaven
  and swear, As I live forever,
41 if I sharpen my flashing sword
  and my hand takes hold on judg-
    ment,
I will take vengeance on my adversar-
    ies
  and will repay those who hate me.
42 I will make my arrows drunk with
    blood,
  and my sword shall devour flesh—
with the blood of the slain and the
    captives,
  from the long-haired heads of the
    enemy.'

43 "Rejoice with him, O heavens;
  bow down to him, all gods,
for he avenges the blood of his chil-
    dren
  and takes vengeance on his adver-
    saries.
He repays those who hate him
  and cleanses his people's land."

44 Moses came and recited all the words
of this song in the hearing of the people,

he and Joshua the son of Nun. **45** And when Moses had finished speaking all these words to all Israel, **46** he said to them, "Take to heart all the words by which I am warning you today, that you may command them to your children, that they may be careful to do all the words of this law. **47** For it is no empty word for you, but your very life, and by this word you shall live long in the land that you are going over the Jordan to possess."

Moses' Death Foretold

48 That very day the LORD spoke to Moses, **49** "Go up this mountain of the Abarim, Mount Nebo, which is in the land of Moab, opposite Jericho, and view the land of Canaan, which I am giving to the people of Israel for a possession. **50** And die on the mountain which you go up, and be gathered to your people, as Aaron your brother died in Mount Hor and was gathered to his people, **51** because you broke faith with me in the midst of the people of Israel at the waters of Meribah-kadesh, in the wilderness of Zin, and because you did not treat me as holy in the midst of the people of Israel. **52** For you shall see the land before you, but you shall not go there, into the land that I am giving to the people of Israel."

Moses' Final Blessing on Israel

33 This is the blessing with which Moses the man of God blessed the people of Israel before his death. **2** He said,

"The LORD came from Sinai
  and dawned from Seir upon us;
  he shone forth from Mount Paran;
  he came from the ten thousands of
    holy ones,
  with flaming fire at his right hand.
3 Yes, he loved his people,
  all his holy ones were in his hand;
so they followed in your steps,
  receiving direction from you,
4 when Moses commanded us a law,
  as a possession for the assembly of
    Jacob.
5 Thus the LORD became king in
    Jeshurun,
  when the heads of the people were
    gathered,
  all the tribes of Israel together.

6 "Let Reuben live, and not die,
  but let his men be few."

7 And this he said of Judah:

"Hear, O LORD, the voice of Judah,
  and bring him in to his people.
With your hands contend for him,
  and be a help against his adversaries."

8 And of Levi he said,

"Give to Levi your Thummim,
  and your Urim to your godly one,
whom you tested at Massah,
  with whom you quarreled at the
    waters of Meribah;
9 who said of his father and mother,
  'I regard them not';
he disowned his brothers
  and ignored his children.
For they observed your word
  and kept your covenant.
10 They shall teach Jacob your rules
  and Israel your law;
they shall put incense before you
  and whole burnt offerings on your
    altar.

11 Bless, O LORD, his substance,
  and accept the work of his hands;
crush the loins of his adversaries,
  of those who hate him, that they
    rise not again."

12 Of Benjamin he said,

"The beloved of the LORD dwells in
    safety.
The High God surrounds him all day
    long,
  and dwells between his shoulders."

13 And of Joseph he said,

"Blessed by the LORD be his land,
  with the choicest gifts of heaven
    above,
  and of the deep that crouches
    beneath,
14 with the choicest fruits of the sun
  and the rich yield of the months,

15   with the finest produce of the ancient
          mountains
             and the abundance of the everlast-
             ing hills,
16   with the best gifts of the earth and its
          fullness
             and the favor of him who dwells in
             the bush.
       May these rest on the head of Joseph,
          on the pate of him who is prince
          among his brothers.
17   A firstborn bull—he has majesty,
          and his horns are the horns of a
          wild ox;
       with them he shall gore the peoples,
          all of them, to the ends of the earth;
       they are the ten thousands of
          Ephraim,
          and they are the thousands of
          Manasseh."

18 And of Zebulun he said,

       "Rejoice, Zebulun, in your going out,
          and Issachar, in your tents.
19   They shall call peoples to their moun-
          tain;
             there they offer right sacrifices;
       for they draw from the abundance of
          the seas
             and the hidden treasures of the
             sand."

20 And of Gad he said,

       "Blessed be he who enlarges Gad!
          Gad crouches like a lion;
          he tears off arm and scalp.
21   He chose the best of the land for him-
          self,
             for there a commander's portion
             was reserved;
       and he came with the heads of the
          people,
       with Israel he executed the justice
          of the LORD,
          and his judgments for Israel."

22 And of Dan he said,

       "Dan is a lion's cub
          that leaps from Bashan."

23 And of Naphtali he said,

       "O Naphtali, sated with favor,
          and full of the blessing of the LORD,
          possess the lake and the south."

24 And of Asher he said,

       "Most blessed of sons be Asher;
          let him be the favorite of his broth-
          ers,
          and let him dip his foot in oil.
25   Your bars shall be iron and bronze,
          and as your days, so shall your
          strength be.
26   "There is none like God, O Jeshurun,
          who rides through the heavens to
          your help,
          through the skies in his majesty.
27   The eternal God is your dwelling place,
          and underneath are the everlasting
          arms.
       And he thrust out the enemy before
          you
          and said, 'Destroy.'
28   So Israel lived in safety,
          Jacob lived alone,
       in a land of grain and wine,
          whose heavens drop down dew.
29   Happy are you, O Israel! Who is like
          you,
          a people saved by the LORD,
       the shield of your help,
          and the sword of your triumph!
       Your enemies shall come fawning to
          you,
          and you shall tread upon their
          backs."

The Death of Moses

34 Then Moses went up from the plains
of Moab to Mount Nebo, to the top
of Pisgah, which is opposite Jericho. And the
LORD showed him all the land, Gilead as far
as Dan, 2 all Naphtali, the land of Ephraim
and Manasseh, all the land of Judah as far as
the western sea, 3 the Negeb, and the Plain,
that is, the Valley of Jericho the city of palm
trees, as far as Zoar. 4 And the LORD said to
him, "This is the land of which I swore to
Abraham, to Isaac, and to Jacob, 'I will give
it to your offspring.' I have let you see it with
your eyes, but you shall not go over there."
5 So Moses the servant of the LORD died there
in the land of Moab, according to the word
of the LORD, 6 and he buried him in the valley in the land of Moab opposite Beth-peor;
but no one knows the place of his burial to
this day. 7 Moses was 120 years old when he
died. His eye was undimmed, and his vigor
unabated. 8 And the people of Israel wept

for Moses in the plains of Moab thirty days. Then the days of weeping and mourning for Moses were ended.

⁹ And Joshua the son of Nun was full of the spirit of wisdom, for Moses had laid his hands on him. So the people of Israel obeyed him and did as the LORD had commanded Moses. ¹⁰ And there has not arisen a prophet since in Israel like Moses, whom the LORD knew face to face, ¹¹ none like him for all the signs and the wonders that the LORD sent him to do in the land of Egypt, to Pharaoh and to all his servants and to all his land, ¹² and for all the mighty power and all the great deeds of terror that Moses did in the sight of all Israel.

INTRODUCTION TO JOSHUA

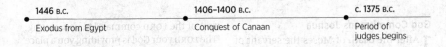

1446 B.C.	1406–1400 B.C.	c. 1375 B.C.
Exodus from Egypt	Conquest of Canaan	Period of judges begins

AUTHOR AND DATE

While this book mentions Joshua writing (8:32; 24:26), it does not claim he wrote the book. The repeated references to something existing "to this day" (see 4:9; 5:9; 6:25; etc.) seem to suggest that there was a significant lapse of time between the events recorded in the book and the time when the writing of the book was completed. The final writing may have taken place in the time of the exile (post-587 B.C.), but the writing probably began much earlier.

THEME

Joshua records part two of God's grandest work of redemption in the OT period. In part one (the Pentateuch), the Lord redeemed his people out of slavery in Egypt and formalized his covenantal love for them at Sinai. Moses led the people during that time. Now in part two, under the leadership of Joshua, the Lord brings his people into the Land of Promise and gives them rest.

PURPOSE AND BACKGROUND

The book of Joshua seeks to explain God's purpose in the events surrounding Israel's capture of and settlement in Canaan. Those events are seen as the fulfillment of God's promises to Abraham, Isaac, and Jacob. Such an account would have been relevant to ancient Israel from its earliest arrival in Canaan, and to every generation of God's people to the present day.

Joshua comes immediately after the Pentateuch and in many ways completes its story. The theme of the first five books of the Bible is the progressive fulfillment of the "patriarchal promise," made first to Abraham (Gen. 12:1–3) and repeated to his son Isaac (Gen. 26:2–4) and his grandson Jacob (Gen. 28:13–15; etc.). The Lord promised Abraham and his descendants that they would be blessed and would become a blessing to others, that they would grow to become a great nation, and that they would be given a land of their own—and that these blessings would be enjoyed within a close covenant relationship with God.

By the end of the Pentateuch, Israel has been brought into a covenant relationship with the Lord and has become a great people. But they remain outside the Land of Promise, on the plains of Moab. Forty years before, the Lord had chosen Moses to lead his people out of slavery in Egypt and to bring them to the land he had promised (Ex. 3:6–8; 6:2–8). Now, after so many years of wandering, Joshua, the "new Moses" (Josh. 1:1–9), is to lead God's people into the land, take it, and divide it among them as their inheritance from the Lord.

KEY THEMES

1. The Lord's continuing presence as the key to strength and courage (e.g., 1:5, 9).

2. The importance of the Lord's instructions for succeeding in one's mission and acting with wisdom (1:7–8).

3. The ability of the Lord to save the "outsider" (Rahab), and the danger of the "insider" falling away (Achan; see chs. 2 and 7).

4. The Lord as divine Warrior and the reality of judgment (e.g., 10:42; 11:19–20).

5. The danger of failing to ask the Lord (e.g., 9:14).

6. The Lord as Protector of the covenant (e.g., 10:1–15, especially v. 11).

7. The unity of the people of God (18:1–10; 22:34).

8. The sovereignty of God in giving his people a place and rest (1:13; 11:23; 21:43–45).

9. The faithfulness of God in fulfilling all his good promises (1:2; 21:43–45).

10. The necessity of removing false gods and worshiping God alone (ch. 24).

OUTLINE

I. Crossing into the Land (1:1–5:15)

II. Taking the Land (6:1–12:24)

III. Dividing the Land (13:1–21:45)

IV. Serving the Lord in the Land (22:1–24:33)

JOSHUA

God Commissions Joshua

1 After the death of Moses the servant of the LORD, the LORD said to Joshua the son of Nun, Moses' assistant, ² "Moses my servant is dead. Now therefore arise, go over this Jordan, you and all this people, into the land that I am giving to them, to the people of Israel. ³ Every place that the sole of your foot will tread upon I have given to you, just as I promised to Moses. ⁴ From the wilderness and this Lebanon as far as the great river, the river Euphrates, all the land of the Hittites to the Great Sea toward the going down of the sun shall be your territory. ⁵ No man shall be able to stand before you all the days of your life. Just as I was with Moses, so I will be with you. I will not leave you or forsake you. ⁶ Be strong and courageous, for you shall cause this people to inherit the land that I swore to their fathers to give them. ⁷ Only be strong and very courageous, being careful to do according to all the law that Moses my servant commanded you. Do not turn from it to the right hand or to the left, that you may have good success wherever you go. ⁸ This Book of the Law shall not depart from your mouth, but you shall meditate on it day and night, so that you may be careful to do according to all that is written in it. For then you will make your way prosperous, and then you will have good success. ⁹ Have I not commanded you? Be strong and courageous. Do not be frightened, and do not be dismayed, for the LORD your God is with you wherever you go."

Joshua Assumes Command

¹⁰ And Joshua commanded the officers of the people, ¹¹ "Pass through the midst of the camp and command the people, 'Prepare your provisions, for within three days you are to pass over this Jordan to go in to take possession of the land that the LORD your God is giving you to possess.'"

¹² And to the Reubenites, the Gadites, and the half-tribe of Manasseh Joshua said, ¹³ "Remember the word that Moses the ser- vant of the LORD commanded you, saying, 'The LORD your God is providing you a place of rest and will give you this land.' ¹⁴ Your wives, your little ones, and your livestock shall remain in the land that Moses gave you beyond the Jordan, but all the men of valor among you shall pass over armed before your brothers and shall help them, ¹⁵ until the LORD gives rest to your brothers as he has to you, and they also take possession of the land that the LORD your God is giving them. Then you shall return to the land of your possession and shall possess it, the

> ### GETTING THE MESSAGE
>
> **The Historical Books.** Joshua begins the section of the Bible known as the Historical Books. There are 12 Historical Books: Joshua, Judges, Ruth, 1–2 Samuel, 1–2 Kings, 1–2 Chronicles, Ezra, Nehemiah, and Esther.

land that Moses the servant of the LORD gave you beyond the Jordan toward the sunrise."

¹⁶ And they answered Joshua, "All that you have commanded us we will do, and wher- ever you send us we will go. ¹⁷ Just as we obeyed Moses in all things, so we will obey you. Only may the LORD your God be with you, as he was with Moses! ¹⁸ Whoever rebels against your commandment and disobeys your words, whatever you command him, shall be put to death. Only be strong and courageous."

Rahab Hides the Spies

2 And Joshua the son of Nun sent two men secretly from Shittim as spies, say- ing, "Go, view the land, especially Jericho." And they went and came into the house of a prostitute whose name was Rahab and lodged there. ² And it was told to the king of Jericho, "Behold, men of Israel have come here tonight to search out the land." ³ Then the king of Jericho sent to Rahab, saying,

"Bring out the men who have come to you, who entered your house, for they have come to search out all the land." ⁴ But the woman had taken the two men and hidden them. And she said, "True, the men came to me, but I did not know where they were from. ⁵ And when the gate was about to be closed at dark, the men went out. I do not know where the men went. Pursue them quickly, for you will overtake them." ⁶ But she had brought them up to the roof and hid them with the stalks of flax that she had laid in order on the roof. ⁷ So the men pursued after

---

PROFILE

JOSHUA

Joshua was a spiritual and military leader of Israel. He accompanied Moses part of the way up Mount Sinai and also assisted him at the tent of meeting. He was one of the 12 spies sent to explore the land of Canaan. Upon their return, most of the spies said it would be impossible to conquer the land, but Joshua and Caleb encouraged the people to trust the Lord for victory. Because of their obedience and faith, Joshua and Caleb were the only two men of their generation allowed to enter Canaan. The Lord appointed Joshua to lead Israel into the Promised Land. He was also put in charge of dividing the land among the tribes.

KEY REFERENCE: NUMBERS 27:18–23

---

them on the way to the Jordan as far as the fords. And the gate was shut as soon as the pursuers had gone out.

⁸ Before the men lay down, she came up to them on the roof ⁹ and said to the men, "I know that the LORD has given you the land, and that the fear of you has fallen upon us, and that all the inhabitants of the land melt away before you. ¹⁰ For we have heard how the LORD dried up the water of the Red Sea before you when you came out of Egypt, and what you did to the two kings of the Amorites who were beyond the

Jordan, to Sihon and Og, whom you devoted to destruction.[1] ¹¹ And as soon as we heard it, our hearts melted, and there was no spirit left in any man because of you, for the LORD your God, he is God in the heavens above and on the earth beneath. ¹² Now then, please swear to me by the LORD that, as I have dealt kindly with you, you also will deal kindly with my father's house, and give me a sure sign ¹³ that you will save alive my father and mother, my brothers and sisters, and all who belong to them, and deliver our lives from death." ¹⁴ And the men said to her, "Our life for yours even to death! If you do not tell this business of ours, then when the LORD gives us the land we will deal kindly and faithfully with you."

¹⁵ Then she let them down by a rope through the window, for her house was built into the city wall, so that she lived in the wall. ¹⁶ And she said to them, "Go into the

---

GETTING THE MESSAGE

Double walls. Like several other ancient cities, Jericho was most likely protected by a double wall. Poorer citizens of the city often built their homes between the inner and outer walls (2:15).

---

hills, or the pursuers will encounter you, and hide there three days until the pursuers have returned. Then afterward you may go your way." ¹⁷ The men said to her, "We will be guiltless with respect to this oath of yours that you have made us swear. ¹⁸ Behold, when we come into the land, you shall tie this scarlet cord in the window through which you let us down, and you shall gather into your house your father and mother, your brothers, and all your father's household. ¹⁹ Then if anyone goes out of the doors of your house into the street, his blood shall be on his own head, and we shall be guiltless. But if a hand is laid on anyone who is with you in the house, his blood shall be on our head. ²⁰ But if you tell this business of ours, then we shall be guiltless with respect to your oath that you have made us swear." ²¹ And she said, "According to your words, so be it." Then she sent them away,

---

[1] That is, destroyed or made an offering because of sin, at God's command; also 6:17, 18, 21; 7:12; 8:26; 10:1, 28, 35, 37, 39, 40; 11:11, 12, 20, 21

and they departed. And she tied the scarlet cord in the window. ²²They departed and went into the hills and remained there three days until the pursuers returned, and the pursuers searched all along the way and found nothing. ²³Then the two men returned. They came down from the hills and passed over and came to Joshua the son of Nun, and they told him all that had happened to them. ²⁴And they said to Joshua, "Truly the LORD has given all the land into our hands. And also, all the inhabitants of the land melt away because of us."

Israel Crosses the Jordan

3 Then Joshua rose early in the morning and they set out from Shittim. And they came to the Jordan, he and all the people of Israel, and lodged there before they passed over. ²At the end of three days the officers went through the camp ³and commanded the people, "As soon as you see the ark of the covenant of the LORD your God being carried by the Levitical priests, then you shall set out from your place and follow it. ⁴Yet there shall be a distance between you and it, about 2,000 cubits in length. Do not come near it, in order that you may know the way you shall go, for you have not passed this way before." ⁵Then Joshua said to the people, "Consecrate yourselves, for tomorrow the LORD will do wonders among you." ⁶And Joshua said to the priests, "Take up the ark of the covenant and pass on before the people." So they took up the ark of the covenant and went before the people.

⁷The LORD said to Joshua, "Today I will begin to exalt you in the sight of all Israel, that they may know that, as I was with Moses, so I will be with you. ⁸And as for you, command the priests who bear the ark of the covenant, 'When you come to the brink of the waters of the Jordan, you shall stand still in the Jordan.'" ⁹And Joshua said to the people of Israel, "Come here and listen to the words of the LORD your God." ¹⁰And Joshua said, "Here is how you shall know that the living God is among you and that he will without fail drive out from before you the Canaanites, the Hittites, the Hivites, the Perizzites, the Girgashites, the Amorites, and the Jebusites. ¹¹Behold, the ark of the covenant of the Lord of all the earth is passing over before you into the Jordan. ¹²Now therefore take twelve men from the tribes of Israel, from each tribe a man. ¹³And when the soles of the feet of the priests bearing the ark of the LORD, the Lord of all the earth, shall rest in the waters of the Jordan, the waters of the Jordan shall be cut off from flowing, and the waters coming down from above shall stand in one heap."

¹⁴So when the people set out from their tents to pass over the Jordan with the priests bearing the ark of the covenant before the people, ¹⁵and as soon as those bearing the ark had come as far as the Jordan, and the feet of the priests bearing the ark were dipped in the brink of the water (now the Jordan overflows all its banks throughout the time of harvest), ¹⁶the waters coming down from above stood and rose up in a heap very far away, at Adam, the city that is beside Zarethan, and those flowing down toward the Sea of the Arabah, the Salt Sea,

were completely cut off. And the people passed over opposite Jericho. ¹⁷Now the priests bearing the ark of the covenant of the LORD stood firmly on dry ground in the midst of the Jordan, and all Israel was passing over on dry ground until all the nation finished passing over the Jordan.

Twelve Memorial Stones from the Jordan

4 When all the nation had finished passing over the Jordan, the LORD said to Joshua, ²"Take twelve men from the people, from each tribe a man, ³and command them, saying, 'Take twelve stones from here out of the midst of the Jordan, from the very place where the priests' feet stood firmly, and bring them over with you and lay them down in the place where you lodge tonight.'" ⁴Then Joshua called the twelve men from the people of Israel, whom he had appointed, a man from each tribe. ⁵And Joshua said to them, "Pass on before the ark

of the LORD your God into the midst of the Jordan, and take up each of you a stone upon his shoulder, according to the number of the tribes of the people of Israel, **6** that this may be a sign among you. When your children ask in time to come, 'What do those stones mean to you?' **7** then you shall tell them that the waters of the Jordan were cut off before the ark of the covenant of the LORD. When it passed over the Jordan, the waters of the Jordan were cut off. So these stones shall be to the people of Israel a memorial forever."

8 And the people of Israel did just as Joshua commanded and took up twelve stones out of the midst of the Jordan, according to the number of the tribes of the people of Israel, just as the LORD told Joshua. And they carried them over with them to the place where they lodged and laid them down there. **9** And Joshua set up twelve stones in the midst of

---

GETTING THE MESSAGE

Circumcision was widely practiced in the ancient Near East, though not by every people group. In Egypt, it was considered a rite of passage. For the people of Israel, however, it was a sign of the nation's covenant with God. Flint or obsidian knives were generally used to perform circumcision.

---

the Jordan, in the place where the feet of the priests bearing the ark of the covenant had stood; and they are there to this day. **10** For the priests bearing the ark stood in the midst of the Jordan until everything was finished that the LORD commanded Joshua to tell the people, according to all that Moses had commanded Joshua.

The people passed over in haste. **11** And when all the people had finished passing over, the ark of the LORD and the priests passed over before the people. **12** The sons of Reuben and the sons of Gad and the half-tribe of Manasseh passed over armed before the people of Israel, as Moses had told them. **13** About 40,000 ready for war passed over before the LORD for battle, to the plains of Jericho. **14** On that day the LORD exalted Joshua in the sight of all Israel, and they stood in awe of him just as they had stood in awe of Moses, all the days of his life.

15 And the LORD said to Joshua, **16** "Command the priests bearing the ark of the testimony to come up out of the Jordan." **17** So Joshua commanded the priests, "Come up out of the Jordan." **18** And when the priests bearing the ark of the covenant of the LORD came up from the midst of the Jordan, and the soles of the priests' feet were lifted up on dry ground, the waters of the Jordan returned to their place and overflowed all its banks, as before.

19 The people came up out of the Jordan on the tenth day of the first month, and they encamped at Gilgal on the east border of Jericho. **20** And those twelve stones, which they took out of the Jordan, Joshua set up at Gilgal. **21** And he said to the people of Israel, "When your children ask their fathers in times to come, 'What do these stones mean?' **22** then you shall let your children know, 'Israel passed over this Jordan on dry ground.' **23** For the LORD your God dried up the waters of the Jordan for you until you passed over, as the LORD your God did to the Red Sea, which he dried up for us until we passed over, **24** so that all the peoples of the earth may know that the hand of the LORD is mighty, that you may fear the LORD your God forever."

The New Generation Circumcised

5 As soon as all the kings of the Amorites who were beyond the Jordan to the west, and all the kings of the Canaanites who were by the sea, heard that the LORD had dried up the waters of the Jordan for the people of Israel until they had crossed over, their hearts melted and there was no longer any spirit in them because of the people of Israel.

2 At that time the LORD said to Joshua, "Make flint knives and circumcise the sons of Israel a second time." **3** So Joshua made flint knives and circumcised the sons of Israel at Gibeath-haaraloth. **4** And this is the reason why Joshua circumcised them: all the males of the people who came out of Egypt, all the men of war, had died in the wilderness on the way after they had come out of Egypt. **5** Though all the people who came out had been circumcised, yet all the people who were born on the way in the wilderness after they had come out of Egypt had not been circumcised. **6** For the people of Israel walked forty years in the wilderness, until all the nation, the men of war who came out of Egypt, perished, because they did not obey the voice of the LORD; the LORD swore to them that he would not let them see the land that the LORD had sworn to their fathers to give to us, a land flowing with milk and honey. ⁷ So it was their children, whom he raised up in their place, that Joshua circumcised. For they were uncircumcised, because they had not been circumcised on the way.

⁸ When the circumcising of the whole nation was finished, they remained in their places in the camp until they were healed. ⁹ And the LORD said to Joshua, "Today I have rolled away the reproach of Egypt from you." And so the name of that place is called Gilgal¹ to this day.

First Passover in Canaan

¹⁰ While the people of Israel were encamped at Gilgal, they kept the Passover on the fourteenth day of the month in the evening on the plains of Jericho. ¹¹ And the day after the Passover, on that very day, they ate of the produce of the land, unleavened cakes and parched grain. ¹² And the manna ceased the day after they ate of the produce of the land. And there was no longer manna for the people of Israel, but they ate of the fruit of the land of Canaan that year.

The Commander of the LORD's Army

¹³ When Joshua was by Jericho, he lifted up his eyes and looked, and behold, a man was standing before him with his drawn sword in his hand. And Joshua went to him and said to him, "Are you for us, or for our adversaries?" ¹⁴ And he said, "No; but I am the commander of the army of the LORD. Now I have come." And Joshua fell on his face to the earth and worshiped and said to him, "What does my lord say to his servant?" ¹⁵ And the commander of the LORD's army said to Joshua, "Take off your sandals from your feet, for the place where you are standing is holy." And Joshua did so.

The Fall of Jericho

6 Now Jericho was shut up inside and outside because of the people of Israel. None went out, and none came in. ² And the LORD said to Joshua, "See, I have given Jericho into your hand, with its king and

mighty men of valor. ³ You shall march around the city, all the men of war going around the city once. Thus shall you do for six days. ⁴ Seven priests shall bear seven trumpets of rams' horns before the ark. On the seventh day you shall march around the city seven times, and the priests shall blow the trumpets. ⁵ And when they make a long blast with the ram's horn, when you hear the sound of the trumpet, then all the people shall shout with a great shout, and the wall of the city will fall down flat, and the people shall go up, everyone straight before him." ⁶ So Joshua the son of Nun called the priests and said to them, "Take up the ark of the covenant and let seven priests bear seven trumpets of rams' horns before the ark of the LORD." ⁷ And he said to the people,

---

GETTING THE MESSAGE

Jericho is one of the oldest cities in the world. At about 750 feet (229 m) below sea level, it is also one of the lowest cities in the world. Jericho receives only a few inches of rainfall each year, and yet it was an oasis for travelers because of its abundant supply of spring water. Jericho is often referred to as the "city of palms" (see Deut. 34:3).

"Go forward. March around the city and let the armed men pass on before the ark of the LORD."

⁸ And just as Joshua had commanded the people, the seven priests bearing the seven trumpets of rams' horns before the LORD went forward, blowing the trumpets, with the ark of the covenant of the LORD following them. ⁹ The armed men were walking before the priests who were blowing the trumpets, and the rear guard was walking after the ark, while the trumpets blew continually. ¹⁰ But Joshua commanded the people, "You shall not shout or make your voice heard, neither shall any word go out of your mouth, until the day I tell you to shout. Then you shall shout." ¹¹ So he caused the ark of the LORD to circle the city, going about it once. And they came into the camp and spent the night in the camp.

¹ *Gilgal* sounds like the Hebrew for *to roll*

¹² Then Joshua rose early in the morning, and the priests took up the ark of the LORD. ¹³ And the seven priests bearing the seven trumpets of rams' horns before the ark of the LORD walked on, and they blew the trumpets continually. And the armed men were walking before them, and the rear guard was walking after the ark of the LORD, while the trumpets blew continually. ¹⁴ And the second day they marched around the city once, and returned into the camp. So they did for six days.

PROFILE
RAHAB

Rahab was a Gentile prostitute who lived in Jericho. When Joshua sent two spies to gather information about the city, she hid the men from the king. She also deceived the men who came looking for the spies. She convinced them to leave the city in pursuit of the spies, who were actually hidden on her roof. She demonstrated a remarkable awareness of Israel's history and of the Lord's intention to give Israel the land of Canaan. In response to her kindness, Joshua spared Rahab and her household when Israel destroyed Jericho. Rahab was Boaz's mother and is one of four women listed in the genealogy of Jesus. She is commended in the New Testament for her faith and for her good works.

KEY REFERENCE: JOSHUA 2:10–11

¹⁵ On the seventh day they rose early, at the dawn of day, and marched around the city in the same manner seven times. It was only on that day that they marched around the city seven times. ¹⁶ And at the seventh time, when the priests had blown the trumpets, Joshua said to the people, "Shout, for the LORD has given you the city. ¹⁷ And the city and all that is within it shall be devoted to the LORD for destruction. Only Rahab the prostitute and all who are with her in her house shall live, because she hid the messengers whom we sent. ¹⁸ But you, keep yourselves from the things devoted to destruction, lest when you have devoted them you take any of the devoted things and make the camp of Israel a thing for destruction and bring trouble upon it. ¹⁹ But all silver and gold, and every vessel of bronze and iron, are holy to the LORD; they shall go into the treasury of the LORD." ²⁰ So the people shouted, and the trumpets were blown. As soon as the people heard the sound of the trumpet, the people shouted a great shout, and the wall fell down flat, so that the people went up into the city, every man straight before him, and they captured the city. ²¹ Then they devoted all in the city to destruction, both men and women, young and old, oxen, sheep, and donkeys, with the edge of the sword.

²² But to the two men who had spied out the land, Joshua said, "Go into the prostitute's house and bring out from there the woman and all who belong to her, as you swore to her." ²³ So the young men who had been spies went in and brought out Rahab and her father and mother and brothers and all who belonged to her. And they brought all her relatives and put them outside the camp of Israel. ²⁴ And they burned the city with fire, and everything in it. Only the silver and gold, and the vessels of bronze and of iron, they put into the treasury of the house of the LORD. ²⁵ But Rahab the prostitute and her father's household and all who belonged to her, Joshua saved alive. And she has lived in Israel to this day, because she hid the messengers whom Joshua sent to spy out Jericho.

²⁶ Joshua laid an oath on them at that time, saying, "Cursed before the LORD be the man who rises up and rebuilds this city, Jericho.

"At the cost of his firstborn shall he
    lay its foundation,
and at the cost of his youngest son
    shall he set up its gates."

²⁷ So the LORD was with Joshua, and his fame was in all the land.

Israel Defeated at Ai

7 But the people of Israel broke faith in regard to the devoted things, for Achan the son of Carmi, son of Zabdi, son of Zerah, of the tribe of Judah, took some of the devoted things. And the anger of the LORD burned against the people of Israel.

² Joshua sent men from Jericho to Ai, which is near Beth-aven, east of Bethel, and said to them, "Go up and spy out the land." And the men went up and spied out Ai. ³ And they returned to Joshua and said to him, "Do not have all the people go up, but let about two or three thousand men go up and attack Ai. Do not make the whole people toil up there, for they are few." ⁴ So about three thousand men went up there from the people. And they fled before the men of Ai, ⁵ and the men of Ai killed about thirty-six of their men and chased them before the gate as far as Shebarim and struck them at the descent. And the hearts of the people melted and became as water.

⁶ Then Joshua tore his clothes and fell to the earth on his face before the ark of the LORD until the evening, he and the elders of Israel. And they put dust on their heads. ⁷ And Joshua said, "Alas, O Lord GOD, why have you brought this people over the Jordan at all, to give us into the hands of the Amorites, to destroy us? Would that we had been content to dwell beyond the Jordan! ⁸ O Lord, what can I say, when Israel has turned their backs before their enemies! ⁹ For the Canaanites and all the inhabitants of the land will hear of it and will surround us and cut off our name from the earth. And what will you do for your great name?"

The Sin of Achan

¹⁰ The LORD said to Joshua, "Get up! Why have you fallen on your face? ¹¹ Israel has sinned; they have transgressed my covenant that I commanded them; they have taken some of the devoted things; they have stolen and lied and put them among their own belongings. ¹² Therefore the people of Israel cannot stand before their enemies. They turn their backs before their enemies, because they have become devoted for destruction. I will be with you no more, unless you destroy the devoted things from among you. ¹³ Get up! Consecrate the people and say, 'Consecrate yourselves for tomorrow; for thus says the LORD, God of Israel, "There are devoted things in your midst, O Israel. You cannot stand before your enemies until you take away the devoted things from among you." ¹⁴ In the morning therefore you shall be brought near by your tribes. And the tribe that the LORD takes by lot shall come near by clans. And the clan

that the LORD takes shall come near by households. And the household that the LORD takes shall come near man by man. ¹⁵ And he who is taken with the devoted things shall be burned with fire, he and all that he has, because he has transgressed the covenant of the LORD, and because he has done an outrageous thing in Israel.'"

¹⁶ So Joshua rose early in the morning and brought Israel near tribe by tribe, and the tribe of Judah was taken. ¹⁷ And he brought near the clans of Judah, and the clan of the Zerahites was taken. And he brought near the clan of the Zerahites man by man, and Zabdi was taken. ¹⁸ And he brought near his household man by man, and Achan the son of Carmi, son of Zabdi, son of Zerah, of the tribe of Judah, was taken. ¹⁹ Then Joshua said to Achan, "My son, give glory to the LORD God of Israel and give praise to him. And tell

GETTING THE MESSAGE

How did the people of Israel consecrate themselves? The people of Israel were often instructed to consecrate themselves in preparation to meet with God. Sanctifying, or "separating" oneself included washing one's clothes and temporarily abstaining from sexual relations (3:5; 7:13; Ex. 19:14–15).

me now what you have done; do not hide it from me." ²⁰ And Achan answered Joshua, "Truly I have sinned against the LORD God of Israel, and this is what I did: ²¹ when I saw among the spoil a beautiful cloak from Shinar, and 200 shekels of silver, and a bar of gold weighing 50 shekels, then I coveted them and took them. And see, they are hidden in the earth inside my tent, with the silver underneath."

²² So Joshua sent messengers, and they ran to the tent; and behold, it was hidden in his tent with the silver underneath. ²³ And they took them out of the tent and brought them to Joshua and to all the people of Israel. And they laid them down before the LORD. ²⁴ And Joshua and all Israel with him took Achan the son of Zerah, and the silver and the cloak and the bar of gold, and his sons and daughters and his oxen and donkeys and sheep and his tent and all that he had. And

they brought them up to the Valley of Achor. **25** And Joshua said, "Why did you bring trouble on us? The LORD brings trouble on you today." And all Israel stoned him with stones. They burned them with fire and stoned them with stones. **26** And they raised over him a great heap of stones that remains to this day. Then the LORD turned from his burning anger. Therefore, to this day the name of that place is called the Valley of Achor.[1]

The Fall of Ai

8 And the LORD said to Joshua, "Do not fear and do not be dismayed. Take all the fighting men with you, and arise, go up to Ai. See, I have given into your hand the king of Ai, and his people, his city, and his land. **2** And you shall do to Ai and its king as you did to Jericho and its king. Only its spoil and its livestock you shall take as plunder for yourselves. Lay an ambush against the city, behind it."

> **GETTING THE MESSAGE**
>
> **Ambush.** Battles were sometimes won by deceptive military strategy rather than by brute strength. If an army had smaller numbers or was unfamiliar with the territory, an ambush (8:2) was a great way to "even the odds."

3 So Joshua and all the fighting men arose to go up to Ai. And Joshua chose 30,000 mighty men of valor and sent them out by night. **4** And he commanded them, "Behold, you shall lie in ambush against the city, behind it. Do not go very far from the city, but all of you remain ready. **5** And I and all the people who are with me will approach the city. And when they come out against us just as before, we shall flee before them. **6** And they will come out after us, until we have drawn them away from the city. For they will say, 'They are fleeing from us, just as before.' So we will flee before them. **7** Then you shall rise up from the ambush and seize the city, for the LORD your God will give it into your hand. **8** And as soon as you have taken the city, you shall set the city on fire. You shall do according to the word of the LORD. See, I have commanded you." **9** So Joshua sent them out. And they went to

the place of ambush and lay between Bethel and Ai, to the west of Ai, but Joshua spent that night among the people.

10 Joshua arose early in the morning and mustered the people and went up, he and the elders of Israel, before the people to Ai. **11** And all the fighting men who were with him went up and drew near before the city and encamped on the north side of Ai, with a ravine between them and Ai. **12** He took about 5,000 men and set them in ambush between Bethel and Ai, to the west of the city. **13** So they stationed the forces, the main encampment that was north of the city and its rear guard west of the city. But Joshua spent that night in the valley. **14** And as soon as the king of Ai saw this, he and all his people, the men of the city, hurried and went out early to the appointed place toward the Arabah to meet Israel in battle. But he did not know that there was an ambush against him behind the city. **15** And Joshua and all Israel pretended to be beaten before them and fled in the direction of the wilderness. **16** So all the people who were in the city were called together to pursue them, and as they pursued Joshua they were drawn away from the city. **17** Not a man was left in Ai or Bethel who did not go out after Israel. They left the city open and pursued Israel.

18 Then the LORD said to Joshua, "Stretch out the javelin that is in your hand toward Ai, for I will give it into your hand." And Joshua stretched out the javelin that was in his hand toward the city. **19** And the men in the ambush rose quickly out of their place, and as soon as he had stretched out his hand, they ran and entered the city and captured it. And they hurried to set the city on fire. **20** So when the men of Ai looked back, behold, the smoke of the city went up to heaven, and they had no power to flee this way or that, for the people who fled to the wilderness turned back against the pursuers. **21** And when Joshua and all Israel saw that the ambush had captured the city, and that the smoke of the city went up, then they turned back and struck down the men of Ai. **22** And the others came out from the city against them, so they were in the midst of Israel, some on this side, and some on that side. And Israel struck them down, until there was left none that survived or

[1] *Achor* means *trouble*

escaped. ²³ But the king of Ai they took alive, and brought him near to Joshua.

²⁴ When Israel had finished killing all the inhabitants of Ai in the open wilderness where they pursued them, and all of them to the very last had fallen by the edge of the sword, all Israel returned to Ai and struck it down with the edge of the sword. ²⁵ And all who fell that day, both men and women, were 12,000, all the people of Ai. ²⁶ But Joshua did not draw back his hand with which he stretched out the javelin until he had devoted all the inhabitants of Ai to destruction. ²⁷ Only the livestock and the spoil of that city Israel took as their plunder, according to the word of the LORD that he commanded Joshua. ²⁸ So Joshua burned Ai and made it forever a heap of ruins, as it is to this day. ²⁹ And he hanged the king of Ai on a tree until evening. And at sunset Joshua commanded, and they took his body down from the tree and threw it at the entrance of the gate of the city and raised over it a great heap of stones, which stands there to this day.

Joshua Renews the Covenant

³⁰ At that time Joshua built an altar to the LORD, the God of Israel, on Mount Ebal, ³¹ just as Moses the servant of the LORD had commanded the people of Israel, as it is written in the Book of the Law of Moses, "an altar of uncut stones, upon which no man has wielded an iron tool." And they offered on it burnt offerings to the LORD and sacrificed peace offerings. ³² And there, in the presence of the people of Israel, he wrote on the stones a copy of the law of Moses, which he had written. ³³ And all Israel, sojourner as well as native born, with their elders and officers and their judges, stood on opposite sides of the ark before the Levitical priests who carried the ark of the covenant of the LORD, half of them in front of Mount Gerizim and half of them in front of Mount Ebal, just as Moses the servant of the LORD had commanded at the first, to bless the people of Israel. ³⁴ And afterward he read all the words of the law, the blessing and the curse, according to all that is written in the Book of the Law. ³⁵ There was not a word of all that Moses commanded that Joshua did not read before all the assembly of Israel, and the women, and the little ones, and the sojourners who lived among them.

The Gibeonite Deception

9 As soon as all the kings who were beyond the Jordan in the hill country and in the lowland all along the coast of the Great Sea toward Lebanon, the Hittites, the Amorites, the Canaanites, the Perizzites, the Hivites, and the Jebusites, heard of this, ² they gathered together as one to fight against Joshua and Israel.

³ But when the inhabitants of Gibeon heard what Joshua had done to Jericho and to Ai, ⁴ they on their part acted with cunning and went and made ready provisions and took worn-out sacks for their donkeys, and wineskins, worn-out and torn and mended, ⁵ with worn-out, patched sandals on their feet, and worn-out clothes. And all their provisions were dry and crumbly. ⁶ And they went to Joshua in the camp at Gilgal and said to him and to the men of Israel, "We have

GETTING THE MESSAGE

Wineskins used for storing and pouring wine (9:13) were made from the skin of a goat or other animal. Jesus uses wineskins as a metaphor to contrast the outdated religious rules of the Pharisees and the new life that he brings (Matt. 9:17).

come from a distant country, so now make a covenant with us." ⁷ But the men of Israel said to the Hivites, "Perhaps you live among us; then how can we make a covenant with you?" ⁸ They said to Joshua, "We are your servants." And Joshua said to them, "Who are you? And where do you come from?" ⁹ They said to him, "From a very distant country your servants have come, because of the name of the LORD your God. For we have heard a report of him, and all that he did in Egypt, ¹⁰ and all that he did to the two kings of the Amorites who were beyond the Jordan, to Sihon the king of Heshbon, and to Og king of Bashan, who lived in Ashtaroth. ¹¹ So our elders and all the inhabitants of our country said to us, 'Take provisions in your hand for the journey and go to meet them and say to them, "We are your servants. Come now, make a covenant with us." ' ¹² Here is our bread. It was still warm when we took it from our houses as our food for the journey on the day we set out to come to you, but now, behold, it is dry and crumbly. ¹³ These wineskins were new when we filled them, and behold, they have burst. And these garments and sandals of ours are worn out from the very long journey." ¹⁴ So the men took some of their provisions, but did not ask counsel from the LORD. ¹⁵ And Joshua made peace with them and made a covenant with them, to let them live, and the leaders of the congregation swore to them.

¹⁶ At the end of three days after they had made a covenant with them, they heard that they were their neighbors and that they lived among them. ¹⁷ And the people of Israel set out and reached their cities on the third day. Now their cities were Gibeon, Chephirah, Beeroth, and Kiriath-jearim. ¹⁸ But the people of Israel did not attack them, because the leaders of the congregation had sworn to them by the LORD, the God of Israel. Then all the congregation murmured against the leaders. ¹⁹ But all the leaders said to all the congregation, "We have sworn to them by the LORD, the God of Israel, and now we may not touch them. ²⁰ This we will do to them: let them live, lest wrath be upon us, because of the oath that we swore to them." ²¹ And the leaders said to them, "Let them live." So they became cutters of wood and drawers of water for all the congregation, just as the leaders had said of them.

²² Joshua summoned them, and he said to them, "Why did you deceive us, saying, 'We are very far from you,' when you dwell among us? ²³ Now therefore you are cursed, and some of you shall never be anything but servants, cutters of wood and drawers of water for the house of my God." ²⁴ They answered Joshua, "Because it was told to your servants for a certainty that the LORD your God had commanded his servant Moses to give you all the land and to destroy all the inhabitants of the land from before you—so we feared greatly for our lives because of you and did this thing. ²⁵ And now, behold, we are in your hand. Whatever seems good and right in your sight to do to us, do it." ²⁶ So he did this to them and delivered them out of the hand of the people of Israel, and they did not kill them. ²⁷ But Joshua made them that day cutters of wood and drawers of water for the congregation

and for the altar of the LORD, to this day, in the place that he should choose.

The Sun Stands Still

10 As soon as Adoni-zedek, king of Jerusalem, heard how Joshua had captured Ai and had devoted it to destruction, doing to Ai and its king as he had done to Jericho and its king, and how the inhabitants of Gibeon had made peace with Israel and were among them, ² he feared greatly, because Gibeon was a great city, like one of the royal cities, and because it was greater than Ai, and all its men were warriors. ³ So Adoni-zedek king of Jerusalem sent to Hoham king of Hebron, to Piram king of Jarmuth, to Japhia king of Lachish, and to Debir king of Eglon, saying, ⁴ "Come up to me and help me, and let us strike Gibeon. For it has made peace with Joshua and with the people of Israel." ⁵ Then the five kings of the Amorites, the king of Jerusalem, the king of Hebron, the king of Jarmuth, the king of Lachish, and the king of Eglon, gathered their forces and went up with all their armies and encamped against Gibeon and made war against it.

⁶ And the men of Gibeon sent to Joshua at the camp in Gilgal, saying, "Do not relax your hand from your servants. Come up to us quickly and save us and help us, for all the kings of the Amorites who dwell in the hill country are gathered against us." ⁷ So Joshua went up from Gilgal, he and all the people of war with him, and all the mighty men of valor. ⁸ And the LORD said to Joshua, "Do not fear them, for I have given them into your hands. Not a man of them shall stand before you." ⁹ So Joshua came upon them suddenly, having marched up all night from Gilgal. ¹⁰ And the LORD threw them into a panic before Israel, who struck them with a great blow at Gibeon and chased them by the way of the ascent of Beth-horon and struck them as far as Azekah and Makkedah. ¹¹ And as they fled before Israel, while they were going down the ascent of Beth-horon, the LORD threw down large stones from heaven on them as far as Azekah, and they died. There were more who died because of the hailstones than the sons of Israel killed with the sword.

¹² At that time Joshua spoke to the LORD in the day when the LORD gave the Amorites

over to the sons of Israel, and he said in the sight of Israel,

> "Sun, stand still at Gibeon,
>   and moon, in the Valley of Aijalon."
> ¹³   And the sun stood still, and the moon
>   stopped,
>   until the nation took vengeance on
>   their enemies.

Is this not written in the Book of Jashar? The sun stopped in the midst of heaven and did not hurry to set for about a whole day. ¹⁴ There has been no day like it before or since, when the LORD heeded the voice of a man, for the LORD fought for Israel.

¹⁵ So Joshua returned, and all Israel with him, to the camp at Gilgal.

Five Amorite Kings Executed

¹⁶ These five kings fled and hid themselves in the cave at Makkedah. ¹⁷ And it was told to Joshua, "The five kings have been found, hidden in the cave at Makkedah." ¹⁸ And Joshua said, "Roll large stones against the mouth of the cave and set men by it to guard them, ¹⁹ but do not stay there yourselves. Pursue your enemies; attack their rear guard. Do not let them enter their cities, for the LORD your God has given them into your hand." ²⁰ When Joshua and the sons of Israel had finished striking them with a great blow until they were wiped out, and when the remnant that remained of them had entered into the fortified cities, ²¹ then all the people returned safe to Joshua in the camp at Makkedah. Not a man moved his tongue against any of the people of Israel. ²² Then Joshua said, "Open the mouth of the cave and bring those five kings out to me from the cave." ²³ And they did so, and brought those five kings out to him from the cave, the king of Jerusalem, the king of Hebron, the king of Jarmuth, the king of Lachish, and the king of Eglon. ²⁴ And when they brought those kings out to Joshua, Joshua summoned all the men of Israel and said to the chiefs of the men of war who had gone with him, "Come near; put your feet on the necks of these kings." Then they came near and put their feet on their necks. ²⁵ And Joshua said to them, "Do not be afraid or dismayed; be strong and courageous. For thus the LORD will do to all your enemies against whom you fight." ²⁶ And afterward Joshua struck them and put them to death, and he

hanged them on five trees. And they hung on the trees until evening. ²⁷ But at the time of the going down of the sun, Joshua commanded, and they took them down from the trees and threw them into the cave where they had hidden themselves, and they set large stones against the mouth of the cave, which remain to this very day.

²⁸ As for Makkedah, Joshua captured it on that day and struck it, and its king, with the edge of the sword. He devoted to destruction every person in it; he left none remaining. And he did to the king of Makkedah just as he had done to the king of Jericho.

Conquest of Southern Canaan

²⁹ Then Joshua and all Israel with him passed on from Makkedah to Libnah and fought against Libnah. ³⁰ And the LORD gave it also and its king into the hand of Israel. And he struck it with the edge of the sword,

---

GETTING THE MESSAGE

Royal humiliation. In the ancient Near East, victors would often put their feet on the necks of defeated foes (10:24). This was usually done to people in positions of leadership. The act was meant to show dominance over the defeated foe.

---

and every person in it; he left none remaining in it. And he did to its king as he had done to the king of Jericho.

³¹ Then Joshua and all Israel with him passed on from Libnah to Lachish and laid siege to it and fought against it. ³² And the LORD gave Lachish into the hand of Israel, and he captured it on the second day and struck it with the edge of the sword, and every person in it, as he had done to Libnah.

³³ Then Horam king of Gezer came up to help Lachish. And Joshua struck him and his people, until he left none remaining.

³⁴ Then Joshua and all Israel with him passed on from Lachish to Eglon. And they laid siege to it and fought against it. ³⁵ And they captured it on that day, and struck it with the edge of the sword. And he devoted every person in it to destruction that day, as he had done to Lachish.

³⁶ Then Joshua and all Israel with him went up from Eglon to Hebron. And they

fought against it [37] and captured it and struck it with the edge of the sword, and its king and its towns, and every person in it. He left none remaining, as he had done to Eglon, and devoted it to destruction and every person in it.

[38] Then Joshua and all Israel with him turned back to Debir and fought against it [39] and he captured it with its king and all its towns. And they struck them with the edge of the sword and devoted to destruction every person in it; he left none remaining. Just as he had done to Hebron and to Libnah and its king, so he did to Debir and to its king.

[40] So Joshua struck the whole land, the hill country and the Negeb and the lowland and the slopes, and all their kings. He left none remaining, but devoted to destruction all that breathed, just as the LORD God of Israel commanded. [41] And Joshua struck

them from Kadesh-barnea as far as Gaza, and all the country of Goshen, as far as Gibeon. [42] And Joshua captured all these kings and their land at one time, because the LORD God of Israel fought for Israel. [43] Then Joshua returned, and all Israel with him, to the camp at Gilgal.

Conquests in Northern Canaan

11 When Jabin, king of Hazor, heard of this, he sent to Jobab king of Madon, and to the king of Shimron, and to the king of Achshaph, [2] and to the kings who were in the northern hill country, and in the Arabah south of Chinneroth, and in the lowland, and in Naphoth-dor on the west, [3] to the Canaanites in the east and the west, the Amorites, the Hittites, the Perizzites, and the Jebusites in the hill country, and the Hivites under Hermon in the land of Mizpah. [4] And they came out with all their troops, a great horde, in number like the sand that is on the seashore, with very many horses and chariots. [5] And all these kings

joined their forces and came and encamped together at the waters of Merom to fight against Israel.

[6] And the LORD said to Joshua, "Do not be afraid of them, for tomorrow at this time I will give over all of them, slain, to Israel. You shall hamstring their horses and burn their chariots with fire." [7] So Joshua and all his warriors came suddenly against them by the waters of Merom and fell upon them. [8] And the LORD gave them into the hand of Israel, who struck them and chased them as far as Great Sidon and Misrephoth-maim, and eastward as far as the Valley of Mizpeh. And they struck them until he left none remaining. [9] And Joshua did to them just as the LORD said to him: he hamstrung their horses and burned their chariots with fire.

[10] And Joshua turned back at that time and captured Hazor and struck its king with the sword, for Hazor formerly was the head of all those kingdoms. [11] And they struck with the sword all who were in it, devoting them to destruction; there was none left that breathed. And he burned Hazor with fire. [12] And all the cities of those kings, and all their kings, Joshua captured, and struck them with the edge of the sword, devoting them to destruction, just as Moses the servant of the LORD had commanded. [13] But none of the cities that stood on mounds did Israel burn, except Hazor alone; that Joshua burned. [14] And all the spoil of these cities and the livestock, the people of Israel took for their plunder. But every person they struck with the edge of the sword until they had destroyed them, and they did not leave any who breathed. [15] Just as the LORD had commanded Moses his servant, so Moses commanded Joshua, and so Joshua did. He left nothing undone of all that the LORD had commanded Moses.

[16] So Joshua took all that land, the hill country and all the Negeb and all the land of Goshen and the lowland and the Arabah and the hill country of Israel and its lowland [17] from Mount Halak, which rises toward Seir, as far as Baal-gad in the Valley of Lebanon below Mount Hermon. And he captured all their kings and struck them and put them to death. [18] Joshua made war a long time with all those kings. [19] There was not a city that made peace with the people of Israel except the Hivites, the inhabitants

of Gibeon. They took them all in battle. ²⁰ For it was the Lord's doing to harden their hearts that they should come against Israel in battle, in order that they should be devoted to destruction and should receive no mercy but be destroyed, just as the Lord commanded Moses.

²¹ And Joshua came at that time and cut off the Anakim from the hill country, from Hebron, from Debir, from Anab, and from all the hill country of Judah, and from all the hill country of Israel. Joshua devoted them to destruction with their cities. ²² There was none of the Anakim left in the land of the people of Israel. Only in Gaza, in Gath, and in Ashdod did some remain. ²³ So Joshua took the whole land, according to all that the Lord had spoken to Moses. And Joshua gave it for an inheritance to Israel according to their tribal allotments. And the land had rest from war.

Kings Defeated by Moses

12 Now these are the kings of the land whom the people of Israel defeated and took possession of their land beyond the Jordan toward the sunrise, from the Valley of the Arnon to Mount Hermon, with all the Arabah eastward: ² Sihon king of the Amorites who lived at Heshbon and ruled from Aroer, which is on the edge of the Valley of the Arnon, and from the middle of the valley as far as the river Jabbok, the boundary of the Ammonites, that is, half of Gilead, ³ and the Arabah to the Sea of Chinneroth eastward, and in the direction of Beth-jeshimoth, to the Sea of the Arabah, the Salt Sea, southward to the foot of the slopes of Pisgah; ⁴ and Og king of Bashan, one of the remnant of the Rephaim, who lived at Ashtaroth and at Edrei ⁵ and ruled over Mount Hermon and Salecah and all Bashan to the boundary of the Geshurites and the Maacathites, and over half of Gilead to the boundary of Sihon king of Heshbon. ⁶ Moses, the servant of the Lord, and the people of Israel defeated them. And Moses the servant of the Lord gave their land for a possession to the Reubenites and the Gadites and the half-tribe of Manasseh.

Kings Defeated by Joshua

⁷ And these are the kings of the land whom Joshua and the people of Israel defeated on the west side of the Jordan, from Baal-gad

in the Valley of Lebanon to Mount Halak, that rises toward Seir (and Joshua gave their land to the tribes of Israel as a possession according to their allotments, ⁸ in the hill country, in the lowland, in the Arabah, in the slopes, in the wilderness, and in the Negeb, the land of the Hittites, the Amorites, the Canaanites, the Perizzites, the Hivites, and the Jebusites): ⁹ the king of Jericho, one; the king of Ai, which is beside Bethel, one; ¹⁰ the king of Jerusalem, one; the king of Hebron, one; ¹¹ the king of Jarmuth, one; the king of Lachish, one; ¹² the king of Eglon, one; the king of Gezer, one; ¹³ the king of Debir, one; the king of Geder, one; ¹⁴ the king of Hormah, one; the king of Arad, one; ¹⁵ the king of Libnah, one; the king of Adullam, one; ¹⁶ the king of Makkedah, one; the king of Bethel, one; ¹⁷ the king of Tappuah, one; the king of Hepher, one; ¹⁸ the king of Aphek, one; the king of Lasharon, one; ¹⁹ the king of Madon, one; the king of Hazor, one; ²⁰ the king of Shimron-meron, one; the king of Achshaph, one; ²¹ the king of Taanach, one; the king of Megiddo, one; ²² the king of Kedesh, one; the king of Jokneam in Carmel, one; ²³ the king of Dor in Naphath-dor, one; the king of Goiim in Galilee, one; ²⁴ the king of Tirzah, one: in all, thirty-one kings.

Land Still to Be Conquered

13 Now Joshua was old and advanced in years, and the Lord said to him, "You are old and advanced in years, and there remains yet very much land to possess. ² This is the land that yet remains: all the regions of the Philistines, and all those of the Geshurites ³ (from the Shihor, which is east of Egypt, northward to the boundary of Ekron, it is counted as Canaanite; there are five rulers of the Philistines, those of Gaza, Ashdod, Ashkelon, Gath, and Ekron), and those of the Avvim, ⁴ in the south, all the land of the Canaanites, and Mearah that belongs to the Sidonians, to Aphek, to the boundary of the Amorites, ⁵ and the land of the Gebalites, and all Lebanon, toward the sunrise, from Baal-gad below Mount Hermon to Lebo-hamath, ⁶ all the inhabitants of the hill country from Lebanon to Misrephoth-maim, even all the Sidonians. I myself will drive them out from before the people of Israel. Only allot the land to Israel for an inheritance, as I have commanded you. ⁷ Now therefore divide this land for an inheritance to the nine tribes and half the tribe of Manasseh."

The Inheritance East of the Jordan

8 With the other half of the tribe of Manasseh the Reubenites and the Gadites received their inheritance, which Moses gave them, beyond the Jordan eastward, as Moses the servant of the LORD gave them: **9** from Aroer, which is on the edge of the Valley of the Arnon, and the city that is in the middle of the valley, and all the tableland of Medeba as far as Dibon; **10** and all the cities of Sihon king of the Amorites, who reigned in Heshbon, as far as the boundary of the Ammonites; **11** and Gilead, and the region of the Geshurites and Maacathites, and all Mount Hermon, and all Bashan to Salecah; **12** all the kingdom of Og in Bashan, who reigned in Ashtaroth and in Edrei (he alone was left of the remnant of the Rephaim); these Moses had struck and

> ## GETTING THE MESSAGE
>
> **Mount Hermon** (13:5) represented the northern boundary of the Promised Land. At over 9,000 feet (2,743 m), its snowy peak and thick forests were home to leopards and lions.

driven out. **13** Yet the people of Israel did not drive out the Geshurites or the Maacathites, but Geshur and Maacath dwell in the midst of Israel to this day.

14 To the tribe of Levi alone Moses gave no inheritance. The offerings by fire to the LORD God of Israel are their inheritance, as he said to him.

15 And Moses gave an inheritance to the tribe of the people of Reuben according to their clans. **16** So their territory was from Aroer, which is on the edge of the Valley of the Arnon, and the city that is in the middle of the valley, and all the tableland by Medeba; **17** with Heshbon, and all its cities that are in the tableland; Dibon, and Bamoth-baal, and Beth-baal-meon, **18** and Jahaz, and Kedemoth, and Mephaath, **19** and Kiriathaim, and Sibmah, and Zereth-shahar on the hill of the valley, **20** and Beth-peor, and the slopes of Pisgah, and Beth-jeshimoth, **21** that is, all the cities of the tableland, and all the kingdom of Sihon king

of the Amorites, who reigned in Heshbon, whom Moses defeated with the leaders of Midian, Evi and Rekem and Zur and Hur and Reba, the princes of Sihon, who lived in the land. **22** Balaam also, the son of Beor, the one who practiced divination, was killed with the sword by the people of Israel among the rest of their slain. **23** And the border of the people of Reuben was the Jordan as a boundary. This was the inheritance of the people of Reuben, according to their clans with their cities and villages.

24 Moses gave an inheritance also to the tribe of Gad, to the people of Gad, according to their clans. **25** Their territory was Jazer, and all the cities of Gilead, and half the land of the Ammonites, to Aroer, which is east of Rabbah, **26** and from Heshbon to Ramath-mizpeh and Betonim, and from Mahanaim to the territory of Debir, **27** and in the valley Beth-haram, Beth-nimrah, Succoth, and Zaphon, the rest of the kingdom of Sihon king of Heshbon, having the Jordan as a boundary, to the lower end of the Sea of Chinnereth, eastward beyond the Jordan. **28** This is the inheritance of the people of Gad according to their clans, with their cities and villages.

29 And Moses gave an inheritance to the half-tribe of Manasseh. It was allotted to the half-tribe of the people of Manasseh according to their clans. **30** Their region extended from Mahanaim, through all Bashan, the whole kingdom of Og king of Bashan, and all the towns of Jair, which are in Bashan, sixty cities, **31** and half Gilead, and Ashtaroth, and Edrei, the cities of the kingdom of Og in Bashan. These were allotted to the people of Machir the son of Manasseh for the half of the people of Machir according to their clans.

32 These are the inheritances that Moses distributed in the plains of Moab, beyond the Jordan east of Jericho. **33** But to the tribe of Levi Moses gave no inheritance; the LORD God of Israel is their inheritance, just as he said to them.

The Inheritance West of the Jordan

14 These are the inheritances that the people of Israel received in the land of Canaan, which Eleazar the priest and Joshua the son of Nun and the heads of the fathers' houses of the tribes of the people of Israel gave them to inherit. **2** Their inheritance was by lot, just as the LORD had commanded by the hand of Moses for the nine and one-half tribes. ³ For Moses had given an inheritance to the two and one-half tribes beyond the Jordan, but to the Levites he gave no inheritance among them. ⁴ For the people of Joseph were two tribes, Manasseh and Ephraim. And no portion was given to the Levites in the land, but only cities to dwell in, with their pasturelands for their livestock and their substance. ⁵ The people of Israel did as the LORD commanded Moses; they allotted the land.

Caleb's Request and Inheritance

⁶ Then the people of Judah came to Joshua at Gilgal. And Caleb the son of Jephunneh the Kenizzite said to him, "You know what the LORD said to Moses the man of God in Kadesh-barnea concerning you and me. ⁷ I was forty years old when Moses the servant of the LORD sent me from Kadesh-barnea to spy out the land, and I brought him word again as it was in my heart. ⁸ But my brothers who went up with me made the heart of the people melt; yet I wholly followed the LORD my God. ⁹ And Moses swore on that day, saying, 'Surely the land on which your foot has trodden shall be an inheritance for you and your children forever, because you have wholly followed the LORD my God.' ¹⁰ And now, behold, the LORD has kept me alive, just as he said, these forty-five years since the time that the LORD spoke this word to Moses, while Israel walked in the wilderness. And now, behold, I am this day eighty-five years old. ¹¹ I am still as strong today as I was in the day that Moses sent me; my strength now is as my strength was then, for war and for going and coming. ¹² So now give me this hill country of which the LORD spoke on that day, for you heard on that day how the Anakim were there, with great fortified cities. It may be that the LORD will be with me, and I shall drive them out just as the LORD said."

¹³ Then Joshua blessed him, and he gave Hebron to Caleb the son of Jephunneh for an inheritance. ¹⁴ Therefore Hebron became the inheritance of Caleb the son of Jephunneh the Kenizzite to this day, because he wholly followed the LORD, the God of Israel. ¹⁵ Now the name of Hebron formerly was Kiriath-arba.[1] (Arba was the greatest man among the Anakim.) And the land had rest from war.

The Allotment for Judah

15 The allotment for the tribe of the people of Judah according to their clans reached southward to the boundary of Edom, to the wilderness of Zin at the farthest south. ² And their south boundary ran from the end of the Salt Sea, from the bay that faces southward. ³ It goes out southward of the ascent of Akrabbim, passes along to Zin, and goes up south of Kadesh-barnea, along by Hezron, up to Addar, turns about to Karka, ⁴ passes along to Azmon, goes out by the Brook of Egypt, and comes to its end at the sea. This shall be your south boundary. ⁵ And the east boundary is the Salt Sea, to the mouth of the Jordan. And the boundary on the north side runs from the bay of the sea at the mouth of the Jordan. ⁶ And

> ### GETTING THE MESSAGE
>
> **Anakim** (14:12) were apparently a race of very tall people, descended from Anak. After the Israelites conquered Canaan, many of the Anakim took up residence with the Philistines. Because of this, many assume that Goliath was descended from the Anakim.

the boundary goes up to Beth-hoglah and passes along north of Beth-arabah. And the boundary goes up to the stone of Bohan the son of Reuben. ⁷ And the boundary goes up to Debir from the Valley of Achor, and so northward, turning toward Gilgal, which is opposite the ascent of Adummim, which is on the south side of the valley. And the boundary passes along to the waters of En-shemesh and ends at En-rogel. ⁸ Then the boundary goes up by the Valley of the Son of Hinnom at the southern shoulder of the Jebusite (that is, Jerusalem). And the boundary goes up to the top of the mountain that lies over against the Valley of Hinnom, on the west, at the northern end of the Valley of Rephaim. ⁹ Then the boundary extends from the top of the mountain to the spring of the waters of Nephtoah, and from there to the cities of Mount Ephron. Then the boundary bends around to Baalah

---

[1] Kiriath-arba means the city of Arba

(that is, Kiriath-jearim). ¹⁰ And the boundary circles west of Baalah to Mount Seir, passes along to the northern shoulder of Mount Jearim (that is, Chesalon), and goes down to Beth-shemesh and passes along by Timnah. ¹¹ The boundary goes out to the shoulder of the hill north of Ekron, then the boundary bends around to Shikkeron and passes along to Mount Baalah and goes out to Jabneel. Then the boundary comes to an end at the sea. ¹² And the west boundary was the Great Sea with its coastline. This is the boundary around the people of Judah according to their clans.

¹³ According to the commandment of the LORD to Joshua, he gave to Caleb the son of Jephunneh a portion among the people of Judah, Kiriath-arba, that is, Hebron (Arba was the father of Anak). ¹⁴ And Caleb drove out from there the three sons of Anak, Sheshai and Ahiman and Talmai, the descendants of Anak. ¹⁵ And he went up from there against the inhabitants of Debir. Now the name of Debir formerly was Kiriath-sepher. ¹⁶ And Caleb said, "Whoever strikes Kiriath-sepher and captures it, to him will I give Achsah my daughter as wife." ¹⁷ And Othniel the son of Kenaz, the brother of Caleb, captured it. And he gave him Achsah his daughter as wife. ¹⁸ When she came to him, she urged him to ask her father for a field. And she got off her donkey, and Caleb said to her, "What do you want?" ¹⁹ She said to him, "Give me a blessing. Since you have given me the land of the Negeb, give me also springs of water." And he gave her the upper springs and the lower springs.

²⁰ This is the inheritance of the tribe of the people of Judah according to their clans. ²¹ The cities belonging to the tribe of the people of Judah in the extreme south, toward the boundary of Edom, were Kabzeel, Eder, Jagur, ²² Kinah, Dimonah, Adadah, ²³ Kedesh, Hazor, Ithnan, ²⁴ Ziph, Telem, Bealoth, ²⁵ Hazor-hadattah, Kerioth-hezron (that is, Hazor), ²⁶ Amam, Shema, Moladah, ²⁷ Hazar-gaddah, Heshmon, Beth-pelet, ²⁸ Hazar-shual, Beersheba, Biziothiah, ²⁹ Baalah, Iim, Ezem, ³⁰ Eltolad, Chesil, Hormah, ³¹ Ziklag, Madmannah, Sansannah, ³² Lebaoth, Shilhim, Ain, and Rimmon: in all, twenty-nine cities with their villages.

³³ And in the lowland, Eshtaol, Zorah, Ashnah, ³⁴ Zanoah, En-gannim, Tappuah, Enam, ³⁵ Jarmuth, Adullam, Socoh, Azekah, ³⁶ Shaaraim, Adithaim, Gederah, Gederothaim: fourteen cities with their villages.

³⁷ Zenan, Hadashah, Migdal-gad, ³⁸ Dilean, Mizpeh, Joktheel, ³⁹ Lachish, Bozkath, Eglon, ⁴⁰ Cabbon, Lahmam, Chitlish, ⁴¹ Gederoth, Beth-dagon, Naamah, and Makkedah: sixteen cities with their villages.

⁴² Libnah, Ether, Ashan, ⁴³ Iphtah, Ashnah, Nezib, ⁴⁴ Keilah, Achzib, and Mareshah: nine cities with their villages.

⁴⁵ Ekron, with its towns and its villages; ⁴⁶ from Ekron to the sea, all that were by the side of Ashdod, with their villages.

⁴⁷ Ashdod, its towns and its villages; Gaza, its towns and its villages; to the Brook of Egypt, and the Great Sea with its coastline.

⁴⁸ And in the hill country, Shamir, Jattir, Socoh, ⁴⁹ Dannah, Kiriath-sannah (that is, Debir), ⁵⁰ Anab, Eshtemoh, Anim, ⁵¹ Goshen, Holon, and Giloh: eleven cities with their villages.

⁵² Arab, Dumah, Eshan, ⁵³ Janim, Beth-tappuah, Aphekah, ⁵⁴ Humtah, Kiriath-arba (that is, Hebron), and Zior: nine cities with their villages.

⁵⁵ Maon, Carmel, Ziph, Juttah, ⁵⁶ Jezreel, Jokdeam, Zanoah, ⁵⁷ Kain, Gibeah, and Timnah: ten cities with their villages.

⁵⁸ Halhul, Beth-zur, Gedor, ⁵⁹ Maarath, Beth-anoth, and Eltekon: six cities with their villages.

⁶⁰ Kiriath-baal (that is, Kiriath-jearim), and Rabbah: two cities with their villages.

⁶¹ In the wilderness, Beth-arabah, Middin, Secacah, ⁶² Nibshan, the City of Salt, and Engedi: six cities with their villages.

⁶³ But the Jebusites, the inhabitants of Jerusalem, the people of Judah could not drive out, so the Jebusites dwell with the people of Judah at Jerusalem to this day.

The Allotment for Ephraim and Manasseh

16 The allotment of the people of Joseph went from the Jordan by Jericho, east of the waters of Jericho, into the wilderness, going up from Jericho into the hill country to Bethel. ² Then going from Bethel to Luz, it passes along to Ataroth, the territory of the Archites. ³ Then it goes down westward to the territory of the Japhletites, as far as the territory of Lower Beth-horon, then to Gezer, and it ends at the sea.

⁴ The people of Joseph, Manasseh and Ephraim, received their inheritance.

⁵ The territory of the people of Ephraim by their clans was as follows: the boundary of their inheritance on the east was Ataroth-addar as far as Upper Beth-horon, ⁶ and the boundary goes from there to the sea. On the north is Michmethath. Then on the east the boundary turns around toward Taanath-shiloh and passes along beyond it on the east to Janoah, ⁷ then it goes down from Janoah to Ataroth and to Naarah, and touches Jericho, ending at the Jordan. ⁸ From Tappuah the boundary goes westward to the brook Kanah and ends at the sea. Such is the inheritance of the tribe of the people of Ephraim by their clans, ⁹ together with the towns that were set apart for the people of Ephraim within the inheritance of the Manassites, all those towns with their villages. ¹⁰ However, they did not drive out the Canaanites who lived in Gezer, so the Canaanites have lived in the midst of Ephraim to this day but have been made to do forced labor.

17 Then allotment was made to the people of Manasseh, for he was the first-born of Joseph. To Machir the firstborn of Manasseh, the father of Gilead, were allotted Gilead and Bashan, because he was a man of war. ² And allotments were made to the rest of the people of Manasseh by their clans, Abiezer, Helek, Asriel, Shechem, Hepher, and Shemida. These were the male descendants of Manasseh the son of Joseph, by their clans.

³ Now Zelophehad the son of Hepher, son of Gilead, son of Machir, son of Manasseh, had no sons, but only daughters, and these are the names of his daughters: Mahlah, Noah, Hoglah, Milcah, and Tirzah. ⁴ They approached Eleazar the priest and Joshua the son of Nun and the leaders and said, "The LORD commanded Moses to give us an inheritance along with our brothers." So according to the mouth of the LORD he gave them an inheritance among the brothers of their father. ⁵ Thus there fell to Manasseh ten portions, besides the land of Gilead and Bashan, which is on the other side of the Jordan, ⁶ because the daughters of Manasseh received an inheritance along with his sons. The land of Gilead was allotted to the rest of the people of Manasseh.

⁷ The territory of Manasseh reached from Asher to Michmethath, which is east of Shechem. Then the boundary goes along southward to the inhabitants of En-tappuah. ⁸ The land of Tappuah belonged to Manasseh, but the town of Tappuah on the boundary of Manasseh belonged to the people of Ephraim. ⁹ Then the boundary went down to the brook Kanah. These cities, to the south of the brook, among the cities of Manasseh, belong to Ephraim. Then the boundary of Manasseh goes on the north side of the brook and ends at the sea, ¹⁰ the land to the south being Ephraim's and that to the north being Manasseh's, with the sea forming its boundary. On the north Asher is reached, and on the east Issachar. ¹¹ Also in Issachar and in Asher Manasseh had Beth-shean and

GETTING THE MESSAGE

Megiddo (17:11) was the site of many important Old Testament battles. It was a walled city that guarded the main road that linked Egypt and Syria. Its setting made Megiddo a strategic military stronghold. In John's visions in Revelation, Megiddo represents the global combat zone where the final battle between Christ and Satan will be fought. The word Armageddon means "Mount Megiddo" (Zech. 12:11; Rev. 16:16).

its villages, and Ibleam and its villages, and the inhabitants of Dor and its villages, and the inhabitants of En-dor and its villages, and the inhabitants of Taanach and its villages, and the inhabitants of Megiddo and its villages; the third is Naphath. ¹² Yet the people of Manasseh could not take possession of those cities, but the Canaanites persisted in dwelling in that land. ¹³ Now when the people of Israel grew strong, they put the Canaanites to forced labor, but did not utterly drive them out.

¹⁴ Then the people of Joseph spoke to Joshua, saying, "Why have you given me but one lot and one portion as an inheritance, although I am a numerous people, since all along the LORD has blessed me?" ¹⁵ And Joshua said to them, "If you are a numerous people, go up by yourselves to the forest, and there clear ground for yourselves in

the land of the Perizzites and the Rephaim, since the hill country of Ephraim is too narrow for you." **16** The people of Joseph said, "The hill country is not enough for us. Yet all the Canaanites who dwell in the plain have chariots of iron, both those in Beth-shean and its villages and those in the Valley of Jezreel." **17** Then Joshua said to the house of Joseph, to Ephraim and Manasseh, "You are a numerous people and have great power. You shall not have one allotment only, **18** but the hill country shall be yours, for though it is a forest, you shall clear it and possess it to its farthest borders. For you shall drive out the Canaanites, though they have chariots of iron, and though they are strong."

Allotment of the Remaining Land

18 Then the whole congregation of the people of Israel assembled at Shiloh and set up the tent of meeting there. The land lay subdued before them.

2 There remained among the people of Israel seven tribes whose inheritance had not yet been apportioned. **3** So Joshua said to the people of Israel, "How long will you put off going in to take possession of the land, which the LORD, the God of your fathers, has given you? **4** Provide three men from each tribe, and I will send them out that they may set out and go up and down the land. They shall write a description of it with a view to their inheritances, and then come to me. **5** They shall divide it into seven portions. Judah shall continue in his territory on the south, and the house of Joseph shall continue in their territory on the north. **6** And you shall describe the land in seven divisions and bring the description here to me. And I will cast lots for you here before the LORD our God. **7** The Levites have no portion among you, for the priesthood of the LORD is their heritage. And Gad and Reuben and half the tribe of Manasseh have received their inheritance beyond the Jordan eastward, which Moses the servant of the LORD gave them."

8 So the men arose and went, and Joshua charged those who went to write the description of the land, saying, "Go up and down in the land and write a description and return to me. And I will cast lots for you here before the LORD in Shiloh." **9** So the men went and passed up and down in the land and wrote in a book a description of it by towns in seven divisions. Then they came to Joshua to the camp at Shiloh, **10** and Joshua cast lots for them in Shiloh before the LORD. And there Joshua apportioned the land to the people of Israel, to each his portion.

The Inheritance for Benjamin

11 The lot of the tribe of the people of Benjamin according to its clans came up, and the territory allotted to it fell between the people of Judah and the people of Joseph. **12** On the north side their boundary began at the Jordan. Then the boundary goes up to the shoulder north of Jericho, then up through the hill country westward, and it ends at the wilderness of Beth-aven. **13** From there the boundary passes along southward in the direction of Luz, to the shoulder of Luz (that is, Bethel), then the boundary goes down to Ataroth-addar, on the mountain that lies south of Lower Beth-horon. **14** Then the boundary goes in another direction, turning on the western side southward from the mountain that lies to the south, opposite Beth-horon, and it ends at Kiriath-baal (that is, Kiriath-jearim), a city belonging to the people of Judah. This forms the western side. **15** And the southern side begins at the outskirts of Kiriath-jearim. And the boundary goes from there to Ephron, to the spring of the waters of Nephtoah. **16** Then the boundary goes down to the border of the mountain that overlooks the Valley of the Son of Hinnom, which is at the north end of the Valley of Rephaim. And it then goes down the Valley of Hinnom, south of the shoulder of the Jebusites, and downward to En-rogel. **17** Then it bends in a northerly direction going on to En-shemesh, and from there goes to Geliloth, which is opposite the ascent of Adummim. Then it goes down to the stone of Bohan the son of Reuben, **18** and passing on to the north of the shoulder of Beth-arabah it goes down to the Arabah. **19** Then the boundary passes on to the north of the shoulder of Beth-hoglah. And the boundary ends at the northern bay of the Salt Sea, at the south end of the Jordan: this is the southern border. **20** The Jordan forms its boundary on the eastern side. This is the inheritance of the people of Benjamin, according to their clans, boundary by boundary all around.

21 Now the cities of the tribe of the people of Benjamin according to their clans were

Jericho, Beth-hoglah, Emek-keziz, ²² Beth-arabah, Zemaraim, Bethel, ²³ Avvim, Parah, Ophrah, ²⁴ Chephar-ammoni, Ophni, Geba—twelve cities with their villages: ²⁵ Gibeon, Ramah, Beeroth, ²⁶ Mizpeh, Chephirah, Mozah, ²⁷ Rekem, Irpeel, Taralah, ²⁸ Zela, Haeleph, Jebus (that is, Jerusalem), Gibeah and Kiriath-jearim—fourteen cities with their villages. This is the inheritance of the people of Benjamin according to its clans.

The Inheritance for Simeon

19 The second lot came out for Simeon, for the tribe of the people of Simeon, according to their clans, and their inheritance was in the midst of the inheritance of the people of Judah. ² And they had for their inheritance Beersheba, Sheba, Moladah, ³ Hazar-shual, Balah, Ezem, ⁴ Eltolad, Bethul, Hormah, ⁵ Ziklag, Beth-marcaboth, Hazar-susah, ⁶ Beth-lebaoth, and Sharuhen—thirteen cities with their villages; ⁷ Ain, Rimmon, Ether, and Ashan—four cities with their villages, ⁸ together with all the villages around these cities as far as Baalath-beer, Ramah of the Negeb. This was the inheritance of the tribe of the people of Simeon according to their clans. ⁹ The inheritance of the people of Simeon formed part of the territory of the people of Judah. Because the portion of the people of Judah was too large for them, the people of Simeon obtained an inheritance in the midst of their inheritance.

The Inheritance for Zebulun

¹⁰ The third lot came up for the people of Zebulun, according to their clans. And the territory of their inheritance reached as far as Sarid. ¹¹ Then their boundary goes up westward and on to Mareal and touches Dabbesheth, then the brook that is east of Jokneam. ¹² From Sarid it goes in the other direction eastward toward the sunrise to the boundary of Chisloth-tabor. From there it goes to Daberath, then up to Japhia. ¹³ From there it passes along on the east toward the sunrise to Gath-hepher, to Eth-kazin, and going on to Rimmon it bends toward Neah, ¹⁴ then on the north the boundary turns about to Hannathon, and it ends at the Valley of Iphtahel; ¹⁵ and Kattath, Nahalal, Shimron, Idalah, and Bethlehem—twelve cities with their villages. ¹⁶ This is the inheritance of the people of Zebulun, according to their clans—these cities with their villages.

The Inheritance for Issachar

¹⁷ The fourth lot came out for Issachar, for the people of Issachar, according to their clans. ¹⁸ Their territory included Jezreel, Chesulloth, Shunem, ¹⁹ Hapharaim, Shion, Anaharath, ²⁰ Rabbith, Kishion, Ebez, ²¹ Remeth, En-gannim, En-haddah, Beth-pazzez. ²² The boundary also touches Tabor, Shahazumah, and Beth-shemesh, and its boundary ends at the Jordan—sixteen cities with their villages. ²³ This is the inheritance of the tribe of the people of Issachar, according to their clans—the cities with their villages.

The Inheritance for Asher

²⁴ The fifth lot came out for the tribe of the people of Asher according to their clans. ²⁵ Their territory included Helkath, Hali, Beten, Achshaph, ²⁶ Allammelech, Amad, and Mishal. On the west it touches Carmel and Shihor-libnath, ²⁷ then it turns eastward, it goes to Beth-dagon, and touches Zebulun and the Valley of Iphtahel northward to Beth-emek and Neiel. Then it continues in the north to Cabul, ²⁸ Ebron, Rehob, Hammon, Kanah, as far as Sidon the Great. ²⁹ Then the boundary turns to Ramah, reaching to the fortified city of Tyre. Then the boundary turns to Hosah, and it ends at the sea; Mahalab, Achzib, ³⁰ Ummah, Aphek and Rehob—twenty-two cities with their villages. ³¹ This is the inheritance of the tribe of the people of Asher according to their clans—these cities with their villages.

The Inheritance for Naphtali

³² The sixth lot came out for the people of Naphtali, for the people of Naphtali, according to their clans. ³³ And their boundary ran from Heleph, from the oak in Zaanannim,

> ### GETTING THE MESSAGE
>
> **Bethlehem?** There are actually two places called Bethlehem in the Bible. The town where Ruth lived and where Jesus was born was about 5 miles (8 km) south of Jerusalem. The one mentioned in 19:15 was about 7 miles (11 km) northwest of Nazareth, the town where Jesus spent his childhood years.

and Adami-nekeb, and Jabneel, as far as Lakkum, and it ended at the Jordan. ³⁴ Then the boundary turns westward to Aznoth-tabor and goes from there to Hukkok, touching Zebulun at the south and Asher on the west and Judah on the east at the Jordan. ³⁵ The fortified cities are Ziddim, Zer, Hammath, Rakkath, Chinnereth, ³⁶ Adamah, Ramah, Hazor, ³⁷ Kedesh, Edrei, En-hazor, ³⁸ Yiron, Migdal-el, Horem, Beth-anath, and Beth-shemesh—nineteen cities with their villages. ³⁹ This is the inheritance of the tribe of the people of Naphtali according to their clans—the cities with their villages.

The Inheritance for Dan

⁴⁰ The seventh lot came out for the tribe of the people of Dan, according to their clans. ⁴¹ And the territory of its inheritance included Zorah, Eshtaol, Ir-shemesh,

---

GETTING THE MESSAGE

A **manslayer** was a person who unintentionally took another person's life. Such a person could flee to a "city of refuge" (20:1–6) for safety until his case was heard. The term "manslayer" corresponds to the modern use of the term "manslaughter" for unintentional killing.

---

⁴² Shaalabbin, Aijalon, Ithlah, ⁴³ Elon, Timnah, Ekron, ⁴⁴ Eltekeh, Gibbethon, Baalath, ⁴⁵ Jehud, Bene-berak, Gath-rimmon, ⁴⁶ and Me-jarkon and Rakkon with the territory over against Joppa. ⁴⁷ When the territory of the people of Dan was lost to them, the people of Dan went up and fought against Leshem, and after capturing it and striking it with the sword they took possession of it and settled in it, calling Leshem, Dan, after the name of Dan their ancestor. ⁴⁸ This is the inheritance of the tribe of the people of Dan, according to their clans—these cities with their villages.

The Inheritance for Joshua

⁴⁹ When they had finished distributing the several territories of the land as inheritances, the people of Israel gave an inheritance among them to Joshua the son of Nun. ⁵⁰ By command of the LORD they gave him

the city that he asked, Timnath-serah in the hill country of Ephraim. And he rebuilt the city and settled in it.

⁵¹ These are the inheritances that Eleazar the priest and Joshua the son of Nun and the heads of the fathers' houses of the tribes of the people of Israel distributed by lot at Shiloh before the LORD, at the entrance of the tent of meeting. So they finished dividing the land.

The Cities of Refuge

20 Then the LORD said to Joshua, ² "Say to the people of Israel, 'Appoint the cities of refuge, of which I spoke to you through Moses, ³ that the manslayer who strikes any person without intent or unknowingly may flee there. They shall be for you a refuge from the avenger of blood. ⁴ He shall flee to one of these cities and shall stand at the entrance of the gate of the city and explain his case to the elders of that city. Then they shall take him into the city and give him a place, and he shall remain with them. ⁵ And if the avenger of blood pursues him, they shall not give up the manslayer into his hand, because he struck his neighbor unknowingly, and did not hate him in the past. ⁶ And he shall remain in that city until he has stood before the congregation for judgment, until the death of him who is high priest at the time. Then the manslayer may return to his own town and his own home, to the town from which he fled.'"

⁷ So they set apart Kedesh in Galilee in the hill country of Naphtali, and Shechem in the hill country of Ephraim, and Kiriath-arba (that is, Hebron) in the hill country of Judah. ⁸ And beyond the Jordan east of Jericho, they appointed Bezer in the wilderness on the tableland, from the tribe of Reuben, and Ramoth in Gilead, from the tribe of Gad, and Golan in Bashan, from the tribe of Manasseh. ⁹ These were the cities designated for all the people of Israel and for the stranger sojourning among them, that anyone who killed a person without intent could flee there, so that he might not die by the hand of the avenger of blood, till he stood before the congregation.

Cities and Pasturelands Allotted to Levi

21 Then the heads of the fathers' houses of the Levites came to Eleazar the priest and to Joshua the son of Nun and to

the heads of the fathers' houses of the tribes of the people of Israel. ² And they said to them at Shiloh in the land of Canaan, "The LORD commanded through Moses that we be given cities to dwell in, along with their pasturelands for our livestock." ³ So by command of the LORD the people of Israel gave to the Levites the following cities and pasturelands out of their inheritance.

⁴ The lot came out for the clans of the Kohathites. So those Levites who were descendants of Aaron the priest received by lot from the tribes of Judah, Simeon, and Benjamin, thirteen cities.

⁵ And the rest of the Kohathites received by lot from the clans of the tribe of Ephraim, from the tribe of Dan and the half-tribe of Manasseh, ten cities.

⁶ The Gershonites received by lot from the clans of the tribe of Issachar, from the tribe of Asher, from the tribe of Naphtali, and from the half-tribe of Manasseh in Bashan, thirteen cities.

⁷ The Merarites according to their clans received from the tribe of Reuben, the tribe of Gad, and the tribe of Zebulun, twelve cities.

⁸ These cities and their pasturelands the people of Israel gave by lot to the Levites, as the LORD had commanded through Moses.

⁹ Out of the tribe of the people of Judah and the tribe of the people of Simeon they gave the following cities mentioned by name, ¹⁰ which went to the descendants of Aaron, one of the clans of the Kohathites who belonged to the people of Levi; since the lot fell to them first. ¹¹ They gave them Kiriath-arba (Arba being the father of Anak), that is Hebron, in the hill country of Judah, along with the pasturelands around it. ¹² But the fields of the city and its villages had been given to Caleb the son of Jephunneh as his possession.

¹³ And to the descendants of Aaron the priest they gave Hebron, the city of refuge for the manslayer, with its pasturelands, Libnah with its pasturelands, ¹⁴ Jattir with its pasturelands, Eshtemoa with its pasturelands, ¹⁵ Holon with its pasturelands, Debir with its pasturelands, ¹⁶ Ain with its pasturelands, Juttah with its pasturelands, Beth-shemesh with its pasturelands—nine cities out of these two tribes; ¹⁷ then out of the tribe of Benjamin, Gibeon with its pasturelands, Geba with its pasturelands,

¹⁸ Anathoth with its pasturelands, and Almon with its pasturelands—four cities. ¹⁹ The cities of the descendants of Aaron, the priests, were in all thirteen cities with their pasturelands.

²⁰ As to the rest of the Kohathites belonging to the Kohathite clans of the Levites, the cities allotted to them were out of the tribe of Ephraim. ²¹ To them were given Shechem, the city of refuge for the manslayer, with its pasturelands in the hill country of Ephraim, Gezer with its pasturelands, ²² Kibzaim with its pasturelands, Beth-horon with its pasturelands—four cities; ²³ and out of the tribe of Dan, Elteke with its pasturelands, Gibbethon with its pasturelands, ²⁴ Aijalon with its pasturelands, Gath-rimmon with its pasturelands—four cities; ²⁵ and out of the half-tribe of Manasseh, Taanach with its pasturelands, and Gath-rimmon with its pasturelands—two cities. ²⁶ The cities of the clans of the rest of the Kohathites were ten in all with their pasturelands.

²⁷ And to the Gershonites, one of the clans of the Levites, were given out of the half-tribe of Manasseh, Golan in Bashan with its pasturelands, the city of refuge for the manslayer, and Beeshterah with its pasturelands—two cities; ²⁸ and out of the tribe of Issachar, Kishion with its pasturelands, Daberath with its pasturelands, ²⁹ Jarmuth with its pasturelands, En-gannim with its pasturelands—four cities; ³⁰ and out of the tribe of Asher, Mishal with its pasturelands, Abdon with its pasturelands, ³¹ Helkath with its pasturelands, and Rehob with its pasturelands—four cities; ³² and out of the tribe of Naphtali, Kedesh in Galilee with its pasturelands, the city of refuge for the manslayer, Hammoth-dor with its pasturelands, and Kartan with its pasturelands—three cities. ³³ The cities of the several clans of the Gershonites were in all thirteen cities with their pasturelands.

³⁴ And to the rest of the Levites, the Merarite clans, were given out of the tribe of Zebulun, Jokneam with its pasturelands, Kartah with its pasturelands, ³⁵ Dimnah with its pasturelands, Nahalal with its pasturelands—four cities; ³⁶ and out of the tribe of Reuben, Bezer with its pasturelands, Jahaz with its pasturelands, ³⁷ Kedemoth with its pasturelands, and Mephaath with its pasturelands—four cities; ³⁸ and out

of the tribe of Gad, Ramoth in Gilead with its pasturelands, the city of refuge for the manslayer, Mahanaim with its pasturelands, [39] Heshbon with its pasturelands, Jazer with its pasturelands—four cities in all. [40] As for the cities of the several Merarite clans, that is, the remainder of the clans of the Levites, those allotted to them were in all twelve cities.

[41] The cities of the Levites in the midst of the possession of the people of Israel were in all forty-eight cities with their pasturelands. [42] These cities each had its pasturelands around it. So it was with all these cities.

[43] Thus the LORD gave to Israel all the land that he swore to give to their fathers. And they took possession of it, and they settled there. [44] And the LORD gave them rest on

GETTING THE MESSAGE

Dividing the spoils after a war or battle was a very common practice. Livestock, precious metals, clothing, and even people could be taken as spoils. These things were considered gifts from the victor's gods. In the case of the Israelites, they were considered gifts from the Lord. All gifts were to be shared with allies no matter how much or how little they helped in winning the victory (22:8).

every side just as he had sworn to their fathers. Not one of all their enemies had withstood them, for the LORD had given all their enemies into their hands. [45] Not one word of all the good promises that the LORD had made to the house of Israel had failed; all came to pass.

The Eastern Tribes Return Home

22 At that time Joshua summoned the Reubenites and the Gadites and the half-tribe of Manasseh, [2] and said to them, "You have kept all that Moses the servant of the LORD commanded you and have obeyed my voice in all that I have commanded you. [3] You have not forsaken your brothers these many days, down to this day, but have been careful to keep the charge of the LORD your God. [4] And now the LORD your God has given rest to your brothers, as he promised them. Therefore turn and go to your tents in the land where your possession lies, which Moses the servant of the LORD gave you on the other side of the Jordan. [5] Only be very careful to observe the commandment and the law that Moses the servant of the LORD commanded you, to love the LORD your God, and to walk in all his ways and to keep his commandments and to cling to him and to serve him with all your heart and with all your soul." [6] So Joshua blessed them and sent them away, and they went to their tents.

[7] Now to the one half of the tribe of Manasseh Moses had given a possession in Bashan, but to the other half Joshua had given a possession beside their brothers in the land west of the Jordan. And when Joshua sent them away to their homes and blessed them, [8] he said to them, "Go back to your tents with much wealth and with very much livestock, with silver, gold, bronze, and iron, and with much clothing. Divide the spoil of your enemies with your brothers." [9] So the people of Reuben and the people of Gad and the half-tribe of Manasseh returned home, parting from the people of Israel at Shiloh, which is in the land of Canaan, to go to the land of Gilead, their own land of which they had possessed themselves by command of the LORD through Moses.

The Eastern Tribes' Altar of Witness

[10] And when they came to the region of the Jordan that is in the land of Canaan, the people of Reuben and the people of Gad and the half-tribe of Manasseh built there an altar by the Jordan, an altar of imposing size. [11] And the people of Israel heard it said, "Behold, the people of Reuben and the people of Gad and the half-tribe of Manasseh have built the altar at the frontier of the land of Canaan, in the region about the Jordan, on the side that belongs to the people of Israel." [12] And when the people of Israel heard of it, the whole assembly of the people of Israel gathered at Shiloh to make war against them.

[13] Then the people of Israel sent to the people of Reuben and the people of Gad and the half-tribe of Manasseh, in the land of Gilead, Phinehas the son of Eleazar the priest, [14] and with him ten chiefs, one from each of the tribal families of Israel, every one of them the head of a family among the clans of Israel. [15] And they came to the

people of Reuben, the people of Gad, and the half-tribe of Manasseh, in the land of Gilead, and they said to them, [16] "Thus says the whole congregation of the LORD, 'What is this breach of faith that you have committed against the God of Israel in turning away this day from following the LORD by building yourselves an altar this day in rebellion against the LORD? [17] Have we not had enough of the sin at Peor from which even yet we have not cleansed ourselves, and for which there came a plague upon the congregation of the LORD, [18] that you too must turn away this day from following the LORD? And if you too rebel against the LORD today then tomorrow he will be angry with the whole congregation of Israel. [19] But now, if the land of your possession is unclean, pass over into the LORD's land where the LORD's tabernacle stands, and take for yourselves a possession among us. Only do not rebel against the LORD or make us as rebels by building for yourselves an altar other than the altar of the LORD our God. [20] Did not Achan the son of Zerah break faith in the matter of the devoted things, and wrath fell upon all the congregation of Israel? And he did not perish alone for his iniquity.'"

[21] Then the people of Reuben, the people of Gad, and the half-tribe of Manasseh said in answer to the heads of the families of Israel, [22] "The Mighty One, God, the LORD! The Mighty One, God, the LORD! He knows; and let Israel itself know! If it was in rebellion or in breach of faith against the LORD, do not spare us today [23] for building an altar to turn away from following the LORD. Or if we did so to offer burnt offerings or grain offerings or peace offerings on it, may the LORD himself take vengeance. [24] No, but we did it from fear that in time to come your children might say to our children, 'What have you to do with the LORD, the God of Israel? [25] For the LORD has made the Jordan a boundary between us and you, you people of Reuben and people of Gad. You have no portion in the LORD.' So your children might make our children cease to worship the LORD. [26] Therefore we said, 'Let us now build an altar, not for burnt offering, nor for sacrifice, [27] but to be a witness between us and you, and between our generations after us, that we do perform the service of the LORD in his presence with our burnt

offerings and sacrifices and peace offerings, so your children will not say to our children in time to come, "You have no portion in the LORD."' [28] And we thought, 'If this should be said to us or to our descendants in time to come, we should say, "Behold, the copy of the altar of the LORD, which our fathers made, not for burnt offerings, nor for sacrifice, but to be a witness between us and you."' [29] Far be it from us that we should rebel against the LORD and turn away this day from following the LORD by building an altar for burnt offering, grain offering, or sacrifice, other than the altar of the LORD our God that stands before his tabernacle!"

[30] When Phinehas the priest and the chiefs of the congregation, the heads of the families of Israel who were with him, heard the words that the people of Reuben and the people of Gad and the people of Manasseh spoke, it was good in their eyes. [31] And Phinehas the son of Eleazar the priest said to the people of Reuben and the people of Gad and the people of Manasseh, "Today we know that the LORD is in our midst, because you have not committed this breach of faith against the LORD. Now you have delivered the people of Israel from the hand of the LORD."

[32] Then Phinehas the son of Eleazar the priest, and the chiefs, returned from the people of Reuben and the people of Gad in the land of Gilead to the land of Canaan, to the people of Israel, and brought back word to them. [33] And the report was good in the eyes of the people of Israel. And the people of Israel blessed God and spoke no more of making war against them to destroy the land where the people of Reuben and the people of Gad were settled. [34] The people of Reuben and the people of Gad called the altar Witness, "For," they said, "it is a witness between us that the LORD is God."

Joshua's Charge to Israel's Leaders

23 A long time afterward, when the LORD had given rest to Israel from all their surrounding enemies, and Joshua was old and well advanced in years, [2] Joshua summoned all Israel, its elders and heads, its judges and officers, and said to them, "I am now old and well advanced in years. [3] And you have seen all that the LORD your God has done to all these nations for your sake, for it is the LORD your God who has fought for you. [4] Behold, I have allotted to

you as an inheritance for your tribes those nations that remain, along with all the nations that I have already cut off, from the Jordan to the Great Sea in the west. **5** The LORD your God will push them back before you and drive them out of your sight. And you shall possess their land, just as the LORD your God promised you. **6** Therefore, be very strong to keep and to do all that is written in the Book of the Law of Moses, turning aside from it neither to the right hand nor to the left, **7** that you may not mix with these nations remaining among you or make mention of the names of their gods or swear by them or serve them or bow down to them, **8** but you shall cling to the LORD your God just as you have done to this day. **9** For the LORD has driven out before you great and strong nations. And as for you, no man has been able to stand before you to this day. **10** One man of you puts to flight

GETTING THE MESSAGE

Shechem was an important center of pagan worship before and during the time of Joshua. It also became important for Israel as the place where they renewed their covenant with the Lord.

a thousand, since it is the LORD your God who fights for you, just as he promised you. **11** Be very careful, therefore, to love the LORD your God. **12** For if you turn back and cling to the remnant of these nations remaining among you and make marriages with them, so that you associate with them and they with you, **13** know for certain that the LORD your God will no longer drive out these nations before you, but they shall be a snare and a trap for you, a whip on your sides and thorns in your eyes, until you perish from off this good ground that the LORD your God has given you.

14 "And now I am about to go the way of all the earth, and you know in your hearts and souls, all of you, that not one word has failed of all the good things that the LORD your God promised concerning you. All have come to pass for you; not one of them has failed. **15** But just as all the good things that the LORD your God promised concerning you have been fulfilled for you, so the LORD

will bring upon you all the evil things, until he has destroyed you from off this good land that the LORD your God has given you, **16** if you transgress the covenant of the LORD your God, which he commanded you, and go and serve other gods and bow down to them. Then the anger of the LORD will be kindled against you, and you shall perish quickly from off the good land that he has given to you."

The Covenant Renewal at Shechem

24 Joshua gathered all the tribes of Israel to Shechem and summoned the elders, the heads, the judges, and the officers of Israel. And they presented themselves before God. **2** And Joshua said to all the people, "Thus says the LORD, the God of Israel, 'Long ago, your fathers lived beyond the Euphrates, Terah, the father of Abraham and of Nahor; and they served other gods. **3** Then I took your father Abraham from beyond the River and led him through all the land of Canaan, and made his offspring many. I gave him Isaac. **4** And to Isaac I gave Jacob and Esau. And I gave Esau the hill country of Seir to possess, but Jacob and his children went down to Egypt. **5** And I sent Moses and Aaron, and I plagued Egypt with what I did in the midst of it, and afterward I brought you out.

6 "'Then I brought your fathers out of Egypt, and you came to the sea. And the Egyptians pursued your fathers with chariots and horsemen to the Red Sea. **7** And when they cried to the LORD, he put darkness between you and the Egyptians and made the sea come upon them and cover them; and your eyes saw what I did in Egypt. And you lived in the wilderness a long time. **8** Then I brought you to the land of the Amorites, who lived on the other side of the Jordan. They fought with you, and I gave them into your hand, and you took possession of their land, and I destroyed them before you. **9** Then Balak the son of Zippor, king of Moab, arose and fought against Israel. And he sent and invited Balaam the son of Beor to curse you, **10** but I would not listen to Balaam. Indeed, he blessed you. So I delivered you out of his hand. **11** And you went over the Jordan and came to Jericho, and the leaders of Jericho fought against you, and also the Amorites, the Perizzites, the Canaanites, the Hittites, the Girgashites, the Hivites, and the Jebusites. And I gave them into your hand. [12] And I sent the hornet before you, which drove them out before you, the two kings of the Amorites; it was not by your sword or by your bow. [13] I gave you a land on which you had not labored and cities that you had not built, and you dwell in them. You eat the fruit of vineyards and olive orchards that you did not plant.'

Choose Whom You Will Serve

[14] "Now therefore fear the LORD and serve him in sincerity and in faithfulness. Put away the gods that your fathers served beyond the River and in Egypt, and serve the LORD. [15] And if it is evil in your eyes to serve the LORD, choose this day whom you will serve, whether the gods your fathers served in the region beyond the River, or the gods of the Amorites in whose land you dwell. But as for me and my house, we will serve the LORD."

[16] Then the people answered, "Far be it from us that we should forsake the LORD to serve other gods, [17] for it is the LORD our God who brought us and our fathers up from the land of Egypt, out of the house of slavery, and who did those great signs in our sight and preserved us in all the way that we went, and among all the peoples through whom we passed. [18] And the LORD drove out before us all the peoples, the Amorites who lived in the land. Therefore we also will serve the LORD, for he is our God."

[19] But Joshua said to the people, "You are not able to serve the LORD, for he is a holy God. He is a jealous God; he will not forgive your transgressions or your sins. [20] If you forsake the LORD and serve foreign gods, then he will turn and do you harm and consume you, after having done you good." [21] And the people said to Joshua, "No, but we will serve the LORD." [22] Then Joshua said to the people, "You are witnesses against

yourselves that you have chosen the LORD, to serve him." And they said, "We are witnesses." [23] He said, "Then put away the foreign gods that are among you, and incline your heart to the LORD, the God of Israel." [24] And the people said to Joshua, "The LORD our God we will serve, and his voice we will obey." [25] So Joshua made a covenant with the people that day, and put in place statutes and rules for them at Shechem. [26] And Joshua wrote these words in the Book of the Law of God. And he took a large stone and set it up there under the terebinth that was by the sanctuary of the LORD. [27] And Joshua said to all the people, "Behold, this stone shall be a witness against us, for it has heard all the words of the LORD that he spoke to us. Therefore it shall be a witness against you, lest you deal falsely with your God." [28] So Joshua sent the people away, every man to his inheritance.

Joshua's Death and Burial

[29] After these things Joshua the son of Nun, the servant of the LORD, died, being 110 years old. [30] And they buried him in his own inheritance at Timnath-serah, which is in the hill country of Ephraim, north of the mountain of Gaash.

[31] Israel served the LORD all the days of Joshua, and all the days of the elders who outlived Joshua and had known all the work that the LORD did for Israel.

[32] As for the bones of Joseph, which the people of Israel brought up from Egypt, they buried them at Shechem, in the piece of land that Jacob bought from the sons of Hamor the father of Shechem for a hundred pieces of money. It became an inheritance of the descendants of Joseph.

[33] And Eleazar the son of Aaron died, and they buried him at Gibeah, the town of Phinehas his son, which had been given him in the hill country of Ephraim.

INTRODUCTION TO JUDGES

c. 1375 B.C.	1209 B.C.	c. 1162 B.C.	c. 1100 B.C.
Period of the judges begins	Deborah, Barak defeat Canaanites	Gideon defeats Midianites	Birth of Samuel

AUTHOR AND DATE

Nowhere in Scripture is an author of this book named. The events in Judges took place in the period between Joshua's death and the rise of Samuel and Saul. Most of the book was likely written by David's time (1010–970 B.C.).

THEME

The theme of Judges is the downward spiral of Israel's national and spiritual life into chaos and rebellion against God, showing the need for a godly king (17:6; 21:25).

PURPOSE AND PATTERN

The book of Judges was written to show the consequences of religious unfaithfulness and to point the way to a king who, if righteous, would lead the people to God. In the book of Joshua, the people of Israel seemed to want to follow the Lord and obey his commands. The book of Judges reveals, however, that the people had been rebelling even in Joshua's time. This disobedience continued and grew more serious throughout the period of the judges. As summarized in Judges 2:16–23, time and again Israel turned its back on God and embraced the gods and ways of the Canaanites. Israel's history unfolds in a repetitive way, with each cycle taking Israel further away from God. By the end of the book, Israel had violated its covenant with God in almost every way imaginable.

KEY THEMES

1. Israel's existence in the land, which had been promised by God, was threatened by its continuing rebellion. Israel had not conquered the land completely (ch. 1), because of its unfaithfulness (2:1–3, 20–22). Therefore, the day would come when the nation would be taken captive, away from the land (18:30).

2. The oppressions, chaos, and generally negative picture in the book are due to Israel's repeated sin. Time and again the Israelites broke the covenant, turning to the Canaanite gods and "doing evil" (2:3, 11–13, 17, 19; 3:6, 7, 12; 4:1; 6:1, 10; 8:24–27, 33; 10:6; 13:1; 17:6; 21:25), and they repeatedly suffered the consequences.

3. Despite Israel's repeated falling away, God in his faithfulness continually delivered them. This was not due to Israel's merits or its repentance. Instead it was because of God's compassion and pity (2:16, 18) and his faithfulness to his promises to Abraham (Deut. 6:10–11; compare Gen. 12:7; 15:7, 18–21; 26:2–3; 35:12).

4. The judges were not able to stop the peoples' unfaithfulness. If anything, they made it worse. Major judges such as Gideon (8:24–27), Jephthah (11:30–31, 34–40), and Samson (chs. 14–16) were guilty of significant sin. The shining exception was Deborah (chs. 4–5).

5. Israel needed a godly king to lead it in doing right *in the Lord's eyes* rather than a leader who "did what was right in his own eyes" (compare 17:6; 21:25). God had promised from the beginning that there would be kings (Gen. 17:6, 16; 35:11; 49:10), and had explained what a godly king would look like (Deut. 17:14–20). The book of Judges shows the depths to which the people of Israel descended in the absence of a godly king.

OUTLINE

I. The Roots of Israel's Unfaithfulness (1:1–3:6)

II. The Downward Spiral of Israel's Unfaithfulness (3:7–16:31)

III. The Depths of Israel's Unfaithfulness (17:1–21:25)

JUDGES

The Continuing Conquest of Canaan

1 After the death of Joshua, the people of Israel inquired of the LORD, "Who shall go up first for us against the Canaanites, to fight against them?" **2** The LORD said, "Judah shall go up; behold, I have given the land into his hand." **3** And Judah said to Simeon his brother, "Come up with me into the territory allotted to me, that we may fight against the Canaanites. And I likewise will go with you into the territory allotted to you." So Simeon went with him. **4** Then Judah went up and the LORD gave the Canaanites and the Perizzites into their hand, and they defeated 10,000 of them at Bezek. **5** They found Adoni-bezek at Bezek and fought against him and defeated the Canaanites and the Perizzites. **6** Adoni-bezek fled, but they pursued him and caught him and cut off his thumbs and his big toes. **7** And Adoni-bezek said, "Seventy kings with their thumbs and their big toes cut off used to pick up scraps under my table. As I have done, so God has repaid me." And they brought him to Jerusalem, and he died there.

8 And the men of Judah fought against Jerusalem and captured it and struck it with the edge of the sword and set the city on fire. **9** And afterward the men of Judah went down to fight against the Canaanites who lived in the hill country, in the Negeb, and in the lowland. **10** And Judah went against the Canaanites who lived in Hebron (now the name of Hebron was formerly Kiriath-arba), and they defeated Sheshai and Ahiman and Talmai.

11 From there they went against the inhabitants of Debir. The name of Debir was formerly Kiriath-sepher. **12** And Caleb said, "He who attacks Kiriath-sepher and captures it, I will give him Achsah my daughter for a wife." **13** And Othniel the son of Kenaz, Caleb's younger brother, captured it. And he gave him Achsah his daughter for a wife. **14** When she came to him, she urged him to ask her father for a field. And she dismounted from her donkey, and Caleb said to her, "What do you want?" **15** She said to him, "Give me a blessing. Since you have set me in the land of the Negeb, give me also springs of water." And Caleb gave her the upper springs and the lower springs.

16 And the descendants of the Kenite, Moses' father-in-law, went up with the people of Judah from the city of palms into the wilderness of Judah, which lies in the Negeb near Arad, and they went and settled with the people. **17** And Judah went with

---

GETTING THE MESSAGE

Toes and Thumbs. Victors in ancient battles would often cut off the thumbs and toes of their foes (1:6–7). This would allow their enemies to live but would prevent them from ever participating in another battle.

Simeon his brother, and they defeated the Canaanites who inhabited Zephath and devoted it to destruction. So the name of the city was called Hormah.[1] **18** Judah also captured Gaza with its territory, and Ashkelon with its territory, and Ekron with its territory. **19** And the LORD was with Judah, and he took possession of the hill country, but he could not drive out the inhabitants of the plain because they had chariots of iron. **20** And Hebron was given to Caleb, as Moses had said. And he drove out from it the three sons of Anak. **21** But the people of Benjamin did not drive out the Jebusites who lived in Jerusalem, so the Jebusites have lived with the people of Benjamin in Jerusalem to this day.

22 The house of Joseph also went up against Bethel, and the LORD was with them. **23** And the house of Joseph scouted out Bethel. (Now the name of the city was formerly Luz.) **24** And the spies saw a man coming out of the city, and they said to him,

---

[1] *Hormah means destruction*

"Please show us the way into the city, and we will deal kindly with you." 25 And he showed them the way into the city. And they struck the city with the edge of the sword, but they let the man and all his family go. 26 And the man went to the land of the Hittites and built a city and called its name Luz. That is its name to this day.

Failure to Complete the Conquest

27 Manasseh did not drive out the inhabitants of Beth-shean and its villages, or Taanach and its villages, or the inhabitants of Dor and its villages, or the inhabitants of Ibleam and its villages, or the inhabitants of Megiddo and its villages, for the Canaanites persisted in dwelling in that land. 28 When Israel grew strong, they put the Canaanites to forced labor, but did not drive them out completely.

> **GETTING THE MESSAGE**
>
> **Ashtoreth** (2:13) was the goddess of fertility, love, and war in Canaanite culture. Canaanite legends portray her as Baal's wife or sister. She is also known by her Greek name, Astarte, and in Mesopotamian texts as Ishtar.

29 And Ephraim did not drive out the Canaanites who lived in Gezer, so the Canaanites lived in Gezer among them. 30 Zebulun did not drive out the inhabitants of Kitron, or the inhabitants of Nahalol, so the Canaanites lived among them, but became subject to forced labor. 31 Asher did not drive out the inhabitants of Acco, or the inhabitants of Sidon or of Ahlab or of Achzib or of Helbah or of Aphik or of Rehob, 32 so the Asherites lived among the Canaanites, the inhabitants of the land, for they did not drive them out. 33 Naphtali did not drive out the inhabitants of Beth-shemesh, or the inhabitants of Beth-anath, so they lived among the Canaanites, the inhabitants of the land. Nevertheless, the inhabitants of Beth-shemesh and of Beth-anath became subject to forced labor for them. 34 The Amorites pressed the people of Dan back into the hill country, for they did not allow them to come down to the plain.

35 The Amorites persisted in dwelling in Mount Heres, in Aijalon, and in Shaalbim, but the hand of the house of Joseph rested heavily on them, and they became subject to forced labor. 36 And the border of the Amorites ran from the ascent of Akrabbim, from Sela and upward.

Israel's Disobedience

2 Now the angel of the LORD went up from Gilgal to Bochim. And he said, "I brought you up from Egypt and brought you into the land that I swore to give to your fathers. I said, 'I will never break my covenant with you, 2 and you shall make no covenant with the inhabitants of this land; you shall break down their altars.' But you have not obeyed my voice. What is this you have done? 3 So now I say, I will not drive them out before you, but they shall become thorns in your sides, and their gods shall be a snare to you." 4 As soon as the angel of the LORD spoke these words to all the people of Israel, the people lifted up their voices and wept. 5 And they called the name of that place Bochim.[1] And they sacrificed there to the LORD.

The Death of Joshua

6 When Joshua dismissed the people, the people of Israel went each to his inheritance to take possession of the land. 7 And the people served the LORD all the days of Joshua, and all the days of the elders who outlived Joshua, who had seen all the great work that the LORD had done for Israel. 8 And Joshua the son of Nun, the servant of the LORD, died at the age of 110 years. 9 And they buried him within the boundaries of his inheritance in Timnath-heres, in the hill country of Ephraim, north of the mountain of Gaash. 10 And all that generation also were gathered to their fathers. And there arose another generation after them who did not know the LORD or the work that he had done for Israel.

Israel's Unfaithfulness

11 And the people of Israel did what was evil in the sight of the LORD and served the Baals. 12 And they abandoned the LORD, the God of their fathers, who had brought them out of the land of Egypt. They went after other gods, from among the gods of the peoples who were around them, and bowed

---

[1] Bochim means weepers

down to them. And they provoked the LORD to anger. ¹³ They abandoned the LORD and served the Baals and the Ashtaroth. ¹⁴ So the anger of the LORD was kindled against Israel, and he gave them over to plunderers, who plundered them. And he sold them into the hand of their surrounding enemies, so that they could no longer withstand their enemies. ¹⁵ Whenever they marched out, the hand of the LORD was against them for harm, as the LORD had warned, and as the LORD had sworn to them. And they were in terrible distress.

The LORD Raises Up Judges

¹⁶ Then the LORD raised up judges, who saved them out of the hand of those who plundered them. ¹⁷ Yet they did not listen to their judges, for they whored after other gods and bowed down to them. They soon turned aside from the way in which their fathers had walked, who had obeyed the commandments of the LORD, and they did not do so. ¹⁸ Whenever the LORD raised up judges for them, the LORD was with the judge, and he saved them from the hand of their enemies all the days of the judge. For the LORD was moved to pity by their groaning because of those who afflicted and oppressed them. ¹⁹ But whenever the judge died, they turned back and were more corrupt than their fathers, going after other gods, serving them and bowing down to them. They did not drop any of their practices or their stubborn ways. ²⁰ So the anger of the LORD was kindled against Israel, and he said, "Because this people have transgressed my covenant that I commanded their fathers and have not obeyed my voice, ²¹ I will no longer drive out before them any of the nations that Joshua left when he died, ²² in order to test Israel by them, whether they will take care to walk in the way of the LORD as their fathers did, or not." ²³ So the LORD left those nations, not driving them out quickly, and he did not give them into the hand of Joshua.

3 Now these are the nations that the LORD left, to test Israel by them, that is, all in Israel who had not experienced all the wars in Canaan. ² It was only in order that the generations of the people of Israel might know war, to teach war to those who had not known it before. ³ These are the nations: the five lords of the Philistines and all the Canaanites and the Sidonians and the Hivites who lived on Mount Lebanon, from Mount Baal-hermon as far as Lebo-hamath. ⁴ They were for the testing of Israel, to know whether Israel would obey the commandments of the LORD, which he commanded their fathers by the hand of Moses. ⁵ So the people of Israel lived among the Canaanites, the Hittites, the Amorites, the Perizzites, the Hivites, and the Jebusites. ⁶ And their daughters they took to themselves for wives, and their own daughters they gave to their sons, and they served their gods.

PROFILE

EHUD

The story of Ehud begins by saying that he was "a left-handed man" (3:15), and in fact the Lord used Ehud's left-handedness to defeat Israel's enemy. Ehud led a delegation to pay tribute to Eglon, king of Moab, who was ruling over Israel. Because he was left-handed, Ehud was able to conceal a sword on his right thigh, where it would not be expected. He pretended to have a secret message for the king. While he was alone with King Eglon, Ehud killed him, then managed to escape before the king's servants realized what had happened. The graphic details in this account show the rough nature of this time in Israel's history and the earthy character of many of its "heroes."

KEY REFERENCE: JUDGES 3:28

Othniel

⁷ And the people of Israel did what was evil in the sight of the LORD. They forgot the LORD their God and served the Baals and the Asheroth. ⁸ Therefore the anger of the LORD was kindled against Israel, and he sold them into the hand of Cushan-rishathaim king of Mesopotamia. And the people of Israel served Cushan-rishathaim eight years. ⁹ But when the people of Israel cried out to the LORD, the LORD raised up a deliverer for the people of Israel, who saved them, Othniel the son of Kenaz, Caleb's younger brother.

10 The Spirit of the LORD was upon him, and he judged Israel. He went out to war, and the LORD gave Cushan-rishathaim king of Mesopotamia into his hand. And his hand prevailed over Cushan-rishathaim. 11 So the land had rest forty years. Then Othniel the son of Kenaz died.

Ehud

12 And the people of Israel again did what was evil in the sight of the LORD, and the LORD strengthened Eglon the king of Moab against Israel, because they had done what was evil in the sight of the LORD. 13 He gathered to himself the Ammonites and the Amalekites, and went and defeated Israel. And they took possession of the city of palms. 14 And the people of Israel served Eglon the king of Moab eighteen years.

> ### GETTING THE MESSAGE
>
> **Cool breezes** were rare in the arid climate of ancient Israel. Usually the best place to feel a nice breeze was on the roof of the house (3:20). Roofs served many purposes. They provided a place to dry grain and fruit and to store the harvest. They were also a good place to sleep on hot summer nights.

15 Then the people of Israel cried out to the LORD, and the LORD raised up for them a deliverer, Ehud, the son of Gera, the Benjaminite, a left-handed man. The people of Israel sent tribute by him to Eglon the king of Moab. 16 And Ehud made for himself a sword with two edges, a cubit in length, and he bound it on his right thigh under his clothes. 17 And he presented the tribute to Eglon king of Moab. Now Eglon was a very fat man. 18 And when Ehud had finished presenting the tribute, he sent away the people who carried the tribute. 19 But he himself turned back at the idols near Gilgal and said, "I have a secret message for you, O king." And he commanded, "Silence." And all his attendants went out from his presence. 20 And Ehud came to him as he was sitting alone in his cool roof chamber. And Ehud said, "I have a message from God for you." And he arose from his seat. 21 And Ehud reached with his left hand, took the sword from his right thigh, and thrust it

into his belly. 22 And the hilt also went in after the blade, and the fat closed over the blade, for he did not pull the sword out of his belly; and the dung came out. 23 Then Ehud went out into the porch and closed the doors of the roof chamber behind him and locked them.

24 When he had gone, the servants came, and when they saw that the doors of the roof chamber were locked, they thought, "Surely he is relieving himself in the closet of the cool chamber." 25 And they waited till they were embarrassed. But when he still did not open the doors of the roof chamber, they took the key and opened them, and there lay their lord dead on the floor.

26 Ehud escaped while they delayed, and he passed beyond the idols and escaped to Seirah. 27 When he arrived, he sounded the trumpet in the hill country of Ephraim. Then the people of Israel went down with him from the hill country, and he was their leader. 28 And he said to them, "Follow after me, for the LORD has given your enemies the Moabites into your hand." So they went down after him and seized the fords of the Jordan against the Moabites and did not allow anyone to pass over. 29 And they killed at that time about 10,000 of the Moabites, all strong, able-bodied men; not a man escaped. 30 So Moab was subdued that day under the hand of Israel. And the land had rest for eighty years.

Shamgar

31 After him was Shamgar the son of Anath, who killed 600 of the Philistines with an oxgoad, and he also saved Israel.

Deborah and Barak

4 And the people of Israel again did what was evil in the sight of the LORD after Ehud died. 2 And the LORD sold them into the hand of Jabin king of Canaan, who reigned in Hazor. The commander of his army was Sisera, who lived in Harosheth-hagoyim. 3 Then the people of Israel cried out to the LORD for help, for he had 900 chariots of iron and he oppressed the people of Israel cruelly for twenty years.

4 Now Deborah, a prophetess, the wife of Lappidoth, was judging Israel at that time. 5 She used to sit under the palm of Deborah between Ramah and Bethel in the hill country of Ephraim, and the people of Israel

came up to her for judgment. **6** She sent and summoned Barak the son of Abinoam from Kedesh-naphtali and said to him, "Has not the LORD, the God of Israel, commanded you, 'Go, gather your men at Mount Tabor, taking 10,000 from the people of Naphtali and the people of Zebulun. **7** And I will draw out Sisera, the general of Jabin's army, to meet you by the river Kishon with his chariots and his troops, and I will give him into your hand'?" **8** Barak said to her, "If you will go with me, I will go, but if you will not go with me, I will not go." **9** And she said, "I will surely go with you. Nevertheless, the road on which you are going will not lead to your glory, for the LORD will sell Sisera into the hand of a woman." Then Deborah arose and went with Barak to Kedesh. **10** And Barak called out Zebulun and Naphtali to Kedesh.

GETTING THE MESSAGE

Chariots of iron. Iron chariots were the equivalent of tanks in the ancient Near East. They were greatly feared by enemy foot soldiers. Charioteers could run over them, and archers riding in the chariots could hit them from a distance. The only real problem with chariots was that their wheels could get mired in mud.

And 10,000 men went up at his heels, and Deborah went up with him.

11 Now Heber the Kenite had separated from the Kenites, the descendants of Hobab the father-in-law of Moses, and had pitched his tent as far away as the oak in Zaanannim, which is near Kedesh.

12 When Sisera was told that Barak the son of Abinoam had gone up to Mount Tabor, **13** Sisera called out all his chariots, 900 chariots of iron, and all the men who were with him, from Harosheth-hagoyim to the river Kishon. **14** And Deborah said to Barak, "Up! For this is the day in which the LORD has given Sisera into your hand. Does not the LORD go out before you?" So Barak went down from Mount Tabor with 10,000 men following him. **15** And the LORD routed Sisera and all his chariots and all his army before Barak by the edge of the sword. And Sisera got down from his chariot and fled away on

foot. **16** And Barak pursued the chariots and the army to Harosheth-hagoyim, and all the army of Sisera fell by the edge of the sword; not a man was left.

17 But Sisera fled away on foot to the tent of Jael, the wife of Heber the Kenite, for there was peace between Jabin the king of Hazor and the house of Heber the Kenite. **18** And Jael came out to meet Sisera and said to him, "Turn aside, my lord; turn aside to me; do not be afraid." So he turned aside to her into the tent, and she covered him with

PROFILE

DEBORAH

When the Canaanite king Jabin, with his 900 chariots of iron, oppressed Israel, the Lord raised up a woman to save them. Deborah, a prophetess, was called to lead the nation as a judge and deliverer. Since women did not usually go into battle, Deborah called upon Barak to lead the army against Jabin, but then Barak insisted that Deborah go into battle with him. Following the victory, Deborah and Barak sang a song of praise to the Lord. The defeat of Jabin ushered in a period of 40 years of peace for the people of Israel. Although many of the judges made poor choices during their rule, Deborah's actions and words consistently pointed to God.

KEY REFERENCE: JUDGES 4:4-7

a rug. **19** And he said to her, "Please give me a little water to drink, for I am thirsty." So she opened a skin of milk and gave him a drink and covered him. **20** And he said to her, "Stand at the opening of the tent, and if any man comes and asks you, 'Is anyone here?' say, 'No.'" **21** But Jael the wife of Heber took a tent peg, and took a hammer in her hand. Then she went softly to him and drove the peg into his temple until it went down into the ground while he was lying fast asleep from weariness. So he died. **22** And behold, as Barak was pursuing Sisera, Jael went out to meet him and said to him, "Come, and I will show you the man whom

you are seeking." So he went in to her tent,
and there lay Sisera dead, with the tent peg
in his temple.

²³ So on that day God subdued Jabin the
king of Canaan before the people of Israel.
²⁴ And the hand of the people of Israel
pressed harder and harder against Jabin the
king of Canaan, until they destroyed Jabin
king of Canaan.

The Song of Deborah and Barak

5 Then sang Deborah and Barak the son
of Abinoam on that day:

² "That the leaders took the lead in Israel,
  that the people offered themselves
      willingly,
    bless the LORD!

³ "Hear, O kings; give ear, O princes;
    to the LORD I will sing;
  I will make melody to the LORD, the
      God of Israel.

GETTING THE MESSAGE

Donkeys played many roles in the
ancient Near East. They provided much
of the heavy labor in agriculture and
provided personal transportation. The
number of donkeys a man possessed
often determined his wealth. White
donkeys were highly prized (5:10)
because they were rare.

⁴ "LORD, when you went out from Seir,
    when you marched from the region
        of Edom,
  the earth trembled
    and the heavens dropped,
      yes, the clouds dropped water.
⁵ The mountains quaked before the
      LORD,
    even Sinai before the LORD, the God
        of Israel.

⁶ "In the days of Shamgar, son of Anath,
    in the days of Jael, the highways
        were abandoned,
  and travelers kept to the byways.
⁷ The villagers ceased in Israel;
    they ceased to be until I arose;
  I, Deborah, arose as a mother in
      Israel.

⁸ When new gods were chosen,
    then war was in the gates.
  Was shield or spear to be seen
    among forty thousand in Israel?
⁹ My heart goes out to the commanders
        of Israel
  who offered themselves willingly
      among the people.
    Bless the LORD.

¹⁰ "Tell of it, you who ride on white don-
        keys,
  you who sit on rich carpets
    and you who walk by the way.
¹¹ To the sound of musicians at the
        watering places,
    there they repeat the righteous
        triumphs of the LORD,
      the righteous triumphs of his vil-
          lagers in Israel.

"Then down to the gates marched the
    people of the LORD.

¹² "Awake, awake, Deborah!
    Awake, awake, break out in a song!
  Arise, Barak, lead away your captives,
      O son of Abinoam.
¹³ Then down marched the remnant of
        the noble;
    the people of the LORD marched
        down for me against the mighty.
¹⁴ From Ephraim their root they
        marched down into the valley,
    following you, Benjamin, with your
        kinsmen;
  from Machir marched down the com-
        manders,
    and from Zebulun those who bear
        the lieutenant's staff;
¹⁵ the princes of Issachar came with
        Deborah,
    and Issachar faithful to Barak;
  into the valley they rushed at his
        heels.
  Among the clans of Reuben
    there were great searchings of heart.
¹⁶ Why did you sit still among the
        sheepfolds,
    to hear the whistling for the flocks?
  Among the clans of Reuben
    there were great searchings of heart.
¹⁷ Gilead stayed beyond the Jordan;
    and Dan, why did he stay with the
        ships?

Asher sat still at the coast of the sea,
    staying by his landings.

18 Zebulun is a people who risked their
    lives to the death;
    Naphtali, too, on the heights of the
    field.

19 "The kings came, they fought;
    then fought the kings of Canaan,
    at Taanach, by the waters of Megiddo;
    they got no spoils of silver.

20 From heaven the stars fought,
    from their courses they fought
    against Sisera.

21 The torrent Kishon swept them away,
    the ancient torrent, the torrent
    Kishon.
    March on, my soul, with might!

22 "Then loud beat the horses' hoofs
    with the galloping, galloping of his
    steeds.

23 "Curse Meroz, says the angel of the
    LORD,
    curse its inhabitants thoroughly,
    because they did not come to the help
    of the LORD,
    to the help of the LORD against the
    mighty.

24 "Most blessed of women be Jael,
    the wife of Heber the Kenite,
    of tent-dwelling women most
    blessed.

25 He asked for water and she gave him
    milk;
    she brought him curds in a noble's
    bowl.

26 She sent her hand to the tent peg
    and her right hand to the work-
    men's mallet;
    she struck Sisera;
    she crushed his head;
    she shattered and pierced his tem-
    ple.

27 Between her feet
    he sank, he fell, he lay still;
    between her feet
    he sank, he fell;
    where he sank,
    there he fell—dead.

28 "Out of the window she peered,
    the mother of Sisera wailed through
    the lattice:

'Why is his chariot so long in coming?
    Why tarry the hoofbeats of his char-
    iots?'

29 Her wisest princesses answer,
    indeed, she answers herself,

30 'Have they not found and divided the
    spoil?—
    A womb or two for every man;
    spoil of dyed materials for Sisera,
    spoil of dyed materials embroidered,
    two pieces of dyed work embroi-
    dered for the neck as spoil?'

31 "So may all your enemies perish,
    O LORD!
    But your friends be like the sun as
    he rises in his might."

And the land had rest for forty years.

GETTING THE MESSAGE

Camels at war? The Midianites were among the first to use camels in warfare (6:5). Their camels were most likely the single-humped dromedary, which could travel more than 150 miles (240 km) in one day. The two-humped Bactrian camel was slower but could carry more weight than the dromedary. It was therefore ideal for trade caravans. Camels could be dangerous and unpredictable. If they became angry, they could wreck an entire campsite.

Midian Oppresses Israel

6 The people of Israel did what was evil in the sight of the LORD, and the LORD gave them into the hand of Midian seven years. ² And the hand of Midian overpowered Israel, and because of Midian the people of Israel made for themselves the dens that are in the mountains and the caves and the strongholds. ³ For whenever the Israelites planted crops, the Midianites and the Amalekites and the people of the East would come up against them. ⁴ They would encamp against them and devour the produce of the land, as far as Gaza, and leave no sustenance in Israel and no sheep or ox or donkey. ⁵ For they would come up with their livestock and their tents; they would come like locusts in number—both they and their camels could not be counted—so

that they laid waste the land as they came in. ⁶ And Israel was brought very low because of Midian. And the people of Israel cried out for help to the LORD.

⁷ When the people of Israel cried out to the LORD on account of the Midianites, ⁸ the LORD sent a prophet to the people of Israel. And he said to them, "Thus says the LORD, the God of Israel: I led you up from Egypt and brought you out of the house of slavery. ⁹ And I delivered you from the hand of the Egyptians and from the hand of all who

---

GIDEON

Gideon was called by God to free the Israelites from oppression by the Midianites. After destroying an altar of Baal, he was given the name Jerubbaal, which means, "let Baal contend." The name was a mocking challenge to this powerless false god. The God of Israel proved his own power by leading Gideon to choose his army in a very unusual way, reducing it from 32,000 to only 300 men. Those 300 men defeated the Midianites, not with the sword but with trumpets, torches, and pitchers! Gideon was viewed as a hero, and the people tried to make him king. He refused their request, rightly declaring that "the LORD will rule over you" (8:23). Sadly, however, Gideon went on to do things that suggested a heart filled with pride rather than humility.

KEY REFERENCE: JUDGES 6:36–40

---

oppressed you, and drove them out before you and gave you their land. ¹⁰ And I said to you, 'I am the LORD your God; you shall not fear the gods of the Amorites in whose land you dwell.' But you have not obeyed my voice."

The Call of Gideon

¹¹ Now the angel of the LORD came and sat under the terebinth at Ophrah, which belonged to Joash the Abiezrite, while his son Gideon was beating out wheat in the winepress to hide it from the Midianites.

¹² And the angel of the LORD appeared to him and said to him, "The LORD is with you, O mighty man of valor." ¹³ And Gideon said to him, "Please, sir, if the LORD is with us, why then has all this happened to us? And where are all his wonderful deeds that our fathers recounted to us, saying, 'Did not the LORD bring us up from Egypt?' But now the LORD has forsaken us and given us into the hand of Midian." ¹⁴ And the LORD turned to him and said, "Go in this might of yours and save Israel from the hand of Midian; do not I send you?" ¹⁵ And he said to him, "Please, Lord, how can I save Israel? Behold, my clan is the weakest in Manasseh, and I am the least in my father's house." ¹⁶ And the LORD said to him, "But I will be with you, and you shall strike the Midianites as one man." ¹⁷ And he said to him, "If now I have found favor in your eyes, then show me a sign that it is you who speak with me. ¹⁸ Please do not depart from here until I come to you and bring out my present and set it before you." And he said, "I will stay till you return."

¹⁹ So Gideon went into his house and prepared a young goat and unleavened cakes from an ephah of flour. The meat he put in a basket, and the broth he put in a pot, and brought them to him under the terebinth and presented them. ²⁰ And the angel of God said to him, "Take the meat and the unleavened cakes, and put them on this rock, and pour the broth over them." And he did so. ²¹ Then the angel of the LORD reached out the tip of the staff that was in his hand and touched the meat and the unleavened cakes. And fire sprang up from the rock and consumed the meat and the unleavened cakes. And the angel of the LORD vanished from his sight. ²² Then Gideon perceived that he was the angel of the LORD. And Gideon said, "Alas, O Lord GOD! For now I have seen the angel of the LORD face to face." ²³ But the LORD said to him, "Peace be to you. Do not fear; you shall not die." ²⁴ Then Gideon built an altar there to the LORD and called it, The LORD Is Peace. To this day it still stands at Ophrah, which belongs to the Abiezrites.

²⁵ That night the LORD said to him, "Take your father's bull, and the second bull seven years old, and pull down the altar of Baal that your father has, and cut down the Asherah that is beside it ²⁶ and build an altar to the LORD your God on the top

of the stronghold here, with stones laid in due order. Then take the second bull and offer it as a burnt offering with the wood of the Asherah that you shall cut down." ²⁷ So Gideon took ten men of his servants and did as the LORD had told him. But because he was too afraid of his family and the men of the town to do it by day, he did it by night.

Gideon Destroys the Altar of Baal

²⁸ When the men of the town rose early in the morning, behold, the altar of Baal was broken down, and the Asherah beside it was cut down, and the second bull was offered on the altar that had been built. ²⁹ And they said to one another, "Who has done this thing?" And after they had searched and inquired, they said, "Gideon the son of Joash has done this thing." ³⁰ Then the men of the town said to Joash, "Bring out your son, that he may die, for he has broken down the altar of Baal and cut down the Asherah beside it." ³¹ But Joash said to all who stood against him, "Will you contend for Baal? Or will you save him? Whoever contends for him shall be put to death by morning. If he is a god, let him contend for himself, because his altar has been broken down." ³² Therefore on that day Gideon was called Jerubbaal, that is to say, "Let Baal contend against him," because he broke down his altar.

³³ Now all the Midianites and the Amalekites and the people of the East came together, and they crossed the Jordan and encamped in the Valley of Jezreel. ³⁴ But the Spirit of the LORD clothed Gideon, and he sounded the trumpet, and the Abiezrites were called out to follow him. ³⁵ And he sent messengers throughout all Manasseh, and they too were called out to follow him. And he sent messengers to Asher, Zebulun, and Naphtali, and they went up to meet them.

The Sign of the Fleece

³⁶ Then Gideon said to God, "If you will save Israel by my hand, as you have said, ³⁷ behold, I am laying a fleece of wool on the threshing floor. If there is dew on the fleece alone, and it is dry on all the ground, then I shall know that you will save Israel by my hand, as you have said." ³⁸ And it was so. When he rose early next morning and squeezed the fleece, he wrung enough dew from the fleece to fill a bowl with water. ³⁹ Then Gideon said to God, "Let not your anger burn against me; let me speak just once more. Please let me test just once more with the fleece. Please let it be dry on the fleece only, and on all the ground let there be dew." ⁴⁰ And God did so that night; and it was dry on the fleece only, and on all the ground there was dew.

Gideon's Three Hundred Men

7 Then Jerubbaal (that is, Gideon) and all the people who were with him rose early and encamped beside the spring of Harod. And the camp of Midian was north of them, by the hill of Moreh, in the valley.

² The LORD said to Gideon, "The people with you are too many for me to give the Midianites into their hand, lest Israel boast over me, saying, 'My own hand has saved me.' ³ Now therefore proclaim in the ears of the people, saying, 'Whoever is fearful and trembling, let him return home and hurry away from Mount Gilead.'" Then 22,000 of the people returned, and 10,000 remained.

⁴ And the LORD said to Gideon, "The people are still too many. Take them down to the water, and I will test them for you there, and anyone of whom I say to you, 'This one shall go with you,' shall go with you, and anyone of whom I say to you, 'This one shall not go with you,' shall not go." ⁵ So he brought the people down to the water. And the LORD said to Gideon, "Every one who laps the water with his tongue, as a dog laps, you shall set by himself. Likewise, every one who kneels down to drink." ⁶ And the number of those who lapped, putting their hands to their mouths, was 300 men, but all the rest of the people knelt down to drink water. ⁷ And the LORD said to Gideon, "With the 300 men who lapped I will save you and give the Midianites into your hand, and let all the others go every man to his home." ⁸ So the people took provisions in their hands, and their trumpets. And he sent all the rest of Israel every man to his tent, but retained the 300 men. And the camp of Midian was below him in the valley.

⁹ That same night the LORD said to him, "Arise, go down against the camp, for I have given it into your hand. ¹⁰ But if you are afraid to go down, go down to the camp with Purah your servant. ¹¹ And you shall hear what they say, and afterward your hands shall be strengthened to go down against the camp." Then he went down with Purah

his servant to the outposts of the armed men who were in the camp. ¹²And the Midianites and the Amalekites and all the people of the East lay along the valley like locusts in abundance, and their camels were without number, as the sand that is on the seashore in abundance. ¹³When Gideon came, behold, a man was telling a dream to his comrade. And he said, "Behold, I dreamed a dream, and behold, a cake of barley bread tumbled into the camp of Midian and came to the tent and struck it so that it fell and turned it upside down, so that the tent lay flat." ¹⁴And his comrade answered, "This is no other than the sword of Gideon the son of Joash, a man of Israel; God has given into his hand Midian and all the camp."

¹⁵As soon as Gideon heard the telling of the dream and its interpretation, he worshiped. And he returned to the camp of Israel and said, "Arise, for the LORD has

GETTING THE MESSAGE

The night watch. Watchmen were an important part of life in Bible times. They provided night-time protection both for soldiers in their tents and for ordinary people in their homes.

given the host of Midian into your hand." ¹⁶And he divided the 300 men into three companies and put trumpets into the hands of all of them and empty jars, with torches inside the jars. ¹⁷And he said to them, "Look at me, and do likewise. When I come to the outskirts of the camp, do as I do. ¹⁸When I blow the trumpet, I and all who are with me, then blow the trumpets also on every side of all the camp and shout, 'For the LORD and for Gideon.'"

Gideon Defeats Midian

¹⁹So Gideon and the hundred men who were with him came to the outskirts of the camp at the beginning of the middle watch, when they had just set the watch. And they blew the trumpets and smashed the jars that were in their hands. ²⁰Then the three companies blew the trumpets and broke the jars. They held in their left hands the torches, and in their right hands the trumpets to blow. And they cried out, "A sword for the

LORD and for Gideon!" ²¹Every man stood in his place around the camp, and all the army ran. They cried out and fled. ²²When they blew the 300 trumpets, the LORD set every man's sword against his comrade and against all the army. And the army fled as far as Beth-shittah toward Zererah, as far as the border of Abel-meholah, by Tabbath. ²³And the men of Israel were called out from Naphtali and from Asher and from all Manasseh, and they pursued after Midian.

²⁴Gideon sent messengers throughout all the hill country of Ephraim, saying, "Come down against the Midianites and capture the waters against them, as far as Beth-barah, and also the Jordan." So all the men of Ephraim were called out, and they captured the waters as far as Beth-barah, and also the Jordan. ²⁵And they captured the two princes of Midian, Oreb and Zeeb. They killed Oreb at the rock of Oreb, and Zeeb they killed at the winepress of Zeeb. Then they pursued Midian, and they brought the heads of Oreb and Zeeb to Gideon across the Jordan.

Gideon Defeats Zebah and Zalmunna

8 Then the men of Ephraim said to him, "What is this that you have done to us, not to call us when you went to fight against Midian?" And they accused him fiercely. ²And he said to them, "What have I done now in comparison with you? Is not the gleaning of the grapes of Ephraim better than the grape harvest of Abiezer? ³God has given into your hands the princes of Midian, Oreb and Zeeb. What have I been able to do in comparison with you?" Then their anger against him subsided when he said this.

⁴And Gideon came to the Jordan and crossed over, he and the 300 men who were with him, exhausted yet pursuing. ⁵So he said to the men of Succoth, "Please give loaves of bread to the people who follow me, for they are exhausted, and I am pursuing after Zebah and Zalmunna, the kings of Midian." ⁶And the officials of Succoth said, "Are the hands of Zebah and Zalmunna already in your hand, that we should give bread to your army?" ⁷So Gideon said, "Well then, when the LORD has given Zebah and Zalmunna into my hand, I will flail your flesh with the thorns of the wilderness and with briers." ⁸And from there he went up to Penuel, and spoke to them in the same way, and the men of Penuel answered him

as the men of Succoth had answered. **9** And he said to the men of Penuel, "When I come again in peace, I will break down this tower."

10 Now Zebah and Zalmunna were in Karkor with their army, about 15,000 men, all who were left of all the army of the people of the East, for there had fallen 120,000 men who drew the sword. **11** And Gideon went up by the way of the tent dwellers east of Nobah and Jogbehah and attacked the army, for the army felt secure. **12** And Zebah and Zalmunna fled, and he pursued them and captured the two kings of Midian, Zebah and Zalmunna, and he threw all the army into a panic.

13 Then Gideon the son of Joash returned from the battle by the ascent of Heres. **14** And he captured a young man of Succoth and questioned him. And he wrote down for him the officials and elders of Succoth, seventy-seven men. **15** And he came to the men of Succoth and said, "Behold Zebah and Zalmunna, about whom you taunted me, saying, 'Are the hands of Zebah and Zalmunna already in your hand, that we should give bread to your men who are exhausted?'" **16** And he took the elders of the city, and he took thorns of the wilderness and briers and with them taught the men of Succoth a lesson. **17** And he broke down the tower of Penuel and killed the men of the city.

18 Then he said to Zebah and Zalmunna, "Where are the men whom you killed at Tabor?" They answered, "As you are, so were they. Every one of them resembled the son of a king." **19** And he said, "They were my brothers, the sons of my mother. As the LORD lives, if you had saved them alive, I would not kill you." **20** So he said to Jether his firstborn, "Rise and kill them!" But the young man did not draw his sword, for he was afraid, because he was still a young man. **21** Then Zebah and Zalmunna said, "Rise yourself and fall upon us, for as the man is, so is his strength." And Gideon arose and killed Zebah and Zalmunna, and he took the crescent ornaments that were on the necks of their camels.

Gideon's Ephod

22 Then the men of Israel said to Gideon, "Rule over us, you and your son and your grandson also, for you have saved us from the hand of Midian." **23** Gideon said to them,

"I will not rule over you, and my son will not rule over you; the LORD will rule over you." **24** And Gideon said to them, "Let me make a request of you: every one of you give me the earrings from his spoil." (For they had golden earrings, because they were Ishmaelites.) **25** And they answered, "We will willingly give them." And they spread a cloak, and every man threw in it the earrings of his spoil. **26** And the weight of the golden earrings that he requested was 1,700 shekels of gold, besides the crescent ornaments and the pendants and the purple garments worn by the kings of Midian, and besides the collars that were around the necks of their camels. **27** And Gideon made an ephod of it and put it in his city, in Ophrah. And all Israel whored after it there, and it became

GETTING THE MESSAGE

Crescents. Midianite kings often decorated their camels with gold or silver pendants in the shape of a crescent moon (8:21). They may have believed the crescents were magic, since many of Israel's neighbors worshiped the moon. Crescents are mentioned in Isaiah 3:16–18 as part of the "finery" that the Lord will take away from the "daughters of Zion."

a snare to Gideon and to his family. **28** So Midian was subdued before the people of Israel, and they raised their heads no more. And the land had rest forty years in the days of Gideon.

The Death of Gideon

29 Jerubbaal the son of Joash went and lived in his own house. **30** Now Gideon had seventy sons, his own offspring, for he had many wives. **31** And his concubine who was in Shechem also bore him a son, and he called his name Abimelech. **32** And Gideon the son of Joash died in a good old age and was buried in the tomb of Joash his father, at Ophrah of the Abiezrites.

33 As soon as Gideon died, the people of Israel turned again and whored after the Baals and made Baal-berith their god. **34** And the people of Israel did not remember the LORD their God, who had delivered them from the hand of all their enemies on every side, **35** and they did not show steadfast love to the family of Jerubbaal (that is, Gideon) in return for all the good that he had done to Israel.

Abimelech's Conspiracy

9 Now Abimelech the son of Jerubbaal went to Shechem to his mother's relatives and said to them and to the whole clan of his mother's family, **2** "Say in the ears of all the leaders of Shechem, 'Which is better for

---

PROFILE

ABIMELECH

Gideon's son Abimelech became king over the city of Shechem thanks to his family's successful campaign to influence the city's leaders. He then removed his strongest competition for leadership by ruthlessly killing 70 of his own brothers. Abimelech's youngest brother Jotham, who alone had escaped the murderous rampage, courageously condemned Abimelech and the leaders. He told a fable that predicted the judgment that would fall on Abimelech and the leaders for the deaths of Gideon's sons. When the people of Shechem later turned against Abimelech, he successfully resisted their rebellion by killing many people and destroying their city. But then, as he tried to capture a nearby city, a woman dropped a millstone on his head, crushing his skull. This episode in Israel's history shows some of the consequences of Israel's unfaithfulness to the Lord (8:33–34).

KEY REFERENCE: JUDGES 9:5–6

---

you, that all seventy of the sons of Jerubbaal rule over you, or that one rule over you?' Remember also that I am your bone and your flesh."

3 And his mother's relatives spoke all these words on his behalf in the ears of all the leaders of Shechem, and their hearts inclined to follow Abimelech, for they said, "He is our brother." **4** And they gave him seventy pieces of silver out of the house of Baal-berith with which Abimelech hired worthless and reck-

less fellows, who followed him. **5** And he went to his father's house at Ophrah and killed his brothers the sons of Jerubbaal, seventy men, on one stone. But Jotham the youngest son of Jerubbaal was left, for he hid himself. **6** And all the leaders of Shechem came together, and all Beth-millo, and they went and made Abimelech king, by the oak of the pillar at Shechem.

7 When it was told to Jotham, he went and stood on top of Mount Gerizim and cried aloud and said to them, "Listen to me, you leaders of Shechem, that God may listen to you. **8** The trees once went out to anoint a king over them, and they said to the olive tree, 'Reign over us.' **9** But the olive tree said to them, 'Shall I leave my abundance, by

---

GETTING THE MESSAGE

Mount Gerizim and Mount Ebal make up the sides of the east-west pass into the Valley of Shechem. When Joshua conquered central Israel, he used these mountains as symbols, pronouncing blessings from Mount Gerizim and punishments from Mount Ebal (Josh. 8:30–35). Perhaps because of its historical importance, Jotham chose Mount Gerizim as the place to tell his prophetic story about the trees and the bramble bush (Judg. 9:7–21).

---

which gods and men are honored, and go hold sway over the trees?' **10** And the trees said to the fig tree, 'You come and reign over us.' **11** But the fig tree said to them, 'Shall I leave my sweetness and my good fruit and go hold sway over the trees?' **12** And the trees said to the vine, 'You come and reign over us.' **13** But the vine said to them, 'Shall I leave my wine that cheers God and men and go hold sway over the trees?' **14** Then all the trees said to the bramble, 'You come and reign over us.' **15** And the bramble said to the trees, 'If in good faith you are anointing me king over you, then come and take refuge in my shade, but if not, let fire come out of the bramble and devour the cedars of Lebanon.'

16 "Now therefore, if you acted in good faith and integrity when you made Abimelech king, and if you have dealt well with

Jerubbaal and his house and have done to him as his deeds deserved— ¹⁷ for my father fought for you and risked his life and delivered you from the hand of Midian, ¹⁸ and you have risen up against my father's house this day and have killed his sons, seventy men on one stone, and have made Abimelech, the son of his female servant, king over the leaders of Shechem, because he is your relative— ¹⁹ if you then have acted in good faith and integrity with Jerubbaal and with his house this day, then rejoice in Abimelech, and let him also rejoice in you. ²⁰ But if not, let fire come out from Abimelech and devour the leaders of Shechem and Beth-millo; and let fire come out from the leaders of Shechem and from Beth-millo and devour Abimelech." ²¹ And Jotham ran away and fled and went to Beer and lived there, because of Abimelech his brother.

The Downfall of Abimelech

²² Abimelech ruled over Israel three years. ²³ And God sent an evil spirit between Abimelech and the leaders of Shechem, and the leaders of Shechem dealt treacherously with Abimelech, ²⁴ that the violence done to the seventy sons of Jerubbaal might come, and their blood be laid on Abimelech their brother, who killed them, and on the men of Shechem, who strengthened his hands to kill his brothers. ²⁵ And the leaders of Shechem put men in ambush against him on the mountaintops, and they robbed all who passed by them along that way. And it was told to Abimelech.

²⁶ And Gaal the son of Ebed moved into Shechem with his relatives, and the leaders of Shechem put confidence in him. ²⁷ And they went out into the field and gathered the grapes from their vineyards and trod them and held a festival; and they went into the house of their god and ate and drank and reviled Abimelech. ²⁸ And Gaal the son of Ebed said, "Who is Abimelech, and who are we of Shechem, that we should serve him? Is he not the son of Jerubbaal, and is not Zebul his officer? Serve the men of Hamor the father of Shechem; but why should we serve him? ²⁹ Would that this people were under my hand! Then I would remove Abimelech. I would say to Abimelech, 'Increase your army, and come out.'"

³⁰ When Zebul the ruler of the city heard the words of Gaal the son of Ebed, his anger was kindled. ³¹ And he sent messengers to Abimelech secretly, saying, "Behold, Gaal the son of Ebed and his relatives have come to Shechem, and they are stirring up the city against you. ³² Now therefore, go by night, you and the people who are with you, and set an ambush in the field. ³³ Then in the morning, as soon as the sun is up, rise early and rush upon the city. And when he and the people who are with him come out against you, you may do to them as your hand finds to do."

³⁴ So Abimelech and all the men who were with him rose up by night and set an ambush against Shechem in four companies. ³⁵ And Gaal the son of Ebed went out and stood in the entrance of the gate of the city, and Abimelech and the people who were with him rose from the ambush. ³⁶ And when Gaal saw the people, he said to Zebul, "Look, people are coming down from the mountaintops!" And Zebul said to him, "You mistake the shadow of the mountains for men." ³⁷ Gaal spoke again and said, "Look, people are coming down from the center of the land, and one company is coming from the direction of the Diviners' Oak." ³⁸ Then Zebul said to him, "Where is your mouth now, you who said, 'Who is Abimelech, that we should serve him?' Are not these the people whom you despised? Go out now and fight with them." ³⁹ And Gaal went out at the head of the leaders of Shechem and fought with Abimelech. ⁴⁰ And Abimelech chased him, and he fled before him. And many fell wounded, up to the entrance of the gate. ⁴¹ And Abimelech lived at Arumah, and Zebul drove out Gaal and his relatives, so that they could not dwell at Shechem.

⁴² On the following day, the people went out into the field, and Abimelech was told. ⁴³ He took his people and divided them into three companies and set an ambush in the fields. And he looked and saw the people coming out of the city. So he rose against them and killed them. ⁴⁴ Abimelech and the company that was with him rushed forward and stood at the entrance of the gate of the city, while the two companies rushed upon all who were in the field and killed them. ⁴⁵ And Abimelech fought against the city all that day. He captured the city and killed the people who were in it, and he razed the city and sowed it with salt.

46 When all the leaders of the Tower of Shechem heard of it, they entered the stronghold of the house of El-berith. 47 Abimelech was told that all the leaders of the Tower of Shechem were gathered together. 48 And Abimelech went up to Mount Zalmon, he and all the people who were with him. And Abimelech took an axe in his hand and cut down a bundle of brushwood and took it up and laid it on his shoulder. And he said to the men who were with him, "What you have seen me do, hurry and do as I have done." 49 So every one of the people cut down his bundle and following Abimelech put it against the stronghold, and they set the stronghold on fire over them, so that all the people of the Tower of Shechem also died, about 1,000 men and women.

50 Then Abimelech went to Thebez and encamped against Thebez and captured it. 51 But there was a strong tower within the city, and all the men and women and all the leaders of the city fled to it and shut themselves in, and they went up to the roof of the tower. 52 And Abimelech came to the tower and fought against it and drew near to the door of the tower to burn it with fire. 53 And a certain woman threw an upper millstone on Abimelech's head and crushed his skull. 54 Then he called quickly to the young man his armor-bearer and said to him, "Draw your sword and kill me, lest they say of me, 'A woman killed him.'" And his young man thrust him through, and he died. 55 And when the men of Israel saw that Abimelech was dead, everyone departed to his home. 56 Thus God returned the evil of Abimelech, which he committed against his father in killing his seventy brothers. 57 And God also made all the evil of the men of Shechem return on their heads, and upon them came the curse of Jotham the son of Jerubbaal.

Tola and Jair

10 After Abimelech there arose to save Israel Tola the son of Puah, son of Dodo, a man of Issachar, and he lived at Shamir in the hill country of Ephraim. 2 And he judged Israel twenty-three years. Then he died and was buried at Shamir.

3 After him arose Jair the Gileadite, who judged Israel twenty-two years. 4 And he had thirty sons who rode on thirty donkeys, and they had thirty cities, called Havvoth-jair to this day, which are in the land of Gilead. 5 And Jair died and was buried in Kamon.

Further Disobedience and Oppression

6 The people of Israel again did what was evil in the sight of the LORD and served the Baals and the Ashtaroth, the gods of Syria, the gods of Sidon, the gods of Moab, the gods of the Ammonites, and the gods of the Philistines. And they forsook the LORD and did not serve him. 7 So the anger of the LORD was kindled against Israel, and he sold them into the hand of the Philistines and into the hand of the Ammonites, 8 and they crushed and oppressed the people of Israel that year. For eighteen years they oppressed all the people of Israel who were beyond the Jordan in the land of the Amorites, which is in Gilead. 9 And the Ammonites crossed the Jordan to fight also against Judah and against Benjamin and against the house of Ephraim, so that Israel was severely distressed.

10 And the people of Israel cried out to the LORD, saying, "We have sinned against you, because we have forsaken our God and have served the Baals." 11 And the LORD said to the people of Israel, "Did I not save you from the Egyptians and from the Amorites, from the Ammonites and from the Philistines? 12 The Sidonians also, and the Amalekites and the Maonites oppressed you, and you cried out to me, and I saved you out of their hand. 13 Yet you have forsaken me and served other gods; therefore I will save you no more. 14 Go and cry out to the gods whom you have chosen; let them save you in the time of your distress." 15 And the people of Israel said to the LORD, "We have sinned; do to us whatever seems good to you. Only please deliver us this day." 16 So they put away the foreign gods from among them and served the LORD, and he became impatient over the misery of Israel.

17 Then the Ammonites were called to arms, and they encamped in Gilead. And the people of Israel came together, and they encamped at Mizpah. 18 And the people, the leaders of Gilead, said one to another, "Who is the man who will begin to fight against the Ammonites? He shall be head over all the inhabitants of Gilead."

Jephthah Delivers Israel

11 Now Jephthah the Gileadite was a mighty warrior, but he was the son of a prostitute. Gilead was the father of Jephthah. ² And Gilead's wife also bore him sons. And when his wife's sons grew up, they drove Jephthah out and said to him, "You shall not have an inheritance in our father's house, for you are the son of another woman." ³ Then Jephthah fled from his brothers and lived in the land of Tob, and worthless fellows collected around Jephthah and went out with him.

⁴ After a time the Ammonites made war against Israel. ⁵ And when the Ammonites made war against Israel, the elders of Gilead went to bring Jephthah from the land of Tob. ⁶ And they said to Jephthah, "Come and be our leader, that we may fight against the Ammonites." ⁷ But Jephthah said to the elders of Gilead, "Did you not hate me and drive me out of my father's house? Why have you come to me now when you are in distress?" ⁸ And the elders of Gilead said to Jephthah, "That is why we have turned to you now, that you may go with us and fight against the Ammonites and be our head over all the inhabitants of Gilead." ⁹ Jephthah said to the elders of Gilead, "If you bring me home again to fight against the Ammonites, and the LORD gives them over to me, I will be your head." ¹⁰ And the elders of Gilead said to Jephthah, "The LORD will be witness between us, if we do not do as you say." ¹¹ So Jephthah went with the elders of Gilead, and the people made him head and leader over them. And Jephthah spoke all his words before the LORD at Mizpah.

¹² Then Jephthah sent messengers to the king of the Ammonites and said, "What do you have against me, that you have come to me to fight against my land?" ¹³ And the king of the Ammonites answered the messengers of Jephthah, "Because Israel on coming up from Egypt took away my land, from the Arnon to the Jabbok and to the Jordan; now therefore restore it peaceably." ¹⁴ Jephthah again sent messengers to the king of the Ammonites ¹⁵ and said to him, "Thus says Jephthah: Israel did not take away the land of Moab or the land of the Ammonites, ¹⁶ but when they came up from Egypt, Israel went through the wilderness to the Red Sea and came to Kadesh. ¹⁷ Israel then sent messengers to the king of Edom, saying, 'Please let us pass through your land,' but the king of Edom would not listen. And they sent also to the king of Moab, but he would not consent. So Israel remained at Kadesh.

¹⁸ "Then they journeyed through the wilderness and went around the land of Edom and the land of Moab and arrived on the east side of the land of Moab and camped on the other side of the Arnon. But they did not enter the territory of Moab, for the Arnon

was the boundary of Moab. ¹⁹ Israel then sent messengers to Sihon king of the Amorites, king of Heshbon, and Israel said to him, 'Please let us pass through your land to our country,' ²⁰ but Sihon did not trust Israel to pass through his territory, so Sihon gathered all his people together and encamped at Jahaz and fought with Israel. ²¹ And the LORD, the God of Israel, gave Sihon and all his people into the hand of Israel, and they defeated them. So Israel took possession of all the land of the Amorites, who inhabited that country. ²² And they took possession of all the territory of the Amorites from the Arnon to the Jabbok and from the wilderness to the Jordan. ²³ So then the LORD, the God of Israel, dispossessed the Amorites from before his people Israel; and are you to take possession of them? ²⁴ Will you not possess what Chemosh your god gives you to possess? And all that the LORD our God has dispossessed before us, we will possess. ²⁵ Now are you any better than Balak the son of Zippor, king of Moab? Did he ever contend against Israel, or did he ever go to war with them? ²⁶ While Israel lived in Heshbon and its villages, and in Aroer and its villages, and in all the cities that are on the banks of the Arnon, 300 years, why did you not deliver them within that time? ²⁷ I therefore have not sinned against you, and you do me wrong by making war on me. The LORD, the Judge, decide this day between the people

---

GETTING THE MESSAGE

Foolish vows. When Jephthah realized that his foolish vow could result in the death of his daughter (11:29–40), he could have broken the vow. For whatever reason, however, he chose not to break the vow.

---

of Israel and the people of Ammon." ²⁸ But the king of the Ammonites did not listen to the words of Jephthah that he sent to him.

Jephthah's Tragic Vow

²⁹ Then the Spirit of the LORD was upon Jephthah, and he passed through Gilead and Manasseh and passed on to Mizpah of Gilead, and from Mizpah of Gilead he passed on to the Ammonites. ³⁰ And Jephthah made a vow to the LORD and said, "If you will give the Ammonites into my hand, ³¹ then whatever comes out from the doors of my house to meet me when I return in peace from the Ammonites shall be the LORD's, and I will offer it up for a burnt offering." ³² So Jephthah crossed over to the Ammonites to fight against them, and the LORD gave them into his hand. ³³ And he struck them from Aroer to the neighborhood of Minnith, twenty cities, and as far as Abel-keramim, with a great blow. So the Ammonites were subdued before the people of Israel.

³⁴ Then Jephthah came to his home at Mizpah. And behold, his daughter came out to meet him with tambourines and with dances. She was his only child; besides her he had neither son nor daughter. ³⁵ And as soon as he saw her, he tore his clothes and said, "Alas, my daughter! You have brought me very low, and you have become the cause of great trouble to me. For I have opened my mouth to the LORD, and I cannot take back my vow." ³⁶ And she said to him, "My father, you have opened your mouth to the LORD; do to me according to what has gone out of your mouth, now that the LORD has avenged you on your enemies, on the Ammonites." ³⁷ So she said to her father, "Let this thing be done for me: leave me alone two months, that I may go up and down on the mountains and weep for my virginity, I and my companions." ³⁸ So he said, "Go." Then he sent her away for two months, and she departed, she and her companions, and wept for her virginity on the mountains. ³⁹ And at the end of two months, she returned to her father, who did with her according to his vow that he had made. She had never known a man, and it became a custom in Israel ⁴⁰ that the daughters of Israel went year by year to lament the daughter of Jephthah the Gileadite four days in the year.

Jephthah's Conflict with Ephraim

12 The men of Ephraim were called to arms, and they crossed to Zaphon and said to Jephthah, "Why did you cross over to fight against the Ammonites and did not call us to go with you? We will burn your house over you with fire." ² And Jephthah said to them, "I and my people had a great dispute with the Ammonites, and when I called you, you did not save me from their hand. ³ And when I saw that you would not save me, I took my life in my hand and crossed over against the Ammonites, and the LORD gave them into my hand. Why then have you come up to me this day to fight against me?" ⁴ Then Jephthah gathered all the men of Gilead and fought with Ephraim. And the men of Gilead struck Ephraim, because they said, "You are fugitives of Ephraim, you Gileadites, in the midst of Ephraim and Manasseh." ⁵ And the Gileadites captured the fords of the Jordan against the Ephraimites. And when any of the fugitives of Ephraim

said, "Let me go over," the men of Gilead said to him, "Are you an Ephraimite?" When he said, "No," **6** they said to him, "Then say Shibboleth," and he said, "Sibboleth," for he could not pronounce it right. Then they seized him and slaughtered him at the fords of the Jordan. At that time 42,000 of the Ephraimites fell.

7 Jephthah judged Israel six years. Then Jephthah the Gileadite died and was buried in his city in Gilead.

Ibzan, Elon, and Abdon

8 After him Ibzan of Bethlehem judged Israel. **9** He had thirty sons, and thirty daughters he gave in marriage outside his clan, and thirty daughters he brought in from outside for his sons. And he judged Israel seven years. **10** Then Ibzan died and was buried at Bethlehem.

11 After him Elon the Zebulunite judged Israel, and he judged Israel ten years. **12** Then Elon the Zebulunite died and was buried at Aijalon in the land of Zebulun.

13 After him Abdon the son of Hillel the Pirathonite judged Israel. **14** He had forty sons and thirty grandsons, who rode on seventy donkeys, and he judged Israel eight years. **15** Then Abdon the son of Hillel the Pirathonite died and was buried at Pirathon in the land of Ephraim, in the hill country of the Amalekites.

The Birth of Samson

13 And the people of Israel again did what was evil in the sight of the LORD, so the LORD gave them into the hand of the Philistines for forty years.

2 There was a certain man of Zorah, of the tribe of the Danites, whose name was Manoah. And his wife was barren and had no children. **3** And the angel of the LORD appeared to the woman and said to her, "Behold, you are barren and have not borne children, but you shall conceive and bear a son. **4** Therefore be careful and drink no wine or strong drink, and eat nothing unclean, **5** for behold, you shall conceive and bear a son. No razor shall come upon his head, for the child shall be a Nazirite to God from the womb, and he shall begin to save Israel from the hand of the Philistines." **6** Then the woman came and told her husband, "A man of God came to me, and his appearance was like the appearance of the angel of God, very

awesome. I did not ask him where he was from, and he did not tell me his name, **7** but he said to me, 'Behold, you shall conceive and bear a son. So then drink no wine or strong drink, and eat nothing unclean, for the child shall be a Nazirite to God from the womb to the day of his death.'"

8 Then Manoah prayed to the LORD and said, "O Lord, please let the man of God whom you sent come again to us and teach us what we are to do with the child who will be born." **9** And God listened to the voice of Manoah, and the angel of God came again to the woman as she sat in the field. But Manoah her husband was not with her. **10** So

> ### GETTING THE MESSAGE
>
> **Is it "Shibboleth" or "Sibboleth"?**
> The Gileadites came up with a clever test to distinguish between their friends and their enemies (12:1–6). Knowing that the rival Ephraimites spoke a slightly different dialect, they asked them to say the word "Shibboleth." The Ephraimites pronounced the word with an "s" rather than a "sh" sound, thus making them easy to spot. Today, a "shibboleth" is a word or expression of belief that "insiders" use to determine who is an "outsider." Thus, if a person doesn't express his beliefs using just the right words, he may be rejected by a particular group.

the woman ran quickly and told her husband, "Behold, the man who came to me the other day has appeared to me." **11** And Manoah arose and went after his wife and came to the man and said to him, "Are you the man who spoke to this woman?" And he said, "I am." **12** And Manoah said, "Now when your words come true, what is to be the child's manner of life, and what is his mission?" **13** And the angel of the LORD said to Manoah, "Of all that I said to the woman let her be careful. **14** She may not eat of anything that comes from the vine, neither let her drink wine or strong drink, or eat any unclean thing. All that I commanded her let her observe."

15 Manoah said to the angel of the LORD, "Please let us detain you and prepare a young goat for you." **16** And the angel of the LORD said to Manoah, "If you detain me, I will not eat of your food. But if you prepare a burnt offering, then offer it to the LORD." (For Manoah did not know that he was the angel of the LORD.) **17** And Manoah said to the angel of the LORD, "What is your name, so that, when your words come true, we may honor you?" **18** And the angel of the LORD said to him, "Why do you ask my name, seeing it is wonderful?" **19** So Manoah took the young

PROFILE
SAMSON

Samson was the twelfth and final judge of Israel. God raised him up to deliver Israel from the Philistines. Possessing great strength, he often battled the Philistines single-handedly. Samson was a life-long Nazirite, but he broke every one of his vows. He made particularly bad decisions regarding his relationships with women. This is most evident in his relationship with Delilah, to whom he revealed the secret of his strength. Paid by the Philistines to seduce Samson, Delilah cut off his hair while he slept. He was attacked and blinded by a group of Philistines lying in wait, and taken as their prisoner. His final feat of strength was to bring down a Philistine temple, killing about 3,000 Philistines along with himself. Despite Samson's sinful life and continued unfaithfulness, God used him to save Israel.

KEY REFERENCE: JUDGES 15:14–17

goat with the grain offering, and offered it on the rock to the LORD, to the one who works wonders, and Manoah and his wife were watching. **20** And when the flame went up toward heaven from the altar, the angel of the LORD went up in the flame of the altar. Now Manoah and his wife were watching, and they fell on their faces to the ground. **21** The angel of the LORD appeared no more to Manoah and to his wife. Then Manoah knew that he was the angel of the LORD. **22** And Manoah said to his wife, "We shall surely die, for we have seen God." **23** But his

wife said to him, "If the LORD had meant to kill us, he would not have accepted a burnt offering and a grain offering at our hands, or shown us all these things, or now announced to us such things as these." **24** And the woman bore a son and called his name Samson. And the young man grew, and the LORD blessed him. **25** And the Spirit of the LORD began to stir him in Mahaneh-dan, between Zorah and Eshtaol.

Samson's Marriage

14 Samson went down to Timnah, and at Timnah he saw one of the daughters of the Philistines. **2** Then he came up and told his father and mother, "I saw one of the daughters of the Philistines at Timnah. Now get her for me as my wife." **3** But his father and mother said to him, "Is there not a woman among the daughters of your relatives, or among all our people, that you must

> **GETTING THE MESSAGE**
>
> **Riddles** were as popular in ancient Near Eastern cultures as they are today. Samson's riddle about the lion and the honey (14:5–18) is the best example of a riddle in Scripture.

go to take a wife from the uncircumcised Philistines?" But Samson said to his father, "Get her for me, for she is right in my eyes." **4** His father and mother did not know that it was from the LORD, for he was seeking an opportunity against the Philistines. At that time the Philistines ruled over Israel. **5** Then Samson went down with his father and mother to Timnah, and they came to the vineyards of Timnah. And behold, a young lion came toward him roaring. **6** Then the Spirit of the LORD rushed upon him, and although he had nothing in his hand, he tore the lion in pieces as one tears a young goat. But he did not tell his father or his mother what he had done. **7** Then he went down and talked with the woman, and she was right in Samson's eyes. **8** After some days he returned to take her. And he turned aside to see the carcass of the lion, and behold, there was a swarm of bees in the body of the lion, and honey. **9** He scraped it out into his hands and went on, eating as he went. And he came to his father and mother and gave some to them, and they ate. But he did not tell them that he had scraped the honey from the carcass of the lion.

10 His father went down to the woman, and Samson prepared a feast there, for so the young men used to do. **11** As soon as the people saw him, they brought thirty companions to be with him. **12** And Samson said to them, "Let me now put a riddle to you. If you can tell me what it is, within the seven days of the feast, and find it out, then I will give you thirty linen garments and thirty changes of clothes, **13** but if you cannot tell me what it is, then you shall give me thirty linen garments and thirty changes of clothes." And they said to him, "Put your riddle, that we may hear it." **14** And he said to them,

"Out of the eater came something to eat.
Out of the strong came something
    sweet."

And in three days they could not solve the riddle.

15 On the fourth day they said to Samson's wife, "Entice your husband to tell us what the riddle is, lest we burn you and your father's house with fire. Have you invited us here to impoverish us?" **16** And Samson's wife wept over him and said, "You only hate me; you do not love me. You have put a riddle to my people, and you have not told me what it is." And he said to her, "Behold, I have not told my father nor my mother, and shall I tell you?" **17** She wept before him the seven days that their feast lasted, and on the seventh day he told her, because she pressed him hard. Then she told the riddle to her people. **18** And the men of the city said to him on the seventh day before the sun went down,

"What is sweeter than honey?
What is stronger than a lion?"

And he said to them,

"If you had not plowed with my heifer,
you would not have found out my
    riddle."

19 And the Spirit of the LORD rushed upon him, and he went down to Ashkelon and struck down thirty men of the town and took their spoil and gave the garments to those who had told the riddle. In hot anger

he went back to his father's house. **20** And Samson's wife was given to his companion, who had been his best man.

Samson Defeats the Philistines

15 After some days, at the time of wheat harvest, Samson went to visit his wife with a young goat. And he said, "I will go in to my wife in the chamber." But her father would not allow him to go in. **2** And her father said, "I really thought that you utterly hated her, so I gave her to your companion. Is not her younger sister more beautiful than she? Please take her instead." **3** And Samson said to them, "This time I shall be innocent in regard to the Philistines, when I do them harm." **4** So Samson went and caught 300 foxes and took torches. And

---

> **GETTING THE MESSAGE**

Were the "foxes" actually jackals?
The same Hebrew word can mean either "fox" or "jackal." While foxes usually travel alone, jackals can often be seen roaming in small packs around nightfall. They can be instantly recognized by their wailing, even if they are not seen. It would have been easier for Samson to round up 300 jackals than to catch 300 foxes (15:4), though neither task would have been easy!

---

he turned them tail to tail and put a torch between each pair of tails. **5** And when he had set fire to the torches, he let the foxes go into the standing grain of the Philistines and set fire to the stacked grain and the standing grain, as well as the olive orchards. **6** Then the Philistines said, "Who has done this?" And they said, "Samson, the son-in-law of the Timnite, because he has taken his wife and given her to his companion." And the Philistines came up and burned her and her father with fire. **7** And Samson said to them, "If this is what you do, I swear I will be avenged on you, and after that I will quit." **8** And he struck them hip and thigh with a great blow, and he went down and stayed in the cleft of the rock of Etam.

9 Then the Philistines came up and encamped in Judah and made a raid on Lehi. **10** And the men of Judah said, "Why have you come up against us?" They said, "We have come up to bind Samson, to do to him as he did to us." **11** Then 3,000 men of Judah went down to the cleft of the rock of Etam, and said to Samson, "Do you not know that the Philistines are rulers over us? What then is this that you have done to us?" And he said to them, "As they did to me, so have I done to them." **12** And they said to him, "We have come down to bind you, that we may give you into the hands of the Philistines." And Samson said to them, "Swear to me that you will not attack me yourselves." **13** They said to him, "No; we will only bind you and give you into their hands. We will surely not kill you." So they bound him with two new ropes and brought him up from the rock.

GETTING THE MESSAGE

City gates (16:3) in Bible times were often very elaborate. Many of them were two stories high or even higher. The actual opening would be narrow, with guardrooms on each side. The gateposts were anchored deep in the ground to support the doors. City gates would often have multiple doors and entrances as well as sharp turns. These were designed to slow down enemies if they tried to get through the gate. They were also the place where business transactions and judicial decisions were made.

14 When he came to Lehi, the Philistines came shouting to meet him. Then the Spirit of the LORD rushed upon him, and the ropes that were on his arms became as flax that has caught fire, and his bonds melted off his hands. **15** And he found a fresh jawbone of a donkey, and put out his hand and took it, and with it he struck 1,000 men. **16** And Samson said,

"With the jawbone of a donkey,
     heaps upon heaps,
with the jawbone of a donkey
     have I struck down a thousand men."

17 As soon as he had finished speaking, he threw away the jawbone out of his hand. And that place was called Ramath-lehi.[1]

18 And he was very thirsty, and he called upon the LORD and said, "You have granted this great salvation by the hand of your servant, and shall I now die of thirst and fall into the hands of the uncircumcised?" **19** And God split open the hollow place that is at Lehi, and water came out from it. And when he drank, his spirit returned, and he revived. Therefore the name of it was called En-hakkore;[2] it is at Lehi to this day. **20** And he judged Israel in the days of the Philistines twenty years.

Samson and Delilah

16 Samson went to Gaza, and there he saw a prostitute, and he went in to her. **2** The Gazites were told, "Samson has come here." And they surrounded the place and set an ambush for him all night at the gate of the city. They kept quiet all night, saying, "Let us wait till the light of the morning; then we will kill him." **3** But Samson lay till midnight, and at midnight he arose and took hold of the doors of the gate of the city and the two posts, and pulled them up, bar and all, and put them on his shoulders and carried them to the top of the hill that is in front of Hebron.

4 After this he loved a woman in the Valley of Sorek, whose name was Delilah. **5** And the lords of the Philistines came up to her and said to her, "Seduce him, and see where his great strength lies, and by what means we may overpower him, that we may bind him to humble him. And we will each give you 1,100 pieces of silver." **6** So Delilah said to Samson, "Please tell me where your great strength lies, and how you might be bound, that one could subdue you."

7 Samson said to her, "If they bind me with seven fresh bowstrings that have not been dried, then I shall become weak and be like any other man." **8** Then the lords of the Philistines brought up to her seven fresh bowstrings that had not been dried, and she bound him with them. **9** Now she had men lying in ambush in an inner chamber. And she said to him, "The Philistines are upon you, Samson!" But he snapped the bowstrings, as a thread of flax snaps when it touches the fire. So the secret of his strength was not known.

10 Then Delilah said to Samson, "Behold, you have mocked me and told me lies. Please tell me how you might be bound." **11** And he said to her, "If they bind me with

[1] *Ramath-lehi* means *the hill of the jawbone* [2] *En-hakkore* means *the spring of him who called*

new ropes that have not been used, then I shall become weak and be like any other man." ¹² So Delilah took new ropes and bound him with them and said to him, "The Philistines are upon you, Samson!" And the men lying in ambush were in an inner chamber. But he snapped the ropes off his arms like a thread.

¹³ Then Delilah said to Samson, "Until now you have mocked me and told me lies. Tell me how you might be bound." And he said to her, "If you weave the seven locks of my head with the web and fasten it tight with the pin, then I shall become weak and be like any other man." ¹⁴ So while he slept, Delilah took the seven locks of his head and wove them into the web. And she made them tight with the pin and said to him, "The Philistines are upon you, Samson!" But he awoke from his sleep and pulled away the pin, the loom, and the web.

¹⁵ And she said to him, "How can you say, 'I love you,' when your heart is not with me? You have mocked me these three times, and you have not told me where your great strength lies." ¹⁶ And when she pressed him hard with her words day after day, and urged him, his soul was vexed to death. ¹⁷ And he told her all his heart, and said to her, "A razor has never come upon my head, for I have been a Nazirite to God from my mother's womb. If my head is shaved, then my strength will leave me, and I shall become weak and be like any other man."

¹⁸ When Delilah saw that he had told her all his heart, she sent and called the lords of the Philistines, saying, "Come up again, for he has told me all his heart." Then the lords of the Philistines came up to her and brought the money in their hands. ¹⁹ She made him sleep on her knees. And she called a man and had him shave off the seven locks of his head. Then she began to torment him, and his strength left him. ²⁰ And she said, "The Philistines are upon you, Samson!" And he awoke from his sleep and said, "I will go out as at other times and shake myself free." But he did not know that the LORD had left him. ²¹ And the Philistines seized him and gouged out his eyes and brought him down to Gaza and bound him with bronze shackles. And he ground at the mill in the prison. ²² But the hair of his head began to grow again after it had been shaved.

The Death of Samson

²³ Now the lords of the Philistines gathered to offer a great sacrifice to Dagon their god and to rejoice, and they said, "Our god has given Samson our enemy into our hand." ²⁴ And when the people saw him, they praised their god. For they said, "Our god has given our enemy into our hand, the ravager of our country, who has killed many of us." ²⁵ And when their hearts were merry, they said, "Call Samson, that he may entertain us." So they called Samson out of the prison, and he entertained them. They made him stand between the pillars. ²⁶ And Samson said to the young man who held him by the hand, "Let me feel the pillars on which the house rests, that I may lean against them." ²⁷ Now the house was full of men and women. All the lords of the Philistines were there, and on the roof

GETTING THE MESSAGE

Blinding a prisoner and forcing him to grind grain at a mill (16:21) was a common form of punishment in the ancient Near East. This is one more example of how the Bible presents an accurate record of the events of its day.

there were about 3,000 men and women, who looked on while Samson entertained. ²⁸ Then Samson called to the LORD and said, "O Lord GOD, please remember me and please strengthen me only this once, O God, that I may be avenged on the Philistines for my two eyes." ²⁹ And Samson grasped the two middle pillars on which the house rested, and he leaned his weight against them, his right hand on the one and his left hand on the other. ³⁰ And Samson said, "Let me die with the Philistines." Then he bowed with all his strength, and the house fell upon the lords and upon all the people who were in it. So the dead whom he killed at his death were more than those whom he had killed during his life. ³¹ Then his brothers and all his family came down and took him and brought him up and buried him between Zorah and Eshtaol in the tomb of Manoah his father. He had judged Israel twenty years.

Micah and the Levite

17 There was a man of the hill country of Ephraim, whose name was Micah. [2] And he said to his mother, "The 1,100 pieces of silver that were taken from you, about which you uttered a curse, and also spoke it in my ears, behold, the silver is with me; I took it." And his mother said, "Blessed be my son by the LORD." [3] And he restored the 1,100 pieces of silver to his mother. And his mother said, "I dedicate the silver to the LORD from my hand for my son, to make a carved image and a metal image. Now therefore I will restore it to you." [4] So when he restored the money to his mother, his mother took 200 pieces of silver and gave it to the silversmith, who made it into a carved image and a metal image. And it was in the house of Micah. [5] And the man

> ### GETTING THE MESSAGE
>
> **Laish** was about 25 miles (40 km) north of the Sea of Galilee. The Danites would have traveled about a hundred miles (161 km) to reach the city (18:7). After they invaded and destroyed Laish, the city was renamed Dan (18:29). For many years thereafter, this city would be considered the northern border of Israel. The nation was often described as extending "from Dan to Beersheba" (20:1).

Micah had a shrine, and he made an ephod and household gods, and ordained one of his sons, who became his priest. [6] In those days there was no king in Israel. Everyone did what was right in his own eyes.

[7] Now there was a young man of Bethlehem in Judah, of the family of Judah, who was a Levite, and he sojourned there. [8] And the man departed from the town of Bethlehem in Judah to sojourn where he could find a place. And as he journeyed, he came to the hill country of Ephraim to the house of Micah. [9] And Micah said to him, "Where do you come from?" And he said to him, "I am a Levite of Bethlehem in Judah, and I am going to sojourn where I may find a place." [10] And Micah said to him, "Stay with me, and be to me a father and a priest, and I will give you ten pieces of silver a year and a suit of clothes and your living." And the

Levite went in. [11] And the Levite was content to dwell with the man, and the young man became to him like one of his sons. [12] And Micah ordained the Levite, and the young man became his priest, and was in the house of Micah. [13] Then Micah said, "Now I know that the LORD will prosper me, because I have a Levite as priest."

Danites Take the Levite and the Idol

18 In those days there was no king in Israel. And in those days the tribe of the people of Dan was seeking for itself an inheritance to dwell in, for until then no inheritance among the tribes of Israel had fallen to them. [2] So the people of Dan sent five able men from the whole number of their tribe, from Zorah and from Eshtaol, to spy out the land and to explore it. And they said to them, "Go and explore the land." And they came to the hill country of Ephraim, to the house of Micah, and lodged there. [3] When they were by the house of Micah, they recognized the voice of the young Levite. And they turned aside and said to him, "Who brought you here? What are you doing in this place? What is your business here?" [4] And he said to them, "This is how Micah dealt with me: he has hired me, and I have become his priest." [5] And they said to him, "Inquire of God, please, that we may know whether the journey on which we are setting out will succeed." [6] And the priest said to them, "Go in peace. The journey on which you go is under the eye of the LORD."

[7] Then the five men departed and came to Laish and saw the people who were there, how they lived in security, after the manner of the Sidonians, quiet and unsuspecting, lacking nothing that is in the earth and possessing wealth, and how they were far from the Sidonians and had no dealings with anyone. [8] And when they came to their brothers at Zorah and Eshtaol, their brothers said to them, "What do you report?" [9] They said, "Arise, and let us go up against them, for we have seen the land, and behold, it is very good. And will you do nothing? Do not be slow to go, to enter in and possess the land. [10] As soon as you go, you will come to an unsuspecting people. The land is spacious, for God has given it into your hands, a place where there is no lack of anything that is in the earth."

[11] So 600 men of the tribe of Dan, armed with weapons of war, set out from Zorah and Eshtaol, [12] and went up and encamped at Kiriath-jearim in Judah. On this account that place is called Mahaneh-dan[1] to this day; behold, it is west of Kiriath-jearim. [13] And they passed on from there to the hill country of Ephraim, and came to the house of Micah.

[14] Then the five men who had gone to scout out the country of Laish said to their brothers, "Do you know that in these houses there are an ephod, household gods, a carved image, and a metal image? Now therefore consider what you will do." [15] And they turned aside there and came to the house of the young Levite, at the home of Micah, and asked him about his welfare. [16] Now the 600 men of the Danites, armed with their weapons of war, stood by the entrance of the gate. [17] And the five men who had gone to scout out the land went up and entered and took the carved image, the ephod, the household gods, and the metal image, while the priest stood by the entrance of the gate with the 600 men armed with weapons of war. [18] And when these went into Micah's house and took the carved image, the ephod, the household gods, and the metal image, the priest said to them, "What are you doing?" [19] And they said to him, "Keep quiet; put your hand on your mouth and come with us and be to us a father and a priest. Is it better for you to be priest to the house of one man, or to be priest to a tribe and clan in Israel?" [20] And the priest's heart was glad. He took the ephod and the household gods and the carved image and went along with the people.

[21] So they turned and departed, putting the little ones and the livestock and the goods in front of them. [22] When they had gone a distance from the home of Micah, the men who were in the houses near Micah's house were called out, and they overtook the people of Dan. [23] And they shouted to the people of Dan, who turned around and said to Micah, "What is the matter with you, that you come with such a company?" [24] And he said, "You take my gods that I made and the priest, and go away, and what have I left? How then do you ask me, 'What is the matter with you?'" [25] And the people of Dan said to him, "Do not

let your voice be heard among us, lest angry fellows fall upon you, and you lose your life with the lives of your household." [26] Then the people of Dan went their way. And when Micah saw that they were too strong for him, he turned and went back to his home.

[27] But the people of Dan took what Micah had made, and the priest who belonged to him, and they came to Laish, to a people quiet and unsuspecting, and struck them with the edge of the sword and burned the city with fire. [28] And there was no deliverer because it was far from Sidon, and they had no dealings with anyone. It was in the valley that belongs to Beth-rehob. Then they rebuilt the city and lived in it. [29] And they named the city Dan, after the name of Dan their ancestor, who was born to Israel; but the name of the city was Laish at the first. [30] And the people of Dan set up the carved image for themselves, and Jonathan the son of Gershom, son of Moses, and his sons were priests to the tribe of the Danites until the day of the captivity of the land. [31] So they set up Micah's carved image that he made, as long as the house of God was at Shiloh.

A Levite and His Concubine

19 In those days, when there was no king in Israel, a certain Levite was sojourning in the remote parts of the hill country of Ephraim, who took to himself a concubine from Bethlehem in Judah. [2] And his concubine was unfaithful to him, and she went away from him to her father's house at Bethlehem in Judah, and was there some four months. [3] Then her husband arose and went after her, to speak kindly to her and bring her back. He had with him his servant and a couple of donkeys. And she brought him into her father's house. And when the girl's father saw him, he came with joy to meet him. [4] And his father-in-law, the girl's father, made him stay, and he remained with him three days. So they ate and drank and spent the night there. [5] And on the fourth day they arose early in the morning, and he prepared to go, but the girl's father said to his son-in-law, "Strengthen your heart with a morsel of bread, and after that you may go." [6] So the two of them sat and ate and drank together. And the girl's father said to the man, "Be pleased to spend the night, and let your heart be merry." [7] And

---

[1] Mahaneh-dan means camp of Dan

when the man rose up to go, his father-in-law pressed him, till he spent the night there again. ⁸ And on the fifth day he arose early in the morning to depart. And the girl's father said, "Strengthen your heart and wait until the day declines." So they ate, both of them. ⁹ And when the man and his concubine and his servant rose up to depart, his father-in-law, the girl's father, said to him, "Behold, now the day has waned toward evening. Please, spend the night. Behold, the day draws to its close. Lodge here and let your heart be merry, and tomorrow you shall arise early in the morning for your journey, and go home."

¹⁰ But the man would not spend the night. He rose up and departed and arrived opposite Jebus (that is, Jerusalem). He had with him a couple of saddled donkeys, and his concubine was with him. ¹¹ When they were

> ### GETTING THE MESSAGE
>
> **Jebus** (19:11) was the name of Jerusalem during this time because it was still under the control of the Jebusites. It would stay in the hands of the Jebusites until David conquered it and claimed it for Israel (2 Sam. 5:6–10).

near Jebus, the day was nearly over, and the servant said to his master, "Come now, let us turn aside to this city of the Jebusites and spend the night in it." ¹² And his master said to him, "We will not turn aside into the city of foreigners, who do not belong to the people of Israel, but we will pass on to Gibeah." ¹³ And he said to his young man, "Come and let us draw near to one of these places and spend the night at Gibeah or at Ramah." ¹⁴ So they passed on and went their way. And the sun went down on them near Gibeah, which belongs to Benjamin, ¹⁵ and they turned aside there, to go in and spend the night at Gibeah. And he went in and sat down in the open square of the city, for no one took them into his house to spend the night.

¹⁶ And behold, an old man was coming from his work in the field at evening. The man was from the hill country of Ephraim, and he was sojourning in Gibeah. The men of the place were Benjaminites. ¹⁷ And he lifted up his eyes and saw the traveler in the open square of the city. And the old man said, "Where are you going? And where do you come from?" ¹⁸ And he said to him, "We are passing from Bethlehem in Judah to the remote parts of the hill country of Ephraim, from which I come. I went to Bethlehem in Judah, and I am going to the house of the Lord, but no one has taken me into his house. ¹⁹ We have straw and feed for our donkeys, with bread and wine for me and your female servant and the young man with your servants. There is no lack of anything." ²⁰ And the old man said, "Peace be to you; I will care for all your wants. Only, do not spend the night in the square." ²¹ So he brought him into his house and gave the donkeys feed. And they washed their feet, and ate and drank.

Gibeah's Crime

²² As they were making their hearts merry, behold, the men of the city, worthless fellows, surrounded the house, beating on the door. And they said to the old man, the master of the house, "Bring out the man who came into your house, that we may know him." ²³ And the man, the master of the house, went out to them and said to them, "No, my brothers, do not act so wickedly; since this man has come into my house, do not do this vile thing. ²⁴ Behold, here are my virgin daughter and his concubine. Let me bring them out now. Violate them and do with them what seems good to you, but against this man do not do this outrageous thing." ²⁵ But the men would not listen to him. So the man seized his concubine and made her go out to them. And they knew her and abused her all night until the morning. And as the dawn began to break, they let her go. ²⁶ And as morning appeared, the woman came and fell down at the door of the man's house where her master was, until it was light.

²⁷ And her master rose up in the morning, and when he opened the doors of the house and went out to go on his way, behold, there was his concubine lying at the door of the house, with her hands on the threshold. ²⁸ He said to her, "Get up, let us be going." But there was no answer. Then he put her on the donkey, and the man rose up and went away to his home. ²⁹ And when he entered his house, he took a knife, and taking hold of his

concubine he divided her, limb by limb, into twelve pieces, and sent her throughout all the territory of Israel. **30** And all who saw it said, "Such a thing has never happened or been seen from the day that the people of Israel came up out of the land of Egypt until this day; consider it, take counsel, and speak."

Israel's War with the Tribe of Benjamin

20 Then all the people of Israel came out, from Dan to Beersheba, including the land of Gilead, and the congregation assembled as one man to the LORD at Mizpah. **2** And the chiefs of all the people, of all the tribes of Israel, presented themselves in the assembly of the people of God, 400,000 men on foot that drew the sword. **3** (Now the people of Benjamin heard that the people of Israel had gone up to Mizpah.) And the people of Israel said, "Tell us, how did this evil happen?" **4** And the Levite, the husband of the woman who was murdered, answered and said, "I came to Gibeah that belongs to Benjamin, I and my concubine, to spend the night. **5** And the leaders of Gibeah rose against me and surrounded the house against me by night. They meant to kill me, and they violated my concubine, and she is dead. **6** So I took hold of my concubine and cut her in pieces and sent her throughout all the country of the inheritance of Israel, for they have committed abomination and outrage in Israel. **7** Behold, you people of Israel, all of you, give your advice and counsel here."

8 And all the people arose as one man, saying, "None of us will go to his tent, and none of us will return to his house. **9** But now this is what we will do to Gibeah: we will go up against it by lot, **10** and we will take ten men of a hundred throughout all the tribes of Israel, and a hundred of a thousand, and a thousand of ten thousand, to bring provisions for the people, that when they come they may repay Gibeah of Benjamin, for all the outrage that they have committed in Israel." **11** So all the men of Israel gathered against the city, united as one man.

12 And the tribes of Israel sent men through all the tribe of Benjamin, saying, "What evil is this that has taken place among you? **13** Now therefore give up the men, the worthless fellows in Gibeah, that we may put them to death and purge evil from Israel." But the Benjaminites would not

listen to the voice of their brothers, the people of Israel. **14** Then the people of Benjamin came together out of the cities to Gibeah to go out to battle against the people of Israel. **15** And the people of Benjamin mustered out of their cities on that day 26,000 men who drew the sword, besides the inhabitants of Gibeah, who mustered 700 chosen men. **16** Among all these were 700 chosen men who were left-handed; every one could sling a stone at a hair and not miss. **17** And the men of Israel, apart from Benjamin, mustered 400,000 men who drew the sword; all these were men of war.

18 The people of Israel arose and went up to Bethel and inquired of God, "Who shall go up first for us to fight against the people of Benjamin?" And the LORD said, "Judah shall go up first."

> ### GETTING THE MESSAGE
>
> **Slings** (20:16) were weapons made of two long straps, usually either leather or cloth. These were attached to a wider pocket in the middle, where the thrower would place a rock or some other object. The sling was then swung above the head until one of the straps was let go, releasing the rock. Slings were designed to incapacitate the enemy. A fellow soldier with a sword or spear could then deliver the fatal blow.

19 Then the people of Israel rose in the morning and encamped against Gibeah. **20** And the men of Israel went out to fight against Benjamin, and the men of Israel drew up the battle line against them at Gibeah. **21** The people of Benjamin came out of Gibeah and destroyed on that day 22,000 men of the Israelites. **22** But the people, the men of Israel, took courage, and again formed the battle line in the same place where they had formed it on the first day. **23** And the people of Israel went up and wept before the LORD until the evening. And they inquired of the LORD, "Shall we again draw near to fight against our brothers, the people of Benjamin?" And the LORD said, "Go up against them."

24 So the people of Israel came near against the people of Benjamin the second day. 25 And Benjamin went against them out of Gibeah the second day, and destroyed 18,000 men of the people of Israel. All these were men who drew the sword. 26 Then all the people of Israel, the whole army, went up and came to Bethel and wept. They sat there before the LORD and fasted that day until evening, and offered burnt offerings and peace offerings before the LORD. 27 And the people of Israel inquired of the LORD (for the ark of the covenant of God was there in those days, 28 and Phinehas the son of Eleazar, son of Aaron, ministered before it in those days), saying, "Shall we go out once more to battle against our brothers, the people of Benjamin, or shall we cease?" And the LORD said, "Go up, for tomorrow I will give them into your hand."

29 So Israel set men in ambush around Gibeah. 30 And the people of Israel went up against the people of Benjamin on the third day and set themselves in array against Gibeah, as at other times. 31 And the people of Benjamin went out against the people and were drawn away from the city. And as at other times they began to strike and kill some of the people in the highways, one of which goes up to Bethel and the other to Gibeah, and in the open country, about thirty men of Israel. 32 And the people of Benjamin said, "They are routed before us, as at the first." But the people of Israel said, "Let us flee and draw them away from the city to the highways." 33 And all the men of Israel rose up out of their place and set themselves in array at Baal-tamar, and the men of Israel who were in ambush rushed out of their place from Maareh-geba. 34 And there came against Gibeah 10,000 chosen men out of all Israel, and the battle was hard, but the Benjaminites did not know that disaster was close upon them. 35 And the LORD defeated Benjamin before Israel, and the people of Israel destroyed 25,100 men of Benjamin that day. All these were men who drew the sword. 36 So the people of Benjamin saw that they were defeated.

The men of Israel gave ground to Benjamin, because they trusted the men in ambush whom they had set against Gibeah. 37 Then the men in ambush hurried and rushed against Gibeah; the men in ambush moved out and struck all the city with the edge of the sword. 38 Now the appointed signal between the men of Israel and the men in the main ambush was that when they made a great cloud of smoke rise up out of the city 39 the men of Israel should turn in battle. Now Benjamin had begun to strike and kill about thirty men of Israel. They said, "Surely they are defeated before us, as in the first battle." 40 But when the signal began to rise out of the city in a column of smoke, the Benjaminites looked behind them, and behold, the whole of the city went up in smoke to heaven. 41 Then the men of Israel turned, and the men of Benjamin were dismayed, for they saw that disaster was close upon them. 42 Therefore they turned their backs before the men of Israel in the direction of the wilderness, but the battle overtook them. And those who came out of the cities were destroying them in their midst. 43 Surrounding the Benjaminites, they pursued them and trod them down from Nohah as far as opposite Gibeah on the east. 44 Eighteen thousand men of Benjamin fell, all of them men of valor. 45 And they turned and fled toward the wilderness to the rock of Rimmon. Five thousand men of them were cut down in the highways. And they were pursued hard to Gidom, and 2,000 men of them were struck down. 46 So all who fell that day of Benjamin were 25,000 men who drew the sword, all of them men of valor. 47 But 600 men turned and fled toward the wilderness to the rock of Rimmon and remained at the rock of Rimmon four months. 48 And the men of Israel turned back against the people of Benjamin and struck them with the edge of the sword, the city, men and beasts and all that they found. And all the towns that they found they set on fire.

Wives Provided for the Tribe of Benjamin

21 Now the men of Israel had sworn at Mizpah, "No one of us shall give his daughter in marriage to Benjamin." 2 And the people came to Bethel and sat there till evening before God, and they lifted up their voices and wept bitterly. 3 And they said, "O LORD, the God of Israel, why has this happened in Israel, that today there should be one tribe lacking in Israel?" 4 And the next day the people rose early and built there an altar and offered burnt offerings and peace offerings. 5 And the people of Israel

said, "Which of all the tribes of Israel did not come up in the assembly to the LORD?" For they had taken a great oath concerning him who did not come up to the LORD to Mizpah, saying, "He shall surely be put to death." ⁶ And the people of Israel had compassion for Benjamin their brother and said, "One tribe is cut off from Israel this day. ⁷ What shall we do for wives for those who are left, since we have sworn by the LORD that we will not give them any of our daughters for wives?"

⁸ And they said, "What one is there of the tribes of Israel that did not come up to the LORD to Mizpah?" And behold, no one had come to the camp from Jabesh-gilead, to the assembly. ⁹ For when the people were mustered, behold, not one of the inhabitants of Jabesh-gilead was there. ¹⁰ So the congregation sent 12,000 of their bravest men there and commanded them, "Go and strike the inhabitants of Jabesh-gilead with the edge of the sword; also the women and the little ones. ¹¹ This is what you shall do: every male and every woman that has lain with a male you shall devote to destruction." ¹² And they found among the inhabitants of Jabesh-gilead 400 young virgins who had not known a man by lying with him, and they brought them to the camp at Shiloh, which is in the land of Canaan.

¹³ Then the whole congregation sent word to the people of Benjamin who were at the rock of Rimmon and proclaimed peace to them. ¹⁴ And Benjamin returned at that time. And they gave them the women whom they had saved alive of the women of Jabesh-gilead, but they were not enough for them. ¹⁵ And the people had compassion on Benjamin because the LORD had made a breach in the tribes of Israel.

¹⁶ Then the elders of the congregation said, "What shall we do for wives for those who are left, since the women are destroyed out of Benjamin?" ¹⁷ And they said, "There must be an inheritance for the survivors of Benjamin, that a tribe not be blotted out from Israel. ¹⁸ Yet we cannot give them wives from our daughters." For the people of Israel had sworn, "Cursed be he who gives a wife to Benjamin." ¹⁹ So they said, "Behold, there is the yearly feast of the LORD at Shiloh, which is north of Bethel, on the east of the highway that goes up from Bethel to Shechem, and south of Lebonah." ²⁰ And they commanded the people of Benjamin, saying, "Go and lie in ambush in the vineyards ²¹ and watch. If the daughters of Shiloh come out to dance in the dances, then come out of the vineyards and snatch each man his wife from the daughters of Shiloh, and go to the land of Benjamin. ²² And when their fathers or their brothers come to complain to us, we will say to them, 'Grant them graciously to us, because we did not take for each man of them his wife in battle, neither did you give them to them, else you would now be guilty.'" ²³ And the people of Benjamin did so and took their wives, according to their number, from the dancers whom they carried off. Then they went and returned to their inheritance and rebuilt the towns and lived in them. ²⁴ And the people of Israel departed from there at that time, every man to his tribe and family, and they went out from there every man to his inheritance.

²⁵ In those days there was no king in Israel. Everyone did what was right in his own eyes.

INTRODUCTION TO RUTH

c. 1375 B.C.

Period of the
judges begins

Events of Ruth

c. 1040 B.C.

Birth of David,
descendant of Ruth

AUTHOR AND DATE

The story of Ruth takes place in the time of
the judges (after the conquest of Canaan and
before c. 1050 B.C.). No author is named, but the
mention of David and his genealogy (4:17–22)
places the writing sometime after David
became king (2 Samuel 2) in c. 1010 B.C.

THEME

Ruth shows how God's people can experience
his sovereignty, wisdom, and covenant kindness.
These often come in hard circumstances and are
expressed through the kindness of others.

KEY THEMES

1. *Kindness.* Ruth shows kindness to her mother-
in-law, Naomi, by leaving her homeland to care
for her (1:16–17; 2:11, 18, 23). Boaz shows kindness
to Ruth as he welcomes her to Israel, acts as
her kinsman-redeemer (4:9–10), and marries
her (4:13). Human kindness reflects the Lord's
kindness toward his people (see Ex. 15:13; Deut.
7:8–9; Psalm 136).

2. *Redemption.* Redemption is linked to
kindness and is at the heart of the story (2:20).
The book of Ruth describes two legal practices
combined into one: property redemption by a
near kinsman and levirate marriage. Property
redemption by a relative assured that land
would not remain outside the family (see
Lev. 25:23–25). Levirate marriage involved a
childless widow marrying her husband's brother

to provide an heir for the deceased husband
(Deut. 25:5–6). Boaz, a close relative of Ruth,
redeemed the family property for her (Ruth
4:9), married her (4:10, 13), and fathered Obed
(4:13, 17), who became heir to the property of
Ruth's deceased first husband.

Ruth and Naomi's desperate conditions
changed for the better (4:13–17) when Boaz
agreed to be their kinsman-redeemer (4:9–10).
This resulted in blessing for Ruth (marriage and
motherhood; 4:13) and for Naomi (happiness in
her old age; 4:14–15). Redemption also brought
blessing to the community (4:11–12) and, through
David, to the nation (4:14, 17). Ultimate redemption would finally come through David's "son,"
Jesus the Christ. In him, redeemed people of all
nations, no longer strangers and aliens, become
fellow citizens in God's household (Eph. 2:11–22).

OUTLINE

    I. Introduction: Naomi's Family Dies (1:1–5)

   II. Scene 1: Naomi Returns to Bethlehem with
       Ruth (1:6–22)

  III. Scene 2: Ruth Gleans in Boaz's Field (2:1–23)

   IV. Scene 3: Ruth, at the Threshing Floor, Asks
       Boaz to Marry Her (3:1–18)

    V. Scene 4: Boaz Arranges Redemption at
       the Gate (4:1–12)

   VI. Conclusion: Naomi Blessed with a New
       Family (4:13–17)

  VII. Genealogy: Extended Blessing (4:18–22)

RUTH

Naomi Widowed

1 In the days when the judges ruled there was a famine in the land, and a man of Bethlehem in Judah went to sojourn in the country of Moab, he and his wife and his two sons. ² The name of the man was Elimelech and the name of his wife Naomi, and the names of his two sons were Mahlon and Chilion. They were Ephrathites from Bethlehem in Judah. They went into the country of Moab and remained there. ³ But Elimelech, the husband of Naomi, died, and she was left with her two sons. ⁴ These took Moabite wives; the name of the one was Orpah and the name of the other Ruth. They lived there about ten years, ⁵ and both Mahlon and Chilion died, so that the woman was left without her two sons and her husband.

Ruth's Loyalty to Naomi

⁶ Then she arose with her daughters-in-law to return from the country of Moab, for she had heard in the fields of Moab that the LORD had visited his people and given them food. ⁷ So she set out from the place where she was with her two daughters-in-law, and they went on the way to return to the land of Judah. ⁸ But Naomi said to her two daughters-in-law, "Go, return each of you to her mother's house. May the LORD deal kindly with you, as you have dealt with the dead and with me. ⁹ The LORD grant that you may find rest, each of you in the house of her husband!" Then she kissed them, and they lifted up their voices and wept. ¹⁰ And they said to her, "No, we will return with you to your people." ¹¹ But Naomi said, "Turn back, my daughters; why will you go with me? Have I yet sons in my womb that they may become your husbands? ¹² Turn back, my daughters; go your way, for I am too old to have a husband. If I should say I have hope, even if I should have a husband this night and should bear sons, ¹³ would you therefore wait till they were grown? Would you therefore refrain from marrying? No, my daughters, for it is exceedingly bitter to me for your sake that the hand of the LORD has gone out against me." ¹⁴ Then they lifted up their voices and wept again. And Orpah kissed her mother-in-law, but Ruth clung to her.

¹⁵ And she said, "See, your sister-in-law has gone back to her people and to her gods; return after your sister-in-law." ¹⁶ But Ruth said, "Do not urge me to leave you or to return from following you. For where you go I will go, and where you lodge I will lodge. Your people shall be my people, and your God my God. ¹⁷ Where you die I will die, and there will I be buried. May the LORD do so to me and more also if anything but death parts me from you." ¹⁸ And when Naomi saw that she was determined to go with her, she said no more.

Naomi and Ruth Return

¹⁹ So the two of them went on until they came to Bethlehem. And when they came to Bethlehem, the whole town was stirred because of them. And the women said, "Is this Naomi?" ²⁰ She said to them, "Do not call me Naomi;[1] call me Mara,[2] for the Almighty has dealt very bitterly with me. ²¹ I went away full, and the LORD has brought me back empty. Why call me Naomi, when the LORD has testified against me and the Almighty has brought calamity upon me?" ²² So Naomi returned, and Ruth the Moabite her daughter-in-law with her, who returned from the country of Moab. And they came to Bethlehem at the beginning of barley harvest.

GETTING THE MESSAGE

Gleaning was the Hebrew practice of allowing the poor to follow behind those harvesting crops to gather any food or grain left by the harvesters. Gleaners often worked from morning to evening, to gather enough to sustain themselves and their families. After sundown they would take the gathered grain and thresh it to separate the edible portion from the husk.

Ruth Meets Boaz

2 Now Naomi had a relative of her husband's, a worthy man of the clan of Elimelech, whose name was Boaz. ² And Ruth the Moabite said to Naomi, "Let me go to the field and glean among the ears of grain after him in whose sight I shall find favor." And she said to her, "Go, my daughter." ³ So she set out and went and gleaned in the field after the reapers, and she happened to come to the part of the field belonging to Boaz, who was of the clan of Elimelech. ⁴ And behold, Boaz came from Bethlehem. And he said to the reapers, "The LORD be with you!" And they answered, "The LORD bless you." ⁵ Then Boaz said to his young man who was in charge of the reapers, "Whose young woman is this?" ⁶ And the servant who was in charge of the reapers answered, "She is the young Moabite woman, who came back with Naomi from the country of Moab. ⁷ She said, 'Please let me glean and gather among

the sheaves after the reapers.' So she came, and she has continued from early morning until now, except for a short rest."

⁸ Then Boaz said to Ruth, "Now, listen, my daughter, do not go to glean in another field or leave this one, but keep close to my young women. ⁹ Let your eyes be on the field that they are reaping, and go after them. Have I not charged the young men not to touch you? And when you are thirsty, go to the vessels and drink what the young men have drawn." ¹⁰ Then she fell on her face, bowing to the ground, and said to him, "Why have I found favor in your eyes, that you should take notice of me, since I am a foreigner?" ¹¹ But Boaz answered her, "All that you have done for your mother-in-law since the death of your husband has been fully told to me, and how you left your father and mother and your native land and came to a people that you did not know before. ¹² The LORD repay you for what you have done, and a full reward be given you by the LORD, the God of Israel, under whose wings you have come to take refuge!" ¹³ Then she said, "I have found favor in your eyes, my lord, for you have comforted me and spoken kindly to your servant, though I am not one of your servants."

¹⁴ And at mealtime Boaz said to her, "Come here and eat some bread and dip your morsel in the wine." So she sat beside the reapers, and he passed to her roasted grain. And she ate until she was satisfied, and she had some left over. ¹⁵ When she rose to glean, Boaz instructed his young men, saying, "Let her glean even among the sheaves, and do not reproach her. ¹⁶ And also pull out some from the bundles for her and leave it for her to glean, and do not rebuke her."

¹⁷ So she gleaned in the field until evening. Then she beat out what she had gleaned, and it was about an ephah of barley. ¹⁸ And she took it up and went into the city. Her mother-in-law saw what she had gleaned. She also brought out and gave her what food she had left over after being satisfied. ¹⁹ And her mother-in-law said to her, "Where did you glean today? And where have you worked? Blessed be the man who took notice of you." So she told her mother-in-law with whom she had worked and said, "The man's name with whom I worked today is Boaz." ²⁰ And

---

¹ *Naomi* means *pleasant* ² *Mara* means *bitter*

Naomi said to her daughter-in-law, "May he be blessed by the LORD, whose kindness has not forsaken the living or the dead!" Naomi also said to her, "The man is a close relative of ours, one of our redeemers." **21** And Ruth the Moabite said, "Besides, he said to me, 'You shall keep close by my young men until they have finished all my harvest.'" **22** And Naomi said to Ruth, her daughter-in-law, "It is good, my daughter, that you go out with his young women, lest in another field you be assaulted." **23** So she kept close to the young women of Boaz, gleaning until the end of the barley and wheat harvests. And she lived with her mother-in-law.

Ruth and Boaz at the Threshing Floor

3 Then Naomi her mother-in-law said to her, "My daughter, should I not seek rest for you, that it may be well with you? **2** Is not Boaz our relative, with whose young women you were? See, he is winnowing barley tonight at the threshing floor. **3** Wash therefore and anoint yourself, and put on your cloak and go down to the threshing floor, but do not make yourself known to the man until he has finished eating and drinking. **4** But when he lies down, observe the place where he lies. Then go and uncover his feet and lie down, and he will tell you what to do." **5** And she replied, "All that you say I will do."

6 So she went down to the threshing floor and did just as her mother-in-law had commanded her. **7** And when Boaz had eaten and drunk, and his heart was merry, he went to lie down at the end of the heap of grain. Then she came softly and uncovered his feet and lay down. **8** At midnight the man was startled and turned over, and behold, a woman lay at his feet! **9** He said, "Who are you?" And she answered, "I am Ruth, your servant. Spread your wings over your servant, for you are a redeemer." **10** And he said, "May you be blessed by the LORD, my daughter. You have made this last kindness greater than the first in that you have not gone after young men, whether poor or rich. **11** And now, my daughter, do not fear. I will do for you all that you ask, for all my fellow townsmen know that you are a worthy woman. **12** And now it is true that I am a redeemer. Yet there is a redeemer nearer than I. **13** Remain tonight, and in the morning, if he will redeem you, good; let him do

it. But if he is not willing to redeem you, then, as the LORD lives, I will redeem you. Lie down until the morning."

14 So she lay at his feet until the morning, but arose before one could recognize another. And he said, "Let it not be known that the woman came to the threshing floor." **15** And he said, "Bring the garment you are wearing and hold it out." So she held it, and he measured out six measures of barley and put it on her. Then she went into the city. **16** And when she came to her mother-in-law, she said, "How did you fare, my daughter?" Then she told her all that the man had done for her, **17** saying, "These six measures of barley he gave to me, for he said to me, 'You must not go back empty-handed to your

mother-in-law.'" **18** She replied, "Wait, my daughter, until you learn how the matter turns out, for the man will not rest but will settle the matter today."

Boaz Redeems Ruth

4 Now Boaz had gone up to the gate and sat down there. And behold, the redeemer, of whom Boaz had spoken, came by. So Boaz said, "Turn aside, friend; sit down here." And he turned aside and sat down. **2** And he took ten men of the elders of the city and said, "Sit down here." So they sat down. **3** Then he said to the redeemer, "Naomi, who has come back from the country of Moab, is selling the parcel of land that belonged to our relative Elimelech. **4** So I thought I would tell you of it and say, 'Buy it in the presence of those sitting here and in the presence of the elders of my people.' If you will redeem it, redeem it. But if you

will not, tell me, that I may know, for there is no one besides you to redeem it, and I come after you." And he said, "I will redeem it." **5** Then Boaz said, "The day you buy the field from the hand of Naomi, you also acquire Ruth the Moabite, the widow of the dead, in order to perpetuate the name of the dead in his inheritance." **6** Then the redeemer

---

PROFILE

BOAZ

When Naomi and her Moabite daughter-in-law Ruth came to Bethlehem as childless widows to start a new life, they encountered Boaz, a relative of Naomi's deceased husband. He was a good man who allowed the poor to glean in his field, as God commanded in the Law. The report of Ruth's loyalty to Naomi and to the Lord impressed him, and he protected Ruth while she worked in his field. By Israelite tradition, Boaz was among those who could rescue Naomi and Ruth from poverty. He could do so by redeeming Naomi's ancestral land and by marrying Ruth, thus providing heirs for Naomi's and Ruth's deceased husbands. After Ruth revealed her interest in Boaz, he agreed to do all of this. As he and Ruth moved toward marriage, Boaz was very careful to make sure that everything was done in an orderly and honorable way. Boaz and Ruth became the parents of Obed, who became King David's grandfather.

KEY REFERENCE: RUTH 4:9–10

---

said, "I cannot redeem it for myself, lest I impair my own inheritance. Take my right of redemption yourself, for I cannot redeem it." **7** Now this was the custom in former times in Israel concerning redeeming and exchanging: to confirm a transaction, the one drew off his sandal and gave it to the other, and this was the manner of attesting in Israel. **8** So when the redeemer said to Boaz, "Buy it for yourself," he drew off his sandal. **9** Then Boaz said to the elders and all the people, "You are witnesses this day that I have bought from the hand of Naomi

all that belonged to Elimelech and all that belonged to Chilion and to Mahlon. **10** Also Ruth the Moabite, the widow of Mahlon, I have bought to be my wife, to perpetuate the name of the dead in his inheritance, that the name of the dead may not be cut off from among his brothers and from the gate of his native place. You are witnesses this day." **11** Then all the people who were at the gate and the elders said, "We are witnesses. May the LORD make the woman, who is coming into your house, like Rachel and Leah, who together built up the house of Israel. May you act worthily in Ephrathah and be renowned in Bethlehem, **12** and may your house be like the house of Perez, whom Tamar bore to Judah, because of the offspring that the LORD will give you by this young woman."

GETTING THE MESSAGE

Redemption is a key theme in the book of Ruth. The words "redeem," "redeemer," and "redemption" appear 23 times.

Ruth and Boaz Marry

13 So Boaz took Ruth, and she became his wife. And he went in to her, and the LORD gave her conception, and she bore a son. **14** Then the women said to Naomi, "Blessed be the LORD, who has not left you this day without a redeemer, and may his name be renowned in Israel! **15** He shall be to you a restorer of life and a nourisher of your old age, for your daughter-in-law who loves you, who is more to you than seven sons, has given birth to him." **16** Then Naomi took the child and laid him on her lap and became his nurse. **17** And the women of the neighborhood gave him a name, saying, "A son has been born to Naomi." They named him Obed. He was the father of Jesse, the father of David.

The Genealogy of David

18 Now these are the generations of Perez: Perez fathered Hezron, **19** Hezron fathered Ram, Ram fathered Amminadab, **20** Amminadab fathered Nahshon, Nahshon fathered Salmon, **21** Salmon fathered Boaz, Boaz fathered Obed, **22** Obed fathered Jesse, and Jesse fathered David.

INTRODUCTION TO 1–2 SAMUEL

c. 1100 B.C.	1050/1030 B.C.?	1010 B.C.
Birth of Samuel	Reign of Saul begins	Reign of David begins

AUTHOR AND DATE

The author or authors of 1 and 2 Samuel are not known. These books recount the stories of Samuel, Saul, and David. Saul's reign began between 1050–1030 B.C. and ended in 1010. David then reigned until 971. The books were probably written soon after the end of his reign.

THEME

The central theme of the books of Samuel is how the Lord (1) established a dynasty ("house") in Israel for David rather than Saul and (2) how he chose Jerusalem as the place where David's successor would establish the temple ("house") for the worship of the divine King Yahweh.

PURPOSE

The purpose of 1 Samuel is to highlight two major events: the establishment of the monarchy in Israel (chs. 8–12); and the rise of David to be king after Saul (chs. 16–31). After ruling for a while, Saul was rejected by the Lord in favor of David (chs. 15–16), though Saul stayed on the throne until his death at Mount Gilboa (ch. 31). Later, in 2 Samuel 7, God promises David and his house an eternal dynasty. The book of 1 Samuel establishes the principle that obedience to the word of God is the necessary condition for a king to be acceptable to the God of Israel.

First and Second Samuel deal with a transitional period in the history of ancient Israel. There is a transition of leadership first from the priest Eli to the judge Samuel, then from the judge Samuel to the king Saul, and then from Saul to David. Samuel thus is the link between the judgeship and the kingship in Israel. He is the prophet God uses to anoint both Saul and David. The kingdom of Saul was also transitional. Under Saul, Israel was more than a loose confederation that gathered together whenever there was a common threat, but there was no strong central rule such as existed later. The story of the rise of David in the second half of 1 Samuel prepares for the full-scale kingship of David in 2 Samuel.

1 SAMUEL KEY THEMES

1. *God's kingship.* God is King of the universe and always has been. No human king can assume kingship except as a deputy of the divine King.

2. *God's providential guidance.* God providentially and individually guided the lives of chosen people such as Hannah, Samuel, and David. Even the life of Saul was in God's providential care (see 1 Sam. 9:16). God's timing is always perfect (see 1 Samuel 9 and the end of 1 Samuel 23), for he is the Lord of history.

3. *God's sovereign will and power.* God chooses or rejects people according to his absolute sovereign will and purpose. He may change his way of dealing with individuals according to his plan and purpose, but his decision is always just and right. At the same time, he is merciful and gracious.

Therefore, obedience to God's word is of prime importance. Only God's grace allows sinful human beings to be in relationship with the holy God. Only the God-given way of approaching him through sacrifice can prepare humans to come closer to God. Believers can only wait on God, who will do his will according to his own purpose. What is impossible for humans is possible for God. This should encourage believers to put their faith in the one who is sovereign over the entire creation.

2 SAMUEL KEY THEMES

The themes of 1 Samuel are related to the themes of 2 Samuel: the sovereign God, who has guided David's life, chooses David as the ruler of God's people. God pledges to David an eternal covenant. David thus becomes the prototype of the future Messiah, Jesus Christ.

1. *Davidic covenant.* See 2 Samuel 7.

2. *Messianic promise.* Second Samuel 7 is a turning point in the history of salvation. God chose David to be the beginning of an enduring dynasty, from which the ultimate Ruler, Jesus, would come. God used David to fulfill his eternal plan of salvation, not because he was perfect

from a human viewpoint, but because the Lord was "with him" and showed grace to him.

1 SAMUEL OUTLINE

2 SAMUEL OUTLINE

1 SAMUEL

The Birth of Samuel

1 There was a certain man of Ramathaim-zophim of the hill country of Ephraim whose name was Elkanah the son of Jeroham, son of Elihu, son of Tohu, son of Zuph, an Ephrathite. ² He had two wives. The name of the one was Hannah, and the name of the other, Peninnah. And Peninnah had children, but Hannah had no children.

³ Now this man used to go up year by year from his city to worship and to sacrifice to the LORD of hosts at Shiloh, where the two sons of Eli, Hophni and Phinehas, were priests of the LORD. ⁴ On the day when Elkanah sacrificed, he would give portions to Peninnah his wife and to all her sons and daughters. ⁵ But to Hannah he gave a double portion, because he loved her, though the LORD had closed her womb. ⁶ And her rival used to provoke her grievously to irritate her, because the LORD had closed her womb. ⁷ So it went on year by year. As often as she went up to the house of the LORD, she used to provoke her. Therefore Hannah wept and would not eat. ⁸ And Elkanah, her husband, said to her, "Hannah, why do you weep? And why do you not eat? And why is your heart sad? Am I not more to you than ten sons?"

⁹ After they had eaten and drunk in Shiloh, Hannah rose. Now Eli the priest was sitting on the seat beside the doorpost of the temple of the LORD. ¹⁰ She was deeply distressed and prayed to the LORD and wept bitterly. ¹¹ And she vowed a vow and said, "O LORD of hosts, if you will indeed look on the affliction of your servant and remember me and not forget your servant, but will give to your servant a son, then I will give him to the LORD all the days of his life, and no razor shall touch his head."

¹² As she continued praying before the LORD, Eli observed her mouth. ¹³ Hannah was speaking in her heart; only her lips moved, and her voice was not heard. Therefore Eli took her to be a drunken woman.

¹⁴ And Eli said to her, "How long will you go on being drunk? Put your wine away from you." ¹⁵ But Hannah answered, "No, my lord, I am a woman troubled in spirit. I have drunk neither wine nor strong drink, but I have been pouring out my soul before the LORD. ¹⁶ Do not regard your servant as a worthless woman, for all along I have been speaking out of my great anxiety and vexation." ¹⁷ Then Eli answered, "Go in peace, and the God of Israel grant your petition that you have made to him." ¹⁸ And she said, "Let

> ### GETTING THE MESSAGE
>
> **Children** were of great importance in ancient times for several reasons. They carried on the family name and helped to care for the family's flocks and herds. Women who could not have children were often looked down upon because children were considered a blessing from the Lord. It was common for children to die as infants, so couples would often have many children, knowing some would not survive.

your servant find favor in your eyes." Then the woman went her way and ate, and her face was no longer sad.

¹⁹ They rose early in the morning and worshiped before the LORD; then they went back to their house at Ramah. And Elkanah knew Hannah his wife, and the LORD remembered her. ²⁰ And in due time Hannah conceived and bore a son, and she called his name Samuel, for she said, "I have asked for him from the LORD."¹

Samuel Given to the LORD

²¹ The man Elkanah and all his house went up to offer to the LORD the yearly sacrifice and to pay his vow. ²² But Hannah did not go up, for she said to her husband, "As soon as the child is weaned, I will bring him, so that he may appear in the presence of the

---

¹ *Samuel* sounds like the Hebrew for *heard of God*

LORD and dwell there forever." **23** Elkanah her husband said to her, "Do what seems best to you; wait until you have weaned him; only, may the LORD establish his word." So the woman remained and nursed her son until she weaned him. **24** And when she had weaned him, she took him up with her, along with a three-year-old bull, an ephah of flour, and a skin of wine, and she brought him to the house of the LORD at Shiloh. And the child was young. **25** Then they slaughtered the bull, and they brought the child to Eli. **26** And she said, "Oh, my lord! As you live, my lord, I am the woman who was standing here in your presence, praying to the LORD. **27** For this child I prayed, and the LORD has granted me my petition that I made to him. **28** Therefore I have lent him to the LORD. As long as he lives, he is lent to the LORD."

And he worshiped the LORD there.

Hannah's Prayer

2 And Hannah prayed and said,

"My heart exults in the LORD;
  my horn is exalted in the LORD.
My mouth derides my enemies,
  because I rejoice in your salvation.

2 "There is none holy like the LORD:
  for there is none besides you;
  there is no rock like our God.
3 Talk no more so very proudly,
  let not arrogance come from your
    mouth;
  for the LORD is a God of knowledge,
  and by him actions are weighed.
4 The bows of the mighty are broken,
  but the feeble bind on strength.
5 Those who were full have hired them-
    selves out for bread,
  but those who were hungry have
    ceased to hunger.
The barren has borne seven,
  but she who has many children is
    forlorn.
6 The LORD kills and brings to life;
  he brings down to Sheol and raises
    up.
7 The LORD makes poor and makes rich;
  he brings low and he exalts.
8 He raises up the poor from the dust;
  he lifts the needy from the ash heap
to make them sit with princes
  and inherit a seat of honor.

For the pillars of the earth are the
  LORD's,
  and on them he has set the world.
9 "He will guard the feet of his faithful
    ones,
  but the wicked shall be cut off in
    darkness,
  for not by might shall a man prevail.
10 The adversaries of the LORD shall be
    broken to pieces;
  against them he will thunder in
    heaven.

PROFILE
HANNAH

Hannah was one of Elkanah's two wives. Although his other wife, Peninnah, had children, Hannah did not. While at the temple in Shiloh, Hannah wept bitterly because of her inability to have a child. Deeply distressed, she prayed to the Lord. She vowed that if he gave her a son, she would dedicate the child to God. Eli the priest observed Hannah praying and thought that she was drunk. When he realized that her display of emotion was genuine, however, he blessed Hannah. God answered Hannah's prayer, and she gave birth to Samuel. When the child was weaned, she took him to Eli at the temple in fulfillment of her vow. Hannah's song, praising God for her new son, is very similar to the prayer of Mary in Luke 1:46–55 as she looked forward to the birth of her son Jesus.

KEY REFERENCE: 1 SAMUEL 1:9–11

The LORD will judge the ends of the
  earth;
  he will give strength to his king
  and exalt the horn of his anointed."

11 Then Elkanah went home to Ramah. And the boy was ministering to the LORD in the presence of Eli the priest.

Eli's Worthless Sons

12 Now the sons of Eli were worthless men. They did not know the LORD. **13** The custom of the priests with the people was that when any man offered sacrifice, the priest's servant would come, while the meat was boiling, with a three-pronged fork in his hand, **14** and he would thrust it into the pan or kettle or cauldron or pot. All that the fork brought up the priest would take for himself. This is what they did at Shiloh to all the Israelites who came there. **15** Moreover, before the fat was burned, the priest's servant would come and say to the man who was sacrificing, "Give meat for the priest to roast, for he will not accept boiled meat from you but only raw." **16** And if the man said to him, "Let them burn the fat first, and then take as much as you wish," he would say, "No, you must give it now, and if not, I will take it by force." **17** Thus the sin of the young men was very great in the sight of the LORD, for the men treated the offering of the LORD with contempt.

> ### GETTING THE MESSAGE
>
> **"Thus says the Lord."** Ancient messengers would begin their message by stating the sender's name and saying, "[The sender's name] has spoken thus." The message would then be delivered in the first person as if the sender were saying it himself (2:27).

18 Samuel was ministering before the LORD, a boy clothed with a linen ephod. **19** And his mother used to make for him a little robe and take it to him each year when she went up with her husband to offer the yearly sacrifice. **20** Then Eli would bless Elkanah and his wife, and say, "May the LORD give you children by this woman for the petition she asked of the LORD." So then they would return to their home.

21 Indeed the LORD visited Hannah, and she conceived and bore three sons and two daughters. And the boy Samuel grew in the presence of the LORD.

Eli Rebukes His Sons

22 Now Eli was very old, and he kept hearing all that his sons were doing to all Israel, and how they lay with the women who were serving at the entrance to the tent of meeting. **23** And he said to them, "Why do you do such things? For I hear of your evil dealings from all these people.

24 No, my sons; it is no good report that I hear the people of the LORD spreading abroad. **25** If someone sins against a man, God will mediate for him, but if someone sins against the LORD, who can intercede for him?" But they would not listen to the voice of their father, for it was the will of the LORD to put them to death.

26 Now the boy Samuel continued to grow both in stature and in favor with the LORD and also with man.

The LORD Rejects Eli's Household

27 And there came a man of God to Eli and said to him, "Thus says the LORD, 'Did I indeed reveal myself to the house of your father when they were in Egypt subject to the house of Pharaoh? **28** Did I choose him out of all the tribes of Israel to be my priest, to go up to my altar, to burn incense, to wear an ephod before me? I gave to the house of your father all my offerings by fire from the people of Israel. **29** Why then do you scorn my sacrifices and my offerings that I commanded for my dwelling, and honor your sons above me by fattening yourselves on the choicest parts of every offering of my people Israel?' **30** Therefore the LORD, the God of Israel, declares: 'I promised that your house and the house of your father should go in and out before me forever,' but now the LORD declares: 'Far be it from me, for those who honor me I will honor, and those who despise me shall be lightly esteemed. **31** Behold, the days are coming when I will cut off your strength and the strength of your father's house, so that there will not be an old man in your house. **32** Then in distress you will look with envious eye on all the prosperity that shall be bestowed on Israel, and there shall not be an old man in your house forever. **33** The only one of you whom I shall not cut off from my altar shall be spared to weep his eyes out to grieve his heart, and all the descendants of your house shall die by the sword of men. **34** And this that shall come upon your two sons, Hophni and Phinehas, shall be the sign to you: both of them shall die on the same day. **35** And I will raise up for myself a faithful priest, who shall do according to what is in my heart and in my mind. And I will build him a sure house, and he shall go in and out before my anointed forever. **36** And everyone who is left in your house shall come to implore him for a piece of silver or a loaf of bread and shall say, "Please put me in one of the priests' places, that I may eat a morsel of bread."'"

The LORD Calls Samuel

3 Now the boy Samuel was ministering to the LORD in the presence of Eli. And the word of the LORD was rare in those days; there was no frequent vision.

² At that time Eli, whose eyesight had begun to grow dim so that he could not see, was lying down in his own place. ³ The lamp of God had not yet gone out, and Samuel was lying down in the temple of the LORD, where the ark of God was.

⁴ Then the LORD called Samuel, and he said, "Here I am!" ⁵ and ran to Eli and said, "Here I am, for you called me." But he said, "I did not call; lie down again." So he went and lay down.

> ### GETTING THE MESSAGE
>
> **Samuel! Samuel!** When God called Samuel to his service, he called out his name twice (3:10). Abraham, Jacob, and Moses also heard the Lord speak their name twice at a crucial point in their lives.

⁶ And the LORD called again, "Samuel!" and Samuel arose and went to Eli and said, "Here I am, for you called me." But he said, "I did not call, my son; lie down again." ⁷ Now Samuel did not yet know the LORD, and the word of the LORD had not yet been revealed to him.

⁸ And the LORD called Samuel again the third time. And he arose and went to Eli and said, "Here I am, for you called me." Then Eli perceived that the LORD was calling the boy. ⁹ Therefore Eli said to Samuel, "Go, lie down, and if he calls you, you shall say, 'Speak, LORD, for your servant hears.'" So Samuel went and lay down in his place.

¹⁰ And the LORD came and stood, calling as at other times, "Samuel! Samuel!" And Samuel said, "Speak, for your servant hears." ¹¹ Then the LORD said to Samuel, "Behold, I am about to do a thing in Israel at which the two ears of everyone who hears it will tingle. ¹² On that day I will fulfill against Eli all that I have spoken concerning his house, from beginning to end. ¹³ And I declare to

him that I am about to punish his house forever, for the iniquity that he knew, because his sons were blaspheming God, and he did not restrain them. ¹⁴ Therefore I swear to the house of Eli that the iniquity of Eli's house shall not be atoned for by sacrifice or offering forever."

¹⁵ Samuel lay until morning; then he opened the doors of the house of the LORD. And Samuel was afraid to tell the vision to Eli. ¹⁶ But Eli called Samuel and said, "Samuel, my son." And he said, "Here I am."

PROFILE
ELI

Eli was a priest at Shiloh and a judge of Israel. He became Samuel's guardian after Hannah brought her son to the temple. When God spoke to Samuel, it was Eli who realized the voice was the Lord's, and he told Samuel how to respond. Eli had two sons, Hophni and Phinehas, who also served as priests. Both of them were wicked and blasphemed God. Although Eli rebuked his sons, they did not listen. A messenger from God announced to Eli that his household had been rejected by the Lord. Eli died after receiving news that both of his sons had been killed in battle and the ark of the Lord had been captured.

KEY REFERENCE: 1 SAMUEL 4:12–18

¹⁷ And Eli said, "What was it that he told you? Do not hide it from me. May God do so to you and more also if you hide anything from me of all that he told you." ¹⁸ So Samuel told him everything and hid nothing from him. And he said, "It is the LORD. Let him do what seems good to him."

¹⁹ And Samuel grew, and the LORD was with him and let none of his words fall to the ground. ²⁰ And all Israel from Dan to Beersheba knew that Samuel was established as a prophet of the LORD. ²¹ And the LORD appeared again at Shiloh, for the LORD revealed himself to Samuel at Shiloh by the word of the LORD.

The Philistines Capture the Ark

4 And the word of Samuel came to all Israel.

Now Israel went out to battle against the Philistines. They encamped at Ebenezer, and the Philistines encamped at Aphek. ² The Philistines drew up in line against Israel, and when the battle spread, Israel was defeated before the Philistines, who killed about four thousand men on the field of battle. ³ And when the people came to the camp, the elders of Israel said, "Why has the LORD defeated us today before the Philistines? Let us bring the ark of the covenant of the LORD here from Shiloh, that it may come among us and save us from the power of our enemies." ⁴ So the people sent to Shiloh and brought from there the ark of the covenant of the LORD of hosts,

> ### GETTING THE MESSAGE
>
> **The term "Hebrews"** is used in 4:6 by the Philistines to describe the Israelites as an ethnic group. The term literally means "descendants of Eber" (Gen. 10:21–25). After David established the monarchy, the nation was referred to as "Israel" rather than "the Hebrews."

who is enthroned on the cherubim. And the two sons of Eli, Hophni and Phinehas, were there with the ark of the covenant of God.

⁵ As soon as the ark of the covenant of the LORD came into the camp, all Israel gave a mighty shout, so that the earth resounded. ⁶ And when the Philistines heard the noise of the shouting, they said, "What does this great shouting in the camp of the Hebrews mean?" And when they learned that the ark of the LORD had come to the camp, ⁷ the Philistines were afraid, for they said, "A god has come into the camp." And they said, "Woe to us! For nothing like this has happened before. ⁸ Woe to us! Who can deliver us from the power of these mighty gods? These are the gods who struck the Egyptians with every sort of plague in the wilderness. ⁹ Take courage, and be men, O Philistines, lest you become slaves to the Hebrews as they have been to you; be men and fight."

¹⁰ So the Philistines fought, and Israel was defeated, and they fled, every man to his home. And there was a very great slaughter, for thirty thousand foot soldiers of Israel fell. ¹¹ And the ark of God was captured, and the two sons of Eli, Hophni and Phinehas, died.

The Death of Eli

¹² A man of Benjamin ran from the battle line and came to Shiloh the same day, with his clothes torn and with dirt on his head. ¹³ When he arrived, Eli was sitting on his seat by the road watching, for his heart trembled for the ark of God. And when the man came into the city and told the news, all the city cried out. ¹⁴ When Eli heard the sound of the outcry, he said, "What is this uproar?" Then the man hurried and came and told Eli. ¹⁵ Now Eli was ninety-eight years old and his eyes were set so that he could not see. ¹⁶ And the man said to Eli, "I am he who has come from the battle; I fled from the battle today." And he said, "How did it go, my son?" ¹⁷ He who brought the news answered and said, "Israel has fled before the Philistines, and there has also been a great defeat among the people. Your two sons also, Hophni and Phinehas, are dead, and the ark of God has been captured." ¹⁸ As soon as he mentioned the ark of God, Eli fell over backward from his seat by the side of the gate, and his neck was broken and he died, for the man was old and heavy. He had judged Israel forty years.

¹⁹ Now his daughter-in-law, the wife of Phinehas, was pregnant, about to give birth. And when she heard the news that the ark of God was captured, and that her father-in-law and her husband were dead, she bowed and gave birth, for her pains came upon her. ²⁰ And about the time of her death the women attending her said to her, "Do not be afraid, for you have borne a son." But she did not answer or pay attention. ²¹ And she named the child Ichabod, saying, "The glory has departed from Israel!" because the ark of God had been captured and because of her father-in-law and her husband. ²² And she said, "The glory has departed from Israel, for the ark of God has been captured."

The Philistines and the Ark

5 When the Philistines captured the ark of God, they brought it from Ebenezer to Ashdod. ² Then the Philistines took the ark of God and brought it into the house of Dagon and set it up beside Dagon. ³ And when the people of Ashdod rose early the

next day, behold, Dagon had fallen face downward on the ground before the ark of the LORD. So they took Dagon and put him back in his place. ⁴ But when they rose early on the next morning, behold, Dagon had fallen face downward on the ground before the ark of the LORD, and the head of Dagon and both his hands were lying cut off on the threshold. Only the trunk of Dagon was left to him. ⁵ This is why the priests of Dagon and all who enter the house of Dagon do not tread on the threshold of Dagon in Ashdod to this day.

⁶ The hand of the LORD was heavy against the people of Ashdod, and he terrified and afflicted them with tumors, both Ashdod and its territory. ⁷ And when the men of Ashdod saw how things were, they said, "The ark of the God of Israel must not remain with us, for his hand is hard against us and against Dagon our god." ⁸ So they sent and gathered together all the lords of the Philistines and said, "What shall we do with the ark of the God of Israel?" They answered, "Let the ark of the God of Israel be brought around to Gath." So they brought the ark of the God of Israel there. ⁹ But after they had brought it around, the hand of the LORD was against the city, causing a very great panic, and he afflicted the men of the city, both young and old, so that tumors broke out on them. ¹⁰ So they sent the ark of God to Ekron. But as soon as the ark of God came to Ekron, the people of Ekron cried out, "They have brought around to us the ark of the God of Israel to kill us and our people." ¹¹ They sent therefore and gathered together all the lords of the Philistines and said, "Send away the ark of the God of Israel, and let it return to its own place, that it may not kill us and our people." For there was a deathly panic throughout the whole city. The hand of God was very heavy there. ¹² The men who did not die were struck with tumors, and the cry of the city went up to heaven.

The Ark Returned to Israel

6 The ark of the LORD was in the country of the Philistines seven months. ² And the Philistines called for the priests and the diviners and said, "What shall we do with the ark of the LORD? Tell us with what we shall send it to its place." ³ They said, "If you send away the ark of the God of Israel, do not send it empty, but by all means return him

a guilt offering. Then you will be healed, and it will be known to you why his hand does not turn away from you." ⁴ And they said, "What is the guilt offering that we shall return to him?" They answered, "Five golden tumors and five golden mice, according to the number of the lords of the Philistines, for the same plague was on all of you and on your lords. ⁵ So you must make images of your tumors and images of your mice that ravage the land, and give glory to the God of Israel. Perhaps he will lighten his hand from off you and your gods and your land. ⁶ Why should you harden your hearts as the Egyptians and Pharaoh hardened their hearts? After he had dealt severely with them, did they not send the people away, and they departed? ⁷ Now then, take and prepare a new cart and two milk cows on which

GETTING THE MESSAGE

Why the offering of golden mice and tumors? The tumors that afflicted the Philistines were most likely inflamed lymph nodes. This is the most common symptom of bubonic plague, which is often spread through rodents such as mice. Therefore, in order to appease the God of Israel, the Philistines sent gold replicas of the mice and tumors (6:17).

there has never come a yoke, and yoke the cows to the cart, but take their calves home, away from them. ⁸ And take the ark of the LORD and place it on the cart and put in a box at its side the figures of gold, which you are returning to him as a guilt offering. Then send it off and let it go its way ⁹ and watch. If it goes up on the way to its own land, to Beth-shemesh, then it is he who has done us this great harm, but if not, then we shall know that it is not his hand that struck us; it happened to us by coincidence."

¹⁰ The men did so, and took two milk cows and yoked them to the cart and shut up their calves at home. ¹¹ And they put the ark of the LORD on the cart and the box with the golden mice and the images of their tumors. ¹² And the cows went straight in the direction of Beth-shemesh along one highway, lowing as they went. They turned neither to the right nor to the left, and the lords of

the Philistines went after them as far as the border of Beth-shemesh. **13** Now the people of Beth-shemesh were reaping their wheat harvest in the valley. And when they lifted up their eyes and saw the ark, they rejoiced to see it. **14** The cart came into the field of Joshua of Beth-shemesh and stopped there. A great stone was there. And they split up the wood of the cart and offered the cows as a burnt offering to the LORD. **15** And the Levites took down the ark of the LORD and the box that was beside it, in which were

SAMUEL

Samuel's birth was God's answer to Hannah's prayer for a son. Dedicated to the Lord as a small child, he lived and ministered at Shiloh. When he was a young man, the Lord spoke to him and established him as a prophet. Samuel called the people of Israel to repent and put aside idolatry. During Samuel's lifetime, Israel changed from a collection of tribes ruled by various temporary "judges" to a nation ruled by a king. As the last judge of Israel, Samuel anointed Saul as Israel's first king. When Saul disobeyed God and was rejected as king, Samuel anointed David as his successor. Samuel acted as a faithful judge, prophet, and priest, foreshadowing the work of Christ as king, prophet, and priest (Heb. 1:1–3).

KEY REFERENCE: 1 SAMUEL 3:19–21

the golden figures, and set them upon the great stone. And the men of Beth-shemesh offered burnt offerings and sacrificed sacrifices on that day to the LORD. **16** And when the five lords of the Philistines saw it, they returned that day to Ekron.

17 These are the golden tumors that the Philistines returned as a guilt offering to the LORD: one for Ashdod, one for Gaza, one for Ashkelon, one for Gath, one for Ekron, **18** and the golden mice, according to the number of all the cities of the Philistines belonging to the five lords, both fortified cities and unwalled villages. The great stone beside

which they set down the ark of the LORD is a witness to this day in the field of Joshua of Beth-shemesh.

19 And he struck some of the men of Beth-shemesh, because they looked upon the ark of the LORD. He struck seventy men of them, and the people mourned because the LORD had struck the people with a great blow. **20** Then the men of Beth-shemesh said, "Who is able to stand before the LORD, this holy God? And to whom shall he go up away from us?" **21** So they sent messengers to the inhabitants of Kiriath-jearim, saying, "The Philistines have returned the ark of the LORD. Come down and take it up to you."

7 And the men of Kiriath-jearim came and took up the ark of the LORD and brought it to the house of Abinadab on the hill. And they consecrated his son Eleazar to have charge of the ark of the LORD. **2** From the day that the ark was lodged at Kiriath-jearim, a long time passed, some twenty years, and all the house of Israel lamented after the LORD.

Samuel Judges Israel

3 And Samuel said to all the house of Israel, "If you are returning to the LORD with all your heart, then put away the foreign gods and the Ashtaroth from among you and direct your heart to the LORD and serve him only, and he will deliver you out of the hand of the Philistines." **4** So the people of Israel put away the Baals and the Ashtaroth, and they served the LORD only.

5 Then Samuel said, "Gather all Israel at Mizpah, and I will pray to the LORD for you." **6** So they gathered at Mizpah and drew water and poured it out before the LORD and fasted on that day and said there, "We have sinned against the LORD." And Samuel judged the people of Israel at Mizpah. **7** Now when the Philistines heard that the people of Israel had gathered at Mizpah, the lords of the Philistines went up against Israel. And when the people of Israel heard of it, they were afraid of the Philistines. **8** And the people of Israel said to Samuel, "Do not cease to cry out to the LORD our God for us, that he may save us from the hand of the Philistines." **9** So Samuel took a nursing lamb and offered it as a whole burnt offering to the LORD. And Samuel cried out to the LORD for Israel, and the LORD answered him. **10** As Samuel was offering up the burnt offering, the Philistines drew near to attack Israel.

But the LORD thundered with a mighty sound that day against the Philistines and threw them into confusion, and they were defeated before Israel. ¹¹ And the men of Israel went out from Mizpah and pursued the Philistines and struck them, as far as below Beth-car.

¹² Then Samuel took a stone and set it up between Mizpah and Shen and called its name Ebenezer;¹ for he said, "Till now the LORD has helped us." ¹³ So the Philistines were subdued and did not again enter the territory of Israel. And the hand of the LORD was against the Philistines all the days of Samuel. ¹⁴ The cities that the Philistines had taken from Israel were restored to Israel, from Ekron to Gath, and Israel delivered their territory from the hand of the Philistines. There was peace also between Israel and the Amorites.

¹⁵ Samuel judged Israel all the days of his life. ¹⁶ And he went on a circuit year by year to Bethel, Gilgal, and Mizpah. And he judged Israel in all these places. ¹⁷ Then he would return to Ramah, for his home was there, and there also he judged Israel. And he built there an altar to the LORD.

Israel Demands a King

8 When Samuel became old, he made his sons judges over Israel. ² The name of his firstborn son was Joel, and the name of his second, Abijah; they were judges in Beersheba. ³ Yet his sons did not walk in his ways but turned aside after gain. They took bribes and perverted justice.

⁴ Then all the elders of Israel gathered together and came to Samuel at Ramah ⁵ and said to him, "Behold, you are old and your sons do not walk in your ways. Now appoint for us a king to judge us like all the nations." ⁶ But the thing displeased Samuel when they said, "Give us a king to judge us." And Samuel prayed to the LORD. ⁷ And the LORD said to Samuel, "Obey the voice of the people in all that they say to you, for they have not rejected you, but they have rejected me from being king over them. ⁸ According to all the deeds that they have done, from the day I brought them up out of Egypt even to this day, forsaking me and serving other gods, so they are also doing to you. ⁹ Now then, obey their voice; only you shall sol-emnly warn them and show them the ways of the king who shall reign over them."

Samuel's Warning Against Kings

¹⁰ So Samuel told all the words of the LORD to the people who were asking for a king from him. ¹¹ He said, "These will be the ways of the king who will reign over you: he will take your sons and appoint them to his chariots and to be his horsemen and to run before his chariots. ¹² And he will appoint for himself commanders of thousands and commanders of fifties, and some to plow his ground and to reap his harvest, and to make his implements of war and the equipment of his chariots. ¹³ He will take your daughters to be perfumers and cooks and bakers. ¹⁴ He will take the best of your fields and vineyards and olive orchards and give them

> ### GETTING THE MESSAGE
>
> **Ebenezer** (7:12) means "stone of help." The monument was raised to remember the victory of the Israelites over the Philistines. Samuel chose to name it after the place where the Philistines first defeated the Israelites. This monument represented a chance of a fresh start for Israel because God had changed their circumstances and restored them as a nation.

to his servants. ¹⁵ He will take the tenth of your grain and of your vineyards and give it to his officers and to his servants. ¹⁶ He will take your male servants and female servants and the best of your young men and your donkeys, and put them to his work. ¹⁷ He will take the tenth of your flocks, and you shall be his slaves. ¹⁸ And in that day you will cry out because of your king, whom you have chosen for yourselves, but the LORD will not answer you in that day."

The LORD Grants Israel's Request

¹⁹ But the people refused to obey the voice of Samuel. And they said, "No! But there shall be a king over us, ²⁰ that we also may be like all the nations, and that our king may judge us and go out before us and fight our battles." ²¹ And when Samuel had heard all the words of the people, he repeated them in

¹ Ebenezer means *stone of help*

the ears of the LORD. [22] And the LORD said to Samuel, "Obey their voice and make them a king." Samuel then said to the men of Israel, "Go every man to his city."

Saul Chosen to Be King

9 There was a man of Benjamin whose name was Kish, the son of Abiel, son of Zeror, son of Becorath, son of Aphiah, a Benjaminite, a man of wealth. [2] And he had a son whose name was Saul, a handsome young man. There was not a man among the people of Israel more handsome than he. From his shoulders upward he was taller than any of the people.

[3] Now the donkeys of Kish, Saul's father, were lost. So Kish said to Saul his son, "Take one of the young men with you, and arise, go and look for the donkeys." [4] And he passed through the hill country of Ephraim and passed through the land of Shalishah,

---

> **GETTING THE MESSAGE**
>
> **A gift for the prophet.** Gift-giving was an important custom in the social dealings of the ancient world. It was expected that a person seeking knowledge from a prophet would give a gift in exchange (9:6–8).

---

but they did not find them. And they passed through the land of Shaalim, but they were not there. Then they passed through the land of Benjamin, but did not find them. [5] When they came to the land of Zuph, Saul said to his servant who was with him, "Come, let us go back, lest my father cease to care about the donkeys and become anxious about us." [6] But he said to him, "Behold, there is a man of God in this city, and he is a man who is held in honor; all that he says comes true. So now let us go there. Perhaps he can tell us the way we should go." [7] Then Saul said to his servant, "But if we go, what can we bring the man? For the bread in our sacks is gone, and there is no present to bring to the man of God. What do we have?" [8] The servant answered Saul again, "Here, I have with me a quarter of a shekel of silver, and I will give it to the man of God to tell us our way." [9] (Formerly in Israel, when a man went to inquire of God, he said, "Come, let us go to the seer," for today's "prophet" was

formerly called a seer.) [10] And Saul said to his servant, "Well said; come, let us go." So they went to the city where the man of God was.

[11] As they went up the hill to the city, they met young women coming out to draw water and said to them, "Is the seer here?" [12] They answered, "He is; behold, he is just ahead of you. Hurry. He has come just now to the city, because the people have a sacrifice today on the high place. [13] As soon as you enter the city you will find him, before he goes up to the high place to eat. For the people will not eat till he comes, since he must bless the sacrifice; afterward those who are invited will eat. Now go up, for you will meet him immediately." [14] So they went up to the city. As they were entering the city, they saw Samuel coming out toward them on his way up to the high place.

[15] Now the day before Saul came, the LORD had revealed to Samuel: [16] "Tomorrow about this time I will send to you a man from the land of Benjamin, and you shall anoint him to be prince over my people Israel. He shall save my people from the hand of the Philistines. For I have seen my people, because their cry has come to me." [17] When Samuel saw Saul, the LORD told him, "Here is the man of whom I spoke to you! It is he who shall restrain my people." [18] Then Saul approached Samuel in the gate and said, "Tell me where is the house of the seer?" [19] Samuel answered Saul, "I am the seer. Go up before me to the high place, for today you shall eat with me, and in the morning I will let you go and will tell you all that is on your mind. [20] As for your donkeys that were lost three days ago, do not set your mind on them, for they have been found. And for whom is all that is desirable in Israel? Is it not for you and for all your father's house?" [21] Saul answered, "Am I not a Benjaminite, from the least of the tribes of Israel? And is not my clan the humblest of all the clans of the tribe of Benjamin? Why then have you spoken to me in this way?"

[22] Then Samuel took Saul and his young man and brought them into the hall and gave them a place at the head of those who had been invited, who were about thirty persons. [23] And Samuel said to the cook, "Bring the portion I gave you, of which I said to you, 'Put it aside.'" [24] So the cook took up the leg and what was on it and set them before Saul.

And Samuel said, "See, what was kept is set before you. Eat, because it was kept for you until the hour appointed, that you might eat with the guests."

So Saul ate with Samuel that day. 25 And when they came down from the high place into the city, a bed was spread for Saul on the roof, and he lay down to sleep. 26 Then at the break of dawn Samuel called to Saul on the roof, "Up, that I may send you on your way." So Saul arose, and both he and Samuel went out into the street.

27 As they were going down to the outskirts of the city, Samuel said to Saul, "Tell the servant to pass on before us, and when he has passed on, stop here yourself for a while, that I may make known to you the word of God."

Saul Anointed King

10 Then Samuel took a flask of oil and poured it on his head and kissed him and said, "Has not the LORD anointed you to be prince over his people Israel? And you shall reign over the people of the LORD and you will save them from the hand of their surrounding enemies. And this shall be the sign to you that the LORD has anointed you to be prince over his heritage. 2 When you depart from me today, you will meet two men by Rachel's tomb in the territory of Benjamin at Zelzah, and they will say to you, 'The donkeys that you went to seek are found, and now your father has ceased to care about the donkeys and is anxious about you, saying, "What shall I do about my son?"' 3 Then you shall go on from there farther and come to the oak of Tabor. Three men going up to God at Bethel will meet you there, one carrying three young goats, another carrying three loaves of bread, and another carrying a skin of wine. 4 And they will greet you and give you two loaves of bread, which you shall accept from their hand. 5 After that you shall come to Gibeath-elohim, where there is a garrison of the Philistines. And there, as soon as you come to the city, you will meet a group of prophets coming down from the high place with harp, tambourine, flute, and lyre before them, prophesying. 6 Then the Spirit of the LORD will rush upon you, and you will prophesy with them and be turned into another man. 7 Now when these signs meet you, do what your hand finds to do, for God is with you.

8 Then go down before me to Gilgal. And behold, I am coming down to you to offer burnt offerings and to sacrifice peace offerings. Seven days you shall wait, until I come to you and show you what you shall do."

9 When he turned his back to leave Samuel, God gave him another heart. And all these signs came to pass that day. 10 When they came to Gibeah, behold, a group of prophets met him, and the Spirit of God rushed upon him, and he prophesied among them. 11 And when all who knew him previously saw how he prophesied with the prophets, the people said to one another, "What has come over the son of Kish? Is Saul also among the prophets?" 12 And a man of the place answered, "And who is their father?" Therefore it became a proverb, "Is Saul also among the prophets?" 13 When he had finished prophesying, he came to the high place.

> **GETTING THE MESSAGE**

Though **musical instruments** were used to induce trances in pagan worship, the Israelites used them for pleasing the Lord. The instruments used by the prophets in 10:5 were the same ones used during feasts (Isa. 5:12).

---

14 Saul's uncle said to him and to his servant, "Where did you go?" And he said, "To seek the donkeys. And when we saw they were not to be found, we went to Samuel." 15 And Saul's uncle said, "Please tell me what Samuel said to you." 16 And Saul said to his uncle, "He told us plainly that the donkeys had been found." But about the matter of the kingdom, of which Samuel had spoken, he did not tell him anything.

Saul Proclaimed King

17 Now Samuel called the people together to the LORD at Mizpah. 18 And he said to the people of Israel, "Thus says the LORD, the God of Israel, 'I brought up Israel out of Egypt, and I delivered you from the hand of the Egyptians and from the hand of all the kingdoms that were oppressing you.' 19 But today you have rejected your God, who saves you from all your calamities and your distresses, and you have said to him, 'Set a king over us.' Now therefore present yourselves

before the Lord by your tribes and by your thousands."

²⁰ Then Samuel brought all the tribes of Israel near, and the tribe of Benjamin was taken by lot. ²¹ He brought the tribe of Benjamin near by its clans, and the clan of the Matrites was taken by lot; and Saul the son of Kish was taken by lot. But when they sought him, he could not be found. ²² So they inquired again of the Lord, "Is there a man still to come?" and the Lord said, "Behold, he has hidden himself among the baggage."

PROFILE
SAUL

God chose Saul to be the first king of Israel. Soon after Samuel anointed him privately, the entire nation discovered by means of casting lots that he was to be their king. Saul was a gifted military leader who won the confidence of Israel by saving the city of Jabesh-gilead from the Ammonites. The Bible describes him as a tall, handsome man. Although Saul was chosen by God, he was not faithful to the Lord. He eventually grew proud and disobedient, and God rejected him as king. Tormented into paranoia by a harmful spirit, Saul became insanely jealous of David's popularity and success and sought to kill him. He was wounded in a battle against the Philistines, and ultimately took his own life to avoid capture.

KEY REFERENCE: 1 SAMUEL 11:15

²³ Then they ran and took him from there. And when he stood among the people, he was taller than any of the people from his shoulders upward. ²⁴ And Samuel said to all the people, "Do you see him whom the Lord has chosen? There is none like him among all the people." And all the people shouted, "Long live the king!"

²⁵ Then Samuel told the people the rights and duties of the kingship, and he wrote them in a book and laid it up before the Lord. Then Samuel sent all the people away, each one to his home. ²⁶ Saul also went to his home at Gibeah, and with him went men

of valor whose hearts God had touched. ²⁷ But some worthless fellows said, "How can this man save us?" And they despised him and brought him no present. But he held his peace.

Saul Defeats the Ammonites

11 Then Nahash the Ammonite went up and besieged Jabesh-gilead, and all the men of Jabesh said to Nahash, "Make a treaty with us, and we will serve you." ² But Nahash the Ammonite said to them, "On this condition I will make a treaty with you, that I gouge out all your right eyes, and thus bring disgrace on all Israel." ³ The elders of Jabesh said to him, "Give us seven days' respite that we may send messengers through all the territory of Israel. Then, if there is no one to save us, we will give ourselves up to you." ⁴ When the messengers came to Gibeah of Saul, they reported the matter in the ears of the people, and all the people wept aloud.

⁵ Now, behold, Saul was coming from the field behind the oxen. And Saul said, "What is wrong with the people, that they are weeping?" So they told him the news of the men of Jabesh. ⁶ And the Spirit of God rushed upon Saul when he heard these words, and his anger was greatly kindled. ⁷ He took a yoke of oxen and cut them in pieces and sent them throughout all the territory of Israel by the hand of the messengers, saying, "Whoever does not come out after Saul and Samuel, so shall it be done to his oxen!" Then the dread of the Lord fell upon the people, and they came out as one man. ⁸ When he mustered them at Bezek, the people of Israel were three hundred thousand, and the men of Judah thirty thousand. ⁹ And they said to the messengers who had come, "Thus shall you say to the men of Jabesh-gilead: 'Tomorrow, by the time the sun is hot, you shall have salvation.'" When the messengers came and told the men of Jabesh, they were glad. ¹⁰ Therefore the men of Jabesh said, "Tomorrow we will give ourselves up to you, and you may do to us whatever seems good to you." ¹¹ And the next day Saul put the people in three companies. And they came into the midst of the camp in the morning watch and struck down the Ammonites until the heat of the day. And those who survived were scattered, so that no two of them were left together.

The Kingdom Is Renewed

[12] Then the people said to Samuel, "Who is it that said, 'Shall Saul reign over us?' Bring the men, that we may put them to death." [13] But Saul said, "Not a man shall be put to death this day, for today the LORD has worked salvation in Israel." [14] Then Samuel said to the people, "Come, let us go to Gilgal and there renew the kingdom." [15] So all the people went to Gilgal, and there they made Saul king before the LORD in Gilgal. There they sacrificed peace offerings before the LORD, and there Saul and all the men of Israel rejoiced greatly.

Samuel's Farewell Address

12 And Samuel said to all Israel, "Behold, I have obeyed your voice in all that you have said to me and have made a king over you. [2] And now, behold, the king walks before you, and I am old and gray; and behold, my sons are with you. I have walked before you from my youth until this day. [3] Here I am; testify against me before the LORD and before his anointed. Whose ox have I taken? Or whose donkey have I taken? Or whom have I defrauded? Whom have I oppressed? Or from whose hand have I taken a bribe to blind my eyes with it? Testify against me and I will restore it to you." [4] They said, "You have not defrauded us or oppressed us or taken anything from any man's hand." [5] And he said to them, "The LORD is witness against you, and his anointed is witness this day, that you have not found anything in my hand." And they said, "He is witness."

[6] And Samuel said to the people, "The LORD is witness, who appointed Moses and Aaron and brought your fathers up out of the land of Egypt. [7] Now therefore stand still that I may plead with you before the LORD concerning all the righteous deeds of the LORD that he performed for you and for your fathers. [8] When Jacob went into Egypt, and the Egyptians oppressed them, then your fathers cried out to the LORD and the LORD sent Moses and Aaron, who brought your fathers out of Egypt and made them dwell in this place. [9] But they forgot the LORD their God. And he sold them into the hand of Sisera, commander of the army of Hazor, and into the hand of the Philistines, and into the hand of the king of Moab. And they fought against them. [10] And they cried

out to the LORD and said, 'We have sinned, because we have forsaken the LORD and have served the Baals and the Ashtaroth. But now deliver us out of the hand of our enemies, that we may serve you.' [11] And the LORD sent Jerubbaal and Barak and Jephthah and Samuel and delivered you out of the hand of your enemies on every side, and you lived in safety. [12] And when you saw that Nahash the king of the Ammonites came against you, you said to me, 'No, but a king shall reign over us,' when the LORD your God was your king. [13] And now behold the king whom you have chosen, for whom you have asked; behold, the LORD has set a king over you. [14] If you will fear the LORD and serve him and obey his voice and not rebel against the commandment of the LORD, and if both you and the king who reigns over you will follow the LORD your God, it will be well.

> ## GETTING THE MESSAGE
>
> **A king is crowned.** Saul becomes the first king of all 12 tribes of Israel in ch. 12. Only three kings (Saul, David, and Solomon) ruled the entire nation before the people divided into the nations of Israel and Judah.

[15] But if you will not obey the voice of the LORD, but rebel against the commandment of the LORD, then the hand of the LORD will be against you and your king. [16] Now therefore stand still and see this great thing that the LORD will do before your eyes. [17] Is it not wheat harvest today? I will call upon the LORD, that he may send thunder and rain. And you shall know and see that your wickedness is great, which you have done in the sight of the LORD, in asking for yourselves a king." [18] So Samuel called upon the LORD, and the LORD sent thunder and rain that day, and all the people greatly feared the LORD and Samuel.

[19] And all the people said to Samuel, "Pray for your servants to the LORD your God, that we may not die, for we have added to all our sins this evil, to ask for ourselves a king." [20] And Samuel said to the people, "Do not be afraid; you have done all this evil. Yet do not turn aside from following the LORD, but serve the LORD with all your heart.

21 And do not turn aside after empty things that cannot profit or deliver, for they are empty. 22 For the LORD will not forsake his people, for his great name's sake, because it has pleased the LORD to make you a people for himself. 23 Moreover, as for me, far be it from me that I should sin against the LORD by ceasing to pray for you, and I will instruct you in the good and the right way. 24 Only fear the LORD and serve him faithfully with all your heart. For consider what great things he has done for you. 25 But if you still do wickedly, you shall be swept away, both you and your king."

Saul Fights the Philistines

13 Saul lived for one year and then became king, and when he had reigned for two years over Israel, 2 Saul chose three thousand men of Israel. Two thousand

GETTING THE MESSAGE

Lord of lords. Beginning with Saul and David, kings ruled over Israel. But kings did not have supreme authority. That position still belonged to the Lord. Any king who undermined the authority of the Lord or the words he sent through his prophets would eventually see his kingdom fail.

were with Saul in Michmash and the hill country of Bethel, and a thousand were with Jonathan in Gibeah of Benjamin. The rest of the people he sent home, every man to his tent. 3 Jonathan defeated the garrison of the Philistines that was at Geba, and the Philistines heard of it. And Saul blew the trumpet throughout all the land, saying, "Let the Hebrews hear." 4 And all Israel heard it said that Saul had defeated the garrison of the Philistines, and also that Israel had become a stench to the Philistines. And the people were called out to join Saul at Gilgal.

5 And the Philistines mustered to fight with Israel, thirty thousand chariots and six thousand horsemen and troops like the sand on the seashore in multitude. They came up and encamped in Michmash, to the east of Beth-aven. 6 When the men of Israel saw that they were in trouble (for the people were hard pressed), the people hid themselves in caves and in holes and in rocks and in

tombs and in cisterns, 7 and some Hebrews crossed the fords of the Jordan to the land of Gad and Gilead. Saul was still at Gilgal, and all the people followed him trembling.

Saul's Unlawful Sacrifice

8 He waited seven days, the time appointed by Samuel. But Samuel did not come to Gilgal, and the people were scattering from him. 9 So Saul said, "Bring the burnt offering here to me, and the peace offerings." And he offered the burnt offering. 10 As soon as he had finished offering the burnt offering, behold, Samuel came. And Saul went out to meet him and greet him. 11 Samuel said, "What have you done?" And Saul said, "When I saw that the people were scattering from me, and that you did not come within the days appointed, and that the Philistines had mustered at Michmash, 12 I said, 'Now the Philistines will come down against me at Gilgal, and I have not sought the favor of the LORD.' So I forced myself, and offered the burnt offering." 13 And Samuel said to Saul, "You have done foolishly. You have not kept the command of the LORD your God, with which he commanded you. For then the LORD would have established your kingdom over Israel forever. 14 But now your kingdom shall not continue. The LORD has sought out a man after his own heart, and the LORD has commanded him to be prince over his people, because you have not kept what the LORD commanded you." 15 And Samuel arose and went up from Gilgal. The rest of the people went up after Saul to meet the army; they went up from Gilgal to Gibeah of Benjamin.

And Saul numbered the people who were present with him, about six hundred men. 16 And Saul and Jonathan his son and the people who were present with them stayed in Geba of Benjamin, but the Philistines encamped in Michmash. 17 And raiders came out of the camp of the Philistines in three companies. One company turned toward Ophrah, to the land of Shual; 18 another company turned toward Beth-horon; and another company turned toward the border that looks down on the Valley of Zeboim toward the wilderness.

19 Now there was no blacksmith to be found throughout all the land of Israel, for the Philistines said, "Lest the Hebrews make themselves swords or spears." 20 But

every one of the Israelites went down to the Philistines to sharpen his plowshare, his mattock, his axe, or his sickle, ²¹and the charge was two-thirds of a shekel for the plowshares and for the mattocks, and a third of a shekel for sharpening the axes and for setting the goads. ²²So on the day of the battle there was neither sword nor spear found in the hand of any of the people with Saul and Jonathan, but Saul and Jonathan his son had them. ²³And the garrison of the Philistines went out to the pass of Michmash.

Jonathan Defeats the Philistines

14 One day Jonathan the son of Saul said to the young man who carried his armor, "Come, let us go over to the Philistine garrison on the other side." But he did not tell his father. ²Saul was staying in the outskirts of Gibeah in the pomegranate cave at Migron. The people who were with him were about six hundred men, ³including Ahijah the son of Ahitub, Ichabod's brother, son of Phinehas, son of Eli, the priest of the LORD in Shiloh, wearing an ephod. And the people did not know that Jonathan had gone. ⁴Within the passes, by which Jonathan sought to go over to the Philistine garrison, there was a rocky crag on the one side and a rocky crag on the other side. The name of the one was Bozez, and the name of the other Seneh. ⁵The one crag rose on the north in front of Michmash, and the other on the south in front of Geba.

⁶Jonathan said to the young man who carried his armor, "Come, let us go over to the garrison of these uncircumcised. It may be that the LORD will work for us, for nothing can hinder the LORD from saving by many or by few." ⁷And his armor-bearer said to him, "Do all that is in your heart. Do as you wish. Behold, I am with you heart and soul." ⁸Then Jonathan said, "Behold, we will cross over to the men, and we will show ourselves to them. ⁹If they say to us, 'Wait until we come to you,' then we will stand still in our place, and we will not go up to them. ¹⁰But if they say, 'Come up to us,' then we will go up, for the LORD has given them into our hand. And this shall be the sign to us." ¹¹So both of them showed themselves to the garrison of the Philistines. And the Philistines said, "Look, Hebrews are coming out of the holes where they have hidden themselves." ¹²And

the men of the garrison hailed Jonathan and his armor-bearer and said, "Come up to us, and we will show you a thing." And Jonathan said to his armor-bearer, "Come up after me, for the LORD has given them into the hand of Israel." ¹³Then Jonathan climbed up on his hands and feet, and his armor-bearer after him. And they fell before Jonathan, and his armor-bearer killed them after him. ¹⁴And that first strike, which Jonathan and his armor-bearer made, killed about twenty men within as it were half a furrow's length in an acre of land. ¹⁵And there was a panic in the camp, in the field, and among all the people. The garrison and even the raiders trembled, the earth quaked, and it became a very great panic.

¹⁶And the watchmen of Saul in Gibeah of Benjamin looked, and behold, the multitude was dispersing here and there. ¹⁷Then Saul said to the people who were with him,

GETTING THE MESSAGE

Jonathan shows his trust in God when he says, "nothing can hinder the LORD from saving by many or by few" (14:6). The Lord blesses him and gives him victory over the Philistine army (14:1–23). In contrast, Saul disobeys God and loses his kingship.

"Count and see who has gone from us." And when they had counted, behold, Jonathan and his armor-bearer were not there. ¹⁸So Saul said to Ahijah, "Bring the ark of God here." For the ark of God went at that time with the people of Israel. ¹⁹Now while Saul was talking to the priest, the tumult in the camp of the Philistines increased more and more. So Saul said to the priest, "Withdraw your hand." ²⁰Then Saul and all the people who were with him rallied and went into the battle. And behold, every Philistine's sword was against his fellow, and there was very great confusion. ²¹Now the Hebrews who had been with the Philistines before that time and who had gone up with them into the camp, even they also turned to be with the Israelites who were with Saul and Jonathan. ²²Likewise, when all the men of Israel who had hidden themselves in the hill country of Ephraim heard that the Philistines were fleeing, they too followed hard after them in the battle. ²³ So the LORD saved Israel that day. And the battle passed beyond Beth-aven.

Saul's Rash Vow

²⁴ And the men of Israel had been hard pressed that day, so Saul had laid an oath on the people, saying, "Cursed be the man who eats food until it is evening and I am avenged on my enemies." So none of the people had tasted food. ²⁵ Now when all the people came to the forest, behold, there was honey on the ground. ²⁶ And when the people entered the forest, behold, the honey was dropping, but no one put his hand to his mouth, for the people feared the oath. ²⁷ But Jonathan had not heard his father charge the people with the oath, so he put out the tip of the staff that was in his hand and dipped it in the honeycomb and put his hand to his mouth, and his eyes became bright. ²⁸ Then one of the people said, "Your father strictly charged the people with an oath, saying, 'Cursed be the man who eats food this day.'" And the people were faint. ²⁹ Then Jonathan said, "My father has troubled the land. See how my eyes have become bright because I tasted a little of this honey. ³⁰ How much better if the people had eaten freely today of the spoil of their enemies that they found. For now the defeat among the Philistines has not been great."

³¹ They struck down the Philistines that day from Michmash to Aijalon. And the people were very faint. ³² The people pounced on the spoil and took sheep and oxen and calves and slaughtered them on the ground. And the people ate them with the blood. ³³ Then they told Saul, "Behold, the people are sinning against the LORD by eating with the blood." And he said, "You have dealt treacherously; roll a great stone to me here." ³⁴ And Saul said, "Disperse yourselves among the people and say to them, 'Let every man bring his ox or his sheep and slaughter them here and eat, and do not sin against the LORD by eating with the blood.'" So every one of the people brought his ox with him that night and they slaughtered them there. ³⁵ And Saul built an altar to the LORD; it was the first altar that he built to the LORD.

³⁶ Then Saul said, "Let us go down after the Philistines by night and plunder them until the morning light; let us not leave a man of them." And they said, "Do whatever seems good to you." But the priest said, "Let us draw near to God here." ³⁷ And Saul inquired of God, "Shall I go down after the Philistines? Will you give them into the hand of Israel?" But he did not answer him that day. ³⁸ And Saul said, "Come here, all you leaders of the people, and know and see how this sin has arisen today. ³⁹ For as the LORD lives who saves Israel, though it be in Jonathan my son, he shall surely die." But there was not a man among all the people who answered him. ⁴⁰ Then he said to all Israel, "You shall be on one side, and I and Jonathan my son will be on the other side." And the people said to Saul, "Do what seems good to you." ⁴¹ Therefore Saul said, "O LORD God of Israel, why have you not answered your servant this day? If this guilt is in me or in Jonathan my son, O LORD, God of Israel, give Urim. But if this guilt is in your people Israel, give Thummim." And Jonathan and Saul were taken, but the people escaped. ⁴² Then Saul said, "Cast the lot between me and my son Jonathan." And Jonathan was taken.

⁴³ Then Saul said to Jonathan, "Tell me what you have done." And Jonathan told him, "I tasted a little honey with the tip of the staff that was in my hand. Here I am; I will die." ⁴⁴ And Saul said, "God do so to me and more also; you shall surely die, Jonathan." ⁴⁵ Then the people said to Saul, "Shall Jonathan die, who has worked this great salvation in Israel? Far from it! As the LORD lives, there shall not one hair of his head fall to the ground, for he has worked with God this day." So the people ransomed Jonathan, so that he did not die. ⁴⁶ Then Saul went up from pursuing the Philistines, and the Philistines went to their own place.

Saul Fights Israel's Enemies

⁴⁷ When Saul had taken the kingship over Israel, he fought against all his enemies on every side, against Moab, against the Ammonites, against Edom, against the kings of Zobah, and against the Philistines. Wherever he turned he routed them. ⁴⁸ And he did valiantly and struck the Amalekites and delivered Israel out of the hands of those who plundered them.

⁴⁹ Now the sons of Saul were Jonathan, Ishvi, and Malchi-shua. And the names of his two daughters were these: the name of the firstborn was Merab, and the name of the younger Michal. ⁵⁰ And the name of Saul's wife was Ahinoam the daughter of Ahimaaz. And the name of the commander of his army was Abner the son of Ner, Saul's uncle. ⁵¹ Kish was the father of Saul, and Ner the father of Abner was the son of Abiel.

⁵² There was hard fighting against the Philistines all the days of Saul. And when Saul saw any strong man, or any valiant man, he attached him to himself.

The Lord Rejects Saul

15 And Samuel said to Saul, "The Lord sent me to anoint you king over his people Israel; now therefore listen to the words of the Lord. ² Thus says the Lord of hosts, 'I have noted what Amalek did to Israel in opposing them on the way when they came up out of Egypt. ³ Now go and strike Amalek and devote to destruction[1] all that they have. Do not spare them, but kill both man and woman, child and infant, ox and sheep, camel and donkey.'"

⁴ So Saul summoned the people and numbered them in Telaim, two hundred thousand men on foot, and ten thousand men of Judah. ⁵ And Saul came to the city of Amalek and lay in wait in the valley. ⁶ Then Saul said to the Kenites, "Go, depart; go down from among the Amalekites, lest I destroy you with them. For you showed kindness to all the people of Israel when they came up out of Egypt." So the Kenites departed from among the Amalekites. ⁷ And Saul defeated the Amalekites from Havilah as far as Shur, which is east of Egypt. ⁸ And he took Agag the king of the Amalekites alive and devoted to destruction all the people with the edge of the sword. ⁹ But Saul and the people spared Agag and the best of the sheep and of the oxen and of the fattened calves and the lambs, and all that was good, and would not utterly destroy them. All that was despised and worthless they devoted to destruction.

¹⁰ The word of the Lord came to Samuel: ¹¹ "I regret that I have made Saul king, for he has turned back from following me and has not performed my commandments." And Samuel was angry, and he cried to the Lord all night. ¹² And Samuel rose early to meet Saul in the morning. And it was told Samuel, "Saul came to Carmel, and behold, he set up a monument for himself and turned and passed on and went down to Gilgal." ¹³ And Samuel came to Saul, and Saul said to him, "Blessed be you to the Lord. I have performed the commandment of the Lord." ¹⁴ And Samuel said, "What then is this bleating of the sheep in my ears and the lowing of the oxen that I hear?" ¹⁵ Saul said, "They have brought them from the Amalekites, for the people spared the best of the sheep and of the oxen to sacrifice to the Lord your God, and the rest we have devoted to destruction." ¹⁶ Then Samuel said to Saul, "Stop! I will tell you what the Lord said to me this night." And he said to him, "Speak."

¹⁷ And Samuel said, "Though you are little in your own eyes, are you not the head of the tribes of Israel? The Lord anointed

GETTING THE MESSAGE

Why did Saul spare the Kenites? Moses' father-in-law Jethro was a Kenite. Jethro and his son were helpful and kind to the Israelites when they came out of Egypt. Because of this, David also showed favor to the Kenites when he became king.

you king over Israel. ¹⁸ And the Lord sent you on a mission and said, 'Go, devote to destruction the sinners, the Amalekites, and fight against them until they are consumed.' ¹⁹ Why then did you not obey the voice of the Lord? Why did you pounce on the spoil and do what was evil in the sight of the Lord?" ²⁰ And Saul said to Samuel, "I have obeyed the voice of the Lord. I have gone on the mission on which the Lord sent me. I have brought Agag the king of Amalek, and I have devoted the Amalekites to destruction. ²¹ But the people took of the spoil, sheep and oxen, the best of the things devoted to destruction, to sacrifice to the Lord your God in Gilgal." ²² And Samuel said,

"Has the Lord as great delight in burnt offerings and sacrifices,
    as in obeying the voice of the Lord?
Behold, to obey is better than sacrifice,
    and to listen than the fat of rams.

[1] That is, destroy or make an offering because of sin, at God's command; also 15:8, 9, 15, 18, 20, 21

23 For rebellion is as the sin of divination,
and presumption is as iniquity and
idolatry.
Because you have rejected the word of
the Lord,
he has also rejected you from being
king."

24 Saul said to Samuel, "I have sinned, for I have transgressed the commandment of the Lord and your words, because I feared the people and obeyed their voice. 25 Now therefore, please pardon my sin and return with

---

PROFILE
DAVID

David was the youngest son of Jesse of Bethlehem. When Saul was rejected as king, God chose David as his successor. A handsome and gifted man, David played the lyre to soothe Saul, gaining his favor and eventually becoming his armor-bearer. On a mission to deliver food to his older brothers, David fought and killed the giant Goliath. He became Israel's greatest king, and made Jerusalem the nation's capital city. Although he was a godly man, David fell into sin with Bathsheba. God used him not because he was mighty or perfect, but because he found favor in God's sight. The Lord promised David an eternal throne (2 Sam. 7:16), and through his lineage came Jesus the Messiah.

KEY REFERENCE: 2 SAMUEL 7:1–29

---

me that I may bow before the Lord." 26 And Samuel said to Saul, "I will not return with you. For you have rejected the word of the Lord, and the Lord has rejected you from being king over Israel." 27 As Samuel turned to go away, Saul seized the skirt of his robe, and it tore. 28 And Samuel said to him, "The Lord has torn the kingdom of Israel from you this day and has given it to a neighbor of yours, who is better than you. 29 And also the Glory of Israel will not lie or have regret, for he is not a man, that he should have regret." 30 Then he said, "I have sinned;

yet honor me now before the elders of my people and before Israel, and return with me, that I may bow before the Lord your God." 31 So Samuel turned back after Saul, and Saul bowed before the Lord.

32 Then Samuel said, "Bring here to me Agag the king of the Amalekites." And Agag came to him cheerfully. Agag said, "Surely the bitterness of death is past." 33 And Samuel said, "As your sword has made women childless, so shall your mother be childless among women." And Samuel hacked Agag to pieces before the Lord in Gilgal.

34 Then Samuel went to Ramah, and Saul went up to his house in Gibeah of Saul. 35 And Samuel did not see Saul again until the day of his death, but Samuel grieved over Saul. And the Lord regretted that he had made Saul king over Israel.

David Anointed King

16 The Lord said to Samuel, "How long will you grieve over Saul, since I have rejected him from being king over Israel? Fill your horn with oil, and go. I will send you to Jesse the Bethlehemite, for I have provided for myself a king among his sons." 2 And Samuel said, "How can I go? If Saul hears it, he will kill me." And the Lord said, "Take a heifer with you and say, 'I have come to sacrifice to the Lord.' 3 And invite Jesse to the sacrifice, and I will show you what you shall do. And you shall anoint for me him whom I declare to you." 4 Samuel did what the Lord commanded and came to Bethlehem. The elders of the city came to meet him trembling and said, "Do you come peaceably?" 5 And he said, "Peaceably; I have come to sacrifice to the Lord. Consecrate yourselves, and come with me to the sacrifice." And he consecrated Jesse and his sons and invited them to the sacrifice.

6 When they came, he looked on Eliab and thought, "Surely the Lord's anointed is before him." 7 But the Lord said to Samuel, "Do not look on his appearance or on the height of his stature, because I have rejected him. For the Lord sees not as man sees: man looks on the outward appearance, but the Lord looks on the heart." 8 Then Jesse called Abinadab and made him pass before Samuel. And he said, "Neither has the Lord chosen this one." 9 Then Jesse made Shammah pass by. And he said, "Neither has the Lord chosen this one." 10 And Jesse

made seven of his sons pass before Samuel. And Samuel said to Jesse, "The LORD has not chosen these." ¹¹ Then Samuel said to Jesse, "Are all your sons here?" And he said, "There remains yet the youngest, but behold, he is keeping the sheep." And Samuel said to Jesse, "Send and get him, for we will not sit down till he comes here." ¹² And he sent and brought him in. Now he was ruddy and had beautiful eyes and was handsome. And the LORD said, "Arise, anoint him, for this is he." ¹³ Then Samuel took the horn of oil and anointed him in the midst of his brothers. And the Spirit of the LORD rushed upon David from that day forward. And Samuel rose up and went to Ramah.

David in Saul's Service

¹⁴ Now the Spirit of the LORD departed from Saul, and a harmful spirit from the LORD tormented him. ¹⁵ And Saul's servants said to him, "Behold now, a harmful spirit from God is tormenting you. ¹⁶ Let our lord now command your servants who are before you to seek out a man who is skillful in playing the lyre, and when the harmful spirit from God is upon you, he will play it, and you will be well." ¹⁷ So Saul said to his servants, "Provide for me a man who can play well and bring him to me." ¹⁸ One of the young men answered, "Behold, I have seen a son of Jesse the Bethlehemite, who is skillful in playing, a man of valor, a man of war, prudent in speech, and a man of good presence, and the LORD is with him." ¹⁹ Therefore Saul sent messengers to Jesse and said, "Send me David your son, who is with the sheep." ²⁰ And Jesse took a donkey laden with bread and a skin of wine and a young goat and sent them by David his son to Saul. ²¹ And David came to Saul and entered his service. And Saul loved him greatly, and he became his armor-bearer. ²² And Saul sent to Jesse, saying, "Let David remain in my service, for he has found favor in my sight." ²³ And whenever the harmful spirit from God was upon Saul, David took the lyre and played it with his hand. So Saul was refreshed and was well, and the harmful spirit departed from him.

David and Goliath

17 Now the Philistines gathered their armies for battle. And they were gathered at Socoh, which belongs to Judah, and encamped between Socoh and Azekah, in Ephes-dammim. ² And Saul and the men of Israel were gathered, and encamped in the Valley of Elah, and drew up in line of battle against the Philistines. ³ And the Philistines stood on the mountain on the one side, and Israel stood on the mountain on the other side, with a valley between them. ⁴ And there came out from the camp of the Philistines a champion named Goliath of Gath, whose height was six cubits and a span. ⁵ He had a helmet of bronze on his head, and he was armed with a coat of mail, and the weight of the coat was five thousand shekels of bronze. ⁶ And he had bronze armor on his legs, and a javelin of bronze slung between his shoulders. ⁷ The shaft of his spear was like a weaver's beam, and his spear's head weighed six hundred shekels of iron. And his shield-bearer went

GETTING THE MESSAGE

A battle of champions. To save lives, the outcomes of battles were at times decided by one-on-one combat (17:4). A champion was selected from the opposing armies to fight each other. Both sides assumed that the gods had thereby determined the winning side.

before him. ⁸ He stood and shouted to the ranks of Israel, "Why have you come out to draw up for battle? Am I not a Philistine, and are you not servants of Saul? Choose a man for yourselves, and let him come down to me. ⁹ If he is able to fight with me and kill me, then we will be your servants. But if I prevail against him and kill him, then you shall be our servants and serve us." ¹⁰ And the Philistine said, "I defy the ranks of Israel this day. Give me a man, that we may fight together." ¹¹ When Saul and all Israel heard these words of the Philistine, they were dismayed and greatly afraid.

¹² Now David was the son of an Ephrathite of Bethlehem in Judah, named Jesse, who had eight sons. In the days of Saul the man was already old and advanced in years. ¹³ The three oldest sons of Jesse had followed Saul to the battle. And the names of his three sons who went to the battle were Eliab the firstborn, and next to him Abinadab, and the

third Shammah. ¹⁴David was the youngest. The three eldest followed Saul, ¹⁵but David went back and forth from Saul to feed his father's sheep at Bethlehem. ¹⁶For forty days the Philistine came forward and took his stand, morning and evening.

¹⁷And Jesse said to David his son, "Take for your brothers an ephah of this parched grain, and these ten loaves, and carry them quickly to the camp to your brothers. ¹⁸Also take these ten cheeses to the commander of their thousand. See if your brothers are well, and bring some token from them."

¹⁹Now Saul and they and all the men of Israel were in the Valley of Elah, fighting with the Philistines. ²⁰And David rose early in the morning and left the sheep with a keeper and took the provisions and went, as Jesse had commanded him. And he came to the encampment as the host was going out to the battle line, shouting the war cry. ²¹And Israel and the Philistines drew up for battle, army against army. ²²And David left the things in charge of the keeper of the baggage and ran to the ranks and went and greeted his brothers. ²³As he talked with them, behold, the champion, the Philistine of Gath, Goliath by name, came up out of the ranks of the Philistines and spoke the same words as before. And David heard him.

²⁴All the men of Israel, when they saw the man, fled from him and were much afraid. ²⁵And the men of Israel said, "Have you seen this man who has come up? Surely he has come up to defy Israel. And the king will enrich the man who kills him with great riches and will give him his daughter and make his father's house free in Israel." ²⁶And David said to the men who stood by him, "What shall be done for the man who kills this Philistine and takes away the reproach from Israel? For who is this uncircumcised Philistine, that he should defy the armies of the living God?" ²⁷And the people answered him in the same way, "So shall it be done to the man who kills him."

²⁸Now Eliab his eldest brother heard when he spoke to the men. And Eliab's anger was kindled against David, and he said, "Why have you come down? And with whom have you left those few sheep in the wilderness? I know your presumption and the evil of your heart, for you have come down to see the battle." ²⁹And David said, "What have I

done now? Was it not but a word?" ³⁰And he turned away from him toward another, and spoke in the same way, and the people answered him again as before.

³¹When the words that David spoke were heard, they repeated them before Saul, and he sent for him. ³²And David said to Saul, "Let no man's heart fail because of him. Your servant will go and fight with this Philistine." ³³And Saul said to David, "You are not able to go against this Philistine to fight with him, for you are but a youth, and he has been a man of war from his youth." ³⁴But David said to Saul, "Your servant used to keep sheep for his father. And when there came a lion, or a bear, and took a lamb from the flock, ³⁵I went after him and struck him and delivered it out of his mouth. And if he arose against me, I caught him by his beard and struck him and killed him. ³⁶Your servant has struck down both lions and bears, and this uncircumcised Philistine shall be like one of them, for he has defied the armies of the living God." ³⁷And David said, "The LORD who delivered me from the paw of the lion and from the paw of the bear will deliver me from the hand of this Philistine." And Saul said to David, "Go, and the LORD be with you!"

³⁸Then Saul clothed David with his armor. He put a helmet of bronze on his head and clothed him with a coat of mail, ³⁹and David strapped his sword over his armor. And he tried in vain to go, for he had not tested them. Then David said to Saul, "I cannot go with these, for I have not tested them." So David put them off. ⁴⁰Then he took his staff in his hand and chose five smooth stones from the brook and put them in his shepherd's pouch. His sling was in his hand, and he approached the Philistine.

⁴¹And the Philistine moved forward and came near to David, with his shield-bearer in front of him. ⁴²And when the Philistine looked and saw David, he disdained him, for he was but a youth, ruddy and handsome in appearance. ⁴³And the Philistine said to David, "Am I a dog, that you come to me with sticks?" And the Philistine cursed David by his gods. ⁴⁴The Philistine said to David, "Come to me, and I will give your flesh to the birds of the air and to the beasts of the field." ⁴⁵Then David said to the Philistine, "You come to me with a

sword and with a spear and with a javelin, but I come to you in the name of the LORD of hosts, the God of the armies of Israel, whom you have defied. ⁴⁶ This day the LORD will deliver you into my hand, and I will strike you down and cut off your head. And I will give the dead bodies of the host of the Philistines this day to the birds of the air and to the wild beasts of the earth, that all the earth may know that there is a God in Israel, ⁴⁷ and that all this assembly may know that the LORD saves not with sword and spear. For the battle is the LORD's, and he will give you into our hand."

⁴⁸ When the Philistine arose and came and drew near to meet David, David ran quickly toward the battle line to meet the Philistine. ⁴⁹ And David put his hand in his bag and took out a stone and slung it and struck the Philistine on his forehead. The stone sank into his forehead, and he fell on his face to the ground.

⁵⁰ So David prevailed over the Philistine with a sling and with a stone, and struck the Philistine and killed him. There was no sword in the hand of David. ⁵¹ Then David ran and stood over the Philistine and took his sword and drew it out of its sheath and killed him and cut off his head with it. When the Philistines saw that their champion was dead, they fled. ⁵² And the men of Israel and Judah rose with a shout and pursued the Philistines as far as Gath and the gates of Ekron, so that the wounded Philistines fell on the way from Shaaraim as far as Gath and Ekron. ⁵³ And the people of Israel came back from chasing the Philistines, and they plundered their camp. ⁵⁴ And David took the head of the Philistine and brought it to Jerusalem, but he put his armor in his tent.

⁵⁵ As soon as Saul saw David go out against the Philistine, he said to Abner, the commander of the army, "Abner, whose son is this youth?" And Abner said, "As your soul lives, O king, I do not know." ⁵⁶ And the king said, "Inquire whose son the boy is." ⁵⁷ And as soon as David returned from the striking down of the Philistine, Abner took him, and brought him before Saul with the head of the Philistine in his hand. ⁵⁸ And Saul said to him, "Whose son are you, young man?" And David answered, "I am the son of your servant Jesse the Bethlehemite."

David and Jonathan's Friendship

18 As soon as he had finished speaking to Saul, the soul of Jonathan was knit to the soul of David, and Jonathan loved him as his own soul. ² And Saul took him that day and would not let him return to his father's house. ³ Then Jonathan made a covenant with David, because he loved him as his own soul. ⁴ And Jonathan stripped himself of the robe that was on him and gave it to David, and his armor, and even his sword and his bow and his belt. ⁵ And David went out and was successful wherever Saul sent him, so that Saul set him over the men of war. And this was good in the sight of all the people and also in the sight of Saul's servants.

Saul's Jealousy of David

⁶ As they were coming home, when David returned from striking down the Philistine, the women came out of all the cities of Israel,

GETTING THE MESSAGE

Fed to the birds and beasts. In Israel, being killed and left for scavenger birds, like vultures, was considered shameful (17:46). It deprived a person of a meaningful burial where family members could properly mourn.

singing and dancing, to meet King Saul, with tambourines, with songs of joy, and with musical instruments. ⁷ And the women sang to one another as they celebrated,

"Saul has struck down his thousands,
    and David his ten thousands."

⁸ And Saul was very angry, and this saying displeased him. He said, "They have ascribed to David ten thousands, and to me they have ascribed thousands, and what more can he have but the kingdom?" ⁹ And Saul eyed David from that day on.

¹⁰ The next day a harmful spirit from God rushed upon Saul, and he raved within his house while David was playing the lyre, as he did day by day. Saul had his spear in his hand. ¹¹ And Saul hurled the spear, for he thought, "I will pin David to the wall." But David evaded him twice.

¹² Saul was afraid of David because the LORD was with him but had departed from Saul. ¹³ So Saul removed him from his

presence and made him a commander of a thousand. And he went out and came in before the people. ¹⁴ And David had success in all his undertakings, for the LORD was with him. ¹⁵ And when Saul saw that he had great success, he stood in fearful awe of him. ¹⁶ But all Israel and Judah loved David, for he went out and came in before them.

David Marries Michal

¹⁷ Then Saul said to David, "Here is my elder daughter Merab. I will give her to you for a wife. Only be valiant for me and fight the LORD's battles." For Saul thought, "Let not my hand be against him, but let the hand of the Philistines be against him." ¹⁸ And David said to Saul, "Who am I, and who are my relatives, my father's clan in Israel, that I should be son-in-law to the king?" ¹⁹ But at the time when Merab, Saul's

> **GETTING THE MESSAGE**
>
> **The sound of victory.** The sight of women singing, dancing, and playing tambourines was very common following a military victory (18:6). Ancient clay figurines or plaques showing women playing tambourines have been found in Israel.

daughter, should have been given to David, she was given to Adriel the Meholathite for a wife.

²⁰ Now Saul's daughter Michal loved David. And they told Saul, and the thing pleased him. ²¹ Saul thought, "Let me give her to him, that she may be a snare for him and that the hand of the Philistines may be against him." Therefore Saul said to David a second time, "You shall now be my son-in-law." ²² And Saul commanded his servants, "Speak to David in private and say, 'Behold, the king has delight in you, and all his servants love you. Now then become the king's son-in-law.'" ²³ And Saul's servants spoke those words in the ears of David. And David said, "Does it seem to you a little thing to become the king's son-in-law, since I am a poor man and have no reputation?" ²⁴ And the servants of Saul told him, "Thus and so did David speak." ²⁵ Then Saul said, "Thus shall you say to David, 'The king desires no bride-price except a hundred foreskins

of the Philistines, that he may be avenged of the king's enemies.'" Now Saul thought to make David fall by the hand of the Philistines. ²⁶ And when his servants told David these words, it pleased David well to be the king's son-in-law. Before the time had expired, ²⁷ David arose and went, along with his men, and killed two hundred of the Philistines. And David brought their foreskins, which were given in full number to the king, that he might become the king's son-in-law. And Saul gave him his daughter Michal for a wife. ²⁸ But when Saul saw and knew that the LORD was with David, and that Michal, Saul's daughter, loved him, ²⁹ Saul was even more afraid of David. So Saul was David's enemy continually.

³⁰ Then the commanders of the Philistines came out to battle, and as often as they came out David had more success than all the servants of Saul, so that his name was highly esteemed.

Saul Tries to Kill David

19 And Saul spoke to Jonathan his son and to all his servants, that they should kill David. But Jonathan, Saul's son, delighted much in David. ² And Jonathan told David, "Saul my father seeks to kill you. Therefore be on your guard in the morning. Stay in a secret place and hide yourself. ³ And I will go out and stand beside my father in the field where you are, and I will speak to my father about you. And if I learn anything I will tell you." ⁴ And Jonathan spoke well of David to Saul his father and said to him, "Let not the king sin against his servant David, because he has not sinned against you, and because his deeds have brought good to you. ⁵ For he took his life in his hand and he struck down the Philistine, and the LORD worked a great salvation for all Israel. You saw it, and rejoiced. Why then will you sin against innocent blood by killing David without cause?" ⁶ And Saul listened to the voice of Jonathan. Saul swore, "As the LORD lives, he shall not be put to death." ⁷ And Jonathan called David, and Jonathan reported to him all these things. And Jonathan brought David to Saul, and he was in his presence as before.

⁸ And there was war again. And David went out and fought with the Philistines and struck them with a great blow, so that they fled before him. ⁹ Then a harmful spirit

from the LORD came upon Saul, as he sat in his house with his spear in his hand. And David was playing the lyre. **¹⁰** And Saul sought to pin David to the wall with the spear, but he eluded Saul, so that he struck the spear into the wall. And David fled and escaped that night.

¹¹ Saul sent messengers to David's house to watch him, that he might kill him in the morning. But Michal, David's wife, told him, "If you do not escape with your life tonight, tomorrow you will be killed." **¹²** So Michal let David down through the window, and he fled away and escaped. **¹³** Michal took an image¹ and laid it on the bed and put a pillow of goats' hair at its head and covered it with the clothes. **¹⁴** And when Saul sent messengers to take David, she said, "He is sick." **¹⁵** Then Saul sent the messengers to see David, saying, "Bring him up to me in the bed, that I may kill him." **¹⁶** And when the messengers came in, behold, the image was in the bed, with the pillow of goats' hair at its head. **¹⁷** Saul said to Michal, "Why have you deceived me thus and let my enemy go, so that he has escaped?" And Michal answered Saul, "He said to me, 'Let me go. Why should I kill you?'"

¹⁸ Now David fled and escaped, and he came to Samuel at Ramah and told him all that Saul had done to him. And he and Samuel went and lived at Naioth. **¹⁹** And it was told Saul, "Behold, David is at Naioth in Ramah." **²⁰** Then Saul sent messengers to take David, and when they saw the company of the prophets prophesying, and Samuel standing as head over them, the Spirit of God came upon the messengers of Saul, and they also prophesied. **²¹** When it was told Saul, he sent other messengers, and they also prophesied. And Saul sent messengers again the third time, and they also prophesied. **²²** Then he himself went to Ramah and came to the great well that is in Secu. And he asked, "Where are Samuel and David?" And one said, "Behold, they are at Naioth in Ramah." **²³** And he went there to Naioth in Ramah. And the Spirit of God came upon him also, and as he went he prophesied until he came to Naioth in Ramah. **²⁴** And he too stripped off his clothes, and he too prophesied before Samuel and lay naked all that day and all

that night. Thus it is said, "Is Saul also among the prophets?"

Jonathan Warns David

20 Then David fled from Naioth in Ramah and came and said before Jonathan, "What have I done? What is my guilt? And what is my sin before your father, that he seeks my life?" **²** And he said to him, "Far from it! You shall not die. Behold, my father does nothing either great or small without disclosing it to me. And why should my father hide this from me? It is not so." **³** But David vowed again, saying, "Your father knows well that I have found favor in your eyes, and he thinks, 'Do not let Jonathan know this, lest he be grieved.' But truly, as the LORD lives and as your soul lives, there is but a step between me

▶ **GETTING THE MESSAGE**

What was the significance of the new moon? The new moon (20:5) was the day of the first appearance of the crescent moon in the western sky at sunset. This marked the beginning of the month in the lunar calendar. One of the main festivals in Israelite society was held at the time of the new moon.

and death." **⁴** Then Jonathan said to David, "Whatever you say, I will do for you." **⁵** David said to Jonathan, "Behold, tomorrow is the new moon, and I should not fail to sit at table with the king. But let me go, that I may hide myself in the field till the third day at evening. **⁶** If your father misses me at all, then say, 'David earnestly asked leave of me to run to Bethlehem his city, for there is a yearly sacrifice there for all the clan.' **⁷** If he says, 'Good!' it will be well with your servant, but if he is angry, then know that harm is determined by him. **⁸** Therefore deal kindly with your servant, for you have brought your servant into a covenant of the LORD with you. But if there is guilt in me, kill me yourself, for why should you bring me to your father?" **⁹** And Jonathan said, "Far be it from you! If I knew that it was determined by my father that harm should come to you, would I not tell you?" **¹⁰** Then David said to Jonathan, "Who will tell me

¹ Or a household god

if your father answers you roughly?" ¹¹ And Jonathan said to David, "Come, let us go out into the field." So they both went out into the field.

¹² And Jonathan said to David, "The LORD, the God of Israel, be witness! When I have sounded out my father, about this time tomorrow, or the third day, behold, if he is well disposed toward David, shall I not then send and disclose it to you? ¹³ But should it please my father to do you harm, the LORD do so to Jonathan and more also if I do not

---

PROFILE

JONATHAN

Jonathan was King Saul's oldest son. He showed great trust in God at Michmash (14:6), where he led a daring raid that brought an Israelite victory over the Philistines. Jonathan became a close friend of David. The Bible says that he loved David "as his own soul" (18:1). When his father sought to kill David, Jonathan warned his friend and helped him escape. As Saul's popular eldest son, Jonathan would have been easily accepted as Saul's heir. He showed radical self-denial, however, in giving up any right to the throne of Israel. He gave his absolute support to David as the Lord's choice to succeed Saul as king. Jonathan remained devoted to his father, dying alongside him at Mount Gilboa.

KEY REFERENCE: 1 SAMUEL 18:1-4

---

disclose it to you and send you away, that you may go in safety. May the LORD be with you, as he has been with my father. ¹⁴ If I am still alive, show me the steadfast love of the LORD, that I may not die; ¹⁵ and do not cut off your steadfast love from my house forever, when the LORD cuts off every one of the enemies of David from the face of the earth." ¹⁶ And Jonathan made a covenant with the house of David, saying, "May the LORD take vengeance on David's enemies." ¹⁷ And Jonathan made David swear again by his love for him, for he loved him as he loved his own soul.

¹⁸ Then Jonathan said to him, "Tomorrow is the new moon, and you will be missed, because your seat will be empty. ¹⁹ On the third day go down quickly to the place where you hid yourself when the matter was in hand, and remain beside the stone heap. ²⁰ And I will shoot three arrows to the side of it, as though I shot at a mark. ²¹ And behold, I will send the boy, saying, 'Go, find the arrows.' If I say to the boy, 'Look, the arrows are on this side of you, take them,' then you are to come, for, as the LORD lives, it is safe for you and there is no danger. ²² But if I say to the youth, 'Look, the arrows are beyond you,' then go, for the LORD has sent you away. ²³ And as for the matter of which you and I have spoken, behold, the LORD is between you and me forever."

²⁴ So David hid himself in the field. And when the new moon came, the king sat down to eat food. ²⁵ The king sat on his seat, as at other times, on the seat by the wall. Jonathan sat opposite, and Abner sat by Saul's side, but David's place was empty. ²⁶ Yet Saul did not say anything that day, for he thought, "Something has happened to him. He is not clean; surely he is not clean." ²⁷ But on the second day, the day after the new moon, David's place was empty. And Saul said to Jonathan his son, "Why has not the son of Jesse come to the meal, either yesterday or today?" ²⁸ Jonathan answered Saul, "David earnestly asked leave of me to go to Bethlehem. ²⁹ He said, 'Let me go, for our clan holds a sacrifice in the city, and my brother has commanded me to be there. So now, if I have found favor in your eyes, let me get away and see my brothers.' For this reason he has not come to the king's table."

³⁰ Then Saul's anger was kindled against Jonathan, and he said to him, "You son of a perverse, rebellious woman, do I not know that you have chosen the son of Jesse to your own shame, and to the shame of your mother's nakedness? ³¹ For as long as the son of Jesse lives on the earth, neither you nor your kingdom shall be established. Therefore send and bring him to me, for he shall surely die." ³² Then Jonathan answered Saul his father, "Why should he be put to death? What has he done?" ³³ But Saul hurled his spear at him to strike him. So Jonathan knew that his father was determined to put David to death. ³⁴ And Jonathan rose from

the table in fierce anger and ate no food the second day of the month, for he was grieved for David, because his father had disgraced him.

³⁵ In the morning Jonathan went out into the field to the appointment with David, and with him a little boy. ³⁶ And he said to his boy, "Run and find the arrows that I shoot." As the boy ran, he shot an arrow beyond him. ³⁷ And when the boy came to the place of the arrow that Jonathan had shot, Jonathan called after the boy and said, "Is not the arrow beyond you?" ³⁸ And Jonathan called after the boy, "Hurry! Be quick! Do not stay!" So Jonathan's boy gathered up the arrows and came to his master. ³⁹ But the boy knew nothing. Only Jonathan and David knew the matter. ⁴⁰ And Jonathan gave his weapons to his boy and said to him, "Go and carry them to the city." ⁴¹ And as soon as the boy had gone, David rose from beside the stone heap and fell on his face to the ground and bowed three times. And they kissed one another and wept with one another, David weeping the most. ⁴² Then Jonathan said to David, "Go in peace, because we have sworn both of us in the name of the LORD, saying, 'The LORD shall be between me and you, and between my offspring and your offspring, forever.'" And he rose and departed, and Jonathan went into the city.

David and the Holy Bread

21 Then David came to Nob to Ahimelech the priest. And Ahimelech came to meet David trembling and said to him, "Why are you alone, and no one with you?" ² And David said to Ahimelech the priest, "The king has charged me with a matter and said to me, 'Let no one know anything of the matter about which I send you, and with which I have charged you.' I have made an appointment with the young men for such and such a place. ³ Now then, what do you have on hand? Give me five loaves of bread, or whatever is here." ⁴ And the priest answered David, "I have no common bread on hand, but there is holy bread—if the young men have kept themselves from women." ⁵ And David answered the priest, "Truly women have been kept from us as always when I go on an expedition. The vessels of the young men are holy even when it is an ordinary journey. How much more today will their vessels be holy?" ⁶ So the priest gave him the holy bread, for there was no bread there but the bread of the Presence, which is removed from before the LORD, to be replaced by hot bread on the day it is taken away.

⁷ Now a certain man of the servants of Saul was there that day, detained before the LORD. His name was Doeg the Edomite, the chief of Saul's herdsmen.

⁸ Then David said to Ahimelech, "Then have you not here a spear or a sword at hand? For I have brought neither my sword nor my weapons with me, because the king's business required haste." ⁹ And the priest said, "The sword of Goliath the Philistine, whom you struck down in the Valley of Elah, behold, it is here wrapped in a cloth behind the ephod. If you will take that, take it, for there is none but that here." And David said, "There is none like that; give it to me."

GETTING THE MESSAGE

After the destruction of Shiloh, **Nob** apparently became the city where the priests and Levites lived (21:1). Although its exact location is unknown, it was probably a mile or two north of Jerusalem. After the building of the temple, Jerusalem became the nation's official religious center.

David Flees to Gath

¹⁰ And David rose and fled that day from Saul and went to Achish the king of Gath. ¹¹ And the servants of Achish said to him, "Is not this David the king of the land? Did they not sing to one another of him in dances,

'Saul has struck down his thousands, and David his ten thousands'?"

¹² And David took these words to heart and was much afraid of Achish the king of Gath. ¹³ So he changed his behavior before them and pretended to be insane in their hands and made marks on the doors of the gate and let his spittle run down his beard. ¹⁴ Then Achish said to his servants, "Behold, you see the man is mad. Why then have you brought him to me? ¹⁵ Do I lack madmen, that you have brought this fellow to behave as a madman in my presence? Shall this fellow come into my house?"

David at the Cave of Adullam

22 David departed from there and escaped to the cave of Adullam. And when his brothers and all his father's house heard it, they went down there to him. ²And everyone who was in distress, and everyone who was in debt, and everyone who was bitter in soul, gathered to him. And he became commander over them. And there were with him about four hundred men.

³And David went from there to Mizpeh of Moab. And he said to the king of Moab, "Please let my father and my mother stay with you, till I know what God will do for me." ⁴And he left them with the king of Moab, and they stayed with him all the time that David was in the stronghold. ⁵Then the prophet Gad said to David, "Do not remain in the stronghold; depart, and go into the land of Judah." So David departed and went into the forest of Hereth.

Saul Kills the Priests at Nob

⁶Now Saul heard that David was discovered, and the men who were with him. Saul was sitting at Gibeah under the tamarisk tree on the height with his spear in his hand, and all his servants were standing about him. ⁷And Saul said to his servants who stood about him, "Hear now, people of Benjamin; will the son of Jesse give every one of you fields and vineyards, will he make you all commanders of thousands and commanders of hundreds, ⁸that all of you have conspired against me? No one discloses to me when my son makes a covenant with the son of Jesse. None of you is sorry for me or discloses to me that my son has stirred up my servant against me, to lie in wait, as at this day." ⁹Then answered Doeg the Edomite, who stood by the servants of Saul, "I saw the son of Jesse coming to Nob, to Ahimelech the son of Ahitub, ¹⁰and he inquired of the LORD for him and gave him provisions and gave him the sword of Goliath the Philistine."

¹¹Then the king sent to summon Ahimelech the priest, the son of Ahitub, and all his father's house, the priests who were at Nob, and all of them came to the king. ¹²And Saul said, "Hear now, son of Ahitub." And he answered, "Here I am, my lord." ¹³And Saul said to him, "Why have you conspired against me, you and the son of Jesse, in that you have given him bread and a sword

and have inquired of God for him, so that he has risen against me, to lie in wait, as at this day?" ¹⁴Then Ahimelech answered the king, "And who among all your servants is so faithful as David, who is the king's son-in-law, and captain over your bodyguard, and honored in your house? ¹⁵Is today the first time that I have inquired of God for him? No! Let not the king impute anything to his servant or to all the house of my father, for your servant has known nothing of all this, much or little." ¹⁶And the king said, "You shall surely die, Ahimelech, you and all your father's house." ¹⁷And the king said to the guard who stood about him, "Turn and kill the priests of the LORD, because their hand also is with David, and they knew that he fled and did not disclose it to me." But the servants of the king would not put out their hand to strike the priests of the LORD. ¹⁸Then the king said to Doeg, "You turn and strike the priests." And Doeg the Edomite turned and struck down the priests, and he killed on that day eighty-five persons who wore the linen ephod. ¹⁹And Nob, the city of the priests, he put to the sword; both man and woman, child and infant, ox, donkey and sheep, he put to the sword.

²⁰But one of the sons of Ahimelech the son of Ahitub, named Abiathar, escaped and fled after David. ²¹And Abiathar told David that Saul had killed the priests of the LORD. ²²And David said to Abiathar, "I knew on that day, when Doeg the Edomite was there, that he would surely tell Saul. I have occasioned the death of all the persons of your father's house. ²³Stay with me; do not be afraid, for he who seeks my life seeks your life. With me you shall be in safekeeping."

David Saves the City of Keilah

23 Now they told David, "Behold, the Philistines are fighting against Keilah and are robbing the threshing floors." ²Therefore David inquired of the LORD, "Shall I go and attack these Philistines?" And the LORD said to David, "Go and attack the Philistines and save Keilah." ³But David's men said to him, "Behold, we are afraid here in Judah; how much more then if we go to Keilah against the armies of the Philistines?" ⁴Then David inquired of the LORD again. And the LORD answered him, "Arise, go down to Keilah, for I will give the Philistines into your hand." ⁵And David and his men went to Keilah and fought with the Philistines and brought away their livestock and struck them with a great blow. So David saved the inhabitants of Keilah.

⁶ When Abiathar the son of Ahimelech had fled to David to Keilah, he had come down with an ephod in his hand. ⁷ Now it was told Saul that David had come to Keilah. And Saul said, "God has given him into my hand, for he has shut himself in by entering a town that has gates and bars." ⁸ And Saul summoned all the people to war, to go down to Keilah, to besiege David and his men. ⁹ David knew that Saul was plotting harm against him. And he said to Abiathar the priest, "Bring the ephod here." ¹⁰ Then David said, "O LORD, the God of Israel, your servant has surely heard that Saul seeks to come to Keilah, to destroy the city on my account. ¹¹ Will the men of Keilah surrender me into his hand? Will Saul come down, as your servant has heard? O LORD, the God of Israel, please tell your servant." And the LORD said, "He will come down." ¹² Then David said, "Will the men of Keilah surrender me and my men into the hand of Saul?" And the LORD said, "They will surrender you." ¹³ Then David and his men, who were about six hundred, arose and departed from Keilah, and they went wherever they could go. When Saul was told that David had escaped from Keilah, he gave up the expedition. ¹⁴ And David remained in the strongholds in the wilderness, in the hill country of the wilderness of Ziph. And Saul sought him every day, but God did not give him into his hand.

Saul Pursues David

¹⁵ David saw that Saul had come out to seek his life. David was in the wilderness of Ziph at Horesh. ¹⁶ And Jonathan, Saul's son, rose and went to David at Horesh, and strengthened his hand in God. ¹⁷ And he said to him, "Do not fear, for the hand of Saul my father shall not find you. You shall be king over Israel, and I shall be next to you. Saul my father also knows this." ¹⁸ And the two of them made a covenant before the LORD. David remained at Horesh, and Jonathan went home.

¹⁹ Then the Ziphites went up to Saul at Gibeah, saying, "Is not David hiding among us in the strongholds at Horesh, on the hill of Hachilah, which is south of Jeshimon?

²⁰ Now come down, O king, according to all your heart's desire to come down, and our part shall be to surrender him into the king's hand." ²¹ And Saul said, "May you be blessed by the LORD, for you have had compassion on me. ²² Go, make yet more sure. Know and see the place where his foot is, and who has seen him there, for it is told me that he is very cunning. ²³ See therefore and take note of all the lurking places where he hides, and come back to me with sure information. Then I will go with you. And if he is in the land, I will search him out among all the thousands of Judah." ²⁴ And they arose and went to Ziph ahead of Saul.

Now David and his men were in the wilderness of Maon, in the Arabah to the south of Jeshimon. ²⁵ And Saul and his men went to seek him. And David was told, so he went down to the rock and lived in the wilderness of Maon. And when Saul heard that, he pursued after David in the wilderness of Maon.

²⁶ Saul went on one side of the mountain, and David and his men on the other side of the mountain. And David was hurrying to get away from Saul. As Saul and his men were closing in on David and his men to capture them, ²⁷ a messenger came to Saul, saying, "Hurry and come, for the Philistines have made a raid against the land." ²⁸ So Saul returned from pursuing after David and went against the Philistines. Therefore that place was called the Rock of Escape. ²⁹ And David went up from there and lived in the strongholds of Engedi.

David Spares Saul's Life

24 When Saul returned from following the Philistines, he was told, "Behold, David is in the wilderness of Engedi." ² Then Saul took three thousand chosen men out of all Israel and went to seek David and his men in front of the Wildgoats' Rocks. ³ And he came to the sheepfolds by the way, where there was a cave, and Saul went in to relieve himself. Now David and his men were sitting in the innermost parts of the cave. ⁴ And

the men of David said to him, "Here is the day of which the LORD said to you, 'Behold, I will give your enemy into your hand, and you shall do to him as it shall seem good to you.'" Then David arose and stealthily cut off a corner of Saul's robe. [5] And afterward David's heart struck him, because he had cut off a corner of Saul's robe. [6] He said to his men, "The LORD forbid that I should do this thing to my lord, the LORD's anointed, to put out my hand against him, seeing he is the LORD's anointed." [7] So David persuaded his men with these words and did not permit them to attack Saul. And Saul rose up and left the cave and went on his way.

[8] Afterward David also arose and went out of the cave, and called after Saul, "My lord the king!" And when Saul looked behind him, David bowed with his face to the earth

and paid homage. [9] And David said to Saul, "Why do you listen to the words of men who say, 'Behold, David seeks your harm'? [10] Behold, this day your eyes have seen how the LORD gave you today into my hand in the cave. And some told me to kill you, but I spared you. I said, 'I will not put out my hand against my lord, for he is the LORD's anointed.' [11] See, my father, see the corner of your robe in my hand. For by the fact that I cut off the corner of your robe and did not kill you, you may know and see that there is no wrong or treason in my hands. I have not sinned against you, though you hunt my life to take it. [12] May the LORD judge between me and you, may the LORD avenge me against you, but my hand shall not be against you. [13] As the proverb of the ancients says, 'Out of the wicked comes wickedness.' But my hand shall not be against you. [14] After whom has the king of Israel come out? After whom do

you pursue? After a dead dog! After a flea! [15] May the LORD therefore be judge and give sentence between me and you, and see to it and plead my cause and deliver me from your hand."

[16] As soon as David had finished speaking these words to Saul, Saul said, "Is this your voice, my son David?" And Saul lifted up his voice and wept. [17] He said to David, "You are more righteous than I, for you have repaid me good, whereas I have repaid you evil. [18] And you have declared this day how you have dealt well with me, in that you did not kill me when the LORD put me into your hands. [19] For if a man finds his enemy, will he let him go away safe? So may the LORD reward you with good for what you have done to me this day. [20] And now, behold, I know that you shall surely be king, and that the kingdom of Israel shall be established in your hand. [21] Swear to me therefore by the LORD that you will not cut off my offspring after me, and that you will not destroy my name out of my father's house." [22] And David swore this to Saul. Then Saul went home, but David and his men went up to the stronghold.

The Death of Samuel

25 Now Samuel died. And all Israel assembled and mourned for him, and they buried him in his house at Ramah.

David and Abigail

Then David rose and went down to the wilderness of Paran. [2] And there was a man in Maon whose business was in Carmel. The man was very rich; he had three thousand sheep and a thousand goats. He was shearing his sheep in Carmel. [3] Now the name of the man was Nabal, and the name of his wife Abigail. The woman was discerning and beautiful, but the man was harsh and badly behaved; he was a Calebite. [4] David heard in the wilderness that Nabal was shearing his sheep. [5] So David sent ten young men. And David said to the young men, "Go up to Carmel, and go to Nabal and greet him in my name. [6] And thus you shall greet him: 'Peace be to you, and peace be to your house, and peace be to all that you have. [7] I hear that you have shearers. Now your shepherds have been with us, and we did them no harm, and they missed nothing all the time they were in Carmel. [8] Ask your young men, and they will tell you. Therefore let my young men find favor in your eyes, for we come on a feast day. Please give whatever you have at hand to your servants and to your son David.'"

⁹ When David's young men came, they said all this to Nabal in the name of David, and then they waited. ¹⁰ And Nabal answered David's servants, "Who is David? Who is the son of Jesse? There are many servants these days who are breaking away from their masters. ¹¹ Shall I take my bread and my water and my meat that I have killed for my shearers and give it to men who come from I do not know where?" ¹² So David's young men turned away and came back and told him all this. ¹³ And David said to his men, "Every man strap on his sword!" And every man of them strapped on his sword. David also strapped on his sword. And about four hundred men went up after David, while two hundred remained with the baggage.

¹⁴ But one of the young men told Abigail, Nabal's wife, "Behold, David sent messengers out of the wilderness to greet our master, and he railed at them. ¹⁵ Yet the men were very good to us, and we suffered no harm, and we did not miss anything when we were in the fields, as long as we went with them. ¹⁶ They were a wall to us both by night and by day, all the while we were with them keeping the sheep. ¹⁷ Now therefore know this and consider what you should do, for harm is determined against our master and against all his house, and he is such a worthless man that one cannot speak to him."

¹⁸ Then Abigail made haste and took two hundred loaves and two skins of wine and five sheep already prepared and five seahs of parched grain and a hundred clusters of raisins and two hundred cakes of figs, and laid them on donkeys. ¹⁹ And she said to her young men, "Go on before me; behold, I come after you." But she did not tell her husband Nabal. ²⁰ And as she rode on the donkey and came down under cover of the mountain, behold, David and his men came down toward her, and she met them. ²¹ Now David had said, "Surely in vain have I guarded all that this fellow has in the wilderness, so that nothing was missed of all that belonged to him, and he has returned me evil for good. ²² God do so to the enemies of David and more also, if by morning I leave so much as one male of all who belong to him."

²³ When Abigail saw David, she hurried and got down from the donkey and fell before David on her face and bowed to the ground. ²⁴ She fell at his feet and said, "On me alone, my lord, be the guilt. Please let your servant speak in your ears, and hear the words of your servant. ²⁵ Let not my lord regard this worthless fellow, Nabal, for as his name is, so is he. Nabal[1] is his name, and folly is with him. But I your servant did

---

PROFILE

ABIGAIL

Abigail was the wife of Nabal, a wealthy but extremely foolish man. Nabal insulted David by refusing to care for and feed David and his men. His rudeness made David very angry, but Abigail wisely convinced David not to take vengeance. She sent food to David and spoke humbly and respectfully to him. Abigail calmed David's anger and persuaded him not to kill her wicked husband and his household. Impressed by Abigail's wisdom and discernment, David blessed Abigail and sent her home in peace. When she told Nabal what had happened, his "heart died within him" (25:37). A few days later, the Lord struck Nabal and he died. Following his death, David married Abigail.

KEY REFERENCE: 1 SAMUEL 25:32–35

---

not see the young men of my lord, whom you sent. ²⁶ Now then, my lord, as the LORD lives, and as your soul lives, because the LORD has restrained you from bloodguilt and from saving with your own hand, now then let your enemies and those who seek to do evil to my lord be as Nabal. ²⁷ And now let this present that your servant has brought to my lord be given to the young men who follow my lord. ²⁸ Please forgive the trespass of your servant. For the LORD will certainly make my lord a sure house, because my lord is fighting the battles of the LORD, and evil

---

[1] Nabal means fool

shall not be found in you so long as you live. ²⁹ If men rise up to pursue you and to seek your life, the life of my lord shall be bound in the bundle of the living in the care of the LORD your God. And the lives of your enemies he shall sling out as from the hollow of a sling. ³⁰ And when the LORD has done to my lord according to all the good that he has spoken concerning you and has appointed you prince over Israel, ³¹ my lord shall have no cause of grief or pangs of conscience for having shed blood without cause or for my lord working salvation himself. And when the LORD has dealt well with my lord, then remember your servant."

³² And David said to Abigail, "Blessed be the LORD, the God of Israel, who sent you this day to meet me! ³³ Blessed be your discretion, and blessed be you, who have kept me this day from bloodguilt and from working salvation with my own hand! ³⁴ For as surely as the LORD, the God of Israel, lives, who has restrained me from hurting you, unless you had hurried and come to meet me, truly by morning there had not been left to Nabal so much as one male." ³⁵ Then David received from her hand what she had brought him. And he said to her, "Go up in peace to your house. See, I have obeyed your voice, and I have granted your petition."

³⁶ And Abigail came to Nabal, and behold, he was holding a feast in his house, like the feast of a king. And Nabal's heart was merry within him, for he was very drunk. So she told him nothing at all until the morning light. ³⁷ In the morning, when the wine had gone out of Nabal, his wife told him these things, and his heart died within him, and he became as a stone. ³⁸ And about ten days later the LORD struck Nabal, and he died.

³⁹ When David heard that Nabal was dead, he said, "Blessed be the LORD who has avenged the insult I received at the hand of Nabal, and has kept back his servant from wrongdoing. The LORD has returned the evil of Nabal on his own head." Then David sent and spoke to Abigail, to take her as his wife. ⁴⁰ When the servants of David came to Abigail at Carmel, they said to her, "David has sent us to you to take you to him as his wife." ⁴¹ And she rose and bowed with her face to the ground and said, "Behold, your handmaid is a servant to wash the feet of the servants of my lord." ⁴² And Abigail

hurried and rose and mounted a donkey, and her five young women attended her. She followed the messengers of David and became his wife.

⁴³ David also took Ahinoam of Jezreel, and both of them became his wives. ⁴⁴ Saul had given Michal his daughter, David's wife, to Palti the son of Laish, who was of Gallim.

David Spares Saul Again

26 Then the Ziphites came to Saul at Gibeah, saying, "Is not David hiding himself on the hill of Hachilah, which is on the east of Jeshimon?" ² So Saul arose and went down to the wilderness of Ziph with three thousand chosen men of Israel to seek David in the wilderness of Ziph. ³ And Saul encamped on the hill of Hachilah, which is beside the road on the east of Jeshimon. But David remained in the wilderness. When he saw that Saul came after him into the wilderness, ⁴ David sent out spies and learned that Saul had indeed come. ⁵ Then David rose and came to the place where Saul had encamped. And David saw the place where Saul lay, with Abner the son of Ner, the commander of his army. Saul was lying within the encampment, while the army was encamped around him.

⁶ Then David said to Ahimelech the Hittite, and to Joab's brother Abishai the son of Zeruiah, "Who will go down with me into the camp to Saul?" And Abishai said, "I will go down with you." ⁷ So David and Abishai went to the army by night. And there lay Saul sleeping within the encampment, with his spear stuck in the ground at his head, and Abner and the army lay around him. ⁸ Then Abishai said to David, "God has given your enemy into your hand this day. Now please let me pin him to the earth with one stroke of the spear, and I will not strike him twice." ⁹ But David said to Abishai, "Do not destroy him, for who can put out his hand against the LORD's anointed and be guiltless?" ¹⁰ And David said, "As the LORD lives, the LORD will strike him, or his day will come to die, or he will go down into battle and perish. ¹¹ The LORD forbid that I should put out my hand against the LORD's anointed. But take now the spear that is at his head and the jar of water, and let us go." ¹² So David took the spear and the jar of water from Saul's head, and they went away. No man saw it or knew it, nor did any awake,

for they were all asleep, because a deep sleep from the LORD had fallen upon them. ¹³ Then David went over to the other side and stood far off on the top of the hill, with a great space between them. ¹⁴ And David called to the army, and to Abner the son of Ner, saying, "Will you not answer, Abner?" Then Abner answered, "Who are you who calls to the king?" ¹⁵ And David said to Abner, "Are you not a man? Who is like you in Israel? Why then have you not kept watch over your lord the king? For one of the people came in to destroy the king your lord. ¹⁶ This thing that you have done is not good. As the LORD lives, you deserve to die, because you have not kept watch over your lord, the LORD's anointed. And now see where the king's spear is and the jar of water that was at his head."

¹⁷ Saul recognized David's voice and said, "Is this your voice, my son David?" And David said, "It is my voice, my lord, O king." ¹⁸ And he said, "Why does my lord pursue after his servant? For what have I done? What evil is on my hands? ¹⁹ Now therefore let my lord the king hear the words of his servant. If it is the LORD who has stirred you up against me, may he accept an offering, but if it is men, may they be cursed before the LORD, for they have driven me out this day that I should have no share in the heritage of the LORD, saying, 'Go, serve other gods.' ²⁰ Now therefore, let not my blood fall to the earth away from the presence of the LORD, for the king of Israel has come out to seek a single flea like one who hunts a partridge in the mountains."

²¹ Then Saul said, "I have sinned. Return, my son David, for I will no more do you harm, because my life was precious in your eyes this day. Behold, I have acted foolishly, and have made a great mistake." ²² And David answered and said, "Here is the spear, O king! Let one of the young men come over and take it. ²³ The LORD rewards every man for his righteousness and his faithfulness, for the LORD gave you into my hand today, and I would not put out my hand against the LORD's anointed. ²⁴ Behold, as your life was precious this day in my sight, so may my life be precious in the sight of the LORD, and may he deliver me out of all tribulation." ²⁵ Then Saul said to David, "Blessed be you, my son David! You will do many things and

will succeed in them." So David went his way, and Saul returned to his place.

David Flees to the Philistines

27 Then David said in his heart, "Now I shall perish one day by the hand of Saul. There is nothing better for me than that I should escape to the land of the Philistines. Then Saul will despair of seeking me any longer within the borders of Israel, and I shall escape out of his hand." ² So David arose and went over, he and the six hundred men who were with him, to Achish the son of Maoch, king of Gath. ³ And David lived with Achish at Gath, he and his men, every man with his household, and David with his two wives, Ahinoam of Jezreel, and Abigail of Carmel, Nabal's widow. ⁴ And when it was told Saul that David had fled to Gath, he no longer sought him.

⁵ Then David said to Achish, "If I have found favor in your eyes, let a place be given me in one of the country towns, that I may dwell there. For why should your servant dwell in the royal city with you?" ⁶ So that day Achish gave him Ziklag. Therefore Ziklag has belonged to the kings of Judah to this day. ⁷ And the number of the days that David lived in the country of the Philistines was a year and four months.

⁸ Now David and his men went up and made raids against the Geshurites, the Girzites, and the Amalekites, for these were the inhabitants of the land from of old, as far as Shur, to the land of Egypt. ⁹ And David would strike the land and would leave neither man nor woman alive, but would take away the sheep, the oxen, the donkeys, the camels, and the garments, and come back to Achish. ¹⁰ When Achish asked, "Where have you made a raid today?" David would say, "Against the Negeb of Judah," or, "Against the Negeb of the Jerahmeelites," or, "Against the

Negeb of the Kenites." ¹¹ And David would leave neither man nor woman alive to bring news to Gath, thinking, "lest they should tell about us and say, 'So David has done.'" Such was his custom all the while he lived in the country of the Philistines. ¹² And Achish trusted David, thinking, "He has made himself an utter stench to his people Israel; therefore he shall always be my servant."

Saul and the Medium of En-dor

28 In those days the Philistines gathered their forces for war, to fight against Israel. And Achish said to David, "Understand that you and your men are to go out with me in the army." ² David said to Achish, "Very well, you shall know what your servant can do." And Achish said to David, "Very well, I will make you my bodyguard for life."

> ### GETTING THE MESSAGE
>
> **How is a fattened calf different from a regular calf?** A fattened calf (28:24) was one that had been set aside for a special occasion. While most cattle simply grazed in fields, these select animals were fed in a stall. The extra food and the inability to roam freely meant that they would gain more weight.

³ Now Samuel had died, and all Israel had mourned for him and buried him in Ramah, his own city. And Saul had put the mediums and the necromancers out of the land. ⁴ The Philistines assembled and came and encamped at Shunem. And Saul gathered all Israel, and they encamped at Gilboa. ⁵ When Saul saw the army of the Philistines, he was afraid, and his heart trembled greatly. ⁶ And when Saul inquired of the LORD, the LORD did not answer him, either by dreams, or by Urim, or by prophets. ⁷ Then Saul said to his servants, "Seek out for me a woman who is a medium, that I may go to her and inquire of her." And his servants said to him, "Behold, there is a medium at En-dor."

⁸ So Saul disguised himself and put on other garments and went, he and two men with him. And they came to the woman by night. And he said, "Divine for me by a spirit and bring up for me whomever I shall name to you." ⁹ The woman said to him, "Surely you know what Saul has done, how he has cut off the mediums and the necromancers from the land. Why then are you laying a trap for my life to bring about my death?" ¹⁰ But Saul swore to her by the LORD, "As the LORD lives, no punishment shall come upon you for this thing." ¹¹ Then the woman said, "Whom shall I bring up for you?" He said, "Bring up Samuel for me." ¹² When the woman saw Samuel, she cried out with a loud voice. And the woman said to Saul, "Why have you deceived me? You are Saul." ¹³ The king said to her, "Do not be afraid. What do you see?" And the woman said to Saul, "I see a god coming up out of the earth." ¹⁴ He said to her, "What is his appearance?" And she said, "An old man is coming up, and he is wrapped in a robe." And Saul knew that it was Samuel, and he bowed with his face to the ground and paid homage.

¹⁵ Then Samuel said to Saul, "Why have you disturbed me by bringing me up?" Saul answered, "I am in great distress, for the Philistines are warring against me, and God has turned away from me and answers me no more, either by prophets or by dreams. Therefore I have summoned you to tell me what I shall do." ¹⁶ And Samuel said, "Why then do you ask me, since the LORD has turned from you and become your enemy? ¹⁷ The LORD has done to you as he spoke by me, for the LORD has torn the kingdom out of your hand and given it to your neighbor, David. ¹⁸ Because you did not obey the voice of the LORD and did not carry out his fierce wrath against Amalek, therefore the LORD has done this thing to you this day. ¹⁹ Moreover, the LORD will give Israel also with you into the hand of the Philistines, and tomorrow you and your sons shall be with me. The LORD will give the army of Israel also into the hand of the Philistines."

²⁰ Then Saul fell at once full length on the ground, filled with fear because of the words of Samuel. And there was no strength in him, for he had eaten nothing all day and all night. ²¹ And the woman came to Saul, and when she saw that he was terrified, she said to him, "Behold, your servant has obeyed you. I have taken my life in my hand and have listened to what you have said to me. ²² Now therefore, you also obey your servant. Let me set a morsel of bread before you; and eat, that you may have strength

when you go on your way." **23** He refused and said, "I will not eat." But his servants, together with the woman, urged him, and he listened to their words. So he arose from the earth and sat on the bed. **24** Now the woman had a fattened calf in the house, and she quickly killed it, and she took flour and kneaded it and baked unleavened bread of it, **25** and she put it before Saul and his servants, and they ate. Then they rose and went away that night.

The Philistines Reject David

29 Now the Philistines had gathered all their forces at Aphek. And the Israelites were encamped by the spring that is in Jezreel. **2** As the lords of the Philistines were passing on by hundreds and by thousands, and David and his men were passing on in the rear with Achish, **3** the commanders of the Philistines said, "What are these Hebrews doing here?" And Achish said to the commanders of the Philistines, "Is this not David, the servant of Saul, king of Israel, who has been with me now for days and years, and since he deserted to me I have found no fault in him to this day." **4** But the commanders of the Philistines were angry with him. And the commanders of the Philistines said to him, "Send the man back, that he may return to the place to which you have assigned him. He shall not go down with us to battle, lest in the battle he become an adversary to us. For how could this fellow reconcile himself to his lord? Would it not be with the heads of the men here? **5** Is not this David, of whom they sing to one another in dances,

'Saul has struck down his thousands,
    and David his ten thousands'?"

6 Then Achish called David and said to him, "As the LORD lives, you have been honest, and to me it seems right that you should march out and in with me in the campaign. For I have found nothing wrong in you from the day of your coming to me to this day. Nevertheless, the lords do not approve of you. **7** So go back now; and go peaceably, that you may not displease the lords of the Philistines." **8** And David said to Achish, "But what have I done? What have you found in your servant from the day I entered your service until now, that I may not go and fight against the enemies of my lord the

king?" **9** And Achish answered David and said, "I know that you are as blameless in my sight as an angel of God. Nevertheless, the commanders of the Philistines have said, 'He shall not go up with us to the battle.' **10** Now then rise early in the morning with the servants of your lord who came with you, and start early in the morning, and depart as soon as you have light." **11** So David set out with his men early in the morning to return to the land of the Philistines. But the Philistines went up to Jezreel.

David's Wives Are Captured

30 Now when David and his men came to Ziklag on the third day, the Amalekites had made a raid against the Negeb and against Ziklag. They had overcome Ziklag and burned it with fire **2** and taken captive the women and all who were in it, both small and great. They killed no one, but carried them off and went their way. **3** And when David and his men came to the city, they found it burned with fire, and their wives and sons and daughters taken captive. **4** Then David and the people who were with him raised their voices and wept until they had no more strength to weep. **5** David's two wives also had been taken captive, Ahinoam of Jezreel and Abigail the widow of Nabal of Carmel. **6** And David was greatly distressed, for the people spoke of stoning him, because all the people were bitter in soul, each for his sons and daughters. But David strengthened himself in the LORD his God.

7 And David said to Abiathar the priest, the son of Ahimelech, "Bring me the ephod." So Abiathar brought the ephod to David. **8** And David inquired of the LORD, "Shall I pursue after this band? Shall I overtake them?" He answered him, "Pursue, for you shall surely overtake and shall surely rescue." **9** So David set out, and the six hundred men who were with him, and they came to the brook Besor, where those who were left behind stayed. **10** But David pursued, he and four hundred men. Two hundred stayed behind, who were too exhausted to cross the brook Besor.

11 They found an Egyptian in the open country and brought him to David. And they gave him bread and he ate. They gave him water to drink, **12** and they gave him a piece of a cake of figs and two clusters of raisins.

And when he had eaten, his spirit revived, for he had not eaten bread or drunk water for three days and three nights. ¹³ And David said to him, "To whom do you belong? And where are you from?" He said, "I am a young man of Egypt, servant to an Amalekite, and my master left me behind because I fell sick three days ago. ¹⁴ We had made a raid against the Negeb of the Cherethites and against that which belongs to Judah and against the Negeb of Caleb, and we burned Ziklag with fire." ¹⁵ And David said to him, "Will you take me down to this band?" And he said, "Swear to me by God that you will not kill me or deliver me into the hands of my master, and I will take you down to this band."

David Defeats the Amalekites

¹⁶ And when he had taken him down, behold, they were spread abroad over all the land, eating and drinking and dancing, because of all the great spoil they had taken

> **GETTING THE MESSAGE**
>
> **Pressed fig cakes** were a common food for travelers (30:12). The dried figs would not spoil, and their sugar content made them an ideal energy food.

from the land of the Philistines and from the land of Judah. ¹⁷ And David struck them down from twilight until the evening of the next day, and not a man of them escaped, except four hundred young men, who mounted camels and fled. ¹⁸ David recovered all that the Amalekites had taken, and David rescued his two wives. ¹⁹ Nothing was missing, whether small or great, sons or daughters, spoil or anything that had been taken. David brought back all. ²⁰ David also captured all the flocks and herds, and the people drove the livestock before him, and said, "This is David's spoil."

²¹ Then David came to the two hundred men who had been too exhausted to follow David, and who had been left at the brook Besor. And they went out to meet David and to meet the people who were with him. And when David came near to the people he greeted them. ²² Then all the wicked and worthless fellows among the men who had gone with David said, "Because they did not

go with us, we will not give them any of the spoil that we have recovered, except that each man may lead away his wife and children, and depart." ²³ But David said, "You shall not do so, my brothers, with what the LORD has given us. He has preserved us and given into our hand the band that came against us. ²⁴ Who would listen to you in this matter? For as his share is who goes down into the battle, so shall his share be who stays by the baggage. They shall share alike." ²⁵ And he made it a statute and a rule for Israel from that day forward to this day.

²⁶ When David came to Ziklag, he sent part of the spoil to his friends, the elders of Judah, saying, "Here is a present for you from the spoil of the enemies of the LORD." ²⁷ It was for those in Bethel, in Ramoth of the Negeb, in Jattir, ²⁸ in Aroer, in Siphmoth, in Eshtemoa, ²⁹ in Racal, in the cities of the Jerahmeelites, in the cities of the Kenites, ³⁰ in Hormah, in Bor-ashan, in Athach, ³¹ in Hebron, for all the places where David and his men had roamed.

The Death of Saul

31 Now the Philistines were fighting against Israel, and the men of Israel fled before the Philistines and fell slain on Mount Gilboa. ² And the Philistines overtook Saul and his sons, and the Philistines struck down Jonathan and Abinadab and Malchi-shua, the sons of Saul. ³ The battle pressed hard against Saul, and the archers found him, and he was badly wounded by the archers. ⁴ Then Saul said to his armor-bearer, "Draw your sword, and thrust me through with it, lest these uncircumcised come and thrust me through, and mistreat me." But his armor-bearer would not, for he feared greatly. Therefore Saul took his own sword and fell upon it. ⁵ And when his armor-bearer saw that Saul was dead, he also fell upon his sword and died with him. ⁶ Thus Saul died, and his three sons, and his armor-bearer, and all his men, on the same day together. ⁷ And when the men of Israel who were on the other side of the valley and those beyond the Jordan saw that the men of Israel had fled and that Saul and his sons were dead, they abandoned their cities and fled. And the Philistines came and lived in them.

⁸ The next day, when the Philistines came to strip the slain, they found Saul and his

three sons fallen on Mount Gilboa. ⁹So they cut off his head and stripped off his armor and sent messengers throughout the land of the Philistines, to carry the good news to the house of their idols and to the people. ¹⁰They put his armor in the temple of Ashtaroth, and they fastened his body to the wall of Beth-shan. ¹¹But when the inhabitants of Jabesh-gilead heard what the Philistines had done to Saul, ¹²all the valiant men arose and went all night and took the body of Saul and the bodies of his sons from the wall of Beth-shan, and they came to Jabesh and burned them there. ¹³And they took their bones and buried them under the tamarisk tree in Jabesh and fasted seven days.

2 SAMUEL

David Hears of Saul's Death

1 After the death of Saul, when David had returned from striking down the Amalekites, David remained two days in Ziklag. ² And on the third day, behold, a man came from Saul's camp, with his clothes torn and dirt on his head. And when he came to David, he fell to the ground and paid homage. ³ David said to him, "Where do you come from?" And he said to him, "I have escaped from the camp of Israel." ⁴ And David said to him, "How did it go? Tell me." And he answered, "The people fled from the battle, and also many of the people have fallen and are dead, and Saul and his son Jonathan are also dead." ⁵ Then David said to the young man who told him, "How do you know that Saul and his son Jonathan are dead?" ⁶ And the young man who told him said, "By chance I happened to be on Mount Gilboa, and there was Saul leaning on his spear, and behold, the chariots and the horsemen were close upon him. ⁷ And when he looked behind him, he saw me, and called to me. And I answered, 'Here I am.' ⁸ And he said to me, 'Who are you?' I answered him, 'I am an Amalekite.' ⁹ And he said to me, 'Stand beside me and kill me, for anguish has seized me, and yet my life still lingers.' ¹⁰ So I stood beside him and killed him, because I was sure that he could not live after he had fallen. And I took the crown that was on his head and the armlet that was on his arm, and I have brought them here to my lord."

¹¹ Then David took hold of his clothes and tore them, and so did all the men who were with him. ¹² And they mourned and wept and fasted until evening for Saul and for Jonathan his son and for the people of the LORD and for the house of Israel, because they had fallen by the sword. ¹³ And David said to the young man who told him, "Where do you come from?" And he answered, "I am the son of a sojourner, an Amalekite." ¹⁴ David said to him, "How is it you were not afraid to put out your hand to destroy the LORD's anointed?" ¹⁵ Then David called one of the young men and said, "Go, execute him." And he struck him down so that he died. ¹⁶ And David said to him, "Your blood be on your head, for your own mouth has testified against you, saying, 'I have killed the LORD's anointed.'"

David's Lament for Saul and Jonathan

¹⁷ And David lamented with this lamentation over Saul and Jonathan his son, ¹⁸ and he said it should be taught to the people of Judah; behold, it is written in the Book of Jashar. He said:

¹⁹ "Your glory, O Israel, is slain on your
        high places!
    How the mighty have fallen!

> ### GETTING THE MESSAGE
>
> **Laments** were a common way of showing grief and mourning for the dead. They could poetically capture a person's feelings toward the departed.

²⁰ Tell it not in Gath,
        publish it not in the streets of
            Ashkelon,
    lest the daughters of the Philistines
        rejoice,
    lest the daughters of the uncircumcised exult.

²¹ "You mountains of Gilboa,
        let there be no dew or rain upon you,
        nor fields of offerings!
    For there the shield of the mighty was
        defiled,
        the shield of Saul, not anointed
            with oil.

²² "From the blood of the slain,
        from the fat of the mighty,
    the bow of Jonathan turned not back,
        and the sword of Saul returned not
            empty.

²³ "Saul and Jonathan, beloved and lovely!
    In life and in death they were not
        divided;

they were swifter than eagles;
they were stronger than lions.

24 "You daughters of Israel, weep over Saul,
who clothed you luxuriously in
scarlet,
who put ornaments of gold on your
apparel.

25 "How the mighty have fallen
in the midst of the battle!

"Jonathan lies slain on your high places.
26 I am distressed for you, my brother
Jonathan;
very pleasant have you been to me;
your love to me was extraordinary,
surpassing the love of women.

27 "How the mighty have fallen,
and the weapons of war perished!"

GETTING THE MESSAGE

The pool of Gibeon (2:13) was probably
a huge round cistern cut into limestone
rock. Since the water was about 80 feet
(24 m) below ground, nearly 30 feet
(9 m) of stairs were carved into the side
of the shaft. These stairs led to a tunnel
about 40 feet (12 m) long. At the end of
this tunnel was the pool, where a person
could draw water for daily use.

David Anointed King of Judah

2 After this David inquired of the LORD,
"Shall I go up into any of the cities of
Judah?" And the LORD said to him, "Go up."
David said, "To which shall I go up?" And
he said, "To Hebron." ² So David went up
there, and his two wives also, Ahinoam of
Jezreel and Abigail the widow of Nabal of
Carmel. ³ And David brought up his men
who were with him, everyone with his
household, and they lived in the towns of
Hebron. ⁴ And the men of Judah came, and
there they anointed David king over the
house of Judah.

When they told David, "It was the men of
Jabesh-gilead who buried Saul," ⁵ David sent
messengers to the men of Jabesh-gilead
and said to them, "May you be blessed by
the LORD, because you showed this loyalty
to Saul your lord and buried him. ⁶ Now
may the LORD show steadfast love and

faithfulness to you. And I will do good
to you because you have done this thing.
⁷ Now therefore let your hands be strong,
and be valiant, for Saul your lord is dead,
and the house of Judah has anointed me
king over them."

Ish-bosheth Made King of Israel

⁸ But Abner the son of Ner, commander
of Saul's army, took Ish-bosheth the son of
Saul and brought him over to Mahanaim,
⁹ and he made him king over Gilead and
the Ashurites and Jezreel and Ephraim and
Benjamin and all Israel. ¹⁰ Ish-bosheth,

PROFILE

ABNER

Abner was the commander of Saul's army.
When Saul died, Abner took the king's son,
Ish-bosheth, and made him king of Israel.
During the Battle of Gibeon, Abner killed
Asahel, one of David's mighty men. This led
to hostility between himself and Asahel's
brothers, Joab and Abishai. After a quarrel
with Ish-bosheth, Abner convinced the
elders of Israel that they should side with
David. He was welcomed by David but was
then murdered by Joab. David cursed Joab
for killing Abner and held a public funeral for
the murdered warrior. David called Abner "a
prince and a great man" (3:38).

KEY REFERENCE: 2 SAMUEL 3:38

Saul's son, was forty years old when he
began to reign over Israel, and he reigned
two years. But the house of Judah followed
David. ¹¹ And the time that David was king in
Hebron over the house of Judah was seven
years and six months.

The Battle of Gibeon

¹² Abner the son of Ner, and the servants of
Ish-bosheth the son of Saul, went out from
Mahanaim to Gibeon. ¹³ And Joab the son of
Zeruiah and the servants of David went out
and met them at the pool of Gibeon. And
they sat down, the one on the one side of the
pool, and the other on the other side of

the pool. **14** And Abner said to Joab, "Let the young men arise and compete before us." And Joab said, "Let them arise." **15** Then they arose and passed over by number, twelve for Benjamin and Ish-bosheth the son of Saul, and twelve of the servants of David. **16** And each caught his opponent by the head and thrust his sword in his opponent's side, so they fell down together. Therefore that place was called Helkath-hazzurim,[1] which is at Gibeon. **17** And the battle was very fierce that day. And Abner and the men of Israel were beaten before the servants of David.

18 And the three sons of Zeruiah were there, Joab, Abishai, and Asahel. Now Asahel was as swift of foot as a wild gazelle. **19** And Asahel pursued Abner, and as he went, he turned neither to the right hand nor to the left from following Abner. **20** Then Abner

> ### GETTING THE MESSAGE
>
> **Dogs** are mentioned 40 times in Scripture, and few of the references are positive. Dogs were viewed as unclean animals because they were scavengers, not pets. To compare someone to a dog was a great insult (3:8).

looked behind him and said, "Is it you, Asahel?" And he answered, "It is I." **21** Abner said to him, "Turn aside to your right hand or to your left, and seize one of the young men and take his spoil." But Asahel would not turn aside from following him. **22** And Abner said again to Asahel, "Turn aside from following me. Why should I strike you to the ground? How then could I lift up my face to your brother Joab?" **23** But he refused to turn aside. Therefore Abner struck him in the stomach with the butt of his spear, so that the spear came out at his back. And he fell there and died where he was. And all who came to the place where Asahel had fallen and died, stood still. **24** But Joab and Abishai pursued Abner. And as the sun was going down they came to the hill of Ammah, which lies before Giah on the way to the wilderness of Gibeon. **25** And the people of Benjamin gathered themselves together behind Abner and

became one group and took their stand on the top of a hill. **26** Then Abner called to Joab, "Shall the sword devour forever? Do you not know that the end will be bitter? How long will it be before you tell your people to turn from the pursuit of their brothers?" **27** And Joab said, "As God lives, if you had not spoken, surely the men would not have given up the pursuit of their brothers until the morning." **28** So Joab blew the trumpet, and all the men stopped and pursued Israel no more, nor did they fight anymore.

29 And Abner and his men went all that night through the Arabah. They crossed the Jordan, and marching the whole morning, they came to Mahanaim. **30** Joab returned from the pursuit of Abner. And when he had gathered all the people together, there were missing from David's servants nineteen men besides Asahel. **31** But the servants of David had struck down of Benjamin 360 of Abner's men. **32** And they took up Asahel and buried him in the tomb of his father, which was at Bethlehem. And Joab and his men marched all night, and the day broke upon them at Hebron.

Abner Joins David

3 There was a long war between the house of Saul and the house of David. And David grew stronger and stronger, while the house of Saul became weaker and weaker.

2 And sons were born to David at Hebron: his firstborn was Amnon, of Ahinoam of Jezreel; **3** and his second, Chileab, of Abigail the widow of Nabal of Carmel; and the third, Absalom the son of Maacah the daughter of Talmai king of Geshur; **4** and the fourth, Adonijah the son of Haggith; and the fifth, Shephatiah the son of Abital; **5** and the sixth, Ithream, of Eglah, David's wife. These were born to David in Hebron.

6 While there was war between the house of Saul and the house of David, Abner was making himself strong in the house of Saul. **7** Now Saul had a concubine whose name was Rizpah, the daughter of Aiah. And Ish-bosheth said to Abner, "Why have you gone in to my father's concubine?" **8** Then Abner was very angry over the words of Ish-bosheth and said, "Am I a dog's head of Judah? To this day I keep showing steadfast love to the house of Saul your father, to his brothers, and to his friends, and have not

---

[1] Helkath-hazzurim means *the field of sword-edges*

given you into the hand of David. And yet you charge me today with a fault concerning a woman. ⁹ God do so to Abner and more also, if I do not accomplish for David what the LORD has sworn to him, ¹⁰ to transfer the kingdom from the house of Saul and set up the throne of David over Israel and over Judah, from Dan to Beersheba." ¹¹ And Ish-bosheth could not answer Abner another word, because he feared him.

¹² And Abner sent messengers to David on his behalf, saying, "To whom does the land belong? Make your covenant with me, and behold, my hand shall be with you to bring over all Israel to you." ¹³ And he said, "Good; I will make a covenant with you. But one thing I require of you; that is, you shall not see my face unless you first bring Michal, Saul's daughter, when you come to see my face." ¹⁴ Then David sent messengers to Ish-bosheth, Saul's son, saying, "Give me my wife Michal, for whom I paid the bridal price of a hundred foreskins of the Philistines." ¹⁵ And Ish-bosheth sent and took her from her husband Paltiel the son of Laish. ¹⁶ But her husband went with her, weeping after her all the way to Bahurim. Then Abner said to him, "Go, return." And he returned.

¹⁷ And Abner conferred with the elders of Israel, saying, "For some time past you have been seeking David as king over you. ¹⁸ Now then bring it about, for the LORD has promised David, saying, 'By the hand of my servant David I will save my people Israel from the hand of the Philistines, and from the hand of all their enemies.'" ¹⁹ Abner also spoke to Benjamin. And then Abner went to tell David at Hebron all that Israel and the whole house of Benjamin thought good to do.

²⁰ When Abner came with twenty men to David at Hebron, David made a feast for Abner and the men who were with him. ²¹ And Abner said to David, "I will arise and go and will gather all Israel to my lord the king, that they may make a covenant with you, and that you may reign over all that your heart desires." So David sent Abner away, and he went in peace.

²² Just then the servants of David arrived with Joab from a raid, bringing much spoil with them. But Abner was not with David at Hebron, for he had sent him away, and he had gone in peace. ²³ When Joab and all the army that was with him came, it was told Joab, "Abner the son of Ner came to the king, and he has let him go, and he has gone in peace." ²⁴ Then Joab went to the king and said, "What have you done? Behold, Abner came to you. Why is it that you have sent him away, so that he is gone? ²⁵ You know that Abner the son of Ner came to deceive you and to know your going out and your coming in, and to know all that you are doing."

Joab Murders Abner

²⁶ When Joab came out from David's presence, he sent messengers after Abner, and they brought him back from the cistern of Sirah. But David did not know about it. ²⁷ And when Abner returned to Hebron, Joab took him aside into the midst of the gate to speak with him privately, and there he struck him in the stomach, so that he died, for the blood of Asahel his brother. ²⁸ Afterward, when David heard of it, he said, "I and my kingdom are forever guiltless before the LORD for the blood of Abner the son of Ner. ²⁹ May it fall upon the head of Joab and upon all his father's house, and may the house of Joab never be without one who has a discharge or who is leprous or who holds a spindle or who falls by the sword or who lacks bread!" ³⁰ So Joab and Abishai his brother killed Abner, because he had put their brother Asahel to death in the battle at Gibeon.

David Mourns Abner

³¹ Then David said to Joab and to all the people who were with him, "Tear your clothes and put on sackcloth and mourn before Abner." And King David followed the bier. ³² They buried Abner at Hebron. And the king lifted up his voice and wept at the grave of Abner, and all the people wept. ³³ And the king lamented for Abner, saying,

"Should Abner die as a fool dies?
³⁴   Your hands were not bound;
          your feet were not fettered;
     as one falls before the wicked
          you have fallen."

And all the people wept again over him. ³⁵ Then all the people came to persuade David to eat bread while it was yet day. But David swore, saying, "God do so to me and more also, if I taste bread or anything else till the sun goes down!" ³⁶ And all the people took notice of it, and it pleased them, as everything that the king did pleased all the people. [37] So all the people and all Israel understood that day that it had not been the king's will to put to death Abner the son of Ner. [38] And the king said to his servants, "Do you not know that a prince and a great man has fallen this day in Israel? [39] And I was gentle today, though anointed king. These men, the sons of Zeruiah, are more severe than I. The LORD repay the evildoer according to his wickedness!"

Ish-bosheth Murdered

4 When Ish-bosheth, Saul's son, heard that Abner had died at Hebron, his courage failed, and all Israel was dismayed. [2] Now Saul's son had two men who were captains of raiding bands; the name of the one was Baanah, and the name of the other Rechab, sons of Rimmon a man of Benjamin

GETTING THE MESSAGE

Hanging by the neck was never used as a form of execution in ancient Israel. However, the hanging of a person's body after execution was a common practice (4:12). This was done to cast shame on the criminal and to warn others not to commit similar crimes.

from Beeroth (for Beeroth also is counted part of Benjamin; [3] the Beerothites fled to Gittaim and have been sojourners there to this day).

[4] Jonathan, the son of Saul, had a son who was crippled in his feet. He was five years old when the news about Saul and Jonathan came from Jezreel, and his nurse took him up and fled, and as she fled in her haste, he fell and became lame. And his name was Mephibosheth.

[5] Now the sons of Rimmon the Beerothite, Rechab and Baanah, set out, and about the heat of the day they came to the house of Ish-bosheth as he was taking his noonday rest. [6] And they came into the midst of the house as if to get wheat, and they stabbed him in the stomach. Then Rechab and Baanah his brother escaped. [7] When they came into the house, as he lay on his bed in his bedroom, they struck him and put him to death and beheaded him. They

took his head and went by the way of the Arabah all night, [8] and brought the head of Ish-bosheth to David at Hebron. And they said to the king, "Here is the head of Ish-bosheth, the son of Saul, your enemy, who sought your life. The LORD has avenged my lord the king this day on Saul and on his offspring." [9] But David answered Rechab and Baanah his brother, the sons of Rimmon the Beerothite, "As the LORD lives, who has redeemed my life out of every adversity, [10] when one told me, 'Behold, Saul is dead,' and thought he was bringing good news, I seized him and killed him at Ziklag, which was the reward I gave him for his news. [11] How much more, when wicked men have killed a righteous man in his own house on his bed, shall I not now require his blood at your hand and destroy you from the earth?" [12] And David commanded his young men, and they killed them and cut off their hands and feet and hanged them beside the pool at Hebron. But they took the head of Ish-bosheth and buried it in the tomb of Abner at Hebron.

David Anointed King of Israel

5 Then all the tribes of Israel came to David at Hebron and said, "Behold, we are your bone and flesh. [2] In times past, when Saul was king over us, it was you who led out and brought in Israel. And the LORD said to you, 'You shall be shepherd of my people Israel, and you shall be prince over Israel.'" [3] So all the elders of Israel came to the king at Hebron, and King David made a covenant with them at Hebron before the LORD, and they anointed David king over Israel. [4] David was thirty years old when he began to reign, and he reigned forty years. [5] At Hebron he reigned over Judah seven years and six months, and at Jerusalem he reigned over all Israel and Judah thirty-three years.

[6] And the king and his men went to Jerusalem against the Jebusites, the inhabitants of the land, who said to David, "You will not come in here, but the blind and the lame will ward you off"—thinking, "David cannot come in here." [7] Nevertheless, David took the stronghold of Zion, that is, the city of David. [8] And David said on that day, "Whoever would strike the Jebusites, let him get up the water shaft to attack 'the lame and the blind,' who are hated by David's soul."

Therefore it is said, "The blind and the lame shall not come into the house." ⁹ And David lived in the stronghold and called it the city of David. And David built the city all around from the Millo inward. ¹⁰ And David became greater and greater, for the LORD, the God of hosts, was with him.

¹¹ And Hiram king of Tyre sent messengers to David, and cedar trees, also carpenters and masons who built David a house. ¹² And David knew that the LORD had established him king over Israel, and that he had exalted his kingdom for the sake of his people Israel.

¹³ And David took more concubines and wives from Jerusalem, after he came from Hebron, and more sons and daughters were born to David. ¹⁴ And these are the names of those who were born to him in Jerusalem: Shammua, Shobab, Nathan, Solomon, ¹⁵ Ibhar, Elishua, Nepheg, Japhia, ¹⁶ Elishama, Eliada, and Eliphelet.

David Defeats the Philistines

¹⁷ When the Philistines heard that David had been anointed king over Israel, all the Philistines went up to search for David. But David heard of it and went down to the stronghold. ¹⁸ Now the Philistines had come and spread out in the Valley of Rephaim. ¹⁹ And David inquired of the LORD, "Shall I go up against the Philistines? Will you give them into my hand?" And the LORD said to David, "Go up, for I will certainly give the Philistines into your hand." ²⁰ And David came to Baal-perazim, and David defeated them there. And he said, "The LORD has broken through my enemies before me like a breaking flood." Therefore the name of that place is called Baal-perazim.¹ ²¹ And the Philistines left their idols there, and David and his men carried them away.

²² And the Philistines came up yet again and spread out in the Valley of Rephaim. ²³ And when David inquired of the LORD, he said, "You shall not go up; go around to their rear, and come against them opposite the balsam trees. ²⁴ And when you hear the sound of marching in the tops of the balsam trees, then rouse yourself, for then the LORD has gone out before you to strike down the army of the Philistines." ²⁵ And David did as the LORD commanded him, and struck down the Philistines from Geba to Gezer.

The Ark Brought to Jerusalem

6 David again gathered all the chosen men of Israel, thirty thousand. ² And David arose and went with all the people who were with him from Baale-judah to bring up from there the ark of God, which is called by the name of the LORD of hosts who sits enthroned on the cherubim. ³ And they carried the ark of God on a new cart and brought it out of the house of Abinadab, which was on the hill. And Uzzah and Ahio, the sons of Abinadab, were driving the new cart, ⁴ with the ark of God, and Ahio went before the ark.

Uzzah and the Ark

⁵ And David and all the house of Israel were celebrating before the LORD, with songs and lyres and harps and tambourines and castanets and cymbals. ⁶ And when they came to

> **GETTING THE MESSAGE**
>
> **Millo** means "fill" in Hebrew. The Millo (5:9) was a series of terraces built so that houses and other structures could rest on flat areas of land. A retaining wall would first be built and then workers would "fill" dirt in behind it, piling it up until it formed a raised terrace.

the threshing floor of Nacon, Uzzah put out his hand to the ark of God and took hold of it, for the oxen stumbled. ⁷ And the anger of the LORD was kindled against Uzzah, and God struck him down there because of his error, and he died there beside the ark of God. ⁸ And David was angry because the LORD had broken out against Uzzah. And that place is called Perez-uzzah² to this day. ⁹ And David was afraid of the LORD that day, and he said, "How can the ark of the LORD come to me?" ¹⁰ So David was not willing to take the ark of the LORD into the city of David. But David took it aside to the house of Obed-edom the Gittite. ¹¹ And the ark of the LORD remained in the house of Obed-edom the Gittite three months, and the LORD blessed Obed-edom and all his household.

¹² And it was told King David, "The LORD has blessed the household of Obed-edom and all that belongs to him, because of the ark of God." So David went and brought up

---

¹ *Baal-perazim* means *lord of breaking through* ² *Perez-uzzah* means *the breaking out against Uzzah*

the ark of God from the house of Obed-edom to the city of David with rejoicing. [13] And when those who bore the ark of the LORD had gone six steps, he sacrificed an ox and a fattened animal. [14] And David danced before the LORD with all his might. And David was wearing a linen ephod. [15] So David and all the house of Israel brought up the ark of the LORD with shouting and with the sound of the horn.

PROFILE

MICHAL

Saul's daughter Michal loved David, and Saul hoped to use this to his advantage. Saul offered David the right to marry Michal, but he asked for a very unusual "bride-price" which he assumed would lead to David's death (1 Sam. 18:20–25). The scheme didn't work, and Michal became David's wife. When Saul once again tried to kill David, Michal warned him and helped him escape. Saul then gave Michal to another man even though she was still married to David. After Saul's death, David arranged for Michal to be returned to him. But the story of David and Michal had a sad ending. When David brought the ark of the covenant to Jerusalem, he celebrated by dancing before the Lord. This caused Michal to despise him, and she remained childless throughout her life.

KEY REFERENCE: 2 SAMUEL 6:16–19

David and Michal

[16] As the ark of the LORD came into the city of David, Michal the daughter of Saul looked out of the window and saw King David leaping and dancing before the LORD, and she despised him in her heart. [17] And they brought in the ark of the LORD and set it in its place, inside the tent that David had pitched for it. And David offered burnt offerings and peace offerings before the LORD. [18] And when David had finished offering the burnt offerings and the peace offerings, he blessed the people in the name of the LORD of hosts [19] and distributed among all the people, the whole multitude of Israel,

both men and women, a cake of bread, a portion of meat, and a cake of raisins to each one. Then all the people departed, each to his house.

[20] And David returned to bless his household. But Michal the daughter of Saul came out to meet David and said, "How the king of Israel honored himself today, uncovering himself today before the eyes of his servants' female servants, as one of the vulgar fellows shamelessly uncovers himself!" [21] And David said to Michal, "It was before the LORD, who chose me above your father and above all his house, to appoint me as prince over Israel, the people of the LORD— and I will celebrate before the LORD. [22] I will make myself yet more contemptible than this, and I will be abased in your eyes. But by the female servants of whom you have

GETTING THE MESSAGE

Dancing was a vital part of both worship and celebration (6:14). The Hebrew word for dance can mean to twist or whirl about in circular movements or to leap or skip. Performed by both males and females, it was quite similar to folk dancing today.

spoken, by them I shall be held in honor." [23] And Michal the daughter of Saul had no child to the day of her death.

The LORD's Covenant with David

7 Now when the king lived in his house and the LORD had given him rest from all his surrounding enemies, [2] the king said to Nathan the prophet, "See now, I dwell in a house of cedar, but the ark of God dwells in a tent." [3] And Nathan said to the king, "Go, do all that is in your heart, for the LORD is with you."

[4] But that same night the word of the LORD came to Nathan, [5] "Go and tell my servant David, 'Thus says the LORD: Would you build me a house to dwell in? [6] I have not lived in a house since the day I brought up the people of Israel from Egypt to this day, but I have been moving about in a tent for my dwelling. [7] In all places where I have moved with all the people of Israel, did I speak a word with any of the judges of Israel, whom I commanded to shepherd my people Israel,

saying, "Why have you not built me a house of cedar?" ' **8** Now, therefore, thus you shall say to my servant David, 'Thus says the LORD of hosts, I took you from the pasture, from following the sheep, that you should be prince over my people Israel. **9** And I have been with you wherever you went and have cut off all your enemies from before you. And I will make for you a great name, like the name of the great ones of the earth. **10** And I will appoint a place for my people Israel and will plant them, so that they may dwell in their own place and be disturbed no more. And violent men shall afflict them no more, as formerly, **11** from the time that I appointed judges over my people Israel. And I will give you rest from all your enemies. Moreover, the LORD declares to you that the LORD will make you a house. **12** When your days are fulfilled and you lie down with your fathers, I will raise up your offspring after you, who shall come from your body, and I will establish his kingdom. **13** He shall build a house for my name, and I will establish the throne of his kingdom forever. **14** I will be to him a father, and he shall be to me a son. When he commits iniquity, I will discipline him with the rod of men, with the stripes of the sons of men, **15** but my steadfast love will not depart from him, as I took it from Saul, whom I put away from before you. **16** And your house and your kingdom shall be made sure forever before me. Your throne shall be established forever.' " **17** In accordance with all these words, and in accordance with all this vision, Nathan spoke to David.

David's Prayer of Gratitude

18 Then King David went in and sat before the LORD and said, "Who am I, O Lord GOD, and what is my house, that you have brought me thus far? **19** And yet this was a small thing in your eyes, O Lord GOD. You have spoken also of your servant's house for a great while to come, and this is instruction for mankind, O Lord GOD! **20** And what more can David say to you? For you know your servant, O Lord GOD! **21** Because of your promise, and according to your own heart, you have brought about all this greatness, to make your servant know it. **22** Therefore you are great, O LORD God. For there is none like you, and there is no God besides you, according to all that we have heard with our ears. **23** And who is like your people Israel, the one nation on earth whom God went to redeem to be his people, making himself a name and doing for them great and awesome things by driving out before your people, whom you redeemed for yourself from Egypt, a nation and its gods? **24** And you established for yourself your people Israel to be your people forever. And you, O LORD, became their God. **25** And now, O LORD God, confirm forever the word that you have spoken concerning your servant and concerning his house, and do as you have spoken. **26** And your name will be magnified forever, saying, 'The LORD of hosts is God over Israel,' and the house of your servant David will be established before you. **27** For you, O LORD of hosts, the God of Israel, have made this revelation to your servant, saying, 'I will build you a house.' Therefore

> ### GETTING THE MESSAGE
>
> **Building a house for gods** was a common thing for a king or leader to do in the ancient Near East. David's desire to build a temple for the Lord (7:6–7) may have been influenced by this tradition. Ultimately, however, the temple was built only because the Lord directed that David's son Solomon "shall build a house for my name" (7:13).

your servant has found courage to pray this prayer to you. **28** And now, O Lord GOD, you are God, and your words are true, and you have promised this good thing to your servant. **29** Now therefore may it please you to bless the house of your servant, so that it may continue forever before you. For you, O Lord GOD, have spoken, and with your blessing shall the house of your servant be blessed forever."

David's Victories

8 After this David defeated the Philistines and subdued them, and David took Metheg-ammah out of the hand of the Philistines.

2 And he defeated Moab and he measured them with a line, making them lie down on the ground. Two lines he measured to be put to death, and one full line to be spared. And the Moabites became servants to David and brought tribute.

³ David also defeated Hadadezer the son of Rehob, king of Zobah, as he went to restore his power at the river Euphrates. ⁴ And David took from him 1,700 horsemen, and 20,000 foot soldiers. And David hamstrung all the chariot horses but left enough for 100 chariots. ⁵ And when the Syrians of Damascus came to help Hadadezer king of Zobah, David struck down 22,000 men of the Syrians. ⁶ Then David put garrisons in Aram of Damascus, and the Syrians became servants to David and brought tribute. And the LORD gave victory to David wherever he went. ⁷ And David took the shields of gold that were carried by the servants of Hadadezer and brought them to Jerusalem. ⁸ And from Betah and from Berothai, cities of Hadadezer, King David took very much bronze.

> **GETTING THE MESSAGE**
>
> **Hamstringing horses** (8:4) was a practice used by victorious armies to ensure that their enemy's horses could not be used in battle again. It involved severing the leg tendon on the horse so that it could not gallop. Though it was a cruel act, many of the horses could still be used for farming.

⁹ When Toi king of Hamath heard that David had defeated the whole army of Hadadezer, ¹⁰ Toi sent his son Joram to King David, to ask about his health and to bless him because he had fought against Hadadezer and defeated him, for Hadadezer had often been at war with Toi. And Joram brought with him articles of silver, of gold, and of bronze. ¹¹ These also King David dedicated to the LORD, together with the silver and gold that he dedicated from all the nations he subdued, ¹² from Edom, Moab, the Ammonites, the Philistines, Amalek, and from the spoil of Hadadezer the son of Rehob, king of Zobah.

¹³ And David made a name for himself when he returned from striking down 18,000 Edomites in the Valley of Salt. ¹⁴ Then he put garrisons in Edom; throughout all Edom he put garrisons, and all the Edomites became David's servants. And the LORD gave victory to David wherever he went.

David's Officials

¹⁵ So David reigned over all Israel. And David administered justice and equity to all his people. ¹⁶ Joab the son of Zeruiah was over the army, and Jehoshaphat the son of Ahilud was recorder, ¹⁷ and Zadok the son of Ahitub and Ahimelech the son of Abiathar were priests, and Seraiah was secretary, ¹⁸ and Benaiah the son of Jehoiada was over the Cherethites and the Pelethites, and David's sons were priests.

David's Kindness to Mephibosheth

9 And David said, "Is there still anyone left of the house of Saul, that I may show him kindness for Jonathan's sake?" ² Now there was a servant of the house of Saul whose name was Ziba, and they called him to David. And the king said to him, "Are you Ziba?" And he said, "I am your servant." ³ And the king said, "Is there not still someone of the house of Saul, that I may show the kindness of God to him?" Ziba said to the king, "There is still a son of Jonathan; he is crippled in his feet." ⁴ The king said to him, "Where is he?" And Ziba said to the king, "He is in the house of Machir the son of Ammiel, at Lo-debar." ⁵ Then King David sent and brought him from the house of Machir the son of Ammiel, at Lo-debar. ⁶ And Mephibosheth the son of Jonathan, son of Saul, came to David and fell on his face and paid homage. And David said, "Mephibosheth!" And he answered, "Behold, I am your servant." ⁷ And David said to him, "Do not fear, for I will show you kindness for the sake of your father Jonathan, and I will restore to you all the land of Saul your father, and you shall eat at my table always." ⁸ And he paid homage and said, "What is your servant, that you should show regard for a dead dog such as I?"

⁹ Then the king called Ziba, Saul's servant, and said to him, "All that belonged to Saul and to all his house I have given to your master's grandson. ¹⁰ And you and your sons and your servants shall till the land for him and shall bring in the produce, that your master's grandson may have bread to eat. But Mephibosheth your master's grandson shall always eat at my table." Now Ziba had fifteen sons and twenty servants. ¹¹ Then Ziba said to the king, "According to all that my lord the king commands his servant, so will your servant do." So Mephibosheth

ate at David's table, like one of the king's sons. ¹² And Mephibosheth had a young son, whose name was Mica. And all who lived in Ziba's house became Mephibosheth's servants. ¹³ So Mephibosheth lived in Jerusalem, for he ate always at the king's table. Now he was lame in both his feet.

David Defeats Ammon and Syria

10 After this the king of the Ammonites died, and Hanun his son reigned in his place. ² And David said, "I will deal loyally with Hanun the son of Nahash, as his father dealt loyally with me." So David sent by his servants to console him concerning his father. And David's servants came into the land of the Ammonites. ³ But the princes of the Ammonites said to Hanun their lord, "Do you think, because David has sent comforters to you, that he is honoring your father? Has not David sent his servants to you to search the city and to spy it out and to overthrow it?" ⁴ So Hanun took David's servants and shaved off half the beard of each and cut off their garments in the middle, at their hips, and sent them away. ⁵ When it was told David, he sent to meet them, for the men were greatly ashamed. And the king said, "Remain at Jericho until your beards have grown and then return."

⁶ When the Ammonites saw that they had become a stench to David, the Ammonites sent and hired the Syrians of Beth-rehob, and the Syrians of Zobah, 20,000 foot soldiers, and the king of Maacah with 1,000 men, and the men of Tob, 12,000 men. ⁷ And when David heard of it, he sent Joab and all the host of the mighty men. ⁸ And the Ammonites came out and drew up in battle array at the entrance of the gate, and the Syrians of Zobah and of Rehob and the men of Tob and Maacah were by themselves in the open country.

⁹ When Joab saw that the battle was set against him both in front and in the rear, he chose some of the best men of Israel and arrayed them against the Syrians. ¹⁰ The rest of his men he put in the charge of Abishai his brother, and he arrayed them against the Ammonites. ¹¹ And he said, "If the Syrians are too strong for me, then you shall help me, but if the Ammonites are too strong for you, then I will come and help you. ¹² Be of good courage, and let us be courageous for our people, and for the cities of our God, and may

the Lord do what seems good to him." ¹³ So Joab and the people who were with him drew near to battle against the Syrians, and they fled before him. ¹⁴ And when the Ammonites saw that the Syrians fled, they likewise fled before Abishai and entered the city. Then Joab returned from fighting against the Ammonites and came to Jerusalem.

¹⁵ But when the Syrians saw that they had been defeated by Israel, they gathered themselves together. ¹⁶ And Hadadezer sent and brought out the Syrians who were beyond the Euphrates. They came to Helam, with Shobach the commander of the army of Hadadezer at their head. ¹⁷ And when it was told David, he gathered all Israel together and crossed the Jordan and came to Helam. The Syrians arrayed themselves against David and fought with him. ¹⁸ And the Syrians fled before Israel, and David

> ## GETTING THE MESSAGE
>
> **Sexual activity while on military duty** was expressly forbidden by law in ancient Israel (11:11). It brought about ritual impurity and therefore forced a soldier to undergo purification rituals. This would prevent him from performing his military duty.

killed of the Syrians the men of 700 chariots, and 40,000 horsemen, and wounded Shobach the commander of their army, so that he died there. ¹⁹ And when all the kings who were servants of Hadadezer saw that they had been defeated by Israel, they made peace with Israel and became subject to them. So the Syrians were afraid to save the Ammonites anymore.

David and Bathsheba

11 In the spring of the year, the time when kings go out to battle, David sent Joab, and his servants with him, and all Israel. And they ravaged the Ammonites and besieged Rabbah. But David remained at Jerusalem.

² It happened, late one afternoon, when David arose from his couch and was walking on the roof of the king's house, that he saw from the roof a woman bathing; and the woman was very beautiful. ³ And David sent and inquired about the woman. And

one said, "Is not this Bathsheba, the daughter of Eliam, the wife of Uriah the Hittite?" **4** So David sent messengers and took her, and she came to him, and he lay with her. (Now she had been purifying herself from her uncleanness.) Then she returned to her house. **5** And the woman conceived, and she sent and told David, "I am pregnant."

6 So David sent word to Joab, "Send me Uriah the Hittite." And Joab sent Uriah to David. **7** When Uriah came to him, David asked how Joab was doing and how the people were doing and how the war was going. **8** Then David said to Uriah, "Go down to your house and wash your feet." And Uriah went out of the king's house, and there followed him a present from the king. **9** But Uriah slept at the door of the king's house with all the servants of his lord, and did not go down

> ### GETTING THE MESSAGE
>
> **David's disobedience.** David broke three of the Ten Commandments in his relationship with Bathsheba. He broke the tenth commandment by coveting another man's wife, then the seventh commandment by committing adultery. He broke the sixth commandment by arranging the death of Bathsheba's husband, Uriah.

to his house. **10** When they told David, "Uriah did not go down to his house," David said to Uriah, "Have you not come from a journey? Why did you not go down to your house?" **11** Uriah said to David, "The ark and Israel and Judah dwell in booths, and my lord Joab and the servants of my lord are camping in the open field. Shall I then go to my house, to eat and to drink and to lie with my wife? As you live, and as your soul lives, I will not do this thing." **12** Then David said to Uriah, "Remain here today also, and tomorrow I will send you back." So Uriah remained in Jerusalem that day and the next. **13** And David invited him, and he ate in his presence and drank, so that he made him drunk. And in the evening he went out to lie on his couch with the servants of his lord, but he did not go down to his house.

14 In the morning David wrote a letter to Joab and sent it by the hand of Uriah. **15** In the letter he wrote, "Set Uriah in the forefront of the hardest fighting, and then draw back from him, that he may be struck down, and die." **16** And as Joab was besieging the city, he assigned Uriah to the place where he knew there were valiant men. **17** And the men of the city came out and fought with Joab, and some of the servants of David among the people fell. Uriah the Hittite also died. **18** Then Joab sent and told David all the news about the fighting. **19** And he instructed the messenger, "When you have finished telling all the news about the fighting to the king, **20** then, if the king's anger rises, and if he says to you, 'Why did you go so near the city to fight? Did you not know that they would shoot from the wall? **21** Who killed Abimelech the son of Jerubbesheth? Did not a woman cast an upper millstone on him from the wall, so that he died at Thebez? Why did you go so near the wall?' then you shall say, 'Your servant Uriah the Hittite is dead also.'"

22 So the messenger went and came and told David all that Joab had sent him to tell. **23** The messenger said to David, "The men gained an advantage over us and came out against us in the field, but we drove them back to the entrance of the gate. **24** Then the archers shot at your servants from the wall. Some of the king's servants are dead, and your servant Uriah the Hittite is dead also." **25** David said to the messenger, "Thus shall you say to Joab, 'Do not let this matter displease you, for the sword devours now one and now another. Strengthen your attack against the city and overthrow it.' And encourage him."

26 When the wife of Uriah heard that Uriah her husband was dead, she lamented over her husband. **27** And when the mourning was over, David sent and brought her to his house, and she became his wife and bore him a son. But the thing that David had done displeased the LORD.

Nathan Rebukes David

12 And the LORD sent Nathan to David. He came to him and said to him, "There were two men in a certain city, the one rich and the other poor. **2** The rich man had very many flocks and herds, **3** but the poor man had nothing but one little ewe lamb, which he had bought. And he brought it up, and it grew up with him and with his children. It used to eat of his morsel and drink from his cup and lie in his arms, and it was like a daughter to him. ⁴ Now there came a traveler to the rich man, and he was unwilling to take one of his own flock or herd to prepare for the guest who had come to him, but he took the poor man's lamb and prepared it for the man who had come to him." ⁵ Then David's anger was greatly kindled against the man, and he said to Nathan, "As the LORD lives, the man who has done this deserves to die, ⁶ and he shall restore the lamb fourfold, because he did this thing, and because he had no pity."

⁷ Nathan said to David, "You are the man! Thus says the LORD, the God of Israel, 'I anointed you king over Israel, and I delivered you out of the hand of Saul. ⁸ And I gave you your master's house and your master's wives into your arms and gave you the house of Israel and of Judah. And if this were too little, I would add to you as much more. ⁹ Why have you despised the word of the LORD, to do what is evil in his sight? You have struck down Uriah the Hittite with the sword and have taken his wife to be your wife and have killed him with the sword of the Ammonites. ¹⁰ Now therefore the sword shall never depart from your house, because you have despised me and have taken the wife of Uriah the Hittite to be your wife.' ¹¹ Thus says the LORD, 'Behold, I will raise up evil against you out of your own house. And I will take your wives before your eyes and give them to your neighbor, and he shall lie with your wives in the sight of this sun. ¹² For you did it secretly, but I will do this thing before all Israel and before the sun.'" ¹³ David said to Nathan, "I have sinned against the LORD." And Nathan said to David, "The LORD also has put away your sin; you shall not die. ¹⁴ Nevertheless, because by this deed you have utterly scorned the LORD, the child who is born to you shall die." ¹⁵ Then Nathan went to his house.

David's Child Dies

And the LORD afflicted the child that Uriah's wife bore to David, and he became sick. ¹⁶ David therefore sought God on behalf of the child. And David fasted and went in and lay all night on the ground. ¹⁷ And the elders of his house stood beside him, to raise him from the ground, but he would not, nor did he eat food with them. ¹⁸ On the seventh day the child died. And the servants of David were afraid to tell him that the child was dead, for they said, "Behold, while the child was yet alive, we spoke to him, and he did not listen to us. How then can we say to him the child is dead? He may do himself some harm." ¹⁹ But when David saw that his servants were whispering together, David understood that the child was dead. And David said to his servants, "Is the child dead?" They said, "He is dead." ²⁰ Then David arose from the earth and washed and anointed himself

PROFILE
NATHAN

Nathan was a prophet during the reigns of David and Solomon. When David desired to build a temple, he asked for Nathan's counsel. At first, Nathan told him to go ahead, with the Lord's blessing. But then, after hearing directly from the Lord, Nathan told David that one of his sons, rather than David himself, would be the one to build the temple. Through Nathan God also promised to establish the house and the kingdom of David forever. After David sinned with Bathsheba, God sent Nathan to rebuke him. To show David how wrong it was for him to take another man's wife, Nathan told a parable about a rich man who took the only lamb belonging to a poor man. It was a powerful story, and David repented of his sin.

KEY REFERENCE: 2 SAMUEL 12:1-15

and changed his clothes. And he went into the house of the LORD and worshiped. He then went to his own house. And when he asked, they set food before him, and he ate. ²¹ Then his servants said to him, "What is this thing that you have done? You fasted and wept for the child while he was alive; but when the child died, you arose and ate food." ²² He said, "While the child was still alive, I fasted and wept, for I said, 'Who knows whether the LORD will be gracious to me, that the child may live?' ²³ But now he is dead. Why should I fast? Can I bring him back again? I shall go to him, but he will not return to me."

Solomon's Birth

24 Then David comforted his wife, Bathsheba, and went in to her and lay with her, and she bore a son, and he called his name Solomon. And the LORD loved him 25 and sent a message by Nathan the prophet. So he called his name Jedidiah,[1] because of the LORD.

Rabbah Is Captured

26 Now Joab fought against Rabbah of the Ammonites and took the royal city. 27 And Joab sent messengers to David and said, "I have fought against Rabbah; moreover, I have taken the city of waters. 28 Now then gather the rest of the people together and

> ### GETTING THE MESSAGE
>
> **Why did Tamar not want to be sent away?** Although Amnon raped her, Tamar knew that the Mosaic Law said he must now marry her or pay damages for what he had done. Though she told her father David what had happened, he did nothing to punish Amnon (13:20–22). Both Amnon and David ignored God's standards in this sad episode.

encamp against the city and take it, lest I take the city and it be called by my name." 29 So David gathered all the people together and went to Rabbah and fought against it and took it. 30 And he took the crown of their king from his head. The weight of it was a talent of gold, and in it was a precious stone, and it was placed on David's head. And he brought out the spoil of the city, a very great amount. 31 And he brought out the people who were in it and set them to labor with saws and iron picks and iron axes and made them toil at the brick kilns. And thus he did to all the cities of the Ammonites. Then David and all the people returned to Jerusalem.

Amnon and Tamar

13 Now Absalom, David's son, had a beautiful sister, whose name was Tamar. And after a time Amnon, David's son, loved her. 2 And Amnon was so tormented

that he made himself ill because of his sister Tamar, for she was a virgin, and it seemed impossible to Amnon to do anything to her. 3 But Amnon had a friend, whose name was Jonadab, the son of Shimeah, David's brother. And Jonadab was a very crafty man. 4 And he said to him, "O son of the king, why are you so haggard morning after morning? Will you not tell me?" Amnon said to him, "I love Tamar, my brother Absalom's sister." 5 Jonadab said to him, "Lie down on your bed and pretend to be ill. And when your father comes to see you, say to him, 'Let my sister Tamar come and give me bread to eat, and prepare the food in my sight, that I may see it and eat it from her hand.'" 6 So Amnon lay down and pretended to be ill. And when the king came to see him, Amnon said to the king, "Please let my sister Tamar come and make a couple of cakes in my sight, that I may eat from her hand."

7 Then David sent home to Tamar, saying, "Go to your brother Amnon's house and prepare food for him." 8 So Tamar went to her brother Amnon's house, where he was lying down. And she took dough and kneaded it and made cakes in his sight and baked the cakes. 9 And she took the pan and emptied it out before him, but he refused to eat. And Amnon said, "Send out everyone from me." So everyone went out from him. 10 Then Amnon said to Tamar, "Bring the food into the chamber, that I may eat from your hand." And Tamar took the cakes she had made and brought them into the chamber to Amnon her brother. 11 But when she brought them near him to eat, he took hold of her and said to her, "Come, lie with me, my sister." 12 She answered him, "No, my brother, do not violate me, for such a thing is not done in Israel; do not do this outrageous thing. 13 As for me, where could I carry my shame? And as for you, you would be as one of the outrageous fools in Israel. Now therefore, please speak to the king, for he will not withhold me from you." 14 But he would not listen to her, and being stronger than she, he violated her and lay with her.

15 Then Amnon hated her with very great hatred, so that the hatred with which he hated her was greater than the love with which he had loved her. And Amnon said to her, "Get up! Go!" 16 But she said to him,

1 Jedidiah means beloved of the LORD

"No, my brother, for this wrong in sending me away is greater than the other that you did to me." But he would not listen to her. [17] He called the young man who served him and said, "Put this woman out of my presence and bolt the door after her." [18] Now she was wearing a long robe with sleeves, for thus were the virgin daughters of the king dressed. So his servant put her out and bolted the door after her. [19] And Tamar put ashes on her head and tore the long robe that she wore. And she laid her hand on her head and went away, crying aloud as she went.

[20] And her brother Absalom said to her, "Has Amnon your brother been with you? Now hold your peace, my sister. He is your brother; do not take this to heart." So Tamar lived, a desolate woman, in her brother Absalom's house. [21] When King David heard of all these things, he was very angry. [22] But Absalom spoke to Amnon neither good nor bad, for Absalom hated Amnon, because he had violated his sister Tamar.

Absalom Murders Amnon

[23] After two full years Absalom had sheepshearers at Baal-hazor, which is near Ephraim, and Absalom invited all the king's sons. [24] And Absalom came to the king and said, "Behold, your servant has sheepshearers. Please let the king and his servants go with your servant." [25] But the king said to Absalom, "No, my son, let us not all go, lest we be burdensome to you." He pressed him, but he would not go but gave him his blessing. [26] Then Absalom said, "If not, please let my brother Amnon go with us." And the king said to him, "Why should he go with you?" [27] But Absalom pressed him until he let Amnon and all the king's sons go with him. [28] Then Absalom commanded his servants, "Mark when Amnon's heart is merry with wine, and when I say to you, 'Strike Amnon,' then kill him. Do not fear; have I not commanded you? Be courageous and be valiant." [29] So the servants of Absalom did to Amnon as Absalom had commanded. Then all the king's sons arose, and each mounted his mule and fled.

[30] While they were on the way, news came to David, "Absalom has struck down all the king's sons, and not one of them is left." [31] Then the king arose and tore his garments and lay on the earth. And all his servants who were standing by tore their garments. [32] But Jonadab the son of Shimeah, David's brother, said, "Let not my lord suppose that they have killed all the young men, the king's sons, for Amnon alone is dead. For by the command of Absalom this has been determined from the day he violated his sister Tamar. [33] Now therefore let not my lord the king so take it to heart as to suppose that all the king's sons are dead, for Amnon alone is dead."

Absalom Flees to Geshur

[34] But Absalom fled. And the young man who kept the watch lifted up his eyes and looked, and behold, many people were coming from the road behind him by the side of the mountain. [35] And Jonadab said to the king, "Behold, the king's sons have come; as your servant said, so it has come about." [36] And as soon as he had finished speaking, behold, the king's sons came and lifted up their voice and wept. And the king also and all his servants wept very bitterly.

> ### GETTING THE MESSAGE
>
> **Geshur** was a border town between the nation of Israel and Aram to the north. David's wife and Absalom's mother, Maacah, was from this city, which may explain why Absalom fled there.

[37] But Absalom fled and went to Talmai the son of Ammihud, king of Geshur. And David mourned for his son day after day. [38] So Absalom fled and went to Geshur, and was there three years. [39] And the spirit of the king longed to go out to Absalom, because he was comforted about Amnon, since he was dead.

Absalom Returns to Jerusalem

14 Now Joab the son of Zeruiah knew that the king's heart went out to Absalom. [2] And Joab sent to Tekoa and brought from there a wise woman and said to her, "Pretend to be a mourner and put on mourning garments. Do not anoint yourself with oil, but behave like a woman who has been mourning many days for the dead. [3] Go to the king and speak thus to him." So Joab put the words in her mouth.

[4] When the woman of Tekoa came to the king, she fell on her face to the ground and

paid homage and said, "Save me, O king." ⁵ And the king said to her, "What is your trouble?" She answered, "Alas, I am a widow; my husband is dead. ⁶ And your servant had two sons, and they quarreled with one another in the field. There was no one to separate them, and one struck the other and killed him. ⁷ And now the whole clan has risen against your servant, and they say, 'Give up the man who struck his brother, that we may put him to death for the life of his brother whom he killed.' And so they would destroy the heir also. Thus they would quench my coal that is left and leave to my husband neither name nor remnant on the face of the earth."

⁸ Then the king said to the woman, "Go to your house, and I will give orders concerning you." ⁹ And the woman of Tekoa said to the king, "On me be the guilt, my lord the king, and on my father's house; let the king and his throne be guiltless." ¹⁰ The king said, "If anyone says anything to you, bring him to me, and he shall never touch you again." ¹¹ Then she said, "Please let the king invoke the LORD your God, that the avenger of blood kill no more, and my son be not destroyed." He said, "As the LORD lives, not one hair of your son shall fall to the ground."

¹² Then the woman said, "Please let your servant speak a word to my lord the king." He said, "Speak." ¹³ And the woman said, "Why then have you planned such a thing against the people of God? For in giving this decision the king convicts himself, inasmuch as the king does not bring his banished one home again. ¹⁴ We must all die; we are like water spilled on the ground, which cannot be gathered up again. But God will not take away life, and he devises means so that the banished one will not remain an outcast. ¹⁵ Now I have come to say this to my lord the king because the people have made me afraid, and your servant thought, 'I will speak to the king; it may be that the king will perform the request of his servant. ¹⁶ For the king will hear and deliver his servant from the hand of the man who would destroy me and my son together from the heritage of God.' ¹⁷ And your servant thought, 'The word of my lord the king will set me at rest,' for my lord the king is like the angel of God to discern good and evil. The LORD your God be with you!"

¹⁸ Then the king answered the woman, "Do not hide from me anything I ask you." And the woman said, "Let my lord the king speak." ¹⁹ The king said, "Is the hand of Joab with you in all this?" The woman answered and said, "As surely as you live, my lord the king, one cannot turn to the right hand or to the left from anything that my lord the king has said. It was your servant Joab who commanded me; it was he who put all these words in the mouth of your servant. ²⁰ In order to change the course of things your servant Joab did this. But my lord has wisdom like the wisdom of the angel of God to know all things that are on the earth."

²¹ Then the king said to Joab, "Behold now, I grant this; go, bring back the young man Absalom." ²² And Joab fell on his face to the ground and paid homage and blessed the king. And Joab said, "Today your servant knows that I have found favor in your sight, my lord the king, in that the king has granted the request of his servant." ²³ So Joab arose and went to Geshur and brought Absalom to Jerusalem. ²⁴ And the king said, "Let him dwell apart in his own house; he is not to come into my presence." So Absalom lived apart in his own house and did not come into the king's presence.

²⁵ Now in all Israel there was no one so much to be praised for his handsome appearance as Absalom. From the sole of his foot to the crown of his head there was no blemish in him. ²⁶ And when he cut the hair of his head (for at the end of every year he used to cut it; when it was heavy on him, he cut it), he weighed the hair of his head, two hundred shekels by the king's weight. ²⁷ There were born to Absalom three sons, and one daughter whose name was Tamar. She was a beautiful woman.

²⁸ So Absalom lived two full years in Jerusalem, without coming into the king's presence. ²⁹ Then Absalom sent for Joab, to send him to the king, but Joab would not come to him. And he sent a second time, but Joab would not come. ³⁰ Then he said to his servants, "See, Joab's field is next to mine, and he has barley there; go and set it on fire." So Absalom's servants set the field on fire. ³¹ Then Joab arose and went to Absalom at his house and said to him, "Why have your servants set my field on fire?" ³² Absalom answered Joab, "Behold, I sent word to you,

'Come here, that I may send you to the king, to ask, "Why have I come from Geshur? It would be better for me to be there still." Now therefore let me go into the presence of the king, and if there is guilt in me, let him put me to death.'" **33** Then Joab went to the king and told him, and he summoned Absalom. So he came to the king and bowed himself on his face to the ground before the king, and the king kissed Absalom.

Absalom's Conspiracy

15 After this Absalom got himself a chariot and horses, and fifty men to run before him. **2** And Absalom used to rise early and stand beside the way of the gate. And when any man had a dispute to come before the king for judgment, Absalom would call to him and say, "From what city are you?" And when he said, "Your servant is of such and such a tribe in Israel," **3** Absalom would say to him, "See, your claims are good and right, but there is no man designated by the king to hear you." **4** Then Absalom would say, "Oh that I were judge in the land! Then every man with a dispute or cause might come to me, and I would give him justice." **5** And whenever a man came near to pay homage to him, he would put out his hand and take hold of him and kiss him. **6** Thus Absalom did to all of Israel who came to the king for judgment. So Absalom stole the hearts of the men of Israel.

7 And at the end of four years Absalom said to the king, "Please let me go and pay my vow, which I have vowed to the LORD, in Hebron. **8** For your servant vowed a vow while I lived at Geshur in Aram, saying, 'If the LORD will indeed bring me back to Jerusalem, then I will offer worship to the LORD.'" **9** The king said to him, "Go in peace." So he arose and went to Hebron. **10** But Absalom sent secret messengers throughout all the tribes of Israel, saying, "As soon as you hear the sound of the trumpet, then say, 'Absalom is king at Hebron!'" **11** With Absalom went two hundred men from Jerusalem who were invited guests, and they went in their innocence and knew nothing. **12** And while Absalom was offering the sacrifices, he sent for Ahithophel the Gilonite, David's counselor, from his city Giloh. And the conspiracy grew strong, and the people with Absalom kept increasing.

David Flees Jerusalem

13 And a messenger came to David, saying, "The hearts of the men of Israel have gone after Absalom." **14** Then David said to all his servants who were with him at Jerusalem, "Arise, and let us flee, or else there will be no escape for us from Absalom. Go quickly, lest he overtake us quickly and bring down ruin on us and strike the city with the edge of the sword." **15** And the king's servants said to the king, "Behold, your servants are ready to do whatever my lord the king decides." **16** So the king went out, and all his household after him. And the king left ten concubines to keep the house. **17** And the king went out, and all the people after him. And they halted at the last house.

18 And all his servants passed by him, and all the Cherethites, and all the Pelethites, and all the six hundred Gittites who had followed him from Gath, passed on before the king. **19** Then the king said to Ittai the

> ### GETTING THE MESSAGE
>
> **Regicide** is the act of murdering a king. In most cases, a person who killed a king was trying to place himself on the throne.

Gittite, "Why do you also go with us? Go back and stay with the king, for you are a foreigner and also an exile from your home. **20** You came only yesterday, and shall I today make you wander about with us, since I go I know not where? Go back and take your brothers with you, and may the LORD show steadfast love and faithfulness to you." **21** But Ittai answered the king, "As the LORD lives, and as my lord the king lives, wherever my lord the king shall be, whether for death or for life, there also will your servant be." **22** And David said to Ittai, "Go then, pass on." So Ittai the Gittite passed on with all his men and all the little ones who were with him. **23** And all the land wept aloud as all the people passed by, and the king crossed the brook Kidron, and all the people passed on toward the wilderness.

24 And Abiathar came up, and behold, Zadok came also with all the Levites, bearing the ark of the covenant of God. And they set down the ark of God until the people had all passed out of the city. ²⁵ Then the king said to Zadok, "Carry the ark of God back into the city. If I find favor in the eyes of the LORD, he will bring me back and let me see both it and his dwelling place. ²⁶ But if he says, 'I have no pleasure in you,' behold, here I am, let him do to me what seems good to him." ²⁷ The king also said to Zadok the priest, "Are you not a seer? Go back to the city in peace, with your two sons, Ahimaaz your son, and Jonathan the son of Abiathar. ²⁸ See,

PROFILE

ABSALOM

David's son Absalom was a handsome man with the personality of a strong leader. When Absalom's half brother Amnon raped Absalom's sister Tamar, Absalom retaliated by killing Amnon. He then fled into exile. Three years later he returned to Jerusalem and was reconciled with David. But then he led a rebellion against David, and David himself was forced to flee the city. While battling David's men, Absalom's long hair became stuck in the branches of an oak tree, enabling David's commander Joab to kill him. Absalom's death allowed David to return to Jerusalem, but he mourned bitterly for his fallen son. Absalom's betrayal of his father helped fulfill Nathan's prophecy (12:10–12) that, because of his sin with Bathsheba, the "sword shall never depart" from David's house.

KEY REFERENCE: 2 SAMUEL 15:1–6

I will wait at the fords of the wilderness until word comes from you to inform me." ²⁹ So Zadok and Abiathar carried the ark of God back to Jerusalem, and they remained there.

³⁰ But David went up the ascent of the Mount of Olives, weeping as he went, barefoot and with his head covered. And all the people who were with him covered their heads, and they went up, weeping as they went. ³¹ And it was told David, "Ahithophel is among the conspirators with Absalom." And David said, "O LORD, please turn the counsel of Ahithophel into foolishness."

³² While David was coming to the summit, where God was worshiped, behold, Hushai the Archite came to meet him with his coat torn and dirt on his head. ³³ David said to him, "If you go on with me, you will be a burden to me. ³⁴ But if you return to the city and say to Absalom, 'I will be your servant, O king; as I have been your father's servant in time past, so now I will be your servant,' then you will defeat for me the counsel of Ahithophel. ³⁵ Are not Zadok and Abiathar the priests with you there? So whatever you hear from the king's house, tell it to Zadok and Abiathar the priests. ³⁶ Behold, their two sons are with them there, Ahimaaz, Zadok's son, and Jonathan, Abiathar's son, and by them you shall send to me everything you hear." ³⁷ So Hushai, David's friend, came into the city, just as Absalom was entering Jerusalem.

David and Ziba

16 When David had passed a little beyond the summit, Ziba the servant of Mephibosheth met him, with a couple of donkeys saddled, bearing two hundred loaves of bread, a hundred bunches of raisins, a hundred of summer fruits, and a skin of wine. ² And the king said to Ziba, "Why have you brought these?" Ziba answered, "The donkeys are for the king's household to ride on, the bread and summer fruit for the young men to eat, and the wine for those who faint in the wilderness to drink." ³ And the king said, "And where is your master's son?" Ziba said to the king, "Behold, he remains in Jerusalem, for he said, 'Today the house of Israel will give me back the kingdom of my father.'" ⁴ Then the king said to Ziba, "Behold, all that belonged to Mephibosheth is now yours." And Ziba said, "I pay homage; let me ever find favor in your sight, my lord the king."

Shimei Curses David

⁵ When King David came to Bahurim, there came out a man of the family of the house of Saul, whose name was Shimei, the son of Gera, and as he came he cursed continually. ⁶ And he threw stones at David and at all the servants of King David, and all the people and all the mighty men were on his right hand and on his left. ⁷ And Shimei said as he cursed, "Get out, get out, you man of blood, you worthless man! ⁸ The LORD has

avenged on you all the blood of the house of Saul, in whose place you have reigned, and the LORD has given the kingdom into the hand of your son Absalom. See, your evil is on you, for you are a man of blood."

⁹ Then Abishai the son of Zeruiah said to the king, "Why should this dead dog curse my lord the king? Let me go over and take off his head." ¹⁰ But the king said, "What have I to do with you, you sons of Zeruiah? If he is cursing because the LORD has said to him, 'Curse David,' who then shall say, 'Why have you done so?'" ¹¹ And David said to Abishai and to all his servants, "Behold, my own son seeks my life; how much more now may this Benjaminite! Leave him alone, and let him curse, for the LORD has told him to. ¹² It may be that the LORD will look on the wrong done to me, and that the LORD will repay me with good for his cursing today." ¹³ So David and his men went on the road, while Shimei went along on the hillside opposite him and cursed as he went and threw stones at him and flung dust. ¹⁴ And the king, and all the people who were with him, arrived weary at the Jordan. And there he refreshed himself.

Absalom Enters Jerusalem

¹⁵ Now Absalom and all the people, the men of Israel, came to Jerusalem, and Ahithophel with him. ¹⁶ And when Hushai the Archite, David's friend, came to Absalom, Hushai said to Absalom, "Long live the king! Long live the king!" ¹⁷ And Absalom said to Hushai, "Is this your loyalty to your friend? Why did you not go with your friend?" ¹⁸ And Hushai said to Absalom, "No, for whom the LORD and this people and all the men of Israel have chosen, his I will be, and with him I will remain. ¹⁹ And again, whom should I serve? Should it not be his son? As I have served your father, so I will serve you."

²⁰ Then Absalom said to Ahithophel, "Give your counsel. What shall we do?" ²¹ Ahithophel said to Absalom, "Go in to your father's concubines, whom he has left to keep the house, and all Israel will hear that you have made yourself a stench to your father, and the hands of all who are with you will be strengthened." ²² So they pitched a tent for Absalom on the roof. And Absalom went in to his father's concubines in the sight of all Israel. ²³ Now in those days the counsel that Ahithophel gave was as if one consulted the word of God; so was all the counsel of Ahithophel esteemed, both by David and by Absalom.

Hushai Saves David

17 Moreover, Ahithophel said to Absalom, "Let me choose twelve thousand men, and I will arise and pursue David tonight. ² I will come upon him while he is weary and discouraged and throw him into a panic, and all the people who are with him will flee. I will strike down only the king, ³ and I will bring all the people back to you as a bride comes home to her husband. You seek the life of only one man, and all the people will be at peace." ⁴ And the advice seemed right in the eyes of Absalom and all the elders of Israel.

⁵ Then Absalom said, "Call Hushai the Archite also, and let us hear what he has to say." ⁶ And when Hushai came to Absalom, Absalom said to him, "Thus has Ahithophel

> ### GETTING THE MESSAGE
>
> **A stiff penalty.** The punishment for cursing God (Lev. 24:10–23), the king (Ex. 22:28), or one's parents (Lev. 20:9) was death. Shimei cursed King David (2 Sam. 16:5–14), but later begged David's forgiveness, and David forgave him (19:16–23).

spoken; shall we do as he says? If not, you speak." ⁷ Then Hushai said to Absalom, "This time the counsel that Ahithophel has given is not good." ⁸ Hushai said, "You know that your father and his men are mighty men, and that they are enraged, like a bear robbed of her cubs in the field. Besides, your father is expert in war; he will not spend the night with the people. ⁹ Behold, even now he has hidden himself in one of the pits or in some other place. And as soon as some of the people fall at the first attack, whoever hears it will say, 'There has been a slaughter among the people who follow Absalom.' ¹⁰ Then even the valiant man, whose heart is like the heart of a lion, will utterly melt with fear, for all Israel knows that your father is a mighty man, and that those who are with him are valiant men. ¹¹ But my counsel is that all Israel be gathered to you, from Dan to Beersheba, as the sand by the sea for multitude, and that you go to battle in person.

¹²So we shall come upon him in some place where he is to be found, and we shall light upon him as the dew falls on the ground, and of him and all the men with him not one will be left. ¹³ If he withdraws into a city, then all Israel will bring ropes to that city, and we shall drag it into the valley, until not even a pebble is to be found there." ¹⁴ And Absalom and all the men of Israel said, "The counsel of Hushai the Archite is better than the counsel of Ahithophel." For the LORD had ordained to defeat the good counsel of Ahithophel, so that the LORD might bring harm upon Absalom.

¹⁵ Then Hushai said to Zadok and Abiathar the priests, "Thus and so did Ahithophel counsel Absalom and the elders of Israel, and thus and so have I counseled. ¹⁶ Now therefore send quickly and tell David, 'Do not stay tonight at the fords of the wilderness, but by all means pass over, lest the

GETTING THE MESSAGE

When attacking a city, **ropes with grappling hooks** were often used to bring down its walls (17:13). Since most cities were built on hills, the attackers could simply pull the walls away and down the slopes of the hill.

king and all the people who are with him be swallowed up.'" ¹⁷ Now Jonathan and Ahimaaz were waiting at En-rogel. A female servant was to go and tell them, and they were to go and tell King David, for they were not to be seen entering the city. ¹⁸ But a young man saw them and told Absalom. So both of them went away quickly and came to the house of a man at Bahurim, who had a well in his courtyard. And they went down into it. ¹⁹ And the woman took and spread a covering over the well's mouth and scattered grain on it, and nothing was known of it. ²⁰ When Absalom's servants came to the woman at the house, they said, "Where are Ahimaaz and Jonathan?" And the woman said to them, "They have gone over the brook of water." And when they had sought and could not find them, they returned to Jerusalem.

²¹ After they had gone, the men came up out of the well, and went and told King

David. They said to David, "Arise, and go quickly over the water, for thus and so has Ahithophel counseled against you." ²² Then David arose, and all the people who were with him, and they crossed the Jordan. By daybreak not one was left who had not crossed the Jordan.

²³ When Ahithophel saw that his counsel was not followed, he saddled his donkey and went off home to his own city. He set his house in order and hanged himself, and he died and was buried in the tomb of his father.

²⁴ Then David came to Mahanaim. And Absalom crossed the Jordan with all the men of Israel. ²⁵ Now Absalom had set Amasa over the army instead of Joab. Amasa was the son of a man named Ithra the Ishmaelite, who had married Abigal the daughter of Nahash, sister of Zeruiah, Joab's mother. ²⁶ And Israel and Absalom encamped in the land of Gilead.

²⁷ When David came to Mahanaim, Shobi the son of Nahash from Rabbah of the Ammonites, and Machir the son of Ammiel from Lo-debar, and Barzillai the Gileadite from Rogelim, ²⁸ brought beds, basins, and earthen vessels, wheat, barley, flour, parched grain, beans and lentils, ²⁹ honey and curds and sheep and cheese from the herd, for David and the people with him to eat, for they said, "The people are hungry and weary and thirsty in the wilderness."

Absalom Killed

18 Then David mustered the men who were with him and set over them commanders of thousands and commanders of hundreds. ² And David sent out the army, one third under the command of Joab, one third under the command of Abishai the son of Zeruiah, Joab's brother, and one third under the command of Ittai the Gittite. And the king said to the men, "I myself will also go out with you." ³ But the men said, "You shall not go out. For if we flee, they will not care about us. If half of us die, they will not care about us. But you are worth ten thousand of us. Therefore it is better that you send us help from the city." ⁴ The king said to them, "Whatever seems best to you I will do." So the king stood at the side of the gate, while all the army marched out by hundreds and by thousands. ⁵ And the king ordered Joab and Abishai and Ittai, "Deal gently for my sake with the young man

Absalom." And all the people heard when the king gave orders to all the commanders about Absalom.

⁶ So the army went out into the field against Israel, and the battle was fought in the forest of Ephraim. ⁷ And the men of Israel were defeated there by the servants of David, and the loss there was great on that day, twenty thousand men. ⁸ The battle spread over the face of all the country, and the forest devoured more people that day than the sword.

⁹ And Absalom happened to meet the servants of David. Absalom was riding on his mule, and the mule went under the thick branches of a great oak, and his head caught fast in the oak, and he was suspended between heaven and earth, while the mule that was under him went on. ¹⁰ And a certain man saw it and told Joab, "Behold, I saw Absalom hanging in an oak." ¹¹ Joab said to the man who told him, "What, you saw him! Why then did you not strike him there to the ground? I would have been glad to give you ten pieces of silver and a belt." ¹² But the man said to Joab, "Even if I felt in my hand the weight of a thousand pieces of silver, I would not reach out my hand against the king's son, for in our hearing the king commanded you and Abishai and Ittai, 'For my sake protect the young man Absalom.' ¹³ On the other hand, if I had dealt treacherously against his life (and there is nothing hidden from the king), then you yourself would have stood aloof." ¹⁴ Joab said, "I will not waste time like this with you." And he took three javelins in his hand and thrust them into the heart of Absalom while he was still alive in the oak. ¹⁵ And ten young men, Joab's armor-bearers, surrounded Absalom and struck him and killed him.

¹⁶ Then Joab blew the trumpet, and the troops came back from pursuing Israel, for Joab restrained them. ¹⁷ And they took Absalom and threw him into a great pit in the forest and raised over him a very great heap of stones. And all Israel fled every one to his own home. ¹⁸ Now Absalom in his lifetime had taken and set up for himself the pillar that is in the King's Valley, for he said, "I have no son to keep my name in remembrance." He called the pillar after his own name, and it is called Absalom's monument to this day.

David Hears of Absalom's Death

¹⁹ Then Ahimaaz the son of Zadok said, "Let me run and carry news to the king that the LORD has delivered him from the hand of his enemies." ²⁰ And Joab said to him, "You are not to carry news today. You may carry news another day, but today you shall carry no news, because the king's son is dead." ²¹ Then Joab said to the Cushite, "Go, tell the king what you have seen." The Cushite bowed before Joab, and ran. ²² Then Ahimaaz the son of Zadok said again to Joab, "Come what may, let me also run after the Cushite." And Joab said, "Why will you run, my son, seeing that you will have no reward for the news?" ²³ "Come what may," he said, "I will run." So he said to him, "Run." Then Ahimaaz ran by the way of the plain, and outran the Cushite.

²⁴ Now David was sitting between the two gates, and the watchman went up to the roof

GETTING THE MESSAGE

The forest of Ephraim (18:6) was east of the Jordan River in Gilead. Gilead was known for its forests, and there David's men would have a tactical advantage against a larger force.

of the gate by the wall, and when he lifted up his eyes and looked, he saw a man running alone. ²⁵ The watchman called out and told the king. And the king said, "If he is alone, there is news in his mouth." And he drew nearer and nearer. ²⁶ The watchman saw another man running. And the watchman called to the gate and said, "See, another man running alone!" The king said, "He also brings news." ²⁷ The watchman said, "I think the running of the first is like the running of Ahimaaz the son of Zadok." And the king said, "He is a good man and comes with good news."

²⁸ Then Ahimaaz cried out to the king, "All is well." And he bowed before the king with his face to the earth and said, "Blessed be the LORD your God, who has delivered up the men who raised their hand against my lord the king." ²⁹ And the king said, "Is it well with the young man Absalom?" Ahimaaz answered, "When Joab sent the king's servant, your servant, I saw a great commotion,

but I do not know what it was." **30** And the king said, "Turn aside and stand here." So he turned aside and stood still.

David's Grief

31 And behold, the Cushite came, and the Cushite said, "Good news for my lord the king! For the LORD has delivered you this day from the hand of all who rose up against you." **32** The king said to the Cushite, "Is it well with the young man Absalom?" And the Cushite answered, "May the enemies of my

---

PROFILE

JOAB

Joab was the commander of David's army. He was a complicated person, showing both strong faith and chilling ruthlessness in battle. In retaliation for the death of his brother Asahel, Joab murdered Abner, Saul's general. He helped to bring about David's reconciliation with Absalom. But later, after Absalom rebelled against David, Joab killed Absalom even though David had told him not to do so. Then, Joab rebuked David for mourning for his rebellious son rather than rejoicing with his victorious troops. As Joab so memorably expressed it, "you love those who hate you and hate those who love you" (19:6). Later, Joab supported Adonijah instead of Solomon as David's successor. David advised Solomon to have Joab put to death. Joab was killed as he hid in the sanctuary.

KEY REFERENCE: 2 SAMUEL 19:1-8

---

lord the king and all who rise up against you for evil be like that young man." **33** And the king was deeply moved and went up to the chamber over the gate and wept. And as he went, he said, "O my son Absalom, my son, my son Absalom! Would I had died instead of you, O Absalom, my son, my son!"

Joab Rebukes David

19 It was told Joab, "Behold, the king is weeping and mourning for Absalom." **2** So the victory that day was turned into mourning for all the people, for the peo-

ple heard that day, "The king is grieving for his son." **3** And the people stole into the city that day as people steal in who are ashamed when they flee in battle. **4** The king covered his face, and the king cried with a loud voice, "O my son Absalom, O Absalom, my son, my son!" **5** Then Joab came into the house to the king and said, "You have today covered with shame the faces of all your servants, who have this day saved your life and the lives of your sons and your daughters and the lives of your wives and your concubines, **6** because you love those who hate you and hate those who love you. For you have made it clear today that commanders and servants are nothing to you, for today I know that if Absalom were alive and all of us were dead today, then you would be pleased. **7** Now therefore arise, go out and speak kindly to your servants, for I swear by the LORD, if you do not go, not a man will stay with you this night, and this will be worse for you than all the evil that has come upon you from your youth until now." **8** Then the king arose and took his seat in the gate. And the people were all told, "Behold, the king is sitting in the gate." And all the people came before the king.

David Returns to Jerusalem

Now Israel had fled every man to his own home. **9** And all the people were arguing throughout all the tribes of Israel, saying, "The king delivered us from the hand of our enemies and saved us from the hand of the Philistines, and now he has fled out of the land from Absalom. **10** But Absalom, whom we anointed over us, is dead in battle. Now therefore why do you say nothing about bringing the king back?"

11 And King David sent this message to Zadok and Abiathar the priests: "Say to the elders of Judah, 'Why should you be the last to bring the king back to his house, when the word of all Israel has come to the king? **12** You are my brothers; you are my bone and my flesh. Why then should you be the last to bring back the king?' **13** And say to Amasa, 'Are you not my bone and my flesh? God do so to me and more also, if you are not commander of my army from now on in place of Joab.'" **14** And he swayed the heart of all the men of Judah as one man, so that they sent word to the king, "Return, both you and all your servants." **15** So the king came back to the Jordan, and Judah came to Gilgal to meet the king and to bring the king over the Jordan.

David Pardons His Enemies

¹⁶ And Shimei the son of Gera, the Benjaminite, from Bahurim, hurried to come down with the men of Judah to meet King David. ¹⁷ And with him were a thousand men from Benjamin. And Ziba the servant of the house of Saul, with his fifteen sons and his twenty servants, rushed down to the Jordan before the king, ¹⁸ and they crossed the ford to bring over the king's household and to do his pleasure. And Shimei the son of Gera fell down before the king, as he was about to cross the Jordan, ¹⁹ and said to the king, "Let not my lord hold me guilty or remember how your servant did wrong on the day my lord the king left Jerusalem. Do not let the king take it to heart. ²⁰ For your servant knows that I have sinned. Therefore, behold, I have come this day, the first of all the house of Joseph to come down to meet my lord the king." ²¹ Abishai the son of Zeruiah answered, "Shall not Shimei be put to death for this, because he cursed the LORD's anointed?" ²² But David said, "What have I to do with you, you sons of Zeruiah, that you should this day be as an adversary to me? Shall anyone be put to death in Israel this day? For do I not know that I am this day king over Israel?" ²³ And the king said to Shimei, "You shall not die." And the king gave him his oath.

²⁴ And Mephibosheth the son of Saul came down to meet the king. He had neither taken care of his feet nor trimmed his beard nor washed his clothes, from the day the king departed until the day he came back in safety. ²⁵ And when he came to Jerusalem to meet the king, the king said to him, "Why did you not go with me, Mephibosheth?" ²⁶ He answered, "My lord, O king, my servant deceived me, for your servant said to him, 'I will saddle a donkey for myself, that I may ride on it and go with the king.' For your servant is lame. ²⁷ He has slandered your servant to my lord the king. But my lord the king is like the angel of God; do therefore what seems good to you. ²⁸ For all my father's house were but men doomed to death before my lord the king, but you set your servant among those who eat at your table. What further right have I, then, to cry

to the king?" ²⁹ And the king said to him, "Why speak any more of your affairs? I have decided: you and Ziba shall divide the land." ³⁰ And Mephibosheth said to the king, "Oh, let him take it all, since my lord the king has come safely home."

³¹ Now Barzillai the Gileadite had come down from Rogelim, and he went on with the king to the Jordan, to escort him over the Jordan. ³² Barzillai was a very aged man, eighty years old. He had provided the king with food while he stayed at Mahanaim, for he was a very wealthy man. ³³ And the king said to Barzillai, "Come over with me, and I will provide for you with me in Jerusalem." ³⁴ But Barzillai said to the king, "How many years have I still to live, that I should go up with the king to Jerusalem? ³⁵ I am this day eighty years old. Can I discern what is pleasant and what is not? Can your servant taste

GETTING THE MESSAGE

Kissing was a cultural means of showing respect, friendship, or reverence, as it is in many places today. A kiss was often given as a form of greeting or farewell (19:39). There are only three places in all of Scripture where kissing is connected with romance (Prov. 7:13, Song 1:2; 8:1.).

what he eats or what he drinks? Can I still listen to the voice of singing men and singing women? Why then should your servant be an added burden to my lord the king? ³⁶ Your servant will go a little way over the Jordan with the king. Why should the king repay me with such a reward? ³⁷ Please let your servant return, that I may die in my own city near the grave of my father and my mother. But here is your servant Chimham. Let him go over with my lord the king, and do for him whatever seems good to you." ³⁸ And the king answered, "Chimham shall go over with me, and I will do for him whatever seems good to you, and all that you desire of me I will do for you." ³⁹ Then all the people went over the Jordan, and the king went over. And the king kissed Barzillai and blessed him, and he returned to his own home. ⁴⁰ The king went on to Gilgal, and Chimham went on with him. All the people of Judah, and also half the people of Israel, brought the king on his way.

⁴¹ Then all the men of Israel came to the king and said to the king, "Why have our brothers the men of Judah stolen you away and brought the king and his household over the Jordan, and all David's men with him?" ⁴² All the men of Judah answered the men of Israel, "Because the king is our close relative. Why then are you angry over this matter? Have we eaten at all at the king's expense? Or has he given us any gift?" ⁴³ And the men of Israel answered the men of Judah, "We have ten shares in the king, and in David also we have more than you. Why then did you despise us? Were we not the first to speak of bringing back our king?" But the words of the men of Judah were fiercer than the words of the men of Israel.

The Rebellion of Sheba

20 Now there happened to be there a worthless man, whose name was Sheba, the son of Bichri, a Benjaminite. And he blew the trumpet and said,

"We have no portion in David,
    and we have no inheritance in the son of Jesse;
every man to his tents, O Israel!"

² So all the men of Israel withdrew from David and followed Sheba the son of Bichri. But the men of Judah followed their king steadfastly from the Jordan to Jerusalem.

³ And David came to his house at Jerusalem. And the king took the ten concubines whom he had left to care for the house and put them in a house under guard and provided for them, but did not go in to them. So they were shut up until the day of their death, living as if in widowhood.

⁴ Then the king said to Amasa, "Call the men of Judah together to me within three days, and be here yourself." ⁵ So Amasa went to summon Judah, but he delayed beyond the set time that had been appointed him. ⁶ And David said to Abishai, "Now Sheba the son of Bichri will do us more harm than Absalom. Take your lord's servants and pursue him, lest he get himself to fortified cities and escape from us." ⁷ And there went out after him Joab's men and the Cherethites and the Pelethites, and all the mighty men. They went out from Jerusalem to pursue Sheba the son of Bichri. ⁸ When they were

at the great stone that is in Gibeon, Amasa came to meet them. Now Joab was wearing a soldier's garment, and over it was a belt with a sword in its sheath fastened on his thigh, and as he went forward it fell out. ⁹ And Joab said to Amasa, "Is it well with you, my brother?" And Joab took Amasa by the beard with his right hand to kiss him. ¹⁰ But Amasa did not observe the sword that was in Joab's hand. So Joab struck him with it in the stomach and spilled his entrails to the ground without striking a second blow, and he died.

Then Joab and Abishai his brother pursued Sheba the son of Bichri. ¹¹ And one of Joab's young men took his stand by Amasa and said, "Whoever favors Joab, and whoever is for David, let him follow Joab." ¹² And Amasa lay wallowing in his blood in the highway. And anyone who came by, seeing him, stopped. And when the man saw that all the people stopped, he carried Amasa out of the highway into the field and threw a garment over him. ¹³ When he was taken out of the highway, all the people went on after Joab to pursue Sheba the son of Bichri.

¹⁴ And Sheba passed through all the tribes of Israel to Abel of Beth-maacah, and all the Bichrites assembled and followed him in. ¹⁵ And all the men who were with Joab came and besieged him in Abel of Beth-maacah. They cast up a mound against the city, and it stood against the rampart, and they were battering the wall to throw it down. ¹⁶ Then a wise woman called from the city, "Listen! Listen! Tell Joab, 'Come here, that I may speak to you.'" ¹⁷ And he came near her, and the woman said, "Are you Joab?" He answered, "I am." Then she said to him, "Listen to the words of your servant." And he answered, "I am listening." ¹⁸ Then she said, "They used to say in former times, 'Let them but ask counsel at Abel,' and so they settled a matter. ¹⁹ I am one of those who are peaceable and faithful in Israel. You seek to destroy a city that is a mother in Israel. Why will you swallow up the heritage of the LORD?" ²⁰ Joab answered, "Far be it from me, far be it, that I should swallow up or destroy! ²¹ That is not true. But a man of the hill country of Ephraim, called Sheba the son of Bichri, has lifted up his hand against King David. Give up him alone, and I will withdraw from the city." And the woman

said to Joab, "Behold, his head shall be thrown to you over the wall." ²² Then the woman went to all the people in her wisdom. And they cut off the head of Sheba the son of Bichri and threw it out to Joab. So he blew the trumpet, and they dispersed from the city, every man to his home. And Joab returned to Jerusalem to the king.

²³ Now Joab was in command of all the army of Israel; and Benaiah the son of Jehoiada was in command of the Cherethites and the Pelethites; ²⁴ and Adoram was in charge of the forced labor; and Jehoshaphat the son of Ahilud was the recorder; ²⁵ and Sheva was secretary; and Zadok and Abiathar were priests; ²⁶ and Ira the Jairite was also David's priest.

David Avenges the Gibeonites

21 Now there was a famine in the days of David for three years, year after year. And David sought the face of the LORD. And the LORD said, "There is bloodguilt on Saul and on his house, because he put the Gibeonites to death." ² So the king called the Gibeonites and spoke to them. Now the Gibeonites were not of the people of Israel but of the remnant of the Amorites. Although the people of Israel had sworn to spare them, Saul had sought to strike them down in his zeal for the people of Israel and Judah. ³ And David said to the Gibeonites, "What shall I do for you? And how shall I make atonement, that you may bless the heritage of the LORD?" ⁴ The Gibeonites said to him, "It is not a matter of silver or gold between us and Saul or his house; neither is it for us to put any man to death in Israel." And he said, "What do you say that I shall do for you?" ⁵ They said to the king, "The man who consumed us and planned to destroy us, so that we should have no place in all the territory of Israel, ⁶ let seven of his sons be given to us, so that we may hang them before the LORD at Gibeah of Saul, the chosen of the LORD." And the king said, "I will give them."

⁷ But the king spared Mephibosheth, the son of Saul's son Jonathan, because of the oath of the LORD that was between them, between David and Jonathan the son of Saul. ⁸ The king took the two sons of Rizpah the daughter of Aiah, whom she bore to Saul, Armoni and Mephibosheth; and the five sons of Merab the daughter of Saul, whom she bore to Adriel the son of Barzillai the Meholathite; ⁹ and he gave them into the hands of the Gibeonites, and they hanged them on the mountain before the LORD, and the seven of them perished together. They were put to death in the first days of harvest, at the beginning of barley harvest.

¹⁰ Then Rizpah the daughter of Aiah took sackcloth and spread it for herself on the rock, from the beginning of harvest until rain fell upon them from the heavens. And she did not allow the birds of the air to come upon them by day, or the beasts of the field by night. ¹¹ When David was told what Rizpah the daughter of Aiah, the concubine of Saul, had done, ¹² David went and took the bones of Saul and the bones of his son Jonathan from the men of Jabesh-gilead, who had stolen them from the public

> ## GETTING THE MESSAGE
>
> **Barley** was an essential grain for the Israelite people and their livestock (21:9). A failed barley crop could spell disaster for a whole community.

square of Beth-shan, where the Philistines had hanged them, on the day the Philistines killed Saul on Gilboa. ¹³ And he brought up from there the bones of Saul and the bones of his son Jonathan; and they gathered the bones of those who were hanged. ¹⁴ And they buried the bones of Saul and his son Jonathan in the land of Benjamin in Zela, in the tomb of Kish his father. And they did all that the king commanded. And after that God responded to the plea for the land.

War with the Philistines

¹⁵ There was war again between the Philistines and Israel, and David went down together with his servants, and they fought against the Philistines. And David grew weary. ¹⁶ And Ishbi-benob, one of the descendants of the giants, whose spear weighed three hundred shekels of bronze, and who was armed with a new sword, thought to kill David. ¹⁷ But Abishai the son of Zeruiah came to his aid and attacked the Philistine and killed him. Then David's men swore to him, "You shall no longer go out with us to battle, lest you quench the lamp of Israel."

¹⁸ After this there was again war with the Philistines at Gob. Then Sibbecai the Hushathite struck down Saph, who was one of the descendants of the giants. ¹⁹ And there was again war with the Philistines at Gob, and Elhanan the son of Jaare-oregim, the Bethlehemite, struck down Goliath the Gittite, the shaft of whose spear was like a weaver's beam. ²⁰ And there was again war at Gath, where there was a man of great stature, who had six fingers on each hand, and six toes on each foot, twenty-four in number, and he also was descended from the giants. ²¹ And when he taunted Israel, Jonathan the son of Shimei, David's brother, struck him down. ²² These four were descended from the giants in Gath, and they fell by the hand of David and by the hand of his servants.

GETTING THE MESSAGE

David's **Song of Deliverance** is nearly identical to Psalm 18. Perhaps 2 Samuel 22 was meant to be read aloud for instruction and Psalm 18 was meant to be sung or prayed as part of worship.

David's Song of Deliverance

22 And David spoke to the LORD the words of this song on the day when the LORD delivered him from the hand of all his enemies, and from the hand of Saul. ² He said,

"The LORD is my rock and my fortress and my deliverer,
³   my God, my rock, in whom I take refuge,
   my shield, and the horn of my salvation,
      my stronghold and my refuge,
   my savior; you save me from violence.
⁴ I call upon the LORD, who is worthy to be praised,
   and I am saved from my enemies.

⁵ "For the waves of death encompassed me,
   the torrents of destruction assailed me;
⁶   the cords of Sheol entangled me;
   the snares of death confronted me.

⁷ "In my distress I called upon the LORD;
   to my God I called.
From his temple he heard my voice,
   and my cry came to his ears.

⁸ "Then the earth reeled and rocked;
   the foundations of the heavens trembled
   and quaked, because he was angry.
⁹   Smoke went up from his nostrils,
   and devouring fire from his mouth;
   glowing coals flamed forth from him.
¹⁰   He bowed the heavens and came down;
   thick darkness was under his feet.
¹¹   He rode on a cherub and flew;
   he was seen on the wings of the wind.
¹²   He made darkness around him his canopy,
   thick clouds, a gathering of water.
¹³   Out of the brightness before him
   coals of fire flamed forth.
¹⁴   The LORD thundered from heaven,
   and the Most High uttered his voice.
¹⁵   And he sent out arrows and scattered them;
   lightning, and routed them.
¹⁶   Then the channels of the sea were seen;
   the foundations of the world were laid bare,
   at the rebuke of the LORD,
   at the blast of the breath of his nostrils.

¹⁷ "He sent from on high, he took me;
   he drew me out of many waters.
¹⁸   He rescued me from my strong enemy,
   from those who hated me,
   for they were too mighty for me.
¹⁹   They confronted me in the day of my calamity,
   but the LORD was my support.
²⁰   He brought me out into a broad place;
   he rescued me, because he delighted in me.

²¹ "The LORD dealt with me according to my righteousness;
   according to the cleanness of my hands he rewarded me.
²²   For I have kept the ways of the LORD
   and have not wickedly departed from my God.

23 For all his rules were before me,
    and from his statutes I did not turn
     aside.
24 I was blameless before him,
    and I kept myself from guilt.
25 And the LORD has rewarded me
     according to my righteousness,
    according to my cleanness in his
     sight.

26 "With the merciful you show yourself
     merciful;
    with the blameless man you show
     yourself blameless;
27 with the purified you deal purely,
    and with the crooked you make
     yourself seem tortuous.
28 You save a humble people,
    but your eyes are on the haughty to
     bring them down.
29 For you are my lamp, O LORD,
    and my God lightens my darkness.
30 For by you I can run against a troop,
    and by my God I can leap over a
     wall.
31 This God—his way is perfect;
    the word of the LORD proves true;
    he is a shield for all those who take
     refuge in him.

32 "For who is God, but the LORD?
    And who is a rock, except our God?
33 This God is my strong refuge
    and has made my way blameless.
34 He made my feet like the feet of a
     deer
    and set me secure on the heights.
35 He trains my hands for war,
    so that my arms can bend a bow of
     bronze.
36 You have given me the shield of your
     salvation,
    and your gentleness made me
     great.
37 You gave a wide place for my steps
     under me,
    and my feet did not slip;
38 I pursued my enemies and destroyed
     them,
    and did not turn back until they
     were consumed.
39 I consumed them; I thrust them
     through, so that they did
     not rise;
    they fell under my feet.

40 For you equipped me with strength
     for the battle;
    you made those who rise against
     me sink under me.
41 You made my enemies turn their
     backs to me,
    those who hated me, and I
     destroyed them.
42 They looked, but there was none to
     save;
    they cried to the LORD, but he did
     not answer them.
43 I beat them fine as the dust of the
     earth;
    I crushed them and stamped them
     down like the mire of the streets.

44 "You delivered me from strife with my
     people;
    you kept me as the head of the
     nations;
    people whom I had not known
     served me.
45 Foreigners came cringing to me;
    as soon as they heard of me, they
     obeyed me.
46 Foreigners lost heart
    and came trembling out of their
     fortresses.

47 "The LORD lives, and blessed be my rock,
    and exalted be my God, the rock of
     my salvation,
48 the God who gave me vengeance
    and brought down peoples under
     me,
49 who brought me out from my enemies;
    you exalted me above those who
     rose against me;
    you delivered me from men of
     violence.

50 "For this I will praise you, O LORD,
     among the nations,
    and sing praises to your name.
51 Great salvation he brings to his king,
    and shows steadfast love to his
     anointed,
    to David and his offspring forever."

The Last Words of David

23 Now these are the last words of
David:

The oracle of David, the son of Jesse,
    the oracle of the man who was
     raised on high,

the anointed of the God of Jacob,
the sweet psalmist of Israel:

2 "The Spirit of the LORD speaks by me;
his word is on my tongue.
3 The God of Israel has spoken;
the Rock of Israel has said to me:
When one rules justly over men,
ruling in the fear of God,
4 he dawns on them like the morning
light,
like the sun shining forth on a
cloudless morning,
like rain that makes grass to sprout
from the earth.

PROFILE

ABISHAI

Abishai was David's nephew and became the commander of David's "thirty men." Like his brothers Joab and Asahel, Abishai was a loyal but ruthless warrior. He killed 18,000 Edomites in the Valley of Salt. He urged David to allow him to kill Saul, but David refused to let him kill "the LORD's anointed" (1 Sam. 26:8–9). He fought alongside his brothers at the Battle of Gibeon, where Abner killed Asahel. Abishai later helped Joab kill Abner in revenge. When Shimei cursed David, Abishai thought he should be put to death, but again David refused his request. He helped lead David's troops against Absalom, and again fought for David when Sheba led a rebellion against him. Abishai also saved David's life by killing the Philistine giant Ishbi-benob.

KEY REFERENCE: 2 SAMUEL 23:18–19

---

5 "For does not my house stand so with
God?
For he has made with me an everlasting covenant,
ordered in all things and secure.
For will he not cause to prosper
all my help and my desire?
6 But worthless men are all like thorns
that are thrown away,
for they cannot be taken with the
hand;

7 but the man who touches them
arms himself with iron and the
shaft of a spear,
and they are utterly consumed with
fire."

David's Mighty Men

8 These are the names of the mighty men whom David had: Josheb-basshebeth a Tahchemonite; he was chief of the three. He wielded his spear against eight hundred whom he killed at one time.

9 And next to him among the three mighty men was Eleazar the son of Dodo, son of Ahohi. He was with David when they defied the Philistines who were gathered there for battle, and the men of Israel withdrew. 10 He rose and struck down the Philistines until his hand was weary, and his hand clung to the sword. And the LORD brought about a great victory that day, and the men returned after him only to strip the slain.

11 And next to him was Shammah, the son of Agee the Hararite. The Philistines gathered together at Lehi, where there was a plot of ground full of lentils, and the men fled from the Philistines. 12 But he took his stand in the midst of the plot and defended it and struck down the Philistines, and the LORD worked a great victory.

13 And three of the thirty chief men went down and came about harvest time to David at the cave of Adullam, when a band of Philistines was encamped in the Valley of Rephaim. 14 David was then in the stronghold, and the garrison of the Philistines was then at Bethlehem. 15 And David said longingly, "Oh, that someone would give me water to drink from the well of Bethlehem that is by the gate!" 16 Then the three mighty men broke through the camp of the Philistines and drew water out of the well of Bethlehem that was by the gate and carried and brought it to David. But he would not drink of it. He poured it out to the LORD 17 and said, "Far be it from me, O LORD, that I should do this. Shall I drink the blood of the men who went at the risk of their lives?" Therefore he would not drink it. These things the three mighty men did.

18 Now Abishai, the brother of Joab, the son of Zeruiah, was chief of the thirty. And he wielded his spear against three hundred men and killed them and won a name beside the three. 19 He was the most renowned of

the thirty and became their commander, but he did not attain to the three.

²⁰ And Benaiah the son of Jehoiada was a valiant man of Kabzeel, a doer of great deeds. He struck down two ariels of Moab. He also went down and struck down a lion in a pit on a day when snow had fallen. ²¹ And he struck down an Egyptian, a handsome man. The Egyptian had a spear in his hand, but Benaiah went down to him with a staff and snatched the spear out of the Egyptian's hand and killed him with his own spear. ²² These things did Benaiah the son of Jehoiada, and won a name beside the three mighty men. ²³ He was renowned among the thirty, but he did not attain to the three. And David set him over his bodyguard.

²⁴ Asahel the brother of Joab was one of the thirty; Elhanan the son of Dodo of Bethlehem, ²⁵ Shammah of Harod, Elika of Harod, ²⁶ Helez the Paltite, Ira the son of Ikkesh of Tekoa, ²⁷ Abiezer of Anathoth, Mebunnai the Hushathite, ²⁸ Zalmon the Ahohite, Maharai of Netophah, ²⁹ Heleb the son of Baanah of Netophah, Ittai the son of Ribai of Gibeah of the people of Benjamin, ³⁰ Benaiah of Pirathon, Hiddai of the brooks of Gaash, ³¹ Abi-albon the Arbathite, Azmaveth of Bahurim, ³² Eliahba the Shaalbonite, the sons of Jashen, Jonathan, ³³ Shammah the Hararite, Ahiam the son of Sharar the Hararite, ³⁴ Eliphelet the son of Ahasbai of Maacah, Eliam the son of Ahithophel of Gilo, ³⁵ Hezro of Carmel, Paarai the Arbite, ³⁶ Igal the son of Nathan of Zobah, Bani the Gadite, ³⁷ Zelek the Ammonite, Naharai of Beeroth, the armorbearer of Joab the son of Zeruiah, ³⁸ Ira the Ithrite, Gareb the Ithrite, ³⁹ Uriah the Hittite: thirty-seven in all.

David's Census

24 Again the anger of the LORD was kindled against Israel, and he incited David against them, saying, "Go, number Israel and Judah." ² So the king said to Joab, the commander of the army, who was with him, "Go through all the tribes of Israel, from Dan to Beersheba, and number the people, that I may know the number of the people." ³ But Joab said to the king, "May the LORD your God add to the people a hundred times as many as they are, while the eyes of my lord the king still see it, but why does my lord the king delight in this thing?"

⁴ But the king's word prevailed against Joab and the commanders of the army. So Joab and the commanders of the army went out from the presence of the king to number the people of Israel. ⁵ They crossed the Jordan and began from Aroer, and from the city that is in the middle of the valley, toward Gad and on to Jazer. ⁶ Then they came to Gilead, and to Kadesh in the land of the Hittites; and they came to Dan, and from Dan they went around to Sidon, ⁷ and came to the fortress of Tyre and to all the cities of the Hivites and Canaanites; and they went out to the Negeb of Judah at Beersheba. ⁸ So when they had gone through all the land, they came to Jerusalem at the end of nine months and twenty days. ⁹ And Joab gave the sum of the numbering of the people to the

GETTING THE MESSAGE

David's census was most likely a military census. Its purpose would have been to find the age and location of potential new draftees for service in the army. It was either intended to give David pride in the number of his supporters or was a sign of his fear of another rebellion. Either way, it showed his lack of faith in God.

king: in Israel there were 800,000 valiant men who drew the sword, and the men of Judah were 500,000.

The LORD's Judgment of David's Sin

¹⁰ But David's heart struck him after he had numbered the people. And David said to the LORD, "I have sinned greatly in what I have done. But now, O LORD, please take away the iniquity of your servant, for I have done very foolishly." ¹¹ And when David arose in the morning, the word of the LORD came to the prophet Gad, David's seer, saying, ¹² "Go and say to David, 'Thus says the LORD, Three things I offer you. Choose one of them, that I may do it to you.' " ¹³ So Gad came to David and told him, and said to him, "Shall three years of famine come to you in your land? Or will you flee three months before your foes while they pursue you? Or shall there be three days' pestilence in your land? Now consider, and decide what answer I shall return to him who sent me." ¹⁴ Then David

said to Gad, "I am in great distress. Let us fall into the hand of the LORD, for his mercy is great; but let me not fall into the hand of man."

¹⁵ So the LORD sent a pestilence on Israel from the morning until the appointed time. And there died of the people from Dan to Beersheba 70,000 men. ¹⁶ And when the angel stretched out his hand toward Jerusalem to destroy it, the LORD relented from the calamity and said to the angel who was working destruction among the people, "It is enough; now stay your hand." And the angel of the LORD was by the threshing floor of Araunah the Jebusite. ¹⁷ Then David spoke to the LORD when he saw the angel who was striking the people, and said, "Behold, I have sinned, and I have done wickedly. But these sheep, what have they done? Please let your hand be against me and against my father's house."

David Builds an Altar

¹⁸ And Gad came that day to David and said to him, "Go up, raise an altar to the LORD on the threshing floor of Araunah the Jebusite." ¹⁹ So David went up at Gad's word, as the LORD commanded. ²⁰ And when Araunah looked down, he saw the king and his servants coming on toward him. And Araunah went out and paid homage to the king with his face to the ground. ²¹ And Araunah said, "Why has my lord the king come to his servant?" David said, "To buy the threshing floor from you, in order to build an altar to the LORD, that the plague may be averted from the people." ²² Then Araunah said to David, "Let my lord the king take and offer up what seems good to him. Here are the oxen for the burnt offering and the threshing sledges and the yokes of the oxen for the wood. ²³ All this, O king, Araunah gives to the king." And Araunah said to the king, "May the LORD your God accept you." ²⁴ But the king said to Araunah, "No, but I will buy it from you for a price. I will not offer burnt offerings to the LORD my God that cost me nothing." So David bought the threshing floor and the oxen for fifty shekels of silver. ²⁵ And David built there an altar to the LORD and offered burnt offerings and peace offerings. So the LORD responded to the plea for the land, and the plague was averted from Israel.

INTRODUCTION TO 1–2 KINGS

971, 931 B.C.	722 B.C.	586 B.C.
Reign of Solomon, Israel divided	Fall of Israel	Fall of Judah

AUTHOR AND DATE

The author or authors of these two books is unknown. As the titles of the books indicate, 1–2 Kings describe the period of the monarchy in ancient Israel (970–586 B.C.), concentrating on the kings who ruled after David.

THEME

The books show that Israel suffers again and again because of its great sinfulness (2 Kings 17:7–23; 24:1–4). Yet there is still hope for the nation, because God's chosen family of kings has not come to an end (2 Kings 25:27–30), and God remains ready to forgive those who repent (1 Kings 8:22–61).

PURPOSE, OCCASION, AND BACKGROUND

The fall of Jerusalem to Babylon in 586 B.C. raised several questions: Was Israel's God not in fact in control of history, as Moses had claimed? If the God of Moses did exist, and was good and all-powerful, how was it that God's chosen city and temple had been destroyed, and his chosen royal family had all but come to its end?

The books of Kings respond to such questions, explaining why Israel was defeated. Israel's God is indeed in control of nature and history. There are no other true gods anywhere. It is this good and all-powerful God who has overseen the destruction of his chosen city and his temple, and Israel's exile to Babylon. Israel's sin has caused these punishments.

After the division of the kingdom, the northern kingdom of Israel lasted slightly more than 200 years (931–722 B.C.), with 19 different kings, all of whom were wicked. The southern kingdom of Judah had the same number of kings, but many of them were good, and Judah lasted almost 150 years longer (931–586 B.C.). Toward the end of Judah's monarchy came two of its best kings: Hezekiah (2 Kings 18:1–20:21) and Josiah (2 Kings 22:1–23:30). Yet

the people still rebelled against the Lord, and Judah, like Israel, eventually went into exile as punishment for its sin. But hope remained, for God's chosen royal line had not come to a complete end (2 Kings 25:27–30), and God remained ready to forgive those who repented.

KEY THEMES

1. *Yahweh is the only true God, and he controls nature.* There is only one living God, and he is the Lord. He alone controls the natural order (1 Kings 17–19; 2 Kings 1:2–17; 4:8–37; 5:1–18; 6:1–7, 27).

2. *Yahweh controls history.* The Lord rules over the past, present, and future. He alone controls the historical process (1 Kings 11:14, 23; 14:1–18; 22:1–38; 2 Kings 5:1–18; 10:32–33; 18:17–19:37).

3. *Yahweh demands exclusive worship.* As the only God, the Lord demands exclusive worship. He alone will be worshiped, by Israelite and foreigner alike (1 Kings 8:41–43, 60; 2 Kings 5:15–18; 17:24–41).

4. *The content and place of true worship.* Much of 1–2 Kings is concerned with exposing false religion. It speaks out against the *content* of false worship (1 Kings 11:1–40; 12:25–13:34; 14:22–24; 16:29–33; 2 Kings 16:1–4; 17:7–23; 21:1–9). It also exposes the wrongful *place* of such false worship (1 Kings 3:2; 5:1–9:9; 15:14; 22:43; 2 Kings 18:4; 23:1–20).

5. *The consequences of false worship.* True worship of God includes obedience to the law of God. The worship of something other than God always leads to mistreating other people.

6. *Yahweh is the just and gracious Lawgiver.* The Lord gave the law, which defines true worship, right thinking, and correct behavior. The Lord is also the one who punishes wrongdoers.

7. *Yahweh is the promise-giver.* Israel's God is a promise-giver. The divine promises given to the patriarchs and to David are an important theme in 1–2 Kings.

1 KINGS OUTLINE

2 KINGS OUTLINE

1 KINGS

David in His Old Age

1 Now King David was old and advanced in years. And although they covered him with clothes, he could not get warm. ² Therefore his servants said to him, "Let a young woman be sought for my lord the king, and let her wait on the king and be in his service. Let her lie in your arms, that my lord the king may be warm." ³ So they sought for a beautiful young woman throughout all the territory of Israel, and found Abishag the Shunammite, and brought her to the king. ⁴ The young woman was very beautiful, and she was of service to the king and attended to him, but the king knew her not.

> ### GETTING THE MESSAGE
>
> God promised to establish David's kingdom **forever** (2 Sam. 7:1–17). Although Adonijah was David's eldest living son, Nathan and Bathsheba's actions ensured that Solomon's claim to the throne was stronger (ch. 1). Solomon became king at David's death.

Adonijah Sets Himself Up as King

⁵ Now Adonijah the son of Haggith exalted himself, saying, "I will be king." And he prepared for himself chariots and horsemen, and fifty men to run before him. ⁶ His father had never at any time displeased him by asking, "Why have you done thus and so?" He was also a very handsome man, and he was born next after Absalom. ⁷ He conferred with Joab the son of Zeruiah and with Abiathar the priest. And they followed Adonijah and helped him. ⁸ But Zadok the priest and Benaiah the son of Jehoiada and Nathan the prophet and Shimei and Rei and David's mighty men were not with Adonijah.

⁹ Adonijah sacrificed sheep, oxen, and fattened cattle by the Serpent's Stone, which is beside En-rogel, and he invited all his brothers, the king's sons, and all the royal officials of Judah, ¹⁰ but he did not invite Nathan the prophet or Benaiah or the mighty men or Solomon his brother.

Nathan and Bathsheba Before David

¹¹ Then Nathan said to Bathsheba the mother of Solomon, "Have you not heard that Adonijah the son of Haggith has become king and David our lord does not know it? ¹² Now therefore come, let me give you advice, that you may save your own life and the life of your son Solomon. ¹³ Go in at once to King David, and say to him, 'Did you not, my lord the king, swear to your servant, saying, "Solomon your son shall reign after me, and he shall sit on my throne"? Why then is Adonijah king?' ¹⁴ Then while you are still speaking with the king, I also will come in after you and confirm your words."

¹⁵ So Bathsheba went to the king in his chamber (now the king was very old, and Abishag the Shunammite was attending to the king). ¹⁶ Bathsheba bowed and paid homage to the king, and the king said, "What do you desire?" ¹⁷ She said to him, "My lord, you swore to your servant by the LORD your God, saying, 'Solomon your son shall reign after me, and he shall sit on my throne.' ¹⁸ And now, behold, Adonijah is king, although you, my lord the king, do not know it. ¹⁹ He has sacrificed oxen, fattened cattle, and sheep in abundance, and has invited all the sons of the king, Abiathar the priest, and Joab the commander of the army, but Solomon your servant he has not invited. ²⁰ And now, my lord the king, the eyes of all Israel are on you, to tell them who shall sit on the throne of my lord the king after him. ²¹ Otherwise it will come to pass, when my lord the king sleeps with his fathers, that I and my son Solomon will be counted offenders."

²² While she was still speaking with the king, Nathan the prophet came in. ²³ And they told the king, "Here is Nathan the prophet." And when he came in before the king, he bowed before the king, with his face to the ground. ²⁴ And Nathan said, "My lord the king, have you said, 'Adonijah shall reign after me, and he shall sit on my

throne'? **25** For he has gone down this day and has sacrificed oxen, fattened cattle, and sheep in abundance, and has invited all the king's sons, the commanders of the army, and Abiathar the priest. And behold, they are eating and drinking before him, and saying, 'Long live King Adonijah!' **26** But me, your servant, and Zadok the priest, and Benaiah the son of Jehoiada, and your servant Solomon he has not invited. **27** Has this thing been brought about by my lord the king and you have not told your servants who should sit on the throne of my lord the king after him?"

Solomon Anointed King

28 Then King David answered, "Call Bathsheba to me." So she came into the king's presence and stood before the king. **29** And the king swore, saying, "As the LORD lives, who has redeemed my soul out of every adversity, **30** as I swore to you by the LORD, the God of Israel, saying, 'Solomon your son shall reign after me, and he shall sit on my throne in my place,' even so will I do this day." **31** Then Bathsheba bowed with her face to the ground and paid homage to the king and said, "May my lord King David live forever!"

32 King David said, "Call to me Zadok the priest, Nathan the prophet, and Benaiah the son of Jehoiada." So they came before the king. **33** And the king said to them, "Take with you the servants of your lord and have Solomon my son ride on my own mule, and bring him down to Gihon. **34** And let Zadok the priest and Nathan the prophet there anoint him king over Israel. Then blow the trumpet and say, 'Long live King Solomon!' **35** You shall then come up after him, and he shall come and sit on my throne, for he shall be king in my place. And I have appointed him to be ruler over Israel and over Judah." **36** And Benaiah the son of Jehoiada answered the king, "Amen! May the LORD, the God of my lord the king, say so. **37** As the LORD has been with my lord the king, even so may he be with Solomon, and make his throne greater than the throne of my lord King David."

38 So Zadok the priest, Nathan the prophet, and Benaiah the son of Jehoiada, and the Cherethites and the Pelethites went down and had Solomon ride on King David's mule and brought him to Gihon. **39** There Zadok the priest took the horn of oil from the tent and anointed Solomon. Then they blew the trumpet, and all the people said, "Long live King Solomon!" **40** And all the people went up after him, playing on pipes, and rejoicing with great joy, so that the earth was split by their noise.

41 Adonijah and all the guests who were with him heard it as they finished feasting. And when Joab heard the sound of the trumpet, he said, "What does this uproar in the city mean?" **42** While he was still speaking, behold, Jonathan the son of Abiathar the

---

PROFILE

BATHSHEBA

Bathsheba was the beautiful wife of Uriah the Hittite, one of David's warriors. While walking on his roof one afternoon, David saw Bathsheba bathing. He sent messengers to take her and bring her to him, and he committed adultery with her. Bathsheba became pregnant, and David desperately attempted to cover his sin. He first tried to make it appear that the child was Uriah's, but when that failed, he plotted the murder of his faithful soldier. After Uriah's death, David married Bathsheba. His sin brought evil upon his household, including the death of his and Bathsheba's first child. God had mercy on David, who repented of his sin. Bathsheba bore him four sons, including Solomon.

KEY REFERENCE: 1 KINGS 1:15–21

---

priest came. And Adonijah said, "Come in, for you are a worthy man and bring good news." **43** Jonathan answered Adonijah, "No, for our lord King David has made Solomon king, **44** and the king has sent with him Zadok the priest, Nathan the prophet, and Benaiah the son of Jehoiada, and the Cherethites and the Pelethites. And they had him ride on the king's mule. **45** And Zadok the priest and Nathan the prophet have anointed him king at Gihon, and they have gone up from there rejoicing, so that the city is in an uproar. This is the noise that you have heard. ⁴⁶ Solomon sits on the royal throne. ⁴⁷ Moreover, the king's servants came to congratulate our lord King David, saying, 'May your God make the name of Solomon more famous than yours, and make his throne greater than your throne.' And the king bowed himself on the bed. ⁴⁸ And the king also said, 'Blessed be the LORD, the God of Israel, who has granted someone to sit on my throne this day, my own eyes seeing it.'"

⁴⁹ Then all the guests of Adonijah trembled and rose, and each went his own way. ⁵⁰ And Adonijah feared Solomon. So he arose and went and took hold of the horns of the altar. ⁵¹ Then it was told Solomon, "Behold, Adonijah fears King Solomon, for behold, he has laid hold of the horns of the altar, saying, 'Let King Solomon swear to me first that he will not put his servant to death with

the sword.'" ⁵² And Solomon said, "If he will show himself a worthy man, not one of his hairs shall fall to the earth, but if wickedness is found in him, he shall die." ⁵³ So King Solomon sent, and they brought him down from the altar. And he came and paid homage to King Solomon, and Solomon said to him, "Go to your house."

David's Instructions to Solomon

2 When David's time to die drew near, he commanded Solomon his son, saying, ² "I am about to go the way of all the earth. Be strong, and show yourself a man, ³ and keep the charge of the LORD your God, walking in his ways and keeping his statutes, his commandments, his rules, and his testimonies, as it is written in the Law of Moses, that you may prosper in all that you do and wherever you turn, ⁴ that the LORD may establish his word that he spoke concerning me, saying, 'If your sons pay close attention to their way,

to walk before me in faithfulness with all their heart and with all their soul, you shall not lack a man on the throne of Israel.'

⁵ "Moreover, you also know what Joab the son of Zeruiah did to me, how he dealt with the two commanders of the armies of Israel, Abner the son of Ner, and Amasa the son of Jether, whom he killed, avenging in time of peace for blood that had been shed in war, and putting the blood of war on the belt around his waist and on the sandals on his feet. ⁶ Act therefore according to your wisdom, but do not let his gray head go down to Sheol in peace. ⁷ But deal loyally with the sons of Barzillai the Gileadite, and let them be among those who eat at your table, for with such loyalty they met me when I fled from Absalom your brother. ⁸ And there is also with you Shimei the son of Gera, the Benjaminite from Bahurim, who cursed me with a grievous curse on the day when I went to Mahanaim. But when he came down to meet me at the Jordan, I swore to him by the LORD, saying, 'I will not put you to death with the sword.' ⁹ Now therefore do not hold him guiltless, for you are a wise man. You will know what you ought to do to him, and you shall bring his gray head down with blood to Sheol."

The Death of David

¹⁰ Then David slept with his fathers and was buried in the city of David. ¹¹ And the time that David reigned over Israel was forty years. He reigned seven years in Hebron and thirty-three years in Jerusalem. ¹² So Solomon sat on the throne of David his father, and his kingdom was firmly established.

Solomon's Reign Established

¹³ Then Adonijah the son of Haggith came to Bathsheba the mother of Solomon. And she said, "Do you come peacefully?" He said, "Peacefully." ¹⁴ Then he said, "I have something to say to you." She said, "Speak." ¹⁵ He said, "You know that the kingdom was mine, and that all Israel fully expected me to reign. However, the kingdom has turned about and become my brother's, for it was his from the LORD. ¹⁶ And now I have one request to make of you; do not refuse me." She said to him, "Speak." ¹⁷ And he said, "Please ask King Solomon—he will not refuse you—to give me Abishag the Shunammite as my wife."

¹⁸ Bathsheba said, "Very well; I will speak for you to the king."

¹⁹ So Bathsheba went to King Solomon to speak to him on behalf of Adonijah. And the king rose to meet her and bowed down to her. Then he sat on his throne and had a seat brought for the king's mother, and she sat on his right. ²⁰ Then she said, "I have one small request to make of you; do not refuse me." And the king said to her, "Make your request, my mother, for I will not refuse you." ²¹ She said, "Let Abishag the Shunammite be given to Adonijah your brother as his wife." ²² King Solomon answered his mother, "And why do you ask Abishag the Shunammite for Adonijah? Ask for him the kingdom also, for he is my older brother, and on his side are Abiathar the priest and Joab the son of Zeruiah." ²³ Then King Solomon swore by the LORD, saying, "God do so to me and more also if this word does not cost Adonijah his life! ²⁴ Now therefore as the LORD lives, who has established me and placed me on the throne of David my father, and who has made me a house, as he promised, Adonijah shall be put to death today." ²⁵ So King Solomon sent Benaiah the son of Jehoiada, and he struck him down, and he died.

²⁶ And to Abiathar the priest the king said, "Go to Anathoth, to your estate, for you deserve death. But I will not at this time put you to death, because you carried the ark of the Lord GOD before David my father, and because you shared in all my father's affliction." ²⁷ So Solomon expelled Abiathar from being priest to the LORD, thus fulfilling the word of the LORD that he had spoken concerning the house of Eli in Shiloh.

²⁸ When the news came to Joab—for Joab had supported Adonijah although he had not supported Absalom—Joab fled to the tent of the LORD and caught hold of the horns of the altar. ²⁹ And when it was told King Solomon, "Joab has fled to the tent of the LORD, and behold, he is beside the altar," Solomon sent Benaiah the son of Jehoiada, saying, "Go, strike him down." ³⁰ So Benaiah came to the tent of the LORD and said to him, "The king commands, 'Come out.'" But he said, "No, I will die here." Then Benaiah brought the king word again, saying, "Thus said Joab, and thus he answered me." ³¹ The king replied to him, "Do as he has said, strike him down and bury him, and thus take away from me and from my father's house the guilt for the blood that Joab shed without cause. ³² The LORD will bring back his bloody deeds on his own head, because, without the knowledge of my father David, he attacked and killed with the sword two men more righteous and better than himself, Abner the son of Ner, commander of the army of Israel, and Amasa the son of Jether, commander of the army of Judah. ³³ So shall their blood come back on the head of Joab and on the head of his descendants forever. But for David and for his descendants and for his house and for his throne there shall be peace from the LORD forevermore." ³⁴ Then Benaiah the son of Jehoiada went up and struck him down and put him to death. And he was buried in his own house in the wilderness. ³⁵ The king put Benaiah the son of Jehoiada over the army in place

GETTING THE MESSAGE

Why did Adonijah ask for Abishag?
Marrying David's concubine (2:17) would have given Adonijah a claim to the throne.

of Joab, and the king put Zadok the priest in the place of Abiathar.

³⁶ Then the king sent and summoned Shimei and said to him, "Build yourself a house in Jerusalem and dwell there, and do not go out from there to any place whatever. ³⁷ For on the day you go out and cross the brook Kidron, know for certain that you shall die. Your blood shall be on your own head." ³⁸ And Shimei said to the king, "What you say is good; as my lord the king has said, so will your servant do." So Shimei lived in Jerusalem many days.

³⁹ But it happened at the end of three years that two of Shimei's servants ran away to Achish, son of Maacah, king of Gath. And when it was told Shimei, "Behold, your servants are in Gath," ⁴⁰ Shimei arose and saddled a donkey and went to Gath to Achish to seek his servants. Shimei went and brought his servants from Gath. ⁴¹ And when Solomon was told that Shimei had gone from Jerusalem to Gath and returned, ⁴² the king sent and summoned Shimei and

said to him, "Did I not make you swear by the LORD and solemnly warn you, saying, 'Know for certain that on the day you go out and go to any place whatever, you shall die'? And you said to me, 'What you say is good; I will obey.' **43** Why then have you not kept your oath to the LORD and the commandment with which I commanded you?" **44** The king also said to Shimei, "You know in your own heart all the harm that you did to David my father. So the LORD will bring back your harm on your own head. **45** But King Solomon shall be blessed, and the throne of David shall be established before the LORD forever." **46** Then the king commanded Benaiah the son of Jehoiada, and he went out and struck him down, and he died.

So the kingdom was established in the hand of Solomon.

GETTING THE MESSAGE

No witnesses. Under normal circumstances, priests and judges would have presided over the case between the two prostitutes (3:16–28). However, because there were no witnesses to the case, the law required them to go before Solomon. The king was considered to be the highest court of appeal.

Solomon's Prayer for Wisdom

3 Solomon made a marriage alliance with Pharaoh king of Egypt. He took Pharaoh's daughter and brought her into the city of David until he had finished building his own house and the house of the LORD and the wall around Jerusalem. **2** The people were sacrificing at the high places, however, because no house had yet been built for the name of the LORD. **3** Solomon loved the LORD, walking in the statutes of David his father, only he sacrificed and made offerings at the high places. **4** And the king went to Gibeon to sacrifice there, for that was the great high place. Solomon used to offer a thousand burnt offerings on that altar. **5** At Gibeon the LORD appeared to Solomon in a dream by night, and God said, "Ask what I shall give you." **6** And Solomon said, "You have shown great and steadfast love to your servant David my father, because he walked before you in faithfulness, in righteousness,

and in uprightness of heart toward you. And you have kept for him this great and steadfast love and have given him a son to sit on his throne this day. **7** And now, O LORD my God, you have made your servant king in place of David my father, although I am but a little child. I do not know how to go out or come in. **8** And your servant is in the midst of your people whom you have chosen, a great people, too many to be numbered or counted for multitude. **9** Give your servant therefore an understanding mind to govern your people, that I may discern between good and evil, for who is able to govern this your great people?"

10 It pleased the Lord that Solomon had asked this. **11** And God said to him, "Because you have asked this, and have not asked for yourself long life or riches or the life of your enemies, but have asked for yourself understanding to discern what is right, **12** behold, I now do according to your word. Behold, I give you a wise and discerning mind, so that none like you has been before you and none like you shall arise after you. **13** I give you also what you have not asked, both riches and honor, so that no other king shall compare with you, all your days. **14** And if you will walk in my ways, keeping my statutes and my commandments, as your father David walked, then I will lengthen your days."

15 And Solomon awoke, and behold, it was a dream. Then he came to Jerusalem and stood before the ark of the covenant of the Lord, and offered up burnt offerings and peace offerings, and made a feast for all his servants.

Solomon's Wisdom

16 Then two prostitutes came to the king and stood before him. **17** The one woman said, "Oh, my lord, this woman and I live in the same house, and I gave birth to a child while she was in the house. **18** Then on the third day after I gave birth, this woman also gave birth. And we were alone. There was no one else with us in the house; only we two were in the house. **19** And this woman's son died in the night, because she lay on him. **20** And she arose at midnight and took my son from beside me, while your servant slept, and laid him at her breast, and laid her dead son at my breast. **21** When I rose in the morning to nurse my child, behold, he was dead. But when I looked at him closely in the morning, behold, he was not the child that I had borne." ²² But the other woman said, "No, the living child is mine, and the dead child is yours." The first said, "No, the dead child is yours, and the living child is mine." Thus they spoke before the king.

²³ Then the king said, "The one says, 'This is my son that is alive, and your son is dead'; and the other says, 'No; but your son is dead, and my son is the living one.'" ²⁴ And the king said, "Bring me a sword." So a sword was brought before the king. ²⁵ And the king said, "Divide the living child in two, and give half to the one and half to the other." ²⁶ Then the woman whose son was alive said to the king, because her heart yearned for her son, "Oh, my lord, give her the living child, and by no means put him to death." But the other said, "He shall be neither mine nor yours; divide him." ²⁷ Then the king answered and said, "Give the living child to the first woman, and by no means put him to death; she is his mother." ²⁸ And all Israel heard of the judgment that the king had rendered, and they stood in awe of the king, because they perceived that the wisdom of God was in him to do justice.

Solomon's Officials

4 King Solomon was king over all Israel, ² and these were his high officials: Azariah the son of Zadok was the priest; ³ Elihoreph and Ahijah the sons of Shisha were secretaries; Jehoshaphat the son of Ahilud was recorder; ⁴ Benaiah the son of Jehoiada was in command of the army; Zadok and Abiathar were priests; ⁵ Azariah the son of Nathan was over the officers; Zabud the son of Nathan was priest and king's friend; ⁶ Ahishar was in charge of the palace; and Adoniram the son of Abda was in charge of the forced labor.

⁷ Solomon had twelve officers over all Israel, who provided food for the king and his household. Each man had to make provision for one month in the year. ⁸ These were their names: Ben-hur, in the hill country of Ephraim; ⁹ Ben-deker, in Makaz, Shaalbim, Beth-shemesh, and Elonbeth-hanan; ¹⁰ Ben-hesed, in Arubboth (to him belonged Socoh and all the land of Hepher); ¹¹ Ben-abinadab, in all Naphath-dor (he had Taphath the daughter of Solomon as his wife); ¹² Baana the son of Ahilud, in Taanach, Megiddo, and all Beth-shean that is beside Zarethan below Jezreel, and from Beth-shean to Abel-meholah, as far as the other side of Jokmeam; ¹³ Ben-geber, in Ramoth-gilead (he had the villages of Jair the son of Manasseh, which are in Gilead, and he had the region of Argob, which is in Bashan, sixty great cities with walls and bronze bars); ¹⁴ Ahinadab the son of Iddo, in Mahanaim; ¹⁵ Ahimaaz, in Naphtali (he had taken Basemath the daughter of Solomon as his wife); ¹⁶ Baana the son of Hushai, in Asher and Bealoth; ¹⁷ Jehoshaphat the son of Paruah, in Issachar; ¹⁸ Shimei the son of Ela, in Benjamin; ¹⁹ Geber the son of Uri, in the land of Gilead, the country of Sihon king of the Amorites and of Og king of Bashan. And there was one governor who was over the land.

> ### GETTING THE MESSAGE
>
> **How large was Israel under Solomon's rule?** During the reign of Solomon, Israel extended into the Sinai desert near Egypt in the south and to the Euphrates River in the north. It was roughly three times the size of Israel today and would have included parts of present-day Lebanon, Jordan, and Syria.

Solomon's Wealth and Wisdom

²⁰ Judah and Israel were as many as the sand by the sea. They ate and drank and were happy. ²¹ Solomon ruled over all the kingdoms from the Euphrates to the land of the Philistines and to the border of Egypt. They brought tribute and served Solomon all the days of his life.

²² Solomon's provision for one day was thirty cors of fine flour and sixty cors of meal, ²³ ten fat oxen, and twenty pasture-fed cattle, a hundred sheep, besides deer, gazelles, roebucks, and fattened fowl. ²⁴ For he had dominion over all the region west of the Euphrates from Tiphsah to Gaza, over all the kings west of the Euphrates. And he had peace on all sides around him. ²⁵ And Judah and Israel lived in safety, from Dan even to Beersheba, every man under his vine and under his fig tree, all the days of Solomon. ²⁶ Solomon also had 40,000 stalls of horses for his chariots, and 12,000

horsemen. **27** And those officers supplied provisions for King Solomon, and for all who came to King Solomon's table, each one in his month. They let nothing be lacking. **28** Barley also and straw for the horses and swift steeds they brought to the place where it was required, each according to his duty.

29 And God gave Solomon wisdom and understanding beyond measure, and breadth of mind like the sand on the seashore, **30** so that Solomon's wisdom surpassed the wisdom of all the people of the east and all the wisdom of Egypt. **31** For he was wiser than all other men, wiser than Ethan the Ezrahite, and Heman, Calcol, and Darda, the sons of Mahol, and his fame was in all the surrounding nations. **32** He also spoke 3,000 proverbs, and his songs were 1,005. **33** He spoke of trees, from the cedar that is in Lebanon to the hyssop that grows out of the

GETTING THE MESSAGE

Dressed stones (5:17) are stones that have been cut and polished so that they have smooth faces and edges. This type of masonry was time-consuming and expensive, so it was used primarily for palaces and temples.

wall. He spoke also of beasts, and of birds, and of reptiles, and of fish. **34** And people of all nations came to hear the wisdom of Solomon, and from all the kings of the earth, who had heard of his wisdom.

Preparations for Building the Temple

5 Now Hiram king of Tyre sent his servants to Solomon when he heard that they had anointed him king in place of his father, for Hiram always loved David. **2** And Solomon sent word to Hiram, **3** "You know that David my father could not build a house for the name of the LORD his God because of the warfare with which his enemies surrounded him, until the LORD put them under the soles of his feet. **4** But now the LORD my God has given me rest on every side. There is neither adversary nor misfortune. **5** And so I intend to build a house for the name of the LORD my God, as the LORD said to David my father, 'Your son, whom I will set on your throne in your place, shall

build the house for my name.' **6** Now therefore command that cedars of Lebanon be cut for me. And my servants will join your servants, and I will pay you for your servants such wages as you set, for you know that there is no one among us who knows how to cut timber like the Sidonians."

7 As soon as Hiram heard the words of Solomon, he rejoiced greatly and said, "Blessed be the LORD this day, who has given to David a wise son to be over this great people." **8** And Hiram sent to Solomon, saying, "I have heard the message that you have sent to me. I am ready to do all you desire in the matter of cedar and cypress timber. **9** My servants shall bring it down to the sea from Lebanon, and I will make it into rafts to go by sea to the place you direct. And I will have them broken up there, and you shall receive it. And you shall meet my wishes by providing food for my household." **10** So Hiram supplied Solomon with all the timber of cedar and cypress that he desired, **11** while Solomon gave Hiram 20,000 cors of wheat as food for his household, and 20,000 cors of beaten oil. Solomon gave this to Hiram year by year. **12** And the LORD gave Solomon wisdom, as he promised him. And there was peace between Hiram and Solomon, and the two of them made a treaty.

13 King Solomon drafted forced labor out of all Israel, and the draft numbered 30,000 men. **14** And he sent them to Lebanon, 10,000 a month in shifts. They would be a month in Lebanon and two months at home. Adoniram was in charge of the draft. **15** Solomon also had 70,000 burden-bearers and 80,000 stonecutters in the hill country, **16** besides Solomon's 3,300 chief officers who were over the work, who had charge of the people who carried on the work. **17** At the king's command they quarried out great, costly stones in order to lay the foundation of the house with dressed stones. **18** So Solomon's builders and Hiram's builders and the men of Gebal did the cutting and prepared the timber and the stone to build the house.

Solomon Builds the Temple

6 In the four hundred and eightieth year after the people of Israel came out of the land of Egypt, in the fourth year of Solomon's reign over Israel, in the month of Ziv, which is the second month, he began

to build the house of the LORD. ²The house that King Solomon built for the LORD was sixty cubits long, twenty cubits wide, and thirty cubits high. ³The vestibule in front of the nave of the house was twenty cubits long, equal to the width of the house, and ten cubits deep in front of the house. ⁴And he made for the house windows with recessed frames. ⁵He also built a structure against the wall of the house, running around the walls of the house, both the nave and the inner sanctuary. And he made side chambers all around. ⁶The lowest story was five cubits broad, the middle one was six cubits broad, and the third was seven cubits broad. For around the outside of the house he made offsets on the wall in order that the supporting beams should not be inserted into the walls of the house.

⁷When the house was built, it was with stone prepared at the quarry, so that neither hammer nor axe nor any tool of iron was heard in the house while it was being built.

⁸The entrance for the lowest story was on the south side of the house, and one went up by stairs to the middle story, and from the middle story to the third. ⁹So he built the house and finished it, and he made the ceiling of the house of beams and planks of cedar. ¹⁰He built the structure against the whole house, five cubits high, and it was joined to the house with timbers of cedar.

¹¹Now the word of the LORD came to Solomon, ¹²"Concerning this house that you are building, if you will walk in my statutes and obey my rules and keep all my commandments and walk in them, then I will establish my word with you, which I spoke to David your father. ¹³And I will dwell among the children of Israel and will not forsake my people Israel."

¹⁴So Solomon built the house and finished it. ¹⁵He lined the walls of the house on the inside with boards of cedar. From the floor of the house to the walls of the ceiling, he covered them on the inside with wood, and he covered the floor of the house with boards of cypress. ¹⁶He built twenty cubits of the rear of the house with boards of cedar from the floor to the walls, and he built this within as an inner sanctuary, as the Most Holy Place. ¹⁷The house, that is, the nave in front of the inner sanctuary, was forty cubits long. ¹⁸The cedar within

the house was carved in the form of gourds and open flowers. All was cedar; no stone was seen. ¹⁹The inner sanctuary he prepared in the innermost part of the house, to set there the ark of the covenant of the LORD. ²⁰The inner sanctuary was twenty cubits long, twenty cubits wide, and twenty cubits high, and he overlaid it with pure gold. He also overlaid an altar of cedar. ²¹And Solomon overlaid the inside of the house with pure gold, and he drew chains of gold across, in front of the inner sanctuary, and overlaid it with gold. ²²And he overlaid the whole house with gold, until all the house was finished. Also the whole altar that belonged to the inner sanctuary he overlaid with gold.

²³In the inner sanctuary he made two cherubim of olivewood, each ten cubits

GETTING THE MESSAGE

No tools of iron? The Lord had forbidden the use of iron tools in the construction of altars (Ex. 20:25). As they built the temple, the Israelites used iron tools on the stones only at the quarry, never at the construction site. They probably did this as an expression of reverence for the temple (1 Kings 6:7).

high. ²⁴Five cubits was the length of one wing of the cherub, and five cubits the length of the other wing of the cherub; it was ten cubits from the tip of one wing to the tip of the other. ²⁵The other cherub also measured ten cubits; both cherubim had the same measure and the same form. ²⁶The height of one cherub was ten cubits, and so was that of the other cherub. ²⁷He put the cherubim in the innermost part of the house. And the wings of the cherubim were spread out so that a wing of one touched the one wall, and a wing of the other cherub touched the other wall; their other wings touched each other in the middle of the house. ²⁸And he overlaid the cherubim with gold.

²⁹Around all the walls of the house he carved engraved figures of cherubim and palm trees and open flowers, in the inner and outer rooms. ³⁰The floor of the house

he overlaid with gold in the inner and outer rooms. [31] For the entrance to the inner sanctuary he made doors of olivewood; the lintel and the doorposts were five-sided. [32] He covered the two doors of olivewood with carvings of cherubim, palm trees, and open flowers. He overlaid them with gold and spread gold on the cherubim and on the palm trees.

[33] So also he made for the entrance to the nave doorposts of olivewood, in the form of a square, [34] and two doors of cypress wood. The two leaves of the one door were folding, and the two leaves of the other door were folding. [35] On them he carved cherubim and palm trees and open flowers, and he overlaid them with gold evenly applied on the carved work. [36] He built the inner court with three courses of cut stone and one course of cedar beams.

GETTING THE MESSAGE

The House of the Forest of Lebanon (7:2) was part of Solomon's palace. It was much larger than the temple and designed to be a treasury or an armory. It got its name from the large amounts of cedar timber used to build it.

[37] In the fourth year the foundation of the house of the LORD was laid, in the month of Ziv. [38] And in the eleventh year, in the month of Bul, which is the eighth month, the house was finished in all its parts, and according to all its specifications. He was seven years in building it.

Solomon Builds His Palace

7 Solomon was building his own house thirteen years, and he finished his entire house.

[2] He built the House of the Forest of Lebanon. Its length was a hundred cubits and its breadth fifty cubits and its height thirty cubits, and it was built on four rows of cedar pillars, with cedar beams on the pillars. [3] And it was covered with cedar above the chambers that were on the forty-five pillars, fifteen in each row. [4] There were window frames in three rows, and window opposite window in three tiers. [5] All the doorways and windows had square frames, and window was opposite window in three tiers.

[6] And he made the Hall of Pillars; its length was fifty cubits, and its breadth thirty cubits. There was a porch in front with pillars, and a canopy in front of them.

[7] And he made the Hall of the Throne where he was to pronounce judgment, even the Hall of Judgment. It was finished with cedar from floor to rafters.

[8] His own house where he was to dwell, in the other court back of the hall, was of like workmanship. Solomon also made a house like this hall for Pharaoh's daughter whom he had taken in marriage.

[9] All these were made of costly stones, cut according to measure, sawed with saws, back and front, even from the foundation to the coping, and from the outside to the great court. [10] The foundation was of costly stones, huge stones, stones of eight and ten cubits. [11] And above were costly stones, cut according to measurement, and cedar. [12] The great court had three courses of cut stone all around, and a course of cedar beams; so had the inner court of the house of the LORD and the vestibule of the house.

The Temple Furnishings

[13] And King Solomon sent and brought Hiram from Tyre. [14] He was the son of a widow of the tribe of Naphtali, and his father was a man of Tyre, a worker in bronze. And he was full of wisdom, understanding, and skill for making any work in bronze. He came to King Solomon and did all his work.

[15] He cast two pillars of bronze. Eighteen cubits was the height of one pillar, and a line of twelve cubits measured its circumference. It was hollow, and its thickness was four fingers. The second pillar was the same. [16] He also made two capitals of cast bronze to set on the tops of the pillars. The height of the one capital was five cubits, and the height of the other capital was five cubits. [17] There were lattices of checker work with wreaths of chain work for the capitals on the tops of the pillars, a lattice for the one capital and a lattice for the other capital. [18] Likewise he made pomegranates in two rows around the one latticework to cover the capital that was on the top of the pillar, and he did the same with the other capital. [19] Now the capitals that were on the tops of the pillars in the vestibule were of lily-work, four cubits. [20] The capitals were on the two pillars and also above the rounded

projection which was beside the lattice-work. There were two hundred pomegranates in two rows all around, and so with the other capital. ²¹ He set up the pillars at the vestibule of the temple. He set up the pillar on the south and called its name Jachin, and he set up the pillar on the north and called its name Boaz. ²² And on the tops of the pillars was lily-work. Thus the work of the pillars was finished.

²³ Then he made the sea of cast metal. It was round, ten cubits from brim to brim, and five cubits high, and a line of thirty cubits measured its circumference. ²⁴ Under its brim were gourds, for ten cubits, compassing the sea all around. The gourds were in two rows, cast with it when it was cast. ²⁵ It stood on twelve oxen, three facing north, three facing west, three facing south, and three facing east. The sea was set on them, and all their rear parts were inward. ²⁶ Its thickness was a handbreadth, and its brim was made like the brim of a cup, like the flower of a lily. It held two thousand baths.

²⁷ He also made the ten stands of bronze. Each stand was four cubits long, four cubits wide, and three cubits high. ²⁸ This was the construction of the stands: they had panels, and the panels were set in the frames, ²⁹ and on the panels that were set in the frames were lions, oxen, and cherubim. On the frames, both above and below the lions and oxen, there were wreaths of beveled work. ³⁰ Moreover, each stand had four bronze wheels and axles of bronze, and at the four corners were supports for a basin. The supports were cast with wreaths at the side of each. ³¹ Its opening was within a crown that projected upward one cubit. Its opening was round, as a pedestal is made, a cubit and a half deep. At its opening there were carvings, and its panels were square, not round. ³² And the four wheels were underneath the panels. The axles of the wheels were of one piece with the stands, and the height of a wheel was a cubit and a half. ³³ The wheels were made like a chariot wheel; their axles, their rims, their spokes, and their hubs were all cast. ³⁴ There were four supports at the four corners of each stand. The supports were of one piece with the stands. ³⁵ And on the top of the stand there was a round band half a cubit high; and on the top of the

stand its stays and its panels were of one piece with it. ³⁶ And on the surfaces of its stays and on its panels, he carved cherubim, lions, and palm trees, according to the space of each, with wreaths all around. ³⁷ After this manner he made the ten stands. All of them were cast alike, of the same measure and the same form.

³⁸ And he made ten basins of bronze. Each basin held forty baths, each basin measured four cubits, and there was a basin for each of the ten stands. ³⁹ And he set the stands, five on the south side of the house, and five

---

PROFILE

SOLOMON

The son of David and Bathsheba, Solomon succeeded his father as king of Israel. Rather than ask God for riches or power, Solomon asked for wisdom. His request pleased God, who granted him not only what he asked for but also what he did not ask—riches and honor such as the world had never known. Among the king's most significant building projects were the first temple in Jerusalem and a magnificent palace. But riches and wisdom were not the only things Solomon had in abundance—he also had over 700 wives! He was a great king when he obeyed God, but sadly his marriages to women outside the people of God proved to be his downfall. Solomon's reign ended in tragedy when "his wives turned away his heart" (11:3) by influencing him to worship pagan gods.

KEY REFERENCE: 1 KINGS 3:10–14

---

on the north side of the house. And he set the sea at the southeast corner of the house.

⁴⁰ Hiram also made the pots, the shovels, and the basins. So Hiram finished all the work that he did for King Solomon on the house of the LORD: ⁴¹ the two pillars, the two bowls of the capitals that were on the tops of the pillars, and the two latticeworks to cover the two bowls of the capitals that were on the tops of the pillars; ⁴² and the four hundred pomegranates for the two

latticeworks, two rows of pomegranates for each latticework, to cover the two bowls of the capitals that were on the pillars; **43** the ten stands, and the ten basins on the stands; **44** and the one sea, and the twelve oxen underneath the sea.

45 Now the pots, the shovels, and the basins, all these vessels in the house of the Lord, which Hiram made for King Solomon, were of burnished bronze. **46** In the plain of the Jordan the king cast them, in the clay ground between Succoth and Zarethan. **47** And Solomon left all the vessels unweighed, because there were so many of them; the weight of the bronze was not ascertained.

48 So Solomon made all the vessels that were in the house of the Lord: the golden altar, the golden table for the bread of the

Presence, **49** the lampstands of pure gold, five on the south side and five on the north, before the inner sanctuary; the flowers, the lamps, and the tongs, of gold; **50** the cups, snuffers, basins, dishes for incense, and fire pans, of pure gold; and the sockets of gold, for the doors of the innermost part of the house, the Most Holy Place, and for the doors of the nave of the temple.

51 Thus all the work that King Solomon did on the house of the Lord was finished. And Solomon brought in the things that David his father had dedicated, the silver, the gold, and the vessels, and stored them in the treasuries of the house of the Lord.

The Ark Brought into the Temple

8 Then Solomon assembled the elders of Israel and all the heads of the tribes, the leaders of the fathers' houses of the people of Israel, before King Solomon in Jerusalem, to bring up the ark of the covenant of the Lord out of the city of David, which is Zion. **2** And all the men of Israel assembled to King

Solomon at the feast in the month Ethanim, which is the seventh month. **3** And all the elders of Israel came, and the priests took up the ark. **4** And they brought up the ark of the Lord, the tent of meeting, and all the holy vessels that were in the tent; the priests and the Levites brought them up. **5** And King Solomon and all the congregation of Israel, who had assembled before him, were with him before the ark, sacrificing so many sheep and oxen that they could not be counted or numbered. **6** Then the priests brought the ark of the covenant of the Lord to its place in the inner sanctuary of the house, in the Most Holy Place, underneath the wings of the cherubim. **7** For the cherubim spread out their wings over the place of the ark, so that the cherubim overshadowed the ark and its poles. **8** And the poles were so long that the ends of the poles were seen from the Holy Place before the inner sanctuary; but they could not be seen from outside. And they are there to this day. **9** There was nothing in the ark except the two tablets of stone that Moses put there at Horeb, where the Lord made a covenant with the people of Israel, when they came out of the land of Egypt. **10** And when the priests came out of the Holy Place, a cloud filled the house of the Lord, **11** so that the priests could not stand to minister because of the cloud, for the glory of the Lord filled the house of the Lord.

Solomon Blesses the Lord

12 Then Solomon said, "The Lord has said that he would dwell in thick darkness. **13** I have indeed built you an exalted house, a place for you to dwell in forever." **14** Then the king turned around and blessed all the assembly of Israel, while all the assembly of Israel stood. **15** And he said, "Blessed be the Lord, the God of Israel, who with his hand has fulfilled what he promised with his mouth to David my father, saying, **16** 'Since the day that I brought my people Israel out of Egypt, I chose no city out of all the tribes of Israel in which to build a house, that my name might be there. But I chose David to be over my people Israel.' **17** Now it was in the heart of David my father to build a house for the name of the Lord, the God of Israel. **18** But the Lord said to David my father, 'Whereas it was in your heart to build a house for my name, you did well that it was in your heart. **19** Nevertheless, you shall not build the house, but your son who shall be born to you shall build the house for my name.' **20** Now the LORD has fulfilled his promise that he made. For I have risen in the place of David my father, and sit on the throne of Israel, as the LORD promised, and I have built the house for the name of the LORD, the God of Israel. **21** And there I have provided a place for the ark, in which is the covenant of the LORD that he made with our fathers, when he brought them out of the land of Egypt."

Solomon's Prayer of Dedication

22 Then Solomon stood before the altar of the LORD in the presence of all the assembly of Israel and spread out his hands toward heaven, **23** and said, "O LORD, God of Israel, there is no God like you, in heaven above or on earth beneath, keeping covenant and showing steadfast love to your servants who walk before you with all their heart; **24** you have kept with your servant David my father what you declared to him. You spoke with your mouth, and with your hand have fulfilled it this day. **25** Now therefore, O LORD, God of Israel, keep for your servant David my father what you have promised him, saying, 'You shall not lack a man to sit before me on the throne of Israel, if only your sons pay close attention to their way, to walk before me as you have walked before me.' **26** Now therefore, O God of Israel, let your word be confirmed, which you have spoken to your servant David my father.

27 "But will God indeed dwell on the earth? Behold, heaven and the highest heaven cannot contain you; how much less this house that I have built! **28** Yet have regard to the prayer of your servant and to his plea, O LORD my God, listening to the cry and to the prayer that your servant prays before you this day, **29** that your eyes may be open night and day toward this house, the place of which you have said, 'My name shall be there,' that you may listen to the prayer that your servant offers toward this place. **30** And listen to the plea of your servant and of your people Israel, when they pray toward this place. And listen in heaven your dwelling place, and when you hear, forgive.

31 "If a man sins against his neighbor and is made to take an oath and comes and

swears his oath before your altar in this house, **32** then hear in heaven and act and judge your servants, condemning the guilty by bringing his conduct on his own head, and vindicating the righteous by rewarding him according to his righteousness.

33 "When your people Israel are defeated before the enemy because they have sinned against you, and if they turn again to you and acknowledge your name and pray and plead with you in this house, **34** then hear in heaven and forgive the sin of your people Israel and bring them again to the land that you gave to their fathers.

35 "When heaven is shut up and there is no rain because they have sinned against you, if they pray toward this place and acknowledge your name and turn from their sin, when you afflict them, **36** then

> ### GETTING THE MESSAGE
>
> **Praying toward Jerusalem** (8:29) was a practice started by Solomon that many Jews still follow today. It comes from Solomon's prayer of dedication, where he stated that God is too great to dwell in a temple. However, the Lord stated himself that his name would dwell in the temple forever (9:3), thus providing a symbolic place to which people could direct their prayers.

hear in heaven and forgive the sin of your servants, your people Israel, when you teach them the good way in which they should walk, and grant rain upon your land, which you have given to your people as an inheritance.

37 "If there is famine in the land, if there is pestilence or blight or mildew or locust or caterpillar, if their enemy besieges them in the land at their gates, whatever plague, whatever sickness there is, **38** whatever prayer, whatever plea is made by any man or by all your people Israel, each knowing the affliction of his own heart and stretching out his hands toward this house, **39** then hear in heaven your dwelling place and forgive and act and render to each whose heart you know, according to all his ways (for you, you only, know the hearts of all the children of mankind), **40** that they may fear you all the days that they live in the land that you gave to our fathers.

⁴¹"Likewise, when a foreigner, who is not of your people Israel, comes from a far country for your name's sake ⁴²(for they shall hear of your great name and your mighty hand, and of your outstretched arm), when he comes and prays toward this house, ⁴³ hear in heaven your dwelling place and do according to all for which the foreigner calls to you, in order that all the peoples of the earth may know your name and fear you, as do your people Israel, and that they may know that this house that I have built is called by your name.

⁴⁴"If your people go out to battle against their enemy, by whatever way you shall send them, and they pray to the Lord toward the city that you have chosen and the house that I have built for your name, ⁴⁵then hear in heaven their prayer and their plea, and maintain their cause.

⁴⁶"If they sin against you—for there is no one who does not sin—and you are angry with them and give them to an enemy, so that they are carried away captive to the land of the enemy, far off or near, ⁴⁷yet if they turn their heart in the land to which they have been carried captive, and repent and plead with you in the land of their captors, saying, 'We have sinned and have acted perversely and wickedly,' ⁴⁸if they repent with all their mind and with all their heart in the land of their enemies, who carried them captive, and pray to you toward their land, which you gave to their fathers, the city that you have chosen, and the house that I have built for your name, ⁴⁹then hear in heaven your dwelling place their prayer and their plea, and maintain their cause ⁵⁰and forgive your people who have sinned against you, and all their transgressions that they have committed against you, and grant them compassion in the sight of those who carried them captive, that they may have compassion on them ⁵¹(for they are your people, and your heritage, which you brought out of Egypt, from the midst of the iron furnace). ⁵²Let your eyes be open to the plea of your servant and to the plea of your people Israel, giving ear to them whenever they call to you. ⁵³For you separated them from among all the peoples of the earth to be your heritage, as you declared through

Moses your servant, when you brought our fathers out of Egypt, O Lord God."

Solomon's Benediction

⁵⁴ Now as Solomon finished offering all this prayer and plea to the Lord, he arose from before the altar of the Lord, where he had knelt with hands outstretched toward heaven. ⁵⁵ And he stood and blessed all the assembly of Israel with a loud voice, saying, ⁵⁶"Blessed be the Lord who has given rest to his people Israel, according to all that he promised. Not one word has failed of all his good promise, which he spoke by Moses his servant. ⁵⁷ The Lord our God be with us, as he was with our fathers. May he not leave us or forsake us, ⁵⁸ that he may incline our hearts to him, to walk in all his ways and to keep his commandments, his statutes, and his rules, which he commanded our fathers. ⁵⁹ Let these words of mine, with which I have pleaded before the Lord, be near to the Lord our God day and night, and may he maintain the cause of his servant and the cause of his people Israel, as each day requires, ⁶⁰ that all the peoples of the earth may know that the Lord is God; there is no other. ⁶¹ Let your heart therefore be wholly true to the Lord our God, walking in his statutes and keeping his commandments, as at this day."

Solomon's Sacrifices

⁶² Then the king, and all Israel with him, offered sacrifice before the Lord. ⁶³ Solomon offered as peace offerings to the Lord 22,000 oxen and 120,000 sheep. So the king and all the people of Israel dedicated the house of the Lord. ⁶⁴ The same day the king consecrated the middle of the court that was before the house of the Lord, for there he offered the burnt offering and the grain offering and the fat pieces of the peace offerings, because the bronze altar that was before the Lord was too small to receive the burnt offering and the grain offering and the fat pieces of the peace offerings.

⁶⁵ So Solomon held the feast at that time, and all Israel with him, a great assembly, from Lebo-hamath to the Brook of Egypt, before the Lord our God, seven days. ⁶⁶ On the eighth day he sent the people away, and they blessed the king and went to their homes joyful and glad of heart for all the goodness that the Lord had shown to David his servant and to Israel his people.

The Lord Appears to Solomon

9 As soon as Solomon had finished building the house of the Lord and the king's house and all that Solomon desired to build, ² the Lord appeared to Solomon a second time, as he had appeared to him at Gibeon. ³ And the Lord said to him, "I have heard your prayer and your plea, which you have made before me. I have consecrated this house that you have built, by putting my name there forever. My eyes and my heart will be there for all time. ⁴ And as for you, if you will walk before me, as David your father walked, with integrity of heart and uprightness, doing according to all that I have commanded you, and keeping my statutes and my rules, ⁵ then I will establish your royal throne over Israel forever, as I promised David your father, saying, 'You shall not lack a man on the throne of Israel.' ⁶ But if you turn aside from following me, you or your children, and do not keep my commandments and my statutes that I have set before you, but go and serve other gods and worship them, ⁷ then I will cut off Israel from the land that I have given them, and the house that I have consecrated for my name I will cast out of my sight, and Israel will become a proverb and a byword among all peoples. ⁸ And this house will become a heap of ruins. Everyone passing by it will be astonished and will hiss, and they will say, 'Why has the Lord done thus to this land and to this house?' ⁹ Then they will say, 'Because they abandoned the Lord their God who brought their fathers out of the land of Egypt and laid hold on other gods and worshiped them and served them. Therefore the Lord has brought all this disaster on them.'"

Solomon's Other Acts

¹⁰ At the end of twenty years, in which Solomon had built the two houses, the house of the Lord and the king's house, ¹¹ and Hiram king of Tyre had supplied Solomon with cedar and cypress timber and gold, as much as he desired, King Solomon gave to Hiram twenty cities in the land of Galilee. ¹² But when Hiram came from Tyre to see the cities that Solomon had given him, they did not please him. ¹³ Therefore he said, "What kind of cities are these that you have given me, my brother?" So they are called the land of Cabul to this day. ¹⁴ Hiram had sent to the king 120 talents of gold.

¹⁵ And this is the account of the forced labor that King Solomon drafted to build the house of the Lord and his own house and the Millo and the wall of Jerusalem and Hazor and Megiddo and Gezer ¹⁶ (Pharaoh king of Egypt had gone up and captured Gezer and burned it with fire, and had killed the Canaanites who lived in the city, and had given it as dowry to his daughter, Solomon's wife; ¹⁷ so Solomon rebuilt Gezer) and Lower Beth-horon ¹⁸ and Baalath and Tamar in the wilderness, in the land of Judah, ¹⁹ and all the store cities that Solomon had, and the cities for his chariots, and the cities for his horsemen, and whatever Solomon desired to build in Jerusalem, in Lebanon, and in all

GETTING THE MESSAGE

The city of **Megiddo** (9:15) was located on one of the most important trade routes of the ancient Near East. In fact, it was so important that when Egypt's Pharaoh Thutmose III conquered the city in 1482 B.C. he said that capturing it was like capturing a thousand cities. It was so strategic that Israel's King Ahab (869–850 B.C.) dug a 120-foot (37-m) deep shaft and a 215-foot-long tunnel to provide water for the city in case it came under siege.

the land of his dominion. ²⁰ All the people who were left of the Amorites, the Hittites, the Perizzites, the Hivites, and the Jebusites, who were not of the people of Israel — ²¹ their descendants who were left after them in the land, whom the people of Israel were unable to devote to destruction[1] — these Solomon drafted to be slaves, and so they are to this day. ²² But of the people of Israel Solomon made no slaves. They were the soldiers, they were his officials, his commanders, his captains, his chariot commanders and his horsemen.

²³ These were the chief officers who were over Solomon's work: 550 who had charge of the people who carried on the work.

²⁴ But Pharaoh's daughter went up from the city of David to her own house that

[1] That is, destroy or make an offering because of sin, at God's command; also 20:42

Solomon had built for her. Then he built the Millo.

²⁵ Three times a year Solomon used to offer up burnt offerings and peace offerings on the altar that he built to the LORD, making offerings with it before the LORD. So he finished the house.

²⁶ King Solomon built a fleet of ships at Ezion-geber, which is near Eloth on the shore of the Red Sea, in the land of Edom.

THE QUEEN OF SHEBA

When word of Solomon's extraordinary wisdom reached the ears of the queen of Sheba, she traveled from Arabia to Jerusalem to test him with hard questions. She came to Jerusalem with a remarkable entourage, including camels bearing spices and gold and precious stones. The queen was deeply impressed by Solomon's wisdom and wealth. This Gentile queen recognized that Solomon's greatness was from the true God of Israel, and that God himself had put Solomon on his throne. Although the queen gave Solomon a tremendous gift—about 9,000 pounds (4 kg) of gold—it paled in comparison to the riches that he presented to her. Solomon gave the queen all she desired and more, after which she returned to her own land.

KEY REFERENCE: 1 KINGS 10:1–13

²⁷ And Hiram sent with the fleet his servants, seamen who were familiar with the sea, together with the servants of Solomon. ²⁸ And they went to Ophir and brought from there gold, 420 talents, and they brought it to King Solomon.

The Queen of Sheba

10 Now when the queen of Sheba heard of the fame of Solomon concerning the name of the LORD, she came to test him with hard questions. ² She came to Jerusalem with a very great retinue, with camels bearing spices and very much gold and precious stones. And when she came

to Solomon, she told him all that was on her mind. ³ And Solomon answered all her questions; there was nothing hidden from the king that he could not explain to her. ⁴ And when the queen of Sheba had seen all the wisdom of Solomon, the house that he had built, ⁵ the food of his table, the seating of his officials, and the attendance of his servants, their clothing, his cupbearers, and his burnt offerings that he offered at the house of the LORD, there was no more breath in her.

⁶ And she said to the king, "The report was true that I heard in my own land of your words and of your wisdom, ⁷ but I did not believe the reports until I came and my own eyes had seen it. And behold, the half was not told me. Your wisdom and prosperity surpass the report that I heard. ⁸ Happy are your men! Happy are your servants, who continually stand before you and hear your wisdom! ⁹ Blessed be the LORD your God, who has delighted in you and set you on the throne of Israel! Because the LORD loved Israel forever, he has made you king, that you may execute justice and righteousness." ¹⁰ Then she gave the king 120 talents of gold, and a very great quantity of spices and precious stones. Never again came such an abundance of spices as these that the queen of Sheba gave to King Solomon.

¹¹ Moreover, the fleet of Hiram, which brought gold from Ophir, brought from Ophir a very great amount of almug wood and precious stones. ¹² And the king made of the almug wood supports for the house of the LORD and for the king's house, also lyres and harps for the singers. No such almug wood has come or been seen to this day.

¹³ And King Solomon gave to the queen of Sheba all that she desired, whatever she asked besides what was given her by the bounty of King Solomon. So she turned and went back to her own land with her servants.

Solomon's Great Wealth

¹⁴ Now the weight of gold that came to Solomon in one year was 666 talents of gold, ¹⁵ besides that which came from the explorers and from the business of the merchants, and from all the kings of the west and from the governors of the land. ¹⁶ King Solomon made 200 large shields of beaten gold; 600 shekels of gold went into each shield. ¹⁷ And he made 300 shields of beaten gold; three

minas of gold went into each shield. And the king put them in the House of the Forest of Lebanon. ¹⁸ The king also made a great ivory throne and overlaid it with the finest gold. ¹⁹ The throne had six steps, and the throne had a round top, and on each side of the seat were armrests and two lions standing beside the armrests, ²⁰ while twelve lions stood there, one on each end of a step on the six steps. The like of it was never made in any kingdom. ²¹ All King Solomon's drinking vessels were of gold, and all the vessels of the House of the Forest of Lebanon were of pure gold. None were of silver; silver was not considered as anything in the days of Solomon. ²² For the king had a fleet of ships of Tarshish at sea with the fleet of Hiram. Once every three years the fleet of ships of Tarshish used to come bringing gold, silver, ivory, apes, and peacocks.

²³ Thus King Solomon excelled all the kings of the earth in riches and in wisdom. ²⁴ And the whole earth sought the presence of Solomon to hear his wisdom, which God had put into his mind. ²⁵ Every one of them brought his present, articles of silver and gold, garments, myrrh, spices, horses, and mules, so much year by year.

²⁶ And Solomon gathered together chariots and horsemen. He had 1,400 chariots and 12,000 horsemen, whom he stationed in the chariot cities and with the king in Jerusalem. ²⁷ And the king made silver as common in Jerusalem as stone, and he made cedar as plentiful as the sycamore of the Shephelah. ²⁸ And Solomon's import of horses was from Egypt and Kue, and the king's traders received them from Kue at a price. ²⁹ A chariot could be imported from Egypt for 600 shekels of silver and a horse for 150, and so through the king's traders they were exported to all the kings of the Hittites and the kings of Syria.

Solomon Turns from the Lord

11 Now King Solomon loved many foreign women, along with the daughter of Pharaoh: Moabite, Ammonite, Edomite, Sidonian, and Hittite women, ² from the nations concerning which the Lord had said to the people of Israel, "You shall not enter into marriage with them, neither shall they with you, for surely they will turn away your heart after their gods." Solomon clung to these in love. ³ He had 700 wives, who were princesses, and 300 concubines. And his wives turned away his heart. ⁴ For when Solomon was old his wives turned away his heart after other gods, and his heart was not wholly true to the Lord his God, as was the heart of David his father. ⁵ For Solomon went after Ashtoreth the goddess of the Sidonians, and after Milcom the abomination of the Ammonites. ⁶ So Solomon did what was evil in the sight of the Lord and did not wholly follow the Lord, as David his father had done. ⁷ Then Solomon built a high place for Chemosh the abomination of Moab, and for Molech the abomination of the Ammonites, on the mountain east of Jerusalem. ⁸ And so he did for all his foreign wives, who made offerings and sacrificed to their gods.

The Lord Raises Adversaries

⁹ And the Lord was angry with Solomon, because his heart had turned away from the Lord, the God of Israel, who had appeared to him twice ¹⁰ and had commanded him concerning this thing, that he should not go after other gods. But he did not keep what the Lord commanded. ¹¹ Therefore the Lord said to Solomon, "Since this has been your practice and you have not kept my covenant and my statutes that I have commanded you, I will surely tear the kingdom from you and will give it to your servant. ¹² Yet for the sake of David your father I will not do it in your days, but I will tear it out of the hand of your son. ¹³ However, I will not tear away all the kingdom, but I will give one tribe to your son, for the sake of David my servant and for the sake of Jerusalem that I have chosen."

¹⁴ And the Lord raised up an adversary against Solomon, Hadad the Edomite. He was of the royal house in Edom. ¹⁵ For when David was in Edom, and Joab the commander of the army went up to bury the slain, he struck down every male in Edom

¹⁶ (for Joab and all Israel remained there six months, until he had cut off every male in Edom). ¹⁷ But Hadad fled to Egypt, together with certain Edomites of his father's servants, Hadad still being a little child. ¹⁸ They set out from Midian and came to Paran and took men with them from Paran and came to Egypt, to Pharaoh king of Egypt, who gave him a house and assigned him an allowance of food and gave him land. ¹⁹ And Hadad found great favor in the sight of Pharaoh, so that he gave him in marriage the sister of his own wife, the sister of Tahpenes the queen. ²⁰ And the sister of Tahpenes bore him Genubath his son, whom Tahpenes weaned in Pharaoh's house. And Genubath was in Pharaoh's house among the sons of

GETTING THE MESSAGE

From ancient times, **Damascus** (11:24) has been a strategic location. It was a primary stopping point along the main caravan route that ran from Africa to Mesopotamia. When it became the capital of the Aramean kingdom (modern Syria), it served as a military outpost to prevent Israel from expanding northward.

Pharaoh. ²¹ But when Hadad heard in Egypt that David slept with his fathers and that Joab the commander of the army was dead, Hadad said to Pharaoh, "Let me depart, that I may go to my own country." ²² But Pharaoh said to him, "What have you lacked with me that you are now seeking to go to your own country?" And he said to him, "Only let me depart."

²³ God also raised up as an adversary to him, Rezon the son of Eliada, who had fled from his master Hadadezer king of Zobah. ²⁴ And he gathered men about him and became leader of a marauding band, after the killing by David. And they went to Damascus and lived there and made him king in Damascus. ²⁵ He was an adversary of Israel all the days of Solomon, doing harm as Hadad did. And he loathed Israel and reigned over Syria.

²⁶ Jeroboam the son of Nebat, an Ephraimite of Zeredah, a servant of Solomon, whose mother's name was Zeruah, a widow, also

lifted up his hand against the king. ²⁷ And this was the reason why he lifted up his hand against the king. Solomon built the Millo, and closed up the breach of the city of David his father. ²⁸ The man Jeroboam was very able, and when Solomon saw that the young man was industrious he gave him charge over all the forced labor of the house of Joseph. ²⁹ And at that time, when Jeroboam went out of Jerusalem, the prophet Ahijah the Shilonite found him on the road. Now Ahijah had dressed himself in a new garment, and the two of them were alone in the open country. ³⁰ Then Ahijah laid hold of the new garment that was on him, and tore it into twelve pieces. ³¹ And he said to Jeroboam, "Take for yourself ten pieces, for thus says the LORD, the God of Israel, 'Behold, I am about to tear the kingdom from the hand of Solomon and will give you ten tribes ³² (but he shall have one tribe, for the sake of my servant David and for the sake of Jerusalem, the city that I have chosen out of all the tribes of Israel), ³³ because they have forsaken me and worshiped Ashtoreth the goddess of the Sidonians, Chemosh the god of Moab, and Milcom the god of the Ammonites, and they have not walked in my ways, doing what is right in my sight and keeping my statutes and my rules, as David his father did. ³⁴ Nevertheless, I will not take the whole kingdom out of his hand, but I will make him ruler all the days of his life, for the sake of David my servant whom I chose, who kept my commandments and my statutes. ³⁵ But I will take the kingdom out of his son's hand and will give it to you, ten tribes. ³⁶ Yet to his son I will give one tribe, that David my servant may always have a lamp before me in Jerusalem, the city where I have chosen to put my name. ³⁷ And I will take you, and you shall reign over all that your soul desires, and you shall be king over Israel. ³⁸ And if you will listen to all that I command you, and will walk in my ways, and do what is right in my eyes by keeping my statutes and my commandments, as David my servant did, I will be with you and will build you a sure house, as I built for David, and I will give Israel to you. ³⁹ And I will afflict the offspring of David because of this, but not forever.'" ⁴⁰ Solomon sought therefore to kill Jeroboam. But Jeroboam arose and fled into Egypt, to Shishak king of Egypt, and was in Egypt until the death of Solomon.

⁴¹ Now the rest of the acts of Solomon, and all that he did, and his wisdom, are they not written in the Book of the Acts of Solomon? ⁴² And the time that Solomon reigned in Jerusalem over all Israel was forty years. ⁴³ And Solomon slept with his fathers and was buried in the city of David his father. And Rehoboam his son reigned in his place.

Rehoboam's Folly

12 Rehoboam went to Shechem, for all Israel had come to Shechem to make him king. ² And as soon as Jeroboam the son of Nebat heard of it (for he was still in Egypt, where he had fled from King Solomon), then Jeroboam returned from Egypt. ³ And they sent and called him, and Jeroboam and all the assembly of Israel came and said to Rehoboam, ⁴ "Your father made our yoke heavy. Now therefore lighten the hard service of your father and his heavy yoke on us, and we will serve you." ⁵ He said to them, "Go away for three days, then come again to me." So the people went away.

⁶ Then King Rehoboam took counsel with the old men, who had stood before Solomon his father while he was yet alive, saying, "How do you advise me to answer this people?" ⁷ And they said to him, "If you will be a servant to this people today and serve them, and speak good words to them when you answer them, then they will be your servants forever." ⁸ But he abandoned the counsel that the old men gave him and took counsel with the young men who had grown up with him and stood before him. ⁹ And he said to them, "What do you advise that we answer this people who have said to me, 'Lighten the yoke that your father put on us'?" ¹⁰ And the young men who had grown up with him said to him, "Thus shall you speak to this people who said to you, 'Your father made our yoke heavy, but you lighten it for us,' thus shall you say to them, 'My little finger is thicker than my father's thighs. ¹¹ And now, whereas my father laid on you a heavy yoke, I will add to your yoke. My father disciplined you with whips, but I will discipline you with scorpions.'"

¹² So Jeroboam and all the people came to Rehoboam the third day, as the king said, "Come to me again the third day." ¹³ And the king answered the people harshly, and

forsaking the counsel that the old men had given him, ¹⁴ he spoke to them according to the counsel of the young men, saying, "My father made your yoke heavy, but I will add to your yoke. My father disciplined you with whips, but I will discipline you with scorpions." ¹⁵ So the king did not listen to the people, for it was a turn of affairs brought about by the LORD that he might fulfill his word, which the LORD spoke by Ahijah the Shilonite to Jeroboam the son of Nebat.

The Kingdom Divided

¹⁶ And when all Israel saw that the king did not listen to them, the people answered the king, "What portion do we have in David? We have no inheritance in the son of Jesse. To your tents, O Israel! Look now to your own house, David." So Israel went to their tents. ¹⁷ But Rehoboam reigned over the people

> **GETTING THE MESSAGE**
>
> **How long did the United Kingdom of Israel last?** All 12 tribes of Israel were together as one nation for a total of 120 years: 40 years under Saul, 40 years under David, and 40 years under Solomon (c. 1050–930 B.C.).

of Israel who lived in the cities of Judah. ¹⁸ Then King Rehoboam sent Adoram, who was taskmaster over the forced labor, and all Israel stoned him to death with stones. And King Rehoboam hurried to mount his chariot to flee to Jerusalem. ¹⁹ So Israel has been in rebellion against the house of David to this day. ²⁰ And when all Israel heard that Jeroboam had returned, they sent and called him to the assembly and made him king over all Israel. There was none that followed the house of David but the tribe of Judah only.

²¹ When Rehoboam came to Jerusalem, he assembled all the house of Judah and the tribe of Benjamin, 180,000 chosen warriors, to fight against the house of Israel, to restore the kingdom to Rehoboam the son of Solomon. ²² But the word of God came to Shemaiah the man of God: ²³ "Say to Rehoboam the son of Solomon, king of Judah, and to all the house of Judah and Benjamin, and to the rest of the people, ²⁴ 'Thus says the LORD, You shall not go up or fight against your relatives the people of

Israel. Every man return to his home, for this thing is from me.'" So they listened to the word of the LORD and went home again, according to the word of the LORD.

Jeroboam's Golden Calves

25 Then Jeroboam built Shechem in the hill country of Ephraim and lived there. And he went out from there and built Penuel. 26 And Jeroboam said in his heart, "Now the kingdom will turn back to the house of David. 27 If this people go up to offer sacrifices in the temple of the LORD at

PROFILE
JEROBOAM

Jeroboam, a servant of Solomon, was in charge of the forced labor doing construction work in Jerusalem. He was approached by the prophet Ahijah, who prophesied that he would one day be king over 10 of the tribes of Israel. This prophecy came true when, after Solomon's death, his son Rehoboam refused to lighten his father's heavy tax burden on the people. The 10 northern tribes revolted. They broke away from the two southern tribes and made Jeroboam their king. To prevent his people from returning to Jerusalem to worship, Jeroboam built competing centers of worship in Bethel and Dan. By inventing his own system of worship, he led the people of Israel astray.

KEY REFERENCE: 1 KINGS 11:29–40

Jerusalem, then the heart of this people will turn again to their lord, to Rehoboam king of Judah, and they will kill me and return to Rehoboam king of Judah." 28 So the king took counsel and made two calves of gold. And he said to the people, "You have gone up to Jerusalem long enough. Behold your gods, O Israel, who brought you up out of the land of Egypt." 29 And he set one in Bethel, and the other he put in Dan. 30 Then this thing became a sin, for the people went as far as Dan to be before one. 31 He also made temples on high places and appointed priests from among all the people, who were not

of the Levites. 32 And Jeroboam appointed a feast on the fifteenth day of the eighth month like the feast that was in Judah, and he offered sacrifices on the altar. So he did in Bethel, sacrificing to the calves that he made. And he placed in Bethel the priests of the high places that he had made. 33 He went up to the altar that he had made in Bethel on the fifteenth day in the eighth month, in the month that he had devised from his own heart. And he instituted a feast for the people of Israel and went up to the altar to make offerings.

A Man of God Confronts Jeroboam

13 And behold, a man of God came out of Judah by the word of the LORD to Bethel. Jeroboam was standing by the altar to make offerings. 2 And the man cried against the altar by the word of the LORD

GETTING THE MESSAGE

"Man of God," meaning "prophet," is used 37 times in 1–2 Kings. Though God judged the Judean prophet's disobedience (13:1–32), his prophecy against the temple in Bethel was fulfilled, and King Josiah preserved his burial place (2 Kings 23:15–20).

and said, "O altar, altar, thus says the LORD: 'Behold, a son shall be born to the house of David, Josiah by name, and he shall sacrifice on you the priests of the high places who make offerings on you, and human bones shall be burned on you.'" 3 And he gave a sign the same day, saying, "This is the sign that the LORD has spoken: 'Behold, the altar shall be torn down, and the ashes that are on it shall be poured out.'" 4 And when the king heard the saying of the man of God, which he cried against the altar at Bethel, Jeroboam stretched out his hand from the altar, saying, "Seize him." And his hand, which he stretched out against him, dried up, so that he could not draw it back to himself. 5 The altar also was torn down, and the ashes poured out from the altar, according to the sign that the man of God had given by the word of the LORD. 6 And the king said to the man of God, "Entreat now the favor of the LORD your God, and pray for me, that my hand may be restored to me." And the man of God entreated the LORD, and the king's hand was restored to him and became as it was before. ⁷ And the king said to the man of God, "Come home with me, and refresh yourself, and I will give you a reward." ⁸ And the man of God said to the king, "If you give me half your house, I will not go in with you. And I will not eat bread or drink water in this place, ⁹ for so was it commanded me by the word of the LORD, saying, 'You shall neither eat bread nor drink water nor return by the way that you came.'" ¹⁰ So he went another way and did not return by the way that he came to Bethel.

The Prophet's Disobedience

¹¹ Now an old prophet lived in Bethel. And his sons came and told him all that the man of God had done that day in Bethel. They also told to their father the words that he had spoken to the king. ¹² And their father said to them, "Which way did he go?" And his sons showed him the way that the man of God who came from Judah had gone. ¹³ And he said to his sons, "Saddle the donkey for me." So they saddled the donkey for him and he mounted it. ¹⁴ And he went after the man of God and found him sitting under an oak. And he said to him, "Are you the man of God who came from Judah?" And he said, "I am." ¹⁵ Then he said to him, "Come home with me and eat bread." ¹⁶ And he said, "I may not return with you, or go in with you, neither will I eat bread nor drink water with you in this place, ¹⁷ for it was said to me by the word of the LORD, 'You shall neither eat bread nor drink water there, nor return by the way that you came.'" ¹⁸ And he said to him, "I also am a prophet as you are, and an angel spoke to me by the word of the LORD, saying, 'Bring him back with you into your house that he may eat bread and drink water.'" But he lied to him. ¹⁹ So he went back with him and ate bread in his house and drank water.

²⁰ And as they sat at the table, the word of the LORD came to the prophet who had brought him back. ²¹ And he cried to the man of God who came from Judah, "Thus says the LORD, 'Because you have disobeyed the word of the LORD and have not kept the command that the LORD your God commanded you, ²² but have come back and have eaten bread and drunk water in the place of which he said to you, "Eat no bread and drink no

water," your body shall not come to the tomb of your fathers.'" ²³ And after he had eaten bread and drunk, he saddled the donkey for the prophet whom he had brought back. ²⁴ And as he went away a lion met him on the road and killed him. And his body was thrown in the road, and the donkey stood beside it; the lion also stood beside the body. ²⁵ And behold, men passed by and saw the body thrown in the road and the lion standing by the body. And they came and told it in the city where the old prophet lived.

²⁶ And when the prophet who had brought him back from the way heard of it, he said, "It is the man of God who disobeyed the word of the LORD; therefore the LORD has given him to the lion, which has torn him and killed him, according to the word that the LORD spoke to him." ²⁷ And he said to his sons, "Saddle the donkey for me." And

they saddled it. ²⁸ And he went and found his body thrown in the road, and the donkey and the lion standing beside the body. The lion had not eaten the body or torn the donkey. ²⁹ And the prophet took up the body of the man of God and laid it on the donkey and brought it back to the city to mourn and to bury him. ³⁰ And he laid the body in his own grave. And they mourned over him, saying, "Alas, my brother!" ³¹ And after he had buried him, he said to his sons, "When I die, bury me in the grave in which the man of God is buried; lay my bones beside his bones. ³² For the saying that he called out by the word of the LORD against the altar in Bethel and against all the houses of the high places that are in the cities of Samaria shall surely come to pass."

³³ After this thing Jeroboam did not turn from his evil way, but made priests for the high places again from among all the people. Any who would, he ordained to be priests of the high places. ³⁴ And this thing became sin to the house of Jeroboam, so as

to cut it off and to destroy it from the face of the earth.

Prophecy Against Jeroboam

14 At that time Abijah the son of Jeroboam fell sick. ²And Jeroboam said to his wife, "Arise, and disguise yourself, that it not be known that you are the wife of Jeroboam, and go to Shiloh. Behold, Ahijah the prophet is there, who said of me that I should be king over this people. ³Take with you ten loaves, some cakes, and a jar of honey, and go to him. He will tell you what shall happen to the child."

⁴Jeroboam's wife did so. She arose and went to Shiloh and came to the house of Ahijah. Now Ahijah could not see, for his eyes were dim because of his age. ⁵And the LORD said to Ahijah, "Behold, the wife of

---

GETTING THE MESSAGE

What were high places? High places (14:23) were worship sites for local pagan gods. Before the temple was built in Jerusalem, Israelites often offered sacrifices in such places. After the temple was built, however, people were required to sacrifice there instead of at the high places.

Jeroboam is coming to inquire of you concerning her son, for he is sick. Thus and thus shall you say to her."

When she came, she pretended to be another woman. ⁶But when Ahijah heard the sound of her feet, as she came in at the door, he said, "Come in, wife of Jeroboam. Why do you pretend to be another? For I am charged with unbearable news for you. ⁷Go, tell Jeroboam, 'Thus says the LORD, the God of Israel: "Because I exalted you from among the people and made you leader over my people Israel ⁸and tore the kingdom away from the house of David and gave it to you, and yet you have not been like my servant David, who kept my commandments and followed me with all his heart, doing only that which was right in my eyes, ⁹but you have done evil above all who were before you and have gone and made for yourself other gods and metal images, provoking me to anger, and have cast me behind your

back, ¹⁰therefore behold, I will bring harm upon the house of Jeroboam and will cut off from Jeroboam every male, both bond and free in Israel, and will burn up the house of Jeroboam, as a man burns up dung until it is all gone. ¹¹Anyone belonging to Jeroboam who dies in the city the dogs shall eat, and anyone who dies in the open country the birds of the heavens shall eat, for the LORD has spoken it."' ¹²Arise therefore, go to your house. When your feet enter the city, the child shall die. ¹³And all Israel shall mourn for him and bury him, for he only of Jeroboam shall come to the grave, because in him there is found something pleasing to the LORD, the God of Israel, in the house of Jeroboam. ¹⁴Moreover, the LORD will raise up for himself a king over Israel who shall cut off the house of Jeroboam today. And henceforth, ¹⁵the LORD will strike Israel as a reed is shaken in the water, and root up Israel out of this good land that he gave to their fathers and scatter them beyond the Euphrates, because they have made their Asherim, provoking the LORD to anger. ¹⁶And he will give Israel up because of the sins of Jeroboam, which he sinned and made Israel to sin."

¹⁷Then Jeroboam's wife arose and departed and came to Tirzah. And as she came to the threshold of the house, the child died. ¹⁸And all Israel buried him and mourned for him, according to the word of the LORD, which he spoke by his servant Ahijah the prophet.

The Death of Jeroboam

¹⁹Now the rest of the acts of Jeroboam, how he warred and how he reigned, behold, they are written in the Book of the Chronicles of the Kings of Israel. ²⁰And the time that Jeroboam reigned was twenty-two years. And he slept with his fathers, and Nadab his son reigned in his place.

Rehoboam Reigns in Judah

²¹Now Rehoboam the son of Solomon reigned in Judah. Rehoboam was forty-one years old when he began to reign, and he reigned seventeen years in Jerusalem, the city that the LORD had chosen out of all the tribes of Israel, to put his name there. His mother's name was Naamah the Ammonite. ²²And Judah did what was evil in the sight of the LORD, and they provoked him to jealousy

with their sins that they committed, more than all that their fathers had done. ²³ For they also built for themselves high places and pillars and Asherim on every high hill and under every green tree, ²⁴ and there were also male cult prostitutes in the land. They did according to all the abominations of the nations that the LORD drove out before the people of Israel.

²⁵ In the fifth year of King Rehoboam, Shishak king of Egypt came up against Jerusalem. ²⁶ He took away the treasures of the house of the LORD and the treasures of the king's house. He took away everything. He also took away all the shields of gold that Solomon had made, ²⁷ and King Rehoboam made in their place shields of bronze, and committed them to the hands of the officers of the guard, who kept the door of the king's house. ²⁸ And as often as the king went into the house of the LORD, the guard carried them and brought them back to the guardroom.

²⁹ Now the rest of the acts of Rehoboam and all that he did, are they not written in the Book of the Chronicles of the Kings of Judah? ³⁰ And there was war between Rehoboam and Jeroboam continually. ³¹ And Rehoboam slept with his fathers and was buried with his fathers in the city of David. His mother's name was Naamah the Ammonite. And Abijam his son reigned in his place.

Abijam Reigns in Judah

15 Now in the eighteenth year of King Jeroboam the son of Nebat, Abijam began to reign over Judah. ² He reigned for three years in Jerusalem. His mother's name was Maacah the daughter of Abishalom. ³ And he walked in all the sins that his father did before him, and his heart was not wholly true to the LORD his God, as the heart of David his father. ⁴ Nevertheless, for David's sake the LORD his God gave him a lamp in Jerusalem, setting up his son after him, and establishing Jerusalem, ⁵ because David did what was right in the eyes of the LORD and did not turn aside from anything that he commanded him all the days of his life, except in the matter of Uriah the Hittite. ⁶ Now there was war between Rehoboam and Jeroboam all the days of his life. ⁷ The rest of the acts of Abijam and all that he did, are they not written in the Book of the Chronicles of the Kings of Judah? And there

was war between Abijam and Jeroboam. ⁸ And Abijam slept with his fathers, and they buried him in the city of David. And Asa his son reigned in his place.

Asa Reigns in Judah

⁹ In the twentieth year of Jeroboam king of Israel, Asa began to reign over Judah, ¹⁰ and he reigned forty-one years in Jerusalem. His mother's name was Maacah the daughter of Abishalom. ¹¹ And Asa did what was right in the eyes of the LORD, as David his father had done. ¹² He put away the male cult prostitutes out of the land and removed all the idols that his fathers had made. ¹³ He also removed Maacah his mother from being queen mother because she had made an abominable image for Asherah. And Asa cut down her image and burned it at the brook Kidron. ¹⁴ But the high places were not taken away. Nevertheless, the heart of Asa was wholly true to the LORD all his days.

> ### GETTING THE MESSAGE
>
> The role of the **queen mother** (15:13) was an important one in the royal court. She might serve as an adviser to the king and also as a teacher for his children.

¹⁵ And he brought into the house of the LORD the sacred gifts of his father and his own sacred gifts, silver, and gold, and vessels.

¹⁶ And there was war between Asa and Baasha king of Israel all their days. ¹⁷ Baasha king of Israel went up against Judah and built Ramah, that he might permit no one to go out or come in to Asa king of Judah. ¹⁸ Then Asa took all the silver and the gold that were left in the treasures of the house of the LORD and the treasures of the king's house and gave them into the hands of his servants. And King Asa sent them to Ben-hadad the son of Tabrimmon, the son of Hezion, king of Syria, who lived in Damascus, saying, ¹⁹ "Let there be a covenant between me and you, as there was between my father and your father. Behold, I am sending to you a present of silver and gold. Go, break your covenant with Baasha king of Israel, that he may withdraw from me." ²⁰ And Ben-hadad listened to King Asa and sent the commanders of his armies against the cities of Israel and conquered Ijon, Dan,

Abel-beth-maacah, and all Chinneroth, with all the land of Naphtali. [21] And when Baasha heard of it, he stopped building Ramah, and he lived in Tirzah. [22] Then King Asa made a proclamation to all Judah, none was exempt, and they carried away the stones of Ramah and its timber, with which Baasha had been building, and with them King Asa built Geba of Benjamin and Mizpah. [23] Now the rest of all the acts of Asa, all his might, and all that he did, and the cities that he built, are they not written in the Book of the Chronicles of the Kings of Judah? But in his old age he was diseased in his feet. [24] And Asa slept with his fathers and was buried with his fathers in the city of David his father, and Jehoshaphat his son reigned in his place.

Nadab Reigns in Israel

[25] Nadab the son of Jeroboam began to reign over Israel in the second year of Asa king of Judah, and he reigned over Israel two years. [26] He did what was evil in the sight of the LORD and walked in the way of his father, and in his sin which he made Israel to sin.

[27] Baasha the son of Ahijah, of the house of Issachar, conspired against him. And Baasha struck him down at Gibbethon, which belonged to the Philistines, for Nadab and all Israel were laying siege to Gibbethon. [28] So Baasha killed him in the third year of Asa king of Judah and reigned in his place. [29] And as soon as he was king, he killed all the house of Jeroboam. He left to the house of Jeroboam not one that breathed, until he had destroyed it, according to the word of the LORD that he spoke by his servant Ahijah the Shilonite. [30] It was for the sins of Jeroboam that he sinned and that he made Israel to sin, and because of the anger to which he provoked the LORD, the God of Israel.

[31] Now the rest of the acts of Nadab and all that he did, are they not written in the Book of the Chronicles of the Kings of Israel? [32] And there was war between Asa and Baasha king of Israel all their days.

Baasha Reigns in Israel

[33] In the third year of Asa king of Judah, Baasha the son of Ahijah began to reign over all Israel at Tirzah, and he reigned twenty-four years. [34] He did what was evil in the sight of the LORD and walked in the way of Jeroboam and in his sin which he made Israel to sin.

16 And the word of the LORD came to Jehu the son of Hanani against Baasha, saying, [2] "Since I exalted you out of the dust and made you leader over my people Israel, and you have walked in the way of Jeroboam and have made my people Israel to sin, provoking me to anger with their sins, [3] behold, I will utterly sweep away Baasha and his house, and I will make your house like the house of Jeroboam the son of Nebat. [4] Anyone belonging to Baasha who dies in the city the dogs shall eat, and anyone of his who dies in the field the birds of the heavens shall eat."

[5] Now the rest of the acts of Baasha and what he did, and his might, are they not written in the Book of the Chronicles of the Kings of Israel? [6] And Baasha slept with his fathers and was buried at Tirzah, and Elah his son reigned in his place. [7] Moreover, the word of the LORD came by the prophet Jehu the son of Hanani against Baasha and his house, both because of all the evil that he did in the sight of the LORD, provoking him to anger with the work of his hands, in being like the house of Jeroboam, and also because he destroyed it.

Elah Reigns in Israel

[8] In the twenty-sixth year of Asa king of Judah, Elah the son of Baasha began to reign over Israel in Tirzah, and he reigned two years. [9] But his servant Zimri, commander of half his chariots, conspired against him. When he was at Tirzah, drinking himself drunk in the house of Arza, who was over the household in Tirzah, [10] Zimri came in and struck him down and killed him, in the twenty-seventh year of Asa king of Judah, and reigned in his place.

[11] When he began to reign, as soon as he had seated himself on his throne, he struck down all the house of Baasha. He did not leave him a single male of his relatives or his friends. [12] Thus Zimri destroyed all the house of Baasha, according to the word of the LORD, which he spoke against Baasha by Jehu the prophet, [13] for all the sins of Baasha and the sins of Elah his son, which they sinned and which they made Israel to sin, provoking the LORD God of Israel to anger with their idols. [14] Now the rest of the acts of Elah and all that he did, are they not written in the Book of the Chronicles of the Kings of Israel?

Zimri Reigns in Israel

¹⁵ In the twenty-seventh year of Asa king of Judah, Zimri reigned seven days in Tirzah. Now the troops were encamped against Gibbethon, which belonged to the Philistines, ¹⁶ and the troops who were encamped heard it said, "Zimri has conspired, and he has killed the king." Therefore all Israel made Omri, the commander of the army, king over Israel that day in the camp. ¹⁷ So Omri went up from Gibbethon, and all Israel with him, and they besieged Tirzah. ¹⁸ And when Zimri saw that the city was taken, he went into the citadel of the king's house and burned the king's house over him with fire and died, ¹⁹ because of his sins that he committed, doing evil in the sight of the LORD, walking in the way of Jeroboam, and for his sin which he committed, making Israel to sin. ²⁰ Now the rest of the acts of Zimri, and the conspiracy that he made, are they not written in the Book of the Chronicles of the Kings of Israel?

Omri Reigns in Israel

²¹ Then the people of Israel were divided into two parts. Half of the people followed Tibni the son of Ginath, to make him king, and half followed Omri. ²² But the people who followed Omri overcame the people who followed Tibni the son of Ginath. So Tibni died, and Omri became king. ²³ In the thirty-first year of Asa king of Judah, Omri began to reign over Israel, and he reigned for twelve years; six years he reigned in Tirzah. ²⁴ He bought the hill of Samaria from Shemer for two talents of silver, and he fortified the hill and called the name of the city that he built Samaria, after the name of Shemer, the owner of the hill.

²⁵ Omri did what was evil in the sight of the LORD, and did more evil than all who were before him. ²⁶ For he walked in all the way of Jeroboam the son of Nebat, and in the sins that he made Israel to sin, provoking the LORD, the God of Israel, to anger by their idols. ²⁷ Now the rest of the acts of Omri that he did, and the might that he showed, are they not written in the Book of the Chronicles of the Kings of Israel? ²⁸ And Omri slept with his fathers and was buried in Samaria, and Ahab his son reigned in his place.

Ahab Reigns in Israel

²⁹ In the thirty-eighth year of Asa king of Judah, Ahab the son of Omri began to reign over Israel, and Ahab the son of Omri reigned over Israel in Samaria twenty-two years. ³⁰ And Ahab the son of Omri did evil in the sight of the LORD, more than all who were before him. ³¹ And as if it had been a light thing for him to walk in the sins of Jeroboam the son of Nebat, he took for his wife Jezebel the daughter of Ethbaal king of the Sidonians, and went and served Baal and worshiped him. ³² He erected an altar for Baal in the house of Baal, which he built in Samaria. ³³ And Ahab made an Asherah. Ahab did more to provoke the LORD, the God of Israel, to anger than all the kings of Israel who were before him. ³⁴ In his days Hiel of Bethel built Jericho. He laid its foundation

GETTING THE MESSAGE

Though the story of **King Omri** is told in just eight verses (16:21-28), politically speaking he was one of Israel's most important kings. He built the capital city of Samaria in a place that gave Israel a strategic advantage over its enemies. After his time, the Assyrians referred to Israel as "the land of Omri."

at the cost of Abiram his firstborn, and set up its gates at the cost of his youngest son Segub, according to the word of the LORD, which he spoke by Joshua the son of Nun.

Elijah Predicts a Drought

17 Now Elijah the Tishbite, of Tishbe in Gilead, said to Ahab, "As the LORD, the God of Israel, lives, before whom I stand, there shall be neither dew nor rain these years, except by my word." ² And the word of the LORD came to him: ³ "Depart from here and turn eastward and hide yourself by the brook Cherith, which is east of the Jordan. ⁴ You shall drink from the brook, and I have commanded the ravens to feed you there." ⁵ So he went and did according to the word of the LORD. He went and lived by the brook Cherith that is east of the Jordan. ⁶ And the ravens brought him bread and meat in the morning, and bread and meat in the evening, and he drank from the brook. ⁷ And after a while the brook dried up, because there was no rain in the land.

The Widow of Zarephath

8 Then the word of the LORD came to him, **9** "Arise, go to Zarephath, which belongs to Sidon, and dwell there. Behold, I have commanded a widow there to feed you." **10** So he arose and went to Zarephath. And when he came to the gate of the city, behold, a widow was there gathering sticks. And he called to her and said, "Bring me a little water in a vessel, that I may drink." **11** And as she was going to bring it, he called to her and said, "Bring me a morsel of bread in your hand." **12** And she said, "As the LORD your God lives, I have nothing baked, only a handful of flour in a jar and a little oil in a jug. And now I am gathering a couple of sticks that I may go in and prepare it for myself and my son, that we may eat it and die." **13** And Elijah said to her, "Do not fear; go and do as you have said. But first make me a little cake of it and bring it to me, and afterward make something for yourself and your son. **14** For thus says the LORD, the God of Israel, 'The jar of flour shall not be spent, and the jug of oil shall not be empty, until the day that the LORD sends rain upon the earth.'" **15** And she went and did as Elijah said. And she and he and her household ate for many days. **16** The jar of flour was not spent, neither did the jug of oil become empty, according to the word of the LORD that he spoke by Elijah.

Elijah Raises the Widow's Son

17 After this the son of the woman, the mistress of the house, became ill. And his illness was so severe that there was no breath left in him. **18** And she said to Elijah, "What have you against me, O man of God? You have come to me to bring my sin to remembrance and to cause the death of my son!" **19** And he said to her, "Give me your son." And he took him from her arms and carried him up into the upper chamber where he lodged, and laid him on his own bed. **20** And he cried to the LORD, "O LORD my God, have you brought calamity even upon the widow with whom I sojourn, by killing her son?" **21** Then he stretched himself upon the child three times and cried to the LORD, "O LORD my God, let this child's life come into him again." **22** And the LORD listened to the voice of Elijah. And the life of the child came into him again, and he revived. **23** And Elijah took the child and brought him down from the upper chamber into the house and delivered him to his mother. And Elijah said, "See, your son lives." **24** And the woman said to Elijah, "Now I know that you are a man of God, and that the word of the LORD in your mouth is truth."

PROFILE
ELIJAH

Elijah, one of the greatest prophets of the Old Testament, ministered in the northern kingdom of Israel. He prophesied against the wicked king Ahab, who along with his wife Jezebel promoted Baal worship throughout Israel and persecuted the prophets of the Lord. Elijah challenged Ahab and the prophets of Baal to a contest on Mount Carmel. He instructed the prophets of Baal to call upon their gods to send down fire from heaven. In an almost humorous way, the Bible records the prophets' utter failure to get a response from their false god. When Elijah called upon the Lord, however, he sent fire from heaven to consume his altar. Following their humiliating defeat, Elijah slaughtered all 450 of the prophets of Baal. Elijah did not die, but rather was carried into heaven by chariots and horses of fire, as his successor, Elisha, watched.

KEY REFERENCE: 1 KINGS 18:36–40

GETTING THE MESSAGE

Life for a widow was not easy in the ancient Near East. Widows had difficulty protecting themselves and their children economically, legally, or physically. If the widow became childless, her situation would be even more difficult, since she would have no one to care for her in her old age (see 17:8–24).

Elijah Confronts Ahab

18 After many days the word of the LORD came to Elijah, in the third year, saying, "Go, show yourself to Ahab, and I will send rain upon the earth." ²So Elijah went to show himself to Ahab. Now the famine was severe in Samaria. ³And Ahab called Obadiah, who was over the household. (Now Obadiah feared the LORD greatly, ⁴and when Jezebel cut off the prophets of the LORD, Obadiah took a hundred prophets and hid them by fifties in a cave and fed them with bread and water.) ⁵And Ahab said to Obadiah, "Go through the land to all the springs of water and to all the valleys. Perhaps we may find grass and save the horses and mules alive, and not lose some of the animals." ⁶So they divided the land between them to pass through it. Ahab went in one direction by himself, and Obadiah went in another direction by himself.

⁷And as Obadiah was on the way, behold, Elijah met him. And Obadiah recognized him and fell on his face and said, "Is it you, my lord Elijah?" ⁸And he answered him, "It is I. Go, tell your lord, 'Behold, Elijah is here.'" ⁹And he said, "How have I sinned, that you would give your servant into the hand of Ahab, to kill me? ¹⁰As the LORD your God lives, there is no nation or kingdom where my lord has not sent to seek you. And when they would say, 'He is not here,' he would take an oath of the kingdom or nation, that they had not found you. ¹¹And now you say, 'Go, tell your lord, "Behold, Elijah is here."' ¹²And as soon as I have gone from you, the Spirit of the LORD will carry you I know not where. And so, when I come and tell Ahab and he cannot find you, he will kill me, although I your servant have feared the LORD from my youth. ¹³Has it not been told my lord what I did when Jezebel killed the prophets of the LORD, how I hid a hundred men of the LORD's prophets by fifties in a cave and fed them with bread and water? ¹⁴And now you say, 'Go, tell your lord, "Behold, Elijah is here"'; and he will kill me." ¹⁵And Elijah said, "As the LORD of hosts lives, before whom I stand, I will surely show myself to him today." ¹⁶So Obadiah went to meet Ahab, and told him. And Ahab went to meet Elijah.

¹⁷When Ahab saw Elijah, Ahab said to him, "Is it you, you troubler of Israel?" ¹⁸And he answered, "I have not troubled Israel, but you have, and your father's house, because you have abandoned the commandments of the LORD and followed the Baals. ¹⁹Now therefore send and gather all Israel to me at Mount Carmel, and the 450 prophets of Baal and the 400 prophets of Asherah, who eat at Jezebel's table."

The Prophets of Baal Defeated

²⁰So Ahab sent to all the people of Israel and gathered the prophets together at Mount Carmel. ²¹And Elijah came near to all the people and said, "How long will you go limping between two different opinions? If the LORD is God, follow him; but if Baal, then follow him." And the people did not answer him a word. ²²Then Elijah said to the people, "I, even I only, am left a prophet of the LORD, but Baal's prophets are 450 men.

GETTING THE MESSAGE

Why did the prophets of Baal cut themselves? According to one ancient Canaanite myth, the father of Baal slashes his chest, arms, and back upon learning of his son's death. In the myth, Baal returns to life when the rains come. The prophets may have hoped that their actions would bring rain and end the drought.

---

²³Let two bulls be given to us, and let them choose one bull for themselves and cut it in pieces and lay it on the wood, but put no fire to it. And I will prepare the other bull and lay it on the wood and put no fire to it. ²⁴And you call upon the name of your god, and I will call upon the name of the LORD, and the God who answers by fire, he is God." And all the people answered, "It is well spoken." ²⁵Then Elijah said to the prophets of Baal, "Choose for yourselves one bull and prepare it first, for you are many, and call upon the name of your god, but put no fire to it." ²⁶And they took the bull that was given them, and they prepared it and called upon the name of Baal from morning until noon, saying, "O Baal, answer us!" But there was no voice, and no one answered. And they limped around the altar that they had made. ²⁷And at noon Elijah mocked them, saying, "Cry aloud, for he is a god. Either he

is musing, or he is relieving himself, or he is on a journey, or perhaps he is asleep and must be awakened." ²⁸ And they cried aloud and cut themselves after their custom with swords and lances, until the blood gushed out upon them. ²⁹ And as midday passed, they raved on until the time of the offering of the oblation, but there was no voice. No one answered; no one paid attention.

³⁰ Then Elijah said to all the people, "Come near to me." And all the people came near to him. And he repaired the altar of the LORD

PROFILE
AHAB

Ahab, the son and successor of King Omri, reigned over Israel for 22 years. Ahab married a Phoenician princess named Jezebel, who persuaded her husband and all of Israel to worship Baal. Ahab even built a house and altar for Baal. He was confronted by the prophet Elijah, who challenged Ahab and the prophets of Baal to a "contest" on Mount Carmel (18:20–40). The Lord repeatedly revealed himself to Ahab through prophets despite Ahab's idolatry. When Elijah prophesied the destruction of Ahab's family, Ahab briefly humbled himself before the Lord and found mercy, only to return to his old ways afterward. Ahab's reign was marked by conflict with Ben-hadad of Syria, whom he defeated in battle twice.

KEY REFERENCE: 1 KINGS 21:25

that had been thrown down. ³¹ Elijah took twelve stones, according to the number of the tribes of the sons of Jacob, to whom the word of the LORD came, saying, "Israel shall be your name," ³² and with the stones he built an altar in the name of the LORD. And he made a trench about the altar, as great as would contain two seahs of seed. ³³ And he put the wood in order and cut the bull in pieces and laid it on the wood. And he said, "Fill four jars with water and pour it on the burnt offering and on the wood." ³⁴ And he said, "Do it a second time." And they did it a second time. And he said, "Do it a third

time." And they did it a third time. ³⁵ And the water ran around the altar and filled the trench also with water.

³⁶ And at the time of the offering of the oblation, Elijah the prophet came near and said, "O LORD, God of Abraham, Isaac, and Israel, let it be known this day that you are God in Israel, and that I am your servant, and that I have done all these things at your word. ³⁷ Answer me, O LORD, answer me, that this people may know that you, O LORD, are God, and that you have turned their hearts back." ³⁸ Then the fire of the LORD fell and consumed the burnt offering and the wood and the stones and the dust, and licked up the water that was in the trench. ³⁹ And when all the people saw it, they fell on their faces and said, "The LORD, he is God; the LORD, he is God." ⁴⁰ And Elijah said to them, "Seize the prophets of Baal; let not one of them escape." And they seized them. And Elijah brought them down to the brook Kishon and slaughtered them there.

The LORD Sends Rain

⁴¹ And Elijah said to Ahab, "Go up, eat and drink, for there is a sound of the rushing of rain." ⁴² So Ahab went up to eat and to drink. And Elijah went up to the top of Mount Carmel. And he bowed himself down on the earth and put his face between his knees. ⁴³ And he said to his servant, "Go up now, look toward the sea." And he went up and looked and said, "There is nothing." And he said, "Go again," seven times. ⁴⁴ And at the seventh time he said, "Behold, a little cloud like a man's hand is rising from the sea." And he said, "Go up, say to Ahab, 'Prepare your chariot and go down, lest the rain stop you.'" ⁴⁵ And in a little while the heavens grew black with clouds and wind, and there was a great rain. And Ahab rode and went to Jezreel. ⁴⁶ And the hand of the LORD was on Elijah, and he gathered up his garment and ran before Ahab to the entrance of Jezreel.

Elijah Flees Jezebel

19 Ahab told Jezebel all that Elijah had done, and how he had killed all the prophets with the sword. ² Then Jezebel sent a messenger to Elijah, saying, "So may the gods do to me and more also, if I do not make your life as the life of one of them by this time tomorrow." ³ Then he was afraid, and he arose and ran for his life and came to Beersheba, which belongs to Judah, and left his servant there.

⁴ But he himself went a day's journey into the wilderness and came and sat down under a broom tree. And he asked that he might die, saying, "It is enough; now, O LORD, take away my life, for I am no better than my fathers." ⁵ And he lay down and slept under a broom tree. And behold, an angel touched him and said to him, "Arise and eat." ⁶ And he looked, and behold, there was at his head a cake baked on hot stones and a jar of water. And he ate and drank and lay down again. ⁷ And the angel of the LORD came again a second time and touched him and said, "Arise and eat, for the journey is too great for you." ⁸ And he arose and ate and drank, and went in the strength of that food forty days and forty nights to Horeb, the mount of God.

The LORD Speaks to Elijah

⁹ There he came to a cave and lodged in it. And behold, the word of the LORD came to him, and he said to him, "What are you doing here, Elijah?" ¹⁰ He said, "I have been very jealous for the LORD, the God of hosts. For the people of Israel have forsaken your covenant, thrown down your altars, and killed your prophets with the sword, and I, even I only, am left, and they seek my life, to take it away." ¹¹ And he said, "Go out and stand on the mount before the LORD." And behold, the LORD passed by, and a great and strong wind tore the mountains and broke in pieces the rocks before the LORD, but the LORD was not in the wind. And after the wind an earthquake, but the LORD was not in the earthquake. ¹² And after the earthquake a fire, but the LORD was not in the fire. And after the fire the sound of a low whisper. ¹³ And when Elijah heard it, he wrapped his face in his cloak and went out and stood at the entrance of the cave. And behold, there came a voice to him and said, "What are you doing here, Elijah?" ¹⁴ He said, "I have been very jealous for the LORD, the God of hosts. For the people of Israel have forsaken your covenant, thrown down your altars, and killed your prophets with the sword, and I, even I only, am left, and they seek my life, to take it away." ¹⁵ And the LORD said to him, "Go, return on your way to the wilderness of Damascus. And when you arrive, you shall anoint Hazael to be king over Syria. ¹⁶ And

Jehu the son of Nimshi you shall anoint to be king over Israel, and Elisha the son of Shaphat of Abel-meholah you shall anoint to be prophet in your place. ¹⁷ And the one who escapes from the sword of Hazael shall Jehu put to death, and the one who escapes from the sword of Jehu shall Elisha put to death. ¹⁸ Yet I will leave seven thousand in Israel, all the knees that have not bowed to Baal, and every mouth that has not kissed him."

The Call of Elisha

¹⁹ So he departed from there and found Elisha the son of Shaphat, who was plowing with twelve yoke of oxen in front of him, and he was with the twelfth. Elijah passed by him and cast his cloak upon him. ²⁰ And he left the oxen and ran after Elijah and said, "Let me kiss my father and my mother, and then I will follow you." And he said to him, "Go back again, for what have I done to you?"

> **GETTING THE MESSAGE**
>
> **Broom trees** (19:5) are a type of desert shrub common in Palestine, Arabia, and Egypt. Its long branches form a bush that grows to about 12 feet (3.7 m) high. Wood from broom trees makes excellent charcoal.

²¹ And he returned from following him and took the yoke of oxen and sacrificed them and boiled their flesh with the yokes of the oxen and gave it to the people, and they ate. Then he arose and went after Elijah and assisted him.

Ahab's Wars with Syria

20 Ben-hadad the king of Syria gathered all his army together. Thirty-two kings were with him, and horses and chariots. And he went up and closed in on Samaria and fought against it. ² And he sent messengers into the city to Ahab king of Israel and said to him, "Thus says Ben-hadad: ³ 'Your silver and your gold are mine; your best wives and children also are mine.'" ⁴ And the king of Israel answered, "As you say, my lord, O king, I am yours, and all that I have." ⁵ The messengers came again and said, "Thus says Ben-hadad: 'I sent to you, saying, "Deliver to me your silver and your gold, your wives and your children."

⁶ Nevertheless I will send my servants to you tomorrow about this time, and they shall search your house and the houses of your servants and lay hands on whatever pleases you and take it away.'"

⁷ Then the king of Israel called all the elders of the land and said, "Mark, now, and see how this man is seeking trouble, for he sent to me for my wives and my children, and for my silver and my gold, and I did not refuse him." ⁸ And all the elders and all the people said to him, "Do not listen or consent." ⁹ So he said to the messengers of Ben-hadad, "Tell my lord the king, 'All that you first demanded of your servant I will do, but this thing I cannot do.'" And the messengers departed and brought him word again. ¹⁰ Ben-hadad sent to him and said, "The gods do so to me and more also, if the dust of Samaria shall suffice for handfuls for all the people who follow me." ¹¹ And the king of Israel answered, "Tell him, 'Let not him who straps on his armor boast himself as he who takes it off.'" ¹² When Ben-hadad heard this message as he was drinking with the kings in the booths, he said to his men, "Take your positions." And they took their positions against the city.

Ahab Defeats Ben-hadad

¹³ And behold, a prophet came near to Ahab king of Israel and said, "Thus says the LORD, Have you seen all this great multitude? Behold, I will give it into your hand this day, and you shall know that I am the LORD." ¹⁴ And Ahab said, "By whom?" He said, "Thus says the LORD, By the servants of the governors of the districts." Then he said, "Who shall begin the battle?" He answered, "You." ¹⁵ Then he mustered the servants of the governors of the districts, and they were 232. And after them he mustered all the people of Israel, seven thousand.

¹⁶ And they went out at noon, while Ben-hadad was drinking himself drunk in the booths, he and the thirty-two kings who helped him. ¹⁷ The servants of the governors of the districts went out first. And Ben-hadad sent out scouts, and they reported to him, "Men are coming out from Samaria." ¹⁸ He said, "If they have come out for peace, take them alive. Or if they have come out for war, take them alive."

¹⁹ So these went out of the city, the servants of the governors of the districts and the army that followed them. ²⁰ And each struck down his man. The Syrians fled, and Israel pursued them, but Ben-hadad king of Syria escaped on a horse with horsemen. ²¹ And the king of Israel went out and struck the horses and chariots, and struck the Syrians with a great blow.

²² Then the prophet came near to the king of Israel and said to him, "Come, strengthen yourself, and consider well what you have to do, for in the spring the king of Syria will come up against you."

²³ And the servants of the king of Syria said to him, "Their gods are gods of the hills, and so they were stronger than we. But let us fight against them in the plain, and surely we shall be stronger than they. ²⁴ And do this: remove the kings, each from his post, and put commanders in their places, ²⁵ and muster an army like the army that you have lost, horse for horse, and chariot for chariot. Then we will fight against them in the plain, and surely we shall be stronger than they." And he listened to their voice and did so.

Ahab Defeats Ben-hadad Again

²⁶ In the spring, Ben-hadad mustered the Syrians and went up to Aphek to fight against Israel. ²⁷ And the people of Israel were mustered and were provisioned and went against them. The people of Israel encamped before them like two little flocks of goats, but the Syrians filled the country. ²⁸ And a man of God came near and said to the king of Israel, "Thus says the LORD, 'Because the Syrians have said, "The LORD is a god of the hills but he is not a god of the valleys," therefore I will give all this great multitude into your hand, and you shall know that I am the LORD.'" ²⁹ And they encamped opposite one another seven days. Then on the seventh day the battle was joined. And the people of Israel struck down of the Syrians 100,000 foot soldiers in one day. ³⁰ And the rest fled into the city of Aphek, and the wall fell upon 27,000 men who were left.

Ben-hadad also fled and entered an inner chamber in the city. ³¹ And his servants said to him, "Behold now, we have heard that the kings of the house of Israel are merciful kings. Let us put sackcloth around our waists and ropes on our heads and go out to the king of Israel. Perhaps he will spare your life." ³² So they tied sackcloth around their waists and put ropes on their heads and went to the king of Israel and said, "Your servant Ben-hadad says, 'Please, let me live.'" And he said, "Does he still live? He is my brother." **33** Now the men were watching for a sign, and they quickly took it up from him and said, "Yes, your brother Ben-hadad." Then he said, "Go and bring him." Then Ben-hadad came out to him, and he caused him to come up into the chariot. **34** And Ben-hadad said to him, "The cities that my father took from your father I will restore, and you may establish bazaars for yourself in Damascus, as my father did in Samaria." And Ahab said, "I will let you go on these terms." So he made a covenant with him and let him go.

The word **bazaar** (20:34) meant "place of prices" in Persian. Bazaars were permanent places designated for merchants and traders to buy and sell goods. Either a part of one street or a whole district of a city would be used as a bazaar.

A Prophet Condemns Ben-hadad's Release

35 And a certain man of the sons of the prophets said to his fellow at the command of the LORD, "Strike me, please." But the man refused to strike him. **36** Then he said to him, "Because you have not obeyed the voice of the LORD, behold, as soon as you have gone from me, a lion shall strike you down." And as soon as he had departed from him, a lion met him and struck him down. **37** Then he found another man and said, "Strike me, please." And the man struck him—struck him and wounded him. **38** So the prophet departed and waited for the king by the way, disguising himself with a bandage over his eyes. **39** And as the king passed, he cried to the king and said, "Your servant went out into the midst of the battle, and behold, a soldier turned and brought a man to me and said, 'Guard this man; if by any means he is missing, your life shall be for his life, or else you shall pay a talent of silver.' **40** And as your servant was busy here and there, he was gone." The king of Israel said to him,

"So shall your judgment be; you yourself have decided it." **41** Then he hurried to take the bandage away from his eyes, and the king of Israel recognized him as one of the prophets. **42** And he said to him, "Thus says the LORD, 'Because you have let go out of your hand the man whom I had devoted to destruction, therefore your life shall be for his life, and your people for his people.'" **43** And the king of Israel went to his house vexed and sullen and came to Samaria.

PROFILE
JEZEBEL

Jezebel was the wife of King Ahab and the daughter of Ethbaal, king of Sidon. Because she was so wicked, her name, "Jezebel," has become synonymous with evil (Rev. 2:20). As queen of Israel, Jezebel acted with power and influenced King Ahab. She promoted the worship of Baal and ruthlessly killed many prophets of God. When she learned of the defeat of her false god on Mount Carmel (1 Kings 18:20–40), she tried to kill Elijah, forcing him to flee into the wilderness. When Ahab sulked because Naboth would not sell his vineyard to him, Jezebel arranged the murder of Naboth. Jezebel met a gruesome end when she was thrown from a window by her own servants and was eaten by dogs, in fulfillment of Elijah's prophecy (2 Kings 9:30–37).

KEY REFERENCE: 2 KINGS 9:36-37

Naboth's Vineyard

21 Now Naboth the Jezreelite had a vineyard in Jezreel, beside the palace of Ahab king of Samaria. **2** And after this Ahab said to Naboth, "Give me your vineyard, that I may have it for a vegetable garden, because it is near my house, and I will give you a better vineyard for it; or, if it seems good to you, I will give you its value in money." **3** But Naboth said to Ahab, "The LORD forbid that I should give you the inheritance of my fathers." **4** And Ahab went into his house vexed and sullen because of what Naboth the Jezreelite had said to him, for he had said, "I will not give you the inheritance of my fathers." And he lay down on his bed and turned away his face and would eat no food.

⁵ But Jezebel his wife came to him and said to him, "Why is your spirit so vexed that you eat no food?" ⁶ And he said to her, "Because I spoke to Naboth the Jezreelite and said to him, 'Give me your vineyard for money, or else, if it please you, I will give you another vineyard for it.' And he answered, 'I will not give you my vineyard.'" ⁷ And Jezebel his wife said to him, "Do you now govern Israel? Arise and eat bread and let your heart be cheerful; I will give you the vineyard of Naboth the Jezreelite."

⁸ So she wrote letters in Ahab's name and sealed them with his seal, and she sent the letters to the elders and the leaders who lived with Naboth in his city. ⁹ And she

> ### GETTING THE MESSAGE
>
> **Confiscation of land.** Israelite law did not allow the king to confiscate the land of an executed criminal. This was, however, a common practice outside of Israel. Perhaps Jezebel, who came from Tyre, based her plan to seize Naboth's vineyard on this practice.

wrote in the letters, "Proclaim a fast, and set Naboth at the head of the people. ¹⁰ And set two worthless men opposite him, and let them bring a charge against him, saying, 'You have cursed God and the king.' Then take him out and stone him to death." ¹¹ And the men of his city, the elders and the leaders who lived in his city, did as Jezebel had sent word to them. As it was written in the letters that she had sent to them, ¹² they proclaimed a fast and set Naboth at the head of the people. ¹³ And the two worthless men came in and sat opposite him. And the worthless men brought a charge against Naboth in the presence of the people, saying, "Naboth cursed God and the king." So they took him outside the city and stoned him to death with stones. ¹⁴ Then they sent to Jezebel, saying, "Naboth has been stoned; he is dead."

¹⁵ As soon as Jezebel heard that Naboth had been stoned and was dead, Jezebel said to Ahab, "Arise, take possession of the vineyard of Naboth the Jezreelite, which he refused to give you for money, for Naboth is not alive, but dead." ¹⁶ And as soon as Ahab heard that Naboth was dead, Ahab arose to go down to the vineyard of Naboth the Jezreelite, to take possession of it.

The LORD Condemns Ahab

¹⁷ Then the word of the LORD came to Elijah the Tishbite, saying, ¹⁸ "Arise, go down to meet Ahab king of Israel, who is in Samaria; behold, he is in the vineyard of Naboth, where he has gone to take possession. ¹⁹ And you shall say to him, 'Thus says the LORD, "Have you killed and also taken possession?"' And you shall say to him, 'Thus says the LORD: "In the place where dogs licked up the blood of Naboth shall dogs lick your own blood."'"

²⁰ Ahab said to Elijah, "Have you found me, O my enemy?" He answered, "I have found you, because you have sold yourself to do what is evil in the sight of the LORD. ²¹ Behold, I will bring disaster upon you. I will utterly burn you up, and will cut off from Ahab every male, bond or free, in Israel. ²² And I will make your house like the house of Jeroboam the son of Nebat, and like the house of Baasha the son of Ahijah, for the anger to which you have provoked me, and because you have made Israel to sin. ²³ And of Jezebel the LORD also said, 'The dogs shall eat Jezebel within the walls of Jezreel.' ²⁴ Anyone belonging to Ahab who dies in the city the dogs shall eat, and anyone of his who dies in the open country the birds of the heavens shall eat."

Ahab's Repentance

²⁵ (There was none who sold himself to do what was evil in the sight of the LORD like Ahab, whom Jezebel his wife incited. ²⁶ He acted very abominably in going after idols, as the Amorites had done, whom the LORD cast out before the people of Israel.)

²⁷ And when Ahab heard those words, he tore his clothes and put sackcloth on his flesh and fasted and lay in sackcloth and went about dejectedly. ²⁸ And the word of the LORD came to Elijah the Tishbite, saying, ²⁹ "Have you seen how Ahab has humbled himself before me? Because he has humbled himself before me, I will not bring the disaster in his days; but in his son's days I will bring the disaster upon his house."

Ahab and the False Prophets

22 For three years Syria and Israel continued without war. ² But in the third year Jehoshaphat the king of Judah came down to the king of Israel. ³ And the king of Israel said to his servants, "Do you know that Ramoth-gilead belongs to us, and we keep quiet and do not take it out of the hand of the king of Syria?" ⁴ And he said to Jehoshaphat, "Will you go with me to battle at Ramoth-gilead?" And Jehoshaphat said to the king of Israel, "I am as you are, my people as your people, my horses as your horses."

⁵ And Jehoshaphat said to the king of Israel, "Inquire first for the word of the LORD." ⁶ Then the king of Israel gathered the prophets together, about four hundred men, and said to them, "Shall I go to battle against Ramoth-gilead, or shall I refrain?" And they said, "Go up, for the Lord will give it into the hand of the king." ⁷ But Jehoshaphat said, "Is there not here another prophet of the LORD of whom we may inquire?" ⁸ And the king of Israel said to Jehoshaphat, "There is yet one man by whom we may inquire of the LORD, Micaiah the son of Imlah, but I hate him, for he never prophesies good concerning me, but evil." And Jehoshaphat said, "Let not the king say so." ⁹ Then the king of Israel summoned an officer and said, "Bring quickly Micaiah the son of Imlah." ¹⁰ Now the king of Israel and Jehoshaphat the king of Judah were sitting on their thrones, arrayed in their robes, at the threshing floor at the entrance of the gate of Samaria, and all the prophets were prophesying before them. ¹¹ And Zedekiah the son of Chenaanah made for himself horns of iron and said, "Thus says the LORD, 'With these you shall push the Syrians until they are destroyed.'" ¹² And all the prophets prophesied so and said, "Go up to Ramoth-gilead and triumph; the LORD will give it into the hand of the king."

Micaiah Prophesies Against Ahab

¹³ And the messenger who went to summon Micaiah said to him, "Behold, the words of the prophets with one accord are favorable to the king. Let your word be like the word of one of them, and speak favorably." ¹⁴ But Micaiah said, "As the LORD lives, what the LORD says to me, that I will speak." ¹⁵ And when he had come to the king, the king said to him, "Micaiah, shall we go to Ramoth-gilead to battle, or shall we refrain?" And he answered him, "Go up and triumph; the LORD will give it into the hand of the king." ¹⁶ But the king said to him, "How many times shall I make you swear that you speak to me nothing but the truth in the name of the LORD?" ¹⁷ And he said, "I saw all Israel scattered on the mountains, as sheep that have no shepherd. And the LORD said, 'These have no master; let each return to his home in peace.'" ¹⁸ And the king of Israel said to Jehoshaphat, "Did I not tell you that he would not prophesy good concerning me, but evil?" ¹⁹ And Micaiah said, "Therefore hear the word of the LORD: I saw the LORD sitting on his throne, and all the host of heaven standing beside him on his right hand and on his left; ²⁰ and the LORD said, 'Who will entice Ahab, that he may go up and fall at Ramoth-gilead?' And one said one thing, and another said another. ²¹ Then a spirit came forward and stood before the LORD, saying, 'I will entice him.' ²² And the LORD said to him, 'By what means?' And he said, 'I will go out, and will be a lying spirit in the mouth of all his prophets.' And he said, 'You are to entice him, and you shall succeed; go out and do so.' ²³ Now therefore behold, the LORD has put a lying spirit in the mouth of all these your prophets; the LORD has declared disaster for you."

²⁴ Then Zedekiah the son of Chenaanah came near and struck Micaiah on the cheek and said, "How did the Spirit of the LORD go from me to speak to you?" ²⁵ And Micaiah said, "Behold, you shall see on that day when you go into an inner chamber to hide yourself." ²⁶ And the king of Israel said, "Seize Micaiah, and take him back to Amon the governor of the city and to Joash the king's son, ²⁷ and say, 'Thus says the king, "Put this fellow in prison and feed him meager rations of bread and water, until I come in peace."'" ²⁸ And Micaiah said, "If you return in peace, the LORD has not spoken by me." And he said, "Hear, all you peoples!"

Ahab Killed in Battle

²⁹ So the king of Israel and Jehoshaphat the king of Judah went up to Ramoth-gilead. ³⁰ And the king of Israel said to Jehoshaphat, "I will disguise myself and go into battle, but you wear your robes." And the king of Israel disguised himself and went into

battle. **31** Now the king of Syria had commanded the thirty-two captains of his chariots, "Fight with neither small nor great, but only with the king of Israel." **32** And when the captains of the chariots saw Jehoshaphat, they said, "It is surely the king of Israel." So they turned to fight against him. And Jehoshaphat cried out. **33** And when the captains of the chariots saw that it was not the king of Israel, they turned back from pursuing him. **34** But a certain man drew his bow at random and struck the king of Israel between the scale armor and the breastplate. Therefore he said to the driver of his chariot, "Turn around and carry me out of the battle, for I am wounded." **35** And the battle continued that day, and the king was propped

> ### ▶ GETTING THE MESSAGE

Ahab's ivory palace. Archaeologists have discovered remains of Ahab's palace (22:39) in Samaria. Beautifully carved ivory fragments with Egyptian and Phoenician designs were found where its main floors and courtyard would have been.

up in his chariot facing the Syrians, until at evening he died. And the blood of the wound flowed into the bottom of the chariot. **36** And about sunset a cry went through the army, "Every man to his city, and every man to his country!"

37 So the king died, and was brought to Samaria. And they buried the king in Samaria. **38** And they washed the chariot by the pool of Samaria, and the dogs licked up his blood, and the prostitutes washed themselves in it, according to the word of the LORD that he had spoken. **39** Now the rest of the acts of Ahab and all that he did, and the ivory house that he built and all the cities that he built, are they not written in the Book of the Chronicles of the Kings of

Israel? **40** So Ahab slept with his fathers, and Ahaziah his son reigned in his place.

Jehoshaphat Reigns in Judah

41 Jehoshaphat the son of Asa began to reign over Judah in the fourth year of Ahab king of Israel. **42** Jehoshaphat was thirty-five years old when he began to reign, and he reigned twenty-five years in Jerusalem. His mother's name was Azubah the daughter of Shilhi. **43** He walked in all the way of Asa his father. He did not turn aside from it, doing what was right in the sight of the LORD. Yet the high places were not taken away, and the people still sacrificed and made offerings on the high places. **44** Jehoshaphat also made peace with the king of Israel.

45 Now the rest of the acts of Jehoshaphat, and his might that he showed, and how he warred, are they not written in the Book of the Chronicles of the Kings of Judah? **46** And from the land he exterminated the remnant of the male cult prostitutes who remained in the days of his father Asa.

47 There was no king in Edom; a deputy was king. **48** Jehoshaphat made ships of Tarshish to go to Ophir for gold, but they did not go, for the ships were wrecked at Ezion-geber. **49** Then Ahaziah the son of Ahab said to Jehoshaphat, "Let my servants go with your servants in the ships," but Jehoshaphat was not willing. **50** And Jehoshaphat slept with his fathers and was buried with his fathers in the city of David his father, and Jehoram his son reigned in his place.

Ahaziah Reigns in Israel

51 Ahaziah the son of Ahab began to reign over Israel in Samaria in the seventeenth year of Jehoshaphat king of Judah, and he reigned two years over Israel. **52** He did what was evil in the sight of the LORD and walked in the way of his father and in the way of his mother and in the way of Jeroboam the son of Nebat, who made Israel to sin. **53** He served Baal and worshiped him and provoked the LORD, the God of Israel, to anger in every way that his father had done.

2 KINGS

Elijah Denounces Ahaziah

1 After the death of Ahab, Moab rebelled against Israel.

2 Now Ahaziah fell through the lattice in his upper chamber in Samaria, and lay sick; so he sent messengers, telling them, "Go, inquire of Baal-zebub, the god of Ekron, whether I shall recover from this sickness." 3 But the angel of the LORD said to Elijah the Tishbite, "Arise, go up to meet the messengers of the king of Samaria, and say to them, 'Is it because there is no God in Israel that you are going to inquire of Baal-zebub, the god of Ekron? 4 Now therefore thus says the LORD, You shall not come down from the bed to which you have gone up, but you shall surely die.'" So Elijah went.

5 The messengers returned to the king, and he said to them, "Why have you returned?" 6 And they said to him, "There came a man to meet us, and said to us, 'Go back to the king who sent you, and say to him, Thus says the LORD, Is it because there is no God in Israel that you are sending to inquire of Baal-zebub, the god of Ekron? Therefore you shall not come down from the bed to which you have gone up, but you shall surely die.'" 7 He said to them, "What kind of man was he who came to meet you and told you these things?" 8 They answered him, "He wore a garment of hair, with a belt of leather about his waist." And he said, "It is Elijah the Tishbite."

9 Then the king sent to him a captain of fifty men with his fifty. He went up to Elijah, who was sitting on the top of a hill, and said to him, "O man of God, the king says, 'Come down.'" 10 But Elijah answered the captain of fifty, "If I am a man of God, let fire come down from heaven and consume you and your fifty." Then fire came down from heaven and consumed him and his fifty.

11 Again the king sent to him another captain of fifty men with his fifty. And he answered and said to him, "O man of God, this is the king's order, 'Come down quickly!'" 12 But Elijah answered them, "If I am a man of God, let fire come down from heaven and consume you and your fifty." Then the fire of God came down from heaven and consumed him and his fifty.

13 Again the king sent the captain of a third fifty with his fifty. And the third captain of fifty went up and came and fell on his knees before Elijah and entreated him, "O man of God, please let my life, and the life of these fifty servants of yours, be precious in your sight. 14 Behold, fire came down from heaven and consumed the two former captains of fifty men with their fifties, but now let my life be precious in your sight." 15 Then the angel of the LORD said to Elijah, "Go down with him; do not be afraid of

him." So he arose and went down with him to the king 16 and said to him, "Thus says the LORD, 'Because you have sent messengers to inquire of Baal-zebub, the god of Ekron—is it because there is no God in Israel to inquire of his word?—therefore you shall not come down from the bed to which you have gone up, but you shall surely die.'"

17 So he died according to the word of the LORD that Elijah had spoken. Jehoram became king in his place in the second year of Jehoram the son of Jehoshaphat, king of Judah, because Ahaziah had no son. 18 Now the rest of the acts of Ahaziah that he did, are they not written in the Book of the Chronicles of the Kings of Israel?

Elijah Taken to Heaven

2 Now when the LORD was about to take Elijah up to heaven by a whirlwind, Elijah and Elisha were on their way from Gilgal. 2 And Elijah said to Elisha, "Please

stay here, for the LORD has sent me as far as Bethel." But Elisha said, "As the LORD lives, and as you yourself live, I will not leave you." So they went down to Bethel. ³ And the sons of the prophets who were in Bethel came out to Elisha and said to him, "Do you know that today the LORD will take away your master from over you?" And he said, "Yes, I know it; keep quiet."

⁴ Elijah said to him, "Elisha, please stay here, for the LORD has sent me to Jericho." But he said, "As the LORD lives, and as you yourself live, I will not leave you." So they came to Jericho. ⁵ The sons of the prophets who were at Jericho drew near to Elisha and said to him, "Do you know that today the LORD will take away your master from over you?" And he answered, "Yes, I know it; keep quiet."

GETTING THE MESSAGE

Though **bears** no longer live in the region of Palestine, the bear God used to punish the disrespectful boys (2:24) was probably of a type that could grow up to 7 feet (2 m) tall and reach 500 pounds (227 kg).

⁶ Then Elijah said to him, "Please stay here, for the LORD has sent me to the Jordan." But he said, "As the LORD lives, and as you yourself live, I will not leave you." So the two of them went on. ⁷ Fifty men of the sons of the prophets also went and stood at some distance from them, as they both were standing by the Jordan. ⁸ Then Elijah took his cloak and rolled it up and struck the water, and the water was parted to the one side and to the other, till the two of them could go over on dry ground.

⁹ When they had crossed, Elijah said to Elisha, "Ask what I shall do for you, before I am taken from you." And Elisha said, "Please let there be a double portion of your spirit on me." ¹⁰ And he said, "You have asked a hard thing; yet, if you see me as I am being taken from you, it shall be so for you, but if you do not see me, it shall not be so." ¹¹ And as they still went on and talked, behold, chariots of fire and horses of fire separated the two of them. And Elijah went up by a whirlwind into heaven. ¹² And Elisha saw

it and he cried, "My father, my father! The chariots of Israel and its horsemen!" And he saw him no more.

Then he took hold of his own clothes and tore them in two pieces. ¹³ And he took up the cloak of Elijah that had fallen from him and went back and stood on the bank of the Jordan. ¹⁴ Then he took the cloak of Elijah that had fallen from him and struck the water, saying, "Where is the LORD, the God of Elijah?" And when he had struck the water, the water was parted to the one side and to the other, and Elisha went over.

PROFILE
ELISHA

Elisha was Elijah's disciple and assistant and, eventually, his successor. He served as a prophet for 55 years and became famous for the many miracles he performed. Among these miracles was the healing of Naaman, the commander of the Syrian army. Naaman was a leper and came to Israel seeking to be healed. Elisha told him to wash in the Jordan River seven times. At first, Naaman felt insulted by these simple instructions, but when he finally obeyed, he was healed instantly. Elisha's God-given power did not end at his death. When a fallen soldier was thrown into Elisha's grave, the soldier came back to life as soon as his body came into contact with the prophet's bones (13:20–21).

KEY REFERENCE: 2 KINGS 5:8-14

Elisha Succeeds Elijah

¹⁵ Now when the sons of the prophets who were at Jericho saw him opposite them, they said, "The spirit of Elijah rests on Elisha." And they came to meet him and bowed to the ground before him. ¹⁶ And they said to him, "Behold now, there are with your servants fifty strong men. Please let them go and seek your master. It may be that the Spirit of the LORD has caught him up and cast him upon some mountain or into some valley." And he said, "You shall not send." ¹⁷ But when they urged him till he was ashamed, he said, "Send." They sent

therefore fifty men. And for three days they sought him but did not find him. [18] And they came back to him while he was staying at Jericho, and he said to them, "Did I not say to you, 'Do not go'?"

[19] Now the men of the city said to Elisha, "Behold, the situation of this city is pleasant, as my lord sees, but the water is bad, and the land is unfruitful." [20] He said, "Bring me a new bowl, and put salt in it." So they brought it to him. [21] Then he went to the spring of water and threw salt in it and said, "Thus says the LORD, I have healed this water; from now on neither death nor miscarriage shall come from it." [22] So the water has been healed to this day, according to the word that Elisha spoke.

GETTING THE MESSAGE

The Moabite Stone is a small monument inscribed with details about the conflict between the Israelites and the Moabites (3:4–27). Written by the Moabites, it emphasizes their victories over Israel. More importantly, it features the earliest known reference to the Lord's personal name (YHWH; see footnote on Gen. 2:4) outside of the Bible.

[23] He went up from there to Bethel, and while he was going up on the way, some small boys came out of the city and jeered at him, saying, "Go up, you baldhead! Go up, you baldhead!" [24] And he turned around, and when he saw them, he cursed them in the name of the LORD. And two she-bears came out of the woods and tore forty-two of the boys. [25] From there he went on to Mount Carmel, and from there he returned to Samaria.

Moab Rebels Against Israel

3 In the eighteenth year of Jehoshaphat king of Judah, Jehoram the son of Ahab became king over Israel in Samaria, and he reigned twelve years. [2] He did what was evil in the sight of the LORD, though not like his father and mother, for he put away the pillar of Baal that his father had made. [3] Nevertheless, he clung to the sin of Jeroboam the son of Nebat, which he made Israel to sin; he did not depart from it.

[4] Now Mesha king of Moab was a sheep breeder, and he had to deliver to the king of Israel 100,000 lambs and the wool of 100,000 rams. [5] But when Ahab died, the king of Moab rebelled against the king of Israel. [6] So King Jehoram marched out of Samaria at that time and mustered all Israel. [7] And he went and sent word to Jehoshaphat king of Judah, "The king of Moab has rebelled against me. Will you go with me to battle against Moab?" And he said, "I will go. I am as you are, my people as your people, my horses as your horses." [8] Then he said, "By which way shall we march?" Jehoram answered, "By the way of the wilderness of Edom."

[9] So the king of Israel went with the king of Judah and the king of Edom. And when they had made a circuitous march of seven days, there was no water for the army or for the animals that followed them. [10] Then the king of Israel said, "Alas! The LORD has called these three kings to give them into the hand of Moab." [11] And Jehoshaphat said, "Is there no prophet of the LORD here, through whom we may inquire of the LORD?" Then one of the king of Israel's servants answered, "Elisha the son of Shaphat is here, who poured water on the hands of Elijah." [12] And Jehoshaphat said, "The word of the LORD is with him." So the king of Israel and Jehoshaphat and the king of Edom went down to him.

[13] And Elisha said to the king of Israel, "What have I to do with you? Go to the prophets of your father and to the prophets of your mother." But the king of Israel said to him, "No; it is the LORD who has called these three kings to give them into the hand of Moab." [14] And Elisha said, "As the LORD of hosts lives, before whom I stand, were it not that I have regard for Jehoshaphat the king of Judah, I would neither look at you nor see you. [15] But now bring me a musician." And when the musician played, the hand of the LORD came upon him. [16] And he said, "Thus says the LORD, 'I will make this dry streambed full of pools.' [17] For thus says the LORD, 'You shall not see wind or rain, but that streambed shall be filled with water, so that you shall drink, you, your livestock, and your animals.' [18] This is a light thing in the sight of the LORD. He will also give the Moabites into your hand, [19] and you shall attack every fortified city and every choice

city, and shall fell every good tree and stop up all springs of water and ruin every good piece of land with stones." ²⁰ The next morning, about the time of offering the sacrifice, behold, water came from the direction of Edom, till the country was filled with water.

²¹ When all the Moabites heard that the kings had come up to fight against them, all who were able to put on armor, from the youngest to the oldest, were called out and were drawn up at the border. ²² And when they rose early in the morning and the sun shone on the water, the Moabites saw the water opposite them as red as blood. ²³ And they said, "This is blood; the kings have surely fought together and struck one another down. Now then, Moab, to the spoil!" ²⁴ But when they came to the camp of Israel, the Israelites rose and struck the Moabites, till they fled before them. And they went forward, striking the Moabites as they went. ²⁵ And they overthrew the cities, and on every good piece of land every man threw a stone until it was covered. They stopped every spring of water and felled all the good trees, till only its stones were left in Kir-hareseth, and the slingers surrounded and attacked it. ²⁶ When the king of Moab saw that the battle was going against him, he took with him 700 swordsmen to break through, opposite the king of Edom, but they could not. ²⁷ Then he took his oldest son who was to reign in his place and offered him for a burnt offering on the wall. And there came great wrath against Israel. And they withdrew from him and returned to their own land.

Elisha and the Widow's Oil

4 Now the wife of one of the sons of the prophets cried to Elisha, "Your servant my husband is dead, and you know that your servant feared the LORD, but the creditor has come to take my two children to be his slaves." ² And Elisha said to her, "What shall I do for you? Tell me; what have you in the house?" And she said, "Your servant has nothing in the house except a jar of oil." ³ Then he said, "Go outside, borrow vessels from all your neighbors, empty vessels and not too few. ⁴ Then go in and shut the door behind yourself and your sons and pour into all these vessels. And when one is full, set it aside." ⁵ So she went from him and shut the door behind herself and her sons. And

as she poured they brought the vessels to her. ⁶ When the vessels were full, she said to her son, "Bring me another vessel." And he said to her, "There is not another." Then the oil stopped flowing. ⁷ She came and told the man of God, and he said, "Go, sell the oil and pay your debts, and you and your sons can live on the rest."

Elisha and the Shunammite Woman

⁸ One day Elisha went on to Shunem, where a wealthy woman lived, who urged him to eat some food. So whenever he passed that way, he would turn in there to eat food. ⁹ And she said to her husband, "Behold now, I know that this is a holy man of God who is continually passing our way. ¹⁰ Let us make a small room on the roof with walls and put there for him a bed, a table, a chair, and a lamp, so that whenever he comes to us, he can go in there."

¹¹ One day he came there, and he turned into the chamber and rested there. ¹² And he said to Gehazi his servant, "Call this Shunammite." When he had called her, she stood before him. ¹³ And he said to him, "Say now to her, 'See, you have taken all this trouble for us; what is to be done for you? Would you have a word spoken on your behalf to the king or to the commander of the army?'" She answered, "I dwell among my own people." ¹⁴ And he said, "What then is to be done for her?" Gehazi answered, "Well, she has no son, and her husband is old." ¹⁵ He said, "Call her." And when he had called her, she stood in the doorway. ¹⁶ And he said, "At this season, about this time next year, you shall embrace a son." And she said, "No, my lord, O man of God; do not lie to your servant." ¹⁷ But the woman conceived, and she bore a son about that time the following spring, as Elisha had said to her.

Elisha Raises the Shunammite's Son

¹⁸ When the child had grown, he went out one day to his father among the reapers. ¹⁹ And he said to his father, "Oh, my head, my head!" The father said to his servant, "Carry him to his mother." ²⁰ And when he had lifted him and brought him to his mother, the child sat on her lap till noon, and then he died. ²¹ And she went up and laid him on the bed of the man of God and shut the door behind him and went out. ²² Then she called to her husband and said,

"Send me one of the servants and one of the donkeys, that I may quickly go to the man of God and come back again." **23** And he said, "Why will you go to him today? It is neither new moon nor Sabbath." She said, "All is well." **24** Then she saddled the donkey, and she said to her servant, "Urge the animal on; do not slacken the pace for me unless I tell you." **25** So she set out and came to the man of God at Mount Carmel.

When the man of God saw her coming, he said to Gehazi his servant, "Look, there is the Shunammite. **26** Run at once to meet her and say to her, 'Is all well with you? Is all well with your husband? Is all well with the child?'" And she answered, "All is well." **27** And when she came to the mountain to the man of God, she caught hold of his feet. And Gehazi came to push her away. But the man of God said, "Leave her alone, for she is in bitter distress, and the LORD has hidden

GETTING THE MESSAGE

The **wild gourds** gathered by the prophet (4:38–41) were poisonous. The prophet, of course, did not realize this. He added the gourds to the stew, "not knowing what they were" (4:39).

it from me and has not told me." **28** Then she said, "Did I ask my lord for a son? Did I not say, 'Do not deceive me?'" **29** He said to Gehazi, "Tie up your garment and take my staff in your hand and go. If you meet anyone, do not greet him, and if anyone greets you, do not reply. And lay my staff on the face of the child." **30** Then the mother of the child said, "As the LORD lives and as you yourself live, I will not leave you." So he arose and followed her. **31** Gehazi went on ahead and laid the staff on the face of the child, but there was no sound or sign of life. Therefore he returned to meet him and told him, "The child has not awakened." **32** When Elisha came into the house, he saw the child lying dead on his bed. **33** So he went in and shut the door behind the two of them and prayed to the LORD. **34** Then he went up and lay on the child, putting his mouth on his mouth, his eyes on his eyes, and his hands on his hands. And as

he stretched himself upon him, the flesh of the child became warm. **35** Then he got up again and walked once back and forth in the house, and went up and stretched himself upon him. The child sneezed seven times, and the child opened his eyes. **36** Then he summoned Gehazi and said, "Call this Shunammite." So he called her. And when she came to him, he said, "Pick up your son." **37** She came and fell at his feet, bowing to the ground. Then she picked up her son and went out.

Elisha Purifies the Deadly Stew

38 And Elisha came again to Gilgal when there was a famine in the land. And as the sons of the prophets were sitting before him, he said to his servant, "Set on the large pot, and boil stew for the sons of the prophets." **39** One of them went out into the field to gather herbs, and found a wild vine and gathered from it his lap full of wild gourds, and came and cut them up into the pot of stew, not knowing what they were. **40** And they poured out some for the men to eat. But while they were eating of the stew, they cried out, "O man of God, there is death in the pot!" And they could not eat it. **41** He said, "Then bring flour." And he threw it into the pot and said, "Pour some out for the men, that they may eat." And there was no harm in the pot.

42 A man came from Baal-shalishah, bringing the man of God bread of the first-fruits, twenty loaves of barley and fresh ears of grain in his sack. And Elisha said, "Give to the men, that they may eat." **43** But his servant said, "How can I set this before a hundred men?" So he repeated, "Give them to the men, that they may eat, for thus says the LORD, 'They shall eat and have some left.'" **44** So he set it before them. And they ate and had some left, according to the word of the LORD.

Naaman Healed of Leprosy

5 Naaman, commander of the army of the king of Syria, was a great man with his master and in high favor, because by him the LORD had given victory to Syria. He was a mighty man of valor, but he was a leper.[1] **2** Now the Syrians on one of their raids had carried off a little girl from the land of Israel, and she worked in the service of Naaman's

[1] *Leprosy* was a term for several skin diseases (see Leviticus 13)

wife. [3] She said to her mistress, "Would that my lord were with the prophet who is in Samaria! He would cure him of his leprosy." [4] So Naaman went in and told his lord, "Thus and so spoke the girl from the land of Israel." [5] And the king of Syria said, "Go now, and I will send a letter to the king of Israel."

So he went, taking with him ten talents of silver, six thousand shekels of gold, and ten changes of clothing. [6] And he brought the letter to the king of Israel, which read, "When this letter reaches you, know that I have sent to you Naaman my servant, that you may cure him of his leprosy." [7] And when the king of Israel read the letter, he tore his clothes and said, "Am I God, to kill and to make alive, that this man sends word to me to cure a man of his leprosy? Only consider, and see how he is seeking a quarrel with me."

[8] But when Elisha the man of God heard that the king of Israel had torn his clothes, he sent to the king, saying, "Why have you torn your clothes? Let him come now to me, that he may know that there is a prophet in Israel." [9] So Naaman came with his horses and chariots and stood at the door of Elisha's house. [10] And Elisha sent a messenger to him, saying, "Go and wash in the Jordan seven times, and your flesh shall be restored, and you shall be clean." [11] But Naaman was angry and went away, saying, "Behold, I thought that he would surely come out to me and stand and call upon the name of the LORD his God, and wave his hand over the place and cure the leper. [12] Are not Abana and Pharpar, the rivers of Damascus, better than all the waters of Israel? Could I not wash in them and be clean?" So he turned and went away in a rage. [13] But his servants came near and said to him, "My father, it is a great word the prophet has spoken to you; will you not do it? Has he actually said to you, 'Wash, and be clean'?" [14] So he went down and dipped himself seven times in the Jordan, according to the word of the man of God, and his flesh was restored like the flesh of a little child, and he was clean.

Gehazi's Greed and Punishment

[15] Then he returned to the man of God, he and all his company, and he came and stood before him. And he said, "Behold, I know that there is no God in all the earth but in Israel; so accept now a present from your servant." [16] But he said, "As the LORD lives, before whom I stand, I will receive none." And he urged him to take it, but he refused. [17] Then Naaman said, "If not, please let there be given to your servant two mule loads of earth, for from now on your servant will not offer burnt offering or sacrifice to any god but the LORD. [18] In this matter may the LORD pardon your servant: when my master goes into the house of Rimmon to worship there, leaning on my arm, and I bow myself in the house of Rimmon, when I bow myself in the house of Rimmon, the LORD pardon your servant in this matter." [19] He said to him, "Go in peace."

But when Naaman had gone from him a short distance, [20] Gehazi, the servant of Elisha the man of God, said, "See, my master has spared this Naaman the Syrian, in not

accepting from his hand what he brought. As the LORD lives, I will run after him and get something from him." [21] So Gehazi followed Naaman. And when Naaman saw someone running after him, he got down from the chariot to meet him and said, "Is all well?" [22] And he said, "All is well. My master has sent me to say, 'There have just now come to me from the hill country of Ephraim two young men of the sons of the prophets. Please give them a talent of silver and two changes of clothing.'" [23] And Naaman said, "Be pleased to accept two talents." And he urged him and tied up two talents of silver in two bags, with two changes of clothing, and laid them on two of his servants. And they carried them before Gehazi. [24] And when he came to the hill, he took them from their hand and put them in the house, and he sent the men away, and they departed. [25] He went in and stood before his master, and Elisha said to him, "Where have you been, Gehazi?" And he said, "Your servant went nowhere." **26** But he said to him, "Did not my heart go when the man turned from his chariot to meet you? Was it a time to accept money and garments, olive orchards and vineyards, sheep and oxen, male servants and female servants? **27** Therefore the leprosy of Naaman shall cling to you and to your descendants forever." So he went out from his presence a leper, like snow.

The Axe Head Recovered

6 Now the sons of the prophets said to Elisha, "See, the place where we dwell under your charge is too small for us. **2** Let us go to the Jordan and each of us get there a log, and let us make a place for us to dwell there." And he answered, "Go." **3** Then one of them said, "Be pleased to go with your servants." And he answered, "I will go." **4** So he went with them. And when they came to the Jordan, they cut down trees. **5** But as one was felling a log, his axe head fell into the water, and he cried out, "Alas, my master! It was borrowed." **6** Then the man of God said, "Where did it fall?" When he showed him the place, he cut off a stick and threw it in there and made the iron float. **7** And he said, "Take it up." So he reached out his hand and took it.

Horses and Chariots of Fire

8 Once when the king of Syria was warring against Israel, he took counsel with his servants, saying, "At such and such a place shall be my camp." **9** But the man of God sent word to the king of Israel, "Beware that you do not pass this place, for the Syrians are going down there." **10** And the king of Israel sent to the place about which the man of God told him. Thus he used to warn him, so that he saved himself there more than once or twice.

11 And the mind of the king of Syria was greatly troubled because of this thing, and he called his servants and said to them, "Will you not show me who of us is for the king of Israel?" **12** And one of his servants said, "None, my lord, O king; but Elisha, the prophet who is in Israel, tells the king of Israel the words that you speak in your bedroom." **13** And he said, "Go and see where he is, that I may send and seize him." It was told him, "Behold, he is in Dothan." **14** So he sent there horses and chariots and a

great army, and they came by night and surrounded the city.

15 When the servant of the man of God rose early in the morning and went out, behold, an army with horses and chariots was all around the city. And the servant said, "Alas, my master! What shall we do?" **16** He said, "Do not be afraid, for those who are with us are more than those who are with them." **17** Then Elisha prayed and said, "O Lord, please open his eyes that he may see." So the Lord opened the eyes of the young man, and he saw, and behold, the mountain was full of horses and chariots of fire all around Elisha. **18** And when the Syrians came down against him, Elisha prayed to the Lord and said, "Please strike this people with blindness." So he struck them with blindness in accordance with the prayer of Elisha. **19** And Elisha said to them, "This is not the way, and this is not the city. Follow me, and I will bring you to the man whom you seek." And he led them to Samaria.

20 As soon as they entered Samaria, Elisha said, "O Lord, open the eyes of these men, that they may see." So the Lord opened their eyes and they saw, and behold, they were in the midst of Samaria. **21** As soon as the king of Israel saw them, he said to Elisha, "My father, shall I strike them down? Shall I strike them down?" **22** He answered, "You shall not strike them down. Would you strike down those whom you have taken captive with your sword and with your bow? Set bread and water before them, that they may eat and drink and go to their master." **23** So he prepared for them a great feast, and when they had eaten and drunk, he sent them away, and they went to their master. And the Syrians did not come again on raids into the land of Israel.

Ben-hadad's Siege of Samaria

24 Afterward Ben-hadad king of Syria mustered his entire army and went up and besieged Samaria. **25** And there was a great famine in Samaria, as they besieged it, until a donkey's head was sold for eighty shekels of silver, and the fourth part of a kab of dove's dung for five shekels of silver. **26** Now as the king of Israel was passing by on the wall, a woman cried out to him, saying, "Help, my lord, O king!" **27** And he said, "If the Lord will not help you, how shall I help you? From the threshing floor, or from the winepress?" **28** And the king asked her, "What is your trouble?" She answered, "This woman said to me, 'Give your son, that we may eat him today, and we will eat my son tomorrow.' **29** So we boiled my son and ate him. And on the next day I said to her, 'Give your son, that we may eat him.' But she has hidden her son." **30** When the king heard the words of the woman, he tore his clothes—now he was passing by on the wall—and the people looked, and behold, he had sackcloth beneath on his body— **31** and he said, "May God do so to me and more also, if the head of Elisha the son of Shaphat remains on his shoulders today."

32 Elisha was sitting in his house, and the elders were sitting with him. Now the king had dispatched a man from his presence, but before the messenger arrived Elisha said to the elders, "Do you see how this murderer has sent to take off my head? Look, when the messenger comes, shut the door and hold the door fast against him. Is not the sound of his master's feet behind him?" **33** And while he was still speaking with them, the messenger came down to him and said, "This trouble is from the LORD! Why should I wait for the LORD any longer?"

Elisha Promises Food

7 But Elisha said, "Hear the word of the LORD: thus says the LORD, Tomorrow about this time a seah of fine flour shall be sold for a shekel, and two seahs of barley for a shekel, at the gate of Samaria." **2** Then the captain on whose hand the king leaned said to the man of God, "If the LORD himself should make windows in heaven, could this thing be?" But he said, "You shall see it with your own eyes, but you shall not eat of it."

The Syrians Flee

3 Now there were four men who were lepers[1] at the entrance to the gate. And they said to one another, "Why are we sitting here until we die? **4** If we say, 'Let us enter the city,' the famine is in the city, and we shall die there. And if we sit here, we die also. So now come, let us go over to the camp of the Syrians. If they spare our lives we shall live, and if they kill us we shall but die." **5** So they arose at twilight to go to the camp of the Syrians. But when they came to the edge of the camp of the Syrians, behold, there was

no one there. **6** For the Lord had made the army of the Syrians hear the sound of chariots and of horses, the sound of a great army, so that they said to one another, "Behold, the king of Israel has hired against us the kings of the Hittites and the kings of Egypt to come against us." **7** So they fled away in the twilight and abandoned their tents, their horses, and their donkeys, leaving the camp as it was, and fled for their lives. **8** And when these lepers came to the edge of the camp, they went into a tent and ate and drank, and they carried off silver and gold and clothing and went and hid them. Then they came back and entered another tent and carried off things from it and went and hid them.

9 Then they said to one another, "We are not doing right. This day is a day of good

> ### GETTING THE MESSAGE
>
> **What is a siege?** In ancient times, a "siege" occurred when an enemy army surrounded a city and demanded that it surrender. If the city refused, the invaders cut off food and water supplies and attempted to tear down the city's defensive walls. Cities usually surrendered when they ran out of water. Those who fought to the end faced terrible consequences when their enemies finally overwhelmed them (6:24–7:20; 17:5; 25:1–2).

news. If we are silent and wait until the morning light, punishment will overtake us. Now therefore come; let us go and tell the king's household." **10** So they came and called to the gatekeepers of the city and told them, "We came to the camp of the Syrians, and behold, there was no one to be seen or heard there, nothing but the horses tied and the donkeys tied and the tents as they were." **11** Then the gatekeepers called out, and it was told within the king's household. **12** And the king rose in the night and said to his servants, "I will tell you what the Syrians have done to us. They know that we are hungry. Therefore they have gone out of the camp to hide themselves in the open country, thinking, 'When they come out of the city, we shall take them alive and get into the

---

[1] *Leprosy* was a term for several skin diseases (see Leviticus 13)

city.'" ¹³ And one of his servants said, "Let some men take five of the remaining horses, seeing that those who are left here will fare like the whole multitude of Israel who have already perished. Let us send and see." ¹⁴ So they took two horsemen, and the king sent them after the army of the Syrians, saying, "Go and see." ¹⁵ So they went after them as far as the Jordan, and behold, all the way was littered with garments and equipment that the Syrians had thrown away in their haste. And the messengers returned and told the king.

¹⁶ Then the people went out and plundered the camp of the Syrians. So a seah of fine flour was sold for a shekel, and two seahs of barley for a shekel, according to the word of the LORD. ¹⁷ Now the king had appointed the captain on whose hand he leaned to have charge of the gate. And the people trampled him in the gate, so that he died, as the man of God had said when the king came down to him. ¹⁸ For when the man of God

> **GETTING THE MESSAGE**
>
> A **seah** is a dry measurement equal to about 7 quarts or 7.7 liters.

had said to the king, "Two seahs of barley shall be sold for a shekel, and a seah of fine flour for a shekel, about this time tomorrow in the gate of Samaria," ¹⁹ the captain had answered the man of God, "If the LORD himself should make windows in heaven, could such a thing be?" And he had said, "You shall see it with your own eyes, but you shall not eat of it." ²⁰ And so it happened to him, for the people trampled him in the gate and he died.

The Shunammite's Land Restored

8 Now Elisha had said to the woman whose son he had restored to life, "Arise, and depart with your household, and sojourn wherever you can, for the LORD has called for a famine, and it will come upon the land for seven years." ² So the woman arose and did according to the word of the man of God. She went with her household and sojourned in the land of the Philistines seven years. ³ And at the end of the seven years, when the woman returned from the land of the Philistines, she went to appeal to the king for her house and her land. ⁴ Now the king was talking with Gehazi the servant of the man of God, saying, "Tell me all the great things that Elisha has done." ⁵ And while he was telling the king how Elisha had restored the dead to life, behold, the woman whose son he had restored to life appealed to the king for her house and her land. And Gehazi said, "My lord, O king, here is the woman, and here is her son whom Elisha restored to life." ⁶ And when the king asked the woman, she told him. So the king appointed an official for her, saying, "Restore all that was hers, together with all the produce of the fields from the day that she left the land until now."

Hazael Murders Ben-hadad

⁷ Now Elisha came to Damascus. Ben-hadad the king of Syria was sick. And when it was told him, "The man of God has come here," ⁸ the king said to Hazael, "Take a present with you and go to meet the man of God, and inquire of the LORD through him, saying, 'Shall I recover from this sickness?'" ⁹ So Hazael went to meet him, and took a present with him, all kinds of goods of Damascus, forty camels' loads. When he came and stood before him, he said, "Your son Ben-hadad king of Syria has sent me to you, saying, 'Shall I recover from this sickness?'" ¹⁰ And Elisha said to him, "Go, say to him, 'You shall certainly recover,' but the LORD has shown me that he shall certainly die." ¹¹ And he fixed his gaze and stared at him, until he was embarrassed. And the man of God wept. ¹² And Hazael said, "Why does my lord weep?" He answered, "Because I know the evil that you will do to the people of Israel. You will set on fire their fortresses, and you will kill their young men with the sword and dash in pieces their little ones and rip open their pregnant women." ¹³ And Hazael said, "What is your servant, who is but a dog, that he should do this great thing?" Elisha answered, "The LORD has shown me that you are to be king over Syria." ¹⁴ Then he departed from Elisha and came to his master, who said to him, "What did Elisha say to you?" And he answered, "He told me that you would certainly recover." ¹⁵ But the next day he took the bed cloth and dipped it in water and spread it over his face, till he died. And Hazael became king in his place.

Jehoram Reigns in Judah

[16] In the fifth year of Joram the son of Ahab, king of Israel, when Jehoshaphat was king of Judah, Jehoram the son of Jehoshaphat, king of Judah, began to reign. [17] He was thirty-two years old when he became king, and he reigned eight years in Jerusalem. [18] And he walked in the way of the kings of Israel, as the house of Ahab had done, for the daughter of Ahab was his wife. And he did what was evil in the sight of the LORD. [19] Yet the LORD was not willing to destroy Judah, for the sake of David his servant, since he promised to give a lamp to him and to his sons forever.

[20] In his days Edom revolted from the rule of Judah and set up a king of their own. [21] Then Joram[1] passed over to Zair with all his chariots and rose by night, and he and his chariot commanders struck the Edomites who had surrounded him, but his army fled home. [22] So Edom revolted from the rule of Judah to this day. Then Libnah revolted at the same time. [23] Now the rest of the acts of Joram, and all that he did, are they not written in the Book of the Chronicles of the Kings of Judah? [24] So Joram slept with his fathers and was buried with his fathers in the city of David, and Ahaziah his son reigned in his place.

Ahaziah Reigns in Judah

[25] In the twelfth year of Joram the son of Ahab, king of Israel, Ahaziah the son of Jehoram, king of Judah, began to reign. [26] Ahaziah was twenty-two years old when he began to reign, and he reigned one year in Jerusalem. His mother's name was Athaliah; she was a granddaughter of Omri king of Israel. [27] He also walked in the way of the house of Ahab and did what was evil in the sight of the LORD, as the house of Ahab had done, for he was son-in-law to the house of Ahab.

[28] He went with Joram the son of Ahab to make war against Hazael king of Syria at Ramoth-gilead, and the Syrians wounded Joram. [29] And King Joram returned to be healed in Jezreel of the wounds that the Syrians had given him at Ramah, when he fought against Hazael king of Syria. And Ahaziah the son of Jehoram king of Judah went down to see Joram the son of Ahab in Jezreel, because he was sick.

Jehu Anointed King of Israel

9 Then Elisha the prophet called one of the sons of the prophets and said to him, "Tie up your garments, and take this flask of oil in your hand, and go to Ramoth-gilead. [2] And when you arrive, look there for Jehu the son of Jehoshaphat, son of Nimshi. And go in and have him rise from among his fellows, and lead him to an inner chamber. [3] Then take the flask of oil and pour it on his head and say, 'Thus says the LORD, I anoint you king over Israel.' Then open the door and flee; do not linger."

[4] So the young man, the servant of the prophet, went to Ramoth-gilead. [5] And when he came, behold, the commanders of the army were in council. And he said, "I have a word for you, O commander." And Jehu said, "To which of us all?" And he said, "To

---

▶ GETTING THE MESSAGE

Was it Joram or Jehoram? At about the same time, Israel had a king named Joram who was sometimes called Jehoram, while Judah had a king named Jehoram who was sometimes called Joram. King Joram of Israel was a son of Ahab while King Jehoram of Judah married a daughter of Ahab.

---

you, O commander." [6] So he arose and went into the house. And the young man poured the oil on his head, saying to him, "Thus says the LORD, the God of Israel, I anoint you king over the people of the LORD, over Israel. [7] And you shall strike down the house of Ahab your master, so that I may avenge on Jezebel the blood of my servants the prophets, and the blood of all the servants of the LORD. [8] For the whole house of Ahab shall perish, and I will cut off from Ahab every male, bond or free, in Israel. [9] And I will make the house of Ahab like the house of Jeroboam the son of Nebat, and like the house of Baasha the son of Ahijah. [10] And the dogs shall eat Jezebel in the territory of Jezreel, and none shall bury her." Then he opened the door and fled.

[11] When Jehu came out to the servants of his master, they said to him, "Is all well?

---

[1] *Joram* is an alternate spelling of *Jehoram* (the son of Jehoshaphat) as in 8:16; also 8:23, 24

Why did this mad fellow come to you?" And he said to them, "You know the fellow and his talk." ¹² And they said, "That is not true; tell us now." And he said, "Thus and so he spoke to me, saying, 'Thus says the LORD, I anoint you king over Israel.'" ¹³ Then in haste every man of them took his garment and put it under him on the bare steps, and they blew the trumpet and proclaimed, "Jehu is king."

PROFILE
JEHU

Jehu was an army commander who became king of Israel. He was famous for his reckless driving (9:20) but also for his great zeal for the Lord. He set out to destroy every trace of Baal worship in Israel. He killed the kings of both Israel and Judah, and then the entire household of Ahab. He killed the wicked queen Jezebel and then all Ahab's sons, royal officials, and priests. Jehu then brought together all the followers of Baal by pretending that he himself wanted to worship their false god. Once all the Baal worshipers had assembled, Jehu killed them all. He destroyed the temple of Baal, turning it into a latrine. Sadly, though God used Jehu to completely eradicate Baal worship in Israel, he continued to worship the golden calves that Jeroboam had set up.

KEY REFERENCE: 2 KINGS 10:28–31

Jehu Assassinates Joram and Ahaziah

¹⁴ Thus Jehu the son of Jehoshaphat the son of Nimshi conspired against Joram. (Now Joram with all Israel had been on guard at Ramoth-gilead against Hazael king of Syria, ¹⁵ but King Joram had returned to be healed in Jezreel of the wounds that the Syrians had given him, when he fought with Hazael king of Syria.) So Jehu said, "If this is your decision, then let no one slip out of the city to go and tell the news in Jezreel." ¹⁶ Then Jehu mounted his chariot and went to Jezreel, for Joram lay there. And Ahaziah king of Judah had come down to visit Joram.

¹⁷ Now the watchman was standing on the tower in Jezreel, and he saw the company of Jehu as he came and said, "I see a company." And Joram said, "Take a horseman and send to meet them, and let him say, 'Is it peace?'" ¹⁸ So a man on horseback went to meet him and said, "Thus says the king, 'Is it peace?'" And Jehu said, "What do you have to do with peace? Turn around and ride behind me." And the watchman reported, saying, "The messenger reached them, but he is not coming back." ¹⁹ Then he sent out a second horseman, who came to them and said, "Thus the king has said, 'Is it peace?'" And Jehu answered, "What do you have to do with peace? Turn around and ride behind me." ²⁰ Again the watchman reported, "He reached them, but he is not coming back. And the driving is like the driving of Jehu the son of Nimshi, for he drives furiously."

²¹ Joram said, "Make ready." And they made ready his chariot. Then Joram king of Israel and Ahaziah king of Judah set out, each in his chariot, and went to meet Jehu, and met him at the property of Naboth the Jezreelite. ²² And when Joram saw Jehu, he said, "Is it peace, Jehu?" He answered, "What peace can there be, so long as the whorings and the sorceries of your mother Jezebel are so many?" ²³ Then Joram reined about and fled, saying to Ahaziah, "Treachery, O Ahaziah!" ²⁴ And Jehu drew his bow with his full strength, and shot Joram between the shoulders, so that the arrow pierced his heart, and he sank in his chariot. ²⁵ Jehu said to Bidkar his aide, "Take him up and throw him on the plot of ground belonging to Naboth the Jezreelite. For remember, when you and I rode side by side behind Ahab his father, how the LORD made this pronouncement against him: ²⁶ 'As surely as I saw yesterday the blood of Naboth and the blood of his

sons—declares the LORD—I will repay you on this plot of ground.' Now therefore take him up and throw him on the plot of ground, in accordance with the word of the LORD."

²⁷ When Ahaziah the king of Judah saw this, he fled in the direction of Beth-haggan. And Jehu pursued him and said, "Shoot him also." And they shot him in the chariot at the ascent of Gur, which is by Ibleam. And he fled to Megiddo and died there. ²⁸ His servants carried him in a chariot to Jerusalem, and buried him in his tomb with his fathers in the city of David.

²⁹ In the eleventh year of Joram the son of Ahab, Ahaziah began to reign over Judah.

Jehu Executes Jezebel

³⁰ When Jehu came to Jezreel, Jezebel heard of it. And she painted her eyes and adorned her head and looked out of the window. ³¹ And as Jehu entered the gate, she said, "Is it peace, you Zimri, murderer of your master?" ³² And he lifted up his face to the window and said, "Who is on my side? Who?" Two or three eunuchs looked out at him. ³³ He said, "Throw her down." So they threw her down. And some of her blood spattered on the wall and on the horses, and they trampled on her. ³⁴ Then he went in and ate and drank. And he said, "See now to this cursed woman and bury her, for she is a king's daughter." ³⁵ But when they went to bury her, they found no more of her than the skull and the feet and the palms of her hands. ³⁶ When they came back and told him, he said, "This is the word of the LORD, which he spoke by his servant Elijah the Tishbite: 'In the territory of Jezreel the dogs shall eat the flesh of Jezebel, ³⁷ and the corpse of Jezebel shall be as dung on the face of the field in the territory of Jezreel, so that no one can say, This is Jezebel.'"

Jehu Slaughters Ahab's Descendants

10 Now Ahab had seventy sons in Samaria. So Jehu wrote letters and sent them to Samaria, to the rulers of the city, to the elders, and to the guardians of the sons of Ahab, saying, ² "Now then, as soon as this letter comes to you, seeing your master's sons are with you, and there are with you chariots and horses, fortified cities also, and weapons, ³ select the best and fittest of your master's sons and set him on his father's throne and fight for your master's house." ⁴ But they were exceedingly afraid and said, "Behold, the two kings could not stand before him. How then can we stand?" ⁵ So he who was over the palace, and he who was over the city, together with the elders and the guardians, sent to Jehu, saying, "We are your servants, and we will do all that you tell us. We will not make anyone king. Do whatever is good in your eyes." ⁶ Then he wrote to them a second letter, saying, "If you are on my side, and if you are ready to obey me, take the heads of your master's sons and come to me at Jezreel tomorrow at this time." Now the king's sons, seventy persons, were with the great men of the city, who were bringing them up. ⁷ And as soon as the letter came to them, they took the king's sons and slaughtered them, seventy persons, and put their heads in baskets and sent them to him

at Jezreel. ⁸ When the messenger came and told him, "They have brought the heads of the king's sons," he said, "Lay them in two heaps at the entrance of the gate until the morning." ⁹ Then in the morning, when he went out, he stood and said to all the people, "You are innocent. It was I who conspired against my master and killed him, but who struck down all these? ¹⁰ Know then that there shall fall to the earth nothing of the word of the LORD, which the LORD spoke concerning the house of Ahab, for the LORD has done what he said by his servant Elijah." ¹¹ So Jehu struck down all who remained of the house of Ahab in Jezreel, all his great men and his close friends and his priests, until he left him none remaining.

¹² Then he set out and went to Samaria. On the way, when he was at Beth-eked of the Shepherds, ¹³ Jehu met the relatives of Ahaziah king of Judah, and he said, "Who are you?" And they answered, "We are the relatives of Ahaziah, and we came down to

visit the royal princes and the sons of the queen mother." **14** He said, "Take them alive." And they took them alive and slaughtered them at the pit of Beth-eked, forty-two persons, and he spared none of them.

15 And when he departed from there, he met Jehonadab the son of Rechab coming to meet him. And he greeted him and said to him, "Is your heart true to my heart as mine is to yours?" And Jehonadab answered, "It is." Jehu said, "If it is, give me your hand." So he gave him his hand. And Jehu took him up with him into the chariot. **16** And he said, "Come with me, and see my zeal for the LORD." So he had him ride in his chariot. **17** And when he came to Samaria, he struck down all who remained to Ahab in Samaria, till he had wiped them out, according to the word of the LORD that he spoke to Elijah.

Jehu Strikes Down the Prophets of Baal

18 Then Jehu assembled all the people and said to them, "Ahab served Baal a little, but Jehu will serve him much. **19** Now therefore call to me all the prophets of Baal, all his worshipers and all his priests. Let none be missing, for I have a great sacrifice to offer to Baal. Whoever is missing shall not live." But Jehu did it with cunning in order to destroy the worshipers of Baal. **20** And Jehu ordered, "Sanctify a solemn assembly for Baal." So they proclaimed it. **21** And Jehu sent throughout all Israel, and all the worshipers of Baal came, so that there was not a man left who did not come. And they entered the house of Baal, and the house of Baal was filled from one end to the other. **22** He said to him who was in charge of the wardrobe, "Bring out the vestments for all the worshipers of Baal." So he brought out the vestments for them. **23** Then Jehu went into the house of Baal with Jehonadab the son of Rechab, and he said to the worshipers of Baal, "Search,

and see that there is no servant of the LORD here among you, but only the worshipers of Baal." **24** Then they went in to offer sacrifices and burnt offerings.

Now Jehu had stationed eighty men outside and said, "The man who allows any of those whom I give into your hands to escape shall forfeit his life." **25** So as soon as he had made an end of offering the burnt offering, Jehu said to the guard and to the officers, "Go in and strike them down; let not a man escape." So when they put them to the sword, the guard and the officers cast them out and went into the inner room of the house of Baal, **26** and they brought out the pillar that was in the house of Baal and burned it. **27** And they demolished the pillar of Baal, and demolished the house of Baal, and made it a latrine to this day.

Jehu Reigns in Israel

28 Thus Jehu wiped out Baal from Israel. **29** But Jehu did not turn aside from the sins of Jeroboam the son of Nebat, which he made Israel to sin—that is, the golden calves that were in Bethel and in Dan. **30** And the LORD said to Jehu, "Because you have done well in carrying out what is right in my eyes, and have done to the house of Ahab according to all that was in my heart, your sons of the fourth generation shall sit on the throne of Israel." **31** But Jehu was not careful to walk in the law of the LORD, the God of Israel, with all his heart. He did not turn from the sins of Jeroboam, which he made Israel to sin.

32 In those days the LORD began to cut off parts of Israel. Hazael defeated them throughout the territory of Israel: **33** from the Jordan eastward, all the land of Gilead, the Gadites, and the Reubenites, and the Manassites, from Aroer, which is by the Valley of the Arnon, that is, Gilead and Bashan. **34** Now the rest of the acts of Jehu and all that he did, and all his might, are they not written in the Book of the Chronicles of the Kings of Israel? **35** So Jehu slept with his fathers, and they buried him in Samaria. And Jehoahaz his son reigned in his place. **36** The time that Jehu reigned over Israel in Samaria was twenty-eight years.

Athaliah Reigns in Judah

11 Now when Athaliah the mother of Ahaziah saw that her son was dead, she arose and destroyed all the royal family.

² But Jehosheba, the daughter of King Joram, sister of Ahaziah, took Joash the son of Ahaziah and stole him away from among the king's sons who were being put to death, and she put him and his nurse in a bedroom. Thus they hid him from Athaliah, so that he was not put to death. ³ And he remained with her six years, hidden in the house of the Lord, while Athaliah reigned over the land.

Joash Anointed King in Judah

⁴ But in the seventh year Jehoiada sent and brought the captains of the Carites and of the guards, and had them come to him in the house of the Lord. And he made a covenant with them and put them under oath in the house of the Lord, and he showed them the king's son. ⁵ And he commanded them, "This is the thing that you shall do: one third of you, those who come off duty

> **GETTING THE MESSAGE**
>
> **Joash** (or Jehoash) became King of Judah at the age of seven. Joash listened to the godly instruction of Jehoiada the priest and obeyed the Lord. But after Jehoiada died, Joash took advice from idolaters and forgot the Lord.

on the Sabbath and guard the king's house ⁶ (another third being at the gate Sur and a third at the gate behind the guards) shall guard the palace. ⁷ And the two divisions of you, which come on duty in force on the Sabbath and guard the house of the Lord on behalf of the king, ⁸ shall surround the king, each with his weapons in his hand. And whoever approaches the ranks is to be put to death. Be with the king when he goes out and when he comes in."

⁹ The captains did according to all that Jehoiada the priest commanded, and they each brought his men who were to go off duty on the Sabbath, with those who were to come on duty on the Sabbath, and came to Jehoiada the priest. ¹⁰ And the priest gave to the captains the spears and shields that had been King David's, which were in the house of the Lord. ¹¹ And the guards stood, every man with his weapons in his hand, from the south side of the house to the north side of the house, around the altar and the house

on behalf of the king. ¹² Then he brought out the king's son and put the crown on him and gave him the testimony. And they proclaimed him king and anointed him, and they clapped their hands and said, "Long live the king!"

¹³ When Athaliah heard the noise of the guard and of the people, she went into the house of the Lord to the people. ¹⁴ And when she looked, there was the king standing by the pillar, according to the custom, and the

PROFILE

JOASH

Joash (also spelled Jehoash) was just an infant when his father, King Ahaziah of Judah, was murdered. Following the king's death, Joash's wicked grandmother Athaliah tried to kill everyone in the royal family so that she could claim the throne. Joash was spared when his aunt, Jehosheba, hid him in the temple. When Joash was seven years old, Jehoiada, the chief priest, revealed that the young boy was alive. Joash was proclaimed king, and Athaliah was put to death. Joash was a good king as long as Jehoiada was there to guide him. Probably his greatest achievement was making some much-needed repairs to the temple. After Jehoiada died, however, Joash listened to ungodly advice and disobeyed the Lord. His life ended tragically as he was murdered by his own men.

KEY REFERENCE: 2 KINGS 12:1–3

captains and the trumpeters beside the king, and all the people of the land rejoicing and blowing trumpets. And Athaliah tore her clothes and cried, "Treason! Treason!" ¹⁵ Then Jehoiada the priest commanded the captains who were set over the army, "Bring her out between the ranks, and put to death with the sword anyone who follows her." For the priest said, "Let her not be put to death in the house of the Lord." ¹⁶ So they laid hands on her; and she went through the horses' entrance to the king's house, and there she was put to death.

[17] And Jehoiada made a covenant between the LORD and the king and people, that they should be the LORD's people, and also between the king and the people. [18] Then all the people of the land went to the house of Baal and tore it down; his altars and his images they broke in pieces, and they killed Mattan the priest of Baal before the altars. And the priest posted watchmen over the house of the LORD. [19] And he took the captains, the Carites, the guards, and all the people of the land, and they brought the king down from the house of the LORD, marching through the gate of the guards to the king's house. And he took his seat on the throne of the kings. [20] So all the people of the land rejoiced, and the city was quiet after Athaliah had been put to death with the sword at the king's house.

GETTING THE MESSAGE

Hazael (12:17) was king of Syria from 843–796 B.C. He threatened Israel during the reigns of Jehu (1 Kings 19:17), Joram (8:28), and Jehoahaz (13:22).

Jehoash Reigns in Judah

[21] Jehoash[1] was seven years old when he began to reign.

12 In the seventh year of Jehu, Jehoash began to reign, and he reigned forty years in Jerusalem. His mother's name was Zibiah of Beersheba. [2] And Jehoash did what was right in the eyes of the LORD all his days, because Jehoiada the priest instructed him. [3] Nevertheless, the high places were not taken away; the people continued to sacrifice and make offerings on the high places.

Jehoash Repairs the Temple

[4] Jehoash said to the priests, "All the money of the holy things that is brought into the house of the LORD, the money for which each man is assessed—the money from the assessment of persons—and the money that a man's heart prompts him to bring into the house of the LORD, [5] let the priests take, each from his donor, and let them repair the house wherever any need of repairs is discovered." [6] But by the twenty-third year of King Jehoash, the priests had made no repairs on the house. [7] Therefore King Jehoash summoned Jehoiada the priest and the other priests and said to them, "Why are you not repairing the house? Now therefore take no more money from your donors, but hand it over for the repair of the house." [8] So the priests agreed that they should take no more money from the people, and that they should not repair the house.

[9] Then Jehoiada the priest took a chest and bored a hole in the lid of it and set it beside the altar on the right side as one entered the house of the LORD. And the priests who guarded the threshold put in it all the money that was brought into the house of the LORD. [10] And whenever they saw that there was much money in the chest, the king's secretary and the high priest came up and they bagged and counted the money that was found in the house of the LORD. [11] Then they would give the money that was weighed out into the hands of the workmen who had the oversight of the house of the LORD. And they paid it out to the carpenters and the builders who worked on the house of the LORD, [12] and to the masons and the stonecutters, as well as to buy timber and quarried stone for making repairs on the house of the LORD, and for any outlay for the repairs of the house. [13] But there were not made for the house of the LORD basins of silver, snuffers, bowls, trumpets, or any vessels of gold, or of silver, from the money that was brought into the house of the LORD, [14] for that was given to the workmen who were repairing the house of the LORD with it. [15] And they did not ask for an accounting from the men into whose hand they delivered the money to pay out to the workmen, for they dealt honestly. [16] The money from the guilt offerings and the money from the sin offerings was not brought into the house of the LORD; it belonged to the priests.

[17] At that time Hazael king of Syria went up and fought against Gath and took it. But when Hazael set his face to go up against Jerusalem, [18] Jehoash king of Judah took all the sacred gifts that Jehoshaphat and Jehoram and Ahaziah his fathers, the kings of Judah, had dedicated, and his own sacred gifts, and all the gold that was found in the treasuries of the house of the LORD and of the king's house, and sent these to Hazael

[1] Jehoash is an alternate spelling of Joash (son of Ahaziah) as in 11:2; also 12:1, 2, 4, 6, 7, 18

king of Syria. Then Hazael went away from Jerusalem.

The Death of Joash

¹⁹ Now the rest of the acts of Joash and all that he did, are they not written in the Book of the Chronicles of the Kings of Judah? ²⁰ His servants arose and made a conspiracy and struck down Joash in the house of Millo, on the way that goes down to Silla. ²¹ It was Jozacar the son of Shimeath and Jehozabad the son of Shomer, his servants, who struck him down, so that he died. And they buried him with his fathers in the city of David, and Amaziah his son reigned in his place.

Jehoahaz Reigns in Israel

13 In the twenty-third year of Joash the son of Ahaziah, king of Judah, Jehoahaz the son of Jehu began to reign over Israel in Samaria, and he reigned seventeen years. ² He did what was evil in the sight of the LORD and followed the sins of Jeroboam the son of Nebat, which he made Israel to sin; he did not depart from them. ³ And the anger of the LORD was kindled against Israel, and he gave them continually into the hand of Hazael king of Syria and into the hand of Benhadad the son of Hazael. ⁴ Then Jehoahaz sought the favor of the LORD, and the LORD listened to him, for he saw the oppression of Israel, how the king of Syria oppressed them. ⁵ (Therefore the LORD gave Israel a savior, so that they escaped from the hand of the Syrians, and the people of Israel lived in their homes as formerly. ⁶ Nevertheless, they did not depart from the sins of the house of Jeroboam, which he made Israel to sin, but walked in them; and the Asherah also remained in Samaria.) ⁷ For there was not left to Jehoahaz an army of more than fifty horsemen and ten chariots and ten thousand footmen, for the king of Syria had destroyed them and made them like the dust at threshing. ⁸ Now the rest of the acts of Jehoahaz and all that he did, and his might, are they not written in the Book of the Chronicles of the Kings of Israel? ⁹ So Jehoahaz slept with his fathers, and they buried him in Samaria, and Joash his son reigned in his place.

Jehoash Reigns in Israel

¹⁰ In the thirty-seventh year of Joash king of Judah, Jehoash[1] the son of Jehoahaz began to reign over Israel in Samaria, and he reigned sixteen years. ¹¹ He also did what was evil in the sight of the LORD. He did not depart from all the sins of Jeroboam the son of Nebat, which he made Israel to sin, but he walked in them. ¹² Now the rest of the acts of Joash and all that he did, and the might with which he fought against Amaziah king of Judah, are they not written in the Book of the Chronicles of the Kings of Israel? ¹³ So Joash slept with his fathers, and Jeroboam sat on his throne. And Joash was buried in Samaria with the kings of Israel.

The Death of Elisha

¹⁴ Now when Elisha had fallen sick with the illness of which he was to die, Joash king of Israel went down to him and wept before him, crying, "My father, my father! The chariots of Israel and its horsemen!" ¹⁵ And Elisha said to him, "Take a bow and arrows." So he took a bow and arrows. ¹⁶ Then he said to the king of Israel, "Draw the bow," and he drew it. And Elisha laid his hands on the king's hands. ¹⁷ And he said, "Open the window eastward," and he opened it. Then Elisha said, "Shoot," and he shot. And he said, "The LORD's arrow of victory, the arrow of victory over Syria! For you shall fight the Syrians in Aphek until you have made an end of them." ¹⁸ And he said, "Take the arrows," and he took them. And he said to the king of Israel, "Strike the ground with them." And he struck three times and stopped. ¹⁹ Then the man of God was angry with him and said, "You should have struck five or six times; then you would have struck down Syria until you had made an end of it, but now you will strike down Syria only three times."

²⁰ So Elisha died, and they buried him. Now bands of Moabites used to invade the land in the spring of the year. ²¹ And as a man was being buried, behold, a marauding band was seen and the man was thrown into the grave of Elisha, and as soon as the man touched the bones of Elisha, he revived and stood on his feet.

²² Now Hazael king of Syria oppressed Israel all the days of Jehoahaz. ²³ But the LORD was gracious to them and had compassion on them, and he turned toward them, because of his covenant with Abraham, Isaac, and Jacob, and would not destroy

---

[1] *Jehoash* is an alternate spelling of *Joash* (son of Jehoahaz) as in 13:9, 12-14

them, nor has he cast them from his presence until now.

²⁴ When Hazael king of Syria died, Benhadad his son became king in his place. ²⁵ Then Jehoash[1] the son of Jehoahaz took again from Ben-hadad the son of Hazael the cities that he had taken from Jehoahaz his father in war. Three times Joash defeated him and recovered the cities of Israel.

Amaziah Reigns in Judah

14 In the second year of Joash the son of Joahaz, king of Israel, Amaziah the son of Joash, king of Judah, began to reign. ² He was twenty-five years old when he began to reign, and he reigned twenty-nine years in Jerusalem. His mother's name was Jehoaddin of Jerusalem. ³ And he did what was right in the eyes of the LORD, yet not like David his father. He did in all things as Joash his father had done. ⁴ But the high places were not removed; the people still sacrificed

GETTING THE MESSAGE

Elath (14:22) was a strategic seaport on the northernmost tip of the Red Sea. It was located at the southern end of the King's Highway, which ran north all the way to Damascus.

and made offerings on the high places. ⁵ And as soon as the royal power was firmly in his hand, he struck down his servants who had struck down the king his father. ⁶ But he did not put to death the children of the murderers, according to what is written in the Book of the Law of Moses, where the LORD commanded, "Fathers shall not be put to death because of their children, nor shall children be put to death because of their fathers. But each one shall die for his own sin."

⁷ He struck down ten thousand Edomites in the Valley of Salt and took Sela by storm, and called it Joktheel, which is its name to this day.

⁸ Then Amaziah sent messengers to Jehoash the son of Jehoahaz, son of Jehu, king of Israel, saying, "Come, let us look one another in the face." ⁹ And Jehoash king of Israel sent word to Amaziah king of Judah, "A thistle on Lebanon sent to a cedar on Lebanon, saying, 'Give your daughter to my

son for a wife,' and a wild beast of Lebanon passed by and trampled down the thistle. ¹⁰ You have indeed struck down Edom, and your heart has lifted you up. Be content with your glory, and stay at home, for why should you provoke trouble so that you fall, you and Judah with you?"

¹¹ But Amaziah would not listen. So Jehoash king of Israel went up, and he and Amaziah king of Judah faced one another in battle at Beth-shemesh, which belongs to Judah. ¹² And Judah was defeated by Israel, and every man fled to his home. ¹³ And Jehoash king of Israel captured Amaziah king of Judah, the son of Jehoash, son of Ahaziah, at Beth-shemesh, and came to Jerusalem and broke down the wall of Jerusalem for four hundred cubits, from the Ephraim Gate to the Corner Gate. ¹⁴ And he seized all the gold and silver, and all the vessels that were found in the house of the LORD and in the treasuries of the king's house, also hostages, and he returned to Samaria.

¹⁵ Now the rest of the acts of Jehoash that he did, and his might, and how he fought with Amaziah king of Judah, are they not written in the Book of the Chronicles of the Kings of Israel? ¹⁶ And Jehoash slept with his fathers and was buried in Samaria with the kings of Israel, and Jeroboam his son reigned in his place.

¹⁷ Amaziah the son of Joash, king of Judah, lived fifteen years after the death of Jehoash son of Jehoahaz, king of Israel. ¹⁸ Now the rest of the deeds of Amaziah, are they not written in the Book of the Chronicles of the Kings of Judah? ¹⁹ And they made a conspiracy against him in Jerusalem, and he fled to Lachish. But they sent after him to Lachish and put him to death there. ²⁰ And they brought him on horses; and he was buried in Jerusalem with his fathers in the city of David. ²¹ And all the people of Judah took Azariah, who was sixteen years old, and made him king instead of his father Amaziah. ²² He built Elath and restored it to Judah, after the king slept with his fathers.

Jeroboam II Reigns in Israel

²³ In the fifteenth year of Amaziah the son of Joash, king of Judah, Jeroboam the son of Joash, king of Israel, began to reign in Samaria, and he reigned forty-one years. ²⁴ And he did what was evil in the sight of

[1] *Jehoash* is an alternate spelling of *Joash* (son of Jehoahaz) as in 13:9, 12–14; also 14:8, 9, 11, 13, 15, 16

the LORD. He did not depart from all the sins of Jeroboam the son of Nebat, which he made Israel to sin. **25** He restored the border of Israel from Lebo-hamath as far as the Sea of the Arabah, according to the word of the LORD, the God of Israel, which he spoke by his servant Jonah the son of Amittai, the prophet, who was from Gath-hepher. **26** For the LORD saw that the affliction of Israel was very bitter, for there was none left, bond or free, and there was none to help Israel. **27** But the LORD had not said that he would blot out the name of Israel from under heaven, so he saved them by the hand of Jeroboam the son of Joash.

28 Now the rest of the acts of Jeroboam and all that he did, and his might, how he fought, and how he restored Damascus and Hamath to Judah in Israel, are they not written in the Book of the Chronicles of the Kings of Israel? **29** And Jeroboam slept with his fathers, the kings of Israel, and Zechariah his son reigned in his place.

Azariah Reigns in Judah

15 In the twenty-seventh year of Jeroboam king of Israel, Azariah the son of Amaziah, king of Judah, began to reign. **2** He was sixteen years old when he began to reign, and he reigned fifty-two years in Jerusalem. His mother's name was Jecoliah of Jerusalem. **3** And he did what was right in the eyes of the LORD, according to all that his father Amaziah had done. **4** Nevertheless, the high places were not taken away. The people still sacrificed and made offerings on the high places. **5** And the LORD touched the king, so that he was a leper[1] to the day of his death, and he lived in a separate house. And Jotham the king's son was over the household, governing the people of the land. **6** Now the rest of the acts of Azariah, and all that he did, are they not written in the Book of the Chronicles of the Kings of Judah? **7** And Azariah slept with his fathers, and they buried him with his fathers in the city of David, and Jotham his son reigned in his place.

Zechariah Reigns in Israel

8 In the thirty-eighth year of Azariah king of Judah, Zechariah the son of Jeroboam reigned over Israel in Samaria six months.

9 And he did what was evil in the sight of the LORD, as his fathers had done. He did not depart from the sins of Jeroboam the son of Nebat, which he made Israel to sin. **10** Shallum the son of Jabesh conspired against him and struck him down at Ibleam and put him to death and reigned in his place. **11** Now the rest of the deeds of Zechariah, behold, they are written in the Book of the Chronicles of the Kings of Israel. **12** (This was the promise of the LORD that he gave to Jehu, "Your sons shall sit on the throne of Israel to the fourth generation." And so it came to pass.)

Shallum Reigns in Israel

13 Shallum the son of Jabesh began to reign in the thirty-ninth year of Uzziah[2] king of Judah, and he reigned one month in Samaria. **14** Then Menahem the son of Gadi came up from Tirzah and came to Samaria, and he struck down Shallum the son of Jabesh in Samaria and put him to death and reigned in his place. **15** Now the rest of the deeds of Shallum, and the conspiracy that he made, behold, they are written in the Book of the Chronicles of the Kings of Israel. **16** At that time Menahem sacked Tiphsah and all who were in it and its territory from Tirzah on, because they did not open it to him. Therefore he sacked it, and he ripped open all the women in it who were pregnant.

Menahem Reigns in Israel

17 In the thirty-ninth year of Azariah king of Judah, Menahem the son of Gadi began to reign over Israel, and he reigned ten years in Samaria. **18** And he did what was evil in the sight of the LORD. He did not depart all his days from all the sins of Jeroboam the son of Nebat, which he made Israel to sin. **19** Pul[3] the king of Assyria came against the land, and Menahem gave Pul a thousand talents of silver, that he might help him to confirm his hold on the royal power. **20** Menahem exacted the money from Israel, that is, from all the wealthy men, fifty shekels of silver from every man, to give to the king of Assyria. So the king of Assyria turned back and did not stay there in the land. **21** Now the rest of the deeds of Menahem and all that he did, are they not written in the Book of the Chronicles of the Kings of Israel?

[1] *Leprosy* was a term for several skin diseases (see Leviticus 13) [2] Another name for *Azariah* [3] Another name for *Tiglath-pileser III* (compare 15:29)

22 And Menahem slept with his fathers, and Pekahiah his son reigned in his place.

Pekahiah Reigns in Israel

23 In the fiftieth year of Azariah king of Judah, Pekahiah the son of Menahem began to reign over Israel in Samaria, and he reigned two years. 24 And he did what was evil in the sight of the LORD. He did not turn away from the sins of Jeroboam the son of Nebat, which he made Israel to sin. 25 And Pekah the son of Remaliah, his captain, conspired against him with fifty men of the people of Gilead, and struck him down in Samaria, in the citadel of the king's house with Argob and Arieh; he put him to death and reigned in his place. 26 Now the rest of the deeds of Pekahiah and all that he did, behold, they are written in the Book of the Chronicles of the Kings of Israel.

Pekah Reigns in Israel

27 In the fifty-second year of Azariah king of Judah, Pekah the son of Remaliah began to reign over Israel in Samaria, and he reigned twenty years. 28 And he did what was evil in the sight of the LORD. He did not depart from the sins of Jeroboam the son of Nebat, which he made Israel to sin.

29 In the days of Pekah king of Israel, Tiglath-pileser king of Assyria came and captured Ijon, Abel-beth-maacah, Janoah, Kedesh, Hazor, Gilead, and Galilee, all the land of Naphtali, and he carried the people captive to Assyria. 30 Then Hoshea the son of Elah made a conspiracy against Pekah the son of Remaliah and struck him down and put him to death and reigned in his place, in the twentieth year of Jotham the son of Uzziah. 31 Now the rest of the acts of Pekah and all that he did, behold, they are written

in the Book of the Chronicles of the Kings of Israel.

Jotham Reigns in Judah

32 In the second year of Pekah the son of Remaliah, king of Israel, Jotham the son of Uzziah, king of Judah, began to reign. 33 He was twenty-five years old when he began to reign, and he reigned sixteen years in Jerusalem. His mother's name was Jerusha the daughter of Zadok. 34 And he did what was right in the eyes of the LORD, according to all that his father Uzziah had done. 35 Nevertheless, the high places were not removed. The people still sacrificed and made offerings on the high places. He built the upper gate of the house of the LORD. 36 Now the rest of the acts of Jotham and all that he did, are they not written in the Book of the Chronicles of the Kings of Judah? 37 In those days the LORD began to send Rezin the king of Syria and Pekah the son of Remaliah against Judah. 38 Jotham slept with his fathers and was buried with his fathers in the city of David his father, and Ahaz his son reigned in his place.

Ahaz Reigns in Judah

16 In the seventeenth year of Pekah the son of Remaliah, Ahaz the son of Jotham, king of Judah, began to reign. 2 Ahaz was twenty years old when he began to reign, and he reigned sixteen years in Jerusalem. And he did not do what was right in the eyes of the LORD his God, as his father David had done, 3 but he walked in the way of the kings of Israel. He even burned his son as an offering, according to the despicable practices of the nations whom the LORD drove out before the people of Israel. 4 And he sacrificed and made offerings on the high places and on the hills and under every green tree.

5 Then Rezin king of Syria and Pekah the son of Remaliah, king of Israel, came up to wage war on Jerusalem, and they besieged Ahaz but could not conquer him. 6 At that time Rezin the king of Syria recovered Elath for Syria and drove the men of Judah from Elath, and the Edomites came to Elath, where they dwell to this day. 7 So Ahaz sent messengers to Tiglath-pileser king of Assyria, saying, "I am your servant and your son. Come up and rescue me from the hand of the king of Syria and from the hand of the

king of Israel, who are attacking me." [8] Ahaz also took the silver and gold that was found in the house of the LORD and in the treasures of the king's house and sent a present to the king of Assyria. [9] And the king of Assyria listened to him. The king of Assyria marched up against Damascus and took it, carrying its people captive to Kir, and he killed Rezin.

[10] When King Ahaz went to Damascus to meet Tiglath-pileser king of Assyria, he saw the altar that was at Damascus. And King Ahaz sent to Uriah the priest a model of the altar, and its pattern, exact in all its details. [11] And Uriah the priest built the altar; in accordance with all that King Ahaz had sent from Damascus, so Uriah the priest made it, before King Ahaz arrived from Damascus. [12] And when the king came from Damascus, the king viewed the altar. Then the king drew near to the altar and went up on it [13] and burned his burnt offering and his grain offering and poured his drink offering and threw the blood of his peace offerings on the altar. [14] And the bronze altar that was before the LORD he removed from the front of the house, from the place between his altar and the house of the LORD, and put it on the north side of his altar. [15] And King Ahaz commanded Uriah the priest, saying, "On the great altar burn the morning burnt offering and the evening grain offering and the king's burnt offering and his grain offering, with the burnt offering of all the people of the land, and their grain offering and their drink offering. And throw on it all the blood of the burnt offering and all the blood of the sacrifice, but the bronze altar shall be for me to inquire by." [16] Uriah the priest did all this, as King Ahaz commanded.

[17] And King Ahaz cut off the frames of the stands and removed the basin from them, and he took down the sea from off the bronze oxen that were under it and put it on a stone pedestal. [18] And the covered way for the Sabbath that had been built inside the house and the outer entrance for the king he caused to go around the house of the LORD, because of the king of Assyria. [19] Now the rest of the acts of Ahaz that he did, are they not written in the Book of the Chronicles of the Kings of Judah? [20] And Ahaz slept with his fathers and was buried with his fathers in the city of David, and Hezekiah his son reigned in his place.

Hoshea Reigns in Israel

17 In the twelfth year of Ahaz king of Judah, Hoshea the son of Elah began to reign in Samaria over Israel, and he reigned nine years. [2] And he did what was evil in the sight of the LORD, yet not as the kings of Israel who were before him. [3] Against him came up Shalmaneser king of Assyria. And Hoshea became his vassal and paid him tribute. [4] But the king of Assyria found treachery in Hoshea, for he had sent messengers to So, king of Egypt, and offered no tribute to the king of Assyria, as he had done year by year. Therefore the king of Assyria shut him up and bound him in prison. [5] Then the king of Assyria invaded all the land and came to Samaria, and for three years he besieged it.

The Fall of Israel

[6] In the ninth year of Hoshea, the king of Assyria captured Samaria, and he carried the Israelites away to Assyria and placed them in Halah, and on the Habor, the river of Gozan, and in the cities of the Medes.

Exile Because of Idolatry

[7] And this occurred because the people of Israel had sinned against the LORD their God, who had brought them up out of the land of Egypt from under the hand of Pharaoh king of Egypt, and had feared other gods [8] and walked in the customs of the nations whom the LORD drove out before the people of Israel, and in the customs that the kings of Israel had practiced. [9] And the people of Israel did secretly against the LORD their God things that were not right. They built for themselves high places in all their towns, from watchtower to fortified city. [10] They set up for themselves pillars and Asherim on every high hill and under every green tree, [11] and there they made offerings on all the high places, as the nations did whom the LORD carried away before them. And they did wicked things, provoking the LORD to anger, [12] and they served idols, of which the LORD had said to them, "You shall not do this." [13] Yet the LORD warned Israel and Judah by every prophet and every seer, saying, "Turn from your evil ways and keep my commandments and my statutes, in accordance with all the Law that I commanded your fathers, and that I sent to you by my servants the prophets."

14 But they would not listen, but were stubborn, as their fathers had been, who did not believe in the LORD their God. 15 They despised his statutes and his covenant that he made with their fathers and the warnings that he gave them. They went after false idols and became false, and they followed the nations that were around them, concerning whom the LORD had commanded them that they should not do like them. 16 And they abandoned all the commandments of the LORD their God, and made for themselves metal images of two calves; and they made an Asherah and worshiped all the host of heaven and served Baal. 17 And they burned their sons and their daughters as offerings and used divination and omens and sold themselves to do evil in the sight of

> ### GETTING THE MESSAGE
>
> **Why were the Israelites deported?**
> The Babylonians had learned that destroying an enemy's land but allowing them to remain in it was a bad idea. It ruined potential crop resources and gave an opportunity for the conquered people to regroup and rebel. Instead, they deported the conquered people to other lands, and brought in people from other places to live in the conquered territory. This mixing of ethnic groups made any organized rebellion less likely.

the LORD, provoking him to anger. 18 Therefore the LORD was very angry with Israel and removed them out of his sight. None was left but the tribe of Judah only.

19 Judah also did not keep the commandments of the LORD their God, but walked in the customs that Israel had introduced. 20 And the LORD rejected all the descendants of Israel and afflicted them and gave them into the hand of plunderers, until he had cast them out of his sight.

21 When he had torn Israel from the house of David, they made Jeroboam the son of Nebat king. And Jeroboam drove Israel from following the LORD and made them commit great sin. 22 The people of Israel walked in all the sins that Jeroboam did. They did not depart from them, 23 until the LORD removed Israel out of his sight, as he had spoken by

all his servants the prophets. So Israel was exiled from their own land to Assyria until this day.

Assyria Resettles Samaria

24 And the king of Assyria brought people from Babylon, Cuthah, Avva, Hamath, and Sepharvaim, and placed them in the cities of Samaria instead of the people of Israel. And they took possession of Samaria and lived in its cities. 25 And at the beginning of their dwelling there, they did not fear the LORD. Therefore the LORD sent lions among them, which killed some of them. 26 So the king of Assyria was told, "The nations that you have carried away and placed in the cities of Samaria do not know the law of the god of the land. Therefore he has sent lions among them, and behold, they are killing them, because they do not know the law of the god of the land." 27 Then the king of Assyria commanded, "Send there one of the priests whom you carried away from there, and let him go and dwell there and teach them the law of the god of the land." 28 So one of the priests whom they had carried away from Samaria came and lived in Bethel and taught them how they should fear the LORD.

29 But every nation still made gods of its own and put them in the shrines of the high places that the Samaritans had made, every nation in the cities in which they lived. 30 The men of Babylon made Succoth-benoth, the men of Cuth made Nergal, the men of Hamath made Ashima, 31 and the Avvites made Nibhaz and Tartak; and the Sepharvites burned their children in the fire to Adrammelech and Anammelech, the gods of Sepharvaim. 32 They also feared the LORD and appointed from among themselves all sorts of people as priests of the high places, who sacrificed for them in the shrines of the high places. 33 So they feared the LORD but also served their own gods, after the manner of the nations from among whom they had been carried away.

34 To this day they do according to the former manner. They do not fear the LORD, and they do not follow the statutes or the rules or the law or the commandment that the LORD commanded the children of Jacob, whom he named Israel. 35 The LORD made a covenant with them and commanded them, "You shall not fear other gods or bow yourselves to them or serve them or sacrifice to

them, 36 but you shall fear the LORD, who brought you out of the land of Egypt with great power and with an outstretched arm. You shall bow yourselves to him, and to him you shall sacrifice. 37 And the statutes and the rules and the law and the commandment that he wrote for you, you shall always be careful to do. You shall not fear other gods, 38 and you shall not forget the covenant that I have made with you. You shall not fear other gods, 39 but you shall fear the LORD your God, and he will deliver you out of the hand of all your enemies." 40 However, they would not listen, but they did according to their former manner.

41 So these nations feared the LORD and also served their carved images. Their children did likewise, and their children's children—as their fathers did, so they do to this day.

Hezekiah Reigns in Judah

18 In the third year of Hoshea son of Elah, king of Israel, Hezekiah the son of Ahaz, king of Judah, began to reign. 2 He was twenty-five years old when he began to reign, and he reigned twenty-nine years in Jerusalem. His mother's name was Abi the daughter of Zechariah. 3 And he did what was right in the eyes of the LORD, according to all that David his father had done. 4 He removed the high places and broke the pillars and cut down the Asherah. And he broke in pieces the bronze serpent that Moses had made, for until those days the people of Israel had made offerings to it (it was called Nehushtan).¹ 5 He trusted in the LORD, the God of Israel, so that there was none like him among all the kings of Judah after him, nor among those who were before him. 6 For he held fast to the LORD. He did not depart from following him, but kept the commandments that the LORD commanded Moses. 7 And the LORD was with him; wherever he went out, he prospered. He rebelled against the king of Assyria and would not serve him. 8 He struck down the Philistines as far as Gaza and its territory, from watchtower to fortified city.

9 In the fourth year of King Hezekiah, which was the seventh year of Hoshea son of Elah, king of Israel, Shalmaneser king of Assyria came up against Samaria and besieged it, 10 and at the end of three years

he took it. In the sixth year of Hezekiah, which was the ninth year of Hoshea king of Israel, Samaria was taken. 11 The king of Assyria carried the Israelites away to Assyria and put them in Halah, and on the Habor, the river of Gozan, and in the cities of the Medes, 12 because they did not obey the voice of the LORD their God but transgressed his covenant, even all that Moses the servant of the LORD commanded. They neither listened nor obeyed.

PROFILE

HEZEKIAH

Hezekiah was king of the southern kingdom, Judah, at the time when the Assyrians defeated the northern kingdom of Israel. Hezekiah was a good king who followed God throughout his life. He began his reign by completely reforming Judean worship. He removed the high places and all the idols that previous kings had allowed. At one point Hezekiah became very sick and was at the point of death, so he prayed that the Lord would heal him. God honored his prayer, promising to give him another 15 years of life. He also delivered Hezekiah and Jerusalem from the Assyrians. Hezekiah resembled King David more closely than any other Davidic king thus far. He is listed in the genealogy of Jesus (Matt. 1:9–10).

KEY REFERENCE: 2 KINGS 18:3–8

Sennacherib Attacks Judah

13 In the fourteenth year of King Hezekiah, Sennacherib king of Assyria came up against all the fortified cities of Judah and took them. 14 And Hezekiah king of Judah sent to the king of Assyria at Lachish, saying, "I have done wrong; withdraw from me. Whatever you impose on me I will bear." And the king of Assyria required of Hezekiah king of Judah three hundred talents of silver and thirty talents of gold. 15 And Hezekiah gave him all the silver that was found in the house of the LORD and in the treasuries of the king's house. 16 At that time Hezekiah

---

¹ Nehushtan sounds like the Hebrew for both bronze and serpent

stripped the gold from the doors of the temple of the LORD and from the doorposts that Hezekiah king of Judah had overlaid and gave it to the king of Assyria. ¹⁷ And the king of Assyria sent the Tartan, the Rab-saris, and the Rabshakeh with a great army from Lachish to King Hezekiah at Jerusalem. And they went up and came to Jerusalem. When they arrived, they came and stood by the conduit of the upper pool, which is on the highway to the Washer's Field. ¹⁸ And when they called for the king, there came out to them Eliakim the son of Hilkiah, who was over the household, and Shebnah the secretary, and Joah the son of Asaph, the recorder.

¹⁹ And the Rabshakeh said to them, "Say to Hezekiah, 'Thus says the great king, the

---

GETTING THE MESSAGE

"Please speak in Aramaic." As Assyria tried to conquer Judah, they sent a delegation to Jerusalem to engage in "psychological warfare" (18:17–37). They made public proclamations intended to turn the Judeans against their king. The Judean officials begged the Assyrians to speak only in Aramaic (v. 26), which these officials would have understood but which the ordinary bystanders did not understand. But the Assyrians went on speaking in Hebrew, seeking to demoralize all those who were listening.

---

king of Assyria: On what do you rest this trust of yours? ²⁰ Do you think that mere words are strategy and power for war? In whom do you now trust, that you have rebelled against me? ²¹ Behold, you are trusting now in Egypt, that broken reed of a staff, which will pierce the hand of any man who leans on it. Such is Pharaoh king of Egypt to all who trust in him. ²² But if you say to me, "We trust in the LORD our God," is it not he whose high places and altars Hezekiah has removed, saying to Judah and to Jerusalem, "You shall worship before this altar in Jerusalem"? ²³ Come now, make a wager with my master the king of Assyria: I will give you two thousand horses, if you are able on your part to set riders on them. ²⁴ How then can you repulse a single captain among the least of my master's servants,

when you trust in Egypt for chariots and for horsemen? ²⁵ Moreover, is it without the LORD that I have come up against this place to destroy it? The LORD said to me, Go up against this land, and destroy it.'"

²⁶ Then Eliakim the son of Hilkiah, and Shebnah, and Joah, said to the Rabshakeh, "Please speak to your servants in Aramaic, for we understand it. Do not speak to us in the language of Judah within the hearing of the people who are on the wall." ²⁷ But the Rabshakeh said to them, "Has my master sent me to speak these words to your master and to you, and not to the men sitting on the wall, who are doomed with you to eat their own dung and to drink their own urine?"

²⁸ Then the Rabshakeh stood and called out in a loud voice in the language of Judah: "Hear the word of the great king, the king of Assyria! ²⁹ Thus says the king: 'Do not let Hezekiah deceive you, for he will not be able to deliver you out of my hand. ³⁰ Do not let Hezekiah make you trust in the LORD by saying, The LORD will surely deliver us, and this city will not be given into the hand of the king of Assyria.' ³¹ Do not listen to Hezekiah, for thus says the king of Assyria: 'Make your peace with me and come out to me. Then each one of you will eat of his own vine, and each one of his own fig tree, and each one of you will drink the water of his own cistern, ³² until I come and take you away to a land like your own land, a land of grain and wine, a land of bread and vineyards, a land of olive trees and honey, that you may live, and not die. And do not listen to Hezekiah when he misleads you by saying, "The LORD will deliver us." ³³ Has any of the gods of the nations ever delivered his land out of the hand of the king of Assyria? ³⁴ Where are the gods of Hamath and Arpad? Where are the gods of Sepharvaim, Hena, and Ivvah? Have they delivered Samaria out of my hand? ³⁵ Who among all the gods of the lands have delivered their lands out of my hand, that the LORD should deliver Jerusalem out of my hand?'"

³⁶ But the people were silent and answered him not a word, for the king's command was, "Do not answer him." ³⁷ Then Eliakim the son of Hilkiah, who was over the household, and Shebna the secretary, and Joah the son of Asaph, the recorder, came to

Hezekiah with their clothes torn and told him the words of the Rabshakeh.

Isaiah Reassures Hezekiah

19 As soon as King Hezekiah heard it, he tore his clothes and covered himself with sackcloth and went into the house of the LORD. ² And he sent Eliakim, who was over the household, and Shebna the secretary, and the senior priests, covered with sackcloth, to the prophet Isaiah the son of Amoz. ³ They said to him, "Thus says Hezekiah, This day is a day of distress, of rebuke, and of disgrace; children have come to the point of birth, and there is no strength to bring them forth. ⁴ It may be that the LORD your God heard all the words of the Rabshakeh, whom his master the king of Assyria has sent to mock the living God, and will rebuke the words that the LORD your God has heard; therefore lift up your prayer for the remnant that is left." ⁵ When the servants of King Hezekiah came to Isaiah, ⁶ Isaiah said to them, "Say to your master, 'Thus says the LORD: Do not be afraid because of the words that you have heard, with which the servants of the king of Assyria have reviled me. ⁷ Behold, I will put a spirit in him, so that he shall hear a rumor and return to his own land, and I will make him fall by the sword in his own land.'"

Sennacherib Defies the LORD

⁸ The Rabshakeh returned, and found the king of Assyria fighting against Libnah, for he heard that the king had left Lachish. ⁹ Now the king heard concerning Tirhakah king of Cush, "Behold, he has set out to fight against you." So he sent messengers again to Hezekiah, saying, ¹⁰ "Thus shall you speak to Hezekiah king of Judah: 'Do not let your God in whom you trust deceive you by promising that Jerusalem will not be given into the hand of the king of Assyria. ¹¹ Behold, you have heard what the kings of Assyria have done to all lands, devoting them to destruction. And shall you be delivered? ¹² Have the gods of the nations delivered them, the nations that my fathers destroyed, Gozan, Haran, Rezeph, and the people of Eden who were in Telassar? ¹³ Where is the king of Hamath, the king of Arpad, the king of the city of Sepharvaim, the king of Hena, or the king of Ivvah?'"

Hezekiah's Prayer

¹⁴ Hezekiah received the letter from the hand of the messengers and read it; and Hezekiah went up to the house of the LORD and spread it before the LORD. ¹⁵ And Hezekiah prayed before the LORD and said: "O LORD, the God of Israel, enthroned above the cherubim, you are the God, you alone, of all the kingdoms of the earth; you have made heaven and earth. ¹⁶ Incline your ear, O LORD, and hear; open your eyes, O LORD, and see;

PROFILE

SENNACHERIB

Sennacherib became king of the powerful Assyrian Empire following the death of his father, Sargon II. After defeating Babylon, Sennacherib began attacking the area of Syria and Palestine. His official records claim that he captured 46 strong-walled cities in Israel. Following a major victory at Lachish, he laid siege to Jerusalem. Sennacherib forced Hezekiah to pay a huge tribute. He mocked God, urging Hezekiah to turn his back on the Lord. Instead, Hezekiah prayed for God's deliverance. God answered the king's prayer, and the siege of Jerusalem was broken when the angel of the Lord killed 185,000 Assyrians in a single night. Sennacherib withdrew and returned to Nineveh, only to be killed by his own sons as he worshiped in the temple of the false god Nisroch.

KEY REFERENCE: 2 KINGS 19:35–37

and hear the words of Sennacherib, which he has sent to mock the living God. ¹⁷ Truly, O LORD, the kings of Assyria have laid waste the nations and their lands ¹⁸ and have cast their gods into the fire, for they were not gods, but the work of men's hands, wood and stone. Therefore they were destroyed. ¹⁹ So now, O LORD our God, save us, please, from his hand, that all the kingdoms of the earth may know that you, O LORD, are God alone."

Isaiah Prophesies Sennacherib's Fall

²⁰ Then Isaiah the son of Amoz sent to Hezekiah, saying, "Thus says the LORD,

the God of Israel: Your prayer to me about Sennacherib king of Assyria I have heard. ²¹ This is the word that the LORD has spoken concerning him:

> "She despises you, she scorns you—
>   the virgin daughter of Zion;
>   she wags her head behind you—
>   the daughter of Jerusalem.

²² "Whom have you mocked and reviled?
>   Against whom have you raised your
>   voice
>   and lifted your eyes to the heights?
>   Against the Holy One of Israel!
²³ By your messengers you have mocked
>   the Lord,
>   and you have said, 'With my many
>   chariots

> **GETTING THE MESSAGE**
>
> **Siege mounds** (19:32) were mounds or ramps built out of dirt, rubble, and timbers. They were designed so that soldiers could batter down a city's walls and fortifications. The Assyrians were the first to use wheeled towers with these mounds. Protected inside the tower as it was moved up the ramp to the wall, the soldiers could then exit the tower and invade the city. A siege mound can still be found today at Masada.

> I have gone up the heights of the
>   mountains,
>   to the far recesses of Lebanon;
>   I felled its tallest cedars,
>   its choicest cypresses;
>   I entered its farthest lodging place,
>   its most fruitful forest.
²⁴ I dug wells
>   and drank foreign waters,
>   and I dried up with the sole of my foot
>   all the streams of Egypt.'

²⁵ "Have you not heard
>   that I determined it long ago?
>   I planned from days of old
>   what now I bring to pass,
>   that you should turn fortified cities
>   into heaps of ruins,
²⁶ while their inhabitants, shorn of
>   strength,
>   are dismayed and confounded,

and have become like plants of the field
>   and like tender grass,
>   like grass on the housetops,
>   blighted before it is grown.

²⁷ "But I know your sitting down
>   and your going out and coming in,
>   and your raging against me.
²⁸ Because you have raged against me
>   and your complacency has come
>   into my ears,
>   I will put my hook in your nose
>   and my bit in your mouth,
>   and I will turn you back on the way
>   by which you came.

²⁹ "And this shall be the sign for you: this year eat what grows of itself, and in the second year what springs of the same. Then in the third year sow and reap and plant vineyards, and eat their fruit. ³⁰ And the surviving remnant of the house of Judah shall again take root downward and bear fruit upward. ³¹ For out of Jerusalem shall go a remnant, and out of Mount Zion a band of survivors. The zeal of the LORD will do this.

³² "Therefore thus says the LORD concerning the king of Assyria: He shall not come into this city or shoot an arrow there, or come before it with a shield or cast up a siege mound against it. ³³ By the way that he came, by the same he shall return, and he shall not come into this city, declares the LORD. ³⁴ For I will defend this city to save it, for my own sake and for the sake of my servant David."

³⁵ And that night the angel of the LORD went out and struck down 185,000 in the camp of the Assyrians. And when people arose early in the morning, behold, these were all dead bodies. ³⁶ Then Sennacherib king of Assyria departed and went home and lived at Nineveh. ³⁷ And as he was worshiping in the house of Nisroch his god, Adrammelech and Sharezer, his sons, struck him down with the sword and escaped into the land of Ararat. And Esarhaddon his son reigned in his place.

Hezekiah's Illness and Recovery

20 In those days Hezekiah became sick and was at the point of death. And Isaiah the prophet the son of Amoz came to him and said to him, "Thus says the LORD, 'Set your house in order, for you shall die; you shall not recover.'" ² Then

Hezekiah turned his face to the wall and prayed to the LORD, saying, ³"Now, O LORD, please remember how I have walked before you in faithfulness and with a whole heart, and have done what is good in your sight." And Hezekiah wept bitterly. ⁴And before Isaiah had gone out of the middle court, the word of the LORD came to him: ⁵"Turn back, and say to Hezekiah the leader of my people, Thus says the LORD, the God of David your father: I have heard your prayer; I have seen your tears. Behold, I will heal you. On the third day you shall go up to the house of the LORD, ⁶and I will add fifteen years to your life. I will deliver you and this city out of the hand of the king of Assyria, and I will defend this city for my own sake and for my servant David's sake." ⁷And Isaiah said, "Bring a cake of figs. And let them take and lay it on the boil, that he may recover."

⁸And Hezekiah said to Isaiah, "What shall be the sign that the LORD will heal me, and that I shall go up to the house of the LORD on the third day?" ⁹And Isaiah said, "This shall be the sign to you from the LORD, that the LORD will do the thing that he has promised: shall the shadow go forward ten steps, or go back ten steps?" ¹⁰And Hezekiah answered, "It is an easy thing for the shadow to lengthen ten steps. Rather let the shadow go back ten steps." ¹¹And Isaiah the prophet called to the LORD, and he brought the shadow back ten steps, by which it had gone down on the steps of Ahaz.

Hezekiah and the Babylonian Envoys

¹²At that time Merodach-baladan the son of Baladan, king of Babylon, sent envoys with letters and a present to Hezekiah, for he heard that Hezekiah had been sick. ¹³And Hezekiah welcomed them, and he showed them all his treasure house, the silver, the gold, the spices, the precious oil, his armory, all that was found in his storehouses. There was nothing in his house or in all his realm that Hezekiah did not show them. ¹⁴Then Isaiah the prophet came to King Hezekiah, and said to him, "What did these men say? And from where did they come to you?" And Hezekiah said, "They have come from a far country, from Babylon." ¹⁵He said, "What have they seen in your house?" And Hezekiah answered, "They have seen all that is in my house;

there is nothing in my storehouses that I did not show them."

¹⁶Then Isaiah said to Hezekiah, "Hear the word of the LORD: ¹⁷Behold, the days are coming, when all that is in your house, and that which your fathers have stored up till this day, shall be carried to Babylon. Nothing shall be left, says the LORD. ¹⁸And some of your own sons, who shall be born to you, shall be taken away, and they shall be eunuchs in the palace of the king of Babylon." ¹⁹Then Hezekiah said to Isaiah, "The word of the LORD that you have spoken is good." For he thought, "Why not, if there will be peace and security in my days?"

²⁰The rest of the deeds of Hezekiah and all his might and how he made the pool and the conduit and brought water into the city, are they not written in the Book

GETTING THE MESSAGE

Hezekiah's tunnel. As Assyria prepared to attack Jerusalem, the city faced a crisis, since its water supply was outside the city walls. King Hezekiah responded by ordering the construction of a tunnel from the water source to the Pool of Siloam, within the city walls (20:20).

of the Chronicles of the Kings of Judah? ²¹And Hezekiah slept with his fathers, and Manasseh his son reigned in his place.

Manasseh Reigns in Judah

21 Manasseh was twelve years old when he began to reign, and he reigned fifty-five years in Jerusalem. His mother's name was Hephzibah. ²And he did what was evil in the sight of the LORD, according to the despicable practices of the nations whom the LORD drove out before the people of Israel. ³For he rebuilt the high places that Hezekiah his father had destroyed, and he erected altars for Baal and made an Asherah, as Ahab king of Israel had done, and worshiped all the host of heaven and served them. ⁴And he built altars in the house of the LORD, of which the LORD had said, "In Jerusalem will I put my name." ⁵And he built altars for all the host of heaven in the two courts of the house of the LORD. ⁶And he burned his son as an offering and used fortune-telling and omens and dealt with mediums and with necromancers. He did much evil in the sight of the LORD, provoking him to anger. **7** And the carved image of Asherah that he had made he set in the house of which the LORD said to David and to Solomon his son, "In this house, and in Jerusalem, which I have chosen out of all the tribes of Israel, I will put my name forever. **8** And I will not cause the feet of Israel to wander anymore out of the land that I gave to their fathers, if only they will be careful to do according to all that I have commanded them, and according to all the Law that my servant Moses commanded them." **9** But they did not listen, and Manasseh led them astray to do more evil than the nations had done whom the LORD destroyed before the people of Israel.

Manasseh's Idolatry Denounced

10 And the LORD said by his servants the prophets, **11** "Because Manasseh king of Judah has committed these abominations and has done things more evil than all that the Amorites did, who were before him, and has made Judah also to sin with his idols, **12** therefore thus says the LORD, the God of Israel: Behold, I am bringing upon Jerusalem and Judah such disaster that the ears of everyone who hears of it will tingle. **13** And I will stretch over Jerusalem the measuring line of Samaria, and the plumb line of the house of Ahab, and I will wipe Jerusalem as one wipes a dish, wiping it and turning it upside down. **14** And I will forsake the remnant of my heritage and give them into the hand of their enemies, and they shall become a prey and a spoil to all their enemies, **15** because they have done what is evil in my sight and have provoked me to anger, since the day their fathers came out of Egypt, even to this day."

16 Moreover, Manasseh shed very much innocent blood, till he had filled Jerusalem from one end to another, besides the sin that he made Judah to sin so that they did what was evil in the sight of the LORD.

17 Now the rest of the acts of Manasseh and all that he did, and the sin that he committed, are they not written in the Book of the Chronicles of the Kings of Judah? **18** And Manasseh slept with his fathers and was buried in the garden of his house, in the garden of Uzza, and Amon his son reigned in his place.

Amon Reigns in Judah

19 Amon was twenty-two years old when he began to reign, and he reigned two years in Jerusalem. His mother's name was Meshullemeth the daughter of Haruz of Jotbah. **20** And he did what was evil in the sight of the LORD, as Manasseh his father had done. **21** He walked in all the way in which his father walked and served the idols that his father served and worshiped them. **22** He abandoned the LORD, the God of his fathers, and did not walk in the way of the LORD. **23** And the servants of Amon conspired against him and put the king to death in his house. **24** But the people of the land struck down all those who had conspired against King Amon, and the people of the land made Josiah his son king in his place. **25** Now the rest of the acts of Amon that he did, are they not written in the Book of the Chronicles of the Kings of Judah? **26** And he was buried in his tomb in the garden of Uzza, and Josiah his son reigned in his place.

Josiah Reigns in Judah

22 Josiah was eight years old when he began to reign, and he reigned thirty-one years in Jerusalem. His mother's name was Jedidah the daughter of Adaiah of Bozkath. **2** And he did what was right in the eyes of the LORD and walked in all the way of David his father, and he did not turn aside to the right or to the left.

Josiah Repairs the Temple

3 In the eighteenth year of King Josiah, the king sent Shaphan the son of Azaliah, son of Meshullam, the secretary, to the house of the LORD, saying, **4** "Go up to Hilkiah the high priest, that he may count the money that has been brought into the house of the LORD, which the keepers of the threshold have collected from the people. **5** And let it be given into the hand of the workmen who have the oversight of the house of the LORD, and let them give it to the workmen who are at the house of the LORD, repairing the house **6** (that is, to the carpenters, and to the builders, and to the masons), and let them use it for buying timber and quarried stone to repair the house. **7** But no accounting shall be asked from them for the money that is delivered into their hand, for they deal honestly."

Hilkiah Finds the Book of the Law

⁸ And Hilkiah the high priest said to Shaphan the secretary, "I have found the Book of the Law in the house of the LORD." And Hilkiah gave the book to Shaphan, and he read it. ⁹ And Shaphan the secretary came to the king, and reported to the king, "Your servants have emptied out the money that was found in the house and have delivered it into the hand of the workmen who have the oversight of the house of the LORD." ¹⁰ Then Shaphan the secretary told the king, "Hilkiah the priest has given me a book." And Shaphan read it before the king.

¹¹ When the king heard the words of the Book of the Law, he tore his clothes. ¹² And the king commanded Hilkiah the priest, and

GETTING THE MESSAGE

Why did Josiah tear his clothes when the Law was read? As the Book of the Law was read in public for the first time in nearly 60 years, King Josiah tore his clothes as a sign of his grief. He grieved when he realized that he, as the nation's leader, had not been fulfilling the commandments of the Lord.

Ahikam the son of Shaphan, and Achbor the son of Micaiah, and Shaphan the secretary, and Asaiah the king's servant, saying, ¹³ "Go, inquire of the LORD for me, and for the people, and for all Judah, concerning the words of this book that has been found. For great is the wrath of the LORD that is kindled against us, because our fathers have not obeyed the words of this book, to do according to all that is written concerning us."

¹⁴ So Hilkiah the priest, and Ahikam, and Achbor, and Shaphan, and Asaiah went to Huldah the prophetess, the wife of Shallum the son of Tikvah, son of Harhas, keeper of the wardrobe (now she lived in Jerusalem in the Second Quarter), and they talked with her. ¹⁵ And she said to them, "Thus says the LORD, the God of Israel: 'Tell the man who sent you to me, ¹⁶ Thus says the LORD, Behold, I will bring disaster upon this place and upon its inhabitants, all the words of the book that the king of Judah

has read. ¹⁷ Because they have forsaken me and have made offerings to other gods, that they might provoke me to anger with all the work of their hands, therefore my wrath will be kindled against this place, and it will not be quenched. ¹⁸ But to the king of Judah, who sent you to inquire of the LORD, thus shall you say to him, Thus says the LORD, the God of Israel: Regarding the words that you have heard, ¹⁹ because your heart was penitent, and you humbled yourself before the LORD, when you heard how I spoke against this

PROFILE

JOSIAH

Josiah was only eight years old when he became king of Judah. He had been ruling Judah for 18 years when Hilkiah, the high priest, found the Book of the Law. As soon as Josiah heard the commands of God, he tore his clothes in grief and despair. He launched a massive effort to abolish pagan worship throughout Judah and Israel. After organizing a covenant-renewal ceremony, he destroyed all the buildings associated with idol worship. Among his most significant deeds was restoring the celebration of the Passover, which had not been observed since the days of the judges. Josiah was more faithful to the Lord than even David and Hezekiah. He was like the ideal king described in Deut. 17:19–20.

KEY REFERENCE: 2 KINGS 23:25

place and against its inhabitants, that they should become a desolation and a curse, and you have torn your clothes and wept before me, I also have heard you, declares the LORD. ²⁰ Therefore, behold, I will gather you to your fathers, and you shall be gathered to your grave in peace, and your eyes shall not see all the disaster that I will bring upon this place.'" And they brought back word to the king.

Josiah's Reforms

23 Then the king sent, and all the elders of Judah and Jerusalem were gathered to him. ² And the king went up to the house of the LORD, and with him all the men of Judah and all the inhabitants of Jerusalem and the priests and the prophets, all the people, both small and great. And he read in their hearing all the words of the Book of the Covenant that had been found in the house of the LORD. ³ And the king stood by the pillar and made a covenant before the LORD, to walk after the LORD and to keep his commandments and his testimonies and his statutes with all his heart and all his soul, to perform the words of this covenant that were written in this book. And all the people joined in the covenant.

⁴ And the king commanded Hilkiah the high priest and the priests of the second order and the keepers of the threshold to bring out of the temple of the LORD all the vessels made for Baal, for Asherah, and for all the host of heaven. He burned them outside Jerusalem in the fields of the Kidron

GETTING THE MESSAGE

The host of heaven refers in 23:4 to false gods, represented by celestial bodies such as the sun, moon, and planets. King Josiah ordered the destruction of all these symbols of pagan worship.

and carried their ashes to Bethel. ⁵ And he deposed the priests whom the kings of Judah had ordained to make offerings in the high places at the cities of Judah and around Jerusalem; those also who burned incense to Baal, to the sun and the moon and the constellations and all the host of the heavens. ⁶ And he brought out the Asherah from the house of the LORD, outside Jerusalem, to the brook Kidron, and burned it at the brook Kidron and beat it to dust and cast the dust of it upon the graves of the common people. ⁷ And he broke down the houses of the male cult prostitutes who were in the house of the LORD, where the women wove hangings for the Asherah. ⁸ And he brought all the priests out of the cities of Judah, and defiled the high places where the priests had made offerings, from Geba to Beersheba. And he broke down the high places of the gates that were at the entrance of the gate of Joshua the gover-

nor of the city, which were on one's left at the gate of the city. ⁹ However, the priests of the high places did not come up to the altar of the LORD in Jerusalem, but they ate unleavened bread among their brothers. ¹⁰ And he defiled Topheth, which is in the Valley of the Son of Hinnom, that no one might burn his son or his daughter as an offering to Molech. ¹¹ And he removed the horses that the kings of Judah had dedicated to the sun, at the entrance to the house of the LORD, by the chamber of Nathan-melech the chamberlain, which was in the precincts. And he burned the chariots of the sun with fire. ¹² And the altars on the roof of the upper chamber of Ahaz, which the kings of Judah had made, and the altars that Manasseh had made in the two courts of the house of the LORD, he pulled down and broke in pieces and cast the dust of them into the brook Kidron. ¹³ And the king defiled the high places that were east of Jerusalem, to the south of the mount of corruption, which Solomon the king of Israel had built for Ashtoreth the abomination of the Sidonians, and for Chemosh the abomination of Moab, and for Milcom the abomination of the Ammonites. ¹⁴ And he broke in pieces the pillars and cut down the Asherim and filled their places with the bones of men.

¹⁵ Moreover, the altar at Bethel, the high place erected by Jeroboam the son of Nebat, who made Israel to sin, that altar with the high place he pulled down and burned, reducing it to dust. He also burned the Asherah. ¹⁶ And as Josiah turned, he saw the tombs there on the mount. And he sent and took the bones out of the tombs and burned them on the altar and defiled it, according to the word of the LORD that the man of God proclaimed, who had predicted these things. ¹⁷ Then he said, "What is that monument that I see?" And the men of the city told him, "It is the tomb of the man of God who came from Judah and predicted these things that you have done against the altar at Bethel." ¹⁸ And he said, "Let him be; let no man move his bones." So they let his bones alone, with the bones of the prophet who came out of Samaria. ¹⁹ And Josiah removed all the shrines also of the high places that were in the cities of Samaria, which kings of Israel had made, provoking

the LORD to anger. He did to them according to all that he had done at Bethel. **20** And he sacrificed all the priests of the high places who were there, on the altars, and burned human bones on them. Then he returned to Jerusalem.

Josiah Restores the Passover

21 And the king commanded all the people, "Keep the Passover to the LORD your God, as it is written in this Book of the Covenant." **22** For no such Passover had been kept since the days of the judges who judged Israel, or during all the days of the kings of Israel or of the kings of Judah. **23** But in the eighteenth year of King Josiah this Passover was kept to the LORD in Jerusalem.

24 Moreover, Josiah put away the mediums and the necromancers and the household gods and the idols and all the abominations that were seen in the land of Judah and in Jerusalem, that he might establish the words of the law that were written in the book that Hilkiah the priest found in the house of the LORD. **25** Before him there was no king like him, who turned to the LORD with all his heart and with all his soul and with all his might, according to all the Law of Moses, nor did any like him arise after him.

26 Still the LORD did not turn from the burning of his great wrath, by which his anger was kindled against Judah, because of all the provocations with which Manasseh had provoked him. **27** And the LORD said, "I will remove Judah also out of my sight, as I have removed Israel, and I will cast off this city that I have chosen, Jerusalem, and the house of which I said, My name shall be there."

Josiah's Death in Battle

28 Now the rest of the acts of Josiah and all that he did, are they not written in the Book of the Chronicles of the Kings of Judah? **29** In his days Pharaoh Neco king of Egypt went up to the king of Assyria to the river Euphrates. King Josiah went to meet him, and Pharaoh Neco killed him at Megiddo, as soon as he saw him. **30** And his servants carried him dead in a chariot from Megiddo and brought him to Jerusalem and buried him in his own tomb. And the people of the land took Jehoahaz the son of Josiah, and anointed him, and made him king in his father's place.

Jehoahaz's Reign and Captivity

31 Jehoahaz was twenty-three years old when he began to reign, and he reigned three months in Jerusalem. His mother's name was Hamutal the daughter of Jeremiah of Libnah. **32** And he did what was evil in the sight of the LORD, according to all that his fathers had done. **33** And Pharaoh Neco put him in bonds at Riblah in the land of Hamath, that he might not reign in Jerusalem, and laid on the land a tribute of a hundred talents of silver and a talent of gold. **34** And Pharaoh Neco made Eliakim the son of Josiah king in the place of Josiah his father, and changed his name to Jehoiakim. But he took Jehoahaz away, and he came to Egypt and died there. **35** And Jehoiakim gave the silver and the gold to Pharaoh, but he taxed the land to give the money according to the command of Pharaoh. He exacted the

silver and the gold of the people of the land, from everyone according to his assessment, to give it to Pharaoh Neco.

Jehoiakim Reigns in Judah

36 Jehoiakim was twenty-five years old when he began to reign, and he reigned eleven years in Jerusalem. His mother's name was Zebidah the daughter of Pedaiah of Rumah. **37** And he did what was evil in the sight of the LORD, according to all that his fathers had done.

24 In his days, Nebuchadnezzar king of Babylon came up, and Jehoiakim became his servant for three years. Then he turned and rebelled against him. **2** And the LORD sent against him bands of the Chaldeans and bands of the Syrians and bands of the Moabites and bands of the Ammonites, and sent them against Judah to destroy it, according to the word of the LORD that he spoke by his servants the prophets. **3** Surely this came upon Judah at the command of the LORD, to remove them out of his sight, for the sins of Manasseh, according to all that he had done, [4] and also for the innocent blood that he had shed. For he filled Jerusalem with innocent blood, and the LORD would not pardon. [5] Now the rest of the deeds of Jehoiakim and all that he did, are they not written in the Book of the Chronicles of the Kings of Judah? [6] So Jehoiakim slept with his fathers, and Jehoiachin his son reigned in his place. [7] And the king of Egypt did not come again out of his land, for the king of Babylon had taken all that belonged to the king of Egypt from the Brook of Egypt to the river Euphrates.

Jehoiachin Reigns in Judah

[8] Jehoiachin was eighteen years old when he became king, and he reigned three months in Jerusalem. His mother's name was Nehushta the daughter of Elnathan of Jerusalem. [9] And he did what was evil in the sight of the LORD, according to all that his father had done.

Jerusalem Captured

[10] At that time the servants of Nebuchadnezzar king of Babylon came up to Jerusalem, and the city was besieged. [11] And Nebuchadnezzar king of Babylon came to the city while his servants were besieging it, [12] and Jehoiachin the king of Judah gave himself up to the king of Babylon, himself and his mother and his servants and his officials and his palace officials. The king of Babylon took him prisoner in the eighth year of his reign [13] and carried off all the treasures of the house of the LORD and the treasures of the king's house, and cut in pieces all the vessels of gold in the temple of the LORD, which Solomon king of Israel had made, as the LORD had foretold. [14] He carried away all Jerusalem and all the officials and all the mighty men of valor, 10,000 captives, and all the craftsmen and the smiths. None remained, except the poorest people of the land. [15] And he carried away Jehoiachin to Babylon. The king's mother, the king's wives, his officials, and the chief men of the land he took into captivity from Jerusalem to Babylon. [16] And the king of Babylon brought captive to Babylon all the men of valor, 7,000, and the craftsmen and the metal workers, 1,000, all of them strong and fit for war. [17] And the king of Babylon made

Mattaniah, Jehoiachin's uncle, king in his place, and changed his name to Zedekiah.

Zedekiah Reigns in Judah

[18] Zedekiah was twenty-one years old when he became king, and he reigned eleven years in Jerusalem. His mother's name was Hamutal the daughter of Jeremiah of Libnah. [19] And he did what was evil in the sight of the LORD, according to all that Jehoiakim had done. [20] For because of the anger of the LORD it came to the point in Jerusalem and Judah that he cast them out from his presence.

And Zedekiah rebelled against the king of Babylon.

Fall and Captivity of Judah

25 And in the ninth year of his reign, in the tenth month, on the tenth day of the month, Nebuchadnezzar king of Babylon came with all his army against Jerusalem and laid siege to it. And they built siegeworks all around it. [2] So the city was besieged till the eleventh year of King Zedekiah. [3] On the ninth day of the fourth month the famine was so severe in the city that there was no food for the people of the land. [4] Then a breach was made in the city, and all the men of war fled by night by the way of the gate between the two walls, by the king's garden, and the Chaldeans were around the city. And they went in the direction of the Arabah. [5] But the army of the Chaldeans pursued the king and overtook him in the plains of Jericho, and all his army was scattered from him. [6] Then they captured the king and brought him up to the king of Babylon at Riblah, and they passed sentence on him. [7] They slaughtered the sons of Zedekiah before his eyes, and put out the eyes of Zedekiah and bound him in chains and took him to Babylon.

[8] In the fifth month, on the seventh day of the month—that was the nineteenth year of King Nebuchadnezzar, king of Babylon—Nebuzaradan, the captain of the bodyguard, a servant of the king of Babylon, came to Jerusalem. [9] And he burned the house of the LORD and the king's house and all the houses of Jerusalem; every great house he burned down. [10] And all the army of the Chaldeans, who were with the captain of the guard, broke down the walls around Jerusalem. [11] And the rest of the people who were left in the city and the deserters who

had deserted to the king of Babylon, together with the rest of the multitude, Nebuzaradan the captain of the guard carried into exile. ¹² But the captain of the guard left some of the poorest of the land to be vinedressers and plowmen.

¹³ And the pillars of bronze that were in the house of the LORD, and the stands and the bronze sea that were in the house of the LORD, the Chaldeans broke in pieces and carried the bronze to Babylon. ¹⁴ And they took away the pots and the shovels and the snuffers and the dishes for incense and all the vessels of bronze used in the temple service, ¹⁵ the fire pans also and the bowls. What was of gold the captain of the guard took away as gold, and what was of silver, as silver. ¹⁶ As for the two pillars, the one sea, and the stands that Solomon had made for the house of the LORD, the bronze of all these vessels was beyond weight. ¹⁷ The height of the one pillar was eighteen cubits, and on it was a capital of bronze. The height of the capital was three cubits. A latticework and pomegranates, all of bronze, were all around the capital. And the second pillar had the same, with the latticework.

¹⁸ And the captain of the guard took Seraiah the chief priest and Zephaniah the second priest and the three keepers of the threshold; ¹⁹ and from the city he took an officer who had been in command of the men of war, and five men of the king's council who were found in the city; and the secretary of the commander of the army, who mustered the people of the land; and sixty men of the people of the land, who were found in the city. ²⁰ And Nebuzaradan the captain of the guard took them and brought them to the king of Babylon at Riblah. ²¹ And the king of Babylon struck them down and put them to death at Riblah in the land of Hamath. So Judah was taken into exile out of its land.

Gedaliah Made Governor of Judah

²² And over the people who remained in the land of Judah, whom Nebuchadnezzar king of Babylon had left, he appointed Gedaliah the son of Ahikam, son of Shaphan,

governor. ²³ Now when all the captains and their men heard that the king of Babylon had appointed Gedaliah governor, they came with their men to Gedaliah at Mizpah, namely, Ishmael the son of Nethaniah, and Johanan the son of Kareah, and Seraiah the son of Tanhumeth the Netophathite, and Jaazaniah the son of the Maacathite. ²⁴ And Gedaliah swore to them and their men, saying, "Do not be afraid because of the Chaldean officials. Live in the land and serve the king of Babylon, and it shall be well with you." ²⁵ But in the seventh month, Ishmael the son of Nethaniah, son of Elishama, of the royal family, came with ten men and struck down Gedaliah and put him to death along with the Jews and the Chaldeans who

GETTING THE MESSAGE

What happened to the ark of the covenant? After the fall of Jerusalem, the ark completely disappeared from historical records. It is unlikely that the Babylonians took it because there is no mention of it in Babylonian records.

were with him at Mizpah. ²⁶ Then all the people, both small and great, and the captains of the forces arose and went to Egypt, for they were afraid of the Chaldeans.

Jehoiachin Released from Prison

²⁷ And in the thirty-seventh year of the exile of Jehoiachin king of Judah, in the twelfth month, on the twenty-seventh day of the month, Evil-merodach king of Babylon, in the year that he began to reign, graciously freed Jehoiachin king of Judah from prison. ²⁸ And he spoke kindly to him and gave him a seat above the seats of the kings who were with him in Babylon. ²⁹ So Jehoiachin put off his prison garments. And every day of his life he dined regularly at the king's table, ³⁰ and for his allowance, a regular allowance was given him by the king, according to his daily needs, as long as he lived.

INTRODUCTION TO 1–2 CHRONICLES

1010 B.C.	931 B.C.	722 B.C.	586 B.C.
Reign of David begins	Israel divided	Fall of Israel	Fall of Judah

AUTHOR AND DATE

The text nowhere directly identifies its author, but traditionally he has been called "the Chronicler." He was either a priest or Levite who was employed in the service of the temple during the Persian period (539–332 B.C.). He had scribal training and access to the temple records.

THEME

The central theme of Chronicles is God's covenant with David as the basis of Israel's life and hope. The Davidic covenant is expressed in two institutions: the monarchy and the temple. These institutions are related (1 Chron. 17:10b–14), and together they represent God's kingdom in Israel (2 Chron. 13:5, 8). The Davidic covenant does not replace the Mosaic covenant but builds on it for the new age of the monarchy and the temple.

PURPOSE, OCCASION, AND BACKGROUND

Judah and Benjamin, the only surviving tribes of Israel, had returned to the land after the Babylonian exile. They had rebuilt the temple in Jerusalem. But in many ways it seemed like they were still in exile (see Ezra 9:6–15; Neh. 9:32–36). There were questions about Israel's place in God's purposes and the meaning of his ancient promises to David. With such questions in mind, the Chronicler wrote his books to promote spiritual and social renewal. He presented an interpretation of Israel's past, drawing mainly on the books of Samuel and Kings. He showed how the nation's unfaithfulness to God had led to disaster but also how its faithful kings and people had experienced God's blessing.

KEY THEMES

1. *The Davidic covenant.* God's covenant with David preserved the nation and enabled Solomon to build the temple. God is committed to preserving the line of David's descendants even through spiritual unfaithfulness (2 Chron. 21:13) and exile (1 Chron. 3:17–24). Being heirs of God's covenant with David also involves living according to God's earlier covenant with Moses.

2. *The temple.* The temple is an expression of the Davidic covenant. David provided for the construction of the temple and organized its personnel. His faithful successors should ensure that the worship is maintained, and that the building is kept in repair and is purified after defilement. The temple personnel should come to the aid of the Davidic dynasty in times of crisis. The Levites played an essential role in maintaining the whole system of worship, and in many ways they are the forerunners of the Christian ministry.

3. *The people of Israel.* The Chronicler sought to address some urgent questions of his day concerning the identity of Israel. He wanted to instill fresh confidence in the people. The genealogies of Israel that begin the work (1 Chronicles 1–9) start by tracing the people's ancestry back to Adam, a striking reminder that Israel was at the center of God's purpose from the very beginning of creation.

Second, the genealogies makes it clear that all 12 tribes were descended from Jacob's sons (1 Chron. 2:1). The Chronicler's history of the divided kingdom (2 Chronicles 10–36) focuses mainly on Judah and Benjamin. But he tries to show that the northern tribes are still a part of

BASIC CHRONOLOGY OF 1–2 CHRONICLES

Events	Dates	Passages
Foundation of the Davidic monarchy	c. 1010–931 B.C.	1 Chronicles 10–2 Chronicles 9
History of Judah from the division of the kingdom until its fall	931–586	2 Chron. 10:1–36:21
Babylonian captivity	586–538	2 Chron. 36:17–21
Cyrus's decree	538	2 Chron. 36:22–23

Israel, even though they rebelled against the rightful Davidic king (2 Chron. 13:5).

While the Chronicler does focus on the nation's kings and its priesthood, he also includes many stories that highlight the participation of ordinary people in the life of the nation.

OUTLINE FOR 1–2 CHRONICLES

1 CHRONICLES

From Adam to Abraham

1 Adam, Seth, Enosh; ² Kenan, Mahalalel, Jared; ³ Enoch, Methuselah, Lamech; ⁴ Noah, Shem, Ham, and Japheth.

⁵ The sons of Japheth: Gomer, Magog, Madai, Javan, Tubal, Meshech, and Tiras. ⁶ The sons of Gomer: Ashkenaz, Riphath, and Togarmah. ⁷ The sons of Javan: Elishah, Tarshish, Kittim, and Rodanim.

⁸ The sons of Ham: Cush, Egypt, Put, and Canaan. ⁹ The sons of Cush: Seba, Havilah, Sabta, Raama, and Sabteca. The sons of Raamah: Sheba and Dedan. ¹⁰ Cush fathered Nimrod. He was the first on earth to be a mighty man.

> ### GETTING THE MESSAGE
>
> **Why begin with Adam?** By beginning with Adam, the Chronicler shows that God planned to make Israel his chosen people since the very beginning of human history.

¹¹ Egypt fathered Ludim, Anamim, Lehabim, Naphtuhim, ¹² Pathrusim, Casluhim (from whom the Philistines came), and Caphtorim.

¹³ Canaan fathered Sidon his firstborn and Heth, ¹⁴ and the Jebusites, the Amorites, the Girgashites, ¹⁵ the Hivites, the Arkites, the Sinites, ¹⁶ the Arvadites, the Zemarites, and the Hamathites.

¹⁷ The sons of Shem: Elam, Asshur, Arpachshad, Lud, and Aram. And the sons of Aram: Uz, Hul, Gether, and Meshech. ¹⁸ Arpachshad fathered Shelah, and Shelah fathered Eber. ¹⁹ To Eber were born two sons: the name of the one was Peleg (for in his days the earth was divided), and his brother's name was Joktan. ²⁰ Joktan fathered Almodad, Sheleph, Hazarmaveth, Jerah, ²¹ Hadoram, Uzal, Diklah, ²² Obal, Abimael, Sheba, ²³ Ophir, Havilah, and Jobab; all these were the sons of Joktan.

²⁴ Shem, Arpachshad, Shelah; ²⁵ Eber, Peleg, Reu; ²⁶ Serug, Nahor, Terah; ²⁷ Abram, that is, Abraham.

From Abraham to Jacob

²⁸ The sons of Abraham: Isaac and Ishmael. ²⁹ These are their genealogies: the firstborn of Ishmael, Nebaioth, and Kedar, Adbeel, Mibsam, ³⁰ Mishma, Dumah, Massa, Hadad, Tema, ³¹ Jetur, Naphish, and Kedemah. These are the sons of Ishmael. ³² The sons of Keturah, Abraham's concubine: she bore Zimran, Jokshan, Medan, Midian, Ishbak, and Shuah. The sons of Jokshan: Sheba and Dedan. ³³ The sons of Midian: Ephah, Epher, Hanoch, Abida, and Eldaah. All these were the descendants of Keturah.

³⁴ Abraham fathered Isaac. The sons of Isaac: Esau and Israel. ³⁵ The sons of Esau: Eliphaz, Reuel, Jeush, Jalam, and Korah. ³⁶ The sons of Eliphaz: Teman, Omar, Zepho, Gatam, Kenaz, and of Timna, Amalek. ³⁷ The sons of Reuel: Nahath, Zerah, Shammah, and Mizzah.

³⁸ The sons of Seir: Lotan, Shobal, Zibeon, Anah, Dishon, Ezer, and Dishan. ³⁹ The sons of Lotan: Hori and Hemam; and Lotan's sister was Timna. ⁴⁰ The sons of Shobal: Alvan, Manahath, Ebal, Shepho, and Onam. The sons of Zibeon: Aiah and Anah. ⁴¹ The son of Anah: Dishon. The sons of Dishon: Hemdan, Eshban, Ithran, and Cheran. ⁴² The sons of Ezer: Bilhan, Zaavan, and Akan. The sons of Dishan: Uz and Aran.

⁴³ These are the kings who reigned in the land of Edom before any king reigned over the people of Israel: Bela the son of Beor, the name of his city being Dinhabah. ⁴⁴ Bela died, and Jobab the son of Zerah of Bozrah reigned in his place. ⁴⁵ Jobab died, and Husham of the land of the Temanites reigned in his place. ⁴⁶ Husham died, and Hadad the son of Bedad, who defeated Midian in the country of Moab, reigned in his place, the name of his city being Avith. ⁴⁷ Hadad died, and Samlah of Masrekah reigned in his place. ⁴⁸ Samlah died, and Shaul of Rehoboth on the Euphrates reigned

in his place. ⁴⁹Shaul died, and Baal-hanan, the son of Achbor, reigned in his place. ⁵⁰Baal-hanan died, and Hadad reigned in his place, the name of his city being Pai; and his wife's name was Mehetabel, the daughter of Matred, the daughter of Mezahab. ⁵¹And Hadad died.

The chiefs of Edom were: chiefs Timna, Alvah, Jetheth, ⁵²Oholibamah, Elah, Pinon, ⁵³Kenaz, Teman, Mibzar, ⁵⁴Magdiel, and Iram; these are the chiefs of Edom.

A Genealogy of David

2 These are the sons of Israel: Reuben, Simeon, Levi, Judah, Issachar, Zebulun, ²Dan, Joseph, Benjamin, Naphtali, Gad, and Asher. ³The sons of Judah: Er, Onan and Shelah; these three Bath-shua the Canaanite bore to him. Now Er, Judah's firstborn, was evil in the sight of the LORD, and he put him to death. ⁴His daughter-in-law Tamar also bore him Perez and Zerah. Judah had five sons in all.

⁵The sons of Perez: Hezron and Hamul. ⁶The sons of Zerah: Zimri, Ethan, Heman, Calcol, and Dara, five in all. ⁷The son of Carmi: Achan, the troubler of Israel, who broke faith in the matter of the devoted thing; ⁸and Ethan's son was Azariah.

⁹The sons of Hezron that were born to him: Jerahmeel, Ram, and Chelubai. ¹⁰Ram fathered Amminadab, and Amminadab fathered Nahshon, prince of the sons of Judah. ¹¹Nahshon fathered Salmon, Salmon fathered Boaz, ¹²Boaz fathered Obed, Obed fathered Jesse. ¹³Jesse fathered Eliab his firstborn, Abinadab the second, Shimea the third, ¹⁴Nethanel the fourth, Raddai the fifth, ¹⁵Ozem the sixth, David the seventh. ¹⁶And their sisters were Zeruiah and Abigail. The sons of Zeruiah: Abishai, Joab, and Asahel, three. ¹⁷Abigail bore Amasa, and the father of Amasa was Jether the Ishmaelite.

¹⁸Caleb the son of Hezron fathered children by his wife Azubah, and by Jerioth; and these were her sons: Jesher, Shobab, and Ardon. ¹⁹When Azubah died, Caleb married Ephrath, who bore him Hur. ²⁰Hur fathered Uri, and Uri fathered Bezalel.

²¹Afterward Hezron went in to the daughter of Machir the father of Gilead, whom he married when he was sixty years old, and she bore him Segub. ²²And Segub fathered Jair, who had twenty-three cities in the land of Gilead. ²³But Geshur and Aram took from them Havvoth-jair, Kenath, and its villages, sixty towns. All these were descendants of Machir, the father of Gilead. ²⁴After the death of Hezron, Caleb went in to Ephrathah, the wife of Hezron his father, and she bore him Ashhur, the father of Tekoa.

²⁵The sons of Jerahmeel, the firstborn of Hezron: Ram, his firstborn, Bunah, Oren, Ozem, and Ahijah. ²⁶Jerahmeel also had another wife, whose name was Atarah; she was the mother of Onam. ²⁷The sons of Ram, the firstborn of Jerahmeel: Maaz, Jamin, and Eker. ²⁸The sons of Onam: Shammai and Jada. The sons of Shammai: Nadab and Abishur. ²⁹The name of Abishur's wife was Abihail, and she bore him Ahban and Molid. ³⁰The sons of Nadab: Seled and Appaim; and Seled died childless. ³¹The son of Appaim: Ishi. The son of Ishi:

> ### GETTING THE MESSAGE
>
> **Why so many genealogies?** The first readers of 1 Chronicles were Israelites living after the Babylonian exile. The genealogies showed them that they were still God's people. For Christians, the genealogies also show how God preserved the line of David's descendants that eventually led to Jesus the Messiah.

Sheshan. The son of Sheshan: Ahlai. ³²The sons of Jada, Shammai's brother: Jether and Jonathan; and Jether died childless. ³³The sons of Jonathan: Peleth and Zaza. These were the descendants of Jerahmeel. ³⁴Now Sheshan had no sons, only daughters, but Sheshan had an Egyptian slave whose name was Jarha. ³⁵So Sheshan gave his daughter in marriage to Jarha his slave, and she bore him Attai. ³⁶Attai fathered Nathan, and Nathan fathered Zabad. ³⁷Zabad fathered Ephlal, and Ephlal fathered Obed. ³⁸Obed fathered Jehu, and Jehu fathered Azariah. ³⁹Azariah fathered Helez, and Helez fathered Eleasah. ⁴⁰Eleasah fathered Sismai, and Sismai fathered Shallum. ⁴¹Shallum fathered Jekamiah, and Jekamiah fathered Elishama.

⁴²The sons of Caleb the brother of Jerahmeel: Mareshah his firstborn, who fathered Ziph. The son of Mareshah: Hebron. ⁴³The sons of Hebron: Korah, Tappuah, Rekem and Shema. ⁴⁴Shema

fathered Raham, the father of Jorkeam; and Rekem fathered Shammai. **45** The son of Shammai: Maon; and Maon fathered Beth-zur. **46** Ephah also, Caleb's concubine, bore Haran, Moza, and Gazez; and Haran fathered Gazez. **47** The sons of Jahdai: Regem, Jotham, Geshan, Pelet, Ephah, and Shaaph. **48** Maacah, Caleb's concubine, bore Sheber and Tirhanah. **49** She also bore Shaaph the father of Madmannah, Sheva the father of Machbenah and the father of Gibea; and the daughter of Caleb was Achsah. **50** These were the descendants of Caleb.

The sons of Hur the firstborn of Ephrathah: Shobal the father of Kiriath-jearim, **51** Salma, the father of Bethlehem, and Hareph the father of Beth-gader. **52** Shobal the father of Kiriath-jearim had other sons: Haroeh, half of the Menuhoth. **53** And the clans of Kiriath-jearim: the Ithrites, the

GETTING THE MESSAGE

Do the books of Chronicles have a main theme? The central theme of 1–2 Chronicles is how God's covenant with David provided an enduring hope for Israel, even in its darkest hours.

Puthites, the Shumathites, and the Mishraites; from these came the Zorathites and the Eshtaolites. **54** The sons of Salma: Bethlehem, the Netophathites, Atroth-beth-joab and half of the Manahathites, the Zorites. **55** The clans also of the scribes who lived at Jabez: the Tirathites, the Shimeathites and the Sucathites. These are the Kenites who came from Hammath, the father of the house of Rechab.

Descendants of David

3 These are the sons of David who were born to him in Hebron: the firstborn, Amnon, by Ahinoam the Jezreelite; the second, Daniel, by Abigail the Carmelite, **2** the third, Absalom, whose mother was Maacah, the daughter of Talmai, king of Geshur; the fourth, Adonijah, whose mother was Haggith; **3** the fifth, Shephatiah, by Abital; the sixth, Ithream, by his wife Eglah; **4** six were born to him in Hebron, where he reigned for seven years and six months. And he reigned thirty-three years in Jerusalem. **5** These were born to him in

Jerusalem: Shimea, Shobab, Nathan and Solomon, four by Bath-shua, the daughter of Ammiel; **6** then Ibhar, Elishama, Eliphelet, **7** Nogah, Nepheg, Japhia, **8** Elishama, Eliada, and Eliphelet, nine. **9** All these were David's sons, besides the sons of the concubines, and Tamar was their sister.

10 The son of Solomon was Rehoboam, Abijah his son, Asa his son, Jehoshaphat his son, **11** Joram his son, Ahaziah his son, Joash his son, **12** Amaziah his son, Azariah his son, Jotham his son, **13** Ahaz his son, Hezekiah his son, Manasseh his son, **14** Amon his son, Josiah his son. **15** The sons of Josiah: Johanan the firstborn, the second Jehoiakim, the third Zedekiah, the fourth Shallum. **16** The descendants of Jehoiakim: Jeconiah his son, Zedekiah his son; **17** and the sons of Jeconiah, the captive: Shealtiel his son, **18** Malchiram, Pedaiah, Shenazzar, Jekamiah, Hoshama and Nedabiah; **19** and the sons of Pedaiah: Zerubbabel and Shimei; and the sons of Zerubbabel: Meshullam and Hananiah, and Shelomith was their sister; **20** and Hashubah, Ohel, Berechiah, Hasadiah, and Jushabhesed, five. **21** The sons of Hananiah: Pelatiah and Jeshaiah, his son Rephaiah, his son Arnan, his son Obadiah, his son Shecaniah. **22** The son of Shecaniah: Shemaiah. And the sons of Shemaiah: Hattush, Igal, Bariah, Neariah, and Shaphat, six. **23** The sons of Neariah: Elioenai, Hizkiah, and Azrikam, three. **24** The sons of Elioenai: Hodaviah, Eliashib, Pelaiah, Akkub, Johanan, Delaiah, and Anani, seven.

Descendants of Judah

4 The sons of Judah: Perez, Hezron, Carmi, Hur, and Shobal. **2** Reaiah the son of Shobal fathered Jahath, and Jahath fathered Ahumai and Lahad. These were the clans of the Zorathites. **3** These were the sons of Etam: Jezreel, Ishma, and Idbash; and the name of their sister was Hazzelelponi, **4** and Penuel fathered Gedor, and Ezer fathered Hushah. These were the sons of Hur, the firstborn of Ephrathah, the father of Bethlehem. **5** Ashhur, the father of Tekoa, had two wives, Helah and Naarah; **6** Naarah bore him Ahuzzam, Hepher, Temeni, and Haahashtari. These were the sons of Naarah. **7** The sons of Helah: Zereth, Izhar, and Ethnan. **8** Koz fathered Anub, Zobebah, and the clans of Aharhel, the son of Harum. **9** Jabez was more honorable than

his brothers; and his mother called his name Jabez, saying, "Because I bore him in pain."[1] [10] Jabez called upon the God of Israel, saying, "Oh that you would bless me and enlarge my border, and that your hand might be with me, and that you would keep me from harm so that it might not bring me pain!" And God granted what he asked. [11] Chelub, the brother of Shuhah, fathered Mehir, who fathered Eshton. [12] Eshton fathered Beth-rapha, Paseah, and Tehinnah, the father of Ir-nahash. These are the men of Recah. [13] The sons of Kenaz: Othniel and Seraiah; and the sons of Othniel: Hathath and Meonothai. [14] Meonothai fathered Ophrah; and Seraiah fathered Joab, the father of Ge-harashim,[2] so-called because they were craftsmen. [15] The sons of Caleb the son of Jephunneh: Iru, Elah, and Naam; and the son of Elah: Kenaz. [16] The sons of Jehallelel: Ziph, Ziphah, Tiria, and Asarel. [17] The sons of Ezrah: Jether, Mered, Epher, and Jalon. These are the sons of Bithiah, the daughter of Pharaoh, whom Mered married; and she conceived and bore Miriam, Shammai, and Ishbah, the father of Eshtemoa. [18] And his Judahite wife bore Jered the father of Gedor, Heber the father of Soco, and Jekuthiel the father of Zanoah. [19] The sons of the wife of Hodiah, the sister of Naham, were the fathers of Keilah the Garmite and Eshtemoa the Maacathite. [20] The sons of Shimon: Amnon, Rinnah, Ben-hanan, and Tilon. The sons of Ishi: Zoheth and Ben-zoheth. [21] The sons of Shelah the son of Judah: Er the father of Lecah, Laadah the father of Mareshah, and the clans of the house of linen workers at Beth-ashbea; [22] and Jokim, and the men of Cozeba, and Joash, and Saraph, who ruled in Moab and returned to Lehem (now the records are ancient). [23] These were the potters who were inhabitants of Netaim and Gederah. They lived there in the king's service.

Descendants of Simeon

[24] The sons of Simeon: Nemuel, Jamin, Jarib, Zerah, Shaul; [25] Shallum was his son, Mibsam his son, Mishma his son. [26] The sons of Mishma: Hammuel his son, Zaccur his son, Shimei his son. [27] Shimei had sixteen sons and six daughters; but his brothers did not have many children, nor did all their clan multiply like the men of Judah. [28] They lived in Beersheba, Moladah, Hazar-shual, [29] Bilhah, Ezem, Tolad, [30] Bethuel, Hormah, Ziklag, [31] Beth-marcaboth, Hazar-susim, Beth-biri, and Shaaraim. These were their cities until David reigned. [32] And their villages were Etam, Ain, Rimmon, Tochen, and Ashan, five cities, [33] along with all their villages that were around these cities as far as Baal. These were their settlements, and they kept a genealogical record.

[34] Meshobab, Jamlech, Joshah the son of Amaziah, [35] Joel, Jehu the son of Joshibiah, son of Seraiah, son of Asiel, [36] Elioenai, Jaakobah, Jeshohaiah, Asaiah, Adiel, Jesimiel, Benaiah, [37] Ziza the son of Shiphi, son of Allon, son of Jedaiah, son of Shimri, son of Shemaiah — [38] these mentioned by name were princes in their clans, and their fathers' houses increased greatly. [39] They journeyed to the entrance of Gedor, to the east side of the valley, to seek pasture for their flocks, [40] where they found rich, good pasture, and the land was very broad, quiet, and peaceful, for the former inhabitants there belonged to Ham. [41] These, registered by name, came in the days of Hezekiah, king of Judah, and destroyed their tents and the Meunites who were found there, and marked them for destruction to this day, and settled in their place, because there was pasture there for their flocks. [42] And some of them, five hundred men of the Simeonites, went to Mount Seir, having as their leaders Pelatiah, Neariah, Rephaiah, and Uzziel, the sons of Ishi. [43] And they defeated the remnant of the Amalekites who had escaped, and they have lived there to this day.

Descendants of Reuben

5 The sons of Reuben the firstborn of Israel (for he was the firstborn, but because he defiled his father's couch, his birthright was given to the sons of Joseph the son of Israel, so that he could not be enrolled as the oldest son; [2] though Judah became strong among his brothers and a chief came from him, yet the birthright belonged to Joseph), [3] the sons of Reuben, the firstborn of Israel: Hanoch, Pallu, Hezron, and Carmi. [4] The sons of Joel: Shemaiah his son, Gog his son, Shimei his son, [5] Micah his son, Reaiah his son, Baal his son, [6] Beerah his son, whom Tiglath-pileser king of Assyria carried away into exile; he was a chief of the Reubenites. [7] And his kinsmen by their clans, when the genealogy of

---

[1] *Jabez* sounds like the Hebrew for *pain* [2] *Ge-harashim* means *valley of craftsmen*

their generations was recorded: the chief, Jeiel, and Zechariah, ⁸ and Bela the son of Azaz, son of Shema, son of Joel, who lived in Aroer, as far as Nebo and Baal-meon. ⁹ He also lived to the east as far as the entrance of the desert this side of the Euphrates, because their livestock had multiplied in the land of Gilead. ¹⁰ And in the days of Saul they waged war against the Hagrites, who fell into their hand. And they lived in their tents throughout all the region east of Gilead.

Descendants of Gad

¹¹ The sons of Gad lived over against them in the land of Bashan as far as Salecah: ¹² Joel the chief, Shapham the second, Janai, and Shaphat in Bashan. ¹³ And their kinsmen according to their fathers' houses: Michael, Meshullam, Sheba, Jorai, Jacan, Zia and Eber, seven. ¹⁴ These were the sons of Abihail the son of Huri, son of Jaroah, son of Gilead, son of Michael, son of Jeshishai, son of Jahdo, son of Buz. ¹⁵ Ahi the son of Abdiel, son of Guni, was chief in their fathers' houses, ¹⁶ and they lived in Gilead, in Bashan and in its towns, and in all the pasturelands of Sharon to their limits. ¹⁷ All of these were recorded in genealogies in the days of Jotham king of Judah, and in the days of Jeroboam king of Israel.

¹⁸ The Reubenites, the Gadites, and the half-tribe of Manasseh had valiant men who carried shield and sword, and drew the bow, expert in war, 44,760, able to go to war. ¹⁹ They waged war against the Hagrites, Jetur, Naphish, and Nodab. ²⁰ And when they prevailed over them, the Hagrites and all who were with them were given into their hands, for they cried out to God in the battle, and he granted their urgent plea because they trusted in him. ²¹ They carried

off their livestock: 50,000 of their camels, 250,000 sheep, 2,000 donkeys, and 100,000 men alive. ²² For many fell, because the war was of God. And they lived in their place until the exile.

The Half-Tribe of Manasseh

²³ The members of the half-tribe of Manasseh lived in the land. They were very numerous from Bashan to Baal-hermon, Senir, and Mount Hermon. ²⁴ These were the heads of their fathers' houses: Epher, Ishi, Eliel, Azriel, Jeremiah, Hodaviah, and Jahdiel, mighty warriors, famous men, heads of their fathers' houses. ²⁵ But they broke faith with the God of their fathers, and whored after the gods of the peoples of the land, whom God had destroyed before them. ²⁶ So the God of Israel stirred up the spirit of Pul king of Assyria, the spirit of Tiglath-pileser king of Assyria, and he took them into exile, namely, the Reubenites, the Gadites, and the half-tribe of Manasseh, and brought them to Halah, Habor, Hara, and the river Gozan, to this day.

Descendants of Levi

6 The sons of Levi: Gershon, Kohath, and Merari. ² The sons of Kohath: Amram, Izhar, Hebron, and Uzziel. ³ The children of Amram: Aaron, Moses, and Miriam. The sons of Aaron: Nadab, Abihu, Eleazar, and Ithamar. ⁴ Eleazar fathered Phinehas, Phinehas fathered Abishua, ⁵ Abishua fathered Bukki, Bukki fathered Uzzi, ⁶ Uzzi fathered Zerahiah, Zerahiah fathered Meraioth, ⁷ Meraioth fathered Amariah, Amariah fathered Ahitub, ⁸ Ahitub fathered Zadok, Zadok fathered Ahimaaz, ⁹ Ahimaaz fathered Azariah, Azariah fathered Johanan, ¹⁰ and Johanan fathered Azariah (it was he who served as priest in the house that Solomon built in Jerusalem). ¹¹ Azariah fathered Amariah, Amariah fathered Ahitub, ¹² Ahitub fathered Zadok, Zadok fathered Shallum, ¹³ Shallum fathered Hilkiah, Hilkiah fathered Azariah, ¹⁴ Azariah fathered Seraiah, Seraiah fathered Jehozadak; ¹⁵ and Jehozadak went into exile when the LORD sent Judah and Jerusalem into exile by the hand of Nebuchadnezzar.

¹⁶ The sons of Levi: Gershom, Kohath, and Merari. ¹⁷ And these are the names of the sons of Gershom: Libni and Shimei. ¹⁸ The sons of Kohath: Amram, Izhar, Hebron and

Uzziel. ¹⁹ The sons of Merari: Mahli and Mushi. These are the clans of the Levites according to their fathers. ²⁰ Of Gershom: Libni his son, Jahath his son, Zimmah his son, ²¹ Joah his son, Iddo his son, Zerah his son, Jeatherai his son. ²² The sons of Kohath: Amminadab his son, Korah his son, Assir his son, ²³ Elkanah his son, Ebiasaph his son, Assir his son, ²⁴ Tahath his son, Uriel his son, Uzziah his son, and Shaul his son. ²⁵ The sons of Elkanah: Amasai and Ahimoth, ²⁶ Elkanah his son, Zophai his son, Nahath his son, ²⁷ Eliab his son, Jeroham his son, Elkanah his son. ²⁸ The sons of Samuel: Joel his firstborn, the second Abijah. ²⁹ The sons of Merari: Mahli, Libni his son, Shimei his son, Uzzah his son, ³⁰ Shimea his son, Haggiah his son, and Asaiah his son.

³¹ These are the men whom David put in charge of the service of song in the house of the LORD after the ark rested there. ³² They ministered with song before the tabernacle of the tent of meeting until Solomon built the house of the LORD in Jerusalem, and they performed their service according to their order. ³³ These are the men who served and their sons. Of the sons of the Kohathites: Heman the singer the son of Joel, son of Samuel, ³⁴ son of Elkanah, son of Jeroham, son of Eliel, son of Toah, ³⁵ son of Zuph, son of Elkanah, son of Mahath, son of Amasai, ³⁶ son of Elkanah, son of Joel, son of Azariah, son of Zephaniah, ³⁷ son of Tahath, son of Assir, son of Ebiasaph, son of Korah, ³⁸ son of Izhar, son of Kohath, son of Levi, son of Israel; ³⁹ and his brother Asaph, who stood on his right hand, namely, Asaph the son of Berechiah, son of Shimea, ⁴⁰ son of Michael, son of Baaseiah, son of Malchijah, ⁴¹ son of Ethni, son of Zerah, son of Adaiah, ⁴² son of Ethan, son of Zimmah, son of Shimei, ⁴³ son of Jahath, son of Gershom, son of Levi. ⁴⁴ On the left hand were their brothers, the sons of Merari: Ethan the son of Kishi, son of Abdi, son of Malluch, ⁴⁵ son of Hashabiah, son of Amaziah, son of Hilkiah, ⁴⁶ son of Amzi, son of Bani, son of Shemer, ⁴⁷ son of Mahli, son of Mushi, son of Merari, son of Levi. ⁴⁸ And their brothers the Levites were appointed for all the service of the tabernacle of the house of God.

⁴⁹ But Aaron and his sons made offerings on the altar of burnt offering and on the altar of incense for all the work of the Most Holy Place, and to make atonement for Israel, according to all that Moses the servant of God had commanded. ⁵⁰ These are the sons of Aaron: Eleazar his son, Phinehas his son, Abishua his son, ⁵¹ Bukki his son, Uzzi his son, Zerahiah his son, ⁵² Meraioth his son, Amariah his son, Ahitub his son, ⁵³ Zadok his son, Ahimaaz his son.

⁵⁴ These are their dwelling places according to their settlements within their borders: to the sons of Aaron of the clans of Kohathites, for theirs was the first lot, ⁵⁵ to them they gave Hebron in the land of Judah and its surrounding pasturelands, ⁵⁶ but the fields of the city and its villages they gave to Caleb the son of Jephunneh. ⁵⁷ To the sons of Aaron they gave the cities of refuge: Hebron, Libnah with its pasturelands, Jattir, Eshtemoa with its pasturelands, ⁵⁸ Hilen with its pasturelands, Debir with its pasturelands, ⁵⁹ Ashan with its pasturelands, and Beth-shemesh with its pasturelands; ⁶⁰ and from the tribe of Benjamin, Gibeon, Geba with its pasturelands, Alemeth with its pasturelands, and Anathoth with its pasturelands. All their cities throughout their clans were thirteen.

⁶¹ To the rest of the Kohathites were given by lot out of the clan of the tribe, out of the half-tribe, the half of Manasseh, ten cities. ⁶² To the Gershomites according to their clans were allotted thirteen cities out of the tribes of Issachar, Asher, Naphtali and Manasseh in Bashan. ⁶³ To the Merarites according to their clans were allotted twelve cities out of the tribes of Reuben, Gad, and Zebulun. ⁶⁴ So the people of Israel gave the Levites the cities with their pasturelands. ⁶⁵ They gave by lot out of the tribes of Judah, Simeon, and Benjamin these cities that are mentioned by name.

⁶⁶ And some of the clans of the sons of Kohath had cities of their territory out of the tribe of Ephraim. ⁶⁷ They were given the cities of refuge: Shechem with its pasturelands in the hill country of Ephraim, Gezer with its pasturelands, ⁶⁸ Jokmeam with its pasturelands, Beth-horon with its pasturelands, ⁶⁹ Aijalon with its pasturelands, Gath-rimmon with its pasturelands, ⁷⁰ and out of the half-tribe of Manasseh, Aner with its pasturelands, and Bileam with its pasturelands, for the rest of the clans of the Kohathites.

71 To the Gershomites were given out of the clan of the half-tribe of Manasseh: Golan in Bashan with its pasturelands and Ashtaroth with its pasturelands; **72** and out of the tribe of Issachar: Kedesh with its pasturelands, Daberath with its pasturelands, **73** Ramoth with its pasturelands, and Anem with its pasturelands; **74** out of the tribe of Asher: Mashal with its pasturelands, Abdon with its pasturelands, **75** Hukok with its pasturelands, and Rehob with its pasturelands; **76** and out of the tribe of Naphtali: Kedesh in Galilee with its pasturelands, Hammon with its pasturelands, and Kiriathaim with its pasturelands. **77** To the rest of the Merarites were allotted out of the tribe of Zebulun: Rimmono with its pasturelands, Tabor with its pasturelands, **78** and beyond the Jordan at Jericho, on the east side of the Jordan, out of the tribe of Reuben: Bezer

GETTING THE MESSAGE

Why is the genealogy for Naphtali so short? The Chronicler was writing more than a thousand years after the beginning of Israel's tribes. During that time, all the tribes had gone into exile. This made it difficult to find genealogies for all the tribes.

in the wilderness with its pasturelands, Jahzah with its pasturelands, **79** Kedemoth with its pasturelands, and Mephaath with its pasturelands; **80** and out of the tribe of Gad: Ramoth in Gilead with its pasturelands, Mahanaim with its pasturelands, **81** Heshbon with its pasturelands, and Jazer with its pasturelands.

Descendants of Issachar

7 The sons of Issachar: Tola, Puah, Jashub, and Shimron, four. **2** The sons of Tola: Uzzi, Rephaiah, Jeriel, Jahmai, Ibsam, and Shemuel, heads of their fathers' houses, namely of Tola, mighty warriors of their generations, their number in the days of David being 22,600. **3** The son of Uzzi: Izrahiah. And the sons of Izrahiah: Michael, Obadiah, Joel, and Isshiah, all five of them were chief men. **4** And along with them, by their generations, according to their fathers' houses, were units of the army for war, 36,000, for they had many wives and sons.

5 Their kinsmen belonging to all the clans of Issachar were in all 87,000 mighty warriors, enrolled by genealogy.

Descendants of Benjamin

6 The sons of Benjamin: Bela, Becher, and Jediael, three. **7** The sons of Bela: Ezbon, Uzzi, Uzziel, Jerimoth, and Iri, five, heads of fathers' houses, mighty warriors. And their enrollment by genealogies was 22,034. **8** The sons of Becher: Zemirah, Joash, Eliezer, Elioenai, Omri, Jeremoth, Abijah, Anathoth, and Alemeth. All these were the sons of Becher. **9** And their enrollment by genealogies, according to their generations, as heads of their fathers' houses, mighty warriors, was 20,200. **10** The son of Jediael: Bilhan. And the sons of Bilhan: Jeush, Benjamin, Ehud, Chenaanah, Zethan, Tarshish, and Ahishahar. **11** All these were the sons of Jediael according to the heads of their fathers' houses, mighty warriors, 17,200, able to go to war. **12** And Shuppim and Huppim were the sons of Ir, Hushim the son of Aher.

Descendants of Naphtali

13 The sons of Naphtali: Jahziel, Guni, Jezer and Shallum, the descendants of Bilhah.

Descendants of Manasseh

14 The sons of Manasseh: Asriel, whom his Aramean concubine bore; she bore Machir the father of Gilead. **15** And Machir took a wife for Huppim and for Shuppim. The name of his sister was Maacah. And the name of the second was Zelophehad, and Zelophehad had daughters. **16** And Maacah the wife of Machir bore a son, and she called his name Peresh; and the name of his brother was Sheresh; and his sons were Ulam and Rakem. **17** The son of Ulam: Bedan. These were the sons of Gilead the son of Machir, son of Manasseh. **18** And his sister Hammolecheth bore Ishhod, Abiezer and Mahlah. **19** The sons of Shemida were Ahian, Shechem, Likhi, and Aniam.

Descendants of Ephraim

20 The sons of Ephraim: Shuthelah, and Bered his son, Tahath his son, Eleadah his son, Tahath his son, **21** Zabad his son, Shuthelah his son, and Ezer and Elead, whom the men of Gath who were born in the land killed, because they came down to raid their livestock. **22** And Ephraim their father mourned many days, and his brothers came to comfort him. ²³ And Ephraim went in to his wife, and she conceived and bore a son. And he called his name Beriah, because disaster had befallen his house.[1] ²⁴ His daughter was Sheerah, who built both Lower and Upper Beth-horon, and Uzzensheerah. ²⁵ Rephah was his son, Resheph his son, Telah his son, Tahan his son, ²⁶ Ladan his son, Ammihud his son, Elishama his son, ²⁷ Nun his son, Joshua his son. ²⁸ Their possessions and settlements were Bethel and its towns, and to the east Naaran, and to the west Gezer and its towns, Shechem and its towns, and Ayyah and its towns; ²⁹ also in possession of the Manassites, Beth-shean and its towns, Taanach and its towns, Megiddo and its towns, Dor and its towns. In these lived the sons of Joseph the son of Israel.

Descendants of Asher

³⁰ The sons of Asher: Imnah, Ishvah, Ishvi, Beriah, and their sister Serah. ³¹ The sons of Beriah: Heber, and Malchiel, who fathered Birzaith. ³² Heber fathered Japhlet, Shomer, Hotham, and their sister Shua. ³³ The sons of Japhlet: Pasach, Bimhal, and Ashvath. These are the sons of Japhlet. ³⁴ The sons of Shemer his brother: Rohgah, Jehubbah, and Aram. ³⁵ The sons of Helem his brother: Zophah, Imna, Shelesh, and Amal. ³⁶ The sons of Zophah: Suah, Harnepher, Shual, Beri, Imrah. ³⁷ Bezer, Hod, Shamma, Shilshah, Ithran, and Beera. ³⁸ The sons of Jether: Jephunneh, Pispa, and Ara. ³⁹ The sons of Ulla: Arah, Hanniel, and Rizia. ⁴⁰ All of these were men of Asher, heads of fathers' houses, approved, mighty warriors, chiefs of the princes. Their number enrolled by genealogies, for service in war, was 26,000 men.

A Genealogy of Saul

8 Benjamin fathered Bela his firstborn, Ashbel the second, Aharah the third, ² Nohah the fourth, and Rapha the fifth. ³ And Bela had sons: Addar, Gera, Abihud, ⁴ Abishua, Naaman, Ahoah, ⁵ Gera, Shephuphan, and Huram. ⁶ These are the sons of Ehud (they were heads of fathers' houses of the inhabitants of Geba, and they were carried into exile to Manahath): ⁷ Naaman, Ahijah, and Gera, that is, Heglam, who fathered Uzza and Ahihud. ⁸ And Shaharaim

fathered sons in the country of Moab after he had sent away Hushim and Baara his wives. ⁹ He fathered sons by Hodesh his wife: Jobab, Zibia, Mesha, Malcam, ¹⁰ Jeuz, Sachia, and Mirmah. These were his sons, heads of fathers' houses. ¹¹ He also fathered sons by Hushim: Abitub and Elpaal. ¹² The sons of Elpaal: Eber, Misham, and Shemed, who built Ono and Lod with its towns, ¹³ and Beriah and Shema (they were heads of fathers' houses of the inhabitants of Aijalon, who caused the inhabitants of Gath to flee); ¹⁴ and Ahio, Shashak, and Jeremoth. ¹⁵ Zebadiah, Arad, Eder, ¹⁶ Michael, Ishpah, and Joha were sons of Beriah. ¹⁷ Zebadiah, Meshullam, Hizki, Heber, ¹⁸ Ishmerai, Izliah, and Jobab were the sons of Elpaal. ¹⁹ Jakim, Zichri, Zabdi, ²⁰ Elienai, Zillethai, Eliel, ²¹ Adaiah, Beraiah, and Shimrath were the sons of Shimei. ²² Ishpan, Eber, Eliel, ²³ Abdon, Zichri, Hanan, ²⁴ Hananiah,

GETTING THE MESSAGE

How many genealogies are there in the Bible? There are about 25 genealogical lists in the Bible. These genealogies show how God protected his covenant people through the centuries.

Elam, Anthothijah, ²⁵ Iphdeiah, and Penuel were the sons of Shashak. ²⁶ Shamsherai, Shehariah, Athaliah, ²⁷ Jaareshiah, Elijah, and Zichri were the sons of Jeroham. ²⁸ These were the heads of fathers' houses, according to their generations, chief men. These lived in Jerusalem.

²⁹ Jeiel the father of Gibeon lived in Gibeon, and the name of his wife was Maacah. ³⁰ His firstborn son: Abdon, then Zur, Kish, Baal, Nadab, ³¹ Gedor, Ahio, Zecher, ³² and Mikloth (he fathered Shimeah). Now these also lived opposite their kinsmen in Jerusalem, with their kinsmen. ³³ Ner was the father of Kish, Kish of Saul, Saul of Jonathan, Malchi-shua, Abinadab and Eshbaal; ³⁴ and the son of Jonathan was Merib-baal; and Merib-baal was the father of Micah. ³⁵ The sons of Micah: Pithon, Melech, Tarea, and Ahaz. ³⁶ Ahaz fathered Jehoaddah, and Jehoaddah fathered Alemeth, Azmaveth, and Zimri. Zimri fathered Moza. ³⁷ Moza fathered

---

[1] *Beriah* sounds like the Hebrew for *disaster*

Binea; Raphah was his son, Eleasah his son, Azel his son. **38** Azel had six sons, and these are their names: Azrikam, Bocheru, Ishmael, Sheariah, Obadiah, and Hanan. All these were the sons of Azel. **39** The sons of Eshek his brother: Ulam his firstborn, Jeush the second, and Eliphelet the third. **40** The sons of Ulam were men who were mighty warriors, bowmen, having many sons and grandsons, 150. All these were Benjaminites.

A Genealogy of the Returned Exiles

9 So all Israel was recorded in genealogies, and these are written in the Book of the Kings of Israel. And Judah was taken into exile in Babylon because of their breach of faith. **2** Now the first to dwell again in their possessions in their cities were Israel, the priests, the Levites, and the temple servants. **3** And some of the people of Judah, Benjamin, Ephraim, and Manasseh lived in Jerusalem: **4** Uthai the son of Ammihud, son of Omri, son of Imri, son of Bani, from the sons of Perez the son of Judah. **5** And of the Shilonites: Asaiah the firstborn, and his sons. **6** Of the sons of Zerah: Jeuel and their kinsmen, 690. **7** Of the Benjaminites: Sallu the son of Meshullam, son of Hodaviah, son of Hassenuah, **8** Ibneiah the son of Jeroham, Elah the son of Uzzi, son of Michri, and Meshullam the son of Shephatiah, son of Reuel, son of Ibnijah; **9** and their kinsmen according to their generations, 956. All these were heads of fathers' houses according to their fathers' houses.

10 Of the priests: Jedaiah, Jehoiarib, Jachin, **11** and Azariah the son of Hilkiah, son of Meshullam, son of Zadok, son of Meraioth, son of Ahitub, the chief officer of the house of God; **12** and Adaiah the son of Jeroham, son of Pashhur, son of Malchijah, and Maasai the son of Adiel, son of Jahzerah, son of Meshullam, son of Meshillemith, son of Immer; **13** besides their kinsmen, heads of their fathers' houses, 1,760, mighty men for the work of the service of the house of God.

14 Of the Levites: Shemaiah the son of Hasshub, son of Azrikam, son of Hashabiah, of the sons of Merari; **15** and Bakbakkar, Heresh, Galal and Mattaniah the son of Mica, son of Zichri, son of Asaph; **16** and Obadiah the son of Shemaiah, son of Galal, son of Jeduthun, and Berechiah the son of Asa, son of Elkanah, who lived in the villages of the Netophathites.

17 The gatekeepers were Shallum, Akkub, Talmon, Ahiman, and their kinsmen (Shallum was the chief); **18** until then they were in the king's gate on the east side as the gatekeepers of the camps of the Levites. **19** Shallum the son of Kore, son of Ebiasaph, son of Korah, and his kinsmen of his fathers' house, the Korahites, were in charge of the work of the service, keepers of the thresholds of the tent, as their fathers had been in charge of the camp of the LORD, keepers of the entrance. **20** And Phinehas the son of Eleazar was the chief officer over them in time past; the LORD was with him. **21** Zechariah the son of Meshelemiah was gatekeeper at the entrance of the tent of meeting. **22** All these, who were chosen as gatekeepers at the thresholds, were 212. They were enrolled by genealogies in their villages. David and Samuel the seer established them in their office of trust. **23** So they and their sons were in charge of the gates of the house of the LORD, that is, the house of the tent, as guards. **24** The gatekeepers were on the four sides, east, west, north, and south. **25** And their kinsmen who were in their villages were obligated to come in every seven days, in turn, to be with these, **26** for the four chief gatekeepers, who were Levites, were entrusted to be over the chambers and the treasures of the house of God. **27** And they lodged around the house of God, for on them lay the duty of watching, and they had charge of opening it every morning.

28 Some of them had charge of the utensils of service, for they were required to count them when they were brought in and taken out. **29** Others of them were appointed over the furniture and over all the holy utensils, also over the fine flour, the wine, the oil, the incense, and the spices. **30** Others, of the sons of the priests, prepared the mixing of the spices, **31** and Mattithiah, one of the Levites, the firstborn of Shallum the Korahite, was entrusted with making the flat cakes. **32** Also some of their kinsmen of the Kohathites had charge of the showbread, to prepare it every Sabbath.

33 Now these, the singers, the heads of fathers' houses of the Levites, were in the chambers of the temple free from other service, for they were on duty day and night. **34** These were heads of fathers' houses of the Levites, according to their generations, leaders. These lived in Jerusalem.

Saul's Genealogy Repeated

35 In Gibeon lived the father of Gibeon, Jeiel, and the name of his wife was Maacah, 36 and his firstborn son Abdon, then Zur, Kish, Baal, Ner, Nadab, 37 Gedor, Ahio, Zechariah, and Mikloth; 38 and Mikloth was the father of Shimeam; and these also lived opposite their kinsmen in Jerusalem, with their kinsmen. 39 Ner fathered Kish, Kish fathered Saul, Saul fathered Jonathan, Malchi-shua, Abinadab, and Eshbaal. 40 And the son of Jonathan was Merib-baal, and Merib-baal fathered Micah. 41 The sons of Micah: Pithon, Melech, Tahrea, and Ahaz. 42 And Ahaz fathered Jarah, and Jarah fathered Alemeth, Azmaveth, and Zimri. And Zimri fathered Moza. 43 Moza fathered Binea, and Rephaiah was his son, Eleasah his son, Azel his son. 44 Azel had six sons and these are their names: Azrikam, Bocheru, Ishmael, Sheariah, Obadiah, and Hanan; these were the sons of Azel.

The Death of Saul and His Sons

10 Now the Philistines fought against Israel, and the men of Israel fled before the Philistines and fell slain on Mount Gilboa. 2 And the Philistines overtook Saul and his sons, and the Philistines struck down Jonathan and Abinadab and Malchi-shua, the sons of Saul. 3 The battle pressed hard against Saul, and the archers found him, and he was wounded by the archers. 4 Then Saul said to his armor-bearer, "Draw your sword and thrust me through with it, lest these uncircumcised come and mistreat me." But his armor-bearer would not, for he feared greatly. Therefore Saul took his own sword and fell upon it. 5 And when his armor-bearer saw that Saul was dead, he also fell upon his sword and died. 6 Thus Saul died; he and his three sons and all his house died together. 7 And when all the men of Israel who were in the valley saw that the army had fled and that Saul and his sons were dead, they abandoned their cities and fled, and the Philistines came and lived in them.

8 The next day, when the Philistines came to strip the slain, they found Saul and his sons fallen on Mount Gilboa. 9 And they stripped him and took his head and his armor, and sent messengers throughout the land of the Philistines to carry the good news to their idols and to the people. 10 And they put his armor in the temple of their gods and fastened his head in the temple of Dagon. 11 But when all Jabesh-gilead heard all that the Philistines had done to Saul, 12 all the valiant men arose and took away the body of Saul and the bodies of his sons, and brought them to Jabesh. And they buried their bones under the oak in Jabesh and fasted seven days.

13 So Saul died for his breach of faith. He broke faith with the LORD in that he did not keep the command of the LORD, and also consulted a medium, seeking guidance. 14 He did not seek guidance from the LORD. Therefore the LORD put him to death and turned the kingdom over to David the son of Jesse.

GETTING THE MESSAGE

How did David conquer Jerusalem?
The Chronicler tells of David's conquest of Jerusalem in 11:4–9. Second Samuel 5:8 provides an additional interesting detail: David and his men were able to enter the city through an underground water shaft.

David Anointed King

11 Then all Israel gathered together to David at Hebron and said, "Behold, we are your bone and flesh. 2 In times past, even when Saul was king, it was you who led out and brought in Israel. And the LORD your God said to you, 'You shall be shepherd of my people Israel, and you shall be prince over my people Israel.'" 3 So all the elders of Israel came to the king at Hebron, and David made a covenant with them at Hebron before the LORD. And they anointed David king over Israel, according to the word of the LORD by Samuel.

David Takes Jerusalem

4 And David and all Israel went to Jerusalem, that is, Jebus, where the Jebusites were, the inhabitants of the land. 5 The inhabitants of Jebus said to David, "You will not come in here." Nevertheless, David took the stronghold of Zion, that is, the city of David. 6 David said, "Whoever strikes the Jebusites

first shall be chief and commander." And Joab the son of Zeruiah went up first, so he became chief. ⁷ And David lived in the stronghold; therefore it was called the city of David. ⁸ And he built the city all around from the Millo in complete circuit, and Joab repaired the rest of the city. ⁹ And David became greater and greater, for the LORD of hosts was with him.

David's Mighty Men

¹⁰ Now these are the chiefs of David's mighty men, who gave him strong support in his kingdom, together with all Israel, to make him king, according to the word of the LORD concerning Israel. ¹¹ This is an account of David's mighty men: Jashobeam, a Hachmonite, was chief of the three. He wielded his spear against 300 whom he killed at one time.

¹² And next to him among the three mighty men was Eleazar the son of Dodo, the Ahohite. ¹³ He was with David at Pasdammim when the Philistines were gathered there for battle. There was a plot of ground full of barley, and the men fled from the Philistines. ¹⁴ But he took his stand in the midst of the plot and defended it and killed the Philistines. And the LORD saved them by a great victory.

¹⁵ Three of the thirty chief men went down to the rock to David at the cave of Adullam, when the army of Philistines was encamped in the Valley of Rephaim. ¹⁶ David was then in the stronghold, and the garrison of the Philistines was then at Bethlehem. ¹⁷ And David said longingly, "Oh that someone would give me water to drink from the well of Bethlehem that is by the gate!" ¹⁸ Then the three mighty men broke through the camp of the Philistines and drew water out of the well of Bethlehem that was by the gate and took it and brought it to David. But David would not drink it. He poured it out to the LORD ¹⁹ and said, "Far be it from me before my God that I should do this. Shall I drink the lifeblood of these men? For at the risk of their lives they brought it." Therefore he would not drink it. These things did the three mighty men.

²⁰ Now Abishai, the brother of Joab, was chief of the thirty. And he wielded his spear against 300 men and killed them and won a name beside the three. ²¹ He was the most renowned of the thirty and became

their commander, but he did not attain to the three.

²² And Benaiah the son of Jehoiada was a valiant man of Kabzeel, a doer of great deeds. He struck down two heroes of Moab. He also went down and struck down a lion in a pit on a day when snow had fallen. ²³ And he struck down an Egyptian, a man of great stature, five cubits tall. The Egyptian had in his hand a spear like a weaver's beam, but Benaiah went down to him with a staff and snatched the spear out of the Egyptian's hand and killed him with his own spear. ²⁴ These things did Benaiah the son of Jehoiada and won a name beside the three mighty men. ²⁵ He was renowned among the thirty, but he did not attain to the three. And David set him over his bodyguard.

²⁶ The mighty men were Asahel the brother of Joab, Elhanan the son of Dodo of Bethlehem, ²⁷ Shammoth of Harod, Helez the Pelonite, ²⁸ Ira the son of Ikkesh of Tekoa, Abiezer of Anathoth, ²⁹ Sibbecai the Hushathite, Ilai the Ahohite, ³⁰ Maharai of Netophah, Heled the son of Baanah of Netophah, ³¹ Ithai the son of Ribai of Gibeah of the people of Benjamin, Benaiah of Pirathon, ³² Hurai of the brooks of Gaash, Abiel the Arbathite, ³³ Azmaveth of Baharum, Eliahba the Shaalbonite, ³⁴ Hashem the Gizonite, Jonathan the son of Shagee the Hararite, ³⁵ Ahiam the son of Sachar the Hararite, Eliphal the son of Ur, ³⁶ Hepher the Mecherathite, Ahijah the Pelonite, ³⁷ Hezro of Carmel, Naarai the son of Ezbai, ³⁸ Joel the brother of Nathan, Mibhar the son of Hagri, ³⁹ Zelek the Ammonite, Naharai of Beeroth, the armor-bearer of Joab the son of Zeruiah, ⁴⁰ Ira the Ithrite, Gareb the Ithrite, ⁴¹ Uriah the Hittite, Zabad the son of Ahlai, ⁴² Adina the son of Shiza the Reubenite, a leader of the Reubenites, and thirty with him, ⁴³ Hanan the son of Maacah, and Joshaphat the Mithnite, ⁴⁴ Uzzia the Ashterathite, Shama and Jeiel the sons of Hotham the Aroerite, ⁴⁵ Jediael the son of Shimri, and Joha his brother, the Tizite, ⁴⁶ Eliel the Mahavite, and Jeribai, and Joshaviah, the sons of Elnaam, and Ithmah the Moabite, ⁴⁷ Eliel, and Obed, and Jaasiel the Mezobaite.

The Mighty Men Join David

12 Now these are the men who came to David at Ziklag, while he could not move about freely because of Saul the son of Kish. And they were among the mighty men who helped him in war. ²They were bowmen and could shoot arrows and sling stones with either the right or the left hand; they were Benjaminites, Saul's kinsmen. ³The chief was Ahiezer, then Joash, both sons of Shemaah of Gibeah; also Jeziel and Pelet, the sons of Azmaveth; Beracah, Jehu of Anathoth, ⁴Ishmaiah of Gibeon, a mighty man among the thirty and a leader over the thirty; Jeremiah, Jahaziel, Johanan, Jozabad of Gederah, ⁵Eluzai, Jerimoth, Bealiah, Shemariah, Shephatiah the Haruphite; ⁶Elkanah, Isshiah, Azarel, Joezer, and Jashobeam, the Korahites; ⁷And Joelah and Zebadiah, the sons of Jeroham of Gedor.

⁸From the Gadites there went over to David at the stronghold in the wilderness mighty and experienced warriors, expert with shield and spear, whose faces were like the faces of lions and who were swift as gazelles upon the mountains: ⁹Ezer the chief, Obadiah second, Eliab third, ¹⁰Mishmannah fourth, Jeremiah fifth, ¹¹Attai sixth, Eliel seventh, ¹²Johanan eighth, Elzabad ninth, ¹³Jeremiah tenth, Machbannai eleventh. ¹⁴These Gadites were officers of the army; the least was a match for a hundred men and the greatest for a thousand. ¹⁵These are the men who crossed the Jordan in the first month, when it was overflowing all its banks, and put to flight all those in the valleys, to the east and to the west.

¹⁶And some of the men of Benjamin and Judah came to the stronghold to David. ¹⁷David went out to meet them and said to them, "If you have come to me in friendship to help me, my heart will be joined to you; but if to betray me to my adversaries, although there is no wrong in my hands, then may the God of our fathers see and rebuke you." ¹⁸Then the Spirit clothed Amasai, chief of the thirty, and he said,

"We are yours, O David,
    and with you, O son of Jesse!
Peace, peace to you,
    and peace to your helpers!
For your God helps you."

Then David received them and made them officers of his troops.

¹⁹Some of the men of Manasseh deserted to David when he came with the Philistines for the battle against Saul. (Yet he did not help them, for the rulers of the Philistines took counsel and sent him away, saying, "At peril to our heads he will desert to his master Saul.") ²⁰As he went to Ziklag, these men of Manasseh deserted to him: Adnah, Jozabad, Jediael, Michael, Jozabad, Elihu, and Zillethai, chiefs of thousands in Manasseh. ²¹They helped David against the band of raiders, for they were all mighty men of valor and were commanders in the army. ²²For from day to day men came to David to help him, until there was a great army, like an army of God.

²³These are the numbers of the divisions of the armed troops who came to David in Hebron to turn the kingdom of Saul over to him, according to the word of the LORD. ²⁴The men of Judah bearing shield and spear were 6,800 armed troops. ²⁵Of the

GETTING THE MESSAGE

Bows and arrows were widely used in Bible times (12:2). Bows were made with single pieces of wood or by gluing layers of wood, horn, and sinew together. They were between 3 and 6 feet (0.9 and 1.8 m) long. Arrows were made of wood shafts or reeds that were tipped with metal heads. Bird feathers were added to guide the arrows.

Simeonites, mighty men of valor for war, 7,100. ²⁶Of the Levites 4,600. ²⁷The prince Jehoiada, of the house of Aaron, and with him 3,700. ²⁸Zadok, a young man mighty in valor, and twenty-two commanders from his own fathers' house. ²⁹Of the Benjaminites, the kinsmen of Saul, 3,000, of whom the majority had to that point kept their allegiance to the house of Saul. ³⁰Of the Ephraimites 20,800, mighty men of valor, famous men in their fathers' houses. ³¹Of the half-tribe of Manasseh 18,000, who were expressly named to come and make David king. ³²Of Issachar, men who had understanding of the times, to know what Israel ought to do, 200 chiefs, and all their kinsmen under their command. ³³Of Zebulun 50,000 seasoned troops, equipped for battle with all the weapons of war, to help David with singleness of purpose. ³⁴Of Naphtali 1,000 commanders with whom were 37,000 men armed with shield and spear. ³⁵ Of the Danites 28,600 men equipped for battle. ³⁶ Of Asher 40,000 seasoned troops ready for battle. ³⁷ Of the Reubenites and Gadites and the half-tribe of Manasseh from beyond the Jordan, 120,000 men armed with all the weapons of war.

³⁸ All these, men of war, arrayed in battle order, came to Hebron with a whole heart to make David king over all Israel. Likewise, all the rest of Israel were of a single mind to make David king. ³⁹ And they were there with David for three days, eating and drinking, for their brothers had made preparation for them. ⁴⁰ And also their relatives, from as far as Issachar and Zebulun and Naphtali, came bringing food on donkeys and on camels and on mules and on oxen, abundant

GETTING THE MESSAGE

Why couldn't the ark be carried on an oxcart? The Lord had commanded that the ark should be carried with long poles (Ex. 25:12–15). Transporting the ark on an oxcart instead demonstrated a lack of reverence for this representation of God's presence. When the oxen stumbled, Uzzah touched the ark to steady it, and the Lord struck him dead. Even those whose job it was to carry the ark were forbidden to touch it (Num. 4:15).

provisions of flour, cakes of figs, clusters of raisins, and wine and oil, oxen and sheep, for there was joy in Israel.

The Ark Brought from Kiriath-Jearim

13 David consulted with the commanders of thousands and of hundreds, with every leader. ² And David said to all the assembly of Israel, "If it seems good to you and from the LORD our God, let us send abroad to our brothers who remain in all the lands of Israel, as well as to the priests and Levites in the cities that have pasturelands, that they may be gathered to us. ³ Then let us bring again the ark of our God to us, for we did not seek it in the days of Saul." ⁴ All the assembly agreed to do so, for the thing was right in the eyes of all the people.

Uzzah and the Ark

⁵ So David assembled all Israel from the Nile of Egypt to Lebo-hamath, to bring the ark of God from Kiriath-jearim. ⁶ And David and all Israel went up to Baalah, that is, to Kiriath-jearim that belongs to Judah, to bring up from there the ark of God, which is called by the name of the LORD who sits enthroned above the cherubim. ⁷ And they carried the ark of God on a new cart, from the house of Abinadab, and Uzzah and Ahio were driving the cart. ⁸ And David and all Israel were celebrating before God with all their might, with song and lyres and harps and tambourines and cymbals and trumpets.

⁹ And when they came to the threshing floor of Chidon, Uzzah put out his hand to take hold of the ark, for the oxen stumbled. ¹⁰ And the anger of the LORD was kindled against Uzzah, and he struck him down because he put out his hand to the ark, and he died there before God. ¹¹ And David was angry because the LORD had broken out against Uzzah. And that place is called Perez-uzza¹ to this day. ¹² And David was afraid of God that day, and he said, "How can I bring the ark of God home to me?" ¹³ So David did not take the ark home into the city of David, but took it aside to the house of Obed-edom the Gittite. ¹⁴ And the ark of God remained with the household of Obed-edom in his house three months. And the LORD blessed the household of Obed-edom and all that he had.

David's Wives and Children

14 And Hiram king of Tyre sent messengers to David, and cedar trees, also masons and carpenters to build a house for him. ² And David knew that the LORD had established him as king over Israel, and that his kingdom was highly exalted for the sake of his people Israel.

³ And David took more wives in Jerusalem, and David fathered more sons and daughters. ⁴ These are the names of the children born to him in Jerusalem: Shammua, Shobab, Nathan, Solomon, ⁵ Ibhar, Elishua, Elpelet, ⁶ Nogah, Nepheg, Japhia, ⁷ Elishama, Beeliada and Eliphelet.

Philistines Defeated

⁸ When the Philistines heard that David had been anointed king over all Israel, all

¹ Perez-uzza means the breaking out against Uzzah

the Philistines went up to search for David. But David heard of it and went out against them. ⁹ Now the Philistines had come and made a raid in the Valley of Rephaim. ¹⁰ And David inquired of God, "Shall I go up against the Philistines? Will you give them into my hand?" And the LORD said to him, "Go up, and I will give them into your hand." ¹¹ And he went up to Baal-perazim, and David struck them down there. And David said, "God has broken through¹ my enemies by my hand, like a bursting flood." Therefore the name of that place is called Baal-perazim. ¹² And they left their gods there, and David gave command, and they were burned.

¹³ And the Philistines yet again made a raid in the valley. ¹⁴ And when David again inquired of God, God said to him, "You shall not go up after them; go around and come against them opposite the balsam trees. ¹⁵ And when you hear the sound of marching in the tops of the balsam trees, then go out to battle, for God has gone out before you to strike down the army of the Philistines." ¹⁶ And David did as God commanded him, and they struck down the Philistine army from Gibeon to Gezer. ¹⁷ And the fame of David went out into all lands, and the LORD brought the fear of him upon all nations.

The Ark Brought to Jerusalem

15 David built houses for himself in the city of David. And he prepared a place for the ark of God and pitched a tent for it. ² Then David said that no one but the Levites may carry the ark of God, for the LORD had chosen them to carry the ark of the LORD and to minister to him forever. ³ And David assembled all Israel at Jerusalem to bring up the ark of the LORD to its place, which he had prepared for it. ⁴ And David gathered together the sons of Aaron and the Levites: ⁵ of the sons of Kohath, Uriel the chief, with 120 of his brothers; ⁶ of the sons of Merari, Asaiah the chief, with 220 of his brothers; ⁷ of the sons of Gershom, Joel the chief, with 130 of his brothers; ⁸ of the sons of Elizaphan, Shemaiah the chief, with 200 of his brothers; ⁹ of the sons of Hebron, Eliel the chief, with 80 of his brothers; ¹⁰ of the sons of Uzziel, Amminadab the chief, with 112 of his brothers. ¹¹ Then David summoned

the priests Zadok and Abiathar, and the Levites Uriel, Asaiah, Joel, Shemaiah, Eliel, and Amminadab, ¹² and said to them, "You are the heads of the fathers' houses of the Levites. Consecrate yourselves, you and your brothers, so that you may bring up the ark of the LORD, the God of Israel, to the place that I have prepared for it. ¹³ Because you did not carry it the first time, the LORD our God broke out against us, because we did not seek him according to the rule." ¹⁴ So the priests and the Levites consecrated themselves to bring up the ark of the LORD, the God of Israel. ¹⁵ And the Levites carried the ark of God on their shoulders with the poles, as Moses had commanded according to the word of the LORD.

¹⁶ David also commanded the chiefs of the Levites to appoint their brothers as the

GETTING THE MESSAGE

How does Chronicles differ from Samuel and Kings? The books of 1–2 Samuel and 1–2 Kings show that the Lord drove Israel and Judah from their land because of their sin. The books of 1–2 Chronicles agree that Israel sinned and suffered exile as a result. They also show that God still had a purpose for his people.

singers who should play loudly on musical instruments, on harps and lyres and cymbals, to raise sounds of joy. ¹⁷ So the Levites appointed Heman the son of Joel; and of his brothers Asaph the son of Berechiah; and of the sons of Merari, their brothers, Ethan the son of Kushaiah; ¹⁸ and with them their brothers of the second order, Zechariah, Jaaziel, Shemiramoth, Jehiel, Unni, Eliab, Benaiah, Maaseiah, Mattithiah, Eliphelehu, and Mikneiah, and the gatekeepers Obed-edom and Jeiel. ¹⁹ The singers, Heman, Asaph, and Ethan, were to sound bronze cymbals; ²⁰ Zechariah, Aziel, Shemiramoth, Jehiel, Unni, Eliab, Maaseiah, and Benaiah were to play harps according to Alamoth; ²¹ but Mattithiah, Eliphelehu, Mikneiah, Obed-edom, Jeiel, and Azaziah were to lead with lyres according to the Sheminith. ²² Chenaniah, leader of the Levites in music,

---

¹ Baal-perazim means lord of breaking through

should direct the music, for he understood it. ²³ Berechiah and Elkanah were to be gatekeepers for the ark. ²⁴ Shebaniah, Joshaphat, Nethanel, Amasai, Zechariah, Benaiah, and Eliezer, the priests, should blow the trumpets before the ark of God. Obed-edom and Jehiah were to be gatekeepers for the ark.

²⁵ So David and the elders of Israel and the commanders of thousands went to bring up the ark of the covenant of the Lord from the house of Obed-edom with rejoicing. ²⁶ And because God helped the Levites who were carrying the ark of the covenant of the Lord, they sacrificed seven bulls and seven rams. ²⁷ David was clothed with a robe of fine linen, as also were all the Levites who were carrying the ark, and the singers and Chenaniah the leader of the music of the singers. And David wore a linen ephod. ²⁸ So all Israel brought up the ark of the covenant of the Lord with shouting, to the sound of the horn, trumpets, and cymbals, and made loud music on harps and lyres.

²⁹ And as the ark of the covenant of the Lord came to the city of David, Michal the daughter of Saul looked out of the window and saw King David dancing and celebrating, and she despised him in her heart.

The Ark Placed in a Tent

16 And they brought in the ark of God and set it inside the tent that David had pitched for it, and they offered burnt offerings and peace offerings before God. ² And when David had finished offering the burnt offerings and the peace offerings, he blessed the people in the name of the Lord ³ and distributed to all Israel, both men and women, to each a loaf of bread, a portion of meat, and a cake of raisins.

⁴ Then he appointed some of the Levites as ministers before the ark of the Lord, to invoke, to thank, and to praise the Lord, the God of Israel. ⁵ Asaph was the chief, and second to him were Zechariah, Jeiel, Shemiramoth, Jehiel, Mattithiah, Eliab, Benaiah, Obed-edom, and Jeiel, who were to play harps and lyres; Asaph was to sound the cymbals, ⁶ and Benaiah and Jahaziel the priests were to blow trumpets regularly before the ark of the covenant of God. ⁷ Then on that day David first appointed that thanksgiving be sung to the Lord by Asaph and his brothers.

David's Song of Thanks

⁸ Oh give thanks to the Lord; call upon his name;
  make known his deeds among the peoples!
⁹ Sing to him, sing praises to him;
  tell of all his wondrous works!
¹⁰ Glory in his holy name;
  let the hearts of those who seek the Lord rejoice!
¹¹ Seek the Lord and his strength;
  seek his presence continually!
¹² Remember the wondrous works that he has done,
  his miracles and the judgments he uttered,
¹³ O offspring of Israel his servant,
  children of Jacob, his chosen ones!

¹⁴ He is the Lord our God;
  his judgments are in all the earth.
¹⁵ Remember his covenant forever,
  the word that he commanded, for a thousand generations,
¹⁶ the covenant that he made with Abraham,
  his sworn promise to Isaac,
¹⁷ which he confirmed to Jacob as a statute,
  to Israel as an everlasting covenant,
¹⁸ saying, "To you I will give the land of Canaan,
  as your portion for an inheritance."

¹⁹ When you were few in number,
  of little account, and sojourners in it,
²⁰ wandering from nation to nation,
  from one kingdom to another people,
²¹ he allowed no one to oppress them;
  he rebuked kings on their account,
²² saying, "Touch not my anointed ones,
  do my prophets no harm!"

²³ Sing to the Lord, all the earth!
  Tell of his salvation from day to day.
²⁴ Declare his glory among the nations,
  his marvelous works among all the peoples!
²⁵ For great is the Lord, and greatly to be praised,
  and he is to be feared above all gods.
²⁶ For all the gods of the peoples are worthless idols,
  but the Lord made the heavens.

27 Splendor and majesty are before him;
   strength and joy are in his place.
28 Ascribe to the LORD, O families of the
      peoples,
   ascribe to the LORD glory and
      strength!
29 Ascribe to the LORD the glory due his
      name;
   bring an offering and come before
      him!
   Worship the LORD in the splendor of
      holiness;
30   tremble before him, all the earth;
   yes, the world is established; it shall
      never be moved.
31 Let the heavens be glad, and let the
      earth rejoice,
   and let them say among the
      nations, "The LORD reigns!"
32 Let the sea roar, and all that fills it;
   let the field exult, and everything in
      it!
33 Then shall the trees of the forest sing
      for joy
   before the LORD, for he comes to
      judge the earth.
34 Oh give thanks to the LORD, for he is
      good;
   for his steadfast love endures for-
      ever!
35 Say also:

   "Save us, O God of our salvation,
      and gather and deliver us from
         among the nations,
   that we may give thanks to your holy
      name
   and glory in your praise.
36 Blessed be the LORD, the God of Israel,
   from everlasting to everlasting!"

Then all the people said, "Amen!" and
praised the LORD.

Worship Before the Ark

37 So David left Asaph and his brothers
there before the ark of the covenant of the
LORD to minister regularly before the ark as
each day required, 38 and also Obed-edom
and his sixty-eight brothers, while Obed-
edom, the son of Jeduthun, and Hosah were
to be gatekeepers. 39 And he left Zadok the
priest and his brothers the priests before
the tabernacle of the LORD in the high place
that was at Gibeon 40 to offer burnt offerings

to the LORD on the altar of burnt offering
regularly morning and evening, to do all
that is written in the Law of the LORD that
he commanded Israel. 41 With them were
Heman and Jeduthun and the rest of those
chosen and expressly named to give thanks
to the LORD, for his steadfast love endures
forever. 42 Heman and Jeduthun had trumpets and cymbals for the music and instruments for sacred song. The sons of Jeduthun
were appointed to the gate.

43 Then all the people departed each to
his house, and David went home to bless
his household.

The LORD's Covenant with David

17 Now when David lived in his house,
   David said to Nathan the prophet,
"Behold, I dwell in a house of cedar, but the
ark of the covenant of the LORD is under a
tent." 2 And Nathan said to David, "Do all
that is in your heart, for God is with you."

> ### GETTING THE MESSAGE
>
> **King David** is the main character in
> 1 Chronicles. The writer presents a very
> positive picture of him, leaving out many
> of the tragic details of his life that the
> writer of 2 Samuel describes.

3 But that same night the word of the LORD
came to Nathan, 4 "Go and tell my servant
David, 'Thus says the LORD: It is not you
who will build me a house to dwell in. 5 For
I have not lived in a house since the day
I brought up Israel to this day, but I have
gone from tent to tent and from dwelling to
dwelling. 6 In all places where I have moved
with all Israel, did I speak a word with any
of the judges of Israel, whom I commanded
to shepherd my people, saying, "Why have
you not built me a house of cedar?"' 7 Now,
therefore, thus shall you say to my servant
David, 'Thus says the LORD of hosts, I took
you from the pasture, from following the
sheep, to be prince over my people Israel,
8 and I have been with you wherever you
have gone and have cut off all your enemies
from before you. And I will make for you a
name, like the name of the great ones of
the earth. 9 And I will appoint a place for
my people Israel and will plant them, that
they may dwell in their own place and be

disturbed no more. And violent men shall waste them no more, as formerly, [10] from the time that I appointed judges over my people Israel. And I will subdue all your enemies. Moreover, I declare to you that the LORD will build you a house. [11] When your days are fulfilled to walk with your fathers, I will raise up your offspring after you, one of your own sons, and I will establish his kingdom. [12] He shall build a house for me, and I will establish his throne forever. [13] I will be to him a father, and he shall be to me a son. I will not take my steadfast love from him, as I took it from him who was before you, [14] but I will confirm him in my house and in my kingdom forever, and his throne shall be established forever.'" [15] In accordance with all these words, and in accordance with all this vision, Nathan spoke to David.

David's Prayer

[16] Then King David went in and sat before the LORD and said, "Who am I, O LORD God, and what is my house, that you have brought me thus far? [17] And this was a small thing in your eyes, O God. You have also spoken of your servant's house for a great while to come, and have shown me future generations, O LORD God! [18] And what more can David say to you for honoring your servant? For you know your servant. [19] For your servant's sake, O LORD, and according to your own heart, you have done all this greatness, in making known all these great things. [20] There is none like you, O LORD, and there is no God besides you, according to all that we have heard with our ears. [21] And who is like your people Israel, the one nation on earth whom God went to redeem to be his people, making for yourself a name for great and awesome things, in driving out nations before your people whom you redeemed from Egypt? [22] And you made your people Israel to be your people forever, and you, O LORD, became their God. [23] And now, O LORD, let the word that you have spoken concerning your servant and concerning his house be established forever, and do as you have spoken, [24] and your name will be established and magnified forever, saying, 'The LORD of hosts, the God of Israel, is Israel's God,' and the house of your servant David will be established before you. [25] For you, my God, have revealed to your servant that you will build a house for him. Therefore your servant has found courage to pray before you. [26] And now, O LORD, you are God, and you have promised this good thing to your servant. [27] Now you have been pleased to bless the house of your servant, that it may continue forever before you, for it is you, O LORD, who have blessed, and it is blessed forever."

David Defeats His Enemies

18 After this David defeated the Philistines and subdued them, and he took Gath and its villages out of the hand of the Philistines.

[2] And he defeated Moab, and the Moabites became servants to David and brought tribute.

[3] David also defeated Hadadezer king of Zobah-Hamath, as he went to set up his monument at the river Euphrates. [4] And David took from him 1,000 chariots, 7,000 horsemen, and 20,000 foot soldiers. And David hamstrung all the chariot horses, but left enough for 100 chariots. [5] And when the Syrians of Damascus came to help Hadadezer king of Zobah, David struck down 22,000 men of the Syrians. [6] Then David put garrisons in Syria of Damascus, and the Syrians became servants to David and brought tribute. And the LORD gave victory to David wherever he went. [7] And David took the shields of gold that were carried by the servants of Hadadezer and brought them to Jerusalem. [8] And from Tibhath and from Cun, cities of Hadadezer, David took a large amount of bronze. With it Solomon made the bronze sea and the pillars and the vessels of bronze.

[9] When Tou king of Hamath heard that David had defeated the whole army of Hadadezer, king of Zobah, [10] he sent his son Hadoram to King David, to ask about his health and to bless him because he had fought against Hadadezer and defeated him; for Hadadezer had often been at war with Tou. And he sent all sorts of articles of gold, of silver, and of bronze. [11] These also King David dedicated to the LORD, together with the silver and gold that he had carried off from all the nations, from Edom, Moab, the Ammonites, the Philistines, and Amalek.

[12] And Abishai, the son of Zeruiah, killed 18,000 Edomites in the Valley of Salt. [13] Then he put garrisons in Edom, and all the Edomites became David's servants. And the LORD gave victory to David wherever he went.

David's Administration

¹⁴ So David reigned over all Israel, and he administered justice and equity to all his people. ¹⁵ And Joab the son of Zeruiah was over the army; and Jehoshaphat the son of Ahilud was recorder; ¹⁶ and Zadok the son of Ahitub and Ahimelech the son of Abiathar were priests; and Shavsha was secretary; ¹⁷ and Benaiah the son of Jehoiada was over the Cherethites and the Pelethites; and David's sons were the chief officials in the service of the king.

The Ammonites Disgrace David's Men

19 Now after this Nahash the king of the Ammonites died, and his son reigned in his place. ² And David said, "I will deal kindly with Hanun the son of Nahash, for his father dealt kindly with me." So David sent messengers to console him concerning his father. And David's servants came to the land of the Ammonites to Hanun to console him. ³ But the princes of the Ammonites said to Hanun, "Do you think, because David has sent comforters to you, that he is honoring your father? Have not his servants come to you to search and to overthrow and to spy out the land?" ⁴ So Hanun took David's servants and shaved them and cut off their garments in the middle, at their hips, and sent them away; ⁵ and they departed. When David was told concerning the men, he sent messengers to meet them, for the men were greatly ashamed. And the king said, "Remain at Jericho until your beards have grown and then return."

⁶ When the Ammonites saw that they had become a stench to David, Hanun and the Ammonites sent 1,000 talents of silver to hire chariots and horsemen from Mesopotamia, from Aram-maacah, and from Zobah. ⁷ They hired 32,000 chariots and the king of Maacah with his army, who came and encamped before Medeba. And the Ammonites were mustered from their cities and came to battle. ⁸ When David heard of it, he sent Joab and all the army of the mighty men. ⁹ And the Ammonites came out and drew up in battle array at the entrance of the city, and the kings who had come were by themselves in the open country.

Ammonites and Syrians Defeated

¹⁰ When Joab saw that the battle was set against him both in front and in the rear, he chose some of the best men of Israel and arrayed them against the Syrians. ¹¹ The rest of his men he put in the charge of Abishai his brother, and they were arrayed against the Ammonites. ¹² And he said, "If the Syrians are too strong for me, then you shall help me, but if the Ammonites are too strong for you, then I will help you. ¹³ Be strong, and let us use our strength for our people and for the cities of our God, and may the LORD do what seems good to him." ¹⁴ So Joab and the people who were with him drew near before the Syrians for battle, and they fled before him. ¹⁵ And when the Ammonites saw that the Syrians fled, they likewise fled before Abishai, Joab's brother, and entered the city. Then Joab came to Jerusalem.

¹⁶ But when the Syrians saw that they had been defeated by Israel, they sent messengers and brought out the Syrians who were beyond the Euphrates, with Shophach the commander of the army of Hadadezer at their head. ¹⁷ And when it was told to David, he gathered all Israel together and crossed the Jordan and came to them and drew up his forces against them. And when David set the battle in array against the Syrians, they fought with him. ¹⁸ And the Syrians fled before Israel, and David killed of the Syrians the men of 7,000 chariots and 40,000 foot soldiers, and put to death also Shophach the commander of their army. ¹⁹ And when the servants of Hadadezer saw that they had been defeated by Israel, they made peace with David and became subject to him. So the Syrians were not willing to save the Ammonites anymore.

The Capture of Rabbah

20 In the spring of the year, the time when kings go out to battle, Joab led out the army and ravaged the country of the Ammonites and came and besieged Rabbah. But David remained at Jerusalem. And Joab struck down Rabbah and overthrew it. ² And David took the crown of their king from his head. He found that it weighed a talent of gold, and in it was a precious stone. And it was placed on David's head. And he brought out the spoil of the city, a very great amount. ³ And he brought out the people who were in it and set them to labor with saws and iron picks and axes. And thus David did to all the cities of the Ammonites. Then David and all the people returned to Jerusalem.

Philistine Giants Killed

4 And after this there arose war with the Philistines at Gezer. Then Sibbecai the Hushathite struck down Sippai, who was one of the descendants of the giants, and the Philistines were subdued. **5** And there was again war with the Philistines, and Elhanan the son of Jair struck down Lahmi the brother of Goliath the Gittite, the shaft of whose spear was like a weaver's beam. **6** And there was again war at Gath, where there was a man of great stature, who had six fingers on each hand and six toes on each foot, twenty-four in number, and he also was descended from the giants. **7** And when he taunted Israel, Jonathan the son of Shimea, David's brother, struck him down. **8** These were descended from the giants in Gath, and they fell by the hand of David and by the hand of his servants.

GETTING THE MESSAGE

Why did ancient kings go to war in the spring? In Palestine, crops such as barley and wheat were harvested in the spring. An invading army could live off harvested grains (20:1).

David's Census Brings Pestilence

21 Then Satan stood against Israel and incited David to number Israel. **2** So David said to Joab and the commanders of the army, "Go, number Israel, from Beersheba to Dan, and bring me a report, that I may know their number." **3** But Joab said, "May the LORD add to his people a hundred times as many as they are! Are they not, my lord the king, all of them my lord's servants? Why then should my lord require this? Why should it be a cause of guilt for Israel?" **4** But the king's word prevailed against Joab. So Joab departed and went throughout all Israel and came back to Jerusalem. **5** And Joab gave the sum of the numbering of the people to David. In all Israel there were 1,100,000 men who drew the sword, and in Judah 470,000 who drew the sword. **6** But he did not include Levi and Benjamin in the numbering, for the king's command was abhorrent to Joab.

7 But God was displeased with this thing, and he struck Israel. **8** And David said to God,

"I have sinned greatly in that I have done this thing. But now, please take away the iniquity of your servant, for I have acted very foolishly." **9** And the LORD spoke to Gad, David's seer, saying, **10** "Go and say to David, 'Thus says the LORD, Three things I offer you; choose one of them, that I may do it to you.'" **11** So Gad came to David and said to him, "Thus says the LORD, 'Choose what you will: **12** either three years of famine, or three months of devastation by your foes while the sword of your enemies overtakes you, or else three days of the sword of the LORD, pestilence on the land, with the angel of the LORD destroying throughout all the territory of Israel.' Now decide what answer I shall return to him who sent me." **13** Then David said to Gad, "I am in great distress. Let me fall into the hand of the LORD, for his mercy is very great, but do not let me fall into the hand of man."

14 So the LORD sent a pestilence on Israel, and 70,000 men of Israel fell. **15** And God sent the angel to Jerusalem to destroy it, but as he was about to destroy it, the LORD saw, and he relented from the calamity. And he said to the angel who was working destruction, "It is enough; now stay your hand." And the angel of the LORD was standing by the threshing floor of Ornan the Jebusite. **16** And David lifted his eyes and saw the angel of the LORD standing between earth and heaven, and in his hand a drawn sword stretched out over Jerusalem. Then David and the elders, clothed in sackcloth, fell upon their faces. **17** And David said to God, "Was it not I who gave command to number the people? It is I who have sinned and done great evil. But these sheep, what have they done? Please let your hand, O LORD my God, be against me and against my father's house. But do not let the plague be on your people."

David Builds an Altar

18 Now the angel of the LORD had commanded Gad to say to David that David should go up and raise an altar to the LORD on the threshing floor of Ornan the Jebusite. **19** So David went up at Gad's word, which he had spoken in the name of the LORD. **20** Now Ornan was threshing wheat. He turned and saw the angel, and his four sons who were with him hid themselves. **21** As David came to Ornan, Ornan looked and saw David and went out from the threshing floor and paid homage to David with his face to the ground. ²² And David said to Ornan, "Give me the site of the threshing floor that I may build on it an altar to the LORD—give it to me at its full price—that the plague may be averted from the people." ²³ Then Ornan said to David, "Take it, and let my lord the king do what seems good to him. See, I give the oxen for burnt offerings and the threshing sledges for the wood and the wheat for a grain offering; I give it all." ²⁴ But King David said to Ornan, "No, but I will buy them for the full price. I will not take for the LORD what is yours, nor offer burnt offerings that cost me nothing." ²⁵ So David paid Ornan 600 shekels of gold by weight for the site. ²⁶ And David built there an altar to the LORD and presented burnt offerings and peace offerings and called on the LORD, and the LORD answered him with fire from heaven upon the altar of burnt offering. ²⁷ Then the LORD commanded the angel, and he put his sword back into its sheath.

²⁸ At that time, when David saw that the LORD had answered him at the threshing floor of Ornan the Jebusite, he sacrificed there. ²⁹ For the tabernacle of the LORD, which Moses had made in the wilderness, and the altar of burnt offering were at that time in the high place at Gibeon, ³⁰ but David could not go before it to inquire of God, for he was afraid of the sword of the angel of the LORD.

22 Then David said, "Here shall be the house of the LORD God and here the altar of burnt offering for Israel."

David Prepares for Temple Building

² David commanded to gather together the resident aliens who were in the land of Israel, and he set stonecutters to prepare dressed stones for building the house of God. ³ David also provided great quantities of iron for nails for the doors of the gates and for clamps, as well as bronze in quantities beyond weighing, ⁴ and cedar timbers without number, for the Sidonians and Tyrians brought great quantities of cedar to David. ⁵ For David said, "Solomon my son is young and inexperienced, and the house that is to be built for the LORD must be exceedingly magnificent, of fame and glory throughout all lands. I will therefore make preparation for it." So David provided materials in great quantity before his death.

Solomon Charged to Build the Temple

⁶ Then he called for Solomon his son and charged him to build a house for the LORD, the God of Israel. ⁷ David said to Solomon, "My son, I had it in my heart to build a house to the name of the LORD my God. ⁸ But the word of the LORD came to me, saying, 'You have shed much blood and have waged great wars. You shall not build a house to my name, because you have shed so much blood before me on the earth. ⁹ Behold, a son shall be born to you who shall be a man of rest. I will give him rest from all his surrounding enemies. For his name shall be Solomon, and I will give peace and quiet to Israel in his days. ¹⁰ He shall build a house for my name. He shall be my son, and I will be his father, and I will establish his royal throne in Israel forever.'

¹¹ "Now, my son, the LORD be with you, so that you may succeed in building the house of the LORD your God, as he has spoken concerning you. ¹² Only, may the LORD grant you discretion and understanding, that when he gives you charge over Israel you may keep the law of the LORD your God. ¹³ Then you will prosper if you are careful to observe the statutes and the rules that the LORD commanded Moses for Israel. Be strong and courageous. Fear not; do not be dismayed. ¹⁴ With great pains I have provided for the house of the LORD 100,000 talents of gold, a million talents of silver, and bronze and iron beyond weighing, for there is so much of it; timber and stone, too, I have provided. To these you must add. ¹⁵ You have an abundance of workmen: stonecutters, masons, carpenters, and all kinds of craftsmen without number, skilled in working ¹⁶ gold, silver, bronze, and iron. Arise and work! The LORD be with you!"

¹⁷ David also commanded all the leaders of Israel to help Solomon his son, saying, ¹⁸ "Is not the LORD your God with you? And has he not given you peace on every side? For he has delivered the inhabitants of the land into my hand, and the land is subdued before the LORD and his people. ¹⁹ Now set your mind and heart to seek the LORD your God. Arise and build the sanctuary of the LORD God, so that the ark of the covenant of the LORD and the holy vessels of God may be brought into a house built for the name of the LORD."

David Organizes the Levites

23 When David was old and full of days, he made Solomon his son king over Israel.

² David assembled all the leaders of Israel and the priests and the Levites. ³ The Levites, thirty years old and upward, were numbered, and the total was 38,000 men. ⁴ "Twenty-four thousand of these," David said, "shall have charge of the work in the house of the LORD, 6,000 shall be officers and judges, ⁵ 4,000 gatekeepers, and 4,000 shall offer praises to the LORD with the instruments that I have made for praise." ⁶ And David organized them in divisions corresponding to the sons of Levi: Gershon, Kohath, and Merari.

⁷ The sons of Gershon were Ladan and Shimei. ⁸ The sons of Ladan: Jehiel the chief,

GETTING THE MESSAGE

New job descriptions for the Levites.
For nearly 500 years a specific group of Levites had taken care of the portable tabernacle and its furniture, including the ark. Whenever the tabernacle was moved, each Levite had a specific job to do. Now that there would be a permanent temple, David gave new instructions to these faithful workers.

and Zetham, and Joel, three. ⁹ The sons of Shimei: Shelomoth, Haziel, and Haran, three. These were the heads of the fathers' houses of Ladan. ¹⁰ And the sons of Shimei: Jahath, Zina, and Jeush and Beriah. These four were the sons of Shimei. ¹¹ Jahath was the chief, and Zizah the second; but Jeush and Beriah did not have many sons, therefore they became counted as a single father's house.

¹² The sons of Kohath: Amram, Izhar, Hebron, and Uzziel, four. ¹³ The sons of Amram: Aaron and Moses. Aaron was set apart to dedicate the most holy things, that he and his sons forever should make offerings before the LORD and minister to him and pronounce blessings in his name forever. ¹⁴ But the sons of Moses the man of God were named among the tribe of Levi. ¹⁵ The sons of Moses: Gershom and Eliezer. ¹⁶ The sons of Gershom: Shebuel the chief.

¹⁷ The sons of Eliezer: Rehabiah the chief. Eliezer had no other sons, but the sons of Rehabiah were very many. ¹⁸ The sons of Izhar: Shelomith the chief. ¹⁹ The sons of Hebron: Jeriah the chief, Amariah the second, Jahaziel the third, and Jekameam the fourth. ²⁰ The sons of Uzziel: Micah the chief and Isshiah the second.

²¹ The sons of Merari: Mahli and Mushi. The sons of Mahli: Eleazar and Kish. ²² Eleazar died having no sons, but only daughters; their kinsmen, the sons of Kish, married them. ²³ The sons of Mushi: Mahli, Eder, and Jeremoth, three.

²⁴ These were the sons of Levi by their fathers' houses, the heads of fathers' houses as they were listed according to the number of the names of the individuals from twenty years old and upward who were to do the work for the service of the house of the LORD. ²⁵ For David said, "The LORD, the God of Israel, has given rest to his people, and he dwells in Jerusalem forever. ²⁶ And so the Levites no longer need to carry the tabernacle or any of the things for its service." ²⁷ For by the last words of David the sons of Levi were numbered from twenty years old and upward. ²⁸ For their duty was to assist the sons of Aaron for the service of the house of the LORD, having the care of the courts and the chambers, the cleansing of all that is holy, and any work for the service of the house of God. ²⁹ Their duty was also to assist with the showbread, the flour for the grain offering, the wafers of unleavened bread, the baked offering, the offering mixed with oil, and all measures of quantity or size. ³⁰ And they were to stand every morning, thanking and praising the LORD, and likewise at evening, ³¹ and whenever burnt offerings were offered to the LORD on Sabbaths, new moons, and feast days, according to the number required of them, regularly before the LORD. ³² Thus they were to keep charge of the tent of meeting and the sanctuary, and to attend the sons of Aaron, their brothers, for the service of the house of the LORD.

David Organizes the Priests

24 The divisions of the sons of Aaron were these. The sons of Aaron: Nadab, Abihu, Eleazar, and Ithamar. ² But Nadab and Abihu died before their father and had no children, so Eleazar and Ithamar became the priests. ³ With the help of Zadok of the sons of Eleazar, and Ahimelech of the sons of Ithamar, David organized them according to the appointed duties in their service. ⁴ Since more chief men were found among the sons of Eleazar than among the sons of Ithamar, they organized them under sixteen heads of fathers' houses of the sons of Eleazar, and eight of the sons of Ithamar. ⁵ They divided them by lot, all alike, for there were sacred officers and officers of God among both the sons of Eleazar and the sons of Ithamar. ⁶ And the scribe Shemaiah, the son of Nethanel, a Levite, recorded them in the presence of the king and the princes and Zadok the priest and Ahimelech the son of Abiathar and the heads of the fathers' houses of the priests and of the Levites, one father's house being chosen for Eleazar and one chosen for Ithamar.

⁷ The first lot fell to Jehoiarib, the second to Jedaiah, ⁸ the third to Harim, the fourth to Seorim, ⁹ the fifth to Malchijah, the sixth to Mijamin, ¹⁰ the seventh to Hakkoz, the eighth to Abijah, ¹¹ the ninth to Jeshua, the tenth to Shecaniah, ¹² the eleventh to Eliashib, the twelfth to Jakim, ¹³ the thirteenth to Huppah, the fourteenth to Jeshebeab, ¹⁴ the fifteenth to Bilgah, the sixteenth to Immer, ¹⁵ the seventeenth to Hezir, the eighteenth to Happizzez, ¹⁶ the nineteenth to Pethahiah, the twentieth to Jehezkel, ¹⁷ the twenty-first to Jachin, the twenty-second to Gamul, ¹⁸ the twenty-third to Delaiah, the twenty-fourth to Maaziah. ¹⁹ These had as their appointed duty in their service to come into the house of the LORD according to the procedure established for them by Aaron their father, as the LORD God of Israel had commanded him.

²⁰ And of the rest of the sons of Levi: of the sons of Amram, Shubael; of the sons of Shubael, Jehdeiah. ²¹ Of Rehabiah: of the sons of Rehabiah, Isshiah the chief. ²² Of the Izharites, Shelomoth; of the sons of Shelomoth, Jahath. ²³ The sons of Hebron: Jeriah the chief, Amariah the second, Jahaziel the third, Jekameam the fourth. ²⁴ The sons of Uzziel, Micah; of the sons of Micah, Shamir. ²⁵ The brother of Micah, Isshiah; of the sons of Isshiah, Zechariah. ²⁶ The sons of Merari: Mahli and Mushi. The sons of Jaaziah: Beno. ²⁷ The sons of Merari: of Jaaziah, Beno, Shoham, Zaccur, and Ibri.

²⁸ Of Mahli: Eleazar, who had no sons. ²⁹ Of Kish, the sons of Kish: Jerahmeel. ³⁰ The sons of Mushi: Mahli, Eder, and Jerimoth. These were the sons of the Levites according to their fathers' houses. ³¹ These also, the head of each father's house and his younger brother alike, cast lots, just as their brothers the sons of Aaron, in the presence of King David, Zadok, Ahimelech, and the heads of fathers' houses of the priests and of the Levites.

David Organizes the Musicians

25 David and the chiefs of the service also set apart for the service the sons of Asaph, and of Heman, and of Jeduthun, who prophesied with lyres, with harps, and with cymbals. The list of those who did the work and of their duties was: ² Of the sons of Asaph: Zaccur, Joseph, Nethaniah, and Asharelah, sons of Asaph, under the direction of Asaph, who prophesied under the

> ### GETTING THE MESSAGE
>
> **What is a lyre?** The lyre (25:3) is a triangular stringed musical instrument, with anywhere from 3 to 12 strings. It is held like a guitar and strummed with either the fingers or a pick.

direction of the king. ³ Of Jeduthun, the sons of Jeduthun: Gedaliah, Zeri, Jeshaiah, Shimei, Hashabiah, and Mattithiah, six, under the direction of their father Jeduthun, who prophesied with the lyre in thanksgiving and praise to the LORD. ⁴ Of Heman, the sons of Heman: Bukkiah, Mattaniah, Uzziel, Shebuel and Jerimoth, Hananiah, Hanani, Eliathah, Giddalti, and Romamti-ezer, Joshbekashah, Mallothi, Hothir, Mahazioth. ⁵ All these were the sons of Heman the king's seer, according to the promise of God to exalt him, for God had given Heman fourteen sons and three daughters. ⁶ They were all under the direction of their father in the music in the house of the LORD with cymbals, harps, and lyres for the service of the house of God. Asaph, Jeduthun, and Heman were under the order of the king. ⁷ The number of them along with their brothers, who were trained in singing to the LORD, all who were skillful, was 288. ⁸ And they cast lots for their duties, small and great, teacher and pupil alike.

⁹ The first lot fell for Asaph to Joseph; the second to Gedaliah, to him and his brothers and his sons, twelve; ¹⁰ the third to Zaccur, his sons and his brothers, twelve; ¹¹ the fourth to Izri, his sons and his brothers, twelve; ¹² the fifth to Nethaniah, his sons and his brothers, twelve; ¹³ the sixth to Bukkiah, his sons and his brothers, twelve; ¹⁴ the seventh to Jesharelah, his sons and his brothers, twelve; ¹⁵ the eighth to Jeshaiah, his sons and his brothers, twelve; ¹⁶ the ninth to Mattaniah, his sons and his brothers, twelve; ¹⁷ the tenth to Shimei, his sons and his brothers, twelve; ¹⁸ the eleventh to Azarel, his sons and his brothers, twelve; ¹⁹ the twelfth to Hashabiah, his sons and his brothers, twelve; ²⁰ to the thirteenth, Shubael, his sons and his brothers, twelve; ²¹ to the fourteenth, Mattithiah, his sons and his brothers, twelve; ²² to the fifteenth, to Jeremoth, his sons and his brothers, twelve; ²³ to the sixteenth, to Hananiah, his sons and his brothers, twelve; ²⁴ to the seventeenth, to Joshbekashah, his sons and his brothers, twelve; ²⁵ to the eighteenth, to Hanani, his sons and his brothers, twelve; ²⁶ to the nineteenth, to Mallothi, his sons and his brothers, twelve; ²⁷ to the twentieth, to Eliathah, his sons and his brothers, twelve; ²⁸ to the twenty-first, to Hothir, his sons and his brothers, twelve; ²⁹ to the twenty-second, to Giddalti, his sons and his brothers, twelve; ³⁰ to the twenty-third, to Mahazioth, his sons and his brothers, twelve; ³¹ to the twenty-fourth, to Romamti-ezer, his sons and his brothers, twelve.

Divisions of the Gatekeepers

26 As for the divisions of the gatekeepers: of the Korahites, Meshelemiah the son of Kore, of the sons of Asaph. ² And Meshelemiah had sons: Zechariah the firstborn, Jediael the second, Zebadiah the third, Jathniel the fourth, ³ Elam the fifth, Jehohanan the sixth, Eliehoenai the seventh. ⁴ And Obed-edom had sons: Shemaiah the firstborn, Jehozabad the second, Joah the third, Sachar the fourth, Nethanel the fifth, ⁵ Ammiel the sixth, Issachar the seventh, Peullethai the eighth, for God blessed him. ⁶ Also to his son Shemaiah were sons born who were rulers in their fathers' houses, for they were men of great ability. ⁷ The sons of Shemaiah: Othni, Rephael, Obed and Elzabad, whose brothers were

able men, Elihu and Semachiah. ⁸ All these were of the sons of Obed-edom with their sons and brothers, able men qualified for the service; sixty-two of Obed-edom. ⁹ And Meshelemiah had sons and brothers, able men, eighteen. ¹⁰ And Hosah, of the sons of Merari, had sons: Shimri the chief (for though he was not the firstborn, his father made him chief), ¹¹ Hilkiah the second, Tebaliah the third, Zechariah the fourth: all the sons and brothers of Hosah were thirteen.

¹² These divisions of the gatekeepers, corresponding to their chief men, had duties, just as their brothers did, ministering in the house of the LORD. ¹³ And they cast lots by fathers' houses, small and great alike, for their gates. ¹⁴ The lot for the east fell to Shelemiah. They cast lots also for his son Zechariah, a shrewd counselor, and his lot came out for the north. ¹⁵ Obed-edom's came out for the south, and to his sons was allotted the gatehouse. ¹⁶ For Shuppim and Hosah it came out for the west, at the gate of Shallecheth on the road that goes up. Watch corresponded to watch. ¹⁷ On the east there were six each day, on the north four each day, on the south four each day, as well as two and two at the gatehouse. ¹⁸ And for the colonnade on the west there were four at the road and two at the colonnade. ¹⁹ These were the divisions of the gatekeepers among the Korahites and the sons of Merari.

Treasurers and Other Officials

²⁰ And of the Levites, Ahijah had charge of the treasuries of the house of God and the treasuries of the dedicated gifts. ²¹ The sons of Ladan, the sons of the Gershonites belonging to Ladan, the heads of the fathers' houses belonging to Ladan the Gershonite: Jehieli. ²² The sons of Jehieli, Zetham, and Joel his brother, were in charge of the treasuries of the house of the LORD. ²³ Of the Amramites, the Izharites, the Hebronites, and the Uzzielites— ²⁴ and Shebuel the son of Gershom, son of Moses, was chief officer in charge of the treasuries. ²⁵ His brothers: from Eliezer were his son Rehabiah, and his son Jeshaiah, and his son Joram, and his son Zichri, and his son Shelomoth. ²⁶ This Shelomoth and his brothers were in charge of all the treasuries of the dedicated gifts that David the king and the heads of the fathers' houses and the officers of

the thousands and the hundreds and the commanders of the army had dedicated. ²⁷ From spoil won in battles they dedicated gifts for the maintenance of the house of the LORD. ²⁸ Also all that Samuel the seer and Saul the son of Kish and Abner the son of Ner and Joab the son of Zeruiah had dedicated—all dedicated gifts were in the care of Shelomoth and his brothers.

²⁹ Of the Izharites, Chenaniah and his sons were appointed to external duties for Israel, as officers and judges. ³⁰ Of the Hebronites, Hashabiah and his brothers, 1,700 men of ability, had the oversight of Israel westward of the Jordan for all the work of the LORD and for the service of the king. ³¹ Of the Hebronites, Jerijah was chief of the Hebronites of whatever genealogy or fathers' houses. (In the fortieth year of David's reign search was made and men of great ability among them were found at Jazer in Gilead.) ³² King David appointed him and his brothers, 2,700 men of ability, heads of fathers' houses, to have the oversight of the Reubenites, the Gadites and the half-tribe of the Manassites for everything pertaining to God and for the affairs of the king.

Military Divisions

27 This is the number of the people of Israel, the heads of fathers' houses, the commanders of thousands and hundreds, and their officers who served the king in all matters concerning the divisions that came and went, month after month throughout the year, each division numbering 24,000:

² Jashobeam the son of Zabdiel was in charge of the first division in the first month; in his division were 24,000. ³ He was a descendant of Perez and was chief of all the commanders. He served for the first month. ⁴ Dodai the Ahohite was in charge of the division of the second month; in his division were 24,000. ⁵ The third commander, for the third month, was Benaiah, the son of Jehoiada the chief priest; in his division were 24,000. ⁶ This is the Benaiah who was a mighty man of the thirty and in command of the thirty; Ammizabad his son was in charge of his division. ⁷ Asahel the brother of Joab was fourth, for the fourth month, and his son Zebadiah after him; in his division were 24,000. ⁸ The fifth commander, for the fifth month, was

Shamhuth the Izrahite; in his division were 24,000. ⁹ Sixth, for the sixth month, was Ira, the son of Ikkesh the Tekoite; in his division were 24,000. ¹⁰ Seventh, for the seventh month, was Helez the Pelonite, of the sons of Ephraim; in his division were 24,000. ¹¹ Eighth, for the eighth month, was Sibbecai the Hushathite, of the Zerahites; in his division were 24,000. ¹² Ninth, for the ninth month, was Abiezer of Anathoth, a Benjaminite; in his division were 24,000. ¹³ Tenth, for the tenth month, was Maharai of Netophah, of the Zerahites; in his division were 24,000. ¹⁴ Eleventh, for the eleventh month, was Benaiah of Pirathon, of the sons of Ephraim; in his division were 24,000. ¹⁵ Twelfth, for the twelfth month, was Heldai the Netophathite, of Othniel; in his division were 24,000.

Leaders of Tribes

¹⁶ Over the tribes of Israel, for the Reubenites, Eliezer the son of Zichri was chief officer; for the Simeonites, Shephatiah the son of Maacah; ¹⁷ for Levi, Hashabiah the son of Kemuel; for Aaron, Zadok; ¹⁸ for Judah, Elihu, one of David's brothers; for Issachar, Omri the son of Michael; ¹⁹ for Zebulun, Ishmaiah the son of Obadiah; for Naphtali, Jeremoth the son of Azriel; ²⁰ for the Ephraimites, Hoshea the son of Azaziah; for the half-tribe of Manasseh, Joel the son of Pedaiah; ²¹ for the half-tribe of Manasseh in Gilead, Iddo the son of Zechariah; for Benjamin, Jaasiel the son of Abner; ²² for Dan, Azarel the son of Jeroham. These were the leaders of the tribes of Israel. ²³ David did not count those below twenty years of age, for the LORD had promised to make Israel as many as the stars of heaven. ²⁴ Joab the son of Zeruiah began to count, but did not finish. Yet wrath came upon Israel for this, and the number was not entered in the chronicles of King David.

²⁵ Over the king's treasuries was Azmaveth the son of Adiel; and over the treasuries in the country, in the cities, in the villages, and in the towers, was Jonathan the son of Uzziah; ²⁶ and over those who did the work of the field for tilling the soil was Ezri the son of Chelub; ²⁷ and over the vineyards was Shimei the Ramathite; and over the produce of the vineyards for the wine cellars was Zabdi the Shiphmite. ²⁸ Over the olive and sycamore trees in the Shephelah was

Baal-hanan the Gederite; and over the stores of oil was Joash. ²⁹ Over the herds that pastured in Sharon was Shitrai the Sharonite; over the herds in the valleys was Shaphat the son of Adlai. ³⁰ Over the camels was Obil the Ishmaelite; and over the donkeys was Jehdeiah the Meronothite. Over the flocks was Jaziz the Hagrite. ³¹ All these were stewards of King David's property.

³² Jonathan, David's uncle, was a counselor, being a man of understanding and a scribe. He and Jehiel the son of Hachmoni attended the king's sons. ³³ Ahithophel was the king's counselor, and Hushai the Archite was the king's friend. ³⁴ Ahithophel was succeeded by Jehoiada the son of Benaiah, and Abiathar. Joab was commander of the king's army.

David's Charge to Israel

28 David assembled at Jerusalem all the officials of Israel, the officials of the tribes, the officers of the divisions that served the king, the commanders of thousands, the commanders of hundreds, the stewards of all the property and livestock of the king and his sons, together with the palace officials, the mighty men and all the seasoned warriors. ² Then King David rose to his feet and said: "Hear me, my brothers and my people. I had it in my heart to build a house of rest for the ark of the covenant of the LORD and for the footstool of our God, and I made preparations for building. ³ But God said to me, 'You may not build a house for my name, for you are a man of war and have shed blood.' ⁴ Yet the LORD God of Israel chose me from all my father's house to be king over Israel forever. For he chose Judah as leader, and in the house of Judah my father's house, and among my father's sons he took pleasure in me to make me king over all Israel. ⁵ And of all my sons (for the LORD has given me many sons) he has chosen Solomon my son to sit on the throne of the kingdom of the LORD over Israel. ⁶ He said to me, 'It is Solomon your son who shall build my house and my courts, for I have chosen him to be my son, and I will be his father. ⁷ I will establish his kingdom forever if he continues strong in keeping my commandments and my rules, as he is today.' ⁸ Now therefore in the sight of all Israel, the assembly of the LORD, and in the hearing of our God, observe and seek out all the commandments of the LORD your God, that you may possess this good land and leave it for an inheritance to your children after you forever.

David's Charge to Solomon

⁹ "And you, Solomon my son, know the God of your father and serve him with a whole heart and with a willing mind, for the LORD searches all hearts and understands every plan and thought. If you seek him, he will be found by you, but if you forsake him, he will cast you off forever. ¹⁰ Be careful now, for the LORD has chosen you to build a house for the sanctuary; be strong and do it."

¹¹ Then David gave Solomon his son the plan of the vestibule of the temple, and of its houses, its treasuries, its upper rooms, and its inner chambers, and of the room for the mercy seat; ¹² and the plan of all that he had in mind for the courts of the house of the LORD, all the surrounding chambers, the treasuries of the house of God, and the treasuries for dedicated gifts; ¹³ for the divisions of the priests and of the Levites, and all the work of the service in the house of the LORD; for all the vessels for the service in the house of the LORD, ¹⁴ the weight of gold for all golden vessels for each service, the weight of silver vessels for each service, ¹⁵ the weight of the golden lampstands and their lamps, the weight of gold for each lampstand and its lamps, the weight of silver for a lampstand and its lamps, according to the use of each lampstand in the service, ¹⁶ the weight of gold for each table for the showbread, the silver for the silver tables, ¹⁷ and pure gold for the forks, the basins and the cups; for the golden bowls and the weight of each; for the silver bowls and the weight of each; ¹⁸ for the altar of incense made of refined gold, and its weight; also his plan for the golden chariot of the cherubim that spread their wings and covered the ark of the covenant of the LORD. ¹⁹ "All this he made clear to me in writing from the hand of the LORD, all the work to be done according to the plan."

²⁰ Then David said to Solomon his son, "Be strong and courageous and do it. Do not be afraid and do not be dismayed, for the LORD God, even my God, is with you. He will not leave you or forsake you, until all the work for the service of the house of the LORD is finished. ²¹ And behold the divisions

of the priests and the Levites for all the service of the house of God; and with you in all the work will be every willing man who has skill for any kind of service; also the officers and all the people will be wholly at your command."

Offerings for the Temple

29 And David the king said to all the assembly, "Solomon my son, whom alone God has chosen, is young and inexperienced, and the work is great, for the palace will not be for man but for the LORD God. ² So I have provided for the house of my God, so far as I was able, the gold for the things of gold, the silver for the things of silver, and the bronze for the things of bronze, the iron for the things of iron, and wood for the things of wood, besides great quantities of onyx and stones for setting, antimony, colored stones, all sorts of precious stones and marble. ³ Moreover, in addition to all that I have provided for the holy house, I have a treasure of my own of gold and silver, and because of my devotion to the house of my God I give it to the house of my God: ⁴ 3,000 talents of gold, of the gold of Ophir, and 7,000 talents of refined silver, for overlaying the walls of the house, ⁵ and for all the work to be done by craftsmen, gold for the things of gold and silver for the things of silver. Who then will offer willingly, consecrating himself today to the LORD?"

⁶ Then the leaders of fathers' houses made their freewill offerings, as did also the leaders of the tribes, the commanders of thousands and of hundreds, and the officers over the king's work. ⁷ They gave for the service of the house of God 5,000 talents and 10,000 darics of gold, 10,000 talents of silver, 18,000 talents of bronze and 100,000 talents of iron. ⁸ And whoever had precious stones gave them to the treasury of the house of the LORD, in the care of Jehiel the Gershonite. ⁹ Then the people rejoiced because they had given willingly, for with a whole heart they had offered freely to the LORD. David the king also rejoiced greatly.

David Prays in the Assembly

¹⁰ Therefore David blessed the LORD in the presence of all the assembly. And David said: "Blessed are you, O LORD, the God of Israel our father, forever and ever. ¹¹ Yours, O LORD, is the greatness and the power and the glory and the victory and the majesty, for all that is in the heavens and in the earth is yours. Yours is the kingdom, O LORD, and you are exalted as head above all. ¹² Both riches and honor come from you, and you rule over all. In your hand are power and might, and in your hand it is to make great and to give strength to all. ¹³ And now we thank you, our God, and praise your glorious name.

¹⁴ "But who am I, and what is my people, that we should be able thus to offer willingly? For all things come from you, and of your own have we given you. ¹⁵ For we are strangers before you and sojourners, as all our fathers were. Our days on the earth are like a shadow, and there is no abiding. ¹⁶ O LORD our God, all this abundance that we have provided for building you a house for your holy name comes from your hand and is all your own. ¹⁷ I know, my God, that you test the heart and have pleasure

> ### GETTING THE MESSAGE
>
> **David reigned for 40 years.** He ruled over Judah for 7 years in Hebron, and then over all twelve tribes for 33 years in Jerusalem (29:27).

in uprightness. In the uprightness of my heart I have freely offered all these things, and now I have seen your people, who are present here, offering freely and joyously to you. ¹⁸ O LORD, the God of Abraham, Isaac, and Israel, our fathers, keep forever such purposes and thoughts in the hearts of your people, and direct their hearts toward you. ¹⁹ Grant to Solomon my son a whole heart that he may keep your commandments, your testimonies, and your statutes, performing all, and that he may build the palace for which I have made provision."

²⁰ Then David said to all the assembly, "Bless the LORD your God." And all the assembly blessed the LORD, the God of their fathers, and bowed their heads and paid homage to the LORD and to the king. ²¹ And they offered sacrifices to the LORD, and on the next day offered burnt offerings to the LORD, 1,000 bulls, 1,000 rams, and 1,000 lambs, with their drink offerings, and sacrifices in abundance for all Israel.

[22] And they ate and drank before the LORD on that day with great gladness.

Solomon Anointed King

And they made Solomon the son of David king the second time, and they anointed him as prince for the LORD, and Zadok as priest. [23] Then Solomon sat on the throne of the LORD as king in place of David his father. And he prospered, and all Israel obeyed him. [24] All the leaders and the mighty men, and also all the sons of King David, pledged their allegiance to King Solomon. [25] And the LORD made Solomon very great in the sight of all Israel and bestowed on him such royal majesty as had not been on any king before him in Israel.

The Death of David

[26] Thus David the son of Jesse reigned over all Israel. [27] The time that he reigned over Israel was forty years. He reigned seven years in Hebron and thirty-three years in Jerusalem. [28] Then he died at a good age, full of days, riches, and honor. And Solomon his son reigned in his place. [29] Now the acts of King David, from first to last, are written in the Chronicles of Samuel the seer, and in the Chronicles of Nathan the prophet, and in the Chronicles of Gad the seer, [30] with accounts of all his rule and his might and of the circumstances that came upon him and upon Israel and upon all the kingdoms of the countries.

2 CHRONICLES

Solomon Worships at Gibeon

1 Solomon the son of David established himself in his kingdom, and the LORD his God was with him and made him exceedingly great.

2 Solomon spoke to all Israel, to the commanders of thousands and of hundreds, to the judges, and to all the leaders in all Israel, the heads of fathers' houses. 3 And Solomon, and all the assembly with him, went to the high place that was at Gibeon, for the tent of meeting of God, which Moses the servant of the LORD had made in the wilderness, was

there. 4 (But David had brought up the ark of God from Kiriath-jearim to the place that David had prepared for it, for he had pitched a tent for it in Jerusalem.) 5 Moreover, the bronze altar that Bezalel the son of Uri, son of Hur, had made, was there before the tabernacle of the LORD. And Solomon and the assembly sought it out. 6 And Solomon went up there to the bronze altar before the LORD, which was at the tent of meeting, and offered a thousand burnt offerings on it.

Solomon Prays for Wisdom

7 In that night God appeared to Solomon, and said to him, "Ask what I shall give you." 8 And Solomon said to God, "You have shown great and steadfast love to David my father, and have made me king in his place. 9 O LORD God, let your word to David my father be now fulfilled, for you have made me king over a people as numerous as the dust of the earth. 10 Give me now wisdom

and knowledge to go out and come in before this people, for who can govern this people of yours, which is so great?" 11 God answered Solomon, "Because this was in your heart, and you have not asked for possessions, wealth, honor, or the life of those who hate you, and have not even asked for long life, but have asked for wisdom and knowledge for yourself that you may govern my people over whom I have made you king, 12 wisdom and knowledge are granted to you. I will also give you riches, possessions, and honor, such as none of the kings had who were before you, and none after you shall have the like." 13 So Solomon came from the high place at Gibeon, from before the tent of meeting, to Jerusalem. And he reigned over Israel.

Solomon Given Wealth

14 Solomon gathered together chariots and horsemen. He had 1,400 chariots and 12,000 horsemen, whom he stationed in the chariot cities and with the king in Jerusalem. 15 And the king made silver and gold as common in Jerusalem as stone, and he made cedar as plentiful as the sycamore of the Shephelah. 16 And Solomon's import of horses was from Egypt and Kue, and the king's traders would buy them from Kue for a price. 17 They imported a chariot from Egypt for 600 shekels of silver, and a horse for 150. Likewise through them these were exported to all the kings of the Hittites and the kings of Syria.

Preparing to Build the Temple

2 Now Solomon purposed to build a temple for the name of the LORD, and a royal palace for himself. 2 And Solomon assigned 70,000 men to bear burdens and 80,000 to quarry in the hill country, and 3,600 to oversee them. 3 And Solomon sent word to Hiram the king of Tyre: "As you dealt with David my father and sent him cedar to build himself a house to dwell in, so deal with me. 4 Behold, I am about to build a house for the name of the LORD my God and dedicate it to him for the

burning of incense of sweet spices before him, and for the regular arrangement of the showbread, and for burnt offerings morning and evening, on the Sabbaths and the new moons and the appointed feasts of the LORD our God, as ordained forever for Israel. **5** The house that I am to build will be great, for our God is greater than all gods. **6** But who is able to build him a house, since heaven, even highest heaven, cannot contain him? Who am I to build a house for him, except as a place to make offerings before him? **7** So now send me a man skilled to work in gold, silver, bronze, and iron, and in purple, crimson, and blue fabrics, trained also in engraving, to be with the skilled workers who are with me in Judah and Jerusalem, whom David my father provided. **8** Send me also cedar, cypress, and algum timber from Lebanon, for I know that your servants know how to cut timber in Lebanon. And my servants will be with your servants, **9** to prepare timber for me in abundance, for the house I am to build will be great and wonderful. **10** I will give for your servants, the woodsmen who cut timber, 20,000 cors of crushed wheat, 20,000 cors of barley, 20,000 baths of wine, and 20,000 baths of oil."

11 Then Hiram the king of Tyre answered in a letter that he sent to Solomon, "Because the LORD loves his people, he has made you king over them." **12** Hiram also said, "Blessed be the LORD God of Israel, who made heaven and earth, who has given King David a wise son, who has discretion and understanding, who will build a temple for the LORD and a royal palace for himself.

13 "Now I have sent a skilled man, who has understanding, Huram-abi, **14** the son of a woman of the daughters of Dan, and his father was a man of Tyre. He is trained to work in gold, silver, bronze, iron, stone, and wood, and in purple, blue, and crimson fabrics and fine linen, and to do all sorts of engraving and execute any design that may be assigned him, with your craftsmen, the craftsmen of my lord, David your father. **15** Now therefore the wheat and barley, oil and wine, of which my lord has spoken, let him send to his servants. **16** And we will cut whatever timber you need from Lebanon and bring it to you in rafts by sea to Joppa, so that you may take it up to Jerusalem."

17 Then Solomon counted all the resident aliens who were in the land of Israel, after the census of them that David his father had taken, and there were found 153,600. **18** Seventy thousand of them he assigned to bear burdens, 80,000 to quarry in the hill country, and 3,600 as overseers to make the people work.

Solomon Builds the Temple

3 Then Solomon began to build the house of the LORD in Jerusalem on Mount Moriah, where the LORD had appeared to David his father, at the place that David had appointed, on the threshing floor of Ornan the Jebusite. **2** He began to build in the second month of the fourth year of his reign. **3** These are Solomon's measurements for building the house of God: the length, in cubits of the old standard, was sixty cubits,

---

> **GETTING THE MESSAGE**
>
> **Why did the pillars of the temple have names?** Jachin means "he establishes,", while Boaz means "in him is strength" (3:17). The names may have been a way of reminding worshipers that the Lord establishes his covenant through the temple.

---

and the breadth twenty cubits. **4** The vestibule in front of the nave of the house was twenty cubits long, equal to the width of the house, and its height was 120 cubits. He overlaid it on the inside with pure gold. **5** The nave he lined with cypress and covered it with fine gold and made palms and chains on it. **6** He adorned the house with settings of precious stones. The gold was gold of Parvaim. **7** So he lined the house with gold — its beams, its thresholds, its walls, and its doors — and he carved cherubim on the walls.

8 And he made the Most Holy Place. Its length, corresponding to the breadth of the house, was twenty cubits, and its breadth was twenty cubits. He overlaid it with 600 talents of fine gold. **9** The weight of gold for the nails was fifty shekels. And he overlaid the upper chambers with gold.

10 In the Most Holy Place he made two cherubim of wood and overlaid them with gold. **11** The wings of the cherubim together extended twenty cubits: one wing of the one, of five cubits, touched the wall of the house, and its other wing, of five cubits, touched the wing of the other cherub; ¹² and of this cherub, one wing, of five cubits, touched the wall of the house, and the other wing, also of five cubits, was joined to the wing of the first cherub. ¹³ The wings of these cherubim extended twenty cubits. The cherubim stood on their feet, facing the nave. ¹⁴ And he made the veil of blue and purple and crimson fabrics and fine linen, and he worked cherubim on it.

¹⁵ In front of the house he made two pillars thirty-five cubits high, with a capital of five cubits on the top of each. ¹⁶ He made chains like a necklace and put them on the tops of the pillars, and he made a hundred pomegranates and put them on the chains.

GETTING THE MESSAGE

What was the "sea" in the temple court? The sea (4:2) was a bronze water tank outside the southeast corner of the temple. The priests used it for ceremonial washing before entering the temple and to clean the area where sacrifices were made. It held at least 12,000 gallons (55,000 liters) of water.

¹⁷ He set up the pillars in front of the temple, one on the south, the other on the north; that on the south he called Jachin, and that on the north Boaz.

The Temple's Furnishings

4 He made an altar of bronze, twenty cubits long and twenty cubits wide and ten cubits high. ² Then he made the sea of cast metal. It was round, ten cubits from brim to brim, and five cubits high, and a line of thirty cubits measured its circumference. ³ Under it were figures of gourds, for ten cubits, compassing the sea all around. The gourds were in two rows, cast with it when it was cast. ⁴ It stood on twelve oxen, three facing north, three facing west, three facing south, and three facing east. The sea was set on them, and all their rear parts were inward. ⁵ Its thickness was a handbreadth. And its brim was made like the brim of a cup, like the flower of a lily. It held 3,000 baths. ⁶ He also made ten basins in which to

wash, and set five on the south side, and five on the north side. In these they were to rinse off what was used for the burnt offering, and the sea was for the priests to wash in.

⁷ And he made ten golden lampstands as prescribed, and set them in the temple, five on the south side and five on the north. ⁸ He also made ten tables and placed them in the temple, five on the south side and five on the north. And he made a hundred basins of gold. ⁹ He made the court of the priests and the great court and doors for the court and overlaid their doors with bronze. ¹⁰ And he set the sea at the southeast corner of the house.

¹¹ Hiram also made the pots, the shovels, and the basins. So Hiram finished the work that he did for King Solomon on the house of God: ¹² the two pillars, the bowls, and the two capitals on the top of the pillars; and the two latticeworks to cover the two bowls of the capitals that were on the top of the pillars; ¹³ and the 400 pomegranates for the two latticeworks, two rows of pomegranates for each latticework, to cover the two bowls of the capitals that were on the pillars. ¹⁴ He made the stands also, and the basins on the stands, ¹⁵ and the one sea, and the twelve oxen underneath it. ¹⁶ The pots, the shovels, the forks, and all the equipment for these Huram-abi made of burnished bronze for King Solomon for the house of the LORD. ¹⁷ In the plain of the Jordan the king cast them, in the clay ground between Succoth and Zeredah. ¹⁸ Solomon made all these things in great quantities, for the weight of the bronze was not sought.

¹⁹ So Solomon made all the vessels that were in the house of God: the golden altar, the tables for the bread of the Presence, ²⁰ the lampstands and their lamps of pure gold to burn before the inner sanctuary, as prescribed; ²¹ the flowers, the lamps, and the tongs, of purest gold; ²² the snuffers, basins, dishes for incense, and fire pans, of pure gold, and the sockets of the temple, for the inner doors to the Most Holy Place and for the doors of the nave of the temple were of gold.

5 Thus all the work that Solomon did for the house of the LORD was finished. And Solomon brought in the things that David his father had dedicated, and stored the silver, the gold, and all the vessels in the treasuries of the house of God.

The Ark Brought to the Temple

2 Then Solomon assembled the elders of Israel and all the heads of the tribes, the leaders of the fathers' houses of the people of Israel, in Jerusalem, to bring up the ark of the covenant of the LORD out of the city of David, which is Zion. **3** And all the men of Israel assembled before the king at the feast that is in the seventh month. **4** And all the elders of Israel came, and the Levites took up the ark. **5** And they brought up the ark, the tent of meeting, and all the holy vessels that were in the tent; the Levitical priests brought them up. **6** And King Solomon and all the congregation of Israel, who had assembled before him, were before the ark, sacrificing so many sheep and oxen that they could not be counted or numbered. **7** Then the priests brought the ark of the covenant of the LORD to its place, in the inner sanctuary of the house, in the Most Holy Place, underneath the wings of the cherubim. **8** The cherubim spread out their wings over the place of the ark, so that the cherubim made a covering above the ark and its poles. **9** And the poles were so long that the ends of the poles were seen from the Holy Place before the inner sanctuary, but they could not be seen from outside. And they are there to this day. **10** There was nothing in the ark except the two tablets that Moses put there at Horeb, where the LORD made a covenant with the people of Israel, when they came out of Egypt. **11** And when the priests came out of the Holy Place (for all the priests who were present had consecrated themselves, without regard to their divisions, **12** and all the Levitical singers, Asaph, Heman, and Jeduthun, their sons and kinsmen, arrayed in fine linen, with cymbals, harps, and lyres, stood east of the altar with 120 priests who were trumpeters; **13** and it was the duty of the trumpeters and singers to make themselves heard in unison in praise and thanksgiving to the LORD), and when the song was raised, with trumpets and cymbals and other musical instruments, in praise to the LORD,

"For he is good,
for his steadfast love endures forever,"

the house, the house of the LORD, was filled with a cloud, **14** so that the priests could not stand to minister because of the cloud, for the glory of the LORD filled the house of God.

Solomon Blesses the People

6 Then Solomon said, "The LORD has said that he would dwell in thick darkness. **2** But I have built you an exalted house, a place for you to dwell in forever." **3** Then the king turned around and blessed all the assembly of Israel, while all the assembly of Israel stood. **4** And he said, "Blessed be the LORD, the God of Israel, who with his hand has fulfilled what he promised with his mouth to David my father, saying, **5** 'Since the day that I brought my people out of the land of Egypt, I chose no city out of all the tribes of Israel in which to build a house, that my name might be there, and I chose no man as prince over my people Israel; **6** but I have chosen Jerusalem that my name may be there, and I have chosen David to be over my people Israel.' **7** Now it was in the heart of David my father to build a house for the name of the LORD, the God of Israel. **8** But the LORD said to David my father, 'Whereas it was in your heart to build a house for my name, you did well that it was in your heart. **9** Nevertheless, it is not you who shall build the house, but your son who shall be born to you shall build the house for my name.' **10** Now the LORD has fulfilled his promise that he made. For I have risen in the place of David my father and sit on the throne of Israel, as the LORD promised, and I have built the house for the name of the LORD, the God of Israel. **11** And there I have set the ark, in which is the covenant of the LORD that he made with the people of Israel."

Solomon's Prayer of Dedication

12 Then Solomon stood before the altar of the LORD in the presence of all the assembly of Israel and spread out his hands. **13** Solomon had made a bronze platform five cubits long, five cubits wide, and three cubits high, and had set it in the court, and he stood on it. Then he knelt on his knees in the presence of all the assembly of Israel, and spread out his hands toward heaven, **14** and said, "O LORD, God of Israel, there is no God like you, in heaven or on earth, keeping covenant and showing steadfast love to your servants who walk before you with all their heart, **15** who have kept with your servant David my father what you declared to him. You spoke with your mouth, and with your hand have fulfilled it this day. **16** Now therefore, O Lᴏʀᴅ, God of Israel, keep for your servant David my father what you have promised him, saying, 'You shall not lack a man to sit before me on the throne of Israel, if only your sons pay close attention to their way, to walk in my law as you have walked before me.' **17** Now therefore, O Lᴏʀᴅ, God of Israel, let your word be confirmed, which you have spoken to your servant David.

18 "But will God indeed dwell with man on the earth? Behold, heaven and the highest heaven cannot contain you, how much less this house that I have built! **19** Yet have regard to the prayer of your servant and to his plea, O Lᴏʀᴅ my God, listening to the cry and to the prayer that your servant prays before you, **20** that your eyes may be open day and night toward this house, the place where you have promised to set your name, that you may listen to the prayer that your servant offers toward this place. **21** And listen to the pleas of your servant and of your people Israel, when they pray toward this place. And listen from heaven your dwelling place, and when you hear, forgive.

22 "If a man sins against his neighbor and is made to take an oath and comes and swears his oath before your altar in this house, **23** then hear from heaven and act and judge your servants, repaying the guilty by bringing his conduct on his own head, and vindicating the righteous by rewarding him according to his righteousness.

24 "If your people Israel are defeated before the enemy because they have sinned against you, and they turn again and acknowledge your name and pray and plead with you in this house, **25** then hear from heaven and forgive the sin of your people Israel and bring them again to the land that you gave to them and to their fathers.

26 "When heaven is shut up and there is no rain because they have sinned against you, if they pray toward this place and acknowledge your name and turn from their sin, when you afflict them, **27** then hear in heaven and forgive the sin of your servants, your people Israel, when you teach them the good way in which they should walk, and grant rain upon your land, which you have given to your people as an inheritance.

28 "If there is famine in the land, if there is pestilence or blight or mildew or locust or caterpillar, if their enemies besiege them in the land at their gates, whatever plague, whatever sickness there is, **29** whatever prayer, whatever plea is made by any man or by all your people Israel, each knowing his own affliction and his own sorrow and stretching out his hands toward this house, **30** then hear from heaven your dwelling place and forgive and render to each whose heart you know, according to all his ways, for you, you only, know the hearts of the children of mankind, **31** that they may fear you and walk in your ways all the days that they live in the land that you gave to our fathers.

32 "Likewise, when a foreigner, who is not of your people Israel, comes from a far country for the sake of your great name and your mighty hand and your outstretched arm, when he comes and prays toward this house, **33** hear from heaven your dwelling place and do according to all for which the foreigner calls to you, in order that all the peoples of the earth may know your name and fear you, as do your people Israel, and that they may know that this house that I have built is called by your name.

34 "If your people go out to battle against their enemies, by whatever way you shall send them, and they pray to you toward this city that you have chosen and the house that I have built for your name, **35** then hear from heaven their prayer and their plea, and maintain their cause.

36 "If they sin against you—for there is no one who does not sin—and you are angry with them and give them to an enemy, so that they are carried away captive to a land far or near, **37** yet if they turn their heart in the land to which they have been carried captive, and repent and plead with you in the land of their captivity, saying, 'We have sinned and have acted perversely and wickedly,' **38** if they repent with all their mind and with all their heart in the land of their captivity to which they were carried captive, and pray toward their land, which you gave to their fathers, the city that you have chosen and the house that I have built for your name, **39** then hear from heaven your dwelling place their prayer and their pleas, and maintain their cause and forgive your people who have sinned against you. **40** Now,

O my God, let your eyes be open and your ears attentive to the prayer of this place.

41 "And now arise, O LORD God, and go to your resting place,
  you and the ark of your might.
Let your priests, O LORD God, be clothed with salvation,
  and let your saints rejoice in your goodness.
42 O LORD God, do not turn away the face of your anointed one!
  Remember your steadfast love for David your servant."

Fire from Heaven

7 As soon as Solomon finished his prayer, fire came down from heaven and consumed the burnt offering and the sacrifices, and the glory of the LORD filled the temple. ² And the priests could not enter the house of the LORD, because the glory of the LORD filled the LORD's house. ³ When all the people of Israel saw the fire come down and the glory of the LORD on the temple, they bowed down with their faces to the ground on the pavement and worshiped and gave thanks to the LORD, saying, "For he is good, for his steadfast love endures forever."

The Dedication of the Temple

⁴ Then the king and all the people offered sacrifice before the LORD. ⁵ King Solomon offered as a sacrifice 22,000 oxen and 120,000 sheep. So the king and all the people dedicated the house of God. ⁶ The priests stood at their posts; the Levites also, with the instruments for music to the LORD that King David had made for giving thanks to the LORD—for his steadfast love endures forever—whenever David offered praises by their ministry; opposite them the priests sounded trumpets, and all Israel stood.

⁷ And Solomon consecrated the middle of the court that was before the house of the LORD, for there he offered the burnt offering and the fat of the peace offerings, because the bronze altar Solomon had made could not hold the burnt offering and the grain offering and the fat.

⁸ At that time Solomon held the feast for seven days, and all Israel with him, a very great assembly, from Lebo-hamath to the Brook of Egypt. ⁹ And on the eighth day they held a solemn assembly, for they had kept the dedication of the altar seven days and the feast seven days. ¹⁰ On the twenty-third day of the seventh month he sent the people away to their homes, joyful and glad of heart for the prosperity that the LORD had granted to David and to Solomon and to Israel his people.

If My People Pray

¹¹ Thus Solomon finished the house of the LORD and the king's house. All that Solomon had planned to do in the house of the LORD and in his own house he successfully accomplished. ¹² Then the LORD appeared to Solomon in the night and said to him: "I have heard your prayer and have chosen this place for myself as a house of sacrifice. ¹³ When I shut up the heavens so that there is no rain, or command the locust to devour the land, or send pestilence among my people, ¹⁴ if my people who are called by my name humble themselves,

---

GETTING THE MESSAGE

Trumpets were important instruments in Israel (7:6). They were constructed from metals such as bronze, copper, silver, or gold. They were used for a variety of purposes, for instance, to gather the congregation and to announce festivals.

---

and pray and seek my face and turn from their wicked ways, then I will hear from heaven and will forgive their sin and heal their land. ¹⁵ Now my eyes will be open and my ears attentive to the prayer that is made in this place. ¹⁶ For now I have chosen and consecrated this house that my name may be there forever. My eyes and my heart will be there for all time. ¹⁷ And as for you, if you will walk before me as David your father walked, doing according to all that I have commanded you and keeping my statutes and my rules, ¹⁸ then I will establish your royal throne, as I covenanted with David your father, saying, 'You shall not lack a man to rule Israel.'

¹⁹ "But if you turn aside and forsake my statutes and my commandments that I have set before you, and go and serve other gods and worship them, ²⁰ then I will pluck you up from my land that I have given you, and this house that I have consecrated for my name, I will cast out of my sight, and I will

make it a proverb and a byword among all peoples. **21** And at this house, which was exalted, everyone passing by will be astonished and say, 'Why has the LORD done thus to this land and to this house?' **22** Then they will say, 'Because they abandoned the LORD, the God of their fathers who brought them out of the land of Egypt, and laid hold on other gods and worshiped them and served them. Therefore he has brought all this disaster on them.'"

Solomon's Accomplishments

8 At the end of twenty years, in which Solomon had built the house of the LORD and his own house, **2** Solomon rebuilt the cities that Hiram had given to him, and settled the people of Israel in them.

3 And Solomon went to Hamath-zobah and took it. **4** He built Tadmor in the wilderness and all the store cities that he built in

> ### GETTING THE MESSAGE
>
> **Which took longer to build: Solomon's palace, or the temple?**
> Although Solomon spent seven years building the temple, he spent 13 years building his own palace (8:1; 1 Kings 6:38; 7:1). This may have been an early sign that he was more devoted to his own causes than to the Lord.

Hamath. **5** He also built Upper Beth-horon and Lower Beth-horon, fortified cities with walls, gates, and bars, **6** and Baalath, and all the store cities that Solomon had and all the cities for his chariots and the cities for his horsemen, and whatever Solomon desired to build in Jerusalem, in Lebanon, and in all the land of his dominion. **7** All the people who were left of the Hittites, the Amorites, the Perizzites, the Hivites, and the Jebusites, who were not of Israel, **8** from their descendants who were left after them in the land, whom the people of Israel had not destroyed—these Solomon drafted as forced labor, and so they are to this day. **9** But of the people of Israel Solomon made no slaves for his work; they were soldiers, and his officers, the commanders of his chariots, and his horsemen. **10** And these were the chief officers of King Solomon, 250, who exercised authority over the people.

11 Solomon brought Pharaoh's daughter up from the city of David to the house that he had built for her, for he said, "My wife shall not live in the house of David king of Israel, for the places to which the ark of the LORD has come are holy."

12 Then Solomon offered up burnt offerings to the LORD on the altar of the LORD that he had built before the vestibule, **13** as the duty of each day required, offering according to the commandment of Moses for the Sabbaths, the new moons, and the three annual feasts—the Feast of Unleavened Bread, the Feast of Weeks, and the Feast of Booths. **14** According to the ruling of David his father, he appointed the divisions of the priests for their service, and the Levites for their offices of praise and ministry before the priests as the duty of each day required, and the gatekeepers in their divisions at each gate, for so David the man of God had commanded. **15** And they did not turn aside from what the king had commanded the priests and Levites concerning any matter and concerning the treasuries.

16 Thus was accomplished all the work of Solomon from the day the foundation of the house of the LORD was laid until it was finished. So the house of the LORD was completed.

17 Then Solomon went to Ezion-geber and Eloth on the shore of the sea, in the land of Edom. **18** And Hiram sent to him by the hand of his servants ships and servants familiar with the sea, and they went to Ophir together with the servants of Solomon and brought from there 450 talents of gold and brought it to King Solomon.

The Queen of Sheba

9 Now when the queen of Sheba heard of the fame of Solomon, she came to Jerusalem to test him with hard questions, having a very great retinue and camels bearing spices and very much gold and precious stones. And when she came to Solomon, she told him all that was on her mind. **2** And Solomon answered all her questions. There was nothing hidden from Solomon that he could not explain to her. **3** And when the queen of Sheba had seen the wisdom of Solomon, the house that he had built, **4** the food of his table, the seating of his officials, and the attendance of his servants, and their clothing, his cupbearers, and their clothing,

and his burnt offerings that he offered at the house of the LORD, there was no more breath in her.

5 And she said to the king, "The report was true that I heard in my own land of your words and of your wisdom, 6 but I did not believe the reports until I came and my own eyes had seen it. And behold, half the greatness of your wisdom was not told me; you surpass the report that I heard. 7 Happy are your wives! Happy are these your servants, who continually stand before you and hear your wisdom! 8 Blessed be the LORD your God, who has delighted in you and set you on his throne as king for the LORD your God! Because your God loved Israel and would establish them forever, he has made you king over them, that you may execute justice and righteousness." 9 Then she gave the king 120 talents of gold, and a very great quantity of spices, and precious stones. There were no spices such as those that the queen of Sheba gave to King Solomon.

10 Moreover, the servants of Hiram and the servants of Solomon, who brought gold from Ophir, brought algum wood and precious stones. 11 And the king made from the algum wood supports for the house of the LORD and for the king's house, lyres also and harps for the singers. There never was seen the like of them before in the land of Judah.

12 And King Solomon gave to the queen of Sheba all that she desired, whatever she asked besides what she had brought to the king. So she turned and went back to her own land with her servants.

Solomon's Wealth

13 Now the weight of gold that came to Solomon in one year was 666 talents of gold, 14 besides that which the explorers and merchants brought. And all the kings of Arabia and the governors of the land brought gold and silver to Solomon. 15 King Solomon made 200 large shields of beaten gold; 600 shekels of beaten gold went into each shield. 16 And he made 300 shields of beaten gold; 300 shekels of gold went into each shield; and the king put them in the House of the Forest of Lebanon. 17 The king also made a great ivory throne and overlaid it with pure gold. 18 The throne had six steps and a footstool of gold, which were attached to the throne, and on each side of the seat were armrests and two lions standing beside the armrests, 19 while

twelve lions stood there, one on each end of a step on the six steps. Nothing like it was ever made for any kingdom. 20 All King Solomon's drinking vessels were of gold, and all the vessels of the House of the Forest of Lebanon were of pure gold. Silver was not considered as anything in the days of Solomon. 21 For the king's ships went to Tarshish with the servants of Hiram. Once every three years the ships of Tarshish used to come bringing gold, silver, ivory, apes, and peacocks.

22 Thus King Solomon excelled all the kings of the earth in riches and in wisdom. 23 And all the kings of the earth sought the presence of Solomon to hear his wisdom, which God had put into his mind. 24 Every one of them brought his present, articles of silver and of gold, garments, myrrh, spices, horses, and mules, so much year by year. 25 And Solomon had 4,000 stalls for horses and chariots, and 12,000 horsemen, whom he stationed in the chariot cities and with

GETTING THE MESSAGE

Second Chronicles covers a span of more than 400 years and the reigns of 20 different kings.

the king in Jerusalem. 26 And he ruled over all the kings from the Euphrates to the land of the Philistines and to the border of Egypt. 27 And the king made silver as common in Jerusalem as stone, and he made cedar as plentiful as the sycamore of the Shephelah. 28 And horses were imported for Solomon from Egypt and from all lands.

Solomon's Death

29 Now the rest of the acts of Solomon, from first to last, are they not written in the history of Nathan the prophet, and in the prophecy of Ahijah the Shilonite, and in the visions of Iddo the seer concerning Jeroboam the son of Nebat? 30 Solomon reigned in Jerusalem over all Israel forty years. 31 And Solomon slept with his fathers and was buried in the city of David his father, and Rehoboam his son reigned in his place.

The Revolt Against Rehoboam

10 Rehoboam went to Shechem, for all Israel had come to Shechem to make him king. 2 And as soon as Jeroboam the son

of Nebat heard of it (for he was in Egypt, where he had fled from King Solomon), then Jeroboam returned from Egypt. ³ And they sent and called him. And Jeroboam and all Israel came and said to Rehoboam, ⁴ "Your father made our yoke heavy. Now therefore lighten the hard service of your father and his heavy yoke on us, and we will serve you." ⁵ He said to them, "Come to me again in three days." So the people went away.

PROFILE
REHOBOAM

Following the death of King Solomon, the people of Israel gathered at Shechem to make Solomon's son, Rehoboam, their king. The people made one request: that Rehoboam lighten the heavy tax burden that his father had forced upon them. Rather than honor their request, however, Rehoboam vowed to make life even harder for the people of Israel. Disregarding the wise advice of his older counselors, Rehoboam followed the younger men's counsel and warned the people: "My father disciplined you with whips, but I will discipline you with scorpions" (10:14). His plan for more oppressive control backfired, however, when the 10 northern tribes revolted and set up Jeroboam as their king. The northern kingdom would now be known as Israel and the southern kingdom would be called Judah.

KEY REFERENCE:
2 CHRONICLES 12:13–14

⁶ Then King Rehoboam took counsel with the old men, who had stood before Solomon his father while he was yet alive, saying, "How do you advise me to answer this people?" ⁷ And they said to him, "If you will be good to this people and please them and speak good words to them, then they will be your servants forever." ⁸ But he abandoned the counsel that the old men gave him, and took counsel with the young men who had grown up with him and stood before him. ⁹ And he said to them, "What do you advise

that we answer this people who have said to me, 'Lighten the yoke that your father put on us'?" ¹⁰ And the young men who had grown up with him said to him, "Thus shall you speak to the people who said to you, 'Your father made our yoke heavy, but you lighten it for us'; thus shall you say to them, 'My little finger is thicker than my father's thighs. ¹¹ And now, whereas my father laid on you a heavy yoke, I will add to your yoke. My father disciplined you with whips, but I will discipline you with scorpions.'"

¹² So Jeroboam and all the people came to Rehoboam the third day, as the king said, "Come to me again the third day." ¹³ And the king answered them harshly; and forsaking the counsel of the old men, ¹⁴ King Rehoboam spoke to them according to the counsel of the young men, saying, "My father made your yoke heavy, but I will add to it. My father disciplined you with whips, but I will discipline you with scorpions." ¹⁵ So the king did not listen to the people, for it was a turn of affairs brought about by God that the LORD might fulfill his word, which he spoke by Ahijah the Shilonite to Jeroboam the son of Nebat.

¹⁶ And when all Israel saw that the king did not listen to them, the people answered the king, "What portion have we in David? We have no inheritance in the son of Jesse. Each of you to your tents, O Israel! Look now to your own house, David." So all Israel went to their tents. ¹⁷ But Rehoboam reigned over the people of Israel who lived in the cities of Judah. ¹⁸ Then King Rehoboam sent Hadoram, who was taskmaster over the forced labor, and the people of Israel stoned him to death with stones. And King Rehoboam quickly mounted his chariot to flee to Jerusalem. ¹⁹ So Israel has been in rebellion against the house of David to this day.

Rehoboam Secures His Kingdom

11 When Rehoboam came to Jerusalem, he assembled the house of Judah and Benjamin, 180,000 chosen warriors, to fight against Israel, to restore the kingdom to Rehoboam. ² But the word of the LORD came to Shemaiah the man of God: ³ "Say to Rehoboam the son of Solomon, king of Judah, and to all Israel in Judah and Benjamin, ⁴ Thus says the LORD, You shall not go up or fight against your relatives. Return every man to his home, for this thing

is from me.'" So they listened to the word of the Lord and returned and did not go against Jeroboam.

5 Rehoboam lived in Jerusalem, and he built cities for defense in Judah. 6 He built Bethlehem, Etam, Tekoa, 7 Beth-zur, Soco, Adullam, 8 Gath, Mareshah, Ziph, 9 Adoraim, Lachish, Azekah, 10 Zorah, Aijalon, and Hebron, fortified cities that are in Judah and in Benjamin. 11 He made the fortresses strong, and put commanders in them, and stores of food, oil, and wine. 12 And he put shields and spears in all the cities and made them very strong. So he held Judah and Benjamin.

Priests and Levites Come to Jerusalem

13 And the priests and the Levites who were in all Israel presented themselves to him from all places where they lived. 14 For the Levites left their common lands and their holdings and came to Judah and Jerusalem, because Jeroboam and his sons cast them out from serving as priests of the Lord, 15 and he appointed his own priests for the high places and for the goat idols and for the calves that he had made. 16 And those who had set their hearts to seek the Lord God of Israel came after them from all the tribes of Israel to Jerusalem to sacrifice to the Lord, the God of their fathers. 17 They strengthened the kingdom of Judah, and for three years they made Rehoboam the son of Solomon secure, for they walked for three years in the way of David and Solomon.

Rehoboam's Family

18 Rehoboam took as wife Mahalath the daughter of Jerimoth the son of David, and of Abihail the daughter of Eliab the son of Jesse, 19 and she bore him sons, Jeush, Shemariah, and Zaham. 20 After her he took Maacah the daughter of Absalom, who bore him Abijah, Attai, Ziza, and Shelomith. 21 Rehoboam loved Maacah the daughter of Absalom above all his wives and concubines (he took eighteen wives and sixty concubines, and fathered twenty-eight sons and sixty daughters). 22 And Rehoboam appointed Abijah the son of Maacah as chief prince among his brothers, for he intended to make him king. 23 And he dealt wisely and distributed some of his sons through all the districts of Judah and Benjamin, in all the fortified cities, and he gave them abundant provisions and procured wives for them.

Egypt Plunders Jerusalem

12 When the rule of Rehoboam was established and he was strong, he abandoned the law of the Lord, and all Israel with him. 2 In the fifth year of King Rehoboam, because they had been unfaithful to the Lord, Shishak king of Egypt came up against Jerusalem 3 with 1,200 chariots and 60,000 horsemen. And the people were without number who came with him from Egypt—Libyans, Sukkiim, and Ethiopians. 4 And he took the fortified cities of Judah and came as far as Jerusalem. 5 Then Shemaiah the prophet came to Rehoboam and to the princes of Judah, who had gathered at Jerusalem because of Shishak, and said to them, "Thus says the Lord, 'You abandoned me, so I have abandoned you to the hand of

> ### GETTING THE MESSAGE
>
> The title of **chief prince** (11:22–23) was most likely an administrative position. Members of the royal family were sometimes appointed to such positions to help them learn how to lead a kingdom.

Shishak.'" 6 Then the princes of Israel and the king humbled themselves and said, "The Lord is righteous." 7 When the Lord saw that they humbled themselves, the word of the Lord came to Shemaiah: "They have humbled themselves. I will not destroy them, but I will grant them some deliverance, and my wrath shall not be poured out on Jerusalem by the hand of Shishak. 8 Nevertheless, they shall be servants to him, that they may know my service and the service of the kingdoms of the countries."

9 So Shishak king of Egypt came up against Jerusalem. He took away the treasures of the house of the Lord and the treasures of the king's house. He took away everything. He also took away the shields of gold that Solomon had made, 10 and King Rehoboam made in their place shields of bronze and committed them to the hands of the officers of the guard, who kept the door of the king's house. 11 And as often as the king went into the house of the Lord, the guard came and

carried them and brought them back to the guardroom. ¹² And when he humbled himself the wrath of the Lord turned from him, so as not to make a complete destruction. Moreover, conditions were good in Judah.

¹³ So King Rehoboam grew strong in Jerusalem and reigned. Rehoboam was forty-one years old when he began to reign, and he reigned seventeen years in Jerusalem, the city that the Lord had chosen out of all the tribes of Israel to put his name there. His mother's name was Naamah the Ammonite. ¹⁴ And he did evil, for he did not set his heart to seek the Lord.

¹⁵ Now the acts of Rehoboam, from first to last, are they not written in the chronicles of Shemaiah the prophet and of Iddo the seer? There were continual wars between Rehoboam and Jeroboam. ¹⁶ And Rehoboam slept with his fathers and was buried in the city of David, and Abijah his son reigned in his place.

Abijah Reigns in Judah

13 In the eighteenth year of King Jeroboam, Abijah began to reign over Judah. ² He reigned for three years in Jerusalem. His mother's name was Micaiah the daughter of Uriel of Gibeah.

Now there was war between Abijah and Jeroboam. ³ Abijah went out to battle, having an army of valiant men of war, 400,000 chosen men. And Jeroboam drew up his line of battle against him with 800,000 chosen mighty warriors. ⁴ Then Abijah stood up on Mount Zemaraim that is in the hill country of Ephraim and said, "Hear me, O Jeroboam and all Israel! ⁵ Ought you not to know that the Lord God of Israel gave the kingship over Israel forever to David and his sons by a covenant of salt? ⁶ Yet Jeroboam the son of Nebat, a servant of Solomon the son of David, rose up and rebelled against his lord, ⁷ and certain worthless scoundrels gathered about him and defied Rehoboam the son of Solomon, when Rehoboam was young and irresolute and could not withstand them.

⁸ "And now you think to withstand the kingdom of the Lord in the hand of the sons of David, because you are a great multitude and have with you the golden calves that Jeroboam made you for gods. ⁹ Have you not driven out the priests of the Lord, the sons of Aaron, and the Levites, and made priests for yourselves like the peoples of other lands? Whoever comes for ordination with a young bull or seven rams becomes a priest of what are no gods. ¹⁰ But as for us, the Lord is our God, and we have not forsaken him. We have priests ministering to the Lord who are sons of Aaron, and Levites for their service. ¹¹ They offer to the Lord every morning and every evening burnt offerings and incense of sweet spices, set out the showbread on the table of pure gold, and care for the golden lampstand that its lamps may burn every evening. For we keep the charge of the Lord our God, but you have forsaken him. ¹² Behold, God is with us at our head, and his priests with their battle trumpets to sound the call to battle against you. O sons of Israel, do not fight against the Lord, the God of your fathers, for you cannot succeed."

¹³ Jeroboam had sent an ambush around to come upon them from behind. Thus his troops were in front of Judah, and the ambush was behind them. ¹⁴ And when Judah looked, behold, the battle was in front of and behind them. And they cried to the Lord, and the priests blew the trumpets. ¹⁵ Then the men of Judah raised the battle shout. And when the men of Judah shouted, God defeated Jeroboam and all Israel before Abijah and Judah. ¹⁶ The men of Israel fled before Judah, and God gave them into their hand. ¹⁷ Abijah and his people struck them with great force, so there fell slain of Israel 500,000 chosen men. ¹⁸ Thus the men of Israel were subdued at that time, and the men of Judah prevailed, because they relied on the Lord, the God of their fathers. ¹⁹ And Abijah pursued Jeroboam and took cities from him, Bethel with its villages and Jeshanah with its villages and Ephron with its villages. ²⁰ Jeroboam did not recover his power in the days of Abijah. And the Lord struck him down, and he died. ²¹ But Abijah grew mighty. And he took fourteen wives and had twenty-two sons and sixteen daughters. ²² The rest of the acts of Abijah, his ways and his sayings, are written in the story of the prophet Iddo.

Asa Reigns in Judah

14 Abijah slept with his fathers, and they buried him in the city of David. And Asa his son reigned in his place. In his days the land had rest for ten years. ² And Asa did what was good and right in the eyes of the

LORD his God. ³ He took away the foreign altars and the high places and broke down the pillars and cut down the Asherim ⁴ and commanded Judah to seek the LORD, the God of their fathers, and to keep the law and the commandment. ⁵ He also took out of all the cities of Judah the high places and the incense altars. And the kingdom had rest under him. ⁶ He built fortified cities in Judah, for the land had rest. He had no war in those years, for the LORD gave him peace. ⁷ And he said to Judah, "Let us build these cities and surround them with walls and towers, gates and bars. The land is still ours, because we have sought the LORD our God. We have sought him, and he has given us peace on every side." So they built and prospered. ⁸ And Asa had an army of 300,000 from Judah, armed with large shields and spears, and 280,000 men from Benjamin that carried shields and drew bows. All these were mighty men of valor.

⁹ Zerah the Ethiopian came out against them with an army of a million men and 300 chariots, and came as far as Mareshah. ¹⁰ And Asa went out to meet him, and they drew up their lines of battle in the Valley of Zephathah at Mareshah. ¹¹ And Asa cried to the LORD his God, "O LORD, there is none like you to help, between the mighty and the weak. Help us, O LORD our God, for we rely on you, and in your name we have come against this multitude. O LORD, you are our God; let not man prevail against you." ¹² So the LORD defeated the Ethiopians before Asa and before Judah, and the Ethiopians fled. ¹³ Asa and the people who were with him pursued them as far as Gerar, and the Ethiopians fell until none remained alive, for they were broken before the LORD and his army. The men of Judah carried away very much spoil. ¹⁴ And they attacked all the cities around Gerar, for the fear of the LORD was upon them. They plundered all the cities, for there was much plunder in them. ¹⁵ And they struck down the tents of those who had livestock and carried away sheep in abundance and camels. Then they returned to Jerusalem.

Asa's Religious Reforms

15 The Spirit of God came upon Azariah the son of Oded, ² and he went out to meet Asa and said to him, "Hear me, Asa, and all Judah and Benjamin: The LORD is with you while you are with him. If you seek him, he will be found by you, but if you forsake him, he will forsake you. ³ For a long time Israel was without the true God, and without a teaching priest and without law, ⁴ but when in their distress they turned to the LORD, the God of Israel, and sought him, he was found by them. ⁵ In those times there was no peace to him who went out or to him who came in, for great disturbances afflicted all the inhabitants of the lands. ⁶ They were broken in pieces. Nation was crushed by nation and city by city, for God troubled them with every sort of distress. ⁷ But you, take courage! Do not let your hands be weak, for your work shall be rewarded."

⁸ As soon as Asa heard these words, the prophecy of Azariah the son of Oded, he took courage and put away the detestable idols

> ### GETTING THE MESSAGE
>
> **An unreported defeat?** Scholars believe that Zerah the Ethiopian (14:9), who suffered a humiliating defeat by King Asa, may have been fighting on behalf of Egypt. There is no record of the battle in Egyptian history, but that does not mean the defeat did not occur, since the Pharaohs did not always record their defeats.

from all the land of Judah and Benjamin and from the cities that he had taken in the hill country of Ephraim, and he repaired the altar of the LORD that was in front of the vestibule of the house of the LORD. ⁹ And he gathered all Judah and Benjamin, and those from Ephraim, Manasseh, and Simeon who were residing with them, for great numbers had deserted to him from Israel when they saw that the LORD his God was with him. ¹⁰ They were gathered at Jerusalem in the third month of the fifteenth year of the reign of Asa. ¹¹ They sacrificed to the LORD on that day from the spoil that they had brought 700 oxen and 7,000 sheep. ¹² And they entered into a covenant to seek the LORD, the God of their fathers, with all their heart and with all their soul, ¹³ but that whoever would not seek the LORD, the God of Israel, should be put to death, whether young or old, man or woman. ¹⁴ They swore an oath to the LORD with a loud voice and with shouting and with trumpets and with horns. ¹⁵ And all Judah rejoiced over the oath, for they had sworn with all their heart and had sought him with their whole desire, and he was found by them, and the LORD gave them rest all around.

¹⁶ Even Maacah, his mother, King Asa removed from being queen mother because she had made a detestable image for Asherah. Asa cut down her image, crushed

PROFILE
ASA

Asa became king following the death of his father, Abijah. As a result of his faithful leadership, Judah lived at peace during the first 10 years of his reign. The prophet Azariah prophesied concerning Asa, "The LORD is with you while you are with him. If you seek him, he will be found by you, but if you forsake him, he will forsake you" (15:2). Asa took the prophet's words to heart and immediately set about making religious reforms, including repair of the altar in the temple. He gathered the people together to make a covenant, commanding that anyone who would not seek the Lord would be put to death. Sadly, the last five years of Asa's reign were marked by spiritual and physical decline, as the king began to trust human alliances and ability rather than God.

KEY REFERENCE: 2 CHRONICLES 15:8–19

it, and burned it at the brook Kidron. ¹⁷ But the high places were not taken out of Israel. Nevertheless, the heart of Asa was wholly true all his days. ¹⁸ And he brought into the house of God the sacred gifts of his father and his own sacred gifts, silver, and gold, and vessels. ¹⁹ And there was no more war until the thirty-fifth year of the reign of Asa.

Asa's Last Years

16 In the thirty-sixth year of the reign of Asa, Baasha king of Israel went up against Judah and built Ramah, that he might permit no one to go out or come in

to Asa king of Judah. ² Then Asa took silver and gold from the treasures of the house of the LORD and the king's house and sent them to Ben-hadad king of Syria, who lived in Damascus, saying, ³ "There is a covenant between me and you, as there was between my father and your father. Behold, I am sending to you silver and gold. Go, break your covenant with Baasha king of Israel, that he may withdraw from me." ⁴ And Ben-hadad listened to King Asa and sent the commanders of his armies against the cities of Israel, and they conquered Ijon, Dan, Abel-maim, and all the store cities of Naphtali. ⁵ And when Baasha heard of it, he stopped building Ramah and let his work cease. ⁶ Then King Asa took all Judah, and they carried away the stones of Ramah and its timber, with which Baasha had been building, and with them he built Geba and Mizpah.

⁷ At that time Hanani the seer came to Asa king of Judah and said to him, "Because you relied on the king of Syria, and did not rely on the LORD your God, the army of the king of Syria has escaped you. ⁸ Were not the Ethiopians and the Libyans a huge army with very many chariots and horsemen? Yet because you relied on the LORD, he gave them into your hand. ⁹ For the eyes of the LORD run to and fro throughout the whole earth, to give strong support to those whose heart is blameless toward him. You have done foolishly in this, for from now on you will have wars." ¹⁰ Then Asa was angry with the seer and put him in the stocks in prison, for he was in a rage with him because of this. And Asa inflicted cruelties upon some of the people at the same time.

¹¹ The acts of Asa, from first to last, are written in the Book of the Kings of Judah and Israel. ¹² In the thirty-ninth year of his reign Asa was diseased in his feet, and his disease became severe. Yet even in his disease he did not seek the LORD, but sought help from physicians. ¹³ And Asa slept with his fathers, dying in the forty-first year of his reign. ¹⁴ They buried him in the tomb that he had cut for himself in the city of David. They laid him on a bier that had been filled with various kinds of spices prepared by the perfumer's art, and they made a very great fire in his honor.

Jehoshaphat Reigns in Judah

17 Jehoshaphat his son reigned in his place and strengthened himself against Israel. ² He placed forces in all the fortified cities of Judah and set garrisons in the land of Judah, and in the cities of Ephraim that Asa his father had captured. ³ The Lord was with Jehoshaphat, because he walked in the earlier ways of his father David. He did not seek the Baals, ⁴ but sought the God of his father and walked in his commandments, and not according to the practices of Israel. ⁵ Therefore the Lord established the kingdom in his hand. And all Judah brought tribute to Jehoshaphat, and he had great riches and honor. ⁶ His heart was courageous in the ways of the Lord. And furthermore, he took the high places and the Asherim out of Judah.

⁷ In the third year of his reign he sent his officials, Ben-hail, Obadiah, Zechariah, Nethanel, and Micaiah, to teach in the cities of Judah; ⁸ and with them the Levites, Shemaiah, Nethaniah, Zebadiah, Asahel, Shemiramoth, Jehonathan, Adonijah, Tobijah, and Tobadonijah; and with these Levites, the priests Elishama and Jehoram. ⁹ And they taught in Judah, having the Book of the Law of the Lord with them. They went about through all the cities of Judah and taught among the people.

¹⁰ And the fear of the Lord fell upon all the kingdoms of the lands that were around Judah, and they made no war against Jehoshaphat. ¹¹ Some of the Philistines brought Jehoshaphat presents and silver for tribute, and the Arabians also brought him 7,700 rams and 7,700 goats. ¹² And Jehoshaphat grew steadily greater. He built in Judah fortresses and store cities, ¹³ and he had large supplies in the cities of Judah. He had soldiers, mighty men of valor, in Jerusalem. ¹⁴ This was the muster of them by fathers' houses: Of Judah, the commanders of thousands: Adnah the commander, with 300,000 mighty men of valor; ¹⁵ and next to him Jehohanan the commander, with 280,000; ¹⁶ and next to him Amasiah the son of Zichri, a volunteer for the service of the Lord, with 200,000 mighty men of valor. ¹⁷ Of Benjamin: Eliada, a mighty man of valor, with 200,000 men armed with bow and shield; ¹⁸ and next to him Jehozabad with 180,000 armed for war. ¹⁹ These were in the service of the king, besides those whom the king had placed in the fortified cities throughout all Judah.

Jehoshaphat Allies with Ahab

18 Now Jehoshaphat had great riches and honor, and he made a marriage alliance with Ahab. ² After some years he went down to Ahab in Samaria. And Ahab killed an abundance of sheep and oxen for him and for the people who were with him, and induced him to go up against Ramoth-gilead. ³ Ahab king of Israel said to Jehoshaphat king of Judah, "Will you go with me to Ramoth-gilead?" He answered him, "I am as you are, my people as your people. We will be with you in the war."

⁴ And Jehoshaphat said to the king of Israel, "Inquire first for the word of the Lord." ⁵ Then the king of Israel gathered the

> **GETTING THE MESSAGE**
>
> **Co-regency** was the common practice of two kings ruling a country at the same time. The first king in the Bible to do this was David when he anointed his son Solomon to rule. Asa and Jehoshaphat reigned together for three years (chs. 16–17). Co-regency allowed the son to learn from the father as he ruled. It also protected the throne from being claimed by another heir.

prophets together, four hundred men, and said to them, "Shall we go to battle against Ramoth-gilead, or shall I refrain?" And they said, "Go up, for God will give it into the hand of the king." ⁶ But Jehoshaphat said, "Is there not here another prophet of the Lord of whom we may inquire?" ⁷ And the king of Israel said to Jehoshaphat, "There is yet one man by whom we may inquire of the Lord, Micaiah the son of Imlah; but I hate him, for he never prophesies good concerning me, but always evil." And Jehoshaphat said, "Let not the king say so." ⁸ Then the king of Israel summoned an officer and said, "Bring quickly Micaiah the son of Imlah." ⁹ Now the king of Israel and Jehoshaphat the king of Judah were sitting on their thrones, arrayed in their robes. And they were sitting at the threshing floor at the entrance of the gate of Samaria, and all the prophets were prophesying before them. ¹⁰ And Zedekiah the son of Chenaanah made for himself horns of iron and said, "Thus says the LORD, 'With these you shall push the Syrians until they are destroyed.'" ¹¹ And all the prophets prophesied so and said, "Go up to Ramoth-gilead and triumph. The LORD will give it into the hand of the king."

¹² And the messenger who went to summon Micaiah said to him, "Behold, the words of the prophets with one accord are favorable to the king. Let your word be like the word of one of them, and speak favorably." ¹³ But Micaiah said, "As the LORD lives, what my God says, that I will speak." ¹⁴ And when he had come to the king, the king said to him, "Micaiah, shall we go to Ramoth-gilead to battle, or shall I refrain?" And he answered, "Go up and triumph; they will be given into your hand." ¹⁵ But the king said

> ### GETTING THE MESSAGE
>
> **Ramoth-gilead** was a commercial center and an important border town between Israel and Syria. This made it a prime target for capture. It had already changed hands several times between the two nations before the events described in ch. 18.

to him, "How many times shall I make you swear that you speak to me nothing but the truth in the name of the LORD?" ¹⁶ And he said, "I saw all Israel scattered on the mountains, as sheep that have no shepherd. And the LORD said, 'These have no master; let each return to his home in peace.'" ¹⁷ And the king of Israel said to Jehoshaphat, "Did I not tell you that he would not prophesy good concerning me, but evil?" ¹⁸ And Micaiah said, "Therefore hear the word of the LORD: I saw the LORD sitting on his throne, and all the host of heaven standing on his right hand and on his left. ¹⁹ And the LORD said, 'Who will entice Ahab the king of Israel, that he may go up and fall at Ramoth-gilead?' And one said one thing, and another said another. ²⁰ Then a spirit came forward and stood before the LORD, saying, 'I will entice him.' And the LORD said to him, 'By what means?' ²¹ And he said, 'I will go out, and will be a lying spirit in the mouth of all his

prophets.' And he said, 'You are to entice him, and you shall succeed; go out and do so.' ²² Now therefore behold, the LORD has put a lying spirit in the mouth of these your prophets. The LORD has declared disaster concerning you."

²³ Then Zedekiah the son of Chenaanah came near and struck Micaiah on the cheek and said, "Which way did the Spirit of the LORD go from me to speak to you?" ²⁴ And Micaiah said, "Behold, you shall see on that day when you go into an inner chamber to hide yourself." ²⁵ And the king of Israel said, "Seize Micaiah and take him back to Amon the governor of the city and to Joash the king's son, ²⁶ and say, 'Thus says the king, Put this fellow in prison and feed him with meager rations of bread and water until I return in peace.'" ²⁷ And Micaiah said, "If you return in peace, the LORD has not spoken by me." And he said, "Hear, all you peoples!"

The Defeat and Death of Ahab

²⁸ So the king of Israel and Jehoshaphat the king of Judah went up to Ramoth-gilead. ²⁹ And the king of Israel said to Jehoshaphat, "I will disguise myself and go into battle, but you wear your robes." And the king of Israel disguised himself, and they went into battle. ³⁰ Now the king of Syria had commanded the captains of his chariots, "Fight with neither small nor great, but only with the king of Israel." ³¹ As soon as the captains of the chariots saw Jehoshaphat, they said, "It is the king of Israel." So they turned to fight against him. And Jehoshaphat cried out, and the LORD helped him; God drew them away from him. ³² For as soon as the captains of the chariots saw that it was not the king of Israel, they turned back from pursuing him. ³³ But a certain man drew his bow at random and struck the king of Israel between the scale armor and the breastplate. Therefore he said to the driver of his chariot, "Turn around and carry me out of the battle, for I am wounded." ³⁴ And the battle continued that day, and the king of Israel was propped up in his chariot facing the Syrians until evening. Then at sunset he died.

Jehoshaphat's Reforms

19 Jehoshaphat the king of Judah returned in safety to his house in Jerusalem. ² But Jehu the son of Hanani the seer went out to meet him and said to

King Jehoshaphat, "Should you help the wicked and love those who hate the LORD? Because of this, wrath has gone out against you from the LORD. ³ Nevertheless, some good is found in you, for you destroyed the Asheroth out of the land, and have set your heart to seek God."

⁴ Jehoshaphat lived at Jerusalem. And he went out again among the people, from Beersheba to the hill country of Ephraim, and brought them back to the LORD, the God of their fathers. ⁵ He appointed judges in the land in all the fortified cities of Judah, city by city, ⁶ and said to the judges, "Consider what you do, for you judge not for man but for the LORD. He is with you in giving judgment. ⁷ Now then, let the fear of the LORD be upon you. Be careful what you do, for there is no injustice with the LORD our God, or partiality or taking bribes."

⁸ Moreover, in Jerusalem Jehoshaphat appointed certain Levites and priests and heads of families of Israel, to give judgment for the LORD and to decide disputed cases. They had their seat at Jerusalem. ⁹ And he charged them: "Thus you shall do in the fear of the LORD, in faithfulness, and with your whole heart: ¹⁰ whenever a case comes to you from your brothers who live in their cities, concerning bloodshed, law or commandment, statutes or rules, then you shall warn them, that they may not incur guilt before the LORD and wrath may not come upon you and your brothers. Thus you shall do, and you will not incur guilt. ¹¹ And behold, Amariah the chief priest is over you in all matters of the LORD; and Zebadiah the son of Ishmael, the governor of the house of Judah, in all the king's matters, and the Levites will serve you as officers. Deal courageously, and may the LORD be with the upright!"

Jehoshaphat's Prayer

20 After this the Moabites and Ammonites, and with them some of the Meunites, came against Jehoshaphat for battle. ² Some men came and told Jehoshaphat, "A great multitude is coming against you from Edom, from beyond the sea; and, behold, they are in Hazazon-tamar" (that is, Engedi). ³ Then Jehoshaphat was afraid and set his face to seek the LORD, and proclaimed a fast throughout all Judah. ⁴ And Judah assembled to seek help from the LORD;

from all the cities of Judah they came to seek the LORD.

⁵ And Jehoshaphat stood in the assembly of Judah and Jerusalem, in the house of the LORD, before the new court, ⁶ and said, "O LORD, God of our fathers, are you not God in heaven? You rule over all the kingdoms of the nations. In your hand are power and might, so that none is able to withstand you. ⁷ Did you not, our God, drive out the inhabitants of this land before your people Israel,

PROFILE
JEHOSHAPHAT

Like his father, Asa, King Jehoshaphat was faithful to the Lord and received God's blessings. He strengthened his kingdom both spiritually and militarily, and appointed teachers to go throughout Judah and teach the people concerning the Book of the Law. Large armies served Jehoshaphat, and he built up fortresses and store cities in Judah. He had great riches and honor. Jehoshaphat is criticized, however, for his association with the ungodly northern kingdom, including a marriage alliance with King Ahab. Such alliances caused the king to "help the wicked and love those who hate the LORD" (19:2). Despite his shortcomings, Jehoshaphat is remembered primarily for his great faith and leadership and as one who did "what was right in the sight of the LORD" (20:32).

KEY REFERENCE: 2 CHRONICLES 19:4

and give it forever to the descendants of Abraham your friend? ⁸ And they have lived in it and have built for you in it a sanctuary for your name, saying, ⁹ 'If disaster comes upon us, the sword, judgment, or pestilence, or famine, we will stand before this house and before you—for your name is in this house—and cry out to you in our affliction, and you will hear and save.' ¹⁰ And now behold, the men of Ammon and Moab and Mount Seir, whom you would not let Israel invade when they came from the land of Egypt, and whom they avoided and did not destroy— [11] behold, they reward us by coming to drive us out of your possession, which you have given us to inherit. [12] O our God, will you not execute judgment on them? For we are powerless against this great horde that is coming against us. We do not know what to do, but our eyes are on you."

[13] Meanwhile all Judah stood before the LORD, with their little ones, their wives, and their children. [14] And the Spirit of the LORD came upon Jahaziel the son of Zechariah, son of Benaiah, son of Jeiel, son of Mattaniah, a Levite of the sons of Asaph, in the midst of the assembly. [15] And he said, "Listen, all Judah and inhabitants of Jerusalem and King Jehoshaphat: Thus says the LORD to you, 'Do not be afraid and do not be dismayed at this great horde, for the battle is not yours but God's. [16] Tomorrow go down against them. Behold, they will come up by the ascent of Ziz. You will find them at the end of the valley, east of the wilderness of Jeruel. [17] You will not need to fight in this battle. Stand firm, hold your position, and see the salvation of the LORD on your behalf, O Judah and Jerusalem.' Do not be afraid and do not be dismayed. Tomorrow go out against them, and the LORD will be with you."

[18] Then Jehoshaphat bowed his head with his face to the ground, and all Judah and the inhabitants of Jerusalem fell down before the LORD, worshiping the LORD. [19] And the Levites, of the Kohathites and the Korahites, stood up to praise the LORD, the God of Israel, with a very loud voice.

[20] And they rose early in the morning and went out into the wilderness of Tekoa. And when they went out, Jehoshaphat stood and said, "Hear me, Judah and inhabitants of Jerusalem! Believe in the LORD your God, and you will be established; believe his prophets, and you will succeed." [21] And when he had taken counsel with the people, he appointed those who were to sing to the LORD and praise him in holy attire, as they went before the army, and say,

"Give thanks to the LORD,
    for his steadfast love endures forever."

[22] And when they began to sing and praise, the LORD set an ambush against the men of Ammon, Moab, and Mount Seir, who had come against Judah, so that they were routed. [23] For the men of Ammon and Moab rose against the inhabitants of Mount Seir, devoting them to destruction, and when they had made an end of the inhabitants of Seir, they all helped to destroy one another.

The LORD Delivers Judah

[24] When Judah came to the watchtower of the wilderness, they looked toward the horde, and behold, there were dead bodies lying on the ground; none had escaped. [25] When Jehoshaphat and his people came to take their spoil, they found among them, in great numbers, goods, clothing, and precious things, which they took for themselves until they could carry no more. They were three days in taking the spoil, it was so much. [26] On the fourth day they assembled in the Valley of Beracah,[1] for there they blessed the LORD. Therefore the name of that place has been called the Valley of Beracah to this day. [27] Then they returned, every man of Judah and Jerusalem, and Jehoshaphat at their head, returning to Jerusalem with joy, for the LORD had made them rejoice over their enemies. [28] They came to Jerusalem with harps and lyres and trumpets, to the house of the LORD. [29] And the fear of God came on all the kingdoms of the countries when they heard that the LORD had fought against the enemies of Israel. [30] So the realm of Jehoshaphat was quiet, for his God gave him rest all around.

[31] Thus Jehoshaphat reigned over Judah. He was thirty-five years old when he began to reign, and he reigned twenty-five years in Jerusalem. His mother's name was Azubah the daughter of Shilhi. [32] He walked in the way of Asa his father and did not turn aside from it, doing what was right in the sight of the LORD. [33] The high places, however, were not taken away; the people had not yet set their hearts upon the God of their fathers.

[34] Now the rest of the acts of Jehoshaphat, from first to last, are written in the chronicles of Jehu the son of Hanani, which are recorded in the Book of the Kings of Israel.

The End of Jehoshaphat's Reign

[35] After this Jehoshaphat king of Judah joined with Ahaziah king of Israel, who acted

---

[1] Beracah means blessing

wickedly. **36** He joined him in building ships to go to Tarshish, and they built the ships in Ezion-geber. **37** Then Eliezer the son of Dodavahu of Mareshah prophesied against Jehoshaphat, saying, "Because you have joined with Ahaziah, the LORD will destroy what you have made." And the ships were wrecked and were not able to go to Tarshish.

Jehoram Reigns in Judah

21 Jehoshaphat slept with his fathers and was buried with his fathers in the city of David, and Jehoram his son reigned in his place. **2** He had brothers, the sons of Jehoshaphat: Azariah, Jehiel, Zechariah, Azariah, Michael, and Shephatiah; all these were the sons of Jehoshaphat king of Israel. **3** Their father gave them great gifts of silver, gold, and valuable possessions, together with fortified cities in Judah, but he gave the kingdom to Jehoram, because he was the firstborn. **4** When Jehoram had ascended the throne of his father and was established, he killed all his brothers with the sword, and also some of the princes of Israel. **5** Jehoram was thirty-two years old when he became king, and he reigned eight years in Jerusalem. **6** And he walked in the way of the kings of Israel, as the house of Ahab had done, for the daughter of Ahab was his wife. And he did what was evil in the sight of the LORD. **7** Yet the LORD was not willing to destroy the house of David, because of the covenant that he had made with David, and since he had promised to give a lamp to him and to his sons forever.

8 In his days Edom revolted from the rule of Judah and set up a king of their own. **9** Then Jehoram passed over with his commanders and all his chariots, and he rose by night and struck the Edomites who had surrounded him and his chariot commanders. **10** So Edom revolted from the rule of Judah to this day. At that time Libnah also revolted from his rule, because he had forsaken the LORD, the God of his fathers.

11 Moreover, he made high places in the hill country of Judah and led the inhabitants of Jerusalem into whoredom and made Judah go astray. **12** And a letter came to him from Elijah the prophet, saying, "Thus says the LORD, the God of David your father, 'Because you have not walked in the ways of Jehoshaphat your father, or in the ways of Asa king of Judah, **13** but have walked in the

way of the kings of Israel and have enticed Judah and the inhabitants of Jerusalem into whoredom, as the house of Ahab led Israel into whoredom, and also you have killed your brothers, of your father's house, who were better than you, **14** behold, the LORD will bring a great plague on your people, your children, your wives, and all your possessions, **15** and you yourself will have a severe sickness with a disease of your bowels, until your bowels come out because of the disease, day by day.'"

16 And the LORD stirred up against Jehoram the anger of the Philistines and of the Arabians who are near the Ethiopians. **17** And they came up against Judah and invaded it and carried away all the possessions they found that belonged to the king's house, and also his sons and his wives, so that no son was left to him except Jehoahaz, his youngest son.

> ### ▶ GETTING THE MESSAGE
>
> **Tarshish** (20:36) was a city at the western end of the Mediterranean Sea, possibly in Spain. It was famous for building ships to carry gold and silver to the Near East. Jonah tried to flee to Tarshish to avoid his responsibilities as a prophet.

18 And after all this the LORD struck him in his bowels with an incurable disease. **19** In the course of time, at the end of two years, his bowels came out because of the disease, and he died in great agony. His people made no fire in his honor, like the fires made for his fathers. **20** He was thirty-two years old when he began to reign, and he reigned eight years in Jerusalem. And he departed with no one's regret. They buried him in the city of David, but not in the tombs of the kings.

Ahaziah Reigns in Judah

22 And the inhabitants of Jerusalem made Ahaziah, his youngest son, king in his place, for the band of men that came with the Arabians to the camp had killed all the older sons. So Ahaziah the son of Jehoram king of Judah reigned. **2** Ahaziah was twenty-two years old when he began to reign, and he reigned one year in Jerusalem. His mother's name was Athaliah, the granddaughter of Omri. ³ He also walked in the ways of the house of Ahab, for his mother was his counselor in doing wickedly. ⁴ He did what was evil in the sight of the LORD, as the house of Ahab had done. For after the death of his father they were his counselors, to his undoing. ⁵ He even followed their counsel and went with Jehoram the son of Ahab king of Israel to make war against Hazael king of Syria at Ramoth-gilead. And the Syrians wounded Joram, ⁶ and he returned to be healed in Jezreel of the wounds that he had received at Ramah, when he fought against Hazael king of Syria. And Ahaziah the son of Jehoram king of Judah went down to see Joram the son of Ahab in Jezreel, because he was wounded.

> ## GETTING THE MESSAGE
>
> **Athaliah** was the only woman to rule over Judah. She was the granddaughter of Omri and the daughter of Ahab. After seizing the throne and murdering the rest of the royal family, she reigned for six years before being overthrown. The young child Joash was hidden during her reign and became king after her death.

⁷ But it was ordained by God that the downfall of Ahaziah should come about through his going to visit Joram. For when he came there, he went out with Jehoram to meet Jehu the son of Nimshi, whom the LORD had anointed to destroy the house of Ahab. ⁸ And when Jehu was executing judgment on the house of Ahab, he met the princes of Judah and the sons of Ahaziah's brothers, who attended Ahaziah, and he killed them. ⁹ He searched for Ahaziah, and he was captured while hiding in Samaria, and he was brought to Jehu and put to death. They buried him, for they said, "He is the grandson of Jehoshaphat, who sought the LORD with all his heart." And the house of Ahaziah had no one able to rule the kingdom.

Athaliah Reigns in Judah

¹⁰ Now when Athaliah the mother of Ahaziah saw that her son was dead, she arose and destroyed all the royal family of the house of Judah. ¹¹ But Jehoshabeath, the daughter of the king, took Joash the son of Ahaziah and stole him away from among the king's sons who were about to be put to death, and she put him and his nurse in a bedroom. Thus Jehoshabeath, the daughter of King Jehoram and wife of Jehoiada the priest, because she was a sister of Ahaziah, hid him¹ from Athaliah, so that she did not put him to death. ¹² And he remained with them six years, hidden in the house of God, while Athaliah reigned over the land.

Joash Made King

23 But in the seventh year Jehoiada took courage and entered into a covenant with the commanders of hundreds, Azariah the son of Jeroham, Ishmael the son of Jehohanan, Azariah the son of Obed, Maaseiah the son of Adaiah, and Elishaphat the son of Zichri. ² And they went about through Judah and gathered the Levites from all the cities of Judah, and the heads of fathers' houses of Israel, and they came to Jerusalem. ³ And all the assembly made a covenant with the king in the house of God. And Jehoiada said to them, "Behold, the king's son! Let him reign, as the LORD spoke concerning the sons of David. ⁴ This is the thing that you shall do: of you priests and Levites who come off duty on the Sabbath, one third shall be gatekeepers, ⁵ and one third shall be at the king's house and one third at the Gate of the Foundation. And all the people shall be in the courts of the house of the LORD. ⁶ Let no one enter the house of the LORD except the priests and ministering Levites. They may enter, for they are holy, but all the people shall keep the charge of the LORD. ⁷ The Levites shall surround the king, each with his weapons in his hand. And whoever enters the house shall be put to death. Be with the king when he comes in and when he goes out."

⁸ The Levites and all Judah did according to all that Jehoiada the priest commanded, and they each brought his men, who were to go off duty on the Sabbath, with those who were to come on duty on the Sabbath, for Jehoiada the priest did not dismiss the divisions. ⁹ And Jehoiada the priest gave to the captains the spears and the large and small shields that had been King David's,

¹ That is, Joash

which were in the house of God. ¹⁰ And he set all the people as a guard for the king, every man with his weapon in his hand, from the south side of the house to the north side of the house, around the altar and the house. ¹¹ Then they brought out the king's son and put the crown on him and gave him the testimony. And they proclaimed him king, and Jehoiada and his sons anointed him, and they said, "Long live the king."

Athaliah Executed

¹² When Athaliah heard the noise of the people running and praising the king, she went into the house of the LORD to the people. ¹³ And when she looked, there was the king standing by his pillar at the entrance, and the captains and the trumpeters beside the king, and all the people of the land rejoicing and blowing trumpets, and the singers with their musical instruments leading in the celebration. And Athaliah tore her clothes and cried, "Treason! Treason!" ¹⁴ Then Jehoiada the priest brought out the captains who were set over the army, saying to them, "Bring her out between the ranks, and anyone who follows her is to be put to death with the sword." For the priest said, "Do not put her to death in the house of the LORD." ¹⁵ So they laid hands on her, and she went into the entrance of the horse gate of the king's house, and they put her to death there.

Jehoiada's Reforms

¹⁶ And Jehoiada made a covenant between himself and all the people and the king that they should be the LORD's people. ¹⁷ Then all the people went to the house of Baal and tore it down; his altars and his images they broke in pieces, and they killed Mattan the priest of Baal before the altars. ¹⁸ And Jehoiada posted watchmen for the house of the LORD under the direction of the Levitical priests and the Levites whom David had organized to be in charge of the house of the LORD, to offer burnt offerings to the LORD, as it is written in the Law of Moses, with rejoicing and with singing, according to the order of David. ¹⁹ He stationed the gatekeepers at the gates of the house of the LORD so that no one should enter who was in any way unclean. ²⁰ And he took the captains, the nobles, the governors of the people, and all the people of the land, and they brought the king down from the house of the LORD, marching through the upper gate to the king's house. And they set the king on the royal throne. ²¹ So all the people of the land rejoiced, and the city was quiet after Athaliah had been put to death with the sword.

Joash Repairs the Temple

24 Joash was seven years old when he began to reign, and he reigned forty years in Jerusalem. His mother's name was Zibiah of Beersheba. ² And Joash did what was right in the eyes of the LORD all the days of Jehoiada the priest. ³ Jehoiada got for him two wives, and he had sons and daughters.

⁴ After this Joash decided to restore the house of the LORD. ⁵ And he gathered the priests and the Levites and said to them, "Go out to the cities of Judah and gather from all Israel money to repair the house of your God from year to year, and see that

> ### GETTING THE MESSAGE
>
> **Why did the guards carry King David's spears?** Even though King David's spears (23:9) were around 150 years old, they served an important purpose. Having the guards hold the spears at the coronation of Joash, who was only seven years old, symbolized his right to David's throne.

you act quickly." But the Levites did not act quickly. ⁶ So the king summoned Jehoiada the chief and said to him, "Why have you not required the Levites to bring in from Judah and Jerusalem the tax levied by Moses, the servant of the LORD, and the congregation of Israel for the tent of testimony?" ⁷ For the sons of Athaliah, that wicked woman, had broken into the house of God, and had also used all the dedicated things of the house of the LORD for the Baals.

⁸ So the king commanded, and they made a chest and set it outside the gate of the house of the LORD. ⁹ And proclamation was made throughout Judah and Jerusalem to bring in for the LORD the tax that Moses the servant of God laid on Israel in the wilderness. ¹⁰ And all the princes and all the people rejoiced and brought their tax and dropped it into the chest until they had finished. ¹¹ And whenever the chest was brought to the king's officers by the Levites, when they saw that there was much money in it, the king's

secretary and the officer of the chief priest would come and empty the chest and take it and return it to its place. Thus they did day after day, and collected money in abundance. ¹² And the king and Jehoiada gave it to those who had charge of the work of the house of the LORD, and they hired masons and carpenters to restore the house of the LORD, and also workers in iron and bronze to repair the house of the LORD. ¹³ So those who were engaged in the work labored, and the repairing went forward in their hands, and they restored the house of God to its proper condition and strengthened it. ¹⁴ And when they had finished, they brought the rest of the money before the king and Jehoiada, and with it were made utensils for the house of the LORD, both for the service and for the burnt offerings, and dishes for incense and vessels of gold and silver. And they offered burnt offerings in the house of the LORD regularly all the days of Jehoiada.

¹⁵ But Jehoiada grew old and full of days, and died. He was 130 years old at his death. ¹⁶ And they buried him in the city of David among the kings, because he had done good in Israel, and toward God and his house.

¹⁷ Now after the death of Jehoiada the princes of Judah came and paid homage to the king. Then the king listened to them. ¹⁸ And they abandoned the house of the LORD, the God of their fathers, and served the Asherim and the idols. And wrath came upon Judah and Jerusalem for this guilt of theirs. ¹⁹ Yet he sent prophets among them to bring them back to the LORD. These testified against them, but they would not pay attention.

Joash's Treachery

²⁰ Then the Spirit of God clothed Zechariah the son of Jehoiada the priest, and he stood above the people, and said to them, "Thus says God, 'Why do you break the commandments of the LORD, so that you cannot prosper? Because you have forsaken the LORD, he has forsaken you.'" ²¹ But they conspired against him, and by command of the king they stoned him with stones in the court of the house of the LORD. ²² Thus Joash the king did not remember the kindness that Jehoiada, Zechariah's father, had shown him, but killed his son. And when he was dying, he said, "May the LORD see and avenge!"

Joash Assassinated

²³ At the end of the year the army of the Syrians came up against Joash. They came to Judah and Jerusalem and destroyed all the princes of the people from among the people and sent all their spoil to the king of Damascus. ²⁴ Though the army of the Syrians had come with few men, the LORD delivered into their hand a very great army, because Judah had forsaken the LORD, the God of their fathers. Thus they executed judgment on Joash.

²⁵ When they had departed from him, leaving him severely wounded, his servants conspired against him because of the blood of the son of Jehoiada the priest, and killed him on his bed. So he died, and they buried him in the city of David, but they did not bury him in the tombs of the kings. ²⁶ Those who conspired against him were Zabad the son of Shimeath the Ammonite, and Jehozabad the son of Shimrith the Moabite. ²⁷ Accounts of his sons and of the many oracles against him and of the rebuilding of the house of God are written in the Story of the Book of the Kings. And Amaziah his son reigned in his place.

Amaziah Reigns in Judah

25 Amaziah was twenty-five years old when he began to reign, and he reigned twenty-nine years in Jerusalem. His mother's name was Jehoaddan of Jerusalem. ² And he did what was right in the eyes of the LORD, yet not with a whole heart. ³ And as soon as the royal power was firmly his, he killed his servants who had struck down the king his father. ⁴ But he did not put their children to death, according to what is written in the Law, in the Book of Moses, where the LORD commanded, "Fathers shall not die because of their children, nor children die because of their fathers, but each one shall die for his own sin."

Amaziah's Victories

⁵ Then Amaziah assembled the men of Judah and set them by fathers' houses under commanders of thousands and of hundreds for all Judah and Benjamin. He mustered those twenty years old and upward, and found that they were 300,000 choice men, fit for war, able to handle spear and shield. ⁶ He hired also 100,000 mighty men of valor from Israel for 100 talents of

silver. **7** But a man of God came to him and said, "O king, do not let the army of Israel go with you, for the LORD is not with Israel, with all these Ephraimites. **8** But go, act, be strong for the battle. Why should you suppose that God will cast you down before the enemy? For God has power to help or to cast down." **9** And Amaziah said to the man of God, "But what shall we do about the hundred talents that I have given to the army of Israel?" The man of God answered, "The LORD is able to give you much more than this." **10** Then Amaziah discharged the army that had come to him from Ephraim to go home again. And they became very angry with Judah and returned home in fierce anger. **11** But Amaziah took courage and led out his people and went to the Valley of Salt and struck down 10,000 men of Seir. **12** The men of Judah captured another 10,000 alive and took them to the top of a rock and threw them down from the top of the rock, and they were all dashed to pieces. **13** But the men of the army whom Amaziah sent back, not letting them go with him to battle, raided the cities of Judah, from Samaria to Beth-horon, and struck down 3,000 people in them and took much spoil.

Amaziah's Idolatry

14 After Amaziah came from striking down the Edomites, he brought the gods of the men of Seir and set them up as his gods and worshiped them, making offerings to them. **15** Therefore the LORD was angry with Amaziah and sent to him a prophet, who said to him, "Why have you sought the gods of a people who did not deliver their own people from your hand?" **16** But as he was speaking, the king said to him, "Have we made you a royal counselor? Stop! Why should you be struck down?" So the prophet stopped, but said, "I know that God has determined to destroy you, because you have done this and have not listened to my counsel."

Israel Defeats Amaziah

17 Then Amaziah king of Judah took counsel and sent to Joash the son of Jehoahaz, son of Jehu, king of Israel, saying, "Come, let us look one another in the face." **18** And Joash the king of Israel sent word to Amaziah king of Judah, "A thistle on Lebanon sent to a cedar on Lebanon, saying, 'Give your daughter to my son for a wife,' and a wild beast of Lebanon passed by and trampled down the thistle. **19** You say, 'See, I have struck down Edom,' and your heart has lifted you up in boastfulness. But now stay at home. Why should you provoke trouble so that you fall, you and Judah with you?"

20 But Amaziah would not listen, for it was of God, in order that he might give them into the hand of their enemies, because they had sought the gods of Edom. **21** So Joash king of Israel went up, and he and Amaziah king of Judah faced one another in battle at Beth-shemesh, which belongs to Judah. **22** And Judah was defeated by Israel, and every man fled to his home. **23** And Joash king of Israel captured Amaziah king of Judah, the son of Joash, son of Ahaziah, at Beth-shemesh, and brought him to Jerusalem and broke down the wall of Jerusalem for 400 cubits, from the Ephraim Gate to the Corner Gate. **24** And he seized all the gold and silver, and all the

> **GETTING THE MESSAGE**

Thistles (25:18) are flowering plants known for their sharp outer edges. This discourages animals from feeding on the plant. In the Bible, thistles often represent God's curse on the land.

vessels that were found in the house of God, in the care of Obed-edom. He seized also the treasuries of the king's house, also hostages, and he returned to Samaria.

25 Amaziah the son of Joash, king of Judah, lived fifteen years after the death of Joash the son of Jehoahaz, king of Israel. **26** Now the rest of the deeds of Amaziah, from first to last, are they not written in the Book of the Kings of Judah and Israel? **27** From the time when he turned away from the LORD they made a conspiracy against him in Jerusalem, and he fled to Lachish. But they sent after him to Lachish and put him to death there. **28** And they brought him upon horses, and he was buried with his fathers in the city of David.

Uzziah Reigns in Judah

26 And all the people of Judah took Uzziah, who was sixteen years old, and made him king instead of his father Amaziah. **2** He built Eloth and restored it to Judah, after the king slept with his fathers.

³ Uzziah was sixteen years old when he began to reign, and he reigned fifty-two years in Jerusalem. His mother's name was Jecoliah of Jerusalem. ⁴ And he did what was right in the eyes of the LORD, according to all that his father Amaziah had done. ⁵ He set himself to seek God in the days of Zechariah, who instructed him in the fear of God, and as long as he sought the LORD, God made him prosper.

PROFILE
UZZIAH

Uzziah was 16 years old when he became king, following the assassination of his father, Amaziah. Like many kings before him, Uzziah's reign began with a period of faithfulness and blessing: "as long as he sought the LORD, God made him prosper" (26:5). But this was followed by a period of sin, leading to punishment from the Lord. Uzziah successfully battled the Philistines and demanded tribute from the Ammonites. His fame spread far and wide. Sadly, Uzziah's success led to pride, and he began to desire spiritual as well as political authority over the people. Ignoring God's law, he entered the temple to burn incense and was confronted by the priests. Rather than repent of his actions, Uzziah grew angry. The Lord immediately struck him with leprosy, forcing him to withdraw from his royal duties.

KEY REFERENCE: 2 CHRONICLES 26:3–5

⁶ He went out and made war against the Philistines and broke through the wall of Gath and the wall of Jabneh and the wall of Ashdod, and he built cities in the territory of Ashdod and elsewhere among the Philistines. ⁷ God helped him against the Philistines and against the Arabians who lived in Gurbaal and against the Meunites. ⁸ The Ammonites paid tribute to Uzziah, and his fame spread even to the border of Egypt, for he became very strong. ⁹ Moreover, Uzziah built towers in Jerusalem at the Corner Gate and at the Valley Gate and at the Angle, and fortified them. ¹⁰ And he built towers in the wilderness and cut out many cisterns, for he had large herds, both in the Shephelah and in the plain, and he had farmers and vinedressers in the hills and in the fertile lands, for he loved the soil. ¹¹ Moreover, Uzziah had an army of soldiers, fit for war, in divisions according to the numbers in the muster made by Jeiel the secretary and Maaseiah the officer, under the direction of Hananiah, one of the king's commanders. ¹² The whole number of the heads of fathers' houses of mighty men of valor was 2,600. ¹³ Under their command was an army of 307,500, who could make war with mighty power, to help the king against the enemy. ¹⁴ And Uzziah prepared for all the army shields, spears, helmets, coats of mail, bows, and stones for slinging. ¹⁵ In Jerusalem he made machines, invented by skillful men, to be on the towers and the corners, to shoot arrows and great stones. And his fame spread far, for he was marvelously helped, till he was strong.

Uzziah's Pride and Punishment

¹⁶ But when he was strong, he grew proud, to his destruction. For he was unfaithful to the LORD his God and entered the temple of the LORD to burn incense on the altar of incense. ¹⁷ But Azariah the priest went in after him, with eighty priests of the LORD who were men of valor, ¹⁸ and they withstood King Uzziah and said to him, "It is not for you, Uzziah, to burn incense to the LORD, but for the priests, the sons of Aaron, who are consecrated to burn incense. Go out of the sanctuary, for you have done wrong, and it will bring you no honor from the LORD God." ¹⁹ Then Uzziah was angry. Now he had a censer in his hand to burn incense, and when he became angry with the priests, leprosy¹ broke out on his forehead in the presence of the priests in the house of the LORD, by the altar of incense. ²⁰ And Azariah the chief priest and all the priests looked at him, and behold, he was leprous in his forehead! And they rushed him out quickly, and he himself hurried to go out, because the LORD had struck him. ²¹ And King Uzziah was a leper to the day of his death, and being a leper lived in a separate house, for he was excluded from the house of the LORD. And

¹ *Leprosy* was a term for several skin diseases (see Leviticus 13)

Jotham his son was over the king's household, governing the people of the land.

²² Now the rest of the acts of Uzziah, from first to last, Isaiah the prophet the son of Amoz wrote. ²³ And Uzziah slept with his fathers, and they buried him with his fathers in the burial field that belonged to the kings, for they said, "He is a leper." And Jotham his son reigned in his place.

Jotham Reigns in Judah

27 Jotham was twenty-five years old when he began to reign, and he reigned sixteen years in Jerusalem. His mother's name was Jerushah the daughter of Zadok. ² And he did what was right in the eyes of the LORD according to all that his father Uzziah had done, except he did not enter the temple of the LORD. But the people still followed corrupt practices. ³ He built the upper gate of the house of the LORD and did much building on the wall of Ophel. ⁴ Moreover, he built cities in the hill country of Judah, and forts and towers on the wooded hills. ⁵ He fought with the king of the Ammonites and prevailed against them. And the Ammonites gave him that year 100 talents of silver, and 10,000 cors of wheat and 10,000 of barley. The Ammonites paid him the same amount in the second and the third years. ⁶ So Jotham became mighty, because he ordered his ways before the LORD his God. ⁷ Now the rest of the acts of Jotham, and all his wars and his ways, behold, they are written in the Book of the Kings of Israel and Judah. ⁸ He was twenty-five years old when he began to reign, and he reigned sixteen years in Jerusalem. ⁹ And Jotham slept with his fathers, and they buried him in the city of David, and Ahaz his son reigned in his place.

Ahaz Reigns in Judah

28 Ahaz was twenty years old when he began to reign, and he reigned sixteen years in Jerusalem. And he did not do what was right in the eyes of the LORD, as his father David had done, ² but he walked in the ways of the kings of Israel. He even made metal images for the Baals, ³ and he made offerings in the Valley of the Son of Hinnom and burned his sons as an offering, according to the abominations of the nations whom the LORD drove out before the people of Israel. ⁴ And he sacrificed and made offerings on the high places and on the hills and under every green tree.

Judah Defeated

⁵ Therefore the LORD his God gave him into the hand of the king of Syria, who defeated him and took captive a great number of his people and brought them to Damascus. He was also given into the hand of the king of Israel, who struck him with great force. ⁶ For Pekah the son of Remaliah

PROFILE

AHAZ

Ahaz was a wicked king whose apostasy led Judah astray and brought the nation to ruin. Rather than worship the God of Israel, Ahaz made images of Baal. He even sacrificed his own children to the false god, a practice strongly condemned by the Lord. Because of his wickedness, God allowed both Syria and Israel to successfully attack Judah. Ahaz did not repent and turn to the Lord for help in his time of distress, but rather sought help from the king of Assyria. The plan backfired, however, when the Assyrians "came against him and afflicted him instead of strengthening him" (28:20). Even then, Ahaz still turned away from the Lord. Not only did he close the doors of the temple, but also "in every city of Judah he made high places to make offerings to other gods" (28:25).

KEY REFERENCE:
2 CHRONICLES 28:22–27

killed 120,000 from Judah in one day, all of them men of valor, because they had forsaken the LORD, the God of their fathers. ⁷ And Zichri, a mighty man of Ephraim, killed Maaseiah the king's son and Azrikam the commander of the palace and Elkanah the next in authority to the king.

⁸ The men of Israel took captive 200,000 of their relatives, women, sons, and daughters. They also took much spoil from them and brought the spoil to Samaria. ⁹ But a prophet of the LORD was there, whose name was Oded, and he went out to meet the army that

came to Samaria and said to them, "Behold, because the Lord, the God of your fathers, was angry with Judah, he gave them into your hand, but you have killed them in a rage that has reached up to heaven. ¹⁰ And now you intend to subjugate the people of Judah and Jerusalem, male and female, as your slaves. Have you not sins of your own against the Lord your God? ¹¹ Now hear me, and send back the captives from your relatives whom you have taken, for the fierce wrath of the Lord is upon you."

¹² Certain chiefs also of the men of Ephraim, Azariah the son of Johanan, Berechiah the son of Meshillemoth, Jehizkiah the son of Shallum, and Amasa the son of Hadlai, stood up against those who were coming from the war ¹³ and said to them, "You shall not bring the captives in here, for you propose to bring upon us guilt against

GETTING THE MESSAGE

Ten Hebrew kings are mentioned among the records of the Assyrian Empire, which helps to show the reliability of biblical history. King Ahaz asked the Assyrians for help (28:16) but ended up becoming their servant (28:20–21).

the Lord in addition to our present sins and guilt. For our guilt is already great, and there is fierce wrath against Israel." ¹⁴ So the armed men left the captives and the spoil before the princes and all the assembly. ¹⁵ And the men who have been mentioned by name rose and took the captives, and with the spoil they clothed all who were naked among them. They clothed them, gave them sandals, provided them with food and drink, and anointed them, and carrying all the feeble among them on donkeys, they brought them to their kinsfolk at Jericho, the city of palm trees. Then they returned to Samaria.

¹⁶ At that time King Ahaz sent to the king of Assyria for help. ¹⁷ For the Edomites had again invaded and defeated Judah and carried away captives. ¹⁸ And the Philistines had made raids on the cities in the Shephelah and the Negeb of Judah, and had taken Beth-shemesh, Aijalon, Gederoth, Soco with its villages, Timnah with its villages, and Gimzo with its villages. And they set-

tled there. ¹⁹ For the Lord humbled Judah because of Ahaz king of Israel, for he had made Judah act sinfully and had been very unfaithful to the Lord. ²⁰ So Tiglath-pileser king of Assyria came against him and afflicted him instead of strengthening him. ²¹ For Ahaz took a portion from the house of the Lord and the house of the king and of the princes, and gave tribute to the king of Assyria, but it did not help him.

Ahaz's Idolatry

²² In the time of his distress he became yet more faithless to the Lord—this same King Ahaz. ²³ For he sacrificed to the gods of Damascus that had defeated him and said, "Because the gods of the kings of Syria helped them, I will sacrifice to them that they may help me." But they were the ruin of him and of all Israel. ²⁴ And Ahaz gathered together the vessels of the house of God and cut in pieces the vessels of the house of God, and he shut up the doors of the house of the Lord, and he made himself altars in every corner of Jerusalem. ²⁵ In every city of Judah he made high places to make offerings to other gods, provoking to anger the Lord, the God of his fathers. ²⁶ Now the rest of his acts and all his ways, from first to last, behold, they are written in the Book of the Kings of Judah and Israel. ²⁷ And Ahaz slept with his fathers, and they buried him in the city, in Jerusalem, for they did not bring him into the tombs of the kings of Israel. And Hezekiah his son reigned in his place.

Hezekiah Reigns in Judah

29 Hezekiah began to reign when he was twenty-five years old, and he reigned twenty-nine years in Jerusalem. His mother's name was Abijah the daughter of Zechariah. ² And he did what was right in the eyes of the Lord, according to all that David his father had done.

Hezekiah Cleanses the Temple

³ In the first year of his reign, in the first month, he opened the doors of the house of the Lord and repaired them. ⁴ He brought in the priests and the Levites and assembled them in the square on the east ⁵ and said to them, "Hear me, Levites! Now consecrate yourselves, and consecrate the house of the Lord, the God of your fathers, and carry out the filth from the Holy Place. ⁶ For our fathers have been unfaithful and have

done what was evil in the sight of the LORD our God. They have forsaken him and have turned away their faces from the habitation of the LORD and turned their backs. ⁷ They also shut the doors of the vestibule and put out the lamps and have not burned incense or offered burnt offerings in the Holy Place to the God of Israel. ⁸ Therefore the wrath of the LORD came on Judah and Jerusalem, and he has made them an object of horror, of astonishment, and of hissing, as you see with your own eyes. ⁹ For behold, our fathers have fallen by the sword, and our sons and our daughters and our wives are in captivity for this. ¹⁰ Now it is in my heart to make a covenant with the LORD, the God of Israel, in order that his fierce anger may turn away from us. ¹¹ My sons, do not now be negligent, for the LORD has chosen you to stand in his presence, to minister to him and to be his ministers and make offerings to him."

¹² Then the Levites arose, Mahath the son of Amasai, and Joel the son of Azariah, of the sons of the Kohathites; and of the sons of Merari, Kish the son of Abdi, and Azariah the son of Jehallelel; and of the Gershonites, Joah the son of Zimmah, and Eden the son of Joah; ¹³ and of the sons of Elizaphan, Shimri and Jeuel; and of the sons of Asaph, Zechariah and Mattaniah; ¹⁴ and of the sons of Heman, Jehuel and Shimei; and of the sons of Jeduthun, Shemaiah and Uzziel. ¹⁵ They gathered their brothers and consecrated themselves and went in as the king had commanded, by the words of the LORD, to cleanse the house of the LORD. ¹⁶ The priests went into the inner part of the house of the LORD to cleanse it, and they brought out all the uncleanness that they found in the temple of the LORD into the court of the house of the LORD. And the Levites took it and carried it out to the brook Kidron. ¹⁷ They began to consecrate on the first day of the first month, and on the eighth day of the month they came to the vestibule of the LORD. Then for eight days they consecrated the house of the LORD, and on the sixteenth day of the first month they finished. ¹⁸ Then they went in to Hezekiah the king and said, "We have cleansed all the house of the LORD, the altar of burnt offering and all its utensils, and the table for the showbread and all its utensils. ¹⁹ All the utensils that King Ahaz discarded in his reign when he was faithless, we have made ready and consecrated, and behold, they are before the altar of the LORD."

Hezekiah Restores Temple Worship

²⁰ Then Hezekiah the king rose early and gathered the officials of the city and went up to the house of the LORD. ²¹ And they brought seven bulls, seven rams, seven lambs, and seven male goats for a sin offering for the kingdom and for the sanctuary and for Judah. And he commanded the priests, the sons of Aaron, to offer them on the altar of the LORD. ²² So they slaughtered the bulls, and the priests received the blood and threw it against the altar. And they slaughtered the rams, and their blood was thrown against the altar. And they slaughtered the lambs, and their blood was thrown against the altar.

> ### GETTING THE MESSAGE
>
> **What is a scapegoat?** Laying hands on a sacrificial animal (29:23–24) was a symbolic act. It meant that human sin was being placed on the animal and taken away. On the Day of Atonement the people sacrificed a goat in this manner (see Lev. 16:20–22). Thus, today, when a person takes the blame for someone else, he or she may be referred to as a "scapegoat."

²³ Then the goats for the sin offering were brought to the king and the assembly, and they laid their hands on them, ²⁴ and the priests slaughtered them and made a sin offering with their blood on the altar, to make atonement for all Israel. For the king commanded that the burnt offering and the sin offering should be made for all Israel.

²⁵ And he stationed the Levites in the house of the LORD with cymbals, harps, and lyres, according to the commandment of David and of Gad the king's seer and of Nathan the prophet, for the commandment was from the LORD through his prophets. ²⁶ The Levites stood with the instruments of David, and the priests with the trumpets. ²⁷ Then Hezekiah commanded that the burnt offering be offered on the altar. And when the burnt offering began, the song to the LORD began also, and the trumpets, accompanied by the instruments of David

king of Israel. ²⁸ The whole assembly worshiped, and the singers sang, and the trumpeters sounded. All this continued until the burnt offering was finished. ²⁹ When the offering was finished, the king and all who were present with him bowed themselves and worshiped. ³⁰ And Hezekiah the king and the officials commanded the Levites to sing praises to the LORD with the words of David and of Asaph the seer. And they sang praises with gladness, and they bowed down and worshiped.

³¹ Then Hezekiah said, "You have now consecrated yourselves to the LORD. Come near; bring sacrifices and thank offerings to the house of the LORD." And the assembly brought sacrifices and thank offerings, and all who were of a willing heart brought burnt offerings. ³² The number of the burnt offerings that the assembly brought was 70 bulls, 100 rams, and 200 lambs; all these were for a burnt offering to the LORD. ³³ And the consecrated offerings were 600 bulls and 3,000 sheep. ³⁴ But the priests were too few and could not flay all the burnt offerings, so until other priests had consecrated themselves, their brothers the Levites helped them, until the work was finished—for the Levites were more upright in heart than the priests in consecrating themselves. ³⁵ Besides the great number of burnt offerings, there was the fat of the peace offerings, and there were the drink offerings for the burnt offerings. Thus the service of the house of the LORD was restored. ³⁶ And Hezekiah and all the people rejoiced because God had provided for the people, for the thing came about suddenly.

Passover Celebrated

30 Hezekiah sent to all Israel and Judah, and wrote letters also to Ephraim and Manasseh, that they should come to the house of the LORD at Jerusalem to keep the Passover to the LORD, the God of Israel. ² For the king and his princes and all the assembly in Jerusalem had taken counsel to keep the Passover in the second month— ³ for they could not keep it at that time because the priests had not consecrated themselves in sufficient number, nor had the people assembled in Jerusalem— ⁴ and the plan seemed right to the king and all the assembly. ⁵ So they decreed to make a proclamation throughout all Israel, from Beersheba to Dan, that the people should come and keep the Passover to the LORD, the God of Israel, at Jerusalem, for they had not kept it as often as prescribed. ⁶ So couriers went throughout all Israel and Judah with letters from the king and his princes, as the king had commanded, saying, "O people of Israel, return to the LORD, the God of Abraham, Isaac, and Israel, that he may turn again to the remnant of you who have escaped from the hand of the kings of Assyria. ⁷ Do not be like your fathers and your brothers, who were faithless to the LORD God of their fathers, so that he made them a desolation, as you see. ⁸ Do not now be stiff-necked as your fathers were, but yield yourselves to the LORD and come to his sanctuary, which he has consecrated forever, and serve the LORD your God, that his fierce anger may turn away from you. ⁹ For if you return to the LORD, your brothers and your children will find compassion with their captors and return to this land. For the LORD your God is gracious and merciful and will not turn away his face from you, if you return to him."

¹⁰ So the couriers went from city to city through the country of Ephraim and Manasseh, and as far as Zebulun, but they laughed them to scorn and mocked them. ¹¹ However, some men of Asher, of Manasseh, and of Zebulun humbled themselves and came to Jerusalem. ¹² The hand of God was also on Judah to give them one heart to do what the king and the princes commanded by the word of the LORD.

¹³ And many people came together in Jerusalem to keep the Feast of Unleavened Bread in the second month, a very great assembly. ¹⁴ They set to work and removed the altars that were in Jerusalem, and all the altars for burning incense they took away and threw into the brook Kidron. ¹⁵ And they slaughtered the Passover lamb on the fourteenth day of the second month. And the priests and the Levites were ashamed, so that they consecrated themselves and brought burnt offerings into the house of the LORD. ¹⁶ They took their accustomed posts according to the Law of Moses the man of God. The priests threw the blood that they received from the hand of the Levites. ¹⁷ For there were many in the assembly who had not consecrated themselves. Therefore the Levites had to slaughter the

Passover lamb for everyone who was not clean, to consecrate it to the LORD. ¹⁸ For a majority of the people, many of them from Ephraim, Manasseh, Issachar, and Zebulun, had not cleansed themselves, yet they ate the Passover otherwise than as prescribed. For Hezekiah had prayed for them, saying, "May the good LORD pardon everyone ¹⁹ who sets his heart to seek God, the LORD, the God of his fathers, even though not according to the sanctuary's rules of cleanness." ²⁰ And the LORD heard Hezekiah and healed the people. ²¹ And the people of Israel who were present at Jerusalem kept the Feast of Unleavened Bread seven days with great gladness, and the Levites and the priests praised the LORD day by day, singing with all their might to the LORD. ²² And Hezekiah spoke encouragingly to all the Levites who showed good skill in the service of the LORD. So they ate the food of the festival for seven days, sacrificing peace offerings and giving thanks to the LORD, the God of their fathers.

²³ Then the whole assembly agreed together to keep the feast for another seven days. So they kept it for another seven days with gladness. ²⁴ For Hezekiah king of Judah gave the assembly 1,000 bulls and 7,000 sheep for offerings, and the princes gave the assembly 1,000 bulls and 10,000 sheep. And the priests consecrated themselves in great numbers. ²⁵ The whole assembly of Judah, and the priests and the Levites, and the whole assembly that came out of Israel, and the sojourners who came out of the land of Israel, and the sojourners who lived in Judah, rejoiced. ²⁶ So there was great joy in Jerusalem, for since the time of Solomon the son of David king of Israel there had been nothing like this in Jerusalem. ²⁷ Then the priests and the Levites arose and blessed the people, and their voice was heard, and their prayer came to his holy habitation in heaven.

Hezekiah Organizes the Priests

31 Now when all this was finished, all Israel who were present went out to the cities of Judah and broke in pieces the pillars and cut down the Asherim and broke down the high places and the altars throughout all Judah and Benjamin, and in Ephraim and Manasseh, until they had destroyed them all. Then all the people of Israel returned to their cities, every man to his possession.

² And Hezekiah appointed the divisions of the priests and of the Levites, division by division, each according to his service, the priests and the Levites, for burnt offerings and peace offerings, to minister in the gates of the camp of the LORD and to give thanks and praise. ³ The contribution of the king from his own possessions was for the burnt offerings: the burnt offerings of morning and evening, and the burnt offerings for the Sabbaths, the new moons, and the appointed feasts, as it is written in the Law of the LORD. ⁴ And he commanded the people who lived in Jerusalem to give the portion due to the priests and the Levites, that they might give themselves to the Law of the LORD. ⁵ As soon as the command was spread abroad, the people of Israel gave in abundance the firstfruits of grain, wine, oil, honey, and of

> ### GETTING THE MESSAGE
>
> **Generous givers.** When Hezekiah asked the people to contribute financially to his temple restoration project, they gave generously (31:5). Their response recalls the time of the tabernacle's construction. The people gave so freely that Moses actually asked them to stop giving (Ex. 36:3–7).

all the produce of the field. And they brought in abundantly the tithe of everything. ⁶ And the people of Israel and Judah who lived in the cities of Judah also brought in the tithe of cattle and sheep, and the tithe of the dedicated things that had been dedicated to the LORD their God, and laid them in heaps. ⁷ In the third month they began to pile up the heaps, and finished them in the seventh month. ⁸ When Hezekiah and the princes came and saw the heaps, they blessed the LORD and his people Israel. ⁹ And Hezekiah questioned the priests and the Levites about the heaps. ¹⁰ Azariah the chief priest, who was of the house of Zadok, answered him, "Since they began to bring the contributions into the house of the LORD, we have eaten and had enough and have plenty left, for the LORD has blessed his people, so that we have this large amount left."

¹¹ Then Hezekiah commanded them to prepare chambers in the house of the

LORD, and they prepared them. [12] And they faithfully brought in the contributions, the tithes, and the dedicated things. The chief officer in charge of them was Conaniah the Levite, with Shimei his brother as second, [13] while Jehiel, Azaziah, Nahath, Asahel, Jerimoth, Jozabad, Eliel, Ismachiah, Mahath, and Benaiah were overseers assisting Conaniah and Shimei his brother, by the appointment of Hezekiah the king and Azariah the chief officer of the house of God. [14] And Kore the son of Imnah the Levite, keeper of the east gate, was over the freewill offerings to God, to apportion the contribution reserved for the LORD and the most holy offerings. [15] Eden, Miniamin, Jeshua, Shemaiah, Amariah, and Shecaniah were faithfully assisting him in the cities of the priests, to distribute the portions to their brothers, old and young alike, by divisions, [16] except those enrolled by genealogy, males

GETTING THE MESSAGE

Hezekiah's wall (32:5) was one of his many efforts to defend Jerusalem from the invading Assyrians. Archaeologists have uncovered a 650-foot (200-m) portion of this wall.

from three years old and upward—all who entered the house of the LORD as the duty of each day required—for their service according to their offices, by their divisions. [17] The enrollment of the priests was according to their fathers' houses; that of the Levites from twenty years old and upward was according to their offices, by their divisions. [18] They were enrolled with all their little children, their wives, their sons, and their daughters, the whole assembly, for they were faithful in keeping themselves holy. [19] And for the sons of Aaron, the priests, who were in the fields of common land belonging to their cities, there were men in the several cities who were designated by name to distribute portions to every male among the priests and to everyone among the Levites who was enrolled.

[20] Thus Hezekiah did throughout all Judah, and he did what was good and right and faithful before the LORD his God. [21] And every work that he undertook in the service

of the house of God and in accordance with the law and the commandments, seeking his God, he did with all his heart, and prospered.

Sennacherib Invades Judah

32 After these things and these acts of faithfulness, Sennacherib king of Assyria came and invaded Judah and encamped against the fortified cities, thinking to win them for himself. [2] And when Hezekiah saw that Sennacherib had come and intended to fight against Jerusalem, [3] he planned with his officers and his mighty men to stop the water of the springs that were outside the city; and they helped him. [4] A great many people were gathered, and they stopped all the springs and the brook that flowed through the land, saying, "Why should the kings of Assyria come and find much water?" [5] He set to work resolutely and built up all the wall that was broken down and raised towers upon it, and outside it he built another wall, and he strengthened the Millo in the city of David. He also made weapons and shields in abundance. [6] And he set combat commanders over the people and gathered them together to him in the square at the gate of the city and spoke encouragingly to them, saying, [7] "Be strong and courageous. Do not be afraid or dismayed before the king of Assyria and all the horde that is with him, for there are more with us than with him. [8] With him is an arm of flesh, but with us is the LORD our God, to help us and to fight our battles." And the people took confidence from the words of Hezekiah king of Judah.

Sennacherib Blasphemes

[9] After this, Sennacherib king of Assyria, who was besieging Lachish with all his forces, sent his servants to Jerusalem to Hezekiah king of Judah and to all the people of Judah who were in Jerusalem, saying, [10] "Thus says Sennacherib king of Assyria, 'On what are you trusting, that you endure the siege in Jerusalem? [11] Is not Hezekiah misleading you, that he may give you over to die by famine and by thirst, when he tells you, "The LORD our God will deliver us from the hand of the king of Assyria"? [12] Has not this same Hezekiah taken away his high places and his altars and commanded Judah and Jerusalem, "Before one altar you shall worship, and on it you shall burn your

sacrifices"? [13] Do you not know what I and my fathers have done to all the peoples of other lands? Were the gods of the nations of those lands at all able to deliver their lands out of my hand? [14] Who among all the gods of those nations that my fathers devoted to destruction was able to deliver his people from my hand, that your God should be able to deliver you from my hand? [15] Now, therefore, do not let Hezekiah deceive you or mislead you in this fashion, and do not believe him, for no god of any nation or kingdom has been able to deliver his people from my hand or from the hand of my fathers. How much less will your God deliver you out of my hand!'"

[16] And his servants said still more against the LORD God and against his servant Hezekiah. [17] And he wrote letters to cast contempt on the LORD, the God of Israel, and to speak against him, saying, "Like the gods of the nations of the lands who have not delivered their people from my hands, so the God of Hezekiah will not deliver his people from my hand." [18] And they shouted it with a loud voice in the language of Judah to the people of Jerusalem who were on the wall, to frighten and terrify them, in order that they might take the city. [19] And they spoke of the God of Jerusalem as they spoke of the gods of the peoples of the earth, which are the work of men's hands.

The LORD Delivers Jerusalem

[20] Then Hezekiah the king and Isaiah the prophet, the son of Amoz, prayed because of this and cried to heaven. [21] And the LORD sent an angel, who cut off all the mighty warriors and commanders and officers in the camp of the king of Assyria. So he returned with shame of face to his own land. And when he came into the house of his god, some of his own sons struck him down there with the sword. [22] So the LORD saved Hezekiah and the inhabitants of Jerusalem from the hand of Sennacherib king of Assyria and from the hand of all his enemies, and he provided for them on every side. [23] And many brought gifts to the LORD to Jerusalem and precious things to Hezekiah king of Judah, so that he was exalted in the sight of all nations from that time onward.

Hezekiah's Pride and Achievements

[24] In those days Hezekiah became sick and was at the point of death, and he prayed to the LORD, and he answered him and gave him a sign. [25] But Hezekiah did not make return according to the benefit done to him, for his heart was proud. Therefore wrath came upon him and Judah and Jerusalem. [26] But Hezekiah humbled himself for the pride of his heart, both he and the inhabitants of Jerusalem, so that the wrath of the LORD did not come upon them in the days of Hezekiah.

[27] And Hezekiah had very great riches and honor, and he made for himself treasuries for silver, for gold, for precious stones, for spices, for shields, and for all kinds of costly vessels; [28] storehouses also for the yield of grain, wine, and oil; and stalls for all kinds of cattle, and sheepfolds. [29] He likewise provided cities for himself, and flocks and herds in abundance, for God had given him very great possessions. [30] This same Hezekiah closed the upper outlet of the waters of Gihon and directed them down to the west side of the city of David. And Hezekiah prospered in all his works. [31] And so in the matter of the envoys of the princes of Babylon, who had been sent to him to inquire about the sign that had been done in the land, God left him to himself, in order to test him and to know all that was in his heart.

[32] Now the rest of the acts of Hezekiah and his good deeds, behold, they are written in the vision of Isaiah the prophet the son of Amoz, in the Book of the Kings of Judah and Israel. [33] And Hezekiah slept with his fathers, and they buried him in the upper part of the tombs of the sons of David, and all Judah and the inhabitants of Jerusalem did him honor at his death. And Manasseh his son reigned in his place.

Manasseh Reigns in Judah

33 Manasseh was twelve years old when he began to reign, and he reigned fifty-five years in Jerusalem. [2] And he did what was evil in the sight of the LORD, according to the abominations of the nations whom the LORD drove out before the people of Israel. [3] For he rebuilt the high places that his father Hezekiah had broken down, and he erected altars to the Baals, and made Asheroth, and worshiped all the host of heaven and served them. [4] And he built altars in the house of the LORD, of which the LORD had said, "In Jerusalem shall my name be forever." [5] And he built altars for

all the host of heaven in the two courts of the house of the LORD. **6** And he burned his sons as an offering in the Valley of the Son of Hinnom, and used fortune-telling and omens and sorcery, and dealt with mediums and with necromancers. He did much evil in the sight of the LORD, provoking him to anger. **7** And the carved image of the idol that he had made he set in the house of God, of which God said to David and to Solomon his son, "In this house, and in Jerusalem, which I have chosen out of all the tribes of

---

PROFILE

MANASSEH

Manasseh, son of Hezekiah, ruled over Judah for 55 years. He was the longest reigning king in the nation's history. Unlike his father, who honored the Lord, Manasseh was perhaps the worst of Judah's kings. He actively pursued practices forbidden by God, and even built altars to false gods inside the temple. Manasseh burned his sons as child sacrifices, and practiced fortune-telling and sorcery. Unlike other evil kings, however, when Manasseh faced the judgment of the Lord for his actions, he repented. When he was taken as a captive to Babylon, he "entreated the favor of the LORD his God and humbled himself greatly before the God of his fathers" (33:12). God heard Manasseh's prayer, and restored him to his kingdom.

KEY REFERENCE: 2 CHRONICLES 33:9–14

Israel, I will put my name forever, **8** and I will no more remove the foot of Israel from the land that I appointed for your fathers, if only they will be careful to do all that I have commanded them, all the law, the statutes, and the rules given through Moses." **9** Manasseh led Judah and the inhabitants of Jerusalem astray, to do more evil than the nations whom the LORD destroyed before the people of Israel.

Manasseh's Repentance

10 The LORD spoke to Manasseh and to his people, but they paid no attention.

11 Therefore the LORD brought upon them the commanders of the army of the king of Assyria, who captured Manasseh with hooks and bound him with chains of bronze and brought him to Babylon. **12** And when he was in distress, he entreated the favor of the LORD his God and humbled himself greatly before the God of his fathers. **13** He prayed to him, and God was moved by his entreaty and heard his plea and brought him again to Jerusalem into his kingdom. Then Manasseh knew that the LORD was God.

14 Afterward he built an outer wall for the city of David west of Gihon, in the valley, and for the entrance into the Fish Gate, and carried it around Ophel, and raised it to a very great height. He also put commanders of the army in all the fortified cities in Judah. **15** And he took away the foreign gods and the idol from the house of the LORD, and all the altars that he had built on the mountain of the house of the LORD and in Jerusalem, and he threw them outside of the city. **16** He also restored the altar of the LORD and offered on it sacrifices of peace offerings and of thanksgiving, and he commanded Judah to serve the LORD, the God of Israel. **17** Nevertheless, the people still sacrificed at the high places, but only to the LORD their God.

18 Now the rest of the acts of Manasseh, and his prayer to his God, and the words of the seers who spoke to him in the name of the LORD, the God of Israel, behold, they are in the Chronicles of the Kings of Israel. **19** And his prayer, and how God was moved by his entreaty, and all his sin and his faithlessness, and the sites on which he built high places and set up the Asherim and the images, before he humbled himself, behold, they are written in the Chronicles of the Seers. **20** So Manasseh slept with his fathers, and they buried him in his house, and Amon his son reigned in his place.

Amon's Reign and Death

21 Amon was twenty-two years old when he began to reign, and he reigned two years in Jerusalem. **22** And he did what was evil in the sight of the LORD, as Manasseh his father had done. Amon sacrificed to all the images that Manasseh his father had made, and served them. **23** And he did not humble himself before the LORD, as Manasseh his father had humbled himself, but this

Amon incurred guilt more and more. **24** And his servants conspired against him and put him to death in his house. **25** But the people of the land struck down all those who had conspired against King Amon. And the people of the land made Josiah his son king in his place.

Josiah Reigns in Judah

34 Josiah was eight years old when he began to reign, and he reigned thirty-one years in Jerusalem. **2** And he did what was right in the eyes of the LORD, and walked in the ways of David his father; and he did not turn aside to the right hand or to the left. **3** For in the eighth year of his reign, while he was yet a boy, he began to seek the God of David his father, and in the twelfth year he began to purge Judah and Jerusalem of the high places, the Asherim, and the carved and the metal images. **4** And they chopped down the altars of the Baals in his presence, and he cut down the incense altars that stood above them. And he broke in pieces the Asherim and the carved and the metal images, and he made dust of them and scattered it over the graves of those who had sacrificed to them. **5** He also burned the bones of the priests on their altars and cleansed Judah and Jerusalem. **6** And in the cities of Manasseh, Ephraim, and Simeon, and as far as Naphtali, in their ruins all around, **7** he broke down the altars and beat the Asherim and the images into powder and cut down all the incense altars throughout all the land of Israel. Then he returned to Jerusalem.

The Book of the Law Found

8 Now in the eighteenth year of his reign, when he had cleansed the land and the house, he sent Shaphan the son of Azaliah, and Maaseiah the governor of the city, and Joah the son of Joahaz, the recorder, to repair the house of the LORD his God. **9** They came to Hilkiah the high priest and gave him the money that had been brought into the house of God, which the Levites, the keepers of the threshold, had collected from Manasseh and Ephraim and from all the remnant of Israel and from all Judah and Benjamin and from the inhabitants of Jerusalem. **10** And they gave it to the workmen who were working in the house of the LORD. And the workmen who were working in the house of the LORD

gave it for repairing and restoring the house. **11** They gave it to the carpenters and the builders to buy quarried stone, and timber for binders and beams for the buildings that the kings of Judah had let go to ruin. **12** And the men did the work faithfully. Over them were set Jahath and Obadiah the Levites, of the sons of Merari, and Zechariah and Meshullam, of the sons of the Kohathites, to have oversight. The Levites, all who were skillful with instruments of music, **13** were over the burden-bearers and directed all who did work in every kind of service, and some of the Levites were scribes and officials and gatekeepers.

14 While they were bringing out the money that had been brought into the house of the LORD, Hilkiah the priest found the Book of the Law of the LORD given through Moses. **15** Then Hilkiah answered and said

---

GETTING THE MESSAGE

The Book of the Law of the Lord.
The high priest discovered this forgotten book while the temple was being repaired (34:14). After reading the Law, King Josiah called the nation to further measures of repentance and reform. The book may have included part or all of Deuteronomy.

---

to Shaphan the secretary, "I have found the Book of the Law in the house of the LORD." And Hilkiah gave the book to Shaphan. **16** Shaphan brought the book to the king, and further reported to the king, "All that was committed to your servants they are doing. **17** They have emptied out the money that was found in the house of the LORD and have given it into the hand of the overseers and the workmen." **18** Then Shaphan the secretary told the king, "Hilkiah the priest has given me a book." And Shaphan read from it before the king.

19 And when the king heard the words of the Law, he tore his clothes. **20** And the king commanded Hilkiah, Ahikam the son of Shaphan, Abdon the son of Micah, Shaphan the secretary, and Asaiah the king's servant, saying, **21** "Go, inquire of the LORD for me and for those who are left in Israel and in Judah, concerning the words of the book that has been found. For great is the wrath of the LORD that is poured out on us, because our fathers have not kept the word of the LORD, to do according to all that is written in this book."

Huldah Prophesies Disaster

²² So Hilkiah and those whom the king had sent went to Huldah the prophetess, the wife of Shallum the son of Tokhath, son of Hasrah, keeper of the wardrobe (now she lived in Jerusalem in the Second Quarter) and spoke to her to that effect. ²³ And she said to them, "Thus says the LORD, the God of Israel: 'Tell the man who sent you to me, ²⁴ Thus says the LORD, Behold, I will bring disaster upon this place and upon its inhabitants, all the curses that are written in the book that was read before the king of Judah. ²⁵ Because they have forsaken me and have made offerings to other gods, that they might provoke me to anger with all the works of their hands, therefore my wrath will be poured out on this place and will not be quenched. ²⁶ But to the king of Judah, who sent you to inquire of the LORD, thus shall you say to him, Thus says the LORD, the God of Israel: Regarding the words that you have heard, ²⁷ because your heart was tender and you humbled yourself before God when you heard his words against this place and its inhabitants, and you have humbled yourself before me and have torn your clothes and wept before me, I also have heard you, declares the LORD. ²⁸ Behold, I will gather you to your fathers, and you shall be gathered to your grave in peace, and your eyes shall not see all the disaster that I will bring upon this place and its inhabitants.'" And they brought back word to the king.

²⁹ Then the king sent and gathered together all the elders of Judah and Jerusalem. ³⁰ And the king went up to the house of the LORD, with all the men of Judah and the inhabitants of Jerusalem and the priests and the Levites, all the people both great and small. And he read in their hearing all the words of the Book of the Covenant that had been found in the house of the LORD. ³¹ And the king stood in his place and made a covenant before the LORD, to walk after the LORD and to keep his commandments and his testimonies and his statutes, with all his heart and all his soul, to perform the words of the covenant that were written in

this book. ³² Then he made all who were present in Jerusalem and in Benjamin join in it. And the inhabitants of Jerusalem did according to the covenant of God, the God of their fathers. ³³ And Josiah took away all the abominations from all the territory that belonged to the people of Israel and made all who were present in Israel serve the LORD their God. All his days they did not turn away from following the LORD, the God of their fathers.

Josiah Keeps the Passover

35 Josiah kept a Passover to the LORD in Jerusalem. And they slaughtered the Passover lamb on the fourteenth day of the first month. ² He appointed the priests to their offices and encouraged them in the service of the house of the LORD. ³ And he said to the Levites who taught all Israel and who were holy to the LORD, "Put the holy ark in the house that Solomon the son of David, king of Israel, built. You need not carry it on your shoulders. Now serve the LORD your God and his people Israel. ⁴ Prepare yourselves according to your fathers' houses by your divisions, as prescribed in the writing of David king of Israel and the document of Solomon his son. ⁵ And stand in the Holy Place according to the groupings of the fathers' houses of your brothers the lay people, and according to the division of the Levites by fathers' household. ⁶ And slaughter the Passover lamb, and consecrate yourselves, and prepare for your brothers, to do according to the word of the LORD by Moses."

⁷ Then Josiah contributed to the lay people, as Passover offerings for all who were present, lambs and young goats from the flock to the number of 30,000, and 3,000 bulls; these were from the king's possessions. ⁸ And his officials contributed willingly to the people, to the priests, and to the Levites. Hilkiah, Zechariah, and Jehiel, the chief officers of the house of God, gave to the priests for the Passover offerings 2,600 Passover lambs and 300 bulls. ⁹ Conaniah also, and Shemaiah and Nethanel his brothers, and Hashabiah and Jeiel and Jozabad, the chiefs of the Levites, gave to the Levites for the Passover offerings 5,000 lambs and young goats and 500 bulls.

¹⁰ When the service had been prepared for, the priests stood in their place, and the Levites in their divisions according to the

king's command. **11** And they slaughtered the Passover lamb, and the priests threw the blood that they received from them while the Levites flayed the sacrifices. **12** And they set aside the burnt offerings that they might distribute them according to the groupings of the fathers' houses of the lay people, to offer to the LORD, as it is written in the Book of Moses. And so they did with the bulls. **13** And they roasted the Passover lamb with fire according to the rule; and they boiled the holy offerings in pots, in cauldrons, and in pans, and carried them quickly to all the lay people. **14** And afterward they prepared for themselves and for the priests, because the priests, the sons of Aaron, were offering the burnt offerings and the fat parts until night; so the Levites prepared for themselves and for the priests, the sons of Aaron. **15** The singers, the sons of Asaph, were in their place according to the command of David, and Asaph, and Heman, and Jeduthun the king's seer; and the gatekeepers were at each gate. They did not need to depart from their service, for their brothers the Levites prepared for them.

16 So all the service of the LORD was prepared that day, to keep the Passover and to offer burnt offerings on the altar of the LORD, according to the command of King Josiah. **17** And the people of Israel who were present kept the Passover at that time, and the Feast of Unleavened Bread seven days. **18** No Passover like it had been kept in Israel since the days of Samuel the prophet. None of the kings of Israel had kept such a Passover as was kept by Josiah, and the priests and the Levites, and all Judah and Israel who were present, and the inhabitants of Jerusalem. **19** In the eighteenth year of the reign of Josiah this Passover was kept.

Josiah Killed in Battle

20 After all this, when Josiah had prepared the temple, Neco king of Egypt went up to fight at Carchemish on the Euphrates, and Josiah went out to meet him. **21** But he sent envoys to him, saying, "What have we to do with each other, king of Judah? I am not coming against you this day, but against the house with which I am at war. And God has commanded me to hurry. Cease opposing God, who is with me, lest he destroy you." **22** Nevertheless, Josiah did not turn away from him, but disguised himself in order to fight with him. He did not listen to the words of Neco from the mouth of God, but came to fight in the plain of Megiddo. **23** And the archers shot King Josiah. And the king said to his servants, "Take me away, for I am badly wounded." **24** So his servants took him out of the chariot and carried him in his second chariot and brought him to Jerusalem. And he died and was buried in the tombs of his fathers. All Judah and Jerusalem mourned for Josiah. **25** Jeremiah also uttered a lament for Josiah; and all the singing men and singing women have spoken of Josiah in their laments to this day. They made these a rule in Israel; behold, they are written in the Laments. **26** Now the rest of the acts of Josiah, and his good deeds according to what is written in the Law of the LORD, **27** and his acts, first and last, behold, they are written in the Book of the Kings of Israel and Judah.

GETTING THE MESSAGE

Passover is a feast remembering Israel's exodus from Egypt. It recalls their final meal in Egypt before deliverance. The most important element is the lamb (Ex. 12:5). It reminds participants of the blood smeared on the doorposts to protect them from the plague of the firstborn. Bitter herbs are eaten with the lamb, symbolizing the bitterness of Egyptian captivity.

Judah's Decline

36 The people of the land took Jehoahaz the son of Josiah and made him king in his father's place in Jerusalem. **2** Jehoahaz was twenty-three years old when he began to reign, and he reigned three months in Jerusalem. **3** Then the king of Egypt deposed him in Jerusalem and laid on the land a tribute of a hundred talents of silver and a talent of gold. **4** And the king of Egypt made Eliakim his brother king over Judah and Jerusalem, and changed his name to Jehoiakim. But Neco took Jehoahaz his brother and carried him to Egypt.

5 Jehoiakim was twenty-five years old when he began to reign, and he reigned eleven years in Jerusalem. He did what was evil in the sight of the LORD his God.

⁶ Against him came up Nebuchadnezzar king of Babylon and bound him in chains to take him to Babylon. ⁷ Nebuchadnezzar also carried part of the vessels of the house of the LORD to Babylon and put them in his palace in Babylon. ⁸ Now the rest of the acts of Jehoiakim, and the abominations that he did, and what was found against him, behold, they are written in the Book of the Kings of Israel and Judah. And Jehoiachin his son reigned in his place.

⁹ Jehoiachin was eighteen years old when he became king, and he reigned three months and ten days in Jerusalem. He did what was evil in the sight of the LORD. ¹⁰ In the spring of the year King Nebuchadnezzar sent and brought him to Babylon, with the precious vessels of the house of the LORD, and made his brother Zedekiah king over Judah and Jerusalem.

¹¹ Zedekiah was twenty-one years old when he began to reign, and he reigned eleven years in Jerusalem. ¹² He did what was evil in the sight of the LORD his God. He did not humble himself before Jeremiah the prophet, who spoke from the mouth of the LORD. ¹³ He also rebelled against King Nebuchadnezzar, who had made him swear by God. He stiffened his neck and hardened his heart against turning to the LORD, the God of Israel. ¹⁴ All the officers of the priests and the people likewise were exceedingly unfaithful, following all the abominations of the nations. And they polluted the house of the LORD that he had made holy in Jerusalem.

¹⁵ The LORD, the God of their fathers, sent persistently to them by his messengers, because he had compassion on his people and on his dwelling place. ¹⁶ But they kept mocking the messengers of God, despising his words and scoffing at his prophets, until the wrath of the LORD rose against his people, until there was no remedy.

Jerusalem Captured and Burned

¹⁷ Therefore he brought up against them the king of the Chaldeans, who killed their young men with the sword in the house of their sanctuary and had no compassion on young man or virgin, old man or aged. He gave them all into his hand. ¹⁸ And all the vessels of the house of God, great and small, and the treasures of the house of the LORD, and the treasures of the king and of his princes, all these he brought to Babylon. ¹⁹ And they burned the house of God and broke down the wall of Jerusalem and burned all its palaces with fire and destroyed all its precious vessels. ²⁰ He took into exile in Babylon those who had escaped from the sword, and they became servants to him and to his sons until the establishment of the kingdom of Persia, ²¹ to fulfill the word of the LORD by the mouth of Jeremiah, until the land had enjoyed its Sabbaths. All the days that it lay desolate it kept Sabbath, to fulfill seventy years.

The Proclamation of Cyrus

²² Now in the first year of Cyrus king of Persia, that the word of the LORD by the mouth of Jeremiah might be fulfilled, the LORD stirred up the spirit of Cyrus king of Persia, so that he made a proclamation throughout all his kingdom and also put it in writing: ²³ "Thus says Cyrus king of Persia, 'The LORD, the God of heaven, has given me all the kingdoms of the earth, and he has charged me to build him a house at Jerusalem, which is in Judah. Whoever is among you of all his people, may the LORD his God be with him. Let him go up.'"

INTRODUCTION TO EZRA

586 B.C.	538 B.C.	516 B.C.	458 B.C.
Fall of Judah/temple destroyed	Decree of Cyrus/end of exile	Temple rebuilt	Ezra arrives in Jerusalem

AUTHOR AND DATE

The book of Ezra never declares its author, and the book's contents make it difficult to determine when it was written. Ezra 1–6 recounts events that occurred long before Ezra's time. Ezra 7:27–9:15 clearly comes from Ezra's own hand, since it is written in the first person. Ezra 7:1–26 and 10:1–44 describe events in Ezra's time, but are written in the third person. It is possible Ezra may have combined the other materials with his autobiographical writings to form the book. Or, a later historian may have collected all the portions to describe Israelite history from c. 538–433 B.C. Many scholars believe that the same author wrote Ezra, Nehemiah, and 1–2 Chronicles. In ancient times, Ezra and Nehemiah were counted as one book. The events narrated in Ezra–Nehemiah occur over a century: Ezra 1–6 covers 538–515 B.C.; Ezra 7–Nehemiah 13 covers 458–433 B.C.

THEME

The theme of Ezra is faithfulness to the Lord, both in keeping the Mosaic law (7:6) and in worship. Because of his concern about worship, Ezra stresses the importance of rebuilding the temple.

PURPOSE, OCCASION, AND BACKGROUND

As the people return from exile in Babylon to the Promised Land, they are under threat from the non-Jews living there. Having been driven from the land previously because of their sin, they also need to learn once again how to live in covenant with God. The land must be restored through the physical presence of God's people, and the people must revive a spiritual commitment to serve God alone. As the temple is rebuilt and more exiles come back to the land, the people start to reestablish the nation that God had promised Abraham. As the priests return and begin to teach the people how to love God and live according to his ways, the people recommit themselves to the Lord.

The book of Ezra encourages the postexilic community toward pure worship and holy behavior. Ezra calls the people back to covenant loyalty and obedience to the Mosaic law. The book rejoices in God's provision in returning them to the land, rebuilding the temple, and calling his people back to himself. The book also warns against falling away again through sin and against serving other gods. The remnant of Israel should persevere in hope, repent in humility, and live in obedience.

KEY THEMES

1. The Lord is faithful to his promises, and his mercy is greater than his anger (9:13).

2. The Lord works providentially by all means, especially through powerful rulers, to bring about his greater purposes (e.g., 6:22).

3. The exiles are the remnant of Israel, the "holy race" (9:2, 8). They are bound by covenant to guard their identity and character as the people of the Lord by obeying his law.

4. People belong to the Lord by willingly accepting his covenant. Membership in the covenant community is open to the people of any nation who meet this requirement (6:21).

5. Faithfulness to the Lord is demonstrated by proper attention to worship. In Ezra, this is shown especially in the rebuilding of the temple and in the proper ordering of its services. The priests, Levites, gatekeepers, musicians, and other temple servants once again perform their duties (2:36–58; 3:10–11).

6. The heart of worship is joy (6:22).

OUTLINE

I. Cyrus's Decree and the Return of Exiles from Babylon (1:1–2:70)
   A. The decree (1:1–4)
   B. The exiles respond to the decree (1:5–11)
   C. The exiles live again in their ancestral homes (2:1–70)

II. The Returned Exiles Rebuild the Temple on Its Original Site (3:1–6:22)

EZRA

The Proclamation of Cyrus

1 In the first year of Cyrus king of Persia, that the word of the LORD by the mouth of Jeremiah might be fulfilled, the LORD stirred up the spirit of Cyrus king of Persia, so that he made a proclamation throughout all his kingdom and also put it in writing:

2 "Thus says Cyrus king of Persia: The LORD, the God of heaven, has given me all the kingdoms of the earth, and he has charged me to build him a house at Jerusalem, which is in Judah. 3 Whoever is among you of all his people, may his God be

with him, and let him go up to Jerusalem, which is in Judah, and rebuild the house of the LORD, the God of Israel—he is the God who is in Jerusalem. 4 And let each survivor, in whatever place he sojourns, be assisted by the men of his place with silver and gold, with goods and with beasts, besides freewill offerings for the house of God that is in Jerusalem."

5 Then rose up the heads of the fathers' houses of Judah and Benjamin, and the priests and the Levites, everyone whose spirit God had stirred to go up to rebuild the house of the LORD that is in Jerusalem. 6 And all who were about them aided them with vessels of silver, with gold, with goods, with beasts, and with costly wares, besides all that was freely offered. 7 Cyrus the king also brought out the vessels of the house of the LORD that Nebuchadnezzar had carried away

from Jerusalem and placed in the house of his gods. 8 Cyrus king of Persia brought these out in the charge of Mithredath the treasurer, who counted them out to Sheshbazzar the prince of Judah. 9 And this was the number of them: 30 basins of gold, 1,000 basins of silver, 29 censers, 10 30 bowls of gold, 410 bowls of silver, and 1,000 other vessels; 11 all the vessels of gold and of silver were 5,400. All these did Sheshbazzar bring up, when the exiles were brought up from Babylonia to Jerusalem.

The Exiles Return

2 Now these were the people of the province who came up out of the captivity of those exiles whom Nebuchadnezzar the king of Babylon had carried captive to Babylonia. They returned to Jerusalem and Judah, each to his own town. 2 They came with Zerubbabel, Jeshua, Nehemiah, Seraiah, Reelaiah, Mordecai, Bilshan, Mispar, Bigvai, Rehum, and Baanah.

The number of the men of the people of Israel: 3 the sons of Parosh, 2,172. 4 The sons of Shephatiah, 372. 5 The sons of Arah, 775. 6 The sons of Pahath-moab, namely the sons of Jeshua and Joab, 2,812. 7 The sons of Elam, 1,254. 8 The sons of Zattu, 945. 9 The sons of Zaccai, 760. 10 The sons of Bani, 642. 11 The sons of Bebai, 623. 12 The sons of Azgad, 1,222. 13 The sons of Adonikam, 666. 14 The sons of Bigvai, 2,056. 15 The sons of Adin, 454. 16 The sons of Ater, namely of Hezekiah, 98. 17 The sons of Bezai, 323. 18 The sons of Jorah, 112. 19 The sons of Hashum, 223. 20 The sons of Gibbar, 95. 21 The sons of Bethlehem, 123. 22 The men of Netophah, 56. 23 The men of Anathoth, 128. 24 The sons of Azmaveth, 42. 25 The sons of Kiriath-arim, Chephirah, and Beeroth, 743. 26 The sons of Ramah and Geba, 621. 27 The men of Michmas, 122. 28 The men of Bethel and Ai, 223. 29 The sons of Nebo, 52. 30 The sons of Magbish, 156. 31 The sons of the other Elam, 1,254. 32 The sons of Harim, 320. 33 The sons of Lod, Hadid, and Ono, 725. 34 The sons of Jericho, 345. 35 The sons of Senaah, 3,630.

36 The priests: the sons of Jedaiah, of the house of Jeshua, 973. 37 The sons of Immer, 1,052. 38 The sons of Pashhur, 1,247. 39 The sons of Harim, 1,017.

40 The Levites: the sons of Jeshua and Kadmiel, of the sons of Hodaviah, 74. 41 The singers: the sons of Asaph, 128. 42 The sons of the gatekeepers: the sons of Shallum, the sons of Ater, the sons of Talmon, the sons of Akkub, the sons of Hatita, and the sons of Shobai, in all 139.

43 The temple servants: the sons of Ziha, the sons of Hasupha, the sons of Tabbaoth, 44 the sons of Keros, the sons of Siaha, the sons of Padon, 45 the sons of Lebanah, the sons of Hagabah, the sons of Akkub, 46 the sons of Hagab, the sons of Shamlai, the sons of Hanan, 47 the sons of Giddel, the sons of Gahar, the sons of Reaiah, 48 the sons of Rezin, the sons of Nekoda, the sons of Gazzam, 49 the sons of Uzza, the sons of Paseah, the sons of Besai, 50 the sons of Asnah, the sons of Meunim, the sons of Nephisim, 51 the sons of Bakbuk, the sons of Hakupha, the sons of Harhur, 52 the sons of Bazluth, the sons of Mehida, the sons of Harsha, 53 the sons of Barkos, the sons of Sisera, the sons of Temah, 54 the sons of Neziah, and the sons of Hatipha.

55 The sons of Solomon's servants: the sons of Sotai, the sons of Hassophereth, the sons of Peruda, 56 the sons of Jaalah, the sons of Darkon, the sons of Giddel, 57 the sons of Shephatiah, the sons of Hattil, the sons of Pochereth-hazzebaim, and the sons of Ami.

58 All the temple servants and the sons of Solomon's servants were 392.

59 The following were those who came up from Tel-melah, Tel-harsha, Cherub, Addan, and Immer, though they could not prove their fathers' houses or their descent, whether they belonged to Israel: 60 the sons of Delaiah, the sons of Tobiah, and the sons of Nekoda, 652. 61 Also, of the sons of the priests: the sons of Habaiah, the sons of Hakkoz, and the sons of Barzillai (who had taken a wife from the daughters of Barzillai the Gileadite, and was called by their name). 62 These sought their registration among those enrolled in the genealogies, but they were not found there, and so they were excluded from the priesthood as unclean. 63 The governor told them that they were not to partake of the most holy food, until

there should be a priest to consult Urim and Thummim.

64 The whole assembly together was 42,360, 65 besides their male and female servants, of whom there were 7,337, and they had 200 male and female singers. 66 Their horses were 736, their mules were 245, 67 their camels were 435, and their donkeys were 6,720.

68 Some of the heads of families, when they came to the house of the LORD that is in Jerusalem, made freewill offerings for the house of God, to erect it on its site. 69 According to their ability they gave to the treasury of the work 61,000 darics of gold, 5,000 minas of silver, and 100 priests' garments.

70 Now the priests, the Levites, some of the people, the singers, the gatekeepers, and the temple servants lived in their towns, and all the rest of Israel in their towns.

GETTING THE MESSAGE

Darics (2:69) were gold coins used throughout the Persian Empire. These coins were often called "archers" because of the image of an archer stamped on the face. When one particular king remarked that 30,000 archers had run him out of his kingdom, he was implying that he had been bribed to give up his throne.

Rebuilding the Altar

3 When the seventh month came, and the children of Israel were in the towns, the people gathered as one man to Jerusalem. 2 Then arose Jeshua the son of Jozadak, with his fellow priests, and Zerubbabel the son of Shealtiel with his kinsmen, and they built the altar of the God of Israel, to offer burnt offerings on it, as it is written in the Law of Moses the man of God. 3 They set the altar in its place, for fear was on them because of the peoples of the lands, and they offered burnt offerings on it to the LORD, burnt offerings morning and evening. 4 And they kept the Feast of Booths, as it is written, and offered the daily burnt offerings by number according to the rule, as each day required, 5 and after that the regular burnt offerings, the offerings at the new moon and at all the appointed feasts of the LORD, and the

offerings of everyone who made a freewill offering to the LORD. **6** From the first day of the seventh month they began to offer burnt offerings to the LORD. But the foundation of the temple of the LORD was not yet laid. **7** So they gave money to the masons and the carpenters, and food, drink, and oil to the Sidonians and the Tyrians to bring cedar trees from Lebanon to the sea, to Joppa, according to the grant that they had from Cyrus king of Persia.

PROFILE

ZERUBBABEL

King Cyrus of Persia decreed that the Jewish exiles in Babylon should return to Jerusalem and rebuild the destroyed temple. Zerubbabel, whom the prophet Haggai refers to as "governor of Judah" (Hag. 1:1), was one of the first exiles to return. Along with the priest Jeshua, he rebuilt the altar of the Lord so that sacrifices could once again be made. The following year, under the guidance and supervision of Zerubbabel and Jeshua, work began on the temple itself. The foundations of the temple were laid, but opposition from local governors prevented its completion for more than 20 years. With the support of the prophets Haggai and Zechariah, Zerubbabel and Jeshua resumed and completed the reconstruction of the temple during the reign of King Darius.

KEY REFERENCE: EZRA 5:2

Rebuilding the Temple

8 Now in the second year after their coming to the house of God at Jerusalem, in the second month, Zerubbabel the son of Shealtiel and Jeshua the son of Jozadak made a beginning, together with the rest of their kinsmen, the priests and the Levites and all who had come to Jerusalem from the captivity. They appointed the Levites, from twenty years old and upward, to supervise the work of the house of the LORD. **9** And Jeshua with his sons and his brothers, and Kadmiel and his sons, the sons of Judah, together supervised the workmen in the house of God,

along with the sons of Henadad and the Levites, their sons and brothers.

10 And when the builders laid the foundation of the temple of the LORD, the priests in their vestments came forward with trumpets, and the Levites, the sons of Asaph, with cymbals, to praise the LORD, according to the directions of David king of Israel. **11** And they sang responsively, praising and giving thanks to the LORD,

"For he is good,
for his steadfast love endures forever toward Israel."

And all the people shouted with a great shout when they praised the LORD, because the foundation of the house of the LORD was laid. **12** But many of the priests and Levites and heads of fathers' houses, old men who

> **GETTING THE MESSAGE**

Joppa was 35 miles (56 km) northwest of Jerusalem on the Mediterranean Sea and was a major seaport (3:7). Joppa had the only natural harbor in all of Palestine. Though the surrounding reefs made it dangerous for ships to enter the harbor, it was still greatly valued because of its strategic location for trade with the west.

had seen the first house, wept with a loud voice when they saw the foundation of this house being laid, though many shouted aloud for joy, **13** so that the people could not distinguish the sound of the joyful shout from the sound of the people's weeping, for the people shouted with a great shout, and the sound was heard far away.

Adversaries Oppose the Rebuilding

4 Now when the adversaries of Judah and Benjamin heard that the returned exiles were building a temple to the LORD, the God of Israel, **2** they approached Zerubbabel and the heads of fathers' houses and said to them, "Let us build with you, for we worship your God as you do, and we have been sacrificing to him ever since the days of Esarhaddon king of Assyria who brought us here." **3** But Zerubbabel, Jeshua, and the rest of the heads of fathers' houses in Israel said to them, "You have nothing to do with us in building a house to our God; but we alone will build to the LORD, the God of Israel, as King Cyrus the king of Persia has commanded us."

⁴ Then the people of the land discouraged the people of Judah and made them afraid to build ⁵ and bribed counselors against them to frustrate their purpose, all the days of Cyrus king of Persia, even until the reign of Darius king of Persia.

⁶ And in the reign of Ahasuerus, in the beginning of his reign, they wrote an accusation against the inhabitants of Judah and Jerusalem.

The Letter to King Artaxerxes

⁷ In the days of Artaxerxes, Bishlam and Mithredath and Tabeel and the rest of their associates wrote to Artaxerxes king of Persia. The letter was written in Aramaic and translated. ⁸ Rehum the commander and Shimshai the scribe wrote a letter against Jerusalem to Artaxerxes the king as follows: ⁹ Rehum the commander, Shimshai the scribe, and the rest of their associates, the judges, the governors, the officials, the Persians, the men of Erech, the Babylonians, the men of Susa, that is, the Elamites, ¹⁰ and the rest of the nations whom the great and noble Osnappar deported and settled in the cities of Samaria and in the rest of the province Beyond the River. ¹¹ (This is a copy of the letter that they sent.) "To Artaxerxes the king: Your servants, the men of the province Beyond the River, send greeting. And now ¹² be it known to the king that the Jews who came up from you to us have gone to Jerusalem. They are rebuilding that rebellious and wicked city. They are finishing the walls and repairing the foundations. ¹³ Now be it known to the king that if this city is rebuilt and the walls finished, they will not pay tribute, custom, or toll, and the royal revenue will be impaired. ¹⁴ Now because we eat the salt of the palace and it is not fitting for us to witness the king's dishonor, therefore we send and inform the king, ¹⁵ in order that search may be made in the book of the records of your fathers. You will find in the book of the records and learn that this city is a rebellious city, hurtful to kings and provinces, and that sedition was stirred up in it from of old. That was why this city was laid waste. ¹⁶ We make known to the king that if this city is

rebuilt and its walls finished, you will then have no possession in the province Beyond the River."

The King Orders the Work to Cease

¹⁷ The king sent an answer: "To Rehum the commander and Shimshai the scribe and the rest of their associates who live in Samaria and in the rest of the province Beyond the River, greeting. And now ¹⁸ the letter that you sent to us has been plainly read before me. ¹⁹ And I made a decree, and search has been made, and it has been found that this city from of old has risen against kings, and that rebellion and sedition have been made in it. ²⁰ And mighty kings have been over Jerusalem, who ruled over the whole province Beyond the River, to whom tribute, custom, and toll were paid. ²¹ Therefore make a decree that these men be made to cease, and

---

GETTING THE MESSAGE

Beyond the River was the name given by Persian rulers to their province that included Judah and Israel (4:11). The "River" refers to the Euphrates River, running through present-day Iraq. From the perspective of people living in Persia, Israel was indeed "beyond the river."

---

that this city be not rebuilt, until a decree is made by me. ²² And take care not to be slack in this matter. Why should damage grow to the hurt of the king?"

²³ Then, when the copy of King Artaxerxes' letter was read before Rehum and Shimshai the scribe and their associates, they went in haste to the Jews at Jerusalem and by force and power made them cease. ²⁴ Then the work on the house of God that is in Jerusalem stopped, and it ceased until the second year of the reign of Darius king of Persia.

Rebuilding Begins Anew

5 Now the prophets, Haggai and Zechariah the son of Iddo, prophesied to the Jews who were in Judah and Jerusalem, in the name of the God of Israel who was over them. ² Then Zerubbabel the son of Shealtiel and Jeshua the son of Jozadak arose and began to rebuild the house of God that is in Jerusalem, and the prophets of God were with them, supporting them.

³ At the same time Tattenai the governor of the province Beyond the River and Shethar-bozenai and their associates came to them and spoke to them thus: "Who gave you a decree to build this house and to finish this structure?" ⁴ They also asked them this: "What are the names of the men who are building this building?" ⁵ But the eye of their God was on the elders of the Jews, and they did not stop them until the report should reach Darius and then an answer be returned by letter concerning it.

Tattenai's Letter to King Darius

⁶ This is a copy of the letter that Tattenai the governor of the province Beyond the River and Shethar-bozenai and his associates, the governors who were in the province Beyond the River, sent to Darius the king. ⁷ They sent him a report, in which was written as follows: "To Darius the king, all

> ### GETTING THE MESSAGE
>
> **The Behistun Inscription.** This 50-by-80-foot (15-by-24 m) inscription was carved into the face of a cliff in western Iran. Using various languages, it provides an autobiography of Darius's life, lineage, and victories as king of Persia.

peace. ⁸ Be it known to the king that we went to the province of Judah, to the house of the great God. It is being built with huge stones, and timber is laid in the walls. This work goes on diligently and prospers in their hands. ⁹ Then we asked those elders and spoke to them thus: 'Who gave you a decree to build this house and to finish this structure?' ¹⁰ We also asked them their names, for your information, that we might write down the names of their leaders. ¹¹ And this was their reply to us: 'We are the servants of the God of heaven and earth, and we are rebuilding the house that was built many years ago, which a great king of Israel built and finished. ¹² But because our fathers had angered the God of heaven, he gave them into the hand of Nebuchadnezzar king of Babylon, the Chaldean, who destroyed this house and carried away the people to Babylonia. ¹³ However, in the first year of Cyrus king of Babylon, Cyrus the king made a decree that this house of God should be

rebuilt. ¹⁴ And the gold and silver vessels of the house of God, which Nebuchadnezzar had taken out of the temple that was in Jerusalem and brought into the temple of Babylon, these Cyrus the king took out of the temple of Babylon, and they were delivered to one whose name was Sheshbazzar, whom he had made governor; ¹⁵ and he said to him, "Take these vessels, go and put them in the temple that is in Jerusalem, and let the house of God be rebuilt on its site." ¹⁶ Then this Sheshbazzar came and laid the foundations of the house of God that is in Jerusalem, and from that time until now it has been in building, and it is not yet finished.' ¹⁷ Therefore, if it seems good to the king, let search be made in the royal archives there in Babylon, to see whether a decree was issued by Cyrus the king for the rebuilding of this house of God in Jerusalem. And let the king send us his pleasure in this matter."

The Decree of Darius

6 Then Darius the king made a decree, and search was made in Babylonia, in the house of the archives where the documents were stored. ² And in Ecbatana, the citadel that is in the province of Media, a scroll was found on which this was written: "A record. ³ In the first year of Cyrus the king, Cyrus the king issued a decree: Concerning the house of God at Jerusalem, let the house be rebuilt, the place where sacrifices were offered, and let its foundations be retained. Its height shall be sixty cubits and its breadth sixty cubits, ⁴ with three layers of great stones and one layer of timber. Let the cost be paid from the royal treasury. ⁵ And also let the gold and silver vessels of the house of God, which Nebuchadnezzar took out of the temple that is in Jerusalem and brought to Babylon, be restored and brought back to the temple that is in Jerusalem, each to its place. You shall put them in the house of God."

⁶ "Now therefore, Tattenai, governor of the province Beyond the River, Shethar-bozenai, and your associates the governors who are in the province Beyond the River, keep away. ⁷ Let the work on this house of God alone. Let the governor of the Jews and the elders of the Jews rebuild this house of God on its site. ⁸ Moreover, I make a decree regarding what you shall do for these elders

of the Jews for the rebuilding of this house of God. The cost is to be paid to these men in full and without delay from the royal revenue, the tribute of the province from Beyond the River. ⁹ And whatever is needed — bulls, rams, or sheep for burnt offerings to the God of heaven, wheat, salt, wine, or oil, as the priests at Jerusalem require — let that be given to them day by day without fail, ¹⁰ that they may offer pleasing sacrifices to the God of heaven and pray for the life of the king and his sons. ¹¹ Also I make a decree that if anyone alters this edict, a beam shall be pulled out of his house, and he shall be impaled on it, and his house shall be made a dunghill. ¹² May the God who has caused his name to dwell there overthrow any king or people who shall put out a hand to alter this,

GETTING THE MESSAGE

How long did it take to rebuild the temple? The Jews returning from exile faced many obstacles in rebuilding the temple. The non-Jewish people now living in the land resisted their efforts, and the returned exiles often lacked the motivation to work. The temple took 20 years to complete, and it fell far short of the grandeur of Solomon's temple.

or to destroy this house of God that is in Jerusalem. I Darius make a decree; let it be done with all diligence."

The Temple Finished and Dedicated

¹³ Then, according to the word sent by Darius the king, Tattenai, the governor of the province Beyond the River, Shethar-bozenai, and their associates did with all diligence what Darius the king had ordered. ¹⁴ And the elders of the Jews built and prospered through the prophesying of Haggai the prophet and Zechariah the son of Iddo. They finished their building by decree of the God of Israel and by decree of Cyrus and Darius and Artaxerxes king of Persia; ¹⁵ and this house was finished on the third day of the month of Adar, in the sixth year of the reign of Darius the king.

¹⁶ And the people of Israel, the priests and the Levites, and the rest of the returned exiles, celebrated the dedication of this house of God with joy. ¹⁷ They offered at the dedication of this house of God 100 bulls, 200 rams, 400 lambs, and as a sin offering for all Israel 12 male goats, according to the number of the tribes of Israel. ¹⁸ And they set the priests in their divisions and the Levites in their divisions, for the service of God at Jerusalem, as it is written in the Book of Moses.

Passover Celebrated

¹⁹ On the fourteenth day of the first month, the returned exiles kept the Passover. ²⁰ For the priests and the Levites had

PROFILE
EZRA

Ezra is described as "a man learned in matters of the commandments of the LORD and his statutes for Israel" (7:11). Both a priest and scribe, Ezra was commissioned by King Artaxerxes of Persia to establish the Law of Moses in Jerusalem. The king also gave him money from the royal treasury to beautify the temple. Arriving in Jerusalem 57 years after the temple was rebuilt, Ezra appointed judges to administer the law. Seventy years of Babylonian exile had had a negative effect on the people's relationship with the Lord. The Lord enabled Ezra to guide Israel as they sought once again to live according to the law.

KEY REFERENCE: EZRA 7:1-6

purified themselves together; all of them were clean. So they slaughtered the Passover lamb for all the returned exiles, for their fellow priests, and for themselves. ²¹ It was eaten by the people of Israel who had returned from exile, and also by every one who had joined them and separated himself from the uncleanness of the peoples of the land to worship the LORD, the God of Israel. ²² And they kept the Feast of Unleavened Bread seven days with joy, for the LORD had made them joyful and had turned the heart of the king of Assyria to them, so that he aided them in the work of the house of God, the God of Israel.

Ezra Sent to Teach the People

7 Now after this, in the reign of Artaxerxes king of Persia, Ezra the son of Seraiah, son of Azariah, son of Hilkiah, ² son of Shallum, son of Zadok, son of Ahitub, ³ son of Amariah, son of Azariah, son of Meraioth, ⁴ son of Zerahiah, son of Uzzi, son of Bukki, ⁵ son of Abishua, son of Phinehas, son of Eleazar, son of Aaron the chief priest— ⁶ this Ezra went up from Babylonia. He was a scribe skilled in the Law of Moses that the LORD, the God of Israel, had given, and the king granted him all that he asked, for the hand of the LORD his God was on him.

⁷ And there went up also to Jerusalem, in the seventh year of Artaxerxes the king, some of the people of Israel, and some of the priests and Levites, the singers and gate-keepers, and the temple servants. ⁸ And Ezra

How long was the journey from Babylon to Jerusalem? It took Ezra and the caravan he was traveling with four months to traverse the nearly 900 miles (1,448 km) from Babylon to Jerusalem. An army could have traveled much faster, but Ezra's entourage probably included children and elderly people.

came to Jerusalem in the fifth month, which was in the seventh year of the king. ⁹ For on the first day of the first month he began to go up from Babylonia, and on the first day of the fifth month he came to Jerusalem, for the good hand of his God was on him. ¹⁰ For Ezra had set his heart to study the Law of the LORD, and to do it and to teach his statutes and rules in Israel.

¹¹ This is a copy of the letter that King Artaxerxes gave to Ezra the priest, the scribe, a man learned in matters of the commandments of the LORD and his statutes for Israel: ¹² "Artaxerxes, king of kings, to Ezra the priest, the scribe of the Law of the God of heaven. Peace. And now ¹³ I make a decree that anyone of the people of Israel or their priests or Levites in my kingdom, who freely offers to go to Jerusalem, may go with you. ¹⁴ For you are sent by the king and his seven counselors to make inquiries about Judah and Jerusalem according to the Law of your

God, which is in your hand, ¹⁵ and also to carry the silver and gold that the king and his counselors have freely offered to the God of Israel, whose dwelling is in Jerusalem, ¹⁶ with all the silver and gold that you shall find in the whole province of Babylonia, and with the freewill offerings of the people and the priests, vowed willingly for the house of their God that is in Jerusalem. ¹⁷ With this money, then, you shall with all diligence buy bulls, rams, and lambs, with their grain offerings and their drink offerings, and you shall offer them on the altar of the house of your God that is in Jerusalem. ¹⁸ Whatever seems good to you and your brothers to do with the rest of the silver and gold, you may do, according to the will of your God. ¹⁹ The vessels that have been given you for the service of the house of your God, you shall deliver before the God of Jerusalem. ²⁰ And whatever else is required for the house of your God, which it falls to you to provide, you may provide it out of the king's treasury.

²¹ "And I, Artaxerxes the king, make a decree to all the treasurers in the province Beyond the River: Whatever Ezra the priest, the scribe of the Law of the God of heaven, requires of you, let it be done with all diligence, ²² up to 100 talents of silver, 100 cors of wheat, 100 baths of wine, 100 baths of oil, and salt without prescribing how much. ²³ Whatever is decreed by the God of heaven, let it be done in full for the house of the God of heaven, lest his wrath be against the realm of the king and his sons. ²⁴ We also notify you that it shall not be lawful to impose tribute, custom, or toll on anyone of the priests, the Levites, the singers, the doorkeepers, the temple servants, or other servants of this house of God.

²⁵ "And you, Ezra, according to the wisdom of your God that is in your hand, appoint magistrates and judges who may judge all the people in the province Beyond the River, all such as know the laws of your God. And those who do not know them, you shall teach. ²⁶ Whoever will not obey the law of your God and the law of the king, let judgment be strictly executed on him, whether for death or for banishment or for confiscation of his goods or for imprisonment."

²⁷ Blessed be the LORD, the God of our fathers, who put such a thing as this into the heart of the king, to beautify the house

of the LORD that is in Jerusalem, [28] and who extended to me his steadfast love before the king and his counselors, and before all the king's mighty officers. I took courage, for the hand of the LORD my God was on me, and I gathered leading men from Israel to go up with me.

Genealogy of Those Who Returned with Ezra

8 These are the heads of their fathers' houses, and this is the genealogy of those who went up with me from Babylonia, in the reign of Artaxerxes the king: [2] Of the sons of Phinehas, Gershom. Of the sons of Ithamar, Daniel. Of the sons of David, Hattush. [3] Of the sons of Shecaniah, who was of the sons of Parosh, Zechariah, with whom were registered 150 men. [4] Of the sons of Pahath-moab, Eliehoenai the son of Zerahiah, and with him 200 men. [5] Of the sons of Zattu, Shecaniah the son of Jahaziel, and with him 300 men. [6] Of the sons of Adin, Ebed the son of Jonathan, and with him 50 men. [7] Of the sons of Elam, Jeshaiah the son of Athaliah, and with him 70 men. [8] Of the sons of Shephatiah, Zebadiah the son of Michael, and with him 80 men. [9] Of the sons of Joab, Obadiah the son of Jehiel, and with him 218 men. [10] Of the sons of Bani, Shelomith the son of Josiphiah, and with him 160 men. [11] Of the sons of Bebai, Zechariah, the son of Bebai, and with him 28 men. [12] Of the sons of Azgad, Johanan the son of Hakkatan, and with him 110 men. [13] Of the sons of Adonikam, those who came later, their names being Eliphelet, Jeuel, and Shemaiah, and with them 60 men. [14] Of the sons of Bigvai, Uthai and Zaccur, and with them 70 men.

Ezra Sends for Levites

[15] I gathered them to the river that runs to Ahava, and there we camped three days. As I reviewed the people and the priests, I found there none of the sons of Levi. [16] Then I sent for Eliezer, Ariel, Shemaiah, Elnathan, Jarib, Elnathan, Nathan, Zechariah, and Meshullam, leading men, and for Joiarib and Elnathan, who were men of insight, [17] and sent them to Iddo, the leading man at the place Casiphia, telling them what to say to Iddo and his brothers and the temple servants at the place Casiphia, namely, to send us ministers for the house of our God. [18] And by the good hand of our God on us, they brought us a man of discretion, of the sons of Mahli the son of Levi, son of Israel, namely Sherebiah with his sons and kinsmen, 18; [19] also Hashabiah, and with him Jeshaiah of the sons of Merari, with his kinsmen and their sons, 20; [20] besides 220 of the temple servants, whom David and his officials had set apart to attend the Levites. These were all mentioned by name.

Fasting and Prayer for Protection

[21] Then I proclaimed a fast there, at the river Ahava, that we might humble ourselves before our God, to seek from him a safe journey for ourselves, our children, and all our goods. [22] For I was ashamed to ask the king for a band of soldiers and horsemen to protect us against the enemy on our way, since we had told the king, "The hand of our God is for good on all who seek him, and the power of his wrath is against all who forsake him." [23] So we fasted and implored our God for this, and he listened to our entreaty.

Priests to Guard Offerings

[24] Then I set apart twelve of the leading priests: Sherebiah, Hashabiah, and ten of their kinsmen with them. [25] And I weighed out to them the silver and the gold and the vessels, the offering for the house of our God that the king and his counselors and his lords and all Israel there present had offered. [26] I weighed out into their hand 650 talents of silver, and silver vessels worth 200 talents, and 100 talents of gold, [27] 20 bowls of gold worth 1,000 darics, and two vessels of fine bright bronze as precious as gold. [28] And I said to them, "You are holy to the LORD, and the vessels are holy, and the silver and the gold are a freewill offering to the LORD, the God of your fathers. [29] Guard them and keep them until you weigh them before the chief priests and the Levites and the heads of fathers' houses in Israel at Jerusalem, within the chambers of the house of the LORD." [30] So the priests and the Levites took over the weight of the silver and the gold and the vessels, to bring them to Jerusalem, to the house of our God.

[31] Then we departed from the river Ahava on the twelfth day of the first month, to go to Jerusalem. The hand of our God was on us, and he delivered us from the hand of the enemy and from ambushes by the way. [32] We

came to Jerusalem, and there we remained three days. [33] On the fourth day, within the house of our God, the silver and the gold and the vessels were weighed into the hands of Meremoth the priest, son of Uriah, and with him was Eleazar the son of Phinehas, and with them were the Levites, Jozabad the son of Jeshua and Noadiah the son of Binnui. [34] The whole was counted and weighed, and the weight of everything was recorded.

[35] At that time those who had come from captivity, the returned exiles, offered burnt offerings to the God of Israel, twelve bulls for all Israel, ninety-six rams, seventy-seven lambs, and as a sin offering twelve male goats. All this was a burnt offering to the LORD. [36] They also delivered the king's commissions to the king's satraps[1] and to the governors of the province Beyond the River, and they aided the people and the house of God.

Ezra Prays About Intermarriage

9 After these things had been done, the officials approached me and said, "The people of Israel and the priests and the Levites have not separated themselves from the peoples of the lands with their abominations, from the Canaanites, the Hittites, the Perizzites, the Jebusites, the Ammonites, the Moabites, the Egyptians, and the Amorites. [2] For they have taken some of their daughters to be wives for themselves and for their sons, so that the holy race has mixed itself with the peoples of the lands. And in this faithlessness the hand of the officials and chief men has been foremost." [3] As soon as I heard this, I tore my garment and my cloak and pulled hair from my head and beard and sat appalled. [4] Then all who trembled at the words of the God of Israel, because of the faithlessness of the returned exiles, gathered around me while I sat appalled until the evening sacrifice. [5] And at the evening sacrifice I rose from my fasting, with my garment and my cloak torn, and fell upon my knees and spread out my hands to the LORD my God, [6] saying:

"O my God, I am ashamed and blush to lift my face to you, my God, for our iniquities have risen higher than our heads, and our guilt has mounted up to the heavens. [7] From the days of our fathers to this day we have been in great guilt. And for our iniquities

we, our kings, and our priests have been given into the hand of the kings of the lands, to the sword, to captivity, to plundering, and to utter shame, as it is today. [8] But now for a brief moment favor has been shown by the LORD our God, to leave us a remnant and to give us a secure hold within his holy place, that our God may brighten our eyes and grant us a little reviving in our slavery. [9] For we are slaves. Yet our God has not forsaken us in our slavery, but has extended to us his steadfast love before the kings of Persia, to grant us some reviving to set up the house of our God, to repair its ruins, and to give us protection in Judea and Jerusalem.

[10] "And now, O our God, what shall we say after this? For we have forsaken your commandments, [11] which you commanded by your servants the prophets, saying, 'The land that you are entering, to take possession of it, is a land impure with the impurity of the peoples of the lands, with their abominations that have filled it from end to end with their uncleanness. [12] Therefore do not give your daughters to their sons, neither take their daughters for your sons, and never seek their peace or prosperity, that you may be strong and eat the good of the land and leave it for an inheritance to your children forever.' [13] And after all that has come upon us for our evil deeds and for our great guilt, seeing that you, our God, have punished us less than our iniquities deserved and have given us such a remnant as this, [14] shall we break your commandments again and intermarry with the peoples who practice these abominations? Would you not be angry with us until you consumed us, so that there should be no remnant, nor any to escape? [15] O LORD, the God of Israel, you are just, for we are left a remnant that has escaped, as it is today. Behold, we are before you in our guilt, for none can stand before you because of this."

The People Confess Their Sin

10 While Ezra prayed and made confession, weeping and casting himself down before the house of God, a very great assembly of men, women, and children, gathered to him out of Israel, for the people wept bitterly. [2] And Shecaniah the son of Jehiel, of the sons of Elam, addressed Ezra: "We have broken faith with our God and

---

[1] A *satrap* was a Persian official

have married foreign women from the peoples of the land, but even now there is hope for Israel in spite of this. ³ Therefore let us make a covenant with our God to put away all these wives and their children, according to the counsel of my lord and of those who tremble at the commandment of our God, and let it be done according to the Law. ⁴ Arise, for it is your task, and we are with you; be strong and do it." ⁵ Then Ezra arose and made the leading priests and Levites and all Israel take an oath that they would do as had been said. So they took the oath.

⁶ Then Ezra withdrew from before the house of God and went to the chamber of Jehohanan the son of Eliashib, where he spent the night, neither eating bread nor drinking water, for he was mourning over the faithlessness of the exiles. ⁷ And a proclamation was made throughout Judah and Jerusalem to all the returned exiles that they should assemble at Jerusalem, ⁸ and that if anyone did not come within three days, by order of the officials and the elders all his property should be forfeited, and he himself banned from the congregation of the exiles.

⁹ Then all the men of Judah and Benjamin assembled at Jerusalem within the three days. It was the ninth month, on the twentieth day of the month. And all the people sat in the open square before the house of God, trembling because of this matter and because of the heavy rain. ¹⁰ And Ezra the priest stood up and said to them, "You have broken faith and married foreign women, and so increased the guilt of Israel. ¹¹ Now then make confession to the LORD, the God of your fathers and do his will. Separate yourselves from the peoples of the land and from the foreign wives." ¹² Then all the assembly answered with a loud voice, "It is so; we must do as you have said. ¹³ But the people are many, and it is a time of heavy rain; we cannot stand in the open. Nor is this a task for one day or for two, for we have greatly transgressed in this matter. ¹⁴ Let our officials stand for the whole assembly. Let all in our cities who have taken foreign wives come at appointed times, and with them the elders and judges of every city, until the fierce wrath of our God over this matter is turned away from us." ¹⁵ Only Jonathan the son of Asahel and

Jahzeiah the son of Tikvah opposed this, and Meshullam and Shabbethai the Levite supported them.

¹⁶ Then the returned exiles did so. Ezra the priest selected men, heads of fathers' houses, according to their fathers' houses, each of them designated by name. On the first day of the tenth month they sat down to examine the matter; ¹⁷ and by the first day of the first month they had come to the end of all the men who had married foreign women.

Those Guilty of Intermarriage

¹⁸ Now there were found some of the sons of the priests who had married foreign women: Maaseiah, Eliezer, Jarib, and Gedaliah, some of the sons of Jeshua the son of Jozadak and his brothers. ¹⁹ They pledged themselves to put away their wives, and their

GETTING THE MESSAGE

An unscheduled assembly in Jerusalem. Three times each year, all the people of Israel were to gather in Jerusalem: Passover, Pentecost, and the Feast of Tabernacles. The unscheduled meeting in 10:9 took place in early winter, when it would have been cold and rainy in Jerusalem.

guilt offering was a ram of the flock for their guilt. ²⁰ Of the sons of Immer: Hanani and Zebadiah. ²¹ Of the sons of Harim: Maaseiah, Elijah, Shemaiah, Jehiel, and Uzziah. ²² Of the sons of Pashhur: Elioenai, Maaseiah, Ishmael, Nethanel, Jozabad, and Elasah.

²³ Of the Levites: Jozabad, Shimei, Kelaiah (that is, Kelita), Pethahiah, Judah, and Eliezer. ²⁴ Of the singers: Eliashib. Of the gatekeepers: Shallum, Telem, and Uri.

²⁵ And of Israel: of the sons of Parosh: Ramiah, Izziah, Malchijah, Mijamin, Eleazar, Hashabiah, and Benaiah. ²⁶ Of the sons of Elam: Mattaniah, Zechariah, Jehiel, Abdi, Jeremoth, and Elijah. ²⁷ Of the sons of Zattu: Elioenai, Eliashib, Mattaniah, Jeremoth, Zabad, and Aziza. ²⁸ Of the sons of Bebai were Jehohanan, Hananiah, Zabbai, and Athlai. ²⁹ Of the sons of Bani were Meshullam, Malluch, Adaiah, Jashub, Sheal, and Jeremoth. ³⁰ Of the sons of Pahath-moab: Adna, Chelal, Benaiah,

Maaseiah, Mattaniah, Bezalel, Binnui, and Manasseh. ³¹Of the sons of Harim: Eliezer, Isshijah, Malchijah, Shemaiah, Shimeon, ³²Benjamin, Malluch, and Shemariah. ³³Of the sons of Hashum: Mattenai, Mattattah, Zabad, Eliphelet, Jeremai, Manasseh, and Shimei. ³⁴Of the sons of Bani: Maadai, Amram, Uel, ³⁵Benaiah, Bedeiah, Cheluhi, ³⁶Vaniah, Meremoth, Eliashib, ³⁷Mattaniah, Mattenai, Jaasu. ³⁸Of the sons of Binnui: Shimei, ³⁹Shelemiah, Nathan, Adaiah, ⁴⁰Machnadebai, Shashai, Sharai, ⁴¹Azarel, Shelemiah, Shemariah, ⁴²Shallum, Amariah, and Joseph. ⁴³Of the sons of Nebo: Jeiel, Mattithiah, Zabad, Zebina, Jaddai, Joel, and Benaiah. ⁴⁴All these had married foreign women, and some of the women had even borne children.

INTRODUCTION TO NEHEMIAH

516 B.C.	458 B.C.	445 B.C.
Temple rebuilt	Ezra arrives in Jerusalem	Nehemiah rebuilds walls

AUTHOR AND DATE

Nehemiah is the central figure in the book. It contains some of his own records, but he is not the author of the entire book. The same author probably wrote Nehemiah and portions of Ezra. Nehemiah arrived in Jerusalem in 445 B.C., 13 years after Ezra arrived. He returned for a further visit sometime between 433 and 423 B.C. He may have made several journeys between Persian capitals and Jerusalem in this period of 20 years.

THEME

The theme of Nehemiah is the Lord's protection of his people and their need to be faithful in worship and in keeping the Mosaic law.

PURPOSE AND BACKGROUND

The basic purpose and background of Nehemiah are the same as that for Ezra (see Introduction to Ezra). Ezra, "a scribe skilled in the Law of Moses" (Ezra 7:6), called the returning exiles back to covenant loyalty and obedience to the law. Nehemiah rebuilt the city walls so that the community could be protected from enemies who might take advantage of them.

KEY THEMES

1. The Lord hears prayer (1:4–6).

2. The Lord works providentially, especially through powerful rulers, to bring about his greater purposes (e.g., 2:8).

3. The Lord protects his people. Because of this, they need not be afraid (4:14).

4. The Lord is merciful and faithful to his promises despite his people's ongoing sin (9:32–35).

5. Worship is at the center of the life of God's people. It includes the willing, joyful giving of resources (10:32–39).

6. God's people need to be on their guard against their own moral weakness (ch. 13).

OUTLINE

NEHEMIAH

Report from Jerusalem

1 The words of Nehemiah the son of Hacaliah.

Now it happened in the month of Chislev, in the twentieth year, as I was in Susa the citadel, ² that Hanani, one of my brothers, came with certain men from Judah. And I asked them concerning the Jews who escaped, who had survived the exile, and concerning Jerusalem. ³ And they said to me, "The remnant there in the province who had survived the exile is in great trouble and shame. The wall of Jerusalem is broken down, and its gates are destroyed by fire."

Nehemiah's Prayer

⁴ As soon as I heard these words I sat down and wept and mourned for days, and I continued fasting and praying before the God of heaven. ⁵ And I said, "O LORD God of heaven, the great and awesome God who keeps covenant and steadfast love with those who love him and keep his commandments, ⁶ let your ear be attentive and your eyes open, to hear the prayer of your servant that I now pray before you day and night for the people of Israel your servants, confessing the sins of the people of Israel, which we have sinned against you. Even I and my father's house have sinned. ⁷ We have acted very corruptly against you and have not kept the commandments, the statutes, and the rules that you commanded your servant Moses. ⁸ Remember the word that you commanded your servant Moses, saying, 'If you are unfaithful, I will scatter you among the peoples, ⁹ but if you return to me and keep my commandments and do them, though your outcasts are in the uttermost parts of heaven, from there I will gather them and bring them to the place that I have chosen, to make my name dwell there.' ¹⁰ They are your servants and your people, whom you have redeemed by your great power and by your strong hand. ¹¹ O Lord, let your ear be attentive to the prayer of your servant, and to the prayer of your servants who delight to fear your name, and give success to your servant today, and grant him mercy in the sight of this man."

Now I was cupbearer to the king.

Nehemiah Sent to Judah

2 In the month of Nisan, in the twentieth year of King Artaxerxes, when wine was before him, I took up the wine and gave it to the king. Now I had not been sad in his presence. ² And the king said to me, "Why is your face sad, seeing you are not sick? This is nothing but sadness of the heart." Then I was very much afraid. ³ I said to the king,

"Let the king live forever! Why should not my face be sad, when the city, the place of my fathers' graves, lies in ruins, and its gates have been destroyed by fire?" ⁴ Then the king said to me, "What are you requesting?" So I prayed to the God of heaven. ⁵ And I said to the king, "If it pleases the king, and if your servant has found favor in your sight, that you send me to Judah, to the city of my fathers' graves, that I may rebuild it." ⁶ And the king said to me (the queen sitting beside him), "How long will you be gone, and when will you return?" So it pleased the king to send me when I had given him a time. ⁷ And I said to the king, "If it pleases the king, let letters be given me to the governors of the province Beyond the River, that they may let me pass through until I come to Judah, ⁸ and a letter to Asaph, the keeper of the king's forest, that he may give me timber to make beams for the gates of the fortress of the temple, and for the wall of the city, and for the house that I shall occupy." And the king granted me what I asked, for the good hand of my God was upon me.

Nehemiah Inspects Jerusalem's Walls

⁹ Then I came to the governors of the province Beyond the River and gave them the king's letters. Now the king had sent with me officers of the army and horsemen. ¹⁰ But

PROFILE
NEHEMIAH

As a Jewish captive in Babylon, Nehemiah held the distinguished position of cupbearer to King Artaxerxes. He was devastated to hear that the Jews who had returned to Jerusalem were in "great trouble and shame" (1:3). He expressed his concern to the king, and the king allowed him to return to Jerusalem to rebuild the city's walls. Many of the non-Jewish people in Judah opposed the rebuilding effort, and the returned exiles soon became disheartened. Nehemiah encouraged the men, saying, "Do not be afraid of them. Remember the Lord, who is great and awesome, and fight for your brothers, your sons, your daughters, your wives, and your homes" (4:14). Under his leadership, the walls were rebuilt despite the difficult circumstances. As governor of Judah, Nehemiah was used mightily by God to bring the Jews back into a life of covenant faithfulness.

KEY REFERENCE: NEHEMIAH 2:17–18

when Sanballat the Horonite and Tobiah the Ammonite servant heard this, it displeased them greatly that someone had come to seek the welfare of the people of Israel.

¹¹ So I went to Jerusalem and was there three days. ¹² Then I arose in the night, I and a few men with me. And I told no one what my God had put into my heart to do for Jerusalem. There was no animal with me but the one on which I rode. ¹³ I went out by night by the Valley Gate to the Dragon Spring and to the Dung Gate, and I inspected the

walls of Jerusalem that were broken down and its gates that had been destroyed by fire. ¹⁴ Then I went on to the Fountain Gate and to the King's Pool, but there was no room for the animal that was under me to pass. ¹⁵ Then I went up in the night by the valley and inspected the wall, and I turned back and entered by the Valley Gate, and so returned. ¹⁶ And the officials did not know where I had gone or what I was doing, and I had not yet told the Jews, the priests, the nobles, the officials, and the rest who were to do the work.

¹⁷ Then I said to them, "You see the trouble we are in, how Jerusalem lies in ruins with its gates burned. Come, let us build the wall of Jerusalem, that we may no longer suffer derision." ¹⁸ And I told them of the hand of my God that had been upon me for good,

GETTING THE MESSAGE

The fortress of the temple (2:8) provided extra defense for the temple area, since this section of Jerusalem was very vulnerable to attack. Many other governors of Jerusalem after Nehemiah built fortresses here, including Herod the Great, whose famous Antonia Fortress can be visited today.

and also of the words that the king had spoken to me. And they said, "Let us rise up and build." So they strengthened their hands for the good work. ¹⁹ But when Sanballat the Horonite and Tobiah the Ammonite servant and Geshem the Arab heard of it, they jeered at us and despised us and said, "What is this thing that you are doing? Are you rebelling against the king?" ²⁰ Then I replied to them, "The God of heaven will make us prosper, and we his servants will arise and build, but you have no portion or right or claim in Jerusalem."

Rebuilding the Wall

3 Then Eliashib the high priest rose up with his brothers the priests, and they built the Sheep Gate. They consecrated it and set its doors. They consecrated it as far as the Tower of the Hundred, as far as the Tower of Hananel. ² And next to him the men of Jericho built. And next to them Zaccur the son of Imri built.

3 The sons of Hassenaah built the Fish Gate. They laid its beams and set its doors, its bolts, and its bars. **4** And next to them Meremoth the son of Uriah, son of Hakkoz repaired. And next to them Meshullam the son of Berechiah, son of Meshezabel repaired. And next to them Zadok the son of Baana repaired. **5** And next to them the Tekoites repaired, but their nobles would not stoop to serve their Lord.

6 Joiada the son of Paseah and Meshullam the son of Besodeiah repaired the Gate of Yeshanah. They laid its beams and set its doors, its bolts, and its bars. **7** And next to them repaired Melatiah the Gibeonite and Jadon the Meronothite, the men of Gibeon and of Mizpah, the seat of the governor of the province Beyond the River. **8** Next to them Uzziel the son of Harhaiah, goldsmiths, repaired. Next to him Hananiah, one of the perfumers, repaired, and they restored Jerusalem as far as the Broad Wall. **9** Next to them Rephaiah the son of Hur, ruler of half the district of Jerusalem, repaired. **10** Next to them Jedaiah the son of Harumaph repaired opposite his house. And next to him Hattush the son of Hashabneiah repaired. **11** Malchijah the son of Harim and Hasshub the son of Pahath-moab repaired another section and the Tower of the Ovens. **12** Next to him Shallum the son of Hallohesh, ruler of half the district of Jerusalem, repaired, he and his daughters.

13 Hanun and the inhabitants of Zanoah repaired the Valley Gate. They rebuilt it and set its doors, its bolts, and its bars, and repaired a thousand cubits of the wall, as far as the Dung Gate.

14 Malchijah the son of Rechab, ruler of the district of Beth-haccherem, repaired the Dung Gate. He rebuilt it and set its doors, its bolts, and its bars.

15 And Shallum the son of Col-hozeh, ruler of the district of Mizpah, repaired the Fountain Gate. He rebuilt it and covered it and set its doors, its bolts, and its bars. And he built the wall of the Pool of Shelah of the king's garden, as far as the stairs that go down from the city of David. **16** After him Nehemiah the son of Azbuk, ruler of half the district of Beth-zur, repaired to a point opposite the tombs of David, as far as the artificial pool, and as far as the house of the mighty men. **17** After him the Levites repaired: Rehum the son of Bani. Next to him Hashabiah, ruler of half the district of Keilah, repaired for his district. **18** After him their brothers repaired: Bavvai the son of Henadad, ruler of half the district of Keilah. **19** Next to him Ezer the son of Jeshua, ruler of Mizpah, repaired another section opposite the ascent to the armory at the buttress.[1] **20** After him Baruch the son of Zabbai repaired another section from the buttress to the door of the house of Eliashib the high priest. **21** After him Meremoth the son of Uriah, son of Hakkoz repaired another section from the door of the house of Eliashib to the end of the house of Eliashib. **22** After him the priests, the men of the surrounding area, repaired. **23** After them Benjamin and Hasshub repaired opposite their house.

> ### GETTING THE MESSAGE

What was the Ophel? The Ophel (3:26) was a hill in Jerusalem between the Kidron and Central Valleys. It was northeast of the older City of David and just south of the Temple Mount. The oldest part of Jerusalem was built long before David captured the city from the Jebusites.

After them Azariah the son of Maaseiah, son of Ananiah repaired beside his own house. **24** After him Binnui the son of Henadad repaired another section, from the house of Azariah to the buttress **25** and to the corner. Palal the son of Uzai repaired opposite the buttress and the tower projecting from the upper house of the king at the court of the guard. After him Pedaiah the son of Parosh **26** and the temple servants living on Ophel repaired to a point opposite the Water Gate on the east and the projecting tower. **27** After him the Tekoites repaired another section opposite the great projecting tower as far as the wall of Ophel.

28 Above the Horse Gate the priests repaired, each one opposite his own house. **29** After them Zadok the son of Immer repaired opposite his own house. After him Shemaiah the son of Shecaniah, the keeper of the East Gate, repaired. **30** After him Hananiah

[1] Or corner; also 3:20, 24, 25

the son of Shelemiah and Hanun the sixth son of Zalaph repaired another section. After him Meshullam the son of Berechiah repaired opposite his chamber. ³¹ After him Malchijah, one of the goldsmiths, repaired as far as the house of the temple servants and of the merchants, opposite the Muster Gate, and to the upper chamber of the corner. ³² And between the upper chamber of the corner and the Sheep Gate the goldsmiths and the merchants repaired.

Opposition to the Work

4 Now when Sanballat heard that we were building the wall, he was angry and greatly enraged, and he jeered at the Jews. ² And he said in the presence of his brothers and of the army of Samaria, "What are these feeble Jews doing? Will they restore

Why did so many local people oppose Nehemiah? After the exile, people who had been living in Judah for over a hundred years saw it as belonging to them and not to the returning Jews. Nehemiah had the blessing of King Artaxerxes to rebuild the walls, but the king was in Persia, more than 1,100 miles (1,770 km) away. This made Nehemiah's enemies bolder in their opposition to him.

it for themselves? Will they sacrifice? Will they finish up in a day? Will they revive the stones out of the heaps of rubbish, and burned ones at that?" ³ Tobiah the Ammonite was beside him, and he said, "Yes, what they are building—if a fox goes up on it he will break down their stone wall!" ⁴ Hear, O our God, for we are despised. Turn back their taunt on their own heads and give them up to be plundered in a land where they are captives. ⁵ Do not cover their guilt, and let not their sin be blotted out from your sight, for they have provoked you to anger in the presence of the builders.

⁶ So we built the wall. And all the wall was joined together to half its height, for the people had a mind to work.

⁷ But when Sanballat and Tobiah and the Arabs and the Ammonites and the Ashdodites heard that the repairing of the walls of Jerusalem was going forward and

that the breaches were beginning to be closed, they were very angry. ⁸ And they all plotted together to come and fight against Jerusalem and to cause confusion in it. ⁹ And we prayed to our God and set a guard as a protection against them day and night.

¹⁰ In Judah it was said, "The strength of those who bear the burdens is failing. There is too much rubble. By ourselves we will not be able to rebuild the wall." ¹¹ And our enemies said, "They will not know or see till we come among them and kill them and stop the work." ¹² At that time the Jews who lived near them came from all directions and said to us ten times, "You must return to us." ¹³ So in the lowest parts of the space behind the wall, in open places, I stationed the people by their clans, with their swords, their spears, and their bows. ¹⁴ And I looked and arose and said to the nobles and to the officials and to the rest of the people, "Do not be afraid of them. Remember the Lord, who is great and awesome, and fight for your brothers, your sons, your daughters, your wives, and your homes."

The Work Resumes

¹⁵ When our enemies heard that it was known to us and that God had frustrated their plan, we all returned to the wall, each to his work. ¹⁶ From that day on, half of my servants worked on construction, and half held the spears, shields, bows, and coats of mail. And the leaders stood behind the whole house of Judah, ¹⁷ who were building on the wall. Those who carried burdens were loaded in such a way that each labored on the work with one hand and held his weapon with the other. ¹⁸ And each of the builders had his sword strapped at his side while he built. The man who sounded the trumpet was beside me. ¹⁹ And I said to the nobles and to the officials and to the rest of the people, "The work is great and widely spread, and we are separated on the wall, far from one another. ²⁰ In the place where you hear the sound of the trumpet, rally to us there. Our God will fight for us."

²¹ So we labored at the work, and half of them held the spears from the break of dawn until the stars came out. ²² I also said to the people at that time, "Let every man and his servant pass the night within Jerusalem, that they may be a guard for us by night and may labor by day." ²³ So neither I nor

my brothers nor my servants nor the men of the guard who followed me, none of us took off our clothes; each kept his weapon at his right hand.

Nehemiah Stops Oppression of the Poor

5 Now there arose a great outcry of the people and of their wives against their Jewish brothers. ²For there were those who said, "With our sons and our daughters, we are many. So let us get grain, that we may eat and keep alive." ³There were also those who said, "We are mortgaging our fields, our vineyards, and our houses to get grain because of the famine." ⁴And there were those who said, "We have borrowed money for the king's tax on our fields and our vineyards. ⁵Now our flesh is as the flesh of our brothers, our children are as their children. Yet we are forcing our sons and our daughters to be slaves, and some of our daughters have already been enslaved, but it is not in our power to help it, for other men have our fields and our vineyards."

⁶I was very angry when I heard their outcry and these words. ⁷I took counsel with myself, and I brought charges against the nobles and the officials. I said to them, "You are exacting interest, each from his brother." And I held a great assembly against them ⁸and said to them, "We, as far as we are able, have bought back our Jewish brothers who have been sold to the nations, but you even sell your brothers that they may be sold to us!" They were silent and could not find a word to say. ⁹So I said, "The thing that you are doing is not good. Ought you not to walk in the fear of our God to prevent the taunts of the nations our enemies? ¹⁰Moreover, I and my brothers and my servants are lending them money and grain. Let us abandon this exacting of interest. ¹¹Return to them this very day their fields, their vineyards, their olive orchards, and their houses, and the percentage of money, grain, wine, and oil that you have been exacting from them." ¹²Then they said, "We will restore these and require nothing from them. We will do as you say." And I called the priests and made them swear to do as they had promised. ¹³I also shook out the fold of my garment and said, "So may God shake out every man from his house and from his labor who does not keep this promise. So may he be shaken out and emptied." And all the assembly said "Amen" and praised the LORD. And the people did as they had promised.

Nehemiah's Generosity

¹⁴Moreover, from the time that I was appointed to be their governor in the land of Judah, from the twentieth year to the thirty-second year of Artaxerxes the king, twelve years, neither I nor my brothers ate the food allowance of the governor. ¹⁵The former governors who were before me laid heavy burdens on the people and took from them for their daily ration forty shekels of silver. Even their servants lorded it over the people. But I did not do so, because of the fear of God. ¹⁶I also persevered in the work on this wall, and we acquired no land, and all my servants were gathered there for the work. ¹⁷Moreover, there were at my table

GETTING THE MESSAGE

The returned exiles would sometimes **mortgage their property** (5:3) to raise money for the heavy taxes imposed on them. This mortgaging would have involved temporarily forfeiting the use of one's property and any fruit it produced to wealthier people who could afford to pay the taxes. The Mosaic law forbade such practices, and Nehemiah was quick to oppose it.

150 men, Jews and officials, besides those who came to us from the nations that were around us. ¹⁸Now what was prepared at my expense for each day was one ox and six choice sheep and birds, and every ten days all kinds of wine in abundance. Yet for all this I did not demand the food allowance of the governor, because the service was too heavy on this people. ¹⁹Remember for my good, O my God, all that I have done for this people.

Conspiracy Against Nehemiah

6 Now when Sanballat and Tobiah and Geshem the Arab and the rest of our enemies heard that I had built the wall and that there was no breach left in it (although up to that time I had not set up the doors in the gates), ²Sanballat and Geshem sent to me, saying, "Come and let us meet together at Hakkephirim in the plain of Ono." But

they intended to do me harm. **3** And I sent messengers to them, saying, "I am doing a great work and I cannot come down. Why should the work stop while I leave it and come down to you?" **4** And they sent to me four times in this way, and I answered them in the same manner. **5** In the same way Sanballat for the fifth time sent his servant to me with an open letter in his hand. **6** In it was written, "It is reported among the nations, and Geshem also says it, that you and the Jews intend to rebel; that is why you are building the wall. And according to these reports you wish to become their king. **7** And you have also set up prophets to proclaim concerning you in Jerusalem, 'There is a king in Judah.' And now the king will hear of these reports. So now come and let us take counsel together." **8** Then I sent to him, saying, "No such things as you say have

GETTING THE MESSAGE

An **open letter** (6:5) was one that was read to the entire public, not just the individual to whom it was addressed. By publicly claiming that Artaxerxes would be angry about the rebuilding of the walls, Sanballat was hoping to frighten the laborers into ceasing their work.

been done, for you are inventing them out of your own mind." **9** For they all wanted to frighten us, thinking, "Their hands will drop from the work, and it will not be done." But now, O God, strengthen my hands.

10 Now when I went into the house of Shemaiah the son of Delaiah, son of Mehetabel, who was confined to his home, he said, "Let us meet together in the house of God, within the temple. Let us close the doors of the temple, for they are coming to kill you. They are coming to kill you by night." **11** But I said, "Should such a man as I run away? And what man such as I could go into the temple and live? I will not go in." **12** And I understood and saw that God had not sent him, but he had pronounced the prophecy against me because Tobiah and Sanballat had hired him. **13** For this purpose he was hired, that I should be afraid and act in this way and sin, and so they could give me a bad name in order to taunt me.

14 Remember Tobiah and Sanballat, O my God, according to these things that they did, and also the prophetess Noadiah and the rest of the prophets who wanted to make me afraid.

The Wall Is Finished

15 So the wall was finished on the twenty-fifth day of the month Elul, in fifty-two days. **16** And when all our enemies heard of it, all the nations around us were afraid and fell greatly in their own esteem, for they perceived that this work had been accomplished with the help of our God. **17** Moreover, in those days the nobles of Judah sent many letters to Tobiah, and Tobiah's letters came to them. **18** For many in Judah were bound by oath to him, because he was the son-in-law of Shecaniah the son of Arah: and his son Jehohanan had taken the daughter of Meshullam the son of Berechiah as his wife. **19** Also they spoke of his good deeds in my presence and reported my words to him. And Tobiah sent letters to make me afraid.

7 Now when the wall had been built and I had set up the doors, and the gatekeepers, the singers, and the Levites had been appointed, **2** I gave my brother Hanani and Hananiah the governor of the castle charge over Jerusalem, for he was a more faithful and God-fearing man than many. **3** And I said to them, "Let not the gates of Jerusalem be opened until the sun is hot. And while they are still standing guard, let them shut and bar the doors. Appoint guards from among the inhabitants of Jerusalem, some at their guard posts and some in front of their own homes." **4** The city was wide and large, but the people within it were few, and no houses had been rebuilt.

Lists of Returned Exiles

5 Then my God put it into my heart to assemble the nobles and the officials and the people to be enrolled by genealogy. And I found the book of the genealogy of those who came up at the first, and I found written in it:

6 These were the people of the province who came up out of the captivity of those exiles whom Nebuchadnezzar the king of Babylon had carried into exile. They returned to Jerusalem and Judah, each to his town. **7** They came with Zerubbabel,

Jeshua, Nehemiah, Azariah, Raamiah, Nahamani, Mordecai, Bilshan, Mispereth, Bigvai, Nehum, Baanah.

The number of the men of the people of Israel: **8** the sons of Parosh, 2,172. **9** The sons of Shephatiah, 372. **10** The sons of Arah, 652. **11** The sons of Pahath-moab, namely the sons of Jeshua and Joab, 2,818. **12** The sons of Elam, 1,254. **13** The sons of Zattu, 845. **14** The sons of Zaccai, 760. **15** The sons of Binnui, 648. **16** The sons of Bebai, 628. **17** The sons of Azgad, 2,322. **18** The sons of Adonikam, 667. **19** The sons of Bigvai, 2,067. **20** The sons of Adin, 655. **21** The sons of Ater, namely of Hezekiah, 98. **22** The sons of Hashum, 328. **23** The sons of Bezai, 324. **24** The sons of Hariph, 112. **25** The sons of Gibeon, 95. **26** The men of Bethlehem and Netophah, 188. **27** The men of Anathoth, 128. **28** The men of Beth-azmaveth, 42. **29** The men of Kiriath-jearim, Chephirah, and Beeroth, 743. **30** The men of Ramah and Geba, 621. **31** The men of Michmas, 122. **32** The men of Bethel and Ai, 123. **33** The men of the other Nebo, 52. **34** The sons of the other Elam, 1,254. **35** The sons of Harim, 320. **36** The sons of Jericho, 345. **37** The sons of Lod, Hadid, and Ono, 721. **38** The sons of Senaah, 3,930.

39 The priests: the sons of Jedaiah, namely the house of Jeshua, 973. **40** The sons of Immer, 1,052. **41** The sons of Pashhur, 1,247. **42** The sons of Harim, 1,017.

43 The Levites: the sons of Jeshua, namely of Kadmiel of the sons of Hodevah, 74. **44** The singers: the sons of Asaph, 148. **45** The gate-keepers: the sons of Shallum, the sons of Ater, the sons of Talmon, the sons of Akkub, the sons of Hatita, the sons of Shobai, 138.

46 The temple servants: the sons of Ziha, the sons of Hasupha, the sons of Tabbaoth, **47** the sons of Keros, the sons of Sia, the sons of Padon, **48** the sons of Lebana, the sons of Hagaba, the sons of Shalmai, **49** the sons of Hanan, the sons of Giddel, the sons of Gahar, **50** the sons of Reaiah, the sons of Rezin, the sons of Nekoda, **51** the sons of Gazzam, the sons of Uzza, the sons of Paseah, **52** the sons of Besai, the sons of Meunim, the sons of Nephushesim, **53** the sons of Bakbuk, the sons of Hakupha, the sons of Harhur, **54** the sons of Bazlith, the sons of Mehida, the sons of Harsha, **55** the sons of Barkos, the sons of Sisera, the sons of Temah, **56** the sons of Neziah, the sons of Hatipha.

57 The sons of Solomon's servants: the sons of Sotai, the sons of Sophereth, the sons of Perida, **58** the sons of Jaala, the sons of Darkon, the sons of Giddel, **59** the sons of Shephatiah, the sons of Hattil, the sons of Pochereth-hazzebaim, the sons of Amon.

60 All the temple servants and the sons of Solomon's servants were 392.

61 The following were those who came up from Tel-melah, Tel-harsha, Cherub, Addon, and Immer, but they could not prove their fathers' houses nor their descent, whether they belonged to Israel: **62** the sons of Delaiah, the sons of Tobiah, the sons of Nekoda, 642. **63** Also, of the priests: the sons of Hobaiah, the sons of Hakkoz, the sons of Barzillai (who had taken a wife of the daughters of Barzillai the Gileadite and was called by their name). **64** These sought their registration among those enrolled in

the genealogies, but it was not found there, so they were excluded from the priesthood as unclean. **65** The governor told them that they were not to partake of the most holy food until a priest with Urim and Thummim should arise.

Totals of People and Gifts

66 The whole assembly together was 42,360, **67** besides their male and female servants, of whom there were 7,337. And they had 245 singers, male and female. **68** Their horses were 736, their mules 245, **69** their camels 435, and their donkeys 6,720.

70 Now some of the heads of fathers' houses gave to the work. The governor gave to the treasury 1,000 darics of gold, 50 basins, 30 priests' garments and 500 minas of silver. **71** And some of the heads of fathers' houses gave into the treasury of the work 20,000 darics of gold and 2,200 minas of silver. **72** And what the rest of the people gave was 20,000 darics of gold, 2,000 minas of silver, and 67 priests' garments.

⁷³ So the priests, the Levites, the gatekeepers, the singers, some of the people, the temple servants, and all Israel, lived in their towns.

And when the seventh month had come, the people of Israel were in their towns.

Ezra Reads the Law

8 And all the people gathered as one man into the square before the Water Gate. And they told Ezra the scribe to bring the Book of the Law of Moses that the LORD had commanded Israel. ² So Ezra the priest brought the Law before the assembly, both men and women and all who could understand what they heard, on the first day of the seventh month. ³ And he read from it facing the square before the Water Gate from

> ### GETTING THE MESSAGE
>
> **The Feast of Booths** (8:2) marked the end of the agricultural year. It was a time to celebrate God's provision and to ask his blessing for the next year's crops. Once every seven years, the Book of the Law of Moses was to be read during the festival. This was done to instruct the children and as a reminder for the adults.

early morning until midday, in the presence of the men and the women and those who could understand. And the ears of all the people were attentive to the Book of the Law. ⁴ And Ezra the scribe stood on a wooden platform that they had made for the purpose. And beside him stood Mattithiah, Shema, Anaiah, Uriah, Hilkiah, and Maaseiah on his right hand, and Pedaiah, Mishael, Malchijah, Hashum, Hashbaddanah, Zechariah, and Meshullam on his left hand. ⁵ And Ezra opened the book in the sight of all the people, for he was above all the people, and as he opened it all the people stood. ⁶ And Ezra blessed the LORD, the great God, and all the people answered, "Amen, Amen," lifting up their hands. And they bowed their heads and worshiped the LORD with their faces to the ground. ⁷ Also Jeshua, Bani, Sherebiah, Jamin, Akkub, Shabbethai, Hodiah, Maaseiah, Kelita, Azariah, Jozabad, Hanan, Pelaiah, the Levites, helped the peo-

ple to understand the Law, while the people remained in their places. ⁸ They read from the book, from the Law of God, clearly, and they gave the sense, so that the people understood the reading.

This Day Is Holy

⁹ And Nehemiah, who was the governor, and Ezra the priest and scribe, and the Levites who taught the people said to all the people, "This day is holy to the LORD your God; do not mourn or weep." For all the people wept as they heard the words of the Law. ¹⁰ Then he said to them, "Go your way. Eat the fat and drink sweet wine and send portions to anyone who has nothing ready, for this day is holy to our Lord. And do not be grieved, for the joy of the LORD is your strength." ¹¹ So the Levites calmed all the people, saying, "Be quiet, for this day is holy; do not be grieved." ¹² And all the people went their way to eat and drink and to send portions and to make great rejoicing, because they had understood the words that were declared to them.

Feast of Booths Celebrated

¹³ On the second day the heads of fathers' houses of all the people, with the priests and the Levites, came together to Ezra the scribe in order to study the words of the Law. ¹⁴ And they found it written in the Law that the LORD had commanded by Moses that the people of Israel should dwell in booths during the feast of the seventh month, ¹⁵ and that they should proclaim it and publish it in all their towns and in Jerusalem, "Go out to the hills and bring branches of olive, wild olive, myrtle, palm, and other leafy trees to make booths, as it is written." ¹⁶ So the people went out and brought them and made booths for themselves, each on his roof, and in their courts and in the courts of the house of God, and in the square at the Water Gate and in the square at the Gate of Ephraim. ¹⁷ And all the assembly of those who had returned from the captivity made booths and lived in the booths, for from the days of Jeshua the son of Nun to that day the people of Israel had not done so. And there was very great rejoicing. ¹⁸ And day by day, from the first day to the last day, he read from the Book of the Law of God. They kept the feast seven days, and on the eighth day there was a solemn assembly, according to the rule.

The People of Israel Confess Their Sin

9 Now on the twenty-fourth day of this month the people of Israel were assembled with fasting and in sackcloth, and with earth on their heads. ² And the Israelites separated themselves from all foreigners and stood and confessed their sins and the iniquities of their fathers. ³ And they stood up in their place and read from the Book of the Law of the LORD their God for a quarter of the day; for another quarter of it they made confession and worshiped the LORD their God. ⁴ On the stairs of the Levites stood Jeshua, Bani, Kadmiel, Shebaniah, Bunni, Sherebiah, Bani, and Chenani; and they cried with a loud voice to the LORD their God. ⁵ Then the Levites, Jeshua, Kadmiel, Bani, Hashabneiah, Sherebiah, Hodiah, Shebaniah, and Pethahiah, said, "Stand up and bless the LORD your God from everlasting to everlasting. Blessed be your glorious name, which is exalted above all blessing and praise.

⁶ "You are the LORD, you alone. You have made heaven, the heaven of heavens, with all their host, the earth and all that is on it, the seas and all that is in them; and you preserve all of them; and the host of heaven worships you. ⁷ You are the LORD, the God who chose Abram and brought him out of Ur of the Chaldeans and gave him the name Abraham. ⁸ You found his heart faithful before you, and made with him the covenant to give to his offspring the land of the Canaanite, the Hittite, the Amorite, the Perizzite, the Jebusite, and the Girgashite. And you have kept your promise, for you are righteous.

⁹ "And you saw the affliction of our fathers in Egypt and heard their cry at the Red Sea, ¹⁰ and performed signs and wonders against Pharaoh and all his servants and all the people of his land, for you knew that they acted arrogantly against our fathers. And you made a name for yourself, as it is to this day. ¹¹ And you divided the sea before them, so that they went through the midst of the sea on dry land, and you cast their pursuers into the depths, as a stone into mighty waters. ¹² By a pillar of cloud you led them in the day, and by a pillar of fire in the night to light for them the way in which they should go. ¹³ You came down on Mount Sinai and spoke with them from heaven and gave them right rules and true laws, good statutes and commandments, ¹⁴ and you made known to them your holy Sabbath and commanded them commandments and statutes and a law by Moses your servant. ¹⁵ You gave them bread from heaven for their hunger and brought water for them out of the rock for their thirst, and you told them to go in to possess the land that you had sworn to give them.

¹⁶ "But they and our fathers acted presumptuously and stiffened their neck and did not obey your commandments. ¹⁷ They refused to obey and were not mindful of the wonders that you performed among them, but they stiffened their neck and appointed a leader to return to their slavery in Egypt. But you are a God ready to forgive, gracious

---

GETTING THE MESSAGE

Word pictures for worship and teaching. Religious images were strictly forbidden under the Mosaic law, but Israel's leaders often used vivid imagery in their story-telling to teach the people and to help them worship. Chapter 9 gives an example of this, as the Levites publicly recite the nation's history, from creation to the present.

---

and merciful, slow to anger and abounding in steadfast love, and did not forsake them. ¹⁸ Even when they had made for themselves a golden calf and said, 'This is your God who brought you up out of Egypt,' and had committed great blasphemies, ¹⁹ you in your great mercies did not forsake them in the wilderness. The pillar of cloud to lead them in the way did not depart from them by day, nor the pillar of fire by night to light for them the way by which they should go. ²⁰ You gave your good Spirit to instruct them and did not withhold your manna from their mouth and gave them water for their thirst. ²¹ Forty years you sustained them in the wilderness, and they lacked nothing. Their clothes did not wear out and their feet did not swell.

²² "And you gave them kingdoms and peoples and allotted to them every corner. So they took possession of the land of Sihon king of Heshbon and the land of Og king of

Bashan. ²³ You multiplied their children as the stars of heaven, and you brought them into the land that you had told their fathers to enter and possess. ²⁴ So the descendants went in and possessed the land, and you subdued before them the inhabitants of the land, the Canaanites, and gave them into their hand, with their kings and the peoples of the land, that they might do with them as they would. ²⁵ And they captured fortified cities and a rich land, and took possession of houses full of all good things, cisterns already hewn, vineyards, olive orchards and fruit trees in abundance. So they ate and were filled and became fat and delighted themselves in your great goodness.

²⁶ "Nevertheless, they were disobedient and rebelled against you and cast your law behind their back and killed your prophets, who had warned them in order to turn them back to you, and they committed great blasphemies. ²⁷ Therefore you gave them into

GETTING THE MESSAGE

Seals in the ancient Near East (e.g., 10:1) were stamps pressed into soft wax on documents that demonstrated ownership or authorship.

the hand of their enemies, who made them suffer. And in the time of their suffering they cried out to you and you heard them from heaven, and according to your great mercies you gave them saviors who saved them from the hand of their enemies. ²⁸ But after they had rest they did evil again before you, and you abandoned them to the hand of their enemies, so that they had dominion over them. Yet when they turned and cried to you, you heard from heaven, and many times you delivered them according to your mercies. ²⁹ And you warned them in order to turn them back to your law. Yet they acted presumptuously and did not obey your commandments, but sinned against your rules, which if a person does them, he shall live by them, and they turned a stubborn shoulder and stiffened their neck and would not obey. ³⁰ Many years you bore with them and warned them by your Spirit through your prophets. Yet they would not give ear. Therefore you gave them into the hand of

the peoples of the lands. ³¹ Nevertheless, in your great mercies you did not make an end of them or forsake them, for you are a gracious and merciful God.

³² "Now, therefore, our God, the great, the mighty, and the awesome God, who keeps covenant and steadfast love, let not all the hardship seem little to you that has come upon us, upon our kings, our princes, our priests, our prophets, our fathers, and all your people, since the time of the kings of Assyria until this day. ³³ Yet you have been righteous in all that has come upon us, for you have dealt faithfully and we have acted wickedly. ³⁴ Our kings, our princes, our priests, and our fathers have not kept your law or paid attention to your commandments and your warnings that you gave them. ³⁵ Even in their own kingdom, and amid your great goodness that you gave them, and in the large and rich land that you set before them, they did not serve you or turn from their wicked works. ³⁶ Behold, we are slaves this day; in the land that you gave to our fathers to enjoy its fruit and its good gifts, behold, we are slaves. ³⁷ And its rich yield goes to the kings whom you have set over us because of our sins. They rule over our bodies and over our livestock as they please, and we are in great distress.

³⁸ "Because of all this we make a firm covenant in writing; on the sealed document are the names of our princes, our Levites, and our priests.

The People Who Sealed the Covenant

10 "On the seals are the names of Nehemiah the governor, the son of Hacaliah, Zedekiah, ² Seraiah, Azariah, Jeremiah, ³ Pashhur, Amariah, Malchijah, ⁴ Hattush, Shebaniah, Malluch, ⁵ Harim, Meremoth, Obadiah, ⁶ Daniel, Ginnethon, Baruch, ⁷ Meshullam, Abijah, Mijamin, ⁸ Maaziah, Bilgai, Shemaiah; these are the priests. ⁹ And the Levites: Jeshua the son of Azaniah, Binnui of the sons of Henadad, Kadmiel; ¹⁰ and their brothers, Shebaniah, Hodiah, Kelita, Pelaiah, Hanan, ¹¹ Mica, Rehob, Hashabiah, ¹² Zaccur, Sherebiah, Shebaniah, ¹³ Hodiah, Bani, Beninu. ¹⁴ The chiefs of the people: Parosh, Pahath-moab, Elam, Zattu, Bani, ¹⁵ Bunni, Azgad, Bebai, ¹⁶ Adonijah, Bigvai, Adin, ¹⁷ Ater, Hezekiah, Azzur, ¹⁸ Hodiah, Hashum, Bezai, ¹⁹ Hariph, Anathoth, Nebai, ²⁰ Magpiash, Meshullam,

Hezir, ²¹ Meshezabel, Zadok, Jaddua, ²² Pelatiah, Hanan, Anaiah, ²³ Hoshea, Hananiah, Hasshub, ²⁴ Hallohesh, Pilha, Shobek, ²⁵ Rehum, Hashabnah, Maaseiah, ²⁶ Ahiah, Hanan, Anan, ²⁷ Malluch, Harim, Baanah.

The Obligations of the Covenant

²⁸ "The rest of the people, the priests, the Levites, the gatekeepers, the singers, the temple servants, and all who have separated themselves from the peoples of the lands to the Law of God, their wives, their sons, their daughters, all who have knowledge and understanding, ²⁹ join with their brothers, their nobles, and enter into a curse and an oath to walk in God's Law that was given by Moses the servant of God, and to observe and do all the commandments of the LORD our Lord and his rules and his statutes. ³⁰ We will not give our daughters to the peoples of the land or take their daughters for our sons. ³¹ And if the peoples of the land bring in goods or any grain on the Sabbath day to sell, we will not buy from them on the Sabbath or on a holy day. And we will forego the crops of the seventh year and the exaction of every debt.

³² "We also take on ourselves the obligation to give yearly a third part of a shekel for the service of the house of our God: ³³ for the showbread, the regular grain offering, the regular burnt offering, the Sabbaths, the new moons, the appointed feasts, the holy things, and the sin offerings to make atonement for Israel, and for all the work of the house of our God. ³⁴ We, the priests, the Levites, and the people, have likewise cast lots for the wood offering, to bring it into the house of our God, according to our fathers' houses, at times appointed, year by year, to burn on the altar of the LORD our God, as it is written in the Law. ³⁵ We obligate ourselves to bring the firstfruits of our ground and the firstfruits of all fruit of every tree, year by year, to the house of the LORD; ³⁶ also to bring to the house of our God, to the priests who minister in the house of our God, the firstborn of our sons and of our cattle, as it is written in the Law, and the firstborn of our herds and of our flocks; ³⁷ and to bring the first of our dough, and our contributions, the fruit of every tree, the wine and the oil, to the priests, to the chambers of the house of our God; and to bring to the Levites the tithes from our ground, for it is the Levites who collect the tithes in all our towns where we labor. ³⁸ And the priest, the son of Aaron, shall be with the Levites when the Levites receive the tithes. And the Levites shall bring up the tithe of the tithes to the house of our God, to the chambers of the storehouse. ³⁹ For the people of Israel and the sons of Levi shall bring the contribution of grain, wine, and oil to the chambers, where the vessels of the sanctuary are, as well as the priests who minister, and the gatekeepers and the singers. We will not neglect the house of our God."

The Leaders in Jerusalem

11 Now the leaders of the people lived in Jerusalem. And the rest of the people cast lots to bring one out of ten to live in Jerusalem the holy city, while nine out of

GETTING THE MESSAGE

Why did the small towns of Judah send people to live in Jerusalem?
In Nehemiah's time, Jerusalem was only one-fourth the size it had been before the exile. No one wanted to live in a city without defensive walls. Once the walls were completed, however, the community leaders wanted Jerusalem to become a thriving capital city once again. This meant transplanting citizens from the small towns (11:1–2).

ten remained in the other towns. ² And the people blessed all the men who willingly offered to live in Jerusalem.

³ These are the chiefs of the province who lived in Jerusalem; but in the towns of Judah everyone lived on his property in their towns: Israel, the priests, the Levites, the temple servants, and the descendants of Solomon's servants. ⁴ And in Jerusalem lived certain of the sons of Judah and of the sons of Benjamin. Of the sons of Judah: Athaiah the son of Uzziah, son of Zechariah, son of Amariah, son of Shephatiah, son of Mahalalel, of the sons of Perez; ⁵ and Maaseiah the son of Baruch, son of Colhozeh, son of Hazaiah, son of Adaiah, son of Joiarib, son of Zechariah, son of the Shilonite. ⁶ All the sons of Perez who lived in Jerusalem were 468 valiant men.

7 And these are the sons of Benjamin: Sallu the son of Meshullam, son of Joed, son of Pedaiah, son of Kolaiah, son of Maaseiah, son of Ithiel, son of Jeshaiah, 8 and his brothers, men of valor, 928. 9 Joel the son of Zichri was their overseer; and Judah the son of Hassenuah was second over the city.

10 Of the priests: Jedaiah the son of Joiarib, Jachin, 11 Seraiah the son of Hilkiah, son of Meshullam, son of Zadok, son of Meraioth, son of Ahitub, ruler of the house of God, 12 and their brothers who did the work of the house, 822; and Adaiah the son of Jeroham, son of Pelaliah, son of Amzi, son of Zechariah, son of Pashhur, son of Malchijah, 13 and his brothers, heads of fathers' houses, 242; and Amashsai, the son of Azarel, son of Ahzai, son of Meshillemoth, son of Immer, 14 and their brothers, mighty men of valor, 128; their overseer was Zabdiel the son of Haggedolim.

15 And of the Levites: Shemaiah the son of Hasshub, son of Azrikam, son of Hashabiah, son of Bunni; 16 and Shabbethai and Jozabad, of the chiefs of the Levites, who were over the outside work of the house of God; 17 and Mattaniah the son of Mica, son of Zabdi, son of Asaph, who was the leader of the praise, who gave thanks, and Bakbukiah, the second among his brothers; and Abda the son of Shammua, son of Galal, son of Jeduthun. 18 All the Levites in the holy city were 284.

19 The gatekeepers, Akkub, Talmon and their brothers, who kept watch at the gates, were 172. 20 And the rest of Israel, and of the priests and the Levites, were in all the towns of Judah, every one in his inheritance. 21 But the temple servants lived on Ophel; and Ziha and Gishpa were over the temple servants.

22 The overseer of the Levites in Jerusalem was Uzzi the son of Bani, son of Hashabiah, son of Mattaniah, son of Mica, of the sons of Asaph, the singers, over the work of the house of God. 23 For there was a command from the king concerning them, and a fixed provision for the singers, as every day required. 24 And Pethahiah the son of Meshezabel, of the sons of Zerah the son of Judah, was at the king's side in all matters concerning the people.

Villages Outside Jerusalem

25 And as for the villages, with their fields, some of the people of Judah lived in Kiriath-arba and its villages, and in Dibon and its villages, and in Jekabzeel and its villages, 26 and in Jeshua and in Moladah and Beth-pelet, 27 in Hazar-shual, in Beersheba and its villages, 28 in Ziklag, in Meconah and its villages, 29 in En-rimmon, in Zorah, in Jarmuth, 30 Zanoah, Adullam, and their villages, Lachish and its fields, and Azekah and its villages. So they encamped from Beersheba to the Valley of Hinnom. 31 The people of Benjamin also lived from Geba onward, at Michmash, Aija, Bethel and its villages, 32 Anathoth, Nob, Ananiah, 33 Hazor, Ramah, Gittaim, 34 Hadid, Zeboim, Neballat, 35 Lod, and Ono, the valley of craftsmen. 36 And certain divisions of the Levites in Judah were assigned to Benjamin.

Priests and Levites

12 These are the priests and the Levites who came up with Zerubbabel the son of Shealtiel, and Jeshua: Seraiah, Jeremiah, Ezra, 2 Amariah, Malluch, Hattush, 3 Shecaniah, Rehum, Meremoth, 4 Iddo, Ginnethoi, Abijah, 5 Mijamin, Maadiah, Bilgah, 6 Shemaiah, Joiarib, Jedaiah, 7 Sallu, Amok, Hilkiah, Jedaiah. These were the chiefs of the priests and of their brothers in the days of Jeshua.

8 And the Levites: Jeshua, Binnui, Kadmiel, Sherebiah, Judah, and Mattaniah, who with his brothers was in charge of the songs of thanksgiving. 9 And Bakbukiah and Unni and their brothers stood opposite them in the service. 10 And Jeshua was the father of Joiakim, Joiakim the father of Eliashib, Eliashib the father of Joiada, 11 Joiada the father of Jonathan, and Jonathan the father of Jaddua.

12 And in the days of Joiakim were priests, heads of fathers' houses: of Seraiah, Meraiah; of Jeremiah, Hananiah; 13 of Ezra, Meshullam; of Amariah, Jehohanan; 14 of Malluchi, Jonathan; of Shebaniah, Joseph; 15 of Harim, Adna; of Meraioth, Helkai; 16 of Iddo, Zechariah; of Ginnethon, Meshullam; 17 of Abijah, Zichri; of Miniamin, of Moadiah, Piltai; 18 of Bilgah, Shammua; of Shemaiah, Jehonathan; 19 of Joiarib, Mattenai; of Jedaiah, Uzzi; 20 of Sallai, Kallai; of Amok, Eber; 21 of Hilkiah, Hashabiah; of Jedaiah, Nethanel.

22 In the days of Eliashib, Joiada, Johanan, and Jaddua, the Levites were recorded as heads of fathers' houses; so too were the priests in the reign of Darius the Persian. 23 As for the sons of Levi, their heads of

fathers' houses were written in the Book of the Chronicles until the days of Johanan the son of Eliashib. ²⁴ And the chiefs of the Levites: Hashabiah, Sherebiah, and Jeshua the son of Kadmiel, with their brothers who stood opposite them, to praise and to give thanks, according to the commandment of David the man of God, watch by watch. ²⁵ Mattaniah, Bakbukiah, Obadiah, Meshullam, Talmon, and Akkub were gatekeepers standing guard at the storehouses of the gates. ²⁶ These were in the days of Joiakim the son of Jeshua son of Jozadak, and in the days of Nehemiah the governor and of Ezra, the priest and scribe.

Dedication of the Wall

²⁷ And at the dedication of the wall of Jerusalem they sought the Levites in all their places, to bring them to Jerusalem to celebrate the dedication with gladness, with thanksgivings and with singing, with cymbals, harps, and lyres. ²⁸ And the sons of the singers gathered together from the district surrounding Jerusalem and from the villages of the Netophathites; ²⁹ also from Beth-gilgal and from the region of Geba and Azmaveth, for the singers had built for themselves villages around Jerusalem. ³⁰ And the priests and the Levites purified themselves, and they purified the people and the gates and the wall.

³¹ Then I brought the leaders of Judah up onto the wall and appointed two great choirs that gave thanks. One went to the south on the wall to the Dung Gate. ³² And after them went Hoshaiah and half of the leaders of Judah, ³³ and Azariah, Ezra, Meshullam, ³⁴ Judah, Benjamin, Shemaiah, and Jeremiah, ³⁵ and certain of the priests' sons with trumpets: Zechariah the son of Jonathan, son of Shemaiah, son of Mattaniah, son of Micaiah, son of Zaccur, son of Asaph; ³⁶ and his relatives, Shemaiah, Azarel, Milalai, Gilalai, Maai, Nethanel, Judah, and Hanani, with the musical instruments of David the man of God. And Ezra the scribe went before them. ³⁷ At the Fountain Gate they went up straight before them by the stairs of the city of David, at the ascent of the wall, above the house of David, to the Water Gate on the east.

³⁸ The other choir of those who gave thanks went to the north, and I followed them with half of the people, on the wall, above the Tower of the Ovens, to the Broad Wall, ³⁹ and above the Gate of Ephraim, and by the Gate of Yeshanah, and by the Fish Gate and the Tower of Hananel and the Tower of the Hundred, to the Sheep Gate; and they came to a halt at the Gate of the Guard. ⁴⁰ So both choirs of those who gave thanks stood in the house of God, and I and half of the officials with me; ⁴¹ and the priests Eliakim, Maaseiah, Miniamin, Micaiah, Elioenai, Zechariah, and Hananiah, with trumpets; ⁴² and Maaseiah, Shemaiah, Eleazar, Uzzi, Jehohanan, Malchijah, Elam, and Ezer. And the singers sang with Jezrahiah as their leader. ⁴³ And they offered great sacrifices that day and rejoiced, for God had made them rejoice with great joy; the women and children also rejoiced. And the joy of Jerusalem was heard far away.

Service at the Temple

⁴⁴ On that day men were appointed over the storerooms, the contributions, the first-fruits, and the tithes, to gather into them the portions required by the Law for the priests and for the Levites according to the fields of the towns, for Judah rejoiced over the priests and the Levites who ministered. ⁴⁵ And they performed the service of their God and the service of purification, as did the singers and the gatekeepers, according to the command of David and his son Solomon. ⁴⁶ For long ago in the days of David and Asaph there were directors of the singers, and there were songs of praise and thanksgiving to God. ⁴⁷ And all Israel in the days of Zerubbabel and in the days of Nehemiah gave the daily portions for the singers and the gatekeepers; and they set apart that which was for the Levites; and the Levites set apart that which was for the sons of Aaron.

Nehemiah's Final Reforms

13 On that day they read from the Book of Moses in the hearing of the people. And in it was found written that no Ammonite or Moabite should ever enter the assembly of God, ² for they did not meet the people of Israel with bread and water, but hired Balaam against them to curse them—yet our God turned the curse into a blessing. ³ As soon as the people heard the law, they separated from Israel all those of foreign descent.

⁴ Now before this, Eliashib the priest, who was appointed over the chambers of the house of our God, and who was related to Tobiah, ⁵ prepared for Tobiah a large chamber where they had previously put the grain offering, the frankincense, the vessels, and the tithes of grain, wine, and oil, which were given by commandment to the Levites, singers, and gatekeepers, and the contributions for the priests. ⁶ While this was taking place, I was not in Jerusalem, for in the thirty-second year of Artaxerxes king of Babylon I went to the king. And after some time I asked leave of the king ⁷ and came to Jerusalem, and I then discovered the evil that Eliashib had done for Tobiah, preparing for him a chamber in the courts of the house of God. ⁸ And I was very angry, and I threw all the household furniture of Tobiah out of the chamber. ⁹ Then I gave orders, and they cleansed the chambers, and I brought back there the vessels of the house of God, with the grain offering and the frankincense.

¹⁰ I also found out that the portions of the Levites had not been given to them, so that the Levites and the singers, who did the work, had fled each to his field. ¹¹ So I confronted the officials and said, "Why is the house of God forsaken?" And I gathered them together and set them in their stations. ¹² Then all Judah brought the tithe of the grain, wine, and oil into the storehouses. ¹³ And I appointed as treasurers over the storehouses Shelemiah the priest, Zadok the scribe, and Pedaiah of the Levites, and as their assistant Hanan the son of Zaccur, son of Mattaniah, for they were considered reliable, and their duty was to distribute to their brothers. ¹⁴ Remember me, O my God, concerning this, and do not wipe out my good deeds that I have done for the house of my God and for his service.

¹⁵ In those days I saw in Judah people treading winepresses on the Sabbath, and bringing in heaps of grain and loading them on donkeys, and also wine, grapes, figs, and all kinds of loads, which they brought into Jerusalem on the Sabbath day. And I warned them on the day when they sold food. ¹⁶ Tyrians also, who lived in the city, brought in fish and all kinds of goods and sold them on the Sabbath to the people of Judah, in Jerusalem itself! ¹⁷ Then I confronted the nobles of Judah and said to them, "What is this evil thing that you are doing, profaning the Sabbath day? ¹⁸ Did not your fathers act in this way, and did not our God bring all this disaster¹ on us and on this city? Now you are bringing more wrath on Israel by profaning the Sabbath."

¹⁹ As soon as it began to grow dark at the gates of Jerusalem before the Sabbath, I commanded that the doors should be shut and gave orders that they should not be opened until after the Sabbath. And I stationed some of my servants at the gates, that no load might be brought in on the Sabbath day. ²⁰ Then the merchants and sellers of all kinds of wares lodged outside Jerusalem once or twice. ²¹ But I warned them and said to them, "Why do you lodge outside the wall? If you do so again, I will lay hands on you." From that time on they did not come on the Sabbath. ²² Then I commanded the Levites that they should purify themselves and come and guard the gates, to keep the Sabbath day holy. Remember this also in my favor, O my God, and spare me according to the greatness of your steadfast love.

²³ In those days also I saw the Jews who had married women of Ashdod, Ammon, and Moab. ²⁴ And half of their children spoke the language of Ashdod, and they could not speak the language of Judah, but only the language of each people. ²⁵ And I confronted them and cursed them and beat some of them and pulled out their hair. And I made them take an oath in the name of God, saying, "You shall not give your daughters to their sons, or take their daughters for your sons or for yourselves. ²⁶ Did not Solomon king of Israel sin on account of such women? Among the many nations there was no king like him, and he was beloved by his God, and God made him king over all Israel. Nevertheless, foreign women made even him to sin. ²⁷ Shall we then listen to you and do all this great evil and act treacherously against our God by marrying foreign women?"

²⁸ And one of the sons of Jehoiada, the son of Eliashib the high priest, was the son-in-law of Sanballat the Horonite. Therefore I chased him from me. ²⁹ Remember them, O my God, because they have desecrated the

¹ The Hebrew word can mean *evil, harm,* or *disaster,* depending on the context

priesthood and the covenant of the priesthood and the Levites.

³⁰ Thus I cleansed them from everything foreign, and I established the duties of the priests and Levites, each in his work; ³¹ and I provided for the wood offering at appointed times, and for the firstfruits.

Remember me, O my God, for good.

INTRODUCTION TO ESTHER

516 B.C.	478–473 B.C.	445 B.C.
Temple rebuilt (in Jerusalem)	Events of Esther (in Persia)	Walls rebuilt (in Jerusalem)

AUTHOR AND DATE

Like many OT books, Esther is an anonymous work. It is possible that the author was someone like Mordecai, who had access to historical documents (2:23; 6:1) and an interest in Jewish affairs.

Esther belongs to the period after the Babylonian exile, when Persia had replaced Babylon as the ruling power. The story is set in Susa, one of the Persian capitals, during the reign of King Ahasuerus, better known by his Greek name, Xerxes I (486–464 B.C.). Some Jews had returned to Jerusalem, where they enjoyed a reasonable amount of control over their own affairs. Others, like Esther and Mordecai, were still in exile. As a minority group, the Jews were viewed with suspicion and sometimes faced threats to their existence.

OVERVIEW AND PURPOSE

The book of Esther tells how a Jewish girl became the queen of Persia and saved her people from a plot to destroy them. She is assisted in this by Mordecai, her cousin and guardian.

Esther was written to explain the origin of the Feast of Purim and to ensure that it would be observed by all future generations of the Jewish people (9:28). It has clearly achieved this purpose, since Jews have continued to observe Purim to the present day. The book of Esther is read as part of the celebration of Purim.

Esther is part of a much larger story that runs all the way from Abraham to Christ and, through him, to the church. If Haman had succeeded, the Jewish people as a whole would have been destroyed, and the story of God's saving work in and through Abraham's descendants would have come to an end. There would have been

no fulfillment in Christ, and therefore no gospel and no Christian church. Christians should read the book of Esther, not just as a story about the Jews but as part of their own heritage. Christians are not obliged to observe the Feast of Purim, but they are to take to heart the truth that God providentially watches over his own (Rom. 8:28).

KEY THEMES

Esther is an entertaining historical story that also reveals important truths about how and why the Jews survived such an overwhelming threat:

1. *Divine providence.* God is not mentioned by name in the book of Esther. But it shows clearly that, even when God is most hidden, he is still working to protect his chosen people.

2. *Human responsibility.* Esther and Mordecai show great initiative and courage. Their actions are obviously significant. The providence of God does not negate the responsibility of people to act with courage and resolve when circumstances require it.

3. *The absurdity of wickedness.* Ahasuerus and Haman were important people who had considerable power. But the story of Esther often causes laughter at their expense. The proud people of this world are not nearly as powerful as they think they are. When they oppose God's people they bring about their own destruction. God laughs at such people (Ps. 2:4). The story of Esther invites us to laugh with him.

OUTLINE

   I. Introduction (1:1–2:23)

  II. Main Action (3:1–9:19)

 III. Conclusion (9:20–10:3)

ESTHER

The King's Banquets

1 Now in the days of Ahasuerus, the Ahasuerus who reigned from India to Ethiopia over 127 provinces, ² in those days when King Ahasuerus sat on his royal throne in Susa, the citadel, ³ in the third year of his reign he gave a feast for all his officials and servants. The army of Persia and Media and the nobles and governors of the provinces were before him, ⁴ while he showed the riches of his royal glory and the splendor and pomp of his greatness for many days, 180 days. ⁵ And when these days were completed, the king gave for all the people present in Susa the citadel, both great and small, a feast lasting for seven days in the court of the garden of the king's palace. ⁶ There were white cotton curtains and violet hangings fastened with cords of fine linen and purple to silver rods and marble pillars, and also couches of gold and silver on a mosaic pavement of porphyry, marble, mother-of-pearl and precious stones. ⁷ Drinks were served in golden vessels, vessels of different kinds, and the royal wine was lavished according to the bounty of the king. ⁸ And drinking was according to this edict: "There is no compulsion." For the king had given orders to all the staff of his palace to do as each man desired. ⁹ Queen Vashti also gave a feast for the women in the palace that belonged to King Ahasuerus.

Queen Vashti's Refusal

¹⁰ On the seventh day, when the heart of the king was merry with wine, he commanded Mehuman, Biztha, Harbona, Bigtha and Abagtha, Zethar and Carkas, the seven eunuchs who served in the presence of King Ahasuerus, ¹¹ to bring Queen Vashti before the king with her royal crown, in order to show the peoples and the princes her beauty, for she was lovely to look at. ¹² But Queen Vashti refused to come at the king's command delivered by the eunuchs. At this the king became enraged, and his anger burned within him.

¹³ Then the king said to the wise men who knew the times (for this was the king's procedure toward all who were versed in law and judgment, ¹⁴ the men next to him being Carshena, Shethar, Admatha, Tarshish, Meres, Marsena, and Memucan, the seven princes of Persia and Media, who saw the king's face, and sat first in the kingdom): ¹⁵ "According to the law, what is to be done to Queen Vashti, because she has not performed the command of King Ahasuerus delivered by the eunuchs?" ¹⁶ Then Memucan said in the presence of the king and the officials, "Not only against the

GETTING THE MESSAGE

Persian drinking vessels. The Persians were famous for making elaborate, expensive drinking cups and vessels (1:7). In fact, no two were alike. When the Greeks crushed the Persian Empire, the Persian drinking vessels were among the most highly valued spoils.

king has Queen Vashti done wrong, but also against all the officials and all the peoples who are in all the provinces of King Ahasuerus. ¹⁷ For the queen's behavior will be made known to all women, causing them to look at their husbands with contempt, since they will say, 'King Ahasuerus commanded Queen Vashti to be brought before him, and she did not come.' ¹⁸ This very day the noble women of Persia and Media who have heard of the queen's behavior will say the same to all the king's officials, and there will be contempt and wrath in plenty. ¹⁹ If it please the king, let a royal order go out from him, and let it be written among the laws of the Persians and the Medes so that it may not be repealed, that Vashti is never again to come before King Ahasuerus. And let the king give her royal position to another who is better than she. ²⁰ So when the decree made by the king is proclaimed throughout all his kingdom, for it is vast, all women will give honor to their husbands, high and low alike." **21** This advice pleased the king and the princes, and the king did as Memucan proposed. **22** He sent letters to all the royal provinces, to every province in its own script and to every people in its own language, that every man be master in his own household and speak according to the language of his people.

Esther Chosen Queen

2 After these things, when the anger of King Ahasuerus had abated, he remembered Vashti and what she had done and what had been decreed against her. **2** Then the king's young men who attended him said, "Let beautiful young virgins be sought out for the king. **3** And let the king appoint officers in all the provinces of his kingdom to gather all the beautiful young virgins to the harem in Susa the citadel, under custody of Hegai, the king's eunuch, who is in

> **GETTING THE MESSAGE**
>
> **Absolute authority.** Once the king wrote a law, it could not be overturned (1:19–20). But it could be modified by an additional law (8:8–9:1).

charge of the women. Let their cosmetics be given them. **4** And let the young woman who pleases the king be queen instead of Vashti." This pleased the king, and he did so.

5 Now there was a Jew in Susa the citadel whose name was Mordecai, the son of Jair, son of Shimei, son of Kish, a Benjaminite, **6** who had been carried away from Jerusalem among the captives carried away with Jeconiah king of Judah, whom Nebuchadnezzar king of Babylon had carried away. **7** He was bringing up Hadassah, that is Esther, the daughter of his uncle, for she had neither father nor mother. The young woman had a beautiful figure and was lovely to look at, and when her father and her mother died, Mordecai took her as his own daughter. **8** So when the king's order and his edict were proclaimed, and when many young women were gathered in Susa the citadel in custody of Hegai, Esther also was taken into the king's palace and put in custody of Hegai, who had charge of the women. **9** And the young woman pleased

him and won his favor. And he quickly provided her with her cosmetics and her portion of food, and with seven chosen young women from the king's palace, and advanced her and her young women to the best place in the harem. **10** Esther had not made known her people or kindred, for Mordecai had commanded her not to make it known. **11** And every day Mordecai walked in front of the court of the harem to learn how Esther was and what was happening to her.

12 Now when the turn came for each young woman to go in to King Ahasuerus, after being twelve months under the regulations for the women, since this was the regular period of their beautifying, six months with oil of myrrh and six months with spices and ointments for women— **13** when the young woman went in to the king in this way, she was given whatever she desired to take with her from the harem to the king's palace. **14** In the evening she would go in, and in the morning she would return to the second harem in custody of Shaashgaz, the king's eunuch, who was in charge of the concubines. She would not go in to the king again, unless the king delighted in her and she was summoned by name.

15 When the turn came for Esther the daughter of Abihail the uncle of Mordecai, who had taken her as his own daughter, to go in to the king, she asked for nothing except what Hegai the king's eunuch, who had charge of the women, advised. Now Esther was winning favor in the eyes of all who saw her. **16** And when Esther was taken to King Ahasuerus, into his royal palace, in the tenth month, which is the month of Tebeth, in the seventh year of his reign, **17** the king loved Esther more than all the women, and she won grace and favor in his sight more than all the virgins, so that he set the royal crown on her head and made her queen instead of Vashti. **18** Then the king gave a great feast for all his officials and servants; it was Esther's feast. He also granted a remission of taxes to the provinces and gave gifts with royal generosity.

Mordecai Discovers a Plot

19 Now when the virgins were gathered together the second time, Mordecai was sitting at the king's gate. **20** Esther had not made known her kindred or her people, as Mordecai had commanded her, for Esther obeyed Mordecai just as when she was brought up by him. ²¹ In those days, as Mordecai was sitting at the king's gate, Bigthan and Teresh, two of the king's eunuchs, who guarded the threshold, became angry and sought to lay hands on King Ahasuerus. ²² And this came to the knowledge of Mordecai, and he told it to Queen Esther, and Esther told the king in the name of Mordecai. ²³ When the affair was investigated and found to be so, the men were both hanged on the gallows. And it was recorded in the book of the chronicles in the presence of the king.

Haman Plots Against the Jews

3 After these things King Ahasuerus promoted Haman the Agagite, the son of Hammedatha, and advanced him and set his throne above all the officials who were with him. ² And all the king's servants who were at the king's gate bowed down and paid homage to Haman, for the king had so commanded concerning him. But Mordecai did not bow down or pay homage. ³ Then the king's servants who were at the king's gate said to Mordecai, "Why do you transgress the king's command?" ⁴ And when they spoke to him day after day and he would not listen to them, they told Haman, in order to see whether Mordecai's words would stand, for he had told them that he was a Jew. ⁵ And when Haman saw that Mordecai did not bow down or pay homage to him, Haman was filled with fury. ⁶ But he disdained to lay hands on Mordecai alone. So, as they had made known to him the people of Mordecai, Haman sought to destroy all the Jews, the people of Mordecai, throughout the whole kingdom of Ahasuerus.

⁷ In the first month, which is the month of Nisan, in the twelfth year of King Ahasuerus, they cast Pur (that is, they cast lots) before Haman day after day; and they cast it month after month till the twelfth month, which is the month of Adar. ⁸ Then Haman said to King Ahasuerus, "There is a certain people scattered abroad and dispersed among the peoples in all the provinces of your kingdom. Their laws are different from those of every other people, and they do not keep the king's laws, so that it is not to the king's profit to tolerate them. ⁹ If it please the king, let it be decreed that they be destroyed, and

I will pay 10,000 talents of silver into the hands of those who have charge of the king's business, that they may put it into the king's treasuries." ¹⁰ So the king took his signet ring from his hand and gave it to Haman the Agagite, the son of Hammedatha, the enemy of the Jews. ¹¹ And the king said to Haman, "The money is given to you, the people also, to do with them as it seems good to you."

¹² Then the king's scribes were summoned on the thirteenth day of the first month, and an edict, according to all that Haman commanded, was written to the king's satraps and to the governors over all the provinces and to the officials of all the peoples, to every province in its own script and every people in its own language. It was written in the name of King Ahasuerus and sealed with the king's signet ring. ¹³ Letters were sent by couriers to all the king's provinces

with instruction to destroy, to kill, and to annihilate all Jews, young and old, women and children, in one day, the thirteenth day of the twelfth month, which is the month of Adar, and to plunder their goods. ¹⁴ A copy of the document was to be issued as a decree in every province by proclamation to all the peoples to be ready for that day. ¹⁵ The couriers went out hurriedly by order of the king, and the decree was issued in Susa the citadel. And the king and Haman sat down to drink, but the city of Susa was thrown into confusion.

Esther Agrees to Help the Jews

4 When Mordecai learned all that had been done, Mordecai tore his clothes and put on sackcloth and ashes, and went out into the midst of the city, and he cried out with a loud and bitter cry. ² He went up to the entrance of the king's gate, for no one was allowed to enter the king's gate clothed in sackcloth. ³ And in every province, wherever the king's command and his

decree reached, there was great mourning among the Jews, with fasting and weeping and lamenting, and many of them lay in sackcloth and ashes.

⁴ When Esther's young women and her eunuchs came and told her, the queen was deeply distressed. She sent garments to clothe Mordecai, so that he might take off his sackcloth, but he would not accept them. ⁵ Then Esther called for Hathach, one of the king's eunuchs, who had been appointed to attend her, and ordered him to go to Mordecai to learn what this was and why it was. ⁶ Hathach went out to Mordecai in

the open square of the city in front of the king's gate, ⁷ and Mordecai told him all that had happened to him, and the exact sum of money that Haman had promised to pay into the king's treasuries for the destruction of the Jews. ⁸ Mordecai also gave him a copy of the written decree issued in Susa for their destruction, that he might show it to Esther and explain it to her and command her to go to the king to beg his favor and plead with him on behalf of her people. ⁹ And Hathach went and told Esther what Mordecai had said. ¹⁰ Then Esther spoke to Hathach and commanded him to go to Mordecai and say, ¹¹ "All the king's servants and the people of the king's provinces know that if any man

or woman goes to the king inside the inner court without being called, there is but one law—to be put to death, except the one to whom the king holds out the golden scepter so that he may live. But as for me, I have not been called to come in to the king these thirty days."

¹² And they told Mordecai what Esther had said. ¹³ Then Mordecai told them to reply to Esther, "Do not think to yourself that in the king's palace you will escape any more than all the other Jews. ¹⁴ For if you keep silent at this time, relief and deliverance will rise for the Jews from another place, but you and your father's house will perish. And who knows whether you have not come to the kingdom for such a time as this?" ¹⁵ Then Esther told them to reply to Mordecai, ¹⁶ "Go, gather all the Jews to be found in Susa, and hold a fast on my behalf, and do not eat or drink for three days, night or day. I and my young women will also fast as you do. Then I will go to the king, though it is against the law, and if I perish, I perish." ¹⁷ Mordecai then went away and did everything as Esther had ordered him.

Esther Prepares a Banquet

5 On the third day Esther put on her royal robes and stood in the inner court of the king's palace, in front of the king's quarters, while the king was sitting on his royal throne inside the throne room opposite the entrance to the palace. ² And when the king saw Queen Esther standing in the court, she won favor in his sight, and he held out to Esther the golden scepter that was in his hand. Then Esther approached and touched the tip of the scepter. ³ And the king said to her, "What is it, Queen Esther? What is your request? It shall be given you, even to the half of my kingdom." ⁴ And Esther said, "If it please the king, let the king and Haman come today to a feast that I have prepared for the king." ⁵ Then the king said, "Bring Haman quickly, so that we may do as Esther has asked." So the king and Haman came to the feast that Esther had prepared. ⁶ And as they were drinking wine after the feast, the king said to Esther, "What is your wish? It shall be granted you. And what is your request? Even to the half of my kingdom, it shall be fulfilled." ⁷ Then Esther answered, "My wish and my request is: ⁸ If I have found favor in the sight of the king, and if it please

PROFILE
ESTHER

Esther was a Jew living among the exiles in Persia, during the reign of King Ahasuerus. Following the death of her parents, Esther was raised by her cousin, Mordecai. Esther was a beautiful woman, and she won favor in the eyes of all who saw her. When the reigning queen was removed from power, a beauty contest was held to choose her replacement, and Esther was chosen. As queen of Persia, Esther risked her life to save the Jewish people from annihilation. She and Mordecai instituted the Feast of Purim to commemorate their deliverance.

KEY REFERENCE: ESTHER 4:14

the king to grant my wish and fulfill my request, let the king and Haman come to the feast that I will prepare for them, and tomorrow I will do as the king has said."

Haman Plans to Hang Mordecai

9 And Haman went out that day joyful and glad of heart. But when Haman saw Mordecai in the king's gate, that he neither rose nor trembled before him, he was filled with wrath against Mordecai. 10 Nevertheless, Haman restrained himself and went home, and he sent and brought his friends and his wife Zeresh. 11 And Haman recounted to them the splendor of his riches, the number of his sons, all the promotions with which the king had honored him, and how he had advanced him above the officials and the servants of the king. 12 Then Haman said, "Even Queen Esther let no one but me come with the king to the feast she prepared. And tomorrow also I am invited by her together with the king. 13 Yet all this is worth nothing to me, so long as I see Mordecai the Jew sitting at the king's gate." 14 Then his wife Zeresh and all his friends said to him, "Let a gallows fifty cubits high be made, and in the morning tell the king to have Mordecai hanged upon it. Then go joyfully with the king to the feast." This idea pleased Haman, and he had the gallows made.

The King Honors Mordecai

6 On that night the king could not sleep. And he gave orders to bring the book of memorable deeds, the chronicles, and they were read before the king. 2 And it was found written how Mordecai had told about Bigthana and Teresh, two of the king's eunuchs, who guarded the threshold, and who had sought to lay hands on King Ahasuerus. 3 And the king said, "What honor or distinction has been bestowed on Mordecai for this?" The king's young men who attended him said, "Nothing has been done for him." 4 And the king said, "Who is in the court?" Now Haman had just entered the outer court of the king's palace to speak to the king about having Mordecai hanged on the gallows that he had prepared for him. 5 And the king's young men told him, "Haman is there, standing in the court." And the king said, "Let him come in." 6 So Haman came in, and the king said to him,

"What should be done to the man whom the king delights to honor?" And Haman said to himself, "Whom would the king delight to honor more than me?" 7 And Haman said to the king, "For the man whom the king delights to honor, 8 let royal robes be brought, which the king has worn, and the horse that the king has ridden, and on whose head a royal crown is set. 9 And let the robes and the horse be handed over to one of the king's most noble officials. Let them dress the man whom the king delights to honor, and let them lead him on the horse through the square of the city, proclaiming before him: 'Thus shall it be done to the man whom the king delights to honor.'" 10 Then the king said to Haman, "Hurry; take the robes and the horse, as you have said, and do so to Mordecai the Jew, who sits at the king's gate. Leave out nothing that you have mentioned." 11 So Haman took the robes and the

---

GETTING THE MESSAGE

The invisible God. The book of Esther does not directly mention God, but his providential hand is evident throughout the story.

---

horse, and he dressed Mordecai and led him through the square of the city, proclaiming before him, "Thus shall it be done to the man whom the king delights to honor."

12 Then Mordecai returned to the king's gate. But Haman hurried to his house, mourning and with his head covered. 13 And Haman told his wife Zeresh and all his friends everything that had happened to him. Then his wise men and his wife Zeresh said to him, "If Mordecai, before whom you have begun to fall, is of the Jewish people, you will not overcome him but will surely fall before him."

Esther Reveals Haman's Plot

14 While they were yet talking with him, the king's eunuchs arrived and hurried to bring Haman to the feast that Esther had prepared.

7 So the king and Haman went in to feast with Queen Esther. 2 And on the second day, as they were drinking wine after the feast, the king again said to Esther, "What is your wish, Queen Esther? It shall be granted you. And what is your request? Even to the

half of my kingdom, it shall be fulfilled." ³ Then Queen Esther answered, "If I have found favor in your sight, O king, and if it please the king, let my life be granted me for my wish, and my people for my request. ⁴ For we have been sold, I and my people, to be destroyed, to be killed, and to be annihilated. If we had been sold merely as slaves, men and women, I would have been silent, for our affliction is not to be compared with the loss to the king." ⁵ Then King Ahasuerus said to Queen Esther, "Who is he, and where

is he, who has dared to do this?" ⁶ And Esther said, "A foe and enemy! This wicked Haman!" Then Haman was terrified before the king and the queen.

Haman Is Hanged

⁷ And the king arose in his wrath from the wine-drinking and went into the palace garden, but Haman stayed to beg for his life from Queen Esther, for he saw that harm was determined against him by the king. ⁸ And the king returned from the palace garden to the place where they were drinking wine, as Haman was falling on the couch where Esther was. And the king said, "Will

he even assault the queen in my presence, in my own house?" As the word left the mouth of the king, they covered Haman's face. ⁹ Then Harbona, one of the eunuchs in attendance on the king, said, "Moreover, the gallows that Haman has prepared for Mordecai, whose word saved the king, is standing at Haman's house, fifty cubits high." ¹⁰ And the king said, "Hang him on that." So they hanged Haman on the gallows that he had prepared for Mordecai. Then the wrath of the king abated.

Esther Saves the Jews

8 On that day King Ahasuerus gave to Queen Esther the house of Haman, the enemy of the Jews. And Mordecai came before the king, for Esther had told what he was to her. ² And the king took off his signet ring, which he had taken from Haman, and gave it to Mordecai. And Esther set Mordecai over the house of Haman.

³ Then Esther spoke again to the king. She fell at his feet and wept and pleaded with him to avert the evil plan of Haman the Agagite and the plot that he had devised against the Jews. ⁴ When the king held out the golden scepter to Esther, ⁵ Esther rose and stood before the king. And she said, "If it please the king, and if I have found favor in his sight, and if the thing seems right before the king, and I am pleasing in his eyes, let an order be written to revoke the letters devised by Haman the Agagite, the son of Hammedatha, which he wrote to destroy the Jews who are in all the provinces of the king. ⁶ For how can I bear to see the calamity that is coming to my people? Or how can I bear to see the destruction of my kindred?" ⁷ Then King Ahasuerus said to Queen Esther and to Mordecai the Jew, "Behold, I have given Esther the house of Haman, and they have hanged him on the gallows, because he intended to lay hands on the Jews. ⁸ But you may write as you please with regard to the Jews, in the name of the king, and seal it with the king's ring, for an edict written in the name of the king and sealed with the king's ring cannot be revoked."

⁹ The king's scribes were summoned at that time, in the third month, which is the month of Sivan, on the twenty-third day. And an edict was written, according to all that Mordecai commanded concerning the Jews, to the satraps and the governors and

the officials of the provinces from India to Ethiopia, 127 provinces, to each province in its own script and to each people in its own language, and also to the Jews in their script and their language. ¹⁰ And he wrote in the name of King Ahasuerus and sealed it with the king's signet ring. Then he sent the letters by mounted couriers riding on swift horses that were used in the king's service, bred from the royal stud, ¹¹ saying that the king allowed the Jews who were in every city to gather and defend their lives, to destroy, to kill, and to annihilate any armed force of any people or province that might attack them, children and women included, and to plunder their goods, ¹² on one day throughout all the provinces of King Ahasuerus, on the thirteenth day of the twelfth month, which is the month of Adar. ¹³ A copy of what was written was to be issued as a decree in every province, being publicly displayed to all peoples, and the Jews were to be ready on that day to take vengeance on their enemies. ¹⁴ So the couriers, mounted on their swift horses that were used in the king's service, rode out hurriedly, urged by the king's command. And the decree was issued in Susa the citadel.

¹⁵ Then Mordecai went out from the presence of the king in royal robes of blue and white, with a great golden crown and a robe of fine linen and purple, and the city of Susa shouted and rejoiced. ¹⁶ The Jews had light and gladness and joy and honor. ¹⁷ And in every province and in every city, wherever the king's command and his edict reached, there was gladness and joy among the Jews, a feast and a holiday. And many from the peoples of the country declared themselves Jews, for fear of the Jews had fallen on them.

The Jews Destroy Their Enemies

9 Now in the twelfth month, which is the month of Adar, on the thirteenth day of the same, when the king's command and edict were about to be carried out, on the very day when the enemies of the Jews hoped to gain the mastery over them, the reverse occurred: the Jews gained mastery over those who hated them. ² The Jews gathered in their cities throughout all the provinces of King Ahasuerus to lay hands on those who sought their harm. And no one could stand against them, for the fear of them had fallen on all peoples. ³ All the

officials of the provinces and the satraps and the governors and the royal agents also helped the Jews, for the fear of Mordecai had fallen on them. ⁴ For Mordecai was great in the king's house, and his fame spread throughout all the provinces, for the man Mordecai grew more and more powerful. ⁵ The Jews struck all their enemies with the sword, killing and destroying them, and did as they pleased to those who hated them. ⁶ In Susa the citadel itself the Jews killed and destroyed 500 men, ⁷ and also killed Parshandatha and Dalphon and Aspatha ⁸ and Poratha and Adalia and Aridatha ⁹ and Parmashta and Arisai and Aridai and Vaizatha, ¹⁰ the ten sons of Haman the son of Hammedatha, the enemy of the Jews, but they laid no hand on the plunder.

GETTING THE MESSAGE

Ancient Pony Express. The Persian Empire may have had the world's first postal service. Carriers rode on horseback to various stations throughout the empire, where they would deliver messages to other waiting carriers (8:14).

¹¹ That very day the number of those killed in Susa the citadel was reported to the king. ¹² And the king said to Queen Esther, "In Susa the citadel the Jews have killed and destroyed 500 men and also the ten sons of Haman. What then have they done in the rest of the king's provinces! Now what is your wish? It shall be granted you. And what further is your request? It shall be fulfilled." ¹³ And Esther said, "If it please the king, let the Jews who are in Susa be allowed tomorrow also to do according to this day's edict. And let the ten sons of Haman be hanged on the gallows." ¹⁴ So the king commanded this to be done. A decree was issued in Susa, and the ten sons of Haman were hanged. ¹⁵ The Jews who were in Susa gathered also on the fourteenth day of the month of Adar and they killed 300 men in Susa, but they laid no hands on the plunder.

¹⁶ Now the rest of the Jews who were in the king's provinces also gathered to defend their lives, and got relief from their enemies and killed 75,000 of those who hated them, but they laid no hands on the plunder.

17 This was on the thirteenth day of the month of Adar, and on the fourteenth day they rested and made that a day of feasting and gladness. **18** But the Jews who were in Susa gathered on the thirteenth day and on the fourteenth, and rested on the fifteenth day, making that a day of feasting and gladness. **19** Therefore the Jews of the villages, who live in the rural towns, hold the fourteenth day of the month of Adar as a day for gladness and feasting, as a holiday, and as a day on which they send gifts of food to one another.

The Feast of Purim Inaugurated

20 And Mordecai recorded these things and sent letters to all the Jews who were in all the provinces of King Ahasuerus, both near and far, **21** obliging them to keep the fourteenth day of the month Adar and also the fifteenth day of the same, year by year, **22** as the days on which the Jews got relief from their enemies, and as the month that had been turned for them from sorrow into gladness and from mourning into a holiday; that they should make them days of feasting and gladness, days for sending gifts of food to one another and gifts to the poor.

23 So the Jews accepted what they had started to do, and what Mordecai had written to them. **24** For Haman the Agagite, the son of Hammedatha, the enemy of all the Jews, had plotted against the Jews to destroy them, and had cast Pur (that is, cast lots), to crush and to destroy them. **25** But when it came before the king, he gave orders in writing that his evil plan that he had devised against the Jews should return on his own head, and that he and his sons should be hanged on the gallows. **26** Therefore they called these days Purim, after the term Pur. Therefore, because of all that was written

in this letter, and of what they had faced in this matter, and of what had happened to them, **27** the Jews firmly obligated themselves and their offspring and all who joined them, that without fail they would keep these two days according to what was written and at the time appointed every year, **28** that these days should be remembered and kept throughout every generation, in every clan, province, and city, and that these days of Purim should never fall into disuse among the Jews, nor should the commemoration of these days cease among their descendants.

29 Then Queen Esther, the daughter of Abihail, and Mordecai the Jew gave full written authority, confirming this second letter about Purim. **30** Letters were sent to all the Jews, to the 127 provinces of the kingdom of Ahasuerus, in words of peace and truth, **31** that these days of Purim should be observed at their appointed seasons, as Mordecai the Jew and Queen Esther obligated them, and as they had obligated themselves and their offspring, with regard to their fasts and their lamenting. **32** The command of Queen Esther confirmed these practices of Purim, and it was recorded in writing.

The Greatness of Mordecai

10 King Ahasuerus imposed tax on the land and on the coastlands of the sea. **2** And all the acts of his power and might, and the full account of the high honor of Mordecai, to which the king advanced him, are they not written in the Book of the Chronicles of the kings of Media and Persia? **3** For Mordecai the Jew was second in rank to King Ahasuerus, and he was great among the Jews and popular with the multitude of his brothers, for he sought the welfare of his people and spoke peace to all his people.

INTRODUCTION TO JOB

Abraham born   Events of Job   Exodus from Egypt

1446 B.C.

AUTHOR AND DATE

The unknown Israelite author of this book presents Job as a person living in Uz. Job's godliness (1:1) matches the ideals of Israelite wisdom literature. He clearly knows Yahweh (1:21). The events of the book seem to be set in the times of the patriarchs (Abraham, Isaac, and Jacob).

THEOLOGICAL THEMES

The book of Job concerns itself with the question of faith in a sovereign God. Can God be trusted? Is he good and just in his rule of the world? The book shows that the reasons for human suffering often remain a secret to human beings.

In the book of Job, God seems both too close and too far away. On the one hand, Job complains that God is watching him every moment so that he cannot even swallow his spit (7:19). On the other hand, Job finds God elusive (9:11). Though God is greatly concerned about humans, he does not always answer their most agonizing questions.

At the same time, Job's friends offer no real help. They come to "comfort" him (2:11), but Job ends up declaring them "miserable comforters" who would console him "with empty nothings" (21:34). These friends represent an oversimplified view of faith. They think that all human troubles are divine punishments for wrongdoing. Their "comfort" consists largely of urging Job to identify his sin and repent of it. These friends are negative examples of how to comfort those who are suffering.

The book illustrates that one does not need to fully understand God's will in order to be faithful while suffering. Those who suffer need not be afraid to express to God their confusion and questions.

PURPOSE

The book of Job was written to those who struggle with the question of how God can be good when the world is filled with suffering.

The author does not provide a formal defense of God's justice. Rather, as Job's friends offer their inadequate answers, the author shows how their reasoning fails. Then, in chs. 38–41, the Lord speaks in his own defense, bringing Job to fuller understanding (ch. 42).

Even during his suffering and confusion, before God finally speaks, Job can triumphantly declare, "I know that my Redeemer lives" (19:25).

OUTLINE

I. Prologue: Job's Character and the Circumstances of His Test (1:1–2:13)

II. Dialogue: Job, His Suffering, and His Standing before God (3:1–42:6)

   A. Job: despair for the day of his birth (3:1–26)

   B. The friends and Job: can Job be right before God? (4:1–25:6)

      1. First cycle (4:1–14:22)

      2. Second cycle (15:1–21:34)

      3. Third cycle (22:1–25:6)

   C. Job: the power of God, place of wisdom, and path of integrity (26:1–31:40)

   D. Elihu: suffering as a discipline (32:1–37:24)

   E. Challenge: the Lord answers Job (38:1–42:6)

III. Epilogue: The Vindication, Intercession, and Restoration of Job (42:7–17)

JOB

Job's Character and Wealth

1 There was a man in the land of Uz whose name was Job, and that man was blameless and upright, one who feared God and turned away from evil. **2** There were born to him seven sons and three daughters. **3** He possessed 7,000 sheep, 3,000 camels, 500 yoke of oxen, and 500 female donkeys, and very many servants, so that this man was the greatest of all the people of the east. **4** His sons used to go and hold a feast in the house of each one on his day, and they would send and invite their three sisters to eat and drink with them. **5** And when the days of the feast had run their course, Job would send and consecrate them, and he would rise early in the morning and offer burnt offerings according to the number of them all. For Job said, "It may be that my children have sinned, and cursed God in their hearts." Thus Job did continually.

Satan Allowed to Test Job

6 Now there was a day when the sons of God came to present themselves before the Lord, and Satan[1] also came among them. **7** The Lord said to Satan, "From where have you come?" Satan answered the Lord and said, "From going to and fro on the earth, and from walking up and down on it." **8** And the Lord said to Satan, "Have you considered my servant Job, that there is none like him on the earth, a blameless and upright man, who fears God and turns away from evil?" **9** Then Satan answered the Lord and said, "Does Job fear God for no reason? **10** Have you not put a hedge around him and his house and all that he has, on every side? You have blessed the work of his hands, and his possessions have increased in the land. **11** But stretch out your hand and touch all that he has, and he will curse you to your face." **12** And the Lord said to Satan, "Behold, all that he has is in your hand. Only against him do not stretch out your hand." So Satan went out from the presence of the Lord.

Satan Takes Job's Property and Children

13 Now there was a day when his sons and daughters were eating and drinking wine in their oldest brother's house, **14** and there came a messenger to Job and said, "The oxen were plowing and the donkeys feeding beside them, **15** and the Sabeans fell upon them and took them and struck down the servants with the edge of the sword, and I alone have escaped to tell you." **16** While he was yet speaking, there came another and said, "The fire of God fell from heaven and burned up the sheep and the servants and consumed them, and I alone

GETTING THE MESSAGE

Comfort (2:11) is a key word in the book of Job. When faced with personal tragedies, Job receives no comfort from his friends (16:2). But when God answers him (see chs. 38–41), he finds the comfort he needs.

have escaped to tell you." **17** While he was yet speaking, there came another and said, "The Chaldeans formed three groups and made a raid on the camels and took them and struck down the servants with the edge of the sword, and I alone have escaped to tell you." **18** While he was yet speaking, there came another and said, "Your sons and daughters were eating and drinking wine in their oldest brother's house, **19** and behold, a great wind came across the wilderness and struck the four corners of the house, and it fell upon the young people, and they are dead, and I alone have escaped to tell you." **20** Then Job arose and tore his robe and shaved his head and fell on the ground and worshiped. **21** And he said, "Naked I came from my mother's womb, and naked shall I return. The Lord gave, and the Lord has taken away; blessed be the name of the Lord."

---

[1] Hebrew *the Accuser* or *the Adversary*; so throughout chapters 1–2

²² In all this Job did not sin or charge God with wrong.

Satan Attacks Job's Health

2 Again there was a day when the sons of God came to present themselves before the LORD, and Satan also came among them to present himself before the LORD. ² And the LORD said to Satan, "From where have you come?" Satan answered the LORD and said,

---

PROFILE

JOB

Job was a wealthy man whom the Bible describes as "blameless and upright" (1:1). When God pointed out Job's faithfulness, Satan responded that Job feared God only because the Lord had protected and blessed him. To test Job's integrity, God allowed Satan to take away all of Job's possessions and his children. In a single day Job lost everything, yet he responded faithfully (1:21). Next God gave Satan permission to attack Job's health. He struck Job with painful sores (2:7). Job's wife then urged him to "curse God and die" (2:9). Job's friends wrongly concluded that his sins caused his suffering, but Job refused to accept this. Instead, Job asked God to explain why he was suffering. God eventually answered Job's cries, and Job humbly submitted to God's sovereignty. The Lord then restored Job's fortune, giving him "twice as much as he had before" (42:10), and blessed him with more children.

KEY REFERENCE: JOB 19:25

"From going to and fro on the earth, and from walking up and down on it." ³ And the LORD said to Satan, "Have you considered my servant Job, that there is none like him on the earth, a blameless and upright man, who fears God and turns away from evil? He still holds fast his integrity, although you incited me against him to destroy him without reason." ⁴ Then Satan answered the LORD and said, "Skin for skin! All that a man has he will give for his life. ⁵ But stretch out

your hand and touch his bone and his flesh, and he will curse you to your face." ⁶ And the LORD said to Satan, "Behold, he is in your hand; only spare his life."

⁷ So Satan went out from the presence of the LORD and struck Job with loathsome sores from the sole of his foot to the crown of his head. ⁸ And he took a piece of broken pottery with which to scrape himself while he sat in the ashes.

⁹ Then his wife said to him, "Do you still hold fast your integrity? Curse God and die." ¹⁰ But he said to her, "You speak as one of the foolish women would speak. Shall we receive good from God, and shall we not receive evil?"¹ In all this Job did not sin with his lips.

Job's Three Friends

¹¹ Now when Job's three friends heard of all this evil that had come upon him, they came each from his own place, Eliphaz the Temanite, Bildad the Shuhite, and Zophar

---

GETTING THE MESSAGE

Seven days and seven nights was a traditional period for mourning in the ancient Near East (2:13).

---

the Naamathite. They made an appointment together to come to show him sympathy and comfort him. ¹² And when they saw him from a distance, they did not recognize him. And they raised their voices and wept, and they tore their robes and sprinkled dust on their heads toward heaven. ¹³ And they sat with him on the ground seven days and seven nights, and no one spoke a word to him, for they saw that his suffering was very great.

Job Laments His Birth

3 After this Job opened his mouth and cursed the day of his birth. ² And Job said:

³   "Let the day perish on which I was born,
        and the night that said,
        'A man is conceived.'
⁴   Let that day be darkness!
        May God above not seek it,
        nor light shine upon it.

¹ Or *disaster*; also 2:11

5 Let gloom and deep darkness claim it.
  Let clouds dwell upon it;
    let the blackness of the day terrify it.
6 That night—let thick darkness seize it!
  Let it not rejoice among the days of
    the year;
    let it not come into the number of
    the months.
7 Behold, let that night be barren;
  let no joyful cry enter it.
8 Let those curse it who curse the day,
  who are ready to rouse up Leviathan.
9 Let the stars of its dawn be dark;
  let it hope for light, but have none,
    nor see the eyelids of the morning,
10 because it did not shut the doors of
  my mother's womb,
    nor hide trouble from my eyes.

11 "Why did I not die at birth,
  come out from the womb and expire?
12 Why did the knees receive me?
  Or why the breasts, that I should
    nurse?
13 For then I would have lain down and
    been quiet;
  I would have slept; then I would
    have been at rest,
14 with kings and counselors of the earth
  who rebuilt ruins for themselves,
15 or with princes who had gold,
  who filled their houses with silver.
16 Or why was I not as a hidden stillborn
    child,
  as infants who never see the light?
17 There the wicked cease from troubling,
  and there the weary are at rest.
18 There the prisoners are at ease
    together;
  they hear not the voice of the task-
    master.
19 The small and the great are there,
  and the slave is free from his master.

20 "Why is light given to him who is in
    misery,
  and life to the bitter in soul,
21 who long for death, but it comes not,
  and dig for it more than for hidden
    treasures,
22 who rejoice exceedingly
  and are glad when they find the
    grave?
23 Why is light given to a man whose
    way is hidden,
  whom God has hedged in?

24 For my sighing comes instead of my
    bread,
  and my groanings are poured out
    like water.
25 For the thing that I fear comes upon
    me,
  and what I dread befalls me.
26 I am not at ease, nor am I quiet;
  I have no rest, but trouble comes."

Eliphaz Speaks: The Innocent Prosper

4 Then Eliphaz the Temanite answered
  and said:

2 "If one ventures a word with you, will
    you be impatient?
  Yet who can keep from speaking?
3 Behold, you have instructed many,
  and you have strengthened the
    weak hands.

GETTING THE MESSAGE

Was Job a real person? It is not known
exactly when Job lived, but he was a real
person. Ezekiel 14:14, 20 and James 5:11
refer to him as a historical figure.

4 Your words have upheld him who was
    stumbling,
  and you have made firm the feeble
    knees.
5 But now it has come to you, and you
    are impatient;
  it touches you, and you are dis-
    mayed.
6 Is not your fear of God your confi-
    dence,
  and the integrity of your ways your
    hope?

7 "Remember: who that was innocent
    ever perished?
  Or where were the upright cut off?
8 As I have seen, those who plow iniq-
    uity
  and sow trouble reap the same.
9 By the breath of God they perish,
  and by the blast of his anger they
    are consumed.
10 The roar of the lion, the voice of the
    fierce lion,
  the teeth of the young lions are
    broken.

11 The strong lion perishes for lack of prey,
   and the cubs of the lioness are scattered.
12 "Now a word was brought to me
   stealthily;
   my ear received the whisper of it.
13 Amid thoughts from visions of the
   night,
   when deep sleep falls on men,

PROFILE

ELIPHAZ, BILDAD, AND ZOPHAR

After the Lord allowed Satan to afflict Job, three of his friends, Eliphaz, Bildad, and Zophar, came to comfort him. However, all three wrongly assumed that Job's suffering was the result of some hidden sin. Each man urged Job to repent so that God would have mercy on him. But Job insisted that he was innocent. Although it is true that some suffering is a result of sin, Eliphaz, Bildad, and Zophar oversimplified this truth. They believed that all troubles are punishments for wrongdoing, which was not the case for Job. The wrong actions of Job's three friends should remind believers today to be wise and sensitive when dealing with people in distress. The Lord rebuked Job's three friends and instructed Job to pray for them.

KEY REFERENCE: JOB 42:7–9

---

14 dread came upon me, and trembling,
   which made all my bones shake.
15 A spirit glided past my face;
   the hair of my flesh stood up.
16 It stood still,
   but I could not discern its appearance.
   A form was before my eyes;
   there was silence, then I heard a
   voice:
17 'Can mortal man be in the right before
   God?
   Can a man be pure before his Maker?

18 Even in his servants he puts no trust,
   and his angels he charges with error;
19 how much more those who dwell in
   houses of clay,
   whose foundation is in the dust,
   who are crushed like the moth.
20 Between morning and evening they
   are beaten to pieces;
   they perish forever without anyone
   regarding it.
21 Is not their tent-cord plucked up
   within them,
   do they not die, and that without
   wisdom?'

5 "Call now; is there anyone who will
   answer you?
   To which of the holy ones will you
   turn?
2 Surely vexation kills the fool,
   and jealousy slays the simple.
3 I have seen the fool taking root,
   but suddenly I cursed his dwelling.
4 His children are far from safety;
   they are crushed in the gate,
   and there is no one to deliver them.
5 The hungry eat his harvest,
   and he takes it even out of thorns,
   and the thirsty pant after his wealth.
6 For affliction does not come from the
   dust,
   nor does trouble sprout from the
   ground,
7 but man is born to trouble
   as the sparks fly upward.

8 "As for me, I would seek God,
   and to God would I commit my
   cause,
9 who does great things and unsearchable,
   marvelous things without number:
10 he gives rain on the earth
   and sends waters on the fields;
11 he sets on high those who are lowly,
   and those who mourn are lifted to
   safety.
12 He frustrates the devices of the crafty,
   so that their hands achieve no success.
13 He catches the wise in their own craftiness,
   and the schemes of the wily are
   brought to a quick end.

14 They meet with darkness in the daytime
     and grope at noonday as in the night.
15 But he saves the needy from the
   sword of their mouth
     and from the hand of the mighty.
16 So the poor have hope,
     and injustice shuts her mouth.

17 "Behold, blessed is the one whom God
   reproves;
     therefore despise not the discipline
       of the Almighty.
18 For he wounds, but he binds up;
     he shatters, but his hands heal.
19 He will deliver you from six troubles;
     in seven no evil[1] shall touch you.
20 In famine he will redeem you from
   death,
     and in war from the power of the
       sword.
21 You shall be hidden from the lash of
   the tongue,
     and shall not fear destruction when
       it comes.
22 At destruction and famine you shall
   laugh,
     and shall not fear the beasts of the
       earth.
23 For you shall be in league with the
   stones of the field,
     and the beasts of the field shall be
       at peace with you.
24 You shall know that your tent is at
   peace,
     and you shall inspect your fold and
       miss nothing.
25 You shall know also that your offspring shall be many,
     and your descendants as the grass
       of the earth.
26 You shall come to your grave in ripe
   old age,
     like a sheaf gathered up in its season.
27 Behold, this we have searched out; it
   is true.
     Hear, and know it for your good."

Job Replies: My Complaint Is Just

6 Then Job answered and said:

2 "Oh that my vexation were weighed,
     and all my calamity laid in the
       balances!

3 For then it would be heavier than the
   sand of the sea;
     therefore my words have been rash.
4 For the arrows of the Almighty are in
   me;
     my spirit drinks their poison;
     the terrors of God are arrayed
       against me.
5 Does the wild donkey bray when he
   has grass,
     or the ox low over his fodder?
6 Can that which is tasteless be eaten
   without salt,
     or is there any taste in the juice of
       the mallow?
7 My appetite refuses to touch them;
     they are as food that is loathsome to
       me.

8 "Oh that I might have my request,
     and that God would fulfill my hope,
9 that it would please God to crush me,
     that he would let loose his hand
       and cut me off!
10 This would be my comfort;
     I would even exult in pain unspar-
       ing,
     for I have not denied the words of
       the Holy One.
11 What is my strength, that I should wait?
     And what is my end, that I should
       be patient?
12 Is my strength the strength of stones,
     or is my flesh bronze?
13 Have I any help in me,
     when resource is driven from me?

14 "He who withholds kindness from a
   friend
     forsakes the fear of the Almighty.
15 My brothers are treacherous as a
   torrent-bed,
     as torrential streams that pass away,
16 which are dark with ice,
     and where the snow hides itself.
17 When they melt, they disappear;
     when it is hot, they vanish from
       their place.
18 The caravans turn aside from their
   course;
     they go up into the waste and per-
       ish.
19 The caravans of Tema look,
     the travelers of Sheba hope.

[1] Or disaster

20 They are ashamed because they were
      confident;
   they come there and are disap-
      pointed.
21 For you have now become nothing;
   you see my calamity and are afraid.
22 Have I said, 'Make me a gift'?
   Or, 'From your wealth offer a bribe
      for me'?
23 Or, 'Deliver me from the adversary's
      hand'?
   Or, 'Redeem me from the hand of
      the ruthless'?

24 "Teach me, and I will be silent;
   make me understand how I have
      gone astray.
25 How forceful are upright words!
   But what does reproof from you
      reprove?

GETTING THE MESSAGE

What is Sheol? In the Old Testament,
Sheol (7:9–10) is where the dead reside.
It is a place of rest for believers (1 Sam.
28:14), but a place of punishment for the
wicked (Isa. 14:3–23).

26 Do you think that you can reprove
      words,
   when the speech of a despairing
      man is wind?
27 You would even cast lots over the
      fatherless,
   and bargain over your friend.
28 "But now, be pleased to look at me,
   for I will not lie to your face.
29 Please turn; let no injustice be done.
   Turn now; my vindication is at
      stake.
30 Is there any injustice on my tongue?
   Cannot my palate discern the cause
      of calamity?

Job Continues: My Life Has No Hope

7 "Has not man a hard service on earth,
   and are not his days like the days of a
      hired hand?
2 Like a slave who longs for the shadow,
   and like a hired hand who looks for
      his wages,
3 so I am allotted months of emptiness,
   and nights of misery are appor-
      tioned to me.
4 When I lie down I say, 'When shall I
      arise?'
   But the night is long,
   and I am full of tossing till the dawn.
5 My flesh is clothed with worms and
      dirt;
   my skin hardens, then breaks out
      afresh.
6 My days are swifter than a weaver's
      shuttle
   and come to their end without hope.

7 "Remember that my life is a breath;
   my eye will never again see good.
8 The eye of him who sees me will
      behold me no more;
   while your eyes are on me, I shall be
      gone.
9 As the cloud fades and vanishes,
   so he who goes down to Sheol does
      not come up;
10 he returns no more to his house,
   nor does his place know him any-
      more.

11 "Therefore I will not restrain my
      mouth;
   I will speak in the anguish of my
      spirit;
   I will complain in the bitterness of
      my soul.
12 Am I the sea, or a sea monster,
   that you set a guard over me?
13 When I say, 'My bed will comfort me,
   my couch will ease my complaint,'
14 then you scare me with dreams
   and terrify me with visions,
15 so that I would choose strangling
   and death rather than my bones.
16 I loathe my life; I would not live for-
      ever.
   Leave me alone, for my days are a
      breath.
17 What is man, that you make so much
      of him,
   and that you set your heart on him,
18 visit him every morning
   and test him every moment?
19 How long will you not look away from
      me,
   nor leave me alone till I swallow my
      spit?

²⁰ If I sin, what do I do to you, you
      watcher of mankind?
    Why have you made me your mark?
    Why have I become a burden to you?
²¹ Why do you not pardon my transgres-
      sion
    and take away my iniquity?
    For now I shall lie in the earth;
      you will seek me, but I shall not be."

Bildad Speaks: Job Should Repent

8 Then Bildad the Shuhite answered and
said:

² "How long will you say these things,
    and the words of your mouth be a
      great wind?
³ Does God pervert justice?
    Or does the Almighty pervert the
      right?
⁴ If your children have sinned against
      him,
    he has delivered them into the hand
      of their transgression.
⁵ If you will seek God
    and plead with the Almighty for
      mercy,
⁶ if you are pure and upright,
    surely then he will rouse himself
      for you
    and restore your rightful habitation.
⁷ And though your beginning was
      small,
    your latter days will be very great.

⁸ "For inquire, please, of bygone ages,
    and consider what the fathers have
      searched out.
⁹ For we are but of yesterday and know
      nothing,
    for our days on earth are a shadow.
¹⁰ Will they not teach you and tell you
    and utter words out of their under-
      standing?
¹¹ "Can papyrus grow where there is no
      marsh?
    Can reeds flourish where there is
      no water?
¹² While yet in flower and not cut down,
    they wither before any other plant.
¹³ Such are the paths of all who forget
      God;
    the hope of the godless shall perish.
¹⁴ His confidence is severed,
    and his trust is a spider's web.

¹⁵ He leans against his house, but it does
      not stand;
    he lays hold of it, but it does not
      endure.
¹⁶ He is a lush plant before the sun,
    and his shoots spread over his gar-
      den.
¹⁷ His roots entwine the stone heap;
    he looks upon a house of stones.
¹⁸ If he is destroyed from his place,
    then it will deny him, saying, 'I have
      never seen you.'
¹⁹ Behold, this is the joy of his way,
    and out of the soil others will
      spring.

²⁰ "Behold, God will not reject a blame-
      less man,
    nor take the hand of evildoers.
²¹ He will yet fill your mouth with
      laughter,
    and your lips with shouting.

> ### GETTING THE MESSAGE
>
> In the literature of the ancient Near East,
> **the sea** (9:8) is often seen as a threat
> to the order of nature. People looked
> upon the sea as something that could
> not be contained or conquered.

²² Those who hate you will be clothed
      with shame,
    and the tent of the wicked will be
      no more."

Job Replies: There Is No Arbiter

9 Then Job answered and said:

² "Truly I know that it is so:
    But how can a man be in the right
      before God?
³ If one wished to contend with him,
    one could not answer him once in a
      thousand times.
⁴ He is wise in heart and mighty in
      strength
    —who has hardened himself
      against him, and succeeded?—
⁵ he who removes mountains, and they
      know it not,
    when he overturns them in his
      anger,

6 who shakes the earth out of its place,
  and its pillars tremble;
7 who commands the sun, and it does
    not rise;
  who seals up the stars;
8 who alone stretched out the heavens
  and trampled the waves of the sea;
9 who made the Bear and Orion,
  the Pleiades and the chambers of
    the south;
10 who does great things beyond search-
    ing out,
  and marvelous things beyond num-
    ber.
11 Behold, he passes by me, and I see
    him not;
  he moves on, but I do not perceive
    him.
12 Behold, he snatches away; who can
    turn him back?
  Who will say to him, 'What are you
    doing?'
13 "God will not turn back his anger;
  beneath him bowed the helpers of
    Rahab.
14 How then can I answer him,
  choosing my words with him?
15 Though I am in the right, I cannot
    answer him;
  I must appeal for mercy to my
    accuser.
16 If I summoned him and he answered
    me,
  I would not believe that he was
    listening to my voice.
17 For he crushes me with a tempest
  and multiplies my wounds without
    cause;
18 he will not let me get my breath,
  but fills me with bitterness.
19 If it is a contest of strength, behold, he
    is mighty!
  If it is a matter of justice, who can
    summon him?
20 Though I am in the right, my own
    mouth would condemn me;
  though I am blameless, he would
    prove me perverse.
21 I am blameless; I regard not myself;
  I loathe my life.
22 It is all one; therefore I say,
  'He destroys both the blameless and
    the wicked.'

23 When disaster brings sudden death,
  he mocks at the calamity of the
    innocent.
24 The earth is given into the hand of the
    wicked;
  he covers the faces of its judges—
  if it is not he, who then is it?

25 "My days are swifter than a runner;
  they flee away; they see no good.
26 They go by like skiffs of reed,
  like an eagle swooping on the prey.
27 If I say, 'I will forget my complaint,
  I will put off my sad face, and be of
    good cheer,'
28 I become afraid of all my suffering,
  for I know you will not hold me
    innocent.
29 I shall be condemned;
  why then do I labor in vain?
30 If I wash myself with snow
  and cleanse my hands with lye,
31 yet you will plunge me into a pit,
  and my own clothes will abhor me.
32 For he is not a man, as I am, that I
    might answer him,
  that we should come to trial
    together.
33 There is no arbiter between us,
  who might lay his hand on us both.
34 Let him take his rod away from me,
  and let not dread of him terrify me.
35 Then I would speak without fear of
    him,
  for I am not so in myself.

Job Continues: A Plea to God

10 "I loathe my life;
  I will give free utterance to my
    complaint;
  I will speak in the bitterness of my
    soul.
2 I will say to God, Do not condemn me;
  let me know why you contend
    against me.
3 Does it seem good to you to oppress,
  to despise the work of your hands
  and favor the designs of the
    wicked?
4 Have you eyes of flesh?
  Do you see as man sees?
5 Are your days as the days of man,
  or your years as a man's years,
6 that you seek out my iniquity
  and search for my sin,

⁷ although you know that I am not guilty,
   and there is none to deliver out of
      your hand?
⁸ Your hands fashioned and made me,
   and now you have destroyed me
      altogether.
⁹ Remember that you have made me
      like clay;
   and will you return me to the dust?
¹⁰ Did you not pour me out like milk
   and curdle me like cheese?
¹¹ You clothed me with skin and flesh,
   and knit me together with bones
      and sinews.
¹² You have granted me life and steadfast
      love,
   and your care has preserved my
      spirit.
¹³ Yet these things you hid in your
      heart;
   I know that this was your purpose.
¹⁴ If I sin, you watch me
   and do not acquit me of my iniq-
      uity.
¹⁵ If I am guilty, woe to me!
   If I am in the right, I cannot lift up
      my head,
   for I am filled with disgrace
   and look on my affliction.
¹⁶ And were my head lifted up, you
      would hunt me like a lion
   and again work wonders against
      me.
¹⁷ You renew your witnesses against me
   and increase your vexation toward
      me;
   you bring fresh troops against me.
¹⁸ "Why did you bring me out from the
      womb?
   Would that I had died before any
      eye had seen me
¹⁹ and were as though I had not been,
   carried from the womb to the grave.
²⁰ Are not my days few?
   Then cease, and leave me alone,
      that I may find a little cheer
²¹ before I go—and I shall not return—
   to the land of darkness and deep
      shadow,
²² the land of gloom like thick darkness,
   like deep shadow without any
      order,
   where light is as thick darkness."

Zophar Speaks: You Deserve Worse

11 Then Zophar the Naamathite answered and said:

² "Should a multitude of words go unan-
      swered,
   and a man full of talk be judged right?
³ Should your babble silence men,
   and when you mock, shall no one
      shame you?
⁴ For you say, 'My doctrine is pure,
   and I am clean in God's eyes.'
⁵ But oh, that God would speak
   and open his lips to you,
⁶ and that he would tell you the secrets
      of wisdom!
   For he is manifold in understanding.
   Know then that God exacts of you less
      than your guilt deserves.

GETTING THE MESSAGE

Clay was one of the most readily available materials in ancient times. It was used to construct buildings and to make everyday household items. Job describes himself as having been made "like clay" (10:9) and says that he will someday return to dust. This should remind readers of Genesis 2:7, where the Lord created man from dust.

⁷ "Can you find out the deep things of
      God?
   Can you find out the limit of the
      Almighty?
⁸ It is higher than heaven—what can
      you do?
   Deeper than Sheol—what can you
      know?
⁹ Its measure is longer than the earth
   and broader than the sea.
¹⁰ If he passes through and imprisons
   and summons the court, who can
      turn him back?
¹¹ For he knows worthless men;
   when he sees iniquity, will he not
      consider it?
¹² But a stupid man will get understand-
      ing
   when a wild donkey's colt is born a
      man!

13 "If you prepare your heart,
    you will stretch out your hands
        toward him.
14 If iniquity is in your hand, put it far
        away,
    and let not injustice dwell in your
        tents.
15 Surely then you will lift up your face
        without blemish;
    you will be secure and will not fear.
16 You will forget your misery;
    you will remember it as waters that
        have passed away.
17 And your life will be brighter than the
        noonday;
    its darkness will be like the morning.
18 And you will feel secure, because
        there is hope;
    you will look around and take your
        rest in security.
19 You will lie down, and none will make
        you afraid;
    many will court your favor.
20 But the eyes of the wicked will fail;
    all way of escape will be lost to them,
    and their hope is to breathe their
        last."

Job Replies: The Lord Has Done This

12 Then Job answered and said:

2 "No doubt you are the people,
    and wisdom will die with you.
3 But I have understanding as well as
        you;
    I am not inferior to you.
    Who does not know such things as
        these?
4 I am a laughingstock to my friends;
    I, who called to God and he
        answered me,
    a just and blameless man, am a
        laughingstock.
5 In the thought of one who is at ease
        there is contempt for misfortune;
    it is ready for those whose feet slip.
6 The tents of robbers are at peace,
    and those who provoke God are
        secure,
    who bring their god in their hand.

7 "But ask the beasts, and they will teach
        you;
    the birds of the heavens, and they
        will tell you;

8 or the bushes of the earth, and they
        will teach you;
    and the fish of the sea will declare
        to you.
9 Who among all these does not know
    that the hand of the Lord has done
        this?
10 In his hand is the life of every living
        thing
    and the breath of all mankind.
11 Does not the ear test words
    as the palate tastes food?
12 Wisdom is with the aged,
    and understanding in length of
        days.

13 "With God are wisdom and might;
    he has counsel and understanding.
14 If he tears down, none can rebuild;
    if he shuts a man in, none can open.
15 If he withholds the waters, they dry
        up;
    if he sends them out, they over-
        whelm the land.
16 With him are strength and sound
        wisdom;
    the deceived and the deceiver are
        his.
17 He leads counselors away stripped,
    and judges he makes fools.
18 He looses the bonds of kings
    and binds a waistcloth on their
        hips.
19 He leads priests away stripped
    and overthrows the mighty.
20 He deprives of speech those who are
        trusted
    and takes away the discernment of
        the elders.
21 He pours contempt on princes
    and loosens the belt of the strong.
22 He uncovers the deeps out of darkness
    and brings deep darkness to light.
23 He makes nations great, and he
        destroys them;
    he enlarges nations, and leads them
        away.
24 He takes away understanding from the
        chiefs of the people of the earth
    and makes them wander in a track-
        less waste.
25 They grope in the dark without light,
    and he makes them stagger like a
        drunken man.

Job Continues: Still I Will Hope in God

13 "Behold, my eye has seen all this,
my ear has heard and understood
it.

2 What you know, I also know;
I am not inferior to you.

3 But I would speak to the Almighty,
and I desire to argue my case with
God.

4 As for you, you whitewash with lies;
worthless physicians are you all.

5 Oh that you would keep silent,
and it would be your wisdom!

6 Hear now my argument
and listen to the pleadings of my
lips.

7 Will you speak falsely for God
and speak deceitfully for him?

8 Will you show partiality toward him?
Will you plead the case for God?

9 Will it be well with you when he
searches you out?
Or can you deceive him, as one
deceives a man?

10 He will surely rebuke you
if in secret you show partiality.

11 Will not his majesty terrify you,
and the dread of him fall upon you?

12 Your maxims are proverbs of ashes;
your defenses are defenses of clay.

13 "Let me have silence, and I will speak,
and let come on me what may.

14 Why should I take my flesh in my
teeth
and put my life in my hand?

15 Though he slay me, I will hope in him;
yet I will argue my ways to his face.

16 This will be my salvation,
that the godless shall not come
before him.

17 Keep listening to my words,
and let my declaration be in your
ears.

18 Behold, I have prepared my case;
I know that I shall be in the right.

19 Who is there who will contend with
me?
For then I would be silent and die.

20 Only grant me two things,
then I will not hide myself from
your face:

21 withdraw your hand far from me,
and let not dread of you terrify me.

22 Then call, and I will answer;
or let me speak, and you reply to me.

23 How many are my iniquities and my
sins?
Make me know my transgression
and my sin.

24 Why do you hide your face
and count me as your enemy?

25 Will you frighten a driven leaf
and pursue dry chaff?

26 For you write bitter things against me
and make me inherit the iniquities
of my youth.

27 You put my feet in the stocks
and watch all my paths;
you set a limit for the soles of my
feet.

28 Man wastes away like a rotten thing,
like a garment that is moth-eaten.

GETTING THE MESSAGE

The book of Job includes **three cycles of conversations** in which the friends of Job offer their comfort and advice, and then listen as Job responds. The first cycle covers chs. 4–14.

Job Continues: Death Comes Soon to All

14 "Man who is born of a woman
is few of days and full of trouble.

2 He comes out like a flower and withers;
he flees like a shadow and continues not.

3 And do you open your eyes on such a
one
and bring me into judgment with
you?

4 Who can bring a clean thing out of an
unclean?
There is not one.

5 Since his days are determined,
and the number of his months is
with you,
and you have appointed his limits
that he cannot pass,

6 look away from him and leave him
alone,
that he may enjoy, like a hired
hand, his day.

7 "For there is hope for a tree,
      if it be cut down, that it will sprout
          again,
      and that its shoots will not cease.
8 Though its root grow old in the earth,
      and its stump die in the soil,
9 yet at the scent of water it will bud
      and put out branches like a young
          plant.
10 But a man dies and is laid low;
      man breathes his last, and where is
          he?
11 As waters fail from a lake
      and a river wastes away and dries up,
12 so a man lies down and rises not again;
      till the heavens are no more he will
          not awake
      or be roused out of his sleep.
13 Oh that you would hide me in Sheol,
      that you would conceal me until
          your wrath be past,
      that you would appoint me a set
          time, and remember me!
14 If a man dies, shall he live again?
      All the days of my service I would
          wait,
      till my renewal should come.
15 You would call, and I would answer
          you;
      you would long for the work of your
          hands.
16 For then you would number my steps;
      you would not keep watch over my
          sin;
17 my transgression would be sealed up
          in a bag,
      and you would cover over my iniq-
          uity.

18 "But the mountain falls and crumbles
          away,
      and the rock is removed from its
          place;
19 the waters wear away the stones;
      the torrents wash away the soil of
          the earth;
      so you destroy the hope of man.
20 You prevail forever against him, and
          he passes;
      you change his countenance, and
          send him away.
21 His sons come to honor, and he does
          not know it;
      they are brought low, and he per-
          ceives it not.

22 He feels only the pain of his own
          body,
      and he mourns only for himself."

Eliphaz Accuses: Job Does Not Fear God

15 Then Eliphaz the Temanite answered
      and said:

2 "Should a wise man answer with
          windy knowledge,
      and fill his belly with the east wind?
3 Should he argue in unprofitable talk,
      or in words with which he can do
          no good?
4 But you are doing away with the fear
          of God
      and hindering meditation before
          God.
5 For your iniquity teaches your mouth,
      and you choose the tongue of the
          crafty.
6 Your own mouth condemns you, and
          not I;
      your own lips testify against you.

7 "Are you the first man who was born?
      Or were you brought forth before
          the hills?
8 Have you listened in the council of
          God?
      And do you limit wisdom to your-
          self?
9 What do you know that we do not
          know?
      What do you understand that is not
          clear to us?
10 Both the gray-haired and the aged are
          among us,
      older than your father.
11 Are the comforts of God too small for
          you,
      or the word that deals gently with
          you?
12 Why does your heart carry you away,
      and why do your eyes flash,
13 that you turn your spirit against God
      and bring such words out of your
          mouth?
14 What is man, that he can be pure?
      Or he who is born of a woman, that
          he can be righteous?
15 Behold, God puts no trust in his holy
          ones,
      and the heavens are not pure in his
          sight;

16 how much less one who is abominable and corrupt,
  a man who drinks injustice like water!

17 "I will show you; hear me,
  and what I have seen I will declare

18 (what wise men have told,
  without hiding it from their fathers,

19 to whom alone the land was given,
  and no stranger passed among them).

20 The wicked man writhes in pain all his days,
  through all the years that are laid up for the ruthless.

21 Dreadful sounds are in his ears;
  in prosperity the destroyer will come upon him.

22 He does not believe that he will return out of darkness,
  and he is marked for the sword.

23 He wanders abroad for bread, saying, 'Where is it?'
  He knows that a day of darkness is ready at his hand;

24 distress and anguish terrify him;
  they prevail against him, like a king ready for battle.

25 Because he has stretched out his hand against God
  and defies the Almighty,

26 running stubbornly against him
  with a thickly bossed shield;

27 because he has covered his face with his fat
  and gathered fat upon his waist

28 and has lived in desolate cities,
  in houses that none should inhabit,
  which were ready to become heaps of ruins;

29 he will not be rich, and his wealth will not endure,
  nor will his possessions spread over the earth;

30 he will not depart from darkness;
  the flame will dry up his shoots,
  and by the breath of his mouth he will depart.

31 Let him not trust in emptiness, deceiving himself,
  for emptiness will be his payment.

32 It will be paid in full before his time,
  and his branch will not be green.

33 He will shake off his unripe grape like the vine,
  and cast off his blossom like the olive tree.

34 For the company of the godless is barren,
  and fire consumes the tents of bribery.

35 They conceive trouble and give birth to evil,
  and their womb prepares deceit."

Job Replies: Miserable Comforters Are You

16 Then Job answered and said:

2 "I have heard many such things;
  miserable comforters are you all.

GETTING THE MESSAGE

Sackcloth (16:15) was an outward sign of grieving. It was a coarse fabric used for grain sacks. It was very uncomfortable to wear and thus showed that the person was truly grieving. It was also worn to show repentance.

3 Shall windy words have an end?
  Or what provokes you that you answer?

4 I also could speak as you do,
  if you were in my place;
  I could join words together against you
  and shake my head at you.

5 I could strengthen you with my mouth,
  and the solace of my lips would assuage your pain.

6 "If I speak, my pain is not assuaged,
  and if I forbear, how much of it leaves me?

7 Surely now God has worn me out;
  he has made desolate all my company.

8 And he has shriveled me up,
  which is a witness against me,
  and my leanness has risen up against me;
  it testifies to my face.

9 He has torn me in his wrath and hated
       me;
   he has gnashed his teeth at me;
   my adversary sharpens his eyes
       against me.
10 Men have gaped at me with their
       mouth;
   they have struck me insolently on
       the cheek;
   they mass themselves together
       against me.
11 God gives me up to the ungodly
   and casts me into the hands of the
       wicked.
12 I was at ease, and he broke me apart;
   he seized me by the neck and
       dashed me to pieces;

> **GETTING THE MESSAGE**

Proverbs in Job. In 17:5, Job may have
been quoting a proverb to warn his
friends not to make false accusations
against him. Proverbs are an effective
and memorable way of stating a truth.
The book of Proverbs is a rich resource
of such wisdom.

   he set me up as his target;
13   his archers surround me.
   He slashes open my kidneys and does
       not spare;
   he pours out my gall on the ground.
14 He breaks me with breach upon breach;
   he runs upon me like a warrior.
15 I have sewed sackcloth upon my skin
   and have laid my strength in the
       dust.
16 My face is red with weeping,
   and on my eyelids is deep darkness,
17 although there is no violence in my
       hands,
   and my prayer is pure.
18 "O earth, cover not my blood,
   and let my cry find no resting place.
19 Even now, behold, my witness is in
       heaven,
   and he who testifies for me is on
       high.
20 My friends scorn me;
   my eye pours out tears to God,
21 that he would argue the case of a man
       with God,
   as a son of man does with his
       neighbor.
22 For when a few years have come
   I shall go the way from which I shall
       not return.

Job Continues: Where Then Is My Hope?

17 "My spirit is broken; my days are
       extinct;
   the graveyard is ready for me.
2 Surely there are mockers about me,
   and my eye dwells on their provo-
       cation.

3 "Lay down a pledge for me with you;
   who is there who will put up secu-
       rity for me?
4 Since you have closed their hearts to
       understanding,
   therefore you will not let them
       triumph.
5 He who informs against his friends to
       get a share of their property—
   the eyes of his children will fail.

6 "He has made me a byword of the peo-
       ples,
   and I am one before whom men spit.
7 My eye has grown dim from vexation,
   and all my members are like a
       shadow.
8 The upright are appalled at this,
   and the innocent stirs himself up
       against the godless.
9 Yet the righteous holds to his way,
   and he who has clean hands grows
       stronger and stronger.
10 But you, come on again, all of you,
   and I shall not find a wise man
       among you.
11 My days are past; my plans are broken
       off,
   the desires of my heart.
12 They make night into day:
   'The light,' they say, 'is near to the
       darkness.'
13 If I hope for Sheol as my house,
   if I make my bed in darkness,
14 if I say to the pit, 'You are my father,'
   and to the worm, 'My mother,' or
       'My sister,'
15 where then is my hope?
   Who will see my hope?

16 Will it go down to the bars of Sheol?
    Shall we descend together into the
        dust?"

Bildad Speaks: God Punishes the Wicked

18 Then Bildad the Shuhite answered
   and said:

2 "How long will you hunt for words?
    Consider, and then we will speak.
3 Why are we counted as cattle?
    Why are we stupid in your sight?
4 You who tear yourself in your anger,
    shall the earth be forsaken for you,
    or the rock be removed out of its
        place?

5 "Indeed, the light of the wicked is put
        out,
    and the flame of his fire does not
        shine.
6 The light is dark in his tent,
    and his lamp above him is put out.
7 His strong steps are shortened,
    and his own schemes throw him
        down.
8 For he is cast into a net by his own
        feet,
    and he walks on its mesh.
9 A trap seizes him by the heel;
    a snare lays hold of him.
10 A rope is hidden for him in the
        ground,
    a trap for him in the path.
11 Terrors frighten him on every side,
    and chase him at his heels.
12 His strength is famished,
    and calamity is ready for his stum-
        bling.
13 It consumes the parts of his skin;
    the firstborn of death consumes his
        limbs.
14 He is torn from the tent in which he
        trusted
    and is brought to the king of terrors.
15 In his tent dwells that which is none
        of his;
    sulfur is scattered over his habita-
        tion.
16 His roots dry up beneath,
    and his branches wither above.
17 His memory perishes from the earth,
    and he has no name in the street.
18 He is thrust from light into darkness,
    and driven out of the world.

19 He has no posterity or progeny among
        his people,
    and no survivor where he used to
        live.
20 They of the west are appalled at his
        day,
    and horror seizes them of the east.
21 Surely such are the dwellings of the
        unrighteous,
    such is the place of him who knows
        not God."

Job Replies: My Redeemer Lives

19 Then Job answered and said:

2 "How long will you torment me
    and break me in pieces with words?
3 These ten times you have cast
        reproach upon me;
    are you not ashamed to wrong me?
4 And even if it be true that I have erred,
    my error remains with myself.
5 If indeed you magnify yourselves
        against me
    and make my disgrace an argument
        against me,
6 know then that God has put me in the
        wrong
    and closed his net about me.
7 Behold, I cry out, 'Violence!' but I am
        not answered;
    I call for help, but there is no justice.
8 He has walled up my way, so that I
        cannot pass,
    and he has set darkness upon my
        paths.
9 He has stripped from me my glory
    and taken the crown from my head.
10 He breaks me down on every side, and
        I am gone,
    and my hope has he pulled up like a
        tree.
11 He has kindled his wrath against me
    and counts me as his adversary.
12 His troops come on together;
    they have cast up their siege ramp
        against me
    and encamp around my tent.
13 "He has put my brothers far from me,
    and those who knew me are wholly
        estranged from me.
14 My relatives have failed me,
    my close friends have forgotten me.

¹⁵ The guests in my house and my maid-
 servants count me as a stranger;
 I have become a foreigner in their
 eyes.
¹⁶ I call to my servant, but he gives me
 no answer;
 I must plead with him with my
 mouth for mercy.
¹⁷ My breath is strange to my wife,
 and I am a stench to the children of
 my own mother.
¹⁸ Even young children despise me;
 when I rise they talk against me.
¹⁹ All my intimate friends abhor me,
 and those whom I loved have
 turned against me.
²⁰ My bones stick to my skin and to my
 flesh,
 and I have escaped by the skin of
 my teeth.

GETTING THE MESSAGE

Honey is mentioned often in the Bible
(see 20:17). People probably gathered
the honey from wild bees. The gathering
of wild honey led to an interesting
episode in the life of Samson (Judg.
14:8–20).

²¹ Have mercy on me, have mercy on
 me, O you my friends,
 for the hand of God has touched me!
²² Why do you, like God, pursue me?
 Why are you not satisfied with my
 flesh?
²³ "Oh that my words were written!
 Oh that they were inscribed in a
 book!
²⁴ Oh that with an iron pen and lead
 they were engraved in the rock
 forever!
²⁵ For I know that my Redeemer lives,
 and at the last he will stand upon
 the earth.
²⁶ And after my skin has been thus
 destroyed,
 yet in my flesh I shall see God,
²⁷ whom I shall see for myself,
 and my eyes shall behold, and not
 another.
 My heart faints within me!

²⁸ If you say, 'How we will pursue him!'
 and, 'The root of the matter is found
 in him,'
²⁹ be afraid of the sword,
 for wrath brings the punishment of
 the sword,
 that you may know there is a judgment.'"

Zophar Speaks: The Wicked Will Suffer

20 Then Zophar the Naamathite answered and said:

² "Therefore my thoughts answer me,
 because of my haste within me.
³ I hear censure that insults me,
 and out of my understanding a
 spirit answers me.
⁴ Do you not know this from of old,
 since man was placed on earth,
⁵ that the exulting of the wicked is short,
 and the joy of the godless but for a
 moment?
⁶ Though his height mount up to the
 heavens,
 and his head reach to the clouds,
⁷ he will perish forever like his own
 dung;
 those who have seen him will say,
 'Where is he?'
⁸ He will fly away like a dream and not
 be found;
 he will be chased away like a vision
 of the night.
⁹ The eye that saw him will see him no
 more,
 nor will his place any more behold
 him.
¹⁰ His children will seek the favor of the
 poor,
 and his hands will give back his
 wealth.
¹¹ His bones are full of his youthful vigor,
 but it will lie down with him in the
 dust.
¹² "Though evil is sweet in his mouth,
 though he hides it under his tongue,
¹³ though he is loath to let it go
 and holds it in his mouth,
¹⁴ yet his food is turned in his stomach;
 it is the venom of cobras within him.
¹⁵ He swallows down riches and vomits
 them up again;
 God casts them out of his belly.

16 He will suck the poison of cobras;
   the tongue of a viper will kill him.
17 He will not look upon the rivers,
   the streams flowing with honey and
   curds.
18 He will give back the fruit of his toil
   and will not swallow it down;
   from the profit of his trading
   he will get no enjoyment.
19 For he has crushed and abandoned
   the poor;
   he has seized a house that he did
   not build.

20 "Because he knew no contentment in
   his belly,
   he will not let anything in which he
   delights escape him.
21 There was nothing left after he had
   eaten;
   therefore his prosperity will not
   endure.
22 In the fullness of his sufficiency he
   will be in distress;
   the hand of everyone in misery will
   come against him.
23 To fill his belly to the full,
   God will send his burning anger
   against him
   and rain it upon him into his body.
24 He will flee from an iron weapon;
   a bronze arrow will strike him
   through.
25 It is drawn forth and comes out of his
   body;
   the glittering point comes out of his
   gallbladder;
   terrors come upon him.
26 Utter darkness is laid up for his treasures;
   a fire not fanned will devour him;
   what is left in his tent will be consumed.
27 The heavens will reveal his iniquity,
   and the earth will rise up against
   him.
28 The possessions of his house will be
   carried away,
   dragged off in the day of God's
   wrath.
29 This is the wicked man's portion from
   God,
   the heritage decreed for him by
   God."

Job Replies: The Wicked Do Prosper

21 Then Job answered and said:

2 "Keep listening to my words,
   and let this be your comfort.
3 Bear with me, and I will speak,
   and after I have spoken, mock on.
4 As for me, is my complaint against
   man?
   Why should I not be impatient?
5 Look at me and be appalled,
   and lay your hand over your mouth.
6 When I remember, I am dismayed,
   and shuddering seizes my flesh.
7 Why do the wicked live,
   reach old age, and grow mighty in
   power?
8 Their offspring are established in
   their presence,
   and their descendants before their
   eyes.
9 Their houses are safe from fear,
   and no rod of God is upon them.
10 Their bull breeds without fail;
   their cow calves and does not miscarry.
11 They send out their little boys like a
   flock,
   and their children dance.
12 They sing to the tambourine and the
   lyre
   and rejoice to the sound of the
   pipe.
13 They spend their days in prosperity,
   and in peace they go down to
   Sheol.
14 They say to God, 'Depart from us!
   We do not desire the knowledge of
   your ways.
15 What is the Almighty, that we should
   serve him?
   And what profit do we get if we pray
   to him?'
16 Behold, is not their prosperity in their
   hand?
   The counsel of the wicked is far
   from me.

17 "How often is it that the lamp of the
   wicked is put out?
   That their calamity comes upon
   them?
   That God distributes pains in his
   anger?

18 That they are like straw before the
        wind,
            and like chaff that the storm carries
                away?
19 You say, 'God stores up their iniquity
        for their children.'
            Let him pay it out to them, that they
                may know it.
20 Let their own eyes see their destruc-
        tion,
            and let them drink of the wrath of
                the Almighty.
21 For what do they care for their houses
        after them,
            when the number of their months
                is cut off?
22 Will any teach God knowledge,
        seeing that he judges those who are
            on high?

GETTING THE MESSAGE

A **pledge** (22:6) was an object of
worth given as a down payment on
a debt. Israelites were not to take in
pledge essential items such as clothing
(Ex. 22:26) or tools a person needed for
their work (Deut. 24:6).

23 One dies in his full vigor,
        being wholly at ease and secure,
24 his pails full of milk
        and the marrow of his bones moist.
25 Another dies in bitterness of soul,
        never having tasted of prosperity.
26 They lie down alike in the dust,
        and the worms cover them.

27 "Behold, I know your thoughts
        and your schemes to wrong me.
28 For you say, 'Where is the house of the
        prince?
            Where is the tent in which the
                wicked lived?'
29 Have you not asked those who travel
        the roads,
            and do you not accept their testi-
                mony
30 that the evil man is spared in the day
        of calamity,
            that he is rescued in the day of
                wrath?

31 Who declares his way to his face,
        and who repays him for what he
            has done?
32 When he is carried to the grave,
        watch is kept over his tomb.
33 The clods of the valley are sweet to
        him;
            all mankind follows after him,
            and those who go before him are
                innumerable.
34 How then will you comfort me with
        empty nothings?
            There is nothing left of your
                answers but falsehood."

Eliphaz Speaks: Job's Wickedness Is Great

22 Then Eliphaz the Temanite answered
    and said:

2 "Can a man be profitable to God?
        Surely he who is wise is profitable
            to himself.
3 Is it any pleasure to the Almighty if
        you are in the right,
            or is it gain to him if you make your
                ways blameless?
4 Is it for your fear of him that he
        reproves you
            and enters into judgment with you?
5 Is not your evil abundant?
        There is no end to your iniquities.
6 For you have exacted pledges of your
        brothers for nothing
            and stripped the naked of their
                clothing.
7 You have given no water to the weary
        to drink,
            and you have withheld bread from
                the hungry.
8 The man with power possessed the
        land,
            and the favored man lived in it.
9 You have sent widows away empty,
        and the arms of the fatherless were
            crushed.
10 Therefore snares are all around you,
        and sudden terror overwhelms
            you,
11 or darkness, so that you cannot see,
        and a flood of water covers you.

12 "Is not God high in the heavens?
        See the highest stars, how lofty they
            are!

13 But you say, 'What does God know?
　　Can he judge through the deep
　　　darkness?
14 Thick clouds veil him, so that he does
　　　not see,
　　and he walks on the vault of heaven.'
15 Will you keep to the old way
　　that wicked men have trod?
16 They were snatched away before their
　　　time;
　　their foundation was washed away.
17 They said to God, 'Depart from us,'
　　and 'What can the Almighty do to
　　　us?'
18 Yet he filled their houses with good
　　　things—
　　but the counsel of the wicked is far
　　　from me.
19 The righteous see it and are glad;
　　the innocent one mocks at them,
20 saying, 'Surely our adversaries are cut
　　　off,
　　and what they left the fire has con-
　　　sumed.'

21 "Agree with God, and be at peace;
　　thereby good will come to you.
22 Receive instruction from his mouth,
　　and lay up his words in your heart.
23 If you return to the Almighty you will
　　　be built up;
　　if you remove injustice far from
　　　your tents,
24 if you lay gold in the dust,
　　and gold of Ophir among the stones
　　　of the torrent-bed,
25 then the Almighty will be your gold
　　and your precious silver.
26 For then you will delight yourself in
　　　the Almighty
　　and lift up your face to God.
27 You will make your prayer to him, and
　　　he will hear you,
　　and you will pay your vows.
28 You will decide on a matter, and it will
　　　be established for you,
　　and light will shine on your ways.
29 For when they are humbled you say,
　　'It is because of pride';
　　but he saves the lowly.
30 He delivers even the one who is not
　　　innocent,
　　who will be delivered through the
　　　cleanness of your hands."

Job Replies: Where Is God?

23 Then Job answered and said:

2 "Today also my complaint is bitter;
　　my hand is heavy on account of my
　　　groaning.
3 Oh, that I knew where I might find
　　　him,
　　that I might come even to his seat!
4 I would lay my case before him
　　and fill my mouth with arguments.
5 I would know what he would
　　　answer me
　　and understand what he would say
　　　to me.
6 Would he contend with me in the
　　　greatness of his power?
　　No; he would pay attention to me.
7 There an upright man could argue
　　　with him,
　　and I would be acquitted forever by
　　　my judge.

8 "Behold, I go forward, but he is not
　　　there,
　　and backward, but I do not perceive
　　　him;
9 on the left hand when he is working,
　　　I do not behold him;
　　he turns to the right hand, but I do
　　　not see him.
10 But he knows the way that I take;
　　when he has tried me, I shall come
　　　out as gold.
11 My foot has held fast to his steps;
　　I have kept his way and have not
　　　turned aside.
12 I have not departed from the com-
　　　mandment of his lips;
　　I have treasured the words of his
　　　mouth more than my portion of
　　　food.
13 But he is unchangeable, and who can
　　　turn him back?
　　What he desires, that he does.
14 For he will complete what he appoints
　　　for me,
　　and many such things are in his
　　　mind.
15 Therefore I am terrified at his presence;
　　when I consider, I am in dread of
　　　him.
16 God has made my heart faint;
　　the Almighty has terrified me;

17 yet I am not silenced because of the
        darkness,
     nor because thick darkness covers
        my face.

24 "Why are not times of judgment
        kept by the Almighty,
     and why do those who know him
        never see his days?
2 Some move landmarks;
     they seize flocks and pasture them.
3 They drive away the donkey of the
        fatherless;
     they take the widow's ox for a
        pledge.
4 They thrust the poor off the road;
     the poor of the earth all hide them-
        selves.

> **GETTING THE MESSAGE**

Those who rebel against the light is
how Job describes people who oppose
wisdom and righteousness (24:13). They
sleep during the day and do their evil
deeds at night.

5 Behold, like wild donkeys in the desert
     the poor go out to their toil, seeking
        game;
     the wasteland yields food for their
        children.
6 They gather their fodder in the field,
     and they glean the vineyard of the
        wicked man.
7 They lie all night naked, without
        clothing,
     and have no covering in the cold.
8 They are wet with the rain of the
        mountains
     and cling to the rock for lack of
        shelter.
9 (There are those who snatch the
        fatherless child from the breast,
     and they take a pledge against the
        poor.)
10 They go about naked, without clothing;
     hungry, they carry the sheaves;
11 among the olive rows of the wicked
        they make oil;
     they tread the winepresses, but
        suffer thirst.

12 From out of the city the dying groan,
     and the soul of the wounded cries
        for help;
     yet God charges no one with wrong.
13 "There are those who rebel against the
        light,
     who are not acquainted with its
        ways,
     and do not stay in its paths.
14 The murderer rises before it is light,
     that he may kill the poor and needy,
     and in the night he is like a thief.
15 The eye of the adulterer also waits for
        the twilight,
     saying, 'No eye will see me';
     and he veils his face.
16 In the dark they dig through houses;
     by day they shut themselves up;
     they do not know the light.
17 For deep darkness is morning to all of
        them;
     for they are friends with the terrors
        of deep darkness.

18 "You say, 'Swift are they on the face of
        the waters;
     their portion is cursed in the land;
     no treader turns toward their vine-
        yards.
19 Drought and heat snatch away the
        snow waters;
     so does Sheol those who have
        sinned.
20 The womb forgets them;
     the worm finds them sweet;
     they are no longer remembered,
     so wickedness is broken like a tree.'
21 "They wrong the barren, childless
        woman,
     and do no good to the widow.
22 Yet God prolongs the life of the
        mighty by his power;
     they rise up when they despair of
        life.
23 He gives them security, and they are
        supported,
     and his eyes are upon their ways.
24 They are exalted a little while, and
        then are gone;
     they are brought low and gathered
        up like all others;
     they are cut off like the heads of
        grain.

25   If it is not so, who will prove me a liar
        and show that there is nothing in
            what I say?"

Bildad Speaks: Man Cannot Be Righteous

25 Then Bildad the Shuhite answered and said:

2   "Dominion and fear are with God;
        he makes peace in his high heaven.
3   Is there any number to his armies?
        Upon whom does his light not arise?
4   How then can man be in the right
            before God?
        How can he who is born of woman
            be pure?
5   Behold, even the moon is not bright,
        and the stars are not pure in his eyes;
6   how much less man, who is a maggot,
        and the son of man, who is a worm!"

Job Replies: God's Majesty Is Unsearchable

26 Then Job answered and said:

2   "How you have helped him who has no
            power!
        How you have saved the arm that
            has no strength!
3   How you have counseled him who
            has no wisdom,
        and plentifully declared sound
            knowledge!
4   With whose help have you uttered
            words,
        and whose breath has come out
            from you?
5   The dead tremble
        under the waters and their inhabi-
            tants.
6   Sheol is naked before God,
        and Abaddon has no covering.
7   He stretches out the north over the void
        and hangs the earth on nothing.
8   He binds up the waters in his thick
            clouds,
        and the cloud is not split open
            under them.
9   He covers the face of the full moon
        and spreads over it his cloud.
10 He has inscribed a circle on the face of
            the waters
        at the boundary between light and
            darkness.

11 The pillars of heaven tremble
        and are astounded at his rebuke.
12 By his power he stilled the sea;
        by his understanding he shattered
            Rahab.
13 By his wind the heavens were made
            fair;
        his hand pierced the fleeing serpent.
14 Behold, these are but the outskirts of
            his ways,
        and how small a whisper do we
            hear of him!
        But the thunder of his power who
            can understand?"

Job Continues: I Will Maintain My Integrity

27 And Job again took up his discourse, and said:

2   "As God lives, who has taken away my
            right,

        and the Almighty, who has made
            my soul bitter,
3   as long as my breath is in me,
        and the spirit of God is in my nos-
            trils,
4   my lips will not speak falsehood,
        and my tongue will not utter deceit.
5   Far be it from me to say that you are
            right;
        till I die I will not put away my
            integrity from me.
6   I hold fast my righteousness and will
            not let it go;
        my heart does not reproach me for
            any of my days.
7   "Let my enemy be as the wicked,
        and let him who rises up against
            me be as the unrighteous.
8   For what is the hope of the godless
            when God cuts him off,
        when God takes away his life?

⁹ Will God hear his cry
    when distress comes upon him?
¹⁰ Will he take delight in the Almighty?
    Will he call upon God at all times?
¹¹ I will teach you concerning the hand
    of God,
    what is with the Almighty I will not
    conceal.
¹² Behold, all of you have seen it your-
    selves;
    why then have you become alto-
    gether vain?

¹³ "This is the portion of a wicked man
    with God,
    and the heritage that oppressors
    receive from the Almighty:
¹⁴ If his children are multiplied, it is for
    the sword,
    and his descendants have not
    enough bread.
¹⁵ Those who survive him the pestilence
    buries,
    and his widows do not weep.
¹⁶ Though he heap up silver like dust,
    and pile up clothing like clay,
¹⁷ he may pile it up, but the righteous
    will wear it,
    and the innocent will divide the
    silver.
¹⁸ He builds his house like a moth's,
    like a booth that a watchman
    makes.
¹⁹ He goes to bed rich, but will do so no
    more;
    he opens his eyes, and his wealth is
    gone.
²⁰ Terrors overtake him like a flood;
    in the night a whirlwind carries
    him off.
²¹ The east wind lifts him up and he is
    gone;
    it sweeps him out of his place.
²² It hurls at him without pity;
    he flees from its power in headlong
    flight.
²³ It claps its hands at him
    and hisses at him from its place.

Job Continues: Where Is Wisdom?

28 "Surely there is a mine for silver,
    and a place for gold that they
    refine.
² Iron is taken out of the earth,
    and copper is smelted from the ore.

³ Man puts an end to darkness
    and searches out to the farthest limit
    the ore in gloom and deep darkness.
⁴ He opens shafts in a valley away from
    where anyone lives;
    they are forgotten by travelers;
    they hang in the air, far away from
    mankind; they swing to and fro.
⁵ As for the earth, out of it comes bread,
    but underneath it is turned up as by
    fire.
⁶ Its stones are the place of sapphires,
    and it has dust of gold.

⁷ "That path no bird of prey knows,
    and the falcon's eye has not seen it.
⁸ The proud beasts have not trodden it;
    the lion has not passed over it.

⁹ "Man puts his hand to the flinty rock
    and overturns mountains by the
    roots.
¹⁰ He cuts out channels in the rocks,
    and his eye sees every precious
    thing.
¹¹ He dams up the streams so that they
    do not trickle,
    and the thing that is hidden he
    brings out to light.

¹² "But where shall wisdom be found?
    And where is the place of under-
    standing?
¹³ Man does not know its worth,
    and it is not found in the land of the
    living.
¹⁴ The deep says, 'It is not in me,'
    and the sea says, 'It is not with me.'
¹⁵ It cannot be bought for gold,
    and silver cannot be weighed as its
    price.
¹⁶ It cannot be valued in the gold of
    Ophir,
    in precious onyx or sapphire.
¹⁷ Gold and glass cannot equal it,
    nor can it be exchanged for jewels
    of fine gold.
¹⁸ No mention shall be made of coral or
    of crystal;
    the price of wisdom is above pearls.
¹⁹ The topaz of Ethiopia cannot equal it,
    nor can it be valued in pure gold.

²⁰ "From where, then, does wisdom come?
    And where is the place of under-
    standing?

21 It is hidden from the eyes of all living
    and concealed from the birds of the
        air.
22 Abaddon and Death say,
    'We have heard a rumor of it with
        our ears.'

23 "God understands the way to it,
    and he knows its place.
24 For he looks to the ends of the earth
    and sees everything under the heav-
        ens.
25 When he gave to the wind its weight
    and apportioned the waters by
        measure,
26 when he made a decree for the rain
    and a way for the lightning of the
        thunder,
27 then he saw it and declared it;
    he established it, and searched it out.
28 And he said to man,
    'Behold, the fear of the Lord, that is
        wisdom,
    and to turn away from evil is under-
        standing.'"

Job's Summary Defense

29 And Job again took up his discourse,
    and said:

2 "Oh, that I were as in the months of old,
    as in the days when God watched
        over me,
3 when his lamp shone upon my head,
    and by his light I walked through
        darkness,
4 as I was in my prime,
    when the friendship of God was
        upon my tent,
5 when the Almighty was yet with me,
    when my children were all around
        me,
6 when my steps were washed with
        butter,
    and the rock poured out for me
        streams of oil!
7 When I went out to the gate of the city,
    when I prepared my seat in the
        square,
8 the young men saw me and withdrew,
    and the aged rose and stood;
9 the princes refrained from talking
    and laid their hand on their mouth;
10 the voice of the nobles was hushed,
    and their tongue stuck to the roof of
        their mouth.

11 When the ear heard, it called me
        blessed,
    and when the eye saw, it approved,
12 because I delivered the poor who
        cried for help,
    and the fatherless who had none to
        help him.
13 The blessing of him who was about to
        perish came upon me,
    and I caused the widow's heart to
        sing for joy.
14 I put on righteousness, and it clothed
        me;
    my justice was like a robe and a
        turban.
15 I was eyes to the blind
    and feet to the lame.
16 I was a father to the needy,
    and I searched out the cause of him
        whom I did not know.

GETTING THE MESSAGE

Rocks pouring out streams of oil (29:6)
is a reference to olive trees. They are one
of the few trees that thrive in rocky soil.
It can be 10 years or more before an olive
tree yields fruit, but then it can produce
olives for hundreds of years. Some
olive trees are more than a thousand
years old.

17 I broke the fangs of the unrighteous
    and made him drop his prey from
        his teeth.
18 Then I thought, 'I shall die in my
        nest,
    and I shall multiply my days as the
        sand,
19 my roots spread out to the waters,
    with the dew all night on my
        branches,
20 my glory fresh with me,
    and my bow ever new in my hand.'

21 "Men listened to me and waited
    and kept silence for my counsel.
22 After I spoke they did not speak
        again,
    and my word dropped upon them.
23 They waited for me as for the rain,
    and they opened their mouths as
        for the spring rain.

24 I smiled on them when they had no
confidence,
and the light of my face they did not
cast down.
25 I chose their way and sat as chief,
and I lived like a king among his
troops,
like one who comforts mourners.

30 "But now they laugh at me,
men who are younger than I,
whose fathers I would have disdained
to set with the dogs of my flock.
2 What could I gain from the strength of
their hands,
men whose vigor is gone?
3 Through want and hard hunger
they gnaw the dry ground by night
in waste and desolation;
4 they pick saltwort and the leaves of
bushes,
and the roots of the broom tree for
their food.
5 They are driven out from human
company;
they shout after them as after a thief.
6 In the gullies of the torrents they
must dwell,
in holes of the earth and of the rocks.
7 Among the bushes they bray;
under the nettles they huddle
together.
8 A senseless, a nameless brood,
they have been whipped out of the
land.

9 "And now I have become their song;
I am a byword to them.
10 They abhor me; they keep aloof from
me;
they do not hesitate to spit at the
sight of me.
11 Because God has loosed my cord and
humbled me,
they have cast off restraint in my
presence.
12 On my right hand the rabble rise;
they push away my feet;
they cast up against me their ways
of destruction.
13 They break up my path;
they promote my calamity;
they need no one to help them.
14 As through a wide breach they come;
amid the crash they roll on.

15 Terrors are turned upon me;
my honor is pursued as by the wind,
and my prosperity has passed away
like a cloud.

16 "And now my soul is poured out
within me;
days of affliction have taken hold of
me.
17 The night racks my bones,
and the pain that gnaws me takes
no rest.
18 With great force my garment is disfig-
ured;
it binds me about like the collar of
my tunic.
19 God has cast me into the mire,
and I have become like dust and
ashes.
20 I cry to you for help and you do not
answer me;
I stand, and you only look at me.
21 You have turned cruel to me;
with the might of your hand you
persecute me.
22 You lift me up on the wind; you make
me ride on it,
and you toss me about in the roar of
the storm.
23 For I know that you will bring me to
death
and to the house appointed for all
living.

24 "Yet does not one in a heap of ruins
stretch out his hand,
and in his disaster cry for help?
25 Did not I weep for him whose day was
hard?
Was not my soul grieved for the
needy?
26 But when I hoped for good, evil came,
and when I waited for light, darkness came.
27 My inward parts are in turmoil and
never still;
days of affliction come to meet me.
28 I go about darkened, but not by the
sun;
I stand up in the assembly and cry
for help.
29 I am a brother of jackals
and a companion of ostriches.
30 My skin turns black and falls from me,
and my bones burn with heat.

31 My lyre is turned to mourning,
  and my pipe to the voice of those
    who weep.

Job's Final Appeal

31 "I have made a covenant with my
    eyes;
  how then could I gaze at a virgin?
2 What would be my portion from God
    above
  and my heritage from the Almighty
    on high?
3 Is not calamity for the unrighteous,
  and disaster for the workers of
    iniquity?
4 Does not he see my ways
  and number all my steps?

5 "If I have walked with falsehood
  and my foot has hastened to deceit;
6 (Let me be weighed in a just balance,
  and let God know my integrity!)
7 if my step has turned aside from the
    way
  and my heart has gone after my eyes,
  and if any spot has stuck to my
    hands,
8 then let me sow, and another eat,
  and let what grows for me be rooted
    out.

9 "If my heart has been enticed toward a
    woman,
  and I have lain in wait at my neigh-
    bor's door,
10 then let my wife grind for another,
  and let others bow down on her.
11 For that would be a heinous crime;
  that would be an iniquity to be
    punished by the judges;
12 for that would be a fire that consumes
    as far as Abaddon,
  and it would burn to the root all my
    increase.

13 "If I have rejected the cause of my
    manservant or my maidservant,
  when they brought a complaint
    against me,
14 what then shall I do when God rises up?
  When he makes inquiry, what shall
    I answer him?
15 Did not he who made me in the womb
    make him?
  And did not one fashion us in the
    womb?

16 "If I have withheld anything that the
    poor desired,
  or have caused the eyes of the
    widow to fail,
17 or have eaten my morsel alone,
  and the fatherless has not eaten
    of it
18 (for from my youth the fatherless
    grew up with me as with a
    father,
  and from my mother's womb I
    guided the widow),
19 if I have seen anyone perish for lack of
    clothing,
  or the needy without covering,
20 if his body has not blessed me,
  and if he was not warmed with the
    fleece of my sheep,
21 if I have raised my hand against the
    fatherless,
  because I saw my help in the gate,
22 then let my shoulder blade fall from
    my shoulder,
  and let my arm be broken from its
    socket.
23 For I was in terror of calamity from
    God,
  and I could not have faced his maj-
    esty.

24 "If I have made gold my trust
  or called fine gold my confidence,
25 if I have rejoiced because my wealth
    was abundant
  or because my hand had found
    much,
26 if I have looked at the sun when it
    shone,
  or the moon moving in splendor,
27 and my heart has been secretly
    enticed,
  and my mouth has kissed my hand,
28 this also would be an iniquity to be
    punished by the judges,
  for I would have been false to God
    above.

29 "If I have rejoiced at the ruin of him
    who hated me,
  or exulted when evil overtook him
30 (I have not let my mouth sin
  by asking for his life with a curse),
31 if the men of my tent have not said,
  'Who is there that has not been
    filled with his meat?'

32 (the sojourner has not lodged in the street;
I have opened my doors to the traveler),

33 if I have concealed my transgressions as others do
by hiding my iniquity in my heart,

34 because I stood in great fear of the multitude,
and the contempt of families terrified me,
so that I kept silence, and did not go out of doors—

PROFILE
ELIHU

Elihu rebuked both Job and his three friends. He was angry at Job for defending himself rather than God, and he was angry at Eliphaz, Bildad, and Zophar for failing to provide an answer for Job. During his lengthy speech, Elihu shifted the focus away from Job to God as the only source of certainty and hope. At the same time, he seemed to overestimate his own understanding, even claiming to speak "on God's behalf" (36:2). Actually, Elihu didn't understand the reasons for Job's suffering any more than the three friends did, and his statements were often similar to theirs. Although there was some truth in Elihu's argument, his application of those truths and the conclusions he drew about Job were often incorrect.

KEY REFERENCE: JOB 32:1–5

35 Oh, that I had one to hear me!
(Here is my signature! Let the Almighty answer me!)
Oh, that I had the indictment written by my adversary!

36 Surely I would carry it on my shoulder;
I would bind it on me as a crown;

37 I would give him an account of all my steps;
like a prince I would approach him.

38 "If my land has cried out against me
and its furrows have wept together,

39 if I have eaten its yield without payment
and made its owners breathe their last,

40 let thorns grow instead of wheat,
and foul weeds instead of barley."

The words of Job are ended.

Elihu Rebukes Job's Three Friends

32 So these three men ceased to answer Job, because he was righteous in his own eyes. ² Then Elihu the son of Barachel the Buzite, of the family of Ram, burned with anger. He burned with anger at Job because he justified himself rather than God. ³ He burned with anger also at Job's three friends because they had found no answer, although they had declared Job to be in the wrong. ⁴ Now Elihu had waited to speak to Job because they were older than he. ⁵ And when Elihu saw that there was no answer in the mouth of these three men, he burned with anger.

⁶ And Elihu the son of Barachel the Buzite answered and said:

"I am young in years,
and you are aged;
therefore I was timid and afraid
to declare my opinion to you.

7 I said, 'Let days speak,
and many years teach wisdom.'

8 But it is the spirit in man,
the breath of the Almighty, that makes him understand.

9 It is not the old who are wise,
nor the aged who understand what is right.

10 Therefore I say, 'Listen to me;
let me also declare my opinion.'

11 "Behold, I waited for your words,
I listened for your wise sayings,
while you searched out what to say.

12 I gave you my attention,
and, behold, there was none among you who refuted Job
or who answered his words.

13 Beware lest you say, 'We have found wisdom;
God may vanquish him, not a man.'

14 He has not directed his words against me,
and I will not answer him with your speeches.

15 "They are dismayed; they answer no
  more;
  　they have not a word to say.
16 And shall I wait, because they do not
  speak,
  　because they stand there, and
  　answer no more?
17 I also will answer with my share;
  　I also will declare my opinion.
18 For I am full of words;
  　the spirit within me constrains me.
19 Behold, my belly is like wine that has
  no vent;
  　like new wineskins ready to burst.
20 I must speak, that I may find relief;
  　I must open my lips and answer.
21 I will not show partiality to any man
  　or use flattery toward any person.
22 For I do not know how to flatter,
  　else my Maker would soon take me
  　away.

Elihu Rebukes Job

33 "But now, hear my speech, O Job,
  　and listen to all my words.
2 Behold, I open my mouth;
  　the tongue in my mouth speaks.
3 My words declare the uprightness of
  my heart,
  　and what my lips know they speak
  　sincerely.
4 The Spirit of God has made me,
  　and the breath of the Almighty
  　gives me life.
5 Answer me, if you can;
  　set your words in order before me;
  　take your stand.
6 Behold, I am toward God as you are;
  　I too was pinched off from a piece
  　of clay.
7 Behold, no fear of me need terrify you;
  　my pressure will not be heavy upon
  　you.
8 "Surely you have spoken in my ears,
  　and I have heard the sound of your
  　words.
9 You say, 'I am pure, without transgression;
  　I am clean, and there is no iniquity
  　in me.
10 Behold, he finds occasions against me,
  　he counts me as his enemy,
11 he puts my feet in the stocks
  　and watches all my paths.'

12 "Behold, in this you are not right. I will
  answer you,
  　for God is greater than man.
13 Why do you contend against him,
  　saying, 'He will answer none of
  　man's words'?
14 For God speaks in one way,
  　and in two, though man does not
  　perceive it.
15 In a dream, in a vision of the night,
  　when deep sleep falls on men,
  　while they slumber on their beds,
16 then he opens the ears of men
  　and terrifies them with warnings,
17 that he may turn man aside from his
  deed
  　and conceal pride from a man;
18 he keeps back his soul from the pit,
  　his life from perishing by the sword.

19 "Man is also rebuked with pain on his
  bed
  　and with continual strife in his
  　bones,
20 so that his life loathes bread,
  　and his appetite the choicest food.
21 His flesh is so wasted away that it
  cannot be seen,
  　and his bones that were not seen
  　stick out.
22 His soul draws near the pit,
  　and his life to those who bring
  　death.
23 If there be for him an angel,
  　a mediator, one of the thousand,
  　to declare to man what is right for
  　him,
24 and he is merciful to him, and says,
  　'Deliver him from going down into
  　the pit;
  　I have found a ransom;

25 let his flesh become fresh with youth;
    let him return to the days of his
        youthful vigor';
26 then man prays to God, and he accepts
        him;
    he sees his face with a shout of joy,
    and he restores to man his righteous-
        ness.
27 He sings before men and says:
    'I sinned and perverted what was right,
        and it was not repaid to me.
28 He has redeemed my soul from going
        down into the pit,
    and my life shall look upon the light.'

29 "Behold, God does all these things,
        twice, three times, with a man,
30 to bring back his soul from the pit,
        that he may be lighted with the
            light of life.
31 Pay attention, O Job, listen to me;
        be silent, and I will speak.

> ### GETTING THE MESSAGE

Elihu is the only character in the book of
Job with a Hebrew name.

32 If you have any words, answer me;
        speak, for I desire to justify you.
33 If not, listen to me;
        be silent, and I will teach you wis-
            dom."

Elihu Asserts God's Justice

34 Then Elihu answered and said:

2 "Hear my words, you wise men,
        and give ear to me, you who know;
3 for the ear tests words
        as the palate tastes food.
4 Let us choose what is right;
        let us know among ourselves what
            is good.
5 For Job has said, 'I am in the right,
        and God has taken away my right;
6 in spite of my right I am counted a liar;
        my wound is incurable, though I
            am without transgression.'
7 What man is like Job,
        who drinks up scoffing like water,
8 who travels in company with evildoers
        and walks with wicked men?

9 For he has said, 'It profits a man noth-
        ing
    that he should take delight in God.'
10 "Therefore, hear me, you men of
        understanding:
    far be it from God that he should do
        wickedness,
    and from the Almighty that he
        should do wrong.
11 For according to the work of a man he
        will repay him,
    and according to his ways he will
        make it befall him.
12 Of a truth, God will not do wickedly,
        and the Almighty will not pervert
            justice.
13 Who gave him charge over the earth,
        and who laid on him the whole
            world?
14 If he should set his heart to it
        and gather to himself his spirit and
            his breath,
15 all flesh would perish together,
        and man would return to dust.

16 "If you have understanding, hear this;
        listen to what I say.
17 Shall one who hates justice govern?
        Will you condemn him who is righ-
            teous and mighty,
18 who says to a king, 'Worthless one,'
        and to nobles, 'Wicked man,'
19 who shows no partiality to princes,
        nor regards the rich more than the
            poor,
    for they are all the work of his hands?
20 In a moment they die;
        at midnight the people are shaken
            and pass away,
    and the mighty are taken away by
        no human hand.

21 "For his eyes are on the ways of a man,
        and he sees all his steps.
22 There is no gloom or deep darkness
        where evildoers may hide them-
            selves.
23 For God has no need to consider a
        man further,
    that he should go before God in
        judgment.
24 He shatters the mighty without inves-
        tigation
    and sets others in their place.

25 Thus, knowing their works,
     he overturns them in the night, and
          they are crushed.
26 He strikes them for their wickedness
     in a place for all to see,
27 because they turned aside from fol-
     lowing him
     and had no regard for any of his
          ways,
28 so that they caused the cry of the poor
     to come to him,
     and he heard the cry of the
          afflicted—
29 When he is quiet, who can condemn?
     When he hides his face, who can
          behold him,
     whether it be a nation or a man?—
30 that a godless man should not reign,
     that he should not ensnare the
          people.

31 "For has anyone said to God,
     'I have borne punishment; I will not
          offend any more;
32 teach me what I do not see;
     if I have done iniquity, I will do it
          no more'?
33 Will he then make repayment to suit
          you,
     because you reject it?
     For you must choose, and not I;
          therefore declare what you know.
34 Men of understanding will say to me,
     and the wise man who hears me
          will say:
35 'Job speaks without knowledge;
     his words are without insight.'
36 Would that Job were tried to the end,
     because he answers like wicked
          men.
37 For he adds rebellion to his sin;
     he claps his hands among us
     and multiplies his words against
          God."

Elihu Condemns Job

35 And Elihu answered and said:

2 "Do you think this to be just?
     Do you say, 'It is my right before God,'
3 that you ask, 'What advantage have I?
     How am I better off than if I had
          sinned?'
4 I will answer you
     and your friends with you.

5 Look at the heavens, and see;
     and behold the clouds, which are
          higher than you.
6 If you have sinned, what do you
          accomplish against him?
     And if your transgressions are mul-
          tiplied, what do you do to him?
7 If you are righteous, what do you give
          to him?
     Or what does he receive from your
          hand?
8 Your wickedness concerns a man like
          yourself,
     and your righteousness a son of
          man.

9 "Because of the multitude of oppres-
          sions people cry out;
     they call for help because of the arm
          of the mighty.

10 But none says, 'Where is God my Maker,
     who gives songs in the night,
11 who teaches us more than the beasts
          of the earth
     and makes us wiser than the birds
          of the heavens?'
12 There they cry out, but he does not
          answer,
     because of the pride of evil men.
13 Surely God does not hear an empty cry,
     nor does the Almighty regard it.
14 How much less when you say that you
          do not see him,
     that the case is before him, and you
          are waiting for him!
15 And now, because his anger does not
          punish,
     and he does not take much note of
          transgression,
16 Job opens his mouth in empty talk;
     he multiplies words without knowl-
          edge."

Elihu Extols God's Greatness

36 And Elihu continued, and said:

2 "Bear with me a little, and I will show
you,
for I have yet something to say on
God's behalf.
3 I will get my knowledge from afar
and ascribe righteousness to my
Maker.
4 For truly my words are not false;
one who is perfect in knowledge is
with you.

5 "Behold, God is mighty, and does not
despise any;
he is mighty in strength of understanding.
6 He does not keep the wicked alive,
but gives the afflicted their right.
7 He does not withdraw his eyes from
the righteous,
but with kings on the throne
he sets them forever, and they are
exalted.
8 And if they are bound in chains
and caught in the cords of affliction,
9 then he declares to them their work
and their transgressions, that they
are behaving arrogantly.
10 He opens their ears to instruction
and commands that they return
from iniquity.
11 If they listen and serve him,
they complete their days in prosperity,
and their years in pleasantness.
12 But if they do not listen, they perish
by the sword
and die without knowledge.

13 "The godless in heart cherish anger;
they do not cry for help when he
binds them.
14 They die in youth,
and their life ends among the cult
prostitutes.
15 He delivers the afflicted by their
affliction
and opens their ear by adversity.
16 He also allured you out of distress
into a broad place where there was
no cramping,
and what was set on your table was
full of fatness.

17 "But you are full of the judgment on
the wicked;
judgment and justice seize you.
18 Beware lest wrath entice you into
scoffing,
and let not the greatness of the
ransom turn you aside.
19 Will your cry for help avail to keep
you from distress,
or all the force of your strength?
20 Do not long for the night,
when peoples vanish in their place.
21 Take care; do not turn to iniquity,
for this you have chosen rather than
affliction.
22 Behold, God is exalted in his power;
who is a teacher like him?
23 Who has prescribed for him his way,
or who can say, 'You have done
wrong'?

24 "Remember to extol his work,
of which men have sung.
25 All mankind has looked on it;
man beholds it from afar.
26 Behold, God is great, and we know
him not;
the number of his years is
unsearchable.
27 For he draws up the drops of water;
they distill his mist in rain,
28 which the skies pour down
and drop on mankind abundantly.
29 Can anyone understand the spreading
of the clouds,
the thunderings of his pavilion?
30 Behold, he scatters his lightning
about him
and covers the roots of the sea.
31 For by these he judges peoples;
he gives food in abundance.
32 He covers his hands with the lightning
and commands it to strike the
mark.
33 Its crashing declares his presence;
the cattle also declare that he rises.

Elihu Proclaims God's Majesty

37 "At this also my heart trembles
and leaps out of its place.
2 Keep listening to the thunder of his
voice
and the rumbling that comes from
his mouth.

3 Under the whole heaven he lets it go,
   and his lightning to the corners of
     the earth.
4 After it his voice roars;
   he thunders with his majestic voice,
   and he does not restrain the light-
     nings when his voice is heard.
5 God thunders wondrously with his
     voice;
   he does great things that we cannot
     comprehend.
6 For to the snow he says, 'Fall on the
     earth,'
   likewise to the downpour, his
     mighty downpour.
7 He seals up the hand of every man,
   that all men whom he made may
     know it.
8 Then the beasts go into their lairs,
   and remain in their dens.
9 From its chamber comes the whirl-
     wind,
   and cold from the scattering winds.
10 By the breath of God ice is given,
   and the broad waters are frozen fast.
11 He loads the thick cloud with moisture;
   the clouds scatter his lightning.
12 They turn around and around by his
     guidance,
   to accomplish all that he com-
     mands them
   on the face of the habitable world.
13 Whether for correction or for his land
   or for love, he causes it to happen.

14 "Hear this, O Job;
   stop and consider the wondrous
     works of God.
15 Do you know how God lays his com-
     mand upon them
   and causes the lightning of his
     cloud to shine?
16 Do you know the balancings of the
     clouds,
   the wondrous works of him who is
     perfect in knowledge,
17 you whose garments are hot
   when the earth is still because of
     the south wind?
18 Can you, like him, spread out the
     skies,
   hard as a cast metal mirror?
19 Teach us what we shall say to him;
   we cannot draw up our case
     because of darkness.

20 Shall it be told him that I would speak?
   Did a man ever wish that he would
     be swallowed up?

21 "And now no one looks on the light
   when it is bright in the skies,
   when the wind has passed and
     cleared them.
22 Out of the north comes golden splen-
     dor;
   God is clothed with awesome maj-
     esty.
23 The Almighty—we cannot find him;
   he is great in power;
   justice and abundant righteousness
     he will not violate.
24 Therefore men fear him;
   he does not regard any who are wise
     in their own conceit."

GETTING THE MESSAGE

The **snow from Mount Hermon** is an important water source for the Jordan River, but the climate in much of Israel is too mild for regular snowfall. In Job, snow is a symbol of purity (37:6).

The LORD Answers Job

38 Then the LORD answered Job out of the whirlwind and said:

2 "Who is this that darkens counsel by
     words without knowledge?
3 Dress for action like a man;
   I will question you, and you make it
     known to me.

4 "Where were you when I laid the foun-
     dation of the earth?
   Tell me, if you have understanding.
5 Who determined its measurements—
     surely you know!
   Or who stretched the line upon it?
6 On what were its bases sunk,
   or who laid its cornerstone,
7 when the morning stars sang together
   and all the sons of God shouted for
     joy?

8 "Or who shut in the sea with doors
   when it burst out from the womb,
9 when I made clouds its garment
   and thick darkness its swaddling
     band,

10   and prescribed limits for it
     and set bars and doors,
11   and said, 'Thus far shall you come,
         and no farther,
     and here shall your proud waves be
         stayed'?
12   "Have you commanded the morning
         since your days began,
     and caused the dawn to know its
         place,
13   that it might take hold of the skirts of
         the earth,
     and the wicked be shaken out of it?
14   It is changed like clay under the seal,
     and its features stand out like a
         garment.
15   From the wicked their light is withheld,
     and their uplifted arm is broken.

> ### GETTING THE MESSAGE
>
> God's great **majesty** shines forth in poetic
> language in chs. 38–39. These are some of
> the Bible's most awe-inspiring passages
> about God.

16   "Have you entered into the springs of
         the sea,
     or walked in the recesses of the deep?
17   Have the gates of death been revealed
         to you,
     or have you seen the gates of deep
         darkness?
18   Have you comprehended the expanse
         of the earth?
     Declare, if you know all this.
19   "Where is the way to the dwelling of
         light,
     and where is the place of darkness,
20   that you may take it to its territory
     and that you may discern the paths
         to its home?
21   You know, for you were born then,
     and the number of your days is great!
22   "Have you entered the storehouses of
         the snow,
     or have you seen the storehouses of
         the hail,
23   which I have reserved for the time of
         trouble,
     for the day of battle and war?

24   What is the way to the place where the
         light is distributed,
     or where the east wind is scattered
         upon the earth?
25   "Who has cleft a channel for the tor-
         rents of rain
     and a way for the thunderbolt,
26   to bring rain on a land where no man
         is,
     on the desert in which there is no
         man,
27   to satisfy the waste and desolate land,
     and to make the ground sprout with
         grass?
28   "Has the rain a father,
     or who has begotten the drops of
         dew?
29   From whose womb did the ice come
         forth,
     and who has given birth to the frost
         of heaven?
30   The waters become hard like stone,
     and the face of the deep is frozen.
31   "Can you bind the chains of the Pleiades
     or loose the cords of Orion?
32   Can you lead forth the Mazzaroth in
         their season,
     or can you guide the Bear with its
         children?
33   Do you know the ordinances of the
         heavens?
     Can you establish their rule on the
         earth?
34   "Can you lift up your voice to the clouds,
     that a flood of waters may cover you?
35   Can you send forth lightnings, that
         they may go
     and say to you, 'Here we are'?
36   Who has put wisdom in the inward
         parts
     or given understanding to the mind?
37   Who can number the clouds by wis-
         dom?
     Or who can tilt the waterskins of
         the heavens,
38   when the dust runs into a mass
     and the clods stick fast together?
39   "Can you hunt the prey for the lion,
     or satisfy the appetite of the young
         lions,
40   when they crouch in their dens
     or lie in wait in their thicket?

41 Who provides for the raven its prey,
  when its young ones cry to God for
    help,
  and wander about for lack of food?

39 "Do you know when the mountain goats give birth?
  Do you observe the calving of the
    does?
2 Can you number the months that they
    fulfill,
  and do you know the time when
    they give birth,
3 when they crouch, bring forth their
    offspring,
  and are delivered of their young?
4 Their young ones become strong; they
    grow up in the open;
  they go out and do not return to
    them.

5 "Who has let the wild donkey go free?
  Who has loosed the bonds of the
    swift donkey,
6 to whom I have given the arid plain
    for his home
  and the salt land for his dwelling
    place?
7 He scorns the tumult of the city;
  he hears not the shouts of the driver.
8 He ranges the mountains as his pasture,
  and he searches after every green
    thing.

9 "Is the wild ox willing to serve you?
  Will he spend the night at your
    manger?
10 Can you bind him in the furrow with
    ropes,
  or will he harrow the valleys after
    you?
11 Will you depend on him because his
    strength is great,
  and will you leave to him your labor?
12 Do you have faith in him that he will
    return your grain
  and gather it to your threshing floor?

13 "The wings of the ostrich wave proudly,
  but are they the pinions and plumage of love?
14 For she leaves her eggs to the earth
  and lets them be warmed on the
    ground,
15 forgetting that a foot may crush them
  and that the wild beast may trample
    them.

16 She deals cruelly with her young, as if
    they were not hers;
  though her labor be in vain, yet she
    has no fear,
17 because God has made her forget
    wisdom
  and given her no share in understanding.
18 When she rouses herself to flee,
  she laughs at the horse and his
    rider.

19 "Do you give the horse his might?
  Do you clothe his neck with a
    mane?
20 Do you make him leap like the locust?
  His majestic snorting is terrifying.
21 He paws in the valley and exults in his
    strength;
  he goes out to meet the weapons.
22 He laughs at fear and is not dismayed;
  he does not turn back from the
    sword.
23 Upon him rattle the quiver,
  the flashing spear, and the javelin.
24 With fierceness and rage he swallows
    the ground;
  he cannot stand still at the sound of
    the trumpet.
25 When the trumpet sounds, he says
    'Aha!'
  He smells the battle from afar,
  the thunder of the captains, and the
    shouting.

26 "Is it by your understanding that the
    hawk soars
  and spreads his wings toward the
    south?
27 Is it at your command that the eagle
    mounts up
  and makes his nest on high?
28 On the rock he dwells and makes his
    home,
  on the rocky crag and stronghold.
29 From there he spies out the prey;
  his eyes behold it from far away.
30 His young ones suck up blood,
  and where the slain are, there is he."

40 And the LORD said to Job:

2 "Shall a faultfinder contend with the
    Almighty?
  He who argues with God, let him
    answer it."

Job Promises Silence

[3] Then Job answered the LORD and said:

[4] "Behold, I am of small account; what
  shall I answer you?
  I lay my hand on my mouth.
[5] I have spoken once, and I will not
  answer;
  twice, but I will proceed no further."

The LORD Challenges Job

[6] Then the LORD answered Job out of the
whirlwind and said:

[7] "Dress for action like a man;
  I will question you, and you make it
  known to me.
[8] Will you even put me in the wrong?
  Will you condemn me that you may
  be in the right?
[9] Have you an arm like God,
  and can you thunder with a voice
  like his?

[10] "Adorn yourself with majesty and
  dignity;
  clothe yourself with glory and
  splendor.
[11] Pour out the overflowings of your
  anger,
  and look on everyone who is proud
  and abase him.
[12] Look on everyone who is proud and
  bring him low
  and tread down the wicked where
  they stand.
[13] Hide them all in the dust together;
  bind their faces in the world below.
[14] Then will I also acknowledge to you
  that your own right hand can save
  you.

[15] "Behold, Behemoth,[1]
  which I made as I made you;
  he eats grass like an ox.
[16] Behold, his strength in his loins,
  and his power in the muscles of his
  belly.

[17] He makes his tail stiff like a cedar;
  the sinews of his thighs are knit
  together.
[18] His bones are tubes of bronze,
  his limbs like bars of iron.
[19] "He is the first of the works of God;
  let him who made him bring near
  his sword!
[20] For the mountains yield food for him
  where all the wild beasts play.
[21] Under the lotus plants he lies,
  in the shelter of the reeds and in the
  marsh.
[22] For his shade the lotus trees cover
  him;
  the willows of the brook surround
  him.
[23] Behold, if the river is turbulent he is
  not frightened;
  he is confident though Jordan
  rushes against his mouth.
[24] Can one take him by his eyes,
  or pierce his nose with a snare?

41 "Can you draw out Leviathan[2] with
  a fishhook
  or press down his tongue with a
  cord?
[2] Can you put a rope in his nose
  or pierce his jaw with a hook?
[3] Will he make many pleas to you?
  Will he speak to you soft words?
[4] Will he make a covenant with you
  to take him for your servant forever?
[5] Will you play with him as with a bird,
  or will you put him on a leash for
  your girls?
[6] Will traders bargain over him?
  Will they divide him up among the
  merchants?
[7] Can you fill his skin with harpoons
  or his head with fishing spears?
[8] Lay your hands on him;
  remember the battle—you will not
  do it again!
[9] Behold, the hope of a man is false;
  he is laid low even at the sight of
  him.
[10] No one is so fierce that he dares to stir
  him up.
  Who then is he who can stand
  before me?

[1] A large animal, exact identity unknown [2] A large sea animal, exact identity unknown

11 Who has first given to me, that I
    should repay him?
    Whatever is under the whole
      heaven is mine.

12 "I will not keep silence concerning his
    limbs,
    or his mighty strength, or his
      goodly frame.
13 Who can strip off his outer garment?
    Who would come near him with a
      bridle?
14 Who can open the doors of his face?
    Around his teeth is terror.
15 His back is made of rows of shields,
    shut up closely as with a seal.
16 One is so near to another
    that no air can come between
      them.
17 They are joined one to another;
    they clasp each other and cannot be
      separated.
18 His sneezings flash forth light,
    and his eyes are like the eyelids of
      the dawn.
19 Out of his mouth go flaming torches;
    sparks of fire leap forth.
20 Out of his nostrils comes forth
    smoke,
    as from a boiling pot and burning
      rushes.
21 His breath kindles coals,
    and a flame comes forth from his
      mouth.
22 In his neck abides strength,
    and terror dances before him.
23 The folds of his flesh stick together,
    firmly cast on him and immovable.
24 His heart is hard as a stone,
    hard as the lower millstone.
25 When he raises himself up the mighty
    are afraid;
    at the crashing they are beside
      themselves.
26 Though the sword reaches him, it
    does not avail,
    nor the spear, the dart, or the javelin.
27 He counts iron as straw,
    and bronze as rotten wood.
28 The arrow cannot make him flee;
    for him sling stones are turned to
      stubble.
29 Clubs are counted as stubble;
    he laughs at the rattle of javelins.

30 His underparts are like sharp pot-
    sherds;
    he spreads himself like a threshing
      sledge on the mire.
31 He makes the deep boil like a pot;
    he makes the sea like a pot of oint-
      ment.
32 Behind him he leaves a shining wake;
    one would think the deep to be
      white-haired.
33 On earth there is not his like,
    a creature without fear.
34 He sees everything that is high;
    he is king over all the sons of
      pride."

Job's Confession and Repentance

42 Then Job answered the LORD and
said:

2 "I know that you can do all things,
    and that no purpose of yours can be
      thwarted.
3 'Who is this that hides counsel with-
    out knowledge?'
    Therefore I have uttered what I did
      not understand,
    things too wonderful for me, which
      I did not know.
4 'Hear, and I will speak;
    I will question you, and you make it
      known to me.'
5 I had heard of you by the hearing of
    the ear,
    but now my eye sees you;
6 therefore I despise myself,
    and repent in dust and ashes."

The LORD Rebukes Job's Friends

7 After the LORD had spoken these words to Job, the LORD said to Eliphaz the Temanite: "My anger burns against you and against your two friends, for you have not spoken of me what is right, as my servant Job has. 8 Now therefore take seven bulls and seven rams and go to my servant Job and offer up a burnt offering for yourselves. And my servant Job shall pray for you, for I will accept his prayer not to deal with you according to your folly. For you have not spoken of me what is right, as my servant Job has." 9 So Eliphaz the Temanite and Bildad the Shuhite and Zophar the Naamathite went and did what the LORD had told them, and the LORD accepted Job's prayer.

The Lord Restores Job's Fortunes

¹⁰ And the Lord restored the fortunes of Job, when he had prayed for his friends. And the Lord gave Job twice as much as he had before. ¹¹ Then came to him all his brothers and sisters and all who had known him before, and ate bread with him in his house. And they showed him sympathy and comforted him for all the evil[1] that the Lord had brought upon him. And each of them gave him a piece of money and a ring of gold.

¹² And the Lord blessed the latter days of Job more than his beginning. And he had 14,000 sheep, 6,000 camels, 1,000 yoke of oxen, and 1,000 female donkeys. ¹³ He had also seven sons and three daughters. ¹⁴ And he called the name of the first daughter Jemimah, and the name of the second Keziah, and the name of the third Keren-happuch. ¹⁵ And in all the land there were no women so beautiful as Job's daughters. And their father gave them an inheritance among their brothers. ¹⁶ And after this Job lived 140 years, and saw his sons, and his sons' sons, four generations. ¹⁷ And Job died, an old man, and full of days.

---

[1] Or disaster

INTRODUCTION TO THE PSALMS

1050/1030–1010 B.C.	1010–971 B.C.	971–931 B.C.	586 B.C.
Reign of Saul	Reign of David	Reign of Solomon	Fall of Judah/exile

AUTHOR AND DATE

Individual psalms come from diverse periods of Israel's history, but at every stage they served as the songbook of God's people. David wrote about half of the Psalms. His role as king was more than that of a ruler. He was to represent and even embody the people, and their well-being was tied to his faithfulness. David, then, writes as a representative, and the readers must discern whether the emphasis of a psalm is more on his role as ruler or more on his role as ideal Israelite, in which he is an example for all. The historical occasions mentioned in the psalm titles help the reader see how faith applies to real-life situations.

KEY THEMES

The Psalter is fundamentally the hymnbook of God's people. It takes the basic themes of OT theology and turns them into song:

1. *Monotheism.* The one God, Maker and Ruler of all, will vindicate his goodness and justice in his own time. Everyone must know and love this God, whose purity, power, wisdom, faithfulness, and unceasing love are breathtakingly beautiful.

2. *Creation and fall.* Though God made man with dignity and purpose, all people since the fall are beset with sins and weaknesses that only God's grace can heal.

3. *Election and covenant.* The one true God chose a people for himself and bound himself to them by his covenant. This covenant expressed God's intention to save his people, and through them to bring light to the world.

4. *Covenant membership.* In his covenant, God offers grace to his people: forgiveness of their sins, the shaping of their lives to reflect his own glory, and a part to play as light to the Gentiles. Each member of God's people is responsible to believe God's promises and to grow in obeying his commands. Those who do this enjoy the full benefits of God's love and find delight in knowing him. The well-being of God's people as a whole affects the well-being of each member.

Each one shares the joys and sorrows of the others. When believers suffer, they should not seek revenge but should pray. They can be confident that God will make all things right in his own time.

5. *Eschatology.* The story of God's people is headed toward a glorious future, in which all kinds of people will come to know the Lord. The personal faithfulness of God's people contributes to his ultimate purpose. The Messiah, the ultimate heir of David, will lead his people in the great task of bringing light to the Gentiles.

TYPES OF PSALMS

The Psalms can be identified according to some basic categories:

• ***Laments,*** which lay a troubled situation before the Lord, asking him for help. There are community (Psalm 12) and individual (Psalm 13) laments. This category is the largest by far, including up to a third of all Psalms.

• ***Hymns of praise,*** which call God's people to admire his great attributes and deeds. Examples include Psalms 8; 93; and 145.

• ***Hymns of thanksgiving.*** As with laments, there are community (Psalm 9) and individual (Psalm 30) thanksgiving psalms.

• ***Hymns celebrating God's law*** (Psalm 119).

• ***Wisdom psalms*** (Psalms 1; 37), which reflect themes from the Wisdom Books (Job, Proverbs, Ecclesiastes, Song of Solomon).

• ***Songs of confidence,*** which enable worshipers to deepen their trust in God amid difficult circumstances (Psalm 23).

• ***Royal psalms,*** which present the Davidic monarchy as the vehicle of blessing for God's people. Some of these are prayers (Psalm 20), some are thanksgivings (Psalm 21). All relate to the Messiah, the ultimate heir of David, either by setting a pattern (Psalms 20–21) or by portraying the king's reign in such a way that only the Messiah can completely fulfill it (Psalms 2; 72), or by focusing on the future (Psalm 110).

• **Historical psalms,** which take lessons from the history of God's dealings with his people (Psalm 78).

• **Prophetic hymns,** which echo the Prophets, calling people to covenant faithfulness (Psalm 81).

STRUCTURE

The standard Hebrew text divides the Psalms into five "books," perhaps in imitation of the five books of the Pentateuch.

Book 1	Psalms 1–41	Psalms 1–2 provide an introduction to the Psalms as a whole. Except for Psalms 10 and 33, the remaining psalms of Book 1 are psalms of David. Most of them are prayers of distress. Others are statements of confidence in the God who alone can save (e.g., 9; 11; 16; 18), striking the note that concludes the book (40–41). Reflections on ethics and worship are found in Psalms 1; 14–15; 19; 24; and 26.
Book 2	Psalms 42–72	Book 2 introduces the first group of psalms by the "sons of Korah" (42; 44–49; 50). There are also more psalms of David (51–65; 68–69), including most of the "historical" psalms (51–52; 54; 56–57; 59–60; 63). Once again, lament and distress dominate these prayers, which now also include a communal voice (e.g., 44; compare 67; 68). The lone psalm attributed to Solomon concludes Book 2 with a look at God's ideal for Israel's kings—ultimately pointing to Christ as the final great King of God's people.
Book 3	Psalms 73–89	The tone darkens further in Book 3. The opening Psalm 73 starkly questions the justice of God before seeing light in God's presence. That light has almost escaped the psalmist in Psalm 88, the bleakest of all psalms. Book 2 ended with the high point of royal aspirations; Book 3 concludes in Psalm 89 with these expectations badly threatened. Sharp rays of hope occasionally pierce the darkness (e.g., 75; 85; 87). The brief third book contains most of the psalms of Asaph (73–83), as well as another set of Korah psalms (84–85; 87–88).
Book 4	Psalms 90–106	Psalm 90 opens the fourth book of the psalms. It may be seen as the first response to the problems raised by Book 3. Psalm 90, attributed to Moses, reminds the worshiper that God was active on Israel's behalf long before David. This theme is taken up in Psalms 103–106, which summarize God's dealings with his people before any kings reigned. In between there is a group of psalms (93–100) characterized by the refrain "The LORD reigns." This truth refutes the doubts of Psalm 89.
Book 5	Psalms 107–150	The structure of Book 5 reflects the closing petition of Book 4 in 106:47. It declares that God does answer prayer (107) and concludes with five Hallelujah psalms (146–150). In between there are several psalms affirming the validity of the promises to David (110; 132; 144), two collections of Davidic psalms (108–110; 138–145); the longest psalm, celebrating the value of God's law (119); and 15 psalms of ascent for use by pilgrims to Jerusalem (120–134).

THE PSALMS

BOOK ONE

The Way of the Righteous and the Wicked

1 Blessed is the man[1]
who walks not in the counsel of the
wicked,
nor stands in the way of sinners,
nor sits in the seat of scoffers;
² but his delight is in the law of the LORD,
and on his law he meditates day
and night.

---

³ He is like a tree
planted by streams of water
that yields its fruit in its season,
and its leaf does not wither.
In all that he does, he prospers.
⁴ The wicked are not so,
but are like chaff that the wind
drives away.

⁵ Therefore the wicked will not stand in
the judgment,
nor sinners in the congregation of
the righteous;
⁶ for the LORD knows the way of the
righteous,
but the way of the wicked will perish.

The Reign of the LORD's Anointed

2 Why do the nations rage
and the peoples plot in vain?
² The kings of the earth set themselves,

and the rulers take counsel
together,
against the LORD and against his
Anointed, saying,
³ "Let us burst their bonds apart
and cast away their cords from us."

⁴ He who sits in the heavens laughs;
the Lord holds them in derision.
⁵ Then he will speak to them in his
wrath,
and terrify them in his fury, saying,
⁶ "As for me, I have set my King
on Zion, my holy hill."

⁷ I will tell of the decree:
The LORD said to me, "You are my
Son;
today I have begotten you.
⁸ Ask of me, and I will make the nations
your heritage,
and the ends of the earth your possession.
⁹ You shall break them with a rod of
iron
and dash them in pieces like a potter's vessel."

¹⁰ Now therefore, O kings, be wise;
be warned, O rulers of the earth.
¹¹ Serve the LORD with fear,
and rejoice with trembling.
¹² Kiss the Son,
lest he be angry, and you perish in
the way,
for his wrath is quickly kindled.
Blessed are all who take refuge in
him.

Save Me, O My God

3 A PSALM OF DAVID, WHEN HE FLED FROM
ABSALOM HIS SON.

¹ O LORD, how many are my foes!
Many are rising against me;
² many are saying of my soul,
there is no salvation for him in God.
Selah[2]

---

[1] The Hebrew word for *man* refers here to both men and women [2] The meaning of *Selah* throughout the Psalms is uncertain;
it may be a musical term

3 But you, O LORD, are a shield about me,
      my glory, and the lifter of my head.
4 I cried aloud to the LORD,
      and he answered me from his holy
          hill.   *Selah*

5 I lay down and slept;
      I woke again, for the LORD sus-
          tained me.
6 I will not be afraid of many thousands
          of people
      who have set themselves against
          me all around.

7 Arise, O LORD!
      Save me, O my God!
   For you strike all my enemies on the
          cheek;
      you break the teeth of the wicked.

8 Salvation belongs to the LORD;
      your blessing be on your people!
                                       Selah

Answer Me When I Call

4 TO THE CHOIRMASTER: WITH STRINGED
   INSTRUMENTS. A PSALM OF DAVID.

1 Answer me when I call, O God of my
          righteousness!
      You have given me relief when I
          was in distress.
      Be gracious to me and hear my prayer!

2 O men, how long shall my honor be
          turned into shame?
      How long will you love vain words
          and seek after lies?   *Selah*
3 But know that the LORD has set apart
          the godly for himself;
      the LORD hears when I call to him.

4 Be angry, and do not sin;
      ponder in your own hearts on your
          beds, and be silent.   *Selah*
5 Offer right sacrifices,
      and put your trust in the LORD.

6 There are many who say, "Who will
          show us some good?
      Lift up the light of your face upon
          us, O LORD!"
7 You have put more joy in my heart
      than they have when their grain and
          wine abound.

8 In peace I will both lie down and sleep;
      for you alone, O LORD, make me
          dwell in safety.

Lead Me in Your Righteousness

5 TO THE CHOIRMASTER: FOR THE FLUTES.
   A PSALM OF DAVID.

1 Give ear to my words, O LORD;
      consider my groaning.
2 Give attention to the sound of my
          cry,
      my King and my God,
      for to you do I pray.
3 O LORD, in the morning you hear my
          voice;
      in the morning I prepare a sacrifice
          for you and watch.

4 For you are not a God who delights in
          wickedness;
      evil may not dwell with you.
5 The boastful shall not stand before
          your eyes;
      you hate all evildoers.

GETTING THE MESSAGE

A shield for his people. Without the proper shield, an ancient warrior had little chance in battle. Psalms uses the term "shield" (3:3) to describe God's protection of his people.

6 You destroy those who speak lies;
      the LORD abhors the bloodthirsty
          and deceitful man.

7 But I, through the abundance of your
          steadfast love,
      will enter your house.
   I will bow down toward your holy
          temple
      in the fear of you.
8 Lead me, O LORD, in your righteous-
          ness
      because of my enemies;
      make your way straight before me.

9 For there is no truth in their mouth;
      their inmost self is destruction;
   their throat is an open grave;
      they flatter with their tongue.
10 Make them bear their guilt, O God;
      let them fall by their own counsels;
   because of the abundance of their
          transgressions cast them out,
      for they have rebelled against you.

[11] But let all who take refuge in you
      rejoice;
   let them ever sing for joy,
and spread your protection over them,
      that those who love your name may
      exult in you.
[12] For you bless the righteous, O Lord;
   you cover him with favor as with a
      shield.

O Lord, Deliver My Life

6 To the choirmaster: with stringed instruments; according to The Sheminith.[1] A Psalm of David.

[1] O Lord, rebuke me not in your anger,
   nor discipline me in your wrath.
[2] Be gracious to me, O Lord, for I am
      languishing;
   heal me, O Lord, for my bones are
      troubled.

GETTING THE MESSAGE

How are the Psalms divided?
The Psalms are divided into five books:
1–41; 42–72; 73–89; 90–106; 107–150.
Each book ends with a "doxology,"
a hymn of praise to God.

---

[3] My soul also is greatly troubled.
   But you, O Lord—how long?

[4] Turn, O Lord, deliver my life;
   save me for the sake of your stead-
      fast love.
[5] For in death there is no remembrance
      of you;
   in Sheol who will give you praise?

[6] I am weary with my moaning;
   every night I flood my bed with
      tears;
   I drench my couch with my weeping.
[7] My eye wastes away because of grief;
   it grows weak because of all my foes.

[8] Depart from me, all you workers of
      evil,
   for the Lord has heard the sound of
      my weeping.
[9] The Lord has heard my plea;
   the Lord accepts my prayer.

[10] All my enemies shall be ashamed and
      greatly troubled;
   they shall turn back and be put to
      shame in a moment.

In You Do I Take Refuge

7 A Shiggaion[2] of David, which he sang to the Lord concerning the words of Cush, a Benjaminite.

[1] O Lord my God, in you do I take ref-
      uge;
   save me from all my pursuers and
      deliver me,
[2] lest like a lion they tear my soul
      apart,
   rending it in pieces, with none to
      deliver.

[3] O Lord my God, if I have done this,
   if there is wrong in my hands,
[4] if I have repaid my friend with evil
      or plundered my enemy without
      cause,
[5] let the enemy pursue my soul and
      overtake it,
   and let him trample my life to the
      ground
   and lay my glory in the dust.   *Selah*

[6] Arise, O Lord, in your anger;
   lift yourself up against the fury of
      my enemies;
   awake for me; you have appointed a
      judgment.
[7] Let the assembly of the peoples be
      gathered about you;
   over it return on high.

[8] The Lord judges the peoples;
   judge me, O Lord, according to my
      righteousness
   and according to the integrity that
      is in me.
[9] Oh, let the evil of the wicked come to
      an end,
   and may you establish the righ-
      teous—
you who test the minds and hearts,
   O righteous God!
[10] My shield is with God,
   who saves the upright in heart.
[11] God is a righteous judge,
   and a God who feels indignation
      every day.

[1] Probably a musical term; also 12:1 [2] Probably a musical term

¹² If a man does not repent, God will
  whet his sword;
    he has bent and readied his bow;
¹³ he has prepared for him his deadly
  weapons,
    making his arrows fiery shafts.
¹⁴ Behold, the wicked man conceives evil
  and is pregnant with mischief
    and gives birth to lies.
¹⁵ He makes a pit, digging it out,
    and falls into the hole that he has
    made.
¹⁶ His mischief returns upon his own
  head,
    and on his own skull his violence
    descends.

¹⁷ I will give to the LORD the thanks due
  to his righteousness,
    and I will sing praise to the name of
    the LORD, the Most High.

How Majestic Is Your Name

8 TO THE CHOIRMASTER: ACCORDING TO
THE GITTITH.¹ A PSALM OF DAVID.

¹ O LORD, our Lord,
    how majestic is your name in all
    the earth!
  You have set your glory above the
  heavens.
² Out of the mouth of babies and
  infants,
  you have established strength because
    of your foes,
    to still the enemy and the avenger.

³ When I look at your heavens, the work
  of your fingers,
    the moon and the stars, which you
    have set in place,
⁴ what is man that you are mindful of
  him,
    and the son of man that you care
    for him?

⁵ Yet you have made him a little lower
  than the heavenly beings
    and crowned him with glory and
    honor.
⁶ You have given him dominion over
  the works of your hands;
    you have put all things under his
    feet,
⁷ all sheep and oxen,
    and also the beasts of the field,

⁸ the birds of the heavens, and the fish
  of the sea,
    whatever passes along the paths of
    the seas.

⁹ O LORD, our Lord,
    how majestic is your name in all
    the earth!

I Will Recount Your Wonderful Deeds

9 TO THE CHOIRMASTER: ACCORDING TO
MUTH-LABBEN.² A PSALM OF DAVID.

¹ I will give thanks to the LORD with my
  whole heart;
    I will recount all of your wonderful
    deeds.
² I will be glad and exult in you;
    I will sing praise to your name,
      O Most High.

³ When my enemies turn back,
    they stumble and perish before
      your presence.
⁴ For you have maintained my just
  cause;
    you have sat on the throne, giving
    righteous judgment.
⁵ You have rebuked the nations; you
  have made the wicked perish;
    you have blotted out their name
    forever and ever.
⁶ The enemy came to an end in everlasting ruins;
    their cities you rooted out;
    the very memory of them has per-
    ished.
⁷ But the LORD sits enthroned forever;
    he has established his throne for
    justice,
⁸ and he judges the world with righteousness;
    he judges the peoples with upright-
    ness.

¹ Probably a musical term; also 81:1; 84:1 ² Probably a musical term

9 The LORD is a stronghold for the
oppressed,
  a stronghold in times of trouble.
10 And those who know your name put
their trust in you,
  for you, O LORD, have not forsaken
those who seek you.
11 Sing praises to the LORD, who sits
enthroned in Zion!
  Tell among the peoples his deeds!
12 For he who avenges blood is mindful
of them;
  he does not forget the cry of the
afflicted.
13 Be gracious to me, O LORD!
  See my affliction from those who
hate me,
  O you who lift me up from the gates
of death,

GETTING THE MESSAGE

What is "Sheol"? In the Old Testament,
the Hebrew word "Sheol" (9:17) refers to
the place where people go when they die.
It is similar to the Greek word "Hades."
Both words are usually translated "death"
or "the grave."

---

14 that I may recount all your praises,
  that in the gates of the daughter of
Zion
  I may rejoice in your salvation.
15 The nations have sunk in the pit that
they made;
  in the net that they hid, their own
foot has been caught.
16 The LORD has made himself known;
  he has executed judgment;
  the wicked are snared in the work of
their own hands. *Higgaion.*[1] *Selah*
17 The wicked shall return to Sheol,
  all the nations that forget God.
18 For the needy shall not always be
forgotten,
  and the hope of the poor shall not
perish forever.
19 Arise, O LORD! Let not man prevail;
  let the nations be judged before you!

20 Put them in fear, O LORD!
  Let the nations know that they are
but men!   *Selah*

Why Do You Hide Yourself?

10 Why, O LORD, do you stand far
away?
  Why do you hide yourself in times
of trouble?

2 In arrogance the wicked hotly pursue
the poor;
  let them be caught in the schemes
that they have devised.
3 For the wicked boasts of the desires of
his soul,
  and the one greedy for gain curses
and renounces the LORD.
4 In the pride of his face the wicked
does not seek him;
  all his thoughts are, "There is no
God."
5 His ways prosper at all times;
  your judgments are on high, out of
his sight;
  as for all his foes, he puffs at them.
6 He says in his heart, "I shall not be
moved;
  throughout all generations I shall
not meet adversity."
7 His mouth is filled with cursing and
deceit and oppression;
  under his tongue are mischief and
iniquity.
8 He sits in ambush in the villages;
  in hiding places he murders the
innocent.
His eyes stealthily watch for the helpless;
9 he lurks in ambush like a lion in his
thicket;
he lurks that he may seize the poor;
  he seizes the poor when he draws
him into his net.
10 The helpless are crushed, sink down,
  and fall by his might.
11 He says in his heart, "God has forgotten,
  he has hidden his face, he will
never see it."
12 Arise, O LORD; O God, lift up your hand;
  forget not the afflicted.

---

[1] Probably a musical term

13 Why does the wicked renounce God
      and say in his heart, "You will not
         call to account"?
14 But you do see, for you note mischief
      and vexation,
         that you may take it into your
            hands;
      to you the helpless commits himself;
      you have been the helper of the
         fatherless.
15 Break the arm of the wicked and evil-
      doer;
         call his wickedness to account till
            you find none.

16 The LORD is king forever and ever;
      the nations perish from his land.
17 O LORD, you hear the desire of the
      afflicted;
         you will strengthen their heart;
         you will incline your ear
18 to do justice to the fatherless and
      the oppressed,
         so that man who is of the earth
            may strike terror no more.

The LORD Is in His Holy Temple

11 TO THE CHOIRMASTER. OF DAVID.
      In the LORD I take refuge;
   how can you say to my soul,
      "Flee like a bird to your mountain,
2 for behold, the wicked bend the
      bow;
         they have fitted their arrow to the
            string
         to shoot in the dark at the upright
            in heart;
3 if the foundations are destroyed,
      what can the righteous do?"

4 The LORD is in his holy temple;
      the LORD's throne is in heaven;
         his eyes see, his eyelids test the
            children of man.
5 The LORD tests the righteous,
      but his soul hates the wicked and
         the one who loves violence.
6 Let him rain coals on the wicked;
      fire and sulfur and a scorching
         wind shall be the portion of
            their cup.
7 For the LORD is righteous;
   he loves righteous deeds;
      the upright shall behold his
         face.

The Faithful Have Vanished

12 TO THE CHOIRMASTER: ACCORDING TO
      THE SHEMINITH. A PSALM OF DAVID.
1 Save, O LORD, for the godly one is
      gone;
         for the faithful have vanished from
            among the children of man.
2 Everyone utters lies to his neighbor;
      with flattering lips and a double
         heart they speak.

3 May the LORD cut off all flattering
      lips,
         the tongue that makes great boasts,
4 those who say, "With our tongue we
      will prevail,
         our lips are with us; who is master
            over us?"

> ### GETTING THE MESSAGE
>
> **What is a psalm of lament?** The main
> purpose of a psalm of lament is to tell
> the Lord about a difficult situation, to ask
> him for his help, and to praise him for
> helping. Some laments are community,
> congregational psalms. Others are
> individual, personal laments. One third
> of all the Psalms are psalms of lament.

5 "Because the poor are plundered,
      because the needy groan,
   I will now arise," says the LORD;
      "I will place him in the safety for
         which he longs."
6 The words of the LORD are pure
      words,
         like silver refined in a furnace on
            the ground,
         purified seven times.
7 You, O LORD, will keep them;
      you will guard us from this genera-
         tion forever.
8 On every side the wicked prowl,
      as vileness is exalted among the
         children of man.

How Long, O LORD?

13 TO THE CHOIRMASTER. A PSALM OF
      DAVID.
1 How long, O LORD? Will you forget me
      forever?

How long will you hide your face
from me?
2 How long must I take counsel in my
soul
and have sorrow in my heart all the
day?
How long shall my enemy be exalted
over me?

3 Consider and answer me, O LORD my
God;
light up my eyes, lest I sleep the
sleep of death,
4 lest my enemy say, "I have prevailed
over him,"
lest my foes rejoice because I am
shaken.

5 But I have trusted in your steadfast love;
my heart shall rejoice in your salvation.

GETTING THE MESSAGE

**How many of the Psalms were written
by David?** David is the author of about
half of the Psalms. Other authors include
Asaph, Solomon, Moses, and the sons
of Korah.

6 I will sing to the LORD,
because he has dealt bountifully
with me.

The Fool Says, There Is No God

14 TO THE CHOIRMASTER. OF DAVID.
The fool says in his heart, "There
is no God."
They are corrupt, they do abominable deeds,
there is none who does good.

2 The LORD looks down from heaven on
the children of man,
to see if there are any who understand,
who seek after God.
3 They have all turned aside; together
they have become corrupt;
there is none who does good,
not even one.

4 Have they no knowledge, all the evildoers

who eat up my people as they eat
bread
and do not call upon the LORD?
5 There they are in great terror,
for God is with the generation of the
righteous.
6 You would shame the plans of the poor,
but the LORD is his refuge.
7 Oh, that salvation for Israel would
come out of Zion!
When the LORD restores the fortunes of his people,
let Jacob rejoice, let Israel be glad.

Who Shall Dwell on Your Holy Hill?

15 A PSALM OF DAVID.
O LORD, who shall sojourn in your
tent?
Who shall dwell on your holy hill?

2 He who walks blamelessly and does
what is right
and speaks truth in his heart;
3 who does not slander with his tongue
and does no evil to his neighbor,
nor takes up a reproach against his
friend;
4 in whose eyes a vile person is despised,
but who honors those who fear the
LORD;
who swears to his own hurt and does
not change;
5 who does not put out his money at
interest
and does not take a bribe against
the innocent.
He who does these things shall never
be moved.

You Will Not Abandon My Soul

16 A MIKTAM[1] OF DAVID.
Preserve me, O God, for in you I
take refuge.
2 I say to the LORD, "You are my Lord;
I have no good apart from you."

3 As for the saints in the land, they are
the excellent ones,
in whom is all my delight.

4 The sorrows of those who run after
another god shall multiply;
their drink offerings of blood I will
not pour out
or take their names on my lips.

[1] Probably a musical term, throughout the Psalms

5 The LORD is my chosen portion and
   my cup;
   you hold my lot.
6 The lines have fallen for me in pleasant places;
   indeed, I have a beautiful inheritance.
7 I bless the LORD who gives me counsel;
   in the night also my heart instructs
   me.
8 I have set the LORD always before me;
   because he is at my right hand,
   I shall not be shaken.
9 Therefore my heart is glad, and my
   whole being rejoices;
   my flesh also dwells secure.
10 For you will not abandon my soul to
   Sheol,
   or let your holy one see corruption.
11 You make known to me the path of life;
   in your presence there is fullness of
   joy;
   at your right hand are pleasures
   forevermore.

In the Shadow of Your Wings

17 A PRAYER OF DAVID.
   Hear a just cause, O LORD; attend
   to my cry!
   Give ear to my prayer from lips free
   of deceit!
2 From your presence let my vindication come!
   Let your eyes behold the right!
3 You have tried my heart, you have
   visited me by night,
   you have tested me, and you will
   find nothing;
   I have purposed that my mouth will
   not transgress.
4 With regard to the works of man, by
   the word of your lips
   I have avoided the ways of the violent.
5 My steps have held fast to your paths;
   my feet have not slipped.
6 I call upon you, for you will answer
   me, O God;
   incline your ear to me; hear my
   words.
7 Wondrously show your steadfast love,
   O Savior of those who seek refuge
   from their adversaries at your right
   hand.

8 Keep me as the apple of your eye;
   hide me in the shadow of your wings,
9 from the wicked who do me violence,
   my deadly enemies who surround
   me.
10 They close their hearts to pity;
   with their mouths they speak arrogantly.
11 They have now surrounded our steps;
   they set their eyes to cast us to the
   ground.
12 He is like a lion eager to tear,
   as a young lion lurking in ambush.
13 Arise, O LORD! Confront him, subdue
   him!
   Deliver my soul from the wicked by
   your sword,
14 from men by your hand, O LORD,
   from men of the world whose portion is in this life.

GETTING THE MESSAGE

What is parallelism? Parallelism is one of
the main features of Hebrew poetry. All
150 Psalms include parallelism. Typically,
the main lines in a psalm are followed
by secondary lines that either repeat or
expand upon an idea in the main line.

You fill their womb with treasure;
   they are satisfied with children,
   and they leave their abundance to
   their infants.
15 As for me, I shall behold your face in
   righteousness;
   when I awake, I shall be satisfied
   with your likeness.

The LORD Is My Rock and My Fortress

18 TO THE CHOIRMASTER. A PSALM OF
   DAVID, THE SERVANT OF THE LORD,
   WHO ADDRESSED THE WORDS OF THIS
   SONG TO THE LORD ON THE DAY WHEN
   THE LORD RESCUED HIM FROM THE
   HAND OF ALL HIS ENEMIES, AND FROM
   THE HAND OF SAUL. HE SAID:

1 I love you, O LORD, my strength.
2 The LORD is my rock and my fortress
   and my deliverer,
   my God, my rock, in whom I take
   refuge,

my shield, and the horn of my
salvation, my stronghold.
³ I call upon the LORD, who is worthy to
be praised,
and I am saved from my enemies.

⁴ The cords of death encompassed me;
the torrents of destruction assailed
me;
⁵ the cords of Sheol entangled me;
the snares of death confronted me.

⁶ In my distress I called upon the LORD;
to my God I cried for help.
From his temple he heard my voice,
and my cry to him reached his ears.

⁷ Then the earth reeled and rocked;
the foundations also of the mountains trembled
and quaked, because he was angry.

GETTING THE MESSAGE

**What defined someone as an "enemy"
of the people of Israel?** The "enemies"
mentioned in the Psalms (e.g., 18:17)
were people hostile to the faith of God's
people. Sometimes they expressed their
hatred by physically attacking the people
of Israel, while other times they merely
rejoiced when Israel faced misfortunes.

⁸ Smoke went up from his nostrils,
and devouring fire from his mouth;
glowing coals flamed forth from
him.
⁹ He bowed the heavens and came
down;
thick darkness was under his feet.
¹⁰ He rode on a cherub and flew;
he came swiftly on the wings of the
wind.
¹¹ He made darkness his covering, his
canopy around him,
thick clouds dark with water.
¹² Out of the brightness before him
hailstones and coals of fire broke
through his clouds.
¹³ The LORD also thundered in the heavens,
and the Most High uttered his voice,
hailstones and coals of fire.

¹⁴ And he sent out his arrows and scattered them;
he flashed forth lightnings and
routed them.
¹⁵ Then the channels of the sea were seen,
and the foundations of the world
were laid bare
at your rebuke, O LORD,
at the blast of the breath of your
nostrils.
¹⁶ He sent from on high, he took me;
he drew me out of many waters.
¹⁷ He rescued me from my strong enemy
and from those who hated me,
for they were too mighty for me.
¹⁸ They confronted me in the day of my
calamity,
but the LORD was my support.
¹⁹ He brought me out into a broad place;
he rescued me, because he
delighted in me.

²⁰ The LORD dealt with me according to
my righteousness;
according to the cleanness of my
hands he rewarded me.
²¹ For I have kept the ways of the LORD,
and have not wickedly departed
from my God.
²² For all his rules were before me,
and his statutes I did not put away
from me.
²³ I was blameless before him,
and I kept myself from my guilt.
²⁴ So the LORD has rewarded me according to my righteousness,
according to the cleanness of my
hands in his sight.

²⁵ With the merciful you show yourself
merciful;
with the blameless man you show
yourself blameless;
²⁶ with the purified you show yourself
pure;
and with the crooked you make
yourself seem tortuous.
²⁷ For you save a humble people,
but the haughty eyes you bring
down.
²⁸ For it is you who light my lamp;
the LORD my God lightens my darkness.
²⁹ For by you I can run against a troop,
and by my God I can leap over a wall.

30 This God—his way is perfect;
    the word of the LORD proves true;
   he is a shield for all those who take
       refuge in him.

31 For who is God, but the LORD?
    And who is a rock, except our God?—
32 the God who equipped me with
       strength
    and made my way blameless.
33 He made my feet like the feet of a deer
    and set me secure on the heights.
34 He trains my hands for war,
    so that my arms can bend a bow of
       bronze.
35 You have given me the shield of your
       salvation,
    and your right hand supported me,
    and your gentleness made me great.
36 You gave a wide place for my steps
       under me,
    and my feet did not slip.
37 I pursued my enemies and overtook
       them,
    and did not turn back till they were
       consumed.
38 I thrust them through, so that they
       were not able to rise;
    they fell under my feet.
39 For you equipped me with strength
       for the battle;
    you made those who rise against
       me sink under me.
40 You made my enemies turn their
       backs to me,
    and those who hated me I
       destroyed.
41 They cried for help, but there was
       none to save;
    they cried to the LORD, but he did
       not answer them.
42 I beat them fine as dust before the
       wind;
    I cast them out like the mire of the
       streets.
43 You delivered me from strife with the
       people;
    you made me the head of the
       nations;
    people whom I had not known
       served me.
44 As soon as they heard of me they
       obeyed me;
    foreigners came cringing to me.

45 Foreigners lost heart
    and came trembling out of their
       fortresses.
46 The LORD lives, and blessed be my rock,
    and exalted be the God of my salva-
       tion—
47 the God who gave me vengeance
    and subdued peoples under me,
48 who delivered me from my enemies;
    yes, you exalted me above those
       who rose against me;
    you rescued me from the man of
       violence.
49 For this I will praise you, O LORD,
       among the nations,
    and sing to your name.
50 Great salvation he brings to his king,
    and shows steadfast love to his
       anointed,
    to David and his offspring forever.

GETTING THE MESSAGE

Are the Psalms poetry? The Psalms
often reflect the feelings or emotions of
the person who wrote the psalm. The
book of Psalms includes poetry that
covers all kinds of emotional feelings and
experiences, from anguish and sorrow to
great joy and thanksgiving.

The Law of the LORD Is Perfect

19 TO THE CHOIRMASTER. A PSALM OF
    DAVID.

1 The heavens declare the glory of God,
    and the sky above proclaims his
       handiwork.
2 Day to day pours out speech,
    and night to night reveals knowl-
       edge.
3 There is no speech, nor are there words,
    whose voice is not heard.
4 Their voice goes out through all the
       earth,
    and their words to the end of the
       world.
  In them he has set a tent for the sun,
5   which comes out like a bridegroom
       leaving his chamber,
    and, like a strong man, runs its
       course with joy.

6 Its rising is from the end of the heav-
        ens,
    and its circuit to the end of them,
    and there is nothing hidden from
        its heat.

7 The law of the LORD is perfect,
        reviving the soul;
    the testimony of the LORD is sure,
        making wise the simple;

8 the precepts of the LORD are right,
        rejoicing the heart;
    the commandment of the LORD is pure,
        enlightening the eyes;

9 the fear of the LORD is clean,
        enduring forever;
    the rules of the LORD are true,
        and righteous altogether.

10 More to be desired are they than gold,
        even much fine gold;

> ## GETTING THE MESSAGE
>
> **What are royal psalms?** Royal psalms
> (e.g., 18) emphasize God's promise to
> David that he would have an eternal
> kingdom (2 Samuel 7; 1 Chronicles 17).
> David and his descendants are called
> to bless Israel and the nations. Some
> of these psalms are praises, some are
> thanksgivings, and some are confessions
> of sin. The promises to David point to the
> Messiah, the ultimate heir of David.

    sweeter also than honey
    and drippings of the honeycomb.

11 Moreover, by them is your servant
        warned;
    in keeping them there is great
        reward.

12 Who can discern his errors?
    Declare me innocent from hidden
        faults.

13 Keep back your servant also from
        presumptuous sins;
    let them not have dominion over me!
    Then I shall be blameless,
        and innocent of great transgression.

14 Let the words of my mouth and the
        meditation of my heart
    be acceptable in your sight,
    O LORD, my rock and my redeemer.

Trust in the Name of the LORD Our God

20 To the choirmaster. A Psalm of
David.

1 May the LORD answer you in the day
        of trouble!
    May the name of the God of Jacob
        protect you!

2 May he send you help from the sanc-
        tuary
    and give you support from Zion!

3 May he remember all your offerings
    and regard with favor your burnt
        sacrifices!   *Selah*

4 May he grant you your heart's desire
    and fulfill all your plans!

5 May we shout for joy over your salva-
        tion,
    and in the name of our God set up
        our banners!
    May the LORD fulfill all your petitions!

6 Now I know that the LORD saves his
        anointed;
    he will answer him from his holy
        heaven
    with the saving might of his right
        hand.

7 Some trust in chariots and some in
        horses,
    but we trust in the name of the
        LORD our God.

8 They collapse and fall,
    but we rise and stand upright.

9 O LORD, save the king!
    May he answer us when we call.

The King Rejoices in the LORD's Strength

21 To the choirmaster. A Psalm of
David.

1 O LORD, in your strength the king
        rejoices,
    and in your salvation how greatly
        he exults!

2 You have given him his heart's desire
    and have not withheld the request
        of his lips.   *Selah*

3 For you meet him with rich blessings;
    you set a crown of fine gold upon
        his head.

4 He asked life of you; you gave it to
        him,
    length of days forever and ever.

5 His glory is great through your salva-
      tion;
    splendor and majesty you bestow
      on him.
6 For you make him most blessed for-
      ever;
    you make him glad with the joy of
      your presence.
7 For the king trusts in the Lord,
    and through the steadfast love of
      the Most High he shall not be
      moved.

8 Your hand will find out all your ene-
      mies;
    your right hand will find out those
      who hate you.
9 You will make them as a blazing oven
      when you appear.
    The Lord will swallow them up in his
      wrath,
    and fire will consume them.
10 You will destroy their descendants
      from the earth,
    and their offspring from among the
      children of man.
11 Though they plan evil against you,
    though they devise mischief, they
      will not succeed.
12 For you will put them to flight;
    you will aim at their faces with your
      bows.

13 Be exalted, O Lord, in your strength!
    We will sing and praise your power.

Why Have You Forsaken Me?

22 To the choirmaster: according
    to The Doe of the Dawn. A Psalm
    of David.

1 My God, my God, why have you for-
      saken me?
    Why are you so far from saving me,
      from the words of my groaning?
2 O my God, I cry by day, but you do not
      answer,
    and by night, but I find no rest.

3 Yet you are holy,
    enthroned on the praises of Israel.
4 In you our fathers trusted;
    they trusted, and you delivered
      them.
5 To you they cried and were rescued;
    in you they trusted and were not
      put to shame.

6 But I am a worm and not a man,
    scorned by mankind and despised
      by the people.
7 All who see me mock me;
    they make mouths at me; they wag
      their heads;
8 "He trusts in the Lord; let him deliver
      him;
    let him rescue him, for he delights
      in him!"

9 Yet you are he who took me from the
      womb;
    you made me trust you at my moth-
      er's breasts.
10 On you was I cast from my birth,
    and from my mother's womb you
      have been my God.
11 Be not far from me,
      for trouble is near,
    and there is none to help.

GETTING THE MESSAGE

**How often does the New Testament
quote from the Psalms?** Of all the Old
Testament books, the Psalms and Isaiah
are by far the two most widely quoted in
the New Testament.

12 Many bulls encompass me;
    strong bulls of Bashan surround me;
13 they open wide their mouths at me,
    like a ravening and roaring lion.

14 I am poured out like water,
    and all my bones are out of joint;
    my heart is like wax;
      it is melted within my breast;
15 my strength is dried up like a pot-
      sherd,
    and my tongue sticks to my jaws;
    you lay me in the dust of death.

16 For dogs encompass me;
    a company of evildoers encircles me;
    they have pierced my hands and feet—
17 I can count all my bones—
    they stare and gloat over me;
18 they divide my garments among them,
    and for my clothing they cast lots.

19 But you, O Lord, do not be far off!
    O you my help, come quickly to my
      aid!

20 Deliver my soul from the sword,
    my precious life from the power of
        the dog!
21   Save me from the mouth of the lion!
    You have rescued me from the horns
        of the wild oxen!

22 I will tell of your name to my brothers;
    in the midst of the congregation I
        will praise you:
23 You who fear the LORD, praise him!
    All you offspring of Jacob, glorify
        him,
    and stand in awe of him, all you
        offspring of Israel!
24 For he has not despised or abhorred
    the affliction of the afflicted,
    and he has not hidden his face from
        him,
    but has heard, when he cried to
        him.

25 From you comes my praise in the
    great congregation;
    my vows I will perform before those
        who fear him.
26 The afflicted shall eat and be satisfied;
    those who seek him shall praise the
        LORD!
    May your hearts live forever!

27 All the ends of the earth shall remem-
    ber
    and turn to the LORD,
    and all the families of the nations
        shall worship before you.
28 For kingship belongs to the LORD,
    and he rules over the nations.

29 All the prosperous of the earth eat and
    worship;
    before him shall bow all who go
        down to the dust,
    even the one who could not keep
        himself alive.
30 Posterity shall serve him;
    it shall be told of the Lord to the
        coming generation;
31 they shall come and proclaim his
    righteousness to a people yet
        unborn,
    that he has done it.

The LORD Is My Shepherd

23 A PSALM OF DAVID.
The LORD is my shepherd; I shall
    not want.

2   He makes me lie down in green
        pastures.
    He leads me beside still waters.
3   He restores my soul.
    He leads me in paths of righteousness
        for his name's sake.

4   Even though I walk through the valley
        of the shadow of death,
    I will fear no evil,
    for you are with me;
        your rod and your staff,
        they comfort me.

5   You prepare a table before me
        in the presence of my enemies;
    you anoint my head with oil;
        my cup overflows.
6   Surely goodness and mercy shall
        follow me
        all the days of my life,
    and I shall dwell in the house of the
        LORD
        forever.

The King of Glory

24 A PSALM OF DAVID.
The earth is the LORD's and the
    fullness thereof,
    the world and those who dwell
        therein,
2   for he has founded it upon the seas
        and established it upon the rivers.

3   Who shall ascend the hill of the LORD?
        And who shall stand in his holy
            place?
4   He who has clean hands and a pure
        heart,
        who does not lift up his soul to
            what is false
        and does not swear deceitfully.
5   He will receive blessing from the LORD
        and righteousness from the God of
            his salvation.
6   Such is the generation of those who
        seek him,
        who seek the face of the God of
            Jacob.   Selah

7   Lift up your heads, O gates!
        And be lifted up, O ancient doors,
        that the King of glory may come in.
8   Who is this King of glory?
        The LORD, strong and mighty,
        the LORD, mighty in battle!

9   Lift up your heads, O gates!
      And lift them up, O ancient doors,
      that the King of glory may come in.
10 Who is this King of glory?
      The LORD of hosts,
      he is the King of glory!   *Selah*

Teach Me Your Paths

25 OF DAVID.
      To you, O LORD, I lift up my soul.
2   O my God, in you I trust;
      let me not be put to shame;
      let not my enemies exult over me.
3   Indeed, none who wait for you shall
          be put to shame;
      they shall be ashamed who are
          wantonly treacherous.

4   Make me to know your ways, O LORD;
      teach me your paths.
5   Lead me in your truth and teach me,
      for you are the God of my salvation;
      for you I wait all the day long.

6   Remember your mercy, O LORD, and
          your steadfast love,
      for they have been from of old.
7   Remember not the sins of my youth
          or my transgressions;
      according to your steadfast love
          remember me,
      for the sake of your goodness,
          O LORD!

8   Good and upright is the LORD;
      therefore he instructs sinners in the
          way.
9   He leads the humble in what is right,
      and teaches the humble his way.
10 All the paths of the LORD are steadfast
          love and faithfulness,
      for those who keep his covenant
          and his testimonies.

11 For your name's sake, O LORD,
      pardon my guilt, for it is great.
12 Who is the man who fears the LORD?
      Him will he instruct in the way that
          he should choose.
13 His soul shall abide in well-being,
      and his offspring shall inherit the
          land.
14 The friendship of the LORD is for
          those who fear him,
      and he makes known to them his
          covenant.

15 My eyes are ever toward the LORD,
      for he will pluck my feet out of the
          net.
16 Turn to me and be gracious to me,
      for I am lonely and afflicted.
17 The troubles of my heart are enlarged;
      bring me out of my distresses.
18 Consider my affliction and my trou-
          ble,
      and forgive all my sins.
19 Consider how many are my foes,
      and with what violent hatred they
          hate me.
20 Oh, guard my soul, and deliver me!
      Let me not be put to shame, for I
          take refuge in you.
21 May integrity and uprightness pre-
          serve me,
      for I wait for you.

22 Redeem Israel, O God,
      out of all his troubles.

GETTING THE MESSAGE

What does *Selah* mean? Although the
word *Selah* is found 39 times in the book
of Psalms, its exact meaning is uncertain.
Most scholars believe it is a musical term
or a term to be used by a worship leader,
possibly to mark a pause.

I Will Bless the LORD

26 OF DAVID.
      Vindicate me, O LORD,
      for I have walked in my integrity,
      and I have trusted in the LORD with-
          out wavering.
2   Prove me, O LORD, and try me;
      test my heart and my mind.
3   For your steadfast love is before my
          eyes,
      and I walk in your faithfulness.

4   I do not sit with men of falsehood,
      nor do I consort with hypocrites.
5   I hate the assembly of evildoers,
      and I will not sit with the wicked.

6   I wash my hands in innocence
      and go around your altar, O LORD,
7   proclaiming thanksgiving aloud,
      and telling all your wondrous
          deeds.

8 O Lord, I love the habitation of your
    house
  and the place where your glory
    dwells.
9 Do not sweep my soul away with
    sinners,
  nor my life with bloodthirsty men,
10 in whose hands are evil devices,
  and whose right hands are full of
    bribes.
11 But as for me, I shall walk in my integ-
    rity;
  redeem me, and be gracious to me.
12 My foot stands on level ground;
  in the great assembly I will bless the
    Lord.

The Lord Is My Light and My Salvation

27 Of David.
        The Lord is my light and my
        salvation;
  whom shall I fear?
  The Lord is the stronghold of my life;
  of whom shall I be afraid?

> **GETTING THE MESSAGE**
>
> The term **house of the Lord** (27:4)
> always refers to the temple, where God
> in Old Testament times lived among his
> people.

2 When evildoers assail me
    to eat up my flesh,
  my adversaries and foes,
    it is they who stumble and fall.
3 Though an army encamp against me,
    my heart shall not fear;
  though war arise against me,
    yet I will be confident.
4 One thing have I asked of the Lord,
    that will I seek after:
  that I may dwell in the house of the
    Lord
    all the days of my life,
  to gaze upon the beauty of the Lord
    and to inquire in his temple.
5 For he will hide me in his shelter
    in the day of trouble;
  he will conceal me under the cover of
    his tent;
  he will lift me high upon a rock.

6 And now my head shall be lifted up
    above my enemies all around me,
  and I will offer in his tent
    sacrifices with shouts of joy;
  I will sing and make melody to the
    Lord.
7 Hear, O Lord, when I cry aloud;
    be gracious to me and answer me!
8 You have said, "Seek my face."
  My heart says to you,
    "Your face, Lord, do I seek."
9 Hide not your face from me.
  Turn not your servant away in anger,
    O you who have been my help.
  Cast me not off; forsake me not,
    O God of my salvation!
10 For my father and my mother have
    forsaken me,
  but the Lord will take me in.
11 Teach me your way, O Lord,
    and lead me on a level path
    because of my enemies.
12 Give me not up to the will of my
    adversaries;
  for false witnesses have risen
    against me,
  and they breathe out violence.
13 I believe that I shall look upon the
    goodness of the Lord
    in the land of the living!
14 Wait for the Lord;
  be strong, and let your heart take
    courage;
  wait for the Lord!

The Lord Is My Strength and My Shield

28 Of David.
        To you, O Lord, I call;
  my rock, be not deaf to me,
  lest, if you be silent to me,
    I become like those who go down to
      the pit.
2 Hear the voice of my pleas for mercy,
    when I cry to you for help,
  when I lift up my hands
    toward your most holy sanctuary.
3 Do not drag me off with the wicked,
    with the workers of evil,
  who speak peace with their neighbors
    while evil is in their hearts.
4 Give to them according to their work
    and according to the evil of their
      deeds;

give to them according to the work of
their hands;
render them their due reward.
5 Because they do not regard the works
of the LORD
or the work of his hands,
he will tear them down and build
them up no more.

6 Blessed be the LORD!
For he has heard the voice of my
pleas for mercy.
7 The LORD is my strength and my shield;
in him my heart trusts, and I am
helped;
my heart exults,
and with my song I give thanks to
him.

8 The LORD is the strength of his people;
he is the saving refuge of his
anointed.
9 Oh, save your people and bless your
heritage!
Be their shepherd and carry them
forever.

Ascribe to the LORD Glory

29 A PSALM OF DAVID.
Ascribe to the LORD, O heavenly
beings,
ascribe to the LORD glory and
strength.
2 Ascribe to the LORD the glory due his
name;
worship the LORD in the splendor of
holiness.

3 The voice of the LORD is over the
waters;
the God of glory thunders,
the LORD, over many waters.
4 The voice of the LORD is powerful;
the voice of the LORD is full of majesty.
5 The voice of the LORD breaks the cedars;
the LORD breaks the cedars of
Lebanon.
6 He makes Lebanon to skip like a calf,
and Sirion like a young wild ox.
7 The voice of the LORD flashes forth
flames of fire.
8 The voice of the LORD shakes the
wilderness;
the LORD shakes the wilderness of
Kadesh.

9 The voice of the LORD makes the deer
give birth
and strips the forests bare,
and in his temple all cry, "Glory!"
10 The LORD sits enthroned over the
flood;
the LORD sits enthroned as king
forever.
11 May the LORD give strength to his
people!
May the LORD bless his people with
peace!

Joy Comes with the Morning

30 A PSALM OF DAVID. A SONG AT THE
DEDICATION OF THE TEMPLE.
1 I will extol you, O LORD, for you have
drawn me up
and have not let my foes rejoice
over me.
2 O LORD my God, I cried to you for help,
and you have healed me.
3 O LORD, you have brought up my soul
from Sheol;
you restored me to life from among
those who go down to the pit.

4 Sing praises to the LORD, O you his
saints,
and give thanks to his holy name.
5 For his anger is but for a moment,
and his favor is for a lifetime.
Weeping may tarry for the night,
but joy comes with the morning.

6 As for me, I said in my prosperity,
"I shall never be moved."
7 By your favor, O LORD,
you made my mountain stand
strong;
you hid your face;
I was dismayed.

8 To you, O LORD, I cry,
and to the Lord I plead for mercy:
9 "What profit is there in my death,
if I go down to the pit?
Will the dust praise you?
Will it tell of your faithfulness?
10 Hear, O LORD, and be merciful to me!
O LORD, be my helper!"

11 You have turned for me my mourning
into dancing;
you have loosed my sackcloth
and clothed me with gladness,

12 that my glory may sing your praise
and not be silent.
O Lord my God, I will give thanks
to you forever!

Into Your Hand I Commit My Spirit

31 To the choirmaster. A Psalm of
David.

1 In you, O Lord, do I take refuge;
let me never be put to shame;
in your righteousness deliver me!
2 Incline your ear to me;
rescue me speedily!
Be a rock of refuge for me,
a strong fortress to save me!
3 For you are my rock and my fortress;
and for your name's sake you lead
me and guide me;
4 you take me out of the net they have
hidden for me,
for you are my refuge.
5 Into your hand I commit my spirit;
you have redeemed me, O Lord,
faithful God.

6 I hate those who pay regard to worthless idols,
but I trust in the Lord.
7 I will rejoice and be glad in your
steadfast love,
because you have seen my affliction;
you have known the distress of my
soul,
8 and you have not delivered me into
the hand of the enemy;
you have set my feet in a broad
place.

9 Be gracious to me, O Lord, for I am in
distress;
my eye is wasted from grief;
my soul and my body also.
10 For my life is spent with sorrow,
and my years with sighing;
my strength fails because of my iniquity,
and my bones waste away.
11 Because of all my adversaries I have
become a reproach,
especially to my neighbors,
and an object of dread to my acquaintances;
those who see me in the street flee
from me.

12 I have been forgotten like one who is
dead;
I have become like a broken vessel.
13 For I hear the whispering of many—
terror on every side!—
as they scheme together against me,
as they plot to take my life.
14 But I trust in you, O Lord;
I say, "You are my God."
15 My times are in your hand;
rescue me from the hand of my enemies and from my persecutors!
16 Make your face shine on your servant;
save me in your steadfast love!
17 O Lord, let me not be put to shame,
for I call upon you;
let the wicked be put to shame;
let them go silently to Sheol.
18 Let the lying lips be mute,
which speak insolently against the
righteous
in pride and contempt.

19 Oh, how abundant is your goodness,
which you have stored up for those
who fear you
and worked for those who take refuge
in you,
in the sight of the children of mankind!
20 In the cover of your presence you hide
them
from the plots of men;
you store them in your shelter
from the strife of tongues.
21 Blessed be the Lord,
for he has wondrously shown his
steadfast love to me
when I was in a besieged city.
22 I had said in my alarm,
"I am cut off from your sight."
But you heard the voice of my pleas
for mercy
when I cried to you for help.

23 Love the Lord, all you his saints!
The Lord preserves the faithful
but abundantly repays the one who
acts in pride.
24 Be strong, and let your heart take
courage,
all you who wait for the Lord!

Blessed Are the Forgiven

32 A MASKIL[1] OF DAVID.

Blessed is the one whose transgression is forgiven,
  whose sin is covered.
2 Blessed is the man against whom the
    LORD counts no iniquity,
  and in whose spirit there is no deceit.

3 For when I kept silent, my bones
    wasted away
  through my groaning all day long.
4 For day and night your hand was
    heavy upon me;
  my strength was dried up as by the
    heat of summer.   *Selah*

5 I acknowledged my sin to you,
  and I did not cover my iniquity;
I said, "I will confess my transgressions to the LORD,"
  and you forgave the iniquity of my
    sin.   *Selah*

6 Therefore let everyone who is godly
    offer prayer to you at a time when
    you may be found;
  surely in the rush of great waters,
    they shall not reach him.
7 You are a hiding place for me;
  you preserve me from trouble;
  you surround me with shouts of
    deliverance.   *Selah*

8 I will instruct you and teach you in
    the way you should go;
  I will counsel you with my eye
    upon you.
9 Be not like a horse or a mule, without
    understanding,
  which must be curbed with bit and
    bridle,
  or it will not stay near you.
10 Many are the sorrows of the wicked,
  but steadfast love surrounds the
    one who trusts in the LORD.
11 Be glad in the LORD, and rejoice,
    O righteous,
  and shout for joy, all you upright in
    heart!

The Steadfast Love of the LORD

33 Shout for joy in the LORD, O you
  righteous!
  Praise befits the upright.

2 Give thanks to the LORD with the lyre;
  make melody to him with the harp
    of ten strings!
3 Sing to him a new song;
  play skillfully on the strings, with
    loud shouts.

4 For the word of the LORD is upright,
  and all his work is done in faithfulness.
5 He loves righteousness and justice;
  the earth is full of the steadfast love
    of the LORD.

6 By the word of the LORD the heavens
    were made,
  and by the breath of his mouth all
    their host.
7 He gathers the waters of the sea as a
    heap;
  he puts the deeps in storehouses.

GETTING THE MESSAGE

Summers in Israel can be very hot, depending on where one is (see 32:4). In places like Masada, near the Dead Sea, temperatures can soar past 110 degrees Fahrenheit (43° C) without a drop of rain. However, Jerusalem, with its higher elevation, remains cooler with temperatures between 75 and 85 degrees (24 to 29° C).

8 Let all the earth fear the LORD;
  let all the inhabitants of the world
    stand in awe of him!
9 For he spoke, and it came to be;
  he commanded, and it stood firm.
10 The LORD brings the counsel of the
    nations to nothing;
  he frustrates the plans of the peoples.
11 The counsel of the LORD stands forever,
  the plans of his heart to all generations.
12 Blessed is the nation whose God is the
    LORD,
  the people whom he has chosen as
    his heritage!
13 The LORD looks down from heaven;
  he sees all the children of man;

[1] Probably a musical term, throughout the Psalms

14 from where he sits enthroned he
    looks out
  on all the inhabitants of the earth,
15 he who fashions the hearts of them all
  and observes all their deeds.
16 The king is not saved by his great army;
  a warrior is not delivered by his
    great strength.
17 The war horse is a false hope for sal-
    vation,
  and by its great might it cannot
    rescue.

18 Behold, the eye of the LORD is on
    those who fear him,
  on those who hope in his steadfast
    love,
19 that he may deliver their soul from
    death
  and keep them alive in famine.

20 Our soul waits for the LORD;
  he is our help and our shield.

21 For our heart is glad in him,
  because we trust in his holy name.
22 Let your steadfast love, O LORD, be
    upon us,
  even as we hope in you.

Taste and See That the LORD Is Good

34 OF DAVID, WHEN HE CHANGED HIS
BEHAVIOR BEFORE ABIMELECH, SO
THAT HE DROVE HIM OUT, AND HE
WENT AWAY.

1 I will bless the LORD at all times;
  his praise shall continually be in
    my mouth.
2 My soul makes its boast in the LORD;
  let the humble hear and be glad.
3 Oh, magnify the LORD with me,
  and let us exalt his name together!

4 I sought the LORD, and he answered me
  and delivered me from all my fears.
5 Those who look to him are radiant,
  and their faces shall never be
    ashamed.

6 This poor man cried, and the LORD
    heard him
  and saved him out of all his troubles.
7 The angel of the LORD encamps
  around those who fear him, and
    delivers them.

8 Oh, taste and see that the LORD is
    good!
  Blessed is the man who takes refuge
    in him!
9 Oh, fear the LORD, you his saints,
  for those who fear him have no
    lack!
10 The young lions suffer want and hun-
    ger;
  but those who seek the LORD lack
    no good thing.

11 Come, O children, listen to me;
  I will teach you the fear of the LORD.
12 What man is there who desires life
  and loves many days, that he may
    see good?
13 Keep your tongue from evil
  and your lips from speaking deceit.
14 Turn away from evil and do good;
  seek peace and pursue it.

15 The eyes of the LORD are toward the
    righteous
  and his ears toward their cry.
16 The face of the LORD is against those
    who do evil,
  to cut off the memory of them from
    the earth.
17 When the righteous cry for help, the
    LORD hears
  and delivers them out of all their
    troubles.
18 The LORD is near to the brokenhearted
  and saves the crushed in spirit.

19 Many are the afflictions of the righ-
    teous,
  but the LORD delivers him out of
    them all.
20 He keeps all his bones;
  not one of them is broken.
21 Affliction will slay the wicked,
  and those who hate the righteous
    will be condemned.
22 The LORD redeems the life of his ser-
    vants;
  none of those who take refuge in
    him will be condemned.

Great Is the LORD

35 OF DAVID.

Contend, O LORD, with those
who contend with me;
fight against those who fight
against me!
2 Take hold of shield and buckler
and rise for my help!
3 Draw the spear and javelin
against my pursuers!
Say to my soul,
"I am your salvation!"

4 Let them be put to shame and dishonor
who seek after my life!
Let them be turned back and disappointed
who devise evil against me!
5 Let them be like chaff before the wind,
with the angel of the LORD driving
them away!
6 Let their way be dark and slippery,
with the angel of the LORD pursuing
them!

7 For without cause they hid their net
for me;
without cause they dug a pit for my
life.
8 Let destruction come upon him when
he does not know it!
And let the net that he hid ensnare
him;
let him fall into it—to his destruction!

9 Then my soul will rejoice in the LORD,
exulting in his salvation.
10 All my bones shall say,
"O LORD, who is like you,
delivering the poor
from him who is too strong for him,
the poor and needy from him who
robs him?"

11 Malicious witnesses rise up;
they ask me of things that I do not
know.
12 They repay me evil for good;
my soul is bereft.
13 But I, when they were sick—
I wore sackcloth;
I afflicted myself with fasting;
I prayed with head bowed on my chest.
14 I went about as though I grieved for
my friend or my brother;

as one who laments his mother,
I bowed down in mourning.

15 But at my stumbling they rejoiced and
gathered;
they gathered together against me;
wretches whom I did not know
tore at me without ceasing;
16 like profane mockers at a feast,
they gnash at me with their teeth.

17 How long, O Lord, will you look on?
Rescue me from their destruction,
my precious life from the lions!
18 I will thank you in the great congregation;
in the mighty throng I will praise
you.

> ### GETTING THE MESSAGE
>
> **Strong offense and defense.** The shield
> and buckler (35:2) and the spear and
> javelin (35:3) represented extremes in
> weaponry. While the shield was lighter
> and could be carried without the use of a
> helper, the larger buckler gave the warrior
> more protection. The javelin could be
> hurled at enemies from a distance while
> the spear served better in close combat.

19 Let not those rejoice over me
who are wrongfully my foes,
and let not those wink the eye
who hate me without cause.
20 For they do not speak peace,
but against those who are quiet in
the land
they devise words of deceit.
21 They open wide their mouths against
me;
they say, "Aha, Aha!
Our eyes have seen it!"

22 You have seen, O LORD; be not silent!
O Lord, be not far from me!
23 Awake and rouse yourself for my
vindication,
for my cause, my God and my Lord!
24 Vindicate me, O LORD, my God,
according to your righteousness,
and let them not rejoice over me!
25 Let them not say in their hearts,
"Aha, our heart's desire!"
Let them not say, "We have swallowed
him up."

26 Let them be put to shame and disappointed altogether
   who rejoice at my calamity!
   Let them be clothed with shame and
   dishonor
   who magnify themselves against
   me!
27 Let those who delight in my righteousness
   shout for joy and be glad
   and say evermore,
   "Great is the LORD,
   who delights in the welfare of his
   servant!"
28 Then my tongue shall tell of your
   righteousness
   and of your praise all the day long.

> ## GETTING THE MESSAGE
>
> The phrase **shadow of your wings** (36:7)
> is also found in two other psalms (17:8;
> 57:1). It symbolizes the protection and
> safety of the Lord.

How Precious Is Your Steadfast Love

36 TO THE CHOIRMASTER. OF DAVID,
THE SERVANT OF THE LORD.

1 Transgression speaks to the wicked
   deep in his heart;
   there is no fear of God
   before his eyes.
2 For he flatters himself in his own eyes
   that his iniquity cannot be found
   out and hated.
3 The words of his mouth are trouble
   and deceit;
   he has ceased to act wisely and do
   good.
4 He plots trouble while on his bed;
   he sets himself in a way that is not
   good;
   he does not reject evil.
5 Your steadfast love, O LORD, extends
   to the heavens,
   your faithfulness to the clouds.
6 Your righteousness is like the mountains of God;
   your judgments are like the great
   deep;
   man and beast you save, O LORD.

7 How precious is your steadfast love,
   O God!
   The children of mankind take refuge
   in the shadow of your wings.
8 They feast on the abundance of your
   house,
   and you give them drink from the
   river of your delights.
9 For with you is the fountain of life;
   in your light do we see light.

10 Oh, continue your steadfast love to
   those who know you,
   and your righteousness to the
   upright of heart!
11 Let not the foot of arrogance come
   upon me,
   nor the hand of the wicked drive
   me away.
12 There the evildoers lie fallen;
   they are thrust down, unable to rise.

He Will Not Forsake His Saints

37 OF DAVID.
   Fret not yourself because of evildoers;
   be not envious of wrongdoers!
2 For they will soon fade like the grass
   and wither like the green herb.
3 Trust in the LORD, and do good;
   dwell in the land and befriend
   faithfulness.
4 Delight yourself in the LORD,
   and he will give you the desires of
   your heart.
5 Commit your way to the LORD;
   trust in him, and he will act.
6 He will bring forth your righteousness
   as the light,
   and your justice as the noonday.
7 Be still before the LORD and wait
   patiently for him;
   fret not yourself over the one who
   prospers in his way,
   over the man who carries out evil
   devices!
8 Refrain from anger, and forsake
   wrath!
   Fret not yourself; it tends only to
   evil.
9 For the evildoers shall be cut off,
   but those who wait for the LORD
   shall inherit the land.

10 In just a little while, the wicked will
      be no more;
   though you look carefully at his
      place, he will not be there.
11 But the meek shall inherit the land
   and delight themselves in abundant
      peace.

12 The wicked plots against the righteous
   and gnashes his teeth at him,
13 but the Lord laughs at the wicked,
   for he sees that his day is coming.

14 The wicked draw the sword and bend
      their bows
   to bring down the poor and needy,
   to slay those whose way is upright;
15 their sword shall enter their own heart,
   and their bows shall be broken.

16 Better is the little that the righteous has
   than the abundance of many wicked.
17 For the arms of the wicked shall be
      broken,
   but the LORD upholds the righteous.

18 The LORD knows the days of the
      blameless,
   and their heritage will remain forever;
19 they are not put to shame in evil times;
   in the days of famine they have
      abundance.

20 But the wicked will perish;
   the enemies of the LORD are like the
      glory of the pastures;
   they vanish—like smoke they van-
      ish away.

21 The wicked borrows but does not pay
      back,
   but the righteous is generous and
      gives;
22 for those blessed by the LORD shall
      inherit the land,
   but those cursed by him shall be cut
      off.

23 The steps of a man are established by
      the LORD,
   when he delights in his way;
24 though he fall, he shall not be cast
      headlong,
   for the LORD upholds his hand.

25 I have been young, and now am old,
   yet I have not seen the righteous
      forsaken
   or his children begging for bread.

26 He is ever lending generously,
   and his children become a bless-
      ing.
27 Turn away from evil and do good;
   so shall you dwell forever.
28 For the LORD loves justice;
   he will not forsake his saints.
   They are preserved forever,
   but the children of the wicked shall
      be cut off.
29 The righteous shall inherit the land
   and dwell upon it forever.

30 The mouth of the righteous utters
      wisdom,
   and his tongue speaks justice.
31 The law of his God is in his heart;
   his steps do not slip.

32 The wicked watches for the righteous
   and seeks to put him to death.

GETTING THE MESSAGE

The **laurel tree** (37:35) may be the
sweet-bay tree, which is found all over
the Mediterranean and can grow up to
60 feet (18 m) in height. Parts of the
tree can be used for medicinal purposes
while its leaves (bay leaves) can be used
for seasoning food.

33 The LORD will not abandon him to his
      power
   or let him be condemned when he
      is brought to trial.
34 Wait for the LORD and keep his way,
   and he will exalt you to inherit the
      land;
   you will look on when the wicked
      are cut off.

35 I have seen a wicked, ruthless man,
   spreading himself like a green lau-
      rel tree.
36 But he passed away, and behold, he
      was no more;
   though I sought him, he could not
      be found.
37 Mark the blameless and behold the
      upright,
   for there is a future for the man of
      peace.

38 But transgressors shall be altogether
destroyed;
   the future of the wicked shall be cut
   off.
39 The salvation of the righteous is from
the LORD;
   he is their stronghold in the time of
   trouble.
40 The LORD helps them and delivers
them;
   he delivers them from the wicked
   and saves them,
   because they take refuge in him.

Do Not Forsake Me, O Lord

38
A PSALM OF DAVID, FOR THE
MEMORIAL OFFERING.

1 O LORD, rebuke me not in your anger,
   nor discipline me in your wrath!

GETTING THE MESSAGE

Snares (38:12) were traps used to catch
birds and animals. Some snares used
ropes or nets that would be triggered
as soon as the bait was touched. Pits
disguised with sticks and leaves were
also used as snares. In the Psalms, snares
serve as symbols of danger or death at
the hands of the wicked.

2 For your arrows have sunk into me,
   and your hand has come down on
   me.
3 There is no soundness in my flesh
   because of your indignation;
   there is no health in my bones
   because of my sin.
4 For my iniquities have gone over my
   head;
   like a heavy burden, they are too
   heavy for me.
5 My wounds stink and fester
   because of my foolishness,
6 I am utterly bowed down and prostrate;
   all the day I go about mourning.
7 For my sides are filled with burning,
   and there is no soundness in my
   flesh.
8 I am feeble and crushed;
   I groan because of the tumult of my
   heart.

9 O Lord, all my longing is before you;
   my sighing is not hidden from you.
10 My heart throbs; my strength fails me,
   and the light of my eyes—it also
   has gone from me.
11 My friends and companions stand
   aloof from my plague,
   and my nearest kin stand far off.
12 Those who seek my life lay their
   snares;
   those who seek my hurt speak of
   ruin
   and meditate treachery all day long.
13 But I am like a deaf man; I do not hear,
   like a mute man who does not open
   his mouth.
14 I have become like a man who does
   not hear,
   and in whose mouth are no rebukes.
15 But for you, O LORD, do I wait;
   it is you, O Lord my God, who will
   answer.
16 For I said, "Only let them not rejoice
   over me,
   who boast against me when my foot
   slips!"
17 For I am ready to fall,
   and my pain is ever before me.
18 I confess my iniquity;
   I am sorry for my sin.
19 But my foes are vigorous, they are
   mighty,
   and many are those who hate me
   wrongfully.
20 Those who render me evil for good
   accuse me because I follow after
   good.
21 Do not forsake me, O LORD!
   O my God, be not far from me!
22 Make haste to help me,
   O Lord, my salvation!

What Is the Measure of My Days?

39
TO THE CHOIRMASTER: TO
JEDUTHUN. A PSALM OF DAVID.

1 I said, "I will guard my ways,
   that I may not sin with my tongue;
   I will guard my mouth with a muzzle,
   so long as the wicked are in my
   presence."
2 I was mute and silent;
   I held my peace to no avail,

and my distress grew worse.
3   My heart became hot within me.
    As I mused, the fire burned;
        then I spoke with my tongue:

4   "O LORD, make me know my end
        and what is the measure of my
            days;
        let me know how fleeting I am!
5   Behold, you have made my days a few
            handbreadths,
        and my lifetime is as nothing
            before you.
    Surely all mankind stands as a mere
            breath!   *Selah*
6   Surely a man goes about as a shadow!
    Surely for nothing they are in turmoil;
        man heaps up wealth and does not
            know who will gather!

7   "And now, O Lord, for what do I wait?
        My hope is in you.
8   Deliver me from all my transgressions.
        Do not make me the scorn of the
            fool!
9   I am mute; I do not open my mouth,
        for it is you who have done it.
10 Remove your stroke from me;
        I am spent by the hostility of your
            hand.
11 When you discipline a man
        with rebukes for sin,
    you consume like a moth what is dear
            to him;
        surely all mankind is a mere breath!
                                       Selah

12 "Hear my prayer, O LORD,
        and give ear to my cry;
        hold not your peace at my tears!
    For I am a sojourner with you,
        a guest, like all my fathers.
13 Look away from me, that I may smile
            again,
        before I depart and am no more!"

My Help and My Deliverer

40 TO THE CHOIRMASTER. A PSALM OF
    DAVID.

1   I waited patiently for the LORD;
        he inclined to me and heard my cry.
2   He drew me up from the pit of
            destruction,
        out of the miry bog,
    and set my feet upon a rock,
        making my steps secure.

3   He put a new song in my mouth,
        a song of praise to our God.
    Many will see and fear,
        and put their trust in the LORD.

4   Blessed is the man who makes
        the LORD his trust,
    who does not turn to the proud,
        to those who go astray after a lie!
5   You have multiplied, O LORD my God,
        your wondrous deeds and your
            thoughts toward us;
        none can compare with you!
    I will proclaim and tell of them,
        yet they are more than can be told.

6   In sacrifice and offering you have not
            delighted,
        but you have given me an open ear.
    Burnt offering and sin offering
        you have not required.

GETTING THE MESSAGE

How long is a handbreadth? A handbreadth (39:5) was considered to be the
width of the four fingers on one hand, or
roughly 4 inches (10 cm).

7   Then I said, "Behold, I have come;
        in the scroll of the book it is written
            of me:
8   I delight to do your will, O my God;
        your law is within my heart."
9   I have told the glad news of deliverance
            in the great congregation;
    behold, I have not restrained my lips,
        as you know, O LORD.
10 I have not hidden your deliverance
            within my heart;
    I have spoken of your faithfulness
            and your salvation;
    I have not concealed your steadfast
            love and your faithfulness
        from the great congregation.

11 As for you, O LORD, you will not restrain
        your mercy from me;
    your steadfast love and your faithful-
            ness will
        ever preserve me!
12 For evils have encompassed me
            beyond number;
    my iniquities have overtaken me,
        and I cannot see;

they are more than the hairs of my head;
  my heart fails me.
13 Be pleased, O LORD, to deliver me!
  O LORD, make haste to help me!
14 Let those be put to shame and disappointed altogether
  who seek to snatch away my life;
  let those be turned back and brought to dishonor
  who delight in my hurt!
15 Let those be appalled because of their shame
  who say to me, "Aha, Aha!"

16 But may all who seek you
  rejoice and be glad in you;
  may those who love your salvation
  say continually, "Great is the LORD!"

GETTING THE MESSAGE

There were at least three known species of **deer** (42:1) in ancient Palestine. The red deer was the largest. The male could weigh up to 500 pounds (225 kg) while the female weighed up to 350 pounds (160 kg).

17 As for me, I am poor and needy,
  but the Lord takes thought for me.
  You are my help and my deliverer;
  do not delay, O my God!

O LORD, Be Gracious to Me

41 To THE CHOIRMASTER. A PSALM OF DAVID.

1 Blessed is the one who considers the poor!
  In the day of trouble the LORD delivers him;
2 the LORD protects him and keeps him alive;
  he is called blessed in the land;
  you do not give him up to the will of his enemies.
3 The LORD sustains him on his sickbed;
  in his illness you restore him to full health.

4 As for me, I said, "O LORD, be gracious to me;
  heal me, for I have sinned against you!"

5 My enemies say of me in malice,
  "When will he die, and his name perish?"
6 And when one comes to see me, he utters empty words,
  while his heart gathers iniquity;
  when he goes out, he tells it abroad.
7 All who hate me whisper together about me;
  they imagine the worst for me.
8 They say, "A deadly thing is poured out on him;
  he will not rise again from where he lies."
9 Even my close friend in whom I trusted,
  who ate my bread, has lifted his heel against me.
10 But you, O LORD, be gracious to me,
  and raise me up, that I may repay them!

11 By this I know that you delight in me:
  my enemy will not shout in triumph over me.
12 But you have upheld me because of my integrity,
  and set me in your presence forever.

13 Blessed be the LORD, the God of Israel,
  from everlasting to everlasting!
  Amen and Amen.

BOOK TWO

Why Are You Cast Down, O My Soul?

42 To THE CHOIRMASTER. A MASKIL OF THE SONS OF KORAH.

1 As a deer pants for flowing streams,
  so pants my soul for you, O God.
2 My soul thirsts for God,
  for the living God.
  When shall I come and appear before God?
3 My tears have been my food day and night,
  while they say to me all the day long,
  "Where is your God?"
4 These things I remember,
  as I pour out my soul:
  how I would go with the throng
  and lead them in procession to the house of God
  with glad shouts and songs of praise,
  a multitude keeping festival.

5 Why are you cast down, O my soul,
　　and why are you in turmoil within
　　　me?
　Hope in God; for I shall again praise
　　him,
　　my salvation 6 and my God.

My soul is cast down within me;
　therefore I remember you
from the land of Jordan and of
　　Hermon,
　from Mount Mizar.
7 Deep calls to deep
　at the roar of your waterfalls;
all your breakers and your waves
　have gone over me.
8 By day the LORD commands his stead-
　　fast love,
　　and at night his song is with me,
　　a prayer to the God of my life.
9 I say to God, my rock:
　"Why have you forgotten me?
Why do I go mourning
　　because of the oppression of the
　　　enemy?"
10 As with a deadly wound in my bones,
　my adversaries taunt me,
while they say to me all the day long,
　"Where is your God?"
11 Why are you cast down, O my soul,
　　and why are you in turmoil within
　　　me?
　Hope in God; for I shall again praise
　　him,
　　my salvation and my God.

Send Out Your Light and Your Truth

43 Vindicate me, O God, and defend
　　my cause
　against an ungodly people,
from the deceitful and unjust man
　deliver me!
2 For you are the God in whom I take
　　refuge;
　why have you rejected me?
Why do I go about mourning
　　because of the oppression of the
　　　enemy?
3 Send out your light and your truth;
　let them lead me;
let them bring me to your holy hill
　and to your dwelling!
4 Then I will go to the altar of God,
　to God my exceeding joy,

and I will praise you with the lyre,
　O God, my God.

5 Why are you cast down, O my soul,
　　and why are you in turmoil within
　　　me?
　Hope in God; for I shall again praise
　　him,
　　my salvation and my God.

Come to Our Help

44 TO THE CHOIRMASTER. A MASKIL OF
　　THE SONS OF KORAH.

1 O God, we have heard with our ears,
　　our fathers have told us,
　what deeds you performed in their
　　days,
　　in the days of old:

GETTING THE MESSAGE

Forgetting the name of God (44:20).
Many of the pagan religions of Old
Testament times taught that a god's
power was tied directly to its name.
The false prophets of Jeremiah's time
believed that, if they could erase God's
name from the people's memory, they
would follow Baal instead (Jer. 23:26–27).
However, God does not forget his people,
even when they have forgotten him
(Deut. 4:31).

2 you with your own hand drove out the
　　nations,
　but them you planted;
you afflicted the peoples,
　but them you set free;
3 for not by their own sword did they
　　win the land,
　nor did their own arm save them,
but your right hand and your arm,
　and the light of your face,
　for you delighted in them.

4 You are my King, O God;
　ordain salvation for Jacob!
5 Through you we push down our foes;
　through your name we tread down
　　those who rise up against us.
6 For not in my bow do I trust,
　nor can my sword save me.

7 But you have saved us from our foes
    and have put to shame those who
        hate us.
8 In God we have boasted continually,
    and we will give thanks to your
        name forever. *Selah*

9 But you have rejected us and dis-
        graced us
    and have not gone out with our
        armies.
10 You have made us turn back from the
        foe,
    and those who hate us have gotten
        spoil.
11 You have made us like sheep for
        slaughter
    and have scattered us among the
        nations.

12 You have sold your people for a trifle,
    demanding no high price for them.
13 You have made us the taunt of our
        neighbors,
    the derision and scorn of those
        around us.
14 You have made us a byword among
        the nations,
    a laughingstock among the peoples.
15 All day long my disgrace is before me,
    and shame has covered my face
16 at the sound of the taunter and reviler,
    at the sight of the enemy and the
        avenger.

17 All this has come upon us,
    though we have not forgotten you,
    and we have not been false to your
        covenant.
18 Our heart has not turned back,
    nor have our steps departed from
        your way;

19 yet you have broken us in the place of
        jackals
    and covered us with the shadow of
        death.
20 If we had forgotten the name of our
        God
    or spread out our hands to a foreign
        god,
21 would not God discover this?
    For he knows the secrets of the
        heart.
22 Yet for your sake we are killed all the
        day long;
    we are regarded as sheep to be
        slaughtered.
23 Awake! Why are you sleeping, O Lord?
    Rouse yourself! Do not reject us
        forever!
24 Why do you hide your face?
    Why do you forget our affliction
        and oppression?
25 For our soul is bowed down to the
        dust;
    our belly clings to the ground.
26 Rise up; come to our help!
    Redeem us for the sake of your
        steadfast love!

Your Throne, O God, Is Forever

45 TO THE CHOIRMASTER: ACCORDING
TO LILIES. A MASKIL OF THE SONS OF
KORAH; A LOVE SONG.

1 My heart overflows with a pleasing
        theme;
    I address my verses to the king;
    my tongue is like the pen of a ready
        scribe.

2 You are the most handsome of the
        sons of men;
    grace is poured upon your lips;
    therefore God has blessed you for-
        ever.
3 Gird your sword on your thigh,
        O mighty one,
    in your splendor and majesty!

4 In your majesty ride out victoriously
    for the cause of truth and meekness
        and righteousness;
    let your right hand teach you awe-
        some deeds!
5 Your arrows are sharp
    in the heart of the king's enemies;
    the peoples fall under you.

6   Your throne, O God, is forever and ever.
     The scepter of your kingdom is a
       scepter of uprightness;
7   you have loved righteousness and
      hated wickedness.
  Therefore God, your God, has
     anointed you
    with the oil of gladness beyond
      your companions;
8   your robes are all fragrant with
      myrrh and aloes and cassia.
  From ivory palaces stringed instru-
     ments make you glad;
9   daughters of kings are among your
      ladies of honor;
    at your right hand stands the queen
      in gold of Ophir.

10 Hear, O daughter, and consider, and
     incline your ear:
    forget your people and your father's
      house,
11 and the king will desire your beauty.
  Since he is your lord, bow to him.
12 The people of Tyre will seek your
     favor with gifts,
    the richest of the people.

13 All glorious is the princess in her
     chamber, with robes interwo-
     ven with gold.
14 In many-colored robes she is led to
     the king,
    with her virgin companions follow-
     ing behind her.
15 With joy and gladness they are led
     along
    as they enter the palace of the king.

16 In place of your fathers shall be your
     sons;
    you will make them princes in all
     the earth.
17 I will cause your name to be remem-
     bered in all generations;
    therefore nations will praise you
     forever and ever.

God Is Our Fortress

46 To the choirmaster. Of the
Sons of Korah. According to
Alamoth.[1] A Song.

1   God is our refuge and strength,
    a very present help in trouble.

---

[1] Probably a musical term

2   Therefore we will not fear though the
     earth gives way,
    though the mountains be moved
     into the heart of the sea,
3   though its waters roar and foam,
    though the mountains tremble at
     its swelling.   Selah

4   There is a river whose streams make
     glad the city of God,
    the holy habitation of the Most High.
5   God is in the midst of her; she shall
     not be moved;
    God will help her when morning
     dawns.
6   The nations rage, the kingdoms totter;
    he utters his voice, the earth melts.
7   The Lord of hosts is with us;
    the God of Jacob is our fortress. Selah

8   Come, behold the works of the Lord,
    how he has brought desolations on
     the earth.
9   He makes wars cease to the end of the
     earth;
    he breaks the bow and shatters the
     spear;
    he burns the chariots with fire.
10 "Be still, and know that I am God.
    I will be exalted among the nations,
    I will be exalted in the earth!"
11 The Lord of hosts is with us;
    the God of Jacob is our fortress. Selah

God Is King over All the Earth

47 To the choirmaster. A Psalm of
the Sons of Korah.

1   Clap your hands, all peoples!
    Shout to God with loud songs of joy!
2   For the Lord, the Most High, is to be
     feared,
    a great king over all the earth.
3   He subdued peoples under us,
    and nations under our feet.
4   He chose our heritage for us,
    the pride of Jacob whom he loves.
                      Selah

5   God has gone up with a shout,
    the Lord with the sound of a trum-
     pet.
6   Sing praises to God, sing praises!
    Sing praises to our King, sing praises!
7   For God is the King of all the earth;
    sing praises with a psalm!

8 God reigns over the nations;
   God sits on his holy throne.
9 The princes of the peoples gather
   as the people of the God of Abraham.
For the shields of the earth belong to
   God;
   he is highly exalted!

Zion, the City of Our God

48 A Song. A Psalm of the Sons of Korah.

1 Great is the LORD and greatly to be
   praised
   in the city of our God!
His holy mountain, **2** beautiful in
   elevation,
   is the joy of all the earth,
Mount Zion, in the far north,
   the city of the great King.
3 Within her citadels God
   has made himself known as a fortress.

4 For behold, the kings assembled;
   they came on together.
5 As soon as they saw it, they were
   astounded;
   they were in panic; they took to
   flight.
6 Trembling took hold of them there,
   anguish as of a woman in labor.
7 By the east wind you shattered
   the ships of Tarshish.
8 As we have heard, so have we seen
   in the city of the LORD of hosts,
in the city of our God,
   which God will establish forever.
                    Selah

9 We have thought on your steadfast
   love, O God,
   in the midst of your temple.
10 As your name, O God,
   so your praise reaches to the ends
   of the earth.
Your right hand is filled with righteousness.
11 Let Mount Zion be glad!
Let the daughters of Judah rejoice
   because of your judgments!

12 Walk about Zion, go around her,
   number her towers,
13 consider well her ramparts,
   go through her citadels,

that you may tell the next generation
14   that this is God,
our God forever and ever.
   He will guide us forever.

Why Should I Fear in Times of Trouble?

49 To the choirmaster. A Psalm of the Sons of Korah.

1 Hear this, all peoples!
   Give ear, all inhabitants of the world,
2 both low and high,
   rich and poor together!
3 My mouth shall speak wisdom;
   the meditation of my heart shall be
   understanding.
4 I will incline my ear to a proverb;
   I will solve my riddle to the music
   of the lyre.

5 Why should I fear in times of trouble,
   when the iniquity of those who
   cheat me surrounds me,
6 those who trust in their wealth
   and boast of the abundance of their
   riches?
7 Truly no man can ransom another,
   or give to God the price of his life,
8 for the ransom of their life is costly
   and can never suffice,
9 that he should live on forever
   and never see the pit.

10 For he sees that even the wise die;
   the fool and the stupid alike must
   perish
   and leave their wealth to others.
11 Their graves are their homes forever,
   their dwelling places to all generations,
   though they called lands by their
   own names.
12 Man in his pomp will not remain;
   he is like the beasts that perish.

13 This is the path of those who have
   foolish confidence;
   yet after them people approve of
   their boasts.   *Selah*
14 Like sheep they are appointed for
   Sheol;
   death shall be their shepherd,
and the upright shall rule over them
   in the morning.
   Their form shall be consumed in
   Sheol, with no place to dwell.

15 But God will ransom my soul from the
   power of Sheol,
     for he will receive me.   *Selah*

16 Be not afraid when a man becomes
   rich,
     when the glory of his house
       increases.
17 For when he dies he will carry nothing
   away;
     his glory will not go down after him.
18 For though, while he lives, he counts
   himself blessed
     —and though you get praise when
       you do well for yourself—
19 his soul will go to the generation of
   his fathers,
     who will never again see light.
20 Man in his pomp yet without understanding is like the beasts that
     perish.

God Himself Is Judge

50 A PSALM OF ASAPH.
   The Mighty One, God the LORD,
   speaks and summons the earth
   from the rising of the sun to its
     setting.
2 Out of Zion, the perfection of beauty,
   God shines forth.

3 Our God comes; he does not keep
   silence;
     before him is a devouring fire,
     around him a mighty tempest.
4 He calls to the heavens above
   and to the earth, that he may judge
     his people:
5 "Gather to me my faithful ones,
   who made a covenant with me by
     sacrifice!"
6 The heavens declare his righteousness,
     for God himself is judge!   *Selah*

7 "Hear, O my people, and I will speak;
   O Israel, I will testify against you.
   I am God, your God.
8 Not for your sacrifices do I rebuke you;
   your burnt offerings are continually
     before me.
9 I will not accept a bull from your
   house
     or goats from your folds.
10 For every beast of the forest is mine,
   the cattle on a thousand hills.

11 I know all the birds of the hills,
   and all that moves in the field is
     mine.
12 "If I were hungry, I would not tell you,
   for the world and its fullness are
     mine.
13 Do I eat the flesh of bulls
   or drink the blood of goats?
14 Offer to God a sacrifice of thanksgiving,
   and perform your vows to the Most
     High,
15 and call upon me in the day of trouble;
   I will deliver you, and you shall
     glorify me."

16 But to the wicked God says:
   "What right have you to recite my
     statutes
   or take my covenant on your lips?
17 For you hate discipline,
   and you cast my words behind you.
18 If you see a thief, you are pleased with
   him,
     and you keep company with adul-
       terers.

19 "You give your mouth free rein for evil,
   and your tongue frames deceit.
20 You sit and speak against your brother;
   you slander your own mother's son.
21 These things you have done, and I
   have been silent;
     you thought that I was one like
       yourself.
   But now I rebuke you and lay the
     charge before you.

22 "Mark this, then, you who forget God,
   lest I tear you apart, and there be
     none to deliver!
23 The one who offers thanksgiving as
   his sacrifice glorifies me;
     to one who orders his way rightly
   I will show the salvation of God!"

Create in Me a Clean Heart, O God

51 TO THE CHOIRMASTER. A PSALM OF
   DAVID, WHEN NATHAN THE PROPHET
   WENT TO HIM, AFTER HE HAD GONE IN
   TO BATHSHEBA.

1 Have mercy on me, O God,
   according to your steadfast love;
   according to your abundant mercy
     blot out my transgressions.
2 Wash me thoroughly from my iniquity,
   and cleanse me from my sin!

3 For I know my transgressions,
    and my sin is ever before me.
4 Against you, you only, have I sinned
      and done what is evil in your sight,
    so that you may be justified in your
        words
      and blameless in your judgment.
5 Behold, I was brought forth in iniquity,
    and in sin did my mother conceive
        me.
6 Behold, you delight in truth in the
        inward being,
    and you teach me wisdom in the
        secret heart.
7 Purge me with hyssop, and I shall be
        clean;
    wash me, and I shall be whiter than
        snow.

8 Let me hear joy and gladness;
    let the bones that you have broken
        rejoice.
9 Hide your face from my sins,
    and blot out all my iniquities.
10 Create in me a clean heart, O God,
    and renew a right spirit within me.
11 Cast me not away from your presence,
    and take not your Holy Spirit from
        me.
12 Restore to me the joy of your salva-
        tion,
    and uphold me with a willing spirit.
13 Then I will teach transgressors your
        ways,
    and sinners will return to you.
14 Deliver me from bloodguiltiness,
        O God,
    O God of my salvation,
    and my tongue will sing aloud of
        your righteousness.

15 O Lord, open my lips,
    and my mouth will declare your
        praise.
16 For you will not delight in sacrifice, or
        I would give it;
    you will not be pleased with a burnt
        offering.
17 The sacrifices of God are a broken
        spirit;
    a broken and contrite heart, O God,
        you will not despise.

18 Do good to Zion in your good pleasure;
    build up the walls of Jerusalem;
19 then will you delight in right sacrifices,
    in burnt offerings and whole burnt
        offerings;
    then bulls will be offered on your
        altar.

The Steadfast Love of God Endures

52 TO THE CHOIRMASTER. A MASKIL OF
DAVID, WHEN DOEG, THE EDOMITE,
CAME AND TOLD SAUL, "DAVID HAS
COME TO THE HOUSE OF AHIMELECH."

1 Why do you boast of evil, O mighty
        man?
    The steadfast love of God endures
        all the day.
2 Your tongue plots destruction,
    like a sharp razor, you worker of
        deceit.
3 You love evil more than good,
    and lying more than speaking what
        is right.   Selah
4 You love all words that devour,
    O deceitful tongue.

5 But God will break you down forever;
    he will snatch and tear you from
        your tent;
    he will uproot you from the land of
        the living.   Selah
6 The righteous shall see and fear,
    and shall laugh at him, saying,
7 "See the man who would not make
        God his refuge,
    but trusted in the abundance of his
        riches
    and sought refuge in his own
        destruction!"

8 But I am like a green olive tree
    in the house of God.
    I trust in the steadfast love of God
        forever and ever.

9 I will thank you forever,
   because you have done it.
I will wait for your name, for it is good,
   in the presence of the godly.

There Is None Who Does Good

53
TO THE CHOIRMASTER: ACCORDING TO MAHALATH. A MASKIL OF DAVID.

1 The fool says in his heart, "There is no God."
   They are corrupt, doing abominable iniquity;
   there is none who does good.

2 God looks down from heaven
   on the children of man
to see if there are any who understand,
   who seek after God.

3 They have all fallen away;
   together they have become corrupt;
there is none who does good,
   not even one.

4 Have those who work evil no knowledge,
   who eat up my people as they eat bread,
   and do not call upon God?

5 There they are, in great terror,
   where there is no terror!
For God scatters the bones of him who encamps against you;
   you put them to shame, for God has rejected them.

6 Oh, that salvation for Israel would come out of Zion!
   When God restores the fortunes of his people,
   let Jacob rejoice, let Israel be glad.

The Lord Upholds My Life

54
TO THE CHOIRMASTER: WITH STRINGED INSTRUMENTS. A MASKIL OF DAVID, WHEN THE ZIPHITES WENT AND TOLD SAUL, "IS NOT DAVID HIDING AMONG US?"

1 O God, save me by your name,
   and vindicate me by your might.
2 O God, hear my prayer;
   give ear to the words of my mouth.

3 For strangers have risen against me;
   ruthless men seek my life;
they do not set God before themselves.   *Selah*

4 Behold, God is my helper;
   the Lord is the upholder of my life.
5 He will return the evil to my enemies;
   in your faithfulness put an end to them.

6 With a freewill offering I will sacrifice to you;
   I will give thanks to your name,
   O LORD, for it is good.
7 For he has delivered me from every trouble,
   and my eye has looked in triumph on my enemies.

Cast Your Burden on the LORD

55
TO THE CHOIRMASTER: WITH STRINGED INSTRUMENTS. A MASKIL OF DAVID.

1 Give ear to my prayer, O God,
   and hide not yourself from my plea for mercy!

GETTING THE MESSAGE

There is none who does good. In Rom. 3:10–12, the apostle Paul cites Ps. 53:1–3 to explain the universal human condition of sin. No person on his own seeks for God or does any good that merits salvation. Everyone needs the perfect Savior, Jesus Christ.

2 Attend to me, and answer me;
   I am restless in my complaint and I moan,
3 because of the noise of the enemy,
   because of the oppression of the wicked.
For they drop trouble upon me,
   and in anger they bear a grudge against me.

4 My heart is in anguish within me;
   the terrors of death have fallen upon me.
5 Fear and trembling come upon me,
   and horror overwhelms me.
6 And I say, "Oh, that I had wings like a dove!
   I would fly away and be at rest;
7 yes, I would wander far away;
   I would lodge in the wilderness;   *Selah*

8   I would hurry to find a shelter
      from the raging wind and tempest."

9   Destroy, O Lord, divide their tongues;
      for I see violence and strife in the
         city.

10 Day and night they go around it
      on its walls,
  and iniquity and trouble are within it;

11   ruin is in its midst;
  oppression and fraud
      do not depart from its marketplace.

12 For it is not an enemy who taunts me—
      then I could bear it;
  it is not an adversary who deals inso-
        lently with me—
      then I could hide from him.

13 But it is you, a man, my equal,
      my companion, my familiar friend.

14 We used to take sweet counsel
      together;

GETTING THE MESSAGE

A helpful guide. The writers of the Psalms understood the importance of constant communication with God. They knew that God would hear their prayers, and they trusted him to act on their behalf. Believers today can benefit greatly by patterning their prayers after specific psalms.

      within God's house we walked in
      the throng.

15 Let death steal over them;
      let them go down to Sheol alive;
  for evil is in their dwelling place
      and in their heart.

16 But I call to God,
      and the Lord will save me.

17 Evening and morning and at noon
      I utter my complaint and moan,
      and he hears my voice.

18 He redeems my soul in safety
      from the battle that I wage,
      for many are arrayed against me.

19 God will give ear and humble them,
      he who is enthroned from of old,
                   Selah
  because they do not change
      and do not fear God.

20 My companion stretched out his hand
      against his friends;
  he violated his covenant.

21 His speech was smooth as butter,
      yet war was in his heart;
  his words were softer than oil,
      yet they were drawn swords.

22 Cast your burden on the Lord,
      and he will sustain you;
  he will never permit
      the righteous to be moved.

23 But you, O God, will cast them down
      into the pit of destruction;
  men of blood and treachery
      shall not live out half their days.
  But I will trust in you.

In God I Trust

56

To the choirmaster: according to The Dove on Far-off Terebinths. A Miktam of David, when the Philistines seized him in Gath.

1   Be gracious to me, O God, for man
      tramples on me;
  all day long an attacker oppresses
      me;

2   my enemies trample on me all day
      long,
  for many attack me proudly.

3   When I am afraid,
      I put my trust in you.

4   In God, whose word I praise,
      in God I trust; I shall not be afraid.
      What can flesh do to me?

5   All day long they injure my cause;
      all their thoughts are against me for
      evil.

6   They stir up strife, they lurk;
      they watch my steps,
      as they have waited for my life.

7   For their crime will they escape?
      In wrath cast down the peoples,
      O God!

8   You have kept count of my tossings;
      put my tears in your bottle.
      Are they not in your book?

9   Then my enemies will turn back
      in the day when I call.
      This I know, that God is for me.

10 In God, whose word I praise,
      in the Lord, whose word I praise,

11 in God I trust; I shall not be afraid.
     What can man do to me?

12 I must perform my vows to you, O God;
     I will render thank offerings to you.

13 For you have delivered my soul from
     death,
         yes, my feet from falling,
     that I may walk before God
         in the light of life.

Let Your Glory Be over All the Earth

57 To the choirmaster: according to Do Not Destroy. A Miktam of David, when he fled from Saul, in the cave.

1 Be merciful to me, O God, be merciful
     to me,
         for in you my soul takes refuge;
     in the shadow of your wings I will
         take refuge,
     till the storms of destruction pass
         by.

2 I cry out to God Most High,
     to God who fulfills his purpose for
         me.

3 He will send from heaven and save me;
     he will put to shame him who tram-
         ples on me.   Selah
     God will send out his steadfast love
         and his faithfulness!

4 My soul is in the midst of lions;
     I lie down amid fiery beasts—
     the children of man, whose teeth are
         spears and arrows,
         whose tongues are sharp swords.

5 Be exalted, O God, above the heavens!
     Let your glory be over all the earth!

6 They set a net for my steps;
     my soul was bowed down.
     They dug a pit in my way,
         but they have fallen into it them-
         selves.   Selah

7 My heart is steadfast, O God,
     my heart is steadfast!
     I will sing and make melody!

8   Awake, my glory!
     Awake, O harp and lyre!
         I will awake the dawn!

9 I will give thanks to you, O Lord,
         among the peoples;
     I will sing praises to you among the
         nations.

10 For your steadfast love is great to the
     heavens,
         your faithfulness to the clouds.

11 Be exalted, O God, above the heavens!
     Let your glory be over all the earth!

God Who Judges the Earth

58 To the choirmaster: according to Do Not Destroy. A Miktam of David.

1 Do you indeed decree what is right,
         you gods?
     Do you judge the children of man
         uprightly?

2 No, in your hearts you devise wrongs;
     your hands deal out violence on
         earth.

3 The wicked are estranged from the
     womb;
         they go astray from birth, speaking
         lies.

> ## GETTING THE MESSAGE
>
> **Memorizing the Psalms.** The poetic style of the Psalms make them easy to memorize. Throughout the centuries, many believers have memorized all 150 Psalms.

4 They have venom like the venom of a
     serpent,
         like the deaf adder that stops its ear,

5 so that it does not hear the voice of
         charmers
     or of the cunning enchanter.

6 O God, break the teeth in their mouths;
     tear out the fangs of the young
         lions, O Lord!

7 Let them vanish like water that runs
     away;
         when he aims his arrows, let them
         be blunted.

8 Let them be like the snail that dis-
     solves into slime,
         like the stillborn child who never
         sees the sun.

9 Sooner than your pots can feel the
     heat of thorns,
         whether green or ablaze, may he
         sweep them away!

10   The righteous will rejoice when he
         sees the vengeance;
     he will bathe his feet in the blood of
         the wicked.
11   Mankind will say, "Surely there is a
         reward for the righteous;
     surely there is a God who judges on
         earth."

Deliver Me from My Enemies

59 To the choirmaster: according
to Do Not Destroy. A Miktam of
David, when Saul sent men to
watch his house in order to
kill him.

1   Deliver me from my enemies, O my
         God;
     protect me from those who rise up
         against me;
2   deliver me from those who work evil,
     and save me from bloodthirsty men.

GETTING THE MESSAGE

Pride (59:12) is the opposite of humility.
It means putting excessive confidence in
one's own abilities, wealth, or position.
Pride causes a person to crave the glory
and honor that belong only to God.

3   For behold, they lie in wait for my
         life;
     fierce men stir up strife against me.
     For no transgression or sin of mine,
         O Lord,
4   for no fault of mine, they run and
         make ready.
     Awake, come to meet me, and see!
5   You, Lord God of hosts, are God of
         Israel.
     Rouse yourself to punish all the
         nations;
         spare none of those who treacher-
         ously plot evil.   *Selah*

6   Each evening they come back,
         howling like dogs
         and prowling about the city.
7   There they are, bellowing with their
         mouths
         with swords in their lips—
     for "Who," they think, "will hear us?"

8   But you, O Lord, laugh at them;
         you hold all the nations in derision.
9   O my Strength, I will watch for you,
         for you, O God, are my fortress.
10   My God in his steadfast love will meet
         me;
     God will let me look in triumph on
         my enemies.

11   Kill them not, lest my people forget;
         make them totter by your power
         and bring them down,
     O Lord, our shield!
12   For the sin of their mouths, the words
         of their lips,
     let them be trapped in their pride.
     For the cursing and lies that they utter,
13   consume them in wrath;
     consume them till they are no more,
     that they may know that God rules
         over Jacob
     to the ends of the earth.   *Selah*

14   Each evening they come back,
         howling like dogs
         and prowling about the city.
15   They wander about for food
         and growl if they do not get their fill.

16   But I will sing of your strength;
     I will sing aloud of your steadfast
         love in the morning.
     For you have been to me a fortress
         and a refuge in the day of my dis-
         tress.
17   O my Strength, I will sing praises to
         you,
     for you, O God, are my fortress,
     the God who shows me steadfast
         love.

He Will Tread Down Our Foes

60 To the choirmaster: according
to Shushan Eduth. A Miktam of
David; for instruction; when
he strove with Aram-naharaim
and with Aram-zobah, and
when Joab on his return struck
down twelve thousand of Edom
in the Valley of Salt.

1   O God, you have rejected us, broken
         our defenses;
     you have been angry; oh, restore us.
2   You have made the land to quake; you
         have torn it open;
     repair its breaches, for it totters.

3 You have made your people see hard
        things;
    you have given us wine to drink
        that made us stagger.

4 You have set up a banner for those
        who fear you,
    that they may flee to it from the
        bow.   *Selah*
5 That your beloved ones may be deliv-
        ered,
    give salvation by your right hand
        and answer us!

6 God has spoken in his holiness:
    "With exultation I will divide up
        Shechem
    and portion out the Vale of Succoth.
7 Gilead is mine; Manasseh is mine;
    Ephraim is my helmet;
        Judah is my scepter;
8 Moab is my washbasin;
    upon Edom I cast my shoe;
    over Philistia I shout in triumph."

9 Who will bring me to the fortified city?
    Who will lead me to Edom?
10 Have you not rejected us, O God?
    You do not go forth, O God, with our
        armies.
11 Oh, grant us help against the foe,
    for vain is the salvation of man!
12 With God we shall do valiantly;
    it is he who will tread down our foes.

Lead Me to the Rock

61 TO THE CHOIRMASTER: WITH STRINGED
     INSTRUMENTS. OF DAVID.

1 Hear my cry, O God,
    listen to my prayer;
2 from the end of the earth I call to you
        when my heart is faint.
    Lead me to the rock
        that is higher than I,
3 for you have been my refuge,
    a strong tower against the enemy.

4 Let me dwell in your tent forever!
    Let me take refuge under the shelter
        of your wings!   *Selah*
5 For you, O God, have heard my vows;
    you have given me the heritage of
        those who fear your name.

6 Prolong the life of the king;
    may his years endure to all genera-
        tions!

7 May he be enthroned forever before
        God;
    appoint steadfast love and faithful-
        ness to watch over him!
8 So will I ever sing praises to your name,
    as I perform my vows day after day.

My Soul Waits for God Alone

62 TO THE CHOIRMASTER: ACCORDING
     TO JEDUTHUN. A PSALM OF DAVID.

1 For God alone my soul waits in silence;
    from him comes my salvation.
2 He alone is my rock and my salvation,
    my fortress; I shall not be greatly
        shaken.
3 How long will all of you attack a man
        to batter him,
    like a leaning wall, a tottering fence?

GETTING THE MESSAGE

Banners served as battle flags in ancient wars. Attached to poles, they were used to signal troop movements or to serve as rallying points. Banners could be actual flags or they could be carved figures, often depicting a bird or animal. Each of the Israelite tribes may have had a banner to help organize the mass exodus out of Sinai. In Psalm 60:4, the banner is a symbol of God's protection over those who trust him.

4 They only plan to thrust him down
        from his high position.
    They take pleasure in falsehood.
    They bless with their mouths,
        but inwardly they curse.   *Selah*
5 For God alone, O my soul, wait in
        silence,
    for my hope is from him.
6 He only is my rock and my salvation,
    my fortress; I shall not be shaken.
7 On God rests my salvation and my
        glory;
    my mighty rock, my refuge is God.
8 Trust in him at all times, O people;
    pour out your heart before him;
    God is a refuge for us.   *Selah*
9 Those of low estate are but a breath;
    those of high estate are a delusion;

in the balances they go up;
they are together lighter than a
breath.
10 Put no trust in extortion;
set no vain hopes on robbery;
if riches increase, set not your heart
on them.
11 Once God has spoken;
twice have I heard this:
that power belongs to God,
12 and that to you, O Lord, belongs
steadfast love.
For you will render to a man
according to his work.

My Soul Thirsts for You

63
A Psalm of David, when he was in
the wilderness of Judah.

1 O God, you are my God; earnestly I
seek you;
my soul thirsts for you;

GETTING THE MESSAGE

The term **fortress** (62:2) could describe
the city walls of ancient times. These
walls, usually stone, included towers at
strategic points so that the soldiers could
see if anyone was trying to breach the
wall. God is the believer's true fortress,
the only real source of protection.

---

my flesh faints for you,
as in a dry and weary land where
there is no water.
2 So I have looked upon you in the
sanctuary,
beholding your power and glory.
3 Because your steadfast love is better
than life,
my lips will praise you.
4 So I will bless you as long as I live;
in your name I will lift up my
hands.
5 My soul will be satisfied as with fat
and rich food,
and my mouth will praise you with
joyful lips,
6 when I remember you upon my bed,
and meditate on you in the watches
of the night;

7 for you have been my help,
and in the shadow of your wings I
will sing for joy.
8 My soul clings to you;
your right hand upholds me.
9 But those who seek to destroy my life
shall go down into the depths of the
earth;
10 they shall be given over to the power
of the sword;
they shall be a portion for jackals.
11 But the king shall rejoice in God;
all who swear by him shall exult,
for the mouths of liars will be
stopped.

Hide Me from the Wicked

64
To the choirmaster. A Psalm of
David.

1 Hear my voice, O God, in my complaint;
preserve my life from dread of the
enemy.
2 Hide me from the secret plots of the
wicked,
from the throng of evildoers,
3 who whet their tongues like swords,
who aim bitter words like arrows,
4 shooting from ambush at the blameless,
shooting at him suddenly and without fear.
5 They hold fast to their evil purpose;
they talk of laying snares secretly,
thinking, "Who can see them?"
6 They search out injustice,
saying, "We have accomplished a
diligent search."
For the inward mind and heart of a
man are deep.
7 But God shoots his arrow at them;
they are wounded suddenly.
8 They are brought to ruin, with their
own tongues turned against
them;
all who see them will wag their
heads.
9 Then all mankind fears;
they tell what God has brought about
and ponder what he has done.
10 Let the righteous one rejoice in the
Lord
and take refuge in him!
Let all the upright in heart exult!

O God of Our Salvation

65 To the choirmaster. A Psalm of David. A Song.

¹ Praise is due to you, O God, in Zion,
  and to you shall vows be performed.
² O you who hear prayer,
  to you shall all flesh come.
³ When iniquities prevail against me,
  you atone for our transgressions.
⁴ Blessed is the one you choose and
  bring near,
  to dwell in your courts!
We shall be satisfied with the goodness of your house,
  the holiness of your temple!

⁵ By awesome deeds you answer us
  with righteousness,
  O God of our salvation,
the hope of all the ends of the earth
  and of the farthest seas;
⁶ the one who by his strength established the mountains,
  being girded with might;
⁷ who stills the roaring of the seas,
  the roaring of their waves,
  the tumult of the peoples,
⁸ so that those who dwell at the ends
  of the earth are in awe at your
  signs.
You make the going out of the morning
  and the evening to shout for joy.

⁹ You visit the earth and water it;
  you greatly enrich it;
the river of God is full of water;
  you provide their grain,
  for so you have prepared it.
¹⁰ You water its furrows abundantly,
  settling its ridges,
softening it with showers,
  and blessing its growth.
¹¹ You crown the year with your bounty;
  your wagon tracks overflow with
  abundance.
¹² The pastures of the wilderness overflow,
  the hills gird themselves with joy,
¹³ the meadows clothe themselves with
  flocks,
  the valleys deck themselves with
  grain,
  they shout and sing together for
  joy.

How Awesome Are Your Deeds

66 To the choirmaster. A Song. A Psalm.

¹ Shout for joy to God, all the earth;
² sing the glory of his name;
  give to him glorious praise!
³ Say to God, "How awesome are your
  deeds!
So great is your power that your
  enemies come cringing to you.
⁴ All the earth worships you
  and sings praises to you;
  they sing praises to your name." *Selah*

⁵ Come and see what God has done:
  he is awesome in his deeds toward
  the children of man.
⁶ He turned the sea into dry land;
  they passed through the river on
  foot.

GETTING THE MESSAGE

The psalmist David's desire to **dwell in God's courts** (65:4), that is, in the sanctuary, recalls his closing words in Psalm 23: "and I shall dwell in the house of the Lord forever."

⁷ There did we rejoice in him,
  who rules by his might forever,
whose eyes keep watch on the
  nations—
  let not the rebellious exalt themselves.   *Selah*

⁸ Bless our God, O peoples;
  let the sound of his praise be heard,
⁹ who has kept our soul among the living
  and has not let our feet slip.
¹⁰ For you, O God, have tested us;
  you have tried us as silver is tried.
¹¹ You brought us into the net;
  you laid a crushing burden on our
  backs;
¹² you let men ride over our heads;
  we went through fire and through
  water;
yet you have brought us out to a place
  of abundance.
¹³ I will come into your house with
  burnt offerings;
  I will perform my vows to you,

14 that which my lips uttered
   and my mouth promised when I
      was in trouble.
15 I will offer to you burnt offerings of
      fattened animals,
   with the smoke of the sacrifice of
      rams;
   I will make an offering of bulls and
      goats.   *Selah*

16 Come and hear, all you who fear God,
   and I will tell what he has done for
      my soul.
17 I cried to him with my mouth,
   and high praise was on my tongue.
18 If I had cherished iniquity in my heart,
   the Lord would not have listened.
19 But truly God has listened;
   he has attended to the voice of my
      prayer.

> **GETTING THE MESSAGE**

Wanting God's blessing. Psalm 67 echoes the priestly blessing in Num. 6:24–26. Israel desires God's blessing so that all nations may know of his saving power. God called Abram in order to bless him and his descendants and to make them a means of blessing to the Gentiles (Gen. 12:2–3).

20 Blessed be God,
   because he has not rejected my
      prayer
   or removed his steadfast love from
      me!

Make Your Face Shine upon Us

67 To the choirmaster: with stringed instruments. A Psalm. A Song.

1 May God be gracious to us and bless us
   and make his face to shine upon us,
                               Selah
2 that your way may be known on earth,
   your saving power among all nations.
3 Let the peoples praise you, O God;
   let all the peoples praise you!

4 Let the nations be glad and sing for joy,
   for you judge the peoples with equity
   and guide the nations upon earth.
                               Selah

5 Let the peoples praise you, O God;
   let all the peoples praise you!

6 The earth has yielded its increase;
   God, our God, shall bless us.
7 God shall bless us;
   let all the ends of the earth fear
      him!

God Shall Scatter His Enemies

68 To the choirmaster. A Psalm of David. A Song.

1 God shall arise, his enemies shall be
      scattered;
   and those who hate him shall flee
      before him!
2 As smoke is driven away, so you shall
      drive them away;
   as wax melts before fire,
   so the wicked shall perish before
      God!
3 But the righteous shall be glad;
   they shall exult before God;
   they shall be jubilant with joy!

4 Sing to God, sing praises to his
      name;
   lift up a song to him who rides
      through the deserts;
   his name is the Lord;
   exult before him!
5 Father of the fatherless and protector
      of widows
   is God in his holy habitation.
6 God settles the solitary in a home;
   he leads out the prisoners to pros-
      perity,
   but the rebellious dwell in a
      parched land.

7 O God, when you went out before
      your people,
   when you marched through the
      wilderness,   *Selah*
8 the earth quaked, the heavens poured
      down rain,
   before God, the One of Sinai,
   before God, the God of Israel.
9 Rain in abundance, O God, you shed
      abroad;
   you restored your inheritance as it
      languished;
10 your flock found a dwelling in it;
   in your goodness, O God, you pro-
      vided for the needy.

11 The Lord gives the word;
   the women who announce the
       news are a great host:
12 "The kings of the armies—they flee,
       they flee!"
   The women at home divide the spoil—
13 though you men lie among the
       sheepfolds—
   the wings of a dove covered with silver,
       its pinions with shimmering gold.
14 When the Almighty scatters kings
       there,
   let snow fall on Zalmon.

15 O mountain of God, mountain of
       Bashan;
   O many-peaked mountain, moun-
       tain of Bashan!
16 Why do you look with hatred,
       O many-peaked mountain,
   at the mount that God desired for
       his abode,
   yes, where the LORD will dwell
       forever?
17 The chariots of God are twice ten
       thousand,
   thousands upon thousands;
   the Lord is among them; Sinai is
       now in the sanctuary.
18 You ascended on high,
   leading a host of captives in your
       train
   and receiving gifts among men,
   even among the rebellious, that the
       LORD God may dwell there.

19 Blessed be the Lord,
   who daily bears us up;
   God is our salvation.   Selah
20 Our God is a God of salvation,
   and to GOD, the Lord, belong deliv-
       erances from death.
21 But God will strike the heads of his
       enemies,
   the hairy crown of him who walks
       in his guilty ways.
22 The Lord said,
   "I will bring them back from Bashan,
   I will bring them back from the
       depths of the sea,
23 that you may strike your feet in their
       blood,
   that the tongues of your dogs may
       have their portion from the foe."

24 Your procession is seen, O God,
   the procession of my God, my King,
       into the sanctuary—
25 the singers in front, the musicians
       last,
   between them virgins playing tam-
       bourines:
26 "Bless God in the great congregation,
   the LORD, O you who are of Israel's
       fountain!"
27 There is Benjamin, the least of them,
       in the lead,
   the princes of Judah in their
       throng,
   the princes of Zebulun, the princes
       of Naphtali.

28 Summon your power, O God,
   the power, O God, by which you
       have worked for us.

GETTING THE MESSAGE

Ancient worship leaders. Psalm 68:24–27 mentions singers and musicians leading worship. Other passages, such as 1 Chron. 15:16–22, give details about some of the musical instruments that were used in Israelite worship.

29 Because of your temple at Jerusalem
   kings shall bear gifts to you.
30 Rebuke the beasts that dwell among
       the reeds,
   the herd of bulls with the calves of
       the peoples.
   Trample underfoot those who lust
       after tribute;
   scatter the peoples who delight in
       war.
31 Nobles shall come from Egypt;
   Cush shall hasten to stretch out her
       hands to God.
32 O kingdoms of the earth, sing to God;
   sing praises to the Lord,   Selah
33 to him who rides in the heavens, the
       ancient heavens;
   behold, he sends out his voice, his
       mighty voice.
34 Ascribe power to God,
   whose majesty is over Israel,
   and whose power is in the skies.

35 Awesome is God from his sanctuary;
    the God of Israel — he is the one
        who gives power and strength
            to his people.
    Blessed be God!

Save Me, O God

69 TO THE CHOIRMASTER: ACCORDING
    TO LILIES. OF DAVID.

1 Save me, O God!
    For the waters have come up to my
        neck.
2 I sink in deep mire,
    where there is no foothold;
  I have come into deep waters,
    and the flood sweeps over me.
3 I am weary with my crying out;
    my throat is parched.
  My eyes grow dim
    with waiting for my God.

GETTING THE MESSAGE

The deep. In Ps. 69:15, "the deep" is
a striking picture of the problems of
life that can seem so frightening and
overpowering. But the Lord, who created
the world out of "the deep" (Gen. 1:2),
can rescue his people from all such
problems.

---

4 More in number than the hairs of my
        head
    are those who hate me without
        cause;
  mighty are those who would destroy
        me,
    those who attack me with lies.
  What I did not steal
    must I now restore?
5 O God, you know my folly;
    the wrongs I have done are not
        hidden from you.
6 Let not those who hope in you be put
        to shame through me,
    O Lord GOD of hosts;
  let not those who seek you be brought
        to dishonor through me,
    O God of Israel.
7 For it is for your sake that I have borne
        reproach,
    that dishonor has covered my face.

8 I have become a stranger to my broth-
        ers,
    an alien to my mother's sons.
9 For zeal for your house has consumed
        me,
    and the reproaches of those who
        reproach you have fallen on me.
10 When I wept and humbled my soul
        with fasting,
    it became my reproach.
11 When I made sackcloth my clothing,
    I became a byword to them.
12 I am the talk of those who sit in the
        gate,
    and the drunkards make songs
        about me.
13 But as for me, my prayer is to you,
        O LORD.
    At an acceptable time, O God,
        in the abundance of your steadfast
        love answer me in your saving
        faithfulness.
14 Deliver me
    from sinking in the mire;
  let me be delivered from my enemies
    and from the deep waters.
15 Let not the flood sweep over me,
    or the deep swallow me up,
    or the pit close its mouth over me.

16 Answer me, O LORD, for your steadfast
        love is good;
    according to your abundant mercy,
        turn to me.
17 Hide not your face from your servant;
    for I am in distress; make haste to
        answer me.
18 Draw near to my soul, redeem me;
    ransom me because of my enemies!
19 You know my reproach,
    and my shame and my dishonor;
  my foes are all known to you.
20 Reproaches have broken my heart,
    so that I am in despair.
  I looked for pity, but there was none,
    and for comforters, but I found none.
21 They gave me poison for food,
    and for my thirst they gave me sour
        wine to drink.

22 Let their own table before them
        become a snare;
    and when they are at peace, let it
        become a trap.

23 Let their eyes be darkened, so that
         they cannot see,
     and make their loins tremble con-
         tinually.
24 Pour out your indignation upon them,
     and let your burning anger overtake
         them.
25 May their camp be a desolation;
     let no one dwell in their tents.
26 For they persecute him whom you
         have struck down,
     and they recount the pain of those
         you have wounded.
27 Add to them punishment upon pun-
         ishment;
     may they have no acquittal from you.
28 Let them be blotted out of the book of
         the living;
     let them not be enrolled among the
         righteous.

29 But I am afflicted and in pain;
     let your salvation, O God, set me on
         high!

30 I will praise the name of God with a
         song;
     I will magnify him with thanksgiving.
31 This will please the Lord more than
         an ox
     or a bull with horns and hoofs.
32 When the humble see it they will be
         glad;
     you who seek God, let your hearts
         revive.
33 For the Lord hears the needy
     and does not despise his own peo-
         ple who are prisoners.

34 Let heaven and earth praise him,
     the seas and everything that moves
         in them.
35 For God will save Zion
     and build up the cities of Judah,
     and people shall dwell there and pos-
         sess it;
36 the offspring of his servants shall
         inherit it,
     and those who love his name shall
         dwell in it.

O Lord, Do Not Delay

70 To the choirmaster. Of David,
     for the memorial offering.

1 Make haste, O God, to deliver me!
     O Lord, make haste to help me!

2 Let them be put to shame and confu-
         sion
     who seek my life!
Let them be turned back and brought
         to dishonor
     who delight in my hurt!
3 Let them turn back because of their
         shame
     who say, "Aha, Aha!"

4 May all who seek you
     rejoice and be glad in you!
May those who love your salvation
     say evermore, "God is great!"
5 But I am poor and needy;
     hasten to me, O God!
You are my help and my deliverer;
     O Lord, do not delay!

Forsake Me Not When My Strength Is Spent

71 In you, O Lord, do I take refuge;
     let me never be put to shame!
2 In your righteousness deliver me and
         rescue me;
     incline your ear to me, and save me!
3 Be to me a rock of refuge,
     to which I may continually come;
you have given the command to save
         me,
     for you are my rock and my fortress.

4 Rescue me, O my God, from the hand
         of the wicked,
     from the grasp of the unjust and
         cruel man.
5 For you, O Lord, are my hope,
     my trust, O Lord, from my youth.
6 Upon you I have leaned from before
         my birth;
     you are he who took me from my
         mother's womb.
My praise is continually of you.

7 I have been as a portent to many,
     but you are my strong refuge.
8 My mouth is filled with your praise,
     and with your glory all the day.
9 Do not cast me off in the time of old
         age;
     forsake me not when my strength is
         spent.
10 For my enemies speak concerning
         me;
     those who watch for my life consult
         together

11 and say, "God has forsaken him;
    pursue and seize him,
        for there is none to deliver him."
12 O God, be not far from me;
    O my God, make haste to help me!
13 May my accusers be put to shame and
        consumed;
    with scorn and disgrace may they
        be covered
    who seek my hurt.
14 But I will hope continually
    and will praise you yet more and
        more.
15 My mouth will tell of your righteous
        acts,
    of your deeds of salvation all the day,
    for their number is past my knowl-
        edge.

> **GETTING THE MESSAGE**
>
> **Hope** means putting one's full
> confidence in God, who always keeps
> his promises. Believers can have hope
> for the future because of what God has
> done in the past. Created things will
> always ultimately disappoint. God alone
> is the source of true hope (71:5).

---

16 With the mighty deeds of the Lord
    GOD I will come;
    I will remind them of your righ-
        teousness, yours alone.
17 O God, from my youth you have
        taught me,
    and I still proclaim your wondrous
        deeds.
18 So even to old age and gray hairs,
    O God, do not forsake me,
    until I proclaim your might to another
        generation,
    your power to all those to come.
19 Your righteousness, O God,
    reaches the high heavens.
    You who have done great things,
    O God, who is like you?
20 You who have made me see many
        troubles and calamities
    will revive me again;
    from the depths of the earth
        you will bring me up again.
21 You will increase my greatness
    and comfort me again.

22 I will also praise you with the harp
    for your faithfulness, O my God;
    I will sing praises to you with the lyre,
    O Holy One of Israel.
23 My lips will shout for joy,
    when I sing praises to you;
    my soul also, which you have
        redeemed.
24 And my tongue will talk of your righ-
        teous help all the day long,
    for they have been put to shame and
        disappointed
    who sought to do me hurt.

Give the King Your Justice

72 OF SOLOMON.
    Give the king your justice, O God,
    and your righteousness to the royal
        son!
2 May he judge your people with righ-
        teousness,
    and your poor with justice!
3 Let the mountains bear prosperity for
        the people,
    and the hills, in righteousness!
4 May he defend the cause of the poor
        of the people,
    give deliverance to the children of
        the needy,
    and crush the oppressor!

5 May they fear you while the sun
        endures,
    and as long as the moon, through-
        out all generations!
6 May he be like rain that falls on the
        mown grass,
    like showers that water the earth!
7 In his days may the righteous flourish,
    and peace abound, till the moon be
        no more!

8 May he have dominion from sea to
        sea,
    and from the River to the ends of
        the earth!
9 May desert tribes bow down before
        him,
    and his enemies lick the dust!
10 May the kings of Tarshish and of the
        coastlands
    render him tribute;
    may the kings of Sheba and Seba
        bring gifts!
11 May all kings fall down before him,
    all nations serve him!

12 For he delivers the needy when he calls,
      the poor and him who has no helper.
13 He has pity on the weak and the needy,
      and saves the lives of the needy.
14 From oppression and violence he
          redeems their life,
      and precious is their blood in his
          sight.

15 Long may he live;
      may gold of Sheba be given to him!
    May prayer be made for him continu-
          ally,
      and blessings invoked for him all
          the day!
16 May there be abundance of grain in
          the land;
      on the tops of the mountains may it
          wave;
      may its fruit be like Lebanon;
    and may people blossom in the cities
      like the grass of the field!
17 May his name endure forever,
      his fame continue as long as the sun!
    May people be blessed in him,
      all nations call him blessed!

18 Blessed be the LORD, the God of Israel,
      who alone does wondrous things.
19 Blessed be his glorious name forever;
      may the whole earth be filled with
          his glory!
            Amen and Amen!

20 The prayers of David, the son of Jesse,
      are ended.

BOOK THREE

God Is My Strength and Portion Forever

73 A PSALM OF ASAPH.
      Truly God is good to Israel,
    to those who are pure in heart.
2   But as for me, my feet had almost
          stumbled,
      my steps had nearly slipped.
3   For I was envious of the arrogant
      when I saw the prosperity of the
          wicked.
4   For they have no pangs until death;
      their bodies are fat and sleek.
5   They are not in trouble as others are;
      they are not stricken like the rest of
          mankind.
6   Therefore pride is their necklace;
      violence covers them as a garment.

7   Their eyes swell out through fatness;
      their hearts overflow with follies.
8   They scoff and speak with malice;
      loftily they threaten oppression.
9   They set their mouths against the
          heavens,
      and their tongue struts through the
          earth.
10 Therefore his people turn back to
          them,
      and find no fault in them.
11 And they say, "How can God know?
      Is there knowledge in the Most
          High?"
12 Behold, these are the wicked;
      always at ease, they increase in
          riches.
13 All in vain have I kept my heart clean
      and washed my hands in innocence.

GETTING THE MESSAGE

What does it mean to be "pure in heart"? Those who are pure in heart (73:1) love God wholeheartedly (Deut. 6:5). Their pursuit of purity and upright-ness affects every area of life (Matt. 5:8).

14 For all the day long I have been
          stricken
      and rebuked every morning.
15 If I had said, "I will speak thus,"
      I would have betrayed the genera-
          tion of your children.
16 But when I thought how to under-
          stand this,
      it seemed to me a wearisome task,
17 until I went into the sanctuary of God;
      then I discerned their end.
18 Truly you set them in slippery places;
      you make them fall to ruin.
19 How they are destroyed in a moment,
      swept away utterly by terrors!
20 Like a dream when one awakes,
      O Lord, when you rouse yourself,
          you despise them as phantoms.
21 When my soul was embittered,
      when I was pricked in heart,
22 I was brutish and ignorant;
      I was like a beast toward you.

23 Nevertheless, I am continually with
   you;
   you hold my right hand.
24 You guide me with your counsel,
   and afterward you will receive me
   to glory.
25 Whom have I in heaven but you?
   And there is nothing on earth that I
   desire besides you.
26 My flesh and my heart may fail,
   but God is the strength of my heart
   and my portion forever.
27 For behold, those who are far from
   you shall perish;
   you put an end to everyone who is
   unfaithful to you.
28 But for me it is good to be near God;
   I have made the Lord GOD my refuge,
   that I may tell of all your works.

Arise, O God, Defend Your Cause

74 A MASKIL OF ASAPH.
   O God, why do you cast us off
   forever?
   Why does your anger smoke against
   the sheep of your pasture?
2 Remember your congregation, which
   you have purchased of old,
   which you have redeemed to be the
   tribe of your heritage!
   Remember Mount Zion, where you
   have dwelt.
3 Direct your steps to the perpetual
   ruins;
   the enemy has destroyed everything
   in the sanctuary!

4 Your foes have roared in the midst of
   your meeting place;
   they set up their own signs for signs.
5 They were like those who swing axes
   in a forest of trees.
6 And all its carved wood
   they broke down with hatchets and
   hammers.
7 They set your sanctuary on fire;
   they profaned the dwelling place of
   your name,
   bringing it down to the ground.
8 They said to themselves, "We will
   utterly subdue them";
   they burned all the meeting places
   of God in the land.

9 We do not see our signs;
   there is no longer any prophet,
   and there is none among us who
   knows how long.
10 How long, O God, is the foe to scoff?
   Is the enemy to revile your name
   forever?
11 Why do you hold back your hand,
   your right hand?
   Take it from the fold of your garment and destroy them!

12 Yet God my King is from of old,
   working salvation in the midst of
   the earth.
13 You divided the sea by your might;
   you broke the heads of the sea mon-
   sters[1] on the waters.
14 You crushed the heads of Leviathan;
   you gave him as food for the creatures of the wilderness.
15 You split open springs and brooks;
   you dried up ever-flowing streams.
16 Yours is the day, yours also the night;
   you have established the heavenly
   lights and the sun.
17 You have fixed all the boundaries of
   the earth;
   you have made summer and winter.

18 Remember this, O LORD, how the
   enemy scoffs,
   and a foolish people reviles your
   name.
19 Do not deliver the soul of your dove to
   the wild beasts;
   do not forget the life of your poor
   forever.
20 Have regard for the covenant,
   for the dark places of the land are full
   of the habitations of violence.
21 Let not the downtrodden turn back in
   shame;
   let the poor and needy praise your
   name.

22 Arise, O God, defend your cause;
   remember how the foolish scoff at
   you all the day!
23 Do not forget the clamor of your foes,
   the uproar of those who rise
   against you, which goes up
   continually!

[1] Or large sea creatures

God Will Judge with Equity

75 To the choirmaster: according to Do Not Destroy. A Psalm of Asaph. A Song.

1 We give thanks to you, O God;
    we give thanks, for your name is near.
We recount your wondrous deeds.

2 "At the set time that I appoint
    I will judge with equity.
3 When the earth totters, and all its
        inhabitants,
    it is I who keep steady its pillars.
                                        Selah
4 I say to the boastful, 'Do not boast,'
    and to the wicked, 'Do not lift up
        your horn;
5 do not lift up your horn on high,
    or speak with haughty neck.'"

6 For not from the east or from the west
    and not from the wilderness comes
        lifting up,
7 but it is God who executes judgment,
    putting down one and lifting up
        another.
8 For in the hand of the LORD there is a
        cup
    with foaming wine, well mixed,
and he pours out from it,
    and all the wicked of the earth
    shall drain it down to the dregs.

9 But I will declare it forever;
    I will sing praises to the God of
        Jacob.
10 All the horns of the wicked I will cut
        off,
    but the horns of the righteous shall
        be lifted up.

Who Can Stand Before You?

76 To the choirmaster: with stringed instruments. A Psalm of Asaph. A Song.

1 In Judah God is known;
    his name is great in Israel.
2 His abode has been established in
        Salem,
    his dwelling place in Zion.
3 There he broke the flashing arrows,
    the shield, the sword, and the
        weapons of war.   *Selah*

4 Glorious are you, more majestic
    than the mountains full of prey.

5 The stouthearted were stripped of
        their spoil;
    they sank into sleep;
all the men of war
    were unable to use their hands.
6 At your rebuke, O God of Jacob,
    both rider and horse lay stunned.

7 But you, you are to be feared!
    Who can stand before you
    when once your anger is roused?
8 From the heavens you uttered judg-
        ment;
    the earth feared and was still,
9 when God arose to establish judgment,
    to save all the humble of the earth.
                                        Selah

10 Surely the wrath of man shall praise
        you;
    the remnant of wrath you will put
        on like a belt.

> ### GETTING THE MESSAGE
>
> The **horn** could be a symbol of power and military strength, and thus to lift up or exalt it was to publicly assert power. God warns the ungodly not to lift up their horns (75:4), and promises that he will lift up the horn of the faithful.

11 Make your vows to the LORD your God
        and perform them;
    let all around him bring gifts
    to him who is to be feared,
12 who cuts off the spirit of princes,
    who is to be feared by the kings of
        the earth.

In the Day of Trouble I Seek the Lord

77 To the choirmaster: according to Jeduthun. A Psalm of Asaph.

1 I cry aloud to God,
    aloud to God, and he will hear me.
2 In the day of my trouble I seek the Lord;
    in the night my hand is stretched
        out without wearying;
    my soul refuses to be comforted.
3 When I remember God, I moan;
    when I meditate, my spirit faints.
                                        Selah

4 You hold my eyelids open;
    I am so troubled that I cannot speak.

5 I consider the days of old,
  the years long ago.
6 I said, "Let me remember my song in
  the night;
  let me meditate in my heart."
  Then my spirit made a diligent
  search:
7 "Will the Lord spurn forever,
  and never again be favorable?
8 Has his steadfast love forever ceased?
  Are his promises at an end for all
  time?
9 Has God forgotten to be gracious?
  Has he in anger shut up his compassion?"   *Selah*

10 Then I said, "I will appeal to this,
   to the years of the right hand of the
   Most High."

> ### GETTING THE MESSAGE

Zoan (78:12) is the ancient Egyptian
city of Tanis, one of many cities in the
area where the Israelites lived around
the time of Moses. The city's ruins were
surveyed by Napoleon Bonaparte in the
late 1700s.

11 I will remember the deeds of the
   LORD;
   yes, I will remember your wonders
   of old.
12 I will ponder all your work,
   and meditate on your mighty
   deeds.
13 Your way, O God, is holy.
   What god is great like our God?
14 You are the God who works wonders;
   you have made known your might
   among the peoples.
15 You with your arm redeemed your
   people,
   the children of Jacob and Joseph.
                                     Selah

16 When the waters saw you, O God,
   when the waters saw you, they were
   afraid;
   indeed, the deep trembled.
17 The clouds poured out water;
   the skies gave forth thunder;
   your arrows flashed on every side.

18 The crash of your thunder was in the
   whirlwind;
   your lightnings lighted up the world;
   the earth trembled and shook.
19 Your way was through the sea,
   your path through the great waters;
   yet your footprints were unseen.
20 You led your people like a flock
   by the hand of Moses and Aaron.

Tell the Coming Generation

78 A MASKIL OF ASAPH.
   Give ear, O my people, to my
   teaching;
   incline your ears to the words of my
   mouth!
2 I will open my mouth in a parable;
  I will utter dark sayings from of old,
3 things that we have heard and known,
  that our fathers have told us.
4 We will not hide them from their
  children,
  but tell to the coming generation
  the glorious deeds of the LORD, and
  his might,
  and the wonders that he has done.

5 He established a testimony in Jacob
  and appointed a law in Israel,
  which he commanded our fathers
  to teach to their children,
6 that the next generation might know
  them,
  the children yet unborn,
  and arise and tell them to their children,
7 so that they should set their hope in
  God
  and not forget the works of God,
  but keep his commandments;
8 and that they should not be like their
  fathers,
  a stubborn and rebellious generation,
  a generation whose heart was not
  steadfast,
  whose spirit was not faithful to God.

9 The Ephraimites, armed with the bow,
  turned back on the day of battle.
10 They did not keep God's covenant,
   but refused to walk according to his
   law.
11 They forgot his works
   and the wonders that he had shown
   them.

¹² In the sight of their fathers he per-
        formed wonders
      in the land of Egypt, in the fields of
        Zoan.
¹³ He divided the sea and let them pass
        through it,
      and made the waters stand like a
        heap.
¹⁴ In the daytime he led them with a
        cloud,
      and all the night with a fiery light.
¹⁵ He split rocks in the wilderness
      and gave them drink abundantly as
        from the deep.
¹⁶ He made streams come out of the rock
      and caused waters to flow down
        like rivers.

¹⁷ Yet they sinned still more against him,
      rebelling against the Most High in
        the desert.
¹⁸ They tested God in their heart
      by demanding the food they craved.
¹⁹ They spoke against God, saying,
      "Can God spread a table in the wil-
        derness?
²⁰ He struck the rock so that water
        gushed out
      and streams overflowed.
      Can he also give bread
        or provide meat for his people?"

²¹ Therefore, when the LORD heard, he
        was full of wrath;
      a fire was kindled against Jacob;
        his anger rose against Israel,
²² because they did not believe in God
      and did not trust his saving power.
²³ Yet he commanded the skies above
      and opened the doors of heaven,
²⁴ and he rained down on them manna
        to eat
      and gave them the grain of heaven.
²⁵ Man ate of the bread of the angels;
      he sent them food in abundance.
²⁶ He caused the east wind to blow in
        the heavens,
      and by his power he led out the
        south wind;
²⁷ he rained meat on them like dust,
      winged birds like the sand of the
        seas;
²⁸ he let them fall in the midst of their
        camp,
      all around their dwellings.

²⁹ And they ate and were well filled,
      for he gave them what they craved.
³⁰ But before they had satisfied their
        craving,
      while the food was still in their
        mouths,
³¹ the anger of God rose against them,
      and he killed the strongest of them
      and laid low the young men of Israel.

³² In spite of all this, they still sinned;
      despite his wonders, they did not
        believe.
³³ So he made their days vanish like a
        breath,
      and their years in terror.
³⁴ When he killed them, they sought him;
      they repented and sought God ear-
        nestly.
³⁵ They remembered that God was their
        rock,
      the Most High God their redeemer.
³⁶ But they flattered him with their
        mouths;
      they lied to him with their tongues.
³⁷ Their heart was not steadfast toward
        him;
      they were not faithful to his cov-
        enant.
³⁸ Yet he, being compassionate,
      atoned for their iniquity
      and did not destroy them;
    he restrained his anger often
      and did not stir up all his wrath.
³⁹ He remembered that they were but
        flesh,
      a wind that passes and comes not
        again.
⁴⁰ How often they rebelled against him
        in the wilderness
      and grieved him in the desert!
⁴¹ They tested God again and again
      and provoked the Holy One of Israel.
⁴² They did not remember his power
      or the day when he redeemed them
        from the foe,
⁴³ when he performed his signs in Egypt
      and his marvels in the fields of Zoan.
⁴⁴ He turned their rivers to blood,
      so that they could not drink of their
        streams.
⁴⁵ He sent among them swarms of flies,
      which devoured them,
      and frogs, which destroyed them.

46 He gave their crops to the destroying
      locust
    and the fruit of their labor to the
      locust.
47 He destroyed their vines with hail
    and their sycamores with frost.
48 He gave over their cattle to the hail
    and their flocks to thunderbolts.
49 He let loose on them his burning anger,
    wrath, indignation, and distress,
    a company of destroying angels.
50 He made a path for his anger;
    he did not spare them from death,
    but gave their lives over to the
      plague.
51 He struck down every firstborn in
      Egypt,
    the firstfruits of their strength in
      the tents of Ham.
52 Then he led out his people like sheep
    and guided them in the wilderness
      like a flock.

GETTING THE MESSAGE

How long? This question (79:5) occurs
nearly twenty times in the Psalms, more
than any other question. It is almost
always associated with a psalm of
lament, such as Psalm 79.

53 He led them in safety, so that they
      were not afraid,
    but the sea overwhelmed their
      enemies.
54 And he brought them to his holy land,
    to the mountain which his right
      hand had won.
55 He drove out nations before them;
    he apportioned them for a posses-
      sion
    and settled the tribes of Israel in
      their tents.
56 Yet they tested and rebelled against
      the Most High God
    and did not keep his testimonies,
57 but turned away and acted treacher-
      ously like their fathers;
    they twisted like a deceitful bow.
58 For they provoked him to anger with
      their high places;
    they moved him to jealousy with
      their idols.

59 When God heard, he was full of wrath,
    and he utterly rejected Israel.
60 He forsook his dwelling at Shiloh,
    the tent where he dwelt among
      mankind,
61 and delivered his power to captivity,
    his glory to the hand of the foe.
62 He gave his people over to the sword
    and vented his wrath on his heritage.
63 Fire devoured their young men,
    and their young women had no
      marriage song.
64 Their priests fell by the sword,
    and their widows made no lamen-
      tation.
65 Then the Lord awoke as from sleep,
    like a strong man shouting because
      of wine.
66 And he put his adversaries to rout;
    he put them to everlasting shame.
67 He rejected the tent of Joseph;
    he did not choose the tribe of
      Ephraim,
68 but he chose the tribe of Judah,
    Mount Zion, which he loves.
69 He built his sanctuary like the high
      heavens,
    like the earth, which he has
      founded forever.
70 He chose David his servant
    and took him from the sheepfolds;
71 from following the nursing ewes he
      brought him
    to shepherd Jacob his people,
    Israel his inheritance.
72 With upright heart he shepherded them
    and guided them with his skillful
      hand.

How Long, O Lord?

79

A PSALM OF ASAPH.
    O God, the nations have come
      into your inheritance;
    they have defiled your holy temple;
    they have laid Jerusalem in ruins.
2 They have given the bodies of your
      servants
    to the birds of the heavens for food,
    the flesh of your faithful to the
      beasts of the earth.
3 They have poured out their blood like
      water
    all around Jerusalem,
    and there was no one to bury them.

4   We have become a taunt to our neigh-
        bors,
        mocked and derided by those
            around us.

5   How long, O LORD? Will you be angry
        forever?
    Will your jealousy burn like fire?
6   Pour out your anger on the nations
        that do not know you,
    and on the kingdoms
        that do not call upon your name!
7   For they have devoured Jacob
        and laid waste his habitation.

8   Do not remember against us our for-
        mer iniquities;
        let your compassion come speedily
            to meet us,
        for we are brought very low.
9   Help us, O God of our salvation,
        for the glory of your name;
    deliver us, and atone for our sins,
        for your name's sake!
10 Why should the nations say,
        "Where is their God?"
    Let the avenging of the outpoured
        blood of your servants
        be known among the nations before
            our eyes!

11 Let the groans of the prisoners come
        before you;
        according to your great power,
            preserve those doomed to die!
12 Return sevenfold into the lap of our
        neighbors
        the taunts with which they have
            taunted you, O Lord!
13 But we your people, the sheep of your
        pasture,
        will give thanks to you forever;
        from generation to generation we
            will recount your praise.

Restore Us, O God

80 TO THE CHOIRMASTER: ACCORDING
    TO LILIES. A TESTIMONY. OF ASAPH,
    A PSALM.

1   Give ear, O Shepherd of Israel,
        you who lead Joseph like a flock.
    You who are enthroned upon the
        cherubim, shine forth.
2   Before Ephraim and Benjamin and
            Manasseh,

    stir up your might
        and come to save us!
3   Restore us, O God;
        let your face shine, that we may be
            saved!

4   O LORD God of hosts,
        how long will you be angry with
            your people's prayers?
5   You have fed them with the bread of
        tears
        and given them tears to drink in full
            measure.
6   You make us an object of contention
        for our neighbors,
        and our enemies laugh among
            themselves.

7   Restore us, O God of hosts;
        let your face shine, that we may be
            saved!

8   You brought a vine out of Egypt;
        you drove out the nations and
            planted it.
9   You cleared the ground for it;
        it took deep root and filled the land.
10 The mountains were covered with its
        shade,
        the mighty cedars with its branches.
11 It sent out its branches to the sea
        and its shoots to the River.
12 Why then have you broken down its
        walls,
        so that all who pass along the way
            pluck its fruit?
13 The boar from the forest ravages it,
        and all that move in the field feed
            on it.

14 Turn again, O God of hosts!
        Look down from heaven, and see;
    have regard for this vine,
15   the stock that your right hand
            planted,
        and for the son whom you made
            strong for yourself.
16 They have burned it with fire; they
        have cut it down;
        may they perish at the rebuke of
            your face!
17 But let your hand be on the man of
        your right hand,
        the son of man whom you have
            made strong for yourself!

18 Then we shall not turn back from you;
    give us life, and we will call upon
        your name!

19 Restore us, O LORD God of hosts!
    Let your face shine, that we may be
        saved!

Oh, That My People Would Listen to Me

81 TO THE CHOIRMASTER: ACCORDING TO
THE GITTITH. OF ASAPH.

1 Sing aloud to God our strength;
    shout for joy to the God of Jacob!
2 Raise a song; sound the tambourine,
    the sweet lyre with the harp.
3 Blow the trumpet at the new moon,
    at the full moon, on our feast day.

4 For it is a statute for Israel,
    a rule of the God of Jacob.
5 He made it a decree in Joseph
    when he went out over the land of
        Egypt.
    I hear a language I had not known:
6 "I relieved your shoulder of the burden;
    your hands were freed from the
        basket.
7 In distress you called, and I delivered
        you;
    I answered you in the secret place
        of thunder;
    I tested you at the waters of
        Meribah.   *Selah*
8 Hear, O my people, while I admonish
        you!
    O Israel, if you would but listen to
        me!
9 There shall be no strange god among
        you;
    you shall not bow down to a foreign
        god.
10 I am the LORD your God,
    who brought you up out of the land
        of Egypt.
    Open your mouth wide, and I will
        fill it.

11 "But my people did not listen to my
        voice;
    Israel would not submit to me.
12 So I gave them over to their stubborn
        hearts,
    to follow their own counsels.
13 Oh, that my people would listen to me,
    that Israel would walk in my ways!

14 I would soon subdue their enemies
    and turn my hand against their
        foes.
15 Those who hate the LORD would
    cringe toward him,
    and their fate would last forever.
16 But he would feed you with the finest
    of the wheat,
    and with honey from the rock I
        would satisfy you."

Rescue the Weak and Needy

82 A PSALM OF ASAPH.
God has taken his place in the
    divine council;
    in the midst of the gods he holds
        judgment:
2 "How long will you judge unjustly
    and show partiality to the wicked?
                                Selah
3 Give justice to the weak and the
        fatherless;
    maintain the right of the afflicted
        and the destitute.
4 Rescue the weak and the needy;
    deliver them from the hand of the
        wicked."

5 They have neither knowledge nor
        understanding,
    they walk about in darkness;
    all the foundations of the earth are
        shaken.

6 I said, "You are gods,
    sons of the Most High, all of you;
7 nevertheless, like men you shall die,
    and fall like any prince."

8 Arise, O God, judge the earth;
    for you shall inherit all the
        nations!

O God, Do Not Keep Silence

83 A SONG. A PSALM OF ASAPH.
O God, do not keep silence;
    do not hold your peace or be still,
        O God!
2 For behold, your enemies make an
        uproar;
    those who hate you have raised
        their heads.
3 They lay crafty plans against your
        people;
    they consult together against your
        treasured ones.

4 They say, "Come, let us wipe them out
       as a nation;
     let the name of Israel be remem-
       bered no more!"
5 For they conspire with one accord;
     against you they make a covenant—
6 the tents of Edom and the Ishmaelites,
     Moab and the Hagrites,
7 Gebal and Ammon and Amalek,
     Philistia with the inhabitants of
       Tyre;
8 Asshur also has joined them;
     they are the strong arm of the chil-
       dren of Lot.   *Selah*

9 Do to them as you did to Midian,
     as to Sisera and Jabin at the river
       Kishon,
10 who were destroyed at En-dor,
     who became dung for the ground.
11 Make their nobles like Oreb and Zeeb,
     all their princes like Zebah and
       Zalmunna,
12 who said, "Let us take possession for
       ourselves
     of the pastures of God."

13 O my God, make them like whirling
       dust,
     like chaff before the wind.
14 As fire consumes the forest,
     as the flame sets the mountains
       ablaze,
15 so may you pursue them with your
       tempest
     and terrify them with your hurri-
       cane!
16 Fill their faces with shame,
     that they may seek your name,
       O LORD.
17 Let them be put to shame and dis-
       mayed forever;
     let them perish in disgrace,
18 that they may know that you alone,
     whose name is the LORD,
     are the Most High over all the earth.

My Soul Longs for the Courts of the LORD

84
TO THE CHOIRMASTER: ACCORDING
TO THE GITTITH. A PSALM OF THE
SONS OF KORAH.

1 How lovely is your dwelling place,
     O LORD of hosts!
2 My soul longs, yes, faints
     for the courts of the LORD;

my heart and flesh sing for joy
     to the living God.
3 Even the sparrow finds a home,
     and the swallow a nest for herself,
     where she may lay her young,
   at your altars, O LORD of hosts,
     my King and my God.
4 Blessed are those who dwell in your
       house,
     ever singing your praise!   *Selah*

5 Blessed are those whose strength is in
       you,
     in whose heart are the highways to
       Zion.
6 As they go through the Valley of Baca
     they make it a place of springs;
     the early rain also covers it with
       pools.
7 They go from strength to strength;
     each one appears before God in Zion.

GETTING THE MESSAGE

The word **blessed** (84:4, 5, 12, etc.) refers to someone who has received—or who will receive—something good from the Lord. It is not just a temporary feeling of happiness but a state of well-being in relationship to God.

8 O LORD God of hosts, hear my prayer;
     give ear, O God of Jacob!   *Selah*
9 Behold our shield, O God;
     look on the face of your anointed!

10 For a day in your courts is better
     than a thousand elsewhere.
   I would rather be a doorkeeper in the
     house of my God
     than dwell in the tents of wickedness.
11 For the LORD God is a sun and shield;
     the LORD bestows favor and honor.
   No good thing does he withhold
     from those who walk uprightly.
12 O LORD of hosts,
     blessed is the one who trusts in you!

Revive Us Again

85
TO THE CHOIRMASTER. A PSALM OF
THE SONS OF KORAH.

1 LORD, you were favorable to your land;
     you restored the fortunes of Jacob.

² You forgave the iniquity of your people;
  you covered all their sin.   *Selah*
³ You withdrew all your wrath;
  you turned from your hot anger.

⁴ Restore us again, O God of our salvation,
  and put away your indignation
  toward us!
⁵ Will you be angry with us forever?
  Will you prolong your anger to all
  generations?
⁶ Will you not revive us again,
  that your people may rejoice in you?
⁷ Show us your steadfast love, O Lᴏʀᴅ,
  and grant us your salvation.

⁸ Let me hear what God the Lᴏʀᴅ will
  speak,
  for he will speak peace to his people, to his saints;
  but let them not turn back to folly.

▶ GETTING THE MESSAGE

The words of Ps. 86:9 are incorporated
into the **song of the Lamb** in Rev. 15:4.
All nations will someday worship
the Lord.

⁹ Surely his salvation is near to those
  who fear him,
  that glory may dwell in our land.
¹⁰ Steadfast love and faithfulness meet;
  righteousness and peace kiss each
  other.
¹¹ Faithfulness springs up from the
  ground,
  and righteousness looks down from
  the sky.
¹² Yes, the Lᴏʀᴅ will give what is good,
  and our land will yield its increase.
¹³ Righteousness will go before him
  and make his footsteps a way.

Great Is Your Steadfast Love

86
A Pʀᴀʏᴇʀ ᴏꜰ Dᴀᴠɪᴅ.
Incline your ear, O Lᴏʀᴅ, and
answer me,
  for I am poor and needy.
² Preserve my life, for I am godly;
  save your servant, who trusts in
  you—you are my God.

³ Be gracious to me, O Lord,
  for to you do I cry all the day.
⁴ Gladden the soul of your servant,
  for to you, O Lord, do I lift up my
  soul.
⁵ For you, O Lord, are good and forgiving,
  abounding in steadfast love to all
  who call upon you.
⁶ Give ear, O Lᴏʀᴅ, to my prayer;
  listen to my plea for grace.
⁷ In the day of my trouble I call upon
  you,
  for you answer me.

⁸ There is none like you among the
  gods, O Lord,
  nor are there any works like yours.
⁹ All the nations you have made shall
  come
  and worship before you, O Lord,
  and shall glorify your name.
¹⁰ For you are great and do wondrous
  things;
  you alone are God.
¹¹ Teach me your way, O Lᴏʀᴅ,
  that I may walk in your truth;
  unite my heart to fear your name.
¹² I give thanks to you, O Lord my God,
  with my whole heart,
  and I will glorify your name forever.
¹³ For great is your steadfast love toward
  me;
  you have delivered my soul from
  the depths of Sheol.

¹⁴ O God, insolent men have risen up
  against me;
  a band of ruthless men seeks my
  life,
  and they do not set you before
  them.
¹⁵ But you, O Lord, are a God merciful
  and gracious,
  slow to anger and abounding in
  steadfast love and faithfulness.
¹⁶ Turn to me and be gracious to me;
  give your strength to your servant,
  and save the son of your maidservant.
¹⁷ Show me a sign of your favor,
  that those who hate me may see
  and be put to shame
  because you, Lᴏʀᴅ, have helped me
  and comforted me.

Glorious Things of You Are Spoken

87
A PSALM OF THE SONS OF KORAH.
A SONG.

1 On the holy mount stands the city he
     founded;
2   the LORD loves the gates of Zion
     more than all the dwelling places of
     Jacob.
3 Glorious things of you are spoken,
     O city of God.   *Selah*

4 Among those who know me I men-
     tion Rahab and Babylon;
     behold, Philistia and Tyre, with
     Cush—
     "This one was born there," they say.
5 And of Zion it shall be said,
     "This one and that one were born in
     her";
     for the Most High himself will
     establish her.
6 The LORD records as he registers the
     peoples,
     "This one was born there."   *Selah*

7 Singers and dancers alike say,
     "All my springs are in you."

I Cry Out Day and Night Before You

88
A SONG. A PSALM OF THE SONS OF
KORAH. TO THE CHOIRMASTER:
ACCORDING TO MAHALATH
LEANNOTH. A MASKIL OF HEMAN
THE EZRAHITE.

1 O LORD, God of my salvation;
     I cry out day and night before you.
2 Let my prayer come before you;
     incline your ear to my cry!

3 For my soul is full of troubles,
     and my life draws near to Sheol.
4 I am counted among those who go
     down to the pit;
     I am a man who has no strength,
5 like one set loose among the dead,
     like the slain that lie in the grave,
     like those whom you remember no
     more,
     for they are cut off from your hand.
6 You have put me in the depths of the
     pit,
     in the regions dark and deep.
7 Your wrath lies heavy upon me,
     and you overwhelm me with all
     your waves.   *Selah*

8 You have caused my companions to
     shun me;
     you have made me a horror to
     them.
     I am shut in so that I cannot escape;
9   my eye grows dim through sorrow.
     Every day I call upon you, O LORD;
     I spread out my hands to you.
10 Do you work wonders for the dead?
     Do the departed rise up to praise
     you?   *Selah*
11 Is your steadfast love declared in the
     grave,
     or your faithfulness in Abaddon?
12 Are your wonders known in the dark-
     ness,
     or your righteousness in the land of
     forgetfulness?

GETTING THE MESSAGE

Keeping a record of the population
(87:6) was a very important task in the
ancient world. In fact, sometimes entire
cities were employed for this purpose.
People who performed such royal duties
were sometimes rewarded by being
exempt from imprisonment and military
service, and from having to pay taxes.

13 But I, O LORD, cry to you;
     in the morning my prayer comes
     before you.
14 O LORD, why do you cast my soul away?
     Why do you hide your face from me?
15 Afflicted and close to death from my
     youth up,
     I suffer your terrors; I am helpless.
16 Your wrath has swept over me;
     your dreadful assaults destroy me.
17 They surround me like a flood all day
     long;
     they close in on me together.
18 You have caused my beloved and my
     friend to shun me;
     my companions have become dark-
     ness.

I Will Sing of the Steadfast Love of the LORD

89
A MASKIL OF ETHAN THE EZRAHITE.
I will sing of the steadfast love of
the LORD, forever;

with my mouth I will make known
 your faithfulness to all generations.
2 For I said, "Steadfast love will be built
 up forever;
 in the heavens you will establish
 your faithfulness."
3 You have said, "I have made a covenant with my chosen one;
 I have sworn to David my servant:
4 'I will establish your offspring forever,
 and build your throne for all generations.'"   *Selah*

5 Let the heavens praise your wonders,
 O Lord,
 your faithfulness in the assembly of
 the holy ones!
6 For who in the skies can be compared
 to the Lord?
 Who among the heavenly beings is
 like the Lord,

> ### GETTING THE MESSAGE
>
> **Abaddon** (88:11) means "place of
> destruction." In Rev. 9:11, Abaddon
> is king of "the bottomless pit."

7 a God greatly to be feared in the council of the holy ones,
 and awesome above all who are
 around him?
8 O Lord God of hosts,
 who is mighty as you are, O Lord,
 with your faithfulness all around
 you?
9 You rule the raging of the sea;
 when its waves rise, you still them.
10 You crushed Rahab like a carcass;
 you scattered your enemies with
 your mighty arm.
11 The heavens are yours; the earth also
 is yours;
 the world and all that is in it, you
 have founded them.
12 The north and the south, you have
 created them;
 Tabor and Hermon joyously praise
 your name.
13 You have a mighty arm;
 strong is your hand, high your right
 hand.

14 Righteousness and justice are the
 foundation of your throne;
 steadfast love and faithfulness go
 before you.
15 Blessed are the people who know the
 festal shout,
 who walk, O Lord, in the light of
 your face,
16 who exult in your name all the day
 and in your righteousness are
 exalted.
17 For you are the glory of their strength;
 by your favor our horn is exalted.
18 For our shield belongs to the Lord,
 our king to the Holy One of Israel.
19 Of old you spoke in a vision to your
 godly one, and said:
 "I have granted help to one who is
 mighty;
 I have exalted one chosen from the
 people.
20 I have found David, my servant;
 with my holy oil I have anointed
 him,
21 so that my hand shall be established
 with him;
 my arm also shall strengthen him.
22 The enemy shall not outwit him;
 the wicked shall not humble him.
23 I will crush his foes before him
 and strike down those who hate him.
24 My faithfulness and my steadfast love
 shall be with him,
 and in my name shall his horn be
 exalted.
25 I will set his hand on the sea
 and his right hand on the rivers.
26 He shall cry to me, 'You are my Father,
 my God, and the Rock of my salvation.'
27 And I will make him the firstborn,
 the highest of the kings of the earth.
28 My steadfast love I will keep for him
 forever,
 and my covenant will stand firm for
 him.
29 I will establish his offspring forever
 and his throne as the days of the
 heavens.
30 If his children forsake my law
 and do not walk according to my
 rules,
31 if they violate my statutes
 and do not keep my commandments,

32 then I will punish their transgression
        with the rod
    and their iniquity with stripes,
33 but I will not remove from him my
        steadfast love
    or be false to my faithfulness.
34 I will not violate my covenant
    or alter the word that went forth
        from my lips.
35 Once for all I have sworn by my holi-
        ness;
    I will not lie to David.
36 His offspring shall endure forever,
    his throne as long as the sun before
        me.
37 Like the moon it shall be established
        forever,
    a faithful witness in the skies."
                                        Selah

38 But now you have cast off and
        rejected;
    you are full of wrath against your
        anointed.
39 You have renounced the covenant
        with your servant;
    you have defiled his crown in the
        dust.
40 You have breached all his walls;
    you have laid his strongholds in
        ruins.
41 All who pass by plunder him;
    he has become the scorn of his
        neighbors.
42 You have exalted the right hand of his
        foes;
    you have made all his enemies
        rejoice.
43 You have also turned back the edge of
        his sword,
    and you have not made him stand
        in battle.
44 You have made his splendor to cease
    and cast his throne to the ground.
45 You have cut short the days of his
        youth;
    you have covered him with shame.
                                        Selah

46 How long, O LORD? Will you hide
        yourself forever?
    How long will your wrath burn like
        fire?
47 Remember how short my time is!
    For what vanity you have created all
        the children of man!

48 What man can live and never see
        death?
    Who can deliver his soul from the
        power of Sheol?   *Selah*

49 Lord, where is your steadfast love of
        old,
    which by your faithfulness you
        swore to David?
50 Remember, O Lord, how your servants
        are mocked,
    and how I bear in my heart the
        insults of all the many nations,
51 with which your enemies mock,
        O LORD,
    with which they mock the footsteps
        of your anointed.

52 Blessed be the LORD forever!
    Amen and Amen.

> **GETTING THE MESSAGE**

How old? Psalm 90:10 suggests that
Israelites were living to be 70 or 80
years old in the days of Moses. While life
expectancy has varied somewhat over
the centuries, it is about the same today.

BOOK FOUR

From Everlasting to Everlasting

90 A PRAYER OF MOSES, THE MAN OF GOD.

1 Lord, you have been our dwelling
        place
    in all generations.
2 Before the mountains were brought
        forth,
    or ever you had formed the earth
        and the world,
    from everlasting to everlasting you
        are God.
3 You return man to dust
    and say, "Return, O children of
        man!"
4 For a thousand years in your sight
    are but as yesterday when it is past,
    or as a watch in the night.
5 You sweep them away as with a flood;
        they are like a dream,
    like grass that is renewed in the
        morning:

6 in the morning it flourishes and is
    renewed;
      in the evening it fades and withers.

7 For we are brought to an end by your
    anger;
      by your wrath we are dismayed.
8 You have set our iniquities before
    you,
      our secret sins in the light of your
      presence.

9 For all our days pass away under your
    wrath;
      we bring our years to an end like a
      sigh.
10 The years of our life are seventy,
    or even by reason of strength
      eighty;

GETTING THE MESSAGE

Satan knows the Scriptures. Psalm 91:11–12 was quoted by Satan when he tempted Jesus in the desert (Matt. 4:6). Of course, he misapplied it for his own evil purposes. In no way do these verses mean that believers should put themselves in unnecessary danger.

    yet their span is but toil and trouble;
      they are soon gone, and we fly
      away.
11 Who considers the power of your
    anger,
      and your wrath according to the
      fear of you?

12 So teach us to number our days
    that we may get a heart of wisdom.
13 Return, O Lord! How long?
    Have pity on your servants!
14 Satisfy us in the morning with your
    steadfast love,
      that we may rejoice and be glad all
      our days.
15 Make us glad for as many days as you
    have afflicted us,
      and for as many years as we have
      seen evil.
16 Let your work be shown to your ser-
    vants,
      and your glorious power to their
      children.

17 Let the favor of the Lord our God be
    upon us,
      and establish the work of our hands
      upon us;
      yes, establish the work of our hands!

My Refuge and My Fortress

91 He who dwells in the shelter of
    the Most High
      will abide in the shadow of the
      Almighty.
2 I will say to the Lord, "My refuge and
    my fortress,
      my God, in whom I trust."

3 For he will deliver you from the snare
    of the fowler
      and from the deadly pestilence.
4 He will cover you with his pinions,
    and under his wings you will find
      refuge;
      his faithfulness is a shield and
      buckler.
5 You will not fear the terror of the night,
    nor the arrow that flies by day,
6 nor the pestilence that stalks in dark-
    ness,
      nor the destruction that wastes at
      noonday.

7 A thousand may fall at your side,
    ten thousand at your right hand,
      but it will not come near you.
8 You will only look with your eyes
    and see the recompense of the
      wicked.

9 Because you have made the Lord your
    dwelling place—
      the Most High, who is my refuge—
10 no evil shall be allowed to befall you,
    no plague come near your tent.

11 For he will command his angels con-
    cerning you
      to guard you in all your ways.
12 On their hands they will bear you up,
    lest you strike your foot against a
      stone.
13 You will tread on the lion and the
    adder;
      the young lion and the serpent you
      will trample underfoot.

14 "Because he holds fast to me in love,
    I will deliver him;
      I will protect him, because he
      knows my name.

15 When he calls to me, I will answer him;
   I will be with him in trouble;
   I will rescue him and honor him.
16 With long life I will satisfy him
   and show him my salvation."

How Great Are Your Works

92 A PSALM. A SONG FOR THE SABBATH.
   It is good to give thanks to the
   LORD,
   to sing praises to your name,
   O Most High;
2 to declare your steadfast love in the
   morning,
   and your faithfulness by night,
3 to the music of the lute and the harp,
   to the melody of the lyre.
4 For you, O LORD, have made me glad
   by your work;
   at the works of your hands I sing for
   joy.

5 How great are your works, O LORD!
   Your thoughts are very deep!
6 The stupid man cannot know;
   the fool cannot understand this:
7 that though the wicked sprout like
   grass
   and all evildoers flourish,
   they are doomed to destruction forever;
8 but you, O LORD, are on high forever.
9 For behold, your enemies, O LORD,
   for behold, your enemies shall
   perish;
   all evildoers shall be scattered.

10 But you have exalted my horn like
   that of the wild ox;
   you have poured over me fresh oil.
11 My eyes have seen the downfall of my
   enemies;
   my ears have heard the doom of my
   evil assailants.

12 The righteous flourish like the palm
   tree
   and grow like a cedar in Lebanon.
13 They are planted in the house of the
   LORD;
   they flourish in the courts of our
   God.
14 They still bear fruit in old age;
   they are ever full of sap and green,
15 to declare that the LORD is upright;
   he is my rock, and there is no
   unrighteousness in him.

The LORD Reigns

93 The LORD reigns; he is robed in
   majesty;
   the LORD is robed; he has put on
   strength as his belt.
   Yes, the world is established; it shall
   never be moved.
2 Your throne is established from of old;
   you are from everlasting.

3 The floods have lifted up, O LORD,
   the floods have lifted up their voice;
   the floods lift up their roaring.
4 Mightier than the thunders of many
   waters,
   mightier than the waves of the sea,
   the LORD on high is mighty!

5 Your decrees are very trustworthy;
   holiness befits your house,
   O LORD, forevermore.

GETTING THE MESSAGE

The word **vengeance** is used in Ps. 94:1 to describe one way in which the Lord brings about justice in the world. Individual Israelites were forbidden to seek personal vengeance (Lev. 19:18). However, it was the duty of the civil government to ensure just retribution against wrongdoers (Ex. 21:20).

The LORD Will Not Forsake His People

94 O LORD, God of vengeance,
   O God of vengeance, shine forth!
2 Rise up, O judge of the earth;
   repay to the proud what they
   deserve!
3 O LORD, how long shall the wicked,
   how long shall the wicked exult?
4 They pour out their arrogant words;
   all the evildoers boast.
5 They crush your people, O LORD,
   and afflict your heritage.
6 They kill the widow and the sojourner,
   and murder the fatherless;
7 and they say, "The LORD does not see;
   the God of Jacob does not perceive."

8 Understand, O dullest of the people!
   Fools, when will you be wise?
9 He who planted the ear, does he not
   hear?

He who formed the eye, does he not see?

10 He who disciplines the nations, does he not rebuke?
He who teaches man knowledge—
11 the LORD—knows the thoughts of man,
that they are but a breath.

12 Blessed is the man whom you discipline, O LORD,
and whom you teach out of your law,
13 to give him rest from days of trouble,
until a pit is dug for the wicked.
14 For the LORD will not forsake his people;
he will not abandon his heritage;
15 for justice will return to the righteous,
and all the upright in heart will follow it.

GETTING THE MESSAGE

Maker of heaven and earth. Psalm 95 is one of several psalms that focus on God's rule over all of creation. God is the ultimate king because he created everything that exists. The Psalms frequently remind God's people that we owe him our worship and allegiance because it is he who made us.

16 Who rises up for me against the wicked?
Who stands up for me against evil-doers?
17 If the LORD had not been my help,
my soul would soon have lived in the land of silence.
18 When I thought, "My foot slips,"
your steadfast love, O LORD, held me up.
19 When the cares of my heart are many,
your consolations cheer my soul.
20 Can wicked rulers be allied with you,
those who frame injustice by statute?
21 They band together against the life of the righteous
and condemn the innocent to death.
22 But the LORD has become my stronghold,
and my God the rock of my refuge.

23 He will bring back on them their iniquity
and wipe them out for their wickedness;
the LORD our God will wipe them out.

Let Us Sing Songs of Praise

95 Oh come, let us sing to the LORD;
let us make a joyful noise to the rock of our salvation!
2 Let us come into his presence with thanksgiving;
let us make a joyful noise to him with songs of praise!
3 For the LORD is a great God,
and a great King above all gods.
4 In his hand are the depths of the earth;
the heights of the mountains are his also.
5 The sea is his, for he made it,
and his hands formed the dry land.

6 Oh come, let us worship and bow down;
let us kneel before the LORD, our Maker!
7 For he is our God,
and we are the people of his pasture,
and the sheep of his hand.
Today, if you hear his voice,
8 do not harden your hearts, as at Meribah,
as on the day at Massah in the wilderness,
9 when your fathers put me to the test
and put me to the proof, though they had seen my work.
10 For forty years I loathed that generation
and said, "They are a people who go astray in their heart,
and they have not known my ways."
11 Therefore I swore in my wrath,
"They shall not enter my rest."

Worship in the Splendor of Holiness

96 Oh sing to the LORD a new song;
sing to the LORD, all the earth!
2 Sing to the LORD, bless his name;
tell of his salvation from day to day.
3 Declare his glory among the nations,
his marvelous works among all the peoples!
4 For great is the LORD, and greatly to be praised;
he is to be feared above all gods.

5 For all the gods of the peoples are
    worthless idols,
  but the LORD made the heavens.
6 Splendor and majesty are before him;
    strength and beauty are in his sanc-
    tuary.

7 Ascribe to the LORD, O families of the
    peoples,
  ascribe to the LORD glory and
    strength!
8 Ascribe to the LORD the glory due his
    name;
  bring an offering, and come into his
    courts!
9 Worship the LORD in the splendor of
    holiness;
  tremble before him, all the earth!

10 Say among the nations, "The LORD
    reigns!
  Yes, the world is established; it shall
    never be moved;
  he will judge the peoples with
    equity."

11 Let the heavens be glad, and let the
    earth rejoice;
  let the sea roar, and all that fills it;
12 let the field exult, and everything in
    it!
  Then shall all the trees of the forest
    sing for joy
13 before the LORD, for he comes,
  for he comes to judge the earth.
  He will judge the world in righteous-
    ness,
  and the peoples in his faithfulness.

The LORD Reigns

97 The LORD reigns, let the earth
    rejoice;
  let the many coastlands be glad!
2 Clouds and thick darkness are all
    around him;
  righteousness and justice are the
    foundation of his throne.
3 Fire goes before him
  and burns up his adversaries all
    around.
4 His lightnings light up the world;
  the earth sees and trembles.
5 The mountains melt like wax before
    the LORD,
  before the Lord of all the earth.

6 The heavens proclaim his righteous-
    ness,
  and all the peoples see his glory.
7 All worshipers of images are put to
    shame,
  who make their boast in worthless
    idols;
  worship him, all you gods!

8 Zion hears and is glad,
  and the daughters of Judah rejoice,
  because of your judgments,
    O LORD.
9 For you, O LORD, are most high over
    all the earth;
  you are exalted far above all gods.

10 O you who love the LORD, hate evil!
  He preserves the lives of his saints;
  he delivers them from the hand of
    the wicked.

GETTING THE MESSAGE

Joy to the world! Psalm 98:4–9
inspired Isaac Watts to write his famous
Christmas hymn, "Joy to the World," in
1719. The song celebrates not only the
birth of Christ but how creation itself
rejoices at the return of her King, who
"comes to judge the earth . . . with
righteousness" (98:9).

---

11 Light is sown for the righteous,
  and joy for the upright in heart.
12 Rejoice in the LORD, O you righteous,
  and give thanks to his holy name!

Make a Joyful Noise to the LORD

98 A PSALM.
  Oh sing to the LORD a new song,
  for he has done marvelous things!
  His right hand and his holy arm
  have worked salvation for him.
2 The LORD has made known his salva-
    tion;
  he has revealed his righteousness
    in the sight of the nations.
3 He has remembered his steadfast love
    and faithfulness
  to the house of Israel.
  All the ends of the earth have seen
  the salvation of our God.

4 Make a joyful noise to the Lord, all
    the earth;
        break forth into joyous song and
        sing praises!
5 Sing praises to the Lord with the lyre,
        with the lyre and the sound of mel-
        ody!
6 With trumpets and the sound of the
        horn
        make a joyful noise before the King,
        the Lord!

7 Let the sea roar, and all that fills it;
        the world and those who dwell in it!
8 Let the rivers clap their hands;
        let the hills sing for joy together
9 before the Lord, for he comes
        to judge the earth.
    He will judge the world with righ-
        teousness,
        and the peoples with equity.

> ### GETTING THE MESSAGE
>
> **What is integrity?** When the Bible
> describes someone as having "integrity"
> (101:2), it means that the person is
> characterized by good moral behavior.
> The Bible might also describe this person
> as "blameless" in the sight of God.

The Lord Our God Is Holy

99
The Lord reigns; let the peoples
tremble!
    He sits enthroned upon the cheru-
        bim; let the earth quake!
2 The Lord is great in Zion;
        he is exalted over all the peoples.
3 Let them praise your great and awe-
        some name!
        Holy is he!

4 The King in his might loves justice.
        You have established equity;
    you have executed justice
        and righteousness in Jacob.
5 Exalt the Lord our God;
        worship at his footstool!
        Holy is he!

6 Moses and Aaron were among his
        priests,
        Samuel also was among those who
        called upon his name.

They called to the Lord, and he
        answered them.
7 In the pillar of the cloud he spoke to
        them;
        they kept his testimonies
        and the statute that he gave them.

8 O Lord our God, you answered them;
        you were a forgiving God to them,
        but an avenger of their wrongdoings.
9 Exalt the Lord our God,
        and worship at his holy mountain;
        for the Lord our God is holy!

His Steadfast Love Endures Forever

100
A Psalm for giving thanks.
Make a joyful noise to the
Lord, all the earth!
2   Serve the Lord with gladness!
        Come into his presence with singing!

3 Know that the Lord, he is God!
        It is he who made us, and we are his;
        we are his people, and the sheep of
        his pasture.

4 Enter his gates with thanksgiving,
        and his courts with praise!
        Give thanks to him; bless his name!

5 For the Lord is good;
        his steadfast love endures forever,
        and his faithfulness to all genera-
        tions.

I Will Walk with Integrity

101
A Psalm of David.
I will sing of steadfast love and
justice;
        to you, O Lord, I will make music.
2 I will ponder the way that is blameless.
        Oh when will you come to me?
    I will walk with integrity of heart
        within my house;
3 I will not set before my eyes
        anything that is worthless.
    I hate the work of those who fall away;
        it shall not cling to me.
4 A perverse heart shall be far from me;
        I will know nothing of evil.

5 Whoever slanders his neighbor secretly
        I will destroy.
    Whoever has a haughty look and an
        arrogant heart
        I will not endure.

6 I will look with favor on the faithful in
the land,
that they may dwell with me;
he who walks in the way that is
blameless
shall minister to me.

7 No one who practices deceit
shall dwell in my house;
no one who utters lies
shall continue before my eyes.

8 Morning by morning I will destroy
all the wicked in the land,
cutting off all the evildoers
from the city of the LORD.

Do Not Hide Your Face from Me

102 A PRAYER OF ONE AFFLICTED,
WHEN HE IS FAINT AND POURS
OUT HIS COMPLAINT BEFORE
THE LORD.

1 Hear my prayer, O LORD;
let my cry come to you!
2 Do not hide your face from me
in the day of my distress!
Incline your ear to me;
answer me speedily in the day
when I call!

3 For my days pass away like smoke,
and my bones burn like a furnace.
4 My heart is struck down like grass and
has withered;
I forget to eat my bread.
5 Because of my loud groaning
my bones cling to my flesh.
6 I am like a desert owl of the wilderness,
like an owl of the waste places;
7 I lie awake;
I am like a lonely sparrow on the
housetop.
8 All the day my enemies taunt me;
those who deride me use my name
for a curse.
9 For I eat ashes like bread
and mingle tears with my drink,
10 because of your indignation and anger;
for you have taken me up and
thrown me down.
11 My days are like an evening shadow;
I wither away like grass.

12 But you, O LORD, are enthroned forever;
you are remembered throughout all
generations.

13 You will arise and have pity on Zion;
it is the time to favor her;
the appointed time has come.
14 For your servants hold her stones dear
and have pity on her dust.
15 Nations will fear the name of the LORD,
and all the kings of the earth will
fear your glory.
16 For the LORD builds up Zion;
he appears in his glory;
17 he regards the prayer of the destitute
and does not despise their prayer.
18 Let this be recorded for a generation
to come,
so that a people yet to be created
may praise the LORD:
19 that he looked down from his holy
height;
from heaven the LORD looked at the
earth,

GETTING THE MESSAGE

Ashes were often used in the Old
Testament to express sorrow, humiliation,
or feelings of worthlessness. In Ps. 102:9,
they are a sign of mourning, as indicated
by their mention along with tears. The
prophet Jeremiah encouraged Israel to
"roll in ashes" to mourn the destruction
that would soon befall her (Jer. 6:26).

20 to hear the groans of the prisoners,
to set free those who were doomed
to die,
21 that they may declare in Zion the
name of the LORD,
and in Jerusalem his praise,
22 when peoples gather together,
and kingdoms, to worship the LORD.

23 He has broken my strength in mid-
course;
he has shortened my days.
24 "O my God," I say, "take me not away
in the midst of my days—
you whose years endure
throughout all generations!"

25 Of old you laid the foundation of the
earth,
and the heavens are the work of
your hands.

26 They will perish, but you will remain;
     they will all wear out like a gar-
        ment.
   You will change them like a robe, and
        they will pass away,
27 but you are the same, and your
        years have no end.
28 The children of your servants shall
        dwell secure;
     their offspring shall be established
        before you.

Bless the LORD, O My Soul

103 OF DAVID.
     Bless the LORD, O my soul,
   and all that is within me,
     bless his holy name!
2 Bless the LORD, O my soul,
     and forget not all his benefits,
3 who forgives all your iniquity,
     who heals all your diseases,
4 who redeems your life from the pit,
     who crowns you with steadfast love
        and mercy,
5 who satisfies you with good
     so that your youth is renewed like
        the eagle's.

6 The LORD works righteousness
     and justice for all who are
        oppressed.
7 He made known his ways to Moses,
     his acts to the people of Israel.
8 The LORD is merciful and gracious,
     slow to anger and abounding in
        steadfast love.
9 He will not always chide,
     nor will he keep his anger forever.
10 He does not deal with us according to
        our sins,
     nor repay us according to our iniq-
        uities.
11 For as high as the heavens are above
        the earth,
     so great is his steadfast love toward
        those who fear him;
12 as far as the east is from the west,
     so far does he remove our trans-
        gressions from us.
13 As a father shows compassion to his
        children,
     so the LORD shows compassion to
        those who fear him.
14 For he knows our frame;
     he remembers that we are dust.

15 As for man, his days are like grass;
     he flourishes like a flower of the
        field;
16 for the wind passes over it, and it is
        gone,
     and its place knows it no more.
17 But the steadfast love of the LORD is
        from everlasting to everlasting
        on those who fear him,
     and his righteousness to children's
        children,
18 to those who keep his covenant
     and remember to do his command-
        ments.
19 The LORD has established his throne
        in the heavens,
     and his kingdom rules over all.

20 Bless the LORD, O you his angels,
     you mighty ones who do his word,
        obeying the voice of his word!
21 Bless the LORD, all his hosts,
     his ministers, who do his will!
22 Bless the LORD, all his works,
     in all places of his dominion.
   Bless the LORD, O my soul!

O LORD My God, You Are Very Great

104 Bless the LORD, O my soul!
     O LORD my God, you are very
        great!
   You are clothed with splendor and
        majesty,
2 covering yourself with light as with
        a garment,
     stretching out the heavens like a tent.
3 He lays the beams of his chambers on
        the waters;
     he makes the clouds his chariot;
     he rides on the wings of the wind;
4 he makes his messengers winds,
     his ministers a flaming fire.

5 He set the earth on its foundations,
     so that it should never be moved.
6 You covered it with the deep as with a
        garment;
     the waters stood above the moun-
        tains.
7 At your rebuke they fled;
     at the sound of your thunder they
        took to flight.
8 The mountains rose, the valleys sank
        down
     to the place that you appointed for
        them.

9 You set a boundary that they may not
    pass,
  so that they might not again cover
    the earth.
10 You make springs gush forth in the
    valleys;
  they flow between the hills;
11 they give drink to every beast of the
    field;
  the wild donkeys quench their thirst.
12 Beside them the birds of the heavens
    dwell;
  they sing among the branches.
13 From your lofty abode you water the
    mountains;
  the earth is satisfied with the fruit
    of your work.
14 You cause the grass to grow for the
    livestock
  and plants for man to cultivate,
  that he may bring forth food from the
    earth
15 and wine to gladden the heart of
    man,
  oil to make his face shine
  and bread to strengthen man's heart.
16 The trees of the Lord are watered
    abundantly,
  the cedars of Lebanon that he
    planted.
17 In them the birds build their nests;
  the stork has her home in the fir
    trees.
18 The high mountains are for the wild
    goats;
  the rocks are a refuge for the rock
    badgers.
19 He made the moon to mark the sea-
    sons;
  the sun knows its time for setting.
20 You make darkness, and it is night,
  when all the beasts of the forest
    creep about.
21 The young lions roar for their prey,
  seeking their food from God.
22 When the sun rises, they steal away
  and lie down in their dens.
23 Man goes out to his work
  and to his labor until the evening.
24 O Lord, how manifold are your works!
  In wisdom have you made them all;
  the earth is full of your creatures.

25 Here is the sea, great and wide,
  which teems with creatures innu-
    merable,
  living things both small and great.
26 There go the ships,
  and Leviathan, which you formed
    to play in it.
27 These all look to you,
  to give them their food in due sea-
    son.
28 When you give it to them, they gather
    it up;
  when you open your hand, they are
    filled with good things.
29 When you hide your face, they are dis-
    mayed;
  when you take away their breath,
    they die
  and return to their dust.
30 When you send forth your Spirit, they
    are created,
  and you renew the face of the
    ground.
31 May the glory of the Lord endure
    forever;
  may the Lord rejoice in his works,
32 who looks on the earth and it trembles,
  who touches the mountains and
    they smoke!
33 I will sing to the Lord as long as I live;
  I will sing praise to my God while I
    have being.
34 May my meditation be pleasing to
    him,
  for I rejoice in the Lord.
35 Let sinners be consumed from the
    earth,
  and let the wicked be no more!
  Bless the Lord, O my soul!
  Praise the Lord!

Tell of All His Wonderful Works

105 Oh give thanks to the Lord;
  call upon his name;
  make known his deeds among the
    peoples!
2 Sing to him, sing praises to him;
  tell of all his wondrous works!
3 Glory in his holy name;
  let the hearts of those who seek the
    Lord rejoice!
4 Seek the Lord and his strength;
  seek his presence continually!

5 Remember the wondrous works that
    he has done,
    his miracles, and the judgments he
        uttered,
6 O offspring of Abraham, his servant,
    children of Jacob, his chosen ones!

7 He is the LORD our God;
    his judgments are in all the earth.
8 He remembers his covenant forever,
    the word that he commanded, for a
        thousand generations,
9 the covenant that he made with
        Abraham,
    his sworn promise to Isaac,
10 which he confirmed to Jacob as a
        statute,
    to Israel as an everlasting covenant,
11 saying, "To you I will give the land of
        Canaan
    as your portion for an inheritance."

GETTING THE MESSAGE

Psalms 105 and 106 **celebrate** God's faithfulness to his people. They recall his promises to Abraham, Isaac, and Jacob. Those who sing the psalms should see themselves as the beneficiaries of all the amazing things God has done in the past.

12 When they were few in number,
    of little account, and sojourners in it,
13 wandering from nation to nation,
    from one kingdom to another peo-
        ple,
14 he allowed no one to oppress them;
    he rebuked kings on their account,
15 saying, "Touch not my anointed ones,
    do my prophets no harm!"

16 When he summoned a famine on the
        land
    and broke all supply of bread,
17 he had sent a man ahead of them,
    Joseph, who was sold as a slave.
18 His feet were hurt with fetters;
    his neck was put in a collar of iron;
19 until what he had said came to pass,
    the word of the LORD tested him.
20 The king sent and released him;
    the ruler of the peoples set him free;
21 he made him lord of his house
    and ruler of all his possessions,

22 to bind his princes at his pleasure
    and to teach his elders wisdom.
23 Then Israel came to Egypt;
    Jacob sojourned in the land of Ham.
24 And the LORD made his people very
        fruitful
    and made them stronger than their
        foes.
25 He turned their hearts to hate his
        people,
    to deal craftily with his servants.

26 He sent Moses, his servant,
    and Aaron, whom he had chosen.
27 They performed his signs among
        them
    and miracles in the land of Ham.
28 He sent darkness, and made the land
        dark;
    they did not rebel against his words.
29 He turned their waters into blood
    and caused their fish to die.
30 Their land swarmed with frogs,
    even in the chambers of their kings.
31 He spoke, and there came swarms of
        flies,
    and gnats throughout their country.
32 He gave them hail for rain,
    and fiery lightning bolts through
        their land.
33 He struck down their vines and fig
        trees,
    and shattered the trees of their
        country.
34 He spoke, and the locusts came,
    young locusts without number,
35 which devoured all the vegetation in
        their land
    and ate up the fruit of their ground.
36 He struck down all the firstborn in
        their land,
    the firstfruits of all their strength.

37 Then he brought out Israel with silver
        and gold,
    and there was none among his
        tribes who stumbled.
38 Egypt was glad when they departed,
    for dread of them had fallen upon it.
39 He spread a cloud for a covering,
    and fire to give light by night.
40 They asked, and he brought quail,
    and gave them bread from heaven
        in abundance.

41 He opened the rock, and water gushed
　　out;
　　it flowed through the desert like a
　　river.
42 For he remembered his holy promise,
　　and Abraham, his servant.

43 So he brought his people out with joy,
　　his chosen ones with singing.
44 And he gave them the lands of the
　　nations,
　　and they took possession of the
　　fruit of the peoples' toil,
45 that they might keep his statutes
　　and observe his laws.
　　Praise the LORD!

Give Thanks to the LORD, for He Is Good

106 Praise the LORD!
　　Oh give thanks to the LORD,
　　for he is good,
　　for his steadfast love endures for-
　　ever!
2 Who can utter the mighty deeds of the
　　LORD,
　　or declare all his praise?
3 Blessed are they who observe justice,
　　who do righteousness at all times!

4 Remember me, O LORD, when you
　　show favor to your people;
　　help me when you save them,
5 that I may look upon the prosperity of
　　your chosen ones,
　　that I may rejoice in the gladness of
　　your nation,
　　that I may glory with your inheri-
　　tance.

6 Both we and our fathers have sinned;
　　we have committed iniquity; we
　　have done wickedness.
7 Our fathers, when they were in Egypt,
　　did not consider your wondrous
　　works;
　　they did not remember the abundance
　　of your steadfast love,
　　but rebelled by the sea, at the Red
　　Sea.
8 Yet he saved them for his name's sake,
　　that he might make known his
　　mighty power.
9 He rebuked the Red Sea, and it
　　became dry,
　　and he led them through the deep
　　as through a desert.

10 So he saved them from the hand of
　　the foe
　　and redeemed them from the power
　　of the enemy.
11 And the waters covered their adver-
　　saries;
　　not one of them was left.
12 Then they believed his words;
　　they sang his praise.

13 But they soon forgot his works;
　　they did not wait for his counsel.
14 But they had a wanton craving in the
　　wilderness,
　　and put God to the test in the desert;
15 he gave them what they asked,
　　but sent a wasting disease among
　　them.

16 When men in the camp were jealous
　　of Moses
　　and Aaron, the holy one of the LORD,

GETTING THE MESSAGE

Despite all the faithfulness and steadfast
love God showed to his people, as Psalm
105 recounts, they **murmured** (106:25),
displaying a lack of contentment and
trust in him. Such murmuring amounts
to disobeying a gracious God who leads
his people.

17 the earth opened and swallowed up
　　Dathan,
　　and covered the company of Abiram.
18 Fire also broke out in their company;
　　the flame burned up the wicked.

19 They made a calf in Horeb
　　and worshiped a metal image.
20 They exchanged the glory of God
　　for the image of an ox that eats grass.
21 They forgot God, their Savior,
　　who had done great things in Egypt,
22 wondrous works in the land of Ham,
　　and awesome deeds by the Red Sea.
23 Therefore he said he would destroy
　　them—
　　had not Moses, his chosen one,
　　stood in the breach before him,
　　to turn away his wrath from
　　destroying them.

24 Then they despised the pleasant land,
　　having no faith in his promise.

25 They murmured in their tents,
     and did not obey the voice of the
        LORD.
26 Therefore he raised his hand and
        swore to them
     that he would make them fall in the
        wilderness,
27 and would make their offspring fall
        among the nations,
     scattering them among the lands.

28 Then they yoked themselves to the
        Baal of Peor,
     and ate sacrifices offered to the dead;
29 they provoked the LORD to anger with
        their deeds,
     and a plague broke out among them.
30 Then Phinehas stood up and inter-
        vened,
     and the plague was stayed.

GETTING THE MESSAGE

What is God's **steadfast love** to his
people, for which Psalm 107 repeatedly
says they should thank him? It is the
enduring faithfulness, care, and kindness
that he has promised to them. Even
after their repeated disobedience, which
brought his discipline, they cried out to
him and he forgave them.

31 And that was counted to him as righ-
        teousness
     from generation to generation
        forever.
32 They angered him at the waters of
        Meribah,
     and it went ill with Moses on their
        account,
33 for they made his spirit bitter,
     and he spoke rashly with his lips.
34 They did not destroy the peoples,
     as the LORD commanded them,
35 but they mixed with the nations
     and learned to do as they did.
36 They served their idols,
     which became a snare to them.
37 They sacrificed their sons
     and their daughters to the demons;
38 they poured out innocent blood,
     the blood of their sons and daugh-
        ters,

whom they sacrificed to the idols of
        Canaan,
     and the land was polluted with
        blood.
39 Thus they became unclean by their
        acts,
     and played the whore in their
        deeds.
40 Then the anger of the LORD was kin-
        dled against his people,
     and he abhorred his heritage;
41 he gave them into the hand of the
        nations,
     so that those who hated them ruled
        over them.
42 Their enemies oppressed them,
     and they were brought into subjec-
        tion under their power.
43 Many times he delivered them,
     but they were rebellious in their
        purposes
     and were brought low through their
        iniquity.
44 Nevertheless, he looked upon their
        distress,
     when he heard their cry.
45 For their sake he remembered his cov-
        enant,
     and relented according to the abun-
        dance of his steadfast love.
46 He caused them to be pitied
     by all those who held them captive.
47 Save us, O LORD our God,
     and gather us from among the
        nations,
     that we may give thanks to your holy
        name
     and glory in your praise.
48 Blessed be the LORD, the God of Israel,
     from everlasting to everlasting!
     And let all the people say, "Amen!"
     Praise the LORD!

BOOK FIVE

Let the Redeemed of the LORD Say So

107
Oh give thanks to the LORD,
        for he is good,
     for his steadfast love endures for-
        ever!
2 Let the redeemed of the LORD say so,
     whom he has redeemed from trou-
        ble

3 and gathered in from the lands,
  from the east and from the west,
  from the north and from the
    south.

4 Some wandered in desert wastes,
  finding no way to a city to dwell
    in;
5 hungry and thirsty,
  their soul fainted within them.
6 Then they cried to the LORD in their
    trouble,
  and he delivered them from their
    distress.
7 He led them by a straight way
  till they reached a city to dwell in.
8 Let them thank the LORD for his
    steadfast love,
  for his wondrous works to the
    children of man!
9 For he satisfies the longing soul,
  and the hungry soul he fills with
    good things.

10 Some sat in darkness and in the
    shadow of death,
  prisoners in affliction and in
    irons,
11 for they had rebelled against the
    words of God,
  and spurned the counsel of the
    Most High.
12 So he bowed their hearts down with
    hard labor;
  they fell down, with none to help.
13 Then they cried to the LORD in their
    trouble,
  and he delivered them from their
    distress.
14 He brought them out of darkness and
    the shadow of death,
  and burst their bonds apart.
15 Let them thank the LORD for his stead-
    fast love,
  for his wondrous works to the chil-
    dren of man!
16 For he shatters the doors of bronze
  and cuts in two the bars of iron.
17 Some were fools through their sinful
    ways,
  and because of their iniquities
    suffered affliction;
18 they loathed any kind of food,
  and they drew near to the gates of
    death.

19 Then they cried to the LORD in their
    trouble,
  and he delivered them from their
    distress.
20 He sent out his word and healed them,
  and delivered them from their
    destruction.
21 Let them thank the LORD for his stead-
    fast love,
  for his wondrous works to the chil-
    dren of man!
22 And let them offer sacrifices of
    thanksgiving,
  and tell of his deeds in songs of joy!

23 Some went down to the sea in ships,
  doing business on the great waters;
24 they saw the deeds of the LORD,
  his wondrous works in the deep.
25 For he commanded and raised the
    stormy wind,
  which lifted up the waves of the sea.
26 They mounted up to heaven; they
    went down to the depths;
  their courage melted away in their
    evil plight;
27 they reeled and staggered like
    drunken men
  and were at their wits' end.
28 Then they cried to the LORD in their
    trouble,
  and he delivered them from their
    distress.
29 He made the storm be still,
  and the waves of the sea were
    hushed.
30 Then they were glad that the waters
    were quiet,
  and he brought them to their
    desired haven.
31 Let them thank the LORD for his stead-
    fast love,
  for his wondrous works to the chil-
    dren of man!
32 Let them extol him in the congrega-
    tion of the people,
  and praise him in the assembly of
    the elders.

33 He turns rivers into a desert,
  springs of water into thirsty ground,
34 a fruitful land into a salty waste,
  because of the evil of its inhabitants.
35 He turns a desert into pools of water,
  a parched land into springs of water.

36 And there he lets the hungry dwell,
    and they establish a city to live in;
37 they sow fields and plant vineyards
    and get a fruitful yield.
38 By his blessing they multiply greatly,
    and he does not let their livestock
    diminish.
39 When they are diminished and
    brought low
    through oppression, evil, and sor-
    row,
40 he pours contempt on princes
    and makes them wander in track-
    less wastes;
41 but he raises up the needy out of
    affliction
    and makes their families like flocks.
42 The upright see it and are glad,
    and all wickedness shuts its mouth.

GETTING THE MESSAGE

"Upon Edom I cast my shoe" (108:9). In ancient times, people would sometimes lay claim to a parcel of land by walking its boundaries and then offering the shoes they had worn as their title of ownership. Here, the Lord is claiming Edom as his own.

43 Whoever is wise, let him attend to
    these things;
    let them consider the steadfast love
    of the LORD.

With God We Shall Do Valiantly

108
A SONG. A PSALM OF DAVID.
My heart is steadfast, O God!
I will sing and make melody with
    all my being!
2 Awake, O harp and lyre!
    I will awake the dawn!
3 I will give thanks to you, O LORD,
    among the peoples;
    I will sing praises to you among the
    nations.
4 For your steadfast love is great above
    the heavens;
    your faithfulness reaches to the
    clouds.
5 Be exalted, O God, above the heavens!
    Let your glory be over all the earth!

6 That your beloved ones may be deliv-
    ered,
    give salvation by your right hand
    and answer me!
7 God has promised in his holiness:
    "With exultation I will divide up
    Shechem
    and portion out the Valley of
    Succoth.
8 Gilead is mine; Manasseh is mine;
    Ephraim is my helmet,
    Judah my scepter.
9 Moab is my washbasin;
    upon Edom I cast my shoe;
    over Philistia I shout in triumph."
10 Who will bring me to the fortified city?
    Who will lead me to Edom?
11 Have you not rejected us, O God?
    You do not go out, O God, with our
    armies.
12 Oh grant us help against the foe,
    for vain is the salvation of man!
13 With God we shall do valiantly;
    it is he who will tread down our foes.

Help Me, O LORD My God

109
TO THE CHOIRMASTER. A PSALM
OF DAVID.
1 Be not silent, O God of my praise!
2 For wicked and deceitful mouths are
    opened against me,
    speaking against me with lying
    tongues.
3 They encircle me with words of hate,
    and attack me without cause.
4 In return for my love they accuse me,
    but I give myself to prayer.
5 So they reward me evil for good,
    and hatred for my love.

6 Appoint a wicked man against him;
    let an accuser stand at his right
    hand.
7 When he is tried, let him come forth
    guilty;
    let his prayer be counted as sin!
8 May his days be few;
    may another take his office!
9 May his children be fatherless
    and his wife a widow!
10 May his children wander about and
    beg,
    seeking food far from the ruins they
    inhabit!

11 May the creditor seize all that he has;
    may strangers plunder the fruits of
        his toil!
12 Let there be none to extend kindness
        to him,
    nor any to pity his fatherless chil-
        dren!
13 May his posterity be cut off;
    may his name be blotted out in the
        second generation!
14 May the iniquity of his fathers be
        remembered before the LORD,
    and let not the sin of his mother be
        blotted out!
15 Let them be before the LORD continu-
        ally,
    that he may cut off the memory of
        them from the earth!
16 For he did not remember to show
        kindness,
    but pursued the poor and needy
    and the brokenhearted, to put them
        to death.
17 He loved to curse; let curses come
        upon him!
    He did not delight in blessing; may
        it be far from him!
18 He clothed himself with cursing as
        his coat;
    may it soak into his body like water,
        like oil into his bones!
19 May it be like a garment that he wraps
        around him,
    like a belt that he puts on every day!
20 May this be the reward of my accusers
        from the LORD,
    of those who speak evil against my
        life!
21 But you, O GOD my Lord,
    deal on my behalf for your name's
        sake;
    because your steadfast love is good,
        deliver me!
22 For I am poor and needy,
    and my heart is stricken within me.
23 I am gone like a shadow at evening;
    I am shaken off like a locust.
24 My knees are weak through fasting;
    my body has become gaunt, with no
        fat.
25 I am an object of scorn to my accusers;
    when they see me, they wag their
        heads.

26 Help me, O LORD my God!
    Save me according to your steadfast
        love!
27 Let them know that this is your hand;
    you, O LORD, have done it!
28 Let them curse, but you will bless!
    They arise and are put to shame,
        but your servant will be glad!
29 May my accusers be clothed with
        dishonor;
    may they be wrapped in their own
        shame as in a cloak!
30 With my mouth I will give great
        thanks to the LORD;
    I will praise him in the midst of the
        throng.
31 For he stands at the right hand of the
        needy one,
    to save him from those who con-
        demn his soul to death.

> **GETTING THE MESSAGE**
>
> **The right hand** is often a symbol of
> authority and power. Kings wore their
> signet rings on their right hand (Jer.
> 22:24), and a father blessed his oldest
> son with his right hand (Gen. 48:14, 17).
> In Psalm 110, the right hand describes a
> place of honor and distinction. The Bible
> often refers to God's right hand in his
> acts of blessing and deliverance (Ex. 15:6;
> Ps. 16:11).

Sit at My Right Hand

110 A PSALM OF DAVID.
    The LORD says to my Lord:
    "Sit at my right hand,
until I make your enemies your foot-
        stool."

2 The LORD sends forth from Zion
    your mighty scepter.
    Rule in the midst of your enemies!
3 Your people will offer themselves freely
    on the day of your power,
    in holy garments;
from the womb of the morning,
    the dew of your youth will be yours.
4 The LORD has sworn
    and will not change his mind,
"You are a priest forever
    after the order of Melchizedek."

5 The Lord is at your right hand;
  he will shatter kings on the day of
    his wrath.
6 He will execute judgment among the
    nations,
  filling them with corpses;
  he will shatter chiefs
    over the wide earth.
7 He will drink from the brook by the
    way;
  therefore he will lift up his head.

Great Are the Lord's Works

111 Praise the Lord!
  I will give thanks to the Lord with
    my whole heart,
  in the company of the upright, in
    the congregation.
2 Great are the works of the Lord,
  studied by all who delight in them.
3 Full of splendor and majesty is his
    work,

> ## GETTING THE MESSAGE
>
> **Two acrostic poems.** Because of
> their similar themes, Psalms 111 and 112
> can be seen as companion psalms. Both
> are also acrostic poems. In the acrostics
> of the Old Testament, each line or verse
> begins with successive letters of the
> Hebrew alphabet.

  and his righteousness endures
    forever.
4 He has caused his wondrous works to
    be remembered;
  the Lord is gracious and merciful.
5 He provides food for those who fear
    him;
  he remembers his covenant for-
    ever.
6 He has shown his people the power
    of his works,
  in giving them the inheritance of
    the nations.
7 The works of his hands are faithful
    and just;
  all his precepts are trustworthy;
8 they are established forever and
    ever,
  to be performed with faithfulness
    and uprightness.

9 He sent redemption to his people;
  he has commanded his covenant
    forever.
  Holy and awesome is his name!
10 The fear of the Lord is the beginning
    of wisdom;
  all those who practice it have a good
    understanding.
  His praise endures forever!

The Righteous Will Never Be Moved

112 Praise the Lord!
  Blessed is the man who fears the
    Lord,
  who greatly delights in his com-
    mandments!
2 His offspring will be mighty in the
    land;
  the generation of the upright will be
    blessed.
3 Wealth and riches are in his house,
  and his righteousness endures
    forever.
4 Light dawns in the darkness for the
    upright;
  he is gracious, merciful, and righ-
    teous.
5 It is well with the man who deals
    generously and lends;
  who conducts his affairs with justice.
6 For the righteous will never be moved;
  he will be remembered forever.
7 He is not afraid of bad news;
  his heart is firm, trusting in the
    Lord.
8 His heart is steady; he will not be
    afraid,
  until he looks in triumph on his
    adversaries.
9 He has distributed freely; he has given
    to the poor;
  his righteousness endures forever;
  his horn is exalted in honor.
10 The wicked man sees it and is angry;
  he gnashes his teeth and melts
    away;
  the desire of the wicked will perish!

Who Is like the Lord Our God?

113 Praise the Lord!
  Praise, O servants of the Lord,
  praise the name of the Lord!

2 Blessed be the name of the Lord
  from this time forth and forever-
    more!

3 From the rising of the sun to its setting,
  the name of the LORD is to be
    praised!

4 The LORD is high above all nations,
  and his glory above the heavens!
5 Who is like the LORD our God,
  who is seated on high,
6 who looks far down
  on the heavens and the earth?
7 He raises the poor from the dust
  and lifts the needy from the ash
    heap,
8 to make them sit with princes,
  with the princes of his people.
9 He gives the barren woman a home,
  making her the joyous mother of
    children.
  Praise the LORD!

Tremble at the Presence of the Lord

114 When Israel went out from
  Egypt,
  the house of Jacob from a people of
    strange language,
2 Judah became his sanctuary,
  Israel his dominion.

3 The sea looked and fled;
  Jordan turned back.
4 The mountains skipped like rams,
  the hills like lambs.

5 What ails you, O sea, that you flee?
  O Jordan, that you turn back?
6 O mountains, that you skip like rams?
  O hills, like lambs?

7 Tremble, O earth, at the presence of
    the Lord,
  at the presence of the God of Jacob,
8 who turns the rock into a pool of
    water,
  the flint into a spring of water.

To Your Name Give Glory

115 Not to us, O LORD, not to us, but
  to your name give glory,
  for the sake of your steadfast love
    and your faithfulness!

2 Why should the nations say,
  "Where is their God?"
3 Our God is in the heavens;
  he does all that he pleases.

4 Their idols are silver and gold,
  the work of human hands.

5 They have mouths, but do not speak;
  eyes, but do not see.
6 They have ears, but do not hear;
  noses, but do not smell.
7 They have hands, but do not feel;
  feet, but do not walk;
  and they do not make a sound in
    their throat.
8 Those who make them become like
    them;
  so do all who trust in them.

9 O Israel, trust in the LORD!
  He is their help and their shield.
10 O house of Aaron, trust in the LORD!
  He is their help and their shield.
11 You who fear the LORD, trust in the
    LORD!
  He is their help and their shield.

GETTING THE MESSAGE

Flint is a very hard variety of quartz that was plentiful in the land of the Bible. It could be broken into sharp pieces and used to make tools and weapons. Knives, arrowheads, sickle blades, and saws were all made from flint. The Bible often uses flint as a picture of strength and determination (Isa. 50:7; Ezek. 3:9). In Psalm 114, it provides a picture of God's power over what he has created.

12 The LORD has remembered us; he will
    bless us;
  he will bless the house of Israel;
  he will bless the house of Aaron;
13 he will bless those who fear the LORD,
  both the small and the great.

14 May the LORD give you increase,
  you and your children!
15 May you be blessed by the LORD,
  who made heaven and earth!

16 The heavens are the LORD's heavens,
  but the earth he has given to the
    children of man.
17 The dead do not praise the LORD,
  nor do any who go down into silence.
18 But we will bless the LORD
  from this time forth and forever-
    more.
  Praise the LORD!

I Love the Lord

116 I love the Lord, because he has heard
my voice and my pleas for mercy.
2 Because he inclined his ear to me,
therefore I will call on him as long
as I live.
3 The snares of death encompassed me;
the pangs of Sheol laid hold on me;
I suffered distress and anguish.
4 Then I called on the name of the
Lord:
"O Lord, I pray, deliver my soul!"

5 Gracious is the Lord, and righteous;
our God is merciful.
6 The Lord preserves the simple;
when I was brought low, he saved
me.

> ### GETTING THE MESSAGE
>
> **Idols** (115:4) represent anything allowed
> to compete with God for ultimate loyalty,
> robbing him of the devotion and glory
> he alone deserves. Idolatry is evil and
> foolish. God deserves our wholehearted
> love because nothing else compares
> with him.

7 Return, O my soul, to your rest;
for the Lord has dealt bountifully
with you.

8 For you have delivered my soul from
death,
my eyes from tears,
my feet from stumbling;
9 I will walk before the Lord
in the land of the living.
10 I believed, even when I spoke:
"I am greatly afflicted";
11 I said in my alarm,
"All mankind are liars."

12 What shall I render to the Lord
for all his benefits to me?
13 I will lift up the cup of salvation
and call on the name of the Lord,
14 I will pay my vows to the Lord
in the presence of all his people.
15 Precious in the sight of the Lord
is the death of his saints.

16 O Lord, I am your servant;
I am your servant, the son of your
maidservant.
You have loosed my bonds.
17 I will offer to you the sacrifice of
thanksgiving
and call on the name of the Lord.
18 I will pay my vows to the Lord
in the presence of all his people,
19 in the courts of the house of the
Lord,
in your midst, O Jerusalem.
Praise the Lord!

The Lord's Faithfulness Endures Forever

117 Praise the Lord, all nations!
Extol him, all peoples!
2 For great is his steadfast love toward us,
and the faithfulness of the Lord
endures forever.
Praise the Lord!

His Steadfast Love Endures Forever

118 Oh give thanks to the Lord, for
he is good;
for his steadfast love endures forever!

2 Let Israel say,
"His steadfast love endures forever."
3 Let the house of Aaron say,
"His steadfast love endures forever."
4 Let those who fear the Lord say,
"His steadfast love endures forever."

5 Out of my distress I called on the Lord;
the Lord answered me and set me
free.
6 The Lord is on my side; I will not fear.
What can man do to me?
7 The Lord is on my side as my helper;
I shall look in triumph on those
who hate me.

8 It is better to take refuge in the Lord
than to trust in man.
9 It is better to take refuge in the Lord
than to trust in princes.

10 All nations surrounded me;
in the name of the Lord I cut them
off!
11 They surrounded me, surrounded me
on every side;
in the name of the Lord I cut them
off!

12 They surrounded me like bees;
    they went out like a fire among
        thorns;
    in the name of the LORD I cut them
        off!
13 I was pushed hard, so that I was falling,
    but the LORD helped me.
14 The LORD is my strength and my song;
    he has become my salvation.
15 Glad songs of salvation
    are in the tents of the righteous:
    "The right hand of the LORD does val-
        iantly,
16 the right hand of the LORD exalts,
    the right hand of the LORD does
        valiantly!"
17 I shall not die, but I shall live,
    and recount the deeds of the LORD.
18 The LORD has disciplined me severely,
    but he has not given me over to
        death.
19 Open to me the gates of righteousness,
    that I may enter through them
    and give thanks to the LORD.
20 This is the gate of the LORD;
    the righteous shall enter through it.
21 I thank you that you have answered me
    and have become my salvation.
22 The stone that the builders rejected
    has become the cornerstone.
23 This is the LORD's doing;
    it is marvelous in our eyes.
24 This is the day that the LORD has made;
    let us rejoice and be glad in it.
25 Save us, we pray, O LORD!
    O LORD, we pray, give us success!
26 Blessed is he who comes in the name
    of the LORD!
    We bless you from the house of the
        LORD.
27 The LORD is God,
    and he has made his light to shine
        upon us.
    Bind the festal sacrifice with cords,
    up to the horns of the altar!
28 You are my God, and I will give thanks
    to you;
    you are my God; I will extol you.
29 Oh give thanks to the LORD, for he is
    good;
    for his steadfast love endures for-
        ever!

Your Word Is a Lamp to My Feet

ALEPH

119 Blessed are those whose way is
    blameless,
    who walk in the law of the LORD!
2 Blessed are those who keep his testi-
    monies,
    who seek him with their whole heart,
3 who also do no wrong,
    but walk in his ways!
4 You have commanded your precepts
    to be kept diligently.
5 Oh that my ways may be steadfast
    in keeping your statutes!
6 Then I shall not be put to shame,
    having my eyes fixed on all your
        commandments.
7 I will praise you with an upright heart,
    when I learn your righteous rules.
8 I will keep your statutes;
    do not utterly forsake me!

GETTING THE MESSAGE

The **cornerstone** (118:22) is the large shaped stone at the corner of the building's foundation. It is essential to a structure's stability. Several New Testament writers compared Jesus Christ to a cornerstone (e.g., Matt. 21:42; Eph. 2:20; 1 Pet. 2:4–8).

BETH

9 How can a young man keep his way
    pure?
    By guarding it according to your
        word.
10 With my whole heart I seek you;
    let me not wander from your com-
        mandments!
11 I have stored up your word in my heart,
    that I might not sin against you.
12 Blessed are you, O LORD;
    teach me your statutes!
13 With my lips I declare
    all the rules of your mouth.
14 In the way of your testimonies I delight
    as much as in all riches.
15 I will meditate on your precepts
    and fix my eyes on your ways.
16 I will delight in your statutes;
    I will not forget your word.

GIMEL

17 Deal bountifully with your servant,
  that I may live and keep your word.
18 Open my eyes, that I may behold
  wondrous things out of your law.
19 I am a sojourner on the earth;
  hide not your commandments from
  me!
20 My soul is consumed with longing
  for your rules at all times.
21 You rebuke the insolent, accursed ones,
  who wander from your commandments.
22 Take away from me scorn and contempt,
  for I have kept your testimonies.
23 Even though princes sit plotting
  against me,
  your servant will meditate on your
  statutes.
24 Your testimonies are my delight;
  they are my counselors.

> **GETTING THE MESSAGE**

Aside from being **the longest psalm**, Psalm 119 is also the longest and most carefully structured chapter in the Bible. The psalm is an acrostic poem of 22 stanzas, following the 22 letters of the Hebrew alphabet. Within each stanza, each verse begins with the same Hebrew letter.

DALETH

25 My soul clings to the dust;
  give me life according to your
  word!
26 When I told of my ways, you
  answered me;
  teach me your statutes!
27 Make me understand the way of your
  precepts,
  and I will meditate on your wondrous works.
28 My soul melts away for sorrow;
  strengthen me according to your
  word!
29 Put false ways far from me
  and graciously teach me your law!
30 I have chosen the way of faithfulness;
  I set your rules before me.

31 I cling to your testimonies, O LORD;
  let me not be put to shame!
32 I will run in the way of your commandments
  when you enlarge my heart!

HE

33 Teach me, O LORD, the way of your
  statutes;
  and I will keep it to the end.
34 Give me understanding, that I may
  keep your law
  and observe it with my whole heart.
35 Lead me in the path of your commandments,
  for I delight in it.
36 Incline my heart to your testimonies,
  and not to selfish gain!
37 Turn my eyes from looking at worthless things;
  and give me life in your ways.
38 Confirm to your servant your promise,
  that you may be feared.
39 Turn away the reproach that I dread,
  for your rules are good.
40 Behold, I long for your precepts;
  in your righteousness give me life!

WAW

41 Let your steadfast love come to me,
  O LORD,
  your salvation according to your
  promise;
42 then shall I have an answer for him
  who taunts me,
  for I trust in your word.
43 And take not the word of truth utterly
  out of my mouth,
  for my hope is in your rules.
44 I will keep your law continually,
  forever and ever,
45 and I shall walk in a wide place,
  for I have sought your precepts.
46 I will also speak of your testimonies
  before kings
  and shall not be put to shame,
47 for I find my delight in your commandments,
  which I love.
48 I will lift up my hands toward your
  commandments, which I love,
  and I will meditate on your statutes.

ZAYIN

49 Remember your word to your servant,
  in which you have made me hope.

50 This is my comfort in my affliction,
  that your promise gives me life.
51 The insolent utterly deride me,
  but I do not turn away from your law.
52 When I think of your rules from of old,
  I take comfort, O Lord.
53 Hot indignation seizes me because of
  the wicked,
  who forsake your law.
54 Your statutes have been my songs
  in the house of my sojourning.
55 I remember your name in the night,
  O Lord,
  and keep your law.
56 This blessing has fallen to me,
  that I have kept your precepts.

Heth

57 The Lord is my portion;
  I promise to keep your words.
58 I entreat your favor with all my heart;
  be gracious to me according to your
  promise.
59 When I think on my ways,
  I turn my feet to your testimonies;
60 I hasten and do not delay
  to keep your commandments.
61 Though the cords of the wicked
  ensnare me,
  I do not forget your law.
62 At midnight I rise to praise you,
  because of your righteous rules.
63 I am a companion of all who fear you,
  of those who keep your precepts.
64 The earth, O Lord, is full of your
  steadfast love;
  teach me your statutes!

Teth

65 You have dealt well with your servant,
  O Lord, according to your word.
66 Teach me good judgment and knowledge,
  for I believe in your commandments.
67 Before I was afflicted I went astray,
  but now I keep your word.
68 You are good and do good;
  teach me your statutes.
69 The insolent smear me with lies,
  but with my whole heart I keep your
  precepts;
70 their heart is unfeeling like fat,
  but I delight in your law.
71 It is good for me that I was afflicted,
  that I might learn your statutes.

72 The law of your mouth is better to me
  than thousands of gold and silver
  pieces.

Yodh

73 Your hands have made and fashioned
  me;
  give me understanding that I may
  learn your commandments.
74 Those who fear you shall see me and
  rejoice,
  because I have hoped in your word.
75 I know, O Lord, that your rules are
  righteous,
  and that in faithfulness you have
  afflicted me.
76 Let your steadfast love comfort me
  according to your promise to your
  servant.
77 Let your mercy come to me, that I may
  live;
  for your law is my delight.
78 Let the insolent be put to shame,
  because they have wronged me with
  falsehood;
  as for me, I will meditate on your
  precepts.
79 Let those who fear you turn to me,
  that they may know your testimonies.
80 May my heart be blameless in your
  statutes,
  that I may not be put to shame!

Kaph

81 My soul longs for your salvation;
  I hope in your word.
82 My eyes long for your promise;
  I ask, "When will you comfort me?"
83 For I have become like a wineskin in
  the smoke,
  yet I have not forgotten your statutes.
84 How long must your servant endure?
  When will you judge those who persecute me?
85 The insolent have dug pitfalls for me;
  they do not live according to your
  law.
86 All your commandments are sure;
  they persecute me with falsehood;
  help me!
87 They have almost made an end of me
  on earth,
  but I have not forsaken your precepts.

88 In your steadfast love give me life,
    that I may keep the testimonies of
        your mouth.

LAMEDH

89 Forever, O LORD, your word
    is firmly fixed in the heavens.
90 Your faithfulness endures to all gener-
        ations;
    you have established the earth, and
        it stands fast.
91 By your appointment they stand this
        day,
    for all things are your servants.
92 If your law had not been my delight,
    I would have perished in my afflic-
        tion.
93 I will never forget your precepts,
    for by them you have given me life.
94 I am yours; save me,
    for I have sought your precepts.
95 The wicked lie in wait to destroy me,
    but I consider your testimonies.
96 I have seen a limit to all perfection,
    but your commandment is exceed-
        ingly broad.

MEM

97 Oh how I love your law!
    It is my meditation all the day.
98 Your commandment makes me wiser
        than my enemies,
    for it is ever with me.
99 I have more understanding than all
        my teachers,
    for your testimonies are my medita-
        tion.
100 I understand more than the aged,
    for I keep your precepts.
101 I hold back my feet from every evil
        way,
    in order to keep your word.
102 I do not turn aside from your rules,
    for you have taught me.
103 How sweet are your words to my taste,
    sweeter than honey to my mouth!
104 Through your precepts I get under-
        standing;
    therefore I hate every false way.

NUN

105 Your word is a lamp to my feet
    and a light to my path.
106 I have sworn an oath and confirmed it,
    to keep your righteous rules.

107 I am severely afflicted;
    give me life, O LORD, according to
        your word!
108 Accept my freewill offerings of praise,
        O LORD,
    and teach me your rules.
109 I hold my life in my hand continually,
    but I do not forget your law.
110 The wicked have laid a snare for me,
    but I do not stray from your precepts.
111 Your testimonies are my heritage
        forever,
    for they are the joy of my heart.
112 I incline my heart to perform your
        statutes
    forever, to the end.

SAMEKH

113 I hate the double-minded,
    but I love your law.
114 You are my hiding place and my shield;
    I hope in your word.
115 Depart from me, you evildoers,
    that I may keep the commandments
        of my God.
116 Uphold me according to your prom-
        ise, that I may live,
    and let me not be put to shame in
        my hope!
117 Hold me up, that I may be safe
    and have regard for your statutes
        continually!
118 You spurn all who go astray from your
        statutes,
    for their cunning is in vain.
119 All the wicked of the earth you discard
        like dross,
    therefore I love your testimonies.
120 My flesh trembles for fear of you,
    and I am afraid of your judgments.

AYIN

121 I have done what is just and right;
    do not leave me to my oppressors.
122 Give your servant a pledge of good;
    let not the insolent oppress me.
123 My eyes long for your salvation
    and for the fulfillment of your righ-
        teous promise.
124 Deal with your servant according to
        your steadfast love,
    and teach me your statutes.
125 I am your servant; give me under-
        standing,
    that I may know your testimonies!

126 It is time for the LORD to act,
    for your law has been broken.
127 Therefore I love your commandments
    above gold, above fine gold.
128 Therefore I consider all your precepts
    to be right;
    I hate every false way.

PE

129 Your testimonies are wonderful;
    therefore my soul keeps them.
130 The unfolding of your words gives
    light;
    it imparts understanding to the
    simple.
131 I open my mouth and pant,
    because I long for your command-
    ments.
132 Turn to me and be gracious to me,
    as is your way with those who love
    your name.
133 Keep steady my steps according to
    your promise,
    and let no iniquity get dominion
    over me.
134 Redeem me from man's oppression,
    that I may keep your precepts.
135 Make your face shine upon your ser-
    vant,
    and teach me your statutes.
136 My eyes shed streams of tears,
    because people do not keep your
    law.

TSADHE

137 Righteous are you, O LORD,
    and right are your rules.
138 You have appointed your testimonies
    in righteousness
    and in all faithfulness.
139 My zeal consumes me,
    because my foes forget your words.
140 Your promise is well tried,
    and your servant loves it.
141 I am small and despised,
    yet I do not forget your precepts.
142 Your righteousness is righteous forever,
    and your law is true.
143 Trouble and anguish have found me
    out,
    but your commandments are my
    delight.
144 Your testimonies are righteous forever;
    give me understanding that I may
    live.

QOPH

145 With my whole heart I cry; answer
    me, O LORD!
    I will keep your statutes.
146 I call to you; save me,
    that I may observe your testimonies.
147 I rise before dawn and cry for help;
    I hope in your words.
148 My eyes are awake before the watches
    of the night,
    that I may meditate on your promise.
149 Hear my voice according to your
    steadfast love;
    O LORD, according to your justice
    give me life.
150 They draw near who persecute me
    with evil purpose;
    they are far from your law.
151 But you are near, O LORD,
    and all your commandments are
    true.

GETTING THE MESSAGE

Unique verses. Out of the 176 verses
in Psalm 119, only seven lack an explicit
mention of God's Word: vv. 84, 90–91,
120, 122, 132, and 149.

152 Long have I known from your testi-
    monies
    that you have founded them forever.

RESH

153 Look on my affliction and deliver me,
    for I do not forget your law.
154 Plead my cause and redeem me;
    give me life according to your
    promise!
155 Salvation is far from the wicked,
    for they do not seek your statutes.
156 Great is your mercy, O LORD;
    give me life according to your rules.
157 Many are my persecutors and my
    adversaries,
    but I do not swerve from your testi-
    monies.
158 I look at the faithless with disgust,
    because they do not keep your com-
    mands.
159 Consider how I love your precepts!
    Give me life according to your
    steadfast love.

160 The sum of your word is truth,
    and every one of your righteous
        rules endures forever.

SIN AND SHIN

161 Princes persecute me without cause,
    but my heart stands in awe of
        your words.
162 I rejoice at your word
    like one who finds great spoil.
163 I hate and abhor falsehood,
    but I love your law.
164 Seven times a day I praise you
    for your righteous rules.
165 Great peace have those who love
        your law;
    nothing can make them stumble.
166 I hope for your salvation, O LORD,
    and I do your commandments.
167 My soul keeps your testimonies;
    I love them exceedingly.

GETTING THE MESSAGE

The wood of the **broom tree** makes excellent **charcoal** (120:4). Charcoal was an ideal source of fuel in Bible times because it was lightweight and created a hot fire that retained its heat for a long time.

168 I keep your precepts and testimo-
        nies,
    for all my ways are before you.

TAW

169 Let my cry come before you, O LORD;
    give me understanding according
        to your word!
170 Let my plea come before you;
    deliver me according to your
        word.
171 My lips will pour forth praise,
    for you teach me your statutes.
172 My tongue will sing of your word,
    for all your commandments are
        right.
173 Let your hand be ready to help me,
    for I have chosen your precepts.
174 I long for your salvation, O LORD,
    and your law is my delight.
175 Let my soul live and praise you,
    and let your rules help me.

176 I have gone astray like a lost sheep;
    seek your servant,
    for I do not forget your command-
        ments.

Deliver Me, O LORD

120 A SONG OF ASCENTS.
In my distress I called to the
    LORD,
and he answered me.
2 Deliver me, O LORD,
    from lying lips,
    from a deceitful tongue.

3 What shall be given to you,
    and what more shall be done to you,
    you deceitful tongue?
4 A warrior's sharp arrows,
    with glowing coals of the broom tree!

5 Woe to me, that I sojourn in Meshech,
    that I dwell among the tents of
        Kedar!
6 Too long have I had my dwelling
    among those who hate peace.
7 I am for peace,
    but when I speak, they are for war!

My Help Comes from the LORD

121 A SONG OF ASCENTS.
I lift up my eyes to the hills.
From where does my help come?
2 My help comes from the LORD,
    who made heaven and earth.

3 He will not let your foot be moved;
    he who keeps you will not slumber.
4 Behold, he who keeps Israel
    will neither slumber nor sleep.

5 The LORD is your keeper;
    the LORD is your shade on your
        right hand.
6 The sun shall not strike you by day,
    nor the moon by night.

7 The LORD will keep you from all evil;
    he will keep your life.
8 The LORD will keep
    your going out and your coming in
    from this time forth and forever-
        more.

Let Us Go to the House of the LORD

122 A SONG OF ASCENTS. OF DAVID.
I was glad when they said to
    me,
"Let us go to the house of the LORD!"

2 Our feet have been standing
   within your gates, O Jerusalem!

3 Jerusalem—built as a city
   that is bound firmly together,
4 to which the tribes go up,
   the tribes of the LORD,
   as was decreed for Israel,
     to give thanks to the name of the
     LORD.
5 There thrones for judgment were set,
   the thrones of the house of David.

6 Pray for the peace of Jerusalem!
   "May they be secure who love you!
7 Peace be within your walls
   and security within your towers!"
8 For my brothers and companions'
     sake
   I will say, "Peace be within you!"
9 For the sake of the house of the LORD
     our God,
   I will seek your good.

Our Eyes Look to the LORD Our God

123 A SONG OF ASCENTS.
   To you I lift up my eyes,
   O you who are enthroned in the
     heavens!
2 Behold, as the eyes of servants
   look to the hand of their master,
   as the eyes of a maidservant
   to the hand of her mistress,
   so our eyes look to the LORD our God,
   till he has mercy upon us.

3 Have mercy upon us, O LORD, have
     mercy upon us,
   for we have had more than enough
     of contempt.
4 Our soul has had more than enough
   of the scorn of those who are at
     ease,
   of the contempt of the proud.

Our Help Is in the Name of the LORD

124 A SONG OF ASCENTS. OF DAVID.
   If it had not been the LORD
   who was on our side—
   let Israel now say—
2 if it had not been the LORD who was
     on our side
   when people rose up against us,
3 then they would have swallowed us
     up alive,
   when their anger was kindled
     against us;

4 then the flood would have swept us
     away,
   the torrent would have gone over
     us;
5 then over us would have gone
   the raging waters.

6 Blessed be the LORD,
   who has not given us
   as prey to their teeth!
7 We have escaped like a bird
   from the snare of the fowlers;
   the snare is broken,
   and we have escaped!
8 Our help is in the name of the LORD,
   who made heaven and earth.

The LORD Surrounds His People

125 A SONG OF ASCENTS.
   Those who trust in the LORD
   are like Mount Zion,
   which cannot be moved, but abides
     forever.

GETTING THE MESSAGE

Psalm 122 is one of the 15 **Songs of Ascents**, which were sung by worshipers who were on their way up to the temple. It reflects the joy of seeing God's chosen city, Jerusalem, and being in the house of God to worship. The Songs of Ascents include Psalms 120–134.

---

2 As the mountains surround
     Jerusalem,
   so the LORD surrounds his people,
   from this time forth and forever-
     more.
3 For the scepter of wickedness shall
     not rest
   on the land allotted to the righ-
     teous,
   lest the righteous stretch out
   their hands to do wrong.
4 Do good, O LORD, to those who are
     good,
   and to those who are upright in
     their hearts!
5 But those who turn aside to their
     crooked ways
   the LORD will lead away with evil-
     doers!
   Peace be upon Israel!

Restore Our Fortunes, O Lord

126 A Song of Ascents.
When the Lord restored the fortunes of Zion,
we were like those who dream.
2 Then our mouth was filled with laughter,
and our tongue with shouts of joy;
then they said among the nations,
"The Lord has done great things for them."
3 The Lord has done great things for us;
we are glad.

4 Restore our fortunes, O Lord,
like streams in the Negeb!
5 Those who sow in tears
shall reap with shouts of joy!
6 He who goes out weeping,
bearing the seed for sowing,
shall come home with shouts of joy,
bringing his sheaves with him.

GETTING THE MESSAGE

What are fowlers? A "fowler" is someone who traps birds. In the Scriptures, it is used figuratively to describe active enemies of God's people. The psalmist describes God as delivering his people from the fowler's snare (91:3; 124:7).

Unless the Lord Builds the House

127 A Song of Ascents. Of Solomon.
Unless the Lord builds the house,
those who build it labor in vain.
Unless the Lord watches over the city,
the watchman stays awake in vain.
2 It is in vain that you rise up early
and go late to rest,
eating the bread of anxious toil;
for he gives to his beloved sleep.

3 Behold, children are a heritage from the Lord,
the fruit of the womb a reward.
4 Like arrows in the hand of a warrior
are the children of one's youth.
5 Blessed is the man
who fills his quiver with them!

He shall not be put to shame
when he speaks with his enemies
in the gate.

Blessed Is Everyone Who Fears the Lord

128 A Song of Ascents.
Blessed is everyone who fears the Lord,
who walks in his ways!
2 You shall eat the fruit of the labor of your hands;
you shall be blessed, and it shall be well with you.

3 Your wife will be like a fruitful vine within your house;
your children will be like olive shoots around your table.
4 Behold, thus shall the man be blessed who fears the Lord.

5 The Lord bless you from Zion!
May you see the prosperity of Jerusalem
all the days of your life!
6 May you see your children's children!
Peace be upon Israel!

They Have Afflicted Me from My Youth

129 A Song of Ascents.
"Greatly have they afflicted me from my youth"—
let Israel now say—
2 "Greatly have they afflicted me from my youth,
yet they have not prevailed against me.
3 The plowers plowed upon my back;
they made long their furrows."
4 The Lord is righteous;
he has cut the cords of the wicked.
5 May all who hate Zion
be put to shame and turned backward!
6 Let them be like the grass on the housetops,
which withers before it grows up,
7 with which the reaper does not fill his hand
nor the binder of sheaves his arms,
8 nor do those who pass by say,
"The blessing of the Lord be upon you!
We bless you in the name of the Lord!"

My Soul Waits for the Lord

130 A SONG OF ASCENTS.
Out of the depths I cry to you,
O LORD!
2 O Lord, hear my voice!
Let your ears be attentive
to the voice of my pleas for mercy!

3 If you, O LORD, should mark iniquities,
O Lord, who could stand?
4 But with you there is forgiveness,
that you may be feared.

5 I wait for the LORD, my soul waits,
and in his word I hope;
6 my soul waits for the Lord
more than watchmen for the morning,
more than watchmen for the morning.

7 O Israel, hope in the LORD!
For with the LORD there is steadfast
love,
and with him is plentiful redemption.
8 And he will redeem Israel
from all his iniquities.

I Have Calmed and Quieted My Soul

131 A SONG OF ASCENTS. OF DAVID.
O LORD, my heart is not lifted up;
my eyes are not raised too high;
I do not occupy myself with things
too great and too marvelous for me.
2 But I have calmed and quieted my
soul,
like a weaned child with its mother;
like a weaned child is my soul
within me.

3 O Israel, hope in the LORD
from this time forth and forevermore.

The LORD Has Chosen Zion

132 A SONG OF ASCENTS.
Remember, O LORD, in David's
favor,
all the hardships he endured,
2 how he swore to the LORD
and vowed to the Mighty One of
Jacob,
3 "I will not enter my house
or get into my bed,
4 I will not give sleep to my eyes
or slumber to my eyelids,

5 until I find a place for the LORD,
a dwelling place for the Mighty One
of Jacob."

6 Behold, we heard of it in Ephrathah;
we found it in the fields of Jaar.
7 "Let us go to his dwelling place;
let us worship at his footstool!"

8 Arise, O LORD, and go to your resting
place,
you and the ark of your might.
9 Let your priests be clothed with righteousness,
and let your saints shout for joy.
10 For the sake of your servant David,
do not turn away the face of your
anointed one.

GETTING THE MESSAGE

What does it mean to "redeem" someone? The word "redeem" expresses the idea of rescue and protection. The Psalms speak of God redeeming Israel (44:26; 111:9; 130:8). God's acts of redemption in the Old Testament anticipate redemption from sin through the death of Jesus Christ (Col. 1:13–14).

11 The LORD swore to David a sure oath
from which he will not turn back:
"One of the sons of your body
I will set on your throne.
12 If your sons keep my covenant
and my testimonies that I shall
teach them,
their sons also forever
shall sit on your throne."

13 For the LORD has chosen Zion;
he has desired it for his dwelling
place:
14 "This is my resting place forever;
here I will dwell, for I have desired it.
15 I will abundantly bless her provisions;
I will satisfy her poor with bread.
16 Her priests I will clothe with salvation,
and her saints will shout for joy.
17 There I will make a horn to sprout for
David;
I have prepared a lamp for my
anointed.

18   His enemies I will clothe with shame,
        but on him his crown will shine."

When Brothers Dwell in Unity

133   A SONG OF ASCENTS. OF DAVID.
        Behold, how good and pleasant
        it is
    when brothers dwell in unity!
2   It is like the precious oil on the head,
        running down on the beard,
    on the beard of Aaron,
        running down on the collar of his
        robes!
3   It is like the dew of Hermon,
        which falls on the mountains of
        Zion!
    For there the LORD has commanded
        the blessing,
        life forevermore.

> **GETTING THE MESSAGE**
>
> **Anointing with oil.** It was common
> during festivals for people to have their
> foreheads anointed with fragrant oils.
> This not only provided a pleasant aroma
> but gave the person a glistening look of
> good health. (See 133:2.)

Come, Bless the LORD

134   A SONG OF ASCENTS.
        Come, bless the LORD, all you
        servants of the LORD,
    who stand by night in the house of
        the LORD!
2   Lift up your hands to the holy place
        and bless the LORD!

3   May the LORD bless you from Zion,
        he who made heaven and earth!

Your Name, O LORD, Endures Forever

135   Praise the LORD!
        Praise the name of the LORD,
        give praise, O servants of the LORD,
2   who stand in the house of the LORD,
        in the courts of the house of our God!
3   Praise the LORD, for the LORD is good;
        sing to his name, for it is pleasant!
4   For the LORD has chosen Jacob for
        himself,
    Israel as his own possession.

5   For I know that the LORD is great,
        and that our Lord is above all gods.

6   Whatever the LORD pleases, he does,
        in heaven and on earth,
        in the seas and all deeps.
7   He it is who makes the clouds rise at
        the end of the earth,
    who makes lightnings for the rain
        and brings forth the wind from his
        storehouses.
8   He it was who struck down the first-
        born of Egypt,
        both of man and of beast;
9   who in your midst, O Egypt,
        sent signs and wonders
        against Pharaoh and all his servants;
10   who struck down many nations
        and killed mighty kings,
11   Sihon, king of the Amorites,
        and Og, king of Bashan,
        and all the kingdoms of Canaan,
12   and gave their land as a heritage,
        a heritage to his people Israel.

13   Your name, O LORD, endures forever,
        your renown, O LORD, throughout
        all ages.
14   For the LORD will vindicate his people
        and have compassion on his ser-
        vants.

15   The idols of the nations are silver and
        gold,
        the work of human hands.
16   They have mouths, but do not speak;
        they have eyes, but do not see;
17   they have ears, but do not hear,
        nor is there any breath in their
        mouths.
18   Those who make them become like
        them,
        so do all who trust in them.

19   O house of Israel, bless the LORD!
        O house of Aaron, bless the LORD!
20   O house of Levi, bless the LORD!
        You who fear the LORD, bless the
        LORD!
21   Blessed be the LORD from Zion,
        he who dwells in Jerusalem!
    Praise the LORD!

His Steadfast Love Endures Forever

136   Give thanks to the LORD, for he
        is good,
        for his steadfast love endures forever.
2   Give thanks to the God of gods,
        for his steadfast love endures forever.

³ Give thanks to the Lord of lords,
  for his steadfast love endures forever;

⁴ to him who alone does great wonders,
  for his steadfast love endures forever;

⁵ to him who by understanding made
    the heavens,
  for his steadfast love endures forever;

⁶ to him who spread out the earth
    above the waters,
  for his steadfast love endures forever;

⁷ to him who made the great lights,
  for his steadfast love endures forever;

⁸ the sun to rule over the day,
  for his steadfast love endures forever;

⁹ the moon and stars to rule over the
    night,
  for his steadfast love endures forever;

¹⁰ to him who struck down the firstborn
    of Egypt,
  for his steadfast love endures forever;

¹¹ and brought Israel out from among
    them,
  for his steadfast love endures forever;

¹² with a strong hand and an out-
    stretched arm,
  for his steadfast love endures forever;

¹³ to him who divided the Red Sea in two,
  for his steadfast love endures forever;

¹⁴ and made Israel pass through the
    midst of it,
  for his steadfast love endures forever;

¹⁵ but overthrew Pharaoh and his host in
    the Red Sea,
  for his steadfast love endures forever;

¹⁶ to him who led his people through the
    wilderness,
  for his steadfast love endures forever;

¹⁷ to him who struck down great kings,
  for his steadfast love endures forever;

¹⁸ and killed mighty kings,
  for his steadfast love endures forever;

¹⁹ Sihon, king of the Amorites,
  for his steadfast love endures forever;

²⁰ and Og, king of Bashan,
  for his steadfast love endures forever;

²¹ and gave their land as a heritage,
  for his steadfast love endures forever;

²² a heritage to Israel his servant,
  for his steadfast love endures forever.

²³ It is he who remembered us in our
    low estate,
  for his steadfast love endures forever;

²⁴ and rescued us from our foes,
  for his steadfast love endures forever;

²⁵ he who gives food to all flesh,
  for his steadfast love endures forever.

²⁶ Give thanks to the God of heaven,
  for his steadfast love endures forever.

How Shall We Sing the LORD's Song?

137 By the waters of Babylon,
    there we sat down and wept,
  when we remembered Zion.

² On the willows there
    we hung up our lyres.

³ For there our captors
    required of us songs,
  and our tormentors, mirth, saying,
    "Sing us one of the songs of Zion!"

GETTING THE MESSAGE

Wonders can also be translated "marvels." The word is often used to describe God's works of rescuing his people and protecting and caring for them (9:1; 78:11; 98:1; Ex. 3:20; 34:10). In Ps. 136:4, it describes creation, showing that God's work as Creator should fill us with awe and wonder.

⁴ How shall we sing the LORD's song
  in a foreign land?

⁵ If I forget you, O Jerusalem,
  let my right hand forget its skill!

⁶ Let my tongue stick to the roof of my
    mouth,
  if I do not remember you,
  if I do not set Jerusalem
    above my highest joy!

⁷ Remember, O LORD, against the
    Edomites
  the day of Jerusalem,
  how they said, "Lay it bare, lay it
    bare,
  down to its foundations!"

⁸ O daughter of Babylon, doomed to
    be destroyed,
  blessed shall he be who repays you
    with what you have done to us!

⁹ Blessed shall he be who takes your
    little ones
  and dashes them against the rock!

Give Thanks to the Lord

138

Of David.

I give you thanks, O Lord, with
my whole heart;
   before the gods I sing your praise;
2 I bow down toward your holy temple
   and give thanks to your name for
      your steadfast love and your
      faithfulness,
   for you have exalted above all
      things
   your name and your word.
3 On the day I called, you answered me;
   my strength of soul you increased.

4 All the kings of the earth shall give
      you thanks, O Lord,
   for they have heard the words of
      your mouth,

GETTING THE MESSAGE

The Lord protects his people. Psalm 138
tells of God's constant care for everyone
who loves him. Singing this psalm helps
believers be more aware of the ways in
which God preserves and protects them.

5 and they shall sing of the ways of the
      Lord,
   for great is the glory of the Lord.
6 For though the Lord is high, he
      regards the lowly,
   but the haughty he knows from
      afar.

7 Though I walk in the midst of trouble,
      you preserve my life;
   you stretch out your hand against the
      wrath of my enemies,
   and your right hand delivers me.
8 The Lord will fulfill his purpose for
      me;
   your steadfast love, O Lord,
      endures forever.
   Do not forsake the work of your
      hands.

Search Me, O God, and Know My Heart

139

To the choirmaster. A Psalm
of David.

1 O Lord, you have searched me and
      known me!

2 You know when I sit down and when I
      rise up;
   you discern my thoughts from afar.
3 You search out my path and my lying
      down
   and are acquainted with all my ways.
4 Even before a word is on my tongue,
   behold, O Lord, you know it alto-
      gether.
5 You hem me in, behind and before,
   and lay your hand upon me.
6 Such knowledge is too wonderful for
      me;
   it is high; I cannot attain it.

7 Where shall I go from your Spirit?
   Or where shall I flee from your pres-
      ence?
8 If I ascend to heaven, you are there!
   If I make my bed in Sheol, you are
      there!
9 If I take the wings of the morning
   and dwell in the uttermost parts of
      the sea,
10 even there your hand shall lead me,
   and your right hand shall hold me.
11 If I say, "Surely the darkness shall
      cover me,
   and the light about me be night,"
12 even the darkness is not dark to you;
   the night is bright as the day,
   for darkness is as light with you.

13 For you formed my inward parts;
   you knitted me together in my
      mother's womb.
14 I praise you, for I am fearfully and
      wonderfully made.
   Wonderful are your works;
   my soul knows it very well.
15 My frame was not hidden from you,
   when I was being made in secret,
   intricately woven in the depths of
      the earth.
16 Your eyes saw my unformed substance;
   in your book were written, every one
      of them,
   the days that were formed for me,
   when as yet there was none of them.

17 How precious to me are your
      thoughts, O God!
   How vast is the sum of them!
18 If I would count them, they are more
      than the sand.
   I awake, and I am still with you.

19 Oh that you would slay the wicked,
O God!
   O men of blood, depart from me!
20 They speak against you with malicious intent;
   your enemies take your name in vain.
21 Do I not hate those who hate you,
O LORD?
   And do I not loathe those who rise
up against you?
22 I hate them with complete hatred;
   I count them my enemies.

23 Search me, O God, and know my heart!
   Try me and know my thoughts!
24 And see if there be any grievous way
in me,
   and lead me in the way everlasting!

Deliver Me, O LORD, from Evil Men

140 TO THE CHOIRMASTER. A PSALM
OF DAVID.

1 Deliver me, O LORD, from evil men;
   preserve me from violent men,
2 who plan evil things in their heart
   and stir up wars continually.
3 They make their tongue sharp as a
serpent's,
   and under their lips is the venom of
asps.   *Selah*

4 Guard me, O LORD, from the hands of
the wicked;
   preserve me from violent men,
   who have planned to trip up my feet.
5 The arrogant have hidden a trap for me,
   and with cords they have spread a
net;
   beside the way they have set snares
for me.   *Selah*

6 I say to the LORD, You are my God;
   give ear to the voice of my pleas for
mercy, O LORD!
7 O LORD, my Lord, the strength of my
salvation,
   you have covered my head in the
day of battle.
8 Grant not, O LORD, the desires of the
wicked;
   do not further their evil plot, or
they will be exalted!   *Selah*

9 As for the head of those who surround
me,
   let the mischief of their lips overwhelm them!

10 Let burning coals fall upon them!
   Let them be cast into fire,
      into miry pits, no more to rise!
11 Let not the slanderer be established in
the land;
   let evil hunt down the violent man
speedily!

12 I know that the LORD will maintain
the cause of the afflicted,
   and will execute justice for the
needy.
13 Surely the righteous shall give thanks
to your name;
   the upright shall dwell in your presence.

> **GETTING THE MESSAGE**
>
> In the Old Testament, **salvation** (140:7)
> generally refers to deliverance from both
> physical and spiritual danger. Because
> God had been a faithful Savior in the past,
> Israel trusted that they could look forward
> to his greater salvation in the future. The
> ultimate salvation for all mankind would
> come through Jesus the Messiah.

Give Ear to My Voice

141 A PSALM OF DAVID.
O LORD, I call upon you; hasten
to me!
   Give ear to my voice when I call to
you!
2 Let my prayer be counted as incense
before you,
   and the lifting up of my hands as
the evening sacrifice!

3 Set a guard, O LORD, over my mouth;
   keep watch over the door of my lips!
4 Do not let my heart incline to any evil,
   to busy myself with wicked deeds
in company with men who work iniquity,
   and let me not eat of their delicacies!

5 Let a righteous man strike me—it is a
kindness;
   let him rebuke me—it is oil for my
head;
   let my head not refuse it.
Yet my prayer is continually against
their evil deeds.

6   When their judges are thrown over
      the cliff,
      then they shall hear my words, for
      they are pleasant.
7   As when one plows and breaks up the
      earth,
      so shall our bones be scattered at
      the mouth of Sheol.
8   But my eyes are toward you, O GOD,
      my Lord;
      in you I seek refuge; leave me not
      defenseless!
9   Keep me from the trap that they have
      laid for me
      and from the snares of evildoers!
10 Let the wicked fall into their own
      nets,
      while I pass by safely.

You Are My Refuge

142
A MASKIL OF DAVID, WHEN HE
WAS IN THE CAVE. A PRAYER.

1   With my voice I cry out to the LORD;
      with my voice I plead for mercy to
      the LORD.
2   I pour out my complaint before him;
      I tell my trouble before him.
3   When my spirit faints within me,
      you know my way!
    In the path where I walk
      they have hidden a trap for me.
4   Look to the right and see:
      there is none who takes notice of me;
    no refuge remains to me;
      no one cares for my soul.
5   I cry to you, O LORD;
      I say, "You are my refuge,
      my portion in the land of the living."
6   Attend to my cry,
      for I am brought very low!
    Deliver me from my persecutors,
      for they are too strong for me!
7   Bring me out of prison,
      that I may give thanks to your name!
    The righteous will surround me,
      for you will deal bountifully with me.

My Soul Thirsts for You

143
A PSALM OF DAVID.
Hear my prayer, O LORD;
give ear to my pleas for mercy!
In your faithfulness answer me, in
your righteousness!

2   Enter not into judgment with your
      servant,
      for no one living is righteous before
      you.
3   For the enemy has pursued my soul;
      he has crushed my life to the
      ground;
      he has made me sit in darkness like
      those long dead.
4   Therefore my spirit faints within me;
      my heart within me is appalled.
5   I remember the days of old;
      I meditate on all that you have
      done;
      I ponder the work of your hands.
6   I stretch out my hands to you;
      my soul thirsts for you like a
      parched land.   Selah
7   Answer me quickly, O LORD!
      My spirit fails!
    Hide not your face from me,
      lest I be like those who go down to
      the pit.
8   Let me hear in the morning of your
      steadfast love,
      for in you I trust.
    Make me know the way I should go,
      for to you I lift up my soul.
9   Deliver me from my enemies,
      O LORD!
      I have fled to you for refuge.
10 Teach me to do your will,
      for you are my God!
    Let your good Spirit lead me
      on level ground!
11 For your name's sake, O LORD, pre-
      serve my life!
      In your righteousness bring my
      soul out of trouble!
12 And in your steadfast love you will cut
      off my enemies,
      and you will destroy all the adver-
      saries of my soul,
      for I am your servant.

My Rock and My Fortress

144
OF DAVID.
Blessed be the LORD, my rock,
who trains my hands for war,
and my fingers for battle;
2   he is my steadfast love and my fortress,
      my stronghold and my deliverer,

my shield and he in whom I take
    refuge,
  who subdues peoples under me.

3 O Lord, what is man that you regard
    him,
  or the son of man that you think of
    him?
4 Man is like a breath;
  his days are like a passing shadow.

5 Bow your heavens, O Lord, and come
    down!
  Touch the mountains so that they
    smoke!
6 Flash forth the lightning and scatter
    them;
  send out your arrows and rout them!
7 Stretch out your hand from on high;
  rescue me and deliver me from the
    many waters,
  from the hand of foreigners,
8 whose mouths speak lies
  and whose right hand is a right
    hand of falsehood.

9 I will sing a new song to you, O God;
  upon a ten-stringed harp I will play
    to you,
10 who gives victory to kings,
  who rescues David his servant from
    the cruel sword.

11 Rescue me and deliver me
  from the hand of foreigners,
  whose mouths speak lies
  and whose right hand is a right
    hand of falsehood.

12 May our sons in their youth
  be like plants full grown,
  our daughters like corner pillars
  cut for the structure of a palace;
13 may our granaries be full,
  providing all kinds of produce;
  may our sheep bring forth thousands
  and ten thousands in our fields;
14 may our cattle be heavy with young,
  suffering no mishap or failure in
    bearing;
  may there be no cry of distress in our
    streets!
15 Blessed are the people to whom such
    blessings fall!
  Blessed are the people whose God is
    the Lord!

Great Is the Lord

145 A Song of Praise. Of David.
  I will extol you, my God and
    King,
  and bless your name forever and
    ever.
2 Every day I will bless you
  and praise your name forever and
    ever.
3 Great is the Lord, and greatly to be
    praised,
  and his greatness is unsearchable.

4 One generation shall commend your
    works to another,
  and shall declare your mighty acts.
5 On the glorious splendor of your maj-
    esty,
  and on your wondrous works, I will
    meditate.
6 They shall speak of the might of your
    awesome deeds,
  and I will declare your greatness.
7 They shall pour forth the fame of your
    abundant goodness
  and shall sing aloud of your righ-
    teousness.

8 The Lord is gracious and merciful,
  slow to anger and abounding in
    steadfast love.
9 The Lord is good to all,
  and his mercy is over all that he has
    made.

10 All your works shall give thanks to
    you, O Lord,
  and all your saints shall bless you!
11 They shall speak of the glory of your
    kingdom
  and tell of your power,
12 to make known to the children of
    man your mighty deeds,
  and the glorious splendor of your
    kingdom.
13 Your kingdom is an everlasting king-
    dom,
  and your dominion endures
    throughout all generations.

[The Lord is faithful in all his words
  and kind in all his works.][1]
14 The Lord upholds all who are falling
  and raises up all who are bowed
    down.

---

[1] These two lines are in brackets because they appear in most but not all ancient manuscripts (see Preface)

15 The eyes of all look to you,
       and you give them their food in due
         season.
16 You open your hand;
       you satisfy the desire of every living
         thing.
17 The LORD is righteous in all his ways
       and kind in all his works.
18 The LORD is near to all who call on
         him,
       to all who call on him in truth.
19 He fulfills the desire of those who fear
         him;
       he also hears their cry and saves
         them.
20 The LORD preserves all who love him,
       but all the wicked he will destroy.

GETTING THE MESSAGE

Who are the saints? The term "saints"
is used in both the Old Testament
and New Testament to describe God's
people. In the Old Testament it describes
the faithful among God's people Israel
(37:28; 145:10). In the New Testament,
the Greek word translated "saints"
means "holy," in the sense of being set
apart for God. This includes all those
who have put their trust in Jesus, the
only one who can truly make them holy.

21 My mouth will speak the praise of the
         LORD,
       and let all flesh bless his holy name
         forever and ever.

Put Not Your Trust in Princes

146 Praise the LORD!
       Praise the LORD, O my soul!
2   I will praise the LORD as long as I live;
       I will sing praises to my God while I
         have my being.
3   Put not your trust in princes,
       in a son of man, in whom there is
         no salvation.
4   When his breath departs, he returns
         to the earth;
       on that very day his plans perish.
5   Blessed is he whose help is the God of
         Jacob,
       whose hope is in the LORD his God,

6   who made heaven and earth,
       the sea, and all that is in them,
     who keeps faith forever;
7   who executes justice for the
         oppressed,
       who gives food to the hungry.

    The LORD sets the prisoners free;
8   the LORD opens the eyes of the blind.
    The LORD lifts up those who are
         bowed down;
       the LORD loves the righteous.
9   The LORD watches over the sojourners;
       he upholds the widow and the
         fatherless,
       but the way of the wicked he brings
         to ruin.
10   The LORD will reign forever,
       your God, O Zion, to all generations.
     Praise the LORD!

He Heals the Brokenhearted

147 Praise the LORD!
       For it is good to sing praises to
         our God;
       for it is pleasant, and a song of
         praise is fitting.
2   The LORD builds up Jerusalem;
       he gathers the outcasts of Israel.
3   He heals the brokenhearted
       and binds up their wounds.
4   He determines the number of the
         stars;
       he gives to all of them their names.
5   Great is our Lord, and abundant in
         power;
       his understanding is beyond mea-
         sure.
6   The LORD lifts up the humble;
       he casts the wicked to the ground.
7   Sing to the LORD with thanksgiving;
       make melody to our God on the lyre!
8   He covers the heavens with clouds;
       he prepares rain for the earth;
       he makes grass grow on the hills.
9   He gives to the beasts their food,
       and to the young ravens that cry.
10   His delight is not in the strength of
         the horse,
       nor his pleasure in the legs of a man,
11   but the LORD takes pleasure in those
         who fear him,
       in those who hope in his steadfast
         love.

12 Praise the LORD, O Jerusalem!
    Praise your God, O Zion!
13 For he strengthens the bars of your
       gates;
    he blesses your children within you.
14 He makes peace in your borders;
    he fills you with the finest of the
       wheat.
15 He sends out his command to the
       earth;
    his word runs swiftly.
16 He gives snow like wool;
    he scatters frost like ashes.
17 He hurls down his crystals of ice like
       crumbs;
    who can stand before his cold?
18 He sends out his word, and melts
       them;
    he makes his wind blow and the
       waters flow.
19 He declares his word to Jacob,
    his statutes and rules to Israel.
20 He has not dealt thus with any other
       nation;
    they do not know his rules.
    Praise the LORD!

Praise the Name of the LORD

148 Praise the LORD!
    Praise the LORD from the heav-
       ens;
    praise him in the heights!
2 Praise him, all his angels;
    praise him, all his hosts!

3 Praise him, sun and moon,
    praise him, all you shining stars!
4 Praise him, you highest heavens,
    and you waters above the heavens!

5 Let them praise the name of the LORD!
    For he commanded and they were
       created.
6 And he established them forever and
       ever;
    he gave a decree, and it shall not
       pass away.

7 Praise the LORD from the earth,
    you great sea creatures and all deeps,
8 fire and hail, snow and mist,
    stormy wind fulfilling his word!
9 Mountains and all hills,
    fruit trees and all cedars!
10 Beasts and all livestock,
    creeping things and flying birds!

11 Kings of the earth and all peoples,
    princes and all rulers of the earth!
12 Young men and maidens together,
    old men and children!

13 Let them praise the name of the LORD,
    for his name alone is exalted;
    his majesty is above earth and
       heaven.
14 He has raised up a horn for his people,
    praise for all his saints,
    for the people of Israel who are near
       to him.
    Praise the LORD!

Sing to the LORD a New Song

149 Praise the LORD!
    Sing to the LORD a new song,
    his praise in the assembly of the
       godly!

> ### GETTING THE MESSAGE
>
> **Two-edged swords** (149:6) were made
> of bronze or iron and were filed on each
> side, so that the blade could more readily
> and deeply penetrate enemy armor. In
> the New Testament, the word of God is
> said to be "sharper than any two-edged
> sword" (Heb. 4:12) because of the way
> it exposes the deepest "thoughts and
> intentions" of a person's heart.

2 Let Israel be glad in his Maker;
    let the children of Zion rejoice in
       their King!
3 Let them praise his name with danc-
       ing,
    making melody to him with tam-
       bourine and lyre!
4 For the LORD takes pleasure in his
       people;
    he adorns the humble with salvation.
5 Let the godly exult in glory;
    let them sing for joy on their beds.
6 Let the high praises of God be in their
       throats
    and two-edged swords in their
       hands,
7 to execute vengeance on the nations
    and punishments on the peoples,
8 to bind their kings with chains
    and their nobles with fetters of iron,

9 to execute on them the judgment
       written!
     This is honor for all his godly ones.
   Praise the LORD!

Let Everything Praise the LORD

150 Praise the LORD!
        Praise God in his sanctuary;
   praise him in his mighty heavens!
2 Praise him for his mighty deeds;
     praise him according to his excel-
       lent greatness!

3 Praise him with trumpet sound;
     praise him with lute and harp!
4 Praise him with tambourine and
       dance;
     praise him with strings and pipe!
5 Praise him with sounding cymbals;
     praise him with loud clashing cym-
       bals!
6 Let everything that has breath praise
       the LORD!
   Praise the LORD!

INTRODUCTION TO PROVERBS

1010–971 B.C.	971–931 B.C.	715–686 B.C.
Reign of David	Reign of Solomon	Reign of Hezekiah

AUTHOR AND DATE

Proverbs itself mentions Solomon (reigned c. 971–931 B.C.) as author or collector of its contents (1:1; 10:1), including the proverbs copied by Hezekiah's men (25:1). There are also two batches of sayings from a group called "the wise" (22:17–24:22; 24:23–34), and "oracles" from Agur (30:1–33) and Lemuel (31:1–9). No author is named for the song in praise of the excellent wife that ends the book (31:10–31). Although Proverbs was begun in the time of Solomon, it probably was not in its present form until the time of Hezekiah (reigned c. 715–686 B.C.).

THEME

The goal of the book is stated right at the beginning (1:1–7): to describe what wisdom is and to help God's people become wise. Wisdom is founded in the "fear of the LORD," and it enables believers to express their faith in the practical details of everyday life.

AUDIENCE

The book is addressed to a young man. The situations he will face while he is young receive much attention. These situations supply concrete examples from which all readers can apply lessons to their own lives. Anyone who is wise and who pays attention will benefit (1:5) from this instruction.

READING PROVERBS

The reader of Proverbs must seek to understand the various types of people the book describes. The most obvious characters in the book are the wise, the fool, and the simple. Proverbs urges its readers to be wise, which means embracing God's covenant and living out the covenant in everyday situations (compare 2:2; 10:1). The fool is the person who constantly opposes God's covenant (1:7b). The simple is the person who is not firmly committed, either to wisdom or to folly; he is easily misled (14:15).

The first nine chapters of Proverbs are "wisdom poems" that urge the reader to pursue wisdom. The main section of Proverbs—the concise, memorable statements of two or three lines—begins in 10:1. Proverbs often seem to be mere observations about life, but their deeper meanings will reveal themselves if the following questions are kept in mind: (1) What virtue does this proverb commend? (2) What vice does it disapprove of? (3) What value does it affirm?

KEY THEMES

Proverbs offers wisdom on a wide array of topics from daily life: diligence and laziness (6:6–11); friendship (3:27–28; 18:24); speech (10:19–21); marriage (18:22; 19:14); child rearing (22:6); domestic peace (15:17; 17:1); work (11:1); getting along and good manners (23:1–2; 25:16–17; 26:17–19; 27:14); eternity (14:32; 23:17–18); and much more. It shows that "godliness is of value in every way, as it holds promise for the present life and also for the life to come" (1 Tim. 4:8).

1. God's will is intensely practical, applying to every aspect of life. A proper relation to God involves trying hard to understand his truth, and then embracing and obeying that truth.

2. A life lived by God's will is a happy life (3:21–26).

3. A life lived by God's will is a useful life (3:27–28; 12:18, 25).

4. A life lived by God's will does not just happen. One must seek after it (9:1–6).

OUTLINE

PROVERBS

The Beginning of Knowledge

1 The proverbs of Solomon, son of David, king of Israel:

2 To know wisdom and instruction,
  to understand words of insight,
3 to receive instruction in wise dealing,
  in righteousness, justice, and equity;
4 to give prudence to the simple,
  knowledge and discretion to the
  youth—
5 Let the wise hear and increase in
  learning,
  and the one who understands
  obtain guidance,
6 to understand a proverb and a saying,
  the words of the wise and their
  riddles.

7 The fear of the LORD is the beginning
  of knowledge;
  fools despise wisdom and instruction.

The Enticement of Sinners

8 Hear, my son, your father's instruction,
  and forsake not your mother's
  teaching,
9 for they are a graceful garland for your
  head
  and pendants for your neck.
10 My son, if sinners entice you,
  do not consent.
11 If they say, "Come with us, let us lie in
  wait for blood;
  let us ambush the innocent without
  reason;
12 like Sheol let us swallow them alive,
  and whole, like those who go down
  to the pit;
13 we shall find all precious goods,
  we shall fill our houses with plunder;
14 throw in your lot among us;
  we will all have one purse"—
15 my son, do not walk in the way with
  them;
  hold back your foot from their paths,
16 for their feet run to evil,
  and they make haste to shed blood.

17 For in vain is a net spread
  in the sight of any bird,
18 but these men lie in wait for their
  own blood;
  they set an ambush for their own
  lives.
19 Such are the ways of everyone who is
  greedy for unjust gain;
  it takes away the life of its possessors.

The Call of Wisdom

20 Wisdom cries aloud in the street,
  in the markets she raises her voice;

GETTING THE MESSAGE

Wisdom is a key term in Job, Proverbs, and Ecclesiastes. The word can mean "skilled at making sound decisions in life." Proverbs 9:10 states that "the fear of the LORD is the beginning of wisdom."

21 at the head of the noisy streets she
  cries out;
  at the entrance of the city gates she
  speaks:
22 "How long, O simple ones, will you
  love being simple?
  How long will scoffers delight in their
  scoffing
  and fools hate knowledge?
23 If you turn at my reproof,
  behold, I will pour out my spirit to
  you;
  I will make my words known to
  you.
24 Because I have called and you refused
  to listen,
  have stretched out my hand and no
  one has heeded,
25 because you have ignored all my
  counsel
  and would have none of my reproof,
26 I also will laugh at your calamity;
  I will mock when terror strikes you,

27 when terror strikes you like a storm
   and your calamity comes like a
      whirlwind,
   when distress and anguish come
      upon you.
28 Then they will call upon me, but I will
      not answer;
   they will seek me diligently but will
      not find me.
29 Because they hated knowledge
   and did not choose the fear of the
      LORD,
30 would have none of my counsel
   and despised all my reproof,
31 therefore they shall eat the fruit of
      their way,
   and have their fill of their own
      devices.
32 For the simple are killed by their turn-
      ing away,
   and the complacency of fools
      destroys them;

GETTING THE MESSAGE

In biblical times, **proverbs** were often
used as a means of instruction for young
people.

33 but whoever listens to me will dwell
      secure
   and will be at ease, without dread
      of disaster."

The Value of Wisdom

2 My son, if you receive my words
   and treasure up my commandments
      with you,
2 making your ear attentive to wisdom
   and inclining your heart to under-
      standing;
3 yes, if you call out for insight
   and raise your voice for under-
      standing,
4 if you seek it like silver
   and search for it as for hidden trea-
      sures,
5 then you will understand the fear of
      the LORD
   and find the knowledge of God.
6 For the LORD gives wisdom;
   from his mouth come knowledge
      and understanding;

7 he stores up sound wisdom for the
      upright;
   he is a shield to those who walk in
      integrity,
8 guarding the paths of justice
   and watching over the way of his
      saints.
9 Then you will understand righteous-
      ness and justice
   and equity, every good path;
10 for wisdom will come into your heart,
   and knowledge will be pleasant to
      your soul;
11 discretion will watch over you,
   understanding will guard you,
12 delivering you from the way of evil,
   from men of perverted speech,
13 who forsake the paths of uprightness
   to walk in the ways of darkness,
14 who rejoice in doing evil
   and delight in the perverseness of
      evil,
15 men whose paths are crooked,
   and who are devious in their ways.

16 So you will be delivered from the
      forbidden woman,
   from the adulteress with her
      smooth words,
17 who forsakes the companion of her
      youth
   and forgets the covenant of her God;
18 for her house sinks down to death,
   and her paths to the departed;
19 none who go to her come back,
   nor do they regain the paths of life.

20 So you will walk in the way of the
      good
   and keep to the paths of the righ-
      teous.
21 For the upright will inhabit the land,
   and those with integrity will remain
      in it,
22 but the wicked will be cut off from the
      land,
   and the treacherous will be rooted
      out of it.

Trust in the LORD with All Your Heart

3 My son, do not forget my teaching,
   but let your heart keep my com-
      mandments,
2 for length of days and years of life
   and peace they will add to you.

³ Let not steadfast love and faithfulness
forsake you;
bind them around your neck;
write them on the tablet of your
heart.
⁴ So you will find favor and good success
in the sight of God and man.

⁵ Trust in the LORD with all your heart,
and do not lean on your own understanding.
⁶ In all your ways acknowledge him,
and he will make straight your paths.
⁷ Be not wise in your own eyes;
fear the LORD, and turn away from
evil.
⁸ It will be healing to your flesh
and refreshment to your bones.

⁹ Honor the LORD with your wealth
and with the firstfruits of all your
produce;
¹⁰ then your barns will be filled with
plenty,
and your vats will be bursting with
wine.

¹¹ My son, do not despise the LORD's
discipline
or be weary of his reproof,
¹² for the LORD reproves him whom he
loves,
as a father the son in whom he
delights.

Blessed Is the One Who Finds Wisdom
¹³ Blessed is the one who finds wisdom,
and the one who gets understanding,
¹⁴ for the gain from her is better than
gain from silver
and her profit better than gold.
¹⁵ She is more precious than jewels,
and nothing you desire can compare with her.
¹⁶ Long life is in her right hand;
in her left hand are riches and honor.
¹⁷ Her ways are ways of pleasantness,
and all her paths are peace.
¹⁸ She is a tree of life to those who lay
hold of her;
those who hold her fast are called
blessed.
¹⁹ The LORD by wisdom founded the
earth;
by understanding he established
the heavens;

²⁰ by his knowledge the deeps broke
open,
and the clouds drop down the dew.

²¹ My son, do not lose sight of these—
keep sound wisdom and discretion,
²² and they will be life for your soul
and adornment for your neck.
²³ Then you will walk on your way
securely,
and your foot will not stumble.
²⁴ If you lie down, you will not be afraid;
when you lie down, your sleep will
be sweet.
²⁵ Do not be afraid of sudden terror
or of the ruin of the wicked, when it
comes,
²⁶ for the LORD will be your confidence
and will keep your foot from being
caught.

GETTING THE MESSAGE

The Hebrew word for peace is **shalom**. It means much more than just the absence of conflict and turmoil. It means that "all is well" in a person's life (3:17).

²⁷ Do not withhold good from those to
whom it is due,
when it is in your power to do it.
²⁸ Do not say to your neighbor, "Go, and
come again,
tomorrow I will give it"—when you
have it with you.
²⁹ Do not plan evil against your neighbor,
who dwells trustingly beside you.
³⁰ Do not contend with a man for no
reason,
when he has done you no harm.
³¹ Do not envy a man of violence
and do not choose any of his ways,
³² for the devious person is an abomination to the LORD,
but the upright are in his confidence.
³³ The LORD's curse is on the house of
the wicked,
but he blesses the dwelling of the
righteous.
³⁴ Toward the scorners he is scornful,
but to the humble he gives favor.
³⁵ The wise will inherit honor,
but fools get disgrace.

A Father's Wise Instruction

4 Hear, O sons, a father's instruction,
and be attentive, that you may gain insight,

² for I give you good precepts;
do not forsake my teaching.

³ When I was a son with my father,
tender, the only one in the sight of my mother,

⁴ he taught me and said to me,
"Let your heart hold fast my words;
keep my commandments, and live.

⁵ Get wisdom; get insight;
do not forget, and do not turn away
from the words of my mouth.

⁶ Do not forsake her, and she will keep you;
love her, and she will guard you.

GETTING THE MESSAGE

Garlands were wreaths woven from leaves and flowers. They were worn around the head or neck during various celebrations such as weddings. They were also symbols of honor for military success. In Proverbs, they symbolize the honor that comes from following the way of wisdom (4:9).

⁷ The beginning of wisdom is this: Get wisdom,
and whatever you get, get insight.

⁸ Prize her highly, and she will exalt you;
she will honor you if you embrace her.

⁹ She will place on your head a graceful garland;
she will bestow on you a beautiful crown."

¹⁰ Hear, my son, and accept my words,
that the years of your life may be many.

¹¹ I have taught you the way of wisdom;
I have led you in the paths of uprightness.

¹² When you walk, your step will not be hampered,
and if you run, you will not stumble.

¹³ Keep hold of instruction; do not let go;
guard her, for she is your life.

¹⁴ Do not enter the path of the wicked,
and do not walk in the way of the evil.

¹⁵ Avoid it; do not go on it;
turn away from it and pass on.

¹⁶ For they cannot sleep unless they have done wrong;
they are robbed of sleep unless they have made someone stumble.

¹⁷ For they eat the bread of wickedness
and drink the wine of violence.

¹⁸ But the path of the righteous is like the light of dawn,
which shines brighter and brighter until full day.

¹⁹ The way of the wicked is like deep darkness;
they do not know over what they stumble.

²⁰ My son, be attentive to my words;
incline your ear to my sayings.

²¹ Let them not escape from your sight;
keep them within your heart.

²² For they are life to those who find them,
and healing to all their flesh.

²³ Keep your heart with all vigilance,
for from it flow the springs of life.

²⁴ Put away from you crooked speech,
and put devious talk far from you.

²⁵ Let your eyes look directly forward,
and your gaze be straight before you.

²⁶ Ponder the path of your feet;
then all your ways will be sure.

²⁷ Do not swerve to the right or to the left;
turn your foot away from evil.

Warning Against Adultery

5 My son, be attentive to my wisdom;
incline your ear to my understanding,

² that you may keep discretion,
and your lips may guard knowledge.

³ For the lips of a forbidden woman drip honey,
and her speech is smoother than oil,

⁴ but in the end she is bitter as wormwood,
sharp as a two-edged sword.

⁵ Her feet go down to death;
her steps follow the path to Sheol;

⁶ she does not ponder the path of life;
her ways wander, and she does not know it.

7 And now, O sons, listen to me,
  and do not depart from the words
    of my mouth.
8 Keep your way far from her,
  and do not go near the door of her
    house,
9 lest you give your honor to others
  and your years to the merciless,
10 lest strangers take their fill of your
    strength,
  and your labors go to the house of a
    foreigner,
11 and at the end of your life you groan,
  when your flesh and body are con-
    sumed,
12 and you say, "How I hated discipline,
  and my heart despised reproof!
13 I did not listen to the voice of my
    teachers
  or incline my ear to my instructors.
14 I am at the brink of utter ruin
  in the assembled congregation."

15 Drink water from your own cistern,
  flowing water from your own well.
16 Should your springs be scattered
    abroad,
  streams of water in the streets?
17 Let them be for yourself alone,
  and not for strangers with you.
18 Let your fountain be blessed,
  and rejoice in the wife of your youth,
19 a lovely deer, a graceful doe.
  Let her breasts fill you at all times
    with delight;
  be intoxicated always in her love.
20 Why should you be intoxicated, my
    son, with a forbidden woman
  and embrace the bosom of an adul-
    teress?
21 For a man's ways are before the eyes
    of the LORD,
  and he ponders all his paths.
22 The iniquities of the wicked ensnare
    him,
  and he is held fast in the cords of
    his sin.
23 He dies for lack of discipline,
  and because of his great folly he is
    led astray.

Practical Warnings

6 My son, if you have put up security
  for your neighbor,
    have given your pledge for a stranger,

2 if you are snared in the words of your
    mouth,
  caught in the words of your mouth,
3 then do this, my son, and save yourself,
  for you have come into the hand of
    your neighbor:
  go, hasten, and plead urgently with
    your neighbor.
4 Give your eyes no sleep
  and your eyelids no slumber;
5 save yourself like a gazelle from the
    hand of the hunter,
  like a bird from the hand of the
    fowler.

6 Go to the ant, O sluggard;
  consider her ways, and be wise.
7 Without having any chief,
  officer, or ruler,

GETTING THE MESSAGE

Despite their small size, **ants** are a picture of wisdom and initiative (6:6–8; 30:25). Ant colonies can reach populations of more than half a million, and will work tirelessly during the harvest season to store food for the winter.

8 she prepares her bread in summer
  and gathers her food in harvest.
9 How long will you lie there, O sluggard?
  When will you arise from your sleep?
10 A little sleep, a little slumber,
  a little folding of the hands to rest,
11 and poverty will come upon you like a
    robber,
  and want like an armed man.

12 A worthless person, a wicked man,
  goes about with crooked speech,
13 winks with his eyes, signals with his
    feet,
  points with his finger,
14 with perverted heart devises evil,
  continually sowing discord;
15 therefore calamity will come upon
    him suddenly;
  in a moment he will be broken
    beyond healing.

16 There are six things that the LORD
    hates,
  seven that are an abomination to
    him:

17 haughty eyes, a lying tongue,
   and hands that shed innocent blood,
18 a heart that devises wicked plans,
   feet that make haste to run to evil,
19 a false witness who breathes out lies,
   and one who sows discord among
      brothers.

Warnings Against Adultery

20 My son, keep your father's command-
      ment,
   and forsake not your mother's
      teaching.
21 Bind them on your heart always;
   tie them around your neck.
22 When you walk, they will lead you;
   when you lie down, they will watch
      over you;
   and when you awake, they will talk
      with you.

> ### GETTING THE MESSAGE
>
> **The simple person** (7:7) is one of the
> primary character types described in the
> book of Proverbs. The term describes
> someone who is immature and easily
> misled (14:15).

23 For the commandment is a lamp and
      the teaching a light,
   and the reproofs of discipline are
      the way of life,
24 to preserve you from the evil woman,
   from the smooth tongue of the
      adulteress.
25 Do not desire her beauty in your heart,
   and do not let her capture you with
      her eyelashes;
26 for the price of a prostitute is only a
      loaf of bread,
   but a married woman hunts down a
      precious life.
27 Can a man carry fire next to his chest
   and his clothes not be burned?
28 Or can one walk on hot coals
   and his feet not be scorched?
29 So is he who goes in to his neighbor's
      wife;
   none who touches her will go
      unpunished.
30 People do not despise a thief if he steals
   to satisfy his appetite when he is
      hungry,

31 but if he is caught, he will pay seven-
      fold;
   he will give all the goods of his
      house.
32 He who commits adultery lacks sense;
   he who does it destroys himself.
33 He will get wounds and dishonor,
   and his disgrace will not be wiped
      away.
34 For jealousy makes a man furious,
   and he will not spare when he takes
      revenge.
35 He will accept no compensation;
   he will refuse though you multiply
      gifts.

Warning Against the Adulteress

7 My son, keep my words
   and treasure up my commandments
      with you;
2 keep my commandments and live;
   keep my teaching as the apple of
      your eye;
3 bind them on your fingers;
   write them on the tablet of your
      heart.
4 Say to wisdom, "You are my sister,"
   and call insight your intimate
      friend,
5 to keep you from the forbidden
      woman,
   from the adulteress with her
      smooth words.
6 For at the window of my house
   I have looked out through my lattice,
7 and I have seen among the simple,
   I have perceived among the youths,
   a young man lacking sense,
8 passing along the street near her
      corner,
   taking the road to her house
9 in the twilight, in the evening,
   at the time of night and darkness.
10 And behold, the woman meets him,
   dressed as a prostitute, wily of heart.
11 She is loud and wayward;
   her feet do not stay at home;
12 now in the street, now in the market,
   and at every corner she lies in wait.
13 She seizes him and kisses him,
   and with bold face she says to him,
14 "I had to offer sacrifices,
   and today I have paid my vows;

15 so now I have come out to meet you,
  to seek you eagerly, and I have
    found you.
16 I have spread my couch with coverings,
  colored linens from Egyptian linen;
17 I have perfumed my bed with myrrh,
  aloes, and cinnamon.
18 Come, let us take our fill of love till
    morning;
  let us delight ourselves with love.
19 For my husband is not at home;
  he has gone on a long journey;
20 he took a bag of money with him;
  at full moon he will come home."

21 With much seductive speech she
    persuades him;
  with her smooth talk she compels
    him.
22 All at once he follows her,
  as an ox goes to the slaughter,
  or as a stag is caught fast
23   till an arrow pierces its liver;
  as a bird rushes into a snare;
  he does not know that it will cost
    him his life.

24 And now, O sons, listen to me,
  and be attentive to the words of my
    mouth.
25 Let not your heart turn aside to her
    ways;
  do not stray into her paths,
26 for many a victim has she laid low,
  and all her slain are a mighty
    throng.
27 Her house is the way to Sheol,
  going down to the chambers of
    death.

The Blessings of Wisdom

8 Does not wisdom call?
  Does not understanding raise her
    voice?
2 On the heights beside the way,
  at the crossroads she takes her stand;
3 beside the gates in front of the town,
  at the entrance of the portals she
    cries aloud:
4 "To you, O men, I call,
  and my cry is to the children of man.
5 O simple ones, learn prudence;
  O fools, learn sense.
6 Hear, for I will speak noble things,
  and from my lips will come what is
    right,

7 for my mouth will utter truth;
  wickedness is an abomination to
    my lips.
8 All the words of my mouth are righ-
    teous;
  there is nothing twisted or crooked
    in them.
9 They are all straight to him who
    understands,
  and right to those who find knowl-
    edge.
10 Take my instruction instead of silver,
  and knowledge rather than choice
    gold,
11 for wisdom is better than jewels,
  and all that you may desire cannot
    compare with her.

12 "I, wisdom, dwell with prudence,
  and I find knowledge and discretion.
13 The fear of the LORD is hatred of evil.
  Pride and arrogance and the way of evil
  and perverted speech I hate.
14 I have counsel and sound wisdom;
  I have insight; I have strength.
15 By me kings reign,
  and rulers decree what is just;
16 by me princes rule,
  and nobles, all who govern justly.
17 I love those who love me,
  and those who seek me diligently
    find me.
18 Riches and honor are with me,
  enduring wealth and righteousness.
19 My fruit is better than gold, even fine
    gold,
  and my yield than choice silver.
20 I walk in the way of righteousness,
  in the paths of justice,
21 granting an inheritance to those who
    love me,
  and filling their treasuries.

22 "The LORD possessed me at the begin-
    ning of his work,
  the first of his acts of old.
23 Ages ago I was set up,
  at the first, before the beginning of
    the earth.
24 When there were no depths I was
    brought forth,
  when there were no springs
    abounding with water.
25 Before the mountains had been
    shaped,
  before the hills, I was brought forth,

26 before he had made the earth with its
      fields,
    or the first of the dust of the world.
27 When he established the heavens,
      I was there;
      when he drew a circle on the face of
        the deep,
28 when he made firm the skies above,
      when he established the fountains
        of the deep,
29 when he assigned to the sea its limit,
      so that the waters might not trans-
        gress his command,
    when he marked out the foundations
      of the earth,
30   then I was beside him, like a master
        workman,
    and I was daily his delight,
      rejoicing before him always,

GETTING THE MESSAGE

The fact that the house of Wisdom
has **seven pillars** (9:1) could signify
perfection. Or, it could simply mean that
Wisdom's house is large and impressive.

---

31 rejoicing in his inhabited world
      and delighting in the children of
        man.
32 "And now, O sons, listen to me:
      blessed are those who keep my ways.
33 Hear instruction and be wise,
      and do not neglect it.
34 Blessed is the one who listens to me,
      watching daily at my gates,
      waiting beside my doors.
35 For whoever finds me finds life
      and obtains favor from the LORD,
36 but he who fails to find me injures
        himself;
      all who hate me love death."

The Way of Wisdom

9 Wisdom has built her house;
      she has hewn her seven pillars.
2   She has slaughtered her beasts; she
        has mixed her wine;
      she has also set her table.
3   She has sent out her young women to
        call
      from the highest places in the town,

4   "Whoever is simple, let him turn in
        here!"
      To him who lacks sense she says,
5   "Come, eat of my bread
      and drink of the wine I have mixed.
6   Leave your simple ways, and live,
      and walk in the way of insight."

7   Whoever corrects a scoffer gets him-
        self abuse,
      and he who reproves a wicked man
        incurs injury.
8   Do not reprove a scoffer, or he will
        hate you;
      reprove a wise man, and he will
        love you.
9   Give instruction to a wise man, and
        he will be still wiser;
      teach a righteous man, and he will
        increase in learning.
10 The fear of the LORD is the beginning
        of wisdom,
      and the knowledge of the Holy One
        is insight.
11 For by me your days will be multiplied,
      and years will be added to your life.
12 If you are wise, you are wise for your-
        self;
      if you scoff, you alone will bear it.

The Way of Folly

13 The woman Folly is loud;
      she is seductive and knows nothing.
14 She sits at the door of her house;
      she takes a seat on the highest
        places of the town,
15 calling to those who pass by,
      who are going straight on their way,
16 "Whoever is simple, let him turn in
        here!"
      And to him who lacks sense she
        says,
17 "Stolen water is sweet,
      and bread eaten in secret is pleasant."
18 But he does not know that the dead
        are there,
      that her guests are in the depths of
        Sheol.

The Proverbs of Solomon

10 The proverbs of Solomon.

    A wise son makes a glad father,
      but a foolish son is a sorrow to his
        mother.

2 Treasures gained by wickedness do
   not profit,
      but righteousness delivers from
      death.
3 The LORD does not let the righteous
   go hungry,
      but he thwarts the craving of the
      wicked.
4 A slack hand causes poverty,
      but the hand of the diligent makes
      rich.
5 He who gathers in summer is a prudent son,
      but he who sleeps in harvest is a
      son who brings shame.
6 Blessings are on the head of the righteous,
      but the mouth of the wicked con-
      ceals violence.
7 The memory of the righteous is a
   blessing,
      but the name of the wicked will rot.
8 The wise of heart will receive commandments,
      but a babbling fool will come to
      ruin.
9 Whoever walks in integrity walks
   securely,
      but he who makes his ways crooked
      will be found out.
10 Whoever winks the eye causes trouble,
      and a babbling fool will come to
      ruin.
11 The mouth of the righteous is a fountain of life,
      but the mouth of the wicked con-
      ceals violence.
12 Hatred stirs up strife,
      but love covers all offenses.
13 On the lips of him who has understanding, wisdom is found,
      but a rod is for the back of him who
      lacks sense.
14 The wise lay up knowledge,
      but the mouth of a fool brings ruin
      near.
15 A rich man's wealth is his strong city;
      the poverty of the poor is their ruin.
16 The wage of the righteous leads to life,
      the gain of the wicked to sin.
17 Whoever heeds instruction is on the
   path to life,
      but he who rejects reproof leads
      others astray.
18 The one who conceals hatred has
   lying lips,
      and whoever utters slander is a
      fool.
19 When words are many, transgression
   is not lacking,
      but whoever restrains his lips is
      prudent.
20 The tongue of the righteous is choice
   silver;
      the heart of the wicked is of little
      worth.
21 The lips of the righteous feed many,
      but fools die for lack of sense.
22 The blessing of the LORD makes rich,
      and he adds no sorrow with it.
23 Doing wrong is like a joke to a fool,
      but wisdom is pleasure to a man of
      understanding.

GETTING THE MESSAGE

Vinegar (10:26) is wine that has soured.
Though generally made from grapes,
vinegar can be made with many different
fruits. It was often used for seasoning
food and bread (Ruth 2:14).

24 What the wicked dreads will come
   upon him,
      but the desire of the righteous will
      be granted.
25 When the tempest passes, the wicked
   is no more,
      but the righteous is established
      forever.
26 Like vinegar to the teeth and smoke to
   the eyes,
      so is the sluggard to those who send
      him.
27 The fear of the LORD prolongs life,
      but the years of the wicked will be
      short.
28 The hope of the righteous brings joy,
      but the expectation of the wicked
      will perish.
29 The way of the LORD is a stronghold to
   the blameless,
      but destruction to evildoers.
30 The righteous will never be removed,
      but the wicked will not dwell in the
      land.

31 The mouth of the righteous brings
      forth wisdom,
   but the perverse tongue will be cut
      off.
32 The lips of the righteous know what is
      acceptable,
   but the mouth of the wicked, what
      is perverse.

11 A false balance is an abomination to
   the LORD,
      but a just weight is his delight.
2 When pride comes, then comes disgrace,
      but with the humble is wisdom.
3 The integrity of the upright guides
      them,
   but the crookedness of the treacher-
      ous destroys them.

> ### GETTING THE MESSAGE
>
> **A different kind of security.** In biblical
> times, if a person was unable to pay his
> debt, the consequences could be serious.
> The whole family could be sold into
> slavery. If someone put up "security" for
> another person, he promised to pay that
> person's debt if he was unable to do so
> himself. Proverbs teaches that putting up
> security for another person is generally
> unwise, since those who do so risk losing
> everything if the other person cannot
> pay his debt (11:15).

4 Riches do not profit in the day of
      wrath,
   but righteousness delivers from
      death.
5 The righteousness of the blameless
      keeps his way straight,
   but the wicked falls by his own
      wickedness.
6 The righteousness of the upright
      delivers them,
   but the treacherous are taken cap-
      tive by their lust.
7 When the wicked dies, his hope will
      perish,
   and the expectation of wealth per-
      ishes too.
8 The righteous is delivered from trou-
      ble,
   and the wicked walks into it instead.

9 With his mouth the godless man
      would destroy his neighbor,
   but by knowledge the righteous are
      delivered.
10 When it goes well with the righteous,
      the city rejoices,
   and when the wicked perish there
      are shouts of gladness.
11 By the blessing of the upright a city is
      exalted,
   but by the mouth of the wicked it is
      overthrown.
12 Whoever belittles his neighbor lacks
      sense,
   but a man of understanding
      remains silent.
13 Whoever goes about slandering
      reveals secrets,
   but he who is trustworthy in spirit
      keeps a thing covered.
14 Where there is no guidance, a people
      falls,
   but in an abundance of counselors
      there is safety.
15 Whoever puts up security for a
      stranger will surely suffer
      harm,
   but he who hates striking hands in
      pledge is secure.
16 A gracious woman gets honor,
      and violent men get riches.
17 A man who is kind benefits himself,
      but a cruel man hurts himself.
18 The wicked earns deceptive wages,
      but one who sows righteousness
         gets a sure reward.
19 Whoever is steadfast in righteousness
      will live,
   but he who pursues evil will die.
20 Those of crooked heart are an abomi-
      nation to the LORD,
   but those of blameless ways are his
      delight.
21 Be assured, an evil person will not go
      unpunished,
   but the offspring of the righteous
      will be delivered.
22 Like a gold ring in a pig's snout
      is a beautiful woman without dis-
         cretion.
23 The desire of the righteous ends only
      in good;
   the expectation of the wicked in
      wrath.

24 One gives freely, yet grows all the
     richer;
   another withholds what he should
     give, and only suffers want.
25 Whoever brings blessing will be
     enriched,
   and one who waters will himself be
     watered.
26 The people curse him who holds back
     grain,
   but a blessing is on the head of him
     who sells it.
27 Whoever diligently seeks good seeks
     favor,
   but evil comes to him who searches
     for it.
28 Whoever trusts in his riches will fall,
   but the righteous will flourish like a
     green leaf.
29 Whoever troubles his own household
     will inherit the wind,
   and the fool will be servant to the
     wise of heart.
30 The fruit of the righteous is a tree of
     life,
   and whoever captures souls is wise.
31 If the righteous is repaid on earth,
   how much more the wicked and the
     sinner!

12 Whoever loves discipline loves
     knowledge,
   but he who hates reproof is stupid.
2 A good man obtains favor from the
     LORD,
   but a man of evil devices he con-
     demns.
3 No one is established by wickedness,
   but the root of the righteous will
     never be moved.
4 An excellent wife is the crown of her
     husband,
   but she who brings shame is like
     rottenness in his bones.
5 The thoughts of the righteous are just;
   the counsels of the wicked are
     deceitful.
6 The words of the wicked lie in wait for
     blood,
   but the mouth of the upright deliv-
     ers them.
7 The wicked are overthrown and are no
     more,
   but the house of the righteous will
     stand.

8 A man is commended according to
     his good sense,
   but one of twisted mind is despised.
9 Better to be lowly and have a servant
   than to play the great man and lack
     bread.
10 Whoever is righteous has regard for
     the life of his beast,
   but the mercy of the wicked is cruel.
11 Whoever works his land will have
     plenty of bread,
   but he who follows worthless pur-
     suits lacks sense.
12 Whoever is wicked covets the spoil of
     evildoers,
   but the root of the righteous bears
     fruit.
13 An evil man is ensnared by the trans-
     gression of his lips,

▶ GETTING THE MESSAGE

What is an "abomination"? When
the Bible refers to something as an
"abomination" (12:22), it means that
it is repulsive or detestable to the
Lord. Things that are an abomination
are contrary to the will of God and his
commandments.

   but the righteous escapes from
     trouble.
14 From the fruit of his mouth a man is
     satisfied with good,
   and the work of a man's hand
     comes back to him.
15 The way of a fool is right in his own
     eyes,
   but a wise man listens to advice.
16 The vexation of a fool is known at
     once,
   but the prudent ignores an insult.
17 Whoever speaks the truth gives hon-
     est evidence,
   but a false witness utters deceit.
18 There is one whose rash words are
     like sword thrusts,
   but the tongue of the wise brings
     healing.
19 Truthful lips endure forever,
   but a lying tongue is but for a
     moment.

20 Deceit is in the heart of those who
    devise evil,
  but those who plan peace have joy.
21 No ill befalls the righteous,
  but the wicked are filled with trou-
    ble.
22 Lying lips are an abomination to the
    LORD,
  but those who act faithfully are his
    delight.
23 A prudent man conceals knowledge,
  but the heart of fools proclaims folly.
24 The hand of the diligent will rule,
  while the slothful will be put to
    forced labor.
25 Anxiety in a man's heart weighs him
    down,
  but a good word makes him glad.

GETTING THE MESSAGE

What does it mean to be prudent?
The "prudent" person (13:16) is one
who uses good sense. A prudent person
carefully thinks through situations and
their possible consequences and acts
accordingly. Prudence also involves
carefully managing resources so that
one has what is needed in the future.

26 One who is righteous is a guide to his
    neighbor,
  but the way of the wicked leads
    them astray.
27 Whoever is slothful will not roast his
    game,
  but the diligent man will get pre-
    cious wealth.
28 In the path of righteousness is life,
  and in its pathway there is no death.

13 A wise son hears his father's
    instruction,
  but a scoffer does not listen to
    rebuke.
2 From the fruit of his mouth a man
    eats what is good,
  but the desire of the treacherous is
    for violence.
3 Whoever guards his mouth preserves
    his life;
  he who opens wide his lips comes
    to ruin.

4 The soul of the sluggard craves and
    gets nothing,
  while the soul of the diligent is
    richly supplied.
5 The righteous hates falsehood,
  but the wicked brings shame and
    disgrace.
6 Righteousness guards him whose way
    is blameless,
  but sin overthrows the wicked.
7 One pretends to be rich, yet has noth-
    ing;
  another pretends to be poor, yet has
    great wealth.
8 The ransom of a man's life is his wealth,
  but a poor man hears no threat.
9 The light of the righteous rejoices,
  but the lamp of the wicked will be
    put out.
10 By insolence comes nothing but strife,
  but with those who take advice is
    wisdom.
11 Wealth gained hastily will dwindle,
  but whoever gathers little by little
    will increase it.
12 Hope deferred makes the heart sick,
  but a desire fulfilled is a tree of life.
13 Whoever despises the word brings
    destruction on himself,
  but he who reveres the command-
    ment will be rewarded.
14 The teaching of the wise is a fountain
    of life,
  that one may turn away from the
    snares of death.
15 Good sense wins favor,
  but the way of the treacherous is
    their ruin.
16 In everything the prudent acts with
    knowledge,
  but a fool flaunts his folly.
17 A wicked messenger falls into trouble,
  but a faithful envoy brings healing.
18 Poverty and disgrace come to him
    who ignores instruction,
  but whoever heeds reproof is hon-
    ored.
19 A desire fulfilled is sweet to the soul,
  but to turn away from evil is an
    abomination to fools.
20 Whoever walks with the wise
    becomes wise,
  but the companion of fools will
    suffer harm.

21 Disaster pursues sinners,
    but the righteous are rewarded with
        good.
22 A good man leaves an inheritance to
        his children's children,
    but the sinner's wealth is laid up for
        the righteous.
23 The fallow ground of the poor would
        yield much food,
    but it is swept away through injus-
        tice.
24 Whoever spares the rod hates his son,
    but he who loves him is diligent to
        discipline him.
25 The righteous has enough to satisfy
        his appetite,
    but the belly of the wicked suffers
        want.

14 The wisest of women builds her
    house,
    but folly with her own hands tears
        it down.
2 Whoever walks in uprightness fears
        the LORD,
    but he who is devious in his ways
        despises him.
3 By the mouth of a fool comes a rod for
        his back,
    but the lips of the wise will preserve
        them.
4 Where there are no oxen, the manger
        is clean,
    but abundant crops come by the
        strength of the ox.
5 A faithful witness does not lie,
    but a false witness breathes out
        lies.
6 A scoffer seeks wisdom in vain,
    but knowledge is easy for a man of
        understanding.
7 Leave the presence of a fool,
    for there you do not meet words of
        knowledge.
8 The wisdom of the prudent is to dis-
        cern his way,
    but the folly of fools is deceiving.
9 Fools mock at the guilt offering,
    but the upright enjoy acceptance.
10 The heart knows its own bitterness,
    and no stranger shares its joy.
11 The house of the wicked will be
        destroyed,
    but the tent of the upright will
        flourish.

12 There is a way that seems right to a
        man,
    but its end is the way to death.
13 Even in laughter the heart may ache,
    and the end of joy may be grief.
14 The backslider in heart will be filled
        with the fruit of his ways,
    and a good man will be filled with
        the fruit of his ways.
15 The simple believes everything,
    but the prudent gives thought to his
        steps.
16 One who is wise is cautious and turns
        away from evil,
    but a fool is reckless and careless.
17 A man of quick temper acts foolishly,
    and a man of evil devices is hated.

GETTING THE MESSAGE

Tents were the most common type of
housing in biblical times (14:11). The
simple structure and sparse furnishings
made them easy to move from place to
place. Tents were made by setting poles
in the ground, then stretching animal
skin or cloth over the poles. Curtains
could be used inside the tent to divide it
into rooms. Mats often covered the floor,
with an open area left in the middle for
building a fire.

18 The simple inherit folly,
    but the prudent are crowned with
        knowledge.
19 The evil bow down before the good,
    the wicked at the gates of the righ-
        teous.
20 The poor is disliked even by his
        neighbor,
    but the rich has many friends.
21 Whoever despises his neighbor is a
        sinner,
    but blessed is he who is generous to
        the poor.
22 Do they not go astray who devise evil?
    Those who devise good meet stead-
        fast love and faithfulness.
23 In all toil there is profit,
    but mere talk tends only to poverty.
24 The crown of the wise is their wealth,
    but the folly of fools brings folly.

25 A truthful witness saves lives,
   but one who breathes out lies is
      deceitful.
26 In the fear of the LORD one has strong
      confidence,
   and his children will have a refuge.
27 The fear of the LORD is a fountain of
      life,
   that one may turn away from the
      snares of death.
28 In a multitude of people is the glory of
      a king,
   but without people a prince is
      ruined.
29 Whoever is slow to anger has great
      understanding,
   but he who has a hasty temper
      exalts folly.

> **GETTING THE MESSAGE**

Thorns grew abundantly in the lands
of the Bible (15:19). In both the Old
Testament and New Testament, thorns
were used as instruments of torture
and punishment. During the crucifixion,
Roman soldiers mocked Jesus by placing
a crown made from thorns on his head
(Matt. 27:29).

30 A tranquil heart gives life to the
      flesh,
   but envy makes the bones rot.
31 Whoever oppresses a poor man
      insults his Maker,
   but he who is generous to the
      needy honors him.
32 The wicked is overthrown through
      his evildoing,
   but the righteous finds refuge in
      his death.
33 Wisdom rests in the heart of a man
      of understanding,
   but it makes itself known even in
      the midst of fools.
34 Righteousness exalts a nation,
   but sin is a reproach to any people.
35 A servant who deals wisely has the
      king's favor,
   but his wrath falls on one who acts
      shamefully.

15 A soft answer turns away wrath,
   but a harsh word stirs up anger.
2 The tongue of the wise commends
      knowledge,
   but the mouths of fools pour out
      folly.
3 The eyes of the LORD are in every place,
   keeping watch on the evil and the
      good.
4 A gentle tongue is a tree of life,
   but perverseness in it breaks the
      spirit.
5 A fool despises his father's instruction,
   but whoever heeds reproof is pru-
      dent.
6 In the house of the righteous there is
      much treasure,
   but trouble befalls the income of
      the wicked.
7 The lips of the wise spread knowledge;
   not so the hearts of fools.
8 The sacrifice of the wicked is an
      abomination to the LORD,
   but the prayer of the upright is
      acceptable to him.
9 The way of the wicked is an abomina-
      tion to the LORD,
   but he loves him who pursues righ-
      teousness.
10 There is severe discipline for him who
      forsakes the way;
   whoever hates reproof will die.
11 Sheol and Abaddon lie open before
      the LORD;
   how much more the hearts of the
      children of man!
12 A scoffer does not like to be reproved;
   he will not go to the wise.
13 A glad heart makes a cheerful face,
   but by sorrow of heart the spirit is
      crushed.
14 The heart of him who has under-
      standing seeks knowledge,
   but the mouths of fools feed on folly.
15 All the days of the afflicted are evil,
   but the cheerful of heart has a con-
      tinual feast.
16 Better is a little with the fear of the
      LORD
   than great treasure and trouble with
      it.
17 Better is a dinner of herbs where love is
   than a fattened ox and hatred with it.

¹⁸ A hot-tempered man stirs up strife,
  but he who is slow to anger quiets
    contention.

¹⁹ The way of a sluggard is like a hedge
    of thorns,
  but the path of the upright is a level
    highway.

²⁰ A wise son makes a glad father,
  but a foolish man despises his
    mother.

²¹ Folly is a joy to him who lacks sense,
  but a man of understanding walks
    straight ahead.

²² Without counsel plans fail,
  but with many advisers they suc-
    ceed.

²³ To make an apt answer is a joy to a
    man,
  and a word in season, how good it is!

²⁴ The path of life leads upward for the
    prudent,
  that he may turn away from Sheol
    beneath.

²⁵ The LORD tears down the house of the
    proud
  but maintains the widow's bound-
    aries.

²⁶ The thoughts of the wicked are an
    abomination to the LORD,
  but gracious words are pure.

²⁷ Whoever is greedy for unjust gain
    troubles his own household,
  but he who hates bribes will live.

²⁸ The heart of the righteous ponders
    how to answer,
  but the mouth of the wicked pours
    out evil things.

²⁹ The LORD is far from the wicked,
  but he hears the prayer of the righ-
    teous.

³⁰ The light of the eyes rejoices the
    heart,
  and good news refreshes the bones.

³¹ The ear that listens to life-giving
    reproof
  will dwell among the wise.

³² Whoever ignores instruction despises
    himself,
  but he who listens to reproof gains
    intelligence.

³³ The fear of the LORD is instruction in
    wisdom,
  and humility comes before honor.

16 The plans of the heart belong to
    man,
  but the answer of the tongue is
    from the LORD.

² All the ways of a man are pure in his
    own eyes,
  but the LORD weighs the spirit.

³ Commit your work to the LORD,
  and your plans will be established.

⁴ The LORD has made everything for its
    purpose,
  even the wicked for the day of trou-
    ble.

⁵ Everyone who is arrogant in heart is
    an abomination to the LORD;
  be assured, he will not go unpun-
    ished.

⁶ By steadfast love and faithfulness
    iniquity is atoned for,
  and by the fear of the LORD one
    turns away from evil.

⁷ When a man's ways please the LORD,
  he makes even his enemies to be at
    peace with him.

⁸ Better is a little with righteousness
  than great revenues with injustice.

⁹ The heart of man plans his way,
  but the LORD establishes his steps.

¹⁰ An oracle is on the lips of a king;
  his mouth does not sin in judgment.

¹¹ A just balance and scales are the
    LORD's;
  all the weights in the bag are his
    work.

¹² It is an abomination to kings to do evil,
  for the throne is established by
    righteousness.

¹³ Righteous lips are the delight of a king,
  and he loves him who speaks what
    is right.

¹⁴ A king's wrath is a messenger of death,
  and a wise man will appease it.

¹⁵ In the light of a king's face there is life,
  and his favor is like the clouds that
    bring the spring rain.

¹⁶ How much better to get wisdom than
    gold!
  To get understanding is to be cho-
    sen rather than silver.

¹⁷ The highway of the upright turns
    aside from evil;
  whoever guards his way preserves
    his life.

18 Pride goes before destruction,
   and a haughty spirit before a fall.
19 It is better to be of a lowly spirit with
      the poor
   than to divide the spoil with the
      proud.
20 Whoever gives thought to the word
      will discover good,
   and blessed is he who trusts in the
      LORD.
21 The wise of heart is called discerning,
   and sweetness of speech increases
      persuasiveness.
22 Good sense is a fountain of life to him
      who has it,
   but the instruction of fools is folly.
23 The heart of the wise makes his
      speech judicious
   and adds persuasiveness to his lips.

GETTING THE MESSAGE

The **fountains** of ancient Israel (16:22)
were not the decorative kind seen today.
A fountain was a natural spring-fed pool
and was considered a treasure in the arid
climate. Cities were often built around
such water sources.

24 Gracious words are like a honeycomb,
   sweetness to the soul and health to
      the body.
25 There is a way that seems right to a
      man,
   but its end is the way to death.
26 A worker's appetite works for him;
   his mouth urges him on.
27 A worthless man plots evil,
   and his speech is like a scorching
      fire.
28 A dishonest man spreads strife,
   and a whisperer separates close
      friends.
29 A man of violence entices his neighbor
   and leads him in a way that is not
      good.
30 Whoever winks his eyes plans dis-
      honest things;
   he who purses his lips brings evil to
      pass.
31 Gray hair is a crown of glory;
   it is gained in a righteous life.

32 Whoever is slow to anger is better
      than the mighty,
   and he who rules his spirit than he
      who takes a city.
33 The lot is cast into the lap,
   but its every decision is from the
      LORD.

17 Better is a dry morsel with quiet
   than a house full of feasting with
      strife.
2 A servant who deals wisely will rule
      over a son who acts shamefully
   and will share the inheritance as
      one of the brothers.
3 The crucible is for silver, and the
      furnace is for gold,
   and the LORD tests hearts.
4 An evildoer listens to wicked lips,
   and a liar gives ear to a mischievous
      tongue.
5 Whoever mocks the poor insults his
      Maker;
   he who is glad at calamity will not
      go unpunished.
6 Grandchildren are the crown of the
      aged,
   and the glory of children is their
      fathers.
7 Fine speech is not becoming to a fool;
   still less is false speech to a prince.
8 A bribe is like a magic stone in the
      eyes of the one who gives it;
   wherever he turns he prospers.
9 Whoever covers an offense seeks love,
   but he who repeats a matter sepa-
      rates close friends.
10 A rebuke goes deeper into a man of
      understanding
   than a hundred blows into a fool.
11 An evil man seeks only rebellion,
   and a cruel messenger will be sent
      against him.
12 Let a man meet a she-bear robbed of
      her cubs
   rather than a fool in his folly.
13 If anyone returns evil for good,
   evil will not depart from his house.
14 The beginning of strife is like letting
      out water,
   so quit before the quarrel breaks out.
15 He who justifies the wicked and he
      who condemns the righteous
   are both alike an abomination to
      the LORD.

16 Why should a fool have money in his
    hand to buy wisdom
    when he has no sense?
17 A friend loves at all times,
    and a brother is born for adversity.
18 One who lacks sense gives a pledge
    and puts up security in the pres-
    ence of his neighbor.
19 Whoever loves transgression loves
    strife;
    he who makes his door high seeks
    destruction.
20 A man of crooked heart does not
    discover good,
    and one with a dishonest tongue
    falls into calamity.
21 He who sires a fool gets himself sor-
    row,
    and the father of a fool has no joy.
22 A joyful heart is good medicine,
    but a crushed spirit dries up the
    bones.
23 The wicked accepts a bribe in secret
    to pervert the ways of justice.
24 The discerning sets his face toward
    wisdom,
    but the eyes of a fool are on the
    ends of the earth.
25 A foolish son is a grief to his father
    and bitterness to her who bore
    him.
26 To impose a fine on a righteous man
    is not good,
    nor to strike the noble for their
    uprightness.
27 Whoever restrains his words has
    knowledge,
    and he who has a cool spirit is a
    man of understanding.
28 Even a fool who keeps silent is con-
    sidered wise;
    when he closes his lips, he is
    deemed intelligent.

18

Whoever isolates himself seeks
his own desire;
    he breaks out against all sound
    judgment.
2 A fool takes no pleasure in under-
    standing,
    but only in expressing his opinion.
3 When wickedness comes, contempt
    comes also,
    and with dishonor comes disgrace.

4 The words of a man's mouth are deep
    waters;
    the fountain of wisdom is a bub-
    bling brook.
5 It is not good to be partial to the wicked
    or to deprive the righteous of justice.
6 A fool's lips walk into a fight,
    and his mouth invites a beating.
7 A fool's mouth is his ruin,
    and his lips are a snare to his soul.
8 The words of a whisperer are like
    delicious morsels;
    they go down into the inner parts of
    the body.
9 Whoever is slack in his work
    is a brother to him who destroys.
10 The name of the LORD is a strong tower;
    the righteous man runs into it and
    is safe.

GETTING THE MESSAGE

A **bribe** is anything that is given with the
intent of persuading someone to act in a
person's favor. Bribes were forbidden in
Ex. 23:8. The poor often lost their cases
in court because they could not afford to
bribe the judge (Prov. 17:23).

11 A rich man's wealth is his strong city,
    and like a high wall in his imagina-
    tion.
12 Before destruction a man's heart is
    haughty,
    but humility comes before honor.
13 If one gives an answer before he hears,
    it is his folly and shame.
14 A man's spirit will endure sickness,
    but a crushed spirit who can bear?
15 An intelligent heart acquires knowl-
    edge,
    and the ear of the wise seeks knowl-
    edge.
16 A man's gift makes room for him
    and brings him before the great.
17 The one who states his case first
    seems right,
    until the other comes and examines
    him.
18 The lot puts an end to quarrels
    and decides between powerful
    contenders.

19 A brother offended is more unyielding than a strong city,
and quarreling is like the bars of a castle.

20 From the fruit of a man's mouth his stomach is satisfied;
he is satisfied by the yield of his lips.

21 Death and life are in the power of the tongue,
and those who love it will eat its fruits.

22 He who finds a wife finds a good thing
and obtains favor from the LORD.

23 The poor use entreaties,
but the rich answer roughly.

24 A man of many companions may come to ruin,
but there is a friend who sticks closer than a brother.

GETTING THE MESSAGE

Casting lots. Though quarrels were often settled by a judge's decision, sometimes there was not enough evidence to reach a verdict. In such cases, the parties involved might cast lots, trusting that the Lord himself would decide the result (18:18). Lots were like the dice used in various games today.

19

1 Better is a poor person who walks in his integrity
than one who is crooked in speech and is a fool.

2 Desire without knowledge is not good,
and whoever makes haste with his feet misses his way.

3 When a man's folly brings his way to ruin,
his heart rages against the LORD.

4 Wealth brings many new friends,
but a poor man is deserted by his friend.

5 A false witness will not go unpunished,
and he who breathes out lies will not escape.

6 Many seek the favor of a generous man,
and everyone is a friend to a man who gives gifts.

7 All a poor man's brothers hate him;
how much more do his friends go far from him!
He pursues them with words, but does not have them.

8 Whoever gets sense loves his own soul;
he who keeps understanding will discover good.

9 A false witness will not go unpunished,
and he who breathes out lies will perish.

10 It is not fitting for a fool to live in luxury,
much less for a slave to rule over princes.

11 Good sense makes one slow to anger,
and it is his glory to overlook an offense.

12 A king's wrath is like the growling of a lion,
but his favor is like dew on the grass.

13 A foolish son is ruin to his father,
and a wife's quarreling is a continual dripping of rain.

14 House and wealth are inherited from fathers,
but a prudent wife is from the LORD.

15 Slothfulness casts into a deep sleep,
and an idle person will suffer hunger.

16 Whoever keeps the commandment keeps his life;
he who despises his ways will die.

17 Whoever is generous to the poor lends to the LORD,
and he will repay him for his deed.

18 Discipline your son, for there is hope;
do not set your heart on putting him to death.

19 A man of great wrath will pay the penalty,
for if you deliver him, you will only have to do it again.

20 Listen to advice and accept instruction,
that you may gain wisdom in the future.

21 Many are the plans in the mind of a man,
but it is the purpose of the LORD that will stand.

22 What is desired in a man is steadfast love,
and a poor man is better than a liar.

23 The fear of the LORD leads to life,
    and whoever has it rests satisfied;
    he will not be visited by harm.

24 The sluggard buries his hand in the
    dish
    and will not even bring it back to
    his mouth.

25 Strike a scoffer, and the simple will
    learn prudence;
    reprove a man of understanding,
    and he will gain knowledge.

26 He who does violence to his father
    and chases away his mother
    is a son who brings shame and
    reproach.

27 Cease to hear instruction, my son,
    and you will stray from the words of
    knowledge.

28 A worthless witness mocks at justice,
    and the mouth of the wicked
    devours iniquity.

29 Condemnation is ready for scoffers,
    and beating for the backs of fools.

20 Wine is a mocker, strong drink a
    brawler,
    and whoever is led astray by it is
    not wise.

2 The terror of a king is like the growl-
    ing of a lion;
    whoever provokes him to anger
    forfeits his life.

3 It is an honor for a man to keep aloof
    from strife,
    but every fool will be quarreling.

4 The sluggard does not plow in the
    autumn;
    he will seek at harvest and have
    nothing.

5 The purpose in a man's heart is like
    deep water,
    but a man of understanding will
    draw it out.

6 Many a man proclaims his own stead-
    fast love,
    but a faithful man who can find?

7 The righteous who walks in his integ-
    rity—
    blessed are his children after him!

8 A king who sits on the throne of judg-
    ment
    winnows all evil with his eyes.

9 Who can say, "I have made my heart
    pure;
    I am clean from my sin"?

10 Unequal weights and unequal mea-
    sures
    are both alike an abomination to
    the LORD.

11 Even a child makes himself known by
    his acts,
    by whether his conduct is pure and
    upright.

12 The hearing ear and the seeing eye,
    the LORD has made them both.

13 Love not sleep, lest you come to pov-
    erty;
    open your eyes, and you will have
    plenty of bread.

14 "Bad, bad," says the buyer,
    but when he goes away, then he
    boasts.

15 There is gold and abundance of costly
    stones,
    but the lips of knowledge are a
    precious jewel.

GETTING THE MESSAGE

Unequal weights. The price for some goods was fixed according to their weight. If the seller's scales were unequal (20:23), the buyer could be charged far more than the fair price of the goods.

16 Take a man's garment when he has
    put up security for a stranger,
    and hold it in pledge when he puts
    up security for foreigners.

17 Bread gained by deceit is sweet to a
    man,
    but afterward his mouth will be full
    of gravel.

18 Plans are established by counsel;
    by wise guidance wage war.

19 Whoever goes about slandering
    reveals secrets;
    therefore do not associate with a
    simple babbler.

20 If one curses his father or his mother,
    his lamp will be put out in utter
    darkness.

21 An inheritance gained hastily in the
    beginning
    will not be blessed in the end.

22 Do not say, "I will repay evil";
    wait for the LORD, and he will
    deliver you.

23 Unequal weights are an abomination
   to the LORD,
      and false scales are not good.
24 A man's steps are from the LORD;
      how then can man understand his
      way?
25 It is a snare to say rashly, "It is holy,"
      and to reflect only after making
      vows.
26 A wise king winnows the wicked
      and drives the wheel over them.
27 The spirit of man is the lamp of the
   LORD,
      searching all his innermost parts.
28 Steadfast love and faithfulness preserve the king,
      and by steadfast love his throne is
      upheld.

GETTING THE MESSAGE

The concept of **weighing the heart**
(21:2) originated in Egypt. Egyptians
believed that when a person died, the
gods placed that person's heart on a set
of golden scales along with the Feather
of Truth. If the heart weighed less than
the feather, the person was admitted
into the afterlife. It is possible that the
Israelites brought this imagery with them
when they left Egypt and replaced the
Egyptian gods with Yahweh, who is the
true judge of the heart.

29 The glory of young men is their
   strength,
      but the splendor of old men is their
      gray hair.
30 Blows that wound cleanse away evil;
      strokes make clean the innermost
      parts.

21 The king's heart is a stream of
   water in the hand of the LORD;
      he turns it wherever he will.
2 Every way of a man is right in his own
   eyes,
      but the LORD weighs the heart.
3 To do righteousness and justice
      is more acceptable to the LORD than
      sacrifice.
4 Haughty eyes and a proud heart,
      the lamp of the wicked, are sin.

5 The plans of the diligent lead surely to
   abundance,
      but everyone who is hasty comes
      only to poverty.
6 The getting of treasures by a lying
   tongue
      is a fleeting vapor and a snare of
      death.
7 The violence of the wicked will sweep
   them away,
      because they refuse to do what is
      just.
8 The way of the guilty is crooked,
      but the conduct of the pure is
      upright.
9 It is better to live in a corner of the
   housetop
      than in a house shared with a quar-
      relsome wife.
10 The soul of the wicked desires evil;
      his neighbor finds no mercy in his
      eyes.
11 When a scoffer is punished, the simple becomes wise;
      when a wise man is instructed, he
      gains knowledge.
12 The Righteous One observes the
   house of the wicked;
      he throws the wicked down to ruin.
13 Whoever closes his ear to the cry of
   the poor
      will himself call out and not be
      answered.
14 A gift in secret averts anger,
      and a concealed bribe, strong wrath.
15 When justice is done, it is a joy to the
   righteous
      but terror to evildoers.
16 One who wanders from the way of
   good sense
      will rest in the assembly of the dead.
17 Whoever loves pleasure will be a poor
   man;
      he who loves wine and oil will not
      be rich.
18 The wicked is a ransom for the righteous,
      and the traitor for the upright.
19 It is better to live in a desert land
      than with a quarrelsome and fretful
      woman.
20 Precious treasure and oil are in a wise
   man's dwelling,
      but a foolish man devours it.

²¹ Whoever pursues righteousness and
kindness
     will find life, righteousness, and
honor.
²² A wise man scales the city of the
mighty
     and brings down the stronghold in
which they trust.
²³ Whoever keeps his mouth and his
tongue
     keeps himself out of trouble.
²⁴ "Scoffer" is the name of the arrogant,
haughty man
     who acts with arrogant pride.
²⁵ The desire of the sluggard kills him,
     for his hands refuse to labor.
²⁶ All day long he craves and craves,
     but the righteous gives and does
not hold back.
²⁷ The sacrifice of the wicked is an
abomination;
     how much more when he brings it
with evil intent.
²⁸ A false witness will perish,
     but the word of a man who hears
will endure.
²⁹ A wicked man puts on a bold face,
     but the upright gives thought to his
ways.
³⁰ No wisdom, no understanding, no
counsel
     can avail against the Lord.
³¹ The horse is made ready for the day of
battle,
     but the victory belongs to the Lord.

22 A good name is to be chosen
rather than great riches,
     and favor is better than silver or gold.
² The rich and the poor meet together;
     the Lord is the maker of them all.
³ The prudent sees danger and hides
himself,
     but the simple go on and suffer for it.
⁴ The reward for humility and fear of
the Lord
     is riches and honor and life.
⁵ Thorns and snares are in the way of
the crooked;
     whoever guards his soul will keep
far from them.
⁶ Train up a child in the way he should
go;
     even when he is old he will not
depart from it.

⁷ The rich rules over the poor,
     and the borrower is the slave of the
lender.
⁸ Whoever sows injustice will reap
calamity,
     and the rod of his fury will fail.
⁹ Whoever has a bountiful eye will be
blessed,
     for he shares his bread with the poor.
¹⁰ Drive out a scoffer, and strife will go
out,
     and quarreling and abuse will cease.
¹¹ He who loves purity of heart,
     and whose speech is gracious, will
have the king as his friend.
¹² The eyes of the Lord keep watch over
knowledge,
     but he overthrows the words of the
traitor.
¹³ The sluggard says, "There is a lion
outside!
     I shall be killed in the streets!"
¹⁴ The mouth of forbidden women is a
deep pit;
     he with whom the Lord is angry
will fall into it.
¹⁵ Folly is bound up in the heart of a child,
     but the rod of discipline drives it far
from him.
¹⁶ Whoever oppresses the poor to
increase his own wealth,
     or gives to the rich, will only come
to poverty.

Words of the Wise

¹⁷ Incline your ear, and hear the words
of the wise,
     and apply your heart to my knowl-
edge,
¹⁸ for it will be pleasant if you keep them
within you,
     if all of them are ready on your lips.
¹⁹ That your trust may be in the Lord,
     I have made them known to you
today, even to you.
²⁰ Have I not written for you thirty say-
ings
     of counsel and knowledge,
²¹ to make you know what is right and
true,
     that you may give a true answer to
those who sent you?

²² Do not rob the poor, because he is poor,
     or crush the afflicted at the gate,

23 for the LORD will plead their cause
   and rob of life those who rob them.
24 Make no friendship with a man given
   to anger,
   nor go with a wrathful man,
25 lest you learn his ways
   and entangle yourself in a snare.
26 Be not one of those who give pledges,
   who put up security for debts.
27 If you have nothing with which to
   pay,
   why should your bed be taken from
   under you?
28 Do not move the ancient landmark
   that your fathers have set.
29 Do you see a man skillful in his
   work?
   He will stand before kings;
   he will not stand before obscure
   men.

> **GETTING THE MESSAGE**

Landmarks (22:28) were boundary stones placed on each corner of a person's property to show where it began and ended.

23

When you sit down to eat with a ruler,
   observe carefully what is before you,
2 and put a knife to your throat
   if you are given to appetite.
3 Do not desire his delicacies,
   for they are deceptive food.
4 Do not toil to acquire wealth;
   be discerning enough to desist.
5 When your eyes light on it, it is gone,
   for suddenly it sprouts wings,
   flying like an eagle toward heaven.
6 Do not eat the bread of a man who is
   stingy;
   do not desire his delicacies,
7 for he is like one who is inwardly
   calculating.
   "Eat and drink!" he says to you,
   but his heart is not with you.
8 You will vomit up the morsels that
   you have eaten,
   and waste your pleasant words.
9 Do not speak in the hearing of a fool,
   for he will despise the good sense of
   your words.

10 Do not move an ancient landmark
    or enter the fields of the fatherless,
11 for their Redeemer is strong;
    he will plead their cause against you.
12 Apply your heart to instruction
    and your ear to words of knowledge.
13 Do not withhold discipline from a
    child;
    if you strike him with a rod, he will
    not die.
14 If you strike him with the rod,
    you will save his soul from Sheol.
15 My son, if your heart is wise,
    my heart too will be glad.
16 My inmost being will exult
    when your lips speak what is right.
17 Let not your heart envy sinners,
    but continue in the fear of the LORD
    all the day.
18 Surely there is a future,
    and your hope will not be cut off.
19 Hear, my son, and be wise,
    and direct your heart in the way.
20 Be not among drunkards
    or among gluttonous eaters of meat,
21 for the drunkard and the glutton will
    come to poverty,
    and slumber will clothe them with
    rags.
22 Listen to your father who gave you life,
    and do not despise your mother
    when she is old.
23 Buy truth, and do not sell it;
    buy wisdom, instruction, and
    understanding.
24 The father of the righteous will greatly
    rejoice;
    he who fathers a wise son will be
    glad in him.
25 Let your father and mother be glad;
    let her who bore you rejoice.
26 My son, give me your heart,
    and let your eyes observe my ways.
27 For a prostitute is a deep pit;
    an adulteress is a narrow well.
28 She lies in wait like a robber
    and increases the traitors among
    mankind.
29 Who has woe? Who has sorrow?
    Who has strife? Who has complain-
    ing?
    Who has wounds without cause?
    Who has redness of eyes?

30 Those who tarry long over wine;
  those who go to try mixed wine.
31 Do not look at wine when it is red,
  when it sparkles in the cup
  and goes down smoothly.
32 In the end it bites like a serpent
  and stings like an adder.
33 Your eyes will see strange things,
  and your heart utter perverse things.
34 You will be like one who lies down in
  the midst of the sea,
  like one who lies on the top of a
  mast.
35 "They struck me," you will say, "but I
  was not hurt;
  they beat me, but I did not feel it.
  When shall I awake?
  I must have another drink."

24 Be not envious of evil men,
  nor desire to be with them,
2 for their hearts devise violence,
  and their lips talk of trouble.

3 By wisdom a house is built,
  and by understanding it is established;
4 by knowledge the rooms are filled
  with all precious and pleasant riches.
5 A wise man is full of strength,
  and a man of knowledge enhances
  his might,
6 for by wise guidance you can wage
  your war,
  and in abundance of counselors
  there is victory.
7 Wisdom is too high for a fool;
  in the gate he does not open his
  mouth.
8 Whoever plans to do evil
  will be called a schemer.
9 The devising of folly is sin,
  and the scoffer is an abomination
  to mankind.
10 If you faint in the day of adversity,
  your strength is small.
11 Rescue those who are being taken
  away to death;
  hold back those who are stumbling
  to the slaughter.
12 If you say, "Behold, we did not know
  this,"
  does not he who weighs the heart
  perceive it?

Does not he who keeps watch over
  your soul know it,
  and will he not repay man according to his work?
13 My son, eat honey, for it is good,
  and the drippings of the honeycomb are sweet to your taste.
14 Know that wisdom is such to your soul;
  if you find it, there will be a future,
  and your hope will not be cut off.
15 Lie not in wait as a wicked man against
  the dwelling of the righteous;
  do no violence to his home;
16 for the righteous falls seven times and
  rises again,
  but the wicked stumble in times of
  calamity.

GETTING THE MESSAGE

Mixed wine. Since the process of
distillation had not yet been invented,
the wine of ancient Palestine had a low
alcoholic content. Sometimes, people
added various herbs and spices to
the wine to increase its potency. The
drunkenness described in 23:29–35
could have been caused by drinking
such "mixed wine" (v. 30).

17 Do not rejoice when your enemy falls,
  and let not your heart be glad when
  he stumbles,
18 lest the LORD see it and be displeased,
  and turn away his anger from him.
19 Fret not yourself because of evildoers,
  and be not envious of the wicked,
20 for the evil man has no future;
  the lamp of the wicked will be put
  out.
21 My son, fear the LORD and the king,
  and do not join with those who do
  otherwise,
22 for disaster will arise suddenly from
  them,
  and who knows the ruin that will
  come from them both?

More Sayings of the Wise
23 These also are sayings of the wise.

  Partiality in judging is not good.

24 Whoever says to the wicked, "You are
      in the right,"
   will be cursed by peoples, abhorred
      by nations,
25 but those who rebuke the wicked will
      have delight,
   and a good blessing will come upon
      them.
26 Whoever gives an honest answer
   kisses the lips.

27 Prepare your work outside;
   get everything ready for yourself in
      the field,
   and after that build your house.

28 Be not a witness against your neigh-
      bor without cause,
   and do not deceive with your lips.

The phrase **kisses the lips** in 24:26
probably has more to do with respect
and friendly affection than with any idea
of romance. The proverb teaches that
speaking honestly to a person is one way
of showing respect and affection.

29 Do not say, "I will do to him as he has
      done to me;
   I will pay the man back for what he
      has done."
30 I passed by the field of a sluggard,
   by the vineyard of a man lacking
      sense,
31 and behold, it was all overgrown with
      thorns;
   the ground was covered with net-
      tles,
   and its stone wall was broken
      down.
32 Then I saw and considered it;
   I looked and received instruction.
33 A little sleep, a little slumber,
   a little folding of the hands to rest,
34 and poverty will come upon you like a
      robber,
   and want like an armed man.

More Proverbs of Solomon

25 These also are proverbs of Solomon
which the men of Hezekiah king of
Judah copied.

2 It is the glory of God to conceal things,
   but the glory of kings to search
      things out.
3 As the heavens for height, and the
      earth for depth,
   so the heart of kings is unsearchable.
4 Take away the dross from the silver,
   and the smith has material for a
      vessel;
5 take away the wicked from the pres-
      ence of the king,
   and his throne will be established
      in righteousness.
6 Do not put yourself forward in the
      king's presence
   or stand in the place of the great,
7 for it is better to be told, "Come up
      here,"
   than to be put lower in the presence
      of a noble.

   What your eyes have seen
8   do not hastily bring into court,
   for what will you do in the end,
      when your neighbor puts you to
         shame?
9 Argue your case with your neighbor
      himself,
   and do not reveal another's secret,
10 lest he who hears you bring shame
      upon you,
   and your ill repute have no end.

11 A word fitly spoken
   is like apples of gold in a setting of
      silver.
12 Like a gold ring or an ornament of
      gold
   is a wise reprover to a listening ear.
13 Like the cold of snow in the time of
      harvest
   is a faithful messenger to those who
      send him;
   he refreshes the soul of his masters.
14 Like clouds and wind without rain
   is a man who boasts of a gift he
      does not give.
15 With patience a ruler may be per-
      suaded,
   and a soft tongue will break a bone.
16 If you have found honey, eat only
      enough for you,
   lest you have your fill of it and
      vomit it.

17 Let your foot be seldom in your neigh-
        bor's house,
        lest he have his fill of you and hate
        you.
18 A man who bears false witness
        against his neighbor
        is like a war club, or a sword, or a
        sharp arrow.
19 Trusting in a treacherous man in time
        of trouble
        is like a bad tooth or a foot that slips.
20 Whoever sings songs to a heavy heart
        is like one who takes off a garment
        on a cold day,
        and like vinegar on soda.
21 If your enemy is hungry, give him
        bread to eat,
        and if he is thirsty, give him water
        to drink,
22 for you will heap burning coals on his
        head,
        and the LORD will reward you.
23 The north wind brings forth rain,
        and a backbiting tongue, angry looks.
24 It is better to live in a corner of the
        housetop
        than in a house shared with a quar-
        relsome wife.
25 Like cold water to a thirsty soul,
        so is good news from a far country.
26 Like a muddied spring or a polluted
        fountain
        is a righteous man who gives way
        before the wicked.
27 It is not good to eat much honey,
        nor is it glorious to seek one's own
        glory.
28 A man without self-control
        is like a city broken into and left
        without walls.

26 Like snow in summer or rain in
        harvest,
        so honor is not fitting for a fool.
2 Like a sparrow in its flitting, like a
        swallow in its flying,
        a curse that is causeless does not
        alight.
3 A whip for the horse, a bridle for the
        donkey,
        and a rod for the back of fools.
4 Answer not a fool according to his folly,
        lest you be like him yourself.
5 Answer a fool according to his folly,
        lest he be wise in his own eyes.

6 Whoever sends a message by the hand
        of a fool
        cuts off his own feet and drinks
        violence.
7 Like a lame man's legs, which hang
        useless,
        is a proverb in the mouth of fools.
8 Like one who binds the stone in the
        sling
        is one who gives honor to a fool.
9 Like a thorn that goes up into the
        hand of a drunkard
        is a proverb in the mouth of fools.
10 Like an archer who wounds everyone
        is one who hires a passing fool or
        drunkard.
11 Like a dog that returns to his vomit
        is a fool who repeats his folly.

> **GETTING THE MESSAGE**

Rains from the north. In Palestine, winds from the north usually bring good weather. When the north wind brings rain, as in 25:23, the rain can be sudden and damaging. Thus it is compared here to a "backbiting tongue."

12 Do you see a man who is wise in his
        own eyes?
        There is more hope for a fool than
        for him.
13 The sluggard says, "There is a lion in
        the road!
        There is a lion in the streets!"
14 As a door turns on its hinges,
        so does a sluggard on his bed.
15 The sluggard buries his hand in the
        dish;
        it wears him out to bring it back to
        his mouth.
16 The sluggard is wiser in his own eyes
        than seven men who can answer
        sensibly.
17 Whoever meddles in a quarrel not his
        own
        is like one who takes a passing dog
        by the ears.
18 Like a madman who throws fire-
        brands, arrows, and death
19 is the man who deceives his neighbor
        and says, "I am only joking!"

20 For lack of wood the fire goes out,
    and where there is no whisperer,
      quarreling ceases.
21 As charcoal to hot embers and wood
    to fire,
    so is a quarrelsome man for kin-
      dling strife.
22 The words of a whisperer are like
    delicious morsels;
    they go down into the inner parts of
      the body.
23 Like the glaze covering an earthen
    vessel
    are fervent lips with an evil heart.
24 Whoever hates disguises himself with
    his lips
    and harbors deceit in his heart;

GETTING THE MESSAGE

Glazing over the truth? As in modern times, clay pottery was often glazed to improve its appearance. But glaze could also be used to hide poor craftsmanship. It is this dishonest use that is described in 26:23.

25 when he speaks graciously, believe
    him not,
    for there are seven abominations in
      his heart;
26 though his hatred be covered with
    deception,
    his wickedness will be exposed in
      the assembly.
27 Whoever digs a pit will fall into it,
    and a stone will come back on him
      who starts it rolling.
28 A lying tongue hates its victims,
    and a flattering mouth works ruin.

27 Do not boast about tomorrow,
    for you do not know what a day
      may bring.
2 Let another praise you, and not your
    own mouth;
    a stranger, and not your own lips.
3 A stone is heavy, and sand is weighty,
    but a fool's provocation is heavier
      than both.
4 Wrath is cruel, anger is overwhelming,
    but who can stand before jealousy?

5 Better is open rebuke
    than hidden love.
6 Faithful are the wounds of a friend;
    profuse are the kisses of an enemy.
7 One who is full loathes honey,
    but to one who is hungry every-
      thing bitter is sweet.
8 Like a bird that strays from its nest
    is a man who strays from his
      home.
9 Oil and perfume make the heart glad,
    and the sweetness of a friend
      comes from his earnest
      counsel.
10 Do not forsake your friend and your
    father's friend,
    and do not go to your brother's
      house in the day of your
      calamity.
    Better is a neighbor who is near
    than a brother who is far away.
11 Be wise, my son, and make my heart
    glad,
    that I may answer him who
      reproaches me.
12 The prudent sees danger and hides
    himself,
    but the simple go on and suffer for
      it.
13 Take a man's garment when he has
    put up security for a stranger,
    and hold it in pledge when he puts
      up security for an adulteress.
14 Whoever blesses his neighbor with a
    loud voice,
    rising early in the morning,
    will be counted as cursing.
15 A continual dripping on a rainy day
    and a quarrelsome wife are alike;
16 to restrain her is to restrain the wind
    or to grasp oil in one's right hand.
17 Iron sharpens iron,
    and one man sharpens another.
18 Whoever tends a fig tree will eat its
    fruit,
    and he who guards his master will
      be honored.
19 As in water face reflects face,
    so the heart of man reflects the
      man.
20 Sheol and Abaddon are never satis-
    fied,
    and never satisfied are the eyes of
      man.

21 The crucible is for silver, and the
     furnace is for gold,
       and a man is tested by his praise.
22 Crush a fool in a mortar with a pestle
     along with crushed grain,
       yet his folly will not depart from
         him.
23 Know well the condition of your flocks,
       and give attention to your herds,
24 for riches do not last forever;
       and does a crown endure to all
         generations?
25 When the grass is gone and the new
     growth appears
       and the vegetation of the moun-
         tains is gathered,
26 the lambs will provide your clothing,
       and the goats the price of a field.
27 There will be enough goats' milk for
     your food,
       for the food of your household
       and maintenance for your girls.

28 The wicked flee when no one
       pursues,
       but the righteous are bold as a lion.
2 When a land transgresses, it has many
     rulers,
       but with a man of understanding
         and knowledge,
       its stability will long continue.
3 A poor man who oppresses the poor
       is a beating rain that leaves no food.
4 Those who forsake the law praise the
     wicked,
       but those who keep the law strive
         against them.
5 Evil men do not understand justice,
       but those who seek the LORD under-
         stand it completely.
6 Better is a poor man who walks in his
     integrity
       than a rich man who is crooked in
         his ways.
7 The one who keeps the law is a son
     with understanding,
       but a companion of gluttons
         shames his father.
8 Whoever multiplies his wealth by
     interest and profit
       gathers it for him who is generous
         to the poor.
9 If one turns away his ear from hearing
     the law,
       even his prayer is an abomination.

10 Whoever misleads the upright into an
     evil way
       will fall into his own pit,
       but the blameless will have a goodly
         inheritance.
11 A rich man is wise in his own eyes,
       but a poor man who has under-
         standing will find him out.
12 When the righteous triumph, there is
     great glory,
       but when the wicked rise, people
         hide themselves.
13 Whoever conceals his transgressions
     will not prosper,
       but he who confesses and forsakes
         them will obtain mercy.
14 Blessed is the one who fears the LORD
     always,
       but whoever hardens his heart will
         fall into calamity.

GETTING THE MESSAGE

What is a crucible? In the ancient world,
a crucible (27:21) was a bowl-shaped
instrument used to hold metals such as
gold and silver for the refining process.
The crucible had to withstand the high
temperatures needed to melt out the
impurities within the metals. Materials
such as clay or stone were used as
crucibles.

15 Like a roaring lion or a charging bear
       is a wicked ruler over a poor peo-
         ple.
16 A ruler who lacks understanding is a
     cruel oppressor,
       but he who hates unjust gain will
         prolong his days.
17 If one is burdened with the blood of
     another,
       he will be a fugitive until death;
       let no one help him.
18 Whoever walks in integrity will be
     delivered,
       but he who is crooked in his ways
         will suddenly fall.
19 Whoever works his land will have
     plenty of bread,
       but he who follows worthless pur-
         suits will have plenty of poverty.

20 A faithful man will abound with
   blessings,
      but whoever hastens to be rich will
      not go unpunished.
21 To show partiality is not good,
      but for a piece of bread a man will
      do wrong.
22 A stingy man hastens after wealth
   and does not know that poverty will
   come upon him.
23 Whoever rebukes a man will afterward find more favor
      than he who flatters with his
      tongue.
24 Whoever robs his father or his
   mother
   and says, "That is no transgression,"
   is a companion to a man who
   destroys.

> **GETTING THE MESSAGE**

Gluttony (28:7) refers to excessive
eating. The Bible condemns gluttony as
well as drunkenness. Proverbs teaches
that eating and drinking in excess can
lead to poverty (23:19–21).

25 A greedy man stirs up strife,
      but the one who trusts in the LORD
      will be enriched.
26 Whoever trusts in his own mind is a
   fool,
      but he who walks in wisdom will be
      delivered.
27 Whoever gives to the poor will not
   want,
      but he who hides his eyes will get
      many a curse.
28 When the wicked rise, people hide
   themselves,
      but when they perish, the righteous
      increase.

29 He who is often reproved, yet
   stiffens his neck,
      will suddenly be broken beyond
      healing.
2 When the righteous increase, the
   people rejoice,
      but when the wicked rule, the peo-
      ple groan.

3 He who loves wisdom makes his
   father glad,
      but a companion of prostitutes
      squanders his wealth.
4 By justice a king builds up the land,
      but he who exacts gifts tears it down.
5 A man who flatters his neighbor
   spreads a net for his feet.
6 An evil man is ensnared in his transgression,
      but a righteous man sings and
      rejoices.
7 A righteous man knows the rights of
   the poor;
      a wicked man does not understand
      such knowledge.
8 Scoffers set a city aflame,
      but the wise turn away wrath.
9 If a wise man has an argument with a
   fool,
      the fool only rages and laughs, and
      there is no quiet.
10 Bloodthirsty men hate one who is
   blameless
   and seek the life of the upright.
11 A fool gives full vent to his spirit,
      but a wise man quietly holds it back.
12 If a ruler listens to falsehood,
   all his officials will be wicked.
13 The poor man and the oppressor meet
      together;
      the LORD gives light to the eyes of
      both.
14 If a king faithfully judges the poor,
      his throne will be established for-
      ever.
15 The rod and reproof give wisdom,
      but a child left to himself brings
      shame to his mother.
16 When the wicked increase, transgression increases,
      but the righteous will look upon
      their downfall.
17 Discipline your son, and he will give
      you rest;
      he will give delight to your heart.
18 Where there is no prophetic vision
      the people cast off restraint,
      but blessed is he who keeps the law.
19 By mere words a servant is not disciplined,
      for though he understands, he will
      not respond.

20 Do you see a man who is hasty in his
words?
There is more hope for a fool than
for him.

21 Whoever pampers his servant from
childhood
will in the end find him his heir.

22 A man of wrath stirs up strife,
and one given to anger causes
much transgression.

23 One's pride will bring him low,
but he who is lowly in spirit will
obtain honor.

24 The partner of a thief hates his own life;
he hears the curse, but discloses
nothing.

25 The fear of man lays a snare,
but whoever trusts in the LORD is
safe.

26 Many seek the face of a ruler,
but it is from the LORD that a man
gets justice.

27 An unjust man is an abomination to
the righteous,
but one whose way is straight is an
abomination to the wicked.

The Words of Agur

30 The words of Agur son of Jakeh.
The oracle.

The man declares, I am weary, O God;
I am weary, O God, and worn out.

2 Surely I am too stupid to be a man.
I have not the understanding of a
man.

3 I have not learned wisdom,
nor have I knowledge of the Holy One.

4 Who has ascended to heaven and
come down?
Who has gathered the wind in his
fists?
Who has wrapped up the waters in a
garment?
Who has established all the ends of
the earth?
What is his name, and what is his
son's name?
Surely you know!

5 Every word of God proves true;
he is a shield to those who take
refuge in him.

6 Do not add to his words,
lest he rebuke you and you be
found a liar.

7 Two things I ask of you;
deny them not to me before I die:

8 Remove far from me falsehood and
lying;
give me neither poverty nor riches;
feed me with the food that is need-
ful for me,

9 lest I be full and deny you
and say, "Who is the LORD?"
or lest I be poor and steal
and profane the name of my God.

10 Do not slander a servant to his master,
lest he curse you, and you be held
guilty.

11 There are those who curse their
fathers
and do not bless their mothers.

12 There are those who are clean in their
own eyes
but are not washed of their filth.

> **GETTING THE MESSAGE**

Hezekiah's contribution to Proverbs.
Although most of the Proverbs were
collected or written by King Solomon,
who reigned from 971–931 B.C., the book
of Proverbs did not exist in its present
form until the time of King Hezekiah,
some 200 years later. Hezekiah and
"his men," probably his scribes, recorded
chs. 25–29.

---

13 There are those—how lofty are their
eyes,
how high their eyelids lift!

14 There are those whose teeth are
swords,
whose fangs are knives,
to devour the poor from off the earth,
the needy from among mankind.

15 The leech has two daughters:
Give and Give.
Three things are never satisfied;
four never say, "Enough":

16 Sheol, the barren womb,
the land never satisfied with water,
and the fire that never says,
"Enough."

17 The eye that mocks a father
and scorns to obey a mother

will be picked out by the ravens of the
    valley
  and eaten by the vultures.

18 Three things are too wonderful for me;
  four I do not understand:
19 the way of an eagle in the sky,
  the way of a serpent on a rock,
the way of a ship on the high seas,
  and the way of a man with a virgin.

20 This is the way of an adulteress:
  she eats and wipes her mouth
and says, "I have done no wrong."

21 Under three things the earth trembles;
  under four it cannot bear up:
22 a slave when he becomes king,
  and a fool when he is filled with
    food;
23 an unloved woman when she gets a
    husband,
  and a maidservant when she dis-
    places her mistress.

GETTING THE MESSAGE

Rock badgers are small cliff-dwelling animals closely resembling guinea pigs. They live and forage for food in large groups and are good at hiding. They are best known for posting sentries that alert the group when danger is near. Perhaps it was this mark of wisdom that earned them a mention in Proverbs (30:26).

24 Four things on earth are small,
  but they are exceedingly wise:
25 the ants are a people not strong,
  yet they provide their food in the
    summer;
26 the rock badgers are a people not
    mighty,
  yet they make their homes in the
    cliffs;
27 the locusts have no king,
  yet all of them march in rank;
28 the lizard you can take in your hands,
  yet it is in kings' palaces.

29 Three things are stately in their tread;
  four are stately in their stride:
30 the lion, which is mightiest among
    beasts
  and does not turn back before any;

31 the strutting rooster, the he-goat,
  and a king whose army is with him.

32 If you have been foolish, exalting
    yourself,
  or if you have been devising evil,
  put your hand on your mouth.
33 For pressing milk produces curds,
  pressing the nose produces blood,
  and pressing anger produces strife.

The Words of King Lemuel

31 The words of King Lemuel. An oracle
that his mother taught him:

2 What are you doing, my son? What are
    you doing, son of my womb?
  What are you doing, son of my vows?
3 Do not give your strength to women,
  your ways to those who destroy
    kings.
4 It is not for kings, O Lemuel,
  it is not for kings to drink wine,
  or for rulers to take strong drink,
5 lest they drink and forget what has
    been decreed
  and pervert the rights of all the
    afflicted.
6 Give strong drink to the one who is
    perishing,
  and wine to those in bitter distress;
7 let them drink and forget their poverty
  and remember their misery no more.
8 Open your mouth for the mute,
  for the rights of all who are destitute.
9 Open your mouth, judge righteously,
  defend the rights of the poor and
    needy.

The Woman Who Fears the Lord

10 An excellent wife who can find?
  She is far more precious than jewels.
11 The heart of her husband trusts in her,
  and he will have no lack of gain.
12 She does him good, and not harm,
  all the days of her life.
13 She seeks wool and flax,
  and works with willing hands.
14 She is like the ships of the merchant;
  she brings her food from afar.
15 She rises while it is yet night
  and provides food for her household
  and portions for her maidens.
16 She considers a field and buys it;
  with the fruit of her hands she
    plants a vineyard.

¹⁷ She dresses herself with strength
 and makes her arms strong.

¹⁸ She perceives that her merchandise is
  profitable.
 Her lamp does not go out at night.

¹⁹ She puts her hands to the distaff,
 and her hands hold the spindle.

²⁰ She opens her hand to the poor
 and reaches out her hands to the
  needy.

²¹ She is not afraid of snow for her
  household,
 for all her household are clothed in
  scarlet.

²² She makes bed coverings for herself;
 her clothing is fine linen and purple.

²³ Her husband is known in the gates
 when he sits among the elders of
  the land.

²⁴ She makes linen garments and sells
  them;
 she delivers sashes to the merchant.

²⁵ Strength and dignity are her clothing,
 and she laughs at the time to come.

²⁶ She opens her mouth with wisdom,
 and the teaching of kindness is on
  her tongue.

²⁷ She looks well to the ways of her
  household
 and does not eat the bread of idleness.

²⁸ Her children rise up and call her
  blessed;
 her husband also, and he praises
  her:

²⁹ "Many women have done excellently,
 but you surpass them all."

³⁰ Charm is deceitful, and beauty is
  vain,
 but a woman who fears the LORD is
  to be praised.

³¹ Give her of the fruit of her hands,
 and let her works praise her in the
  gates.

INTRODUCTION TO ECCLESIASTES

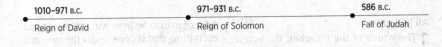

1010–971 B.C.	971–931 B.C.	586 B.C.
Reign of David	Reign of Solomon	Fall of Judah

AUTHOR

The author of Ecclesiastes calls himself "the Preacher" (1:1). Some interpreters have concluded that this was Solomon, while others think he was a role-playing writer later than Solomon. Either way, the book claims that its wisdom comes from the "one Shepherd" (12:11), the Lord himself.

THEME AND INTERPRETATION OF ECCLESIASTES

The theme of Ecclesiastes is the necessity of fearing God in this fallen, confusing world. Each human being wants to understand all the ways God is acting in the world, but he cannot, because he is not God. And yet the faithful do not despair but cling to God, even when they cannot see what God is doing. The Lord deserves his people's trust. They can leave everything to him while they seek to understand what it means to "fear God and keep his commandments" (12:13). This is true wisdom.

KEY THEMES

1. *The tragic reality of the fall.* The Preacher is painfully aware that the creation has been damaged by sin (7:29; Rom. 8:20, 22). He speaks as one who eagerly awaits the resurrection age (Rom. 8:23).

2. *The "vanity" of life.* The book begins and ends with the exclamation, "Vanity of vanities! All is vanity" (Eccles. 1:2; 12:8). The phrase pictures something fleeting and elusive. All the endeavors and pleasures of earthly life are only temporary. When one sees the consequences of sin in this fallen world, one is left in utter frustration, anger, and sorrow. The more one tries to understand life, the more mysterious it becomes (1:12–18).

3. *Sin and death.* By sinning, human beings forfeited the righteousness they originally had

before God (7:29), and thus all people are sinners (7:20). Death was a result of the fall. The Preacher is only too aware of this dreadful reality that affects everyone (e.g., 2:14–17; 3:18–21; 6:6).

4. *The joy and the frustration of work.* God gave Adam work to accomplish prior to the fall, but part of the punishment of his sin was that his work would become difficult (Gen. 2:15; 3:17–19). Both realities are seen in the Preacher's experience, as he finds his work to be both satisfying (Eccles. 2:10, 24; 3:22; 5:18–20; 9:9–10) and aggravating (2:18–23; 4:4–8).

5. *The grateful enjoyment of God's good gifts.* The Preacher spends a great deal of time commenting on the twisted realities of a fallen world, but this does not blind him to the beauty of God's world (3:11). Nor does it cause him to despise God's good gifts of human relationships, food, drink, and satisfying labor (5:18–20; 8:15; 9:7, 9). These are to be received humbly and enjoyed fully as blessings from God.

6. *The fear of God.* The fact that "all is vanity" should drive people to take refuge in God, fearing and revering him (7:18; 8:12–13; 12:13–14).

OUTLINE

ECCLESIASTES

All Is Vanity

1 The words of the Preacher, the son of David, king in Jerusalem.

2 Vanity[1] of vanities, says the Preacher,
  vanity of vanities! All is vanity.
3 What does man gain by all the toil
  at which he toils under the sun?
4 A generation goes, and a generation comes,
  but the earth remains forever.
5 The sun rises, and the sun goes down,
  and hastens to the place where it rises.
6 The wind blows to the south
  and goes around to the north;
  around and around goes the wind,
  and on its circuits the wind returns.
7 All streams run to the sea,
  but the sea is not full;
  to the place where the streams flow,
  there they flow again.
8 All things are full of weariness;
  a man cannot utter it;
  the eye is not satisfied with seeing,
  nor the ear filled with hearing.
9 What has been is what will be,
  and what has been done is what will be done,
  and there is nothing new under the sun.
10 Is there a thing of which it is said,
  "See, this is new"?
  It has been already
  in the ages before us.
11 There is no remembrance of former things,
  nor will there be any remembrance
  of later things yet to be
  among those who come after.

The Vanity of Wisdom

12 I the Preacher have been king over Israel in Jerusalem. 13 And I applied my heart to seek and to search out by wisdom all that is done under heaven. It is an unhappy business that God has given to the children of man to be busy with. 14 I have seen everything that is done under the sun, and behold, all is vanity and a striving after wind.

15 What is crooked cannot be made straight,
  and what is lacking cannot be counted.

16 I said in my heart, "I have acquired great wisdom, surpassing all who were over Jerusalem before me, and my heart has had great experience of wisdom and knowledge." 17 And I applied my heart to know wisdom and to know madness and folly. I perceived that this also is but a striving after wind.

18 For in much wisdom is much vexation,
  and he who increases knowledge increases sorrow.

The Vanity of Self-Indulgence

2 I said in my heart, "Come now, I will test you with pleasure; enjoy yourself." But behold, this also was vanity. 2 I said of laughter, "It is mad," and of pleasure, "What use is it?" 3 I searched with my heart how to cheer my body with wine—my heart still guiding me with wisdom—and how to lay hold on folly, till I might see what was good for the children of man to do under heaven during the few days of their life. 4 I made great works. I built houses and planted vineyards for myself. 5 I made myself gardens and parks, and planted in them all kinds of fruit trees. 6 I made myself pools from which to water the forest of growing trees.

---

[1] Throughout Ecclesiastes, the Hebrew word for *vanity* or *vain* can refer to a "mist," "vapor," or "mere breath." It shows that many things in life are temporary

⁷ I bought male and female slaves, and had slaves who were born in my house. I had also great possessions of herds and flocks, more than any who had been before me in Jerusalem. ⁸ I also gathered for myself silver and gold and the treasure of kings and provinces. I got singers, both men and women, and many concubines, the delight of the sons of man.

⁹ So I became great and surpassed all who were before me in Jerusalem. Also my wisdom remained with me. ¹⁰ And whatever my eyes desired I did not keep from them. I kept my heart from no pleasure, for my heart found pleasure in all my toil, and this was my reward for all my toil. ¹¹ Then I considered all that my hands had done and the toil I had expended in doing it, and behold, all was vanity and a striving after wind, and there was nothing to be gained under the sun.

> **GETTING THE MESSAGE**
>
> The words **vanity, vanities,** and **vain** occur nearly 40 times in Ecclesiastes. Their literal meaning is "vapor" or "breath," so they are used to describe things that can be fleeting or elusive, like the search for meaning and purpose in life.

The Vanity of Living Wisely

¹² So I turned to consider wisdom and madness and folly. For what can the man do who comes after the king? Only what has already been done. ¹³ Then I saw that there is more gain in wisdom than in folly, as there is more gain in light than in darkness. ¹⁴ The wise person has his eyes in his head, but the fool walks in darkness. And yet I perceived that the same event happens to all of them. ¹⁵ Then I said in my heart, "What happens to the fool will happen to me also. Why then have I been so very wise?" And I said in my heart that this also is vanity. ¹⁶ For of the wise as of the fool there is no enduring remembrance, seeing that in the days to come all will have been long forgotten. How the wise dies just like the fool! ¹⁷ So I hated life, because what is done under the sun was grievous to me, for all is vanity and a striving after wind.

The Vanity of Toil

¹⁸ I hated all my toil in which I toil under the sun, seeing that I must leave it to the man who will come after me, ¹⁹ and who knows whether he will be wise or a fool? Yet he will be master of all for which I toiled and used my wisdom under the sun. This also is vanity. ²⁰ So I turned about and gave my heart up to despair over all the toil of my labors under the sun, ²¹ because sometimes a person who has toiled with wisdom and knowledge and skill must leave everything to be enjoyed by someone who did not toil for it. This also is vanity and a great evil. ²² What has a man from all the toil and striving of heart with which he toils beneath the sun? ²³ For all his days are full of sorrow, and his work is a vexation. Even in the night his heart does not rest. This also is vanity.

²⁴ There is nothing better for a person than that he should eat and drink and find enjoyment in his toil. This also, I saw, is from the hand of God, ²⁵ for apart from him who can eat or who can have enjoyment? ²⁶ For to the one who pleases him God has given wisdom and knowledge and joy, but to the sinner he has given the business of gathering and collecting, only to give to one who pleases God. This also is vanity and a striving after wind.

A Time for Everything

3 For everything there is a season, and a time for every matter under heaven:

2   a time to be born, and a time to die;
     a time to plant, and a time to pluck up
          what is planted;
3   a time to kill, and a time to heal;
     a time to break down, and a time to
          build up;
4   a time to weep, and a time to laugh;
     a time to mourn, and a time to dance;
5   a time to cast away stones, and a time
          to gather stones together;
     a time to embrace, and a time to
          refrain from embracing;
6   a time to seek, and a time to lose;
     a time to keep, and a time to cast
          away;
7   a time to tear, and a time to sew;
     a time to keep silence, and a time to
          speak;
8   a time to love, and a time to hate;
     a time for war, and a time for peace.

The God-Given Task

⁹ What gain has the worker from his toil? ¹⁰ I have seen the business that God has given to the children of man to be busy with. ¹¹ He has made everything beautiful in its time. Also, he has put eternity into man's heart, yet so that he cannot find out what God has done from the beginning to the end. ¹² I perceived that there is nothing better for them than to be joyful and to do good as long as they live; ¹³ also that everyone should eat and drink and take pleasure in all his toil—this is God's gift to man.

¹⁴ I perceived that whatever God does endures forever; nothing can be added to it, nor anything taken from it. God has done it, so that people fear before him. ¹⁵ That which is, already has been; that which is to be, already has been; and God seeks what has been driven away.

From Dust to Dust

¹⁶ Moreover, I saw under the sun that in the place of justice, even there was wickedness, and in the place of righteousness, even there was wickedness. ¹⁷ I said in my heart, God will judge the righteous and the wicked, for there is a time for every matter and for every work. ¹⁸ I said in my heart with regard to the children of man that God is testing them that they may see that they themselves are but beasts. ¹⁹ For what happens to the children of man and what happens to the beasts is the same; as one dies, so dies the other. They all have the same breath, and man has no advantage over the beasts, for all is vanity. ²⁰ All go to one place. All are from the dust, and to dust all return. ²¹ Who knows whether the spirit of man goes upward and the spirit of the beast goes down into the earth? ²² So I saw that there is nothing better than that a man should rejoice in his work, for that is his lot. Who can bring him to see what will be after him?

Evil Under the Sun

4 Again I saw all the oppressions that are done under the sun. And behold, the tears of the oppressed, and they had no one to comfort them! On the side of their oppressors there was power, and there was no one to comfort them. ² And I thought the dead who are already dead more fortunate than the living who are still alive. ³ But better

than both is he who has not yet been and has not seen the evil deeds that are done under the sun.

⁴ Then I saw that all toil and all skill in work come from a man's envy of his neighbor. This also is vanity and a striving after wind.

⁵ The fool folds his hands and eats his own flesh.

⁶ Better is a handful of quietness than two hands full of toil and a striving after wind.

⁷ Again, I saw vanity under the sun: ⁸ one person who has no other, either son or brother, yet there is no end to all his toil, and his eyes are never satisfied with riches, so that he never asks, "For whom am I toiling and depriving myself of pleasure?" This also is vanity and an unhappy business.

⁹ Two are better than one, because they have a good reward for their toil. ¹⁰ For if they fall, one will lift up his fellow. But woe to him who is alone when he falls and has not another to lift him up! ¹¹ Again, if two lie together, they keep warm, but how can one keep warm alone? ¹² And though a man might prevail against one who is alone, two will withstand him—a threefold cord is not quickly broken.

¹³ Better was a poor and wise youth than an old and foolish king who no longer knew how to take advice. ¹⁴ For he went from prison to the throne, though in his own kingdom he had been born poor. ¹⁵ I saw all the living who move about under the sun, along with that youth who was to stand in the king's place. ¹⁶ There was no end of all the people, all of whom he led. Yet those who come later will not rejoice in him. Surely this also is vanity and a striving after wind.

Fear God

5 Guard your steps when you go to the house of God. To draw near to listen is better than to offer the sacrifice of fools, for they do not know that they are doing evil. [2] Be not rash with your mouth, nor let your heart be hasty to utter a word before God, for God is in heaven and you are on earth. Therefore let your words be few. [3] For a dream comes with much business, and a fool's voice with many words.

[4] When you vow a vow to God, do not delay paying it, for he has no pleasure in fools. Pay what you vow. [5] It is better that you should not vow than that you should vow and not pay. [6] Let not your mouth lead you into sin, and do not say before the messenger that it was a mistake. Why should God be angry at your voice and destroy the work of your hands? [7] For when dreams increase and words grow many, there is vanity; but God is the one you must fear.

The Vanity of Wealth and Honor

[8] If you see in a province the oppression of the poor and the violation of justice and righteousness, do not be amazed at the matter, for the high official is watched by a higher, and there are yet higher ones over them. [9] But this is gain for a land in every way: a king committed to cultivated fields.

[10] He who loves money will not be satisfied with money, nor he who loves wealth with his income; this also is vanity. [11] When goods increase, they increase who eat them, and what advantage has their owner but to see them with his eyes? [12] Sweet is the sleep of a laborer, whether he eats little or much, but the full stomach of the rich will not let him sleep.

[13] There is a grievous evil that I have seen under the sun: riches were kept by their owner to his hurt, [14] and those riches were lost in a bad venture. And he is father of a son, but he has nothing in his hand. [15] As he came from his mother's womb he shall go again, naked as he came, and shall take nothing for his toil that he may carry away in his hand. [16] This also is a grievous evil: just as he came, so shall he go, and what gain is there to him who toils for the wind? [17] Moreover, all his days he eats in darkness in much vexation and sickness and anger.

[18] Behold, what I have seen to be good and fitting is to eat and drink and find enjoyment in all the toil with which one toils under the sun the few days of his life that God has given him, for this is his lot. [19] Everyone also to whom God has given wealth and possessions and power to enjoy them, and to accept his lot and rejoice in his toil—this is the gift of God. [20] For he will not much remember the days of his life because God keeps him occupied with joy in his heart.

6 There is an evil that I have seen under the sun, and it lies heavy on mankind: [2] a man to whom God gives wealth, possessions, and honor, so that he lacks nothing of all that he desires, yet God does not give him power to enjoy them, but a stranger enjoys them. This is vanity; it is a grievous evil. [3] If a man fathers a hundred children and lives many years, so that the days of his years are many, but his soul is not satisfied with life's good things, and he also has no burial, I say that a stillborn child is better off than he. [4] For it comes in vanity and goes in darkness, and in darkness its name is covered. [5] Moreover, it has not seen the sun or known anything, yet it finds rest rather than he. [6] Even though he should live a thousand years twice over, yet enjoy no good—do not all go to the one place?

[7] All the toil of man is for his mouth, yet his appetite is not satisfied. [8] For what advantage has the wise man over the fool? And what does the poor man have who knows how to conduct himself before the living? [9] Better is the sight of the eyes than the wandering of the appetite: this also is vanity and a striving after wind.

[10] Whatever has come to be has already been named, and it is known what man is, and that he is not able to dispute with one stronger than he. [11] The more words, the more vanity, and what is the advantage to man? [12] For who knows what is good for man while he lives the few days of his vain life, which he passes like a shadow? For who can tell man what will be after him under the sun?

The Contrast of Wisdom and Folly

7 A good name is better than precious ointment,
　　and the day of death than the day of birth.
[2]　It is better to go to the house of mourning
　　than to go to the house of feasting,

for this is the end of all mankind,
    and the living will lay it to heart.
3 Sorrow is better than laughter,
    for by sadness of face the heart is
      made glad.
4 The heart of the wise is in the house
    of mourning,
    but the heart of fools is in the house
      of mirth.
5 It is better for a man to hear the
    rebuke of the wise
    than to hear the song of fools.
6 For as the crackling of thorns under a
    pot,
    so is the laughter of the fools;
    this also is vanity.
7 Surely oppression drives the wise into
    madness,
    and a bribe corrupts the heart.
8 Better is the end of a thing than its
    beginning,
    and the patient in spirit is better
      than the proud in spirit.
9 Be not quick in your spirit to become
    angry,
    for anger lodges in the heart of
      fools.
10 Say not, "Why were the former days
    better than these?"
    For it is not from wisdom that you
      ask this.
11 Wisdom is good with an inheritance,
    an advantage to those who see the
      sun.
12 For the protection of wisdom is like
    the protection of money,
    and the advantage of knowledge is
      that wisdom preserves the life
      of him who has it.
13 Consider the work of God:
    who can make straight what he has
      made crooked?

14 In the day of prosperity be joyful, and in the day of adversity consider: God has made the one as well as the other, so that man may not find out anything that will be after him.

15 In my vain life I have seen everything. There is a righteous man who perishes in his righteousness, and there is a wicked man who prolongs his life in his evildoing. 16 Be not overly righteous, and do not make yourself too wise. Why should you destroy yourself? 17 Be not overly wicked, neither be a fool. Why should you die before your time?

18 It is good that you should take hold of this, and from that withhold not your hand, for the one who fears God shall come out from both of them.

19 Wisdom gives strength to the wise man more than ten rulers who are in a city.

20 Surely there is not a righteous man on earth who does good and never sins.

21 Do not take to heart all the things that people say, lest you hear your servant cursing you. 22 Your heart knows that many times you yourself have cursed others.

23 All this I have tested by wisdom. I said, "I will be wise," but it was far from me. 24 That which has been is far off, and deep, very deep; who can find it out?

25 I turned my heart to know and to search out and to seek wisdom and the scheme of things, and to know the wickedness of folly and the foolishness that is madness. 26 And I find something more bitter than death: the

woman whose heart is snares and nets, and whose hands are fetters. He who pleases God escapes her, but the sinner is taken by her. 27 Behold, this is what I found, says the Preacher, while adding one thing to another to find the scheme of things — 28 which my soul has sought repeatedly, but I have not found. One man among a thousand I found, but a woman among all these I have not found. 29 See, this alone I found, that God made man upright, but they have sought out many schemes.

Keep the King's Command

8 Who is like the wise?
    And who knows the interpretation
      of a thing?
    A man's wisdom makes his face shine,
    and the hardness of his face is
      changed.

2 I say: Keep the king's command, because of God's oath to him. 3 Be not hasty to go from

his presence. Do not take your stand in an evil cause, for he does whatever he pleases. ⁴ For the word of the king is supreme, and who may say to him, "What are you doing?" ⁵ Whoever keeps a command will know no evil thing, and the wise heart will know the proper time and the just way. ⁶ For there is a time and a way for everything, although man's trouble lies heavy on him. ⁷ For he does not know what is to be, for who can tell him how it will be? ⁸ No man has power to retain the spirit, or power over the day of death. There is no discharge from war, nor will wickedness deliver those who are given to it. ⁹ All this I observed while applying my heart to all that is done under the sun, when man had power over man to his hurt.

Those Who Fear God Will Do Well

¹⁰ Then I saw the wicked buried. They used to go in and out of the holy place and were praised in the city where they had done such

GETTING THE MESSAGE

"Eat, drink, and be merry"? Ecclesiastes advises those who serve God to enjoy his gifts of food, drink, comfort, married life, and honest work (9:7–9; compare 2:24–26; 3:13; 5:19–20).

things. This also is vanity. ¹¹ Because the sentence against an evil deed is not executed speedily, the heart of the children of man is fully set to do evil. ¹² Though a sinner does evil a hundred times and prolongs his life, yet I know that it will be well with those who fear God, because they fear before him. ¹³ But it will not be well with the wicked, neither will he prolong his days like a shadow, because he does not fear before God.

Man Cannot Know God's Ways

¹⁴ There is a vanity that takes place on earth, that there are righteous people to whom it happens according to the deeds of the wicked, and there are wicked people to whom it happens according to the deeds of the righteous. I said that this also is vanity. ¹⁵ And I commend joy, for man has nothing better under the sun but to eat and drink and be joyful, for this will go with him in his toil through the days of his life that God has given him under the sun.

¹⁶ When I applied my heart to know wisdom, and to see the business that is done on earth, how neither day nor night do one's eyes see sleep, ¹⁷ then I saw all the work of God, that man cannot find out the work that is done under the sun. However much man may toil in seeking, he will not find it out. Even though a wise man claims to know, he cannot find it out.

Death Comes to All

9 But all this I laid to heart, examining it all, how the righteous and the wise and their deeds are in the hand of God. Whether it is love or hate, man does not know; both are before him. ² It is the same for all, since the same event happens to the righteous and the wicked, to the good and the evil, to the clean and the unclean, to him who sacrifices and him who does not sacrifice. As the good one is, so is the sinner, and he who swears is as he who shuns an oath. ³ This is an evil in all that is done under the sun, that the same event happens to all. Also, the hearts of the children of man are full of evil, and madness is in their hearts while they live, and after that they go to the dead. ⁴ But he who is joined with all the living has hope, for a living dog is better than a dead lion. ⁵ For the living know that they will die, but the dead know nothing, and they have no more reward, for the memory of them is forgotten. ⁶ Their love and their hate and their envy have already perished, and forever they have no more share in all that is done under the sun.

Enjoy Life with the One You Love

⁷ Go, eat your bread with joy, and drink your wine with a merry heart, for God has already approved what you do.

⁸ Let your garments be always white. Let not oil be lacking on your head.

⁹ Enjoy life with the wife whom you love, all the days of your vain life that he has given you under the sun, because that is your portion in life and in your toil at which you toil under the sun. ¹⁰ Whatever your hand finds to do, do it with your might, for there is no work or thought or knowledge or wisdom in Sheol, to which you are going.

Wisdom Better than Folly

¹¹ Again I saw that under the sun the race is not to the swift, nor the battle to the strong, nor bread to the wise, nor riches

to the intelligent, nor favor to those with knowledge, but time and chance happen to them all. ¹²For man does not know his time. Like fish that are taken in an evil net, and like birds that are caught in a snare, so the children of man are snared at an evil time, when it suddenly falls upon them.

¹³I have also seen this example of wisdom under the sun, and it seemed great to me. ¹⁴There was a little city with few men in it, and a great king came against it and besieged it, building great siegeworks against it. ¹⁵But there was found in it a poor, wise man, and he by his wisdom delivered the city. Yet no one remembered that poor man. ¹⁶But I say that wisdom is better than might, though the poor man's wisdom is despised and his words are not heard.

¹⁷The words of the wise heard in quiet are better than the shouting of a ruler among fools. ¹⁸Wisdom is better than weapons of war, but one sinner destroys much good.

10 Dead flies make the perfumer's
ointment give off a stench;
    so a little folly outweighs wisdom
        and honor.
² A wise man's heart inclines him to the
        right,
    but a fool's heart to the left.
³ Even when the fool walks on the road,
        he lacks sense,
    and he says to everyone that he is a
        fool.
⁴ If the anger of the ruler rises against
        you, do not leave your place,
    for calmness will lay great offenses
        to rest.

⁵There is an evil that I have seen under the sun, as it were an error proceeding from the ruler: ⁶folly is set in many high places, and the rich sit in a low place. ⁷I have seen slaves on horses, and princes walking on the ground like slaves.

⁸ He who digs a pit will fall into it,
    and a serpent will bite him who
        breaks through a wall.
⁹ He who quarries stones is hurt by them,
    and he who splits logs is endan-
        gered by them.
¹⁰ If the iron is blunt, and one does not
        sharpen the edge,
    he must use more strength,
    but wisdom helps one to succeed.

¹¹ If the serpent bites before it is charmed,
    there is no advantage to the charmer.
¹² The words of a wise man's mouth win
        him favor,
    but the lips of a fool consume him.
¹³ The beginning of the words of his
        mouth is foolishness,
    and the end of his talk is evil mad-
        ness.
¹⁴ A fool multiplies words,
    though no man knows what is to be,
    and who can tell him what will be
        after him?
¹⁵ The toil of a fool wearies him,
    for he does not know the way to the
        city.
¹⁶ Woe to you, O land, when your king is
        a child,
    and your princes feast in the morn-
        ing!
¹⁷ Happy are you, O land, when your
        king is the son of the nobility,
    and your princes feast at the proper
        time,
    for strength, and not for drunken-
        ness!
¹⁸ Through sloth the roof sinks in,
    and through indolence the house
        leaks.
¹⁹ Bread is made for laughter,
    and wine gladdens life,
    and money answers everything.
²⁰ Even in your thoughts, do not curse
        the king,
    nor in your bedroom curse the rich,
    for a bird of the air will carry your
        voice,
    or some winged creature tell the
        matter.

Cast Your Bread upon the Waters

11 Cast your bread upon the waters,
    for you will find it after many days.
² Give a portion to seven, or even to
        eight,
    for you know not what disaster may
        happen on earth.
³ If the clouds are full of rain,
    they empty themselves on the
        earth,
    and if a tree falls to the south or to the
        north,
    in the place where the tree falls,
        there it will lie.

4   He who observes the wind will not sow,
        and he who regards the clouds will
            not reap.

5 As you do not know the way the spirit comes to the bones in the womb of a woman with child, so you do not know the work of God who makes everything.

6 In the morning sow your seed, and at evening withhold not your hand, for you do not know which will prosper, this or that, or whether both alike will be good.

7 Light is sweet, and it is pleasant for the eyes to see the sun.

8 So if a person lives many years, let him rejoice in them all; but let him remember that the days of darkness will be many. All that comes is vanity.

9 Rejoice, O young man, in your youth, and let your heart cheer you in the days of your youth. Walk in the ways of your heart and the sight of your eyes. But know that for all these things God will bring you into judgment.

10 Remove vexation from your heart, and put away pain from your body, for youth and the dawn of life are vanity.

Remember Your Creator in Your Youth

12 Remember also your Creator in the days of your youth, before the evil days come and the years draw near of which you will say, "I have no pleasure in them"; 2 before the sun and the light and the moon and the stars are darkened and the clouds return after the rain, 3 in the day when the keepers of the house tremble, and the strong men are bent, and the grinders cease because they are few, and those who look through the windows are dimmed, 4 and the doors on the street are shut—when the sound of the grinding is low, and one rises up at the sound of a bird, and all the daughters of song are brought low— 5 they are afraid also of what is high, and terrors are in the way; the almond tree blossoms, the grasshopper drags itself along, and desire fails, because man is going to his eternal home, and the mourners go about the streets— 6 before the silver cord is snapped, or the golden bowl is broken, or the pitcher is shattered at the fountain, or the wheel broken at the cistern, 7 and the dust returns to the earth as it was, and the spirit returns to God who gave it. 8 Vanity of vanities, says the Preacher; all is vanity.

Fear God and Keep His Commandments

9 Besides being wise, the Preacher also taught the people knowledge, weighing and studying and arranging many proverbs with great care. 10 The Preacher sought to find words of delight, and uprightly he wrote words of truth.

11 The words of the wise are like goads, and like nails firmly fixed are the collected sayings; they are given by one Shepherd. 12 My son, beware of anything beyond these. Of making many books there is no end, and much study is a weariness of the flesh.

13 The end of the matter; all has been heard. Fear God and keep his commandments, for this is the whole duty of man. 14 For God will bring every deed into judgment, with every secret thing, whether good or evil.

INTRODUCTION TO THE SONG OF SOLOMON

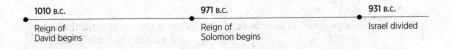

AUTHOR AND DATE

The wording of the first verse in Song of Solomon (or Song of Songs; 1:1) does not necessarily mean that Solomon wrote the book. It may have been written by Solomon himself, or it could have been written in his honor. When he is mentioned (1:5; 3:7, 9, 11; 8:11–12), it is generally as a distant, even idealized figure. What is known about Solomon suggests that he probably was not the writer himself (1 Kings 3:1; 11:1–8). However, the book was probably composed during Solomon's time, perhaps under his oversight, between c. 960 and 931 B.C.

THEME

The Song of Solomon contains beautiful poetry expressing romantic love between a young man and a young woman in ancient Israel. He is a shepherd (1:7) and she is a shepherdess (1:8). They are looking forward to their marriage and the pleasure it will bring.

INTERPRETING LITERARY IMAGES

The Song of Solomon includes several extravagant comparisons. For example, the woman is compared to a horse in Pharaoh's court (1:9), and her hair is compared to a flock of goats (4:1). It is helpful to remember that (1) the comparisons are figurative rather than literal, and (2) what the person has in common with what he or she is compared with is a certain quality, usually the quality of excellence, or of being the best of its kind.

STRUCTURE

The author has presented the Song of Solomon as a series of exchanges, mostly between the shepherdess and the shepherd, with the chorus-like "others" sprinkled in. These others usually pick up items from the lovers' speeches and urge the two forward in love. There is also a refrain, "I adjure you, O daughters of Jerusalem, . . . that you not stir up or awaken love until it pleases" (2:7; 3:5; 8:4; variation in 5:8), spoken by the shepherdess. This is understood as her urging the other women not to push this love too fast, in order to let it reach its consummation at the right time (the marriage bed, which seems to begin in 8:5).

KEY THEMES

1. God's law commands sexual purity. Marriage provides the right framework within which his people may properly enjoy the gift of sexual intimacy (see Gen. 2:23–24). Thus God's people honor him and commend him to the world when they demonstrate with their lives that obedience in such matters brings genuine delight.

2. Marriage is a gift of God, and is to be founded on loyalty and commitment (see Gen. 2:24, "hold fast"), which allows delight to flourish. As such, it is a fitting image for God's relationship with his people.

OUTLINE

   I. Title: The Best of Songs (1:1)

  II. The Lovers Yearn for Each Other (1:2–2:17)

 III. The Shepherdess Dreams (3:1–6:3)

 IV. The Lovers Yearn for Each Other Again (6:4–8:4)

  V. The Lovers Join in Marriage (8:5–14)

THE SONG OF SOLOMON

1 The Song of Songs, which is Solomon's.

The Bride Confesses Her Love

SHE[1]

2 Let him kiss me with the kisses of his
   mouth!
For your love is better than wine;
3   your anointing oils are fragrant;
your name is oil poured out;
   therefore virgins love you.
4 Draw me after you; let us run.
   The king has brought me into his
   chambers.

OTHERS

We will exult and rejoice in you;
   we will extol your love more than
   wine;
rightly do they love you.

SHE

5 I am very dark, but lovely,
   O daughters of Jerusalem,
like the tents of Kedar,
   like the curtains of Solomon.
6 Do not gaze at me because I am dark,
   because the sun has looked upon
   me.
My mother's sons were angry with
   me;
   they made me keeper of the vineyards,
   but my own vineyard I have not
   kept!
7 Tell me, you whom my soul loves,
   where you pasture your flock,
   where you make it lie down at noon;
for why should I be like one who veils
   herself
   beside the flocks of your companions?

Solomon and His Bride Delight in Each Other

HE

8 If you do not know,
   O most beautiful among women,

follow in the tracks of the flock,
   and pasture your young goats
   beside the shepherds' tents.

9 I compare you, my love,
   to a mare among Pharaoh's chariots.
10 Your cheeks are lovely with ornaments,
   your neck with strings of jewels.

OTHERS

11 We will make for you ornaments of
   gold,
   studded with silver.

GETTING THE MESSAGE

The man in this love story compared his
beloved to a **mare among Pharaoh's
chariots** (1:9). Only the best and most
handsome of mares would have been
chosen for important processions, and
they would have been well-adorned
with jewels and ornaments. This was the
man's way of saying that his beloved's
beauty is incomparable.

SHE

12 While the king was on his couch,
   my nard gave forth its fragrance.
13 My beloved is to me a sachet of myrrh
   that lies between my breasts.
14 My beloved is to me a cluster of henna
   blossoms
   in the vineyards of Engedi.

HE

15 Behold, you are beautiful, my love;
   behold, you are beautiful;
   your eyes are doves.

SHE

16 Behold, you are beautiful, my beloved,
   truly delightful.
Our couch is green;
17   the beams of our house are cedar;
   our rafters are pine.

---

[1] Throughout the Song of Solomon, the speakers (HE, SHE, and OTHERS) have been noted to help readers follow the story

2

I am a rose of Sharon,
  a lily of the valleys.

HE

2 As a lily among brambles,
     so is my love among the young
       women.

SHE

3 As an apple tree among the trees of
       the forest,
     so is my beloved among the young
       men.
   With great delight I sat in his shadow,
     and his fruit was sweet to my taste.
4 He brought me to the banqueting
       house,
     and his banner over me was love.
5 Sustain me with raisins;
     refresh me with apples,
   for I am sick with love.
6 His left hand is under my head,
     and his right hand embraces me!
7 I adjure you, O daughters of
       Jerusalem,
     by the gazelles or the does of the
       field,
   that you not stir up or awaken love
     until it pleases.

The Bride Adores Her Beloved

8 The voice of my beloved!
     Behold, he comes,
   leaping over the mountains,
     bounding over the hills.
9 My beloved is like a gazelle
     or a young stag.
   Behold, there he stands
     behind our wall,
   gazing through the windows,
     looking through the lattice.
10 My beloved speaks and says to me:
   "Arise, my love, my beautiful one,
     and come away,
11   for behold, the winter is past;
       the rain is over and gone.
12 The flowers appear on the earth,
     the time of singing has come,
   and the voice of the turtledove
     is heard in our land.
13 The fig tree ripens its figs,
     and the vines are in blossom;
       they give forth fragrance.
   Arise, my love, my beautiful one,
     and come away.

14 O my dove, in the clefts of the rock,
     in the crannies of the cliff,
   let me see your face,
     let me hear your voice,
   for your voice is sweet,
     and your face is lovely.
15 Catch the foxes for us,
     the little foxes
   that spoil the vineyards,
     for our vineyards are in blossom."

16 My beloved is mine, and I am his;
     he grazes among the lilies.
17 Until the day breathes
     and the shadows flee,
   turn, my beloved, be like a gazelle
     or a young stag on cleft moun-
       tains.

The Bride's Dream

3

On my bed by night
  I sought him whom my soul loves;
   I sought him, but found him not.
2 I will rise now and go about the city,
     in the streets and in the squares;
   I will seek him whom my soul loves.
   I sought him, but found him not.
3 The watchmen found me
     as they went about in the city.
   "Have you seen him whom my soul
     loves?"
4 Scarcely had I passed them
     when I found him whom my soul
       loves.
   I held him, and would not let him go
     until I had brought him into my
       mother's house,
     and into the chamber of her who
       conceived me.
5 I adjure you, O daughters of
       Jerusalem,
     by the gazelles or the does of the
       field,
   that you not stir up or awaken love
     until it pleases.

Solomon Arrives for the Wedding

6 What is that coming up from the
       wilderness
     like columns of smoke,
   perfumed with myrrh and frankin-
       cense,
     with all the fragrant powders of a
       merchant?
7 Behold, it is the litter of Solomon!

Around it are sixty mighty men,
   some of the mighty men of Israel,
8 all of them wearing swords
   and expert in war,
each with his sword at his thigh,
   against terror by night.
9 King Solomon made himself a carriage
   from the wood of Lebanon.
10 He made its posts of silver,
   its back of gold, its seat of purple;
its interior was inlaid with love
   by the daughters of Jerusalem.
11 Go out, O daughters of Zion,
   and look upon King Solomon,
with the crown with which his
     mother crowned him
   on the day of his wedding,
   on the day of the gladness of his
     heart.

Solomon Admires His Bride's Beauty

He

4 Behold, you are beautiful, my love,
   behold, you are beautiful!
Your eyes are doves
   behind your veil.
Your hair is like a flock of goats
   leaping down the slopes of Gilead.
2 Your teeth are like a flock of shorn
     ewes
   that have come up from the wash-
     ing,
all of which bear twins,
   and not one among them has lost
     its young.
3 Your lips are like a scarlet thread,
   and your mouth is lovely.
Your cheeks are like halves of a pome-
     granate
   behind your veil.
4 Your neck is like the tower of David,
   built in rows of stone;
on it hang a thousand shields,
   all of them shields of warriors.
5 Your two breasts are like two fawns,
   twins of a gazelle,
   that graze among the lilies.
6 Until the day breathes
   and the shadows flee,
I will go away to the mountain of
     myrrh
   and the hill of frankincense.
7 You are altogether beautiful, my love;
   there is no flaw in you.

8 Come with me from Lebanon, my
     bride;
   come with me from Lebanon.
Depart from the peak of Amana,
   from the peak of Senir and Hermon,
from the dens of lions,
   from the mountains of leopards.
9 You have captivated my heart, my
     sister, my bride;
   you have captivated my heart with
     one glance of your eyes,
   with one jewel of your necklace.
10 How beautiful is your love, my sister,
     my bride!
   How much better is your love than
     wine,
   and the fragrance of your oils than
     any spice!

GETTING THE MESSAGE

Purple cloth was associated with royalty because the purple dye was very difficult to produce in large quantities (3:10). Most of the purple dye came from a shellfish called the murex. It took more than 8,000 murex shellfish to extract one gram of dye.

11 Your lips drip nectar, my bride;
   honey and milk are under your
     tongue;
   the fragrance of your garments is
     like the fragrance of Lebanon.
12 A garden locked is my sister, my bride,
   a spring locked, a fountain sealed.
13 Your shoots are an orchard of pome-
     granates
   with all choicest fruits,
   henna with nard,
14 nard and saffron, calamus and cinna-
     mon,
   with all trees of frankincense,
myrrh and aloes,
   with all choice spices—
15 a garden fountain, a well of living
     water,
   and flowing streams from Lebanon.

16 Awake, O north wind,
   and come, O south wind!
Blow upon my garden,
   let its spices flow.

Together in the Garden of Love

SHE

Let my beloved come to his garden,
and eat its choicest fruits.

HE

5 I came to my garden, my sister, my bride,
I gathered my myrrh with my spice,
I ate my honeycomb with my honey,
I drank my wine with my milk.

OTHERS

Eat, friends, drink,
and be drunk with love!

The Bride Searches for Her Beloved

SHE

2 I slept, but my heart was awake.
A sound! My beloved is knocking.

> ### GETTING THE MESSAGE
>
> The woman addresses the **daughters of Jerusalem** four times throughout this book, creating a refrain that ties her "songs" together (2:7; 3:5; 5:8; 8:4). She urges them not to "stir up or awaken love until it pleases." In other words, they should wait until the appropriate time to enjoy romantic love.

"Open to me, my sister, my love,
my dove, my perfect one,
for my head is wet with dew,
my locks with the drops of the night."
3 I had put off my garment;
how could I put it on?
I had bathed my feet;
how could I soil them?
4 My beloved put his hand to the latch,
and my heart was thrilled within me.
5 I arose to open to my beloved,
and my hands dripped with myrrh,
my fingers with liquid myrrh,
on the handles of the bolt.
6 I opened to my beloved,
but my beloved had turned and gone.
My soul failed me when he spoke.
I sought him, but found him not;
I called him, but he gave no answer.
7 The watchmen found me
as they went about in the city;

they beat me, they bruised me,
they took away my veil,
those watchmen of the walls.
8 I adjure you, O daughters of Jerusalem,
if you find my beloved,
that you tell him
I am sick with love.

OTHERS

9 What is your beloved more than
another beloved,
O most beautiful among women?
What is your beloved more than
another beloved,
that you thus adjure us?

The Bride Praises Her Beloved

SHE

10 My beloved is radiant and ruddy,
distinguished among ten thousand.
11 His head is the finest gold;
his locks are wavy,
black as a raven.
12 His eyes are like doves
beside streams of water,
bathed in milk,
sitting beside a full pool.
13 His cheeks are like beds of spices,
mounds of sweet-smelling herbs.
His lips are lilies,
dripping liquid myrrh.
14 His arms are rods of gold,
set with jewels.
His body is polished ivory,
bedecked with sapphires.
15 His legs are alabaster columns,
set on bases of gold.
His appearance is like Lebanon,
choice as the cedars.
16 His mouth is most sweet,
and he is altogether desirable.
This is my beloved and this is my friend,
O daughters of Jerusalem.

OTHERS

6 Where has your beloved gone,
O most beautiful among women?
Where has your beloved turned,
that we may seek him with you?

Together in the Garden of Love

SHE

2 My beloved has gone down to his garden
to the beds of spices,

to graze in the gardens
  and to gather lilies.
³ I am my beloved's and my beloved is
    mine;
  he grazes among the lilies.

Solomon and His Bride Delight in Each Other

HE

⁴ You are beautiful as Tirzah, my love,
    lovely as Jerusalem,
    awesome as an army with banners.
⁵ Turn away your eyes from me,
    for they overwhelm me—
  Your hair is like a flock of goats
    leaping down the slopes of Gilead.
⁶ Your teeth are like a flock of ewes
    that have come up from the washing;
  all of them bear twins;
    not one among them has lost its
      young.
⁷ Your cheeks are like halves of a pome-
    granate
  behind your veil.
⁸ There are sixty queens and eighty
    concubines,
    and virgins without number.
⁹ My dove, my perfect one, is the only
    one,
  the only one of her mother,
    pure to her who bore her.
  The young women saw her and called
    her blessed;
  the queens and concubines also,
    and they praised her.
¹⁰ "Who is this who looks down like the
    dawn,
  beautiful as the moon, bright as the
    sun,
  awesome as an army with banners?"

SHE

¹¹ I went down to the nut orchard
    to look at the blossoms of the valley,
  to see whether the vines had budded,
    whether the pomegranates were in
      bloom.
¹² Before I was aware, my desire set me
    among the chariots of my kinsman,
    a prince.

OTHERS

¹³ Return, return, O Shulammite,
    return, return, that we may look
      upon you.

HE

Why should you look upon the
    Shulammite,
    as upon a dance before two armies?

7 How beautiful are your feet in san-
    dals,
    O noble daughter!
  Your rounded thighs are like jewels,
    the work of a master hand.
² Your navel is a rounded bowl
    that never lacks mixed wine.
  Your belly is a heap of wheat,
    encircled with lilies.
³ Your two breasts are like two fawns,
    twins of a gazelle.
⁴ Your neck is like an ivory tower.
  Your eyes are pools in Heshbon,
    by the gate of Bath-rabbim.
  Your nose is like a tower of Lebanon,
    which looks toward Damascus.

GETTING THE MESSAGE

Vineyards, fields, and palm trees.
The Song of Solomon takes place in
a rural setting, and the lovers describe
each other using images drawn from this
context. The man is a shepherd, and the
woman works in her family's vineyard.

⁵ Your head crowns you like Carmel,
    and your flowing locks are like
      purple;
  a king is held captive in the tresses.

⁶ How beautiful and pleasant you are,
    O loved one, with all your delights!
⁷ Your stature is like a palm tree,
    and your breasts are like its clusters.
⁸ I say I will climb the palm tree
    and lay hold of its fruit.
  Oh may your breasts be like clusters
    of the vine,
    and the scent of your breath like
      apples,
⁹ and your mouth like the best wine.

SHE

It goes down smoothly for my
    beloved,
    gliding over lips and teeth.

¹⁰ I am my beloved's,
    and his desire is for me.

The Bride Gives Her Love

11 Come, my beloved,
     let us go out into the fields
     and lodge in the villages;
12 let us go out early to the vineyards
     and see whether the vines have
        budded,
   whether the grape blossoms have
        opened
     and the pomegranates are in
        bloom.
   There I will give you my love.
13 The mandrakes give forth fragrance,
     and beside our doors are all choice
        fruits,
   new as well as old,
     which I have laid up for you, O my
        beloved.

Longing for Her Beloved

8 Oh that you were like a brother to me
     who nursed at my mother's breasts!
   If I found you outside, I would kiss you,
     and none would despise me.
2 I would lead you and bring you
     into the house of my mother—
     she who used to teach me.
   I would give you spiced wine to drink,
     the juice of my pomegranate.
3 His left hand is under my head,
     and his right hand embraces me!
4 I adjure you, O daughters of Jerusalem,
     that you not stir up or awaken love
     until it pleases.

5 Who is that coming up from the wil-
        derness,
     leaning on her beloved?

   Under the apple tree I awakened you.
   There your mother was in labor with
        you;
     there she who bore you was in
        labor.

6 Set me as a seal upon your heart,
     as a seal upon your arm,
   for love is strong as death,
     jealousy is fierce as the grave.

Its flashes are flashes of fire,
     the very flame of the LORD.
7 Many waters cannot quench love,
     neither can floods drown it.
   If a man offered for love
     all the wealth of his house,
     he would be utterly despised.

Final Advice

OTHERS
8 We have a little sister,
     and she has no breasts.
   What shall we do for our sister
     on the day when she is spoken for?
9 If she is a wall,
     we will build on her a battlement of
        silver,
   but if she is a door,
     we will enclose her with boards of
        cedar.

SHE
10 I was a wall,
     and my breasts were like towers;
   then I was in his eyes
     as one who finds peace.

11 Solomon had a vineyard at Baal-
        hamon;
     he let out the vineyard to keepers;
     each one was to bring for its fruit a
        thousand pieces of silver.
12 My vineyard, my very own, is before
        me;
     you, O Solomon, may have the
        thousand,
     and the keepers of the fruit two
        hundred.

HE
13 O you who dwell in the gardens,
     with companions listening for your
        voice;
     let me hear it.

SHE
14 Make haste, my beloved,
     and be like a gazelle
   or a young stag
     on the mountains of spices.

INTRODUCTION TO ISAIAH

767 B.C.	740 B.C.	722 B.C.	715 B.C.
Reign of Uzziah begins	Prophetic ministry of Isaiah begins	Fall of Israel	Reign of Hezekiah begins

AUTHOR AND DATE

Isaiah was called to his prophetic ministry "in the year that King Uzziah died" (6:1), around 740 B.C. He lived long enough to record the death of Sennacherib (37:38), in 681. However, most of the book can be dated only in very general terms because few specific dates are given.

THEME

The central theme of the book is God himself, who does all things for his own glory (48:11). Isaiah defines everything else by how it relates to God: is it rightly related to him as the center of all reality (45:22–25)? God's people find strength only as they rest in the promises of their God (30:15). They find refreshment only as they delight themselves in his word (55:1–2). To serve his cause is their worthy devotion (ch. 62), but to rebel against him is endless death (66:24).

KEY THEMES

1. God is offended by religious practices that come from an empty heart or a careless life (1:10–17; 58:1–12; 66:1–4).

2. God's true people will someday become a multinational community of worship and peace that will last forever (2:2–4; 56:3–8; 66:18–23). They will be the predominant culture of a new world (14:1–2; 41:8–16; 43:3–7; 60:1–22).

3. God opposes human pride (2:10–17; 13:11; 23:9).

4. The foolish idols that man creates are destined for destruction (2:20–21; 44:9–20; 46:1–7).

5. God's judgment will reduce Israel to a remnant. From this remnant he will raise up a holy people (1:9; 6:1–12:6; 40:1–2).

6. God sometimes judges people by making them deaf and blind to his saving word (29:9–14).

7. The only hope of the world is in one man. He is the promised Davidic king (7:14; 9:2–7; 11:1–10), the servant of the Lord (42:1–9; 52:13–53:12), the anointed preacher of the gospel (61:1–3), and the victor over all evil (63:1–6).

8. God uses everything, even human sin, for his own glory (44:24–45:13).

9. All people are called to repent of sin and trust in God alone (12:2; 26:3–4; 32:17–18; 50:10; 66:2).

10. Often, when God's people feel abandoned by him (40:27), they foolishly trust in worldly powers (31:1–3; 39:1–8).

11. God will vindicate his cause with a world-transforming display of his glory (11:10; 40:3–5; 52:10; 59:19).

12. God is guiding all of human history (41:1–4; 44:6–8; 46:8–11).

SIMPLIFIED OVERVIEW OF ISAIAH

	Isaiah 1–39	Isaiah 40–55	Isaiah 56–66
Date and Setting	The eighth century B.C. (700s); the Assyrian threat	Prophecies for the sixth century B.C. (500s); the Babylonian exile	Prophecies about all times and occasions until the end
Audience	God's rebellious people craving worldly security	God's defeated people under worldly domination	All who hold fast to God's covenant
Actions	God purifies a remnant of his apostate people through judgment	God encourages his discouraged people in exile	God prepares all of his true people for his promised salvation
Message	"In returning and rest you shall be saved; . . . But you were unwilling" (30:15)	"the glory of the LORD shall be revealed" (40:5)	"Keep justice, and do righteousness" (56:1)

13. God's faithfulness and the certainty of his final victory should motivate his people to pray and to be obedient (56:1–2; 62:1–64:12).

14. The wrath of God is to be feared above all else (9:19; 13:9, 13; 30:27; 34:2; 66:15–16).

OUTLINE

ISAIAH

1 The vision of Isaiah the son of Amoz, which he saw concerning Judah and Jerusalem in the days of Uzziah, Jotham, Ahaz, and Hezekiah, kings of Judah.

The Wickedness of Judah

2 Hear, O heavens, and give ear,
O earth;
for the LORD has spoken:
"Children have I reared and brought up,
but they have rebelled against me.
3 The ox knows its owner,
and the donkey its master's crib,
but Israel does not know,
my people do not understand."

> ▶ GETTING THE MESSAGE
>
> **The Holy One of Israel** (1:4) is Isaiah's main title for God. The phrase occurs 25 times in the book, but rarely elsewhere in the Bible. The word "holy" describes the Lord's absolute moral purity and his being far greater than all that he has created.

4 Ah, sinful nation,
a people laden with iniquity,
offspring of evildoers,
children who deal corruptly!
They have forsaken the LORD,
they have despised the Holy One of Israel,
they are utterly estranged.

5 Why will you still be struck down?
Why will you continue to rebel?
The whole head is sick,
and the whole heart faint.
6 From the sole of the foot even to the head,
there is no soundness in it,
but bruises and sores
and raw wounds;
they are not pressed out or bound up
or softened with oil.

7 Your country lies desolate;
your cities are burned with fire;
in your very presence
foreigners devour your land;
it is desolate, as overthrown by foreigners.
8 And the daughter of Zion is left
like a booth in a vineyard,
like a lodge in a cucumber field,
like a besieged city.
9 If the LORD of hosts
had not left us a few survivors,
we should have been like Sodom,
and become like Gomorrah.

10 Hear the word of the LORD,
you rulers of Sodom!
Give ear to the teaching of our God,
you people of Gomorrah!
11 "What to me is the multitude of your sacrifices?
says the LORD;
I have had enough of burnt offerings of rams
and the fat of well-fed beasts;
I do not delight in the blood of bulls,
or of lambs, or of goats.

12 "When you come to appear before me,
who has required of you
this trampling of my courts?
13 Bring no more vain offerings;
incense is an abomination to me.
New moon and Sabbath and the calling of convocations—
I cannot endure iniquity and solemn assembly.
14 Your new moons and your appointed feasts
my soul hates;
they have become a burden to me;
I am weary of bearing them.
15 When you spread out your hands,
I will hide my eyes from you;
even though you make many prayers,
I will not listen;
your hands are full of blood.

16 Wash yourselves; make yourselves
        clean;
    remove the evil of your deeds from
        before my eyes;
    cease to do evil,
17   learn to do good;
    seek justice,
        correct oppression;
    bring justice to the fatherless,
        plead the widow's cause.

18 "Come now, let us reason together,
        says the LORD:
    though your sins are like scarlet,
        they shall be as white as snow;
    though they are red like crimson,
        they shall become like wool.
19 If you are willing and obedient,
        you shall eat the good of the land;
20 but if you refuse and rebel,
        you shall be eaten by the sword;
    for the mouth of the LORD has spo-
        ken."

The Unfaithful City

21 How the faithful city
        has become a whore,
        she who was full of justice!
    Righteousness lodged in her,
        but now murderers.
22 Your silver has become dross,
        your best wine mixed with water.
23 Your princes are rebels
        and companions of thieves.
    Everyone loves a bribe
        and runs after gifts.
    They do not bring justice to the
        fatherless,
        and the widow's cause does not
        come to them.
24 Therefore the Lord declares,
        the LORD of hosts,
        the Mighty One of Israel:
    "Ah, I will get relief from my enemies
        and avenge myself on my foes.
25 I will turn my hand against you
        and will smelt away your dross as
        with lye
        and remove all your alloy.
26 And I will restore your judges as at
        the first,
        and your counselors as at the begin-
        ning.

    Afterward you shall be called the city
        of righteousness,
        the faithful city."
27 Zion shall be redeemed by justice,
        and those in her who repent, by
        righteousness.
28 But rebels and sinners shall be broken
        together,
        and those who forsake the LORD
        shall be consumed.
29 For they shall be ashamed of the oaks
        that you desired;
    and you shall blush for the gardens
        that you have chosen.
30 For you shall be like an oak
        whose leaf withers,
        and like a garden without water.
31 And the strong shall become tinder,
        and his work a spark,
    and both of them shall burn together,
        with none to quench them.

GETTING THE MESSAGE

Pruning hooks (2:4) were used to cut
away newly formed leaves and shoots
from grape vines. The blade curved into
a sharp hook at the tip, allowing it to
capture and cut new growth more easily
than a straight blade.

The Mountain of the LORD

2 The word that Isaiah the son of Amoz
    saw concerning Judah and Jerusalem.

2   It shall come to pass in the latter days
        that the mountain of the house of
        the LORD
    shall be established as the highest of
        the mountains,
        and shall be lifted up above the hills;
    and all the nations shall flow to it,
3   and many peoples shall come, and
        say:
    "Come, let us go up to the mountain of
        the LORD,
        to the house of the God of Jacob,
    that he may teach us his ways
        and that we may walk in his paths."
    For out of Zion shall go the law,
        and the word of the LORD from
        Jerusalem.

4 He shall judge between the nations,
  and shall decide disputes for many
    peoples;
and they shall beat their swords into
    plowshares,
  and their spears into pruning hooks;
nation shall not lift up sword against
    nation,
  neither shall they learn war anymore.

5 O house of Jacob,
  come, let us walk
  in the light of the LORD.

The Day of the LORD

6 For you have rejected your people,
    the house of Jacob,
  because they are full of things from
    the east
    and of fortune-tellers like the
      Philistines,
    and they strike hands with the
      children of foreigners.
7 Their land is filled with silver and gold,
    and there is no end to their treasures;
  their land is filled with horses,
    and there is no end to their chariots.
8 Their land is filled with idols;
    they bow down to the work of their
      hands,
    to what their own fingers have made.
9 So man is humbled,
    and each one is brought low—
    do not forgive them!
10 Enter into the rock
    and hide in the dust
  from before the terror of the LORD,
    and from the splendor of his majesty.
11 The haughty looks of man shall be
      brought low,
    and the lofty pride of men shall be
      humbled,
  and the LORD alone will be exalted in
    that day.

12 For the LORD of hosts has a day
    against all that is proud and lofty,
    against all that is lifted up—and it
      shall be brought low;
13 against all the cedars of Lebanon,
    lofty and lifted up;
    and against all the oaks of Bashan;
14 against all the lofty mountains,
    and against all the uplifted hills;
15 against every high tower,
    and against every fortified wall;

16 against all the ships of Tarshish,
    and against all the beautiful craft.
17 And the haughtiness of man shall be
      humbled,
    and the lofty pride of men shall be
      brought low,
    and the LORD alone will be exalted
      in that day.
18 And the idols shall utterly pass away.
19 And people shall enter the caves of
      the rocks
    and the holes of the ground,
  from before the terror of the LORD,
    and from the splendor of his majesty,
    when he rises to terrify the earth.

20 In that day mankind will cast away
    their idols of silver and their idols
      of gold,
  which they made for themselves to
    worship,
    to the moles and to the bats,
21 to enter the caverns of the rocks
    and the clefts of the cliffs,
  from before the terror of the LORD,
    and from the splendor of his majesty,
    when he rises to terrify the earth.
22 Stop regarding man
    in whose nostrils is breath,
    for of what account is he?

Judgment on Judah and Jerusalem

3 For behold, the Lord GOD of hosts
  is taking away from Jerusalem and
      from Judah
support and supply,
    all support of bread,
    and all support of water;
2 the mighty man and the soldier,
    the judge and the prophet,
    the diviner and the elder,
3 the captain of fifty
    and the man of rank,
  the counselor and the skillful magician
    and the expert in charms.
4 And I will make boys their princes,
    and infants shall rule over them.
5 And the people will oppress one
      another,
    every one his fellow
    and every one his neighbor;
  the youth will be insolent to the
      elder,
    and the despised to the honorable.

6 For a man will take hold of his brother
    in the house of his father, saying:
"You have a cloak;
    you shall be our leader,
and this heap of ruins
    shall be under your rule";
7 in that day he will speak out, saying:
"I will not be a healer;
    in my house there is neither bread
        nor cloak;
you shall not make me
    leader of the people."
8 For Jerusalem has stumbled,
    and Judah has fallen,
because their speech and their deeds
    are against the LORD,
    defying his glorious presence.
9 For the look on their faces bears wit-
        ness against them;
    they proclaim their sin like Sodom;
    they do not hide it.
Woe to them!
    For they have brought evil on them-
        selves.
10 Tell the righteous that it shall be well
        with them,
    for they shall eat the fruit of their
        deeds.
11 Woe to the wicked! It shall be ill with
        him,
    for what his hands have dealt out
        shall be done to him.
12 My people—infants are their oppres-
        sors,
    and women rule over them.
O my people, your guides mislead
        you
    and they have swallowed up the
        course of your paths.
13 The LORD has taken his place to con-
        tend;
    he stands to judge peoples.
14 The LORD will enter into judgment
    with the elders and princes of his
        people:
"It is you who have devoured the vine-
        yard,
    the spoil of the poor is in your
        houses.
15 What do you mean by crushing my
        people,
    by grinding the face of the poor?"
        declares the Lord GOD of hosts.

16 The LORD said:
Because the daughters of Zion are
        haughty
    and walk with outstretched necks,
    glancing wantonly with their eyes,
mincing along as they go,
    tinkling with their feet,
17 therefore the Lord will strike with a
        scab
    the heads of the daughters of Zion,
    and the LORD will lay bare their
        secret parts.

18 In that day the Lord will take away the
finery of the anklets, the headbands, and
the crescents; 19 the pendants, the bracelets,
and the scarves; 20 the headdresses, the armlets, the sashes, the perfume boxes, and the
amulets; 21 the signet rings and nose rings;
22 the festal robes, the mantles, the cloaks,
and the handbags; 23 the mirrors, the linen
garments, the turbans, and the veils.

> ### GETTING THE MESSAGE
>
> The **tinkling of feet** mentioned in 3:16
> is probably the ankle bracelets many
> women wore in the ancient world. They
> were usually made of bronze and were
> attached permanently.

24 Instead of perfume there will be rot-
        tenness;
    and instead of a belt, a rope;
and instead of well-set hair, baldness;
    and instead of a rich robe, a skirt of
        sackcloth;
    and branding instead of beauty.
25 Your men shall fall by the sword
    and your mighty men in battle.
26 And her gates shall lament and
        mourn;
    empty, she shall sit on the ground.

4 And seven women shall take hold
of one man in that day, saying, "We
will eat our own bread and wear our own
clothes, only let us be called by your name;
take away our reproach."

The Branch of the LORD Glorified

2 In that day the branch of the LORD shall
be beautiful and glorious, and the fruit of
the land shall be the pride and honor of

the survivors of Israel. ³ And he who is left in Zion and remains in Jerusalem will be called holy, everyone who has been recorded for life in Jerusalem, ⁴ when the Lord shall have washed away the filth of the daughters of Zion and cleansed the bloodstains of Jerusalem from its midst by a spirit of judgment and by a spirit of burning. ⁵ Then the LORD will create over the whole site of Mount Zion and over her assemblies a cloud by day, and smoke and the shining of a flaming fire by night; for over all the glory there will be a canopy. ⁶ There will be a booth for shade by day from the heat, and for a refuge and a shelter from the storm and rain.

The Vineyard of the LORD Destroyed

5 Let me sing for my beloved
    my love song concerning his vineyard:

My beloved had a vineyard
    on a very fertile hill.
² He dug it and cleared it of stones,
    and planted it with choice vines;
he built a watchtower in the midst of it,
    and hewed out a wine vat in it;
and he looked for it to yield grapes,
    but it yielded wild grapes.

³ And now, O inhabitants of Jerusalem
    and men of Judah,
judge between me and my vineyard.
⁴ What more was there to do for my
        vineyard,
    that I have not done in it?
When I looked for it to yield grapes,
    why did it yield wild grapes?

⁵ And now I will tell you
    what I will do to my vineyard.
I will remove its hedge,
    and it shall be devoured;

I will break down its wall,
    and it shall be trampled down.
⁶ I will make it a waste;
    it shall not be pruned or hoed,
    and briers and thorns shall grow up;
I will also command the clouds
    that they rain no rain upon it.

⁷ For the vineyard of the LORD of hosts
    is the house of Israel,
and the men of Judah
    are his pleasant planting;
and he looked for justice,
    but behold, bloodshed;¹
for righteousness,
    but behold, an outcry!²

Woe to the Wicked

⁸ Woe to those who join house to house,
    who add field to field,
until there is no more room,
    and you are made to dwell alone
    in the midst of the land.
⁹ The LORD of hosts has sworn in my
        hearing:
"Surely many houses shall be desolate,
    large and beautiful houses, without
        inhabitant.
¹⁰ For ten acres of vineyard shall yield
        but one bath,
    and a homer of seed shall yield but
        an ephah."

¹¹ Woe to those who rise early in the
        morning,
    that they may run after strong
        drink,
who tarry late into the evening
    as wine inflames them!
¹² They have lyre and harp,
    tambourine and flute and wine at
        their feasts,
but they do not regard the deeds of
        the LORD,
    or see the work of his hands.

¹³ Therefore my people go into exile
    for lack of knowledge;
their honored men go hungry,
    and their multitude is parched with
        thirst.
¹⁴ Therefore Sheol has enlarged its appetite
    and opened its mouth beyond measure,

¹ The Hebrew words for *justice* and *bloodshed* sound alike ² The Hebrew words for *righteous* and *outcry* sound alike

and the nobility of Jerusalem and her
　multitude will go down,
　her revelers and he who exults in her.

15 Man is humbled, and each one is
　brought low,
　and the eyes of the haughty are
　brought low.

16 But the Lord of hosts is exalted in
　justice,
　and the Holy God shows himself
　holy in righteousness.

17 Then shall the lambs graze as in their
　pasture,
　and nomads shall eat among the
　ruins of the rich.

18 Woe to those who draw iniquity with
　cords of falsehood,
　who draw sin as with cart ropes,

19 who say: "Let him be quick,
　let him speed his work
　that we may see it;
　let the counsel of the Holy One of
　Israel draw near,
　and let it come, that we may know it!"

20 Woe to those who call evil good
　and good evil,
　who put darkness for light
　and light for darkness,
　who put bitter for sweet
　and sweet for bitter!

21 Woe to those who are wise in their
　own eyes,
　and shrewd in their own sight!

22 Woe to those who are heroes at drink-
　ing wine,
　and valiant men in mixing strong
　drink,

23 who acquit the guilty for a bribe,
　and deprive the innocent of his right!

24 Therefore, as the tongue of fire
　devours the stubble,
　and as dry grass sinks down in the
　flame,
　so their root will be as rottenness,
　and their blossom go up like dust;
　for they have rejected the law of the
　Lord of hosts,
　and have despised the word of the
　Holy One of Israel.

25 Therefore the anger of the Lord was
　kindled against his people,
　and he stretched out his hand
　against them and struck them,
　and the mountains quaked;

and their corpses were as refuse
　in the midst of the streets.
For all this his anger has not turned
　away,
　and his hand is stretched out still.

26 He will raise a signal for nations far
　away,
　and whistle for them from the ends
　of the earth;
　and behold, quickly, speedily they
　come!

PROFILE

ISAIAH

The book of Isaiah reveals few details about the prophet himself. We know that he was the son of Amoz, that he was a husband and a father, and that at God's command he used some rather unusual methods of getting his point across (20:2–6)! With the exception of a few details such as these, the Bible focuses exclusively on the prophet's message. God called Isaiah to be a prophet in a time when the people of Judah were no longer faithful to the covenant. The nation's disobedience meant that their prospects for the future involved God's judgment rather than his blessing. Isaiah denounced the people's hypocrisy, greed, and idolatry. The heart of his message, however, is found in the meaning of his name: "Yahweh is salvation." Isaiah's vision is ultimately a message of hope for sinners through the coming Messiah.

KEY REFERENCE: ISAIAH 6:8-13

---

27 None is weary, none stumbles,
　none slumbers or sleeps,
　not a waistband is loose,
　not a sandal strap broken;

28 their arrows are sharp,
　all their bows bent,
　their horses' hoofs seem like flint,
　and their wheels like the whirlwind.

29 Their roaring is like a lion,
　like young lions they roar;
　they growl and seize their prey;
　they carry it off, and none can rescue.

30 They will growl over it on that day,
  like the growling of the sea.
And if one looks to the land,
  behold, darkness and distress;
and the light is darkened by its clouds.

Isaiah's Vision of the Lord

6 In the year that King Uzziah died I saw the Lord sitting upon a throne, high and lifted up; and the train of his robe filled the temple. ² Above him stood the seraphim. Each had six wings: with two he covered his face, and with two he covered his feet, and with two he flew. ³ And one called to another and said:

"Holy, holy, holy is the LORD of hosts;
  the whole earth is full of his glory!"

⁴ And the foundations of the thresholds shook at the voice of him who called, and the house was filled with smoke. ⁵ And I said: "Woe is me! For I am lost; for I am a man of unclean lips, and I dwell in the midst of a people of unclean lips; for my eyes have seen the King, the LORD of hosts!"

⁶ Then one of the seraphim flew to me, having in his hand a burning coal that he had taken with tongs from the altar. ⁷ And he touched my mouth and said: "Behold, this has touched your lips; your guilt is taken away, and your sin atoned for."

Isaiah's Commission from the Lord

⁸ And I heard the voice of the Lord saying, "Whom shall I send, and who will go for us?" Then I said, "Here I am! Send me." ⁹ And he said, "Go, and say to this people:

"'Keep on hearing, but do not under-
    stand;
keep on seeing, but do not perceive.'

10 Make the heart of this people dull,
    and their ears heavy,
    and blind their eyes;
  lest they see with their eyes,
    and hear with their ears,
  and understand with their hearts,
    and turn and be healed."

11 Then I said, "How long, O Lord?"
And he said:
"Until cities lie waste
    without inhabitant,
  and houses without people,
    and the land is a desolate waste,

12 and the LORD removes people far away,
    and the forsaken places are many in
      the midst of the land.
13 And though a tenth remain in it,
    it will be burned again,
  like a terebinth or an oak,
    whose stump remains
    when it is felled."
The holy seed is its stump.

Isaiah Sent to King Ahaz

7 In the days of Ahaz the son of Jotham, son of Uzziah, king of Judah, Rezin the king of Syria and Pekah the son of Remaliah the king of Israel came up to Jerusalem to wage war against it, but could not yet mount an attack against it. ² When the house of David was told, "Syria is in league with Ephraim," the heart of Ahaz and the heart of his people shook as the trees of the forest shake before the wind.

³ And the LORD said to Isaiah, "Go out to meet Ahaz, you and Shear-jashub¹ your son, at the end of the conduit of the upper pool on the highway to the Washer's Field. ⁴ And say to him, 'Be careful, be quiet, do not fear, and do not let your heart be faint because of these two smoldering stumps of firebrands, at the fierce anger of Rezin and Syria and the son of Remaliah. ⁵ Because Syria, with Ephraim and the son of Remaliah, has devised evil against you, saying, ⁶ "Let us go up against Judah and terrify it, and let us conquer it for ourselves, and set up the son of Tabeel as king in the midst of it," ⁷ thus says the Lord GOD:

"'It shall not stand,
    and it shall not come to pass.
8 For the head of Syria is Damascus,
    and the head of Damascus is Rezin.
And within sixty-five years
    Ephraim will be shattered from
      being a people.
9 And the head of Ephraim is Samaria,
    and the head of Samaria is the son
      of Remaliah.
If you are not firm in faith,
    you will not be firm at all.'"

The Sign of Immanuel

10 Again the LORD spoke to Ahaz, 11 "Ask a sign of the LORD your God; let it be deep as Sheol or high as heaven." 12 But Ahaz said, "I will not ask, and I will not put the LORD to

---

¹ Shear-jashub means A remnant shall return

the test." [13] And he said, "Hear then, O house of David! Is it too little for you to weary men, that you weary my God also? [14] Therefore the Lord himself will give you a sign. Behold, the virgin shall conceive and bear a son, and shall call his name Immanuel.[1] [15] He shall eat curds and honey when he knows how to refuse the evil and choose the good. [16] For before the boy knows how to refuse the evil and choose the good, the land whose two kings you dread will be deserted. [17] The LORD will bring upon you and upon your people and upon your father's house such days as have not come since the day that Ephraim departed from Judah—the king of Assyria."

[18] In that day the LORD will whistle for the fly that is at the end of the streams of Egypt, and for the bee that is in the land of Assyria. [19] And they will all come and settle in the steep ravines, and in the clefts of the rocks, and on all the thornbushes, and on all the pastures.

[20] In that day the Lord will shave with a razor that is hired beyond the River— with the king of Assyria—the head and the hair of the feet, and it will sweep away the beard also.

[21] In that day a man will keep alive a young cow and two sheep, [22] and because of the abundance of milk that they give, he will eat curds, for everyone who is left in the land will eat curds and honey.

[23] In that day every place where there used to be a thousand vines, worth a thousand shekels of silver, will become briers and thorns. [24] With bow and arrows a man will come there, for all the land will be briers and thorns. [25] And as for all the hills that used to be hoed with a hoe, you will not come there for fear of briers and thorns, but they will become a place where cattle are let loose and where sheep tread.

The Coming Assyrian Invasion

8 Then the LORD said to me, "Take a large tablet and write on it in common characters, 'Belonging to Maher-shalal-hash-baz.' [2] And I will get reliable witnesses, Uriah the priest and Zechariah the son of Jeberechiah, to attest for me."

[3] And I went to the prophetess, and she conceived and bore a son. Then the LORD said to me, "Call his name Maher-shalal-hash-baz; [4] for before the boy knows how to cry 'My father' or 'My mother,' the wealth of Damascus and the spoil of Samaria will be carried away before the king of Assyria."

[5] The LORD spoke to me again: [6] "Because this people has refused the waters of Shiloah that flow gently, and rejoice over Rezin and the son of Remaliah, [7] therefore, behold, the Lord is bringing up against them the waters of the River, mighty and many, the king of Assyria and all his glory. And it will rise over all its channels and go over all its banks, [8] and it will sweep on into Judah, it will overflow and pass on, reaching even to the neck, and its outspread wings will fill the breadth of your land, O Immanuel."

[9]　Be broken, you peoples, and be shattered;
　　　give ear, all you far countries;

GETTING THE MESSAGE

Shaving. Being forced to shave was a mark of humiliation (7:20). In some nations of that time, the hair of slaves was shaved in a particular way to identify them as their owner's property.

　　　strap on your armor and be shattered;
　　　strap on your armor and be shattered.
[10]　Take counsel together, but it will come to nothing;
　　　speak a word, but it will not stand,
　　　for God is with us.[2]

Fear God, Wait for the LORD

[11] For the LORD spoke thus to me with his strong hand upon me, and warned me not to walk in the way of this people, saying: [12] "Do not call conspiracy all that this people calls conspiracy, and do not fear what they fear, nor be in dread. [13] But the LORD of hosts, him you shall honor as holy. Let him be your fear, and let him be your dread. [14] And he will become a sanctuary and a stone of offense and a rock of stumbling to both houses of Israel, a trap and a snare to the inhabitants of Jerusalem. [15] And many shall stumble on it. They shall fall and be broken; they shall be snared and taken."

---

[1] Immanuel means God is with us　[2] The Hebrew for God is with us is Immanuel

¹⁶ Bind up the testimony; seal the teaching among my disciples. ¹⁷ I will wait for the Lord, who is hiding his face from the house of Jacob, and I will hope in him. ¹⁸ Behold, I and the children whom the Lord has given me are signs and portents in Israel from the Lord of hosts, who dwells on Mount Zion. ¹⁹ And when they say to you, "Inquire of the mediums and the necromancers who chirp and mutter," should not a people inquire of their God? Should they inquire of the dead on behalf of the living? ²⁰ To the teaching and to the testimony! If they will not speak according to this word, it is because they have no dawn. ²¹ They will pass through the land, greatly distressed and hungry. And when they are hungry, they will be enraged and

will speak contemptuously against their king and their God, and turn their faces upward. ²² And they will look to the earth, but behold, distress and darkness, the gloom of anguish. And they will be thrust into thick darkness.

For to Us a Child Is Born

9 But there will be no gloom for her who was in anguish. In the former time he brought into contempt the land of Zebulun and the land of Naphtali, but in the latter time he has made glorious the way of the sea, the land beyond the Jordan, Galilee of the nations.

² The people who walked in darkness
have seen a great light;
those who dwelt in a land of deep
darkness,
on them has light shone.
³ You have multiplied the nation;
you have increased its joy;

they rejoice before you
as with joy at the harvest,
as they are glad when they divide
the spoil.
⁴ For the yoke of his burden,
and the staff for his shoulder,
the rod of his oppressor,
you have broken as on the day of
Midian.
⁵ For every boot of the tramping warrior
in battle tumult
and every garment rolled in blood
will be burned as fuel for the fire.
⁶ For to us a child is born,
to us a son is given;
and the government shall be upon his
shoulder,
and his name shall be called
Wonderful Counselor, Mighty God,
Everlasting Father, Prince of Peace.
⁷ Of the increase of his government and
of peace
there will be no end,
on the throne of David and over his
kingdom,
to establish it and to uphold it
with justice and with righteousness
from this time forth and forevermore.
The zeal of the Lord of hosts will do
this.

Judgment on Arrogance and Oppression

⁸ The Lord has sent a word against
Jacob,
and it will fall on Israel;
⁹ and all the people will know,
Ephraim and the inhabitants of
Samaria,
who say in pride and in arrogance
of heart:
¹⁰ "The bricks have fallen,
but we will build with dressed
stones;
the sycamores have been cut down,
but we will put cedars in their place."
¹¹ But the Lord raises the adversaries of
Rezin against him,
and stirs up his enemies.
¹² The Syrians on the east and the
Philistines on the west
devour Israel with open mouth.
For all this his anger has not turned
away,
and his hand is stretched out still.

13 The people did not turn to him who
       struck them,
     nor inquire of the LORD of hosts.
14 So the LORD cut off from Israel head
       and tail,
     palm branch and reed in one day—
15 the elder and honored man is the head,
     and the prophet who teaches lies is
       the tail;
16 for those who guide this people have
       been leading them astray,
     and those who are guided by them
       are swallowed up.
17 Therefore the Lord does not rejoice
       over their young men,
     and has no compassion on their
       fatherless and widows;
   for everyone is godless and an evildoer,
     and every mouth speaks folly.
   For all this his anger has not turned
       away,
     and his hand is stretched out still.

18 For wickedness burns like a fire;
     it consumes briers and thorns;
   it kindles the thickets of the forest,
     and they roll upward in a column of
       smoke.
19 Through the wrath of the LORD of
       hosts
     the land is scorched,
   and the people are like fuel for the fire;
     no one spares another.
20 They slice meat on the right, but are
       still hungry,
     and they devour on the left, but are
       not satisfied;
   each devours the flesh of his own arm,
21 Manasseh devours Ephraim, and
       Ephraim devours Manasseh;
     together they are against Judah.
   For all this his anger has not turned
       away,
     and his hand is stretched out still.

10 Woe to those who decree iniqui-
       tous decrees,
     and the writers who keep writing
       oppression,
2 to turn aside the needy from justice
     and to rob the poor of my people of
       their right,
   that widows may be their spoil,
     and that they may make the father-
       less their prey!

3 What will you do on the day of pun-
       ishment,
     in the ruin that will come from afar?
   To whom will you flee for help,
     and where will you leave your
       wealth?
4 Nothing remains but to crouch
       among the prisoners
     or fall among the slain.
   For all this his anger has not turned
       away,
     and his hand is stretched out still.

Judgment on Arrogant Assyria

5 Ah, Assyria, the rod of my anger;
     the staff in their hands is my fury!
6 Against a godless nation I send him,
     and against the people of my wrath
       I command him,
   to take spoil and seize plunder,
     and to tread them down like the
       mire of the streets.
7 But he does not so intend,
     and his heart does not so think;
   but it is in his heart to destroy,
     and to cut off nations not a few;
8 for he says:
   "Are not my commanders all kings?
9 Is not Calno like Carchemish?
     Is not Hamath like Arpad?
     Is not Samaria like Damascus?
10 As my hand has reached to the king-
       doms of the idols,
     whose carved images were greater
       than those of Jerusalem and
       Samaria,
11 shall I not do to Jerusalem and her idols
     as I have done to Samaria and her
       images?"

12 When the Lord has finished all his work
on Mount Zion and on Jerusalem, he will
punish the speech of the arrogant heart of
the king of Assyria and the boastful look in
his eyes. 13 For he says:

   "By the strength of my hand I have
       done it,
     and by my wisdom, for I have
       understanding;
   I remove the boundaries of peoples,
     and plunder their treasures;
     like a bull I bring down those who
       sit on thrones.
14 My hand has found like a nest
     the wealth of the peoples;

and as one gathers eggs that have
    been forsaken,
    so I have gathered all the earth;
and there was none that moved a wing
    or opened the mouth or chirped."

15 Shall the axe boast over him who
    hews with it,
    or the saw magnify itself against
    him who wields it?
As if a rod should wield him who lifts
    it,
    or as if a staff should lift him who is
    not wood!
16 Therefore the Lord GOD of hosts
    will send wasting sickness among
    his stout warriors,
and under his glory a burning will be
    kindled,
    like the burning of fire.

GETTING THE MESSAGE

Yokes were wooden frames placed on work animals such as oxen to harness their power. When Israelites heard prophets like Isaiah speak of the yokes placed on them by their oppressors (10:27), they would readily understand what he meant.

17 The light of Israel will become a fire,
    and his Holy One a flame,
and it will burn and devour
    his thorns and briers in one day.
18 The glory of his forest and of his fruit-
    ful land
    the LORD will destroy, both soul and
    body,
    and it will be as when a sick man
    wastes away.
19 The remnant of the trees of his forest
    will be so few
    that a child can write them down.

The Remnant of Israel Will Return

20 In that day the remnant of Israel and the survivors of the house of Jacob will no more lean on him who struck them, but will lean on the LORD, the Holy One of Israel, in truth. 21 A remnant will return, the remnant of Jacob, to the mighty God. 22 For though your people Israel be as the sand of the sea, only a remnant of them will return.

Destruction is decreed, overflowing with righteousness. 23 For the Lord GOD of hosts will make a full end, as decreed, in the midst of all the earth.

24 Therefore thus says the Lord GOD of hosts: "O my people, who dwell in Zion, be not afraid of the Assyrians when they strike with the rod and lift up their staff against you as the Egyptians did. 25 For in a very little while my fury will come to an end, and my anger will be directed to their destruction. 26 And the LORD of hosts will wield against them a whip, as when he struck Midian at the rock of Oreb. And his staff will be over the sea, and he will lift it as he did in Egypt. 27 And in that day his burden will depart from your shoulder, and his yoke from your neck; and the yoke will be broken because of the fat."

28 He has come to Aiath;
    he has passed through Migron;
    at Michmash he stores his bag-
        gage;
29 they have crossed over the pass;
    at Geba they lodge for the night;
Ramah trembles;
    Gibeah of Saul has fled.
30 Cry aloud, O daughter of Gallim!
    Give attention, O Laishah!
    O poor Anathoth!
31 Madmenah is in flight;
    the inhabitants of Gebim flee for
    safety.
32 This very day he will halt at Nob;
    he will shake his fist
    at the mount of the daughter of
    Zion,
    the hill of Jerusalem.
33 Behold, the Lord GOD of hosts
    will lop the boughs with terrifying
    power;
the great in height will be hewn
    down,
    and the lofty will be brought low.
34 He will cut down the thickets of the
    forest with an axe,
    and Lebanon will fall by the
    Majestic One.

The Righteous Reign of the Branch

11 There shall come forth a shoot from
    the stump of Jesse,
    and a branch from his roots shall
    bear fruit.

2 And the Spirit of the LORD shall rest
   upon him,
   the Spirit of wisdom and under-
      standing,
   the Spirit of counsel and might,
   the Spirit of knowledge and the fear
      of the LORD.
3 And his delight shall be in the fear of
   the LORD.
He shall not judge by what his eyes
   see,
   or decide disputes by what his ears
      hear,
4 but with righteousness he shall judge
   the poor,
   and decide with equity for the meek
      of the earth;
and he shall strike the earth with the
   rod of his mouth,
   and with the breath of his lips he
      shall kill the wicked.
5 Righteousness shall be the belt of his
   waist,
   and faithfulness the belt of his loins.

6 The wolf shall dwell with the lamb,
   and the leopard shall lie down with
      the young goat,
and the calf and the lion and the
   fattened calf together;
   and a little child shall lead them.
7 The cow and the bear shall graze;
   their young shall lie down together;
   and the lion shall eat straw like the
      ox.
8 The nursing child shall play over the
   hole of the cobra,
   and the weaned child shall put his
      hand on the adder's den.
9 They shall not hurt or destroy
   in all my holy mountain;
   for the earth shall be full of the
      knowledge of the LORD
   as the waters cover the sea.

10 In that day the root of Jesse, who shall
stand as a signal for the peoples—of him
shall the nations inquire, and his resting
place shall be glorious.

11 In that day the Lord will extend his hand
yet a second time to recover the remnant
that remains of his people, from Assyria,
from Egypt, from Pathros, from Cush, from
Elam, from Shinar, from Hamath, and from
the coastlands of the sea.

12 He will raise a signal for the nations
   and will assemble the banished of
      Israel,
and gather the dispersed of Judah
   from the four corners of the earth.
13 The jealousy of Ephraim shall depart,
   and those who harass Judah shall be
      cut off;
Ephraim shall not be jealous of
   Judah,
   and Judah shall not harass
      Ephraim.
14 But they shall swoop down on the
   shoulder of the Philistines in
      the west,
   and together they shall plunder the
      people of the east.
They shall put out their hand against
   Edom and Moab,
   and the Ammonites shall obey them.

GETTING THE MESSAGE

The idea of tame **farm animals** living
in harmony with **wild animals** such as
lions and bears (11:6–9) would have been
a startling thought for the people of
Isaiah's day, for whom such predators
were a frequent threat (see also
65:17–25).

15 And the LORD will utterly destroy
   the tongue of the Sea of Egypt,
and will wave his hand over the River
   with his scorching breath,
and strike it into seven channels,
   and he will lead people across in
      sandals.
16 And there will be a highway from
   Assyria
   for the remnant that remains of his
      people,
as there was for Israel
   when they came up from the land
      of Egypt.

The LORD Is My Strength and My Song

12 You will say in that day:
   "I will give thanks to you, O LORD,
   for though you were angry with me,
   your anger turned away,
      that you might comfort me.

² "Behold, God is my salvation;
  I will trust, and will not be afraid;
for the Lord God is my strength and
    my song,
  and he has become my salvation."

³ With joy you will draw water from the
wells of salvation. ⁴ And you will say in
that day:

"Give thanks to the Lord,
  call upon his name,
make known his deeds among the
    peoples,
  proclaim that his name is exalted.

⁵ "Sing praises to the Lord, for he has
    done gloriously;
  let this be made known in all the
    earth.
⁶ Shout, and sing for joy, O inhabitant
    of Zion,
  for great in your midst is the Holy
    One of Israel."

The Judgment of Babylon

13 The oracle concerning Babylon which
Isaiah the son of Amoz saw.

² On a bare hill raise a signal;
    cry aloud to them;
  wave the hand for them to enter
    the gates of the nobles.
³ I myself have commanded my conse-
    crated ones,
  and have summoned my mighty
    men to execute my anger,
  my proudly exulting ones.

⁴ The sound of a tumult is on the
    mountains
    as of a great multitude!
  The sound of an uproar of kingdoms,
    of nations gathering together!
  The Lord of hosts is mustering
    a host for battle.
⁵ They come from a distant land,
    from the end of the heavens,
  the Lord and the weapons of his
    indignation,
    to destroy the whole land.

⁶ Wail, for the day of the Lord is near;
    as destruction from the Almighty it
    will come!
⁷ Therefore all hands will be feeble,
  and every human heart will melt.

⁸ They will be dismayed:
    pangs and agony will seize them;
  they will be in anguish like a
    woman in labor.
  They will look aghast at one another;
    their faces will be aflame.

⁹ Behold, the day of the Lord comes,
    cruel, with wrath and fierce anger,
  to make the land a desolation
    and to destroy its sinners from it.
¹⁰ For the stars of the heavens and their
    constellations
    will not give their light;
  the sun will be dark at its rising,
    and the moon will not shed its light.
¹¹ I will punish the world for its evil,
    and the wicked for their iniquity;
  I will put an end to the pomp of the
    arrogant,
    and lay low the pompous pride of
    the ruthless.
¹² I will make people more rare than fine
    gold,
    and mankind than the gold of Ophir.
¹³ Therefore I will make the heavens
    tremble,
    and the earth will be shaken out of
    its place,
  at the wrath of the Lord of hosts
    in the day of his fierce anger.
¹⁴ And like a hunted gazelle,
    or like sheep with none to gather
    them,
  each will turn to his own people,
    and each will flee to his own land.
¹⁵ Whoever is found will be thrust
    through,
    and whoever is caught will fall by
    the sword.
¹⁶ Their infants will be dashed in pieces
    before their eyes;
  their houses will be plundered
    and their wives ravished.

¹⁷ Behold, I am stirring up the Medes
    against them,
  who have no regard for silver
    and do not delight in gold.
¹⁸ Their bows will slaughter the young
    men;
  they will have no mercy on the fruit
    of the womb;
  their eyes will not pity children.

¹⁹ And Babylon, the glory of kingdoms,
  the splendor and pomp of the
      Chaldeans,
will be like Sodom and Gomorrah
  when God overthrew them.
²⁰ It will never be inhabited
  or lived in for all generations;
no Arab will pitch his tent there;
  no shepherds will make their flocks
      lie down there.
²¹ But wild animals will lie down there,
  and their houses will be full of
      howling creatures;
there ostriches will dwell,
  and there wild goats will dance.
²² Hyenas will cry in its towers,
  and jackals in the pleasant palaces;
its time is close at hand
  and its days will not be prolonged.

The Restoration of Jacob

14 For the Lord will have compassion on Jacob and will again choose Israel, and will set them in their own land, and sojourners will join them and will attach themselves to the house of Jacob. ² And the peoples will take them and bring them to their place, and the house of Israel will possess them in the Lord's land as male and female slaves.[1] They will take captive those who were their captors, and rule over those who oppressed them.

Israel's Remnant Taunts Babylon

³ When the Lord has given you rest from your pain and turmoil and the hard service with which you were made to serve, ⁴ you will take up this taunt against the king of Babylon:

"How the oppressor has ceased,
  the insolent fury ceased!
⁵ The Lord has broken the staff of the
      wicked,
  the scepter of rulers,
⁶ that struck the peoples in wrath
  with unceasing blows,
that ruled the nations in anger
  with unrelenting persecution.
⁷ The whole earth is at rest and quiet;
  they break forth into singing.
⁸ The cypresses rejoice at you,
  the cedars of Lebanon, saying,
'Since you were laid low,
  no woodcutter comes up against us.'

⁹ Sheol beneath is stirred up
  to meet you when you come;
it rouses the shades to greet you,
  all who were leaders of the earth;
it raises from their thrones
  all who were kings of the nations.
¹⁰ All of them will answer
  and say to you:
'You too have become as weak as we!
  You have become like us!'
¹¹ Your pomp is brought down to Sheol,
  the sound of your harps;
maggots are laid as a bed beneath you,
  and worms are your covers.

¹² "How you are fallen from heaven,
  O Day Star, son of Dawn!
How you are cut down to the ground,
  you who laid the nations low!
¹³ You said in your heart,
  'I will ascend to heaven;

above the stars of God
  I will set my throne on high;
I will sit on the mount of assembly
  in the far reaches of the north;
¹⁴ I will ascend above the heights of the
      clouds;
  I will make myself like the Most
      High.'
¹⁵ But you are brought down to Sheol,
  to the far reaches of the pit.
¹⁶ Those who see you will stare at you
  and ponder over you:
'Is this the man who made the earth
      tremble,
  who shook kingdoms,
¹⁷ who made the world like a desert
  and overthrew its cities,
who did not let his prisoners go
      home?'
¹⁸ All the kings of the nations lie in
      glory,
  each in his own tomb;

---

[1] Or *servants*; the Hebrew word (*ebed*) can mean either voluntary service or forced service (see Preface)

19 but you are cast out, away from your
      grave,
    like a loathed branch,
  clothed with the slain, those pierced
      by the sword,
  who go down to the stones of the
      pit,
  like a dead body trampled underfoot.
20 You will not be joined with them in
      burial,
    because you have destroyed your
      land,
    you have slain your people.

  "May the offspring of evildoers
      nevermore be named!
21 Prepare slaughter for his sons
      because of the guilt of their fathers,
  lest they rise and possess the earth,
    and fill the face of the world with
      cities."

22 "I will rise up against them," declares
the LORD of hosts, "and will cut off from
Babylon name and remnant, descendants
and posterity," declares the LORD. 23 "And
I will make it a possession of the hedgehog, and pools of water, and I will sweep
it with the broom of destruction," declares
the LORD of hosts.

An Oracle Concerning Assyria

24 The LORD of hosts has sworn:
  "As I have planned,
      so shall it be,
  and as I have purposed,
      so shall it stand,
25 that I will break the Assyrian in my
      land,
    and on my mountains trample him
      underfoot;
  and his yoke shall depart from them,
    and his burden from their shoulder."
26 This is the purpose that is purposed
    concerning the whole earth,
  and this is the hand that is stretched
      out
    over all the nations.
27 For the LORD of hosts has purposed,
    and who will annul it?
  His hand is stretched out,
    and who will turn it back?

An Oracle Concerning Philistia

28 In the year that King Ahaz died came
this oracle:

29 Rejoice not, O Philistia, all of you,
    that the rod that struck you is bro-
      ken,
  for from the serpent's root will come
      forth an adder,
    and its fruit will be a flying fiery
      serpent.
30 And the firstborn of the poor will graze,
    and the needy lie down in safety;
  but I will kill your root with famine,
    and your remnant it will slay.
31 Wail, O gate; cry out, O city;
    melt in fear, O Philistia, all of you!
  For smoke comes out of the north,
    and there is no straggler in his ranks.

32 What will one answer the messengers
      of the nation?
  "The LORD has founded Zion,
    and in her the afflicted of his people
      find refuge."

An Oracle Concerning Moab

15 An oracle concerning Moab.

  Because Ar of Moab is laid waste in a
      night,
    Moab is undone;
  because Kir of Moab is laid waste in a
      night,
    Moab is undone.
2 He has gone up to the temple, and to
      Dibon,
    to the high places to weep;
  over Nebo and over Medeba
    Moab wails.
  On every head is baldness;
    every beard is shorn;
3 in the streets they wear sackcloth;
    on the housetops and in the squares
    everyone wails and melts in tears.
4 Heshbon and Elealeh cry out;
    their voice is heard as far as Jahaz;
  therefore the armed men of Moab cry
      aloud;
    his soul trembles.
5 My heart cries out for Moab;
    her fugitives flee to Zoar,
    to Eglath-shelishiyah.
  For at the ascent of Luhith
    they go up weeping;
  on the road to Horonaim
    they raise a cry of destruction;
6 the waters of Nimrim
    are a desolation;

the grass is withered, the vegetation
fails,
the greenery is no more.
7 Therefore the abundance they have
gained
and what they have laid up
they carry away
over the Brook of the Willows.
8 For a cry has gone
around the land of Moab;
her wailing reaches to Eglaim;
her wailing reaches to Beer-elim.
9 For the waters of Dibon are full of
blood;
for I will bring upon Dibon even
more,
a lion for those of Moab who escape,
for the remnant of the land.

16 Send the lamb to the ruler of the
land,
from Sela, by way of the desert,
to the mount of the daughter of Zion.
2 Like fleeing birds,
like a scattered nest,
so are the daughters of Moab
at the fords of the Arnon.

3 "Give counsel;
grant justice;
make your shade like night
at the height of noon;
shelter the outcasts;
do not reveal the fugitive;
4 let the outcasts of Moab
sojourn among you;
be a shelter to them
from the destroyer.
When the oppressor is no more,
and destruction has ceased,
and he who tramples underfoot has
vanished from the land,
5 then a throne will be established in
steadfast love,
and on it will sit in faithfulness
in the tent of David
one who judges and seeks justice
and is swift to do righteousness."

6 We have heard of the pride of Moab—
how proud he is!—
of his arrogance, his pride, and his
insolence;
in his idle boasting he is not right.
7 Therefore let Moab wail for Moab,
let everyone wail.

Mourn, utterly stricken,
for the raisin cakes of Kir-hareseth.
8 For the fields of Heshbon languish,
and the vine of Sibmah;
the lords of the nations
have struck down its branches,
which reached to Jazer
and strayed to the desert;
its shoots spread abroad
and passed over the sea.
9 Therefore I weep with the weeping of
Jazer
for the vine of Sibmah;
I drench you with my tears,
O Heshbon and Elealeh;
for over your summer fruit and your
harvest
the shout has ceased.
10 And joy and gladness are taken away
from the fruitful field,

> **GETTING THE MESSAGE**
>
> **Payment in lambs.** The people of Moab
> offered to pay the Israelites to protect
> them from their enemies. Such tribute
> was often paid in goods rather than with
> money; since the Moabites had many
> sheep, that's how they paid (16:1).

and in the vineyards no songs are
sung,
no cheers are raised;
no treader treads out wine in the
presses;
I have put an end to the shouting.
11 Therefore my inner parts moan like a
lyre for Moab,
and my inmost self for Kir-
hareseth.

12 And when Moab presents himself, when
he wearies himself on the high place, when
he comes to his sanctuary to pray, he will
not prevail.

13 This is the word that the LORD spoke
concerning Moab in the past. 14 But now the
LORD has spoken, saying, "In three years,
like the years of a hired worker, the glory
of Moab will be brought into contempt, in
spite of all his great multitude, and those
who remain will be very few and feeble."

An Oracle Concerning Damascus

17 An oracle concerning Damascus.

> Behold, Damascus will cease to be a
>   city
> and will become a heap of ruins.
> 2 The cities of Aroer are deserted;
>   they will be for flocks,
> which will lie down, and none will
>   make them afraid.
> 3 The fortress will disappear from
>   Ephraim,
>   and the kingdom from Damascus;
> and the remnant of Syria will be
>   like the glory of the children of Israel,
>   declares the LORD of hosts.
>
> 4 And in that day the glory of Jacob will
>   be brought low,
>   and the fat of his flesh will grow
>   lean.

GETTING THE MESSAGE

Olive harvesting was very similar to
grain harvesting. The olive harvesters
would beat the branches of the tree with
long poles, knocking the olives to the
ground. The uppermost branches were
left untouched so that the poor could
gather what remained (17:6).

> 5 And it shall be as when the reaper
>   gathers standing grain
> and his arm harvests the ears,
> and as when one gleans the ears of
>   grain
>   in the Valley of Rephaim.
> 6 Gleanings will be left in it,
>   as when an olive tree is beaten—
> two or three berries
>   in the top of the highest bough,
> four or five
>   on the branches of a fruit tree,
>   declares the LORD God of Israel.

7 In that day man will look to his Maker,
and his eyes will look on the Holy One of
Israel. 8 He will not look to the altars, the
work of his hands, and he will not look on
what his own fingers have made, either the
Asherim or the altars of incense.

9 In that day their strong cities will be like
the deserted places of the wooded heights
and the hilltops, which they deserted
because of the children of Israel, and there
will be desolation.

> 10 For you have forgotten the God of
>   your salvation
>   and have not remembered the Rock
>   of your refuge;
> therefore, though you plant pleasant
>   plants
>   and sow the vine-branch of a
>   stranger,
> 11 though you make them grow on the
>   day that you plant them,
>   and make them blossom in the
>   morning that you sow,
> yet the harvest will flee away
>   in a day of grief and incurable pain.
>
> 12 Ah, the thunder of many peoples;
>   they thunder like the thundering of
>   the sea!
> Ah, the roar of nations;
>   they roar like the roaring of mighty
>   waters!
> 13 The nations roar like the roaring of
>   many waters,
>   but he will rebuke them, and they
>   will flee far away,
> chased like chaff on the mountains
>   before the wind
> and whirling dust before the storm.
> 14 At evening time, behold, terror!
>   Before morning, they are no more!
> This is the portion of those who loot us,
>   and the lot of those who plunder us.

An Oracle Concerning Cush

18 Ah, land of whirring wings
>   that is beyond the rivers of Cush,
> 2 which sends ambassadors by the sea,
>   in vessels of papyrus on the waters!
> Go, you swift messengers,
>   to a nation tall and smooth,
> to a people feared near and far,
>   a nation mighty and conquering,
>   whose land the rivers divide.
>
> 3 All you inhabitants of the world,
>   you who dwell on the earth,
> when a signal is raised on the moun-
>   tains, look!
>   When a trumpet is blown, hear!
> 4 For thus the LORD said to me:
> "I will quietly look from my dwelling
>   like clear heat in sunshine,

like a cloud of dew in the heat of
harvest."
5 For before the harvest, when the blossom is over,
and the flower becomes a ripening
grape,
he cuts off the shoots with pruning
hooks,
and the spreading branches he lops
off and clears away.
6 They shall all of them be left
to the birds of prey of the mountains
and to the beasts of the earth.
And the birds of prey will summer on
them,
and all the beasts of the earth will
winter on them.

7 At that time tribute will be brought to
the Lord of hosts

from a people tall and smooth,
from a people feared near and far,
a nation mighty and conquering,
whose land the rivers divide,

to Mount Zion, the place of the name of the
Lord of hosts.

An Oracle Concerning Egypt

19

An oracle concerning Egypt.

Behold, the Lord is riding on a swift
cloud
and comes to Egypt;
and the idols of Egypt will tremble at
his presence,
and the heart of the Egyptians will
melt within them.
2 And I will stir up Egyptians against
Egyptians,
and they will fight, each against
another
and each against his neighbor,
city against city, kingdom against
kingdom;
3 and the spirit of the Egyptians within
them will be emptied out,
and I will confound their counsel;
and they will inquire of the idols and
the sorcerers,
and the mediums and the necromancers;
4 and I will give over the Egyptians
into the hand of a hard master,

and a fierce king will rule over them,
declares the Lord God of hosts.

5 And the waters of the sea will be dried
up,
and the river will be dry and parched,
6 and its canals will become foul,
and the branches of Egypt's Nile
will diminish and dry up,
reeds and rushes will rot away.
7 There will be bare places by the Nile,
on the brink of the Nile,
and all that is sown by the Nile will be
parched,
will be driven away, and will be no
more.
8 The fishermen will mourn and lament,
all who cast a hook in the Nile;
and they will languish
who spread nets on the water.
9 The workers in combed flax will be in
despair,
and the weavers of white cotton.

> ### GETTING THE MESSAGE

Competing Pharaohs. Beginning in
about 1000 B.C., Egypt fell into a period
of decline and royal feuding that lasted
nearly 400 years. During Isaiah's time,
there were four rival pharaohs claiming
the Egyptian throne (19:13).

10 Those who are the pillars of the land
will be crushed,
and all who work for pay will be
grieved.

11 The princes of Zoan are utterly foolish;
the wisest counselors of Pharaoh
give stupid counsel.
How can you say to Pharaoh,
"I am a son of the wise,
a son of ancient kings"?
12 Where then are your wise men?
Let them tell you
that they might know what the
Lord of hosts has purposed
against Egypt.
13 The princes of Zoan have become fools,
and the princes of Memphis are
deluded;
those who are the cornerstones of her
tribes
have made Egypt stagger.

14 The LORD has mingled within her a
     spirit of confusion,
and they will make Egypt stagger in
     all its deeds,
     as a drunken man staggers in his
          vomit.
15 And there will be nothing for Egypt
     that head or tail, palm branch or
     reed, may do.

Egypt, Assyria, Israel Blessed

16 In that day the Egyptians will be like women, and tremble with fear before the hand that the LORD of hosts shakes over them. 17 And the land of Judah will become a terror to the Egyptians. Everyone to whom it is mentioned will fear because of the purpose that the LORD of hosts has purposed against them.

18 In that day there will be five cities in the land of Egypt that speak the language of Canaan and swear allegiance to the LORD of hosts. One of these will be called the City of Destruction.

19 In that day there will be an altar to the LORD in the midst of the land of Egypt, and a pillar to the LORD at its border. 20 It will be a sign and a witness to the LORD of hosts in the land of Egypt. When they cry to the LORD because of oppressors, he will send them a savior and defender, and deliver them. 21 And the LORD will make himself known to the Egyptians, and the Egyptians will know the LORD in that day and worship with sacrifice and offering, and they will make vows to the LORD and perform them. 22 And the LORD will strike Egypt, striking and healing, and they will return to the LORD, and he will listen to their pleas for mercy and heal them.

23 In that day there will be a highway from Egypt to Assyria, and Assyria will come into Egypt, and Egypt into Assyria, and the Egyptians will worship with the Assyrians.

24 In that day Israel will be the third with Egypt and Assyria, a blessing in the midst of the earth, 25 whom the LORD of hosts has blessed, saying, "Blessed be Egypt my people, and Assyria the work of my hands, and Israel my inheritance."

A Sign Against Egypt and Cush

20 In the year that the commander in chief, who was sent by Sargon the king of Assyria, came to Ashdod and fought against it and captured it— 2 at that time the LORD spoke by Isaiah the son of Amoz, saying, "Go, and loose the sackcloth from your waist and take off your sandals from your feet," and he did so, walking naked and barefoot.

3 Then the LORD said, "As my servant Isaiah has walked naked and barefoot for three years as a sign and a portent against Egypt and Cush, 4 so shall the king of Assyria lead away the Egyptian captives and the Cushite exiles, both the young and the old, naked and barefoot, with buttocks uncovered, the nakedness of Egypt. 5 Then they shall be dismayed and ashamed because of Cush their hope and of Egypt their boast. 6 And the inhabitants of this coastland will say in that day, 'Behold, this is what has happened to those in whom we hoped and to whom we fled for help to be delivered from the king of Assyria! And we, how shall we escape?'"

Fallen, Fallen Is Babylon

21 The oracle concerning the wilderness of the sea.

As whirlwinds in the Negeb sweep on,
     it comes from the wilderness,
     from a terrible land.
2 A stern vision is told to me;
     the traitor betrays,
     and the destroyer destroys.
Go up, O Elam;
     lay siege, O Media;
all the sighing she has caused
     I bring to an end.
3 Therefore my loins are filled with
          anguish;
     pangs have seized me,
     like the pangs of a woman in labor;
I am bowed down so that I cannot
     hear;
     I am dismayed so that I cannot see.
4 My heart staggers; horror has appalled
          me;
     the twilight I longed for
     has been turned for me into trem-
          bling.
5 They prepare the table,
     they spread the rugs,
     they eat, they drink.
Arise, O princes;
     oil the shield!
6 For thus the Lord said to me:
"Go, set a watchman;
     let him announce what he sees.

7 When he sees riders, horsemen in
    pairs,
    riders on donkeys, riders on camels,
let him listen diligently,
    very diligently."
8 Then he who saw cried out:
"Upon a watchtower I stand, O Lord,
    continually by day,
and at my post I am stationed
    whole nights.
9 And behold, here come riders,
    horsemen in pairs!"
And he answered,
    "Fallen, fallen is Babylon;
and all the carved images of her gods
    he has shattered to the ground."
10 O my threshed and winnowed one,
    what I have heard from the LORD of
    hosts,
    the God of Israel, I announce to you.

11 The oracle concerning Dumah.

One is calling to me from Seir,
    "Watchman, what time of the night?
    Watchman, what time of the night?"
12 The watchman says:
"Morning comes, and also the night.
    If you will inquire, inquire;
    come back again."

13 The oracle concerning Arabia.

In the thickets in Arabia you will lodge,
    O caravans of Dedanites.
14 To the thirsty bring water;
    meet the fugitive with bread,
O inhabitants of the land of Tema.
15 For they have fled from the swords,
    from the drawn sword,
from the bent bow,
    and from the press of battle.

16 For thus the Lord said to me, "Within a year, according to the years of a hired worker, all the glory of Kedar will come to an end. 17 And the remainder of the archers of the mighty men of the sons of Kedar will be few, for the LORD, the God of Israel, has spoken."

An Oracle Concerning Jerusalem

22 The oracle concerning the valley of vision.

What do you mean that you have gone
    up,
    all of you, to the housetops,

2 you who are full of shoutings,
    tumultuous city, exultant town?
Your slain are not slain with the sword
    or dead in battle.
3 All your leaders have fled together;
    without the bow they were cap-
    tured.
All of you who were found were cap-
    tured,
    though they had fled far away.
4 Therefore I said:
"Look away from me;
    let me weep bitter tears;
do not labor to comfort me
    concerning the destruction of the
    daughter of my people."
5 For the Lord GOD of hosts has a day
    of tumult and trampling and confu-
    sion
    in the valley of vision,

GETTING THE MESSAGE

The **key to the house of David** was carried by the steward, and it opened every door and gate in the palace. It was probably bronze and was large enough that it had to be worn around the neck ("on his shoulder," 22:22). For the steward, it was a status symbol.

    a battering down of walls
    and a shouting to the mountains.
6 And Elam bore the quiver
    with chariots and horsemen,
    and Kir uncovered the shield.
7 Your choicest valleys were full of
    chariots,
    and the horsemen took their stand
    at the gates.
8 He has taken away the covering of
    Judah.

In that day you looked to the weapons of the House of the Forest, 9 and you saw that the breaches of the city of David were many. You collected the waters of the lower pool, 10 and you counted the houses of Jerusalem, and you broke down the houses to fortify the wall. 11 You made a reservoir between the two walls for the water of the old pool. But you did not look to him who did it, or see him who planned it long ago.

¹² In that day the Lord God of hosts
       called for weeping and mourning,
       for baldness and wearing sackcloth;
¹³ and behold, joy and gladness,
       killing oxen and slaughtering
           sheep,
       eating flesh and drinking wine.
   "Let us eat and drink,
       for tomorrow we die."
¹⁴ The Lord of hosts has revealed him-
       self in my ears:
   "Surely this iniquity will not be atoned
       for you until you die,"
       says the Lord God of hosts.

¹⁵ Thus says the Lord God of hosts, "Come, go to this steward, to Shebna, who is over the household, and say to him: ¹⁶ What have you to do here, and whom have you here, that you have cut out here a tomb for yourself, you who cut out a tomb on the height and carve a dwelling for yourself in the rock?

GETTING THE MESSAGE

Cyprus (23:1) is the third largest island in the Mediterranean Sea. Seafarers like the people of Sidon (23:12) would have valued it as both a seaport and a place of refuge.

¹⁷ Behold, the Lord will hurl you away violently, O you strong man. He will seize firm hold on you ¹⁸ and whirl you around and around, and throw you like a ball into a wide land. There you shall die, and there shall be your glorious chariots, you shame of your master's house. ¹⁹ I will thrust you from your office, and you will be pulled down from your station. ²⁰ In that day I will call my servant Eliakim the son of Hilkiah, ²¹ and I will clothe him with your robe, and will bind your sash on him, and will commit your authority to his hand. And he shall be a father to the inhabitants of Jerusalem and to the house of Judah. ²² And I will place on his shoulder the key of the house of David. He shall open, and none shall shut; and he shall shut, and none shall open. ²³ And I will fasten him like a peg in a secure place, and he will become a throne of honor to his father's house. ²⁴ And they will hang on him the whole honor of his father's house, the offspring and issue, every small vessel,

from the cups to all the flagons. ²⁵ In that day, declares the Lord of hosts, the peg that was fastened in a secure place will give way, and it will be cut down and fall, and the load that was on it will be cut off, for the Lord has spoken."

An Oracle Concerning Tyre and Sidon

23 The oracle concerning Tyre.

   Wail, O ships of Tarshish,
       for Tyre is laid waste, without
           house or harbor!
   From the land of Cyprus
       it is revealed to them.
² Be still, O inhabitants of the coast;
       the merchants of Sidon, who cross
           the sea, have filled you.
³ And on many waters
   your revenue was the grain of Shihor,
       the harvest of the Nile;
       you were the merchant of the
           nations.
⁴ Be ashamed, O Sidon, for the sea has
           spoken,
       the stronghold of the sea, saying:
   "I have neither labored nor given birth,
       I have neither reared young men
       nor brought up young women."
⁵ When the report comes to Egypt,
       they will be in anguish over the
           report about Tyre.
⁶ Cross over to Tarshish;
       wail, O inhabitants of the coast!
⁷ Is this your exultant city
       whose origin is from days of old,
   whose feet carried her
       to settle far away?
⁸ Who has purposed this
       against Tyre, the bestower of crowns,
   whose merchants were princes,
       whose traders were the honored of
           the earth?
⁹ The Lord of hosts has purposed it,
       to defile the pompous pride of all
           glory,
       to dishonor all the honored of the
           earth.
¹⁰ Cross over your land like the Nile,
       O daughter of Tarshish;
       there is no restraint anymore.
¹¹ He has stretched out his hand over
           the sea;
       he has shaken the kingdoms;

the Lord has given command concerning Canaan
to destroy its strongholds.
[12] And he said:
"You will no more exult,
  O oppressed virgin daughter of
    Sidon;
arise, cross over to Cyprus,
  even there you will have no rest."

[13] Behold the land of the Chaldeans! This is the people that was not; Assyria destined it for wild beasts. They erected their siege towers, they stripped her palaces bare, they made her a ruin.

[14] Wail, O ships of Tarshish,
  for your stronghold is laid waste.

[15] In that day Tyre will be forgotten for seventy years, like the days of one king. At the end of seventy years, it will happen to Tyre as in the song of the prostitute:

[16] "Take a harp;
  go about the city,
  O forgotten prostitute!
Make sweet melody;
  sing many songs,
  that you may be remembered."

[17] At the end of seventy years, the Lord will visit Tyre, and she will return to her wages and will prostitute herself with all the kingdoms of the world on the face of the earth. [18] Her merchandise and her wages will be holy to the Lord. It will not be stored or hoarded, but her merchandise will supply abundant food and fine clothing for those who dwell before the Lord.

Judgment on the Whole Earth

24 Behold, the Lord will empty the earth[1] and make it desolate,
  and he will twist its surface and
    scatter its inhabitants.
[2] And it shall be, as with the people, so
    with the priest;
  as with the slave, so with his master;
  as with the maid, so with her mis-
    tress;
  as with the buyer, so with the seller;
  as with the lender, so with the bor-
    rower;
  as with the creditor, so with the
    debtor.

[3] The earth shall be utterly empty and
    utterly plundered;
  for the Lord has spoken this word.
[4] The earth mourns and withers;
  the world languishes and withers;
  the highest people of the earth
    languish.
[5] The earth lies defiled
  under its inhabitants;
for they have transgressed the laws,
  violated the statutes,
  broken the everlasting covenant.
[6] Therefore a curse devours the earth,
  and its inhabitants suffer for their
    guilt;
therefore the inhabitants of the earth
    are scorched,
  and few men are left.
[7] The wine mourns,
  the vine languishes,
  all the merry-hearted sigh.
[8] The mirth of the tambourines is stilled,
  the noise of the jubilant has ceased,
  the mirth of the lyre is stilled.
[9] No more do they drink wine with
    singing;
  strong drink is bitter to those who
    drink it.
[10] The wasted city is broken down;
  every house is shut up so that none
    can enter.
[11] There is an outcry in the streets for
    lack of wine;
  all joy has grown dark;
  the gladness of the earth is banished.
[12] Desolation is left in the city;
  the gates are battered into ruins.
[13] For thus it shall be in the midst of the
    earth
  among the nations,
as when an olive tree is beaten,
  as at the gleaning when the grape
    harvest is done.
[14] They lift up their voices, they sing for
    joy;
  over the majesty of the Lord they
    shout from the west.
[15] Therefore in the east give glory to the
    Lord;
  in the coastlands of the sea, give
    glory to the name of the Lord,
    the God of Israel.

[1] Or *land*; so throughout this chapter

16 From the ends of the earth we hear
   songs of praise,
      of glory to the Righteous One.
   But I say, "I waste away,
      I waste away. Woe is me!
   For the traitors have betrayed,
      with betrayal the traitors have
         betrayed."

17 Terror and the pit and the snare[1]
      are upon you, O inhabitant of the
         earth!
18 He who flees at the sound of the ter-
      ror
      shall fall into the pit,
   and he who climbs out of the pit
      shall be caught in the snare.
   For the windows of heaven are
      opened,
      and the foundations of the earth
         tremble.
19 The earth is utterly broken,
      the earth is split apart,
      the earth is violently shaken.
20 The earth staggers like a drunken
      man;
      it sways like a hut;
   its transgression lies heavy upon it,
      and it falls, and will not rise again.
21 On that day the LORD will punish
      the host of heaven, in heaven,
      and the kings of the earth, on the
         earth.
22 They will be gathered together
      as prisoners in a pit;
   they will be shut up in a prison,
      and after many days they will be
         punished.
23 Then the moon will be confounded
      and the sun ashamed,
   for the LORD of hosts reigns
      on Mount Zion and in Jerusalem,
   and his glory will be before his elders.

God Will Swallow Up Death Forever

25 O LORD, you are my God;
      I will exalt you; I will praise your
         name,
   for you have done wonderful things,
      plans formed of old, faithful and
         sure.
2 For you have made the city a heap,
      the fortified city a ruin;

the foreigners' palace is a city no more;
   it will never be rebuilt.
3 Therefore strong peoples will glorify
      you;
   cities of ruthless nations will fear
      you.
4 For you have been a stronghold to the
      poor,
      a stronghold to the needy in his
         distress,
      a shelter from the storm and a
         shade from the heat;
   for the breath of the ruthless is like a
      storm against a wall,
5   like heat in a dry place.
   You subdue the noise of the foreign-
      ers;
      as heat by the shade of a cloud,
      so the song of the ruthless is put
         down.

6 On this mountain the LORD of hosts
      will make for all peoples
      a feast of rich food, a feast of well-
         aged wine,
      of rich food full of marrow, of aged
         wine well refined.
7 And he will swallow up on this moun-
      tain
      the covering that is cast over all
         peoples,
      the veil that is spread over all
         nations.
8   He will swallow up death forever;
   and the Lord GOD will wipe away tears
      from all faces,
      and the reproach of his people he
         will take away from all the earth,
   for the LORD has spoken.
9 It will be said on that day,
   "Behold, this is our God; we have
      waited for him, that he might
         save us.
   This is the LORD; we have waited
      for him;
      let us be glad and rejoice in his
         salvation."
10 For the hand of the LORD will rest on
      this mountain,
      and Moab shall be trampled down
         in his place,
      as straw is trampled down in a
         dunghill.

[1] The Hebrew words for *terror*, *pit*, and *snare* sound alike

¹¹ And he will spread out his hands in
the midst of it
as a swimmer spreads his hands out
to swim,
but the LORD will lay low his pomp-
ous pride together with the skill
of his hands.
¹² And the high fortifications of his
walls he will bring down,
lay low, and cast to the ground, to
the dust.

You Keep Him in Perfect Peace

26 In that day this song will be sung in
the land of Judah:

"We have a strong city;
he sets up salvation
as walls and bulwarks.
² Open the gates,
that the righteous nation that keeps
faith may enter in.
³ You keep him in perfect peace
whose mind is stayed on you,
because he trusts in you.
⁴ Trust in the LORD forever,
for the LORD GOD is an everlasting
rock.
⁵ For he has humbled
the inhabitants of the height,
the lofty city.
He lays it low, lays it low to the
ground,
casts it to the dust.
⁶ The foot tramples it,
the feet of the poor,
the steps of the needy."

⁷ The path of the righteous is level;
you make level the way of the righteous.
⁸ In the path of your judgments,
O LORD, we wait for you;
your name and remembrance
are the desire of our soul.
⁹ My soul yearns for you in the night;
my spirit within me earnestly seeks
you.
For when your judgments are in the
earth,
the inhabitants of the world learn
righteousness.
¹⁰ If favor is shown to the wicked,
he does not learn righteousness;

in the land of uprightness he deals
corruptly
and does not see the majesty of the
LORD.
¹¹ O LORD, your hand is lifted up,
but they do not see it.
Let them see your zeal for your people, and be ashamed.
Let the fire for your adversaries
consume them.
¹² O LORD, you will ordain peace for us,
for you have indeed done for us all
our works.
¹³ O LORD our God,
other lords besides you have ruled
over us,
but your name alone we bring to
remembrance.
¹⁴ They are dead, they will not live;
they are shades, they will not arise;
to that end you have visited them
with destruction
and wiped out all remembrance of
them.
¹⁵ But you have increased the nation,
O LORD,
you have increased the nation; you
are glorified;
you have enlarged all the borders of
the land.
¹⁶ O LORD, in distress they sought you;
they poured out a whispered
prayer
when your discipline was upon
them.
¹⁷ Like a pregnant woman
who writhes and cries out in her
pangs
when she is near to giving birth,
so were we because of you, O LORD;
¹⁸ we were pregnant, we writhed,
but we have given birth to wind.
We have accomplished no deliverance
in the earth,
and the inhabitants of the world
have not fallen.
¹⁹ Your dead shall live; their bodies shall
rise.
You who dwell in the dust, awake
and sing for joy!
For your dew is a dew of light,
and the earth will give birth to the
dead.

20 Come, my people, enter your chambers,
    and shut your doors behind you;
  hide yourselves for a little while
    until the fury has passed by.
21 For behold, the LORD is coming out
      from his place
    to punish the inhabitants of the
      earth for their iniquity,
  and the earth will disclose the blood
    shed on it,
    and will no more cover its slain.

The Redemption of Israel

27 In that day the LORD with his hard
    and great and strong sword will pun-
ish Leviathan the fleeing serpent, Leviathan
the twisting serpent, and he will slay the
dragon that is in the sea.

2   In that day,
  "A pleasant vineyard, sing of it!

> ### GETTING THE MESSAGE
>
> **Chalkstone** is a type of limestone that,
> when crushed, can be used for things
> such as whitewashing and as mortar for
> brick-laying. Because it was so easy to
> crush, Isaiah used it as a visual example
> of how the Lord will destroy the altars
> and high places of idol worship (27:9).

3   I, the LORD, am its keeper;
      every moment I water it.
    Lest anyone punish it,
    I keep it night and day;
4   I have no wrath.
    Would that I had thorns and briers to
      battle!
      I would march against them,
      I would burn them up together.
5   Or let them lay hold of my protection,
    let them make peace with me,
    let them make peace with me."
6   In days to come Jacob shall take root,
    Israel shall blossom and put forth
      shoots
    and fill the whole world with fruit.
7   Has he struck them as he struck those
      who struck them?
    Or have they been slain as their
      slayers were slain?

8   Measure by measure, by exile you
      contended with them;
    he removed them with his fierce
      breath in the day of the east
      wind.
9   Therefore by this the guilt of Jacob
      will be atoned for,
    and this will be the full fruit of the
      removal of his sin:
  when he makes all the stones of the
      altars
    like chalkstones crushed to pieces,
    no Asherim or incense altars will
      remain standing.
10 For the fortified city is solitary,
    a habitation deserted and forsaken,
      like the wilderness;
  there the calf grazes;
    there it lies down and strips its
      branches.
11 When its boughs are dry, they are
      broken;
    women come and make a fire of
      them.
  For this is a people without discern-
      ment;
    therefore he who made them will
      not have compassion on them;
    he who formed them will show
      them no favor.

12 In that day from the river Euphrates to
the Brook of Egypt the LORD will thresh out
the grain, and you will be gleaned one by
one, O people of Israel. 13 And in that day a
great trumpet will be blown, and those who
were lost in the land of Assyria and those
who were driven out to the land of Egypt
will come and worship the LORD on the holy
mountain at Jerusalem.

Judgment on Ephraim and Jerusalem

28 Ah, the proud crown of the
    drunkards of Ephraim,
    and the fading flower of its glorious
      beauty,
    which is on the head of the rich
      valley of those overcome with
      wine!
2   Behold, the Lord has one who is
      mighty and strong;
    like a storm of hail, a destroying
      tempest,

like a storm of mighty, overflowing
waters,
he casts down to the earth with his
hand.

3 The proud crown of the drunkards of
Ephraim
will be trodden underfoot;
4 and the fading flower of its glorious
beauty,
which is on the head of the rich
valley,
will be like a first-ripe fig before the
summer:
when someone sees it, he swallows it
as soon as it is in his hand.

5 In that day the LORD of hosts will be a
crown of glory,
and a diadem of beauty, to the remnant of his people,
6 and a spirit of justice to him who sits
in judgment,
and strength to those who turn
back the battle at the gate.

7 These also reel with wine
and stagger with strong drink;
the priest and the prophet reel with
strong drink,
they are swallowed by wine,
they stagger with strong drink,
they reel in vision,
they stumble in giving judgment.
8 For all tables are full of filthy vomit,
with no space left.

9 "To whom will he teach knowledge,
and to whom will he explain the
message?
Those who are weaned from the milk,
those taken from the breast?
10 For it is precept upon precept, precept
upon precept,
line upon line, line upon line,
here a little, there a little."

11 For by people of strange lips
and with a foreign tongue
the LORD will speak to this people,
12 to whom he has said,
"This is rest;
give rest to the weary;
and this is repose";
yet they would not hear.
13 And the word of the LORD will be to
them

precept upon precept, precept upon
precept,
line upon line, line upon line,
here a little, there a little,
that they may go, and fall backward,
and be broken, and snared, and
taken.

A Cornerstone in Zion

14 Therefore hear the word of the LORD,
you scoffers,
who rule this people in Jerusalem!
15 Because you have said, "We have
made a covenant with death,
and with Sheol we have an agreement,
when the overwhelming whip passes
through
it will not come to us,

GETTING THE MESSAGE

Details about farming. While a farmer
"scatters" seeds like dill and cumin,
other seeds, such as wheat and barley,
had to be planted "in rows . . . in its
proper place" (28:25). The Bible is
accurate and trustworthy, even in
such agricultural details.

for we have made lies our refuge,
and in falsehood we have taken
shelter";
16 therefore thus says the Lord GOD,
"Behold, I am the one who has laid as a
foundation in Zion,
a stone, a tested stone,
a precious cornerstone, of a sure
foundation:
'Whoever believes will not be in
haste.'
17 And I will make justice the line,
and righteousness the plumb line;
and hail will sweep away the refuge of
lies,
and waters will overwhelm the
shelter."
18 Then your covenant with death will
be annulled,
and your agreement with Sheol will
not stand;
when the overwhelming scourge
passes through,
you will be beaten down by it.

19 As often as it passes through it will
    take you;
    for morning by morning it will pass
       through,
    by day and by night;
and it will be sheer terror to under-
    stand the message.

20 For the bed is too short to stretch
    oneself on,
    and the covering too narrow to
       wrap oneself in.

21 For the Lord will rise up as on Mount
    Perazim;
    as in the Valley of Gibeon he will be
       roused;
to do his deed—strange is his deed!
    and to work his work—alien is his
       work!

22 Now therefore do not scoff,
    lest your bonds be made strong;

> **GETTING THE MESSAGE**
>
> Hebrew schoolchildren were taught
> the **yearly "round" of feasts** (29:1)
> at an early age. But the Lord is never
> impressed by insincere religious
> observances.

for I have heard a decree of destruction
    from the Lord God of hosts against
       the whole land.

23 Give ear, and hear my voice;
    give attention, and hear my speech.

24 Does he who plows for sowing plow
    continually?
    Does he continually open and har-
       row his ground?

25 When he has leveled its surface,
    does he not scatter dill, sow cumin,
and put in wheat in rows
    and barley in its proper place,
    and emmer as the border?

26 For he is rightly instructed;
    his God teaches him.

27 Dill is not threshed with a threshing
    sledge,
    nor is a cart wheel rolled over cumin,
but dill is beaten out with a stick,
    and cumin with a rod.

28 Does one crush grain for bread?
    No, he does not thresh it forever;
when he drives his cart wheel over it
    with his horses, he does not crush it.

29 This also comes from the Lord of
    hosts;
    he is wonderful in counsel
    and excellent in wisdom.

The Siege of Jerusalem

29 Ah, Ariel, Ariel,
    the city where David encamped!
Add year to year;
    let the feasts run their round.

2 Yet I will distress Ariel,
    and there shall be moaning and
       lamentation,
    and she shall be to me like an
       Ariel.[1]

3 And I will encamp against you all
    around,
    and will besiege you with towers
    and I will raise siegeworks against
       you.

4 And you will be brought low; from the
    earth you shall speak,
    and from the dust your speech will
       be bowed down;
your voice shall come from the
       ground like the voice of a ghost,
    and from the dust your speech shall
       whisper.

5 But the multitude of your foreign foes
    shall be like small dust,
    and the multitude of the ruthless
       like passing chaff.
And in an instant, suddenly,

6   you will be visited by the Lord of
       hosts
with thunder and with earthquake
    and great noise,
    with whirlwind and tempest, and
       the flame of a devouring fire.

7 And the multitude of all the nations
    that fight against Ariel,
    all that fight against her and her
       stronghold and distress her,
shall be like a dream, a vision of the
       night.

8 As when a hungry man dreams, and
    behold, he is eating
    and awakes with his hunger not
       satisfied,

---

[1] *Ariel* could mean *lion of God*, or *hero* (2 Samuel 23:20), or *altar hearth* (Ezekiel 43:15–16)

or as when a thirsty man dreams, and
behold, he is drinking
and awakes faint, with his thirst not
quenched,
so shall the multitude of all the
nations be
that fight against Mount Zion.

9   Astonish yourselves and be astonished;
blind yourselves and be blind!
Be drunk, but not with wine;
stagger, but not with strong drink!
10 For the LORD has poured out upon
you
a spirit of deep sleep,
and has closed your eyes (the prophets),
and covered your heads (the seers).

¹¹ And the vision of all this has become to
you like the words of a book that is sealed.
When men give it to one who can read, saying, "Read this," he says, "I cannot, for it is
sealed." ¹² And when they give the book to
one who cannot read, saying, "Read this,"
he says, "I cannot read."

13 And the Lord said:
"Because this people draw near with
their mouth
and honor me with their lips,
while their hearts are far from me,
and their fear of me is a commandment taught by men,
14 therefore, behold, I will again
do wonderful things with this people,
with wonder upon wonder;
and the wisdom of their wise men
shall perish,
and the discernment of their discerning men shall be hidden."

15 Ah, you who hide deep from the LORD
your counsel,
whose deeds are in the dark,
and who say, "Who sees us? Who
knows us?"
16 You turn things upside down!
Shall the potter be regarded as the clay,
that the thing made should say of its
maker,
"He did not make me";
or the thing formed say of him who
formed it,
"He has no understanding"?

17 Is it not yet a very little while
until Lebanon shall be turned into a
fruitful field,
and the fruitful field shall be
regarded as a forest?
18 In that day the deaf shall hear
the words of a book,
and out of their gloom and darkness
the eyes of the blind shall see.
19 The meek shall obtain fresh joy in the
LORD,
and the poor among mankind shall
exult in the Holy One of Israel.
20 For the ruthless shall come to nothing
and the scoffer cease,
and all who watch to do evil shall be
cut off,
21 who by a word make a man out to be
an offender,
and lay a snare for him who
reproves in the gate,
and with an empty plea turn aside
him who is in the right.

²² Therefore thus says the LORD, who
redeemed Abraham, concerning the house
of Jacob:

"Jacob shall no more be ashamed,
no more shall his face grow pale.
23 For when he sees his children,
the work of my hands, in his midst,
they will sanctify my name;
they will sanctify the Holy One of
Jacob
and will stand in awe of the God of
Israel.
24 And those who go astray in spirit will
come to understanding,
and those who murmur will accept
instruction."

Do Not Go Down to Egypt

30 "Ah, stubborn children," declares
the LORD,
"who carry out a plan, but not mine,
and who make an alliance, but not of
my Spirit,
that they may add sin to sin;
2   who set out to go down to Egypt,
without asking for my direction,
to take refuge in the protection of
Pharaoh
and to seek shelter in the shadow of
Egypt!

3   Therefore shall the protection of
         Pharaoh turn to your shame,
      and the shelter in the shadow of
         Egypt to your humiliation.
4   For though his officials are at Zoan
         and his envoys reach Hanes,
5   everyone comes to shame
         through a people that cannot profit
            them,
      that brings neither help nor profit,
         but shame and disgrace."

6 An oracle on the beasts of the Negeb.

      Through a land of trouble and anguish,
         from where come the lioness and
            the lion,
         the adder and the flying fiery serpent,
      they carry their riches on the backs of
            donkeys,
         and their treasures on the humps of
            camels,
      to a people that cannot profit them.
7   Egypt's help is worthless and empty;
         therefore I have called her
      "Rahab who sits still."

A Rebellious People

8   And now, go, write it before them on a
         tablet
         and inscribe it in a book,
      that it may be for the time to come
         as a witness forever.
9   For they are a rebellious people,
         lying children,
      children unwilling to hear
         the instruction of the LORD;
10   who say to the seers, "Do not see,"
         and to the prophets, "Do not proph-
            esy to us what is right;
      speak to us smooth things,
         prophesy illusions,
11   leave the way, turn aside from the path,
         let us hear no more about the Holy
            One of Israel."

12   Therefore thus says the Holy One of
         Israel,
      "Because you despise this word
         and trust in oppression and per-
            verseness
         and rely on them,
13   therefore this iniquity shall be to you
         like a breach in a high wall, bulging
            out, and about to collapse,
         whose breaking comes suddenly, in
            an instant;

14   and its breaking is like that of a pot-
         ter's vessel
      that is smashed so ruthlessly
      that among its fragments not a shard
         is found
      with which to take fire from the
         hearth,
      or to dip up water out of the cistern."

15   For thus said the Lord GOD, the Holy
         One of Israel,
      "In returning and rest you shall be
         saved;
         in quietness and in trust shall be
            your strength."
      But you were unwilling, 16 and you said,
      "No! We will flee upon horses";
         therefore you shall flee away;
      and, "We will ride upon swift steeds";
         therefore your pursuers shall be
            swift.
17   A thousand shall flee at the threat of
         one;
         at the threat of five you shall flee,
      till you are left
         like a flagstaff on the top of a
            mountain,
         like a signal on a hill.

The LORD Will Be Gracious

18   Therefore the LORD waits to be gra-
         cious to you,
         and therefore he exalts himself to
            show mercy to you.
      For the LORD is a God of justice;
         blessed are all those who wait for
            him.

19 For a people shall dwell in Zion, in
Jerusalem; you shall weep no more. He will
surely be gracious to you at the sound of
your cry. As soon as he hears it, he answers
you. 20 And though the Lord give you the
bread of adversity and the water of affliction, yet your Teacher will not hide himself anymore, but your eyes shall see your
Teacher. 21 And your ears shall hear a word
behind you, saying, "This is the way, walk in
it," when you turn to the right or when you
turn to the left. 22 Then you will defile your
carved idols overlaid with silver and your
gold-plated metal images. You will scatter
them as unclean things. You will say to
them, "Be gone!"

23 And he will give rain for the seed with
which you sow the ground, and bread, the

produce of the ground, which will be rich and plenteous. In that day your livestock will graze in large pastures, ²⁴ and the oxen and the donkeys that work the ground will eat seasoned fodder, which has been winnowed with shovel and fork. ²⁵ And on every lofty mountain and every high hill there will be brooks running with water, in the day of the great slaughter, when the towers fall. ²⁶ Moreover, the light of the moon will be as the light of the sun, and the light of the sun will be sevenfold, as the light of seven days, in the day when the LORD binds up the brokenness of his people, and heals the wounds inflicted by his blow.

²⁷ Behold, the name of the LORD comes from afar,
    burning with his anger, and in thick rising smoke;
his lips are full of fury,
    and his tongue is like a devouring fire;
²⁸ his breath is like an overflowing stream
    that reaches up to the neck;
to sift the nations with the sieve of destruction,
    and to place on the jaws of the peoples a bridle that leads astray.

²⁹ You shall have a song as in the night when a holy feast is kept, and gladness of heart, as when one sets out to the sound of the flute to go to the mountain of the LORD, to the Rock of Israel. ³⁰ And the LORD will cause his majestic voice to be heard and the descending blow of his arm to be seen, in furious anger and a flame of devouring fire, with a cloudburst and storm and hailstones. ³¹ The Assyrians will be terror-stricken at the voice of the LORD, when he strikes with his rod. ³² And every stroke of the appointed staff that the LORD lays on them will be to the sound of tambourines and lyres. Battling with brandished arm, he will fight with them. ³³ For a burning place has long been prepared; indeed, for the king it is made ready, its pyre made deep and wide, with fire and wood in abundance; the breath of the LORD, like a stream of sulfur, kindles it.

Woe to Those Who Go Down to Egypt

31 Woe to those who go down to Egypt for help
    and rely on horses,

who trust in chariots because they are many
    and in horsemen because they are very strong,
but do not look to the Holy One of Israel
    or consult the LORD!
² And yet he is wise and brings disaster;
    he does not call back his words,
but will arise against the house of the evildoers
    and against the helpers of those who work iniquity.
³ The Egyptians are man, and not God,
    and their horses are flesh, and not spirit.
When the LORD stretches out his hand,
    the helper will stumble, and he who is helped will fall,
and they will all perish together.

GETTING THE MESSAGE

The sieve of destruction. Farmers used two different kinds of sieves when working in the fields. The larger sieve was used to sift out big rocks and stones from the fields. A smaller one was used to sift out smaller particles from the grain being harvested. This smaller sieve is the one mentioned in 30:28; the Lord is separating those who are his people (the grain) from those who are not.

⁴ For thus the LORD said to me,
"As a lion or a young lion growls over his prey,
    and when a band of shepherds is called out against him
he is not terrified by their shouting
    or daunted at their noise,
so the LORD of hosts will come down
    to fight on Mount Zion and on its hill.
⁵ Like birds hovering, so the LORD of hosts
    will protect Jerusalem;
he will protect and deliver it;
    he will spare and rescue it."

⁶ Turn to him from whom people have deeply revolted, O children of Israel. ⁷ For in that day everyone shall cast away his idols of silver and his idols of gold, which your hands have sinfully made for you.

8 "And the Assyrian shall fall by a sword,
    not of man;
  and a sword, not of man, shall
    devour him;
  and he shall flee from the sword,
    and his young men shall be put to
      forced labor.
9 His rock shall pass away in terror,
    and his officers desert the standard
      in panic,"
  declares the LORD, whose fire is in Zion,
    and whose furnace is in Jerusalem.

A King Will Reign in Righteousness

32 Behold, a king will reign in righ-
      teousness,
  and princes will rule in justice.
2 Each will be like a hiding place from
    the wind,
    a shelter from the storm,

GETTING THE MESSAGE

Watchtowers (32:14) sometimes served
as signal beacons when an invading
force was approaching. By lighting small
fires at the tops of the towers, watchmen
could signal other towns that danger
was near.

---

like streams of water in a dry place,
  like the shade of a great rock in a
    weary land.
3 Then the eyes of those who see will
    not be closed,
  and the ears of those who hear will
    give attention.
4 The heart of the hasty will understand
    and know,
  and the tongue of the stammerers
    will hasten to speak distinctly.
5 The fool will no more be called noble,
  nor the scoundrel said to be honor-
    able.
6 For the fool speaks folly,
    and his heart is busy with iniquity,
  to practice ungodliness,
    to utter error concerning the LORD,
  to leave the craving of the hungry
    unsatisfied,
    and to deprive the thirsty of drink.
7 As for the scoundrel—his devices are
    evil;
  he plans wicked schemes

to ruin the poor with lying words,
  even when the plea of the needy is
    right.
8 But he who is noble plans noble things,
  and on noble things he stands.

Complacent Women Warned of Disaster

9 Rise up, you women who are at ease,
    hear my voice;
  you complacent daughters, give ear
    to my speech.
10 In little more than a year
    you will shudder, you complacent
      women;
  for the grape harvest fails,
    the fruit harvest will not come.
11 Tremble, you women who are at ease,
    shudder, you complacent ones;
  strip, and make yourselves bare,
    and tie sackcloth around your waist.
12 Beat your breasts for the pleasant
      fields,
    for the fruitful vine,
13 for the soil of my people
    growing up in thorns and briers,
  yes, for all the joyous houses
    in the exultant city.
14 For the palace is forsaken,
    the populous city deserted;
  the hill and the watchtower
    will become dens forever,
  a joy of wild donkeys,
    a pasture of flocks;
15 until the Spirit is poured upon us
      from on high,
    and the wilderness becomes a fruit-
      ful field,
    and the fruitful field is deemed a
      forest.
16 Then justice will dwell in the wilder-
      ness,
    and righteousness abide in the
      fruitful field.
17 And the effect of righteousness will be
      peace,
    and the result of righteousness,
      quietness and trust forever.
18 My people will abide in a peaceful
      habitation,
    in secure dwellings, and in quiet
      resting places.
19 And it will hail when the forest falls
      down,
    and the city will be utterly laid low.

20 Happy are you who sow beside all
    waters,
        who let the feet of the ox and the
        donkey range free.

O Lord, Be Gracious to Us

33 Ah, you destroyer,
    who yourself have not been
    destroyed,
you traitor,
    whom none has betrayed!
When you have ceased to destroy,
    you will be destroyed;
and when you have finished betray-
    ing,
    they will betray you.

2 O Lord, be gracious to us; we wait for
    you.
    Be our arm every morning,
    our salvation in the time of trouble.
3 At the tumultuous noise peoples flee;
    when you lift yourself up, nations
    are scattered,
4 and your spoil is gathered as the cat-
    erpillar gathers;
    as locusts leap, it is leapt upon.

5 The Lord is exalted, for he dwells on
    high;
    he will fill Zion with justice and
    righteousness,
6 and he will be the stability of your
    times,
    abundance of salvation, wisdom,
    and knowledge;
    the fear of the Lord is Zion's trea-
    sure.

7 Behold, their heroes cry in the streets;
    the envoys of peace weep bitterly.
8 The highways lie waste;
    the traveler ceases.
    Covenants are broken;
    cities are despised;
    there is no regard for man.
9 The land mourns and languishes;
    Lebanon is confounded and with-
    ers away;
    Sharon is like a desert,
    and Bashan and Carmel shake off
    their leaves.

10 "Now I will arise," says the Lord,
    "now I will lift myself up;
    now I will be exalted.

11 You conceive chaff; you give birth to
    stubble;
    your breath is a fire that will con-
    sume you.
12 And the peoples will be as if burned to
    lime,
    like thorns cut down, that are
    burned in the fire."

13 Hear, you who are far off, what I have
    done;
    and you who are near, acknowledge
    my might.
14 The sinners in Zion are afraid;
    trembling has seized the godless:
    "Who among us can dwell with the
    consuming fire?
    Who among us can dwell with ever-
    lasting burnings?"
15 He who walks righteously and speaks
    uprightly,
    who despises the gain of oppres-
    sions,
    who shakes his hands, lest they hold a
    bribe,
    who stops his ears from hearing of
    bloodshed
    and shuts his eyes from looking on
    evil,
16 he will dwell on the heights;
    his place of defense will be the
    fortresses of rocks;
    his bread will be given him; his
    water will be sure.

17 Your eyes will behold the king in his
    beauty;
    they will see a land that stretches
    afar.
18 Your heart will muse on the terror:
    "Where is he who counted, where is
    he who weighed the tribute?
    Where is he who counted the tow-
    ers?"
19 You will see no more the insolent
    people,
    the people of an obscure speech
    that you cannot comprehend,
    stammering in a tongue that you
    cannot understand.
20 Behold Zion, the city of our appointed
    feasts!
    Your eyes will see Jerusalem,
    an untroubled habitation, an
    immovable tent,

whose stakes will never be plucked up,
    nor will any of its cords be broken.
21 But there the LORD in majesty will be
    for us
    a place of broad rivers and streams,
where no galley with oars can go,
    nor majestic ship can pass.
22 For the LORD is our judge; the LORD is
    our lawgiver;
    the LORD is our king; he will save us.

23 Your cords hang loose;
    they cannot hold the mast firm in
      its place
    or keep the sail spread out.
Then prey and spoil in abundance will
    be divided;
    even the lame will take the prey.
24 And no inhabitant will say, "I am sick";
    the people who dwell there will be
      forgiven their iniquity.

GETTING THE MESSAGE

"He who counted" (33:18) refers to tax
collectors. If people couldn't pay their
taxes, their property might be seized or
they might become forced laborers. If
the official failed to collect all the taxes
due, he himself was punished.

Judgment on the Nations

34
Draw near, O nations, to hear,
    and give attention, O peoples!
Let the earth hear, and all that fills it;
    the world, and all that comes from it.
2 For the LORD is enraged against all the
    nations,
    and furious against all their host;
he has devoted them to destruc-
    tion,[1] has given them over for
    slaughter.
3 Their slain shall be cast out,
    and the stench of their corpses shall
      rise;
    the mountains shall flow with their
      blood.
4 All the host of heaven shall rot away,
    and the skies roll up like a scroll.
All their host shall fall,
    as leaves fall from the vine,
    like leaves falling from the fig tree.

5 For my sword has drunk its fill in the
    heavens;
    behold, it descends for judgment
      upon Edom,
    upon the people I have devoted to
      destruction.
6 The LORD has a sword; it is sated with
    blood;
    it is gorged with fat,
    with the blood of lambs and goats,
    with the fat of the kidneys of rams.
For the LORD has a sacrifice in Bozrah,
    a great slaughter in the land of
      Edom.
7 Wild oxen shall fall with them,
    and young steers with the mighty
      bulls.
Their land shall drink its fill of blood,
    and their soil shall be gorged with
      fat.

8 For the LORD has a day of vengeance,
    a year of recompense for the cause
      of Zion.
9 And the streams of Edom shall be
      turned into pitch,
    and her soil into sulfur;
    her land shall become burning pitch.
10 Night and day it shall not be quenched;
    its smoke shall go up forever.
From generation to generation it shall
    lie waste;
    none shall pass through it forever
      and ever.
11 But the hawk and the porcupine shall
      possess it,
    the owl and the raven shall dwell in
      it.
He shall stretch the line of confusion
      over it,
    and the plumb line of emptiness.
12 Its nobles—there is no one there to
      call it a kingdom,
    and all its princes shall be nothing.
13 Thorns shall grow over its strongholds,
    nettles and thistles in its fortresses.
It shall be the haunt of jackals,
    an abode for ostriches.
14 And wild animals shall meet with
      hyenas;
    the wild goat shall cry to his fellow;
indeed, there the night bird settles
    and finds for herself a resting place.

---

[1] That is, destroyed or made an offering because of sin, at God's command; also 34:5

15 There the owl nests and lays
   and hatches and gathers her young
      in her shadow;
indeed, there the hawks are gathered,
   each one with her mate.
16 Seek and read from the book of the
      LORD:
   Not one of these shall be missing;
   none shall be without her mate.
For the mouth of the LORD has com-
      manded,
   and his Spirit has gathered them.
17 He has cast the lot for them;
   his hand has portioned it out to
      them with the line;
they shall possess it forever;
   from generation to generation they
      shall dwell in it.

The Ransomed Shall Return

35 The wilderness and the dry land
      shall be glad;
   the desert shall rejoice and blossom
      like the crocus;
2 it shall blossom abundantly
   and rejoice with joy and singing.
The glory of Lebanon shall be given to
      it,
   the majesty of Carmel and Sharon.
They shall see the glory of the LORD,
   the majesty of our God.

3 Strengthen the weak hands,
   and make firm the feeble knees.
4 Say to those who have an anxious
      heart,
   "Be strong; fear not!
Behold, your God
   will come with vengeance,
with the recompense of God.
   He will come and save you."

5 Then the eyes of the blind shall be
      opened,
   and the ears of the deaf unstopped;
6 then shall the lame man leap like a
      deer,
   and the tongue of the mute sing for
      joy.
For waters break forth in the wilder-
      ness,
   and streams in the desert;
7 the burning sand shall become a pool,
   and the thirsty ground springs of
      water;

in the haunt of jackals, where they lie
      down,
   the grass shall become reeds and
      rushes.

8 And a highway shall be there,
   and it shall be called the Way of
      Holiness;
the unclean shall not pass over it.
   It shall belong to those who walk on
      the way;
   even if they are fools, they shall not
      go astray.
9 No lion shall be there,
   nor shall any ravenous beast come
      up on it;
they shall not be found there,
   but the redeemed shall walk there.
10 And the ransomed of the LORD shall
      return
   and come to Zion with singing;
everlasting joy shall be upon their
      heads;
   they shall obtain gladness and joy,
   and sorrow and sighing shall flee
      away.

Sennacherib Invades Judah

36 In the fourteenth year of King Hezekiah, Sennacherib king of Assyria
came up against all the fortified cities of
Judah and took them. 2 And the king of
Assyria sent the Rabshakeh[1] from Lachish
to King Hezekiah at Jerusalem, with a great
army. And he stood by the conduit of the
upper pool on the highway to the Washer's
Field. 3 And there came out to him Eliakim
the son of Hilkiah, who was over the household, and Shebna the secretary, and Joah the
son of Asaph, the recorder.

4 And the Rabshakeh said to them, "Say to
Hezekiah, 'Thus says the great king, the king
of Assyria: On what do you rest this trust
of yours? 5 Do you think that mere words
are strategy and power for war? In whom
do you now trust, that you have rebelled
against me? 6 Behold, you are trusting in
Egypt, that broken reed of a staff, which will
pierce the hand of any man who leans on
it. Such is Pharaoh king of Egypt to all who
trust in him. 7 But if you say to me, "We trust
in the LORD our God," is it not he whose high
places and altars Hezekiah has removed,
saying to Judah and to Jerusalem, "You shall

---

[1] *Rabshakeh* is the title of a high-ranking Assyrian military officer

worship before this altar"? ⁸ Come now, make a wager with my master the king of Assyria: I will give you two thousand horses, if you are able on your part to set riders on them. ⁹ How then can you repulse a single captain among the least of my master's servants, when you trust in Egypt for chariots and for horsemen? ¹⁰ Moreover, is it without the LORD that I have come up against this land to destroy it? The LORD said to me, Go up against this land and destroy it.'"

¹¹ Then Eliakim, Shebna, and Joah said to the Rabshakeh, "Please speak to your servants in Aramaic, for we understand it. Do not speak to us in the language of Judah within the hearing of the people who are on the wall." ¹² But the Rabshakeh said, "Has my master sent me to speak these words to your master and to you, and not to the

GETTING THE MESSAGE

To eat of your own vine and fig tree was a traditional blessing found in both the historical and prophetic books of Israel (36:16; 1 Kings 4:25). It was a reward for trusting in the Lord. On the other hand, to lose those precious resources was a sign of God's disfavor (Jer. 5:17).

men sitting on the wall, who are doomed with you to eat their own dung and drink their own urine?"

¹³ Then the Rabshakeh stood and called out in a loud voice in the language of Judah: "Hear the words of the great king, the king of Assyria! ¹⁴ Thus says the king: 'Do not let Hezekiah deceive you, for he will not be able to deliver you. ¹⁵ Do not let Hezekiah make you trust in the LORD by saying, "The LORD will surely deliver us. This city will not be given into the hand of the king of Assyria." ¹⁶ Do not listen to Hezekiah. For thus says the king of Assyria: Make your peace with me and come out to me. Then each one of you will eat of his own vine, and each one of his own fig tree, and each one of you will drink the water of his own cistern, ¹⁷ until I come and take you away to a land like your own land, a land of grain and wine, a land of bread and vineyards. ¹⁸ Beware lest Hezekiah mislead you by say-

ing, "The LORD will deliver us." Has any of the gods of the nations delivered his land out of the hand of the king of Assyria? ¹⁹ Where are the gods of Hamath and Arpad? Where are the gods of Sepharvaim? Have they delivered Samaria out of my hand? ²⁰ Who among all the gods of these lands have delivered their lands out of my hand, that the LORD should deliver Jerusalem out of my hand?'"

²¹ But they were silent and answered him not a word, for the king's command was, "Do not answer him." ²² Then Eliakim the son of Hilkiah, who was over the household, and Shebna the secretary, and Joah the son of Asaph, the recorder, came to Hezekiah with their clothes torn, and told him the words of the Rabshakeh.

Hezekiah Seeks Isaiah's Help

37 As soon as King Hezekiah heard it, he tore his clothes and covered himself with sackcloth and went into the house of the LORD. ² And he sent Eliakim, who was over the household, and Shebna the secretary, and the senior priests, covered with sackcloth, to the prophet Isaiah the son of Amoz. ³ They said to him, "Thus says Hezekiah, 'This day is a day of distress, of rebuke, and of disgrace; children have come to the point of birth, and there is no strength to bring them forth. ⁴ It may be that the LORD your God will hear the words of the Rabshakeh, whom his master the king of Assyria has sent to mock the living God, and will rebuke the words that the LORD your God has heard; therefore lift up your prayer for the remnant that is left.'"

⁵ When the servants of King Hezekiah came to Isaiah, ⁶ Isaiah said to them, "Say to your master, 'Thus says the LORD: Do not be afraid because of the words that you have heard, with which the young men of the king of Assyria have reviled me. ⁷ Behold, I will put a spirit in him, so that he shall hear a rumor and return to his own land, and I will make him fall by the sword in his own land.'"

⁸ The Rabshakeh returned, and found the king of Assyria fighting against Libnah, for he had heard that the king had left Lachish. ⁹ Now the king heard concerning Tirhakah king of Cush, "He has set out to fight against you." And when he heard it, he sent messengers to Hezekiah, saying, ¹⁰ "Thus shall

you speak to Hezekiah king of Judah: 'Do not let your God in whom you trust deceive you by promising that Jerusalem will not be given into the hand of the king of Assyria. ¹¹ Behold, you have heard what the kings of Assyria have done to all lands, devoting them to destruction. And shall you be delivered? ¹² Have the gods of the nations delivered them, the nations that my fathers destroyed, Gozan, Haran, Rezeph, and the people of Eden who were in Telassar? ¹³ Where is the king of Hamath, the king of Arpad, the king of the city of Sepharvaim, the king of Hena, or the king of Ivvah?'"

Hezekiah's Prayer for Deliverance

¹⁴ Hezekiah received the letter from the hand of the messengers, and read it; and Hezekiah went up to the house of the LORD, and spread it before the LORD. ¹⁵ And Hezekiah prayed to the LORD: ¹⁶ "O LORD of hosts, God of Israel, enthroned above the cherubim, you are the God, you alone, of all the kingdoms of the earth; you have made heaven and earth. ¹⁷ Incline your ear, O LORD, and hear; open your eyes, O LORD, and see; and hear all the words of Sennacherib, which he has sent to mock the living God. ¹⁸ Truly, O LORD, the kings of Assyria have laid waste all the nations and their lands, ¹⁹ and have cast their gods into the fire. For they were no gods, but the work of men's hands, wood and stone. Therefore they were destroyed. ²⁰ So now, O LORD our God, save us from his hand, that all the kingdoms of the earth may know that you alone are the LORD."

Sennacherib's Fall

²¹ Then Isaiah the son of Amoz sent to Hezekiah, saying, "Thus says the LORD, the God of Israel: Because you have prayed to me concerning Sennacherib king of Assyria, ²² this is the word that the LORD has spoken concerning him:

"'She despises you, she scorns you—
    the virgin daughter of Zion;
she wags her head behind you—
    the daughter of Jerusalem.

²³ "'Whom have you mocked and reviled?
    Against whom have you raised your
        voice
and lifted your eyes to the heights?
    Against the Holy One of Israel!

²⁴ By your servants you have mocked the
        Lord,
    and you have said, With my many
        chariots
I have gone up the heights of the
        mountains,
    to the far recesses of Lebanon,
to cut down its tallest cedars,
    its choicest cypresses,
to come to its remotest height,
    its most fruitful forest.

²⁵ I dug wells
    and drank waters,
to dry up with the sole of my foot
    all the streams of Egypt.

²⁶ "'Have you not heard
    that I determined it long ago?
I planned from days of old
    what now I bring to pass,
that you should make fortified cities
    crash into heaps of ruins,

²⁷ while their inhabitants, shorn of
        strength,
    are dismayed and confounded,
and have become like plants of the
        field
    and like tender grass,
like grass on the housetops,
    blighted before it is grown.

²⁸ "'I know your sitting down
    and your going out and coming in,
    and your raging against me.

²⁹ Because you have raged against me
    and your complacency has come to
        my ears,
I will put my hook in your nose
    and my bit in your mouth,
and I will turn you back on the way
    by which you came.'

³⁰ "And this shall be the sign for you: this year you shall eat what grows of itself, and in the second year what springs from that. Then in the third year sow and reap, and plant vineyards, and eat their fruit. ³¹ And the surviving remnant of the house of Judah shall again take root downward and bear fruit upward. ³² For out of Jerusalem shall go a remnant, and out of Mount Zion a band of survivors. The zeal of the LORD of hosts will do this.

³³ "Therefore thus says the LORD concerning the king of Assyria: He shall not come into this city or shoot an arrow there

or come before it with a shield or cast up a siege mound against it. ³⁴ By the way that he came, by the same he shall return, and he shall not come into this city, declares the LORD. ³⁵ For I will defend this city to save it, for my own sake and for the sake of my servant David."

³⁶ And the angel of the LORD went out and struck down 185,000 in the camp of the Assyrians. And when people arose early in the morning, behold, these were all dead bodies. ³⁷ Then Sennacherib king of Assyria departed and returned home and lived at Nineveh. ³⁸ And as he was worshiping in the house of Nisroch his god, Adrammelech and Sharezer, his sons, struck him down with the sword. And after they escaped into the land of Ararat, Esarhaddon his son reigned in his place.

> ### GETTING THE MESSAGE
>
> **Cut off from the loom.** Weaving on a loom involves warp threads, which are attached to the top and bottom of the loom, and weft threads, which are woven through the warp. When the weaver finishes a piece, he cuts the warp threads from the loom. When Hezekiah was ill, he felt as if he had been cut off from the loom of God's presence (38:12).

Hezekiah's Sickness and Recovery

38 In those days Hezekiah became sick and was at the point of death. And Isaiah the prophet the son of Amoz came to him, and said to him, "Thus says the LORD: Set your house in order, for you shall die, you shall not recover." ² Then Hezekiah turned his face to the wall and prayed to the LORD, ³ and said, "Please, O LORD, remember how I have walked before you in faithfulness and with a whole heart, and have done what is good in your sight." And Hezekiah wept bitterly.

⁴ Then the word of the LORD came to Isaiah: ⁵ "Go and say to Hezekiah, Thus says the LORD, the God of David your father: I have heard your prayer; I have seen your tears. Behold, I will add fifteen years to your life. ⁶ I will deliver you and this city out of the hand of the king of Assyria, and will defend this city.

⁷ "This shall be the sign to you from the LORD, that the LORD will do this thing that he has promised: ⁸ Behold, I will make the shadow cast by the declining sun on the dial of Ahaz turn back ten steps." So the sun turned back on the dial the ten steps by which it had declined.

⁹ A writing of Hezekiah king of Judah, after he had been sick and had recovered from his sickness:

¹⁰   I said, In the middle of my days
         I must depart;
     I am consigned to the gates of Sheol
         for the rest of my years.
¹¹   I said, I shall not see the LORD,
         the LORD in the land of the living;
     I shall look on man no more
         among the inhabitants of the world.
¹²   My dwelling is plucked up and
             removed from me
         like a shepherd's tent;
     like a weaver I have rolled up my life;
         he cuts me off from the loom;
     from day to night you bring me to an
             end;
¹³   I calmed myself until morning;
     like a lion he breaks all my bones;
         from day to night you bring me to
             an end.
¹⁴   Like a swallow or a crane I chirp;
         I moan like a dove.
     My eyes are weary with looking
             upward.
         O Lord, I am oppressed; be my
             pledge of safety!
¹⁵   What shall I say? For he has spoken to
             me,
         and he himself has done it.
     I walk slowly all my years
         because of the bitterness of my soul.
¹⁶   O Lord, by these things men live,
         and in all these is the life of my
             spirit.
     Oh restore me to health and make
             me live!
¹⁷   Behold, it was for my welfare
         that I had great bitterness;
     but in love you have delivered my life
         from the pit of destruction,
     for you have cast all my sins
         behind your back.
¹⁸   For Sheol does not thank you;
         death does not praise you;

those who go down to the pit do not
hope
for your faithfulness.
¹⁹ The living, the living, he thanks you,
as I do this day;
the father makes known to the children
your faithfulness.

²⁰ The LORD will save me,
and we will play my music on
stringed instruments
all the days of our lives,
at the house of the LORD.

²¹ Now Isaiah had said, "Let them take a cake of figs and apply it to the boil, that he may recover." ²² Hezekiah also had said, "What is the sign that I shall go up to the house of the LORD?"

Envoys from Babylon

39 At that time Merodach-baladan the son of Baladan, king of Babylon, sent envoys with letters and a present to Hezekiah, for he heard that he had been sick and had recovered. ² And Hezekiah welcomed them gladly. And he showed them his treasure house, the silver, the gold, the spices, the precious oil, his whole armory, all that was found in his storehouses. There was nothing in his house or in all his realm that Hezekiah did not show them. ³ Then Isaiah the prophet came to King Hezekiah, and said to him, "What did these men say? And from where did they come to you?" Hezekiah said, "They have come to me from a far country, from Babylon." ⁴ He said, "What have they seen in your house?" Hezekiah answered, "They have seen all that is in my house. There is nothing in my storehouses that I did not show them."

⁵ Then Isaiah said to Hezekiah, "Hear the word of the LORD of hosts: ⁶ Behold, the days are coming, when all that is in your house, and that which your fathers have stored up till this day, shall be carried to Babylon. Nothing shall be left, says the LORD. ⁷ And some of your own sons, who will come from you, whom you will father, shall be taken away, and they shall be eunuchs in the palace of the king of Babylon." ⁸ Then Hezekiah said to Isaiah, "The word of the LORD that you have spoken is good." For he thought, "There will be peace and security in my days."

Comfort for God's People

40 Comfort, comfort my people,
says your God.
² Speak tenderly to Jerusalem,
and cry to her
that her warfare is ended,
that her iniquity is pardoned,
that she has received from the LORD's
hand
double for all her sins.

³ A voice cries:
"In the wilderness prepare the way of
the LORD;
make straight in the desert a highway for our God.
⁴ Every valley shall be lifted up,
and every mountain and hill be
made low;
the uneven ground shall become level,
and the rough places a plain.

GETTING THE MESSAGE

The **highways** of the ancient Near East were not paved by professionals like modern highways. Rather, they were maintained by the people living along the roads. They did their best to keep the roads level and free of obstacles (see 40:3).

⁵ And the glory of the LORD shall be
revealed,
and all flesh shall see it together,
for the mouth of the LORD has spoken."

The Word of God Stands Forever

⁶ A voice says, "Cry!"
And I said, "What shall I cry?"
All flesh is grass,
and all its beauty is like the flower
of the field.
⁷ The grass withers, the flower fades
when the breath of the LORD blows
on it;
surely the people are grass.
⁸ The grass withers, the flower fades,
but the word of our God will stand
forever.

The Greatness of God

⁹ Go on up to a high mountain,
O Zion, herald of good news;

lift up your voice with strength,
O Jerusalem, herald of good news;
lift it up, fear not;
say to the cities of Judah,
"Behold your God!"
10 Behold, the Lord GOD comes with
might,
and his arm rules for him;
behold, his reward is with him,
and his recompense before him.
11 He will tend his flock like a shepherd;
he will gather the lambs in his arms;
he will carry them in his bosom,
and gently lead those that are with
young.

12 Who has measured the waters in the
hollow of his hand
and marked off the heavens with a
span,
enclosed the dust of the earth in a
measure
and weighed the mountains in scales
and the hills in a balance?
13 Who has measured the Spirit of the
LORD,
or what man shows him his counsel?
14 Whom did he consult,
and who made him understand?
Who taught him the path of justice,
and taught him knowledge,
and showed him the way of understanding?
15 Behold, the nations are like a drop
from a bucket,
and are accounted as the dust on
the scales;
behold, he takes up the coastlands
like fine dust.
16 Lebanon would not suffice for fuel,
nor are its beasts enough for a burnt
offering.
17 All the nations are as nothing before
him,
they are accounted by him as less
than nothing and emptiness.

18 To whom then will you liken God,
or what likeness compare with him?
19 An idol! A craftsman casts it,
and a goldsmith overlays it with gold
and casts for it silver chains.
20 He who is too impoverished for an
offering
chooses wood that will not rot;

he seeks out a skillful craftsman
to set up an idol that will not move.

21 Do you not know? Do you not hear?
Has it not been told you from the
beginning?
Have you not understood from the
foundations of the earth?
22 It is he who sits above the circle of the
earth,
and its inhabitants are like grasshoppers;
who stretches out the heavens like a
curtain,
and spreads them like a tent to
dwell in;
23 who brings princes to nothing,
and makes the rulers of the earth as
emptiness.

24 Scarcely are they planted, scarcely
sown,
scarcely has their stem taken root
in the earth,
when he blows on them, and they
wither,
and the tempest carries them off
like stubble.
25 To whom then will you compare me,
that I should be like him? says the
Holy One.
26 Lift up your eyes on high and see:
who created these?
He who brings out their host by number,
calling them all by name,
by the greatness of his might,
and because he is strong in power
not one is missing.

27 Why do you say, O Jacob,
and speak, O Israel,
"My way is hidden from the LORD,
and my right is disregarded by my
God"?
28 Have you not known? Have you not
heard?
The LORD is the everlasting God,
the Creator of the ends of the earth.
He does not faint or grow weary;
his understanding is unsearchable.
29 He gives power to the faint,
and to him who has no might he
increases strength.
30 Even youths shall faint and be weary,
and young men shall fall exhausted;

31 but they who wait for the LORD shall
        renew their strength;
    they shall mount up with wings like
        eagles;
    they shall run and not be weary;
    they shall walk and not faint.

Fear Not, for I Am with You

41 Listen to me in silence, O coast-
        lands;
    let the peoples renew their strength;
    let them approach, then let them
        speak;
    let us together draw near for judg-
        ment.

2 Who stirred up one from the east
        whom victory meets at every step?
    He gives up nations before him,
        so that he tramples kings underfoot;
    he makes them like dust with his
        sword,
    like driven stubble with his bow.

3 He pursues them and passes on
        safely,
    by paths his feet have not trod.

4 Who has performed and done this,
        calling the generations from the
        beginning?
    I, the LORD, the first,
        and with the last; I am he.

5 The coastlands have seen and are
        afraid;
    the ends of the earth tremble;
    they have drawn near and come.

6 Everyone helps his neighbor
        and says to his brother, "Be strong!"

7 The craftsman strengthens the gold-
        smith,
    and he who smooths with the ham-
        mer him who strikes the anvil,
    saying of the soldering, "It is good";
    and they strengthen it with nails so
        that it cannot be moved.

8 But you, Israel, my servant,
        Jacob, whom I have chosen,
    the offspring of Abraham, my
        friend;

9 you whom I took from the ends of the
        earth,
    and called from its farthest corners,
    saying to you, "You are my servant,
    I have chosen you and not cast you
        off";

10 fear not, for I am with you;
        be not dismayed, for I am your God;
    I will strengthen you, I will help you,
        I will uphold you with my righteous
        right hand.

11 Behold, all who are incensed against
        you
    shall be put to shame and con-
        founded;
    those who strive against you
        shall be as nothing and shall per-
        ish.

12 You shall seek those who contend
        with you,
    but you shall not find them;
    those who war against you
        shall be as nothing at all.

13 For I, the LORD your God,
        hold your right hand;

GETTING THE MESSAGE

The **craftsmen and goldsmiths**
mentioned in 41:7 were fashioning idols.
The craftsman would begin by making a
mold from an existing image. He would
then cast the new image in metal. The
goldsmith would then add gold plating,
smooth it out with a hammer, and
burnish it to give it a shine.

it is I who say to you, "Fear not,
    I am the one who helps you."

14 Fear not, you worm Jacob,
        you men of Israel!
    I am the one who helps you, declares
        the LORD;
        your Redeemer is the Holy One of
        Israel.

15 Behold, I make of you a threshing
        sledge,
    new, sharp, and having teeth;
    you shall thresh the mountains and
        crush them,
    and you shall make the hills like
        chaff;

16 you shall winnow them, and the wind
        shall carry them away,
    and the tempest shall scatter them.
    And you shall rejoice in the LORD;
        in the Holy One of Israel you shall
        glory.

17 When the poor and needy seek water,
  and there is none,
  and their tongue is parched with
  thirst,
  I the LORD will answer them;
  I the God of Israel will not forsake
  them.
18 I will open rivers on the bare heights,
  and fountains in the midst of the
  valleys.
  I will make the wilderness a pool of
  water,
  and the dry land springs of water.
19 I will put in the wilderness the cedar,
  the acacia, the myrtle, and the olive.
  I will set in the desert the cypress,
  the plane and the pine together,
20 that they may see and know,
  may consider and understand
  together,
  that the hand of the LORD has done
  this,
  the Holy One of Israel has created it.

The Futility of Idols

21 Set forth your case, says the LORD;
  bring your proofs, says the King of
  Jacob.
22 Let them bring them, and tell us
  what is to happen.
  Tell us the former things, what they
  are,
  that we may consider them,
  that we may know their outcome;
  or declare to us the things to come.
23 Tell us what is to come hereafter,
  that we may know that you are gods;
  do good, or do harm,
  that we may be dismayed and terrified.
24 Behold, you are nothing,
  and your work is less than nothing;
  an abomination is he who chooses
  you.

25 I stirred up one from the north, and
  he has come,
  from the rising of the sun, and he
  shall call upon my name;
  he shall trample on rulers as on mortar,
  as the potter treads clay.
26 Who declared it from the beginning,
  that we might know,
  and beforehand, that we might say,
  "He is right"?

There was none who declared it, none
  who proclaimed,
  none who heard your words.
27 I was the first to say to Zion, "Behold,
  here they are!"
  and I give to Jerusalem a herald of
  good news.
28 But when I look, there is no one;
  among these there is no counselor
  who, when I ask, gives an answer.
29 Behold, they are all a delusion;
  their works are nothing;
  their metal images are empty wind.

The LORD's Chosen Servant

42 Behold my servant, whom I
  uphold,
  my chosen, in whom my soul
  delights;
  I have put my Spirit upon him;
  he will bring forth justice to the
  nations.
2 He will not cry aloud or lift up his
  voice,
  or make it heard in the street;
3 a bruised reed he will not break,
  and a faintly burning wick he will
  not quench;
  he will faithfully bring forth justice.
4 He will not grow faint or be discouraged
  till he has established justice in the
  earth;
  and the coastlands wait for his law.

5 Thus says God, the LORD,
  who created the heavens and
  stretched them out,
  who spread out the earth and what
  comes from it,
  who gives breath to the people on it
  and spirit to those who walk in it:
6 "I am the LORD; I have called you in
  righteousness;
  I will take you by the hand and keep
  you;
  I will give you as a covenant for the
  people,
  a light for the nations,
7 to open the eyes that are blind,
  to bring out the prisoners from the
  dungeon,
  from the prison those who sit in
  darkness.

8 I am the Lord; that is my name;
  my glory I give to no other,
  nor my praise to carved idols.
9 Behold, the former things have come
    to pass,
  and new things I now declare;
  before they spring forth
  I tell you of them."

Sing to the Lord a New Song

10 Sing to the Lord a new song,
  his praise from the end of the earth,
  you who go down to the sea, and all
    that fills it,
  the coastlands and their inhabitants.
11 Let the desert and its cities lift up
    their voice,
  the villages that Kedar inhabits;
  let the habitants of Sela sing for joy,
  let them shout from the top of the
    mountains.
12 Let them give glory to the Lord,
  and declare his praise in the coast-
    lands.
13 The Lord goes out like a mighty man,
  like a man of war he stirs up his
    zeal;
  he cries out, he shouts aloud,
  he shows himself mighty against
    his foes.
14 For a long time I have held my peace;
  I have kept still and restrained
    myself;
  now I will cry out like a woman in
    labor;
  I will gasp and pant.
15 I will lay waste mountains and hills,
  and dry up all their vegetation;
  I will turn the rivers into islands,
  and dry up the pools.
16 And I will lead the blind
  in a way that they do not know,
  in paths that they have not known
  I will guide them.
  I will turn the darkness before them
    into light,
  the rough places into level ground.
  These are the things I do,
  and I do not forsake them.
17 They are turned back and utterly put
    to shame,
  who trust in carved idols,
  who say to metal images,
  "You are our gods."

Israel's Failure to Hear and See

18 Hear, you deaf,
  and look, you blind, that you may
    see!
19 Who is blind but my servant,
  or deaf as my messenger whom I
    send?
  Who is blind as my dedicated one,
  or blind as the servant of the Lord?
20 He sees many things, but does not
    observe them;
  his ears are open, but he does not
    hear.
21 The Lord was pleased, for his righ-
    teousness' sake,
  to magnify his law and make it
    glorious.
22 But this is a people plundered and
    looted;

GETTING THE MESSAGE

Long-term imprisonment was not as common in the ancient world as it is today. Prisons housed criminals awaiting trial. If there was no room in the jail, a pit or hole would be dug to hold the prisoner until his fate was decided (42:22).

  they are all of them trapped in holes
  and hidden in prisons;
  they have become plunder with none
    to rescue,
  spoil with none to say, "Restore!"
23 Who among you will give ear to this,
  will attend and listen for the time to
    come?
24 Who gave up Jacob to the looter,
  and Israel to the plunderers?
  Was it not the Lord, against whom we
    have sinned,
  in whose ways they would not walk,
  and whose law they would not
    obey?
25 So he poured on him the heat of his
    anger
  and the might of battle;
  it set him on fire all around, but he
    did not understand;
  it burned him up, but he did not
    take it to heart.

Israel's Only Savior

43 But now thus says the LORD,
    he who created you, O Jacob,
    he who formed you, O Israel:
"Fear not, for I have redeemed you;
    I have called you by name, you are
        mine.
2 When you pass through the waters,
    I will be with you;
    and through the rivers, they shall
        not overwhelm you;
when you walk through fire you shall
        not be burned,
    and the flame shall not consume
        you.
3 For I am the LORD your God,
    the Holy One of Israel, your Savior.
I give Egypt as your ransom,
    Cush and Seba in exchange for you.
4 Because you are precious in my eyes,
    and honored, and I love you,
I give men in return for you,
    peoples in exchange for your life.
5 Fear not, for I am with you;
    I will bring your offspring from the
        east,
    and from the west I will gather you.
6 I will say to the north, Give up,
    and to the south, Do not withhold;
bring my sons from afar
    and my daughters from the end of
        the earth,
7 everyone who is called by my name,
    whom I created for my glory,
    whom I formed and made."

8 Bring out the people who are blind,
    yet have eyes,
    who are deaf, yet have ears!
9 All the nations gather together,
    and the peoples assemble.
Who among them can declare this,
    and show us the former things?
Let them bring their witnesses to
        prove them right,
    and let them hear and say, It is true.
10 "You are my witnesses," declares the
        LORD,
    "and my servant whom I have chosen,
that you may know and believe me
    and understand that I am he.
Before me no god was formed,
    nor shall there be any after me.
11 I, I am the LORD,
    and besides me there is no savior.

12 I declared and saved and proclaimed,
    when there was no strange god
        among you;
    and you are my witnesses," declares
        the LORD, "and I am God.
13 Also henceforth I am he;
    there is none who can deliver from
        my hand;
    I work, and who can turn it back?"

14 Thus says the LORD,
    your Redeemer, the Holy One of
        Israel:
"For your sake I send to Babylon
    and bring them all down as fugitives,
    even the Chaldeans, in the ships in
        which they rejoice.
15 I am the LORD, your Holy One,
    the Creator of Israel, your King."

16 Thus says the LORD,
    who makes a way in the sea,
    a path in the mighty waters,
17 who brings forth chariot and horse,
    army and warrior;
they lie down, they cannot rise,
    they are extinguished, quenched
        like a wick:
18 "Remember not the former things,
    nor consider the things of old.
19 Behold, I am doing a new thing;
    now it springs forth, do you not
        perceive it?
I will make a way in the wilderness
    and rivers in the desert.
20 The wild beasts will honor me,
    the jackals and the ostriches,
for I give water in the wilderness,
    rivers in the desert,
to give drink to my chosen people,
21   the people whom I formed for
        myself
that they might declare my praise.

22 "Yet you did not call upon me, O Jacob;
    but you have been weary of me,
        O Israel!
23 You have not brought me your sheep
    for burnt offerings,
    or honored me with your sacrifices.
I have not burdened you with offerings,
    or wearied you with frankincense.
24 You have not bought me sweet cane
    with money,
    or satisfied me with the fat of your
        sacrifices.

But you have burdened me with your
      sins;
  you have wearied me with your
      iniquities.
25 "I, I am he
  who blots out your transgressions
      for my own sake,
  and I will not remember your sins.
26 Put me in remembrance; let us argue
      together;
  set forth your case, that you may be
      proved right.
27 Your first father sinned,
  and your mediators transgressed
      against me.
28 Therefore I will profane the princes of
      the sanctuary,
  and deliver Jacob to utter destruction
      and Israel to reviling.

Israel the LORD's Chosen

44 "But now hear, O Jacob my servant,
      Israel whom I have chosen!
2 Thus says the LORD who made you,
  who formed you from the womb
      and will help you:
  Fear not, O Jacob my servant,
  Jeshurun whom I have chosen.
3 For I will pour water on the thirsty
      land,
  and streams on the dry ground;
  I will pour my Spirit upon your off-
      spring,
  and my blessing on your descen-
      dants.
4 They shall spring up among the grass
  like willows by flowing streams.
5 This one will say, 'I am the LORD's,'
  another will call on the name of
      Jacob,
  and another will write on his hand,
      'The LORD's,'
  and name himself by the name of
      Israel."

Besides Me There Is No God

6 Thus says the LORD, the King of Israel
  and his Redeemer, the LORD of hosts:
"I am the first and I am the last;
  besides me there is no god.
7 Who is like me? Let him proclaim it.
  Let him declare and set it before me,
  since I appointed an ancient people.
  Let them declare what is to come,
  and what will happen.

8 Fear not, nor be afraid;
  have I not told you from of old and
      declared it?
  And you are my witnesses!
  Is there a God besides me?
  There is no Rock; I know not any."

The Folly of Idolatry

9 All who fashion idols are nothing,
and the things they delight in do not profit.
Their witnesses neither see nor know, that
they may be put to shame. 10 Who fashions
a god or casts an idol that is profitable for
nothing? 11 Behold, all his companions shall
be put to shame, and the craftsmen are only
human. Let them all assemble, let them
stand forth. They shall be terrified; they
shall be put to shame together.

12 The ironsmith takes a cutting tool and
works it over the coals. He fashions it with
hammers and works it with his strong arm.
He becomes hungry, and his strength fails;
he drinks no water and is faint. 13 The carpenter stretches a line; he marks it out with
a pencil. He shapes it with planes and marks
it with a compass. He shapes it into the figure of a man, with the beauty of a man, to
dwell in a house. 14 He cuts down cedars, or
he chooses a cypress tree or an oak and lets
it grow strong among the trees of the forest.
He plants a cedar and the rain nourishes it.
15 Then it becomes fuel for a man. He takes
a part of it and warms himself; he kindles
a fire and bakes bread. Also he makes a god
and worships it; he makes it an idol and falls
down before it. 16 Half of it he burns in the
fire. Over the half he eats meat; he roasts it
and is satisfied. Also he warms himself and
says, "Aha, I am warm, I have seen the fire!"
17 And the rest of it he makes into a god, his
idol, and falls down to it and worships it.
He prays to it and says, "Deliver me, for you
are my god!"

18 They know not, nor do they discern, for
he has shut their eyes, so that they cannot
see, and their hearts, so that they cannot
understand. 19 No one considers, nor is there
knowledge or discernment to say, "Half of
it I burned in the fire; I also baked bread on
its coals; I roasted meat and have eaten. And
shall I make the rest of it an abomination?
Shall I fall down before a block of wood?"
20 He feeds on ashes; a deluded heart has led
him astray, and he cannot deliver himself
or say, "Is there not a lie in my right hand?"

The Lord Redeems Israel

21 Remember these things, O Jacob,
    and Israel, for you are my servant;
I formed you; you are my servant;
    O Israel, you will not be forgotten
        by me.
22 I have blotted out your transgressions
        like a cloud
    and your sins like mist;
return to me, for I have redeemed you.

23 Sing, O heavens, for the Lord has
        done it;
    shout, O depths of the earth;
break forth into singing, O mountains,
    O forest, and every tree in it!
For the Lord has redeemed Jacob,
    and will be glorified in Israel.

24 Thus says the Lord, your Redeemer,
    who formed you from the womb:

> ### GETTING THE MESSAGE
>
> **The prophecy about Cyrus.** King Cyrus
> of Persia would one day make it possible
> for the Jews to return home from their
> exile in Babylon (see the book of Ezra).
> Isaiah predicted this great event, even
> mentioning Cyrus by name (Isa. 44:28;
> 45:1), some 150 years before Cyrus's time.

"I am the Lord, who made all things,
    who alone stretched out the heav-
        ens,
    who spread out the earth by myself,
25 who frustrates the signs of liars
    and makes fools of diviners,
who turns wise men back
    and makes their knowledge foolish,
26 who confirms the word of his servant
    and fulfills the counsel of his mes-
        sengers,
who says of Jerusalem, 'She shall be
        inhabited,'
    and of the cities of Judah, 'They
        shall be built,
    and I will raise up their ruins';
27 who says to the deep, 'Be dry;
    I will dry up your rivers';
28 who says of Cyrus, 'He is my shep-
        herd,
    and he shall fulfill all my purpose';

saying of Jerusalem, 'She shall be built,'
    and of the temple, 'Your foundation
        shall be laid.'"

Cyrus, God's Instrument

45 Thus says the Lord to his
    anointed, to Cyrus,
    whose right hand I have grasped,
to subdue nations before him
    and to loose the belts of kings,
to open doors before him
    that gates may not be closed:
2 "I will go before you
    and level the exalted places,
I will break in pieces the doors of
        bronze
    and cut through the bars of iron,
3 I will give you the treasures of darkness
    and the hoards in secret places,
that you may know that it is I, the
        Lord,
    the God of Israel, who call you by
        your name.
4 For the sake of my servant Jacob,
    and Israel my chosen,
I call you by your name,
    I name you, though you do not
        know me.
5 I am the Lord, and there is no other,
    besides me there is no God;
    I equip you, though you do not
        know me,
6 that people may know, from the rising
        of the sun
    and from the west, that there is
        none besides me;
    I am the Lord, and there is no other.
7 I form light and create darkness,
    I make well-being and create calam-
        ity,
    I am the Lord, who does all these
        things.
8 "Shower, O heavens, from above,
    and let the clouds rain down righ-
        teousness;
let the earth open, that salvation and
        righteousness may bear fruit;
    let the earth cause them both to
        sprout;
    I the Lord have created it.

9 "Woe to him who strives with him who
        formed him,
    a pot among earthen pots!

Does the clay say to him who forms it,
'What are you making?'
or 'Your work has no handles'?
¹⁰ Woe to him who says to a father,
'What are you begetting?'
or to a woman, 'With what are you
in labor?'"

¹¹ Thus says the LORD,
the Holy One of Israel, and the one
who formed him:
"Ask me of things to come;
will you command me concerning
my children and the work of my
hands?
¹² I made the earth
and created man on it;
it was my hands that stretched out the
heavens,
and I commanded all their host.
¹³ I have stirred him up in righteousness,
and I will make all his ways level;
he shall build my city
and set my exiles free,
not for price or reward,"
says the LORD of hosts.

The LORD, the Only Savior

¹⁴ Thus says the LORD:
"The wealth of Egypt and the merchandise of Cush,
and the Sabeans, men of stature,
shall come over to you and be yours;
they shall follow you;
they shall come over in chains and
bow down to you.
They will plead with you, saying:
'Surely God is in you, and there is no
other,
no god besides him.'"

¹⁵ Truly, you are a God who hides himself,
O God of Israel, the Savior.
¹⁶ All of them are put to shame and
confounded;
the makers of idols go in confusion
together.
¹⁷ But Israel is saved by the LORD
with everlasting salvation;
you shall not be put to shame or confounded
to all eternity.

¹⁸ For thus says the LORD,
who created the heavens
(he is God!),

who formed the earth and made it
(he established it;
he did not create it empty,
he formed it to be inhabited!):
"I am the LORD, and there is no other.
¹⁹ I did not speak in secret,
in a land of darkness;
I did not say to the offspring of Jacob,
'Seek me in vain.'
I the LORD speak the truth;
I declare what is right.

²⁰ "Assemble yourselves and come;
draw near together,
you survivors of the nations!
They have no knowledge
who carry about their wooden idols,
and keep on praying to a god
that cannot save.
²¹ Declare and present your case;
let them take counsel together!

GETTING THE MESSAGE

Feeding idols? In Isaiah's day, people treated idols almost as if they were human. Some even fed, bathed, and dressed their idols. Isaiah spoke of how foolish it was for people to worship something that they themselves had made (46:6).

Who told this long ago?
Who declared it of old?
Was it not I, the LORD?
And there is no other god besides
me,
a righteous God and a Savior;
there is none besides me.

²² "Turn to me and be saved,
all the ends of the earth!
For I am God, and there is no other.
²³ By myself I have sworn;
from my mouth has gone out in
righteousness
a word that shall not return:
'To me every knee shall bow,
every tongue shall swear allegiance.'

²⁴ "Only in the LORD, it shall be said
of me,
are righteousness and strength;
to him shall come and be ashamed
all who were incensed against him.

²⁵ In the LORD all the offspring of Israel
shall be justified and shall glory.”

The Idols of Babylon and the One True God

46 Bel bows down; Nebo stoops;
their idols are on beasts and
livestock;
these things you carry are borne
as burdens on weary beasts.
² They stoop; they bow down together;
they cannot save the burden,
but themselves go into captivity.

³ “Listen to me, O house of Jacob,
all the remnant of the house of
Israel,
who have been borne by me from
before your birth,
carried from the womb;

⁴ even to your old age I am he,
and to gray hairs I will carry you.
I have made, and I will bear;
I will carry and will save.
⁵ “To whom will you liken me and make
me equal,
and compare me, that we may be
alike?
⁶ Those who lavish gold from the
purse,
and weigh out silver in the scales,
hire a goldsmith, and he makes it into
a god;
then they fall down and worship!
⁷ They lift it to their shoulders, they
carry it,
they set it in its place, and it stands
there;
it cannot move from its place.
If one cries to it, it does not answer
or save him from his trouble.

⁸ “Remember this and stand firm,
recall it to mind, you transgressors,
⁹ remember the former things of old;
for I am God, and there is no other;
I am God, and there is none like me,
¹⁰ declaring the end from the beginning
and from ancient times things not
yet done,
saying, ‘My counsel shall stand,
and I will accomplish all my purpose,’
¹¹ calling a bird of prey from the east,
the man of my counsel from a far
country.
I have spoken, and I will bring it to
pass;
I have purposed, and I will do it.

¹² “Listen to me, you stubborn of heart,
you who are far from righteousness:
¹³ I bring near my righteousness; it is
not far off,
and my salvation will not delay;
I will put salvation in Zion,
for Israel my glory.”

The Humiliation of Babylon

47 Come down and sit in the dust,
O virgin daughter of Babylon;
sit on the ground without a throne,
O daughter of the Chaldeans!
For you shall no more be called
tender and delicate.
² Take the millstones and grind flour,
put off your veil,
strip off your robe, uncover your legs,
pass through the rivers.
³ Your nakedness shall be uncovered,
and your disgrace shall be seen.
I will take vengeance,
and I will spare no one.
⁴ Our Redeemer—the LORD of hosts is
his name—
is the Holy One of Israel.

⁵ Sit in silence, and go into darkness,
O daughter of the Chaldeans;
for you shall no more be called
the mistress of kingdoms.
⁶ I was angry with my people;
I profaned my heritage;
I gave them into your hand;
you showed them no mercy;
on the aged you made your yoke
exceedingly heavy.

7 You said, "I shall be mistress forever,"
  so that you did not lay these things
      to heart
  or remember their end.

8 Now therefore hear this, you lover of
      pleasures,
  who sit securely,
who say in your heart,
  "I am, and there is no one besides me;
I shall not sit as a widow
  or know the loss of children":

9 These two things shall come to you
  in a moment, in one day;
the loss of children and widowhood
  shall come upon you in full mea-
    sure,
in spite of your many sorceries
  and the great power of your
    enchantments.

10 You felt secure in your wickedness,
  you said, "No one sees me";
your wisdom and your knowledge led
    you astray,
and you said in your heart,
  "I am, and there is no one besides
    me."

11 But evil shall come upon you,
  which you will not know how to
    charm away;
disaster shall fall upon you,
  for which you will not be able to
    atone;
and ruin shall come upon you sud-
    denly,
  of which you know nothing.

12 Stand fast in your enchantments
  and your many sorceries,
    with which you have labored from
      your youth;
perhaps you may be able to succeed;
  perhaps you may inspire terror.

13 You are wearied with your many
    counsels;
  let them stand forth and save you,
those who divide the heavens,
  who gaze at the stars,
who at the new moons make known
  what shall come upon you.

14 Behold, they are like stubble;
  the fire consumes them;
they cannot deliver themselves
  from the power of the flame.

No coal for warming oneself is this,
  no fire to sit before!

15 Such to you are those with whom you
    have labored,
  who have done business with you
    from your youth;
they wander about, each in his own
    direction;
  there is no one to save you.

Israel Refined for God's Glory

48 Hear this, O house of Jacob,
  who are called by the name of
    Israel,
  and who came from the waters of
    Judah,
who swear by the name of the LORD
  and confess the God of Israel,
  but not in truth or right.

2 For they call themselves after the holy
    city,
  and stay themselves on the God of
    Israel;
  the LORD of hosts is his name.

3 "The former things I declared of old;
  they went out from my mouth, and
    I announced them;
  then suddenly I did them, and they
    came to pass.

4 Because I know that you are obstinate,
  and your neck is an iron sinew
  and your forehead brass,

5 I declared them to you from of old,
  before they came to pass I
    announced them to you,
lest you should say, 'My idol did them,
  my carved image and my metal
    image commanded them.'

6 "You have heard; now see all this;
  and will you not declare it?
From this time forth I announce to
    you new things,
  hidden things that you have not
    known.

7 They are created now, not long ago;
  before today you have never heard
    of them,
  lest you should say, 'Behold, I knew
    them.'

8 You have never heard, you have never
    known,
  from of old your ear has not been
    opened.

For I knew that you would surely deal
treacherously,
and that from before birth you were
called a rebel.
9 "For my name's sake I defer my anger,
for the sake of my praise I restrain it
for you,
that I may not cut you off.
10 Behold, I have refined you, but not as
silver;
I have tried you in the furnace of
affliction.
11 For my own sake, for my own sake,
I do it,
for how should my name be profaned?
My glory I will not give to another.

GETTING THE MESSAGE

A mouth like a sharp sword. The Bible
often describes either the mouth or
words coming from the mouth as a
sword (49:2). One Hebrew word for
mouth actually means "edge," as in
"edge of a sword." It is certainly an
accurate picture of the power of words,
for good or ill (James 3:1–12).

The LORD's Call to Israel
12 "Listen to me, O Jacob,
and Israel, whom I called!
I am he; I am the first,
and I am the last.
13 My hand laid the foundation of the
earth,
and my right hand spread out the
heavens;
when I call to them,
they stand forth together.

14 "Assemble, all of you, and listen!
Who among them has declared
these things?
The LORD loves him;
he shall perform his purpose on
Babylon,
and his arm shall be against the
Chaldeans.
15 I, even I, have spoken and called him;
I have brought him, and he will
prosper in his way.

16 Draw near to me, hear this:
from the beginning I have not spoken in secret,
from the time it came to be I have
been there."
And now the Lord GOD has sent me,
and his Spirit.

17 Thus says the LORD,
your Redeemer, the Holy One of
Israel:
"I am the LORD your God,
who teaches you to profit,
who leads you in the way you
should go.
18 Oh that you had paid attention to my
commandments!
Then your peace would have been
like a river,
and your righteousness like the
waves of the sea;
19 your offspring would have been like
the sand,
and your descendants like its grains;
their name would never be cut off
or destroyed from before me."

20 Go out from Babylon, flee from
Chaldea,
declare this with a shout of joy,
proclaim it,
send it out to the end of the earth;
say, "The LORD has redeemed his
servant Jacob!"
21 They did not thirst when he led them
through the deserts;
he made water flow for them from
the rock;
he split the rock and the water
gushed out.
22 "There is no peace," says the LORD, "for
the wicked."

The Servant of the LORD
49 Listen to me, O coastlands,
and give attention, you peoples
from afar.
The LORD called me from the womb,
from the body of my mother he
named my name.
2 He made my mouth like a sharp
sword;
in the shadow of his hand he hid me;
he made me a polished arrow;
in his quiver he hid me away.

3 And he said to me, "You are my servant,
  Israel, in whom I will be glorified."
4 But I said, "I have labored in vain;
  I have spent my strength for nothing and vanity;
yet surely my right is with the Lord,
  and my recompense with my God."

5 And now the Lord says,
  he who formed me from the womb
to be his servant,
to bring Jacob back to him;
  and that Israel might be gathered to
him—
for I am honored in the eyes of the
Lord,
  and my God has become my
strength—
6 he says:
"It is too light a thing that you should
be my servant
  to raise up the tribes of Jacob
  and to bring back the preserved of
Israel;
I will make you as a light for the
nations,
  that my salvation may reach to the
end of the earth."

7 Thus says the Lord,
  the Redeemer of Israel and his Holy
One,
to one deeply despised, abhorred by
the nation,
  the servant of rulers:
"Kings shall see and arise;
  princes, and they shall prostrate
themselves;
because of the Lord, who is faithful,
  the Holy One of Israel, who has
chosen you."

The Restoration of Israel

8 Thus says the Lord:
"In a time of favor I have answered
you;
  in a day of salvation I have helped
you;
I will keep you and give you
as a covenant to the people,
to establish the land,
  to apportion the desolate heritages,
9 saying to the prisoners, 'Come out,'
  to those who are in darkness,
'Appear.'

They shall feed along the ways;
  on all bare heights shall be their
pasture;
10 they shall not hunger or thirst,
  neither scorching wind nor sun
shall strike them,
for he who has pity on them will lead
them,
  and by springs of water will guide
them.
11 And I will make all my mountains a
road,
  and my highways shall be raised up.
12 Behold, these shall come from afar,
  and behold, these from the north
and from the west,
  and these from the land of Syene."

13 Sing for joy, O heavens, and exult,
O earth;
  break forth, O mountains, into singing!
For the Lord has comforted his people
  and will have compassion on his
afflicted.

14 But Zion said, "The Lord has forsaken
me;
  my Lord has forgotten me."
15 "Can a woman forget her nursing child,
  that she should have no compassion on the son of her womb?
Even these may forget,
  yet I will not forget you.
16 Behold, I have engraved you on the
palms of my hands;
  your walls are continually before me.
17 Your builders make haste;
  your destroyers and those who laid
you waste go out from you.
18 Lift up your eyes around and see;
  they all gather, they come to you.
As I live, declares the Lord,
  you shall put them all on as an
ornament;
  you shall bind them on as a bride
does.
19 "Surely your waste and your desolate
places
  and your devastated land—
surely now you will be too narrow for
your inhabitants,
  and those who swallowed you up
will be far away.

20 The children of your bereavement
     will yet say in your ears:
   'The place is too narrow for me;
     make room for me to dwell in.'
21 Then you will say in your heart:
   'Who has borne me these?
   I was bereaved and barren,
     exiled and put away,
     but who has brought up these?
   Behold, I was left alone;
     from where have these come?'"

22 Thus says the Lord GOD:
   "Behold, I will lift up my hand to the
     nations,
     and raise my signal to the peoples;
   and they shall bring your sons in their
     arms,
     and your daughters shall be carried
     on their shoulders.
23 Kings shall be your foster fathers,
     and their queens your nursing
     mothers.
   With their faces to the ground they
     shall bow down to you,
     and lick the dust of your feet.
   Then you will know that I am the LORD;
     those who wait for me shall not be
     put to shame."

24 Can the prey be taken from the mighty,
     or the captives of a tyrant be rescued?
25 For thus says the LORD:
   "Even the captives of the mighty shall
     be taken,
     and the prey of the tyrant be rescued,
   for I will contend with those who
     contend with you,
     and I will save your children.
26 I will make your oppressors eat their
     own flesh,
     and they shall be drunk with their
     own blood as with wine.
   Then all flesh shall know
     that I am the LORD your Savior,
     and your Redeemer, the Mighty One
     of Jacob."

Israel's Sin and the Servant's Obedience

50 Thus says the LORD:
   "Where is your mother's certifi-
     cate of divorce,
   with which I sent her away?
   Or which of my creditors is it
     to whom I have sold you?

Behold, for your iniquities you were
     sold,
   and for your transgressions your
     mother was sent away.
2 Why, when I came, was there no man;
     why, when I called, was there no
     one to answer?
   Is my hand shortened, that it cannot
     redeem?
     Or have I no power to deliver?
   Behold, by my rebuke I dry up the sea,
     I make the rivers a desert;
   their fish stink for lack of water
     and die of thirst.
3 I clothe the heavens with blackness
     and make sackcloth their covering."

4 The Lord GOD has given me
     the tongue of those who are taught,
   that I may know how to sustain with a
     word
     him who is weary.
   Morning by morning he awakens;
     he awakens my ear
     to hear as those who are taught.
5 The Lord GOD has opened my ear,
     and I was not rebellious;
     I turned not backward.
6 I gave my back to those who strike,
     and my cheeks to those who pull
     out the beard;
   I hid not my face
     from disgrace and spitting.

7 But the Lord GOD helps me;
     therefore I have not been disgraced;
   therefore I have set my face like a flint,
     and I know that I shall not be put to
     shame.
8 He who vindicates me is near.
   Who will contend with me?
     Let us stand up together.
   Who is my adversary?
     Let him come near to me.
9 Behold, the Lord GOD helps me;
     who will declare me guilty?
   Behold, all of them will wear out like a
     garment;
     the moth will eat them up.

10 Who among you fears the LORD
     and obeys the voice of his servant?
   Let him who walks in darkness
     and has no light
   trust in the name of the LORD
     and rely on his God.

¹¹   Behold, all you who kindle a fire,
           who equip yourselves with burning
               torches!
       Walk by the light of your fire,
           and by the torches that you have
               kindled!
       This you have from my hand:
           you shall lie down in torment.

The LORD's Comfort for Zion

51 "Listen to me, you who pursue righ-
       teousness,
       you who seek the LORD:
   look to the rock from which you were
       hewn,
           and to the quarry from which you
               were dug.
²   Look to Abraham your father
           and to Sarah who bore you;
       for he was but one when I called him,
           that I might bless him and multiply
               him.
³   For the LORD comforts Zion;
           he comforts all her waste places
       and makes her wilderness like Eden,
           her desert like the garden of the
               LORD;
       joy and gladness will be found in her,
           thanksgiving and the voice of song.

⁴   "Give attention to me, my people,
           and give ear to me, my nation;
       for a law will go out from me,
           and I will set my justice for a light
               to the peoples.
⁵   My righteousness draws near,
           my salvation has gone out,
           and my arms will judge the peoples;
       the coastlands hope for me,
           and for my arm they wait.
⁶   Lift up your eyes to the heavens,
           and look at the earth beneath;
       for the heavens vanish like smoke,
           the earth will wear out like a gar-
               ment,
           and they who dwell in it will die in
               like manner;
       but my salvation will be forever,
           and my righteousness will never be
               dismayed.
⁷   "Listen to me, you who know righ-
           teousness,
           the people in whose heart is my law;
       fear not the reproach of man,
           nor be dismayed at their revilings.

⁸   For the moth will eat them up like a
           garment,
           and the worm will eat them like
               wool;
       but my righteousness will be forever,
           and my salvation to all generations."

⁹   Awake, awake, put on strength,
           O arm of the LORD;
       awake, as in days of old,
           the generations of long ago.
       Was it not you who cut Rahab in
           pieces,
           who pierced the dragon?
¹⁰   Was it not you who dried up the sea,
           the waters of the great deep,
       who made the depths of the sea a way
           for the redeemed to pass over?
¹¹   And the ransomed of the LORD shall
           return
           and come to Zion with singing;

GETTING THE MESSAGE

The **head of the street** (51:20) referred to
prominent corners or intersections within
a city. Few cities were laid out according
to a specific plan. Most had buildings
scattered randomly, with narrow streets
and dead-end alleys.

       everlasting joy shall be upon their
           heads;
           they shall obtain gladness and joy,
           and sorrow and sighing shall flee
               away.

¹²   "I, I am he who comforts you;
           who are you that you are afraid of
               man who dies,
           of the son of man who is made like
               grass,
¹³   and have forgotten the LORD, your
           Maker,
           who stretched out the heavens
           and laid the foundations of the
               earth,
       and you fear continually all the day
           because of the wrath of the oppres-
               sor,
       when he sets himself to destroy?
           And where is the wrath of the
               oppressor?

14 He who is bowed down shall speedily
        be released;
    he shall not die and go down to the
        pit,
    neither shall his bread be lacking.
15 I am the LORD your God,
    who stirs up the sea so that its
        waves roar—
    the LORD of hosts is his name.
16 And I have put my words in your
        mouth
        and covered you in the shadow of
        my hand,
    establishing the heavens
        and laying the foundations of the
        earth,
        and saying to Zion, 'You are my
        people.'"
17 Wake yourself, wake yourself,
    stand up, O Jerusalem,

    you who have drunk from the hand of
        the LORD
        the cup of his wrath,
    who have drunk to the dregs
        the bowl, the cup of staggering.
18 There is none to guide her
        among all the sons she has borne;
    there is none to take her by the hand
        among all the sons she has brought
        up.
19 These two things have happened to
        you—
    who will console you?—
    devastation and destruction, famine
        and sword;
    who will comfort you?
20 Your sons have fainted;
    they lie at the head of every street
        like an antelope in a net;
    they are full of the wrath of the LORD,
        the rebuke of your God.

21 Therefore hear this, you who are
        afflicted,
    who are drunk, but not with wine:
22 Thus says your Lord, the LORD,
        your God who pleads the cause of
        his people:
    "Behold, I have taken from your hand
        the cup of staggering;
    the bowl of my wrath you shall drink
        no more;
23 and I will put it into the hand of your
        tormentors,
    who have said to you,
    'Bow down, that we may pass over';
    and you have made your back like the
        ground
        and like the street for them to pass
        over."

The LORD's Coming Salvation

52 Awake, awake,
        put on your strength, O Zion;
    put on your beautiful garments,
        O Jerusalem, the holy city;
    for there shall no more come into you
        the uncircumcised and the unclean.
2   Shake yourself from the dust and
        arise;
        be seated, O Jerusalem;
    loose the bonds from your neck,
        O captive daughter of Zion.

3 For thus says the LORD: "You were sold
for nothing, and you shall be redeemed
without money." 4 For thus says the Lord
GOD: "My people went down at the first into
Egypt to sojourn there, and the Assyrian
oppressed them for nothing. 5 Now therefore
what have I here," declares the LORD, "seeing
that my people are taken away for nothing?
Their rulers wail," declares the LORD, "and
continually all the day my name is despised.
6 Therefore my people shall know my name.
Therefore in that day they shall know that
it is I who speak; here I am."

7   How beautiful upon the mountains
        are the feet of him who brings good
        news,
    who publishes peace, who brings
        good news of happiness,
    who publishes salvation,
        who says to Zion, "Your God reigns."
8   The voice of your watchmen—they
        lift up their voice;
        together they sing for joy;

for eye to eye they see
  the return of the LORD to Zion.
9 Break forth together into singing,
  you waste places of Jerusalem,
for the LORD has comforted his peo-
    ple;
  he has redeemed Jerusalem.
10 The LORD has bared his holy arm
  before the eyes of all the nations,
and all the ends of the earth shall see
  the salvation of our God.

11 Depart, depart, go out from there;
  touch no unclean thing;
go out from the midst of her; purify
    yourselves,
  you who bear the vessels of the
    LORD.
12 For you shall not go out in haste,
  and you shall not go in flight,
for the LORD will go before you,
  and the God of Israel will be your
    rear guard.

He Was Pierced for Our Transgressions

13 Behold, my servant shall act wisely;
  he shall be high and lifted up,
  and shall be exalted.
14 As many were astonished at you—
  his appearance was so marred,
    beyond human semblance,
  and his form beyond that of the
    children of mankind—
15 so shall he sprinkle many nations;
  kings shall shut their mouths
    because of him;
for that which has not been told them
    they see,
  and that which they have not heard
    they understand.

53 Who has believed what he has
  heard from us?
  And to whom has the arm of the
    LORD been revealed?
2 For he grew up before him like a
    young plant,
  and like a root out of dry ground;
he had no form or majesty that we
    should look at him,
  and no beauty that we should desire
    him.
3 He was despised and rejected by
    men;
  a man of sorrows, and acquainted
    with grief;

and as one from whom men hide
    their faces
  he was despised, and we esteemed
    him not.

4 Surely he has borne our griefs
  and carried our sorrows;
yet we esteemed him stricken,
  smitten by God, and afflicted.
5 But he was pierced for our transgres-
    sions;
  he was crushed for our iniquities;
upon him was the chastisement that
    brought us peace,
  and with his wounds we are
    healed.
6 All we like sheep have gone astray;
  we have turned—every one—to his
    own way;
and the LORD has laid on him
  the iniquity of us all.

7 He was oppressed, and he was
    afflicted,
  yet he opened not his mouth;
like a lamb that is led to the slaughter,
  and like a sheep that before its
    shearers is silent,
  so he opened not his mouth.
8 By oppression and judgment he was
    taken away;
  and as for his generation, who con-
    sidered
that he was cut off out of the land of
    the living,
  stricken for the transgression of my
    people?
9 And they made his grave with the
    wicked
  and with a rich man in his death,
although he had done no violence,
  and there was no deceit in his
    mouth.

10 Yet it was the will of the LORD to crush
    him;
  he has put him to grief;
when his soul makes an offering for
    guilt,
  he shall see his offspring; he shall
    prolong his days;
the will of the LORD shall prosper in
    his hand.
11 Out of the anguish of his soul he shall
  see and be satisfied;

by his knowledge shall the righteous
  one, my servant,
    make many to be accounted righ-
      teous,
  and he shall bear their iniquities.
12 Therefore I will divide him a portion
    with the many,
  and he shall divide the spoil with
    the strong,
because he poured out his soul to
    death
  and was numbered with the trans-
    gressors;
yet he bore the sin of many,
  and makes intercession for the
    transgressors.

The Eternal Covenant of Peace

54 "Sing, O barren one, who did not
    bear;
  break forth into singing and cry
    aloud,

you who have not been in labor!
For the children of the desolate one
  will be more
  than the children of her who is
    married," says the LORD.
2 "Enlarge the place of your tent,
    and let the curtains of your habita-
      tions be stretched out;
  do not hold back; lengthen your
    cords
  and strengthen your stakes.
3 For you will spread abroad to the right
    and to the left,
  and your offspring will possess the
    nations
  and will people the desolate cities.
4 "Fear not, for you will not be ashamed;
    be not confounded, for you will not
      be disgraced;

for you will forget the shame of your
    youth,
  and the reproach of your widowhood
    you will remember no more.
5 For your Maker is your husband,
    the LORD of hosts is his name;
and the Holy One of Israel is your
    Redeemer,
  the God of the whole earth he is
    called.
6 For the LORD has called you
  like a wife deserted and grieved in
    spirit,
  like a wife of youth when she is cast
    off,
    says your God.
7 For a brief moment I deserted you,
    but with great compassion I will
      gather you.
8 In overflowing anger for a moment
    I hid my face from you,
  but with everlasting love I will have
    compassion on you,"
    says the LORD, your Redeemer.

9 "This is like the days of Noah to me:
    as I swore that the waters of Noah
    should no more go over the earth,
so I have sworn that I will not be
    angry with you,
  and will not rebuke you.
10 For the mountains may depart
    and the hills be removed,
  but my steadfast love shall not depart
    from you,
  and my covenant of peace shall not
    be removed,"
    says the LORD, who has compassion
      on you.

11 "O afflicted one, storm-tossed and not
    comforted,
  behold, I will set your stones in
    antimony,
  and lay your foundations with sap-
    phires.
12 I will make your pinnacles of agate,
    your gates of carbuncles,
  and all your wall of precious
    stones.
13 All your children shall be taught by
    the LORD,
  and great shall be the peace of your
    children.

14 In righteousness you shall be established;
   you shall be far from oppression,
     for you shall not fear;
   and from terror, for it shall not
     come near you.
15 If anyone stirs up strife,
   it is not from me;
   whoever stirs up strife with you
     shall fall because of you.
16 Behold, I have created the smith
   who blows the fire of coals
     and produces a weapon for its pur-
     pose.
   I have also created the ravager to
     destroy;
17   no weapon that is fashioned against
     you shall succeed,
   and you shall refute every tongue that
     rises against you in judgment.
   This is the heritage of the servants of
     the LORD
   and their vindication from me,
     declares the LORD."

The Compassion of the LORD

55 "Come, everyone who thirsts,
   come to the waters;
  and he who has no money,
   come, buy and eat!
  Come, buy wine and milk
   without money and without price.
2 Why do you spend your money for
     that which is not bread,
   and your labor for that which does
     not satisfy?
  Listen diligently to me, and eat what
     is good,
   and delight yourselves in rich food.
3 Incline your ear, and come to me;
   hear, that your soul may live;
  and I will make with you an everlast-
     ing covenant,
   my steadfast, sure love for David.
4 Behold, I made him a witness to the
     peoples,
   a leader and commander for the
     peoples.
5 Behold, you shall call a nation that
     you do not know,
   and a nation that did not know you
     shall run to you,
  because of the LORD your God, and of
     the Holy One of Israel,
   for he has glorified you.

6 "Seek the LORD while he may be found;
   call upon him while he is near;
7   let the wicked forsake his way,
   and the unrighteous man his
     thoughts;
  let him return to the LORD, that he
     may have compassion on him,
   and to our God, for he will abun-
     dantly pardon.
8 For my thoughts are not your thoughts,
   neither are your ways my ways,
     declares the LORD.
9 For as the heavens are higher than the
     earth,
   so are my ways higher than your
     ways
   and my thoughts than your thoughts.

10 "For as the rain and the snow come
     down from heaven
   and do not return there but water
     the earth,
  making it bring forth and sprout,
   giving seed to the sower and bread
     to the eater,
11 so shall my word be that goes out
     from my mouth;
   it shall not return to me empty,
  but it shall accomplish that which I
     purpose,
   and shall succeed in the thing for
     which I sent it.

12 "For you shall go out in joy
   and be led forth in peace;
  the mountains and the hills before you
     shall break forth into singing,
   and all the trees of the field shall
     clap their hands.
13 Instead of the thorn shall come up the
     cypress;
   instead of the brier shall come up
     the myrtle;
  and it shall make a name for the LORD,
   an everlasting sign that shall not be
     cut off."

Salvation for Foreigners

56 Thus says the LORD:
   "Keep justice, and do righteous-
     ness,
  for soon my salvation will come,
   and my righteousness be revealed.
2 Blessed is the man who does this,
   and the son of man who holds it fast,

who keeps the Sabbath, not profaning
it,
   and keeps his hand from doing any
   evil."

3 Let not the foreigner who has joined
   himself to the LORD say,
   "The LORD will surely separate me
      from his people";
   and let not the eunuch say,
   "Behold, I am a dry tree."
4 For thus says the LORD:
   "To the eunuchs who keep my Sabbaths,
      who choose the things that
      please me
   and hold fast my covenant,
5 I will give in my house and within my
      walls
   a monument and a name
   better than sons and daughters;

GETTING THE MESSAGE

Keeping the Sabbath was an important
expression of faith for Israelites (56:2).
All of life was organized around the
weekly Sabbath. It also set them apart
from the surrounding nations, none of
whom kept the seventh day of the week
as a holy day.

I will give them an everlasting name
   that shall not be cut off.

6 "And the foreigners who join them-
      selves to the LORD,
   to minister to him, to love the name
      of the LORD,
   and to be his servants,
   everyone who keeps the Sabbath and
      does not profane it,
   and holds fast my covenant—
7 these I will bring to my holy mountain,
   and make them joyful in my house
      of prayer;
   their burnt offerings and their sacri-
      fices
   will be accepted on my altar;
   for my house shall be called a house
      of prayer
   for all peoples."
8 The Lord GOD,
   who gathers the outcasts of Israel,
      declares,

"I will gather yet others to him
   besides those already gathered."

Israel's Irresponsible Leaders

9 All you beasts of the field, come to
      devour—
   all you beasts in the forest.
10 His watchmen are blind;
   they are all without knowledge;
   they are all silent dogs;
      they cannot bark,
   dreaming, lying down,
      loving to slumber.
11 The dogs have a mighty appetite;
      they never have enough.
   But they are shepherds who have no
      understanding;
   they have all turned to their own
      way,
   each to his own gain, one and all.
12 "Come," they say, "let me get wine;
   let us fill ourselves with strong drink;
   and tomorrow will be like this day,
      great beyond measure."

Israel's Futile Idolatry

57 The righteous man perishes,
   and no one lays it to heart;
   devout men are taken away,
      while no one understands.
   For the righteous man is taken away
      from calamity;
2   he enters into peace;
   they rest in their beds
   who walk in their uprightness.
3 But you, draw near,
   sons of the sorceress,
   offspring of the adulterer and the
      loose woman.
4 Whom are you mocking?
   Against whom do you open your
      mouth wide
   and stick out your tongue?
   Are you not children of transgression,
      the offspring of deceit,
5 you who burn with lust among the
      oaks,
   under every green tree,
   who slaughter your children in the
      valleys,
   under the clefts of the rocks?
6 Among the smooth stones of the
      valley is your portion;
   they, they, are your lot;

to them you have poured out a drink
offering,
you have brought a grain offering.
Shall I relent for these things?

7 On a high and lofty mountain
you have set your bed,
and there you went up to offer
sacrifice.

8 Behind the door and the doorpost
you have set up your memorial;
for, deserting me, you have uncovered
your bed,
you have gone up to it,
you have made it wide;
and you have made a covenant for
yourself with them,
you have loved their bed,
you have looked on nakedness.

9 You journeyed to the king with oil
and multiplied your perfumes;
you sent your envoys far off,
and sent down even to Sheol.

10 You were wearied with the length of
your way,
but you did not say, "It is hopeless";
you found new life for your strength,
and so you were not faint.

11 Whom did you dread and fear,
so that you lied,
and did not remember me,
did not lay it to heart?
Have I not held my peace, even for a
long time,
and you do not fear me?

12 I will declare your righteousness and
your deeds,
but they will not profit you.

13 When you cry out, let your collection
of idols deliver you!
The wind will carry them all off,
a breath will take them away.
But he who takes refuge in me shall
possess the land
and shall inherit my holy mountain.

Comfort for the Contrite

14 And it shall be said,
"Build up, build up, prepare the way,
remove every obstruction from my
people's way."

15 For thus says the One who is high and
lifted up,
who inhabits eternity, whose name
is Holy:

"I dwell in the high and holy place,
and also with him who is of a con-
trite and lowly spirit,
to revive the spirit of the lowly,
and to revive the heart of the con-
trite.

16 For I will not contend forever,
nor will I always be angry;
for the spirit would grow faint before
me,
and the breath of life that I made.

17 Because of the iniquity of his unjust
gain I was angry,
I struck him; I hid my face and was
angry,
but he went on backsliding in the
way of his own heart.

18 I have seen his ways, but I will heal
him;
I will lead him and restore comfort
to him and his mourners,

19 creating the fruit of the lips.
Peace, peace, to the far and to the
near," says the LORD,
"and I will heal him.

20 But the wicked are like the tossing sea;
for it cannot be quiet,
and its waters toss up mire and dirt.

21 There is no peace," says my God, "for
the wicked."

True and False Fasting

58 "Cry aloud; do not hold back;
lift up your voice like a trumpet;
declare to my people their transgression,
to the house of Jacob their sins.

2 Yet they seek me daily
and delight to know my ways,
as if they were a nation that did righteousness
and did not forsake the judgment of
their God;
they ask of me righteous judgments;
they delight to draw near to God.

3 'Why have we fasted, and you see it not?
Why have we humbled ourselves,
and you take no knowledge of it?'
Behold, in the day of your fast you
seek your own pleasure,
and oppress all your workers.

4 Behold, you fast only to quarrel and to
fight
and to hit with a wicked fist.

Fasting like yours this day
   will not make your voice to be
      heard on high.
5 Is such the fast that I choose,
   a day for a person to humble him-
      self?
Is it to bow down his head like a reed,
   and to spread sackcloth and ashes
      under him?
Will you call this a fast,
   and a day acceptable to the LORD?
6 "Is not this the fast that I choose:
   to loose the bonds of wickedness,
   to undo the straps of the yoke,
to let the oppressed go free,
   and to break every yoke?
7 Is it not to share your bread with the
      hungry
   and bring the homeless poor into
      your house;

when you see the naked, to cover him,
   and not to hide yourself from your
      own flesh?
8 Then shall your light break forth like
      the dawn,
   and your healing shall spring up
      speedily;
your righteousness shall go before
      you;
   the glory of the LORD shall be your
      rear guard.
9 Then you shall call, and the LORD will
      answer;
   you shall cry, and he will say, 'Here I
      am.'
If you take away the yoke from your
      midst,
   the pointing of the finger, and
      speaking wickedness,
10 if you pour yourself out for the hungry
   and satisfy the desire of the afflicted,

then shall your light rise in the dark-
      ness
   and your gloom be as the noonday.
11 And the LORD will guide you continu-
      ally
   and satisfy your desire in scorched
      places
   and make your bones strong;
and you shall be like a watered garden,
   like a spring of water,
      whose waters do not fail.
12 And your ancient ruins shall be
      rebuilt;
   you shall raise up the foundations
      of many generations;
you shall be called the repairer of the
      breach,
   the restorer of streets to dwell in.
13 "If you turn back your foot from the
      Sabbath,
   from doing your pleasure on my
      holy day,
and call the Sabbath a delight
   and the holy day of the LORD honor-
      able;
if you honor it, not going your own
      ways,
   or seeking your own pleasure, or
      talking idly;
14 then you shall take delight in the LORD,
   and I will make you ride on the
      heights of the earth;
I will feed you with the heritage of
      Jacob your father,
   for the mouth of the LORD has spo-
      ken."

Evil and Oppression

59 Behold, the LORD's hand is not
      shortened, that it cannot save,
   or his ear dull, that it cannot hear;
2 but your iniquities have made a sepa-
      ration
   between you and your God,
and your sins have hidden his face
      from you
   so that he does not hear.
3 For your hands are defiled with blood
   and your fingers with iniquity;
your lips have spoken lies;
   your tongue mutters wickedness.
4 No one enters suit justly;
   no one goes to law honestly;

they rely on empty pleas, they speak lies,
  they conceive mischief and give birth to iniquity.
5 They hatch adders' eggs;
  they weave the spider's web;
he who eats their eggs dies,
  and from one that is crushed a viper is hatched.
6 Their webs will not serve as clothing;
  men will not cover themselves with what they make.
Their works are works of iniquity,
  and deeds of violence are in their hands.
7 Their feet run to evil,
  and they are swift to shed innocent blood;
their thoughts are thoughts of iniquity;
  desolation and destruction are in their highways.
8 The way of peace they do not know,
  and there is no justice in their paths;
they have made their roads crooked;
  no one who treads on them knows peace.

9 Therefore justice is far from us,
  and righteousness does not overtake us;
we hope for light, and behold, darkness,
  and for brightness, but we walk in gloom.
10 We grope for the wall like the blind;
  we grope like those who have no eyes;
we stumble at noon as in the twilight,
  among those in full vigor we are like dead men.
11 We all growl like bears;
  we moan and moan like doves;
we hope for justice, but there is none;
  for salvation, but it is far from us.
12 For our transgressions are multiplied before you,
  and our sins testify against us;
for our transgressions are with us,
  and we know our iniquities:
13 transgressing, and denying the LORD,
  and turning back from following our God,
speaking oppression and revolt,
  conceiving and uttering from the heart lying words.

Judgment and Redemption

14 Justice is turned back,
  and righteousness stands far away;
for truth has stumbled in the public squares,
  and uprightness cannot enter.
15 Truth is lacking,
  and he who departs from evil makes himself a prey.

The LORD saw it, and it displeased him
  that there was no justice.
16 He saw that there was no man,
  and wondered that there was no one to intercede;
then his own arm brought him salvation,
  and his righteousness upheld him.
17 He put on righteousness as a breastplate,
  and a helmet of salvation on his head;
he put on garments of vengeance for clothing,
  and wrapped himself in zeal as a cloak.
18 According to their deeds, so will he repay,
  wrath to his adversaries, repayment to his enemies;
  to the coastlands he will render repayment.
19 So they shall fear the name of the LORD from the west,
  and his glory from the rising of the sun;
for he will come like a rushing stream,
  which the wind of the LORD drives.

20 "And a Redeemer will come to Zion,
  to those in Jacob who turn from transgression," declares the LORD.

21 "And as for me, this is my covenant with them," says the LORD: "My Spirit that is upon you, and my words that I have put in your mouth, shall not depart out of your mouth, or out of the mouth of your offspring, or out of the mouth of your children's offspring," says the LORD, "from this time forth and forevermore."

The Future Glory of Israel

60

Arise, shine, for your light has come,
and the glory of the LORD has risen
upon you.
2 For behold, darkness shall cover the
earth,
and thick darkness the peoples;
but the LORD will arise upon you,
and his glory will be seen upon you.
3 And nations shall come to your light,
and kings to the brightness of your
rising.

4 Lift up your eyes all around, and see;
they all gather together, they come
to you;
your sons shall come from afar,
and your daughters shall be carried
on the hip.

GETTING THE MESSAGE

The phrase **ships of Tarshish** (60:9)
describes huge ships, able to go on
voyages as long as three years (1 Kings
10:22). Isaiah says that ships like these
will someday bring the nations to Israel
to worship the Lord.

5 Then you shall see and be radiant;
your heart shall thrill and exult,
because the abundance of the sea
shall be turned to you,
the wealth of the nations shall
come to you.
6 A multitude of camels shall cover you,
the young camels of Midian and
Ephah;
all those from Sheba shall come.
They shall bring gold and frankincense,
and shall bring good news, the
praises of the LORD.
7 All the flocks of Kedar shall be gathered to you;
the rams of Nebaioth shall minister
to you;
they shall come up with acceptance
on my altar,
and I will beautify my beautiful
house.
8 Who are these that fly like a cloud,
and like doves to their windows?

9 For the coastlands shall hope for me,
the ships of Tarshish first,
to bring your children from afar,
their silver and gold with them,
for the name of the LORD your God,
and for the Holy One of Israel,
because he has made you beautiful.
10 Foreigners shall build up your walls,
and their kings shall minister to you;
for in my wrath I struck you,
but in my favor I have had mercy on
you.
11 Your gates shall be open continually;
day and night they shall not be shut,
that people may bring to you the
wealth of the nations,
with their kings led in procession.
12 For the nation and kingdom
that will not serve you shall perish;
those nations shall be utterly laid
waste.
13 The glory of Lebanon shall come to you,
the cypress, the plane, and the pine,
to beautify the place of my sanctuary,
and I will make the place of my feet
glorious.
14 The sons of those who afflicted you
shall come bending low to you,
and all who despised you
shall bow down at your feet;
they shall call you the City of the LORD,
the Zion of the Holy One of Israel.

15 Whereas you have been forsaken and
hated,
with no one passing through,
I will make you majestic forever,
a joy from age to age.
16 You shall suck the milk of nations;
you shall nurse at the breast of kings;
and you shall know that I, the LORD,
am your Savior
and your Redeemer, the Mighty One
of Jacob.
17 Instead of bronze I will bring gold,
and instead of iron I will bring silver;
instead of wood, bronze,
instead of stones, iron.
I will make your overseers peace
and your taskmasters righteousness.
18 Violence shall no more be heard in
your land,
devastation or destruction within
your borders;

you shall call your walls Salvation,
    and your gates Praise.
19 The sun shall be no more
        your light by day,
    nor for brightness shall the moon
        give you light;
    but the LORD will be your everlasting
        light,
        and your God will be your glory.
20 Your sun shall no more go down,
        nor your moon withdraw itself;
    for the LORD will be your everlasting
        light,
        and your days of mourning shall be
            ended.
21 Your people shall all be righteous;
        they shall possess the land forever,
    the branch of my planting, the work
        of my hands,
        that I might be glorified.
22 The least one shall become a clan,
        and the smallest one a mighty
            nation;
    I am the LORD;
        in its time I will hasten it.

The Year of the LORD's Favor

61 The Spirit of the Lord GOD is upon
        me,
    because the LORD has anointed me
    to bring good news to the poor;
        he has sent me to bind up the bro-
            kenhearted,
    to proclaim liberty to the captives,
        and the opening of the prison to
            those who are bound;
2   to proclaim the year of the LORD's
        favor,
        and the day of vengeance of our God;
        to comfort all who mourn;
3   to grant to those who mourn in Zion—
        to give them a beautiful headdress
            instead of ashes,
    the oil of gladness instead of mourn-
        ing,
        the garment of praise instead of a
            faint spirit;
    that they may be called oaks of righ-
        teousness,
        the planting of the LORD, that he
            may be glorified.
4   They shall build up the ancient ruins;
        they shall raise up the former dev-
            astations;

they shall repair the ruined cities,
    the devastations of many genera-
        tions.
5   Strangers shall stand and tend your
        flocks;
        foreigners shall be your plowmen
            and vinedressers;
6   but you shall be called the priests of
        the LORD;
        they shall speak of you as the min-
            isters of our God;
    you shall eat the wealth of the nations,
        and in their glory you shall boast.
7   Instead of your shame there shall be a
        double portion;
        instead of dishonor they shall
            rejoice in their lot;
    therefore in their land they shall pos-
        sess a double portion;
        they shall have everlasting joy.

8   For I the LORD love justice;
        I hate robbery and wrong;
    I will faithfully give them their rec-
        ompense,
        and I will make an everlasting cov-
            enant with them.
9   Their offspring shall be known among
        the nations,
        and their descendants in the midst
            of the peoples;
    all who see them shall acknowledge
        them,
        that they are an offspring the LORD
            has blessed.
10 I will greatly rejoice in the LORD;
        my soul shall exult in my God,
    for he has clothed me with the gar-
        ments of salvation;
        he has covered me with the robe of
            righteousness,
    as a bridegroom decks himself like a
        priest with a beautiful headdress,
        and as a bride adorns herself with
            her jewels.

11   For as the earth brings forth its sprouts,
     and as a garden causes what is
        sown in it to sprout up,
  so the Lord GOD will cause righteous-
     ness and praise
     to sprout up before all the nations.

Zion's Coming Salvation

62 For Zion's sake I will not keep
    silent,
  and for Jerusalem's sake I will not
    be quiet,
until her righteousness goes forth as
    brightness,
  and her salvation as a burning torch.
2   The nations shall see your righteous-
    ness,
  and all the kings your glory,
and you shall be called by a new
    name
    that the mouth of the LORD will
     give.
3   You shall be a crown of beauty in the
    hand of the LORD,
  and a royal diadem in the hand of
    your God.
4   You shall no more be termed Forsaken,
  and your land shall no more be
    termed Desolate,
but you shall be called My Delight Is
    in Her,
  and your land Married;
for the LORD delights in you,
  and your land shall be married.
5   For as a young man marries a young
    woman,
  so shall your sons marry you,
and as the bridegroom rejoices over
    the bride,
  so shall your God rejoice over you.
6   On your walls, O Jerusalem,
  I have set watchmen;
all the day and all the night
  they shall never be silent.
You who put the LORD in remem-
    brance,
  take no rest,
7   and give him no rest
  until he establishes Jerusalem
  and makes it a praise in the earth.
8   The LORD has sworn by his right hand
  and by his mighty arm:
"I will not again give your grain
  to be food for your enemies,

and foreigners shall not drink your
    wine
  for which you have labored;
9   but those who garner it shall eat it
  and praise the LORD,
and those who gather it shall drink it
  in the courts of my sanctuary."

10   Go through, go through the gates;
  prepare the way for the people;
build up, build up the highway;
  clear it of stones;
  lift up a signal over the peoples.
11   Behold, the LORD has proclaimed
  to the end of the earth:
Say to the daughter of Zion,
  "Behold, your salvation comes;
behold, his reward is with him,
  and his recompense before him."
12   And they shall be called The Holy
    People,
  The Redeemed of the LORD;
and you shall be called Sought Out,
  A City Not Forsaken.

The LORD's Day of Vengeance

63 Who is this who comes from
    Edom,
  in crimsoned garments from Bozrah,
he who is splendid in his apparel,
  marching in the greatness of his
    strength?
"It is I, speaking in righteousness,
  mighty to save."

2   Why is your apparel red,
  and your garments like his who
    treads in the winepress?

3   "I have trodden the winepress alone,
  and from the peoples no one was
    with me;
I trod them in my anger
  and trampled them in my wrath;
their lifeblood spattered on my gar-
    ments,
  and stained all my apparel.
4   For the day of vengeance was in my
    heart,
  and my year of redemption had
    come.
5   I looked, but there was no one to help;
  I was appalled, but there was no
    one to uphold;
so my own arm brought me salvation,
  and my wrath upheld me.

6 I trampled down the peoples in my
    anger;
  I made them drunk in my wrath,
  and I poured out their lifeblood on
    the earth."

The Lord's Mercy Remembered

7 I will recount the steadfast love of the
    Lord,
  the praises of the Lord,
  according to all that the Lord has
    granted us,
  and the great goodness to the house
    of Israel
  that he has granted them according to
    his compassion,
  according to the abundance of his
    steadfast love.
8 For he said, "Surely they are my people,
  children who will not deal falsely."
  And he became their Savior.
9 In all their affliction he was afflicted,
  and the angel of his presence saved
    them;
  in his love and in his pity he
    redeemed them;
  he lifted them up and carried them
    all the days of old.

10 But they rebelled
  and grieved his Holy Spirit;
  therefore he turned to be their enemy,
  and himself fought against them.
11 Then he remembered the days of old,
    of Moses and his people.
  Where is he who brought them up out
    of the sea
  with the shepherds of his flock?
  Where is he who put in the midst of
    them
  his Holy Spirit,
12 who caused his glorious arm
  to go at the right hand of Moses,
  who divided the waters before them
  to make for himself an everlasting
    name,
13 who led them through the depths?
  Like a horse in the desert,
  they did not stumble.
14 Like livestock that go down into the
    valley,
  the Spirit of the Lord gave them rest.
  So you led your people,
  to make for yourself a glorious name.

Prayer for Mercy

15 Look down from heaven and see,
  from your holy and beautiful habi-
    tation.
  Where are your zeal and your might?
  The stirring of your inner parts and
    your compassion
  are held back from me.
16 For you are our Father,
  though Abraham does not know us,
  and Israel does not acknowledge us;
  you, O Lord, are our Father,
  our Redeemer from of old is your
    name.
17 O Lord, why do you make us wander
    from your ways
  and harden our heart, so that we
    fear you not?
  Return for the sake of your servants,
  the tribes of your heritage.
18 Your holy people held possession for
    a little while;
  our adversaries have trampled
    down your sanctuary.
19 We have become like those over
    whom you have never ruled,
  like those who are not called by
    your name.

64 Oh that you would rend the
  heavens and come down,
  that the mountains might quake at
    your presence—
2 as when fire kindles brushwood
  and the fire causes water to boil—
  to make your name known to your
    adversaries,
  and that the nations might tremble
    at your presence!
3 When you did awesome things that
    we did not look for,
  you came down, the mountains
    quaked at your presence.
4 From of old no one has heard
  or perceived by the ear,
  no eye has seen a God besides you,
  who acts for those who wait for him.
5 You meet him who joyfully works
    righteousness,
  those who remember you in your
    ways.
  Behold, you were angry, and we
    sinned;
  in our sins we have been a long
    time, and shall we be saved?

⁶ We have all become like one who is unclean,
  and all our righteous deeds are like a polluted garment.
We all fade like a leaf,
  and our iniquities, like the wind, take us away.
⁷ There is no one who calls upon your name,
  who rouses himself to take hold of you;
for you have hidden your face from us,
  and have made us melt in the hand of our iniquities.

⁸ But now, O LORD, you are our Father;
  we are the clay, and you are our potter;
  we are all the work of your hand.

> **GETTING THE MESSAGE**
>
> The Israelites were not the only ones who did not eat or sacrifice **pig flesh**. The Assyrians found the pig to be equally offensive. However, many other people groups ate and sacrificed them to their gods (65:4).

⁹ Be not so terribly angry, O LORD,
  and remember not iniquity forever.
  Behold, please look, we are all your people.
¹⁰ Your holy cities have become a wilderness;
  Zion has become a wilderness,
  Jerusalem a desolation.
¹¹ Our holy and beautiful house,
  where our fathers praised you,
has been burned by fire,
  and all our pleasant places have become ruins.
¹² Will you restrain yourself at these things, O LORD?
  Will you keep silent, and afflict us so terribly?

Judgment and Salvation

65 I was ready to be sought by those who did not ask for me;
  I was ready to be found by those who did not seek me.

I said, "Here I am, here I am,"
  to a nation that was not called by my name.
² I spread out my hands all the day
  to a rebellious people,
who walk in a way that is not good,
  following their own devices;
³ a people who provoke me
  to my face continually,
sacrificing in gardens
  and making offerings on bricks;
⁴ who sit in tombs,
  and spend the night in secret places;
who eat pig's flesh,
  and broth of tainted meat is in their vessels;
⁵ who say, "Keep to yourself,
  do not come near me, for I am too holy for you."
These are a smoke in my nostrils,
  a fire that burns all the day.
⁶ Behold, it is written before me:
  "I will not keep silent, but I will repay;
I will indeed repay into their lap
⁷   both your iniquities and your fathers' iniquities together,
            says the LORD;
because they made offerings on the mountains
  and insulted me on the hills,
I will measure into their lap
  payment for their former deeds."

⁸ Thus says the LORD:
"As the new wine is found in the cluster,
  and they say, 'Do not destroy it,
  for there is a blessing in it,'
so I will do for my servants' sake,
  and not destroy them all.
⁹ I will bring forth offspring from Jacob,
  and from Judah possessors of my mountains;
my chosen shall possess it,
  and my servants shall dwell there.
¹⁰ Sharon shall become a pasture for flocks,
  and the Valley of Achor a place for herds to lie down,
  for my people who have sought me.
¹¹ But you who forsake the LORD,
  who forget my holy mountain,
who set a table for Fortune
  and fill cups of mixed wine for Destiny,

12 I will destine you to the sword,
      and all of you shall bow down to the
         slaughter,
    because, when I called, you did not
         answer;
      when I spoke, you did not listen,
    but you did what was evil in my eyes
      and chose what I did not delight in."

13 Therefore thus says the Lord God:
    "Behold, my servants shall eat,
      but you shall be hungry;
    behold, my servants shall drink,
      but you shall be thirsty;
    behold, my servants shall rejoice,
      but you shall be put to shame;
14 behold, my servants shall sing for
         gladness of heart,
      but you shall cry out for pain of heart
      and shall wail for breaking of spirit.
15 You shall leave your name to my cho-
         sen for a curse,
      and the Lord God will put you to
         death,
      but his servants he will call by
         another name.
16 So that he who blesses himself in the
         land
      shall bless himself by the God of
         truth,
    and he who takes an oath in the land
      shall swear by the God of truth;
    because the former troubles are for-
         gotten
      and are hidden from my eyes.

New Heavens and a New Earth

17 "For behold, I create new heavens
      and a new earth,
    and the former things shall not be
         remembered
      or come into mind.
18 But be glad and rejoice forever
      in that which I create;
    for behold, I create Jerusalem to be a joy,
      and her people to be a gladness.
19 I will rejoice in Jerusalem
      and be glad in my people;
    no more shall be heard in it the sound
         of weeping
      and the cry of distress.
20 No more shall there be in it
      an infant who lives but a few days,
      or an old man who does not fill out
         his days,

    for the young man shall die a hundred
         years old,
      and the sinner a hundred years old
         shall be accursed.
21 They shall build houses and inhabit
         them;
      they shall plant vineyards and eat
         their fruit.
22 They shall not build and another
         inhabit;
      they shall not plant and another eat;
    for like the days of a tree shall the
         days of my people be,
      and my chosen shall long enjoy the
         work of their hands.
23 They shall not labor in vain
      or bear children for calamity,
    for they shall be the offspring of the
         blessed of the Lord,
      and their descendants with them.
24 Before they call I will answer;
      while they are yet speaking I will
         hear.
25 The wolf and the lamb shall graze
         together;
      the lion shall eat straw like the ox,
      and dust shall be the serpent's food.
    They shall not hurt or destroy
    in all my holy mountain,"
                          says the Lord.

The Humble and Contrite in Spirit

66 Thus says the Lord:
    "Heaven is my throne,
      and the earth is my footstool;
    what is the house that you would
         build for me,
      and what is the place of my rest?
2   All these things my hand has made,
      and so all these things came to be,
                          declares the Lord.
    But this is the one to whom I will look:
      he who is humble and contrite in
         spirit
      and trembles at my word.

3   "He who slaughters an ox is like one
         who kills a man;
      he who sacrifices a lamb, like one
         who breaks a dog's neck;
    he who presents a grain offering, like
         one who offers pig's blood;
      he who makes a memorial offering
         of frankincense, like one who
         blesses an idol.

These have chosen their own ways,
    and their soul delights in their
        abominations;
4 I also will choose harsh treatment for
        them
    and bring their fears upon them,
because when I called, no one
        answered,
    when I spoke, they did not listen;
but they did what was evil in my eyes
    and chose that in which I did not
        delight."

5 Hear the word of the LORD,
    you who tremble at his word:
"Your brothers who hate you
    and cast you out for my name's
        sake
have said, 'Let the LORD be glorified,
    that we may see your joy';
    but it is they who shall be put to
        shame.

GETTING THE MESSAGE

The land of **Javan** was probably the
Ionian region of Greece, which is the
western coast of present-day Turkey.
Isaiah says that even this far-off land
would someday declare God's glory
among the nations (66:19).

6 "The sound of an uproar from the city!
    A sound from the temple!
The sound of the LORD,
    rendering recompense to his ene-
        mies!

Rejoice with Jerusalem
7 "Before she was in labor
        she gave birth;
    before her pain came upon her
        she delivered a son.
8 Who has heard such a thing?
    Who has seen such things?
Shall a land be born in one day?
    Shall a nation be brought forth in
        one moment?
For as soon as Zion was in labor
    she brought forth her children.
9 Shall I bring to the point of birth and
        not cause to bring forth?"
    says the LORD;

"shall I, who cause to bring forth, shut
        the womb?"
    says your God.

10 "Rejoice with Jerusalem, and be glad
        for her,
    all you who love her;
rejoice with her in joy,
    all you who mourn over her;
11 that you may nurse and be satisfied
        from her consoling breast;
    that you may drink deeply with
        delight
    from her glorious abundance."

12 For thus says the LORD:
"Behold, I will extend peace to her like
        a river,
    and the glory of the nations like an
        overflowing stream;
and you shall nurse, you shall be
        carried upon her hip,
    and bounced upon her knees.
13 As one whom his mother comforts,
        so I will comfort you;
    you shall be comforted in
        Jerusalem.
14 You shall see, and your heart shall
        rejoice;
    your bones shall flourish like the
        grass;
and the hand of the LORD shall be
        known to his servants,
    and he shall show his indignation
        against his enemies.

Final Judgment and Glory of the LORD
15 "For behold, the LORD will come in
        fire,
    and his chariots like the whirlwind,
to render his anger in fury,
    and his rebuke with flames of fire.
16 For by fire will the LORD enter into
        judgment,
    and by his sword, with all flesh;
    and those slain by the LORD shall be
        many.

17 "Those who sanctify and purify themselves to go into the gardens, following
one in the midst, eating pig's flesh and the
abomination and mice, shall come to an end
together, declares the LORD.
18 "For I know their works and their
thoughts, and the time is coming to gather
all nations and tongues. And they shall

come and shall see my glory, ¹⁹ and I will set a sign among them. And from them I will send survivors to the nations, to Tarshish, Pul, and Lud, who draw the bow, to Tubal and Javan, to the coastlands far away, that have not heard my fame or seen my glory. And they shall declare my glory among the nations. ²⁰ And they shall bring all your brothers from all the nations as an offering to the LORD, on horses and in chariots and in litters and on mules and on dromedaries, to my holy mountain Jerusalem, says the LORD, just as the Israelites bring their grain offering in a clean vessel to the house of the LORD. ²¹ And some of them also I will take for priests and for Levites, says the LORD.

²² "For as the new heavens and the new
    earth
    that I make
shall remain before me, says the LORD,
    so shall your offspring and your
    name remain.
²³ From new moon to new moon,
    and from Sabbath to Sabbath,
all flesh shall come to worship before
    me,
declares the LORD.

²⁴ "And they shall go out and look on the dead bodies of the men who have rebelled against me. For their worm shall not die, their fire shall not be quenched, and they shall be an abhorrence to all flesh."

INTRODUCTION TO JEREMIAH

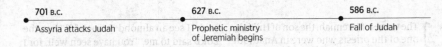

701 B.C.	627 B.C.	586 B.C.
Assyria attacks Judah	Prophetic ministry of Jeremiah begins	Fall of Judah

AUTHOR AND DATE

Jeremiah was called to be a prophet c. 627 B.C., when he was young (1:6). He served for more than 40 years (1:2–3). Jeremiah had a difficult life. His messages of repentance delivered at the temple were not well received (7:1–8:3; 26:1–11). His hometown plotted against him (11:18–23), and he endured much persecution (20:1–6; 37:11–38:13; 43:1–7). At God's command, he never married (16:1–4). Although he preached God's word faithfully, he apparently had only two converts: Baruch, his scribe (32:12; 36:1–4; 45:1–5); and Ebed-melech, an Ethiopian eunuch who served the king (38:7–13; 39:15–18). Though the book does not reveal the time or place of Jeremiah's death, he probably died in Egypt, where he had been taken by his countrymen against his will after the fall of Jerusalem (43:1–7). He most likely did not live to see the devastation he mentions in chs. 46–51.

PURPOSE

Jeremiah and Baruch left a record of the difficult times in which they lived, God's message for those times, and God's message for the future of Israel and the nations.

KEY THEMES

1. *God and humanity.* God alone is a living God. God alone made the world. All other so-called gods are mere idols (10:1–16). This Creator God called Israel to a special relationship (chs. 2–6), gave her his holy word, and promised to bless her temple with his name and presence (7:1–8:3). God rules both the present and the future (1:4–16; 29:1–10), protects his chosen ones (1:17–19; 29:11–14; 39:15–18; 45:1–5), and saves those who turn to him (12:14–17). Because God is absolutely trustworthy and always keeps his promises, his grace triumphs over sin and judgment when people repent and turn to him.

The human heart is sick, and no one except God can cure it (17:9–10). The nations worship idols instead of their Creator (10:1–16). Israel, God's covenant people, went after other gods (chs. 2–6), defiled the temple by their unwillingness to repent (7:1–8:3; 26:1–11), and oppressed one another (34:8–16). Since Israel and the nations have sinned against God (25:1–26), God the Creator is also the *Judge* of every nation on the earth he created (chs. 46–51).

2. *Old covenant, Messiah, and new covenant.* God made a covenant with Israel, based on his promises to Abraham, Isaac, and Jacob (Genesis 12–50). As time passed, God's covenant with Israel included his promise to David of an eternal kingdom (2 Samuel 7; 1 Chronicles 17). God used Jeremiah to deliver the good news that God would one day "make a new covenant with the house of Israel and the house of Judah" (Jer. 31:31). This covenant would be different in one major way. The new covenant partners would not break the covenant, as most of the old partners did even though God was completely faithful (31:32). Instead, the new covenant partners would have the word of God so ingrained in their hearts through God's power that they would know and follow God all their lives (31:33–34).

Thus, all the new covenant partners would be believers who were forgiven and empowered by God; he would "remember their sin no more" (31:34). Hebrews 8:8–12 quotes Jer. 31:31–34 as evidence that the new covenant has come through the life, death, and resurrection of Jesus Christ. The coming of Jesus the Messiah fulfills God's promises to Abraham, Moses, David, and the prophets.

OUTLINE

JEREMIAH

1 The words of Jeremiah, the son of Hilkiah, one of the priests who were in Anathoth in the land of Benjamin, ²to whom the word of the LORD came in the days of Josiah the son of Amon, king of Judah, in the thirteenth year of his reign. ³It came also in the days of Jehoiakim the son of Josiah, king of Judah, and until the end of the eleventh year of Zedekiah, the son of Josiah, king of Judah, until the captivity of Jerusalem in the fifth month.

The Call of Jeremiah

⁴Now the word of the LORD came to me, saying,

⁵ "Before I formed you in the womb I
        knew you,
    and before you were born I conse-
        crated you;
    I appointed you a prophet to the
        nations."

⁶Then I said, "Ah, Lord GOD! Behold, I do not know how to speak, for I am only a youth." ⁷But the LORD said to me,

    "Do not say, 'I am only a youth';
        for to all to whom I send you, you
            shall go,
    and whatever I command you, you
        shall speak.
⁸   Do not be afraid of them,
        for I am with you to deliver you,
            declares the LORD."

⁹Then the LORD put out his hand and touched my mouth. And the LORD said to me,

    "Behold, I have put my words in your
        mouth.
¹⁰   See, I have set you this day over
        nations and over kingdoms,
    to pluck up and to break down,
    to destroy and to overthrow,
    to build and to plant."

¹¹And the word of the LORD came to me, saying, "Jeremiah, what do you see?" And I said, "I see an almond¹ branch." ¹²Then the LORD said to me, "You have seen well, for I am watching over my word to perform it."

¹³The word of the LORD came to me a second time, saying, "What do you see?" And I said, "I see a boiling pot, facing away from the north." ¹⁴Then the LORD said to me, "Out of the north disaster² shall be let loose upon all the inhabitants of the land. ¹⁵For behold, I am calling all the tribes of the kingdoms of the north, declares the LORD, and they shall come, and every one

> ### GETTING THE MESSAGE
>
> **Watching like an almond tree.**
> The Hebrew words for "almond" and "watching" are very similar. Because the almond tree was the first tree to bud in spring, it was said to be "watching for spring." God used the almond branch to teach Jeremiah that he is always watching over his word (1:11–12), so Jeremiah can trust him.

shall set his throne at the entrance of the gates of Jerusalem, against all its walls all around and against all the cities of Judah. ¹⁶And I will declare my judgments against them, for all their evil in forsaking me. They have made offerings to other gods and worshiped the works of their own hands. ¹⁷But you, dress yourself for work; arise, and say to them everything that I command you. Do not be dismayed by them, lest I dismay you before them. ¹⁸And I, behold, I make you this day a fortified city, an iron pillar, and bronze walls, against the whole land, against the kings of Judah, its officials, its priests, and the people of the land. ¹⁹They will fight against you, but they shall not prevail against you, for I am with you, declares the LORD, to deliver you."

¹ *Almond* sounds like the Hebrew for *watching* (compare 1:12) ² The Hebrew word can mean *evil, harm,* or *disaster,* depending on the context; so throughout Jeremiah

Israel Forsakes the LORD

2 The word of the LORD came to me, saying, ² "Go and proclaim in the hearing of Jerusalem, Thus says the LORD,

> "I remember the devotion of your
>   youth,
>   your love as a bride,
> how you followed me in the wilderness,
>   in a land not sown.

PROFILE

JEREMIAH

Jeremiah was born in Anathoth, a small town outside of Jerusalem. Called by God as a young man, he served as a prophet for more than 40 years. Jeremiah had a difficult life. By God's command, he never married, and he apparently had only two converts during his entire ministry. The nation of Judah did not respond favorably to his messages of repentance. He was scorned in his own hometown and even falsely imprisoned on charges that he was collaborating with the Babylonian invaders. Like many of the Lord's prophets, Jeremiah suffered public mockery and physical abuse. Yet God used his faithful servant to deliver the good news that in future days God would make a new, unbreakable covenant with his people (31:31). Hebrews 8:8–12 quotes Jeremiah 31:31–34 as evidence that this new covenant has come through the life, death, and resurrection of Jesus Christ.

KEY REFERENCE: JEREMIAH 31:31–34

³ Israel was holy to the LORD,
>   the firstfruits of his harvest.
> All who ate of it incurred guilt;
>   disaster came upon them,
>   declares the LORD."

⁴ Hear the word of the LORD, O house of Jacob, and all the clans of the house of Israel. ⁵ Thus says the LORD:

> "What wrong did your fathers find
>   in me
> that they went far from me,

and went after worthlessness, and
    became worthless?
⁶ They did not say, 'Where is the LORD
    who brought us up from the land of
        Egypt,
who led us in the wilderness,
    in a land of deserts and pits,
in a land of drought and deep darkness,
    in a land that none passes through,
    where no man dwells?'
⁷ And I brought you into a plentiful land
    to enjoy its fruits and its good
        things.
But when you came in, you defiled my
    land
    and made my heritage an abomination.
⁸ The priests did not say, 'Where is the
    LORD?'
Those who handle the law did not
    know me;

GETTING THE MESSAGE

Fresh water that flows from a spring or stream was known as **living water** in Palestine (2:12–13). It was the best and purest water. Jesus says that he is the source of true living water (John 4:10–14; 7:38).

the shepherds transgressed against me;
    the prophets prophesied by Baal
and went after things that do not
    profit.
⁹ "Therefore I still contend with you,
        declares the LORD,
    and with your children's children I
        will contend.
¹⁰ For cross to the coasts of Cyprus and
        see,
    or send to Kedar and examine with
        care;
    see if there has been such a thing.
¹¹ Has a nation changed its gods,
    even though they are no gods?
But my people have changed their glory
    for that which does not profit.
¹² Be appalled, O heavens, at this;
    be shocked, be utterly desolate,
        declares the LORD,
¹³ for my people have committed two
        evils:

they have forsaken me,
   the fountain of living waters,
and hewed out cisterns for themselves,
   broken cisterns that can hold no
      water.

14 "Is Israel a slave? Is he a homeborn
      servant?
   Why then has he become a prey?
15 The lions have roared against him;
   they have roared loudly.
They have made his land a waste;
   his cities are in ruins, without
      inhabitant.
16 Moreover, the men of Memphis and
      Tahpanhes
   have shaved the crown of your head.
17 Have you not brought this upon your-
      self
   by forsaking the LORD your God,
   when he led you in the way?
18 And now what do you gain by going to
      Egypt
   to drink the waters of the Nile?
Or what do you gain by going to Assyria
   to drink the waters of the Euphrates?
19 Your evil will chastise you,
   and your apostasy will reprove you.
Know and see that it is evil and bitter
   for you to forsake the LORD your God;
   the fear of me is not in you,
      declares the Lord GOD of hosts.

20 "For long ago I broke your yoke
   and burst your bonds;
   but you said, 'I will not serve.'
Yes, on every high hill
   and under every green tree
   you bowed down like a whore.
21 Yet I planted you a choice vine,
   wholly of pure seed.
How then have you turned degenerate
   and become a wild vine?
22 Though you wash yourself with lye
   and use much soap,
   the stain of your guilt is still before
      me,
      declares the Lord GOD.
23 How can you say, 'I am not unclean,
   I have not gone after the Baals'?
Look at your way in the valley;
   know what you have done—
a restless young camel running here
      and there,
24   a wild donkey used to the wilder-
      ness,

in her heat sniffing the wind!
   Who can restrain her lust?
None who seek her need weary them-
      selves;
   in her month they will find her.
25 Keep your feet from going unshod
   and your throat from thirst.
But you said, 'It is hopeless,
   for I have loved foreigners,
   and after them I will go.'

26 "As a thief is shamed when caught,
   so the house of Israel shall be
      shamed:
they, their kings, their officials,
   their priests, and their prophets,
27 who say to a tree, 'You are my father,'
   and to a stone, 'You gave me birth.'
For they have turned their back to me,
   and not their face.
But in the time of their trouble they
      say,
   'Arise and save us!'
28 But where are your gods
   that you made for yourself?
Let them arise, if they can save you,
   in your time of trouble;
for as many as your cities
   are your gods, O Judah.

29 "Why do you contend with me?
   You have all transgressed against me,
      declares the LORD.
30 In vain have I struck your children;
   they took no correction;
your own sword devoured your
      prophets
   like a ravening lion.
31 And you, O generation, behold the
      word of the LORD.
Have I been a wilderness to Israel,
   or a land of thick darkness?
Why then do my people say, 'We are
      free,
   we will come no more to you'?
32 Can a virgin forget her ornaments,
   or a bride her attire?
Yet my people have forgotten me
   days without number.

33 "How well you direct your course
   to seek love!
So that even to wicked women
   you have taught your ways.
34 Also on your skirts is found
   the lifeblood of the guiltless poor;

you did not find them breaking in.
    Yet in spite of all these things
35 you say, 'I am innocent;
    surely his anger has turned from me.'
Behold, I will bring you to judgment
    for saying, 'I have not sinned.'
36 How much you go about,
    changing your way!
You shall be put to shame by Egypt
    as you were put to shame by
      Assyria.
37 From it too you will come away
    with your hands on your head,
for the LORD has rejected those in
      whom you trust,
    and you will not prosper by them.

3 "If a man divorces his wife
    and she goes from him
and becomes another man's wife,
    will he return to her?

▶ GETTING THE MESSAGE

Jeremiah lived during **troubled times**.
He became a prophet during the reign
of Josiah, who was the last faithful king
in Judah's history. Josiah's death marked
the beginning of the end for the nation
of Judah. It would fall within two short
decades.

Would not that land be greatly pol-
    luted?
You have played the whore with many
    lovers;
    and would you return to me?
        declares the LORD.
2 Lift up your eyes to the bare heights,
    and see!
    Where have you not been ravished?
By the waysides you have sat awaiting
    lovers
    like an Arab in the wilderness.
You have polluted the land
    with your vile whoredom.
3 Therefore the showers have been
    withheld,
    and the spring rain has not come;
yet you have the forehead of a whore;
    you refuse to be ashamed.
4 Have you not just now called to me,
    'My father, you are the friend of my
      youth—

5 will he be angry forever,
    will he be indignant to the end?'
Behold, you have spoken,
    but you have done all the evil that
      you could."

Faithless Israel Called to Repentance

6 The LORD said to me in the days of King
Josiah: "Have you seen what she did, that
faithless one, Israel, how she went up on
every high hill and under every green tree,
and there played the whore? 7 And I thought,
'After she has done all this she will return to
me,' but she did not return, and her treacherous sister Judah saw it. 8 She saw that
for all the adulteries of that faithless one,
Israel, I had sent her away with a decree of
divorce. Yet her treacherous sister Judah did
not fear, but she too went and played the
whore. 9 Because she took her whoredom
lightly, she polluted the land, committing
adultery with stone and tree. 10 Yet for all
this her treacherous sister Judah did not
return to me with her whole heart, but in
pretense, declares the LORD."

11 And the LORD said to me, "Faithless
Israel has shown herself more righteous
than treacherous Judah. 12 Go, and proclaim
these words toward the north, and say,

"'Return, faithless Israel,
        declares the LORD.
I will not look on you in anger,
    for I am merciful,
        declares the LORD;
I will not be angry forever.
13 Only acknowledge your guilt,
    that you rebelled against the LORD
      your God
and scattered your favors among for-
      eigners under every green tree,
    and that you have not obeyed my
      voice,
        declares the LORD.
14 Return, O faithless children,
        declares the LORD;
for I am your master;
    I will take you, one from a city and
      two from a family,
    and I will bring you to Zion.

15 "'And I will give you shepherds after my
own heart, who will feed you with knowledge and understanding. 16 And when you
have multiplied and been fruitful in the
land, in those days, declares the LORD, they

shall no more say, "The ark of the covenant of the LORD." It shall not come to mind or be remembered or missed; it shall not be made again. ¹⁷ At that time Jerusalem shall be called the throne of the LORD, and all nations shall gather to it, to the presence of the LORD in Jerusalem, and they shall no more stubbornly follow their own evil heart. ¹⁸ In those days the house of Judah shall join the house of Israel, and together they shall come from the land of the north to the land that I gave your fathers for a heritage.

¹⁹ " 'I said,

How I would set you among my sons,
  and give you a pleasant land,
    a heritage most beautiful of all
      nations.
And I thought you would call me, My
  Father,
    and would not turn from following
      me.
²⁰ Surely, as a treacherous wife leaves
      her husband,
    so have you been treacherous to
      me, O house of Israel,
        declares the LORD.' "
²¹ A voice on the bare heights is heard,
      the weeping and pleading of Israel's
        sons
    because they have perverted their way;
      they have forgotten the LORD their
        God.
²² "Return, O faithless sons;
      I will heal your faithlessness."
    "Behold, we come to you,
      for you are the LORD our God.
²³ Truly the hills are a delusion,
      the orgies on the mountains.
    Truly in the LORD our God
      is the salvation of Israel.

²⁴ "But from our youth the shameful thing has devoured all for which our fathers labored, their flocks and their herds, their sons and their daughters. ²⁵ Let us lie down in our shame, and let our dishonor cover us. For we have sinned against the LORD our God, we and our fathers, from our youth even to this day, and we have not obeyed the voice of the LORD our God."

4 "If you return, O Israel,
        declares the LORD,
    to me you should return.

If you remove your detestable things
      from my presence,
    and do not waver,
²   and if you swear, 'As the LORD lives,'
      in truth, in justice, and in righ-
        teousness,
    then nations shall bless themselves in
      him,
    and in him shall they glory."

³ For thus says the LORD to the men of Judah and Jerusalem:

"Break up your fallow ground,
      and sow not among thorns.
⁴   Circumcise yourselves to the LORD;
      remove the foreskin of your hearts,
    O men of Judah and inhabitants of
      Jerusalem;
    lest my wrath go forth like fire,
      and burn with none to quench it,
    because of the evil of your deeds."

Disaster from the North

⁵ Declare in Judah, and proclaim in Jerusalem, and say,

"Blow the trumpet through the land;
      cry aloud and say,
    'Assemble, and let us go
      into the fortified cities!'
⁶   Raise a standard toward Zion,
      flee for safety, stay not,
    for I bring disaster from the north,
      and great destruction.
⁷   A lion has gone up from his thicket,
      a destroyer of nations has set out;
      he has gone out from his place
    to make your land a waste;
      your cities will be ruins
        without inhabitant.
⁸   For this put on sackcloth,
      lament and wail,
    for the fierce anger of the LORD
      has not turned back from us."

⁹ "In that day, declares the LORD, courage shall fail both king and officials. The priests shall be appalled and the prophets astounded." ¹⁰ Then I said, "Ah, Lord GOD, surely you have utterly deceived this people and Jerusalem, saying, 'It shall be well with you,' whereas the sword has reached their very life."

¹¹ At that time it will be said to this people and to Jerusalem, "A hot wind from the bare heights in the desert toward the daughter of

my people, not to winnow or cleanse, ¹² a wind too full for this comes for me. Now it is I who speak in judgment upon them."

¹³ Behold, he comes up like clouds;
 his chariots like the whirlwind;
his horses are swifter than eagles—
 woe to us, for we are ruined!
¹⁴ O Jerusalem, wash your heart from evil,
 that you may be saved.
How long shall your wicked thoughts
 lodge within you?
¹⁵ For a voice declares from Dan
 and proclaims trouble from Mount
 Ephraim.
¹⁶ Warn the nations that he is coming;
 announce to Jerusalem,
"Besiegers come from a distant land;
 they shout against the cities of
 Judah.

GETTING THE MESSAGE

A sad but faithful servant. Jeremiah was very open about the anguish he suffered as a prophet (4:19–26). In addition to being devastated by the wickedness of his beloved people, he also suffered much abuse from them. Yet despite his struggles, Jeremiah trusted in the Lord.

¹⁷ Like keepers of a field are they against
 her all around,
 because she has rebelled against me,
 declares the LORD.
¹⁸ Your ways and your deeds
 have brought this upon you.
This is your doom, and it is bitter;
 it has reached your very heart."

Anguish over Judah's Desolation

¹⁹ My anguish, my anguish! I writhe in
 pain!
 Oh the walls of my heart!
My heart is beating wildly;
 I cannot keep silent,
for I hear the sound of the trumpet,
 the alarm of war.
²⁰ Crash follows hard on crash;
 the whole land is laid waste.
Suddenly my tents are laid waste,
 my curtains in a moment.
²¹ How long must I see the standard
 and hear the sound of the trumpet?

²² "For my people are foolish;
 they know me not;
they are stupid children;
 they have no understanding.
They are 'wise'—in doing evil!
 But how to do good they know not."

²³ I looked on the earth, and behold, it
 was without form and void;
 and to the heavens, and they had no
 light.
²⁴ I looked on the mountains, and
 behold, they were quaking,
 and all the hills moved to and fro.
²⁵ I looked, and behold, there was no
 man,
 and all the birds of the air had fled.
²⁶ I looked, and behold, the fruitful land
 was a desert,
 and all its cities were laid in ruins
 before the LORD, before his fierce
 anger.

²⁷ For thus says the LORD, "The whole land shall be a desolation; yet I will not make a full end.

²⁸ "For this the earth shall mourn,
 and the heavens above be dark;
for I have spoken; I have purposed;
 I have not relented, nor will I turn
 back."

²⁹ At the noise of horseman and archer
 every city takes to flight;
they enter thickets; they climb among
 rocks;
 all the cities are forsaken,
 and no man dwells in them.
³⁰ And you, O desolate one,
what do you mean that you dress in
 scarlet,
 that you adorn yourself with ornaments of gold,
 that you enlarge your eyes with
 paint?
In vain you beautify yourself.
 Your lovers despise you;
 they seek your life.
³¹ For I heard a cry as of a woman in labor,
 anguish as of one giving birth to her
 first child,
the cry of the daughter of Zion gasp-
 ing for breath,
 stretching out her hands,
"Woe is me! I am fainting before murderers."

Jerusalem Refused to Repent

5 Run to and fro through the streets of
    Jerusalem,
      look and take note!
Search her squares to see
    if you can find a man,
one who does justice
    and seeks truth,
that I may pardon her.
² Though they say, "As the Lord lives,"
    yet they swear falsely.
³ O Lord, do not your eyes look for truth?
You have struck them down,
    but they felt no anguish;
you have consumed them,
    but they refused to take correction.
They have made their faces harder
      than rock;
    they have refused to repent.

⁴ Then I said, "These are only the poor;
    they have no sense;
for they do not know the way of the
      Lord,
    the justice of their God.
⁵ I will go to the great
    and will speak to them,
for they know the way of the Lord,
    the justice of their God."
But they all alike had broken the yoke;
    they had burst the bonds.

⁶ Therefore a lion from the forest shall
      strike them down;
    a wolf from the desert shall devas-
      tate them.
A leopard is watching their cities;
    everyone who goes out of them
      shall be torn in pieces,
because their transgressions are many,
    their apostasies are great.

⁷ "How can I pardon you?
    Your children have forsaken me
    and have sworn by those who are
      no gods.
When I fed them to the full,
    they committed adultery
    and trooped to the houses of whores.
⁸ They were well-fed, lusty stallions,
    each neighing for his neighbor's wife.
⁹ Shall I not punish them for these
      things?
                declares the Lord;
    and shall I not avenge myself
on a nation such as this?

¹⁰ "Go up through her vine rows and
      destroy,
    but make not a full end;
strip away her branches,
    for they are not the Lord's.
¹¹ For the house of Israel and the house
      of Judah
    have been utterly treacherous to me,
                declares the Lord.
¹² They have spoken falsely of the Lord
    and have said, 'He will do nothing;
no disaster will come upon us,
    nor shall we see sword or famine.
¹³ The prophets will become wind;
    the word is not in them.
Thus shall it be done to them!'"

The Lord Proclaims Judgment

¹⁴ Therefore thus says the Lord, the God
    of hosts:

GETTING THE MESSAGE

Yokes are made of wooden bars tied to animals by leather thongs around their necks. This ensured that the two animals would work together to pull a plow. Jeremiah uses the yoke in 5:5 as a symbol of God's rule in his people's lives.

"Because you have spoken this word,
behold, I am making my words in
      your mouth a fire,
    and this people wood, and the fire
      shall consume them.
¹⁵ Behold, I am bringing against you
    a nation from afar, O house of Israel,
                declares the Lord.
It is an enduring nation;
    it is an ancient nation,
a nation whose language you do not
      know,
    nor can you understand what they
      say.
¹⁶ Their quiver is like an open tomb;
    they are all mighty warriors.
¹⁷ They shall eat up your harvest and
      your food;
    they shall eat up your sons and your
      daughters;
they shall eat up your flocks and your
      herds;
    they shall eat up your vines and
      your fig trees;

your fortified cities in which you trust
  they shall beat down with the
    sword."

¹⁸ "But even in those days, declares the
LORD, I will not make a full end of you.
¹⁹ And when your people say, 'Why has the
LORD our God done all these things to us?'
you shall say to them, 'As you have forsaken
me and served foreign gods in your land, so
you shall serve foreigners in a land that is
not yours.'"

²⁰ Declare this in the house of Jacob;
      proclaim it in Judah:
²¹ "Hear this, O foolish and senseless
        people,
      who have eyes, but see not,
      who have ears, but hear not.
²² Do you not fear me? declares the LORD.
      Do you not tremble before me?

GETTING THE MESSAGE

A faithful prophet. Despite persistent
rejection, Jeremiah proclaimed the word
of God for at least 40 years. His ministry
lasted from a time when Judah still had
the opportunity to change its ways and
avoid punishment, to the time when
judgment finally came as Jerusalem was
destroyed and the people went into exile
(586 B.C.).

   I placed the sand as the boundary for
     the sea,
       a perpetual barrier that it cannot
         pass;
     though the waves toss, they cannot
       prevail;
       though they roar, they cannot pass
         over it.
²³ But this people has a stubborn and
      rebellious heart;
      they have turned aside and gone
        away.
²⁴ They do not say in their hearts,
      'Let us fear the LORD our God,
    who gives the rain in its season,
       the autumn rain and the spring rain,
    and keeps for us
       the weeks appointed for the harvest.'
²⁵ Your iniquities have turned these away,
      and your sins have kept good from
        you.

²⁶ For wicked men are found among my
      people;
      they lurk like fowlers lying in wait.
    They set a trap;
      they catch men.
²⁷ Like a cage full of birds,
      their houses are full of deceit;
    therefore they have become great and
      rich;
²⁸   they have grown fat and sleek.
    They know no bounds in deeds of
      evil;
      they judge not with justice
    the cause of the fatherless, to make it
      prosper,
      and they do not defend the rights of
        the needy.
²⁹ Shall I not punish them for these
      things?
                      declares the LORD,
      and shall I not avenge myself
    on a nation such as this?"

³⁰ An appalling and horrible thing
      has happened in the land:
³¹ the prophets prophesy falsely,
      and the priests rule at their direc-
        tion;
    my people love to have it so,
      but what will you do when the end
        comes?

Impending Disaster for Jerusalem

6 Flee for safety, O people of Benjamin,
   from the midst of Jerusalem!
   Blow the trumpet in Tekoa,
     and raise a signal on Beth-
       haccherem,
   for disaster looms out of the north,
     and great destruction.
² The lovely and delicately bred I will
     destroy,
     the daughter of Zion.
³ Shepherds with their flocks shall
     come against her;
     they shall pitch their tents around
       her;
     they shall pasture, each in his place.
⁴ "Prepare war against her;
     arise, and let us attack at noon!
   Woe to us, for the day declines,
     for the shadows of evening
       lengthen!
⁵ Arise, and let us attack by night
     and destroy her palaces!"

6 For thus says the LORD of hosts:
"Cut down her trees;
　　cast up a siege mound against
　　　Jerusalem.
This is the city that must be pun-
　　ished;
　　there is nothing but oppression
　　　within her.
7 As a well keeps its water fresh,
　　so she keeps fresh her evil;
　violence and destruction are heard
　　　within her;
　　sickness and wounds are ever
　　　before me.
8 Be warned, O Jerusalem,
　　lest I turn from you in disgust,
　lest I make you a desolation,
　　an uninhabited land."

9 Thus says the LORD of hosts:
"They shall glean thoroughly as a vine
　　the remnant of Israel;
　like a grape gatherer pass your hand
　　again
　　　over its branches."
10 To whom shall I speak and give warn-
　　ing,
　　that they may hear?
Behold, their ears are uncircumcised,
　　they cannot listen;
behold, the word of the LORD is to
　　them an object of scorn;
　they take no pleasure in it.
11 Therefore I am full of the wrath of the
　　LORD;
　I am weary of holding it in.
"Pour it out upon the children in the
　　street,
　　and upon the gatherings of young
　　　men, also;
both husband and wife shall be
　　taken,
　the elderly and the very aged.
12 Their houses shall be turned over to
　　others,
　　their fields and wives together,
for I will stretch out my hand
　　against the inhabitants of the
　　　land,"
　　　　　　　　　　declares the LORD.
13 "For from the least to the greatest of
　　them,
　　everyone is greedy for unjust gain;
and from prophet to priest,
　　everyone deals falsely.

14 They have healed the wound of my
　　people lightly,
　　saying, 'Peace, peace,'
　when there is no peace.
15 Were they ashamed when they com-
　　mitted abomination?
No, they were not at all ashamed;
　　they did not know how to blush.
Therefore they shall fall among those
　　who fall;
　at the time that I punish them, they
　　shall be overthrown,"
　　　　　　　　　　　　says the LORD.

16 Thus says the LORD:
"Stand by the roads, and look,
　　and ask for the ancient paths,
　where the good way is; and walk in it,
　　and find rest for your souls.
But they said, 'We will not walk in it.'
17 I set watchmen over you, saying,
　　'Pay attention to the sound of the
　　　trumpet!'
But they said, 'We will not pay atten-
　　tion.'
18 Therefore hear, O nations,
　　and know, O congregation, what
　　　will happen to them.
19 Hear, O earth; behold, I am bringing
　　disaster upon this people,
　　the fruit of their devices,
because they have not paid attention
　　to my words;
　and as for my law, they have
　　rejected it.
20 What use to me is frankincense that
　　comes from Sheba,
　　or sweet cane from a distant land?
Your burnt offerings are not acceptable,
　　nor your sacrifices pleasing to me.
21 Therefore thus says the LORD:
'Behold, I will lay before this people
　　stumbling blocks against which
　　　they shall stumble;
fathers and sons together,
　　neighbor and friend shall perish.'"

22 Thus says the LORD:
"Behold, a people is coming from the
　　north country,
　a great nation is stirring from the
　　farthest parts of the earth.
23 They lay hold on bow and javelin;
　　they are cruel and have no mercy;
　the sound of them is like the roar-
　　ing sea;

they ride on horses,
   set in array as a man for battle,
   against you, O daughter of Zion!"
24 We have heard the report of it;
   our hands fall helpless;
anguish has taken hold of us,
   pain as of a woman in labor.
25 Go not out into the field,
   nor walk on the road,
for the enemy has a sword;
   terror is on every side.
26 O daughter of my people, put on sackcloth,
   and roll in ashes;
make mourning as for an only son,
   most bitter lamentation,
for suddenly the destroyer
   will come upon us.

GETTING THE MESSAGE

Judah considered their **temple** a guarantee of God's favor, despite their idolatry and wickedness (7:4). They accused Jeremiah of blasphemy when he prophesied against Jerusalem. Sadly, Judah's corrupt worship and failure to repent would eventually lead to the destruction of the temple.

27 "I have made you a tester of metals
   among my people,
   that you may know and test their
   ways.
28 They are all stubbornly rebellious,
   going about with slanders;
they are bronze and iron;
   all of them act corruptly.
29 The bellows blow fiercely;
   the lead is consumed by the fire;
in vain the refining goes on,
   for the wicked are not removed.
30 Rejected silver they are called,
   for the LORD has rejected them."

Evil in the Land

7 The word that came to Jeremiah from the LORD: 2 "Stand in the gate of the LORD's house, and proclaim there this word, and say, Hear the word of the LORD, all you men of Judah who enter these gates to worship the LORD. 3 Thus says the LORD of hosts, the God of Israel: Amend your ways and your deeds, and I will let you dwell in this place. 4 Do not trust in these deceptive words: 'This is the temple of the LORD, the temple of the LORD, the temple of the LORD.'

5 "For if you truly amend your ways and your deeds, if you truly execute justice one with another, 6 if you do not oppress the sojourner, the fatherless, or the widow, or shed innocent blood in this place, and if you do not go after other gods to your own harm, 7 then I will let you dwell in this place, in the land that I gave of old to your fathers forever.

8 "Behold, you trust in deceptive words to no avail. 9 Will you steal, murder, commit adultery, swear falsely, make offerings to Baal, and go after other gods that you have not known, 10 and then come and stand before me in this house, which is called by my name, and say, 'We are delivered!'— only to go on doing all these abominations? 11 Has this house, which is called by my name, become a den of robbers in your eyes? Behold, I myself have seen it, declares the LORD. 12 Go now to my place that was in Shiloh, where I made my name dwell at first, and see what I did to it because of the evil of my people Israel. 13 And now, because you have done all these things, declares the LORD, and when I spoke to you persistently you did not listen, and when I called you, you did not answer, 14 therefore I will do to the house that is called by my name, and in which you trust, and to the place that I gave to you and to your fathers, as I did to Shiloh. 15 And I will cast you out of my sight, as I cast out all your kinsmen, all the offspring of Ephraim.

16 "As for you, do not pray for this people, or lift up a cry or prayer for them, and do not intercede with me, for I will not hear you. 17 Do you not see what they are doing in the cities of Judah and in the streets of Jerusalem? 18 The children gather wood, the fathers kindle fire, and the women knead dough, to make cakes for the queen of heaven. And they pour out drink offerings to other gods, to provoke me to anger. 19 Is it I whom they provoke? declares the LORD. Is it not themselves, to their own shame? 20 Therefore thus says the Lord GOD: Behold, my anger and my wrath will be poured out on this place, upon man and beast, upon the trees of the field and the fruit of the ground; it will burn and not be quenched."

²¹ Thus says the LORD of hosts, the God of Israel: "Add your burnt offerings to your sacrifices, and eat the flesh. ²² For in the day that I brought them out of the land of Egypt, I did not speak to your fathers or command them concerning burnt offerings and sacrifices. ²³ But this command I gave them: 'Obey my voice, and I will be your God, and you shall be my people. And walk in all the way that I command you, that it may be well with you.' ²⁴ But they did not obey or incline their ear, but walked in their own counsels and the stubbornness of their evil hearts, and went backward and not forward. ²⁵ From the day that your fathers came out of the land of Egypt to this day, I have persistently sent all my servants the prophets to them, day after day. ²⁶ Yet they did not listen to me or incline their ear, but stiffened their neck. They did worse than their fathers.

²⁷ "So you shall speak all these words to them, but they will not listen to you. You shall call to them, but they will not answer you. ²⁸ And you shall say to them, 'This is the nation that did not obey the voice of the LORD their God, and did not accept discipline; truth has perished; it is cut off from their lips.'

²⁹ "'Cut off your hair and cast it away;
    raise a lamentation on the bare
        heights,
    for the LORD has rejected and forsaken
        the generation of his wrath.'

The Valley of Slaughter

³⁰ "For the sons of Judah have done evil in my sight, declares the LORD. They have set their detestable things in the house that is called by my name, to defile it. ³¹ And they have built the high places of Topheth, which is in the Valley of the Son of Hinnom, to burn their sons and their daughters in the fire, which I did not command, nor did it come into my mind. ³² Therefore, behold, the days are coming, declares the LORD, when it will no more be called Topheth, or the Valley of the Son of Hinnom, but the Valley of Slaughter; for they will bury in Topheth, because there is no room elsewhere. ³³ And the dead bodies of this people will be food for the birds of the air, and for the beasts of the earth, and none will frighten them away. ³⁴ And I will silence in the cities of Judah and in the streets of Jerusalem the voice of mirth and the voice of gladness, the voice of the bridegroom and the voice of the bride, for the land shall become a waste.

8 "At that time, declares the LORD, the bones of the kings of Judah, the bones of its officials, the bones of the priests, the bones of the prophets, and the bones of the inhabitants of Jerusalem shall be brought out of their tombs. ² And they shall be spread before the sun and the moon and all the host of heaven, which they have loved and served, which they have gone after, and which they have sought and worshiped. And they shall not be gathered or buried. They shall be as dung on the surface of the ground. ³ Death shall be preferred to life by all the remnant that remains of this evil family in all the places where I have driven them, declares the LORD of hosts.

Sin and Treachery

⁴ "You shall say to them, Thus says the
        LORD:
    When men fall, do they not rise again?
        If one turns away, does he not return?
⁵   Why then has this people turned away
        in perpetual backsliding?
    They hold fast to deceit;
        they refuse to return.
⁶   I have paid attention and listened,
        but they have not spoken rightly;
    no man relents of his evil,
        saying, 'What have I done?'
    Everyone turns to his own course,
        like a horse plunging headlong into
            battle.
⁷   Even the stork in the heavens
        knows her times,
    and the turtledove, swallow, and crane
        keep the time of their coming,
    but my people know not
        the rules of the LORD.

⁸   "How can you say, 'We are wise,
        and the law of the LORD is with us'?
    But behold, the lying pen of the scribes
        has made it into a lie.
⁹   The wise men shall be put to shame;
        they shall be dismayed and taken;
    behold, they have rejected the word of
        the LORD,
        so what wisdom is in them?
¹⁰ Therefore I will give their wives to
            others
        and their fields to conquerors,

because from the least to the greatest
    everyone is greedy for unjust gain;
from prophet to priest,
    everyone deals falsely.
11 They have healed the wound of my
    people lightly,
    saying, 'Peace, peace,'
    when there is no peace.
12 Were they ashamed when they com-
    mitted abomination?
    No, they were not at all ashamed;
    they did not know how to blush.
Therefore they shall fall among the
    fallen;
    when I punish them, they shall be
    overthrown,
    says the LORD.
13 When I would gather them, declares
    the LORD,
there are no grapes on the vine,
    nor figs on the fig tree;
even the leaves are withered,
    and what I gave them has passed
    away from them."
14 Why do we sit still?
Gather together; let us go into the
    fortified cities
    and perish there,
for the LORD our God has doomed us
    to perish
    and has given us poisoned water to
    drink,
because we have sinned against the
    LORD.
15 We looked for peace, but no good came;
    for a time of healing, but behold,
    terror.
16 "The snorting of their horses is heard
    from Dan;
    at the sound of the neighing of their
    stallions
    the whole land quakes.
They come and devour the land and
    all that fills it,
    the city and those who dwell in it.
17 For behold, I am sending among you
    serpents,
    adders that cannot be charmed,
    and they shall bite you,"
    declares the LORD.

Jeremiah Grieves for His People

18 My joy is gone; grief is upon me;
    my heart is sick within me.

19 Behold, the cry of the daughter of my
    people
    from the length and breadth of the
    land:
"Is the LORD not in Zion?
    Is her King not in her?"
"Why have they provoked me to anger
    with their carved images
    and with their foreign idols?"
20 "The harvest is past, the summer is
    ended,
    and we are not saved."
21 For the wound of the daughter of my
    people is my heart wounded;
    I mourn, and dismay has taken hold
    on me.
22 Is there no balm in Gilead?
    Is there no physician there?
Why then has the health of the daugh-
    ter of my people
    not been restored?

9 Oh that my head were waters,
    and my eyes a fountain of tears,
that I might weep day and night
    for the slain of the daughter of my
    people!
2 Oh that I had in the desert
    a travelers' lodging place,
that I might leave my people
    and go away from them!
For they are all adulterers,
    a company of treacherous men.
3 They bend their tongue like a bow;
    falsehood and not truth has grown
    strong in the land;
for they proceed from evil to evil,
    and they do not know me, declares
    the LORD.

4 Let everyone beware of his neighbor,
    and put no trust in any brother,
for every brother is a deceiver,
    and every neighbor goes about as a
    slanderer.
5 Everyone deceives his neighbor,
    and no one speaks the truth;
they have taught their tongue to speak
    lies;
    they weary themselves committing
    iniquity.
6 Heaping oppression upon oppression,
    and deceit upon deceit,
    they refuse to know me, declares
    the LORD.

7 Therefore thus says the Lord of hosts:
"Behold, I will refine them and test
them,
for what else can I do, because of
my people?
8 Their tongue is a deadly arrow;
it speaks deceitfully;
with his mouth each speaks peace to
his neighbor,
but in his heart he plans an ambush
for him.
9 Shall I not punish them for these
things? declares the Lord,
and shall I not avenge myself
on a nation such as this?

10 "I will take up weeping and wailing for
the mountains,
and a lamentation for the pastures
of the wilderness,
because they are laid waste so that no
one passes through,
and the lowing of cattle is not
heard;
both the birds of the air and the beasts
have fled and are gone.
11 I will make Jerusalem a heap of ruins,
a lair of jackals,
and I will make the cities of Judah a
desolation,
without inhabitant."

12 Who is the man so wise that he can
understand this? To whom has the mouth
of the Lord spoken, that he may declare it?
Why is the land ruined and laid waste like a
wilderness, so that no one passes through?
13 And the Lord says: "Because they have forsaken my law that I set before them, and have
not obeyed my voice or walked in accord with
it, 14 but have stubbornly followed their own
hearts and have gone after the Baals, as their
fathers taught them. 15 Therefore thus says
the Lord of hosts, the God of Israel: Behold,
I will feed this people with bitter food, and
give them poisonous water to drink. 16 I will
scatter them among the nations whom neither they nor their fathers have known, and
I will send the sword after them, until I have
consumed them."

17 Thus says the Lord of hosts:
"Consider, and call for the mourning
women to come;
send for the skillful women to
come;

18 let them make haste and raise a wailing over us,
that our eyes may run down with
tears
and our eyelids flow with water.
19 For a sound of wailing is heard from
Zion:
'How we are ruined!
We are utterly shamed,
because we have left the land,
because they have cast down our
dwellings.'"
20 Hear, O women, the word of the Lord,
and let your ear receive the word of
his mouth;
teach to your daughters a lament,
and each to her neighbor a dirge.
21 For death has come up into our windows;
it has entered our palaces,

GETTING THE MESSAGE

The **wailing women** mentioned in 9:17
were probably professional mourners.
In many ancient cultures, such people
were paid to sing or deliver eulogies at
funerals.

cutting off the children from the streets
and the young men from the
squares.
22 Speak: "Thus declares the Lord,
'The dead bodies of men shall fall
like dung upon the open field,
like sheaves after the reaper,
and none shall gather them.'"

23 Thus says the Lord: "Let not the wise
man boast in his wisdom, let not the mighty
man boast in his might, let not the rich man
boast in his riches, 24 but let him who boasts
boast in this, that he understands and
knows me, that I am the Lord who practices
steadfast love, justice, and righteousness
in the earth. For in these things I delight,
declares the Lord."
25 "Behold, the days are coming, declares
the Lord, when I will punish all those
who are circumcised merely in the flesh—
26 Egypt, Judah, Edom, the sons of Ammon,
Moab, and all who dwell in the desert who
cut the corners of their hair, for all these

nations are uncircumcised, and all the house of Israel are uncircumcised in heart."

Idols and the Living God

10 Hear the word that the LORD speaks to you, O house of Israel. ² Thus says the LORD:

"Learn not the way of the nations,
    nor be dismayed at the signs of the heavens
        because the nations are dismayed at them,
³ for the customs of the peoples are vanity.
A tree from the forest is cut down
    and worked with an axe by the hands of a craftsman.
⁴ They decorate it with silver and gold;
    they fasten it with hammer and nails
        so that it cannot move.

GETTING THE MESSAGE

God's storehouses. Just like today, people in Bible times needed places to store things. The Lord also has "store-houses" (10:13), for things like rain and lightning and wind!

---

⁵ Their idols are like scarecrows in a cucumber field,
    and they cannot speak;
they have to be carried,
    for they cannot walk.
Do not be afraid of them,
    for they cannot do evil,
        neither is it in them to do good."

⁶ There is none like you, O LORD;
    you are great, and your name is great in might.
⁷ Who would not fear you, O King of the nations?
    For this is your due;
for among all the wise ones of the nations
    and in all their kingdoms
        there is none like you.
⁸ They are both stupid and foolish;
    the instruction of idols is but wood!
⁹ Beaten silver is brought from Tarshish,
    and gold from Uphaz.

They are the work of the craftsman and of the hands of the goldsmith;
    their clothing is violet and purple;
        they are all the work of skilled men.
¹⁰ But the LORD is the true God;
    he is the living God and the ever-lasting King.
At his wrath the earth quakes,
    and the nations cannot endure his indignation.

¹¹ Thus shall you say to them: "The gods who did not make the heavens and the earth shall perish from the earth and from under the heavens."

¹² It is he who made the earth by his power,
    who established the world by his wisdom,
        and by his understanding stretched out the heavens.
¹³ When he utters his voice, there is a tumult of waters in the heavens,
    and he makes the mist rise from the ends of the earth.
He makes lightning for the rain,
    and he brings forth the wind from his storehouses.
¹⁴ Every man is stupid and without knowledge;
    every goldsmith is put to shame by his idols,
for his images are false,
    and there is no breath in them.
¹⁵ They are worthless, a work of delusion;
    at the time of their punishment they shall perish.
¹⁶ Not like these is he who is the portion of Jacob,
    for he is the one who formed all things,
and Israel is the tribe of his inheritance;
    the LORD of hosts is his name.

¹⁷ Gather up your bundle from the ground,
    O you who dwell under siege!
¹⁸ For thus says the LORD:
"Behold, I am slinging out the inhabitants of the land
    at this time,
and I will bring distress on them,
    that they may feel it."

¹⁹ Woe is me because of my hurt!
    My wound is grievous.

But I said, "Truly this is an affliction,
      and I must bear it."
20 My tent is destroyed,
      and all my cords are broken;
   my children have gone from me,
      and they are not;
   there is no one to spread my tent again
      and to set up my curtains.
21 For the shepherds are stupid
      and do not inquire of the LORD;
   therefore they have not prospered,
      and all their flock is scattered.

22 A voice, a rumor! Behold, it comes!—
      a great commotion out of the north
         country
   to make the cities of Judah a desola-
         tion,
      a lair of jackals.

23 I know, O LORD, that the way of man is
         not in himself,
      that it is not in man who walks to
         direct his steps.
24 Correct me, O LORD, but in justice;
      not in your anger, lest you bring me
         to nothing.
25 Pour out your wrath on the nations
      that know you not,
   and on the peoples that call not on
      your name,
   for they have devoured Jacob;
      they have devoured him and con-
         sumed him,
      and have laid waste his habitation.

The Broken Covenant

11 The word that came to Jeremiah from the LORD: ² "Hear the words of this covenant, and speak to the men of Judah and the inhabitants of Jerusalem. ³ You shall say to them, Thus says the LORD, the God of Israel: Cursed be the man who does not hear the words of this covenant ⁴ that I commanded your fathers when I brought them out of the land of Egypt, from the iron furnace, saying, Listen to my voice, and do all that I command you. So shall you be my people, and I will be your God, ⁵ that I may confirm the oath that I swore to your fathers, to give them a land flowing with milk and honey, as at this day." Then I answered, "So be it, LORD."

⁶ And the LORD said to me, "Proclaim all these words in the cities of Judah and in the streets of Jerusalem: Hear the words of this covenant and do them. ⁷ For I solemnly warned your fathers when I brought them up out of the land of Egypt, warning them persistently, even to this day, saying, Obey my voice. ⁸ Yet they did not obey or incline their ear, but everyone walked in the stubbornness of his evil heart. Therefore I brought upon them all the words of this covenant, which I commanded them to do, but they did not."

⁹ Again the LORD said to me, "A conspiracy exists among the men of Judah and the inhabitants of Jerusalem. ¹⁰ They have turned back to the iniquities of their forefathers, who refused to hear my words. They have gone after other gods to serve them. The house of Israel and the house of Judah have broken my covenant that I made with their fathers. ¹¹ Therefore, thus says the

---

GETTING THE MESSAGE

Judah's good king **Josiah** rediscovered the Book of the Law, reinstituted the Passover, and destroyed foreign idols. And yet Jeremiah had to declare that the end was coming for Judah (11:11), just as it had for Israel a hundred years before.

LORD, Behold, I am bringing disaster upon them that they cannot escape. Though they cry to me, I will not listen to them. ¹² Then the cities of Judah and the inhabitants of Jerusalem will go and cry to the gods to whom they make offerings, but they cannot save them in the time of their trouble. ¹³ For your gods have become as many as your cities, O Judah, and as many as the streets of Jerusalem are the altars you have set up to shame, altars to make offerings to Baal.

¹⁴ "Therefore do not pray for this people, or lift up a cry or prayer on their behalf, for I will not listen when they call to me in the time of their trouble. ¹⁵ What right has my beloved in my house, when she has done many vile deeds? Can even sacrificial flesh avert your doom? Can you then exult? ¹⁶ The LORD once called you 'a green olive tree, beautiful with good fruit.' But with the roar of a great tempest he will set fire to it, and its branches will be consumed. ¹⁷ The LORD of hosts, who planted you, has

decreed disaster against you, because of the evil that the house of Israel and the house of Judah have done, provoking me to anger by making offerings to Baal."

18 The LORD made it known to me and I
      knew;
      then you showed me their deeds.
19 But I was like a gentle lamb
      led to the slaughter.
   I did not know it was against me
      they devised schemes, saying,
   "Let us destroy the tree with its fruit,
      let us cut him off from the land of
         the living,
      that his name be remembered no
         more."
20 But, O LORD of hosts, who judges
      righteously,
   who tests the heart and the mind,
   let me see your vengeance upon them,
      for to you have I committed my
         cause.

21 Therefore thus says the LORD concerning the men of Anathoth, who seek your life, and say, "Do not prophesy in the name of the LORD, or you will die by our hand"— 22 therefore thus says the LORD of hosts: "Behold, I will punish them. The young men shall die by the sword, their sons and their daughters shall die by famine, 23 and none of them shall be left. For I will bring disaster upon the men of Anathoth, the year of their punishment."

Jeremiah's Complaint

12 Righteous are you, O LORD,
      when I complain to you;
   yet I would plead my case before you.
   Why does the way of the wicked pros-
      per?
   Why do all who are treacherous
      thrive?
2 You plant them, and they take root;
      they grow and produce fruit;
   you are near in their mouth
      and far from their heart.
3 But you, O LORD, know me;
      you see me, and test my heart
         toward you.
   Pull them out like sheep for the
      slaughter,
      and set them apart for the day of
         slaughter.
4 How long will the land mourn
      and the grass of every field wither?

For the evil of those who dwell in it
   the beasts and the birds are swept
      away,
      because they said, "He will not see
         our latter end."

The LORD Answers Jeremiah

5 "If you have raced with men on foot,
      and they have wearied you,
      how will you compete with horses?
   And if in a safe land you are so trusting,
      what will you do in the thicket of
         the Jordan?
6 For even your brothers and the house
      of your father,
      even they have dealt treacherously
         with you;
      they are in full cry after you;
   do not believe them,
      though they speak friendly words to
         you."

7 "I have forsaken my house;
      I have abandoned my heritage;
   I have given the beloved of my soul
      into the hands of her enemies.
8 My heritage has become to me
      like a lion in the forest;
   she has lifted up her voice against me;
      therefore I hate her.
9 Is my heritage to me like a hyena's lair?
      Are the birds of prey against her all
         around?
   Go, assemble all the wild beasts;
      bring them to devour.
10 Many shepherds have destroyed my
      vineyard;
      they have trampled down my por-
         tion;
   they have made my pleasant portion
      a desolate wilderness.
11 They have made it a desolation;
      desolate, it mourns to me.
   The whole land is made desolate,
      but no man lays it to heart.
12 Upon all the bare heights in the desert
      destroyers have come,
   for the sword of the LORD devours
      from one end of the land to the
         other;
      no flesh has peace.
13 They have sown wheat and have
      reaped thorns;
      they have tired themselves out but
         profit nothing.

They shall be ashamed of their harvests
because of the fierce anger of the
LORD."

¹⁴ Thus says the LORD concerning all my evil neighbors who touch the heritage that I have given my people Israel to inherit: "Behold, I will pluck them up from their land, and I will pluck up the house of Judah from among them. ¹⁵ And after I have plucked them up, I will again have compassion on them, and I will bring them again each to his heritage and each to his land. ¹⁶ And it shall come to pass, if they will diligently learn the ways of my people, to swear by my name, 'As the LORD lives,' even as they taught my people to swear by Baal, then they shall be built up in the midst of my people. ¹⁷ But if any nation will not listen, then I will utterly pluck it up and destroy it, declares the LORD."

The Ruined Loincloth

13 Thus says the LORD to me, "Go and buy a linen loincloth and put it around your waist, and do not dip it in water." ² So I bought a loincloth according to the word of the LORD, and put it around my waist. ³ And the word of the LORD came to me a second time, ⁴ "Take the loincloth that you have bought, which is around your waist, and arise, go to the Euphrates and hide it there in a cleft of the rock." ⁵ So I went and hid it by the Euphrates, as the LORD commanded me. ⁶ And after many days the LORD said to me, "Arise, go to the Euphrates, and take from there the loincloth that I commanded you to hide there." ⁷ Then I went to the Euphrates, and dug, and I took the loincloth from the place where I had hidden it. And behold, the loincloth was spoiled; it was good for nothing.

⁸ Then the word of the LORD came to me: ⁹ "Thus says the LORD: Even so will I spoil the pride of Judah and the great pride of Jerusalem. ¹⁰ This evil people, who refuse to hear my words, who stubbornly follow their own heart and have gone after other gods to serve them and worship them, shall be like this loincloth, which is good for nothing. ¹¹ For as the loincloth clings to the waist of a man, so I made the whole house of Israel and the whole house of Judah cling to me, declares the LORD, that they might be for me a people, a name, a praise, and a glory, but they would not listen.

The Jars Filled with Wine

¹² "You shall speak to them this word: 'Thus says the LORD, the God of Israel, "Every jar shall be filled with wine."' And they will say to you, 'Do we not indeed know that every jar will be filled with wine?' ¹³ Then you shall say to them, 'Thus says the LORD: Behold, I will fill with drunkenness all the inhabitants of this land: the kings who sit on David's throne, the priests, the prophets, and all the inhabitants of Jerusalem. ¹⁴ And I will dash them one against another, fathers and sons together, declares the LORD. I will not pity or spare or have compassion, that I should not destroy them.'"

Exile Threatened

¹⁵   Hear and give ear; be not proud,
        for the LORD has spoken.
¹⁶   Give glory to the LORD your God
        before he brings darkness,
    before your feet stumble
        on the twilight mountains,
    and while you look for light
        he turns it into gloom
        and makes it deep darkness.
¹⁷   But if you will not listen,
        my soul will weep in secret for your
            pride;
    my eyes will weep bitterly and run
            down with tears,
        because the LORD's flock has been
            taken captive.
¹⁸   Say to the king and the queen mother:
        "Take a lowly seat,
    for your beautiful crown
        has come down from your head."
¹⁹   The cities of the Negeb are shut up,
        with none to open them;
    all Judah is taken into exile,
        wholly taken into exile.

²⁰   "Lift up your eyes and see
        those who come from the north.
    Where is the flock that was given you,
        your beautiful flock?
²¹   What will you say when they set as
            head over you
        those whom you yourself have
            taught to be friends to you?
    Will not pangs take hold of you
        like those of a woman in labor?
²²   And if you say in your heart,
        'Why have these things come upon
            me?'

it is for the greatness of your iniquity
    that your skirts are lifted up
    and you suffer violence.
23 Can the Ethiopian change his skin
    or the leopard his spots?
    Then also you can do good
    who are accustomed to do evil.
24 I will scatter you like chaff
    driven by the wind from the desert.
25 This is your lot,
    the portion I have measured out to
      you, declares the LORD,
because you have forgotten me
    and trusted in lies.
26 I myself will lift up your skirts over
    your face,
    and your shame will be seen.

> ### GETTING THE MESSAGE
>
> **The primary calling of the prophet** was
> to serve as God's spokesperson. There
> were many prophets, however, and
> they sometimes declared conflicting
> messages (14:13). The way to determine
> if a prophet was speaking God's words
> was to see if the prophecy was actually
> fulfilled (see Deut. 18:18–22).

27 I have seen your abominations,
    your adulteries and neighings, your
      lewd whorings,
    on the hills in the field.
Woe to you, O Jerusalem!
    How long will it be before you are
      made clean?"

Famine, Sword, and Pestilence

14 The word of the LORD that came to
Jeremiah concerning the drought:

2 "Judah mourns,
    and her gates languish;
    her people lament on the ground,
    and the cry of Jerusalem goes up.
3 Her nobles send their servants for
    water;
    they come to the cisterns;
    they find no water;
    they return with their vessels empty;
    they are ashamed and confounded
    and cover their heads.
4 Because of the ground that is dismayed,
    since there is no rain on the land,

the farmers are ashamed;
    they cover their heads.
5 Even the doe in the field forsakes her
    newborn fawn
    because there is no grass.
6 The wild donkeys stand on the bare
    heights;
    they pant for air like jackals;
    their eyes fail
    because there is no vegetation.
7 "Though our iniquities testify against
    us,
    act, O LORD, for your name's sake;
for our backslidings are many;
    we have sinned against you.
8 O you hope of Israel,
    its savior in time of trouble,
why should you be like a stranger in
    the land,
    like a traveler who turns aside to
      tarry for a night?
9 Why should you be like a man con-
    fused,
    like a mighty warrior who cannot
      save?
Yet you, O LORD, are in the midst of us,
    and we are called by your name;
    do not leave us."

10 Thus says the LORD concerning this
    people:
"They have loved to wander thus;
    they have not restrained their feet;
therefore the LORD does not accept
    them;
    now he will remember their iniquity
    and punish their sins."

11 The LORD said to me: "Do not pray for the
welfare of this people. 12 Though they fast,
I will not hear their cry, and though they
offer burnt offering and grain offering, I will
not accept them. But I will consume them
by the sword, by famine, and by pestilence."

Lying Prophets

13 Then I said: "Ah, Lord GOD, behold, the
prophets say to them, 'You shall not see
the sword, nor shall you have famine, but I
will give you assured peace in this place.'"
14 And the LORD said to me: "The prophets
are prophesying lies in my name. I did not
send them, nor did I command them or
speak to them. They are prophesying to you
a lying vision, worthless divination, and

the deceit of their own minds. ¹⁵ Therefore thus says the LORD concerning the prophets who prophesy in my name although I did not send them, and who say, 'Sword and famine shall not come upon this land': By sword and famine those prophets shall be consumed. ¹⁶ And the people to whom they prophesy shall be cast out in the streets of Jerusalem, victims of famine and sword, with none to bury them—them, their wives, their sons, and their daughters. For I will pour out their evil upon them.

¹⁷ "You shall say to them this word:
'Let my eyes run down with tears night and day,
and let them not cease,
for the virgin daughter of my people is shattered with a great wound,
with a very grievous blow.
¹⁸ If I go out into the field,
behold, those pierced by the sword!
And if I enter the city,
behold, the diseases of famine!
For both prophet and priest ply their trade through the land
and have no knowledge.'"

¹⁹ Have you utterly rejected Judah?
Does your soul loathe Zion?
Why have you struck us down
so that there is no healing for us?
We looked for peace, but no good came;
for a time of healing, but behold, terror.
²⁰ We acknowledge our wickedness, O LORD,
and the iniquity of our fathers,
for we have sinned against you.
²¹ Do not spurn us, for your name's sake;
do not dishonor your glorious throne;
remember and do not break your covenant with us.
²² Are there any among the false gods of the nations that can bring rain?
Or can the heavens give showers?
Are you not he, O LORD our God?
We set our hope on you,
for you do all these things.

The LORD Will Not Relent

15 Then the LORD said to me, "Though Moses and Samuel stood before me, yet my heart would not turn toward this people. Send them out of my sight, and let

them go! ² And when they ask you, 'Where shall we go?' you shall say to them, 'Thus says the LORD:

"'Those who are for pestilence, to pestilence,
and those who are for the sword, to the sword;
those who are for famine, to famine,
and those who are for captivity, to captivity.'

³ I will appoint over them four kinds of destroyers, declares the LORD: the sword to kill, the dogs to tear, and the birds of the air and the beasts of the earth to devour and destroy. ⁴ And I will make them a horror to all the kingdoms of the earth because of what Manasseh the son of Hezekiah, king of Judah, did in Jerusalem.

⁵ "Who will have pity on you, O Jerusalem,
or who will grieve for you?
Who will turn aside
to ask about your welfare?
⁶ You have rejected me, declares the LORD;
you keep going backward,
so I have stretched out my hand against you and destroyed you—
I am weary of relenting.
⁷ I have winnowed them with a winnowing fork
in the gates of the land;
I have bereaved them; I have destroyed my people;
they did not turn from their ways.
⁸ I have made their widows more in number
than the sand of the seas;
I have brought against the mothers of young men
a destroyer at noonday;

I have made anguish and terror
    fall upon them suddenly.
9 She who bore seven has grown feeble;
    she has fainted away;
her sun went down while it was yet
    day;
    she has been shamed and disgraced.
And the rest of them I will give to the
    sword
    before their enemies,
        declares the LORD."

Jeremiah's Complaint

10 Woe is me, my mother, that you bore me, a man of strife and contention to the whole land! I have not lent, nor have I borrowed, yet all of them curse me. 11 The LORD said, "Have I not set you free for their good? Have I not pleaded for you before the enemy in the time of trouble and in the time of

GETTING THE MESSAGE

Singleness for a prophetic purpose.
The Lord told Jeremiah not to get married. This was probably intended as a symbolic warning that life would soon be very difficult for people with children (16:1–4).

distress? 12 Can one break iron, iron from the north, and bronze? 13 "Your wealth and your treasures I will give as spoil, without price, for all your sins, throughout all your territory. 14 I will make you serve your enemies in a land that you do not know, for in my anger a fire is kindled that shall burn forever."

15 O LORD, you know;
    remember me and visit me,
    and take vengeance for me on my
        persecutors.
In your forbearance take me not away;
    know that for your sake I bear
        reproach.
16 Your words were found, and I ate
    them,
    and your words became to me a joy
    and the delight of my heart,
for I am called by your name,
    O LORD, God of hosts.
17 I did not sit in the company of revelers,
    nor did I rejoice;

I sat alone, because your hand was
    upon me,
    for you had filled me with indigna-
        tion.
18 Why is my pain unceasing,
    my wound incurable,
    refusing to be healed?
Will you be to me like a deceitful brook,
    like waters that fail?

19 Therefore thus says the LORD:
"If you return, I will restore you,
    and you shall stand before me.
If you utter what is precious, and not
        what is worthless,
    you shall be as my mouth.
They shall turn to you,
    but you shall not turn to them.
20 And I will make you to this people
    a fortified wall of bronze;
they will fight against you,
    but they shall not prevail over you,
for I am with you
    to save you and deliver you,
        declares the LORD.
21 I will deliver you out of the hand of
    the wicked,
    and redeem you from the grasp of
    the ruthless."

Famine, Sword, and Death

16 The word of the LORD came to me: 2 "You shall not take a wife, nor shall you have sons or daughters in this place. 3 For thus says the LORD concerning the sons and daughters who are born in this place, and concerning the mothers who bore them and the fathers who fathered them in this land: 4 They shall die of deadly diseases. They shall not be lamented, nor shall they be buried. They shall be as dung on the surface of the ground. They shall perish by the sword and by famine, and their dead bodies shall be food for the birds of the air and for the beasts of the earth.

5 "For thus says the LORD: Do not enter the house of mourning, or go to lament or grieve for them, for I have taken away my peace from this people, my steadfast love and mercy, declares the LORD. 6 Both great and small shall die in this land. They shall not be buried, and no one shall lament for them or cut himself or make himself bald for them. 7 No one shall break bread for the mourner, to comfort him for the dead, nor

shall anyone give him the cup of consolation to drink for his father or his mother. ⁸ You shall not go into the house of feasting to sit with them, to eat and drink. ⁹ For thus says the LORD of hosts, the God of Israel: Behold, I will silence in this place, before your eyes and in your days, the voice of mirth and the voice of gladness, the voice of the bridegroom and the voice of the bride.

¹⁰ "And when you tell this people all these words, and they say to you, 'Why has the LORD pronounced all this great evil against us? What is our iniquity? What is the sin that we have committed against the LORD our God?' ¹¹ then you shall say to them: 'Because your fathers have forsaken me, declares the LORD, and have gone after other gods and have served and worshiped them, and have forsaken me and have not kept my law, ¹² and because you have done worse than your fathers, for behold, every one of you follows his stubborn, evil will, refusing to listen to me. ¹³ Therefore I will hurl you out of this land into a land that neither you nor your fathers have known, and there you shall serve other gods day and night, for I will show you no favor.'

The LORD Will Restore Israel

¹⁴ "Therefore, behold, the days are coming, declares the LORD, when it shall no longer be said, 'As the LORD lives who brought up the people of Israel out of the land of Egypt,' ¹⁵ but 'As the LORD lives who brought up the people of Israel out of the north country and out of all the countries where he had driven them.' For I will bring them back to their own land that I gave to their fathers.

¹⁶ "Behold, I am sending for many fishers, declares the LORD, and they shall catch them. And afterward I will send for many hunters, and they shall hunt them from every mountain and every hill, and out of the clefts of the rocks. ¹⁷ For my eyes are on all their ways. They are not hidden from me, nor is their iniquity concealed from my eyes. ¹⁸ But first I will doubly repay their iniquity and their sin, because they have polluted my land with the carcasses of their detestable idols, and have filled my inheritance with their abominations."

¹⁹   O LORD, my strength and my stronghold,
      my refuge in the day of trouble,

to you shall the nations come
    from the ends of the earth and say:
"Our fathers have inherited nothing
      but lies,
    worthless things in which there is
      no profit.
²⁰   Can man make for himself gods?
    Such are not gods!"

²¹ "Therefore, behold, I will make them know, this once I will make them know my power and my might, and they shall know that my name is the LORD."

The Sin of Judah

17 "The sin of Judah is written with a pen of iron; with a point of diamond it is engraved on the tablet of their heart, and on the horns of their altars, ² while their children remember their altars and their Asherim, beside every green tree and on the high hills, ³ on the mountains in the open country. Your wealth and all your treasures I will give for spoil as the price of your high places for sin throughout all your territory. ⁴ You shall loosen your hand from your heritage that I gave to you, and I will make you serve your enemies in a land that you do not know, for in my anger a fire is kindled that shall burn forever."

⁵   Thus says the LORD:
"Cursed is the man who trusts in man
    and makes flesh his strength,
    whose heart turns away from the
      LORD.
⁶   He is like a shrub in the desert,
    and shall not see any good come.
He shall dwell in the parched places
      of the wilderness,
    in an uninhabited salt land.

⁷   "Blessed is the man who trusts in the
      LORD,
    whose trust is the LORD.
⁸   He is like a tree planted by water,
    that sends out its roots by the
      stream,
and does not fear when heat comes,
    for its leaves remain green,
and is not anxious in the year of
      drought,
    for it does not cease to bear fruit."

⁹   The heart is deceitful above all things,
    and desperately sick;
    who can understand it?

¹⁰ "I the Lord search the heart
    and test the mind,
to give every man according to his
        ways,
    according to the fruit of his deeds."

¹¹ Like the partridge that gathers a brood
        that she did not hatch,
    so is he who gets riches but not by
        justice;
in the midst of his days they will leave
        him,
    and at his end he will be a fool.

¹² A glorious throne set on high from the
        beginning
    is the place of our sanctuary.

¹³ O Lord, the hope of Israel,
    all who forsake you shall be put to
        shame;
those who turn away from you shall
        be written in the earth,
    for they have forsaken the Lord, the
        fountain of living water.

Jeremiah Prays for Deliverance

¹⁴ Heal me, O Lord, and I shall be healed;
    save me, and I shall be saved,
    for you are my praise.

¹⁵ Behold, they say to me,
    "Where is the word of the Lord?
        Let it come!"

¹⁶ I have not run away from being your
        shepherd,
    nor have I desired the day of sick-
        ness.
You know what came out of my lips;
    it was before your face.

¹⁷ Be not a terror to me;
    you are my refuge in the day of
        disaster.

¹⁸ Let those be put to shame who perse-
        cute me,
    but let me not be put to shame;
let them be dismayed,
    but let me not be dismayed;
bring upon them the day of disaster;
    destroy them with double destruc-
        tion!

Keep the Sabbath Holy

¹⁹ Thus said the Lord to me: "Go and stand
in the People's Gate, by which the kings of
Judah enter and by which they go out, and in
all the gates of Jerusalem, ²⁰ and say: 'Hear the
word of the Lord, you kings of Judah, and all

Judah, and all the inhabitants of Jerusalem,
who enter by these gates. ²¹ Thus says the
Lord: Take care for the sake of your lives, and
do not bear a burden on the Sabbath day or
bring it in by the gates of Jerusalem. ²² And do
not carry a burden out of your houses on the
Sabbath or do any work, but keep the Sabbath
day holy, as I commanded your fathers. ²³ Yet
they did not listen or incline their ear, but
stiffened their neck, that they might not hear
and receive instruction.

²⁴ "'But if you listen to me, declares the
Lord, and bring in no burden by the gates
of this city on the Sabbath day, but keep
the Sabbath day holy and do no work on it,
²⁵ then there shall enter by the gates of this
city kings and princes who sit on the throne
of David, riding in chariots and on horses,
they and their officials, the men of Judah
and the inhabitants of Jerusalem. And this
city shall be inhabited forever. ²⁶ And people
shall come from the cities of Judah and the
places around Jerusalem, from the land of
Benjamin, from the Shephelah, from the hill
country, and from the Negeb, bringing burnt
offerings and sacrifices, grain offerings and
frankincense, and bringing thank offerings
to the house of the Lord. ²⁷ But if you do not
listen to me, to keep the Sabbath day holy,
and not to bear a burden and enter by the
gates of Jerusalem on the Sabbath day, then
I will kindle a fire in its gates, and it shall
devour the palaces of Jerusalem and shall
not be quenched.'"

The Potter and the Clay

18 The word that came to Jeremiah from
the Lord: ² "Arise, and go down to the
potter's house, and there I will let you hear
my words." ³ So I went down to the potter's
house, and there he was working at his
wheel. ⁴ And the vessel he was making of
clay was spoiled in the potter's hand, and he
reworked it into another vessel, as it seemed
good to the potter to do.

⁵ Then the word of the Lord came to me:
⁶ "O house of Israel, can I not do with you
as this potter has done? declares the Lord.
Behold, like the clay in the potter's hand, so
are you in my hand, O house of Israel. ⁷ If at
any time I declare concerning a nation or a
kingdom, that I will pluck up and break down
and destroy it, ⁸ and if that nation, concerning which I have spoken, turns from its evil,
I will relent of the disaster that I intended to

do to it. ⁹ And if at any time I declare concerning a nation or a kingdom that I will build and plant it, ¹⁰ and if it does evil in my sight, not listening to my voice, then I will relent of the good that I had intended to do to it. ¹¹ Now, therefore, say to the men of Judah and the inhabitants of Jerusalem: 'Thus says the LORD, Behold, I am shaping disaster against you and devising a plan against you. Return, every one from his evil way, and amend your ways and your deeds.'

¹² "But they say, 'That is in vain! We will follow our own plans, and will every one act according to the stubbornness of his evil heart.'

¹³ "Therefore thus says the LORD:
Ask among the nations,
 Who has heard the like of this?
The virgin Israel
 has done a very horrible thing.
¹⁴ Does the snow of Lebanon leave
 the crags of Sirion?
Do the mountain waters run dry,
 the cold flowing streams?
¹⁵ But my people have forgotten me;
 they make offerings to false gods;
they made them stumble in their ways,
 in the ancient roads,
and to walk into side roads,
 not the highway,
¹⁶ making their land a horror,
 a thing to be hissed at forever.
Everyone who passes by it is horrified
 and shakes his head.
¹⁷ Like the east wind I will scatter them
 before the enemy.
I will show them my back, not my face,
 in the day of their calamity."

¹⁸ Then they said, "Come, let us make plots against Jeremiah, for the law shall not perish from the priest, nor counsel from the wise, nor the word from the prophet. Come, let us strike him with the tongue, and let us not pay attention to any of his words."

¹⁹ Hear me, O LORD,
 and listen to the voice of my adversaries.
²⁰ Should good be repaid with evil?
 Yet they have dug a pit for my life.
Remember how I stood before you
 to speak good for them,
 to turn away your wrath from them.

²¹ Therefore deliver up their children to famine;
 give them over to the power of the sword;
let their wives become childless and widowed.
 May their men meet death by pestilence,
 their youths be struck down by the sword in battle.
²² May a cry be heard from their houses,
 when you bring the plunderer suddenly upon them!
For they have dug a pit to take me
 and laid snares for my feet.
²³ Yet you, O LORD, know
 all their plotting to kill me.
Forgive not their iniquity,
 nor blot out their sin from your sight.

GETTING THE MESSAGE

Repentance is mentioned more than a hundred times in Jeremiah. The Lord promised to forgive and heal the people if they turned from their sins (18:5–11). Few responded to Jeremiah's call for repentance, but the Lord promised that someday they would respond (33:14–26).

Let them be overthrown before you;
 deal with them in the time of your anger.

The Broken Flask

19 Thus says the LORD, "Go, buy a potter's earthenware flask, and take some of the elders of the people and some of the elders of the priests, ² and go out to the Valley of the Son of Hinnom at the entry of the Potsherd Gate, and proclaim there the words that I tell you. ³ You shall say, 'Hear the word of the LORD, O kings of Judah and inhabitants of Jerusalem. Thus says the LORD of hosts, the God of Israel: Behold, I am bringing such disaster upon this place that the ears of everyone who hears of it will tingle. ⁴ Because the people have forsaken me and have profaned this place by making offerings in it to other gods whom neither they nor their fathers nor the kings of Judah have known; and because they have filled this place with the blood of innocents, ⁵ and

have built the high places of Baal to burn their sons in the fire as burnt offerings to Baal, which I did not command or decree, nor did it come into my mind — ⁶ therefore, behold, days are coming, declares the LORD, when this place shall no more be called Topheth, or the Valley of the Son of Hinnom, but the Valley of Slaughter. ⁷ And in this place I will make void the plans of Judah and Jerusalem, and will cause their people to fall by the sword before their enemies, and by the hand of those who seek their life. I will give their dead bodies for food to the birds of the air and to the beasts of the earth. ⁸ And I will make this city a horror, a thing to be hissed at. Everyone who passes by it will be horrified and will hiss because of all its wounds. ⁹ And I will make them eat the flesh of their sons and their daughters, and everyone shall eat the flesh of his neighbor in the siege and in the distress, with which their enemies and those who seek their life afflict them.'

¹⁰ "Then you shall break the flask in the sight of the men who go with you, ¹¹ and shall say to them, 'Thus says the LORD of hosts: So will I break this people and this city, as one breaks a potter's vessel, so that it can never be mended. Men shall bury in Topheth because there will be no place else to bury. ¹² Thus will I do to this place, declares the LORD, and to its inhabitants, making this city like Topheth. ¹³ The houses of Jerusalem and the houses of the kings of Judah — all the houses on whose roofs offerings have been offered to all the host of heaven, and drink offerings have been poured out to other gods — shall be defiled like the place of Topheth.'"

¹⁴ Then Jeremiah came from Topheth, where the LORD had sent him to prophesy, and he stood in the court of the LORD's house and said to all the people: ¹⁵ "Thus says the LORD of hosts, the God of Israel, behold, I am bringing upon this city and upon all its towns all the disaster that I have pronounced against it, because they have stiffened their neck, refusing to hear my words."

Jeremiah Persecuted by Pashhur

20 Now Pashhur the priest, the son of Immer, who was chief officer in the house of the LORD, heard Jeremiah prophesying these things. ² Then Pashhur beat Jeremiah the prophet, and put him in the stocks that were in the upper Benjamin Gate of the house of the LORD. ³ The next day, when Pashhur released Jeremiah from the stocks, Jeremiah said to him, "The LORD does not call your name Pashhur, but Terror on Every Side. ⁴ For thus says the LORD: Behold, I will make you a terror to yourself and to all your friends. They shall fall by the sword of their enemies while you look on. And I will give all Judah into the hand of the king of Babylon. He shall carry them captive to Babylon, and shall strike them down with the sword. ⁵ Moreover, I will give all the wealth of the city, all its gains, all its prized belongings, and all the treasures of the kings of Judah into the hand of their enemies, who shall plunder them and seize them and carry them to Babylon. ⁶ And you, Pashhur, and all who dwell in your house, shall go into captivity. To Babylon you shall go, and there you shall die, and there you shall be buried, you and all your friends, to whom you have prophesied falsely."

⁷   O LORD, you have deceived me,
         and I was deceived;
     you are stronger than I,
         and you have prevailed.
     I have become a laughingstock all the
         day;
         everyone mocks me.
⁸   For whenever I speak, I cry out,
         I shout, "Violence and destruc-
             tion!"
     For the word of the LORD has become
         for me
         a reproach and derision all day
             long.
⁹   If I say, "I will not mention him,
         or speak any more in his name,"
     there is in my heart as it were a burn-
             ing fire
         shut up in my bones,
     and I am weary with holding it in,
         and I cannot.
¹⁰   For I hear many whispering.
         Terror is on every side!
     "Denounce him! Let us denounce
             him!"
         say all my close friends,
         watching for my fall.
     "Perhaps he will be deceived;
         then we can overcome him
         and take our revenge on him."

But the Lord is with me as a dread
warrior;
therefore my persecutors will stumble;
they will not overcome me.
They will be greatly shamed,
for they will not succeed.
Their eternal dishonor
will never be forgotten.
O Lord of hosts, who tests the righteous,
who sees the heart and the mind,
let me see your vengeance upon them,
for to you have I committed my
cause.
Sing to the Lord;
praise the Lord!
For he has delivered the life of the
needy
from the hand of evildoers.

Cursed be the day
on which I was born!
The day when my mother bore me,
let it not be blessed!
Cursed be the man who brought the
news to my father,
"A son is born to you,"
making him very glad.
Let that man be like the cities
that the Lord overthrew without
pity;
let him hear a cry in the morning
and an alarm at noon,
because he did not kill me in the
womb;
so my mother would have been my
grave,
and her womb forever great.
Why did I come out from the womb
to see toil and sorrow,
and spend my days in shame?

Jerusalem Will Fall to Nebuchadnezzar

21 This is the word that came to Jeremiah
from the Lord, when King Zedekiah
sent to him Pashhur the son of Malchiah and
Zephaniah the priest, the son of Maaseiah,
saying, ² "Inquire of the Lord for us, for
Nebuchadnezzar king of Babylon is making
war against us. Perhaps the Lord will deal
with us according to all his wonderful deeds
and will make him withdraw from us."

³ Then Jeremiah said to them: "Thus
you shall say to Zedekiah, ⁴ 'Thus says the
Lord, the God of Israel: Behold, I will turn
back the weapons of war that are in your
hands and with which you are fighting
against the king of Babylon and against the
Chaldeans who are besieging you outside
the walls. And I will bring them together
into the midst of this city. ⁵ I myself will
fight against you with outstretched hand
and strong arm, in anger and in fury and
in great wrath. ⁶ And I will strike down
the inhabitants of this city, both man and
beast. They shall die of a great pestilence.
⁷ Afterward, declares the Lord, I will give
Zedekiah king of Judah and his servants and
the people in this city who survive the pestilence, sword, and famine into the hand of
Nebuchadnezzar king of Babylon and into
the hand of their enemies, into the hand of
those who seek their lives. He shall strike
them down with the edge of the sword. He

> **GETTING THE MESSAGE**
>
> **Mind or kidneys?** The word translated
> "mind" in 20:12 is actually the Hebrew
> word for "kidneys." Because the kidneys
> were hidden deep within the body, they
> were seen as the source of emotions and
> even wisdom.

shall not pity them or spare them or have
compassion.'

⁸ "And to this people you shall say: 'Thus
says the Lord: Behold, I set before you the
way of life and the way of death. ⁹ He who
stays in this city shall die by the sword, by
famine, and by pestilence, but he who goes
out and surrenders to the Chaldeans who
are besieging you shall live and shall have
his life as a prize of war. ¹⁰ For I have set my
face against this city for harm and not for
good, declares the Lord: it shall be given
into the hand of the king of Babylon, and
he shall burn it with fire.'

Message to the House of David

¹¹ "And to the house of the king of Judah
say, 'Hear the word of the Lord, ¹² O house
of David! Thus says the Lord:

"'Execute justice in the morning,
and deliver from the hand of the
oppressor
him who has been robbed,

lest my wrath go forth like fire,
    and burn with none to quench it,
    because of your evil deeds.'"

13 "Behold, I am against you, O inhabitant
    of the valley,
    O rock of the plain,
        declares the LORD;
you who say, 'Who shall come down
    against us,
    or who shall enter our habitations?'
14 I will punish you according to the
    fruit of your deeds,
        declares the LORD;
    I will kindle a fire in her forest,
    and it shall devour all that is around
    her."

22 Thus says the LORD: "Go down to the house of the king of Judah and speak there this word, ² and say, 'Hear the word of the LORD, O king of Judah, who sits on the throne of David, you, and your servants, and your people who enter these gates. ³ Thus says the LORD: Do justice and righteousness, and deliver from the hand of the oppressor him who has been robbed. And do no wrong or violence to the resident alien, the fatherless, and the widow, nor shed innocent blood in this place. ⁴ For if you will indeed obey this word, then there shall enter the gates of this house kings who sit on the throne of David, riding in chariots and on horses, they and their servants and their people. ⁵ But if you will not obey these words, I swear by myself, declares the LORD, that this house shall become a desolation. ⁶ For thus says the LORD concerning the house of the king of Judah:

"'You are like Gilead to me,
    like the summit of Lebanon,
yet surely I will make you a desert,
    an uninhabited city.
7 I will prepare destroyers against you,
    each with his weapons,
and they shall cut down your choicest
    cedars
    and cast them into the fire.

8 "'And many nations will pass by this city, and every man will say to his neighbor, "Why has the LORD dealt thus with this great city?" 9 And they will answer, "Because they have forsaken the covenant of the LORD their God and worshiped other gods and served them."'"

10 Weep not for him who is dead,
    nor grieve for him,
but weep bitterly for him who goes
    away,
    for he shall return no more
    to see his native land.

Message to the Sons of Josiah

11 For thus says the LORD concerning Shallum the son of Josiah, king of Judah, who reigned instead of Josiah his father, and who went away from this place: "He shall return here no more, 12 but in the place where they have carried him captive, there shall he die, and he shall never see this land again."

13 "Woe to him who builds his house by
    unrighteousness,
    and his upper rooms by injustice,
who makes his neighbor serve him for
    nothing
    and does not give him his wages,
14 who says, 'I will build myself a great
    house
    with spacious upper rooms,'
who cuts out windows for it,
    paneling it with cedar
    and painting it with vermilion.
15 Do you think you are a king
    because you compete in cedar?
Did not your father eat and drink
    and do justice and righteousness?
    Then it was well with him.
16 He judged the cause of the poor and
    needy;
    then it was well.
Is not this to know me?
    declares the LORD.
17 But you have eyes and heart
    only for your dishonest gain,
for shedding innocent blood,
    and for practicing oppression and
    violence."

18 Therefore thus says the LORD concerning Jehoiakim the son of Josiah, king of Judah:

"They shall not lament for him, saying,
    'Ah, my brother!' or 'Ah, sister!'
They shall not lament for him, saying,
    'Ah, lord!' or 'Ah, his majesty!'
19 With the burial of a donkey he shall
    be buried,
    dragged and dumped beyond the
    gates of Jerusalem."

20 "Go up to Lebanon, and cry out,
    and lift up your voice in Bashan;
  cry out from Abarim,
    for all your lovers are destroyed.
21 I spoke to you in your prosperity,
    but you said, 'I will not listen.'
  This has been your way from your
      youth,
    that you have not obeyed my voice.
22 The wind shall shepherd all your
      shepherds,
    and your lovers shall go into captiv-
      ity;
  then you will be ashamed and con-
      founded
    because of all your evil.
23 O inhabitant of Lebanon,
    nested among the cedars,
  how you will be pitied when pangs
      come upon you,
    pain as of a woman in labor!"

24 "As I live, declares the LORD, though Coniah the son of Jehoiakim, king of Judah, were the signet ring on my right hand, yet I would tear you off 25 and give you into the hand of those who seek your life, into the hand of those of whom you are afraid, even into the hand of Nebuchadnezzar king of Babylon and into the hand of the Chaldeans. 26 I will hurl you and the mother who bore you into another country, where you were not born, and there you shall die. 27 But to the land to which they will long to return, there they shall not return."

28 Is this man Coniah a despised, broken
      pot,
    a vessel no one cares for?
  Why are he and his children hurled
      and cast
    into a land that they do not know?
29 O land, land, land,
    hear the word of the LORD!
30 Thus says the LORD:
  "Write this man down as childless,
    a man who shall not succeed in his
      days,
  for none of his offspring shall succeed
    in sitting on the throne of David
    and ruling again in Judah."

The Righteous Branch

23 "Woe to the shepherds who destroy and scatter the sheep of my pasture!" declares the LORD. 2 Therefore thus says the LORD, the God of Israel, concerning the shepherds who care for my people: "You have scattered my flock and have driven them away, and you have not attended to them. Behold, I will attend to you for your evil deeds, declares the LORD. 3 Then I will gather the remnant of my flock out of all the countries where I have driven them, and I will bring them back to their fold, and they shall be fruitful and multiply. 4 I will set shepherds over them who will care for them, and they shall fear no more, nor be dismayed, neither shall any be missing, declares the LORD.

5 "Behold, the days are coming, declares the LORD, when I will raise up for David a righteous Branch, and he shall reign as king and deal wisely, and shall execute justice and righteousness in the land. 6 In his days Judah will be saved, and Israel will dwell securely.

GETTING THE MESSAGE

The faithful remnant. In many places, the Bible speaks of a "remnant," that is, a relatively small group of people, who will remain faithful to the Lord (23:3; compare Ezra 9:8; Isa. 10:20; Rom. 11:5).

And this is the name by which he will be called: 'The LORD is our righteousness.'

7 "Therefore, behold, the days are coming, declares the LORD, when they shall no longer say, 'As the LORD lives who brought up the people of Israel out of the land of Egypt,' 8 but 'As the LORD lives who brought up and led the offspring of the house of Israel out of the north country and out of all the countries where he had driven them.' Then they shall dwell in their own land."

Lying Prophets

9 Concerning the prophets:

  My heart is broken within me;
    all my bones shake;
  I am like a drunken man,
    like a man overcome by wine,
  because of the LORD
    and because of his holy words.
10 For the land is full of adulterers;
    because of the curse the land mourns,
    and the pastures of the wilderness
      are dried up.

Their course is evil,
  and their might is not right.
11 "Both prophet and priest are ungodly;
  even in my house I have found their
    evil,
        declares the LORD.
12 Therefore their way shall be to them
  like slippery paths in the darkness,
  into which they shall be driven and
    fall,
  for I will bring disaster upon them
  in the year of their punishment,
        declares the LORD.
13 In the prophets of Samaria
  I saw an unsavory thing:
  they prophesied by Baal
  and led my people Israel astray.
14 But in the prophets of Jerusalem
  I have seen a horrible thing:
  they commit adultery and walk in lies;
  they strengthen the hands of evil-
    doers,
  so that no one turns from his evil;
  all of them have become like Sodom
    to me,
  and its inhabitants like Gomorrah."
15 Therefore thus says the LORD of hosts
    concerning the prophets:
  "Behold, I will feed them with bitter
    food
  and give them poisoned water to
    drink,
  for from the prophets of Jerusalem
  ungodliness has gone out into all
    the land."

16 Thus says the LORD of hosts: "Do not listen to the words of the prophets who prophesy to you, filling you with vain hopes. They
speak visions of their own minds, not from
the mouth of the LORD. 17 They say continually to those who despise the word of the
LORD, 'It shall be well with you'; and to everyone who stubbornly follows his own heart,
they say, 'No disaster shall come upon you.'"

18 For who among them has stood in the
    council of the LORD
  to see and to hear his word,
  or who has paid attention to his
    word and listened?
19 Behold, the storm of the LORD!
  Wrath has gone forth,
  a whirling tempest;
  it will burst upon the head of the
    wicked.
20 The anger of the LORD will not turn
    back
  until he has executed and accom-
    plished
  the intents of his heart.
  In the latter days you will understand
    it clearly.

21 "I did not send the prophets,
    yet they ran;
  I did not speak to them,
    yet they prophesied.
22 But if they had stood in my council,
  then they would have proclaimed
    my words to my people,
  and they would have turned them
    from their evil way,
  and from the evil of their deeds.

23 "Am I a God at hand, declares the LORD,
and not a God far away? 24 Can a man hide
himself in secret places so that I cannot see
him? declares the LORD. Do I not fill heaven
and earth? declares the LORD. 25 I have heard
what the prophets have said who prophesy
lies in my name, saying, 'I have dreamed,
I have dreamed!' 26 How long shall there
be lies in the heart of the prophets who
prophesy lies, and who prophesy the deceit
of their own heart, 27 who think to make
my people forget my name by their dreams
that they tell one another, even as their
fathers forgot my name for Baal? 28 Let the
prophet who has a dream tell the dream,
but let him who has my word speak my
word faithfully. What has straw in common
with wheat? declares the LORD. 29 Is not my
word like fire, declares the LORD, and like
a hammer that breaks the rock in pieces?
30 Therefore, behold, I am against the prophets, declares the LORD, who steal my words
from one another. 31 Behold, I am against the
prophets, declares the LORD, who use their
tongues and declare, 'declares the LORD.'
32 Behold, I am against those who prophesy
lying dreams, declares the LORD, and who
tell them and lead my people astray by their
lies and their recklessness, when I did not
send them or charge them. So they do not
profit this people at all, declares the LORD.

33 "When one of this people, or a prophet
or a priest asks you, 'What is the burden
of the LORD?' you shall say to them, 'You are
the burden, and I will cast you off, declares
the LORD.' 34 And as for the prophet, priest,
or one of the people who says, 'The burden

of the LORD,' I will punish that man and his household. ³⁵ Thus shall you say, every one to his neighbor and every one to his brother, 'What has the LORD answered?' or 'What has the LORD spoken?' ³⁶ But 'the burden of the LORD' you shall mention no more, for the burden is every man's own word, and you pervert the words of the living God, the LORD of hosts, our God. ³⁷ Thus you shall say to the prophet, 'What has the LORD answered you?' or 'What has the LORD spoken?' ³⁸ But if you say, 'The burden of the LORD,' thus says the LORD, 'Because you have said these words, "The burden of the LORD," when I sent to you, saying, "You shall not say, 'The burden of the LORD,'" ³⁹ therefore, behold, I will surely lift you up and cast you away from my presence, you and the city that I gave to you and your fathers. ⁴⁰ And I will bring upon you everlasting reproach and perpetual shame, which shall not be forgotten.'"

The Good Figs and the Bad Figs

24 After Nebuchadnezzar king of Babylon had taken into exile from Jerusalem Jeconiah the son of Jehoiakim, king of Judah, together with the officials of Judah, the craftsmen, and the metal workers, and had brought them to Babylon, the LORD showed me this vision: behold, two baskets of figs placed before the temple of the LORD. ² One basket had very good figs, like first-ripe figs, but the other basket had very bad figs, so bad that they could not be eaten. ³ And the LORD said to me, "What do you see, Jeremiah?" I said, "Figs, the good figs very good, and the bad figs very bad, so bad that they cannot be eaten."

⁴ Then the word of the LORD came to me: ⁵ "Thus says the LORD, the God of Israel: Like these good figs, so I will regard as good the exiles from Judah, whom I have sent away from this place to the land of the Chaldeans. ⁶ I will set my eyes on them for good, and I will bring them back to this land. I will build them up, and not tear them down; I will plant them, and not pluck them up. ⁷ I will give them a heart to know that I am the LORD, and they shall be my people and I will be their God, for they shall return to me with their whole heart.

⁸ "But thus says the LORD: Like the bad figs that are so bad they cannot be eaten, so will I treat Zedekiah the king of Judah, his officials, the remnant of Jerusalem who

remain in this land, and those who dwell in the land of Egypt. ⁹ I will make them a horror to all the kingdoms of the earth, to be a reproach, a byword, a taunt, and a curse in all the places where I shall drive them. ¹⁰ And I will send sword, famine, and pestilence upon them, until they shall be utterly destroyed from the land that I gave to them and their fathers."

Seventy Years of Captivity

25 The word that came to Jeremiah concerning all the people of Judah, in the fourth year of Jehoiakim the son of Josiah, king of Judah (that was the first year of Nebuchadnezzar king of Babylon), ² which Jeremiah the prophet spoke to all the people of Judah and all the inhabitants of Jerusalem: ³ "For twenty-three years, from the thirteenth year of Josiah the son of Amon, king of Judah, to this day, the word

> ### GETTING THE MESSAGE
>
> **Seventy years in Babylon.** Jeremiah saw many of his fellow Judeans exiled to Babylon during his lifetime. He predicted that they would remain there for 70 years (25:11–12), and Ezra 1:1 records the precise fulfillment of that prophecy.

of the LORD has come to me, and I have spoken persistently to you, but you have not listened. ⁴ You have neither listened nor inclined your ears to hear, although the LORD persistently sent to you all his servants the prophets, ⁵ saying, 'Turn now, every one of you, from his evil way and evil deeds, and dwell upon the land that the LORD has given to you and your fathers from of old and forever. ⁶ Do not go after other gods to serve and worship them, or provoke me to anger with the work of your hands. Then I will do you no harm.' ⁷ Yet you have not listened to me, declares the LORD, that you might provoke me to anger with the work of your hands to your own harm.

⁸ "Therefore thus says the LORD of hosts: Because you have not obeyed my words, ⁹ behold, I will send for all the tribes of the north, declares the LORD, and for Nebuchadnezzar the king of Babylon, my servant, and I will bring them against this land and its inhabitants, and against all

these surrounding nations. I will devote them to destruction, and make them a horror, a hissing, and an everlasting desolation. ¹⁰ Moreover, I will banish from them the voice of mirth and the voice of gladness, the voice of the bridegroom and the voice of the bride, the grinding of the millstones and the light of the lamp. ¹¹ This whole land shall become a ruin and a waste, and these nations shall serve the king of Babylon seventy years. ¹² Then after seventy years are completed, I will punish the king of Babylon and that nation, the land of the Chaldeans, for their iniquity, declares the LORD, making the land an everlasting waste. ¹³ I will bring upon that land all the words that I have uttered against it, everything written in this book, which Jeremiah prophesied against all the nations. ¹⁴ For many nations and great kings shall make slaves even of them, and I will recompense them according to their deeds and the work of their hands."

The Cup of the LORD's Wrath

¹⁵ Thus the LORD, the God of Israel, said to me: "Take from my hand this cup of the wine of wrath, and make all the nations to whom I send you drink it. ¹⁶ They shall drink and stagger and be crazed because of the sword that I am sending among them."

¹⁷ So I took the cup from the LORD's hand, and made all the nations to whom the LORD sent me drink it: ¹⁸ Jerusalem and the cities of Judah, its kings and officials, to make them a desolation and a waste, a hissing and a curse, as at this day; ¹⁹ Pharaoh king of Egypt, his servants, his officials, all his people, ²⁰ and all the mixed tribes among them; all the kings of the land of Uz and all the kings of the land of the Philistines (Ashkelon, Gaza, Ekron, and the remnant of Ashdod); ²¹ Edom, Moab, and the sons of Ammon; ²² all the kings of Tyre, all the kings of Sidon, and the kings of the coastland across the sea; ²³ Dedan, Tema, Buz, and all who cut the corners of their hair; ²⁴ all the kings of Arabia and all the kings of the mixed tribes who dwell in the desert; ²⁵ all the kings of Zimri, all the kings of Elam, and all the kings of Media; ²⁶ all the kings of the north, far and near, one after another, and all the kingdoms of the world that are on the face of the earth. And after them the king of Babylon shall drink.

²⁷ "Then you shall say to them, 'Thus says the LORD of hosts, the God of Israel: Drink, be drunk and vomit, fall and rise no more, because of the sword that I am sending among you.'

²⁸ "And if they refuse to accept the cup from your hand to drink, then you shall say to them, 'Thus says the LORD of hosts: You must drink! ²⁹ For behold, I begin to work disaster at the city that is called by my name, and shall you go unpunished? You shall not go unpunished, for I am summoning a sword against all the inhabitants of the earth, declares the LORD of hosts.'

³⁰ "You, therefore, shall prophesy against them all these words, and say to them:

"'The LORD will roar from on high,
    and from his holy habitation utter
        his voice;
he will roar mightily against his fold,
    and shout, like those who tread
        grapes,
    against all the inhabitants of the
        earth.
³¹ The clamor will resound to the ends
        of the earth,
    for the LORD has an indictment
        against the nations;
he is entering into judgment with all
        flesh,
    and the wicked he will put to the
        sword,
                declares the LORD.'

³² "Thus says the LORD of hosts:
Behold, disaster is going forth
    from nation to nation,
and a great tempest is stirring
    from the farthest parts of the earth!

³³ "And those pierced by the LORD on that day shall extend from one end of the earth to the other. They shall not be lamented, or gathered, or buried; they shall be dung on the surface of the ground.

³⁴ "Wail, you shepherds, and cry out,
    and roll in ashes, you lords of the
        flock,
for the days of your slaughter and
        dispersion have come,
    and you shall fall like a choice vessel.
³⁵ No refuge will remain for the shep-
        herds,
    nor escape for the lords of the flock.

36 A voice—the cry of the shepherds,
　　and the wail of the lords of the flock!
　　For the Lord is laying waste their
　　　　pasture,
37 and the peaceful folds are devastated
　　because of the fierce anger of the
　　　　Lord.
38 Like a lion he has left his lair,
　　for their land has become a waste
　　because of the sword of the oppressor,
　　and because of his fierce anger."

Jeremiah Threatened with Death

26 In the beginning of the reign of Jehoiakim the son of Josiah, king of Judah, this word came from the Lord: ² "Thus says the Lord: Stand in the court of the Lord's house, and speak to all the cities of Judah that come to worship in the house of the Lord all the words that I command you to speak to them; do not hold back a word. ³ It may be they will listen, and every one turn from his evil way, that I may relent of the disaster that I intend to do to them because of their evil deeds. ⁴ You shall say to them, 'Thus says the Lord: If you will not listen to me, to walk in my law that I have set before you, ⁵ and to listen to the words of my servants the prophets whom I send to you urgently, though you have not listened, ⁶ then I will make this house like Shiloh, and I will make this city a curse for all the nations of the earth.'"

⁷ The priests and the prophets and all the people heard Jeremiah speaking these words in the house of the Lord. ⁸ And when Jeremiah had finished speaking all that the Lord had commanded him to speak to all the people, then the priests and the prophets and all the people laid hold of him, saying, "You shall die! ⁹ Why have you prophesied in the name of the Lord, saying, 'This house shall be like Shiloh, and this city shall be desolate, without inhabitant'?" And all the people gathered around Jeremiah in the house of the Lord.

¹⁰ When the officials of Judah heard these things, they came up from the king's house to the house of the Lord and took their seat in the entry of the New Gate of the house of the Lord. ¹¹ Then the priests and the prophets said to the officials and to all the people, "This man deserves the sentence of death, because he has prophesied against this city, as you have heard with your own ears."

¹² Then Jeremiah spoke to all the officials and all the people, saying, "The Lord sent me to prophesy against this house and this city all the words you have heard. ¹³ Now therefore mend your ways and your deeds, and obey the voice of the Lord your God, and the Lord will relent of the disaster that he has pronounced against you. ¹⁴ But as for me, behold, I am in your hands. Do with me as seems good and right to you. ¹⁵ Only know for certain that if you put me to death, you will bring innocent blood upon yourselves and upon this city and its inhabitants, for in truth the Lord sent me to you to speak all these words in your ears."

Jeremiah Spared from Death

¹⁶ Then the officials and all the people said to the priests and the prophets, "This man does not deserve the sentence of death, for he has spoken to us in the name of the Lord our God." ¹⁷ And certain of the elders of the land arose and spoke to all the assembled people, saying, ¹⁸ "Micah of Moresheth prophesied in the days of Hezekiah king of Judah, and said to all the people of Judah: 'Thus says the Lord of hosts,

　"'Zion shall be plowed as a field;
　　Jerusalem shall become a heap of
　　　　ruins,
　　and the mountain of the house a
　　　　wooded height.'

¹⁹ Did Hezekiah king of Judah and all Judah put him to death? Did he not fear the Lord and entreat the favor of the Lord, and did not the Lord relent of the disaster that he had pronounced against them? But we are about to bring great disaster upon ourselves."

²⁰ There was another man who prophesied in the name of the Lord, Uriah the son of Shemaiah from Kiriath-jearim. He prophesied against this city and against this land in words like those of Jeremiah. ²¹ And when King Jehoiakim, with all his warriors and all the officials, heard his words, the king sought to put him to death. But when Uriah heard of it, he was afraid and fled and escaped to Egypt. ²² Then King Jehoiakim sent to Egypt certain men, Elnathan the son of Achbor and others with him, ²³ and they took Uriah from Egypt and brought him to King Jehoiakim, who struck him down with the sword and dumped his dead body into the burial place of the common people.

24 But the hand of Ahikam the son of Shaphan was with Jeremiah so that he was not given over to the people to be put to death.

The Yoke of Nebuchadnezzar

27 In the beginning of the reign of Zedekiah the son of Josiah, king of Judah, this word came to Jeremiah from the LORD. **2** Thus the LORD said to me: "Make yourself straps and yoke-bars, and put them on your neck. **3** Send word to the king of Edom, the king of Moab, the king of the sons of Ammon, the king of Tyre, and the king of Sidon by the hand of the envoys who have come to Jerusalem to Zedekiah king of Judah. **4** Give them this charge for their masters: 'Thus says the LORD of hosts, the God of Israel: This is what you shall say to your

> ### GETTING THE MESSAGE
>
> **Jeremiah's unpopular message.** While all the other prophets were predicting victory over Babylon, Jeremiah told the people it was God's will that they serve Babylon for a certain number of years. Then, God would rescue them and would judge Babylon (ch. 27). Needless to say, Jeremiah's message did not make him very popular with either the people or the king.

masters: **5** "It is I who by my great power and my outstretched arm have made the earth, with the men and animals that are on the earth, and I give it to whomever it seems right to me. **6** Now I have given all these lands into the hand of Nebuchadnezzar, the king of Babylon, my servant, and I have given him also the beasts of the field to serve him. **7** All the nations shall serve him and his son and his grandson, until the time of his own land comes. Then many nations and great kings shall make him their slave. **8** "'But if any nation or kingdom will not serve this Nebuchadnezzar king of Babylon, and put its neck under the yoke of the king of Babylon, I will punish that nation with the sword, with famine, and with pestilence, declares the LORD, until I have consumed it by his hand. **9** So do not listen to your prophets, your diviners, your dreamers, your fortune-tellers, or your sorcerers, who

are saying to you, 'You shall not serve the king of Babylon.' **10** For it is a lie that they are prophesying to you, with the result that you will be removed far from your land, and I will drive you out, and you will perish. **11** But any nation that will bring its neck under the yoke of the king of Babylon and serve him, I will leave on its own land, to work it and dwell there, declares the LORD."'"

12 To Zedekiah king of Judah I spoke in like manner: "Bring your necks under the yoke of the king of Babylon, and serve him and his people and live. **13** Why will you and your people die by the sword, by famine, and by pestilence, as the LORD has spoken concerning any nation that will not serve the king of Babylon? **14** Do not listen to the words of the prophets who are saying to you, 'You shall not serve the king of Babylon,' for it is a lie that they are prophesying to you. **15** I have not sent them, declares the LORD, but they are prophesying falsely in my name, with the result that I will drive you out and you will perish, you and the prophets who are prophesying to you."

16 Then I spoke to the priests and to all this people, saying, "Thus says the LORD: Do not listen to the words of your prophets who are prophesying to you, saying, 'Behold, the vessels of the LORD's house will now shortly be brought back from Babylon,' for it is a lie that they are prophesying to you. **17** Do not listen to them; serve the king of Babylon and live. Why should this city become a desolation? **18** If they are prophets, and if the word of the LORD is with them, then let them intercede with the LORD of hosts, that the vessels that are left in the house of the LORD, in the house of the king of Judah, and in Jerusalem may not go to Babylon. **19** For thus says the LORD of hosts concerning the pillars, the sea, the stands, and the rest of the vessels that are left in this city, **20** which Nebuchadnezzar king of Babylon did not take away, when he took into exile from Jerusalem to Babylon Jeconiah the son of Jehoiakim, king of Judah, and all the nobles of Judah and Jerusalem — **21** thus says the LORD of hosts, the God of Israel, concerning the vessels that are left in the house of the LORD, in the house of the king of Judah, and in Jerusalem: **22** They shall be carried to Babylon and remain there until the day when I visit them, declares the LORD. Then

I will bring them back and restore them to this place."

Hananiah the False Prophet

28 In that same year, at the beginning of the reign of Zedekiah king of Judah, in the fifth month of the fourth year, Hananiah the son of Azzur, the prophet from Gibeon, spoke to me in the house of the LORD, in the presence of the priests and all the people, saying, ² "Thus says the LORD of hosts, the God of Israel: I have broken the yoke of the king of Babylon. ³ Within two years I will bring back to this place all the vessels of the LORD's house, which Nebuchadnezzar king of Babylon took away from this place and carried to Babylon. ⁴ I will also bring back to this place Jeconiah the son of Jehoiakim, king of Judah, and all the exiles from Judah who went to Babylon, declares the LORD, for I will break the yoke of the king of Babylon."

⁵ Then the prophet Jeremiah spoke to Hananiah the prophet in the presence of the priests and all the people who were standing in the house of the LORD, ⁶ and the prophet Jeremiah said, "Amen! May the LORD do so; may the LORD make the words that you have prophesied come true, and bring back to this place from Babylon the vessels of the house of the LORD, and all the exiles. ⁷ Yet hear now this word that I speak in your hearing and in the hearing of all the people. ⁸ The prophets who preceded you and me from ancient times prophesied war, famine, and pestilence against many countries and great kingdoms. ⁹ As for the prophet who prophesies peace, when the word of that prophet comes to pass, then it will be known that the LORD has truly sent the prophet."

¹⁰ Then the prophet Hananiah took the yoke-bars from the neck of Jeremiah the prophet and broke them. ¹¹ And Hananiah spoke in the presence of all the people, saying, "Thus says the LORD: Even so will I break the yoke of Nebuchadnezzar king of Babylon from the neck of all the nations within two years." But Jeremiah the prophet went his way.

¹² Sometime after the prophet Hananiah had broken the yoke-bars from off the neck of Jeremiah the prophet, the word of the LORD came to Jeremiah: ¹³ "Go, tell Hananiah, 'Thus says the LORD: You have

broken wooden bars, but you have made in their place bars of iron. ¹⁴ For thus says the LORD of hosts, the God of Israel: I have put upon the neck of all these nations an iron yoke to serve Nebuchadnezzar king of Babylon, and they shall serve him, for I have given to him even the beasts of the field.'" ¹⁵ And Jeremiah the prophet said to the prophet Hananiah, "Listen, Hananiah, the LORD has not sent you, and you have made this people trust in a lie. ¹⁶ Therefore thus says the LORD: 'Behold, I will remove you from the face of the earth. This year you shall die, because you have uttered rebellion against the LORD.'"

¹⁷ In that same year, in the seventh month, the prophet Hananiah died.

Jeremiah's Letter to the Exiles

29 These are the words of the letter that Jeremiah the prophet sent from Jerusalem to the surviving elders of the

GETTING THE MESSAGE

Why were Israel's craftsmen taken?
Craftsmen were highly prized by conquering kings (29:2). They could provide assistance with the king's projects as well as offer secrets of the trade that had been passed down through the generations.

exiles, and to the priests, the prophets, and all the people, whom Nebuchadnezzar had taken into exile from Jerusalem to Babylon. ² This was after King Jeconiah and the queen mother, the eunuchs, the officials of Judah and Jerusalem, the craftsmen, and the metal workers had departed from Jerusalem. ³ The letter was sent by the hand of Elasah the son of Shaphan and Gemariah the son of Hilkiah, whom Zedekiah king of Judah sent to Babylon to Nebuchadnezzar king of Babylon. It said: ⁴ "Thus says the LORD of hosts, the God of Israel, to all the exiles whom I have sent into exile from Jerusalem to Babylon: ⁵ Build houses and live in them; plant gardens and eat their produce. ⁶ Take wives and have sons and daughters; take wives for your sons, and give your daughters in marriage, that they may bear sons and daughters; multiply there, and do not decrease. ⁷ But seek the welfare of the city where I have sent you into exile, and pray to the LORD on its behalf, for in its welfare you will find your welfare. **8** For thus says the LORD of hosts, the God of Israel: Do not let your prophets and your diviners who are among you deceive you, and do not listen to the dreams that they dream, **9** for it is a lie that they are prophesying to you in my name; I did not send them, declares the LORD.

10 "For thus says the LORD: When seventy years are completed for Babylon, I will visit you, and I will fulfill to you my promise and bring you back to this place. **11** For I know the plans I have for you, declares the LORD, plans for welfare and not for evil, to give you a future and a hope. **12** Then you will call upon me and come and pray to me, and I will hear you. **13** You will seek me and find me, when you seek me with all your heart. **14** I will be found by you, declares the LORD, and I will restore your fortunes and gather you from all the nations and all the places where I have driven you, declares the LORD, and I will bring you back to the place from which I sent you into exile.

15 "Because you have said, 'The LORD has raised up prophets for us in Babylon,' **16** thus says the LORD concerning the king who sits on the throne of David, and concerning all the people who dwell in this city, your kinsmen who did not go out with you into exile: **17** 'Thus says the LORD of hosts, behold, I am sending on them sword, famine, and pestilence, and I will make them like vile figs that are so rotten they cannot be eaten. **18** I will pursue them with sword, famine, and pestilence, and will make them a horror to all the kingdoms of the earth, to be a curse, a terror, a hissing, and a reproach among all the nations where I have driven them, **19** because they did not pay attention to my words, declares the LORD, that I persistently sent to you by my servants the prophets, but you would not listen, declares the LORD.' **20** Hear the word of the LORD, all you exiles whom I sent away from Jerusalem to Babylon: **21** 'Thus says the LORD of hosts, the God of Israel, concerning Ahab the son of Kolaiah and Zedekiah the son of Maaseiah, who are prophesying a lie to you in my name: Behold, I will deliver them into the hand of Nebuchadnezzar king of Babylon, and he shall strike them down before your

eyes. **22** Because of them this curse shall be used by all the exiles from Judah in Babylon: "The LORD make you like Zedekiah and Ahab, whom the king of Babylon roasted in the fire," **23** because they have done an outrageous thing in Israel, they have committed adultery with their neighbors' wives, and they have spoken in my name lying words that I did not command them. I am the one who knows, and I am witness, declares the LORD.'"

Shemaiah's False Prophecy

24 To Shemaiah of Nehelam you shall say: **25** "Thus says the LORD of hosts, the God of Israel: You have sent letters in your name to all the people who are in Jerusalem, and to Zephaniah the son of Maaseiah the priest, and to all the priests, saying, **26** 'The LORD has made you priest instead of Jehoiada the priest, to have charge in the house of the LORD over every madman who prophesies, to put him in the stocks and neck irons. **27** Now why have you not rebuked Jeremiah of Anathoth who is prophesying to you? **28** For he has sent to us in Babylon, saying, "Your exile will be long; build houses and live in them, and plant gardens and eat their produce."'" **29** Zephaniah the priest read this letter in the hearing of Jeremiah the prophet. **30** Then the word of the LORD came to Jeremiah: **31** "Send to all the exiles, saying, 'Thus says the LORD concerning Shemaiah of Nehelam: Because Shemaiah had prophesied to you when I did not send him, and has made you trust in a lie, **32** therefore thus says the LORD: Behold, I will punish Shemaiah of Nehelam and his descendants. He shall not have anyone living among this people, and he shall not see the good that I will do to my people, declares the LORD, for he has spoken rebellion against the LORD.'"

Restoration for Israel and Judah

30 The word that came to Jeremiah from the LORD: **2** "Thus says the LORD, the God of Israel: Write in a book all the words that I have spoken to you. **3** For behold, days are coming, declares the LORD, when I will restore the fortunes of my people, Israel and Judah, says the LORD, and I will bring them back to the land that I gave to their fathers, and they shall take possession of it."

4 These are the words that the LORD spoke concerning Israel and Judah:

5 "Thus says the LORD:
We have heard a cry of panic,
   of terror, and no peace.
6 Ask now, and see,
   can a man bear a child?
Why then do I see every man
   with his hands on his stomach like
     a woman in labor?
   Why has every face turned pale?
7 Alas! That day is so great
   there is none like it;
it is a time of distress for Jacob;
   yet he shall be saved out of it.

8 "And it shall come to pass in that day, declares the LORD of hosts, that I will break his yoke from off your neck, and I will burst your bonds, and foreigners shall no more make a servant of him. **9** But they shall serve the LORD their God and David their king, whom I will raise up for them.

10 "Then fear not, O Jacob my servant,
     declares the LORD,
   nor be dismayed, O Israel;
for behold, I will save you from far
     away,
   and your offspring from the land of
     their captivity.
Jacob shall return and have quiet and
     ease,
   and none shall make him afraid.
11 For I am with you to save you,
     declares the LORD;
I will make a full end of all the nations
   among whom I scattered you,
   but of you I will not make a full
     end.
I will discipline you in just measure,
   and I will by no means leave you
     unpunished.

12 "For thus says the LORD:
Your hurt is incurable,
   and your wound is grievous.
13 There is none to uphold your cause,
   no medicine for your wound,
   no healing for you.
14 All your lovers have forgotten you;
   they care nothing for you;
for I have dealt you the blow of an
     enemy,
   the punishment of a merciless foe,

because your guilt is great,
   because your sins are flagrant.
15 Why do you cry out over your hurt?
   Your pain is incurable.
Because your guilt is great,
   because your sins are flagrant,
I have done these things to you.
16 Therefore all who devour you shall be
     devoured,
   and all your foes, every one of
     them, shall go into captivity;
those who plunder you shall be
     plundered,
   and all who prey on you I will make
     a prey.
17 For I will restore health to you,
   and your wounds I will heal,
       declares the LORD,

GETTING THE MESSAGE

Books in the Old Testament could refer to any written material (see 30:2). Usually this was in the form of papyrus scrolls. Pages were glued together end to end so they could be rolled up. A typical papyrus page was similar to the pages used in printers today. Scrolls were usually around 20 pages long, or roughly 15 feet (4.5 m).

because they have called you an out-
     cast:
   'It is Zion, for whom no one cares!'

18 "Thus says the LORD:
Behold, I will restore the fortunes of
     the tents of Jacob
   and have compassion on his dwell-
     ings;
the city shall be rebuilt on its
     mound,
   and the palace shall stand where it
     used to be.
19 Out of them shall come songs of
     thanksgiving,
   and the voices of those who cele-
     brate.
I will multiply them, and they shall
     not be few;
   I will make them honored, and they
     shall not be small.

20 Their children shall be as they were of
          old,
       and their congregation shall be
          established before me,
       and I will punish all who oppress
          them.
21 Their prince shall be one of them-
          selves;
       their ruler shall come out from
          their midst;
    I will make him draw near, and he
          shall approach me,
       for who would dare of himself to
          approach me?
                    declares the LORD.
22 And you shall be my people,
       and I will be your God."

23 Behold the storm of the LORD!
       Wrath has gone forth,
    a whirling tempest;
       it will burst upon the head of the
          wicked.
24 The fierce anger of the LORD will not
          turn back
       until he has executed and accom-
          plished
       the intentions of his mind.
    In the latter days you will understand
          this.

The LORD Will Turn Mourning to Joy

31 "At that time, declares the LORD, I will
    be the God of all the clans of Israel,
and they shall be my people."

2 Thus says the LORD:
    "The people who survived the sword
       found grace in the wilderness;
    when Israel sought for rest,
3   the LORD appeared to him from far
          away.
    I have loved you with an everlasting
          love;
       therefore I have continued my
          faithfulness to you.
4 Again I will build you, and you shall
          be built,
       O virgin Israel!
    Again you shall adorn yourself with
          tambourines
       and shall go forth in the dance of
          the merrymakers.
5 Again you shall plant vineyards
       on the mountains of Samaria;

    the planters shall plant
       and shall enjoy the fruit.
6 For there shall be a day when watch-
          men will call
       in the hill country of Ephraim:
    'Arise, and let us go up to Zion,
       to the LORD our God.'"

7 For thus says the LORD:
    "Sing aloud with gladness for Jacob,
       and raise shouts for the chief of the
          nations;
    proclaim, give praise, and say,
       'O LORD, save your people,
       the remnant of Israel.'
8 Behold, I will bring them from the
          north country
       and gather them from the farthest
          parts of the earth,
    among them the blind and the lame,
       the pregnant woman and she who
          is in labor, together;
    a great company, they shall return
          here.
9 With weeping they shall come,
       and with pleas for mercy I will lead
          them back,
    I will make them walk by brooks of
          water,
       in a straight path in which they
          shall not stumble,
    for I am a father to Israel,
       and Ephraim is my firstborn.

10 "Hear the word of the LORD, O nations,
       and declare it in the coastlands far
          away;
    say, 'He who scattered Israel will
          gather him,
       and will keep him as a shepherd
          keeps his flock.'
11 For the LORD has ransomed Jacob
       and has redeemed him from hands
          too strong for him.
12 They shall come and sing aloud on
          the height of Zion,
       and they shall be radiant over the
          goodness of the LORD,
    over the grain, the wine, and the oil,
       and over the young of the flock and
          the herd;
    their life shall be like a watered gar-
          den,
       and they shall languish no more.

13 Then shall the young women rejoice
    in the dance,
  and the young men and the old
    shall be merry.
I will turn their mourning into joy;
  I will comfort them, and give them
    gladness for sorrow.
14 I will feast the soul of the priests with
    abundance,
  and my people shall be satisfied
    with my goodness,
             declares the LORD."

15 Thus says the LORD:
"A voice is heard in Ramah,
  lamentation and bitter weeping.
Rachel is weeping for her children;
  she refuses to be comforted for her
    children,
  because they are no more."

16 Thus says the LORD:
"Keep your voice from weeping,
  and your eyes from tears,
for there is a reward for your work,
             declares the LORD,
and they shall come back from the
    land of the enemy.
17 There is hope for your future,
             declares the LORD,
and your children shall come back
    to their own country.
18 I have heard Ephraim grieving,
'You have disciplined me, and I was
    disciplined,
  like an untrained calf;
bring me back that I may be restored,
  for you are the LORD my God.
19 For after I had turned away, I relented,
  and after I was instructed, I struck
    my thigh;
I was ashamed, and I was confounded,
  because I bore the disgrace of my
    youth.'
20 Is Ephraim my dear son?
  Is he my darling child?
For as often as I speak against him,
  I do remember him still.
Therefore my heart yearns for him;
  I will surely have mercy on him,
            declares the LORD.

21 "Set up road markers for yourself;
  make yourself guideposts;
consider well the highway,
  the road by which you went.
Return, O virgin Israel,
  return to these your cities.
22 How long will you waver,
  O faithless daughter?
For the LORD has created a new thing
    on the earth:
  a woman encircles a man."

23 Thus says the LORD of hosts, the God
of Israel: "Once more they shall use these
words in the land of Judah and in its cities,
when I restore their fortunes:

" 'The LORD bless you, O habitation of
    righteousness,
  O holy hill!'

24 And Judah and all its cities shall dwell
there together, and the farmers and those
who wander with their flocks. 25 For I will

GETTING THE MESSAGE

Jeremiah said that Jerusalem would
someday be rebuilt **from the Tower of
Hananel to the Corner Gate** (31:38). This
is probably where the Babylonian army
broke through the walls of Jerusalem. It
was on the north side of the city, where
the land was flat. There were steep
valleys around the rest of the city, which
would have made it harder to invade.

satisfy the weary soul, and every languishing soul I will replenish."

26 At this I awoke and looked, and my
sleep was pleasant to me.

27 "Behold, the days are coming, declares
the LORD, when I will sow the house of Israel
and the house of Judah with the seed of man
and the seed of beast. 28 And it shall come
to pass that as I have watched over them
to pluck up and break down, to overthrow,
destroy, and bring harm, so I will watch
over them to build and to plant, declares
the LORD. 29 In those days they shall no
longer say:

" 'The fathers have eaten sour grapes,
  and the children's teeth are set on
    edge.'

30 But everyone shall die for his own iniquity. Each man who eats sour grapes, his
teeth shall be set on edge.

The New Covenant

³¹"Behold, the days are coming, declares the LORD, when I will make a new covenant with the house of Israel and the house of Judah, ³²not like the covenant that I made with their fathers on the day when I took them by the hand to bring them out of the land of Egypt, my covenant that they broke, though I was their husband, declares the LORD. ³³For this is the covenant that I will make with the house of Israel after those days, declares the LORD: I will put my law within them, and I will write it on their hearts. And I will be their God, and they shall be my people. ³⁴And no longer shall each one teach his neighbor and each his brother, saying, 'Know the LORD,' for they shall all know me, from the least of them to the greatest, declares the LORD. For I will forgive their iniquity, and I will remember their sin no more."

³⁵ Thus says the LORD,
　 who gives the sun for light by day
　　 and the fixed order of the moon and
　　　 the stars for light by night,
　 who stirs up the sea so that its waves
　　 roar—
　 the LORD of hosts is his name:
³⁶ "If this fixed order departs
　　 from before me, declares the LORD,
　 then shall the offspring of Israel cease
　　 from being a nation before me
　　　 forever."

³⁷ Thus says the LORD:
　 "If the heavens above can be mea-
　　 sured,
　 and the foundations of the earth
　　 below can be explored,
　 then I will cast off all the offspring of
　　 Israel
　　 for all that they have done,
　　　　　　　 declares the LORD."

³⁸"Behold, the days are coming, declares the LORD, when the city shall be rebuilt for the LORD from the Tower of Hananel to the Corner Gate. ³⁹And the measuring line shall go out farther, straight to the hill Gareb, and shall then turn to Goah. ⁴⁰The whole valley of the dead bodies and the ashes, and all the fields as far as the brook Kidron, to the corner of the Horse Gate toward the east, shall be sacred to the LORD. It shall not be plucked up or overthrown anymore forever."

Jeremiah Buys a Field During the Siege

32 The word that came to Jeremiah from the LORD in the tenth year of Zedekiah king of Judah, which was the eighteenth year of Nebuchadnezzar. ²At that time the army of the king of Babylon was besieging Jerusalem, and Jeremiah the prophet was shut up in the court of the guard that was in the palace of the king of Judah. ³For Zedekiah king of Judah had imprisoned him, saying, "Why do you prophesy and say, 'Thus says the LORD: Behold, I am giving this city into the hand of the king of Babylon, and he shall capture it; ⁴Zedekiah king of Judah shall not escape out of the hand of the Chaldeans, but shall surely be given into the hand of the king of Babylon, and shall speak with him face to face and see him eye to eye. ⁵And he shall take Zedekiah to Babylon, and there he shall remain until I visit him, declares the LORD. Though you fight against the Chaldeans, you shall not succeed'?"

⁶Jeremiah said, "The word of the LORD came to me: ⁷Behold, Hanamel the son of Shallum your uncle will come to you and say, 'Buy my field that is at Anathoth, for the right of redemption by purchase is yours.' ⁸Then Hanamel my cousin came to me in the court of the guard, in accordance with the word of the LORD, and said to me, 'Buy my field that is at Anathoth in the land of Benjamin, for the right of possession and redemption is yours; buy it for yourself.' Then I knew that this was the word of the LORD.

⁹"And I bought the field at Anathoth from Hanamel my cousin, and weighed out the money to him, seventeen shekels of silver. ¹⁰I signed the deed, sealed it, got witnesses, and weighed the money on scales. ¹¹Then I took the sealed deed of purchase, containing the terms and conditions and the open copy. ¹²And I gave the deed of purchase to Baruch the son of Neriah son of Mahseiah, in the presence of Hanamel my cousin, in the presence of the witnesses who signed the deed of purchase, and in the presence of all the Judeans who were sitting in the court of the guard. ¹³I charged Baruch in their presence, saying, ¹⁴'Thus says the LORD of hosts, the God of Israel: Take these deeds, both this sealed deed of purchase and this open deed, and put them in an earthenware vessel, that they may last for a long time.

¹⁵ For thus says the LORD of hosts, the God of Israel: Houses and fields and vineyards shall again be bought in this land.'

Jeremiah Prays for Understanding

¹⁶ "After I had given the deed of purchase to Baruch the son of Neriah, I prayed to the LORD, saying: ¹⁷ 'Ah, Lord GOD! It is you who have made the heavens and the earth by your great power and by your outstretched arm! Nothing is too hard for you. ¹⁸ You show steadfast love to thousands, but you repay the guilt of fathers to their children after them, O great and mighty God, whose name is the LORD of hosts, ¹⁹ great in counsel and mighty in deed, whose eyes are open to all the ways of the children of man, rewarding each one according to his ways and according to the fruit of his deeds. ²⁰ You have shown signs and wonders in the land of Egypt, and to this day in Israel and among all mankind, and have made a name for yourself, as at this day. ²¹ You brought your people Israel out of the land of Egypt with signs and wonders, with a strong hand and outstretched arm, and with great terror. ²² And you gave them this land, which you swore to their fathers to give them, a land flowing with milk and honey. ²³ And they entered and took possession of it. But they did not obey your voice or walk in your law. They did nothing of all you commanded them to do. Therefore you have made all this disaster come upon them. ²⁴ Behold, the siege mounds have come up to the city to take it, and because of sword and famine and pestilence the city is given into the hands of the Chaldeans who are fighting against it. What you spoke has come to pass, and behold, you see it. ²⁵ Yet you, O Lord GOD, have said to me, "Buy the field for money and get witnesses"—though the city is given into the hands of the Chaldeans.' "

²⁶ The word of the LORD came to Jeremiah: ²⁷ "Behold, I am the LORD, the God of all flesh. Is anything too hard for me? ²⁸ Therefore, thus says the LORD: Behold, I am giving this city into the hands of the Chaldeans and into the hand of Nebuchadnezzar king of Babylon, and he shall capture it. ²⁹ The Chaldeans who are fighting against this city shall come and set this city on fire and burn it, with the houses on whose roofs offerings have been made to Baal and drink offerings have been poured out to other gods, to pro-

voke me to anger. ³⁰ For the children of Israel and the children of Judah have done nothing but evil in my sight from their youth. The children of Israel have done nothing but provoke me to anger by the work of their hands, declares the LORD. ³¹ This city has aroused my anger and wrath, from the day it was built to this day, so that I will remove it from my sight ³² because of all the evil of the children of Israel and the children of Judah that they did to provoke me to anger—their kings and their officials, their priests and their prophets, the men of Judah and the inhabitants of Jerusalem. ³³ They have turned to me their back and not their face. And though I have taught them persistently, they have not listened to receive instruction. ³⁴ They set up their abominations in the house that is called by my name, to defile it. ³⁵ They built the high places of

Baal in the Valley of the Son of Hinnom, to offer up their sons and daughters to Molech, though I did not command them, nor did it enter into my mind, that they should do this abomination, to cause Judah to sin.

They Shall Be My People; I Will Be Their God

³⁶ "Now therefore thus says the LORD, the God of Israel, concerning this city of which you say, 'It is given into the hand of the king of Babylon by sword, by famine, and by pestilence': ³⁷ Behold, I will gather them from all the countries to which I drove them in my anger and my wrath and in great indignation. I will bring them back to this place, and I will make them dwell in safety. ³⁸ And they shall be my people, and I will be their God. ³⁹ I will give them one heart and one way, that they may fear me forever, for their own good and the good of their children after them. ⁴⁰ I will make with them an everlasting covenant, that I will not turn

away from doing good to them. And I will put the fear of me in their hearts, that they may not turn from me. ⁴¹ I will rejoice in doing them good, and I will plant them in this land in faithfulness, with all my heart and all my soul.

⁴² "For thus says the Lord: Just as I have brought all this great disaster upon this people, so I will bring upon them all the good that I promise them. ⁴³ Fields shall be bought in this land of which you are saying, 'It is a desolation, without man or beast; it is given into the hand of the Chaldeans.' ⁴⁴ Fields shall be bought for money, and deeds shall be signed and sealed and witnessed, in the land of Benjamin, in the places about Jerusalem, and in the cities of Judah, in the cities of the hill country, in the cities of the Shephelah, and in the cities of the Negeb; for I will restore their fortunes, declares the Lord."

The Lord Promises Peace

33 The word of the Lord came to Jeremiah a second time, while he was still shut up in the court of the guard: ² "Thus says the Lord who made the earth, the Lord who formed it to establish it—the Lord is his name: ³ Call to me and I will answer you, and will tell you great and hidden things that you have not known. ⁴ For thus says the Lord, the God of Israel, concerning the houses of this city and the houses of the kings of Judah that were torn down to make a defense against the siege mounds and against the sword: ⁵ They are coming in to fight against the Chaldeans and to fill them[1] with the dead bodies of men whom I shall strike down in my anger and my wrath, for I have hidden my face from this city because of all their evil. ⁶ Behold, I will bring to it health and healing, and I will heal them and reveal to them abundance of prosperity and security. ⁷ I will restore the fortunes of Judah and the fortunes of Israel, and rebuild them as they were at first. ⁸ I will cleanse them from all the guilt of their sin against me, and I will forgive all the guilt of their sin and rebellion against me. ⁹ And this city shall be to me a name of joy, a praise and a glory before all the nations of the earth who shall hear of all the good that I do for them. They shall fear and tremble because

of all the good and all the prosperity I provide for it.

¹⁰ "Thus says the Lord: In this place of which you say, 'It is a waste without man or beast,' in the cities of Judah and the streets of Jerusalem that are desolate, without man or inhabitant or beast, there shall be heard again ¹¹ the voice of mirth and the voice of gladness, the voice of the bridegroom and the voice of the bride, the voices of those who sing, as they bring thank offerings to the house of the Lord:

" 'Give thanks to the Lord of hosts,
   for the Lord is good,
     for his steadfast love endures forever!'

For I will restore the fortunes of the land as at first, says the Lord.

¹² "Thus says the Lord of hosts: In this place that is waste, without man or beast, and in all of its cities, there shall again be habitations of shepherds resting their flocks. ¹³ In the cities of the hill country, in the cities of the Shephelah, and in the cities of the Negeb, in the land of Benjamin, the places about Jerusalem, and in the cities of Judah, flocks shall again pass under the hands of the one who counts them, says the Lord.

The Lord's Eternal Covenant with David

¹⁴ "Behold, the days are coming, declares the Lord, when I will fulfill the promise I made to the house of Israel and the house of Judah. ¹⁵ In those days and at that time I will cause a righteous Branch to spring up for David, and he shall execute justice and righteousness in the land. ¹⁶ In those days Judah will be saved, and Jerusalem will dwell securely. And this is the name by which it will be called: 'The Lord is our righteousness.'

¹⁷ "For thus says the Lord: David shall never lack a man to sit on the throne of the house of Israel, ¹⁸ and the Levitical priests shall never lack a man in my presence to offer burnt offerings, to burn grain offerings, and to make sacrifices forever."

¹⁹ The word of the Lord came to Jeremiah: ²⁰ "Thus says the Lord: If you can break my covenant with the day and my covenant with the night, so that day and night will not come at their appointed time, ²¹ then also my covenant with David my servant

[1] That is, the torn-down houses

may be broken, so that he shall not have a son to reign on his throne, and my covenant with the Levitical priests my ministers. ²² As the host of heaven cannot be numbered and the sands of the sea cannot be measured, so I will multiply the offspring of David my servant, and the Levitical priests who minister to me."

²³ The word of the LORD came to Jeremiah: ²⁴ "Have you not observed that these people are saying, 'The LORD has rejected the two clans that he chose'? Thus they have despised my people so that they are no longer a nation in their sight. ²⁵ Thus says the LORD: If I have not established my covenant with day and night and the fixed order of heaven and earth, ²⁶ then I will reject the offspring of Jacob and David my servant and will not choose one of his offspring to rule over the offspring of Abraham, Isaac, and Jacob. For I will restore their fortunes and will have mercy on them."

Zedekiah to Die in Babylon

34 The word that came to Jeremiah from the LORD, when Nebuchadnezzar king of Babylon and all his army and all the kingdoms of the earth under his dominion and all the peoples were fighting against Jerusalem and all of its cities: ² "Thus says the LORD, the God of Israel: Go and speak to Zedekiah king of Judah and say to him, 'Thus says the LORD: Behold, I am giving this city into the hand of the king of Babylon, and he shall burn it with fire. ³ You shall not escape from his hand but shall surely be captured and delivered into his hand. You shall see the king of Babylon eye to eye and speak with him face to face. And you shall go to Babylon.' ⁴ Yet hear the word of the LORD, O Zedekiah king of Judah! Thus says the LORD concerning you: 'You shall not die by the sword. ⁵ You shall die in peace. And as spices were burned for your fathers, the former kings who were before you, so people shall burn spices for you and lament for you, saying, "Alas, lord!"' For I have spoken the word, declares the LORD."

⁶ Then Jeremiah the prophet spoke all these words to Zedekiah king of Judah, in Jerusalem, ⁷ when the army of the king of Babylon was fighting against Jerusalem and against all the cities of Judah that were left, Lachish and Azekah, for these were the only fortified cities of Judah that remained.

⁸ The word that came to Jeremiah from the LORD, after King Zedekiah had made a covenant with all the people in Jerusalem to make a proclamation of liberty to them, ⁹ that everyone should set free his Hebrew slaves, male and female, so that no one should enslave a Jew, his brother. ¹⁰ And they obeyed, all the officials and all the people who had entered into the covenant that everyone would set free his slave, male or female, so that they would not be enslaved again. They obeyed and set them free. ¹¹ But afterward they turned around and took back the male and female slaves they had set free, and brought them into subjection as slaves. ¹² The word of the LORD came to Jeremiah from the LORD: ¹³ "Thus says the LORD, the God of Israel: I myself made a covenant with your fathers when I brought them out of the

> ### GETTING THE MESSAGE
>
> **Burning of spices during funerals** (34:5) served a number of purposes. If a burial was delayed, spices would mask any unpleasant odors. Since they were expensive, spices were also a way of displaying wealth and honoring the memory of the deceased.

land of Egypt, out of the house of slavery, saying, ¹⁴ 'At the end of seven years each of you must set free the fellow Hebrew who has been sold to you and has served you six years; you must set him free from your service.' But your fathers did not listen to me or incline their ears to me. ¹⁵ You recently repented and did what was right in my eyes by proclaiming liberty, each to his neighbor, and you made a covenant before me in the house that is called by my name, ¹⁶ but then you turned around and profaned my name when each of you took back his male and female slaves, whom you had set free according to their desire, and you brought them into subjection to be your slaves.

¹⁷ "Therefore, thus says the LORD: You have not obeyed me by proclaiming liberty, every one to his brother and to his neighbor; behold, I proclaim to you liberty to the sword, to pestilence, and to famine, declares the LORD. I will make you a horror to all the kingdoms of the earth. ¹⁸ And the men who

transgressed my covenant and did not keep the terms of the covenant that they made before me, I will make them like the calf that they cut in two and passed between its parts — **19** the officials of Judah, the officials of Jerusalem, the eunuchs, the priests, and all the people of the land who passed between the parts of the calf. **20** And I will give them into the hand of their enemies and into the hand of those who seek their lives. Their dead bodies shall be food for the birds of the air and the beasts of the earth. **21** And Zedekiah king of Judah and his officials I will give into the hand of their enemies and into the hand of those who seek their lives, into the hand of the army of the king of Babylon which has withdrawn from you. **22** Behold, I will command, declares

> **GETTING THE MESSAGE**
>
> The Lord commended the **Rechabites** for keeping the commandments of their founder (ch. 35), which included abstaining from wine and not building permanent houses. The Rechabites obeyed after being told only once, while the people of Judah continued to disobey the Lord after being warned many times.

the LORD, and will bring them back to this city. And they will fight against it and take it and burn it with fire. I will make the cities of Judah a desolation without inhabitant."

The Obedience of the Rechabites

35 The word that came to Jeremiah from the LORD in the days of Jehoiakim the son of Josiah, king of Judah: **2** "Go to the house of the Rechabites and speak with them and bring them to the house of the LORD, into one of the chambers; then offer them wine to drink." **3** So I took Jaazaniah the son of Jeremiah, son of Habazziniah and his brothers and all his sons and the whole house of the Rechabites. **4** I brought them to the house of the LORD into the chamber of the sons of Hanan the son of Igdaliah, the man of God, which was near the chamber of the officials, above the chamber of Maaseiah the son of Shallum, keeper of the threshold. **5** Then I set before the Rechabites pitchers full of wine, and cups, and I said to

them, "Drink wine." **6** But they answered, "We will drink no wine, for Jonadab the son of Rechab, our father, commanded us, 'You shall not drink wine, neither you nor your sons forever. **7** You shall not build a house; you shall not sow seed; you shall not plant or have a vineyard; but you shall live in tents all your days, that you may live many days in the land where you sojourn.' **8** We have obeyed the voice of Jonadab the son of Rechab, our father, in all that he commanded us, to drink no wine all our days, ourselves, our wives, our sons, or our daughters, **9** and not to build houses to dwell in. We have no vineyard or field or seed, **10** but we have lived in tents and have obeyed and done all that Jonadab our father commanded us. **11** But when Nebuchadnezzar king of Babylon came up against the land, we said, 'Come, and let us go to Jerusalem for fear of the army of the Chaldeans and the army of the Syrians.' So we are living in Jerusalem."

12 Then the word of the LORD came to Jeremiah: **13** "Thus says the LORD of hosts, the God of Israel: Go and say to the people of Judah and the inhabitants of Jerusalem, Will you not receive instruction and listen to my words? declares the LORD. **14** The command that Jonadab the son of Rechab gave to his sons, to drink no wine, has been kept, and they drink none to this day, for they have obeyed their father's command. I have spoken to you persistently, but you have not listened to me. **15** I have sent to you all my servants the prophets, sending them persistently, saying, 'Turn now every one of you from his evil way, and amend your deeds, and do not go after other gods to serve them, and then you shall dwell in the land that I gave to you and your fathers.' But you did not incline your ear or listen to me. **16** The sons of Jonadab the son of Rechab have kept the command that their father gave them, but this people has not obeyed me. **17** Therefore, thus says the LORD, the God of hosts, the God of Israel: Behold, I am bringing upon Judah and all the inhabitants of Jerusalem all the disaster that I have pronounced against them, because I have spoken to them and they have not listened, I have called to them and they have not answered."

18 But to the house of the Rechabites Jeremiah said, "Thus says the LORD of hosts, the God of Israel: Because you have obeyed the command of Jonadab your father and kept all his precepts and done all that he commanded you, ¹⁹ therefore thus says the LORD of hosts, the God of Israel: Jonadab the son of Rechab shall never lack a man to stand before me.'"

Jehoiakim Burns Jeremiah's Scroll

36 In the fourth year of Jehoiakim the son of Josiah, king of Judah, this word came to Jeremiah from the LORD: ² "Take a scroll and write on it all the words that I have spoken to you against Israel and Judah and all the nations, from the day I spoke to you, from the days of Josiah until today. ³ It may be that the house of Judah will hear all the disaster that I intend to do to them, so that every one may turn from his evil way, and that I may forgive their iniquity and their sin."

⁴ Then Jeremiah called Baruch the son of Neriah, and Baruch wrote on a scroll at the dictation of Jeremiah all the words of the LORD that he had spoken to him. ⁵ And Jeremiah ordered Baruch, saying, "I am banned from going to the house of the LORD, ⁶ so you are to go, and on a day of fasting in the hearing of all the people in the LORD's house you shall read the words of the LORD from the scroll that you have written at my dictation. You shall read them also in the hearing of all the men of Judah who come out of their cities. ⁷ It may be that their plea for mercy will come before the LORD, and that every one will turn from his evil way, for great is the anger and wrath that the LORD has pronounced against this people." ⁸ And Baruch the son of Neriah did all that Jeremiah the prophet ordered him about reading from the scroll the words of the LORD in the LORD's house.

⁹ In the fifth year of Jehoiakim the son of Josiah, king of Judah, in the ninth month, all the people in Jerusalem and all the people who came from the cities of Judah to Jerusalem proclaimed a fast before the LORD. ¹⁰ Then, in the hearing of all the people, Baruch read the words of Jeremiah from the scroll, in the house of the LORD, in the chamber of Gemariah the son of Shaphan the secretary, which was in the upper court, at the entry of the New Gate of the LORD's house.

¹¹ When Micaiah the son of Gemariah, son of Shaphan, heard all the words of the LORD from the scroll, ¹² he went down to the king's house, into the secretary's chamber, and all the officials were sitting there: Elishama the secretary, Delaiah the son of Shemaiah, Elnathan the son of Achbor, Gemariah the son of Shaphan, Zedekiah the son of Hananiah, and all the officials. ¹³ And Micaiah told them all the words that he had heard, when Baruch read the scroll in the

PROFILE
BARUCH

Baruch, whose name means "blessed," was Jeremiah's friend, scribe, and disciple. Like Jeremiah, Baruch was a faithful servant of God. He helped Jeremiah purchase a field from one of the prophet's relatives. The Lord would use this as a symbol of hope despite the disaster that was to befall Judah: since the field had been bought and paid for, they could be assured that, after the exile, some of the people would return to the land. Baruch also recorded Jeremiah's prophecies on a scroll, and because Jeremiah had been barred from entering the temple, it was Baruch himself who read the words of the scroll. It was a warning from God to the nation of Judah. These prophecies angered the king so much that he burned the scroll. Baruch experienced serious persecution alongside Jeremiah.

KEY REFERENCE: JEREMIAH 36:4–10

hearing of the people. ¹⁴ Then all the officials sent Jehudi the son of Nethaniah, son of Shelemiah, son of Cushi, to say to Baruch, "Take in your hand the scroll that you read in the hearing of the people, and come." So Baruch the son of Neriah took the scroll in his hand and came to them. ¹⁵ And they said to him, "Sit down and read it." So Baruch read it to them. ¹⁶ When they heard all the words, they turned one to another in fear. And they said to Baruch, "We must report all these words to the king." ¹⁷ Then they asked Baruch, "Tell us, please, how did you write all these words? Was it at his dictation?" [18] Baruch answered them, "He dictated all these words to me, while I wrote them with ink on the scroll." [19] Then the officials said to Baruch, "Go and hide, you and Jeremiah, and let no one know where you are."

[20] So they went into the court to the king, having put the scroll in the chamber of Elishama the secretary, and they reported all the words to the king. [21] Then the king sent Jehudi to get the scroll, and he took it from the chamber of Elishama the secretary. And Jehudi read it to the king and all the officials who stood beside the king. [22] It was the ninth month, and the king was sitting in the winter house, and there was a fire burning in the fire pot before him. [23] As Jehudi read three or four columns, the king would cut them off with a knife and throw them into the fire in the fire pot, until the entire scroll was consumed in the fire that was in the fire pot. [24] Yet neither the king nor any of his servants who heard all these words was afraid, nor did they tear their garments. [25] Even when Elnathan and Delaiah and Gemariah urged the king not to burn the scroll, he would not listen to them. [26] And the king commanded Jerahmeel the king's son and Seraiah the son of Azriel and Shelemiah the son of Abdeel to seize Baruch the secretary and Jeremiah the prophet, but the LORD hid them.

[27] Now after the king had burned the scroll with the words that Baruch wrote at Jeremiah's dictation, the word of the LORD came to Jeremiah: [28] "Take another scroll and write on it all the former words that were in the first scroll, which Jehoiakim the king of Judah has burned. [29] And concerning Jehoiakim king of Judah you shall say, 'Thus says the LORD, You have burned this scroll, saying, "Why have you written in it that the king of Babylon will certainly come and destroy this land, and will cut off from it man and beast?" [30] Therefore thus says the LORD concerning Jehoiakim king of Judah: He shall have none to sit on the throne of David, and his dead body shall be cast out to the heat by day and the frost by night. [31] And I will punish him and his offspring and his servants for their iniquity. I will bring upon them and upon the inhabitants of Jerusalem and upon the people of Judah all the disaster that I have pronounced against them, but they would not hear.'"

[32] Then Jeremiah took another scroll and gave it to Baruch the scribe, the son of Neriah, who wrote on it at the dictation of Jeremiah all the words of the scroll that Jehoiakim king of Judah had burned in the fire. And many similar words were added to them.

Jeremiah Warns Zedekiah

37 Zedekiah the son of Josiah, whom Nebuchadnezzar king of Babylon made king in the land of Judah, reigned instead of Coniah the son of Jehoiakim. [2] But neither he nor his servants nor the people of the land listened to the words of the LORD that he spoke through Jeremiah the prophet.

[3] King Zedekiah sent Jehucal the son of Shelemiah, and Zephaniah the priest, the son of Maaseiah, to Jeremiah the prophet, saying, "Please pray for us to the LORD our God." [4] Now Jeremiah was still going in and out among the people, for he had not yet been put in prison. [5] The army of Pharaoh had come out of Egypt. And when the Chaldeans who were besieging Jerusalem heard news about them, they withdrew from Jerusalem.

[6] Then the word of the LORD came to Jeremiah the prophet: [7] "Thus says the LORD, God of Israel: Thus shall you say to the king of Judah who sent you to me to inquire of me, 'Behold, Pharaoh's army that came to help you is about to return to Egypt, to its own land. [8] And the Chaldeans shall come back and fight against this city. They shall capture it and burn it with fire. [9] Thus says the LORD, Do not deceive yourselves, saying, "The Chaldeans will surely go away from us," for they will not go away. [10] For even if you should defeat the whole army of Chaldeans who are fighting against you, and there remained of them only wounded men, every man in his tent, they would rise up and burn this city with fire.'"

Jeremiah Imprisoned

[11] Now when the Chaldean army had withdrawn from Jerusalem at the approach of Pharaoh's army, [12] Jeremiah set out from Jerusalem to go to the land of Benjamin to receive his portion there among the people. [13] When he was at the Benjamin Gate, a sentry there named Irijah the son of Shelemiah, son of Hananiah, seized Jeremiah the prophet, saying, "You are deserting to the

Chaldeans." ¹⁴ And Jeremiah said, "It is a lie; I am not deserting to the Chaldeans." But Irijah would not listen to him, and seized Jeremiah and brought him to the officials. ¹⁵ And the officials were enraged at Jeremiah, and they beat him and imprisoned him in the house of Jonathan the secretary, for it had been made a prison.

¹⁶ When Jeremiah had come to the dungeon cells and remained there many days, ¹⁷ King Zedekiah sent for him and received him. The king questioned him secretly in his house and said, "Is there any word from the LORD?" Jeremiah said, "There is." Then he said, "You shall be delivered into the hand of the king of Babylon." ¹⁸ Jeremiah also said to King Zedekiah, "What wrong have I done to you or your servants or this people, that you have put me in prison? ¹⁹ Where are your prophets who prophesied to you, saying, 'The king of Babylon will not come against you and against this land'? ²⁰ Now hear, please, O my lord the king: let my humble plea come before you and do not send me back to the house of Jonathan the secretary, lest I die there." ²¹ So King Zedekiah gave orders, and they committed Jeremiah to the court of the guard. And a loaf of bread was given him daily from the bakers' street, until all the bread of the city was gone. So Jeremiah remained in the court of the guard.

Jeremiah Cast into the Cistern

38 Now Shephatiah the son of Mattan, Gedaliah the son of Pashhur, Jucal the son of Shelemiah, and Pashhur the son of Malchiah heard the words that Jeremiah was saying to all the people, ² "Thus says the LORD: He who stays in this city shall die by the sword, by famine, and by pestilence, but he who goes out to the Chaldeans shall live. He shall have his life as a prize of war, and live. ³ Thus says the LORD: This city shall surely be given into the hand of the army of the king of Babylon and be taken." ⁴ Then the officials said to the king, "Let this man be put to death, for he is weakening the hands of the soldiers who are left in this city, and the hands of all the people, by speaking such words to them. For this man is not seeking the welfare of this people, but their harm." ⁵ King Zedekiah said, "Behold, he is in your hands, for the king can do nothing against you." ⁶ So they took Jeremiah and cast him

into the cistern of Malchiah, the king's son, which was in the court of the guard, letting Jeremiah down by ropes. And there was no water in the cistern, but only mud, and Jeremiah sank in the mud.

Jeremiah Rescued from the Cistern

⁷ When Ebed-melech the Ethiopian, a eunuch who was in the king's house, heard that they had put Jeremiah into the cistern—the king was sitting in the Benjamin Gate— ⁸ Ebed-melech went from the king's house and said to the king, ⁹ "My lord the king, these men have done evil in all that they did to Jeremiah the prophet by casting him into the cistern, and he will die there of hunger, for there is no bread left in the city." ¹⁰ Then the king commanded Ebed-melech the Ethiopian, "Take thirty men with you from here, and lift Jeremiah the

prophet out of the cistern before he dies." ¹¹ So Ebed-melech took the men with him and went to the house of the king, to a wardrobe in the storehouse, and took from there old rags and worn-out clothes, which he let down to Jeremiah in the cistern by ropes. ¹² Then Ebed-melech the Ethiopian said to Jeremiah, "Put the rags and clothes between your armpits and the ropes." Jeremiah did so. ¹³ Then they drew Jeremiah up with ropes and lifted him out of the cistern. And Jeremiah remained in the court of the guard.

Jeremiah Warns Zedekiah Again

¹⁴ King Zedekiah sent for Jeremiah the prophet and received him at the third entrance of the temple of the LORD. The king said to Jeremiah, "I will ask you a question; hide nothing from me." ¹⁵ Jeremiah said to Zedekiah, "If I tell you, will you not surely put me to death? And if I give you counsel, you will not listen to me." ¹⁶ Then King

Zedekiah swore secretly to Jeremiah, "As the LORD lives, who made our souls, I will not put you to death or deliver you into the hand of these men who seek your life."

[17] Then Jeremiah said to Zedekiah, "Thus says the LORD, the God of hosts, the God of Israel: If you will surrender to the officials of the king of Babylon, then your life shall be spared, and this city shall not be burned with fire, and you and your house shall live. [18] But if you do not surrender to the officials of the king of Babylon, then this city shall be given into the hand of the Chaldeans, and they shall burn it with fire, and you shall not escape from their hand." [19] King Zedekiah said to Jeremiah, "I am afraid of the Judeans who have deserted to the Chaldeans, lest I be handed over to them and they deal cruelly with me." [20] Jeremiah said, "You shall not

▶ GETTING THE MESSAGE

Free vineyards. After they conquered Judah and shipped all the leading citizens to Babylon, the Babylonians gave vineyards to some of the poor Judeans who remained in the land (39:10). This would have made the people less likely to rebel and would allow them to resume farming after many years of war.

be given to them. Obey now the voice of the LORD in what I say to you, and it shall be well with you, and your life shall be spared. [21] But if you refuse to surrender, this is the vision which the LORD has shown to me: [22] Behold, all the women left in the house of the king of Judah were being led out to the officials of the king of Babylon and were saying,

"'Your trusted friends have deceived you
    and prevailed against you;
now that your feet are sunk in the mud,
    they turn away from you.'

[23] All your wives and your sons shall be led out to the Chaldeans, and you yourself shall not escape from their hand, but shall be seized by the king of Babylon, and this city shall be burned with fire."

[24] Then Zedekiah said to Jeremiah, "Let no one know of these words, and you shall not die. [25] If the officials hear that I have spoken with you and come to you and say to you,

'Tell us what you said to the king and what the king said to you; hide nothing from us and we will not put you to death,' [26] then you shall say to them, 'I made a humble plea to the king that he would not send me back to the house of Jonathan to die there.'" [27] Then all the officials came to Jeremiah and asked him, and he answered them as the king had instructed him. So they stopped speaking with him, for the conversation had not been overheard. [28] And Jeremiah remained in the court of the guard until the day that Jerusalem was taken.

The Fall of Jerusalem

39 In the ninth year of Zedekiah king of Judah, in the tenth month, Nebuchadnezzar king of Babylon and all his army came against Jerusalem and besieged it. [2] In the eleventh year of Zedekiah, in the fourth month, on the ninth day of the month, a breach was made in the city. [3] Then all the officials of the king of Babylon came and sat in the middle gate: Nergal-sar-ezer of Samgar, Nebu-sar-sekim the Rab-saris, Nergal-sar-ezer the Rab-mag, with all the rest of the officers of the king of Babylon. [4] When Zedekiah king of Judah and all the soldiers saw them, they fled, going out of the city at night by way of the king's garden through the gate between the two walls; and they went toward the Arabah. [5] But the army of the Chaldeans pursued them and overtook Zedekiah in the plains of Jericho. And when they had taken him, they brought him up to Nebuchadnezzar king of Babylon, at Riblah, in the land of Hamath; and he passed sentence on him. [6] The king of Babylon slaughtered the sons of Zedekiah at Riblah before his eyes, and the king of Babylon slaughtered all the nobles of Judah. [7] He put out the eyes of Zedekiah and bound him in chains to take him to Babylon. [8] The Chaldeans burned the king's house and the house of the people, and broke down the walls of Jerusalem. [9] Then Nebuzaradan, the captain of the guard, carried into exile to Babylon the rest of the people who were left in the city, those who had deserted to him, and the people who remained. [10] Nebuzaradan, the captain of the guard, left in the land of Judah some of the poor people who owned nothing, and gave them vineyards and fields at the same time.

The Lord Delivers Jeremiah

¹¹ Nebuchadnezzar king of Babylon gave command concerning Jeremiah through Nebuzaradan, the captain of the guard, saying, ¹² "Take him, look after him well, and do him no harm, but deal with him as he tells you." ¹³ So Nebuzaradan the captain of the guard, Nebushazban the Rab-saris, Nergal-sar-ezer the Rab-mag, and all the chief officers of the king of Babylon ¹⁴ sent and took Jeremiah from the court of the guard. They entrusted him to Gedaliah the son of Ahikam, son of Shaphan, that he should take him home. So he lived among the people.

¹⁵ The word of the Lord came to Jeremiah while he was shut up in the court of the guard: ¹⁶ "Go, and say to Ebed-melech the Ethiopian, 'Thus says the Lord of hosts, the God of Israel: Behold, I will fulfill my words against this city for harm and not for good, and they shall be accomplished before you on that day. ¹⁷ But I will deliver you on that day, declares the Lord, and you shall not be given into the hand of the men of whom you are afraid. ¹⁸ For I will surely save you, and you shall not fall by the sword, but you shall have your life as a prize of war, because you have put your trust in me, declares the Lord.'"

Jeremiah Remains in Judah

40 The word that came to Jeremiah from the Lord after Nebuzaradan the captain of the guard had let him go from Ramah, when he took him bound in chains along with all the captives of Jerusalem and Judah who were being exiled to Babylon. ² The captain of the guard took Jeremiah and said to him, "The Lord your God pronounced this disaster against this place. ³ The Lord has brought it about, and has done as he said. Because you sinned against the Lord and did not obey his voice, this thing has come upon you. ⁴ Now, behold, I release you today from the chains on your hands. If it seems good to you to come with me to Babylon, come, and I will look after you well, but if it seems wrong to you to come with me to Babylon, do not come. See, the whole land is before you; go wherever you think it good and right to go. ⁵ If you remain, then return to Gedaliah the son of Ahikam, son of Shaphan, whom the king of Babylon appointed governor of the cities

of Judah, and dwell with him among the people. Or go wherever you think it right to go." So the captain of the guard gave him an allowance of food and a present, and let him go. ⁶ Then Jeremiah went to Gedaliah the son of Ahikam, at Mizpah, and lived with him among the people who were left in the land.

⁷ When all the captains of the forces in the open country and their men heard that the king of Babylon had appointed Gedaliah the son of Ahikam governor in the land and had committed to him men, women, and children, those of the poorest of the land who had not been taken into exile to Babylon, ⁸ they went to Gedaliah at Mizpah—Ishmael the son of Nethaniah, Johanan the son of Kareah, Seraiah the son of Tanhumeth, the sons of Ephai the Netophathite, Jezaniah the son of the Maacathite, they and their men. ⁹ Gedaliah the son of Ahikam, son of Shaphan, swore to them and their men, saying, "Do not be afraid to serve the Chaldeans. Dwell in the land and serve the king of Babylon, and it shall be well with you. ¹⁰ As for me, I will dwell at Mizpah, to represent you before the Chaldeans who will come to us. But as for you, gather wine and summer fruits and oil, and store them in your vessels, and dwell in your cities that you have taken." ¹¹ Likewise, when all the Judeans who were in Moab and among the Ammonites and in Edom and in other lands heard that the king of Babylon had left a remnant in Judah and had appointed Gedaliah the son of Ahikam, son of Shaphan, as governor over them, ¹² then all the Judeans returned from all the places to which they had been driven and came to the land of Judah, to Gedaliah at Mizpah. And they gathered wine and summer fruits in great abundance.

¹³ Now Johanan the son of Kareah and all the leaders of the forces in the open country came to Gedaliah at Mizpah ¹⁴ and said to him, "Do you know that Baalis the king of the Ammonites has sent Ishmael the son of Nethaniah to take your life?" But Gedaliah the son of Ahikam would not believe them. ¹⁵ Then Johanan the son of Kareah spoke secretly to Gedaliah at Mizpah, "Please let me go and strike down Ishmael the son of Nethaniah, and no one will know it. Why should he take your life, so that all the Judeans who are gathered about you would be scattered, and the remnant of

Judah would perish?" ¹⁶ But Gedaliah the son of Ahikam said to Johanan the son of Kareah, "You shall not do this thing, for you are speaking falsely of Ishmael."

Gedaliah Murdered

41 In the seventh month, Ishmael the son of Nethaniah, son of Elishama, of the royal family, one of the chief officers of the king, came with ten men to Gedaliah the son of Ahikam, at Mizpah. As they ate bread together there at Mizpah, ² Ishmael the son of Nethaniah and the ten men with him rose up and struck down Gedaliah the son of Ahikam, son of Shaphan, with the sword, and killed him, whom the king of Babylon had appointed governor in the land. ³ Ishmael also struck down all the Judeans who were with Gedaliah at Mizpah, and the Chaldean soldiers who happened to be there.

GETTING THE MESSAGE

The town of **Geruth Chimham** (41:17) may have been named after the Chimham mentioned in 2 Sam. 19:37–40 (see also "sons of Barzillai," 1 Kings 2:7), who apparently served King David in a time of great need. It was common for members of the royal court to be paid for their services in land rather than money.

⁴ On the day after the murder of Gedaliah, before anyone knew of it, ⁵ eighty men arrived from Shechem and Shiloh and Samaria, with their beards shaved and their clothes torn, and their bodies gashed, bringing grain offerings and incense to present at the temple of the LORD. ⁶ And Ishmael the son of Nethaniah came out from Mizpah to meet them, weeping as he came. As he met them, he said to them, "Come in to Gedaliah the son of Ahikam." ⁷ When they came into the city, Ishmael the son of Nethaniah and the men with him slaughtered them and cast them into a cistern. ⁸ But there were ten men among them who said to Ishmael, "Do not put us to death, for we have stores of wheat, barley, oil, and honey hidden in the fields." So he refrained and did not put them to death with their companions.

⁹ Now the cistern into which Ishmael had thrown all the bodies of the men whom he had struck down along with Gedaliah was the large cistern that King Asa had made for defense against Baasha king of Israel; Ishmael the son of Nethaniah filled it with the slain. ¹⁰ Then Ishmael took captive all the rest of the people who were in Mizpah, the king's daughters and all the people who were left at Mizpah, whom Nebuzaradan, the captain of the guard, had committed to Gedaliah the son of Ahikam. Ishmael the son of Nethaniah took them captive and set out to cross over to the Ammonites.

¹¹ But when Johanan the son of Kareah and all the leaders of the forces with him heard of all the evil that Ishmael the son of Nethaniah had done, ¹² they took all their men and went to fight against Ishmael the son of Nethaniah. They came upon him at the great pool that is in Gibeon. ¹³ And when all the people who were with Ishmael saw Johanan the son of Kareah and all the leaders of the forces with him, they rejoiced. ¹⁴ So all the people whom Ishmael had carried away captive from Mizpah turned around and came back, and went to Johanan the son of Kareah. ¹⁵ But Ishmael the son of Nethaniah escaped from Johanan with eight men, and went to the Ammonites. ¹⁶ Then Johanan the son of Kareah and all the leaders of the forces with him took from Mizpah all the rest of the people whom he had recovered from Ishmael the son of Nethaniah, after he had struck down Gedaliah the son of Ahikam—soldiers, women, children, and eunuchs, whom Johanan brought back from Gibeon. ¹⁷ And they went and stayed at Geruth Chimham near Bethlehem, intending to go to Egypt ¹⁸ because of the Chaldeans. For they were afraid of them, because Ishmael the son of Nethaniah had struck down Gedaliah the son of Ahikam, whom the king of Babylon had made governor over the land.

Warning Against Going to Egypt

42 Then all the commanders of the forces, and Johanan the son of Kareah and Jezaniah the son of Hoshaiah, and all the people from the least to the greatest, came near ² and said to Jeremiah the prophet, "Let our plea for mercy come before you, and pray to the LORD your God for us, for all this remnant—because we are left with but a few, as your eyes see us— ³ that the LORD your God may show us the

way we should go, and the thing that we should do." ⁴Jeremiah the prophet said to them, "I have heard you. Behold, I will pray to the LORD your God according to your request, and whatever the LORD answers you I will tell you. I will keep nothing back from you." ⁵Then they said to Jeremiah, "May the LORD be a true and faithful witness against us if we do not act according to all the word with which the LORD your God sends you to us. ⁶Whether it is good or bad, we will obey the voice of the LORD our God to whom we are sending you, that it may be well with us when we obey the voice of the LORD our God."

⁷At the end of ten days the word of the LORD came to Jeremiah. ⁸Then he summoned Johanan the son of Kareah and all the commanders of the forces who were with him, and all the people from the least to the greatest, ⁹and said to them, "Thus says the LORD, the God of Israel, to whom you sent me to present your plea for mercy before him: ¹⁰If you will remain in this land, then I will build you up and not pull you down; I will plant you, and not pluck you up; for I relent of the disaster that I did to you. ¹¹Do not fear the king of Babylon, of whom you are afraid. Do not fear him, declares the LORD, for I am with you, to save you and to deliver you from his hand. ¹²I will grant you mercy, that he may have mercy on you and let you remain in your own land. ¹³But if you say, 'We will not remain in this land,' disobeying the voice of the LORD your God ¹⁴and saying, 'No, we will go to the land of Egypt, where we shall not see war or hear the sound of the trumpet or be hungry for bread, and we will dwell there,' ¹⁵then hear the word of the LORD, O remnant of Judah. Thus says the LORD of hosts, the God of Israel: If you set your faces to enter Egypt and go to live there, ¹⁶then the sword that you fear shall overtake you there in the land of Egypt, and the famine of which you are afraid shall follow close after you to Egypt, and there you shall die. ¹⁷All the men who set their faces to go to Egypt to live there shall die by the sword, by famine, and by pestilence. They shall have no remnant or survivor from the disaster that I will bring upon them.

¹⁸"For thus says the LORD of hosts, the God of Israel: As my anger and my wrath were poured out on the inhabitants of Jerusalem, so my wrath will be poured out on you when you go to Egypt. You shall become an execration, a horror, a curse, and a taunt. You shall see this place no more. ¹⁹The LORD has said to you, O remnant of Judah, 'Do not go to Egypt.' Know for a certainty that I have warned you this day ²⁰that you have gone astray at the cost of your lives. For you sent me to the LORD your God, saying, 'Pray for us to the LORD our God, and whatever the LORD our God says declare to us and we will do it.' ²¹And I have this day declared it to you, but you have not obeyed the voice of the LORD your God in anything that he sent me to tell you. ²²Now therefore know for a certainty that you shall die by the sword, by famine, and by pestilence in the place where you desire to go to live."

Jeremiah Taken to Egypt

43 When Jeremiah finished speaking to all the people all these words of the LORD their God, with which the LORD their God had sent him to them, ²Azariah the son of Hoshaiah and Johanan the son of Kareah and all the insolent men said to Jeremiah, "You are telling a lie. The LORD our God did not send us to say, 'Do not go to Egypt to live there,' ³but Baruch the son of Neriah has set you against us, to deliver us into the hand of the Chaldeans, that they may kill us or take us into exile in Babylon." ⁴So Johanan the son of Kareah and all the commanders of the forces and all the people did not obey the voice of the LORD, to remain in the land of Judah. ⁵But Johanan the son of Kareah and all the commanders of the forces took all the remnant of Judah who had returned to live in the land of Judah from all the nations to which they had been driven— ⁶the men, the women, the children, the princesses, and every person whom Nebuzaradan the captain of the guard had left with Gedaliah the son of Ahikam, son of Shaphan; also Jeremiah the prophet and Baruch the son of Neriah. ⁷And they came into the land of Egypt, for they did not obey the voice of the LORD. And they arrived at Tahpanhes.

⁸Then the word of the LORD came to Jeremiah in Tahpanhes: ⁹"Take in your hands large stones and hide them in the mortar in the pavement that is at the entrance to Pharaoh's palace in Tahpanhes, in the sight

of the men of Judah, **10** and say to them, 'Thus says the LORD of hosts, the God of Israel: Behold, I will send and take Nebuchadnezzar the king of Babylon, my servant, and I will set his throne above these stones that I have hidden, and he will spread his royal canopy over them. **11** He shall come and strike the land of Egypt, giving over to the pestilence those who are doomed to the pestilence, to captivity those who are doomed to captivity, and to the sword those who are doomed to the sword. **12** I shall kindle a fire in the temples of the gods of Egypt, and he shall burn them and carry them away captive. And he shall clean the land of Egypt as a shepherd cleans his cloak of vermin, and he shall go away from there in peace. **13** He shall break the obelisks of Heliopolis, which is in the land of Egypt, and the temples of the gods of Egypt he shall burn with fire.'"

GETTING THE MESSAGE

Tahpanhes (43:7) was a fortified city in the eastern part of the Nile delta, near what is now the Suez Canal. Archaeologists have found a large building that may have served as a governor's residence. Since all such buildings would have belonged to the state, this may be the "Pharaoh's palace" mentioned in v. 9.

Judgment for Idolatry

44 The word that came to Jeremiah concerning all the Judeans who lived in the land of Egypt, at Migdol, at Tahpanhes, at Memphis, and in the land of Pathros, **2** "Thus says the LORD of hosts, the God of Israel: You have seen all the disaster that I brought upon Jerusalem and upon all the cities of Judah. Behold, this day they are a desolation, and no one dwells in them, **3** because of the evil that they committed, provoking me to anger, in that they went to make offerings and serve other gods that they knew not, neither they, nor you, nor your fathers. **4** Yet I persistently sent to you all my servants the prophets, saying, 'Oh, do not do this abomination that I hate!' **5** But they did not listen or incline their ear, to turn from their evil and make no offerings to other gods. **6** Therefore my wrath and my anger were poured out and kindled in the cities of Judah and in the streets of Jerusalem, and they became a waste and a desolation, as at this day. **7** And now thus says the LORD God of hosts, the God of Israel: Why do you commit this great evil against yourselves, to cut off from you man and woman, infant and child, from the midst of Judah, leaving you no remnant? **8** Why do you provoke me to anger with the works of your hands, making offerings to other gods in the land of Egypt where you have come to live, so that you may be cut off and become a curse and a taunt among all the nations of the earth? **9** Have you forgotten the evil of your fathers, the evil of the kings of Judah, the evil of their wives, your own evil, and the evil of your wives, which they committed in the land of Judah and in the streets of Jerusalem? **10** They have not humbled themselves even to this day, nor have they feared, nor walked in my law and my statutes that I set before you and before your fathers.

11 "Therefore thus says the LORD of hosts, the God of Israel: Behold, I will set my face against you for harm, to cut off all Judah. **12** I will take the remnant of Judah who have set their faces to come to the land of Egypt to live, and they shall all be consumed. In the land of Egypt they shall fall; by the sword and by famine they shall be consumed. From the least to the greatest, they shall die by the sword and by famine, and they shall become an oath, a horror, a curse, and a taunt. **13** I will punish those who dwell in the land of Egypt, as I have punished Jerusalem, with the sword, with famine, and with pestilence, **14** so that none of the remnant of Judah who have come to live in the land of Egypt shall escape or survive or return to the land of Judah, to which they desire to return to dwell there. For they shall not return, except some fugitives."

15 Then all the men who knew that their wives had made offerings to other gods, and all the women who stood by, a great assembly, all the people who lived in Pathros in the land of Egypt, answered Jeremiah: **16** "As for the word that you have spoken to us in the name of the LORD, we will not listen to you. **17** But we will do everything that we have vowed, make offerings to the queen of heaven and pour out drink offerings to her, as we did, both we and our fathers, our kings and our officials, in the cities of

Judah and in the streets of Jerusalem. For then we had plenty of food, and prospered, and saw no disaster. ¹⁸ But since we left off making offerings to the queen of heaven and pouring out drink offerings to her, we have lacked everything and have been consumed by the sword and by famine." ¹⁹ And the women said, "When we made offerings to the queen of heaven and poured out drink offerings to her, was it without our husbands' approval that we made cakes for her bearing her image and poured out drink offerings to her?"

²⁰ Then Jeremiah said to all the people, men and women, all the people who had given him this answer: ²¹ "As for the offerings that you offered in the cities of Judah and in the streets of Jerusalem, you and your fathers, your kings and your officials, and the people of the land, did not the LORD remember them? Did it not come into his mind? ²² The LORD could no longer bear your evil deeds and the abominations that you committed. Therefore your land has become a desolation and a waste and a curse, without inhabitant, as it is this day. ²³ It is because you made offerings and because you sinned against the LORD and did not obey the voice of the LORD or walk in his law and in his statutes and in his testimonies that this disaster has happened to you, as at this day."

²⁴ Jeremiah said to all the people and all the women, "Hear the word of the LORD, all you of Judah who are in the land of Egypt. ²⁵ Thus says the LORD of hosts, the God of Israel: You and your wives have declared with your mouths, and have fulfilled it with your hands, saying, 'We will surely perform our vows that we have made, to make offerings to the queen of heaven and to pour out drink offerings to her.' Then confirm your vows and perform your vows! ²⁶ Therefore hear the word of the LORD, all you of Judah who dwell in the land of Egypt: Behold, I have sworn by my great name, says the LORD, that my name shall no more be invoked by the mouth of any man of Judah in all the land of Egypt, saying, 'As the Lord GOD lives.' ²⁷ Behold, I am watching over them for disaster and not for good. All the men of Judah who are in the land of Egypt shall be consumed by the sword and by famine, until there is an end of them. ²⁸ And those who escape the sword shall return from the land

of Egypt to the land of Judah, few in number; and all the remnant of Judah, who came to the land of Egypt to live, shall know whose word will stand, mine or theirs. ²⁹ This shall be the sign to you, declares the LORD, that I will punish you in this place, in order that you may know that my words will surely stand against you for harm: ³⁰ Thus says the LORD, Behold, I will give Pharaoh Hophra king of Egypt into the hand of his enemies and into the hand of those who seek his life, as I gave Zedekiah king of Judah into the hand of Nebuchadnezzar king of Babylon, who was his enemy and sought his life."

Message to Baruch

45 The word that Jeremiah the prophet spoke to Baruch the son of Neriah, when he wrote these words in a book at the dictation of Jeremiah, in the fourth year of Jehoiakim the son of Josiah, king of Judah:

GETTING THE MESSAGE

Pharaoh Hophra had a tumultuous nineteen-year reign. To the northeast he faced the Babylonians as they invaded Israel; to the west, the armies of Greece were invading Libya. He sent an army to Jerusalem to assist the Israelites but they were defeated, as were his forces in Libya. His own general overthrew him in 570 B.C., and he was killed in battle three years later, thus fulfilling Jeremiah's prophesy (44:30).

²"Thus says the LORD, the God of Israel, to you, O Baruch: ³ You said, 'Woe is me! For the LORD has added sorrow to my pain. I am weary with my groaning, and I find no rest.' ⁴ Thus shall you say to him, Thus says the LORD: Behold, what I have built I am breaking down, and what I have planted I am plucking up—that is, the whole land. ⁵ And do you seek great things for yourself? Seek them not, for behold, I am bringing disaster upon all flesh, declares the LORD. But I will give you your life as a prize of war in all places to which you may go."

Judgment on Egypt

46 The word of the LORD that came to Jeremiah the prophet concerning the nations.

²About Egypt. Concerning the army of Pharaoh Neco, king of Egypt, which was by the river Euphrates at Carchemish and which Nebuchadnezzar king of Babylon defeated in the fourth year of Jehoiakim the son of Josiah, king of Judah:

³ "Prepare buckler and shield,
　　and advance for battle!
⁴ Harness the horses;
　　mount, O horsemen!
　Take your stations with your hel-
　　mets,
　　polish your spears,
　　put on your armor!
⁵ Why have I seen it?
　They are dismayed
　　and have turned backward.
　Their warriors are beaten down
　　and have fled in haste;
　they look not back—
　　terror on every side!
　　　　　　　　declares the LORD.

GETTING THE MESSAGE

When Nebuchadnezzar defeated the Egyptian army at **Carchemish** in 605 B.C., it marked the beginning of Egypt's decline as a power in the region and the beginning of Babylon's rise (see 46:2). Judah fell to Babylon in 586.

⁶ "The swift cannot flee away,
　　nor the warrior escape;
　in the north by the river Euphrates
　　they have stumbled and fallen.

⁷ "Who is this, rising like the Nile,
　　like rivers whose waters surge?
⁸ Egypt rises like the Nile,
　　like rivers whose waters surge.
　He said, 'I will rise, I will cover the
　　earth,
　I will destroy cities and their inhab-
　　itants.'
⁹ Advance, O horses,
　　and rage, O chariots!
　Let the warriors go out:
　　men of Cush and Put who handle
　　the shield,
　　men of Lud, skilled in handling the
　　bow.

¹⁰ That day is the day of the Lord GOD of
　　hosts,
　　a day of vengeance,
　　to avenge himself on his foes.
　The sword shall devour and be sated
　　and drink its fill of their blood.
　For the Lord GOD of hosts holds a
　　sacrifice
　　in the north country by the river
　　Euphrates.
¹¹ Go up to Gilead, and take balm,
　　O virgin daughter of Egypt!
　In vain you have used many medi-
　　cines;
　　there is no healing for you.
¹² The nations have heard of your shame,
　　and the earth is full of your cry;
　for warrior has stumbled against
　　warrior;
　　they have both fallen together."

¹³ The word that the LORD spoke to Jeremiah the prophet about the coming of Nebuchadnezzar king of Babylon to strike the land of Egypt:

¹⁴ "Declare in Egypt, and proclaim in
　　Migdol;
　　proclaim in Memphis and
　　Tahpanhes;
　say, 'Stand ready and be prepared,
　　for the sword shall devour around
　　you.'
¹⁵ Why are your mighty ones face down?
　They do not stand
　　because the LORD thrust them down.
¹⁶ He made many stumble, and they fell,
　　and they said one to another,
　'Arise, and let us go back to our own
　　people
　　and to the land of our birth,
　　because of the sword of the oppres-
　　sor.'
¹⁷ Call the name of Pharaoh, king of
　　Egypt,
　　'Noisy one who lets the hour go by.'
¹⁸ "As I live, declares the King,
　　whose name is the LORD of hosts,
　like Tabor among the mountains
　　and like Carmel by the sea, shall
　　one come.
¹⁹ Prepare yourselves baggage for exile,
　　O inhabitants of Egypt!
　For Memphis shall become a waste,
　　a ruin, without inhabitant.

²⁰ "A beautiful heifer is Egypt,
   but a biting fly from the north has
      come upon her.
²¹ Even her hired soldiers in her midst
      are like fattened calves;
   yes, they have turned and fled together;
      they did not stand,
   for the day of their calamity has come
      upon them,
   the time of their punishment.

²² "She makes a sound like a serpent
      gliding away;
   for her enemies march in force
   and come against her with axes
      like those who fell trees.
²³ They shall cut down her forest,
                  declares the LORD,
   though it is impenetrable,
   because they are more numerous than
      locusts;
   they are without number.
²⁴ The daughter of Egypt shall be put to
      shame;
   she shall be delivered into the hand
      of a people from the north."

²⁵ The LORD of hosts, the God of Israel, said: "Behold, I am bringing punishment upon Amon of Thebes, and Pharaoh and Egypt and her gods and her kings, upon Pharaoh and those who trust in him. ²⁶ I will deliver them into the hand of those who seek their life, into the hand of Nebuchadnezzar king of Babylon and his officers. Afterward Egypt shall be inhabited as in the days of old, declares the LORD.

²⁷ "But fear not, O Jacob my servant,
   nor be dismayed, O Israel,
   for behold, I will save you from far
      away,
   and your offspring from the land of
      their captivity.
   Jacob shall return and have quiet and
      ease,
   and none shall make him afraid.
²⁸ Fear not, O Jacob my servant,
                  declares the LORD,
   for I am with you.
   I will make a full end of all the nations
      to which I have driven you,
   but of you I will not make a full end.
   I will discipline you in just measure,
   and I will by no means leave you
      unpunished."

Judgment on the Philistines

47 The word of the LORD that came to Jeremiah the prophet concerning the Philistines, before Pharaoh struck down Gaza.

² "Thus says the LORD:
   Behold, waters are rising out of the
      north,
   and shall become an overflowing
      torrent;
   they shall overflow the land and all
      that fills it,
   the city and those who dwell in it.
   Men shall cry out,
   and every inhabitant of the land
      shall wail.
³ At the noise of the stamping of the
      hoofs of his stallions,
   at the rushing of his chariots, at the
      rumbling of their wheels,

GETTING THE MESSAGE

The balm of Gilead (46:11) was an ointment used to treat wounds. It was probably made from the sap of a tree.

   the fathers look not back to their
      children,
   so feeble are their hands,
⁴ because of the day that is coming to
      destroy
   all the Philistines,
   to cut off from Tyre and Sidon
      every helper that remains.
   For the LORD is destroying the
      Philistines,
   the remnant of the coastland of
      Caphtor.
⁵ Baldness has come upon Gaza;
   Ashkelon has perished.
   O remnant of their valley,
   how long will you gash yourselves?
⁶ Ah, sword of the LORD!
   How long till you are quiet?
   Put yourself into your scabbard;
   rest and be still!
⁷ How can it be quiet
   when the LORD has given it a
      charge?
   Against Ashkelon and against the
      seashore
   he has appointed it."

Judgment on Moab

48 Concerning Moab.
Thus says the LORD of hosts, the God of Israel:

"Woe to Nebo, for it is laid waste!
    Kiriathaim is put to shame, it is
      taken;
the fortress is put to shame and bro-
    ken down;
²   the renown of Moab is no more.
In Heshbon they planned disaster
    against her:
'Come, let us cut her off from being
    a nation!'
You also, O Madmen, shall be brought
    to silence;
the sword shall pursue you.

³ "A voice! A cry from Horonaim,
    'Desolation and great destruction!'
⁴ Moab is destroyed;
    her little ones have made a cry.
⁵ For at the ascent of Luhith
    they go up weeping;
for at the descent of Horonaim
    they have heard the distressed cry
     of destruction.
⁶ Flee! Save yourselves!
    You will be like a juniper in the
     desert!
⁷ For, because you trusted in your
     works and your treasures,
    you also shall be taken;
and Chemosh shall go into exile
    with his priests and his officials.
⁸ The destroyer shall come upon every
    city,
    and no city shall escape;
the valley shall perish,
    and the plain shall be destroyed,
as the LORD has spoken.

⁹ "Give wings to Moab,
    for she would fly away;
her cities shall become a desolation,
    with no inhabitant in them.

¹⁰ "Cursed is he who does the work of the LORD with slackness, and cursed is he who keeps back his sword from bloodshed.

¹¹ "Moab has been at ease from his youth
    and has settled on his dregs;
he has not been emptied from vessel
    to vessel,
    nor has he gone into exile;

so his taste remains in him,
    and his scent is not changed.

¹² "Therefore, behold, the days are coming, declares the LORD, when I shall send to him pourers who will pour him, and empty his vessels and break his jars in pieces. ¹³ Then Moab shall be ashamed of Chemosh, as the house of Israel was ashamed of Bethel, their confidence.

¹⁴ "How do you say, 'We are heroes
    and mighty men of war'?
¹⁵ The destroyer of Moab and his cities
    has come up,
    and the choicest of his young men
     have gone down to slaughter,
declares the King, whose name is
    the LORD of hosts.
¹⁶ The calamity of Moab is near at hand,
    and his affliction hastens swiftly.
¹⁷ Grieve for him, all you who are
    around him,
    and all who know his name;
say, 'How the mighty scepter is broken,
    the glorious staff.'

¹⁸ "Come down from your glory,
    and sit on the parched ground,
    O inhabitant of Dibon!
For the destroyer of Moab has come
    up against you;
    he has destroyed your strongholds.
¹⁹ Stand by the way and watch,
    O inhabitant of Aroer!
Ask him who flees and her who
    escapes;
    say, 'What has happened?'
²⁰ Moab is put to shame, for it is broken;
    wail and cry!
Tell it beside the Arnon,
    that Moab is laid waste.

²¹ "Judgment has come upon the tableland, upon Holon, and Jahzah, and Mephaath, ²² and Dibon, and Nebo, and Beth-diblathaim, ²³ and Kiriathaim, and Beth-gamul, and Beth-meon, ²⁴ and Kerioth, and Bozrah, and all the cities of the land of Moab, far and near. ²⁵ The horn of Moab is cut off, and his arm is broken, declares the LORD.

²⁶ "Make him drunk, because he magnified himself against the LORD, so that Moab shall wallow in his vomit, and he too shall be held in derision. ²⁷ Was not Israel a derision to you? Was he found among thieves,

that whenever you spoke of him you wagged your head?

28 "Leave the cities, and dwell in the rock,
  O inhabitants of Moab!
Be like the dove that nests
  in the sides of the mouth of a gorge.
29 We have heard of the pride of Moab—
  he is very proud—
of his loftiness, his pride, and his
  arrogance,
  and the haughtiness of his heart.
30 I know his insolence, declares the
  LORD;
  his boasts are false,
  his deeds are false.
31 Therefore I wail for Moab;
  I cry out for all Moab;
  for the men of Kir-hareseth I mourn.
32 More than for Jazer I weep for you,
  O vine of Sibmah!
Your branches passed over the sea,
  reached to the Sea of Jazer;
on your summer fruits and your grapes
  the destroyer has fallen.
33 Gladness and joy have been taken away
  from the fruitful land of Moab;
I have made the wine cease from the
  winepresses;
  no one treads them with shouts of
  joy;
  the shouting is not the shout of joy.

34 "From the outcry at Heshbon even to Elealeh, as far as Jahaz they utter their voice, from Zoar to Horonaim and Eglath-shelishiyah. For the waters of Nimrim also have become desolate. 35 And I will bring to an end in Moab, declares the LORD, him who offers sacrifice in the high place and makes offerings to his god. 36 Therefore my heart moans for Moab like a flute, and my heart moans like a flute for the men of Kir-hareseth. Therefore the riches they gained have perished.

37 "For every head is shaved and every beard cut off. On all the hands are gashes, and around the waist is sackcloth. 38 On all the housetops of Moab and in the squares there is nothing but lamentation, for I have broken Moab like a vessel for which no one cares, declares the LORD. 39 How it is broken! How they wail! How Moab has turned his back in shame! So Moab has become a derision and a horror to all that are around him."

40 For thus says the LORD:
"Behold, one shall fly swiftly like an
  eagle
  and spread his wings against Moab;
41 the cities shall be taken
  and the strongholds seized.
The heart of the warriors of Moab
  shall be in that day
  like the heart of a woman in her
  birth pains;
42 Moab shall be destroyed and be no
  longer a people,
  because he magnified himself
  against the LORD.
43 Terror, pit, and snare
  are before you, O inhabitant of Moab!
  declares the LORD.
44 He who flees from the terror
  shall fall into the pit,
and he who climbs out of the pit
  shall be caught in the snare.

For I will bring these things upon Moab,
  the year of their punishment,
  declares the LORD.
45 "In the shadow of Heshbon
  fugitives stop without strength,
for fire came out from Heshbon,
  flame from the house of Sihon;
it has destroyed the forehead of Moab,
  the crown of the sons of tumult.
46 Woe to you, O Moab!
  The people of Chemosh are undone,
for your sons have been taken captive,
  and your daughters into captivity.
47 Yet I will restore the fortunes of Moab
  in the latter days, declares the LORD."
Thus far is the judgment on Moab.

Judgment on Ammon

49 Concerning the Ammonites.
  Thus says the LORD:

"Has Israel no sons?
  Has he no heir?
Why then has Milcom dispossessed
  Gad,
  and his people settled in its cities?

² Therefore, behold, the days are com-
　　ing,
　　　declares the LORD,
　when I will cause the battle cry to be
　　heard
　　　against Rabbah of the Ammonites;
　it shall become a desolate mound,
　　and its villages shall be burned
　　　with fire;
　then Israel shall dispossess those
　　who dispossessed him,
　　　says the LORD.

³ "Wail, O Heshbon, for Ai is laid waste!
　　Cry out, O daughters of Rabbah!
　Put on sackcloth,
　　lament, and run to and fro among
　　　the hedges!
　For Milcom shall go into exile,
　　with his priests and his officials.

⁴ Why do you boast of your valleys,
　　O faithless daughter,
　who trusted in her treasures, saying,
　　'Who will come against me?'
⁵ Behold, I will bring terror upon you,
　　declares the Lord GOD of hosts,
　　from all who are around you,
　and you shall be driven out, every
　　man straight before him,
　　with none to gather the fugitives.

⁶ "But afterward I will restore the fortunes
of the Ammonites, declares the LORD."

Judgment on Edom

⁷ Concerning Edom.
Thus says the LORD of hosts:

　"Is wisdom no more in Teman?
　　Has counsel perished from the
　　　prudent?
　　Has their wisdom vanished?
⁸ Flee, turn back, dwell in the depths,
　　O inhabitants of Dedan!

For I will bring the calamity of Esau
　　upon him,
　　the time when I punish him.
⁹ If grape gatherers came to you,
　　would they not leave gleanings?
　If thieves came by night,
　　would they not destroy only
　　　enough for themselves?
¹⁰ But I have stripped Esau bare;
　　I have uncovered his hiding places,
　　and he is not able to conceal himself.
　His children are destroyed, and his
　　brothers,
　　and his neighbors; and he is no
　　　more.
¹¹ Leave your fatherless children; I will
　　keep them alive;
　　and let your widows trust in me."

¹² For thus says the LORD: "If those who
did not deserve to drink the cup must drink
it, will you go unpunished? You shall not
go unpunished, but you must drink. ¹³ For
I have sworn by myself, declares the LORD,
that Bozrah shall become a horror, a taunt,
a waste, and a curse, and all her cities shall
be perpetual wastes."

¹⁴ I have heard a message from the LORD,
　　and an envoy has been sent among
　　　the nations:
　"Gather yourselves together and come
　　against her,
　　and rise up for battle!
¹⁵ For behold, I will make you small
　　among the nations,
　　despised among mankind.
¹⁶ The horror you inspire has deceived
　　you,
　　and the pride of your heart,
　you who live in the clefts of the rock,
　　who hold the height of the hill.
　Though you make your nest as high as
　　the eagle's,
　　I will bring you down from there,
　　　　declares the LORD.

¹⁷ "Edom shall become a horror. Everyone
who passes by it will be horrified and will
hiss because of all its disasters. ¹⁸ As when
Sodom and Gomorrah and their neighboring
cities were overthrown, says the LORD, no
man shall dwell there, no man shall sojourn
in her. ¹⁹ Behold, like a lion coming up from
the jungle of the Jordan against a perennial
pasture, I will suddenly make him run away

from her. And I will appoint over her whomever I choose. For who is like me? Who will summon me? What shepherd can stand before me? **20** Therefore hear the plan that the LORD has made against Edom and the purposes that he has formed against the inhabitants of Teman: Even the little ones of the flock shall be dragged away. Surely their fold shall be appalled at their fate. **21** At the sound of their fall the earth shall tremble; the sound of their cry shall be heard at the Red Sea. **22** Behold, one shall mount up and fly swiftly like an eagle and spread his wings against Bozrah, and the heart of the warriors of Edom shall be in that day like the heart of a woman in her birth pains."

Judgment on Damascus

23 Concerning Damascus:

"Hamath and Arpad are confounded,
for they have heard bad news;
they melt in fear,
they are troubled like the sea that
cannot be quiet.
24 Damascus has become feeble, she
turned to flee,
and panic seized her;
anguish and sorrows have taken hold
of her,
as of a woman in labor.
25 How is the famous city not forsaken,
the city of my joy?
26 Therefore her young men shall fall in
her squares,
and all her soldiers shall be
destroyed in that day,
declares the LORD of hosts.
27 And I will kindle a fire in the wall of
Damascus,
and it shall devour the strongholds
of Ben-hadad."

Judgment on Kedar and Hazor

28 Concerning Kedar and the kingdoms of Hazor that Nebuchadnezzar king of Babylon struck down.

Thus says the LORD:
"Rise up, advance against Kedar!
Destroy the people of the east!
29 Their tents and their flocks shall be
taken,
their curtains and all their goods;
their camels shall be led away from
them,

and men shall cry to them: 'Terror
on every side!'
30 Flee, wander far away, dwell in the
depths,
O inhabitants of Hazor!
declares the LORD.
For Nebuchadnezzar king of Babylon
has made a plan against you
and formed a purpose against you.

31 "Rise up, advance against a nation at
ease,
that dwells securely,
declares the LORD,
that has no gates or bars,
that dwells alone.
32 Their camels shall become plunder,
their herds of livestock a spoil.
I will scatter to every wind
those who cut the corners of their
hair,
and I will bring their calamity
from every side of them,
declares the LORD.
33 Hazor shall become a haunt of jackals,
an everlasting waste;
no man shall dwell there;
no man shall sojourn in her."

Judgment on Elam

34 The word of the LORD that came to Jeremiah the prophet concerning Elam, in the beginning of the reign of Zedekiah king of Judah.

35 Thus says the LORD of hosts: "Behold, I will break the bow of Elam, the mainstay of their might. **36** And I will bring upon Elam the four winds from the four quarters of heaven. And I will scatter them to all those winds, and there shall be no nation to which those driven out of Elam shall not come. **37** I will terrify Elam before their enemies and before those who seek their life. I will bring disaster upon them, my fierce anger, declares the LORD. I will send the sword after them, until I have consumed them, **38** and I will set my throne in Elam and destroy their king and officials, declares the LORD.

39 "But in the latter days I will restore the fortunes of Elam, declares the LORD."

Judgment on Babylon

50 The word that the LORD spoke concerning Babylon, concerning the land of the Chaldeans, by Jeremiah the prophet:

² "Declare among the nations and pro-
      claim,
   set up a banner and proclaim,
      conceal it not, and say:
   'Babylon is taken,
      Bel is put to shame,
      Merodach is dismayed.
   Her images are put to shame,
      her idols are dismayed.'

³ "For out of the north a nation has come
up against her, which shall make her land a
desolation, and none shall dwell in it; both
man and beast shall flee away.

⁴ "In those days and in that time, declares
the LORD, the people of Israel and the people of Judah shall come together, weeping
as they come, and they shall seek the LORD
their God. ⁵ They shall ask the way to Zion,
with faces turned toward it, saying, 'Come,

How Babylon fell. Cyrus captured the
well-fortified city of Babylon using a
simple but clever plan. The Euphrates
River ran directly through the city,
and there were spiked gates where it
entered and exited. Cyrus's army dug
canals upstream to divert the flow of the
river. With the water level lowered, his
soldiers slipped under the spiked gates
and took the city during the night.

let us join ourselves to the LORD in an everlasting covenant that will never be forgotten.'

⁶ "My people have been lost sheep. Their
shepherds have led them astray, turning them
away on the mountains. From mountain to
hill they have gone. They have forgotten their
fold. ⁷ All who found them have devoured
them, and their enemies have said, 'We are
not guilty, for they have sinned against the
LORD, their habitation of righteousness, the
LORD, the hope of their fathers.'

⁸ "Flee from the midst of Babylon, and go
out of the land of the Chaldeans, and be as
male goats before the flock. ⁹ For behold,
I am stirring up and bringing against
Babylon a gathering of great nations, from
the north country. And they shall array
themselves against her. From there she shall
be taken. Their arrows are like a skilled war-

rior who does not return empty-handed.
¹⁰ Chaldea shall be plundered; all who plunder her shall be sated, declares the LORD.

¹¹ "Though you rejoice, though you exult,
      O plunderers of my heritage,
   though you frolic like a heifer in the
      pasture,
      and neigh like stallions,
¹² your mother shall be utterly shamed,
      and she who bore you shall be dis-
         graced.
   Behold, she shall be the last of the
      nations,
      a wilderness, a dry land, and a desert.
¹³ Because of the wrath of the LORD she
      shall not be inhabited
   but shall be an utter desolation;
   everyone who passes by Babylon shall
      be appalled,
      and hiss because of all her wounds.
¹⁴ Set yourselves in array against
      Babylon all around,
   all you who bend the bow;
   shoot at her, spare no arrows,
      for she has sinned against the LORD.
¹⁵ Raise a shout against her all around;
      she has surrendered;
   her bulwarks have fallen;
      her walls are thrown down.
   For this is the vengeance of the LORD:
      take vengeance on her;
      do to her as she has done.
¹⁶ Cut off from Babylon the sower,
      and the one who handles the sickle
         in time of harvest;
   because of the sword of the oppressor,
      every one shall turn to his own
         people,
      and every one shall flee to his own
         land.

¹⁷ "Israel is a hunted sheep driven away
by lions. First the king of Assyria devoured
him, and now at last Nebuchadnezzar
king of Babylon has gnawed his bones.
¹⁸ Therefore, thus says the LORD of hosts,
the God of Israel: Behold, I am bringing
punishment on the king of Babylon and
his land, as I punished the king of Assyria.
¹⁹ I will restore Israel to his pasture, and he
shall feed on Carmel and in Bashan, and
his desire shall be satisfied on the hills of
Ephraim and in Gilead. ²⁰ In those days and
in that time, declares the LORD, iniquity
shall be sought in Israel, and there shall be

none, and sin in Judah, and none shall be found, for I will pardon those whom I leave as a remnant.

21 "Go up against the land of Merathaim,[1]
    and against the inhabitants of
        Pekod.[2]
Kill, and devote them to destruction,[3]
                    declares the LORD,
    and do all that I have commanded
        you.
22 The noise of battle is in the land,
    and great destruction!
23 How the hammer of the whole earth
    is cut down and broken!
How Babylon has become
    a horror among the nations!
24 I set a snare for you and you were
        taken, O Babylon,
    and you did not know it;
you were found and caught,
    because you opposed the LORD.
25 The LORD has opened his armory
    and brought out the weapons of his
        wrath,
for the Lord GOD of hosts has a work
        to do
    in the land of the Chaldeans.
26 Come against her from every quarter;
    open her granaries;
pile her up like heaps of grain, and
        devote her to destruction;
    let nothing be left of her.
27 Kill all her bulls;
    let them go down to the slaughter.
Woe to them, for their day has come,
    the time of their punishment.

28 "A voice! They flee and escape from the land of Babylon, to declare in Zion the vengeance of the LORD our God, vengeance for his temple.

29 "Summon archers against Babylon, all those who bend the bow. Encamp around her; let no one escape. Repay her according to her deeds; do to her according to all that she has done. For she has proudly defied the LORD, the Holy One of Israel. 30 Therefore her young men shall fall in her squares, and all her soldiers shall be destroyed on that day, declares the LORD.

31 "Behold, I am against you, O proud one,
    declares the Lord GOD of hosts,

for your day has come,
    the time when I will punish you.
32 The proud one shall stumble and fall,
    with none to raise him up,
and I will kindle a fire in his cities,
    and it will devour all that is around
        him.

33 "Thus says the LORD of hosts: The people of Israel are oppressed, and the people of Judah with them. All who took them captive have held them fast; they refuse to let them go. 34 Their Redeemer is strong; the LORD of hosts is his name. He will surely plead their cause, that he may give rest to the earth, but unrest to the inhabitants of Babylon.

35 "A sword against the Chaldeans,
        declares the LORD,
    and against the inhabitants of
        Babylon,
    and against her officials and her
        wise men!

36 A sword against the diviners,
    that they may become fools!
A sword against her warriors,
    that they may be destroyed!
37 A sword against her horses and
        against her chariots,
    and against all the foreign troops in
        her midst,
    that they may become women!
A sword against all her treasures,
    that they may be plundered!
38 A drought against her waters,
    that they may be dried up!
For it is a land of images,
    and they are mad over idols.

39 "Therefore wild beasts shall dwell with hyenas in Babylon, and ostriches shall dwell in her. She shall never again have people, nor be inhabited for all generations. 40 As

---

[1] Merathaim means double rebellion [2] Pekod means punishment [3] That is, destroy or make an offering because of sin, at God's command; also 51:3

when God overthrew Sodom and Gomorrah and their neighboring cities, declares the LORD, so no man shall dwell there, and no son of man shall sojourn in her.

41 "Behold, a people comes from the north;
    a mighty nation and many kings
    are stirring from the farthest parts
        of the earth.
42 They lay hold of bow and spear;
    they are cruel and have no mercy.
    The sound of them is like the roaring
        of the sea;
    they ride on horses,
    arrayed as a man for battle
    against you, O daughter of Babylon!

43 "The king of Babylon heard the report
        of them,
    and his hands fell helpless;
    anguish seized him,
    pain as of a woman in labor.

44 "Behold, like a lion coming up from the thicket of the Jordan against a perennial pasture, I will suddenly make them run away from her, and I will appoint over her whomever I choose. For who is like me? Who will summon me? What shepherd can stand before me? 45 Therefore hear the plan that the LORD has made against Babylon, and the purposes that he has formed against the land of the Chaldeans: Surely the little ones of their flock shall be dragged away; surely their fold shall be appalled at their fate. 46 At the sound of the capture of Babylon the earth shall tremble, and her cry shall be heard among the nations."

The Utter Destruction of Babylon

51 Thus says the LORD:
    "Behold, I will stir up the spirit of a
        destroyer
    against Babylon,
    against the inhabitants of Leb-kamai,
2 and I will send to Babylon winnowers,
    and they shall winnow her,
    and they shall empty her land,
    when they come against her from
        every side
    on the day of trouble.
3 Let not the archer bend his bow,
    and let him not stand up in his
        armor.
    Spare not her young men;
    devote to destruction all her army.

4 They shall fall down slain in the land
        of the Chaldeans,
    and wounded in her streets.
5 For Israel and Judah have not been
        forsaken
    by their God, the LORD of hosts,
    but the land of the Chaldeans is full of
        guilt
    against the Holy One of Israel.

6 "Flee from the midst of Babylon;
    let every one save his life!
    Be not cut off in her punishment,
    for this is the time of the LORD's
        vengeance,
    the repayment he is rendering her.
7 Babylon was a golden cup in the
        LORD's hand,
    making all the earth drunken;
    the nations drank of her wine;
    therefore the nations went mad.
8 Suddenly Babylon has fallen and been
        broken;
    wail for her!
    Take balm for her pain;
    perhaps she may be healed.
9 We would have healed Babylon,
    but she was not healed.
    Forsake her, and let us go
    each to his own country,
    for her judgment has reached up to
        heaven
    and has been lifted up even to the
        skies.
10 The LORD has brought about our vin-
        dication;
    come, let us declare in Zion
    the work of the LORD our God.

11 "Sharpen the arrows!
    Take up the shields!
The LORD has stirred up the spirit of the kings of the Medes, because his purpose concerning Babylon is to destroy it, for that is the vengeance of the LORD, the vengeance for his temple.

12 "Set up a standard against the walls of
        Babylon;
    make the watch strong;
    set up watchmen;
    prepare the ambushes;
    for the LORD has both planned and
        done
    what he spoke concerning the
        inhabitants of Babylon.

13 O you who dwell by many waters,
   rich in treasures,
   your end has come;
   the thread of your life is cut.
14 The LORD of hosts has sworn by himself:
   Surely I will fill you with men, as
   many as locusts,
   and they shall raise the shout of
   victory over you.

15 "It is he who made the earth by his
   power,
   who established the world by his
   wisdom,
   and by his understanding stretched
   out the heavens.
16 When he utters his voice there is a
   tumult of waters in the heavens,
   and he makes the mist rise from the
   ends of the earth.
   He makes lightning for the rain,
   and he brings forth the wind from
   his storehouses.
17 Every man is stupid and without
   knowledge;
   every goldsmith is put to shame by
   his idols,
   for his images are false,
   and there is no breath in them.
18 They are worthless, a work of delusion;
   at the time of their punishment
   they shall perish.
19 Not like these is he who is the portion
   of Jacob,
   for he is the one who formed all
   things,
   and Israel is the tribe of his inheritance;
   the LORD of hosts is his name.

20 "You are my hammer and weapon of war:
   with you I break nations in pieces;
   with you I destroy kingdoms;
21 with you I break in pieces the horse
   and his rider;
   with you I break in pieces the chariot and the charioteer;
22 with you I break in pieces man and
   woman;
   with you I break in pieces the old
   man and the youth;
   with you I break in pieces the young
   man and the young woman;
23 with you I break in pieces the shepherd and his flock;

with you I break in pieces the farmer
   and his team;
   with you I break in pieces governors
   and commanders.

24 "I will repay Babylon and all the inhabitants of Chaldea before your very eyes for all
the evil that they have done in Zion, declares
the LORD.

25 "Behold, I am against you, O destroying mountain,
                    declares the LORD,
   which destroys the whole earth;
   I will stretch out my hand against you,
   and roll you down from the crags,
   and make you a burnt mountain.
26 No stone shall be taken from you for a
   corner
   and no stone for a foundation,
   but you shall be a perpetual waste,
   declares the LORD.

> ## GETTING THE MESSAGE

The **Ashkenaz** (51:27) were also known
as the Scythians. They were nomads
famed for their horseback-riding
abilities. Most Scythians lived north of
the Black Sea but some migrated as far
away as northern Iran. It is believed that
Attila the Hun was a direct descendant
of the Scythians.

27 "Set up a standard on the earth;
   blow the trumpet among the nations;
   prepare the nations for war against her;
   summon against her the kingdoms,
   Ararat, Minni, and Ashkenaz;
   appoint a marshal against her;
   bring up horses like bristling locusts.
28 Prepare the nations for war against her,
   the kings of the Medes, with their
   governors and deputies,
   and every land under their dominion.
29 The land trembles and writhes in pain,
   for the LORD's purposes against
   Babylon stand,
   to make the land of Babylon a desolation,
   without inhabitant.
30 The warriors of Babylon have ceased
   fighting;
   they remain in their strongholds;

their strength has failed;
    they have become women;
her dwellings are on fire;
    her bars are broken.
31 One runner runs to meet another,
    and one messenger to meet another,
to tell the king of Babylon
    that his city is taken on every side;
32 the fords have been seized,
    the marshes are burned with fire,
    and the soldiers are in panic.
33 For thus says the LORD of hosts, the
    God of Israel:
The daughter of Babylon is like a
    threshing floor
    at the time when it is trodden;
yet a little while
    and the time of her harvest will
    come."

34 "Nebuchadnezzar the king of Babylon
    has devoured me;
    he has crushed me;
he has made me an empty vessel;
    he has swallowed me like a monster;
he has filled his stomach with my
    delicacies;
    he has rinsed me out.
35 The violence done to me and to my
    kinsmen be upon Babylon,"
    let the inhabitant of Zion say.
"My blood be upon the inhabitants of
    Chaldea,"
    let Jerusalem say.
36 Therefore thus says the LORD:
"Behold, I will plead your cause
    and take vengeance for you.
I will dry up her sea
    and make her fountain dry,
37 and Babylon shall become a heap of
    ruins,
    the haunt of jackals,
a horror and a hissing,
    without inhabitant.

38 "They shall roar together like lions;
    they shall growl like lions' cubs.
39 While they are inflamed I will prepare
    them a feast
    and make them drunk, that they
    may become merry,
then sleep a perpetual sleep
    and not wake, declares the LORD.
40 I will bring them down like lambs to
    the slaughter,
    like rams and male goats.

41 "How Babylon is taken,
    the praise of the whole earth seized!
How Babylon has become
    a horror among the nations!
42 The sea has come up on Babylon;
    she is covered with its tumultuous
    waves.
43 Her cities have become a horror,
    a land of drought and a desert,
a land in which no one dwells,
    and through which no son of man
    passes.
44 And I will punish Bel in Babylon,
    and take out of his mouth what he
    has swallowed.
The nations shall no longer flow to
    him;
    the wall of Babylon has fallen.

45 "Go out of the midst of her, my people!
    Let every one save his life
    from the fierce anger of the LORD!
46 Let not your heart faint, and be not
    fearful
    at the report heard in the land,
when a report comes in one year
    and afterward a report in another
    year,
and violence is in the land,
    and ruler is against ruler.

47 "Therefore, behold, the days are coming
    when I will punish the images of
    Babylon;
her whole land shall be put to shame,
    and all her slain shall fall in the
    midst of her.
48 Then the heavens and the earth,
    and all that is in them,
shall sing for joy over Babylon,
    for the destroyers shall come
    against them out of the north,
        declares the LORD.
49 Babylon must fall for the slain of
    Israel,
    just as for Babylon have fallen the
    slain of all the earth.

50 "You who have escaped from the sword,
    go, do not stand still!
Remember the LORD from far away,
    and let Jerusalem come into your
    mind:
51 'We are put to shame, for we have
    heard reproach;
    dishonor has covered our face,

for foreigners have come
    into the holy places of the LORD's
      house.'

52 "Therefore, behold, the days are com-
    ing, declares the LORD,
    when I will execute judgment upon
      her images,
and through all her land
    the wounded shall groan.
53 Though Babylon should mount up to
      heaven,
    and though she should fortify her
      strong height,
yet destroyers would come from me
    against her,
    declares the LORD.

54 "A voice! A cry from Babylon!
    The noise of great destruction from
      the land of the Chaldeans!
55 For the LORD is laying Babylon waste
    and stilling her mighty voice.
Their waves roar like many waters;
    the noise of their voice is raised,
56 for a destroyer has come upon her,
    upon Babylon;
her warriors are taken;
    their bows are broken in pieces,
for the LORD is a God of recompense;
    he will surely repay.
57 I will make drunk her officials and her
      wise men,
    her governors, her commanders,
      and her warriors;
they shall sleep a perpetual sleep and
      not wake,
    declares the King, whose name is
      the LORD of hosts.

58 "Thus says the LORD of hosts:
The broad wall of Babylon
    shall be leveled to the ground,
and her high gates
    shall be burned with fire.
The peoples labor for nothing,
    and the nations weary themselves
      only for fire."

59 The word that Jeremiah the prophet commanded Seraiah the son of Neriah, son of Mahseiah, when he went with Zedekiah king of Judah to Babylon, in the fourth year of his reign. Seraiah was the quartermaster. 60 Jeremiah wrote in a book all the disaster that should come upon Babylon, all these words that are written concerning Babylon.

61 And Jeremiah said to Seraiah: "When you come to Babylon, see that you read all these words, 62 and say, 'O LORD, you have said concerning this place that you will cut it off, so that nothing shall dwell in it, neither man nor beast, and it shall be desolate forever.' 63 When you finish reading this book, tie a stone to it and cast it into the midst of the Euphrates, 64 and say, 'Thus shall Babylon sink, to rise no more, because of the disaster that I am bringing upon her, and they shall become exhausted.'"

Thus far are the words of Jeremiah.

The Fall of Jerusalem Recounted

52 Zedekiah was twenty-one years old when he became king, and he reigned eleven years in Jerusalem. His mother's name was Hamutal the daughter of Jeremiah of Libnah. 2 And he did what

GETTING THE MESSAGE

Sieges were designed with one purpose in mind: to get the citizens of a city to give up without a fight. By surrounding a city, an invader could cut off not only a city's food and water supply but also any means of escape. Once this was done, it was only a matter of time before thirst and hunger set in.

was evil in the sight of the LORD, according to all that Jehoiakim had done. 3 For because of the anger of the LORD it came to the point in Jerusalem and Judah that he cast them out from his presence.

And Zedekiah rebelled against the king of Babylon. 4 And in the ninth year of his reign, in the tenth month, on the tenth day of the month, Nebuchadnezzar king of Babylon came with all his army against Jerusalem, and laid siege to it. And they built siegeworks all around it. 5 So the city was besieged till the eleventh year of King Zedekiah. 6 On the ninth day of the fourth month the famine was so severe in the city that there was no food for the people of the land. 7 Then a breach was made in the city, and all the men of war fled and went out from the city by night by the way of a gate between the two walls, by the king's garden, and the Chaldeans were around the city. And they went in the direction of the Arabah.

⁸ But the army of the Chaldeans pursued the king and overtook Zedekiah in the plains of Jericho, and all his army was scattered from him. ⁹ Then they captured the king and brought him up to the king of Babylon at Riblah in the land of Hamath, and he passed sentence on him. ¹⁰ The king of Babylon slaughtered the sons of Zedekiah before his eyes, and also slaughtered all the officials of Judah at Riblah. ¹¹ He put out the eyes of Zedekiah, and bound him in chains, and the king of Babylon took him to Babylon, and put him in prison till the day of his death.

The Temple Burned

¹² In the fifth month, on the tenth day of the month—that was the nineteenth year of King Nebuchadnezzar, king of Babylon—Nebuzaradan the captain of the bodyguard, who served the king of Babylon, entered Jerusalem. ¹³ And he burned the house of the LORD, and the king's house and all the houses of Jerusalem; every great house he burned down. ¹⁴ And all the army of the Chaldeans, who were with the captain of the guard, broke down all the walls around Jerusalem. ¹⁵ And Nebuzaradan the captain of the guard carried away captive some of the poorest of the people and the rest of the people who were left in the city and the deserters who had deserted to the king of Babylon, together with the rest of the artisans. ¹⁶ But Nebuzaradan the captain of the guard left some of the poorest of the land to be vinedressers and plowmen.

¹⁷ And the pillars of bronze that were in the house of the LORD, and the stands and the bronze sea that were in the house of the LORD, the Chaldeans broke in pieces, and carried all the bronze to Babylon. ¹⁸ And they took away the pots and the shovels and the snuffers and the basins and the dishes for incense and all the vessels of bronze used in the temple service; ¹⁹ also the small bowls and the fire pans and the basins and the pots and the lampstands and the dishes for incense and the bowls for drink offerings. What was of gold the captain of the guard took away as gold, and what was of silver, as silver. ²⁰ As for the two pillars, the one sea, the twelve bronze bulls that were under the sea, and the stands, which Solomon the king had made for the house of the LORD, the bronze of all these things was beyond weight. ²¹ As for the pillars, the height of the one pillar was eighteen cubits, its circumference was twelve cubits, and its thickness was four fingers, and it was hollow. ²² On it was a capital of bronze. The height of the one capital was five cubits. A network and pomegranates, all of bronze, were around the capital. And the second pillar had the same, with pomegranates. ²³ There were ninety-six pomegranates on the sides; all the pomegranates were a hundred upon the network all around.

The People Exiled to Babylon

²⁴ And the captain of the guard took Seraiah the chief priest, and Zephaniah the second priest and the three keepers of the threshold; ²⁵ and from the city he took an officer who had been in command of the men of war, and seven men of the king's council, who were found in the city; and the secretary of the commander of the army, who mustered the people of the land; and sixty men of the people of the land, who were found in the midst of the city. ²⁶ And Nebuzaradan the captain of the guard took them and brought them to the king of Babylon at Riblah. ²⁷ And the king of Babylon struck them down and put them to death at Riblah in the land of Hamath. So Judah was taken into exile out of its land.

²⁸ This is the number of the people whom Nebuchadnezzar carried away captive: in the seventh year, 3,023 Judeans; ²⁹ in the eighteenth year of Nebuchadnezzar he carried away captive from Jerusalem 832 persons; ³⁰ in the twenty-third year of Nebuchadnezzar, Nebuzaradan the captain of the guard carried away captive of the Judeans 745 persons; all the persons were 4,600.

Jehoiachin Released from Prison

³¹ And in the thirty-seventh year of the exile of Jehoiachin king of Judah, in the twelfth month, on the twenty-fifth day of the month, Evil-merodach king of Babylon, in the year that he began to reign, graciously freed Jehoiachin king of Judah and brought him out of prison. ³² And he spoke kindly to him and gave him a seat above the seats of the kings who were with him in Babylon. ³³ So Jehoiachin put off his prison garments. And every day of his life he dined regularly at the king's table, ³⁴ and for his allowance, a regular allowance was given him by the king, according to his daily needs, until the day of his death, as long as he lived.

INTRODUCTION TO LAMENTATIONS

701 B.C.	627 B.C.	586 B.C.
Assyria attacks Judah	Prophetic ministry of Jeremiah begins	Fall of Judah

AUTHOR AND DATE

The author of this literary masterpiece is unknown. Lamentations provides eyewitness testimony of Babylon's destruction of Jerusalem in 586 B.C. in vivid, poetic detail. It was likely written between 586 and 516 B.C., with an early date being more probable.

THEME

The key passage in Lamentations is 3:19–24, which affirms that belief in God's mercy and faithfulness is the key to a restored relationship with God. Forgiveness is possible even for people who have deserved God's judgment (1:18). Hope, not despair, is the central theme in Lamentations.

PURPOSE

Lamentations was most likely written to be prayed or sung in worship services devoted to asking God's forgiveness. Such services began as early as the months after the temple's destruction in 586 B.C. (Jer. 41:4–5). They continued after the temple was rebuilt during Zechariah's time (c. 520 B.C.; see Zech. 7:3–5; 8:19). In later years, Lamentations was read and sung as part of annual observances marking the temple's destruction.

KEY THEMES

Lamentations presents many key theological realities from an important era in Israel's history:

1. It includes memorable prayers that confess sin, express renewed hope, and declare total dependence on God's grace.

2. It is the only book in the Bible written by a person who actually lived through the divine

judgment the Bible often refers to as "the day of the Lord" (see Joel 2:1–2; Amos 5:18; Zeph. 1:14–16).

3. It provides great insight into the nature of pain, sin, and redemption.

4. Like so many other OT passages, Lamentations teaches that Jerusalem fell:
   a. because of the people's sins (1:18);
   b. because they rejected God's word sent through the prophets (2:8, 14, 17);
   c. because their leaders led them astray (4:13).

5. It affirms God's never-ceasing mercy (3:19–24; compare Deut. 30:1–10). Readers can know that God never gives up on his people, even when they sin greatly.

6. Lamentations agrees with the Psalms that prayer is the way to restore a broken relationship with God. It also shares the Psalms' emphasis on God's sovereignty (see Ps. 103:19).

7. Like many of the prophets, Lamentations warns of the "day of the Lord." This is the day when God judges sin. That day has already occurred in historical events like the destruction of Jerusalem in 586 B.C. It will occur again at the end of time as the final "day of the Lord." People need to take seriously the warnings about such days of judgment.

OUTLINE

LAMENTATIONS

How Lonely Sits the City

1 How lonely sits the city
  that was full of people!
  How like a widow has she become,
    she who was great among the
      nations!
  She who was a princess among the
    provinces
    has become a slave.

2 She weeps bitterly in the night,
    with tears on her cheeks;
  among all her lovers
    she has none to comfort her;
  all her friends have dealt treacher-
      ously with her;
    they have become her enemies.

3 Judah has gone into exile because of
      affliction
    and hard servitude;
  she dwells now among the nations,
    but finds no resting place;
  her pursuers have all overtaken her
    in the midst of her distress.

4 The roads to Zion mourn,
    for none come to the festival;
  all her gates are desolate;
    her priests groan;
  her virgins have been afflicted,
    and she herself suffers bitterly.

5 Her foes have become the head;
    her enemies prosper,
  because the LORD has afflicted her
    for the multitude of her transgres-
      sions;
  her children have gone away,
    captives before the foe.

6 From the daughter of Zion
    all her majesty has departed.
  Her princes have become like deer
    that find no pasture;
  they fled without strength
    before the pursuer.

7 Jerusalem remembers
    in the days of her affliction and
      wandering
  all the precious things
    that were hers from days of old.
  When her people fell into the hand of
      the foe,
    and there was none to help her,
  her foes gloated over her;
    they mocked at her downfall.

8 Jerusalem sinned grievously;
    therefore she became filthy;
  all who honored her despise her,
    for they have seen her nakedness;
  she herself groans
    and turns her face away.

9 Her uncleanness was in her skirts;
    she took no thought of her future;
  therefore her fall is terrible;
    she has no comforter.
  "O LORD, behold my affliction,
    for the enemy has triumphed!"

10 The enemy has stretched out his
      hands
    over all her precious things;
  for she has seen the nations
    enter her sanctuary,
  those whom you forbade
    to enter your congregation.

11 All her people groan
    as they search for bread;
  they trade their treasures for food
    to revive their strength.
  "Look, O LORD, and see,
    for I am despised."

12 "Is it nothing to you, all you who pass
      by?
    Look and see
  if there is any sorrow like my sorrow,
    which was brought upon me,
  which the LORD inflicted
    on the day of his fierce anger.

13 "From on high he sent fire;
    into my bones he made it descend;
  he spread a net for my feet;
    he turned me back;
  he has left me stunned,
    faint all the day long.

14 "My transgressions were bound into a
        yoke;
    by his hand they were fastened
        together;
they were set upon my neck;
    he caused my strength to fail;
the Lord gave me into the hands
    of those whom I cannot withstand.

15 "The Lord rejected
    all my mighty men in my midst;
he summoned an assembly against me
    to crush my young men;
the Lord has trodden as in a winepress
    the virgin daughter of Judah.

16 "For these things I weep;
    my eyes flow with tears;
for a comforter is far from me,
    one to revive my spirit;
my children are desolate,
    for the enemy has prevailed."

17 Zion stretches out her hands,
    but there is none to comfort her;
the LORD has commanded against
        Jacob
    that his neighbors should be his
        foes;
Jerusalem has become
    a filthy thing among them.

18 "The LORD is in the right,
    for I have rebelled against his word;
but hear, all you peoples,
    and see my suffering;
my young women and my young men
    have gone into captivity.

19 "I called to my lovers,
    but they deceived me;
my priests and elders
    perished in the city,
while they sought food
    to revive their strength.

20 "Look, O LORD, for I am in distress;
    my stomach churns;
my heart is wrung within me,
    because I have been very rebellious.
In the street the sword bereaves;
    in the house it is like death.

21 "They heard my groaning,
    yet there is no one to comfort me.
All my enemies have heard of my
        trouble;
    they are glad that you have done it.
You have brought the day you
        announced;
    now let them be as I am.

22 "Let all their evildoing come before you,
    and deal with them
as you have dealt with me
    because of all my transgressions;
for my groans are many,
    and my heart is faint."

The Lord Has Destroyed Without Pity

2 How the Lord in his anger
    has set the daughter of Zion under a
        cloud!
He has cast down from heaven to earth
    the splendor of Israel;
he has not remembered his footstool
    in the day of his anger.

2 The Lord has swallowed up without
        mercy
    all the habitations of Jacob;
in his wrath he has broken down
    the strongholds of the daughter of
        Judah;
he has brought down to the ground in
        dishonor
    the kingdom and its rulers.

3 He has cut down in fierce anger
    all the might of Israel;
he has withdrawn from them his right
        hand
    in the face of the enemy;
he has burned like a flaming fire in
        Jacob,
    consuming all around.

4 He has bent his bow like an enemy,
    with his right hand set like a foe;
and he has killed all who were
        delightful in our eyes
    in the tent of the daughter of Zion;
he has poured out his fury like fire.

5 The Lord has become like an enemy;
   he has swallowed up Israel;
he has swallowed up all its palaces;
   he has laid in ruins its strongholds,
and he has multiplied in the daughter
      of Judah
   mourning and lamentation.

6 He has laid waste his booth like a
      garden,
   laid in ruins his meeting place;
the LORD has made Zion forget
   festival and Sabbath,
and in his fierce indignation has
   spurned king and priest.

7 The Lord has scorned his altar,
   disowned his sanctuary;
he has delivered into the hand of the
      enemy
   the walls of her palaces;
they raised a clamor in the house of
      the LORD
   as on the day of festival.

8 The LORD determined to lay in ruins
   the wall of the daughter of Zion;
he stretched out the measuring line;
   he did not restrain his hand from
      destroying;
he caused rampart and wall to
      lament;
   they languished together.

9 Her gates have sunk into the ground;
   he has ruined and broken her bars;
her king and princes are among the
      nations;
   the law is no more,
and her prophets find
   no vision from the LORD.

10 The elders of the daughter of Zion
   sit on the ground in silence;
they have thrown dust on their heads
   and put on sackcloth;
the young women of Jerusalem
   have bowed their heads to the
      ground.

11 My eyes are spent with weeping;
   my stomach churns;
my bile is poured out to the ground
   because of the destruction of the
      daughter of my people,
because infants and babies faint
   in the streets of the city.

12 They cry to their mothers,
   "Where is bread and wine?"
as they faint like a wounded man
   in the streets of the city,
as their life is poured out
   on their mothers' bosom.

13 What can I say for you, to what com-
      pare you,
   O daughter of Jerusalem?
What can I liken to you, that I may
      comfort you,
   O virgin daughter of Zion?
For your ruin is vast as the sea;
   who can heal you?

14 Your prophets have seen for you
   false and deceptive visions;
they have not exposed your iniquity
   to restore your fortunes,
but have seen for you oracles
   that are false and misleading.

> **GETTING THE MESSAGE**

Stretching out the measuring line (2:8)
is a military action. If the army did not
have enough troops to guard a captured
city, they might measure out certain
lengths of wall to destroy. By doing this,
they ensured that the city could not
defend itself if it tried to rebel against
its new captors.

15 All who pass along the way
   clap their hands at you;
they hiss and wag their heads
   at the daughter of Jerusalem:
"Is this the city that was called
   the perfection of beauty,
   the joy of all the earth?"

16 All your enemies
   rail against you;
they hiss, they gnash their teeth,
   they cry: "We have swallowed her!
Ah, this is the day we longed for;
   now we have it; we see it!"

17 The LORD has done what he pur-
      posed;
   he has carried out his word,
which he commanded long ago;
   he has thrown down without pity;

he has made the enemy rejoice over
    you
and exalted the might of your foes.

18 Their heart cried to the Lord.
    O wall of the daughter of Zion,
let tears stream down like a torrent
    day and night!
Give yourself no rest,
    your eyes no respite!

19 "Arise, cry out in the night,
    at the beginning of the night watches!
Pour out your heart like water
    before the presence of the Lord!
Lift your hands to him
    for the lives of your children,
who faint for hunger
    at the head of every street."

20 Look, O LORD, and see!
    With whom have you dealt thus?
Should women eat the fruit of their
    womb,
    the children of their tender care?

GETTING THE MESSAGE

Wormwood (3:15) was a bitter-tasting shrub that grew wild along the rocky slopes of Palestine. In Scripture, its bitter taste is often symbolic of hardship and sorrow.

Should priest and prophet be killed
    in the sanctuary of the Lord?

21 In the dust of the streets
    lie the young and the old;
my young women and my young men
    have fallen by the sword;
you have killed them in the day of
    your anger,
    slaughtering without pity.

22 You summoned as if to a festival day
    my terrors on every side,
and on the day of the anger of the LORD
    no one escaped or survived;
those whom I held and raised
    my enemy destroyed.

Great Is Your Faithfulness

3 I am the man who has seen affliction
    under the rod of his wrath;
2 he has driven and brought me
    into darkness without any light;

3 surely against me he turns his hand
    again and again the whole day long.

4 He has made my flesh and my skin
    waste away;
he has broken my bones;
5 he has besieged and enveloped me
    with bitterness and tribulation;
6 he has made me dwell in darkness
    like the dead of long ago.

7 He has walled me about so that I can-
    not escape;
he has made my chains heavy;
8 though I call and cry for help,
    he shuts out my prayer;
9 he has blocked my ways with blocks
    of stones;
    he has made my paths crooked.

10 He is a bear lying in wait for me,
    a lion in hiding;
11 he turned aside my steps and tore me
    to pieces;
    he has made me desolate;
12 he bent his bow and set me
    as a target for his arrow.

13 He drove into my kidneys
    the arrows of his quiver;
14 I have become the laughingstock of all
    peoples,
    the object of their taunts all day long.
15 He has filled me with bitterness;
    he has sated me with wormwood.
16 He has made my teeth grind on gravel,
    and made me cower in ashes;
17 my soul is bereft of peace;
    I have forgotten what happiness is;
18 so I say, "My endurance has perished;
    so has my hope from the LORD."

19 Remember my affliction and my wan-
    derings,
    the wormwood and the gall!
20 My soul continually remembers it
    and is bowed down within me.
21 But this I call to mind,
    and therefore I have hope:

22 The steadfast love of the LORD never
    ceases;
    his mercies never come to an end;
23 they are new every morning;
    great is your faithfulness.
24 "The LORD is my portion," says my soul,
    "therefore I will hope in him."

25 The LORD is good to those who wait
for him,
to the soul who seeks him.
26 It is good that one should wait quietly
for the salvation of the LORD.
27 It is good for a man that he bear
the yoke in his youth.

28 Let him sit alone in silence
when it is laid on him;
29 let him put his mouth in the dust—
there may yet be hope;
30 let him give his cheek to the one who
strikes,
and let him be filled with insults.

31 For the Lord will not
cast off forever,
32 but, though he cause grief, he will
have compassion
according to the abundance of his
steadfast love;
33 for he does not afflict from his heart
or grieve the children of men.

34 To crush underfoot
all the prisoners of the earth,
35 to deny a man justice
in the presence of the Most High,
36 to subvert a man in his lawsuit,
the Lord does not approve.

37 Who has spoken and it came to pass,
unless the Lord has commanded it?
38 Is it not from the mouth of the Most
High
that good and bad come?
39 Why should a living man complain,
a man, about the punishment of his
sins?

40 Let us test and examine our ways,
and return to the LORD!
41 Let us lift up our hearts and hands
to God in heaven:
42 "We have transgressed and rebelled,
and you have not forgiven.

43 "You have wrapped yourself with anger
and pursued us,
killing without pity;
44 you have wrapped yourself with a cloud
so that no prayer can pass through.
45 You have made us scum and garbage
among the peoples.

46 "All our enemies
open their mouths against us;
47 panic and pitfall have come upon us,
devastation and destruction;
48 my eyes flow with rivers of tears
because of the destruction of the
daughter of my people.

49 "My eyes will flow without ceasing,
without respite,
50 until the LORD from heaven
looks down and sees;
51 my eyes cause me grief
at the fate of all the daughters of my
city.

52 "I have been hunted like a bird
by those who were my enemies
without cause;
53 they flung me alive into the pit
and cast stones on me;
54 water closed over my head;
I said, 'I am lost.'

55 "I called on your name, O LORD,
from the depths of the pit;
56 you heard my plea, 'Do not close
your ear to my cry for help!'
57 You came near when I called on you;
you said, 'Do not fear!'

58 "You have taken up my cause, O Lord;
you have redeemed my life.
59 You have seen the wrong done to me,
O LORD;
judge my cause.
60 You have seen all their vengeance,
all their plots against me.

61 "You have heard their taunts, O LORD,
all their plots against me.
62 The lips and thoughts of my assailants
are against me all the day long.
63 Behold their sitting and their rising;
I am the object of their taunts.

64 "You will repay them, O LORD,
according to the work of their
hands.
65 You will give them dullness of heart;
your curse will be on them.
66 You will pursue them in anger and
destroy them
from under your heavens, O LORD."

The Holy Stones Lie Scattered

4 How the gold has grown dim,
how the pure gold is changed!
The holy stones lie scattered
at the head of every street.

2 The precious sons of Zion,
    worth their weight in fine gold,
how they are regarded as earthen pots,
    the work of a potter's hands!

3 Even jackals offer the breast;
    they nurse their young,
but the daughter of my people has
      become cruel,
    like the ostriches in the wilderness.

4 The tongue of the nursing infant
      sticks
    to the roof of its mouth for thirst;
the children beg for food,
    but no one gives to them.

5 Those who once feasted on delicacies
    perish in the streets;
those who were brought up in purple
    embrace ash heaps.

GETTING THE MESSAGE

The fall of Jerusalem. Jerusalem had been invaded several times, but had always survived. Finally, however, because of the people's continued rebellion, the Lord allowed the Babylonians to conquer Jerusalem in 586 B.C. Chapter 4 contrasts Judah's glory days with its pitiful state after judgment.

6 For the chastisement of the daughter
      of my people has been greater
    than the punishment of Sodom,
which was overthrown in a moment,
    and no hands were wrung for her.

7 Her princes were purer than snow,
    whiter than milk;
their bodies were more ruddy than
      coral,
    the beauty of their form was like
      sapphire.

8 Now their face is blacker than soot;
    they are not recognized in the
      streets;
their skin has shriveled on their bones;
    it has become as dry as wood.

9 Happier were the victims of the sword
    than the victims of hunger,
who wasted away, pierced
    by lack of the fruits of the field.

10 The hands of compassionate women
    have boiled their own children;
they became their food
    during the destruction of the
      daughter of my people.

11 The LORD gave full vent to his wrath;
    he poured out his hot anger,
and he kindled a fire in Zion
    that consumed its foundations.

12 The kings of the earth did not believe,
    nor any of the inhabitants of the
      world,
that foe or enemy could enter
    the gates of Jerusalem.

13 This was for the sins of her prophets
    and the iniquities of her priests,
who shed in the midst of her
    the blood of the righteous.

14 They wandered, blind, through the
      streets;
    they were so defiled with blood
that no one was able to touch
    their garments.

15 "Away! Unclean!" people cried at
      them.
    "Away! Away! Do not touch!"
So they became fugitives and wander-
      ers;
    people said among the nations,
"They shall stay with us no longer."

16 The LORD himself has scattered
      them;
    he will regard them no more;
no honor was shown to the priests,
    no favor to the elders.

17 Our eyes failed, ever watching
    vainly for help;
in our watching we watched
    for a nation which could not save.

18 They dogged our steps
    so that we could not walk in our
      streets;
our end drew near; our days were
      numbered,
    for our end had come.

19 Our pursuers were swifter
    than the eagles in the heavens;
they chased us on the mountains;
    they lay in wait for us in the wilder-
      ness.

20 The breath of our nostrils, the LORD's
      anointed,
    was captured in their pits,
  of whom we said, "Under his shadow
    we shall live among the nations."

21 Rejoice and be glad, O daughter of
      Edom,
    you who dwell in the land of Uz;
  but to you also the cup shall pass;
    you shall become drunk and strip
      yourself bare.

22 The punishment of your iniquity,
      O daughter of Zion, is accom-
      plished;
    he will keep you in exile no longer;
  but your iniquity, O daughter of
      Edom, he will punish;
    he will uncover your sins.

Restore Us to Yourself, O LORD

5 Remember, O LORD, what has
    befallen us;
    look, and see our disgrace!
2 Our inheritance has been turned over
      to strangers,
    our homes to foreigners.
3 We have become orphans, fatherless;
    our mothers are like widows.
4 We must pay for the water we drink;
    the wood we get must be bought.
5 Our pursuers are at our necks;
    we are weary; we are given no rest.
6 We have given the hand to Egypt, and
      to Assyria,
    to get bread enough.
7 Our fathers sinned, and are no more;
    and we bear their iniquities.
8 Slaves rule over us;
    there is none to deliver us from
      their hand.
9 We get our bread at the peril of our
      lives,
    because of the sword in the wilder-
      ness.
10 Our skin is hot as an oven
    with the burning heat of famine.

11 Women are raped in Zion,
    young women in the towns of
      Judah.
12 Princes are hung up by their hands;
    no respect is shown to the elders.
13 Young men are compelled to grind at
      the mill,
    and boys stagger under loads of
      wood.
14 The old men have left the city gate,
    the young men their music.
15 The joy of our hearts has ceased;
    our dancing has been turned to
      mourning.
16 The crown has fallen from our head;
    woe to us, for we have sinned!

GETTING THE MESSAGE

Lamentations contains five poems that
mourn the fall of Judah and the sin that
caused it. Chapters 1–3 and 4 are acrostic
poems. This means that each verse starts
with a different letter of the Hebrew
alphabet, in alphabetical order. Psalm 119
is another example of an acrostic poem.

17 For this our heart has become sick,
    for these things our eyes have
      grown dim,
18 for Mount Zion which lies desolate;
    jackals prowl over it.
19 But you, O LORD, reign forever;
    your throne endures to all genera-
      tions.
20 Why do you forget us forever,
    why do you forsake us for so many
      days?
21 Restore us to yourself, O LORD, that
    we may be restored!
    Renew our days as of old—
22 unless you have utterly rejected us,
    and you remain exceedingly angry
      with us.

INTRODUCTION TO EZEKIEL

593 B.C.	586 B.C.	573 B.C.
Ezekiel's first vision	Fall of Judah/ temple destroyed	Ezekiel's vision of second temple

AUTHOR AND DATE

The first dated message in Ezekiel is from the summer of 593 B.C., four years after Nebuchadnezzar deported the first group of exiles to Babylon. The latest dated oracle is 22 years later, in April 571 B.C. If Ezekiel was 30 years old when his ministry began (1:1), the final vision of the book came when he was about 50.

THEME AND PURPOSE

Ezekiel spoke to a people forced from their home because they had broken faith with their God. As the spokesman for the Lord, Ezekiel spoke oracles that defended his reputation as a holy God (see especially 36:22–23). The primary purpose of Ezekiel's message was to restore God's glory before Israel, who had rejected him in front of the watching nations.

BACKGROUND

Ezekiel prophesied during a time of great confusion following Israel's exile to Babylon in 597 B.C. A former Judean king was among the exiles (the 18-year-old Jehoiachin), and the Babylonians had appointed a puppet king to the throne in Jerusalem (Jehoiachin's uncle, Zedekiah).

In times of crisis, God sent prophets to bring his message to his people. Judah's exile was therefore a period of intense prophetic activity. (Jeremiah also served during this time.)

Ezekiel's fellow exiles were his main audience, but his oracles also communicated to people who remained in Judah.

KEY THEMES

1. As a priest, Ezekiel was deeply concerned with restoring God's people to holiness. His understanding of the depth of Israel's sin is clear in his version of Israel's history (ch. 20). Even the oracles about a restored Israel (chs. 40–48) include a way to deal with the people's sin so they can survive in the presence of a holy God. Ezekiel's concern with sin also accounts for the many places where the book echoes the laws given in the Pentateuch, as well as the similarities between Ezekiel's new temple (chs. 40–42) and the Exodus tabernacle.

2. Israel was subject to its national God. However, this God is no tribal deity. He is supreme over all nations. Therefore Nebuchadnezzar, king of mighty Babylon, was simply a tool in God's hand to accomplish God's purpose (e.g., 21:19–23; 30:25). God's absolute supremacy is most clearly demonstrated in the battle against Gog, the final enemy (chs. 38–39), where God alone crushes Gog's vast hostile forces.

3. Ezekiel declares judgment on those clinging to false hope, but offers true hope to those who accept God's judgment (37:11). He linked God's judgment with the hope of a new heart and spirit (36:22–32).

4. The condemnation of Israel's "princes" (e.g., ch. 19) finds its hopeful counterpart in the promise of a future "prince" who would rule with justice (34:23–24) and connect the people to God (46:1–18).

OUTLINE

EZEKIEL

Ezekiel in Babylon

1 In the thirtieth year, in the fourth month, on the fifth day of the month, as I was among the exiles by the Chebar canal, the heavens were opened, and I saw visions of God. ²On the fifth day of the month (it was the fifth year of the exile of King Jehoiachin), ³the word of the LORD came to Ezekiel the priest, the son of Buzi, in the land of the Chaldeans by the Chebar canal, and the hand of the LORD was upon him there.

The Glory of the LORD

⁴As I looked, behold, a stormy wind came out of the north, and a great cloud, with brightness around it, and fire flashing forth continually, and in the midst of the fire, as it were gleaming metal. ⁵And from the midst of it came the likeness of four living creatures. And this was their appearance: they had a human likeness, ⁶but each had four faces, and each of them had four wings. ⁷Their legs were straight, and the soles of their feet were like the sole of a calf's foot. And they sparkled like burnished bronze. ⁸Under their wings on their four sides they had human hands. And the four had their faces and their wings thus: ⁹their wings touched one another. Each one of them went straight forward, without turning as they went. ¹⁰As for the likeness of their faces, each had a human face. The four had the face of a lion on the right side, the four had the face of an ox on the left side, and the four had the face of an eagle. ¹¹Such were their faces. And their wings were spread out above. Each creature had two wings, each of which touched the wing of another, while two covered their bodies. ¹²And each went straight forward. Wherever the spirit[1] would go, they went, without turning as they went. ¹³As for the likeness of the living creatures, their appearance was like burning coals of fire, like the appearance of torches moving to and fro among the living creatures. And the fire was bright, and out of the fire went forth lightning. ¹⁴And the living creatures darted to and fro, like the appearance of a flash of lightning.

¹⁵Now as I looked at the living creatures, I saw a wheel on the earth beside the living creatures, one for each of the four of them. ¹⁶As for the appearance of the wheels and their construction: their appearance was like the gleaming of beryl. And the four had the same likeness, their appearance and construction being as it were a wheel within a wheel. ¹⁷When they went, they went in any of their four directions without turning as they went. ¹⁸And their rims were tall and awesome, and the rims of all four were full

of eyes all around. ¹⁹And when the living creatures went, the wheels went beside them; and when the living creatures rose from the earth, the wheels rose. ²⁰Wherever the spirit wanted to go, they went, and the wheels rose along with them, for the spirit of the living creatures was in the wheels. ²¹When those went, these went; and when those stood, these stood; and when those rose from the earth, the wheels rose along with them, for the spirit of the living creatures was in the wheels.

²²Over the heads of the living creatures there was the likeness of an expanse, shining like awe-inspiring crystal, spread out above their heads. ²³And under the expanse their wings were stretched out straight, one toward another. And each creature had two wings covering its body. ²⁴And when they went, I heard the sound of their wings like the sound of many waters, like the sound

¹ Or *Spirit*; also 1:20, 21

of the Almighty, a sound of tumult like the sound of an army. When they stood still, they let down their wings. ²⁵ And there came a voice from above the expanse over their heads. When they stood still, they let down their wings.

²⁶ And above the expanse over their heads there was the likeness of a throne, in appearance like sapphire; and seated above the likeness of a throne was a likeness

PROFILE

EZEKIEL

Ezekiel ministered during the same troubled times as the prophet Jeremiah. He was among the thousands of Judeans exiled to Babylon, where he probably spent the remainder of his life. About five years into the exile, at the age of 30, Ezekiel was called as a prophet. God commanded him to speak the word of God fearlessly to the people, regardless of whether or not they listened. He was appointed as a "watchman" for Israel (3:17; 33:1–9), whose task it was to warn the people that God would punish them unless they repented. Courageous sermons, dramatic visions, and symbolic actions characterized Ezekiel's ministry. God asked Ezekiel to enact difficult messages, often at a great personal cost. When his wife died, Ezekiel was commanded not to mourn for her, as a sign to Israel (24:15–27). Like Jeremiah, Ezekiel remained a faithful, humble servant despite his difficult life as a prophet.

KEY REFERENCE: EZEKIEL 33:1–9

with a human appearance. ²⁷ And upward from what had the appearance of his waist I saw as it were gleaming metal, like the appearance of fire enclosed all around. And downward from what had the appearance of his waist I saw as it were the appearance of fire, and there was brightness around him. ²⁸ Like the appearance of the bow that is in the cloud on the day of rain, so was the appearance of the brightness all around.

¹ Or *Son of Adam*; so throughout Ezekiel

Such was the appearance of the likeness of the glory of the LORD. And when I saw it, I fell on my face, and I heard the voice of one speaking.

Ezekiel's Call

2 And he said to me, "Son of man,¹ stand on your feet, and I will speak with you." ² And as he spoke to me, the Spirit entered into me and set me on my feet, and I heard him speaking to me. ³ And he said to me, "Son of man, I send you to the people of Israel, to nations of rebels, who have rebelled against me. They and their fathers have transgressed against me to this very day. ⁴ The descendants also are impudent and stubborn: I send you to them, and you shall say to them, 'Thus says the Lord GOD.' ⁵ And whether they hear or refuse to hear (for they are a rebellious house) they will know that a prophet has been

GETTING THE MESSAGE

Son of man (or "son of Adam") highlights the prophet's humanity before the holy God. Ezekiel is called "son of man" 93 times in this book.

among them. ⁶ And you, son of man, be not afraid of them, nor be afraid of their words, though briers and thorns are with you and you sit on scorpions. Be not afraid of their words, nor be dismayed at their looks, for they are a rebellious house. ⁷ And you shall speak my words to them, whether they hear or refuse to hear, for they are a rebellious house.

⁸ "But you, son of man, hear what I say to you. Be not rebellious like that rebellious house; open your mouth and eat what I give you." ⁹ And when I looked, behold, a hand was stretched out to me, and behold, a scroll of a book was in it. ¹⁰ And he spread it before me. And it had writing on the front and on the back, and there were written on it words of lamentation and mourning and woe.

3 And he said to me, "Son of man, eat whatever you find here. Eat this scroll, and go, speak to the house of Israel." ² So I opened my mouth, and he gave me this scroll to eat. ³ And he said to me, "Son of

man, feed your belly with this scroll that I give you and fill your stomach with it." Then I ate it, and it was in my mouth as sweet as honey.

⁴ And he said to me, "Son of man, go to the house of Israel and speak with my words to them. ⁵ For you are not sent to a people of foreign speech and a hard language, but to the house of Israel — ⁶ not to many peoples of foreign speech and a hard language, whose words you cannot understand. Surely, if I sent you to such, they would listen to you. ⁷ But the house of Israel will not be willing to listen to you, for they are not willing to listen to me: because all the house of Israel have a hard forehead and a stubborn heart. ⁸ Behold, I have made your face as hard as their faces, and your forehead as hard as their foreheads. ⁹ Like emery harder than flint have I made your forehead. Fear them not, nor be dismayed at their looks, for they are a rebellious house." ¹⁰ Moreover, he said to me, "Son of man, all my words that I shall speak to you receive in your heart, and hear with your ears. ¹¹ And go to the exiles, to your people, and speak to them and say to them, 'Thus says the Lord GOD,' whether they hear or refuse to hear."

¹² Then the Spirit lifted me up, and I heard behind me the voice of a great earthquake: "Blessed be the glory of the LORD from its place!" ¹³ It was the sound of the wings of the living creatures as they touched one another, and the sound of the wheels beside them, and the sound of a great earthquake. ¹⁴ The Spirit lifted me up and took me away, and I went in bitterness in the heat of my spirit, the hand of the LORD being strong upon me. ¹⁵ And I came to the exiles at Tel-abib, who were dwelling by the Chebar canal, and I sat where they were dwelling. And I sat there overwhelmed among them seven days.

A Watchman for Israel

¹⁶ And at the end of seven days, the word of the LORD came to me: ¹⁷ "Son of man, I have made you a watchman for the house of Israel. Whenever you hear a word from my mouth, you shall give them warning from me. ¹⁸ If I say to the wicked, 'You shall surely die,' and you give him no warning, nor speak to warn the wicked from his wicked way, in order to save his life, that wicked person shall die for his iniquity, but his blood I will require

at your hand. ¹⁹ But if you warn the wicked, and he does not turn from his wickedness, or from his wicked way, he shall die for his iniquity, but you will have delivered your soul. ²⁰ Again, if a righteous person turns from his righteousness and commits injustice, and I lay a stumbling block before him, he shall die. Because you have not warned him, he shall die for his sin, and his righteous deeds that he has done shall not be remembered, but his blood I will require at your hand. ²¹ But if you warn the righteous person not to sin, and he does not sin, he shall surely live, because he took warning, and you will have delivered your soul."

²² And the hand of the LORD was upon me there. And he said to me, "Arise, go out into the valley, and there I will speak with you." ²³ So I arose and went out into the valley, and behold, the glory of the LORD stood

GETTING THE MESSAGE

Tel-abib was located along the Chebar canal near Babylon. Ezekiel settled there with a community of fellow deportees from Judah (3:15). Many exiles prospered in Babylon, and when the Persians allowed them to return to Jerusalem, many decided to stay.

there, like the glory that I had seen by the Chebar canal, and I fell on my face. ²⁴ But the Spirit entered into me and set me on my feet, and he spoke with me and said to me, "Go, shut yourself within your house. ²⁵ And you, O son of man, behold, cords will be placed upon you, and you shall be bound with them, so that you cannot go out among the people. ²⁶ And I will make your tongue cling to the roof of your mouth, so that you shall be mute and unable to reprove them, for they are a rebellious house. ²⁷ But when I speak with you, I will open your mouth, and you shall say to them, 'Thus says the Lord GOD.' He who will hear, let him hear; and he who will refuse to hear, let him refuse, for they are a rebellious house.

The Siege of Jerusalem Symbolized

4 "And you, son of man, take a brick and lay it before you, and engrave on it a city, even Jerusalem. ² And put siegeworks against it, and build a siege wall against it,

and cast up a mound against it. Set camps also against it, and plant battering rams against it all around. ³ And you, take an iron griddle, and place it as an iron wall between you and the city; and set your face toward it, and let it be in a state of siege, and press the siege against it. This is a sign for the house of Israel.

⁴ "Then lie on your left side, and place the punishment of the house of Israel upon it. For the number of the days that you lie on it, you shall bear their punishment. ⁵ For I assign to you a number of days, 390 days, equal to the number of the years of their punishment. So long shall you bear the punishment of the house of Israel. ⁶ And when you have completed these, you shall lie down a second time, but on your right side, and bear the punishment of the house of Judah. Forty days I assign you, a day for

> ### GETTING THE MESSAGE
>
> God sometimes asked Ezekiel to **act out his prophetic message**. In ch. 4, God asks him to lie on his side for 430 days. In ch. 5, Ezekiel shaves his beard, a shameful act for a priest, to warn the people that God would judge Jerusalem for its rebellion.

each year. ⁷ And you shall set your face toward the siege of Jerusalem, with your arm bared, and you shall prophesy against the city. ⁸ And behold, I will place cords upon you, so that you cannot turn from one side to the other, till you have completed the days of your siege.

⁹ "And you, take wheat and barley, beans and lentils, millet and emmer, and put them into a single vessel and make your bread from them. During the number of days that you lie on your side, 390 days, you shall eat it. ¹⁰ And your food that you eat shall be by weight, twenty shekels a day; from day to day you shall eat it. ¹¹ And water you shall drink by measure, the sixth part of a hin; from day to day you shall drink. ¹² And you shall eat it as a barley cake, baking it in their sight on human dung." ¹³ And the LORD said, "Thus shall the people of Israel eat their bread unclean, among the nations where I will drive them." ¹⁴ Then I said, "Ah, Lord

GOD! Behold, I have never defiled myself. From my youth up till now I have never eaten what died of itself or was torn by beasts, nor has tainted meat come into my mouth." ¹⁵ Then he said to me, "See, I assign to you cow's dung instead of human dung, on which you may prepare your bread." ¹⁶ Moreover, he said to me, "Son of man, behold, I will break the supply of bread in Jerusalem. They shall eat bread by weight and with anxiety, and they shall drink water by measure and in dismay. ¹⁷ I will do this that they may lack bread and water, and look at one another in dismay, and rot away because of their punishment.

Jerusalem Will Be Destroyed

5 "And you, O son of man, take a sharp sword. Use it as a barber's razor and pass it over your head and your beard. Then take balances for weighing and divide the hair. ² A third part you shall burn in the fire in the midst of the city, when the days of the siege are completed. And a third part you shall take and strike with the sword all around the city. And a third part you shall scatter to the wind, and I will unsheathe the sword after them. ³ And you shall take from these a small number and bind them in the skirts of your robe. ⁴ And of these again you shall take some and cast them into the midst of the fire and burn them in the fire. From there a fire will come out into all the house of Israel.

⁵ "Thus says the Lord GOD: This is Jerusalem. I have set her in the center of the nations, with countries all around her. ⁶ And she has rebelled against my rules by doing wickedness more than the nations, and against my statutes more than the countries all around her; for they have rejected my rules and have not walked in my statutes. ⁷ Therefore thus says the Lord GOD: Because you are more turbulent than the nations that are all around you, and have not walked in my statutes or obeyed my rules, and have not even acted according to the rules of the nations that are all around you, ⁸ therefore thus says the Lord GOD: Behold, I, even I, am against you. And I will execute judgments in your midst in the sight of the nations. ⁹ And because of all your abominations I will do with you what I have never yet done, and the like of which I will never do again. ¹⁰ Therefore fathers shall eat their sons in your midst, and sons shall eat their fathers.

And I will execute judgments on you, and any of you who survive I will scatter to all the winds. ¹¹ Therefore, as I live, declares the Lord God, surely, because you have defiled my sanctuary with all your detestable things and with all your abominations, therefore I will withdraw. My eye will not spare, and I will have no pity. ¹² A third part of you shall die of pestilence and be consumed with famine in your midst; a third part shall fall by the sword all around you; and a third part I will scatter to all the winds and will unsheathe the sword after them.

¹³ "Thus shall my anger spend itself, and I will vent my fury upon them and satisfy myself. And they shall know that I am the Lord—that I have spoken in my jealousy—when I spend my fury upon them. ¹⁴ Moreover, I will make you a desolation and an object of reproach among the nations all around you and in the sight of all who pass by. ¹⁵ You shall be a reproach and a taunt, a warning and a horror, to the nations all around you, when I execute judgments on you in anger and fury, and with furious rebukes—I am the Lord; I have spoken— ¹⁶ when I send against you the deadly arrows of famine, arrows for destruction, which I will send to destroy you, and when I bring more and more famine upon you and break your supply of bread. ¹⁷ I will send famine and wild beasts against you, and they will rob you of your children. Pestilence and blood shall pass through you, and I will bring the sword upon you. I am the Lord; I have spoken."

Judgment Against Idolatry

6 The word of the Lord came to me: ² "Son of man, set your face toward the mountains of Israel, and prophesy against them, ³ and say, You mountains of Israel, hear the word of the Lord God! Thus says the Lord God to the mountains and the hills, to the ravines and the valleys: Behold, I, even I, will bring a sword upon you, and I will destroy your high places. ⁴ Your altars shall become desolate, and your incense altars shall be broken, and I will cast down your slain before your idols. ⁵ And I will lay the dead bodies of the people of Israel before their idols, and I will scatter your bones around your altars. ⁶ Wherever you dwell, the cities shall be waste and the high places ruined, so that your altars will be waste and

ruined, your idols broken and destroyed, your incense altars cut down, and your works wiped out. ⁷ And the slain shall fall in your midst, and you shall know that I am the Lord.

⁸ "Yet I will leave some of you alive. When you have among the nations some who escape the sword, and when you are scattered through the countries, ⁹ then those of you who escape will remember me among the nations where they are carried captive, how I have been broken over their whoring heart that has departed from me and over their eyes that go whoring after their idols. And they will be loathsome in their own sight for the evils that they have committed, for all their abominations. ¹⁰ And they shall know that I am the Lord. I have not said in vain that I would do this evil to them."

¹¹ Thus says the Lord God: "Clap your hands and stamp your foot and say, Alas, because of all the evil abominations of the house of Israel, for they shall fall by the sword, by famine, and by pestilence. ¹² He who is far off shall die of pestilence, and he who is near shall fall by the sword, and he who is left and is preserved shall die of famine. Thus I will spend my fury upon them. ¹³ And you shall know that I am the Lord, when their slain lie among their idols around their altars, on every high hill, on all the mountaintops, under every green tree, and under every leafy oak, wherever they offered pleasing aroma to all their idols. ¹⁴ And I will stretch out my hand against them and make the land desolate and waste, in all their dwelling places, from the wilderness to Riblah. Then they will know that I am the Lord."

The Day of the Wrath of the Lord

7 The word of the Lord came to me: ² "And you, O son of man, thus says the Lord God to the land of Israel: An end! The end has come upon the four corners of the land. ³ Now the end is upon you, and I will send my anger upon you; I will judge you according to your ways, and I will punish you for all your abominations. ⁴ And my eye will not spare you, nor will I have pity, but I will punish you for your ways, while your abominations are in your midst. Then you will know that I am the Lord.

⁵ "Thus says the Lord God: Disaster after disaster! Behold, it comes. ⁶ An end has

come; the end has come; it has awakened against you. Behold, it comes. [7] Your doom has come to you, O inhabitant of the land. The time has come; the day is near, a day of tumult, and not of joyful shouting on the mountains. [8] Now I will soon pour out my wrath upon you, and spend my anger against you, and judge you according to your ways, and I will punish you for all your abominations. [9] And my eye will not spare, nor will I have pity. I will punish you according to your ways, while your abominations are in your midst. Then you will know that I am the LORD, who strikes.

[10] "Behold, the day! Behold, it comes! Your doom has come; the rod has blossomed; pride has budded. [11] Violence has grown up into a rod of wickedness. None of them shall remain, nor their abundance, nor their wealth; neither shall there be preeminence

among them. [12] The time has come; the day has arrived. Let not the buyer rejoice, nor the seller mourn, for wrath is upon all their multitude. [13] For the seller shall not return to what he has sold, while they live. For the vision concerns all their multitude; it shall not turn back; and because of his iniquity, none can maintain his life.

[14] "They have blown the trumpet and made everything ready, but none goes to battle, for my wrath is upon all their multitude. [15] The sword is without; pestilence and famine are within. He who is in the field dies by the sword, and him who is in the city famine and pestilence devour. [16] And if any survivors escape, they will be on the mountains, like doves of the valleys, all of them moaning, each one over his iniquity. [17] All hands are feeble, and all knees turn to water. [18] They put on sackcloth, and horror covers them. Shame is on all faces, and baldness on all their heads. [19] They cast

their silver into the streets, and their gold is like an unclean thing. Their silver and gold are not able to deliver them in the day of the wrath of the LORD. They cannot satisfy their hunger or fill their stomachs with it. For it was the stumbling block of their iniquity. [20] His beautiful ornament they used for pride, and they made their abominable images and their detestable things of it. Therefore I make it an unclean thing to them. [21] And I will give it into the hands of foreigners for prey, and to the wicked of the earth for spoil, and they shall profane it. [22] I will turn my face from them, and they shall profane my treasured place. Robbers shall enter and profane it.

[23] "Forge a chain! For the land is full of bloody crimes and the city is full of violence. [24] I will bring the worst of the nations to take possession of their houses. I will put an end to the pride of the strong, and their holy places shall be profaned. [25] When anguish comes, they will seek peace, but there shall be none. [26] Disaster comes upon disaster; rumor follows rumor. They seek a vision from the prophet, while the law perishes from the priest and counsel from the elders. [27] The king mourns, the prince is wrapped in despair, and the hands of the people of the land are paralyzed by terror. According to their way I will do to them, and according to their judgments I will judge them, and they shall know that I am the LORD."

Abominations in the Temple

8 In the sixth year, in the sixth month, on the fifth day of the month, as I sat in my house, with the elders of Judah sitting before me, the hand of the Lord GOD fell upon me there. [2] Then I looked, and behold, a form that had the appearance of a man. Below what appeared to be his waist was fire, and above his waist was something like the appearance of brightness, like gleaming metal. [3] He put out the form of a hand and took me by a lock of my head, and the Spirit lifted me up between earth and heaven and brought me in visions of God to Jerusalem, to the entrance of the gateway of the inner court that faces north, where was the seat of the image of jealousy, which provokes to jealousy. [4] And behold, the glory of the God of Israel was there, like the vision that I saw in the valley.

⁵Then he said to me, "Son of man, lift up your eyes now toward the north." So I lifted up my eyes toward the north, and behold, north of the altar gate, in the entrance, was this image of jealousy. ⁶And he said to me, "Son of man, do you see what they are doing, the great abominations that the house of Israel are committing here, to drive me far from my sanctuary? But you will see still greater abominations."

⁷And he brought me to the entrance of the court, and when I looked, behold, there was a hole in the wall. ⁸Then he said to me, "Son of man, dig in the wall." So I dug in the wall, and behold, there was an entrance. ⁹And he said to me, "Go in, and see the vile abominations that they are committing here." ¹⁰So I went in and saw. And there, engraved on the wall all around, was every form of creeping things and loathsome beasts, and all the idols of the house of Israel. ¹¹And before them stood seventy men of the elders of the house of Israel, with Jaazaniah the son of Shaphan standing among them. Each had his censer in his hand, and the smoke of the cloud of incense went up. ¹²Then he said to me, "Son of man, have you seen what the elders of the house of Israel are doing in the dark, each in his room of pictures? For they say, 'The LORD does not see us, the LORD has forsaken the land.'" ¹³He said also to me, "You will see still greater abominations that they commit."

¹⁴Then he brought me to the entrance of the north gate of the house of the LORD, and behold, there sat women weeping for Tammuz. ¹⁵Then he said to me, "Have you seen this, O son of man? You will see still greater abominations than these."

¹⁶And he brought me into the inner court of the house of the LORD. And behold, at the entrance of the temple of the LORD, between the porch and the altar, were about twenty-five men, with their backs to the temple of the LORD, and their faces toward the east, worshiping the sun toward the east. ¹⁷Then he said to me, "Have you seen this, O son of man? Is it too light a thing for the house of Judah to commit the abominations that they commit here, that they should fill the land with violence and provoke me still further to anger? Behold, they put the branch to their nose. ¹⁸Therefore I will act in wrath. My eye will not spare, nor will I have pity.

And though they cry in my ears with a loud voice, I will not hear them."

Idolaters Killed

9 Then he cried in my ears with a loud voice, saying, "Bring near the executioners of the city, each with his destroying weapon in his hand." ²And behold, six men came from the direction of the upper gate, which faces north, each with his weapon for slaughter in his hand, and with them was a man clothed in linen, with a writing case at his waist. And they went in and stood beside the bronze altar.

³Now the glory of the God of Israel had gone up from the cherub on which it rested to the threshold of the house. And he called to the man clothed in linen, who had the writing case at his waist. ⁴And the LORD said to him, "Pass through the city, through Jerusalem, and put a mark on the foreheads

GETTING THE MESSAGE

A **writing case** (9:2) was standard equipment for scribes. The case provided a surface for writing upon and a place for storing pens and ink. It also contained a knife for keeping the pens sharp.

of the men who sigh and groan over all the abominations that are committed in it." ⁵And to the others he said in my hearing, "Pass through the city after him, and strike. Your eye shall not spare, and you shall show no pity. ⁶Kill old men outright, young men and maidens, little children and women, but touch no one on whom is the mark. And begin at my sanctuary." So they began with the elders who were before the house. ⁷Then he said to them, "Defile the house, and fill the courts with the slain. Go out." So they went out and struck in the city. ⁸And while they were striking, and I was left alone, I fell upon my face, and cried, "Ah, Lord GOD! Will you destroy all the remnant of Israel in the outpouring of your wrath on Jerusalem?"

⁹Then he said to me, "The guilt of the house of Israel and Judah is exceedingly great. The land is full of blood, and the city full of injustice. For they say, 'The LORD has forsaken the land, and the LORD does not see.' ¹⁰As for me, my eye will not spare, nor

will I have pity; I will bring their deeds upon their heads."

¹¹ And behold, the man clothed in linen, with the writing case at his waist, brought back word, saying, "I have done as you commanded me."

The Glory of the Lord Leaves the Temple

10 Then I looked, and behold, on the expanse that was over the heads of the cherubim there appeared above them something like a sapphire, in appearance like a throne. ² And he said to the man clothed in linen, "Go in among the whirling wheels underneath the cherubim. Fill your hands with burning coals from between the cherubim, and scatter them over the city."

And he went in before my eyes. ³ Now the cherubim were standing on the south side of the house, when the man went in, and a cloud filled the inner court. ⁴ And the glory of the Lord went up from the cherub to the threshold of the house, and the house was filled with the cloud, and the court was filled with the brightness of the glory of the Lord. ⁵ And the sound of the wings of the cherubim was heard as far as the outer court, like the voice of God Almighty when he speaks.

⁶ And when he commanded the man clothed in linen, "Take fire from between the whirling wheels, from between the cherubim," he went in and stood beside a wheel. ⁷ And a cherub stretched out his hand from between the cherubim to the fire that was between the cherubim, and took some of it and put it into the hands of the man clothed in linen, who took it and went out. ⁸ The cherubim appeared to have the form of a human hand under their wings.

⁹ And I looked, and behold, there were four wheels beside the cherubim, one beside each cherub, and the appearance of the wheels was like sparkling beryl. ¹⁰ And as for their appearance, the four had the same likeness, as if a wheel were within a wheel. ¹¹ When they went, they went in any of their four directions without turning as they went, but in whatever direction the front wheel faced, the others followed without turning as they went. ¹² And their whole body, their rims, and their spokes, their wings, and the wheels were full of eyes all around—the wheels that the four of them had. ¹³ As for the wheels, they were

called in my hearing "the whirling wheels." ¹⁴ And every one had four faces: the first face was the face of the cherub, and the second face was a human face, and the third the face of a lion, and the fourth the face of an eagle.

¹⁵ And the cherubim mounted up. These were the living creatures that I saw by the Chebar canal. ¹⁶ And when the cherubim went, the wheels went beside them. And when the cherubim lifted up their wings to mount up from the earth, the wheels did not turn from beside them. ¹⁷ When they stood still, these stood still, and when they mounted up, these mounted up with them, for the spirit of the living creatures was in them.

¹⁸ Then the glory of the Lord went out from the threshold of the house, and stood over the cherubim. ¹⁹ And the cherubim lifted up their wings and mounted up from the earth before my eyes as they went out, with the wheels beside them. And they stood at the entrance of the east gate of the house of the Lord, and the glory of the God of Israel was over them.

²⁰ These were the living creatures that I saw underneath the God of Israel by the Chebar canal; and I knew that they were cherubim. ²¹ Each had four faces, and each four wings, and underneath their wings the likeness of human hands. ²² And as for the likeness of their faces, they were the same faces whose appearance I had seen by the Chebar canal. Each one of them went straight forward.

Judgment on Wicked Counselors

11 The Spirit lifted me up and brought me to the east gate of the house of the Lord, which faces east. And behold, at the entrance of the gateway there were twenty-five men. And I saw among them Jaazaniah the son of Azzur, and Pelatiah the son of Benaiah, princes of the people. ² And he said to me, "Son of man, these are the men who devise iniquity and who give wicked counsel in this city; ³ who say, 'The time is not near to build houses. This city is the cauldron, and we are the meat.' ⁴ Therefore prophesy against them, prophesy, O son of man."

⁵ And the Spirit of the Lord fell upon me, and he said to me, "Say, Thus says the Lord: So you think, O house of Israel. For I know the things that come into your

mind. **6** You have multiplied your slain in this city and have filled its streets with the slain. **7** Therefore thus says the Lord GOD: Your slain whom you have laid in the midst of it, they are the meat, and this city is the cauldron, but you shall be brought out of the midst of it. **8** You have feared the sword, and I will bring the sword upon you, declares the Lord GOD. **9** And I will bring you out of the midst of it, and give you into the hands of foreigners, and execute judgments upon you. **10** You shall fall by the sword. I will judge you at the border of Israel, and you shall know that I am the LORD. **11** This city shall not be your cauldron, nor shall you be the meat in the midst of it. I will judge you at the border of Israel, **12** and you shall know that I am the LORD. For you have not walked in my statutes, nor obeyed my rules, but have acted according to the rules of the nations that are around you."

13 And it came to pass, while I was prophesying, that Pelatiah the son of Benaiah died. Then I fell down on my face and cried out with a loud voice and said, "Ah, Lord GOD! Will you make a full end of the remnant of Israel?"

Israel's New Heart and Spirit

14 And the word of the LORD came to me: **15** "Son of man, your brothers, even your brothers, your kinsmen, the whole house of Israel, all of them, are those of whom the inhabitants of Jerusalem have said, 'Go far from the LORD; to us this land is given for a possession.' **16** Therefore say, 'Thus says the Lord GOD: Though I removed them far off among the nations, and though I scattered them among the countries, yet I have been a sanctuary to them for a while in the countries where they have gone.' **17** Therefore say, 'Thus says the Lord GOD: I will gather you from the peoples and assemble you out of the countries where you have been scattered, and I will give you the land of Israel.' **18** And when they come there, they will remove from it all its detestable things and all its abominations. **19** And I will give them one heart, and a new spirit I will put within them. I will remove the heart of stone from their flesh and give them a heart of flesh, **20** that they may walk in my statutes and keep my rules and obey them. And they shall be my people, and I will be their God. **21** But as for those whose heart goes after

their detestable things and their abominations, I will bring their deeds upon their own heads, declares the Lord GOD."

22 Then the cherubim lifted up their wings, with the wheels beside them, and the glory of the God of Israel was over them. **23** And the glory of the LORD went up from the midst of the city and stood on the mountain that is on the east side of the city. **24** And the Spirit lifted me up and brought me in the vision by the Spirit of God into Chaldea, to the exiles. Then the vision that I had seen went up from me. **25** And I told the exiles all the things that the LORD had shown me.

Judah's Captivity Symbolized

12 The word of the LORD came to me: **2** "Son of man, you dwell in the midst of a rebellious house, who have eyes to see, but see not, who have ears to hear, but hear

GETTING THE MESSAGE

Hearts of flesh to replace hearts of stone. The Lord says that his rebellious people have a "heart of stone" (11:19), but he promises to someday give them a "heart of flesh," enabling them to love and obey him.

not, for they are a rebellious house. **3** As for you, son of man, prepare for yourself an exile's baggage, and go into exile by day in their sight. You shall go like an exile from your place to another place in their sight. Perhaps they will understand, though they are a rebellious house. **4** You shall bring out your baggage by day in their sight, as baggage for exile, and you shall go out yourself at evening in their sight, as those do who must go into exile. **5** In their sight dig through the wall, and bring your baggage out through it. **6** In their sight you shall lift the baggage upon your shoulder and carry it out at dusk. You shall cover your face that you may not see the land, for I have made you a sign for the house of Israel."

7 And I did as I was commanded. I brought out my baggage by day, as baggage for exile, and in the evening I dug through the wall with my own hands. I brought out my baggage at dusk, carrying it on my shoulder in their sight.

⁸ In the morning the word of the LORD came to me: ⁹ "Son of man, has not the house of Israel, the rebellious house, said to you, 'What are you doing?' ¹⁰ Say to them, 'Thus says the Lord GOD: This oracle concerns the prince in Jerusalem and all the house of Israel who are in it.' ¹¹ Say, 'I am a sign for you: as I have done, so shall it be done to them. They shall go into exile, into captivity.' ¹² And the prince who is among them shall lift his baggage upon his shoulder at dusk, and shall go out. They shall dig through the wall to bring him out through it. He shall cover his face, that he may not see the land with his eyes. ¹³ And I will spread my net over him, and he shall be taken in my snare. And I will bring him to Babylon, the land of the Chaldeans, yet he shall not see it, and he shall die there. ¹⁴ And I will scatter toward every wind all who are around

GETTING THE MESSAGE

Though **Zedekiah** was king of Judah at the time, Ezekiel refused to call him king. Instead, he calls him "the prince in Jerusalem" (12:10). This is because Zedekiah was a "puppet king" placed on the throne by the Babylonians.

him, his helpers and all his troops, and I will unsheathe the sword after them. ¹⁵ And they shall know that I am the LORD, when I disperse them among the nations and scatter them among the countries. ¹⁶ But I will let a few of them escape from the sword, from famine and pestilence, that they may declare all their abominations among the nations where they go, and may know that I am the LORD."

¹⁷ And the word of the LORD came to me: ¹⁸ "Son of man, eat your bread with quaking, and drink water with trembling and with anxiety. ¹⁹ And say to the people of the land, Thus says the Lord GOD concerning the inhabitants of Jerusalem in the land of Israel: They shall eat their bread with anxiety, and drink water in dismay. In this way her land will be stripped of all it contains, on account of the violence of all those who dwell in it. ²⁰ And the inhabited cities shall be laid waste, and the land shall become a desolation; and you shall know that I am the LORD."

²¹ And the word of the LORD came to me: ²² "Son of man, what is this proverb that you have about the land of Israel, saying, 'The days grow long, and every vision comes to nothing'? ²³ Tell them therefore, 'Thus says the Lord GOD: I will put an end to this proverb, and they shall no more use it as a proverb in Israel.' But say to them, The days are near, and the fulfillment of every vision. ²⁴ For there shall be no more any false vision or flattering divination within the house of Israel. ²⁵ For I am the LORD; I will speak the word that I will speak, and it will be performed. It will no longer be delayed, but in your days, O rebellious house, I will speak the word and perform it, declares the Lord GOD."

²⁶ And the word of the LORD came to me: ²⁷ "Son of man, behold, they of the house of Israel say, 'The vision that he sees is for many days from now, and he prophesies of times far off.' ²⁸ Therefore say to them, Thus says the Lord GOD: None of my words will be delayed any longer, but the word that I speak will be performed, declares the Lord GOD."

False Prophets Condemned

13 The word of the LORD came to me: ² "Son of man, prophesy against the prophets of Israel, who are prophesying, and say to those who prophesy from their own hearts: 'Hear the word of the LORD!' ³ Thus says the Lord GOD, Woe to the foolish prophets who follow their own spirit, and have seen nothing! ⁴ Your prophets have been like jackals among ruins, O Israel. ⁵ You have not gone up into the breaches, or built up a wall for the house of Israel, that it might stand in battle in the day of the LORD. ⁶ They have seen false visions and lying divinations. They say, 'Declares the LORD,' when the LORD has not sent them, and yet they expect him to fulfill their word. ⁷ Have you not seen a false vision and uttered a lying divination, whenever you have said, 'Declares the LORD,' although I have not spoken?"

⁸ Therefore thus says the Lord GOD: "Because you have uttered falsehood and seen lying visions, therefore behold, I am against you, declares the Lord GOD. ⁹ My hand will be against the prophets who see false visions and who give lying divinations. They shall not be in the council of my people, nor be enrolled in the register

of the house of Israel, nor shall they enter the land of Israel. And you shall know that I am the Lord God. ¹⁰ Precisely because they have misled my people, saying, 'Peace,' when there is no peace, and because, when the people build a wall, these prophets smear it with whitewash, ¹¹ say to those who smear it with whitewash that it shall fall! There will be a deluge of rain, and you, O great hailstones, will fall, and a stormy wind break out. ¹² And when the wall falls, will it not be said to you, 'Where is the coating with which you smeared it?' ¹³ Therefore thus says the Lord God: I will make a stormy wind break out in my wrath, and there shall be a deluge of rain in my anger, and great hailstones in wrath to make a full end. ¹⁴ And I will break down the wall that you have smeared with whitewash, and bring it down to the ground, so that its foundation will be laid bare. When it falls, you shall perish in the midst of it, and you shall know that I am the Lord. ¹⁵ Thus will I spend my wrath upon the wall and upon those who have smeared it with whitewash, and I will say to you, The wall is no more, nor those who smeared it, ¹⁶ the prophets of Israel who prophesied concerning Jerusalem and saw visions of peace for her, when there was no peace, declares the Lord God.

¹⁷ "And you, son of man, set your face against the daughters of your people, who prophesy out of their own hearts. Prophesy against them ¹⁸ and say, Thus says the Lord God: Woe to the women who sew magic bands upon all wrists, and make veils for the heads of persons of every stature, in the hunt for souls! Will you hunt down souls belonging to my people and keep your own souls alive? ¹⁹ You have profaned me among my people for handfuls of barley and for pieces of bread, putting to death souls who should not die and keeping alive souls who should not live, by your lying to my people, who listen to lies.

²⁰ "Therefore thus says the Lord God: Behold, I am against your magic bands with which you hunt the souls like birds, and I will tear them from your arms, and I will let the souls whom you hunt go free, the souls like birds. ²¹ Your veils also I will tear off and deliver my people out of your hand, and they shall be no more in your hand as prey, and you shall know that I am the Lord.

²² Because you have disheartened the righteous falsely, although I have not grieved him, and you have encouraged the wicked, that he should not turn from his evil way to save his life, ²³ therefore you shall no more see false visions nor practice divination. I will deliver my people out of your hand. And you shall know that I am the Lord."

Idolatrous Elders Condemned

14 Then certain of the elders of Israel came to me and sat before me. ² And the word of the Lord came to me: ³ "Son of man, these men have taken their idols into their hearts, and set the stumbling block of their iniquity before their faces. Should I indeed let myself be consulted by them? ⁴ Therefore speak to them and say to them, Thus says the Lord God: Any one of the house of Israel who takes his idols into his heart and sets the stumbling block of his

GETTING THE MESSAGE

The women in 13:17 who **"prophesy out of their own hearts"** were false prophets and magicians. Unlike Miriam (Ex. 15:20), Deborah (Judg. 4:4), and Huldah (2 Kings 22:14), these female prophets did not speak God's words.

iniquity before his face, and yet comes to the prophet, I the Lord will answer him as he comes with the multitude of his idols, ⁵ that I may lay hold of the hearts of the house of Israel, who are all estranged from me through their idols.

⁶ "Therefore say to the house of Israel, Thus says the Lord God: Repent and turn away from your idols, and turn away your faces from all your abominations. ⁷ For any one of the house of Israel, or of the strangers who sojourn in Israel, who separates himself from me, taking his idols into his heart and putting the stumbling block of his iniquity before his face, and yet comes to a prophet to consult me through him, I the Lord will answer him myself. ⁸ And I will set my face against that man; I will make him a sign and a byword and cut him off from the midst of my people, and you shall know that I am the Lord. ⁹ And if the prophet is deceived and speaks a word, I, the Lord, have deceived that prophet, and I will stretch out my hand

against him and will destroy him from the midst of my people Israel. ¹⁰ And they shall bear their punishment — the punishment of the prophet and the punishment of the inquirer shall be alike — ¹¹ that the house of Israel may no more go astray from me, nor defile themselves anymore with all their transgressions, but that they may be my people and I may be their God, declares the Lord GOD."

Jerusalem Will Not Be Spared

¹² And the word of the LORD came to me: ¹³ "Son of man, when a land sins against me by acting faithlessly, and I stretch out my hand against it and break its supply of bread and send famine upon it, and cut off from it man and beast, ¹⁴ even if these three men, Noah, Daniel, and Job, were in it, they would deliver but their own lives by their righteousness, declares the Lord GOD.

> ### GETTING THE MESSAGE
>
> Ezekiel compares the Jerusalemites to a **vine** that can only be used as fuel for a fire (ch. 15). In the Bible, the people of God are often compared to a vine. Jesus describes his relationship with his followers using vine imagery in John 15:1-11.

¹⁵ "If I cause wild beasts to pass through the land, and they ravage it, and it be made desolate, so that no one may pass through because of the beasts, ¹⁶ even if these three men were in it, as I live, declares the Lord GOD, they would deliver neither sons nor daughters. They alone would be delivered, but the land would be desolate. ¹⁷ "Or if I bring a sword upon that land and say, Let a sword pass through the land, and I cut off from it man and beast, ¹⁸ though these three men were in it, as I live, declares the Lord GOD, they would deliver neither sons nor daughters, but they alone would be delivered. ¹⁹ "Or if I send a pestilence into that land and pour out my wrath upon it with blood, to cut off from it man and beast, ²⁰ even if Noah, Daniel, and Job were in it, as I live, declares the Lord GOD, they would deliver neither son nor daughter. They would deliver but their own lives by their righteousness.

²¹ "For thus says the Lord GOD: How much more when I send upon Jerusalem my four disastrous acts of judgment, sword, famine, wild beasts, and pestilence, to cut off from it man and beast! ²² But behold, some survivors will be left in it, sons and daughters who will be brought out; behold, when they come out to you, and you see their ways and their deeds, you will be consoled for the disaster that I have brought upon Jerusalem, for all that I have brought upon it. ²³ They will console you, when you see their ways and their deeds, and you shall know that I have not done without cause all that I have done in it, declares the Lord GOD."

Jerusalem, a Useless Vine

15 And the word of the LORD came to me: ² "Son of man, how does the wood of the vine surpass any wood, the vine branch that is among the trees of the forest? ³ Is wood taken from it to make anything? Do people take a peg from it to hang any vessel on it? ⁴ Behold, it is given to the fire for fuel. When the fire has consumed both ends of it, and the middle of it is charred, is it useful for anything? ⁵ Behold, when it was whole, it was used for nothing. How much less, when the fire has consumed it and it is charred, can it ever be used for anything! ⁶ Therefore thus says the Lord GOD: Like the wood of the vine among the trees of the forest, which I have given to the fire for fuel, so have I given up the inhabitants of Jerusalem. ⁷ And I will set my face against them. Though they escape from the fire, the fire shall yet consume them, and you will know that I am the LORD, when I set my face against them. ⁸ And I will make the land desolate, because they have acted faithlessly, declares the Lord GOD."

The LORD's Faithless Bride

16 Again the word of the LORD came to me: ² "Son of man, make known to Jerusalem her abominations, ³ and say, Thus says the Lord GOD to Jerusalem: Your origin and your birth are of the land of the Canaanites; your father was an Amorite and your mother a Hittite. ⁴ And as for your birth, on the day you were born your cord was not cut, nor were you washed with water to cleanse you, nor rubbed with salt, nor wrapped in swaddling cloths. ⁵ No eye pitied you, to do any of these things to you

out of compassion for you, but you were cast out on the open field, for you were abhorred, on the day that you were born.

⁶ "And when I passed by you and saw you wallowing in your blood, I said to you in your blood, 'Live!' I said to you in your blood, 'Live!' ⁷ I made you flourish like a plant of the field. And you grew up and became tall and arrived at full adornment. Your breasts were formed, and your hair had grown; yet you were naked and bare.

⁸ "When I passed by you again and saw you, behold, you were at the age for love, and I spread the corner of my garment over you and covered your nakedness; I made my vow to you and entered into a covenant with you, declares the Lord GOD, and you became mine. ⁹ Then I bathed you with water and washed off your blood from you and anointed you with oil. ¹⁰ I clothed you also with embroidered cloth and shod you with fine leather. I wrapped you in fine linen and covered you with silk. ¹¹ And I adorned you with ornaments and put bracelets on your wrists and a chain on your neck. ¹² And I put a ring on your nose and earrings in your ears and a beautiful crown on your head. ¹³ Thus you were adorned with gold and silver, and your clothing was of fine linen and silk and embroidered cloth. You ate fine flour and honey and oil. You grew exceedingly beautiful and advanced to royalty. ¹⁴ And your renown went forth among the nations because of your beauty, for it was perfect through the splendor that I had bestowed on you, declares the Lord GOD.

¹⁵ "But you trusted in your beauty and played the whore because of your renown and lavished your whorings on any passerby; your beauty became his. ¹⁶ You took some of your garments and made for yourself colorful shrines, and on them played the whore. The like has never been, nor ever shall be. ¹⁷ You also took your beautiful jewels of my gold and of my silver, which I had given you, and made for yourself images of men, and with them played the whore. ¹⁸ And you took your embroidered garments to cover them, and set my oil and my incense before them. ¹⁹ Also my bread that I gave you—I fed you with fine flour and oil and honey—you set before them for a pleasing aroma; and so it was, declares the Lord GOD. ²⁰ And you took your sons and your daughters, whom you had borne to me, and these you sacrificed to them to be devoured. Were your whorings so small a matter ²¹ that you slaughtered my children and delivered them up as an offering by fire to them? ²² And in all your abominations and your whorings you did not remember the days of your youth, when you were naked and bare, wallowing in your blood.

²³ "And after all your wickedness (woe, woe to you! declares the Lord GOD), ²⁴ you built yourself a vaulted chamber and made yourself a lofty place in every square. ²⁵ At the head of every street you built your lofty place and made your beauty an abomination, offering yourself to any passerby and multiplying your whoring. ²⁶ You also played the whore with the Egyptians, your lustful neighbors, multiplying your whoring, to provoke me to anger. ²⁷ Behold, therefore, I stretched out my hand against you and diminished your allotted portion and delivered you to the greed of your enemies, the daughters of the Philistines, who were ashamed of your lewd behavior. ²⁸ You played the whore also with the Assyrians, because you were not satisfied; yes, you played the whore with them, and still you were not satisfied. ²⁹ You multiplied your whoring also with the trading land of Chaldea, and even with this you were not satisfied.

³⁰ "How sick is your heart, declares the Lord GOD, because you did all these things, the deeds of a brazen prostitute, ³¹ building your vaulted chamber at the head of every street, and making your lofty place in every square. Yet you were not like a prostitute, because you scorned payment. ³² Adulterous wife, who receives strangers instead of her husband! ³³ Men give gifts to all prostitutes, but you gave your gifts to all your lovers, bribing them to come to you from every side with your whorings. ³⁴ So you were different from other women in your whorings. No one solicited you to play the whore, and you gave payment, while no payment was given to you; therefore you were different.

³⁵ "Therefore, O prostitute, hear the word of the LORD: ³⁶ Thus says the Lord GOD, Because your lust was poured out and your nakedness uncovered in your whorings with your lovers, and with all

your abominable idols, and because of the blood of your children that you gave to them, **37** therefore, behold, I will gather all your lovers with whom you took pleasure, all those you loved and all those you hated. I will gather them against you from every side and will uncover your nakedness to them, that they may see all your nakedness. **38** And I will judge you as women who commit adultery and shed blood are judged, and bring upon you the blood of wrath and jealousy. **39** And I will give you into their hands, and they shall throw down your vaulted chamber and break down your lofty places. They shall strip you of your clothes and take your beautiful jewels and leave you naked and bare. **40** They shall bring up a crowd against you, and they shall stone you and cut you to pieces with their swords. **41** And they shall burn your houses and execute judgments upon you in the sight of many women. I will make you stop playing the whore, and you shall also give payment no more. **42** So will I satisfy my wrath on you, and my jealousy shall depart from you. I will be calm and will no more be angry. **43** Because you have not remembered the days of your youth, but have enraged me with all these things, therefore, behold, I have returned your deeds upon your head, declares the Lord God. Have you not committed lewdness in addition to all your abominations?

44 "Behold, everyone who uses proverbs will use this proverb about you: 'Like mother, like daughter.' **45** You are the daughter of your mother, who loathed her husband and her children; and you are the sister of your sisters, who loathed their husbands and their children. Your mother was a Hittite and your father an Amorite. **46** And your elder sister is Samaria, who lived with her daughters to the north of you; and your younger sister, who lived to the south of you, is Sodom with her daughters. **47** Not only did you walk in their ways and do according to their abominations; within a very little time you were more corrupt than they in all your ways. **48** As I live, declares the Lord God, your sister Sodom and her daughters have not done as you and your daughters have done. **49** Behold, this was the guilt of your sister Sodom: she and her daughters had pride, excess of food, and prosperous ease, but did not aid the poor and needy. **50** They were haughty and did an abomination before me. So I removed them, when I saw it. **51** Samaria has not committed half your sins. You have committed more abominations than they, and have made your sisters appear righteous by all the abominations that you have committed. **52** Bear your disgrace, you also, for you have intervened on behalf of your sisters. Because of your sins in which you acted more abominably than they, they are more in the right than you. So be ashamed, you also, and bear your disgrace, for you have made your sisters appear righteous.

53 "I will restore their fortunes, both the fortunes of Sodom and her daughters, and the fortunes of Samaria and her daughters, and I will restore your own fortunes in their midst, **54** that you may bear your disgrace and be ashamed of all that you have done, becoming a consolation to them. **55** As for your sisters, Sodom and her daughters shall return to their former state, and Samaria and her daughters shall return to their former state, and you and your daughters shall return to your former state. **56** Was not your sister Sodom a byword in your mouth in the day of your pride, **57** before your wickedness was uncovered? Now you have become an object of reproach for the daughters of Syria and all those around her, and for the daughters of the Philistines, those all around who despise you. **58** You bear the penalty of your lewdness and your abominations, declares the Lord.

The Lord's Everlasting Covenant

59 "For thus says the Lord God: I will deal with you as you have done, you who have despised the oath in breaking the covenant, **60** yet I will remember my covenant with you in the days of your youth, and I will establish for you an everlasting covenant. **61** Then you will remember your ways and be ashamed when you take your sisters, both your elder and your younger, and I give them to you as daughters, but not on account of the covenant with you. **62** I will establish my covenant with you, and you shall know that I am the Lord, **63** that you may remember and be confounded, and never open your mouth again because of your shame, when I atone for you for all that you have done, declares the Lord God."

Parable of Two Eagles and a Vine

17 The word of the LORD came to me: ² "Son of man, propound a riddle, and speak a parable to the house of Israel; ³ say, Thus says the Lord GOD: A great eagle with great wings and long pinions, rich in plumage of many colors, came to Lebanon and took the top of the cedar. ⁴ He broke off the topmost of its young twigs and carried it to a land of trade and set it in a city of merchants. ⁵ Then he took of the seed of the land and planted it in fertile soil. He placed it beside abundant waters. He set it like a willow twig, ⁶ and it sprouted and became a low spreading vine, and its branches turned toward him, and its roots remained where it stood. So it became a vine and produced branches and put out boughs.

⁷ "And there was another great eagle with great wings and much plumage, and behold, this vine bent its roots toward him and shot forth its branches toward him from the bed where it was planted, that he might water it. ⁸ It had been planted on good soil by abundant waters, that it might produce branches and bear fruit and become a noble vine.

⁹ "Say, Thus says the Lord GOD: Will it thrive? Will he not pull up its roots and cut off its fruit, so that it withers, so that all its fresh sprouting leaves wither? It will not take a strong arm or many people to pull it from its roots. ¹⁰ Behold, it is planted; will it thrive? Will it not utterly wither when the east wind strikes it—wither away on the bed where it sprouted?"

¹¹ Then the word of the LORD came to me: ¹² "Say now to the rebellious house, Do you not know what these things mean? Tell them, behold, the king of Babylon came to Jerusalem, and took her king and her princes and brought them to him to Babylon. ¹³ And he took one of the royal offspring and made a covenant with him, putting him under oath (the chief men of the land he had taken away), ¹⁴ that the kingdom might be humble and not lift itself up, and keep his covenant that it might stand. ¹⁵ But he rebelled against him by sending his ambassadors to Egypt, that they might give him horses and a large army. Will he thrive? Can one escape who does such things? Can he break the covenant and yet escape?

¹⁶ "As I live, declares the Lord GOD, surely in the place where the king dwells who made

him king, whose oath he despised, and whose covenant with him he broke, in Babylon he shall die. ¹⁷ Pharaoh with his mighty army and great company will not help him in war, when mounds are cast up and siege walls built to cut off many lives. ¹⁸ He despised the oath in breaking the covenant, and behold, he gave his hand and did all these things; he shall not escape. ¹⁹ Therefore thus says the Lord GOD: As I live, surely it is my oath that he despised, and my covenant that he broke. I will return it upon his head. ²⁰ I will spread my net over him, and he shall be taken in my snare, and I will bring him to Babylon and enter into judgment with him there for the treachery he has committed against me. ²¹ And all the pick of his troops shall fall by the sword, and the survivors shall be scattered to every wind, and you shall know that I am the LORD; I have spoken."

GETTING THE MESSAGE

A "fable" with an important message. Ezekiel's story about the two eagles, the cedar tree, and the vine could be considered a type of "fable." A fable is a story in which animals or plants are the main characters. Though they are sometimes entertaining to read, biblical fables teach important lessons.

²² Thus says the Lord GOD: "I myself will take a sprig from the lofty top of the cedar and will set it out. I will break off from the topmost of its young twigs a tender one, and I myself will plant it on a high and lofty mountain. ²³ On the mountain height of Israel will I plant it, that it may bear branches and produce fruit and become a noble cedar. And under it will dwell every kind of bird; in the shade of its branches birds of every sort will nest. ²⁴ And all the trees of the field shall know that I am the LORD; I bring low the high tree, and make high the low tree, dry up the green tree, and make the dry tree flourish. I am the LORD; I have spoken, and I will do it."

The Soul Who Sins Shall Die

18 The word of the LORD came to me: ² "What do you mean by repeating this proverb concerning the land of Israel, 'The fathers have eaten sour grapes, and the children's teeth are set on edge'? ³ As I live, declares the Lord GOD, this proverb shall no more be used by you in Israel. ⁴ Behold, all souls are mine; the soul of the father as well as the soul of the son is mine: the soul who sins shall die.

⁵ "If a man is righteous and does what is just and right— ⁶ if he does not eat upon the mountains or lift up his eyes to the idols of the house of Israel, does not defile his neighbor's wife or approach a woman in her time of menstrual impurity, ⁷ does not oppress anyone, but restores to the debtor his pledge, commits no robbery, gives his bread to the hungry and covers the naked with a garment, ⁸ does not lend at interest or take any profit, withholds his hand from injustice, executes true justice between man and man, ⁹ walks in my statutes, and

GETTING THE MESSAGE

Are God's judgments fair? Some of the exiles complained that God was punishing them for their parents' sins (ch. 18). Ezekiel replies that God will not judge on the basis of a parent's sins; neither will he forgive because of a parent's righteousness. God's judgement is fair.

keeps my rules by acting faithfully—he is righteous; he shall surely live, declares the Lord GOD.

¹⁰ "If he fathers a son who is violent, a shedder of blood, who does any of these things ¹¹ (though he himself did none of these things), who even eats upon the mountains, defiles his neighbor's wife, ¹² oppresses the poor and needy, commits robbery, does not restore the pledge, lifts up his eyes to the idols, commits abomination, ¹³ lends at interest, and takes profit; shall he then live? He shall not live. He has done all these abominations; he shall surely die; his blood shall be upon himself.

¹⁴ "Now suppose this man fathers a son who sees all the sins that his father has done; he sees, and does not do likewise: ¹⁵ he does not eat upon the mountains or lift up his eyes to the idols of the house of Israel, does not defile his neighbor's wife, ¹⁶ does not oppress anyone, exacts no pledge, com-

mits no robbery, but gives his bread to the hungry and covers the naked with a garment, ¹⁷ withholds his hand from iniquity, takes no interest or profit, obeys my rules, and walks in my statutes; he shall not die for his father's iniquity; he shall surely live. ¹⁸ As for his father, because he practiced extortion, robbed his brother, and did what is not good among his people, behold, he shall die for his iniquity.

¹⁹ "Yet you say, 'Why should not the son suffer for the iniquity of the father?' When the son has done what is just and right, and has been careful to observe all my statutes, he shall surely live. ²⁰ The soul who sins shall die. The son shall not suffer for the iniquity of the father, nor the father suffer for the iniquity of the son. The righteousness of the righteous shall be upon himself, and the wickedness of the wicked shall be upon himself.

²¹ "But if a wicked person turns away from all his sins that he has committed and keeps all my statutes and does what is just and right, he shall surely live; he shall not die. ²² None of the transgressions that he has committed shall be remembered against him; for the righteousness that he has done he shall live. ²³ Have I any pleasure in the death of the wicked, declares the Lord GOD, and not rather that he should turn from his way and live? ²⁴ But when a righteous person turns away from his righteousness and does injustice and does the same abominations that the wicked person does, shall he live? None of the righteous deeds that he has done shall be remembered; for the treachery of which he is guilty and the sin he has committed, for them he shall die.

²⁵ "Yet you say, 'The way of the Lord is not just.' Hear now, O house of Israel: Is my way not just? Is it not your ways that are not just? ²⁶ When a righteous person turns away from his righteousness and does injustice, he shall die for it; for the injustice that he has done he shall die. ²⁷ Again, when a wicked person turns away from the wickedness he has committed and does what is just and right, he shall save his life. ²⁸ Because he considered and turned away from all the transgressions that he had committed, he shall surely live; he shall not die. ²⁹ Yet the house of Israel says, 'The way of the Lord is

not just.' O house of Israel, are my ways not just? Is it not your ways that are not just? ³⁰ "Therefore I will judge you, O house of Israel, every one according to his ways, declares the Lord GOD. Repent and turn from all your transgressions, lest iniquity be your ruin. ³¹ Cast away from you all the transgressions that you have committed, and make yourselves a new heart and a new spirit! Why will you die, O house of Israel? ³² For I have no pleasure in the death of anyone, declares the Lord GOD; so turn, and live."

A Lament for the Princes of Israel

19 And you, take up a lamentation for the princes of Israel, ² and say:

What was your mother? A lioness!
    Among lions she crouched;
in the midst of young lions
    she reared her cubs.
³ And she brought up one of her cubs;
    he became a young lion,
and he learned to catch prey;
    he devoured men.
⁴ The nations heard about him;
    he was caught in their pit,
and they brought him with hooks
    to the land of Egypt.
⁵ When she saw that she waited in vain,
    that her hope was lost,
she took another of her cubs
    and made him a young lion.
⁶ He prowled among the lions;
    he became a young lion,
and he learned to catch prey;
    he devoured men,
⁷ and seized their widows.
    He laid waste their cities,
and the land was appalled and all who
        were in it
    at the sound of his roaring.
⁸ Then the nations set against him
    from provinces on every side;
they spread their net over him;
    he was taken in their pit.
⁹ With hooks they put him in a cage
    and brought him to the king of
        Babylon;
they brought him into custody,
    that his voice should no more be heard
        on the mountains of Israel.

¹⁰ Your mother was like a vine in a vineyard
    planted by the water,
fruitful and full of branches
    by reason of abundant water.
¹¹ Its strong stems became
    rulers' scepters;
it towered aloft
    among the thick boughs;
it was seen in its height
    with the mass of its branches.
¹² But the vine was plucked up in fury,
    cast down to the ground;
the east wind dried up its fruit;
    they were stripped off and withered.
As for its strong stem,
    fire consumed it.
¹³ Now it is planted in the wilderness,
    in a dry and thirsty land.
¹⁴ And fire has gone out from the stem
        of its shoots,
    has consumed its fruit,
so that there remains in it no strong
        stem,
    no scepter for ruling.

GETTING THE MESSAGE

The Hebrew word for **swearing an oath** (20:5) literally means "I raised my hand." In courtrooms today, people are asked to raise their right hand as they take an oath, promising to tell the truth.

This is a lamentation and has become a lamentation.

Israel's Continuing Rebellion

20 In the seventh year, in the fifth month, on the tenth day of the month, certain of the elders of Israel came to inquire of the LORD, and sat before me. ² And the word of the LORD came to me: ³ "Son of man, speak to the elders of Israel, and say to them, Thus says the Lord GOD, Is it to inquire of me that you come? As I live, declares the Lord GOD, I will not be inquired of by you. ⁴ Will you judge them, son of man, will you judge them? Let them know the abominations of their fathers, ⁵ and say to them, Thus says the Lord GOD: On the day when I chose Israel, I swore to the offspring of the house of Jacob, making myself known to them in the land of Egypt; I swore to them, saying, I am the LORD your God. ⁶ On that day I swore to them that I would bring them out of the land of Egypt into a land that I had searched out for them, a land flowing with milk and honey, the most glorious of all lands. ⁷ And I said to them, Cast away the detestable things your eyes feast on, every one of you, and do not defile yourselves with the idols of Egypt; I am the LORD your God. ⁸ But they rebelled against me and were not willing to listen to me. None of them cast away the detestable things their eyes feasted on, nor did they forsake the idols of Egypt.

"Then I said I would pour out my wrath upon them and spend my anger against them in the midst of the land of Egypt. ⁹ But I acted for the sake of my name, that it should not be profaned in the sight of the nations among whom they lived, in whose sight I made myself known to them in bringing them out of the land of Egypt. ¹⁰ So I led them out of the land of Egypt and brought them into the wilderness. ¹¹ I gave them my statutes and made known to them my rules, by which, if a person does them, he shall live. ¹² Moreover, I gave them my Sabbaths, as a sign between me and them, that they might know that I am the LORD who sanctifies them. ¹³ But the house of Israel rebelled against me in the wilderness. They did not walk in my statutes but rejected my rules, by which, if a person does them, he shall live; and my Sabbaths they greatly profaned.

"Then I said I would pour out my wrath upon them in the wilderness, to make a full end of them. ¹⁴ But I acted for the sake of my name, that it should not be profaned in the sight of the nations, in whose sight I had brought them out. ¹⁵ Moreover, I swore to them in the wilderness that I would not bring them into the land that I had given them, a land flowing with milk and honey, the most glorious of all lands, ¹⁶ because they rejected my rules and did not walk in my statutes, and profaned my Sabbaths; for their heart went after their idols. ¹⁷ Nevertheless, my eye spared them, and I did not destroy them or make a full end of them in the wilderness.

¹⁸ "And I said to their children in the wilderness, Do not walk in the statutes of your fathers, nor keep their rules, nor defile yourselves with their idols. ¹⁹ I am

the LORD your God; walk in my statutes, and be careful to obey my rules, ²⁰ and keep my Sabbaths holy that they may be a sign between me and you, that you may know that I am the LORD your God. ²¹ But the children rebelled against me. They did not walk in my statutes and were not careful to obey my rules, by which, if a person does them, he shall live; they profaned my Sabbaths.

"Then I said I would pour out my wrath upon them and spend my anger against them in the wilderness. ²² But I withheld my hand and acted for the sake of my name, that it should not be profaned in the sight of the nations, in whose sight I had brought them out. ²³ Moreover, I swore to them in the wilderness that I would scatter them among the nations and disperse them through the countries, ²⁴ because they had not obeyed my rules, but had rejected my statutes and profaned my Sabbaths, and their eyes were set on their fathers' idols. ²⁵ Moreover, I gave them statutes that were not good and rules by which they could not have life, ²⁶ and I defiled them through their very gifts in their offering up all their firstborn, that I might devastate them. I did it that they might know that I am the LORD.

²⁷ "Therefore, son of man, speak to the house of Israel and say to them, Thus says the Lord GOD: In this also your fathers blasphemed me, by dealing treacherously with me. ²⁸ For when I had brought them into the land that I swore to give them, then wherever they saw any high hill or any leafy tree, there they offered their sacrifices and there they presented the provocation of their offering; there they sent up their pleasing aromas, and there they poured out their drink offerings. ²⁹ (I said to them, What is the high place to which you go? So its name is called Bamah¹ to this day.)

³⁰ "Therefore say to the house of Israel, Thus says the Lord GOD: Will you defile yourselves after the manner of your fathers and go whoring after their detestable things? ³¹ When you present your gifts and offer up your children in fire, you defile yourselves with all your idols to this day. And shall I be inquired of by you, O house of Israel? As I live, declares the Lord GOD, I will not be inquired of by you.

³² "What is in your mind shall never

¹ Bamah means high place

happen—the thought, 'Let us be like the nations, like the tribes of the countries, and worship wood and stone.'

The Lord Will Restore Israel

³³ "As I live, declares the Lord GOD, surely with a mighty hand and an outstretched arm and with wrath poured out I will be king over you. ³⁴ I will bring you out from the peoples and gather you out of the countries where you are scattered, with a mighty hand and an outstretched arm, and with wrath poured out. ³⁵ And I will bring you into the wilderness of the peoples, and there I will enter into judgment with you face to face. ³⁶ As I entered into judgment with your fathers in the wilderness of the land of Egypt, so I will enter into judgment with you, declares the Lord GOD. ³⁷ I will make you pass under the rod, and I will bring you into the bond of the covenant. ³⁸ I will purge out the rebels from among you, and those who transgress against me. I will bring them out of the land where they sojourn, but they shall not enter the land of Israel. Then you will know that I am the LORD.

³⁹ "As for you, O house of Israel, thus says the Lord GOD: Go serve every one of you his idols, now and hereafter, if you will not listen to me; but my holy name you shall no more profane with your gifts and your idols. ⁴⁰ "For on my holy mountain, the mountain height of Israel, declares the Lord GOD, there all the house of Israel, all of them, shall serve me in the land. There I will accept them, and there I will require your contributions and the choicest of your gifts, with all your sacred offerings. ⁴¹ As a pleasing aroma I will accept you, when I bring you out from the peoples and gather you out of the countries where you have been scattered. And I will manifest my holiness among you in the sight of the nations. ⁴² And you shall know that I am the LORD, when I bring you into the land of Israel, the country that I swore to give to your fathers. ⁴³ And there you shall remember your ways and all your deeds with which you have defiled yourselves, and you shall loathe yourselves for all the evils that you have committed. ⁴⁴ And you shall know that I am the LORD, when I deal with you for my name's sake, not according to your evil ways, nor according to your corrupt deeds, O house of Israel, declares the Lord GOD."

⁴⁵ And the word of the LORD came to me: ⁴⁶ "Son of man, set your face toward the southland; preach against the south, and prophesy against the forest land in the Negeb. ⁴⁷ Say to the forest of the Negeb, Hear the word of the LORD: Thus says the Lord GOD, Behold, I will kindle a fire in you, and it shall devour every green tree in you and every dry tree. The blazing flame shall not be quenched, and all faces from south to north shall be scorched by it. ⁴⁸ All flesh shall see that I the LORD have kindled it; it shall not be quenched." ⁴⁹ Then I said, "Ah, Lord GOD! They are saying of me, 'Is he not a maker of parables?'"

The Lord Has Drawn His Sword

21 The word of the LORD came to me: ² "Son of man, set your face toward Jerusalem and preach against the sanctuaries. Prophesy against the land of Israel ³ and

say to the land of Israel, Thus says the LORD: Behold, I am against you and will draw my sword from its sheath and will cut off from you both righteous and wicked. ⁴ Because I will cut off from you both righteous and wicked, therefore my sword shall be drawn from its sheath against all flesh from south to north. ⁵ And all flesh shall know that I am the LORD. I have drawn my sword from its sheath; it shall not be sheathed again.

⁶ "As for you, son of man, groan; with breaking heart and bitter grief, groan before their eyes. ⁷ And when they say to you, 'Why do you groan?' you shall say, 'Because of the news that it is coming. Every heart will melt, and all hands will be feeble; every spirit will faint, and all knees will be weak as water. Behold, it is coming, and it will be fulfilled,'" declares the Lord GOD.

⁸ And the word of the LORD came to me: ⁹ "Son of man, prophesy and say, Thus says the Lord, say:

"A sword, a sword is sharpened
　　　and also polished,
¹⁰　　sharpened for slaughter,
　　　polished to flash like lightning!

(Or shall we rejoice? You have despised the rod, my son, with everything of wood.) ¹¹ So the sword is given to be polished, that it may be grasped in the hand. It is sharpened and polished to be given into the hand of the slayer. ¹² Cry out and wail, son of man, for it is against my people. It is against all the princes of Israel. They are delivered over to the sword with my people. Strike therefore upon your thigh. ¹³ For it will not be a testing—what could it do if you despise the rod?" declares the Lord GOD.

¹⁴ "As for you, son of man, prophesy. Clap your hands and let the sword come down twice, yes, three times, the sword for those to

GETTING THE MESSAGE

Strange religious practices. The pagan King Nebuchadnezzar employed three means of divination to decide what he should do (21:21). Shaking arrows is similar to casting lots. The teraphim are household gods (small figurines). "Looking at the liver" means examining the liver of a sacrificed animal.

be slain. It is the sword for the great slaughter, which surrounds them, ¹⁵ that their hearts may melt, and many stumble. At all their gates I have given the glittering sword. Ah, it is made like lightning; it is taken up for slaughter. ¹⁶ Cut sharply to the right; set yourself to the left, wherever your face is directed. ¹⁷ I also will clap my hands, and I will satisfy my fury; I the LORD have spoken."

¹⁸ The word of the LORD came to me again: ¹⁹ "As for you, son of man, mark two ways for the sword of the king of Babylon to come. Both of them shall come from the same land. And make a signpost; make it at the head of the way to a city. ²⁰ Mark a way for the sword to come to Rabbah of the Ammonites and to Judah, into Jerusalem the fortified. ²¹ For the king of Babylon stands at the parting of the way, at the head of the two ways, to use divination. He shakes the arrows; he consults the teraphim; he looks at the liver. ²² Into his right hand comes the divination

for Jerusalem, to set battering rams, to open the mouth with murder, to lift up the voice with shouting, to set battering rams against the gates, to cast up mounds, to build siege towers. ²³ But to them it will seem like a false divination. They have sworn solemn oaths, but he brings their guilt to remembrance, that they may be taken.

²⁴ "Therefore thus says the Lord GOD: Because you have made your guilt to be remembered, in that your transgressions are uncovered, so that in all your deeds your sins appear—because you have come to remembrance, you shall be taken in hand. ²⁵ And you, O profane wicked one, prince of Israel, whose day has come, the time of your final punishment, ²⁶ thus says the Lord GOD: Remove the turban and take off the crown. Things shall not remain as they are. Exalt that which is low, and bring low that which is exalted. ²⁷ A ruin, ruin, ruin I will make it. This also shall not be, until he comes, the one to whom judgment belongs, and I will give it to him.

²⁸ "And you, son of man, prophesy, and say, Thus says the Lord GOD concerning the Ammonites and concerning their reproach; say, A sword, a sword is drawn for the slaughter. It is polished to consume and to flash like lightning— ²⁹ while they see for you false visions, while they divine lies for you—to place you on the necks of the profane wicked, whose day has come, the time of their final punishment. ³⁰ Return it to its sheath. In the place where you were created, in the land of your origin, I will judge you. ³¹ And I will pour out my indignation upon you; I will blow upon you with the fire of my wrath, and I will deliver you into the hands of brutish men, skillful to destroy. ³² You shall be fuel for the fire. Your blood shall be in the midst of the land. You shall be no more remembered, for I the LORD have spoken."

Israel's Shedding of Blood

22 And the word of the LORD came to me, saying, ² "And you, son of man, will you judge, will you judge the bloody city? Then declare to her all her abominations. ³ You shall say, Thus says the Lord GOD: A city that sheds blood in her midst, so that her time may come, and that makes idols to defile herself! ⁴ You have become guilty by the blood that you have shed, and defiled by the idols that you have made,

and you have brought your days near, the appointed time of your years has come. Therefore I have made you a reproach to the nations, and a mockery to all the countries. ⁵ Those who are near and those who are far from you will mock you; your name is defiled; you are full of tumult.

⁶ "Behold, the princes of Israel in you, every one according to his power, have been bent on shedding blood. ⁷ Father and mother are treated with contempt in you; the sojourner suffers extortion in your midst; the fatherless and the widow are wronged in you. ⁸ You have despised my holy things and profaned my Sabbaths. ⁹ There are men in you who slander to shed blood, and people in you who eat on the mountains; they commit lewdness in your midst. ¹⁰ In you men uncover their fathers' nakedness; in you they violate women who are unclean in their menstrual impurity. ¹¹ One commits abomination with his neighbor's wife; another lewdly defiles his daughter-in-law; another in you violates his sister, his father's daughter. ¹² In you they take bribes to shed blood; you take interest and profit and make gain of your neighbors by extortion; but me you have forgotten, declares the Lord GOD.

¹³ "Behold, I strike my hand at the dishonest gain that you have made, and at the blood that has been in your midst. ¹⁴ Can your courage endure, or can your hands be strong, in the days that I shall deal with you? I the LORD have spoken, and I will do it. ¹⁵ I will scatter you among the nations and disperse you through the countries, and I will consume your uncleanness out of you. ¹⁶ And you shall be profaned by your own doing in the sight of the nations, and you shall know that I am the LORD."

¹⁷ And the word of the LORD came to me: ¹⁸ "Son of man, the house of Israel has become dross to me; all of them are bronze and tin and iron and lead in the furnace; they are dross of silver. ¹⁹ Therefore thus says the Lord GOD: Because you have all become dross, therefore, behold, I will gather you into the midst of Jerusalem. ²⁰ As one gathers silver and bronze and iron and lead and tin into a furnace, to blow the fire on it in order to melt it, so I will gather you in my anger and in my wrath, and I will put you in and melt you. ²¹ I will gather you and blow on you with the fire of my wrath, and

you shall be melted in the midst of it. ²² As silver is melted in a furnace, so you shall be melted in the midst of it, and you shall know that I am the LORD; I have poured out my wrath upon you."

²³ And the word of the LORD came to me: ²⁴ "Son of man, say to her, You are a land that is not cleansed or rained upon in the day of indignation. ²⁵ The conspiracy of her prophets in her midst is like a roaring lion tearing the prey; they have devoured human lives; they have taken treasure and precious things; they have made many widows in her midst. ²⁶ Her priests have done violence to my law and have profaned my holy things. They have made no distinction between the holy and the common, neither have they taught the difference between the unclean and the clean, and they have disregarded my Sabbaths, so that I am profaned among them. ²⁷ Her princes in her midst are like wolves tearing the prey, shedding blood, destroying lives to get dishonest gain. ²⁸ And her prophets have smeared whitewash for them, seeing false visions and divining lies for them, saying, 'Thus says the Lord GOD,' when the LORD has not spoken. ²⁹ The people of the land have practiced extortion and committed robbery. They have oppressed the poor and needy, and have extorted from the sojourner without justice. ³⁰ And I sought for a man among them who should build up the wall and stand in the breach before me for the land, that I should not destroy it, but I found none. ³¹ Therefore I have poured out my indignation upon them. I have consumed them with the fire of my wrath. I have returned their way upon their heads, declares the Lord GOD."

Oholah and Oholibah

23 The word of the LORD came to me: ² "Son of man, there were two women, the daughters of one mother. ³ They played the whore in Egypt; they played the whore in their youth; there their breasts were pressed and their virgin bosoms handled. ⁴ Oholah was the name of the elder and Oholibah the name of her sister. They became mine, and they bore sons and daughters. As for their names, Oholah is Samaria, and Oholibah is Jerusalem.

⁵ "Oholah played the whore while she was mine, and she lusted after her lovers the Assyrians, warriors ⁶ clothed in purple,

governors and commanders, all of them desirable young men, horsemen riding on horses. ⁷ She bestowed her whoring upon them, the choicest men of Assyria all of them, and she defiled herself with all the idols of everyone after whom she lusted. ⁸ She did not give up her whoring that she had begun in Egypt; for in her youth men had lain with her and handled her virgin bosom and poured out their whoring lust upon her. ⁹ Therefore I delivered her into the hands of her lovers, into the hands of the Assyrians, after whom she lusted. ¹⁰ These uncovered her nakedness; they seized her sons and her daughters; and as for her, they killed her with the sword; and she became a byword among women, when judgment had been executed on her.

¹¹ "Her sister Oholibah saw this, and she became more corrupt than her sister in her lust and in her whoring, which was worse

GETTING THE MESSAGE

Samaria was defeated by the Assyrians in 722 B.C., bringing the northern kingdom of Israel to an end. Judah's final defeat came in 587 B.C. Ezekiel portrays the two kingdoms as two sisters (ch. 23). Their unfaithfulness to God caused their defeat.

than that of her sister. ¹² She lusted after the Assyrians, governors and commanders, warriors clothed in full armor, horsemen riding on horses, all of them desirable young men. ¹³ And I saw that she was defiled; they both took the same way. ¹⁴ But she carried her whoring further. She saw men portrayed on the wall, the images of the Chaldeans portrayed in vermilion, ¹⁵ wearing belts on their waists, with flowing turbans on their heads, all of them having the appearance of officers, a likeness of Babylonians whose native land was Chaldea. ¹⁶ When she saw them, she lusted after them and sent messengers to them in Chaldea. ¹⁷ And the Babylonians came to her into the bed of love, and they defiled her with their whoring lust. And after she was defiled by them, she turned from them in disgust. ¹⁸ When she carried on her whoring so openly and flaunted her nakedness, I turned in disgust

from her, as I had turned in disgust from her sister. ¹⁹ Yet she increased her whoring, remembering the days of her youth, when she played the whore in the land of Egypt ²⁰ and lusted after her lovers there, whose members were like those of donkeys, and whose issue was like that of horses. ²¹ Thus you longed for the lewdness of your youth, when the Egyptians handled your bosom and pressed your young breasts."

²² Therefore, O Oholibah, thus says the Lord God: "Behold, I will stir up against you your lovers from whom you turned in disgust, and I will bring them against you from every side: ²³ the Babylonians and all the Chaldeans, Pekod and Shoa and Koa, and all the Assyrians with them, desirable young men, governors and commanders all of them, officers and men of renown, all of them riding on horses. ²⁴ And they shall come against you from the north with chariots and wagons and a host of peoples. They shall set themselves against you on every side with buckler, shield, and helmet; and I will commit the judgment to them, and they shall judge you according to their judgments. ²⁵ And I will direct my jealousy against you, that they may deal with you in fury. They shall cut off your nose and your ears, and your survivors shall fall by the sword. They shall seize your sons and your daughters, and your survivors shall be devoured by fire. ²⁶ They shall also strip you of your clothes and take away your beautiful jewels. ²⁷ Thus I will put an end to your lewdness and your whoring begun in the land of Egypt, so that you shall not lift up your eyes to them or remember Egypt anymore.

²⁸ "For thus says the Lord God: Behold, I will deliver you into the hands of those whom you hate, into the hands of those from whom you turned in disgust, ²⁹ and they shall deal with you in hatred and take away all the fruit of your labor and leave you naked and bare, and the nakedness of your whoring shall be uncovered. Your lewdness and your whoring ³⁰ have brought this upon you, because you played the whore with the nations and defiled yourself with their idols. ³¹ You have gone the way of your sister; therefore I will give her cup into your hand. ³² Thus says the Lord God:

"You shall drink your sister's cup
    that is deep and large;

you shall be laughed at and held in
  derision,
    for it contains much;
³³ you will be filled with drunkenness
    and sorrow.
A cup of horror and desolation,
  the cup of your sister Samaria;
³⁴ you shall drink it and drain it out,
    and gnaw its shards,
    and tear your breasts;

for I have spoken, declares the Lord GOD.
³⁵ Therefore thus says the Lord GOD: Because
you have forgotten me and cast me behind
your back, you yourself must bear the consequences of your lewdness and whoring."

³⁶ The LORD said to me: "Son of man, will
you judge Oholah and Oholibah? Declare to
them their abominations. ³⁷ For they have
committed adultery, and blood is on their
hands. With their idols they have committed adultery, and they have even offered up
to them for food the children whom they
had borne to me. ³⁸ Moreover, this they have
done to me: they have defiled my sanctuary
on the same day and profaned my Sabbaths.
³⁹ For when they had slaughtered their children in sacrifice to their idols, on the same
day they came into my sanctuary to profane
it. And behold, this is what they did in my
house. ⁴⁰ They even sent for men to come
from afar, to whom a messenger was sent;
and behold, they came. For them you bathed
yourself, painted your eyes, and adorned
yourself with ornaments. ⁴¹ You sat on a
stately couch, with a table spread before it
on which you had placed my incense and
my oil. ⁴² The sound of a carefree multitude
was with her; and with men of the common sort, drunkards were brought from the
wilderness; and they put bracelets on the
hands of the women, and beautiful crowns
on their heads.

⁴³ "Then I said of her who was worn out by
adultery, Now they will continue to use her
for a whore, even her! ⁴⁴ For they have gone
in to her, as men go in to a prostitute. Thus
they went in to Oholah and to Oholibah,
lewd women! ⁴⁵ But righteous men shall
pass judgment on them with the sentence
of adulteresses, and with the sentence of
women who shed blood, because they are
adulteresses, and blood is on their hands."

⁴⁶ For thus says the Lord GOD: "Bring up
a vast host against them, and make them

an object of terror and a plunder. ⁴⁷ And
the host shall stone them and cut them
down with their swords. They shall kill
their sons and their daughters, and burn
up their houses. ⁴⁸ Thus will I put an end to
lewdness in the land, that all women may
take warning and not commit lewdness as
you have done. ⁴⁹ And they shall return your
lewdness upon you, and you shall bear the
penalty for your sinful idolatry, and you
shall know that I am the Lord GOD."

The Siege of Jerusalem

24 In the ninth year, in the tenth month,
on the tenth day of the month, the
word of the LORD came to me: ² "Son of man,
write down the name of this day, this very
day. The king of Babylon has laid siege to
Jerusalem this very day. ³ And utter a parable
to the rebellious house and say to them,
Thus says the Lord GOD:

"Set on the pot, set it on;
  pour in water also;
⁴ put in it the pieces of meat,
    all the good pieces, the thigh and
      the shoulder;
    fill it with choice bones.
⁵ Take the choicest one of the flock;
    pile the logs under it;
  boil it well;
    seethe also its bones in it.

⁶ "Therefore thus says the Lord GOD: Woe
to the bloody city, to the pot whose corrosion is in it, and whose corrosion has not
gone out of it! Take out of it piece after piece,
without making any choice. ⁷ For the blood
she has shed is in her midst; she put it on
the bare rock; she did not pour it out on
the ground to cover it with dust. ⁸ To rouse
my wrath, to take vengeance, I have set on
the bare rock the blood she has shed, that
it may not be covered. ⁹ Therefore thus says
the Lord GOD: Woe to the bloody city! I also
will make the pile great. ¹⁰ Heap on the logs,
kindle the fire, boil the meat well, mix in
the spices, and let the bones be burned up.
¹¹ Then set it empty upon the coals, that it
may become hot, and its copper may burn,
that its uncleanness may be melted in it,
its corrosion consumed. ¹² She has wearied
herself with toil; its abundant corrosion
does not go out of it. Into the fire with its
corrosion! ¹³ On account of your unclean
lewdness, because I would have cleansed

you and you were not cleansed from your uncleanness, you shall not be cleansed anymore till I have satisfied my fury upon you. ¹⁴ I am the Lᴏʀᴅ. I have spoken; it shall come to pass; I will do it. I will not go back; I will not spare; I will not relent; according to your ways and your deeds you will be judged, declares the Lord Gᴏᴅ."

Ezekiel's Wife Dies

¹⁵ The word of the Lᴏʀᴅ came to me: ¹⁶ "Son of man, behold, I am about to take the delight of your eyes away from you at a stroke; yet you shall not mourn or weep, nor shall your tears run down. ¹⁷ Sigh, but not aloud; make no mourning for the dead. Bind on your turban, and put your shoes on your feet; do not cover your lips, nor eat the bread of men." ¹⁸ So I spoke to the people in the morning, and at evening my wife died. And on the next morning I did as I was commanded.

> ### GETTING THE MESSAGE
>
> When Ezekiel's wife suddenly dies, God tells him not to **mourn**. This was to be a sign to the people that they should not mourn when their beloved temple is destroyed. God asked Ezekiel to do difficult things in order to warn his people.

¹⁹ And the people said to me, "Will you not tell us what these things mean for us, that you are acting thus?" ²⁰ Then I said to them, "The word of the Lᴏʀᴅ came to me: ²¹ 'Say to the house of Israel, Thus says the Lord Gᴏᴅ: Behold, I will profane my sanctuary, the pride of your power, the delight of your eyes, and the yearning of your soul, and your sons and your daughters whom you left behind shall fall by the sword. ²² And you shall do as I have done; you shall not cover your lips, nor eat the bread of men. ²³ Your turbans shall be on your heads and your shoes on your feet; you shall not mourn or weep, but you shall rot away in your iniquities and groan to one another. ²⁴ Thus shall Ezekiel be to you a sign; according to all that he has done you shall do. When this comes, then you will know that I am the Lord Gᴏᴅ.'

²⁵ "As for you, son of man, surely on the day when I take from them their stronghold, their joy and glory, the delight of their eyes and their soul's desire, and also their sons and daughters, ²⁶ on that day a fugitive will come to you to report to you the news. ²⁷ On that day your mouth will be opened to the fugitive, and you shall speak and be no longer mute. So you will be a sign to them, and they will know that I am the Lᴏʀᴅ."

Prophecy Against Ammon

25 The word of the Lᴏʀᴅ came to me: ² "Son of man, set your face toward the Ammonites and prophesy against them. ³ Say to the Ammonites, Hear the word of the Lord Gᴏᴅ: Thus says the Lord Gᴏᴅ, Because you said, 'Aha!' over my sanctuary when it was profaned, and over the land of Israel when it was made desolate, and over the house of Judah when they went into exile, ⁴ therefore behold, I am handing you over to the people of the East for a possession, and they shall set their encampments among you and make their dwellings in your midst. They shall eat your fruit, and they shall drink your milk. ⁵ I will make Rabbah a pasture for camels and Ammon a fold for flocks. Then you will know that I am the Lᴏʀᴅ. ⁶ For thus says the Lord Gᴏᴅ: Because you have clapped your hands and stamped your feet and rejoiced with all the malice within your soul against the land of Israel, ⁷ therefore, behold, I have stretched out my hand against you, and will hand you over as plunder to the nations. And I will cut you off from the peoples and will make you perish out of the countries; I will destroy you. Then you will know that I am the Lᴏʀᴅ.

Prophecy Against Moab and Seir

⁸ "Thus says the Lord Gᴏᴅ: Because Moab and Seir said, 'Behold, the house of Judah is like all the other nations,' ⁹ therefore I will lay open the flank of Moab from the cities, from its cities on its frontier, the glory of the country, Beth-jeshimoth, Baal-meon, and Kiriathaim. ¹⁰ I will give it along with the Ammonites to the people of the East as a possession, that the Ammonites may be remembered no more among the nations, ¹¹ and I will execute judgments upon Moab. Then they will know that I am the Lᴏʀᴅ.

Prophecy Against Edom

¹² "Thus says the Lord Gᴏᴅ: Because Edom acted revengefully against the house of Judah and has grievously offended in taking vengeance on them, ¹³ therefore thus

says the Lord God, I will stretch out my hand against Edom and cut off from it man and beast. And I will make it desolate; from Teman even to Dedan they shall fall by the sword. **14** And I will lay my vengeance upon Edom by the hand of my people Israel, and they shall do in Edom according to my anger and according to my wrath, and they shall know my vengeance, declares the Lord God.

Prophecy Against Philistia

15 "Thus says the Lord God: Because the Philistines acted revengefully and took vengeance with malice of soul to destroy in never-ending enmity, **16** therefore thus says the Lord God, Behold, I will stretch out my hand against the Philistines, and I will cut off the Cherethites and destroy the rest of the seacoast. **17** I will execute great vengeance on them with wrathful rebukes. Then they will know that I am the Lord, when I lay my vengeance upon them."

Prophecy Against Tyre

26 In the eleventh year, on the first day of the month, the word of the Lord came to me: **2** "Son of man, because Tyre said concerning Jerusalem, 'Aha, the gate of the peoples is broken; it has swung open to me. I shall be replenished, now that she is laid waste,' **3** therefore thus says the Lord God: Behold, I am against you, O Tyre, and will bring up many nations against you, as the sea brings up its waves. **4** They shall destroy the walls of Tyre and break down her towers, and I will scrape her soil from her and make her a bare rock. **5** She shall be in the midst of the sea a place for the spreading of nets, for I have spoken, declares the Lord God. And she shall become plunder for the nations, **6** and her daughters on the mainland shall be killed by the sword. Then they will know that I am the Lord.

7 "For thus says the Lord God: Behold, I will bring against Tyre from the north Nebuchadnezzar king of Babylon, king of kings, with horses and chariots, and with horsemen and a host of many soldiers. **8** He will kill with the sword your daughters on the mainland. He will set up a siege wall against you and throw up a mound against you, and raise a roof of shields against you. **9** He will direct the shock of his battering rams against your walls, and with his axes he will break down your towers. **10** His horses will be so many that their dust will cover you. Your walls will shake at the noise of the horsemen and wagons and chariots, when he enters your gates as men enter a city that has been breached. **11** With the hoofs of his horses he will trample all your streets. He will kill your people with the sword, and your mighty pillars will fall to the ground. **12** They will plunder your riches and loot your merchandise. They will break down your walls and destroy your pleasant houses. Your stones and timber and soil they will cast into the midst of the waters. **13** And I will stop the music of your songs, and the sound of your lyres shall be heard no more. **14** I will make you a bare rock. You

---

GETTING THE MESSAGE

A prophecy fulfilled. The city of Tyre was on an island about a half mile from the coast, with some of its people living in villages on the mainland. Alexander the Great conquered Tyre by first destroying those villages and then using the rubble to build a causeway to the island fortress. This fulfilled Ezekiel's prophecy that Tyre's stones, timber, and soil would be cast into the midst of the water (26:12).

---

shall be a place for the spreading of nets. You shall never be rebuilt, for I am the Lord; I have spoken, declares the Lord God.

15 "Thus says the Lord God to Tyre: Will not the coastlands shake at the sound of your fall, when the wounded groan, when slaughter is made in your midst? **16** Then all the princes of the sea will step down from their thrones and remove their robes and strip off their embroidered garments. They will clothe themselves with trembling; they will sit on the ground and tremble every moment and be appalled at you. **17** And they will raise a lamentation over you and say to you,

"'How you have perished,
     you who were inhabited from the
          seas,
     O city renowned,
          who was mighty on the sea;

she and her inhabitants imposed their
    terror
    on all her inhabitants!
18 Now the coastlands tremble
    on the day of your fall,
and the coastlands that are on the sea
    are dismayed at your passing.'

19 "For thus says the Lord GOD: When I make you a city laid waste, like the cities that are not inhabited, when I bring up the deep over you, and the great waters cover you, 20 then I will make you go down with those who go down to the pit, to the people of old, and I will make you to dwell in the world below, among ruins from of old, with those who go down to the pit, so that you will not be inhabited; but I will set beauty in the land of the living. 21 I will bring you to a dreadful end, and you shall be no more. Though you be sought for, you will never be found again, declares the Lord GOD."

A Lament for Tyre

27 The word of the LORD came to me: 2 "Now you, son of man, raise a lamentation over Tyre, 3 and say to Tyre, who dwells at the entrances to the sea, merchant of the peoples to many coastlands, thus says the Lord GOD:

   "O Tyre, you have said,
    'I am perfect in beauty.'
4   Your borders are in the heart of the
      seas;
    your builders made perfect your
      beauty.
5   They made all your planks
    of fir trees from Senir;
    they took a cedar from Lebanon
    to make a mast for you.
6   Of oaks of Bashan
    they made your oars;
    they made your deck of pines
      from the coasts of Cyprus,
    inlaid with ivory.
7   Of fine embroidered linen from Egypt
    was your sail,
    serving as your banner;
    blue and purple from the coasts of
      Elishah
    was your awning.
8   The inhabitants of Sidon and Arvad
    were your rowers;
    your skilled men, O Tyre, were in you;
    they were your pilots.

9   The elders of Gebal and her skilled
      men were in you,
    caulking your seams;
    all the ships of the sea with their mar-
      iners were in you
    to barter for your wares.

10 "Persia and Lud and Put were in your army as your men of war. They hung the shield and helmet in you; they gave you splendor. 11 Men of Arvad and Helech were on your walls all around, and men of Gamad were in your towers. They hung their shields on your walls all around; they made perfect your beauty.

12 "Tarshish did business with you because of your great wealth of every kind; silver, iron, tin, and lead they exchanged for your wares. 13 Javan, Tubal, and Meshech traded with you; they exchanged human beings and vessels of bronze for your merchandise. 14 From Beth-togarmah they exchanged horses, war horses, and mules for your wares. 15 The men of Dedan traded with you. Many coastlands were your own special markets; they brought you in payment ivory tusks and ebony. 16 Syria did business with you because of your abundant goods; they exchanged for your wares emeralds, purple, embroidered work, fine linen, coral, and ruby. 17 Judah and the land of Israel traded with you; they exchanged for your merchandise wheat of Minnith, meal, honey, oil, and balm. 18 Damascus did business with you for your abundant goods, because of your great wealth of every kind; wine of Helbon and wool of Sahar 19 and casks of wine from Uzal they exchanged for your wares; wrought iron, cassia, and calamus were bartered for your merchandise. 20 Dedan traded with you in saddlecloths for riding. 21 Arabia and all the princes of Kedar were your favored dealers in lambs, rams, and goats; in these they did business with you. 22 The traders of Sheba and Raamah traded with you; they exchanged for your wares the best of all kinds of spices and all precious stones and gold. 23 Haran, Canneh, Eden, traders of Sheba, Asshur, and Chilmad traded with you. 24 In your market these traded with you in choice garments, in clothes of blue and embroidered work, and in carpets of colored material, bound with cords and made secure. 25 The ships of Tarshish traveled for you with your

merchandise. So you were filled and heavily
laden in the heart of the seas.

26 "Your rowers have brought you out
        into the high seas.
    The east wind has wrecked you
        in the heart of the seas.
27 Your riches, your wares, your mer-
        chandise,
    your mariners and your pilots,
    your caulkers, your dealers in mer-
        chandise,
    and all your men of war who are in
        you,
    with all your crew
        that is in your midst,
    sink into the heart of the seas
        on the day of your fall.
28 At the sound of the cry of your pilots
        the countryside shakes,
29 and down from their ships
        come all who handle the oar.
    The mariners and all the pilots of the
        sea
    stand on the land
30 and shout aloud over you
        and cry out bitterly.
    They cast dust on their heads
        and wallow in ashes;
31 they make themselves bald for you
        and put sackcloth on their waist,
    and they weep over you in bitterness
        of soul,
    with bitter mourning.
32 In their wailing they raise a lamenta-
        tion for you
        and lament over you:
    'Who is like Tyre,
        like one destroyed in the midst of
        the sea?
33 When your wares came from the seas,
        you satisfied many peoples;
    with your abundant wealth and mer-
        chandise
    you enriched the kings of the earth.
34 Now you are wrecked by the seas,
        in the depths of the waters;
    your merchandise and all your crew
        in your midst
    have sunk with you.
35 All the inhabitants of the coastlands
        are appalled at you,
    and the hair of their kings bristles
        with horror;
    their faces are convulsed.

36 The merchants among the peoples
        hiss at you;
    you have come to a dreadful end
    and shall be no more forever.'"

Prophecy Against the Prince of Tyre

28 The word of the LORD came to me:
2 "Son of man, say to the prince of
Tyre, Thus says the Lord GOD:

"Because your heart is proud,
    and you have said, 'I am a god,
I sit in the seat of the gods,
    in the heart of the seas,'
yet you are but a man, and no god,
    though you make your heart like
    the heart of a god—
3 you are indeed wiser than Daniel;
    no secret is hidden from you;
4 by your wisdom and your under-
        standing
    you have made wealth for yourself,

GETTING THE MESSAGE

Tyre's wealth came through its port,
where it received goods from all around
the Mediterranean—often items other
nations did not have access to (28:1-10).
Their pride in their wealth would lead to
their destruction.

and have gathered gold and silver
    into your treasuries;
5 by your great wisdom in your trade
    you have increased your wealth,
    and your heart has become proud
        in your wealth—
6 therefore thus says the Lord GOD:
Because you make your heart
    like the heart of a god,
7 therefore, behold, I will bring foreign-
        ers upon you,
    the most ruthless of the nations;
and they shall draw their swords
        against the beauty of your wis-
        dom
    and defile your splendor.
8 They shall thrust you down into the
        pit,
    and you shall die the death of the
        slain
    in the heart of the seas.

9   Will you still say, 'I am a god,'
        in the presence of those who kill
           you,
     though you are but a man, and no god,
        in the hands of those who slay you?
10   You shall die the death of the uncir-
        cumcised
        by the hand of foreigners;
        for I have spoken, declares the Lord
           God."

A Lament over the King of Tyre

11 Moreover, the word of the LORD came
to me: 12 "Son of man, raise a lamentation
over the king of Tyre, and say to him, Thus
says the Lord GOD:

     "You were the signet of perfection,
        full of wisdom and perfect in beauty.
13   You were in Eden, the garden of God;
        every precious stone was your cov-
           ering,
        sardius, topaz, and diamond,
        beryl, onyx, and jasper,
        sapphire, emerald, and carbuncle;
        and crafted in gold were your set-
           tings
        and your engravings.
     On the day that you were created
        they were prepared.
14   You were an anointed guardian
           cherub.
        I placed you; you were on the holy
           mountain of God;
        in the midst of the stones of fire
           you walked.
15   You were blameless in your ways
        from the day you were created,
        till unrighteousness was found in
           you.
16   In the abundance of your trade
        you were filled with violence in
           your midst, and you sinned;
        so I cast you as a profane thing from
           the mountain of God,
        and I destroyed you, O guardian
           cherub,
        from the midst of the stones of fire.
17   Your heart was proud because of your
           beauty;
        you corrupted your wisdom for the
           sake of your splendor.
     I cast you to the ground;
        I exposed you before kings,
        to feast their eyes on you.

18   By the multitude of your iniquities,
        in the unrighteousness of your trade
           you profaned your sanctuaries;
        so I brought fire out from your midst;
           it consumed you,
        and I turned you to ashes on the earth
           in the sight of all who saw you.
19   All who know you among the peoples
        are appalled at you;
        you have come to a dreadful end
        and shall be no more forever."

Prophecy Against Sidon

20 The word of the LORD came to me:
21 "Son of man, set your face toward Sidon,
and prophesy against her 22 and say, Thus
says the Lord GOD:

     "Behold, I am against you, O Sidon,
        and I will manifest my glory in your
           midst.
     And they shall know that I am the LORD
        when I execute judgments in her
        and manifest my holiness in her;
23   for I will send pestilence into her,
        and blood into her streets;
        and the slain shall fall in her midst,
           by the sword that is against her on
              every side.
     Then they will know that I am the
        LORD.

24 "And for the house of Israel there shall
be no more a brier to prick or a thorn to hurt
them among all their neighbors who have
treated them with contempt. Then they will
know that I am the Lord GOD.

Israel Gathered in Security

25 "Thus says the Lord GOD: When I gather
the house of Israel from the peoples among
whom they are scattered, and manifest my
holiness in them in the sight of the nations,
then they shall dwell in their own land that
I gave to my servant Jacob. 26 And they shall
dwell securely in it, and they shall build
houses and plant vineyards. They shall
dwell securely, when I execute judgments
upon all their neighbors who have treated
them with contempt. Then they will know
that I am the LORD their God."

Prophecy Against Egypt

29 In the tenth year, in the tenth
month, on the twelfth day of the
month, the word of the LORD came to me:
2 "Son of man, set your face against Pharaoh

king of Egypt, and prophesy against him and against all Egypt; ³ speak, and say, Thus says the Lord God:

"Behold, I am against you,
    Pharaoh king of Egypt,
the great dragon that lies
    in the midst of his streams,
that says, 'My Nile is my own;
    I made it for myself.'
⁴   I will put hooks in your jaws,
    and make the fish of your streams
        stick to your scales;
and I will draw you up out of the
        midst of your streams,
    with all the fish of your streams
    that stick to your scales.
⁵   And I will cast you out into the wil-
        derness,
    you and all the fish of your streams;
you shall fall on the open field,
    and not be brought together or
        gathered.
To the beasts of the earth and to the
        birds of the heavens
    I give you as food.

⁶ Then all the inhabitants of Egypt shall know that I am the Lord.

"Because you have been a staff of reed to the house of Israel, ⁷ when they grasped you with the hand, you broke and tore all their shoulders; and when they leaned on you, you broke and made all their loins to shake. ⁸ Therefore thus says the Lord God: Behold, I will bring a sword upon you, and will cut off from you man and beast, ⁹ and the land of Egypt shall be a desolation and a waste. Then they will know that I am the Lord.

"Because you said, 'The Nile is mine, and I made it,' ¹⁰ therefore, behold, I am against you and against your streams, and I will make the land of Egypt an utter waste and desolation, from Migdol to Syene, as far as the border of Cush. ¹¹ No foot of man shall pass through it, and no foot of beast shall pass through it; it shall be uninhabited forty years. ¹² And I will make the land of Egypt a desolation in the midst of desolated countries, and her cities shall be a desolation forty years among cities that are laid waste. I will scatter the Egyptians among the nations, and disperse them through the countries.

¹³ "For thus says the Lord God: At the end of forty years I will gather the Egyptians from the peoples among whom they were scattered, ¹⁴ and I will restore the fortunes of Egypt and bring them back to the land of Pathros, the land of their origin, and there they shall be a lowly kingdom. ¹⁵ It shall be the most lowly of the kingdoms, and never again exalt itself above the nations. And I will make them so small that they will never again rule over the nations. ¹⁶ And it shall never again be the reliance of the house of Israel, recalling their iniquity, when they turn to them for aid. Then they will know that I am the Lord God."

¹⁷ In the twenty-seventh year, in the first month, on the first day of the month, the word of the Lord came to me: ¹⁸ "Son of man, Nebuchadnezzar king of Babylon made his army labor hard against Tyre. Every head was made bald, and every shoulder was rubbed bare, yet neither he nor his army got anything from Tyre to pay for the labor that

GETTING THE MESSAGE

Hooks in your jaws (29:4) is a reference to crocodile hunting. Large hooks were baited with pork and cast into the river. When a crocodile bit the baited hook, it was quickly hauled to shore.

he had performed against her. ¹⁹ Therefore thus says the Lord God: Behold, I will give the land of Egypt to Nebuchadnezzar king of Babylon; and he shall carry off its wealth and despoil it and plunder it; and it shall be the wages for his army. ²⁰ I have given him the land of Egypt as his payment for which he labored, because they worked for me, declares the Lord God.

²¹ "On that day I will cause a horn to spring up for the house of Israel, and I will open your lips among them. Then they will know that I am the Lord."

A Lament for Egypt

30 The word of the Lord came to me: ² "Son of man, prophesy, and say, Thus says the Lord God:

"Wail, 'Alas for the day!'
³   For the day is near,
        the day of the Lord is near;
    it will be a day of clouds,
        a time of doom for the nations.

⁴ A sword shall come upon Egypt,
   and anguish shall be in Cush,
when the slain fall in Egypt,
   and her wealth is carried away,
   and her foundations are torn down.

⁵ Cush, and Put, and Lud, and all Arabia, and Libya, and the people of the land that is in league, shall fall with them by the sword.

⁶ "Thus says the LORD:
   Those who support Egypt shall fall,
     and her proud might shall come
      down;
   from Migdol to Syene
     they shall fall within her by the
      sword,
   declares the Lord GOD.
⁷ And they shall be desolated in the
     midst of desolated countries,
   and their cities shall be in the midst
     of cities that are laid waste.
⁸ Then they will know that I am the
   LORD,
   when I have set fire to Egypt,
   and all her helpers are broken.

⁹ "On that day messengers shall go out from me in ships to terrify the unsuspecting people of Cush, and anguish shall come upon them on the day of Egypt's doom; for, behold, it comes!

¹⁰ "Thus says the Lord GOD:

   "I will put an end to the wealth of
     Egypt,
   by the hand of Nebuchadnezzar
     king of Babylon.
¹¹ He and his people with him, the most
     ruthless of nations,
   shall be brought in to destroy the
     land,
   and they shall draw their swords
     against Egypt
   and fill the land with the slain.
¹² And I will dry up the Nile
     and will sell the land into the hand
     of evildoers;
   I will bring desolation upon the land
     and everything in it,
   by the hand of foreigners;
   I am the LORD; I have spoken.

¹³ "Thus says the Lord GOD:

   "I will destroy the idols
     and put an end to the images in
     Memphis;

there shall no longer be a prince from
   the land of Egypt;
so I will put fear in the land of Egypt.
¹⁴ I will make Pathros a desolation
   and will set fire to Zoan
   and will execute judgments on
     Thebes.
¹⁵ And I will pour out my wrath on
     Pelusium,
   the stronghold of Egypt,
   and cut off the multitude of Thebes.
¹⁶ And I will set fire to Egypt;
   Pelusium shall be in great agony;
Thebes shall be breached,
   and Memphis shall face enemies by
     day.
¹⁷ The young men of On and of Pi-beseth
   shall fall by the sword,
   and the women shall go into captiv-
     ity.
¹⁸ At Tehaphnehes the day shall be dark,
   when I break there the yoke bars of
     Egypt,
and her proud might shall come to an
     end in her;
   she shall be covered by a cloud,
   and her daughters shall go into
     captivity.
¹⁹ Thus I will execute judgments on
     Egypt.
   Then they will know that I am the
     LORD."

Egypt Shall Fall to Babylon

²⁰ In the eleventh year, in the first month, on the seventh day of the month, the word of the LORD came to me: ²¹ "Son of man, I have broken the arm of Pharaoh king of Egypt, and behold, it has not been bound up, to heal it by binding it with a bandage, so that it may become strong to wield the sword. ²² Therefore thus says the Lord GOD: Behold, I am against Pharaoh king of Egypt and will break his arms, both the strong arm and the one that was broken, and I will make the sword fall from his hand. ²³ I will scatter the Egyptians among the nations and disperse them through the countries. ²⁴ And I will strengthen the arms of the king of Babylon and put my sword in his hand, but I will break the arms of Pharaoh, and he will groan before him like a man mortally wounded. ²⁵ I will strengthen the arms of the king of Babylon, but the arms of Pharaoh shall fall. Then they shall know that I am the

LORD, when I put my sword into the hand of the king of Babylon and he stretches it out against the land of Egypt. ²⁶ And I will scatter the Egyptians among the nations and disperse them throughout the countries. Then they will know that I am the LORD."

Pharaoh to Be Slain

31 In the eleventh year, in the third month, on the first day of the month, the word of the LORD came to me: ² "Son of man, say to Pharaoh king of Egypt and to his multitude:

"Whom are you like in your greatness?
³   Behold, Assyria was a cedar in
Lebanon,
with beautiful branches and forest
shade,
and of towering height,
its top among the clouds.
⁴   The waters nourished it;
the deep made it grow tall,
making its rivers flow
around the place of its planting,
sending forth its streams
to all the trees of the field.
⁵   So it towered high
above all the trees of the field;
its boughs grew large
and its branches long
from abundant water in its shoots.
⁶   All the birds of the heavens
made their nests in its boughs;
under its branches all the beasts of
the field
gave birth to their young,
and under its shadow
lived all great nations.
⁷   It was beautiful in its greatness,
in the length of its branches;
for its roots went down
to abundant waters.
⁸   The cedars in the garden of God could
not rival it,
nor the fir trees equal its boughs;
neither were the plane trees
like its branches;
no tree in the garden of God
was its equal in beauty.
⁹   I made it beautiful
in the mass of its branches,
and all the trees of Eden envied it,
that were in the garden of God.

¹⁰ "Therefore thus says the Lord GOD: Because it towered high and set its top among the clouds, and its heart was proud of its height, ¹¹ I will give it into the hand of a mighty one of the nations. He shall surely deal with it as its wickedness deserves. I have cast it out. ¹² Foreigners, the most ruthless of nations, have cut it down and left it. On the mountains and in all the valleys its branches have fallen, and its boughs have been broken in all the ravines of the land, and all the peoples of the earth have gone away from its shadow and left it. ¹³ On its fallen trunk dwell all the birds of the heavens, and on its branches are all the beasts of the field. ¹⁴ All this is in order that no trees by the waters may grow to towering height or set their tops among the clouds, and that no trees that drink water may reach up to them in height. For they are all given

GETTING THE MESSAGE

A tree cut down. The Assyrians believed that a sacred tree, whose roots were fed by a vast underground ocean, brought life to its nation. When Ezekiel talked about this "tree" being cut down (31:1–18), he was symbolically describing the end of once-mighty Assyria.

over to death, to the world below, among the children of man, with those who go down to the pit.

¹⁵ "Thus says the Lord GOD: On the day the cedar went down to Sheol I caused mourning; I closed the deep over it, and restrained its rivers, and many waters were stopped. I clothed Lebanon in gloom for it, and all the trees of the field fainted because of it. ¹⁶ I made the nations quake at the sound of its fall, when I cast it down to Sheol with those who go down to the pit. And all the trees of Eden, the choice and best of Lebanon, all that drink water, were comforted in the world below. ¹⁷ They also went down to Sheol with it, to those who are slain by the sword; yes, those who were its arm, who lived under its shadow among the nations.

¹⁸ "Whom are you thus like in glory and in greatness among the trees of Eden? You shall be brought down with the trees of Eden

to the world below. You shall lie among the uncircumcised, with those who are slain by the sword.

"This is Pharaoh and all his multitude, declares the Lord GOD."

A Lament over Pharaoh and Egypt

32 In the twelfth year, in the twelfth month, on the first day of the month, the word of the LORD came to me: **2** "Son of man, raise a lamentation over Pharaoh king of Egypt and say to him:

"You consider yourself a lion of the
          nations,
    but you are like a dragon in the
          seas;
    you burst forth in your rivers,
      trouble the waters with your feet,
      and foul their rivers.

> **GETTING THE MESSAGE**
>
> **Lions and dragons.** Egypt saw itself as a lion, a nation that hunted and devoured other nations. But Ezekiel compares Egypt to a dragon—a near-sighted crocodile that stirs up muddy waters, attracting attention to itself (32:2). Egypt's boasting will be its downfall, as the Lord sends Babylon to conquer and humiliate it.

3   Thus says the Lord GOD:
      I will throw my net over you
        with a host of many peoples,
        and they will haul you up in my
          dragnet.
4   And I will cast you on the ground;
        on the open field I will fling you,
      and will cause all the birds of the
          heavens to settle on you,
      and I will gorge the beasts of the
          whole earth with you.
5   I will strew your flesh upon the
          mountains
      and fill the valleys with your car-
          cass.
6   I will drench the land even to the
          mountains
        with your flowing blood,
      and the ravines will be full of you.
7   When I blot you out, I will cover the
          heavens

and make their stars dark;
    I will cover the sun with a cloud,
      and the moon shall not give its
          light.
8   All the bright lights of heaven
      will I make dark over you,
      and put darkness on your land,
                    declares the Lord GOD.

9 "I will trouble the hearts of many peoples, when I bring your destruction among the nations, into the countries that you have not known. **10** I will make many peoples appalled at you, and the hair of their kings shall bristle with horror because of you, when I brandish my sword before them. They shall tremble every moment, every one for his own life, on the day of your downfall.

11 "For thus says the Lord GOD: The sword of the king of Babylon shall come upon you. **12** I will cause your multitude to fall by the swords of mighty ones, all of them most ruthless of nations.

"They shall bring to ruin the pride of
          Egypt,
      and all its multitude shall perish.
13   I will destroy all its beasts
        from beside many waters;
      and no foot of man shall trouble them
          anymore,
        nor shall the hoofs of beasts trouble
          them.
14   Then I will make their waters clear,
        and cause their rivers to run like
          oil,
                    declares the Lord GOD.
15   When I make the land of Egypt deso-
          late,
      and when the land is desolate of all
          that fills it,
      when I strike down all who dwell in it,
        then they will know that I am the
          LORD.

16 This is a lamentation that shall be chanted; the daughters of the nations shall chant it; over Egypt, and over all her multitude, shall they chant it, declares the Lord GOD."

17 In the twelfth year, in the twelfth month, on the fifteenth day of the month, the word of the LORD came to me: **18** "Son of man, wail over the multitude of Egypt, and send them down, her and the daughters of majestic nations, to the world below, to those who have gone down to the pit:

19 'Whom do you surpass in beauty?
 Go down and be laid to rest with the
 uncircumcised.'

20 They shall fall amid those who are slain by the sword. Egypt is delivered to the sword; drag her away, and all her multitudes. 21 The mighty chiefs shall speak of them, with their helpers, out of the midst of Sheol: 'They have come down, they lie still, the uncircumcised, slain by the sword.'

22 "Assyria is there, and all her company, its graves all around it, all of them slain, fallen by the sword, 23 whose graves are set in the uttermost parts of the pit; and her company is all around her grave, all of them slain, fallen by the sword, who spread terror in the land of the living.

24 "Elam is there, and all her multitude around her grave; all of them slain, fallen by the sword, who went down uncircumcised into the world below, who spread their terror in the land of the living; and they bear their shame with those who go down to the pit. 25 They have made her a bed among the slain with all her multitude, her graves all around it, all of them uncircumcised, slain by the sword; for terror of them was spread in the land of the living, and they bear their shame with those who go down to the pit; they are placed among the slain.

26 "Meshech-Tubal is there, and all her multitude, her graves all around it, all of them uncircumcised, slain by the sword; for they spread their terror in the land of the living. 27 And they do not lie with the mighty, the fallen from among the uncircumcised, who went down to Sheol with their weapons of war, whose swords were laid under their heads, and whose iniquities are upon their bones; for the terror of the mighty men was in the land of the living. 28 But as for you, you shall be broken and lie among the uncircumcised, with those who are slain by the sword.

29 "Edom is there, her kings and all her princes, who for all their might are laid with those who are killed by the sword; they lie with the uncircumcised, with those who go down to the pit.

30 "The princes of the north are there, all of them, and all the Sidonians, who have gone down in shame with the slain, for all the terror that they caused by their might; they lie uncircumcised with those who are slain by the sword, and bear their shame with those who go down to the pit.

31 "When Pharaoh sees them, he will be comforted for all his multitude, Pharaoh and all his army, slain by the sword, declares the Lord GOD. 32 For I spread terror in the land of the living; and he shall be laid to rest among the uncircumcised, with those who are slain by the sword, Pharaoh and all his multitude, declares the Lord GOD."

Ezekiel Is Israel's Watchman

33 The word of the LORD came to me: 2 "Son of man, speak to your people and say to them, If I bring the sword upon a land, and the people of the land take a man from among them, and make him their watchman, 3 and if he sees the sword coming upon the land and blows the trumpet and warns the people, 4 then if anyone who

> ### GETTING THE MESSAGE
>
> **Watchmen.** The Lord appointed Ezekiel to be a "watchman" over Israel (33:7). People depended on the watchman not only to remain vigilant but also to sound the alarm if the city was in danger. It was then up to the people to decide whether to heed these warnings or ignore them.

hears the sound of the trumpet does not take warning, and the sword comes and takes him away, his blood shall be upon his own head. 5 He heard the sound of the trumpet and did not take warning; his blood shall be upon himself. But if he had taken warning, he would have saved his life. 6 But if the watchman sees the sword coming and does not blow the trumpet, so that the people are not warned, and the sword comes and takes any one of them, that person is taken away in his iniquity, but his blood I will require at the watchman's hand.

7 "So you, son of man, I have made a watchman for the house of Israel. Whenever you hear a word from my mouth, you shall give them warning from me. 8 If I say to the wicked, O wicked one, you shall surely die, and you do not speak to warn the wicked to turn from his way, that wicked person shall die in his iniquity, but his blood I will require at your hand. 9 But if you warn the wicked to turn from his way, and he does

not turn from his way, that person shall die in his iniquity, but you will have delivered your soul.

Why Will You Die, Israel?

¹⁰ "And you, son of man, say to the house of Israel, Thus have you said: 'Surely our transgressions and our sins are upon us, and we rot away because of them. How then can we live?' ¹¹ Say to them, As I live, declares the Lord God, I have no pleasure in the death of the wicked, but that the wicked turn from his way and live; turn back, turn back from your evil ways, for why will you die, O house of Israel?

¹² "And you, son of man, say to your people, The righteousness of the righteous shall not deliver him when he transgresses, and as for the wickedness of the wicked, he shall not fall by it when he turns from his wickedness, and the righteous shall not be able to live by his righteousness when he sins. ¹³ Though I say to the righteous that he shall surely live, yet if he trusts in his righteousness and does injustice, none of his righteous deeds shall be remembered, but in his injustice that he has done he shall die. ¹⁴ Again, though I say to the wicked, 'You shall surely die,' yet if he turns from his sin and does what is just and right, ¹⁵ if the wicked restores the pledge, gives back what he has taken by robbery, and walks in the statutes of life, not doing injustice, he shall surely live; he shall not die. ¹⁶ None of the sins that he has committed shall be remembered against him. He has done what is just and right; he shall surely live.

¹⁷ "Yet your people say, 'The way of the Lord is not just,' when it is their own way that is not just. ¹⁸ When the righteous turns from his righteousness and does injustice, he shall die for it. ¹⁹ And when the wicked turns from his wickedness and does what is just and right, he shall live by this. ²⁰ Yet you say, 'The way of the Lord is not just.' O house of Israel, I will judge each of you according to his ways."

Jerusalem Struck Down

²¹ In the twelfth year of our exile, in the tenth month, on the fifth day of the month, a fugitive from Jerusalem came to me and said, "The city has been struck down." ²² Now the hand of the Lord had been upon me the evening before the fugitive came; and he had opened my mouth by the time the man came to me in the morning, so my mouth was opened, and I was no longer mute.

²³ The word of the Lord came to me: ²⁴ "Son of man, the inhabitants of these waste places in the land of Israel keep saying, 'Abraham was only one man, yet he got possession of the land; but we are many; the land is surely given us to possess.' ²⁵ Therefore say to them, Thus says the Lord God: You eat flesh with the blood and lift up your eyes to your idols and shed blood; shall you then possess the land? ²⁶ You rely on the sword, you commit abominations, and each of you defiles his neighbor's wife; shall you then possess the land? ²⁷ Say this to them, Thus says the Lord God: As I live, surely those who are in the waste places shall fall by the sword, and whoever is in the open field I will give to the beasts to be devoured, and those who are in strongholds and in caves shall die by pestilence. ²⁸ And I will make the land a desolation and a waste, and her proud might shall come to an end, and the mountains of Israel shall be so desolate that none will pass through. ²⁹ Then they will know that I am the Lord, when I have made the land a desolation and a waste because of all their abominations that they have committed.

³⁰ "As for you, son of man, your people who talk together about you by the walls and at the doors of the houses, say to one another, each to his brother, 'Come, and hear what the word is that comes from the Lord.' ³¹ And they come to you as people come, and they sit before you as my people, and they hear what you say but they will not do it; for with lustful talk in their mouths they act; their heart is set on their gain. ³² And behold, you are to them like one who sings lustful songs with a beautiful voice and plays well on an instrument, for they hear what you say, but they will not do it. ³³ When this comes—and come it will!—then they will know that a prophet has been among them."

Prophecy Against the Shepherds of Israel

34 The word of the Lord came to me: ² "Son of man, prophesy against the shepherds of Israel; prophesy, and say to them, even to the shepherds, Thus says the Lord God: Ah, shepherds of Israel who have been feeding yourselves! Should not shepherds feed the sheep? ³ You eat the fat, you clothe yourselves with the wool, you slaughter the fat ones, but you do not feed the sheep. ⁴ The weak you have not strengthened, the sick you have not healed, the injured you have not bound up, the strayed you have not brought back, the lost you have not sought, and with force and harshness you have ruled them. ⁵ So they were scattered, because there was no shepherd, and they became food for all the wild beasts. ⁶ My sheep were scattered; they wandered over all the mountains and on every high hill. My sheep were scattered over all the face of the earth, with none to search or seek for them.

⁷ "Therefore, you shepherds, hear the word of the LORD: ⁸ As I live, declares the Lord GOD, surely because my sheep have become a prey, and my sheep have become food for all the wild beasts, since there was no shepherd, and because my shepherds have not searched for my sheep, but the shepherds have fed themselves, and have not fed my sheep, ⁹ therefore, you shepherds, hear the word of the LORD: ¹⁰ Thus says the Lord GOD, Behold, I am against the shepherds, and I will require my sheep at their hand and put a stop to their feeding the sheep. No longer shall the shepherds feed themselves. I will rescue my sheep from their mouths, that they may not be food for them.

The Lord GOD Will Seek Them Out

¹¹ "For thus says the Lord GOD: Behold, I, I myself will search for my sheep and will seek them out. ¹² As a shepherd seeks out his flock when he is among his sheep that have been scattered, so will I seek out my sheep, and I will rescue them from all places where they have been scattered on a day of clouds and thick darkness. ¹³ And I will bring them out from the peoples and gather them from the countries, and will bring them into their own land. And I will feed them on the mountains of Israel, by the ravines, and in all the inhabited places of the country. ¹⁴ I will feed them with good pasture, and on the mountain heights of Israel shall be their grazing land. There they shall lie down in good grazing land, and on rich pasture they shall feed on the mountains of Israel. ¹⁵ I myself will be the shepherd of my sheep, and I myself will make them lie down,

declares the Lord GOD. ¹⁶ I will seek the lost, and I will bring back the strayed, and I will bind up the injured, and I will strengthen the weak, and the fat and the strong I will destroy. I will feed them in justice.

¹⁷ "As for you, my flock, thus says the Lord GOD: Behold, I judge between sheep and sheep, between rams and male goats. ¹⁸ Is it not enough for you to feed on the good pasture, that you must tread down with your feet the rest of your pasture; and to drink of clear water, that you must muddy the rest of the water with your feet? ¹⁹ And must my sheep eat what you have trodden with your feet, and drink what you have muddied with your feet?

²⁰ "Therefore, thus says the Lord GOD to them: Behold, I, I myself will judge between the fat sheep and the lean sheep. ²¹ Because

you push with side and shoulder, and thrust at all the weak with your horns, till you have scattered them abroad, ²² I will rescue my flock; they shall no longer be a prey. And I will judge between sheep and sheep. ²³ And I will set up over them one shepherd, my servant David, and he shall feed them: he shall feed them and be their shepherd. ²⁴ And I, the LORD, will be their God, and my servant David shall be prince among them. I am the LORD; I have spoken.

The LORD's Covenant of Peace

²⁵ "I will make with them a covenant of peace and banish wild beasts from the land, so that they may dwell securely in the wilderness and sleep in the woods. ²⁶ And I will make them and the places all around my hill a blessing, and I will send down the showers in their season; they shall be showers of blessing. ²⁷ And the trees of the field shall yield their fruit, and the earth shall yield its increase, and they shall be secure in their land. And they shall know that I am the

LORD, when I break the bars of their yoke, and deliver them from the hand of those who enslaved them. ²⁸ They shall no more be a prey to the nations, nor shall the beasts of the land devour them. They shall dwell securely, and none shall make them afraid. ²⁹ And I will provide for them renowned plantations so that they shall no more be consumed with hunger in the land, and no longer suffer the reproach of the nations. ³⁰ And they shall know that I am the LORD their God with them, and that they, the house of Israel, are my people, declares the Lord GOD. ³¹ And you are my sheep, human sheep of my pasture, and I am your God, declares the Lord GOD."

Prophecy Against Mount Seir

35 The word of the LORD came to me: ² "Son of man, set your face against Mount Seir, and prophesy against it, ³ and say to it, Thus says the Lord GOD: Behold, I am against you, Mount Seir, and I will stretch out my hand against you, and I will make you a desolation and a waste. ⁴ I will lay your cities waste, and you shall become a desolation, and you shall know that I am the LORD. ⁵ Because you cherished perpetual enmity and gave over the people of Israel to the power of the sword at the time of their calamity, at the time of their final punishment, ⁶ therefore, as I live, declares the Lord GOD, I will prepare you for blood, and blood shall pursue you; because you did not hate bloodshed, therefore blood shall pursue you. ⁷ I will make Mount Seir a waste and a desolation, and I will cut off from it all who come and go. ⁸ And I will fill its mountains with the slain. On your hills and in your valleys and in all your ravines those slain with the sword shall fall. ⁹ I will make you a perpetual desolation, and your cities shall not be inhabited. Then you will know that I am the LORD.

¹⁰ "Because you said, 'These two nations and these two countries shall be mine, and we will take possession of them'—although the LORD was there— ¹¹ therefore, as I live, declares the Lord GOD, I will deal with you according to the anger and envy that you showed because of your hatred against them. And I will make myself known among them, when I judge you. ¹² And you shall know that I am the LORD.

"I have heard all the revilings that you uttered against the mountains of Israel, saying, 'They are laid desolate; they are given us to devour.' ¹³ And you magnified yourselves against me with your mouth, and multiplied your words against me; I heard it. ¹⁴ Thus says the Lord GOD: While the whole earth rejoices, I will make you desolate. ¹⁵ As you rejoiced over the inheritance of the house of Israel, because it was desolate, so I will deal with you; you shall be desolate, Mount Seir, and all Edom, all of it. Then they will know that I am the LORD.

Prophecy to the Mountains of Israel

36 "And you, son of man, prophesy to the mountains of Israel, and say, O mountains of Israel, hear the word of the LORD. ² Thus says the Lord GOD: Because the enemy said of you, 'Aha!' and, 'The ancient heights have become our possession,' ³ therefore prophesy, and say, Thus says the Lord GOD: Precisely because they made you desolate and crushed you from all sides, so that you became the possession of the rest of the nations, and you became the talk and evil gossip of the people, ⁴ therefore, O mountains of Israel, hear the word of the Lord GOD: Thus says the Lord GOD to the mountains and the hills, the ravines and the valleys, the desolate wastes and the deserted cities, which have become a prey and derision to the rest of the nations all around, ⁵ therefore thus says the Lord GOD: Surely I have spoken in my hot jealousy against the rest of the nations and against all Edom, who gave my land to themselves as a possession with wholehearted joy and utter contempt, that they might make its pasturelands a prey. ⁶ Therefore prophesy concerning the land of Israel, and say to the mountains and hills, to the ravines and valleys, Thus says the Lord GOD: Behold, I have spoken in my jealous wrath, because you have suffered the reproach of the nations. ⁷ Therefore thus says the Lord GOD: I swear that the nations that are all around you shall themselves suffer reproach.

⁸ "But you, O mountains of Israel, shall shoot forth your branches and yield your fruit to my people Israel, for they will soon come home. ⁹ For behold, I am for you, and I will turn to you, and you shall be tilled and sown. ¹⁰ And I will multiply people on you, the whole house of Israel, all of it. The cities shall be inhabited and the waste places

rebuilt. **11** And I will multiply on you man and beast, and they shall multiply and be fruitful. And I will cause you to be inhabited as in your former times, and will do more good to you than ever before. Then you will know that I am the LORD. **12** I will let people walk on you, even my people Israel. And they shall possess you, and you shall be their inheritance, and you shall no longer bereave them of children. **13** Thus says the Lord GOD: Because they say to you, 'You devour people, and you bereave your nation of children,' **14** therefore you shall no longer devour people and no longer bereave your nation of children, declares the Lord GOD. **15** And I will not let you hear anymore the reproach of the nations, and you shall no longer bear the disgrace of the peoples and no longer cause your nation to stumble, declares the Lord GOD."

The LORD's Concern for His Holy Name

16 The word of the LORD came to me: **17** "Son of man, when the house of Israel lived in their own land, they defiled it by their ways and their deeds. Their ways before me were like the uncleanness of a woman in her menstrual impurity. **18** So I poured out my wrath upon them for the blood that they had shed in the land, for the idols with which they had defiled it. **19** I scattered them among the nations, and they were dispersed through the countries. In accordance with their ways and their deeds I judged them. **20** But when they came to the nations, wherever they came, they profaned my holy name, in that people said of them, 'These are the people of the LORD, and yet they had to go out of his land.' **21** But I had concern for my holy name, which the house of Israel had profaned among the nations to which they came.

I Will Put My Spirit Within You

22 "Therefore say to the house of Israel, Thus says the Lord GOD: It is not for your sake, O house of Israel, that I am about to act, but for the sake of my holy name, which you have profaned among the nations to which you came. **23** And I will vindicate the holiness of my great name, which has been profaned among the nations, and which you have profaned among them. And the nations will know that I am the LORD, declares the Lord GOD, when through you

I vindicate my holiness before their eyes. **24** I will take you from the nations and gather you from all the countries and bring you into your own land. **25** I will sprinkle clean water on you, and you shall be clean from all your uncleannesses, and from all your idols I will cleanse you. **26** And I will give you a new heart, and a new spirit I will put within you. And I will remove the heart of stone from your flesh and give you a heart of flesh. **27** And I will put my Spirit within you, and cause you to walk in my statutes and be careful to obey my rules. **28** You shall dwell in the land that I gave to your fathers, and you shall be my people, and I will be your God. **29** And I will deliver you from all your uncleannesses. And I will summon the grain and make it abundant and lay no famine upon you. **30** I will make the fruit

GETTING THE MESSAGE

Israel was called to be a **light to the nations** (Isa. 42:6), but instead, their sinful behavior "profaned" God's name before their unbelieving neighbors (Ezek. 36:22–23). The Lord expects his people to bring honor to his name.

of the tree and the increase of the field abundant, that you may never again suffer the disgrace of famine among the nations. **31** Then you will remember your evil ways, and your deeds that were not good, and you will loathe yourselves for your iniquities and your abominations. **32** It is not for your sake that I will act, declares the Lord GOD; let that be known to you. Be ashamed and confounded for your ways, O house of Israel.

33 "Thus says the Lord GOD: On the day that I cleanse you from all your iniquities, I will cause the cities to be inhabited, and the waste places shall be rebuilt. **34** And the land that was desolate shall be tilled, instead of being the desolation that it was in the sight of all who passed by. **35** And they will say, 'This land that was desolate has become like the garden of Eden, and the waste and desolate and ruined cities are now fortified and inhabited.' **36** Then the nations that are left all around you shall know that I am the LORD; I have rebuilt the ruined places and replanted that which was desolate. I am the LORD; I have spoken, and I will do it.

37 "Thus says the Lord GOD: This also I will let the house of Israel ask me to do for them: to increase their people like a flock. **38** Like the flock for sacrifices, like the flock at Jerusalem during her appointed feasts, so shall the waste cities be filled with flocks of people. Then they will know that I am the LORD."

The Valley of Dry Bones

37 The hand of the LORD was upon me, and he brought me out in the Spirit of the LORD and set me down in the middle of the valley; it was full of bones. **2** And he led me around among them, and behold, there were very many on the surface of the valley, and behold, they were very dry. **3** And he said to me, "Son of man, can these

---

> **GETTING THE MESSAGE**
>
> Although Jerusalem was defeated (33:21–22), Ezekiel preaches a message of hope in chs. 33–48. In ch. 37, his vision of a **valley of dry bones** promises that God's Spirit will restore Israel. This is one of the most famous passages in Ezekiel.

---

bones live?" And I answered, "O Lord GOD, you know." **4** Then he said to me, "Prophesy over these bones, and say to them, O dry bones, hear the word of the LORD. **5** Thus says the Lord GOD to these bones: Behold, I will cause breath to enter you, and you shall live. **6** And I will lay sinews upon you, and will cause flesh to come upon you, and cover you with skin, and put breath in you, and you shall live, and you shall know that I am the LORD."

7 So I prophesied as I was commanded. And as I prophesied, there was a sound, and behold, a rattling, and the bones came together, bone to its bone. **8** And I looked, and behold, there were sinews on them, and flesh had come upon them, and skin had covered them. But there was no breath in them. **9** Then he said to me, "Prophesy to the breath; prophesy, son of man, and say to the breath, Thus says the Lord GOD: Come from the four winds, O breath, and breathe on these slain, that they may live." **10** So I prophesied as he commanded me,

and the breath came into them, and they lived and stood on their feet, an exceedingly great army.

11 Then he said to me, "Son of man, these bones are the whole house of Israel. Behold, they say, 'Our bones are dried up, and our hope is lost; we are indeed cut off.' **12** Therefore prophesy, and say to them, Thus says the Lord GOD: Behold, I will open your graves and raise you from your graves, O my people. And I will bring you into the land of Israel. **13** And you shall know that I am the LORD, when I open your graves, and raise you from your graves, O my people. **14** And I will put my Spirit within you, and you shall live, and I will place you in your own land. Then you shall know that I am the LORD; I have spoken, and I will do it, declares the LORD."

I Will Be Their God, They Shall Be My People

15 The word of the LORD came to me: **16** "Son of man, take a stick and write on it, 'For Judah, and the people of Israel associated with him'; then take another stick and write on it, 'For Joseph (the stick of Ephraim) and all the house of Israel associated with him.' **17** And join them one to another into one stick, that they may become one in your hand. **18** And when your people say to you, 'Will you not tell us what you mean by these?' **19** say to them, Thus says the Lord GOD: Behold, I am about to take the stick of Joseph (that is in the hand of Ephraim) and the tribes of Israel associated with him. And I will join with it the stick of Judah, and make them one stick, that they may be one in my hand. **20** When the sticks on which you write are in your hand before their eyes, **21** then say to them, Thus says the Lord GOD: Behold, I will take the people of Israel from the nations among which they have gone, and will gather them from all around, and bring them to their own land. **22** And I will make them one nation in the land, on the mountains of Israel. And one king shall be king over them all, and they shall be no longer two nations, and no longer divided into two kingdoms. **23** They shall not defile themselves anymore with their idols and their detestable things, or with any of their transgressions. But I will save them from all the backslidings in which they have sinned, and will cleanse them; and they shall be my people, and I will be their God.

²⁴ "My servant David shall be king over them, and they shall all have one shepherd. They shall walk in my rules and be careful to obey my statutes. ²⁵ They shall dwell in the land that I gave to my servant Jacob, where your fathers lived. They and their children and their children's children shall dwell there forever, and David my servant shall be their prince forever. ²⁶ I will make a covenant of peace with them. It shall be an everlasting covenant with them. And I will set them in their land and multiply them, and will set my sanctuary in their midst forevermore. ²⁷ My dwelling place shall be with them, and I will be their God, and they shall be my people. ²⁸ Then the nations will know that I am the LORD who sanctifies Israel, when my sanctuary is in their midst forevermore."

Prophecy Against Gog

38 The word of the LORD came to me: ² "Son of man, set your face toward Gog, of the land of Magog, the chief prince of Meshech and Tubal, and prophesy against him ³ and say, Thus says the Lord GOD: Behold, I am against you, O Gog, chief prince of Meshech and Tubal. ⁴ And I will turn you about and put hooks into your jaws, and I will bring you out, and all your army, horses and horsemen, all of them clothed in full armor, a great host, all of them with buckler and shield, wielding swords. ⁵ Persia, Cush, and Put are with them, all of them with shield and helmet; ⁶ Gomer and all his hordes; Beth-togarmah from the uttermost parts of the north with all his hordes— many peoples are with you.

⁷ "Be ready and keep ready, you and all your hosts that are assembled about you, and be a guard for them. ⁸ After many days you will be mustered. In the latter years you will go against the land that is restored from war, the land whose people were gathered from many peoples upon the mountains of Israel, which had been a continual waste. Its people were brought out from the peoples and now dwell securely, all of them. ⁹ You will advance, coming on like a storm. You will be like a cloud covering the land, you and all your hordes, and many peoples with you.

¹⁰ "Thus says the Lord GOD: On that day, thoughts will come into your mind, and you will devise an evil scheme ¹¹ and say,

'I will go up against the land of unwalled villages. I will fall upon the quiet people who dwell securely, all of them dwelling without walls, and having no bars or gates,' ¹² to seize spoil and carry off plunder, to turn your hand against the waste places that are now inhabited, and the people who were gathered from the nations, who have acquired livestock and goods, who dwell at the center of the earth. ¹³ Sheba and Dedan and the merchants of Tarshish and all its leaders will say to you, 'Have you come to seize spoil? Have you assembled your hosts to carry off plunder, to carry away silver and gold, to take away livestock and goods, to seize great spoil?'

¹⁴ "Therefore, son of man, prophesy, and say to Gog, Thus says the Lord GOD: On that day when my people Israel are dwelling securely, will you not know it? ¹⁵ You will

> ### GETTING THE MESSAGE
>
> **Gog and Magog.** In chs. 38–39, Ezekiel prophesies that a mysterious ruler called Gog from an unknown land called Magog will attack Israel. There are many suggestions about who and what Gog and Magog mean, but no agreement has been reached.

come from your place out of the uttermost parts of the north, you and many peoples with you, all of them riding on horses, a great host, a mighty army. ¹⁶ You will come up against my people Israel, like a cloud covering the land. In the latter days I will bring you against my land, that the nations may know me, when through you, O Gog, I vindicate my holiness before their eyes.

¹⁷ "Thus says the Lord GOD: Are you he of whom I spoke in former days by my servants the prophets of Israel, who in those days prophesied for years that I would bring you against them? ¹⁸ But on that day, the day that Gog shall come against the land of Israel, declares the Lord GOD, my wrath will be roused in my anger. ¹⁹ For in my jealousy and in my blazing wrath I declare, On that day there shall be a great earthquake in the land of Israel. ²⁰ The fish of the sea and the birds of the heavens and the beasts of the field and all creeping

things that creep on the ground, and all the people who are on the face of the earth, shall quake at my presence. And the mountains shall be thrown down, and the cliffs shall fall, and every wall shall tumble to the ground. [21] I will summon a sword against Gog on all my mountains, declares the Lord GOD. Every man's sword will be against his brother. [22] With pestilence and bloodshed I will enter into judgment with him, and I will rain upon him and his hordes and the many peoples who are with him torrential rains and hailstones, fire and sulfur. [23] So I will show my greatness and my holiness and make myself known in the eyes of many nations. Then they will know that I am the LORD.

39 "And you, son of man, prophesy against Gog and say, Thus says the Lord GOD: Behold, I am against you, O Gog, chief prince of Meshech and Tubal. [2] And I will turn you about and drive you forward, and bring you up from the uttermost parts of the north, and lead you against the mountains of Israel. [3] Then I will strike your bow from your left hand, and will make your arrows drop out of your right hand. [4] You shall fall on the mountains of Israel, you and all your hordes and the peoples who are with you. I will give you to birds of prey of every sort and to the beasts of the field to be devoured. [5] You shall fall in the open field, for I have spoken, declares the Lord GOD. [6] I will send fire on Magog and on those who dwell securely in the coastlands, and they shall know that I am the LORD.

[7] "And my holy name I will make known in the midst of my people Israel, and I will not let my holy name be profaned anymore. And the nations shall know that I am the LORD, the Holy One in Israel. [8] Behold, it is coming and it will be brought about, declares the Lord GOD. That is the day of which I have spoken.

[9] "Then those who dwell in the cities of Israel will go out and make fires of the weapons and burn them, shields and bucklers, bow and arrows, clubs and spears; and they will make fires of them for seven years, [10] so that they will not need to take wood out of the field or cut down any out of the forests, for they will make their fires of the weapons. They will seize the spoil of those who despoiled them, and plunder those who plundered them, declares the Lord GOD.

[11] "On that day I will give to Gog a place for burial in Israel, the Valley of the Travelers, east of the sea. It will block the travelers, for there Gog and all his multitude will be buried. It will be called the Valley of Hamon-gog.[1] [12] For seven months the house of Israel will be burying them, in order to cleanse the land. [13] All the people of the land will bury them, and it will bring them renown on the day that I show my glory, declares the Lord GOD. [14] They will set apart men to travel through the land regularly and bury those travelers remaining on the face of the land, so as to cleanse it. At the end of seven months they will make their search. [15] And when these travel through the land and anyone sees a human bone, then he shall set up a sign by it, till the buriers have buried it in the Valley of Hamon-gog. [16] (Hamonah[2] is also the name of the city.) Thus shall they cleanse the land.

[17] "As for you, son of man, thus says the Lord GOD: Speak to the birds of every sort and to all beasts of the field, 'Assemble and come, gather from all around to the sacrificial feast that I am preparing for you, a great sacrificial feast on the mountains of Israel, and you shall eat flesh and drink blood. [18] You shall eat the flesh of the mighty, and drink the blood of the princes of the earth—of rams, of lambs, and of he-goats, of bulls, all of them fat beasts of Bashan. [19] And you shall eat fat till you are filled, and drink blood till you are drunk, at the sacrificial feast that I am preparing for you. [20] And you shall be filled at my table with horses and charioteers, with mighty men and all kinds of warriors,' declares the Lord GOD.

[21] "And I will set my glory among the nations, and all the nations shall see my judgment that I have executed, and my hand that I have laid on them. [22] The house of Israel shall know that I am the LORD their God, from that day forward. [23] And the nations shall know that the house of Israel went into captivity for their iniquity, because they dealt so treacherously with me that I hid my face from them and gave them into the hand of their adversaries, and they all fell by the sword. [24] I dealt with them

[1] *Hamon-gog* means the multitude of Gog [2] *Hamonah* means multitude

according to their uncleanness and their transgressions, and hid my face from them.

The Lord Will Restore Israel

25 "Therefore thus says the Lord GOD: Now I will restore the fortunes of Jacob and have mercy on the whole house of Israel, and I will be jealous for my holy name. **26** They shall forget their shame and all the treachery they have practiced against me, when they dwell securely in their land with none to make them afraid, **27** when I have brought them back from the peoples and gathered them from their enemies' lands, and through them have vindicated my holiness in the sight of many nations. **28** Then they shall know that I am the LORD their God, because I sent them into exile among the nations and then assembled them into their own land. I will leave none of them remaining among the nations anymore. **29** And I will not hide my face anymore from them, when I pour out my Spirit upon the house of Israel, declares the Lord GOD."

Vision of the New Temple

40 In the twenty-fifth year of our exile, at the beginning of the year, on the tenth day of the month, in the fourteenth year after the city was struck down, on that very day, the hand of the LORD was upon me, and he brought me to the city. **2** In visions of God he brought me to the land of Israel, and set me down on a very high mountain, on which was a structure like a city to the south. **3** When he brought me there, behold, there was a man whose appearance was like bronze, with a linen cord and a measuring reed in his hand. And he was standing in the gateway. **4** And the man said to me, "Son of man, look with your eyes, and hear with your ears, and set your heart upon all that I shall show you, for you were brought here in order that I might show it to you. Declare all that you see to the house of Israel."

The East Gate to the Outer Court

5 And behold, there was a wall all around the outside of the temple area, and the length of the measuring reed in the man's hand was six long cubits, each being a cubit and a handbreadth in length. So he measured the thickness of the wall, one reed; and the height, one reed. **6** Then he went into the gateway facing east, going up its steps, and measured the threshold of the

gate, one reed deep. **7** And the side rooms, one reed long and one reed broad; and the space between the side rooms, five cubits; and the threshold of the gate by the vestibule of the gate at the inner end, one reed. **8** Then he measured the vestibule of the gateway, on the inside, one reed. **9** Then he measured the vestibule of the gateway, eight cubits; and its jambs, two cubits; and the vestibule of the gate was at the inner end. **10** And there were three side rooms on either side of the east gate. The three were of the same size, and the jambs on either side were of the same size. **11** Then he measured the width of the opening of the gateway, ten cubits; and the length of the gateway, thirteen cubits. **12** There was a barrier before the side rooms, one cubit on either side. And the side rooms were six cubits on either side. **13** Then he measured the gate from the ceiling of the

one side room to the ceiling of the other, a breadth of twenty-five cubits; the openings faced each other. **14** He measured also the vestibule, twenty cubits. And around the vestibule of the gateway was the court. **15** From the front of the gate at the entrance to the front of the inner vestibule of the gate was fifty cubits. **16** And the gateway had windows all around, narrowing inwards toward the side rooms and toward their jambs, and likewise the vestibule had windows all around inside, and on the jambs were palm trees.

The Outer Court

17 Then he brought me into the outer court. And behold, there were chambers and a pavement, all around the court. Thirty chambers faced the pavement. **18** And the pavement ran along the side of the gates, corresponding to the length of the gates. This was the lower pavement. **19** Then he measured the distance from the inner front of the lower gate to the outer front of the inner court, a hundred cubits on the east side and on the north side.

The North Gate

²⁰ As for the gate that faced toward the north, belonging to the outer court, he measured its length and its breadth. ²¹ Its side rooms, three on either side, and its jambs and its vestibule were of the same size as those of the first gate. Its length was fifty cubits, and its breadth twenty-five cubits. ²² And its windows, its vestibule, and its palm trees were of the same size as those of the gate that faced toward the east. And by seven steps people would go up to it, and find its vestibule before them. ²³ And opposite the gate on the north, as on the east, was a gate to the inner court. And he measured from gate to gate, a hundred cubits.

The South Gate

²⁴ And he led me toward the south, and behold, there was a gate on the south. And he measured its jambs and its vestibule; they had the same size as the others. ²⁵ Both it and its vestibule had windows all around, like the windows of the others. Its length was fifty cubits, and its breadth twenty-five cubits. ²⁶ And there were seven steps leading up to it, and its vestibule was before them, and it had palm trees on its jambs, one on either side. ²⁷ And there was a gate on the south of the inner court. And he measured from gate to gate toward the south, a hundred cubits.

The Inner Court

²⁸ Then he brought me to the inner court through the south gate, and he measured the south gate. It was of the same size as the others. ²⁹ Its side rooms, its jambs, and its vestibule were of the same size as the others, and both it and its vestibule had windows all around. Its length was fifty cubits, and its breadth twenty-five cubits. ³⁰ And there were vestibules all around, twenty-five cubits long and five cubits broad. ³¹ Its vestibule faced the outer court, and palm trees were on its jambs, and its stairway had eight steps.

³² Then he brought me to the inner court on the east side, and he measured the gate. It was of the same size as the others. ³³ Its side rooms, its jambs, and its vestibule were of the same size as the others, and both it

and its vestibule had windows all around. Its length was fifty cubits, and its breadth twenty-five cubits. ³⁴ Its vestibule faced the outer court, and it had palm trees on its jambs, on either side, and its stairway had eight steps.

³⁵ Then he brought me to the north gate, and he measured it. It had the same size as the others. ³⁶ Its side rooms, its jambs, and its vestibule were of the same size as the others, and it had windows all around. Its length was fifty cubits, and its breadth twenty-five cubits. ³⁷ Its vestibule faced the outer court, and it had palm trees on its jambs, on either side, and its stairway had eight steps.

³⁸ There was a chamber with its door in the vestibule of the gate, where the burnt offering was to be washed. ³⁹ And in the vestibule of the gate were two tables on either side, on which the burnt offering and the sin offering and the guilt offering were to be slaughtered. ⁴⁰ And off to the side, on the outside as one goes up to the entrance of the north gate, were two tables; and off to the other side of the vestibule of the gate were two tables. ⁴¹ Four tables were on either side of the gate, eight tables, on which to slaughter. ⁴² And there were four tables of hewn stone for the burnt offering, a cubit and a half long, and a cubit and a half broad, and one cubit high, on which the instruments were to be laid with which the burnt offerings and the sacrifices were slaughtered. ⁴³ And hooks, a handbreadth long, were fastened all around within. And on the tables the flesh of the offering was to be laid.

Chambers for the Priests

⁴⁴ On the outside of the inner gateway there were two chambers in the inner court, one at the side of the north gate facing south, the other at the side of the south gate facing north. ⁴⁵ And he said to me, "This chamber that faces south is for the priests who have charge of the temple, ⁴⁶ and the chamber that faces north is for the priests who have charge of the altar. These are the sons of Zadok, who alone among the sons of Levi may come near to the LORD to minister to him." ⁴⁷ And he measured the court, a hundred cubits long and a hundred cubits broad, a square. And the altar was in front of the temple.

The Vestibule of the Temple

⁴⁸ Then he brought me to the vestibule of the temple and measured the jambs of the vestibule, five cubits on either side. And the breadth of the gate was fourteen cubits, and the sidewalls of the gate were three cubits on either side. ⁴⁹ The length of the vestibule was twenty cubits, and the breadth twelve cubits, and people would go up to it by ten steps. And there were pillars beside the jambs, one on either side.

The Inner Temple

41 Then he brought me to the nave and measured the jambs. On each side six cubits was the breadth of the jambs. ² And the breadth of the entrance was ten cubits, and the sidewalls of the entrance were five cubits on either side. And he measured the length of the nave, forty cubits, and its breadth, twenty cubits. ³ Then he went into the inner room and measured the jambs of the entrance, two cubits; and the entrance, six cubits; and the sidewalls on either side of the entrance, seven cubits. ⁴ And he measured the length of the room, twenty cubits, and its breadth, twenty cubits, across the nave. And he said to me, "This is the Most Holy Place."

⁵ Then he measured the wall of the temple, six cubits thick, and the breadth of the side chambers, four cubits, all around the temple. ⁶ And the side chambers were in three stories, one over another, thirty in each story. There were offsets all around the wall of the temple to serve as supports for the side chambers, so that they should not be supported by the wall of the temple. ⁷ And it became broader as it wound upward to the side chambers, because the temple was enclosed upward all around the temple. Thus the temple had a broad area upward, and so one went up from the lowest story to the top story through the middle story. ⁸ I saw also that the temple had a raised platform all around; the foundations of the side chambers measured a full reed of six long cubits. ⁹ The thickness of the outer wall of the side chambers was five cubits. The free space between the side chambers of the temple and the ¹⁰ other chambers was a breadth of twenty cubits all around the temple on every side. ¹¹ And the doors of the side chambers opened on the free space, one door toward the north, and another door toward the south. And the breadth of the free space was five cubits all around.

¹² The building that was facing the separate yard on the west side was seventy cubits broad, and the wall of the building was five cubits thick all around, and its length ninety cubits.

¹³ Then he measured the temple, a hundred cubits long; and the yard and the building with its walls, a hundred cubits long; ¹⁴ also the breadth of the east front of the temple and the yard, a hundred cubits.

¹⁵ Then he measured the length of the building facing the yard that was at the back and its galleries on either side, a hundred cubits.

The inside of the nave and the vestibules of the court, ¹⁶ the thresholds and the narrow windows and the galleries all around the three of them, opposite the threshold, were paneled with wood all around, from the floor up to the windows (now the windows were covered), ¹⁷ to the space above the door, even to the inner room, and on the outside. And on all the walls all around, inside and outside, was a measured pattern. ¹⁸ It was carved of cherubim and palm trees, a palm tree between cherub and cherub. Every cherub had two faces: ¹⁹ a human face toward the palm tree on the one side, and the face of a young lion toward the palm tree on the other side. They were carved on the whole temple all around. ²⁰ From the floor to above the door, cherubim and palm trees were carved; similarly the wall of the nave.

²¹ The doorposts of the nave were squared, and in front of the Holy Place was something resembling ²² an altar of wood, three cubits high, two cubits long, and two cubits broad. Its corners, its base, and its walls were of wood. He said to me, "This is the table that is before the LORD." ²³ The nave and the Holy Place had each a double door. ²⁴ The double doors had two leaves apiece, two swinging leaves for each door. ²⁵ And on the doors of the nave were carved cherubim and palm trees, such as were carved on the walls. And there was a canopy of wood in front of the vestibule outside. ²⁶ And there were narrow windows and palm trees on either side, on the sidewalls of the vestibule, the side chambers of the temple, and the canopies.

The Temple's Chambers

42 Then he led me out into the outer court, toward the north, and he brought me to the chambers that were opposite the separate yard and opposite the building on the north. ² The length of the building whose door faced north was a hundred cubits, and the breadth fifty cubits. ³ Facing the twenty cubits that belonged to the inner court, and facing the pavement that belonged to the outer court, was gallery against gallery in three stories. ⁴ And before the chambers was a passage inward, ten cubits wide and a hundred cubits long, and their doors were on the north. ⁵ Now the upper chambers were narrower, for the galleries took more away from them than from the lower and middle chambers of the building. ⁶ For they were in three stories,

---

GETTING THE MESSAGE

The Lord returns to his temple. Because of the people's rebellion, the glory of the Lord departed from the temple in Ezekiel's vision (10:18–22). But later Ezekiel has a vision in which God returns to the temple (43:1–5), beginning a new era in his relationship with his people. In the New Testament, the apostle Paul teaches that those who believe in Christ are the "temple" in which God is pleased to dwell (1 Cor. 3:16).

---

and they had no pillars like the pillars of the courts. Thus the upper chambers were set back from the ground more than the lower and the middle ones. ⁷ And there was a wall outside parallel to the chambers, toward the outer court, opposite the chambers, fifty cubits long. ⁸ For the chambers on the outer court were fifty cubits long, while those opposite the nave were a hundred cubits long. ⁹ Below these chambers was an entrance on the east side, as one enters them from the outer court.

¹⁰ In the thickness of the wall of the court, on the south also, opposite the yard and opposite the building, there were chambers ¹¹ with a passage in front of them. They were similar to the chambers on the north, of the same length and breadth, with the same exits and arrangements and doors,

¹² as were the entrances of the chambers on the south. There was an entrance at the beginning of the passage, the passage before the corresponding wall on the east as one enters them.

¹³ Then he said to me, "The north chambers and the south chambers opposite the yard are the holy chambers, where the priests who approach the LORD shall eat the most holy offerings. There they shall put the most holy offerings—the grain offering, the sin offering, and the guilt offering—for the place is holy. ¹⁴ When the priests enter the Holy Place, they shall not go out of it into the outer court without laying there the garments in which they minister, for these are holy. They shall put on other garments before they go near to that which is for the people."

¹⁵ Now when he had finished measuring the interior of the temple area, he led me out by the gate that faced east, and measured the temple area all around. ¹⁶ He measured the east side with the measuring reed, 500 cubits by the measuring reed all around. ¹⁷ He measured the north side, 500 cubits by the measuring reed all around. ¹⁸ He measured the south side, 500 cubits by the measuring reed. ¹⁹ Then he turned to the west side and measured, 500 cubits by the measuring reed. ²⁰ He measured it on the four sides. It had a wall around it, 500 cubits long and 500 cubits broad, to make a separation between the holy and the common.

The Glory of the LORD Fills the Temple

43 Then he led me to the gate, the gate facing east. ² And behold, the glory of the God of Israel was coming from the east. And the sound of his coming was like the sound of many waters, and the earth shone with his glory. ³ And the vision I saw was just like the vision that I had seen when he came to destroy the city, and just like the vision that I had seen by the Chebar canal. And I fell on my face. ⁴ As the glory of the LORD entered the temple by the gate facing east, ⁵ the Spirit lifted me up and brought me into the inner court; and behold, the glory of the LORD filled the temple.

⁶ While the man was standing beside me, I heard one speaking to me out of the temple, ⁷ and he said to me, "Son of man, this is the place of my throne and the place of the soles of my feet, where I will dwell in the

midst of the people of Israel forever. And the house of Israel shall no more defile my holy name, neither they, nor their kings, by their whoring and by the dead bodies of their kings at their high places, ⁸ by setting their threshold by my threshold and their doorposts beside my doorposts, with only a wall between me and them. They have defiled my holy name by their abominations that they have committed, so I have consumed them in my anger. ⁹ Now let them put away their whoring and the dead bodies of their kings far from me, and I will dwell in their midst forever.

¹⁰ "As for you, son of man, describe to the house of Israel the temple, that they may be ashamed of their iniquities; and they shall measure the plan. ¹¹ And if they are ashamed of all that they have done, make known to them the design of the temple, its arrangement, its exits and its entrances, that is, its whole design; and make known to them as well all its statutes and its whole design and all its laws, and write it down in their sight, so that they may observe all its laws and all its statutes and carry them out. ¹² This is the law of the temple: the whole territory on the top of the mountain all around shall be most holy. Behold, this is the law of the temple.

The Altar

¹³ "These are the measurements of the altar by cubits (the cubit being a cubit and a handbreadth): its base shall be one cubit high and one cubit broad, with a rim of one span around its edge. And this shall be the height of the altar: ¹⁴ from the base on the ground to the lower ledge, two cubits, with a breadth of one cubit; and from the smaller ledge to the larger ledge, four cubits, with a breadth of one cubit; ¹⁵ and the altar hearth, four cubits; and from the altar hearth projecting upward, four horns. ¹⁶ The altar hearth shall be square, twelve cubits long by twelve cubits broad. ¹⁷ The ledge also shall be square, fourteen cubits long by fourteen broad, with a rim around it half a cubit broad, and its base one cubit all around. The steps of the altar shall face east."

¹⁸ And he said to me, "Son of man, thus says the Lord GOD: These are the ordinances for the altar: On the day when it is erected for offering burnt offerings upon it and for throwing blood against it, ¹⁹ you shall give to the Levitical priests of the family of Zadok,

who draw near to me to minister to me, declares the Lord GOD, a bull from the herd for a sin offering. ²⁰ And you shall take some of its blood and put it on the four horns of the altar and on the four corners of the ledge and upon the rim all around. Thus you shall purify the altar and make atonement for it. ²¹ You shall also take the bull of the sin offering, and it shall be burned in the appointed place belonging to the temple, outside the sacred area. ²² And on the second day you shall offer a male goat without blemish for a sin offering; and the altar shall be purified, as it was purified with the bull. ²³ When you have finished purifying it, you shall offer a bull from the herd without blemish and a ram from the flock without blemish. ²⁴ You shall present them before the LORD, and the priests shall sprinkle salt on them and offer them up as a burnt offering to the LORD.

> ### GETTING THE MESSAGE
>
> **The prince** (44:3) in the visions of restoration is also called God's servant David (34:23–24; 37:24–25). This prince will rule over God's people forever. Jesus' followers viewed him as this promised ruler (Matt. 1:1; Luke 18:38).

²⁵ For seven days you shall provide daily a male goat for a sin offering; also, a bull from the herd and a ram from the flock, without blemish, shall be provided. ²⁶ Seven days shall they make atonement for the altar and cleanse it, and so consecrate it. ²⁷ And when they have completed these days, then from the eighth day onward the priests shall offer on the altar your burnt offerings and your peace offerings, and I will accept you, declares the Lord GOD."

The Gate for the Prince

44 Then he brought me back to the outer gate of the sanctuary, which faces east. And it was shut. ² And the LORD said to me, "This gate shall remain shut; it shall not be opened, and no one shall enter by it, for the LORD, the God of Israel, has entered by it. Therefore it shall remain shut. ³ Only the prince may sit in it to eat bread before the LORD. He shall enter by way of the vestibule of the gate, and shall go out by the same way."

⁴ Then he brought me by way of the north gate to the front of the temple, and I looked, and behold, the glory of the LORD filled the temple of the LORD. And I fell on my face. ⁵ And the LORD said to me, "Son of man, mark well, see with your eyes, and hear with your ears all that I shall tell you concerning all the statutes of the temple of the LORD and all its laws. And mark well the entrance to the temple and all the exits from the sanctuary. ⁶ And say to the rebellious house, to the house of Israel, Thus says the Lord GOD: O house of Israel, enough of all your abominations, ⁷ in admitting foreigners, uncircumcised in heart and flesh, to be in my sanctuary, profaning my temple, when you offer to me my food, the fat and the blood. You have broken my covenant, in addition to all your abominations. ⁸ And you have not kept charge of my holy things, but you have set others to keep my charge for you in my sanctuary.

⁹ "Thus says the Lord GOD: No foreigner, uncircumcised in heart and flesh, of all the foreigners who are among the people of Israel, shall enter my sanctuary. ¹⁰ But the Levites who went far from me, going astray from me after their idols when Israel went astray, shall bear their punishment. ¹¹ They shall be ministers in my sanctuary, having oversight at the gates of the temple and ministering in the temple. They shall slaughter the burnt offering and the sacrifice for the people, and they shall stand before the people, to minister to them. ¹² Because they ministered to them before their idols and became a stumbling block of iniquity to the house of Israel, therefore I have sworn concerning them, declares the Lord GOD, and they shall bear their punishment. ¹³ They shall not come near to me, to serve me as priest, nor come near any of my holy things and the things that are most holy, but they shall bear their shame and the abominations that they have committed. ¹⁴ Yet I will appoint them to keep charge of the temple, to do all its service and all that is to be done in it.

Rules for Levitical Priests

¹⁵ "But the Levitical priests, the sons of Zadok, who kept the charge of my sanctuary when the people of Israel went astray from me, shall come near to me to minister to me. And they shall stand before me to offer me the fat and the blood, declares the Lord GOD. ¹⁶ They shall enter my sanctuary, and they shall approach my table, to minister to me, and they shall keep my charge. ¹⁷ When they enter the gates of the inner court, they shall wear linen garments. They shall have nothing of wool on them, while they minister at the gates of the inner court, and within. ¹⁸ They shall have linen turbans on their heads, and linen undergarments around their waists. They shall not bind themselves with anything that causes sweat. ¹⁹ And when they go out into the outer court to the people, they shall put off the garments in which they have been ministering and lay them in the holy chambers. And they shall put on other garments, lest they transmit holiness to the people with their garments. ²⁰ They shall not shave their heads or let their locks grow long; they shall surely trim the hair of their heads. ²¹ No priest shall drink wine when he enters the inner court. ²² They shall not marry a widow or a divorced woman, but only virgins of the offspring of the house of Israel, or a widow who is the widow of a priest. ²³ They shall teach my people the difference between the holy and the common, and show them how to distinguish between the unclean and the clean. ²⁴ In a dispute, they shall act as judges, and they shall judge it according to my judgments. They shall keep my laws and my statutes in all my appointed feasts, and they shall keep my Sabbaths holy. ²⁵ They shall not defile themselves by going near to a dead person. However, for father or mother, for son or daughter, for brother or unmarried sister they may defile themselves. ²⁶ After he[1] has become clean, they shall count seven days for him. ²⁷ And on the day that he goes into the Holy Place, into the inner court, to minister in the Holy Place, he shall offer his sin offering, declares the Lord GOD.

²⁸ "This shall be their inheritance: I am their inheritance: and you shall give them no possession in Israel; I am their possession. ²⁹ They shall eat the grain offering, the sin offering, and the guilt offering, and every devoted thing in Israel shall be theirs. ³⁰ And the first of all the firstfruits of all kinds, and every offering of all kinds from

---

[1] That is, a priest

all your offerings, shall belong to the priests. You shall also give to the priests the first of your dough, that a blessing may rest on your house. ³¹ The priests shall not eat of anything, whether bird or beast, that has died of itself or is torn by wild animals.

The Holy District

45 "When you allot the land as an inheritance, you shall set apart for the LORD a portion of the land as a holy district, 25,000 cubits long and 20,000 cubits broad. It shall be holy throughout its whole extent. ² Of this a square plot of 500 by 500 cubits shall be for the sanctuary, with fifty cubits for an open space around it. ³ And from this measured district you shall measure off a section 25,000 cubits long and 10,000 broad, in which shall be the sanctuary, the Most Holy Place. ⁴ It shall be the holy portion of the land. It shall be for the priests, who minister in the sanctuary and approach the LORD to minister to him, and it shall be a place for their houses and a holy place for the sanctuary. ⁵ Another section, 25,000 cubits long and 10,000 cubits broad, shall be for the Levites who minister at the temple, as their possession for cities to live in.

⁶ "Alongside the portion set apart as the holy district you shall assign for the property of the city an area 5,000 cubits broad and 25,000 cubits long. It shall belong to the whole house of Israel.

The Portion for the Prince

⁷ "And to the prince shall belong the land on both sides of the holy district and the property of the city, alongside the holy district and the property of the city, on the west and on the east, corresponding in length to one of the tribal portions, and extending from the western to the eastern boundary ⁸ of the land. It is to be his property in Israel. And my princes shall no more oppress my people, but they shall let the house of Israel have the land according to their tribes.

⁹ "Thus says the Lord GOD: Enough, O princes of Israel! Put away violence and oppression, and execute justice and righteousness. Cease your evictions of my people, declares the Lord GOD.

¹⁰ "You shall have just balances, a just ephah, and a just bath. ¹¹ The ephah and the bath shall be of the same measure, the bath containing one tenth of a homer, and the ephah one tenth of a homer; the homer shall be the standard measure. ¹² The shekel shall be twenty gerahs; twenty shekels plus twenty-five shekels plus fifteen shekels shall be your mina.

¹³ "This is the offering that you shall make: one sixth of an ephah from each homer of wheat, and one sixth of an ephah from each homer of barley, ¹⁴ and as the fixed portion of oil, measured in baths, one tenth of a bath from each cor (the cor, like the homer, contains ten baths). ¹⁵ And one sheep from every flock of two hundred, from the watering places of Israel for grain offering, burnt offering, and peace offerings, to make atonement for them, declares the Lord GOD. ¹⁶ All the people of the land shall be obliged to give this offering to the prince in Israel. ¹⁷ It shall be the prince's duty to furnish the burnt offerings, grain offerings, and drink offerings, at the feasts, the new moons, and the Sabbaths, all the appointed feasts of the house of Israel: he shall provide the sin offerings, grain offerings, burnt offerings, and peace offerings, to make atonement on behalf of the house of Israel.

¹⁸ "Thus says the Lord GOD: In the first month, on the first day of the month, you shall take a bull from the herd without blemish, and purify the sanctuary. ¹⁹ The priest shall take some of the blood of the sin offering and put it on the doorposts of the temple, the four corners of the ledge of the altar, and the posts of the gate of the inner court. ²⁰ You shall do the same on the seventh day of the month for anyone who has sinned through error or ignorance; so you shall make atonement for the temple.

²¹ "In the first month, on the fourteenth day of the month, you shall celebrate the Feast of the Passover, and for seven days unleavened bread shall be eaten. ²² On that day the prince shall provide for himself and all the people of the land a young bull for a sin offering. ²³ And on the seven days of the festival he shall provide as a burnt offering to the LORD seven young bulls and seven rams without blemish, on each of the seven days; and a male goat daily for a sin offering. ²⁴ And he shall provide as a grain offering an ephah for each bull, an ephah for each ram, and a hin of oil to each ephah. ²⁵ In the seventh month, on the fifteenth day of the month and for the seven days of the feast,

he shall make the same provision for sin offerings, burnt offerings, and grain offerings, and for the oil.

The Prince and the Feasts

46 "Thus says the Lord GOD: The gate of the inner court that faces east shall be shut on the six working days, but on the Sabbath day it shall be opened, and on the day of the new moon it shall be opened. ² The prince shall enter by the vestibule of the gate from outside, and shall take his stand by the post of the gate. The priests shall offer his burnt offering and his peace offerings, and he shall worship at the threshold of the gate. Then he shall go out, but the gate shall not be shut until evening. ³ The people of the land shall bow down at the entrance of that gate before the LORD on the Sabbaths and on the new moons. ⁴ The burnt offering that the prince

> ### GETTING THE MESSAGE
>
> The **Passover** described by Ezekiel is quite different than the one first observed in Exodus 12. The original Passover was a time to remember how death had passed over the Israelites before their exodus from Egypt. This new Passover emphasizes offerings to atone for sin (45:21–24).

offers to the LORD on the Sabbath day shall be six lambs without blemish and a ram without blemish. ⁵ And the grain offering with the ram shall be an ephah, and the grain offering with the lambs shall be as much as he is able, together with a hin of oil to each ephah. ⁶ On the day of the new moon he shall offer a bull from the herd without blemish, and six lambs and a ram, which shall be without blemish. ⁷ As a grain offering he shall provide an ephah with the bull and an ephah with the ram, and with the lambs as much as he is able, together with a hin of oil to each ephah. ⁸ When the prince enters, he shall enter by the vestibule of the gate, and he shall go out by the same way.

⁹ "When the people of the land come before the LORD at the appointed feasts, he who enters by the north gate to worship shall go out by the south gate, and he who

enters by the south gate shall go out by the north gate: no one shall return by way of the gate by which he entered, but each shall go out straight ahead. ¹⁰ When they enter, the prince shall enter with them, and when they go out, he shall go out.

¹¹ "At the feasts and the appointed festivals, the grain offering with a young bull shall be an ephah, and with a ram an ephah, and with the lambs as much as one is able to give, together with a hin of oil to an ephah. ¹² When the prince provides a freewill offering, either a burnt offering or peace offerings as a freewill offering to the LORD, the gate facing east shall be opened for him. And he shall offer his burnt offering or his peace offerings as he does on the Sabbath day. Then he shall go out, and after he has gone out the gate shall be shut.

¹³ "You shall provide a lamb a year old without blemish for a burnt offering to the LORD daily; morning by morning you shall provide it. ¹⁴ And you shall provide a grain offering with it morning by morning, one sixth of an ephah, and one third of a hin of oil to moisten the flour, as a grain offering to the LORD. This is a perpetual statute. ¹⁵ Thus the lamb and the meal offering and the oil shall be provided, morning by morning, for a regular burnt offering.

¹⁶ "Thus says the Lord GOD: If the prince makes a gift to any of his sons as his inheritance, it shall belong to his sons. It is their property by inheritance. ¹⁷ But if he makes a gift out of his inheritance to one of his servants, it shall be his to the year of liberty. Then it shall revert to the prince; surely it is his inheritance—it shall belong to his sons. ¹⁸ The prince shall not take any of the inheritance of the people, thrusting them out of their property. He shall give his sons their inheritance out of his own property, so that none of my people shall be scattered from his property."

Boiling Places for Offerings

¹⁹ Then he brought me through the entrance, which was at the side of the gate, to the north row of the holy chambers for the priests, and behold, a place was there at the extreme western end of them. ²⁰ And he said to me, "This is the place where the priests shall boil the guilt offering and the sin offering, and where they shall bake the grain offering, in order not to bring them

out into the outer court and so transmit holiness to the people."

²¹ Then he brought me out to the outer court and led me around to the four corners of the court. And behold, in each corner of the court there was another court — ²² in the four corners of the court were small courts, forty cubits long and thirty broad; the four were of the same size. ²³ On the inside, around each of the four courts was a row of masonry, with hearths made at the bottom of the rows all around. ²⁴ Then he said to me, "These are the kitchens where those who minister at the temple shall boil the sacrifices of the people."

Water Flowing from the Temple

47 Then he brought me back to the door of the temple, and behold, water was issuing from below the threshold of the temple toward the east (for the temple faced east). The water was flowing down from below the south end of the threshold of the temple, south of the altar. ² Then he brought me out by way of the north gate and led me around on the outside to the outer gate that faces toward the east; and behold, the water was trickling out on the south side.

³ Going on eastward with a measuring line in his hand, the man measured a thousand cubits, and then led me through the water, and it was ankle-deep. ⁴ Again he measured a thousand, and led me through the water, and it was knee-deep. Again he measured a thousand, and led me through the water, and it was waist-deep. ⁵ Again he measured a thousand, and it was a river that I could not pass through, for the water had risen. It was deep enough to swim in, a river that could not be passed through. ⁶ And he said to me, "Son of man, have you seen this?"

Then he led me back to the bank of the river. ⁷ As I went back, I saw on the bank of the river very many trees on the one side and on the other. ⁸ And he said to me, "This water flows toward the eastern region and goes down into the Arabah, and enters the sea;[1] when the water flows into the sea, the water will become fresh. ⁹ And wherever the river goes, every living creature that swarms will live, and there will be very many fish. For this water goes there, that the waters of the sea may become fresh; so everything will live

where the river goes. ¹⁰ Fishermen will stand beside the sea. From Engedi to Eneglaim it will be a place for the spreading of nets. Its fish will be of very many kinds, like the fish of the Great Sea.[2] ¹¹ But its swamps and marshes will not become fresh; they are to be left for salt. ¹² And on the banks, on both sides of the river, there will grow all kinds of trees for food. Their leaves will not wither, nor their fruit fail, but they will bear fresh fruit every month, because the water for them flows from the sanctuary. Their fruit will be for food, and their leaves for healing."

Division of the Land

¹³ Thus says the Lord GOD: "This is the boundary by which you shall divide the land for inheritance among the twelve tribes of Israel. Joseph shall have two portions. ¹⁴ And you shall divide equally what I swore to give

---

GETTING THE MESSAGE

The Dead Sea is the saltiest body of water in the world. Nearly 35 percent salt, it is six times saltier than the ocean and twice as salty as the Great Salt Lake in Utah. In Ezekiel's vision, the water from the temple turned the Dead Sea into fresh water (47:8). This is a picture of how the Lord Jesus Christ can give life to those who were dead in sin (Eph. 2:1–5).

---

to your fathers. This land shall fall to you as your inheritance.

¹⁵ "This shall be the boundary of the land: On the north side, from the Great Sea by way of Hethlon to Lebo-hamath, and on to Zedad, ¹⁶ Berothah, Sibraim (which lies on the border between Damascus and Hamath), as far as Hazer-hatticon, which is on the border of Hauran. ¹⁷ So the boundary shall run from the sea to Hazar-enan, which is on the northern border of Damascus, with the border of Hamath to the north. This shall be the north side.

¹⁸ "On the east side, the boundary shall run between Hauran and Damascus; along the Jordan between Gilead and the land of Israel; to the eastern sea and as far as Tamar. This shall be the east side.

¹⁹ "On the south side, it shall run from Tamar as far as the waters of Meribah-

---

[1] That is, the Dead Sea [2] That is, the Mediterranean Sea; also 47:15

kadesh, from there along the Brook of Egypt to the Great Sea.[1] This shall be the south side.

20 "On the west side, the Great Sea shall be the boundary to a point opposite Lebo-hamath. This shall be the west side.

21 "So you shall divide this land among you according to the tribes of Israel. 22 You shall allot it as an inheritance for yourselves and for the sojourners who reside among you and have had children among you. They shall be to you as native-born children of Israel. With you they shall be allotted an inheritance among the tribes of Israel. 23 In whatever tribe the sojourner resides, there you shall assign him his inheritance, declares the Lord GOD.

48 "These are the names of the tribes: Beginning at the northern extreme, beside the way of Hethlon to Lebo-hamath, as far as Hazar-enan (which is on the northern border of Damascus over against Hamath), and extending from the east side to the west, Dan, one portion. 2 Adjoining the territory of Dan, from the east side to the west, Asher, one portion. 3 Adjoining the territory of Asher, from the east side to the west, Naphtali, one portion. 4 Adjoining the territory of Naphtali, from the east side to the west, Manasseh, one portion. 5 Adjoining the territory of Manasseh, from the east side to the west, Ephraim, one portion. 6 Adjoining the territory of Ephraim, from the east side to the west, Reuben, one portion. 7 Adjoining the territory of Reuben, from the east side to the west, Judah, one portion.

8 "Adjoining the territory of Judah, from the east side to the west, shall be the portion which you shall set apart, 25,000 cubits in breadth, and in length equal to one of the tribal portions, from the east side to the west, with the sanctuary in the midst of it. 9 The portion that you shall set apart for the LORD shall be 25,000 cubits in length, and 20,000 in breadth. 10 These shall be the allotments of the holy portion: the priests shall have an allotment measuring 25,000 cubits on the northern side, 10,000 cubits in breadth on the western side, 10,000 in breadth on the eastern side, and 25,000 in length on the southern side, with the sanctuary of the LORD in the midst of it. 11 This shall be for the consecrated priests, the sons of Zadok, who kept my charge, who did not go astray when the people of Israel went astray, as the Levites did. 12 And it shall belong to them as a special portion from the holy portion of the land, a most holy place, adjoining the territory of the Levites. 13 And alongside the territory of the priests, the Levites shall have an allotment 25,000 cubits in length and 10,000 in breadth. The whole length shall be 25,000 cubits and the breadth 20,000. 14 They shall not sell or exchange any of it. They shall not alienate this choice portion of the land, for it is holy to the LORD.

15 "The remainder, 5,000 cubits in breadth and 25,000 in length, shall be for common use for the city, for dwellings and for open country. In the midst of it shall be the city, 16 and these shall be its measurements: the north side 4,500 cubits, the south side 4,500, the east side 4,500, and the west side 4,500. 17 And the city shall have open land: on the north 250 cubits, on the south 250, on the east 250, and on the west 250. 18 The remainder of the length alongside the holy portion shall be 10,000 cubits to the east, and 10,000 to the west, and it shall be alongside the holy portion. Its produce shall be food for the workers of the city. 19 And the workers of the city, from all the tribes of Israel, shall till it. 20 The whole portion that you shall set apart shall be 25,000 cubits square, that is, the holy portion together with the property of the city.

21 "What remains on both sides of the holy portion and of the property of the city shall belong to the prince. Extending from the 25,000 cubits of the holy portion to the east border, and westward from the 25,000 cubits to the west border, parallel to the tribal portions, it shall belong to the prince. The holy portion with the sanctuary of the temple shall be in its midst. 22 It shall be separate from the property of the Levites and the property of the city, which are in the midst of that which belongs to the prince. The portion of the prince shall lie between the territory of Judah and the territory of Benjamin.

23 "As for the rest of the tribes: from the east side to the west, Benjamin, one portion. 24 Adjoining the territory of Benjamin, from the east side to the west, Simeon, one portion. 25 Adjoining the territory of Simeon,

[1] That is, the Mediterranean Sea; also 47:20

from the east side to the west, Issachar, one portion. ²⁶ Adjoining the territory of Issachar, from the east side to the west, Zebulun, one portion. ²⁷ Adjoining the territory of Zebulun, from the east side to the west, Gad, one portion. ²⁸ And adjoining the territory of Gad to the south, the boundary shall run from Tamar to the waters of Meribah-kadesh, from there along the Brook of Egypt to the Great Sea.¹ ²⁹ This is the land that you shall allot as an inheritance among the tribes of Israel, and these are their portions, declares the Lord GOD.

The Gates of the City

³⁰ "These shall be the exits of the city: On the north side, which is to be 4,500 cubits by measure, ³¹ three gates, the gate of Reuben, the gate of Judah, and the gate of Levi, the gates of the city being named after the tribes of Israel. ³² On the east side, which is to be 4,500 cubits, three gates, the gate of Joseph, the gate of Benjamin, and the gate of Dan. ³³ On the south side, which is to be 4,500 cubits by measure, three gates, the gate of Simeon, the gate of Issachar, and the gate of Zebulun. ³⁴ On the west side, which is to be 4,500 cubits, three gates, the gate of Gad, the gate of Asher, and the gate of Naphtali. ³⁵ The circumference of the city shall be 18,000 cubits. And the name of the city from that time on shall be, The LORD Is There."

---

¹ That is, the Mediterranean Sea

INTRODUCTION TO DANIEL

c. 605 B.C.	586 B.C.	538 B.C.	522 B.C.
Prophetic ministry of Daniel begins	Fall of Judah	Decree of Cyrus/ end of exile	Reign of Darius begins

AUTHOR AND DATE

Daniel wrote this book in the sixth century B.C. It records the events of Daniel's life and the visions that he saw from the time of his exile in 605 B.C. (1:1) until 536 B.C., the third year of King Cyrus (10:1).

THEME

The book's central theme is God's sovereignty over history, empires, and kings (2:21; 4:34–37). All the kingdoms of this world will come to an end and will be replaced by the Lord's kingdom, which will never pass away (2:44; 7:27). Though trials and difficulties will continue for God's people up until the end, those who are faithful will be raised to glory, honor, and everlasting life in this final kingdom (12:1–3).

KEY THEMES

1. It is possible to live a faithful life while surrounded by pagan influences, if one serves the Lord wholeheartedly (ch. 1).

2. God can give his faithful servants abilities that cause even unbelievers to appreciate them (chs. 2; 3; 6). Nevertheless, believers should not assume that God will always rescue them from harm (3:16–18).

3. God humbles the proud and raises up the humble. Even the hearts of the greatest kings are under his control (chs. 4; 5).

4. This world will be a place of persecution for God's people, getting worse and worse rather than better and better (chs. 2; 7). The Lord will judge the kingdoms of this world and bring them to an end, replacing them with his own kingdom that will never end. This kingdom will be ruled by "one like a son of man" who comes "with the clouds," a figure who combines human and divine traits (7:13).

5. God is sovereign over the course of history,

even over those who rebel against him and seek to destroy his people (ch. 8).

6. The Babylonian exile was not the end of Israel's history of rebellion and judgment. In the future, Israel would continue to sin against the Lord, and Jerusalem would be handed over to her enemies, who would damage her temple and do other offensive things (chs. 8; 9; 12). Eventually, though, the anointed ruler would come to deliver God's people from their sins (9:24–27).

7. These earthly events are reflections of a great conflict between angelic forces of good and evil (ch. 10). Prayer is a significant weapon in that conflict (9:23).

8. God rules over all of these conflicts and events, he limits the damage they do, and he has a precise timetable for the end of his people's persecutions. At that time he will finally intervene to cleanse and deliver his people (ch. 12).

9. In the meantime, believers must be patient and faithful in a hostile world, looking to the Lord alone for deliverance (11:33–35).

OUTLINE

The book of Daniel is made up of two halves, each of which has its own literary style. The first half (chs. 1–6) contains stories from the lives of Daniel and his three friends, Shadrach, Meshach, and Abednego. They show how God's people should live in a world that is not their home (compare Jer. 29:5–7; Heb. 13:14). The second half of the book (Daniel 7–12) contains apocalyptic visions. They are designed to reassure God's people that, in spite of their present persecution and suffering, God is in control and will ultimately be victorious.

   I. Daniel and the Three Friends at the Babylonian Court (1:1–6:28)

   II. The Visions of Daniel (7:1–12:13)

DANIEL

Daniel Taken to Babylon

1 In the third year of the reign of Jehoiakim king of Judah, Nebuchadnezzar king of Babylon came to Jerusalem and besieged it. ² And the Lord gave Jehoiakim king of Judah into his hand, with some of the vessels of the house of God. And he brought them to the land of Shinar, to the house of his god, and placed the vessels in the treasury of his god. ³ Then the king commanded Ashpenaz, his chief eunuch, to bring some of the people of Israel, both of the royal family and of the nobility, ⁴ youths without blemish, of good appearance and skillful in all wisdom, endowed with knowledge, understanding learning, and competent to stand in the king's palace, and to teach them the literature and language of the Chaldeans. ⁵ The king assigned them a daily portion of the food that the king ate, and of the wine that he drank. They were to be educated for three years, and at the end of that time they were to stand before the king. ⁶ Among these were Daniel, Hananiah, Mishael, and Azariah of the tribe of Judah. ⁷ And the chief of the eunuchs gave them names: Daniel he called Belteshazzar, Hananiah he called Shadrach, Mishael he called Meshach, and Azariah he called Abednego.

Daniel's Faithfulness

⁸ But Daniel resolved that he would not defile himself with the king's food, or with the wine that he drank. Therefore he asked the chief of the eunuchs to allow him not to defile himself. ⁹ And God gave Daniel favor and compassion in the sight of the chief of the eunuchs, ¹⁰ and the chief of the eunuchs said to Daniel, "I fear my lord the king, who assigned your food and your drink; for why should he see that you were in worse condition than the youths who are of your own age? So you would endanger my head with the king." ¹¹ Then Daniel said to the steward whom the chief of the eunuchs had assigned over Daniel, Hananiah, Mishael, and Azariah, ¹² "Test your servants for ten days; let us be given vegetables to eat and water

to drink. ¹³ Then let our appearance and the appearance of the youths who eat the king's food be observed by you, and deal with your servants according to what you see." ¹⁴ So he listened to them in this matter, and tested them for ten days. ¹⁵ At the end of ten days it was seen that they were better in appearance and fatter in flesh than all the youths who ate the king's food. ¹⁶ So the steward took away their food and the wine they were to drink, and gave them vegetables.

¹⁷ As for these four youths, God gave them learning and skill in all literature and wisdom, and Daniel had understanding in

all visions and dreams. ¹⁸ At the end of the time, when the king had commanded that they should be brought in, the chief of the eunuchs brought them in before Nebuchadnezzar. ¹⁹ And the king spoke with them, and among all of them none was found like Daniel, Hananiah, Mishael, and Azariah. Therefore they stood before the king. ²⁰ And in every matter of wisdom and understanding about which the king inquired of them, he found them ten times better than all the magicians and enchanters that were in all his kingdom. ²¹ And Daniel was there until the first year of King Cyrus.

Nebuchadnezzar's Dream

2 In the second year of the reign of Nebuchadnezzar, Nebuchadnezzar had dreams; his spirit was troubled, and his sleep left him. ² Then the king commanded that the magicians, the enchanters, the sorcerers, and the Chaldeans be summoned to

tell the king his dreams. So they came in and stood before the king. ³ And the king said to them, "I had a dream, and my spirit is troubled to know the dream." ⁴ Then the Chaldeans said to the king in Aramaic,¹ "O king, live forever! Tell your servants the dream, and we will show the interpretation." ⁵ The king answered and said to the Chaldeans, "The word from me is firm: if

PROFILE

DANIEL

Daniel was a young man from a noble family who was deported from Judah to Babylon by King Nebuchadnezzar (605 B.C.). The Babylonians trained Daniel for three years in their language and culture. The Lord blessed Daniel with exceptional wisdom in these areas. He also gave Daniel the ability to interpret dreams. When Daniel interpreted a dream for Nebuchadnezzar, the grateful king gave him an important position in the royal court. After the fall of the Babylonian Empire, Daniel served in a similar role in the Medo-Persian Empire that succeeded it (6:28). Daniel was a faithful servant of the Lord who consistently refused to disobey God. At the same time, he remained respectful to those in authority over him. Daniel, along with his friends Shadrach, Meshach, and Abednego, did precisely what God had commanded the exiles to do in Jeremiah 29:7: they were a blessing to their captors while at the same time remaining true to their Lord amid extraordinary pressures.

KEY REFERENCE: DANIEL 1:17–21

you do not make known to me the dream and its interpretation, you shall be torn limb from limb, and your houses shall be laid in ruins. ⁶ But if you show the dream and its interpretation, you shall receive from me gifts and rewards and great honor. Therefore show me the dream and its interpretation." ⁷ They answered a second time and said, "Let the king tell his servants the dream, and

we will show its interpretation." ⁸ The king answered and said, "I know with certainty that you are trying to gain time, because you see that the word from me is firm— ⁹ if you do not make the dream known to me, there is but one sentence for you. You have agreed to speak lying and corrupt words before me till the times change. Therefore tell me the dream, and I shall know that you can show me its interpretation." ¹⁰ The Chaldeans answered the king and said, "There is not a man on earth who can meet the king's demand, for no great and powerful king has asked such a thing of any magician or enchanter or Chaldean. ¹¹ The thing that the king asks is difficult, and no one can show it to the king except the gods, whose dwelling is not with flesh."

¹² Because of this the king was angry and very furious, and commanded that all the

GETTING THE MESSAGE

The dreams of a king (2:1) had significance for his nation as a whole because dreams were thought to be the shadows of future events. If the dreams of a king could be correctly interpreted, then the appropriate actions could be taken to preserve the kingdom.

wise men of Babylon be destroyed. ¹³ So the decree went out, and the wise men were about to be killed; and they sought Daniel and his companions, to kill them. ¹⁴ Then Daniel replied with prudence and discretion to Arioch, the captain of the king's guard, who had gone out to kill the wise men of Babylon. ¹⁵ He declared to Arioch, the king's captain, "Why is the decree of the king so urgent?" Then Arioch made the matter known to Daniel. ¹⁶ And Daniel went in and requested the king to appoint him a time, that he might show the interpretation to the king.

God Reveals Nebuchadnezzar's Dream

¹⁷ Then Daniel went to his house and made the matter known to Hananiah, Mishael, and Azariah, his companions, ¹⁸ and told them to seek mercy from the God of heaven concerning this mystery, so that Daniel and

¹ The text from this point to the end of chapter 7 is in Aramaic

his companions might not be destroyed with the rest of the wise men of Babylon. ¹⁹ Then the mystery was revealed to Daniel in a vision of the night. Then Daniel blessed the God of heaven. ²⁰ Daniel answered and said:

"Blessed be the name of God forever
        and ever,
    to whom belong wisdom and might.
²¹   He changes times and seasons;
        he removes kings and sets up kings;
    he gives wisdom to the wise
        and knowledge to those who have
            understanding;
²²   he reveals deep and hidden things;
        he knows what is in the darkness,
        and the light dwells with him.
²³   To you, O God of my fathers,
        I give thanks and praise,
    for you have given me wisdom and
        might,
    and have now made known to me
        what we asked of you,
    for you have made known to us the
        king's matter."

²⁴ Therefore Daniel went in to Arioch, whom the king had appointed to destroy the wise men of Babylon. He went and said thus to him: "Do not destroy the wise men of Babylon; bring me in before the king, and I will show the king the interpretation."

²⁵ Then Arioch brought in Daniel before the king in haste and said thus to him: "I have found among the exiles from Judah a man who will make known to the king the interpretation." ²⁶ The king declared to Daniel, whose name was Belteshazzar, "Are you able to make known to me the dream that I have seen and its interpretation?" ²⁷ Daniel answered the king and said, "No wise men, enchanters, magicians, or astrologers can show to the king the mystery that the king has asked, ²⁸ but there is a God in heaven who reveals mysteries, and he has made known to King Nebuchadnezzar what will be in the latter days. Your dream and the visions of your head as you lay in bed are these: ²⁹ To you, O king, as you lay in bed came thoughts of what would be after this, and he who reveals mysteries made known to you what is to be. ³⁰ But as for me, this mystery has been revealed to me, not because of any wisdom that I have more than all the living, but in order that the interpretation may be made known to the

king, and that you may know the thoughts of your mind.

Daniel Interprets the Dream

³¹ "You saw, O king, and behold, a great image. This image, mighty and of exceeding brightness, stood before you, and its appearance was frightening. ³² The head of this image was of fine gold, its chest and arms of silver, its middle and thighs of bronze, ³³ its legs of iron, its feet partly of iron and partly of clay. ³⁴ As you looked, a stone was cut out by no human hand, and it struck the image on its feet of iron and clay, and broke them in pieces. ³⁵ Then the iron, the clay, the bronze, the silver, and the gold, all together were broken in pieces, and became like the chaff of the summer threshing floors; and the wind carried them away, so that not a trace of them could be found. But the stone that struck the image became a great mountain and filled the whole earth.

> ### GETTING THE MESSAGE
>
> **Daniel's languages.** The book of Daniel was written in both Hebrew (1:1–2:3; 7:1–12:13) and Aramaic (2:4–7:28). In Old Testament times, Aramaic was the language used by several people groups in the Middle East (see 2 Kings 18:26).

³⁶ "This was the dream. Now we will tell the king its interpretation. ³⁷ You, O king, the king of kings, to whom the God of heaven has given the kingdom, the power, and the might, and the glory, ³⁸ and into whose hand he has given, wherever they dwell, the children of man, the beasts of the field, and the birds of the heavens, making you rule over them all—you are the head of gold. ³⁹ Another kingdom inferior to you shall arise after you, and yet a third kingdom of bronze, which shall rule over all the earth. ⁴⁰ And there shall be a fourth kingdom, strong as iron, because iron breaks to pieces and shatters all things. And like iron that crushes, it shall break and crush all these. ⁴¹ And as you saw the feet and toes, partly of potter's clay and partly of iron, it shall be a divided kingdom, but some of the firmness of iron shall be in it, just as you saw iron mixed with the soft clay. ⁴² And as the toes

of the feet were partly iron and partly clay, so the kingdom shall be partly strong and partly brittle. **43** As you saw the iron mixed with soft clay, so they will mix with one another in marriage, but they will not hold together, just as iron does not mix with clay. **44** And in the days of those kings the God of heaven will set up a kingdom that shall never be destroyed, nor shall the kingdom be left to another people. It shall break in pieces all

---

PROFILE
SHADRACH, MESHACH, AND ABEDNEGO

Shadrach, Meshach, and Abednego were Jewish exiles and friends of Daniel in Babylon. As he did for Daniel, God gave them a remarkable understanding of Babylonian literature and culture. They, too, were given positions of great leadership in Babylon. Shadrach, Meshach, and Abednego were always faithful to God and trusted him entirely. While they showed deep respect for King Nebuchadnezzar, they were unwilling to follow any orders that would mean compromising their faith. When commanded to worship a golden image, they refused to do so, even though it meant being cast into a fiery furnace. The three men assured Nebuchadnezzar that their God was able to save them from the furnace, but that even if he chose not to save them, they would still not deny him.

KEY REFERENCE: DANIEL 3:16–18

---

these kingdoms and bring them to an end, and it shall stand forever, **45** just as you saw that a stone was cut from a mountain by no human hand, and that it broke in pieces the iron, the bronze, the clay, the silver, and the gold. A great God has made known to the king what shall be after this. The dream is certain, and its interpretation sure."

Daniel Is Promoted

46 Then King Nebuchadnezzar fell upon his face and paid homage to Daniel, and

commanded that an offering and incense be offered up to him. **47** The king answered and said to Daniel, "Truly, your God is God of gods and Lord of kings, and a revealer of mysteries, for you have been able to reveal this mystery." **48** Then the king gave Daniel high honors and many great gifts, and made him ruler over the whole province of Babylon and chief prefect over all the wise men of Babylon. **49** Daniel made a request of the king, and he appointed Shadrach, Meshach, and Abednego over the affairs of the province of Babylon. But Daniel remained at the king's court.

Nebuchadnezzar's Golden Image

3 King Nebuchadnezzar made an image of gold, whose height was sixty cubits and its breadth six cubits. He set it up on the plain of Dura, in the province of Babylon. **2** Then King Nebuchadnezzar sent to gather the satraps, the prefects, and the governors, the counselors, the treasurers, the justices, the magistrates, and all the officials of the provinces to come to the dedication of the image that King Nebuchadnezzar had set up. **3** Then the satraps, the prefects, and the governors, the counselors, the treasurers, the justices, the magistrates, and all the officials of the provinces gathered for the dedication of the image that King Nebuchadnezzar had set up. And they stood before the image that Nebuchadnezzar had set up. **4** And the herald proclaimed aloud, "You are commanded, O peoples, nations, and languages, **5** that when you hear the sound of the horn, pipe, lyre, trigon, harp, bagpipe, and every kind of music, you are to fall down and worship the golden image that King Nebuchadnezzar has set up. **6** And whoever does not fall down and worship shall immediately be cast into a burning fiery furnace." **7** Therefore, as soon as all the peoples heard the sound of the horn, pipe, lyre, trigon, harp, bagpipe, and every kind of music, all the peoples, nations, and languages fell down and worshiped the golden image that King Nebuchadnezzar had set up.

The Fiery Furnace

8 Therefore at that time certain Chaldeans came forward and maliciously accused the Jews. **9** They declared to King Nebuchadnezzar, "O king, live forever! **10** You, O king, have made a decree, that every man who hears the sound of the horn, pipe, lyre, trigon, harp, bagpipe, and every kind of music, shall fall down and worship the golden image. [11] And whoever does not fall down and worship shall be cast into a burning fiery furnace. [12] There are certain Jews whom you have appointed over the affairs of the province of Babylon: Shadrach, Meshach, and Abednego. These men, O king, pay no attention to you; they do not serve your gods or worship the golden image that you have set up."

[13] Then Nebuchadnezzar in furious rage commanded that Shadrach, Meshach, and Abednego be brought. So they brought these men before the king. [14] Nebuchadnezzar answered and said to them, "Is it true, O Shadrach, Meshach, and Abednego, that you do not serve my gods or worship the golden image that I have set up? [15] Now if you are ready when you hear the sound of the horn, pipe, lyre, trigon, harp, bagpipe, and every kind of music, to fall down and worship the image that I have made, well and good. But if you do not worship, you shall immediately be cast into a burning fiery furnace. And who is the god who will deliver you out of my hands?"

[16] Shadrach, Meshach, and Abednego answered and said to the king, "O Nebuchadnezzar, we have no need to answer you in this matter. [17] If this be so, our God whom we serve is able to deliver us from the burning fiery furnace, and he will deliver us out of your hand, O king. [18] But if not, be it known to you, O king, that we will not serve your gods or worship the golden image that you have set up."

[19] Then Nebuchadnezzar was filled with fury, and the expression of his face was changed against Shadrach, Meshach, and Abednego. He ordered the furnace heated seven times more than it was usually heated. [20] And he ordered some of the mighty men of his army to bind Shadrach, Meshach, and Abednego, and to cast them into the burning fiery furnace. [21] Then these men were bound in their cloaks, their tunics, their hats, and their other garments, and they were thrown into the burning fiery furnace. [22] Because the king's order was urgent and the furnace overheated, the flame of the fire killed those men who took up Shadrach, Meshach, and Abednego.

[23] And these three men, Shadrach, Meshach, and Abednego, fell bound into the burning fiery furnace.

[24] Then King Nebuchadnezzar was astonished and rose up in haste. He declared to his counselors, "Did we not cast three men bound into the fire?" They answered and said to the king, "True, O king." [25] He answered and said, "But I see four men unbound, walking in the midst of the fire, and they are not hurt; and the appearance of the fourth is like a son of the gods."

[26] Then Nebuchadnezzar came near to the door of the burning fiery furnace; he declared, "Shadrach, Meshach, and Abednego, servants of the Most High God, come out, and come here!" Then Shadrach, Meshach, and Abednego came out from the fire. [27] And the satraps, the prefects, the governors, and the king's counselors gathered together and saw that the fire had not had any power over the bodies of those men. The hair of their heads was not singed, their cloaks were not harmed, and no smell of fire had come upon them. [28] Nebuchadnezzar answered and said, "Blessed be the God of Shadrach, Meshach, and Abednego, who has sent his angel and delivered his servants, who trusted in him, and set aside the king's command, and yielded up their bodies rather than serve and worship any god except their own God. [29] Therefore I make a decree: Any people, nation, or language that speaks anything against the God of Shadrach, Meshach, and Abednego shall be torn limb from limb, and their houses laid in ruins, for there is no other god who is able to rescue in this way." [30] Then the king promoted Shadrach, Meshach, and Abednego in the province of Babylon.

Nebuchadnezzar Praises God

4 King Nebuchadnezzar to all peoples, nations, and languages, that dwell in all the earth: Peace be multiplied to you! [2] It has seemed good to me to show the signs and wonders that the Most High God has done for me.

[3]   How great are his signs,
         how mighty his wonders!
     His kingdom is an everlasting kingdom,
         and his dominion endures from
         generation to generation.

Nebuchadnezzar's Second Dream

[4] I, Nebuchadnezzar, was at ease in my house and prospering in my palace. [5] I saw a dream that made me afraid. As I lay in bed the fancies and the visions of my head alarmed me. [6] So I made a decree that all the wise men of Babylon should be brought before me, that they might make known to me the interpretation of the dream. [7] Then the magicians, the enchanters, the Chaldeans, and the astrologers came in, and I told them the dream, but they could not make known to me its interpretation. [8] At last Daniel came in before me—he who was named Belteshazzar after the name of my god, and in whom is the spirit of the holy gods—and I told him the dream, saying, [9] "O Belteshazzar, chief of the magicians, because I know that the spirit of the holy gods is in you and that no mystery is too

GETTING THE MESSAGE

A **tree** represents King Nebuchadnezzar in his dream (4:5–27). Trees can symbolize great kingdoms in the Bible. Ezekiel 31:2–9 compares Assyria to a cedar that shelters the nations. Jesus uses a tree to describe God's kingdom (Mark 4:32).

difficult for you, tell me the visions of my dream that I saw and their interpretation. [10] The visions of my head as I lay in bed were these: I saw, and behold, a tree in the midst of the earth, and its height was great. [11] The tree grew and became strong, and its top reached to heaven, and it was visible to the end of the whole earth. [12] Its leaves were beautiful and its fruit abundant, and in it was food for all. The beasts of the field found shade under it, and the birds of the heavens lived in its branches, and all flesh was fed from it.

[13] "I saw in the visions of my head as I lay in bed, and behold, a watcher, a holy one, came down from heaven. [14] He proclaimed aloud and said thus: 'Chop down the tree and lop off its branches, strip off its leaves and scatter its fruit. Let the beasts flee from under it and the birds from its branches. [15] But leave the stump of its roots in the earth, bound with a band of iron and

bronze, amid the tender grass of the field. Let him be wet with the dew of heaven. Let his portion be with the beasts in the grass of the earth. [16] Let his mind be changed from a man's, and let a beast's mind be given to him; and let seven periods of time pass over him. [17] The sentence is by the decree of the watchers, the decision by the word of the holy ones, to the end that the living may know that the Most High rules the kingdom of men and gives it to whom he will and sets over it the lowliest of men.' [18] This dream I, King Nebuchadnezzar, saw. And you, O Belteshazzar, tell me the interpretation, because all the wise men of my kingdom are not able to make known to me the interpretation, but you are able, for the spirit of the holy gods is in you."

Daniel Interprets the Second Dream

[19] Then Daniel, whose name was Belteshazzar, was dismayed for a while, and his thoughts alarmed him. The king answered and said, "Belteshazzar, let not the dream or the interpretation alarm you." Belteshazzar answered and said, "My lord, may the dream be for those who hate you and its interpretation for your enemies! [20] The tree you saw, which grew and became strong, so that its top reached to heaven, and it was visible to the end of the whole earth, [21] whose leaves were beautiful and its fruit abundant, and in which was food for all, under which beasts of the field found shade, and in whose branches the birds of the heavens lived— [22] it is you, O king, who have grown and become strong. Your greatness has grown and reaches to heaven, and your dominion to the ends of the earth. [23] And because the king saw a watcher, a holy one, coming down from heaven and saying, 'Chop down the tree and destroy it, but leave the stump of its roots in the earth, bound with a band of iron and bronze, in the tender grass of the field, and let him be wet with the dew of heaven, and let his portion be with the beasts of the field, till seven periods of time pass over him,' [24] this is the interpretation, O king: It is a decree of the Most High, which has come upon my lord the king, [25] that you shall be driven from among men, and your dwelling shall be with the beasts of the field. You shall be made to eat grass like an ox, and you shall be wet with the dew of heaven, and seven periods of time shall pass

over you, till you know that the Most High rules the kingdom of men and gives it to whom he will. ²⁶ And as it was commanded to leave the stump of the roots of the tree, your kingdom shall be confirmed for you from the time that you know that Heaven rules. ²⁷ Therefore, O king, let my counsel be acceptable to you: break off your sins by practicing righteousness, and your iniquities by showing mercy to the oppressed, that there may perhaps be a lengthening of your prosperity."

Nebuchadnezzar's Humiliation

²⁸ All this came upon King Nebuchadnezzar. ²⁹ At the end of twelve months he was walking on the roof of the royal palace of Babylon, ³⁰ and the king answered and said, "Is not this great Babylon, which I have built by my mighty power as a royal residence and for the glory of my majesty?" ³¹ While the words were still in the king's mouth, there fell a voice from heaven, "O King Nebuchadnezzar, to you it is spoken: The kingdom has departed from you, ³² and you shall be driven from among men, and your dwelling shall be with the beasts of the field. And you shall be made to eat grass like an ox, and seven periods of time shall pass over you, until you know that the Most High rules the kingdom of men and gives it to whom he will." ³³ Immediately the word was fulfilled against Nebuchadnezzar. He was driven from among men and ate grass like an ox, and his body was wet with the dew of heaven till his hair grew as long as eagles' feathers, and his nails were like birds' claws.

Nebuchadnezzar Restored

³⁴ At the end of the days I, Nebuchadnezzar, lifted my eyes to heaven, and my reason returned to me, and I blessed the Most High, and praised and honored him who lives forever,

> for his dominion is an everlasting dominion,
> and his kingdom endures from generation to generation;
> ³⁵ all the inhabitants of the earth are accounted as nothing,
> and he does according to his will among the host of heaven
> and among the inhabitants of the earth;

and none can stay his hand
> or say to him, "What have you done?"

³⁶ At the same time my reason returned to me, and for the glory of my kingdom, my majesty and splendor returned to me. My counselors and my lords sought me, and I was established in my kingdom, and still more greatness was added to me. ³⁷ Now I, Nebuchadnezzar, praise and extol and honor the King of heaven, for all his works are right and his ways are just; and those who walk in pride he is able to humble.

PROFILE
NEBUCHADNEZZAR

Nebuchadnezzar was the powerful King of Babylon who destroyed Jerusalem and deported a number of the city's inhabitants to his own land. When the king had a dream that only Daniel could interpret, he acknowledged the power of Daniel's God. The mighty king had to be brought very low, however, before he turned to the Lord. After failing to heed a warning from God, Nebuchadnezzar was forced to live in the wilderness, where he ate grass and lived like an animal. At the end of God's appointed time of judgment, however, Nebuchadnezzar turned to the Lord and he regained his sanity. God restored his kingdom to him, demonstrating that the Lord is able to humble the proud and exalt the humble. The great and mighty persecutor of Israel, the destroyer of Jerusalem, was humbled by God's grace and brought to confess God's mercy.

KEY REFERENCE: DANIEL 4:28–37

The Handwriting on the Wall

5 King Belshazzar made a great feast for a thousand of his lords and drank wine in front of the thousand.

² Belshazzar, when he tasted the wine, commanded that the vessels of gold and of silver that Nebuchadnezzar his father had taken out of the temple in Jerusalem be brought, that the king and his lords, his wives, and his concubines might drink from

them. ³ Then they brought in the golden vessels that had been taken out of the temple, the house of God in Jerusalem, and the king and his lords, his wives, and his concubines drank from them. ⁴ They drank wine and praised the gods of gold and silver, bronze, iron, wood, and stone.

⁵ Immediately the fingers of a human hand appeared and wrote on the plaster of the wall of the king's palace, opposite the lampstand. And the king saw the hand as it wrote. ⁶ Then the king's color changed, and his thoughts alarmed him; his limbs gave way, and his knees knocked together. ⁷ The king called loudly to bring in the enchanters, the Chaldeans, and the astrologers. The king declared to the wise men of Babylon, "Whoever reads this writing, and shows me its interpretation, shall be clothed with

> ### ▶ GETTING THE MESSAGE
>
> **The city of Babylon** had some of the most impressive buildings of the ancient Near East. It was home to the famous Hanging Gardens, which was one of the Seven Wonders of the Ancient World. Its outer walls were wide enough for chariots driven by four horses to pass each other.

purple and have a chain of gold around his neck and shall be the third ruler in the kingdom." ⁸ Then all the king's wise men came in, but they could not read the writing or make known to the king the interpretation. ⁹ Then King Belshazzar was greatly alarmed, and his color changed, and his lords were perplexed.

¹⁰ The queen, because of the words of the king and his lords, came into the banqueting hall, and the queen declared, "O king, live forever! Let not your thoughts alarm you or your color change. ¹¹ There is a man in your kingdom in whom is the spirit of the holy gods. In the days of your father, light and understanding and wisdom like the wisdom of the gods were found in him, and King Nebuchadnezzar, your father— your father the king—made him chief of the magicians, enchanters, Chaldeans, and astrologers, ¹² because an excellent spirit, knowledge, and understanding to interpret dreams, explain riddles, and solve problems

were found in this Daniel, whom the king named Belteshazzar. Now let Daniel be called, and he will show the interpretation."

Daniel Interprets the Handwriting

¹³ Then Daniel was brought in before the king. The king answered and said to Daniel, "You are that Daniel, one of the exiles of Judah, whom the king my father brought from Judah. ¹⁴ I have heard of you that the spirit of the gods is in you, and that light and understanding and excellent wisdom are found in you. ¹⁵ Now the wise men, the enchanters, have been brought in before me to read this writing and make known to me its interpretation, but they could not show the interpretation of the matter. ¹⁶ But I have heard that you can give interpretations and solve problems. Now if you can read the writing and make known to me its interpretation, you shall be clothed with purple and have a chain of gold around your neck and shall be the third ruler in the kingdom."

¹⁷ Then Daniel answered and said before the king, "Let your gifts be for yourself, and give your rewards to another. Nevertheless, I will read the writing to the king and make known to him the interpretation. ¹⁸ O king, the Most High God gave Nebuchadnezzar your father kingship and greatness and glory and majesty. ¹⁹ And because of the greatness that he gave him, all peoples, nations, and languages trembled and feared before him. Whom he would, he killed, and whom he would, he kept alive; whom he would, he raised up, and whom he would, he humbled. ²⁰ But when his heart was lifted up and his spirit was hardened so that he dealt proudly, he was brought down from his kingly throne, and his glory was taken from him. ²¹ He was driven from among the children of mankind, and his mind was made like that of a beast, and his dwelling was with the wild donkeys. He was fed grass like an ox, and his body was wet with the dew of heaven, until he knew that the Most High God rules the kingdom of mankind and sets over it whom he will. ²² And you his son, Belshazzar, have not humbled your heart, though you knew all this, ²³ but you have lifted up yourself against the Lord of heaven. And the vessels of his house have been brought in before you, and you and your lords, your wives, and your concubines have drunk wine from them. And you

ption and plea before his God. 12 Then they came near and said before the king, concerning the injunction, "O king! Did you not sign an injunction, that anyone who makes petition to any god or man within thirty days, except to you, O king, shall be cast into the den of lions?" The king answered and said, "The thing stands fast, according to the law of the Medes and Persians, which cannot be revoked." 13 Then they answered and said before the king, "Daniel, who is one of the exiles from Judah, pays no attention to you, O king, or the injunction you have signed, but makes his petition three times a day."

14 Then the king, when he heard these words, was much distressed and set his mind to deliver Daniel. And he labored till the sun went down to rescue him. 15 Then these men came by agreement to the king and said to the king, "Know, O king, that it is a law of the Medes and Persians that no injunction or ordinance that the king establishes can be changed."

16 Then the king commanded, and Daniel was brought and cast into the den of lions. The king declared to Daniel, "May your God,

whom you serve continually, deliver you!" [17] And a stone was brought and laid on the mouth of the den, and the king sealed it with his own signet and with the signet of his lords, that nothing might be changed concerning Daniel. [18] Then the king went to his palace and spent the night fasting; no diversions were brought to him, and sleep fled from him.

[19] Then, at break of day, the king arose and went in haste to the den of lions. [20] As he came near to the den where Daniel was, he cried out in a tone of anguish. The king declared to Daniel, "O Daniel, servant of the living God, has your God, whom you serve continually, been able to deliver you from the lions?" [21] Then Daniel said to the king, "O king, live forever! [22] My God sent his angel and shut the lions' mouths, and they have not harmed me, because I was found

---

GETTING THE MESSAGE

Opening the books. Scribes recorded the daily events and activities of royal courts. These writings served as records for the archives and also could provide testimony for court hearings. Daniel's first readers would have understood quite well his vision of God opening the books (7:10).

---

blameless before him; and also before you, O king, I have done no harm." [23] Then the king was exceedingly glad, and commanded that Daniel be taken up out of the den. So Daniel was taken up out of the den, and no kind of harm was found on him, because he had trusted in his God. [24] And the king commanded, and those men who had maliciously accused Daniel were brought and cast into the den of lions—they, their children, and their wives. And before they reached the bottom of the den, the lions overpowered them and broke all their bones in pieces.

[25] Then King Darius wrote to all the peoples, nations, and languages that dwell in all the earth: "Peace be multiplied to you. [26] I make a decree, that in all my royal dominion people are to tremble and fear before the God of Daniel,

for he is the living God,
        enduring forever;

his kingdom shall never be destroyed,
        and his dominion shall be to the end.
[27]   He delivers and rescues;
        he works signs and wonders
            in heaven and on earth,
        he who has saved Daniel
            from the power of the lions."

[28] So this Daniel prospered during the reign of Darius and the reign of Cyrus the Persian.

Daniel's Vision of the Four Beasts

7 In the first year of Belshazzar king of Babylon, Daniel saw a dream and visions of his head as he lay in his bed. Then he wrote down the dream and told the sum of the matter. [2] Daniel declared, "I saw in my vision by night, and behold, the four winds of heaven were stirring up the great sea. [3] And four great beasts came up out of the sea, different from one another. [4] The first was like a lion and had eagles' wings. Then as I looked its wings were plucked off, and it was lifted up from the ground and made to stand on two feet like a man, and the mind of a man was given to it. [5] And behold, another beast, a second one, like a bear. It was raised up on one side. It had three ribs in its mouth between its teeth; and it was told, 'Arise, devour much flesh.' [6] After this I looked, and behold, another, like a leopard, with four wings of a bird on its back. And the beast had four heads, and dominion was given to it. [7] After this I saw in the night visions, and behold, a fourth beast, terrifying and dreadful and exceedingly strong. It had great iron teeth; it devoured and broke in pieces and stamped what was left with its feet. It was different from all the beasts that were before it, and it had ten horns. [8] I considered the horns, and behold, there came up among them another horn, a little one, before which three of the first horns were plucked up by the roots. And behold, in this horn were eyes like the eyes of a man, and a mouth speaking great things.

The Ancient of Days Reigns

[9] "As I looked,

thrones were placed,
        and the Ancient of Days took his
            seat;
his clothing was white as snow,
        and the hair of his head like pure
            wool;

his throne was fiery flames;
    its wheels were burning fire.
10 A stream of fire issued
    and came out from before him;
a thousand thousands served him,
    and ten thousand times ten thou-
        sand stood before him;
the court sat in judgment,
    and the books were opened.

11 "I looked then because of the sound of the great words that the horn was speaking. And as I looked, the beast was killed, and its body destroyed and given over to be burned with fire. 12 As for the rest of the beasts, their dominion was taken away, but their lives were prolonged for a season and a time.

The Son of Man Is Given Dominion

13 "I saw in the night visions,

and behold, with the clouds of heaven
    there came one like a son of man,
and he came to the Ancient of Days
    and was presented before him.
14 And to him was given dominion
    and glory and a kingdom,
that all peoples, nations, and languages
    should serve him;
his dominion is an everlasting
      dominion,
    which shall not pass away,
and his kingdom one
    that shall not be destroyed.

Daniel's Vision Interpreted

15 "As for me, Daniel, my spirit within me was anxious, and the visions of my head alarmed me. 16 I approached one of those who stood there and asked him the truth concerning all this. So he told me and made known to me the interpretation of the things. 17 'These four great beasts are four kings who shall arise out of the earth. 18 But the saints of the Most High shall receive the kingdom and possess the kingdom forever, forever and ever.'

19 "Then I desired to know the truth about the fourth beast, which was different from all the rest, exceedingly terrifying, with its teeth of iron and claws of bronze, and which devoured and broke in pieces and stamped what was left with its feet, 20 and about the ten horns that were on its head, and the other horn that came up and before which three of them fell, the horn that had eyes

and a mouth that spoke great things, and that seemed greater than its companions. 21 As I looked, this horn made war with the saints and prevailed over them, 22 until the Ancient of Days came, and judgment was given for the saints of the Most High, and the time came when the saints possessed the kingdom.

23 "Thus he said: 'As for the fourth beast,

there shall be a fourth kingdom on
    earth,
    which shall be different from all the
      kingdoms,
and it shall devour the whole earth,
    and trample it down, and break it to
      pieces.
24   As for the ten horns,
out of this kingdom ten kings shall
      arise,
    and another shall arise after them;
he shall be different from the former
      ones,
    and shall put down three kings.
25 He shall speak words against the Most
      High,
    and shall wear out the saints of the
      Most High,
    and shall think to change the times
      and the law;
and they shall be given into his hand
    for a time, times, and half a time.
26 But the court shall sit in judgment,
    and his dominion shall be taken
      away,
    to be consumed and destroyed to
      the end.
27 And the kingdom and the dominion
    and the greatness of the kingdoms
      under the whole heaven
shall be given to the people of the
    saints of the Most High;
his kingdom shall be an everlasting
      kingdom,
    and all dominions shall serve and
      obey him.'

28 "Here is the end of the matter. As for me, Daniel, my thoughts greatly alarmed me, and my color changed, but I kept the matter in my heart."

Daniel's Vision of the Ram and the Goat

8 In the third year of the reign of King Belshazzar a vision appeared to me, Daniel, after that which appeared to me at

the first. [2] And I saw in the vision; and when I saw, I was in Susa the citadel, which is in the province of Elam. And I saw in the vision, and I was at the Ulai canal. [3] I raised my eyes and saw, and behold, a ram standing on the bank of the canal. It had two horns, and both horns were high, but one was higher than the other, and the higher one came up last. [4] I saw the ram charging westward and northward and southward. No beast could stand before him, and there was no one who could rescue from his power. He did as he pleased and became great.

[5] As I was considering, behold, a male goat came from the west across the face of the whole earth, without touching the ground. And the goat had a conspicuous horn between his eyes. [6] He came to the ram with the two horns, which I had seen standing on the bank of the canal, and he ran at

him in his powerful wrath. [7] I saw him come close to the ram, and he was enraged against him and struck the ram and broke his two horns. And the ram had no power to stand before him, but he cast him down to the ground and trampled on him. And there was no one who could rescue the ram from his power. [8] Then the goat became exceedingly great, but when he was strong, the great horn was broken, and instead of it there came up four conspicuous horns toward the four winds of heaven.

[9] Out of one of them came a little horn, which grew exceedingly great toward the south, toward the east, and toward the glorious land. [10] It grew great, even to the host of heaven. And some of the host and some of the stars it threw down to the ground and trampled on them. [11] It became great, even as great as the Prince of the host. And the regular burnt offering was taken away

from him, and the place of his sanctuary was overthrown. [12] And a host will be given over to it together with the regular burnt offering because of transgression, and it will throw truth to the ground, and it will act and prosper. [13] Then I heard a holy one speaking, and another holy one said to the one who spoke, "For how long is the vision concerning the regular burnt offering, the transgression that makes desolate, and the giving over of the sanctuary and host to be trampled underfoot?" [14] And he said to me, "For 2,300 evenings and mornings. Then the sanctuary shall be restored to its rightful state."

The Interpretation of the Vision

[15] When I, Daniel, had seen the vision, I sought to understand it. And behold, there stood before me one having the appearance of a man. [16] And I heard a man's voice between the banks of the Ulai, and it called, "Gabriel, make this man understand the vision." [17] So he came near where I stood. And when he came, I was frightened and fell on my face. But he said to me, "Understand, O son of man, that the vision is for the time of the end."

[18] And when he had spoken to me, I fell into a deep sleep with my face to the ground. But he touched me and made me stand up. [19] He said, "Behold, I will make known to you what shall be at the latter end of the indignation, for it refers to the appointed time of the end. [20] As for the ram that you saw with the two horns, these are the kings of Media and Persia. [21] And the goat is the king of Greece. And the great horn between his eyes is the first king. [22] As for the horn that was broken, in place of which four others arose, four kingdoms shall arise from his nation, but not with his power. [23] And at the latter end of their kingdom, when the transgressors have reached their limit, a king of bold face, one who understands riddles, shall arise. [24] His power shall be great—but not by his own power; and he shall cause fearful destruction and shall succeed in what he does, and destroy mighty men and the people who are the saints. [25] By his cunning he shall make deceit prosper under his hand, and in his own mind he shall become great. Without warning he shall destroy many. And he shall even rise up against the Prince of princes, and he shall

be broken—but by no human hand. ²⁶ The vision of the evenings and the mornings that has been told is true, but seal up the vision, for it refers to many days from now."

²⁷ And I, Daniel, was overcome and lay sick for some days. Then I rose and went about the king's business, but I was appalled by the vision and did not understand it.

Daniel's Prayer for His People

9 In the first year of Darius the son of Ahasuerus, by descent a Mede, who was made king over the realm of the Chaldeans— ² in the first year of his reign, I, Daniel, perceived in the books the number of years that, according to the word of the LORD to Jeremiah the prophet, must pass before the end of the desolations of Jerusalem, namely, seventy years.

³ Then I turned my face to the Lord God, seeking him by prayer and pleas for mercy with fasting and sackcloth and ashes. ⁴ I prayed to the LORD my God and made confession, saying, "O Lord, the great and awesome God, who keeps covenant and steadfast love with those who love him and keep his commandments, ⁵ we have sinned and done wrong and acted wickedly and rebelled, turning aside from your commandments and rules. ⁶ We have not listened to your servants the prophets, who spoke in your name to our kings, our princes, and our fathers, and to all the people of the land. ⁷ To you, O Lord, belongs righteousness, but to us open shame, as at this day, to the men of Judah, to the inhabitants of Jerusalem, and to all Israel, those who are near and those who are far away, in all the lands to which you have driven them, because of the treachery that they have committed against you. ⁸ To us, O LORD, belongs open shame, to our kings, to our princes, and to our fathers, because we have sinned against you. ⁹ To the Lord our God belong mercy and forgiveness, for we have rebelled against him ¹⁰ and have not obeyed the voice of the LORD our God by walking in his laws, which he set before us by his servants the prophets. ¹¹ All Israel has transgressed your law and turned aside, refusing to obey your voice. And the curse and oath that are written in the Law of Moses the servant of God have been poured out upon us, because we have sinned against him. ¹² He has confirmed his words, which he spoke against

us and against our rulers who ruled us, by bringing upon us a great calamity. For under the whole heaven there has not been done anything like what has been done against Jerusalem. ¹³ As it is written in the Law of Moses, all this calamity has come upon us; yet we have not entreated the favor of the LORD our God, turning from our iniquities and gaining insight by your truth. ¹⁴ Therefore the LORD has kept ready the calamity and has brought it upon us, for the LORD our God is righteous in all the works that he has done, and we have not obeyed his voice. ¹⁵ And now, O Lord our God, who brought your people out of the land of Egypt with a mighty hand, and have made a name for yourself, as at this day, we have sinned, we have done wickedly.

¹⁶ "O Lord, according to all your righteous acts, let your anger and your wrath turn away from your city Jerusalem, your holy

GETTING THE MESSAGE

Daniel's prayer. Jeremiah prophesied that God would restore his people after 70 years in Babylon (Jer. 25:11–14; 29:10). With this in mind, Daniel prays for Israel's restoration (Dan. 9:1–19).

hill, because for our sins, and for the iniquities of our fathers, Jerusalem and your people have become a byword among all who are around us. ¹⁷ Now therefore, O our God, listen to the prayer of your servant and to his pleas for mercy, and for your own sake, O Lord, make your face to shine upon your sanctuary, which is desolate. ¹⁸ O my God, incline your ear and hear. Open your eyes and see our desolations, and the city that is called by your name. For we do not present our pleas before you because of our righteousness, but because of your great mercy. ¹⁹ O Lord, hear; O Lord, forgive. O Lord, pay attention and act. Delay not, for your own sake, O my God, because your city and your people are called by your name."

Gabriel Brings an Answer

²⁰ While I was speaking and praying, confessing my sin and the sin of my people Israel, and presenting my plea before the LORD my God for the holy hill of my God,

²¹while I was speaking in prayer, the man Gabriel, whom I had seen in the vision at the first, came to me in swift flight at the time of the evening sacrifice. ²²He made me understand, speaking with me and saying, "O Daniel, I have now come out to give you insight and understanding. ²³At the beginning of your pleas for mercy a word went out, and I have come to tell it to you, for you are greatly loved. Therefore consider the word and understand the vision.

The Seventy Weeks

²⁴ "Seventy weeks are decreed about your people and your holy city, to finish the transgression, to put an end to sin, and to atone for iniquity, to bring in everlasting righteousness, to seal both vision and prophet, and to anoint a most holy place. ²⁵ Know therefore and understand that from the going out of the word to restore and build Jerusalem to the coming of an anointed one, a prince, there shall be seven weeks. Then for sixty-two weeks it shall be built again with squares and moat, but in a troubled time. ²⁶ And after the sixty-two weeks, an anointed one shall be cut off and shall have nothing. And the people of the prince who is to come shall destroy the city and the sanctuary. Its end shall come with a flood, and to the end there shall be war. Desolations are decreed. ²⁷ And he shall make a strong covenant with many for one week, and for half of the week he shall put an end to sacrifice and offering. And on the wing of abominations shall come one who makes desolate, until the decreed end is poured out on the desolator."

Daniel's Terrifying Vision of a Man

10 In the third year of Cyrus king of Persia a word was revealed to Daniel, who was named Belteshazzar. And the word was true, and it was a great conflict. And he understood the word and had understanding of the vision.

²In those days I, Daniel, was mourning for three weeks. ³I ate no delicacies, no meat or wine entered my mouth, nor did I anoint myself at all, for the full three weeks. ⁴On the twenty-fourth day of the first month, as I was standing on the bank of the great river (that is, the Tigris) ⁵I lifted up my eyes and looked, and behold, a man clothed in linen, with a belt of fine gold from Uphaz around his waist. ⁶His body was like beryl, his face like the appearance of lightning, his eyes like flaming torches, his arms and legs like the gleam of burnished bronze, and the sound of his words like the sound of a multitude. ⁷And I, Daniel, alone saw the vision, for the men who were with me did not see the vision, but a great trembling fell upon them, and they fled to hide themselves. ⁸So I was left alone and saw this great vision, and no strength was left in me. My radiant appearance was fearfully changed, and I retained no strength. ⁹Then I heard the sound of his words, and as I heard the sound of his words, I fell on my face in deep sleep with my face to the ground.

¹⁰And behold, a hand touched me and set me trembling on my hands and knees. ¹¹And he said to me, "O Daniel, man greatly loved, understand the words that I speak to you, and stand upright, for now I have been sent to you." And when he had spoken this word to me, I stood up trembling. ¹²Then he said to me, "Fear not, Daniel, for from the first day that you set your heart to understand and humbled yourself before your God, your words have been heard, and I have come because of your words. ¹³The prince of the kingdom of Persia withstood me twenty-one days, but Michael, one of the chief princes, came to help me, for I was left there with the kings of Persia, ¹⁴and came to make you understand what is to happen to your people in the latter days. For the vision is for days yet to come."

¹⁵When he had spoken to me according to these words, I turned my face toward the ground and was mute. ¹⁶And behold, one in the likeness of the children of man touched my lips. Then I opened my mouth and spoke. I said to him who stood before me, "O my lord, by reason of the vision pains have come upon me, and I retain no strength. ¹⁷How can my lord's servant talk with my lord? For now no strength remains in me, and no breath is left in me."

¹⁸Again one having the appearance of a man touched me and strengthened me. ¹⁹And he said, "O man greatly loved, fear not, peace be with you; be strong and of good courage." And as he spoke to me, I was strengthened and said, "Let my lord speak, for you have strengthened me." ²⁰Then he said, "Do you know why I have come to you?

But now I will return to fight against the prince of Persia; and when I go out, behold, the prince of Greece will come. ²¹ But I will tell you what is inscribed in the book of truth: there is none who contends by my side against these except Michael, your prince.

The Kings of the South and the North

11 "And as for me, in the first year of Darius the Mede, I stood up to confirm and strengthen him.

² "And now I will show you the truth. Behold, three more kings shall arise in Persia, and a fourth shall be far richer than all of them. And when he has become strong through his riches, he shall stir up all against the kingdom of Greece. ³ Then a mighty king shall arise, who shall rule with great dominion and do as he wills. ⁴ And as soon as he has arisen, his kingdom shall be broken and divided toward the four winds of heaven, but not to his posterity, nor according to the authority with which he ruled, for his kingdom shall be plucked up and go to others besides these.

⁵ "Then the king of the south shall be strong, but one of his princes shall be stronger than he and shall rule, and his authority shall be a great authority. ⁶ After some years they shall make an alliance, and the daughter of the king of the south shall come to the king of the north to make an agreement. But she shall not retain the strength of her arm, and he and his arm shall not endure, but she shall be given up, and her attendants, he who fathered her, and he who supported her in those times.

⁷ "And from a branch from her roots one shall arise in his place. He shall come against the army and enter the fortress of the king of the north, and he shall deal with them and shall prevail. ⁸ He shall also carry off to Egypt their gods with their metal images and their precious vessels of silver and gold, and for some years he shall refrain from attacking the king of the north. ⁹ Then the latter shall come into the realm of the king of the south but shall return to his own land.

¹⁰ "His sons shall wage war and assemble a multitude of great forces, which shall keep coming and overflow and pass through, and again shall carry the war as far as his fortress. ¹¹ Then the king of the south, moved with rage, shall come out and fight against the king of the north. And he shall raise a great multitude, but it shall be given into his hand. ¹² And when the multitude is taken away, his heart shall be exalted, and he shall cast down tens of thousands, but he shall not prevail. ¹³ For the king of the north shall again raise a multitude, greater than the first. And after some years he shall come on with a great army and abundant supplies.

¹⁴ "In those times many shall rise against the king of the south, and the violent among your own people shall lift themselves up in order to fulfill the vision, but they shall fail. ¹⁵ Then the king of the north shall come and throw up siegeworks and take a well-fortified city. And the forces of the south shall not stand, or even his best troops, for there shall be no strength to stand. ¹⁶ But he who comes against him shall do as he wills, and none shall stand before him. And

GETTING THE MESSAGE

The **mighty king** mentioned in 11:3 is Alexander the Great, who reigned from 336 to 323 B.C. Alexander created one of the largest empires in ancient history, stretching from Greece to India. He brought the Greek language and culture to the Middle East, which is why the New Testament was originally written in Greek.

he shall stand in the glorious land, with destruction in his hand. ¹⁷ He shall set his face to come with the strength of his whole kingdom, and he shall bring terms of an agreement and perform them. He shall give him the daughter of women to destroy the kingdom, but it shall not stand or be to his advantage. ¹⁸ Afterward he shall turn his face to the coastlands and shall capture many of them, but a commander shall put an end to his insolence. Indeed, he shall turn his insolence back upon him. ¹⁹ Then he shall turn his face back toward the fortresses of his own land, but he shall stumble and fall, and shall not be found.

²⁰ "Then shall arise in his place one who shall send an exactor of tribute for the glory of the kingdom. But within a few days he shall be broken, neither in anger nor in battle. ²¹ In his place shall arise a contemptible person to whom royal majesty has not

been given. He shall come in without warning and obtain the kingdom by flatteries. 22 Armies shall be utterly swept away before him and broken, even the prince of the covenant. 23 And from the time that an alliance is made with him he shall act deceitfully, and he shall become strong with a small people. 24 Without warning he shall come into the richest parts of the province, and he shall do what neither his fathers nor his fathers' fathers have done, scattering among them plunder, spoil, and goods. He shall devise plans against strongholds, but only for a time. 25 And he shall stir up his power and his heart against the king of the south with a great army. And the king of the south shall wage war with an exceedingly great and mighty army, but he shall not stand, for plots shall be devised against him. 26 Even

those who eat his food shall break him. His army shall be swept away, and many shall fall down slain. 27 And as for the two kings, their hearts shall be bent on doing evil. They shall speak lies at the same table, but to no avail, for the end is yet to be at the time appointed. 28 And he shall return to his land with great wealth, but his heart shall be set against the holy covenant. And he shall work his will and return to his own land.

29 "At the time appointed he shall return and come into the south, but it shall not be this time as it was before. 30 For ships of Kittim shall come against him, and he shall be afraid and withdraw, and shall turn back and be enraged and take action against the holy covenant. He shall turn back and pay attention to those who forsake the holy covenant. 31 Forces from him shall appear and profane the temple and fortress, and shall take away the regular burnt offering. And they shall set up the abomination that makes desolate. 32 He shall seduce with flattery those who violate the covenant, but the people who know their God shall stand firm and take action. 33 And the wise among the people shall make many understand, though for some days they shall stumble by sword and flame, by captivity and plunder. 34 When they stumble, they shall receive a little help. And many shall join themselves to them with flattery, 35 and some of the wise shall stumble, so that they may be refined, purified, and made white, until the time of the end, for it still awaits the appointed time.

36 "And the king shall do as he wills. He shall exalt himself and magnify himself above every god, and shall speak astonishing things against the God of gods. He shall prosper till the indignation is accomplished; for what is decreed shall be done. 37 He shall pay no attention to the gods of his fathers, or to the one beloved by women. He shall not pay attention to any other god, for he shall magnify himself above all. 38 He shall honor the god of fortresses instead of these. A god whom his fathers did not know he shall honor with gold and silver, with precious stones and costly gifts. 39 He shall deal with the strongest fortresses with the help of a foreign god. Those who acknowledge him he shall load with honor. He shall make them rulers over many and shall divide the land for a price.

40 "At the time of the end, the king of the south shall attack him, but the king of the north shall rush upon him like a whirlwind, with chariots and horsemen, and with many ships. And he shall come into countries and shall overflow and pass through. 41 He shall come into the glorious land. And tens of thousands shall fall, but these shall be delivered out of his hand: Edom and Moab and the main part of the Ammonites. 42 He shall stretch out his hand against the countries, and the land of Egypt shall not escape. 43 He shall become ruler of the treasures of gold and of silver, and all the precious things of Egypt, and the Libyans and the Cushites shall follow in his train. 44 But news from the east and the north shall alarm him, and he shall go out with great fury to destroy and devote many to destruction. 45 And he shall pitch his palatial tents between the sea and the glorious holy mountain. Yet he shall come to his end, with none to help him.

The Time of the End

12 "At that time shall arise Michael, the great prince who has charge of your people. And there shall be a time of trouble, such as never has been since there was a nation till that time. But at that time your people shall be delivered, everyone whose name shall be found written in the book. ²And many of those who sleep in the dust of the earth shall awake, some to everlasting life, and some to shame and everlasting contempt. ³And those who are wise shall shine like the brightness of the sky above; and those who turn many to righteousness, like the stars forever and ever. ⁴But you, Daniel, shut up the words and seal the book, until the time of the end. Many shall run to and fro, and knowledge shall increase."

⁵Then I, Daniel, looked, and behold, two others stood, one on this bank of the stream and one on that bank of the stream. ⁶And someone said to the man clothed in linen, who was above the waters of the stream, "How long shall it be till the end of these wonders?" ⁷And I heard the man clothed in linen, who was above the waters of the stream; he raised his right hand and his left hand toward heaven and swore by him who lives forever that it would be for a time, times, and half a time, and that when the

shattering of the power of the holy people comes to an end all these things would be finished. ⁸I heard, but I did not understand. Then I said, "O my lord, what shall be the outcome of these things?" ⁹He said, "Go your way, Daniel, for the words are shut up and sealed until the time of the end. ¹⁰Many shall purify themselves and make themselves white and be refined, but the

GETTING THE MESSAGE

Purity. In 12:10, "white" symbolizes purity, as in clothing that is clean rather than dirty (see 7:9). "Refined" means purified or cleansed. Revelation similarly pictures saints wearing white clothes (Rev. 4:4; 7:13–14; 19:8).

wicked shall act wickedly. And none of the wicked shall understand, but those who are wise shall understand. ¹¹And from the time that the regular burnt offering is taken away and the abomination that makes desolate is set up, there shall be 1,290 days. ¹²Blessed is he who waits and arrives at the 1,335 days. ¹³But go your way till the end. And you shall rest and shall stand in your allotted place at the end of the days."

INTRODUCTION TO HOSEA

793/781 B.C.	c. 740 B.C.	722 B.C.
Reign of Jeroboam II begins	Prophetic ministry of Hosea	Fall of Israel

AUTHOR AND DATE

Hosea prophesied during the latter half of the eighth century B.C. (c. 753–722 B.C.). This period was an extremely difficult time in Israel's history, just before the northern kingdom went into exile.

AUDIENCE AND PURPOSE

Hosea's primary audience was Ephraim (another name for the northern kingdom, Israel), which is mentioned 35 times in the book. Hosea wanted to see Israel turn back to God.

BACKGROUND AND OVERVIEW

Israel is the Lord's bride, but Israel has instead joined itself to Baal, the false god worshiped in Syria-Palestine. Worshiping Baal violates the first of the Ten Commandments (Ex. 20:3). It is also a betrayal of God's intimate union with his people. Therefore Hosea describes it as spiritual adultery, an offense against the marriage between the Lord and Israel. He compares Israel's spiritual unfaithfulness to the ingratitude of a wayward wife. Such unfaithfulness justifies the Lord's coming judgment. But punishment is not ultimately what the Lord wants for his people. He desires that they leave their sin. He wants them to return to the One who first loved them and who can provide what is best for them.

KEY THEMES

1. Hosea frequently refers to the Pentateuch, the foundation of Israel's relationship to God (e.g., 1:10; 6:7; 7:13; 9:6–10; 11:1–4; 12:2–5, 9–10, 12–13; 13:4–6).

2. Hosea stresses divine sovereignty. God speaks in the first person, "I," almost a hundred times in the book.

3. Hosea's personal life illustrates the Lord's compassion (chs. 1–3).

4. Isolation/exile, which is coming upon Israel, is a way to restoration (1:6–7; 2:14–23; 5:6–6:3; 11:8–11; 12:9).

OUTLINE

Chapters 1–3 use Hosea's own marriage as a parable for the relationship between God and Israel. The dominant image is of Israel as an unfaithful wife. Chapters 4–14 detail the comparison, with its series of accusations, warnings, appeals, and motivations for God's people to return.

I. Biographical: Hosea's Family (1:1–3:5)

II. Accusations, Warnings, and Promises for Israel (4:1–14:9)

HOSEA

1 The word of the LORD that came to Hosea, the son of Beeri, in the days of Uzziah, Jotham, Ahaz, and Hezekiah, kings of Judah, and in the days of Jeroboam the son of Joash, king of Israel.

Hosea's Wife and Children

2 When the LORD first spoke through Hosea, the LORD said to Hosea, "Go, take to yourself a wife of whoredom and have children of whoredom, for the land commits great whoredom by forsaking the LORD." 3 So he went and took Gomer, the daughter of Diblaim, and she conceived and bore him a son.

4 And the LORD said to him, "Call his name Jezreel, for in just a little while I will punish the house of Jehu for the blood of Jezreel, and I will put an end to the kingdom of the house of Israel. 5 And on that day I will break the bow of Israel in the Valley of Jezreel."

6 She conceived again and bore a daughter. And the LORD said to him, "Call her name No Mercy, for I will no more have mercy on the house of Israel, to forgive them at all. 7 But I will have mercy on the house of Judah, and I will save them by the LORD their God. I will not save them by bow or by sword or by war or by horses or by horsemen."

8 When she had weaned No Mercy, she conceived and bore a son. 9 And the LORD said, "Call his name Not My People, for you are not my people, and I am not your God."

10 Yet the number of the children of Israel shall be like the sand of the sea, which cannot be measured or numbered. And in the place where it was said to them, "You are not my people," it shall be said to them, "Children of the living God." 11 And the children of Judah and the children of Israel shall be gathered together, and they shall appoint for themselves one head. And they shall go up from the land, for great shall be the day of Jezreel.

Israel's Unfaithfulness Punished

2 Say to your brothers, "You are my people," and to your sisters, "You have received mercy."

2   "Plead with your mother, plead—
      for she is not my wife,
      and I am not her husband—
    that she put away her whoring from
        her face,
      and her adultery from between her
        breasts;
3   lest I strip her naked
      and make her as in the day she was
        born,
    and make her like a wilderness,
      and make her like a parched land,
      and kill her with thirst.
4   Upon her children also I will have no
        mercy,
      because they are children of whore-
        dom.

5   For their mother has played the
        whore;
      she who conceived them has acted
        shamefully.
    For she said, 'I will go after my lovers,
      who give me my bread and my
        water,
      my wool and my flax, my oil and
        my drink.'
6   Therefore I will hedge up her way
        with thorns,
      and I will build a wall against her,
      so that she cannot find her paths.
7   She shall pursue her lovers
      but not overtake them,
    and she shall seek them
      but shall not find them.
    Then she shall say,
      'I will go and return to my first hus-
        band,
      for it was better for me then than
        now.'

8 And she did not know
   that it was I who gave her
   the grain, the wine, and the oil,
and who lavished on her silver and
      gold,
   which they used for Baal.
9 Therefore I will take back
   my grain in its time,
   and my wine in its season,
and I will take away my wool and my
      flax,
   which were to cover her nakedness.

PROFILE
HOSEA

Hosea ministered to the northern kingdom of Israel during the latter half of the eighth century B.C., the most difficult time the nation had ever faced. Israel had forsaken the Lord and was worshiping Baal instead. Hosea understood that this was why the Lord intended to judge the nation. God commanded Hosea to marry, but warned him that his wife would be unfaithful to him. Hosea married Gomer, who indeed became unfaithful to him. When Gomer left Hosea, God instructed him to reclaim her. This would be a sign to the people that, though their sins were shameful, the Lord still loved Israel, his spiritually unfaithful wife. Hosea's marriage to Gomer, her unfaithfulness, and their eventual restoration were thus a parable of the Lord's relationship to Israel.

KEY REFERENCE: HOSEA 3:1–5

10 Now I will uncover her lewdness
   in the sight of her lovers,
   and no one shall rescue her out of
      my hand.
11 And I will put an end to all her mirth,
   her feasts, her new moons, her
      Sabbaths,
   and all her appointed feasts.
12 And I will lay waste her vines and her
      fig trees,
   of which she said,

1 *Achor* means *trouble*; compare Joshua 7:26

'These are my wages,
   which my lovers have given me.'
I will make them a forest,
   and the beasts of the field shall
      devour them.
13 And I will punish her for the feast
      days of the Baals
   when she burned offerings to them
and adorned herself with her ring and
      jewelry,
   and went after her lovers
   and forgot me, declares the LORD.

The LORD's Mercy on Israel
14 "Therefore, behold, I will allure her,
   and bring her into the wilderness,
   and speak tenderly to her.
15 And there I will give her her vineyards
   and make the Valley of Achor[1] a
      door of hope.

GETTING THE MESSAGE

Public humiliation was a standard punishment for adultery in the ancient world (2:3). Rather than follow that custom, however, Hosea sought to reclaim his wife. This is a picture of the Lord, who seeks to reclaim his people even when they forsake him.

And there she shall answer as in the
      days of her youth,
   as at the time when she came out of
      the land of Egypt.

16 "And in that day, declares the LORD, you will call me 'My Husband,' and no longer will you call me 'My Baal.' 17 For I will remove the names of the Baals from her mouth, and they shall be remembered by name no more. 18 And I will make for them a covenant on that day with the beasts of the field, the birds of the heavens, and the creeping things of the ground. And I will abolish the bow, the sword, and war from the land, and I will make you lie down in safety. 19 And I will betroth you to me forever. I will betroth you to me in righteousness and in justice, in steadfast love and in mercy. 20 I will betroth you to me in faithfulness. And you shall know the LORD.

21 "And in that day I will answer, declares
the Lord,
I will answer the heavens,
and they shall answer the earth,
22 and the earth shall answer the grain,
the wine, and the oil,
and they shall answer Jezreel,[1]
23 and I will sow her for myself in the
land.
And I will have mercy on No Mercy,
and I will say to Not My People, 'You
are my people';
and he shall say, 'You are my God.'"

Hosea Redeems His Wife

3 And the Lord said to me, "Go again, love
a woman who is loved by another man
and is an adulteress, even as the Lord loves
the children of Israel, though they turn to
other gods and love cakes of raisins." 2 So
I bought her for fifteen shekels of silver
and a homer and a lethech of barley. 3 And
I said to her, "You must dwell as mine for
many days. You shall not play the whore, or
belong to another man; so will I also be to
you." 4 For the children of Israel shall dwell
many days without king or prince, without
sacrifice or pillar, without ephod or household gods. 5 Afterward the children of Israel
shall return and seek the Lord their God,
and David their king, and they shall come
in fear to the Lord and to his goodness in
the latter days.

The Lord Accuses Israel

4 Hear the word of the Lord, O children of Israel,
for the Lord has a controversy with
the inhabitants of the land.
There is no faithfulness or steadfast
love,
and no knowledge of God in the
land;
2 there is swearing, lying, murder,
stealing, and committing adultery;
they break all bounds, and bloodshed follows bloodshed.
3 Therefore the land mourns,
and all who dwell in it languish,
and also the beasts of the field
and the birds of the heavens,
and even the fish of the sea are
taken away.

4 Yet let no one contend,
and let none accuse,
for with you is my contention,
O priest.
5 You shall stumble by day;
the prophet also shall stumble with
you by night;
and I will destroy your mother.
6 My people are destroyed for lack of
knowledge;
because you have rejected knowledge,
I reject you from being a priest to
me.
And since you have forgotten the law
of your God,
I also will forget your children.
7 The more they increased,
the more they sinned against me;
I will change their glory into
shame.
8 They feed on the sin of my people;
they are greedy for their iniquity.
9 And it shall be like people, like priest;
I will punish them for their ways
and repay them for their deeds.
10 They shall eat, but not be satisfied;
they shall play the whore, but not
multiply,
because they have forsaken the Lord
to cherish 11 whoredom, wine, and
new wine,
which take away the understanding.
12 My people inquire of a piece of wood,
and their walking staff gives them
oracles.
For a spirit of whoredom has led them
astray,
and they have left their God to play
the whore.
13 They sacrifice on the tops of the
mountains
and burn offerings on the hills,
under oak, poplar, and terebinth,
because their shade is good.
Therefore your daughters play the
whore,
and your brides commit adultery.
14 I will not punish your daughters
when they play the whore,
nor your brides when they commit
adultery;

[1] Jezreel means God will sow

for the men themselves go aside with
  prostitutes
    and sacrifice with cult prostitutes,
and a people without understanding
    shall come to ruin.

15 Though you play the whore, O Israel,
    let not Judah become guilty.
  Enter not into Gilgal,
      nor go up to Beth-aven,
      and swear not, "As the LORD
        lives."
16 Like a stubborn heifer,
    Israel is stubborn;
  can the LORD now feed them
    like a lamb in a broad pasture?
17 Ephraim is joined to idols;
    leave him alone.
18 When their drink is gone, they give
      themselves to whoring;
    their rulers dearly love shame.

19 A wind has wrapped them in its
      wings,
    and they shall be ashamed because
      of their sacrifices.

Punishment Coming for Israel and Judah

5 Hear this, O priests!
  Pay attention, O house of Israel!
  Give ear, O house of the king!
    For the judgment is for you;
  for you have been a snare at
      Mizpah
    and a net spread upon Tabor.
2 And the revolters have gone deep into
      slaughter,
    but I will discipline all of them.

3 I know Ephraim,
    and Israel is not hidden from me;
  for now, O Ephraim, you have played
      the whore;
    Israel is defiled.

4 Their deeds do not permit them
    to return to their God.
  For the spirit of whoredom is within
      them,
    and they know not the LORD.

5 The pride of Israel testifies to his
      face;
    Israel and Ephraim shall stumble in
      his guilt;
  Judah also shall stumble with
      them.
6 With their flocks and herds they
      shall go
    to seek the LORD,
  but they will not find him;
    he has withdrawn from them.
7 They have dealt faithlessly with the
      LORD;
    for they have borne alien children.
  Now the new moon shall devour
      them with their fields.

8 Blow the horn in Gibeah,
    the trumpet in Ramah.
  Sound the alarm at Beth-aven;
    we follow you, O Benjamin!
9 Ephraim shall become a desolation
    in the day of punishment;
  among the tribes of Israel
    I make known what is sure.
10 The princes of Judah have become
    like those who move the landmark;
  upon them I will pour out
    my wrath like water.
11 Ephraim is oppressed, crushed in
      judgment,
    because he was determined to go
      after filth.
12 But I am like a moth to Ephraim,
    and like dry rot to the house of
      Judah.

13 When Ephraim saw his sickness,
    and Judah his wound,
  then Ephraim went to Assyria,
    and sent to the great king.
  But he is not able to cure you
    or heal your wound.
14 For I will be like a lion to Ephraim,
    and like a young lion to the house
      of Judah.
  I, even I, will tear and go away;
    I will carry off, and no one shall
      rescue.

15 I will return again to my place,
   until they acknowledge their guilt
      and seek my face,
   and in their distress earnestly seek
      me.

Israel and Judah Are Unrepentant

6 "Come, let us return to the LORD;
   for he has torn us, that he may heal
      us;
   he has struck us down, and he will
      bind us up.
2 After two days he will revive us;
   on the third day he will raise us up,
   that we may live before him.
3 Let us know; let us press on to know
      the LORD;
   his going out is sure as the dawn;
   he will come to us as the showers,
      as the spring rains that water the
      earth."

4 What shall I do with you, O Ephraim?
   What shall I do with you, O Judah?
   Your love is like a morning cloud,
      like the dew that goes early away.
5 Therefore I have hewn them by the
      prophets;
   I have slain them by the words of
      my mouth,
   and my judgment goes forth as the
      light.
6 For I desire steadfast love and not
      sacrifice,
   the knowledge of God rather than
      burnt offerings.
7 But like Adam they transgressed the
      covenant;
   there they dealt faithlessly with
      me.
8 Gilead is a city of evildoers,
   tracked with blood.
9 As robbers lie in wait for a man,
   so the priests band together;
   they murder on the way to Shechem;
      they commit villainy.
10 In the house of Israel I have seen a
      horrible thing;
   Ephraim's whoredom is there; Israel
      is defiled.

11 For you also, O Judah, a harvest is
      appointed,
   when I restore the fortunes of my
      people.

7 When I would heal Israel,
   the iniquity of Ephraim is revealed,
      and the evil deeds of Samaria;
   for they deal falsely;
      the thief breaks in,
      and the bandits raid outside.
2 But they do not consider
   that I remember all their evil.
   Now their deeds surround them;
      they are before my face.
3 By their evil they make the king glad,
      and the princes by their treachery.
4 They are all adulterers;
   they are like a heated oven
   whose baker ceases to stir the fire,
      from the kneading of the dough
      until it is leavened.
5 On the day of our king, the princes
      became sick with the heat of wine;
   he stretched out his hand with
      mockers.

GETTING THE MESSAGE

To describe the Israelites as a
treacherous bow (7:16) means that they
were undependable and even dangerous
to those who relied on them. If a bow
was improperly stored when not in use,
the dry Mediterranean heat would make
it brittle, causing it to snap and injure
its user.

6 For with hearts like an oven they
      approach their intrigue;
   all night their anger smolders;
   in the morning it blazes like a flam-
      ing fire.
7 All of them are hot as an oven,
   and they devour their rulers.
   All their kings have fallen,
      and none of them calls upon me.

8 Ephraim mixes himself with the peo-
      ples;
   Ephraim is a cake not turned.
9 Strangers devour his strength,
      and he knows it not;
   gray hairs are sprinkled upon him,
      and he knows it not.
10 The pride of Israel testifies to his
      face;

yet they do not return to the LORD
    their God,
  nor seek him, for all this.

11 Ephraim is like a dove,
    silly and without sense,
    calling to Egypt, going to Assyria.
12 As they go, I will spread over them my
      net;
    I will bring them down like birds of
      the heavens;
    I will discipline them according to
      the report made to their congre-
      gation.
13 Woe to them, for they have strayed
      from me!
    Destruction to them, for they have
      rebelled against me!
  I would redeem them,
    but they speak lies against me.
14 They do not cry to me from the heart,
    but they wail upon their beds;

> **GETTING THE MESSAGE**

Worship God alone! Worship of the
calf idol (8:6) violated the First and
Second Commandments: "You shall have
no other gods before me," and "You
shall not make . . . a carved image . . ."
(Ex. 20:3-6). Believers are to worship the
Creator God, rather than created things.

  for grain and wine they gash them-
    selves;
    they rebel against me.
15 Although I trained and strengthened
      their arms,
    yet they devise evil against me.
16 They return, but not upward;
    they are like a treacherous bow;
  their princes shall fall by the sword
    because of the insolence of their
      tongue.
  This shall be their derision in the land
    of Egypt.

Israel Will Reap the Whirlwind

8 Set the trumpet to your lips!
    One like a vulture is over the house
      of the LORD,
  because they have transgressed my
    covenant
    and rebelled against my law.

2 To me they cry,
    "My God, we—Israel—know you."
3 Israel has spurned the good;
    the enemy shall pursue him.

4 They made kings, but not through me.
    They set up princes, but I knew it
      not.
  With their silver and gold they made
    idols
    for their own destruction.
5 I have spurned your calf, O Samaria.
    My anger burns against them.
  How long will they be incapable of
    innocence?
6 For it is from Israel;
  a craftsman made it;
    it is not God.
  The calf of Samaria
    shall be broken to pieces.

7 For they sow the wind,
    and they shall reap the whirlwind.
  The standing grain has no heads;
    it shall yield no flour;
  if it were to yield,
    strangers would devour it.
8 Israel is swallowed up;
    already they are among the nations
      as a useless vessel.
9 For they have gone up to Assyria,
    a wild donkey wandering alone;
    Ephraim has hired lovers.
10 Though they hire allies among the
      nations,
    I will soon gather them up.
  And the king and princes shall soon
    writhe
    because of the tribute.

11 Because Ephraim has multiplied
      altars for sinning,
    they have become to him altars for
      sinning.
12 Were I to write for him my laws by the
      ten thousands,
    they would be regarded as a strange
      thing.
13 As for my sacrificial offerings,
    they sacrifice meat and eat it,
    but the LORD does not accept them.
  Now he will remember their iniquity
    and punish their sins;
    they shall return to Egypt.
14 For Israel has forgotten his Maker
    and built palaces,

and Judah has multiplied fortified
cities;
so I will send a fire upon his cities,
and it shall devour her strongholds.

The LORD Will Punish Israel

9 Rejoice not, O Israel!
Exult not like the peoples;
for you have played the whore, forsaking your God.
You have loved a prostitute's wages
on all threshing floors.
2 Threshing floor and wine vat shall not
feed them,
and the new wine shall fail them.
3 They shall not remain in the land of
the LORD,
but Ephraim shall return to Egypt,
and they shall eat unclean food in
Assyria.

4 They shall not pour drink offerings of
wine to the LORD,
and their sacrifices shall not please
him.
It shall be like mourners' bread to
them;
all who eat of it shall be defiled;
for their bread shall be for their hunger only;
it shall not come to the house of the
LORD.
5 What will you do on the day of the
appointed festival,
and on the day of the feast of the
LORD?
6 For behold, they are going away from
destruction;
but Egypt shall gather them;
Memphis shall bury them.
Nettles shall possess their precious
things of silver;
thorns shall be in their tents.
7 The days of punishment have come;
the days of recompense have come;
Israel shall know it.
The prophet is a fool;
the man of the spirit is mad,
because of your great iniquity
and great hatred.
8 The prophet is the watchman of
Ephraim with my God;
yet a fowler's snare is on all his ways,
and hatred in the house of his God.

9 They have deeply corrupted themselves
as in the days of Gibeah:
he will remember their iniquity;
he will punish their sins.

10 Like grapes in the wilderness,
I found Israel.
Like the first fruit on the fig tree
in its first season,
I saw your fathers.
But they came to Baal-peor
and consecrated themselves to the
thing of shame,
and became detestable like the
thing they loved.
11 Ephraim's glory shall fly away like a
bird—
no birth, no pregnancy, no conception!
12 Even if they bring up children,
I will bereave them till none is left.
Woe to them
when I depart from them!
13 Ephraim, as I have seen, was like
a young palm planted in a
meadow;
but Ephraim must lead his children
out to slaughter.
14 Give them, O LORD—
what will you give?
Give them a miscarrying womb
and dry breasts.

15 Every evil of theirs is in Gilgal;
there I began to hate them.
Because of the wickedness of their
deeds
I will drive them out of my house.
I will love them no more;
all their princes are rebels.
16 Ephraim is stricken;
their root is dried up;
they shall bear no fruit.
Even though they give birth,
I will put their beloved children to
death.
17 My God will reject them
because they have not listened to
him;
they shall be wanderers among the
nations.

10 Israel is a luxuriant vine
that yields its fruit.
The more his fruit increased,
the more altars he built;

as his country improved,
he improved his pillars.
2   Their heart is false;
now they must bear their guilt.
The LORD will break down their altars
and destroy their pillars.

3   For now they will say:
"We have no king,
for we do not fear the LORD;
and a king—what could he do for
us?"
4   They utter mere words;
with empty oaths they make covenants;
so judgment springs up like poisonous weeds
in the furrows of the field.
5   The inhabitants of Samaria tremble
for the calf of Beth-aven.
Its people mourn for it, and so do its
idolatrous priests—
those who rejoiced over it and over
its glory—
for it has departed from them.
6   The thing itself shall be carried to
Assyria
as tribute to the great king.
Ephraim shall be put to shame,
and Israel shall be ashamed of his
idol.

7   Samaria's king shall perish
like a twig on the face of the waters.
8   The high places of Aven, the sin of
Israel,
shall be destroyed.
Thorn and thistle shall grow up
on their altars,
and they shall say to the mountains,
"Cover us,"
and to the hills, "Fall on us."

9   From the days of Gibeah, you have
sinned, O Israel;
there they have continued.
Shall not the war against the unjust
overtake them in Gibeah?
10 When I please, I will discipline them,
and nations shall be gathered
against them
when they are bound up for their
double iniquity.

11 Ephraim was a trained calf
that loved to thresh,
and I spared her fair neck;

but I will put Ephraim to the yoke;
Judah must plow;
Jacob must harrow for himself.
12 Sow for yourselves righteousness;
reap steadfast love;
break up your fallow ground,
for it is the time to seek the LORD,
that he may come and rain righteousness upon you.

13 You have plowed iniquity;
you have reaped injustice;
you have eaten the fruit of lies.
Because you have trusted in your own
way
and in the multitude of your warriors,
14 therefore the tumult of war shall arise
among your people,
and all your fortresses shall be
destroyed,
as Shalman destroyed Beth-arbel on
the day of battle;
mothers were dashed in pieces with
their children.
15 Thus it shall be done to you, O Bethel,
because of your great evil.
At dawn the king of Israel
shall be utterly cut off.

The LORD's Love for Israel

11 When Israel was a child, I loved
him,
and out of Egypt I called my son.
2   The more they were called,
the more they went away;
they kept sacrificing to the Baals
and burning offerings to idols.

3   Yet it was I who taught Ephraim to
walk;
I took them up by their arms,
but they did not know that I healed
them.
4   I led them with cords of kindness,
with the bands of love,
and I became to them as one who
eases the yoke on their jaws,
and I bent down to them and fed
them.

5   They shall not return to the land of
Egypt,
but Assyria shall be their king,
because they have refused to return
to me.

6 The sword shall rage against their
     cities,
  consume the bars of their gates,
  and devour them because of their
     own counsels.
7 My people are bent on turning away
     from me,
  and though they call out to the Most
     High,
  he shall not raise them up at all.

8 How can I give you up, O Ephraim?
  How can I hand you over, O Israel?
How can I make you like Admah?
  How can I treat you like Zeboiim?
My heart recoils within me;
  my compassion grows warm and
     tender.
9 I will not execute my burning anger;
  I will not again destroy Ephraim;
for I am God and not a man,
  the Holy One in your midst,
  and I will not come in wrath.

10 They shall go after the LORD;
   he will roar like a lion;
when he roars,
   his children shall come trembling
      from the west;
11 they shall come trembling like birds
      from Egypt,
   and like doves from the land of
      Assyria,
   and I will return them to their
      homes, declares the LORD.
12 Ephraim has surrounded me with
      lies,
   and the house of Israel with deceit,
but Judah still walks with God
   and is faithful to the Holy One.

12 Ephraim feeds on the wind
   and pursues the east wind all day
      long;
they multiply falsehood and vio-
      lence;
they make a covenant with
      Assyria,
and oil is carried to Egypt.

The LORD's Indictment of Israel and Judah

2 The LORD has an indictment against
      Judah
   and will punish Jacob according to
      his ways;
   he will repay him according to his
      deeds.

3 In the womb he took his brother by
      the heel,
   and in his manhood he strove with
      God.
4 He strove with the angel and pre-
      vailed;
   he wept and sought his favor.
He met God at Bethel,
   and there God spoke with us—
5 the LORD, the God of hosts,
   the LORD is his memorial name:
6 "So you, by the help of your God,
      return,
   hold fast to love and justice,
   and wait continually for your God."

7 A merchant, in whose hands are false
      balances,
   he loves to oppress.
8 Ephraim has said, "Ah, but I am rich;
   I have found wealth for myself;

   in all my labors they cannot find in
      me iniquity or sin."
9 I am the LORD your God
      from the land of Egypt;
   I will again make you dwell in tents,
      as in the days of the appointed
         feast.
10 I spoke to the prophets;
   it was I who multiplied visions,
   and through the prophets gave
      parables.
11 If there is iniquity in Gilead,
   they shall surely come to nothing:
in Gilgal they sacrifice bulls;
   their altars also are like stone heaps
      on the furrows of the field.
12 Jacob fled to the land of Aram;
   there Israel served for a wife,
   and for a wife he guarded sheep.
13 By a prophet the LORD brought Israel
      up from Egypt,
   and by a prophet he was guarded.

14   Ephraim has given bitter provocation;
        so his Lord will leave his bloodguilt
            on him
        and will repay him for his disgrace-
            ful deeds.

The LORD's Relentless Judgment on Israel

13 When Ephraim spoke, there was
        trembling;
    he was exalted in Israel,
    but he incurred guilt through Baal
        and died.

2   And now they sin more and more,
        and make for themselves metal
            images,
    idols skillfully made of their silver,
    all of them the work of craftsmen.
    It is said of them,
        "Those who offer human sacrifice
            kiss calves!"

3   Therefore they shall be like the morn-
        ing mist
        or like the dew that goes early away,
    like the chaff that swirls from the
        threshing floor
        or like smoke from a window.

4   But I am the LORD your God
        from the land of Egypt;
    you know no God but me,
        and besides me there is no savior.

5   It was I who knew you in the wilder-
        ness,
        in the land of drought;

6   but when they had grazed, they
        became full,
        they were filled, and their heart was
            lifted up;
        therefore they forgot me.

7   So I am to them like a lion;
        like a leopard I will lurk beside the
            way.

8   I will fall upon them like a bear
        robbed of her cubs;
    I will tear open their breast,
    and there I will devour them like a lion,
        as a wild beast would rip them open.

9   He destroys you, O Israel,
        for you are against me, against your
            helper.

10 Where now is your king, to save you
        in all your cities?
    Where are all your rulers—
    those of whom you said,
        "Give me a king and princes"?

11 I gave you a king in my anger,
        and I took him away in my wrath.

12 The iniquity of Ephraim is bound up;
        his sin is kept in store.

13 The pangs of childbirth come for him,
        but he is an unwise son,
    for at the right time he does not pre-
        sent himself
        at the opening of the womb.

14 Shall I ransom them from the power
        of Sheol?
    Shall I redeem them from Death?
    O Death, where are your plagues?
        O Sheol, where is your sting?
        Compassion is hidden from my eyes.

15 Though he may flourish among his
        brothers,
        the east wind, the wind of the LORD,
            shall come,
        rising from the wilderness,
    and his fountain shall dry up;
        his spring shall be parched;
    it shall strip his treasury
        of every precious thing.

16 Samaria shall bear her guilt,
        because she has rebelled against
            her God;
    they shall fall by the sword;
        their little ones shall be dashed in
            pieces,
        and their pregnant women ripped
            open.

A Plea to Return to the LORD

14 Return, O Israel, to the LORD your
        God,
        for you have stumbled because of
            your iniquity.

2   Take with you words
        and return to the LORD;

say to him,
  "Take away all iniquity;
accept what is good,
  and we will pay with bulls
  the vows of our lips.
3 Assyria shall not save us;
  we will not ride on horses;
and we will say no more, 'Our God,'
  to the work of our hands.
In you the orphan finds mercy."

4 I will heal their apostasy;
  I will love them freely,
  for my anger has turned from them.
5 I will be like the dew to Israel;
  he shall blossom like the lily;
  he shall take root like the trees of
    Lebanon;
6 his shoots shall spread out;
  his beauty shall be like the olive,
  and his fragrance like Lebanon.

7 They shall return and dwell beneath
    my shadow;
  they shall flourish like the grain;
they shall blossom like the vine;
  their fame shall be like the wine of
    Lebanon.

8 O Ephraim, what have I to do with
    idols?
  It is I who answer and look after
    you.
I am like an evergreen cypress;
  from me comes your fruit.

9 Whoever is wise, let him understand
    these things;
  whoever is discerning, let him
    know them;
for the ways of the LORD are right,
  and the upright walk in them,
  but transgressors stumble in them.

INTRODUCTION TO JOEL

586 B.C.	538 B.C.	c. 500 B.C.?
Fall of Judah/ temple destroyed	Decree of Cyrus/ end of exile	Prophetic ministry of Joel begins

AUTHOR AND DATE

Little is known about Joel, a prophet from Judah (perhaps Jerusalem). Most scholars date the book after the exile to Babylon (586 B.C.).

BACKGROUND

Joel calls the inhabitants of Judah and Jerusalem to lament and return to the Lord during a time of national disaster. A locust plague has destroyed both wine (1:5, 7, 12) and grain (1:10). This threatens the people's ability to present offerings in the temple (1:9, 13, 16).

KEY THEMES

1. *Day of the Lord.* The dominant theme of the book is the "day of the Lord." This describes a time when the presence of the Lord brings judgment and/or deliverance and blessing, depending on the circumstances. Therefore, although the "day" results in destruction for the nations, it can also be seen as a time of salvation for God's people. The Lord remains a refuge in the chaos of judgment (3:15–16).

2. *Repentance.* If the whole community would cry out to the Lord (1:13–20) and look to him—not merely with external actions but in sincerity and commitment (2:12–13)—then judgment may be prevented. However, the Lord is not bound by the acts of the community (2:14). It is his decision to either send or withhold the destruction by the locusts (1:15), just as the army is his to command (2:11).

3. *The Lord in their midst.* The reason the Lord will turn from judgment to blessing is to express his covenant-keeping character (2:13, 18–26; 3:18). His promise to dwell in the midst of his people is prominent not only in Joel (2:27; 3:17, 21) but also throughout the OT (Num. 35:34; Isa. 12:6; Zeph. 3:15, 17; Zech. 2:10–11). God restores what the locusts have destroyed (Joel 2:27) and protects Israel as the world crumbles (3:16–17) so that the people will know his presence. This theme is restated at the end of the book (3:21), showing how important it was for Joel.

4. These three themes come together in the *promise of the future outpouring of the Spirit* (2:28–32). This outpouring is associated with the day of the Lord (2:31) in both its judgmental (2:30–31; see 2:10; 3:15) and its saving (2:32) roles. The outpouring of the Spirit is also related to repentance: those who are saved call "on the name of the LORD" (2:32). The giving of the Spirit is the ultimate evidence of God "in the midst of" his people (Isa. 63:11; see Hag. 2:5).

OUTLINE

I. The Judgment against Judah and the Day of the Lord (1:1–2:17)
  A. Locust invasion: forerunner of the day of the Lord (1:1–20)
  B. Army invasion: the arrival of the day of the Lord (2:1–17)

II. The Mercy of the Lord and Judgment against the Nations (2:18–3:21)
  A. Mercy: the Lord responds by restoring his people (2:18–32)
  B. Judgment: the Lord's judgment against the nations and his dwelling with his people (3:1–21)

JOEL

1 The word of the Lord that came to Joel, the son of Pethuel:

An Invasion of Locusts

2 Hear this, you elders;
  give ear, all inhabitants of the land!
Has such a thing happened in your days,
  or in the days of your fathers?
3 Tell your children of it,
  and let your children tell their children,
  and their children to another generation.

4 What the cutting locust left,
  the swarming locust has eaten.
What the swarming locust left,
  the hopping locust has eaten,
and what the hopping locust left,
  the destroying locust has eaten.

5 Awake, you drunkards, and weep,
  and wail, all you drinkers of wine,
because of the sweet wine,
  for it is cut off from your mouth.
6 For a nation has come up against my land,
  powerful and beyond number;
its teeth are lions' teeth,
  and it has the fangs of a lioness.
7 It has laid waste my vine
  and splintered my fig tree;
it has stripped off their bark and thrown it down;
  their branches are made white.

8 Lament like a virgin wearing sackcloth
  for the bridegroom of her youth.
9 The grain offering and the drink offering are cut off
  from the house of the Lord.
The priests mourn,
  the ministers of the Lord.
10 The fields are destroyed,
  the ground mourns,
because the grain is destroyed,
  the wine dries up,
  the oil languishes.

11 Be ashamed, O tillers of the soil;
  wail, O vinedressers,
for the wheat and the barley,
  because the harvest of the field has perished.
12 The vine dries up;
  the fig tree languishes.
Pomegranate, palm, and apple,
  all the trees of the field are dried up,
and gladness dries up
  from the children of man.

A Call to Repentance

13 Put on sackcloth and lament, O priests;
  wail, O ministers of the altar.

> ### GETTING THE MESSAGE
>
> The **desert locust** has been a destructive force that has plagued agricultural production for thousands of years. Winds from the Sahara have been known to carry them across oceans. Their devastation of crops often leads to famine. Joel compares them to a great army.

Go in, pass the night in sackcloth,
  O ministers of my God!
Because grain offering and drink offering
  are withheld from the house of your God.
14 Consecrate a fast;
  call a solemn assembly.
Gather the elders
  and all the inhabitants of the land
to the house of the Lord your God,
  and cry out to the Lord.
15 Alas for the day!
For the day of the Lord is near,
  and as destruction from the Almighty it comes.
16 Is not the food cut off
  before our eyes,
joy and gladness
  from the house of our God?

17 The seed shrivels under the clods;
    the storehouses are desolate;
the granaries are torn down
    because the grain has dried up.
18 How the beasts groan!
    The herds of cattle are perplexed
because there is no pasture for them;
    even the flocks of sheep suffer.

19 To you, O Lord, I call.
For fire has devoured
    the pastures of the wilderness,
and flame has burned
    all the trees of the field.

PROFILE
JOEL

The name Joel means "Yahweh is God." Little is known about the prophet, who was probably from Judah. It is likely that he ministered during a national calamity sometime after Judah returned from exile in Babylon. The primary theme in the book of Joel is the "day of the Lord"—a time when the presence of the Lord will bring both judgment and deliverance. Joel teaches that, while the day of the Lord will bring destruction on the nations, it will also be a time of salvation for God's people. Judah will be the means through which God pours out his Spirit on all people (2:28–32), and he will preserve them against all who seek to destroy them.

KEY REFERENCE: JOEL 2:11–14

---

20 Even the beasts of the field pant for you
    because the water brooks are dried
      up,
and fire has devoured
    the pastures of the wilderness.

The Day of the Lord

2 Blow a trumpet in Zion;
    sound an alarm on my holy mountain!
Let all the inhabitants of the land
    tremble,
    for the day of the Lord is coming; it
    is near,

2 a day of darkness and gloom,
    a day of clouds and thick darkness!
Like blackness there is spread upon
      the mountains
    a great and powerful people;
their like has never been before,
    nor will be again after them
    through the years of all generations.

3 Fire devours before them,
    and behind them a flame burns.
The land is like the garden of Eden
      before them,
    but behind them a desolate wilder-
      ness,
    and nothing escapes them.

4 Their appearance is like the appear-
      ance of horses,
    and like war horses they run.
5 As with the rumbling of chariots,
    they leap on the tops of the moun-
      tains,
like the crackling of a flame of fire
    devouring the stubble,
like a powerful army
    drawn up for battle.

6 Before them peoples are in anguish;
    all faces grow pale.
7 Like warriors they charge;
    like soldiers they scale the wall.
They march each on his way;
    they do not swerve from their paths.
8 They do not jostle one another;
    each marches in his path;
they burst through the weapons
    and are not halted.
9 They leap upon the city,
    they run upon the walls,
they climb up into the houses,
    they enter through the windows
      like a thief.

10 The earth quakes before them;
    the heavens tremble.
The sun and the moon are darkened,
    and the stars withdraw their shining.
11 The Lord utters his voice
    before his army,
for his camp is exceedingly great;
    he who executes his word is power-
      ful.
For the day of the Lord is great and
      very awesome;
    who can endure it?

Return to the LORD

12 "Yet even now," declares the LORD,
      "return to me with all your heart,
   with fasting, with weeping, and with
      mourning;
13   and rend your hearts and not your
         garments."
   Return to the LORD your God,
      for he is gracious and merciful,
   slow to anger, and abounding in
      steadfast love;
      and he relents over disaster.
14 Who knows whether he will not turn
      and relent,
      and leave a blessing behind him,
   a grain offering and a drink offering
      for the LORD your God?

15 Blow the trumpet in Zion;
      consecrate a fast;
   call a solemn assembly;
16   gather the people.
   Consecrate the congregation;
      assemble the elders;
   gather the children,
      even nursing infants.
   Let the bridegroom leave his room,
      and the bride her chamber.

17 Between the vestibule and the altar
      let the priests, the ministers of the
         LORD, weep
   and say, "Spare your people, O LORD,
      and make not your heritage a
         reproach,
      a byword among the nations.
   Why should they say among the peo-
      ples,
      'Where is their God?'"

The LORD Had Pity

18 Then the LORD became jealous for his
      land
      and had pity on his people.
19 The LORD answered and said to his
      people,
   "Behold, I am sending to you
      grain, wine, and oil,
      and you will be satisfied;
   and I will no more make you
      a reproach among the nations.

20 "I will remove the northerner far from
      you,
      and drive him into a parched and
         desolate land,

his vanguard into the eastern sea,
   and his rear guard into the western
      sea;
the stench and foul smell of him will
   rise,
   for he has done great things.

21 "Fear not, O land;
      be glad and rejoice,
      for the LORD has done great things!
22 Fear not, you beasts of the field,
      for the pastures of the wilderness
         are green;
   the tree bears its fruit;
      the fig tree and vine give their full
         yield.

23 "Be glad, O children of Zion,
      and rejoice in the LORD your God,
   for he has given the early rain for your
      vindication;

GETTING THE MESSAGE

The sun shall be turned to darkness
(2:31) could be describing a solar eclipse,
but more broadly this refers to the
disintegration of the cosmos, which
was understood by Jews to be a sign of
God's judgment. Note that when Jesus
was on the cross, the earth became
dark for three hours, indicating God's
judgment (see Mark 15:33).

he has poured down for you abundant rain,
   the early and the latter rain, as
      before.
24 "The threshing floors shall be full of
      grain;
   the vats shall overflow with wine
      and oil.
25 I will restore to you the years
      that the swarming locust has eaten,
   the hopper, the destroyer, and the
      cutter,
      my great army, which I sent among
         you.
26 "You shall eat in plenty and be satisfied,
      and praise the name of the LORD
         your God,
   who has dealt wondrously with you.
   And my people shall never again be
      put to shame.

27 You shall know that I am in the midst
of Israel,
and that I am the LORD your God
and there is none else.
And my people shall never again be
put to shame.

The LORD Will Pour Out His Spirit

28 "And it shall come to pass afterward,
that I will pour out my Spirit on all
flesh;
your sons and your daughters shall
prophesy,
your old men shall dream dreams,
and your young men shall see
visions.
29 Even on the male and female servants
in those days I will pour out my
Spirit.

30 "And I will show wonders in the heavens and on the earth, blood and fire and

columns of smoke. 31 The sun shall be turned to darkness, and the moon to blood, before the great and awesome day of the LORD comes. 32 And it shall come to pass that everyone who calls on the name of the LORD shall be saved. For in Mount Zion and in Jerusalem there shall be those who escape, as the LORD has said, and among the survivors shall be those whom the LORD calls.

The LORD Judges the Nations

3 "For behold, in those days and at that time, when I restore the fortunes of Judah and Jerusalem, 2 I will gather all the nations and bring them down to the Valley of Jehoshaphat. And I will enter into judgment with them there, on behalf of my people and my heritage Israel, because they have scattered them among the nations and have divided up my land, 3 and have cast lots for my people, and have traded a boy for a prostitute, and have sold a girl for wine and have drunk it.

4 "What are you to me, O Tyre and Sidon, and all the regions of Philistia? Are you paying me back for something? If you are paying me back, I will return your payment on your own head swiftly and speedily. 5 For you have taken my silver and my gold, and have carried my rich treasures into your temples. 6 You have sold the people of Judah and Jerusalem to the Greeks in order to remove them far from their own border. 7 Behold, I will stir them up from the place to which you have sold them, and I will return your payment on your own head. 8 I will sell your sons and your daughters into the hand of the people of Judah, and they will sell them to the Sabeans, to a nation far away, for the LORD has spoken."

9 Proclaim this among the nations:
Consecrate for war;
stir up the mighty men.
Let all the men of war draw near;
let them come up.
10 Beat your plowshares into swords,
and your pruning hooks into spears;
let the weak say, "I am a warrior."

11 Hasten and come,
all you surrounding nations,
and gather yourselves there.
Bring down your warriors, O LORD.
12 Let the nations stir themselves up
and come up to the Valley of
Jehoshaphat;
for there I will sit to judge
all the surrounding nations.

13 Put in the sickle,
for the harvest is ripe.
Go in, tread,
for the winepress is full.
The vats overflow,
for their evil is great.

14 Multitudes, multitudes,
in the valley of decision!
For the day of the LORD is near
in the valley of decision.
15 The sun and the moon are darkened,
and the stars withdraw their shining.

16 The LORD roars from Zion,
and utters his voice from Jerusalem,
and the heavens and the earth
quake.
But the LORD is a refuge to his people,
a stronghold to the people of Israel.

The Glorious Future of Judah

17 "So you shall know that I am the LORD
         your God,
     who dwells in Zion, my holy moun-
         tain.
   And Jerusalem shall be holy,
       and strangers shall never again pass
         through it.

18 "And in that day
   the mountains shall drip sweet
         wine,
       and the hills shall flow with milk,
   and all the streambeds of Judah
       shall flow with water;

and a fountain shall come forth from
       the house of the LORD
   and water the Valley of Shittim.

19 "Egypt shall become a desolation
       and Edom a desolate wilderness,
   for the violence done to the people of
       Judah,
   because they have shed innocent
       blood in their land.

20 But Judah shall be inhabited forever,
       and Jerusalem to all generations.

21 I will avenge their blood,
       blood I have not avenged,
   for the LORD dwells in Zion."

INTRODUCTION TO AMOS

AUTHOR AND DATE

Amos was not a prophet by profession (see 1:1; 7:14–15) but nevertheless was entrusted with bringing a message from the Lord to the northern kingdom of Israel. He prophesied sometime between 793–739 B.C., probably nearer the end of that period.

THEME

The theme of Amos is the universal justice of God. The Israelites clearly expected a "day of the Lord" when all their enemies would be judged (1:2–2:5). What they were not prepared for was that they too would be judged (2:6–9:10). In fact, they would be held more accountable than their neighbors.

PURPOSE, OCCASION, AND BACKGROUND

After about 780–745 B.C., the Assyrian Empire was unable to continue the pressure it had put on the nations of the Canaanite coast during the previous century. At this same time, both Judah and Israel were blessed with fairly stable governments. As a result of these two factors, the two nations (especially Israel) were experiencing a time of wealth and prosperity. But what the Israelites saw as the beginning of a new "Golden Age" was really the end for them. It was Amos's unhappy task to tell them of God's coming judgment. Within just a few years Israel would no longer exist as a nation. They would continue to exist as a scattered

people only by God's unmerited grace (9:11–15). "The day of the Lord," far from being a day of blessing, was going to be a day of darkness. By 722 B.C. Assyria would regain its strength, and the Israelites would be conquered and exiled.

KEY THEMES

1. The Lord is the Creator of the universe. Therefore his ethical norms are universal, and all people are subject to judgment in light of them.

2. Justice and righteousness in the treatment of other people are the key evidences of a right relationship to the Lord.

3. Religious observances in the absence of social justice are disgusting to God.

4. Israel's covenant with the Lord did not guarantee special protection for them when they broke that covenant. Rather, it meant that they would be held to a higher standard of obedience.

5. Thus, the "day of the Lord" would not be a time of miraculous deliverance for unrepentant Israel. Rather, it would be a time of terrible destruction.

6. A faithful remnant of Israel would be preserved and would someday see glorious restoration and blessing.

OUTLINE

I. Superscription (1:1)

II. Oracles of Judgment (1:2–6:14)

III. Visions of Judgment (7:1–9:15)

AMOS

1 The words of Amos, who was among the shepherds of Tekoa, which he saw concerning Israel in the days of Uzziah king of Judah and in the days of Jeroboam the son of Joash, king of Israel, two years before the earthquake.

Judgment on Israel's Neighbors

²And he said:

> "The LORD roars from Zion
>   and utters his voice from
>   Jerusalem;
>   the pastures of the shepherds
>   mourn,
>   and the top of Carmel withers."

³Thus says the LORD:

> "For three transgressions of
>   Damascus,
>   and for four, I will not revoke the
>   punishment,
> because they have threshed Gilead
>   with threshing sledges of iron.
> ⁴ So I will send a fire upon the house of
>   Hazael,
>   and it shall devour the strongholds
>   of Ben-hadad.
> ⁵ I will break the gate-bar of
>   Damascus,
>   and cut off the inhabitants from the
>   Valley of Aven,
> and him who holds the scepter from
>   Beth-eden;
>   and the people of Syria shall go into
>   exile to Kir,"
>   says the LORD.

⁶Thus says the LORD:

> "For three transgressions of Gaza,
>   and for four, I will not revoke the
>   punishment,
> because they carried into exile a
>   whole people
>   to deliver them up to Edom.
> ⁷ So I will send a fire upon the wall of
>   Gaza,
>   and it shall devour her strong-
>   holds.

> ⁸ I will cut off the inhabitants from
>   Ashdod,
>   and him who holds the scepter
>   from Ashkelon;
> I will turn my hand against Ekron,
>   and the remnant of the Philistines
>   shall perish,"
>   says the Lord GOD.

⁹Thus says the LORD:

> "For three transgressions of Tyre,
>   and for four, I will not revoke the
>   punishment,

> because they delivered up a whole
>   people to Edom,
>   and did not remember the covenant
>   of brotherhood.
> ¹⁰ So I will send a fire upon the wall of
>   Tyre,
>   and it shall devour her strongholds."

¹¹Thus says the LORD:

> "For three transgressions of Edom,
>   and for four, I will not revoke the
>   punishment,
> because he pursued his brother with
>   the sword
>   and cast off all pity,
> and his anger tore perpetually,
>   and he kept his wrath forever.
> ¹² So I will send a fire upon Teman,
>   and it shall devour the strongholds
>   of Bozrah."

13 Thus says the LORD:

"For three transgressions of the
        Ammonites,
    and for four, I will not revoke the
        punishment,
because they have ripped open preg-
        nant women in Gilead,
    that they might enlarge their border.
14 So I will kindle a fire in the wall of
        Rabbah,
    and it shall devour her strongholds,

PROFILE
AMOS

Amos was a shepherd from the Judean town of Tekoa, a "herdsman and a dresser of sycamore figs" (7:14). He prophesied primarily to the northern kingdom of Israel during a time of political stability and great wealth. As they often did, the people of Israel saw this prosperity as a sign of God's blessing. But God used Amos to tell them that this was not the case. Much of the nation's wealth had been acquired by oppressing the poor, and so their insincere worship was disgusting to God. Israel had rejected its calling to be a place where God's righteousness and justice was demonstrated to the world. Because of their unfaithfulness, the Israelites would be punished severely. God would remain faithful to his people, however, and would restore what had been destroyed. Peace and blessing would come to Israel—and the world—through the coming of the Messiah.

KEY REFERENCE: AMOS 5:18-24

---

with shouting on the day of battle,
    with a tempest in the day of the
        whirlwind;
15   and their king shall go into exile,
    he and his princes together,"
                            says the LORD.

2 Thus says the LORD:

"For three transgressions of Moab,
    and for four, I will not revoke the
        punishment,

because he burned to lime
    the bones of the king of Edom.
2   So I will send a fire upon Moab,
    and it shall devour the strongholds
        of Kerioth,
and Moab shall die amid uproar,
    amid shouting and the sound of the
        trumpet;
3   I will cut off the ruler from its midst,
    and will kill all its princes with him,"
                            says the LORD.

Judgment on Judah
4 Thus says the LORD:

"For three transgressions of Judah,
    and for four, I will not revoke the
        punishment,
because they have rejected the law of
        the LORD,
    and have not kept his statutes,

but their lies have led them astray,
    those after which their fathers
        walked.
5   So I will send a fire upon Judah,
    and it shall devour the strongholds
        of Jerusalem."

Judgment on Israel
6 Thus says the LORD:

"For three transgressions of Israel,
    and for four, I will not revoke the
        punishment,
because they sell the righteous for
        silver,
    and the needy for a pair of sandals—
7   those who trample the head of the
        poor into the dust of the earth
    and turn aside the way of the
        afflicted;
a man and his father go in to the same
        girl,
    so that my holy name is profaned;

8 they lay themselves down beside
    every altar
  on garments taken in pledge,
  and in the house of their God they
    drink
    the wine of those who have been
      fined.

9 "Yet it was I who destroyed the Amorite
    before them,
  whose height was like the height of
    the cedars
  and who was as strong as the oaks;
  I destroyed his fruit above
  and his roots beneath.

10 Also it was I who brought you up out
    of the land of Egypt
  and led you forty years in the wil-
    derness,
  to possess the land of the Amorite.

11 And I raised up some of your sons for
    prophets,
  and some of your young men for
    Nazirites.
  Is it not indeed so, O people of
    Israel?"
                    declares the Lord.

12 "But you made the Nazirites drink wine,
  and commanded the prophets,
  saying, 'You shall not prophesy.'

13 "Behold, I will press you down in your
    place,
  as a cart full of sheaves presses
    down.

14 Flight shall perish from the swift,
  and the strong shall not retain his
    strength,
  nor shall the mighty save his life;

15 he who handles the bow shall not
    stand,
  and he who is swift of foot shall not
    save himself,
  nor shall he who rides the horse
    save his life;

16 and he who is stout of heart among
    the mighty
  shall flee away naked in that day,"
                    declares the Lord.

Israel's Guilt and Punishment

3 Hear this word that the Lord has spoken
  against you, O people of Israel, against
the whole family that I brought up out of
the land of Egypt:

2 "You only have I known
    of all the families of the earth;
  therefore I will punish you
    for all your iniquities.

3 "Do two walk together,
    unless they have agreed to meet?

4 Does a lion roar in the forest,
    when he has no prey?
  Does a young lion cry out from his
    den,
    if he has taken nothing?

5 Does a bird fall in a snare on the earth,
    when there is no trap for it?
  Does a snare spring up from the
    ground,
    when it has taken nothing?

6 Is a trumpet blown in a city,
    and the people are not afraid?

GETTING THE MESSAGE

The winter house and summer house.
Many wealthy Samarians had two homes.
One would be in the warmer, southern
regions while the other was built in the
cooler north (3:15). This extravagance
made it all the more obvious that Amos
was justified in his criticism of the
wealthy people who ignored the needs
of the poor.

  Does disaster come to a city,
    unless the Lord has done it?

7 "For the Lord God does nothing
    without revealing his secret
    to his servants the prophets.

8 The lion has roared;
    who will not fear?
  The Lord God has spoken;
    who can but prophesy?"

9 Proclaim to the strongholds in Ashdod
    and to the strongholds in the land
      of Egypt,
  and say, "Assemble yourselves on the
      mountains of Samaria,
    and see the great tumults within
      her,
    and the oppressed in her midst."

10 "They do not know how to do right,"
    declares the Lord,
  "those who store up violence and
      robbery in their strongholds."

¹¹Therefore thus says the Lord GOD:

"An adversary shall surround the land
    and bring down your defenses from
    you,
    and your strongholds shall be
    plundered."

¹²Thus says the LORD: "As the shepherd rescues from the mouth of the lion two legs, or a piece of an ear, so shall the people of Israel who dwell in Samaria be rescued, with the corner of a couch and part of a bed.

¹³ "Hear, and testify against the house of
    Jacob,"
    declares the Lord GOD, the God of
    hosts,
¹⁴ "that on the day I punish Israel for his
    transgressions,

GETTING THE MESSAGE

The **blighting** of crops (4:9) was a serious problem for farmers because there was no known way at the time to stop it. Dry winds would blow up from the Sahara at hurricane-like speeds. These dusty winds sucked all moisture out of plant life, leaving the plants themselves brown and wilted.

I will punish the altars of Bethel,
    and the horns of the altar shall be cut
    off
    and fall to the ground.
¹⁵ I will strike the winter house along
    with the summer house,
    and the houses of ivory shall per-
    ish,
    and the great houses shall come to an
    end,"
            declares the LORD.

4 "Hear this word, you cows of Bashan,
    who are on the mountain of
    Samaria,
    who oppress the poor, who crush the
    needy,
    who say to your husbands, 'Bring,
    that we may drink!'
² The Lord GOD has sworn by his holi-
    ness
    that, behold, the days are coming
    upon you,

when they shall take you away with
    hooks,
    even the last of you with fishhooks.
³ And you shall go out through the
    breaches,
    each one straight ahead;
    and you shall be cast out into
    Harmon,"
            declares the LORD.

⁴ "Come to Bethel, and transgress;
    to Gilgal, and multiply transgres-
    sion;
    bring your sacrifices every morning,
    your tithes every three days;
⁵ offer a sacrifice of thanksgiving of
    that which is leavened,
    and proclaim freewill offerings,
    publish them;
    for so you love to do, O people of
    Israel!"
            declares the Lord GOD.

Israel Has Not Returned to the LORD
⁶ "I gave you cleanness of teeth in all
    your cities,
    and lack of bread in all your places,
    yet you did not return to me,"
            declares the LORD.

⁷ "I also withheld the rain from you
    when there were yet three months
    to the harvest;
    I would send rain on one city,
    and send no rain on another city;
    one field would have rain,
    and the field on which it did not
    rain would wither;
⁸ so two or three cities would wander to
    another city
    to drink water, and would not be
    satisfied;
    yet you did not return to me,"
            declares the LORD.

⁹ "I struck you with blight and mildew;
    your many gardens and your vine-
    yards,
    your fig trees and your olive trees
    the locust devoured;
    yet you did not return to me,"
            declares the LORD.

¹⁰ "I sent among you a pestilence after
    the manner of Egypt;
    I killed your young men with the
    sword,

and carried away your horses,
　　and I made the stench of your camp
　　　　go up into your nostrils;
　　yet you did not return to me,"
　　　　　　declares the LORD.

11 "I overthrew some of you,
　　as when God overthrew Sodom and
　　　　Gomorrah,
　　and you were as a brand plucked
　　　　out of the burning;
　　yet you did not return to me,"
　　　　　　declares the LORD.

12 "Therefore thus I will do to you,
　　O Israel;
　　because I will do this to you,
　　　　prepare to meet your God, O Israel!"

13 For behold, he who forms the moun-
　　　　tains and creates the wind,
　　and declares to man what is his
　　　　thought,
　　who makes the morning darkness,
　　　　and treads on the heights of the
　　　　　　earth—
　　　　the LORD, the God of hosts, is his
　　　　　　name!

Seek the LORD and Live

5 Hear this word that I take up over you in
lamentation, O house of Israel:

2 "Fallen, no more to rise,
　　is the virgin Israel;
　　forsaken on her land,
　　　　with none to raise her up."

3 For thus says the Lord GOD:

"The city that went out a thousand
　　shall have a hundred left,
　　and that which went out a hundred
　　　　shall have ten left
　　to the house of Israel."

4 For thus says the LORD to the house of Israel:

"Seek me and live;
5 　　but do not seek Bethel,
　　and do not enter into Gilgal
　　　　or cross over to Beersheba;
　　for Gilgal shall surely go into exile,
　　　　and Bethel shall come to nothing."

6 Seek the LORD and live,
　　lest he break out like fire in the
　　　　house of Joseph,
　　and it devour, with none to quench
　　　　it for Bethel,

7 O you who turn justice to wormwood
　　and cast down righteousness to the
　　　　earth!

8 He who made the Pleiades and Orion,
　　and turns deep darkness into the
　　　　morning
　　and darkens the day into night,
　　who calls for the waters of the sea
　　　　and pours them out on the surface
　　　　　　of the earth,
　　the LORD is his name;

9 who makes destruction flash forth
　　　　against the strong,
　　so that destruction comes upon the
　　　　fortress.

10 They hate him who reproves in the
　　　　gate,
　　and they abhor him who speaks the
　　　　truth.

> ### GETTING THE MESSAGE
>
> Constellations like the **Pleiades** and **Orion** (5:8) were important to pagan cultures, which worshiped them as gods. Images of them could be found on seals and scrolls throughout the ancient Near East. Prophets like Amos believed that these constellations were not gods, but rather were evidence of the scope and majesty of God's creation.

11 Therefore because you trample on the
　　　　poor
　　and you exact taxes of grain from
　　　　him,
　　you have built houses of hewn stone,
　　　　but you shall not dwell in them;
　　you have planted pleasant vineyards,
　　　　but you shall not drink their wine.

12 For I know how many are your trans-
　　　　gressions
　　　　and how great are your sins—
　　you who afflict the righteous, who
　　　　take a bribe,
　　　　and turn aside the needy in the
　　　　　　gate.

13 Therefore he who is prudent will keep
　　　　silent in such a time,
　　for it is an evil time.

14 Seek good, and not evil,
　　that you may live;

and so the LORD, the God of hosts, will
be with you,
as you have said.
15 Hate evil, and love good,
and establish justice in the gate;
it may be that the LORD, the God of
hosts,
will be gracious to the remnant of
Joseph.

16 Therefore thus says the LORD, the God of
hosts, the Lord:

"In all the squares there shall be wailing,
and in all the streets they shall say,
'Alas! Alas!'
They shall call the farmers to mourning
and to wailing those who are skilled
in lamentation,

GETTING THE MESSAGE

Only the very wealthy could afford to
eat the tender meat of **calves from the
midst of the stall** (6:4). These animals
were set aside from other livestock and
fed a strict diet of the more costly grains
like barley in order to fatten them up.
This fattening process ensured that the
animals would bring a higher price when
sold at the market.

17 and in all vineyards there shall be
wailing,
for I will pass through your midst,"
says the LORD.

Let Justice Roll Down

18 Woe to you who desire the day of the
LORD!
Why would you have the day of the
LORD?
It is darkness, and not light,
19 as if a man fled from a lion,
and a bear met him,
or went into the house and leaned his
hand against the wall,
and a serpent bit him.
20 Is not the day of the LORD darkness,
and not light,
and gloom with no brightness in it?

21 "I hate, I despise your feasts,
and I take no delight in your solemn assemblies.

22 Even though you offer me your burnt
offerings and grain offerings,
I will not accept them;
and the peace offerings of your fattened animals,
I will not look upon them.
23 Take away from me the noise of your
songs;
to the melody of your harps I will
not listen.
24 But let justice roll down like waters,
and righteousness like an ever-
flowing stream.

25 "Did you bring to me sacrifices and
offerings during the forty years in the wilderness, O house of Israel? 26 You shall take
up Sikkuth your king, and Kiyyun your
star-god—your images that you made for
yourselves, 27 and I will send you into exile
beyond Damascus," says the LORD, whose
name is the God of hosts.

Woe to Those at Ease in Zion

6 "Woe to those who are at ease in Zion,
and to those who feel secure on the
mountain of Samaria,
the notable men of the first of the
nations,
to whom the house of Israel
comes!
2 Pass over to Calneh, and see,
and from there go to Hamath the
great;
then go down to Gath of the
Philistines.
Are you better than these kingdoms?
Or is their territory greater than
your territory,
3 O you who put far away the day of
disaster
and bring near the seat of violence?

4 "Woe to those who lie on beds of
ivory
and stretch themselves out on their
couches,
and eat lambs from the flock
and calves from the midst of the
stall,
5 who sing idle songs to the sound of
the harp
and like David invent for themselves instruments of music,

6 who drink wine in bowls
and anoint themselves with the
finest oils,
but are not grieved over the ruin of
Joseph!
7 Therefore they shall now be the first
of those who go into exile,
and the revelry of those who
stretch themselves out shall
pass away."

8 The Lord GOD has sworn by himself, declares the LORD, the God of hosts:

"I abhor the pride of Jacob
and hate his strongholds,
and I will deliver up the city and all
that is in it."

9 And if ten men remain in one house, they shall die. 10 And when one's relative, the one who anoints him for burial, shall take him up to bring the bones out of the house, and shall say to him who is in the innermost parts of the house, "Is there still anyone with you?" he shall say, "No"; and he shall say, "Silence! We must not mention the name of the LORD."

11 For behold, the LORD commands,
and the great house shall be struck
down into fragments,
and the little house into bits.
12 Do horses run on rocks?
Does one plow there with oxen?
But you have turned justice into poison
and the fruit of righteousness into
wormwood[1]—
13 you who rejoice in Lo-debar,[2]
who say, "Have we not by our own
strength
captured Karnaim[3] for ourselves?"
14 "For behold, I will raise up against you
a nation,
O house of Israel," declares the
LORD, the God of hosts;
"and they shall oppress you from Lebo-
hamath
to the Brook of the Arabah."

Warning Visions

7 This is what the Lord GOD showed me: behold, he was forming locusts when the latter growth was just beginning to sprout, and behold, it was the latter growth after the king's mowings. 2 When they had finished eating the grass of the land, I said,

"O Lord GOD, please forgive!
How can Jacob stand?
He is so small!"
3 The LORD relented concerning this:
"It shall not be," said the LORD.

4 This is what the Lord GOD showed me: behold, the Lord GOD was calling for a judgment by fire, and it devoured the great deep and was eating up the land. 5 Then I said,

"O Lord GOD, please cease!
How can Jacob stand?
He is so small!"
6 The LORD relented concerning this:
"This also shall not be," said the Lord
GOD.

7 This is what he showed me: behold, the Lord was standing beside a wall built with a plumb line, with a plumb line in his hand. 8 And the LORD said to me, "Amos, what do you see?" And I said, "A plumb line." Then the Lord said,

"Behold, I am setting a plumb line
in the midst of my people Israel;
I will never again pass by them;
9 the high places of Isaac shall be made
desolate,
and the sanctuaries of Israel shall
be laid waste,
and I will rise against the house of
Jeroboam with the sword."

Amos Accused

10 Then Amaziah the priest of Bethel sent to Jeroboam king of Israel, saying, "Amos has conspired against you in the midst of the house of Israel. The land is not able to bear all his words. 11 For thus Amos has said,

"'Jeroboam shall die by the sword,
and Israel must go into exile
away from his land.'"

12 And Amaziah said to Amos, "O seer, go, flee away to the land of Judah, and eat bread there, and prophesy there, 13 but never again prophesy at Bethel, for it is the king's sanctuary, and it is a temple of the kingdom." 14 Then Amos answered and said to Amaziah, "I was no prophet, nor a prophet's son, but I was a herdsman and a dresser of

---

[1] Or into bitter fruit [2] Lo-debar means nothing [3] Karnaim means horns (a symbol of strength)

sycamore figs. 15 But the LORD took me from following the flock, and the LORD said to me, 'Go, prophesy to my people Israel.' 16 Now therefore hear the word of the LORD.

> "You say, 'Do not prophesy against
>   Israel,
>   and do not preach against the house
>   of Isaac.'

17 Therefore thus says the LORD:

> "'Your wife shall be a prostitute in the
>   city,
>   and your sons and your daughters
>   shall fall by the sword,
>   and your land shall be divided up
>   with a measuring line;

GETTING THE MESSAGE

The **annual flooding of the Nile** (8:8) took place from the months of June to September. Monsoon rains from the mountains to the south would overflow the banks of the Nile, bringing with it the fertile silt from the river. Crops could then be sown in October and harvested in February. This cycle went on for thousands of years until 1970, when Egypt completed construction on the Aswan High Dam, which captures the floodwaters for hydroelectric power.

> you yourself shall die in an unclean
>   land,
>   and Israel shall surely go into exile
>   away from its land.'"

The Coming Day of Bitter Mourning

8 This is what the Lord GOD showed me: behold, a basket of summer fruit. 2 And he said, "Amos, what do you see?" And I said, "A basket of summer fruit." Then the LORD said to me,

> "The end has come upon my people
>   Israel;
>   I will never again pass by them.
> 3 The songs of the temple shall become
>   wailings in that day,"
>   declares the Lord GOD.
> "So many dead bodies!"
> "They are thrown everywhere!"
> "Silence!"

4 Hear this, you who trample on the
>   needy
>   and bring the poor of the land to an
>   end,
> 5 saying, "When will the new moon be
>   over,
>   that we may sell grain?
> And the Sabbath,
>   that we may offer wheat for sale,
> that we may make the ephah small
>   and the shekel great
>   and deal deceitfully with false bal-
>   ances,
> 6 that we may buy the poor for silver
>   and the needy for a pair of sandals
>   and sell the chaff of the wheat?"

7 The LORD has sworn by the pride of
>   Jacob:
> "Surely I will never forget any of their
>   deeds.
> 8 Shall not the land tremble on this
>   account,
>   and everyone mourn who dwells in
>   it,
> and all of it rise like the Nile,
>   and be tossed about and sink again,
>   like the Nile of Egypt?"

9 "And on that day," declares the Lord GOD,
>   "I will make the sun go down at noon
>   and darken the earth in broad day-
>   light.
> 10 I will turn your feasts into mourning
>   and all your songs into lamentation;
> I will bring sackcloth on every waist
>   and baldness on every head;
> I will make it like the mourning for an
>   only son
>   and the end of it like a bitter day.

11 "Behold, the days are coming," declares
>   the Lord GOD,
>   "when I will send a famine on the
>   land—
> not a famine of bread, nor a thirst for
>   water,
>   but of hearing the words of the LORD.
> 12 They shall wander from sea to sea,
>   and from north to east;
> they shall run to and fro, to seek the
>   word of the LORD,
>   but they shall not find it.

13 "In that day the lovely virgins and the
>   young men
>   shall faint for thirst.

14   Those who swear by the Guilt of
        Samaria,
    and say, 'As your god lives, O Dan,'
    and, 'As the Way of Beersheba lives,'
        they shall fall, and never rise again."

The Destruction of Israel

9 I saw the Lord standing beside the altar,
and he said:

"Strike the capitals until the thresholds
    shake,
    and shatter them on the heads of all
        the people;
and those who are left of them I will
        kill with the sword;
    not one of them shall flee away;
    not one of them shall escape.

2   "If they dig into Sheol,
    from there shall my hand take
        them;
  if they climb up to heaven,
    from there I will bring them down.
3   If they hide themselves on the top of
        Carmel,
    from there I will search them out
        and take them;
  and if they hide from my sight at the
        bottom of the sea,
    there I will command the serpent,
        and it shall bite them.
4   And if they go into captivity before
        their enemies,
    there I will command the sword,
        and it shall kill them;
  and I will fix my eyes upon them
    for evil and not for good."

5   The Lord GOD of hosts,
  he who touches the earth and it melts,
    and all who dwell in it mourn,
  and all of it rises like the Nile,
    and sinks again, like the Nile of
        Egypt;
6   who builds his upper chambers in the
        heavens
    and founds his vault upon the
        earth;
  who calls for the waters of the sea
    and pours them out upon the sur-
        face of the earth—
  the LORD is his name.

7   "Are you not like the Cushites to me,
    O people of Israel?" declares the
        LORD.

"Did I not bring up Israel from the land
    of Egypt,
  and the Philistines from Caphtor
    and the Syrians from Kir?
8   Behold, the eyes of the Lord GOD are
    upon the sinful kingdom,
    and I will destroy it from the sur-
        face of the ground,
    except that I will not utterly destroy
        the house of Jacob,"
                declares the LORD.
9   "For behold, I will command,
    and shake the house of Israel
        among all the nations
  as one shakes with a sieve,
    but no pebble shall fall to the earth.
10   All the sinners of my people shall die
        by the sword,
    who say, 'Disaster shall not overtake
        or meet us.'

The Restoration of Israel

11   "In that day I will raise up
    the booth of David that is fallen
  and repair its breaches,
    and raise up its ruins
    and rebuild it as in the days of old,
12   that they may possess the remnant of
        Edom
    and all the nations who are called
        by my name,"
  declares the LORD who does this.

13   "Behold, the days are coming," declares
    the LORD,
    "when the plowman shall overtake
        the reaper
    and the treader of grapes him who
        sows the seed;
  the mountains shall drip sweet wine,
    and all the hills shall flow with it.
14   I will restore the fortunes of my peo-
        ple Israel,
    and they shall rebuild the ruined
        cities and inhabit them;
  they shall plant vineyards and drink
        their wine,
    and they shall make gardens and
        eat their fruit.
15   I will plant them on their land,
    and they shall never again be
        uprooted
    out of the land that I have given
        them,"
              says the LORD your God.

INTRODUCTION TO OBADIAH

586 B.C.	c. 570 B.C.	553 B.C.
Fall of Judah	Prophetic ministry of Obadiah	Babylon's campaign against Edom

AUTHOR AND DATE

The book of Obadiah records a prophetic "vision" given by the Lord to a man named Obadiah. The only thing known about this prophet is his name. The book was probably written in the first half of the Babylonian exile, after 586 B.C. (when Babylon destroyed Jerusalem) and before 553 (when Babylon attacked Edom).

BACKGROUND

The people of Jerusalem experienced God's judgment (v. 16a) when the Babylonians invaded and "cast lots for Jerusalem" (v. 11). The Edomites were descended from Jacob's brother Esau and were Israel's eastern neighbors. They should have assisted Israel during the crisis. Instead, they sided with the foreign invaders and even took advantage of Israel's difficulty (vv. 10–14).

Holy Zion had been defiled, and God's people were publicly shamed. Israel was devastated by the exile. Does Israel have a future? Will Zion be defiled forever? Will the plan for Abraham's offspring to bring blessing to the world come to nothing? Will Edom and the hostile nations triumph? Is God indifferent to all of this?

Obadiah proclaimed God's word in response to this situation. The message of Obadiah essentially spells out what Lamentations 4:22 announces: restoration for Zion but doom for Edom.

THEME

Edom, together with all other nations that oppose Israel's God and his people, will experience God's judgment (vv. 1–15). God's own covenant people have been judged by their exile already. God will restore them (vv. 16–21). The book ends with the promise of the kingdom of God.

KEY THEMES

1. Enemies will be put to shame because of their opposition to God's people (v. 10).

2. Every proud human effort at security will ultimately fail before God's coming judgment (vv. 1–9).

3. God's justice is strict and fair, with the punishment corresponding to the sins (v. 15).

4. Reunited Israel will experience God's deliverance (vv. 16–17), possess the Promised Land, and defeat and rule over Edom (vv. 17–21).

5. In the future, Yahweh will definitively establish his eternal kingdom (v. 21).

OUTLINE

I. First Announcement of Judgment to Edom (vv. 1–4)

II. Second Announcement of Judgment to Edom (vv. 5–7)

III. Announcement of Judgment, Accusation, and Warning to Edom (vv. 8–15)

IV. Promise of Restoration and Victory to Israel (vv. 16–18)

V. Promise of Restoration and Yahweh's Kingship (vv. 19–21)

OBADIAH

¹The vision of Obadiah.

Edom Will Be Humbled

Thus says the Lord GOD concerning
  Edom:
We have heard a report from the
  LORD,
  and a messenger has been sent
    among the nations:
"Rise up! Let us rise against her for
  battle!"
² Behold, I will make you small among
    the nations;
  you shall be utterly despised.
³ The pride of your heart has deceived
    you,
  you who live in the clefts of the
    rock,
  in your lofty dwelling,
who say in your heart,
  "Who will bring me down to the
    ground?"
⁴ Though you soar aloft like the eagle,
  though your nest is set among the
    stars,
  from there I will bring you down,
              declares the LORD.
⁵ If thieves came to you,
  if plunderers came by night—
  how you have been destroyed!—
  would they not steal only enough
    for themselves?
If grape gatherers came to you,
  would they not leave gleanings?
⁶ How Esau has been pillaged,
  his treasures sought out!
⁷ All your allies have driven you to your
    border;
  those at peace with you have
    deceived you;
they have prevailed against you;
  those who eat your bread have set a
    trap beneath you—
  you have no understanding.
⁸ Will I not on that day, declares the
    LORD,
  destroy the wise men out of Edom,
and understanding out of Mount
  Esau?
⁹ And your mighty men shall be dis-
    mayed, O Teman,
  so that every man from Mount Esau
    will be cut off by slaughter.

Edom's Violence Against Jacob

¹⁰ Because of the violence done to your
    brother Jacob,
  shame shall cover you,
  and you shall be cut off forever.

---

¹¹ On the day that you stood aloof,
  on the day that strangers carried off
    his wealth
  and foreigners entered his gates
    and cast lots for Jerusalem,
  you were like one of them.

12   But do not gloat over the day of your
          brother
       in the day of his misfortune;
    do not rejoice over the people of Judah
       in the day of their ruin;
    do not boast
       in the day of distress.
13   Do not enter the gate of my people
       in the day of their calamity;
    do not gloat over his disaster
       in the day of his calamity;
    do not loot his wealth
       in the day of his calamity.

GETTING THE MESSAGE

A call to arms. Alliances and treaties
in the ancient world were important in
times of war, just as they are today. Allies
supported each other by combining
forces against the enemy. Messengers
could be sent to allies requesting
soldiers, supplies, and even intelligence
on enemy troop movements and
strength. In vv. 1–14, Obadiah warns
Edom that it will be destroyed by its
former allies.

14   Do not stand at the crossroads
          to cut off his fugitives;
    do not hand over his survivors
       in the day of distress.

The Day of the Lord Is Near

15   For the day of the LORD is near upon
          all the nations.
       As you have done, it shall be done to
          you;
          your deeds shall return on your
             own head.

16   For as you have drunk on my holy
          mountain,
          so all the nations shall drink con-
             tinually;
       they shall drink and swallow,
          and shall be as though they had
             never been.
17   But in Mount Zion there shall be those
          who escape,
          and it shall be holy,
       and the house of Jacob shall possess
             their own possessions.
18   The house of Jacob shall be a fire,
          and the house of Joseph a flame,
          and the house of Esau stubble;
       they shall burn them and consume
             them,
          and there shall be no survivor for
             the house of Esau,
                for the LORD has spoken.

The Kingdom of the Lord

19   Those of the Negeb shall possess
          Mount Esau,
          and those of the Shephelah
             shall possess the land of the
                Philistines;
       they shall possess the land of Ephraim
             and the land of Samaria,
          and Benjamin shall possess Gilead.
20   The exiles of this host of the people of
          Israel
          shall possess the land of the
             Canaanites as far as Zarephath,
       and the exiles of Jerusalem who are in
             Sepharad
          shall possess the cities of the Negeb.
21   Saviors shall go up to Mount Zion
          to rule Mount Esau,
          and the kingdom shall be the
             LORD's.

INTRODUCTION TO JONAH

793/781 B.C.	c. 760 B.C.	722 B.C.
Reign of Jeroboam II begins	Prophetic ministry of Jonah	Fall of Israel

AUTHOR AND DATE

Jonah prophesied during the peaceful and prosperous time of Jeroboam II (2 Kings 14:23–28), who ruled in Israel (the northern kingdom) from 782 to 753 B.C. This was a time when Assyria was not a threat to Israel.

OVERVIEW

The Lord called Jonah to go to the great Assyrian city of Nineveh to pronounce judgment on it. Jonah attempted to escape the Lord's calling by sailing from the seaport of Joppa to Tarshish, which was probably on the shores of the western Mediterranean. Eventually he obeyed the Lord and traveled overland to Nineveh.

THEME

The primary theme in Jonah is that God's compassion is boundless, not limited just to "us" (Jonah and the Israelites) but also available for "them" (the pagan sailors and the Ninevites).

KEY THEMES

1. God is in sovereign control over all events on the earth.

2. God is determined to get his message to the nations.

3. People need to repent from sin in general, and from self-centeredness and hypocrisy in particular.

4. God promises that he will forgive when people repent.

OUTLINE

The story of Jonah includes seven episodes, with the first three paralleled by the second three. The final episode stands alone as the climax of the story:

   A. Jonah's commissioning and flight (1:1–3)

      B. Jonah and the pagan sailors (1:4–16)

         C. Jonah's grateful prayer (1:17–2:10)

   A'. Jonah's recommissioning and compliance (3:1–3a)

      B'. Jonah and the pagan Ninevites (3:3b–10)

         C'. Jonah's angry prayer (4:1–4)

   D. Jonah's lesson about compassion (4:5–11)

JONAH

Jonah Flees the Presence of the Lord

1 Now the word of the Lord came to Jonah the son of Amittai, saying, ² "Arise, go to Nineveh, that great city, and call out against it, for their evil has come up before me." ³ But Jonah rose to flee to Tarshish from the presence of the Lord. He went down to Joppa and found a ship going to Tarshish. So he paid the fare and went down into it, to go with them to Tarshish, away from the presence of the Lord.

⁴ But the Lord hurled a great wind upon the sea, and there was a mighty tempest on the sea, so that the ship threatened to break up. ⁵ Then the mariners were afraid, and each cried out to his god. And they hurled the cargo that was in the ship into the sea to lighten it for them. But Jonah had gone down into the inner part of the ship and had lain down and was fast asleep. ⁶ So the captain came and said to him, "What do you mean, you sleeper? Arise, call out to your god! Perhaps the god will give a thought to us, that we may not perish."

Jonah Is Thrown into the Sea

⁷ And they said to one another, "Come, let us cast lots, that we may know on whose account this evil has come upon us." So they cast lots, and the lot fell on Jonah. ⁸ Then they said to him, "Tell us on whose account this evil has come upon us. What is your occupation? And where do you come from? What is your country? And of what people are you?" ⁹ And he said to them, "I am a Hebrew, and I fear the Lord, the God of heaven, who made the sea and the dry land." ¹⁰ Then the men were exceedingly afraid and said to him, "What is this that you have done!" For the men knew that he was fleeing from the presence of the Lord, because he had told them.

¹¹ Then they said to him, "What shall we do to you, that the sea may quiet down for us?" For the sea grew more and more tempestuous. ¹² He said to them, "Pick me up and hurl me into the sea; then the sea will quiet down for you, for I know it is because

of me that this great tempest has come upon you." ¹³ Nevertheless, the men rowed hard to get back to dry land, but they could not, for the sea grew more and more tempestuous against them. ¹⁴ Therefore they called out to the Lord, "O Lord, let us not perish for this man's life, and lay not on us innocent blood, for you, O Lord, have done as it pleased you." ¹⁵ So they picked up Jonah and hurled him into the sea, and the sea ceased from its raging. ¹⁶ Then the men feared the Lord exceedingly, and they offered a sacrifice to the Lord and made vows.

A Great Fish Swallows Jonah

¹⁷ And the Lord appointed a great fish to swallow up Jonah. And Jonah was in the belly of the fish three days and three nights.

Jonah's Prayer

2 Then Jonah prayed to the Lord his God from the belly of the fish, ² saying,

"I called out to the Lord, out of my
    distress,
    and he answered me;
out of the belly of Sheol I cried,
    and you heard my voice.
³   For you cast me into the deep,
    into the heart of the seas,
    and the flood surrounded me;
all your waves and your billows
    passed over me.
⁴   Then I said, 'I am driven away
    from your sight;
yet I shall again look
    upon your holy temple.'

5 The waters closed in over me to take
    my life;
  the deep surrounded me;
weeds were wrapped about my head
6   at the roots of the mountains.
I went down to the land
  whose bars closed upon me for-
     ever;
yet you brought up my life from the
    pit,
  O LORD my God.

PROFILE
JONAH

God called the prophet Jonah to travel to the city of Nineveh and to speak out against it. Nineveh was an Assyrian city, part of an empire known for its cruelty, that had long threatened Israel. The last thing Jonah wanted was for these particular people to experience the mercy and compassion of the God of Israel. Therefore he rejected the Lord's call and tried to travel as far as he possibly could in the opposite direction from Nineveh! After three days and three nights in the belly of a large fish, however, Jonah repented and went to Nineveh. He delivered a prophetic message against the city, just as the Lord had commanded. Much to Jonah's surprise, the people of Nineveh repented, and the Lord relented from his plans to destroy them. Jonah learned that God is ready to show mercy to all who will turn their hearts to him.

KEY REFERENCE: JONAH 3:6-10

7 When my life was fainting away,
  I remembered the LORD,
and my prayer came to you,
  into your holy temple.
8 Those who pay regard to vain idols
  forsake their hope of steadfast love.
9 But I with the voice of thanksgiving
  will sacrifice to you;
what I have vowed I will pay.
  Salvation belongs to the LORD!"

10 And the LORD spoke to the fish, and it vomited Jonah out upon the dry land.

Jonah Goes to Nineveh

3 Then the word of the LORD came to Jonah the second time, saying, 2 "Arise, go to Nineveh, that great city, and call out against it the message that I tell you." 3 So Jonah arose and went to Nineveh, according to the word of the LORD. Now Nineveh was an exceedingly great city, three days' journey in breadth. 4 Jonah began to go into the city, going a day's journey. And he called out, "Yet forty days, and Nineveh shall be overthrown!" 5 And the people of Nineveh believed God. They called for a fast and put on sackcloth, from the greatest of them to the least of them.

The People of Nineveh Repent

6 The word reached the king of Nineveh, and he arose from his throne, removed his robe, covered himself with sackcloth, and sat in ashes. 7 And he issued a proclamation and published through Nineveh, "By

▶ GETTING THE MESSAGE

Nineveh was located along the Tigris River, across from what is now the city of Mosul in northern Iraq. Its location at the intersection of important trade routes made it strong and wealthy.

the decree of the king and his nobles: Let neither man nor beast, herd nor flock, taste anything. Let them not feed or drink water, 8 but let man and beast be covered with sackcloth, and let them call out mightily to God. Let everyone turn from his evil way and from the violence that is in his hands. 9 Who knows? God may turn and relent and turn from his fierce anger, so that we may not perish." 10 When God saw what they did, how they turned from their evil way, God relented of the disaster that he had said he would do to them, and he did not do it.

Jonah's Anger and the LORD's Compassion

4 But it displeased Jonah exceedingly, and he was angry. 2 And he prayed to the LORD and said, "O LORD, is not this what I said when I was yet in my country? That is why I made haste to flee to Tarshish; for I knew that you are a gracious God and

merciful, slow to anger and abounding in steadfast love, and relenting from disaster. [3] Therefore now, O LORD, please take my life from me, for it is better for me to die than to live." [4] And the LORD said, "Do you do well to be angry?"

[5] Jonah went out of the city and sat to the east of the city and made a booth for himself there. He sat under it in the shade, till he should see what would become of the city. [6] Now the LORD God appointed a plant and made it come up over Jonah, that it might be a shade over his head, to save him from his discomfort. So Jonah was exceedingly glad because of the plant. [7] But when dawn came up the next day, God appointed a worm that attacked the plant, so that it withered. [8] When the sun rose, God appointed a scorching east wind, and the sun beat down on the head of Jonah so that he was faint. And he asked that he might die and said, "It is better for me to die than to live." [9] But God said to Jonah, "Do you do well to be angry for the plant?" And he said, "Yes, I do well to be angry,

angry enough to die." [10] And the LORD said, "You pity the plant, for which you did not labor, nor did you make it grow, which came into being in a night and perished

in a night. [11] And should not I pity Nineveh, that great city, in which there are more than 120,000 persons who do not know their right hand from their left, and also much cattle?"

INTRODUCTION TO MICAH

750 B.C.	c. 742 B.C.	722 B.C.	715 B.C.
Reign of Jotham begins	Prophetic ministry of Micah	Fall of Israel	Reign of Hezekiah begins

AUTHOR AND DATE

Micah prophesied during the reigns of the Judean kings Jotham (750–735 B.C.), Ahaz (735–715), and Hezekiah (715–687). This was about the same time as Hosea and Isaiah, though Micah may have served somewhat later. The length of Micah's public activity may have been about 20 to 25 years.

THEME

The theme of Micah is judgment and forgiveness. The Lord, the Judge who scatters his people for their sins, is also the Shepherd-King who in covenant faithfulness gathers, protects, and forgives them.

PURPOSE AND BACKGROUND

Micah writes to bring God's "lawsuit" against his people (3:8). He indicts Samaria and Jerusalem for their sins (1:2–7). Both Assyria (5:5–6) and Babylon (4:10) stand ready to carry out God's judgment. The reigns of Jotham, Ahaz, and Hezekiah, along with the increasing threat of Assyria, provide the broad background for Micah.

Micah lists specific sins of both the northern and southern kingdoms. These sins include idolatry (1:7; 5:12–14); the seizure of property (2:2, 9); the failure of civil leadership (3:1–3, 9–10; 7:3), religious leadership (3:11), and prophetic leadership (3:5–7, 11); offering sacrifice without truly repenting (6:6–7); and corrupt business practices and violence (6:10–12).

KEY THEMES

1. The Lord's character and the people's sins demand judgment (1:2–5; 2:3; 6:1–2, 9–11). God's "sentence" upon his people comes in the form of an oppressor (1:15; 4:11; 5:1, 5–6) and by means of covenant curses (6:13–15) caused by covenant unfaithfulness (6:16).

2. A Shepherd-King will gather and deliver a faithful remnant of people (2:12–13; 4:6–8; 7:14, 18). This deliverer, functioning as a new David, will come from the very region that was then under Assyrian control (5:2–5a).

3. Practicing justice and mercy shows covenant faithfulness (6:8; compare Matt. 23:23).

4. The Lord is the focus of worship. The nations will come to Zion to learn of the true Lord and to live in peace (Mic. 4:1–5; 7:12; compare Isa. 2:2–5).

5. Grace flowing from the Lord's steadfast love (Mic. 7:18–20) overcomes the penalty due to sin (7:8–9). Forgiveness is possible because of God's faithfulness to his promises (7:20).

6. God's saving acts in the past (6:4–5; 7:14–15) provide hope for his saving acts in the future (7:19–20).

OUTLINE

I. Superscription (1:1)

II. The Announcement of Judgment on Israel and Judah (1:2–2:13)

III. The Present Injustice and the Future Prospect of Just Rule in Jerusalem (3:1–5:15)

IV. The Lord's Indictment and Restoration of His People (6:1–7:20)

MICAH

1 The word of the LORD that came to Micah of Moresheth in the days of Jotham, Ahaz, and Hezekiah, kings of Judah, which he saw concerning Samaria and Jerusalem.

The Coming Destruction

2 Hear, you peoples, all of you;
  pay attention, O earth, and all that
    is in it,
and let the Lord GOD be a witness
    against you,
  the Lord from his holy temple.
3 For behold, the LORD is coming out of
    his place,
  and will come down and tread
    upon the high places of the
    earth.
4 And the mountains will melt under
    him,
  and the valleys will split open,
like wax before the fire,
  like waters poured down a steep
    place.
5 All this is for the transgression of
    Jacob
  and for the sins of the house of
    Israel.
What is the transgression of Jacob?
  Is it not Samaria?
And what is the high place of Judah?
  Is it not Jerusalem?
6 Therefore I will make Samaria a heap
    in the open country,
  a place for planting vineyards,
and I will pour down her stones into
    the valley
  and uncover her foundations.
7 All her carved images shall be beaten
    to pieces,
  all her wages shall be burned with
    fire,
  and all her idols I will lay waste,
for from the fee of a prostitute she
    gathered them,
  and to the fee of a prostitute they
    shall return.
8 For this I will lament and wail;
  I will go stripped and naked;

I will make lamentation like the jack-
    als,
  and mourning like the ostriches.
9 For her wound is incurable,
  and it has come to Judah;
it has reached to the gate of my peo-
    ple,
  to Jerusalem.
10 Tell it not in Gath;
  weep not at all;
in Beth-le-aphrah
  roll yourselves in the dust.
11 Pass on your way,
  inhabitants of Shaphir,
  in nakedness and shame;

> **GETTING THE MESSAGE**

Moresheth, where Micah lived, was a small village 22 miles (35 km) southwest of Jerusalem. It was one of the many military outposts set up to secure the kingdom's borders.

the inhabitants of Zaanan
  do not come out;
the lamentation of Beth-ezel
  shall take away from you its stand-
    ing place.
12 For the inhabitants of Maroth
  wait anxiously for good,
because disaster has come down from
    the LORD
  to the gate of Jerusalem.
13 Harness the steeds to the chariots,
  inhabitants of Lachish;
it was the beginning of sin
  to the daughter of Zion,
for in you were found
  the transgressions of Israel.
14 Therefore you shall give parting gifts
  to Moresheth-gath;
the houses of Achzib shall be a deceit-
    ful thing
  to the kings of Israel.

¹⁵ I will again bring a conqueror to you,
    inhabitants of Mareshah;
the glory of Israel
    shall come to Adullam.
¹⁶ Make yourselves bald and cut off your
        hair,
    for the children of your delight;
make yourselves as bald as the eagle,
    for they shall go from you into exile.

Woe to the Oppressors

2 Woe to those who devise wickedness
    and work evil on their beds!
When the morning dawns, they per-
    form it,

PROFILE
MICAH

Rather than being identified by his father or family, Micah is identified by a location: he is called "Micah of Moresheth" (1:1). The town was 22 miles (35 km) southwest of Jerusalem. Micah's call to prophetic ministry is not recorded, and he is never referred to as "prophet," but he is said to be speaking according to the "Spirit of the LORD" (3:8). The name "Micah" means "Who is like Yahweh?" Similarly, at the end of the book, Micah asks, "Who is a God like you?" (7:18). Both Micah's name and his writings emphasize the matchless character and actions of the Lord. Micah announces God's judgment on Israel for its unfaithfulness, yet he also proclaims God's promise of great blessing through a Messiah—a prophecy fulfilled in Jesus Christ (5:1–15; Eph. 1:3–14).

KEY REFERENCE: MICAH 6:8

because it is in the power of their
    hand.
² They covet fields and seize them,
    and houses, and take them away;
they oppress a man and his house,
    a man and his inheritance.
³ Therefore thus says the LORD:
behold, against this family I am devis-
    ing disaster,
    from which you cannot remove
        your necks,

and you shall not walk haughtily,
    for it will be a time of disaster.
⁴ In that day they shall take up a taunt
        song against you
    and moan bitterly,
and say, "We are utterly ruined;
    he changes the portion of my peo-
        ple;
how he removes it from me!
    To an apostate he allots our fields."
⁵ Therefore you will have none to cast
        the line by lot
    in the assembly of the LORD.

⁶ "Do not preach"—thus they preach—
    "one should not preach of such
        things;
    disgrace will not overtake us."
⁷ Should this be said, O house of Jacob?
    Has the LORD grown impatient?
    Are these his deeds?

GETTING THE MESSAGE

Micah's **list of disasters** (1:10–15) is based on a series of word plays. For example, the city name Beth-le-aphrah means "House of Dust," and its inhabitants will mourn "in the dust" (1:10). Lachish sounds like "steeds," and they will flee on their steeds (1:13).

Do not my words do good
    to him who walks uprightly?
⁸ But lately my people have risen up as
        an enemy;
you strip the rich robe from those
        who pass by trustingly
    with no thought of war.
⁹ The women of my people you drive out
        from their delightful houses;
from their young children you take
        away
    my splendor forever.
¹⁰ Arise and go,
    for this is no place to rest,
because of uncleanness that destroys
    with a grievous destruction.
¹¹ If a man should go about and utter
        wind and lies,
    saying, "I will preach to you of wine
        and strong drink,"
he would be the preacher for this
        people!

12 I will surely assemble all of you,
        O Jacob;
    I will gather the remnant of Israel;
    I will set them together
        like sheep in a fold,
    like a flock in its pasture,
        a noisy multitude of men.
13 He who opens the breach goes up
        before them;
    they break through and pass the gate,
        going out by it.
    Their king passes on before them,
        the LORD at their head.

Rulers and Prophets Denounced

3 And I said:
    Hear, you heads of Jacob
        and rulers of the house of Israel!
    Is it not for you to know justice?—
2   you who hate the good and love the
        evil,
    who tear the skin from off my people
        and their flesh from off their bones,
3   who eat the flesh of my people,
        and flay their skin from off them,
    and break their bones in pieces
        and chop them up like meat in a pot,
        like flesh in a cauldron.

4   Then they will cry to the LORD,
        but he will not answer them;
    he will hide his face from them at that
        time,
    because they have made their deeds
        evil.
5   Thus says the LORD concerning the
        prophets
    who lead my people astray,
    who cry "Peace"
        when they have something to eat,
    but declare war against him
        who puts nothing into their mouths.
6   Therefore it shall be night to you,
        without vision,
    and darkness to you, without divi-
        nation.
    The sun shall go down on the prophets,
        and the day shall be black over them;
7   the seers shall be disgraced,
        and the diviners put to shame;
    they shall all cover their lips,
        for there is no answer from God.
8   But as for me, I am filled with power,
        with the Spirit of the LORD,
        and with justice and might,
    to declare to Jacob his transgression
        and to Israel his sin.

9   Hear this, you heads of the house of
        Jacob
    and rulers of the house of Israel,
    who detest justice
        and make crooked all that is
        straight,
10 who build Zion with blood
        and Jerusalem with iniquity.
11 Its heads give judgment for a bribe;
        its priests teach for a price;
        its prophets practice divination for
        money;
    yet they lean on the LORD and say,
    "Is not the LORD in the midst of us?
        No disaster shall come upon us."
12 Therefore because of you
        Zion shall be plowed as a field;

GETTING THE MESSAGE

The business of prophecy. The life of a
prophet was not an easy one, and few
could carry out its rigorous demands.
False prophets, however, could do
very well for themselves because they
charged money for their prophecies.
Not surprisingly, these "paid prophecies"
usually favored the person paying for
them (3:5).

    Jerusalem shall become a heap of
        ruins,
    and the mountain of the house a
        wooded height.

The Mountain of the LORD

4 It shall come to pass in the latter days
    that the mountain of the house of
        the LORD
    shall be established as the highest of
        the mountains,
    and it shall be lifted up above the
        hills;
    and peoples shall flow to it,
2   and many nations shall come, and
        say:
    "Come, let us go up to the mountain of
        the LORD,
        to the house of the God of Jacob,
    that he may teach us his ways
        and that we may walk in his paths."

For out of Zion shall go forth the law,
    and the word of the LORD from
        Jerusalem.
3   He shall judge between many peoples,
        and shall decide for strong nations
            far away;
    and they shall beat their swords into
        plowshares,
        and their spears into pruning
            hooks;
    nation shall not lift up sword against
        nation,
        neither shall they learn war any-
            more;
4   but they shall sit every man under his
        vine and under his fig tree,
        and no one shall make them afraid,
    for the mouth of the LORD of hosts
        has spoken.
5   For all the peoples walk
        each in the name of its god,
    but we will walk in the name of the
        LORD our God
        forever and ever.

The LORD Shall Rescue Zion

6   In that day, declares the LORD,
        I will assemble the lame
    and gather those who have been
        driven away
    and those whom I have afflicted;
7   and the lame I will make the remnant,
        and those who were cast off, a
            strong nation;
    and the LORD will reign over them in
        Mount Zion
        from this time forth and forever-
            more.

8   And you, O tower of the flock,
        hill of the daughter of Zion,
    to you shall it come,
        the former dominion shall come,
        kingship for the daughter of
            Jerusalem.

9   Now why do you cry aloud?
        Is there no king in you?
    Has your counselor perished,
        that pain seized you like a woman
            in labor?
10 Writhe and groan, O daughter of Zion,
        like a woman in labor,
    for now you shall go out from the city
        and dwell in the open country;
        you shall go to Babylon.

There you shall be rescued;
    there the LORD will redeem you
        from the hand of your enemies.

11 Now many nations
        are assembled against you,
    saying, "Let her be defiled,
        and let our eyes gaze upon Zion."
12 But they do not know
        the thoughts of the LORD;
    they do not understand his plan,
        that he has gathered them as
            sheaves to the threshing floor.
13 Arise and thresh,
        O daughter of Zion,
    for I will make your horn iron,
        and I will make your hoofs bronze;
    you shall beat in pieces many peoples;
        and shall devote their gain to the
            LORD,
        their wealth to the Lord of the
            whole earth.

The Ruler to Be Born in Bethlehem

5   Now muster your troops, O daughter
        of troops;
        siege is laid against us;
    with a rod they strike the judge of
        Israel
        on the cheek.
2   But you, O Bethlehem Ephrathah,
        who are too little to be among the
            clans of Judah,
    from you shall come forth for me
        one who is to be ruler in Israel,
    whose coming forth is from of old,
        from ancient days.
3   Therefore he shall give them up until
        the time
        when she who is in labor has given
            birth;
    then the rest of his brothers shall
        return
        to the people of Israel.
4   And he shall stand and shepherd his
        flock in the strength of the LORD,
        in the majesty of the name of the
            LORD his God.
    And they shall dwell secure, for now
        he shall be great
        to the ends of the earth.
5   And he shall be their peace.

When the Assyrian comes into our
        land
        and treads in our palaces,

then we will raise against him seven
    shepherds
        and eight princes of men;
6   they shall shepherd the land of
        Assyria with the sword,
        and the land of Nimrod at its
            entrances;
    and he shall deliver us from the
        Assyrian
        when he comes into our land
        and treads within our border.

A Remnant Shall Be Delivered

7   Then the remnant of Jacob shall be
        in the midst of many peoples
    like dew from the LORD,
        like showers on the grass,
    which delay not for a man
        nor wait for the children of man.
8   And the remnant of Jacob shall be
        among the nations,
        in the midst of many peoples,
    like a lion among the beasts of the for-
        est,
        like a young lion among the flocks
            of sheep,
    which, when it goes through, treads
        down
        and tears in pieces, and there is
            none to deliver.
9   Your hand shall be lifted up over your
        adversaries,
        and all your enemies shall be cut off.

10 And in that day, declares the LORD,
        I will cut off your horses from
            among you
        and will destroy your chariots;
11 and I will cut off the cities of your land
        and throw down all your strong-
            holds;
12 and I will cut off sorceries from your
        hand,
        and you shall have no more tellers
            of fortunes;
13 and I will cut off your carved images
        and your pillars from among you,
    and you shall bow down no more
        to the work of your hands;
14 and I will root out your Asherah
        images from among you
        and destroy your cities.
15 And in anger and wrath I will execute
        vengeance
        on the nations that did not obey.

The Indictment of the LORD

6   Hear what the LORD says:
        Arise, plead your case before the
            mountains,
        and let the hills hear your voice.
2   Hear, you mountains, the indictment
            of the LORD,
        and you enduring foundations of
            the earth,
    for the LORD has an indictment
        against his people,
        and he will contend with Israel.

3   "O my people, what have I done to you?
        How have I wearied you? Answer me!
4   For I brought you up from the land of
        Egypt
        and redeemed you from the house
            of slavery,
    and I sent before you Moses,
        Aaron, and Miriam.

GETTING THE MESSAGE

The land of Nimrod (5:6) included
Assyria and other parts of Mesopotamia.
Nimrod was the son of Cush and was a
"mighty hunter before the LORD" (Gen.
10:8–14). Many cities of the region claim
him as their founder.

---

5   O my people, remember what Balak
            king of Moab devised,
        and what Balaam the son of Beor
            answered him,
    and what happened from Shittim to
        Gilgal,
        that you may know the righteous
            acts of the LORD."

What Does the LORD Require?

6   "With what shall I come before the
        LORD,
        and bow myself before God on high?
    Shall I come before him with burnt
        offerings,
        with calves a year old?
7   Will the LORD be pleased with thou-
        sands of rams,
        with ten thousands of rivers of oil?
    Shall I give my firstborn for my trans-
        gression,
        the fruit of my body for the sin of
            my soul?"

8 He has told you, O man, what is good;
  and what does the LORD require of
      you
  but to do justice, and to love kindness,
      and to walk humbly with your God?

Destruction of the Wicked

9 The voice of the LORD cries to the city—
  and it is sound wisdom to fear your
      name:
  "Hear of the rod and of him who
      appointed it!
10 Can I forget any longer the treasures
      of wickedness in the house of
      the wicked,
  and the scant measure that is
      accursed?
11 Shall I acquit the man with wicked
      scales
  and with a bag of deceitful weights?
12 Your rich men are full of violence;
  your inhabitants speak lies,
  and their tongue is deceitful in
      their mouth.
13 Therefore I strike you with a grievous
      blow,
  making you desolate because of
      your sins.
14 You shall eat, but not be satisfied,
  and there shall be hunger within
      you;
  you shall put away, but not preserve,
  and what you preserve I will give to
      the sword.
15 You shall sow, but not reap;
  you shall tread olives, but not
      anoint yourselves with oil;
  you shall tread grapes, but not drink
      wine.
16 For you have kept the statutes of Omri,
  and all the works of the house of
      Ahab;
  and you have walked in their coun-
      sels,
  that I may make you a desolation, and
      your inhabitants a hissing;
  so you shall bear the scorn of my
      people."

Wait for the God of Salvation

7 Woe is me! For I have become
  as when the summer fruit has been
      gathered,
  as when the grapes have been
      gleaned:

there is no cluster to eat,
  no first-ripe fig that my soul
      desires.
2 The godly has perished from the
      earth,
  and there is no one upright among
      mankind;
they all lie in wait for blood,
  and each hunts the other with a
      net.
3 Their hands are on what is evil, to do
      it well;
  the prince and the judge ask for a
      bribe,
and the great man utters the evil
      desire of his soul;
  thus they weave it together.
4 The best of them is like a brier,
  the most upright of them a thorn
      hedge.
The day of your watchmen, of your
      punishment, has come;
  now their confusion is at hand.
5 Put no trust in a neighbor;
  have no confidence in a friend;
guard the doors of your mouth
  from her who lies in your arms;
6 for the son treats the father with con-
      tempt,
  the daughter rises up against her
      mother,
the daughter-in-law against her
      mother-in-law;
  a man's enemies are the men of his
      own house.
7 But as for me, I will look to the LORD;
  I will wait for the God of my salva-
      tion;
  my God will hear me.

8 Rejoice not over me, O my enemy;
  when I fall, I shall rise;
when I sit in darkness,
  the LORD will be a light to me.
9 I will bear the indignation of the
      LORD
  because I have sinned against him,
until he pleads my cause
  and executes judgment for me.
He will bring me out to the light;
  I shall look upon his vindication.
10 Then my enemy will see,
  and shame will cover her who said
      to me,
  "Where is the LORD your God?"

My eyes will look upon her;
  now she will be trampled down
  like the mire of the streets.

[11] A day for the building of your walls!
  In that day the boundary shall be far
    extended.
[12] In that day they will come to you,
  from Assyria and the cities of
    Egypt,
and from Egypt to the River,
  from sea to sea and from mountain
    to mountain.
[13] But the earth will be desolate
  because of its inhabitants,
  for the fruit of their deeds.

[14] Shepherd your people with your
    staff,
  the flock of your inheritance,
who dwell alone in a forest
  in the midst of a garden land;
let them graze in Bashan and Gilead
  as in the days of old.
[15] As in the days when you came out of
    the land of Egypt,
  I will show them marvelous things.
[16] The nations shall see and be ashamed
    of all their might;
they shall lay their hands on their
    mouths;
  their ears shall be deaf;
[17] they shall lick the dust like a serpent,
  like the crawling things of the earth;

they shall come trembling out of their
  strongholds;
  they shall turn in dread to the LORD
    our God,
  and they shall be in fear of you.

God's Steadfast Love and Compassion

[18] Who is a God like you, pardoning
    iniquity
  and passing over transgression
    for the remnant of his inheritance?
He does not retain his anger forever,
  because he delights in steadfast
    love.

GETTING THE MESSAGE

God has always been the same. The last verses of Micah describe God the Father as forgiving, compassionate, faithful, and loving (7:18–20). Jesus Christ, who is God the Son, is the living embodiment of these characteristics.

[19] He will again have compassion on us;
  he will tread our iniquities under-
    foot.
You will cast all our sins
  into the depths of the sea.
[20] You will show faithfulness to Jacob
  and steadfast love to Abraham,
as you have sworn to our fathers
  from the days of old.

INTRODUCTION TO NAHUM

686 B.C.	c. 660 B.C.	640 B.C.	612 B.C.
Reign of Manasseh begins	Prophetic ministry of Nahum begins	Reign of Josiah begins	Nineveh destroyed

AUTHOR AND DATE

The prophet Nahum was God's messenger to announce the fall of Nineveh and the complete overthrow of Assyria. Nahum refers to the fall of Thebes as a well-known occurrence (3:8–10). The Assyrian king Ashurbanipal conquered Thebes around 664 B.C. Nahum also predicts the fall of Nineveh, the capital of Assyria, as a future event. Nineveh fell in 612 B.C. The book was composed, therefore, between 664 and 612 B.C.

THEME

Nineveh, the arrogant capital of the Assyrian Empire, will be destroyed.

PURPOSE, OCCASION, AND BACKGROUND

Nahum's book is a sequel to, and a dramatic contrast with, the book of Jonah. Jonah's mission to Nineveh was probably sometime in the first half of the eighth century B.C. (700s). To Jonah's dismay, the Ninevites listened to his message, repented, and were spared God's judgment.

This repentance, however, did not last beyond 745 B.C., when Nineveh became the leading military power in the Near East. In 722 B.C. the Assyrians conquered the northern kingdom of Israel. Nineveh was destroyed in 612 B.C., marking the end of the Assyrian empire.

KEY THEMES

1. The Lord is slow to anger and long-suffering, jealous for his own honor and for his people, but he is wrathful and avenging against his enemies. He controls nature, nations, and history. He is just, righteous, good, merciful, gracious, loving, and faithful. He delivers and protects those who trust in him.

2. God had used Assyria to punish unfaithful Israel and Judah. He also brought well-deserved judgment on Assyria, according to his timetable and method.

3. Nineveh fell because it was a godless and idolatrous city, a city of violence, lust, and greed.

4. The Lord of history is a "stronghold" for "those who take refuge in him" (1:7). He can handle all problems in individual lives. He has defeated powers far greater than Assyria. He grants to his own the ultimate defense and deliverance.

OUTLINE

I. Introduction (1:1)

II. A Psalm Descriptively Praising the Lord (1:2–8)

III. The Lord's Coming Judgment on Nineveh and Deliverance of Judah (1:9–15)

IV. Focus on Nineveh: The Lord's Coming Judgment (2:1–13)

V. Again, Focus on Nineveh: More concerning the Lord's Coming Judgment (3:1–19)

NAHUM

1 An oracle concerning Nineveh. The book of the vision of Nahum of Elkosh.

God's Wrath Against Nineveh

2 The LORD is a jealous and avenging God;
  the LORD is avenging and wrathful;
the LORD takes vengeance on his adversaries
  and keeps wrath for his enemies.
3 The LORD is slow to anger and great in power,
  and the LORD will by no means clear the guilty.
His way is in whirlwind and storm,
  and the clouds are the dust of his feet.
4 He rebukes the sea and makes it dry;
  he dries up all the rivers;
Bashan and Carmel wither;
  the bloom of Lebanon withers.
5 The mountains quake before him;
  the hills melt;
the earth heaves before him,
  the world and all who dwell in it.

6 Who can stand before his indignation?
  Who can endure the heat of his anger?
His wrath is poured out like fire,
  and the rocks are broken into pieces by him.
7 The LORD is good,
  a stronghold in the day of trouble;
he knows those who take refuge in him.
8 But with an overflowing flood
he will make a complete end of the adversaries,
  and will pursue his enemies into darkness.
9 What do you plot against the LORD?
He will make a complete end;
  trouble will not rise up a second time.
10 For they are like entangled thorns,
  like drunkards as they drink;
they are consumed like stubble fully dried.

11 From you came one
  who plotted evil against the LORD,
  a worthless counselor.

12 Thus says the LORD,
"Though they are at full strength and many,
  they will be cut down and pass away.
Though I have afflicted you,
  I will afflict you no more.
13 And now I will break his yoke from off you
  and will burst your bonds apart."

14 The LORD has given commandment about you:
"No more shall your name be perpetuated;
from the house of your gods I will cut off
  the carved image and the metal image.
I will make your grave, for you are vile."

15 Behold, upon the mountains, the feet of him
  who brings good news,
  who publishes peace!
Keep your feasts, O Judah;
  fulfill your vows,
for never again shall the worthless pass through you;
  he is utterly cut off.

The Destruction of Nineveh

2 The scatterer has come up against you.
> Man the ramparts;
> watch the road;
> dress for battle;
> collect all your strength.

2 For the LORD is restoring the majesty
> of Jacob
> as the majesty of Israel,
> for plunderers have plundered them
> and ruined their branches.

PROFILE

NAHUM

All that is known about the prophet Nahum is that he came from Elkosh, probably a town in Judah. Nahum's name means "comfort." The message he received from God—that Nineveh would be destroyed—indeed brought comfort to his hearers. Following Jonah's warning, the cruel Assyrian capital had expressed repentance. That repentance was short-lived, however, and this time God's judgment was unavoidable. Although God had used the Assyrians to punish the wayward southern kingdom, he would not allow Judah to be annihilated. God's plan for the Messiah to come from the line of David could not be defeated. When Nineveh was destroyed in 612 B.C., the once powerful kingdom of Assyria came to an end.

KEY REFERENCE: NAHUM 2:2

3 The shield of his mighty men is red;
> his soldiers are clothed in scarlet.
> The chariots come with flashing metal
> on the day he musters them;
> the cypress spears are brandished.

4 The chariots race madly through the
> streets;
> they rush to and fro through the
> squares;
> they gleam like torches;
> they dart like lightning.

5 He remembers his officers;
> they stumble as they go,

they hasten to the wall;
> the siege tower is set up.

6 The river gates are opened;
> the palace melts away;

7 its mistress is stripped; she is carried
> off,
> her slave girls lamenting,
> moaning like doves
> and beating their breasts.

8 Nineveh is like a pool
> whose waters run away.
> "Halt! Halt!" they cry,
> but none turns back.

9 Plunder the silver,
> plunder the gold!
> There is no end of the treasure
> or of the wealth of all precious
> things.

GETTING THE MESSAGE

The **palace** mentioned in 2:6 was Sennacherib's famous "palace without rival." Built shortly after his reign began, it had more than 80 rooms, many open courts, and even fully irrigated hanging gardens. It is estimated that more than 25 football fields could have fit inside the palace. Yet even this great palace would "melt away" when Nineveh was destroyed.

10 Desolate! Desolation and ruin!
> Hearts melt and knees tremble;
> anguish is in all loins;
> all faces grow pale!

11 Where is the lions' den,
> the feeding place of the young
> lions,
> where the lion and lioness went,
> where his cubs were, with none to
> disturb?

12 The lion tore enough for his cubs
> and strangled prey for his lionesses;
> he filled his caves with prey
> and his dens with torn flesh.

13 Behold, I am against you, declares the LORD of hosts, and I will burn your chariots in smoke, and the sword shall devour your young lions. I will cut off your prey from the earth, and the voice of your messengers shall no longer be heard.

Woe to Nineveh

3 Woe to the bloody city,
all full of lies and plunder—
no end to the prey!

2 The crack of the whip, and rumble of
the wheel,
galloping horse and bounding chariot!

3 Horsemen charging,
flashing sword and glittering
spear,
hosts of slain,
heaps of corpses,
dead bodies without end—
they stumble over the bodies!

4 And all for the countless whorings of
the prostitute,
graceful and of deadly charms,
who betrays nations with her whorings,
and peoples with her charms.

5 Behold, I am against you,
declares the LORD of hosts,
and will lift up your skirts over your
face;
and I will make nations look at your
nakedness
and kingdoms at your shame.

6 I will throw filth at you
and treat you with contempt
and make you a spectacle.

7 And all who look at you will shrink
from you and say,
"Wasted is Nineveh; who will grieve
for her?"
Where shall I seek comforters for
you?

8 Are you better than Thebes
that sat by the Nile,
with water around her,
her rampart a sea,
and water her wall?

9 Cush was her strength;
Egypt too, and that without limit;
Put and the Libyans were her help-
ers.

10 Yet she became an exile;
she went into captivity;
her infants were dashed in pieces
at the head of every street;
for her honored men lots were cast,
and all her great men were bound
in chains.

11 You also will be drunken;
you will go into hiding;
you will seek a refuge from the
enemy.

12 All your fortresses are like fig trees
with first-ripe figs—
if shaken they fall
into the mouth of the eater.

13 Behold, your troops
are women in your midst.
The gates of your land
are wide open to your enemies;
fire has devoured your bars.

14 Draw water for the siege;
strengthen your forts;
go into the clay;
tread the mortar;
take hold of the brick mold!

GETTING THE MESSAGE

As safe as Thebes? The people
of Nineveh thought no one could
destroy their city. Yet they themselves
had destroyed the Egyptian city of
Thebes, which was also considered
indestructible. Nahum reminded the
Ninevites of this (3:8–11) and warned
them that it was now their turn to see
their great city destroyed.

15 There will the fire devour you;
the sword will cut you off.
It will devour you like the locust.
Multiply yourselves like the locust;
multiply like the grasshopper!

16 You increased your merchants
more than the stars of the heavens.
The locust spreads its wings and
flies away.

17 Your princes are like grasshoppers,
your scribes like clouds of locusts
settling on the fences
in a day of cold—
when the sun rises, they fly away;
no one knows where they are.

18 Your shepherds are asleep,
O king of Assyria;
your nobles slumber.
Your people are scattered on the
mountains
with none to gather them.

19 There is no easing your hurt;
  your wound is grievous.
 All who hear the news about you
    clap their hands over you.
  For upon whom has not come
    your unceasing evil?

INTRODUCTION TO HABAKKUK

722 B.C.
Fall of Israel

c. 640 B.C.
Prophetic ministry
of Habakkuk

586 B.C.
Fall of Judah

AUTHOR AND DATE

Habakkuk is unusual as a prophetic book. It never addresses the people of Judah directly. Rather it is a dialogue between the prophet and God. The prophet Habakkuk was probably a contemporary of Zephaniah and Jeremiah, and possibly even of Ezekiel and Daniel. He probably prophesied no later than the end of Josiah's reign (640–609 B.C.).

THEME AND OVERVIEW

The first two chapters are organized around Habakkuk's questions and the Lord's replies. Habakkuk saw Judah's rapid moral and spiritual decline, and this deeply troubled him. Yet God's response puzzled him even more. How could a good and just God use a more wicked nation (Babylon) to punish a less wicked one (Judah)? God makes it clear that both nations are to be judged and appropriately punished for their sin. Although Habakkuk may not fully understand, he has learned to rely totally on God's wisdom and justice. He knows God can resolve issues in ways he could never have imagined. This God is certainly worthy of Habakkuk's praise and worship, which is how the book ends.

Many of the righteous in Judah would have agreed with Habakkuk's words. They wondered what God was doing and struggled with the same issues as Habakkuk. God's words reassured them that he was in control and would deal appropriately with the nations.

KEY THEMES

1. God is just and merciful, even though his people may not always understand his ways (2:4).

2. Wickedness will eventually be punished, and the righteous will ultimately see God's justice (2:5–20).

3. God uses some wicked nations to punish other wicked nations, but ultimately God will judge all nations (1:6; 2:5–20).

4. The key phrase "the righteous shall live by his faith" (2:4) summarizes God's plan for his people. It is quoted three times in the NT (Rom. 1:17; Gal. 3:11; Heb. 10:38). Each time a different aspect of the phrase's meaning is highlighted.

OUTLINE

HABAKKUK

1 The oracle that Habakkuk the prophet saw.

Habakkuk's Complaint

² O Lord, how long shall I cry for help,
and you will not hear?
Or cry to you "Violence!"
and you will not save?
³ Why do you make me see iniquity,
and why do you idly look at wrong?
Destruction and violence are before me;
strife and contention arise.
⁴ So the law is paralyzed,
and justice never goes forth.
For the wicked surround the righteous;
so justice goes forth perverted.

The Lord's Answer

⁵ "Look among the nations, and see;
wonder and be astounded.
For I am doing a work in your days
that you would not believe if told.
⁶ For behold, I am raising up the Chaldeans,
that bitter and hasty nation,
who march through the breadth of the earth,
to seize dwellings not their own.
⁷ They are dreaded and fearsome;
their justice and dignity go forth
from themselves.
⁸ Their horses are swifter than leopards,
more fierce than the evening wolves;
their horsemen press proudly on.
Their horsemen come from afar;
they fly like an eagle swift to devour.
⁹ They all come for violence,
all their faces forward.
They gather captives like sand.
¹⁰ At kings they scoff,
and at rulers they laugh.
They laugh at every fortress,
for they pile up earth and take it.
¹¹ Then they sweep by like the wind and go on,
guilty men, whose own might is their god!"

Habakkuk's Second Complaint

¹² Are you not from everlasting,
O Lord my God, my Holy One?
We shall not die.
O Lord, you have ordained them as a judgment,
and you, O Rock, have established them for reproof.

GETTING THE MESSAGE

The Babylonian horsemen (1:8) were greatly feared by the people they fought against. Taking advantage of their great speed, they would scatter the enemy's foot soldiers and then hunt them down one by one. But even Babylon's horses couldn't save Babylon from the Lord's hand of judgment (3:16).

¹³ You who are of purer eyes than to see evil
and cannot look at wrong,
why do you idly look at traitors
and remain silent when the wicked swallows up
the man more righteous than he?
¹⁴ You make mankind like the fish of the sea,
like crawling things that have no ruler.
¹⁵ He¹ brings all of them up with a hook;
he drags them out with his net;
he gathers them in his dragnet;
so he rejoices and is glad.
¹⁶ Therefore he sacrifices to his net
and makes offerings to his dragnet;
for by them he lives in luxury,
and his food is rich.

¹ That is, the wicked foe

17 Is he then to keep on emptying his
        net
    and mercilessly killing nations
        forever?

2   I will take my stand at my watch-
        post
    and station myself on the tower,
    and look out to see what he will say to
        me,
    and what I will answer concerning
        my complaint.

PROFILE

HABAKKUK

Habakkuk was alarmed by the wickedness of his people, the nation of Judah. He longed for the day when the Lord would bring justice to his nation by punishing sin. He was even more troubled, however, when he learned that the Lord would indeed judge Judah but that he would use the much more wicked nation of Babylon to do so. The book of Habakkuk records the prophet's conversation with God about this perplexing issue. By the end of the book, Habakkuk is convinced that God is sovereign and that his justice is far beyond comprehension. The prophet will wait for and trust in God. Habakkuk's faith serves as an example to believers today, who like the prophet are called to trust that the God of justice will indeed accomplish his purposes for the world.

KEY REFERENCE: HABAKKUK 3:17–19

The Righteous Shall Live by His Faith

²And the Lord answered me:

"Write the vision;
    make it plain on tablets,
    so he may run who reads it.
³   For still the vision awaits its
        appointed time;
    it hastens to the end—it will not
        lie.
    If it seems slow, wait for it;
    it will surely come; it will not
        delay.

4   "Behold, his soul is puffed up; it is not
        upright within him,
    but the righteous shall live by his
        faith.
5   "Moreover, wine is a traitor,
    an arrogant man who is never at rest.
    His greed is as wide as Sheol;
    like death he has never enough.
    He gathers for himself all nations
    and collects as his own all peoples."

Woe to the Chaldeans

⁶ Shall not all these take up their taunt against him, with scoffing and riddles for him, and say,

    "Woe to him who heaps up what is not
        his own—
    for how long?—
    and loads himself with pledges!"
7   Will not your debtors suddenly arise,
    and those awake who will make you
        tremble?

Woe oracles. Verses 6–20 of ch. 2 consist of five "woe oracles" against Babylon. Each of these begins with the word "woe" and condemns the Babylonians for violence and idolatry.

    Then you will be spoil for them.
8   Because you have plundered many
        nations,
    all the remnant of the peoples shall
        plunder you,
    for the blood of man and violence to
        the earth,
    to cities and all who dwell in them.
9   "Woe to him who gets evil gain for his
        house,
    to set his nest on high,
    to be safe from the reach of harm!
10 You have devised shame for your house
    by cutting off many peoples;
    you have forfeited your life.
11 For the stone will cry out from the wall,
    and the beam from the woodwork
        respond.
12 "Woe to him who builds a town with
        blood
    and founds a city on iniquity!

¹³ Behold, is it not from the LORD of hosts
    that peoples labor merely for fire,
    and nations weary themselves for
        nothing?
¹⁴ For the earth will be filled
    with the knowledge of the glory of
        the LORD
    as the waters cover the sea.

¹⁵ "Woe to him who makes his neighbors
        drink—
    you pour out your wrath and make
        them drunk,
    in order to gaze at their nakedness!
¹⁶ You will have your fill of shame
        instead of glory.
    Drink, yourself, and show your
        uncircumcision!
The cup in the LORD's right hand
    will come around to you,
    and utter shame will come upon
        your glory!
¹⁷ The violence done to Lebanon will
        overwhelm you,
    as will the destruction of the beasts
        that terrified them,
for the blood of man and violence to
        the earth,
    to cities and all who dwell in them.

¹⁸ "What profit is an idol
    when its maker has shaped it,
    a metal image, a teacher of lies?
For its maker trusts in his own creation
    when he makes speechless idols!
¹⁹ Woe to him who says to a wooden
        thing, Awake;
    to a silent stone, Arise!
Can this teach?
Behold, it is overlaid with gold and
        silver,
    and there is no breath at all in it.
²⁰ But the LORD is in his holy temple;
    let all the earth keep silence before
        him."

Habakkuk's Prayer

3 A prayer of Habakkuk the prophet,
according to Shigionoth.

² O LORD, I have heard the report of you,
    and your work, O LORD, do I fear.
In the midst of the years revive it;
    in the midst of the years make it
        known;
    in wrath remember mercy.

³ God came from Teman,
    and the Holy One from Mount
        Paran.   *Selah*
His splendor covered the heavens,
    and the earth was full of his praise.
⁴ His brightness was like the light;
    rays flashed from his hand;
    and there he veiled his power.
⁵ Before him went pestilence,
    and plague followed at his heels.
⁶ He stood and measured the earth;
    he looked and shook the nations;
then the eternal mountains were
        scattered;
    the everlasting hills sank low.
    His were the everlasting ways.
⁷ I saw the tents of Cushan in afflic-
        tion;
    the curtains of the land of Midian
        did tremble.

> ### GETTING THE MESSAGE
>
> **Habakkuk's final prayer** (3:1–19) was
> written as a song. The musical term
> "selah," also found in the psalms, occurs
> three times. It closes with a note about
> stringed instruments, which would have
> included harps and lyres (Ps. 33:2).

⁸ Was your wrath against the rivers,
    O LORD?
    Was your anger against the rivers,
    or your indignation against the
        sea,
when you rode on your horses,
    on your chariot of salvation?
⁹ You stripped the sheath from your
        bow,
    calling for many arrows.   *Selah*
You split the earth with rivers.
¹⁰ The mountains saw you and writhed;
    the raging waters swept on;
the deep gave forth its voice;
    it lifted its hands on high.
¹¹ The sun and moon stood still in their
        place
    at the light of your arrows as they
        sped,
    at the flash of your glittering spear.
¹² You marched through the earth in
        fury;
    you threshed the nations in anger.

13 You went out for the salvation of your
        people,
    for the salvation of your anointed.
    You crushed the head of the house of
        the wicked,
        laying him bare from thigh to neck.
                                                    Selah
14 You pierced with his own arrows the
        heads of his warriors,
    who came like a whirlwind to scat-
        ter me,
    rejoicing as if to devour the poor in
        secret.
15 You trampled the sea with your
        horses,
    the surging of mighty waters.

16 I hear, and my body trembles;
    my lips quiver at the sound;
    rottenness enters into my bones;
    my legs tremble beneath me.

Yet I will quietly wait for the day of
        trouble
    to come upon people who invade us.

Habakkuk Rejoices in the Lord

17 Though the fig tree should not blos-
        som,
    nor fruit be on the vines,
    the produce of the olive fail
        and the fields yield no food,
    the flock be cut off from the fold
        and there be no herd in the stalls,
18 yet I will rejoice in the Lord;
    I will take joy in the God of my
        salvation.
19 God, the Lord, is my strength;
    he makes my feet like the deer's;
    he makes me tread on my high
        places.

To the choirmaster: with stringed
    instruments.

INTRODUCTION TO ZEPHANIAH

722 B.C.	c. 620 B.C.	586 B.C.
Fall of Israel	Prophetic ministry of Zephaniah	Fall of Judah

AUTHOR AND DATE

Zephaniah prophesied during the reign of Josiah (640–609 B.C.), a Judean king who sought to reestablish acceptable worship practices (2 Kings 22:1–23:30).

THEME

The theme of Zephaniah is the approaching "day of the Lord." This "day" is one of judgment against those who sin against God, and one of blessing for those who follow him.

PURPOSE AND BACKGROUND

In spite of having seen the destruction and exile of Israel (the northern kingdom), Judah (the southern kingdom) refuses to keep its covenant obligations to God. If Judah repents and abandons its evil ways, "perhaps" God will forgive (2:3). Regardless, God's judgment will lead to renewal for Judah and other peoples (3:9–20).

The book declares judgment on many nations, all of which opposed God through opposition to his people. The last nation warned is Judah herself (3:1–7). God is displeased with those who claimed to be his own people.

KEY THEMES

1. God will judge the whole earth (1:2–3, 17–18; 3:8), including Judah (1:4–16; 3:1–7) and her pagan neighbors (2:4–15) alike.

2. God will bless his people when they return to their covenant relationship with him (3:11–20).

3. God extends blessing and grace to all peoples and nations (3:9–10).

4. Judgment and blessing occur both in the near future for the prophet and his audience (1:4–18; 2:3) and also in the more distant future (3:8–9, 11, 13–17).

5. There is no such thing as a second-generation child of God. Every generation must accept God's covenant, rather than relying on the faith of a previous generation.

OUTLINE

ZEPHANIAH

1 The word of the LORD that came to Zephaniah the son of Cushi, son of Gedaliah, son of Amariah, son of Hezekiah, in the days of Josiah the son of Amon, king of Judah.

The Coming Judgment on Judah

2 "I will utterly sweep away everything
from the face of the earth," declares
the LORD.
3 "I will sweep away man and beast;
I will sweep away the birds of the
heavens
and the fish of the sea,
and the rubble with the wicked.
I will cut off mankind
from the face of the earth," declares
the LORD.
4 "I will stretch out my hand against
Judah
and against all the inhabitants of
Jerusalem;
and I will cut off from this place the
remnant of Baal
and the name of the idolatrous
priests along with the priests,
5 those who bow down on the roofs
to the host of the heavens,
those who bow down and swear to the
LORD
and yet swear by Milcom,
6 those who have turned back from
following the LORD,
who do not seek the LORD or
inquire of him."

The Day of the LORD Is Near

7 Be silent before the Lord GOD!
For the day of the LORD is near;
the LORD has prepared a sacrifice
and consecrated his guests.
8 And on the day of the LORD's sacrifice—
"I will punish the officials and the
king's sons
and all who array themselves in
foreign attire.
9 On that day I will punish
everyone who leaps over the threshold,

and those who fill their master's
house
with violence and fraud.
10 "On that day," declares the LORD,
"a cry will be heard from the Fish
Gate,
a wail from the Second Quarter,
a loud crash from the hills.
11 Wail, O inhabitants of the Mortar!
For all the traders are no more;
all who weigh out silver are cut
off.
12 At that time I will search Jerusalem
with lamps,
and I will punish the men

GETTING THE MESSAGE

The **Mortar** mentioned in 1:11 was probably one of Jerusalem's market districts. It probably got its name from being located in a valley shaped like a mortar that is used for grinding things with a pestle.

who are complacent,
those who say in their hearts,
'The LORD will not do good,
nor will he do ill.'
13 Their goods shall be plundered,
and their houses laid waste.
Though they build houses,
they shall not inhabit them;
though they plant vineyards,
they shall not drink wine from
them."
14 The great day of the LORD is near,
near and hastening fast;
the sound of the day of the LORD is
bitter;
the mighty man cries aloud there.
15 A day of wrath is that day,
a day of distress and anguish,
a day of ruin and devastation,
a day of darkness and gloom,

a day of clouds and thick darkness,
16   a day of trumpet blast and battle
         cry
against the fortified cities
   and against the lofty battlements.

17   I will bring distress on mankind,
      so that they shall walk like the
         blind,
   because they have sinned against
      the LORD;

PROFILE

ZEPHANIAH

The name Zephaniah means "Yahweh has hidden." This is significant in regards to both the prophet's background and his message. The name probably shows that Zephaniah's parents were faithful followers of God. Zephaniah was also the great-great-grandson of the godly king Hezekiah (1:1). Like the prophets Joel and Amos, he prophesied about the coming "day of the LORD" when God would judge his enemies and bless his followers. Zephaniah urged the people of Judah to seek the Lord so that they would be "hidden" from his anger on that day (2:3). Though even God's own people would be judged, at the same time the Lord would preserve a faithful remnant. The book of Zephaniah ends with the promise that, through this remnant, Israel will be restored and the knowledge of God will be brought to all nations.

KEY REFERENCE: ZEPHANIAH 3:9–13

their blood shall be poured out like
      dust,
   and their flesh like dung.
18   Neither their silver nor their gold
      shall be able to deliver them
   on the day of the wrath of the
      LORD.
In the fire of his jealousy,
   all the earth shall be consumed;
for a full and sudden end
   he will make of all the inhabitants
      of the earth.

Judgment on Judah's Enemies

2   Gather together, yes, gather,
      O shameless nation,
2   before the decree takes effect
      —before the day passes away like
         chaff—
before there comes upon you
   the burning anger of the LORD,
before there comes upon you
   the day of the anger of the LORD.
3   Seek the LORD, all you humble of the
         land,
   who do his just commands;
seek righteousness; seek humility;
   perhaps you may be hidden
      on the day of the anger of the LORD.
4   For Gaza shall be deserted,
      and Ashkelon shall become a deso-
         lation;
   Ashdod's people shall be driven out at
         noon,
      and Ekron shall be uprooted.

GETTING THE MESSAGE

Near the end. Zephaniah was written during Josiah's reign (640–609 B.C.), after Assyria had defeated Israel. The prophet warns that God will also judge Judah. Soon thereafter, Babylon invaded Judah, eventually destroying it in 586 B.C.

5   Woe to you inhabitants of the seacoast,
      you nation of the Cherethites!
The word of the LORD is against you,
   O Canaan, land of the Philistines;
   and I will destroy you until no
      inhabitant is left.
6   And you, O seacoast, shall be pastures,
      with meadows for shepherds
      and folds for flocks.
7   The seacoast shall become the posses-
         sion
      of the remnant of the house of Judah,
         on which they shall graze,
   and in the houses of Ashkelon
      they shall lie down at evening.
For the LORD their God will be mind-
      ful of them
   and restore their fortunes.

8   "I have heard the taunts of Moab
      and the revilings of the Ammonites,

how they have taunted my people
    and made boasts against their terri-
        tory.
9 Therefore, as I live," declares the LORD
        of hosts,
    the God of Israel,
"Moab shall become like Sodom,
    and the Ammonites like
        Gomorrah,
a land possessed by nettles and salt
        pits,
    and a waste forever.
The remnant of my people shall plun-
        der them,
    and the survivors of my nation shall
        possess them."
10 This shall be their lot in return for
        their pride,
    because they taunted and boasted
against the people of the LORD of
        hosts.
11 The LORD will be awesome against
        them;
    for he will famish all the gods of the
        earth,
and to him shall bow down,
    each in its place,
    all the lands of the nations.

12 You also, O Cushites,
    shall be slain by my sword.

13 And he will stretch out his hand
        against the north
    and destroy Assyria,
and he will make Nineveh a desola-
        tion,
    a dry waste like the desert.
14 Herds shall lie down in her midst,
    all kinds of beasts;
even the owl and the hedgehog
    shall lodge in her capitals;
a voice shall hoot in the window;
    devastation will be on the thresh-
        old;
    for her cedar work will be laid
        bare.
15 This is the exultant city
    that lived securely,
that said in her heart,
    "I am, and there is no one else."
What a desolation she has become,
    a lair for wild beasts!
Everyone who passes by her
    hisses and shakes his fist.

Judgment on Jerusalem and the Nations

3 Woe to her who is rebellious and
    defiled,
        the oppressing city!
2 She listens to no voice;
        she accepts no correction.
She does not trust in the LORD;
        she does not draw near to her God.
3 Her officials within her
        are roaring lions;
    her judges are evening wolves
        that leave nothing till the morn-
            ing.
4 Her prophets are fickle, treacherous
        men;
    her priests profane what is holy;
        they do violence to the law.
5 The LORD within her is righteous;
    he does no injustice;

▶ GETTING THE MESSAGE

The name **Palestine** is actually derived
from the word Philistine (2:5). The
Philistines migrated to Palestine from
Crete. They are also called Cherethites
(see 1 Sam. 30:14).

every morning he shows forth his
        justice;
    each dawn he does not fail;
        but the unjust knows no shame.

6 "I have cut off nations;
        their battlements are in ruins;
    I have laid waste their streets
        so that no one walks in them;
    their cities have been made desolate,
        without a man, without an inhabi-
            tant.
7 I said, 'Surely you will fear me;
        you will accept correction.
    Then your dwelling would not be cut
        off
        according to all that I have
            appointed against you.'
But all the more they were eager
    to make all their deeds corrupt.

8 "Therefore wait for me," declares the
        LORD,
    "for the day when I rise up to seize
        the prey.

For my decision is to gather nations,
  to assemble kingdoms,
to pour out upon them my indignation,
  all my burning anger;
for in the fire of my jealousy
  all the earth shall be consumed.

The Conversion of the Nations

9 "For at that time I will change the
    speech of the peoples
  to a pure speech,
  that all of them may call upon the
    name of the LORD
  and serve him with one accord.
10 From beyond the rivers of Cush
    my worshipers, the daughter of my
      dispersed ones,
    shall bring my offering.

> ▌ GETTING THE MESSAGE
>
> The **rivers of Cush** mentioned in ch. 3
> are the Blue Nile and the White Nile, the
> two major tributaries of the Nile River,
> which flows northward through Egypt to
> the Mediterranean Sea. The Blue Nile is
> 900 miles (1,450 km) long and begins its
> northward journey in Ethiopia. The White
> Nile is 2,300 miles (3,700 km) long,
> flowing all the way from Lake Victoria
> in Uganda.

11 "On that day you shall not be put to
    shame
    because of the deeds by which you
      have rebelled against me;
  for then I will remove from your midst
    your proudly exultant ones,
  and you shall no longer be haughty
    in my holy mountain.
12 But I will leave in your midst
    a people humble and lowly.
  They shall seek refuge in the name of
    the LORD,
13   those who are left in Israel;

they shall do no injustice
  and speak no lies,
nor shall there be found in their mouth
  a deceitful tongue.
For they shall graze and lie down,
  and none shall make them afraid."

Israel's Joy and Restoration

14 Sing aloud, O daughter of Zion;
    shout, O Israel!
  Rejoice and exult with all your heart,
    O daughter of Jerusalem!
15 The LORD has taken away the judg-
    ments against you;
    he has cleared away your enemies.
  The King of Israel, the LORD, is in your
    midst;
    you shall never again fear evil.
16 On that day it shall be said to
    Jerusalem:
  "Fear not, O Zion;
    let not your hands grow weak.
17 The LORD your God is in your midst,
    a mighty one who will save;
  he will rejoice over you with gladness;
    he will quiet you by his love;
  he will exult over you with loud sing-
    ing.
18 I will gather those of you who mourn
    for the festival,
    so that you will no longer suffer
      reproach.
19 Behold, at that time I will deal
    with all your oppressors.
  And I will save the lame
    and gather the outcast,
  and I will change their shame into
    praise
    and renown in all the earth.
20 At that time I will bring you in,
    at the time when I gather you
      together;
  for I will make you renowned and
    praised
    among all the peoples of the earth,
  when I restore your fortunes
    before your eyes," says the LORD.

INTRODUCTION TO HAGGAI

586 B.C.	538 B.C.	520–516 B.C.
Fall of Judah/ temple destroyed	Decree of Cyrus/ end of exile	Haggai prophesies/ temple rebuilt

AUTHOR AND DATE

The book of Haggai contains messages delivered by the prophet Haggai, and thus it is reasonable to consider Haggai its author. Nothing is known of his genealogy. The specific mention of the "second year of Darius" (1:1) places the book in the year 520 B.C.

HISTORICAL BACKGROUND

Haggai ministered among the Jews who had returned to Judea after some 70 years of exile in Babylon. The Persian ruler Cyrus the Great captured Babylon in 539 B.C. In 538 he permitted the Jews to return to Jerusalem so that they might rebuild the temple (Ezra 1–2). The work of rebuilding stalled, however, when opposition arose (Ezra 3:1–4:5). Haggai prophesied in an effort to motivate the people to renew their work of temple restoration.

THEME

The work of temple restoration highlights the Lord's desire to renew a covenant relationship with his people (1:13; 2:4–5).

KEY THEMES

1. *The restoration of God's house.* A decaying temple signifies a decaying relationship with the Lord. It brings weakness rather than holiness to the people (2:14).

2. *The prophetic word is the divine Word.* The prophecy is delivered "by the hand of Haggai" (1:1, 3; 2:1, 10; see 2:20) but it is God's word (e.g., 1:2, 9, 12, 13).

3. *The Lord is sovereign.* The phrase "LORD of hosts" occurs 14 times in the 38 verses of this short book (see 1:2). The Lord gives the divine word, controls the fortunes of his people (1:9; 2:17, 19) and nations (2:6–8), directs nature (1:10), motivates his people to action (1:14; 2:4), and establishes and removes kingdoms (2:20–23).

4. *The people must work.* A restored house will bring pleasure and glory to the Lord (1:8) and blessing to the people (2:19), but there is work to be done. Physical labor is urged (1:7–8; 2:4–5). But there is also "heart" work to be done (1:5–7; 2:15–19).

5. *The restoration of David's house.* Zerubbabel, the heir of David, is promised high status (2:23). The Lord, who removed the "ring" of the Davidic house (see Jer. 22:24–27), now promises that he will restore David's house. The Messiah will come.

OUTLINE

HAGGAI

The Command to Rebuild the Temple

1 In the second year of Darius the king, in the sixth month, on the first day of the month, the word of the LORD came by the hand of Haggai the prophet to Zerubbabel the son of Shealtiel, governor of Judah, and to Joshua the son of Jehozadak, the high priest: ² "Thus says the LORD of hosts: These people say the time has not yet come to rebuild the house of the LORD." ³ Then the word of the LORD came by the hand of Haggai the prophet, ⁴ "Is it a time for you yourselves to dwell in your paneled houses, while this house lies in ruins? ⁵ Now, therefore, thus says the LORD of hosts: Consider your ways. ⁶ You have sown much, and harvested little. You eat, but you never have enough; you drink, but you never have your fill. You clothe yourselves, but no one is warm. And he who earns wages does so to put them into a bag with holes.

⁷ "Thus says the LORD of hosts: Consider your ways. ⁸ Go up to the hills and bring wood and build the house, that I may take pleasure in it and that I may be glorified, says the LORD. ⁹ You looked for much, and behold, it came to little. And when you brought it home, I blew it away. Why? declares the LORD of hosts. Because of my house that lies in ruins, while each of you busies himself with his own house. ¹⁰ Therefore the heavens above you have withheld the dew, and the earth has withheld its produce. ¹¹ And I have called for a drought on the land and the hills, on the grain, the new wine, the oil, on what the ground brings forth, on man and beast, and on all their labors."

The People Obey the LORD

¹² Then Zerubbabel the son of Shealtiel, and Joshua the son of Jehozadak, the high priest, with all the remnant of the people, obeyed the voice of the LORD their God, and the words of Haggai the prophet, as the LORD their God had sent him. And the people feared the LORD. ¹³ Then Haggai, the messenger of the LORD, spoke to the people with the LORD's message, "I am with you, declares the LORD." ¹⁴ And the LORD stirred up the spirit of Zerubbabel the son of Shealtiel, governor of Judah, and the spirit of Joshua the son of Jehozadak, the high priest, and the spirit of all the remnant of the people. And they came and worked on the house of the LORD of hosts, their God, ¹⁵ on the twenty-fourth day of the month, in the sixth month, in the second year of Darius the king.

The Coming Glory of the Temple

2 In the seventh month, on the twenty-first day of the month, the word of the LORD came by the hand of Haggai the

---

GETTING THE MESSAGE

The **paneled houses** described in 1:4 probably had walls and ceilings covered with cedar wood. Such decoration was a sign of prosperity in a land where wood was scarce. The people were spending freely on their own homes while neglecting the rebuilding of the temple.

---

prophet, ² "Speak now to Zerubbabel the son of Shealtiel, governor of Judah, and to Joshua the son of Jehozadak, the high priest, and to all the remnant of the people, and say, ³ 'Who is left among you who saw this house in its former glory? How do you see it now? Is it not as nothing in your eyes? ⁴ Yet now be strong, O Zerubbabel, declares the LORD. Be strong, O Joshua, son of Jehozadak, the high priest. Be strong, all you people of the land, declares the LORD. Work, for I am with you, declares the LORD of hosts, ⁵ according to the covenant that I made with you when you came out of Egypt. My Spirit remains in your midst. Fear not. ⁶ For thus says the LORD of hosts: Yet once more, in a little while, I will shake the heavens and the earth and the sea and the dry land. ⁷ And I will shake all nations, so that the treasures of all nations shall come in, and I will fill this house with glory, says the LORD of hosts. **8** The silver is mine, and the gold is mine, declares the LORD of hosts. **9** The latter glory of this house shall be greater than the former, says the LORD of hosts. And in this place I will give peace, declares the LORD of hosts.'"

Blessings for a Defiled People

10 On the twenty-fourth day of the ninth month, in the second year of Darius, the word of the LORD came by Haggai the prophet, **11** "Thus says the LORD of hosts:

PROFILE

HAGGAI

When the people of God returned from their lengthy exile in Babylon, Jerusalem was in ruins. Within a short time they laid the foundation for a new temple, but they quickly grew discouraged and began focusing instead on their own homes. By Haggai's time, nearly 20 years later, the temple was still unfinished. God used Haggai to encourage the people to finish rebuilding the temple: "Is it a time for you yourselves to dwell in your paneled houses, while this house lies in ruins?" (1:4). Haggai encouraged the disheartened people of Judah with the message that the God of Israel had not abandoned them. His Spirit was still in their midst, and he would fulfill his promise to bless the whole world through them.

KEY REFERENCE: HAGGAI 2:4–9

Ask the priests about the law: **12** 'If someone carries holy meat in the fold of his garment and touches with his fold bread or stew or wine or oil or any kind of food, does it become holy?'" The priests answered and said, "No." **13** Then Haggai said, "If someone who is unclean by contact with a dead body touches any of these, does it become unclean?" The priests answered and said, "It does become unclean." **14** Then Haggai

answered and said, "So is it with this people, and with this nation before me, declares the LORD, and so with every work of their hands. And what they offer there is unclean. **15** Now then, consider from this day onward. Before stone was placed upon stone in the temple of the LORD, **16** how did you fare? When one came to a heap of twenty measures, there were but ten. When one came to the wine vat to draw fifty measures, there were but twenty. **17** I struck you and all the products of your toil with blight and with mildew and with hail, yet you did not turn to me, declares the LORD. **18** Consider from this day onward, from the twenty-fourth day of the ninth month. Since the day that the foundation of the LORD's temple was laid, consider: **19** Is the seed yet in the barn? Indeed, the vine, the fig tree, the pomegranate, and the olive tree have yielded nothing. But from this day on I will bless you."

GETTING THE MESSAGE

The **temple** was the means through which God dwelt with his people in meaningful fellowship (1:13; 2:4–5). It also brought glory and pleasure to God (1:8). Jesus said that he was the final temple, restoring fellowship once more between God and his people (John 2:19–22; Eph. 2:19–22).

Zerubbabel Chosen as a Signet

20 The word of the LORD came a second time to Haggai on the twenty-fourth day of the month, **21** "Speak to Zerubbabel, governor of Judah, saying, I am about to shake the heavens and the earth, **22** and to overthrow the throne of kingdoms. I am about to destroy the strength of the kingdoms of the nations, and overthrow the chariots and their riders. And the horses and their riders shall go down, every one by the sword of his brother. **23** On that day, declares the LORD of hosts, I will take you, O Zerubbabel my servant, the son of Shealtiel, declares the LORD, and make you like a signet ring, for I have chosen you, declares the LORD of hosts."

INTRODUCTION TO ZECHARIAH

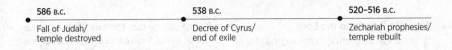

586 B.C.	538 B.C.	520–516 B.C.
Fall of Judah/ temple destroyed	Decree of Cyrus/ end of exile	Zechariah prophesies/ temple rebuilt

AUTHOR AND DATE

Zechariah was a prophet and a priest. He began his ministry in 520 B.C., shortly after Haggai had begun his prophetic work.

BACKGROUND

Nearly 20 years after returning from the Babylonian exile in the time of Cyrus (538 B.C.), God's people were discouraged. The foundation of the temple had been laid shortly after the initial return, in 536 B.C., but powerful opposition had prevented any further progress on rebuilding the temple. And, there was little evidence of the kind of spiritual renewal that the earlier prophets had anticipated. Jewish sovereignty had not been restored. A moral reformation of the people had not occurred. Jerusalem was still only partially rebuilt and had no significance among the surrounding nations. Under the circumstances, many people concluded that theirs was a "day of small things" (4:10) in which God was absent from his people. Many viewed faithful obedience as useless. It seemed to make more sense to forget God and to pursue the best life possible.

KEY THEMES

1. The need for turning to the Lord in repentance (1:1–6) and serving him with sincerity (ch. 7).

2. The Lord's concern and care for his people's difficulties (1:8–17; 4:10).

3. Jerusalem's future expansion and blessing (2:4, 12; 8:1–8; 14:16).

4. The complete and permanent removal of the people's sin (chs. 3; 5), and the removal of false prophecy and idolatry from the land (13:2–6).

5. The importance of the temple as the source of God's blessing (ch. 4).

6. The Lord's wrath at the nations that plundered Judah and Jerusalem (1:18–21; 14:3–5).

7. The Divine Warrior's return to terrorize Israel's foes (9:1–8), and the coming of the Branch, a Davidic ruler who will save his people, cleanse their sins, and establish peace (3:8; 6:9–15; 9:9–10).

8. The pouring out of God's Spirit, resulting in repentance and the opening of a fountain for the cleansing of sin (12:10–13:1).

9. Judgment on the wicked shepherds of God's people and their replacement by a good shepherd (11:1–17).

10. The striking of the good shepherd and the scattering of the flock (13:7–9).

11. The Lord's final triumph over the nations (ch. 14).

OUTLINE

ZECHARIAH

A Call to Return to the LORD

1 In the eighth month, in the second year of Darius, the word of the LORD came to the prophet Zechariah, the son of Berechiah, son of Iddo, saying, ² "The LORD was very angry with your fathers. ³ Therefore say to them, Thus declares the LORD of hosts: Return to me, says the LORD of hosts, and I will return to you, says the LORD of hosts. ⁴ Do not be like your fathers, to whom the former prophets cried out, 'Thus says the LORD of hosts, Return from your evil ways and from your evil deeds.' But they did not hear or pay attention to me, declares the LORD. ⁵ Your fathers, where are they? And the prophets, do they live forever? ⁶ But my words and my statutes, which I commanded my servants the prophets, did they not overtake your fathers? So they repented and said, 'As the LORD of hosts purposed to deal with us for our ways and deeds, so has he dealt with us.'"

A Vision of a Horseman

⁷ On the twenty-fourth day of the eleventh month, which is the month of Shebat, in the second year of Darius, the word of the LORD came to the prophet Zechariah, the son of Berechiah, son of Iddo, saying, ⁸ "I saw in the night, and behold, a man riding on a red horse! He was standing among the myrtle trees in the glen, and behind him were red, sorrel, and white horses. ⁹ Then I said, 'What are these, my lord?' The angel who talked with me said to me, 'I will show you what they are.' ¹⁰ So the man who was standing among the myrtle trees answered, 'These are they whom the LORD has sent to patrol the earth.' ¹¹ And they answered the angel of the LORD who was standing among the myrtle trees, and said, 'We have patrolled the earth, and behold, all the earth remains at rest.' ¹² Then the angel of the LORD said, 'O LORD of hosts, how long will you have no mercy on Jerusalem and the cities of Judah, against which you have been angry these seventy years?' ¹³ And the LORD answered gracious and comforting words to the angel who talked with me. ¹⁴ So the angel who talked with me said to me, 'Cry out, Thus says the LORD of hosts: I am exceedingly jealous for Jerusalem and for Zion. ¹⁵ And I am exceedingly angry with the nations that are at ease; for while I was angry but a little, they furthered the disaster. ¹⁶ Therefore, thus says the LORD, I have returned to Jerusalem with mercy; my house shall be built in it, declares the LORD of hosts, and the measuring line shall be stretched out over Jerusalem. ¹⁷ Cry out again, Thus says the LORD of hosts: My cities shall again overflow with prosperity, and the LORD will again comfort Zion and again choose Jerusalem.'"

A Vision of Horns and Craftsmen

¹⁸ And I lifted my eyes and saw, and behold, four horns! ¹⁹ And I said to the angel who talked with me, "What are these?" And he said to me, "These are the horns that have scattered Judah, Israel, and Jerusalem." ²⁰ Then the LORD showed me four craftsmen. ²¹ And I said, "What are these coming to do?" He said, "These are the horns that scattered Judah, so that no one raised his head. And these have come to terrify them, to cast down the horns of the nations who lifted up their horns against the land of Judah to scatter it."

A Vision of a Man with a Measuring Line

2 And I lifted my eyes and saw, and behold, a man with a measuring line in his hand! ² Then I said, "Where are you going?" And he said to me, "To measure Jerusalem, to see what is its width and what is its length." ³ And behold, the angel who talked with me came forward, and another angel came forward to meet him ⁴ and said to him, "Run, say to that

young man, 'Jerusalem shall be inhabited as villages without walls, because of the multitude of people and livestock in it. ⁵ And I will be to her a wall of fire all around, declares the LORD, and I will be the glory in her midst.'"

⁶ Up! Up! Flee from the land of the north, declares the LORD. For I have spread you abroad as the four winds of the heavens, declares the LORD. ⁷ Up! Escape to Zion, you who dwell with the daughter of Babylon. ⁸ For thus said the LORD of hosts, after his glory sent me to the nations who plundered you,

---

PROFILE

ZECHARIAH

Zechariah was both a priest and a prophet. He was a member of a prominent family who returned from Babylon with Zerubbabel. Like Haggai, who ministered during the same time, Zechariah spoke about the need to rebuild the temple. He reassured Judah that if they would heed the words of the prophets and turn to the Lord, God would bless his people for their faithfulness. God would trouble the nations who were enjoying rest and grant rest to his troubled people, making Jerusalem once again the center of the world. Zechariah also prophesied about the coming of the Messiah. Matthew, Mark, John, Ephesians, and Revelation are among the New Testament books that quote Zechariah, recognizing Jesus as the fulfillment of his prophecies.

KEY REFERENCE: ZECHARIAH 8:1-8

---

for he who touches you touches the apple of his eye: ⁹ "Behold, I will shake my hand over them, and they shall become plunder for those who served them. Then you will know that the LORD of hosts has sent me. ¹⁰ Sing and rejoice, O daughter of Zion, for behold, I come and I will dwell in your midst, declares the LORD. ¹¹ And many nations shall join themselves to the LORD in that day, and shall be my people. And I will dwell in your midst, and you shall know that the LORD of

---

hosts has sent me to you. ¹² And the LORD will inherit Judah as his portion in the holy land, and will again choose Jerusalem."

¹³ Be silent, all flesh, before the LORD, for he has roused himself from his holy dwelling.

A Vision of Joshua the High Priest

3 Then he showed me Joshua the high priest standing before the angel of the LORD, and Satan[1] standing at his right hand to accuse him. ² And the LORD said to Satan, "The LORD rebuke you, O Satan! The LORD who has chosen Jerusalem rebuke you! Is not this a brand plucked from the fire?" ³ Now Joshua was standing before the angel, clothed with filthy garments. ⁴ And the angel said to those who were standing before him, "Remove the filthy garments from him." And to him he said, "Behold,

GETTING THE MESSAGE

The number four in Scripture is often associated with creation or completeness. There are four different directions of the compass, four elements, four seasons of the year, and four times of day (morning, noon, evening, and midnight). In 1:18, four represents all of the world powers responsible for the scattering of Judah. However, the Lord, who is sovereign over his creation, will care for his people and punish their oppressors.

I have taken your iniquity away from you, and I will clothe you with pure vestments." ⁵ And I said, "Let them put a clean turban on his head." So they put a clean turban on his head and clothed him with garments. And the angel of the LORD was standing by.

⁶ And the angel of the LORD solemnly assured Joshua, ⁷ "Thus says the LORD of hosts: If you will walk in my ways and keep my charge, then you shall rule my house and have charge of my courts, and I will give you the right of access among those who are standing here. ⁸ Hear now, O Joshua the high priest, you and your friends who sit before you, for they are men who are a sign: behold, I will bring my servant the Branch. ⁹ For behold, on the stone that I have set before Joshua, on a single stone with seven

---

[1] Hebrew the Accuser or the Adversary

eyes, I will engrave its inscription, declares the LORD of hosts, and I will remove the iniquity of this land in a single day. ¹⁰ In that day, declares the LORD of hosts, every one of you will invite his neighbor to come under his vine and under his fig tree."

A Vision of a Golden Lampstand

4 And the angel who talked with me came again and woke me, like a man who is awakened out of his sleep. ² And he said to me, "What do you see?" I said, "I see, and behold, a lampstand all of gold, with a bowl on the top of it, and seven lamps on it, with seven lips on each of the lamps that are on the top of it. ³ And there are two olive trees by it, one on the right of the bowl and the other on its left." ⁴ And I said to the angel who talked with me, "What are these, my lord?" ⁵ Then the angel who talked with me answered and said to me, "Do you not know what these are?" I said, "No, my lord." ⁶ Then he said to me, "This is the word of the LORD to Zerubbabel: Not by might, nor by power, but by my Spirit, says the LORD of hosts. ⁷ Who are you, O great mountain? Before Zerubbabel you shall become a plain. And he shall bring forward the top stone amid shouts of 'Grace, grace to it!'"

⁸ Then the word of the LORD came to me, saying, ⁹ "The hands of Zerubbabel have laid the foundation of this house; his hands shall also complete it. Then you will know that the LORD of hosts has sent me to you. ¹⁰ For whoever has despised the day of small things shall rejoice, and shall see the plumb line in the hand of Zerubbabel.

"These seven are the eyes of the LORD, which range through the whole earth." ¹¹ Then I said to him, "What are these two olive trees on the right and the left of the lampstand?" ¹² And a second time I answered and said to him, "What are these two branches of the olive trees, which are beside the two golden pipes from which the golden oil is poured out?" ¹³ He said to me, "Do you not know what these are?" I said, "No, my lord." ¹⁴ Then he said, "These are the two anointed ones who stand by the Lord of the whole earth."

A Vision of a Flying Scroll

5 Again I lifted my eyes and saw, and behold, a flying scroll! ² And he said to me, "What do you see?" I answered, "I see a flying scroll. Its length is twenty cubits,

and its width ten cubits." ³ Then he said to me, "This is the curse that goes out over the face of the whole land. For everyone who steals shall be cleaned out according to what is on one side, and everyone who swears falsely shall be cleaned out according to what is on the other side. ⁴ I will send it out, declares the LORD of hosts, and it shall enter the house of the thief, and the house of him who swears falsely by my name. And it shall remain in his house and consume it, both timber and stones."

A Vision of a Woman in a Basket

⁵ Then the angel who talked with me came forward and said to me, "Lift your eyes and see what this is that is going out." ⁶ And I said, "What is it?" He said, "This is the basket that is going out." And he said, "This is their iniquity in all the land." ⁷ And behold, the leaden cover was lifted, and there was a

> ### GETTING THE MESSAGE
>
> **Eight visions.** The book of Zechariah has two major sections: chs. 1–8 and chs. 9–14. The first section contains eight visions that describe what God plans to do. Many of the symbols and images in these visions also appear in Revelation.

woman sitting in the basket! ⁸ And he said, "This is Wickedness." And he thrust her back into the basket, and thrust down the leaden weight on its opening.

⁹ Then I lifted my eyes and saw, and behold, two women coming forward! The wind was in their wings. They had wings like the wings of a stork, and they lifted up the basket between earth and heaven. ¹⁰ Then I said to the angel who talked with me, "Where are they taking the basket?" ¹¹ He said to me, "To the land of Shinar, to build a house for it. And when this is prepared, they will set the basket down there on its base."

A Vision of Four Chariots

6 Again I lifted my eyes and saw, and behold, four chariots came out from between two mountains. And the mountains were mountains of bronze. ² The first chariot had red horses, the second black horses, ³ the third white horses, and the

fourth chariot dappled horses—all of them strong. **4** Then I answered and said to the angel who talked with me, "What are these, my lord?" **5** And the angel answered and said to me, "These are going out to the four winds of heaven, after presenting themselves before the Lord of all the earth. **6** The chariot with the black horses goes toward the north country, the white ones go after them, and the dappled ones go toward the south country." **7** When the strong horses came out, they were impatient to go and patrol the earth. And he said, "Go, patrol the earth." So they patrolled the earth. **8** Then he cried to me, "Behold, those who go toward the north country have set my Spirit at rest in the north country."

The Crown and the Temple

9 And the word of the Lord came to me: **10** "Take from the exiles Heldai, Tobijah, and Jedaiah, who have arrived from Babylon,

> ### ▶ GETTING THE MESSAGE
>
> **Widows, fatherless children, sojourners, and the poor** were vulnerable members of society (7:10). Treating them justly and kindly matters very much to the Lord, and he will punish those who mistreat them (see Ex. 22:21–24; Deut. 10:18–19).

and go the same day to the house of Josiah, the son of Zephaniah. **11** Take from them silver and gold, and make a crown, and set it on the head of Joshua, the son of Jehozadak, the high priest. **12** And say to him, 'Thus says the Lord of hosts, "Behold, the man whose name is the Branch: for he shall branch out from his place, and he shall build the temple of the Lord. **13** It is he who shall build the temple of the Lord and shall bear royal honor, and shall sit and rule on his throne. And there shall be a priest on his throne, and the counsel of peace shall be between them both."' **14** And the crown shall be in the temple of the Lord as a reminder to Helem,[1] Tobijah, Jedaiah, and Hen the son of Zephaniah.

15 "And those who are far off shall come and help to build the temple of the Lord. And you shall know that the Lord of hosts has sent me to you. And this shall come to pass, if you will diligently obey the voice of the Lord your God."

A Call for Justice and Mercy

7 In the fourth year of King Darius, the word of the Lord came to Zechariah on the fourth day of the ninth month, which is Chislev. **2** Now the people of Bethel had sent Sharezer and Regem-melech and their men to entreat the favor of the Lord, **3** saying to the priests of the house of the Lord of hosts and the prophets, "Should I weep and abstain in the fifth month, as I have done for so many years?"

4 Then the word of the Lord of hosts came to me: **5** "Say to all the people of the land and the priests, When you fasted and mourned in the fifth month and in the seventh, for these seventy years, was it for me that you fasted? **6** And when you eat and when you drink, do you not eat for yourselves and drink for yourselves? **7** Were not these the words that the Lord proclaimed by the former prophets, when Jerusalem was inhabited and prosperous, with her cities around her, and the South and the lowland were inhabited?"

8 And the word of the Lord came to Zechariah, saying, **9** "Thus says the Lord of hosts, Render true judgments, show kindness and mercy to one another, **10** do not oppress the widow, the fatherless, the sojourner, or the poor, and let none of you devise evil against another in your heart." **11** But they refused to pay attention and turned a stubborn shoulder and stopped their ears that they might not hear. **12** They made their hearts diamond-hard lest they should hear the law and the words that the Lord of hosts had sent by his Spirit through the former prophets. Therefore great anger came from the Lord of hosts. **13** "As I called, and they would not hear, so they called, and I would not hear," says the Lord of hosts, **14** "and I scattered them with a whirlwind among all the nations that they had not known. Thus the land they left was desolate, so that no one went to and fro, and the pleasant land was made desolate."

The Coming Peace and Prosperity of Zion

8 And the word of the Lord of hosts came, saying, **2** "Thus says the Lord of hosts: I am jealous for Zion with great jealousy, and I am jealous for her with great wrath.

---

[1] An alternate spelling of *Heldai* (6:10)

³ Thus says the LORD: I have returned to Zion and will dwell in the midst of Jerusalem, and Jerusalem shall be called the faithful city, and the mountain of the LORD of hosts, the holy mountain. ⁴ Thus says the LORD of hosts: Old men and old women shall again sit in the streets of Jerusalem, each with staff in hand because of great age. ⁵ And the streets of the city shall be full of boys and girls playing in its streets. ⁶ Thus says the LORD of hosts: If it is marvelous in the sight of the remnant of this people in those days, should it also be marvelous in my sight, declares the LORD of hosts? ⁷ Thus says the LORD of hosts: Behold, I will save my people from the east country and from the west country, ⁸ and I will bring them to dwell in the midst of Jerusalem. And they shall be my people, and I will be their God, in faithfulness and in righteousness."

⁹ Thus says the LORD of hosts: "Let your hands be strong, you who in these days have been hearing these words from the mouth of the prophets who were present on the day that the foundation of the house of the LORD of hosts was laid, that the temple might be built. ¹⁰ For before those days there was no wage for man or any wage for beast, neither was there any safety from the foe for him who went out or came in, for I set every man against his neighbor. ¹¹ But now I will not deal with the remnant of this people as in the former days, declares the LORD of hosts. ¹² For there shall be a sowing of peace. The vine shall give its fruit, and the ground shall give its produce, and the heavens shall give their dew. And I will cause the remnant of this people to possess all these things. ¹³ And as you have been a byword of cursing among the nations, O house of Judah and house of Israel, so will I save you, and you shall be a blessing. Fear not, but let your hands be strong."

¹⁴ For thus says the LORD of hosts: "As I purposed to bring disaster to you when your fathers provoked me to wrath, and I did not relent, says the LORD of hosts, ¹⁵ so again have I purposed in these days to bring good to Jerusalem and to the house of Judah; fear not. ¹⁶ These are the things that you shall do: Speak the truth to one another; render in your gates judgments that are true and make for peace; ¹⁷ do not devise evil in your hearts against one another, and love no false

oath, for all these things I hate, declares the LORD."

¹⁸ And the word of the LORD of hosts came to me, saying, ¹⁹ "Thus says the LORD of hosts: The fast of the fourth month and the fast of the fifth and the fast of the seventh and the fast of the tenth shall be to the house of Judah seasons of joy and gladness and cheerful feasts. Therefore love truth and peace.

²⁰ "Thus says the LORD of hosts: Peoples shall yet come, even the inhabitants of many cities. ²¹ The inhabitants of one city shall go to another, saying, 'Let us go at once to entreat the favor of the LORD and to seek the LORD of hosts; I myself am going.' ²² Many peoples and strong nations shall come to seek the LORD of hosts in Jerusalem and to entreat the favor of the LORD. ²³ Thus says the LORD of hosts: In those days ten

---

GETTING THE MESSAGE

"Your king is coming." In 9:9, Zechariah prophesies about the coming of a future king of Israel. The New Testament quotes this verse when describing Jesus' triumphal entry into Jerusalem, riding on a donkey (Matt. 21:5; John 12:15).

---

men from the nations of every tongue shall take hold of the robe of a Jew, saying, 'Let us go with you, for we have heard that God is with you.'"

Judgment on Israel's Enemies

9 The oracle of the word of the LORD is against the land of Hadrach and Damascus is its resting place.
  For the LORD has an eye on mankind and on all the tribes of Israel,
² and on Hamath also, which borders on it,
  Tyre and Sidon, though they are very wise.
³ Tyre has built herself a rampart and heaped up silver like dust, and fine gold like the mud of the streets.
⁴ But behold, the Lord will strip her of her possessions and strike down her power on the sea, and she shall be devoured by fire.

5 Ashkelon shall see it, and be afraid;
    Gaza too, and shall writhe in
      anguish;
    Ekron also, because its hopes are
      confounded.
The king shall perish from Gaza;
    Ashkelon shall be uninhabited;
6 a mixed people shall dwell in Ashdod,
    and I will cut off the pride of
      Philistia.
7 I will take away its blood from its
      mouth,
    and its abominations from between
      its teeth;
it too shall be a remnant for our God;
    it shall be like a clan in Judah,
    and Ekron shall be like the Jebusites.
8 Then I will encamp at my house as a
      guard,

GETTING THE MESSAGE

When did Israel defeat Greece?
Zechariah predicted that the sons of
Zion would someday defeat the sons
of Greece (9:13). This is probably a
prophecy of the Maccabean revolt in
the second century B.C., when the Jews
defeated the successors of Alexander
the Great who had become their rulers.

    so that none shall march to and fro;
no oppressor shall again march over
      them,
    for now I see with my own eyes.

The Coming King of Zion

9 Rejoice greatly, O daughter of Zion!
    Shout aloud, O daughter of
      Jerusalem!
Behold, your king is coming to you;
    righteous and having salvation is
      he,
humble and mounted on a donkey,
    on a colt, the foal of a donkey.
10 I will cut off the chariot from Ephraim
    and the war horse from Jerusalem;
and the battle bow shall be cut off,
    and he shall speak peace to the
      nations;
his rule shall be from sea to sea,
    and from the River to the ends of
      the earth.

11 As for you also, because of the blood
      of my covenant with you,
    I will set your prisoners free from
      the waterless pit.
12 Return to your stronghold, O prison-
      ers of hope;
    today I declare that I will restore to
      you double.
13 For I have bent Judah as my bow;
    I have made Ephraim its arrow.
I will stir up your sons, O Zion,
    against your sons, O Greece,
    and wield you like a warrior's
      sword.

The LORD Will Save His People

14 Then the LORD will appear over them,
    and his arrow will go forth like
      lightning;
the Lord GOD will sound the trumpet
    and will march forth in the whirl-
      winds of the south.
15 The LORD of hosts will protect them,
    and they shall devour, and tread
      down the sling stones,
and they shall drink and roar as if
      drunk with wine,
    and be full like a bowl,
    drenched like the corners of the
      altar.
16 On that day the LORD their God will
      save them,
    as the flock of his people;
for like the jewels of a crown
    they shall shine on his land.
17 For how great is his goodness, and
      how great his beauty!
Grain shall make the young men
      flourish,
    and new wine the young women.

The Restoration for Judah and Israel

10 Ask rain from the LORD
    in the season of the spring rain,
from the LORD who makes the storm
      clouds,
and he will give them showers of
      rain,
    to everyone the vegetation in the
      field.
2 For the household gods utter non-
      sense,
    and the diviners see lies;
they tell false dreams
    and give empty consolation.

Therefore the people wander like
     sheep;
  they are afflicted for lack of a shep-
     herd.

3 "My anger is hot against the shepherds,
     and I will punish the leaders;
  for the Lord of hosts cares for his
     flock, the house of Judah,
  and will make them like his majes-
     tic steed in battle.
4 From him shall come the cornerstone,
     from him the tent peg,
  from him the battle bow,
     from him every ruler—all of them
     together.
5 They shall be like mighty men in bat-
     tle,
  trampling the foe in the mud of the
     streets;
  they shall fight because the Lord is
     with them,
     and they shall put to shame the
     riders on horses.
6 "I will strengthen the house of Judah,
     and I will save the house of Joseph.
  I will bring them back because I have
     compassion on them,
     and they shall be as though I had
     not rejected them,
  for I am the Lord their God and I
     will answer them.
7 Then Ephraim shall become like a
     mighty warrior,
     and their hearts shall be glad as
     with wine.
  Their children shall see it and be glad;
     their hearts shall rejoice in the
     Lord.
8 "I will whistle for them and gather
     them in,
     for I have redeemed them,
     and they shall be as many as they
     were before.
9 Though I scattered them among the
     nations,
     yet in far countries they shall
     remember me,
  and with their children they shall
     live and return.
10 I will bring them home from the land
     of Egypt,
     and gather them from Assyria,

and I will bring them to the land of
     Gilead and to Lebanon,
     till there is no room for them.
11 He shall pass through the sea of trou-
     bles
     and strike down the waves of the
     sea,
     and all the depths of the Nile shall
     be dried up.
  The pride of Assyria shall be laid low,
     and the scepter of Egypt shall depart.
12 I will make them strong in the Lord,
     and they shall walk in his name,"
                     declares the Lord.

The Flock Doomed to Slaughter

11 Open your doors, O Lebanon,
     that the fire may devour your
        cedars!
2   Wail, O cypress, for the cedar has fallen,
        for the glorious trees are ruined!
    Wail, oaks of Bashan,
        for the thick forest has been felled!
3   The sound of the wail of the shepherds,
        for their glory is ruined!
    The sound of the roar of the lions,
        for the thicket of the Jordan is
           ruined!

4 Thus said the Lord my God: "Become
shepherd of the flock doomed to slaughter.
5 Those who buy them slaughter them and
go unpunished, and those who sell them
say, 'Blessed be the Lord, I have become
rich,' and their own shepherds have no pity
on them. 6 For I will no longer have pity on
the inhabitants of this land, declares the
Lord. Behold, I will cause each of them to
fall into the hand of his neighbor, and each
into the hand of his king, and they shall
crush the land, and I will deliver none from
their hand."

7 So I became the shepherd of the flock
doomed to be slaughtered by the sheep traders. And I took two staffs, one I named Favor,
the other I named Union. And I tended the
sheep. 8 In one month I destroyed the three
shepherds. But I became impatient with
them, and they also detested me. 9 So I said,
"I will not be your shepherd. What is to die,
let it die. What is to be destroyed, let it be
destroyed. And let those who are left devour
the flesh of one another." 10 And I took my
staff Favor, and I broke it, annulling the covenant that I had made with all the peoples.

¹¹ So it was annulled on that day, and the sheep traders, who were watching me, knew that it was the word of the Lord. ¹² Then I said to them, "If it seems good to you, give me my wages; but if not, keep them." And they weighed out as my wages thirty pieces of silver. ¹³ Then the Lord said to me, "Throw it to the potter"—the lordly price at which I was priced by them. So I took the thirty pieces of silver and threw them into the house of the Lord, to the potter. ¹⁴ Then I broke my second staff Union, annulling the brotherhood between Judah and Israel.

¹⁵ Then the Lord said to me, "Take once more the equipment of a foolish shepherd. ¹⁶ For behold, I am raising up in the land a shepherd who does not care for those being destroyed, or seek the young or heal the maimed or nourish the healthy, but devours

> ## GETTING THE MESSAGE
>
> Zechariah promises that when the people of Jerusalem repent, the Lord will provide a **fountain**, or spring, that will cleanse them from their sins (13:1). They were unclean because they had worshiped idols, but when they repented, God would forgive them.

the flesh of the fat ones, tearing off even their hoofs.

¹⁷ "Woe to my worthless shepherd,
 who deserts the flock!
May the sword strike his arm
 and his right eye!
Let his arm be wholly withered,
 his right eye utterly blinded!"

The Lord Will Give Salvation

12 The oracle of the word of the Lord concerning Israel: Thus declares the Lord, who stretched out the heavens and founded the earth and formed the spirit of man within him: ² "Behold, I am about to make Jerusalem a cup of staggering to all the surrounding peoples. The siege of Jerusalem will also be against Judah. ³ On that day I will make Jerusalem a heavy stone for all the peoples. All who lift it will surely hurt themselves. And all the nations of the earth will gather against it. ⁴ On that day, declares the Lord, I will strike every horse

with panic, and its rider with madness. But for the sake of the house of Judah I will keep my eyes open, when I strike every horse of the peoples with blindness. ⁵ Then the clans of Judah shall say to themselves, 'The inhabitants of Jerusalem have strength through the Lord of hosts, their God.'

⁶ "On that day I will make the clans of Judah like a blazing pot in the midst of wood, like a flaming torch among sheaves. And they shall devour to the right and to the left all the surrounding peoples, while Jerusalem shall again be inhabited in its place, in Jerusalem.

⁷ "And the Lord will give salvation to the tents of Judah first, that the glory of the house of David and the glory of the inhabitants of Jerusalem may not surpass that of Judah. ⁸ On that day the Lord will protect the inhabitants of Jerusalem, so that the feeblest among them on that day shall be like David, and the house of David shall be like God, like the angel of the Lord, going before them. ⁹ And on that day I will seek to destroy all the nations that come against Jerusalem.

Him Whom They Have Pierced

¹⁰ "And I will pour out on the house of David and the inhabitants of Jerusalem a spirit of grace and pleas for mercy, so that, when they look on me, on him whom they have pierced, they shall mourn for him, as one mourns for an only child, and weep bitterly over him, as one weeps over a firstborn. ¹¹ On that day the mourning in Jerusalem will be as great as the mourning for Hadad-rimmon in the plain of Megiddo. ¹² The land shall mourn, each family by itself: the family of the house of David by itself, and their wives by themselves; the family of the house of Nathan by itself, and their wives by themselves; ¹³ the family of the house of Levi by itself, and their wives by themselves; the family of the Shimeites by itself, and their wives by themselves; ¹⁴ and all the families that are left, each by itself, and their wives by themselves.

13 "On that day there shall be a fountain opened for the house of David and the inhabitants of Jerusalem, to cleanse them from sin and uncleanness.

Idolatry Cut Off

² "And on that day, declares the Lord of hosts, I will cut off the names of the idols

from the land, so that they shall be remembered no more. And also I will remove from the land the prophets and the spirit of uncleanness. ³ And if anyone again prophesies, his father and mother who bore him will say to him, 'You shall not live, for you speak lies in the name of the LORD.' And his father and mother who bore him shall pierce him through when he prophesies.

⁴ "On that day every prophet will be ashamed of his vision when he prophesies. He will not put on a hairy cloak in order to deceive, ⁵ but he will say, 'I am no prophet, I am a worker of the soil, for a man sold me in my youth.' ⁶ And if one asks him, 'What are these wounds on your back?' he will say, 'The wounds I received in the house of my friends.'

The Shepherd Struck

⁷ "Awake, O sword, against my shepherd,
    against the man who stands next to
    me,"
            declares the LORD of hosts.

"Strike the shepherd, and the sheep
    will be scattered;
I will turn my hand against the little
    ones.
⁸ In the whole land, declares the LORD,
    two thirds shall be cut off and per-
    ish,
and one third shall be left alive.
⁹ And I will put this third into the fire,
    and refine them as one refines silver,
    and test them as gold is tested.
They will call upon my name,
    and I will answer them.
I will say, 'They are my people';
    and they will say, 'The LORD is my
    God.'"

The Coming Day of the LORD

14 Behold, a day is coming for the LORD, when the spoil taken from you will be divided in your midst. ² For I will gather all the nations against Jerusalem to battle, and the city shall be taken and the houses plundered and the women raped. Half of the city shall go out into exile, but the rest of the people shall not be cut off from the city. ³ Then the LORD will go out and fight against those nations as when he fights on a day of battle. ⁴ On that day his feet shall stand on the Mount of Olives that lies before

Jerusalem on the east, and the Mount of Olives shall be split in two from east to west by a very wide valley, so that one half of the Mount shall move northward, and the other half southward. ⁵ And you shall flee to the valley of my mountains, for the valley of the mountains shall reach to Azal. And you shall flee as you fled from the earthquake in the days of Uzziah king of Judah. Then the LORD my God will come, and all the holy ones with him.

⁶ On that day there shall be no light, cold, or frost. ⁷ And there shall be a unique day, which is known to the LORD, neither day nor night, but at evening time there shall be light.

⁸ On that day living waters shall flow out from Jerusalem, half of them to the eastern sea¹ and half of them to the western sea.² It shall continue in summer as in winter.

⁹ And the LORD will be king over all the earth. On that day the LORD will be one and his name one.

¹⁰ The whole land shall be turned into a plain from Geba to Rimmon south of Jerusalem. But Jerusalem shall remain aloft on its site from the Gate of Benjamin to the place of the former gate, to the Corner Gate, and from the Tower of Hananel to the king's winepresses. ¹¹ And it shall be inhabited, for there shall never again be a decree of utter destruction. Jerusalem shall dwell in security.

¹² And this shall be the plague with which the LORD will strike all the peoples that wage war against Jerusalem: their flesh will rot while they are still standing on their feet, their eyes will rot in their sockets, and their tongues will rot in their mouths.

¹³ And on that day a great panic from the LORD shall fall on them, so that each will seize the hand of another, and the hand of the one will be raised against the hand of the other. ¹⁴ Even Judah will fight at Jerusalem. And the wealth of all the surrounding nations shall be collected, gold, silver, and garments in great abundance. ¹⁵ And a plague like this plague shall fall on the horses, the mules, the camels, the donkeys, and whatever beasts may be in those camps.

¹⁶ Then everyone who survives of all the nations that have come against Jerusalem

¹ That is, the Dead Sea ² That is, the Mediterranean Sea

shall go up year after year to worship the King, the LORD of hosts, and to keep the Feast of Booths. ¹⁷ And if any of the families of the earth do not go up to Jerusalem to worship the King, the LORD of hosts, there will be no rain on them. ¹⁸ And if the family of Egypt does not go up and present themselves, then on them there shall be no rain; there shall be the plague with which the LORD afflicts the nations that do not go up to keep the Feast of Booths. ¹⁹ This shall be the punishment to Egypt and the punishment to all the nations that do not go up to keep the Feast of Booths.

²⁰ And on that day there shall be inscribed on the bells of the horses, "Holy to the LORD." And the pots in the house of the LORD shall be as the bowls before the altar. ²¹ And every pot in Jerusalem and Judah shall be holy to the LORD of hosts, so that all who sacrifice may come and take of them and boil the meat of the sacrifice in them. And there shall no longer be a trader in the house of the LORD of hosts on that day.

INTRODUCTION TO MALACHI

516 B.C.	460 B.C.	334–323 B.C.
Temple rebuilt	Prophetic ministry of Malachi	Reign of Alexander the Great

AUTHOR AND DATE

The prophet Malachi (whose name means "my messenger") probably lived at the same time as Ezra and Nehemiah, around 460 B.C.

THEME

Malachi's fellow Israelites were guilty of corrupt worship and unethical behavior. He called the people to renewed covenant obedience.

PURPOSE, OCCASION, AND BACKGROUND

Malachi's ministry took place nearly a hundred years after the decree of Cyrus in 538 B.C., which ended the Babylonian captivity and allowed the Jews to return to their homeland and rebuild the temple (2 Chron. 36:23). This was some 80 years after Haggai and Zechariah encouraged the rebuilding of the temple. Those two earlier prophets had said that the rebuilding of the temple would result in peace, prosperity, the conversion of people from other nations, and the return of God's own glorious presence (see

Haggai 2; Zech. 1:16–17; 2:1–13; 8:1–9:17). To the discouraged people of Malachi's day, these predictions must have seemed a cruel mockery. In contrast to the glowing promises, they faced economic difficulties due to drought and crop failure (Mal. 3:11). They remained an insignificant territory, no longer an independent nation and no longer ruled by a Davidic king. Worst of all, despite the promise of God's presence, they experienced only spiritual decline.

KEY THEMES AND OUTLINE: Malachi's Sixfold Wake-up Call to Renewed Covenant Obedience

The book of Malachi describes six disputations between God and Israel. There is a common pattern in each dispute: (1) God charges his people with bad behavior; (2) he then envisages the people's response to the charge ("But you say"; 1:2, 6, 7, 13; 2:14, 17; 3:7, 8, 13); (3) God then replies to their presumed response and expands the charge. The chart below shows the subject of each dispute and God's response to it.

Disputation	Reference	Summary	Focus
Disputation 1	1:2–5	Malachi defends God's love for Israel. The proper response to his love is covenantal obedience and sincere worship.	Israel must remember the Law of Moses (4:4).
Disputation 2	1:6–2:9	Malachi exposes offenses related to worship and criticizes the priests for allowing them.	
Disputation 3	2:10–16	Malachi condemns marriage to an unbeliever as unfaithfulness to Israel's covenant with God. He also condemns unjust divorce as a violation of the marriage covenant between husband and wife, to which the Lord is witness.	
Disputation 4	2:17–3:5	Malachi promises that God will demonstrate his justice. He will do so when "the messenger of the covenant" comes to judge the wicked and purify his people.	Israel must remember the promise of Elijah and the coming day of the Lord (4:5–6).
Disputation 5	3:6–12	Malachi returns to the subject of Israel's wicked offerings. The difficulties the people are experiencing are punishment for their sin.	
Disputation 6	3:13–4:3	Malachi assures the people that evildoers, who seem to escape divine justice, will be judged. The Lord will deliver his people.	
Summary	4:4–6	Malachi summarizes the main points of his prophecy: keep God's law (the focus of disputes 1–3), and remember the promise of a coming prophet like Elijah and the coming day of the Lord (the focus of disputes 4–6).	

MALACHI

1 The oracle of the word of the LORD to Israel by Malachi.

The LORD's Love for Israel

2 "I have loved you," says the LORD. But you say, "How have you loved us?" "Is not Esau Jacob's brother?" declares the LORD. "Yet I have loved Jacob 3 but Esau I have hated. I have laid waste his hill country and left his heritage to jackals of the desert." 4 If Edom says, "We are shattered but we will rebuild the ruins," the LORD of hosts says, "They may build, but I will tear down, and they will be called 'the wicked country,' and 'the people with whom the LORD is angry forever.'" 5 Your own eyes shall see this, and you shall say, "Great is the LORD beyond the border of Israel!"

The Priests' Polluted Offerings

6 "A son honors his father, and a servant his master. If then I am a father, where is my honor? And if I am a master, where is my fear? says the LORD of hosts to you, O priests, who despise my name. But you say, 'How have we despised your name?' 7 By offering polluted food upon my altar. But you say, 'How have we polluted you?' By saying that the LORD's table may be despised. 8 When you offer blind animals in sacrifice, is that not evil? And when you offer those that are lame or sick, is that not evil? Present that to your governor; will he accept you or show you favor? says the LORD of hosts. 9 And now entreat the favor of God, that he may be gracious to us. With such a gift from your hand, will he show favor to any of you? says the LORD of hosts. 10 Oh that there were one among you who would shut the doors, that you might not kindle fire on my altar in vain! I have no pleasure in you, says the LORD of hosts, and I will not accept an offering from your hand. 11 For from the rising of the sun to its setting my name will be great among the nations, and in every place incense will be offered to my name, and a pure offering. For my name will be great among the nations, says the LORD of hosts. 12 But you profane it when you say that the Lord's table is polluted, and its fruit, that is, its food may be despised. 13 But you say, 'What a weariness this is,' and you snort at it, says the LORD of hosts. You bring what has been taken by violence or is lame or sick, and this you bring as your offering! Shall I accept that from your hand? says the LORD. 14 Cursed be the cheat who has a male in his flock, and vows it, and yet sacrifices to the Lord what is blemished. For I am a great King, says the LORD of hosts, and my name will be feared among the nations.

The LORD Rebukes the Priests

2 "And now, O priests, this command is for you. 2 If you will not listen, if you will not take it to heart to give honor to my name, says the LORD of hosts, then I will send the curse upon you and I will curse your blessings. Indeed, I have already cursed them, because you do not lay it to heart. 3 Behold, I will rebuke your offspring, and spread dung on your faces, the dung of your offerings, and you shall be taken away with it. 4 So shall you know that I have sent this command to you, that my covenant with Levi may stand, says the LORD of hosts. 5 My covenant with him was one of life and peace, and I gave them to him. It was a covenant of fear, and he feared me. He stood in awe of my name. 6 True instruction was in his mouth, and no wrong was found on his lips. He walked with me in peace and uprightness, and he turned many from iniquity. 7 For the lips of a priest should guard knowledge, and people should seek instruc-

tion from his mouth, for he is the messenger of the LORD of hosts. **8** But you have turned aside from the way. You have caused many to stumble by your instruction. You have corrupted the covenant of Levi, says the LORD of hosts, **9** and so I make you despised and abased before all the people, inasmuch as you do not keep my ways but show partiality in your instruction."

MALACHI

Malachi, whose name means "my messenger," probably ministered during the same time as Ezra and Nehemiah. He prophesied to Judah about 80 years after Haggai and Zechariah had encouraged the people to rebuild the temple. Though Haggai and Zechariah had assured Judah that God's blessings would return to his people, bringing peace and prosperity, they had not yet experienced these promised blessings. Instead, they were facing a prolonged period of economic difficulty and hardship. Rather than wait faithfully on the Lord, the people sinned against him with half-hearted worship and imperfect offerings. God used Malachi to reaffirm his love for Israel and to rebuke them for their unfaithfulness to him. Malachi urged Judah to remember the Law of Moses, as well as the promise of Elijah and the coming day of the Lord.

KEY REFERENCE: MALACHI 4:1–6

Judah Profaned the Covenant

10 Have we not all one Father? Has not one God created us? Why then are we faithless to one another, profaning the covenant of our fathers? **11** Judah has been faithless, and abomination has been committed in Israel and in Jerusalem. For Judah has profaned the sanctuary of the LORD, which he loves, and has married the daughter of a foreign god. **12** May the LORD cut off from the tents of Jacob any descendant of the man who does this, who brings an offering to the LORD of hosts! **13** And this second thing you do. You cover the LORD's altar with tears, with weeping and groaning because he no longer regards the offering or accepts it with favor from your hand. **14** But you say, "Why does he not?" Because the LORD was witness between you and the wife of your youth, to whom you have been faithless, though she is your companion and your wife by covenant. **15** Did he not make them one, with a portion of the Spirit in their union? And what was the one God seeking? Godly offspring. So guard yourselves in your spirit, and let none of you be faithless to the wife of your youth. **16** "For the man who does not love his wife but divorces her, says the LORD, the God of Israel, covers his garment with violence, says the LORD of hosts. So guard yourselves in your spirit, and do not be faithless."

> **GETTING THE MESSAGE**

The title **LORD of hosts** appears more frequently in Malachi than in any other Old Testament book. Following the exile, Judah was a very small province within the vast Persian Empire. It had no army of its own, leaving its people painfully aware of how limited their resources were. Malachi wants to remind his people that God is in command of a great heavenly host that stands ready to defend Judah.

The Messenger of the LORD

17 You have wearied the LORD with your words. But you say, "How have we wearied him?" By saying, "Everyone who does evil is good in the sight of the LORD, and he delights in them." Or by asking, "Where is the God of justice?"

3 "Behold, I send my messenger, and he will prepare the way before me. And the Lord whom you seek will suddenly come to his temple; and the messenger of the covenant in whom you delight, behold, he is coming, says the LORD of hosts. **2** But who can endure the day of his coming, and who can stand when he appears? For he is like a refiner's fire and like fullers' soap. **3** He will sit as a refiner and purifier of silver, and he will purify the sons of Levi and refine them like gold and silver, and they will bring offerings in righteousness to the LORD. **4** Then the offering of Judah and Jerusalem will be pleasing to the Lord as in the days of old and as in former years.

⁵ "Then I will draw near to you for judgment. I will be a swift witness against the sorcerers, against the adulterers, against those who swear falsely, against those who oppress the hired worker in his wages, the widow and the fatherless, against those who thrust aside the sojourner, and do not fear me, says the Lord of hosts.

Robbing God

⁶ "For I the Lord do not change; therefore you, O children of Jacob, are not consumed. ⁷ From the days of your fathers you have turned aside from my statutes and have not kept them. Return to me, and I will return to you, says the Lord of hosts. But you say, 'How shall we return?' ⁸ Will man rob God? Yet you are robbing me. But you say, 'How have we robbed you?' In your tithes and contributions. ⁹ You are cursed with a curse, for you are robbing me, the whole nation of you. ¹⁰ Bring the full tithe into the storehouse, that there may be food in my house. And thereby put me to the test, says the Lord of hosts, if I will not open the windows of heaven for you and pour down for you a blessing until there is no more need. ¹¹ I will rebuke the devourer¹ for you, so that it will not destroy the fruits of your soil, and your vine in the field shall not fail to bear, says the Lord of hosts. ¹² Then all nations will call you blessed, for you will be a land of delight, says the Lord of hosts.

¹³ "Your words have been hard against me, says the Lord. But you say, 'How have we spoken against you?' ¹⁴ You have said, 'It is vain to serve God. What is the profit of our keeping his charge or of walking as in mourning before the Lord of hosts? ¹⁵ And now we call the arrogant blessed. Evildoers not only prosper but they put God to the test and they escape.' "

The Book of Remembrance

¹⁶ Then those who feared the Lord spoke with one another. The Lord paid attention and heard them, and a book of remembrance was written before him of those who feared the Lord and esteemed his name. ¹⁷ "They shall be mine, says the Lord of hosts, in the day when I make up my treasured possession, and I will spare them as a man spares his son who serves him. ¹⁸ Then once more you shall see the distinction between the righteous and the wicked, between one who serves God and one who does not serve him.

The Great Day of the Lord

4 "For behold, the day is coming, burning like an oven, when all the arrogant and all evildoers will be stubble. The day that is coming shall set them ablaze, says the Lord of hosts, so that it will leave them neither root nor branch. ² But for you who fear my name, the sun of righteousness shall rise with healing in its wings. You shall go out leaping like calves from the stall. ³ And you shall tread down the wicked, for they will be ashes under the soles of your feet, on the day when I act, says the Lord of hosts.

⁴ "Remember the law of my servant Moses, the statutes and rules that I commanded him at Horeb for all Israel.

⁵ "Behold, I will send you Elijah the prophet before the great and awesome day of the Lord comes. ⁶ And he will turn the hearts of fathers to their children and the hearts of children to their fathers, lest I come and strike the land with a decree of utter destruction."

---

¹ Probably a name for some crop-destroying pest or pests

THE
NEW TESTAMENT

THE THEOLOGY AND TIMELINE
OF THE NEW TESTAMENT

ALREADY—BUT NOT YET

Like John the Baptist before him, Jesus announced the imminent arrival of the kingdom of God (Mark 1:15), which was another way of saying that the saving promises found in the Old Testament were about to be realized. The kingdom of God, however, came in a most unexpected way. The kingdom did not come with apocalyptic power but in a small and almost imperceptible form. It was as small as a mustard seed, and yet it would grow into a great tree that would tower over the entire earth. It was as undetectable as leaven mixed into flour, but the leaven would eventually transform the entire batch of dough (Matt. 13:31–33). In other words, the kingdom was already present in Jesus and his ministry, but it was not yet present in its entirety. It was "already—but not yet." The day of judgment was still to come in the future, even though there would be an interval between God's beginning to fulfill his promises in Jesus (the kingdom inaugurated) and the final realization of his promises (the kingdom consummated). The already-but-not-yet theme dominates the entire New Testament and functions as a key to grasping the whole story.

WHO IS JESUS?

The New Testament highlights the fulfillment of God's saving promises in the Old Testament, but it particularly stresses that those promises and covenants are realized through his Son, Jesus the Christ.

Who is Jesus? According to the New Testament, he is the new and better Moses, declaring God's word as the sovereign interpreter of the Mosaic law (Matt. 5:17–48; Heb. 3:1–6). Jesus is the new Joshua who gives final rest to his people (Heb. 3:7–4:13). He is the true wisdom of God, fulfilling and transcending wisdom themes from the Old Testament (Col. 2:1–3). Jesus is the final prophet predicted by Moses (Deut. 18:15; Acts 3:22–23; 7:37). Jesus' miracles, healings, and authority over demons indicate that the promises of the kingdom are fulfilled in him (Matt. 12:28). His miracles also indicate that he shares God's authority and is himself divine, for only the Creator-Lord can

walk on water and calm the sea (Matt. 8:23–27; compare Ps. 107:29). Jesus is the Messiah, who brings to realization the promise that One would sit on David's throne forever.

Jesus is the Son of Man who will receive the kingdom from the Ancient of Days (Dan. 7:13–14) and will reign forever. His reign, however, has been realized through suffering, for he is also the servant of the Lord who has atoned for the sins of his people (Isa. 52:13–53:12; Mark 14:24; Rom. 4:25; 1 Pet. 2:21–25).

Jesus is the image of God (Col. 1:15; see Heb. 1:3), is in the very form of God, and is equal to God, though he temporarily surrendered some of the privileges of deity by being clothed with humanity so that human beings could be saved (Phil. 2:6–8). Jesus as the Son of God enjoys a unique and eternal relationship with God (see Matt. 28:18; John 20:31; Rom. 8:32), and he is worshiped just as the Father is (see Revelation 4–5). His majestic stature is memorialized by a meal celebrated in his memory (Mark 14:22–25) and by people being baptized in his name (Acts 2:38; 10:48). In a number of texts, Jesus is specifically called "God" (e.g., John 1:1, 18; 20:28; Rom. 9:5; Titus 2:13; Heb. 1:8; 2 Pet. 1:1).

CHRIST'S WORK ON THE CROSS

The New Testament particularly focuses on Jesus' work on the cross, by which he redeemed and saved his people. The narrative of Jesus' suffering and death consumes a significant amount of space in the Gospels. It is the culmination of each of their story lines, indicating that the cross and resurrection are the main point of the story. In Acts we see the growth of the church and the expansion of the mission, as the apostles and others proclaim the crucified and resurrected Lord. The Epistles explain the significance of Jesus' work on the cross and his resurrection, so that believers are enabled to grasp the height, depth, breadth, and width of the love of God (Rom. 8:39). Various themes woven together—creation, adoption, forgiveness of sins, justification, reconciliation, redemption, sanctification, and propitiation—teach that salvation comes from the Lord, and that Jesus as the Christ has redeemed his people from the guilt and bondage of sin.

THE PROMISE OF THE HOLY SPIRIT

Jesus promised to send the Spirit to those who are truly his disciples (John 14:16–17, 26; 15:26), and he poured out the Spirit on his people at Pentecost (Acts 2:1–4, 33) after he had been exalted to the right hand of the Father. The Spirit was given to bring glory to Jesus Christ (John 16:14), so that Christ would be magnified as the great Savior and Redeemer. The Spirit empowers the church to bear witness to Jesus Christ. At the same time, having the Spirit within is the mark of a person belonging to the people of God (Acts 10:44–48; 15:7–9; Rom. 8:9; Gal. 3:1–5). Transformation into Christlikeness is the Spirit's work (Rom. 8:2, 4, 13–14; 2 Cor. 3:18; Gal. 5:16, 18).

SIN, FAITH, AND REPENTANCE

Sin and death are twin powers that rule over all people, so that they stand in need of the redemption Christ brings (see Rom. 1:18–3:20; 5:1–7:25). Sin does not merely constitute failure to keep the law of God. It represents personal rebellion against God's lordship (1 John 3:4). The essence of sin is idolatry, in which people refuse to give thanks and praise to the one and only God, and worship the creature rather than the Creator (Rom. 1:18–25).

But sin is not the last word, since Jesus Christ came to save sinners, thereby high-lighting the mercy and grace of God. The response called for by God's grace is faith and repentance (Mark 1:15; Acts 2:38). Indeed, the whole of the New Testament can be under-stood as a call to repentance and faith (see Hebrews 11). Those who desire to be part of Jesus' new community (the church) and part of the kingdom of God (God's rule in people's hearts and lives) must forsake false gods, renounce self-worship and evil, and turn to Jesus as Lord and Master. The call to repentance is nothing less than a summons to abandonment of sin and to personal faith.

People are called to trust in the saving work of the Lord on their behalf instead of thinking that they can save themselves. Even those who are already believers are to press on in faith and repentance as long as life lasts, for this is the mark of Christ's true disciples.

THE CHURCH AS THE PEOPLE OF GOD

The saving promises of God have begun to be fulfilled in a new community, the church of Jesus Christ. The church is composed of believers in Jesus Christ, both Jews and Gentiles. The laws in the Old Testament that separated Jews from Gentiles (e.g., circumcision, purity laws, special festivals) are no longer in force. The church is God's new temple, indwelt by the Holy Spirit. Christians are called to live out the beauty of the gospel by showing the supreme mark of Christ's disciples: love for one another (John 13:34–35).

The church eagerly awaits the return of Jesus Christ and the consummation of all of God's purposes. Meanwhile, the church is to live out her life in holiness as the radiant bride of Christ, and to herald the good news of salvation to the ends of the earth, so that others may be transferred from Satan's kingdom to the kingdom of the Lord. The church longs for the day when she will behold God face-to-face and worship Jesus Christ forever. The new creation will be a full reality, all things will be new, and the Lord will be praised forever for his love and mercy and grace—for New Testament theology is ultimately about glorifying and praising God.

NEW TESTAMENT TIMELINE

The following pages provide a detailed NT timeline. Most of the dates can be determined precisely by correlating biblical events with extensive historical documents and archaeo-logical evidence. Dates with an asterisk denote approximate or alternative dates. The extensive external confirmation of NT dates and events encourages great confidence in the truth and historicity of both the Old and New Testaments.

5 B.C.*	Jesus is born in Bethlehem.
4 B.C.	Jesus' family flees to Egypt to escape from Herod's plan to kill Jesus (Matt. 2:13–18); Herod dies; Judas (of Sepphoris) and others rebel, requiring the Syrian Governor Varus to intervene throughout Palestine; Sepphoris, a city four miles from Nazareth, is destroyed by Roman soldiers; Judea, Samaria, and Idumea are given to Herod's son, Archelaus; Galilee and Perea are given to his son Antipas; Jesus' family, after returning from Egypt, resides in Nazareth (Matt. 2:19–23), a small village in southern Galilee.
A.D. 6	Archelaus is exiled for incompetence; Judea becomes a Roman province; Judas the Galilean (of Gamla) leads a revolt against the tax census; the governor of Syria, Quirinius (A.D. 6–7), appoints Annas high priest (6–15).
8*	Jesus (age 12) interacts with the teachers in the temple (Luke 2:41–50).
8*–28/30	Jesus works as a carpenter in Nazareth (Matt. 13:55; Mark 6:3) and probably in neighboring villages and Sepphoris, which was being rebuilt.
28–29*	John the Baptist begins his ministry around the Jordan River (John 1:19).
28–30*	Jesus begins his ministry in Judea, but soon focuses his efforts in Galilee. In Jerusalem, Pharisees (like Gamaliel) train disciples (like Paul) in their tradition. They send a delegation to Galilee, but the delegation rejects Jesus' teaching. In Alexandria, Philo (20 B.C.–A.D. 50) attempts to unify Greek philosophy with Hebrew Scripture.
33 (or 30)	Jesus returns to Judea, is crucified, and resurrected. James the brother of Jesus becomes a believer after witnessing the resurrected Jesus (1 Cor. 15:7; Acts 12:17). Jesus ascends to the Father's right hand (Acts 1). Jesus' first followers receive the Holy Spirit at Pentecost and begin to proclaim the gospel (Acts 2).
33/34*	Paul witnesses the resurrected Lord on the way to Damascus and is commissioned as an apostle to the nations (Acts 9; Gal. 1:15–16).
34–37	Paul ministers in Damascus and Arabia (Acts 9:19–22; 26:20; Gal. 1:16–18).
36	Pilate loses his position for incompetence.
36/37*	Paul meets with Peter in Jerusalem (Acts 9:26–30; Gal. 1:18).
37–45	Paul ministers in Syria, Tarsus, and Cilicia (Acts 9:30; Gal. 1:21).
38*	Peter witnesses to Cornelius (Acts 10).
39	Antipas is exiled.
40–45*	James writes his letter to believers outside Palestine (see James 1:1).
41–44	Agrippa, Herod the Great's grandson, rules Palestine; he kills James the brother of John (Acts 12:2) and imprisons Peter (Acts 12:3).
42–44	Paul receives his "thorn in the flesh" (2 Cor. 12:7).
44	Peter leaves Jerusalem; Agrippa is killed by an "angel of the Lord" (Acts 12:23).
44–46	Theudas persuades many Jews to sell their possessions and follow him into the wilderness where he claimed he would miraculously divide the Jordan River; Roman procurator Fadus dispatches his cavalry and beheads the would-be messiah.
44–47*	Paul's Second Visit to Jerusalem; time of famine (Acts 11:27–30; Gal. 2:1–10).
46–47	Paul's First Missionary Journey (with Barnabas) from Antioch to Cyprus, Antioch in Pisidia, Iconium, and Lystra (Acts 13:4–14:26).
46–48	Roman procurator Tiberius Alexander crucifies two sons (Jacob and Simon) of Judas the Galilean.
48*	Paul writes *Galatians*, perhaps from Antioch (see Acts 14:26–28).
48–49*	Paul and Peter return to Jerusalem for the Apostolic Council, which, with the assistance of James, frees Gentile believers from the requirement of circumcision in opposition to Pharisaic believers (Acts 15:1–29); Paul and Barnabas return to Antioch (Acts 15:30) but split over a dispute about John Mark (Acts 15:36–40).
48/49–51*	Paul's Second Missionary Journey (with Silas) from Antioch to Syria, Cilicia, southern Galatia, Macedonia, notably Philippi, Thessalonica, and Berea; and then on to Achaia, notably Athens and Corinth (Acts 15:36–18:22).
49	Claudius expels Jews from Rome because of conflicts about Jesus (Acts 18:2); Paul befriends two refugees, Priscilla and Aquila, in Corinth (Acts 18:2–3).
49–51*	Paul writes *1–2 Thessalonians* from Corinth (Acts 18:1, 11; also compare Acts 18:5 with 1 Thess. 1:8).
51	Paul appears before Gallio, proconsul of Achaia (Acts 18:12–17).
50–54*	Peter comes to Rome.
52–57*	Paul's Third Missionary Journey from Antioch to Galatia, Phrygia, Ephesus, Macedonia, Greece (Acts 18:23–21:17).
52–55	Paul ministers in Ephesus (Acts 19:1–20).
53–55*	Mark writes his Gospel, containing Peter's memories of Jesus; perhaps within a decade, Matthew publishes his Gospel, which relies on Mark and other sources. Paul writes *1 Corinthians* from Ephesus (Acts 19:10).

54	Claudius dies (edict exiling Jews repealed); Priscilla and Aquila return to Rome and host a church in their home (see Rom. 16:3–5).
54–68	Nero reigns.
55–56*	Paul writes *2 Corinthians* from Macedonia (Acts 20:1, 3; 2 Cor. 1:16; 2:13; 7:5; 8:1; 9:2, 4; see 1 Cor. 16:5).
57*	Paul winters in Corinth and writes *Romans* (Acts 20:3; see Rom. 16:1–2; also see Rom. 16:23 with 1 Cor. 1:14); travels to Jerusalem (Acts 21:1–16), visits with James the brother of Jesus (Acts 21:17–26), and is arrested (Acts 21:27–36; 22:22–29).
57–59	Paul is imprisoned and transferred to Caesarea (Acts 23:23–24, 33–34).
60	Paul begins voyage to Rome (Acts 27:1–2); he is shipwrecked for three months on the island of Malta (Acts 27:39–28:10).
60–70*	Letter to the *Hebrews* is written.
62	James the brother of the Lord is executed by the Sadducean high priest Ananus.
62–63*	Peter writes his first letter (*1 Peter*) from Rome (1 Pet. 5:13).
62*	Paul arrives in Rome and remains under house arrest (Acts 28:16–31); he writes *Ephesians* (see verses for Colossians), *Philippians* (Phil. 1:7, 13, 17; 4:22), *Colossians* (Col. 4:3, 10, 18; see Acts 27:2 with Col. 4:10), *Philemon* (see Philem. 23 with Col. 1:7; Philem. 2 with Col. 4:17; Philem. 24 with Col. 4:10; also see Col. 4:9). Luke, Paul's physician and companion (see Col. 4:14), writes *Luke* and *Acts*.
62–64	Paul is released, extends his mission (probably reaching Spain), writes *1 Timothy* from Macedonia (see 1 Tim. 1:3) and *Titus* from Nicopolis (Titus 3:12); he is rearrested in Rome (2 Tim. 1:16–17).
63–64	Work on the temple complex is completed.
64 (July 19)	Fire in Rome; Nero blames and kills many Christians.
64–67*	Peter writes his second letter (*2 Peter*). Jude writes his letter. Paul writes *2 Timothy* (see 2 Tim. 4:6–8). Paul and Peter are martyred in Rome.
66	First Jewish-Roman War begins with a riot between Greeks and Jews at Caesarea; Roman procurator Gesius Florus (A.D. 64–66) is murdered and a Roman garrison wiped out; Menahem, son or grandson of Judas the Galilean, murders the high priest Ananias and seizes control of the temple; Nero dispatches Vespasian with three legions.
67*	Romans destroy the Qumran community, who beforehand hid the so-called Dead Sea Scrolls in nearby caves; the church in Jerusalem flees to Pella (Matt. 24:15–16; Mark 13:14; Luke 21:20–22); John migrates to Ephesus with Mary, Jesus' mother.
68	Nero commits suicide; year of the three emperors.
69	Rebellion quelled in Galilee and Samaria; Vespasian summoned back to Rome to become emperor.
70 (Aug. 30)	Titus, Vespasian's son, after a five-month siege of Jerusalem, destroys the temple after desecrating it; the temple's menorah, Torah, and veil are removed and later put on display in a victory parade in Rome; the influence of the Sadducees ends; the Pharisee Johanan ben Zakkai escapes and convinces the Romans to allow him and others to settle in Jamnia, where they found a school.
73 (May 2)*	Before Roman general Silva breaches the fortress atop Masada following a two-year siege, 936 Jewish rebels commit suicide.
75	Titus has an affair with the Jewish princess Berenice, sister of Agrippa II (Acts 25:13, 23), whom he later abandons because of the scandal.
77	Pliny the Elder writes *Natural History*.
77–78	Josephus publishes *Jewish War* in Rome.
79	Pompeii and Herculaneum are destroyed by eruption of Vesuvius; Pliny the Elder dies attempting to investigate.
81	The Arch of Titus, celebrating his destruction of the temple, is erected in Rome.
81–96	Domitian, Titus's brother, persecutes Christians among the Roman nobility, including his own relatives Clemens and Domitilla.
85–95*	John writes his letters (*1–3 John*), probably in Ephesus.
89–95*	John writes his Gospel, probably in Ephesus.
93–94	Josephus publishes *Jewish Antiquities* in Rome.
94	Domitian exiles philosophers from Rome.
95*	Amidst persecution, Clement, a leader in the Roman church, writes his *Letter to the Corinthians* (*1 Clement*) appealing for peace between the young men and elders.
95–96*	Exiled by Domitian to Patmos, John writes *Revelation* (Rev. 1:9).
96–98	Nerva, the first of five "good" emperors, ends official persecution.

* denotes approximate date; / signifies either/or

INTRODUCTION TO MATTHEW

c. 5 B.C.	c. A.D. 28–33	c. A.D. 55–65
Birth of Jesus	Jesus' ministry, death, resurrection	Matthew's Gospel written

AUTHOR, DATE, AND RECIPIENTS

Matthew was probably written in the late 50s or early 60s A.D. Matthew (also called Levi), the former tax collector who became Jesus' disciple, is the author. The original audience may have been the church in Antioch of Syria. Its members included Jewish and Gentile Christians.

THEME

Matthew tells the story of Jesus of Nazareth, the long-expected Messiah who brought the kingdom of God to earth.

PURPOSE

Matthew writes his Gospel to demonstrate that Jesus is the Messiah, that he has the right to the throne of David as Israel's true King, and that he is the ultimate fulfillment of God's promise to Abraham that his descendants would be a blessing to all the world (1:1; Gen. 12:1–3). Matthew seeks to encourage Jewish Christians (and all future disciples) to stand strong despite opposition. They should feel secure in the knowledge of their citizenship in God's kingdom. Matthew shows that Gentiles also can find salvation through Jesus the Messiah.

KEY THEMES

1. Portrait of Jesus (1:1, 23; 2:2; 14:33; 16:16; 18:20; 21:5–9).

2. The bridge between Old and New Testaments (1:1–17, 22–23; 2:4–5, 15, 17, 23; 5:17–20).

3. God's continuing work of salvation within Israel, extended to all the peoples of the earth through the person and work of Christ (10:5–6; 28:19).

4. The new community of faith (11:28; 16:18–19; 28:19).

5. The church as built and maintained by Jesus' continuing presence (16:18; 18:15–20; 22:10; 28:20).

6. A "great commission" for evangelism and mission (28:19).

7. Jesus' five teachings as a manual on discipleship (chs. 5–7; 10; 13; 18–20; 24–25).

OUTLINE

I. The Arrival of Jesus the Messiah (1:1–2:23)

II. John the Baptist Prepares for the Messianic Kingdom (3:1–17)

III. Jesus the Messiah Begins to Advance the Messianic Kingdom (4:1–25)

IV. The Authoritative Message of the Messiah: Kingdom Life for His Disciples (5:1–7:29)

V. The Authoritative Power of the Messiah: Kingdom Power Demonstrated (8:1–9:38)

VI. The Authoritative Mission of the Messiah's Messengers (10:1–42)

VII. Opposition to the Messiah Increases (11:1–12:50)

VIII. The Messianic Kingdom Revealed in Parables (13:1–53)

IX. The Identity of the Messiah Revealed (13:54–16:20)

X. The Suffering of the Messiah Revealed (16:21–17:27)

XI. The Community of the Messiah Revealed (18:1–20:34)

XII. The Messiah Asserts His Authority over Jerusalem (21:1–23:39)

XIII. The Delay, Return, and Judgment of the Messiah (24:1–25:46)

XIV. The Crucified Messiah (26:1–27:66)

XV. The Resurrection and Commission of the Messiah (28:1–20)

THE GOSPEL ACCORDING TO

MATTHEW

The Genealogy of Jesus Christ

1 The book of the genealogy of Jesus Christ, the son of David, the son of Abraham.

2 Abraham was the father of Isaac, and Isaac the father of Jacob, and Jacob the father of Judah and his brothers, 3 and Judah the father of Perez and Zerah by Tamar, and Perez the father of Hezron, and Hezron the father of Ram, 4 and Ram the father of Amminadab, and Amminadab the father of Nahshon, and Nahshon the father of Salmon, 5 and Salmon the father of Boaz by Rahab, and Boaz the father of Obed by Ruth, and Obed the father of Jesse, 6 and Jesse the father of David the king.

And David was the father of Solomon by the wife of Uriah, 7 and Solomon the father of Rehoboam, and Rehoboam the father of Abijah, and Abijah the father of Asaph, 8 and Asaph the father of Jehoshaphat, and Jehoshaphat the father of Joram, and Joram the father of Uzziah, 9 and Uzziah the father of Jotham, and Jotham the father of Ahaz, and Ahaz the father of Hezekiah, 10 and Hezekiah the father of Manasseh, and Manasseh the father of Amos, and Amos the father of Josiah, 11 and Josiah the father of Jechoniah and his brothers, at the time of the deportation to Babylon.

12 And after the deportation to Babylon: Jechoniah was the father of Shealtiel, and Shealtiel the father of Zerubbabel, 13 and Zerubbabel the father of Abiud, and Abiud the father of Eliakim, and Eliakim the father of Azor, 14 and Azor the father of Zadok, and Zadok the father of Achim, and Achim the father of Eliud, 15 and Eliud the father of Eleazar, and Eleazar the father of Matthan, and Matthan the father of Jacob, 16 and Jacob the father of Joseph the husband of Mary, of whom Jesus was born, who is called Christ.

17 So all the generations from Abraham to David were fourteen generations, and from David to the deportation to Babylon fourteen generations, and from the depor-

tation to Babylon to the Christ fourteen generations.

The Birth of Jesus Christ

18 Now the birth of Jesus Christ took place in this way. When his mother Mary had been betrothed[1] to Joseph, before they came together she was found to be with child from the Holy Spirit. 19 And her husband Joseph, being a just man and unwilling to put her to shame, resolved to divorce her quietly. 20 But as he considered these things, behold,

GETTING THE MESSAGE

From Malachi to Matthew. Malachi, the last book of the Old Testament, was a message of encouragement for the Jews who had returned from exile in Babylon. Matthew wrote his Gospel more than 400 years later. The Jews still lived in their homeland, but under the oppressive rule of Rome. Matthew tells the good news about how Jesus the Messiah fulfills the promises of God in the Old Testament.

an angel of the Lord appeared to him in a dream, saying, "Joseph, son of David, do not fear to take Mary as your wife, for that which is conceived in her is from the Holy Spirit. 21 She will bear a son, and you shall call his name Jesus, for he will save his people from their sins." 22 All this took place to fulfill what the Lord had spoken by the prophet:

23   "Behold, the virgin shall conceive and
          bear a son,
        and they shall call his name
          Immanuel"

(which means, God with us). 24 When Joseph woke from sleep, he did as the angel of the Lord commanded him: he took his wife, 25 but knew her not until she had given birth to a son. And he called his name Jesus.

1 That is, legally committed to be married

The Visit of the Wise Men

2 Now after Jesus was born in Bethlehem of Judea in the days of Herod the king, behold, wise men from the east came to Jerusalem, ² saying, "Where is he who has been born king of the Jews? For we saw his star when it rose and have come to worship him." ³ When Herod the king heard this, he was troubled, and all Jerusalem with him; ⁴ and assembling all the chief priests and scribes of the people, he inquired of them

PROFILE

HEROD THE GREAT

Herod the Great ruled Israel and Judah from 37 to 4 B.C. He was an Idumean (or Edomite), and was appointed king of the Jews under the authority of Rome. Herod ruled firmly and often ruthlessly, murdering any who might challenge his place on the throne. This included his own wife, several sons, and other relatives. It is no surprise, then, that he tried to kill the baby Jesus. Despite his cruelty, Herod was known as "the Great" because Israel and Judah experienced prosperity during his reign. He was a master builder who restored the temple in Jerusalem and built many theaters, cities, palaces, and fortresses. Herod also financed structures—including pagan temples—throughout the Roman Empire. Ravaged by disease, Herod died in his palace at Jericho and was buried at Herodium.

KEY REFERENCE: MATTHEW 2:16–18

where the Christ was to be born. ⁵ They told him, "In Bethlehem of Judea, for so it is written by the prophet:

⁶ "'And you, O Bethlehem, in the land of Judah,
　　are by no means least among the rulers of Judah;
for from you shall come a ruler
　　who will shepherd my people Israel.'"

⁷ Then Herod summoned the wise men

secretly and ascertained from them what time the star had appeared. ⁸ And he sent them to Bethlehem, saying, "Go and search diligently for the child, and when you have found him, bring me word, that I too may come and worship him." ⁹ After listening to the king, they went on their way. And behold, the star that they had seen when it rose went before them until it came to rest over the place where the child was. ¹⁰ When they saw the star, they rejoiced exceedingly with great joy. ¹¹ And going into the house they saw the child with Mary his mother, and they fell down and worshiped him. Then, opening their treasures, they offered him gifts, gold and frankincense and myrrh. ¹² And being warned in a dream not to return to Herod, they departed to their own country by another way.

The Flight to Egypt

¹³ Now when they had departed, behold, an angel of the Lord appeared to Joseph in a dream and said, "Rise, take the child and his mother, and flee to Egypt, and remain there until I tell you, for Herod is about to search for the child, to destroy him." ¹⁴ And he rose and took the child and his mother by night and departed to Egypt ¹⁵ and remained there until the death of Herod. This was to fulfill what the Lord had spoken by the prophet, "Out of Egypt I called my son."

Herod Kills the Children

¹⁶ Then Herod, when he saw that he had been tricked by the wise men, became furious, and he sent and killed all the male children in Bethlehem and in all that region who were two years old or under, according to the time that he had ascertained from the wise men. ¹⁷ Then was fulfilled what was spoken by the prophet Jeremiah:

¹⁸ "A voice was heard in Ramah,
　　weeping and loud lamentation,
Rachel weeping for her children;
　　she refused to be comforted,
　　　　because they are no more."

The Return to Nazareth

¹⁹ But when Herod died, behold, an angel of the Lord appeared in a dream to Joseph in Egypt, ²⁰ saying, "Rise, take the child and his mother and go to the land of Israel, for those who sought the child's life are dead."

²¹ And he rose and took the child and his mother and went to the land of Israel. ²² But when he heard that Archelaus was reigning over Judea in place of his father Herod, he was afraid to go there, and being warned in a dream he withdrew to the district of Galilee. ²³ And he went and lived in a city called Nazareth, so that what was spoken by the prophets might be fulfilled, that he would be called a Nazarene.

John the Baptist Prepares the Way

3 In those days John the Baptist came preaching in the wilderness of Judea, ² "Repent, for the kingdom of heaven is at hand." ³ For this is he who was spoken of by the prophet Isaiah when he said,

> "The voice of one crying in the wilderness:
> 'Prepare the way of the Lord;
> make his paths straight.'"

⁴ Now John wore a garment of camel's hair and a leather belt around his waist, and his food was locusts and wild honey. ⁵ Then Jerusalem and all Judea and all the region about the Jordan were going out to him, ⁶ and they were baptized by him in the river Jordan, confessing their sins.

⁷ But when he saw many of the Pharisees and Sadducees coming to his baptism, he said to them, "You brood of vipers! Who warned you to flee from the wrath to come? ⁸ Bear fruit in keeping with repentance. ⁹ And do not presume to say to yourselves, 'We have Abraham as our father,' for I tell you, God is able from these stones to raise up children for Abraham. ¹⁰ Even now the axe is laid to the root of the trees. Every tree therefore that does not bear good fruit is cut down and thrown into the fire.

¹¹ "I baptize you with water for repentance, but he who is coming after me is mightier than I, whose sandals I am not worthy to carry. He will baptize you with the Holy Spirit and fire. ¹² His winnowing fork is in his hand, and he will clear his threshing floor and gather his wheat into the barn, but the chaff he will burn with unquenchable fire."

The Baptism of Jesus

¹³ Then Jesus came from Galilee to the Jordan to John, to be baptized by him. ¹⁴ John would have prevented him, saying, "I need to be baptized by you, and do you come to me?" ¹⁵ But Jesus answered him, "Let it be so now, for thus it is fitting for us to fulfill all righteousness." Then he consented. ¹⁶ And when Jesus was baptized, immediately he went up from the water, and behold, the heavens were opened to him, and he saw the Spirit of God descending like a dove and coming to rest on him; ¹⁷ and behold, a voice from heaven said, "This is my beloved Son, with whom I am well pleased."

The Temptation of Jesus

4 Then Jesus was led up by the Spirit into the wilderness to be tempted by the devil. ² And after fasting forty days and forty nights, he was hungry. ³ And the tempter came and said to him, "If you are the Son

> ### ▶ GETTING THE MESSAGE
>
> **A humble hometown.** Jesus' parents came from Nazareth, a small town halfway between the Mediterranean Sea and the Sea of Galilee. They returned to Nazareth from Egypt after having fled there from the wrath of Herod (2:19–23). The people of Jesus' day despised Nazareth (John 1:46).

of God, command these stones to become loaves of bread." ⁴ But he answered, "It is written,

> "'Man shall not live by bread alone,
> but by every word that comes from the mouth of God.'"

⁵ Then the devil took him to the holy city and set him on the pinnacle of the temple ⁶ and said to him, "If you are the Son of God, throw yourself down, for it is written,

> "'He will command his angels concerning you,'

and

> "'On their hands they will bear you up,
> lest you strike your foot against a stone.'"

⁷ Jesus said to him, "Again it is written, 'You shall not put the Lord your God to the test.'" ⁸ Again, the devil took him to a very high mountain and showed him all the kingdoms of the world and their glory. ⁹ And he said to

him, "All these I will give you, if you will fall down and worship me." [10] Then Jesus said to him, "Be gone, Satan! For it is written,

> "'You shall worship the Lord your God
> and him only shall you serve.'"

[11] Then the devil left him, and behold, angels came and were ministering to him.

Jesus Begins His Ministry

[12] Now when he heard that John had been arrested, he withdrew into Galilee. [13] And leaving Nazareth he went and lived in Capernaum by the sea, in the territory of Zebulun and Naphtali, [14] so that what was spoken by the prophet Isaiah might be fulfilled:

GETTING THE MESSAGE

At 700 feet (213 m) below sea level, the **Sea of Galilee** is the lowest-lying freshwater lake on earth. Galilee has no natural harbors, and its low elevation coupled with the steep hills surrounding it can cause unpredictable storms. Nonetheless, its wealth of fish made Galilee popular with fishermen, who built artificial harbors to bring in their catch.

[15] "The land of Zebulun and the land of
         Naphtali,
     the way of the sea, beyond the
         Jordan, Galilee of the Gentiles—
[16]   the people dwelling in darkness
     have seen a great light,
     and for those dwelling in the region
         and shadow of death,
     on them a light has dawned."

[17] From that time Jesus began to preach, saying, "Repent, for the kingdom of heaven is at hand."

Jesus Calls the First Disciples

[18] While walking by the Sea of Galilee, he saw two brothers, Simon (who is called Peter) and Andrew his brother, casting a net into the sea, for they were fishermen. [19] And he said to them, "Follow me, and I will make you fishers of men."[1] [20] Immediately they left their nets and followed him. [21] And

going on from there he saw two other brothers, James the son of Zebedee and John his brother, in the boat with Zebedee their father, mending their nets, and he called them. [22] Immediately they left the boat and their father and followed him.

Jesus Ministers to Great Crowds

[23] And he went throughout all Galilee, teaching in their synagogues and proclaiming the gospel of the kingdom and healing every disease and every affliction among the people. [24] So his fame spread throughout all Syria, and they brought him all the sick, those afflicted with various diseases and pains, those oppressed by demons, epileptics, and paralytics, and he healed them. [25] And great crowds followed him from Galilee and the Decapolis, and from Jerusalem and Judea, and from beyond the Jordan.

The Sermon on the Mount

5 Seeing the crowds, he went up on the mountain, and when he sat down, his disciples came to him.

The Beatitudes

[2] And he opened his mouth and taught them, saying:

[3] "Blessed are the poor in spirit, for theirs is the kingdom of heaven.

[4] "Blessed are those who mourn, for they shall be comforted.

[5] "Blessed are the meek, for they shall inherit the earth.

[6] "Blessed are those who hunger and thirst for righteousness, for they shall be satisfied.

[7] "Blessed are the merciful, for they shall receive mercy.

[8] "Blessed are the pure in heart, for they shall see God.

[9] "Blessed are the peacemakers, for they shall be called sons[2] of God.

[10] "Blessed are those who are persecuted for righteousness' sake, for theirs is the kingdom of heaven.

[11] "Blessed are you when others revile you and persecute you and utter all kinds of evil against you falsely on my account. [12] Rejoice and be glad, for your reward is great in heaven, for so they persecuted the prophets who were before you.

---

[1] The Greek word for *men* refers to both men and women (see Preface)   [2] The Greek word for *sons* refers to both sons and daughters (see Preface)

Salt and Light

[13] "You are the salt of the earth, but if salt has lost its taste, how shall its saltiness be restored? It is no longer good for anything except to be thrown out and trampled under people's feet.

[14] "You are the light of the world. A city set on a hill cannot be hidden. [15] Nor do people light a lamp and put it under a basket, but on a stand, and it gives light to all in the house. [16] In the same way, let your light shine before others, so that they may see your good works and give glory to your Father who is in heaven.

Christ Came to Fulfill the Law

[17] "Do not think that I have come to abolish the Law or the Prophets; I have not come to abolish them but to fulfill them. [18] For truly, I say to you, until heaven and earth pass away, not an iota, not a dot, will pass from the Law until all is accomplished. [19] Therefore whoever relaxes one of the least of these commandments and teaches others to do the same will be called least in the kingdom of heaven, but whoever does them and teaches them will be called great in the kingdom of heaven. [20] For I tell you, unless your righteousness exceeds that of the scribes and Pharisees, you will never enter the kingdom of heaven.

Anger

[21] "You have heard that it was said to those of old, 'You shall not murder; and whoever murders will be liable to judgment.' [22] But I say to you that everyone who is angry with his brother will be liable to judgment; whoever insults his brother will be liable to the council; and whoever says, 'You fool!' will be liable to the hell of fire. [23] So if you are offering your gift at the altar and there remember that your brother has something against you, [24] leave your gift there before the altar and go. First be reconciled to your brother, and then come and offer your gift. [25] Come to terms quickly with your accuser while you are going with him to court, lest your accuser hand you over to the judge, and the judge to the guard, and you be put in prison. [26] Truly, I say to you, you will never get out until you have paid the last penny.[1]

Lust

[27] "You have heard that it was said, 'You shall not commit adultery.' [28] But I say to you that everyone who looks at a woman with lustful intent has already committed adultery with her in his heart. [29] If your right eye causes you to sin, tear it out and throw it away. For it is better that you lose one of your members than that your whole body be thrown into hell. [30] And if your right hand causes you to sin, cut it off and throw it away. For it is better that you lose one of your members than that your whole body go into hell.

Divorce

[31] "It was also said, 'Whoever divorces his wife, let him give her a certificate of divorce.' [32] But I say to you that everyone who divorces his wife, except on the ground

of sexual immorality, makes her commit adultery, and whoever marries a divorced woman commits adultery.

Oaths

[33] "Again you have heard that it was said to those of old, 'You shall not swear falsely, but shall perform to the Lord what you have sworn.' [34] But I say to you, Do not take an oath at all, either by heaven, for it is the throne of God, [35] or by the earth, for it is his footstool, or by Jerusalem, for it is the city of the great King. [36] And do not take an oath by your head, for you cannot make one hair white or black. [37] Let what you say be simply 'Yes' or 'No'; anything more than this comes from evil.

Retaliation

[38] "You have heard that it was said, 'An eye for an eye and a tooth for a tooth.' [39] But I say to you, Do not resist the one who is evil. But if anyone slaps you on the right cheek, turn to him the other also. [40] And if anyone would

---

[1] The Greek word refers to about 1/64 of a day's pay for a worker

sue you and take your tunic, let him have your cloak as well. [41] And if anyone forces you to go one mile, go with him two miles. [42] Give to the one who begs from you, and do not refuse the one who would borrow from you.

Love Your Enemies

[43] "You have heard that it was said, 'You shall love your neighbor and hate your enemy.' [44] But I say to you, Love your enemies and pray for those who persecute you, [45] so that you may be sons of your Father who is in heaven. For he makes his sun rise on the evil and on the good, and sends rain on the just and on the unjust. [46] For if you love those who love you, what reward do you have? Do not even the tax collectors do the same? [47] And if you greet only your brothers,[1] what more are you doing than others? Do not even the Gentiles do the

GETTING THE MESSAGE

Jesus encourages his disciples to call God their **Father** (6:6, 9). This reminds believers that God has adopted them as his children because of Jesus (see Rom. 8:15; Gal. 4:6). In Aramaic, the language spoken by Jesus, "Abba" was the word for father (see Mark 14:36).

same? [48] You therefore must be perfect, as your heavenly Father is perfect.

Giving to the Needy

6 "Beware of practicing your righteousness before other people in order to be seen by them, for then you will have no reward from your Father who is in heaven. [2] "Thus, when you give to the needy, sound no trumpet before you, as the hypocrites do in the synagogues and in the streets, that they may be praised by others. Truly, I say to you, they have received their reward. [3] But when you give to the needy, do not let your left hand know what your right hand is doing, [4] so that your giving may be in secret. And your Father who sees in secret will reward you.

The Lord's Prayer

[5] "And when you pray, you must not be like the hypocrites. For they love to stand and pray in the synagogues and at the street corners, that they may be seen by others. Truly, I say to you, they have received their reward. [6] But when you pray, go into your room and shut the door and pray to your Father who is in secret. And your Father who sees in secret will reward you.

[7] "And when you pray, do not heap up empty phrases as the Gentiles do, for they think that they will be heard for their many words. [8] Do not be like them, for your Father knows what you need before you ask him. [9] Pray then like this:

"Our Father in heaven,
hallowed be your name.
[10] Your kingdom come,
your will be done,
on earth as it is in heaven.
[11] Give us this day our daily bread,
[12] and forgive us our debts,
as we also have forgiven our debtors.
[13] And lead us not into temptation,
but deliver us from evil.

[14] For if you forgive others their trespasses, your heavenly Father will also forgive you, [15] but if you do not forgive others their trespasses, neither will your Father forgive your trespasses.

Fasting

[16] "And when you fast, do not look gloomy like the hypocrites, for they disfigure their faces that their fasting may be seen by others. Truly, I say to you, they have received their reward. [17] But when you fast, anoint your head and wash your face, [18] that your fasting may not be seen by others but by your Father who is in secret. And your Father who sees in secret will reward you.

Lay Up Treasures in Heaven

[19] "Do not lay up for yourselves treasures on earth, where moth and rust destroy and where thieves break in and steal, [20] but lay up for yourselves treasures in heaven, where neither moth nor rust destroys and where thieves do not break in and steal. [21] For where your treasure is, there your heart will be also.

[22] "The eye is the lamp of the body. So, if your eye is healthy, your whole body will be full of light, [23] but if your eye is bad, your whole body will be full of darkness. If then

[1] Or brothers and sisters (see Preface)

the light in you is darkness, how great is the darkness!

24 "No one can serve two masters, for either he will hate the one and love the other, or he will be devoted to the one and despise the other. You cannot serve God and money.

Do Not Be Anxious

25 "Therefore I tell you, do not be anxious about your life, what you will eat or what you will drink, nor about your body, what you will put on. Is not life more than food, and the body more than clothing? **26** Look at the birds of the air: they neither sow nor reap nor gather into barns, and yet your heavenly Father feeds them. Are you not of more value than they? **27** And which of you by being anxious can add a single hour to his span of life? **28** And why are you anxious about clothing? Consider the lilies of the field, how they grow: they neither toil nor spin, **29** yet I tell you, even Solomon in all his glory was not arrayed like one of these. **30** But if God so clothes the grass of the field, which today is alive and tomorrow is thrown into the oven, will he not much more clothe you, O you of little faith? **31** Therefore do not be anxious, saying, 'What shall we eat?' or 'What shall we drink?' or 'What shall we wear?' **32** For the Gentiles seek after all these things, and your heavenly Father knows that you need them all. **33** But seek first the kingdom of God and his righteousness, and all these things will be added to you.

34 "Therefore do not be anxious about tomorrow, for tomorrow will be anxious for itself. Sufficient for the day is its own trouble.

Judging Others

7 "Judge not, that you be not judged. **2** For with the judgment you pronounce you will be judged, and with the measure you use it will be measured to you. **3** Why do you see the speck that is in your brother's eye, but do not notice the log that is in your own eye? **4** Or how can you say to your brother, 'Let me take the speck out of your eye,' when there is the log in your own eye? **5** You hypocrite, first take the log out of your own eye, and then you will see clearly to take the speck out of your brother's eye.

6 "Do not give dogs what is holy, and do not throw your pearls before pigs, lest they trample them underfoot and turn to attack you.

Ask, and It Will Be Given

7 "Ask, and it will be given to you; seek, and you will find; knock, and it will be opened to you. **8** For everyone who asks receives, and the one who seeks finds, and to the one who knocks it will be opened. **9** Or which one of you, if his son asks him for bread, will give him a stone? **10** Or if he asks for a fish, will give him a serpent? **11** If you then, who are evil, know how to give good gifts to your children, how much more will your Father who is in heaven give good things to those who ask him!

The Golden Rule

12 "So whatever you wish that others would do to you, do also to them, for this is the Law and the Prophets.

13 "Enter by the narrow gate. For the gate is wide and the way is easy that leads to destruction, and those who enter by it are

GETTING THE MESSAGE

Today **pearls** are often grown in oyster or clam farms, but this was not the case in ancient Palestine. Out of a 6,000-pound (2,700 kg) haul of oysters, one might find only three or four perfect pearls. Such priceless objects certainly shouldn't be thrown to pigs (7:6).

many. **14** For the gate is narrow and the way is hard that leads to life, and those who find it are few.

A Tree and Its Fruit

15 "Beware of false prophets, who come to you in sheep's clothing but inwardly are ravenous wolves. **16** You will recognize them by their fruits. Are grapes gathered from thornbushes, or figs from thistles? **17** So, every healthy tree bears good fruit, but the diseased tree bears bad fruit. **18** A healthy tree cannot bear bad fruit, nor can a diseased tree bear good fruit. **19** Every tree that does not bear good fruit is cut down and thrown into the fire. **20** Thus you will recognize them by their fruits.

I Never Knew You

21 "Not everyone who says to me, 'Lord, Lord,' will enter the kingdom of heaven, but the one who does the will of my Father who is in heaven. **22** On that day many will say to me, 'Lord, Lord, did we not prophesy in your name, and cast out demons in your name, and do many mighty works in your name?' **23** And then will I declare to them, 'I never knew you; depart from me, you workers of lawlessness.'

Build Your House on the Rock

24 "Everyone then who hears these words of mine and does them will be like a wise man who built his house on the rock. **25** And the rain fell, and the floods came, and the winds blew and beat on that house, but it did not fall, because it had been founded on the rock. **26** And everyone who hears these words of mine and does not do them will be like a foolish man who built his house on the sand. **27** And the rain fell, and the floods came, and the winds blew and beat

against that house, and it fell, and great was the fall of it."

The Authority of Jesus

28 And when Jesus finished these sayings, the crowds were astonished at his teaching, **29** for he was teaching them as one who had authority, and not as their scribes.

Jesus Cleanses a Leper

8 When he came down from the mountain, great crowds followed him. **2** And behold, a leper[1] came to him and knelt before him, saying, "Lord, if you will, you can make me clean." **3** And Jesus stretched out his hand and touched him, saying, "I will; be clean." And immediately his leprosy was cleansed. **4** And Jesus said to him, "See that you say nothing to anyone, but go, show

yourself to the priest and offer the gift that Moses commanded, for a proof to them."

The Faith of a Centurion

5 When he had entered Capernaum, a centurion came forward to him, appealing to him, **6** "Lord, my servant is lying paralyzed at home, suffering terribly." **7** And he said to him, "I will come and heal him." **8** But the centurion replied, "Lord, I am not worthy to have you come under my roof, but only say the word, and my servant will be healed. **9** For I too am a man under authority, with soldiers under me. And I say to one, 'Go,' and he goes, and to another, 'Come,' and he comes, and to my servant, 'Do this,' and he does it." **10** When Jesus heard this, he marveled and said to those who followed him, "Truly, I tell you, with no one in Israel have I found such faith. **11** I tell you, many will come from east and west and recline at table with Abraham, Isaac, and Jacob in the kingdom of heaven, **12** while the sons of the kingdom will be thrown into the outer darkness. In that place there will be weeping and gnashing of teeth." **13** And to the centurion Jesus said, "Go; let it be done for you as you have believed." And the servant was healed at that very moment.

Jesus Heals Many

14 And when Jesus entered Peter's house, he saw his mother-in-law lying sick with a fever. **15** He touched her hand, and the fever left her, and she rose and began to serve him. **16** That evening they brought to him many who were oppressed by demons, and he cast out the spirits with a word and healed all who were sick. **17** This was to fulfill what was spoken by the prophet Isaiah: "He took our illnesses and bore our diseases."

The Cost of Following Jesus

18 Now when Jesus saw a crowd around him, he gave orders to go over to the other side. **19** And a scribe came up and said to him, "Teacher, I will follow you wherever you go." **20** And Jesus said to him, "Foxes have holes, and birds of the air have nests, but the Son of Man has nowhere to lay his head." **21** Another of the disciples said to him, "Lord, let me first go and bury my father." **22** And Jesus said to him, "Follow me, and leave the dead to bury their own dead."

[1] *Leprosy* was a term for several skin diseases (see Leviticus 13)

Jesus Calms a Storm

²³ And when he got into the boat, his disciples followed him. ²⁴ And behold, there arose a great storm on the sea, so that the boat was being swamped by the waves; but he was asleep. ²⁵ And they went and woke him, saying, "Save us, Lord; we are perishing." ²⁶ And he said to them, "Why are you afraid, O you of little faith?" Then he rose and rebuked the winds and the sea, and there was a great calm. ²⁷ And the men marveled, saying, "What sort of man is this, that even winds and sea obey him?"

Jesus Heals Two Men with Demons

²⁸ And when he came to the other side, to the country of the Gadarenes, two demon-possessed men met him, coming out of the tombs, so fierce that no one could pass that way. ²⁹ And behold, they cried out, "What have you to do with us, O Son of God? Have you come here to torment us before the time?" ³⁰ Now a herd of many pigs was feeding at some distance from them. ³¹ And the demons begged him, saying, "If you cast us out, send us away into the herd of pigs." ³² And he said to them, "Go." So they came out and went into the pigs, and behold, the whole herd rushed down the steep bank into the sea and drowned in the waters. ³³ The herdsmen fled, and going into the city they told everything, especially what had happened to the demon-possessed men. ³⁴ And behold, all the city came out to meet Jesus, and when they saw him, they begged him to leave their region.

Jesus Heals a Paralytic

9 And getting into a boat he crossed over and came to his own city. ² And behold, some people brought to him a paralytic, lying on a bed. And when Jesus saw their faith, he said to the paralytic, "Take heart, my son; your sins are forgiven." ³ And behold, some of the scribes said to themselves, "This man is blaspheming." ⁴ But Jesus, knowing their thoughts, said, "Why do you think evil in your hearts? ⁵ For which is easier, to say, 'Your sins are forgiven,' or to say, 'Rise and walk'? ⁶ But that you may know that the Son of Man has authority on earth to forgive sins"—he then said to the paralytic—"Rise, pick up your bed and go home." ⁷ And he rose and went home. ⁸ When the crowds saw it, they were afraid, and they glorified God, who had given such authority to men.

Jesus Calls Matthew

⁹ As Jesus passed on from there, he saw a man called Matthew sitting at the tax booth, and he said to him, "Follow me." And he rose and followed him.

¹⁰ And as Jesus reclined at table in the house, behold, many tax collectors and sinners came and were reclining with Jesus and his disciples. ¹¹ And when the Pharisees saw this, they said to his disciples, "Why

---

PROFILE

MATTHEW

Matthew, also called Levi, was one of the 12 disciples and the author of the first Gospel. When Jesus called him, Matthew was sitting in the tax collector's booth collecting taxes for Rome. Other Jews probably considered him a traitor, since collecting taxes meant cooperation with the Roman occupiers of Palestine. Because tax collectors were free to take as much personal profit from people as they liked, they were widely regarded as the worst of sinners, often categorized along with prostitutes (see 21:32). In his Gospel account, Matthew presents Jesus as the Davidic King who has come to fulfill the Old Testament, especially its promises of everlasting salvation.

KEY REFERENCE: MATTHEW 9:9

---

does your teacher eat with tax collectors and sinners?" ¹² But when he heard it, he said, "Those who are well have no need of a physician, but those who are sick. ¹³ Go and learn what this means, 'I desire mercy, and not sacrifice.' For I came not to call the righteous, but sinners."

A Question About Fasting

¹⁴ Then the disciples of John came to him, saying, "Why do we and the Pharisees fast, but your disciples do not fast?" ¹⁵ And Jesus said to them, "Can the wedding guests mourn as long as the bridegroom is with

them? The days will come when the bridegroom is taken away from them, and then they will fast. ¹⁶ No one puts a piece of unshrunk cloth on an old garment, for the patch tears away from the garment, and a worse tear is made. ¹⁷ Neither is new wine put into old wineskins. If it is, the skins burst and the wine is spilled and the skins are destroyed. But new wine is put into fresh wineskins, and so both are preserved."

A Girl Restored to Life and a Woman Healed

¹⁸ While he was saying these things to them, behold, a ruler came in and knelt before him, saying, "My daughter has just died, but come and lay your hand on her, and she will live." ¹⁹ And Jesus rose and followed him, with his disciples. ²⁰ And behold, a woman who had suffered from a discharge of blood for twelve years came

> ### GETTING THE MESSAGE
>
> **How can Jesus cast out demons?**
> Jesus' remarkable supernatural power was obvious. Many believed that his power came from God, but some of the religious leaders denied this (9:34). Matthew's readers understand that Jesus' actions prove that he is the Messiah.

up behind him and touched the fringe of his garment, ²¹ for she said to herself, "If I only touch his garment, I will be made well." ²² Jesus turned, and seeing her he said, "Take heart, daughter; your faith has made you well." And instantly the woman was made well. ²³ And when Jesus came to the ruler's house and saw the flute players and the crowd making a commotion, ²⁴ he said, "Go away, for the girl is not dead but sleeping." And they laughed at him. ²⁵ But when the crowd had been put outside, he went in and took her by the hand, and the girl arose. ²⁶ And the report of this went through all that district.

Jesus Heals Two Blind Men

²⁷ And as Jesus passed on from there, two blind men followed him, crying aloud, "Have mercy on us, Son of David." ²⁸ When

he entered the house, the blind men came to him, and Jesus said to them, "Do you believe that I am able to do this?" They said to him, "Yes, Lord." ²⁹ Then he touched their eyes, saying, "According to your faith be it done to you." ³⁰ And their eyes were opened. And Jesus sternly warned them, "See that no one knows about it." ³¹ But they went away and spread his fame through all that district.

Jesus Heals a Man Unable to Speak

³² As they were going away, behold, a demon-oppressed man who was mute was brought to him. ³³ And when the demon had been cast out, the mute man spoke. And the crowds marveled, saying, "Never was anything like this seen in Israel." ³⁴ But the Pharisees said, "He casts out demons by the prince of demons."

The Harvest Is Plentiful, the Laborers Few

³⁵ And Jesus went throughout all the cities and villages, teaching in their synagogues and proclaiming the gospel of the kingdom and healing every disease and every affliction. ³⁶ When he saw the crowds, he had compassion for them, because they were harassed and helpless, like sheep without a shepherd. ³⁷ Then he said to his disciples, "The harvest is plentiful, but the laborers are few; ³⁸ therefore pray earnestly to the Lord of the harvest to send out laborers into his harvest."

The Twelve Apostles

10 And he called to him his twelve disciples and gave them authority over unclean spirits, to cast them out, and to heal every disease and every affliction. ² The names of the twelve apostles are these: first, Simon, who is called Peter, and Andrew his brother; James the son of Zebedee, and John his brother; ³ Philip and Bartholomew; Thomas and Matthew the tax collector; James the son of Alphaeus, and Thaddaeus; ⁴ Simon the Zealot, and Judas Iscariot, who betrayed him.

Jesus Sends Out the Twelve Apostles

⁵ These twelve Jesus sent out, instructing them, "Go nowhere among the Gentiles and enter no town of the Samaritans, ⁶ but go rather to the lost sheep of the house of Israel. ⁷ And proclaim as you go, saying, 'The kingdom of heaven is at hand.' ⁸ Heal the

sick, raise the dead, cleanse lepers,[1] cast out demons. You received without paying; give without pay. 9 Acquire no gold or silver or copper for your belts, 10 no bag for your journey, or two tunics or sandals or a staff, for the laborer deserves his food. 11 And whatever town or village you enter, find out who is worthy in it and stay there until you depart. 12 As you enter the house, greet it. 13 And if the house is worthy, let your peace come upon it, but if it is not worthy, let your peace return to you. 14 And if anyone will not receive you or listen to your words, shake off the dust from your feet when you leave that house or town. 15 Truly, I say to you, it will be more bearable on the day of judgment for the land of Sodom and Gomorrah than for that town.

Persecution Will Come

16 "Behold, I am sending you out as sheep in the midst of wolves, so be wise as serpents and innocent as doves. 17 Beware of men, for they will deliver you over to courts and flog you in their synagogues, 18 and you will be dragged before governors and kings for my sake, to bear witness before them and the Gentiles. 19 When they deliver you over, do not be anxious how you are to speak or what you are to say, for what you are to say will be given to you in that hour. 20 For it is not you who speak, but the Spirit of your Father speaking through you. 21 Brother will deliver brother over to death, and the father his child, and children will rise against parents and have them put to death, 22 and you will be hated by all for my name's sake. But the one who endures to the end will be saved. 23 When they persecute you in one town, flee to the next, for truly, I say to you, you will not have gone through all the towns of Israel before the Son of Man comes.

24 "A disciple is not above his teacher, nor a servant above his master. 25 It is enough for the disciple to be like his teacher, and the servant like his master. If they have called the master of the house Beelzebul, how much more will they malign those of his household.

Have No Fear

26 "So have no fear of them, for nothing is covered that will not be revealed, or hidden that will not be known. 27 What I tell you in the dark, say in the light, and what you hear whispered, proclaim on the housetops. 28 And do not fear those who kill the body but cannot kill the soul. Rather fear him who can destroy both soul and body in hell. 29 Are not two sparrows sold for a penny?[2] And not one of them will fall to the ground apart from your Father. 30 But even the hairs of your head are all numbered. 31 Fear not, therefore; you are of more value than many sparrows. 32 So everyone who acknowledges me before men, I also will acknowledge before my Father who is in heaven, 33 but whoever denies me before men, I also will deny before my Father who is in heaven.

Not Peace, but a Sword

34 "Do not think that I have come to bring peace to the earth. I have not come to bring peace, but a sword. 35 For I have come to set a man against his father, and a daughter against her mother, and a daughter-in-law against her mother-in-law. 36 And a person's enemies will be those of his own household. 37 Whoever loves father or mother more than me is not worthy of me, and whoever loves son or daughter more than me is not worthy of me. 38 And whoever does not take his cross and follow me is not worthy of me. 39 Whoever finds his life will lose it, and whoever loses his life for my sake will find it.

Rewards

40 "Whoever receives you receives me, and whoever receives me receives him who sent me. 41 The one who receives a prophet because he is a prophet will receive a prophet's reward, and the one who receives a righteous person because he is a righteous person will receive a righteous person's reward. 42 And whoever gives one of these little ones even a cup of cold water because he is a disciple, truly, I say to you, he will by no means lose his reward."

Messengers from John the Baptist

11 When Jesus had finished instructing his twelve disciples, he went on from there to teach and preach in their cities.

2 Now when John heard in prison about the deeds of the Christ, he sent word by his disciples 3 and said to him, "Are you the one who is to come, or shall we look for another?" 4 And Jesus answered them, "Go and tell John what you hear and see: 5 the

---

[1] *Leprosy* was a term for several skin diseases (see Leviticus 13) [2] The Greek word refers to about 1/16 of a day's pay for a worker

blind receive their sight and the lame walk, lepers[1] are cleansed and the deaf hear, and the dead are raised up, and the poor have good news preached to them. **6** And blessed is the one who is not offended by me."

7 As they went away, Jesus began to speak to the crowds concerning John: "What did you go out into the wilderness to see? A reed shaken by the wind? **8** What then did you go out to see? A man dressed in soft clothing? Behold, those who wear soft clothing are in kings' houses. **9** What then did you go out to see? A prophet? Yes, I tell you, and more than a prophet. **10** This is he of whom it is written,

"'Behold, I send my messenger before
            your face,
    who will prepare your way before
            you.'

GETTING THE MESSAGE

John's imprisonment (11:2) was in the **Machaerus fortress**, just east of where the Jordan River flows into the Dead Sea. It sat atop a 1,600-foot-high (490 m) mountain with steep sides and ravines. Along with Masada and the Herodium, it was one of many fortresses that guarded the nation's eastern borders.

11 Truly, I say to you, among those born of women there has arisen no one greater than John the Baptist. Yet the one who is least in the kingdom of heaven is greater than he. **12** From the days of John the Baptist until now the kingdom of heaven has suffered violence, and the violent take it by force. **13** For all the Prophets and the Law prophesied until John, **14** and if you are willing to accept it, he is Elijah who is to come. **15** He who has ears to hear, let him hear.

16 "But to what shall I compare this generation? It is like children sitting in the marketplaces and calling to their playmates,

17 "'We played the flute for you, and you
            did not dance;
    we sang a dirge, and you did not
            mourn.'

18 For John came neither eating nor drinking, and they say, 'He has a demon.' **19** The Son

of Man came eating and drinking, and they say, 'Look at him! A glutton and a drunkard, a friend of tax collectors and sinners!' Yet wisdom is justified by her deeds."

Woe to Unrepentant Cities

20 Then he began to denounce the cities where most of his mighty works had been done, because they did not repent. **21** "Woe to you, Chorazin! Woe to you, Bethsaida! For if the mighty works done in you had been done in Tyre and Sidon, they would have repented long ago in sackcloth and ashes. **22** But I tell you, it will be more bearable on the day of judgment for Tyre and Sidon than for you. **23** And you, Capernaum, will you be exalted to heaven? You will be brought down to Hades. For if the mighty works done in you had been done in Sodom, it would have remained until this day. **24** But I tell you that it will be more tolerable on the day of judgment for the land of Sodom than for you."

Come to Me, and I Will Give You Rest

25 At that time Jesus declared, "I thank you, Father, Lord of heaven and earth, that you have hidden these things from the wise and understanding and revealed them to little children; **26** yes, Father, for such was your gracious will. **27** All things have been handed over to me by my Father, and no one knows the Son except the Father, and no one knows the Father except the Son and anyone to whom the Son chooses to reveal him. **28** Come to me, all who labor and are heavy laden, and I will give you rest. **29** Take my yoke upon you, and learn from me, for I am gentle and lowly in heart, and you will find rest for your souls. **30** For my yoke is easy, and my burden is light."

Jesus Is Lord of the Sabbath

12 At that time Jesus went through the grainfields on the Sabbath. His disciples were hungry, and they began to pluck heads of grain and to eat. **2** But when the Pharisees saw it, they said to him, "Look, your disciples are doing what is not lawful to do on the Sabbath." **3** He said to them, "Have you not read what David did when he was hungry, and those who were with him: **4** how he entered the house of God and ate the bread of the Presence, which it was not lawful for him to eat nor for those who

---

[1] *Leprosy* was a term for several skin diseases (see Leviticus 13)

were with him, but only for the priests? **5** Or have you not read in the Law how on the Sabbath the priests in the temple profane the Sabbath and are guiltless? **6** I tell you, something greater than the temple is here. **7** And if you had known what this means, 'I desire mercy, and not sacrifice,' you would not have condemned the guiltless. **8** For the Son of Man is lord of the Sabbath."

A Man with a Withered Hand

9 He went on from there and entered their synagogue. **10** And a man was there with a withered hand. And they asked him, "Is it lawful to heal on the Sabbath?"—so that they might accuse him. **11** He said to them, "Which one of you who has a sheep, if it falls into a pit on the Sabbath, will not take hold of it and lift it out? **12** Of how much more value is a man than a sheep! So it is lawful to do good on the Sabbath." **13** Then he said to the man, "Stretch out your hand." And the man stretched it out, and it was restored, healthy like the other. **14** But the Pharisees went out and conspired against him, how to destroy him.

God's Chosen Servant

15 Jesus, aware of this, withdrew from there. And many followed him, and he healed them all **16** and ordered them not to make him known. **17** This was to fulfill what was spoken by the prophet Isaiah:

18   "Behold, my servant whom I have
                chosen,
            my beloved with whom my soul is
                well pleased.
        I will put my Spirit upon him,
            and he will proclaim justice to the
                Gentiles.
19   He will not quarrel or cry aloud,
            nor will anyone hear his voice in
                the streets;
20   a bruised reed he will not break,
            and a smoldering wick he will not
                quench,
        until he brings justice to victory;
21   and in his name the Gentiles will
                hope."

Blasphemy Against the Holy Spirit

22 Then a demon-oppressed man who was blind and mute was brought to him, and he healed him, so that the man spoke and saw. **23** And all the people were amazed, and said, "Can this be the Son of David?" **24** But when the Pharisees heard it, they said, "It is only by Beelzebul, the prince of demons, that this man casts out demons." **25** Knowing their thoughts, he said to them, "Every kingdom divided against itself is laid waste, and no city or house divided against itself will stand. **26** And if Satan casts out Satan, he is divided against himself. How then will his kingdom stand? **27** And if I cast out demons by Beelzebul, by whom do your sons cast them out? Therefore they will be your judges. **28** But if it is by the Spirit of God that I cast out demons, then the kingdom of God has come upon you. **29** Or how can someone enter a strong man's house and plunder his goods, unless he first binds the strong man? Then indeed he may plunder his house. **30** Whoever is not with me is against me, and whoever does not gather with me scatters. **31** Therefore I tell you,

GETTING THE MESSAGE

Synagogues (12:9) became a part of Jewish life during the Babylonian exile, when Jews were unable to go to the temple in Jerusalem. The synagogues provided a place for both worship and instruction in the law.

every sin and blasphemy will be forgiven people, but the blasphemy against the Spirit will not be forgiven. **32** And whoever speaks a word against the Son of Man will be forgiven, but whoever speaks against the Holy Spirit will not be forgiven, either in this age or in the age to come.

A Tree Is Known by Its Fruit

33 "Either make the tree good and its fruit good, or make the tree bad and its fruit bad, for the tree is known by its fruit. **34** You brood of vipers! How can you speak good, when you are evil? For out of the abundance of the heart the mouth speaks. **35** The good person out of his good treasure brings forth good, and the evil person out of his evil treasure brings forth evil. **36** I tell you, on the day of judgment people will give account for every careless word they speak, **37** for by your words you will be justified, and by your words you will be condemned."

The Sign of Jonah

38 Then some of the scribes and Pharisees answered him, saying, "Teacher, we wish to see a sign from you." **39** But he answered them, "An evil and adulterous generation seeks for a sign, but no sign will be given to it except the sign of the prophet Jonah. **40** For just as Jonah was three days and three nights in the belly of the great fish, so will the Son of Man be three days and three nights in the heart of the earth. **41** The men of Nineveh will rise up at the judgment with this generation and condemn it, for they repented at the preaching of Jonah, and behold, something greater than Jonah is here. **42** The queen of the South will rise up at the judgment with this generation and condemn it, for she came from the ends of the earth to hear the

> ### GETTING THE MESSAGE
>
> The place where Jesus sat beside the sea (13:1–2) is traditionally called the **Cove of the Parables**. It was a horseshoe-shaped cove that had remarkable acoustics. Anywhere from 5,000 to 7,000 people could fit just along the beach, while twice that many could easily fill the entire hillside. A person sitting at the very top of the hill could hear a speaker standing on the beach, even though they could hardly see him!

wisdom of Solomon, and behold, something greater than Solomon is here.

Return of an Unclean Spirit

43 "When the unclean spirit has gone out of a person, it passes through waterless places seeking rest, but finds none. **44** Then it says, 'I will return to my house from which I came.' And when it comes, it finds the house empty, swept, and put in order. **45** Then it goes and brings with it seven other spirits more evil than itself, and they enter and dwell there, and the last state of that person is worse than the first. So also will it be with this evil generation."

Jesus' Mother and Brothers

46 While he was still speaking to the people, behold, his mother and his brothers stood outside, asking to speak to him. **48** But he replied to the man who told him, "Who

is my mother, and who are my brothers?" **49** And stretching out his hand toward his disciples, he said, "Here are my mother and my brothers! **50** For whoever does the will of my Father in heaven is my brother and sister and mother."

The Parable of the Sower

13 That same day Jesus went out of the house and sat beside the sea. **2** And great crowds gathered about him, so that he got into a boat and sat down. And the whole crowd stood on the beach. **3** And he told them many things in parables, saying: "A sower went out to sow. **4** And as he sowed, some seeds fell along the path, and the birds came and devoured them. **5** Other seeds fell on rocky ground, where they did not have much soil, and immediately they sprang up, since they had no depth of soil, **6** but when the sun rose they were scorched. And since they had no root, they withered away. **7** Other seeds fell among thorns, and the thorns grew up and choked them. **8** Other seeds fell on good soil and produced grain, some a hundredfold, some sixty, some thirty. **9** He who has ears, let him hear."

The Purpose of the Parables

10 Then the disciples came and said to him, "Why do you speak to them in parables?" **11** And he answered them, "To you it has been given to know the secrets of the kingdom of heaven, but to them it has not been given. **12** For to the one who has, more will be given, and he will have an abundance, but from the one who has not, even what he has will be taken away. **13** This is why I speak to them in parables, because seeing they do not see, and hearing they do not hear, nor do they understand. **14** Indeed, in their case the prophecy of Isaiah is fulfilled that says:

> "'You will indeed hear but never understand,
>   and you will indeed see but never perceive.'
> **15**   For this people's heart has grown dull,
>   and with their ears they can barely hear,
>   and their eyes they have closed,
>   lest they should see with their eyes
>   and hear with their ears

and understand with their heart
   and turn, and I would heal them.'

[16] But blessed are your eyes, for they see, and your ears, for they hear. [17] For truly, I say to you, many prophets and righteous people longed to see what you see, and did not see it, and to hear what you hear, and did not hear it.

The Parable of the Sower Explained

[18] "Hear then the parable of the sower: [19] When anyone hears the word of the kingdom and does not understand it, the evil one comes and snatches away what has been sown in his heart. This is what was sown along the path. [20] As for what was sown on rocky ground, this is the one who hears the word and immediately receives it with joy, [21] yet he has no root in himself, but endures for a while, and when tribulation or persecution arises on account of the word, immediately he falls away. [22] As for what was sown among thorns, this is the one who hears the word, but the cares of the world and the deceitfulness of riches choke the word, and it proves unfruitful. [23] As for what was sown on good soil, this is the one who hears the word and understands it. He indeed bears fruit and yields, in one case a hundredfold, in another sixty, and in another thirty."

The Parable of the Weeds

[24] He put another parable before them, saying, "The kingdom of heaven may be compared to a man who sowed good seed in his field, [25] but while his men were sleeping, his enemy came and sowed weeds among the wheat and went away. [26] So when the plants came up and bore grain, then the weeds appeared also. [27] And the servants of the master of the house came and said to him, 'Master, did you not sow good seed in your field? How then does it have weeds?' [28] He said to them, 'An enemy has done this.' So the servants said to him, 'Then do you want us to go and gather them?' [29] But he said, 'No, lest in gathering the weeds you root up the wheat along with them. [30] Let both grow together until the harvest, and at harvest time I will tell the reapers, Gather the weeds first and bind them in bundles to be burned, but gather the wheat into my barn.'"

The Mustard Seed and the Leaven

[31] He put another parable before them, saying, "The kingdom of heaven is like a grain of mustard seed that a man took and sowed in his field. [32] It is the smallest of all seeds, but when it has grown it is larger than all the garden plants and becomes a tree, so that the birds of the air come and make nests in its branches."

[33] He told them another parable. "The kingdom of heaven is like leaven that a woman took and hid in three measures of flour, till it was all leavened."

Prophecy and Parables

[34] All these things Jesus said to the crowds in parables; indeed, he said nothing to them without a parable. [35] This was to fulfill what was spoken by the prophet:

"I will open my mouth in parables;
   I will utter what has been hidden
      since the foundation of the
         world."

The Parable of the Weeds Explained

[36] Then he left the crowds and went into the house. And his disciples came to him, saying, "Explain to us the parable of the weeds of the field." [37] He answered, "The one who sows the good seed is the Son of Man. [38] The field is the world, and the good seed is the sons of the kingdom. The weeds are the sons of the evil one, [39] and the enemy who sowed them is the devil. The harvest is the end of the age, and the reapers are angels. [40] Just as the weeds are gathered and burned with fire, so will it be at the end of the age. [41] The Son of Man will send his angels, and they will gather out of his kingdom all causes of sin and all lawbreakers, [42] and throw them into the fiery furnace. In that place there will be weeping and gnashing of teeth. [43] Then the righteous will shine like the sun in the kingdom of their Father. He who has ears, let him hear.

The Parable of the Hidden Treasure

[44] "The kingdom of heaven is like treasure hidden in a field, which a man found and covered up. Then in his joy he goes and sells all that he has and buys that field.

The Parable of the Pearl of Great Value

[45] "Again, the kingdom of heaven is like a merchant in search of fine pearls, [46] who, on

finding one pearl of great value, went and sold all that he had and bought it.

The Parable of the Net

⁴⁷ "Again, the kingdom of heaven is like a net that was thrown into the sea and gathered fish of every kind. ⁴⁸ When it was full, men drew it ashore and sat down and sorted the good into containers but threw away the bad. ⁴⁹ So it will be at the end of the age. The angels will come out and separate the evil from the righteous ⁵⁰ and throw them into the fiery furnace. In that place there will be weeping and gnashing of teeth.

New and Old Treasures

⁵¹ "Have you understood all these things?" They said to him, "Yes." ⁵² And he said to them, "Therefore every scribe who has been trained for the kingdom of heaven is like a

> ### GETTING THE MESSAGE
>
> **Herod Antipas** (14:1) was the ruler over the region where Jesus ministered. On a trip to Rome, Antipas fell in love with Herodias, the wife of his half brother Herod Phillip I. Both Antipas and Herodias divorced their spouses in order to marry each other. It was for this action that John publicly condemned Antipas, resulting in John's death at Herod's hand.

master of a house, who brings out of his treasure what is new and what is old."

Jesus Rejected at Nazareth

⁵³ And when Jesus had finished these parables, he went away from there, ⁵⁴ and coming to his hometown he taught them in their synagogue, so that they were astonished, and said, "Where did this man get this wisdom and these mighty works? ⁵⁵ Is not this the carpenter's son? Is not his mother called Mary? And are not his brothers James and Joseph and Simon and Judas? ⁵⁶ And are not all his sisters with us? Where then did this man get all these things?" ⁵⁷ And they took offense at him. But Jesus said to them, "A prophet is not without honor except in his hometown and in his own household." ⁵⁸ And he did not do many mighty works there, because of their unbelief.

The Death of John the Baptist

14 At that time Herod the tetrarch heard about the fame of Jesus, ² and he said to his servants, "This is John the Baptist. He has been raised from the dead; that is why these miraculous powers are at work in him." ³ For Herod had seized John and bound him and put him in prison for the sake of Herodias, his brother Philip's wife, ⁴ because John had been saying to him, "It is not lawful for you to have her." ⁵ And though he wanted to put him to death, he feared the people, because they held him to be a prophet. ⁶ But when Herod's birthday came, the daughter of Herodias danced before the company and pleased Herod, ⁷ so that he promised with an oath to give her whatever she might ask. ⁸ Prompted by her mother, she said, "Give me the head of John the Baptist here on a platter." ⁹ And the king was sorry, but because of his oaths and his guests he commanded it to be given. ¹⁰ He sent and had John beheaded in the prison, ¹¹ and his head was brought on a platter and given to the girl, and she brought it to her mother. ¹² And his disciples came and took the body and buried it, and they went and told Jesus.

Jesus Feeds the Five Thousand

¹³ Now when Jesus heard this, he withdrew from there in a boat to a desolate place by himself. But when the crowds heard it, they followed him on foot from the towns. ¹⁴ When he went ashore he saw a great crowd, and he had compassion on them and healed their sick. ¹⁵ Now when it was evening, the disciples came to him and said, "This is a desolate place, and the day is now over; send the crowds away to go into the villages and buy food for themselves." ¹⁶ But Jesus said, "They need not go away; you give them something to eat." ¹⁷ They said to him, "We have only five loaves here and two fish." ¹⁸ And he said, "Bring them here to me." ¹⁹ Then he ordered the crowds to sit down on the grass, and taking the five loaves and the two fish, he looked up to heaven and said a blessing. Then he broke the loaves and gave them to the disciples, and the disciples gave them to the crowds. ²⁰ And they all ate and were satisfied. And they took up twelve baskets full of the broken pieces left over. ²¹ And those who ate were about five thousand men, besides women and children.

Jesus Walks on the Water

22 Immediately he made the disciples get into the boat and go before him to the other side, while he dismissed the crowds. 23 And after he had dismissed the crowds, he went up on the mountain by himself to pray. When evening came, he was there alone, 24 but the boat by this time was a long way from the land, beaten by the waves, for the wind was against them. 25 And in the fourth watch of the night he came to them, walking on the sea. 26 But when the disciples saw him walking on the sea, they were terrified, and said, "It is a ghost!" and they cried out in fear. 27 But immediately Jesus spoke to them, saying, "Take heart; it is I. Do not be afraid." 28 And Peter answered him, "Lord, if it is you, command me to come to you on the water." 29 He said, "Come." So Peter got out of the boat and walked on the water and came to Jesus. 30 But when he saw the wind, he was afraid, and beginning to sink he cried out, "Lord, save me." 31 Jesus immediately reached out his hand and took hold of him, saying to him, "O you of little faith, why did you doubt?" 32 And when they got into the boat, the wind ceased. 33 And those in the boat worshiped him, saying, "Truly you are the Son of God."

Jesus Heals the Sick in Gennesaret

34 And when they had crossed over, they came to land at Gennesaret. 35 And when the men of that place recognized him, they sent around to all that region and brought to him all who were sick 36 and implored him that they might only touch the fringe of his garment. And as many as touched it were made well.

Traditions and Commandments

15 Then Pharisees and scribes came to Jesus from Jerusalem and said, 2 "Why do your disciples break the tradition of the elders? For they do not wash their hands when they eat." 3 He answered them, "And why do you break the commandment of God for the sake of your tradition? 4 For God commanded, 'Honor your father and your mother,' and, 'Whoever reviles father or mother must surely die.' 5 But you say, 'If anyone tells his father or his mother, "What you would have gained from me is given to God," 6 he need not honor his father.' So for the sake of your tradition you have made

void the word of God. 7 You hypocrites! Well did Isaiah prophesy of you, when he said:

8 "'This people honors me with their lips,
    but their heart is far from me;
9 in vain do they worship me,
    teaching as doctrines the com-
        mandments of men.'"

What Defiles a Person

10 And he called the people to him and said to them, "Hear and understand: 11 it is not what goes into the mouth that defiles a person, but what comes out of the mouth; this defiles a person." 12 Then the disciples came and said to him, "Do you know that the Pharisees were offended when they heard this saying?" 13 He answered, "Every plant that my heavenly Father has not planted will be rooted up. 14 Let them alone; they are blind guides. And if the blind lead the blind, both will fall into a pit." 15 But Peter said to him,

> ### GETTING THE MESSAGE
>
> **Fear vs. faith.** Many kinds of fears are understandable and can even keep us from danger. But fears that cause us to doubt God must be overcome by faith. God is trustworthy and able to save us (14:28–33).

"Explain the parable to us." 16 And he said, "Are you also still without understanding? 17 Do you not see that whatever goes into the mouth passes into the stomach and is expelled? 18 But what comes out of the mouth proceeds from the heart, and this defiles a person. 19 For out of the heart come evil thoughts, murder, adultery, sexual immorality, theft, false witness, slander. 20 These are what defile a person. But to eat with unwashed hands does not defile anyone."

The Faith of a Canaanite Woman

21 And Jesus went away from there and withdrew to the district of Tyre and Sidon. 22 And behold, a Canaanite woman from that region came out and was crying, "Have mercy on me, O Lord, Son of David; my daughter is severely oppressed by a demon." 23 But he did not answer her a word. And his disciples came and begged him, saying, "Send her away, for she is crying out after us." 24 He answered, "I was sent only to the

lost sheep of the house of Israel." **25** But she came and knelt before him, saying, "Lord, help me." **26** And he answered, "It is not right to take the children's bread and throw it to the dogs." **27** She said, "Yes, Lord, yet even the dogs eat the crumbs that fall from their masters' table." **28** Then Jesus answered her, "O woman, great is your faith! Be it done for you as you desire." And her daughter was healed instantly.

Jesus Heals Many

29 Jesus went on from there and walked beside the Sea of Galilee. And he went up on the mountain and sat down there. **30** And great crowds came to him, bringing with them the lame, the blind, the crippled, the mute, and many others, and they put them at his feet, and he healed them, **31** so that the crowd wondered, when they saw the

> ### GETTING THE MESSAGE
>
> **Magadan** (15:39) is probably another spelling of Magdala, the home of Mary Magdalene. Magdala was a major fishing center where fishermen would take their catch to be salted for preservation. It was here that archaeologists found the 2,000-year-old "Kinneret boat," which offered a glimpse into the fishing industry of first-century Galilee.

mute speaking, the crippled healthy, the lame walking, and the blind seeing. And they glorified the God of Israel.

Jesus Feeds the Four Thousand

32 Then Jesus called his disciples to him and said, "I have compassion on the crowd because they have been with me now three days and have nothing to eat. And I am unwilling to send them away hungry, lest they faint on the way." **33** And the disciples said to him, "Where are we to get enough bread in such a desolate place to feed so great a crowd?" **34** And Jesus said to them, "How many loaves do you have?" They said, "Seven, and a few small fish." **35** And directing the crowd to sit down on the ground, **36** he took the seven loaves and the fish, and having given thanks he broke them and gave them to the disciples, and the disciples gave them to the crowds. **37** And they all ate and

were satisfied. And they took up seven baskets full of the broken pieces left over. **38** Those who ate were four thousand men, besides women and children. **39** And after sending away the crowds, he got into the boat and went to the region of Magadan.

The Pharisees and Sadducees Demand Signs

16 And the Pharisees and Sadducees came, and to test him they asked him to show them a sign from heaven. **2** He answered them, "When it is evening, you say, 'It will be fair weather, for the sky is red.' **3** And in the morning, 'It will be stormy today, for the sky is red and threatening.' You know how to interpret the appearance of the sky, but you cannot interpret the signs of the times. **4** An evil and adulterous generation seeks for a sign, but no sign will be given to it except the sign of Jonah." So he left them and departed.

The Leaven of the Pharisees and Sadducees

5 When the disciples reached the other side, they had forgotten to bring any bread. **6** Jesus said to them, "Watch and beware of the leaven of the Pharisees and Sadducees." **7** And they began discussing it among themselves, saying, "We brought no bread." **8** But Jesus, aware of this, said, "O you of little faith, why are you discussing among yourselves the fact that you have no bread? **9** Do you not yet perceive? Do you not remember the five loaves for the five thousand, and how many baskets you gathered? **10** Or the seven loaves for the four thousand, and how many baskets you gathered? **11** How is it that you fail to understand that I did not speak about bread? Beware of the leaven of the Pharisees and Sadducees." **12** Then they understood that he did not tell them to beware of the leaven of bread, but of the teaching of the Pharisees and Sadducees.

Peter Confesses Jesus as the Christ

13 Now when Jesus came into the district of Caesarea Philippi, he asked his disciples, "Who do people say that the Son of Man is?" **14** And they said, "Some say John the Baptist, others say Elijah, and others Jeremiah or one of the prophets." **15** He said to them, "But who do you say that I am?" **16** Simon Peter replied, "You are the Christ, the Son of the living God." **17** And Jesus answered him, "Blessed are you, Simon Bar-Jonah! For flesh and blood has not revealed this to you, but my Father who is in heaven. **18** And I tell you, you are Peter, and on this rock[1] I will build my church, and the gates of hell shall not prevail against it. **19** I will give you the keys of the kingdom of heaven, and whatever you bind on earth shall be bound in heaven, and whatever you loose on earth shall be loosed in heaven." **20** Then he strictly charged the disciples to tell no one that he was the Christ.

Jesus Foretells His Death and Resurrection

21 From that time Jesus began to show his disciples that he must go to Jerusalem and suffer many things from the elders and chief priests and scribes, and be killed, and on the third day be raised. **22** And Peter took him aside and began to rebuke him, saying, "Far be it from you, Lord! This shall never happen to you." **23** But he turned and said to Peter, "Get behind me, Satan! You are a hindrance to me. For you are not setting your mind on the things of God, but on the things of man."

Take Up Your Cross and Follow Jesus

24 Then Jesus told his disciples, "If anyone would come after me, let him deny himself and take up his cross and follow me. **25** For whoever would save his life will lose it, but whoever loses his life for my sake will find it. **26** For what will it profit a man if he gains the whole world and forfeits his soul? Or what shall a man give in return for his soul? **27** For the Son of Man is going to come with his angels in the glory of his Father, and then he will repay each person according to what he has done. **28** Truly, I say to you, there are some standing here who will not taste death until they see the Son of Man coming in his kingdom."

The Transfiguration

17 And after six days Jesus took with him Peter and James, and John his brother, and led them up a high mountain by themselves. **2** And he was transfigured before them, and his face shone like the sun, and his clothes became white as light. **3** And behold, there appeared to them Moses and Elijah, talking with him. **4** And Peter said to Jesus, "Lord, it is good that we are

here. If you wish, I will make three tents here, one for you and one for Moses and one for Elijah." **5** He was still speaking when, behold, a bright cloud overshadowed them, and a voice from the cloud said, "This is my beloved Son, with whom I am well pleased; listen to him." **6** When the disciples heard this, they fell on their faces and were terrified. **7** But Jesus came and touched them, saying, "Rise, and have no fear." **8** And when they lifted up their eyes, they saw no one but Jesus only.

9 And as they were coming down the mountain, Jesus commanded them, "Tell no one the vision, until the Son of Man is raised from the dead." **10** And the disciples asked him, "Then why do the scribes say that first Elijah must come?" **11** He answered, "Elijah does come, and he will restore all things. **12** But I tell you that Elijah has already come,

---

GETTING THE MESSAGE

Caesarea Philippi (16:13) was an important city, 25 miles (40 km) north of the Sea of Galilee. It was the center of worship for various pagan deities, including Baal, the Greek god Pan, and even Caesar Augustus himself, who was regarded as a god in the official Roman religion.

---

and they did not recognize him, but did to him whatever they pleased. So also the Son of Man will certainly suffer at their hands." **13** Then the disciples understood that he was speaking to them of John the Baptist.

Jesus Heals a Boy with a Demon

14 And when they came to the crowd, a man came up to him and, kneeling before him, **15** said, "Lord, have mercy on my son, for he is an epileptic and he suffers terribly. For often he falls into the fire, and often into the water. **16** And I brought him to your disciples, and they could not heal him." **17** And Jesus answered, "O faithless and twisted generation, how long am I to be with you? How long am I to bear with you? Bring him here to me." **18** And Jesus rebuked the demon, and it came out of him, and the boy was healed instantly. **19** Then the disciples came to Jesus privately and said, "Why could we

---

[1] The Greek words for *Peter* and *rock* sound similar

not cast it out?" ²⁰ He said to them, "Because of your little faith. For truly, I say to you, if you have faith like a grain of mustard seed, you will say to this mountain, 'Move from here to there,' and it will move, and nothing will be impossible for you."

Jesus Again Foretells Death, Resurrection

²² As they were gathering in Galilee, Jesus said to them, "The Son of Man is about to be

PROFILE

PETER

Peter and his brother Andrew were from the city of Bethsaida. The two fishermen were the first disciples called by Jesus, and they immediately left everything to follow him. Jesus gave Simon the name Cephas, or Peter, which means "rock" (John 1:42). Peter, James, and John became the close inner circle among the 12 disciples. Always listed first among the Twelve, Peter often served as their spokesman and leader. He was with Jesus during the key events of his ministry, including the Transfiguration. Peter was one of Jesus' most outspoken and passionate followers, though at times that enthusiasm was misplaced and needed a word of correction from Jesus (Matt. 19:27–30; 26:31–35, 69–75). Peter preached boldly at Pentecost. He was arrested multiple times, and even imprisoned, for preaching in the name of Jesus, but he remained faithful (Acts 12:1–19). Peter wrote the two New Testament letters that bear his name. He died a martyr in Rome, under Nero.

KEY REFERENCE: MATTHEW 16:13–20

delivered into the hands of men, ²³ and they will kill him, and he will be raised on the third day." And they were greatly distressed.

The Temple Tax

²⁴ When they came to Capernaum, the collectors of the two-drachma tax went up to Peter and said, "Does your teacher not pay the tax?" ²⁵ He said, "Yes." And when he came into the house, Jesus spoke to him

first, saying, "What do you think, Simon? From whom do kings of the earth take toll or tax? From their sons or from others?" ²⁶ And when he said, "From others," Jesus said to him, "Then the sons are free. ²⁷ However, not to give offense to them, go to the sea and cast a hook and take the first fish that comes up, and when you open its mouth you will find a shekel. Take that and give it to them for me and for yourself."

Who Is the Greatest?

18 At that time the disciples came to Jesus, saying, "Who is the greatest in the kingdom of heaven?" ² And calling to him a child, he put him in the midst of them ³ and said, "Truly, I say to you, unless you turn and become like children, you will never enter the kingdom of heaven. ⁴ Whoever humbles himself like this child is the greatest in the kingdom of heaven.

⁵ "Whoever receives one such child in my name receives me, ⁶ but whoever causes one of these little ones who believe in me to sin, it would be better for him to have a great millstone fastened around his neck and to be drowned in the depth of the sea.

Temptations to Sin

⁷ "Woe to the world for temptations to sin! For it is necessary that temptations come, but woe to the one by whom the temptation comes! ⁸ And if your hand or your foot causes you to sin, cut it off and throw it away. It is better for you to enter life crippled or lame than with two hands or two feet to be thrown into the eternal fire. ⁹ And if your eye causes you to sin, tear it out and throw it away. It is better for you to enter life with one eye than with two eyes to be thrown into the hell of fire.

The Parable of the Lost Sheep

¹⁰ "See that you do not despise one of these little ones. For I tell you that in heaven their angels always see the face of my Father who is in heaven. ¹² What do you think? If a man has a hundred sheep, and one of them has gone astray, does he not leave the ninety-nine on the mountains and go in search of the one that went astray? ¹³ And if he finds it, truly, I say to you, he rejoices over it more than over the ninety-nine that never went astray. ¹⁴ So it is not the will of my Father who is in heaven that one of these little ones should perish.

If Your Brother Sins Against You

15 "If your brother sins against you, go and tell him his fault, between you and him alone. If he listens to you, you have gained your brother. 16 But if he does not listen, take one or two others along with you, that every charge may be established by the evidence of two or three witnesses. 17 If he refuses to listen to them, tell it to the church. And if he refuses to listen even to the church, let him be to you as a Gentile and a tax collector. 18 Truly, I say to you, whatever you bind on earth shall be bound in heaven, and whatever you loose on earth shall be loosed in heaven. 19 Again I say to you, if two of you agree on earth about anything they ask, it will be done for them by my Father in heaven. 20 For where two or three are gathered in my name, there am I among them."

The Parable of the Unforgiving Servant

21 Then Peter came up and said to him, "Lord, how often will my brother sin against me, and I forgive him? As many as seven times?" 22 Jesus said to him, "I do not say to you seven times, but seventy-seven times.

23 "Therefore the kingdom of heaven may be compared to a king who wished to settle accounts with his servants. 24 When he began to settle, one was brought to him who owed him ten thousand talents. 25 And since he could not pay, his master ordered him to be sold, with his wife and children and all that he had, and payment to be made. 26 So the servant fell on his knees, imploring him, 'Have patience with me, and I will pay you everything.' 27 And out of pity for him, the master of that servant released him and forgave him the debt. 28 But when that same servant went out, he found one of his fellow servants who owed him a hundred denarii, and seizing him, he began to choke him, saying, 'Pay what you owe.' 29 So his fellow servant fell down and pleaded with him, 'Have patience with me, and I will pay you.' 30 He refused and went and put him in prison until he should pay the debt. 31 When his fellow servants saw what had taken place, they were greatly distressed, and they went and reported to their master all that had taken place. 32 Then his master summoned him and said to him, 'You wicked servant! I forgave you all that debt because you pleaded with me. 33 And should not you have had mercy on your fellow servant, as I had mercy on you?' 34 And in anger his master delivered him to the jailers, until he should pay all his debt. 35 So also my heavenly Father will do to every one of you, if you do not forgive your brother from your heart."

Teaching About Divorce

19 Now when Jesus had finished these sayings, he went away from Galilee and entered the region of Judea beyond the Jordan. 2 And large crowds followed him, and he healed them there.

3 And Pharisees came up to him and tested him by asking, "Is it lawful to divorce one's wife for any cause?" 4 He answered, "Have you not read that he who created them from the beginning made them male and female, 5 and said, 'Therefore a man shall leave his

GETTING THE MESSAGE

The two-drachma temple tax. In Moses' time, each person over the age of 20 was to give a half-shekel offering (the equivalent of two Roman drachmas) for the support of the tabernacle (see Ex. 30:11–16). This practice was still being observed some 1,500 years later, in Jesus' day, to maintain the temple. In Matt. 17:24, Jesus paid the tax for himself and Peter, using a shekel coin retrieved from a fish's mouth!

father and his mother and hold fast to his wife, and the two shall become one flesh'? 6 So they are no longer two but one flesh. What therefore God has joined together, let not man separate." 7 They said to him, "Why then did Moses command one to give a certificate of divorce and to send her away?" 8 He said to them, "Because of your hardness of heart Moses allowed you to divorce your wives, but from the beginning it was not so. 9 And I say to you: whoever divorces his wife, except for sexual immorality, and marries another, commits adultery."

10 The disciples said to him, "If such is the case of a man with his wife, it is better not to marry." 11 But he said to them, "Not everyone can receive this saying, but only those to whom it is given. 12 For there are eunuchs who have been so from birth, and there are eunuchs who have been made eunuchs by

men, and there are eunuchs who have made themselves eunuchs for the sake of the kingdom of heaven. Let the one who is able to receive this receive it."

Let the Children Come to Me

¹³ Then children were brought to him that he might lay his hands on them and pray. The disciples rebuked the people, ¹⁴ but Jesus said, "Let the little children come to me and do not hinder them, for to such belongs the kingdom of heaven." ¹⁵ And he laid his hands on them and went away.

The Rich Young Man

¹⁶ And behold, a man came up to him, saying, "Teacher, what good deed must I do to have eternal life?" ¹⁷ And he said to him, "Why do you ask me about what is good? There is only one who is good. If you would

enter life, keep the commandments." ¹⁸ He said to him, "Which ones?" And Jesus said, "You shall not murder, You shall not commit adultery, You shall not steal, You shall not bear false witness, ¹⁹ Honor your father and mother, and, You shall love your neighbor as yourself." ²⁰ The young man said to him, "All these I have kept. What do I still lack?" ²¹ Jesus said to him, "If you would be perfect, go, sell what you possess and give to the poor, and you will have treasure in heaven; and come, follow me." ²² When the young man heard this he went away sorrowful, for he had great possessions.

²³ And Jesus said to his disciples, "Truly, I say to you, only with difficulty will a rich person enter the kingdom of heaven. ²⁴ Again I tell you, it is easier for a camel to go through the eye of a needle than for a rich person to enter the kingdom of God."

²⁵ When the disciples heard this, they were greatly astonished, saying, "Who then can be saved?" ²⁶ But Jesus looked at them and said, "With man this is impossible, but with God all things are possible." ²⁷ Then Peter said in reply, "See, we have left everything and followed you. What then will we have?" ²⁸ Jesus said to them, "Truly, I say to you, in the new world, when the Son of Man will sit on his glorious throne, you who have followed me will also sit on twelve thrones, judging the twelve tribes of Israel. ²⁹ And everyone who has left houses or brothers or sisters or father or mother or children or lands, for my name's sake, will receive a hundredfold and will inherit eternal life. ³⁰ But many who are first will be last, and the last first.

Laborers in the Vineyard

20 "For the kingdom of heaven is like a master of a house who went out early in the morning to hire laborers for his vineyard. ² After agreeing with the laborers for a denarius a day, he sent them into his vineyard. ³ And going out about the third hour he saw others standing idle in the marketplace, ⁴ and to them he said, 'You go into the vineyard too, and whatever is right I will give you.' ⁵ So they went. Going out again about the sixth hour and the ninth hour, he did the same. ⁶ And about the eleventh hour he went out and found others standing. And he said to them, 'Why do you stand here idle all day?' ⁷ They said to him, 'Because no one has hired us.' He said to them, 'You go into the vineyard too.' ⁸ And when evening came, the owner of the vineyard said to his foreman, 'Call the laborers and pay them their wages, beginning with the last, up to the first.' ⁹ And when those hired about the eleventh hour came, each of them received a denarius. ¹⁰ Now when those hired first came, they thought they would receive more, but each of them also received a denarius. ¹¹ And on receiving it they grumbled at the master of the house, ¹² saying, 'These last worked only one hour, and you have made them equal to us who have borne the burden of the day and the scorching heat.' ¹³ But he replied to one of them, 'Friend, I am doing you no wrong. Did you not agree with me for a denarius? ¹⁴ Take what belongs to you and go. I choose to give to this last worker as I give to you.

¹⁵ Am I not allowed to do what I choose with what belongs to me? Or do you begrudge my generosity?' ¹⁶ So the last will be first, and the first last."

Jesus Foretells His Death a Third Time

¹⁷ And as Jesus was going up to Jerusalem, he took the twelve disciples aside, and on the way he said to them, ¹⁸ "See, we are going up to Jerusalem. And the Son of Man will be delivered over to the chief priests and scribes, and they will condemn him to death ¹⁹ and deliver him over to the Gentiles to be mocked and flogged and crucified, and he will be raised on the third day."

A Mother's Request

²⁰ Then the mother of the sons of Zebedee came up to him with her sons, and kneeling before him she asked him for something. ²¹ And he said to her, "What do you want?" She said to him, "Say that these two sons of mine are to sit, one at your right hand and one at your left, in your kingdom." ²² Jesus answered, "You do not know what you are asking. Are you able to drink the cup that I am to drink?" They said to him, "We are able." ²³ He said to them, "You will drink my cup, but to sit at my right hand and at my left is not mine to grant, but it is for those for whom it has been prepared by my Father." ²⁴ And when the ten heard it, they were indignant at the two brothers. ²⁵ But Jesus called them to him and said, "You know that the rulers of the Gentiles lord it over them, and their great ones exercise authority over them. ²⁶ It shall not be so among you. But whoever would be great among you must be your servant, ²⁷ and whoever would be first among you must be your slave,¹ ²⁸ even as the Son of Man came not to be served but to serve, and to give his life as a ransom for many."

Jesus Heals Two Blind Men

²⁹ And as they went out of Jericho, a great crowd followed him. ³⁰ And behold, there were two blind men sitting by the roadside, and when they heard that Jesus was passing by, they cried out, "Lord, have mercy on us, Son of David!" ³¹ The crowd rebuked them, telling them to be silent, but they cried out all the more, "Lord, have mercy on us, Son of David!" ³² And stopping, Jesus called them

and said, "What do you want me to do for you?" ³³ They said to him, "Lord, let our eyes be opened." ³⁴ And Jesus in pity touched their eyes, and immediately they recovered their sight and followed him.

The Triumphal Entry

21 Now when they drew near to Jerusalem and came to Bethphage, to the Mount of Olives, then Jesus sent two disciples, ² saying to them, "Go into the village in front of you, and immediately you will find a donkey tied, and a colt with her. Untie them and bring them to me. ³ If anyone says anything to you, you shall say, 'The Lord needs them,' and he will send them at once." ⁴ This took place to fulfill what was spoken by the prophet, saying,

GETTING THE MESSAGE

The **Jericho** mentioned in 20:29 was about a mile (1.6 km) south of the Jericho that was destroyed when the Israelites conquered Canaan (Joshua 6). This new Jericho included a palace of Herod the Great. When the winters grew cold and damp in Jerusalem, Herod would go there to enjoy Jericho's warm, dry climate. His palace included gardens, a swimming pool, an amphitheater, and even a chariot race course.

⁵ "Say to the daughter of Zion,
    'Behold, your king is coming to you,
        humble, and mounted on a donkey,
        on a colt, the foal of a beast of burden.'"

⁶ The disciples went and did as Jesus had directed them. ⁷ They brought the donkey and the colt and put on them their cloaks, and he sat on them. ⁸ Most of the crowd spread their cloaks on the road, and others cut branches from the trees and spread them on the road. ⁹ And the crowds that went before him and that followed him were shouting, "Hosanna to the Son of David! Blessed is he who comes in the name of the Lord! Hosanna in the highest!" ¹⁰ And when he entered Jerusalem, the whole city was stirred up, saying, "Who is this?" ¹¹ And

¹ Greek *bondservant* (*doulos*; see Preface)

the crowds said, "This is the prophet Jesus, from Nazareth of Galilee."

Jesus Cleanses the Temple

¹² And Jesus entered the temple and drove out all who sold and bought in the temple, and he overturned the tables of the money-changers and the seats of those who sold pigeons. ¹³ He said to them, "It is written, 'My house shall be called a house of prayer,' but you make it a den of robbers."

¹⁴ And the blind and the lame came to him in the temple, and he healed them. ¹⁵ But when the chief priests and the scribes saw the wonderful things that he did, and the children crying out in the temple, "Hosanna to the Son of David!" they were indignant, ¹⁶ and they said to him, "Do you hear what these are saying?" And Jesus said to them, "Yes; have you never read,

> GETTING THE MESSAGE

Large farming estates were common in Palestine. The landowners frequently rented their vineyards to farmers so they could tend to other interests. Often these vineyards were surrounded by stone walls to prevent wild animals or thieves from entering. Many of the larger vineyards had watchtowers.

"'Out of the mouth of infants and nurs-
    ing babies
    you have prepared praise'?"

¹⁷ And leaving them, he went out of the city to Bethany and lodged there.

Jesus Curses the Fig Tree

¹⁸ In the morning, as he was returning to the city, he became hungry. ¹⁹ And seeing a fig tree by the wayside, he went to it and found nothing on it but only leaves. And he said to it, "May no fruit ever come from you again!" And the fig tree withered at once. ²⁰ When the disciples saw it, they marveled, saying, "How did the fig tree wither at once?" ²¹ And Jesus answered them, "Truly, I say to you, if you have faith and do not doubt, you will not only do what has been done to the fig tree, but even if you say to this mountain, 'Be taken up and thrown into the sea,' it will happen. ²² And whatever

you ask in prayer, you will receive, if you have faith."

The Authority of Jesus Challenged

²³ And when he entered the temple, the chief priests and the elders of the people came up to him as he was teaching, and said, "By what authority are you doing these things, and who gave you this authority?" ²⁴ Jesus answered them, "I also will ask you one question, and if you tell me the answer, then I also will tell you by what authority I do these things. ²⁵ The baptism of John, from where did it come? From heaven or from man?" And they discussed it among themselves, saying, "If we say, 'From heaven,' he will say to us, 'Why then did you not believe him?' ²⁶ But if we say, 'From man,' we are afraid of the crowd, for they all hold that John was a prophet." ²⁷ So they answered Jesus, "We do not know." And he said to them, "Neither will I tell you by what authority I do these things.

The Parable of the Two Sons

²⁸ "What do you think? A man had two sons. And he went to the first and said, 'Son, go and work in the vineyard today.' ²⁹ And he answered, 'I will not,' but afterward he changed his mind and went. ³⁰ And he went to the other son and said the same. And he answered, 'I go, sir,' but did not go. ³¹ Which of the two did the will of his father?" They said, "The first." Jesus said to them, "Truly, I say to you, the tax collectors and the prostitutes go into the kingdom of God before you. ³² For John came to you in the way of righteousness, and you did not believe him, but the tax collectors and the prostitutes believed him. And even when you saw it, you did not afterward change your minds and believe him.

The Parable of the Tenants

³³ "Hear another parable. There was a master of a house who planted a vineyard and put a fence around it and dug a winepress in it and built a tower and leased it to tenants, and went into another country. ³⁴ When the season for fruit drew near, he sent his servants to the tenants to get his fruit. ³⁵ And the tenants took his servants and beat one, killed another, and stoned another. ³⁶ Again he sent other servants, more than the first. And they did the same to them. ³⁷ Finally he sent his son to them, saying, 'They will

respect my son.' **38** But when the tenants saw the son, they said to themselves, 'This is the heir. Come, let us kill him and have his inheritance.' **39** And they took him and threw him out of the vineyard and killed him. **40** When therefore the owner of the vineyard comes, what will he do to those tenants?" **41** They said to him, "He will put those wretches to a miserable death and let out the vineyard to other tenants who will give him the fruits in their seasons."

42 Jesus said to them, "Have you never read in the Scriptures:

"'The stone that the builders rejected
    has become the cornerstone;
this was the Lord's doing,
    and it is marvelous in our eyes'?

43 Therefore I tell you, the kingdom of God will be taken away from you and given to a people producing its fruits. **44** And the one who falls on this stone will be broken to pieces; and when it falls on anyone, it will crush him."

45 When the chief priests and the Pharisees heard his parables, they perceived that he was speaking about them. **46** And although they were seeking to arrest him, they feared the crowds, because they held him to be a prophet.

The Parable of the Wedding Feast

22 And again Jesus spoke to them in parables, saying, **2** "The kingdom of heaven may be compared to a king who gave a wedding feast for his son, **3** and sent his servants to call those who were invited to the wedding feast, but they would not come. **4** Again he sent other servants, saying, 'Tell those who are invited, "See, I have prepared my dinner, my oxen and my fat calves have been slaughtered, and everything is ready. Come to the wedding feast."' **5** But they paid no attention and went off, one to his farm, another to his business, **6** while the rest seized his servants, treated them shamefully, and killed them. **7** The king was angry, and he sent his troops and destroyed those murderers and burned their city. **8** Then he said to his servants, 'The wedding feast is ready, but those invited were not worthy. **9** Go therefore to the main roads and invite to the wedding feast as many as you find.' **10** And those servants went out into the roads and gathered all whom they found,

both bad and good. So the wedding hall was filled with guests.

11 "But when the king came in to look at the guests, he saw there a man who had no wedding garment. **12** And he said to him, 'Friend, how did you get in here without a wedding garment?' And he was speechless. **13** Then the king said to the attendants, 'Bind him hand and foot and cast him into the outer darkness. In that place there will be weeping and gnashing of teeth.' **14** For many are called, but few are chosen."

Paying Taxes to Caesar

15 Then the Pharisees went and plotted how to entangle him in his words. **16** And they sent their disciples to him, along with the Herodians, saying, "Teacher, we know that you are true and teach the way of God

> ### GETTING THE MESSAGE
>
> For the Jews of first-century Palestine, **taxation** was a burdensome problem. The Herodian family, which ruled on behalf of Rome, taxed the people heavily to finance their own building projects. The Jewish religious leaders also taxed the people to maintain the temple. Then there was the large amount of money needed to keep the Roman Empire going. In all, Jewish families paid about half of their income toward various taxes.

truthfully, and you do not care about anyone's opinion, for you are not swayed by appearances. **17** Tell us, then, what you think. Is it lawful to pay taxes to Caesar, or not?" **18** But Jesus, aware of their malice, said, "Why put me to the test, you hypocrites? **19** Show me the coin for the tax." And they brought him a denarius. **20** And Jesus said to them, "Whose likeness and inscription is this?" **21** They said, "Caesar's." Then he said to them, "Therefore render to Caesar the things that are Caesar's, and to God the things that are God's." **22** When they heard it, they marveled. And they left him and went away.

Sadducees Ask About the Resurrection

23 The same day Sadducees came to him, who say that there is no resurrection, and they asked him a question, **24** saying,

"Teacher, Moses said, 'If a man dies having no children, his brother must marry the widow and raise up offspring for his brother.' **25** Now there were seven brothers among us. The first married and died, and having no offspring left his wife to his brother. **26** So too the second and third, down to the seventh. **27** After them all, the woman died. **28** In the resurrection, therefore, of the seven, whose wife will she be? For they all had her."

29 But Jesus answered them, "You are wrong, because you know neither the Scriptures nor the power of God. **30** For in the resurrection they neither marry nor are given in marriage, but are like angels in heaven. **31** And as for the resurrection of the dead, have you not read what was said to you by God: **32** 'I am the God of Abraham,

---

GETTING THE MESSAGE

Phylacteries (23:5) were small cube-shaped leather cases that were tied to the left arms and foreheads of Jewish men attending the synagogue. In the cases were passages of Scripture written on pieces of parchment. This was done in an effort to literally fulfill the Old Testament command to keep the words of the Lord on their hands and between their eyes (Ex. 13:9; Deut. 6:8).

---

and the God of Isaac, and the God of Jacob'? He is not God of the dead, but of the living." **33** And when the crowd heard it, they were astonished at his teaching.

The Great Commandment

34 But when the Pharisees heard that he had silenced the Sadducees, they gathered together. **35** And one of them, a lawyer, asked him a question to test him. **36** "Teacher, which is the great commandment in the Law?" **37** And he said to him, "You shall love the Lord your God with all your heart and with all your soul and with all your mind. **38** This is the great and first commandment. **39** And a second is like it: You shall love your neighbor as yourself. **40** On these two commandments depend all the Law and the Prophets."

Whose Son Is the Christ?

41 Now while the Pharisees were gathered together, Jesus asked them a question, **42** saying, "What do you think about the Christ? Whose son is he?" They said to him, "The son of David." **43** He said to them, "How is it then that David, in the Spirit, calls him Lord, saying,

44 "'The Lord said to my Lord,
"Sit at my right hand,
    until I put your enemies under your feet"'?

45 If then David calls him Lord, how is he his son?" **46** And no one was able to answer him a word, nor from that day did anyone dare to ask him any more questions.

Seven Woes to the Scribes and Pharisees

23 Then Jesus said to the crowds and to his disciples, **2** "The scribes and the Pharisees sit on Moses' seat, **3** so do and observe whatever they tell you, but not the works they do. For they preach, but do not practice. **4** They tie up heavy burdens, hard to bear, and lay them on people's shoulders, but they themselves are not willing to move them with their finger. **5** They do all their deeds to be seen by others. For they make their phylacteries broad and their fringes long, **6** and they love the place of honor at feasts and the best seats in the synagogues **7** and greetings in the marketplaces and being called rabbi[1] by others. **8** But you are not to be called rabbi, for you have one teacher, and you are all brothers.[2] **9** And call no man your father on earth, for you have one Father, who is in heaven. **10** Neither be called instructors, for you have one instructor, the Christ. **11** The greatest among you shall be your servant. **12** Whoever exalts himself will be humbled, and whoever humbles himself will be exalted.

13 "But woe to you, scribes and Pharisees, hypocrites! For you shut the kingdom of heaven in people's faces. For you neither enter yourselves nor allow those who would enter to go in. **15** Woe to you, scribes and Pharisees, hypocrites! For you travel across sea and land to make a single proselyte, and when he becomes a proselyte, you make him twice as much a child of hell as yourselves.

---

[1] *Rabbi* means *my teacher*, or *my master*; also 23:8 [2] Or *brothers and sisters*

¹⁶ "Woe to you, blind guides, who say, 'If anyone swears by the temple, it is nothing, but if anyone swears by the gold of the temple, he is bound by his oath.' ¹⁷ You blind fools! For which is greater, the gold or the temple that has made the gold sacred? ¹⁸ And you say, 'If anyone swears by the altar, it is nothing, but if anyone swears by the gift that is on the altar, he is bound by his oath.' ¹⁹ You blind men! For which is greater, the gift or the altar that makes the gift sacred? ²⁰ So whoever swears by the altar swears by it and by everything on it. ²¹ And whoever swears by the temple swears by it and by him who dwells in it. ²² And whoever swears by heaven swears by the throne of God and by him who sits upon it.

²³ "Woe to you, scribes and Pharisees, hypocrites! For you tithe mint and dill and cumin, and have neglected the weightier matters of the law: justice and mercy and faithfulness. These you ought to have done, without neglecting the others. ²⁴ You blind guides, straining out a gnat and swallowing a camel!

²⁵ "Woe to you, scribes and Pharisees, hypocrites! For you clean the outside of the cup and the plate, but inside they are full of greed and self-indulgence. ²⁶ You blind Pharisee! First clean the inside of the cup and the plate, that the outside also may be clean.

²⁷ "Woe to you, scribes and Pharisees, hypocrites! For you are like whitewashed tombs, which outwardly appear beautiful, but within are full of dead people's bones and all uncleanness. ²⁸ So you also outwardly appear righteous to others, but within you are full of hypocrisy and lawlessness.

²⁹ "Woe to you, scribes and Pharisees, hypocrites! For you build the tombs of the prophets and decorate the monuments of the righteous, ³⁰ saying, 'If we had lived in the days of our fathers, we would not have taken part with them in shedding the blood of the prophets.' ³¹ Thus you witness against yourselves that you are sons of those who murdered the prophets. ³² Fill up, then, the measure of your fathers. ³³ You serpents, you brood of vipers, how are you to escape being sentenced to hell? ³⁴ Therefore I send you prophets and wise men and scribes, some of whom you will kill and crucify, and some you will flog in your synagogues and persecute from town to town, ³⁵ so that on you may come all the righteous blood shed on earth, from the blood of righteous Abel to the blood of Zechariah the son of Barachiah, whom you murdered between the sanctuary and the altar. ³⁶ Truly, I say to you, all these things will come upon this generation.

Lament over Jerusalem

³⁷ "O Jerusalem, Jerusalem, the city that kills the prophets and stones those who are sent to it! How often would I have gathered your children together as a hen gathers her brood under her wings, and you were not willing! ³⁸ See, your house is left to you desolate. ³⁹ For I tell you, you will not see me again, until you say, 'Blessed is he who comes in the name of the Lord.'"

Jesus Foretells Destruction of the Temple

24 Jesus left the temple and was going away, when his disciples came to point out to him the buildings of the temple.

> ### GETTING THE MESSAGE
>
> **Hypocrites!** That's what Jesus called the Pharisees, who followed man-made traditions while often disregarding God's laws. God sees into our hearts. He wants our genuine devotion and obedience (23:13–32).

² But he answered them, "You see all these, do you not? Truly, I say to you, there will not be left here one stone upon another that will not be thrown down."

Signs of the End of the Age

³ As he sat on the Mount of Olives, the disciples came to him privately, saying, "Tell us, when will these things be, and what will be the sign of your coming and of the end of the age?" ⁴ And Jesus answered them, "See that no one leads you astray. ⁵ For many will come in my name, saying, 'I am the Christ,' and they will lead many astray. ⁶ And you will hear of wars and rumors of wars. See that you are not alarmed, for this must take place, but the end is not yet. ⁷ For nation will rise against nation, and kingdom against kingdom, and there will be famines and earthquakes in various places. ⁸ All these are but the beginning of the birth pains.

9 "Then they will deliver you up to tribulation and put you to death, and you will be hated by all nations for my name's sake. **10** And then many will fall away and betray one another and hate one another. **11** And many false prophets will arise and lead many astray. **12** And because lawlessness will be increased, the love of many will grow cold. **13** But the one who endures to the end will be saved. **14** And this gospel of the kingdom will be proclaimed throughout the whole world as a testimony to all nations, and then the end will come.

The Abomination of Desolation

15 "So when you see the abomination of desolation spoken of by the prophet Daniel, standing in the holy place (let the reader understand), **16** then let those who are in Judea flee to the mountains. **17** Let the one who is on the housetop not go down to take what is in his house, **18** and let the one who is in the field not turn back to take his cloak. **19** And alas for women who are pregnant and for those who are nursing infants in those days! **20** Pray that your flight may not be in winter or on a Sabbath. **21** For then there will be great tribulation, such as has not been from the beginning of the world until now, no, and never will be. **22** And if those days had not been cut short, no human being would be saved. But for the sake of the elect those days will be cut short. **23** Then if anyone says to you, 'Look, here is the Christ!' or 'There he is!' do not believe it. **24** For false christs and false prophets will arise and perform great signs and wonders, so as to lead astray, if possible, even the elect. **25** See, I have told you beforehand. **26** So, if they say to you, 'Look, he is in the wilderness,' do not go out. If they say, 'Look, he is in the inner rooms,' do not believe it. **27** For as the lightning comes from the east and shines as far as the west, so will be the coming of the Son of Man. **28** Wherever the corpse is, there the vultures will gather.

The Coming of the Son of Man

29 "Immediately after the tribulation of those days the sun will be darkened, and the moon will not give its light, and the stars will fall from heaven, and the powers of the heavens will be shaken. **30** Then will appear in heaven the sign of the Son of Man, and then all the tribes of the earth will mourn, and they will see the Son of Man coming on the clouds of heaven with power and great glory. **31** And he will send out his angels with a loud trumpet call, and they will gather his elect from the four winds, from one end of heaven to the other.

The Lesson of the Fig Tree

32 "From the fig tree learn its lesson: as soon as its branch becomes tender and puts out its leaves, you know that summer is near. **33** So also, when you see all these things, you know that he is near, at the very gates. **34** Truly, I say to you, this generation will not pass away until all these things take place. **35** Heaven and earth will pass away, but my words will not pass away.

No One Knows That Day and Hour

36 "But concerning that day and hour no one knows, not even the angels of heaven, nor the Son, but the Father only. **37** For as were the days of Noah, so will be the coming of the Son of Man. **38** For as in those days before the flood they were eating and drinking, marrying and giving in marriage, until the day when Noah entered the ark, **39** and they were unaware until the flood came and swept them all away, so will be the coming of the Son of Man. **40** Then two men will be in the field; one will be taken and one left. **41** Two women will be grinding at the mill; one will be taken and one left. **42** Therefore, stay awake, for you do not know on what day your Lord is coming. **43** But know this, that if the master of the house had known in what part of the night the thief was coming, he would have stayed awake and would not have let his house be broken into. **44** Therefore you also must be ready, for the Son of Man is coming at an hour you do not expect.

45 "Who then is the faithful and wise servant, whom his master has set over his household, to give them their food at the proper time? **46** Blessed is that servant whom his master will find so doing when he comes. **47** Truly, I say to you, he will set him over all his possessions. **48** But if that wicked servant says to himself, 'My master is delayed,' **49** and begins to beat his fellow servants and eats and drinks with drunkards, **50** the master of that servant will come on a day when he does not expect him and at an hour he does not know **51** and will cut him in pieces and put him with the hypocrites. In that place there will be weeping and gnashing of teeth.

The Parable of the Ten Virgins

25 "Then the kingdom of heaven will be like ten virgins who took their lamps and went to meet the bridegroom. ² Five of them were foolish, and five were wise. ³ For when the foolish took their lamps, they took no oil with them, ⁴ but the wise took flasks of oil with their lamps. ⁵ As the bridegroom was delayed, they all became drowsy and slept. ⁶ But at midnight there was a cry, 'Here is the bridegroom! Come out to meet him.' ⁷ Then all those virgins rose and trimmed their lamps. ⁸ And the foolish said to the wise, 'Give us some of your oil, for our lamps are going out.' ⁹ But the wise answered, saying, 'Since there will not be enough for us and for you, go rather to the dealers and buy for yourselves.' ¹⁰ And while they were going to buy, the bridegroom came, and those who were ready went in with him to the marriage feast, and the door was shut. ¹¹ Afterward the other virgins came also, saying, 'Lord, lord, open to us.' ¹² But he answered, 'Truly, I say to you, I do not know you.' ¹³ Watch therefore, for you know neither the day nor the hour.

The Parable of the Talents

¹⁴ "For it will be like a man going on a journey, who called his servants and entrusted to them his property. ¹⁵ To one he gave five talents, to another two, to another one, to each according to his ability. Then he went away. ¹⁶ He who had received the five talents went at once and traded with them, and he made five talents more. ¹⁷ So also he who had the two talents made two talents more. ¹⁸ But he who had received the one talent went and dug in the ground and hid his master's money. ¹⁹ Now after a long time the master of those servants came and settled accounts with them. ²⁰ And he who had received the five talents came forward, bringing five talents more, saying, 'Master, you delivered to me five talents; here I have made five talents more.' ²¹ His master said to him, 'Well done, good and faithful servant. You have been faithful over a little; I will set you over much. Enter into the joy of your master.' ²² And he also who had the two talents came forward, saying, 'Master, you delivered to me two talents; here I have

made two talents more.' ²³ His master said to him, 'Well done, good and faithful servant. You have been faithful over a little; I will set you over much. Enter into the joy of your master.' ²⁴ He also who had received the one talent came forward, saying, 'Master, I knew you to be a hard man, reaping where you did not sow, and gathering where you scattered no seed, ²⁵ so I was afraid, and I went and hid your talent in the ground. Here you have what is yours.' ²⁶ But his master answered him, 'You wicked and slothful servant! You knew that I reap where I have not sown and gather where I scattered no seed? ²⁷ Then you ought to have invested my money with the bankers, and at my coming I should have received what was my own with interest. ²⁸ So take the talent from him and give it to him who has the ten talents. ²⁹ For to

GETTING THE MESSAGE

The **bankers** (25:27) were probably money-changers, who would charge for their services. It was rare for people to have money or treasure to invest, but if they did, they buried it (Josh. 7:21), had a friend or neighbor guard it (Ex. 22:7), or kept it in a temple.

everyone who has will more be given, and he will have an abundance. But from the one who has not, even what he has will be taken away. ³⁰ And cast the worthless servant into the outer darkness. In that place there will be weeping and gnashing of teeth.'

The Final Judgment

³¹ "When the Son of Man comes in his glory, and all the angels with him, then he will sit on his glorious throne. ³² Before him will be gathered all the nations, and he will separate people one from another as a shepherd separates the sheep from the goats. ³³ And he will place the sheep on his right, but the goats on the left. ³⁴ Then the King will say to those on his right, 'Come, you who are blessed by my Father, inherit the kingdom prepared for you from the foundation of the world. ³⁵ For I was hungry and you gave me food, I was thirsty and you gave me drink, I was a stranger and you welcomed me, ³⁶ I was naked

and you clothed me, I was sick and you visited me, I was in prison and you came to me.' **37** Then the righteous will answer him, saying, 'Lord, when did we see you hungry and feed you, or thirsty and give you drink? **38** And when did we see you a stranger and welcome you, or naked and clothe you? **39** And when did we see you sick or in prison and visit you?' **40** And the King will answer them, 'Truly, I say to you, as you did it to one of the least of these my brothers,¹ you did it to me.'

41 "Then he will say to those on his left, 'Depart from me, you cursed, into the eternal fire prepared for the devil and his angels. **42** For I was hungry and you gave me no food, I was thirsty and you gave me no drink, **43** I was a stranger and you did not welcome me, naked and you did not clothe me, sick and in prison and you did not visit

> **GETTING THE MESSAGE**
>
> Showing mercy to **the least of** our fellow humans (25:40) is the same as caring about Jesus himself. The care we show (or don't show) to others reveals what is in our heart.

me.' **44** Then they also will answer, saying, 'Lord, when did we see you hungry or thirsty or a stranger or naked or sick or in prison, and did not minister to you?' **45** Then he will answer them, saying, 'Truly, I say to you, as you did not do it to one of the least of these, you did not do it to me.' **46** And these will go away into eternal punishment, but the righteous into eternal life."

The Plot to Kill Jesus

26 When Jesus had finished all these sayings, he said to his disciples, **2** "You know that after two days the Passover is coming, and the Son of Man will be delivered up to be crucified."

3 Then the chief priests and the elders of the people gathered in the palace of the high priest, whose name was Caiaphas, **4** and plotted together in order to arrest Jesus by stealth and kill him. **5** But they said, "Not during the feast, lest there be an uproar among the people."

Jesus Anointed at Bethany

6 Now when Jesus was at Bethany in the house of Simon the leper,² **7** a woman came up to him with an alabaster flask of very expensive ointment, and she poured it on his head as he reclined at table. **8** And when the disciples saw it, they were indignant, saying, "Why this waste? **9** For this could have been sold for a large sum and given to the poor." **10** But Jesus, aware of this, said to them, "Why do you trouble the woman? For she has done a beautiful thing to me. **11** For you always have the poor with you, but you will not always have me. **12** In pouring this ointment on my body, she has done it to prepare me for burial. **13** Truly, I say to you, wherever this gospel is proclaimed in the whole world, what she has done will also be told in memory of her."

Judas to Betray Jesus

14 Then one of the twelve, whose name was Judas Iscariot, went to the chief priests **15** and said, "What will you give me if I deliver him over to you?" And they paid him thirty pieces of silver. **16** And from that moment he sought an opportunity to betray him.

The Passover with the Disciples

17 Now on the first day of Unleavened Bread the disciples came to Jesus, saying, "Where will you have us prepare for you to eat the Passover?" **18** He said, "Go into the city to a certain man and say to him, 'The Teacher says, My time is at hand. I will keep the Passover at your house with my disciples.'" **19** And the disciples did as Jesus had directed them, and they prepared the Passover.

20 When it was evening, he reclined at table with the twelve. **21** And as they were eating, he said, "Truly, I say to you, one of you will betray me." **22** And they were very sorrowful and began to say to him one after another, "Is it I, Lord?" **23** He answered, "He who has dipped his hand in the dish with me will betray me. **24** The Son of Man goes as it is written of him, but woe to that man by whom the Son of Man is betrayed! It would have been better for that man if he had not been born." **25** Judas, who would betray him, answered, "Is it I, Rabbi?" He said to him, "You have said so."

---

¹ Or *brothers and sisters* ² *Leprosy* was a term for several skin diseases (see Leviticus 13)

Institution of the Lord's Supper

26 Now as they were eating, Jesus took bread, and after blessing it broke it and gave it to the disciples, and said, "Take, eat; this is my body." **27** And he took a cup, and when he had given thanks he gave it to them, saying, "Drink of it, all of you, **28** for this is my blood of the covenant, which is poured out for many for the forgiveness of sins. **29** I tell you I will not drink again of this fruit of the vine until that day when I drink it new with you in my Father's kingdom."

Jesus Foretells Peter's Denial

30 And when they had sung a hymn, they went out to the Mount of Olives. **31** Then Jesus said to them, "You will all fall away because of me this night. For it is written, 'I will strike the shepherd, and the sheep of the flock will be scattered.' **32** But after I am raised up, I will go before you to Galilee." **33** Peter answered him, "Though they all fall away because of you, I will never fall away." **34** Jesus said to him, "Truly, I tell you, this very night, before the rooster crows, you will deny me three times." **35** Peter said to him, "Even if I must die with you, I will not deny you!" And all the disciples said the same.

Jesus Prays in Gethsemane

36 Then Jesus went with them to a place called Gethsemane, and he said to his disciples, "Sit here, while I go over there and pray." **37** And taking with him Peter and the two sons of Zebedee, he began to be sorrowful and troubled. **38** Then he said to them, "My soul is very sorrowful, even to death; remain here, and watch with me." **39** And going a little farther he fell on his face and prayed, saying, "My Father, if it be possible, let this cup pass from me; nevertheless, not as I will, but as you will." **40** And he came to the disciples and found them sleeping. And he said to Peter, "So, could you not watch with me one hour? **41** Watch and pray that you may not enter into temptation. The spirit indeed is willing, but the flesh is weak." **42** Again, for the second time, he went away and prayed, "My Father, if this cannot pass unless I drink it, your will be done." **43** And again he came and found them sleeping, for their eyes were heavy. **44** So, leaving them again, he went away and prayed for the third time, saying the same words again. **45** Then he came to the disciples and said to them, "Sleep and take your rest later on. See, the hour is at hand, and the Son of Man is betrayed into the hands of sinners. **46** Rise, let us be going; see, my betrayer is at hand."

Betrayal and Arrest of Jesus

47 While he was still speaking, Judas came, one of the twelve, and with him a great crowd with swords and clubs, from the chief priests and the elders of the people. **48** Now the betrayer had given them a sign, saying, "The one I will kiss is the man; seize him." **49** And he came up to Jesus at once and said, "Greetings, Rabbi!" And he kissed him. **50** Jesus said to him, "Friend, do what you came to do." Then they came up and laid hands on Jesus and seized him. **51** And behold, one of those who were with Jesus stretched out his hand and

GETTING THE MESSAGE

Gethsemane was most likely a garden area among olive tree groves that had an area for pressing the olives into oil. Though the traditional site is now marked by the modern Church of All Nations, many archaeologists believe that a cave located a couple hundred feet north of there is a more likely location.

drew his sword and struck the servant of the high priest and cut off his ear. **52** Then Jesus said to him, "Put your sword back into its place. For all who take the sword will perish by the sword. **53** Do you think that I cannot appeal to my Father, and he will at once send me more than twelve legions of angels? **54** But how then should the Scriptures be fulfilled, that it must be so?" **55** At that hour Jesus said to the crowds, "Have you come out as against a robber, with swords and clubs to capture me? Day after day I sat in the temple teaching, and you did not seize me. **56** But all this has taken place that the Scriptures of the prophets might be fulfilled." Then all the disciples left him and fled.

Jesus Before Caiaphas and the Council

57 Then those who had seized Jesus led him to Caiaphas the high priest, where the scribes and the elders had gathered. [58] And Peter was following him at a distance, as far as the courtyard of the high priest, and going inside he sat with the guards to see the end. [59] Now the chief priests and the whole council were seeking false testimony against Jesus that they might put him to death, [60] but they found none, though many false witnesses came forward. At last two came forward [61] and said, "This man said, 'I am able to destroy the temple of God, and to rebuild it in three days.'" [62] And the high priest stood up and said, "Have you no answer to make? What is it that these men testify against you?" [63] But Jesus remained silent. And the high priest said to him, "I adjure you by the living God, tell us if you are the Christ, the Son of God." [64] Jesus said to him, "You have said so. But I tell you, from now on you will see the Son of Man seated at the right hand of Power and coming on the clouds of heaven." [65] Then the high priest tore his robes and said, "He has uttered blasphemy. What further witnesses do we need? You have now heard his blasphemy. [66] What is your judgment?" They answered, "He deserves death." [67] Then they spit in his face and struck him. And some slapped him, [68] saying, "Prophesy to us, you Christ! Who is it that struck you?"

Peter Denies Jesus

[69] Now Peter was sitting outside in the courtyard. And a servant girl came up to him and said, "You also were with Jesus the Galilean." [70] But he denied it before them all, saying, "I do not know what you mean." [71] And when he went out to the entrance, another servant girl saw him, and she said to the bystanders, "This man was with Jesus of Nazareth." [72] And again he denied it with an oath: "I do not know the man." [73] After a little while the bystanders came up and said to Peter, "Certainly you too are one of them, for your accent betrays you." [74] Then he began to invoke a curse on himself and to swear, "I do not know the man." And immediately the rooster crowed. [75] And Peter remembered the saying of Jesus, "Before the rooster crows, you will deny me three times." And he went out and wept bitterly.

Jesus Delivered to Pilate

27 When morning came, all the chief priests and the elders of the people took counsel against Jesus to put him to death. [2] And they bound him and led him away and delivered him over to Pilate the governor.

Judas Hangs Himself

[3] Then when Judas, his betrayer, saw that Jesus was condemned, he changed his mind and brought back the thirty pieces of silver to the chief priests and the elders, [4] saying, "I have sinned by betraying innocent blood." They said, "What is that to us? See to it yourself." [5] And throwing down the pieces of silver into the temple, he departed, and he went and hanged himself. [6] But the chief priests, taking the pieces of silver, said, "It is not lawful to put them into the treasury, since it is blood money." [7] So they took counsel and bought with them the potter's field as a burial place for strangers. [8] Therefore that field has been called the Field of Blood to this day. [9] Then was fulfilled what had been spoken by the prophet Jeremiah, saying, "And they took the thirty pieces of silver, the price of him on whom a price had been set by some of the sons of Israel, [10] and they gave them for the potter's field, as the Lord directed me."

Jesus Before Pilate

[11] Now Jesus stood before the governor, and the governor asked him, "Are you the King of the Jews?" Jesus said, "You have said so." [12] But when he was accused by the chief priests and elders, he gave no answer. [13] Then Pilate said to him, "Do you not hear how many things they testify against you?" [14] But he gave him no answer, not even to a single charge, so that the governor was greatly amazed.

The Crowd Chooses Barabbas

[15] Now at the feast the governor was accustomed to release for the crowd any one prisoner whom they wanted. [16] And they had then a notorious prisoner called Barabbas. [17] So when they had gathered, Pilate said to them, "Whom do you want me to release for you: Barabbas, or Jesus who is called Christ?" [18] For he knew that it was out of envy that they had delivered him up. [19] Besides, while he was sitting on the judgment seat, his wife sent word to him, "Have nothing to do with that righteous man, for I have suffered much because of him today in a dream." [20] Now the chief priests and the elders persuaded the crowd to ask for Barabbas and

destroy Jesus. [21] The governor again said to them, "Which of the two do you want me to release for you?" And they said, "Barabbas." [22] Pilate said to them, "Then what shall I do with Jesus who is called Christ?" They all said, "Let him be crucified!" [23] And he said, "Why, what evil has he done?" But they shouted all the more, "Let him be crucified!"

Pilate Delivers Jesus to Be Crucified

[24] So when Pilate saw that he was gaining nothing, but rather that a riot was beginning, he took water and washed his hands before the crowd, saying, "I am innocent of this man's blood; see to it yourselves." [25] And all the people answered, "His blood be on us and on our children!" [26] Then he released for them Barabbas, and having scourged[1] Jesus, delivered him to be crucified.

Jesus Is Mocked

[27] Then the soldiers of the governor took Jesus into the governor's headquarters, and they gathered the whole battalion before him. [28] And they stripped him and put a scarlet robe on him, [29] and twisting together a crown of thorns, they put it on his head and put a reed in his right hand. And kneeling before him, they mocked him, saying, "Hail, King of the Jews!" [30] And they spit on him and took the reed and struck him on the head. [31] And when they had mocked him, they stripped him of the robe and put his own clothes on him and led him away to crucify him.

The Crucifixion

[32] As they went out, they found a man of Cyrene, Simon by name. They compelled this man to carry his cross. [33] And when they came to a place called Golgotha (which means Place of a Skull), [34] they offered him wine to drink, mixed with gall, but when he tasted it, he would not drink it. [35] And when they had crucified him, they divided his garments among them by casting lots. [36] Then they sat down and kept watch over him there. [37] And over his head they put the charge against him, which read, "This is Jesus, the King of the Jews." [38] Then two robbers were crucified with him, one on the right and one on the left. [39] And those who passed by derided him, wagging their heads [40] and saying, "You who would destroy the temple and rebuild it in three days, save yourself! If you are the Son of God, come down from the cross." [41] So also the chief priests, with the scribes and elders, mocked him, saying, [42] "He saved others; he cannot save himself. He is the King of Israel; let him come down now from the cross, and we will believe in him. [43] He trusts in God; let God deliver him now, if he desires him. For he said, 'I am the Son of God.'" [44] And the robbers who were crucified with him also reviled him in the same way.

The Death of Jesus

[45] Now from the sixth hour[2] there was darkness over all the land until the ninth hour.[3] [46] And about the ninth hour Jesus cried out with a loud voice, saying, "Eli, Eli, lema sabachthani?" that is, "My God, my God, why have you forsaken me?" [47] And

some of the bystanders, hearing it, said, "This man is calling Elijah." [48] And one of them at once ran and took a sponge, filled it with sour wine, and put it on a reed and gave it to him to drink. [49] But the others said, "Wait, let us see whether Elijah will come to save him." [50] And Jesus cried out again with a loud voice and yielded up his spirit.

[51] And behold, the curtain of the temple was torn in two, from top to bottom. And the earth shook, and the rocks were split. [52] The tombs also were opened. And many bodies of the saints who had fallen asleep were raised, [53] and coming out of the tombs after his resurrection they went into the holy city and appeared to many. [54] When the centurion and those who were with him, keeping watch over Jesus, saw the earthquake and what took place, they were filled with awe and said, "Truly this was the Son of God!"

---

[1] *Scourged* means being beaten with a whip that has metal or bone spikes in it [2] That is, noon [3] That is, 3 P.M.

⁵⁵ There were also many women there, looking on from a distance, who had followed Jesus from Galilee, ministering to him, ⁵⁶ among whom were Mary Magdalene and Mary the mother of James and Joseph and the mother of the sons of Zebedee.

Jesus Is Buried

⁵⁷ When it was evening, there came a rich man from Arimathea, named Joseph, who also was a disciple of Jesus. ⁵⁸ He went to Pilate and asked for the body of Jesus. Then Pilate ordered it to be given to him. ⁵⁹ And Joseph took the body and wrapped it in a clean linen shroud ⁶⁰ and laid it in his own new tomb, which he had cut in the rock. And he rolled a great stone to the entrance of the tomb and went away. ⁶¹ Mary Magdalene and the other Mary were there, sitting opposite the tomb.

GETTING THE MESSAGE

Jesus' **resurrection** is a crucial part of the gospel message. If Jesus did not rise from the dead, we are still in our sins (1 Cor. 15:17). Yet the Jewish leaders chose to make up the story that it never happened (Matt. 28:13–14).

The Guard at the Tomb

⁶² The next day, that is, after the day of Preparation, the chief priests and the Pharisees gathered before Pilate ⁶³ and said, "Sir, we remember how that impostor said, while he was still alive, 'After three days I will rise.' ⁶⁴ Therefore order the tomb to be made secure until the third day, lest his disciples go and steal him away and tell the people, 'He has risen from the dead,' and the last fraud will be worse than the first." ⁶⁵ Pilate said to them, "You have a guard of soldiers. Go, make it as secure as you can." ⁶⁶ So they went and made the tomb secure by sealing the stone and setting a guard.

The Resurrection

28 Now after the Sabbath, toward the dawn of the first day of the week, Mary Magdalene and the other Mary went to see the tomb. ² And behold, there was a great earthquake, for an angel of the Lord descended from heaven and came and rolled back the stone and sat on it. ³ His appearance was like lightning, and his clothing white as snow. ⁴ And for fear of him the guards trembled and became like dead men. ⁵ But the angel said to the women, "Do not be afraid, for I know that you seek Jesus who was crucified. ⁶ He is not here, for he has risen, as he said. Come, see the place where he lay. ⁷ Then go quickly and tell his disciples that he has risen from the dead, and behold, he is going before you to Galilee; there you will see him. See, I have told you." ⁸ So they departed quickly from the tomb with fear and great joy, and ran to tell his disciples. ⁹ And behold, Jesus met them and said, "Greetings!" And they came up and took hold of his feet and worshiped him. ¹⁰ Then Jesus said to them, "Do not be afraid; go and tell my brothers to go to Galilee, and there they will see me."

The Report of the Guard

¹¹ While they were going, behold, some of the guard went into the city and told the chief priests all that had taken place. ¹² And when they had assembled with the elders and taken counsel, they gave a sufficient sum of money to the soldiers ¹³ and said, "Tell people, 'His disciples came by night and stole him away while we were asleep.' ¹⁴ And if this comes to the governor's ears, we will satisfy him and keep you out of trouble." ¹⁵ So they took the money and did as they were directed. And this story has been spread among the Jews to this day.

The Great Commission

¹⁶ Now the eleven disciples went to Galilee, to the mountain to which Jesus had directed them. ¹⁷ And when they saw him they worshiped him, but some doubted. ¹⁸ And Jesus came and said to them, "All authority in heaven and on earth has been given to me. ¹⁹ Go therefore and make disciples of all nations, baptizing them in the name of the Father and of the Son and of the Holy Spirit, ²⁰ teaching them to observe all that I have commanded you. And behold, I am with you always, to the end of the age."

INTRODUCTION TO MARK

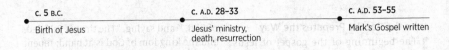

c. 5 B.C.	c. A.D. 28–33	c. A.D. 53–55
Birth of Jesus	Jesus' ministry, death, resurrection	Mark's Gospel written

AUTHOR, DATE, AND RECIPIENTS

The apostle Peter passed on reports of the words and deeds of Jesus to his attendant, John Mark, who wrote this Gospel for the wider church as the record of Peter's apostolic testimony. The book was likely written from Rome during the mid- to late-50s A.D. (though the mid- or late-60s is also possible). Mark's audience, largely unfamiliar with Jewish customs, needed to become familiar with such customs in order to understand the coming of Jesus as the culmination of God's work with Israel and the entire world, so Mark explains them.

PURPOSE AND THEME

The ultimate purpose and theme of Mark's Gospel is to present and defend Jesus' universal call to discipleship. Mark returns often to this theme, categorizing his main audience as either followers or opponents of Jesus. Mark presents and supports this call to discipleship by narrating the identity and teaching of Jesus. For Mark, discipleship is essentially a relationship with Jesus, not merely following a certain code of conduct. Fellowship with Jesus marks the heart of the disciple's life, and this fellowship includes trusting Jesus, confessing him, observing his conduct, following his teaching, and being shaped by a relationship with him. Discipleship also means being prepared to face the kind of rejection that Jesus faced.

KEY THEMES

1. Jesus seeks to correct messianic expectations and misunderstandings (1:25, 34, 44; 3:12; 4:10–12; 5:18–19, 43; 8:30; 9:9).

2. Jesus is man (3:5; 4:38; 6:6; 7:34; 8:12, 33; 10:14; 11:12; 14:33–42).

3. Jesus is the Son of God (1:11; 3:11; 5:7; 8:38; 9:7; 12:6–8; 13:32; 14:36, 61; 15:39).

4. Jesus is the Son of Man with all power and authority (1:16–34; 2:3–12, 23–28; 3:11; 4:35–41; 6:45–52; 7:1–23; 10:1–12).

5. Jesus as the Son of Man must suffer (8:31; 10:45; 14:21, 36).

6. Jesus is Lord (2:28; 12:35–37; 14:62).

7. Jesus calls his followers to imitate him in humble service, self-denial, and suffering (8:34–38; 9:35–37; 10:35–45).

8. Jesus teaches on the kingdom of God, and implies that God continues to call a people to himself (compare 1:15; 9:1; 14:25; 15:43).

OUTLINE

I. Introduction (1:1–15)

II. Demonstration of Jesus' Authority (1:16–8:26)

   A. Jesus' early Galilean ministry (1:16–3:12)

   B. Jesus' later Galilean ministry (3:13–6:6)

   C. Work beyond Galilee (6:7–8:26)

III. Testing Jesus' Authority in Suffering (8:27–16:8)

   A. Journey to Jerusalem (8:27–10:52)

   B. Entering and judging Jerusalem (11:1–13:37)

   C. Death and resurrection in Jerusalem (14:1–16:8)

   [D. "Longer ending of Mark" (16:9–20; see Preface)]

THE GOSPEL ACCORDING TO
MARK

John the Baptist Prepares the Way

1 The beginning of the gospel of Jesus Christ, the Son of God.

2 As it is written in Isaiah the prophet,

"Behold, I send my messenger before
your face,
who will prepare your way,
3 the voice of one crying in the wilderness:
'Prepare the way of the Lord,
make his paths straight,'"

4 John appeared, baptizing in the wilderness and proclaiming a baptism of repentance for the forgiveness of sins. 5 And all the country of Judea and all Jerusalem were going out to him and were being baptized by him in the river Jordan, confessing their sins. 6 Now John was clothed with camel's hair and wore a leather belt around his waist and ate locusts and wild honey. 7 And he preached, saying, "After me comes he who is mightier than I, the strap of whose sandals I am not worthy to stoop down and untie. 8 I have baptized you with water, but he will baptize you with the Holy Spirit."

The Baptism of Jesus

9 In those days Jesus came from Nazareth of Galilee and was baptized by John in the Jordan. 10 And when he came up out of the water, immediately he saw the heavens being torn open and the Spirit descending on him like a dove. 11 And a voice came from heaven, "You are my beloved Son; with you I am well pleased."

The Temptation of Jesus

12 The Spirit immediately drove him out into the wilderness. 13 And he was in the wilderness forty days, being tempted by Satan. And he was with the wild animals, and the angels were ministering to him.

Jesus Begins His Ministry

14 Now after John was arrested, Jesus came into Galilee, proclaiming the gospel of God, 15 and saying, "The time is fulfilled, and the kingdom of God is at hand; repent and believe in the gospel."

Jesus Calls the First Disciples

16 Passing alongside the Sea of Galilee, he saw Simon and Andrew the brother of Simon casting a net into the sea, for they were fishermen. 17 And Jesus said to them, "Follow me, and I will make you become fishers of men."[1] 18 And immediately they left their nets and followed him. 19 And going on a little farther, he saw James the son of Zebedee and John his brother, who

GETTING THE MESSAGE

What is a "Gospel"? "Gospel" literally means "good news." The "Gospel according to Mark," along with the other three Gospels, reports the good news of salvation through the death and resurrection of Jesus Christ.

were in their boat mending the nets. 20 And immediately he called them, and they left their father Zebedee in the boat with the hired servants and followed him.

Jesus Heals a Man with an Unclean Spirit

21 And they went into Capernaum, and immediately on the Sabbath he entered the synagogue and was teaching. 22 And they were astonished at his teaching, for he taught them as one who had authority, and not as the scribes. 23 And immediately there was in their synagogue a man with an unclean spirit. And he cried out, 24 "What have you to do with us, Jesus of Nazareth? Have you come to destroy us? I know who you are—the Holy One of God." 25 But Jesus rebuked him, saying, "Be silent, and come out of him!" 26 And the unclean spirit, convulsing him and crying out with a loud voice, came out of him. 27 And they

[1] The Greek word for *men* refers to both men and women (see Preface)

were all amazed, so that they questioned among themselves, saying, "What is this? A new teaching with authority! He commands even the unclean spirits, and they obey him." 28 And at once his fame spread everywhere throughout all the surrounding region of Galilee.

Jesus Heals Many

29 And immediately he left the synagogue and entered the house of Simon and Andrew, with James and John. 30 Now Simon's mother-in-law lay ill with a fever, and immediately they told him about her. 31 And he came and took her by the hand and lifted her up, and the fever left her, and she began to serve them.

32 That evening at sundown they brought to him all who were sick or oppressed by demons. 33 And the whole city was gathered

GETTING THE MESSAGE

Reclining at the table. During formal dinners in New Testament times, guests reclined on a couch that stretched around three sides of a room (2:15). The host took the central place surrounded by a U-shaped series of tables. The most honored guests reclined on either side of the host, with the guests' heads toward the tables and their feet toward the wall.

together at the door. 34 And he healed many who were sick with various diseases, and cast out many demons. And he would not permit the demons to speak, because they knew him.

Jesus Preaches in Galilee

35 And rising very early in the morning, while it was still dark, he departed and went out to a desolate place, and there he prayed. 36 And Simon and those who were with him searched for him, 37 and they found him and said to him, "Everyone is looking for you." 38 And he said to them, "Let us go on to the next towns, that I may preach there also, for that is why I came out." 39 And he went throughout all Galilee, preaching in their synagogues and casting out demons.

Jesus Cleanses a Leper

40 And a leper[1] came to him, imploring him, and kneeling said to him, "If you will, you can make me clean." 41 Moved with pity, he stretched out his hand and touched him and said to him, "I will; be clean." 42 And immediately the leprosy left him, and he was made clean. 43 And Jesus sternly charged him and sent him away at once, 44 and said to him, "See that you say nothing to anyone, but go, show yourself to the priest and offer for your cleansing what Moses commanded, for a proof to them." 45 But he went out and began to talk freely about it, and to spread the news, so that Jesus could no longer openly enter a town, but was out in desolate places, and people were coming to him from every quarter.

Jesus Heals a Paralytic

2 And when he returned to Capernaum after some days, it was reported that he was at home. 2 And many were gathered together, so that there was no more room, not even at the door. And he was preaching the word to them. 3 And they came, bringing to him a paralytic carried by four men. 4 And when they could not get near him because of the crowd, they removed the roof above him, and when they had made an opening, they let down the bed on which the paralytic lay. 5 And when Jesus saw their faith, he said to the paralytic, "Son, your sins are forgiven." 6 Now some of the scribes were sitting there, questioning in their hearts, 7 "Why does this man speak like that? He is blaspheming! Who can forgive sins but God alone?" 8 And immediately Jesus, perceiving in his spirit that they thus questioned within themselves, said to them, "Why do you question these things in your hearts? 9 Which is easier, to say to the paralytic, 'Your sins are forgiven,' or to say, 'Rise, take up your bed and walk'? 10 But that you may know that the Son of Man has authority on earth to forgive sins"—he said to the paralytic— 11 "I say to you, rise, pick up your bed, and go home." 12 And he rose and immediately picked up his bed and went out before them all, so that they were all amazed and glorified God, saying, "We never saw anything like this!"

---

[1] *Leprosy* was a term for several skin diseases (see Leviticus 13)

Jesus Calls Levi

13 He went out again beside the sea, and all the crowd was coming to him, and he was teaching them. **14** And as he passed by, he saw Levi the son of Alphaeus sitting at the tax booth, and he said to him, "Follow me." And he rose and followed him.

15 And as he reclined at table in his house, many tax collectors and sinners were reclining with Jesus and his disciples, for there were many who followed him. **16** And the scribes of the Pharisees, when they saw that he was eating with sinners and tax collectors, said to his disciples, "Why does he eat with tax collectors and sinners?" **17** And when Jesus heard it, he said to them, "Those who are well have no need of a physician, but those who are sick. I came not to call the righteous, but sinners."

A Question About Fasting

18 Now John's disciples and the Pharisees were fasting. And people came and said to him, "Why do John's disciples and the disciples of the Pharisees fast, but your disciples do not fast?" **19** And Jesus said to them, "Can the wedding guests fast while the bridegroom is with them? As long as they have the bridegroom with them, they cannot fast. **20** The days will come when the bridegroom is taken away from them, and then they will fast in that day. **21** No one sews a piece of unshrunk cloth on an old garment. If he does, the patch tears away from it, the new from the old, and a worse tear is made. **22** And no one puts new wine into old wineskins. If he does, the wine will burst the skins—and the wine is destroyed, and so are the skins. But new wine is for fresh wineskins."

Jesus Is Lord of the Sabbath

23 One Sabbath he was going through the grainfields, and as they made their way, his disciples began to pluck heads of grain. **24** And the Pharisees were saying to him, "Look, why are they doing what is not lawful on the Sabbath?" **25** And he said to them, "Have you never read what David did, when he was in need and was hungry, he and those who were with him: **26** how he entered the house of God, in the time of Abiathar the high priest, and ate the bread of the Presence, which it is not lawful for any but the priests to eat, and also gave it to those who were with him?" **27** And he said to

them, "The Sabbath was made for man, not man for the Sabbath. **28** So the Son of Man is lord even of the Sabbath."

A Man with a Withered Hand

3 Again he entered the synagogue, and a man was there with a withered hand. **2** And they watched Jesus, to see whether he would heal him on the Sabbath, so that they might accuse him. **3** And he said to the man with the withered hand, "Come here." **4** And he said to them, "Is it lawful on the Sabbath to do good or to do harm, to save life or to kill?" But they were silent. **5** And he looked around at them with anger, grieved at their hardness of heart, and said to the man, "Stretch out your hand." He stretched it out, and his hand was restored. **6** The Pharisees went out and immediately held counsel with the Herodians against him, how to destroy him.

GETTING THE MESSAGE

Why does Mark say "immediately" so often? The Greek word translated "immediately" occurs in the Gospel of Mark more often than in the rest of the New Testament combined. The frequent use of the word stresses the importance of an event and helps to show that Christ's ministry has a divine purpose and plan behind it.

A Great Crowd Follows Jesus

7 Jesus withdrew with his disciples to the sea, and a great crowd followed, from Galilee and Judea **8** and Jerusalem and Idumea and from beyond the Jordan and from around Tyre and Sidon. When the great crowd heard all that he was doing, they came to him. **9** And he told his disciples to have a boat ready for him because of the crowd, lest they crush him, **10** for he had healed many, so that all who had diseases pressed around him to touch him. **11** And whenever the unclean spirits saw him, they fell down before him and cried out, "You are the Son of God." **12** And he strictly ordered them not to make him known.

The Twelve Apostles

13 And he went up on the mountain and called to him those whom he desired, and they came to him. ¹⁴ And he appointed twelve (whom he also named apostles) so that they might be with him and he might send them out to preach ¹⁵ and have authority to cast out demons. ¹⁶ He appointed the twelve: Simon (to whom he gave the name Peter); ¹⁷ James the son of Zebedee and John the brother of James (to whom he gave the name Boanerges, that is, Sons of Thunder); ¹⁸ Andrew, and Philip, and Bartholomew, and Matthew, and Thomas, and James the son of Alphaeus, and Thaddaeus, and Simon the Zealot, ¹⁹ and Judas Iscariot, who betrayed him.

²⁰ Then he went home, and the crowd gathered again, so that they could not even eat. ²¹ And when his family heard it, they went out to seize him, for they were saying, "He is out of his mind."

Blasphemy Against the Holy Spirit

²² And the scribes who came down from Jerusalem were saying, "He is possessed by Beelzebul," and "by the prince of demons he casts out the demons." ²³ And he called them to him and said to them in parables, "How can Satan cast out Satan? ²⁴ If a kingdom is divided against itself, that kingdom cannot stand. ²⁵ And if a house is divided against itself, that house will not be able to stand. ²⁶ And if Satan has risen up against himself and is divided, he cannot stand, but is coming to an end. ²⁷ But no one can enter a strong man's house and plunder his goods, unless he first binds the strong man. Then indeed he may plunder his house.

²⁸ "Truly, I say to you, all sins will be forgiven the children of man, and whatever blasphemies they utter, ²⁹ but whoever blasphemes against the Holy Spirit never has forgiveness, but is guilty of an eternal sin"— ³⁰ for they were saying, "He has an unclean spirit."

Jesus' Mother and Brothers

³¹ And his mother and his brothers came, and standing outside they sent to him and called him. ³² And a crowd was sitting around him, and they said to him, "Your mother and your brothers are outside, seeking you." ³³ And he answered them, "Who are my mother and my brothers?" ³⁴ And looking about at those who sat around him, he said, "Here are my mother and my brothers! ³⁵ For whoever does the will of God, he is my brother and sister and mother."

The Parable of the Sower

4 Again he began to teach beside the sea. And a very large crowd gathered about him, so that he got into a boat and sat in it on the sea, and the whole crowd was beside the sea on the land. ² And he was teaching them many things in parables, and in his teaching he said to them: ³ "Listen! Behold, a sower went out to sow. ⁴ And as he sowed, some seed fell along the path, and the birds came and devoured it. ⁵ Other seed fell on rocky ground, where it did not have much soil, and immediately it sprang up, since it had no depth of soil. ⁶ And when the sun rose, it was scorched, and since it had no root, it withered away. ⁷ Other seed fell among thorns, and the thorns grew up and choked it, and it yielded no grain. ⁸ And other seeds fell into good soil and produced grain, growing up and increasing and yielding thirtyfold and sixtyfold and a hundredfold." ⁹ And he said, "He who has ears to hear, let him hear."

The Purpose of the Parables

¹⁰ And when he was alone, those around him with the twelve asked him about the parables. ¹¹ And he said to them, "To you has been given the secret of the kingdom of God, but for those outside everything is in parables, ¹² so that

"'they may indeed see but not perceive,
    and may indeed hear but not understand,
lest they should turn and be forgiven.'"

¹³ And he said to them, "Do you not understand this parable? How then will you understand all the parables? ¹⁴ The sower sows the word. ¹⁵ And these are the ones along the path, where the word is sown: when they hear, Satan immediately comes and takes away the word that is sown in them. ¹⁶ And these are the ones sown on rocky ground: the ones who, when they hear the word, immediately receive it with joy. ¹⁷ And they have no root in themselves, but endure for a while; then, when tribulation or persecution arises on account of the word, immediately they fall away. ¹⁸ And others are the ones sown among thorns. They are those who hear the word, ¹⁹ but the cares of the world and the deceitfulness of riches and the desires for other things enter in and choke the word, and it proves

unfruitful. **20** But those that were sown on the good soil are the ones who hear the word and accept it and bear fruit, thirtyfold and sixtyfold and a hundredfold."

A Lamp Under a Basket

21 And he said to them, "Is a lamp brought in to be put under a basket, or under a bed, and not on a stand? **22** For nothing is hidden except to be made manifest; nor is anything secret except to come to light. **23** If anyone has ears to hear, let him hear." **24** And he said to them, "Pay attention to what you hear: with the measure you use, it will be measured to you, and still more will be added to you. **25** For to the one who has, more will be given, and from the one who has not, even what he has will be taken away."

The Parable of the Seed Growing

26 And he said, "The kingdom of God is as if a man should scatter seed on the ground. **27** He sleeps and rises night and day, and the seed sprouts and grows; he knows not how. **28** The earth produces by itself, first the blade, then the ear, then the full grain in the ear. **29** But when the grain is ripe, at once he puts in the sickle, because the harvest has come."

The Parable of the Mustard Seed

30 And he said, "With what can we compare the kingdom of God, or what parable shall we use for it? **31** It is like a grain of mustard seed, which, when sown on the ground, is the smallest of all the seeds on earth, **32** yet when it is sown it grows up and becomes larger than all the garden plants and puts out large branches, so that the birds of the air can make nests in its shade."

33 With many such parables he spoke the word to them, as they were able to hear it. **34** He did not speak to them without a parable, but privately to his own disciples he explained everything.

Jesus Calms a Storm

35 On that day, when evening had come, he said to them, "Let us go across to the other side." **36** And leaving the crowd, they took him with them in the boat, just as he was. And other boats were with him. **37** And a great windstorm arose, and the waves were breaking into the boat, so that the boat was already filling. **38** But he was in the stern, asleep on the cushion. And they woke him

and said to him, "Teacher, do you not care that we are perishing?" **39** And he awoke and rebuked the wind and said to the sea, "Peace! Be still!" And the wind ceased, and there was a great calm. **40** He said to them, "Why are you so afraid? Have you still no faith?" **41** And they were filled with great fear and said to one another, "Who then is this, that even the wind and the sea obey him?"

Jesus Heals a Man with a Demon

5 They came to the other side of the sea, to the country of the Gerasenes. **2** And when Jesus had stepped out of the boat, immediately there met him out of the tombs a man with an unclean spirit. **3** He lived among the tombs. And no one could bind him anymore, not even with a chain, **4** for he had often been bound with shackles and chains, but he wrenched the chains apart,

---

> **GETTING THE MESSAGE**
>
> **What did people use for lamp fuel?**
> In Old Testament times, people used animal fat as fuel for their lamps. By New Testament times, this had been replaced with olive oil. Olives were usually pressed two or three times. Oil from the first pressing was used for food. Oil from the second and third pressing was used as fuel for lamps.

---

and he broke the shackles in pieces. No one had the strength to subdue him. **5** Night and day among the tombs and on the mountains he was always crying out and cutting himself with stones. **6** And when he saw Jesus from afar, he ran and fell down before him. **7** And crying out with a loud voice, he said, "What have you to do with me, Jesus, Son of the Most High God? I adjure you by God, do not torment me." **8** For he was saying to him, "Come out of the man, you unclean spirit!" **9** And Jesus asked him, "What is your name?" He replied, "My name is Legion, for we are many." **10** And he begged him earnestly not to send them out of the country. **11** Now a great herd of pigs was feeding there on the hillside, **12** and they begged him, saying, "Send us to the pigs; let us enter them." **13** So he gave them permission. And the unclean spirits came out and entered the pigs; and the herd, numbering about two thousand, rushed down the steep bank into the sea and drowned in the sea.

¹⁴ The herdsmen fled and told it in the city and in the country. And people came to see what it was that had happened. ¹⁵ And they came to Jesus and saw the demon-possessed man, the one who had had the legion, sitting there, clothed and in his right mind, and they were afraid. ¹⁶ And those who had seen it described to them what had happened to the demon-possessed man and to the pigs. ¹⁷ And they began to beg Jesus to depart from their region. ¹⁸ As he was getting into the boat, the man who had been possessed with demons begged him that he might be with him. ¹⁹ And he did not permit him but said to him, "Go home to your friends and tell them how much the Lord has done for you, and how he has had mercy on you." ²⁰ And he went away and began to proclaim in the

GETTING THE MESSAGE

The one true God. Mark emphasizes the divine Sonship of Jesus. In New Testament times the Roman emperor was worshiped by many as a god or as a "son of god." It was essential, then, for Mark to make it clear that Jesus was the Son of the one true God.

Decapolis how much Jesus had done for him, and everyone marveled.

Jesus Heals a Woman and Jairus's Daughter

²¹ And when Jesus had crossed again in the boat to the other side, a great crowd gathered about him, and he was beside the sea. ²² Then came one of the rulers of the synagogue, Jairus by name, and seeing him, he fell at his feet ²³ and implored him earnestly, saying, "My little daughter is at the point of death. Come and lay your hands on her, so that she may be made well and live." ²⁴ And he went with him.

And a great crowd followed him and thronged about him. ²⁵ And there was a woman who had had a discharge of blood for twelve years, ²⁶ and who had suffered much under many physicians, and had spent all that she had, and was no better but rather grew worse. ²⁷ She had heard the reports about Jesus and came up behind him

in the crowd and touched his garment. ²⁸ For she said, "If I touch even his garments, I will be made well." ²⁹ And immediately the flow of blood dried up, and she felt in her body that she was healed of her disease. ³⁰ And Jesus, perceiving in himself that power had gone out from him, immediately turned about in the crowd and said, "Who touched my garments?" ³¹ And his disciples said to him, "You see the crowd pressing around you, and yet you say, 'Who touched me?'" ³² And he looked around to see who had done it. ³³ But the woman, knowing what had happened to her, came in fear and trembling and fell down before him and told him the whole truth. ³⁴ And he said to her, "Daughter, your faith has made you well; go in peace, and be healed of your disease."

³⁵ While he was still speaking, there came from the ruler's house some who said, "Your daughter is dead. Why trouble the Teacher any further?" ³⁶ But overhearing what they said, Jesus said to the ruler of the synagogue, "Do not fear, only believe." ³⁷ And he allowed no one to follow him except Peter and James and John the brother of James. ³⁸ They came to the house of the ruler of the synagogue, and Jesus saw a commotion, people weeping and wailing loudly. ³⁹ And when he had entered, he said to them, "Why are you making a commotion and weeping? The child is not dead but sleeping." ⁴⁰ And they laughed at him. But he put them all outside and took the child's father and mother and those who were with him and went in where the child was. ⁴¹ Taking her by the hand he said to her, "Talitha cumi," which means, "Little girl, I say to you, arise." ⁴² And immediately the girl got up and began walking (for she was twelve years of age), and they were immediately overcome with amazement. ⁴³ And he strictly charged them that no one should know this, and told them to give her something to eat.

Jesus Rejected at Nazareth

6 He went away from there and came to his hometown, and his disciples followed him. ² And on the Sabbath he began to teach in the synagogue, and many who heard him were astonished, saying, "Where did this man get these things? What is the wisdom given to him? How are such mighty works done by his hands? ³ Is not this the carpenter, the son of Mary and brother

of James and Joses and Judas and Simon? And are not his sisters here with us?" And they took offense at him. **4** And Jesus said to them, "A prophet is not without honor, except in his hometown and among his relatives and in his own household." **5** And he could do no mighty work there, except that he laid his hands on a few sick people and healed them. **6** And he marveled because of their unbelief.

And he went about among the villages teaching.

Jesus Sends Out the Twelve Apostles

7 And he called the twelve and began to send them out two by two, and gave them authority over the unclean spirits. **8** He charged them to take nothing for their journey except a staff—no bread, no bag, no money in their belts— **9** but to wear sandals and not put on two tunics. **10** And he said to them, "Whenever you enter a house, stay there until you depart from there. **11** And if any place will not receive you and they will not listen to you, when you leave, shake off the dust that is on your feet as a testimony against them." **12** So they went out and proclaimed that people should repent. **13** And they cast out many demons and anointed with oil many who were sick and healed them.

The Death of John the Baptist

14 King Herod heard of it, for Jesus' name had become known. Some said, "John the Baptist has been raised from the dead. That is why these miraculous powers are at work in him." **15** But others said, "He is Elijah." And others said, "He is a prophet, like one of the prophets of old." **16** But when Herod heard of it, he said, "John, whom I beheaded, has been raised." **17** For it was Herod who had sent and seized John and bound him in prison for the sake of Herodias, his brother Philip's wife, because he had married her. **18** For John had been saying to Herod, "It is not lawful for you to have your brother's wife." **19** And Herodias had a grudge against him and wanted to put him to death. But she could not, **20** for Herod feared John, knowing that he was a righteous and holy man, and he kept him safe. When he heard him, he was greatly perplexed, and yet he heard him gladly.

21 But an opportunity came when Herod on his birthday gave a banquet for his nobles and military commanders and the leading men of Galilee. **22** For when Herodias's daughter came in and danced, she pleased Herod and his guests. And the king said to the girl, "Ask me for whatever you wish, and I will give it to you." **23** And he vowed to her, "Whatever you ask me, I will give you, up to half of my kingdom." **24** And she went out and said to her mother, "For what should I ask?" And she said, "The head of John the Baptist." **25** And she came in immediately with haste to the king and asked, saying, "I want you to give me at once the head of John the Baptist on a platter." **26** And the king was exceedingly sorry, but because of his oaths and his guests he did not want to break his word to her. **27** And immediately the king sent an executioner with orders to bring John's head. He went and beheaded

GETTING THE MESSAGE

Shake the dust from your feet.
In ancient times, when Jews returned from a Gentile area, they would sometimes shake the dust off their feet (6:11) to avoid contamination from Gentiles. The act of shaking off the dust illustrates that people who reject God's message are accountable to God alone.

him in the prison **28** and brought his head on a platter and gave it to the girl, and the girl gave it to her mother. **29** When his disciples heard of it, they came and took his body and laid it in a tomb.

Jesus Feeds the Five Thousand

30 The apostles returned to Jesus and told him all that they had done and taught. **31** And he said to them, "Come away by yourselves to a desolate place and rest a while." For many were coming and going, and they had no leisure even to eat. **32** And they went away in the boat to a desolate place by themselves. **33** Now many saw them going and recognized them, and they ran there on foot from all the towns and got there ahead of them. **34** When he went ashore he saw a great crowd, and he had compassion on them, because they were like sheep without a shepherd. And he began to teach them many things. **35** And when

it grew late, his disciples came to him and said, "This is a desolate place, and the hour is now late. **36** Send them away to go into the surrounding countryside and villages and buy themselves something to eat." **37** But he answered them, "You give them something to eat." And they said to him, "Shall we go and buy two hundred denarii worth of bread and give it to them to eat?" **38** And he said to them, "How many loaves do you have? Go and see." And when they had found out,

---

HEROD ANTIPAS

Herod Antipas, son of Herod the Great, was Tetrarch of Galilee during the time of Christ. Although married, Herod fell in love with Herodias, the wife of his half brother, Philip. When Herod and Herodias divorced their spouses and married each other, John the Baptist strongly opposed their adultery. This enraged Herodias, prompting Herod to seize John and put him in prison. He was afraid to take John's life, however, recognizing him as a holy man. Herod finally gave in to Herodias and had John beheaded, but doing so haunted his conscience; later, hearing about the miracles Jesus was performing, Herod feared that it was actually John, resurrected from the dead. Herod participated in the trial of Jesus, mocking him before sending him back to Pilate.

KEY REFERENCE: LUKE 23:11

---

they said, "Five, and two fish." **39** Then he commanded them all to sit down in groups on the green grass. **40** So they sat down in groups, by hundreds and by fifties. **41** And taking the five loaves and the two fish he looked up to heaven and said a blessing and broke the loaves and gave them to the disciples to set before the people. And he divided the two fish among them all. **42** And they all ate and were satisfied. **43** And they took up twelve baskets full of broken pieces and of the fish. **44** And those who ate the loaves were five thousand men.

Jesus Walks on the Water

45 Immediately he made his disciples get into the boat and go before him to the other side, to Bethsaida, while he dismissed the crowd. **46** And after he had taken leave of them, he went up on the mountain to pray. **47** And when evening came, the boat was out on the sea, and he was alone on the land. **48** And he saw that they were making headway painfully, for the wind was against them. And about the fourth watch of the night[1] he came to them, walking on the sea. He meant to pass by them, **49** but when they saw him walking on the sea they thought it was a ghost, and cried out, **50** for they all saw him and were terrified. But immediately he spoke to them and said, "Take heart; it is I. Do not be afraid." **51** And he got into the boat with them, and the wind ceased. And they were utterly astounded, **52** for they did not understand about the loaves, but their hearts were hardened.

Jesus Heals the Sick in Gennesaret

53 When they had crossed over, they came to land at Gennesaret and moored to the shore. **54** And when they got out of the boat, the people immediately recognized him **55** and ran about the whole region and began to bring the sick people on their beds to wherever they heard he was. **56** And wherever he came, in villages, cities, or countryside, they laid the sick in the marketplaces and implored him that they might touch even the fringe of his garment. And as many as touched it were made well.

Traditions and Commandments

7 Now when the Pharisees gathered to him, with some of the scribes who had come from Jerusalem, **2** they saw that some of his disciples ate with hands that were defiled, that is, unwashed. **3** (For the Pharisees and all the Jews do not eat unless they wash their hands properly, holding to the tradition of the elders, **4** and when they come from the marketplace, they do not eat unless they wash. And there are many other traditions that they observe, such as the washing of cups and pots and copper vessels and dining couches.) **5** And the

---

[1] That is, between 3 A.M. and 6 A.M.

Pharisees and the scribes asked him, "Why do your disciples not walk according to the tradition of the elders, but eat with defiled hands?" **6** And he said to them, "Well did Isaiah prophesy of you hypocrites, as it is written,

> "'This people honors me with their lips,
>   but their heart is far from me;
> **7**   in vain do they worship me,
>   teaching as doctrines the com-
>   mandments of men.'

8 You leave the commandment of God and hold to the tradition of men."

9 And he said to them, "You have a fine way of rejecting the commandment of God in order to establish your tradition! **10** For Moses said, 'Honor your father and your mother'; and, 'Whoever reviles father or mother must surely die.' **11** But you say, 'If a man tells his father or his mother, "Whatever you would have gained from me is Corban"' (that is, given to God) — **12** then you no longer permit him to do anything for his father or mother, **13** thus making void the word of God by your tradition that you have handed down. And many such things you do."

What Defiles a Person

14 And he called the people to him again and said to them, "Hear me, all of you, and understand: **15** There is nothing outside a person that by going into him can defile him, but the things that come out of a person are what defile him." **17** And when he had entered the house and left the people, his disciples asked him about the parable. **18** And he said to them, "Then are you also without understanding? Do you not see that whatever goes into a person from outside cannot defile him, **19** since it enters not his heart but his stomach, and is expelled?" (Thus he declared all foods clean.) **20** And he said, "What comes out of a person is what defiles him. **21** For from within, out of the heart of man, come evil thoughts, sexual immorality, theft, murder, adultery, **22** coveting, wickedness, deceit, sensuality, envy, slander, pride, foolishness. **23** All these evil things come from within, and they defile a person."

The Syrophoenician Woman's Faith

24 And from there he arose and went away to the region of Tyre and Sidon. And he entered a house and did not want anyone to know, yet he could not be hidden. **25** But immediately a woman whose little daughter had an unclean spirit heard of him and came and fell down at his feet. **26** Now the woman was a Gentile, a Syrophoenician by birth. And she begged him to cast the demon out of her daughter. **27** And he said to her, "Let the children be fed first, for it is not right to take the children's bread and throw it to the dogs." **28** But she answered him, "Yes, Lord; yet even the dogs under the table eat the children's crumbs." **29** And he said to her, "For this statement you may go your way; the demon has left your daughter." **30** And she went home and found the child lying in bed and the demon gone.

Jesus Heals a Deaf Man

31 Then he returned from the region of Tyre and went through Sidon to the Sea of Galilee,

GETTING THE MESSAGE

What is "Corban"? Corban (7:11) literally means "dedicated to God." Jewish tradition said that money set aside for the care of one's parents could be given to the temple instead. Jesus said that this tradition allowed people to avoid honoring their parents as the law required.

in the region of the Decapolis. **32** And they brought to him a man who was deaf and had a speech impediment, and they begged him to lay his hand on him. **33** And taking him aside from the crowd privately, he put his fingers into his ears, and after spitting touched his tongue. **34** And looking up to heaven, he sighed and said to him, "Ephphatha," that is, "Be opened." **35** And his ears were opened, his tongue was released, and he spoke plainly. **36** And Jesus charged them to tell no one. But the more he charged them, the more zealously they proclaimed it. **37** And they were astonished beyond measure, saying, "He has done all things well. He even makes the deaf hear and the mute speak."

Jesus Feeds the Four Thousand

8 In those days, when again a great crowd had gathered, and they had nothing to eat, he called his disciples to him and said to them, ²"I have compassion on the crowd, because they have been with me now three days and have nothing to eat. ³And if I send them away hungry to their homes, they will faint on the way. And some of them have come from far away." ⁴And his disciples answered him, "How can one feed these people with bread here in this desolate place?" ⁵And he asked them, "How many loaves do you have?" They said, "Seven." ⁶And he directed the crowd to sit down on the ground. And he took the seven loaves, and having given thanks, he broke them and gave them to his disciples to set before the people; and they set them before the crowd. ⁷And they had a few small fish. And having blessed them, he said that these also should be set before them. ⁸And they ate and were satisfied. And they took up the broken pieces left over, seven baskets full. ⁹And there were about four thousand people. And

> ### GETTING THE MESSAGE
>
> **A diet of bread.** For many of the poorer people in New Testament times, bread might be their entire meal. Jesus called himself the "bread of life."

he sent them away. ¹⁰And immediately he got into the boat with his disciples and went to the district of Dalmanutha.

The Pharisees Demand a Sign

¹¹The Pharisees came and began to argue with him, seeking from him a sign from heaven to test him. ¹²And he sighed deeply in his spirit and said, "Why does this generation seek a sign? Truly, I say to you, no sign will be given to this generation." ¹³And he left them, got into the boat again, and went to the other side.

The Leaven of the Pharisees and Herod

¹⁴Now they had forgotten to bring bread, and they had only one loaf with them in the boat. ¹⁵And he cautioned them, saying, "Watch out; beware of the leaven of the Pharisees and the leaven of Herod." ¹⁶And they began discussing with one another the fact that they had no bread. ¹⁷And Jesus, aware of this, said to them, "Why are you discussing the fact that you have no bread?

Do you not yet perceive or understand? Are your hearts hardened? ¹⁸Having eyes do you not see, and having ears do you not hear? And do you not remember? ¹⁹When I broke the five loaves for the five thousand, how many baskets full of broken pieces did you take up?" They said to him, "Twelve." ²⁰"And the seven for the four thousand, how many baskets full of broken pieces did you take up?" And they said to him, "Seven." ²¹And he said to them, "Do you not yet understand?"

Jesus Heals a Blind Man at Bethsaida

²²And they came to Bethsaida. And some people brought to him a blind man and begged him to touch him. ²³And he took the blind man by the hand and led him out of the village, and when he had spit on his eyes and laid his hands on him, he asked him, "Do you see anything?" ²⁴And he looked up and said, "I see people, but they look like trees, walking." ²⁵Then Jesus laid his hands on his eyes again; and he opened his eyes, his sight was restored, and he saw everything clearly. ²⁶And he sent him to his home, saying, "Do not even enter the village."

Peter Confesses Jesus as the Christ

²⁷And Jesus went on with his disciples to the villages of Caesarea Philippi. And on the way he asked his disciples, "Who do people say that I am?" ²⁸And they told him, "John the Baptist; and others say, Elijah; and others, one of the prophets." ²⁹And he asked them, "But who do you say that I am?" Peter answered him, "You are the Christ." ³⁰And he strictly charged them to tell no one about him.

Jesus Foretells His Death and Resurrection

³¹And he began to teach them that the Son of Man must suffer many things and be rejected by the elders and the chief priests and the scribes and be killed, and after three days rise again. ³²And he said this plainly. And Peter took him aside and began to rebuke him. ³³But turning and seeing his disciples, he rebuked Peter and said, "Get behind me, Satan! For you are not setting your mind on the things of God, but on the things of man."

³⁴And calling the crowd to him with his disciples, he said to them, "If anyone would come after me, let him deny himself and take up his cross and follow me.

35 For whoever would save his life will lose it, but whoever loses his life for my sake and the gospel's will save it. **36** For what does it profit a man to gain the whole world and forfeit his soul? **37** For what can a man give in return for his soul? **38** For whoever is ashamed of me and of my words in this adulterous and sinful generation, of him will the Son of Man also be ashamed when he comes in the glory of his Father with the holy angels."

9 And he said to them, "Truly, I say to you, there are some standing here who will not taste death until they see the kingdom of God after it has come with power."

The Transfiguration

2 And after six days Jesus took with him Peter and James and John, and led them up a high mountain by themselves. And he was transfigured before them, **3** and his clothes became radiant, intensely white, as no one on earth could bleach them. **4** And there appeared to them Elijah with Moses, and they were talking with Jesus. **5** And Peter said to Jesus, "Rabbi,[1] it is good that we are here. Let us make three tents, one for you and one for Moses and one for Elijah." **6** For he did not know what to say, for they were terrified. **7** And a cloud overshadowed them, and a voice came out of the cloud, "This is my beloved Son; listen to him." **8** And suddenly, looking around, they no longer saw anyone with them but Jesus only.

9 And as they were coming down the mountain, he charged them to tell no one what they had seen, until the Son of Man had risen from the dead. **10** So they kept the matter to themselves, questioning what this rising from the dead might mean. **11** And they asked him, "Why do the scribes say that first Elijah must come?" **12** And he said to them, "Elijah does come first to restore all things. And how is it written of the Son of Man that he should suffer many things and be treated with contempt? **13** But I tell you that Elijah has come, and they did to him whatever they pleased, as it is written of him."

Jesus Heals a Boy with an Unclean Spirit

14 And when they came to the disciples, they saw a great crowd around them, and scribes arguing with them. **15** And imme-diately all the crowd, when they saw him, were greatly amazed and ran up to him and greeted him. **16** And he asked them, "What are you arguing about with them?" **17** And someone from the crowd answered him, "Teacher, I brought my son to you, for he has a spirit that makes him mute. **18** And whenever it seizes him, it throws him down, and he foams and grinds his teeth and becomes rigid. So I asked your disciples to cast it out, and they were not able." **19** And he answered them, "O faithless generation, how long am I to be with you? How long am I to bear with you? Bring him to me." **20** And they brought the boy to him. And when the spirit saw him, immediately it convulsed the boy, and he fell on the ground and rolled about, foaming at the mouth. **21** And Jesus asked his father, "How long has this been happening to him?" And he said, "From childhood. **22** And it has

---

GETTING THE MESSAGE

A voice from the cloud? In the Bible, clouds are often associated with the presence of God and the mystery and holiness surrounding him (9:7). The prophet Nahum said, "clouds are the dust of his feet" (Nah. 1:3).

---

often cast him into fire and into water, to destroy him. But if you can do anything, have compassion on us and help us." **23** And Jesus said to him, "'If you can'! All things are possible for one who believes." **24** Immediately the father of the child cried out and said, "I believe; help my unbelief!" **25** And when Jesus saw that a crowd came running together, he rebuked the unclean spirit, saying to it, "You mute and deaf spirit, I command you, come out of him and never enter him again." **26** And after crying out and convulsing him terribly, it came out, and the boy was like a corpse, so that most of them said, "He is dead." **27** But Jesus took him by the hand and lifted him up, and he arose. **28** And when he had entered the house, his disciples asked him privately, "Why could we not cast it out?" **29** And he said to them, "This kind cannot be driven out by anything but prayer."

---

[1] Rabbi means *my teacher*, or *my master*

Jesus Again Foretells Death, Resurrection

³⁰ They went on from there and passed through Galilee. And he did not want anyone to know, ³¹ for he was teaching his disciples, saying to them, "The Son of Man is going to be delivered into the hands of men, and they will kill him. And when he is killed, after three days he will rise." ³² But they did not understand the saying, and were afraid to ask him.

Who Is the Greatest?

³³ And they came to Capernaum. And when he was in the house he asked them, "What were you discussing on the way?" ³⁴ But they kept silent, for on the way they had argued with one another about who was the greatest. ³⁵ And he sat down and called the twelve. And he said to them, "If anyone would be first, he must be last of all and servant of all." ³⁶ And he took a child and put him in the midst of them, and taking him in his arms, he said to them, ³⁷ "Whoever receives one such child in my name receives me, and whoever receives me, receives not me but him who sent me."

Anyone Not Against Us Is for Us

³⁸ John said to him, "Teacher, we saw someone casting out demons in your name, and we tried to stop him, because he was not following us." ³⁹ But Jesus said, "Do not stop him, for no one who does a mighty work in my name will be able soon afterward to speak evil of me. ⁴⁰ For the one who is not against us is for us. ⁴¹ For truly, I say to you, whoever gives you a cup of water to drink because you belong to Christ will by no means lose his reward.

Temptations to Sin

⁴² "Whoever causes one of these little ones who believe in me to sin, it would be better for him if a great millstone were hung around his neck and he were thrown into the sea. ⁴³ And if your hand causes you to sin, cut it off. It is better for you to enter life crippled than with two hands to go to hell, to the unquenchable fire. ⁴⁵ And if your foot causes you to sin, cut it off. It is better for you to enter life lame than with two feet to be thrown into hell. ⁴⁷ And if your eye causes you to sin, tear it out. It is better for you to enter the kingdom of God with one eye than with two eyes to be thrown into hell,

⁴⁸ 'where their worm does not die and the fire is not quenched.' ⁴⁹ For everyone will be salted with fire. ⁵⁰ Salt is good, but if the salt has lost its saltiness, how will you make it salty again? Have salt in yourselves, and be at peace with one another."

Teaching About Divorce

10 And he left there and went to the region of Judea and beyond the Jordan, and crowds gathered to him again. And again, as was his custom, he taught them.

² And Pharisees came up and in order to test him asked, "Is it lawful for a man to divorce his wife?" ³ He answered them, "What did Moses command you?" ⁴ They said, "Moses allowed a man to write a certificate of divorce and to send her away." ⁵ And Jesus said to them, "Because of your hardness of heart he wrote you this commandment. ⁶ But from the beginning of creation, 'God made them male and female.' ⁷ 'Therefore a man shall leave his father and mother and hold fast to his wife, ⁸ and the two shall become one flesh.' So they are no longer two but one flesh. ⁹ What therefore God has joined together, let not man separate."

¹⁰ And in the house the disciples asked him again about this matter. ¹¹ And he said to them, "Whoever divorces his wife and marries another commits adultery against her, ¹² and if she divorces her husband and marries another, she commits adultery."

Let the Children Come to Me

¹³ And they were bringing children to him that he might touch them, and the disciples rebuked them. ¹⁴ But when Jesus saw it, he was indignant and said to them, "Let the children come to me; do not hinder them, for to such belongs the kingdom of God. ¹⁵ Truly, I say to you, whoever does not receive the kingdom of God like a child shall not enter it." ¹⁶ And he took them in his arms and blessed them, laying his hands on them.

The Rich Young Man

¹⁷ And as he was setting out on his journey, a man ran up and knelt before him and asked him, "Good Teacher, what must I do to inherit eternal life?" ¹⁸ And Jesus said to him, "Why do you call me good? No one is good except God alone. ¹⁹ You know the commandments: 'Do not murder, Do not commit adultery, Do not steal, Do not bear

false witness, Do not defraud, Honor your father and mother.'" [20] And he said to him, "Teacher, all these I have kept from my youth." [21] And Jesus, looking at him, loved him, and said to him, "You lack one thing: go, sell all that you have and give to the poor, and you will have treasure in heaven; and come, follow me." [22] Disheartened by the saying, he went away sorrowful, for he had great possessions.

[23] And Jesus looked around and said to his disciples, "How difficult it will be for those who have wealth to enter the kingdom of God!" [24] And the disciples were amazed at his words. But Jesus said to them again, "Children, how difficult it is to enter the kingdom of God! [25] It is easier for a camel to go through the eye of a needle than for a rich person to enter the kingdom of God." [26] And they were exceedingly astonished, and said to him, "Then who can be saved?" [27] Jesus looked at them and said, "With man it is impossible, but not with God. For all things are possible with God." [28] Peter began to say to him, "See, we have left everything and followed you." [29] Jesus said, "Truly, I say to you, there is no one who has left house or brothers or sisters or mother or father or children or lands, for my sake and for the gospel, [30] who will not receive a hundredfold now in this time, houses and brothers and sisters and mothers and children and lands, with persecutions, and in the age to come eternal life. [31] But many who are first will be last, and the last first."

Jesus Foretells His Death a Third Time

[32] And they were on the road, going up to Jerusalem, and Jesus was walking ahead of them. And they were amazed, and those who followed were afraid. And taking the twelve again, he began to tell them what was to happen to him, [33] saying, "See, we are going up to Jerusalem, and the Son of Man will be delivered over to the chief priests and the scribes, and they will condemn him to death and deliver him over to the Gentiles. [34] And they will mock him and spit on him, and flog him and kill him. And after three days he will rise."

The Request of James and John

[35] And James and John, the sons of Zebedee, came up to him and said to him,

"Teacher, we want you to do for us whatever we ask of you." [36] And he said to them, "What do you want me to do for you?" [37] And they said to him, "Grant us to sit, one at your right hand and one at your left, in your glory." [38] Jesus said to them, "You do not know what you are asking. Are you able to drink the cup that I drink, or to be baptized with the baptism with which I am baptized?" [39] And they said to him, "We are able." And Jesus said to them, "The cup that I drink you will drink, and with the baptism with which I am baptized, you will be baptized, [40] but to sit at my right hand or at my left is not mine to grant, but it is for those for whom it has been prepared." [41] And when the ten heard it, they began to be indignant at James and John. [42] And Jesus called them to him and said to them, "You know that those who are considered rulers of the Gentiles lord it over them, and their great ones exercise authority over them. [43] But it shall not be so among

GETTING THE MESSAGE

Blindness was a common condition in biblical times. Because they were unable to work, people who were blind often became beggars (10:46–52; see Luke 18:35).

you. But whoever would be great among you must be your servant, [44] and whoever would be first among you must be slave[1] of all. [45] For even the Son of Man came not to be served but to serve, and to give his life as a ransom for many."

Jesus Heals Blind Bartimaeus

[46] And they came to Jericho. And as he was leaving Jericho with his disciples and a great crowd, Bartimaeus, a blind beggar, the son of Timaeus, was sitting by the roadside. [47] And when he heard that it was Jesus of Nazareth, he began to cry out and say, "Jesus, Son of David, have mercy on me!" [48] And many rebuked him, telling him to be silent. But he cried out all the more, "Son of David, have mercy on me!" [49] And Jesus stopped and said, "Call him." And they called the blind man, saying to him, "Take heart. Get up; he is calling you." [50] And throwing off his cloak, he sprang up

---

[1] Greek *bondservant* (*doulos*; see Preface)

and came to Jesus. ⁵¹ And Jesus said to him, "What do you want me to do for you?" And the blind man said to him, "Rabbi, let me recover my sight." ⁵² And Jesus said to him, "Go your way; your faith has made you well." And immediately he recovered his sight and followed him on the way.

The Triumphal Entry

11 Now when they drew near to Jerusalem, to Bethphage and Bethany, at the Mount of Olives, Jesus sent two of his disciples ² and said to them, "Go into the village in front of you, and immediately as you enter it you will find a colt tied, on which no one has ever sat. Untie it and bring it. ³ If anyone says to you, 'Why are you doing this?' say, 'The Lord has need of it and will send it back here immediately.'" ⁴ And they went away and found a colt tied at a door outside in the street, and they untied it. ⁵ And some of those standing there said to them, "What

GETTING THE MESSAGE

Fig trees (11:13) reach an average height of around 10 to 30 feet (3 to 9 m). Figs are harvested twice a year, once in spring or early summer and again in autumn. Figs could be eaten straight from the tree, dried, or made into cakes for the winter.

are you doing, untying the colt?" ⁶ And they told them what Jesus had said, and they let them go. ⁷ And they brought the colt to Jesus and threw their cloaks on it, and he sat on it. ⁸ And many spread their cloaks on the road, and others spread leafy branches that they had cut from the fields. ⁹ And those who went before and those who followed were shouting, "Hosanna! Blessed is he who comes in the name of the Lord! ¹⁰ Blessed is the coming kingdom of our father David! Hosanna in the highest!"

¹¹ And he entered Jerusalem and went into the temple. And when he had looked around at everything, as it was already late, he went out to Bethany with the twelve.

Jesus Curses the Fig Tree

¹² On the following day, when they came from Bethany, he was hungry. ¹³ And seeing in the distance a fig tree in leaf, he went to see if he could find anything on it. When he

came to it, he found nothing but leaves, for it was not the season for figs. ¹⁴ And he said to it, "May no one ever eat fruit from you again." And his disciples heard it.

Jesus Cleanses the Temple

¹⁵ And they came to Jerusalem. And he entered the temple and began to drive out those who sold and those who bought in the temple, and he overturned the tables of the money-changers and the seats of those who sold pigeons. ¹⁶ And he would not allow anyone to carry anything through the temple. ¹⁷ And he was teaching them and saying to them, "Is it not written, 'My house shall be called a house of prayer for all the nations'? But you have made it a den of robbers." ¹⁸ And the chief priests and the scribes heard it and were seeking a way to destroy him, for they feared him, because all the crowd was astonished at his teaching. ¹⁹ And when evening came they went out of the city.

The Lesson from the Withered Fig Tree

²⁰ As they passed by in the morning, they saw the fig tree withered away to its roots. ²¹ And Peter remembered and said to him, "Rabbi, look! The fig tree that you cursed has withered." ²² And Jesus answered them, "Have faith in God. ²³ Truly, I say to you, whoever says to this mountain, 'Be taken up and thrown into the sea,' and does not doubt in his heart, but believes that what he says will come to pass, it will be done for him. ²⁴ Therefore I tell you, whatever you ask in prayer, believe that you have received it, and it will be yours. ²⁵ And whenever you stand praying, forgive, if you have anything against anyone, so that your Father also who is in heaven may forgive you your trespasses."

The Authority of Jesus Challenged

²⁷ And they came again to Jerusalem. And as he was walking in the temple, the chief priests and the scribes and the elders came to him, ²⁸ and they said to him, "By what authority are you doing these things, or who gave you this authority to do them?" ²⁹ Jesus said to them, "I will ask you one question; answer me, and I will tell you by what authority I do these things. ³⁰ Was the baptism of John from heaven or from man? Answer me." ³¹ And they discussed it with one another, saying, "If we say, 'From

heaven,' he will say, 'Why then did you not believe him?' ³² But shall we say, 'From man'?"—they were afraid of the people, for they all held that John really was a prophet. ³³ So they answered Jesus, "We do not know." And Jesus said to them, "Neither will I tell you by what authority I do these things."

The Parable of the Tenants

12 And he began to speak to them in parables. "A man planted a vineyard and put a fence around it and dug a pit for the winepress and built a tower, and leased it to tenants and went into another country. ² When the season came, he sent a servant to the tenants to get from them some of the fruit of the vineyard. ³ And they took him and beat him and sent him away empty-handed. ⁴ Again he sent to them another servant, and they struck him on the head and treated him shamefully. ⁵ And he sent another, and him they killed. And so with many others: some they beat, and some they killed. ⁶ He had still one other, a beloved son. Finally he sent him to them, saying, 'They will respect my son.' ⁷ But those tenants said to one another, 'This is the heir. Come, let us kill him, and the inheritance will be ours.' ⁸ And they took him and killed him and threw him out of the vineyard. ⁹ What will the owner of the vineyard do? He will come and destroy the tenants and give the vineyard to others. ¹⁰ Have you not read this Scripture:

" 'The stone that the builders rejected
    has become the cornerstone;
¹¹   this was the Lord's doing,
    and it is marvelous in our eyes'?"

¹² And they were seeking to arrest him but feared the people, for they perceived that he had told the parable against them. So they left him and went away.

Paying Taxes to Caesar

¹³ And they sent to him some of the Pharisees and some of the Herodians, to trap him in his talk. ¹⁴ And they came and said to him, "Teacher, we know that you are true and do not care about anyone's opinion. For you are not swayed by appearances, but truly teach the way of God. Is it lawful to pay taxes to Caesar, or not? Should we pay them, or should we not?" ¹⁵ But, knowing their hypocrisy, he said to them, "Why put me to the test? Bring me a denarius and let me look

at it." ¹⁶ And they brought one. And he said to them, "Whose likeness and inscription is this?" They said to him, "Caesar's." ¹⁷ Jesus said to them, "Render to Caesar the things that are Caesar's, and to God the things that are God's." And they marveled at him.

The Sadducees Ask About the Resurrection

¹⁸ And Sadducees came to him, who say that there is no resurrection. And they asked him a question, saying, ¹⁹ "Teacher, Moses wrote for us that if a man's brother dies and leaves a wife, but leaves no child, the man must take the widow and raise up offspring for his brother. ²⁰ There were seven brothers; the first took a wife, and when he died left no offspring. ²¹ And the second took her, and died, leaving no offspring. And the third

GETTING THE MESSAGE

The Sadducees were a small but powerful group of Jewish leaders who did not believe in the resurrection (12:18). This may have been because of their emphasis on the Pentateuch (Genesis–Deuteronomy), which does not seem to explicitly mention the resurrection. But Jesus showed them that the idea of resurrection can, in fact, be found in the Pentateuch (Mark 12:26–27).

likewise. ²² And the seven left no offspring. Last of all the woman also died. ²³ In the resurrection, when they rise again, whose wife will she be? For the seven had her as wife."

²⁴ Jesus said to them, "Is this not the reason you are wrong, because you know neither the Scriptures nor the power of God? ²⁵ For when they rise from the dead, they neither marry nor are given in marriage, but are like angels in heaven. ²⁶ And as for the dead being raised, have you not read in the book of Moses, in the passage about the bush, how God spoke to him, saying, 'I am the God of Abraham, and the God of Isaac, and the God of Jacob'? ²⁷ He is not God of the dead, but of the living. You are quite wrong."

The Great Commandment

²⁸ And one of the scribes came up and heard them disputing with one another,

and seeing that he answered them well, asked him, "Which commandment is the most important of all?" **29** Jesus answered, "The most important is, 'Hear, O Israel: The Lord our God, the Lord is one. **30** And you shall love the Lord your God with all your heart and with all your soul and with all your mind and with all your strength.' **31** The second is this: 'You shall love your neighbor as yourself.' There is no other commandment greater than these." **32** And the scribe said to him, "You are right, Teacher. You have truly said that he is one, and there is no other besides him. **33** And to love him with all the heart and with all the understanding and with all the strength, and to love one's neighbor as oneself, is much more than all whole burnt offerings and sacrifices." **34** And when Jesus saw that he answered wisely, he said to him, "You are not far from the kingdom

---

GETTING THE MESSAGE

The Mount of Olives (13:3) gets its name from the olive trees that grow there in abundance. Olive trees were highly valued in Israel as a source of oil and wood. Gethsemane, which was on the Mount of Olives, means "oil press."

---

of God." And after that no one dared to ask him any more questions.

Whose Son Is the Christ?

35 And as Jesus taught in the temple, he said, "How can the scribes say that the Christ is the son of David? **36** David himself, in the Holy Spirit, declared,

" 'The Lord said to my Lord,
  "Sit at my right hand,
      until I put your enemies under your
          feet." '

37 David himself calls him Lord. So how is he his son?" And the great throng heard him gladly.

Beware of the Scribes

38 And in his teaching he said, "Beware of the scribes, who like to walk around in long robes and like greetings in the marketplaces **39** and have the best seats in the synagogues

and the places of honor at feasts, **40** who devour widows' houses and for a pretense make long prayers. They will receive the greater condemnation."

The Widow's Offering

41 And he sat down opposite the treasury and watched the people putting money into the offering box. Many rich people put in large sums. **42** And a poor widow came and put in two small copper coins, which make a penny.[1] **43** And he called his disciples to him and said to them, "Truly, I say to you, this poor widow has put in more than all those who are contributing to the offering box. **44** For they all contributed out of their abundance, but she out of her poverty has put in everything she had, all she had to live on."

Jesus Foretells Destruction of the Temple

13 And as he came out of the temple, one of his disciples said to him, "Look, Teacher, what wonderful stones and what wonderful buildings!" **2** And Jesus said to him, "Do you see these great buildings? There will not be left here one stone upon another that will not be thrown down."

Signs of the Close of the Age

3 And as he sat on the Mount of Olives opposite the temple, Peter and James and John and Andrew asked him privately, **4** "Tell us, when will these things be, and what will be the sign when all these things are about to be accomplished?" **5** And Jesus began to say to them, "See that no one leads you astray. **6** Many will come in my name, saying, 'I am he!' and they will lead many astray. **7** And when you hear of wars and rumors of wars, do not be alarmed. This must take place, but the end is not yet. **8** For nation will rise against nation, and kingdom against kingdom. There will be earthquakes in various places; there will be famines. These are but the beginning of the birth pains.

9 "But be on your guard. For they will deliver you over to councils, and you will be beaten in synagogues, and you will stand before governors and kings for my sake, to bear witness before them. **10** And the gospel must first be proclaimed to all nations. **11** And when they bring you to trial and deliver you over, do not be anxious beforehand what

---

[1] The Greek word refers to about 1/64 of a day's pay for a worker

you are to say, but say whatever is given you in that hour, for it is not you who speak, but the Holy Spirit. **12** And brother will deliver brother over to death, and the father his child, and children will rise against parents and have them put to death. **13** And you will be hated by all for my name's sake. But the one who endures to the end will be saved.

The Abomination of Desolation

14 "But when you see the abomination of desolation standing where he ought not to be (let the reader understand), then let those who are in Judea flee to the mountains. **15** Let the one who is on the housetop not go down, nor enter his house, to take anything out, **16** and let the one who is in the field not turn back to take his cloak. **17** And alas for women who are pregnant and for those who are nursing infants in those days! **18** Pray that it may not happen in winter. **19** For in those days there will be such tribulation as has not been from the beginning of the creation that God created until now, and never will be. **20** And if the Lord had not cut short the days, no human being would be saved. But for the sake of the elect, whom he chose, he shortened the days. **21** And then if anyone says to you, 'Look, here is the Christ!' or 'Look, there he is!' do not believe it. **22** For false christs and false prophets will arise and perform signs and wonders, to lead astray, if possible, the elect. **23** But be on guard; I have told you all things beforehand.

The Coming of the Son of Man

24 "But in those days, after that tribulation, the sun will be darkened, and the moon will not give its light, **25** and the stars will be falling from heaven, and the powers in the heavens will be shaken. **26** And then they will see the Son of Man coming in clouds with great power and glory. **27** And then he will send out the angels and gather his elect from the four winds, from the ends of the earth to the ends of heaven.

The Lesson of the Fig Tree

28 "From the fig tree learn its lesson: as soon as its branch becomes tender and puts out its leaves, you know that summer is near. **29** So also, when you see these things taking place, you know that he is near, at

the very gates. **30** Truly, I say to you, this generation will not pass away until all these things take place. **31** Heaven and earth will pass away, but my words will not pass away.

No One Knows That Day or Hour

32 "But concerning that day or that hour, no one knows, not even the angels in heaven, nor the Son, but only the Father. **33** Be on guard, keep awake. For you do not know when the time will come. **34** It is like a man going on a journey, when he leaves home and puts his servants in charge, each with

his work, and commands the doorkeeper to stay awake. **35** Therefore stay awake—for you do not know when the master of the house will come, in the evening, or at midnight, or when the rooster crows,[1] or in the morning—**36** lest he come suddenly and find you asleep. **37** And what I say to you I say to all: Stay awake."

The Plot to Kill Jesus

14 It was now two days before the Passover and the Feast of Unleavened Bread. And the chief priests and the scribes were seeking how to arrest him by stealth

[1] That is, the third watch of the night, between midnight and 3 A.M.

and kill him, [2] for they said, "Not during the feast, lest there be an uproar from the people."

Jesus Anointed at Bethany

[3] And while he was at Bethany in the house of Simon the leper,[1] as he was reclining at table, a woman came with an alabaster flask of ointment of pure nard, very costly, and she broke the flask and poured it over his head. [4] There were some who said to themselves indignantly, "Why was the ointment wasted like that? [5] For this ointment could have been sold for more than three hundred denarii and given to the poor." And they scolded her. [6] But Jesus said, "Leave her alone. Why do you trouble her? She has done a beautiful thing to me. [7] For you always have the poor with you, and whenever you want, you can do good for them. But you will not always have me. [8] She has done what she could; she has anointed my body beforehand for burial. [9] And truly, I say to you, wherever the gospel is proclaimed in the whole world, what she has done will be told in memory of her."

Judas to Betray Jesus

[10] Then Judas Iscariot, who was one of the twelve, went to the chief priests in order to betray him to them. [11] And when they heard it, they were glad and promised to give him money. And he sought an opportunity to betray him.

The Passover with the Disciples

[12] And on the first day of Unleavened Bread, when they sacrificed the Passover lamb, his disciples said to him, "Where will you have us go and prepare for you to eat the Passover?" [13] And he sent two of his disciples and said to them, "Go into the city, and a man carrying a jar of water will meet you. Follow him, [14] and wherever he enters, say to the master of the house, 'The Teacher says, Where is my guest room, where I may eat the Passover with my disciples?' [15] And he will show you a large upper room furnished and ready; there prepare for us." [16] And the disciples set out and went to the city and found it just as he had told them, and they prepared the Passover.

[17] And when it was evening, he came with the twelve. [18] And as they were reclining at table and eating, Jesus said, "Truly, I say to you, one of you will betray me, one who is eating with me." [19] They began to be sorrowful and to say to him one after another, "Is it I?" [20] He said to them, "It is one of the twelve, one who is dipping bread into the dish with me. [21] For the Son of Man goes as it is written of him, but woe to that man by whom the Son of Man is betrayed! It would have been better for that man if he had not been born."

Institution of the Lord's Supper

[22] And as they were eating, he took bread, and after blessing it broke it and gave it to them, and said, "Take; this is my body." [23] And he took a cup, and when he had given thanks he gave it to them, and they all drank of it. [24] And he said to them, "This is my blood of the covenant, which is poured out for many. [25] Truly, I say to you, I will not drink again of the fruit of the vine until that day when I drink it new in the kingdom of God."

Jesus Foretells Peter's Denial

[26] And when they had sung a hymn, they went out to the Mount of Olives. [27] And Jesus said to them, "You will all fall away, for it is written, 'I will strike the shepherd, and the sheep will be scattered.' [28] But after I am raised up, I will go before you to Galilee." [29] Peter said to him, "Even though they all fall away, I will not." [30] And Jesus said to him, "Truly, I tell you, this very night, before the rooster crows twice, you will deny me three times." [31] But he said emphatically, "If I must die with you, I will not deny you." And they all said the same.

Jesus Prays in Gethsemane

[32] And they went to a place called Gethsemane. And he said to his disciples, "Sit here while I pray." [33] And he took with him Peter and James and John, and began to be greatly distressed and troubled. [34] And he said to them, "My soul is very sorrowful, even to death. Remain here and watch." [35] And going a little farther, he fell on the ground and prayed that, if it were possible, the hour might pass from him. [36] And he said, "Abba, Father, all things are possible for you. Remove this cup from me. Yet not what I will, but what you will." [37] And he came and found them sleeping, and he said to Peter, "Simon, are you asleep?

[1] *Leprosy* was a term for several skin diseases (see Leviticus 13)

Could you not watch one hour? **38** Watch and pray that you may not enter into temptation. The spirit indeed is willing, but the flesh is weak." **39** And again he went away and prayed, saying the same words. **40** And again he came and found them sleeping, for their eyes were very heavy, and they did not know what to answer him. **41** And he came the third time and said to them, "Are you still sleeping and taking your rest? It is enough; the hour has come. The Son of Man is betrayed into the hands of sinners. **42** Rise, let us be going; see, my betrayer is at hand."

Betrayal and Arrest of Jesus

43 And immediately, while he was still speaking, Judas came, one of the twelve, and with him a crowd with swords and clubs, from the chief priests and the scribes and the elders. **44** Now the betrayer had given them a sign, saying, "The one I will kiss is the man. Seize him and lead him away under guard." **45** And when he came, he went up to him at once and said, "Rabbi!" And he kissed him. **46** And they laid hands on him and seized him. **47** But one of those who stood by drew his sword and struck the servant of the high priest and cut off his ear. **48** And Jesus said to them, "Have you come out as against a robber, with swords and clubs to capture me? **49** Day after day I was with you in the temple teaching, and you did not seize me. But let the Scriptures be fulfilled." **50** And they all left him and fled.

A Young Man Flees

51 And a young man followed him, with nothing but a linen cloth about his body. And they seized him, **52** but he left the linen cloth and ran away naked.

Jesus Before the Council

53 And they led Jesus to the high priest. And all the chief priests and the elders and the scribes came together. **54** And Peter had followed him at a distance, right into the courtyard of the high priest. And he was sitting with the guards and warming himself at the fire. **55** Now the chief priests and the whole council were seeking testimony against Jesus to put him to death, but they found none. **56** For many bore false witness against him, but their testimony did not agree. **57** And some stood up and bore false witness against him, saying, **58** "We heard him say, 'I will destroy this temple that is

made with hands, and in three days I will build another, not made with hands.'" **59** Yet even about this their testimony did not agree. **60** And the high priest stood up in the midst and asked Jesus, "Have you no answer to make? What is it that these men testify against you?" **61** But he remained silent and made no answer. Again the high priest asked him, "Are you the Christ, the Son of the Blessed?" **62** And Jesus said, "I am, and you will see the Son of Man seated at the right hand of Power, and coming with the clouds of heaven." **63** And the high priest tore his garments and said, "What further witnesses do we need? **64** You have heard his blasphemy. What is your decision?" And they all condemned him as deserving death. **65** And some began to spit on him and to cover his face and to strike him, saying to him, "Prophesy!" And the guards received him with blows.

GETTING THE MESSAGE

Rabbi (14:45) literally means "my lord." The title was used to address outstanding teachers of the law. Jesus told the disciples that they were not to be called rabbi, because they, like all believers in Christ, have one true teacher—the Lord Jesus himself (Matt. 23:8).

Peter Denies Jesus

66 And as Peter was below in the courtyard, one of the servant girls of the high priest came, **67** and seeing Peter warming himself, she looked at him and said, "You also were with the Nazarene, Jesus." **68** But he denied it, saying, "I neither know nor understand what you mean." And he went out into the gateway and the rooster crowed. **69** And the servant girl saw him and began again to say to the bystanders, "This man is one of them." **70** But again he denied it. And after a little while the bystanders again said to Peter, "Certainly you are one of them, for you are a Galilean." **71** But he began to invoke a curse on himself and to swear, "I do not know this man of whom you speak." **72** And immediately the rooster crowed a second time. And Peter remembered how Jesus had said to him, "Before the rooster crows twice, you will deny me three times." And he broke down and wept.

Jesus Delivered to Pilate

15 And as soon as it was morning, the chief priests held a consultation with the elders and scribes and the whole council. And they bound Jesus and led him away and delivered him over to Pilate. ² And Pilate asked him, "Are you the King of the Jews?" And he answered him, "You have said so." ³ And the chief priests accused him of many things. ⁴ And Pilate again asked him, "Have you no answer to make? See how many charges they bring against you."

PROFILE

PONTIUS PILATE

Pontius Pilate was the Roman governor of Judea during the ministry of Jesus. This position meant that he was the only person who could either pardon a prisoner or sentence him to death. When Jesus was brought before him for judgment, Pilate recognized that Jesus was innocent and was amazed that Jesus refused to defend himself. Even Pilate's wife saw that Jesus was innocent, and warned her husband not to get involved in the case. Pilate was also aware that the Jewish leaders had turned Jesus over to him because they felt threatened by his popularity and his authoritative ministry. Despite all of these warning signs, Pilate gave in to the crowds and handed Jesus over to be crucified.

KEY REFERENCE: MARK 15:15

⁵ But Jesus made no further answer, so that Pilate was amazed.

Pilate Delivers Jesus to Be Crucified

⁶ Now at the feast he used to release for them one prisoner for whom they asked. ⁷ And among the rebels in prison, who had committed murder in the insurrection, there was a man called Barabbas. ⁸ And the crowd came up and began to ask Pilate to do as he usually did for them. ⁹ And he answered them, saying, "Do you want me to release for you the King of the Jews?" ¹⁰ For he perceived that it was out of envy

that the chief priests had delivered him up. ¹¹ But the chief priests stirred up the crowd to have him release for them Barabbas instead. ¹² And Pilate again said to them, "Then what shall I do with the man you call the King of the Jews?" ¹³ And they cried out again, "Crucify him." ¹⁴ And Pilate said to them, "Why, what evil has he done?" But they shouted all the more, "Crucify him." ¹⁵ So Pilate, wishing to satisfy the crowd, released for them Barabbas, and having scourged[1] Jesus, he delivered him to be crucified.

Jesus Is Mocked

¹⁶ And the soldiers led him away inside the palace (that is, the governor's headquarters), and they called together the whole battalion. ¹⁷ And they clothed him in a purple cloak, and twisting together a crown of thorns, they put it on him. ¹⁸ And they began to salute him, "Hail, King of the Jews!" ¹⁹ And

GETTING THE MESSAGE

Releasing prisoners (15:6) was apparently a custom the Roman governor Pilate had instituted as a means of winning favor with the Jewish people. Ironically, in this case, he ended up releasing a man convicted of rebelling against Rome.

they were striking his head with a reed and spitting on him and kneeling down in homage to him. ²⁰ And when they had mocked him, they stripped him of the purple cloak and put his own clothes on him. And they led him out to crucify him.

The Crucifixion

²¹ And they compelled a passerby, Simon of Cyrene, who was coming in from the country, the father of Alexander and Rufus, to carry his cross. ²² And they brought him to the place called Golgotha (which means Place of a Skull). ²³ And they offered him wine mixed with myrrh, but he did not take it. ²⁴ And they crucified him and divided his garments among them, casting lots for them, to decide what each should take. ²⁵ And it was the third hour[2] when they crucified him. ²⁶ And the inscription of the

[1] *Scourged* means being beaten with a whip that has metal or bone spikes in it [2] That is, 9 A.M.

charge against him read, "The King of the Jews." **27** And with him they crucified two robbers, one on his right and one on his left. **29** And those who passed by derided him, wagging their heads and saying, "Aha! You who would destroy the temple and rebuild it in three days, **30** save yourself, and come down from the cross!" **31** So also the chief priests with the scribes mocked him to one another, saying, "He saved others; he cannot save himself. **32** Let the Christ, the King of Israel, come down now from the cross that we may see and believe." Those who were crucified with him also reviled him.

The Death of Jesus

33 And when the sixth hour[1] had come, there was darkness over the whole land until the ninth hour.[2] **34** And at the ninth hour Jesus cried with a loud voice, "Eloi, Eloi, lema sabachthani?" which means, "My God, my God, why have you forsaken me?" **35** And some of the bystanders hearing it said, "Behold, he is calling Elijah." **36** And someone ran and filled a sponge with sour wine, put it on a reed and gave it to him to drink, saying, "Wait, let us see whether Elijah will come to take him down." **37** And Jesus uttered a loud cry and breathed his last. **38** And the curtain of the temple was torn in two, from top to bottom. **39** And when the centurion, who stood facing him, saw that in this way he breathed his last, he said, "Truly this man was the Son of God!"

40 There were also women looking on from a distance, among whom were Mary Magdalene, and Mary the mother of James the younger and of Joses, and Salome. **41** When he was in Galilee, they followed him and ministered to him, and there were also many other women who came up with him to Jerusalem.

Jesus Is Buried

42 And when evening had come, since it was the day of Preparation, that is, the day before the Sabbath, **43** Joseph of Arimathea, a respected member of the council, who was also himself looking for the kingdom of God, took courage and went to Pilate and asked for the body of Jesus. **44** Pilate was surprised to hear that he should have already died. And summoning the centurion, he asked him whether he was already dead. **45** And when he learned from the centurion that he was dead, he granted the corpse to Joseph. **46** And Joseph bought a linen shroud, and taking him down, wrapped him in the linen shroud and laid him in a tomb that had been cut out of the rock. And he rolled a stone against the entrance of the tomb. **47** Mary Magdalene and Mary the mother of Joses saw where he was laid.

The Resurrection

16 When the Sabbath was past, Mary Magdalene, Mary the mother of James, and Salome bought spices, so that they might go and anoint him. **2** And very early on the first day of the week, when the sun had risen, they went to the tomb. **3** And they were saying to one another, "Who will roll away the stone for us from the entrance of the tomb?" **4** And looking up, they saw

> **GETTING THE MESSAGE**
>
> **Scourging** is another term for flogging, a cruel punishment used by the Romans (15:15). Prisoners were tied to a post and beaten with a leather whip that had pieces of bone and metal attached to it. In many cases, scourging was fatal.

that the stone had been rolled back—it was very large. **5** And entering the tomb, they saw a young man sitting on the right side, dressed in a white robe, and they were alarmed. **6** And he said to them, "Do not be alarmed. You seek Jesus of Nazareth, who was crucified. He has risen; he is not here. See the place where they laid him. **7** But go, tell his disciples and Peter that he is going before you to Galilee. There you will see him, just as he told you." **8** And they went out and fled from the tomb, for trembling and astonishment had seized them, and they said nothing to anyone, for they were afraid.

[SOME OF THE EARLIEST MANUSCRIPTS DO NOT INCLUDE 16:9–20.][3]

Jesus Appears to Mary Magdalene

9 [[Now when he rose early on the first day of the week, he appeared first to Mary Magdalene, from whom he had cast out

---

[1] That is, noon [2] That is, 3 P.M. [3] See Preface

seven demons. ¹⁰ She went and told those who had been with him, as they mourned and wept. ¹¹ But when they heard that he was alive and had been seen by her, they would not believe it.

Jesus Appears to Two Disciples

¹² After these things he appeared in another form to two of them, as they were walking into the country. ¹³ And they went back and told the rest, but they did not believe them.

The Great Commission

¹⁴ Afterward he appeared to the eleven themselves as they were reclining at table, and he rebuked them for their unbelief and hardness of heart, because they had not believed those who saw him after he had risen. ¹⁵ And he said to them, "Go into all the world and proclaim the gospel to the whole creation. ¹⁶ Whoever believes and is baptized will be saved, but whoever does not believe will be condemned. ¹⁷ And these signs will accompany those who believe: in my name they will cast out demons; they will speak in new tongues; ¹⁸ they will pick up serpents with their hands; and if they drink any deadly poison, it will not hurt them; they will lay their hands on the sick, and they will recover."

¹⁹ So then the Lord Jesus, after he had spoken to them, was taken up into heaven and sat down at the right hand of God. ²⁰ And they went out and preached everywhere, while the Lord worked with them and confirmed the message by accompanying signs.]]

INTRODUCTION TO LUKE

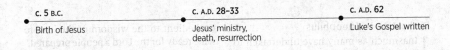

c. 5 B.C.	c. A.D. 28–33	c. A.D. 62
Birth of Jesus	Jesus' ministry, death, resurrection	Luke's Gospel written

AUTHOR, DATE, AND RECIPIENTS

Luke was a physician (Col. 4:14) and a travel companion of the apostle Paul. He wrote this Gospel and its sequel, the book of Acts. The earliest possible date of Luke–Acts is immediately after the events that Luke recorded in Acts 28, which would have been c. A.D. 62. Both Luke and Acts are addressed to "Theophilus" (Luke 1:3; Acts 1:1), about whom nothing more is known. Luke's broader audience consisted primarily of Gentile Christians like Theophilus who had already "been taught" (Luke 1:4) about Jesus.

THEME

The gospel is for all, Jews and Gentiles alike, since Jesus is the promised one of God as prophesied in the OT and as seen in God's saving activity in Jesus' life, death, and resurrection. The Christian traditions Luke's readers have received are true; by believing in Jesus Christ, the Son of God, they will receive the promised Holy Spirit whom he gives to all who follow him.

PURPOSE

Luke probably had several goals in writing: (1) to assure his readers of the truth of what they had been taught; (2) to help them understand how Israel's rejection of Jesus and the Gentiles' entrance into the kingdom of God are part of God's plan; (3) to clarify that Jesus did not teach that his bodily return would come immediately but that there would be a period between his resurrection and his return; and (4) to emphasize that they need not fear any mere earthly power such as Rome.

KEY THEMES

1. God's sovereign rule over history (13:33; 22:22, 42).

2. The arrival and actual presence (though not yet the completion) of the kingdom of God (11:2; 17:20–21; 21:34–36).

3. The coming and presence of the Holy Spirit for Jesus and his followers (1:15–17, 35; 2:25–27; 3:16, 22; 4:1, 18; 24:49).

4. The great reversal taking place in the world, in which the first are becoming last and the last are becoming first, the proud are being brought low and the humble are being exalted (1:48; 6:20–26; 13:30; 14:11).

5. Believers are to live a life of prayer and practice good stewardship with their possessions (6:12; 9:28–29; 11:1–4; 12:33–34; 18:1; 22:40).

6. The danger of riches (6:20–26; 8:14; 12:13–21; 16:10–13, 19–31).

OUTLINE

  I. The Prologue (1:1–4)

  II. The Infancy Narrative (1:5–2:52)

  III. Preparation for the Ministry of Jesus (3:1–4:15)

  IV. The Ministry of Jesus in Galilee (4:16–9:50)

  V. The Journey to Jerusalem (9:51–19:27)

  VI. The Ministry of Jesus in Jerusalem (19:28–21:38)

  VII. The Suffering and Death of Jesus (22:1–23:56)

  VIII. The Resurrection of Jesus (24:1–53)

LUKE

Dedication to Theophilus

1 Inasmuch as many have undertaken to compile a narrative of the things that have been accomplished among us, **2** just as those who from the beginning were eyewitnesses and ministers of the word have delivered them to us, **3** it seemed good to me also, having followed all things closely for some time past, to write an orderly account for you, most excellent Theophilus, **4** that you may have certainty concerning the things you have been taught.

Birth of John the Baptist Foretold

5 In the days of Herod, king of Judea, there was a priest named Zechariah, of the division of Abijah. And he had a wife from the daughters of Aaron, and her name was Elizabeth. **6** And they were both righteous before God, walking blamelessly in all the commandments and statutes of the Lord. **7** But they had no child, because Elizabeth was barren, and both were advanced in years.

8 Now while he was serving as priest before God when his division was on duty, **9** according to the custom of the priesthood, he was chosen by lot to enter the temple of the Lord and burn incense. **10** And the whole multitude of the people were praying outside at the hour of incense. **11** And there appeared to him an angel of the Lord standing on the right side of the altar of incense. **12** And Zechariah was troubled when he saw him, and fear fell upon him. **13** But the angel said to him, "Do not be afraid, Zechariah, for your prayer has been heard, and your wife Elizabeth will bear you a son, and you shall call his name John. **14** And you will have joy and gladness, and many will rejoice at his birth, **15** for he will be great before the Lord. And he must not drink wine or strong drink, and he will be filled with the Holy Spirit, even from his mother's womb. **16** And he will turn many of the children of Israel to the Lord their God, **17** and he will go before him in the spirit and power of Elijah, to turn the hearts of the fathers to the children, and the disobedient to the wisdom of the just, to make ready for the Lord a people prepared."

18 And Zechariah said to the angel, "How shall I know this? For I am an old man, and my wife is advanced in years." **19** And the angel answered him, "I am Gabriel. I stand in the presence of God, and I was sent to speak to you and to bring you this good news. **20** And behold, you will be silent and unable to speak until the day that these things take place, because you did not believe my words, which will be fulfilled in their time." **21** And the people were waiting

---

GETTING THE MESSAGE

Who wrote Luke? Luke wrote both this Gospel account and Acts. He probably traveled with Paul and participated in his ministry (see Col. 4:14; 2 Tim. 4:11; Philem. 24). Luke was also a physician (Col. 4:14).

---

for Zechariah, and they were wondering at his delay in the temple. **22** And when he came out, he was unable to speak to them, and they realized that he had seen a vision in the temple. And he kept making signs to them and remained mute. **23** And when his time of service was ended, he went to his home.

24 After these days his wife Elizabeth conceived, and for five months she kept herself hidden, saying, **25** "Thus the Lord has done for me in the days when he looked on me, to take away my reproach among people."

Birth of Jesus Foretold

26 In the sixth month the angel Gabriel was sent from God to a city of Galilee named Nazareth, **27** to a virgin betrothed[1] to a man whose name was Joseph, of the house of David. And the virgin's name was Mary. **28** And he came to her and said, "Greetings, O favored one, the Lord is with you!" **29** But she was greatly troubled at the saying, and

---

[1] That is, legally committed to be married

tried to discern what sort of greeting this might be. **30** And the angel said to her, "Do not be afraid, Mary, for you have found favor with God. **31** And behold, you will conceive in your womb and bear a son, and you shall call his name Jesus. **32** He will be great and will be called the Son of the Most High. And the Lord God will give to him the throne of his father David, **33** and he will reign over the house of Jacob forever, and of his kingdom there will be no end."

PROFILE

MARY

As a young woman in Nazareth, Mary became betrothed to Joseph, a carpenter. The angel Gabriel visited Mary to announce that she had "found favor with God" (1:30) and would become the mother of the Messiah, whose name would be Jesus. While still a virgin, she would conceive through the power of the Holy Spirit. Though understandably confused by this news, Mary submitted to the Lord's will for her life, saying, "Let it be to me according to your word" (1:38). As she observed the amazing events unfolding around her, Mary "treasured up all these things, pondering them in her heart" (2:19; see also 2:51). This included the warning that a "sword will pierce through your own soul also" (2:35), a prophecy fulfilled as, some 30 years later, she watched with sorrow as her son died on a cross.

KEY REFERENCE: LUKE 1:26–38

34 And Mary said to the angel, "How will this be, since I am a virgin?"

35 And the angel answered her, "The Holy Spirit will come upon you, and the power of the Most High will overshadow you; therefore the child to be born will be called holy— the Son of God. **36** And behold, your relative Elizabeth in her old age has also conceived a son, and this is the sixth month with her who was called barren. **37** For nothing will be impossible with God." **38** And Mary said, "Behold, I am the servant of the Lord; let it

be to me according to your word." And the angel departed from her.

Mary Visits Elizabeth

39 In those days Mary arose and went with haste into the hill country, to a town in Judah, **40** and she entered the house of Zechariah and greeted Elizabeth. **41** And when Elizabeth heard the greeting of Mary, the baby leaped in her womb. And Elizabeth was filled with the Holy Spirit, **42** and she exclaimed with a loud cry, "Blessed are you among women, and blessed is the fruit of your womb! **43** And why is this granted to me that the mother of my Lord should come to me? **44** For behold, when the sound of your greeting came to my ears, the baby in my womb leaped for joy. **45** And blessed is she who believed that there would be a fulfillment of what was spoken to her from the Lord."

GETTING THE MESSAGE

Mary's song includes one of Luke's major themes: the great reversal taking place in the world, in which God will exalt the humble and humble the proud (1:48, 52–53). God often uses seemingly insignificant people to achieve his remarkable purposes.

Mary's Song of Praise: The Magnificat

46 And Mary said,

"My soul magnifies the Lord,
47   and my spirit rejoices in God my Savior,
48 for he has looked on the humble estate of his servant.
    For behold, from now on all generations will call me blessed;
49 for he who is mighty has done great things for me,
    and holy is his name.
50 And his mercy is for those who fear him
    from generation to generation.
51 He has shown strength with his arm;
    he has scattered the proud in the thoughts of their hearts;
52 he has brought down the mighty from their thrones
    and exalted those of humble estate;

⁵³ he has filled the hungry with good
    things,
    and the rich he has sent away empty.
⁵⁴ He has helped his servant Israel,
    in remembrance of his mercy,
⁵⁵ as he spoke to our fathers,
    to Abraham and to his offspring
    forever."

⁵⁶ And Mary remained with her about three months and returned to her home.

The Birth of John the Baptist

⁵⁷ Now the time came for Elizabeth to give birth, and she bore a son. ⁵⁸ And her neighbors and relatives heard that the Lord had shown great mercy to her, and they rejoiced with her. ⁵⁹ And on the eighth day they came to circumcise the child. And they would have called him Zechariah after his father, ⁶⁰ but his mother answered, "No; he shall be called John." ⁶¹ And they said to her, "None of your relatives is called by this name." ⁶² And they made signs to his father, inquiring what he wanted him to be called. ⁶³ And he asked for a writing tablet and wrote, "His name is John." And they all wondered. ⁶⁴ And immediately his mouth was opened and his tongue loosed, and he spoke, blessing God. ⁶⁵ And fear came on all their neighbors. And all these things were talked about through all the hill country of Judea, ⁶⁶ and all who heard them laid them up in their hearts, saying, "What then will this child be?" For the hand of the Lord was with him.

Zechariah's Prophecy

⁶⁷ And his father Zechariah was filled with the Holy Spirit and prophesied, saying,

⁶⁸ "Blessed be the Lord God of Israel,
    for he has visited and redeemed his
    people
⁶⁹ and has raised up a horn of salvation
    for us
    in the house of his servant David,
⁷⁰ as he spoke by the mouth of his holy
    prophets from of old,
⁷¹ that we should be saved from our
    enemies
    and from the hand of all who hate us;
⁷² to show the mercy promised to our
    fathers
    and to remember his holy covenant,

⁷³ the oath that he swore to our father
    Abraham, to grant us
⁷⁴ that we, being delivered from the
    hand of our enemies,
    might serve him without fear,
⁷⁵ in holiness and righteousness
    before him all our days.
⁷⁶ And you, child, will be called the
    prophet of the Most High;
    for you will go before the Lord to
    prepare his ways,
⁷⁷ to give knowledge of salvation to his
    people
    in the forgiveness of their sins,
⁷⁸ because of the tender mercy of our
    God,
    whereby the sunrise shall visit us
    from on high
⁷⁹ to give light to those who sit in dark-
    ness and in the shadow of death,
    to guide our feet into the way of
    peace."

⁸⁰ And the child grew and became strong in spirit, and he was in the wilderness until the day of his public appearance to Israel.

The Birth of Jesus Christ

2 In those days a decree went out from Caesar Augustus that all the world should be registered. ² This was the first registration when Quirinius was governor of Syria. ³ And all went to be registered, each to his own town. ⁴ And Joseph also went up from Galilee, from the town of Nazareth, to Judea, to the city of David, which is called Bethlehem, because he was of the house and lineage of David, ⁵ to be registered with Mary, his betrothed,¹ who was with child. ⁶ And while they were there, the time came for her to give birth. ⁷ And she gave birth to her firstborn son and wrapped him in swaddling cloths and laid him in a manger, because there was no place for them in the inn.

The Shepherds and the Angels

⁸ And in the same region there were shepherds out in the field, keeping watch over their flock by night. ⁹ And an angel of the Lord appeared to them, and the glory of the Lord shone around them, and they were filled with great fear. ¹⁰ And the angel said to them, "Fear not, for behold, I bring you good news of great joy that will be for all the

---

¹ That is, one legally committed to be married

people. ¹¹ For unto you is born this day in the city of David a Savior, who is Christ the Lord. ¹² And this will be a sign for you: you will find a baby wrapped in swaddling cloths and lying in a manger." ¹³ And suddenly there was with the angel a multitude of the heavenly host praising God and saying,

¹⁴ "Glory to God in the highest,
    and on earth peace among those
        with whom he is pleased!"

PROFILE
JOSEPH

Joseph, whom the Bible describes as a "just man" (Matt. 1:19), was a descendant of David and a carpenter by trade. Betrothed to Mary when she was found to be with child, Joseph sought to show compassion and divorce her quietly, even though it looked like Mary had committed adultery. An angel of the Lord appeared to Joseph in a dream, however, assuring him that Mary's child was from the Holy Spirit (Matt. 1:20–21). Joseph trusted God and took Mary as his wife. He traveled with Mary to his ancestral home of Bethlehem, where she gave birth to Jesus. When Herod the Great sought to kill Jesus, Joseph took Mary and the child and escaped to Egypt (Matt. 2:13–18). Following Herod's death, they returned to Palestine and settled in Nazareth. Joseph later fathered at least four other sons and at least two daughters. Since he is not mentioned in the incident related in Matt. 12:46, it is likely that Joseph died before Jesus began his ministry.

KEY REFERENCE: MATTHEW 1:19-21

¹⁵ When the angels went away from them into heaven, the shepherds said to one another, "Let us go over to Bethlehem and see this thing that has happened, which the Lord has made known to us." ¹⁶ And they went with haste and found Mary and Joseph, and the baby lying in a manger. ¹⁷ And when they saw it, they made known the saying that had been told them concerning this child. ¹⁸ And all who heard it wondered at what the shepherds told them. ¹⁹ But Mary

treasured up all these things, pondering them in her heart. ²⁰ And the shepherds returned, glorifying and praising God for all they had heard and seen, as it had been told them.

²¹ And at the end of eight days, when he was circumcised, he was called Jesus, the name given by the angel before he was conceived in the womb.

Jesus Presented at the Temple

²² And when the time came for their purification according to the Law of Moses, they brought him up to Jerusalem to present him to the Lord ²³ (as it is written in the Law of the Lord, "Every male who first opens the womb shall be called holy to the Lord") ²⁴ and to offer a sacrifice according to what is said in the Law of the Lord, "a pair of turtledoves, or two young pigeons." ²⁵ Now there was a man in Jerusalem, whose name was Simeon, and this man was righteous and devout, waiting for the consolation of Israel, and the Holy Spirit was upon him. ²⁶ And it had been revealed to him by the Holy Spirit that he would not see death before he had seen the Lord's Christ. ²⁷ And he came in the Spirit into the temple, and when the parents brought in the child Jesus, to do for him according to the custom of the Law, ²⁸ he took him up in his arms and blessed God and said,

²⁹ "Lord, now you are letting your servant
        depart in peace,
    according to your word;
³⁰ for my eyes have seen your salvation
³¹   that you have prepared in the presence of all peoples,
³² a light for revelation to the Gentiles,
        and for glory to your people Israel."

³³ And his father and his mother marveled at what was said about him. ³⁴ And Simeon blessed them and said to Mary his mother, "Behold, this child is appointed for the fall and rising of many in Israel, and for a sign that is opposed ³⁵ (and a sword will pierce through your own soul also), so that thoughts from many hearts may be revealed."

³⁶ And there was a prophetess, Anna, the daughter of Phanuel, of the tribe of Asher. She was advanced in years, having lived with her husband seven years from when she was a virgin, ³⁷ and then as a widow until she was eighty-four. She did not depart from the

temple, worshiping with fasting and prayer night and day. **38** And coming up at that very hour she began to give thanks to God and to speak of him to all who were waiting for the redemption of Jerusalem.

The Return to Nazareth

39 And when they had performed everything according to the Law of the Lord, they returned into Galilee, to their own town of Nazareth. **40** And the child grew and became strong, filled with wisdom. And the favor of God was upon him.

The Boy Jesus in the Temple

41 Now his parents went to Jerusalem every year at the Feast of the Passover. **42** And when he was twelve years old, they went up according to custom. **43** And when the feast was ended, as they were returning, the boy Jesus stayed behind in Jerusalem. His parents did not know it, **44** but supposing him to be in the group they went a day's journey, but then they began to search for him among their relatives and acquaintances, **45** and when they did not find him, they returned to Jerusalem, searching for him. **46** After three days they found him in the temple, sitting among the teachers, listening to them and asking them questions. **47** And all who heard him were amazed at his understanding and his answers. **48** And when his parents saw him, they were astonished. And his mother said to him, "Son, why have you treated us so? Behold, your father and I have been searching for you in great distress." **49** And he said to them, "Why were you looking for me? Did you not know that I must be in my Father's house?" **50** And they did not understand the saying that he spoke to them. **51** And he went down with them and came to Nazareth and was submissive to them. And his mother treasured up all these things in her heart. **52** And Jesus increased in wisdom and in stature and in favor with God and man.

John the Baptist Prepares the Way

3 In the fifteenth year of the reign of Tiberius Caesar, Pontius Pilate being governor of Judea, and Herod being tetrarch of Galilee, and his brother Philip tetrarch of the region of Ituraea and Trachonitis, and Lysanias tetrarch of Abilene, **2** during the high priesthood of Annas and Caiaphas, the word of God came to John the son of Zechariah in the wilderness. **3** And he went into all the region around the Jordan, proclaiming a baptism of repentance for the forgiveness of sins. **4** As it is written in the book of the words of Isaiah the prophet,

"The voice of one crying in the wilderness:
'Prepare the way of the Lord,
  make his paths straight.
5 Every valley shall be filled,
  and every mountain and hill shall be made low,
and the crooked shall become straight,
  and the rough places shall become level ways,
6 and all flesh shall see the salvation of God.'"

7 He said therefore to the crowds that came out to be baptized by him, "You brood

GETTING THE MESSAGE

Why was Jesus taken to Jerusalem at age 12? At age 13, a Jewish boy was considered a man. It is possible that Joseph and Mary took Jesus to Jerusalem as part of his final preparation for this new stage in his life.

of vipers! Who warned you to flee from the wrath to come? **8** Bear fruits in keeping with repentance. And do not begin to say to yourselves, 'We have Abraham as our father.' For I tell you, God is able from these stones to raise up children for Abraham. **9** Even now the axe is laid to the root of the trees. Every tree therefore that does not bear good fruit is cut down and thrown into the fire."

10 And the crowds asked him, "What then shall we do?" **11** And he answered them, "Whoever has two tunics is to share with him who has none, and whoever has food is to do likewise." **12** Tax collectors also came to be baptized and said to him, "Teacher, what shall we do?" **13** And he said to them, "Collect no more than you are authorized to do." **14** Soldiers also asked him, "And we, what shall we do?" And he said to them, "Do not extort money from anyone by threats or by false accusation, and be content with your wages."

15 As the people were in expectation, and all were questioning in their hearts concerning John, whether he might be the Christ, **16** John answered them all, saying, "I baptize you with water, but he who is mightier than I is coming, the strap of whose sandals I am not worthy to untie. He will baptize you with the Holy Spirit and fire. **17** His winnowing fork is in his hand, to clear his threshing floor and to gather the wheat into his barn, but the chaff he will burn with unquenchable fire."

18 So with many other exhortations he preached good news to the people. **19** But Herod the tetrarch, who had been reproved by him for Herodias, his brother's wife, and for all the evil things that Herod had done, **20** added this to them all, that he locked up John in prison.

21 Now when all the people were baptized, and when Jesus also had been baptized and

was praying, the heavens were opened, **22** and the Holy Spirit descended on him in bodily form, like a dove; and a voice came from heaven, "You are my beloved Son; with you I am well pleased."

The Genealogy of Jesus Christ

23 Jesus, when he began his ministry, was about thirty years of age, being the son (as was supposed) of Joseph, the son of Heli, **24** the son of Matthat, the son of Levi, the son of Melchi, the son of Jannai, the son of Joseph, **25** the son of Mattathias, the son of Amos, the son of Nahum, the son of Esli, the son of Naggai, **26** the son of Maath, the son of Mattathias, the son of Semein, the son of Josech, the son of Joda, **27** the son of Joanan, the son of Rhesa, the son of Zerubbabel, the son of Shealtiel, the son of Neri, **28** the son of Melchi, the son of Addi, the son of Cosam, the son of Elmadam, the son of Er, **29** the son of Joshua, the son of Eliezer, the son of Jorim, the son of Matthat, the son of Levi, **30** the son of Simeon, the son of

Judah, the son of Joseph, the son of Jonam, the son of Eliakim, **31** the son of Melea, the son of Menna, the son of Mattatha, the son of Nathan, the son of David, **32** the son of Jesse, the son of Obed, the son of Boaz, the son of Sala, the son of Nahshon, **33** the son of Amminadab, the son of Admin, the son of Arni, the son of Hezron, the son of Perez, the son of Judah, **34** the son of Jacob, the son of Isaac, the son of Abraham, the son of Terah, the son of Nahor, **35** the son of Serug, the son of Reu, the son of Peleg, the son of Eber, the son of Shelah, **36** the son of Cainan, the son of Arphaxad, the son of Shem, the son of Noah, the son of Lamech, **37** the son of Methuselah, the son of Enoch, the son of Jared, the son of Mahalaleel, the son of Cainan, **38** the son of Enos, the son of Seth, the son of Adam, the son of God.

The Temptation of Jesus

4 And Jesus, full of the Holy Spirit, returned from the Jordan and was led by the Spirit in the wilderness **2** for forty days, being tempted by the devil. And he ate nothing during those days. And when they were ended, he was hungry. **3** The devil said to him, "If you are the Son of God, command this stone to become bread." **4** And Jesus answered him, "It is written, 'Man shall not live by bread alone.'" **5** And the devil took him up and showed him all the kingdoms of the world in a moment of time, **6** and said to him, "To you I will give all this authority and their glory, for it has been delivered to me, and I give it to whom I will. **7** If you, then, will worship me, it will all be yours." **8** And Jesus answered him, "It is written,

"'You shall worship the Lord your
        God,
    and him only shall you serve.'"

9 And he took him to Jerusalem and set him on the pinnacle of the temple and said to him, "If you are the Son of God, throw yourself down from here, **10** for it is written,

"'He will command his angels concerning you,
    to guard you,'

11 and

"'On their hands they will bear you up,
    lest you strike your foot against a
        stone.'"

¹² And Jesus answered him, "It is said, 'You shall not put the Lord your God to the test.'" ¹³ And when the devil had ended every temptation, he departed from him until an opportune time.

Jesus Begins His Ministry

¹⁴ And Jesus returned in the power of the Spirit to Galilee, and a report about him went out through all the surrounding country. ¹⁵ And he taught in their synagogues, being glorified by all.

Jesus Rejected at Nazareth

¹⁶ And he came to Nazareth, where he had been brought up. And as was his custom, he went to the synagogue on the Sabbath day, and he stood up to read. ¹⁷ And the scroll of the prophet Isaiah was given to him. He unrolled the scroll and found the place where it was written,

¹⁸ "The Spirit of the Lord is upon me,
 because he has anointed me
  to proclaim good news to the poor.
 He has sent me to proclaim liberty to
  the captives
   and recovering of sight to the blind,
  to set at liberty those who are
   oppressed,
¹⁹ to proclaim the year of the Lord's
   favor."

²⁰ And he rolled up the scroll and gave it back to the attendant and sat down. And the eyes of all in the synagogue were fixed on him. ²¹ And he began to say to them, "Today this Scripture has been fulfilled in your hearing." ²² And all spoke well of him and marveled at the gracious words that were coming from his mouth. And they said, "Is not this Joseph's son?" ²³ And he said to them, "Doubtless you will quote to me this proverb, 'Physician, heal yourself.' What we have heard you did at Capernaum, do here in your hometown as well." ²⁴ And he said, "Truly, I say to you, no prophet is acceptable in his hometown. ²⁵ But in truth, I tell you, there were many widows in Israel in the days of Elijah, when the heavens were shut up three years and six months, and a great famine came over all the land, ²⁶ and Elijah was sent to none of them but only to Zarephath, in the land of Sidon, to a woman who was a widow. ²⁷ And there were many

lepers¹ in Israel in the time of the prophet Elisha, and none of them was cleansed, but only Naaman the Syrian." ²⁸ When they heard these things, all in the synagogue were filled with wrath. ²⁹ And they rose up and drove him out of the town and brought him to the brow of the hill on which their town was built, so that they could throw him down the cliff. ³⁰ But passing through their midst, he went away.

Jesus Heals a Man with an Unclean Demon

³¹ And he went down to Capernaum, a city of Galilee. And he was teaching them on the Sabbath, ³² and they were astonished at his teaching, for his word possessed authority. ³³ And in the synagogue there was a man who had the spirit of an unclean demon, and he cried out with a loud voice,

> **GETTING THE MESSAGE**
>
> Jesus endured many **temptations** from Satan in the wilderness, designed to discourage him in his ministry. But he met each temptation with a specific Scripture that addressed that particular temptation (4:1–13). We should follow his example.

³⁴ "Ha! What have you to do with us, Jesus of Nazareth? Have you come to destroy us? I know who you are—the Holy One of God." ³⁵ But Jesus rebuked him, saying, "Be silent and come out of him!" And when the demon had thrown him down in their midst, he came out of him, having done him no harm. ³⁶ And they were all amazed and said to one another, "What is this word? For with authority and power he commands the unclean spirits, and they come out!" ³⁷ And reports about him went out into every place in the surrounding region.

Jesus Heals Many

³⁸ And he arose and left the synagogue and entered Simon's house. Now Simon's mother-in-law was ill with a high fever, and they appealed to him on her behalf. ³⁹ And he stood over her and rebuked the fever, and it left her, and immediately she rose and began to serve them.

¹ *Leprosy* was a term for several skin diseases (see Leviticus 13)

40 Now when the sun was setting, all those who had any who were sick with various diseases brought them to him, and he laid his hands on every one of them and healed them. **41** And demons also came out of many, crying, "You are the Son of God!" But he rebuked them and would not allow them to speak, because they knew that he was the Christ.

Jesus Preaches in Synagogues

42 And when it was day, he departed and went into a desolate place. And the people sought him and came to him, and would have kept him from leaving them, **43** but he said to them, "I must preach the good news of the kingdom of God to the other towns as well; for I was sent for this purpose." **44** And he was preaching in the synagogues of Judea.

GETTING THE MESSAGE

The **pinnacle of the temple** (4:9) was probably located at the southeastern corner of the Temple Mount. It overlooked the steep drop into the Kidron Valley, some 300 feet (91 m) below.

Jesus Calls the First Disciples

5 On one occasion, while the crowd was pressing in on him to hear the word of God, he was standing by the lake of Gennesaret, **2** and he saw two boats by the lake, but the fishermen had gone out of them and were washing their nets. **3** Getting into one of the boats, which was Simon's, he asked him to put out a little from the land. And he sat down and taught the people from the boat. **4** And when he had finished speaking, he said to Simon, "Put out into the deep and let down your nets for a catch." **5** And Simon answered, "Master, we toiled all night and took nothing! But at your word I will let down the nets." **6** And when they had done this, they enclosed a large number of fish, and their nets were breaking. **7** They signaled to their partners in the other boat to come and help them. And they came and filled both the boats, so that they began to sink. **8** But when Simon Peter saw it, he fell

down at Jesus' knees, saying, "Depart from me, for I am a sinful man, O Lord." **9** For he and all who were with him were astonished at the catch of fish that they had taken, **10** and so also were James and John, sons of Zebedee, who were partners with Simon. And Jesus said to Simon, "Do not be afraid; from now on you will be catching men."[1] **11** And when they had brought their boats to land, they left everything and followed him.

Jesus Cleanses a Leper

12 While he was in one of the cities, there came a man full of leprosy.[2] And when he saw Jesus, he fell on his face and begged him, "Lord, if you will, you can make me clean." **13** And Jesus stretched out his hand and touched him, saying, "I will; be clean." And immediately the leprosy left him. **14** And he charged him to tell no one, but "go and show yourself to the priest, and make an offering for your cleansing, as Moses commanded, for a proof to them." **15** But now even more the report about him went abroad, and great crowds gathered to hear him and to be healed of their infirmities. **16** But he would withdraw to desolate places and pray.

Jesus Heals a Paralytic

17 On one of those days, as he was teaching, Pharisees and teachers of the law were sitting there, who had come from every village of Galilee and Judea and from Jerusalem. And the power of the Lord was with him to heal. **18** And behold, some men were bringing on a bed a man who was paralyzed, and they were seeking to bring him in and lay him before Jesus, **19** but finding no way to bring him in, because of the crowd, they went up on the roof and let him down with his bed through the tiles into the midst before Jesus. **20** And when he saw their faith, he said, "Man, your sins are forgiven you." **21** And the scribes and the Pharisees began to question, saying, "Who is this who speaks blasphemies? Who can forgive sins but God alone?" **22** When Jesus perceived their thoughts, he answered them, "Why do you question in your hearts? **23** Which is easier, to say, 'Your sins are forgiven you,' or to say, 'Rise and walk'? **24** But that you may know that the Son of Man has authority on earth to

---

[1] The Greek word for *men* refers to both men and women (see Preface) [2] *Leprosy* was a term for several skin diseases (see Leviticus 13)

forgive sins"—he said to the man who was paralyzed—"I say to you, rise, pick up your bed and go home." 25 And immediately he rose up before them and picked up what he had been lying on and went home, glorifying God. 26 And amazement seized them all, and they glorified God and were filled with awe, saying, "We have seen extraordinary things today."

Jesus Calls Levi

27 After this he went out and saw a tax collector named Levi, sitting at the tax booth. And he said to him, "Follow me." 28 And leaving everything, he rose and followed him.

29 And Levi made him a great feast in his house, and there was a large company of tax collectors and others reclining at table with them. 30 And the Pharisees and their scribes grumbled at his disciples, saying, "Why do you eat and drink with tax collectors and sinners?" 31 And Jesus answered them, "Those who are well have no need of a physician, but those who are sick. 32 I have not come to call the righteous but sinners to repentance."

A Question About Fasting

33 And they said to him, "The disciples of John fast often and offer prayers, and so do the disciples of the Pharisees, but yours eat and drink." 34 And Jesus said to them, "Can you make wedding guests fast while the bridegroom is with them? 35 The days will come when the bridegroom is taken away from them, and then they will fast in those days." 36 He also told them a parable: "No one tears a piece from a new garment and puts it on an old garment. If he does, he will tear the new, and the piece from the new will not match the old. 37 And no one puts new wine into old wineskins. If he does, the new wine will burst the skins and it will be spilled, and the skins will be destroyed. 38 But new wine must be put into fresh wineskins. 39 And no one after drinking old wine desires new, for he says, 'The old is good.'"

Jesus Is Lord of the Sabbath

6 On a Sabbath, while he was going through the grainfields, his disciples plucked and ate some heads of grain, rubbing them in their hands. 2 But some of the Pharisees said, "Why are you doing what is not lawful to do on the Sabbath?" 3 And Jesus answered them, "Have you not read what

David did when he was hungry, he and those who were with him: 4 how he entered the house of God and took and ate the bread of the Presence, which is not lawful for any but the priests to eat, and also gave it to those with him?" 5 And he said to them, "The Son of Man is lord of the Sabbath."

A Man with a Withered Hand

6 On another Sabbath, he entered the synagogue and was teaching, and a man was there whose right hand was withered. 7 And the scribes and the Pharisees watched him, to see whether he would heal on the Sabbath, so that they might find a reason to accuse him. 8 But he knew their thoughts, and he said to the man with the withered hand, "Come and stand here." And he rose and stood there. 9 And Jesus said to them, "I ask you, is it lawful on the Sabbath to

> **GETTING THE MESSAGE**
>
> The **Pharisees** may have originated from the *Hasidim*, Jewish separatists who fought for independence in the Maccabean Revolt. Unlike the Sadducees, who controlled the Jewish high court, the Pharisees were heavily involved in the local synagogues. They were popular with the people, but Jesus challenged them on many points.

do good or to do harm, to save life or to destroy it?" 10 And after looking around at them all he said to him, "Stretch out your hand." And he did so, and his hand was restored. 11 But they were filled with fury and discussed with one another what they might do to Jesus.

The Twelve Apostles

12 In these days he went out to the mountain to pray, and all night he continued in prayer to God. 13 And when day came, he called his disciples and chose from them twelve, whom he named apostles: 14 Simon, whom he named Peter, and Andrew his brother, and James and John, and Philip, and Bartholomew, 15 and Matthew, and Thomas, and James the son of Alphaeus, and Simon who was called the Zealot, 16 and Judas the son of James, and Judas Iscariot, who became a traitor.

Jesus Ministers to a Great Multitude

¹⁷ And he came down with them and stood on a level place, with a great crowd of his disciples and a great multitude of people from all Judea and Jerusalem and the seacoast of Tyre and Sidon, ¹⁸ who came to hear him and to be healed of their diseases. And those who were troubled with unclean spirits were cured. ¹⁹ And all the crowd sought to touch him, for power came out from him and healed them all.

The Beatitudes

²⁰ And he lifted up his eyes on his disciples, and said:

"Blessed are you who are poor, for yours is the kingdom of God.

²¹ "Blessed are you who are hungry now, for you shall be satisfied.

"Blessed are you who weep now, for you shall laugh.

²² "Blessed are you when people hate you and when they exclude you and revile you and spurn your name as evil, on account of the Son of Man! ²³ Rejoice in that day, and leap for joy, for behold, your reward is great in heaven; for so their fathers did to the prophets.

Jesus Pronounces Woes

²⁴ "But woe to you who are rich, for you have received your consolation.

²⁵ "Woe to you who are full now, for you shall be hungry.

"Woe to you who laugh now, for you shall mourn and weep.

²⁶ "Woe to you, when all people speak well of you, for so their fathers did to the false prophets.

Love Your Enemies

²⁷ "But I say to you who hear, Love your enemies, do good to those who hate you,

²⁸ bless those who curse you, pray for those who abuse you. ²⁹ To one who strikes you on the cheek, offer the other also, and from one who takes away your cloak do not withhold your tunic either. ³⁰ Give to everyone who begs from you, and from one who takes away your goods do not demand them back. ³¹ And as you wish that others would do to you, do so to them.

³² "If you love those who love you, what benefit is that to you? For even sinners love those who love them. ³³ And if you do good to those who do good to you, what benefit is that to you? For even sinners do the same. ³⁴ And if you lend to those from whom you expect to receive, what credit is that to you? Even sinners lend to sinners, to get back the same amount. ³⁵ But love your enemies, and do good, and lend, expecting nothing in return, and your reward will be great, and you will be sons of the Most High, for he is kind to the ungrateful and the evil. ³⁶ Be merciful, even as your Father is merciful.

Judging Others

³⁷ "Judge not, and you will not be judged; condemn not, and you will not be condemned; forgive, and you will be forgiven; ³⁸ give, and it will be given to you. Good measure, pressed down, shaken together, running over, will be put into your lap. For with the measure you use it will be measured back to you."

³⁹ He also told them a parable: "Can a blind man lead a blind man? Will they not both fall into a pit? ⁴⁰ A disciple is not above his teacher, but everyone when he is fully trained will be like his teacher. ⁴¹ Why do you see the speck that is in your brother's eye, but do not notice the log that is in your own eye? ⁴² How can you say to your brother, 'Brother, let me take out the speck that is in your eye,' when you yourself do not see the log that is in your own eye? You hypocrite, first take the log out of your own eye, and then you will see clearly to take out the speck that is in your brother's eye.

A Tree and Its Fruit

⁴³ "For no good tree bears bad fruit, nor again does a bad tree bear good fruit, ⁴⁴ for each tree is known by its own fruit. For figs are not gathered from thornbushes, nor are grapes picked from a bramble bush. ⁴⁵ The good person out of the good treasure of his

heart produces good, and the evil person out of his evil treasure produces evil, for out of the abundance of the heart his mouth speaks.

Build Your House on the Rock

⁴⁶ "Why do you call me 'Lord, Lord,' and not do what I tell you? ⁴⁷ Everyone who comes to me and hears my words and does them, I will show you what he is like: ⁴⁸ he is like a man building a house, who dug deep and laid the foundation on the rock. And when a flood arose, the stream broke against that house and could not shake it, because it had been well built. ⁴⁹ But the one who hears and does not do them is like a man who built a house on the ground without a foundation. When the stream broke against it, immediately it fell, and the ruin of that house was great."

Jesus Heals a Centurion's Servant

7 After he had finished all his sayings in the hearing of the people, he entered Capernaum. ² Now a centurion had a servant who was sick and at the point of death, who was highly valued by him. ³ When the centurion heard about Jesus, he sent to him elders of the Jews, asking him to come and heal his servant. ⁴ And when they came to Jesus, they pleaded with him earnestly, saying, "He is worthy to have you do this for him, ⁵ for he loves our nation, and he is the one who built us our synagogue." ⁶ And Jesus went with them. When he was not far from the house, the centurion sent friends, saying to him, "Lord, do not trouble yourself, for I am not worthy to have you come under my roof. ⁷ Therefore I did not presume to come to you. But say the word, and let my servant be healed. ⁸ For I too am a man set under authority, with soldiers under me: and I say to one, 'Go,' and he goes; and to another, 'Come,' and he comes; and to my servant, 'Do this,' and he does it." ⁹ When Jesus heard these things, he marveled at him, and turning to the crowd that followed him, said, "I tell you, not even in Israel have I found such faith." ¹⁰ And when those who had been sent returned to the house, they found the servant well.

Jesus Raises a Widow's Son

¹¹ Soon afterward he went to a town called Nain, and his disciples and a great crowd went with him. ¹² As he drew near to the gate of the town, behold, a man who had died was being carried out, the only son of his mother, and she was a widow, and a considerable crowd from the town was with her. ¹³ And when the Lord saw her, he had compassion on her and said to her, "Do not weep." ¹⁴ Then he came up and touched the bier, and the bearers stood still. And he said, "Young man, I say to you, arise." ¹⁵ And the dead man sat up and began to speak, and Jesus gave him to his mother. ¹⁶ Fear seized them all, and they glorified God, saying, "A great prophet has arisen among us!" and "God has visited his people!" ¹⁷ And this report about him spread through the whole of Judea and all the surrounding country.

Messengers from John the Baptist

¹⁸ The disciples of John reported all these things to him. And John, ¹⁹ calling two of

---

GETTING THE MESSAGE

Are you the one who is to come?
John the Baptist sent his disciples to ask Jesus if he was the "mightier one," or the Messiah, who would come after John. In response, Jesus pointed out how his ministry fulfilled Isaiah's prophecies about the Messiah (7:18–23; see 3:16).

---

his disciples to him, sent them to the Lord, saying, "Are you the one who is to come, or shall we look for another?" ²⁰ And when the men had come to him, they said, "John the Baptist has sent us to you, saying, 'Are you the one who is to come, or shall we look for another?'" ²¹ In that hour he healed many people of diseases and plagues and evil spirits, and on many who were blind he bestowed sight. ²² And he answered them, "Go and tell John what you have seen and heard: the blind receive their sight, the lame walk, lepers[1] are cleansed, and the deaf hear, the dead are raised up, the poor have good news preached to them. ²³ And blessed is the one who is not offended by me."

²⁴ When John's messengers had gone, Jesus began to speak to the crowds concerning John: "What did you go out into the wilderness to see? A reed shaken by the wind? ²⁵ What then did you go out to see? A man

---

[1] *Leprosy* was a term for several skin diseases (see Leviticus 13)

dressed in soft clothing? Behold, those who are dressed in splendid clothing and live in luxury are in kings' courts. 26 What then did you go out to see? A prophet? Yes, I tell you, and more than a prophet. 27 This is he of whom it is written,

> "'Behold, I send my messenger before
> your face,
> who will prepare your way before
> you.'

28 I tell you, among those born of women none is greater than John. Yet the one who is least in the kingdom of God is greater than he." 29 (When all the people heard this, and the tax collectors too, they declared God just, having been baptized with the baptism of John, 30 but the Pharisees and the lawyers rejected the purpose of God for themselves, not having been baptized by him.)

31 "To what then shall I compare the people of this generation, and what are they like? 32 They are like children sitting in the marketplace and calling to one another,

> "'We played the flute for you, and you
> did not dance;
> we sang a dirge, and you did not
> weep.'

33 For John the Baptist has come eating no bread and drinking no wine, and you say, 'He has a demon.' 34 The Son of Man has come eating and drinking, and you say, 'Look at him! A glutton and a drunkard, a friend of tax collectors and sinners!' 35 Yet wisdom is justified by all her children."

A Sinful Woman Forgiven

36 One of the Pharisees asked him to eat with him, and he went into the Pharisee's house and reclined at the table. 37 And behold, a woman of the city, who was a sinner, when she learned that he was reclining at table in the Pharisee's house, brought an alabaster flask of ointment, 38 and standing behind him at his feet, weeping, she began to wet his feet with her tears and wiped them with the hair of her head and kissed his feet and anointed them with the ointment. 39 Now when the Pharisee who had invited him saw this, he said to himself, "If this man were a prophet, he would have known who and what sort of woman this is who is touching him, for she is a sinner." 40 And Jesus answering said to him, "Simon,

I have something to say to you." And he answered, "Say it, Teacher."

41 "A certain moneylender had two debtors. One owed five hundred denarii, and the other fifty. 42 When they could not pay, he cancelled the debt of both. Now which of them will love him more?" 43 Simon answered, "The one, I suppose, for whom he cancelled the larger debt." And he said to him, "You have judged rightly." 44 Then turning toward the woman he said to Simon, "Do you see this woman? I entered your house; you gave me no water for my feet, but she has wet my feet with her tears and wiped them with her hair. 45 You gave me no kiss, but from the time I came in she has not ceased to kiss my feet. 46 You did not anoint my head with oil, but she has anointed my feet with ointment. 47 Therefore I tell you, her sins, which are many, are forgiven—for she loved much. But he who is forgiven little, loves little." 48 And he said to her, "Your sins are forgiven." 49 Then those who were at table with him began to say among themselves, "Who is this, who even forgives sins?" 50 And he said to the woman, "Your faith has saved you; go in peace."

Women Accompanying Jesus

8 Soon afterward he went on through cities and villages, proclaiming and bringing the good news of the kingdom of God. And the twelve were with him, 2 and also some women who had been healed of evil spirits and infirmities: Mary, called Magdalene, from whom seven demons had gone out, 3 and Joanna, the wife of Chuza, Herod's household manager, and Susanna, and many others, who provided for them out of their means.

The Parable of the Sower

4 And when a great crowd was gathering and people from town after town came to him, he said in a parable, 5 "A sower went out to sow his seed. And as he sowed, some fell along the path and was trampled underfoot, and the birds of the air devoured it. 6 And some fell on the rock, and as it grew up, it withered away, because it had no moisture. 7 And some fell among thorns, and the thorns grew up with it and choked it. 8 And some fell into good soil and grew and yielded a hundredfold." As he said these

things, he called out, "He who has ears to hear, let him hear."

The Purpose of the Parables

⁹ And when his disciples asked him what this parable meant, ¹⁰ he said, "To you it has been given to know the secrets of the kingdom of God, but for others they are in parables, so that 'seeing they may not see, and hearing they may not understand.' ¹¹ Now the parable is this: The seed is the word of God. ¹² The ones along the path are those who have heard; then the devil comes and takes away the word from their hearts, so that they may not believe and be saved. ¹³ And the ones on the rock are those who, when they hear the word, receive it with joy. But these have no root; they believe for a while, and in time of testing fall away. ¹⁴ And as for what fell among the thorns, they are those who hear, but as they go on their way they are choked by the cares and riches and pleasures of life, and their fruit does not mature. ¹⁵ As for that in the good soil, they are those who, hearing the word, hold it fast in an honest and good heart, and bear fruit with patience.

A Lamp Under a Jar

¹⁶ "No one after lighting a lamp covers it with a jar or puts it under a bed, but puts it on a stand, so that those who enter may see the light. ¹⁷ For nothing is hidden that will not be made manifest, nor is anything secret that will not be known and come to light. ¹⁸ Take care then how you hear, for to the one who has, more will be given, and from the one who has not, even what he thinks that he has will be taken away."

Jesus' Mother and Brothers

¹⁹ Then his mother and his brothers came to him, but they could not reach him because of the crowd. ²⁰ And he was told, "Your mother and your brothers are standing outside, desiring to see you." ²¹ But he answered them, "My mother and my brothers are those who hear the word of God and do it."

Jesus Calms a Storm

²² One day he got into a boat with his disciples, and he said to them, "Let us go across to the other side of the lake." So they set out, ²³ and as they sailed he fell asleep. And a windstorm came down on the lake,

and they were filling with water and were in danger. ²⁴ And they went and woke him, saying, "Master, Master, we are perishing!" And he awoke and rebuked the wind and the raging waves, and they ceased, and there was a calm. ²⁵ He said to them, "Where is your faith?" And they were afraid, and they marveled, saying to one another, "Who then is this, that he commands even winds and water, and they obey him?"

Jesus Heals a Man with a Demon

²⁶ Then they sailed to the country of the Gerasenes, which is opposite Galilee. ²⁷ When Jesus had stepped out on land, there met him a man from the city who had demons. For a long time he had worn no clothes, and he had not lived in a house but among the tombs. ²⁸ When he saw Jesus, he cried out and fell down before him and said with a loud voice, "What have you to do with

GETTING THE MESSAGE

Traveling exorcists tried to **cast out demons** using a variety of spells and devices. Jesus cast out demons using simple commands. This demonstrated his unique authority as the Son of God and showed that Jesus was stronger than any evil power (8:26–39).

me, Jesus, Son of the Most High God? I beg you, do not torment me." ²⁹ For he had commanded the unclean spirit to come out of the man. (For many a time it had seized him. He was kept under guard and bound with chains and shackles, but he would break the bonds and be driven by the demon into the desert.) ³⁰ Jesus then asked him, "What is your name?" And he said, "Legion," for many demons had entered him. ³¹ And they begged him not to command them to depart into the abyss. ³² Now a large herd of pigs was feeding there on the hillside, and they begged him to let them enter these. So he gave them permission. ³³ Then the demons came out of the man and entered the pigs, and the herd rushed down the steep bank into the lake and drowned.

³⁴ When the herdsmen saw what had happened, they fled and told it in the city and in the country. ³⁵ Then people went out to see what had happened, and they came to

Jesus and found the man from whom the demons had gone, sitting at the feet of Jesus, clothed and in his right mind, and they were afraid. ³⁶ And those who had seen it told them how the demon-possessed man had been healed. ³⁷ Then all the people of the surrounding country of the Gerasenes asked him to depart from them, for they were seized with great fear. So he got into the boat and returned. ³⁸ The man from whom the demons had gone begged that he might be with him, but Jesus sent him away, saying, ³⁹ "Return to your home, and declare how much God has done for you." And he went away, proclaiming throughout the whole city how much Jesus had done for him.

Jesus Heals a Woman and Jairus's Daughter

⁴⁰ Now when Jesus returned, the crowd welcomed him, for they were all waiting

for him. ⁴¹ And there came a man named Jairus, who was a ruler of the synagogue. And falling at Jesus' feet, he implored him to come to his house, ⁴² for he had an only daughter, about twelve years of age, and she was dying.

As Jesus went, the people pressed around him. ⁴³ And there was a woman who had had a discharge of blood for twelve years, and though she had spent all her living on physicians, she could not be healed by anyone. ⁴⁴ She came up behind him and touched the fringe of his garment, and immediately her discharge of blood ceased. ⁴⁵ And Jesus said, "Who was it that touched me?" When all denied it, Peter said, "Master, the crowds surround you and are pressing in on you!" ⁴⁶ But Jesus said, "Someone touched me, for I perceive that power has gone out from me." ⁴⁷ And when the woman saw that she was not hidden, she came trembling, and falling down before him declared in the presence

of all the people why she had touched him, and how she had been immediately healed. ⁴⁸ And he said to her, "Daughter, your faith has made you well; go in peace."

⁴⁹ While he was still speaking, someone from the ruler's house came and said, "Your daughter is dead; do not trouble the Teacher any more." ⁵⁰ But Jesus on hearing this answered him, "Do not fear; only believe, and she will be well." ⁵¹ And when he came to the house, he allowed no one to enter with him, except Peter and John and James, and the father and mother of the child. ⁵² And all were weeping and mourning for her, but he said, "Do not weep, for she is not dead but sleeping." ⁵³ And they laughed at him, knowing that she was dead. ⁵⁴ But taking her by the hand he called, saying, "Child, arise." ⁵⁵ And her spirit returned, and she got up at once. And he directed that something should be given her to eat. ⁵⁶ And her parents were amazed, but he charged them to tell no one what had happened.

Jesus Sends Out the Twelve Apostles

9 And he called the twelve together and gave them power and authority over all demons and to cure diseases, ² and he sent them out to proclaim the kingdom of God and to heal. ³ And he said to them, "Take nothing for your journey, no staff, nor bag, nor bread, nor money; and do not have two tunics. ⁴ And whatever house you enter, stay there, and from there depart. ⁵ And wherever they do not receive you, when you leave that town shake off the dust from your feet as a testimony against them." ⁶ And they departed and went through the villages, preaching the gospel and healing everywhere.

Herod Is Perplexed by Jesus

⁷ Now Herod the tetrarch heard about all that was happening, and he was perplexed, because it was said by some that John had been raised from the dead, ⁸ by some that Elijah had appeared, and by others that one of the prophets of old had risen. ⁹ Herod said, "John I beheaded, but who is this about whom I hear such things?" And he sought to see him.

Jesus Feeds the Five Thousand

¹⁰ On their return the apostles told him all that they had done. And he took them and withdrew apart to a town called Bethsaida.

11 When the crowds learned it, they followed him, and he welcomed them and spoke to them of the kingdom of God and cured those who had need of healing. 12 Now the day began to wear away, and the twelve came and said to him, "Send the crowd away to go into the surrounding villages and countryside to find lodging and get provisions, for we are here in a desolate place." 13 But he said to them, "You give them something to eat." They said, "We have no more than five loaves and two fish—unless we are to go and buy food for all these people." 14 For there were about five thousand men. And he said to his disciples, "Have them sit down in groups of about fifty each." 15 And they did so, and had them all sit down. 16 And taking the five loaves and the two fish, he looked up to heaven and said a blessing over them. Then he broke the loaves and gave them to the disciples to set before the crowd. 17 And they all ate and were satisfied. And what was left over was picked up, twelve baskets of broken pieces.

Peter Confesses Jesus as the Christ

18 Now it happened that as he was praying alone, the disciples were with him. And he asked them, "Who do the crowds say that I am?" 19 And they answered, "John the Baptist. But others say, Elijah, and others, that one of the prophets of old has risen." 20 Then he said to them, "But who do you say that I am?" And Peter answered, "The Christ of God."

Jesus Foretells His Death

21 And he strictly charged and commanded them to tell this to no one, 22 saying, "The Son of Man must suffer many things and be rejected by the elders and chief priests and scribes, and be killed, and on the third day be raised."

Take Up Your Cross and Follow Jesus

23 And he said to all, "If anyone would come after me, let him deny himself and take up his cross daily and follow me. 24 For whoever would save his life will lose it, but whoever loses his life for my sake will save it. 25 For what does it profit a man if he gains the whole world and loses or forfeits himself? 26 For whoever is ashamed of me and of my words, of him will the Son of Man be ashamed when he comes in his glory

and the glory of the Father and of the holy angels. 27 But I tell you truly, there are some standing here who will not taste death until they see the kingdom of God."

The Transfiguration

28 Now about eight days after these sayings he took with him Peter and John and James and went up on the mountain to pray. 29 And as he was praying, the appearance of his face was altered, and his clothing became dazzling white. 30 And behold, two men were talking with him, Moses and Elijah, 31 who appeared in glory and spoke of his departure, which he was about to accomplish at Jerusalem. 32 Now Peter and those who were with him were heavy with sleep, but when they became fully awake they saw his glory and the two men who stood with

GETTING THE MESSAGE

Was **Bethsaida** (9:10) actually a fishing village on the Sea of Galilee, as Mark 6:45 suggests? The most likely site for Bethsaida is 1.25 miles (2 km) inland from the Sea. However, recent archaeological research has shown that this can be explained by (1) a lowering of the water level in the Sea, (2) sedimentation, and (3) seismic activity.

him. 33 And as the men were parting from him, Peter said to Jesus, "Master, it is good that we are here. Let us make three tents, one for you and one for Moses and one for Elijah"—not knowing what he said. 34 As he was saying these things, a cloud came and overshadowed them, and they were afraid as they entered the cloud. 35 And a voice came out of the cloud, saying, "This is my Son, my Chosen One; listen to him!" 36 And when the voice had spoken, Jesus was found alone. And they kept silent and told no one in those days anything of what they had seen.

Jesus Heals a Boy with an Unclean Spirit

37 On the next day, when they had come down from the mountain, a great crowd met him. 38 And behold, a man from the crowd cried out, "Teacher, I beg you to look at my son, for he is my only child. 39 And

behold, a spirit seizes him, and he suddenly cries out. It convulses him so that he foams at the mouth, and shatters him, and will hardly leave him. ⁴⁰ And I begged your disciples to cast it out, but they could not." ⁴¹ Jesus answered, "O faithless and twisted generation, how long am I to be with you and bear with you? Bring your son here." ⁴² While he was coming, the demon threw him to the ground and convulsed him. But Jesus rebuked the unclean spirit and healed the boy, and gave him back to his father. ⁴³ And all were astonished at the majesty of God.

PROFILE

JAMES

James and his brother John were fishermen. Together with their father Zebedee, they were mending their nets when Jesus called them to be disciples. Jesus called James and John the "Sons of Thunder" (Mark 3:17; see Luke 9:54). James, along with Peter and John, were the disciples closest to Jesus. They were with the Lord during many of the key moments of his ministry. James was with Jesus at the Transfiguration, where Jesus revealed his divine glory. He was also with Jesus when he healed Jairus's daughter (Mark 5:37). When Jesus prayed at Gethsemane, he asked James, John, and Peter to share with him the agonizing time of anticipation and sorrow as he faced the cross (Matt. 26:37). James was later executed by Herod, becoming the first apostle to die for his faith (Acts 12:1–3).

KEY REFERENCE: MATTHEW 4:21–22

Jesus Again Foretells His Death

But while they were all marveling at everything he was doing, Jesus said to his disciples, ⁴⁴ "Let these words sink into your ears: The Son of Man is about to be delivered into the hands of men." ⁴⁵ But they did not understand this saying, and it was concealed from them, so that they might not perceive it. And they were afraid to ask him about this saying.

Who Is the Greatest?

⁴⁶ An argument arose among them as to which of them was the greatest. ⁴⁷ But Jesus, knowing the reasoning of their hearts, took a child and put him by his side ⁴⁸ and said to them, "Whoever receives this child in my name receives me, and whoever receives me receives him who sent me. For he who is least among you all is the one who is great."

Anyone Not Against Us Is For Us

⁴⁹ John answered, "Master, we saw someone casting out demons in your name, and we tried to stop him, because he does not follow with us." ⁵⁰ But Jesus said to him, "Do not stop him, for the one who is not against you is for you."

A Samaritan Village Rejects Jesus

⁵¹ When the days drew near for him to be taken up, he set his face to go to Jerusalem. ⁵² And he sent messengers ahead of him, who went and entered a village of the Samaritans, to make preparations for him. ⁵³ But the people did not receive him, because his face was set toward Jerusalem. ⁵⁴ And when his disciples James and John saw it, they said, "Lord, do you want us to tell fire to come down from heaven and consume them?" ⁵⁵ But he turned and rebuked them. ⁵⁶ And they went on to another village.

The Cost of Following Jesus

⁵⁷ As they were going along the road, someone said to him, "I will follow you wherever you go." ⁵⁸ And Jesus said to him, "Foxes have holes, and birds of the air have nests, but the Son of Man has nowhere to lay his head." ⁵⁹ To another he said, "Follow me." But he said, "Lord, let me first go and bury my father." ⁶⁰ And Jesus said to him, "Leave the dead to bury their own dead. But as for you, go and proclaim the kingdom of God." ⁶¹ Yet another said, "I will follow you, Lord, but let me first say farewell to those at my home." ⁶² Jesus said to him, "No one who puts his hand to the plow and looks back is fit for the kingdom of God."

Jesus Sends Out the Seventy-Two

10 After this the Lord appointed seventy-two others and sent them on ahead of him, two by two, into every town and place where he himself was about to go. ² And he said to them, "The harvest is plentiful, but the laborers are few. Therefore pray earnestly

to the Lord of the harvest to send out laborers into his harvest. ³ Go your way; behold, I am sending you out as lambs in the midst of wolves. ⁴ Carry no moneybag, no knapsack, no sandals, and greet no one on the road. ⁵ Whatever house you enter, first say, 'Peace be to this house!' ⁶ And if a son of peace is there, your peace will rest upon him. But if not, it will return to you. ⁷ And remain in the same house, eating and drinking what they provide, for the laborer deserves his wages. Do not go from house to house. ⁸ Whenever you enter a town and they receive you, eat what is set before you. ⁹ Heal the sick in it and say to them, 'The kingdom of God has come near to you.' ¹⁰ But whenever you enter a town and they do not receive you, go into its streets and say, ¹¹ 'Even the dust of your town that clings to our feet we wipe off against you. Nevertheless know this, that the kingdom of God has come near.' ¹² I tell you, it will be more bearable on that day for Sodom than for that town.

Woe to Unrepentant Cities

¹³ "Woe to you, Chorazin! Woe to you, Bethsaida! For if the mighty works done in you had been done in Tyre and Sidon, they would have repented long ago, sitting in sackcloth and ashes. ¹⁴ But it will be more bearable in the judgment for Tyre and Sidon than for you. ¹⁵ And you, Capernaum, will you be exalted to heaven? You shall be brought down to Hades.

¹⁶ "The one who hears you hears me, and the one who rejects you rejects me, and the one who rejects me rejects him who sent me."

The Return of the Seventy-Two

¹⁷ The seventy-two returned with joy, saying, "Lord, even the demons are subject to us in your name!" ¹⁸ And he said to them, "I saw Satan fall like lightning from heaven. ¹⁹ Behold, I have given you authority to tread on serpents and scorpions, and over all the power of the enemy, and nothing shall hurt you. ²⁰ Nevertheless, do not rejoice in this, that the spirits are subject to you, but rejoice that your names are written in heaven."

Jesus Rejoices in the Father's Will

²¹ In that same hour he rejoiced in the Holy Spirit and said, "I thank you, Father, Lord of heaven and earth, that you have hidden these things from the wise and understanding and revealed them to little

children; yes, Father, for such was your gracious will. ²² All things have been handed over to me by my Father, and no one knows who the Son is except the Father, or who the Father is except the Son and anyone to whom the Son chooses to reveal him."

²³ Then turning to the disciples he said privately, "Blessed are the eyes that see what you see! ²⁴ For I tell you that many prophets and kings desired to see what you see, and did not see it, and to hear what you hear, and did not hear it."

The Parable of the Good Samaritan

²⁵ And behold, a lawyer stood up to put him to the test, saying, "Teacher, what shall I do to inherit eternal life?" ²⁶ He said to him, "What is written in the Law? How do you read it?" ²⁷ And he answered, "You shall love the Lord your God with all your heart and with all your soul and with all

GETTING THE MESSAGE

Jesus welcomed **children** and sometimes used them as examples of humility (10:21; 18:15–17). He taught that such humility was necessary for his followers (see Matt. 18:3–4). God delights in showing mercy to those who are humble (see Luke 1:52–53).

your strength and with all your mind, and your neighbor as yourself." ²⁸ And he said to him, "You have answered correctly; do this, and you will live."

²⁹ But he, desiring to justify himself, said to Jesus, "And who is my neighbor?" ³⁰ Jesus replied, "A man was going down from Jerusalem to Jericho, and he fell among robbers, who stripped him and beat him and departed, leaving him half dead. ³¹ Now by chance a priest was going down that road, and when he saw him he passed by on the other side. ³² So likewise a Levite, when he came to the place and saw him, passed by on the other side. ³³ But a Samaritan, as he journeyed, came to where he was, and when he saw him, he had compassion. ³⁴ He went to him and bound up his wounds, pouring on oil and wine. Then he set him on his own animal and brought him to an inn and took care of him. ³⁵ And the next day he took out two denarii and gave them to the

innkeeper, saying, 'Take care of him, and whatever more you spend, I will repay you when I come back.' **36** Which of these three, do you think, proved to be a neighbor to the man who fell among the robbers?" **37** He said, "The one who showed him mercy." And Jesus said to him, "You go, and do likewise."

Martha and Mary

38 Now as they went on their way, Jesus entered a village. And a woman named

---

PROFILE

MARTHA

Martha was the sister of Mary and Lazarus. The three of them were close friends of Jesus. Martha welcomed Jesus into her home in Bethany, where she prepared him meals as he taught. A conscientious hostess, Martha busied herself with serving her guests while Mary chose instead to listen to Jesus' teaching. This frustrated Martha, but Jesus gently rebuked her and defended Mary's desire to learn from him (10:38–42). It was Martha and Mary who sent word to Jesus when their brother Lazarus became ill (John 11). Even though Lazarus had died by the time Jesus arrived at their home, Martha believed that God could work a miracle through Jesus. When Jesus gave Martha an opportunity to express her faith, she replied, "Yes, Lord; I believe that you are the Christ, the Son of God, who is coming into the world" (John 11:27).

KEY REFERENCE: LUKE 10:38–42

Martha welcomed him into her house. **39** And she had a sister called Mary, who sat at the Lord's feet and listened to his teaching. **40** But Martha was distracted with much serving. And she went up to him and said, "Lord, do you not care that my sister has left me to serve alone? Tell her then to help me." **41** But the Lord answered her, "Martha, Martha, you are anxious and troubled about many things, **42** but one thing is necessary. Mary has chosen the good portion, which will not be taken away from her."

The Lord's Prayer

11 Now Jesus was praying in a certain place, and when he finished, one of his disciples said to him, "Lord, teach us to pray, as John taught his disciples." **2** And he said to them, "When you pray, say:

"Father, hallowed be your name.
    Your kingdom come.
3   Give us each day our daily bread,
4   and forgive us our sins,
       for we ourselves forgive everyone
           who is indebted to us.
    And lead us not into temptation.'"

5 And he said to them, "Which of you who has a friend will go to him at midnight and say to him, 'Friend, lend me three loaves, **6** for a friend of mine has arrived on a journey, and I have nothing to set before him'; **7** and he will answer from within, 'Do not bother me; the door is now shut, and my children

---

> GETTING THE MESSAGE
>
> **The coming of God's kingdom** (11:2) is an important theme in the Gospels. It refers to the advance of God's rule over all creation, especially as sinful men and women put their trust in Jesus and submit to God's authority in their lives.

---

are with me in bed. I cannot get up and give you anything'? **8** I tell you, though he will not get up and give him anything because he is his friend, yet because of his impudence he will rise and give him whatever he needs. **9** And I tell you, ask, and it will be given to you; seek, and you will find; knock, and it will be opened to you. **10** For everyone who asks receives, and the one who seeks finds, and to the one who knocks it will be opened. **11** What father among you, if his son asks for a fish, will instead of a fish give him a serpent; **12** or if he asks for an egg, will give him a scorpion? **13** If you then, who are evil, know how to give good gifts to your children, how much more will the heavenly Father give the Holy Spirit to those who ask him!"

Jesus and Beelzebul

14 Now he was casting out a demon that was mute. When the demon had gone out, the mute man spoke, and the people marveled. **15** But some of them said, "He casts out demons by Beelzebul, the prince of demons," ¹⁶ while others, to test him, kept seeking from him a sign from heaven. ¹⁷ But he, knowing their thoughts, said to them, "Every kingdom divided against itself is laid waste, and a divided household falls. ¹⁸ And if Satan also is divided against himself, how will his kingdom stand? For you say that I cast out demons by Beelzebul. ¹⁹ And if I cast out demons by Beelzebul, by whom do your sons cast them out? Therefore they will be your judges. ²⁰ But if it is by the finger of God that I cast out demons, then the kingdom of God has come upon you. ²¹ When a strong man, fully armed, guards his own palace, his goods are safe; ²² but when one stronger than he attacks him and overcomes him, he takes away his armor in which he trusted and divides his spoil. ²³ Whoever is not with me is against me, and whoever does not gather with me scatters.

Return of an Unclean Spirit

²⁴ "When the unclean spirit has gone out of a person, it passes through waterless places seeking rest, and finding none it says, 'I will return to my house from which I came.' ²⁵ And when it comes, it finds the house swept and put in order. ²⁶ Then it goes and brings seven other spirits more evil than itself, and they enter and dwell there. And the last state of that person is worse than the first."

True Blessedness

²⁷ As he said these things, a woman in the crowd raised her voice and said to him, "Blessed is the womb that bore you, and the breasts at which you nursed!" ²⁸ But he said, "Blessed rather are those who hear the word of God and keep it!"

The Sign of Jonah

²⁹ When the crowds were increasing, he began to say, "This generation is an evil generation. It seeks for a sign, but no sign will be given to it except the sign of Jonah. ³⁰ For as Jonah became a sign to the people of Nineveh, so will the Son of Man be to this generation. ³¹ The queen of the South will rise up at the judgment with the men of this generation and condemn them, for she came from the ends of the earth to hear the wisdom of Solomon, and behold, something greater than Solomon is here. ³² The men of Nineveh will rise up at the judgment

with this generation and condemn it, for they repented at the preaching of Jonah, and behold, something greater than Jonah is here.

The Light in You

³³ "No one after lighting a lamp puts it in a cellar or under a basket, but on a stand, so that those who enter may see the light. ³⁴ Your eye is the lamp of your body. When your eye is healthy, your whole body is full of light, but when it is bad, your body is full of darkness. ³⁵ Therefore be careful lest the light in you be darkness. ³⁶ If then your whole body is full of light, having no part dark, it will be wholly bright, as when a lamp with its rays gives you light."

Woes to the Pharisees and Lawyers

³⁷ While Jesus was speaking, a Pharisee asked him to dine with him, so he went in and reclined at table. ³⁸ The Pharisee was

> ### GETTING THE MESSAGE
>
> In 11:42–52, Jesus directs six **"woes"** to the Pharisees and the lawyers (or scribes). "Woe" is a way of expressing grief or regret. The Pharisees and scribes took offense, but Jesus' teaching should have led them to repentance.

astonished to see that he did not first wash before dinner. ³⁹ And the Lord said to him, "Now you Pharisees cleanse the outside of the cup and of the dish, but inside you are full of greed and wickedness. ⁴⁰ You fools! Did not he who made the outside make the inside also? ⁴¹ But give as alms those things that are within, and behold, everything is clean for you.

⁴² "But woe to you Pharisees! For you tithe mint and rue and every herb, and neglect justice and the love of God. These you ought to have done, without neglecting the others. ⁴³ Woe to you Pharisees! For you love the best seat in the synagogues and greetings in the marketplaces. ⁴⁴ Woe to you! For you are like unmarked graves, and people walk over them without knowing it."

⁴⁵ One of the lawyers answered him, "Teacher, in saying these things you insult us also." ⁴⁶ And he said, "Woe to you lawyers also! For you load people with burdens hard

to bear, and you yourselves do not touch the burdens with one of your fingers. **47** Woe to you! For you build the tombs of the prophets whom your fathers killed. **48** So you are witnesses and you consent to the deeds of your fathers, for they killed them, and you build their tombs. **49** Therefore also the Wisdom of God said, 'I will send them prophets and apostles, some of whom they will kill and persecute,' **50** so that the blood of all the prophets, shed from the foundation of the world, may be charged against this generation, **51** from the blood of Abel to the blood of Zechariah, who perished between the altar and the sanctuary. Yes, I tell you, it will be required of this generation. **52** Woe to you lawyers! For you have taken away the key of knowledge. You did not enter yourselves, and you hindered those who were entering."

53 As he went away from there, the scribes and the Pharisees began to press him hard

and to provoke him to speak about many things, **54** lying in wait for him, to catch him in something he might say.

Beware of the Leaven of the Pharisees

12 In the meantime, when so many thousands of the people had gathered together that they were trampling one another, he began to say to his disciples first, "Beware of the leaven of the Pharisees, which is hypocrisy. **2** Nothing is covered up that will not be revealed, or hidden that will not be known. **3** Therefore whatever you have said in the dark shall be heard in the light, and what you have whispered in private rooms shall be proclaimed on the housetops.

Have No Fear

4 "I tell you, my friends, do not fear those who kill the body, and after that have noth-

ing more that they can do. **5** But I will warn you whom to fear: fear him who, after he has killed, has authority to cast into hell. Yes, I tell you, fear him! **6** Are not five sparrows sold for two pennies?[1] And not one of them is forgotten before God. **7** Why, even the hairs of your head are all numbered. Fear not; you are of more value than many sparrows.

Acknowledge Christ Before Men

8 "And I tell you, everyone who acknowledges me before men, the Son of Man also will acknowledge before the angels of God, **9** but the one who denies me before men will be denied before the angels of God. **10** And everyone who speaks a word against the Son of Man will be forgiven, but the one who blasphemes against the Holy Spirit will not be forgiven. **11** And when they bring you before the synagogues and the rulers and the authorities, do not be anxious about how you should defend yourself or what you should say, **12** for the Holy Spirit will teach you in that very hour what you ought to say."

The Parable of the Rich Fool

13 Someone in the crowd said to him, "Teacher, tell my brother to divide the inheritance with me." **14** But he said to him, "Man, who made me a judge or arbitrator over you?" **15** And he said to them, "Take care, and be on your guard against all covetousness, for one's life does not consist in the abundance of his possessions." **16** And he told them a parable, saying, "The land of a rich man produced plentifully, **17** and he thought to himself, 'What shall I do, for I have nowhere to store my crops?' **18** And he said, 'I will do this: I will tear down my barns and build larger ones, and there I will store all my grain and my goods. **19** And I will say to my soul, "Soul, you have ample goods laid up for many years; relax, eat, drink, be merry."' **20** But God said to him, 'Fool! This night your soul is required of you, and the things you have prepared, whose will they be?' **21** So is the one who lays up treasure for himself and is not rich toward God."

Do Not Be Anxious

22 And he said to his disciples, "Therefore I tell you, do not be anxious about your life, what you will eat, nor about your body, what you will put on. **23** For life is more than

[1] The Greek word refers to about 1/16 of a day's pay for a worker

food, and the body more than clothing.
²⁴ Consider the ravens: they neither sow nor reap, they have neither storehouse nor barn, and yet God feeds them. Of how much more value are you than the birds! ²⁵ And which of you by being anxious can add a single hour to his span of life? ²⁶ If then you are not able to do as small a thing as that, why are you anxious about the rest? ²⁷ Consider the lilies, how they grow: they neither toil nor spin, yet I tell you, even Solomon in all his glory was not arrayed like one of these. ²⁸ But if God so clothes the grass, which is alive in the field today, and tomorrow is thrown into the oven, how much more will he clothe you, O you of little faith! ²⁹ And do not seek what you are to eat and what you are to drink, nor be worried. ³⁰ For all the nations of the world seek after these things, and your Father knows that you need them. ³¹ Instead, seek his kingdom, and these things will be added to you.

³² "Fear not, little flock, for it is your Father's good pleasure to give you the kingdom. ³³ Sell your possessions, and give to the needy. Provide yourselves with money-bags that do not grow old, with a treasure in the heavens that does not fail, where no thief approaches and no moth destroys. ³⁴ For where your treasure is, there will your heart be also.

You Must Be Ready

³⁵ "Stay dressed for action and keep your lamps burning, ³⁶ and be like men who are waiting for their master to come home from the wedding feast, so that they may open the door to him at once when he comes and knocks. ³⁷ Blessed are those servants whom the master finds awake when he comes. Truly, I say to you, he will dress himself for service and have them recline at table, and he will come and serve them. ³⁸ If he comes in the second watch, or in the third, and finds them awake, blessed are those servants! ³⁹ But know this, that if the master of the house had known at what hour the thief was coming, he would not have left his house to be broken into. ⁴⁰ You also must be ready, for the Son of Man is coming at an hour you do not expect."

⁴¹ Peter said, "Lord, are you telling this parable for us or for all?" ⁴² And the Lord said, "Who then is the faithful and wise manager, whom his master will set over his household, to give them their portion of food at the proper time? ⁴³ Blessed is that servant whom his master will find so doing when he comes. ⁴⁴ Truly, I say to you, he will set him over all his possessions. ⁴⁵ But if that servant says to himself, 'My master is delayed in coming,' and begins to beat the male and female servants, and to eat and drink and get drunk, ⁴⁶ the master of that servant will come on a day when he does not expect him and at an hour he does not know, and will cut him in pieces and put him with the unfaithful. ⁴⁷ And that servant who knew his master's will but did not get ready or act according to his will, will receive a severe beating. ⁴⁸ But the one who did not know, and did what deserved a beating, will receive a light beating. Everyone to whom much was given, of him much will be required, and from him to whom they entrusted much, they will demand the more.

Not Peace, but Division

⁴⁹ "I came to cast fire on the earth, and would that it were already kindled! ⁵⁰ I have a baptism to be baptized with, and how great is my distress until it is accomplished! ⁵¹ Do you think that I have come to give peace on earth? No, I tell you, but rather division. ⁵² For from now on in one house there will be five divided, three against two and two against three. ⁵³ They will be divided, father against son and son against father, mother against daughter and daughter against mother, mother-in-law against her daughter-in-law and daughter-in-law against mother-in-law."

Interpreting the Time

⁵⁴ He also said to the crowds, "When you see a cloud rising in the west, you say at once, 'A shower is coming.' And so it happens. ⁵⁵ And when you see the south wind blowing, you say, 'There will be scorching heat,' and it happens. ⁵⁶ You hypocrites! You know how to interpret the appearance of earth and sky, but why do you not know how to interpret the present time?

Settle with Your Accuser

⁵⁷ "And why do you not judge for yourselves what is right? ⁵⁸ As you go with your accuser before the magistrate, make an effort to settle with him on the way, lest he drag you to the judge, and the judge hand you over to the officer, and the officer put

you in prison. [59] I tell you, you will never get out until you have paid the very last penny." [1]

Repent or Perish

13 There were some present at that very time who told him about the Galileans whose blood Pilate had mingled with their sacrifices. [2] And he answered them, "Do you think that these Galileans were worse sinners than all the other Galileans, because they suffered in this way? [3] No, I tell you; but unless you repent, you will all likewise perish. [4] Or those eighteen on whom the tower in Siloam fell and killed them: do you think that they were worse offenders than all the others who lived in Jerusalem? [5] No, I tell you; but unless you repent, you will all likewise perish."

The Parable of the Barren Fig Tree

[6] And he told this parable: "A man had a fig tree planted in his vineyard, and he

> **GETTING THE MESSAGE**
>
> The synagogue ruler thought that Jesus was wrong to **heal people on the sabbath** (13:14). Keeping the sabbath meant resting from work, and some people thought that healing should be considered work. But there was actually no biblical law against healing on the Sabbath.

came seeking fruit on it and found none. [7] And he said to the vinedresser, 'Look, for three years now I have come seeking fruit on this fig tree, and I find none. Cut it down. Why should it use up the ground?' [8] And he answered him, 'Sir, let it alone this year also, until I dig around it and put on manure. [9] Then if it should bear fruit next year, well and good; but if not, you can cut it down.'"

A Woman with a Disabling Spirit

[10] Now he was teaching in one of the synagogues on the Sabbath. [11] And behold, there was a woman who had had a disabling spirit for eighteen years. She was bent over and could not fully straighten herself. [12] When Jesus saw her, he called her over and said to her, "Woman, you are freed from your disability." [13] And he laid his hands on her,

and immediately she was made straight, and she glorified God. [14] But the ruler of the synagogue, indignant because Jesus had healed on the Sabbath, said to the people, "There are six days in which work ought to be done. Come on those days and be healed, and not on the Sabbath day." [15] Then the Lord answered him, "You hypocrites! Does not each of you on the Sabbath untie his ox or his donkey from the manger and lead it away to water it? [16] And ought not this woman, a daughter of Abraham whom Satan bound for eighteen years, be loosed from this bond on the Sabbath day?" [17] As he said these things, all his adversaries were put to shame, and all the people rejoiced at all the glorious things that were done by him.

The Mustard Seed and the Leaven

[18] He said therefore, "What is the kingdom of God like? And to what shall I compare it? [19] It is like a grain of mustard seed that a man took and sowed in his garden, and it grew and became a tree, and the birds of the air made nests in its branches."

[20] And again he said, "To what shall I compare the kingdom of God? [21] It is like leaven that a woman took and hid in three measures of flour, until it was all leavened."

The Narrow Door

[22] He went on his way through towns and villages, teaching and journeying toward Jerusalem. [23] And someone said to him, "Lord, will those who are saved be few?" And he said to them, [24] "Strive to enter through the narrow door. For many, I tell you, will seek to enter and will not be able. [25] When once the master of the house has risen and shut the door, and you begin to stand outside and to knock at the door, saying, 'Lord, open to us,' then he will answer you, 'I do not know where you come from.' [26] Then you will begin to say, 'We ate and drank in your presence, and you taught in our streets.' [27] But he will say, 'I tell you, I do not know where you come from. Depart from me, all you workers of evil!' [28] In that place there will be weeping and gnashing of teeth, when you see Abraham and Isaac and Jacob and all the prophets in the kingdom of God but you yourselves cast out. [29] And people will come from east and west, and from north and south, and recline at table

---

[1] The Greek word refers to about 1/128 of a day's pay for a worker

in the kingdom of God. ³⁰ And behold, some are last who will be first, and some are first who will be last."

Lament over Jerusalem

³¹ At that very hour some Pharisees came and said to him, "Get away from here, for Herod wants to kill you." ³² And he said to them, "Go and tell that fox, 'Behold, I cast out demons and perform cures today and tomorrow, and the third day I finish my course. ³³ Nevertheless, I must go on my way today and tomorrow and the day following, for it cannot be that a prophet should perish away from Jerusalem.' ³⁴ O Jerusalem, Jerusalem, the city that kills the prophets and stones those who are sent to it! How often would I have gathered your children together as a hen gathers her brood under her wings, and you were not willing! ³⁵ Behold, your house is forsaken. And I tell you, you will not see me until you say, 'Blessed is he who comes in the name of the Lord!'"

Healing of a Man on the Sabbath

14 One Sabbath, when he went to dine at the house of a ruler of the Pharisees, they were watching him carefully. ² And behold, there was a man before him who had dropsy. ³ And Jesus responded to the lawyers and Pharisees, saying, "Is it lawful to heal on the Sabbath, or not?" ⁴ But they remained silent. Then he took him and healed him and sent him away. ⁵ And he said to them, "Which of you, having a son or an ox that has fallen into a well on a Sabbath day, will not immediately pull him out?" ⁶ And they could not reply to these things.

The Parable of the Wedding Feast

⁷ Now he told a parable to those who were invited, when he noticed how they chose the places of honor, saying to them, ⁸ "When you are invited by someone to a wedding feast, do not sit down in a place of honor, lest someone more distinguished than you be invited by him, ⁹ and he who invited you both will come and say to you, 'Give your place to this person,' and then you will begin with shame to take the lowest place. ¹⁰ But when you are invited, go and sit in the lowest place, so that when your host comes he may say to you, 'Friend, move up higher.'

Then you will be honored in the presence of all who sit at table with you. ¹¹ For everyone who exalts himself will be humbled, and he who humbles himself will be exalted."

The Parable of the Great Banquet

¹² He said also to the man who had invited him, "When you give a dinner or a banquet, do not invite your friends or your brothers[1] or your relatives or rich neighbors, lest they also invite you in return and you be repaid. ¹³ But when you give a feast, invite the poor, the crippled, the lame, the blind, ¹⁴ and you will be blessed, because they cannot repay you. For you will be repaid at the resurrection of the just."

¹⁵ When one of those who reclined at table with him heard these things, he said to him, "Blessed is everyone who will eat bread in

GETTING THE MESSAGE

Too late for excuses. Planning a banquet was complicated and expensive. Two invitations were sent. The first would have included an RSVP so the host could determine how much food to prepare. The second would have gone out on the day of the banquet, announcing that the meal was ready. The ungrateful guests in 14:16–24 made their excuses upon receiving the second notice, after the host had already prepared the meal.

the kingdom of God!" ¹⁶ But he said to him, "A man once gave a great banquet and invited many. ¹⁷ And at the time for the banquet he sent his servant to say to those who had been invited, 'Come, for everything is now ready.' ¹⁸ But they all alike began to make excuses. The first said to him, 'I have bought a field, and I must go out and see it. Please have me excused.' ¹⁹ And another said, 'I have bought five yoke of oxen, and I go to examine them. Please have me excused.' ²⁰ And another said, 'I have married a wife, and therefore I cannot come.' ²¹ So the servant came and reported these things to his master. Then the master of the house became angry and said to his servant, 'Go out quickly to the streets and lanes of the city, and bring in the poor and crippled and blind and lame.' ²² And the servant said, 'Sir, what you commanded has

---

[1] Or your brothers and sisters (see Preface)

been done, and still there is room.' ²³ And the master said to the servant, 'Go out to the highways and hedges and compel people to come in, that my house may be filled. ²⁴ For I tell you, none of those men who were invited shall taste my banquet.'"

The Cost of Discipleship

²⁵ Now great crowds accompanied him, and he turned and said to them, ²⁶ "If anyone comes to me and does not hate his own father and mother and wife and children and brothers and sisters, yes, and even his own life, he cannot be my disciple. ²⁷ Whoever does not bear his own cross and come after me cannot be my disciple. ²⁸ For which of you, desiring to build a tower, does not first sit down and count the cost, whether he has enough to complete it? ²⁹ Otherwise, when he has laid a foundation and is not able to finish, all who see it begin to mock him, ³⁰ saying, 'This man began to build and was

GETTING THE MESSAGE

The **pods** mentioned in 15:16 are most likely carob pods. The pods of the carob tree were used for animal feed, but poor people often ate them as well.

not able to finish.' ³¹ Or what king, going out to encounter another king in war, will not sit down first and deliberate whether he is able with ten thousand to meet him who comes against him with twenty thousand? ³² And if not, while the other is yet a great way off, he sends a delegation and asks for terms of peace. ³³ So therefore, any one of you who does not renounce all that he has cannot be my disciple.

Salt Without Taste Is Worthless

³⁴ "Salt is good, but if salt has lost its taste, how shall its saltiness be restored? ³⁵ It is of no use either for the soil or for the manure pile. It is thrown away. He who has ears to hear, let him hear."

The Parable of the Lost Sheep

15 Now the tax collectors and sinners were all drawing near to hear him. ² And the Pharisees and the scribes grum-

bled, saying, "This man receives sinners and eats with them."

³ So he told them this parable: ⁴ "What man of you, having a hundred sheep, if he has lost one of them, does not leave the ninety-nine in the open country, and go after the one that is lost, until he finds it? ⁵ And when he has found it, he lays it on his shoulders, rejoicing. ⁶ And when he comes home, he calls together his friends and his neighbors, saying to them, 'Rejoice with me, for I have found my sheep that was lost.' ⁷ Just so, I tell you, there will be more joy in heaven over one sinner who repents than over ninety-nine righteous persons who need no repentance.

The Parable of the Lost Coin

⁸ "Or what woman, having ten silver coins,¹ if she loses one coin, does not light a lamp and sweep the house and seek diligently until she finds it? ⁹ And when she has found it, she calls together her friends and neighbors, saying, 'Rejoice with me, for I have found the coin that I had lost.' ¹⁰ Just so, I tell you, there is joy before the angels of God over one sinner who repents."

The Parable of the Prodigal Son

¹¹ And he said, "There was a man who had two sons. ¹² And the younger of them said to his father, 'Father, give me the share of property that is coming to me.' And he divided his property between them. ¹³ Not many days later, the younger son gathered all he had and took a journey into a far country, and there he squandered his property in reckless living. ¹⁴ And when he had spent everything, a severe famine arose in that country, and he began to be in need. ¹⁵ So he went and hired himself out to one of the citizens of that country, who sent him into his fields to feed pigs. ¹⁶ And he was longing to be fed with the pods that the pigs ate, and no one gave him anything.

¹⁷ "But when he came to himself, he said, 'How many of my father's hired servants have more than enough bread, but I perish here with hunger! ¹⁸ I will arise and go to my father, and I will say to him, "Father, I have sinned against heaven and before you. ¹⁹ I am no longer worthy to be called your son.' Treat me as one of your hired servants."' ²⁰ And he arose and came to his

¹ The Greek word refers to about ten days' pay for a worker

father. But while he was still a long way off, his father saw him and felt compassion, and ran and embraced him and kissed him. ²¹ And the son said to him, 'Father, I have sinned against heaven and before you. I am no longer worthy to be called your son.' ²² But the father said to his servants, 'Bring quickly the best robe, and put it on him, and put a ring on his hand, and shoes on his feet. ²³ And bring the fattened calf and kill it, and let us eat and celebrate. ²⁴ For this my son was dead, and is alive again; he was lost, and is found.' And they began to celebrate.

²⁵ "Now his older son was in the field, and as he came and drew near to the house, he heard music and dancing. ²⁶ And he called one of the servants and asked what these things meant. ²⁷ And he said to him, 'Your brother has come, and your father has killed the fattened calf, because he has received him back safe and sound.' ²⁸ But he was angry and refused to go in. His father came out and entreated him, ²⁹ but he answered his father, 'Look, these many years I have served you, and I never disobeyed your command, yet you never gave me a young goat, that I might celebrate with my friends. ³⁰ But when this son of yours came, who has devoured your property with prostitutes, you killed the fattened calf for him!' ³¹ And he said to him, 'Son, you are always with me, and all that is mine is yours. ³² It was fitting to celebrate and be glad, for this your brother was dead, and is alive; he was lost, and is found.' "

The Parable of the Dishonest Manager

16 He also said to the disciples, "There was a rich man who had a manager, and charges were brought to him that this man was wasting his possessions. ² And he called him and said to him, 'What is this that I hear about you? Turn in the account of your management, for you can no longer be manager.' ³ And the manager said to himself, 'What shall I do, since my master is taking the management away from me? I am not strong enough to dig, and I am ashamed to beg. ⁴ I have decided what to do, so that when I am removed from management, people may receive me into their houses.' ⁵ So, summoning his master's debtors one by one, he said to the first, 'How much do you owe my master?' ⁶ He said, 'A hundred

measures¹ of oil.' He said to him, 'Take your bill, and sit down quickly and write fifty.' ⁷ Then he said to another, 'And how much do you owe?' He said, 'A hundred measures² of wheat.' He said to him, 'Take your bill, and write eighty.' ⁸ The master commended the dishonest manager for his shrewdness. For the sons of this world are more shrewd in dealing with their own generation than the sons of light. ⁹ And I tell you, make friends for yourselves by means of unrighteous wealth, so that when it fails they may receive you into the eternal dwellings.

¹⁰ "One who is faithful in a very little is also faithful in much, and one who is dishonest in a very little is also dishonest in much. ¹¹ If then you have not been faithful in the unrighteous wealth, who will entrust to you the true riches? ¹² And if you have not been faithful in that which is another's, who will give you that which is your own? ¹³ No servant can serve two masters, for either he will hate the one and love the other, or he will be devoted to the one and despise the other. You cannot serve God and money."

The Law and the Kingdom of God

¹⁴ The Pharisees, who were lovers of money, heard all these things, and they ridiculed him. ¹⁵ And he said to them, "You are those who justify yourselves before men, but God knows your hearts. For what is exalted among men is an abomination in the sight of God.

¹⁶ "The Law and the Prophets were until John; since then the good news of the kingdom of God is preached, and everyone forces his way into it. ¹⁷ But it is easier for heaven and earth to pass away than for one dot of the Law to become void.

Divorce and Remarriage

¹⁸ "Everyone who divorces his wife and marries another commits adultery, and he who marries a woman divorced from her husband commits adultery.

The Rich Man and Lazarus

¹⁹ "There was a rich man who was clothed in purple and fine linen and who feasted sumptuously every day. ²⁰ And at his gate was laid a poor man named Lazarus, covered with sores, ²¹ who desired to be fed with what fell from the rich man's table.

¹ About 875 gallons or 3,200 liters ² Between 1,000 and 1,200 bushels or 37,000 to 45,000 liters

Moreover, even the dogs came and licked his sores. ²² The poor man died and was carried by the angels to Abraham's side. The rich man also died and was buried, ²³ and in Hades, being in torment, he lifted up his eyes and saw Abraham far off and Lazarus at his side. ²⁴ And he called out, 'Father Abraham, have mercy on me, and send Lazarus to dip the end of his finger in water and cool my tongue, for I am in anguish in this flame.' ²⁵ But Abraham said, 'Child, remember that you in your lifetime received your good things, and Lazarus in like manner bad things; but now he is comforted here, and you are in anguish. ²⁶ And besides all this, between us and you a great chasm has been fixed, in order that those who would pass from here to you may not be able, and none may cross from there to us.' ²⁷ And he said, 'Then I beg you, father,

---

> ### GETTING THE MESSAGE
>
> **The rich man and Lazarus.** Luke emphasizes God's love for the poor, outcasts, sinners, and the weak. Many of the stories in his Gospel focus on this theme, including 16:19–31.

---

to send him to my father's house— ²⁸ for I have five brothers[1]—so that he may warn them, lest they also come into this place of torment.' ²⁹ But Abraham said, 'They have Moses and the Prophets; let them hear them.' ³⁰ And he said, 'No, father Abraham, but if someone goes to them from the dead, they will repent.' ³¹ He said to him, 'If they do not hear Moses and the Prophets, neither will they be convinced if someone should rise from the dead.'"

Temptations to Sin

17 And he said to his disciples, "Temptations to sin are sure to come, but woe to the one through whom they come! ² It would be better for him if a millstone were hung around his neck and he were cast into the sea than that he should cause one of these little ones to sin. ³ Pay attention to yourselves! If your brother sins, rebuke him, and if he repents, forgive him, ⁴ and if he sins against you seven times in the day, and

turns to you seven times, saying, 'I repent,' you must forgive him."

Increase Our Faith

⁵ The apostles said to the Lord, "Increase our faith!" ⁶ And the Lord said, "If you had faith like a grain of mustard seed, you could say to this mulberry tree, 'Be uprooted and planted in the sea,' and it would obey you.

Unworthy Servants

⁷ "Will any one of you who has a servant plowing or keeping sheep say to him when he has come in from the field, 'Come at once and recline at table'? ⁸ Will he not rather say to him, 'Prepare supper for me, and dress properly, and serve me while I eat and drink, and afterward you will eat and drink'? ⁹ Does he thank the servant because he did what was commanded? ¹⁰ So you also, when you have done all that you were commanded, say, 'We are unworthy servants; we have only done what was our duty.'"

Jesus Cleanses Ten Lepers

¹¹ On the way to Jerusalem he was passing along between Samaria and Galilee. ¹² And as he entered a village, he was met by ten lepers,[2] who stood at a distance ¹³ and lifted up their voices, saying, "Jesus, Master, have mercy on us." ¹⁴ When he saw them he said to them, "Go and show yourselves to the priests." And as they went they were cleansed. ¹⁵ Then one of them, when he saw that he was healed, turned back, praising God with a loud voice; ¹⁶ and he fell on his face at Jesus' feet, giving him thanks. Now he was a Samaritan. ¹⁷ Then Jesus answered, "Were not ten cleansed? Where are the nine? ¹⁸ Was no one found to return and give praise to God except this foreigner?" ¹⁹ And he said to him, "Rise and go your way; your faith has made you well."

The Coming of the Kingdom

²⁰ Being asked by the Pharisees when the kingdom of God would come, he answered them, "The kingdom of God is not coming in ways that can be observed, ²¹ nor will they say, 'Look, here it is!' or 'There!' for behold, the kingdom of God is in the midst of you."

²² And he said to the disciples, "The days are coming when you will desire to see one of the days of the Son of Man, and you will

---

[1] Or *brothers and sisters* [2] *Leprosy* was a term for several skin diseases (see Leviticus 13)

not see it. 23 And they will say to you, 'Look, there!' or 'Look, here!' Do not go out or follow them. 24 For as the lightning flashes and lights up the sky from one side to the other, so will the Son of Man be in his day. 25 But first he must suffer many things and be rejected by this generation. 26 Just as it was in the days of Noah, so will it be in the days of the Son of Man. 27 They were eating and drinking and marrying and being given in marriage, until the day when Noah entered the ark, and the flood came and destroyed them all. 28 Likewise, just as it was in the days of Lot—they were eating and drinking, buying and selling, planting and building, 29 but on the day when Lot went out from Sodom, fire and sulfur rained from heaven and destroyed them all— 30 so will it be on the day when the Son of Man is revealed. 31 On that day, let the one who is on the housetop, with his goods in the house, not come down to take them away, and likewise let the one who is in the field not turn back. 32 Remember Lot's wife. 33 Whoever seeks to preserve his life will lose it, but whoever loses his life will keep it. 34 I tell you, in that night there will be two in one bed. One will be taken and the other left. 35 There will be two women grinding together. One will be taken and the other left." 37 And they said to him, "Where, Lord?" He said to them, "Where the corpse is, there the vultures will gather."

The Parable of the Persistent Widow

18 And he told them a parable to the effect that they ought always to pray and not lose heart. 2 He said, "In a certain city there was a judge who neither feared God nor respected man. 3 And there was a widow in that city who kept coming to him and saying, 'Give me justice against my adversary.' 4 For a while he refused, but afterward he said to himself, 'Though I neither fear God nor respect man, 5 yet because this widow keeps bothering me, I will give her justice, so that she will not beat me down by her continual coming.'" 6 And the Lord said, "Hear what the unrighteous judge says. 7 And will not God give justice to his elect, who cry to him day and night? Will he delay long over them? 8 I tell you, he will give justice to them speedily. Nevertheless, when the Son of Man comes, will he find faith on earth?"

The Pharisee and the Tax Collector

9 He also told this parable to some who trusted in themselves that they were righteous, and treated others with contempt: 10 "Two men went up into the temple to pray, one a Pharisee and the other a tax collector. 11 The Pharisee, standing by himself, prayed thus: 'God, I thank you that I am not like other men, extortioners, unjust, adulterers, or even like this tax collector. 12 I fast twice a week; I give tithes of all that I get.' 13 But the tax collector, standing far off, would not even lift up his eyes to heaven, but beat his breast, saying, 'God, be merciful to me, a sinner!' 14 I tell you, this man went down to his house justified, rather than the other. For everyone who exalts himself will be humbled, but the one who humbles himself will be exalted."

> ### GETTING THE MESSAGE
>
> **How difficult it is for a rich person.**
> In 18:18–30, Jesus challenges a rich ruler to give his money to the poor. However, the man refuses because his riches matter more to him than obeying Jesus. Elsewhere, Jesus warns that it is impossible to serve both God and money (16:13).

Let the Children Come to Me

15 Now they were bringing even infants to him that he might touch them. And when the disciples saw it, they rebuked them. 16 But Jesus called them to him, saying, "Let the children come to me, and do not hinder them, for to such belongs the kingdom of God. 17 Truly, I say to you, whoever does not receive the kingdom of God like a child shall not enter it."

The Rich Ruler

18 And a ruler asked him, "Good Teacher, what must I do to inherit eternal life?" 19 And Jesus said to him, "Why do you call me good? No one is good except God alone. 20 You know the commandments: 'Do not commit adultery, Do not murder, Do not steal, Do not bear false witness, Honor your father and mother.'" 21 And he said, "All these I have kept from my youth." 22 When Jesus heard this, he said to him, "One thing you

still lack. Sell all that you have and distribute to the poor, and you will have treasure in heaven; and come, follow me." ²³ But when he heard these things, he became very sad, for he was extremely rich. ²⁴ Jesus, seeing that he had become sad, said, "How difficult it is for those who have wealth to enter the kingdom of God! ²⁵ For it is easier for a camel to go through the eye of a needle than for a rich person to enter the kingdom of God." ²⁶ Those who heard it said, "Then who can be saved?" ²⁷ But he said, "What is impossible with man is possible with God." ²⁸ And Peter said, "See, we have left our homes and followed you." ²⁹ And he said to them, "Truly, I say to you, there is no one who has left house or wife or brothers or parents or children, for the sake of the kingdom of God, ³⁰ who will not receive many times more in this time, and in the age to come eternal life."

Jesus Foretells His Death a Third Time

³¹ And taking the twelve, he said to them, "See, we are going up to Jerusalem, and everything that is written about the Son of Man by the prophets will be accomplished. ³² For he will be delivered over to the Gentiles and will be mocked and shamefully treated and spit upon. ³³ And after flogging him, they will kill him, and on the third day he will rise." ³⁴ But they understood none of these things. This saying was hidden from them, and they did not grasp what was said.

Jesus Heals a Blind Beggar

³⁵ As he drew near to Jericho, a blind man was sitting by the roadside begging. ³⁶ And hearing a crowd going by, he inquired what this meant. ³⁷ They told him, "Jesus of Nazareth is passing by." ³⁸ And he cried out, "Jesus, Son of David, have mercy on me!" ³⁹ And those who were in front rebuked him, telling him to be silent. But he cried out all the more, "Son of David, have mercy on me!" ⁴⁰ And Jesus stopped and commanded him to be brought to him. And when he came near, he asked him, ⁴¹ "What do you want me to do for you?" He said, "Lord, let me recover my sight." ⁴² And Jesus said to him, "Recover your sight; your faith has made you well." ⁴³ And immediately he recovered his sight and followed him, glorifying God. And all the people, when they saw it, gave praise to God.

Jesus and Zacchaeus

19 He entered Jericho and was passing through. ² And behold, there was a man named Zacchaeus. He was a chief tax collector and was rich. ³ And he was seeking to see who Jesus was, but on account of the crowd he could not, because he was small in stature. ⁴ So he ran on ahead and climbed up into a sycamore tree to see him, for he was about to pass that way. ⁵ And when Jesus came to the place, he looked up and said to him, "Zacchaeus, hurry and come down, for I must stay at your house today." ⁶ So he hurried and came down and received him joyfully. ⁷ And when they saw it, they all grumbled, "He has gone in to be the guest of a man who is a sinner." ⁸ And Zacchaeus stood and said to the Lord, "Behold, Lord, the half of my goods I give to the poor. And if I have defrauded anyone of anything, I restore it fourfold." ⁹ And Jesus said to him, "Today salvation has come to this house, since he also is a son of Abraham. ¹⁰ For the Son of Man came to seek and to save the lost."

The Parable of the Ten Minas

¹¹ As they heard these things, he proceeded to tell a parable, because he was near to Jerusalem, and because they supposed that the kingdom of God was to appear immediately. ¹² He said therefore, "A nobleman went into a far country to receive for himself a kingdom and then return. ¹³ Calling ten of his servants, he gave them ten minas, and said to them, 'Engage in business until I come.' ¹⁴ But his citizens hated him and sent a delegation after him, saying, 'We do not want this man to reign over us.' ¹⁵ When he returned, having received the kingdom, he ordered these servants to whom he had given the money to be called to him, that he might know what they had gained by doing business. ¹⁶ The first came before him, saying, 'Lord, your mina has made ten minas more.' ¹⁷ And he said to him, 'Well done, good servant! Because you have been faithful in a very little, you shall have authority over ten cities.' ¹⁸ And the second came, saying, 'Lord, your mina has made five minas.' ¹⁹ And he said to him, 'And you are to be over five cities.' ²⁰ Then another came, saying, 'Lord, here is your mina, which I kept laid away in a handkerchief; ²¹ for I was afraid of you, because you are a severe man. You

take what you did not deposit, and reap what you did not sow.' ²² He said to him, 'I will condemn you with your own words, you wicked servant! You knew that I was a severe man, taking what I did not deposit and reaping what I did not sow? ²³ Why then did you not put my money in the bank, and at my coming I might have collected it with interest?' ²⁴ And he said to those who stood by, 'Take the mina from him, and give it to the one who has the ten minas.' ²⁵ And they said to him, 'Lord, he has ten minas!' ²⁶ 'I tell you that to everyone who has, more will be given, but from the one who has not, even what he has will be taken away. ²⁷ But as for these enemies of mine, who did not want me to reign over them, bring them here and slaughter them before me.'"

The Triumphal Entry

²⁸ And when he had said these things, he went on ahead, going up to Jerusalem. ²⁹ When he drew near to Bethphage and Bethany, at the mount that is called Olivet, he sent two of the disciples, ³⁰ saying, "Go into the village in front of you, where on entering you will find a colt tied, on which no one has ever yet sat. Untie it and bring it here. ³¹ If anyone asks you, 'Why are you untying it?' you shall say this: 'The Lord has need of it.'" ³² So those who were sent went away and found it just as he had told them. ³³ And as they were untying the colt, its owners said to them, "Why are you untying the colt?" ³⁴ And they said, "The Lord has need of it." ³⁵ And they brought it to Jesus, and throwing their cloaks on the colt, they set Jesus on it. ³⁶ And as he rode along, they spread their cloaks on the road. ³⁷ As he was drawing near—already on the way down the Mount of Olives—the whole multitude of his disciples began to rejoice and praise God with a loud voice for all the mighty works that they had seen, ³⁸ saying, "Blessed is the King who comes in the name of the Lord! Peace in heaven and glory in the highest!" ³⁹ And some of the Pharisees in the crowd said to him, "Teacher, rebuke your disciples." ⁴⁰ He answered, "I tell you, if these were silent, the very stones would cry out."

Jesus Weeps over Jerusalem

⁴¹ And when he drew near and saw the city, he wept over it, ⁴² saying, "Would that you, even you, had known on this day the things that make for peace! But now they are hidden from your eyes. ⁴³ For the days will come upon you, when your enemies will set up a barricade around you and surround you and hem you in on every side ⁴⁴ and tear you down to the ground, you and your children within you. And they will not leave one stone upon another in you, because you did not know the time of your visitation."

Jesus Cleanses the Temple

⁴⁵ And he entered the temple and began to drive out those who sold, ⁴⁶ saying to them, "It is written, 'My house shall be a house of prayer,' but you have made it a den of robbers."

⁴⁷ And he was teaching daily in the temple. The chief priests and the scribes and the principal men of the people were seeking to

> **GETTING THE MESSAGE**
>
> **Olivet** (19:29), also known as the **Mount of Olives**, is a high mountain ridge stretching some 2.5 miles (4 km) in a north-to-south direction just east of Jerusalem. Throughout Israel's history, it was an ideal location from which to see approaching armies. It is also where Jesus ascended into heaven with the promise to return in the same way (24:51; Acts 1:11–12; see also Zech. 14:4).

destroy him, ⁴⁸ but they did not find anything they could do, for all the people were hanging on his words.

The Authority of Jesus Challenged

20 One day, as Jesus was teaching the people in the temple and preaching the gospel, the chief priests and the scribes with the elders came up ² and said to him, "Tell us by what authority you do these things, or who it is that gave you this authority." ³ He answered them, "I also will ask you a question. Now tell me, ⁴ was the baptism of John from heaven or from man?" ⁵ And they discussed it with one another, saying, "If we say, 'From heaven,' he will say, 'Why did you not believe him?' ⁶ But if we say, 'From man,' all the people will stone us to death, for they are convinced that John was a prophet." ⁷ So they answered that they did not know where it came from. **⁸** And Jesus said to them, "Neither will I tell you by what authority I do these things."

The Parable of the Wicked Tenants

⁹ And he began to tell the people this parable: "A man planted a vineyard and let it out to tenants and went into another country for a long while. **¹⁰** When the time came, he sent a servant to the tenants, so that they would give him some of the fruit of the vineyard. But the tenants beat him and sent him away empty-handed. **¹¹** And he sent another servant. But they also beat and treated him shamefully, and sent him away empty-handed. **¹²** And he sent yet a third. This one also they wounded and cast out. **¹³** Then the owner of the vineyard said, 'What shall I do? I will send my beloved son; perhaps they will respect him.' **¹⁴** But when the tenants saw him, they said to themselves, 'This is the heir. Let us kill him, so that the inheritance may be ours.' **¹⁵** And they threw him out of the vineyard and killed him. What then will the owner of the vineyard do to them? **¹⁶** He will come and destroy those tenants and give the vineyard to others." When they heard this, they said, "Surely not!" **¹⁷** But he looked directly at them and said, "What then is this that is written:

"'The stone that the builders rejected
    has become the cornerstone'?

¹⁸ Everyone who falls on that stone will be broken to pieces, and when it falls on anyone, it will crush him."

Paying Taxes to Caesar

¹⁹ The scribes and the chief priests sought to lay hands on him at that very hour, for they perceived that he had told this parable against them, but they feared the people. **²⁰** So they watched him and sent spies, who pretended to be sincere, that they might catch him in something he said, so as to deliver him up to the authority and jurisdiction of the governor. **²¹** So they asked him, "Teacher, we know that you speak and teach rightly, and show no partiality, but truly teach the way of God. **²²** Is it lawful for us to give tribute to Caesar, or not?" **²³** But he perceived their craftiness, and said to them, **²⁴** "Show me a denarius. Whose likeness and inscription does it

have?" They said, "Caesar's." **²⁵** He said to them, "Then render to Caesar the things that are Caesar's, and to God the things that are God's." **²⁶** And they were not able in the presence of the people to catch him in what he said, but marveling at his answer they became silent.

Sadducees Ask About the Resurrection

²⁷ There came to him some Sadducees, those who deny that there is a resurrection, **²⁸** and they asked him a question, saying, "Teacher, Moses wrote for us that if a man's brother dies, having a wife but no children, the man must take the widow and raise up offspring for his brother. **²⁹** Now there were seven brothers. The first took a wife, and died without children. **³⁰** And the second **³¹** and the third took her, and likewise all seven left no children and died. **³²** Afterward the woman also died. **³³** In the resurrection, therefore, whose wife will the woman be? For the seven had her as wife."

³⁴ And Jesus said to them, "The sons of this age marry and are given in marriage, **³⁵** but those who are considered worthy to attain to that age and to the resurrection from the dead neither marry nor are given in marriage, **³⁶** for they cannot die anymore, because they are equal to angels and are sons of God, being sons of the resurrection. **³⁷** But that the dead are raised, even Moses showed, in the passage about the bush, where he calls the Lord the God of Abraham and the God of Isaac and the God of Jacob. **³⁸** Now he is not God of the dead, but of the living, for all live to him." **³⁹** Then some of the scribes answered, "Teacher, you have spoken well." **⁴⁰** For they no longer dared to ask him any question.

Whose Son Is the Christ?

⁴¹ But he said to them, "How can they say that the Christ is David's son? **⁴²** For David himself says in the Book of Psalms,

"'The Lord said to my Lord,
    "Sit at my right hand,
⁴³   until I make your enemies your
            footstool."'

⁴⁴ David thus calls him Lord, so how is he his son?"

Beware of the Scribes

⁴⁵ And in the hearing of all the people he said to his disciples, **⁴⁶** "Beware of the scribes, who like to walk around in long robes, and love greetings in the market-places and the best seats in the synagogues and the places of honor at feasts, **47** who devour widows' houses and for a pretense make long prayers. They will receive the greater condemnation."

The Widow's Offering

21 Jesus looked up and saw the rich putting their gifts into the offering box, **2** and he saw a poor widow put in two small copper coins. **3** And he said, "Truly, I tell you, this poor widow has put in more than all of them. **4** For they all contributed out of their abundance, but she out of her poverty put in all she had to live on."

Jesus Foretells Destruction of the Temple

5 And while some were speaking of the temple, how it was adorned with noble stones and offerings, he said, **6** "As for these things that you see, the days will come when there will not be left here one stone upon another that will not be thrown down." **7** And they asked him, "Teacher, when will these things be, and what will be the sign when these things are about to take place?" **8** And he said, "See that you are not led astray. For many will come in my name, saying, 'I am he!' and, 'The time is at hand!' Do not go after them. **9** And when you hear of wars and tumults, do not be terrified, for these things must first take place, but the end will not be at once."

Jesus Foretells Wars and Persecution

10 Then he said to them, "Nation will rise against nation, and kingdom against kingdom. **11** There will be great earthquakes, and in various places famines and pestilences. And there will be terrors and great signs from heaven. **12** But before all this they will lay their hands on you and persecute you, delivering you up to the synagogues and prisons, and you will be brought before kings and governors for my name's sake. **13** This will be your opportunity to bear witness. **14** Settle it therefore in your minds not to meditate beforehand how to answer, **15** for I will give you a mouth and wisdom, which none of your adversaries will be able to withstand or contradict. **16** You will be delivered up even by parents and brothers and relatives and friends, and some of you

they will put to death. **17** You will be hated by all for my name's sake. **18** But not a hair of your head will perish. **19** By your endurance you will gain your lives.

Jesus Foretells Destruction of Jerusalem

20 "But when you see Jerusalem surrounded by armies, then know that its desolation has come near. **21** Then let those who are in Judea flee to the mountains, and let those who are inside the city depart, and let not those who are out in the country enter it, **22** for these are days of vengeance, to fulfill all that is written. **23** Alas for women who are pregnant and for those who are nursing infants in those days! For there will be great distress upon the earth and wrath against this people. **24** They will fall by the edge of the sword and be led captive among all nations, and Jerusalem will be trampled

GETTING THE MESSAGE

The widow's offering. There were 13 collection chests for offerings in the temple. The widow's contribution caught Jesus' eye not because it was impressive but because she had given sacrificially. The attitude of the giver is more important to God than the size of the gift.

underfoot by the Gentiles, until the times of the Gentiles are fulfilled.

The Coming of the Son of Man

25 "And there will be signs in sun and moon and stars, and on the earth distress of nations in perplexity because of the roaring of the sea and the waves, **26** people fainting with fear and with foreboding of what is coming on the world. For the powers of the heavens will be shaken. **27** And then they will see the Son of Man coming in a cloud with power and great glory. **28** Now when these things begin to take place, straighten up and raise your heads, because your redemption is drawing near."

The Lesson of the Fig Tree

29 And he told them a parable: "Look at the fig tree, and all the trees. **30** As soon as they come out in leaf, you see for yourselves and know that the summer is already near. **31** So also, when you see these things taking place, you know that the kingdom of God is near. **32** Truly, I say to you, this generation will not pass away until all has taken place. **33** Heaven and earth will pass away, but my words will not pass away.

Watch Yourselves

34 "But watch yourselves lest your hearts be weighed down with dissipation and drunkenness and cares of this life, and that day come upon you suddenly like a trap. **35** For it will come upon all who dwell on the face of the whole earth. **36** But stay awake at all times, praying that you may have strength to escape all these things that are going to take place, and to stand before the Son of Man."

37 And every day he was teaching in the temple, but at night he went out and lodged on the mount called Olivet. **38** And early in

GETTING THE MESSAGE

The **temple** mentioned in the Gospels was the second one. The Babylonians destroyed the first temple, which Solomon had built. The Jews rebuilt it, and Herod the Great fully restored it later. Shortly after Jesus' prophecy (21:6), this temple was destroyed, in A.D. 70.

the morning all the people came to him in the temple to hear him.

The Plot to Kill Jesus

22 Now the Feast of Unleavened Bread drew near, which is called the Passover. **2** And the chief priests and the scribes were seeking how to put him to death, for they feared the people.

Judas to Betray Jesus

3 Then Satan entered into Judas called Iscariot, who was of the number of the twelve. **4** He went away and conferred with the chief priests and officers how he might betray him to them. **5** And they were glad, and agreed to give him money. **6** So he consented and sought an opportunity to betray him to them in the absence of a crowd.

The Passover with the Disciples

7 Then came the day of Unleavened Bread, on which the Passover lamb had to be sacrificed. **8** So Jesus sent Peter and John, saying,

"Go and prepare the Passover for us, that we may eat it." **9** They said to him, "Where will you have us prepare it?" **10** He said to them, "Behold, when you have entered the city, a man carrying a jar of water will meet you. Follow him into the house that he enters **11** and tell the master of the house, 'The Teacher says to you, Where is the guest room, where I may eat the Passover with my disciples?' **12** And he will show you a large upper room furnished; prepare it there." **13** And they went and found it just as he had told them, and they prepared the Passover.

Institution of the Lord's Supper

14 And when the hour came, he reclined at table, and the apostles with him. **15** And he said to them, "I have earnestly desired to eat this Passover with you before I suffer. **16** For I tell you I will not eat it until it is fulfilled in the kingdom of God." **17** And he took a cup, and when he had given thanks he said, "Take this, and divide it among yourselves. **18** For I tell you that from now on I will not drink of the fruit of the vine until the kingdom of God comes." **19** And he took bread, and when he had given thanks, he broke it and gave it to them, saying, "This is my body, which is given for you. Do this in remembrance of me." **20** And likewise the cup after they had eaten, saying, "This cup that is poured out for you is the new covenant in my blood. **21** But behold, the hand of him who betrays me is with me on the table. **22** For the Son of Man goes as it has been determined, but woe to that man by whom he is betrayed!" **23** And they began to question one another, which of them it could be who was going to do this.

Who Is the Greatest?

24 A dispute also arose among them, as to which of them was to be regarded as the greatest. **25** And he said to them, "The kings of the Gentiles exercise lordship over them, and those in authority over them are called benefactors. **26** But not so with you. Rather, let the greatest among you become as the youngest, and the leader as one who serves. **27** For who is the greater, one who reclines at table or one who serves? Is it not the one who reclines at table? But I am among you as the one who serves.

28 "You are those who have stayed with me in my trials, **29** and I assign to you, as my

Father assigned to me, a kingdom, **30** that you may eat and drink at my table in my kingdom and sit on thrones judging the twelve tribes of Israel.

Jesus Foretells Peter's Denial

31 "Simon, Simon, behold, Satan demanded to have you, that he might sift you like wheat, **32** but I have prayed for you that your faith may not fail. And when you have turned again, strengthen your brothers." **33** Peter said to him, "Lord, I am ready to go with you both to prison and to death." **34** Jesus said, "I tell you, Peter, the rooster will not crow this day, until you deny three times that you know me."

Scripture Must Be Fulfilled in Jesus

35 And he said to them, "When I sent you out with no moneybag or knapsack or sandals, did you lack anything?" They said, "Nothing." **36** He said to them, "But now let the one who has a moneybag take it, and likewise a knapsack. And let the one who has no sword sell his cloak and buy one. **37** For I tell you that this Scripture must be fulfilled in me: 'And he was numbered with the transgressors.' For what is written about me has its fulfillment." **38** And they said, "Look, Lord, here are two swords." And he said to them, "It is enough."

Jesus Prays on the Mount of Olives

39 And he came out and went, as was his custom, to the Mount of Olives, and the disciples followed him. **40** And when he came to the place, he said to them, "Pray that you may not enter into temptation." **41** And he withdrew from them about a stone's throw, and knelt down and prayed, **42** saying, "Father, if you are willing, remove this cup from me. Nevertheless, not my will, but yours, be done." **43** And there appeared to him an angel from heaven, strengthening him. **44** And being in an agony he prayed more earnestly; and his sweat became like great drops of blood falling down to the ground. **45** And when he rose from prayer, he came to the disciples and found them sleeping for sorrow, **46** and he said to them, "Why are you sleeping? Rise and pray that you may not enter into temptation."

Betrayal and Arrest of Jesus

47 While he was still speaking, there came a crowd, and the man called Judas, one of the twelve, was leading them. He drew near to Jesus to kiss him, **48** but Jesus said to him, "Judas, would you betray the Son of Man with a kiss?" **49** And when those who were around him saw what would follow, they said, "Lord, shall we strike with the sword?" **50** And one of them struck the servant of the high priest and cut off his right ear. **51** But Jesus said, "No more of this!" And he touched his ear and healed him. **52** Then Jesus said to the chief priests and officers of the temple and elders, who had come out against him, "Have you come out as against a robber, with swords and clubs? **53** When I was with you day after day in the temple, you did not lay hands on me. But this is your hour, and the power of darkness."

Peter Denies Jesus

54 Then they seized him and led him away, bringing him into the high priest's house,

GETTING THE MESSAGE

Jesus knows us. Jesus knew that, in his hour of greatest need, Peter would deny him (22:34). He also knew that Peter would repent and go on to be a great leader in the church (v. 32; see Acts 2:14–41). As Paul declared, "The Lord knows those who are his" (2 Tim. 2:19).

and Peter was following at a distance. **55** And when they had kindled a fire in the middle of the courtyard and sat down together, Peter sat down among them. **56** Then a servant girl, seeing him as he sat in the light and looking closely at him, said, "This man also was with him." **57** But he denied it, saying, "Woman, I do not know him." **58** And a little later someone else saw him and said, "You also are one of them." But Peter said, "Man, I am not." **59** And after an interval of about an hour still another insisted, saying, "Certainly this man also was with him, for he too is a Galilean." **60** But Peter said, "Man, I do not know what you are talking about." And immediately, while he was still speaking, the rooster crowed. **61** And the Lord turned and looked at Peter. And Peter remembered the saying of the Lord, how he had said to him, "Before the rooster crows today, you will deny me three times." **62** And he went out and wept bitterly.

Jesus Is Mocked

63 Now the men who were holding Jesus in custody were mocking him as they beat him. **64** They also blindfolded him and kept asking him, "Prophesy! Who is it that struck you?" **65** And they said many other things against him, blaspheming him.

Jesus Before the Council

66 When day came, the assembly of the elders of the people gathered together, both chief priests and scribes. And they led him away to their council, and they said, **67** "If you are the Christ, tell us." But he said to them, "If I tell you, you will not believe, **68** and if I ask you, you will not answer. **69** But from now on the Son of Man shall be seated at the right hand of the power of God." **70** So they all said, "Are you the Son of God, then?"

> ### GETTING THE MESSAGE
>
> **Take this cup from me.** Drinking cups were often mentioned in the Bible as symbols of God's wrath or judgment. For Jesus to figuratively drink from such a cup meant suffering God's punishment on behalf of sinful people (22:42). This is what he willingly did when he died on the cross.

And he said to them, "You say that I am." **71** Then they said, "What further testimony do we need? We have heard it ourselves from his own lips."

Jesus Before Pilate

23 Then the whole company of them arose and brought him before Pilate. **2** And they began to accuse him, saying, "We found this man misleading our nation and forbidding us to give tribute to Caesar, and saying that he himself is Christ, a king." **3** And Pilate asked him, "Are you the King of the Jews?" And he answered him, "You have said so." **4** Then Pilate said to the chief priests and the crowds, "I find no guilt in this man." **5** But they were urgent, saying, "He stirs up the people, teaching throughout all Judea, from Galilee even to this place."

Jesus Before Herod

6 When Pilate heard this, he asked whether the man was a Galilean. **7** And when he learned that he belonged to Herod's jurisdiction, he sent him over to Herod, who was himself in Jerusalem at that time. **8** When Herod saw Jesus, he was very glad, for he had long desired to see him, because he had heard about him, and he was hoping to see some sign done by him. **9** So he questioned him at some length, but he made no answer. **10** The chief priests and the scribes stood by, vehemently accusing him. **11** And Herod with his soldiers treated him with contempt and mocked him. Then, arraying him in splendid clothing, he sent him back to Pilate. **12** And Herod and Pilate became friends with each other that very day, for before this they had been at enmity with each other.

13 Pilate then called together the chief priests and the rulers and the people, **14** and said to them, "You brought me this man as one who was misleading the people. And after examining him before you, behold, I did not find this man guilty of any of your charges against him. **15** Neither did Herod, for he sent him back to us. Look, nothing deserving death has been done by him. **16** I will therefore punish and release him."

Pilate Delivers Jesus to Be Crucified

18 But they all cried out together, "Away with this man, and release to us Barabbas"— **19** a man who had been thrown into prison for an insurrection started in the city and for murder. **20** Pilate addressed them once more, desiring to release Jesus, **21** but they kept shouting, "Crucify, crucify him!" **22** A third time he said to them, "Why, what evil has he done? I have found in him no guilt deserving death. I will therefore punish and release him." **23** But they were urgent, demanding with loud cries that he should be crucified. And their voices prevailed. **24** So Pilate decided that their demand should be granted. **25** He released the man who had been thrown into prison for insurrection and murder, for whom they asked, but he delivered Jesus over to their will.

The Crucifixion

26 And as they led him away, they seized one Simon of Cyrene, who was coming in from the country, and laid on him the cross, to carry it behind Jesus. **27** And there followed him a great multitude of the people and of women who were mourning and lamenting for him. **28** But turning to them

Jesus said, "Daughters of Jerusalem, do not weep for me, but weep for yourselves and for your children. [29] For behold, the days are coming when they will say, 'Blessed are the barren and the wombs that never bore and the breasts that never nursed!' [30] Then they will begin to say to the mountains, 'Fall on us,' and to the hills, 'Cover us.' [31] For if they do these things when the wood is green, what will happen when it is dry?"

[32] Two others, who were criminals, were led away to be put to death with him. [33] And when they came to the place that is called The Skull, there they crucified him, and the criminals, one on his right and one on his left. [34] And Jesus said, "Father, forgive them, for they know not what they do." And they cast lots to divide his garments. [35] And the people stood by, watching, but the rulers scoffed at him, saying, "He saved others; let him save himself, if he is the Christ of God, his Chosen One!" [36] The soldiers also mocked him, coming up and offering him sour wine [37] and saying, "If you are the King of the Jews, save yourself!" [38] There was also an inscription over him, "This is the King of the Jews."

[39] One of the criminals who were hanged railed at him, saying, "Are you not the Christ? Save yourself and us!" [40] But the other rebuked him, saying, "Do you not fear God, since you are under the same sentence of condemnation? [41] And we indeed justly, for we are receiving the due reward of our deeds; but this man has done nothing wrong." [42] And he said, "Jesus, remember me when you come into your kingdom." [43] And he said to him, "Truly, I say to you, today you will be with me in Paradise."

The Death of Jesus

[44] It was now about the sixth hour,[1] and there was darkness over the whole land until the ninth hour,[2] [45] while the sun's light failed. And the curtain of the temple was torn in two. [46] Then Jesus, calling out with a loud voice, said, "Father, into your hands I commit my spirit!" And having said this he breathed his last. [47] Now when the centurion saw what had taken place, he praised God, saying, "Certainly this man was innocent!" [48] And all the crowds that had assembled for this spectacle, when they saw what had taken place, returned home beating their breasts. [49] And all his acquaintances and the women who had followed him from Galilee stood at a distance watching these things.

Jesus Is Buried

[50] Now there was a man named Joseph, from the Jewish town of Arimathea. He was a member of the council, a good and righteous man, [51] who had not consented to their decision and action; and he was looking for the kingdom of God. [52] This man went to Pilate and asked for the body of Jesus. [53] Then he took it down and wrapped it in a linen shroud and laid him in a tomb cut in stone, where no one had ever yet been laid. [54] It was the day of Preparation, and the Sabbath was beginning. [55] The women who had come with him from Galilee followed and saw the tomb and how his body was laid. [56] Then they returned and prepared spices and ointments.

GETTING THE MESSAGE

The entrance to the tomb where Jesus was buried was probably about 2 feet (0.6 m) wide and 3 feet (0.9 m) tall. It was covered with a stone, perhaps a foot (0.3 m) thick and 4 feet (1.2 m) in diameter. The body would have been placed on a bench until it could be prepared for burial.

On the Sabbath they rested according to the commandment.

The Resurrection

24 But on the first day of the week, at early dawn, they went to the tomb, taking the spices they had prepared. [2] And they found the stone rolled away from the tomb, [3] but when they went in they did not find the body of the Lord Jesus. [4] While they were perplexed about this, behold, two men stood by them in dazzling apparel. [5] And as they were frightened and bowed their faces to the ground, the men said to them, "Why do you seek the living among the dead? [6] He is not here, but has risen. Remember how he told you, while he was still in Galilee, [7] that the Son of Man must be delivered into the hands of sinful men and be crucified and on the third day rise." [8] And they remembered

---

[1] That is, noon [2] That is, 3 P.M.

his words, 9 and returning from the tomb they told all these things to the eleven and to all the rest. 10 Now it was Mary Magdalene and Joanna and Mary the mother of James and the other women with them who told these things to the apostles, 11 but these words seemed to them an idle tale, and they did not believe them. 12 But Peter rose and ran to the tomb; stooping and looking in, he saw the linen cloths by themselves; and he went home marveling at what had happened.

On the Road to Emmaus

13 That very day two of them were going to a village named Emmaus, about seven miles from Jerusalem, 14 and they were talking with each other about all these things that had happened. 15 While they were talking and discussing together, Jesus himself drew near and went with them. 16 But their eyes

---

GETTING THE MESSAGE

Resurrected as real people! After his resurrection, Jesus had a real physical body. He was not just a disembodied spirit. He could eat and be touched (24:39–43). Christians will also experience real, physical resurrection from the dead (1 Corinthians 15).

---

were kept from recognizing him. 17 And he said to them, "What is this conversation that you are holding with each other as you walk?" And they stood still, looking sad. 18 Then one of them, named Cleopas, answered him, "Are you the only visitor to Jerusalem who does not know the things that have happened there in these days?" 19 And he said to them, "What things?" And they said to him, "Concerning Jesus of Nazareth, a man who was a prophet mighty in deed and word before God and all the people, 20 and how our chief priests and rulers delivered him up to be condemned to death, and crucified him. 21 But we had hoped that he was the one to redeem Israel. Yes, and besides all this, it is now the third day since these things happened. 22 Moreover, some women of our company amazed us. They were at the tomb early in the morning, 23 and when they did not find

his body, they came back saying that they had even seen a vision of angels, who said that he was alive. 24 Some of those who were with us went to the tomb and found it just as the women had said, but him they did not see." 25 And he said to them, "O foolish ones, and slow of heart to believe all that the prophets have spoken! 26 Was it not necessary that the Christ should suffer these things and enter into his glory?" 27 And beginning with Moses and all the Prophets, he interpreted to them in all the Scriptures the things concerning himself.

28 So they drew near to the village to which they were going. He acted as if he were going farther, 29 but they urged him strongly, saying, "Stay with us, for it is toward evening and the day is now far spent." So he went in to stay with them. 30 When he was at table with them, he took the bread and blessed and broke it and gave it to them. 31 And their eyes were opened, and they recognized him. And he vanished from their sight. 32 They said to each other, "Did not our hearts burn within us while he talked to us on the road, while he opened to us the Scriptures?" 33 And they rose that same hour and returned to Jerusalem. And they found the eleven and those who were with them gathered together, 34 saying, "The Lord has risen indeed, and has appeared to Simon!" 35 Then they told what had happened on the road, and how he was known to them in the breaking of the bread.

Jesus Appears to His Disciples

36 As they were talking about these things, Jesus himself stood among them, and said to them, "Peace to you!" 37 But they were startled and frightened and thought they saw a spirit. 38 And he said to them, "Why are you troubled, and why do doubts arise in your hearts? 39 See my hands and my feet, that it is I myself. Touch me, and see. For a spirit does not have flesh and bones as you see that I have." 40 And when he had said this, he showed them his hands and his feet. 41 And while they still disbelieved for joy and were marveling, he said to them, "Have you anything here to eat?" 42 They gave him a piece of broiled fish, 43 and he took it and ate before them.

44 Then he said to them, "These are my words that I spoke to you while I was still with you, that everything written about

me in the Law of Moses and the Prophets and the Psalms must be fulfilled." ⁴⁵ Then he opened their minds to understand the Scriptures, ⁴⁶ and said to them, "Thus it is written, that the Christ should suffer and on the third day rise from the dead, ⁴⁷ and that repentance and forgiveness of sins should be proclaimed in his name to all nations, beginning from Jerusalem. ⁴⁸ You are witnesses of these things. ⁴⁹ And behold, I am sending the promise of my Father upon you.

But stay in the city until you are clothed with power from on high."

The Ascension

⁵⁰ Then he led them out as far as Bethany, and lifting up his hands he blessed them. ⁵¹ While he blessed them, he parted from them and was carried up into heaven. ⁵² And they worshiped him and returned to Jerusalem with great joy, ⁵³ and were continually in the temple blessing God.

INTRODUCTION TO JOHN

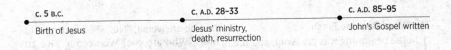

c. 5 B.C.	c. A.D. 28–33	c. A.D. 85–95
Birth of Jesus	Jesus' ministry, death, resurrection	John's Gospel written

AUTHOR, DATE, AND RECIPIENTS

John the son of Zebedee wrote this Gospel. He was a Palestinian Jew, one of the 12 disciples, and a member of Jesus' inner apostolic circle. He was referred to as the disciple "whom Jesus loved" (13:23). John also wrote 1–3 John and Revelation. He likely wrote his Gospel account between A.D. 70 (the date of the destruction of the temple) and A.D. 100 (the reputed end of John's life). It was likely written from Ephesus in Asia Minor (modern-day Turkey), one of the most important cities of the Roman Empire at the time. His original audience consisted of Jews and Gentiles living in the larger Greco-Roman world in Ephesus and beyond, toward the close of the first century A.D.

THEME AND PURPOSE

The theme of John's Gospel is that Jesus is the long-awaited, promised Messiah and Son of God. By believing in Jesus, people have eternal life (see 20:30–31).

As evidence that Jesus is the Messiah, John relies on several selected messianic signs performed by Jesus and a series of witnesses to Jesus. These include the Scriptures, John the Baptist, Jesus himself, God the Father, Jesus' miraculous works, the Holy Spirit, and John himself.

KEY THEMES

1. *Jesus.* Jesus is God, the "I AM." He existed before the creation of the world, and he has supernatural knowledge. He fulfills the Jewish festivals and institutions. As the sent Son of God, he reflects the Sender. Signs and witnesses demonstrate that he is the Messiah.

2. *The Trinity.* Father, Son, and Spirit are united in their work of revelation and redemption.

3. *Salvation.* God is sovereign in salvation. Jesus' death is the basis of salvation, which is obtained through believing in the living Jesus as the Son of God

4. *Eternal Life.* Jesus is the giver of eternal life. Believers can experience some of salvation's benefits during this present evil age.

5. *Mission.* Believers are called to continue Jesus' mission.

OUTLINE

I. Prologue: The Incarnate Word (1:1–18)

II. Signs of the Messiah, with Teaching about Life in Him (1:19–12:50)

III. The Farewell Teaching and the Passion Narrative (13:1–20:31)

IV. Epilogue: The Roles of Peter and of the Disciple Whom Jesus Loved (21:1–25)

THE GOSPEL ACCORDING TO
JOHN

The Word Became Flesh

1 In the beginning was the Word, and the Word was with God, and the Word was God. **2** He was in the beginning with God. **3** All things were made through him, and without him was not any thing made that was made. **4** In him was life, and the life was the light of men. **5** The light shines in the darkness, and the darkness has not overcome it.

6 There was a man sent from God, whose name was John. **7** He came as a witness, to bear witness about the light, that all might believe through him. **8** He was not the light, but came to bear witness about the light.

9 The true light, which gives light to everyone, was coming into the world. **10** He was in the world, and the world was made through him, yet the world did not know him. **11** He came to his own, and his own people did not receive him. **12** But to all who did receive him, who believed in his name, he gave the right to become children of God, **13** who were born, not of blood nor of the will of the flesh nor of the will of man, but of God.

14 And the Word became flesh and dwelt among us, and we have seen his glory, glory as of the only Son from the Father, full of grace and truth. **15** (John bore witness about him, and cried out, "This was he of whom I said, 'He who comes after me ranks before me, because he was before me.'") **16** For from his fullness we have all received, grace upon grace. **17** For the law was given through Moses; grace and truth came through Jesus Christ. **18** No one has ever seen God; the only God, who is at the Father's side, he has made him known.

The Testimony of John the Baptist

19 And this is the testimony of John, when the Jews sent priests and Levites from Jerusalem to ask him, "Who are you?" **20** He confessed, and did not deny, but confessed, "I am not the Christ." **21** And they asked him, "What then? Are you Elijah?" He said, "I am not." "Are you the Prophet?"

And he answered, "No." **22** So they said to him, "Who are you? We need to give an answer to those who sent us. What do you say about yourself?" **23** He said, "I am the voice of one crying out in the wilderness, 'Make straight the way of the Lord,' as the prophet Isaiah said."

24 (Now they had been sent from the Pharisees.) **25** They asked him, "Then why are you baptizing, if you are neither the Christ, nor Elijah, nor the Prophet?" **26** John answered them, "I baptize with water, but among you stands one you do not know, **27** even he who comes after me, the strap

GETTING THE MESSAGE

All things were made through him.
John begins his Gospel in the same way that Genesis begins: with creation (1:1–5; Gen. 1:1). He reveals that Jesus, God's Son, existed eternally with God the Father, and the whole creation was made through him (Col. 1:15–16; compare 1 Cor. 8:6).

of whose sandal I am not worthy to untie." **28** These things took place in Bethany across the Jordan, where John was baptizing.

Behold, the Lamb of God

29 The next day he saw Jesus coming toward him, and said, "Behold, the Lamb of God, who takes away the sin of the world! **30** This is he of whom I said, 'After me comes a man who ranks before me, because he was before me.' **31** I myself did not know him, but for this purpose I came baptizing with water, that he might be revealed to Israel." **32** And John bore witness: "I saw the Spirit descend from heaven like a dove, and it remained on him. **33** I myself did not know him, but he who sent me to baptize with water said to me, 'He on whom you see the Spirit descend and remain, this is he who baptizes with the Holy Spirit.' **34** And I have seen and have borne witness that this is the Son of God."

Jesus Calls the First Disciples

35 The next day again John was standing with two of his disciples, **36** and he looked at Jesus as he walked by and said, "Behold, the Lamb of God!" **37** The two disciples heard him say this, and they followed Jesus. **38** Jesus turned and saw them following and said to them, "What are you seeking?" And they said to him, "Rabbi" (which means Teacher), "where are you staying?" **39** He

---

PROFILE

JOHN THE BAPTIST

Zechariah and Elizabeth were childless and advanced in age when Gabriel announced that Elizabeth would bear a son. The baby would be named John, and he would "be filled with the Holy Spirit, even from his mother's womb" (Luke 1:15). John lived and preached in the wilderness of Judea, where he wore clothes made of camel's hair and ate locusts and wild honey (Mark 1:4–6). John prepared the way for Jesus the Messiah by calling people to repentance, as the Old Testament prophets had predicted (Isa. 40:3; Mal. 3:1). Those who accepted his message were baptized as an outward sign of their inward cleansing from sin. Although Jesus needed no repentance or cleansing, he was baptized by John in order to identify with the sinful people he came to save. After angering the royal Herod family, John was imprisoned and eventually beheaded (Matt. 14:6–12).

KEY REFERENCE: JOHN 1:29–34

---

said to them, "Come and you will see." So they came and saw where he was staying, and they stayed with him that day, for it was about the tenth hour.[1] **40** One of the two who heard John speak and followed Jesus was Andrew, Simon Peter's brother. **41** He first found his own brother Simon and said to him, "We have found the Messiah" (which means Christ). **42** He brought him to

Jesus. Jesus looked at him and said, "You are Simon the son of John. You shall be called Cephas" (which means Peter[2]).

Jesus Calls Philip and Nathanael

43 The next day Jesus decided to go to Galilee. He found Philip and said to him, "Follow me." **44** Now Philip was from Bethsaida, the city of Andrew and Peter. **45** Philip found Nathanael and said to him, "We have found him of whom Moses in the Law and also the prophets wrote, Jesus of Nazareth, the son of Joseph." **46** Nathanael said to him, "Can anything good come out of Nazareth?" Philip said to him, "Come and see." **47** Jesus saw Nathanael coming toward him and said of him, "Behold, an Israelite indeed, in whom there is no deceit!" **48** Nathanael said to him, "How do

---

GETTING THE MESSAGE

Finding their true master. John reports that two of Jesus' disciples had previously followed John the Baptist (1:35–40). One of them was Andrew; the other was probably John himself. They believed John the Baptist's testimony about Jesus, and became his disciples instead.

---

you know me?" Jesus answered him, "Before Philip called you, when you were under the fig tree, I saw you." **49** Nathanael answered him, "Rabbi, you are the Son of God! You are the King of Israel!" **50** Jesus answered him, "Because I said to you, 'I saw you under the fig tree,' do you believe? You will see greater things than these." **51** And he said to him, "Truly, truly, I say to you, you will see heaven opened, and the angels of God ascending and descending on the Son of Man."

The Wedding at Cana

2 On the third day there was a wedding at Cana in Galilee, and the mother of Jesus was there. **2** Jesus also was invited to the wedding with his disciples. **3** When the wine ran out, the mother of Jesus said to him, "They have no wine." **4** And Jesus said to her, "Woman, what does this have to do with me? My hour has not yet come." **5** His

---

[1] That is, about 4 P.M. [2] *Cephas* in Aramaic and *Peter* in Greek both mean *rock*

mother said to the servants, "Do whatever he tells you."

6 Now there were six stone water jars there for the Jewish rites of purification, each holding twenty or thirty gallons. **7** Jesus said to the servants, "Fill the jars with water." And they filled them up to the brim. **8** And he said to them, "Now draw some out and take it to the master of the feast." So they took it. **9** When the master of the feast tasted the water now become wine, and did not know where it came from (though the servants who had drawn the water knew), the master of the feast called the bridegroom **10** and said to him, "Everyone serves the good wine first, and when people have drunk freely, then the poor wine. But you have kept the good wine until now." **11** This, the first of his signs, Jesus did at Cana in Galilee, and manifested his glory. And his disciples believed in him.

12 After this he went down to Capernaum, with his mother and his brothers[1] and his disciples, and they stayed there for a few days.

Jesus Cleanses the Temple

13 The Passover of the Jews was at hand, and Jesus went up to Jerusalem. **14** In the temple he found those who were selling oxen and sheep and pigeons, and the money-changers sitting there. **15** And making a whip of cords, he drove them all out of the temple, with the sheep and oxen. And he poured out the coins of the money-changers and overturned their tables. **16** And he told those who sold the pigeons, "Take these things away; do not make my Father's house a house of trade." **17** His disciples remembered that it was written, "Zeal for your house will consume me."

18 So the Jews said to him, "What sign do you show us for doing these things?" **19** Jesus answered them, "Destroy this temple, and in three days I will raise it up." **20** The Jews then said, "It has taken forty-six years to build this temple, and will you raise it up in three days?" **21** But he was speaking about the temple of his body. **22** When therefore he was raised from the dead, his disciples remembered that he had said this, and they believed the Scripture and the word that Jesus had spoken.

Jesus Knows What Is in Man

23 Now when he was in Jerusalem at the Passover Feast, many believed in his name when they saw the signs that he was doing. **24** But Jesus on his part did not entrust himself to them, because he knew all people **25** and needed no one to bear witness about man, for he himself knew what was in man.

You Must Be Born Again

3 Now there was a man of the Pharisees named Nicodemus, a ruler of the Jews. **2** This man came to Jesus by night and said to him, "Rabbi, we know that you are a teacher come from God, for no one can do these signs that you do unless God is with him." **3** Jesus answered him, "Truly, truly, I say to you, unless one is born again he cannot see the kingdom of God." **4** Nicodemus said to him, "How can a man be born when

> ### GETTING THE MESSAGE
>
> **The master of the feast** (2:9) had an important job. He was both the head-waiter and the master of ceremonies. His primary responsibility was making sure that the guests had enough to eat and drink. If he did a good job, he might be awarded a wreath at the end of the festivities.

he is old? Can he enter a second time into his mother's womb and be born?" **5** Jesus answered, "Truly, truly, I say to you, unless one is born of water and the Spirit, he cannot enter the kingdom of God. **6** That which is born of the flesh is flesh, and that which is born of the Spirit is spirit. **7** Do not marvel that I said to you, 'You must be born again.' **8** The wind blows where it wishes, and you hear its sound, but you do not know where it comes from or where it goes. So it is with everyone who is born of the Spirit."

9 Nicodemus said to him, "How can these things be?" **10** Jesus answered him, "Are you the teacher of Israel and yet you do not understand these things? **11** Truly, truly, I say to you, we speak of what we know, and bear witness to what we have seen, but you do not receive our testimony. **12** If I have told you earthly things and you do not believe, how can you believe if I tell you heavenly

---

[1] Or brothers and sisters (see Preface)

things? [13] No one has ascended into heaven except he who descended from heaven, the Son of Man. [14] And as Moses lifted up the serpent in the wilderness, so must the Son of Man be lifted up, [15] that whoever believes in him may have eternal life.

For God So Loved the World

[16] "For God so loved the world, that he gave his only Son, that whoever believes in him should not perish but have eternal

PROFILE

NICODEMUS

Nicodemus was a Pharisee and a member of the powerful Jewish governing body, the Sanhedrin. He had seen the signs performed by Jesus and recognized that God was with him. Possibly to avoid being seen by his peers, Nicodemus came to Jesus at night to speak with him. Although he was a "teacher of Israel" (3:10) and knew the Old Testament Scriptures, Nicodemus was mystified when Jesus told him that he must be born again. It was while talking with Nicodemus that Jesus made the statement recorded in 3:16, perhaps the most well-known summary of the gospel in all of Scripture. The Bible does not say whether Nicodemus responded to the gospel on this occasion. Later, however, Nicodemus defended Jesus when others wanted to arrest him (7:50–52). After Jesus' death on the cross, Nicodemus helped Joseph of Arimathea prepare Jesus' body for burial (19:39–40).

KEY REFERENCE: JOHN 3:1-21

life. [17] For God did not send his Son into the world to condemn the world, but in order that the world might be saved through him. [18] Whoever believes in him is not condemned, but whoever does not believe is condemned already, because he has not believed in the name of the only Son of God. [19] And this is the judgment: the light has come into the world, and people loved the darkness rather than the light because their works were evil. [20] For everyone who does wicked things hates the light and does not come to the light, lest his works should be exposed. [21] But whoever does what is true comes to the light, so that it may be clearly seen that his works have been carried out in God."

John the Baptist Exalts Christ

[22] After this Jesus and his disciples went into the Judean countryside, and he remained there with them and was baptizing. [23] John also was baptizing at Aenon near Salim, because water was plentiful there, and people were coming and being baptized [24] (for John had not yet been put in prison). [25] Now a discussion arose between some of John's disciples and a Jew over purification. [26] And they came to John and said to him, "Rabbi, he who was with you across the Jordan, to whom you bore witness— look, he is baptizing, and all are going to him." [27] John answered, "A person cannot

GETTING THE MESSAGE

The phrase **born-again Christian** originally comes from 3:1-8. Jesus uses the image of a second birth to explain what happens to believers at conversion. The Holy Spirit cleanses them from sin and makes them new in Christ.

receive even one thing unless it is given him from heaven. [28] You yourselves bear me witness, that I said, 'I am not the Christ, but I have been sent before him.' [29] The one who has the bride is the bridegroom. The friend of the bridegroom, who stands and hears him, rejoices greatly at the bridegroom's voice. Therefore this joy of mine is now complete. [30] He must increase, but I must decrease."

[31] He who comes from above is above all. He who is of the earth belongs to the earth and speaks in an earthly way. He who comes from heaven is above all. [32] He bears witness to what he has seen and heard, yet no one receives his testimony. [33] Whoever receives his testimony sets his seal to this, that God is true. [34] For he whom God has sent utters the words of God, for he gives the Spirit without measure. [35] The Father loves the Son and has given all things into his hand. [36] Whoever believes in the Son has eternal life; whoever

does not obey the Son shall not see life, but the wrath of God remains on him.

Jesus and the Woman of Samaria

4 Now when Jesus learned that the Pharisees had heard that Jesus was making and baptizing more disciples than John ² (although Jesus himself did not baptize, but only his disciples), ³ he left Judea and departed again for Galilee. ⁴ And he had to pass through Samaria. ⁵ So he came to a town of Samaria called Sychar, near the field that Jacob had given to his son Joseph. ⁶ Jacob's well was there; so Jesus, wearied as he was from his journey, was sitting beside the well. It was about the sixth hour.

⁷ A woman from Samaria came to draw water. Jesus said to her, "Give me a drink." ⁸ (For his disciples had gone away into the city to buy food.) ⁹ The Samaritan woman said to him, "How is it that you, a Jew, ask for a drink from me, a woman of Samaria?" (For Jews have no dealings with Samaritans.) ¹⁰ Jesus answered her, "If you knew the gift of God, and who it is that is saying to you, 'Give me a drink,' you would have asked him, and he would have given you living water." ¹¹ The woman said to him, "Sir, you have nothing to draw water with, and the well is deep. Where do you get that living water? ¹² Are you greater than our father Jacob? He gave us the well and drank from it himself, as did his sons and his livestock." ¹³ Jesus said to her, "Everyone who drinks of this water will be thirsty again, ¹⁴ but whoever drinks of the water that I will give him will never be thirsty again. The water that I will give him will become in him a spring of water welling up to eternal life." ¹⁵ The woman said to him, "Sir, give me this water, so that I will not be thirsty or have to come here to draw water."

¹⁶ Jesus said to her, "Go, call your husband, and come here." ¹⁷ The woman answered him, "I have no husband." Jesus said to her, "You are right in saying, 'I have no husband'; ¹⁸ for you have had five husbands, and the one you now have is not your husband. What you have said is true." ¹⁹ The woman said to him, "Sir, I perceive that you are a prophet. ²⁰ Our fathers worshiped on this mountain, but you say that in Jerusalem is the place where people ought to worship." ²¹ Jesus said to her, "Woman, believe me, the hour is coming when neither on this mountain nor in Jerusalem will you worship the Father. ²² You worship what you do not know; we worship what we know, for salvation is from the Jews. ²³ But the hour is coming, and is now here, when the true worshipers will worship the Father in spirit and truth, for the Father is seeking such people to worship him. ²⁴ God is spirit, and those who worship him must worship in spirit and truth." ²⁵ The woman said to him, "I know that Messiah is coming (he who is called Christ). When he comes, he will tell us all things." ²⁶ Jesus said to her, "I who speak to you am he."

²⁷ Just then his disciples came back. They marveled that he was talking with a woman, but no one said, "What do you seek?" or, "Why are you talking with her?" ²⁸ So the

GETTING THE MESSAGE

The Samaritans. When Israel fell to Assyria in 722 B.C., many of the people were taken into exile but others remained in the land. Assyria brought people from other nations to repopulate Israel, and many of the remaining Israelites intermarried with these Gentiles. In New Testament times, their descendants were despised, but Jesus brought them the good news of salvation (4:1–30).

woman left her water jar and went away into town and said to the people, ²⁹ "Come, see a man who told me all that I ever did. Can this be the Christ?" ³⁰ They went out of the town and were coming to him.

³¹ Meanwhile the disciples were urging him, saying, "Rabbi, eat." ³² But he said to them, "I have food to eat that you do not know about." ³³ So the disciples said to one another, "Has anyone brought him something to eat?" ³⁴ Jesus said to them, "My food is to do the will of him who sent me and to accomplish his work. ³⁵ Do you not say, 'There are yet four months, then comes the harvest'? Look, I tell you, lift up your eyes, and see that the fields are white for harvest. ³⁶ Already the one who reaps is receiving wages and gathering fruit for eternal life, so that sower and reaper may rejoice together. ³⁷ For here the saying holds

true, 'One sows and another reaps.' **38** I sent you to reap that for which you did not labor. Others have labored, and you have entered into their labor."

39 Many Samaritans from that town believed in him because of the woman's testimony, "He told me all that I ever did." **40** So when the Samaritans came to him, they asked him to stay with them, and he stayed there two days. **41** And many more believed because of his word. **42** They said to the woman, "It is no longer because of what you said that we believe, for we have heard for ourselves, and we know that this is indeed the Savior of the world."

43 After the two days he departed for Galilee. **44** (For Jesus himself had testified that a prophet has no honor in his own hometown.) **45** So when he came to Galilee, the Galileans welcomed him, having seen all

---

GETTING THE MESSAGE

Jesus and God. In 5:17–29, Jesus claims to be equal with God (vv. 17–19). He claims to have the ability to give life (v. 21) and to judge (v. 22), and the right to be worshiped (v. 23). His opponents denied these claims, but believers recognize them to be true.

---

that he had done in Jerusalem at the feast. For they too had gone to the feast.

Jesus Heals an Official's Son

46 So he came again to Cana in Galilee, where he had made the water wine. And at Capernaum there was an official whose son was ill. **47** When this man heard that Jesus had come from Judea to Galilee, he went to him and asked him to come down and heal his son, for he was at the point of death. **48** So Jesus said to him, "Unless you see signs and wonders you will not believe." **49** The official said to him, "Sir, come down before my child dies." **50** Jesus said to him, "Go; your son will live." The man believed the word that Jesus spoke to him and went on his way. **51** As he was going down, his servants met him and told him that his son was recovering. **52** So he asked them the hour when he began to get better, and they said

to him, "Yesterday at the seventh hour[1] the fever left him." **53** The father knew that was the hour when Jesus had said to him, "Your son will live." And he himself believed, and all his household. **54** This was now the second sign that Jesus did when he had come from Judea to Galilee.

The Healing at the Pool on the Sabbath

5 After this there was a feast of the Jews, and Jesus went up to Jerusalem.

2 Now there is in Jerusalem by the Sheep Gate a pool, in Aramaic called Bethesda, which has five roofed colonnades. **3** In these lay a multitude of invalids—blind, lame, and paralyzed. **5** One man was there who had been an invalid for thirty-eight years. **6** When Jesus saw him lying there and knew that he had already been there a long time, he said to him, "Do you want to be healed?" **7** The sick man answered him, "Sir, I have no one to put me into the pool when the water is stirred up, and while I am going another steps down before me." **8** Jesus said to him, "Get up, take up your bed, and walk." **9** And at once the man was healed, and he took up his bed and walked.

Now that day was the Sabbath. **10** So the Jews[2] said to the man who had been healed, "It is the Sabbath, and it is not lawful for you to take up your bed." **11** But he answered them, "The man who healed me, that man said to me, 'Take up your bed, and walk.'" **12** They asked him, "Who is the man who said to you, 'Take up your bed and walk'?" **13** Now the man who had been healed did not know who it was, for Jesus had withdrawn, as there was a crowd in the place. **14** Afterward Jesus found him in the temple and said to him, "See, you are well! Sin no more, that nothing worse may happen to you." **15** The man went away and told the Jews that it was Jesus who had healed him. **16** And this was why the Jews were persecuting Jesus, because he was doing these things on the Sabbath. **17** But Jesus answered them, "My Father is working until now, and I am working."

Jesus Is Equal with God

18 This was why the Jews were seeking all the more to kill him, because not only was he breaking the Sabbath, but he was even

---

[1] That is, at 1 p.m. [2] The Greek word refers to Jewish religious leaders, and people they influenced, who opposed Jesus; also 5:15, 16, 18; 7:1; 9:18, 22; 18:12, 14, 31, 36, 38; 19:7, 12, 14, 31, 38; 20:19

calling God his own Father, making himself equal with God.

The Authority of the Son

¹⁹ So Jesus said to them, "Truly, truly, I say to you, the Son can do nothing of his own accord, but only what he sees the Father doing. For whatever the Father does, that the Son does likewise. ²⁰ For the Father loves the Son and shows him all that he himself is doing. And greater works than these will he show him, so that you may marvel. ²¹ For as the Father raises the dead and gives them life, so also the Son gives life to whom he will. ²² The Father judges no one, but has given all judgment to the Son, ²³ that all may honor the Son, just as they honor the Father. Whoever does not honor the Son does not honor the Father who sent him. ²⁴ Truly, truly, I say to you, whoever hears my word and believes him who sent me has eternal life. He does not come into judgment, but has passed from death to life.

²⁵ "Truly, truly, I say to you, an hour is coming, and is now here, when the dead will hear the voice of the Son of God, and those who hear will live. ²⁶ For as the Father has life in himself, so he has granted the Son also to have life in himself. ²⁷ And he has given him authority to execute judgment, because he is the Son of Man. ²⁸ Do not marvel at this, for an hour is coming when all who are in the tombs will hear his voice ²⁹ and come out, those who have done good to the resurrection of life, and those who have done evil to the resurrection of judgment.

Witnesses to Jesus

³⁰ "I can do nothing on my own. As I hear, I judge, and my judgment is just, because I seek not my own will but the will of him who sent me. ³¹ If I alone bear witness about myself, my testimony is not true. ³² There is another who bears witness about me, and I know that the testimony that he bears about me is true. ³³ You sent to John, and he has borne witness to the truth. ³⁴ Not that the testimony that I receive is from man, but I say these things so that you may be saved. ³⁵ He was a burning and shining lamp, and you were willing to rejoice for a while in his light. ³⁶ But the testimony that I have is greater than that of John. For the works that the Father has given me to accomplish, the very works that I am doing, bear witness

about me that the Father has sent me. ³⁷ And the Father who sent me has himself borne witness about me. His voice you have never heard, his form you have never seen, ³⁸ and you do not have his word abiding in you, for you do not believe the one whom he has sent. ³⁹ You search the Scriptures because you think that in them you have eternal life; and it is they that bear witness about me, ⁴⁰ yet you refuse to come to me that you may have life. ⁴¹ I do not receive glory from people. ⁴² But I know that you do not have the love of God within you. ⁴³ I have come in my Father's name, and you do not receive me. If another comes in his own name, you will receive him. ⁴⁴ How can you believe, when you receive glory from one another and do not seek the glory that comes from the only God? ⁴⁵ Do not think that I will accuse you to the Father. There is one who accuses you: Moses, on whom you have set

> ### GETTING THE MESSAGE
>
> Each of the four Gospels records **the feeding of the 5,000.** In John, this is Jesus' fourth sign showing that he is the Son of God (6:1-15). Just as God provided manna for Israel, Jesus provided food (see Numbers 11). Jesus wanted people to see that he is the bread of life (John 6:35).

your hope. ⁴⁶ For if you believed Moses, you would believe me; for he wrote of me. ⁴⁷ But if you do not believe his writings, how will you believe my words?"

Jesus Feeds the Five Thousand

6 After this Jesus went away to the other side of the Sea of Galilee, which is the Sea of Tiberias. ² And a large crowd was following him, because they saw the signs that he was doing on the sick. ³ Jesus went up on the mountain, and there he sat down with his disciples. ⁴ Now the Passover, the feast of the Jews, was at hand. ⁵ Lifting up his eyes, then, and seeing that a large crowd was coming toward him, Jesus said to Philip, "Where are we to buy bread, so that these people may eat?" ⁶ He said this to test him, for he himself knew what he would do. ⁷ Philip answered him, "Two hundred denarii worth of bread would not be enough for each of them to get a little." ⁸ One of his

disciples, Andrew, Simon Peter's brother, said to him, 9 "There is a boy here who has five barley loaves and two fish, but what are they for so many?" 10 Jesus said, "Have the people sit down." Now there was much grass in the place. So the men sat down, about five thousand in number. 11 Jesus then took the loaves, and when he had given thanks, he distributed them to those who were seated. So also the fish, as much as they wanted. 12 And when they had eaten their fill, he told his disciples, "Gather up the leftover fragments, that nothing may be lost." 13 So they gathered them up and filled twelve baskets with fragments from the five barley loaves left by those who had eaten. 14 When the people saw the sign that he had done, they said, "This is indeed the Prophet who is to come into the world!"

15 Perceiving then that they were about to come and take him by force to make him king, Jesus withdrew again to the mountain by himself.

Jesus Walks on Water

16 When evening came, his disciples went down to the sea, 17 got into a boat, and started across the sea to Capernaum. It was now dark, and Jesus had not yet come to them. 18 The sea became rough because a strong wind was blowing. 19 When they had rowed about three or four miles, they saw Jesus walking on the sea and coming near the boat, and they were frightened. 20 But he said to them, "It is I; do not be afraid." 21 Then they were glad to take him into the boat, and immediately the boat was at the land to which they were going.

I Am the Bread of Life

22 On the next day the crowd that remained on the other side of the sea saw that there had been only one boat there, and that Jesus had not entered the boat with his disciples, but that his disciples had gone away alone. 23 Other boats from Tiberias came near the place where they had eaten the bread after the Lord had given thanks. 24 So when the crowd saw that Jesus was not there, nor his disciples, they themselves got into the boats and went to Capernaum, seeking Jesus.

25 When they found him on the other side of the sea, they said to him, "Rabbi, when did you come here?" 26 Jesus answered them, "Truly, truly, I say to you, you are seeking me, not because you saw signs, but because you ate your fill of the loaves. 27 Do not work for the food that perishes, but for the food that endures to eternal life, which the Son of Man will give to you. For on him God the Father has set his seal." 28 Then they said to him, "What must we do, to be doing the works of God?" 29 Jesus answered them, "This is the work of God, that you believe in him whom he has sent." 30 So they said to him, "Then what sign do you do, that we may see and believe you? What work do you perform? 31 Our fathers ate the manna in the wilderness; as it is written, 'He gave them bread from heaven to eat.' " 32 Jesus then said to them, "Truly, truly, I say to you, it was not Moses who gave you the bread from heaven, but my Father gives you the true bread from heaven. 33 For the bread of God is he who comes down from heaven and gives life to the world." 34 They said to him, "Sir, give us this bread always."

35 Jesus said to them, "I am the bread of life; whoever comes to me shall not hunger, and whoever believes in me shall never thirst. 36 But I said to you that you have seen me and yet do not believe. 37 All that the Father gives me will come to me, and whoever comes to me I will never cast out. 38 For I have come down from heaven, not to do my own will but the will of him who sent me. 39 And this is the will of him who sent me, that I should lose nothing of all that he has given me, but raise it up on the last day. 40 For this is the will of my Father, that everyone who looks on the Son and believes in him should have eternal life, and I will raise him up on the last day."

41 So the Jews grumbled about him, because he said, "I am the bread that came down from heaven." 42 They said, "Is not this Jesus, the son of Joseph, whose father and mother we know? How does he now say, 'I have come down from heaven'?" 43 Jesus answered them, "Do not grumble among yourselves. 44 No one can come to me unless the Father who sent me draws him. And I will raise him up on the last day. 45 It is written in the Prophets, 'And they will all be taught by God.' Everyone who has heard and learned from the Father comes to me— 46 not that anyone has seen the Father except he who is from God; he has seen the Father. 47 Truly, truly, I say to you, whoever

believes has eternal life. ⁴⁸ I am the bread of life. ⁴⁹ Your fathers ate the manna in the wilderness, and they died. ⁵⁰ This is the bread that comes down from heaven, so that one may eat of it and not die. ⁵¹ I am the living bread that came down from heaven. If anyone eats of this bread, he will live forever. And the bread that I will give for the life of the world is my flesh."

⁵² The Jews then disputed among themselves, saying, "How can this man give us his flesh to eat?" ⁵³ So Jesus said to them, "Truly, truly, I say to you, unless you eat the flesh of the Son of Man and drink his blood, you have no life in you. ⁵⁴ Whoever feeds on my flesh and drinks my blood has eternal life, and I will raise him up on the last day. ⁵⁵ For my flesh is true food, and my blood is true drink. ⁵⁶ Whoever feeds on my flesh and drinks my blood abides in me, and I in him. ⁵⁷ As the living Father sent me, and I live because of the Father, so whoever feeds on me, he also will live because of me. ⁵⁸ This is the bread that came down from heaven, not like the bread the fathers ate, and died. Whoever feeds on this bread will live forever." ⁵⁹ Jesus said these things in the synagogue, as he taught at Capernaum.

The Words of Eternal Life

⁶⁰ When many of his disciples heard it, they said, "This is a hard saying; who can listen to it?" ⁶¹ But Jesus, knowing in himself that his disciples were grumbling about this, said to them, "Do you take offense at this? ⁶² Then what if you were to see the Son of Man ascending to where he was before? ⁶³ It is the Spirit who gives life; the flesh is no help at all. The words that I have spoken to you are spirit and life. ⁶⁴ But there are some of you who do not believe." (For Jesus knew from the beginning who those were who did not believe, and who it was who would betray him.) ⁶⁵ And he said, "This is why I told you that no one can come to me unless it is granted him by the Father."

⁶⁶ After this many of his disciples turned back and no longer walked with him. ⁶⁷ So Jesus said to the Twelve, "Do you want to go away as well?" ⁶⁸ Simon Peter answered him, "Lord, to whom shall we go? You have the words of eternal life, ⁶⁹ and we have believed, and have come to know, that you are the Holy One of God." ⁷⁰ Jesus answered

them, "Did I not choose you, the Twelve? And yet one of you is a devil." ⁷¹ He spoke of Judas the son of Simon Iscariot, for he, one of the Twelve, was going to betray him.

Jesus at the Feast of Booths

7 After this Jesus went about in Galilee. He would not go about in Judea, because the Jews were seeking to kill him. ² Now the Jews' Feast of Booths was at hand. ³ So his brothers¹ said to him, "Leave here and go to Judea, that your disciples also may see the works you are doing. ⁴ For no one works in secret if he seeks to be known openly. If you do these things, show yourself to the world." ⁵ For not even his brothers believed in him. ⁶ Jesus said to them, "My time has not yet come, but your time is always here. ⁷ The world cannot hate you, but it hates me because I testify about it that its works are evil. ⁸ You go up to the feast. I am not going up to this feast, for my time has not yet fully come." ⁹ After saying this, he remained in Galilee.

¹⁰ But after his brothers had gone up to the feast, then he also went up, not publicly but in private. ¹¹ The Jews were looking for him at the feast, and saying, "Where is he?" ¹² And there was much muttering about him among the people. While some said, "He is a good man," others said, "No, he is leading the people astray." ¹³ Yet for fear of the Jews no one spoke openly of him.

¹⁴ About the middle of the feast Jesus went up into the temple and began teaching. ¹⁵ The Jews therefore marveled, saying, "How is it that this man has learning, when he has never studied?" ¹⁶ So Jesus answered them, "My teaching is not mine, but his who sent me. ¹⁷ If anyone's will is to do God's will, he will know whether the teaching is from God or whether I am speaking on my own authority. ¹⁸ The one who speaks on his own authority seeks his own glory; but the one who seeks the glory of him who sent him is true, and in him there is no falsehood. ¹⁹ Has not Moses given you the law? Yet none of you keeps the law. Why do you seek to kill me?" ²⁰ The crowd answered, "You have a demon! Who is seeking to kill you?" ²¹ Jesus answered them, "I did one work, and you all marvel at it. ²² Moses gave you circumcision (not that it is from Moses, but from the fathers), and you circumcise a man on the Sabbath. ²³ If on

¹ Or brothers and sisters; also 7:5, 10

the Sabbath a man receives circumcision, so that the law of Moses may not be broken, are you angry with me because on the Sabbath I made a man's whole body well? **24** Do not judge by appearances, but judge with right judgment."

Can This Be the Christ?

25 Some of the people of Jerusalem therefore said, "Is not this the man whom they seek to kill? **26** And here he is, speaking openly, and they say nothing to him! Can it be that the authorities really know that this is the Christ? **27** But we know where this man comes from, and when the Christ appears, no one will know where he comes from." **28** So Jesus proclaimed, as he taught in the temple, "You know me, and you know where I come from. But I have not come of my own accord. He who sent me is true, and him

> ### GETTING THE MESSAGE
>
> **The Dispersion** (7:35) referred to Jewish people scattered throughout the world. Many Jews were exiled from their homeland in 722 and 586 B.C. Those taken to Babylon in 586 were later allowed to return home, but many stayed in Babylon and others moved west into Greece. After the destruction of the temple in A.D. 70, many Jews were sold into slavery and further scattered abroad.

you do not know. **29** I know him, for I come from him, and he sent me." **30** So they were seeking to arrest him, but no one laid a hand on him, because his hour had not yet come. **31** Yet many of the people believed in him. They said, "When the Christ appears, will he do more signs than this man has done?"

Officers Sent to Arrest Jesus

32 The Pharisees heard the crowd muttering these things about him, and the chief priests and Pharisees sent officers to arrest him. **33** Jesus then said, "I will be with you a little longer, and then I am going to him who sent me. **34** You will seek me and you will not find me. Where I am you cannot come." **35** The Jews said to one another, "Where does this man intend to go that we

will not find him? Does he intend to go to the Dispersion among the Greeks and teach the Greeks? **36** What does he mean by saying, 'You will seek me and you will not find me,' and, 'Where I am you cannot come'?"

Rivers of Living Water

37 On the last day of the feast, the great day, Jesus stood up and cried out, "If anyone thirsts, let him come to me and drink. **38** Whoever believes in me, as the Scripture has said, 'Out of his heart will flow rivers of living water.'" **39** Now this he said about the Spirit, whom those who believed in him were to receive, for as yet the Spirit had not been given, because Jesus was not yet glorified.

Division Among the People

40 When they heard these words, some of the people said, "This really is the Prophet." **41** Others said, "This is the Christ." But some said, "Is the Christ to come from Galilee? **42** Has not the Scripture said that the Christ comes from the offspring of David, and comes from Bethlehem, the village where David was?" **43** So there was a division among the people over him. **44** Some of them wanted to arrest him, but no one laid hands on him.

45 The officers then came to the chief priests and Pharisees, who said to them, "Why did you not bring him?" **46** The officers answered, "No one ever spoke like this man!" **47** The Pharisees answered them, "Have you also been deceived? **48** Have any of the authorities or the Pharisees believed in him? **49** But this crowd that does not know the law is accursed." **50** Nicodemus, who had gone to him before, and who was one of them, said to them, **51** "Does our law judge a man without first giving him a hearing and learning what he does?" **52** They replied, "Are you from Galilee too? Search and see that no prophet arises from Galilee."

[THE EARLIEST MANUSCRIPTS
DO NOT INCLUDE 7:53–8:11.][1]

The Woman Caught in Adultery

8 **53** [[They went each to his own house, **1** but Jesus went to the Mount of Olives. **2** Early in the morning he came again to the temple. All the people came to him, and he sat down and taught them. **3** The scribes and the Pharisees brought a woman who had been caught in adultery, and placing her in the midst ⁴ they said to him, "Teacher, this woman has been caught in the act of adultery. ⁵ Now in the Law Moses commanded us to stone such women. So what do you say?" ⁶ This they said to test him, that they might have some charge to bring against him. Jesus bent down and wrote with his finger on the ground. ⁷ And as they continued to ask him, he stood up and said to them, "Let him who is without sin among you be the first to throw a stone at her." ⁸ And once more he bent down and wrote on the ground. ⁹ But when they heard it, they went away one by one, beginning with the older ones, and Jesus was left alone with the woman standing before him. ¹⁰ Jesus stood up and said to her, "Woman, where are they? Has no one condemned you?" ¹¹ She said, "No one, Lord." And Jesus said, "Neither do I condemn you; go, and from now on sin no more."]]

I Am the Light of the World

¹² Again Jesus spoke to them, saying, "I am the light of the world. Whoever follows me will not walk in darkness, but will have the light of life." ¹³ So the Pharisees said to him, "You are bearing witness about yourself; your testimony is not true." ¹⁴ Jesus answered, "Even if I do bear witness about myself, my testimony is true, for I know where I came from and where I am going, but you do not know where I come from or where I am going. ¹⁵ You judge according to the flesh; I judge no one. ¹⁶ Yet even if I do judge, my judgment is true, for it is not I alone who judge, but I and the Father who sent me. ¹⁷ In your Law it is written that the testimony of two people is true. ¹⁸ I am the one who bears witness about myself, and the Father who sent me bears witness about me." ¹⁹ They said to him therefore, "Where is your Father?" Jesus answered, "You know neither me nor my Father. If you knew me, you would know my Father also." ²⁰ These words he spoke in the treasury, as he taught in the temple; but no one arrested him, because his hour had not yet come.

²¹ So he said to them again, "I am going away, and you will seek me, and you will die in your sin. Where I am going, you cannot come." ²² So the Jews said, "Will he kill himself, since he says, 'Where I am going, you cannot come'?" ²³ He said to them, "You are from below; I am from above. You are of this world; I am not of this world. ²⁴ I told you that you would die in your sins, for unless you believe that I am he you will die in your sins." ²⁵ So they said to him, "Who are you?" Jesus said to them, "Just what I have been telling you from the beginning. ²⁶ I have much to say about you and much to judge, but he who sent me is true, and I declare to the world what I have heard from him." ²⁷ They did not understand that he had been speaking to them about the Father. ²⁸ So Jesus said to them, "When you have lifted up the Son of Man, then you will know that I am he, and that I do nothing on my own authority, but speak just as the Father taught me. ²⁹ And he who sent me is with me. He has not left me alone, for I always do the things that are pleasing to him." ³⁰ As

---

GETTING THE MESSAGE

John wrote his Gospel "**so that you may believe** that Jesus is the Christ, the Son of God, and that by believing you may have life in his name" (20:31). In 8:24, Jesus tells his listeners that faith in him is the only way to find life (see 3:15–16; 11:25).

---

he was saying these things, many believed in him.

The Truth Will Set You Free

³¹ So Jesus said to the Jews who had believed him, "If you abide in my word, you are truly my disciples, ³² and you will know the truth, and the truth will set you free." ³³ They answered him, "We are offspring of Abraham and have never been enslaved to anyone. How is it that you say, 'You will become free'?"

³⁴ Jesus answered them, "Truly, truly, I say to you, everyone who practices sin is a slave¹ to sin. ³⁵ The slave does not remain in the house forever; the son remains forever. ³⁶ So if the Son sets you free, you will be free indeed. ³⁷ I know that you are offspring of Abraham; yet you seek to kill me because my word finds no place in you. ³⁸ I speak of what I have seen with my Father, and you do what you have heard from your father."

---

¹ Greek *doulos* (see Preface); also 8:35

You Are of Your Father the Devil

39 They answered him, "Abraham is our father." Jesus said to them, "If you were Abraham's children, you would be doing the works Abraham did, **40** but now you seek to kill me, a man who has told you the truth that I heard from God. This is not what Abraham did. **41** You are doing the works your father did." They said to him, "We were not born of sexual immorality. We have one Father—even God." **42** Jesus said to them, "If God were your Father, you would love me, for I came from God and I am here. I came not of my own accord, but he sent me. **43** Why do you not understand what I say? It is because you cannot bear to hear my word. **44** You are of your father the devil, and your will is to do your father's desires. He was a murderer from the beginning, and does not stand in the truth, because there is

> ### GETTING THE MESSAGE
>
> **Does sin cause illness?** Many people in Bible times assumed that if a person suffered, it was because that person had sinned (9:2). There are consequences for sin, but suffering is not always directly caused by a person's sin. But God can use suffering to show his power and mercy (9:3).

no truth in him. When he lies, he speaks out of his own character, for he is a liar and the father of lies. **45** But because I tell the truth, you do not believe me. **46** Which one of you convicts me of sin? If I tell the truth, why do you not believe me? **47** Whoever is of God hears the words of God. The reason why you do not hear them is that you are not of God."

Before Abraham Was, I Am

48 The Jews answered him, "Are we not right in saying that you are a Samaritan and have a demon?" **49** Jesus answered, "I do not have a demon, but I honor my Father, and you dishonor me. **50** Yet I do not seek my own glory; there is One who seeks it, and he is the judge. **51** Truly, truly, I say to you, if anyone keeps my word, he will never see death." **52** The Jews said to him, "Now we know that you have a demon! Abraham died, as did the prophets, yet you say, 'If anyone keeps my word, he will never taste death.'

53 Are you greater than our father Abraham, who died? And the prophets died! Who do you make yourself out to be?" **54** Jesus answered, "If I glorify myself, my glory is nothing. It is my Father who glorifies me, of whom you say, 'He is our God.' **55** But you have not known him. I know him. If I were to say that I do not know him, I would be a liar like you, but I do know him and I keep his word. **56** Your father Abraham rejoiced that he would see my day. He saw it and was glad." **57** So the Jews said to him, "You are not yet fifty years old, and have you seen Abraham?" **58** Jesus said to them, "Truly, truly, I say to you, before Abraham was, I am." **59** So they picked up stones to throw at him, but Jesus hid himself and went out of the temple.

Jesus Heals a Man Born Blind

9 As he passed by, he saw a man blind from birth. **2** And his disciples asked him, "Rabbi, who sinned, this man or his parents, that he was born blind?" **3** Jesus answered, "It was not that this man sinned, or his parents, but that the works of God might be displayed in him. **4** We must work the works of him who sent me while it is day; night is coming, when no one can work. **5** As long as I am in the world, I am the light of the world." **6** Having said these things, he spit on the ground and made mud with the saliva. Then he anointed the man's eyes with the mud **7** and said to him, "Go, wash in the pool of Siloam" (which means Sent). So he went and washed and came back seeing.

8 The neighbors and those who had seen him before as a beggar were saying, "Is this not the man who used to sit and beg?" **9** Some said, "It is he." Others said, "No, but he is like him." He kept saying, "I am the man." **10** So they said to him, "Then how were your eyes opened?" **11** He answered, "The man called Jesus made mud and anointed my eyes and said to me, 'Go to Siloam and wash.' So I went and washed and received my sight." **12** They said to him, "Where is he?" He said, "I do not know."

13 They brought to the Pharisees the man who had formerly been blind. **14** Now it was a Sabbath day when Jesus made the mud and opened his eyes. **15** So the Pharisees again asked him how he had received his sight. And he said to them, "He put mud on my eyes, and I washed, and I see." **16** Some of the Pharisees said, "This man is not from God, for he does not keep the Sabbath." But others said, "How can a man who is a sinner do such signs?" And there was a division among them. **17** So they said again to the blind man, "What do you say about him, since he has opened your eyes?" He said, "He is a prophet."

18 The Jews did not believe that he had been blind and had received his sight, until they called the parents of the man who had received his sight **19** and asked them, "Is this your son, who you say was born blind? How then does he now see?" **20** His parents answered, "We know that this is our son and that he was born blind. **21** But how he now sees we do not know, nor do we know who opened his eyes. Ask him; he is of age. He will speak for himself." **22** (His parents said these things because they feared the Jews, for the Jews had already agreed that if anyone should confess Jesus to be Christ, he was to be put out of the synagogue.) **23** Therefore his parents said, "He is of age; ask him."

24 So for the second time they called the man who had been blind and said to him, "Give glory to God. We know that this man is a sinner." **25** He answered, "Whether he is a sinner I do not know. One thing I do know, that though I was blind, now I see." **26** They said to him, "What did he do to you? How did he open your eyes?" **27** He answered them, "I have told you already, and you would not listen. Why do you want to hear it again? Do you also want to become his disciples?" **28** And they reviled him, saying, "You are his disciple, but we are disciples of Moses. **29** We know that God has spoken to Moses, but as for this man, we do not know where he comes from." **30** The man answered, "Why, this is an amazing thing! You do not know where he comes from, and yet he opened my eyes. **31** We know that God does not listen to sinners, but if anyone is a worshiper of God and does his will, God listens to him. **32** Never since the world began has it been heard that anyone opened the eyes of a man born blind. **33** If this man were not from God, he could do nothing." **34** They answered him, "You were born in utter sin, and would you teach us?" And they cast him out.

35 Jesus heard that they had cast him out, and having found him he said, "Do you believe in the Son of Man?" **36** He answered, "And who is he, sir, that I may believe in him?" **37** Jesus said to him, "You have seen him, and it is he who is speaking to you." **38** He said, "Lord, I believe," and he worshiped him. **39** Jesus said, "For judgment I came into this world, that those who do not see may see, and those who see may become blind." **40** Some of the Pharisees near him heard these things, and said to him, "Are we also blind?" **41** Jesus said to them, "If you were blind, you would have no guilt; but now that you say, 'We see,' your guilt remains.

I Am the Good Shepherd

10 "Truly, truly, I say to you, he who does not enter the sheepfold by the door but climbs in by another way, that man is a thief and a robber. **2** But he who enters by the door is the shepherd of the sheep. **3** To him the gatekeeper opens. The sheep hear his voice, and he calls his own sheep by name

GETTING THE MESSAGE

The Feast of Dedication (10:22) commemorated the rededication of the temple in 164 B.C. after Antiochus IV Epiphanes made it unholy. Today, this feast is called Hanukkah.

and leads them out. **4** When he has brought out all his own, he goes before them, and the sheep follow him, for they know his voice. **5** A stranger they will not follow, but they will flee from him, for they do not know the voice of strangers." **6** This figure of speech Jesus used with them, but they did not understand what he was saying to them.

7 So Jesus again said to them, "Truly, truly, I say to you, I am the door of the sheep. **8** All who came before me are thieves and robbers, but the sheep did not listen to them. **9** I am the door. If anyone enters by me, he will be saved and will go in and out and find pasture. **10** The thief comes only to steal and kill and destroy. I came that they may have life and have it abundantly. **11** I am the good shepherd. The good shepherd lays down his life for the sheep. **12** He who is a hired hand and not a shepherd, who does not own the sheep, sees the wolf coming and leaves the sheep and flees, and the wolf snatches them and scatters them. **13** He flees because he is a hired hand and cares nothing for the sheep. [14] I am the good shepherd. I know my own and my own know me, [15] just as the Father knows me and I know the Father; and I lay down my life for the sheep. [16] And I have other sheep that are not of this fold. I must bring them also, and they will listen to my voice. So there will be one flock, one shepherd. [17] For this reason the Father loves me, because I lay down my life that I may take it up again. [18] No one takes it from me, but I lay it down of my own accord. I have authority

---

MARY, SISTER OF LAZARUS

Mary, along with her sister Martha and her brother Lazarus, was a close friend of Jesus. Mary was intensely devoted to Jesus, choosing to sit at his feet and listen to his teaching while Martha struggled to be a good hostess (see Luke 10:38–42). Martha was annoyed that Mary didn't help her, but Jesus praised Mary's decision, saying that it demonstrated her desire for close fellowship with the Lord. On another occasion Mary was scolded by the disciples, who were indignant that she anointed Jesus with costly ointment rather than selling it and giving the money to the poor. Again, Jesus defended Mary's actions of humility and devotion.

KEY REFERENCE: JOHN 12:3

---

to lay it down, and I have authority to take it up again. This charge I have received from my Father."

[19] There was again a division among the Jews because of these words. [20] Many of them said, "He has a demon, and is insane; why listen to him?" [21] Others said, "These are not the words of one who is oppressed by a demon. Can a demon open the eyes of the blind?"

I and the Father Are One

[22] At that time the Feast of Dedication took place at Jerusalem. It was winter, [23] and Jesus was walking in the temple, in the colonnade of Solomon. [24] So the Jews gathered around him and said to him, "How long will you keep us in suspense? If you are the Christ, tell us plainly." [25] Jesus answered them, "I told you, and you do not believe. The works that I do in my Father's name bear witness about me, [26] but you do not believe because you are not among my sheep. [27] My sheep hear my voice, and I know them, and they follow me. [28] I give them eternal life, and they will never perish, and no one will snatch them out of my hand. [29] My Father, who has given them to me, is greater than all, and no one is able to snatch them out of the Father's hand. [30] I and the Father are one."

[31] The Jews picked up stones again to stone him. [32] Jesus answered them, "I have shown you many good works from the Father; for which of them are you going to stone me?" [33] The Jews answered him, "It is not for a good work that we are going to stone you but for blasphemy, because you, being a man, make yourself God." [34] Jesus answered them, "Is it not written in your Law, 'I said, you are gods'? [35] If he called them gods to whom the word of God came—and Scripture cannot be broken— [36] do you say of him whom the Father consecrated and sent into the world, 'You are blaspheming,' because I said, 'I am the Son of God'? [37] If I am not doing the works of my Father, then do not believe me; [38] but if I do them, even though you do not believe me, believe the works, that you may know and understand that the Father is in me and I am in the Father." [39] Again they sought to arrest him, but he escaped from their hands.

[40] He went away again across the Jordan to the place where John had been baptizing at first, and there he remained. [41] And many came to him. And they said, "John did no sign, but everything that John said about this man was true." [42] And many believed in him there.

The Death of Lazarus

11 Now a certain man was ill, Lazarus of Bethany, the village of Mary and her sister Martha. [2] It was Mary who anointed the Lord with ointment and wiped his feet with her hair, whose brother Lazarus was ill. [3] So the sisters sent to him, saying, "Lord, he whom you love is ill." [4] But when Jesus heard it he said, "This illness does not lead to death. It is for the glory of God, so that the Son of God may be glorified through it."

⁵ Now Jesus loved Martha and her sister and Lazarus. ⁶ So, when he heard that Lazarus was ill, he stayed two days longer in the place where he was. ⁷ Then after this he said to the disciples, "Let us go to Judea again." ⁸ The disciples said to him, "Rabbi, the Jews were just now seeking to stone you, and are you going there again?" ⁹ Jesus answered, "Are there not twelve hours in the day? If anyone walks in the day, he does not stumble, because he sees the light of this world. ¹⁰ But if anyone walks in the night, he stumbles, because the light is not in him." ¹¹ After saying these things, he said to them, "Our friend Lazarus has fallen asleep, but I go to awaken him." ¹² The disciples said to him, "Lord, if he has fallen asleep, he will recover." ¹³ Now Jesus had spoken of his death, but they thought that he meant taking rest in sleep. ¹⁴ Then Jesus told them plainly, "Lazarus has died, ¹⁵ and for your sake I am glad that I was not there, so that you may believe. But let us go to him." ¹⁶ So Thomas, called the Twin, said to his fellow disciples, "Let us also go, that we may die with him."

I Am the Resurrection and the Life

¹⁷ Now when Jesus came, he found that Lazarus had already been in the tomb four days. ¹⁸ Bethany was near Jerusalem, about two miles off, ¹⁹ and many of the Jews had come to Martha and Mary to console them concerning their brother. ²⁰ So when Martha heard that Jesus was coming, she went and met him, but Mary remained seated in the house. ²¹ Martha said to Jesus, "Lord, if you had been here, my brother would not have died. ²² But even now I know that whatever you ask from God, God will give you." ²³ Jesus said to her, "Your brother will rise again." ²⁴ Martha said to him, "I know that he will rise again in the resurrection on the last day." ²⁵ Jesus said to her, "I am the resurrection and the life. Whoever believes in me, though he die, yet shall he live, ²⁶ and everyone who lives and believes in me shall never die. Do you believe this?" ²⁷ She said to him, "Yes, Lord; I believe that you are the Christ, the Son of God, who is coming into the world."

Jesus Weeps

²⁸ When she had said this, she went and called her sister Mary, saying in private,

"The Teacher is here and is calling for you." ²⁹ And when she heard it, she rose quickly and went to him. ³⁰ Now Jesus had not yet come into the village, but was still in the place where Martha had met him. ³¹ When the Jews who were with her in the house, consoling her, saw Mary rise quickly and go out, they followed her, supposing that she was going to the tomb to weep there. ³² Now when Mary came to where Jesus was and saw him, she fell at his feet, saying to him, "Lord, if you had been here, my brother would not have died." ³³ When Jesus saw her weeping, and the Jews who had come with her also weeping, he was deeply moved in his spirit and greatly troubled. ³⁴ And he said, "Where have you laid him?" They said to him, "Lord, come and see." ³⁵ Jesus wept. ³⁶ So the Jews said, "See how he loved him!" ³⁷ But some of them said, "Could not he who

opened the eyes of the blind man also have kept this man from dying?"

Jesus Raises Lazarus

³⁸ Then Jesus, deeply moved again, came to the tomb. It was a cave, and a stone lay against it. ³⁹ Jesus said, "Take away the stone." Martha, the sister of the dead man, said to him, "Lord, by this time there will be an odor, for he has been dead four days." ⁴⁰ Jesus said to her, "Did I not tell you that if you believed you would see the glory of God?" ⁴¹ So they took away the stone. And Jesus lifted up his eyes and said, "Father, I thank you that you have heard me. ⁴² I knew that you always hear me, but I said this on account of the people standing around, that they may believe that you sent me." ⁴³ When he had said these things, he cried out with a loud voice, "Lazarus, come out." ⁴⁴ The man who had died came out, his hands and feet bound with linen strips, and

his face wrapped with a cloth. Jesus said to them, "Unbind him, and let him go."

The Plot to Kill Jesus

45 Many of the Jews therefore, who had come with Mary and had seen what he did, believed in him, **46** but some of them went to the Pharisees and told them what Jesus had done. **47** So the chief priests and the Pharisees gathered the council and said, "What are we to do? For this man performs many signs. **48** If we let him go on like this, everyone

---

PROFILE
CAIAPHAS

Caiaphas was the high priest during Jesus' ministry. He consulted frequently with his powerful father-in-law, Annas, who had previously served as high priest. After Jesus raised Lazarus from the dead, the chief priests and Pharisees gathered in great fear to discuss Jesus' growing influence among the Jews. As they contemplated what to do, Caiaphas unwittingly prophesied that Jesus would die for the sins of the world (11:51–52). It was this prophecy that put in motion the plan to have Jesus put to death. When Jesus was arrested before his crucifixion, he was sent first to Annas and then to Caiaphas. As high priest and leader of the Sanhedrin, Caiaphas confirmed the charges against Jesus before handing him over to Pilate to be crucified.

KEY REFERENCE: JOHN 11:49–52

---

will believe in him, and the Romans will come and take away both our place and our nation." **49** But one of them, Caiaphas, who was high priest that year, said to them, "You know nothing at all. **50** Nor do you understand that it is better for you that one man should die for the people, not that the whole nation should perish." **51** He did not say this of his own accord, but being high priest that year he prophesied that Jesus would die for the nation, **52** and not for the nation only, but also to gather into one the children of God who are scattered abroad. **53** So from that day on they made plans to put him to death.

54 Jesus therefore no longer walked openly among the Jews, but went from there to the region near the wilderness, to a town called Ephraim, and there he stayed with the disciples.

55 Now the Passover of the Jews was at hand, and many went up from the country to Jerusalem before the Passover to purify themselves. **56** They were looking for Jesus and saying to one another as they stood in the temple, "What do you think? That he will not come to the feast at all?" **57** Now the chief priests and the Pharisees had given orders that if anyone knew where he was, he should let them know, so that they might arrest him.

Mary Anoints Jesus at Bethany

12 Six days before the Passover, Jesus therefore came to Bethany, where Lazarus was, whom Jesus had raised from the dead. **2** So they gave a dinner for him there. Martha served, and Lazarus was one of those reclining with him at table. **3** Mary therefore took a pound of expensive ointment made from pure nard, and anointed the feet of Jesus and wiped his feet with her hair. The house was filled with the fragrance of the perfume. **4** But Judas Iscariot, one of his disciples (he who was about to betray him), said, **5** "Why was this ointment not sold for three hundred denarii and given to the poor?" **6** He said this, not because he cared about the poor, but because he was a thief, and having charge of the moneybag he used to help himself to what was put into it. **7** Jesus said, "Leave her alone, so that she may keep it for the day of my burial. **8** For the poor you always have with you, but you do not always have me."

The Plot to Kill Lazarus

9 When the large crowd of the Jews learned that Jesus was there, they came, not only on account of him but also to see Lazarus, whom he had raised from the dead. **10** So the chief priests made plans to put Lazarus to death as well, **11** because on account of him many of the Jews were going away and believing in Jesus.

The Triumphal Entry

12 The next day the large crowd that had come to the feast heard that Jesus was coming to Jerusalem. **13** So they took branches of palm trees and went out to meet him, crying out, "Hosanna! Blessed is he who comes in the name of the Lord, even the King of Israel!" **14** And Jesus found a young donkey and sat on it, just as it is written,

15 "Fear not, daughter of Zion;
　　behold, your king is coming,
　　　sitting on a donkey's colt!"

16 His disciples did not understand these things at first, but when Jesus was glorified, then they remembered that these things had been written about him and had been done to him. **17** The crowd that had been with him when he called Lazarus out of the tomb and raised him from the dead continued to bear witness. **18** The reason why the crowd went to meet him was that they heard he had done this sign. **19** So the Pharisees said to one another, "You see that you are gaining nothing. Look, the world has gone after him."

Some Greeks Seek Jesus

20 Now among those who went up to worship at the feast were some Greeks. **21** So these came to Philip, who was from Bethsaida in Galilee, and asked him, "Sir, we wish to see Jesus." **22** Philip went and told Andrew; Andrew and Philip went and told Jesus. **23** And Jesus answered them, "The hour has come for the Son of Man to be glorified. **24** Truly, truly, I say to you, unless a grain of wheat falls into the earth and dies, it remains alone; but if it dies, it bears much fruit. **25** Whoever loves his life loses it, and whoever hates his life in this world will keep it for eternal life. **26** If anyone serves me, he must follow me; and where I am, there will my servant be also. If anyone serves me, the Father will honor him.

The Son of Man Must Be Lifted Up

27 "Now is my soul troubled. And what shall I say? 'Father, save me from this hour'? But for this purpose I have come to this hour. **28** Father, glorify your name." Then a voice came from heaven: "I have glorified it, and I will glorify it again." **29** The crowd that stood there and heard it said that it had thundered. Others said, "An angel has spoken to him." **30** Jesus answered, "This voice has come for your sake, not mine. **31** Now is the judgment of this world; now will the ruler of this world be cast out. **32** And I, when I am lifted up from the earth, will draw all people to myself." **33** He said this to show by

what kind of death he was going to die. **34** So the crowd answered him, "We have heard from the Law that the Christ remains forever. How can you say that the Son of Man must be lifted up? Who is this Son of Man?" **35** So Jesus said to them, "The light is among you for a little while longer. Walk while you have the light, lest darkness overtake you. The one who walks in the darkness does not know where he is going. **36** While you have the light, believe in the light, that you may become sons of light."

The Unbelief of the People

When Jesus had said these things, he departed and hid himself from them. **37** Though he had done so many signs before them, they still did not believe in him, **38** so

> ### GETTING THE MESSAGE
>
> The **Greeks** who came to see Jesus (12:20–21) were not necessarily from Greece. The term could refer to any Gentile in the Greek-speaking world. Like other Greek people such as the centurion in Luke 7:5 or Cornelius in Acts 10, they were attracted to the teachings of the Jewish Scriptures. Now, they wanted to hear more from this man who claimed to be the Messiah.

that the word spoken by the prophet Isaiah might be fulfilled:

"Lord, who has believed what he heard
　　from us,
　　and to whom has the arm of the
　　　Lord been revealed?"

39 Therefore they could not believe. For again Isaiah said,

40 "He has blinded their eyes
　　and hardened their heart,
　　lest they see with their eyes,
　　and understand with their heart,
　　　and turn,
　　and I would heal them."

41 Isaiah said these things because he saw his glory and spoke of him. **42** Nevertheless, many even of the authorities believed in him, but for fear of the Pharisees they did not confess it, so that they would not be put out of the synagogue; **43** for they loved the glory that comes from man more than the glory that comes from God.

Jesus Came to Save the World

44 And Jesus cried out and said, "Whoever believes in me, believes not in me but in him who sent me. **45** And whoever sees me sees him who sent me. **46** I have come into the world as light, so that whoever believes in me may not remain in darkness. **47** If anyone hears my words and does not keep them, I do not judge him; for I did not come to judge the world but to save the world. **48** The one who rejects me and does not receive my words has a judge; the word that I have spoken will judge him on the last day. **49** For I have not spoken on my own authority, but the Father who sent me has himself given me a commandment—what to say and what

> ### GETTING THE MESSAGE
>
> In New Testament times, it was common for a host's servant to **wash the feet** of guests (see Luke 7:44). But in John 13:1-20, Jesus himself performs this task for his disciples, setting an example of humility and service for believers to follow.

to speak. **50** And I know that his commandment is eternal life. What I say, therefore, I say as the Father has told me."

Jesus Washes the Disciples' Feet

13 Now before the Feast of the Passover, when Jesus knew that his hour had come to depart out of this world to the Father, having loved his own who were in the world, he loved them to the end. **2** During supper, when the devil had already put it into the heart of Judas Iscariot, Simon's son, to betray him, **3** Jesus, knowing that the Father had given all things into his hands, and that he had come from God and was going back to God, **4** rose from supper. He laid aside his outer garments, and taking a towel, tied it around his waist. **5** Then he poured water into a basin and began to wash the disciples' feet and to wipe them with the towel that was wrapped around him. **6** He came to Simon Peter, who said to him, "Lord, do you wash my feet?" **7** Jesus

answered him, "What I am doing you do not understand now, but afterward you will understand." **8** Peter said to him, "You shall never wash my feet." Jesus answered him, "If I do not wash you, you have no share with me." **9** Simon Peter said to him, "Lord, not my feet only but also my hands and my head!" **10** Jesus said to him, "The one who has bathed does not need to wash, except for his feet, but is completely clean. And you are clean, but not every one of you." **11** For he knew who was to betray him; that was why he said, "Not all of you are clean."

12 When he had washed their feet and put on his outer garments and resumed his place, he said to them, "Do you understand what I have done to you? **13** You call me Teacher and Lord, and you are right, for so I am. **14** If I then, your Lord and Teacher, have washed your feet, you also ought to wash one another's feet. **15** For I have given you an example, that you also should do just as I have done to you. **16** Truly, truly, I say to you, a servant is not greater than his master, nor is a messenger greater than the one who sent him. **17** If you know these things, blessed are you if you do them. **18** I am not speaking of all of you; I know whom I have chosen. But the Scripture will be fulfilled, 'He who ate my bread has lifted his heel against me.' **19** I am telling you this now, before it takes place, that when it does take place you may believe that I am he. **20** Truly, truly, I say to you, whoever receives the one I send receives me, and whoever receives me receives the one who sent me."

One of You Will Betray Me

21 After saying these things, Jesus was troubled in his spirit, and testified, "Truly, truly, I say to you, one of you will betray me." **22** The disciples looked at one another, uncertain of whom he spoke. **23** One of his disciples, whom Jesus loved, was reclining at table at Jesus' side, **24** so Simon Peter motioned to him to ask Jesus of whom he was speaking. **25** So that disciple, leaning back against Jesus, said to him, "Lord, who is it?" **26** Jesus answered, "It is he to whom I will give this morsel of bread when I have dipped it." So when he had dipped the morsel, he gave it to Judas, the son of Simon Iscariot. **27** Then after he had taken the morsel, Satan entered into him. Jesus said to him, "What you are going to do, do quickly."

²⁸ Now no one at the table knew why he said this to him. ²⁹ Some thought that, because Judas had the moneybag, Jesus was telling him, "Buy what we need for the feast," or that he should give something to the poor. ³⁰ So, after receiving the morsel of bread, he immediately went out. And it was night.

A New Commandment

³¹ When he had gone out, Jesus said, "Now is the Son of Man glorified, and God is glorified in him. ³² If God is glorified in him, God will also glorify him in himself, and glorify him at once. ³³ Little children, yet a little while I am with you. You will seek me, and just as I said to the Jews, so now I also say to you, 'Where I am going you cannot come.' ³⁴ A new commandment I give to you, that you love one another: just as I have loved you, you also are to love one another. ³⁵ By this all people will know that you are my disciples, if you have love for one another."

> **GETTING THE MESSAGE**
>
> Jesus promises his disciples that **the Holy Spirit** will live within them, to teach them and remind them what Jesus has said (14:16–17, 26; see also 16:5–15). The Holy Spirit is also called the "Helper," which can mean "Advocate" or "Counselor."

Jesus Foretells Peter's Denial

³⁶ Simon Peter said to him, "Lord, where are you going?" Jesus answered him, "Where I am going you cannot follow me now, but you will follow afterward." ³⁷ Peter said to him, "Lord, why can I not follow you now? I will lay down my life for you." ³⁸ Jesus answered, "Will you lay down your life for me? Truly, truly, I say to you, the rooster will not crow till you have denied me three times.

I Am the Way, and the Truth, and the Life

14 "Let not your hearts be troubled. Believe in God; believe also in me. ² In my Father's house are many rooms. If it were not so, would I have told you that I go to prepare a place for you? ³ And if I go and prepare a place for you, I will come again and will take you to myself, that where I am you may be also. ⁴ And you know the way to where I

am going." ⁵ Thomas said to him, "Lord, we do not know where you are going. How can we know the way?" ⁶ Jesus said to him, "I am the way, and the truth, and the life. No one comes to the Father except through me. ⁷ If you had known me, you would have known my Father also. From now on you do know him and have seen him."

⁸ Philip said to him, "Lord, show us the Father, and it is enough for us." ⁹ Jesus said to him, "Have I been with you so long, and you still do not know me, Philip? Whoever has seen me has seen the Father. How can

> PROFILE
> # JOHN
>
> John the son of Zebedee was one of Jesus' 12 disciples, along with his brother James. John was a fisherman. He and James were in business with fellow disciples Simon Peter and Andrew (Luke 5:10). John was a close friend of Jesus and one of the inner circle of disciples. He is probably "the other disciple" (John 18:16) and "the one whom Jesus loved" (20:2). This "other disciple" reclined next to Jesus at the Last Supper (13:23). He stood at the foot of the cross, where Jesus entrusted his mother Mary to John's care (19:26–27). Along with Peter he witnessed the empty tomb on the first Easter morning (20:2–10). He also talked with the resurrected Jesus (21:7, 20). In addition to the Gospel bearing his name, John wrote the books of 1, 2, and 3 John, and Revelation.
>
> **KEY REFERENCE:** JOHN 13:23

you say, 'Show us the Father'? ¹⁰ Do you not believe that I am in the Father and the Father is in me? The words that I say to you I do not speak on my own authority, but the Father who dwells in me does his works. ¹¹ Believe me that I am in the Father and the Father is in me, or else believe on account of the works themselves.

¹² "Truly, truly, I say to you, whoever believes in me will also do the works that I do; and greater works than these will he do, because I am going to the Father. ¹³ Whatever

you ask in my name, this I will do, that the Father may be glorified in the Son. ¹⁴ If you ask me anything in my name, I will do it.

Jesus Promises the Holy Spirit

¹⁵ "If you love me, you will keep my commandments. ¹⁶ And I will ask the Father, and he will give you another Helper, to be with you forever, ¹⁷ even the Spirit of truth, whom the world cannot receive, because it neither sees him nor knows him. You know him, for he dwells with you and will be in you.

¹⁸ "I will not leave you as orphans; I will come to you. ¹⁹ Yet a little while and the world will see me no more, but you will see me. Because I live, you also will live. ²⁰ In that day you will know that I am in my Father, and you in me, and I in you. ²¹ Whoever has my commandments and keeps them, he it is who loves me. And he who loves me will be loved by my Father,

> ### GETTING THE MESSAGE
>
> In 13:31–16:33, Jesus prepares his disciples for his departure from them. This is often called **the Farewell Discourse**. Jesus shows his disciples that his death and resurrection will bring them blessing.

and I will love him and manifest myself to him." ²² Judas (not Iscariot) said to him, "Lord, how is it that you will manifest yourself to us, and not to the world?" ²³ Jesus answered him, "If anyone loves me, he will keep my word, and my Father will love him, and we will come to him and make our home with him. ²⁴ Whoever does not love me does not keep my words. And the word that you hear is not mine but the Father's who sent me.

²⁵ "These things I have spoken to you while I am still with you. ²⁶ But the Helper, the Holy Spirit, whom the Father will send in my name, he will teach you all things and bring to your remembrance all that I have said to you. ²⁷ Peace I leave with you; my peace I give to you. Not as the world gives do I give to you. Let not your hearts be troubled, neither let them be afraid. ²⁸ You heard me say to you, 'I am going away, and I will come to you.' If you loved me, you would have rejoiced, because I am going to

the Father, for the Father is greater than I. ²⁹ And now I have told you before it takes place, so that when it does take place you may believe. ³⁰ I will no longer talk much with you, for the ruler of this world is coming. He has no claim on me, ³¹ but I do as the Father has commanded me, so that the world may know that I love the Father. Rise, let us go from here.

I Am the True Vine

15 "I am the true vine, and my Father is the vinedresser. ² Every branch in me that does not bear fruit he takes away, and every branch that does bear fruit he prunes, that it may bear more fruit. ³ Already you are clean because of the word that I have spoken to you. ⁴ Abide in me, and I in you. As the branch cannot bear fruit by itself, unless it abides in the vine, neither can you, unless you abide in me. ⁵ I am the vine; you are the branches. Whoever abides in me and I in him, he it is that bears much fruit, for apart from me you can do nothing. ⁶ If anyone does not abide in me he is thrown away like a branch and withers; and the branches are gathered, thrown into the fire, and burned. ⁷ If you abide in me, and my words abide in you, ask whatever you wish, and it will be done for you. ⁸ By this my Father is glorified, that you bear much fruit and so prove to be my disciples. ⁹ As the Father has loved me, so have I loved you. Abide in my love. ¹⁰ If you keep my commandments, you will abide in my love, just as I have kept my Father's commandments and abide in his love. ¹¹ These things I have spoken to you, that my joy may be in you, and that your joy may be full.

¹² "This is my commandment, that you love one another as I have loved you. ¹³ Greater love has no one than this, that someone lay down his life for his friends. ¹⁴ You are my friends if you do what I command you. ¹⁵ No longer do I call you servants, for the servant does not know what his master is doing; but I have called you friends, for all that I have heard from my Father I have made known to you. ¹⁶ You did not choose me, but I chose you and appointed you that you should go and bear fruit and that your fruit should abide, so that whatever you ask the Father in my name, he may give it to you. ¹⁷ These things I command you, so that you will love one another.

The Hatred of the World

[18] "If the world hates you, know that it has hated me before it hated you. [19] If you were of the world, the world would love you as its own; but because you are not of the world, but I chose you out of the world, therefore the world hates you. [20] Remember the word that I said to you: 'A servant is not greater than his master.' If they persecuted me, they will also persecute you. If they kept my word, they will also keep yours. [21] But all these things they will do to you on account of my name, because they do not know him who sent me. [22] If I had not come and spoken to them, they would not have been guilty of sin, but now they have no excuse for their sin. [23] Whoever hates me hates my Father also. [24] If I had not done among them the works that no one else did, they would not be guilty of sin, but now they have seen and hated both me and my Father. [25] But the word that is written in their Law must be fulfilled: 'They hated me without a cause.'

[26] "But when the Helper comes, whom I will send to you from the Father, the Spirit of truth, who proceeds from the Father, he will bear witness about me. [27] And you also will bear witness, because you have been with me from the beginning.

16

[1] "I have said all these things to you to keep you from falling away. [2] They will put you out of the synagogues. Indeed, the hour is coming when whoever kills you will think he is offering service to God. [3] And they will do these things because they have not known the Father, nor me. [4] But I have said these things to you, that when their hour comes you may remember that I told them to you.

The Work of the Holy Spirit

"I did not say these things to you from the beginning, because I was with you. [5] But now I am going to him who sent me, and none of you asks me, 'Where are you going?' [6] But because I have said these things to you, sorrow has filled your heart. [7] Nevertheless, I tell you the truth: it is to your advantage that I go away, for if I do not go away, the Helper will not come to you. But if I go, I will send him to you. [8] And when he comes, he will convict the world concerning sin and righteousness and judgment: [9] concerning sin, because they do not believe in me; [10] concerning righteousness, because I go to the Father, and you will see me no longer; [11] concerning judgment, because the ruler of this world is judged.

[12] "I still have many things to say to you, but you cannot bear them now. [13] When the Spirit of truth comes, he will guide you into all the truth, for he will not speak on his own authority, but whatever he hears he will speak, and he will declare to you the things that are to come. [14] He will glorify me, for he will take what is mine and declare it to you. [15] All that the Father has is mine; therefore I said that he will take what is mine and declare it to you.

Your Sorrow Will Turn into Joy

[16] "A little while, and you will see me no longer; and again a little while, and you will see me." [17] So some of his disciples said to one another, "What is this that he says to us,

---

GETTING THE MESSAGE

Praying in Jesus' name (16:23; compare 14:13) is not about whether or not the prayer ends with the exact words "in Jesus' name." It means acknowledging that Jesus is our advocate or mediator before God the Father (Rom. 8:34; Heb. 7:25; 1 John 2:1).

'A little while, and you will not see me, and again a little while, and you will see me'; and, 'because I am going to the Father'?" [18] So they were saying, "What does he mean by 'a little while'? We do not know what he is talking about." [19] Jesus knew that they wanted to ask him, so he said to them, "Is this what you are asking yourselves, what I meant by saying, 'A little while and you will not see me, and again a little while and you will see me'? [20] Truly, truly, I say to you, you will weep and lament, but the world will rejoice. You will be sorrowful, but your sorrow will turn into joy. [21] When a woman is giving birth, she has sorrow because her hour has come, but when she has delivered the baby, she no longer remembers the anguish, for joy that a human being has been born into the world. [22] So also you have sorrow now, but I will see you again, and your hearts will rejoice, and no one will take your joy from you. [23] In that day you will ask nothing of me. Truly, truly, I say to you, whatever you ask of the Father in my name, he will give it to you. ²⁴ Until now you have asked nothing in my name. Ask, and you will receive, that your joy may be full.

I Have Overcome the World

²⁵ "I have said these things to you in figures of speech. The hour is coming when I will no longer speak to you in figures of speech but will tell you plainly about the Father. ²⁶ In that day you will ask in my name, and I do not say to you that I will ask the Father on your behalf; ²⁷ for the Father himself loves you, because you have loved me and have believed that I came from God. ²⁸ I came from the Father and have come into the world, and now I am leaving the world and going to the Father."

²⁹ His disciples said, "Ah, now you are speaking plainly and not using figurative

> ### GETTING THE MESSAGE
>
> **Jesus' final prayer.** In 17:1–26, Jesus prays for himself (vv. 1–5) and for his disciples (vv. 6–19). He also prays for people in the future who will believe in Jesus because of the disciples' words (vv. 20–26). He asks God for unity and love among them all.

speech! ³⁰ Now we know that you know all things and do not need anyone to question you; this is why we believe that you came from God." ³¹ Jesus answered them, "Do you now believe? ³² Behold, the hour is coming, indeed it has come, when you will be scattered, each to his own home, and will leave me alone. Yet I am not alone, for the Father is with me. ³³ I have said these things to you, that in me you may have peace. In the world you will have tribulation. But take heart; I have overcome the world."

The High Priestly Prayer

17 When Jesus had spoken these words, he lifted up his eyes to heaven, and said, "Father, the hour has come; glorify your Son that the Son may glorify you, ² since you have given him authority over all flesh, to give eternal life to all whom you have given him. ³ And this is eternal life, that they know you the only true God, and Jesus Christ whom you have sent. ⁴ I glorified you

on earth, having accomplished the work that you gave me to do. ⁵ And now, Father, glorify me in your own presence with the glory that I had with you before the world existed.

⁶ "I have manifested your name to the people whom you gave me out of the world. Yours they were, and you gave them to me, and they have kept your word. ⁷ Now they know that everything that you have given me is from you. ⁸ For I have given them the words that you gave me, and they have received them and have come to know in truth that I came from you; and they have believed that you sent me. ⁹ I am praying for them. I am not praying for the world but for those whom you have given me, for they are yours. ¹⁰ All mine are yours, and yours are mine, and I am glorified in them. ¹¹ And I am no longer in the world, but they are in the world, and I am coming to you. Holy Father, keep them in your name, which you have given me, that they may be one, even as we are one. ¹² While I was with them, I kept them in your name, which you have given me. I have guarded them, and not one of them has been lost except the son of destruction, that the Scripture might be fulfilled. ¹³ But now I am coming to you, and these things I speak in the world, that they may have my joy fulfilled in themselves. ¹⁴ I have given them your word, and the world has hated them because they are not of the world, just as I am not of the world. ¹⁵ I do not ask that you take them out of the world, but that you keep them from the evil one. ¹⁶ They are not of the world, just as I am not of the world. ¹⁷ Sanctify them in the truth; your word is truth. ¹⁸ As you sent me into the world, so I have sent them into the world. ¹⁹ And for their sake I consecrate myself, that they also may be sanctified in truth.

²⁰ "I do not ask for these only, but also for those who will believe in me through their word, ²¹ that they may all be one, just as you, Father, are in me, and I in you, that they also may be in us, so that the world may believe that you have sent me. ²² The glory that you have given me I have given to them, that they may be one even as we are one, ²³ I in them and you in me, that they may become perfectly one, so that the world may know that you sent me and loved them even as you loved me. ²⁴ Father, I desire that they

also, whom you have given me, may be with me where I am, to see my glory that you have given me because you loved me before the foundation of the world. **25** O righteous Father, even though the world does not know you, I know you, and these know that you have sent me. **26** I made known to them your name, and I will continue to make it known, that the love with which you have loved me may be in them, and I in them."

Betrayal and Arrest of Jesus

18 When Jesus had spoken these words, he went out with his disciples across the brook Kidron, where there was a garden, which he and his disciples entered. **2** Now Judas, who betrayed him, also knew the place, for Jesus often met there with his disciples. **3** So Judas, having procured a band of soldiers and some officers from the chief priests and the Pharisees, went there with lanterns and torches and weapons. **4** Then Jesus, knowing all that would happen to him, came forward and said to them, "Whom do you seek?" **5** They answered him, "Jesus of Nazareth." Jesus said to them, "I am he." Judas, who betrayed him, was standing with them. **6** When Jesus said to them, "I am he," they drew back and fell to the ground. **7** So he asked them again, "Whom do you seek?" And they said, "Jesus of Nazareth." **8** Jesus answered, "I told you that I am he. So, if you seek me, let these men go." **9** This was to fulfill the word that he had spoken: "Of those whom you gave me I have lost not one." **10** Then Simon Peter, having a sword, drew it and struck the high priest's servant and cut off his right ear. (The servant's name was Malchus.) **11** So Jesus said to Peter, "Put your sword into its sheath; shall I not drink the cup that the Father has given me?"

Jesus Faces Annas and Caiaphas

12 So the band of soldiers and their captain and the officers of the Jews arrested Jesus and bound him. **13** First they led him to Annas, for he was the father-in-law of Caiaphas, who was high priest that year. **14** It was Caiaphas who had advised the Jews that it would be expedient that one man should die for the people.

Peter Denies Jesus

15 Simon Peter followed Jesus, and so did another disciple. Since that disciple was known to the high priest, he entered with Jesus into the courtyard of the high priest, **16** but Peter stood outside at the door. So the other disciple, who was known to the high priest, went out and spoke to the servant girl who kept watch at the door, and brought Peter in. **17** The servant girl at the door said to Peter, "You also are not one of this man's disciples, are you?" He said, "I am not." **18** Now the servants and officers had made a charcoal fire, because it was cold, and they were standing and warming themselves. Peter also was with them, standing and warming himself.

The High Priest Questions Jesus

19 The high priest then questioned Jesus about his disciples and his teaching. **20** Jesus answered him, "I have spoken openly to the world. I have always taught in synagogues and in the temple, where all Jews come

> ### GETTING THE MESSAGE
>
> The Jews believed that **high priests** were appointed for life, but the Roman authorities replaced them often. Perhaps this is why the Jewish officers consulted Annas, who had been high priest from A.D. 5–15, before consulting his son-in-law Caiaphas, who held the office at that time (18:12–24).

together. I have said nothing in secret. **21** Why do you ask me? Ask those who have heard me what I said to them; they know what I said." **22** When he had said these things, one of the officers standing by struck Jesus with his hand, saying, "Is that how you answer the high priest?" **23** Jesus answered him, "If what I said is wrong, bear witness about the wrong; but if what I said is right, why do you strike me?" **24** Annas then sent him bound to Caiaphas the high priest.

Peter Denies Jesus Again

25 Now Simon Peter was standing and warming himself. So they said to him, "You also are not one of his disciples, are you?" He denied it and said, "I am not." **26** One of the servants of the high priest, a relative of the man whose ear Peter had cut off, asked, "Did I not see you in the garden with him?" **27** Peter again denied it, and at once a rooster crowed.

Jesus Before Pilate

28 Then they led Jesus from the house of Caiaphas to the governor's headquarters. It was early morning. They themselves did not enter the governor's headquarters, so that they would not be defiled, but could eat the Passover. **29** So Pilate went outside to them and said, "What accusation do you bring against this man?" **30** They answered him, "If this man were not doing evil, we would not have delivered him over to you." **31** Pilate said to them, "Take him yourselves and judge him by your own law." The Jews said to him, "It is not lawful for us to put anyone to death." **32** This was to fulfill the word that Jesus had spoken to show by what kind of death he was going to die.

My Kingdom Is Not of This World

33 So Pilate entered his headquarters again and called Jesus and said to him, "Are you the King of the Jews?" **34** Jesus answered, "Do you

> **GETTING THE MESSAGE**
>
> The English word **excruciating** is related to the word **crucify**. It should remind all English-speaking believers of the intense pain Jesus bore on the cross to accomplish their salvation.

say this of your own accord, or did others say it to you about me?" **35** Pilate answered, "Am I a Jew? Your own nation and the chief priests have delivered you over to me. What have you done?" **36** Jesus answered, "My kingdom is not of this world. If my kingdom were of this world, my servants would have been fighting, that I might not be delivered over to the Jews. But my kingdom is not from the world." **37** Then Pilate said to him, "So you are a king?" Jesus answered, "You say that I am a king. For this purpose I was born and for this purpose I have come into the world—to bear witness to the truth. Everyone who is of the truth listens to my voice." **38** Pilate said to him, "What is truth?"

After he had said this, he went back outside to the Jews and told them, "I find no guilt in him. **39** But you have a custom that I should release one man for you at the Passover. So do you want me to release to you the King of the Jews?" **40** They cried out

again, "Not this man, but Barabbas!" Now Barabbas was a robber.

Jesus Delivered to Be Crucified

19 Then Pilate took Jesus and flogged him. **2** And the soldiers twisted together a crown of thorns and put it on his head and arrayed him in a purple robe. **3** They came up to him, saying, "Hail, King of the Jews!" and struck him with their hands. **4** Pilate went out again and said to them, "See, I am bringing him out to you that you may know that I find no guilt in him." **5** So Jesus came out, wearing the crown of thorns and the purple robe. Pilate said to them, "Behold the man!" **6** When the chief priests and the officers saw him, they cried out, "Crucify him, crucify him!" Pilate said to them, "Take him yourselves and crucify him, for I find no guilt in him." **7** The Jews answered him, "We have a law, and according to that law he ought to die because he has made himself the Son of God." **8** When Pilate heard this statement, he was even more afraid. **9** He entered his headquarters again and said to Jesus, "Where are you from?" But Jesus gave him no answer. **10** So Pilate said to him, "You will not speak to me? Do you not know that I have authority to release you and authority to crucify you?" **11** Jesus answered him, "You would have no authority over me at all unless it had been given you from above. Therefore he who delivered me over to you has the greater sin."

12 From then on Pilate sought to release him, but the Jews cried out, "If you release this man, you are not Caesar's friend. Everyone who makes himself a king opposes Caesar." **13** So when Pilate heard these words, he brought Jesus out and sat down on the judgment seat at a place called The Stone Pavement, and in Aramaic Gabbatha. **14** Now it was the day of Preparation of the Passover. It was about the sixth hour.[1] He said to the Jews, "Behold your King!" **15** They cried out, "Away with him, away with him, crucify him!" Pilate said to them, "Shall I crucify your King?" The chief priests answered, "We have no king but Caesar." **16** So he delivered him over to them to be crucified.

The Crucifixion

So they took Jesus, **17** and he went out, bearing his own cross, to the place called

---

[1] That is, about noon

The Place of a Skull, which in Aramaic is called Golgotha. ¹⁸There they crucified him, and with him two others, one on either side, and Jesus between them. ¹⁹Pilate also wrote an inscription and put it on the cross. It read, "Jesus of Nazareth, the King of the Jews." ²⁰Many of the Jews read this inscription, for the place where Jesus was crucified was near the city, and it was written in Aramaic, in Latin, and in Greek. ²¹So the chief priests of the Jews said to Pilate, "Do not write, 'The King of the Jews,' but rather, 'This man said, I am King of the Jews.'" ²²Pilate answered, "What I have written I have written."

²³When the soldiers had crucified Jesus, they took his garments and divided them into four parts, one part for each soldier; also his tunic. But the tunic was seamless, woven in one piece from top to bottom, ²⁴so they said to one another, "Let us not tear it, but cast lots for it to see whose it shall be." This was to fulfill the Scripture which says,

"They divided my garments among them,
and for my clothing they cast lots."

So the soldiers did these things, ²⁵but standing by the cross of Jesus were his mother and his mother's sister, Mary the wife of Clopas, and Mary Magdalene. ²⁶When Jesus saw his mother and the disciple whom he loved standing nearby, he said to his mother, "Woman, behold, your son!" ²⁷Then he said to the disciple, "Behold, your mother!" And from that hour the disciple took her to his own home.

The Death of Jesus

²⁸After this, Jesus, knowing that all was now finished, said (to fulfill the Scripture), "I thirst." ²⁹A jar full of sour wine stood there, so they put a sponge full of the sour wine on a hyssop branch and held it to his mouth. ³⁰When Jesus had received the sour wine, he said, "It is finished," and he bowed his head and gave up his spirit.

Jesus' Side Is Pierced

³¹Since it was the day of Preparation, and so that the bodies would not remain on the cross on the Sabbath (for that Sabbath was a high day), the Jews asked Pilate that their legs might be broken and that they might be taken away. ³²So the soldiers came and broke the legs of the first, and of the other

who had been crucified with him. ³³But when they came to Jesus and saw that he was already dead, they did not break his legs. ³⁴But one of the soldiers pierced his side with a spear, and at once there came out blood and water. ³⁵He who saw it has borne witness—his testimony is true, and he knows that he is telling the truth—that you also may believe. ³⁶For these things took place that the Scripture might be fulfilled: "Not one of his bones will be broken." ³⁷And again another Scripture says, "They will look on him whom they have pierced."

Jesus Is Buried

³⁸After these things Joseph of Arimathea, who was a disciple of Jesus, but secretly for fear of the Jews, asked Pilate that he might take away the body of Jesus, and Pilate gave him permission. So he came and took away

his body. ³⁹Nicodemus also, who earlier had come to Jesus by night, came bringing a mixture of myrrh and aloes, about seventy-five pounds in weight. ⁴⁰So they took the body of Jesus and bound it in linen cloths with the spices, as is the burial custom of the Jews. ⁴¹Now in the place where he was crucified there was a garden, and in the garden a new tomb in which no one had yet been laid. ⁴²So because of the Jewish day of Preparation, since the tomb was close at hand, they laid Jesus there.

The Resurrection

20 Now on the first day of the week Mary Magdalene came to the tomb early, while it was still dark, and saw that the stone had been taken away from the tomb. ²So she ran and went to Simon Peter and the other disciple, the one whom Jesus loved, and said to them, "They have taken

the Lord out of the tomb, and we do not know where they have laid him." ³ So Peter went out with the other disciple, and they were going toward the tomb. ⁴ Both of them were running together, but the other disciple outran Peter and reached the tomb first. ⁵ And stooping to look in, he saw the linen cloths lying there, but he did not go in. ⁶ Then Simon Peter came, following him, and went into the tomb. He saw the linen cloths lying there, ⁷ and the face cloth, which had been on Jesus' head, not lying with the

MARY MAGDALENE

Mary was called Magdalene because she was from Magdala, on the western shore of Galilee. She experienced incredible healing when Jesus drove seven demons from her (Luke 8:2). Mary Magdalene became a faithful and courageous disciple of Jesus. After witnessing the crucifixion, she visited Jesus' tomb to complete burial preparations—only to find the tomb empty. She became the first person to witness the resurrected Jesus when he appeared to her as she stood outside the tomb weeping. Distraught, she first supposed Jesus to be the gardener. But all Jesus had to do was say her name and Mary Magdalene recognized her beloved Lord. It was she who ran to tell the disciples of Jesus' resurrection.

KEY REFERENCE: JOHN 20:1–18

linen cloths but folded up in a place by itself. ⁸ Then the other disciple, who had reached the tomb first, also went in, and he saw and believed; ⁹ for as yet they did not understand the Scripture, that he must rise from the dead. ¹⁰ Then the disciples went back to their homes.

Jesus Appears to Mary Magdalene

¹¹ But Mary stood weeping outside the tomb, and as she wept she stooped to look into the tomb. ¹² And she saw two angels in white, sitting where the body of Jesus had

lain, one at the head and one at the feet. ¹³ They said to her, "Woman, why are you weeping?" She said to them, "They have taken away my Lord, and I do not know where they have laid him." ¹⁴ Having said this, she turned around and saw Jesus standing, but she did not know that it was Jesus. ¹⁵ Jesus said to her, "Woman, why are you weeping? Whom are you seeking?" Supposing him to be the gardener, she said to him, "Sir, if you have carried him away, tell me where you have laid him, and I will take him away." ¹⁶ Jesus said to her, "Mary." She turned and said to him in Aramaic, "Rabboni!" (which means Teacher). ¹⁷ Jesus said to her, "Do not cling to me, for I have not yet ascended to the Father; but go to my brothers and say to them, 'I am ascending to my Father and your Father, to my God and your God.'" ¹⁸ Mary

GETTING THE MESSAGE

Why John believed. Upon seeing the empty tomb, Mary Magdalene thought someone had stolen Jesus' body. If someone had done this, however, they probably would have taken everything of value in the tomb, including the expensive burial linens. Instead, the linens were neatly placed on the bench. When "the other disciple" saw this, he was convinced that Jesus had truly risen from the dead (20:1–8).

Magdalene went and announced to the disciples, "I have seen the Lord"—and that he had said these things to her.

Jesus Appears to the Disciples

¹⁹ On the evening of that day, the first day of the week, the doors being locked where the disciples were for fear of the Jews, Jesus came and stood among them and said to them, "Peace be with you." ²⁰ When he had said this, he showed them his hands and his side. Then the disciples were glad when they saw the Lord. ²¹ Jesus said to them again, "Peace be with you. As the Father has sent me, even so I am sending you." ²² And when he had said this, he breathed on them and said to them, "Receive the Holy Spirit. ²³ If you forgive the sins of any, they are forgiven them; if you withhold forgiveness from any, it is withheld."

Jesus and Thomas

24 Now Thomas, one of the Twelve, called the Twin, was not with them when Jesus came. 25 So the other disciples told him, "We have seen the Lord." But he said to them, "Unless I see in his hands the mark of the nails, and place my finger into the mark of the nails, and place my hand into his side, I will never believe."

26 Eight days later, his disciples were inside again, and Thomas was with them. Although the doors were locked, Jesus came and stood among them and said, "Peace be with you." 27 Then he said to Thomas, "Put your finger here, and see my hands; and put out your hand, and place it in my side. Do not disbelieve, but believe." 28 Thomas answered him, "My Lord and my God!" 29 Jesus said to him, "Have you believed because you have seen me? Blessed are those who have not seen and yet have believed."

GETTING THE MESSAGE

"Stretch out your hands" (21:18–19) refers to the way in which people were crucified. The victim's hands were bound to the horizontal bar of the cross. Jesus predicted that Peter would die in the same horrific way that his Lord and Savior had died.

The Purpose of This Book

30 Now Jesus did many other signs in the presence of the disciples, which are not written in this book; 31 but these are written so that you may believe that Jesus is the Christ, the Son of God, and that by believing you may have life in his name.

Jesus Appears to Seven Disciples

21 After this Jesus revealed himself again to the disciples by the Sea of Tiberias, and he revealed himself in this way. 2 Simon Peter, Thomas (called the Twin), Nathanael of Cana in Galilee, the sons of Zebedee, and two others of his disciples were together. 3 Simon Peter said to them, "I am going fishing." They said to him, "We will go with you." They went out and got into the boat, but that night they caught nothing.

4 Just as day was breaking, Jesus stood on the shore; yet the disciples did not know that it was Jesus. 5 Jesus said to them, "Children, do you have any fish?" They answered him, "No." 6 He said to them, "Cast the net on the right side of the boat, and you will find some." So they cast it, and now they were not able to haul it in, because of the quantity of fish. 7 That disciple whom Jesus loved therefore said to Peter, "It is the Lord!" When Simon Peter heard that it was the Lord, he put on his outer garment, for he was stripped for work, and threw himself into the sea. 8 The other disciples came in the boat, dragging the net full of fish, for

PROFILE

THOMAS

Thomas, one of the 12 disciples, was called "the Twin." He courageously declared that he was willing to die with Jesus (11:16). Unfortunately, however, he is most remembered for displaying doubt rather than bravery. When Jesus first appeared to the disciples following his resurrection, Thomas was not with them. Overcome with uncertainty, he refused to believe the news that Jesus was alive. Thomas declared that he would believe only if he were able to see the scars from Jesus' crucifixion on his hands and side. A few days later, Thomas was with the other disciples when Jesus appeared to them again. When Jesus invited him to see and touch his wounds, Thomas immediately responded, "My Lord and my God!" (20:28).

KEY REFERENCE: JOHN 20:24–28

they were not far from the land, but about a hundred yards off.

9 When they got out on land, they saw a charcoal fire in place, with fish laid out on it, and bread. 10 Jesus said to them, "Bring some of the fish that you have just caught." 11 So Simon Peter went aboard and hauled the net ashore, full of large fish, 153 of them. And although there were so many, the net was not torn. 12 Jesus said to them, "Come and have breakfast." Now none of the disciples dared ask him, "Who are you?" They knew it was the Lord. 13 Jesus came and took

the bread and gave it to them, and so with the fish. [14] This was now the third time that Jesus was revealed to the disciples after he was raised from the dead.

Jesus and Peter

[15] When they had finished breakfast, Jesus said to Simon Peter, "Simon, son of John, do you love me more than these?" He said to him, "Yes, Lord; you know that I love you." He said to him, "Feed my lambs." [16] He said to him a second time, "Simon, son of John, do you love me?" He said to him, "Yes, Lord; you know that I love you." He said to him, "Tend my sheep." [17] He said to him the third time, "Simon, son of John, do you love me?" Peter was grieved because he said to him the third time, "Do you love me?" and he said to him, "Lord, you know everything; you know that I love you." Jesus said to him, "Feed my sheep. [18] Truly, truly, I say to you, when you were young, you used to dress yourself and walk wherever you wanted, but when you are old, you will stretch out your hands, and another will dress you and carry you where you do not want to go." [19] (This he said to show by what kind of death he was to glorify God.) And after saying this he said to him, "Follow me."

Jesus and the Beloved Apostle

[20] Peter turned and saw the disciple whom Jesus loved following them, the one who also had leaned back against him during the supper and had said, "Lord, who is it that is going to betray you?" [21] When Peter saw him, he said to Jesus, "Lord, what about this man?" [22] Jesus said to him, "If it is my will that he remain until I come, what is that to you? You follow me!" [23] So the saying spread abroad among the brothers[1] that this disciple was not to die; yet Jesus did not say to him that he was not to die, but, "If it is my will that he remain until I come, what is that to you?"

[24] This is the disciple who is bearing witness about these things, and who has written these things, and we know that his testimony is true.

[25] Now there are also many other things that Jesus did. Were every one of them to be written, I suppose that the world itself could not contain the books that would be written.

[1] Or *brothers and sisters*

INTRODUCTION TO ACTS

c. A.D. 33/34	c. A.D. 46–57	c. A.D. 64–67
Pentecost, conversion of Paul	Paul's missionary journeys	Peter and Paul martyred in Rome

AUTHOR AND DATE

Acts is a sequel to the Gospel of Luke. Both were written by Luke, a physician who traveled with the apostle Paul. Acts ends with Paul under house arrest, awaiting trial before Caesar, c. A.D. 62. Many scholars assume Acts was written then because it does not record Paul's defense, release, and further gospel preaching.

THEME

The Holy Spirit empowers believers to declare the gospel among both Jews and Gentiles. In doing so they establish the church. The church is the fulfillment of God's promises from the beginning of time.

PURPOSE

Luke's purpose for writing his Gospel (see Luke 1:3–4) applies to Acts as well: to give an "orderly" account of the early church after Christ's resurrection. Dedicating the two-volume work to Theophilus, Luke wanted him to have "certainty" about what he had been taught.

KEY THEMES

Acts tells of the witness of the early church to the truth of the gospel—a theme first introduced in 1:8:

1. The witness is worldwide—Judea, Samaria, the "end of the earth" (1:8).

2. The witness includes all kinds of people (chs. 2–5; 10:1–11:18; 14:8–18; 16:11–15, 25–34; 17:22–31).

3. God guides the church's witness (4:5–22; 23:12–22; 24:1–23; 27:21–26).

4. Faithful witnesses must be prepared to suffer and even die because of their testimony to Christ (5:41–42; 7:54–60).

5. The Holy Spirit empowers the witness (1:8; 2:1–13; 8:17; 13:2–12; 19:6).

6. Effective witness demands unity in the church (2:42–47; 4:32–37; 5:12–14).

7. Jesus' resurrection is a key part of the witness (1:22; 2:22–36; 17:30–31).

8. Acceptance of the message depends both on human response and on God's sovereign will (2:47; 11:18; 13:48).

9. The witness to the gospel calls for a response (26:27–29). It requires repenting of one's sins in the name of Christ. This brings forgiveness of sins (e.g., 2:38).

10. Witnesses must always maintain integrity before the world (18:12–15; 23:29; 25:18; 26:31–32).

11. Christian witnesses continue the ministry that Christ "began" (1:1).

12. Faithful witness can bring great results (4:4; 13:48–49; 17:4; 28:30–31).

OUTLINE

THE
ACTS
OF THE APOSTLES

The Promise of the Holy Spirit

1 In the first book, O Theophilus, I have dealt with all that Jesus began to do and teach, [2] until the day when he was taken up, after he had given commands through the Holy Spirit to the apostles whom he had chosen. [3] He presented himself alive to them after his suffering by many proofs, appearing to them during forty days and speaking about the kingdom of God.

[4] And while staying with them he ordered them not to depart from Jerusalem, but to wait for the promise of the Father, which, he said, "you heard from me; [5] for John baptized with water, but you will be baptized with the Holy Spirit not many days from now."

The Ascension

[6] So when they had come together, they asked him, "Lord, will you at this time restore the kingdom to Israel?" [7] He said to them, "It is not for you to know times or seasons that the Father has fixed by his own authority. [8] But you will receive power when the Holy Spirit has come upon you, and you will be my witnesses in Jerusalem and in all Judea and Samaria, and to the end of the earth." [9] And when he had said these things, as they were looking on, he was lifted up, and a cloud took him out of their sight. [10] And while they were gazing into heaven as he went, behold, two men stood by them in white robes, [11] and said, "Men of Galilee, why do you stand looking into heaven? This Jesus, who was taken up from you into heaven, will come in the same way as you saw him go into heaven."

Matthias Chosen to Replace Judas

[12] Then they returned to Jerusalem from the mount called Olivet, which is near Jerusalem, a Sabbath day's journey away. [13] And when they had entered, they went up to the upper room, where they were staying, Peter and John and James and Andrew, Philip and Thomas, Bartholomew and Matthew, James the son of Alphaeus and Simon the Zealot and Judas the son of James. [14] All these with one accord were devoting themselves to prayer, together with the women and Mary the mother of Jesus, and his brothers.[1]

[15] In those days Peter stood up among the brothers (the company of persons was in all about 120) and said, [16] "Brothers, the Scripture had to be fulfilled, which the Holy Spirit spoke beforehand by the mouth of David concerning Judas, who became a guide to those who arrested Jesus. [17] For he

was numbered among us and was allotted his share in this ministry." [18] (Now this man acquired a field with the reward of his wickedness, and falling headlong he burst open in the middle and all his bowels gushed out. [19] And it became known to all the inhabitants of Jerusalem, so that the field was called in their own language Akeldama, that is, Field of Blood.) [20] "For it is written in the Book of Psalms,

"'May his camp become desolate,
    and let there be no one to dwell in it';

and

"'Let another take his office.'

[21] So one of the men who have accompanied us during all the time that the Lord Jesus went in and out among us, [22] beginning from the baptism of John until the day when he was taken up from us—one of these men must become with us a witness to his resur-

[1] Or brothers and sisters (see Preface); also 1:15

rection." **23** And they put forward two, Joseph called Barsabbas, who was also called Justus, and Matthias. **24** And they prayed and said, "You, Lord, who know the hearts of all, show which one of these two you have chosen **25** to take the place in this ministry and apostleship from which Judas turned aside to go to his own place." **26** And they cast lots for them, and the lot fell on Matthias, and he was numbered with the eleven apostles.

The Coming of the Holy Spirit

2 When the day of Pentecost arrived, they were all together in one place. **2** And suddenly there came from heaven a sound like a mighty rushing wind, and it filled the entire house where they were sitting. **3** And divided tongues as of fire appeared to them and rested on each one of them. **4** And they were all filled with the Holy Spirit and began

---

GETTING THE MESSAGE

Nations at Pentecost. The list of nations in 2:9–11 covers most of the first-century Roman world. Many Jews who lived outside Palestine traveled to Jerusalem to celebrate Pentecost, an annual feast. The Holy Spirit enabled them to hear the disciples speak in their own languages (2:6).

---

to speak in other tongues as the Spirit gave them utterance.

5 Now there were dwelling in Jerusalem Jews, devout men from every nation under heaven. **6** And at this sound the multitude came together, and they were bewildered, because each one was hearing them speak in his own language. **7** And they were amazed and astonished, saying, "Are not all these who are speaking Galileans? **8** And how is it that we hear, each of us in his own native language? **9** Parthians and Medes and Elamites and residents of Mesopotamia, Judea and Cappadocia, Pontus and Asia, **10** Phrygia and Pamphylia, Egypt and the parts of Libya belonging to Cyrene, and visitors from Rome, **11** both Jews and proselytes, Cretans and Arabians—we hear them telling in our own tongues the mighty works of God." **12** And all were amazed and perplexed, saying to one another, "What does this mean?"

13 But others mocking said, "They are filled with new wine."

Peter's Sermon at Pentecost

14 But Peter, standing with the eleven, lifted up his voice and addressed them: "Men of Judea and all who dwell in Jerusalem, let this be known to you, and give ear to my words. **15** For these people are not drunk, as you suppose, since it is only the third hour of the day.[1] **16** But this is what was uttered through the prophet Joel:

17 "'And in the last days it shall be, God declares,
that I will pour out my Spirit on all flesh,
and your sons and your daughters shall prophesy,
and your young men shall see visions,
and your old men shall dream dreams;
18 even on my male servants and female servants
in those days I will pour out my Spirit, and they shall prophesy.
19 And I will show wonders in the heavens above
and signs on the earth below,
blood, and fire, and vapor of smoke;
20 the sun shall be turned to darkness
and the moon to blood,
before the day of the Lord comes,
the great and magnificent day.
21 And it shall come to pass that everyone who calls upon the name of the Lord shall be saved.'

22 "Men of Israel, hear these words: Jesus of Nazareth, a man attested to you by God with mighty works and wonders and signs that God did through him in your midst, as you yourselves know— **23** this Jesus, delivered up according to the definite plan and foreknowledge of God, you crucified and killed by the hands of lawless men. **24** God raised him up, loosing the pangs of death, because it was not possible for him to be held by it. **25** For David says concerning him,

"'I saw the Lord always before me,
for he is at my right hand that I may not be shaken;

[1] That is, 9 A.M.

26 therefore my heart was glad, and my
tongue rejoiced;
my flesh also will dwell in hope.
27 For you will not abandon my soul to
Hades,
or let your Holy One see corruption.
28 You have made known to me the
paths of life;
you will make me full of gladness
with your presence.'

29 "Brothers, I may say to you with confidence about the patriarch David that he
both died and was buried, and his tomb
is with us to this day. 30 Being therefore a
prophet, and knowing that God had sworn
with an oath to him that he would set one
of his descendants on his throne, 31 he fore-
saw and spoke about the resurrection of
the Christ, that he was not abandoned to
Hades, nor did his flesh see corruption.
32 This Jesus God raised up, and of that we all
are witnesses. 33 Being therefore exalted at
the right hand of God, and having received
from the Father the promise of the Holy
Spirit, he has poured out this that you yourselves are seeing and hearing. 34 For David
did not ascend into the heavens, but he
himself says,

"'The Lord said to my Lord,
"Sit at my right hand,
35   until I make your enemies your
footstool."'

36 Let all the house of Israel therefore know
for certain that God has made him both Lord
and Christ, this Jesus whom you crucified."

37 Now when they heard this they were
cut to the heart, and said to Peter and the
rest of the apostles, "Brothers, what shall we
do?" 38 And Peter said to them, "Repent and
be baptized every one of you in the name
of Jesus Christ for the forgiveness of your
sins, and you will receive the gift of the Holy
Spirit. 39 For the promise is for you and for
your children and for all who are far off,
everyone whom the Lord our God calls to
himself." 40 And with many other words he
bore witness and continued to exhort them,
saying, "Save yourselves from this crooked
generation." 41 So those who received his
word were baptized, and there were added
that day about three thousand souls.

The Fellowship of the Believers

42 And they devoted themselves to the
apostles' teaching and the fellowship, to the
breaking of bread and the prayers. 43 And
awe came upon every soul, and many wonders and signs were being done through
the apostles. 44 And all who believed were
together and had all things in common.
45 And they were selling their possessions
and belongings and distributing the proceeds to all, as any had need. 46 And day
by day, attending the temple together and
breaking bread in their homes, they received
their food with glad and generous hearts,
47 praising God and having favor with all the
people. And the Lord added to their number
day by day those who were being saved.

The Lame Beggar Healed

3 Now Peter and John were going up to
the temple at the hour of prayer, the
ninth hour.[1] 2 And a man lame from birth
was being carried, whom they laid daily
at the gate of the temple that is called the
Beautiful Gate to ask alms of those entering
the temple. 3 Seeing Peter and John about
to go into the temple, he asked to receive
alms. 4 And Peter directed his gaze at him,
as did John, and said, "Look at us." 5 And he
fixed his attention on them, expecting to
receive something from them. 6 But Peter
said, "I have no silver and gold, but what I
do have I give to you. In the name of Jesus
Christ of Nazareth, rise up and walk!" 7 And
he took him by the right hand and raised
him up, and immediately his feet and ankles
were made strong. 8 And leaping up he stood
and began to walk, and entered the temple
with them, walking and leaping and praising God. 9 And all the people saw him walking and praising God, 10 and recognized him
as the one who sat at the Beautiful Gate of
the temple, asking for alms. And they were
filled with wonder and amazement at what
had happened to him.

Peter Speaks in Solomon's Portico

11 While he clung to Peter and John, all the
people, utterly astounded, ran together to
them in the portico called Solomon's. 12 And
when Peter saw it he addressed the people:
"Men of Israel, why do you wonder at this,
or why do you stare at us, as though by our
own power or piety we have made him walk?

---

1 That is, 3 P.M.

[13] The God of Abraham, the God of Isaac, and the God of Jacob, the God of our fathers, glorified his servant Jesus, whom you delivered over and denied in the presence of Pilate, when he had decided to release him. [14] But you denied the Holy and Righteous One, and asked for a murderer to be granted to you, [15] and you killed the Author of life, whom God raised from the dead. To this we are witnesses. [16] And his name—by faith in his name—has made this man strong whom you see and know, and the faith that is through Jesus has given the man this perfect health in the presence of you all.

[17] "And now, brothers, I know that you acted in ignorance, as did also your rulers. [18] But what God foretold by the mouth of all the prophets, that his Christ would suffer, he thus fulfilled. [19] Repent therefore, and turn back, that your sins may be blotted

out, [20] that times of refreshing may come from the presence of the Lord, and that he may send the Christ appointed for you, Jesus, [21] whom heaven must receive until the time for restoring all the things about which God spoke by the mouth of his holy prophets long ago. [22] Moses said, 'The Lord God will raise up for you a prophet like me from your brothers. You shall listen to him in whatever he tells you. [23] And it shall be that every soul who does not listen to that prophet shall be destroyed from the people.' [24] And all the prophets who have spoken, from Samuel and those who came after him, also proclaimed these days. [25] You are the sons of the prophets and of the covenant that God made with your fathers, saying to Abraham, 'And in your offspring shall all the families of the earth be blessed.' [26] God, having raised up his servant, sent him to

you first, to bless you by turning every one of you from your wickedness."

Peter and John Before the Council

4 And as they were speaking to the people, the priests and the captain of the temple and the Sadducees came upon them, [2] greatly annoyed because they were teaching the people and proclaiming in Jesus the resurrection from the dead. [3] And they arrested them and put them in custody until the next day, for it was already evening. [4] But many of those who had heard the word believed, and the number of the men came to about five thousand.

[5] On the next day their rulers and elders and scribes gathered together in Jerusalem, [6] with Annas the high priest and Caiaphas and John and Alexander, and all who were of the high-priestly family. [7] And when they had set them in the midst, they inquired, "By what power or by what name did you do this?" [8] Then Peter, filled with the Holy Spirit, said to them, "Rulers of the people and elders, [9] if we are being examined today concerning a good deed done to a crippled man, by what means this man has been healed, [10] let it be known to all of you and to all the people of Israel that by the name of Jesus Christ of Nazareth, whom you crucified, whom God raised from the dead—by him this man is standing before you well. [11] This Jesus is the stone that was rejected by you, the builders, which has become the cornerstone. [12] And there is salvation in no one else, for there is no other name under heaven given among men[1] by which we must be saved."

[13] Now when they saw the boldness of Peter and John, and perceived that they were uneducated, common men, they were astonished. And they recognized that they had been with Jesus. [14] But seeing the man who was healed standing beside them, they had nothing to say in opposition. [15] But when they had commanded them to leave the council, they conferred with one another, [16] saying, "What shall we do with these men? For that a notable sign has been performed through them is evident to all the inhabitants of Jerusalem, and we cannot deny it. [17] But in order that it may spread no further among the people, let us warn them to speak no more to anyone in this

[1] The Greek word for *men* refers to both men and women (see Preface)

name." **18** So they called them and charged them not to speak or teach at all in the name of Jesus. **19** But Peter and John answered them, "Whether it is right in the sight of God to listen to you rather than to God, you must judge, **20** for we cannot but speak of what we have seen and heard." **21** And when they had further threatened them, they let them go, finding no way to punish them, because of the people, for all were praising God for what had happened. **22** For the man on whom this sign of healing was performed was more than forty years old.

The Believers Pray for Boldness

23 When they were released, they went to their friends and reported what the chief priests and the elders had said to them. **24** And when they heard it, they lifted their voices together to God and said, "Sovereign Lord, who made the heaven and the earth and the sea and everything in them, **25** who through the mouth of our father David, your servant, said by the Holy Spirit,

"'Why did the Gentiles rage,
    and the peoples plot in vain?
26   The kings of the earth set themselves,
        and the rulers were gathered
            together,
        against the Lord and against his
            Anointed'—

27 for truly in this city there were gathered together against your holy servant Jesus, whom you anointed, both Herod and Pontius Pilate, along with the Gentiles and the peoples of Israel, **28** to do whatever your hand and your plan had predestined to take place. **29** And now, Lord, look upon their threats and grant to your servants to continue to speak your word with all boldness, **30** while you stretch out your hand to heal, and signs and wonders are performed through the name of your holy servant Jesus." **31** And when they had prayed, the place in which they were gathered together was shaken, and they were all filled with the Holy Spirit and continued to speak the word of God with boldness.

They Had Everything in Common

32 Now the full number of those who believed were of one heart and soul, and no one said that any of the things that belonged to him was his own, but they had everything in common. **33** And with great power

the apostles were giving their testimony to the resurrection of the Lord Jesus, and great grace was upon them all. **34** There was not a needy person among them, for as many as were owners of lands or houses sold them and brought the proceeds of what was sold **35** and laid it at the apostles' feet, and it was distributed to each as any had need. **36** Thus Joseph, who was also called by the apostles Barnabas (which means son of encouragement), a Levite, a native of Cyprus, **37** sold a field that belonged to him and brought the money and laid it at the apostles' feet.

Ananias and Sapphira

5 But a man named Ananias, with his wife Sapphira, sold a piece of property, **2** and with his wife's knowledge he kept back for himself some of the proceeds and brought only a part of it and laid it at the

> ### GETTING THE MESSAGE
>
> **Not a needy person among them.** The earliest Christians in Jerusalem were very generous in helping each other financially (4:34–35). Later, during a severe famine, new believers from all over the Roman Empire contributed to the needs of the Jerusalem church.

apostles' feet. **3** But Peter said, "Ananias, why has Satan filled your heart to lie to the Holy Spirit and to keep back for yourself part of the proceeds of the land? **4** While it remained unsold, did it not remain your own? And after it was sold, was it not at your disposal? Why is it that you have contrived this deed in your heart? You have not lied to man but to God." **5** When Ananias heard these words, he fell down and breathed his last. And great fear came upon all who heard of it. **6** The young men rose and wrapped him up and carried him out and buried him.

7 After an interval of about three hours his wife came in, not knowing what had happened. **8** And Peter said to her, "Tell me whether you sold the land for so much." And she said, "Yes, for so much." **9** But Peter said to her, "How is it that you have agreed together to test the Spirit of the Lord? Behold, the feet of those who have buried your husband are at the door, and they will carry you out." **10** Immediately she fell down at his feet and breathed her last. When the young men came in they found her dead, and they carried her out and buried her beside her husband. ¹¹ And great fear came upon the whole church and upon all who heard of these things.

Many Signs and Wonders Done

¹² Now many signs and wonders were regularly done among the people by the hands of the apostles. And they were all together in Solomon's Portico. ¹³ None of the rest dared join them, but the people held

---

---

them in high esteem. ¹⁴ And more than ever believers were added to the Lord, multitudes of both men and women, ¹⁵ so that they even carried out the sick into the streets and laid them on cots and mats, that as Peter came by at least his shadow might fall on some of them. ¹⁶ The people also gathered from the towns around Jerusalem, bringing the sick and those afflicted with unclean spirits, and they were all healed.

The Apostles Arrested and Freed

¹⁷ But the high priest rose up, and all who were with him (that is, the party of the Sadducees), and filled with jealousy ¹⁸ they arrested the apostles and put them in the public prison. ¹⁹ But during the night an angel of the Lord opened the prison doors and brought them out, and said, ²⁰ "Go and stand in the temple and speak to the people all the words of this Life." ²¹ And when they heard this, they entered the temple at daybreak and began to teach.

Now when the high priest came, and those who were with him, they called together the council, all the senate of the people of Israel, and sent to the prison to have them brought. ²² But when the officers came, they did not find them in the prison, so they returned and reported, ²³ "We found the prison securely locked and the guards standing at the doors, but when we opened them we found no one inside." ²⁴ Now when

the captain of the temple and the chief priests heard these words, they were greatly perplexed about them, wondering what this would come to. ²⁵ And someone came and told them, "Look! The men whom you put in prison are standing in the temple and teaching the people." ²⁶ Then the captain with the officers went and brought them, but not by force, for they were afraid of being stoned by the people.

²⁷ And when they had brought them, they set them before the council. And the high priest questioned them, ²⁸ saying, "We strictly charged you not to teach in this name, yet here you have filled Jerusalem with your teaching, and you intend to bring this man's blood upon us." ²⁹ But Peter and the apostles answered, "We must obey God rather than men. ³⁰ The God of our fathers raised Jesus, whom you killed by hanging

him on a tree. **31** God exalted him at his right hand as Leader and Savior, to give repentance to Israel and forgiveness of sins. **32** And we are witnesses to these things, and so is the Holy Spirit, whom God has given to those who obey him."

33 When they heard this, they were enraged and wanted to kill them. **34** But a Pharisee in the council named Gamaliel, a teacher of the law held in honor by all the people, stood up and gave orders to put the men outside for a little while. **35** And he said to them, "Men of Israel, take care what you are about to do with these men. **36** For before these days Theudas rose up, claiming to be somebody, and a number of men, about four hundred, joined him. He was killed, and all who followed him were dispersed and came to nothing. **37** After him Judas the Galilean rose up in the days of the census and drew away some of the people after him. He too perished, and all who followed him were scattered. **38** So in the present case I tell you, keep away from these men and let them alone, for if this plan or this undertaking is of man, it will fail; **39** but if it is of God, you will not be able to overthrow them. You might even be found opposing God!" So they took his advice, **40** and when they had called in the apostles, they beat them and charged them not to speak in the name of Jesus, and let them go. **41** Then they left the presence of the council, rejoicing that they were counted worthy to suffer dishonor for the name. **42** And every day, in the temple and from house to house, they did not cease teaching and preaching that the Christ is Jesus.

Seven Chosen to Serve

6 Now in these days when the disciples were increasing in number, a complaint by the Hellenists[1] arose against the Hebrews because their widows were being neglected in the daily distribution. **2** And the twelve summoned the full number of the disciples and said, "It is not right that we should give up preaching the word of God to serve tables. **3** Therefore, brothers,[2] pick out from among you seven men of good repute, full of the Spirit and of wisdom, whom we will appoint to this duty. **4** But we will devote ourselves to prayer and to the ministry of the word." **5** And what they said pleased the

whole gathering, and they chose Stephen, a man full of faith and of the Holy Spirit, and Philip, and Prochorus, and Nicanor, and Timon, and Parmenas, and Nicolaus, a proselyte of Antioch. **6** These they set before the apostles, and they prayed and laid their hands on them.

7 And the word of God continued to increase, and the number of the disciples multiplied greatly in Jerusalem, and a great many of the priests became obedient to the faith.

PROFILE
STEPHEN

Stephen was one of seven men chosen by the disciples to care for the Greek-speaking widows in the church (6:5). Like the apostles, Stephen not only ministered to the needy but also proclaimed the gospel. Many of the religious leaders grew angry at Stephen, who was performing signs and wonders and speaking with great wisdom. They dragged him before the Sanhedrin, where he was falsely accused of blasphemy. During his defense, Stephen compared Israel's repeated disobedience in Old Testament times to the nation's present rejection of the Messiah. This made the members of the Sanhedrin so angry that they cast him out of the city and stoned him. Stephen's prayers as he was dying echoed those prayed by Jesus on the cross (7:59–60). His martyrdom led to a time of persecution against the church.

KEY REFERENCE: ACTS 6:8-10

Stephen Is Seized

8 And Stephen, full of grace and power, was doing great wonders and signs among the people. **9** Then some of those who belonged to the synagogue of the Freedmen (as it was called), and of the Cyrenians, and of the Alexandrians, and of those from Cilicia and Asia, rose up and disputed with Stephen. **10** But they could not withstand the wisdom and the Spirit with which he was

[1] That is, Greek-speaking Jews [2] Or brothers and sisters

speaking. **11** Then they secretly instigated men who said, "We have heard him speak blasphemous words against Moses and God." **12** And they stirred up the people and the elders and the scribes, and they came upon him and seized him and brought him before the council, **13** and they set up false witnesses who said, "This man never ceases to speak words against this holy place and the law, **14** for we have heard him say that this Jesus of Nazareth will destroy this place and will change the customs that Moses delivered to us." **15** And gazing at him, all who sat in the council saw that his face was like the face of an angel.

Stephen's Speech

7 And the high priest said, "Are these things so?" **2** And Stephen said:

"Brothers and fathers, hear me. The God of glory appeared to our father Abraham when he was in Mesopotamia, before he

GETTING THE MESSAGE

The speeches in Acts are an important part of Luke's historical account. They make up nearly a third of the book. Ten of these are extended speeches: three by Peter, one by Stephen, and six by Paul.

lived in Haran, **3** and said to him, 'Go out from your land and from your kindred and go into the land that I will show you.' **4** Then he went out from the land of the Chaldeans and lived in Haran. And after his father died, God removed him from there into this land in which you are now living. **5** Yet he gave him no inheritance in it, not even a foot's length, but promised to give it to him as a possession and to his offspring after him, though he had no child. **6** And God spoke to this effect—that his offspring would be sojourners in a land belonging to others, who would enslave them and afflict them four hundred years. **7** 'But I will judge the nation that they serve,' said God, 'and after that they shall come out and worship me in this place.' **8** And he gave him the covenant of circumcision. And so Abraham became the father of Isaac, and circumcised him on the eighth day, and Isaac became the father of Jacob, and Jacob of the twelve patriarchs.

9 "And the patriarchs, jealous of Joseph, sold him into Egypt; but God was with him **10** and rescued him out of all his afflictions and gave him favor and wisdom before Pharaoh, king of Egypt, who made him ruler over Egypt and over all his household. **11** Now there came a famine throughout all Egypt and Canaan, and great affliction, and our fathers could find no food. **12** But when Jacob heard that there was grain in Egypt, he sent out our fathers on their first visit. **13** And on the second visit Joseph made himself known to his brothers, and Joseph's family became known to Pharaoh. **14** And Joseph sent and summoned Jacob his father and all his kindred, seventy-five persons in all. **15** And Jacob went down into Egypt, and he died, he and our fathers, **16** and they were carried back to Shechem and laid in the tomb that Abraham had bought for a sum of silver from the sons of Hamor in Shechem.

17 "But as the time of the promise drew near, which God had granted to Abraham, the people increased and multiplied in Egypt **18** until there arose over Egypt another king who did not know Joseph. **19** He dealt shrewdly with our race and forced our fathers to expose their infants, so that they would not be kept alive. **20** At this time Moses was born; and he was beautiful in God's sight. And he was brought up for three months in his father's house, **21** and when he was exposed, Pharaoh's daughter adopted him and brought him up as her own son. **22** And Moses was instructed in all the wisdom of the Egyptians, and he was mighty in his words and deeds.

23 "When he was forty years old, it came into his heart to visit his brothers, the children of Israel. **24** And seeing one of them being wronged, he defended the oppressed man and avenged him by striking down the Egyptian. **25** He supposed that his brothers would understand that God was giving them salvation by his hand, but they did not understand. **26** And on the following day he appeared to them as they were quarreling and tried to reconcile them, saying, 'Men, you are brothers. Why do you wrong each other?' **27** But the man who was wronging his neighbor thrust him aside, saying, 'Who made you a ruler and a judge over us? **28** Do you want to kill me as you killed the Egyptian yesterday?' **29** At this retort Moses fled and

became an exile in the land of Midian, where he became the father of two sons.

³⁰ "Now when forty years had passed, an angel appeared to him in the wilderness of Mount Sinai, in a flame of fire in a bush. ³¹ When Moses saw it, he was amazed at the sight, and as he drew near to look, there came the voice of the Lord: ³² 'I am the God of your fathers, the God of Abraham and of Isaac and of Jacob.' And Moses trembled and did not dare to look. ³³ Then the Lord said to him, 'Take off the sandals from your feet, for the place where you are standing is holy ground. ³⁴ I have surely seen the affliction of my people who are in Egypt, and have heard their groaning, and I have come down to deliver them. And now come, I will send you to Egypt.'

³⁵ "This Moses, whom they rejected, saying, 'Who made you a ruler and a judge?'—this man God sent as both ruler and redeemer by the hand of the angel who appeared to him in the bush. ³⁶ This man led them out, performing wonders and signs in Egypt and at the Red Sea and in the wilderness for forty years. ³⁷ This is the Moses who said to the Israelites, 'God will raise up for you a prophet like me from your brothers.' ³⁸ This is the one who was in the congregation in the wilderness with the angel who spoke to him at Mount Sinai, and with our fathers. He received living oracles to give to us. ³⁹ Our fathers refused to obey him, but thrust him aside, and in their hearts they turned to Egypt, ⁴⁰ saying to Aaron, 'Make for us gods who will go before us. As for this Moses who led us out from the land of Egypt, we do not know what has become of him.' ⁴¹ And they made a calf in those days, and offered a sacrifice to the idol and were rejoicing in the works of their hands. ⁴² But God turned away and gave them over to worship the host of heaven, as it is written in the book of the prophets:

"'Did you bring to me slain beasts and
    sacrifices,
        during the forty years in the wilder-
            ness, O house of Israel?
⁴³ You took up the tent of Moloch
        and the star of your god Rephan,
    the images that you made to worship;
        and I will send you into exile beyond
            Babylon.'

⁴⁴ "Our fathers had the tent of witness in the wilderness, just as he who spoke to Moses directed him to make it, according to the pattern that he had seen. ⁴⁵ Our fathers in turn brought it in with Joshua when they dispossessed the nations that God drove out before our fathers. So it was until the days of David, ⁴⁶ who found favor in the sight of God and asked to find a dwelling place for the God of Jacob. ⁴⁷ But it was Solomon who built a house for him. ⁴⁸ Yet the Most High does not dwell in houses made by hands, as the prophet says,

⁴⁹ "'Heaven is my throne,
        and the earth is my footstool.
    What kind of house will you build for
        me, says the Lord,
            or what is the place of my rest?
⁵⁰   Did not my hand make all these
            things?'

⁵¹ "You stiff-necked people, uncircumcised in heart and ears, you always resist the Holy Spirit. As your fathers did, so do you. ⁵² Which of the prophets did your fathers not persecute? And they killed those who announced beforehand the coming of the Righteous One, whom you have now betrayed and murdered, ⁵³ you who received the law as delivered by angels and did not keep it."

The Stoning of Stephen

⁵⁴ Now when they heard these things they were enraged, and they ground their teeth at him. ⁵⁵ But he, full of the Holy Spirit, gazed into heaven and saw the glory of God, and Jesus standing at the right hand of God. ⁵⁶ And he said, "Behold, I see the heavens opened, and the Son of Man standing at the right hand of God." ⁵⁷ But they cried out with a loud voice and stopped their ears and rushed together at him. ⁵⁸ Then they cast him out of the city and stoned him. And the witnesses laid down their garments at the feet of a young man named Saul. ⁵⁹ And as they were stoning Stephen, he called out, "Lord Jesus, receive my spirit." ⁶⁰ And falling to his knees he cried out with a loud voice, "Lord, do not hold this sin against them." And when he had said this, he fell asleep.

Saul Ravages the Church

8 And Saul approved of his execution.
    And there arose on that day a great persecution against the church in Jerusalem,

and they were all scattered throughout the regions of Judea and Samaria, except the apostles. ²Devout men buried Stephen and made great lamentation over him. ³But Saul was ravaging the church, and entering house after house, he dragged off men and women and committed them to prison.

Philip Proclaims Christ in Samaria

⁴Now those who were scattered went about preaching the word. ⁵Philip went down to the city of Samaria and proclaimed to them the Christ. ⁶And the crowds with

---

PROFILE
PHILIP

Along with Stephen, Philip was one of the seven men chosen to help the apostles minister to the early church. Referred to as "Philip the evangelist" (21:8), he began his ministry in Samaria, where he proclaimed Christ boldly and with power. Like the apostles, Philip had received the Holy Spirit's power to cast out demons and to heal the sick. The Bible says that as a result of Philip's ministry in Samaria "there was much joy in that city" (8:8). God later led Philip toward Gaza, where he explained the gospel to an Ethiopian royal official. After baptizing the man, Philip was immediately carried away by the Spirit of the Lord to a new area of ministry.

KEY REFERENCE: ACTS 8:5–8

---

one accord paid attention to what was being said by Philip when they heard him and saw the signs that he did. ⁷For unclean spirits, crying out with a loud voice, came out of many who had them, and many who were paralyzed or lame were healed. ⁸So there was much joy in that city.

Simon the Magician Believes

⁹But there was a man named Simon, who had previously practiced magic in the city and amazed the people of Samaria, saying that he himself was somebody great. ¹⁰They all paid attention to him, from the least to the greatest, saying, "This man is the

power of God that is called Great." ¹¹And they paid attention to him because for a long time he had amazed them with his magic. ¹²But when they believed Philip as he preached good news about the kingdom of God and the name of Jesus Christ, they were baptized, both men and women. ¹³Even Simon himself believed, and after being baptized he continued with Philip. And seeing signs and great miracles performed, he was amazed.

¹⁴Now when the apostles at Jerusalem heard that Samaria had received the word of God, they sent to them Peter and John, ¹⁵who came down and prayed for them that they might receive the Holy Spirit, ¹⁶for he had not yet fallen on any of them, but they had only been baptized in the name of the Lord Jesus. ¹⁷Then they laid their hands on them and they received the Holy Spirit. ¹⁸Now when Simon saw that the Spirit was given through the laying on of the apostles' hands, he offered them money, ¹⁹saying, "Give me this power also, so that anyone on whom I lay my hands may receive the Holy Spirit." ²⁰But Peter said to him, "May your silver perish with you, because you thought you could obtain the gift of God with money! ²¹You have neither part nor lot in this matter, for your heart is not right before God. ²²Repent, therefore, of this wickedness of yours, and pray to the Lord that, if possible, the intent of your heart may be forgiven you. ²³For I see that you are in the gall of bitterness and in the bond of iniquity." ²⁴And Simon answered, "Pray for me to the Lord, that nothing of what you have said may come upon me."

²⁵Now when they had testified and spoken the word of the Lord, they returned to Jerusalem, preaching the gospel to many villages of the Samaritans.

Philip and the Ethiopian Eunuch

²⁶Now an angel of the Lord said to Philip, "Rise and go toward the south to the road that goes down from Jerusalem to Gaza." This is a desert place. ²⁷And he rose and went. And there was an Ethiopian, a eunuch, a court official of Candace, queen of the Ethiopians, who was in charge of all her treasure. He had come to Jerusalem to worship ²⁸and was returning, seated in his chariot, and he was reading the prophet Isaiah. ²⁹And the Spirit said to Philip, "Go

over and join this chariot." ³⁰ So Philip ran to him and heard him reading Isaiah the prophet and asked, "Do you understand what you are reading?" ³¹ And he said, "How can I, unless someone guides me?" And he invited Philip to come up and sit with him. ³² Now the passage of the Scripture that he was reading was this:

"Like a sheep he was led to the slaughter
and like a lamb before its shearer is silent,
so he opens not his mouth.
³³ In his humiliation justice was denied him.
Who can describe his generation?
For his life is taken away from the earth."

GETTING THE MESSAGE

The **Ethiopian** mentioned in 8:26–40 was an official in the royal court of Ethiopia, located in what is now Sudan and Ethiopia. Philip found him reading the Old Testament Scriptures, which means he was probably a "God-fearer," that is, a non-Jew who was seeking to know about the God of Israel. His journey to Jerusalem would have taken him three months—a true sign of his sincerity in seeking the Lord.

³⁴ And the eunuch said to Philip, "About whom, I ask you, does the prophet say this, about himself or about someone else?" ³⁵ Then Philip opened his mouth, and beginning with this Scripture he told him the good news about Jesus. ³⁶ And as they were going along the road they came to some water, and the eunuch said, "See, here is water! What prevents me from being baptized?" ³⁸ And he commanded the chariot to stop, and they both went down into the water, Philip and the eunuch, and he baptized him. ³⁹ And when they came up out of the water, the Spirit of the Lord carried Philip away, and the eunuch saw him no more, and went on his way rejoicing. ⁴⁰ But Philip found himself at Azotus, and as he passed through he preached the gospel to all the towns until he came to Caesarea.

The Conversion of Saul

9 But Saul, still breathing threats and murder against the disciples of the Lord, went to the high priest ² and asked him for letters to the synagogues at Damascus, so that if he found any belonging to the Way, men or women, he might bring them bound to Jerusalem. ³ Now as he went on his way, he approached Damascus, and suddenly a

PROFILE
PAUL

Author of 13 out of the 27 New Testament books, Paul is one of the most important people in the history of the Christian faith. Born in Tarsus with the Hebrew name "Saul," he was both a Jew and a Roman citizen. He came to Jerusalem as a young man to be educated by Gamaliel, the most famous rabbinic scholar of that time. After approving the stoning of Stephen, Saul helped lead a great persecution against the church (8:1–3). Then, on his way to Damascus to arrest believers, he was dramatically converted to the faith (9:1–31). Paul would eventually go on three missionary journeys, winning many people to faith in Christ and establishing churches in cities all across the Roman Empire. He was especially effective in explaining the gospel to Gentiles. Paul faced brutal opposition throughout his ministry and eventually was imprisoned. He wrote many of his letters while under house arrest and later in prison in Rome, before being martyred for his faith.

KEY REFERENCE: ACTS 9:1–22

light from heaven shone around him. ⁴ And falling to the ground he heard a voice saying to him, "Saul, Saul, why are you persecuting me?" ⁵ And he said, "Who are you, Lord?" And he said, "I am Jesus, whom you are persecuting. ⁶ But rise and enter the city, and you will be told what you are to do." ⁷ The men who were traveling with him stood speechless, hearing the voice but seeing no one. ⁸ Saul rose from the ground, and although his eyes were opened, he saw nothing. So they led him by the hand and brought him into Damascus. ⁹ And for three days he was without sight, and neither ate nor drank.

¹⁰ Now there was a disciple at Damascus named Ananias. The Lord said to him in a vision, "Ananias." And he said, "Here I am, Lord." ¹¹ And the Lord said to him, "Rise and go to the street called Straight, and at the house of Judas look for a man of Tarsus named Saul, for behold, he is praying, ¹² and he has seen in a vision a man named Ananias come in and lay his hands on him so that he might regain his sight." ¹³ But Ananias answered, "Lord, I have heard from many about this man, how much evil he has done to your saints at Jerusalem. ¹⁴ And here he has authority from the chief priests to bind all who call on your name." ¹⁵ But the Lord

GETTING THE MESSAGE

Ananias. There are three different men named Ananias in the book of Acts (see 5:1; 9:10; 24:1). The Ananias who was apparently the first believer to welcome Paul after his conversion is a positive example of obedience to the Lord (9:10–19).

said to him, "Go, for he is a chosen instrument of mine to carry my name before the Gentiles and kings and the children of Israel. ¹⁶ For I will show him how much he must suffer for the sake of my name." ¹⁷ So Ananias departed and entered the house. And laying his hands on him he said, "Brother Saul, the Lord Jesus who appeared to you on the road by which you came has sent me so that you may regain your sight and be filled with the Holy Spirit." ¹⁸ And immediately something like scales fell from his eyes, and he regained his sight. Then he rose and was baptized; ¹⁹ and taking food, he was strengthened.

Saul Proclaims Jesus in Synagogues

For some days he was with the disciples at Damascus. ²⁰ And immediately he proclaimed Jesus in the synagogues, saying, "He is the Son of God." ²¹ And all who heard him were amazed and said, "Is not this the

man who made havoc in Jerusalem of those who called upon this name? And has he not come here for this purpose, to bring them bound before the chief priests?" ²² But Saul increased all the more in strength, and confounded the Jews who lived in Damascus by proving that Jesus was the Christ.

Saul Escapes from Damascus

²³ When many days had passed, the Jews[1] plotted to kill him, ²⁴ but their plot became known to Saul. They were watching the gates day and night in order to kill him, ²⁵ but his disciples took him by night and let him down through an opening in the wall, lowering him in a basket.

Saul in Jerusalem

²⁶ And when he had come to Jerusalem, he attempted to join the disciples. And they were all afraid of him, for they did not believe that he was a disciple. ²⁷ But Barnabas took him and brought him to the apostles and declared to them how on the road he had seen the Lord, who spoke to him, and how at Damascus he had preached boldly in the name of Jesus. ²⁸ So he went in and out among them at Jerusalem, preaching boldly in the name of the Lord. ²⁹ And he spoke and disputed against the Hellenists.[2] But they were seeking to kill him. ³⁰ And when the brothers learned this, they brought him down to Caesarea and sent him off to Tarsus.

³¹ So the church throughout all Judea and Galilee and Samaria had peace and was being built up. And walking in the fear of the Lord and in the comfort of the Holy Spirit, it multiplied.

The Healing of Aeneas

³² Now as Peter went here and there among them all, he came down also to the saints who lived at Lydda. ³³ There he found a man named Aeneas, bedridden for eight years, who was paralyzed. ³⁴ And Peter said to him, "Aeneas, Jesus Christ heals you; rise and make your bed." And immediately he rose. ³⁵ And all the residents of Lydda and Sharon saw him, and they turned to the Lord.

Dorcas Restored to Life

³⁶ Now there was in Joppa a disciple named Tabitha, which, translated, means Dorcas. She was full of good works and acts

[1] The Greek word refers to Jewish religious leaders, and people they influenced, who opposed the Christian faith; also 13:50; 17:5, 13; 18:12, 14, 28; 20:3, 19; 21:11 [2] That is, Greek-speaking Jews

of charity. 37 In those days she became ill and died, and when they had washed her, they laid her in an upper room. 38 Since Lydda was near Joppa, the disciples, hearing that Peter was there, sent two men to him, urging him, "Please come to us without delay." 39 So Peter rose and went with them. And when he arrived, they took him to the upper room. All the widows stood beside him weeping and showing tunics and other garments that Dorcas made while she was with them. 40 But Peter put them all outside, and knelt down and prayed; and turning to the body he said, "Tabitha, arise." And she opened her eyes, and when she saw Peter she sat up. 41 And he gave her his hand and raised her up. Then calling the saints and widows, he presented her alive. 42 And it became known throughout all Joppa, and many believed in the Lord. 43 And he stayed in Joppa for many days with one Simon, a tanner.

Peter and Cornelius

10 At Caesarea there was a man named Cornelius, a centurion of what was known as the Italian Cohort, 2 a devout man who feared God with all his household, gave alms generously to the people, and prayed continually to God. 3 About the ninth hour of the day[1] he saw clearly in a vision an angel of God come in and say to him, "Cornelius." 4 And he stared at him in terror and said, "What is it, Lord?" And he said to him, "Your prayers and your alms have ascended as a memorial before God. 5 And now send men to Joppa and bring one Simon who is called Peter. 6 He is lodging with one Simon, a tanner, whose house is by the sea." 7 When the angel who spoke to him had departed, he called two of his servants and a devout soldier from among those who attended him, 8 and having related everything to them, he sent them to Joppa.

Peter's Vision

9 The next day, as they were on their journey and approaching the city, Peter went up on the housetop about the sixth hour[2] to pray. 10 And he became hungry and wanted something to eat, but while they were preparing it, he fell into a trance 11 and saw the heavens opened and something like a great sheet descending, being let down by its four corners upon the earth. 12 In it were all kinds

of animals and reptiles and birds of the air. 13 And there came a voice to him: "Rise, Peter; kill and eat." 14 But Peter said, "By no means, Lord; for I have never eaten anything that is common or unclean." 15 And the voice came to him again a second time, "What God has made clean, do not call common." 16 This happened three times, and the thing was taken up at once to heaven.

17 Now while Peter was inwardly perplexed as to what the vision that he had seen might mean, behold, the men who were sent by Cornelius, having made inquiry for Simon's house, stood at the gate 18 and called out to ask whether Simon who was called Peter was lodging there. 19 And while Peter was pondering the vision, the Spirit said to him, "Behold, three men are looking for you. 20 Rise and go down and accompany them

without hesitation, for I have sent them." 21 And Peter went down to the men and said, "I am the one you are looking for. What is the reason for your coming?" 22 And they said, "Cornelius, a centurion, an upright and God-fearing man, who is well spoken of by the whole Jewish nation, was directed by a holy angel to send for you to come to his house and to hear what you have to say." 23 So he invited them in to be his guests.

The next day he rose and went away with them, and some of the brothers from Joppa accompanied him. 24 And on the following day they entered Caesarea. Cornelius was expecting them and had called together his relatives and close friends. 25 When Peter entered, Cornelius met him and fell down at his feet and worshiped him. 26 But Peter lifted him up, saying, "Stand up; I too am a

---

[1] That is, 3 P.M. [2] That is, noon

man." **27** And as he talked with him, he went in and found many persons gathered. **28** And he said to them, "You yourselves know how unlawful it is for a Jew to associate with or to visit anyone of another nation, but God has shown me that I should not call any person common or unclean. **29** So when I was sent for, I came without objection. I ask then why you sent for me."

30 And Cornelius said, "Four days ago, about this hour, I was praying in my house

---

PROFILE
CORNELIUS

Cornelius was a Roman centurion and a "God-fearer"—a Gentile who worshiped Israel's God. As a centurion, Cornelius would have been a socially prominent and wealthy man. The Bible says that he "gave alms generously to the people, and prayed continually to God" (10:2), and that he was held in high regard "by the whole Jewish nation" (10:22). An angel of the Lord appeared to Cornelius in a vision and instructed him to send for the apostle Peter. When Peter arrived, he preached the gospel to Cornelius and his friends and family. While he was still speaking, the Holy Spirit was poured out on these Gentile seekers. Cornelius and his household were baptized, and their conversion convinced the early church that God's promises were for Gentiles as well as for Jews.

KEY REFERENCE: ACTS 10:30–33

---

at the ninth hour,[1] and behold, a man stood before me in bright clothing **31** and said, 'Cornelius, your prayer has been heard and your alms have been remembered before God. **32** Send therefore to Joppa and ask for Simon who is called Peter. He is lodging in the house of Simon, a tanner, by the sea.' **33** So I sent for you at once, and you have been kind enough to come. Now therefore we are all here in the presence of God to hear all that you have been commanded by the Lord."

Gentiles Hear the Good News

34 So Peter opened his mouth and said: "Truly I understand that God shows no partiality, **35** but in every nation anyone who fears him and does what is right is acceptable to him. **36** As for the word that he sent to Israel, preaching good news of peace through Jesus Christ (he is Lord of all), **37** you yourselves know what happened throughout all Judea, beginning from Galilee after the baptism that John proclaimed: **38** how God anointed Jesus of Nazareth with the Holy Spirit and with power. He went about doing good and healing all who were oppressed by the devil, for God was with him. **39** And we are witnesses of all that he did both in the country of the Jews and in Jerusalem. They put him to death by hanging him on a tree, **40** but God raised him on the third day and made him to appear, **41** not to all the people but to us who had been chosen by God as witnesses, who ate and drank with him after he rose from the dead. **42** And he commanded us to preach to the people and to testify that he is the one appointed by God to be judge of the living and the dead. **43** To him all the prophets bear witness that everyone who believes in him receives forgiveness of sins through his name."

The Holy Spirit Falls on the Gentiles

44 While Peter was still saying these things, the Holy Spirit fell on all who heard the word. **45** And the believers from among the circumcised who had come with Peter were amazed, because the gift of the Holy Spirit was poured out even on the Gentiles. **46** For they were hearing them speaking in tongues and extolling God. Then Peter declared, **47** "Can anyone withhold water for baptizing these people, who have received the Holy Spirit just as we have?" **48** And he commanded them to be baptized in the name of Jesus Christ. Then they asked him to remain for some days.

Peter Reports to the Church

11 Now the apostles and the brothers[2] who were throughout Judea heard that the Gentiles also had received the word of God. **2** So when Peter went up to Jerusalem, the circumcision party criticized him, saying, **3** "You went to uncircumcised men and ate with them." **4** But Peter began and explained

---

[1] That is, 3 P.M. [2] Or *brothers and sisters*

it to them in order: [5] "I was in the city of Joppa praying, and in a trance I saw a vision, something like a great sheet descending, being let down from heaven by its four corners, and it came down to me. [6] Looking at it closely, I observed animals and beasts of prey and reptiles and birds of the air. [7] And I heard a voice saying to me, 'Rise, Peter; kill and eat.' [8] But I said, 'By no means, Lord; for nothing common or unclean has ever entered my mouth.' [9] But the voice answered a second time from heaven, 'What God has made clean, do not call common.' [10] This happened three times, and all was drawn up again into heaven. [11] And behold, at that very moment three men arrived at the house in which we were, sent to me from Caesarea. [12] And the Spirit told me to go with them, making no distinction. These six brothers also accompanied me, and we entered the man's house. [13] And he told us how he had seen the angel stand in his house and say, 'Send to Joppa and bring Simon who is called Peter; [14] he will declare to you a message by which you will be saved, you and all your household.' [15] As I began to speak, the Holy Spirit fell on them just as on us at the beginning. [16] And I remembered the word of the Lord, how he said, 'John baptized with water, but you will be baptized with the Holy Spirit.' [17] If then God gave the same gift to them as he gave to us when we believed in the Lord Jesus Christ, who was I that I could stand in God's way?" [18] When they heard these things they fell silent. And they glorified God, saying, "Then to the Gentiles also God has granted repentance that leads to life."

The Church in Antioch

[19] Now those who were scattered because of the persecution that arose over Stephen traveled as far as Phoenicia and Cyprus and Antioch, speaking the word to no one except Jews. [20] But there were some of them, men of Cyprus and Cyrene, who on coming to Antioch spoke to the Hellenists[1] also, preaching the Lord Jesus. [21] And the hand of the Lord was with them, and a great number who believed turned to the Lord. [22] The report of this came to the ears of the church in Jerusalem, and they sent Barnabas to Antioch. [23] When he came and saw the grace of God, he was glad, and he exhorted them all to remain faithful to the Lord with steadfast purpose, [24] for he was a good man, full of the Holy Spirit and of faith. And a great many people were added to the Lord. [25] So Barnabas went to Tarsus to look for Saul, [26] and when he had found him, he brought him to Antioch. For a whole year they met with the church and taught a great many people. And in Antioch the disciples were first called Christians.

[27] Now in these days prophets came down from Jerusalem to Antioch. [28] And one of them named Agabus stood up and foretold by the Spirit that there would be a great famine over all the world (this took place in the days of Claudius). [29] So the disciples determined, every one according to his ability, to send relief to the brothers[2] living in Judea. [30] And they did so, sending it to the elders by the hand of Barnabas and Saul.

> ### GETTING THE MESSAGE
>
> **Antioch in Syria** was the third largest city in the Roman Empire, after Alexandria and mighty Rome. With a population of over a half million, it was the capital of the Syrian province and a major hub for the spread of Christianity throughout the Gentile world.

James Killed and Peter Imprisoned

12 About that time Herod the king laid violent hands on some who belonged to the church. [2] He killed James the brother of John with the sword, [3] and when he saw that it pleased the Jews, he proceeded to arrest Peter also. This was during the days of Unleavened Bread. [4] And when he had seized him, he put him in prison, delivering him over to four squads of soldiers to guard him, intending after the Passover to bring him out to the people. [5] So Peter was kept in prison, but earnest prayer for him was made to God by the church.

Peter Is Rescued

[6] Now when Herod was about to bring him out, on that very night, Peter was sleeping between two soldiers, bound with two chains, and sentries before the door were guarding the prison. [7] And behold,

---

[1] Or *Greeks* (that is, Greek-speaking non-Jews) [2] Or *brothers and sisters*

an angel of the Lord stood next to him, and a light shone in the cell. He struck Peter on the side and woke him, saying, "Get up quickly." And the chains fell off his hands. [8] And the angel said to him, "Dress yourself and put on your sandals." And he did so. And he said to him, "Wrap your cloak around you and follow me." [9] And he went out and followed him. He did not know that what was being done by the angel was

real, but thought he was seeing a vision. [10] When they had passed the first and the second guard, they came to the iron gate leading into the city. It opened for them of its own accord, and they went out and went along one street, and immediately the angel left him. [11] When Peter came to himself, he said, "Now I am sure that the Lord has sent his angel and rescued me from the hand of Herod and from all that the Jewish people were expecting."

[12] When he realized this, he went to the house of Mary, the mother of John whose other name was Mark, where many were gathered together and were praying. [13] And when he knocked at the door of the gateway, a servant girl named Rhoda came to answer. [14] Recognizing Peter's voice, in her joy she did not open the gate but ran in and reported that Peter was standing at the gate. [15] They said to her, "You are out of your mind." But she kept insisting that it was so, and they kept saying, "It is his angel!" [16] But Peter continued knocking, and when they opened, they saw him and were amazed. [17] But motioning to them with his hand to be silent, he described to them how the Lord had brought him out of the prison. And he said, "Tell these things to James and to the brothers."[1] Then he departed and went to another place.

GETTING THE MESSAGE

The death of James. In Mark 10:39, Jesus implies that the brothers James and John would suffer a similar death to his. For James, this was fulfilled when Herod Agrippa I, Roman ruler over Palestine, ordered his execution (Acts 12:2).

[18] Now when day came, there was no little disturbance among the soldiers over what had become of Peter. [19] And after Herod searched for him and did not find him, he examined the sentries and ordered that they should be put to death. Then he went down from Judea to Caesarea and spent time there.

The Death of Herod

[20] Now Herod was angry with the people of Tyre and Sidon, and they came to him with one accord, and having persuaded Blastus, the king's chamberlain, they asked for peace, because their country depended on the king's country for food. [21] On an appointed day Herod put on his royal robes, took his seat upon the throne, and delivered an oration to them. [22] And the people were shouting, "The voice of a god, and not of a man!" [23] Immediately an angel of the Lord struck him down, because he did not give God the glory, and he was eaten by worms and breathed his last.

PROFILE

HEROD AGRIPPA I

Herod Agrippa I was a grandson of Herod the Great. He grew up in Rome, where the future Roman emperors Gaius (Caligula) and Claudius were his childhood playmates. It was largely due to these friendships that Herod was granted rule over various territories in Judea. Herod was a violent persecutor of Christians, perhaps because he believed such persecution would help him gain favor with the Jews (12:3). He executed James, and had Peter put in prison. Following a well-received speech given to the people of Tyre and Sidon, Herod was enthusiastically praised as a god. Rather than reject the people's worship, he embraced it. The Bible says that because of this demonstration of godless pride, an angel of the Lord immediately struck him down, and he died a gruesome death (12:23).

KEY REFERENCE: ACTS 12:1-3

[1] Or brothers and sisters

24 But the word of God increased and multiplied.

25 And Barnabas and Saul returned from Jerusalem when they had completed their service, bringing with them John, whose other name was Mark.

Barnabas and Saul Sent Off

13 Now there were in the church at Antioch prophets and teachers, Barnabas, Simeon who was called Niger, Lucius of Cyrene, Manaen a lifelong friend of Herod the tetrarch, and Saul. **2** While they were worshiping the Lord and fasting, the Holy Spirit said, "Set apart for me Barnabas and Saul for the work to which I have called them." **3** Then after fasting and praying they laid their hands on them and sent them off.

Barnabas and Saul on Cyprus

4 So, being sent out by the Holy Spirit, they went down to Seleucia, and from there they sailed to Cyprus. **5** When they arrived at Salamis, they proclaimed the word of God in the synagogues of the Jews. And they had John to assist them. **6** When they had gone through the whole island as far as Paphos, they came upon a certain magician, a Jewish false prophet named Bar-Jesus. **7** He was with the proconsul, Sergius Paulus, a man of intelligence, who summoned Barnabas and Saul and sought to hear the word of God. **8** But Elymas the magician (for that is the meaning of his name) opposed them, seeking to turn the proconsul away from the faith. **9** But Saul, who was also called Paul, filled with the Holy Spirit, looked intently at him **10** and said, "You son of the devil, you enemy of all righteousness, full of all deceit and villainy, will you not stop making crooked the straight paths of the Lord? **11** And now, behold, the hand of the Lord is upon you, and you will be blind and unable to see the sun for a time." Immediately mist and darkness fell upon him, and he went about seeking people to lead him by the hand. **12** Then the proconsul believed, when he saw what had occurred, for he was astonished at the teaching of the Lord.

Paul and Barnabas at Antioch in Pisidia

13 Now Paul and his companions set sail from Paphos and came to Perga in Pamphylia. And John left them and returned to Jerusalem, **14** but they went on from Perga and came to Antioch in Pisidia. And on the Sabbath day they went into the synagogue and sat down. **15** After the reading from the Law and the Prophets, the rulers of the synagogue sent a message to them, saying, "Brothers, if you have any word of encouragement for the people, say it." **16** So Paul stood up, and motioning with his hand said:

"Men of Israel and you who fear God, listen. **17** The God of this people Israel chose our fathers and made the people great during their stay in the land of Egypt, and with uplifted arm he led them out of it. **18** And for about forty years he put up with them in the wilderness. **19** And after destroying seven nations in the land of Canaan, he

> ### GETTING THE MESSAGE
>
> **Antioch in Pisidia** (13:14) was one of 16 cities that the Syrian king Seleucus named after his father Antiochus. The city had a large Jewish population and the high status of being a Roman colony, probably Asia Minor's most important. Designed to be a smaller version of Rome, it was organized into seven districts and possessed all the amenities that Rome afforded. These included an aqueduct, a bathhouse, and most notably its large sanctuary devoted to emperor worship.

gave them their land as an inheritance. **20** All this took about 450 years. And after that he gave them judges until Samuel the prophet. **21** Then they asked for a king, and God gave them Saul the son of Kish, a man of the tribe of Benjamin, for forty years. **22** And when he had removed him, he raised up David to be their king, of whom he testified and said, 'I have found in David the son of Jesse a man after my heart, who will do all my will.' **23** Of this man's offspring God has brought to Israel a Savior, Jesus, as he promised. **24** Before his coming, John had proclaimed a baptism of repentance to all the people of Israel. **25** And as John was finishing his course, he said, 'What do you suppose that I am? I am not he. No, but behold, after me one is coming, the sandals of whose feet I am not worthy to untie.'

26 "Brothers, sons of the family of Abraham, and those among you who fear God, to us has been sent the message of this salvation. **27** For those who live in Jerusalem and their rulers, because they did not recognize him nor understand the utterances of the prophets, which are read every Sabbath, fulfilled them by condemning him. **28** And though they found in him no guilt worthy of death, they asked Pilate to have him executed. **29** And when they had carried

---

PROFILE

BARNABAS

Barnabas was a Levite from Cyprus. His birth name was Joseph, but the apostles called him Barnabas, which means "son of encouragement." The nickname fit his personality well. Following Paul's conversion, the Christians in Jerusalem were initially afraid of their former persecutor. Barnabas, however, befriended Paul and introduced him to the apostles. He brought Paul to Antioch to help build a church there (11:25–26), and became Paul's companion on his first missionary journey. The two men eventually had a sharp disagreement over John Mark, who had left Paul and Barnabas before the end of the first journey. As a result of the disagreement, Paul and Barnabas went their separate ways. While Paul chose Silas as his companion for his second journey, Barnabas took Mark on a separate mission back to Cyprus to strengthen the church there.

KEY REFERENCE: ACTS 11:22–26

---

out all that was written of him, they took him down from the tree and laid him in a tomb. **30** But God raised him from the dead, **31** and for many days he appeared to those who had come up with him from Galilee to Jerusalem, who are now his witnesses to the people. **32** And we bring you the good news that what God promised to the fathers, **33** this he has fulfilled to us their children by raising Jesus, as also it is written in the second Psalm,

"'You are my Son,
today I have begotten you.'

34 And as for the fact that he raised him from the dead, no more to return to corruption, he has spoken in this way,

"'I will give you the holy and sure blessings of David.'

35 Therefore he says also in another psalm,

"'You will not let your Holy One see corruption.'

36 For David, after he had served the purpose of God in his own generation, fell asleep and was laid with his fathers and saw corruption, **37** but he whom God raised up did not see corruption. **38** Let it be known to you therefore, brothers, that through this man forgiveness of sins is proclaimed to you, **39** and by him everyone who believes is freed from everything from which you could not be freed by the law of Moses. **40** Beware, therefore, lest what is said in the Prophets should come about:

41 "'Look, you scoffers,
be astounded and perish;
for I am doing a work in your days,
a work that you will not believe,
even if one tells it to you.'"

42 As they went out, the people begged that these things might be told them the next Sabbath. **43** And after the meeting of the synagogue broke up, many Jews and devout converts to Judaism followed Paul and Barnabas, who, as they spoke with them, urged them to continue in the grace of God.

44 The next Sabbath almost the whole city gathered to hear the word of the Lord. **45** But when the Jews saw the crowds, they were filled with jealousy and began to contradict what was spoken by Paul, reviling him. **46** And Paul and Barnabas spoke out boldly, saying, "It was necessary that the word of God be spoken first to you. Since you thrust it aside and judge yourselves unworthy of eternal life, behold, we are turning to the Gentiles. **47** For so the Lord has commanded us, saying,

"'I have made you a light for the Gentiles,
that you may bring salvation to the ends of the earth.'"

[48] And when the Gentiles heard this, they began rejoicing and glorifying the word of the Lord, and as many as were appointed to eternal life believed. [49] And the word of the Lord was spreading throughout the whole region. [50] But the Jews incited the devout women of high standing and the leading men of the city, stirred up persecution against Paul and Barnabas, and drove them out of their district. [51] But they shook off the dust from their feet against them and went to Iconium. [52] And the disciples were filled with joy and with the Holy Spirit.

Paul and Barnabas at Iconium

14 Now at Iconium they entered together into the Jewish synagogue and spoke in such a way that a great number of both Jews and Greeks believed. [2] But the unbelieving Jews stirred up the Gentiles and poisoned their minds against the brothers.[1] [3] So they remained for a long time, speaking boldly for the Lord, who bore witness to the word of his grace, granting signs and wonders to be done by their hands. [4] But the people of the city were divided; some sided with the Jews and some with the apostles. [5] When an attempt was made by both Gentiles and Jews, with their rulers, to mistreat them and to stone them, [6] they learned of it and fled to Lystra and Derbe, cities of Lycaonia, and to the surrounding country, [7] and there they continued to preach the gospel.

Paul and Barnabas at Lystra

[8] Now at Lystra there was a man sitting who could not use his feet. He was crippled from birth and had never walked. [9] He listened to Paul speaking. And Paul, looking intently at him and seeing that he had faith to be made well, [10] said in a loud voice, "Stand upright on your feet." And he sprang up and began walking. [11] And when the crowds saw what Paul had done, they lifted up their voices, saying in Lycaonian, "The gods have come down to us in the likeness of men!" [12] Barnabas they called Zeus, and Paul, Hermes, because he was the chief speaker. [13] And the priest of Zeus, whose temple was at the entrance to the city, brought oxen and garlands to the gates and wanted to offer sacrifice with the crowds. [14] But when the apostles Barnabas

and Paul heard of it, they tore their garments and rushed out into the crowd, crying out, [15] "Men, why are you doing these things? We also are men, of like nature with you, and we bring you good news, that you should turn from these vain things to a living God, who made the heaven and the earth and the sea and all that is in them. [16] In past generations he allowed all the nations to walk in their own ways. [17] Yet he did not leave himself without witness, for he did good by giving you rains from heaven and fruitful seasons, satisfying your hearts with food and gladness." [18] Even with these words they scarcely restrained the people from offering sacrifice to them.

Paul Stoned at Lystra

[19] But Jews came from Antioch and Iconium, and having persuaded the crowds,

GETTING THE MESSAGE

Why did they try to worship Paul and Barnabas? When Paul performed a miracle in Lystra, the people treated him and Barnabas as gods (14:8–18). They did this because of a local myth about the gods Hermes and Zeus visiting their region in human form, seeking hospitality. Only one couple gave them shelter, and as a result they were spared when the gods drowned everyone else as punishment.

they stoned Paul and dragged him out of the city, supposing that he was dead. [20] But when the disciples gathered about him, he rose up and entered the city, and on the next day he went on with Barnabas to Derbe. [21] When they had preached the gospel to that city and had made many disciples, they returned to Lystra and to Iconium and to Antioch, [22] strengthening the souls of the disciples, encouraging them to continue in the faith, and saying that through many tribulations we must enter the kingdom of God. [23] And when they had appointed elders for them in every church, with prayer and fasting they committed them to the Lord in whom they had believed.

[1] Or brothers and sisters

Paul and Barnabas Return to Antioch in Syria

24 Then they passed through Pisidia and came to Pamphylia. **25** And when they had spoken the word in Perga, they went down to Attalia, **26** and from there they sailed to Antioch, where they had been commended to the grace of God for the work that they had fulfilled. **27** And when they arrived and gathered the church together, they declared all that God had done with them, and how he had opened a door of faith to the Gentiles. **28** And they remained no little time with the disciples.

The Jerusalem Council

15 But some men came down from Judea and were teaching the brothers, "Unless you are circumcised according to the custom of Moses, you cannot be

GETTING THE MESSAGE

The Jerusalem Council settled some crucial practical issues to enable Jewish and Gentile Christians to worship and minister together (15:1–35).

saved." **2** And after Paul and Barnabas had no small dissension and debate with them, Paul and Barnabas and some of the others were appointed to go up to Jerusalem to the apostles and the elders about this question. **3** So, being sent on their way by the church, they passed through both Phoenicia and Samaria, describing in detail the conversion of the Gentiles, and brought great joy to all the brothers.[1] **4** When they came to Jerusalem, they were welcomed by the church and the apostles and the elders, and they declared all that God had done with them. **5** But some believers who belonged to the party of the Pharisees rose up and said, "It is necessary to circumcise them and to order them to keep the law of Moses." **6** The apostles and the elders were gathered together to consider this matter. **7** And after there had been much debate, Peter stood up and said to them, "Brothers, you know that in the early days God made a choice among you, that by my mouth the Gentiles should hear the word of the gos-

pel and believe. **8** And God, who knows the heart, bore witness to them, by giving them the Holy Spirit just as he did to us, **9** and he made no distinction between us and them, having cleansed their hearts by faith. **10** Now, therefore, why are you putting God to the test by placing a yoke on the neck of the disciples that neither our fathers nor we have been able to bear? **11** But we believe that we will be saved through the grace of the Lord Jesus, just as they will."

12 And all the assembly fell silent, and they listened to Barnabas and Paul as they related what signs and wonders God had done through them among the Gentiles. **13** After they finished speaking, James replied, "Brothers, listen to me. **14** Simeon has related how God first visited the Gentiles, to take from them a people for his name. **15** And with this the words of the prophets agree, just as it is written,

16 "'After this I will return,
and I will rebuild the tent of David
that has fallen;
I will rebuild its ruins,
and I will restore it,
17 that the remnant of mankind may
seek the Lord,
and all the Gentiles who are called
by my name,
says the Lord, who makes these
things **18** known from of old.'

19 Therefore my judgment is that we should not trouble those of the Gentiles who turn to God, **20** but should write to them to abstain from the things polluted by idols, and from sexual immorality, and from what has been strangled, and from blood. **21** For from ancient generations Moses has had in every city those who proclaim him, for he is read every Sabbath in the synagogues."

The Council's Letter to Gentile Believers

22 Then it seemed good to the apostles and the elders, with the whole church, to choose men from among them and send them to Antioch with Paul and Barnabas. They sent Judas called Barsabbas, and Silas, leading men among the brothers, **23** with the following letter: "The brothers, both the apostles and the elders, to the brothers[2] who are of the Gentiles in Antioch and Syria and Cilicia, greetings. **24** Since we have heard that

[1] Or brothers and sisters; also 15:22 [2] Or brothers and sisters

some persons have gone out from us and troubled you with words, unsettling your minds, although we gave them no instructions, ²⁵ it has seemed good to us, having come to one accord, to choose men and send them to you with our beloved Barnabas and Paul, ²⁶ men who have risked their lives for the name of our Lord Jesus Christ. ²⁷ We have therefore sent Judas and Silas, who themselves will tell you the same things by word of mouth. ²⁸ For it has seemed good to the Holy Spirit and to us to lay on you no greater burden than these requirements: ²⁹ that you abstain from what has been sacrificed to idols, and from blood, and from what has been strangled, and from sexual immorality. If you keep yourselves from these, you will do well. Farewell."

³⁰ So when they were sent off, they went down to Antioch, and having gathered the congregation together, they delivered the letter. ³¹ And when they had read it, they rejoiced because of its encouragement. ³² And Judas and Silas, who were themselves prophets, encouraged and strengthened the brothers¹ with many words. ³³ And after they had spent some time, they were sent off in peace by the brothers to those who had sent them. ³⁵ But Paul and Barnabas remained in Antioch, teaching and preaching the word of the Lord, with many others also.

Paul and Barnabas Separate

³⁶ And after some days Paul said to Barnabas, "Let us return and visit the brothers in every city where we proclaimed the word of the Lord, and see how they are." ³⁷ Now Barnabas wanted to take with them John called Mark. ³⁸ But Paul thought best not to take with them one who had withdrawn from them in Pamphylia and had not gone with them to the work. ³⁹ And there arose a sharp disagreement, so that they separated from each other. Barnabas took Mark with him and sailed away to Cyprus, ⁴⁰ but Paul chose Silas and departed, having been commended by the brothers to the grace of the Lord. ⁴¹ And he went through Syria and Cilicia, strengthening the churches.

Timothy Joins Paul and Silas

16 Paul came also to Derbe and to Lystra. A disciple was there, named Timothy, the son of a Jewish woman who

was a believer, but his father was a Greek. ² He was well spoken of by the brothers at Lystra and Iconium. ³ Paul wanted Timothy to accompany him, and he took him and circumcised him because of the Jews who were in those places, for they all knew that his father was a Greek. ⁴ As they went on their way through the cities, they delivered to them for observance the decisions that had been reached by the apostles and elders who were in Jerusalem. ⁵ So the churches were strengthened in the faith, and they increased in numbers daily.

PROFILE
JOHN MARK

John Mark was probably Barnabas's cousin (Col. 4:10). The early church at Jerusalem met at the home of his mother, Mary (Acts 12:12). He accompanied Paul and Barnabas on their first missionary journey, but then chose to leave them. As a result, Paul refused to take him along on his second expedition. However, it seems that Mark eventually regained Paul's favor (2 Tim. 4:11). He ultimately demonstrated his effectiveness and commitment as a missionary pioneer and as the author of the Gospel of Mark. He was closely associated with the apostle Peter, who refers to Mark as his "son" (1 Pet. 5:13).

KEY REFERENCE: 2 TIMOTHY 4:11

The Macedonian Call

⁶ And they went through the region of Phrygia and Galatia, having been forbidden by the Holy Spirit to speak the word in Asia. ⁷ And when they had come up to Mysia, they attempted to go into Bithynia, but the Spirit of Jesus did not allow them. ⁸ So, passing by Mysia, they went down to Troas. ⁹ And a vision appeared to Paul in the night: a man of Macedonia was standing there, urging him and saying, "Come over to Macedonia and help us." ¹⁰ And when Paul had seen the vision, immediately we sought to go on into Macedonia, conclud-

¹ Or brothers and sisters; also 15:33, 36; 16:2

ing that God had called us to preach the gospel to them.

The Conversion of Lydia

¹¹ So, setting sail from Troas, we made a direct voyage to Samothrace, and the following day to Neapolis, ¹² and from there to Philippi, which is a leading city of the district of Macedonia and a Roman colony. We remained in this city some days. ¹³ And on the Sabbath day we went outside the

PROFILE
SILAS

Silas was a Judean Christian and a leader in the Jerusalem church. After Paul and Barnabas parted ways, Silas joined Paul as a coworker on his second missionary journey. While in Philippi, Paul cast out a spirit that was enabling a girl to tell fortunes (ch. 16). The girl's owners were furious, since they had been making money from her demonic powers. They brought Paul and Silas before the magistrates, and they were flogged and jailed. Paul and Silas were miraculously freed from their bonds—but rather than flee, they saw an opportunity to share the gospel. As a result, their jailer and his household became Christians. Silas is known by the name "Silvanus" in the New Testament epistles. He worked closely with the apostle Peter, and delivered Peter's first letter to its recipients in Asia Minor (1 Pet. 5:12).

KEY REFERENCE: ACTS 15:32

gate to the riverside, where we supposed there was a place of prayer, and we sat down and spoke to the women who had come together. ¹⁴ One who heard us was a woman named Lydia, from the city of Thyatira, a seller of purple goods, who was a worshiper of God. The Lord opened her heart to pay attention to what was said by Paul. ¹⁵ And after she was baptized, and her household as well, she urged us, saying, "If you have judged me to be faithful to the Lord, come to my house and stay." And she prevailed upon us.

Paul and Silas in Prison

¹⁶ As we were going to the place of prayer, we were met by a slave girl who had a spirit of divination and brought her owners much gain by fortune-telling. ¹⁷ She followed Paul and us, crying out, "These men are servants of the Most High God, who proclaim to you the way of salvation." ¹⁸ And this she kept doing for many days. Paul, having become greatly annoyed, turned and said to the spirit, "I command you in the name of Jesus Christ to come out of her." And it came out that very hour.

¹⁹ But when her owners saw that their hope of gain was gone, they seized Paul and Silas and dragged them into the marketplace

GETTING THE MESSAGE

Philippi was founded by the Greek king Philip II, father of Alexander the Great, in 356 B.C. Some 300 years later, in 42 B.C., it was in Philippi that Augustus Caesar defeated Brutus and Cassius after they had assassinated Julius Caesar. But the most significant event to occur in Philippi is recorded in 16:6–15, when Paul came to Philippi, making it the first European city to hear the Good News from this great ambassador of Christ.

before the rulers. ²⁰ And when they had brought them to the magistrates, they said, "These men are Jews, and they are disturbing our city. ²¹ They advocate customs that are not lawful for us as Romans to accept or practice." ²² The crowd joined in attacking them, and the magistrates tore the garments off them and gave orders to beat them with rods. ²³ And when they had inflicted many blows upon them, they threw them into prison, ordering the jailer to keep them safely. ²⁴ Having received this order, he put them into the inner prison and fastened their feet in the stocks.

The Philippian Jailer Converted

²⁵ About midnight Paul and Silas were praying and singing hymns to God, and the prisoners were listening to them, ²⁶ and suddenly there was a great earthquake, so that the foundations of the prison were shaken. And immediately all the doors were opened, and everyone's bonds were

unfastened. [27] When the jailer woke and saw that the prison doors were open, he drew his sword and was about to kill himself, supposing that the prisoners had escaped. [28] But Paul cried with a loud voice, "Do not harm yourself, for we are all here." [29] And the jailer called for lights and rushed in, and trembling with fear he fell down before Paul and Silas. [30] Then he brought them out and said, "Sirs, what must I do to be saved?" [31] And they said, "Believe in the Lord Jesus, and you will be saved, you and your household." [32] And they spoke the word of the Lord to him and to all who were in his house. [33] And he took them the same hour of the night and washed their wounds; and he was baptized at once, he and all his family. [34] Then he brought them up into his house and set food before them. And he rejoiced along with his entire household that he had believed in God.

[35] But when it was day, the magistrates sent the police, saying, "Let those men go." [36] And the jailer reported these words to Paul, saying, "The magistrates have sent to let you go. Therefore come out now and go in peace." [37] But Paul said to them, "They have beaten us publicly, uncondemned, men who are Roman citizens, and have thrown us into prison; and do they now throw us out secretly? No! Let them come themselves and take us out." [38] The police reported these words to the magistrates, and they were afraid when they heard that they were Roman citizens. [39] So they came and apologized to them. And they took them out and asked them to leave the city. [40] So they went out of the prison and visited Lydia. And when they had seen the brothers,[1] they encouraged them and departed.

Paul and Silas in Thessalonica

17 Now when they had passed through Amphipolis and Apollonia, they came to Thessalonica, where there was a synagogue of the Jews. [2] And Paul went in, as was his custom, and on three Sabbath days he reasoned with them from the Scriptures, [3] explaining and proving that it was necessary for the Christ to suffer and to rise from the dead, and saying, "This Jesus, whom I proclaim to you, is the Christ." [4] And some of them were persuaded and joined Paul and Silas, as did a great many of the devout

Greeks and not a few of the leading women. [5] But the Jews were jealous, and taking some wicked men of the rabble, they formed a mob, set the city in an uproar, and attacked the house of Jason, seeking to bring them out to the crowd. [6] And when they could not find them, they dragged Jason and some of the brothers before the city authorities, shouting, "These men who have turned the world upside down have come here also, [7] and Jason has received them, and they are all acting against the decrees of Caesar, saying that there is another king, Jesus." [8] And the people and the city authorities were disturbed when they heard these things. [9] And when they had taken money as security from Jason and the rest, they let them go.

GETTING THE MESSAGE

The Court of the Areopagus had authority over the civil and religious life of Athens. In Paul's day, it had a special interest in religion and morality. Paul preached at the Areopagus to a crowd that included philosophers (17:16–34).

Paul and Silas in Berea

[10] The brothers immediately sent Paul and Silas away by night to Berea, and when they arrived they went into the Jewish synagogue. [11] Now these Jews were more noble than those in Thessalonica; they received the word with all eagerness, examining the Scriptures daily to see if these things were so. [12] Many of them therefore believed, with not a few Greek women of high standing as well as men. [13] But when the Jews from Thessalonica learned that the word of God was proclaimed by Paul at Berea also, they came there too, agitating and stirring up the crowds. [14] Then the brothers immediately sent Paul off on his way to the sea, but Silas and Timothy remained there. [15] Those who conducted Paul brought him as far as Athens, and after receiving a command for Silas and Timothy to come to him as soon as possible, they departed.

Paul in Athens

[16] Now while Paul was waiting for them at Athens, his spirit was provoked within

---

[1] Or brothers and sisters; also 17:10, 14

him as he saw that the city was full of idols. ¹⁷ So he reasoned in the synagogue with the Jews and the devout persons, and in the marketplace every day with those who happened to be there. ¹⁸ Some of the Epicurean and Stoic philosophers also conversed with him. And some said, "What does this babbler wish to say?" Others said, "He seems to be a preacher of foreign divinities"—because he was preaching Jesus and the resurrection. ¹⁹ And they took him and

AQUILA AND PRISCILLA

Aquila and his wife, Priscilla (also called Prisca), were close friends and coworkers with the apostle Paul. Forced from Rome by the emperor Claudius, they fled to Corinth (18:1–2). Like Paul, who stayed in their home, they were tentmakers by trade. On his way back to Antioch, Paul left Priscilla and Aquila in Ephesus to establish the church in that city. There the godly couple taught the Christian way "more accurately" to a gifted Alexandrian disciple named Apollos (18:26). They were eventually able to return to Rome, where the church met in their home (Rom. 16:3–5). Paul's deep love and respect for Aquila and Priscilla is obvious in his letter to the Romans, where he declares that the couple "risked their necks" for his life (Rom. 16:3).

KEY REFERENCE: ROMANS 16:3–5

brought him to the Areopagus, saying, "May we know what this new teaching is that you are presenting? ²⁰ For you bring some strange things to our ears. We wish to know therefore what these things mean." ²¹ Now all the Athenians and the foreigners who lived there would spend their time in nothing except telling or hearing something new.

Paul Addresses the Areopagus

²² So Paul, standing in the midst of the Areopagus, said: "Men of Athens, I perceive

that in every way you are very religious. ²³ For as I passed along and observed the objects of your worship, I found also an altar with this inscription, 'To the unknown god.' What therefore you worship as unknown, this I proclaim to you. ²⁴ The God who made the world and everything in it, being Lord of heaven and earth, does not live in temples made by man, ²⁵ nor is he served by human hands, as though he needed anything, since he himself gives to all mankind life and breath and everything. ²⁶ And he made from one man every nation of mankind to live on all the face of the earth, having determined allotted periods and the boundaries of their dwelling place, ²⁷ that they should seek God, and perhaps feel their way toward him and find him. Yet he is actually not far from each one of us, ²⁸ for

"'In him we live and move and have our being';

as even some of your own poets have said,

"'For we are indeed his offspring.'

²⁹ Being then God's offspring, we ought not to think that the divine being is like gold or silver or stone, an image formed by the art and imagination of man. ³⁰ The times of ignorance God overlooked, but now he commands all people everywhere to repent, ³¹ because he has fixed a day on which he will judge the world in righteousness by a man whom he has appointed; and of this he has given assurance to all by raising him from the dead."

³² Now when they heard of the resurrection of the dead, some mocked. But others said, "We will hear you again about this." ³³ So Paul went out from their midst. ³⁴ But some men joined him and believed, among whom also were Dionysius the Areopagite and a woman named Damaris and others with them.

Paul in Corinth

18 After this Paul left Athens and went to Corinth. ² And he found a Jew named Aquila, a native of Pontus, recently come from Italy with his wife Priscilla, because Claudius had commanded all the Jews to leave Rome. And he went to see them, ³ and because he was of the same trade he stayed with them and worked, for they were tentmakers by trade. ⁴ And he reasoned in the synagogue every Sabbath, and tried to persuade Jews and Greeks.

⁵ When Silas and Timothy arrived from Macedonia, Paul was occupied with the word, testifying to the Jews that the Christ was Jesus. ⁶ And when they opposed and reviled him, he shook out his garments and said to them, "Your blood be on your own heads! I am innocent. From now on I will go to the Gentiles." ⁷ And he left there and went to the house of a man named Titius Justus, a worshiper of God. His house was next door to the synagogue. ⁸ Crispus, the ruler of the synagogue, believed in the Lord, together with his entire household. And many of the Corinthians hearing Paul believed and were baptized. ⁹ And the Lord said to Paul one night in a vision, "Do not be afraid, but go on speaking and do not be silent, ¹⁰ for I am with you, and no one will attack you to harm you, for I have many in this city who are my people." ¹¹ And he stayed a year and six months, teaching the word of God among them.

¹² But when Gallio was proconsul of Achaia, the Jews made a united attack on Paul and brought him before the tribunal, ¹³ saying, "This man is persuading people to worship God contrary to the law." ¹⁴ But when Paul was about to open his mouth, Gallio said to the Jews, "If it were a matter of wrongdoing or vicious crime, O Jews, I would have reason to accept your complaint. ¹⁵ But since it is a matter of questions about words and names and your own law, see to it yourselves. I refuse to be a judge of these things." ¹⁶ And he drove them from the tribunal. ¹⁷ And they all seized Sosthenes, the ruler of the synagogue, and beat him in front of the tribunal. But Gallio paid no attention to any of this.

Paul Returns to Antioch

¹⁸ After this, Paul stayed many days longer and then took leave of the brothers[1] and set sail for Syria, and with him Priscilla and Aquila. At Cenchreae he had cut his hair, for he was under a vow. ¹⁹ And they came to Ephesus, and he left them there, but he himself went into the synagogue and reasoned with the Jews. ²⁰ When they asked him to stay for a longer period, he declined. ²¹ But on taking leave of them he said, "I will return to you if God wills," and he set sail from Ephesus.

²² When he had landed at Caesarea, he went up and greeted the church, and then went down to Antioch. ²³ After spending some time there, he departed and went from one place to the next through the region of Galatia and Phrygia, strengthening all the disciples.

Apollos Speaks Boldly in Ephesus

²⁴ Now a Jew named Apollos, a native of Alexandria, came to Ephesus. He was an eloquent man, competent in the Scriptures. ²⁵ He had been instructed in the way of the Lord. And being fervent in spirit, he spoke and taught accurately the things concerning Jesus, though he knew only the baptism of

John. ²⁶ He began to speak boldly in the synagogue, but when Priscilla and Aquila heard him, they took him aside and explained to him the way of God more accurately. ²⁷ And when he wished to cross to Achaia, the brothers encouraged him and wrote to the disciples to welcome him. When he arrived, he greatly helped those who through grace had believed, ²⁸ for he powerfully refuted the Jews in public, showing by the Scriptures that the Christ was Jesus.

Paul in Ephesus

19 And it happened that while Apollos was at Corinth, Paul passed through the inland country and came to Ephesus. There he found some disciples. ² And he said to them, "Did you receive the Holy Spirit when you believed?" And they said, "No, we have not even heard that there is a Holy Spirit." ³ And he said, "Into what then were you baptized?" They said, "Into John's baptism." ⁴ And Paul said, "John baptized with

[1] Or brothers and sisters; also 18:27

the baptism of repentance, telling the people to believe in the one who was to come after him, that is, Jesus." **5** On hearing this, they were baptized in the name of the Lord Jesus. **6** And when Paul had laid his hands on them, the Holy Spirit came on them, and they began speaking in tongues and prophesying. **7** There were about twelve men in all.

8 And he entered the synagogue and for three months spoke boldly, reasoning and persuading them about the kingdom of God. **9** But when some became stubborn and continued in unbelief, speaking evil of the Way before the congregation, he withdrew from them and took the disciples with him, reasoning daily in the hall of Tyrannus. **10** This

GETTING THE MESSAGE

In the Greco-Roman world, many used **magic** to heal, to curse, or to control evil spirits. Paul encountered such magicians on his missionary journeys (8:9–24; 13:6–12). He showed how Jesus' power greatly surpasses any magical spells, and many former magicians became believers (19:17–20).

continued for two years, so that all the residents of Asia heard the word of the Lord, both Jews and Greeks.

The Sons of Sceva

11 And God was doing extraordinary miracles by the hands of Paul, **12** so that even handkerchiefs or aprons that had touched his skin were carried away to the sick, and their diseases left them and the evil spirits came out of them. **13** Then some of the itinerant Jewish exorcists undertook to invoke the name of the Lord Jesus over those who had evil spirits, saying, "I adjure you by the Jesus whom Paul proclaims." **14** Seven sons of a Jewish high priest named Sceva were doing this. **15** But the evil spirit answered them, "Jesus I know, and Paul I recognize, but who are you?" **16** And the man in whom was the evil spirit leaped on them, mastered all of them and overpowered them, so that they fled out of that house naked and wounded. **17** And this became known to all the residents of Ephesus, both Jews

and Greeks. And fear fell upon them all, and the name of the Lord Jesus was extolled. **18** Also many of those who were now believers came, confessing and divulging their practices. **19** And a number of those who had practiced magic arts brought their books together and burned them in the sight of all. And they counted the value of them and found it came to fifty thousand pieces of silver. **20** So the word of the Lord continued to increase and prevail mightily.

A Riot at Ephesus

21 Now after these events Paul resolved in the Spirit to pass through Macedonia and Achaia and go to Jerusalem, saying, "After I have been there, I must also see Rome." **22** And having sent into Macedonia two of his helpers, Timothy and Erastus, he himself stayed in Asia for a while.

23 About that time there arose no little disturbance concerning the Way. **24** For a man named Demetrius, a silversmith, who made silver shrines of Artemis, brought no little business to the craftsmen. **25** These he gathered together, with the workmen in similar trades, and said, "Men, you know that from this business we have our wealth. **26** And you see and hear that not only in Ephesus but in almost all of Asia this Paul has persuaded and turned away a great many people, saying that gods made with hands are not gods. **27** And there is danger not only that this trade of ours may come into disrepute but also that the temple of the great goddess Artemis may be counted as nothing, and that she may even be deposed from her magnificence, she whom all Asia and the world worship."

28 When they heard this they were enraged and were crying out, "Great is Artemis of the Ephesians!" **29** So the city was filled with the confusion, and they rushed together into the theater, dragging with them Gaius and Aristarchus, Macedonians who were Paul's companions in travel. **30** But when Paul wished to go in among the crowd, the disciples would not let him. **31** And even some of the Asiarchs,[1] who were friends of his, sent to him and were urging him not to venture into the theater. **32** Now some cried out one thing, some another, for the assembly was in confusion, and most of them did not know why they had come together. **33** Some

[1] That is, high-ranking officers of the province of Asia

of the crowd prompted Alexander, whom the Jews had put forward. And Alexander, motioning with his hand, wanted to make a defense to the crowd. **34** But when they recognized that he was a Jew, for about two hours they all cried out with one voice, "Great is Artemis of the Ephesians!"

35 And when the town clerk had quieted the crowd, he said, "Men of Ephesus, who is there who does not know that the city of the Ephesians is temple keeper of the great Artemis, and of the sacred stone that fell from the sky? **36** Seeing then that these things cannot be denied, you ought to be quiet and do nothing rash. **37** For you have brought these men here who are neither sacrilegious nor blasphemers of our goddess. **38** If therefore Demetrius and the craftsmen with him have a complaint against anyone, the courts are open, and there are proconsuls. Let them bring charges against one another. **39** But if you seek anything further, it shall be settled in the regular assembly. **40** For we really are in danger of being charged with rioting today, since there is no cause that we can give to justify this commotion." **41** And when he had said these things, he dismissed the assembly.

Paul in Macedonia and Greece

20 After the uproar ceased, Paul sent for the disciples, and after encouraging them, he said farewell and departed for Macedonia. **2** When he had gone through those regions and had given them much encouragement, he came to Greece. **3** There he spent three months, and when a plot was made against him by the Jews as he was about to set sail for Syria, he decided to return through Macedonia. **4** Sopater the Berean, son of Pyrrhus, accompanied him; and of the Thessalonians, Aristarchus and Secundus; and Gaius of Derbe, and Timothy; and the Asians, Tychicus and Trophimus. **5** These went on ahead and were waiting for us at Troas, **6** but we sailed away from Philippi after the days of Unleavened Bread, and in five days we came to them at Troas, where we stayed for seven days.

Eutychus Raised from the Dead

7 On the first day of the week, when we were gathered together to break bread, Paul talked with them, intending to depart on the next day, and he prolonged his speech until midnight. **8** There were many lamps in the upper room where we were gathered. **9** And a young man named Eutychus, sitting at the window, sank into a deep sleep as Paul talked still longer. And being overcome by sleep, he fell down from the third story and was taken up dead. **10** But Paul went down and bent over him, and taking him in his arms, said, "Do not be alarmed, for his life is in him." **11** And when Paul had gone up and had broken bread and eaten, he conversed with them a long while, until daybreak, and so departed. **12** And they took the youth away alive, and were not a little comforted.

13 But going ahead to the ship, we set sail for Assos, intending to take Paul aboard there, for so he had arranged, intending himself to go by land. **14** And when he met us at Assos, we took him on board and went

GETTING THE MESSAGE

Elders and **overseers** (20:17, 28) are probably two different terms for the same kind of church leader. In first-century Israel, an elder would have been an older, more mature person to whom people looked for leadership. An overseer would have been someone who was responsible for people or property. Both words describe a person who takes good care of someone or something.

to Mitylene. **15** And sailing from there we came the following day opposite Chios; the next day we touched at Samos; and the day after that we went to Miletus. **16** For Paul had decided to sail past Ephesus, so that he might not have to spend time in Asia, for he was hastening to be at Jerusalem, if possible, on the day of Pentecost.

Paul Speaks to the Ephesian Elders

17 Now from Miletus he sent to Ephesus and called the elders of the church to come to him. **18** And when they came to him, he said to them:

"You yourselves know how I lived among you the whole time from the first day that I set foot in Asia, **19** serving the Lord with all humility and with tears and with trials that happened to me through the plots of the Jews; **20** how I did not shrink from declaring to you anything that was profitable, and teaching you in public and from house to house, **21** testifying both to Jews and to Greeks of repentance toward God and of faith in our Lord Jesus Christ. **22** And now, behold, I am going to Jerusalem, constrained by the Spirit, not knowing what will happen to me there, **23** except that the Holy Spirit testifies to me in every city that imprisonment and afflictions await me. **24** But I do not account my life of any value nor as precious to myself, if only I may

PROFILE
LUKE

Luke was a doctor (Col. 4:14) and a faithful companion of Paul, accompanying him on several journeys. He was with Paul throughout his two-year imprisonments in both Caesarea and Rome. He is the author of the Gospel bearing his name and the book of Acts, where he records his travels with Paul. Little else is known about Luke. Most scholars believe that he was a Gentile. This is based in part on the fact that Paul does not include Luke among the "men of the circumcision" who were his fellow workers (Col. 4:10–11). How Luke came to know Christ is not revealed, though his thorough acquaintance with the Old Testament suggests that he may have been a "God-fearer" like Cornelius before becoming a Christian.

KEY REFERENCE: ACTS 21:1–8

finish my course and the ministry that I received from the Lord Jesus, to testify to the gospel of the grace of God. **25** And now, behold, I know that none of you among whom I have gone about proclaiming the kingdom will see my face again. **26** Therefore I testify to you this day that I am innocent of the blood of all, **27** for I did not shrink from declaring to you the whole counsel of God. **28** Pay careful attention to yourselves and to all the flock, in which the Holy Spirit has made you overseers, to care for the church

of God, which he obtained with his own blood. **29** I know that after my departure fierce wolves will come in among you, not sparing the flock; **30** and from among your own selves will arise men speaking twisted things, to draw away the disciples after them. **31** Therefore be alert, remembering that for three years I did not cease night or day to admonish every one with tears. **32** And now I commend you to God and to the word of his grace, which is able to build you up and to give you the inheritance among all those who are sanctified. **33** I coveted no one's silver or gold or apparel. **34** You yourselves know that these hands ministered to my necessities and to those who were with me. **35** In all things I have shown you that by working hard in this way we must help the weak and remember

▶ **GETTING THE MESSAGE**

The island of Rhodes, which Paul visited toward the end of his third missionary journey (21:1), was famous for the Colossus of Rhodes, considered one of the Seven Wonders of the Ancient World. This statue, standing nearly 110 feet (34 m) high, was built in about 300 B.C. to commemorate Rhodes's victory over the neighboring island of Cyprus. It stood for only 56 years before being toppled by an earthquake.

the words of the Lord Jesus, how he himself said, 'It is more blessed to give than to receive.'"

36 And when he had said these things, he knelt down and prayed with them all. **37** And there was much weeping on the part of all; they embraced Paul and kissed him, **38** being sorrowful most of all because of the word he had spoken, that they would not see his face again. And they accompanied him to the ship.

Paul Goes to Jerusalem

21 And when we had parted from them and set sail, we came by a straight course to Cos, and the next day to Rhodes, and from there to Patara. **2** And having found a ship crossing to Phoenicia, we went aboard and set sail. **3** When we had come in sight of Cyprus, leaving it on the left we sailed to Syria and landed at Tyre, for there the ship was to unload its cargo. [4] And having sought out the disciples, we stayed there for seven days. And through the Spirit they were telling Paul not to go on to Jerusalem. [5] When our days there were ended, we departed and went on our journey, and they all, with wives and children, accompanied us until we were outside the city. And kneeling down on the beach, we prayed [6] and said farewell to one another. Then we went on board the ship, and they returned home.

[7] When we had finished the voyage from Tyre, we arrived at Ptolemais, and we greeted the brothers[1] and stayed with them for one day. [8] On the next day we departed and came to Caesarea, and we entered the house of Philip the evangelist, who was one of the seven, and stayed with him. [9] He had four unmarried daughters, who prophesied. [10] While we were staying for many days, a prophet named Agabus came down from Judea. [11] And coming to us, he took Paul's belt and bound his own feet and hands and said, "Thus says the Holy Spirit, 'This is how the Jews at Jerusalem will bind the man who owns this belt and deliver him into the hands of the Gentiles.'" [12] When we heard this, we and the people there urged him not to go up to Jerusalem. [13] Then Paul answered, "What are you doing, weeping and breaking my heart? For I am ready not only to be imprisoned but even to die in Jerusalem for the name of the Lord Jesus." [14] And since he would not be persuaded, we ceased and said, "Let the will of the Lord be done."

[15] After these days we got ready and went up to Jerusalem. [16] And some of the disciples from Caesarea went with us, bringing us to the house of Mnason of Cyprus, an early disciple, with whom we should lodge.

Paul Visits James

[17] When we had come to Jerusalem, the brothers received us gladly. [18] On the following day Paul went in with us to James, and all the elders were present. [19] After greeting them, he related one by one the things that God had done among the Gentiles through his ministry. [20] And when they heard it, they glorified God. And they said to him, "You see, brother, how many thousands there are among the Jews of those who have believed. They are all zealous for the law, [21] and they have been told about you that you teach all the Jews who are among the Gentiles to forsake Moses, telling them not to circumcise their children or walk according to our customs. [22] What then is to be done? They will certainly hear that you have come. [23] Do therefore what we tell you. We have four men who are under a vow; [24] take these men and purify yourself along with them and pay their expenses, so that they may shave their heads. Thus all will know that there is nothing in what they have been told about you, but that you yourself also live in observance of the law. [25] But as for the Gentiles who have believed, we have sent a letter with our judgment that they should abstain from what has been sacrificed to idols, and from blood, and from what has been strangled, and from sexual immorality." [26] Then Paul took the men, and the next day he purified himself along with them and went into the temple, giving notice when the days of purification would be fulfilled and the offering presented for each one of them.

Paul Arrested in the Temple

[27] When the seven days were almost completed, the Jews from Asia, seeing him in the temple, stirred up the whole crowd and laid hands on him, [28] crying out, "Men of Israel, help! This is the man who is teaching everyone everywhere against the people and the law and this place. Moreover, he even brought Greeks into the temple and has defiled this holy place." [29] For they had previously seen Trophimus the Ephesian with him in the city, and they supposed that Paul had brought him into the temple. [30] Then all the city was stirred up, and the people ran together. They seized Paul and dragged him out of the temple, and at once the gates were shut. [31] And as they were seeking to kill him, word came to the tribune of the cohort that all Jerusalem was in confusion. [32] He at once took soldiers and centurions and ran down to them. And when they saw the tribune and the soldiers, they stopped beating Paul. [33] Then the tribune came up and arrested him and ordered him to be bound with two chains. He inquired who he was and what he had

[1] Or brothers and sisters; also 21:17

done. [34] Some in the crowd were shouting one thing, some another. And as he could not learn the facts because of the uproar, he ordered him to be brought into the barracks. [35] And when he came to the steps, he was actually carried by the soldiers because of the violence of the crowd, [36] for the mob of the people followed, crying out, "Away with him!"

Paul Speaks to the People

[37] As Paul was about to be brought into the barracks, he said to the tribune, "May I say something to you?" And he said, "Do you know Greek? [38] Are you not the Egyptian, then, who recently stirred up a revolt and led the four thousand men of the Assassins out into the wilderness?" [39] Paul replied, "I am

> ### GETTING THE MESSAGE
>
> Paul says that he was **born in Tarsus** but was **brought up in this city**, referring to Jerusalem (22:3). In Tarsus, Paul would have spoken Greek. As a Jew, he was also fluent in Aramaic. Growing up in Jerusalem, Paul learned from Gamaliel, the greatest Jewish scholar of his day. The Lord used Paul's unique background to reach the Gentiles of the Roman Empire with the good news about the Jewish Messiah who was also the Savior of all people, Jews and Gentiles alike.

a Jew, from Tarsus in Cilicia, a citizen of no obscure city. I beg you, permit me to speak to the people." [40] And when he had given him permission, Paul, standing on the steps, motioned with his hand to the people. And when there was a great hush, he addressed them in the Hebrew language, saying:

22 "Brothers and fathers, hear the defense that I now make before you." [2] And when they heard that he was addressing them in the Hebrew language, they became even more quiet. And he said:

[3] "I am a Jew, born in Tarsus in Cilicia, but brought up in this city, educated at the feet of Gamaliel according to the strict manner of the law of our fathers, being zealous for God as all of you are this day. [4] I persecuted this Way to the death, binding and delivering to prison both men and women, [5] as the high priest and the whole council of elders can bear me witness. From them I received letters to the brothers, and I journeyed toward Damascus to take those also who were there and bring them in bonds to Jerusalem to be punished.

[6] "As I was on my way and drew near to Damascus, about noon a great light from heaven suddenly shone around me. [7] And I fell to the ground and heard a voice saying to me, 'Saul, Saul, why are you persecuting me?' [8] And I answered, 'Who are you, Lord?' And he said to me, 'I am Jesus of Nazareth, whom you are persecuting.' [9] Now those who were with me saw the light but did not understand the voice of the one who was speaking to me. [10] And I said, 'What shall I do, Lord?' And the Lord said to me, 'Rise, and go into Damascus, and there you will be told all that is appointed for you to do.' [11] And since I could not see because of the brightness of that light, I was led by the hand by those who were with me, and came into Damascus.

[12] "And one Ananias, a devout man according to the law, well spoken of by all the Jews who lived there, [13] came to me, and standing by me said to me, 'Brother Saul, receive your sight.' And at that very hour I received my sight and saw him. [14] And he said, 'The God of our fathers appointed you to know his will, to see the Righteous One and to hear a voice from his mouth; [15] for you will be a witness for him to everyone of what you have seen and heard. [16] And now why do you wait? Rise and be baptized and wash away your sins, calling on his name.'

[17] "When I had returned to Jerusalem and was praying in the temple, I fell into a trance [18] and saw him saying to me, 'Make haste and get out of Jerusalem quickly, because they will not accept your testimony about me.' [19] And I said, 'Lord, they themselves know that in one synagogue after another I imprisoned and beat those who believed in you. [20] And when the blood of Stephen your witness was being shed, I myself was standing by and approving and watching over the garments of those who killed him.' [21] And he said to me, 'Go, for I will send you far away to the Gentiles.'"

Paul and the Roman Tribune

[22] Up to this word they listened to him. Then they raised their voices and said, "Away with such a fellow from the earth! For he

should not be allowed to live." **23** And as they were shouting and throwing off their cloaks and flinging dust into the air, **24** the tribune ordered him to be brought into the barracks, saying that he should be examined by flogging, to find out why they were shouting against him like this. **25** But when they had stretched him out for the whips, Paul said to the centurion who was standing by, "Is it lawful for you to flog a man who is a Roman citizen and uncondemned?" **26** When the centurion heard this, he went to the tribune and said to him, "What are you about to do? For this man is a Roman citizen." **27** So the tribune came and said to him, "Tell me, are you a Roman citizen?" And he said, "Yes." **28** The tribune answered, "I bought this citizenship for a large sum." Paul said, "But I am a citizen by birth." **29** So those who were about to examine him withdrew from him immediately, and the tribune also was afraid, for he realized that Paul was a Roman citizen and that he had bound him.

Paul Before the Council

30 But on the next day, desiring to know the real reason why he was being accused by the Jews, he unbound him and commanded the chief priests and all the council to meet, and he brought Paul down and set him before them.

23 And looking intently at the council, Paul said, "Brothers, I have lived my life before God in all good conscience up to this day." **2** And the high priest Ananias commanded those who stood by him to strike him on the mouth. **3** Then Paul said to him, "God is going to strike you, you whitewashed wall! Are you sitting to judge me according to the law, and yet contrary to the law you order me to be struck?" **4** Those who stood by said, "Would you revile God's high priest?" **5** And Paul said, "I did not know, brothers, that he was the high priest, for it is written, 'You shall not speak evil of a ruler of your people.'"

6 Now when Paul perceived that one part were Sadducees and the other Pharisees, he cried out in the council, "Brothers, I am a Pharisee, a son of Pharisees. It is with respect to the hope and the resurrection of the dead that I am on trial." **7** And when he had said this, a dissension arose between the Pharisees and the Sadducees, and the assembly was divided. **8** For the Sadducees

say that there is no resurrection, nor angel, nor spirit, but the Pharisees acknowledge them all. **9** Then a great clamor arose, and some of the scribes of the Pharisees' party stood up and contended sharply, "We find nothing wrong in this man. What if a spirit or an angel spoke to him?" **10** And when the dissension became violent, the tribune, afraid that Paul would be torn to pieces by them, commanded the soldiers to go down and take him away from among them by force and bring him into the barracks.

11 The following night the Lord stood by him and said, "Take courage, for as you have testified to the facts about me in Jerusalem, so you must testify also in Rome."

A Plot to Kill Paul

12 When it was day, the Jews made a plot and bound themselves by an oath neither to eat nor drink till they had killed Paul.

13 There were more than forty who made this conspiracy. **14** They went to the chief priests and elders and said, "We have strictly bound ourselves by an oath to taste no food till we have killed Paul. **15** Now therefore you, along with the council, give notice to the tribune to bring him down to you, as though you were going to determine his case more exactly. And we are ready to kill him before he comes near."

16 Now the son of Paul's sister heard of their ambush, so he went and entered the barracks and told Paul. **17** Paul called one of the centurions and said, "Take this young man to the tribune, for he has something to tell him." **18** So he took him and brought him to the tribune and said, "Paul the prisoner called me and asked me to bring this young man to you, as he has something to say to you." **19** The tribune took him by the hand, and going aside asked him privately, "What is it that you have to tell me?" **20** And he said, "The Jews have agreed to ask you to bring Paul down to the council tomorrow, as though they were going to inquire somewhat more closely about him. **21** But do not be persuaded by them, for more than forty of their men are lying in ambush for him, who have bound themselves by an oath neither to eat nor drink till they have killed him. And now they are ready, waiting for your consent." **22** So the tribune dismissed the young man, charging him, "Tell no one that you have informed me of these things."

Paul Sent to Felix the Governor

23 Then he called two of the centurions and said, "Get ready two hundred soldiers, with seventy horsemen and two hundred spearmen to go as far as Caesarea at the third hour of the night.[1] **24** Also provide mounts for Paul to ride and bring him safely to Felix

> ### GETTING THE MESSAGE
>
> **What is "the Way?"** In Acts, "the Way" appears six times (9:2; 19:9, 23; 22:4; 24:14, 22). People who belonged to the Way were followers of Christ. It means the way of salvation (16:17) and/or the true way of life in relation to God (see 18:25–26).

the governor." **25** And he wrote a letter to this effect:

26 "Claudius Lysias, to his Excellency the governor Felix, greetings. **27** This man was seized by the Jews and was about to be killed by them when I came upon them with the soldiers and rescued him, having learned that he was a Roman citizen. **28** And desiring to know the charge for which they were accusing him, I brought him down to their council. **29** I found that he was being accused about questions of their law, but charged with nothing deserving death or imprisonment. **30** And when it was disclosed to me that there would be a plot against the man, I sent him to you at once, ordering his accusers also to state before you what they have against him."

31 So the soldiers, according to their instructions, took Paul and brought him by night to Antipatris. **32** And on the next

day they returned to the barracks, letting the horsemen go on with him. **33** When they had come to Caesarea and delivered the letter to the governor, they presented Paul also before him. **34** On reading the letter, he asked what province he was from. And when he learned that he was from Cilicia, **35** he said, "I will give you a hearing when your accusers arrive." And he commanded him to be guarded in Herod's praetorium.

Paul Before Felix at Caesarea

24 And after five days the high priest Ananias came down with some elders and a spokesman, one Tertullus. They laid before the governor their case against Paul. **2** And when he had been summoned, Tertullus began to accuse him, saying:

"Since through you we enjoy much peace, and since by your foresight, most excellent Felix, reforms are being made for this nation, **3** in every way and everywhere we accept this with all gratitude. **4** But, to detain you no further, I beg you in your kindness to hear us briefly. **5** For we have found this man a plague, one who stirs up riots among all the Jews throughout the world and is a ringleader of the sect of the Nazarenes. **6** He even tried to profane the temple, but we seized him. **8** By examining him yourself you will be able to find out from him about everything of which we accuse him."

9 The Jews also joined in the charge, affirming that all these things were so.

10 And when the governor had nodded to him to speak, Paul replied:

"Knowing that for many years you have been a judge over this nation, I cheerfully make my defense. **11** You can verify that it is not more than twelve days since I went up to worship in Jerusalem, **12** and they did not find me disputing with anyone or stirring up a crowd, either in the temple or in the synagogues or in the city. **13** Neither can they prove to you what they now bring up against me. **14** But this I confess to you, that according to the Way, which they call a sect, I worship the God of our fathers, believing everything laid down by the Law and written in the Prophets, **15** having a hope in God, which these men themselves accept, that there will be a resurrection of both the just and the unjust. **16** So I always take pains to have a clear conscience toward both God

[1] That is, 9 P.M.

and man. ¹⁷ Now after several years I came to bring alms to my nation and to present offerings. ¹⁸ While I was doing this, they found me purified in the temple, without any crowd or tumult. But some Jews from Asia— ¹⁹ they ought to be here before you and to make an accusation, should they have anything against me. ²⁰ Or else let these men themselves say what wrongdoing they found when I stood before the council, ²¹ other than this one thing that I cried out while standing among them: 'It is with respect to the resurrection of the dead that I am on trial before you this day.'"

Paul Kept in Custody

²² But Felix, having a rather accurate knowledge of the Way, put them off, saying, "When Lysias the tribune comes down, I will decide your case." ²³ Then he gave orders to the centurion that he should be kept in custody but have some liberty, and that none of his friends should be prevented from attending to his needs.

²⁴ After some days Felix came with his wife Drusilla, who was Jewish, and he sent for Paul and heard him speak about faith in Christ Jesus. ²⁵ And as he reasoned about righteousness and self-control and the coming judgment, Felix was alarmed and said, "Go away for the present. When I get an opportunity I will summon you." ²⁶ At the same time he hoped that money would be given him by Paul. So he sent for him often and conversed with him. ²⁷ When two years had elapsed, Felix was succeeded by Porcius Festus. And desiring to do the Jews a favor, Felix left Paul in prison.

Paul Appeals to Caesar

25 Now three days after Festus had arrived in the province, he went up to Jerusalem from Caesarea. ² And the chief priests and the principal men of the Jews laid out their case against Paul, and they urged him, ³ asking as a favor against Paul that he summon him to Jerusalem— because they were planning an ambush to kill him on the way. ⁴ Festus replied that Paul was being kept at Caesarea and that he himself intended to go there shortly. ⁵ "So," said he, "let the men of authority among you go down with me, and if there is anything wrong about the man, let them bring charges against him."

⁶ After he stayed among them not more than eight or ten days, he went down to Caesarea. And the next day he took his seat on the tribunal and ordered Paul to be brought. ⁷ When he had arrived, the Jews who had come down from Jerusalem stood around him, bringing many and serious charges against him that they could not prove. ⁸ Paul argued in his defense, "Neither against the law of the Jews, nor against the temple, nor against Caesar have I committed any offense." ⁹ But Festus, wishing to do the Jews a favor, said to Paul, "Do you wish to go up to Jerusalem and there be tried on these charges before me?" ¹⁰ But Paul said, "I am standing before Caesar's tribunal, where I ought to be tried. To the Jews I have done no wrong, as you yourself know very well. ¹¹ If then I am a wrongdoer and have committed anything for which I deserve to die, I do not seek to escape death. But if there is nothing to their charges against me, no one can give me up to them. I appeal to Caesar." ¹² Then Festus, when he had conferred with his council, answered, "To Caesar you have appealed; to Caesar you shall go."

Paul Before Agrippa and Bernice

¹³ Now when some days had passed, Agrippa the king and Bernice arrived at Caesarea and greeted Festus. ¹⁴ And as they stayed there many days, Festus laid Paul's case before the king, saying, "There is a man left prisoner by Felix, ¹⁵ and when I was at Jerusalem, the chief priests and the elders of the Jews laid out their case against him, asking for a sentence of condemnation against him. ¹⁶ I answered them that it was not the custom of the Romans to give up anyone before the accused met the accusers face to face and had opportunity to make his defense concerning the charge laid against him. ¹⁷ So when they came together here, I made no delay, but on the next day took my seat on the tribunal and ordered the man to be brought. ¹⁸ When the accusers stood up, they brought no charge in his case of such evils as I supposed. ¹⁹ Rather they had certain points of dispute with him about their own religion and about a certain Jesus, who was dead, but whom Paul asserted to be alive. ²⁰ Being at a loss how to investigate these questions, I asked whether he wanted to go to Jerusalem and

be tried there regarding them. ²¹But when Paul had appealed to be kept in custody for the decision of the emperor, I ordered him to be held until I could send him to Caesar." ²²Then Agrippa said to Festus, "I would like to hear the man myself." "Tomorrow," said he, "you will hear him."

²³So on the next day Agrippa and Bernice came with great pomp, and they entered the audience hall with the military tribunes and the prominent men of the city. Then, at the command of Festus, Paul was brought

---

PROFILE

HEROD AGRIPPA II

Herod Agrippa II was the son of Herod Agrippa I and the great-grandson of Herod the Great. Following the death of his father, Agrippa II ruled over several minor territories. He had authority over the temple in Jerusalem, including the right to appoint the high priest. Festus, a Roman unfamiliar with the Jewish faith, sought Agrippa's advice regarding Paul's case (chs. 25–26). While defending himself before Agrippa, Paul presented a detailed explanation of the gospel. Though Agrippa resisted Paul's appeal to believe in Christ, he listened sympathetically to his defense (26:28). He said that if Paul had not appealed to Caesar, he could have been released.

KEY REFERENCE: ACTS 26:27–32

---

in. ²⁴And Festus said, "King Agrippa and all who are present with us, you see this man about whom the whole Jewish people petitioned me, both in Jerusalem and here, shouting that he ought not to live any longer. ²⁵But I found that he had done nothing deserving death. And as he himself appealed to the emperor, I decided to go ahead and send him. ²⁶But I have nothing definite to write to my lord about him. Therefore I have brought him before you all, and especially before you, King Agrippa, so that, after we have examined him, I may

have something to write. ²⁷For it seems to me unreasonable, in sending a prisoner, not to indicate the charges against him."

Paul's Defense Before Agrippa

26 So Agrippa said to Paul, "You have permission to speak for yourself." Then Paul stretched out his hand and made his defense:

²"I consider myself fortunate that it is before you, King Agrippa, I am going to make my defense today against all the accusations of the Jews, ³especially because you are familiar with all the customs and controversies of the Jews. Therefore I beg you to listen to me patiently.

⁴"My manner of life from my youth, spent from the beginning among my own nation and in Jerusalem, is known by all the Jews. ⁵They have known for a long time, if they are willing to testify, that according to the strictest party of our religion I have lived as a Pharisee. ⁶And now I stand here on trial because of my hope in the promise made by God to our fathers, ⁷to which our twelve tribes hope to attain, as they earnestly worship night and day. And for this hope I am accused by Jews, O king! ⁸Why is it thought incredible by any of you that God raises the dead?

⁹"I myself was convinced that I ought to do many things in opposing the name of Jesus of Nazareth. ¹⁰And I did so in Jerusalem. I not only locked up many of the saints in prison after receiving authority from the chief priests, but when they were put to death I cast my vote against them. ¹¹And I punished them often in all the synagogues and tried to make them blaspheme, and in raging fury against them I persecuted them even to foreign cities.

Paul Tells of His Conversion

¹²"In this connection I journeyed to Damascus with the authority and commission of the chief priests. ¹³At midday, O king, I saw on the way a light from heaven, brighter than the sun, that shone around me and those who journeyed with me. ¹⁴And when we had all fallen to the ground, I heard a voice saying to me in the Hebrew language, 'Saul, Saul, why are you persecuting me? It is hard for you to kick against the goads.' ¹⁵And I said, 'Who are you, Lord?' And the Lord said, 'I am Jesus whom you are persecuting.

[16] But rise and stand upon your feet, for I have appeared to you for this purpose, to appoint you as a servant and witness to the things in which you have seen me and to those in which I will appear to you, [17] delivering you from your people and from the Gentiles—to whom I am sending you [18] to open their eyes, so that they may turn from darkness to light and from the power of Satan to God, that they may receive forgiveness of sins and a place among those who are sanctified by faith in me.'

[19] "Therefore, O King Agrippa, I was not disobedient to the heavenly vision, [20] but declared first to those in Damascus, then in Jerusalem and throughout all the region of Judea, and also to the Gentiles, that they should repent and turn to God, performing deeds in keeping with their repentance. [21] For this reason the Jews seized me in the temple and tried to kill me. [22] To this day I have had the help that comes from God, and so I stand here testifying both to small and great, saying nothing but what the prophets and Moses said would come to pass: [23] that the Christ must suffer and that, by being the first to rise from the dead, he would proclaim light both to our people and to the Gentiles."

[24] And as he was saying these things in his defense, Festus said with a loud voice, "Paul, you are out of your mind; your great learning is driving you out of your mind." [25] But Paul said, "I am not out of my mind, most excellent Festus, but I am speaking true and rational words. [26] For the king knows about these things, and to him I speak boldly. For I am persuaded that none of these things has escaped his notice, for this has not been done in a corner. [27] King Agrippa, do you believe the prophets? I know that you believe." [28] And Agrippa said to Paul, "In a short time would you persuade me to be a Christian?" [29] And Paul said, "Whether short or long, I would to God that not only you but also all who hear me this day might become such as I am—except for these chains."

[30] Then the king rose, and the governor and Bernice and those who were sitting with them. [31] And when they had withdrawn, they said to one another, "This man is doing nothing to deserve death or imprisonment." [32] And Agrippa said to Festus, "This man could have been set free if he had not appealed to Caesar."

Paul Sails for Rome

27 And when it was decided that we should sail for Italy, they delivered Paul and some other prisoners to a centurion of the Augustan Cohort named Julius. [2] And embarking in a ship of Adramyttium, which was about to sail to the ports along the coast of Asia, we put to sea, accompanied by Aristarchus, a Macedonian from Thessalonica. [3] The next day we put in at Sidon. And Julius treated Paul kindly and gave him leave to go to his friends and be cared for. [4] And putting out to sea from there we sailed under the lee of Cyprus, because the winds were against us. [5] And when we had sailed across the open sea along the

> ### GETTING THE MESSAGE
>
> **Kicking against the goads.** Goads were long, sharpened sticks used to prod oxen when they were hitched to yokes. Not wanting to be jabbed again with the stick, the ox would kick against it. It would soon learn that it was better to accept the direction of the farmer than to "kick against the goad." In this context of 26:14, the expression means that it is foolish and futile to resist God's will.

coast of Cilicia and Pamphylia, we came to Myra in Lycia. [6] There the centurion found a ship of Alexandria sailing for Italy and put us on board. [7] We sailed slowly for a number of days and arrived with difficulty off Cnidus, and as the wind did not allow us to go farther, we sailed under the lee of Crete off Salmone. [8] Coasting along it with difficulty, we came to a place called Fair Havens, near which was the city of Lasea.

[9] Since much time had passed, and the voyage was now dangerous because even the Fast[1] was already over, Paul advised them, [10] saying, "Sirs, I perceive that the voyage will be with injury and much loss, not only of the cargo and the ship, but also of our lives." [11] But the centurion paid more attention to the pilot and to the owner of the ship than to what Paul said. [12] And because

[1] That is, the Day of Atonement (see Leviticus 16)

the harbor was not suitable to spend the winter in, the majority decided to put out to sea from there, on the chance that somehow they could reach Phoenix, a harbor of Crete, facing both southwest and northwest, and spend the winter there.

The Storm at Sea

13 Now when the south wind blew gently, supposing that they had obtained their purpose, they weighed anchor and sailed along Crete, close to the shore. **14** But soon a tempestuous wind, called the northeaster, struck down from the land. **15** And when the ship was caught and could not face the wind, we gave way to it and were driven along. **16** Running under the lee of a small island called Cauda, we managed with difficulty to secure the ship's boat. **17** After hoisting it up, they used supports to undergird

> ### GETTING THE MESSAGE
>
> Running aground on the **Syrtis** (27:17) was a real fear for mariners on the Mediterranean Sea in New Testament times. The Syrtis was an extensive sandbar off the coast of North Africa. During a storm, if a ship was not properly anchored it could be carried for miles off course and into dangerous shallow waters such as the Syrtis.

the ship. Then, fearing that they would run aground on the Syrtis, they lowered the gear, and thus they were driven along. **18** Since we were violently storm-tossed, they began the next day to jettison the cargo. **19** And on the third day they threw the ship's tackle overboard with their own hands. **20** When neither sun nor stars appeared for many days, and no small tempest lay on us, all hope of our being saved was at last abandoned.

21 Since they had been without food for a long time, Paul stood up among them and said, "Men, you should have listened to me and not have set sail from Crete and incurred this injury and loss. **22** Yet now I urge you to take heart, for there will be no loss of life among you, but only of the ship. **23** For this very night there stood before me an angel of the God to whom I belong and whom I worship, **24** and he said, 'Do not be afraid, Paul; you must stand before Caesar.

And behold, God has granted you all those who sail with you.' **25** So take heart, men, for I have faith in God that it will be exactly as I have been told. **26** But we must run aground on some island."

27 When the fourteenth night had come, as we were being driven across the Adriatic Sea, about midnight the sailors suspected that they were nearing land. **28** So they took a sounding and found twenty fathoms. A little farther on they took a sounding again and found fifteen fathoms. **29** And fearing that we might run on the rocks, they let down four anchors from the stern and prayed for day to come. **30** And as the sailors were seeking to escape from the ship, and had lowered the ship's boat into the sea under pretense of laying out anchors from the bow, **31** Paul said to the centurion and the soldiers, "Unless these men stay in the ship, you cannot be saved." **32** Then the soldiers cut away the ropes of the ship's boat and let it go.

33 As day was about to dawn, Paul urged them all to take some food, saying, "Today is the fourteenth day that you have continued in suspense and without food, having taken nothing. **34** Therefore I urge you to take some food. For it will give you strength, for not a hair is to perish from the head of any of you." **35** And when he had said these things, he took bread, and giving thanks to God in the presence of all he broke it and began to eat. **36** Then they all were encouraged and ate some food themselves. **37** (We were in all 276 persons in the ship.) **38** And when they had eaten enough, they lightened the ship, throwing out the wheat into the sea.

The Shipwreck

39 Now when it was day, they did not recognize the land, but they noticed a bay with a beach, on which they planned if possible to run the ship ashore. **40** So they cast off the anchors and left them in the sea, at the same time loosening the ropes that tied the rudders. Then hoisting the foresail to the wind they made for the beach. **41** But striking a reef, they ran the vessel aground. The bow stuck and remained immovable, and the stern was being broken up by the surf. **42** The soldiers' plan was to kill the prisoners, lest any should swim away and escape. **43** But the centurion, wishing to save Paul, kept them from carrying out their plan. He ordered those who could swim to jump overboard first and make for the land, **44** and the rest on planks or on pieces of the ship. And so it was that all were brought safely to land.

Paul on Malta

28 After we were brought safely through, we then learned that the island was called Malta. **2** The native people showed us unusual kindness, for they kindled a fire and welcomed us all, because it had begun to rain and was cold. **3** When Paul had gathered a bundle of sticks and put them on the fire, a viper came out because of the heat and fastened on his hand. **4** When the native people saw the creature hanging from his hand, they said to one another, "No doubt this man is a murderer. Though he has escaped from the sea, Justice has not allowed him to live." **5** He, however, shook off the creature into the fire and suffered no harm. **6** They were waiting for him to swell up or suddenly fall down dead. But when they had waited a long time and saw no misfortune come to him, they changed their minds and said that he was a god.

7 Now in the neighborhood of that place were lands belonging to the chief man of the island, named Publius, who received us and entertained us hospitably for three days. **8** It happened that the father of Publius lay sick with fever and dysentery. And Paul visited him and prayed, and putting his hands on him healed him. **9** And when this had taken place, the rest of the people on the island who had diseases also came and were cured. **10** They also honored us greatly, and when we were about to sail, they put on board whatever we needed.

Paul Arrives at Rome

11 After three months we set sail in a ship that had wintered in the island, a ship of Alexandria, with the twin gods as a figurehead. **12** Putting in at Syracuse, we stayed there for three days. **13** And from there we made a circuit and arrived at Rhegium. And after one day a south wind sprang up, and on the second day we came to Puteoli. **14** There we found brothers[1] and were invited to stay with them for seven days. And so we came to Rome. **15** And the brothers there, when they heard about us, came as far as the Forum of Appius and Three Taverns to meet us. On seeing them, Paul thanked God and took courage. **16** And when we came into Rome, Paul was allowed to stay by himself, with the soldier who guarded him.

Paul in Rome

17 After three days he called together the local leaders of the Jews, and when they had gathered, he said to them, "Brothers, though I had done nothing against our people or the customs of our fathers, yet I was delivered as a prisoner from Jerusalem into the hands of the Romans. **18** When they had examined me, they wished to set me at liberty, because there was no reason for the death penalty in my case. **19** But because the Jews objected, I was compelled to appeal to Caesar—though I had no charge to bring against my nation. **20** For this reason, therefore, I have asked to see you and speak with you, since it is because of the hope of Israel

> ### GETTING THE MESSAGE
>
> **What happens next?** Acts ends with Paul serving Christ from within a Roman prison. During this time, he wrote Ephesians, Philippians, Colossians, and Philemon. According to the church historian Eusebius, Paul was released, then arrested a second time, and eventually martyred in Rome.

that I am wearing this chain." **21** And they said to him, "We have received no letters from Judea about you, and none of the brothers coming here has reported or spoken any evil about you. **22** But we desire to hear from you what your views are, for with regard to this sect we know that everywhere it is spoken against."

23 When they had appointed a day for him, they came to him at his lodging in greater numbers. From morning till evening he expounded to them, testifying to the kingdom of God and trying to convince them about Jesus both from the Law of Moses and from the Prophets. **24** And some were convinced by what he said, but others disbelieved. **25** And disagreeing among themselves, they departed after Paul had made one statement: "The Holy Spirit was right in saying to your fathers through Isaiah the prophet:

[1] Or *brothers and sisters*; also 28:15, 21

26 "'Go to this people, and say,
   "You will indeed hear but never under-
        stand,
      and you will indeed see but never
        perceive."
27 For this people's heart has grown dull,
      and with their ears they can barely
        hear,
      and their eyes they have closed;
   lest they should see with their eyes
      and hear with their ears

and understand with their heart
   and turn, and I would heal them.'

28 Therefore let it be known to you that this salvation of God has been sent to the Gentiles; they will listen."

30 He lived there two whole years at his own expense, and welcomed all who came to him, 31 proclaiming the kingdom of God and teaching about the Lord Jesus Christ with all boldness and without hindrance.

INTRODUCTION TO ROMANS

c. A.D. **33/34**	c. A.D. **57**	c. A.D. **64–67**
Conversion of Paul	Paul in Corinth, writes Romans	Paul martyred in Rome

AUTHOR, RECIPIENTS, AND DATE

The apostle Paul wrote to the Christians in Rome. He probably did this while he was in Corinth on his third missionary journey, in A.D. 57 (Acts 20:2–3).

THEME

In the cross of Christ, God judges sin and at the same time shows his saving mercy.

PURPOSE

Paul wrote Romans to unite the Jewish and Gentile Christians in Rome in the gospel. He also wanted the church in Rome to become the base of operations from which he could proclaim the gospel in Spain (15:22–24). The ultimate goal of preaching the gospel is the glory of God (11:33–36). Paul longs for the Gentiles to become obedient Christians for the sake of Christ's name (1:5).

KEY THEMES

1. All people are sinners and need to be saved from their sin (1:18–3:20; 5:12–19).

2. The Mosaic law is good and holy, but only Christ can remove sin and overcome its power (2:12–29; 3:9–20; 5:20; 7:1–25; 9:30–10:8).

3. Through the righteousness of God, sin is judged and salvation is provided (3:21–26; 5:12–19; 6:1–10; 7:1–6; 8:1–4).

4. With the coming of Jesus Christ, a new age of redemptive history has begun (1:1–7; 3:21–26; 5:1–8:39).

5. The atoning death of Jesus Christ is central to God's plan of salvation (3:21–26; 4:23–25; 5:6–11, 15–19; 6:1–10; 7:4–6; 8:1–4).

6. Justification is by faith alone (1:16–4:25; 9:30–10:21).

7. Those who are in Christ Jesus have a sure hope of future glory (5:1–8:39).

8. By the power of the Holy Spirit, those who have died with Christ live a new life (2:25–29; 6:1–7:6; 8:1–39).

9. God is sovereign in salvation. He works all things according to his plan (9:1–11:36).

10. God fulfills his promises to both Jews and Gentiles (1:18–4:25; 9:1–11:36; 14:1–15:13).

11. Because of God's grace, Christians should be morally pure, should show love to their neighbors, should be good citizens, and should welcome their fellow believers into fullest fellowship (12:1–15:7).

OUTLINE

THE LETTER OF PAUL TO THE
ROMANS

Greeting

1 Paul, a servant[1] of Christ Jesus, called to be an apostle, set apart for the gospel of God, 2 which he promised beforehand through his prophets in the holy Scriptures, 3 concerning his Son, who was descended from David according to the flesh 4 and was declared to be the Son of God in power according to the Spirit of holiness by his resurrection from the dead, Jesus Christ our Lord, 5 through whom we have received grace and apostleship to bring about the obedience of faith for the sake of his name among all the nations, 6 including you who are called to belong to Jesus Christ,

7 To all those in Rome who are loved by God and called to be saints:

Grace to you and peace from God our Father and the Lord Jesus Christ.

Longing to Go to Rome

8 First, I thank my God through Jesus Christ for all of you, because your faith is proclaimed in all the world. 9 For God is my witness, whom I serve with my spirit in the gospel of his Son, that without ceasing I mention you 10 always in my prayers, asking that somehow by God's will I may now at last succeed in coming to you. 11 For I long to see you, that I may impart to you some spiritual gift to strengthen you— 12 that is, that we may be mutually encouraged by each other's faith, both yours and mine. 13 I do not want you to be unaware, brothers,[2] that I have often intended to come to you (but thus far have been prevented), in order that I may reap some harvest among you as well as among the rest of the Gentiles. 14 I am under obligation both to Greeks and to barbarians, both to the wise and to the foolish. 15 So I am eager to preach the gospel to you also who are in Rome.

The Righteous Shall Live by Faith

16 For I am not ashamed of the gospel, for it is the power of God for salvation to everyone who believes, to the Jew first and also to the Greek. 17 For in it the righteousness of God is revealed from faith for faith, as it is written, "The righteous shall live by faith."

God's Wrath on Unrighteousness

18 For the wrath of God is revealed from heaven against all ungodliness and unrighteousness of men, who by their unrighteousness suppress the truth. 19 For what can be known about God is plain to them, because God has shown it to them. 20 For his invisible attributes, namely, his eternal power and divine nature, have been clearly perceived, ever since the creation of the

GETTING THE MESSAGE

A letter to Rome. Because Romans is Paul's fullest explanation of his theology, it is easy to forget that Paul wrote it to a particular church in Rome. His letter applies the eternal truth of the gospel to their real-life concerns.

world, in the things that have been made. So they are without excuse. 21 For although they knew God, they did not honor him as God or give thanks to him, but they became futile in their thinking, and their foolish hearts were darkened. 22 Claiming to be wise, they became fools, 23 and exchanged the glory of the immortal God for images resembling mortal man and birds and animals and creeping things.

24 Therefore God gave them up in the lusts of their hearts to impurity, to the dishonoring of their bodies among themselves, 25 because they exchanged the truth about God for a lie and worshiped and served the creature rather than the Creator, who is blessed forever! Amen.

26 For this reason God gave them up to dishonorable passions. For their women exchanged natural relations for those that are contrary to nature; 27 and the men like-

---

[1] Or slave (Greek doulos; see Preface) [2] Or brothers and sisters (see Preface)

wise gave up natural relations with women and were consumed with passion for one another, men committing shameless acts with men and receiving in themselves the due penalty for their error.

28 And since they did not see fit to acknowledge God, God gave them up to a debased mind to do what ought not to be done. **29** They were filled with all manner of unrighteousness, evil, covetousness, malice. They are full of envy, murder, strife, deceit, maliciousness. They are gossips, **30** slanderers, haters of God, insolent, haughty, boastful, inventors of evil, disobedient to parents, **31** foolish, faithless, heartless, ruthless. **32** Though they know God's righteous decree that those who practice such things deserve to die, they not only do them but give approval to those who practice them.

GETTING THE MESSAGE

God's judgment. Humanity's rejection of God is the root of all that is wrong with the world. Since Adam and Eve, everyone has responded to God's love by doing things he hates. Everyone deserves punishment, but God offers forgiveness through Christ (see 3:23–24).

God's Righteous Judgment

2 Therefore you have no excuse, O man, every one of you who judges. For in passing judgment on another you condemn yourself, because you, the judge, practice the very same things. **2** We know that the judgment of God rightly falls on those who practice such things. **3** Do you suppose, O man—you who judge those who practice such things and yet do them yourself—that you will escape the judgment of God? **4** Or do you presume on the riches of his kindness and forbearance and patience, not knowing that God's kindness is meant to lead you to repentance? **5** But because of your hard and impenitent heart you are storing up wrath for yourself on the day of wrath when God's righteous judgment will be revealed.

6 He will render to each one according to his works: **7** to those who by patience in well-doing seek for glory and honor and immortality, he will give eternal life; **8** but for those

who are self-seeking and do not obey the truth, but obey unrighteousness, there will be wrath and fury. **9** There will be tribulation and distress for every human being who does evil, the Jew first and also the Greek, **10** but glory and honor and peace for everyone who does good, the Jew first and also the Greek. **11** For God shows no partiality.

God's Judgment and the Law

12 For all who have sinned without the law will also perish without the law, and all who have sinned under the law will be judged by the law. **13** For it is not the hearers of the law who are righteous before God, but the doers of the law who will be justified. **14** For when Gentiles, who do not have the law, by nature do what the law requires, they are a law to themselves, even though they do not have the law. **15** They show that the work of the law is written on their hearts, while their conscience also bears witness, and their conflicting thoughts accuse or even excuse them **16** on that day when, according to my gospel, God judges the secrets of men by Christ Jesus.

17 But if you call yourself a Jew and rely on the law and boast in God **18** and know his will and approve what is excellent, because you are instructed from the law; **19** and if you are sure that you yourself are a guide to the blind, a light to those who are in darkness, **20** an instructor of the foolish, a teacher of children, having in the law the embodiment of knowledge and truth— **21** you then who teach others, do you not teach yourself? While you preach against stealing, do you steal? **22** You who say that one must not commit adultery, do you commit adultery? You who abhor idols, do you rob temples? **23** You who boast in the law dishonor God by breaking the law. **24** For, as it is written, "The name of God is blasphemed among the Gentiles because of you."

25 For circumcision indeed is of value if you obey the law, but if you break the law, your circumcision becomes uncircumcision. **26** So, if a man who is uncircumcised keeps the precepts of the law, will not his uncircumcision be regarded as circumcision? **27** Then he who is physically uncircumcised but keeps the law will condemn you who have the written code and circumcision but break the law. **28** For no one is a Jew who is merely one outwardly, nor is circumcision outward and physical. **29** But a Jew is one inwardly, and circumcision is a matter of the heart, by the Spirit, not by the letter. His praise is not from man but from God.

God's Righteousness Upheld

3 Then what advantage has the Jew? Or what is the value of circumcision? **2** Much in every way. To begin with, the Jews were entrusted with the oracles of God. **3** What if some were unfaithful? Does their faithlessness nullify the faithfulness of God? **4** By no means! Let God be true though every one were a liar, as it is written,

"That you may be justified in your
　　words,
　　and prevail when you are judged."

5 But if our unrighteousness serves to show the righteousness of God, what shall we say? That God is unrighteous to inflict wrath on us? (I speak in a human way.) **6** By no means! For then how could God judge the world? **7** But if through my lie God's truth abounds to his glory, why am I still being condemned as a sinner? **8** And why not do evil that good may come?—as some people slanderously charge us with saying. Their condemnation is just.

No One Is Righteous

9 What then? Are we Jews any better off? No, not at all. For we have already charged that all, both Jews and Greeks, are under sin, **10** as it is written:

"None is righteous, no, not one;
11　no one understands;
　　no one seeks for God.
12　All have turned aside; together they
　　have become worthless;
　　no one does good,
　　not even one."
13　"Their throat is an open grave;
　　they use their tongues to deceive."
　"The venom of asps is under their
　　lips."
14　"Their mouth is full of curses and
　　bitterness."
15　"Their feet are swift to shed blood;
16　in their paths are ruin and misery,
17　and the way of peace they have not
　　known."
18　"There is no fear of God before their
　　eyes."

19 Now we know that whatever the law says it speaks to those who are under the law, so that every mouth may be stopped, and the whole world may be held accountable to God. **20** For by works of the law no human being will be justified in his sight, since through the law comes knowledge of sin.

The Righteousness of God Through Faith

21 But now the righteousness of God has been manifested apart from the law, although the Law and the Prophets bear witness to it— **22** the righteousness of God through faith in Jesus Christ for all who believe. For there is no distinction: **23** for all have sinned and fall short of the glory of God, **24** and are justified by his grace as a gift, through the redemption that is in Christ Jesus, **25** whom God put forward as a propitiation by his blood, to be received by

faith. This was to show God's righteousness, because in his divine forbearance he had passed over former sins. **26** It was to show his righteousness at the present time, so that he might be just and the justifier of the one who has faith in Jesus.

27 Then what becomes of our boasting? It is excluded. By what kind of law? By a law of works? No, but by the law of faith. **28** For we hold that one is justified by faith apart from works of the law. **29** Or is God the God of Jews only? Is he not the God of Gentiles also? Yes, of Gentiles also, **30** since God is one—who will justify the circumcised by faith and the uncircumcised through faith. **31** Do we then overthrow the law by this faith? By no means! On the contrary, we uphold the law.

Abraham Justified by Faith

4 What then shall we say was gained by Abraham, our forefather according to the flesh? **2** For if Abraham was justified by works, he has something to boast about,

but not before God. ³ For what does the Scripture say? "Abraham believed God, and it was counted to him as righteousness." ⁴ Now to the one who works, his wages are not counted as a gift but as his due. ⁵ And to the one who does not work but believes in him who justifies the ungodly, his faith is counted as righteousness, ⁶ just as David also speaks of the blessing of the one to whom God counts righteousness apart from works:

⁷ "Blessed are those whose lawless deeds
      are forgiven,
  and whose sins are covered;
⁸   blessed is the man against whom the
      Lord will not count his sin."

⁹ Is this blessing then only for the circumcised, or also for the uncircumcised? For we say that faith was counted to Abraham as righteousness. ¹⁰ How then was it counted

> ### GETTING THE MESSAGE
>
> Those who trust in Christ have **peace with God** (5:1). God declares them forgiven. They stand securely in God's grace and salvation rather than his judgment (5:2, 8–9).

to him? Was it before or after he had been circumcised? It was not after, but before he was circumcised. ¹¹ He received the sign of circumcision as a seal of the righteousness that he had by faith while he was still uncircumcised. The purpose was to make him the father of all who believe without being circumcised, so that righteousness would be counted to them as well, ¹² and to make him the father of the circumcised who are not merely circumcised but who also walk in the footsteps of the faith that our father Abraham had before he was circumcised.

The Promise Realized Through Faith

¹³ For the promise to Abraham and his offspring that he would be heir of the world did not come through the law but through the righteousness of faith. ¹⁴ For if it is the adherents of the law who are to be the heirs, faith is null and the promise is void. ¹⁵ For the law brings wrath, but where there is no law there is no transgression.

¹⁶ That is why it depends on faith, in order that the promise may rest on grace and be guaranteed to all his offspring — not only to the adherent of the law but also to the one who shares the faith of Abraham, who is the father of us all, ¹⁷ as it is written, "I have made you the father of many nations" — in the presence of the God in whom he believed, who gives life to the dead and calls into existence the things that do not exist. ¹⁸ In hope he believed against hope, that he should become the father of many nations, as he had been told, "So shall your offspring be." ¹⁹ He did not weaken in faith when he considered his own body, which was as good as dead (since he was about a hundred years old), or when he considered the barrenness of Sarah's womb. ²⁰ No unbelief made him waver concerning the promise of God, but he grew strong in his faith as he gave glory to God, ²¹ fully convinced that God was able to do what he had promised. ²² That is why his faith was "counted to him as righteousness." ²³ But the words "it was counted to him" were not written for his sake alone, ²⁴ but for ours also. It will be counted to us who believe in him who raised from the dead Jesus our Lord, ²⁵ who was delivered up for our trespasses and raised for our justification.

Peace with God Through Faith

5 Therefore, since we have been justified by faith, we have peace with God through our Lord Jesus Christ. ² Through him we have also obtained access by faith into this grace in which we stand, and we rejoice in hope of the glory of God. ³ Not only that, but we rejoice in our sufferings, knowing that suffering produces endurance, ⁴ and endurance produces character, and character produces hope, ⁵ and hope does not put us to shame, because God's love has been poured into our hearts through the Holy Spirit who has been given to us.

⁶ For while we were still weak, at the right time Christ died for the ungodly. ⁷ For one will scarcely die for a righteous person — though perhaps for a good person one would dare even to die — ⁸ but God shows his love for us in that while we were still sinners, Christ died for us. ⁹ Since, therefore, we have now been justified by his blood, much more shall we be saved by him from the wrath of God. ¹⁰ For if while we were enemies we were reconciled to God by the death

of his Son, much more, now that we are reconciled, shall we be saved by his life. [11] More than that, we also rejoice in God through our Lord Jesus Christ, through whom we have now received reconciliation.

Death in Adam, Life in Christ

[12] Therefore, just as sin came into the world through one man, and death through sin, and so death spread to all men[1] because all sinned— [13] for sin indeed was in the world before the law was given, but sin is not counted where there is no law. [14] Yet death reigned from Adam to Moses, even over those whose sinning was not like the transgression of Adam, who was a type of the one who was to come.

[15] But the free gift is not like the trespass. For if many died through one man's trespass, much more have the grace of God and the free gift by the grace of that one man Jesus Christ abounded for many. [16] And the free gift is not like the result of that one man's sin. For the judgment following one trespass brought condemnation, but the free gift following many trespasses brought justification. [17] For if, because of one man's trespass, death reigned through that one man, much more will those who receive the abundance of grace and the free gift of righteousness reign in life through the one man Jesus Christ.

[18] Therefore, as one trespass led to condemnation for all men, so one act of righteousness leads to justification and life for all men. [19] For as by the one man's disobedience the many were made sinners, so by the one man's obedience the many will be made righteous. [20] Now the law came in to increase the trespass, but where sin increased, grace abounded all the more, [21] so that, as sin reigned in death, grace also might reign through righteousness leading to eternal life through Jesus Christ our Lord.

Dead to Sin, Alive to God

6 What shall we say then? Are we to continue in sin that grace may abound? [2] By no means! How can we who died to sin still live in it? [3] Do you not know that all of us who have been baptized into Christ Jesus were baptized into his death? [4] We were buried therefore with him by baptism into death, in order that, just as Christ was raised

from the dead by the glory of the Father, we too might walk in newness of life.

[5] For if we have been united with him in a death like his, we shall certainly be united with him in a resurrection like his. [6] We know that our old self was crucified with him in order that the body of sin might be brought to nothing, so that we would no longer be enslaved to sin. [7] For one who has died has been set free from sin. [8] Now if we have died with Christ, we believe that we will also live with him. [9] We know that Christ, being raised from the dead, will never die again; death no longer has dominion over him. [10] For the death he died he died to sin, once for all, but the life he lives he lives to God. [11] So you also must consider yourselves dead to sin and alive to God in Christ Jesus.

GETTING THE MESSAGE

Transgression means to disobey a specific command from God. It could refer to a violation of a command in the written law of God (4:15) or to a verbal command from God, as in the case of Adam (5:14).

[12] Let not sin therefore reign in your mortal body, to make you obey its passions. [13] Do not present your members to sin as instruments for unrighteousness, but present yourselves to God as those who have been brought from death to life, and your members to God as instruments for righteousness. [14] For sin will have no dominion over you, since you are not under law but under grace.

Slaves to Righteousness

[15] What then? Are we to sin because we are not under law but under grace? By no means! [16] Do you not know that if you present yourselves to anyone as obedient slaves,[2] you are slaves of the one whom you obey, either of sin, which leads to death, or of obedience, which leads to righteousness? [17] But thanks be to God, that you who were once slaves of sin have become obedient from the heart to the standard of teaching to which you were committed, [18] and, having been set free from sin, have become slaves of righteousness.

[1] The Greek word for *men* refers to both men and women (see Preface); also 5:18 [2] Greek *doulos* (see Preface); also 6:17

19 I am speaking in human terms, because of your natural limitations. For just as you once presented your members as slaves[1] to impurity and to lawlessness leading to more lawlessness, so now present your members as slaves to righteousness leading to sanctification.

20 For when you were slaves of sin, you were free in regard to righteousness. **21** But what fruit were you getting at that time from the things of which you are now ashamed? For the end of those things is death. **22** But now that you have been set free from sin and have become slaves of God, the fruit you get leads to sanctification and its end, eternal life. **23** For the wages of sin is death, but the free gift of God is eternal life in Christ Jesus our Lord.

> **GETTING THE MESSAGE**
>
> Paul was probably asked, "Does your message about salvation by grace lead people to **continue in sin**?" He explains what baptism symbolizes in the Christian life: Christ's defeat of sin's rule and the gift of new life (6:1–14). God changes believers so that they can obey him "from the heart" (6:17).

Released from the Law

7 Or do you not know, brothers[2]—for I am speaking to those who know the law— that the law is binding on a person only as long as he lives? **2** For a married woman is bound by law to her husband while he lives, but if her husband dies she is released from the law of marriage. **3** Accordingly, she will be called an adulteress if she lives with another man while her husband is alive. But if her husband dies, she is free from that law, and if she marries another man she is not an adulteress.

4 Likewise, my brothers, you also have died to the law through the body of Christ, so that you may belong to another, to him who has been raised from the dead, in order that we may bear fruit for God. **5** For while we were living in the flesh, our sinful passions, aroused by the law, were at work in our members to bear fruit for death. **6** But now we are released from the law, having died to that which held us captive, so that we serve in the new way of the Spirit and not in the old way of the written code.

The Law and Sin

7 What then shall we say? That the law is sin? By no means! Yet if it had not been for the law, I would not have known sin. For I would not have known what it is to covet if the law had not said, "You shall not covet." **8** But sin, seizing an opportunity through the commandment, produced in me all kinds of covetousness. For apart from the law, sin lies dead. **9** I was once alive apart from the law, but when the commandment came, sin came alive and I died. **10** The very commandment that promised life proved to be death to me. **11** For sin, seizing an opportunity through the commandment, deceived me and through it killed me. **12** So the law is holy, and the commandment is holy and righteous and good.

13 Did that which is good, then, bring death to me? By no means! It was sin, producing death in me through what is good, in order that sin might be shown to be sin, and through the commandment might become sinful beyond measure. **14** For we know that the law is spiritual, but I am of the flesh, sold under sin. **15** For I do not understand my own actions. For I do not do what I want, but I do the very thing I hate. **16** Now if I do what I do not want, I agree with the law, that it is good. **17** So now it is no longer I who do it, but sin that dwells within me. **18** For I know that nothing good dwells in me, that is, in my flesh. For I have the desire to do what is right, but not the ability to carry it out. **19** For I do not do the good I want, but the evil I do not want is what I keep on doing. **20** Now if I do what I do not want, it is no longer I who do it, but sin that dwells within me.

21 So I find it to be a law that when I want to do right, evil lies close at hand. **22** For I delight in the law of God, in my inner being, **23** but I see in my members another law waging war against the law of my mind and making me captive to the law of sin that dwells in my members. **24** Wretched man that I am! Who will deliver me from this body of death? **25** Thanks be to God through Jesus Christ our Lord! So then, I myself serve the law of God with my mind, but with my flesh I serve the law of sin.

[1] Greek *doulos* (see Preface); also 6:20 [2] Or *brothers and sisters*; also 7:4

Life in the Spirit

8 There is therefore now no condemnation for those who are in Christ Jesus. [2] For the law of the Spirit of life has set you free in Christ Jesus from the law of sin and death. [3] For God has done what the law, weakened by the flesh, could not do. By sending his own Son in the likeness of sinful flesh and for sin, he condemned sin in the flesh, [4] in order that the righteous requirement of the law might be fulfilled in us, who walk not according to the flesh but according to the Spirit. [5] For those who live according to the flesh set their minds on the things of the flesh, but those who live according to the Spirit set their minds on the things of the Spirit. [6] For to set the mind on the flesh is death, but to set the mind on the Spirit is life and peace. [7] For the mind that is set on the flesh is hostile to God, for it does not submit to God's law; indeed, it cannot. [8] Those who are in the flesh cannot please God.

[9] You, however, are not in the flesh but in the Spirit, if in fact the Spirit of God dwells in you. Anyone who does not have the Spirit of Christ does not belong to him. [10] But if Christ is in you, although the body is dead because of sin, the Spirit is life because of righteousness. [11] If the Spirit of him who raised Jesus from the dead dwells in you, he who raised Christ Jesus from the dead will also give life to your mortal bodies through his Spirit who dwells in you.

Heirs with Christ

[12] So then, brothers,[1] we are debtors, not to the flesh, to live according to the flesh. [13] For if you live according to the flesh you will die, but if by the Spirit you put to death the deeds of the body, you will live. [14] For all who are led by the Spirit of God are sons[2] of God. [15] For you did not receive the spirit of slavery to fall back into fear, but you have received the Spirit of adoption as sons, by whom we cry, "Abba! Father!" [16] The Spirit himself bears witness with our spirit that we are children of God, [17] and if children, then heirs—heirs of God and fellow heirs with Christ, provided we suffer with him in order that we may also be glorified with him.

Future Glory

[18] For I consider that the sufferings of this present time are not worth comparing with the glory that is to be revealed to us. [19] For the creation waits with eager longing for the revealing of the sons of God. [20] For the creation was subjected to futility, not willingly, but because of him who subjected it, in hope [21] that the creation itself will be set free from its bondage to corruption and obtain the freedom of the glory of the children of God. [22] For we know that the whole creation has been groaning together in the pains of childbirth until now. [23] And not only the creation, but we ourselves, who have the firstfruits of the Spirit, groan inwardly as we wait eagerly for adoption as sons, the redemption of our bodies. [24] For in this hope we were saved. Now hope that is seen is not hope. For who hopes for what he sees? [25] But if we hope for what we do not see, we wait for it with patience.

[26] Likewise the Spirit helps us in our weakness. For we do not know what to pray for as

---

GETTING THE MESSAGE

Even Christians often struggle with sinful desires (7:7-25), but they can be confident that **the Spirit lives within them**, helping them to obey God (8:1-11).

---

we ought, but the Spirit himself intercedes for us with groanings too deep for words. [27] And he who searches hearts knows what is the mind of the Spirit, because the Spirit intercedes for the saints according to the will of God. [28] And we know that for those who love God all things work together for good, for those who are called according to his purpose. [29] For those whom he foreknew he also predestined to be conformed to the image of his Son, in order that he might be the firstborn among many brothers. [30] And those whom he predestined he also called, and those whom he called he also justified, and those whom he justified he also glorified.

God's Everlasting Love

[31] What then shall we say to these things? If God is for us, who can be against us? [32] He who did not spare his own Son but gave him up for us all, how will he not also with him graciously give us all things? [33] Who shall

---

[1] Or *brothers and sisters*; also 8:29　[2] The Greek word for *sons* refers to both sons and daughters (see Preface)

bring any charge against God's elect? It is God who justifies. **34** Who is to condemn? Christ Jesus is the one who died—more than that, who was raised—who is at the right hand of God, who indeed is interceding for us. **35** Who shall separate us from the love of Christ? Shall tribulation, or distress, or persecution, or famine, or nakedness, or danger, or sword? **36** As it is written,

> "For your sake we are being killed all
> the day long;
> we are regarded as sheep to be
> slaughtered."

37 No, in all these things we are more than conquerors through him who loved us. **38** For I am sure that neither death nor life, nor angels nor rulers, nor things present nor things to come, nor powers, **39** nor height nor depth, nor anything else in all creation,

GETTING THE MESSAGE

When Christ returns, he will fix everything that is broken and hurting (8:16–39; see Rev. 21:1–22:5). He will restore creation to its original beauty and wholeness. God will bring dead believers back to life and make all his children perfect like Christ (Rom. 8:29; 1 Thess. 4:13–18).

will be able to separate us from the love of God in Christ Jesus our Lord.

God's Sovereign Choice

9 I am speaking the truth in Christ—I am not lying; my conscience bears me witness in the Holy Spirit— **2** that I have great sorrow and unceasing anguish in my heart. **3** For I could wish that I myself were accursed and cut off from Christ for the sake of my brothers,[1] my kinsmen according to the flesh. **4** They are Israelites, and to them belong the adoption, the glory, the covenants, the giving of the law, the worship, and the promises. **5** To them belong the patriarchs, and from their race, according to the flesh, is the Christ, who is God over all, blessed forever. Amen.

6 But it is not as though the word of God has failed. For not all who are descended from Israel belong to Israel, **7** and not all are children of Abraham because they are his offspring, but "Through Isaac shall your offspring be named." **8** This means that it is not the children of the flesh who are the children of God, but the children of the promise are counted as offspring. **9** For this is what the promise said: "About this time next year I will return, and Sarah shall have a son." **10** And not only so, but also when Rebekah had conceived children by one man, our forefather Isaac, **11** though they were not yet born and had done nothing either good or bad—in order that God's purpose of election might continue, not because of works but because of him who calls— **12** she was told, "The older will serve the younger." **13** As it is written, "Jacob I loved, but Esau I hated."

14 What shall we say then? Is there injustice on God's part? By no means! **15** For he says to Moses, "I will have mercy on whom I have mercy, and I will have compassion on whom I have compassion." **16** So then it depends not on human will or exertion, but on God, who has mercy. **17** For the Scripture says to Pharaoh, "For this very purpose I have raised you up, that I might show my power in you, and that my name might be proclaimed in all the earth." **18** So then he has mercy on whomever he wills, and he hardens whomever he wills.

19 You will say to me then, "Why does he still find fault? For who can resist his will?" **20** But who are you, O man, to answer back to God? Will what is molded say to its molder, "Why have you made me like this?" **21** Has the potter no right over the clay, to make out of the same lump one vessel for honorable use and another for dishonorable use? **22** What if God, desiring to show his wrath and to make known his power, has endured with much patience vessels of wrath prepared for destruction, **23** in order to make known the riches of his glory for vessels of mercy, which he has prepared beforehand for glory— **24** even us whom he has called, not from the Jews only but also from the Gentiles? **25** As indeed he says in Hosea,

> "Those who were not my people I will
> call 'my people,'
> and her who was not beloved I will
> call 'beloved.'"

[1] Or brothers and sisters

26 "And in the very place where it was said
         to them, 'You are not my people,'
    there they will be called 'sons of the
         living God.'"

27 And Isaiah cries out concerning Israel:
"Though the number of the sons of Israel
be as the sand of the sea, only a remnant of
them will be saved, 28 for the Lord will carry
out his sentence upon the earth fully and
without delay." 29 And as Isaiah predicted,

    "If the Lord of hosts had not left us
         offspring,
      we would have been like Sodom
      and become like Gomorrah."

Israel's Unbelief

30 What shall we say, then? That Gentiles
who did not pursue righteousness have
attained it, that is, a righteousness that is
by faith; 31 but that Israel who pursued a
law that would lead to righteousness did
not succeed in reaching that law. 32 Why?
Because they did not pursue it by faith,
but as if it were based on works. They have
stumbled over the stumbling stone, 33 as it
is written,

    "Behold, I am laying in Zion a stone of
         stumbling, and a rock of offense;
      and whoever believes in him will
         not be put to shame."

10 Brothers,[1] my heart's desire and
prayer to God for them is that they
may be saved. 2 For I bear them witness that
they have a zeal for God, but not according to knowledge. 3 For, being ignorant of
the righteousness of God, and seeking to
establish their own, they did not submit
to God's righteousness. 4 For Christ is the
end of the law for righteousness to everyone
who believes.

The Message of Salvation to All

5 For Moses writes about the righteousness that is based on the law, that the person who does the commandments shall
live by them. 6 But the righteousness based
on faith says, "Do not say in your heart,
'Who will ascend into heaven?'" (that is, to
bring Christ down) 7 "or 'Who will descend
into the abyss?'" (that is, to bring Christ
up from the dead). 8 But what does it say?
"The word is near you, in your mouth and

in your heart" (that is, the word of faith that
we proclaim); 9 because, if you confess with
your mouth that Jesus is Lord and believe
in your heart that God raised him from the
dead, you will be saved. 10 For with the heart
one believes and is justified, and with the
mouth one confesses and is saved. 11 For the
Scripture says, "Everyone who believes in
him will not be put to shame." 12 For there is
no distinction between Jew and Greek; for
the same Lord is Lord of all, bestowing his
riches on all who call on him. 13 For "everyone who calls on the name of the Lord will
be saved."

14 How then will they call on him in
whom they have not believed? And how
are they to believe in him of whom they
have never heard? And how are they to hear
without someone preaching? 15 And how
are they to preach unless they are sent? As

GETTING THE MESSAGE

Paul's love for God and his compassion
for those who do not know Christ are
clear (see 9:1–5; 10:1, 14–15). Believers'
experience of God's grace should
motivate them to **share the Good News
with others** and to pray that they will
believe.

it is written, "How beautiful are the feet of
those who preach the good news!" 16 But
they have not all obeyed the gospel. For
Isaiah says, "Lord, who has believed what
he has heard from us?" 17 So faith comes
from hearing, and hearing through the
word of Christ.

18 But I ask, have they not heard? Indeed
they have, for

    "Their voice has gone out to all the
         earth,
      and their words to the ends of the
         world."

19 But I ask, did Israel not understand? First
Moses says,

    "I will make you jealous of those who
         are not a nation;
      with a foolish nation I will make
         you angry."

[1] Or Brothers and sisters

20 Then Isaiah is so bold as to say,

"I have been found by those who did
not seek me;
I have shown myself to those who
did not ask for me."

21 But of Israel he says, "All day long I have held out my hands to a disobedient and contrary people."

The Remnant of Israel

11 I ask, then, has God rejected his people? By no means! For I myself am an Israelite, a descendant of Abraham, a member of the tribe of Benjamin. **2** God has not rejected his people whom he foreknew. Do you not know what the Scripture says of Elijah, how he appeals to God against Israel? **3** "Lord, they have killed your prophets, they have demolished your altars, and I alone am

---

GETTING THE MESSAGE

A wild olive branch? Farmers don't usually graft a wild plant onto a cultivated one, but Paul says that is just what God has done in grafting the wild olive branch of the Gentile world onto the cultivated olive tree of his people Israel (11:11–24). He has done this so that all people everywhere can become a part of his family.

---

left, and they seek my life." **4** But what is God's reply to him? "I have kept for myself seven thousand men who have not bowed the knee to Baal." **5** So too at the present time there is a remnant, chosen by grace. **6** But if it is by grace, it is no longer on the basis of works; otherwise grace would no longer be grace.

7 What then? Israel failed to obtain what it was seeking. The elect obtained it, but the rest were hardened, **8** as it is written,

"God gave them a spirit of stupor,
eyes that would not see
and ears that would not hear,
down to this very day."

9 And David says,

"Let their table become a snare and a
trap,
a stumbling block and a retribution
for them;

10   let their eyes be darkened so that they
cannot see,
and bend their backs forever."

Gentiles Grafted In

11 So I ask, did they stumble in order that they might fall? By no means! Rather through their trespass salvation has come to the Gentiles, so as to make Israel jealous. **12** Now if their trespass means riches for the world, and if their failure means riches for the Gentiles, how much more will their full inclusion mean!

13 Now I am speaking to you Gentiles. Inasmuch then as I am an apostle to the Gentiles, I magnify my ministry **14** in order somehow to make my fellow Jews jealous, and thus save some of them. **15** For if their rejection means the reconciliation of the world, what will their acceptance mean but life from the dead? **16** If the dough offered as firstfruits is holy, so is the whole lump, and if the root is holy, so are the branches.

17 But if some of the branches were broken off, and you, although a wild olive shoot, were grafted in among the others and now share in the nourishing root of the olive tree, **18** do not be arrogant toward the branches. If you are, remember it is not you who support the root, but the root that supports you. **19** Then you will say, "Branches were broken off so that I might be grafted in." **20** That is true. They were broken off because of their unbelief, but you stand fast through faith. So do not become proud, but fear. **21** For if God did not spare the natural branches, neither will he spare you. **22** Note then the kindness and the severity of God: severity toward those who have fallen, but God's kindness to you, provided you continue in his kindness. Otherwise you too will be cut off. **23** And even they, if they do not continue in their unbelief, will be grafted in, for God has the power to graft them in again. **24** For if you were cut from what is by nature a wild olive tree, and grafted, contrary to nature, into a cultivated olive tree, how much more will these, the natural branches, be grafted back into their own olive tree.

The Mystery of Israel's Salvation

25 Lest you be wise in your own sight, I do not want you to be unaware of this mystery, brothers:[1] a partial hardening has come upon Israel, until the fullness of the Gentiles has come in. **26** And in this way all Israel will be saved, as it is written,

> "The Deliverer will come from Zion,
>> he will banish ungodliness from Jacob";
27 "and this will be my covenant with them
>> when I take away their sins."

28 As regards the gospel, they are enemies for your sake. But as regards election, they are beloved for the sake of their forefathers. **29** For the gifts and the calling of God are irrevocable. **30** For just as you were at one time disobedient to God but now have received mercy because of their disobedience, **31** so they too have now been disobedient in order that by the mercy shown to you they also may now receive mercy. **32** For God has consigned all to disobedience, that he may have mercy on all.

33 Oh, the depth of the riches and wisdom and knowledge of God! How unsearchable are his judgments and how inscrutable his ways!

34 "For who has known the mind of the Lord,
>> or who has been his counselor?"
35 "Or who has given a gift to him
>> that he might be repaid?"

36 For from him and through him and to him are all things. To him be glory forever. Amen.

A Living Sacrifice

12 I appeal to you therefore, brothers, by the mercies of God, to present your bodies as a living sacrifice, holy and acceptable to God, which is your spiritual worship. **2** Do not be conformed to this world, but be transformed by the renewal of your mind, that by testing you may discern what is the will of God, what is good and acceptable and perfect.

Gifts of Grace

3 For by the grace given to me I say to everyone among you not to think of himself more highly than he ought to think, but to think with sober judgment, each according to the measure of faith that God

has assigned. **4** For as in one body we have many members, and the members do not all have the same function, **5** so we, though many, are one body in Christ, and individually members one of another. **6** Having gifts that differ according to the grace given to us, let us use them: if prophecy, in proportion to our faith; **7** if service, in our serving; the one who teaches, in his teaching; **8** the one who exhorts, in his exhortation; the one who contributes, in generosity; the one who leads, with zeal; the one who does acts of mercy, with cheerfulness.

Marks of the True Christian

9 Let love be genuine. Abhor what is evil; hold fast to what is good. **10** Love one another with brotherly affection. Outdo one another in showing honor. **11** Do not be slothful in zeal, be fervent in spirit, serve the Lord. **12** Rejoice

---

GETTING THE MESSAGE

What does "discern" mean? To discern something means to understand it. For Christians, discernment involves the use of wisdom and the Holy Spirit's guidance to figure out how to apply biblical principles to the concrete issues of life (12:2; see also Eph. 5:10).

---

in hope, be patient in tribulation, be constant in prayer. **13** Contribute to the needs of the saints and seek to show hospitality.

14 Bless those who persecute you; bless and do not curse them. **15** Rejoice with those who rejoice, weep with those who weep. **16** Live in harmony with one another. Do not be haughty, but associate with the lowly. Never be wise in your own sight. **17** Repay no one evil for evil, but give thought to do what is honorable in the sight of all. **18** If possible, so far as it depends on you, live peaceably with all. **19** Beloved, never avenge yourselves, but leave it to the wrath of God, for it is written, "Vengeance is mine, I will repay, says the Lord." **20** To the contrary, "if your enemy is hungry, feed him; if he is thirsty, give him something to drink; for by so doing you will heap burning coals on his head." **21** Do not be overcome by evil, but overcome evil with good.

---

[1] Or brothers and sisters; also 12:1

Submission to the Authorities

13 Let every person be subject to the governing authorities. For there is no authority except from God, and those that exist have been instituted by God. ² Therefore whoever resists the authorities resists what God has appointed, and those who resist will incur judgment. ³ For rulers are not a terror to good conduct, but to bad. Would you have no fear of the one who is in authority? Then do what is good, and you will receive his approval, ⁴ for he is God's servant for your good. But if you do wrong, be afraid, for he does not bear the sword in vain. For he is the servant of God, an avenger who carries out God's wrath on the wrongdoer. ⁵ Therefore one must be in subjection, not only to avoid God's wrath but also for the sake of conscience. ⁶ For because of this you also pay taxes, for the authorities are ministers of

> ### GETTING THE MESSAGE
>
> **Should Christians always pay their taxes?** Paul says that paying taxes is one way in which Christians show honor to the authorities God has placed over them (13:1–7). Christians should obey their government unless doing so means disobeying the Lord (Acts 5:29).

God, attending to this very thing. ⁷ Pay to all what is owed to them: taxes to whom taxes are owed, revenue to whom revenue is owed, respect to whom respect is owed, honor to whom honor is owed.

Fulfilling the Law Through Love

⁸ Owe no one anything, except to love each other, for the one who loves another has fulfilled the law. ⁹ For the commandments, "You shall not commit adultery, You shall not murder, You shall not steal, You shall not covet," and any other commandment, are summed up in this word: "You shall love your neighbor as yourself." ¹⁰ Love does no wrong to a neighbor; therefore love is the fulfilling of the law.

¹¹ Besides this you know the time, that the hour has come for you to wake from sleep. For salvation is nearer to us now than when we first believed. ¹² The night is far gone; the day is at hand. So then let us cast off the works of darkness and put on the armor of light. ¹³ Let us walk properly as in the daytime, not in orgies and drunkenness, not in sexual immorality and sensuality, not in quarreling and jealousy. ¹⁴ But put on the Lord Jesus Christ, and make no provision for the flesh, to gratify its desires.

Do Not Pass Judgment on One Another

14 As for the one who is weak in faith, welcome him, but not to quarrel over opinions. ² One person believes he may eat anything, while the weak person eats only vegetables. ³ Let not the one who eats despise the one who abstains, and let not the one who abstains pass judgment on the one who eats, for God has welcomed him. ⁴ Who are you to pass judgment on the servant of another? It is before his own master that he stands or falls. And he will be upheld, for the Lord is able to make him stand.

⁵ One person esteems one day as better than another, while another esteems all days alike. Each one should be fully convinced in his own mind. ⁶ The one who observes the day, observes it in honor of the Lord. The one who eats, eats in honor of the Lord, since he gives thanks to God, while the one who abstains, abstains in honor of the Lord and gives thanks to God. ⁷ For none of us lives to himself, and none of us dies to himself. ⁸ For if we live, we live to the Lord, and if we die, we die to the Lord. So then, whether we live or whether we die, we are the Lord's. ⁹ For to this end Christ died and lived again, that he might be Lord both of the dead and of the living.

¹⁰ Why do you pass judgment on your brother? Or you, why do you despise your brother? For we will all stand before the judgment seat of God; ¹¹ for it is written,

> "As I live, says the Lord, every knee
> shall bow to me,
> and every tongue shall confess to
> God."

¹² So then each of us will give an account of himself to God.

Do Not Cause Another to Stumble

¹³ Therefore let us not pass judgment on one another any longer, but rather decide never to put a stumbling block or hindrance in the way of a brother. ¹⁴ I know and am persuaded in the Lord Jesus that nothing is unclean in itself, but it is unclean for

anyone who thinks it unclean. [15] For if your brother is grieved by what you eat, you are no longer walking in love. By what you eat, do not destroy the one for whom Christ died. [16] So do not let what you regard as good be spoken of as evil. [17] For the kingdom of God is not a matter of eating and drinking but of righteousness and peace and joy in the Holy Spirit. [18] Whoever thus serves Christ is acceptable to God and approved by men. [19] So then let us pursue what makes for peace and for mutual upbuilding.

[20] Do not, for the sake of food, destroy the work of God. Everything is indeed clean, but it is wrong for anyone to make another stumble by what he eats. [21] It is good not to eat meat or drink wine or do anything that causes your brother to stumble. [22] The faith that you have, keep between yourself and God. Blessed is the one who has no reason to pass judgment on himself for what he approves. [23] But whoever has doubts is condemned if he eats, because the eating is not from faith. For whatever does not proceed from faith is sin.

The Example of Christ

15 We who are strong have an obligation to bear with the failings of the weak, and not to please ourselves. [2] Let each of us please his neighbor for his good, to build him up. [3] For Christ did not please himself, but as it is written, "The reproaches of those who reproached you fell on me." [4] For whatever was written in former days was written for our instruction, that through endurance and through the encouragement of the Scriptures we might have hope. [5] May the God of endurance and encouragement grant you to live in such harmony with one another, in accord with Christ Jesus, [6] that together you may with one voice glorify the God and Father of our Lord Jesus Christ. [7] Therefore welcome one another as Christ has welcomed you, for the glory of God.

Christ the Hope of Jews and Gentiles

[8] For I tell you that Christ became a servant to the circumcised to show God's truthfulness, in order to confirm the promises given to the patriarchs, [9] and in order that the Gentiles might glorify God for his mercy. As it is written,

"Therefore I will praise you among the
    Gentiles,
    and sing to your name."

[10] And again it is said,

"Rejoice, O Gentiles, with his people."

[11] And again,

"Praise the Lord, all you Gentiles,
    and let all the peoples extol him."

[12] And again Isaiah says,

"The root of Jesse will come,
    even he who arises to rule the
        Gentiles;
    in him will the Gentiles hope."

[13] May the God of hope fill you with all joy and peace in believing, so that by the power of the Holy Spirit you may abound in hope.

Paul the Minister to the Gentiles

[14] I myself am satisfied about you, my brothers,[1] that you yourselves are full of goodness, filled with all knowledge and able to instruct one another. [15] But on some points I have written to you very boldly by way of reminder, because of the grace given me by God [16] to be a minister of Christ Jesus to the Gentiles in the priestly service of the gospel of God, so that the offering of the Gentiles may be acceptable, sanctified by the Holy Spirit. [17] In Christ Jesus, then, I have reason to be proud of my work for God. [18] For I will not venture to speak of anything except what Christ has accomplished through me to bring the Gentiles to obedience—by word and deed, [19] by the power of signs and wonders, by the power of the Spirit of God—so that from Jerusalem and all the way around to Illyricum I have fulfilled the ministry of the gospel of Christ; [20] and thus I make it my ambition to preach the gospel, not where Christ has already been named, lest I build on someone else's foundation, [21] but as it is written,

"Those who have never been told of
        him will see,
    and those who have never heard
        will understand."

Paul's Plan to Visit Rome

[22] This is the reason why I have so often been hindered from coming to you. [23] But

---

[1] Or brothers and sisters

now, since I no longer have any room for work in these regions, and since I have longed for many years to come to you, [24] I hope to see you in passing as I go to Spain, and to be helped on my journey there by you, once I have enjoyed your company for a while. [25] At present, however, I am going to Jerusalem bringing aid to the saints. [26] For Macedonia and Achaia have been pleased to make some contribution for the poor among the saints at Jerusalem. [27] For they were pleased to do it, and indeed they owe it to them. For if the Gentiles have come to share in their spiritual blessings, they ought also to be of service to them in material blessings. [28] When therefore I have completed this and have delivered to them what has been collected, I will leave for Spain by way of you. [29] I know that when

GETTING THE MESSAGE

Paul had not visited Rome when he wrote this letter, but he sent personal greetings to more than 25 individually named men and women plus households (16:3-15). **He obviously cared deeply** for his Christian brothers and sisters and appreciated their work for Christ.

I come to you I will come in the fullness of the blessing of Christ.

[30] I appeal to you, brothers,[1] by our Lord Jesus Christ and by the love of the Spirit, to strive together with me in your prayers to God on my behalf, [31] that I may be delivered from the unbelievers in Judea, and that my service for Jerusalem may be acceptable to the saints, [32] so that by God's will I may come to you with joy and be refreshed in your company. [33] May the God of peace be with you all. Amen.

Personal Greetings

16 I commend to you our sister Phoebe, a servant of the church at Cenchreae, [2] that you may welcome her in the Lord in a way worthy of the saints, and help her in whatever she may need from you, for she has been a patron of many and of myself as well.

[3] Greet Prisca and Aquila, my fellow work-ers in Christ Jesus, [4] who risked their necks for my life, to whom not only I give thanks but all the churches of the Gentiles give thanks as well. [5] Greet also the church in their house. Greet my beloved Epaenetus, who was the first convert to Christ in Asia. [6] Greet Mary, who has worked hard for you. [7] Greet Andronicus and Junia, my kinsmen and my fellow prisoners. They are well known to the apostles, and they were in Christ before me. [8] Greet Ampliatus, my beloved in the Lord. [9] Greet Urbanus, our fellow worker in Christ, and my beloved Stachys. [10] Greet Apelles, who is approved in Christ. Greet those who belong to the family of Aristobulus. [11] Greet my kinsman Herodion. Greet those in the Lord who belong to the family of Narcissus. [12] Greet those workers in the Lord, Tryphaena and Tryphosa. Greet the beloved Persis, who has worked hard in the Lord. [13] Greet Rufus, chosen in the Lord; also his mother, who has been a mother to me as well. [14] Greet Asyncritus, Phlegon, Hermes, Patrobas, Hermas, and the brothers who are with them. [15] Greet Philologus, Julia, Nereus and his sister, and Olympas, and all the saints who are with them. [16] Greet one another with a holy kiss. All the churches of Christ greet you.

Final Instructions and Greetings

[17] I appeal to you, brothers, to watch out for those who cause divisions and create obstacles contrary to the doctrine that you have been taught; avoid them. [18] For such persons do not serve our Lord Christ, but their own appetites, and by smooth talk and flattery they deceive the hearts of the naive. [19] For your obedience is known to all, so that I rejoice over you, but I want you to be wise as to what is good and innocent as to what is evil. [20] The God of peace will soon crush Satan under your feet. The grace of our Lord Jesus Christ be with you.

[21] Timothy, my fellow worker, greets you; so do Lucius and Jason and Sosipater, my kinsmen.

[22] I Tertius, who wrote this letter, greet you in the Lord.

[23] Gaius, who is host to me and to the whole church, greets you. Erastus, the city treasurer, and our brother Quartus, greet you.

[1] Or brothers and sisters; also 16:14, 17

Doxology

25 Now to him who is able to strengthen you according to my gospel and the preaching of Jesus Christ, according to the revelation of the mystery that was kept secret for long ages 26 but has now been disclosed and through the prophetic writings has been made known to all nations, according to the command of the eternal God, to bring about the obedience of faith — 27 to the only wise God be glory forevermore through Jesus Christ! Amen.

INTRODUCTION TO 1 CORINTHIANS

c. A.D. 33/34	c. A.D. 48/49–51	c. A.D. 53–55
Conversion of Paul	Paul plants church at Corinth	Paul writes 1 Corinthians

AUTHOR, DATE, AND RECIPIENTS

The apostle Paul wrote this letter to the Corinthian church in the spring of A.D. 53, 54, or 55. This was near the end of his three-year ministry in Ephesus. Altogether Paul wrote four letters to this church: (1) the previous letter mentioned in 1 Corinthians 5:9; (2) 1 Corinthians; (3) the tearful, severe letter mentioned in 2 Corinthians 2:3–4; and (4) 2 Corinthians. Only 1 and 2 Corinthians have survived.

THEME

The Corinthian church, divided because of the arrogance of its more powerful members, should work together for the advancement of the gospel. They should repent of their rivalries, build up the faith of those who are weak, and witness effectively to unbelievers.

PURPOSE

Paul received an oral report and a letter from the Corinthian church. These revealed a church struggling with division, immorality, idolatry, and theological confusion. He wrote them this letter so that they would become a true dwelling place for God's Spirit (3:12, 16), stay faithful to the gospel, and be "guiltless in the day of our Lord Jesus Christ" (1:8).

KEY THEMES

1. The church is the dwelling place of God's Spirit. Thus, the people who make up the church should work for unity by building each other up (1:10–4:21, especially 3:10–16; 14:12).

2. Christians should build up the church in four practical ways:

   a. they should be sensitive to those with fragile faith (8:1–9:18; 10:28, 33).

   b. they should win unbelievers to the faith (9:19–23; 10:27, 32–33).

   c. they should conduct worship services in such a way that unbelievers might come to faith (14:16, 23–25).

   d. their corporate worship should use spiritual gifts not out of personal pride, or for evaluating who has the better gift, but to build up the church (11:2–16; 12:12–30; 14:1–35).

3. Sexual relations form a union between man and woman as deep as the union of the believer with Christ. Therefore sexual activity should be confined to marriage (5:1–13; 6:12–20; 7:5, 9, 36).

4. Baptism and the Lord's Supper are important. Yet both are less important than personal trust in the gospel and living in the way God commands (1:14–17; 10:1–5; 11:17–34; 15:29–34).

5. The bodily resurrection of Jesus (and of his followers) from the dead is a key truth of the Christian faith (6:14; 15:1–58).

OUTLINE

I. Introduction to the Letter's Main Themes (1:1–9)

II. Divisions over Christian Preachers (1:10–4:21)

III. A Report of Sexual Immorality and Lawsuits (5:1–6:20)

IV. Three Issues from the Corinthians' Letter (7:1–11:1)

V. Divisions over Corporate Worship (11:2–14:40)

VI. The Futility of Faith If the Dead Are Not Raised (15:1–58)

VII. The Collection for the Saints and Travel Plans (16:1–12)

VIII. Closing Admonitions and Greetings (16:13–24)

1 CORINTHIANS

Greeting

1 Paul, called by the will of God to be an apostle of Christ Jesus, and our brother Sosthenes,

² To the church of God that is in Corinth, to those sanctified in Christ Jesus, called to be saints together with all those who in every place call upon the name of our Lord Jesus Christ, both their Lord and ours:

³ Grace to you and peace from God our Father and the Lord Jesus Christ.

Thanksgiving

⁴ I give thanks to my God always for you because of the grace of God that was given you in Christ Jesus, ⁵ that in every way you were enriched in him in all speech and all knowledge— ⁶ even as the testimony about Christ was confirmed among you— ⁷ so that you are not lacking in any gift, as you wait for the revealing of our Lord Jesus Christ, ⁸ who will sustain you to the end, guiltless in the day of our Lord Jesus Christ. ⁹ God is faithful, by whom you were called into the fellowship of his Son, Jesus Christ our Lord.

Divisions in the Church

¹⁰ I appeal to you, brothers,[1] by the name of our Lord Jesus Christ, that all of you agree, and that there be no divisions among you, but that you be united in the same mind and the same judgment. ¹¹ For it has been reported to me by Chloe's people that there is quarreling among you, my brothers. ¹² What I mean is that each one of you says, "I follow Paul," or "I follow Apollos," or "I follow Cephas," or "I follow Christ." ¹³ Is Christ divided? Was Paul crucified for you? Or were you baptized in the name of Paul? ¹⁴ I thank God that I baptized none of you except Crispus and Gaius, ¹⁵ so that no one may say that you were baptized in my name. ¹⁶ (I did baptize also the household of Stephanas. Beyond that, I do not know whether I baptized anyone else.) ¹⁷ For Christ did not send me to baptize but to preach the gospel, and not with words of eloquent wisdom, lest the cross of Christ be emptied of its power.

Christ the Wisdom and Power of God

¹⁸ For the word of the cross is folly to those who are perishing, but to us who are being saved it is the power of God. ¹⁹ For it is written,

> "I will destroy the wisdom of the wise,
> and the discernment of the discerning I will thwart."

²⁰ Where is the one who is wise? Where is the scribe? Where is the debater of this age?

> ### GETTING THE MESSAGE
>
> **Apollos** (1:12) was a Jew from the city of Alexandria. He was "an eloquent man, competent in the Scriptures" (Acts 18:24). At Ephesus, Aquila and Priscilla helped Apollos to better understand the gospel. From Ephesus he traveled on to Corinth, where the church benefited greatly from his teaching (1 Cor. 3:6).

Has not God made foolish the wisdom of the world? ²¹ For since, in the wisdom of God, the world did not know God through wisdom, it pleased God through the folly of what we preach to save those who believe. ²² For Jews demand signs and Greeks seek wisdom, ²³ but we preach Christ crucified, a stumbling block to Jews and folly to Gentiles, ²⁴ but to those who are called, both Jews and Greeks, Christ the power of God and the wisdom of God. ²⁵ For the foolishness of God is wiser than men, and the weakness of God is stronger than men.

²⁶ For consider your calling, brothers: not many of you were wise according to worldly standards, not many were powerful, not many were of noble birth; ²⁷ But God chose what is foolish in the world to shame the wise; God chose what is weak in the world to shame the strong; ²⁸ God chose what is

[1] Or brothers and sisters (see Preface); also 1:11, 26

low and despised in the world, even things that are not, to bring to nothing things that are, [29] so that no human being might boast in the presence of God. [30] And because of him you are in Christ Jesus, who became to us wisdom from God, righteousness and sanctification and redemption, [31] so that, as it is written, "Let the one who boasts, boast in the Lord."

Proclaiming Christ Crucified

2 And I, when I came to you, brothers,[1] did not come proclaiming to you the testimony of God with lofty speech or wisdom. [2] For I decided to know nothing among you except Jesus Christ and him crucified. [3] And I was with you in weakness and in fear and much trembling, [4] and my speech and my message were not in plausible words of wisdom, but in demonstration of the Spirit

---

GETTING THE MESSAGE

The wisdom of men and the power of God. Mere intellectual persuasion does not save people. Saving faith is produced by the heart-changing power of the Holy Spirit as the gospel is proclaimed (2:5).

---

and of power, [5] so that your faith might not rest in the wisdom of men[2] but in the power of God.

Wisdom from the Spirit

[6] Yet among the mature we do impart wisdom, although it is not a wisdom of this age or of the rulers of this age, who are doomed to pass away. [7] But we impart a secret and hidden wisdom of God, which God decreed before the ages for our glory. [8] None of the rulers of this age understood this, for if they had, they would not have crucified the Lord of glory. [9] But, as it is written,

"What no eye has seen, nor ear heard,
    nor the heart of man imagined,
what God has prepared for those who
        love him"—

[10] these things God has revealed to us through the Spirit. For the Spirit searches everything, even the depths of God. [11] For who knows a person's thoughts except the spirit of that person, which is in him? So also no one comprehends the thoughts of God except the Spirit of God. [12] Now we have received not the spirit of the world, but the Spirit who is from God, that we might understand the things freely given us by God. [13] And we impart this in words not taught by human wisdom but taught by the Spirit, interpreting spiritual truths to those who are spiritual.

[14] The natural person does not accept the things of the Spirit of God, for they are folly to him, and he is not able to understand them because they are spiritually discerned. [15] The spiritual person judges all things, but is himself to be judged by no one. [16] "For who has understood the mind of the Lord so as to instruct him?" But we have the mind of Christ.

Divisions in the Church

3 But I, brothers, could not address you as spiritual people, but as people of the flesh, as infants in Christ. [2] I fed you with milk, not solid food, for you were not ready for it. And even now you are not yet ready, [3] for you are still of the flesh. For while there is jealousy and strife among you, are you not of the flesh and behaving only in a human way? [4] For when one says, "I follow Paul," and another, "I follow Apollos," are you not being merely human?

[5] What then is Apollos? What is Paul? Servants through whom you believed, as the Lord assigned to each. [6] I planted, Apollos watered, but God gave the growth. [7] So neither he who plants nor he who waters is anything, but only God who gives the growth. [8] He who plants and he who waters are one, and each will receive his wages according to his labor. [9] For we are God's fellow workers. You are God's field, God's building.

[10] According to the grace of God given to me, like a skilled master builder I laid a foundation, and someone else is building upon it. Let each one take care how he builds upon it. [11] For no one can lay a foundation other than that which is laid, which is Jesus Christ. [12] Now if anyone builds on the foundation with gold, silver, precious stones, wood, hay, straw— [13] each one's work will become manifest, for the Day will disclose it, because it will be revealed by fire, and the fire will test what sort of work each one has

---

[1] Or brothers and sisters; also 3:1 [2] The Greek word for men refers to both men and women (see Preface)

done. [14] If the work that anyone has built on the foundation survives, he will receive a reward. [15] If anyone's work is burned up, he will suffer loss, though he himself will be saved, but only as through fire.

[16] Do you not know that you are God's temple and that God's Spirit dwells in you? [17] If anyone destroys God's temple, God will destroy him. For God's temple is holy, and you are that temple.

[18] Let no one deceive himself. If anyone among you thinks that he is wise in this age, let him become a fool that he may become wise. [19] For the wisdom of this world is folly with God. For it is written, "He catches the wise in their craftiness," [20] and again, "The Lord knows the thoughts of the wise, that they are futile." [21] So let no one boast in men. For all things are yours, [22] whether Paul or Apollos or Cephas or the world or life or death or the present or the future—all are yours, [23] and you are Christ's, and Christ is God's.

The Ministry of Apostles

4 This is how one should regard us, as servants of Christ and stewards of the mysteries of God. [2] Moreover, it is required of stewards that they be found faithful. [3] But with me it is a very small thing that I should be judged by you or by any human court. In fact, I do not even judge myself. [4] For I am not aware of anything against myself, but I am not thereby acquitted. It is the Lord who judges me. [5] Therefore do not pronounce judgment before the time, before the Lord comes, who will bring to light the things now hidden in darkness and will disclose the purposes of the heart. Then each one will receive his commendation from God.

[6] I have applied all these things to myself and Apollos for your benefit, brothers,[1] that you may learn by us not to go beyond what is written, that none of you may be puffed up in favor of one against another. [7] For who sees anything different in you? What do you have that you did not receive? If then you received it, why do you boast as if you did not receive it?

[8] Already you have all you want! Already you have become rich! Without us you have become kings! And would that you did reign, so that we might share the rule with you! [9] For I think that God has exhibited us apostles as last of all, like men sentenced to death, because we have become a spectacle to the world, to angels, and to men. [10] We are fools for Christ's sake, but you are wise in Christ. We are weak, but you are strong. You are held in honor, but we in disrepute. [11] To the present hour we hunger and thirst, we are poorly dressed and buffeted and homeless, [12] and we labor, working with our own hands. When reviled, we bless; when persecuted, we endure; [13] when slandered, we entreat. We have become, and are still, like the scum of the world, the refuse of all things.

[14] I do not write these things to make you ashamed, but to admonish you as my beloved children. [15] For though you have countless guides in Christ, you do not have many fathers. For I became your father in

Christ Jesus through the gospel. [16] I urge you, then, be imitators of me. [17] That is why I sent you Timothy, my beloved and faithful child in the Lord, to remind you of my ways in Christ, as I teach them everywhere in every church. [18] Some are arrogant, as though I were not coming to you. [19] But I will come to you soon, if the Lord wills, and I will find out not the talk of these arrogant people but their power. [20] For the kingdom of God does not consist in talk but in power. [21] What do you wish? Shall I come to you with a rod, or with love in a spirit of gentleness?

Sexual Immorality Defiles the Church

5 It is actually reported that there is sexual immorality among you, and of a kind that is not tolerated even among pagans, for a man has his father's wife. [2] And you are arrogant! Ought you not rather to mourn?

[1] Or brothers and sisters

Let him who has done this be removed from among you.

3 For though absent in body, I am present in spirit; and as if present, I have already pronounced judgment on the one who did such a thing. **4** When you are assembled in the name of the Lord Jesus and my spirit is present, with the power of our Lord Jesus, **5** you are to deliver this man to Satan for the destruction of the flesh, so that his spirit may be saved in the day of the Lord.

6 Your boasting is not good. Do you not know that a little leaven leavens the whole lump? **7** Cleanse out the old leaven that you may be a new lump, as you really are unleavened. For Christ, our Passover lamb, has been sacrificed. **8** Let us therefore celebrate the festival, not with the old leaven, the leaven of malice and evil, but with the unleavened bread of sincerity and truth.

> **GETTING THE MESSAGE**
>
> **Leaven** is fermented or soured dough that is added in small amounts to a larger portion in order to make it rise. In the New Testament, leaven often symbolizes sin that goes undisciplined or unchecked and thus negatively affects the church as a whole (5:6–8).

9 I wrote to you in my letter not to associate with sexually immoral people— **10** not at all meaning the sexually immoral of this world, or the greedy and swindlers, or idolaters, since then you would need to go out of the world. **11** But now I am writing to you not to associate with anyone who bears the name of brother if he is guilty of sexual immorality or greed, or is an idolater, reviler, drunkard, or swindler—not even to eat with such a one. **12** For what have I to do with judging outsiders? Is it not those inside the church whom you are to judge? **13** God judges those outside. "Purge the evil person from among you."

Lawsuits Against Believers

6 When one of you has a grievance against another, does he dare go to law before the unrighteous instead of the saints? **2** Or do you not know that the saints will judge the world? And if the world is to be judged by you, are you incompetent to try trivial cases? **3** Do you not know that we are to judge angels? How much more, then, matters pertaining to this life! **4** So if you have such cases, why do you lay them before those who have no standing in the church? **5** I say this to your shame. Can it be that there is no one among you wise enough to settle a dispute between the brothers, **6** but brother goes to law against brother, and that before unbelievers? **7** To have lawsuits at all with one another is already a defeat for you. Why not rather suffer wrong? Why not rather be defrauded? **8** But you yourselves wrong and defraud—even your own brothers![1]

9 Or do you not know that the unrighteous will not inherit the kingdom of God? Do not be deceived: neither the sexually immoral, nor idolaters, nor adulterers, nor men who practice homosexuality, **10** nor thieves, nor the greedy, nor drunkards, nor revilers, nor swindlers will inherit the kingdom of God. **11** And such were some of you. But you were washed, you were sanctified, you were justified in the name of the Lord Jesus Christ and by the Spirit of our God.

Flee Sexual Immorality

12 "All things are lawful for me," but not all things are helpful. "All things are lawful for me," but I will not be dominated by anything. **13** "Food is meant for the stomach and the stomach for food"—and God will destroy both one and the other. The body is not meant for sexual immorality, but for the Lord, and the Lord for the body. **14** And God raised the Lord and will also raise us up by his power. **15** Do you not know that your bodies are members of Christ? Shall I then take the members of Christ and make them members of a prostitute? Never! **16** Or do you not know that he who is joined to a prostitute becomes one body with her? For, as it is written, "The two will become one flesh." **17** But he who is joined to the Lord becomes one spirit with him. **18** Flee from sexual immorality. Every other sin a person commits is outside the body, but the sexually immoral person sins against his own body. **19** Or do you not know that your body is a temple of the Holy Spirit within you, whom you have from God? You are not your own, **20** for you were bought with a price. So glorify God in your body.

[1] Or brothers and sisters

Principles for Marriage

7 Now concerning the matters about which you wrote: "It is good for a man not to have sexual relations with a woman." ² But because of the temptation to sexual immorality, each man should have his own wife and each woman her own husband. ³ The husband should give to his wife her conjugal rights, and likewise the wife to her husband. ⁴ For the wife does not have authority over her own body, but the husband does. Likewise the husband does not have authority over his own body, but the wife does. ⁵ Do not deprive one another, except perhaps by agreement for a limited time, that you may devote yourselves to prayer; but then come together again, so that Satan may not tempt you because of your lack of self-control.

⁶ Now as a concession, not a command, I say this. ⁷ I wish that all were as I myself am. But each has his own gift from God, one of one kind and one of another.

⁸ To the unmarried and the widows I say that it is good for them to remain single as I am. ⁹ But if they cannot exercise self-control, they should marry. For it is better to marry than to burn with passion.

¹⁰ To the married I give this charge (not I, but the Lord): the wife should not separate from her husband ¹¹ (but if she does, she should remain unmarried or else be reconciled to her husband), and the husband should not divorce his wife.

¹² To the rest I say (I, not the Lord) that if any brother has a wife who is an unbeliever, and she consents to live with him, he should not divorce her. ¹³ If any woman has a husband who is an unbeliever, and he consents to live with her, she should not divorce him. ¹⁴ For the unbelieving husband is made holy because of his wife, and the unbelieving wife is made holy because of her husband. Otherwise your children would be unclean, but as it is, they are holy. ¹⁵ But if the unbelieving partner separates, let it be so. In such cases the brother or sister is not enslaved. God has called you to peace. ¹⁶ For how do you know, wife, whether you will save your husband? Or how do you know, husband, whether you will save your wife?

Live as You Are Called

¹⁷ Only let each person lead the life that the Lord has assigned to him, and to which God has called him. This is my rule in all the churches. ¹⁸ Was anyone at the time of his call already circumcised? Let him not seek to remove the marks of circumcision. Was anyone at the time of his call uncircumcised? Let him not seek circumcision. ¹⁹ For neither circumcision counts for anything nor uncircumcision, but keeping the commandments of God. ²⁰ Each one should remain in the condition in which he was called. ²¹ Were you a bondservant when called? Do not be concerned about it. (But if you can gain your freedom, avail yourself of the opportunity.) ²² For he who was called in the Lord as a bondservant is a freedman of the Lord. Likewise he who was free when called is a bondservant of Christ. ²³ You were bought with a price; do not become bondservants of men. ²⁴ So, brothers,¹ in whatever condition each was called, there let him remain with God.

GETTING THE MESSAGE

What is a "freedman"? A released bondservant was officially designated a "freedman" (7:21–22). Bondservants were often paid and some were able eventually to buy their freedom.

The Unmarried and the Widowed

²⁵ Now concerning the betrothed, I have no command from the Lord, but I give my judgment as one who by the Lord's mercy is trustworthy. ²⁶ I think that in view of the present distress it is good for a person to remain as he is. ²⁷ Are you bound to a wife? Do not seek to be free. Are you free from a wife? Do not seek a wife. ²⁸ But if you do marry, you have not sinned, and if a betrothed woman marries, she has not sinned. Yet those who marry will have worldly troubles, and I would spare you that. ²⁹ This is what I mean, brothers: the appointed time has grown very short. From now on, let those who have wives live as though they had none, ³⁰ and those who mourn as though they were not mourning, and those who rejoice as though they were not rejoicing, and those who buy as though they had no goods, ³¹ and those who deal with the world as though they had no deal-

¹ Or brothers and sisters; also 7:29

ings with it. For the present form of this world is passing away.

[32] I want you to be free from anxieties. The unmarried man is anxious about the things of the Lord, how to please the Lord. [33] But the married man is anxious about worldly things, how to please his wife, [34] and his interests are divided. And the unmarried or betrothed woman is anxious about the things of the Lord, how to be holy in body and spirit. But the married woman is anxious about worldly things, how to please her husband. [35] I say this for your own benefit, not to lay any restraint upon you, but to promote good order and to secure your undivided devotion to the Lord.

[36] If anyone thinks that he is not behaving properly toward his betrothed, if his passions are strong, and it has to be, let him do

GETTING THE MESSAGE

First Corinthians is a **pastoral letter** to a spiritually troubled church. Paul deeply loved the church at Corinth, but he was distressed by some of the behavior prevalent among its members. He wrote to the Corinthians to address such issues as the relationship between Christians and the surrounding culture, divisions within the church, and matters of personal morality.

as he wishes: let them marry—it is no sin. [37] But whoever is firmly established in his heart, being under no necessity but having his desire under control, and has determined this in his heart, to keep her as his betrothed, he will do well. [38] So then he who marries his betrothed does well, and he who refrains from marriage will do even better.

[39] A wife is bound to her husband as long as he lives. But if her husband dies, she is free to be married to whom she wishes, only in the Lord. [40] Yet in my judgment she is happier if she remains as she is. And I think that I too have the Spirit of God.

Food Offered to Idols

8 Now concerning food offered to idols: we know that "all of us possess knowledge." This "knowledge" puffs up, but love builds up. [2] If anyone imagines that he

knows something, he does not yet know as he ought to know. [3] But if anyone loves God, he is known by God.

[4] Therefore, as to the eating of food offered to idols, we know that "an idol has no real existence," and that "there is no God but one." [5] For although there may be so-called gods in heaven or on earth—as indeed there are many "gods" and many "lords"— [6] yet for us there is one God, the Father, from whom are all things and for whom we exist, and one Lord, Jesus Christ, through whom are all things and through whom we exist.

[7] However, not all possess this knowledge. But some, through former association with idols, eat food as really offered to an idol, and their conscience, being weak, is defiled. [8] Food will not commend us to God. We are no worse off if we do not eat, and no better off if we do. [9] But take care that this right of yours does not somehow become a stumbling block to the weak. [10] For if anyone sees you who have knowledge eating in an idol's temple, will he not be encouraged, if his conscience is weak, to eat food offered to idols? [11] And so by your knowledge this weak person is destroyed, the brother for whom Christ died. [12] Thus, sinning against your brothers[1] and wounding their conscience when it is weak, you sin against Christ. [13] Therefore, if food makes my brother stumble, I will never eat meat, lest I make my brother stumble.

Paul Surrenders His Rights

9 Am I not free? Am I not an apostle? Have I not seen Jesus our Lord? Are not you my workmanship in the Lord? [2] If to others I am not an apostle, at least I am to you, for you are the seal of my apostleship in the Lord.

[3] This is my defense to those who would examine me. [4] Do we not have the right to eat and drink? [5] Do we not have the right to take along a believing wife, as do the other apostles and the brothers of the Lord and Cephas? [6] Or is it only Barnabas and I who have no right to refrain from working for a living? [7] Who serves as a soldier at his own expense? Who plants a vineyard without eating any of its fruit? Or who tends a flock without getting some of the milk?

[8] Do I say these things on human authority? Does not the Law say the same? [9] For it is

[1] Or brothers and sisters

written in the Law of Moses, "You shall not muzzle an ox when it treads out the grain." Is it for oxen that God is concerned? [10] Does he not certainly speak for our sake? It was written for our sake, because the plowman should plow in hope and the thresher thresh in hope of sharing in the crop. [11] If we have sown spiritual things among you, is it too much if we reap material things from you? [12] If others share this rightful claim on you, do not we even more?

Nevertheless, we have not made use of this right, but we endure anything rather than put an obstacle in the way of the gospel of Christ. [13] Do you not know that those who are employed in the temple service get their food from the temple, and those who serve at the altar share in the sacrificial offerings? [14] In the same way, the Lord commanded that those who proclaim the gospel should get their living by the gospel.

[15] But I have made no use of any of these rights, nor am I writing these things to secure any such provision. For I would rather die than have anyone deprive me of my ground for boasting. [16] For if I preach the gospel, that gives me no ground for boasting. For necessity is laid upon me. Woe to me if I do not preach the gospel! [17] For if I do this of my own will, I have a reward, but if not of my own will, I am still entrusted with a stewardship. [18] What then is my reward? That in my preaching I may present the gospel free of charge, so as not to make full use of my right in the gospel.

[19] For though I am free from all, I have made myself a servant to all, that I might win more of them. [20] To the Jews I became as a Jew, in order to win Jews. To those under the law I became as one under the law (though not being myself under the law) that I might win those under the law. [21] To those outside the law I became as one outside the law (not being outside the law of God but under the law of Christ) that I might win those outside the law. [22] To the weak I became weak, that I might win the weak. I have become all things to all people, that by all means I might save some. [23] I do it all for the sake of the gospel, that I may share with them in its blessings.

[24] Do you not know that in a race all the runners run, but only one receives the prize?

So run that you may obtain it. [25] Every athlete exercises self-control in all things. They do it to receive a perishable wreath, but we an imperishable. [26] So I do not run aimlessly; I do not box as one beating the air. [27] But I discipline my body and keep it under control, lest after preaching to others I myself should be disqualified.

Warning Against Idolatry

10 For I do not want you to be unaware, brothers,[1] that our fathers were all under the cloud, and all passed through the sea, [2] and all were baptized into Moses in the cloud and in the sea, [3] and all ate the same spiritual food, [4] and all drank the same spiritual drink. For they drank from the spiritual Rock that followed them, and the Rock was Christ. [5] Nevertheless, with most of them

---

GETTING THE MESSAGE

Free of charge. Traveling speakers and teachers were a common sight in Paul's day. Some of them openly used their speaking skills to seek fame and fortune. Others claimed to despise materialism while privately pocketing large sums of money. Paul distinguished himself from such dishonest people by earning his own living through manual labor (9:18; compare 1 Thess. 4:11).

God was not pleased, for they were overthrown in the wilderness.

[6] Now these things took place as examples for us, that we might not desire evil as they did. [7] Do not be idolaters as some of them were; as it is written, "The people sat down to eat and drink and rose up to play." [8] We must not indulge in sexual immorality as some of them did, and twenty-three thousand fell in a single day. [9] We must not put Christ to the test, as some of them did and were destroyed by serpents, [10] nor grumble, as some of them did and were destroyed by the Destroyer. [11] Now these things happened to them as an example, but they were written down for our instruction, on whom the end of the ages has come. [12] Therefore let anyone who thinks that he stands take heed lest he fall. [13] No temptation has overtaken

---

[1] Or brothers and sisters

you that is not common to man. God is faithful, and he will not let you be tempted beyond your ability, but with the temptation he will also provide the way of escape, that you may be able to endure it.

14 Therefore, my beloved, flee from idolatry. **15** I speak as to sensible people; judge for yourselves what I say. **16** The cup of blessing that we bless, is it not a participation in the blood of Christ? The bread that we break, is it not a participation in the body of Christ? **17** Because there is one bread, we who are many are one body, for we all partake of the one bread. **18** Consider the people of Israel: are not those who eat the sacrifices participants in the altar? **19** What do I imply then? That food offered to idols is anything, or that an idol is anything? **20** No, I imply that what pagans sacrifice they offer to demons and not to God. I do not want you to be participants with demons. **21** You cannot drink the cup of the Lord and the cup of demons. You cannot partake of the table of the Lord and the table of demons. **22** Shall we provoke the Lord to jealousy? Are we stronger than he?

Do All to the Glory of God

23 "All things are lawful," but not all things are helpful. "All things are lawful," but not all things build up. **24** Let no one seek his own good, but the good of his neighbor. **25** Eat whatever is sold in the meat market without raising any question on the ground of conscience. **26** For "the earth is the Lord's, and the fullness thereof." **27** If one of the unbelievers invites you to dinner and you are disposed to go, eat whatever is set before you without raising any question on the ground of conscience. **28** But if someone says to you, "This has been offered in sacrifice," then do not eat it, for the sake of the one who informed you, and for the sake of conscience— **29** I do not mean your conscience, but his. For why should my liberty be determined by someone else's conscience? **30** If I partake with thankfulness, why am I denounced because of that for which I give thanks?

31 So, whether you eat or drink, or whatever you do, do all to the glory of God. **32** Give no offense to Jews or to Greeks or to the church of God, **33** just as I try to please everyone in everything I do, not seeking my own

advantage, but that of many, that they may be saved.

11 Be imitators of me, as I am of Christ.

Head Coverings

2 Now I commend you because you remember me in everything and maintain the traditions even as I delivered them to you. **3** But I want you to understand that the head of every man is Christ, the head of a wife is her husband, and the head of Christ is God. **4** Every man who prays or prophesies with his head covered dishonors his head, **5** but every wife who prays or prophesies with her head uncovered[1] dishonors her head, since it is the same as if her head were shaven.[2] **6** For if a wife will not cover her head, then she should cut her hair short. But since it is disgraceful for a wife to cut off her hair or shave her head, let her cover her head. **7** For a man ought not to cover his head, since he is the image and glory of God, but woman is the glory of man. **8** For man was not made from woman, but woman from man. **9** Neither was man created for woman, but woman for man. **10** That is why a wife ought to have a symbol of authority on her head, because of the angels. **11** Nevertheless, in the Lord woman is not independent of man nor man of woman; **12** for as woman was made from man, so man is now born of woman. And all things are from God. **13** Judge for yourselves: is it proper for a wife to pray to God with her head uncovered? **14** Does not nature itself teach you that if a man wears long hair[3] it is a disgrace for him, **15** but if a woman has long hair, it is her glory? For her hair is given to her for a covering. **16** If anyone is inclined to be contentious, we have no such practice, nor do the churches of God.

The Lord's Supper

17 But in the following instructions I do not commend you, because when you come together it is not for the better but for the worse. **18** For, in the first place, when you come together as a church, I hear that there are divisions among you. And I believe it in part, **19** for there must be factions among you in order that those who are genuine among you may be recognized. **20** When you come

[1] In ancient times, married women often wore headscarves to show that they were married [2] In ancient times, female prostitutes often shaved their heads [3] In ancient times, male prostitutes often had long hair

together, it is not the Lord's supper that you eat. ²¹For in eating, each one goes ahead with his own meal. One goes hungry, another gets drunk. ²²What! Do you not have houses to eat and drink in? Or do you despise the church of God and humiliate those who have nothing? What shall I say to you? Shall I commend you in this? No, I will not.

²³For I received from the Lord what I also delivered to you, that the Lord Jesus on the night when he was betrayed took bread, ²⁴and when he had given thanks, he broke it, and said, "This is my body which is for you. Do this in remembrance of me." ²⁵In the same way also he took the cup, after supper, saying, "This cup is the new covenant in my blood. Do this, as often as you drink it, in remembrance of me." ²⁶For as often as you eat this bread and drink the cup, you proclaim the Lord's death until he comes.

²⁷Whoever, therefore, eats the bread or drinks the cup of the Lord in an unworthy manner will be guilty concerning the body and blood of the Lord. ²⁸Let a person examine himself, then, and so eat of the bread and drink of the cup. ²⁹For anyone who eats and drinks without discerning the body eats and drinks judgment on himself. ³⁰That is why many of you are weak and ill, and some have died. ³¹But if we judged ourselves truly, we would not be judged. ³²But when we are judged by the Lord, we are disciplined so that we may not be condemned along with the world.

³³So then, my brothers,¹ when you come together to eat, wait for one another— ³⁴if anyone is hungry, let him eat at home—so that when you come together it will not be for judgment. About the other things I will give directions when I come.

Spiritual Gifts

12 Now concerning spiritual gifts, brothers, I do not want you to be uninformed. ²You know that when you were pagans you were led astray to mute idols, however you were led. ³Therefore I want you to understand that no one speaking in the Spirit of God ever says "Jesus is accursed!" and no one can say "Jesus is Lord" except in the Holy Spirit.

⁴Now there are varieties of gifts, but the same Spirit; ⁵and there are varieties of service, but the same Lord; ⁶and there are

varieties of activities, but it is the same God who empowers them all in everyone. ⁷To each is given the manifestation of the Spirit for the common good. ⁸For to one is given through the Spirit the utterance of wisdom, and to another the utterance of knowledge according to the same Spirit, ⁹to another faith by the same Spirit, to another gifts of healing by the one Spirit, ¹⁰to another the working of miracles, to another prophecy, to another the ability to distinguish between spirits, to another various kinds of tongues, to another the interpretation of tongues. ¹¹All these are empowered by one and the same Spirit, who apportions to each one individually as he wills.

One Body with Many Members

¹²For just as the body is one and has many members, and all the members of the body, though many, are one body, so it

---

GETTING THE MESSAGE

The right way to observe the Lord's Supper. Wealthy Corinthians in the church were apparently treating the Lord's Supper as an opportunity to display their elite social status (11:21-23). Paul reminds them of the true meaning of this important Christian observance (vv. 24-34).

---

is with Christ. ¹³For in one Spirit we were all baptized into one body—Jews or Greeks, slaves² or free—and all were made to drink of one Spirit.

¹⁴For the body does not consist of one member but of many. ¹⁵If the foot should say, "Because I am not a hand, I do not belong to the body," that would not make it any less a part of the body. ¹⁶And if the ear should say, "Because I am not an eye, I do not belong to the body," that would not make it any less a part of the body. ¹⁷If the whole body were an eye, where would be the sense of hearing? If the whole body were an ear, where would be the sense of smell? ¹⁸But as it is, God arranged the members in the body, each one of them, as he chose. ¹⁹If all were a single member, where would the body be? ²⁰As it is, there are many parts, yet one body.

---

¹ Or *brothers and sisters*; also 12:1 ² Greek *doulos* (see Preface)

21 The eye cannot say to the hand, "I have no need of you," nor again the head to the feet, "I have no need of you." 22 On the contrary, the parts of the body that seem to be weaker are indispensable, 23 and on those parts of the body that we think less honorable we bestow the greater honor, and our unpresentable parts are treated with greater modesty, 24 which our more presentable parts do not require. But God has so composed the body, giving greater honor to the part that lacked it, 25 that there may be no division in the body, but that the members may have the same care for one another. 26 If one member suffers, all suffer together; if one member is honored, all rejoice together.

27 Now you are the body of Christ and individually members of it. 28 And God has appointed in the church first apostles, second prophets, third teachers, then miracles,

GETTING THE MESSAGE

The greatest is love. Jesus said that Christians should be famous for their love for each other (John 13:34–35), but the Corinthian church was becoming known for its divisions and arguments (see 1 Cor. 3:3; 6:1; 11:18). Paul tells them what Christian love should look like (ch. 13).

then gifts of healing, helping, administrating, and various kinds of tongues. 29 Are all apostles? Are all prophets? Are all teachers? Do all work miracles? 30 Do all possess gifts of healing? Do all speak with tongues? Do all interpret? 31 But earnestly desire the higher gifts.

And I will show you a still more excellent way.

The Way of Love

13 If I speak in the tongues of men and of angels, but have not love, I am a noisy gong or a clanging cymbal. 2 And if I have prophetic powers, and understand all mysteries and all knowledge, and if I have all faith, so as to remove mountains, but have not love, I am nothing. 3 If I give away all I have, and if I deliver up my body to be burned, but have not love, I gain nothing.

4 Love is patient and kind; love does not envy or boast; it is not arrogant 5 or rude. It does not insist on its own way; it is not irritable or resentful; 6 it does not rejoice at wrongdoing, but rejoices with the truth. 7 Love bears all things, believes all things, hopes all things, endures all things.

8 Love never ends. As for prophecies, they will pass away; as for tongues, they will cease; as for knowledge, it will pass away. 9 For we know in part and we prophesy in part, 10 but when the perfect comes, the partial will pass away. 11 When I was a child, I spoke like a child, I thought like a child, I reasoned like a child. When I became a man, I gave up childish ways. 12 For now we see in a mirror dimly, but then face to face. Now I know in part; then I shall know fully, even as I have been fully known.

13 So now faith, hope, and love abide, these three; but the greatest of these is love.

Prophecy and Tongues

14 Pursue love, and earnestly desire the spiritual gifts, especially that you may prophesy. 2 For one who speaks in a tongue speaks not to men but to God; for no one understands him, but he utters mysteries in the Spirit. 3 On the other hand, the one who prophesies speaks to people for their upbuilding and encouragement and consolation. 4 The one who speaks in a tongue builds up himself, but the one who prophesies builds up the church. 5 Now I want you all to speak in tongues, but even more to prophesy. The one who prophesies is greater than the one who speaks in tongues, unless someone interprets, so that the church may be built up.

6 Now, brothers,[1] if I come to you speaking in tongues, how will I benefit you unless I bring you some revelation or knowledge or prophecy or teaching? 7 If even lifeless instruments, such as the flute or the harp, do not give distinct notes, how will anyone know what is played? 8 And if the bugle gives an indistinct sound, who will get ready for battle? 9 So with yourselves, if with your tongue you utter speech that is not intelligible, how will anyone know what is said? For you will be speaking into the air. 10 There are doubtless many different languages in the world, and none is without meaning, 11 but if I do not know the meaning of the language, I will be a foreigner to the

[1] Or brothers and sisters

speaker and the speaker a foreigner to me. [12] So with yourselves, since you are eager for manifestations of the Spirit, strive to excel in building up the church.

[13] Therefore, one who speaks in a tongue should pray that he may interpret. [14] For if I pray in a tongue, my spirit prays but my mind is unfruitful. [15] What am I to do? I will pray with my spirit, but I will pray with my mind also; I will sing praise with my spirit, but I will sing with my mind also. [16] Otherwise, if you give thanks with your spirit, how can anyone in the position of an outsider say "Amen" to your thanksgiving when he does not know what you are saying? [17] For you may be giving thanks well enough, but the other person is not being built up. [18] I thank God that I speak in tongues more than all of you. [19] Nevertheless, in church I would rather speak five words with my mind in order to instruct others, than ten thousand words in a tongue.

[20] Brothers,[1] do not be children in your thinking. Be infants in evil, but in your thinking be mature. [21] In the Law it is written, "By people of strange tongues and by the lips of foreigners will I speak to this people, and even then they will not listen to me, says the Lord." [22] Thus tongues are a sign not for believers but for unbelievers, while prophecy is a sign not for unbelievers but for believers. [23] If, therefore, the whole church comes together and all speak in tongues, and outsiders or unbelievers enter, will they not say that you are out of your minds? [24] But if all prophesy, and an unbeliever or outsider enters, he is convicted by all, he is called to account by all, [25] the secrets of his heart are disclosed, and so, falling on his face, he will worship God and declare that God is really among you.

Orderly Worship

[26] What then, brothers? When you come together, each one has a hymn, a lesson, a revelation, a tongue, or an interpretation. Let all things be done for building up. [27] If any speak in a tongue, let there be only two or at most three, and each in turn, and let someone interpret. [28] But if there is no one to interpret, let each of them keep silent in church and speak to himself and to God. [29] Let two or three prophets speak, and let the others weigh what is said. [30] If a reve-

lation is made to another sitting there, let the first be silent. [31] For you can all prophesy one by one, so that all may learn and all be encouraged, [32] and the spirits of prophets are subject to prophets. [33] For God is not a God of confusion but of peace.

As in all the churches of the saints, [34] the women should keep silent in the churches. For they are not permitted to speak, but should be in submission, as the Law also says. [35] If there is anything they desire to learn, let them ask their husbands at home. For it is shameful for a woman to speak in church.

[36] Or was it from you that the word of God came? Or are you the only ones it has reached? [37] If anyone thinks that he is a prophet, or spiritual, he should acknowledge that the things I am writing to you are a command of the Lord. [38] If anyone does not recognize this, he is not recognized. [39] So,

---

GETTING THE MESSAGE

When the church meets, it should be to worship the Lord and to **build up the church** (14:12, 17). "Building up" includes using words and actions to edify and instruct others, or to make others stronger and more mature in Christ.

---

my brothers, earnestly desire to prophesy, and do not forbid speaking in tongues. [40] But all things should be done decently and in order.

The Resurrection of Christ

15 Now I would remind you, brothers, of the gospel I preached to you, which you received, in which you stand, [2] and by which you are being saved, if you hold fast to the word I preached to you—unless you believed in vain.

[3] For I delivered to you as of first importance what I also received: that Christ died for our sins in accordance with the Scriptures, [4] that he was buried, that he was raised on the third day in accordance with the Scriptures, [5] and that he appeared to Cephas, then to the twelve. [6] Then he appeared to more than five hundred brothers at one time, most of whom are still alive, though some have fallen asleep. [7] Then he

---

[1] Or *Brothers and sisters*; also 14:26, 39; 15:1, 6

appeared to James, then to all the apostles. **8** Last of all, as to one untimely born, he appeared also to me. **9** For I am the least of the apostles, unworthy to be called an apostle, because I persecuted the church of God. **10** But by the grace of God I am what I am, and his grace toward me was not in vain. On the contrary, I worked harder than any of them, though it was not I, but the grace of God that is with me. **11** Whether then it was I or they, so we preach and so you believed.

The Resurrection of the Dead

12 Now if Christ is proclaimed as raised from the dead, how can some of you say that there is no resurrection of the dead? **13** But if there is no resurrection of the dead, then not even Christ has been raised. **14** And if Christ has not been raised, then our preaching is in

> ### GETTING THE MESSAGE
>
> **Speaking the truth in an understandable way.** When Paul said, "Bad company ruins good morals" (15:33), he was probably quoting the words of a famous Athenian playwright. This is similar to Paul's sermon in Athens (Acts 17:22–31), where he quotes from non-Christian writers. Christians can often share God's truth with nonbelievers by relating it to ideas with which they are familiar.

vain and your faith is in vain. **15** We are even found to be misrepresenting God, because we testified about God that he raised Christ, whom he did not raise if it is true that the dead are not raised. **16** For if the dead are not raised, not even Christ has been raised. **17** And if Christ has not been raised, your faith is futile and you are still in your sins. **18** Then those also who have fallen asleep in Christ have perished. **19** If in Christ we have hope in this life only, we are of all people most to be pitied.

20 But in fact Christ has been raised from the dead, the firstfruits of those who have fallen asleep. **21** For as by a man came death, by a man has come also the resurrection of the dead. **22** For as in Adam all die, so also in Christ shall all be made alive. **23** But each in his own order: Christ the firstfruits, then

at his coming those who belong to Christ. **24** Then comes the end, when he delivers the kingdom to God the Father after destroying every rule and every authority and power. **25** For he must reign until he has put all his enemies under his feet. **26** The last enemy to be destroyed is death. **27** For "God has put all things in subjection under his feet." But when it says, "all things are put in subjection," it is plain that he is excepted who put all things in subjection under him. **28** When all things are subjected to him, then the Son himself will also be subjected to him who put all things in subjection under him, that God may be all in all.

29 Otherwise, what do people mean by being baptized on behalf of the dead? If the dead are not raised at all, why are people baptized on their behalf? **30** Why are we in danger every hour? **31** I protest, brothers,[1] by my pride in you, which I have in Christ Jesus our Lord, I die every day! **32** What do I gain if, humanly speaking, I fought with beasts at Ephesus? If the dead are not raised, "Let us eat and drink, for tomorrow we die." **33** Do not be deceived: "Bad company ruins good morals." **34** Wake up from your drunken stupor, as is right, and do not go on sinning. For some have no knowledge of God. I say this to your shame.

The Resurrection Body

35 But someone will ask, "How are the dead raised? With what kind of body do they come?" **36** You foolish person! What you sow does not come to life unless it dies. **37** And what you sow is not the body that is to be, but a bare kernel, perhaps of wheat or of some other grain. **38** But God gives it a body as he has chosen, and to each kind of seed its own body. **39** For not all flesh is the same, but there is one kind for humans, another for animals, another for birds, and another for fish. **40** There are heavenly bodies and earthly bodies, but the glory of the heavenly is of one kind, and the glory of the earthly is of another. **41** There is one glory of the sun, and another glory of the moon, and another glory of the stars; for star differs from star in glory.

42 So is it with the resurrection of the dead. What is sown is perishable; what is raised is imperishable. **43** It is sown in dishonor; it is raised in glory. It is sown

---

[1] Or *brothers and sisters*

in weakness; it is raised in power. ⁴⁴ It is sown a natural body; it is raised a spiritual body. If there is a natural body, there is also a spiritual body. ⁴⁵ Thus it is written, "The first man Adam became a living being"; the last Adam became a life-giving spirit. ⁴⁶ But it is not the spiritual that is first but the natural, and then the spiritual. ⁴⁷ The first man was from the earth, a man of dust; the second man is from heaven. ⁴⁸ As was the man of dust, so also are those who are of the dust, and as is the man of heaven, so also are those who are of heaven. ⁴⁹ Just as we have borne the image of the man of dust, we shall also bear the image of the man of heaven.

Mystery and Victory

⁵⁰ I tell you this, brothers:¹ flesh and blood cannot inherit the kingdom of God, nor does the perishable inherit the imperishable. ⁵¹ Behold! I tell you a mystery. We shall not all sleep, but we shall all be changed, ⁵² in a moment, in the twinkling of an eye, at the last trumpet. For the trumpet will sound, and the dead will be raised imperishable, and we shall be changed. ⁵³ For this perishable body must put on the imperishable, and this mortal body must put on immortality. ⁵⁴ When the perishable puts on the imperishable, and the mortal puts on immortality, then shall come to pass the saying that is written:

"Death is swallowed up in victory."
⁵⁵ "O death, where is your victory?
      O death, where is your sting?"

⁵⁶ The sting of death is sin, and the power of sin is the law. ⁵⁷ But thanks be to God, who gives us the victory through our Lord Jesus Christ.

⁵⁸ Therefore, my beloved brothers, be steadfast, immovable, always abounding in the work of the Lord, knowing that in the Lord your labor is not in vain.

The Collection for the Saints

16 Now concerning the collection for the saints: as I directed the churches of Galatia, so you also are to do. ² On the first day of every week, each of you is to put something aside and store it up, as he may prosper, so that there will be no collecting when I come. ³ And when I arrive, I will send those whom you accredit by letter to carry your gift to Jerusalem. ⁴ If it seems advisable that I should go also, they will accompany me.

Plans for Travel

⁵ I will visit you after passing through Macedonia, for I intend to pass through Macedonia, ⁶ and perhaps I will stay with you or even spend the winter, so that you may help me on my journey, wherever I go. ⁷ For I do not want to see you now just in passing. I hope to spend some time with you, if the Lord permits. ⁸ But I will stay in Ephesus until Pentecost, ⁹ for a wide door for effective work has opened to me, and there are many adversaries.

¹⁰ When Timothy comes, see that you put him at ease among you, for he is doing the work of the Lord, as I am. ¹¹ So let no one despise him. Help him on his way in peace,

that he may return to me, for I am expecting him with the brothers.

Final Instructions

¹² Now concerning our brother Apollos, I strongly urged him to visit you with the other brothers, but it was not at all his will to come now. He will come when he has opportunity.

¹³ Be watchful, stand firm in the faith, act like men, be strong. ¹⁴ Let all that you do be done in love.

¹⁵ Now I urge you, brothers—you know that the household of Stephanas were the first converts in Achaia, and that they have devoted themselves to the service of the saints— ¹⁶ be subject to such as these, and to every fellow worker and laborer. ¹⁷ I rejoice at the coming of Stephanas and Fortunatus and Achaicus, because they have made up for your absence, ¹⁸ for they refreshed my

¹ Or brothers and sisters; also 15:58; 16:15

spirit as well as yours. Give recognition to such people.

Greetings

19 The churches of Asia send you greetings. Aquila and Prisca, together with the church in their house, send you hearty greetings in the Lord. 20 All the brothers[1] send you greetings. Greet one another with a holy kiss.

21 I, Paul, write this greeting with my own hand. 22 If anyone has no love for the Lord, let him be accursed. Our Lord, come! 23 The grace of the Lord Jesus be with you. 24 My love be with you all in Christ Jesus. Amen.

[1] Or brothers and sisters

INTRODUCTION TO 2 CORINTHIANS

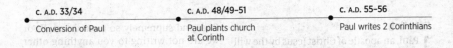

c. A.D. 33/34	c. A.D. 48/49–51	c. A.D. 55–56
Conversion of Paul	Paul plants church at Corinth	Paul writes 2 Corinthians

AUTHOR, DATE, AND RECIPIENTS

The apostle Paul wrote 2 Corinthians from Macedonia around A.D. 55/56. This was approximately a year after he wrote 1 Corinthians and a year before he wrote his letter to the Romans. This is the fourth letter he had written to the Corinthian church (in addition to 1 Corinthians, see the letters mentioned in 1 Cor. 5:9 and 2 Cor. 2:3–4).

THEME

The central theme of 2 Corinthians is the relationship between suffering and the power of the Spirit in Paul's apostolic life, ministry, and message. Paul's opponents had questioned his motives and his personal courage. They argued that he had suffered too much to be a Spirit-filled apostle of the risen Christ. But Paul argues that his suffering is the means God uses to reveal his glory (1:3–4, 11, 20).

PURPOSE

Paul vindicates his apostolic ministry in order to (1) strengthen the faithful majority in Corinth (primarily chs. 1–7); (2) encourage them to contribute to the financial needs of other believers, as an expression of their repentance (primarily chs. 8–9); and (3) offer the rebellious minority in Corinth another chance to repent before he returns to judge those still rejecting him and his message (primarily chs. 10–13).

KEY THEMES

1. Paul's suffering imitates the cross of Christ. Those who reject him because he suffers are "false apostles" and "servants of Satan" (11:13–15).

2. Paul is a servant of the new covenant (3:6). His ministry and message of the cross mediates the Spirit of the living God and God's righteousness to believers (3:3, 6–9; 5:14–15, 21).

3. Endurance through difficulty and Christlike behavior are made possible by the grace of God and are modeled by Paul himself. These qualities are the greatest display of God's presence, power, and glory in this fallen world (1:12–14; 6:14–7:1; 12:7–10; 13:4).

4. The Spirit transforms believers into the image of God, which is seen in Christ. This new creation is characterized by God's righteousness. Believers therefore embody the new creation of the new covenant by living for the sake of others. This is made possible because believers are reconciled with God through the cross (3:18; 5:15, 17–21).

5. Repentance expresses itself in holiness. This is a purity-producing love for God and his church and a unity-creating love for one's neighbor (6:14–7:1; chs. 8–9).

6. Christ, as Savior, is also the universal Judge. He will judge all people according to their deeds. The Spirit transforms those in whom he dwells as a guarantee of the "eternal weight of glory" to come for believers at the resurrection (1:22; 3:18; 5:5, 9–11).

OUTLINE

I. Paul's Defense of His Ministry as an Apostle (1:1–7:16)

II. Paul's Appeal to the Repentant Church Regarding the Collection (8:1–9:15)

III. Paul's Appeal to the Rebellious Minority in Corinth (10:1–13:10)

IV. Closing Greetings (13:11–14)

2 CORINTHIANS

Greeting

1 Paul, an apostle of Christ Jesus by the will of God, and Timothy our brother,

To the church of God that is at Corinth, with all the saints who are in the whole of Achaia:

[2] Grace to you and peace from God our Father and the Lord Jesus Christ.

God of All Comfort

[3] Blessed be the God and Father of our Lord Jesus Christ, the Father of mercies and God of all comfort, [4] who comforts us in all our affliction, so that we may be able to comfort those who are in any affliction, with the comfort with which we ourselves are comforted by God. [5] For as we share abundantly in Christ's sufferings, so through Christ we share abundantly in comfort too. [6] If we are afflicted, it is for your comfort and salvation; and if we are comforted, it is for your comfort, which you experience when you patiently endure the same sufferings that we suffer. [7] Our hope for you is unshaken, for we know that as you share in our sufferings, you will also share in our comfort.

[8] For we do not want you to be unaware, brothers,[1] of the affliction we experienced in Asia. For we were so utterly burdened beyond our strength that we despaired of life itself. [9] Indeed, we felt that we had received the sentence of death. But that was to make us rely not on ourselves but on God who raises the dead. [10] He delivered us from such a deadly peril, and he will deliver us. On him we have set our hope that he will deliver us again. [11] You also must help us by prayer, so that many will give thanks on our behalf for the blessing granted us through the prayers of many.

Paul's Change of Plans

[12] For our boast is this, the testimony of our conscience, that we behaved in the world with simplicity and godly sincerity, not by earthly wisdom but by the grace of God, and supremely so toward you. [13] For we are not writing to you anything other than what you read and understand and I hope you will fully understand — [14] just as you did partially understand us — that on the day of our Lord Jesus you will boast of us as we will boast of you.

[15] Because I was sure of this, I wanted to come to you first, so that you might have a second experience of grace. [16] I wanted to visit you on my way to Macedonia, and to come back to you from Macedonia and have you send me on my way to Judea. [17] Was I vacillating when I wanted to do this? Do

GETTING THE MESSAGE

Amen is the Greek form of the Hebrew word meaning "to confirm." The word is used throughout the Bible to affirm the truth of important statements (see 1:20). Paul often ends his letters with "Amen" (see Rom. 16:27), but here in 2 Corinthians he says it near the beginning of his letter.

I make my plans according to the flesh, ready to say "Yes, yes" and "No, no" at the same time? [18] As surely as God is faithful, our word to you has not been Yes and No. [19] For the Son of God, Jesus Christ, whom we proclaimed among you, Silvanus and Timothy and I, was not Yes and No, but in him it is always Yes. [20] For all the promises of God find their Yes in him. That is why it is through him that we utter our Amen to God for his glory. [21] And it is God who establishes us with you in Christ, and has anointed us, [22] and who has also put his seal on us and given us his Spirit in our hearts as a guarantee.

[23] But I call God to witness against me — it was to spare you that I refrained from coming again to Corinth. [24] Not that we lord it over your faith, but we work with you for your joy, for you stand firm in your faith.

[1] Or brothers and sisters (see Preface)

2 For I made up my mind not to make another painful visit to you. ² For if I cause you pain, who is there to make me glad but the one whom I have pained? ³ And I wrote as I did, so that when I came I might not suffer pain from those who should have made me rejoice, for I felt sure of all of you, that my joy would be the joy of you all. ⁴ For I wrote to you out of much affliction and anguish of heart and with many tears, not to cause you pain but to let you know the abundant love that I have for you.

Forgive the Sinner

⁵ Now if anyone has caused pain, he has caused it not to me, but in some measure— not to put it too severely— to all of you. ⁶ For such a one, this punishment by the majority is enough, ⁷ so you should rather turn to forgive and comfort him, or he may be overwhelmed by excessive sorrow. ⁸ So I beg

> **GETTING THE MESSAGE**
>
> **A new covenant.** God wrote the first covenant, the law, on stone tablets (Ex. 24:12). The new covenant is "written" on hearts (2 Cor. 3:2–3; see Jer. 31:31–34; Ezek. 11:19). In other words, the Spirit changes believers' hearts to enable them to obey God.

you to reaffirm your love for him. ⁹ For this is why I wrote, that I might test you and know whether you are obedient in everything. ¹⁰ Anyone whom you forgive, I also forgive. Indeed, what I have forgiven, if I have forgiven anything, has been for your sake in the presence of Christ, ¹¹ so that we would not be outwitted by Satan; for we are not ignorant of his designs.

Triumph in Christ

¹² When I came to Troas to preach the gospel of Christ, even though a door was opened for me in the Lord, ¹³ my spirit was not at rest because I did not find my brother Titus there. So I took leave of them and went on to Macedonia.

¹⁴ But thanks be to God, who in Christ always leads us in triumphal procession, and through us spreads the fragrance of the knowledge of him everywhere. ¹⁵ For we are

the aroma of Christ to God among those who are being saved and among those who are perishing, ¹⁶ to one a fragrance from death to death, to the other a fragrance from life to life. Who is sufficient for these things? ¹⁷ For we are not, like so many, peddlers of God's word, but as men of sincerity, as commissioned by God, in the sight of God we speak in Christ.

Ministers of the New Covenant

3 Are we beginning to commend ourselves again? Or do we need, as some do, letters of recommendation to you, or from you? ² You yourselves are our letter of recommendation, written on our hearts, to be known and read by all. ³ And you show that you are a letter from Christ delivered by us, written not with ink but with the Spirit of the living God, not on tablets of stone but on tablets of human hearts.

⁴ Such is the confidence that we have through Christ toward God. ⁵ Not that we are sufficient in ourselves to claim anything as coming from us, but our sufficiency is from God, ⁶ who has made us sufficient to be ministers of a new covenant, not of the letter but of the Spirit. For the letter kills, but the Spirit gives life.

⁷ Now if the ministry of death, carved in letters on stone, came with such glory that the Israelites could not gaze at Moses' face because of its glory, which was being brought to an end, ⁸ will not the ministry of the Spirit have even more glory? ⁹ For if there was glory in the ministry of condemnation, the ministry of righteousness must far exceed it in glory. ¹⁰ Indeed, in this case, what once had glory has come to have no glory at all, because of the glory that surpasses it. ¹¹ For if what was being brought to an end came with glory, much more will what is permanent have glory.

¹² Since we have such a hope, we are very bold, ¹³ not like Moses, who would put a veil over his face so that the Israelites might not gaze at the outcome of what was being brought to an end. ¹⁴ But their minds were hardened. For to this day, when they read the old covenant, that same veil remains unlifted, because only through Christ is it taken away. ¹⁵ Yes, to this day whenever Moses is read a veil lies over their hearts. ¹⁶ But when one turns to the Lord, the veil is removed. ¹⁷ Now the Lord is the Spirit,

and where the Spirit of the Lord is, there is freedom. [18] And we all, with unveiled face, beholding the glory of the Lord, are being transformed into the same image from one degree of glory to another. For this comes from the Lord who is the Spirit.

The Light of the Gospel

4 Therefore, having this ministry by the mercy of God, we do not lose heart. [2] But we have renounced disgraceful, underhanded ways. We refuse to practice cunning or to tamper with God's word, but by the open statement of the truth we would commend ourselves to everyone's conscience in the sight of God. [3] And even if our gospel is veiled, it is veiled to those who are perishing. [4] In their case the god of this world has blinded the minds of the unbelievers, to keep them from seeing the light of the gospel of the glory of Christ, who is the image of God. [5] For what we proclaim is not ourselves, but Jesus Christ as Lord, with ourselves as your servants for Jesus' sake. [6] For God, who said, "Let light shine out of darkness," has shone in our hearts to give the light of the knowledge of the glory of God in the face of Jesus Christ.

Treasure in Jars of Clay

[7] But we have this treasure in jars of clay, to show that the surpassing power belongs to God and not to us. [8] We are afflicted in every way, but not crushed; perplexed, but not driven to despair; [9] persecuted, but not forsaken; struck down, but not destroyed; [10] always carrying in the body the death of Jesus, so that the life of Jesus may also be manifested in our bodies. [11] For we who live are always being given over to death for Jesus' sake, so that the life of Jesus also may be manifested in our mortal flesh. [12] So death is at work in us, but life in you.

[13] Since we have the same spirit of faith according to what has been written, "I believed, and so I spoke," we also believe, and so we also speak, [14] knowing that he who raised the Lord Jesus will raise us also with Jesus and bring us with you into his presence. [15] For it is all for your sake, so that as grace extends to more and more people it may increase thanksgiving, to the glory of God.

[16] So we do not lose heart. Though our outer self is wasting away, our inner self is being renewed day by day. [17] For this light momentary affliction is preparing for us an eternal weight of glory beyond all comparison, [18] as we look not to the things that are seen but to the things that are unseen. For the things that are seen are transient, but the things that are unseen are eternal.

Our Heavenly Dwelling

5 For we know that if the tent that is our earthly home is destroyed, we have a building from God, a house not made with hands, eternal in the heavens. [2] For in this tent we groan, longing to put on our heavenly dwelling, [3] if indeed by putting it on we may not be found naked. [4] For while we are still in this tent, we groan, being burdened—not that we would be unclothed, but that we would be further clothed, so that what is mortal may be swallowed up by life. [5] He who has prepared us for this very

thing is God, who has given us the Spirit as a guarantee.

[6] So we are always of good courage. We know that while we are at home in the body we are away from the Lord, [7] for we walk by faith, not by sight. [8] Yes, we are of good courage, and we would rather be away from the body and at home with the Lord. [9] So whether we are at home or away, we make it our aim to please him. [10] For we must all appear before the judgment seat of Christ, so that each one may receive what is due for what he has done in the body, whether good or evil.

The Ministry of Reconciliation

[11] Therefore, knowing the fear of the Lord, we persuade others. But what we are is known to God, and I hope it is known also to your conscience. [12] We are not commending ourselves to you again but giving you cause to boast about us, so that you may be able to answer those who boast about

outward appearance and not about what is in the heart. ¹³ For if we are beside ourselves, it is for God; if we are in our right mind, it is for you. ¹⁴ For the love of Christ controls us, because we have concluded this: that one has died for all, therefore all have died; ¹⁵ and he died for all, that those who live might no longer live for themselves but for him who for their sake died and was raised.

¹⁶ From now on, therefore, we regard no one according to the flesh. Even though we once regarded Christ according to the flesh, we regard him thus no longer. ¹⁷ Therefore, if anyone is in Christ, he is a new creation. The old has passed away; behold, the new has come. ¹⁸ All this is from God, who through Christ reconciled us to himself and gave us the ministry of reconciliation; ¹⁹ that is, in

> ### GETTING THE MESSAGE
>
> **What does it mean to be "reconciled"?**
> To be reconciled means to be reunited with someone from whom one has been alienated. Forgiveness can lead to restored fellowship. Sin leads to alienation from God, but through Christ we can be forgiven and reconciled to God. "Be reconciled to God" (5:20) is thus a wonderful invitation to the gospel (see also Rom. 5:11).

Christ God was reconciling the world to himself, not counting their trespasses against them, and entrusting to us the message of reconciliation. ²⁰ Therefore, we are ambassadors for Christ, God making his appeal through us. We implore you on behalf of Christ, be reconciled to God. ²¹ For our sake he made him to be sin who knew no sin, so that in him we might become the righteousness of God.

6 Working together with him, then, we appeal to you not to receive the grace of God in vain. ² For he says,

"In a favorable time I listened to you,
    and in a day of salvation I have
        helped you."

Behold, now is the favorable time; behold, now is the day of salvation. ³ We put no obstacle in anyone's way, so that no fault may be found with our ministry, ⁴ but as servants of God we commend ourselves in

every way: by great endurance, in afflictions, hardships, calamities, ⁵ beatings, imprisonments, riots, labors, sleepless nights, hunger; ⁶ by purity, knowledge, patience, kindness, the Holy Spirit, genuine love; ⁷ by truthful speech, and the power of God; with the weapons of righteousness for the right hand and for the left; ⁸ through honor and dishonor, through slander and praise. We are treated as impostors, and yet are true; ⁹ as unknown, and yet well known; as dying, and behold, we live; as punished, and yet not killed; ¹⁰ as sorrowful, yet always rejoicing; as poor, yet making many rich; as having nothing, yet possessing everything.

¹¹ We have spoken freely to you, Corinthians; our heart is wide open. ¹² You are not restricted by us, but you are restricted in your own affections. ¹³ In return (I speak as to children) widen your hearts also.

The Temple of the Living God

¹⁴ Do not be unequally yoked with unbelievers. For what partnership has righteousness with lawlessness? Or what fellowship has light with darkness? ¹⁵ What accord has Christ with Belial? Or what portion does a believer share with an unbeliever? ¹⁶ What agreement has the temple of God with idols? For we are the temple of the living God; as God said,

"I will make my dwelling among them
        and walk among them,
    and I will be their God,
        and they shall be my people.
¹⁷ Therefore go out from their midst,
        and be separate from them, says the
            Lord,
    and touch no unclean thing;
        then I will welcome you,
¹⁸ and I will be a father to you,
        and you shall be sons and daughters to me,
    says the Lord Almighty."

7 Since we have these promises, beloved, let us cleanse ourselves from every defilement of body and spirit, bringing holiness to completion in the fear of God.

Paul's Joy

² Make room in your hearts for us. We have wronged no one, we have corrupted no one, we have taken advantage of no one. ³ I do not say this to condemn you, for

I said before that you are in our hearts, to die together and to live together. [4] I am acting with great boldness toward you; I have great pride in you; I am filled with comfort. In all our affliction, I am overflowing with joy.

[5] For even when we came into Macedonia, our bodies had no rest, but we were afflicted at every turn—fighting without and fear within. [6] But God, who comforts the downcast, comforted us by the coming of Titus, [7] and not only by his coming but also by the comfort with which he was comforted by you, as he told us of your longing, your mourning, your zeal for me, so that I rejoiced still more. [8] For even if I made you grieve with my letter, I do not regret it—though I did regret it, for I see that that letter grieved you, though only for a while. [9] As it is, I rejoice, not because you were grieved, but because you were grieved into repenting. For you felt a godly grief, so that you suffered no loss through us.

[10] For godly grief produces a repentance that leads to salvation without regret, whereas worldly grief produces death. [11] For see what earnestness this godly grief has produced in you, but also what eagerness to clear yourselves, what indignation, what fear, what longing, what zeal, what punishment! At every point you have proved yourselves innocent in the matter. [12] So although I wrote to you, it was not for the sake of the one who did the wrong, nor for the sake of the one who suffered the wrong, but in order that your earnestness for us might be revealed to you in the sight of God. [13] Therefore we are comforted.

And besides our own comfort, we rejoiced still more at the joy of Titus, because his spirit has been refreshed by you all. [14] For whatever boasts I made to him about you, I was not put to shame. But just as everything we said to you was true, so also our boasting before Titus has proved true. [15] And his affection for you is even greater, as he remembers the obedience of you all, how you received him with fear and trembling. [16] I rejoice, because I have complete confidence in you.

Encouragement to Give Generously

8 We want you to know, brothers,[1] about the grace of God that has been given among the churches of Macedonia, [2] for in a severe test of affliction, their abundance of joy and their extreme poverty have overflowed in a wealth of generosity on their part. [3] For they gave according to their means, as I can testify, and beyond their means, of their own accord, [4] begging us earnestly for the favor of taking part in the relief of the saints— [5] and this, not as we expected, but they gave themselves first to the Lord and then by the will of God to us. [6] Accordingly, we urged Titus that as he had started, so he should complete among you this act of grace. [7] But as you excel in everything—in faith, in speech, in knowledge, in all earnestness, and in our love for you—see that you excel in this act of grace also.

[8] I say this not as a command, but to prove by the earnestness of others that your love also is genuine. [9] For you know the grace of

our Lord Jesus Christ, that though he was rich, yet for your sake he became poor, so that you by his poverty might become rich. [10] And in this matter I give my judgment: this benefits you, who a year ago started not only to do this work but also to desire to do it. [11] So now finish doing it as well, so that your readiness in desiring it may be matched by your completing it out of what you have. [12] For if the readiness is there, it is acceptable according to what a person has, not according to what he does not have. [13] For I do not mean that others should be eased and you burdened, but that as a matter of fairness [14] your abundance at the present time should supply their need, so that their abundance may supply your need, that there may be fairness. [15] As it is written, "Whoever gathered much had nothing left over, and whoever gathered little had no lack."

[1] Or brothers and sisters

Commendation of Titus

¹⁶ But thanks be to God, who put into the heart of Titus the same earnest care I have for you. ¹⁷ For he not only accepted our appeal, but being himself very earnest he is going to you of his own accord. ¹⁸ With him we are sending the brother who is famous among all the churches for his preaching of the gospel. ¹⁹ And not only that, but he has been appointed by the churches to travel with us as we carry out this act of grace that is being ministered by us, for the glory of the Lord himself and to show our good will. ²⁰ We take this course so that no one should blame us about this generous gift that is being administered by us, ²¹ for we aim at what is honorable not only in the Lord's sight but also in the sight of man. ²² And with them we are sending our brother whom we have often tested and found earnest in

GETTING THE MESSAGE

More than simple charity. From the Jerusalem church, the good news about Christ had spread to the Gentile world. Paul's collection (chs. 8–9) was an opportunity for Gentile believers to show gratitude to their Jewish brothers and sisters in Christ (see Rom. 15:27).

many matters, but who is now more earnest than ever because of his great confidence in you. ²³ As for Titus, he is my partner and fellow worker for your benefit. And as for our brothers, they are messengers of the churches, the glory of Christ. ²⁴ So give proof before the churches of your love and of our boasting about you to these men.

The Collection for Christians in Jerusalem

9 Now it is superfluous for me to write to you about the ministry for the saints, ² for I know your readiness, of which I boast about you to the people of Macedonia, saying that Achaia has been ready since last year. And your zeal has stirred up most of them. ³ But I am sending the brothers so that our boasting about you may not prove empty in this matter, so that you may be ready, as I said you would be. ⁴ Otherwise, if some Macedonians come with me and find that you are not ready, we would be

humiliated—to say nothing of you—for being so confident. ⁵ So I thought it necessary to urge the brothers to go on ahead to you and arrange in advance for the gift you have promised, so that it may be ready as a willing gift, not as an exaction.

The Cheerful Giver

⁶ The point is this: whoever sows sparingly will also reap sparingly, and whoever sows bountifully will also reap bountifully. ⁷ Each one must give as he has decided in his heart, not reluctantly or under compulsion, for God loves a cheerful giver. ⁸ And God is able to make all grace abound to you, so that having all sufficiency in all things at all times, you may abound in every good work. ⁹ As it is written,

"He has distributed freely, he has given to the poor;
    his righteousness endures forever."

¹⁰ He who supplies seed to the sower and bread for food will supply and multiply your seed for sowing and increase the harvest of your righteousness. ¹¹ You will be enriched in every way to be generous in every way, which through us will produce thanksgiving to God. ¹² For the ministry of this service is not only supplying the needs of the saints but is also overflowing in many thanksgivings to God. ¹³ By their approval of this service, they will glorify God because of your submission that comes from your confession of the gospel of Christ, and the generosity of your contribution for them and for all others, ¹⁴ while they long for you and pray for you, because of the surpassing grace of God upon you. ¹⁵ Thanks be to God for his inexpressible gift!

Paul Defends His Ministry

10 I, Paul, myself entreat you, by the meekness and gentleness of Christ—I who am humble when face to face with you, but bold toward you when I am away!— ² I beg of you that when I am present I may not have to show boldness with such confidence as I count on showing against some who suspect us of walking according to the flesh. ³ For though we walk in the flesh, we are not waging war according to the flesh. ⁴ For the weapons of our warfare are not of the flesh but have divine power to destroy strongholds. ⁵ We

destroy arguments and every lofty opinion raised against the knowledge of God, and take every thought captive to obey Christ, ⁶ being ready to punish every disobedience, when your obedience is complete.

⁷ Look at what is before your eyes. If anyone is confident that he is Christ's, let him remind himself that just as he is Christ's, so also are we. ⁸ For even if I boast a little too much of our authority, which the Lord gave for building you up and not for destroying you, I will not be ashamed. ⁹ I do not want to appear to be frightening you with my letters. ¹⁰ For they say, "His letters are weighty and strong, but his bodily presence is weak, and his speech of no account." ¹¹ Let such a person understand that what we say by letter when absent, we do when present. ¹² Not that we dare to classify or compare ourselves with some of those who are commending themselves. But when they measure themselves by one another and compare themselves with one another, they are without understanding.

¹³ But we will not boast beyond limits, but will boast only with regard to the area of influence God assigned to us, to reach even to you. ¹⁴ For we are not overextending ourselves, as though we did not reach you. For we were the first to come all the way to you with the gospel of Christ. ¹⁵ We do not boast beyond limit in the labors of others. But our hope is that as your faith increases, our area of influence among you may be greatly enlarged, ¹⁶ so that we may preach the gospel in lands beyond you, without boasting of work already done in another's area of influence. ¹⁷ "Let the one who boasts, boast in the Lord." ¹⁸ For it is not the one who commends himself who is approved, but the one whom the Lord commends.

Paul and the False Apostles

11 I wish you would bear with me in a little foolishness. Do bear with me! ² For I feel a divine jealousy for you, since I betrothed you to one husband, to present you as a pure virgin to Christ. ³ But I am afraid that as the serpent deceived Eve by his cunning, your thoughts will be led astray from a sincere and pure devotion to Christ. ⁴ For if someone comes and proclaims another Jesus than the one we proclaimed, or if you receive a different spirit from the one you received, or if you

accept a different gospel from the one you accepted, you put up with it readily enough. ⁵ Indeed, I consider that I am not in the least inferior to these super-apostles. ⁶ Even if I am unskilled in speaking, I am not so in knowledge; indeed, in every way we have made this plain to you in all things.

⁷ Or did I commit a sin in humbling myself so that you might be exalted, because I preached God's gospel to you free of charge? ⁸ I robbed other churches by accepting support from them in order to serve you. ⁹ And when I was with you and was in need, I did not burden anyone, for the brothers who came from Macedonia supplied my need. So I refrained and will refrain from burdening you in any way. ¹⁰ As the truth of Christ is in me, this boasting of mine will

GETTING THE MESSAGE

Problems in Corinth. Paul's second visit to Corinth was a painful one. The Corinthians had accepted false teachers, and they openly rebelled against Paul and the gospel. Grieved, he left and sent them a severe letter (now lost). Paul now warns them that during his third visit he will be forced to judge those who have not repented from their sins (10:2; 12:20–21; 13:10).

not be silenced in the regions of Achaia. ¹¹ And why? Because I do not love you? God knows I do!

¹² And what I am doing I will continue to do, in order to undermine the claim of those who would like to claim that in their boasted mission they work on the same terms as we do. ¹³ For such men are false apostles, deceitful workmen, disguising themselves as apostles of Christ. ¹⁴ And no wonder, for even Satan disguises himself as an angel of light. ¹⁵ So it is no surprise if his servants, also, disguise themselves as servants of righteousness. Their end will correspond to their deeds.

Paul's Sufferings as an Apostle

¹⁶ I repeat, let no one think me foolish. But even if you do, accept me as a fool, so that I too may boast a little. ¹⁷ What I am saying with this boastful confidence, I say not as

the Lord would but as a fool. [18] Since many boast according to the flesh, I too will boast. [19] For you gladly bear with fools, being wise yourselves! [20] For you bear it if someone makes slaves of you, or devours you, or takes advantage of you, or puts on airs, or strikes you in the face. [21] To my shame, I must say, we were too weak for that!

But whatever anyone else dares to boast of—I am speaking as a fool—I also dare to boast of that. [22] Are they Hebrews? So am I. Are they Israelites? So am I. Are they offspring of Abraham? So am I. [23] Are they servants of Christ? I am a better one—I am talking like a madman—with far greater labors, far more imprisonments, with countless beatings, and often near death. [24] Five times I received at the hands of the Jews the forty lashes less one. [25] Three times I was beaten with rods. Once I was stoned. Three

GETTING THE MESSAGE

Preaching for free. Some traveling teachers in Paul's day accepted money from their listeners, but Paul worked as a tentmaker to support himself (Acts 18:3; see 1 Cor. 9:4–18). Churches also supported his missions financially (2 Cor. 11:9).

times I was shipwrecked; a night and a day I was adrift at sea; [26] on frequent journeys, in danger from rivers, danger from robbers, danger from my own people, danger from Gentiles, danger in the city, danger in the wilderness, danger at sea, danger from false brothers; [27] in toil and hardship, through many a sleepless night, in hunger and thirst, often without food, in cold and exposure. [28] And, apart from other things, there is the daily pressure on me of my anxiety for all the churches. [29] Who is weak, and I am not weak? Who is made to fall, and I am not indignant?

[30] If I must boast, I will boast of the things that show my weakness. [31] The God and Father of the Lord Jesus, he who is blessed forever, knows that I am not lying. [32] At Damascus, the governor under King Aretas was guarding the city of Damascus in order to seize me, [33] but I was let down in a basket through a window in the wall and escaped his hands.

Paul's Visions and His Thorn

12 I must go on boasting. Though there is nothing to be gained by it, I will go on to visions and revelations of the Lord. [2] I know a man in Christ who fourteen years ago was caught up to the third heaven—whether in the body or out of the body I do not know, God knows. [3] And I know that this man was caught up into paradise—whether in the body or out of the body I do not know, God knows— [4] and he heard things that cannot be told, which man may not utter. [5] On behalf of this man I will boast, but on my own behalf I will not boast, except of my weaknesses— [6] though if I should wish to boast, I would not be a fool, for I would be speaking the truth; but I refrain from it, so that no one may think more of me than he sees in me or hears from me. [7] So to keep me from becoming conceited because of the surpassing greatness of the revelations, a thorn was given me in the flesh, a messenger of Satan to harass me, to keep me from becoming conceited. [8] Three times I pleaded with the Lord about this, that it should leave me. [9] But he said to me, "My grace is sufficient for you, for my power is made perfect in weakness." Therefore I will boast all the more gladly of my weaknesses, so that the power of Christ may rest upon me. [10] For the sake of Christ, then, I am content with weaknesses, insults, hardships, persecutions, and calamities. For when I am weak, then I am strong.

Concern for the Corinthian Church

[11] I have been a fool! You forced me to it, for I ought to have been commended by you. For I was not at all inferior to these super-apostles, even though I am nothing. [12] The signs of a true apostle were performed among you with utmost patience, with signs and wonders and mighty works. [13] For in what were you less favored than the rest of the churches, except that I myself did not burden you? Forgive me this wrong!

[14] Here for the third time I am ready to come to you. And I will not be a burden, for I seek not what is yours but you. For children are not obligated to save up for their parents, but parents for their children. [15] I will most gladly spend and be spent for your souls. If I love you more, am I to be loved less? [16] But granting that I myself did not burden you, I was crafty, you say, and got the better of

you by deceit. [17] Did I take advantage of you through any of those whom I sent to you? [18] I urged Titus to go, and sent the brother with him. Did Titus take advantage of you? Did we not act in the same spirit? Did we not take the same steps?

[19] Have you been thinking all along that we have been defending ourselves to you? It is in the sight of God that we have been speaking in Christ, and all for your upbuilding, beloved. [20] For I fear that perhaps when I come I may find you not as I wish, and that you may find me not as you wish — that perhaps there may be quarreling, jealousy, anger, hostility, slander, gossip, conceit, and disorder. [21] I fear that when I come again my God may humble me before you, and I may have to mourn over many of those who sinned earlier and have not repented of the impurity, sexual immorality, and sensuality that they have practiced.

Final Warnings

13 This is the third time I am coming to you. Every charge must be established by the evidence of two or three witnesses. [2] I warned those who sinned before and all the others, and I warn them now while absent, as I did when present on my second visit, that if I come again I will not spare them — [3] since you seek proof that Christ is speaking in me. He is not weak in dealing with you, but is powerful among

you. [4] For he was crucified in weakness, but lives by the power of God. For we also are weak in him, but in dealing with you we will live with him by the power of God.

[5] Examine yourselves, to see whether you are in the faith. Test yourselves. Or do you not realize this about yourselves, that Jesus Christ is in you?—unless indeed you fail to meet the test! [6] I hope you will find out that we have not failed the test. [7] But we pray to God that you may not do wrong—not that we may appear to have met the test, but that you may do what is right, though we may seem to have failed. [8] For we cannot do anything against the truth, but only for the truth. [9] For we are glad when we are weak and you are strong. Your restoration is what we pray for. [10] For this reason I write these things while I am away from you, that when I come I may not have to be severe in my use of the authority that the Lord has given me for building up and not for tearing down.

Final Greetings

[11] Finally, brothers,[1] rejoice. Aim for restoration, comfort one another, agree with one another, live in peace; and the God of love and peace will be with you. [12] Greet one another with a holy kiss. [13] All the saints greet you.

[14] The grace of the Lord Jesus Christ and the love of God and the fellowship of the Holy Spirit be with you all.

[1] Or brothers and sisters

INTRODUCTION TO GALATIANS

c. A.D. **33/34**	A.D. **48/49–51**	c. A.D. **64–67**
Conversion of Paul	Paul visits, writes to Galatians	Paul martyred in Rome

AUTHOR, DATE, AND RECIPIENTS

The apostle Paul wrote this letter about A.D. 48. The Galatians are probably believers in the churches of the southern region of the Roman province of Galatia. Paul is more critical of his audience here than in any of his other letters.

THEME

Christ's death has brought in the age of the new covenant (3:23–26; 4:4–5, 24). People do not have to become Jews or follow the outward ceremonies of the Mosaic law in order to be Christians (2:3, 11–12, 14; 4:10). To require these things denies the heart of the gospel, which is justification by faith alone and not by keeping the "works of the law" (2:16). In this new age, Christians are to live in the guidance and power of the Spirit (chs. 5–6).

PURPOSE

False teachers have convinced the Galatians that they are required to be circumcised. The result is division within their church (5:15). Paul gives numerous reasons why they should return to the simple truth of the gospel.

KEY THEMES

1. In his sin-bearing death, Christ is a substitute for all Christians. He brings them into a new realm of freedom and life (1:4; 2:20; 3:13).

2. The gospel of Christ comes from God alone—not from any human source. Paul himself is a living example of this. His conversion to Christ and his apostleship were not through human means. They came through direct revelation from Christ (1:1, 11–12, 15–20).

3. Salvation comes not by works of law but by faith, which leads to justification (2:16).

4. To require circumcision and other Mosaic laws as a supplement to faith is to fall back from the realm of grace and freedom and to come under the whole law and its curse, since perfect observance of the law is impossible (2:12–14, 16; 3:10; 4:10; 5:3).

5. Old Testament Scripture itself testifies to the truth of justification by faith (Gen. 15:6; Hab. 2:4).

6. Believers have died with Christ to sin and therefore have renounced the flesh (Gal. 5:24; 6:14).

7. The Spirit is the source of power and guidance in the Christian life. He produces love and faith in the believer (5:6, 16, 18, 25).

8. The Christian life is one of pleasing Christ. This requires willingness to suffer persecution for the sake of his cross (1:10; 6:12, 14).

OUTLINE

I. Opening (1:1–9)

II. Indirect Appeal: Paul's Ministry and the Gospel (1:10–2:21)

III. Direct Appeals to the Galatians (3:1–5:12)

IV. Life in the Spirit and Love (5:13–6:10)

V. Final Warning (6:11–18)

THE LETTER OF PAUL TO THE
GALATIANS

Greeting

1 Paul, an apostle—not from men nor through man, but through Jesus Christ and God the Father, who raised him from the dead— 2 and all the brothers[1] who are with me,

To the churches of Galatia:

3 Grace to you and peace from God our Father and the Lord Jesus Christ, 4 who gave himself for our sins to deliver us from the present evil age, according to the will of our God and Father, 5 to whom be the glory forever and ever. Amen.

No Other Gospel

6 I am astonished that you are so quickly deserting him who called you in the grace of Christ and are turning to a different gospel— 7 not that there is another one, but there are some who trouble you and want to distort the gospel of Christ. 8 But even if we or an angel from heaven should preach to you a gospel contrary to the one we preached to you, let him be accursed. 9 As we have said before, so now I say again: If anyone is preaching to you a gospel contrary to the one you received, let him be accursed.

10 For am I now seeking the approval of man, or of God? Or am I trying to please man? If I were still trying to please man, I would not be a servant[2] of Christ.

Paul Called by God

11 For I would have you know, brothers, that the gospel that was preached by me is not man's gospel. 12 For I did not receive it from any man, nor was I taught it, but I received it through a revelation of Jesus Christ. 13 For you have heard of my former life in Judaism, how I persecuted the church of God violently and tried to destroy it. 14 And I was advancing in Judaism beyond many of my own age among my people, so extremely zealous was I for the traditions of my fathers. 15 But when he who had set me apart before I was born, and who called me by his grace, 16 was pleased to reveal his Son to me, in order that I might preach him among the Gentiles, I did not immediately consult with anyone; 17 nor did I go up to Jerusalem to those who were apostles before me, but I went away into Arabia, and returned again to Damascus.

18 Then after three years I went up to Jerusalem to visit Cephas and remained with him fifteen days. 19 But I saw none of the other apostles except James the Lord's brother. 20 (In what I am writing to you, before God, I do not lie!) 21 Then I went into the regions of Syria and Cilicia. 22 And I was

> ### GETTING THE MESSAGE
>
> **Paul's letter to the Galatians** was likely written to the churches he established in the southern part of Galatia during his first missionary journey (Acts 13:1–14:28). He probably sent the letter from his home church in Antioch, sometime before the Jerusalem council (see Acts 15:1–31).

still unknown in person to the churches of Judea that are in Christ. 23 They only were hearing it said, "He who used to persecute us is now preaching the faith he once tried to destroy." 24 And they glorified God because of me.

Paul Accepted by the Apostles

2 Then after fourteen years I went up again to Jerusalem with Barnabas, taking Titus along with me. 2 I went up because of a revelation and set before them (though privately before those who seemed influential) the gospel that I proclaim among the Gentiles, in order to make sure I was not running or had not run in vain. 3 But even Titus, who was with me, was not forced to be circumcised, though he was a Greek. 4 Yet because of false brothers secretly brought in—who slipped in to spy out our freedom

---

[1] Or brothers and sisters (see Preface); also 1:11 [2] Or slave (Greek doulos; see Preface)

that we have in Christ Jesus, so that they might bring us into slavery— **5** to them we did not yield in submission even for a moment, so that the truth of the gospel might be preserved for you. **6** And from those who seemed to be influential (what they were makes no difference to me; God shows no partiality)—those, I say, who seemed influential added nothing to me. **7** On the contrary, when they saw that I had been entrusted with the gospel to the uncircumcised, just as Peter had been entrusted with the gospel to the circumcised **8** (for he who worked through Peter for his apostolic ministry to the circumcised worked also through me for mine to the Gentiles), **9** and when James and Cephas and John, who seemed to be pillars, perceived the grace that was given to me, they gave the right hand of fellowship to Barnabas and me, that

GETTING THE MESSAGE

Justification by faith alone. False teachers were trying to persuade the Galatians that they needed to practice circumcision and other outward ceremonies of the Mosaic law in order to be right with God. But Paul explains that only through faith in Christ can one be right with God (2:16).

we should go to the Gentiles and they to the circumcised. **10** Only, they asked us to remember the poor, the very thing I was eager to do.

Paul Opposes Peter

11 But when Cephas came to Antioch, I opposed him to his face, because he stood condemned. **12** For before certain men came from James, he was eating with the Gentiles; but when they came he drew back and separated himself, fearing the circumcision party. **13** And the rest of the Jews acted hypocritically along with him, so that even Barnabas was led astray by their hypocrisy. **14** But when I saw that their conduct was not in step with the truth of the gospel, I said to Cephas before them all, "If you, though a Jew, live like a Gentile and not like a Jew, how can you force the Gentiles to live like Jews?"

Justified by Faith

15 We ourselves are Jews by birth and not Gentile sinners; **16** yet we know that a person is not justified by works of the law but through faith in Jesus Christ, so we also have believed in Christ Jesus, in order to be justified by faith in Christ and not by works of the law, because by works of the law no one will be justified.

17 But if, in our endeavor to be justified in Christ, we too were found to be sinners, is Christ then a servant of sin? Certainly not! **18** For if I rebuild what I tore down, I prove myself to be a transgressor. **19** For through the law I died to the law, so that I might live to God. **20** I have been crucified with Christ. It is no longer I who live, but Christ who lives in me. And the life I now live in the flesh I live by faith in the Son of God, who loved me and gave himself for me. **21** I do not nullify the grace of God, for if righteousness were through the law, then Christ died for no purpose.

By Faith, or by Works of the Law?

3 O foolish Galatians! Who has bewitched you? It was before your eyes that Jesus Christ was publicly portrayed as crucified. **2** Let me ask you only this: Did you receive the Spirit by works of the law or by hearing with faith? **3** Are you so foolish? Having begun by the Spirit, are you now being perfected by the flesh? **4** Did you suffer so many things in vain—if indeed it was in vain? **5** Does he who supplies the Spirit to you and works miracles among you do so by works of the law, or by hearing with faith— **6** just as Abraham "believed God, and it was counted to him as righteousness"?

7 Know then that it is those of faith who are the sons of Abraham. **8** And the Scripture, foreseeing that God would justify the Gentiles by faith, preached the gospel beforehand to Abraham, saying, "In you shall all the nations be blessed." **9** So then, those who are of faith are blessed along with Abraham, the man of faith.

The Righteous Shall Live by Faith

10 For all who rely on works of the law are under a curse; for it is written, "Cursed be everyone who does not abide by all things written in the Book of the Law, and do them." **11** Now it is evident that no one is justified before God by the law, for "The righteous shall live by faith." [12] But the law is not of faith, rather "The one who does them shall live by them." [13] Christ redeemed us from the curse of the law by becoming a curse for us—for it is written, "Cursed is everyone who is hanged on a tree"— [14] so that in Christ Jesus the blessing of Abraham might come to the Gentiles, so that we might receive the promised Spirit through faith.

The Law and the Promise

[15] To give a human example, brothers:[1] even with a man-made covenant, no one annuls it or adds to it once it has been ratified. [16] Now the promises were made to Abraham and to his offspring. It does not say, "And to offsprings," referring to many, but referring to one, "And to your offspring," who is Christ. [17] This is what I mean: the law, which came 430 years afterward, does not annul a covenant previously ratified by God, so as to make the promise void. [18] For if the inheritance comes by the law, it no longer comes by promise; but God gave it to Abraham by a promise.

[19] Why then the law? It was added because of transgressions, until the offspring should come to whom the promise had been made, and it was put in place through angels by an intermediary. [20] Now an intermediary implies more than one, but God is one.

[21] Is the law then contrary to the promises of God? Certainly not! For if a law had been given that could give life, then righteousness would indeed be by the law. [22] But the Scripture imprisoned everything under sin, so that the promise by faith in Jesus Christ might be given to those who believe.

[23] Now before faith came, we were held captive under the law, imprisoned until the coming faith would be revealed. [24] So then, the law was our guardian until Christ came, in order that we might be justified by faith. [25] But now that faith has come, we are no longer under a guardian, [26] for in Christ Jesus you are all sons of God, through faith. [27] For as many of you as were baptized into Christ have put on Christ. [28] There is neither Jew nor Greek, there is neither slave[2] nor free, there is no male and female, for you are all one in Christ Jesus. [29] And if you are Christ's, then you are Abraham's offspring, heirs according to promise.

Sons and Heirs

4 I mean that the heir, as long as he is a child, is no different from a slave, though he is the owner of everything, [2] but he is under guardians and managers until the date set by his father. [3] In the same way we also, when we were children, were enslaved to the elementary principles of the world. [4] But when the fullness of time had come, God sent forth his Son, born of woman, born under the law, [5] to redeem those who were under the law, so that we might receive adoption as sons. [6] And because you are sons, God has sent the Spirit of his Son into our hearts, crying, "Abba! Father!" [7] So you are no longer a slave, but a son, and if a son, then an heir through God.

Paul's Concern for the Galatians

[8] Formerly, when you did not know God, you were enslaved to those that by nature

GETTING THE MESSAGE

God's promises to Abraham. When Abraham believed God's promises to him, God counted his faith as righteousness (Gen. 15:6). Paul uses this precedent to show that God's promises to Abraham are for all who "hear with faith," not just the people of Israel (Gal. 3:1–29).

are not gods. [9] But now that you have come to know God, or rather to be known by God, how can you turn back again to the weak and worthless elementary principles of the world, whose slaves you want to be once more? [10] You observe days and months and seasons and years! [11] I am afraid I may have labored over you in vain.

[12] Brothers, I entreat you, become as I am, for I also have become as you are. You did me no wrong. [13] You know it was because of a bodily ailment that I preached the gospel to you at first, [14] and though my condition was a trial to you, you did not scorn or despise me, but received me as an angel of God, as Christ Jesus. [15] What then has become of your blessedness? For I testify to you that, if possible, you would have gouged out your eyes and given them to me. [16] Have I then become your enemy by telling you the truth? [17] They make much of you, but for no good

purpose. They want to shut you out, that you may make much of them. ¹⁸ It is always good to be made much of for a good purpose, and not only when I am present with you, ¹⁹ my little children, for whom I am again in the anguish of childbirth until Christ is formed in you! ²⁰ I wish I could be present with you now and change my tone, for I am perplexed about you.

Example of Hagar and Sarah

²¹ Tell me, you who desire to be under the law, do you not listen to the law? ²² For it is written that Abraham had two sons, one by a slave woman and one by a free woman. ²³ But the son of the slave was born according to the flesh, while the son of the free woman was born through promise. ²⁴ Now this may be interpreted allegorically: these women are two covenants. One is from Mount Sinai, bearing children for slavery;

> **GETTING THE MESSAGE**
>
> "They" in 4:17 refers to the **false teachers** who were trying to persuade the Galatian believers that Paul was wrong about certain important issues. They avoided persecution and gained favor from the Jews by requiring circumcision (6:12–13).

she is Hagar. ²⁵ Now Hagar is Mount Sinai in Arabia; she corresponds to the present Jerusalem, for she is in slavery with her children. ²⁶ But the Jerusalem above is free, and she is our mother. ²⁷ For it is written,

> "Rejoice, O barren one who does not
>   bear;
>   break forth and cry aloud, you who
>   are not in labor!
> For the children of the desolate one
>   will be more
>   than those of the one who has a
>   husband."

²⁸ Now you, brothers,¹ like Isaac, are children of promise. ²⁹ But just as at that time he who was born according to the flesh persecuted him who was born according to the Spirit, so also it is now. ³⁰ But what does the Scripture say? "Cast out the slave woman and her son, for the son of the slave woman

shall not inherit with the son of the free woman." ³¹ So, brothers, we are not children of the slave but of the free woman.

Christ Has Set Us Free

5 For freedom Christ has set us free; stand firm therefore, and do not submit again to a yoke of slavery.

² Look: I, Paul, say to you that if you accept circumcision, Christ will be of no advantage to you. ³ I testify again to every man who accepts circumcision that he is obligated to keep the whole law. ⁴ You are severed from Christ, you who would be justified by the law; you have fallen away from grace. ⁵ For through the Spirit, by faith, we ourselves eagerly wait for the hope of righteousness. ⁶ For in Christ Jesus neither circumcision nor uncircumcision counts for anything, but only faith working through love.

⁷ You were running well. Who hindered you from obeying the truth? ⁸ This persuasion is not from him who calls you. ⁹ A little leaven leavens the whole lump. ¹⁰ I have confidence in the Lord that you will take no other view, and the one who is troubling you will bear the penalty, whoever he is. ¹¹ But if I, brothers, still preach circumcision, why am I still being persecuted? In that case the offense of the cross has been removed. ¹² I wish those who unsettle you would emasculate themselves!

¹³ For you were called to freedom, brothers. Only do not use your freedom as an opportunity for the flesh, but through love serve one another. ¹⁴ For the whole law is fulfilled in one word: "You shall love your neighbor as yourself." ¹⁵ But if you bite and devour one another, watch out that you are not consumed by one another.

Keep in Step with the Spirit

¹⁶ But I say, walk by the Spirit, and you will not gratify the desires of the flesh. ¹⁷ For the desires of the flesh are against the Spirit, and the desires of the Spirit are against the flesh, for these are opposed to each other, to keep you from doing the things you want to do. ¹⁸ But if you are led by the Spirit, you are not under the law. ¹⁹ Now the works of the flesh are evident: sexual immorality, impurity, sensuality, ²⁰ idolatry, sorcery, enmity, strife, jealousy, fits of anger, rivalries, dissensions, divisions, ²¹ envy, drunkenness,

¹ Or *brothers and sisters*; also 4:31; 5:11, 13

orgies, and things like these. I warn you, as I warned you before, that those who do such things will not inherit the kingdom of God. [22] But the fruit of the Spirit is love, joy, peace, patience, kindness, goodness, faithfulness, [23] gentleness, self-control; against such things there is no law. [24] And those who belong to Christ Jesus have crucified the flesh with its passions and desires.

[25] If we live by the Spirit, let us also keep in step with the Spirit. [26] Let us not become conceited, provoking one another, envying one another.

Bear One Another's Burdens

6 Brothers,[1] if anyone is caught in any transgression, you who are spiritual should restore him in a spirit of gentleness. Keep watch on yourself, lest you too be tempted. [2] Bear one another's burdens, and so fulfill the law of Christ. [3] For if anyone thinks he is something, when he is nothing, he deceives himself. [4] But let each one test his own work, and then his reason to boast will be in himself alone and not in his neighbor. [5] For each will have to bear his own load.

[6] Let the one who is taught the word share all good things with the one who teaches. [7] Do not be deceived: God is not mocked, for whatever one sows, that will he also reap. [8] For the one who sows to his own flesh will from the flesh reap corruption, but the one who sows to the Spirit will from the Spirit reap eternal life. [9] And let us not grow weary of doing good, for in due season we will reap, if we do not give up. [10] So then, as we have opportunity, let us do good to every-

one, and especially to those who are of the household of faith.

Final Warning and Benediction

[11] See with what large letters I am writing to you with my own hand. [12] It is those who want to make a good showing in the flesh who would force you to be circumcised, and only in order that they may not be persecuted for the cross of Christ. [13] For even those who are circumcised do not themselves keep the law, but they desire to have you circumcised that they may boast in your flesh. [14] But far be it from

---

GETTING THE MESSAGE

To **walk by the Spirit** means making decisions and choices based on the Holy Spirit's guidance (5:16, 25). It also involves relying on the Spirit's power to conquer sinful desires (5:17–18). The Spirit will produce "fruits" of godliness in the believer's life (5:22–23).

---

me to boast except in the cross of our Lord Jesus Christ, by which the world has been crucified to me, and I to the world. [15] For neither circumcision counts for anything, nor uncircumcision, but a new creation. [16] And as for all who walk by this rule, peace and mercy be upon them, and upon the Israel of God.

[17] From now on let no one cause me trouble, for I bear on my body the marks of Jesus.

[18] The grace of our Lord Jesus Christ be with your spirit, brothers. Amen.

---

[1] Or Brothers and sisters; also 6:18

INTRODUCTION TO EPHESIANS

C. A.D. 33/34	C. A.D. 52–57	C. A.D. 62
Conversion of Paul	Paul's third missionary journey	Paul arrested, writes Ephesians

AUTHOR, DATE, AND RECIPIENTS

The apostle Paul wrote this letter to the churches in Ephesus and the surrounding region c. A.D. 62 while imprisoned in Rome (Acts 28). During this time he also wrote Colossians and Philemon. All three letters were sent with Tychicus and Onesimus.

THEME

There are three main themes of Ephesians: (1) Christ has reconciled all creation to himself and to God; (2) Christ has united people from all nations to himself and to one another in his church; and (3) Christians must live as new people.

PURPOSE

Ephesians offers general instruction in the truths of God's redemptive work in Christ; the unity of the church among diverse peoples; and proper conduct in the church, the home, and the world.

KEY THEMES

1. All people are by nature spiritually dead. They disobey God's law and are ruled by Satan (1:7; 2:1–3, 5, 11–12).

2. God predestined his people to redemption and holiness in Christ (1:3–14; 2:4, 8–9).

3. God's rich mercy in Christ has saved sinners. This free gift is by grace through faith alone (1:7–8; 2:4–14).

4. Jesus' saving work was part of redeeming a fallen creation for God. For this he deserves glory, honor, and authority in this age and the next (1:15–23; 3:1–13).

5. Jesus unites Jews and Gentiles into his one body, the church, as a new creation (1:23; 2:10–22; 3:1–21; 4:1–6).

6. Christ's people are saved to new lives of holiness in thought, word, and deed. They must reject their old, sinful lifestyles (4:1–3, 17–32; 5:1–20).

7. Holiness in life includes submission to proper authorities, in home and family life, and those in authority must care for those in submission to them (5:21–6:9).

8. Jesus has given powerful gifts to his church. These bring unity, maturity, and defense against the devil and his allies (4:7–16; 6:10–19).

OUTLINE

I. Introduction (1:1–14)

II. Paul's Prayer of Thanksgiving (1:15–23)

III. Salvation by Grace through Faith (2:1–10)

IV. Unity and the Peace of Christ (2:11–22)

V. Revelation of the Gospel Mystery (3:1–13)

VI. Paul's Prayer for Strength and Insight (3:14–21)

VII. Unity of the Body of Christ (4:1–16)

VIII. Paul's Testimony (4:17–24)

IX. Encouragement for a Holy Lifestyle (4:25–32)

X. New Life in Love (5:1–20)

XI. Submission to One Another (5:21–6:9)

XII. The Whole Armor of God (6:10–20)

XIII. Conclusion (6:21–24)

EPHESIANS

Greeting

1 Paul, an apostle of Christ Jesus by the will of God,

To the saints who are in Ephesus, and are faithful in Christ Jesus:

[2] Grace to you and peace from God our Father and the Lord Jesus Christ.

Spiritual Blessings in Christ

[3] Blessed be the God and Father of our Lord Jesus Christ, who has blessed us in Christ with every spiritual blessing in the heavenly places, [4] even as he chose us in him before the foundation of the world, that we should be holy and blameless before him. In love [5] he predestined us for adoption as sons through Jesus Christ, according to the purpose of his will, [6] to the praise of his glorious grace, with which he has blessed us in the Beloved. [7] In him we have redemption through his blood, the forgiveness of our trespasses, according to the riches of his grace, [8] which he lavished upon us, in all wisdom and insight [9] making known to us the mystery of his will, according to his purpose, which he set forth in Christ [10] as a plan for the fullness of time, to unite all things in him, things in heaven and things on earth.

[11] In him we have obtained an inheritance, having been predestined according to the purpose of him who works all things according to the counsel of his will, [12] so that we who were the first to hope in Christ might be to the praise of his glory. [13] In him you also, when you heard the word of truth, the gospel of your salvation, and believed in him, were sealed with the promised Holy Spirit, [14] who is the guarantee of our inheritance until we acquire possession of it, to the praise of his glory.

Thanksgiving and Prayer

[15] For this reason, because I have heard of your faith in the Lord Jesus and your love toward all the saints, [16] I do not cease to give thanks for you, remembering you in my prayers, [17] that the God of our Lord Jesus Christ, the Father of glory, may give you the Spirit of wisdom and of revelation in the knowledge of him, [18] having the eyes of your hearts enlightened, that you may know what is the hope to which he has called you, what are the riches of his glorious inheritance in the saints, [19] and what is the immeasurable greatness of his power toward us who believe, according to the working of his great might [20] that he worked in Christ when he raised him from the dead and seated him at his right hand in the heavenly places, [21] far above all rule and authority and power and dominion, and above every name that is named, not only in this age but also in the

GETTING THE MESSAGE

Ephesus was one of the largest cities in the Roman Empire and the primary port for Asia Minor. It boasted an advanced system of aqueducts, a 25,000-seat amphitheater, a major library with more than 12,000 scrolls, and the Temple of Artemis (one of the Seven Wonders of the Ancient World).

one to come. [22] And he put all things under his feet and gave him as head over all things to the church, [23] which is his body, the fullness of him who fills all in all.

By Grace Through Faith

2 And you were dead in the trespasses and sins [2] in which you once walked, following the course of this world, following the prince of the power of the air, the spirit that is now at work in the sons of disobedience— [3] among whom we all once lived in the passions of our flesh, carrying out the desires of the body and the mind, and were by nature children of wrath, like the rest of mankind. [4] But God, being rich in mercy, because of the great love with which he loved us, [5] even when we were dead in our trespasses, made us alive together with Christ—by grace you have been saved— [6] and raised us up with him and seated us with him in the heavenly

places in Christ Jesus, **7** so that in the coming ages he might show the immeasurable riches of his grace in kindness toward us in Christ Jesus. **8** For by grace you have been saved through faith. And this is not your own doing; it is the gift of God, **9** not a result of works, so that no one may boast. **10** For we are his workmanship, created in Christ Jesus for good works, which God prepared beforehand, that we should walk in them.

One in Christ

11 Therefore remember that at one time you Gentiles in the flesh, called "the uncircumcision" by what is called the circumcision, which is made in the flesh by hands— **12** remember that you were at that time separated from Christ, alienated from the commonwealth of Israel and strangers to the covenants of promise, having no hope and without God in the world. **13** But

> **GETTING THE MESSAGE**
>
> **Salvation by grace.** In 2:1–10, Paul eloquently describes how God initiated salvation for undeserving sinners just because he loves them. Through no merit of their own, he rescued them from slavery to sin and graciously gave them new life in Christ (1:5).

now in Christ Jesus you who once were far off have been brought near by the blood of Christ. **14** For he himself is our peace, who has made us both one and has broken down in his flesh the dividing wall of hostility **15** by abolishing the law of commandments expressed in ordinances, that he might create in himself one new man in place of the two, so making peace, **16** and might reconcile us both to God in one body through the cross, thereby killing the hostility. **17** And he came and preached peace to you who were far off and peace to those who were near. **18** For through him we both have access in one Spirit to the Father. **19** So then you are no longer strangers and aliens, but you are fellow citizens with the saints and members of the household of God, **20** built on the foundation of the apostles and prophets, Christ Jesus himself being the cornerstone, **21** in whom the whole structure, being joined together, grows into a holy temple in

the Lord. **22** In him you also are being built together into a dwelling place for God by the Spirit.

The Mystery of the Gospel Revealed

3 For this reason I, Paul, a prisoner for Christ Jesus on behalf of you Gentiles— **2** assuming that you have heard of the stewardship of God's grace that was given to me for you, **3** how the mystery was made known to me by revelation, as I have written briefly. **4** When you read this, you can perceive my insight into the mystery of Christ, **5** which was not made known to the sons of men in other generations as it has now been revealed to his holy apostles and prophets by the Spirit. **6** This mystery is that the Gentiles are fellow heirs, members of the same body, and partakers of the promise in Christ Jesus through the gospel.

7 Of this gospel I was made a minister according to the gift of God's grace, which was given me by the working of his power. **8** To me, though I am the very least of all the saints, this grace was given, to preach to the Gentiles the unsearchable riches of Christ, **9** and to bring to light for everyone what is the plan of the mystery hidden for ages in God who created all things, **10** so that through the church the manifold wisdom of God might now be made known to the rulers and authorities in the heavenly places. **11** This was according to the eternal purpose that he has realized in Christ Jesus our Lord, **12** in whom we have boldness and access with confidence through our faith in him. **13** So I ask you not to lose heart over what I am suffering for you, which is your glory.

Prayer for Spiritual Strength

14 For this reason I bow my knees before the Father, **15** from whom every family in heaven and on earth is named, **16** that according to the riches of his glory he may grant you to be strengthened with power through his Spirit in your inner being, **17** so that Christ may dwell in your hearts through faith— that you, being rooted and grounded in love, **18** may have strength to comprehend with all the saints what is the breadth and length and height and depth, **19** and to know the love of Christ that surpasses knowledge, that you may be filled with all the fullness of God.

20 Now to him who is able to do far more abundantly than all that we ask or think, according to the power at work within us, [21] to him be glory in the church and in Christ Jesus throughout all generations, forever and ever. Amen.

Unity in the Body of Christ

4 I therefore, a prisoner for the Lord, urge you to walk in a manner worthy of the calling to which you have been called, [2] with all humility and gentleness, with patience, bearing with one another in love, [3] eager to maintain the unity of the Spirit in the bond of peace. [4] There is one body and one Spirit—just as you were called to the one hope that belongs to your call— [5] one Lord, one faith, one baptism, [6] one God and Father of all, who is over all and through all and in all. [7] But grace was given to each one of us according to the measure of Christ's gift. [8] Therefore it says,

"When he ascended on high he led a host of captives,
    and he gave gifts to men."[1]

[9] (In saying, "He ascended," what does it mean but that he had also descended into the lower regions, the earth? [10] He who descended is the one who also ascended far above all the heavens, that he might fill all things.) [11] And he gave the apostles, the prophets, the evangelists, the shepherds[2] and teachers, [12] to equip the saints for the work of ministry, for building up the body of Christ, [13] until we all attain to the unity of the faith and of the knowledge of the Son of God, to mature manhood, to the measure of the stature of the fullness of Christ, [14] so that we may no longer be children, tossed to and fro by the waves and carried about by every wind of doctrine, by human cunning, by craftiness in deceitful schemes. [15] Rather, speaking the truth in love, we are to grow up in every way into him who is the head, into Christ, [16] from whom the whole body, joined and held together by every joint with which it is equipped, when each part is working properly, makes the body grow so that it builds itself up in love.

The New Life

[17] Now this I say and testify in the Lord, that you must no longer walk as the Gentiles do, in the futility of their minds. [18] They are darkened in their understanding, alienated from the life of God because of the ignorance that is in them, due to their hardness of heart. [19] They have become callous and have given themselves up to sensuality, greedy to practice every kind of impurity. [20] But that is not the way you learned Christ!— [21] assuming that you have heard about him and were taught in him, as the truth is in Jesus, [22] to put off your old self, which belongs to your former manner of life and is corrupt through deceitful desires, [23] and to be renewed in the spirit of your minds, [24] and to put on the new self, created after the likeness of God in true righteousness and holiness.

[25] Therefore, having put away falsehood, let each one of you speak the truth with his neighbor, for we are members one of another. [26] Be angry and do not sin; do not let the sun go down on your anger, [27] and give

GETTING THE MESSAGE

Renewed minds. Christians sometimes distinguish between "head knowledge" and "heart knowledge." But the Bible clearly teaches that we are to love and serve the Lord with all that we are, including both our hearts and our minds (4:23; see Deut. 6:5; Matt. 22:37).

no opportunity to the devil. [28] Let the thief no longer steal, but rather let him labor, doing honest work with his own hands, so that he may have something to share with anyone in need. [29] Let no corrupting talk come out of your mouths, but only such as is good for building up, as fits the occasion, that it may give grace to those who hear. [30] And do not grieve the Holy Spirit of God, by whom you were sealed for the day of redemption. [31] Let all bitterness and wrath and anger and clamor and slander be put away from you, along with all malice. [32] Be kind to one another, tenderhearted, forgiving one another, as God in Christ forgave you.

Walk in Love

5 Therefore be imitators of God, as beloved children. [2] And walk in love, as Christ loved us and gave himself up for us, a fragrant offering and sacrifice to God.

---

[1] The Greek word for *men* refers to both men and women (see Preface) [2] Or *pastors*

[3] But sexual immorality and all impurity or covetousness must not even be named among you, as is proper among saints. [4] Let there be no filthiness nor foolish talk nor crude joking, which are out of place, but instead let there be thanksgiving. [5] For you may be sure of this, that everyone who is sexually immoral or impure, or who is covetous (that is, an idolater), has no inheritance in the kingdom of Christ and God. [6] Let no one deceive you with empty words, for because of these things the wrath of God comes upon the sons of disobedience. [7] Therefore do not become partners with them; [8] for at one time you were darkness, but now you are light in the Lord. Walk as children of light [9] (for the fruit of light is found in all that is good and right and true), [10] and try to discern what is pleasing to the Lord. [11] Take no part in the unfruitful works

> ### GETTING THE MESSAGE
>
> Paul makes it clear that Christians must live **holy lives** (5:1–21; see 4:17–24). This means rejecting sexual immorality, impurity, idolatry, coveting, and drunkenness. Instead, they should strive to imitate God, because he loves them (5:1–2).

of darkness, but instead expose them. [12] For it is shameful even to speak of the things that they do in secret. [13] But when anything is exposed by the light, it becomes visible, [14] for anything that becomes visible is light. Therefore it says,

"Awake, O sleeper,
    and arise from the dead,
    and Christ will shine on you."

[15] Look carefully then how you walk, not as unwise but as wise, [16] making the best use of the time, because the days are evil. [17] Therefore do not be foolish, but understand what the will of the Lord is. [18] And do not get drunk with wine, for that is debauchery, but be filled with the Spirit, [19] addressing one another in psalms and hymns and spiritual songs, singing and making melody to the Lord with your heart, [20] giving thanks always and for everything to God the Father in the name of our Lord Jesus Christ, [21] submitting to one another out of reverence for Christ.

Wives and Husbands

[22] Wives, submit to your own husbands, as to the Lord. [23] For the husband is the head of the wife even as Christ is the head of the church, his body, and is himself its Savior. [24] Now as the church submits to Christ, so also wives should submit in everything to their husbands.

[25] Husbands, love your wives, as Christ loved the church and gave himself up for her, [26] that he might sanctify her, having cleansed her by the washing of water with the word, [27] so that he might present the church to himself in splendor, without spot or wrinkle or any such thing, that she might be holy and without blemish. [28] In the same way husbands should love their wives as their own bodies. He who loves his wife loves himself. [29] For no one ever hated his own flesh, but nourishes and cherishes it, just as Christ does the church, [30] because we are members of his body. [31] "Therefore a man shall leave his father and mother and hold fast to his wife, and the two shall become one flesh." [32] This mystery is profound, and I am saying that it refers to Christ and the church. [33] However, let each one of you love his wife as himself, and let the wife see that she respects her husband.

Children and Parents

6 Children, obey your parents in the Lord, for this is right. [2] "Honor your father and mother" (this is the first commandment with a promise), [3] "that it may go well with you and that you may live long in the land." [4] Fathers, do not provoke your children to anger, but bring them up in the discipline and instruction of the Lord.

Bondservants and Masters

[5] Bondservants,[1] obey your earthly masters with fear and trembling, with a sincere heart, as you would Christ, [6] not by the way of eye-service, as people-pleasers, but as bondservants of Christ, doing the will of God from the heart, [7] rendering service with a good will as to the Lord and not to man, [8] knowing that whatever good anyone does, this he will receive back from the Lord, whether he is a bondservant or is free.

---

[1] Or *Slaves* (Greek *doulos*; see Preface); also 6:6, 8

⁹ Masters, do the same to them, and stop your threatening, knowing that he who is both their Master and yours is in heaven, and that there is no partiality with him.

The Whole Armor of God

¹⁰ Finally, be strong in the Lord and in the strength of his might. ¹¹ Put on the whole armor of God, that you may be able to stand against the schemes of the devil. ¹² For we do not wrestle against flesh and blood, but against the rulers, against the authorities, against the cosmic powers over this present darkness, against the spiritual forces of evil in the heavenly places. ¹³ Therefore take up the whole armor of God, that you may be able to withstand in the evil day, and having done all, to stand firm. ¹⁴ Stand therefore, having fastened on the belt of truth, and having put on the breastplate of righteousness, ¹⁵ and, as shoes for your feet, having put on the readiness given by the gospel of peace. ¹⁶ In all circumstances take up the shield of faith, with which you can extinguish all the flaming darts of the evil one; ¹⁷ and take the helmet of salvation, and the sword of the Spirit, which is the word of God, ¹⁸ praying at all times in the Spirit, with all prayer and supplication. To that end keep alert with all perseverance, making supplication for all the saints, ¹⁹ and also for me,

that words may be given to me in opening my mouth boldly to proclaim the mystery of the gospel, ²⁰ for which I am an ambassador in chains, that I may declare it boldly, as I ought to speak.

Final Greetings

²¹ So that you also may know how I am and what I am doing, Tychicus the beloved brother and faithful minister in the Lord

GETTING THE MESSAGE

Flaming darts (6:16) were arrows tipped with cloth, then dipped in pitch and set on fire before shooting. They were used to ignite structures and the shields of opposing infantrymen. In defense against such darts, soldiers often covered their shields with leather and soaked them in water.

will tell you everything. ²² I have sent him to you for this very purpose, that you may know how we are, and that he may encourage your hearts.

²³ Peace be to the brothers,[1] and love with faith, from God the Father and the Lord Jesus Christ. ²⁴ Grace be with all who love our Lord Jesus Christ with love incorruptible.

[1] Or brothers and sisters (see Preface)

INTRODUCTION TO PHILIPPIANS

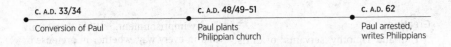

c. A.D. 33/34	c. A.D. 48/49–51	c. A.D. 62
Conversion of Paul	Paul plants Philippian church	Paul arrested, writes Philippians

AUTHOR, DATE, AND RECIPIENTS

The apostle Paul wrote this letter to the Christians in Philippi, probably from Rome c. A.D. 62.

THEME

Paul encourages the Philippians to live as citizens of a heavenly city, growing in their commitment to serve God and one another. Jesus is the supreme example of this way of life. Paul, Timothy, and Epaphroditus try to be good examples as well.

PURPOSE

Paul wrote to the Philippians from prison. He had several purposes in mind: (1) to tell them that Epaphroditus had recovered from a serious illness; (2) to encourage them in their faith; (3) to assure them that he was still in good spirits; and (4) to thank them for their continued support.

KEY THEMES

1. Christians need to keep making spiritual progress (1:12, 25; 3:12–16).

2. Such progress requires a proper spiritual outlook (1:5–11; 2:1–11; 3:7, 15; 4:7–9).

3. Christ is the supreme example for the Christian. Mature Christians can also serve as role models (1:12–26; 2:5–11, 19–30; 3:3–17; 4:9).

4. Suffering will come, but Christians can still be joyful (1:12–26; 2:14–15; 4:4, 11–13, 19).

5. Prayer is crucial for maintaining a joyful Christian life (1:3–11; 4:5–7).

6. Christians can enjoy rich relationships with one another; they can be united in service to promote the gospel (1:4, 7, 24–27; 2:1–4, 19–30; 4:2–4, 14).

7. Keeping the law cannot provide a right standing with God; believers are saved only through their faith in Jesus Christ (3:2–10).

8. Jesus is fully God and fully man. Because of his suffering on the cross, he is now glorified as Lord and Christ (2:5–11).

OUTLINE

I. Greeting and Prayer (1:1–11)

II. Paul's Reflections on His Imprisonment (1:12–30)

III. Encouragement to Humble Service (2:1–30)

IV. Opponents of the Gospel: Where Does Righteousness Come From? (3:1–21)

V. Concluding Encouragement and Thanksgiving (4:1–23)

PHILIPPIANS

Greeting

1 Paul and Timothy, servants[1] of Christ Jesus,

To all the saints in Christ Jesus who are at Philippi, with the overseers and deacons:

[2] Grace to you and peace from God our Father and the Lord Jesus Christ.

Thanksgiving and Prayer

[3] I thank my God in all my remembrance of you, [4] always in every prayer of mine for you all making my prayer with joy, [5] because of your partnership in the gospel from the first day until now. [6] And I am sure of this, that he who began a good work in you will bring it to completion at the day of Jesus Christ. [7] It is right for me to feel this way about you all, because I hold you in my heart, for you are all partakers with me of grace, both in my imprisonment and in the defense and confirmation of the gospel. [8] For God is my witness, how I yearn for you all with the affection of Christ Jesus. [9] And it is my prayer that your love may abound more and more, with knowledge and all discernment, [10] so that you may approve what is excellent, and so be pure and blameless for the day of Christ, [11] filled with the fruit of righteousness that comes through Jesus Christ, to the glory and praise of God.

The Advance of the Gospel

[12] I want you to know, brothers,[2] that what has happened to me has really served to advance the gospel, [13] so that it has become known throughout the whole imperial guard and to all the rest that my imprisonment is for Christ. [14] And most of the brothers, having become confident in the Lord by my imprisonment, are much more bold to speak the word without fear.

[15] Some indeed preach Christ from envy and rivalry, but others from good will. [16] The latter do it out of love, knowing that I am put here for the defense of the gospel. [17] The former proclaim Christ out of selfish ambition, not sincerely but thinking to afflict me

in my imprisonment. [18] What then? Only that in every way, whether in pretense or in truth, Christ is proclaimed, and in that I rejoice.

To Live Is Christ

Yes, and I will rejoice, [19] for I know that through your prayers and the help of the Spirit of Jesus Christ this will turn out for my deliverance, [20] as it is my eager expectation and hope that I will not be at all ashamed, but that with full courage now as always Christ will be honored in my body, whether

GETTING THE MESSAGE

The **imperial guard** that Paul mentions in 1:13 was probably the Roman emperor's group of elite personal bodyguards. Through his imprisonment, Paul was able to tell them about Christ. Because of this, Paul rejoiced even in the midst of his difficult circumstances (1:18).

by life or by death. [21] For to me to live is Christ, and to die is gain. [22] If I am to live in the flesh, that means fruitful labor for me. Yet which I shall choose I cannot tell. [23] I am hard pressed between the two. My desire is to depart and be with Christ, for that is far better. [24] But to remain in the flesh is more necessary on your account. [25] Convinced of this, I know that I will remain and continue with you all, for your progress and joy in the faith, [26] so that in me you may have ample cause to glory in Christ Jesus, because of my coming to you again.

[27] Only let your manner of life be worthy of the gospel of Christ, so that whether I come and see you or am absent, I may hear of you that you are standing firm in one spirit, with one mind striving side by side for the faith of the gospel, [28] and not frightened in anything by your opponents. This is a clear sign to them of their destruction,

[1] Or *slaves* (Greek *doulos*; see Preface) [2] Or *brothers and sisters* (see Preface); also 1:14

but of your salvation, and that from God. **29** For it has been granted to you that for the sake of Christ you should not only believe in him but also suffer for his sake, **30** engaged in the same conflict that you saw I had and now hear that I still have.

Christ's Example of Humility

2 So if there is any encouragement in Christ, any comfort from love, any participation in the Spirit, any affection and sympathy, **2** complete my joy by being of the same mind, having the same love, being in full accord and of one mind. **3** Do nothing from selfish ambition or conceit, but in humility count others more significant than yourselves. **4** Let each of you look not only to his own interests, but also to the interests of others. **5** Have this mind among yourselves,

> ### GETTING THE MESSAGE
>
> The heart of Philippians is the magnificent **"hymn of Christ"** in 2:5–11. Paul poetically describes Jesus' preexistence and equality with God, his incarnation as a man, his death and resurrection. He is the supreme example of humility and personal sacrifice for the sake of others (2:3–5).

which is yours in Christ Jesus, **6** who, though he was in the form of God, did not count equality with God a thing to be grasped, **7** but emptied himself, by taking the form of a servant, being born in the likeness of men. **8** And being found in human form, he humbled himself by becoming obedient to the point of death, even death on a cross. **9** Therefore God has highly exalted him and bestowed on him the name that is above every name, **10** so that at the name of Jesus every knee should bow, in heaven and on earth and under the earth, **11** and every tongue confess that Jesus Christ is Lord, to the glory of God the Father.

Lights in the World

12 Therefore, my beloved, as you have always obeyed, so now, not only as in my presence but much more in my absence, work out your own salvation with fear and trembling, **13** for it is God who works

in you, both to will and to work for his good pleasure.

14 Do all things without grumbling or disputing, **15** that you may be blameless and innocent, children of God without blemish in the midst of a crooked and twisted generation, among whom you shine as lights in the world, **16** holding fast to the word of life, so that in the day of Christ I may be proud that I did not run in vain or labor in vain. **17** Even if I am to be poured out as a drink offering upon the sacrificial offering of your faith, I am glad and rejoice with you all. **18** Likewise you also should be glad and rejoice with me.

Timothy and Epaphroditus

19 I hope in the Lord Jesus to send Timothy to you soon, so that I too may be cheered by news of you. **20** For I have no one like him, who will be genuinely concerned for your welfare. **21** For they all seek their own interests, not those of Jesus Christ. **22** But you know Timothy's proven worth, how as a son with a father he has served with me in the gospel. **23** I hope therefore to send him just as soon as I see how it will go with me, **24** and I trust in the Lord that shortly I myself will come also.

25 I have thought it necessary to send to you Epaphroditus my brother and fellow worker and fellow soldier, and your messenger and minister to my need, **26** for he has been longing for you all and has been distressed because you heard that he was ill. **27** Indeed he was ill, near to death. But God had mercy on him, and not only on him but on me also, lest I should have sorrow upon sorrow. **28** I am the more eager to send him, therefore, that you may rejoice at seeing him again, and that I may be less anxious. **29** So receive him in the Lord with all joy, and honor such men, **30** for he nearly died for the work of Christ, risking his life to complete what was lacking in your service to me.

Righteousness Through Faith in Christ

3 Finally, my brothers,[1] rejoice in the Lord. To write the same things to you is no trouble to me and is safe for you.

2 Look out for the dogs, look out for the evildoers, look out for those who mutilate the flesh. **3** For we are the circumcision, who worship by the Spirit of God and glory

[1] Or brothers and sisters

in Christ Jesus and put no confidence in the flesh— [4] though I myself have reason for confidence in the flesh also. If anyone else thinks he has reason for confidence in the flesh, I have more: [5] circumcised on the eighth day, of the people of Israel, of the tribe of Benjamin, a Hebrew of Hebrews; as to the law, a Pharisee; [6] as to zeal, a persecutor of the church; as to righteousness under the law, blameless. [7] But whatever gain I had, I counted as loss for the sake of Christ. [8] Indeed, I count everything as loss because of the surpassing worth of knowing Christ Jesus my Lord. For his sake I have suffered the loss of all things and count them as rubbish, in order that I may gain Christ [9] and be found in him, not having a righteousness of my own that comes from the law, but that which comes through faith in Christ, the righteousness from God that depends on faith— [10] that I may know him and the power of his resurrection, and may share his sufferings, becoming like him in his death, [11] that by any means possible I may attain the resurrection from the dead.

Straining Toward the Goal

[12] Not that I have already obtained this or am already perfect, but I press on to make it my own, because Christ Jesus has made me his own. [13] Brothers,[1] I do not consider that I have made it my own. But one thing I do: forgetting what lies behind and straining forward to what lies ahead, [14] I press on toward the goal for the prize of the upward call of God in Christ Jesus. [15] Let those of us who are mature think this way, and if in anything you think otherwise, God will reveal that also to you. [16] Only let us hold true to what we have attained.

[17] Brothers, join in imitating me, and keep your eyes on those who walk according to the example you have in us. [18] For many, of whom I have often told you and now tell you even with tears, walk as enemies of the cross of Christ. [19] Their end is destruction, their god is their belly, and they glory in their shame, with minds set on earthly things. [20] But our citizenship is in heaven, and from it we await a Savior, the Lord Jesus Christ, [21] who will transform our lowly body to be like his glorious body, by the power that enables him even to subject all things to himself.

[1] Or Brothers and sisters; also 3:17; 4:1, 8

4 Therefore, my brothers, whom I love and long for, my joy and crown, stand firm thus in the Lord, my beloved.

Exhortation, Encouragement, and Prayer

[2] I entreat Euodia and I entreat Syntyche to agree in the Lord. [3] Yes, I ask you also, true companion, help these women, who have labored side by side with me in the gospel together with Clement and the rest of my fellow workers, whose names are in the book of life.

[4] Rejoice in the Lord always; again I will say, rejoice. [5] Let your reasonableness be known to everyone. The Lord is at hand; [6] do not be anxious about anything, but in everything by prayer and supplication with thanksgiving let your requests be made known to God. [7] And the peace of God, which surpasses all understanding, will guard your hearts and your minds in Christ Jesus.

GETTING THE MESSAGE

Encouragement is an important theme in Paul's letter to the Philippians. The words for "joy" or "rejoice" occur more than a dozen times in this brief letter.

[8] Finally, brothers, whatever is true, whatever is honorable, whatever is just, whatever is pure, whatever is lovely, whatever is commendable, if there is any excellence, if there is anything worthy of praise, think about these things. [9] What you have learned and received and heard and seen in me—practice these things, and the God of peace will be with you.

God's Provision

[10] I rejoiced in the Lord greatly that now at length you have revived your concern for me. You were indeed concerned for me, but you had no opportunity. [11] Not that I am speaking of being in need, for I have learned in whatever situation I am to be content. [12] I know how to be brought low, and I know how to abound. In any and every circumstance, I have learned the secret of facing plenty and hunger, abundance and need. [13] I can do all things through him who strengthens me.

[14] Yet it was kind of you to share my trouble. [15] And you Philippians yourselves know that in the beginning of the gospel, when I left Macedonia, no church entered into partnership with me in giving and receiving, except you only. [16] Even in Thessalonica you sent me help for my needs once and again. [17] Not that I seek the gift, but I seek the fruit that increases to your credit. [18] I have received full payment, and more. I am well supplied, having received from Epaphroditus the gifts you sent, a fragrant offering, a sacrifice acceptable and pleasing to God. [19] And my God will supply every need of yours according to his riches in glory in Christ Jesus. [20] To our God and Father be glory forever and ever. Amen.

Final Greetings

[21] Greet every saint in Christ Jesus. The brothers[1] who are with me greet you. [22] All the saints greet you, especially those of Caesar's household.

[23] The grace of the Lord Jesus Christ be with your spirit.

---

[1] Or brothers and sisters

INTRODUCTION TO COLOSSIANS

c. A.D. **52–57**	c. A.D. **62**	c. A.D. **64–67**
Paul evangelizes Colossae	Paul in Rome, writes Colossians	Paul martyred in Rome

AUTHOR, DATE, AND RECIPIENTS

The apostle Paul wrote this letter to Christians living in the small city of Colossae. It was probably written c. A.D. 62, while Paul was in prison in Rome (Acts 27–28). This was about the same time he wrote Ephesians and Philemon. All three letters were sent with Tychicus and Onesimus.

THEME

Christ is Lord over all of creation, including the invisible realm. He has redeemed his people, enabling them to participate in his death, resurrection, and fullness.

PURPOSE, OCCASION, AND BACKGROUND

A dangerous teaching was threatening the church at Colossae, one that lessened Christ's role and undermined the new identity of believers "in Christ" (1:2, 28). Paul wrote to warn against this false teaching and to encourage the believers in their growth toward Christian maturity. He emphasizes Christ's authority over all evil powers. Christians are united with the risen Christ, and therefore they share in his power and authority. Paul also encourages these believers to fight against sin, pursue holiness, and live as distinctively Christian households.

KEY THEMES

1. Jesus Christ is preeminent over all creation, Lord over all human rulers and cosmic powers (1:15–20; 2:9–10; 3:1).

2. God has acted through Christ to secure redemption and reconciliation for all who put their faith in him (1:13–14, 20–22).

3. Believers are in Christ, and so they share in Christ's death, resurrection, new life, and his fullness (2:9–14; 3:1–4).

4. Christ has defeated the powers of darkness on the cross. Christians share in his power and authority over that realm (2:10, 15; see also 2:8, 20).

5. Jesus is the fulfillment of Jewish expectation. Christians share in the heritage of the old covenant people of God through their union with him (1:12, 21–22, 27).

6. Believers are called to grow in spiritual maturity by getting rid of sinful practices and developing Christian virtues (1:10–12, 28; 3:1–4:6).

OUTLINE

COLOSSIANS

Greeting

1 Paul, an apostle of Christ Jesus by the will of God, and Timothy our brother,

2 To the saints and faithful brothers[1] in Christ at Colossae:

Grace to you and peace from God our Father.

Thanksgiving and Prayer

3 We always thank God, the Father of our Lord Jesus Christ, when we pray for you, 4 since we heard of your faith in Christ Jesus and of the love that you have for all the saints, 5 because of the hope laid up for you in heaven. Of this you have heard before in the word of the truth, the gospel, 6 which has come to you, as indeed in the whole world it is bearing fruit and increasing—as it also does among you, since the day you heard it and understood the grace of God in truth, 7 just as you learned it from Epaphras our beloved fellow servant.[2] He is a faithful minister of Christ on your behalf 8 and has made known to us your love in the Spirit.

9 And so, from the day we heard, we have not ceased to pray for you, asking that you may be filled with the knowledge of his will in all spiritual wisdom and understanding, 10 so as to walk in a manner worthy of the Lord, fully pleasing to him, bearing fruit in every good work and increasing in the knowledge of God. 11 May you be strengthened with all power, according to his glorious might, for all endurance and patience with joy, 12 giving thanks to the Father, who has qualified you to share in the inheritance of the saints in light. 13 He has delivered us from the domain of darkness and transferred us to the kingdom of his beloved Son, 14 in whom we have redemption, the forgiveness of sins.

The Preeminence of Christ

15 He is the image of the invisible God, the firstborn of all creation. 16 For by him all things were created, in heaven and on earth, visible and invisible, whether thrones or dominions or rulers or authorities—all things were created through him and for him. 17 And he is before all things, and in him all things hold together. 18 And he is the head of the body, the church. He is the beginning, the firstborn from the dead, that in everything he might be preeminent. 19 For in him all the fullness of God was pleased to dwell, 20 and through him to reconcile to himself all things, whether on earth or in heaven, making peace by the blood of his cross.

21 And you, who once were alienated and hostile in mind, doing evil deeds, 22 he has

now reconciled in his body of flesh by his death, in order to present you holy and blameless and above reproach before him, 23 if indeed you continue in the faith, stable and steadfast, not shifting from the hope of the gospel that you heard, which has been proclaimed in all creation under heaven, and of which I, Paul, became a minister.

Paul's Ministry to the Church

24 Now I rejoice in my sufferings for your sake, and in my flesh I am filling up what is lacking in Christ's afflictions for the sake of his body, that is, the church, 25 of which I became a minister according to the stewardship from God that was given to me for you, to make the word of God fully known, 26 the mystery hidden for ages and generations but now revealed to his saints. 27 To them God chose to make known how great among the Gentiles are the riches of the glory of this mystery, which is Christ in you, the

---

[1] Or brothers and sisters (see Preface) [2] Or fellow slave (Greek sundoulos; see Preface)

hope of glory. **28** Him we proclaim, warning everyone and teaching everyone with all wisdom, that we may present everyone mature in Christ. **29** For this I toil, struggling with all his energy that he powerfully works within me.

2 For I want you to know how great a struggle I have for you and for those at Laodicea and for all who have not seen me face to face, **2** that their hearts may be encouraged, being knit together in love, to reach all the riches of full assurance of understanding and the knowledge of God's mystery, which is Christ, **3** in whom are hidden all the treasures of wisdom and knowledge. **4** I say this in order that no one may delude you with plausible arguments. **5** For though I am absent in body, yet I am with you in spirit, rejoicing to see your good order and the firmness of your faith in Christ.

> ### GETTING THE MESSAGE
>
> **Worship of angels.** Many Colossians greatly feared evil spirits. In order to control the spirits and to avoid affliction, they called on angels for help and protection (2:18). Paul reminds them of Christ's supremacy in dealing with demonic powers (1:13–14; 2:15).

Alive in Christ

6 Therefore, as you received Christ Jesus the Lord, so walk in him, **7** rooted and built up in him and established in the faith, just as you were taught, abounding in thanksgiving.

8 See to it that no one takes you captive by philosophy and empty deceit, according to human tradition, according to the elemental spirits of the world, and not according to Christ. **9** For in him the whole fullness of deity dwells bodily, **10** and you have been filled in him, who is the head of all rule and authority. **11** In him also you were circumcised with a circumcision made without hands, by putting off the body of the flesh, by the circumcision of Christ, **12** having been buried with him in baptism, in which you were also raised with him through faith in the powerful working of God, who raised him from the dead. **13** And you, who were dead in your trespasses and the uncircum-

cision of your flesh, God made alive together with him, having forgiven us all our trespasses, **14** by canceling the record of debt that stood against us with its legal demands. This he set aside, nailing it to the cross. **15** He disarmed the rulers and authorities and put them to open shame, by triumphing over them in him.

Let No One Disqualify You

16 Therefore let no one pass judgment on you in questions of food and drink, or with regard to a festival or a new moon or a Sabbath. **17** These are a shadow of the things to come, but the substance belongs to Christ. **18** Let no one disqualify you, insisting on asceticism and worship of angels, going on in detail about visions, puffed up without reason by his sensuous mind, **19** and not holding fast to the Head, from whom the whole body, nourished and knit together through its joints and ligaments, grows with a growth that is from God.

20 If with Christ you died to the elemental spirits of the world, why, as if you were still alive in the world, do you submit to regulations— **21** "Do not handle, Do not taste, Do not touch" **22** (referring to things that all perish as they are used)—according to human precepts and teachings? **23** These have indeed an appearance of wisdom in promoting self-made religion and asceticism and severity to the body, but they are of no value in stopping the indulgence of the flesh.

Put On the New Self

3 If then you have been raised with Christ, seek the things that are above, where Christ is, seated at the right hand of God. **2** Set your minds on things that are above, not on things that are on earth. **3** For you have died, and your life is hidden with Christ in God. **4** When Christ who is your life appears, then you also will appear with him in glory.

5 Put to death therefore what is earthly in you: sexual immorality, impurity, passion, evil desire, and covetousness, which is idolatry. **6** On account of these the wrath of God is coming. **7** In these you too once walked, when you were living in them. **8** But now you must put them all away: anger, wrath, malice, slander, and obscene talk from your mouth. **9** Do not lie to one another, seeing that you have put off the old self with its practices [10] and have put on the new self, which is being renewed in knowledge after the image of its creator. [11] Here there is not Greek and Jew, circumcised and uncircumcised, barbarian, Scythian, slave,[1] free; but Christ is all, and in all.

[12] Put on then, as God's chosen ones, holy and beloved, compassionate hearts, kindness, humility, meekness, and patience, [13] bearing with one another and, if one has a complaint against another, forgiving each other; as the Lord has forgiven you, so you also must forgive. [14] And above all these put on love, which binds everything together in perfect harmony. [15] And let the peace of Christ rule in your hearts, to which indeed you were called in one body. And be thankful. [16] Let the word of Christ dwell in you richly, teaching and admonishing one another in all wisdom, singing psalms and hymns and spiritual songs, with thankfulness in your hearts to God. [17] And whatever you do, in word or deed, do everything in the name of the Lord Jesus, giving thanks to God the Father through him.

Rules for Christian Households

[18] Wives, submit to your husbands, as is fitting in the Lord. [19] Husbands, love your wives, and do not be harsh with them. [20] Children, obey your parents in everything, for this pleases the Lord. [21] Fathers, do not provoke your children, lest they become discouraged. [22] Bondservants,[2] obey in everything those who are your earthly masters, not by way of eye-service, as people-pleasers, but with sincerity of heart, fearing the Lord. [23] Whatever you do, work heartily, as for the Lord and not for men, [24] knowing that from the Lord you will receive the inheritance as your reward. You are serving the Lord Christ. [25] For the wrongdoer will be paid back for the wrong he has done, and there is no partiality. 4 Masters, treat your bondservants justly and fairly, knowing that you also have a Master in heaven.

Further Instructions

[2] Continue steadfastly in prayer, being watchful in it with thanksgiving. [3] At the same time, pray also for us, that God may open to us a door for the word, to declare the mystery of Christ, on account of which

I am in prison — [4] that I may make it clear, which is how I ought to speak.

[5] Walk in wisdom toward outsiders, making the best use of the time. [6] Let your speech always be gracious, seasoned with salt, so that you may know how you ought to answer each person.

Final Greetings

[7] Tychicus will tell you all about my activities. He is a beloved brother and faithful minister and fellow servant[3] in the Lord. [8] I have sent him to you for this very purpose, that you may know how we are and that he may encourage your hearts, [9] and with him Onesimus, our faithful and beloved brother, who is one of you. They will tell you of everything that has taken place here.

> ### GETTING THE MESSAGE
>
> The **Scythians** (3:11) lived about 500 miles (805 km) north of Colossae along the Black Sea coast. The Greeks thought of them as violent, uneducated, uncivilized people. In contrast, Paul states that Christ binds all people together in unity through his love. Racial and cultural prejudice has no place among Christians.

[10] Aristarchus my fellow prisoner greets you, and Mark the cousin of Barnabas (concerning whom you have received instructions — if he comes to you, welcome him), [11] and Jesus who is called Justus. These are the only men of the circumcision among my fellow workers for the kingdom of God, and they have been a comfort to me. [12] Epaphras, who is one of you, a servant of Christ Jesus, greets you, always struggling on your behalf in his prayers, that you may stand mature and fully assured in all the will of God. [13] For I bear him witness that he has worked hard for you and for those in Laodicea and in Hierapolis. [14] Luke the beloved physician greets you, as does Demas. [15] Give my greetings to the brothers[4] at Laodicea, and to Nympha and the church in her house. [16] And when this letter has been read among you, have it also read in the church of the Laodiceans; and see that

---

[1] Greek *doulos* (see Preface) [2] Or *Slaves* (Greek *doulos*; see Preface); also 4:1 [3] Or *fellow slave* (Greek *sundoulos*; see Preface)
[4] Or *brothers and sisters*

you also read the letter from Laodicea. ¹⁷ And say to Archippus, "See that you fulfill the ministry that you have received in the Lord."

¹⁸ I, Paul, write this greeting with my own hand. Remember my chains. Grace be with you.

INTRODUCTION TO 1 THESSALONIANS

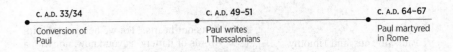

c. A.D. 33/34	c. A.D. 49–51	c. A.D. 64–67
Conversion of Paul	Paul writes 1 Thessalonians	Paul martyred in Rome

AUTHOR, DATE, AND RECIPIENTS

Paul wrote this letter to the church in Thessalonica. He probably wrote in A.D. 49–51 from Corinth during his second missionary journey (Acts 18:1–18).

THEME

The main theme is Jesus' second coming. When he returns, the dead who have believed in Christ will rise and will join the living to meet the Lord in the air (4:15–17). Unbelievers will experience God's wrath, while believers will inherit salvation (1:10; 5:2–4, 9–10). In preparation for that great day, Christians are called to be holy and blameless (3:11–4:8; 5:23). God, who is faithful, will produce in them the holiness he requires (5:24).

PURPOSE

Paul has received a report from Timothy about the Thessalonian church. Paul writes to them to restore their hope, which has been tested by unexpected deaths in the church. He reassures them that both the dead and the living believers will be safe at the second coming (4:13–5:11). In addition, Paul wants (1) to stress the authenticity of himself, Silas, and Timothy as preachers of the gospel (1:5; 2:1–12; 2:17–3:10); (2) to teach them that persecution is normal for Christians (3:3–4); and (3) to challenge them to take responsibility for earning their own living (4:9–12).

KEY THEMES

1. God's wrath comes on those who reject the gospel (2:16; 5:3).

2. Jesus' death and resurrection are the basis for the Christian's hope (4:14; 5:10).

3. Christians are destined not for wrath but for salvation when Christ returns (1:10; 5:4, 9).

4. Christians who die will participate fully in the second coming (4:14–17; 5:10).

5. Those who respond to the gospel have been elected and called by God. They continue to be called by God throughout their lives (1:4; 2:12; 4:7; 5:9, 24).

6. Christians should live lives of complete holiness (3:13; 4:3–8; 5:23).

7. Christians must never ignore their responsibility to work (4:9–12; 5:14).

8. The truth of the gospel is confirmed by the integrity of its preachers (1:5; 2:1–12).

9. Joy, especially in suffering, is a mark of the Christian (1:6; 5:16).

10. Christians experience the realities of the new covenant (4:8–9).

11. Faith, hope, and love are essential traits of the Christian (1:2–3; 5:8).

OUTLINE

1 THESSALONIANS

Greeting

1 Paul, Silvanus, and Timothy,
To the church of the Thessalonians in God the Father and the Lord Jesus Christ:
Grace to you and peace.

The Thessalonians' Faith and Example

² We give thanks to God always for all of you, constantly mentioning you in our prayers, ³ remembering before our God and Father your work of faith and labor of love and steadfastness of hope in our Lord Jesus Christ. ⁴ For we know, brothers,[1] loved by God, that he has chosen you, ⁵ because our gospel came to you not only in word, but also in power and in the Holy Spirit and with full conviction. You know what kind of men we proved to be among you for your sake. ⁶ And you became imitators of us and of the Lord, for you received the word in much affliction, with the joy of the Holy Spirit, ⁷ so that you became an example to all the believers in Macedonia and in Achaia. ⁸ For not only has the word of the Lord sounded forth from you in Macedonia and Achaia, but your faith in God has gone forth everywhere, so that we need not say anything. ⁹ For they themselves report concerning us the kind of reception we had among you, and how you turned to God from idols to serve the living and true God, ¹⁰ and to wait for his Son from heaven, whom he raised from the dead, Jesus who delivers us from the wrath to come.

Paul's Ministry to the Thessalonians

2 For you yourselves know, brothers, that our coming to you was not in vain. ² But though we had already suffered and been shamefully treated at Philippi, as you know, we had boldness in our God to declare to you the gospel of God in the midst of much conflict. ³ For our appeal does not spring from error or impurity or any attempt to deceive, ⁴ but just as we have been approved by God to be entrusted with the gospel, so we speak, not to please man, but to please God who tests our hearts. ⁵ For we never came with words of flattery, as you know, nor with a pretext for greed—God is witness. ⁶ Nor did we seek glory from people, whether from you or from others, though we could have made demands as apostles of Christ. ⁷ But we were gentle among you, like a nursing mother taking care of her own children. ⁸ So, being affectionately desirous of you, we were ready to share with you not only the gospel of God but also our own selves, because you had become very dear to us.

⁹ For you remember, brothers, our labor and toil: we worked night and day, that we might not be a burden to any of you, while

GETTING THE MESSAGE

Thessalonica was the proud capital of the Roman province of Macedonia, with a population of more than 100,000. It was a center of education as well as commerce.

we proclaimed to you the gospel of God. ¹⁰ You are witnesses, and God also, how holy and righteous and blameless was our conduct toward you believers. ¹¹ For you know how, like a father with his children, ¹² we exhorted each one of you and encouraged you and charged you to walk in a manner worthy of God, who calls you into his own kingdom and glory.

¹³ And we also thank God constantly for this, that when you received the word of God, which you heard from us, you accepted it not as the word of men[2] but as what it really is, the word of God, which is at work in you believers. ¹⁴ For you, brothers, became imitators of the churches of God in Christ Jesus that are in Judea. For you suffered the same things from your own countrymen as they did from the Jews,[3] ¹⁵ who killed both the Lord Jesus and the prophets, and drove us out, and displease God and oppose all

---

[1] Or brothers and sisters (see Preface); also 2:1, 9, 14 [2] The Greek word for men refers to both men and women (see Preface)
[3] The Greek word refers to Jewish religious leaders, and people they influenced, who opposed the Christian faith

mankind [16] by hindering us from speaking to the Gentiles that they might be saved—so as always to fill up the measure of their sins. But wrath has come upon them at last!

Paul's Longing to See Them Again

[17] But since we were torn away from you, brothers,[1] for a short time, in person not in heart, we endeavored the more eagerly and with great desire to see you face to face, [18] because we wanted to come to you— I, Paul, again and again—but Satan hindered us. [19] For what is our hope or joy or crown of boasting before our Lord Jesus at his coming? Is it not you? [20] For you are our glory and joy.

3 Therefore when we could bear it no longer, we were willing to be left behind at Athens alone, [2] and we sent Timothy, our brother and God's coworker in the gospel of Christ, to establish and exhort you in your

faith, [3] that no one be moved by these afflictions. For you yourselves know that we are destined for this. [4] For when we were with you, we kept telling you beforehand that we were to suffer affliction, just as it has come to pass, and just as you know. [5] For this reason, when I could bear it no longer, I sent to learn about your faith, for fear that somehow the tempter had tempted you and our labor would be in vain.

Timothy's Encouraging Report

[6] But now that Timothy has come to us from you, and has brought us the good news of your faith and love and reported that you always remember us kindly and long to see us, as we long to see you— [7] for this reason, brothers, in all our distress and affliction we have been comforted about you through your faith. [8] For now we live, if you are standing fast in the Lord. [9] For

what thanksgiving can we return to God for you, for all the joy that we feel for your sake before our God, [10] as we pray most earnestly night and day that we may see you face to face and supply what is lacking in your faith?

[11] Now may our God and Father himself, and our Lord Jesus, direct our way to you, [12] and may the Lord make you increase and abound in love for one another and for all, as we do for you, [13] so that he may establish your hearts blameless in holiness before our God and Father, at the coming of our Lord Jesus with all his saints.

A Life Pleasing to God

4 Finally, then, brothers, we ask and urge you in the Lord Jesus, that as you received from us how you ought to walk and to please God, just as you are doing, that you do so more and more. [2] For you know what instructions we gave you through the Lord Jesus. [3] For this is the will of God, your sanctification: that you abstain from sexual immorality; [4] that each one of you know how to control his own body in holiness and honor, [5] not in the passion of lust like the Gentiles who do not know God; [6] that no one transgress and wrong his brother in this matter, because the Lord is an avenger in all these things, as we told you beforehand and solemnly warned you. [7] For God has not called us for impurity, but in holiness. [8] Therefore whoever disregards this, disregards not man but God, who gives his Holy Spirit to you.

[9] Now concerning brotherly love you have no need for anyone to write to you, for you yourselves have been taught by God to love one another, [10] for that indeed is what you are doing to all the brothers throughout Macedonia. But we urge you, brothers, to do this more and more, [11] and to aspire to live quietly, and to mind your own affairs, and to work with your hands, as we instructed you, [12] so that you may walk properly before outsiders and be dependent on no one.

The Coming of the Lord

[13] But we do not want you to be uninformed, brothers, about those who are asleep, that you may not grieve as others do who have no hope. [14] For since we believe that Jesus died and rose again, even

---

[1] Or brothers and sisters; also 3:7; 4:1, 10, 13

so, through Jesus, God will bring with him those who have fallen asleep. [15] For this we declare to you by a word from the Lord, that we who are alive, who are left until the coming of the Lord, will not precede those who have fallen asleep. [16] For the Lord himself will descend from heaven with a cry of command, with the voice of an archangel, and with the sound of the trumpet of God. And the dead in Christ will rise first. [17] Then we who are alive, who are left, will be caught up together with them in the clouds to meet the Lord in the air, and so we will always be with the Lord. [18] Therefore encourage one another with these words.

The Day of the Lord

5 Now concerning the times and the seasons, brothers,[1] you have no need to have anything written to you. [2] For you yourselves are fully aware that the day of the Lord will come like a thief in the night. [3] While people are saying, "There is peace and security," then sudden destruction will come upon them as labor pains come upon a pregnant woman, and they will not escape. [4] But you are not in darkness, brothers, for that day to surprise you like a thief. [5] For you are all children of light, children of the day. We are not of the night or of the darkness. [6] So then let us not sleep, as others do, but let us keep awake and be sober. [7] For those who sleep, sleep at night, and those who get drunk, are drunk at night. [8] But since we belong to the day, let us be sober, having put on the breastplate of faith and love, and for a helmet the hope of salvation. [9] For God has not destined us for wrath, but to obtain salvation through our Lord Jesus Christ, [10] who died for us so that whether we are awake or asleep we might live with him. [11] Therefore encourage one another and build one another up, just as you are doing.

Final Instructions and Benediction

[12] We ask you, brothers, to respect those who labor among you and are over you in the Lord and admonish you, [13] and to esteem them very highly in love because of their work. Be at peace among yourselves. [14] And we urge you, brothers, admonish the idle, encourage the fainthearted, help the weak, be patient with them all. [15] See that no one repays anyone evil for evil, but always seek to do good to one another and to everyone. [16] Rejoice always, [17] pray without ceasing, [18] give thanks in all circumstances; for this is the will of God in Christ Jesus for you. [19] Do not quench the Spirit. [20] Do not despise prophecies, [21] but test everything;

GETTING THE MESSAGE

The Romans promised **peace and security** to the citizens of their empire. They promoted this message on coins and statues. But Paul warns that, regardless of how secure people may feel, God's day of judgment will come for those who have rejected him (5:3; see Jer. 8:11).

---

hold fast what is good. [22] Abstain from every form of evil.

[23] Now may the God of peace himself sanctify you completely, and may your whole spirit and soul and body be kept blameless at the coming of our Lord Jesus Christ. [24] He who calls you is faithful; he will surely do it.

[25] Brothers, pray for us.

[26] Greet all the brothers with a holy kiss.

[27] I put you under oath before the Lord to have this letter read to all the brothers.

[28] The grace of our Lord Jesus Christ be with you.

---

[1] Or brothers and sisters; also 5:4, 12, 14, 25, 26, 27

INTRODUCTION TO 2 THESSALONIANS

c. A.D. 33/34	c. A.D. 49–51	c. A.D. 64–67
Conversion of Paul	Paul writes 2 Thessalonians	Paul martyred in Rome

AUTHOR, DATE, AND RECIPIENTS

Shortly after writing 1 Thessalonians, the apostle Paul received a report (2 Thess. 3:11) that the Thessalonian church had accepted the strange claim that "the day of the Lord has come" (2:1–2). Paul sent them a second letter in A.D. 49–51. He was probably in Corinth at the time.

THEME

The letter's main theme is Jesus' second coming. Jesus' return will be preceded by an "apostasy" (or rebellion) and by the appearance of the "man of lawlessness," the Antichrist (2:3). When Jesus comes, he will defeat this rebellious world ruler (2:8). He will bring justice to oppressed Christians and wrath to unbelievers (1:5–10; 2:9–15).

PURPOSE, OCCASION, AND BACKGROUND

Paul wrote 2 Thessalonians (1) to reassure those terrified that the day of the Lord had already come (2:1–3:5); (2) to strengthen the Thessalonians in the face of continuing persecution (1:3–12); and (3) to deal with the problem of some of the church members refusing to earn their own living (3:6–15).

Paul assumes that the Thessalonian church knew that the second coming of Jesus Christ would occur at the same time as the coming of the "day of the Lord." Yet the Thessalonians may simply have fallen victim to a belief that the day of the Lord had already come. The persecution they were undergoing may have fueled their confusion about the end times.

Some of the Thessalonians may have stopped working to await and proclaim the second coming. More likely, lazy Christians may have

been exploiting the generosity of wealthier Christians in order to avoid work.

In contrast to the warm emotional tone of 1 Thessalonians, 2 Thessalonians includes some blunt commands as Paul addresses bad behavior and bad thinking. Further, this letter is noteworthy for Paul's tough-mindedness in predicting judgment on the ungodly and in rebuking church members who behave and think incorrectly. Still, there is a regular swing back and forth between reproof and warm encouragement.

KEY THEMES

1. God's righteous judgment will be completed when Jesus returns. Unbelievers will be condemned and believers will be saved (1:5–10; 2:9–14).

2. Christians will share Christ's glory (1:10, 12; 2:14).

3. Jesus will return after the "man of lawlessness" appears and humanity rebels for a final time (2:3–4, 9–12).

4. The man of lawlessness will deceive all those who have rejected the gospel. Jesus will judge them when he returns (2:3, 6–12).

5. Christians must not take advantage of the charity of fellow Christians (3:6–15).

OUTLINE

   I. Opening (1:1–2)

  II. Thanksgiving and Comfort for the Persecuted Thessalonians (1:3–12)

 III. Disproving the False Claim about the Day of the Lord (2:1–17)

 IV. Transition (3:1–5)

  V. The Problem of Lazy Christians (3:6–15)

 VI. Conclusion (3:16–18)

2 THESSALONIANS

Greeting

1 Paul, Silvanus, and Timothy,
To the church of the Thessalonians in God our Father and the Lord Jesus Christ:

² Grace to you and peace from God our Father and the Lord Jesus Christ.

Thanksgiving

³ We ought always to give thanks to God for you, brothers,¹ as is right, because your faith is growing abundantly, and the love of every one of you for one another is increasing. ⁴ Therefore we ourselves boast about you in the churches of God for your steadfastness and faith in all your persecutions and in the afflictions that you are enduring.

The Judgment at Christ's Coming

⁵ This is evidence of the righteous judgment of God, that you may be considered worthy of the kingdom of God, for which you are also suffering— ⁶ since indeed God considers it just to repay with affliction those who afflict you, ⁷ and to grant relief to you who are afflicted as well as to us, when the Lord Jesus is revealed from heaven with his mighty angels ⁸ in flaming fire, inflicting vengeance on those who do not know God and on those who do not obey the gospel of our Lord Jesus. ⁹ They will suffer the punishment of eternal destruction, away from the presence of the Lord and from the glory of his might, ¹⁰ when he comes on that day to be glorified in his saints, and to be marveled at among all who have believed, because our testimony to you was believed. ¹¹ To this end we always pray for you, that our God may make you worthy of his calling and may fulfill every resolve for good and every work of faith by his power, ¹² so that the name of our Lord Jesus may be glorified in you, and you in him, according to the grace of our God and the Lord Jesus Christ.

The Man of Lawlessness

2 Now concerning the coming of our Lord Jesus Christ and our being gathered together to him, we ask you, broth-ers, ² not to be quickly shaken in mind or alarmed, either by a spirit or a spoken word, or a letter seeming to be from us, to the effect that the day of the Lord has come. ³ Let no one deceive you in any way. For that day will not come, unless the rebellion comes first, and the man of lawlessness is revealed, the son of destruction, ⁴ who opposes and exalts himself against every so-called god or object of worship, so that he takes his seat in the temple of God, proclaiming himself to be God. ⁵ Do you not

---

GETTING THE MESSAGE

Why were Christians being persecuted?
The fact that Christians worshiped only one God excluded them from participation in community gatherings, which often focused on other gods. The church's custom of meeting secretly also raised suspicions of disloyalty to the Roman Empire.

---

remember that when I was still with you I told you these things? ⁶ And you know what is restraining him now so that he may be revealed in his time. ⁷ For the mystery of lawlessness is already at work. Only he who now restrains it will do so until he is out of the way. ⁸ And then the lawless one will be revealed, whom the Lord Jesus will kill with the breath of his mouth and bring to nothing by the appearance of his coming. ⁹ The coming of the lawless one is by the activity of Satan with all power and false signs and wonders, ¹⁰ and with all wicked deception for those who are perishing, because they refused to love the truth and so be saved. ¹¹ Therefore God sends them a strong delusion, so that they may believe what is false, ¹² in order that all may be condemned who did not believe the truth but had pleasure in unrighteousness.

¹ Or brothers and sisters (see Preface); also 2:1

Stand Firm

[13] But we ought always to give thanks to God for you, brothers[1] beloved by the Lord, because God chose you as the firstfruits to be saved, through sanctification by the Spirit and belief in the truth. [14] To this he called you through our gospel, so that you may obtain the glory of our Lord Jesus Christ. [15] So then, brothers, stand firm and hold to the traditions that you were taught by us, either by our spoken word or by our letter.

[16] Now may our Lord Jesus Christ himself, and God our Father, who loved us and gave us eternal comfort and good hope through

> ### GETTING THE MESSAGE
>
> **Sanctification** (2:13) refers to the transforming work of the Holy Spirit in a believer's life, whereby the person becomes increasingly more like Christ. This ongoing process continues until the redeemed person is resurrected and made completely holy in heaven (glorification).

grace, [17] comfort your hearts and establish them in every good work and word.

Pray for Us

3 Finally, brothers, pray for us, that the word of the Lord may speed ahead and be honored, as happened among you, [2] and that we may be delivered from wicked and evil men. For not all have faith. [3] But the Lord is faithful. He will establish you and guard you against the evil one. [4] And we have confidence in the Lord about you, that you are doing and will do the things that we

command. [5] May the Lord direct your hearts to the love of God and to the steadfastness of Christ.

Warning Against Idleness

[6] Now we command you, brothers, in the name of our Lord Jesus Christ, that you keep away from any brother who is walking in idleness and not in accord with the tradition that you received from us. [7] For you yourselves know how you ought to imitate us, because we were not idle when we were with you, [8] nor did we eat anyone's bread without paying for it, but with toil and labor we worked night and day, that we might not be a burden to any of you. [9] It was not because we do not have that right, but to give you in ourselves an example to imitate. [10] For even when we were with you, we would give you this command: If anyone is not willing to work, let him not eat. [11] For we hear that some among you walk in idleness, not busy at work, but busybodies. [12] Now such persons we command and encourage in the Lord Jesus Christ to do their work quietly and to earn their own living.

[13] As for you, brothers, do not grow weary in doing good. [14] If anyone does not obey what we say in this letter, take note of that person, and have nothing to do with him, that he may be ashamed. [15] Do not regard him as an enemy, but warn him as a brother.

Benediction

[16] Now may the Lord of peace himself give you peace at all times in every way. The Lord be with you all.

[17] I, Paul, write this greeting with my own hand. This is the sign of genuineness in every letter of mine; it is the way I write. [18] The grace of our Lord Jesus Christ be with you all.

---

[1] Or *brothers and sisters*; also 2:15; 3:1, 6, 13

INTRODUCTION TO 1 TIMOTHY

AUTHOR, DATE, AND RECIPIENT

The apostle Paul probably wrote this letter
to Timothy in the mid-60s A.D., during a
mission trip not recorded in Scripture. This
trip took place after the events described in
Acts, between Paul's first and final Roman
imprisonments.

THEME

The letter's theme is that the gospel leads to
practical, visible change in believers' lives. The
true gospel, in contrast to false teaching, must
and will always lead to godliness.

PURPOSE

Paul wrote 1 Timothy to advise his coworker
Timothy about issues in the church in Ephesus.
False teachers are the main cause for the letter.
Their teaching apparently involved incorrect
assumptions about the law (1:7–11) and not
allowing marriage and certain foods (4:1–5).
Paul's real concern is with the results of the
false teaching. For example, it promotes mere
theories over solid truth (1:4; 6:4). It also leads
to arrogance (6:4) and greed (6:5–10). Paul
focuses on the fact that true Christianity is
shown in lifestyles shaped by the gospel. Those
whose lives are not shaped by the gospel have
turned away from the faith (1:6, 19–20; 4:1; 5:6,
8, 11–12, 15; 6:9–10).

KEY THEMES

1. The gospel produces holiness in the lives
of believers. There is no legitimate separation
between belief and behavior. Thus, those who
profess faith but show no progress in godliness
should question their spiritual health (1:5; 2:8–15;
3:1–16; 4:6–16; 5:4–6, 8; 6:3–5, 11–14, 18–19).

2. Worldwide evangelism is essential. It is
rooted in God's own evangelistic desire (1:15;
2:1–7; 3:16; 4:10).

3. One key evidence of receiving the gospel
is proper behavior in corporate worship, in
matters like evangelistic prayer, unity, modesty,
and submission (2:1–15).

4. Church leaders should be people whose lives
are shaped by the gospel (3:1–13; 4:6–16).

5. Appropriate honor is a key element in how
Christians should relate to one another in the
church (5:1–6:2).

6. Everything God created is good. It is to be
appreciated, but not worshiped (4:4–5; 6:17–19).

7. It is important to protect the purity of the
gospel (1:3–7, 18–20; 4:6–16; 6:2b–3, 12, 20–21).

OUTLINE

1 TIMOTHY

Greeting

1 Paul, an apostle of Christ Jesus by command of God our Savior and of Christ Jesus our hope,

² To Timothy, my true child in the faith:

Grace, mercy, and peace from God the Father and Christ Jesus our Lord.

Warning Against False Teachers

³ As I urged you when I was going to Macedonia, remain at Ephesus so that you may charge certain persons not to teach any different doctrine, ⁴ nor to devote themselves to myths and endless genealogies, which promote speculations rather than the stewardship from God that is by faith. ⁵ The aim of our charge is love that issues from a pure heart and a good conscience and a sincere faith. ⁶ Certain persons, by swerving from these, have wandered away into vain discussion, ⁷ desiring to be teachers of the law, without understanding either what they are saying or the things about which they make confident assertions.

⁸ Now we know that the law is good, if one uses it lawfully, ⁹ understanding this, that the law is not laid down for the just but for the lawless and disobedient, for the ungodly and sinners, for the unholy and profane, for those who strike their fathers and mothers, for murderers, ¹⁰ the sexually immoral, men who practice homosexuality, enslavers,[1] liars, perjurers, and whatever else is contrary to sound doctrine, ¹¹ in accordance with the gospel of the glory of the blessed God with which I have been entrusted.

Christ Jesus Came to Save Sinners

¹² I thank him who has given me strength, Christ Jesus our Lord, because he judged me faithful, appointing me to his service, ¹³ though formerly I was a blasphemer, persecutor, and insolent opponent. But I received mercy because I had acted ignorantly in unbelief, ¹⁴ and the grace of our Lord overflowed for me with the faith and love that are in Christ Jesus. ¹⁵ The saying is trustworthy and deserving of full acceptance, that Christ Jesus came into the world to save sinners, of whom I am the foremost. ¹⁶ But I received mercy for this reason, that in me, as the foremost, Jesus Christ might display his perfect patience as an example to those who were to believe in him for eternal life. ¹⁷ To the King of the ages, immortal, invisible, the only God, be honor and glory forever and ever. Amen.

¹⁸ This charge I entrust to you, Timothy, my child, in accordance with the prophecies previously made about you, that by them

GETTING THE MESSAGE

After Paul established the church in Ephesus, Paul's younger coworker Timothy stayed there to strengthen it against false teaching (1:3). Paul's **first letter to Timothy** provides further instruction about specific issues that the young church faced.

you may wage the good warfare, ¹⁹ holding faith and a good conscience. By rejecting this, some have made shipwreck of their faith, ²⁰ among whom are Hymenaeus and Alexander, whom I have handed over to Satan that they may learn not to blaspheme.

Pray for All People

2 First of all, then, I urge that supplications, prayers, intercessions, and thanksgivings be made for all people, ² for kings and all who are in high positions, that we may lead a peaceful and quiet life, godly and dignified in every way. ³ This is good, and it is pleasing in the sight of God our Savior, ⁴ who desires all people to be saved and to come to the knowledge of the truth. ⁵ For there is one God, and there is one mediator between God and men, the man Christ Jesus, ⁶ who gave himself as a ransom for all, which is the testimony given at the proper

[1] The Greek word refers to kidnapping and selling people as slaves

time. **7** For this I was appointed a preacher and an apostle (I am telling the truth, I am not lying), a teacher of the Gentiles in faith and truth.

8 I desire then that in every place the men should pray, lifting holy hands without anger or quarreling; **9** likewise also that women should adorn themselves in respectable apparel, with modesty and self-control, not with braided hair and gold or pearls or

PROFILE
TIMOTHY

Timothy was from Lystra in South Galatia and was the son of a Jewish mother and a Greek father. Timothy, along with his mother and grandmother, may have been led to Christ during Paul's first visit to Lystra. Timothy joined Paul as a coworker when Paul passed through his hometown early on his second missionary journey. Paul trusted Timothy immensely, and sent him on a number of important missions to strengthen and encourage churches as well as to deal with doctrinal and theological problems. Although he was young, Timothy proved himself to be a godly and effective leader. In Philippians 2:19–24, Paul describes Timothy as an example of a Christ-centered life. Paul also referred to Timothy by the lofty title "God's coworker," emphasizing his credentials (1 Thess. 3:2). Two of the New Testament epistles are letters written from Paul to Timothy.

KEY REFERENCE: PHILIPPIANS 2:19–22

costly attire, **10** but with what is proper for women who profess godliness — with good works. **11** Let a woman learn quietly with all submissiveness. **12** I do not permit a woman to teach or to exercise authority over a man; rather, she is to remain quiet. **13** For Adam was formed first, then Eve; **14** and Adam was not deceived, but the woman was deceived and became a transgressor. **15** Yet she will be saved through childbearing — if they continue in faith and love and holiness, with self-control.

Qualifications for Overseers

3 The saying is trustworthy: If anyone aspires to the office of overseer, he desires a noble task. **2** Therefore an overseer must be above reproach, the husband of one wife, sober-minded, self-controlled, respectable, hospitable, able to teach, **3** not a drunkard, not violent but gentle, not quarrelsome, not a lover of money. **4** He must manage his own household well, with all dignity keeping his children submissive, **5** for if someone does not know how to manage his own household, how will he care for God's church? **6** He must not be a recent convert, or he may become puffed up with conceit and fall into the condemnation of the devil. **7** Moreover, he must be well thought of by outsiders, so that he may not fall into disgrace, into a snare of the devil.

GETTING THE MESSAGE

Hairstyles. In Paul's day, upper-class women showcased their wealth by braiding their hair elaborately and wearing expensive jewelry and clothing. Paul tells believing women to dress modestly and respectably. Godliness is more beautiful than external decoration (2:9–10; see 1 Peter 3:3–4).

Qualifications for Deacons

8 Deacons likewise must be dignified, not double-tongued, not addicted to much wine, not greedy for dishonest gain. **9** They must hold the mystery of the faith with a clear conscience. **10** And let them also be tested first; then let them serve as deacons if they prove themselves blameless. **11** Their wives likewise must be dignified, not slanderers, but sober-minded, faithful in all things. **12** Let deacons each be the husband of one wife, managing their children and their own households well. **13** For those who serve well as deacons gain a good standing for themselves and also great confidence in the faith that is in Christ Jesus.

The Mystery of Godliness

14 I hope to come to you soon, but I am writing these things to you so that, **15** if I delay, you may know how one ought to behave in the household of God, which is the church of the living God, a pillar and buttress of the truth. **16** Great indeed, we confess, is the mystery of godliness:

He was manifested in the flesh,
vindicated by the Spirit,
seen by angels,
proclaimed among the nations,
believed on in the world,
taken up in glory.

Some Will Depart from the Faith

4 Now the Spirit expressly says that in later times some will depart from the faith by devoting themselves to deceitful spirits and teachings of demons, **2** through the insincerity of liars whose consciences are seared, **3** who forbid marriage and require abstinence from foods that God created to be received with thanksgiving by those who believe and know the truth. **4** For everything created by God is good, and nothing is to be rejected if it is received with thanksgiving, **5** for it is made holy by the word of God and prayer.

A Good Servant of Christ Jesus

6 If you put these things before the brothers,[1] you will be a good servant of Christ Jesus, being trained in the words of the faith and of the good doctrine that you have followed. **7** Have nothing to do with irreverent, silly myths. Rather train yourself for godliness; **8** for while bodily training is of some value, godliness is of value in every way, as it holds promise for the present life and also for the life to come. **9** The saying is trustworthy and deserving of full acceptance. **10** For to this end we toil and strive, because we have our hope set on the living God, who is the Savior of all people, especially of those who believe.

11 Command and teach these things. **12** Let no one despise you for your youth, but set the believers an example in speech, in conduct, in love, in faith, in purity. **13** Until I come, devote yourself to the public reading of Scripture, to exhortation, to teaching. **14** Do not neglect the gift you have, which was given you by prophecy when the council of elders laid their hands on you. **15** Practice these things, immerse yourself in them, so that all may see your progress.

16 Keep a close watch on yourself and on the teaching. Persist in this, for by so doing you will save both yourself and your hearers.

Instructions for the Church

5 Do not rebuke an older man but encourage him as you would a father, younger men as brothers, **2** older women as mothers, younger women as sisters, in all purity.

3 Honor widows who are truly widows. **4** But if a widow has children or grandchildren, let them first learn to show godliness to their own household and to make some return to their parents, for this is pleasing in the sight of God. **5** She who is truly a widow, left all alone, has set her hope on God and continues in supplications and prayers night and day, **6** but she who is self-indulgent is dead even while she lives. **7** Command these things as well, so that they may be without reproach. **8** But if

GETTING THE MESSAGE

Paul often describes the church as **the household of God** (3:4–5, 12, 15; see Gal. 6:10; Eph. 2:19). This means that the church is God's family, and its members are brothers and sisters. Also, just like a family, there are certain roles and responsibilities for its members.

anyone does not provide for his relatives, and especially for members of his household, he has denied the faith and is worse than an unbeliever.

9 Let a widow be enrolled if she is not less than sixty years of age, having been the wife of one husband, **10** and having a reputation for good works: if she has brought up children, has shown hospitality, has washed the feet of the saints, has cared for the afflicted, and has devoted herself to every good work. **11** But refuse to enroll younger widows, for when their passions draw them away from Christ, they desire to marry **12** and so incur condemnation for having abandoned their former faith. **13** Besides that, they learn to be idlers, going about from house to house, and not only idlers, but also gossips and busybodies, saying what they should not. **14** So I would have younger widows marry, bear children,

[1] Or brothers and sisters (see Preface)

manage their households, and give the adversary no occasion for slander. ¹⁵ For some have already strayed after Satan. ¹⁶ If any believing woman has relatives who are widows, let her care for them. Let the church not be burdened, so that it may care for those who are truly widows.

¹⁷ Let the elders who rule well be considered worthy of double honor, especially those who labor in preaching and teaching. ¹⁸ For the Scripture says, "You shall not muzzle an ox when it treads out the grain," and, "The laborer deserves his wages." ¹⁹ Do not admit a charge against an elder except on the evidence of two or three witnesses. ²⁰ As for those who persist in sin, rebuke them in the presence of all, so that the rest may stand in fear. ²¹ In the presence of God and of Christ Jesus and of the elect angels I charge you to keep these rules without

GETTING THE MESSAGE

Hospitality was encouraged within the early church (5:10). Peter teaches Christians to "show hospitality to one another without grumbling" (1 Pet. 4:9; see Rom. 12:13). The writer of Hebrews even comments that some who offered hospitality actually "entertained angels" without realizing it (Heb. 13:2).

prejudging, doing nothing from partiality. ²² Do not be hasty in the laying on of hands, nor take part in the sins of others; keep yourself pure. ²³ (No longer drink only water, but use a little wine for the sake of your stomach and your frequent ailments.) ²⁴ The sins of some people are conspicuous, going before them to judgment, but the sins of others appear later. ²⁵ So also good works are conspicuous, and even those that are not cannot remain hidden.

6 Let all who are under a yoke as bondservants[1] regard their own masters as worthy of all honor, so that the name of God and the teaching may not be reviled. ² Those who have believing masters must not be disrespectful on the ground that they are brothers; rather they must serve all the better since those who benefit by their good service are believers and beloved.

False Teachers and True Contentment

Teach and urge these things. ³ If anyone teaches a different doctrine and does not agree with the sound words of our Lord Jesus Christ and the teaching that accords with godliness, ⁴ he is puffed up with conceit and understands nothing. He has an unhealthy craving for controversy and for quarrels about words, which produce envy, dissension, slander, evil suspicions, ⁵ and constant friction among people who are depraved in mind and deprived of the truth, imagining that godliness is a means of gain. ⁶ But godliness with contentment is great gain, ⁷ for we brought nothing into the world, and we cannot take anything out of the world. ⁸ But if we have food and clothing, with these we will be content. ⁹ But those who desire to be rich fall into temptation, into a snare, into many senseless and harmful desires that plunge people into ruin and destruction. ¹⁰ For the love of money is a root of all kinds of evils. It is through this craving that some have wandered away from the faith and pierced themselves with many pangs.

Fight the Good Fight of Faith

¹¹ But as for you, O man of God, flee these things. Pursue righteousness, godliness, faith, love, steadfastness, gentleness. ¹² Fight the good fight of the faith. Take hold of the eternal life to which you were called and about which you made the good confession in the presence of many witnesses. ¹³ I charge you in the presence of God, who gives life to all things, and of Christ Jesus, who in his testimony before Pontius Pilate made the good confession, ¹⁴ to keep the commandment unstained and free from reproach until the appearing of our Lord Jesus Christ, ¹⁵ which he will display at the proper time—he who is the blessed and only Sovereign, the King of kings and Lord of lords, ¹⁶ who alone has immortality, who dwells in unapproachable light, whom no one has ever seen or can see. To him be honor and eternal dominion. Amen.

¹⁷ As for the rich in this present age, charge them not to be haughty, nor to set their hopes on the uncertainty of riches, but on God, who richly provides us with everything to enjoy. ¹⁸ They are to do good, to be rich in good works, to be generous and ready to

[1] Or *slaves* (Greek *doulos*; see Preface)

share, [19] thus storing up treasure for themselves as a good foundation for the future, so that they may take hold of that which is truly life.

[20] O Timothy, guard the deposit entrusted to you. Avoid the irreverent babble and contradictions of what is falsely called "knowledge," [21] for by professing it some have swerved from the faith.

Grace be with you.

INTRODUCTION TO 2 TIMOTHY

AUTHOR, DATE, AND RECIPIENT

Paul wrote this second letter to Timothy during
his second imprisonment in Rome, shortly
before his death. This imprisonment was after
the one recorded in Acts 28. He probably wrote
it in A.D. 64–65, though some would place it as
late as 67.

THEME

Paul gives Timothy a bold, clear call to continue
in the gospel despite suffering.

PURPOSE

Several people have abandoned Paul while he
has been in prison, and several others are away
on assignments (1:15; 4:9–12). In such a time,
Paul's memories of Timothy's sincerity and
devotion are especially touching (1:3–5). Paul
thinks he will die soon (4:6–8), so he writes this
final message to Timothy. Paul urges Timothy
to stand firm and asks him to come for one
final visit before Paul is executed. Though Paul's
death is near, he does not know just when it will
come. Paul also asks Timothy to bring his books
and parchments, so that he can keep studying
and writing until the end.

Second Timothy is very personal. It is a final
letter to a close friend and coworker. Paul
encourages Timothy to continue in faithfulness

and offers his own life as an example for
Timothy to follow. What he calls on Timothy
to do, he himself has done already.

KEY THEMES

1. Suffering is part of the Christian experience
(1:8, 12; 2:3, 9; 3:11–12; 4:5, 14–18).

2. The Christian response to suffering is steady
faith by God's power (1:8; 2:1, 11–13; 4:1–8).

3. The gospel is the basis for the Christian's
endurance (1:9–11; 2:8–10).

4. The Scriptures have power to save and to
preserve (2:15; 3:15–17; 4:1–2).

5. True believers will continue in the faith. Failure
to do so proves one is not truly converted
(2:11–13, 19; 3:14; 4:7, 10).

6. False teaching is deadly and must be dealt
with firmly (2:16–18, 23–26; 3:1–9; 4:3–5).

OUTLINE

I. Opening (1:1–2)

II. Enduring for the Gospel (1:3–2:13)

III. Dealing with False Teachers (2:14–3:9)

IV. Contrasting Timothy with False Teachers
(3:10–4:8)

V. Conclusion (4:9–22)

2 TIMOTHY

Greeting

1 Paul, an apostle of Christ Jesus by the will of God according to the promise of the life that is in Christ Jesus,

² To Timothy, my beloved child:

Grace, mercy, and peace from God the Father and Christ Jesus our Lord.

Guard the Deposit Entrusted to You

³ I thank God whom I serve, as did my ancestors, with a clear conscience, as I remember you constantly in my prayers night and day. ⁴ As I remember your tears, I long to see you, that I may be filled with joy. ⁵ I am reminded of your sincere faith, a faith that dwelt first in your grandmother Lois and your mother Eunice and now, I am sure, dwells in you as well. ⁶ For this reason I remind you to fan into flame the gift of God, which is in you through the laying on of my hands, ⁷ for God gave us a spirit not of fear but of power and love and self-control.

⁸ Therefore do not be ashamed of the testimony about our Lord, nor of me his prisoner, but share in suffering for the gospel by the power of God, ⁹ who saved us and called us to a holy calling, not because of our works but because of his own purpose and grace, which he gave us in Christ Jesus before the ages began, ¹⁰ and which now has been manifested through the appearing of our Savior Christ Jesus, who abolished death and brought life and immortality to light through the gospel, ¹¹ for which I was appointed a preacher and apostle and teacher, ¹² which is why I suffer as I do. But I am not ashamed, for I know whom I have believed, and I am convinced that he is able to guard until that Day what has been entrusted to me. ¹³ Follow the pattern of the sound words that you have heard from me, in the faith and love that are in Christ Jesus. ¹⁴ By the Holy Spirit who dwells within us, guard the good deposit entrusted to you.

¹⁵ You are aware that all who are in Asia turned away from me, among whom are Phygelus and Hermogenes. ¹⁶ May the Lord grant mercy to the household of Onesiphorus, for he often refreshed me and was not ashamed of my chains, ¹⁷ but when he arrived in Rome he searched for me earnestly and found me — ¹⁸ may the Lord grant him to find mercy from the Lord on that Day! — and you well know all the service he rendered at Ephesus.

A Good Soldier of Christ Jesus

2 You then, my child, be strengthened by the grace that is in Christ Jesus, ² and what you have heard from me in the presence of many witnesses entrust to faithful

> ### GETTING THE MESSAGE
>
> The Greek word for **fear** in 1:7 means "cowardice" or "timidity." By contrast, the Holy Spirit enables believers to be brave in all circumstances (see Prov. 28:1; Acts 4:31). Paul wrote these words about bravery while in a Roman prison, facing execution.

men[1] who will be able to teach others also. ³ Share in suffering as a good soldier of Christ Jesus. ⁴ No soldier gets entangled in civilian pursuits, since his aim is to please the one who enlisted him. ⁵ An athlete is not crowned unless he competes according to the rules. ⁶ It is the hard-working farmer who ought to have the first share of the crops. ⁷ Think over what I say, for the Lord will give you understanding in everything.

⁸ Remember Jesus Christ, risen from the dead, the offspring of David, as preached in my gospel, ⁹ for which I am suffering, bound with chains as a criminal. But the word of God is not bound! ¹⁰ Therefore I endure everything for the sake of the elect, that they also may obtain the salvation that is in Christ Jesus with eternal glory. ¹¹ The saying is trustworthy, for:

If we have died with him, we will also
live with him;

[1] The Greek word for *men* refers to both men and women (see Preface)

¹² if we endure, we will also reign with
         him;
   if we deny him, he also will deny us;
¹³ if we are faithless, he remains faith-
         ful—

for he cannot deny himself.

A Worker Approved by God

¹⁴ Remind them of these things, and charge them before God not to quarrel about words, which does no good, but only ruins the hearers. ¹⁵ Do your best to present yourself to God as one approved, a worker who has no need to be ashamed, rightly handling the word of truth. ¹⁶ But avoid irreverent babble, for it will lead people into more and more ungodliness, ¹⁷ and their talk will spread like gangrene. Among them are Hymenaeus and Philetus, ¹⁸ who have swerved from the truth, saying that the resurrection has already

GETTING THE MESSAGE

Gangrene was a serious problem in ancient times, due to the lack of antibiotics. Paul uses the word to describe the danger of false teaching. If it is not dealt with, the false teaching will "spread like gangrene" throughout the church and lead many into ungodliness (2:16–17).

happened. They are upsetting the faith of some. ¹⁹ But God's firm foundation stands, bearing this seal: "The Lord knows those who are his," and, "Let everyone who names the name of the Lord depart from iniquity." ²⁰ Now in a great house there are not only vessels of gold and silver but also of wood and clay, some for honorable use, some for dishonorable. ²¹ Therefore, if anyone cleanses himself from what is dishonorable, he will be a vessel for honorable use, set apart as holy, useful to the master of the house, ready for every good work.

²² So flee youthful passions and pursue righteousness, faith, love, and peace, along with those who call on the Lord from a pure heart. ²³ Have nothing to do with foolish, ignorant controversies; you know that they breed quarrels. ²⁴ And the Lord's servant must not be quarrelsome but kind to everyone, able to teach, patiently enduring evil,

²⁵ correcting his opponents with gentleness. God may perhaps grant them repentance leading to a knowledge of the truth, ²⁶ and they may come to their senses and escape from the snare of the devil, after being captured by him to do his will.

Godlessness in the Last Days

3 But understand this, that in the last days there will come times of difficulty. ² For people will be lovers of self, lovers of money, proud, arrogant, abusive, disobedient to their parents, ungrateful, unholy, ³ heartless, unappeasable, slanderous, without self-control, brutal, not loving good, ⁴ treacherous, reckless, swollen with conceit, lovers of pleasure rather than lovers of God, ⁵ having the appearance of godliness, but denying its power. Avoid such people. ⁶ For among them are those who creep into households and capture weak women, burdened with sins and led astray by various passions, ⁷ always learning and never able to arrive at a knowledge of the truth. ⁸ Just as Jannes and Jambres opposed Moses, so these men also oppose the truth, men corrupted in mind and disqualified regarding the faith. ⁹ But they will not get very far, for their folly will be plain to all, as was that of those two men.

All Scripture Is Breathed Out by God

¹⁰ You, however, have followed my teaching, my conduct, my aim in life, my faith, my patience, my love, my steadfastness, ¹¹ my persecutions and sufferings that happened to me at Antioch, at Iconium, and at Lystra—which persecutions I endured; yet from them all the Lord rescued me. ¹² Indeed, all who desire to live a godly life in Christ Jesus will be persecuted, ¹³ while evil people and impostors will go on from bad to worse, deceiving and being deceived. ¹⁴ But as for you, continue in what you have learned and have firmly believed, knowing from whom you learned it ¹⁵ and how from childhood you have been acquainted with the sacred writings, which are able to make you wise for salvation through faith in Christ Jesus. ¹⁶ All Scripture is breathed out by God and profitable for teaching, for reproof, for correction, and for training in righteousness, ¹⁷ that the man of God may be complete, equipped for every good work.

Preach the Word

4 I charge you in the presence of God and of Christ Jesus, who is to judge the living and the dead, and by his appearing and his kingdom: [2] preach the word; be ready in season and out of season; reprove, rebuke, and exhort, with complete patience and teaching. [3] For the time is coming when people will not endure sound teaching, but having itching ears they will accumulate for themselves teachers to suit their own passions, [4] and will turn away from listening to the truth and wander off into myths. [5] As for you, always be sober-minded, endure suffering, do the work of an evangelist, fulfill your ministry.

[6] For I am already being poured out as a drink offering, and the time of my departure has come. [7] I have fought the good fight, I have finished the race, I have kept the faith. [8] Henceforth there is laid up for me the crown of righteousness, which the Lord, the righteous judge, will award to me on that Day, and not only to me but also to all who have loved his appearing.

Personal Instructions

[9] Do your best to come to me soon. [10] For Demas, in love with this present world, has deserted me and gone to Thessalonica. Crescens has gone to Galatia, Titus to Dalmatia. [11] Luke alone is with me. Get Mark and bring him with you, for he is very useful to me for ministry. [12] Tychicus I have sent to Ephesus. [13] When you come, bring the cloak that I left with Carpus at Troas, also the books, and above all the parchments.

[14] Alexander the coppersmith did me great harm; the Lord will repay him according to his deeds. [15] Beware of him yourself, for he strongly opposed our message. [16] At my first defense no one came to stand by me, but all deserted me. May it not be charged against them! [17] But the Lord stood by me and strengthened me, so that through me the message might be fully proclaimed and all the Gentiles might hear it. So I was rescued from the lion's mouth. [18] The Lord will rescue me from every evil deed and bring me safely into his heavenly kingdom. To him be the glory forever and ever. Amen.

GETTING THE MESSAGE

Parchment (4:13) is writing material usually made from animal skins. It was more durable and practical than papyrus, which was made from plants. Both sides of a sheet of parchment could be written on, and the sheet could be used more than once.

Final Greetings

[19] Greet Prisca and Aquila, and the household of Onesiphorus. [20] Erastus remained at Corinth, and I left Trophimus, who was ill, at Miletus. [21] Do your best to come before winter. Eubulus sends greetings to you, as do Pudens and Linus and Claudia and all the brothers.[1]

[22] The Lord be with your spirit. Grace be with you.

[1] Or brothers and sisters (see Preface)

INTRODUCTION TO TITUS

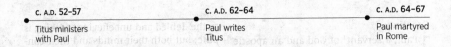

c. A.D. 52–57	c. A.D. 62–64	c. A.D. 64–67
Titus ministers with Paul	Paul writes Titus	Paul martyred in Rome

AUTHOR, DATE, AND RECIPIENT

The apostle Paul wrote this letter to his coworker Titus. The letter was probably written in the mid-60s A.D. between Paul's first imprisonment (Acts 28) and his second imprisonment, which is not mentioned in Acts.

THEME

The letter's theme is the unbreakable link between faith and practice, belief and behavior. This truth is the basis for Paul's criticism of false teaching, his instruction in Christian living, and standards he sets for church leaders.

PURPOSE

Paul had recently completed a journey to Crete. He had left Titus there to teach the new church (see Acts 14:21–23).

False teachers were already a problem in the church (Titus 1:10–16), and the letter focuses primarily on that issue. The description of elders (1:5–9) and of proper Christian living (2:1–10; 3:1–3) appear to be worded for intentional contrast with these false teachers. The content of the false teaching is not fully explained (as in 1 Timothy). There appears to be a significant Jewish element to the teaching. The opponents come from "the circumcision party" (Titus 1:10). They are interested in "Jewish myths" (1:14) and perhaps ritual purity (1:15). Paul's primary concern, however, is with the practical effect of the false teaching. They taught ritual purity, but they lived in a way that proved they did not know God (1:16).

This false teaching would have been welcome in Crete, which was known in the ancient world for immorality. But Paul expected the gospel to produce real godliness in everyday life, even in Crete.

In dealing with the false teaching, Paul also provides Titus with a portrait of a healthy church. He describes proper leadership (1:5–9), proper handling of error (1:10–16; 3:9–11), proper Christian living (especially important for new believers in an immoral setting; 2:1–10; 3:1–2), and the gospel as the source of godliness (2:11–14; 3:3–7).

KEY THEMES

1. The gospel produces godliness in the lives of believers. There is no legitimate separation between belief and behavior (1:1; 2:1, 11–14; 3:4–7).

2. One's deeds will either prove or disprove one's claim to know God (1:16).

3. It is vitally important to have godly men serving as elders/pastors (1:5–9).

4. True Christian living will draw others to the gospel (2:5, 8, 10).

5. Good works have an important place in the lives of believers (2:1–10, 14; 3:1–2, 8, 14).

6. It is important to deal clearly and firmly with doctrinal and moral error in the church (1:10–16; 3:9–11).

7. The gospel is the basis for Christian ethics (2:11–14; 3:3–7).

OUTLINE

  I. Opening (1:1–4)

  II. The Occasion: The Need for Proper Leadership (1:5–9)

  III. The Problem: False Teachers (1:10–16)

  IV. Christian Living in Contrast to the False Teachers (2:1–3:8)

  V. The Problem Restated: False Teachers (3:9–11)

  VI. Closing Encouragement (3:12–15)

THE LETTER OF PAUL TO

TITUS

Greeting

1 Paul, a servant[1] of God and an apostle of Jesus Christ, for the sake of the faith of God's elect and their knowledge of the truth, which accords with godliness, **2** in hope of eternal life, which God, who never lies, promised before the ages began **3** and at the proper time manifested in his word through the preaching with which I have been entrusted by the command of God our Savior;

4 To Titus, my true child in a common faith:

Grace and peace from God the Father and Christ Jesus our Savior.

Qualifications for Elders

5 This is why I left you in Crete, so that you might put what remained into order, and appoint elders in every town as I directed you — **6** if anyone is above reproach, the husband of one wife, and his children are believers and not open to the charge of debauchery or insubordination. **7** For an overseer, as God's steward, must be above reproach. He must not be arrogant or quick-tempered or a drunkard or violent or greedy for gain, **8** but hospitable, a lover of good, self-controlled, upright, holy, and disciplined. **9** He must hold firm to the trustworthy word as taught, so that he may be able to give instruction in sound doctrine and also to rebuke those who contradict it.

10 For there are many who are insubordinate, empty talkers and deceivers, especially those of the circumcision party. **11** They must be silenced, since they are upsetting whole families by teaching for shameful gain what they ought not to teach. **12** One of the Cretans, a prophet of their own, said, "Cretans are always liars, evil beasts, lazy gluttons." **13** This testimony is true. Therefore rebuke them sharply, that they may be sound in the faith, **14** not devoting themselves to Jewish myths and the commands of people who turn away from the truth. **15** To the pure, all things are pure, but to the defiled and unbelieving, nothing is pure; but both their minds and their consciences are defiled. **16** They profess to know God, but they deny him by their works. They are detestable, disobedient, unfit for any good work.

Teach Sound Doctrine

2 But as for you, teach what accords with sound doctrine. **2** Older men are to be sober-minded, dignified, self-controlled, sound in faith, in love, and in steadfastness. **3** Older women likewise are to be reverent in behavior, not slanderers or slaves to much wine. They are to teach what is good, **4** and

so train the young women to love their husbands and children, **5** to be self-controlled, pure, working at home, kind, and submissive to their own husbands, that the word of God may not be reviled. **6** Likewise, urge the younger men to be self-controlled. **7** Show yourself in all respects to be a model of good works, and in your teaching show integrity, dignity, **8** and sound speech that cannot be condemned, so that an opponent may be put to shame, having nothing evil to say about us. **9** Bondservants[2] are to be submissive to their own masters in everything; they are to be well-pleasing, not argumentative, **10** not pilfering, but showing all good faith, so that in everything they may adorn the doctrine of God our Savior.

11 For the grace of God has appeared, bringing salvation for all people, **12** training us to renounce ungodliness and worldly passions, and to live self-controlled, upright,

---

[1] Or *slave* (Greek *doulos*; see Preface) [2] Or *Slaves* (Greek *doulos*; see Preface)

and godly lives in the present age, [13] waiting for our blessed hope, the appearing of the glory of our great God and Savior Jesus Christ, [14] who gave himself for us to redeem us from all lawlessness and to purify for himself a people for his own possession who are zealous for good works.

[15] Declare these things; exhort and rebuke with all authority. Let no one disregard you.

Be Ready for Every Good Work

3 Remind them to be submissive to rulers and authorities, to be obedient, to be ready for every good work, [2] to speak evil of

no one, to avoid quarreling, to be gentle, and to show perfect courtesy toward all people. [3] For we ourselves were once foolish, disobedient, led astray, slaves to various passions and pleasures, passing our days in malice and envy, hated by others and hating one another. [4] But when the goodness and loving kindness of God our Savior appeared, [5] he saved us, not because of works done by us in righteousness, but according to his own mercy, by the washing of regeneration and renewal of the Holy Spirit, [6] whom he poured out on us richly through Jesus Christ our Savior, [7] so that being justified by his grace we might become heirs according to the hope of eternal life. [8] The saying is trustworthy, and I want you to insist on these things, so that those who have believed in God may be careful to devote themselves to good works. These things are excellent and profitable for people. [9] But avoid foolish controversies, genealogies, dissensions, and quarrels about the law, for they are unprofitable and worthless. [10] As for a person who stirs up division, after warning him once and then twice, have nothing more to do with him, [11] knowing that such a person is warped and sinful; he is self-condemned.

Final Instructions and Greetings

[12] When I send Artemas or Tychicus to you, do your best to come to me at Nicopolis, for I have decided to spend the winter there. [13] Do your best to speed Zenas the lawyer and Apollos on their way; see that they lack nothing. [14] And let our people learn to devote themselves to good works, so as to help cases of urgent need, and not be unfruitful.

[15] All who are with me send greetings to you. Greet those who love us in the faith. Grace be with you all.

INTRODUCTION TO PHILEMON

AUTHOR, DATE, AND RECIPIENTS

This is a personal letter from the apostle Paul to Philemon, a wealthy Christian from Colossae. It was also intended for reading to the entire church that met in Philemon's home. It was probably written c. A.D. 62, while Paul was in prison following his voyage to Rome (Acts 27–28).

THEME

The theme of Paul's letter is the power of the gospel to transform individual lives (v. 11) and human relationships (v. 16). Onesimus had experienced that transforming power in his life ("formerly he was useless" but "now he is indeed useful"; v. 11). Paul therefore urged his friend Philemon to form a new relationship with Onesimus, his runaway slave.

PURPOSE

Apparently, during Paul's three-year ministry in Ephesus (A.D. 52–55), Philemon heard the gospel and was saved. He began serving Christ in the Colossian community. He opened his home for a group of Christians to meet there regularly.

At some point, Onesimus, one of Philemon's bondservants, fled to Rome. Before he left, he possibly had stolen money or property from Philemon. While in Rome, Onesimus came into contact with Paul and became a Christian. As he grew in Christ, he was a great help to Paul during Paul's imprisonment.

As much as Paul would like to have retained the services of Onesimus, Paul knew that Onesimus's wrongdoing against his master Philemon needed to be addressed. He wrote this letter urging Philemon to appreciate the transformation that had occurred in Onesimus. Paul asked Philemon to receive Onesimus back not merely as a bondservant but as a "beloved brother" (v. 16).

It is difficult to know if Paul sought Onesimus's full freedom. It is clear, however, that he was seeking a transformed relationship between bondservant and master. This new relationship would defy all of the ingrained status distinctions of the surrounding Greek and Roman culture. It would have been difficult for the kind of servitude practiced by Rome to survive in the atmosphere of Christian love exemplified by the letter. On first-century forms of servitude, see the ESV Preface.

This simplified letter is in the form of letters that people ordinarily write, in contrast to the more stylized and literary five-part format of most NT epistles. The letter is a masterpiece of persuasion as Paul seeks a favorable reception for the returning bondservant, where normally one might expect the master to be vindictive.

Paul's strategy follows that prescribed by Greek and Roman rhetoricians of the day: begin by building rapport and goodwill with an audience (vv. 4–10), then lay out the facts in a way that will convince the mind or intellect (vv. 11–19), and finally appeal to the emotions of the audience (vv. 20–21).

KEY THEMES

1. Reconciliation is the theme of this letter. Onesimus is reconciled to God. He is in the process of being reconciled to a fellow believer.

2. The basis for Paul's appeal to Philemon is the supreme Christian virtue of love. Paul praises Philemon for the love he has shown not just to him but to all the believers in that area.

OUTLINE

THE LETTER OF PAUL TO
PHILEMON

Greeting

¹ Paul, a prisoner for Christ Jesus, and Timothy our brother,

To Philemon our beloved fellow worker ² and Apphia our sister and Archippus our fellow soldier, and the church in your house:

³ Grace to you and peace from God our Father and the Lord Jesus Christ.

Philemon's Love and Faith

⁴ I thank my God always when I remember you in my prayers, ⁵ because I hear of your love and of the faith that you have toward the Lord Jesus and for all the saints, ⁶ and I pray that the sharing of your faith may become effective for the full knowledge of every good thing that is in us for the sake of Christ. ⁷ For I have derived much joy and comfort from your love, my brother, because the hearts of the saints have been refreshed through you.

Paul's Plea for Onesimus

⁸ Accordingly, though I am bold enough in Christ to command you to do what is required, ⁹ yet for love's sake I prefer to appeal to you—I, Paul, an old man and now a prisoner also for Christ Jesus— ¹⁰ I appeal to you for my child, Onesimus,¹ whose father I became in my imprisonment. ¹¹ (Formerly he was useless to you, but now he is indeed useful to you and to me.) ¹² I am sending him back to you, sending my very heart. ¹³ I would have been glad to keep him with me, in order that he might serve me on your behalf during my imprisonment for the gospel, ¹⁴ but I preferred to do nothing without your consent in order that your goodness might not be by compulsion but of your own accord. ¹⁵ For this perhaps is why he was parted from you for a while, that you might have him back forever, ¹⁶ no longer as a bondservant² but more than a bondservant, as a beloved brother—especially to me, but how much more to you, both in the flesh and in the Lord.

¹⁷ So if you consider me your partner, receive him as you would receive me. ¹⁸ If he has wronged you at all, or owes you anything, charge that to my account. ¹⁹ I, Paul, write this with my own hand: I will repay it—to say nothing of your owing me even your own self. ²⁰ Yes, brother, I want some

GETTING THE MESSAGE

How did a person become a bondservant? Being a "bondservant" in New Testament times (v. 16) was different from many of the more recent kinds of slavery. Bondservants were bound to serve their master for a specific period of time. People did not necessarily become slaves because of their race, nor were they completely without legal rights. A person might become a slave as punishment for a crime or as a way to pay off a debt.

benefit from you in the Lord. Refresh my heart in Christ.

²¹ Confident of your obedience, I write to you, knowing that you will do even more than I say. ²² At the same time, prepare a guest room for me, for I am hoping that through your prayers I will be graciously given to you.

Final Greetings

²³ Epaphras, my fellow prisoner in Christ Jesus, sends greetings to you, ²⁴ and so do Mark, Aristarchus, Demas, and Luke, my fellow workers.

²⁵ The grace of the Lord Jesus Christ be with your spirit.

---

¹ Onesimus means *useful* ² Or *slave* (Greek *doulos*; see Preface)

INTRODUCTION TO HEBREWS

AUTHOR, DATE, AND RECIPIENTS

The author of Hebrews is unknown. He knew Timothy (13:23). He was not an eyewitness of Jesus (see 2:1, 3). The letter was probably written before A.D. 70. Early manuscripts bear the title "To the Hebrews," which reflects the ancient assumption that it was written to Jewish Christians as well as Gentile Christians who previously had been drawn to the Jewish religion. The author knew his readers and wanted to see them again (13:19).

THEME

Jesus Christ is greater than any angel, priest, or old covenant practice. Christians must not forsake the great salvation that Jesus has brought about. They must hold on by faith to the true rest found in Christ, and they must encourage others in the church to do the same.

PURPOSE, OCCASION, AND BACKGROUND

Hebrews has two primary purposes: to encourage Christians to endure, and to warn them not to abandon their faith in Christ. These warning passages appear throughout the book (2:1–4; 3:7–4:13; 5:11–6:12; 10:19–39; 12:1–29). The author encourages faithfulness, love, and sound doctrine. He does so by carefully teaching the OT in light of God's revelation in Jesus Christ.

The author shows the superiority of Christ and his new covenant over angels, Moses, the OT priesthood, and the OT sacrificial system. These are so inferior to Christ that it is futile to return to them—or to go anywhere else. Rather, believers should hold fast to their faith, because that faith is grounded in the most superior revelation.

The background of such exhortations must have been the readers' need to continue enduring amid persecution and the trials of life (e.g., ch. 12). They appear to have grown less attentive to Christian instruction (5:11–14), and some apparently have ceased regular attendance at their meetings (10:25). The author reminds them of their past faithfulness and love despite persecution (10:32–34).

Ultimately, the author's words of encouragement and exhortation are rooted in his teaching about Jesus Christ. The Son of God became the heavenly high priest, who offered himself as a sacrifice once for all. Christ obtained salvation for all who approach him in faith (6:1; 11:6; compare 4:2), and such faith perseveres until it receives the promised eternal reward (6:12; 10:22, 38–39).

KEY THEMES

1. Jesus is fully God and fully man (1:1–14; 2:5–18).
2. Jesus, the Son of God, reveals God the Father. He is the creator and he sustains all creation (1:1–14).
3. Jesus is the eternal high priest. As a man, he sympathizes with human weaknesses, and he offered himself as the perfect sacrifice for sin (1:3; 2:10–18; 4:15–16; 9:11–10:19).
4. Jesus is superior to angels, to Moses, to the Mosaic covenant, to the earthly tabernacle, and to the priesthood (1:4–2:18; 3:1–6; 5:1–10; 7:1–10:18).
5. All humanity faces eternal judgment for sin (4:12–13; 9:27–28; 10:26–31).
6. Faith is necessary to please God and to participate in his eternal salvation. Faith requires confidence about the unseen realities of God and his promises. Such faith produces perseverance (6:1; 10:22, 38–39; 11:1–40).
7. Perseverance is necessary in the Christian life; believers are warned against a lack of endurance (2:1–4; 3:7–4:13; 10:19–39; 12:1–29).
8. God's promises are trustworthy, including his promise of eternal salvation (6:13–20).
9. With the coming of Jesus Christ, the last days have begun. They will be completed when he returns (1:2; 9:9–28; 12:22–29).

OUTLINE

I. Jesus Is Superior to Angelic Beings (1:1–2:18)

II. Jesus Is Superior to the Mosaic Law (3:1–10:18)

III. Call to Faith and Endurance (10:19–12:29)

IV. Concluding Encouragements and Remarks (13:1–25)

HEBREWS

The Supremacy of God's Son

1 Long ago, at many times and in many ways, God spoke to our fathers by the prophets, **2** but in these last days he has spoken to us by his Son, whom he appointed the heir of all things, through whom also he created the world. **3** He is the radiance of the glory of God and the exact imprint of his nature, and he upholds the universe by the word of his power. After making purification for sins, he sat down at the right hand of the Majesty on high, **4** having become as much superior to angels as the name he has inherited is more excellent than theirs.

5 For to which of the angels did God ever say,

"You are my Son,
today I have begotten you"?

Or again,

"I will be to him a father,
and he shall be to me a son"?

6 And again, when he brings the firstborn into the world, he says,

"Let all God's angels worship him."

7 Of the angels he says,

"He makes his angels winds,
and his ministers a flame of fire."

8 But of the Son he says,

"Your throne, O God, is forever and
ever,
the scepter of uprightness is the
scepter of your kingdom.
9 You have loved righteousness and
hated wickedness;
therefore God, your God, has anointed
you
with the oil of gladness beyond
your companions."

10 And,

"You, Lord, laid the foundation of the
earth in the beginning,
and the heavens are the work of
your hands;

11 they will perish, but you remain;
they will all wear out like a garment,
12 like a robe you will roll them up,
like a garment they will be changed.
But you are the same,
and your years will have no end."

13 And to which of the angels has he ever said,

"Sit at my right hand
until I make your enemies a footstool for your feet"?

14 Are they not all ministering spirits sent out to serve for the sake of those who are to inherit salvation?

Warning Against Neglecting Salvation

2 Therefore we must pay much closer attention to what we have heard, lest we drift away from it. **2** For since the message declared by angels proved to be reliable, and every transgression or disobedience received a just retribution, **3** how shall we escape if we neglect such a great salvation? It was declared at first by the Lord, and it was attested to us by those who heard, **4** while God also bore witness by signs and wonders and various miracles and by gifts of the Holy Spirit distributed according to his will.

The Founder of Salvation

5 For it was not to angels that God subjected the world to come, of which we are speaking. **6** It has been testified somewhere,

"What is man, that you are mindful of
   him,
   or the son of man, that you care for
     him?
7   You made him for a little while lower
     than the angels;
   you have crowned him with glory
     and honor,
8   putting everything in subjection
     under his feet."

Now in putting everything in subjection to him, he left nothing outside his control. At present, we do not yet see everything in subjection to him. 9 But we see him who for a little while was made lower than the angels, namely Jesus, crowned with glory and honor because of the suffering of death, so that by the grace of God he might taste death for everyone.

GETTING THE MESSAGE

Jesus the master builder. In the era of peace made possible by Roman rule, the building of public buildings and private homes flourished. Working primarily with materials such as marble, bronze, and terra-cotta, architects designed and built large, beautiful structures throughout the empire. However, such buildings were nothing compared to the individual new lives being "built" by Jesus the master builder (3:3–6).

10 For it was fitting that he, for whom and by whom all things exist, in bringing many sons to glory, should make the founder of their salvation perfect through suffering. 11 For he who sanctifies and those who are sanctified all have one source. That is why he is not ashamed to call them brothers,[1] 12 saying,

"I will tell of your name to my brothers;
   in the midst of the congregation I
     will sing your praise."

13 And again,

"I will put my trust in him."

And again,

"Behold, I and the children God has
   given me."

14 Since therefore the children share in flesh and blood, he himself likewise partook of the same things, that through death he might destroy the one who has the power of death, that is, the devil, 15 and deliver all those who through fear of death were subject to lifelong slavery. 16 For surely it is not angels that he helps, but he helps the offspring of Abraham. 17 Therefore he had to be made like his brothers in every respect, so that he might become a merciful and faithful high priest in the service of God, to make propitiation for the sins of the people. 18 For because he himself has suffered when tempted, he is able to help those who are being tempted.

Jesus Greater Than Moses

3 Therefore, holy brothers, you who share in a heavenly calling, consider Jesus, the apostle and high priest of our confession, 2 who was faithful to him who appointed him, just as Moses also was faithful in all God's house. 3 For Jesus has been counted worthy of more glory than Moses — as much more glory as the builder of a house has more honor than the house itself. 4 (For every house is built by someone, but the builder of all things is God.) 5 Now Moses was faithful in all God's house as a servant, to testify to the things that were to be spoken later, 6 but Christ is faithful over God's house as a son. And we are his house if indeed we hold fast our confidence and our boasting in our hope.

A Rest for the People of God

7 Therefore, as the Holy Spirit says,

"Today, if you hear his voice,
8   do not harden your hearts as in the
     rebellion,
   on the day of testing in the wilder-
     ness,
9   where your fathers put me to the test
   and saw my works for forty years.
10   Therefore I was provoked with that
     generation,
   and said, 'They always go astray in
     their heart;
   they have not known my ways.'
11   As I swore in my wrath,
   'They shall not enter my rest.'"

12 Take care, brothers, lest there be in any of you an evil, unbelieving heart, leading

1 Or brothers and sisters (see Preface); also 2:12; 3:1, 12

you to fall away from the living God. ¹³ But exhort one another every day, as long as it is called "today," that none of you may be hardened by the deceitfulness of sin. ¹⁴ For we have come to share in Christ, if indeed we hold our original confidence firm to the end. ¹⁵ As it is said,

"Today, if you hear his voice,
do not harden your hearts as in the rebellion."

¹⁶ For who were those who heard and yet rebelled? Was it not all those who left Egypt led by Moses? ¹⁷ And with whom was he provoked for forty years? Was it not with those who sinned, whose bodies fell in the wilderness? ¹⁸ And to whom did he swear that they would not enter his rest, but to those who were disobedient? ¹⁹ So we see that they were unable to enter because of unbelief.

4 Therefore, while the promise of entering his rest still stands, let us fear lest any of you should seem to have failed to reach it. ² For good news came to us just as to them, but the message they heard did not benefit them, because they were not united by faith with those who listened. ³ For we who have believed enter that rest, as he has said,

"As I swore in my wrath,
'They shall not enter my rest,'"

although his works were finished from the foundation of the world. ⁴ For he has somewhere spoken of the seventh day in this way: "And God rested on the seventh day from all his works." ⁵ And again in this passage he said,

"They shall not enter my rest."

⁶ Since therefore it remains for some to enter it, and those who formerly received the good news failed to enter because of disobedience, ⁷ again he appoints a certain day, "Today," saying through David so long afterward, in the words already quoted,

"Today, if you hear his voice,
do not harden your hearts."

⁸ For if Joshua had given them rest, God would not have spoken of another day later on. ⁹ So then, there remains a Sabbath rest for the people of God, ¹⁰ for whoever has entered God's rest has also rested from his works as God did from his.

¹¹ Let us therefore strive to enter that rest, so that no one may fall by the same sort of disobedience. ¹² For the word of God is living and active, sharper than any two-edged sword, piercing to the division of soul and of spirit, of joints and of marrow, and discerning the thoughts and intentions of the heart. ¹³ And no creature is hidden from his sight, but all are naked and exposed to the eyes of him to whom we must give account.

Jesus the Great High Priest

¹⁴ Since then we have a great high priest who has passed through the heavens, Jesus, the Son of God, let us hold fast our confession. ¹⁵ For we do not have a high priest who is unable to sympathize with our weaknesses, but one who in every respect has been tempted as we are, yet without sin. ¹⁶ Let us then with confidence draw near to the throne of grace, that we may

GETTING THE MESSAGE

Approaching a human ruler's **throne** with a request can be dangerous, especially when one is fully at the mercy of the ruler. In contrast, Christians can expect to find mercy and help when they approach God's throne with a request (4:16).

receive mercy and find grace to help in time of need.

5 For every high priest chosen from among men is appointed to act on behalf of men in relation to God, to offer gifts and sacrifices for sins. ² He can deal gently with the ignorant and wayward, since he himself is beset with weakness. ³ Because of this he is obligated to offer sacrifice for his own sins just as he does for those of the people. ⁴ And no one takes this honor for himself, but only when called by God, just as Aaron was.

⁵ So also Christ did not exalt himself to be made a high priest, but was appointed by him who said to him,

"You are my Son,
today I have begotten you";

⁶ as he says also in another place,

"You are a priest forever,
after the order of Melchizedek."

[7] In the days of his flesh, Jesus offered up prayers and supplications, with loud cries and tears, to him who was able to save him from death, and he was heard because of his reverence. [8] Although he was a son, he learned obedience through what he suffered. [9] And being made perfect, he became the source of eternal salvation to all who obey him, [10] being designated by God a high priest after the order of Melchizedek.

Warning Against Apostasy

[11] About this we have much to say, and it is hard to explain, since you have become dull of hearing. [12] For though by this time you ought to be teachers, you need someone to teach you again the basic principles of the oracles of God. You need milk, not solid food, [13] for everyone who lives on milk is unskilled in the word of righteousness, since he is a child. [14] But solid food is for the

> ### GETTING THE MESSAGE
>
> The safety of sailors depended greatly on a ship's **anchor**. Without it, the likelihood of shipwreck increased dramatically. The anchor therefore became an important emblem of hope and stability for early Christians (6:19).

mature, for those who have their powers of discernment trained by constant practice to distinguish good from evil.

[6] Therefore let us leave the elementary doctrine of Christ and go on to maturity, not laying again a foundation of repentance from dead works and of faith toward God, [2] and of instruction about washings,[1] the laying on of hands, the resurrection of the dead, and eternal judgment. [3] And this we will do if God permits. [4] For it is impossible, in the case of those who have once been enlightened, who have tasted the heavenly gift, and have shared in the Holy Spirit, [5] and have tasted the goodness of the word of God and the powers of the age to come, [6] and then have fallen away, to restore them again to repentance, since they are crucifying once again the Son of God to their own harm and holding him up to contempt. [7] For land that has drunk the rain that often falls on it, and produces a

crop useful to those for whose sake it is cultivated, receives a blessing from God. [8] But if it bears thorns and thistles, it is worthless and near to being cursed, and its end is to be burned.

[9] Though we speak in this way, yet in your case, beloved, we feel sure of better things—things that belong to salvation. [10] For God is not unjust so as to overlook your work and the love that you have shown for his name in serving the saints, as you still do. [11] And we desire each one of you to show the same earnestness to have the full assurance of hope until the end, [12] so that you may not be sluggish, but imitators of those who through faith and patience inherit the promises.

The Certainty of God's Promise

[13] For when God made a promise to Abraham, since he had no one greater by whom to swear, he swore by himself, [14] saying, "Surely I will bless you and multiply you." [15] And thus Abraham, having patiently waited, obtained the promise. [16] For people swear by something greater than themselves, and in all their disputes an oath is final for confirmation. [17] So when God desired to show more convincingly to the heirs of the promise the unchangeable character of his purpose, he guaranteed it with an oath, [18] so that by two unchangeable things, in which it is impossible for God to lie, we who have fled for refuge might have strong encouragement to hold fast to the hope set before us. [19] We have this as a sure and steadfast anchor of the soul, a hope that enters into the inner place behind the curtain, [20] where Jesus has gone as a forerunner on our behalf, having become a high priest forever after the order of Melchizedek.

The Priestly Order of Melchizedek

[7] For this Melchizedek, king of Salem, priest of the Most High God, met Abraham returning from the slaughter of the kings and blessed him, [2] and to him Abraham apportioned a tenth part of everything. He is first, by translation of his name, king of righteousness, and then he is also king of Salem, that is, king of peace. [3] He is without father or mother or genealogy, having neither beginning of days nor end of life, but resembling the Son of God he continues a priest forever.

[1] That is, ceremonial washings (see Exodus 30:19–21)

⁴ See how great this man was to whom Abraham the patriarch gave a tenth of the spoils! ⁵ And those descendants of Levi who receive the priestly office have a commandment in the law to take tithes from the people, that is, from their brothers,[1] though these also are descended from Abraham. ⁶ But this man who does not have his descent from them received tithes from Abraham and blessed him who had the promises. ⁷ It is beyond dispute that the inferior is blessed by the superior. ⁸ In the one case tithes are received by mortal men, but in the other case, by one of whom it is testified that he lives. ⁹ One might even say that Levi himself, who receives tithes, paid tithes through Abraham, ¹⁰ for he was still in the loins of his ancestor when Melchizedek met him.

Jesus Compared to Melchizedek

¹¹ Now if perfection had been attainable through the Levitical priesthood (for under it the people received the law), what further need would there have been for another priest to arise after the order of Melchizedek, rather than one named after the order of Aaron? ¹² For when there is a change in the priesthood, there is necessarily a change in the law as well. ¹³ For the one of whom these things are spoken belonged to another tribe, from which no one has ever served at the altar. ¹⁴ For it is evident that our Lord was descended from Judah, and in connection with that tribe Moses said nothing about priests.

¹⁵ This becomes even more evident when another priest arises in the likeness of Melchizedek, ¹⁶ who has become a priest, not on the basis of a legal requirement concerning bodily descent, but by the power of an indestructible life. ¹⁷ For it is witnessed of him,

"You are a priest forever,
    after the order of Melchizedek."

¹⁸ For on the one hand, a former commandment is set aside because of its weakness and uselessness ¹⁹ (for the law made nothing perfect); but on the other hand, a better hope is introduced, through which we draw near to God.

²⁰ And it was not without an oath. For those who formerly became priests were made such without an oath, ²¹ but this one was made a priest with an oath by the one who said to him:

"The Lord has sworn
    and will not change his mind,
'You are a priest forever.'"

²² This makes Jesus the guarantor of a better covenant.

²³ The former priests were many in number, because they were prevented by death from continuing in office, ²⁴ but he holds his priesthood permanently, because he continues forever. ²⁵ Consequently, he is able to save to the uttermost those who draw near to God through him, since he always lives to make intercession for them.

²⁶ For it was indeed fitting that we should have such a high priest, holy, innocent, unstained, separated from sinners, and exalted above the heavens. ²⁷ He has no

---

GETTING THE MESSAGE

A better covenant. A key theme in the book of Hebrews is the superiority of the new covenant over the old. The words "better," "more," or "greater" to describe the new covenant appear a combined total of 25 times.

---

need, like those high priests, to offer sacrifices daily, first for his own sins and then for those of the people, since he did this once for all when he offered up himself. ²⁸ For the law appoints men in their weakness as high priests, but the word of the oath, which came later than the law, appoints a Son who has been made perfect forever.

Jesus, High Priest of a Better Covenant

8 Now the point in what we are saying is this: we have such a high priest, one who is seated at the right hand of the throne of the Majesty in heaven, ² a minister in the holy places, in the true tent that the Lord set up, not man. ³ For every high priest is appointed to offer gifts and sacrifices; thus it is necessary for this priest also to have something to offer. ⁴ Now if he were on earth, he would not be a priest at all, since there are priests who offer gifts according to the law. ⁵ They serve a copy

---

[1] Or brothers and sisters

and shadow of the heavenly things. For when Moses was about to erect the tent, he was instructed by God, saying, "See that you make everything according to the pattern that was shown you on the mountain." **6** But as it is, Christ has obtained a ministry that is as much more excellent than the old as the covenant he mediates is better, since it is enacted on better promises. **7** For if that first covenant had been faultless, there would have been no occasion to look for a second.

8 For he finds fault with them when he says:

"Behold, the days are coming, declares the Lord,
　when I will establish a new covenant with the house of Israel
　and with the house of Judah,

9 not like the covenant that I made with their fathers
　on the day when I took them by the hand to bring them out of the land of Egypt.
For they did not continue in my covenant,
　and so I showed no concern for them, declares the Lord.
10 For this is the covenant that I will make with the house of Israel after those days, declares the Lord:
I will put my laws into their minds,
　and write them on their hearts,
and I will be their God,
　and they shall be my people.
11 And they shall not teach, each one his neighbor
　and each one his brother, saying, 'Know the Lord,'

for they shall all know me,
　from the least of them to the greatest.
12 For I will be merciful toward their iniquities,
　and I will remember their sins no more."

13 In speaking of a new covenant, he makes the first one obsolete. And what is becoming obsolete and growing old is ready to vanish away.

The Earthly Holy Place

9 Now even the first covenant had regulations for worship and an earthly place of holiness. **2** For a tent was prepared, the first section, in which were the lampstand and the table and the bread of the Presence. It is called the Holy Place. **3** Behind the second curtain was a second section called the Most Holy Place, **4** having the golden altar of incense and the ark of the covenant covered on all sides with gold, in which was a golden urn holding the manna, and Aaron's staff that budded, and the tablets of the covenant. **5** Above it were the cherubim of glory overshadowing the mercy seat. Of these things we cannot now speak in detail.

6 These preparations having thus been made, the priests go regularly into the first section, performing their ritual duties, **7** but into the second only the high priest goes, and he but once a year, and not without taking blood, which he offers for himself and for the unintentional sins of the people. **8** By this the Holy Spirit indicates that the way into the holy places is not yet opened as long as the first section is still standing **9** (which is symbolic for the present age). According to this arrangement, gifts and sacrifices are offered that cannot perfect the conscience of the worshiper, **10** but deal only with food and drink and various washings, regulations for the body imposed until the time of reformation.

Redemption Through the Blood of Christ

11 But when Christ appeared as a high priest of the good things that have come, then through the greater and more perfect tent (not made with hands, that is, not of this creation) **12** he entered once for all into the holy places, not by means of the blood of goats and calves but by means of his own blood, thus securing an eternal redemption. **13** For if the blood of goats and bulls, and the sprinkling of defiled persons with the ashes of a heifer, sanctify for the purification of the flesh, ¹⁴ how much more will the blood of Christ, who through the eternal Spirit offered himself without blemish to God, purify our conscience from dead works to serve the living God.

¹⁵ Therefore he is the mediator of a new covenant, so that those who are called may receive the promised eternal inheritance, since a death has occurred that redeems them from the transgressions committed under the first covenant. ¹⁶ For where a will is involved, the death of the one who made it must be established. ¹⁷ For a will takes effect only at death, since it is not in force as long as the one who made it is alive. ¹⁸ Therefore not even the first covenant was inaugurated without blood. ¹⁹ For when every commandment of the law had been declared by Moses to all the people, he took the blood of calves and goats, with water and scarlet wool and hyssop, and sprinkled both the book itself and all the people, ²⁰ saying, "This is the blood of the covenant that God commanded for you." ²¹ And in the same way he sprinkled with the blood both the tent and all the vessels used in worship. ²² Indeed, under the law almost everything is purified with blood, and without the shedding of blood there is no forgiveness of sins.

²³ Thus it was necessary for the copies of the heavenly things to be purified with these rites, but the heavenly things themselves with better sacrifices than these. ²⁴ For Christ has entered, not into holy places made with hands, which are copies of the true things, but into heaven itself, now to appear in the presence of God on our behalf. ²⁵ Nor was it to offer himself repeatedly, as the high priest enters the holy places every year with blood not his own, ²⁶ for then he would have had to suffer repeatedly since the foundation of the world. But as it is, he has appeared once for all at the end of the ages to put away sin by the sacrifice of himself. ²⁷ And just as it is appointed for man to die once, and after that comes judgment, ²⁸ so Christ, having been offered once to bear the sins of many, will appear a second time, not to deal with sin but to save those who are eagerly waiting for him.

Christ's Sacrifice Once for All

10 For since the law has but a shadow of the good things to come instead of the true form of these realities, it can never, by the same sacrifices that are continually offered every year, make perfect those who draw near. ² Otherwise, would they not have ceased to be offered, since the worshipers, having once been cleansed, would no longer have any consciousness of sins? ³ But in these sacrifices there is a reminder of sins every year. ⁴ For it is impossible for the blood of bulls and goats to take away sins.

⁵ Consequently, when Christ came into the world, he said,

"Sacrifices and offerings you have not desired,
    but a body have you prepared for me;

> ### GETTING THE MESSAGE
>
> **The mercy seat** (9:5) was the place where the high priest sprinkled blood once a year to atone for the people's sins (Lev. 16:14; see Ex. 25:22). In contrast, Jesus' death redeemed our sins "once for all" (Heb. 9:12). His sacrificial death also gives us the freedom to serve God (9:14).

⁶   in burnt offerings and sin offerings
    you have taken no pleasure.
⁷   Then I said, 'Behold, I have come to do your will, O God,
    as it is written of me in the scroll of the book.'"

⁸ When he said above, "You have neither desired nor taken pleasure in sacrifices and offerings and burnt offerings and sin offerings" (these are offered according to the law), ⁹ then he added, "Behold, I have come to do your will." He does away with the first in order to establish the second. ¹⁰ And by that will we have been sanctified through the offering of the body of Jesus Christ once for all.

¹¹ And every priest stands daily at his service, offering repeatedly the same sacrifices, which can never take away sins. ¹² But when Christ had offered for all time a single sacrifice for sins, he sat down at the right hand of God, ¹³ waiting from that time until his enemies should be made a footstool for his feet.

14 For by a single offering he has perfected for all time those who are being sanctified.

15 And the Holy Spirit also bears witness to us; for after saying,

16 "This is the covenant that I will make with them
after those days, declares the Lord:
I will put my laws on their hearts,
and write them on their minds,"

17 then he adds,

"I will remember their sins and their
lawless deeds no more."

18 Where there is forgiveness of these, there is no longer any offering for sin.

The Full Assurance of Faith

19 Therefore, brothers,[1] since we have confidence to enter the holy places by the blood

> **GETTING THE MESSAGE**
>
> **Jesus' perfect sacrifice for sin.** Animal sacrifices symbolized payment for sins under the first covenant (10:1). But Jesus' death paid for sins in a way that animal sacrifices could not (10:1-18). It also made sanctification, the process of conforming into the image of Christ, possible for believers (10:14).

of Jesus, **20** by the new and living way that he opened for us through the curtain, that is, through his flesh, **21** and since we have a great priest over the house of God, **22** let us draw near with a true heart in full assurance of faith, with our hearts sprinkled clean from an evil conscience and our bodies washed with pure water. **23** Let us hold fast the confession of our hope without wavering, for he who promised is faithful. **24** And let us consider how to stir up one another to love and good works, **25** not neglecting to meet together, as is the habit of some, but encouraging one another, and all the more as you see the Day drawing near.

26 For if we go on sinning deliberately after receiving the knowledge of the truth, there no longer remains a sacrifice for sins, **27** but a fearful expectation of judgment, and a fury of fire that will consume the adversaries. **28** Anyone who has set aside

the law of Moses dies without mercy on the evidence of two or three witnesses. **29** How much worse punishment, do you think, will be deserved by the one who has trampled underfoot the Son of God, and has profaned the blood of the covenant by which he was sanctified, and has outraged the Spirit of grace? **30** For we know him who said, "Vengeance is mine; I will repay." And again, "The Lord will judge his people." **31** It is a fearful thing to fall into the hands of the living God.

32 But recall the former days when, after you were enlightened, you endured a hard struggle with sufferings, **33** sometimes being publicly exposed to reproach and affliction, and sometimes being partners with those so treated. **34** For you had compassion on those in prison, and you joyfully accepted the plundering of your property, since you knew that you yourselves had a better possession and an abiding one. **35** Therefore do not throw away your confidence, which has a great reward. **36** For you have need of endurance, so that when you have done the will of God you may receive what is promised. **37** For,

"Yet a little while,
and the coming one will come and
will not delay;
38 but my righteous one shall live by faith,
and if he shrinks back,
my soul has no pleasure in him."

39 But we are not of those who shrink back and are destroyed, but of those who have faith and preserve their souls.

By Faith

11 Now faith is the assurance of things hoped for, the conviction of things not seen. **2** For by it the people of old received their commendation. **3** By faith we understand that the universe was created by the word of God, so that what is seen was not made out of things that are visible.

4 By faith Abel offered to God a more acceptable sacrifice than Cain, through which he was commended as righteous, God commending him by accepting his gifts. And through his faith, though he died, he still speaks. **5** By faith Enoch was taken up so that he should not see death, and he was not found, because God had taken him. Now

[1] Or brothers and sisters

before he was taken he was commended as having pleased God. **6** And without faith it is impossible to please him, for whoever would draw near to God must believe that he exists and that he rewards those who seek him. **7** By faith Noah, being warned by God concerning events as yet unseen, in reverent fear constructed an ark for the saving of his household. By this he condemned the world and became an heir of the righteousness that comes by faith.

8 By faith Abraham obeyed when he was called to go out to a place that he was to receive as an inheritance. And he went out, not knowing where he was going. **9** By faith he went to live in the land of promise, as in a foreign land, living in tents with Isaac and Jacob, heirs with him of the same promise. **10** For he was looking forward to the city that has foundations, whose designer and builder is God. **11** By faith Sarah herself received power to conceive, even when she was past the age, since she considered him faithful who had promised. **12** Therefore from one man, and him as good as dead, were born descendants as many as the stars of heaven and as many as the innumerable grains of sand by the seashore.

13 These all died in faith, not having received the things promised, but having seen them and greeted them from afar, and having acknowledged that they were strangers and exiles on the earth. **14** For people who speak thus make it clear that they are seeking a homeland. **15** If they had been thinking of that land from which they had gone out, they would have had opportunity to return. **16** But as it is, they desire a better country, that is, a heavenly one. Therefore God is not ashamed to be called their God, for he has prepared for them a city.

17 By faith Abraham, when he was tested, offered up Isaac, and he who had received the promises was in the act of offering up his only son, **18** of whom it was said, "Through Isaac shall your offspring be named." **19** He considered that God was able even to raise him from the dead, from which, figuratively speaking, he did receive him back. **20** By faith Isaac invoked future blessings on Jacob and Esau. **21** By faith Jacob, when dying, blessed each of the sons of Joseph, bowing in worship over the head of his staff. **22** By faith Joseph, at the end of his life, made men-

tion of the exodus of the Israelites and gave directions concerning his bones.

23 By faith Moses, when he was born, was hidden for three months by his parents, because they saw that the child was beautiful, and they were not afraid of the king's edict. **24** By faith Moses, when he was grown up, refused to be called the son of Pharaoh's daughter, **25** choosing rather to be mistreated with the people of God than to enjoy the fleeting pleasures of sin. **26** He considered the reproach of Christ greater wealth than the treasures of Egypt, for he was looking to the reward. **27** By faith he left Egypt, not being afraid of the anger of the king, for he endured as seeing him who is invisible. **28** By faith he kept the Passover and sprinkled the blood, so that the Destroyer of the firstborn might not touch them.

GETTING THE MESSAGE

Even under the old covenant, **faith** was essential for a relationship with God. The Old Testament saints believed God and obeyed him even though they did not see his promises fulfilled completely (ch. 11). Christians, however, have the amazing privilege of having seen God's plan fulfilled in Christ.

29 By faith the people crossed the Red Sea as on dry land, but the Egyptians, when they attempted to do the same, were drowned. **30** By faith the walls of Jericho fell down after they had been encircled for seven days. **31** By faith Rahab the prostitute did not perish with those who were disobedient, because she had given a friendly welcome to the spies.

32 And what more shall I say? For time would fail me to tell of Gideon, Barak, Samson, Jephthah, of David and Samuel and the prophets— **33** who through faith conquered kingdoms, enforced justice, obtained promises, stopped the mouths of lions, **34** quenched the power of fire, escaped the edge of the sword, were made strong out of weakness, became mighty in war, put foreign armies to flight. **35** Women received back their dead by resurrection. Some were tortured, refusing to accept release, so that they might rise again to a better life.

36 Others suffered mocking and flogging, and even chains and imprisonment. **37** They were stoned, they were sawn in two, they were killed with the sword. They went about in skins of sheep and goats, destitute, afflicted, mistreated— **38** of whom the world was not worthy—wandering about in deserts and mountains, and in dens and caves of the earth.

39 And all these, though commended through their faith, did not receive what was promised, **40** since God had provided something better for us, that apart from us they should not be made perfect.

Jesus, Founder and Perfecter of Our Faith

12 Therefore, since we are surrounded by so great a cloud of witnesses, let us also lay aside every weight, and sin which clings

so closely, and let us run with endurance the race that is set before us, **2** looking to Jesus, the founder and perfecter of our faith, who for the joy that was set before him endured the cross, despising the shame, and is seated at the right hand of the throne of God.

Do Not Grow Weary

3 Consider him who endured from sinners such hostility against himself, so that you may not grow weary or fainthearted. **4** In your struggle against sin you have not yet resisted to the point of shedding your blood. **5** And have you forgotten the exhortation that addresses you as sons?

"My son, do not regard lightly the discipline of the Lord,
　　nor be weary when reproved by him.
6　For the Lord disciplines the one he loves,
　　and chastises every son whom he receives."

7 It is for discipline that you have to endure. God is treating you as sons. For what son is there whom his father does not discipline? **8** If you are left without discipline, in which all have participated, then you are illegitimate children and not sons. **9** Besides this, we have had earthly fathers who disciplined us and we respected them. Shall we not much more be subject to the Father of spirits and live? **10** For they disciplined us for a short time as it seemed best to them, but he disciplines us for our good, that we may share his holiness. **11** For the moment all discipline seems painful rather than pleasant, but later it yields the peaceful fruit of righteousness to those who have been trained by it.

12 Therefore lift your drooping hands and strengthen your weak knees, **13** and make straight paths for your feet, so that what is lame may not be put out of joint but rather be healed. **14** Strive for peace with everyone, and for the holiness without which no one will see the Lord. **15** See to it that no one fails to obtain the grace of God; that no "root of bitterness" springs up and causes trouble, and by it many become defiled; **16** that no one is sexually immoral or unholy like Esau, who sold his birthright for a single meal. **17** For you know that afterward, when he desired to inherit the blessing, he was rejected, for he found no chance to repent, though he sought it with tears.

A Kingdom That Cannot Be Shaken

18 For you have not come to what may be touched, a blazing fire and darkness and gloom and a tempest **19** and the sound of a trumpet and a voice whose words made the hearers beg that no further messages be spoken to them. **20** For they could not endure the order that was given, "If even a beast touches the mountain, it shall be stoned." **21** Indeed, so terrifying was the sight that Moses said, "I tremble with fear." **22** But you have come to Mount Zion and to the city of the living God, the heavenly Jerusalem, and to innumerable angels in festal gathering, **23** and to the assembly of the firstborn who are enrolled in heaven, and to God, the judge of all, and to the spirits of the righteous made perfect, **24** and to Jesus, the mediator of a new covenant, and to the sprinkled blood that speaks a better word than the blood of Abel.

[25] See that you do not refuse him who is speaking. For if they did not escape when they refused him who warned them on earth, much less will we escape if we reject him who warns from heaven. [26] At that time his voice shook the earth, but now he has promised, "Yet once more I will shake not only the earth but also the heavens." [27] This phrase, "Yet once more," indicates the removal of things that are shaken—that is, things that have been made—in order that the things that cannot be shaken may remain. [28] Therefore let us be grateful for receiving a kingdom that cannot be shaken, and thus let us offer to God acceptable worship, with reverence and awe, [29] for our God is a consuming fire.

Sacrifices Pleasing to God

13 Let brotherly love continue. [2] Do not neglect to show hospitality to strangers, for thereby some have entertained angels unawares. [3] Remember those who are in prison, as though in prison with them, and those who are mistreated, since you also are in the body. [4] Let marriage be held in honor among all, and let the marriage bed be undefiled, for God will judge the sexually immoral and adulterous. [5] Keep your life free from love of money, and be content with what you have, for he has said, "I will never leave you nor forsake you." [6] So we can confidently say,

"The Lord is my helper;
    I will not fear;
what can man do to me?"

[7] Remember your leaders, those who spoke to you the word of God. Consider the outcome of their way of life, and imitate their faith. [8] Jesus Christ is the same yesterday and today and forever. [9] Do not be led away by diverse and strange teachings, for it is good for the heart to be strengthened by grace, not by foods, which have not benefited those devoted to them. [10] We have an altar from which those who serve the tent have no right to eat. [11] For the bodies of those animals whose blood is brought into the holy places by the high priest as a sacrifice for sin are burned outside the camp. [12] So Jesus also suffered outside the gate in order to sanctify the people through his own blood. [13] Therefore let us go to him outside the camp and bear the reproach he endured. [14] For here we have no lasting city, but we seek the city that is to come. [15] Through him then let us continually offer up a sacrifice of praise to God, that is, the fruit of lips that acknowledge his name. [16] Do not neglect to do good and to share what you have, for such sacrifices are pleasing to God.

[17] Obey your leaders and submit to them, for they are keeping watch over your souls, as those who will have to give an account. Let them do this with joy and not with groaning, for that would be of no advantage to you.

[18] Pray for us, for we are sure that we have a clear conscience, desiring to act honorably in all things. [19] I urge you the more earnestly to do this in order that I may be restored to you the sooner.

Benediction

[20] Now may the God of peace who brought again from the dead our Lord Jesus, the great shepherd of the sheep, by the blood of the eternal covenant, [21] equip you with everything good that you may do his will, working in us that which is pleasing in his sight, through Jesus Christ, to whom be glory forever and ever. Amen.

Final Greetings

[22] I appeal to you, brothers,[1] bear with my word of exhortation, for I have written to you briefly. [23] You should know that our brother Timothy has been released, with whom I shall see you if he comes soon. [24] Greet all your leaders and all the saints. Those who come from Italy send you greetings. [25] Grace be with all of you.

[1] Or brothers and sisters

INTRODUCTION TO JAMES

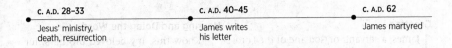

c. A.D. 28–33	c. A.D. 40–45	c. A.D. 62
Jesus' ministry, death, resurrection	James writes his letter	James martyred

AUTHOR, DATE, AND RECIPIENTS

This letter was written by James, the brother of Jesus (Matt. 13:55) and leader of the Jerusalem church (Acts 15). It was probably written about A.D. 40–45 to Jewish Christians living outside Palestine.

THEME

Christians must live out their faith. They should be doers, not just hearers, of God's Word.

PURPOSE

James's readers were suffering persecution and living in poverty. They were in social and spiritual conflict. Many believers were living in a worldly manner. James corrects them and challenges them to seek God's wisdom to work out these problems.

KEY THEMES

1. God is a gracious giver, the unchanging Creator, and merciful and compassionate. He is also a Judge, the one and only God, a jealous God, a gracious God, and a healing God (1:5, 17–18; 2:5, 13, 19; 4:5–6; 5:1–3, 9, 15).

2. Wisdom comes "from above." It enables believers to withstand trials and to have peace rather than divisions among themselves (1:5; 3:13, 17).

3. God allows tests and trials (1:2–4), but temptation comes from self and Satan. The required response is patient endurance (1:3, 13–14; 4:7; 5:7–8).

4. These trials include poverty and mistreatment by the rich. The poor are the special focus of God's care. They must be cared for by his

people. They must not be taken advantage of or ignored. The wealthy are condemned for pride and for stealing from the poor (1:9, 27; 2:1–5, 15–16; 4:13–17; 5:1–6).

5. There is both future judgment and future reward (1:12; 2:5, 12–13; 3:1; 4:12; 5:1–7, 9, 20).

6. What a person says has power both to destroy and to bring peace (3:1–4:12).

7. Rather than merely hearing God's word, believers must obey it in their daily actions (1:19–27; 2:14–26).

8. Prayer is the proper response to trials, but it must not be self-seeking. It is to be central in all of life's circumstances, good or bad. God has great power to heal physical and spiritual problems (1:5–7; 4:2–3; 5:13–18).

9. James and Paul agree that justification comes only by God's grace through faith, and that true faith always results in good works. If no works result, there was no justification in the first place (2:14–26).

OUTLINE

    I. Greeting (1:1)
   II. The Testing of Faith (1:2–18)
  III. Hearing and Doing the Word (1:19–27)
   IV. The Sin of Favoritism (2:1–13)
    V. Faith without Works Is Dead (2:14–26)
   VI. The Sin of Dissension in the Community (3:1–4:12)
  VII. The Sins of the Wealthy (4:13–5:12)
 VIII. The Prayer of Faith (5:13–18)
   IX. Concluding Admonition (5:19–20)

THE LETTER OF
JAMES

Greeting

1 James, a servant[1] of God and of the Lord Jesus Christ,

To the twelve tribes in the Dispersion:

Greetings.

Testing of Your Faith

2 Count it all joy, my brothers,[2] when you meet trials of various kinds, 3 for you know that the testing of your faith produces steadfastness. 4 And let steadfastness have its full effect, that you may be perfect and complete, lacking in nothing.

5 If any of you lacks wisdom, let him ask God, who gives generously to all without reproach, and it will be given him. 6 But let him ask in faith, with no doubting, for the one who doubts is like a wave of the sea that is driven and tossed by the wind. 7 For that person must not suppose that he will receive anything from the Lord; 8 he is a double-minded man, unstable in all his ways.

9 Let the lowly brother boast in his exaltation, 10 and the rich in his humiliation, because like a flower of the grass he will pass away. 11 For the sun rises with its scorching heat and withers the grass; its flower falls, and its beauty perishes. So also will the rich man fade away in the midst of his pursuits.

12 Blessed is the man who remains steadfast under trial, for when he has stood the test he will receive the crown of life, which God has promised to those who love him. 13 Let no one say when he is tempted, "I am being tempted by God," for God cannot be tempted with evil, and he himself tempts no one. 14 But each person is tempted when he is lured and enticed by his own desire. 15 Then desire when it has conceived gives birth to sin, and sin when it is fully grown brings forth death.

16 Do not be deceived, my beloved brothers. 17 Every good gift and every perfect gift is from above, coming down from the Father of lights with whom there is no variation or shadow due to change. 18 Of his own will he brought us forth by the word of truth, that we should be a kind of firstfruits of his creatures.

Hearing and Doing the Word

19 Know this, my beloved brothers: let every person be quick to hear, slow to speak, slow to anger; 20 for the anger of man does not produce the righteousness of God. 21 Therefore put away all filthiness and rampant wickedness and receive with meekness the implanted word, which is able to save your souls.

22 But be doers of the word, and not hearers only, deceiving yourselves. 23 For if anyone is a hearer of the word and not a doer, he is like a man who looks intently at his natural face

GETTING THE MESSAGE

Up until the first century A.D., **mirrors** in the Near East were made of polished bronze or other metals. With the invention of glass in Lebanon, new techniques could be used to create more reflective surfaces. James compares God's Word to a mirror in which people can see themselves in the light of God's truth (1:22–25).

in a mirror. 24 For he looks at himself and goes away and at once forgets what he was like. 25 But the one who looks into the perfect law, the law of liberty, and perseveres, being no hearer who forgets but a doer who acts, he will be blessed in his doing.

26 If anyone thinks he is religious and does not bridle his tongue but deceives his heart, this person's religion is worthless. 27 Religion that is pure and undefiled before God, the Father, is this: to visit orphans and widows in their affliction, and to keep oneself unstained from the world.

The Sin of Partiality

2 My brothers, show no partiality as you hold the faith in our Lord Jesus Christ, the Lord of glory. 2 For if a man wearing a gold ring and fine clothing comes into your assembly, and a poor man in shabby cloth-

---

[1] Or slave (Greek doulos; see Preface) [2] Or brothers and sisters (see Preface); also 1:16, 19; 2:1

ing also comes in, **3** and if you pay attention to the one who wears the fine clothing and say, "You sit here in a good place," while you say to the poor man, "You stand over there," or, "Sit down at my feet," **4** have you not then made distinctions among yourselves and become judges with evil thoughts? **5** Listen, my beloved brothers,[1] has not God chosen those who are poor in the world to be rich in faith and heirs of the kingdom, which he has promised to those who love him? **6** But you have dishonored the poor man. Are not the rich the ones who oppress you, and the ones who drag you into court? **7** Are they not the ones who blaspheme the honorable name by which you were called?

8 If you really fulfill the royal law according to the Scripture, "You shall love your neighbor as yourself," you are doing well. **9** But if you show partiality, you are committing sin

and are convicted by the law as transgressors. **10** For whoever keeps the whole law but fails in one point has become accountable for all of it. **11** For he who said, "Do not commit adultery," also said, "Do not murder." If you do not commit adultery but do murder, you have become a transgressor of the law. **12** So speak and so act as those who are to be judged under the law of liberty. **13** For judgment is without mercy to one who has shown no mercy. Mercy triumphs over judgment.

Faith Without Works Is Dead

14 What good is it, my brothers, if someone says he has faith but does not have works? Can that faith save him? **15** If a brother or sister is poorly clothed and lacking in daily food, **16** and one of you says to them, "Go in peace, be warmed and filled," without giving them the things needed for the body, what

good is that? **17** So also faith by itself, if it does not have works, is dead.

18 But someone will say, "You have faith and I have works." Show me your faith apart from your works, and I will show you my faith by my works. **19** You believe that God is one; you do well. Even the demons believe— and shudder! **20** Do you want to be shown, you foolish person, that faith apart from works is useless? **21** Was not Abraham our father justified by works when he offered up his son Isaac on the altar? **22** You see that faith was active along with his works, and faith was completed by his works; **23** and the Scripture was fulfilled that says, "Abraham believed God, and it was counted to him as righteousness"—and he was called a friend of God. **24** You see that a person is justified by works and not by faith alone. **25** And in the same way was not also Rahab the prostitute justified by works when she received the messengers and sent them out by another way? **26** For as the body apart from the spirit is dead, so also faith apart from works is dead.

Taming the Tongue

3 Not many of you should become teachers, my brothers, for you know that we who teach will be judged with greater strictness. **2** For we all stumble in many ways. And if anyone does not stumble in what he says, he is a perfect man, able also to bridle his whole body. **3** If we put bits into the mouths of horses so that they obey us, we guide their whole bodies as well. **4** Look at the ships also: though they are so large and are driven by strong winds, they are guided by a very small rudder wherever the will of the pilot directs. **5** So also the tongue is a small member, yet it boasts of great things.

How great a forest is set ablaze by such a small fire! **6** And the tongue is a fire, a world of unrighteousness. The tongue is set among our members, staining the whole body, setting on fire the entire course of life, and set on fire by hell. **7** For every kind of beast and bird, of reptile and sea creature, can be tamed and has been tamed by mankind, **8** but no human being can tame the tongue. It is a restless evil, full of deadly poison. **9** With it we bless our Lord and Father, and with it we curse people who are made in the likeness of God. **10** From the same mouth come blessing and cursing. My brothers,

[1] Or *brothers and sisters*; also 2:14; 3:10

these things ought not to be so. **11** Does a spring pour forth from the same opening both fresh and salt water? **12** Can a fig tree, my brothers,[1] bear olives, or a grapevine produce figs? Neither can a salt pond yield fresh water.

Wisdom from Above

13 Who is wise and understanding among you? By his good conduct let him show his works in the meekness of wisdom. **14** But if you have bitter jealousy and selfish ambition in your hearts, do not boast and be false to the truth. **15** This is not the wisdom that comes down from above, but is earthly, unspiritual, demonic. **16** For where jealousy and selfish ambition exist, there will be disorder and every vile practice. **17** But the wisdom from above is first pure, then peaceable, gentle, open to reason, full of mercy and good fruits, impartial and sincere. **18** And a harvest of righteousness is sown in peace by those who make peace.

Warning Against Worldliness

4 What causes quarrels and what causes fights among you? Is it not this, that your passions are at war within you? **2** You desire and do not have, so you murder. You covet and cannot obtain, so you fight and quarrel. You do not have, because you do not ask. **3** You ask and do not receive, because you ask wrongly, to spend it on your passions. **4** You adulterous people! Do you not know that friendship with the world is enmity with God? Therefore whoever wishes to be a friend of the world makes himself an enemy of God. **5** Or do you suppose it is to no purpose that the Scripture says, "He yearns jealously over the spirit that he has made to dwell in us"? **6** But he gives more grace. Therefore it says, "God opposes the proud, but gives grace to the humble." **7** Submit yourselves therefore to God. Resist the devil, and he will flee from you. **8** Draw near to God, and he will draw near to you. Cleanse your hands, you sinners, and purify your hearts, you double-minded. **9** Be wretched and mourn and weep. Let your laughter be turned to mourning and your joy to gloom. **10** Humble yourselves before the Lord, and he will exalt you.

11 Do not speak evil against one another, brothers. The one who speaks against a brother or judges his brother, speaks evil against the law and judges the law. But if you judge the law, you are not a doer of the law but a judge. **12** There is only one lawgiver and judge, he who is able to save and to destroy. But who are you to judge your neighbor?

Boasting About Tomorrow

13 Come now, you who say, "Today or tomorrow we will go into such and such a town and spend a year there and trade and make a profit"— **14** yet you do not know what tomorrow will bring. What is your life? For you are a mist that appears for a little time and then vanishes. **15** Instead you ought to say, "If the Lord wills, we will live and do this or that." **16** As it is, you boast in your arrogance. All such boasting is evil. **17** So whoever knows the right thing to do and fails to do it, for him it is sin.

GETTING THE MESSAGE

Familiar word pictures. The images James uses to describe the power of the tongue (3:1-12) were well chosen to communicate to his original readers. The Greek playwright Sophocles spoke of wild horses being tamed by a small bit in the mouth. The Jewish philosopher Philo compared one's senses to a helmsman steering a boat. And the Roman historian Plutarch compared a loose tongue to a blazing forest fire.

Warning to the Rich

5 Come now, you rich, weep and howl for the miseries that are coming upon you. **2** Your riches have rotted and your garments are moth-eaten. **3** Your gold and silver have corroded, and their corrosion will be evidence against you and will eat your flesh like fire. You have laid up treasure in the last days. **4** Behold, the wages of the laborers who mowed your fields, which you kept back by fraud, are crying out against you, and the cries of the harvesters have reached the ears of the Lord of hosts. **5** You have lived on the earth in luxury and in self-indulgence. You have fattened your hearts in a day of slaughter. **6** You have condemned and murdered the righteous person. He does not resist you.

[1] Or brothers and sisters; also 4:11

Patience in Suffering

[7] Be patient, therefore, brothers,[1] until the coming of the Lord. See how the farmer waits for the precious fruit of the earth, being patient about it, until it receives the early and the late rains. [8] You also, be patient. Establish your hearts, for the coming of the Lord is at hand. [9] Do not grumble against one another, brothers, so that you may not be judged;

behold, the Judge is standing at the door. [10] As an example of suffering and patience, brothers, take the prophets who spoke in the name of the Lord. [11] Behold, we consider those blessed who remained steadfast. You have heard of the steadfastness of Job, and you have seen the purpose of the Lord, how the Lord is compassionate and merciful.

[12] But above all, my brothers, do not swear, either by heaven or by earth or by any other oath, but let your "yes" be yes and your "no" be no, so that you may not fall under condemnation.

The Prayer of Faith

[13] Is anyone among you suffering? Let him pray. Is anyone cheerful? Let him sing praise. [14] Is anyone among you sick? Let him call for the elders of the church, and let them pray over him, anointing him with oil in the name of the Lord. [15] And the prayer of faith will save the one who is sick, and the Lord will raise him up. And if he has committed sins, he will be forgiven. [16] Therefore, confess your sins to one another and pray for one another, that you may be healed. The prayer of a righteous person has great power as it is working. [17] Elijah was a man with a nature like ours, and he prayed fervently that it might not rain, and for three years and six months it did not rain on the earth. [18] Then he prayed again, and heaven gave rain, and the earth bore its fruit.

[19] My brothers, if anyone among you wanders from the truth and someone brings him back, [20] let him know that whoever brings back a sinner from his wandering will save his soul from death and will cover a multitude of sins.

[1] Or *brothers and sisters*; also 5:9, 10, 12, 19

INTRODUCTION TO 1 PETER

c. A.D. 41–44	c. A.D. 62–63	c. A.D. 64–67
Peter jailed in Jerusalem	Peter writes first letter	Peter martyred in Rome

AUTHOR, DATE, AND RECIPIENTS

The apostle Peter wrote this letter (1:1). He was once a fisherman but now was a disciple, a "witness of the sufferings of Christ" (5:1). He probably wrote the letter from Rome (see 5:13; "Babylon" almost certainly refers to Rome) around A.D. 62–63 during Nero's reign. The letter is addressed to Christians scattered in "Pontus, Galatia, Cappadocia, Asia, and Bithynia" (1:1). This is an area north of the Taurus Mountains in Asia Minor (modern-day Turkey). These territories had been impacted by Greco-Roman culture and had been under Roman control from the mid-first century B.C.

THEME

Those who persevere in faith while suffering persecution should be full of hope. They will certainly enjoy end-time salvation, since they already enjoy God's saving promises through Christ's death and resurrection.

PURPOSE

Peter is writing to encourage his readers to endure suffering and persecution (1:6–7; 2:18–20; 3:9, 13–17; 4:1–4, 12–19; 5:9) by giving themselves entirely to God (4:19). They are to remain faithful in times of distress, knowing that God will vindicate them and that they will certainly enjoy the salvation that the Lord has promised. Christ's death and resurrection are the model for believers. Just as Christ suffered

and then entered into glory, so too his followers will suffer before being exalted.

KEY THEMES

1. Those who suffer as Christians will be proven faithful when Christ returns (1:6–9; 2:18–25; 3:13–22; 4:12–19).

2. The church is the new temple, the new Israel, the new people of God (1:1–2; 2:4–10).

3. Believers should set their hope on their end-time inheritance (1:3–9, 13–16).

4. Christ died as a substitute for sinners. His death is the basis for their new life (1:17–21; 2:24; 3:13–22).

5. Christ's suffering is an example to his disciples (2:21–23).

6. At his resurrection, Christ triumphed over his enemies (3:18–22).

7. Christians should live righteously in their homes and in society (2:11–3:7).

8. New life in Christ is the basis for a life of love and holiness (1:3; 1:13–2:3).

OUTLINE

I. Opening (1:1–2)

II. Called to Salvation as Exiles (1:3–2:10)

III. Living as Strangers to Bring Glory to God in a Hostile World (2:11–4:11)

IV. Enduring Suffering (4:12–5:11)

V. Concluding Words (5:12–14)

1 PETER

Greeting

1 Peter, an apostle of Jesus Christ,
To those who are elect exiles of the Dispersion in Pontus, Galatia, Cappadocia, Asia, and Bithynia, ² according to the foreknowledge of God the Father, in the sanctification of the Spirit, for obedience to Jesus Christ and for sprinkling with his blood:

May grace and peace be multiplied to you.

Born Again to a Living Hope

³ Blessed be the God and Father of our Lord Jesus Christ! According to his great mercy, he has caused us to be born again to a living hope through the resurrection of Jesus Christ from the dead, ⁴ to an inheritance that is imperishable, undefiled, and unfading, kept in heaven for you, ⁵ who by God's power are being guarded through faith for a salvation ready to be revealed in the last time. ⁶ In this you rejoice, though now for a little while, if necessary, you have been grieved by various trials, ⁷ so that the tested genuineness of your faith—more precious than gold that perishes though it is tested by fire—may be found to result in praise and glory and honor at the revelation of Jesus Christ. ⁸ Though you have not seen him, you love him. Though you do not now see him, you believe in him and rejoice with joy that is inexpressible and filled with glory, ⁹ obtaining the outcome of your faith, the salvation of your souls.

¹⁰ Concerning this salvation, the prophets who prophesied about the grace that was to be yours searched and inquired carefully, ¹¹ inquiring what person or time the Spirit of Christ in them was indicating when he predicted the sufferings of Christ and the subsequent glories. ¹² It was revealed to them that they were serving not themselves but you, in the things that have now been announced to you through those who preached the good news to you by the Holy Spirit sent from heaven, things into which angels long to look.

Called to Be Holy

¹³ Therefore, preparing your minds for action, and being sober-minded, set your hope fully on the grace that will be brought to you at the revelation of Jesus Christ. ¹⁴ As obedient children, do not be conformed to the passions of your former ignorance, ¹⁵ but as he who called you is holy, you also be holy in all your conduct, ¹⁶ since it is written, "You shall be holy, for I am holy." ¹⁷ And if you call on him as Father who judges impartially according to each one's deeds, conduct yourselves with fear

GETTING THE MESSAGE

The Greek phrase translated **preparing your minds for action** (1:13) was used to describe the action of wrapping one's robes around one's belt before beginning some physical activity. The modern equivalent would be "rolling up your sleeves." Christians should be prepared to fully engage their minds in their service for Christ.

throughout the time of your exile, ¹⁸ knowing that you were ransomed from the futile ways inherited from your forefathers, not with perishable things such as silver or gold, ¹⁹ but with the precious blood of Christ, like that of a lamb without blemish or spot. ²⁰ He was foreknown before the foundation of the world but was made manifest in the last times for the sake of you ²¹ who through him are believers in God, who raised him from the dead and gave him glory, so that your faith and hope are in God.

²² Having purified your souls by your obedience to the truth for a sincere brotherly love, love one another earnestly from a pure heart, ²³ since you have been born again, not of perishable seed but of imperishable, through the living and abiding word of God; ²⁴ for

"All flesh is like grass
  and all its glory like the flower of
     grass.
The grass withers,
  and the flower falls,
25 but the word of the Lord remains
     forever."

And this word is the good news that was
preached to you.

A Living Stone and a Holy People

2 So put away all malice and all deceit
  and hypocrisy and envy and all slander.
² Like newborn infants, long for the pure
spiritual milk, that by it you may grow up
into salvation — ³ if indeed you have tasted
that the Lord is good.

⁴ As you come to him, a living stone
rejected by men but in the sight of God
chosen and precious, ⁵ you yourselves like
living stones are being built up as a spiritual

> ### GETTING THE MESSAGE
>
> **What is God's purpose for civil
> government?** God has established
> civil governments in order to punish
> wrongdoers and promote the good of
> society (Rom. 13:1–4). Peter teaches
> believers to "be subject for the Lord's
> sake to every human institution" (1 Pet.
> 2:13–17; see 1 Tim. 2:1–2).

house, to be a holy priesthood, to offer spiritual sacrifices acceptable to God through
Jesus Christ. ⁶ For it stands in Scripture:

"Behold, I am laying in Zion a stone,
  a cornerstone chosen and precious,
and whoever believes in him will not
     be put to shame."

⁷ So the honor is for you who believe, but for
those who do not believe,

"The stone that the builders rejected
  has become the cornerstone,"

⁸ and

"A stone of stumbling,
  and a rock of offense."

They stumble because they disobey the
word, as they were destined to do.

⁹ But you are a chosen race, a royal priesthood, a holy nation, a people for his own
possession, that you may proclaim the
excellencies of him who called you out of
darkness into his marvelous light. ¹⁰ Once
you were not a people, but now you are
God's people; once you had not received
mercy, but now you have received mercy.

¹¹ Beloved, I urge you as sojourners and
exiles to abstain from the passions of the
flesh, which wage war against your soul.
¹² Keep your conduct among the Gentiles honorable, so that when they speak
against you as evildoers, they may see your
good deeds and glorify God on the day of
visitation.

Submission to Authority

¹³ Be subject for the Lord's sake to every
human institution, whether it be to the
emperor as supreme, ¹⁴ or to governors as
sent by him to punish those who do evil
and to praise those who do good. ¹⁵ For this
is the will of God, that by doing good you
should put to silence the ignorance of foolish people. ¹⁶ Live as people who are free,
not using your freedom as a cover-up for
evil, but living as servants¹ of God. ¹⁷ Honor
everyone. Love the brotherhood. Fear God.
Honor the emperor.

¹⁸ Servants, be subject to your masters
with all respect, not only to the good and
gentle but also to the unjust. ¹⁹ For this is a
gracious thing, when, mindful of God, one
endures sorrows while suffering unjustly.
²⁰ For what credit is it if, when you sin and
are beaten for it, you endure? But if when
you do good and suffer for it you endure,
this is a gracious thing in the sight of God.
²¹ For to this you have been called, because
Christ also suffered for you, leaving you an
example, so that you might follow in his
steps. ²² He committed no sin, neither was
deceit found in his mouth. ²³ When he was
reviled, he did not revile in return; when he
suffered, he did not threaten, but continued
entrusting himself to him who judges justly.
²⁴ He himself bore our sins in his body on
the tree, that we might die to sin and live to
righteousness. By his wounds you have been
healed. ²⁵ For you were straying like sheep,
but have now returned to the Shepherd and
Overseer of your souls.

¹ Or *slaves* (Greek *doulos*; see Preface)

Wives and Husbands

3 Likewise, wives, be subject to your own husbands, so that even if some do not obey the word, they may be won without a word by the conduct of their wives, **2** when they see your respectful and pure conduct. **3** Do not let your adorning be external—the braiding of hair and the putting on of gold jewelry, or the clothing you wear— **4** but let your adorning be the hidden person of the heart with the imperishable beauty of a gentle and quiet spirit, which in God's sight is very precious. **5** For this is how the holy women who hoped in God used to adorn themselves, by submitting to their own husbands, **6** as Sarah obeyed Abraham, calling him lord. And you are her children, if you do good and do not fear anything that is frightening.

7 Likewise, husbands, live with your wives in an understanding way, showing honor to the woman as the weaker vessel, since they are heirs with you of the grace of life, so that your prayers may not be hindered.

Suffering for Righteousness' Sake

8 Finally, all of you, have unity of mind, sympathy, brotherly love, a tender heart, and a humble mind. **9** Do not repay evil for evil or reviling for reviling, but on the contrary, bless, for to this you were called, that you may obtain a blessing. **10** For

> "Whoever desires to love life
>   and see good days,
> let him keep his tongue from evil
>   and his lips from speaking deceit;
> **11** let him turn away from evil and do
>   good;
>   let him seek peace and pursue it.
> **12** For the eyes of the Lord are on the
>   righteous,
>   and his ears are open to their
>   prayer.
> But the face of the Lord is against
>   those who do evil."

13 Now who is there to harm you if you are zealous for what is good? **14** But even if you should suffer for righteousness' sake, you will be blessed. Have no fear of them, nor be troubled, **15** but in your hearts honor Christ the Lord as holy, always being prepared to make a defense to anyone who asks you for a reason for the hope that is in you; yet do it with gentleness and respect,

16 having a good conscience, so that, when you are slandered, those who revile your good behavior in Christ may be put to shame. **17** For it is better to suffer for doing good, if that should be God's will, than for doing evil.

18 For Christ also suffered once for sins, the righteous for the unrighteous, that he might bring us to God, being put to death in the flesh but made alive in the spirit, **19** in which he went and proclaimed to the spirits in prison, **20** because they formerly did not obey, when God's patience waited in the days of Noah, while the ark was being prepared, in which a few, that is, eight persons, were brought safely through water. **21** Baptism, which corresponds to this, now saves you, not as a removal of dirt from the body but as an appeal to God for a good

GETTING THE MESSAGE

Husbands and wives. Peter's statement about wives being heirs with their husbands (3:7) was revolutionary. In Roman tradition, the husband usually decided which religion his family would follow. Christian husbands, however, are to honor their wives as their equals in God's sight (see Gal. 3:28).

conscience, through the resurrection of Jesus Christ, **22** who has gone into heaven and is at the right hand of God, with angels, authorities, and powers having been subjected to him.

Stewards of God's Grace

4 Since therefore Christ suffered in the flesh, arm yourselves with the same way of thinking, for whoever has suffered in the flesh has ceased from sin, **2** so as to live for the rest of the time in the flesh no longer for human passions but for the will of God. **3** For the time that is past suffices for doing what the Gentiles want to do, living in sensuality, passions, drunkenness, orgies, drinking parties, and lawless idolatry. **4** With respect to this they are surprised when you do not join them in the same flood of debauchery, and they malign you; **5** but they will give account to him who is ready to judge the living and the dead. **6** For this is why the gospel was preached even to those who are dead, that though judged in the flesh the way people are, they might live in the spirit the way God does.

⁷ The end of all things is at hand; therefore be self-controlled and sober-minded for the sake of your prayers. ⁸ Above all, keep loving one another earnestly, since love covers a multitude of sins. ⁹ Show hospitality to one another without grumbling. ¹⁰ As each has received a gift, use it to serve one another, as good stewards of God's varied grace: ¹¹ whoever speaks, as one who speaks oracles of God; whoever serves, as one who serves by the strength that God supplies — in order that in everything God may be glorified through Jesus Christ. To him belong glory and dominion forever and ever. Amen.

> ## GETTING THE MESSAGE
>
> A **kiss of love** (5:14) was simply a kiss on the cheek. It was usually practiced among family members. Both Peter and Paul encouraged believers to greet one another in this fashion because it reminded them that they were brothers and sisters in Christ.

Suffering as a Christian

¹² Beloved, do not be surprised at the fiery trial when it comes upon you to test you, as though something strange were happening to you. ¹³ But rejoice insofar as you share Christ's sufferings, that you may also rejoice and be glad when his glory is revealed. ¹⁴ If you are insulted for the name of Christ, you are blessed, because the Spirit of glory and of God rests upon you. ¹⁵ But let none of you suffer as a murderer or a thief or an evildoer or as a meddler. ¹⁶ Yet if anyone suffers as a Christian, let him not be ashamed, but let him glorify God in that name. ¹⁷ For it is time for judgment to begin at the household of God; and if it begins with us, what will be the outcome for those who do not obey the gospel of God? ¹⁸ And

"If the righteous is scarcely saved,
    what will become of the ungodly
        and the sinner?"

¹⁹ Therefore let those who suffer according to God's will entrust their souls to a faithful Creator while doing good.

Shepherd the Flock of God

5 So I exhort the elders among you, as a fellow elder and a witness of the sufferings of Christ, as well as a partaker in the glory that is going to be revealed: ² shepherd the flock of God that is among you, exercising oversight, not under compulsion, but willingly, as God would have you; not for shameful gain, but eagerly; ³ not domineering over those in your charge, but being examples to the flock. ⁴ And when the chief Shepherd appears, you will receive the unfading crown of glory. ⁵ Likewise, you who are younger, be subject to the elders. Clothe yourselves, all of you, with humility toward one another, for "God opposes the proud but gives grace to the humble."

⁶ Humble yourselves, therefore, under the mighty hand of God so that at the proper time he may exalt you, ⁷ casting all your anxieties on him, because he cares for you. ⁸ Be sober-minded; be watchful. Your adversary the devil prowls around like a roaring lion, seeking someone to devour. ⁹ Resist him, firm in your faith, knowing that the same kinds of suffering are being experienced by your brotherhood throughout the world. ¹⁰ And after you have suffered a little while, the God of all grace, who has called you to his eternal glory in Christ, will himself restore, confirm, strengthen, and establish you. ¹¹ To him be the dominion forever and ever. Amen.

Final Greetings

¹² By Silvanus, a faithful brother as I regard him, I have written briefly to you, exhorting and declaring that this is the true grace of God. Stand firm in it. ¹³ She who is at Babylon, who is likewise chosen, sends you greetings, and so does Mark, my son. ¹⁴ Greet one another with the kiss of love.

Peace to all of you who are in Christ.

INTRODUCTION TO 2 PETER

c. A.D. **41–44**	c. A.D. **54**	c. A.D. **64–67**
Peter jailed in Jerusalem	Nero begins reign in Rome	Peter's second letter, martyrdom

AUTHOR, DATE, AND RECIPIENTS

Peter identifies himself as an "apostle of Jesus Christ" (1:1). He specifically mentions that he was an eyewitness of the transfiguration (1:16–18; see Matt. 17:1–8). Peter probably wrote this letter from prison in Rome (see 2 Pet. 1:12–15) not too long before his death by execution, sometime during A.D. 64–67. It is impossible to identify with certainty the churches Peter addresses. He may have been writing to the churches of Asia Minor, because Peter mentions that this is his second letter to these same people (3:1; see 1 Pet. 1:1–2). (On the similarities between 2 Peter 2 and Jude, see Introduction to Jude.)

THEME

God's grace in Christ truly transforms and empowers Christians to live righteously, despite opposition. This grace, introduced in 1:2–4, serves as the foundation for the whole book. The indwelling Holy Spirit produces virtuous qualities in followers of Christ (1:8–12). This results in fruitful lives.

PURPOSE AND OCCASION

Peter writes his brief, final reminder to the churches so that his readers will, by God's grace, live in a way that is pleasing to God. In doing so, Peter must also combat the false teachers who were apparently exerting pressure on the churches to depart from the true knowledge of Christ (see esp. ch. 2). The false teaching is not only a theological challenge but also a moral one, promoting some form of sexual permissiveness as a legitimate Christian lifestyle.

While the false teaching can be described based on what Peter writes, it is historically impossible to identify who the false teachers were. For example, there is no clear historical evidence that these teachers were Gnostics.

Second Peter deals with serious issues, but it is also filled with famous proverbs and wise sayings, as well as vivid poetry and imagery.

KEY THEMES

1. God, through his grace in Jesus Christ, has enabled Christians to partake of the divine nature (1:2–4).

2. God's grace results in godliness (1:5–15).

3. The revelation of truth in Christ and in Scripture is sure because it is from God and not from man (1:16–21).

4. False teachers are handed over for destruction at the hand of God (2:1–10).

5. False teachers are ethically bankrupt (2:11–22).

6. Believers must endure in the face of opposition, knowing that they are living in the last days (3:1–13).

7. The Lord is patient with his creation, but someday he will suddenly return to judge it (3:8–10).

8. God rescues the righteous (2:7–9; 3:13–18).

OUTLINE

   I. Initial Greeting (1:1–2)

  II. God's Grace in Christ Is the Source of Godly Living (1:3–11)

 III. Peter's Reminder to the Churches (1:12–21)

 IV. Evaluation of False Teachers (2:1–22)

  V. The Day of the Lord Will Surely Come (3:1–13)

 VI. Concluding Encouragements (3:14–18)

2 PETER

Greeting

1 Simeon Peter, a servant[1] and apostle of Jesus Christ,

To those who have obtained a faith of equal standing with ours by the righteousness of our God and Savior Jesus Christ:

[2] May grace and peace be multiplied to you in the knowledge of God and of Jesus our Lord.

Confirm Your Calling and Election

[3] His divine power has granted to us all things that pertain to life and godliness, through the knowledge of him who called us to his own glory and excellence, [4] by which he has granted to us his precious and very great promises, so that through them you may become partakers of the divine nature, having escaped from the corruption that is in the world because of sinful desire. [5] For this very reason, make every effort to supplement your faith with virtue, and virtue with knowledge, [6] and knowledge with self-control, and self-control with steadfastness, and steadfastness with godliness, [7] and godliness with brotherly affection, and brotherly affection with love. [8] For if these qualities are yours and are increasing, they keep you from being ineffective or unfruitful in the knowledge of our Lord Jesus Christ. [9] For whoever lacks these qualities is so nearsighted that he is blind, having forgotten that he was cleansed from his former sins. [10] Therefore, brothers,[2] be all the more diligent to confirm your calling and election, for if you practice these qualities you will never fall. [11] For in this way there will be richly provided for you an entrance into the eternal kingdom of our Lord and Savior Jesus Christ.

[12] Therefore I intend always to remind you of these qualities, though you know them and are established in the truth that you have. [13] I think it right, as long as I am in this body, to stir you up by way of reminder, [14] since I know that the putting off of my body will be soon, as our Lord Jesus Christ made clear to me. [15] And I will make every effort so that after my departure you may be able at any time to recall these things.

Christ's Glory and the Prophetic Word

[16] For we did not follow cleverly devised myths when we made known to you the power and coming of our Lord Jesus Christ, but we were eyewitnesses of his majesty. [17] For when he received honor and glory from God the Father, and the voice was borne to him by the Majestic Glory, "This is my beloved Son, with whom I am well pleased," [18] we ourselves heard this very voice borne from heaven, for we were with

GETTING THE MESSAGE

Facing death. As Peter wrote this second letter, apparently he knew that he would die soon (1:14). He was probably martyred during the persecution of Christians following the Great Fire of Rome in A.D. 64. See also 1 Pet. 4:12.

him on the holy mountain. [19] And we have the prophetic word more fully confirmed, to which you will do well to pay attention as to a lamp shining in a dark place, until the day dawns and the morning star rises in your hearts, [20] knowing this first of all, that no prophecy of Scripture comes from someone's own interpretation. [21] For no prophecy was ever produced by the will of man, but men spoke from God as they were carried along by the Holy Spirit.

False Prophets and Teachers

2 But false prophets also arose among the people, just as there will be false teachers among you, who will secretly bring in destructive heresies, even denying the Master who bought them, bringing upon themselves swift destruction. [2] And many will follow their sensuality, and because of them the way of truth will be blasphemed.

[1] Or *slave* (Greek *doulos*; see Preface) [2] Or *brothers and sisters* (see Preface)

[3] And in their greed they will exploit you with false words. Their condemnation from long ago is not idle, and their destruction is not asleep.

[4] For if God did not spare angels when they sinned, but cast them into hell and committed them to chains of gloomy darkness to be kept until the judgment; [5] if he did not spare the ancient world, but preserved Noah, a herald of righteousness, with seven others, when he brought a flood upon the world of the ungodly; [6] if by turning the cities of Sodom and Gomorrah to ashes he condemned them to extinction, making them an example of what is going to happen to the ungodly; [7] and if he rescued righteous Lot, greatly distressed by the sensual conduct of the wicked [8] (for as that righteous man lived among them day after day, he was tormenting his righteous

---

GETTING THE MESSAGE

What is a "heresy"? The word "heresy" (2:1) refers to any doctrine that contradicts the teaching of Scripture. The heresy addressed in 2 Peter also involved sexual permissiveness, greed, and dishonesty. Wrong doctrine often leads to sinful moral choices.

---

soul over their lawless deeds that he saw and heard); [9] then the Lord knows how to rescue the godly from trials, and to keep the unrighteous under punishment until the day of judgment, [10] and especially those who indulge in the lust of defiling passion and despise authority.

Bold and willful, they do not tremble as they blaspheme the glorious ones, [11] whereas angels, though greater in might and power, do not pronounce a blasphemous judgment against them before the Lord. [12] But these, like irrational animals, creatures of instinct, born to be caught and destroyed, blaspheming about matters of which they are ignorant, will also be destroyed in their destruction, [13] suffering wrong as the wage for their wrongdoing. They count it pleasure to revel in the daytime. They are blots and blemishes, reveling in their decep-

tions, while they feast with you. [14] They have eyes full of adultery, insatiable for sin. They entice unsteady souls. They have hearts trained in greed. Accursed children! [15] Forsaking the right way, they have gone astray. They have followed the way of Balaam, the son of Beor, who loved gain from wrongdoing, [16] but was rebuked for his own transgression; a speechless donkey spoke with human voice and restrained the prophet's madness.

[17] These are waterless springs and mists driven by a storm. For them the gloom of utter darkness has been reserved. [18] For, speaking loud boasts of folly, they entice by sensual passions of the flesh those who are barely escaping from those who live in error. [19] They promise them freedom, but they themselves are slaves[1] of corruption. For whatever overcomes a person, to that he is enslaved. [20] For if, after they have escaped the defilements of the world through the knowledge of our Lord and Savior Jesus Christ, they are again entangled in them and overcome, the last state has become worse for them than the first. [21] For it would have been better for them never to have known the way of righteousness than after knowing it to turn back from the holy commandment delivered to them. [22] What the true proverb says has happened to them: "The dog returns to its own vomit, and the sow, after washing herself, returns to wallow in the mire."

The Day of the Lord Will Come

3 This is now the second letter that I am writing to you, beloved. In both of them I am stirring up your sincere mind by way of reminder, [2] that you should remember the predictions of the holy prophets and the commandment of the Lord and Savior through your apostles, [3] knowing this first of all, that scoffers will come in the last days with scoffing, following their own sinful desires. [4] They will say, "Where is the promise of his coming? For ever since the fathers fell asleep, all things are continuing as they were from the beginning of creation." [5] For they deliberately overlook this fact, that the heavens existed long ago, and the earth was formed out of water and through water by the word of God, [6] and that by means of these the world that then existed was deluged with water and perished. [7] But by the

---

[1] Greek *doulos* (see Preface)

same word the heavens and earth that now exist are stored up for fire, being kept until the day of judgment and destruction of the ungodly.

[8] But do not overlook this one fact, beloved, that with the Lord one day is as a thousand years, and a thousand years as one day. [9] The Lord is not slow to fulfill his promise as some count slowness, but is patient toward you, not wishing that any should perish, but that all should reach repentance. [10] But the day of the Lord will come like a thief, and then the heavens will pass away with a roar, and the heavenly bodies will be burned up and dissolved, and the earth and the works that are done on it will be exposed.

[11] Since all these things are thus to be dissolved, what sort of people ought you to be in lives of holiness and godliness, [12] waiting for and hastening the coming of the day of God, because of which the heavens will be set on fire and dissolved, and the heavenly bodies will melt as they burn! [13] But according to his promise we are waiting for new heavens and a new earth in which righteousness dwells.

Final Words

[14] Therefore, beloved, since you are waiting for these, be diligent to be found by him without spot or blemish, and at peace. [15] And count the patience of our Lord as salvation, just as our beloved brother Paul also wrote to you according to the wisdom given him, [16] as he does in all his letters when he speaks in them of these matters. There are some things in them that are hard to understand, which the ignorant and unstable twist to

GETTING THE MESSAGE

Like a thief in the night. Peter says the return of Christ at the end of time will be unexpected, "like a thief" (3:10). Several other New Testament passages describe the Lord's return in this same way (see Matt. 24:43; 1 Thess. 5:2; Rev. 3:3). Christ's return will be a welcome surprise, however, for his true disciples.

their own destruction, as they do the other Scriptures. [17] You therefore, beloved, knowing this beforehand, take care that you are not carried away with the error of lawless people and lose your own stability. [18] But grow in the grace and knowledge of our Lord and Savior Jesus Christ. To him be the glory both now and to the day of eternity. Amen.

INTRODUCTION TO 1–3 JOHN

c. A.D. 28–33	A.D. 70	c. A.D. 85–95
Jesus' ministry, death, resurrection	Temple destroyed	John writes Gospel, letters

AUTHOR, DATE, AND RECIPIENTS

John the son of Zebedee probably wrote his three NT letters no later than the 90s A.D. He wrote from Ephesus (in present-day western Turkey), perhaps to churches like those mentioned in Rev. 2:8–3:22. John also wrote the Fourth Gospel and the book of Revelation.

THEME OF 1 JOHN

First John calls readers back to the three basics of Christian life: true doctrine, obedient living, and faithful devotion. Because "God is light" (1:5), Christ's followers overcome wicked people who oppose them. God's Son lives in and among them. He is greater than the spirit of "the antichrist" now in the world (4:3–4). Those who believe in the Son of God have assurance of eternal life (5:13).

THEME OF 2 JOHN

The focus of 2 John is living in God's love according to the truth of Jesus Christ. This love extends not only to God but to others as well. It is also wise; it does not "go on ahead" of biblical revelation (v. 9). It does not aid enemies of the gospel (vv. 10–11). Instead, Christ's followers "walk according to his commandments" (v. 6). Through faith they "win a full reward" (v. 8).

THEME OF 3 JOHN

The theme of 3 John is faithfulness despite opposition. The man who received the letter, Gaius, faces a troublemaker named Diotrephes. By "walking in the truth" (vv. 3, 4), Christians

can live out the message that John teaches in all his letters.

OUTLINE FOR 1 JOHN

I. God Is Light and Christ Is the Way (1:1–2:6)

II. The Unchanging Commandment in a Changing World (2:7–17)

III. Overcoming the Antichrist by Confessing the Son (2:18–3:10)

IV. Overcoming Evil by Listening to the Apostle (3:11–4:6)

V. The Assurance of God through the Love of God (4:7–21)

VI. Faith in the Son as the Way to Life (5:1–12)

VII. Final Call to Faith and Understanding (5:13–21)

OUTLINE FOR 2 JOHN

I. Greeting: The Elder's Love (vv. 1–3)

II. The Elder's Joy and Request (vv. 4–6)

III. The Elder's Concern (vv. 7–8)

IV. The Elder's Warning (vv. 9–11)

V. Closing: The Elder's Farewell (vv. 12–13)

OUTLINE FOR 3 JOHN

I. Greeting: The Elder's Joy at Gaius's Faithfulness (vv. 1–4)

II. Praise for Gaius's Support for Traveling Christian Workers (vv. 5–8)

III. Concern about Diotrephes (vv. 9–10)

IV. Advice and Commendation of Demetrius (vv. 11–12)

V. Closing: A Promise to Visit (vv. 13–15)

1 JOHN

The Word of Life

1 That which was from the beginning, which we have heard, which we have seen with our eyes, which we looked upon and have touched with our hands, concerning the word of life— [2] the life was made manifest, and we have seen it, and testify to it and proclaim to you the eternal life, which was with the Father and was made manifest to us— [3] that which we have seen and heard we proclaim also to you, so that you too may have fellowship with us; and indeed our fellowship is with the Father and with his Son Jesus Christ. [4] And we are writing these things so that our joy may be complete.

Walking in the Light

[5] This is the message we have heard from him and proclaim to you, that God is light, and in him is no darkness at all. [6] If we say we have fellowship with him while we walk in darkness, we lie and do not practice the truth. [7] But if we walk in the light, as he is in the light, we have fellowship with one another, and the blood of Jesus his Son cleanses us from all sin. [8] If we say we have no sin, we deceive ourselves, and the truth is not in us. [9] If we confess our sins, he is faithful and just to forgive us our sins and to cleanse us from all unrighteousness. [10] If we say we have not sinned, we make him a liar, and his word is not in us.

Christ Our Advocate

2 My little children, I am writing these things to you so that you may not sin. But if anyone does sin, we have an advocate with the Father, Jesus Christ the righteous. [2] He is the propitiation for our sins, and not for ours only but also for the sins of the whole world. [3] And by this we know that we have come to know him, if we keep his commandments. [4] Whoever says "I know him" but does not keep his commandments is a liar, and the truth is not in him, [5] but whoever keeps his word, in him truly the love of God is perfected. By this we may know that we are in him: [6] whoever says he abides in him ought to walk in the same way in which he walked.

The New Commandment

[7] Beloved, I am writing you no new commandment, but an old commandment that you had from the beginning. The old commandment is the word that you have heard. [8] At the same time, it is a new commandment that I am writing to you, which is true in him and in you, because the darkness is passing away and the true light is already shining. [9] Whoever says he is in the light

---

GETTING THE MESSAGE

Propitiation (2:2) is the appeasement of wrath. God's holy anger against sin needed to be appeased before sin could be forgiven. By dying on the cross, Christ bore God's wrath for all who trust in him (see also Rom. 3:25), giving us the ultimate example of love (1 John 4:10).

---

and hates his brother is still in darkness. [10] Whoever loves his brother abides in the light, and in him there is no cause for stumbling. [11] But whoever hates his brother is in the darkness and walks in the darkness, and does not know where he is going, because the darkness has blinded his eyes.

[12] I am writing to you, little children,
    because your sins are forgiven for
        his name's sake.
[13] I am writing to you, fathers,
    because you know him who is from
        the beginning.
I am writing to you, young men,
    because you have overcome the evil
        one.
I write to you, children,
    because you know the Father.
[14] I write to you, fathers,
    because you know him who is from
        the beginning.

I write to you, young men,
  because you are strong,
  and the word of God abides in you,
  and you have overcome the evil
    one.

Do Not Love the World

¹⁵ Do not love the world or the things in the world. If anyone loves the world, the love of the Father is not in him. ¹⁶ For all that is in the world—the desires of the flesh and the desires of the eyes and pride of life—is not from the Father but is from the world. ¹⁷ And the world is passing away along with its desires, but whoever does the will of God abides forever.

Warning Concerning Antichrists

¹⁸ Children, it is the last hour, and as you have heard that antichrist is coming, so now many antichrists have come. Therefore we know that it is the last hour. ¹⁹ They went

---

GETTING THE MESSAGE

The terms **light** and **darkness** come up often in John's writing. The light of God's truth is shining on the darkness of ignorance and sin—and the darkness is passing away (2:8-11).

---

out from us, but they were not of us; for if they had been of us, they would have continued with us. But they went out, that it might become plain that they all are not of us. ²⁰ But you have been anointed by the Holy One, and you all have knowledge. ²¹ I write to you, not because you do not know the truth, but because you know it, and because no lie is of the truth. ²² Who is the liar but he who denies that Jesus is the Christ? This is the antichrist, he who denies the Father and the Son. ²³ No one who denies the Son has the Father. Whoever confesses the Son has the Father also. ²⁴ Let what you heard from the beginning abide in you. If what you heard from the beginning abides in you, then you too will abide in the Son and in the Father. ²⁵ And this is the promise that he made to us—eternal life.

²⁶ I write these things to you about those who are trying to deceive you. ²⁷ But the anointing that you received from him abides in you, and you have no need that

anyone should teach you. But as his anointing teaches you about everything, and is true, and is no lie—just as it has taught you, abide in him.

Children of God

²⁸ And now, little children, abide in him, so that when he appears we may have confidence and not shrink from him in shame at his coming. ²⁹ If you know that he is righteous, you may be sure that everyone who practices righteousness has been born of him.

3 See what kind of love the Father has given to us, that we should be called children of God; and so we are. The reason why the world does not know us is that it did not know him. ² Beloved, we are God's children now, and what we will be has not yet appeared; but we know that when he appears we shall be like him, because we shall see him as he is. ³ And everyone who thus hopes in him purifies himself as he is pure.

⁴ Everyone who makes a practice of sinning also practices lawlessness; sin is lawlessness. ⁵ You know that he appeared in order to take away sins, and in him there is no sin. ⁶ No one who abides in him keeps on sinning; no one who keeps on sinning has either seen him or known him. ⁷ Little children, let no one deceive you. Whoever practices righteousness is righteous, as he is righteous. ⁸ Whoever makes a practice of sinning is of the devil, for the devil has been sinning from the beginning. The reason the Son of God appeared was to destroy the works of the devil. ⁹ No one born of God makes a practice of sinning, for God's seed abides in him, and he cannot keep on sinning because he has been born of God. ¹⁰ By this it is evident who are the children of God, and who are the children of the devil: whoever does not practice righteousness is not of God, nor is the one who does not love his brother.

Love One Another

¹¹ For this is the message that you have heard from the beginning, that we should love one another. ¹² We should not be like Cain, who was of the evil one and murdered his brother. And why did he murder him? Because his own deeds were evil and his brother's righteous. ¹³ Do not be surprised,

brothers,[1] that the world hates you. **14** We know that we have passed out of death into life, because we love the brothers. Whoever does not love abides in death. **15** Everyone who hates his brother is a murderer, and you know that no murderer has eternal life abiding in him.

16 By this we know love, that he laid down his life for us, and we ought to lay down our lives for the brothers. **17** But if anyone has the world's goods and sees his brother in need, yet closes his heart against him, how does God's love abide in him? **18** Little children, let us not love in word or talk but in deed and in truth.

19 By this we shall know that we are of the truth and reassure our heart before him; **20** for whenever our heart condemns us, God is greater than our heart, and he knows everything. **21** Beloved, if our heart does not condemn us, we have confidence before God; **22** and whatever we ask we receive from him, because we keep his commandments and do what pleases him. **23** And this is his commandment, that we believe in the name of his Son Jesus Christ and love one another, just as he has commanded us. **24** Whoever keeps his commandments abides in God, and God in him. And by this we know that he abides in us, by the Spirit whom he has given us.

Test the Spirits

4 Beloved, do not believe every spirit, but test the spirits to see whether they are from God, for many false prophets have gone out into the world. **2** By this you know the Spirit of God: every spirit that confesses that Jesus Christ has come in the flesh is from God, **3** and every spirit that does not confess Jesus is not from God. This is the spirit of the antichrist, which you heard was coming and now is in the world already. **4** Little children, you are from God and have overcome them, for he who is in you is greater than he who is in the world. **5** They are from the world; therefore they speak from the world, and the world listens to them. **6** We are from God. Whoever knows God listens to us; whoever is not from God does not listen to us. By this we know the Spirit of truth and the spirit of error.

God Is Love

7 Beloved, let us love one another, for love is from God, and whoever loves has been born of God and knows God. **8** Anyone who does not love does not know God, because God is love. **9** In this the love of God was made manifest among us, that God sent his only Son into the world, so that we might live through him. **10** In this is love, not that we have loved God but that he loved us and sent his Son to be the propitiation for our sins. **11** Beloved, if God so loved us, we also ought to love one another. **12** No one has ever seen God; if we love one another, God abides in us and his love is perfected in us.

13 By this we know that we abide in him and he in us, because he has given us of his Spirit. **14** And we have seen and testify

GETTING THE MESSAGE

Giving to those in need. Jews in the time of Christ were generous in giving to the needy. In fact, the Jewish historian Josephus remarked that no Jew ever needed to depend on the charity of outsiders. John encourages generosity among Christians as well (3:17).

that the Father has sent his Son to be the Savior of the world. **15** Whoever confesses that Jesus is the Son of God, God abides in him, and he in God. **16** So we have come to know and to believe the love that God has for us. God is love, and whoever abides in love abides in God, and God abides in him. **17** By this is love perfected with us, so that we may have confidence for the day of judgment, because as he is so also are we in this world. **18** There is no fear in love, but perfect love casts out fear. For fear has to do with punishment, and whoever fears has not been perfected in love. **19** We love because he first loved us. **20** If anyone says, "I love God," and hates his brother, he is a liar; for he who does not love his brother whom he has seen cannot love God whom he has not seen. **21** And this commandment we have from him: whoever loves God must also love his brother.

[1] Or brothers and sisters (see Preface); also 3:14, 16

Overcoming the World

5 Everyone who believes that Jesus is the Christ has been born of God, and everyone who loves the Father loves whoever has been born of him. **2** By this we know that we love the children of God, when we love God and obey his commandments. **3** For this is the love of God, that we keep his commandments. And his commandments are not burdensome. **4** For everyone who has been born of God overcomes the world. And this is the victory that has overcome the world—our faith. **5** Who is it that overcomes the world except the one who believes that Jesus is the Son of God?

Testimony Concerning the Son of God

6 This is he who came by water and blood—Jesus Christ; not by the water only but by the water and the blood. And the Spirit is the one who testifies, because the Spirit is the truth. **7** For there are three that testify: **8** the Spirit and the water and the blood; and these three agree. **9** If we receive the testimony of men, the testimony of God is greater, for this is the testimony of God that he has borne concerning his Son.

10 Whoever believes in the Son of God has the testimony in himself. Whoever does not believe God has made him a liar, because he has not believed in the testimony that God has borne concerning his Son. **11** And this is the testimony, that God gave us eternal life, and this life is in his Son. **12** Whoever has the Son has life; whoever does not have the Son of God does not have life.

That You May Know

13 I write these things to you who believe in the name of the Son of God that you may know that you have eternal life. **14** And this is the confidence that we have toward him, that if we ask anything according to his will he hears us. **15** And if we know that he hears us in whatever we ask, we know that we have the requests that we have asked of him.

16 If anyone sees his brother committing a sin not leading to death, he shall ask, and God will give him life—to those who commit sins that do not lead to death. There is sin that leads to death; I do not say that one should pray for that. **17** All wrongdoing is sin, but there is sin that does not lead to death.

18 We know that everyone who has been born of God does not keep on sinning, but he who was born of God protects him, and the evil one does not touch him.

19 We know that we are from God, and the whole world lies in the power of the evil one.

20 And we know that the Son of God has come and has given us understanding, so that we may know him who is true; and we are in him who is true, in his Son Jesus Christ. He is the true God and eternal life. **21** Little children, keep yourselves from idols.

2 JOHN

Greeting

¹ The elder to the elect lady and her children, whom I love in truth, and not only I, but also all who know the truth, ² because of the truth that abides in us and will be with us forever:

³ Grace, mercy, and peace will be with us, from God the Father and from Jesus Christ the Father's Son, in truth and love.

GETTING THE MESSAGE

The elder (v. 1) is clearly a self-description of the apostle John. "Elder" was a common term for a pastoral leader in the early church (see Titus 1:5; 1 Pet. 5:1). Although "elder" does not imply "elderly," John himself was probably quite old when he wrote this letter.

Walking in Truth and Love

⁴ I rejoiced greatly to find some of your children walking in the truth, just as we were commanded by the Father. ⁵ And now I ask you, dear lady—not as though I were writing you a new commandment, but the one we have had from the beginning—that we love one another. ⁶ And this is love, that we walk according to his commandments; this is the commandment, just as you have heard from the beginning, so that you should walk in it. ⁷ For many deceivers have gone out into the world, those who do not confess the coming of Jesus Christ in the flesh. Such a one is the deceiver and the antichrist. ⁸ Watch yourselves, so that you may not lose what we have worked for, but may win a full reward. ⁹ Everyone who goes on ahead and does not abide in the teaching of Christ, does not have God. Whoever abides in the teaching has both the Father and the Son. ¹⁰ If anyone comes to you and does not bring this teaching, do not receive him into your house or give him any greeting, ¹¹ for whoever greets him takes part in his wicked works.

Final Greetings

¹² Though I have much to write to you, I would rather not use paper and ink. Instead I hope to come to you and talk face to face, so that our joy may be complete.

¹³ The children of your elect sister greet you.

3 JOHN

Greeting

¹The elder to the beloved Gaius, whom I love in truth.

²Beloved, I pray that all may go well with you and that you may be in good health, as it goes well with your soul. ³For I rejoiced greatly when the brothers¹ came and testified

to your truth, as indeed you are walking in the truth. ⁴I have no greater joy than to hear that my children are walking in the truth.

Support and Opposition

⁵Beloved, it is a faithful thing you do in all your efforts for these brothers, strangers as they are, ⁶who testified to your love before the church. You will do well to send them on their journey in a manner worthy of God. ⁷For they have gone out for the sake of the name, accepting nothing from the Gentiles. ⁸Therefore we ought to support people like these, that we may be fellow workers for the truth.

⁹I have written something to the church, but Diotrephes, who likes to put himself first, does not acknowledge our authority. ¹⁰So if I come, I will bring up what he is doing, talking wicked nonsense against us. And not content with that, he refuses to welcome the brothers, and also stops those who want to and puts them out of the church.

¹¹Beloved, do not imitate evil but imitate good. Whoever does good is from God; whoever does evil has not seen God. ¹²Demetrius has received a good testimony from everyone, and from the truth itself. We also add our testimony, and you know that our testimony is true.

Final Greetings

¹³I had much to write to you, but I would rather not write with pen and ink. ¹⁴I hope to see you soon, and we will talk face to face.

¹⁵Peace be to you. The friends greet you. Greet the friends, each by name.

---

¹Or brothers and sisters (see Preface); also 5, 10

INTRODUCTION TO JUDE

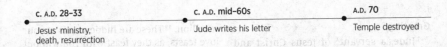

C. A.D. 28–33	C. A.D. mid-60s	A.D. 70
Jesus' ministry, death, resurrection	Jude writes his letter	Temple destroyed

AUTHOR, DATE, AND RECIPIENTS

The book was written by Jude, the brother of James and Jesus (see Matt. 13:55; Mark 6:3, where "Judas" is the same in Greek as "Jude"). Jude was probably written in the mid-60s A.D. Considering the letter's apparent Jewish perspective, Jude's audience was probably Jewish Christians, or a mixture of Jewish and Gentile readers where the Gentiles were familiar with Jewish traditions.

Since Jude addresses a situation similar to the one addressed by 2 Peter and exhibits a literary relationship to ch. 2 of that letter (Jude may have been a source for 2 Peter), the two letters are commonly dated in fairly close proximity, even though evidence for the date of writing within the book of Jude is sparse.

THEME

The church must defend the one true faith (v. 3). Believers must be faithful to the end by resisting false teachers and following the truth.

PURPOSE, OCCASION, AND BACKGROUND

Jude warns against following false teachers who have infiltrated the church and are distorting the one true faith. Jude calls the church to defend the truth aggressively against such false teaching.

While the false teachers of Jude were profoundly libertine (morally unrestrained), it would be historically inaccurate to argue that they were Gnostics. This heretical sect (or group of sects) was influential primarily from the second century A.D. onward.

Jude accomplishes his purpose by drawing analogies with OT events, using the same principles of interpretation found in 2 Peter (and elsewhere in the NT). He also draws on Jewish apocalyptic traditions from nonbiblical literature (he refers to 1 Enoch and the Testament of Moses) in building his case. Thus, as literature, Jude has a distinctively Jewish flavor.

The format is of a NT epistle (letter), with its loose divisions of salutation, body, and closing. But the central unit of the letter (vv. 5–16) fits the style of a judgment oracle: it has an object of attack, an attack coming from several directions, a harsh tone, and an implied standard on which the attack is being conducted ("the faith that was once for all delivered to the saints"; v. 3). The description of those who left the faith (vv. 8–16) provides a picture of their character and actions. The use of images and allusions (e.g., to Sodom and Gomorrah and the archangel Michael) lends a poetic quality to the letter.

The writer displays horror over the apostasy and the false teachers who have caused it. The only NT passage that goes beyond Jude in these traits is Jesus' denunciation of the religious leaders in Matthew 23. But this letter begins with the usual soothing notes of NT epistles, and in the last two verses it becomes one of the most moving benedictions in the NT.

KEY THEMES

1. Christians need to defend the doctrines of the faith (v. 3).

2. False teachers may be identified by their immoral character (vv. 4, 8, 10, 12–13, 16, 18–19).

3. God will judge false teachers (vv. 4, 5–7, 11, 14–15).

4. Saints must endure to be saved (vv. 17–23).

5. As God grants mercy to those who are called, they must show mercy to others (vv. 2, 21–23).

6. God grants the grace to ensure that his people will persevere (vv. 1–2, 24–25).

OUTLINE

THE LETTER OF
JUDE

Greeting

¹Jude, a servant[1] of Jesus Christ and brother of James,

To those who are called, beloved in God the Father and kept for Jesus Christ:

²May mercy, peace, and love be multiplied to you.

Judgment on False Teachers

³Beloved, although I was very eager to write to you about our common salvation, I found it necessary to write appealing to you to contend for the faith that was once for all delivered to the saints. ⁴For certain people have crept in unnoticed who long ago were designated for this condemnation, ungodly people, who pervert the grace of our God into sensuality and deny our only Master and Lord, Jesus Christ.

⁵Now I want to remind you, although you once fully knew it, that Jesus, who saved a people out of the land of Egypt, afterward destroyed those who did not believe. ⁶And the angels who did not stay within their own position of authority, but left their proper dwelling, he has kept in eternal chains under gloomy darkness until the judgment of the great day— ⁷just as Sodom and Gomorrah and the surrounding cities, which likewise indulged in sexual immorality and pursued unnatural desire, serve as an example by undergoing a punishment of eternal fire.

⁸Yet in like manner these people also, relying on their dreams, defile the flesh, reject authority, and blaspheme the glorious ones. ⁹But when the archangel Michael, contending with the devil, was disputing about the body of Moses, he did not presume to pronounce a blasphemous judgment, but said, "The Lord rebuke you." ¹⁰But these people blaspheme all that they do not understand, and they are destroyed by all that they, like unreasoning animals, understand instinctively. ¹¹Woe to them! For they walked in the way of Cain and abandoned themselves for the sake of gain to Balaam's error and perished in Korah's rebellion. ¹²These are hidden reefs at your love feasts, as they feast with you without fear, shepherds feeding themselves; waterless clouds, swept along by winds; fruitless trees in late autumn, twice dead, uprooted; ¹³wild waves of the sea, casting up the foam of their own shame; wandering stars, for whom the gloom of utter darkness has been reserved forever.

¹⁴It was also about these that Enoch, the seventh from Adam, prophesied, saying, "Behold, the Lord comes with ten thousands of his holy ones, ¹⁵to execute judgment on all and to convict all the ungodly of all their

GETTING THE MESSAGE

Michael (v. 9) is the only archangel identified by name in Scripture. In the book of Daniel, he is the guardian of God's people (Dan. 10:13, 21; 12:1). He also leads the heavenly army in the fight against the dragon in Rev. 12:7.

deeds of ungodliness that they have committed in such an ungodly way, and of all the harsh things that ungodly sinners have spoken against him." ¹⁶These are grumblers, malcontents, following their own sinful desires; they are loud-mouthed boasters, showing favoritism to gain advantage.

A Call to Persevere

¹⁷But you must remember, beloved, the predictions of the apostles of our Lord Jesus Christ. ¹⁸They said to you, "In the last time there will be scoffers, following their own ungodly passions." ¹⁹It is these who cause divisions, worldly people, devoid of the Spirit. ²⁰But you, beloved, building yourselves up in your most holy faith and praying in the Holy Spirit, ²¹keep yourselves in the love of God, waiting for the mercy of our Lord Jesus Christ that leads to eternal life. ²²And have mercy on those who doubt; ²³save others by snatching them out of the

---

[1] Or *slave* (Greek *doulos*; see Preface)

fire; to others show mercy with fear, hating even the garment stained by the flesh.

Doxology

24 Now to him who is able to keep you from stumbling and to present you blameless before the presence of his glory with great joy, 25 to the only God, our Savior, through Jesus Christ our Lord, be glory, majesty, dominion, and authority, before all time and now and forever. Amen.

INTRODUCTION TO REVELATION

C. A.D. **28–33**	A.D. **70**	C. A.D. **95–96**
Jesus' ministry, death, resurrection	Temple destroyed	John writes Revelation

AUTHOR AND DATE

Jesus Christ is the divine author of this "revelation" (1:1). He describes coming events to his servant John. John, son of Zebedee, was the "beloved disciple" who also wrote the Fourth Gospel and 1, 2, and 3 John. Most scholars believe John recorded these visions while imprisoned on the island of Patmos in the mid-90s A.D. Revelation is addressed specifically to seven first-century churches in the Roman province of Asia (now western Turkey), but the message is for all churches everywhere.

THEME

The word "Revelation" translates the Greek word *apokalypsis*, which means "disclosure" or "unveiling." Revelation unveils the unseen spiritual war in which the church is engaged: the cosmic conflict between God and his Christ on the one hand, and Satan and his evil allies (both demonic and human) on the other. In this conflict, Jesus the Lamb has already won the decisive victory through his sacrificial death, but his church continues to be assaulted by the dragon, in its death-throes, through persecution (the beast), deceptive heresy (the false prophet), and the allure of material affluence and cultural approval (the prostitute). By revealing the spiritual realities behind the church's trials and temptations, and by affirming the certainty of Christ's triumph in the new heaven and earth, the visions of Revelation fortify believers to endure suffering. The reader of Revelation is encouraged to stay pure from the defiling enticements of the present world order.

KEY THEMES

1. Through his sacrificial death, Jesus Christ has conquered Satan, the accuser. Jesus has redeemed people from every nation to become a kingdom of priests, gladly serving in God's presence (1:5, 18; 5:5–10; 12:1–11).

2. Jesus Christ is present among his churches through his Holy Spirit. He knows their trials, triumphs, and failures (1:12–3:22).

3. World history, including its disasters, is under the control of Jesus, the victorious Lamb (5:1–8:1).

4. God is presently holding back his wrath and preventing his enemies' efforts to destroy the church. He patiently gathers his redeemed people through their witness for Jesus (6:5–11; 7:1–3; 8:6–12; 9:4–6, 18; 11:3–7; 12:6, 13–17).

5. Present disasters are warnings of increasing judgments to come (6:3–17; 8:6–13; 11:13; 16:1–21; 20:11–15).

6. Believers will continue their faithful testimony to the death. They will conquer both the dragon and the beast. The martyrs' victory is now hidden, but it will be obvious when Christ returns (2:10–11, 26–29; 3:11–13; 6:9–11; 7:9–17; 11:7–12, 17–18; 12:10–11; 14:1–5; 15:2–4; 20:4–6).

7. Satan attacks the church's perseverance and purity through persecution, deceptive teaching, and the temptations of wealth and sensual pleasure (2:1–3:22; 13:1–18; 17:1–18:24).

8. At the end of the age, the church's opponents will increase their persecution. Jesus, the triumphant Word of God, will defeat and destroy all his enemies. The old heaven and earth, marked by sin and suffering, will be replaced by the new heaven and earth. The church will be presented as a pure bride to her husband, the Lamb (16:12–16; 19:11–21; 20:7–22:5).

OUTLINE

Revelation contains four series of seven messages or visions. These include letters to churches (chs. 2–3), seals on a scroll (4:1–8:1), trumpets (8:2–11:19), and bowls of wrath (chs. 15–16). There is a general movement from "the things that are" to "the things that are to take place after this." Yet the visions sometimes return to subjects from the previous sections.

The order in which John received the visions does not necessarily indicate the order of the events they symbolize.

THE
REVELATION
TO JOHN

Prologue

1 The revelation of Jesus Christ, which God gave him to show to his servants[1] the things that must soon take place. He made it known by sending his angel to his servant John, [2] who bore witness to the word of God and to the testimony of Jesus Christ, even to all that he saw. [3] Blessed is the one who reads aloud the words of this prophecy, and blessed are those who hear, and who keep what is written in it, for the time is near.

Greeting to the Seven Churches

[4] John to the seven churches that are in Asia:

Grace to you and peace from him who is and who was and who is to come, and from the seven spirits who are before his throne, [5] and from Jesus Christ the faithful witness, the firstborn of the dead, and the ruler of kings on earth.

To him who loves us and has freed us from our sins by his blood [6] and made us a kingdom, priests to his God and Father, to him be glory and dominion forever and ever. Amen. [7] Behold, he is coming with the clouds, and every eye will see him, even those who pierced him, and all tribes of the earth will wail on account of him. Even so. Amen.

[8] "I am the Alpha and the Omega," says the Lord God, "who is and who was and who is to come, the Almighty."

Vision of the Son of Man

[9] I, John, your brother and partner in the tribulation and the kingdom and the patient endurance that are in Jesus, was on the island called Patmos on account of the word of God and the testimony of Jesus. [10] I was in the Spirit on the Lord's day, and I heard behind me a loud voice like a trumpet [11] saying, "Write what you see in a book and send it to the seven churches, to Ephesus and to Smyrna and to Pergamum and to Thyatira and to Sardis and to Philadelphia and to Laodicea."

[12] Then I turned to see the voice that was speaking to me, and on turning I saw seven golden lampstands, [13] and in the midst of the lampstands one like a son of man, clothed with a long robe and with a golden sash around his chest. [14] The hairs of his head were white, like white wool, like snow. His eyes were like a flame of fire, [15] his feet were like burnished bronze, refined in a furnace, and his voice was like the roar of many waters. [16] In his right hand he held seven stars, from his mouth came a sharp two-edged sword, and his face was like the sun shining in full strength.

[17] When I saw him, I fell at his feet as though dead. But he laid his right hand on me, saying, "Fear not, I am the first and the last, [18] and the living one. I died, and behold I am alive forevermore, and I have the keys of Death and Hades. [19] Write therefore the things that you have seen, those that are and those that are to take place after this. [20] As for the mystery of the seven stars that you saw in my right hand, and the seven golden lampstands, the seven stars are the angels of the seven churches, and the seven lampstands are the seven churches.

To the Church in Ephesus

2 "To the angel of the church in Ephesus write: 'The words of him who holds the seven stars in his right hand, who walks among the seven golden lampstands.

[2] "'I know your works, your toil and your patient endurance, and how you cannot bear with those who are evil, but have tested

---

[1] Greek *doulos* (see Preface)

those who call themselves apostles and are not, and found them to be false. ³ I know you are enduring patiently and bearing up for my name's sake, and you have not grown weary. ⁴ But I have this against you, that you have abandoned the love you had at first. ⁵ Remember therefore from where you have fallen; repent, and do the works you did at first. If not, I will come to you and remove your lampstand from its place, unless you repent. ⁶ Yet this you have: you hate the works of the Nicolaitans, which I also hate. ⁷ He who has an ear, let him hear what the Spirit says to the churches. To the one who conquers I will grant to eat of the tree of life, which is in the paradise of God.'

To the Church in Smyrna

⁸ "And to the angel of the church in Smyrna write: 'The words of the first and the last, who died and came to life.

⁹ "'I know your tribulation and your poverty (but you are rich) and the slander of those who say that they are Jews and are not, but are a synagogue of Satan. ¹⁰ Do not fear what you are about to suffer. Behold, the devil is about to throw some of you into prison, that you may be tested, and for ten days you will have tribulation. Be faithful unto death, and I will give you the crown of life. ¹¹ He who has an ear, let him hear what the Spirit says to the churches. The one who conquers will not be hurt by the second death.'

To the Church in Pergamum

¹² "And to the angel of the church in Pergamum write: 'The words of him who has the sharp two-edged sword.

¹³ "'I know where you dwell, where Satan's throne is. Yet you hold fast my name, and you did not deny my faith even in the days of Antipas my faithful witness, who was killed among you, where Satan dwells. ¹⁴ But I have a few things against you: you have some there who hold the teaching of Balaam, who taught Balak to put a stumbling block before the sons of Israel, so that they might eat food sacrificed to idols and practice sexual immorality. ¹⁵ So also you have some who hold the teaching of the Nicolaitans. ¹⁶ Therefore repent. If not, I will come to you soon and war against them with the sword of my mouth. ¹⁷ He

who has an ear, let him hear what the Spirit says to the churches. To the one who conquers I will give some of the hidden manna, and I will give him a white stone, with a new name written on the stone that no one knows except the one who receives it.'

To the Church in Thyatira

¹⁸ "And to the angel of the church in Thyatira write: 'The words of the Son of God, who has eyes like a flame of fire, and whose feet are like burnished bronze.

¹⁹ "'I know your works, your love and faith and service and patient endurance, and that your latter works exceed the first. ²⁰ But I have this against you, that you tolerate that woman Jezebel, who calls herself a prophetess and is teaching and seducing my servants[1] to practice sexual immorality and to eat food sacrificed to idols. ²¹ I gave her time to repent, but she refuses to repent

GETTING THE MESSAGE

Pergamum was an important city in western Asia Minor. Between 150,000 and 200,000 lived there. Located atop a high hill overlooking the Caicus River, it boasted a theater, an impressive library, many temples, and a race track.

of her sexual immorality. ²² Behold, I will throw her onto a sickbed, and those who commit adultery with her I will throw into great tribulation, unless they repent of her works, ²³ and I will strike her children dead. And all the churches will know that I am he who searches mind and heart, and I will give to each of you according to your works. ²⁴ But to the rest of you in Thyatira, who do not hold this teaching, who have not learned what some call the deep things of Satan, to you I say, I do not lay on you any other burden. ²⁵ Only hold fast what you have until I come. ²⁶ The one who conquers and who keeps my works until the end, to him I will give authority over the nations, ²⁷ and he will rule them with a rod of iron, as when earthen pots are broken in pieces, even as I myself have received authority from my Father. ²⁸ And I will give him the morning star. ²⁹ He who has an ear, let him hear what the Spirit says to the churches.'

[1] Greek *doulos* (see Preface)

To the Church in Sardis

3 "And to the angel of the church in Sardis write: 'The words of him who has the seven spirits of God and the seven stars.

" 'I know your works. You have the reputation of being alive, but you are dead. ²Wake up, and strengthen what remains and is about to die, for I have not found your works complete in the sight of my God. ³Remember, then, what you received and heard. Keep it, and repent. If you will not wake up, I will come like a thief, and you will not know at what hour I will come against you. ⁴Yet you have still a few names in Sardis, people who have not soiled their garments, and they will walk with me in white, for they are worthy. ⁵The one who conquers will be clothed thus in white garments, and I will never blot his name out of the book of life. I will confess his name

> ### GETTING THE MESSAGE
>
> **Sardis** was the capital of the ancient kingdom of Lydia and the place where coin minting was invented. After being taken over by Rome, it functioned as the capital of its province and continued to exist until the fifteenth century.

before my Father and before his angels. ⁶He who has an ear, let him hear what the Spirit says to the churches.'

To the Church in Philadelphia

⁷"And to the angel of the church in Philadelphia write: 'The words of the holy one, the true one, who has the key of David, who opens and no one will shut, who shuts and no one opens.

⁸" 'I know your works. Behold, I have set before you an open door, which no one is able to shut. I know that you have but little power, and yet you have kept my word and have not denied my name. ⁹Behold, I will make those of the synagogue of Satan who say that they are Jews and are not, but lie— behold, I will make them come and bow down before your feet, and they will learn that I have loved you. ¹⁰Because you have kept my word about patient endurance, I will keep you from the hour of trial that is coming on the whole world, to try those

who dwell on the earth. ¹¹I am coming soon. Hold fast what you have, so that no one may seize your crown. ¹²The one who conquers, I will make him a pillar in the temple of my God. Never shall he go out of it, and I will write on him the name of my God, and the name of the city of my God, the new Jerusalem, which comes down from my God out of heaven, and my own new name. ¹³He who has an ear, let him hear what the Spirit says to the churches.'

To the Church in Laodicea

¹⁴"And to the angel of the church in Laodicea write: 'The words of the Amen, the faithful and true witness, the beginning of God's creation.

¹⁵" 'I know your works: you are neither cold nor hot. Would that you were either cold or hot! ¹⁶So, because you are lukewarm, and neither hot nor cold, I will spit you out of my mouth. ¹⁷For you say, I am rich, I have prospered, and I need nothing, not realizing that you are wretched, pitiable, poor, blind, and naked. ¹⁸I counsel you to buy from me gold refined by fire, so that you may be rich, and white garments so that you may clothe yourself and the shame of your nakedness may not be seen, and salve to anoint your eyes, so that you may see. ¹⁹Those whom I love, I reprove and discipline, so be zealous and repent. ²⁰Behold, I stand at the door and knock. If anyone hears my voice and opens the door, I will come in to him and eat with him, and he with me. ²¹The one who conquers, I will grant him to sit with me on my throne, as I also conquered and sat down with my Father on his throne. ²²He who has an ear, let him hear what the Spirit says to the churches.' "

The Throne in Heaven

4 After this I looked, and behold, a door standing open in heaven! And the first voice, which I had heard speaking to me like a trumpet, said, "Come up here, and I will show you what must take place after this." ²At once I was in the Spirit, and behold, a throne stood in heaven, with one seated on the throne. ³And he who sat there had the appearance of jasper and carnelian, and around the throne was a rainbow that had the appearance of an emerald. ⁴Around the throne were twenty-four thrones, and seated on the thrones were twenty-four

elders, clothed in white garments, with golden crowns on their heads. **5** From the throne came flashes of lightning, and rumblings and peals of thunder, and before the throne were burning seven torches of fire, which are the seven spirits of God, **6** and before the throne there was as it were a sea of glass, like crystal.

And around the throne, on each side of the throne, are four living creatures, full of eyes in front and behind: **7** the first living creature like a lion, the second living creature like an ox, the third living creature with the face of a man, and the fourth living creature like an eagle in flight. **8** And the four living creatures, each of them with six wings, are full of eyes all around and within, and day and night they never cease to say,

"Holy, holy, holy, is the Lord God
　　　Almighty,
　who was and is and is to come!"

9 And whenever the living creatures give glory and honor and thanks to him who is seated on the throne, who lives forever and ever, **10** the twenty-four elders fall down before him who is seated on the throne and worship him who lives forever and ever. They cast their crowns before the throne, saying,

11　"Worthy are you, our Lord and God,
　　　to receive glory and honor and
　　　　　power,
　　for you created all things,
　　　and by your will they existed and
　　　　　were created."

The Scroll and the Lamb

5 Then I saw in the right hand of him who was seated on the throne a scroll written within and on the back, sealed with seven seals. **2** And I saw a mighty angel proclaiming with a loud voice, "Who is worthy to open the scroll and break its seals?" **3** And no one in heaven or on earth or under the earth was able to open the scroll or to look into it, **4** and I began to weep loudly because no one was found worthy to open the scroll or to look into it. **5** And one of the elders said to me, "Weep no more; behold, the Lion of the tribe of Judah, the Root of David, has conquered, so that he can open the scroll and its seven seals."

6 And between the throne and the four living creatures and among the elders I saw a Lamb standing, as though it had been slain, with seven horns and with seven eyes, which are the seven spirits of God sent out into all the earth. **7** And he went and took the scroll from the right hand of him who was seated on the throne. **8** And when he had taken the scroll, the four living creatures and the twenty-four elders fell down before the Lamb, each holding a harp, and golden bowls full of incense, which are the prayers of the saints. **9** And they sang a new song, saying,

"Worthy are you to take the scroll
　and to open its seals,
　for you were slain, and by your blood
　　you ransomed people for God
　　　from every tribe and language and
　　　　people and nation,

GETTING THE MESSAGE

"Do not harm the oil and wine" suggests that during this time of famine these two basic essentials are still available, although grain is scarce and prices are greatly inflated (6:6). Such a situation would necessarily hurt the poor more than the rich.

10　　and you have made them a kingdom
　　　　and priests to our God,
　　　　and they shall reign on the earth."

11 Then I looked, and I heard around the throne and the living creatures and the elders the voice of many angels, numbering myriads of myriads and thousands of thousands, **12** saying with a loud voice,

"Worthy is the Lamb who was slain,
　to receive power and wealth and wisdom and might
　　and honor and glory and blessing!"

13 And I heard every creature in heaven and on earth and under the earth and in the sea, and all that is in them, saying,

"To him who sits on the throne and to
　　the Lamb
　be blessing and honor and glory and
　　might forever and ever!"

[14] And the four living creatures said, "Amen!" and the elders fell down and worshiped.

The Seven Seals

6 Now I watched when the Lamb opened one of the seven seals, and I heard one of the four living creatures say with a voice like thunder, "Come!" [2] And I looked, and behold, a white horse! And its rider had a bow, and a crown was given to him, and he came out conquering, and to conquer.

[3] When he opened the second seal, I heard the second living creature say, "Come!" [4] And out came another horse, bright red. Its rider was permitted to take peace from the earth, so that people should slay one another, and he was given a great sword.

[5] When he opened the third seal, I heard the third living creature say, "Come!" And I looked, and behold, a black horse! And its rider had a pair of scales in his hand. [6] And

> ### GETTING THE MESSAGE
>
> Kings authenticated documents and marked ownership of an item with their royal signet ring. Similarly, **the seal of the living God** proves God's ownership and protection of his people (7:2; see 14:1). It is the opposite of the mark of the beast (13:16).

I heard what seemed to be a voice in the midst of the four living creatures, saying, "A quart of wheat for a denarius, and three quarts of barley for a denarius, and do not harm the oil and wine!"

[7] When he opened the fourth seal, I heard the voice of the fourth living creature say, "Come!" [8] And I looked, and behold, a pale horse! And its rider's name was Death, and Hades followed him. And they were given authority over a fourth of the earth, to kill with sword and with famine and with pestilence and by wild beasts of the earth.

[9] When he opened the fifth seal, I saw under the altar the souls of those who had been slain for the word of God and for the witness they had borne. [10] They cried out with a loud voice, "O Sovereign Lord, holy and true, how long before you will judge and avenge our blood on those who dwell on the earth?" [11] Then they were each given a white robe and told to rest a little longer, until the number of their fellow servants[1] and their brothers[2] should be complete, who were to be killed as they themselves had been.

[12] When he opened the sixth seal, I looked, and behold, there was a great earthquake, and the sun became black as sackcloth, the full moon became like blood, [13] and the stars of the sky fell to the earth as the fig tree sheds its winter fruit when shaken by a gale. [14] The sky vanished like a scroll that is being rolled up, and every mountain and island was removed from its place. [15] Then the kings of the earth and the great ones and the generals and the rich and the powerful, and everyone, slave[3] and free, hid themselves in the caves and among the rocks of the mountains, [16] calling to the mountains and rocks, "Fall on us and hide us from the face of him who is seated on the throne, and from the wrath of the Lamb, [17] for the great day of their wrath has come, and who can stand?"

The 144,000 of Israel Sealed

7 After this I saw four angels standing at the four corners of the earth, holding back the four winds of the earth, that no wind might blow on earth or sea or against any tree. [2] Then I saw another angel ascending from the rising of the sun, with the seal of the living God, and he called with a loud voice to the four angels who had been given power to harm earth and sea, [3] saying, "Do not harm the earth or the sea or the trees, until we have sealed the servants[4] of our God on their foreheads." [4] And I heard the number of the sealed, 144,000, sealed from every tribe of the sons of Israel:

[5]   12,000 from the tribe of Judah were
            sealed,
        12,000 from the tribe of Reuben,
        12,000 from the tribe of Gad,
[6]   12,000 from the tribe of Asher,
        12,000 from the tribe of Naphtali,
        12,000 from the tribe of Manasseh,
[7]   12,000 from the tribe of Simeon,
        12,000 from the tribe of Levi,
        12,000 from the tribe of Issachar,
[8]   12,000 from the tribe of Zebulun,

---

[1] Greek sundoulos (see Preface) [2] Or brothers and sisters (see Preface) [3] Greek doulos (see Preface) [4] Greek doulos (see Preface)

12,000 from the tribe of Joseph,
 12,000 from the tribe of Benjamin
  were sealed.

A Great Multitude from Every Nation

⁹ After this I looked, and behold, a great multitude that no one could number, from every nation, from all tribes and peoples and languages, standing before the throne and before the Lamb, clothed in white robes, with palm branches in their hands, ¹⁰ and crying out with a loud voice, "Salvation belongs to our God who sits on the throne, and to the Lamb!" ¹¹ And all the angels were standing around the throne and around the elders and the four living creatures, and they fell on their faces before the throne and worshiped God, ¹² saying, "Amen! Blessing and glory and wisdom and thanksgiving and honor and power and might be to our God forever and ever! Amen."

¹³ Then one of the elders addressed me, saying, "Who are these, clothed in white robes, and from where have they come?" ¹⁴ I said to him, "Sir, you know." And he said to me, "These are the ones coming out of the great tribulation. They have washed their robes and made them white in the blood of the Lamb.

¹⁵ "Therefore they are before the throne
  of God,
    and serve him day and night in his
     temple;
    and he who sits on the throne will
     shelter them with his presence.
¹⁶ They shall hunger no more, neither
     thirst anymore;
    the sun shall not strike them,
     nor any scorching heat.
¹⁷ For the Lamb in the midst of the
     throne will be their shepherd,
    and he will guide them to springs of
     living water,
    and God will wipe away every tear
     from their eyes."

The Seventh Seal and the Golden Censer

8 When the Lamb opened the seventh seal, there was silence in heaven for about half an hour. ² Then I saw the seven angels who stand before God, and seven trumpets were given to them. ³ And another angel came and stood at the altar with a golden censer, and he was given much incense to offer with the prayers of all the saints on the golden altar before the throne, ⁴ and the smoke of the incense, with the prayers of the saints, rose before God from the hand of the angel. ⁵ Then the angel took the censer and filled it with fire from the altar and threw it on the earth, and there were peals of thunder, rumblings, flashes of lightning, and an earthquake.

The Seven Trumpets

⁶ Now the seven angels who had the seven trumpets prepared to blow them.

⁷ The first angel blew his trumpet, and there followed hail and fire, mixed with blood, and these were thrown upon the earth. And a third of the earth was burned up, and a third of the trees were burned up, and all green grass was burned up.

> ### GETTING THE MESSAGE
>
> In Old Testament times, **the altar of incense** (8:3–4) stood in the Holy Place of the tabernacle and the temple next to the veil concealing the Most Holy Place. Each morning and evening, the high priest burned incense on the altar (Ex. 30:1–10).

⁸ The second angel blew his trumpet, and something like a great mountain, burning with fire, was thrown into the sea, and a third of the sea became blood. ⁹ A third of the living creatures in the sea died, and a third of the ships were destroyed.

¹⁰ The third angel blew his trumpet, and a great star fell from heaven, blazing like a torch, and it fell on a third of the rivers and on the springs of water. ¹¹ The name of the star is Wormwood.[1] A third of the waters became wormwood, and many people died from the water, because it had been made bitter.

¹² The fourth angel blew his trumpet, and a third of the sun was struck, and a third of the moon, and a third of the stars, so that a third of their light might be darkened, and a third of the day might be kept from shining, and likewise a third of the night.

¹³ Then I looked, and I heard an eagle crying with a loud voice as it flew directly

---

[1] *Wormwood* is the name of a plant and the bitter-tasting liquid that comes from it

overhead, "Woe, woe, woe to those who dwell on the earth, at the blasts of the other trumpets that the three angels are about to blow!"

9 And the fifth angel blew his trumpet, and I saw a star fallen from heaven to earth, and he was given the key to the shaft of the bottomless pit. ² He opened the shaft of the bottomless pit, and from the shaft rose smoke like the smoke of a great furnace, and the sun and the air were darkened with the smoke from the shaft. ³ Then from the smoke came locusts on the earth, and they were given power like the power of scorpions of the earth. ⁴ They were told not to harm the grass of the earth or any green plant or any tree, but only those people who do not have the seal of God on their foreheads. ⁵ They were allowed to torment them for five months, but not to kill them, and their

GETTING THE MESSAGE

About a dozen varieties of **scorpions** exist in Israel. The Lord protected Israel from scorpions during their time in the wilderness (Deut. 8:15). Revelation 9:1–6 compares the demons tormenting the people of earth with scorpions.

torment was like the torment of a scorpion when it stings someone. ⁶ And in those days people will seek death and will not find it. They will long to die, but death will flee from them.

⁷ In appearance the locusts were like horses prepared for battle: on their heads were what looked like crowns of gold; their faces were like human faces, ⁸ their hair like women's hair, and their teeth like lions' teeth; ⁹ they had breastplates like breastplates of iron, and the noise of their wings was like the noise of many chariots with horses rushing into battle. ¹⁰ They have tails and stings like scorpions, and their power to hurt people for five months is in their tails. ¹¹ They have as king over them the angel of the bottomless pit. His name in Hebrew is Abaddon, and in Greek he is called Apollyon.[1]

¹² The first woe has passed; behold, two woes are still to come.

¹³ Then the sixth angel blew his trumpet, and I heard a voice from the four horns of the golden altar before God, ¹⁴ saying to the sixth angel who had the trumpet, "Release the four angels who are bound at the great river Euphrates." ¹⁵ So the four angels, who had been prepared for the hour, the day, the month, and the year, were released to kill a third of mankind. ¹⁶ The number of mounted troops was twice ten thousand times ten thousand; I heard their number. ¹⁷ And this is how I saw the horses in my vision and those who rode them: they wore breastplates the color of fire and of sapphire and of sulfur, and the heads of the horses were like lions' heads, and fire and smoke and sulfur came out of their mouths. ¹⁸ By these three plagues a third of mankind was killed, by the fire and smoke and sulfur coming out of their mouths. ¹⁹ For the power of the horses is in their mouths and in their tails, for their tails are like serpents with heads, and by means of them they wound.

²⁰ The rest of mankind, who were not killed by these plagues, did not repent of the works of their hands nor give up worshiping demons and idols of gold and silver and bronze and stone and wood, which cannot see or hear or walk, ²¹ nor did they repent of their murders or their sorceries or their sexual immorality or their thefts.

The Angel and the Little Scroll

10 Then I saw another mighty angel coming down from heaven, wrapped in a cloud, with a rainbow over his head, and his face was like the sun, and his legs like pillars of fire. ² He had a little scroll open in his hand. And he set his right foot on the sea, and his left foot on the land, ³ and called out with a loud voice, like a lion roaring. When he called out, the seven thunders sounded. ⁴ And when the seven thunders had sounded, I was about to write, but I heard a voice from heaven saying, "Seal up what the seven thunders have said, and do not write it down." ⁵ And the angel whom I saw standing on the sea and on the land raised his right hand to heaven ⁶ and swore by him who lives forever and ever, who created heaven and what is in it, the earth and what is in it, and the sea and what is in it, that there would be no more delay, ⁷ but that in the days of the trumpet call to be sounded

---

[1] Abaddon means *destruction*; Apollyon means *destroyer*

by the seventh angel, the mystery of God would be fulfilled, just as he announced to his servants[1] the prophets.

[8] Then the voice that I had heard from heaven spoke to me again, saying, "Go, take the scroll that is open in the hand of the angel who is standing on the sea and on the land." [9] So I went to the angel and told him to give me the little scroll. And he said to me, "Take and eat it; it will make your stomach bitter, but in your mouth it will be sweet as honey." [10] And I took the little scroll from the hand of the angel and ate it. It was sweet as honey in my mouth, but when I had eaten it my stomach was made bitter. [11] And I was told, "You must again prophesy about many peoples and nations and languages and kings."

The Two Witnesses

11 Then I was given a measuring rod like a staff, and I was told, "Rise and measure the temple of God and the altar and those who worship there, [2] but do not measure the court outside the temple; leave that out, for it is given over to the nations, and they will trample the holy city for forty-two months. [3] And I will grant authority to my two witnesses, and they will prophesy for 1,260 days, clothed in sackcloth."

[4] These are the two olive trees and the two lampstands that stand before the Lord of the earth. [5] And if anyone would harm them, fire pours from their mouth and consumes their foes. If anyone would harm them, this is how he is doomed to be killed. [6] They have the power to shut the sky, that no rain may fall during the days of their prophesying, and they have power over the waters to turn them into blood and to strike the earth with every kind of plague, as often as they desire. [7] And when they have finished their testimony, the beast that rises from the bottomless pit will make war on them and conquer them and kill them, [8] and their dead bodies will lie in the street of the great city that symbolically is called Sodom and Egypt, where their Lord was crucified. [9] For three and a half days some from the peoples and tribes and languages and nations will gaze at their dead bodies and refuse to let them be placed in a tomb, [10] and those who dwell on the earth will rejoice over them and make merry and exchange presents, because these

two prophets had been a torment to those who dwell on the earth. [11] But after the three and a half days a breath of life from God entered them, and they stood up on their feet, and great fear fell on those who saw them. [12] Then they heard a loud voice from heaven saying to them, "Come up here!" And they went up to heaven in a cloud, and their enemies watched them. [13] And at that hour there was a great earthquake, and a tenth of the city fell. Seven thousand people were killed in the earthquake, and the rest were terrified and gave glory to the God of heaven.

[14] The second woe has passed; behold, the third woe is soon to come.

The Seventh Trumpet

[15] Then the seventh angel blew his trumpet, and there were loud voices in heaven, saying, "The kingdom of the world has

GETTING THE MESSAGE

When a lion roars, it can mean that it has caught, or is about to catch, its prey. In 10:3, the lion's roar probably symbolizes God's judgment against the wicked (see Amos 3:8).

become the kingdom of our Lord and of his Christ, and he shall reign forever and ever." [16] And the twenty-four elders who sit on their thrones before God fell on their faces and worshiped God, [17] saying,

"We give thanks to you, Lord God Almighty,
  who is and who was,
  for you have taken your great power
    and begun to reign.
[18] The nations raged,
    but your wrath came,
    and the time for the dead to be judged,
  and for rewarding your servants, the prophets and saints,
    and those who fear your name,
    both small and great,
  and for destroying the destroyers of the earth."

[19] Then God's temple in heaven was opened, and the ark of his covenant was

<hr>

[1] Greek *doulos* (see Preface); also 11:18

seen within his temple. There were flashes of lightning, rumblings, peals of thunder, an earthquake, and heavy hail.

The Woman and the Dragon

12 And a great sign appeared in heaven: a woman clothed with the sun, with the moon under her feet, and on her head a crown of twelve stars. ² She was pregnant and was crying out in birth pains and the agony of giving birth. ³ And another sign appeared in heaven: behold, a great red dragon, with seven heads and ten horns, and on his heads seven diadems. ⁴ His tail swept down a third of the stars of heaven and cast them to the earth. And the dragon stood before the woman who was about to give birth, so that when she bore her child he might devour it. ⁵ She gave birth to a male child, one who is to rule all the nations with

> ### GETTING THE MESSAGE
>
> **The Old Testament in Revelation.**
> Roughly one-seventh of the book of Revelation consists of quotations from the Old Testament. It is a reminder of just how important it is to read and understand the Old Testament as foundational for the New.

a rod of iron, but her child was caught up to God and to his throne, ⁶ and the woman fled into the wilderness, where she has a place prepared by God, in which she is to be nourished for 1,260 days.

Satan Thrown Down to Earth

⁷ Now war arose in heaven, Michael and his angels fighting against the dragon. And the dragon and his angels fought back, ⁸ but he was defeated, and there was no longer any place for them in heaven. ⁹ And the great dragon was thrown down, that ancient serpent, who is called the devil and Satan, the deceiver of the whole world—he was thrown down to the earth, and his angels were thrown down with him. ¹⁰ And I heard a loud voice in heaven, saying, "Now the salvation and the power and the kingdom of our God and the authority of his Christ have come, for the accuser of our brothers[1] has been thrown down, who accuses them

day and night before our God. ¹¹ And they have conquered him by the blood of the Lamb and by the word of their testimony, for they loved not their lives even unto death. ¹² Therefore, rejoice, O heavens and you who dwell in them! But woe to you, O earth and sea, for the devil has come down to you in great wrath, because he knows that his time is short!"

¹³ And when the dragon saw that he had been thrown down to the earth, he pursued the woman who had given birth to the male child. ¹⁴ But the woman was given the two wings of the great eagle so that she might fly from the serpent into the wilderness, to the place where she is to be nourished for a time, and times, and half a time. ¹⁵ The serpent poured water like a river out of his mouth after the woman, to sweep her away with a flood. ¹⁶ But the earth came to the help of the woman, and the earth opened its mouth and swallowed the river that the dragon had poured from his mouth. ¹⁷ Then the dragon became furious with the woman and went off to make war on the rest of her offspring, on those who keep the commandments of God and hold to the testimony of Jesus. And he stood on the sand of the sea.

The First Beast

13 And I saw a beast rising out of the sea, with ten horns and seven heads, with ten diadems on its horns and blasphemous names on its heads. ² And the beast that I saw was like a leopard; its feet were like a bear's, and its mouth was like a lion's mouth. And to it the dragon gave his power and his throne and great authority. ³ One of its heads seemed to have a mortal wound, but its mortal wound was healed, and the whole earth marveled as they followed the beast. ⁴ And they worshiped the dragon, for he had given his authority to the beast, and they worshiped the beast, saying, "Who is like the beast, and who can fight against it?"

⁵ And the beast was given a mouth uttering haughty and blasphemous words, and it was allowed to exercise authority for forty-two months. ⁶ It opened its mouth to utter blasphemies against God, blaspheming his name and his dwelling, that is, those who dwell in heaven. ⁷ Also it was allowed to make war on the saints and to conquer them. And authority was given it over every

---

[1] Or brothers and sisters

tribe and people and language and nation, [8] and all who dwell on earth will worship it, everyone whose name has not been written before the foundation of the world in the book of life of the Lamb who was slain. [9] If anyone has an ear, let him hear:

[10] If anyone is to be taken captive,
       to captivity he goes;
     if anyone is to be slain with the sword,
       with the sword must he be slain.

Here is a call for the endurance and faith of the saints.

The Second Beast

[11] Then I saw another beast rising out of the earth. It had two horns like a lamb and it spoke like a dragon. [12] It exercises all the authority of the first beast in its presence, and makes the earth and its inhabitants worship the first beast, whose mortal wound was healed. [13] It performs great signs, even making fire come down from heaven to earth in front of people, [14] and by the signs that it is allowed to work in the presence of the beast it deceives those who dwell on earth, telling them to make an image for the beast that was wounded by the sword and yet lived. [15] And it was allowed to give breath to the image of the beast, so that the image of the beast might even speak and might cause those who would not worship the image of the beast to be slain. [16] Also it causes all, both small and great, both rich and poor, both free and slave,[1] to be marked on the right hand or the forehead, [17] so that no one can buy or sell unless he has the mark, that is, the name of the beast or the number of its name. [18] This calls for wisdom: let the one who has understanding calculate the number of the beast, for it is the number of a man, and his number is 666.

The Lamb and the 144,000

14 Then I looked, and behold, on Mount Zion stood the Lamb, and with him 144,000 who had his name and his Father's name written on their foreheads. [2] And I heard a voice from heaven like the roar of many waters and like the sound of loud thunder. The voice I heard was like the sound of harpists playing on their harps, [3] and they were singing a new song before the throne and before the four living crea-

tures and before the elders. No one could learn that song except the 144,000 who had been redeemed from the earth. [4] It is these who have not defiled themselves with women, for they are virgins. It is these who follow the Lamb wherever it goes. These have been redeemed from mankind as firstfruits for God and the Lamb, [5] and in their mouth no lie was found, for they are blameless.

The Messages of the Three Angels

[6] Then I saw another angel flying directly overhead, with an eternal gospel to proclaim to those who dwell on earth, to every nation and tribe and language and people. [7] And he said with a loud voice, "Fear God and give him glory, because the hour of his judgment has come, and worship him who made heaven and earth, the sea and the springs of water."

> ### GETTING THE MESSAGE
>
> **A call for endurance.** The churches were facing many threats, including persecution, false teaching, and idolatry. Revelation urges believers to continue (or persevere) in the faith despite difficulties. Christ's victory is secure, and God will richly reward those who suffer for his sake.

[8] Another angel, a second, followed, saying, "Fallen, fallen is Babylon the great, she who made all nations drink the wine of the passion of her sexual immorality."

[9] And another angel, a third, followed them, saying with a loud voice, "If anyone worships the beast and its image and receives a mark on his forehead or on his hand, [10] he also will drink the wine of God's wrath, poured full strength into the cup of his anger, and he will be tormented with fire and sulfur in the presence of the holy angels and in the presence of the Lamb. [11] And the smoke of their torment goes up forever and ever, and they have no rest, day or night, these worshipers of the beast and its image, and whoever receives the mark of its name."

[12] Here is a call for the endurance of the saints, those who keep the commandments of God and their faith in Jesus.

[1] Greek doulos (see Preface)

13 And I heard a voice from heaven saying, "Write this: Blessed are the dead who die in the Lord from now on." "Blessed indeed," says the Spirit, "that they may rest from their labors, for their deeds follow them!"

The Harvest of the Earth

14 Then I looked, and behold, a white cloud, and seated on the cloud one like a son of man, with a golden crown on his head, and a sharp sickle in his hand. **15** And another angel came out of the temple, calling with a loud voice to him who sat on the cloud, "Put in your sickle, and reap, for the hour to reap has come, for the harvest of the earth is fully ripe." **16** So he who sat on the cloud swung his sickle across the earth, and the earth was reaped.

17 Then another angel came out of the temple in heaven, and he too had a sharp sickle. **18** And another angel came out from

---

GETTING THE MESSAGE

The sea of glass (4:6; 15:2) is the transparent pavement surrounding God's throne. Separating heaven above from the earth below, its transparent tranquility shows heaven's peace in contrast to earthly turmoil.

---

the altar, the angel who has authority over the fire, and he called with a loud voice to the one who had the sharp sickle, "Put in your sickle and gather the clusters from the vine of the earth, for its grapes are ripe." **19** So the angel swung his sickle across the earth and gathered the grape harvest of the earth and threw it into the great winepress of the wrath of God. **20** And the winepress was trodden outside the city, and blood flowed from the winepress, as high as a horse's bridle, for 1,600 stadia.

The Seven Angels with Seven Plagues

15 Then I saw another sign in heaven, great and amazing, seven angels with seven plagues, which are the last, for with them the wrath of God is finished.

2 And I saw what appeared to be a sea of glass mingled with fire—and also those who had conquered the beast and its image

and the number of its name, standing beside the sea of glass with harps of God in their hands. **3** And they sing the song of Moses, the servant[1] of God, and the song of the Lamb, saying,

"Great and amazing are your deeds,
  O Lord God the Almighty!
Just and true are your ways,
  O King of the nations!
4 Who will not fear, O Lord,
  and glorify your name?
For you alone are holy.
  All nations will come
  and worship you,
for your righteous acts have been
  revealed."

5 After this I looked, and the sanctuary of the tent of witness in heaven was opened, **6** and out of the sanctuary came the seven angels with the seven plagues, clothed in pure, bright linen, with golden sashes around their chests. **7** And one of the four living creatures gave to the seven angels seven golden bowls full of the wrath of God who lives forever and ever, **8** and the sanctuary was filled with smoke from the glory of God and from his power, and no one could enter the sanctuary until the seven plagues of the seven angels were finished.

The Seven Bowls of God's Wrath

16 Then I heard a loud voice from the temple telling the seven angels, "Go and pour out on the earth the seven bowls of the wrath of God."

2 So the first angel went and poured out his bowl on the earth, and harmful and painful sores came upon the people who bore the mark of the beast and worshiped its image.

3 The second angel poured out his bowl into the sea, and it became like the blood of a corpse, and every living thing died that was in the sea.

4 The third angel poured out his bowl into the rivers and the springs of water, and they became blood. **5** And I heard the angel in charge of the waters say,

"Just are you, O Holy One, who is and who was,
  for you brought these judgments.

---

[1] Greek *doulos* (see Preface)

⁶ For they have shed the blood of saints
        and prophets,
    and you have given them blood to
        drink.
    It is what they deserve!"

⁷ And I heard the altar saying,

"Yes, Lord God the Almighty,
    true and just are your judgments!"

⁸ The fourth angel poured out his bowl on
the sun, and it was allowed to scorch people
with fire. ⁹ They were scorched by the fierce
heat, and they cursed the name of God who
had power over these plagues. They did not
repent and give him glory.

¹⁰ The fifth angel poured out his bowl on
the throne of the beast, and its kingdom was
plunged into darkness. People gnawed their
tongues in anguish ¹¹ and cursed the God of
heaven for their pain and sores. They did
not repent of their deeds.

¹² The sixth angel poured out his bowl on
the great river Euphrates, and its water was
dried up, to prepare the way for the kings
from the east. ¹³ And I saw, coming out of
the mouth of the dragon and out of the
mouth of the beast and out of the mouth of
the false prophet, three unclean spirits like
frogs. ¹⁴ For they are demonic spirits, performing signs, who go abroad to the kings
of the whole world, to assemble them for
battle on the great day of God the Almighty.
¹⁵ ("Behold, I am coming like a thief! Blessed
is the one who stays awake, keeping his garments on, that he may not go about naked
and be seen exposed!") ¹⁶ And they assembled them at the place that in Hebrew is
called Armageddon.

The Seventh Bowl

¹⁷ The seventh angel poured out his bowl
into the air, and a loud voice came out of the
temple, from the throne, saying, "It is done!"
¹⁸ And there were flashes of lightning, rumblings, peals of thunder, and a great earthquake such as there had never been since
man was on the earth, so great was that
earthquake. ¹⁹ The great city was split into
three parts, and the cities of the nations fell,
and God remembered Babylon the great, to
make her drain the cup of the wine of the
fury of his wrath. ²⁰ And every island fled
away, and no mountains were to be found.
²¹ And great hailstones, about one hundred

pounds each, fell from heaven on people;
and they cursed God for the plague of the
hail, because the plague was so severe.

The Great Prostitute and the Beast

17 Then one of the seven angels who
had the seven bowls came and said to
me, "Come, I will show you the judgment of
the great prostitute who is seated on many
waters, ² with whom the kings of the earth
have committed sexual immorality, and
with the wine of whose sexual immorality
the dwellers on earth have become drunk."
³ And he carried me away in the Spirit into
a wilderness, and I saw a woman sitting
on a scarlet beast that was full of blasphemous names, and it had seven heads and ten
horns. ⁴ The woman was arrayed in purple
and scarlet, and adorned with gold and jewels and pearls, holding in her hand a golden

---

GETTING THE MESSAGE

The vision of **the fifth bowl** (16:10–11)
shows that even the very throne of the
beast is not immune to God's just wrath.
It is appropriate that a regime founded
on deceit should be plunged into
darkness (see 13:13–14).

---

cup full of abominations and the impurities of her sexual immorality. ⁵ And on her
forehead was written a name of mystery:
"Babylon the great, mother of prostitutes
and of earth's abominations." ⁶ And I saw the
woman, drunk with the blood of the saints,
the blood of the martyrs of Jesus.

When I saw her, I marveled greatly. ⁷ But
the angel said to me, "Why do you marvel?
I will tell you the mystery of the woman, and
of the beast with seven heads and ten horns
that carries her. ⁸ The beast that you saw
was, and is not, and is about to rise from the
bottomless pit and go to destruction. And
the dwellers on earth whose names have
not been written in the book of life from the
foundation of the world will marvel to see
the beast, because it was and is not and is to
come. ⁹ This calls for a mind with wisdom:
the seven heads are seven mountains on
which the woman is seated; ¹⁰ they are also
seven kings, five of whom have fallen, one
is, the other has not yet come, and when
he does come he must remain only a little

while. [11] As for the beast that was and is not, it is an eighth but it belongs to the seven, and it goes to destruction. [12] And the ten horns that you saw are ten kings who have not yet received royal power, but they are to receive authority as kings for one hour, together with the beast. [13] These are of one mind, and they hand over their power and authority to the beast. [14] They will make war on the Lamb, and the Lamb will conquer them, for he is Lord of lords and King of kings, and those with him are called and chosen and faithful."

[15] And the angel said to me, "The waters that you saw, where the prostitute is seated, are peoples and multitudes and nations and languages. [16] And the ten horns that you saw, they and the beast will hate the

---

GETTING THE MESSAGE

Symbolism is very important in Revelation. Instead of portraying characters and events directly, the author often uses symbols. For example, Jesus is portrayed as a lamb, churches are portrayed as lamps on lampstands, and Satan is portrayed as a dragon with seven heads and ten horns.

---

prostitute. They will make her desolate and naked, and devour her flesh and burn her up with fire, [17] for God has put it into their hearts to carry out his purpose by being of one mind and handing over their royal power to the beast, until the words of God are fulfilled. [18] And the woman that you saw is the great city that has dominion over the kings of the earth."

The Fall of Babylon

18 After this I saw another angel coming down from heaven, having great authority, and the earth was made bright with his glory. [2] And he called out with a mighty voice,

"Fallen, fallen is Babylon the great!
　She has become a dwelling place for
　　demons,
a haunt for every unclean spirit,
a haunt for every unclean bird,
a haunt for every unclean and
　detestable beast.

[3] For all nations have drunk
　the wine of the passion of her sex-
　　ual immorality,
and the kings of the earth have com-
　mitted immorality with her,
and the merchants of the earth have
　grown rich from the power of
　her luxurious living."

[4] Then I heard another voice from heaven saying,

"Come out of her, my people,
　lest you take part in her sins,
lest you share in her plagues;
[5] for her sins are heaped high as heaven,
　and God has remembered her iniq-
　　uities.
[6] Pay her back as she herself has paid
　　back others,
　and repay her double for her deeds;
　mix a double portion for her in the
　　cup she mixed.
[7] As she glorified herself and lived in
　　luxury,
　so give her a like measure of tor-
　　ment and mourning,
since in her heart she says,
　'I sit as a queen,
I am no widow,
　and mourning I shall never see.'
[8] For this reason her plagues will come
　　in a single day,
　death and mourning and famine,
and she will be burned up with fire;
　for mighty is the Lord God who has
　　judged her."

[9] And the kings of the earth, who committed sexual immorality and lived in luxury with her, will weep and wail over her when they see the smoke of her burning. [10] They will stand far off, in fear of her torment, and say,

"Alas! Alas! You great city,
　you mighty city, Babylon!
For in a single hour your judgment
　has come."

[11] And the merchants of the earth weep and mourn for her, since no one buys their cargo anymore, [12] cargo of gold, silver, jewels, pearls, fine linen, purple cloth, silk, scarlet cloth, all kinds of scented wood, all kinds of articles of ivory, all kinds of articles of costly wood, bronze, iron and marble,

[13] cinnamon, spice, incense, myrrh, frankincense, wine, oil, fine flour, wheat, cattle and sheep, horses and chariots, and slaves, that is, human souls.

[14] "The fruit for which your soul longed
has gone from you,
and all your delicacies and your
splendors
are lost to you,
never to be found again!"

[15] The merchants of these wares, who gained wealth from her, will stand far off, in fear of her torment, weeping and mourning aloud,

[16] "Alas, alas, for the great city
that was clothed in fine linen,
in purple and scarlet,
adorned with gold,
with jewels, and with pearls!
[17] For in a single hour all this wealth has
been laid waste."

And all shipmasters and seafaring men, sailors and all whose trade is on the sea, stood far off [18] and cried out as they saw the smoke of her burning,

"What city was like the great city?"

[19] And they threw dust on their heads as they wept and mourned, crying out,

"Alas, alas, for the great city
where all who had ships at sea
grew rich by her wealth!
For in a single hour she has been laid
waste.
[20] Rejoice over her, O heaven,
and you saints and apostles and
prophets,
for God has given judgment for you
against her!"

[21] Then a mighty angel took up a stone like a great millstone and threw it into the sea, saying,

"So will Babylon the great city be
thrown down with violence,
and will be found no more;
[22] and the sound of harpists and
musicians, of flute players and
trumpeters,
will be heard in you no more,
and a craftsman of any craft
will be found in you no more,

and the sound of the mill
will be heard in you no more,
[23] and the light of a lamp
will shine in you no more,
and the voice of bridegroom and
bride
will be heard in you no more,
for your merchants were the great
ones of the earth,
and all nations were deceived by
your sorcery.
[24] And in her was found the blood of
prophets and of saints,
and of all who have been slain on
earth."

Rejoicing in Heaven

19 After this I heard what seemed to be the loud voice of a great multitude in heaven, crying out,

"Hallelujah!
Salvation and glory and power belong
to our God,
[2]   for his judgments are true and
just;
for he has judged the great prostitute
who corrupted the earth with her
immorality,
and has avenged on her the blood of
his servants."[1]

[3] Once more they cried out,

"Hallelujah!
The smoke from her goes up forever
and ever."

[4] And the twenty-four elders and the four living creatures fell down and worshiped God who was seated on the throne, saying, "Amen. Hallelujah!" [5] And from the throne came a voice saying,

[1] Greek doulos (see Preface)

"Praise our God,
    all you his servants,[1]
you who fear him,
    small and great."

The Marriage Supper of the Lamb

6 Then I heard what seemed to be the voice of a great multitude, like the roar of many waters and like the sound of mighty peals of thunder, crying out,

"Hallelujah!
For the Lord our God
    the Almighty reigns.
7 Let us rejoice and exult
    and give him the glory,
for the marriage of the Lamb has come,
    and his Bride has made herself ready;
8 it was granted her to clothe herself
    with fine linen, bright and pure"—

for the fine linen is the righteous deeds of the saints.

> **GETTING THE MESSAGE**
>
> **The rider on the white horse.** Because the color white was associated with victory, military or political leaders often chose white horses. In 19:11, the victorious Jesus rides a white horse.

9 And the angel said to me, "Write this: Blessed are those who are invited to the marriage supper of the Lamb." And he said to me, "These are the true words of God." **10** Then I fell down at his feet to worship him, but he said to me, "You must not do that! I am a fellow servant[2] with you and your brothers who hold to the testimony of Jesus. Worship God." For the testimony of Jesus is the spirit of prophecy.

The Rider on a White Horse

11 Then I saw heaven opened, and behold, a white horse! The one sitting on it is called Faithful and True, and in righteousness he judges and makes war. **12** His eyes are like a flame of fire, and on his head are many diadems, and he has a name written that no one knows but himself. **13** He is clothed in a robe dipped in blood, and the name by which he is called is The Word of God. **14** And the armies of heaven, arrayed in fine linen, white and pure, were following him on white horses. **15** From his mouth comes a sharp sword with which to strike down the nations, and he will rule them with a rod of iron. He will tread the winepress of the fury of the wrath of God the Almighty. **16** On his robe and on his thigh he has a name written, King of kings and Lord of lords.

17 Then I saw an angel standing in the sun, and with a loud voice he called to all the birds that fly directly overhead, "Come, gather for the great supper of God, **18** to eat the flesh of kings, the flesh of captains, the flesh of mighty men, the flesh of horses and their riders, and the flesh of all men, both free and slave,[3] both small and great." **19** And I saw the beast and the kings of the earth with their armies gathered to make war against him who was sitting on the horse and against his army. **20** And the beast was captured, and with it the false prophet who in its presence had done the signs by which he deceived those who had received the mark of the beast and those who worshiped its image. These two were thrown alive into the lake of fire that burns with sulfur. **21** And the rest were slain by the sword that came from the mouth of him who was sitting on the horse, and all the birds were gorged with their flesh.

The Thousand Years

20 Then I saw an angel coming down from heaven, holding in his hand the key to the bottomless pit and a great chain. **2** And he seized the dragon, that ancient serpent, who is the devil and Satan, and bound him for a thousand years, **3** and threw him into the pit, and shut it and sealed it over him, so that he might not deceive the nations any longer, until the thousand years were ended. After that he must be released for a little while.

4 Then I saw thrones, and seated on them were those to whom the authority to judge was committed. Also I saw the souls of those who had been beheaded for the testimony of Jesus and for the word of God, and those who had not worshiped the beast or its image and had not received its mark on their foreheads or their hands. They came to life and reigned with Christ for a thousand years. **5** The rest of the dead did not come to life until the thousand years were ended. This is the first resurrection. **6** Blessed and holy is the one who

---

[1] Greek *doulos* (see Preface)   [2] Greek *sundoulos* (see Preface)   [3] Greek *doulos* (see Preface)

shares in the first resurrection! Over such the second death has no power, but they will be priests of God and of Christ, and they will reign with him for a thousand years.

The Defeat of Satan

⁷ And when the thousand years are ended, Satan will be released from his prison ⁸ and will come out to deceive the nations that are at the four corners of the earth, Gog and Magog, to gather them for battle; their number is like the sand of the sea. ⁹ And they marched up over the broad plain of the earth and surrounded the camp of the saints and the beloved city, but fire came down from heaven and consumed them, ¹⁰ and the devil who had deceived them was thrown into the lake of fire and sulfur where the beast and the false prophet were, and they will be tormented day and night forever and ever.

Judgment Before the Great White Throne

¹¹ Then I saw a great white throne and him who was seated on it. From his presence earth and sky fled away, and no place was found for them. ¹² And I saw the dead, great and small, standing before the throne, and books were opened. Then another book was opened, which is the book of life. And the dead were judged by what was written in the books, according to what they had done. ¹³ And the sea gave up the dead who were in it, Death and Hades gave up the dead who were in them, and they were judged, each one of them, according to what they had done. ¹⁴ Then Death and Hades were thrown into the lake of fire. This is the second death, the lake of fire. ¹⁵ And if anyone's name was not found written in the book of life, he was thrown into the lake of fire.

The New Heaven and the New Earth

21 Then I saw a new heaven and a new earth, for the first heaven and the first earth had passed away, and the sea was no more. ² And I saw the holy city, new Jerusalem, coming down out of heaven from God, prepared as a bride adorned for her husband. ³ And I heard a loud voice from the throne saying, "Behold, the dwelling place of God is with man. He will dwell with them, and they will be his people, and God himself will be with them as their God. ⁴ He will wipe away every tear from their eyes, and death shall be no more, neither shall there

be mourning, nor crying, nor pain anymore, for the former things have passed away."

⁵ And he who was seated on the throne said, "Behold, I am making all things new." Also he said, "Write this down, for these words are trustworthy and true." ⁶ And he said to me, "It is done! I am the Alpha and the Omega, the beginning and the end. To the thirsty I will give from the spring of the water of life without payment. ⁷ The one who conquers will have this heritage, and I will be his God and he will be my son. ⁸ But as for the cowardly, the faithless, the detestable, as for murderers, the sexually immoral, sorcerers, idolaters, and all liars, their portion will be in the lake that burns with fire and sulfur, which is the second death."

The New Jerusalem

⁹ Then came one of the seven angels who had the seven bowls full of the seven last

GETTING THE MESSAGE

Revelation contains seven **benedictions**, or blessings (1:3; 14:13; 16:15; 19:9; 20:6; 22:7, 14). Some other memorable benedictions include Aaron's blessing on Israel (Num. 6:24–26), 2 Corinthians 13:14, and Jude 24–25. These and other blessings are often used in Christian worship.

plagues and spoke to me, saying, "Come, I will show you the Bride, the wife of the Lamb." ¹⁰ And he carried me away in the Spirit to a great, high mountain, and showed me the holy city Jerusalem coming down out of heaven from God, ¹¹ having the glory of God, its radiance like a most rare jewel, like a jasper, clear as crystal. ¹² It had a great, high wall, with twelve gates, and at the gates twelve angels, and on the gates the names of the twelve tribes of the sons of Israel were inscribed — ¹³ on the east three gates, on the north three gates, on the south three gates, and on the west three gates. ¹⁴ And the wall of the city had twelve foundations, and on them were the twelve names of the twelve apostles of the Lamb.

¹⁵ And the one who spoke with me had a measuring rod of gold to measure the city and its gates and walls. ¹⁶ The city lies foursquare, its length the same as its width. And

he measured the city with his rod, 12,000 stadia. Its length and width and height are equal. [17] He also measured its wall, 144 cubits by human measurement, which is also an angel's measurement. [18] The wall was built of jasper, while the city was pure gold, like clear glass. [19] The foundations of the wall of the city were adorned with every kind of jewel. The first was jasper, the second sapphire, the third agate, the fourth emerald, [20] the fifth onyx, the sixth carnelian, the seventh chrysolite, the eighth beryl, the ninth topaz, the tenth chrysoprase, the eleventh jacinth, the twelfth amethyst. [21] And the twelve gates were twelve pearls, each of the gates made of a single pearl, and the street of the city was pure gold, like transparent glass.

[22] And I saw no temple in the city, for its temple is the Lord God the Almighty and the Lamb. [23] And the city has no need of sun or moon to shine on it, for the glory of God

> ### GETTING THE MESSAGE
>
> Revelation refers to the church as **the Bride of Christ** (19:7; 21:2, 9; 22:17). Similarly, Paul uses the relationship between Christ and the church as an example of how husbands and wives should treat each other (Eph. 5:25–27).

gives it light, and its lamp is the Lamb. [24] By its light will the nations walk, and the kings of the earth will bring their glory into it, [25] and its gates will never be shut by day — and there will be no night there. [26] They will bring into it the glory and the honor of the nations. [27] But nothing unclean will ever enter it, nor anyone who does what is detestable or false, but only those who are written in the Lamb's book of life.

The River of Life

22 Then the angel showed me the river of the water of life, bright as crystal, flowing from the throne of God and of the Lamb [2] through the middle of the street of the city; also, on either side of the river, the tree of life with its twelve kinds of fruit, yielding its fruit each month. The leaves of the tree were for the healing of the nations. [3] No longer will there be anything accursed,

but the throne of God and of the Lamb will be in it, and his servants[1] will worship him. [4] They will see his face, and his name will be on their foreheads. [5] And night will be no more. They will need no light of lamp or sun, for the Lord God will be their light, and they will reign forever and ever.

Jesus Is Coming

[6] And he said to me, "These words are trustworthy and true. And the Lord, the God of the spirits of the prophets, has sent his angel to show his servants what must soon take place."

[7] "And behold, I am coming soon. Blessed is the one who keeps the words of the prophecy of this book."

[8] I, John, am the one who heard and saw these things. And when I heard and saw them, I fell down to worship at the feet of the angel who showed them to me, [9] but he said to me, "You must not do that! I am a fellow servant[2] with you and your brothers the prophets, and with those who keep the words of this book. Worship God."

[10] And he said to me, "Do not seal up the words of the prophecy of this book, for the time is near. [11] Let the evildoer still do evil, and the filthy still be filthy, and the righteous still do right, and the holy still be holy."

[12] "Behold, I am coming soon, bringing my recompense with me, to repay each one for what he has done. [13] I am the Alpha and the Omega, the first and the last, the beginning and the end."

[14] Blessed are those who wash their robes, so that they may have the right to the tree of life and that they may enter the city by the gates. [15] Outside are the dogs and sorcerers and the sexually immoral and murderers and idolaters, and everyone who loves and practices falsehood.

[16] "I, Jesus, have sent my angel to testify to you about these things for the churches. I am the root and the descendant of David, the bright morning star."

[17] The Spirit and the Bride say, "Come." And let the one who hears say, "Come." And let the one who is thirsty come; let the one who desires take the water of life without price.

[18] I warn everyone who hears the words of the prophecy of this book: if anyone adds to them, God will add to him the plagues

---

[1] Greek *doulos* (see Preface); also 22:6 [2] Greek *sundoulos* (see Preface)

described in this book, [19] and if anyone takes away from the words of the book of this prophecy, God will take away his share in the tree of life and in the holy city, which are described in this book.

[20] He who testifies to these things says, "Surely I am coming soon." Amen. Come, Lord Jesus!

[21] The grace of the Lord Jesus be with all. Amen.

ARTICLES
AND RESOURCES

GOD'S PLAN OF SALVATION

Two thousand years ago a troubled jailer asked, "what must I do to be saved?" (Acts 16:30). This is the most important question anyone can ask. Why do we need to be saved? Because of the evils in this world, but especially because of our own faults and failures. We often feel guilty for things we've said and things we've done—things that we know are wrong. We sense that we deserve God's judgment. What can be done to save us from our helpless situation?

An Overview
Creation
God made this world and all that is in it: "In the beginning God created the heavens and the earth. . . . God created man in his own image, in the image of God he created him; male and female he created them" (Gen. 1:1, 27). God created human beings to be like him and to have true friendship with him. When his work of creation was finished, God saw that it was "very good" (Gen. 1:31).

Rebellion
Although the first people, Adam and Eve, had complete freedom to live in friendship with God, they chose to rebel against him instead of trusting in him (Gen. 3:1–7). Because God had designed the world so that Adam would represent the entire human race, Adam's sin was catastrophic not only for himself but for us as well: one sin led to the condemnation of all mankind (Rom. 5:18). Our relationship with God was broken. Instead of enjoying his holy pleasure, instead we now face his righteous wrath. Through Adam's sin, we all died spiritually (see Rom. 3:1–20; Eph. 2:1–10) and the entire world was tragically damaged as well: "The creation was subjected to futility" (Rom. 8:20). And we all individually sin against God in our own lives: "for all have sinned and fall short of the glory of God" (Rom. 3:23).

Redemption
God would have been perfectly just and right to leave matters there—with all human beings under his holy judgment. But he didn't do that. Instead, God set in motion a plan to save people from sin and judgment and to set free the entire creation from the tragic effects of sin and the

curse. How? By sending his Son as a true man who would bear the penalty for our sin and die in our place: "Christ died for our sins in accordance with the Scriptures" (1 Cor. 15:3).

The best-known verse in the Bible summarizes the way in which we should respond to this good news: "For God so loved the world, that he gave his only Son, that *whoever believes in him* should not perish but have eternal life" (John 3:16). To "believe in" Jesus includes both a wholehearted *trust* in him for forgiveness of sins and a decision to forsake one's sin or to *repent*: All who truly repent and believe in Jesus will be redeemed (Mark 1:15). They will be restored to a right relationship with God. To "believe in" Jesus also requires trusting in Jesus as he truly is—not just a man in ancient history but also a living Savior who knows our hearts and hears our prayers.

Consummation
God not only rescues lost sinners but will someday fully restore all of creation. We read in Romans 8:21, "the creation itself will be set free from its bondage to corruption and obtain the freedom of the glory of the children of God." The heavens and the earth will "pass away" and will be radically transformed (2 Pet. 3:7–13; Rev. 21:1). We read of the glorious culmination of this in the book of Revelation, where God's people—those whom he has redeemed and saved—are brought into the presence of God to live forever (Rev. 21:1–22:6). This is life as it should be and as God meant it to be.

Filling in the Details
Let's now stop and review this more carefully and specifically, addressing the categories of God, man, Christ, our response, and the result.

God
The God of the Bible is the one and only true God. He is the greatest of all beings. He depends on no other being for his existence. He exists eternally as one God in three persons—Father, Son, and Holy Spirit. He acts according to his own good pleasure. He "works all things according to the counsel of his will" (Eph. 1:11). God created the world and acts in it today in

accordance with his own perfect, holy, good, and loving plan.

In the same way that this perfectly good God created everything according to his own purposes, so also he has acted to save people who have rebelled against him.

Man

People are made *in the image of God* (Gen. 1:27–28). What does that mean? In part it means that we are privileged to act as God's representatives, as sub-rulers over God's creation, reflecting God's good rule over us. Our authority is derived from God's authority (Eph. 3:14–15) and is meant to reflect his good plans for his world. But being in God's image also means that we are *like God* in many ways. Like God, we are spiritual and rational beings. Like God, we communicate and establish relationships. Like God, our souls will endure eternally.

However, the Bible also teaches that there has been an enduring effect of the sin of Adam and Eve recorded in Genesis 3. Because of that sin, we are born morally *fallen*. We are naturally inclined away from God and toward sin in every area of life. We are not as bad as we possibly could be, but we also are not nearly as good as we ought to be. We are all sinners, and we sin in all areas of life (Rom. 3:23). We are corrupted and often make the wrong choices. We are not holy; we do not love God, and therefore we are under the just condemnation of eternal punishment, without defense or excuse. We are guilty of sinning against God. We are fallen from his favor and under the curse of Genesis 3. The promise of God's just judgment of us in the future and forever is guaranteed: "the wages of sin is death" (Rom. 6:23). This is the state from which we need to be saved.

Jesus Christ

When all human beings were desperate and helpless, God "loved us and sent his Son to be the propitiation for our sins" (1 John 4:10). In other words, by his substitutionary sacrifice Jesus turns away the wrath of God that we deserve.

Fully God. Jesus of Nazareth is the Son of God, who has eternally existed with the Father and the Holy Spirit, and who has eternally possessed all the attributes of God. Jesus himself clearly demonstrated his deity by fulfilling prophecy (Mark 14:61–62). Jesus forgave sins, as only God can do (Mark 2:5), he accepted the worship that only God deserves (John 20:28–29), and he taught that, "I and the Father are one" (John 10:30).

Fully man. Jesus was also fully man. He was not a "god" who merely pretended to be human. He had a fully human body. He "grew and became strong, filled with wisdom" (Luke 2:40). He lived in submission to his earthly parents. He learned the trade of carpentry (Mark 6:3). He experienced hunger, felt thirst and grew tired, faced temptation, and eventually suffered even death itself. Jesus Christ was, and is, fully God and fully man. The eternal Son of God became a man in order to save sinners.

Perfect life. Jesus Christ lived a perfect life. He did only what the Father willed that he should do (John 5:19; e.g., Luke 22:42). Therefore, the writer to the Hebrews concludes, "we do not have a high priest who is unable to sympathize with our weaknesses, but one who in every respect has been tempted as we are, yet without sin" (Heb. 4:15). Jesus lived the life of consistent, wholehearted love to the Father that Adam and Eve and Israel—and all of us—should have lived. He deserved no punishment from God because he was never disobedient.

Teaching. Jesus came to teach God's truth, especially about himself (Mark 1:38; Luke 20:42; 24:44). He taught the truth about God, about his relationship with God the Father (John 14), about our sin, about what he had come to do, and about what we must do in response. He explained that the Scriptures of the OT were ultimately about him (Luke 24:44).

Crucifixion. But God sent his Son especially to die for us (Mark 10:45; John 3:16–18). This is how God has shown his love for us (Rom. 5:8; 1 John 4:9–10). Christ gave his life as a ransom for us (Mark 10:45; 1 Tim. 2:6). By his death, Jesus paid the penalty for our sin. Jesus Christ's crucifixion was a horrible act of violence, and yet it was also a display of the self-giving love of God, as the Son of God bore the penalty of God's wrath against us for our sin (Isa. 53:5; Rom. 3:25–26; 4:25; 5:19; 2 Cor. 5:21; Heb. 9:28).

Resurrection, ascension, return. On the third day after his crucifixion, Jesus was raised from the dead by God. This showed God's acceptance of Christ's sacrifice for sin (Rom. 1:4; 4:25). Jesus then ascended to heaven and "will come in the same way as you saw him go into heaven" (Acts 1:11). Christ's return will bring God's plan of salvation to completion.

Response

If God has done all of this through Christ, what are we to do to be saved? We must turn to Christ, which means turning away from sin. If we *repent* of our sin and *trust* in Christ, we will be saved from God's righteous wrath toward our sins. This response of repentance and faith can be explained in more detail as follows:

Turn to God. Paul calls us to "repent and turn to God" (Acts 26:20). To turn to God is to direct all of our life toward him. We are to be like the Prodigal Son who, though conscious of his sin and folly, turns and flees to his loving father (Luke 15:20).

Turn away from sin. Turning to God necessarily means also turning away from sin. We cannot pursue God and sin at the same time. The book of 1 John makes it clear that our basic way of life will be directed either toward God and his light, or toward the darkness of sin. Christians in this life still sin, but when we do so it is against our deepest desires and better judgment. Our lives are not guided and directed by sin as before. We are no longer enslaved to sin. Though we still struggle with it (Gal. 5:17), God has given us the gift of repentance (Acts 11:18), and we have been freed from sin's dominating power.

Believe and trust. We are also called to believe and trust God's promises in Christ and to commit ourselves to being his disciples. Jesus invites us to "repent and believe in the gospel" (Mark 1:15). Paul speaks of "salvation through faith in Christ" (2 Tim. 3:15). We can express our initial repentance and faith to God himself in prayer.

Grow in godliness and seek holiness. Salvation is God's *gift* to us, but the evidence of that salvation must be *lived out* in the continual work of God's Spirit. We can deceive ourselves about being saved, so Paul encourages his readers to "Examine yourselves, to see whether you are in the faith. Test yourselves" (2 Cor. 13:5). Peter encourages Christians to grow in godliness and so become more confident of their election (2 Pet. 1:3–11). We don't create our own salvation by our actions, but we reflect and express it in the things we do and say, and thus grow in our certainty of our salvation. Bible passages such as Jesus' descriptions of his followers in the Sermon of the Mount (Matthew 5–7) or Paul's list of the fruit of the Spirit (Gal. 5:22–23) can act as spiritual maps to reassure us that we are truly on the path of salvation.

The Result

God's plan is to save his people from their sins—and to bring them fully and finally to himself (Matt. 1:21; 2 Tim. 2:10). Christians have been saved from the *penalty* of our sins; we are presently being saved from the *power* of sin; and one day, when God's plan of salvation is completed and we are with Christ in eternity, we shall be like him, and we shall be saved even from the very *presence* of sin. This is God's plan of salvation.

THE IMPORTANCE OF THE CHURCH FOR GROWING IN CHRIST

Mention the church to a group of Christians and you are likely to get a mixed response. Some might say that, while they do love Jesus, they don't love the church. Others might respond, "Of course we love the church." Which view represents the way we should view the church? The real issue here concerns the importance of the church for growing in Christ. To explore this issue, it is necessary to consider what the Bible says about the church.

The Church in the Bible: OT Life and Worship

Before we can look at what the NT teaches about the church, we first need to see what the OT says about life and worship. God instructed Moses to build a tabernacle—a portable tent that represented the presence of God dwelling right in the middle of his people. The tabernacle and later the temple were the places where God ordained the sacrifices to be carried out and the festivals to be celebrated. The tabernacle and temple functioned as the central place of instruction and teaching about God and his will for Israel. From the tabernacle and temple, Israel sounded forth loud and joyful psalms of praise and worship to God.

The instructions for building the tabernacle required it to be at the center of Israel's encampments. Later, Jerusalem, the site of the temple, was seen as representing the center of the land of Israel. The tabernacle and temple were not only to be viewed as the geographical center of Israel; they were also intended to be the spiritual center of Israel. Like spokes of a wheel that fan out from the hub, what occurred at these worship centers was to affect every aspect of Israelite life.

The Church in the Bible: Christ and the Gospels

The church did not officially come into existence until the day of Pentecost, after Jesus had died and had risen. However, even in the Gospels we learn many things from Christ concerning the church. Let's review three. First, we have Jesus' declaration, "I will build my church, and the gates of hell shall not prevail against it" (Matt. 16:18). "Gates" likely represents the power of hell, which is no match whatsoever for Jesus.

Second, Jesus hands the church its mission statement and purpose for existence when he gives the disciples the Great Commission in Matthew 28:16–20. As the church goes out into the world, it is called to make disciples, carrying out the task of baptizing the new disciples and teaching them all that Christ has commanded. These activities must characterize every local church's work and life.

The third thing we learn from Jesus concerning the church comes from his high-priestly prayer in John 17. At the end of the prayer, Jesus expresses to the Father, "I made known to them your name, and I will continue to make it known" (John 17:26). The NT frequently refers to the church as Christ's body. We are literally the presence of Christ on earth. And the church's mission is exactly the same as Christ's mission: to proclaim God's name.

The universal church of Christ's body is visible and manifest in local congregations, or churches. These local churches are to be "incarnational." They are to represent Christ, who was incarnated (that is, born as a human) and walked among us. The incarnational model of the church means that we live and behave with the full realization that we represent Christ to the world and to each other.

The Church in the Bible: The Book of Acts

Acts tells the story of the church, from its inception on the day of Pentecost in Acts 2, to ch. 28 with Paul at Rome. In between, the church experiences tragedies and triumphs, sorrows and joys. The book of Acts tells the story of the young church, persecuted but bold. Two things stand out in the life of the early church. One concerns the power of the Holy Spirit. At the end of the Gospels we see apostles who were scared, even to the point of hiding. Then in the early chapters of Acts these same apostles boldly turn the world upside down.

The key to understanding what happened to them is seen in Acts 1:8 (in Christ's prophecy), then in Acts 2 (the prophecy's fulfillment). The apostles received the Holy Spirit, and with the

Spirit they received power. This same Spirit still binds believers together and brings us into the family of God (Eph. 4:1–7).

The Holy Spirit graciously gives us spiritual gifts, according to Romans 12:3–8 and 1 Corinthians 12:4–11. God has designed the church to be the place where these gifts are discovered, nurtured, and used to build up the body of Christ and bring it to maturity, ultimately for the glory of God (see 1 Corinthians 14).

The same Spirit who worked powerfully in the early church continues to work in and through the church today.

Second, the book of Acts shows how the church functions and what it does. Members of the early church "devoted themselves to the apostles' teaching and the fellowship, to the breaking of bread and the prayers" (Acts 2:42). All these activities are essential to growing in Christ, and all occur within the local church.

The Church in the Bible: The Epistles

Having looked briefly at the tabernacle and temple in the OT, and the church in the Gospels and Acts, we now come to the NT epistles. With a few exceptions, these books were written to churches, stressing again the God-ordained stature of the church. In the Epistles, especially the letters of Paul to Titus and Timothy, Paul clearly could not conceive of living the Christian life apart from the church.

Paul and the other NT writers often use word pictures to describe the church. At one point Paul calls the church the household of God (1 Tim. 3:15). The church is a family (Gal. 3:28;

Heb. 13:1; 1 Pet. 1:22). The church is a building (Eph. 2:20–22; 1 Pet. 2:4–5). The church is pictured as a flock of sheep (1 Pet. 5:1–4). And one of Paul's favorite metaphors is of the church as Christ's body (Eph. 4:11–16; 1 Cor. 12:12–27). All of these metaphors contribute to a fuller understanding of how to live the Christian life as part of the church.

The church is even pictured as a bride (2 Cor. 11:2–4; Rev. 19:7–9; 21:1–4). It is the bride of Christ—a bride for whom Jesus died. In the context of urging husbands to love their wives, Paul writes that "Christ loved the church and gave himself up for her" (Eph. 5:25). What more could be said to underscore and establish the importance of the church for the Christian life?

The Church as the Communion of Saints

From the very beginning of God's dealing with his people, the Bible has stressed community. In fact, biblical discussion of godly living is almost always set in the context of growing together, in community, as God's people. For Christians today, and for the last 2,000 years, God has established the local church as the vehicle for that community. Some current movements seek to replace more traditional understandings of the local church, seeing a group of friends meeting together, for instance, as church. That's not quite the picture that we see in the NT.

In the NT, we see young and old mixing, as older women and men are to teach younger women and men. We see people coming together to worship who come from different

God's Job Description for the Church

proclaim the gospel	Matt. 28:16–20; Acts 2:37–44; 1 Thess. 2:1–12
organize efforts to reach the nations with the message of salvation	Rom. 15:22–33; 2 Cor. 5:18–21
preach the Word	1 Tim. 4:1–5
conduct the ordinances of baptism and the Lord's Supper	Matt. 28:16–20; 1 Cor. 11:17–34
exercise discipline	2 Thess. 3:6–15; 1 Tim. 5:19–25
provide guidance and instruction	1 Timothy 5; Titus 2
provide opportunities to exercise spiritual gifts	Acts 6:1–7; 1 Corinthians 12–14
meet together regularly and encourage one another	Heb. 10:23–25
provide aid for members and others in times of economic need or crisis	1 Cor. 16:1–4
be a voice for common grace and human dignity in the surrounding culture	Gal. 6:9–10
be the body of Christ on earth, modeling love and unity	John 17:20–26
be a place where imperfect people can grow in their knowledge of grace and redemption	1 Pet. 1:3–25

stages in life, different occupations, and different backgrounds. Paul stressed that the social divides typical of most groups in society have no place in the church. The church should be a place of diversity, where each person can contribute to the whole. Limiting oneself to a circle of peers is not sanctioned by Scripture and does not promote spiritual growth.

Sadly, in our day there are churches in which leaders try to dominate their congregations rather than shepherd them in the model of the selfless love of Jesus. But those bad examples do not take away the biblical command to gather and worship as a church. Local churches undoubtedly have their flaws, because they are made up of flawed, sinful people. The Apostles' Creed refers to the church as a "communion of saints." As we come into the church we sometimes imagine that there will be no problems, no conflicts, and no frustrations among our community of saints. But we forget that we are a community of flawed people, still burdened by our imperfections and failures and sins. It is precisely because of our flaws and faults that we need each other.

God has ordained the church, a fellowship of the flawed, to carry out his purpose and will in the world. The following chart lists some things God has ordained for the church to do.

When we consider the biblical teaching on the church, we realize the church is vitally important for growing in Christ. Like a branch that grows because of its connection to the tree, we thrive when we stay connected to the church.

THE AUTHORITY AND RELIABILITY OF THE BIBLE

To Whom Shall We Go?

In the beginning of John 6, a crowd of thousands follows Jesus, hanging on every word he says. By the end of the chapter, after Jesus delivers some hard teachings, the large crowd dwindles and falls away. Jesus turns to the remaining 12 disciples and asks, "Do you want to go away as well?" (John 6:67).

Peter speaks up: "Lord, to whom shall we go? You have the words of eternal life, and we have believed, and have come to know, that you are the Holy One of God" (John 6:68–69).

Peter's question hangs over every one of us. To whom shall we go? In other words, to whom will we listen? What voice will we follow as we live our lives? What *authority* will we follow?

Other Voices

In the early centuries of the church, false Gospels arose, painting a far different portrait of Jesus and of salvation than that found in the Bible. The church fathers responded by affirming orthodox creeds and by recognizing the canon of the Bible consisting of 66 books.

The leaders of the sixteenth-century Protestant Reformation faced a church that had for centuries viewed itself as the final authority in matters of faith, thus obscuring the 66 books of the Bible. The Reformers returned to the Bible as the ultimate authority and drafted statements that summarized biblical teaching.

In the modern age, sometimes called the age of Enlightenment, the rise of science and the overwhelming confidence placed in human reason mounted an assault against belief in the ancient book of Scripture. Instead, reason and science became the authority.

In our pluralistic and postmodern world, choruses of voices vie for attention. Many claim that no one voice has it right. Instead, the prevailing view holds that all opinions are equally valid.

Peter's insightful question, "To whom shall we go?" stands over all of us. Peter's own answer is equally insightful. Jesus is the Holy One, and he speaks the words of eternal life. Scripture alone, the book centered on and permeated by Jesus, is the only true and authentic voice.

Sola Scriptura

As mentioned, the Reformers pointed to Scripture alone as the sole authority. The Latin expression for this is *sola Scriptura*, meaning "Scripture alone." We trust in Scripture because it is the self-disclosure of God. It is God's own revelation of himself. Consequently, we speak of the authority and reliability of Scripture. Let's take a closer look at these crucial concepts.

Authority: This Is the Word of God

From the beginning, the very first verse in Genesis, the Bible makes a number of assertions. Chief among them is the existence and presence of God. The Bible does not attempt to prove that God exists so much as it asserts that he exists. A second assertion concerns God's relationship to the world. God, whom we meet in those opening moments in Genesis, speaks the world into existence, and is now present everywhere within it.

Genesis 1 has a number of poetic features, one being the rhythmic repeating of the phrase, "And God said. . . . And it was so." This repeated phrase reveals God's authority. He speaks, and the universe obeys.

God's authoritative self-disclosure, his written revelation, continues as the books of Scripture unfold. Later in Israel's history, as the prophets come on the scene, these spokespersons for God merely invoke a four-word phrase—"Thus says the Lord"—to establish the credibility and authority of their message.

As we move into the NT, the apostles make similar claims. In fact, Paul tells us directly that his authority as an apostle is derived from his role as a spokesperson for God. Paul wants people to listen to him not because of himself but because he speaks on behalf of God (see Gal. 1:12).

Inspiration

Theologians refer to the Bible as the "inspired word of God." The word "inspired" is a biblical term that literally means "God-breathed" (2 Tim. 3:16; 2 Pet. 1:21). Just as God spoke the universe into existence (Genesis 1), he continued to speak, revealing himself and his plan of salvation

AUTHORITY OF THE BIBLE 1326

through the prophets, the apostles, and all 40 or so divinely inspired human authors of the 66 books of the Bible.

Because of the divine origin of the Bible, it possesses a unique quality among all literature: it alone is true and authoritative in each and every detail. We speak of "verbal, plenary inspiration." "Verbal" means the very words of Scripture are inspired. "Plenary" means the whole, the complete Bible is inspired.

God desired to make himself and his plan of salvation known. He revealed himself. Because it is God's revelation of himself, by himself, we can have full confidence that he superintended the process of the giving of his Word to ensure an exact and accurate record.

The authority of Scripture is established by Scripture's divine origin and authorship. We ultimately come to know this to be true by something more than intellectual argument and persuasion. The Holy Spirit reveals to us that Scripture is God's Word, that it is true, and that we can build and govern our lives by it. Theologians refer to this as the "internal witness of the Holy Spirit." This crucial ministry of the Spirit is explained in 1 Corinthians 2.

But we must recognize that we live in a skeptical age in which people ask, *Who's to say we can really know anything with certainty?* It is also a pluralistic age, raising the question, *Who's to say one religion or one sacred book has a corner on the market of truth?* For an answer to these questions of our age, we need to discuss the reliability of Scripture.

Self-attestation of Scripture

Before considering evidences for Scripture's reliability, we must take into account the self-attestation of Scripture. The Bible's self-claims to be true permeate the pages of Scripture. Psalm 119:89 declares, "Forever, O LORD, your word is firmly fixed in the heavens." In 2 Samuel 7:28 we read, "O Lord GOD, you are God, and your words are true." First John 5:9–12 speaks of the testimony that God has given of Christ. We believe in Christ because what we know of Christ has been told to us by the absolutely certain testimony of God.

Throughout the OT books, God's truthful speech points to his uniqueness and demonstrates that he alone is God. Isaiah 44:6–8 explains that what God declares will happen indeed does happen—when God prophesies of the future, it comes true. Read through Jeremiah 23:23–32 to see what God has to say about false prophets who speak lies, as opposed to the true prophets. God's Word alone is to be trusted because it is true, fixed, and certain.

These self-claims of the Bible to be true may not be all that decisive for the skeptic or for the pluralist, but this is where we must start the discussion. If we look first to external evidences (evidences from history or archaeology that are outside of the Bible) to prove the authority of the Bible, then we are unwittingly placing the Bible in a position of subservience under those things.

Instead of *proving* the Bible to be true, external evidences play a supportive, subordinate role, *demonstrating* the truthfulness inherent in the Bible. The difference between proving and demonstrating is not a mere word game. The Bible does not derive its authority from external evidences. The Bible derives its authority from its own self-claims.

Yet, these external evidences play a crucial role. Only the Holy Spirit can ultimately persuade us to accept God's Word as truth, but the Spirit also uses human means in his work of conviction. In addressing the skeptic or the pluralist, it is helpful to have answers to their questions and to be able to defend the Bible's authority and reliability.

Sometimes Christians have doubts as well. Centuries ago, the medieval theologian Anselm used the phrase "Faith seeking understanding" to declare that evidences and reasons can be a helpful support to our faith. In the words of a father whose son was healed by Jesus, "I believe; help my unbelief!" (Mark 9:24).

Reliability: We Can Know This Is the Word of God

The first line of defense of Scripture's reliability concerns the big picture of the Bible's uniqueness. It is undeniably the most unique book of all time. The Bible was written over a span of some 1,600 years, by approximately 40 authors from all walks of life, in three different languages, on three different continents. Yet, despite all that diversity, the Bible is one unified book, with each of its parts meshing with all the other parts. On that score, the Bible stands in a class all by itself.

Beyond the big picture, consider the textual or manuscript witness, and the historical and archaeological witness to the Bible's factuality.

External Evidences: Textual Matters

Scholars who work with ancient texts regularly practice what they call "conjectural emendation." This is the art of guessing at what's missing in ancient texts. The manuscript witness to the original writings of the ancient philosophers, historians, poets, and politicians is quite spotty. Only a handful of texts remain in existence for many of the major works by figures such as Plato or Herodotus, and those texts can be inconsistent or incomplete, with missing words or lines. Scholars consequently guess (conjecture) as to what's missing and add it to the text (emendation).

No such practice is necessary when it comes to the Bible. Scholars employ three criteria to judge the manuscript witness of ancient texts: *quantity* (the number of manuscripts), *time interval* (between the manuscript and the original writing), and *quality* (how well the scribe did his work on the manuscript). On all three counts the Bible stands apart from every other ancient text. For instance, far more textual evidence exists for the existence of Jesus Christ than for the existence of Julius Caesar.

External Evidences: Archaeological Matters

Consider also the historical or archaeological evidence. Certain scholars questioned the very existence of David and the Davidic line of kings based on the lack of archaeological evidence. Then a discovery was made of the "House of David" inscription, offering hard data of the Davidic dynasty. In addition, consider these archaeological finds:

Merneptah Stele	from the 13th century B.C., containing a reference to Israel
Cyrus Cylinder	confirms the account in Ezra of Israel's return from exile
Moabite Stone	records the interaction between Moab and Israel's King Omri (see 1 Kings 16)
Black Obelisk of Shalmaneser	records King Jehu's defeat in 2 Kings 9-10

The 20th century has witnessed a number of discoveries related to the NT, including the following:

Caiaphas Ossuary	discovered in Old Jerusalem in 1993
Pontius Pilate Inscription	discovered at Caesarea Maritima in 1961
House of Peter(?)	excavated in Capernaum 1968-1986

These finds and many others support the historical reliability of the Bible. In both the big picture and in the details, external evidences point to the uniqueness of the Bible among all books. These evidences offer support for the Bible's self-claim that it is the authoritative, reliable, and true word of God.

Trust and Obey: Listening to the One True Voice

To whom shall we go? Many voices clamor for our attention. May we join in with Peter's heartfelt conviction that there is nowhere else to go but to Jesus and his Word, the words of eternal life.

HOW TO READ AND UNDERSTAND THE BIBLE

The apostle Peter once made a surprising but encouraging confession about reading Paul's epistles: "There are some things in them that are hard to understand" (2 Pet. 3:16). Do you ever feel that way about Scripture? Have you ever felt "lost in the woods" as you try to make sense of a Scripture passage? We have all been there—even Peter.

Over the centuries, church leaders and scholars have offered various guidelines to help readers understand what they are reading, to help them get out of the woods. We have come to call this discipline "hermeneutics."

Herman Who?

In Greek mythology, the figure Hermes carried messages back and forth between the gods. He is also credited with inventing language. From his name we have derived the term "biblical hermeneutics," which means the art and science of interpreting the biblical text.

Perhaps calling it a *science* sends the wrong message. This isn't about test tubes and lab coats. Nevertheless, there is a method involved in understanding Scripture.

However, calling it an *art* actually sends precisely the right message. As an art, interpreting the Bible involves skills and techniques, but as an art it also requires practice and cultivation. Artists may have great natural ability, but they also work hard to become better and better at their craft.

Some Preliminary Principles

So it is with understanding Scripture. We can learn methods and techniques, but we also have to work at it. We don't start off making masterpieces. Over time we mature and become better. But it takes time.

It also takes humble dependence on the Holy Spirit. In 1 Corinthians 2, Paul writes that the Holy Spirit teaches us the deep things of God. He illumines, or sheds light on, Scripture. For those who are saved, who are indwelt by the Holy Spirit, it's like having a new pair of glasses through which to see Scripture more clearly. Maturing in the art of reading the Bible requires an active dependence on the Holy Spirit.

It also takes humble dependence on others. Sometimes we need help in interpreting the Bible. That's why God gave the church the gift of pastor-teachers, as well as the gift of scholars. Study Bibles, encyclopedias, atlases, and commentaries also provide valuable resources for study. We also need to pay careful attention as we listen to sermons and attend Bible studies. Biblical interpretation is not an individual sport. It's a team effort. We need to interpret the Bible as part of a Christian community.

These preliminary principles set the stage. Let's move from here to explore some ways we can better read and understand God's Word to us.

A Three-step Method

One simple method of understanding the Bible consists of the following three steps:

Observe
Interpret
Apply

Observation: Seeing the Bible

We look at a lot of things, but we don't always see them. This is especially true of the things with which we are most familiar. This can also be true when we read the Bible. So the first step is to *observe*, to take the time to see what we're looking at. This involves paying attention to little words, such as "and," "but," or even "or." We also look for signal words, such as "therefore." When we see a "therefore," we should see big arrows that point to what precedes and follows it.

In addition to looking for crucial words, we also need to look for repeated words, clauses, or themes. Biblical authors use repetition to alert us to key themes or ideas. Repetition signals emphasis.

Finally, look for big picture connections. As one example, consider the Bible's emphasis on the *seed to come*. This key idea finds its roots in Genesis 3:15 and comes to full fruit in Christ and his work on the cross. Look for how the various biblical authors interact with this theme. As you grow in reading the Bible, you'll become more adept at seeing and tracing these themes.

Interpretation: Asking the Right Questions

To help you further develop your observation skills, learn the habit of asking questions as you read. You can use the old stand-by questions of *Who? What? When? Where?* and *Why?* These questions help us move from the first step of observation to the second step of interpretation.

Where and When?

Asking the questions of *Where* and *When* helps us get a handle on the physical setting of the text. The physical setting reminds us that God revealed himself in place and time, to real people. We can ask if there are any place names or geographical features mentioned. We can also ask when the events or the action of the text occurs. We can further ask if the time and place of the setting shed any light on understanding what's happening in the text.

There's another setting beyond that of the chronological or geographical. This is the canonical context. As we move from Genesis to Revelation, God reveals his will and his plan progressively. A good question to ask here is, *Where does this particular text fit on the "canonical map"?* That is, *Where are we in the story?*

Who's on First?

In addition to the setting (the questions of *Where* and *When*), look at the characters in the story (the question of *Who*). Who is involved in the passage? What do we know about them from other passages? For instance, you may be reading a passage that mentions the Philistines. What do other passages say about them? One suggestion is to look at the first and last reference to a person or group. Use a concordance or a Bible search program and look for the first time the Philistines come on the biblical stage and the last time they exit.

We can also better read the Bible as we look to people in the Bible as models—models of the good, the bad, and even the ugly. We need to see how they changed, how they followed God in obedience, and also how they disobeyed God. God revealed himself to people just like us. They came from a different place and time, but we share with all of them a common human nature. God gave us their stories to teach us.

God at the Center

The main character of the Bible is the triune God. A God-centered view of Scripture recognizes that the Bible is about God and what he is doing in the world. Be looking for how God is sovereignly at work in the lives of people in the Bible. Ask, *What is the passage teaching about Christ?*

Martin Luther said that while Christ may not be in every verse of the Bible, he is in every passage. Two good questions to ask as we interpret the Bible are, *How does this passage relate to Christ?* and *What does it teach about Christ and his work?* As the Word of God, every passage in the Bible teaches us something about the persons and work of the triune God.

What's the Big Idea?

As we put together the *Where*, *When*, and *Who* of the passage, we begin to get at the *What* of the passage. A helpful question to ask is, *What is the big idea?*

Try to find the main point of the passage. The biblical authors give pointers and clues that help. In the Epistles, we see this in the way paragraphs are formed. Remember English composition and the infamous topic sentence? That's what we're looking for in the paragraphs in the Epistles.

In the narrative or historical books, look at the sections. In the poetic books, look at the poems. These paragraphs, sections, and poems are the literary units of the Bible. They form the context of any given verse.

Context Is King

Too often we take verses out of context, but we shouldn't. A bottom-line rule for understanding the Bible is that *context is king*. First, we encounter the context of the literary unit. These individual units connect with what precedes and what follows. Eventually, these units come together to form the book. Next come groupings of books. Put it all together and we have the Bible.

For instance, the Ten Commandments in Exodus 20 should be read in the context of the book of Exodus; then in the context of the first five books of the Bible (called the Pentateuch); then in the context of the OT; and finally in the context of the entire Bible.

Think of throwing a rock in a pond and watching the concentric circles expand outward. Any given verse is the rock in the middle, and these ever-expanding circles are wider and wider contexts in which the passage fits.

Scripture Interprets Scripture

To interpret a text properly, we may need to look elsewhere in Scripture. This is a time-tested principle: *Scripture interprets Scripture*. We need to connect one passage of Scripture with others and, ultimately, with the whole. The individual pieces of the puzzle make sense when they're connected to the whole.

Application: Be Doers of the Word

James tells us that we haven't really read the Bible until we put it into practice. Application asks the all-important question, *So what?* What difference does what I'm observing and interpreting make in my life? How should I live in light of this passage?

Sometimes we jump too quickly to application in our Bible reading. We ask, What does this text mean *to me*? before we ask, What does *this text* mean? We can also stop too quickly in our Bible reading. We should never be content with just understanding a text. We should always push on until we put what we know into action.

Putting These Principles into Practice

As we read the Bible we should be cultivating good habits as readers, taking time to see (observation), asking and answering questions of the text (interpretation), and living out the text in life (application). To simplify this process, let's summarize some of the principles and guidelines we have sketched out above.

1. *Ask questions as you read.* Ask, *Where? When? Who? What?* and *So what?* Don't be overwhelmed by all these questions. By asking only a few of them you'll be well served in your quest to understand the Bible. Slow down and take your time as you read.
2. *Pay attention to the context.* Remember, context is king. We understand verses far better when we read them in context.
3. *Read prayerfully, dependently, and obediently.* There's far more to understanding Scripture than mental comprehension. We are standing on holy ground every time we open the Bible.

The Psalmist exclaims, "Your word is a lamp to my feet and a light to my path" (Ps. 119:105). God has given us his Word to guide us. May we read, understand, and follow it along our journey through life.

HOW TO APPLY THE BIBLE
IN DAILY LIFE

In the 1920s, J. Gresham Machen, a NT scholar and great defender of the faith, spoke of the ability of the Bible to rise above and break through the noise and chatter and static of his age. Think how many more voices clamor for our attention in the twenty-first century. They seem to bombard us. Yet, above all the noise, the Bible speaks powerfully, poignantly, and clearly. We must listen to it. We must follow its honest and true voice in a world of "sound bites."

Why We Need to Follow God's Word

We need to apply the Bible in daily life because it alone is a sure and certain guide. The Bible tells us how to live. It is not merely an ancient book written to people long ago in places far away. The Bible is God's Word *to us today*.

And as God's Word to us, it asks something of us. In fact, the Bible demands something of us. It demands that we change. We must live it out. The apostle James makes it clear that the one who only reads the Bible, but doesn't do what it says, misses the point (see James 1:22–25).

The Bible in Action

We can live out the Bible in three ways.

First, the Bible speaks to specific situations we face. Consequently, *we need to apply the Bible to specific situations, allowing it to affect our attitudes and actions*.

Second, the Bible offers guidance for the transformation of our lives as we mature in Christ and conform to his image (see Rom. 12:1–2; 2 Cor. 3:16–18). This refers to a process rather than to particular actions. Consequently, *we need to allow the Bible to transform our hearts and minds as we mature in conformity to Christ*.

Third, the Bible addresses not merely individual issues, concerns, and situations, but those of the family, the local church, and the body of Christ. Therefore, *we need to be sensitive to corporate applications of Scripture beyond mere individual applications*.

Let's flesh out each of these three types of application.

The Bible and My Life: Facing Specific Situations

In applying the Bible, we tend to think of specific situations we face. A particular problem or temptation arises, so we turn to the Bible for help. How can we apply what we read in the Bible to these situations?

Keeping First Things First

When reading and then attempting to apply the Bible, we often jump right to our personal lives. This leap to self, however, short-circuits the right order. Remember, the Bible's main emphasis is the glory of God. We need to think of God first, before we think of ourselves. Ask what this passage teaches you about the triune God and what he is doing in the world. Then, in light of that, turn the attention to yourself with questions such as these: (1) How does this passage's teaching about God and his work relate to me? (2) In light of what I learned about God and his work, how should I think and act?

We'll be far better off if we keep God first in everything, even as we seek to apply the Bible to daily life.

Serving Others

We also need to think of others. Jesus gave the Golden Rule: "So whatever you wish that others would do to you, do also to them, for this is the Law and the Prophets" (Matt. 7:12). Going further, he said, "You shall love your neighbor as yourself" (Matt. 22:39). Paul reiterated this principle of humbly considering the needs of others before our own in Philippians 2:1–5. To apply this teaching practically, ask these questions: (1) What does this passage teach about serving others? (2) How can I be a living example of Jesus before others? (3) Based on this passage, is there anything I'm doing that would hinder others from embracing the gospel?

After thinking of God and others, we can look at what the Bible says about our own lives.

Looking into the Mirror

As we read the Bible, we need to let the Bible *read us*. We don't always like what we see in ourselves, but we need to let the light of God's Word shine on our lives, revealing our blind spots and those pesky problem areas.

Here are some beginning questions to ask that will help us become doers of the Word: (1) What character traits does this passage encourage me to develop? (2) What does this passage reveal about me, my thinking, my values, my beliefs, and my actions? (3) As I look in the mirror of God's Word, what needs to change in my life?

Martin Luther said the Word of God both assaults us and comforts us. He's talking about how the Bible both challenges and encourages us. We need to realize that God's Word is the most insightful—and the most true!—book ever written about the human condition. In light of that, here are a few questions to ask ourselves: (1) How does this passage challenge me? (2) What attitudes or actions do I need to change? (3) How does this passage encourage me? (4) What promises of God are found in the passage that give me joy and hope?

When to Kiss, When to Shake Hands

As we apply Scripture to our lives today, we should recognize that some things in the Bible are more culturally bound than others. A classic example of this is, "Greet all the brothers with a holy kiss" (1 Thess. 5:26). A direct application would require us to kiss one another each time we greet. In much of contemporary Western culture we do not follow the custom of greeting one another with a kiss. We use a warm and hearty handshake. Thus, we can apply this passage in daily life by greeting one another warmly, taking time to say hello to others, and showing genuine interest in fellow believers.

It can be difficult to distinguish what in Scripture is bound by culture and what transcends a specific time or culture. One way to cultivate discernment in this area is simply to ask if the biblical command is linked directly to an ancient Near Eastern (OT) or a Greco-Roman (NT) cultural practice. Or we could ask whether the biblical command is addressed to perennial human nature (true for all peoples of all times).

For example, Paul's insistence on pure sexual ethics is not restricted to Christians in the city of Corinth, a city renowned for sexual promiscuity. The commands related to sexual ethics reach all the way back to the garden of Eden and the God-ordained institution of marriage and sex within marriage. These commands for sexual purity are found throughout Scripture. A high sexual ethic applies to all peoples at all times.

The Bible and My Life: The Process of Transformation

The second level of application requires us to dig a little deeper than the first level. Here application concerns the big picture of our lives. Our daily actions, behaviors, and attitudes stem from who we are. The Bible says clearly, "The good person out of the good treasure of his heart produces good, and the evil person out of his evil treasure produces evil, for out of the abundance of the heart his mouth speaks" (Luke 6:45).

We often prefer to focus on the surface (behavior) instead of what lies beneath (the heart). But what lies beneath makes the ultimate difference. We must apply the Bible to the very core of our lives. We don't simply aim to apply the Bible to our lives today or this week. We should also aim to apply the Bible to the entire course of our lives.

Did you ever notice how you become like the people you hang out with? You not only mimic their actions, but you also take on their character qualities. You even start to look alike. But the Bible urges us to become more like Jesus. By spending regular time in the Word as active readers, we begin to look like the picture painted for us in the Bible.

Spending time studying the Bible transforms us. Just as Moses came down from the mountain glowing from his time in the presence of the glory of God, we too will be transformed as we behold the glory of God in prayerful meditation on God's Word (2 Cor. 3:18). Over time, our desire and capacity to apply the Bible will deepen, mature, and grow.

The Bible and My Life: Living Out the Bible as Part of a Community

The third level of application concerns some of our key communities—our family, the local church, and the church worldwide. In Ephesians 4:15–16, Paul presents the idea that our growth as individual Christians is inextricably linked to the growth of the whole body of Christ.

We can get a better handle on this big picture by looking at the local church. Through the ministry of faithful preaching and discipleship, a local church should be applying Scripture and seeing spiritual growth and maturity *as a church*. The Christian life is not an individual effort but a corporate one. How are you contributing to that growth?

We should also think about the application of Scripture in our families. This is difficult in families with both Christians and non-Christians. But in Christian families an attitude that "we're all in this together" should prevail. The whole family should be pursuing the goal of living the Word, with everyone pulling in the same direction.

Applying the Bible: The Dynamic that Makes the Difference

The Bible is not merely human opinion. It is the very Word of God. We may think it asks too much of us. Did Paul really tell us to do everything without complaining? Am I really to remain sexually pure even though cultural voices tell me sexual promiscuity is okay? Do I really have to think of others before I think of myself? Does God really expect me to put his kingdom above everything else?

The truth is that ultimately we can't measure up to these demands. Is this the fine print that gets us all off the hook?

No, our insufficiency does not absolve us of our responsibility to obey God's Word. Rather, it drives us to depend on the Holy Spirit. Just as the Holy Spirit is indispensable to understanding God's Word, so the Holy Spirit is indispensable to applying it.

Application is first a matter of prayer, then a matter of action. God has made us new creatures in Christ (2 Cor. 5:17). He continues the transformation process in our lives as we humbly read and seek to follow his Word. God has also given us the Holy Spirit so that the good work begun at our salvation will continue until it reaches its full and glorious completion (Phil. 1:6). That's why we strive with all our hearts—by God's grace and for his glory—to apply his Word to our lives.

IMPORTANT CHRISTIAN TRUTHS: DOCTRINE

INTRODUCTION

Wearing Your Doctrine

How well do you wear your doctrine? This question might seem strange, but it comes from reading the apostle Paul. In Titus 2:10, Paul says that "in everything" we need to "adorn the doctrine of God our Savior." To see what this means, we have to look at the context.

Chapter 2 of this letter begins with Paul's clear instructions to Pastor Titus: "teach what accords with sound doctrine" (2:1). And this teaching drills down deep into the lives of his congregation. Paul addresses specific groups in the church, such as older men and women, younger men and women, and bondservants. He gives instructions regarding their behavior, attitudes, and character. Then Paul declares: "so that in everything they may *adorn the doctrine* of God our Savior" (2:10). In other words, the way they live should highlight, or adorn, the attractiveness of the gospel.

First, Paul connects doctrine to living the Christian life, telling Titus's congregation on the Island of Crete how to practically live out their faith. They *wear their doctrine* as they live out their faith.

Paul uses two words here that we should look at more closely. The word translated "adorn" is *kosmeō*. The English word "cosmetics" comes from it. It means to wear something—but not in the sense of throwing clothes on because you are running late. It means to arrange carefully. The translation of "adorn" captures this well.

The second word is "doctrine." In the original language it literally means "teachings." Paul used this word more than any other biblical writer to convey the idea of a systematic and organized body of teaching. Again, the translation "doctrine" expresses the original meaning quite well.

This body of teaching is to be adorned "in everything." There is nothing we can be or do or say that falls outside of the bounds of adorning or wearing our doctrine. According to Paul, doctrine should have an effect on every area of life.

It Really Is about God

There's one more word to notice in Titus 2:10 regarding doctrine. This doctrine we are to adorn in everything is the doctrine of God. The subject, the end, the beginning, the middle— *every part of doctrine is about, by, from, and for God*. We humans have a tendency to make everything about *us*. Writing in the Middle Ages, Thomas Aquinas offered a God-focused definition of theology, or doctrine: "Theology is taught by God, theology teaches about God, and theology leads to God." First, God is the *source* of theology and the author of all doctrine. Doctrine comes top-down, from God to us, as he reveals himself and his plan to us through his Word. We are dependent on his revelation for our doctrine.

Not only is God the source of theology, but he is also the *subject* of theology. The phrase "theology teaches about God" means that every subject—every topic and sub-topic in theology— must eventually trace back to God. The word "theology" literally means *the study of God*.

Finally, good theology should be *sung*. It leads to God and ends in worship. We can be good theologians yet fail to see our theological reflection and understanding as an act of worship. The kind of theology worth wearing is that which results in worship.

So again: How well do you wear your doctrine?

Healthy Doctrine

Paul also insists that our doctrine be *sound* (literally "hygienic"). He refers to this healthy or sound doctrine in several places in the Pastoral Epistles (1 Tim. 1:10; 6:3; 2 Tim. 1:13; 4:3; Titus 1:9, 13; 2:1, 2, 8).

Paul reminds both of these younger pastors, Timothy and Titus, of the priority of sound doctrine because false teachings undermine the church. Paul calls these contrary or different teachings—different from the gospel and from the apostles' teaching. So that false teachings do not gain a foothold, fester like a cancer, and destroy the church, young Timothy and

Titus are to preach and teach sound—hygienic and healthy—doctrine (see 1 Tim. 1:3; 6:3; and Rom. 16:17).

That charge to Timothy and Titus has trickled down through the generations and comes directly to each of us. All of us are to be healthy, hygienic theologians who believe, teach, and proclaim sound doctrine.

Why Pay Attention to Doctrine?

Paul calls us to wear our doctrine and live it out. He counsels us to pay attention to sound doctrine and remain committed to knowing the teachings of Jesus and his apostles. Based on Paul's admonitions, we can learn two major reasons why knowing and studying theology is crucial for the life of the church: (1) It keeps us from error, enables us to identify false teaching, and enables us to help others caught up in false teaching. (2) It allows us to know God as he has revealed himself to us, to love God as we should, and to worship God faithfully and truthfully.

What Makes for Sound Doctrine?

How can we know what is sound doctrine? We do not have to guess. The Bible provides what we need to know. We also have the resource of faithful men and women throughout church history. One of the gifts from the early centuries of the church is the Apostles' Creed.

This creed was not written by the apostles but by various church leaders in the generations immediately following the first-century apostles. The early bishops drew up creeds—summaries of the faith that could be memorized and proclaimed—for new converts and for members of the church. Bishops borrowed lines from each other, and eventually patterns began to emerge. By the sixth century these various creeds were all brought together and named the Apostles' Creed.

Bishops wrote these confessions following the model of Scripture. A prime example is 1 Timothy 3:16, where Paul begins with the words, "we confess." Then he offers six rhythmic phrases that summarize the life of Christ from his incarnation to his ascension.

New Testament scholars think Paul is either quoting a creed that had been circulating in the church, or composing a creed for the church to confess. This summary of many teachings about Christ found in the Gospels is presented in a way that can be memorized and recited.

The early bishops also summarized biblical teaching in a way that can be memorized. The Apostles' Creed has been used through

the centuries to express and teach important doctrines of Christianity. It makes basic statements about God, Christ, the Holy Spirit, and the church. As a good starting point, it is worth studying, memorizing, and meditating upon:

I believe in God, the Father Almighty,
Maker of heaven and earth,

And in Jesus Christ, his only Son, our Lord:
who was conceived by the Holy Ghost,
born of the virgin Mary,
suffered under Pontius Pilate,
was crucified, dead, and buried;
he descended into hell.
The third day he arose again from the dead;
he ascended into heaven,
and sitteth on the right hand of God the Father Almighty;
from thence he shall come to judge the quick and the dead.

I believe in the Holy Ghost;
the holy catholic church;
the communion of saints;
the forgiveness of sins;
the resurrection of the body;
and the life everlasting.

Amen.

The word "creed" comes from the Latin word *credo*, meaning "I believe." We should not take lightly these doctrines that we say we believe. Beliefs are important because they lead to behaviors. Our doctrine governs how we look at the world and how we live and act in the world. People have stood firm for their beliefs. Some have suffered. Some have been martyred. When we say "I believe," we are not merely saying words. Let's keep that in mind as we seek to understand what we believe and as we confess and live out our beliefs together.

Building on the Basics

We will build on these basic biblical teachings as we explore important Christian truths. To help us get a handle on the particulars, we will use the following structure, keeping in mind that theology is ultimately about God.

The Word of God: The Doctrine of Scripture
The Person of God: The Doctrines of God the Father, Son, and Holy Spirit
The Work of God: The Doctrines of Creation, Salvation, and Consummation

0

Christianity is not the only religion to claim revelation from God. The Bible, however, possesses a uniqueness that sets it apart from all other religious texts.

The Bible was written over many centuries by a variety of authors, yet it stands as one unified book. The Bible has been confirmed by various historical and archaeological discoveries, as well as by the way it speaks eloquently and truthfully about human experience. All of these lines of evidence bear witness to the Bible as God's written revelation to humanity. It is the true Word of the one true God.

We will unfold the doctrine of Scripture by looking at (1) revelation, (2) inspiration, (3) inerrancy, and (4) the attributes of Scripture.

Revelation

Revelation refers to that which is revealed—in this context, that which God has made known. In talking about this message from God, Peter insists that he and the other apostles did not "follow cleverly devised myths" when they presented Christ (2 Pet. 1:16). Peter is contrasting the Christian message with the messages of the Roman and Greek religions of his time. Those religions followed clever myths, myths that were dreamed up by humans to describe the ways and the will of the gods. But God's revelation is top-down (from him to us), pointing the way back up to him as the source of all truth.

Theologians divide revelation into two categories: general revelation and special revelation. *General revelation* refers to what can be known about God universally through his creation. Paul asserts in Romans 1 that God's "invisible attributes, namely, his eternal power and divine nature, have been clearly perceived, ever since the creation of the world, in the things that have been made" (Rom. 1:20). The psalmist adds, "The heavens declare the glory of God, and the sky above proclaims his handiwork" (Ps. 19:1; see also vv. 2–6).

Creation reveals the Creator, standing as a testimony to the presence and goodness of God. This general revelation is available to all people of all times. Though it is true that sin distorts what we see in creation (see Romans 1), general revelation stands as a witness to God.

Yet general revelation has its limitations. It teaches us about God the Creator, but not about God the Redeemer. God has given us his

world, but he has also given us his Word, which proclaims his work of redemption.

Whereas God's *general* revelation is open to all and is present in creation, God's *special* revelation is specifically directed to individuals or groups and is present through God's supernatural intervention. There are various types of *special revelation*. For example, Scripture speaks of prophets and prophetesses, men and women entrusted with a special word from God. God speaks in visions and dreams, and even through objects, such as the Urim and Thummim (Ex. 28:30), or animals (e.g., the donkey in Num. 22:28). Miracles are another type of special revelation. And then there is the Bible, God's authoritative and direct revelation of himself and his plan of redemption.

God preserved his Word in the 66 books of the Bible, with every word pointing to Christ, the one who is called *the* Word. The author of Hebrews declares, "Long ago, at many times and in many ways, God spoke to our fathers by the prophets, but in these last days he has spoken to us by his Son, whom he appointed the heir of all things, through whom also he created the world" (Heb. 1:1–2). John writes, "And the Word became flesh and dwelt among us, and we have seen his glory, glory as of the only Son from the Father, full of grace and truth" (John 1:14).

Christ is the perfect and ultimate revelation of God—of God's glory, grace, and truth. Christ is the final and ultimate *Word* of and from God. He makes God known; he reveals God. In order to read the Bible as God intended, picture Christ at the very center of the Bible with every part pointing to and flowing from him.

The doctrine of revelation reminds us that God wants to be known. He has made himself known in his world and in his Word. He even made himself known by coming in the flesh and walking and living among us.

Inspiration

Referring to the Bible as the Word of God expresses the crucial doctrine of inspiration. Second Timothy 3:16 declares, "All Scripture is breathed out by God." The words "breathed out" have also been translated as "inspired," from which we get the term "inspiration."

Peter adds that the Holy Spirit plays a unique role within the Godhead in this activity of inspiration. He writes, "For no prophecy was ever produced by the will of man, but men spoke from God as they were carried along by the Holy Spirit" (2 Pet. 1:21).

The result is that the Bible is both a divine and a human book. God used human authors, with their distinct personalities and styles, to give us his Word. Thus inspiration can be defined in this way: *God superintended human authors in the composing of his revelation in a way that utilized the author's personality and ensured the exact and true recording of every word.* This view of inspiration means that the words of the Bible are inspired by God and that all of the Bible, every part of it, is true. This is known as the verbal, plenary view of inspiration.

Inerrancy

The word "inerrancy" means "without error." Applied to the Bible, this means not only that it is free from errors but also that *the Bible is fully and absolutely truthful in all it affirms in the original autographs.* Why is it necessary to add "original autographs" (or manuscripts)? This is added to be careful that we do not treat manuscripts or translations—no matter how good they may be—as inerrant. This doesn't mean that the manuscripts and translations we use today are not to be trusted. Manuscripts are constantly being reevaluated in an effort to get as close to the original autographs as possible. We humbly acknowledge the limitations of our copies and translations, but we also earnestly strive for accuracy.

The doctrines of inspiration and inerrancy offer us a place to stand as we seek to understand what life is all about. These doctrines point us beyond ourselves for the answers to life's most pressing questions. These doctrines point us to God.

Theologians also speak of the attributes of Scripture. They are summarized in five key attributes.

The Attributes of Scripture: Authority, Necessity, Sufficiency, Clarity, and Beauty

Because God is the ultimate authority and standard in the universe, and because the Bible is God's Word, we hold to the *authority of Scripture.* The prophetic books repeatedly use the phrase, "Thus says the LORD." The prophet does not appeal to his own authority. Instead, he steps aside, appealing to God's authority.

The authority of Scripture requires one thing of us: joyful submission as we recognize its claim on all aspects of our lives. That can be hard, especially as we consider the powerful voices in culture that compete for our attention. But God's Word alone stands as the ultimate authority. If we desire to obey and love God, then we must obey his Word.

The *necessity of Scripture* means that Scripture is necessary to understand God's will and his plan of salvation. Paul explains in Romans 10 that those who will be saved are those who have believed. And those who have believed have heard the gospel. And they have heard the gospel because someone explained it to them (Rom. 10:9–15). The Word of God is indispensable to knowing the will of God and the way of salvation.

The Bible teaches us far more than the way of salvation. In fact, the Bible sets before us, in the words of Peter, "all things that pertain to life and godliness" (2 Pet. 1:3). Peter says that we would "do well to pay attention" to the prophetic Word "as to a lamp shining in a dark place" (1:19). We learn from general revelation, and we need that knowledge. But Scripture provides all that we need to know. This is known as the *sufficiency of Scripture.* This is encouraging. One can easily become overloaded with data and feel overcome in the quest to accumulate it. But one must not neglect God's Word. As Psalm 119:105 says, "Your word is a lamp to my feet and a light to my path."

The *clarity of Scripture* means that Scripture can be understood. No decoding device is required to understand it. God revealed his word in the common languages of the time: Hebrew, Greek, and a little Aramaic. We still need teachers, but anyone can read and gain a basic understanding of God's Word. What is especially clear in Scripture is God's plan of salvation—that God loves us so much that he sent his Son to die in our place on the cross.

In addition to Scripture's authority, necessity, sufficiency, and clarity, we cannot forget an often-neglected attribute—the *beauty of Scripture.* The Bible is a beautiful work of art. Consider the poetry and the intense imagery of the prophets. Observe the eloquence of Paul, or the intriguing narratives of the historical books. God could have merely given us bullet points. Instead, he gave us a literary masterpiece that has been esteemed through the ages.

The doctrine of Scripture should fill us with gratitude. God did not leave us alone in the world, groping in the darkness. He gave us his Word as a light for our path. Our gratitude should drive us to study his Word, treasure it, submit to it, and obey it. As you continue to develop your doctrine of Scripture, read Psalm 119, paying attention to how the psalmist views the Word and also to how the Word transforms the Psalmist.

We started with God's Word. Next we turn to God himself.

THE PERSON OF GOD: THE DOCTRINES OF GOD THE FATHER, SON, AND HOLY SPIRIT

It has been said that Christianity is not irrational, but it is supra-rational. When we discuss Christian doctrines we exceed the limits of human intellect—and this is nowhere more true than in the doctrine of the Trinity. Keeping our limitations in mind is a great way to be humble theologians.

One in Three? How Can It Be? Looking at the Trinity

The word "Trinity" was coined by the early church father Tertullian around the year A.D. 200 to capture the massive biblical teaching of God as both one and three. Tertullian used the word "substance" or "essence" to speak of God's oneness, and the word "person" to speak of God's "threeness." Putting these together we get his definition: *God is one substance in three persons.*

God's oneness is seen in such texts as Deuteronomy 6:4, which declares plainly, "the LORD is one." In fact, this oneness is emphasized throughout the OT and carries over into the NT as well. It is seen in James 2:19 and 1 Corinthians 8:4.

But within the oneness of God there is a complexity to his being. The OT refers to the breath or the Spirit of God in a profound way, even in the opening chapters of Genesis (1:2 and 2:7; compare Ezekiel 37). This becomes more complex when we consider the biblical teaching concerning the deity of Christ and of the Holy Spirit. The word "deity" means being divine, or having the essence or nature of God, so the teaching of the deity of Christ affirms that Jesus is fully and completely God. Hebrews 1 makes the case for the deity of Christ, as do many passages in the Gospels. Jesus is explicitly called "God" (*theos*) in a number of passages (John 1:1, 18; 20:28; Rom. 9:5; Titus 2:13; Heb. 1:8; 2 Pet. 1:1). In Acts 5:3–4, lying to the Holy Spirit is used interchangeably with lying to God.

By claiming that Christ is God and the Holy Spirit is God, the Bible teaches that *Christ and the Holy Spirit are what God the Father is.* All three persons of the Godhead (the threeness) are divine (the oneness).

One last place we see the doctrine of the Trinity is in the Trinitarian formulas. We see one of these in Paul's benediction in 2 Corinthians 13:14. Paul also weaves together God, Christ, and the Holy Spirit in Romans 1:1–4 and Ephesians 1:3–14. John also offers this interplay between the three persons of the Godhead (see John 1:33–34; 14:16–31; 20:21–22; 1 John 4:7–21).

Though it is an extremely difficult doctrine for us to wrap our minds around, we must affirm the Bible's teaching about the Trinity. It differentiates Christianity from Islam and Judaism, which do not allow for the *threeness* of God. The doctrine of the Trinity also differentiates Christianity from polytheistic religions, like Hinduism or Shintoism, which do not allow for the *oneness* of God.

Ultimately, the doctrine of the Trinity is a mystery. We must state it as we find it in Scripture. We must teach it. We can even offer illustrations to help people understand it. And then we must stop, being aware of our limitations. The doctrine of the Trinity is certainly a place where Deuteronomy 29:29 applies: "The secret things belong to the LORD our God, but the things that are revealed belong to us and to our children forever."

Why the Doctrine of the Trinity Matters

The doctrine of the Trinity has significant consequences for the Christian life. In addition to the work of salvation, which involves all three members of the Trinity, the Trinity is also at work in our lives as Christians. Consider Romans 8 on the Trinity and prayer. Paul tells us that the "Spirit himself intercedes for us" as we pray (v. 26). He adds that "God is for us" (v. 31) and that Christ is at the Father's right hand, "interceding for us" (v. 34).

So all three members of the Trinity are pulling for us, interceding for us. The triune God is our advocate. And with the triune God on our side we boldly and joyfully conclude with Paul that "we are more than conquerors" (Rom. 8:37). The doctrine of the Trinity is a glorious doctrine indeed, inspiring us to worship. One of the earliest Christian hymns is the "Doxology," which calls us to "praise Father, Son, and Holy Ghost."

The Doctrine of God the Father

Keeping the doctrine of the Trinity in mind, we turn to the teachings of Scripture regarding the three persons of the eternal Godhead. Looking first at God the Father, there are two main areas: the decrees of God and the attributes of God.

The word "Father" invites us to pause and reflect. The God who made everything in the universe invites us to call him Father (Gal. 4:4–6). This is a term of love, protection, and provision (see Matt. 7:7–11). It is our high privilege to call the God of heaven and earth Father. God as Father is only the beginning, however.

The Decrees of God

Since God created all things and is the source of all things, it follows that he controls all things. The "decrees of God" refer to his wise and eternal plans and purposes, which are certain to come to pass. God has not left his world or his creatures to function by chance. Isaiah declares, "The LORD of hosts has sworn: 'As I have planned, so shall it be, and as I have purposed, so shall it stand'" (Isa. 14:24; see also 37:26–29). Paul makes a similar claim in Romans 8:28–30.

God is sovereign over his universe and in control of all that comes to pass (see Eph. 1:11), free to fulfill all his holy will (Ps. 115:3; 135:6). This teaching disturbs some people, but it should comfort us to know that God knows us intimately and that our lives are in his hands.

This view that God has ordained all things that come to pass often gets confused with the view of philosophical determinism or even fatalism, which asserts that blind chance and mere "forces" are at work controlling humanity and the universe. Not so in the decrees of God. Behind the decrees of God stands a person, God the Father, who is all-wise, all-knowing, all-powerful, and all-loving. The Christian doctrine of the divine decrees has nothing in common with blind fate. The end of the divine decrees is God's own glory, or as Paul puts it, everything is "to the praise of his glory" (Eph. 1:14).

The Attributes of God

Who is the God of the decrees? What is he like? The attributes, or characteristics, of God give us abundant reasons to know, love, serve, enjoy, and worship God. Below is a list of attributes with select biblical references, which should be studied in their fuller context. These attributes should be understood in terms of how God relates to us, not just as abstract characteristics.

Glorious	Ex. 33:17–23; Luke 9:28–36
Holy and righteous	Isa. 6; Rev. 4–5
Omniscient	Ps. 139:1–6; Col. 2:1–4
Omnipotent	Isa. 40:25–31; Phil. 4:13
Omnipresent	Ps. 139:7–12; Matt. 1:23
All-good	Ex. 33:17–19; Matt. 7:7–11
Unchanging	Mal. 3:6; James 1:17
Sovereign	Isa. 46:8–11; James 4:13–15
Eternal	Ps. 90:1–4; Rev. 1:8
Loving	Deut. 7:6–10; John 3:16
Just	Ex. 34:6–7; 1 John 1:5–10
Wrathful	Nahum 1; Rev. 18
Patient and longsuffering	Jonah; 2 Pet. 3:9
Merciful	Gen. 16:7–16; Eph. 2:4
Gracious	Psalm 86; Rom. 5:15
Faithful	Lam. 3:19–24; Heb. 10:23
True	2 Sam. 22:31; John 14:6

The Doctrine of God the Son

In the Son, Jesus Christ our Lord, we have the clearest and most riveting revelation of God. John 1:1–18 tells us that Christ came to make the Father known, that is, to reveal the Father. And in Christ we see the fullness of divine grace and truth (John 1:14). Christ also came to accomplish the divine plan of redemption (Mark 1:15). Through Christ's work of redemption, he has begun the good work of "making all things new" (Rev. 21:5), and bringing all things together.

The God-man: The Person of Christ

Paul offers a summary statement about the person of Christ in Colossians 2:9: "For in him the whole fullness of deity dwells bodily." Jesus is both fully God and fully human. In the early centuries of the church's life, even while the NT was being written, the doctrine of the person of Christ came under attack. The first barrage focused on Christ's humanity.

Given the prominence of Platonist philosophy, which looks down on the physical and the earthy, many thought that the idea of God literally taking on flesh was both unbelievable and insulting. But that is exactly what Christ did. He humbled himself, became human, and lived among us here on earth, with both feet firmly in the dust (Phil. 2:5–11 and Matt. 1:21–23).

We know Christ was truly human because he was born, he got hungry (Matt. 4:2), he got tired (John 4:6), and as a human he had limitations. Above all, we know he was human because he died (Matt. 27:45–56). God sent him into this world, to be born of a woman, and to be born to die.

By the 300s A.D., the challenges came from the other direction, attacking the deity of Christ. As a result, the church convened a council at Nicea in 325, and there they affirmed the deity of Christ. The Nicene Creed says Christ is "very God of very God," adding that the Son is of the exact same substance or essence as the Father.

Scripture makes a considerable case for the deity of Christ. First, Christ has the same characteristics or attributes as God (John 1:14; 14:6; Heb. 13:8). Second, Christ is said to be equal with God (John 5:18; 10:30; Heb. 1:1–4). Third, Christ is explicitly called God (John 1:1, 18; 20:28; Rom. 9:5; Titus 2:13; Heb. 1:8; 2 Pet. 1:1). Finally, Christ freely accepts worship, which God alone can rightfully receive (Matt. 14:33; Rev. 5:14).

Later in the church's life, in the first half of the 400s, new challenges arose, namely how these two natures of the deity and humanity of Christ came together. Again, the bishops convened a council, this time at Chalcedon. The Chalcedonian Creed actually doesn't spend much time discussing how the two natures came together. The bishops wisely recognized the mystery of this. Instead, the creed clearly and forcefully states that Christ is 100 percent God and 100 percent human and that these two natures are joined fully and perfectly in *one person*. Theologians refer to this as the "hypostatic union," from the Greek word *hypostasis*, meaning "substance." This takes us right back to Paul's statement in Colossians 2:9. Christ is the God-man. Carefully ponder these texts:

Key Texts on the Two Natures of Christ

Luke 2:11–12	Rom. 1:1–6
John 1:1–18	Phil. 2:5–11
John 20:24–29	1 Tim. 2:3–6
Acts 2:20–36	Heb. 4:14–16

The person of Christ is a central, defining doctrine of Christianity. Compare it to the teaching of Islam regarding Christ and it is clear just how crucial it is. This doctrine is important because the person of Christ has everything to do with the work of Christ, with the gospel. Christ the Lord came down from heaven; he took on flesh "for us and for our salvation," in the words of the Nicene Creed. The author of Hebrews puts it this way: "Therefore he had to be made like his brothers in every respect, so that he might become a merciful and faithful high priest in the service of God" (Heb. 2:17).

Our High Priest: The Work of Christ
The concept of Christ as our high priest begins in the OT. In fact, we need to go back not only to the priests in Israel but all the way back to the beginning, to the garden of Eden. When Adam and Eve disobeyed, that one act of disobedience

plunged all of humanity into sin. The tragic consequence of our sin is separation from God, which brings along enormous misery and sorrow and, eventually, death. (See Genesis 3 and Rom. 5:12–21.)

To undo what Adam did, we need the obedient one who can atone for our sins. God instituted the OT priesthood as the means of intercession for his people so that he could have fellowship with them. But those priests were sinners, as we are. Like us, they were subject to death. But Christ is far superior to those priests. He is the eternal and perfect priest who is able to "make propitiation for the sins of the people" (Heb. 2:17; see Hebrews 7; 10:1–18). His sacrifice paid for our sin, satisfying God's wrath and securing pardon and peace for us.

The Doctrine of God the Holy Spirit
The Person of the Holy Spirit
The third member of the Trinity is the Holy Spirit. Much confusion and disagreement surround the doctrine of the Holy Spirit. This is ironic, given that the Holy Spirit was sent to unite us to the triune God and to each other (Eph. 4:1–6). Let's focus on what we must agree upon.

First, Scripture teaches that the Spirit is a person and is divine. The Holy Spirit is not a mere force or some surging impulse, but a person. The Holy Spirit has the attributes of personhood, including intellect (1 Cor. 2:10–13), will (John 3; Acts 16:6–10), and emotion (Eph. 4:30). The Holy Spirit may be lied to (Acts 5:3) and insulted (Heb. 10:29). The NT authors use personal pronouns, such as "he" and "who," as opposed to impersonal pronouns, such as "that" and "which," to refer to the Holy Spirit (John 16:13–14; Eph. 1:13–14). We relate to him as a person, not as some life force pulsing through us.

The Holy Spirit is God. He has characteristics that only God has. For example, he is eternal (Heb. 9:14), knows all things (1 Cor. 2:10–11), can do all things (Zech. 4:6), and is truth (1 John 5:6). The close associations of the Holy Spirit with God the Father and Christ the Son also demonstrate the deity of the Spirit (see Matt. 28:19; John 14:16). Finally, we see the deity of the Holy Spirit in his work and actions.

Giver of Life: The Work of the Holy Spirit
Scripture highlights the particular work of the Holy Spirit in *creation, inspiration, the incarnation*, and *salvation*. Both Genesis 1:2 and Psalm 104:30 portray the Holy Spirit as life-giver. In Ezekiel's fascinating vision of the dry bones

taking on flesh and coming alive, it is the Spirit, the breath of God, who makes it all happen.

The Spirit plays a unique role in the giving of Scripture, according to 2 Peter 1:21. The Spirit, through inspiration, gives us the Word, the Bible. Through the incarnation, the Spirit also brings forth the Word, Jesus. From Mary's conception (Luke 1:35) throughout the life and ministry of Christ on earth, the Spirit is present and at work (see Luke 4:1, 14).

The Spirit also works to bring us to salvation. He convicts us of sin (John 16:8), regenerates us (John 3:6), and sanctifies us (2 Thess. 2:13). The Holy Spirit indwells every believer. And that indwelling of the Holy Spirit unites us to the triune God (John 14:20), unites us to each other in the family bond as the body of Christ (1 Cor. 12:13), enables us to understand Scripture (1 Cor. 2:12), and empowers us to live the transformed lives of new creatures (Gal. 5:16–25). The Holy Spirit is "the guarantee of our inheritance," sealing us firmly and securely as children of God as we await the consummation of our redemption (Eph. 1:13–14).

The doctrines of the person of God—the doctrine of the Trinity, of God the Father, of Christ the Son, and of the Holy Spirit—set Christianity apart from every other religion. As we come to know the God who has revealed himself in his Word, our hearts respond in thankfulness and we are motivated to serve and worship him.

THE WORK OF GOD: THE DOCTRINES OF CREATION, SALVATION, AND CONSUMMATION

The Doctrine of Creation and Humanity

As with the other doctrines we have explored, the Christian view of humanity offers a unique perspective. Some religions or worldviews stress the spiritual or ideal nature of humanity, even to the extent that the physical is viewed as an illusion. Other worldviews stress the material nature of humanity, arguing that we consist only of flesh and blood and DNA. In Scripture we see that human beings are both physical and spiritual beings (Gen. 2:7; Luke 10:27; 1 Cor. 15:35–48).

But something else sets the Christian view apart: the *image of God* (see Gen. 1:26–31; Psalm 8). Man is created in the image of God, distinguishing us from the rest of God's creation and creatures. The idea of the image of God is why Christians so firmly uphold the sanctity of human life (Ps. 139:13–16). And it is the foundation of how we should treat and relate to other people (see James 3:9). This is how and why we can speak of the dignity of humanity. It is why we must treat each other with love, respect, and kindness.

The Doctrine of Sin

The pristine conditions in the garden of Eden did not last long. Satan tempted Eve, Eve tempted Adam, and because of their sin the whole thing unraveled. Before, Adam and Eve had peace with God, with each other, and with creation itself. Sin ruptured all of that, driving a wedge between humanity and God and steering us into conflict (Genesis 3). Prior to the fall, peace ruled. Now, peace has been replaced with conflict and strife.

Adam's Sin and Our Sin

Our involvment in Adam's fall is known as our "original sin." Once sin came into the world, "death spread to all men" (Rom. 5:12). This is called the *imputation* of Adam's sin. Some reject this doctrine, holding that it is simply not fair to judge all of humanity because of the sin of Adam. Instead, they see Adam only as a bad example for us. This view is contrary to Scripture, which clearly states that when Adam sinned, we all sinned (see Rom. 5:12–21; 1 Cor. 15:20–28). The result is summed up in the doctrine of *total depravity*.

The *total* in total depravity has two meanings. The first is that all of us—every human being except Christ—are sinners (Rom. 3:9–20). The second is that all of us—our whole being of body, mind, soul, spirit, emotions, will—is sinful (Eph. 2:1–3). *Sin is the depraved state of humanity, originating from the fall and continuing in our idolatrous attitudes, thoughts, and actions that are against God and which result in alienation, death, and judgment*. The Bible spells out the effects of our sin:

Condemnation	Rom. 1:18–3:20
Alienation	Eph. 2:12–19
Guilt and shame	Gen. 3:7–10
Bondage/slavery	Exodus 2; Acts 8:23
Death	Gen. 2:17; Rev. 20:11–15

The Sinfulness of Sin

We are born guilty as sinners, but we quickly add our own sins to the mix. Sinners sin, and we have done so ever since Adam and Eve were exiled from the garden. The Bible uses many words to refer to sin, perhaps to show us how tragic, ugly, and deadly sin is. Read Psalm 51 and observe the different words David uses to describe his sin. We run into danger when we take our sin too lightly. Like a tornado, sin destroys everything in its path.

The Doctrine of Salvation

The tragedy of sin sets the stage for the glory, beauty, and sheer joy of salvation. We just saw how Adam's sin was imputed to us—that because of his sin, we stand condemned. Paul offers another equation in Romans 5:12–21. Through Christ's one act of obedience, we may have life. The parallel between Adam and Christ looks like this:

one man Adam	disobedience transgression	death condemnation
one man Christ	obedience righteousness	life justification

Since we are dead in our sins, and dead people cannot save themselves, the work of salvation begins with God. Christ says, "No one can come to me unless the Father who sent me draws him" (John 6:44; see also vv. 60–65). This is known as the "effectual call." This is one of many terms the Bible uses to speak of the work of salvation.

Christ's teaching here shows that God chooses his children. Known as the doctrine of election, God's choosing or election is not based on anything we do or on our own merit. In fact, God chose us "before the foundation of the world" (Eph. 1:4). God's election is based on his sovereign will, and is for his glory alone (Rom. 8:26–30; Eph. 1:3–14).

Scripture stresses that salvation is a glorious work of the triune God from start to finish. God decrees our salvation, Christ accomplished the work of salvation on the cross, and the Holy Spirit applies the work of salvation to us.

Christ's work may be summed up in the word "redemption." This means that we were once slaves to sin and its effects but have been redeemed, or bought back, by the blood of Christ and are now his children (Gal. 4:1–7; 1 Pet. 1:18–21). We now belong to God and are new creatures. We are no longer the people we used

to be. "He has delivered us from the domain of darkness and transferred us to the kingdom of his beloved Son, in whom we have redemption, the forgiveness of sins" (Col. 1:13–14). Paul says that the doctrine of redemption should change the way we live (1 Cor. 6:20).

Another crucial term is "justification," a legal word. God is the holy and righteous judge, and we all stand before him as the guilty party because of our sin. Christ, who became human, is lifted onto the cross, bearing the penalty and enduring God's wrath on our behalf. Because of what Christ has done, the righteous judge declares us not guilty and, instead, declares us righteous and holy (Rom. 3:21–25; 5:17). The chart below lists more words that summarize Christ's work, showing how Christ undid what Adam did.

In Adam	In Christ	Reference
Condemnation	Justification	Rom. 3:21-25
Alienation	Reconciliation	2 Cor. 5:17-21
Wrath/Enmity	Propitiation	1 John 2:1-2
Slavery	Sonship	Gal. 4:1-7
Bondage	Freedom	Gal. 5:1
Guilt/Shame	Peace	Rom. 5:1
Death	Life	John 20:30-31

One other contrast is that in Adam, representing sinful man, the self rules, whereas in Christ, the Holy Spirit rules. The Holy Spirit regenerates us (John 3); cleanses and renews us (Titus 3:4–7); indwells us (1 Cor. 3:16); and seals us until the day of our full and final redemption (Eph. 1:13–14). Further, the Spirit guides and leads us, empowering us to bear the fruit of righteousness (1 Cor. 2:6–16; Gal. 5:16–26).

Salvation provides all of these benefits. Above all, however, salvation unites us to Christ and brings us into the fellowship and bond of the eternal Trinity. In fact, at the time of our salvation, the greatest gift God gives us is himself. Salvation is a work of God from start to finish. So where does that leave us? Our role in all of this is to respond in faith and repentance (Mark 1:15; Acts 16:30–31). Even the act of faith does not come from us, but is a gift of God (Eph. 2:8–10).

Faith and repentance relate not only to the moment of salvation. We are called to a life of faith and repentance and to living through the power of the gospel (Gal. 2:14; Phil. 2:12–18).

The Doctrine of the Church

Christians, however, are not saved to be individuals and Lone Rangers. "No man is an island," wrote the poet John Donne. We are saved to be part of the new community, the church. The NT emphasizes the importance of the church. Jesus ordained the church as the means to spread the gospel, make disciples, and bring God's plan to pass (Matt. 28:16–20). After Christ ascended into heaven, having accomplished his mission, the Holy Spirit descended, empowering the 12 disciples. And so began the church. These early believers "devoted themselves to the apostles' teaching and the fellowship, to the breaking of bread and the prayers" (Acts 2:42). They also put feet to their faith, taking care of the poor and living and acting generously (Acts 2:43–47).

The NT church was and is to be entirely unlike anything else. The social divisions that govern other communities—between rich and poor, between the genders, and among the races and ethnicities—are to be entirely absent in the church (see Eph. 2:11–21; James 2:1–13). The politics that govern other institutions are to be absent in the church.

Christ established one rule for the church: it is to be marked by love (John 17). This love flows from the church's deep roots in the truth (1 Tim. 3:15) and is a powerful witness to the world.

The church's primary function is to preach the Word, proclaiming the gospel and teaching the whole counsel of God (Acts 20:27; 2 Timothy 4; Titus 2). The church is also to practice the two sacraments, or ordinances: the Lord's Supper and baptism (Matt. 28:19; 1 Cor. 11:17–34). These functions are to be carried out in accordance with Scripture and in an orderly manner (Acts 6; 14:23; 1 Timothy 3). God has ordained offices, listed in the following chart, to provide leadership for the church.

New Testament Church Officers

	Office	Biblical Reference
	Apostle (*apostolos* = "sent one")	Acts 1:2; Acts 15; Gal. 2:7-9
P A S T O R	Bishop/Overseer (*episcopos*)	Acts 20:17, 28
	Elder (*presbyteros*)	1 Tim. 3:1-7; Titus 1:5-9
	Pastor/Shepherd (*poimēn*)	1 Pet. 5:1-4
	Deacon (*diakonos* = "servant")	Acts 6:1-6; 1 Tim. 3:8-13

God uses the church to spread "the knowledge of the glory of the LORD as the waters cover the sea" (Hab. 2:14; see Acts 1:8). The church is Christ's body on earth, carrying out the mission he started, which is to make God known (John 17:20–26; 1 Cor. 12:12–29). While the church is ordained by God, it is made up of people and, therefore, is not always perfect. However, that's no reason to give up on it and try to live the Christian life alone. Rather, in humility we recognize our own imperfections and the collective imperfections of local churches, remaining committed to one another in love through the bond and power of the Holy Spirit, growing in grace, truth, and love (Ephesians 4).

The Doctrine of the Future: Consummation

The work that Christ began on the cross, promised back in Genesis 3:15, will someday be complete. There are many different viewpoints, however, regarding the events that will happen before that completion. Some theologians argue that Christ's second coming will be in two parts: (1) the rapture of believers, and (2) the second coming of Christ. Some think there will be a literal seven-year tribulation. Some think there will be a literal 1,000-year reign of Christ on earth (a view called "premillennialism"). Many debate how to interpret Revelation and the other prophetic books of Scripture. The chart below shows the events to come and the differences among the three views as to the order in which these events will occur.

Millennial Views

Historic Premillennialism	Second Coming	1,000-year Millennial Reign	Eternal State
Postmillennialism	1,000-year Millennial Reign	Second Coming	Eternal State
Amillennialism	Second Coming	(no literal 1,000-year reign)	Eternal State

Despite these differences of interpretation, the church has always agreed on three fundamental points regarding the doctrine of the future: (1) Christ will physically, bodily return to earth in victory (the second coming); (2) all of human history is leading up to the culmination of God's purposes for creation (the new heaven and the new earth); and (3) these doctrines are intended to give us hope and to lead us to pursue holiness.

The Second Coming
In Acts 1, the disciples stood gazing into the heavens, having just witnessed the ascension of Christ to the throne of God in heaven. Two angels, described as men in white robes, came to this astonished and befuddled group, declaring, "This Jesus, who was taken up from you into heaven, will come in the same way as you saw him go into heaven" (Acts 1:11). This refers to the second coming, which will be the physical, bodily return of Christ.

This doctrine permeates the NT, as the apostles waited for Christ's return (see, e.g., 2 Thessalonians). Revelation 19 foretells the fulfillment of the single greatest promise of history: the return of Christ to reign on earth. The second coming will be the fruition of the dreams and hopes of the OT prophets, of the NT apostles, and of the people of God through the millennia. It will be the event that makes everything right (Amos 9:11–15).

The second coming will be a time of both victory and judgment. For those who belong to Christ, the second coming will mean eternal life in heaven with the Lord. For those outside of Christ, those who rejected him and the gospel, the second coming will mean being separated from God forever and eternal punishment in the lake of fire (Rev. 20:11–15).

The New Heaven and the New Earth
Following the second coming, we see the new heaven and the new earth described in Revelation 21. Here everything is made new. This is the culmination of the process of restoration that Christ began on the cross. The new heaven and the new earth mark the completion of the work of redemption. As we move into Revelation 22, we see a description of a garden with a river running through it, looking rather similar to Genesis 2. But here, in Revelation 22, sin is gone forever (v. 3) and the glory of God rules supremely and exclusively. When John, author of the book of Revelation, saw and heard all of this in a vision, he fell down and worshiped.

Lives of Hope and Holiness
The doctrines of the future offer hope in times of suffering or trouble and in times when evil seems to prosper. But these doctrines are also intended to spur us on to godliness and lives of holiness. We dare not wait passively for the second coming, but actively. Peter tells us how we should live in light of these doctrines of the future: "Therefore, beloved, since you are waiting for these, be diligent to be found by him without spot or blemish, and at peace" (2 Pet. 3:14).

LIVING THEOLOGY

As Christians, we are a people of beliefs and behaviors. These important doctrines we have been exploring are not merely intended to offer a list of propositions we affirm. These are *living truths*. Powerful and dynamic, these important doctrines change lives.

Doctrine is *both* a matter of getting it right (orthodoxy), *and also* a matter of living it out (orthopraxy). Ultimately, doctrine drives us to a life of worship of the holy, triune God. Paul's prayer for the Ephesian believers captures this well. May it be true of us as followers of Christ

who seek to understand the rich doctrines God has revealed in his Word:

[I pray] that Christ may dwell in your hearts through faith—that you, being rooted and grounded in love, may have strength to comprehend with all the saints what is the breadth and length and height and depth, and to know the love of Christ that surpasses knowledge, that you may be filled with all the fullness of God. (Eph. 3:17–19)

THE BIBLE AND CHRISTIAN LIVING: ETHICS

Why Be Good?

Ethics began in the garden of Eden as God laid down his simple commands for Adam and Eve to follow. On the negative side, the "don'ts," Adam and Eve were given only one rule: they were not to eat the fruit of the tree of the knowledge of good and evil (Gen. 2:16–17). On the positive side, the "dos," Adam and Eve were to follow the creation mandate (Gen. 1:27–31), to work and keep the garden (Gen. 2:15), and to enjoy times of fellowship with God (Gen. 3:8). Clearly, God did not intend to burden them with a long list. But still they disobeyed, giving in to temptation and betraying their God-given charge (Genesis 3).

After the fall, sin became the new reality. Genesis 4:7 pictures sin as "crouching at the door." And sin pounced. It seems that as sinners multiplied and filled the earth, so did human ingenuity to evade and rebel against God. Men devised all sorts of wicked ways to scandalize and violate God's creation and fellow creatures. As a result, the list of "dos and don'ts" is no longer short.

In Exodus 20, the single "don't" of Genesis 2 expanded to a list of ten. Adding the rest of the laws and the commands of the Pentateuch (the first five books of the OT), the number climbs into the hundreds. Additional commands are given in the NT Gospels and Epistles. But why are all these commands necessary? Why follow them? Why, in other words, be good?

Philosophers from the days of Plato have wrestled with ethical questions. (1) *What is the good?* What is justice, what is virtue, what is right, and what is wrong? (2) *Why be good?* What purpose is served by living ethically? (3) *How can we be good?* How can we live ethical lives of virtue and integrity? God did not leave us in the dark. He offers his Word with firm answers to all of these moral questions.

Ethics may be defined as the theory of the nature and basis of morality (what is good? and why be good?). It could also be defined as a set of principles that govern how one lives, or how groups or societies live. The Greek word,

ēthikos, comes from another Greek word, *ēthos*, which originally meant "habits." So the basic meaning of the word "ethics" is moral habits. Habits are funny things. Bad ones seem to come rather easily. Good ones seem to require time and diligence to cultivate. We live by our habits. Consequently, when we talk about ethics, what we are really talking about is how we live, the patterns we live by, the standards we set and aspire to, and the behaviors and actions that stem from our values and beliefs. Ethics has everything to do with living the Christian life.

The Doctrine of Sanctification

In order to think biblically about ethics, we need to consider the doctrine of sanctification. Sanctification refers to the process of being transformed into the likeness and character of Christ. The word literally means *being made holy*. In the OT the priests were *sanctified* so that they could carry out the duties of worship and the service of the sacrificial system (Lev. 21:1–9). We, too, are sanctified, going through the process of being made holy to be used of God in service and in worship (1 Cor. 6:9–11).

Behavior Follows Being

The doctrine of sanctification answers the question of *how* we can be good and *why* we should be good. The answers to both have to do with our new identity in Christ as new creations (Gal. 2:20). Paul has much to say about this new identity and how it affects our behavior. Paul's main idea can be summarized in this way:

Being	Behavior
You are no longer the person you used to be.	You can no longer act the way you used to act.

Our ethics—comprised of our attitudes, motives, behaviors, and actions—stem from our identity, our nature, our being. Behavior (what we do) flows from our being (who we are). "Out of the abundance of the heart," Jesus says, "the mouth speaks" (Matt. 12:34).

But why is reality not as simple, direct, and clean as this equation? Why do we, the redeemed and righteous, struggle with and often give in to sin? To answer this, we need further to explore the idea of sanctification.

Performance-based vs. Grace-based

While we tend to be careful not to "frontload" the gospel with works and merit, we can sometimes "backload" the gospel with them. We emphatically stress that works have nothing to do with coming to Christ. We emphasize that salvation is the exclusive work of God in saving us. We have no room to boast (Rom. 3:21–31; Eph. 2:8–9). We uphold dependence upon God, the regenerating work of the Spirit, and the sovereign good will and pleasure of God.

When we turn to living the Christian life, however, we tend to forget this dependence on God. Instead, we "backload" the gospel by viewing our Christian growth—our sanctification—as something we do on our own. Paul's letter to the Galatians shows that this type of thinking is problematic. Having stressed our new identity in Christ (2:20–21), he asks a rhetorical question: "Are you so foolish? Having begun by the Spirit, are you now being perfected by the flesh?" (3:3). The answer to the second question is a resounding no.

One reason we struggle with and succumb to sin is that we are looking in the wrong place for the strength to resist. We look to the self, rather than confessing dependence on the Holy Spirit. Pride keeps people from the gospel, and even after we are saved, pride still keeps Christians from living by grace. Salvation and sanctification are both the work of God in us. We are saved by grace, and we grow in Christ by grace.

Individual-based vs. Community-based Sanctification

Sin causes us not only to neglect grace and the Spirit but also to neglect each other. One of the impacts of modernity has been the rise of the individual, or individualism. This sometimes spills over into the way we think of Christianity and living the Christian life. We reduce sanctification to personal sanctification only. This individualism runs counter to the biblical emphasis on the body life of Christianity—that we are all members joined together, just as the individual parts of the body make up a person (Eph. 4:11–16; 1 Corinthians 12).

This individualism also runs counter to healthy Christian growth. When we try to "go it alone," we usually fall in our struggle with sin. God placed us in his body—the church—for a reason. Read through the "one anothers"—the places in Scripture that discuss how we connect with and serve one another—to see what we gain by depending on the body of Christ.

A community-based sanctification starts with our union with Christ, which unites us not only to Christ but also to the triune God and to each other. We are commanded to pray for one another, to bear one another's burdens, and to minister to one another (Gal. 6:2; James 5:13–20). If we are united together, growing as the body of Christ, then we will also grow as individuals.

Local churches should be mindful of their collective testimony, not only in their good works to the household of faith but also in their good works to all people (Gal. 6:10). The body of Christ—the sum of all redeemed people—also makes a collective impact. We may look at the various members of the body of Christ and see only differences and division, but we are called to live as "one new man," walking "in a manner worthy of the calling to which [we] have been called" (Eph. 2:14–16; 4:1–6). Healthy local churches that take this seriously advance the gospel, justice, and virtue.

Marathon vs. Sprint

In contrast to the fast pace of our culture's instant downloads, instant food, and instant gratification, the Christian life is more of a marathon than a sprint. Things grow because of a combination of factors—nutrients, air, sunshine, water, and, above all, time. In fact, maturity can be defined as *growth over time*. This natural law rings true of growth in the Christian life. We need nutrients—grace, the Spirit's enablement and empowerment, and other believers. And we need time. Paul instructs Titus to make sure that the older people in the church teach the young precisely because of this dynamic (Titus 2:3–5). The Christian life, as Eugene Peterson calls it, is a "long obedience in the same direction." We're running a marathon, not wind sprints.

This dynamic of growth over time does not offer an excuse for lukewarm living and lackluster obedience. We are obligated to obey. But seeing spiritual progress as a process should serve to encourage us and to remind us that we all have room to grow. We also learn the value of forgiving and showing grace to others and to ourselves, realizing that we won't always be perfect and that we are in a process of change. Finally, this growth process reminds us to cultivate patience, kindness, and gentleness—all fruits of the Spirit—as we deal with one another and as we evaluate our own spiritual progress (Gal. 5:22).

Extrinsic Motivation vs. Intrinsic Motivation

Some serve God out of duty. Some strive for holiness out of misplaced zeal to win God's approval. These approaches tend to result in short-term obedience and success but long-term frustration and disillusionment. We give in to sin when we enter the struggle with wrong motives.

Instead, we ought to strive for holiness out of gratitude for what God has done in making us new creatures in Christ. We ought to fight the good fight of faith by realizing that Christ has accomplished our redemption and has secured our forgiveness. We depend on the indwelling Holy Spirit, who transforms us and enables us to live godly lives in Christ Jesus.

Grace, Gratitude, Growth, Glory

Summarizing this discussion of sanctification, we can put forth this approach to godliness and Christian living:

> **Grace:** We start, live, and end the Christian life by grace. Grace does not stop at salvation. Grace is the arch over all of life. Without grace and apart from grace, we cannot be good and we cannot succeed in our struggle against sin.
> **Gratitude:** We obey and serve God from grateful hearts.
> **Growth:** The dynamic is simple: Maturity comes by growth, which comes from proper nutrients, over time. We are not promised instant sanctification, but we are called to a process of growth.
> **Glory:** The *chief end*, the ultimate purpose, of being good and of living the Christian life, is not for or about us. The ultimate purpose is God's glory. The purpose of God's world is to bring glory to God, and that extends to us as individuals and to our individual lives. We are good for the sake of his glory, not for the sake of our fame.

Work Out Your Own Salvation

While we have been emphasizing grace and God's work of sanctification, we also have to acknowledge our part in obeying the commands in Scripture, such as "work out your own salvation with fear and trembling" (Phil. 2:12), "put on the new self" (Eph. 4:24; Col. 3:10), and "walk in a manner worthy of the calling" (Eph. 4:1). These are all commands that we are called to do. How does this connect with the emphasis on sanctification as God's work?

First, consider that the command to "work out your own salvation" is followed by the declaration, "it is God who works in you, both to will and to work for his good pleasure" (Phil. 2:13). Paul reminds us to depend on God, who both gives those commands and enables us to carry them out.

Once someone has trusted Jesus for salvation, he is a new creation. Christians are not the same after conversion as they were before. We were once dead in sin, unable to do anything (Eph. 2:1–3). But now we have been spiritually raised from the dead and made alive in Christ, and the Holy Spirit lives in us (Eph. 2:4–10). Our eyes have been opened to the truth of Scripture, and we have the gift of fellowship in the body of Christ. To quote from Luther's famous hymn, "A Mighty Fortress Is Our God": "the Spirit and the gifts are ours." So while sanctification is a work of God, upon whom we are entirely dependent, we are to rely on the Spirit and exercise the gifts he gives as we "work out our salvation."

God's Law in the Digital Age: The Bible and Ethics Today

We have been looking at the questions of *why be good* and *how to be good* by exploring the doctrine of sanctification. That leaves the question, *What is the good?* Again, we turn to Scripture. The Bible offers models for thinking about ethics and lays out boundaries for our decision making on specific ethical dilemmas and questions. We'll explore this rich biblical teaching in terms of personal ethics, ethics in the local church, and social ethics.

Integrity

The author of Proverbs tells us that a life of integrity far outranks a life of wealth (Prov. 28:6; 20:7). King David agrees, declaring his intention to walk in integrity before God (Ps. 26:1, 11; 41:12; 101:2). The apostle Paul describes the life of integrity, especially against the backdrop of an ungodly culture: "The grace of God has appeared, bringing salvation for all people, training us to renounce ungodliness and worldly passions, and to live self-controlled, upright, and godly lives in the present age" (Titus 2:11–12). Paul adds that Jesus gave himself for us, in our place, "to redeem us from all lawlessness and to purify for himself a people for his own possession who are zealous for good works" (Titus 2:14).

Paul's challenge to Titus reveals a twofold purpose in Christ's work for us. First, he died to redeem us from our sinful, "lawless" lives. Second, he died for us so we can live holy, "pure" lives. People who are zealous for a cause are single-minded, almost obsessed with their quest. Paul calls us to a zealous quest for good works. We are called to a life of integrity, both inside and out.

Integrity means wholeness, genuineness, soundness. A bridge has integrity when both the surface and what lies beneath are solid and true; it holds firm and sure under the load of traffic. On the surface it may appear sound, but hidden fault lines and cracks may eventually reveal themselves under the weight of traffic. And disaster follows. In the same way, a life has integrity when it holds under pressure. In our new identity as new creatures, reckoned by God to be holy and righteous, we are called to live genuine, whole, and sound lives. Fault lines and cracks may eventually reveal themselves when the pressure comes. As we explore the ethical issues below, consider them all as requiring of us a life of integrity, a sound and whole life able to withstand pressure.

For Further Reflection: Look up verses containing the words "integrity," "sincere/sincerity," and "upright/uprightly/uprightness," paying attention to the context, for more on living a life of integrity.

Loving Our Neighbor

A lawyer asked how he could inherit eternal life. Jesus reiterated the two great commandments to love God and love our neighbor (Luke 10:25–28; see Deut. 6:1–9). This prompted the lawyer to ask, "Who is my neighbor?" (Luke 10:29). Jesus answered with the parable of the good Samaritan. The priest and the Levite passed by the man who had been robbed, beaten, and left for dead alongside the road to Jericho. But a Samaritan stopped and helped, with both compassion and generosity. The Jewish audience that first heard this parable probably found this surprising, since Jews tended to consider Samaritans "unclean" and ungodly (Luke 10:29–37).

This parable teaches that our neighbor is *anyone in proximity who is suffering or in need*. The parable also reminds us that helping and loving our neighbor is costly.

When faced with people in need, we usually ask the wrong question. We ask how helping others might interfere with our lives or what helping others might cost us. Instead we should ask what will happen to others if we don't help. Loving our neighbor requires us to live an others-centered life, not a self-centered life. The priest and the Levite, who should have known better, kept their focus on themselves. The Samaritan looked at the one in need.

Scripture gives further examples of others-centered living. In Acts 2, the new followers of Christ showed love by caring for each other's physical needs (Acts 2:42–47). Boaz instructed his workers to leave behind some barley sheaves for the widows Ruth and Naomi (Ruth 2:15–16). Jesus repeatedly showed love for his neighbor as he healed and performed miracles—and ultimately in laying down his life, as both our sacrifice and example (Rom. 5:8; 1 John 3:16). And the believers at Philippi helped meet Paul's needs (Phil. 4:16). Loving our neighbor—being gracious, generous, and charitable—opens us up to a richly satisfying life of helping others. Because loving our neighbor often seems unnatural, given our worldly and selfish desires, we need God's grace to obey his command.

For Further Reflection: Leviticus 6:1–7; Matthew 5–7; James 2:1–13

Sexual Ethics

First-century Roman life had a rather loose view of sexual ethics. Some of the rituals for the pagan gods went so far as to include sexual acts with temple prostitutes and orgies as part of religious practice. Some cities and places in the empire were worse than others. In fact, the Romans coined the term "to Corinthianize" to describe sexual immorality and lewdness. To the group of believers in that same city Paul declared, "Flee from sexual immorality" (1 Cor. 6:18). Surrounded by a culture of loose morals, with a low view of sexual purity, the believers at Corinth had themselves been tainted by immorality (1 Corinthians 5).

Today we live in a similar culture. Technology provides access to things we shouldn't even know exist, let alone see. In such a time as this, we especially need to guard against making subtle (or not so subtle) compromises in the area of sexual purity. Paul's command to flee from such temptations applies directly to us.

Paul's negative command, to flee from sexual immorality, comes with two positive concepts. The first returns to the idea of our new identity. Jesus bought us with a price, and we belong to him, "So glorify God in your body" (1 Cor. 6:20). The second positive concept concerns marriage, the God-ordained place for sexual fulfillment. In our fallen state, we have misused God's good gift of sexuality (Gen. 2:18–25; compare the Song of Solomon). We have twisted his plan, seeking fulfillment through sexual pleasure outside of the boundaries which God has graciously given us for our good. Within God's plan, however, we have true sexual pleasure and contentment.

Alongside of the "Just say no" approach to sexual immorality, we also need to "Just say yes" to God's good plan for human sexuality and pleasure. We should celebrate marriage and marital fidelity (Heb. 13:4). We should emphasize the pleasure found in living within the wise and good paths God has marked for us (Prov. 18:22; Song 5:1).

Those who fall into sexual immorality or commit adultery say they never intended for it to happen. But it did, and it does. No one wakes up in the morning and decides out of the blue to begin sexually sinning. Little steps down the wrong path and compromises here and there eventually lead away from God's straight path and onto crooked and rough paths of sin (Proverbs 7; 9:13–18). Instead of going such a way, we must commit to a path of glorifying God in our bodies.

For Further Reflection: Exodus 20:14, 17; Proverbs 2; 1 Thessalonians 4:1–8

Workplace Ethics

We sometimes think that work fits into a different compartment in our lives than spirituality. The Bible, however, has a great deal to say about work and how we work. First, we need to see that work preceded the fall. Adam and Eve were commanded to work in the garden (Gen. 2:15). In Psalm 90, Moses asks God to "establish the work of our hands" (Ps. 90:17). Moses repeats this phrase, stressing the importance of God's blessing on our work. Work is not quarantined from our lives as disciples, but woven into it.

Why we work and how we work are important questions. We work for God's glory and honor, in service to him. Our work is "as to the Lord" (Eph. 6:7). That being the case, we should be honest and diligent at our work (2 Thess. 3:6–15). In our era of multitasking we may think we are being good employees, but if our workdays are filled with updating social network pages or sending text messages to friends, we're likely not giving our employers our full attention.

The book of Proverbs offers wise counsel on being diligent at work vs. being lazy and slothful. Such laziness has a way of spilling over into our personal lives and relationships, even affecting our relationship with God. We can also err in the other direction. We were not made to work, as the saying has it, 24/7. In the pattern of creation, God models for us the appropriate rhythms of work and rest (Gen. 1:1–2:3; Ex. 20:8–11). How we work offers a testimony to those around us, pointing either toward or away from the gospel.

For Further Reflection: Psalm 90; Proverbs 22:29; Ephesians 4:28; 6:5–9

Personal Virtues to Cultivate

Humility and meekness	Phil. 2:1–11; 1 Pet.5:5
Patience	Ps. 40:1; 1 Cor. 13:4
Kindness	1 Cor. 13:4; Gal. 5:22–23
Honesty and truthfulness	Prov. 12:22; Col. 3:9
Hard work and diligence	Prov. 6:6; Rom. 12:11
Servant spirit	Matt. 25:31–40; 1 Cor. 9:19
Discretion	Prov. 22:3; Eph. 5:15
Frugality	Prov. 21:20; Luke 16:1–13
Thankfulness	Luke 17:11–19; 1 Thess. 5:18
Contentment	Phil. 4:10–20; Heb. 13:5–6

The gospel is lived out in the context of the local church. Consider the two areas of talking and listening, as lived out in community with other believers.

Taming the Tongue

James reminds us that while the tongue is a small member of our body, "it boasts of great things" (James 3:5). As a small flame can eventually set a whole forest on fire, the tongue wreaks a path of destruction far dispropor- tionate to its size. We can ask forgiveness for our hurtful and spiteful words, but we can't corral those words and put them back into our mouths once we have said them, and we can't always undo the harm our words have done (Matt. 12:36–37).

The power of the tongue leads Paul to say, "Let no corrupting talk come out of your mouths, but only such as is good for building up, as fits the occasion, that it may give grace to those who hear" (Eph. 4:29). Paul calls us to speak appropriate words that edify others in Christ. He also tells us to speak the truth in love (Eph. 4:15, see also Col. 4:6).

The Bible describes some ways the tongue can be misused. The list includes flattery (Rom. 16:18), prideful speech (Ps. 73:8–9), and slander or gossip (Eph. 4:31).

Using our tongue properly can go a long way in cultivating a godly community in an ungodly world. Words possess power, either to build up or to tear down. How we use our tongues gets right to the heart of who we are. A common expression says it's not how you talk the talk, but how you walk the walk. That's not entirely true. Our talk matters a great deal.

For Further Reflection: Proverbs 6:16–19; James 3:1–12; 1 Peter 3:8–12

Listening and Caring: Ministries of Mercy

In *Life Together*, Dietrich Bonhoeffer lists seven ways we minister to each other, and one of them is listening. He says that just as our love for God begins with listening to God in his Word, so our love for each other begins by listening to each other. Brotherly love and brotherly pastoral care begin with listening to others. To listen means to set aside one's own agenda and acknowledge the other person. And as we listen, we can learn how to care for and serve one another.

Bonhoeffer follows listening with the minis- tries of helpfulness and bearing one another's burdens. Both of these tend to come at incon- venient times. People usually need us, both in family life and in the church, when work is pressing. In our former lives we could "sidestep" people with needs and burdens. But this is no longer an option for us as new creatures. We have been commanded to "bear one another's burdens, and so fulfill the law of Christ" (Gal. 6:2)—even at inconvenient times.

Jesus himself followed such a law of loving his neighbor when he bore our burden of sin through his perfect life and agonizing death on the cross. He both commands and models the extent to which we are to serve, care for, and minister to one another.

We minister to one another in the context of the local church, as disciples known by our love (John 17:20–26). From the local church we reach out to our communities and even to people around the world. God has called us to be a people who humbly serve (John 13:1–20). And we can begin such a ministry merely by listening to those around us.

For Further Reflection: Ecclesiastes 5:1–3; John 17; Titus 3:1–11

The theme of *justice* runs throughout Scripture and can be seen as summing up social ethics for the Christian. Justice matters to God primarily because God himself is just. And his people are to live just lives, being an example of justice to the nations. The Bible's call to justice may be applied to the main areas of social ethics. Just as integrity forms the arch over our personal ethics, justice overarches our social ethics.

Sanctity of Life

Atheist and ethicist Peter Singer has predicted that the term "sanctity of life" will collapse by 2040 under the weight of scientific and techno- logical developments. While his pronouncement is likely wide of the mark, we should take note of his thinking. Current cultural movements are radically redefining what it means to be human, with significant consequences for how we value human life.

How a society treats the weak and help-less reveals how much (or how little) they value human life. All human life is valuable, without respect to that person's contribution to society. The value of human life stems from being created in God's image (Gen. 1:26–27). James explains that we shouldn't curse people, because they are made in the image of God (James 3:9). Psalm 139 reminds us of God's intimate involvement in our lives, even in the womb.

These texts are the starting point as we consider the Christian view of abortion, eutha-nasia, and biological or genetic engineering. Reducing human life to merely a material being, to tissue and DNA, leads to the discarding of life. Therefore abortion (killing a baby at the begin-ning of life) and euthanasia (killing someone suffering at the end of life) are categorically and undeniably sins. As Christians, we have an obli-gation to speak up for the helpless who cannot speak for themselves.

We should not only be against abortion and euthanasia, but we should be *for life*—being fully pro-life. In addition to concern for the unborn and the aged, we should also consider others who are vulnerable, such as the malnourished or those living in poverty. If we truly believe that every single life is made in the image of God, then we will live and behave accordingly.

For Further Reflection: Genesis 9:6–7; Psalm 139; Romans 13:8–10

Poverty and Wealth

Perhaps no other barometer reveals more about our love for God and love for neighbor than our attitude toward money. While Scripture chastises those who are poor or needy due to laziness (Prov. 6:6–11; 2 Thess. 3:10), it also calls attention to the plight of those who are poor because of circumstances (James 1:27; also Prov. 14:31; 22:16; and 22:22–23). God's compassion for the poor is seen in the law code for Israel. Leviticus 19 requires that the corners of the field not be harvested nor the vineyards be harvested bare, so that the poor and sojourner may have something to eat (Lev. 19:9–10; see also Deut. 24:19–22; Ruth 2).

Jesus showed compassion to the poor throughout his ministry, beginning with his read-ing of Isaiah 61 in the synagogue at Nazareth (Luke 4:16–19). He taught that we have an obli-gation to care for those in need, declaring that inasmuch as we care for "the least of these," we care for him (Matt. 25:40).

The Bible also has much to say about wealth, and we must be careful to follow "the whole counsel of God" on this theme (Acts 20:27). For example, the book of Luke shows how wealth can be a hindrance to receiving the gospel (Luke 18:18–25), but in Acts (the second half of Luke's two-volume work) we see cases of people using their wealth to further the gospel (Acts 4:32–37). The book of Proverbs endorses thrift and diligence in business and work, along with glad generosity (Prov. 6:6–11; 11:24–26; 14:23). Ephesians 4:28 is instructive as we think about hard work, money, and generosity: "Let the thief no longer steal, but rather let him labor, doing honest work with his own hands, so that he may have something to share with anyone in need." We are to avoid stealing and to work hard, not in order to "have" but in order to share gladly with those who need it.

Whether we have much or little, we are to acknowledge all that we have as a gift from God and be wise stewards over it (Deuteronomy 8). Instead of fostering greed, we should cultivate generosity (1 Thess. 2:1–8). Instead of being consumed with pursuing earthly treasure, we should pursue a heavenly one (Matt. 6:19–21).

For Further Reflection: Leviticus 19; Matthew 25:31–46; Philippians 4:10–20

Creation Care

God created the heavens and the earth (Gen. 1:1), and the purpose of creation is clear: "The heavens declare the glory of God, and the sky above proclaims his handiwork" (Ps. 19:1). This should lead us to marvel at God's great creative work (see Psalm 104). We must also care for God's handiwork by managing the earth and making it productive (Gen. 1:28–30), being careful to avoid unbiblical greed and excess that often lead to an unhealthy consumption and pollution of resources.

Some have blamed misuse of the environ-ment on the creation mandate itself (Gen. 1:28–30). But these problems arise from *abusing* God's command. The mandate comes in the context of a garden that Adam and Eve were to work and to keep (Gen. 2:15). Farmers know that you don't subdue a field by "beating it" into productivity, but by cultivating it. Cultivation yields productivity, whereas abuse yields con-sumption and destruction. So it is with all of creation.

As we live in God's creation we should cultivate, not consume, its God-given resources. Being acutely aware of the world's limited and precarious resources, we should reflect on the global and long-term impact of our land use and our lifestyle. Loving our neighbor requires that we consider how our lifestyle affects others. Just as we await our final redemption from sin and its effects, creation also waits (Rom. 8:18–25).

For Further Reflection: Genesis 1–2; Psalm 19:1–6; Romans 8:18–25

Civil Government

God has ordained human governments to be "a terror" to those who would do harm to others (Rom. 13:3). The political philosopher Thomas Hobbes (1588–1679) may have had this in mind when he argued that human beings are at root sinful creatures, locked in a "war of all against all." So, Hobbes argued, we need governments to restrain us from all-out war with each other. Hobbes also called government a "leviathan," considering it a necessary monster.

John Locke (1632–1704), who disagreed with some of Hobbes's views, saw a positive aim of government: to promote human flourishing. Locke once said government provides for the pursuit of "life, liberty, and the ownership of property." Thomas Jefferson quoted Locke in the United States Declaration of Independence, substituting "happiness" for Locke's last item.

From Scripture we know that God ordained government, that it should be obeyed, and that taxes should be paid (Mark 12:13–17; Rom. 13:1–7). We see believers holding public office (Rom. 16:23). We also see, however, times of *civil disobedience*, the disobeying of government when its laws go against God's law (Ex. 1:15–22; Dan. 3:8–18; Acts 5:12–29). There are laws we are compelled to obey, such as paying taxes. However, prescriptive laws (laws requiring a particular action) that conflict with God's law call for civil disobedience. Consider the story of the birth of Moses. The midwives were being compelled to kill male infants. Those who disobeyed the Egyptian authorities by protecting Moses from this slaughter (Exodus 1) were right to do so. However, prescriptive laws are different from permissive laws, such as laws permitting abortion in the United States or those permitting same-sex unions in some states or municipalities. Government allows for these actions, which are contrary to God's law, but government does not compel these actions. Permissive laws do not warrant civil disobedience.

Proverbs 29:2 declares, "When the righteous increase, the people rejoice, but when the wicked rule, the people groan." Christians have an interest in the promotion of human flourishing, which means we must take an interest in government and politics. (See also the cultural mandate, Gen. 1:26–31.) Our trust must be in God, not in politics, politicians, and positions of power (compare Ps. 20:7). Nevertheless, Peter tells us to "fear God" and "honor the emperor" (1 Pet. 2:17).

For Further Reflection: Job 34:17a; Romans 13:1–7; 1 Peter 2:13–17

Homosexuality

Since the creation of Adam and Eve, physical differentiation between male and female has been at the basis of human sexuality. God ordained sexual activity to be between one man and one woman in the context of marriage (Gen. 2:18–25). At various places, Scripture expressly condemns homosexuality (Lev. 18:22; Rom. 1:26–32; 1 Cor. 6:9).

In recent years some have sought to reinterpret the Bible's understanding of homosexuality. They argue that, while Scripture condemns homosexual promiscuity and pedophilia and coercion to homosexual acts, the Bible does not condemn homosexuality in a monogamous, faithful couple.

This issue becomes a clear case of allowing cultural moods to impact biblical interpretation. Sexual immorality is always condemned in Scripture, whereas sex itself (heterosexual relations within the covenant of marriage) is not condemned but celebrated. This is not the case with homosexuality. Paul categorically declares homosexuality to be "contrary to nature" (Rom. 1:26) and warns that unrepentant homosexual activity is incompatible with inheriting eternal life (1 Cor. 6:9).

Some Christians believe that the discovery of a "homosexual gene" would invalidate the biblical rules against homosexuality. There is no scientific consensus on this issue, but even if such a biological component were found, it would not call into question the biblical worldview. The biblical view is that, while our genes might predispose us to certain wrong behaviors, they never determine that we have to sin. Blaming it on the genes does not justify sinful behavior.

Sadly, Christians are sometimes known only for their hatred toward homosexuals. While Scripture condemns homosexuality, we should show compassion and kindness to homosexuals—as fellow sinners—pointing them to paths of forgiveness, healing, and wholeness. The Christian response to homosexuality will undoubtedly continue to be a pressing issue in the church and in culture. Responding with confidence in Scripture and with compassion and humility is—and will continue to be—our only option.

For Further Reflection: Genesis 2:18–25; Romans 1:26–32

War

Writing from Nazi Germany, the Lutheran theologian and martyr Dietrich Bonhoeffer observed, "So long as the world is without God, there will be wars." Christians are divided on the ugly reality of war. Some hold to *pacifism*, which is opposed to war and argues against Christians serving in the military (known as conscientious objection). Others see military service as legitimate for Christians. In fact, Christian thinkers have led the way in what has come to be known as the *just war theory*. Augustine made significant contributions to this theory by gleaning some principles from Scripture regarding legitimate reasons for governments and nations to wage war. His criteria for going to war boil down to three main points: (1) War should be waged by a legitimate authority (Augustine understood governmental authority to be derived from God [based on Rom. 13:1]). (2) War should be waged to avenge injuries and harms done. (3) Those who wage war should have righteous intentions, while realizing the need for humility and caution in ascribing righteousness to civil actions. Augustine also noted that going to war should be a last resort after efforts of diplomacy. Augustine's criteria for conduct in war concerned protecting civilians and noncombatants from harm and fighting with "proportionality."

Augustine ultimately recognized war as a necessary evil that brings a degree of earthly justice in a sinful world. Regardless of our own views on war, we should uphold principles of humanitarianism in times of war, promote peace, and (to the degree that we can) hold civil authorities accountable to justice in their actions.

For Further Reflection: Exodus 15; Joshua 6; Micah 4:1–4; Romans 13:1–7

Social Virtues to Cultivate

Justice	Amos 5; Mic. 6:6–8; Luke 11:42–44
Hospitality	Lev. 19:33–34; Matt. 25:35; Heb. 13:2–3
Generosity	Lev. 25:35–55; Ruth 3; James 2:1–13
Peace	Matt. 5:9; Rom. 12:18; 1 Tim. 2:1–2
Leadership	Proverbs 29; 1 Pet. 5:1–5

True Virtue and Common Morality: Ethics and Non-Christians

As Christians, we know that anything good in us or done by us is a result of God at work in our lives. Apart from Christ's redemption and the Spirit's conviction, indwelling, and empowering, we would not accomplish the tiniest bit of righteousness. So where does that leave people without the Spirit and outside of redemption in Christ? What about ethics for the non-Christian?

Jonathan Edwards, a colonial American Puritan pastor, addressed this issue by differentiating between *true virtue* on the one hand and *common morality* on the other. God has not left the world without a moral compass. General revelation reveals certain laws governing human behavior. We know this to be true because we have an innate sense of the sanctity of life. We have a built-in, basic sense of right and wrong, of justice and punishment. We don't have to teach children to say, "That's not fair."

Edwards argues that, as Christians, we have the obligation to promote common morality and to celebrate and encourage it when we see it. Only true virtue passes for righteousness before God, and that is developed in us only as the Holy Spirit enables us. But common morality is a good thing. Common morality can even cultivate a seedbed in which the gospel can take root and flourish. As individuals, as families, and as a church, we should applaud and encourage common morality.

"Think on These Things"

We live the Christian life out of love for God. That love leads us to find our joy and satisfaction in God. And that joy instills within us a desire to obey him. God has given us a path for our journey, our walk of obedience. God has shown us in his Word what he requires of us. We need to be aware of Scripture's "don'ts" so we avoid straying from the path. But we also need to cultivate Scripture's "dos," so we not only stay on the path but fully enjoy the journey as well. So we conclude with the words of Paul in Philippians 4:8:

> Finally, brothers, whatever is true, whatever is honorable, whatever is just, whatever is pure, whatever is lovely, whatever is commendable, if there is any excellence, if there is anything worthy of praise, think about these things.

GLOSSARY

A.D.
Abbreviation for *Anno Domini* ("in the year of our Lord"). Refers to the era of history following the birth of Jesus Christ, which immediately follows the era designated B.C. ("before Christ"). See also **B.C.**

ABOMINATION
Something that deeply offends. Often describes something that offends God and his standard of holiness. The Bible also mentions the "abomination of desolation" (or "abomination that makes desolate"), apparently referring to some profane act or object permitted in the temple (Dan. 11:31; 12:11; Matt. 24:15).

ABYSS, THE
Often translated "bottomless pit." The abode of the dead or of demonic forces. Throughout Scripture can refer to both places, although the Bible appears to regard them as distinctly separate (compare Luke 8:31; Rom. 10:7).

ADOPTION
Legal process by which a person gives the status of a son or daughter to another person who is not his or her child by birth. The NT uses the term to describe the act by which God makes believers his children through the atoning death and resurrection of his one and only true Son, Jesus (see Romans 8; Galatians 4).

ADVOCATE
One who acts on another person's behalf as mediator, intercessor, or encourager. In 1 John 2:1, Jesus is described as an advocate for believers before God the Father. The same Greek word (translated "Helper") is used to describe the Holy Spirit in John 14:16, 26.

ALLEGORY
A story that communicates truth through a symbolic understanding of its literal meaning. In allegory characters, objects, and actions specifically represent things from the parallel spiritual or moral context. An example is in Galatians 4, where Paul interpreted the true story of Hagar (Genesis 16–21) as an allegory to make a point about how the Sinai covenant differs from the new covenant in Christ.

ALPHA
First letter of the Greek alphabet (omega is the last letter). Three times in the book of Revelation, Jesus describes himself as "the Alpha and the Omega" (Rev. 1:8; 21:6; 22:13).

AMEN
Greek form of a Hebrew word meaning "to confirm." In Scripture and in Christian life, when uttered after a prayer or statement, it means "let it be so."

ANALOGY
A form of reasoning in which one thing is considered similar to another in a certain respect. An example is Jesus' comparison of his approaching death and burial with Jonah's time in the whale (Matt. 12:40).

ANGEL
A supernatural messenger of God, often sent to carry out his will or to assist human beings in carrying out his will. Though angels are more powerful than humans and often instill awe, they are not to be worshiped (Col. 2:18; Rev. 22:8–9). The Bible does, however, note various appearances of an "angel of the Lord," apparently a physical manifestation of God himself.

ANNUNCIATION, THE
Announcement by an angel to the virgin Mary that she would conceive the Son of God, Jesus, by the power of the Holy Spirit (Luke 1:26–38).

ANOINT
In Scripture, to pour oil (usually olive oil) on someone or something to set the person or thing apart for a special purpose. Anointing was performed for the high priest, for tabernacle vessels, for kings, and for prophets. The Hebrew word *Messiah* and its Greek equivalent *Christ* both mean "anointed one."

ANTICHRIST
This term, found only in the letters of John, describes anyone who denies that Jesus is the Christ, the unique Son of God (1 John 2:22). John and other NT writers may also have foreseen the appearance of one particular "antichrist" in the end times. The "man of lawlessness" (2 Thess. 2:3–4) may have been that person.

ANTINOMIANISM

The false belief that OT moral laws are no longer necessary or binding for those living under grace (see Rom. 6:1–2).

APOCALYPTIC

The distinctive literary form of the book of Revelation and of chs. 7–12 of Daniel. These parts of Scripture include revelation about the future, highly symbolic imagery, and the underlying belief that God himself will one day end the world in its present form and establish his kingdom on earth.

APOCRYPHA

A body of religious writings included in the Septuagint and in Roman Catholic Bibles but not in the Jewish or Protestant canons. See also *canon*.

APOSTASY

Abandonment or renunciation of faith.

APOSTLE

Means "one who is sent" and refers to one who is an official representative of another. In the NT, refers specifically to the those whom Jesus chose to represent him.

ARAMAIC

A language related to Hebrew, spoken throughout much of the ancient Near East. It was the everyday language of most Israelites after their exile to Babylon, and it continued to be spoken by many Jews (including Jesus) living in Palestine during the Roman era. Portions of the books of Ezra and Daniel were written in Aramaic.

ARCHANGEL

A title for the angel Michael in Jude 9, apparently indicating his chief rank among the angels. Paul also mentions that the Lord's return to earth will be accompanied by the voice of an archangel (1 Thess. 4:16). See also *angel*.

ARMAGEDDON

A place name mentioned in Rev. 16:16, where the kings of the earth gather to wage war against God in the last days. Likely means "mountain(s) of Megiddo," referring to a city in northern Israel.

ASCENSION

The departure of the resurrected Jesus to God the Father in heaven (Luke 24:50–51; Acts 1:1–12).

ASTROLOGY

The study of how the position of heavenly bodies supposedly influences earthly activity. Astrology often seeks to predict future events or to provide insight into advisable courses of action. Astrology is akin to other forms of divination condemned in Deut. 18:14. Jeremiah tells his hearers not to fear the signs of the heavens as other nations do (Jer. 10:2).

ATONEMENT

The reconciliation of a person with God, often associated with the offering of a sacrifice. Through his death and resurrection, Jesus Christ made atonement for the sins of believers. His death satisfied God's just wrath against sinful humanity, just as OT sacrifices symbolized substitutionary death as payment for sin. See also *propitiation* and *reconciliation*.

ATTRIBUTES OF GOD

The distinctive characteristics of God as he is described in the Bible. These include eternality, faithfulness, goodness, graciousness, holiness, immutability, infinitude, justice, love, mercy, omnipotence, omnipresence, omniscience, self-existence, self-sufficiency, sovereignty, and wisdom.

B.C.

Abbreviation for "before Christ" in calendars. It immediately precedes the era designated A.D. (*Anno Domini*, meaning "in the year of our Lord") and refers to the number of years before Jesus Christ was born. See also *A.D.*

BAPTIZE

Literally "to immerse" or "to wash." Refers to the Christian practice of immersing a new believer in water as an outward sign of the inward reality of regeneration. This regeneration is the work of the Holy Spirit (see John 3:5, 8; Titus 3:5) and may be received only by grace through faith (see Eph. 2:8). Considerable disagreement exists as to method of baptism (e.g., sprinkling vs. immersion) and who may be baptized (e.g., believers only vs. believers and their infant children).

BEATITUDE

Derived from Latin for "blessedness," refers to various verses in Scripture that declare a person "blessed" or "happy" under certain conditions. Beatitudes appear throughout the Bible but most famously in Matthew 5:1–11 and Luke 6:20–22.

BENEDICTION

A prayer for God's blessing at the end of a letter or a worship service. Many NT letters include a benediction.

BETROTHAL

A formal stage in the marriage process of ancient Near Eastern cultures, in which a couple was pledged to each other but did not yet live together or enjoy physical union. A betrothal could be dissolved only through divorce.

BISHOP

Translation of Greek *episkopos* ("overseer"). A person who exercised authority and oversight within the church. See also *elder*.

BLASPHEMY

Any speech, writing, or action that slanders God. In the OT, the penalty for blasphemy was death (Lev. 24:16), and in the NT, Jesus states that the one who blasphemes against the Holy Spirit will not be forgiven (Luke 12:10).

BLESS

To worship or praise another, especially God; to bestow goodness on another.

BONDSERVANT

See Preface, p. x.

BORN AGAIN

A phrase used by Jesus in John 3 to describe how a person enters the kingdom of heaven. Natural birth is not sufficient. Instead, through the work of the Holy Spirit and the grace of God, a person must experience a second, spiritual birth, in which he or she becomes a new person in Christ

BUSYBODY

Someone who meddles in the affairs of others. Paul exhorted those who were busybodies to mind their own affairs and work hard at earning their own living (2 Thess. 3:11; 1 Tim. 5:13).

CANON

The list of writings recognized as Scripture, that is, regarded as inspired by God and authoritative in all areas of doctrine and practice. Criteria for canonical books include: (1) apostolic authority (was the book written by or associated with an apostle?); (2) universal acceptance by the church; and (3) unity of message (is the message of the book consistent with other books recognized as inspired?). See also *Apocrypha*.

CHRIST

Transliteration of the Greek for "anointed one" (equivalent to Hebrew *Messiah*). The term is used throughout the NT as a title for Jesus, indicating his role as Messiah and Savior.

CHRISTIAN

A follower of Jesus Christ (Acts 11:26).

CHURCH

From a Greek word meaning "assembly." The body of believers in Jesus Christ, referring either to all believers everywhere or to a local gathering of believers.

CIRCUMCISION

The ritual practice of removing the foreskin of an individual, which was commanded for all male Israelites in OT times as a sign of participation in the covenant God established with Abraham (Gen. 17:9–14).

CLEAN/UNCLEAN

The ceremonial, spiritual, or moral state of a person or object, affected by a variety of factors. The terms are primarily related to the concept of holiness and have little to do with actual physical cleanliness. The Mosaic law declared certain foods and animals unclean, and a person became unclean if he or she came in contact with certain substances or objects, such as a dead body. Jesus declared all foods clean (Mark 7:19), and Peter's vision in Acts 10 shows that no person is ceremonially unclean simply because he or she is a Gentile.

COMMANDMENT

In the Bible, an instruction or order given by God. Commandments appear throughout Scripture, but most occur in the Law, the first five books of the Bible. Most famous are the Ten Commandments (Ex. 20:2–17; Deut. 5:6–21).

COMMUNION

The fellowship and unity all believers share as a result of the work of the Holy Spirit in their hearts. Such communion among believers can be expressed in various ways, including worshiping God together, sharing possessions and resources, and partaking of the Lord's Supper, which has also come to be referred to as Communion. See also *Lord's Supper, the*.

CONFESSION

Public acknowledgment of belief (2 Cor. 9:13; Heb. 4:14), or of sin (Ezra 10:1; James 5:16; 1 John 1:9).

CONSCIENCE

The ability to understand the rightness or wrongness of one's actions and motives. The conscience is not identical with the inner witness of the Holy Spirit, although the Holy Spirit often employs the conscience in guiding people and convicting them of sin (Rom. 2:15).

CONSUMMATION

In Christian theology, the final and full establishment of the kingdom of God, when the heavens and earth will be made new and God will rule over all things forever (2 Pet. 3:13; Revelation 11; 19–22).

CONVERSION

The result of turning away from sin, accepting the truth of the gospel of Jesus Christ, and submitting to him.

COVENANT

A binding agreement between two parties, typically involving a formal statement of their relationship, a list of stipulations and obligations for both parties, a list of witnesses to the agreement, and a list of curses for unfaithfulness and blessings for faithfulness to the agreement. The OT is more properly understood as the old covenant, meaning the agreement established between God and his people prior to the coming of Jesus Christ and the establishment of the new covenant (NT).

COVETOUSNESS

The desire to have something (or someone) that belongs to another. Covetousness is forbidden in the Ten Commandments (Ex. 20:17; Deut. 5:21).

CRUCIFIXION

A means of execution in which the person was fastened, by ropes or nails, to a crossbeam that was then raised and attached to a vertical beam, forming a cross (the root meaning of "crucifixion"). The process was designed to maximize pain and humiliation, and to serve as a deterrent for other potential offenders. Jesus suffered this form of execution (Matt. 27:32–56), not for any offense he had committed (Heb. 4:15) but as the atoning sacrifice for all who would believe in him (John 3:16).

DAMNATION

Condemnation by God that results in a person being consigned to suffer forever in hell. All people deserve damnation for sinning against God (Romans 1–3), but God offers redemption through Jesus Christ (Romans 5; Ephesians 2).

DAY OF ATONEMENT

The holiest day in the Israelite calendar, when atonement was made for all the sins of Israel from the past year (Leviticus 16). It occurred on the tenth day of the seventh month (September/October), and all Israel was to fast and do no work. Only on that day each year could someone—the high priest—enter the Most Holy Place of the tabernacle (later, the temple) and offer the necessary sacrifices. A "scapegoat" would also be sent into the wilderness as a sign of Israel's sins being carried away. See also *atonement*.

DEACON

From the Greek for "servant." An officer in the local church (1 Timothy 3) who assists the elders.

DECREE

An official ruling, equivalent to a law. In theology, it can refer to God's foreordained purpose or will regarding future events.

DEDICATION

The setting apart of a person or an object for special or sacred use.

DEITY

God's unique, essential nature as supreme and eternal. Jesus, the Son of God, possesses deity. He is fully God, as is the Holy Spirit.

DEMON

An evil spirit that can inhabit a human being and cause him or her to carry out its will. Demons were created by God and are always limited by God. Jesus and his followers cast out many demons, demonstrating Jesus' superiority over them. All demons will one day be destroyed along with Satan (Matt. 25:41; Rev. 20:10).

DEPRAVITY

The sinful condition of human nature apart from grace, whereby humans are inclined to serve their own will and desires and to reject God's rule.

DEVIL, THE

See *Satan*.

DIASPORA, THE

See *Dispersion, the*.

DISCERNMENT

Wisdom in perception and judgment. Spiritual discernment is a Spirit-enabled capacity in believers to understand God's truths (1 Cor. 2:9–16) as well as to identify spiritual error (1 John 4:1–6).

DISCIPLE
Any person who submits to the teachings of another. In the NT, refers to those who submitted themselves to the teaching of Jesus, especially those who traveled with him during his earthly ministry.

DISPERSION, THE
From the Greek for "scattering," refers to the numerous relocations of large groups of Israelites/Jews throughout the world, including to Assyria and Media (722 B.C.), Babylon (586), Alexandria in Egypt (c. 300), Phrygia (c. 200), and Rome (c. 63). This dispersion resulted in greater exposure of the Jews to other peoples and also laid the groundwork for the worldwide spread of the gospel during the first century.

DIVINATION
The attempt to acquire special knowledge about the future or other naturally unknowable information by interpreting phenomena such as dreams, heavenly bodies, animal intestines, or the casting of lots. All divination is condemned in Deut. 18:14.

DOCTRINE
A body of beliefs or teachings, often in systematic form.

DOXOLOGY
Expression of praise to God. Often included at the end of NT letters. Modern church services often end with doxologies in the form of short hymns.

ECCLESIASTICAL
Having to do with the church (Greek *ekklēsia*). See **church**.

ELDER
A recognized leader charged with oversight of a community or organized body. In the NT, an officer in the local church (Acts 14:23; 1 Tim. 3:1–7) charged primarily with spiritual oversight.

ELECTION
In theology, God's sovereign choice of people for redemption and eternal life. Also referred to as "predestination."

END TIMES
A time associated with events prophesied in Scripture to occur at the end of the world and the second coming of Christ—also known as "the last days." Because the early church expected the return of Christ at any time, the end times can refer to the period from then until Christ returns.

EPICUREANISM
Philosophy based on the teachings of Epicurus (341–270 B.C.), who emphasized tranquility and the absence of pain as the most desirable goals in life.

EPISTLE
Essentially synonymous with "letter." A literary form common in NT times. Epistles typically included: (1) statement of author and recipient; (2) brief greetings and expressions of thanks; (3) the body of the letter; (4) personal greetings and signature; and (5) a closing doxology or blessing. Twenty-one books of the NT are epistles.

ESCHATOLOGY
Study of the end times as described in the Bible. Includes such topics as the return of Christ, the period of tribulation, the resurrection and judgment of all people, and the millennial reign of Christ on earth. See The Doctrine of the Future: Consummation, p. 1343.

ETERNAL LIFE
For believers, the new life that begins with trust in Jesus Christ alone for salvation, and that continues after physical death with an eternity in God's presence in heaven. See also **salvation**.

ETERNAL SECURITY
See **perseverance of the saints**.

ETERNITY
An endless span of time. For humans, eternity has a beginning (the moment of birth) but no end. With God, however, eternity has neither beginning nor end, for he has always existed.

ETHICS
In Christian theology, the study of morality, justice, and virtue in light of the Bible's teachings.

EUCHARIST
From the Greek for "thanksgiving." Synonymous with "the Lord's Supper." See also **Lord's Supper, the**.

EVANGELISM
Proclamation of the gospel (Greek *euangelion*) of Jesus Christ.

EXCOMMUNICATION
In the NT, a form of church discipline that revoked a person's privileges as part of the community of believers. Typically imposed for unrepented sin or heresy, to preserve the community's purity and hopefully to bring

the offender to repentance (Matt. 18:15–18; 1 Corinthians 5; 2 Cor. 2:5–11; 1 Tim. 1:18–20).

EXEGESIS

Examining a text to determine and explain its originally intended meaning. Biblical commentaries are examples of exegesis.

EXHORTATION

A message encouraging someone to follow a particular course of action or to submit to a different way of thinking.

EXILE, THE

Several relocations of large groups of Israelites/ Jews have occurred throughout history (see *Dispersion, the*), but "the exile" typically refers to the Babylonian exile, that is, Nebuchadnezzar's relocation of residents of the southern kingdom of Judah to Babylon in 586 B.C. (Residents of the northern kingdom of Israel had been resettled by Assyria in 722 B.C.) After Babylon came under Persian rule, several waves of Jewish exiles returned and repopulated Judah.

EXODUS, THE

The departure of the people of Israel from Egypt and their journey to Mount Sinai under Moses' leadership (Exodus 1–19; Numbers 33). The exodus demonstrated God's power and providence for his people, who had been enslaved by the Egyptians. The annual festival of Passover commemorates God's final plague upon the Egyptians, resulting in the Israelites' release from Egypt.

EXPIATION

The removal of sin and its consequences.

EXTRABIBLICAL

Pertaining to something not included in the canon of Scripture.

FABLE

A story intended to teach a moral or cultural lesson. Fables are usually relatively brief and portray animals or objects with human abilities such as speech.

FAITH

Trust in or reliance upon something or someone despite a lack of concrete proof. Salvation, which is purely a work of God's grace, can be received only through faith (Rom. 5:2; Eph. 2:8–9). The writer of Hebrews calls on believers to emulate those who lived godly lives by faith (Hebrews 11).

FALL, THE

Adam and Eve's disobedience of God by eating the fruit from the tree of the knowledge of good and evil, resulting in their loss of innocence and favor with God and the introduction of sin and its effects into the world (Genesis 3; Rom. 5:12–21; 1 Cor. 15:21–22).

FASTING

Deliberate abstinence from some or all food for a sustained time.

FEAR

Has both godly and ungodly meanings in the Bible, depending on the context. Fear of the Lord is a godly, wise fear that demonstrates awe and reference for the all-powerful God (Prov. 1:7). Conversely, Jesus taught his disciples not to fear people or situations in a way that shows lack of trust in God's protection (Matt. 10:26–31).

FIGURATIVE

Pertaining to language intended to communicate a meaning other than what is literally expressed. An example is Nahum's description of the Lord's awesome power: "His way is in the whirlwind and storm, and the clouds are the dust of his feet" (Nah. 1:3).

FLESH

Depending on the immediate context, either skin (Lev. 4:11), a living being (Gen. 6:13), or sinful human nature (Rom. 8:3).

FORGIVENESS

Release from guilt and the reestablishment of relationship. Forgiveness can be granted by God to human beings (Luke 24:47; 1 John 1:9) and by human beings to those who have wronged them (Matt. 18:21–22; Col. 3:13).

FORNICATION

Any kind of sexual immorality, that is, any sexual activity other than between a man and a woman in marriage.

GLORIFICATION

The work of God in believers to bring them to the ultimate and perfect stage of salvation—Christlikeness—following his justification and sanctification of them (Rom. 8:29–30). Glorification includes believers receiving imperishable resurrection bodies at Christ's return (1 Cor. 15:42–43). See also *justification* and *sanctification*.

GNOSTICISM

A system of thought prevalent during the second century that combined elements of various philosophies and religions, including Christianity. Some common Gnostic beliefs include (1) a dualistic view of matter and spirit, with matter generally being viewed as evil and spirit as good; (2) the complete transcendence of God, who therefore has nothing to do with the evil material world; (3) a view of salvation in which humans are freed from their physical existence and reunited with God; and (4) an emphasis on special knowledge (Greek *gnosis*) about spiritual realities as the key to salvation.

GOSPEL

A common translation for a Greek word meaning "good news," that is, the good news of Jesus Christ and the salvation he made possible by his crucifixion, burial, and resurrection. *Gospel* with an initial capital letter refers to each of the biblical accounts of Jesus' life on earth (Matthew, Mark, Luke, and John).

GRACE

Unmerited favor, especially the free gift of salvation that God gives to believers through faith in Jesus Christ.

GRECO-ROMAN

Pertaining to the culture, language, religion, or government of the Roman Empire, which was itself greatly influenced by Greek culture and religion.

GUILT

Responsibility for wrongdoing.

HADES

In the NT, the abode of the dead prior to the second coming of Christ. Essentially equivalent to Sheol in the OT. See also **hell** and **Sheol**.

HALLELUJAH

Transliteration of a Hebrew phrase meaning "praise the Lord."

HEAVEN

The sky, or the abode of God (Matt. 6:9), which is commonly regarded as being above the earth and sky. As the abode of God, heaven is also the place where believers live in God's presence after death (1 Thess. 4:16–17).

HELL

A place of eternal torment for those who rebel against God and refuse to repent.

HELLENISM

A modified form of Greek culture, philosophy, religion, politics, and language that was spread throughout the Mediterranean world by the

exploits of Alexander the Great. Hellenism continued to have great influence throughout the time of the Roman Empire.

HERESY

Any teaching incompatible with Christian orthodoxy.

HIGH PLACES

Height may or may not have been a feature of these public sites where offerings were made to God or to false gods. Worshiping the Lord at a high place was legitimate before the time of the temple (1 Kings 3:2, 4). Later "high places," even those where the Lord was worshiped, were forbidden (2 Kings 23:15).

HISTORY OF SALVATION

God's unified plan for all of history, to accomplish the salvation of his people. He accomplished this salvation plan in the work of Jesus Christ on earth, by his life, crucifixion, burial, and resurrection (Eph. 1:10–12). The consummation of God's plan will take place when Jesus Christ comes again to establish the "new heavens and a new earth in which righteousness dwells" (2 Pet. 3:13).

HOLINESS

A quality possessed by something or someone set apart for special use. When applied to God, it refers to his utter perfection and complete transcendence over creation. God's people are called to imitate his holiness (Lev. 19:2), which means being set apart from sin and reserved for his purposes.

HOLY SPIRIT

One of the persons of the Trinity, and thus fully God. The Bible mentions several roles of the Holy Spirit, including convicting people of sin, bringing them to conversion, indwelling them and empowering them to live in righteousness and faithfulness, supporting them in times of trial, and enabling them to understand the Scriptures. The Holy Spirit inspired the writers of Scripture, guiding them to record the very words of God. The Holy Spirit was especially active in Jesus' life and ministry on earth (e.g., Luke 3:22).

HOMOSEXUALITY

Any sexual activity between members of the same sex. Explicitly condemned in both the OT (Lev. 18:22; 20:13) and the NT (Rom. 1:24–32; 1 Cor. 6:9–10).

HYPERBOLE

Rhetorical device for expressing ideas in intentionally exaggerated form for emphasis, where the exaggerated expressions are not intended to be taken literally. An example is Jesus' condemnation of the scribes and Pharisees for straining out a gnat and swallowing a camel (Matt. 23:24).

HYPOCRISY

Falsely presenting oneself to others in order to gain positive regard or praise. Derived from Greek for "actor." Jesus repeatedly condemned the hypocrisy of Jewish religious leaders.

IDIOM

An expression, often of several words that together have a figurative meaning different from the literal meanings of the words themselves. For example, the expression "take it with a grain of salt" means not to take something seriously.

IDOLATRY

In the Bible, usually refers to the worship of a physical object. Paul's comments in Col. 3:5, however, suggest that idolatry can include covetousness, since it is essentially equivalent to worshiping material things.

ILLUMINATION

The process by which God, through the Holy Spirit, enables people to understand Scripture and put it into practice.

IMMANUEL

A Hebrew term meaning "God with us." Mentioned in Isa. 7:14 and 8:8 and then referred to in Matt. 1:23 as another name for Jesus. In both contexts the use of the name was intended to assure the readers of God's presence with them.

IMMORTALITY

Immunity from death. God alone possesses immortality as part of his very being (1 Tim. 6:16), and he will grant believers immortality at the return of Christ (1 Cor. 15:53–54).

IMMUTABILITY

Pertaining to the unchangeable character, will, and promises of God. One of his distinctive attributes (Mal. 3:6).

IMPUTE

To attribute something to someone or credit it to his or her account. Often refers to God's crediting to every believer the righteousness of Jesus Christ.

INCARNATION

Literally "(becoming) in flesh," it refers to God becoming a human being in the person of Jesus of Nazareth.

INDWELLING

In Scripture, refers to the presence of Christ and the Holy Spirit within believers (Rom. 8:9–11; Eph. 3:16–18). This presence enables Christians to love (1 John 4:8–12) and to overcome sin, which also indwells believers (Rom. 8:4–11).

INERRANCY

The doctrine of Biblical inerrancy expresses the Bible's own teaching that it is true, reliable, and trustworthy—without error—in all the matters that it affirms and addresses (2 Tim. 3:16).

INIQUITY

See *sin*.

INSPIRATION

God's work of empowering and directing the writers of Scripture to communicate his authoritative truth to his people (2 Tim. 3:16; 2 Pet. 1:20–21). Belief in the inspiration of the Bible ensures that it represents the very words of God himself.

INTERCESSION

Appealing to one person on behalf of another. Often used with reference to prayer.

INTERMEDIARY

A mediator or messenger between two parties, especially between God and humanity.

INTERMEDIATE STATE

The state of existence believers experience immediately after death and before resurrection. Most Protestant theologians believe that, after death, the souls of believers immediately enter God's presence, although they remain in disembodied form as they await the final resurrection, when they will be reunited with their bodies.

INTERTESTAMENTAL

Pertaining to the time between the end of OT history and beginning of NT history. Roughly 430–5 B.C.

ISRAEL

Originally, another name given to Jacob (Gen. 32:28). Later applied to the nation formed by his descendants, then to the ten northern tribes of that nation, who rejected the anointed king and formed their own nation. In the NT, the name is applied to the church as the spiritual descendants of Abraham (Gal. 6:16).

JEW
A person belonging to one of the tribes of Israel. The term, derived from the word "Judah/Judean," came into being around the time of the Babylonian exile (c. 586 B.C.).

JUDAISM
The religion and culture of the Jewish people after their return from exile in Babylon (c. 538 B.C.), and continuing to modern times.

JUDAIZERS
Though this term is never actually used in the Bible, it refers to those in the early church who sought to compel Gentile believers to adhere to Jewish ceremonial requirements, such as circumcision, as a necessary part of salvation.

JUDGMENT
Any assessment of something or someone, especially moral assessment. The Bible also speaks of a final day of judgment when Christ returns, when all those who have refused to repent will be judged (Rev. 20:12–15).

JUSTIFICATION
The act of God's grace in bringing sinners into a new covenant relationship with himself and counting them as righteous before him through the forgiveness of sins (Rom. 3:20–26).

KINGDOM OF GOD/HEAVEN
The sovereign rule of God. At the present time, the fallen, sinful world does not belong to the kingdom of God, since it does not submit to God's rule. Instead, God's kingdom can be found in heaven and among his people (Matt. 6:9–10; Luke 17:20–21). After Christ returns, however, the kingdoms of the world will become the kingdom of God (Rev. 11:15). Then all people will, either willingly or regretfully, acknowledge his sovereignty (Phil. 2:9–11). Even the natural world will be transformed to operate in perfect harmony with God (Rom. 8:19–23).

KINSMAN-REDEEMER
In OT times, a relative in each extended family who had the responsibility to redeem—that is, to buy back—any relative's land in danger of being sold because of debt. In the book of Ruth, Boaz accepted this responsibility.

LAW
When spelled with an initial capital letter, "Law" refers to the first five books of the Bible (see also **Pentateuch**). The Law contains numerous commands of God to his people, including the Ten Commandments and instructions regarding worship, sacrifice, and life in Israel. The NT often uses "the law" (lower case) to refer to the entire body of precepts set forth in the books of the Law.

LAWYER
In the NT, denotes a religious teacher or scholar considered an authority on the interpretation of Jewish law. See also **scribe**.

LEGALISM
Requirements that go beyond the commands of Scripture; or, the unbiblical belief that works are the means of becoming right with God.

LEPROSY
In OT and NT, refers to several skin diseases. In the OT refers also to a condition affecting garments and houses. It is debated whether the term includes modern leprosy (Hansen's disease).

LESSER-TO-GREATER ARGUMENT
Rhetorical device that takes a recognized truth from one situation and applies it to another situation of greater scope. An example is Jesus' comment that his followers can be certain God will provide for their needs because he provides glorious adornment even for the grass of the field (Matt. 6:30).

LEVIRATE MARRIAGE
In OT times, the obligation for a brother to marry his deceased brother's widow and raise children in the brother's name if he died childless (Deut. 25:5–10). This requirement sought to ensure that no Israelite family line would die out and lose its inheritance in Israel. Derived from *levir*, the Latin word for "brother-in-law."

LEX TALIONIS
Latin for "law of retribution," refers to a system of justice that punishes an offender by inflicting on him the same harm that he inflicted on someone else. Referred to in the Bible as "an eye for an eye" (see Ex. 21:22–27).

LITERAL
A method of communication in which words are intended to be understood according to their normally defined meaning. This is in contrast to figurative, analogical, or symbolic methods of communication.

LITURGICAL

Pertaining to traditional, customary, public readings performed by a church or other religious group.

LOGOS

Greek term literally meaning "word" or "logical principle." Equated with Jesus and God in John's Gospel (John 1:1–18). John is likely drawing upon the rich reservoir of meaning for the term both in Hellenistic thought and in first-century Judaism.

LORD

Someone superior in authority or status to another, similar to "master." It is a common translation for several different Hebrew titles for God in the OT, and in the NT refers to Jesus. When spelled in the OT with small capital letters (Lord) it translates Hebrew *Yahweh* (*YHWH*), the personal name of God. See also *Yahweh.*

LORD'S SUPPER, THE

A meal of remembrance instituted by Jesus on the night of his betrayal. Christians are to observe this meal, also called Communion, in remembrance of Jesus' death. It consists of wine, symbolizing the new covenant in his blood, and bread, symbolizing his body, which was broken for his followers. See also *Communion.*

MACCABEES

A Jewish family who led a successful revolt against the rulers who controlled Israel during the second century B.C. Their story is told in the apocryphal books of *1 and 2 Maccabees.*

MAGIC

In the Bible, refers to the attempt to control events or people through supernatural forces other than God. It is similar to divination and other practices that are condemned in Deut. 18:14. The NT likewise implicitly condemns the practice of magic in Acts 8 and 19. See also *divination.*

MATERIALISM

A sinful love of material things, such as money or possessions. Materialism is sinful in that it looks to material things to provide what only God can truly provide (Col. 3:5).

MEDIATOR

One who intercedes between parties to resolve a conflict or achieve a goal. Jesus is the mediator between God and rebellious humanity (1 Tim. 2:5; compare Heb. 9:15; 12:24).

MEDITATION

Contemplation on something, such as the attributes of God, with focused attention (see Ps. 1:2). Biblical meditation stands in contrast to many forms of Eastern meditation, which seek to empty the mind of rational thought.

MEEKNESS

Humble assurance founded on a deep trust in God's will and providence (Ps. 37:11). Such trust results in a peaceful and gentle disposition even in the face of persecution or difficulty. It frees a person from the temptations of self-reliance and pride.

MERCY

Compassion and kindness toward someone experiencing hardship, sometimes even when such suffering results from the person's own sin or foolishness. God displays mercy toward his people and they, in turn, are called to display mercy toward others (Luke 6:36).

MESSIAH

Transliteration of a Hebrew word meaning "anointed one," the equivalent of the Greek word *Christ*. Originally applied to anyone specially designated for a particular role, such as king or priest. Jesus himself affirmed that he was the Messiah sent from God (Matt. 16:16–17).

METAPHOR

A figure of speech that draws an analogy between two objects by equating them, even though they are not actually the same thing. An example is Ps. 119:105: "Your word is a lamp to my feet and a light to my path." See also *simile.*

MILLENNIUM, THE

See The Doctrine of the Future: Consummation, p. 1343.

MIRACLE

A special act of God that goes beyond natural means, thus demonstrating God's power.

MONOTHEISM

The belief that there is only one true God. One of the distinguishing characteristics of the Israelites in the OT and of Christians, their spiritual heirs. See also *polytheism.*

MYTH

A religious story explaining how the world came to be in its present form and what spiritual entities lie behind the visible world. The NT uses the term exclusively in a negative way (1 Tim. 1:4; 4:7; 2 Tim. 4:4; Titus 1:14; 2 Pet. 1:16).

OATH
Humans were warned in the OT not to swear promises rashly or falsely (Lev. 5:4; 19:11–12). Sometimes oaths were made in God's name, as though to guarantee them, but Jesus told his disciples not to swear oaths at all. Rather, they should let their simple statement of "yes" mean yes and their "no" mean no (Matt. 5:33–37).

OCCULT
Describes any attempt to acquire secret knowledge about the future or other naturally unknowable information through sources other than God and observance of the natural world. Occult practices are similar to divination, which is condemned in Deut. 18:14.

OMEGA
Last letter of the Greek alphabet (alpha is the first letter). Three times in the book of Revelation Jesus describes himself as "the Alpha and the Omega" (Rev. 1:8; 21:6; 22:13).

OMNIPOTENCE
An attribute of God that describes his unlimited power to carry out his will.

OMNIPRESENCE
An attribute of God that describes his presence in all places at all times.

OMNISCIENCE
An attribute of God that describes his complete knowledge and understanding of all things at all times.

ORACLE
From Latin "to speak." In the Bible, refers to a divine pronouncement delivered through a human agent.

ORDINATION
Official investment of religious authority upon a person. In the OT, priests were ordained. Most modern Christian denominations require some form of ordination for those in ministry.

ORIGINAL SIN
A condition of both guilt and a propensity to sin, inherited by all people because of their descent from Adam, who committed the first sin.

ORTHODOXY
Teaching and doctrine regarded as correct and in agreement with essential biblical teachings.

PAGANISM
Any belief system that does not acknowledge the God of the Bible as the one true God.

Atheism, polytheism, pantheism, animism, and humanism, as well as numerous other religious systems, can all be classified as forms of paganism.

PALESTINE
A name often used to refer to the land occupied by the Israelites. Derived from *Philistia*, the stretch of land along the Mediterranean Sea that formed the southwest border of Israel's territory.

PANTHEISM
The heretical belief that all things are part of the essence of God, thus making all things divine.

PAPYRUS
A plant abundant in Middle Eastern marshes. Used for many purposes in ancient times, including the production of writing material. Some of the earliest copies of the Bible were written on papyrus.

PARABLE
A story that uses everyday imagery and activities to communicate a spiritual truth. Jesus often taught in parables (e.g., Matthew 13).

PARADISE
The place of the righteous dead (Luke 23:43; 2 Cor. 12:3; Rev. 2:7), likely the same as heaven.

PARALLELISM
A poetic device, employed in virtually all Hebrew poetry, that places together two or three concepts that are matching, opposing, or progressive in meaning. Essentially it is a "rhyming" of concepts rather than sounds, with the first line being restated in a slightly different way in the second line. An example is Ps. 51:7: "Purge me with hyssop, and I shall be clean; wash me, and I shall be whiter than snow."

PARCHMENT
Writing material, sometimes called *vellum*, produced from animal skin. Some of the earliest known copies of the Bible were written on parchment.

PARDON
See *forgiveness*.

PASSOVER
An annual Israelite festival commemorating God's final plague on the Egyptians, which led to the exodus. In this final plague, the Lord "passed over" the houses of those who spread the blood of a lamb on the doorposts of their homes (Exodus 12). Those who did not obey

this command suffered the death of their firstborn.

PASTOR
A common translation of the Greek for "shepherd," which came to be used of leaders of the church, who are to "shepherd" the "flock" of believers in Christ.

PATRIARCHS
The earliest ancestors of Israel, primarily Abraham, Isaac, and Jacob.

PEACE
In modern use, the absence of tension or conflict. In biblical use, a condition of well-being or wholeness that God grants his people, which also results in harmony with God and others.

PENITENCE
The condition of being repentant and sorrowful for wrongdoing.

PENTATEUCH
The first five books of the Bible.

PERSEVERANCE OF THE SAINTS
According to this doctrine, God enables all true believers to remain faithful to the end. Those who willfully continue in sin reveal that they were never truly believers. Others may for a time *appear* to abandon their faith though they have not in fact done so. This doctrine does not deny the reality that even true believers still sin, nor does it mean that those who have made a profession of faith are free to live sinful, godless lives.

PERSONIFICATION
Rhetorical device attributing human characteristics to non-human things, such as animals, plants, or objects. An example is Isa. 55:12: "The mountains and the hills before you shall break forth into singing, and all the trees of the field shall clap their hands."

PETITION
A request made to someone in authority, such as a citizen to a judge or a person to God in prayer.

PHARISEE
A member of a popular religious/political party in NT times characterized by strict adherence to the law of Moses and also to extrabiblical Jewish traditions. The Pharisees were frequently criticized by Jesus for their legalistic and hypocritical practices. The apostle Paul was a zealous Pharisee prior to his conversion.

PHILOSOPHY
The study of the fundamental questions and principles of any subject or discipline. It is often specifically concerned with topics regarding existence, knowledge, values, and reason and is typically characterized by rational, systematic analysis of its subject of inquiry.

PIETY
Reverential fear of God, often demonstrated by practical deeds. In NT times, many Jews considered prayer, almsgiving, and fasting to be the three primary acts of piety.

POLYTHEISM
Belief in the existence of many gods.

POSTEXILIC
Pertaining to the period following the return from exile in Babylon (c. 538 B.C.). Postexilic life in Israel differed markedly from the time before the exile. There was a greater emphasis on observance of the Law of Moses, a near universal abhorrence of idolatry, and the development of the synagogue as a place for Jews to worship and study the Scriptures.

PREDESTINATION
God's sovereign choice of people for redemption and eternal life. Also referred to as "election."

PREEMINENCE
The quality of being first, foremost, or of highest significance. In the Bible, this quality is attributed supremely to Christ (Col. 1:18).

PRIEST
In OT Israel, the priest represented the people before God, and God before the people. Only those descended from Aaron could be priests. Their prescribed duties also included inspecting and receiving sacrifices from the people and overseeing the daily activities and maintenance of the tabernacle or temple.

PROPITIATION
The appeasement of wrath by the offering of a gift or sacrifice. Jesus made propitiation for the sins of humanity by his suffering and death (Rom. 3:25; Heb. 2:17; 1 John 2:2; 4:10).

PROSELYTE
A convert to a particular religion, as opposed to one who had grown up in that religion. The Law of Moses gave instructions for how Gentiles could become proselytes of the Israelite covenant community. This primarily involved the circumcision of males.

PROVERB

A brief saying that conveys a lesson about how to live wisely and well, usually drawn from observations about nature and life. The book of Proverbs contains the vast majority of biblical proverbs, but they occur in other books as well.

PROVIDENCE

God's good, wise, and sovereign guidance and control of all things, by which he supplies all our needs and accomplishes his holy will.

RABBI

A teacher of Jewish religious law. The term, meaning "my master," originally developed as an expression of respect and later became more formalized as a title. Jesus was often called "Rabbi" by his followers (e.g., Mark 9:5).

RANSOM

A price paid to redeem, or buy back, someone who had become enslaved or something that had been lost to someone else. Jesus described his ministry as serving others and giving his life as a ransom for many (Mark 10:45). See also *redemption*.

RAPTURE, THE

See The Doctrine of the Future: Consummation, p. 1343.

RECONCILIATION

The restoration of relationship and peace between alienated or opposing parties. Through his death and resurrection, Jesus has reconciled believers to God (2 Cor. 5:18–21).

REDEMPTION

In the context of the Bible, the act of buying back someone who had become enslaved or something that had been lost to someone else. Through his death and resurrection, Jesus purchased redemption for all believers (Col. 1:13–14). See also *ransom*.

REGENERATION

The Holy Spirit's work of bringing spiritual life to a person, thus enabling him or her to love and follow God. Essentially equivalent to what is often referred to as being "born again" or "saved."

REINCARNATION

The unbiblical belief that all living beings possess an immortal soul that, upon the death of the physical body, is reborn into another living being. Many also believe that each time this process is repeated the soul moves closer to or further away from some form of ultimate happiness. This belief stands in opposition to the biblical view of human existence and what awaits people after death.

REMNANT

In the Bible, a portion of people who remain after most others are destroyed by some catastrophe. The notion of a "remnant" can be found in various events recorded in Scripture, including the flood (Genesis 6–8) and the return of exiled Judah (Ezra 9).

REPENTANCE

A complete change of heart and mind regarding one's overall attitude toward God or one's individual actions. True regeneration and conversion is always accompanied by repentance.

REPROOF

Rebuke or criticism for wrong or sinful behavior. The book of Proverbs contains many verses commending those willing to listen to rebuke (Prov. 3:11) and condemning those who reject it (Prov. 9:8). Scripture is profitable, among other things, for reproof and correction (2 Tim. 3:16–17).

RESURRECTION

The impartation of new, eternal life to a dead person at the end of time (or in the case of Jesus, on the third day after his death). This new life is not a mere resuscitation of the body (as in the case of Lazarus; John 11:1–44) but a transformation of the body to an eternal state (1 Cor. 15:35–58). Both the righteous and the wicked will be resurrected, the former to eternal life and the latter to judgment (John 5:29).

REVIVAL

A renewed desire for spiritual things, brought about by the work of God.

RHETORIC

The use of language to communicate effectively.

RIGHTEOUSNESS

The quality of being morally right and without sin. One of God's distinctive attributes. God imputes righteousness to (justifies) those who trust in Jesus Christ. See also *justification*.

RITUAL

A symbolic action performed for religious purposes.

SABBATH

Saturday, the seventh day of the week, the Jewish day of worship and rest (Gen. 2:2–3; Ex. 31:13–17). Christians meet for worship on Sunday, the day of Christ's resurrection (Acts 20:7), and regard Sunday, rather than Saturday, as their weekly day of rest. And yet, believers look forward to an eternal Sabbath rest (Heb. 4:1–13).

SABBATICAL
A period of rest. See *Sabbath*.

SACRIFICE
An offering to God, often to signify forgiveness of sin. The Law of Moses gave detailed instructions regarding various kinds of sacrifices. By his death on the cross, Jesus gave himself as a sacrifice to atone for the sins of believers (Eph. 5:2; Heb. 10:12). Believers are to offer their bodies as living sacrifices to God (Rom. 12:1).

SADDUCEE
A member of a religious/political party during Jesus' time characterized by (1) rejection of any OT writings except the five books of Moses, (2) rejection of belief in the resurrection and in angels and demons, (3) an interest in Hellenistic beliefs and ways of life, and (4) affluence, as a result of their influential priestly positions. Jesus criticized the Sadducees for refusing to believe in the resurrection and for demanding a sign from heaven to confirm his authority.

SALVATION
Deliverance from the eternal consequences of sin. Jesus' death and resurrection purchased eternal salvation for believers (Rom. 1:16).

SANCTIFICATION
The process of being conformed to the image of Jesus Christ through the work of the Holy Spirit. This process begins immediately after regeneration and continues throughout a Christian's life.

SANCTUARY
In the Bible, a place set aside as holy because of God's presence there. The inner sanctuary of the tabernacle (and later the temple) was called the Most Holy Place.

SANHEDRIN
Either a local Jewish tribunal ("council," Matt. 5:22; "courts," Matt. 10:17) or the supreme ecclesiastical court in Jerusalem (Matt. 26:59). These Jewish leaders included elders, chief priests, and scribes.

SATAN
A spiritual being whose name means "accuser." As the leader of all the demonic forces, he opposes God's rule and seeks to harm God's people and accuse them of wrongdoing. His power, however, is confined to the bounds that God has set for him, and one day he will be destroyed along with all his demons (Matt. 25:41; Rev. 20:10).

SAVIOR
One who rescues another from destruction. Jesus is the Savior of all believers, rescuing them from sin and eternal punishment (Luke 2:11).

SCAPEGOAT
A goat that was to be sent away into the wilderness on the Day of Atonement as a symbol of Israel's sins being sent away (Leviticus 16).

SCRIBE
Someone trained and authorized to transcribe, teach, and interpret the Scriptures. Jesus often criticized scribes for their pride, their legalistic approach to the Scriptures, and their refusal to believe in him.

SCRIPTURE
Writings regarded by Christians as inspired by God and authoritative in all areas of doctrine and practice.

SELF-RIGHTEOUSNESS
The belief that one is righteous because of moral uprightness or human effort, rather than depending on the grace of God. Self-righteousness is typically accompanied by pride and a judgmental attitude toward others.

SENSUALITY
A strong preference for what can be gained through the physical senses, often leading to indulgence in immoral behavior, such as sexual sin.

SEPTUAGINT
A Greek translation of the Hebrew OT by Jewish scholars in Alexandria, Egypt, around 200 B.C. Its name derives from the belief that 70 translators were involved in the project.

SHEOL
Commonly translated "the grave," this OT term predominantly refers to the abode of the dead prior to the coming of Christ. It was associated with descriptions of a dark, prison-like place in the underworld, where the souls of the deceased resided. See also *Hades* and *hell*.

SIEGE WARFARE
A plan of attack in which an enemy would surround a fortified city and lie in wait until the

city surrendered because of starvation or lack of water. A city under siege would likely fall eventually, apart from divine intervention, as occurred for Jerusalem during the reign of King Hezekiah (2 Kings 19:32–35).

SIMILE
A figure of speech, often seen in poetry, that compares two objects, often using "like" or "as," even though they are not actually the same thing. A biblical example is in Ps. 1:3: "He is like a tree planted by streams of water." See also *metaphor*.

SIN
Any violation of or failure to adhere to the commands of God, or the desire to do so.

SOJOURNER
One living as a non-citizen in a foreign land. In OT times, sojourners had few rights and were especially vulnerable to mistreatment. The Law of Moses protected sojourners and encouraged the Israelites to include them in community life (see Ex. 22:21; Num. 15:15).

SON OF MAN
The title Jesus uses more than any other to refer to himself (e.g., Matt. 8:20; 11:19). While labeling himself this way may underscore Jesus' humanity, the phrase is most significant in relation to the figure in Daniel 7 who receives supreme authority and an everlasting kingdom from God (compare Dan. 7:13–14 and Matt. 26:64; Mark 14:62).

SORCERY
See *magic*.

SOUL
Biblically, there are at least two distinct aspects of a human being: the immaterial or spiritual (spirit/soul) and the material or physical (body). Some interpreters believe that the "soul" and the "spirit" are distinct, and that we are composed of three parts: body, soul, and spirit. Yet most interpreters today believe that "spirit" and "soul" are interchangeable terms for the immaterial aspect of our being. Scripture uses other terms for aspects of our immaterial nature as well, including heart and mind. See also *spirit*.

SOVEREIGNTY
Supreme and independent power and authority. Sovereignty over all things is a distinctive attribute of God (1 Tim. 6:15–16). He directs all things to carry out his purposes (Rom. 8:28–29).

SPIRIT
The innermost, immaterial part of a human being, which corresponds to God, who is Spirit. In the Bible, the term often translates the Hebrew word *ruach* or the Greek word *pneuma*, but these words can also be translated as "breath" or "wind" and can refer to the emotions (e.g., Ps. 34:18; Prov. 17:22) or simply the breath of life (e.g., Gen. 6:17; Job 12:10). See also *soul*.

SPIRITUAL GIFTS
Special abilities given by God to believers for building up the church (Romans 12; 1 Corinthians 12–14; Ephesians 4).

STOICISM
A Hellenistic philosophy that valued logic, asserted that emotions arose from false judgments, and held that the truly wise person would not be subject to such emotions. In modern times it has come to mean being unaffected by either pain or pleasure.

SUBSTITUTIONARY ATONEMENT
A way of understanding the purpose of Jesus' death on the cross: Jesus offered himself to die as a substitute for believers. He took upon himself the punishment they deserve and thereby reconciled them to God.

SUPERNATURAL
Pertaining to anything that is not confined to or explained by the laws of nature as humans understand them.

SUPERSTITION
The belief that an event has a pagan supernatural cause even though it can be explained by other means—either by natural laws or by God's power.

SUPPLICATION
Prayer that asks God to provide something.

SYMBOLISM
The use of natural objects and actions to represent something other than what they actually are. For example, Ps. 23:4: "your rod and your staff, they comfort me." See also *metaphor*.

SYNAGOGUE
In cities other than Jerusalem, the synagogue (meaning "assembly") was the center of Jewish worship during the time of Christ and remains so today. Synagogues were located in most of the leading towns of Israel. See also *tabernacle* and *temple*.

SYNCRETISM

The creation of a new religious system by blending together ideas and practices of various religions.

SYNOPTIC GOSPELS

The Gospels of Matthew, Mark, and Luke, which bear many similarities in their content and basic outline of events ("synoptic" means "same view"). The style and content of the Synoptic Gospels differ in many ways from the Gospel of John.

TABERNACLE

The tent where God dwelled on earth and communed with his people as Israel's divine king. Also referred to as the "tent of meeting" (Lev. 1:5). The temple in Jerusalem later replaced it. See also *synagogue* and *temple*.

TEMPLE

A place set aside as holy because of God's presence there. Solomon built the first temple of the Lord in Jerusalem, to replace the portable tabernacle. This temple was later destroyed by the Babylonians, rebuilt, and destroyed again by the Romans. See also *synagogue* and *tabernacle*.

THEOCRACY

A form of government in which God is recognized as the supreme ruler of a nation or people. Though the Bible never uses the term, it is the form of government that characterized Israel before the time of the kings (see 1 Sam. 10:19).

THEOLOGY

The study of God and religious beliefs.

THEOPHANY

An appearance of God to a human being.

TITHE

The giving of a tenth of one's income to God, typically by giving to those who perform religious services and duties. In the OT, a tithe was required of all Israelites to support the work of the priests and other Levites. The NT neither requires nor repeals the OT tithe, but believers are called on to give generously, with the confidence that God will supply their needs (2 Corinthians 9).

TORAH

The first five books of the Bible, also called the Law. See also *Pentateuch*.

TRANSCENDENCE

A distinctive attribute of God that describes his complete independence from and superiority over creation.

TRANSFIGURATION, THE

An event in the life of Jesus Christ in which his physical appearance was transfigured, or changed to reflect his heavenly glory as the Son of God (Matt. 17:1–13).

TRANSGRESSION

A violation of a command or law.

TRESPASS

To violate a command or boundary—of another human, or of God. See *sin*.

TRIBULATION, THE

See The Doctrine of the Future: Consummation, p. 1343.

TRINITY, THE

The Godhead as it exists in three distinct Persons: Father, Son, and Holy Spirit. There is one God, yet he is three Persons; there are not three Gods, nor do the three Persons merely represent different aspects or modes of a single God. While the term Trinity is not found in the Bible, the concept is repeatedly assumed and affirmed by the writers of Scripture (e.g., Matt. 28:19; Luke 1:35; 3:22; Gal. 4:6; 2 Thess. 2:13–14; Heb. 10:29).

TRIUNE

See *Trinity, the*.

TYPOLOGY

A method of interpretation in which a real, historical object, place, or person is recognized as a pattern or foreshadowing (a "type") of some later object, place, or person. For example, the Bible presents Adam as a "type" of Christ (Rom. 5:14).

UNIVERSALISM

The unbiblical belief that all people will be saved from eternal damnation, regardless of whether or not they come to faith in Christ.

VASSAL

A subservient power who has accepted the terms of a covenant treaty with a superior power. Such treaties usually required the vassal to pledge loyalty to the superior power and to present a monetary tribute.

VICARIOUS ATONEMENT

See *substitutionary atonement*.

VINDICATION

Being cleared of accusation or blame.

WITNESS

In the NT, refers especially to proclaiming the truth of the gospel (Acts 1:8).

WORD, THE

When spelled with an initial capital letter, can refer either to the written Word of God or to Jesus Christ (John 1:1–18). Regarding the latter meaning, see *Logos*.

WORKS

Actions and attitudes, either good or bad. True faith in Christ will inevitably produce good works that are pleasing to God. Good works can never be the basis or means of salvation, which is by grace through faith alone. See *faith* and *grace*.

WORLD

In Scripture, the context determines the meaning of this term. The physical world is God's creation of the earth and everything in it. It can refer to all of humanity (John 3:16) or to the unbelieving, godless world system (John 1:10), often as an adjective, "worldly" (1 Cor. 1:26).

YAHWEH

The likely English form of the name represented by the Hebrew letters *YHWH*. The Lord revealed this unique name for himself to Moses at the burning bush and told him to instruct the Israelites to call on him by this name (Exodus 3). English translations of the Bible usually render this term as "Lᴏʀᴅ," with small capital letters. (*YHWH* can also be translated Gᴏᴅ, in small capitals.)

TABLE OF WEIGHTS AND MEASURES AND MONETARY UNITS

The following table is based on the best generally accepted information available for biblical weights, measures, and monetary units. All equivalents are approximate. Weights and measures also varied somewhat in different times and places in the ancient world.

Biblical Unit	Approximate American and Metric Equivalents	Biblical Equivalent
bath	A *bath* was about 6 gallons or 22 liters	1 ephah
beka	A *beka* was about 1/5 ounce or 5.5 grams	10 gerahs
cor	A *cor* was about 6 bushels or 220 liters	10 ephahs
cubit	A *cubit* was about 18 inches or 45 centimeters	6 handbreadths
daric	A *daric* was a coin of about 1/4 ounce or 8.5 grams	
denarius	A *denarius* was about a day's pay for a worker	
ephah	An *ephah* was about 3/5 bushel or 22 liters	10 omers
fathom	A *fathom* was about 6 feet or 2 meters	
gerah	A *gerah* was about 1/50 ounce or 0.6 gram	1/10 beka
handbreadth	A *handbreadth* was about 3 inches or 7.5 centimeters	1/6 cubit
hin	A *hin* was about 4 quarts or 3.5 liters	1/6 bath
homer	A *homer* was about 6 bushels or 220 liters	10 ephahs
kab	A *kab* was about 1 quart or 1 liter	1/22 ephah
lethech	A *lethech* was about 3 bushels or 110 liters	5 ephahs
log	A *log* was about 1/3 quart or 0.3 liter	1/72 bath
mina	A *mina* was about three months' pay for a worker	50 shekels
omer	An *omer* was about 2 quarts or 2 liters	1/10 ephah
pound	A Roman *pound* was about 11 1/2 ounces or 327 grams	
seah	A *seah* was about 7 quarts or 7.3 liters	1/3 ephah
shekel	A *shekel* was about 2/5 ounce or 11 grams	2 bekas
span	A *span* was about 9 inches or 22 centimeters	3 handbreadths
stadion	A *stadion* (pl. *stadia*) was about 607 feet or 185 meters	
talent	A *talent* was about twenty years' pay for a worker	60 minas

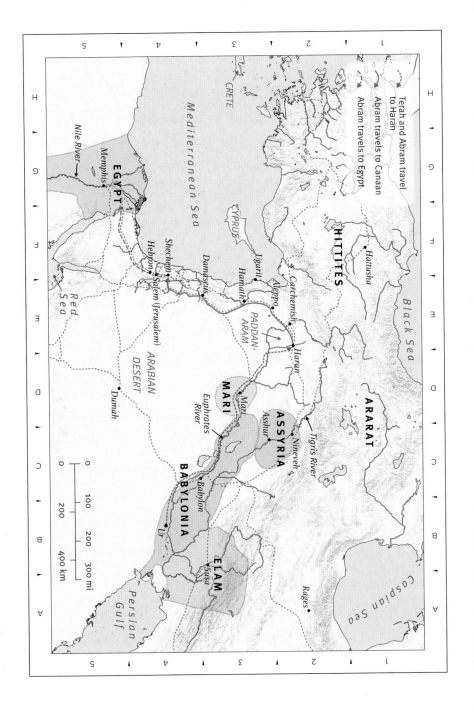

THE WORLD OF THE PATRIARCHS

Terah and Abram travel to Haran
Abram travels to Haran
Abram travels to Canaan
Abram travels to Egypt

Black Sea

Mediterranean Sea

CRETE

CYPRUS

HITTITES

Hattusha

Nile River

Memphis

EGYPT

Red Sea

Ugarit

Hamath

Aleppo

Carchemish

Shechem

Salem (Jerusalem)

Hebron

Damascus

PADDAN-ARAM

Haran

ARABIAN DESERT

Dumah

Euphrates River

MARI

Mari

Asshur

ASSYRIA

Nineveh

Tigris River

ARARAT

Caspian Sea

BABYLONIA

Babylon

Ur

ELAM

Susa

Rages

Persian Gulf

0   100   200   300 km
0   100   200   300 mi
400 km

THE EXODUS FROM EGYPT

Jebel Katarina

Jebel Musa
(traditional
Mount Sinai)

St. Catherine's
Monastery

Ras es-Safsaf

Jebel ed-Deir

Thebes (No-amon)

Traditional route of the exodus

Possible routes of the exodus

0   50   100 mi
0   50   100 Km

Nile River

Mount Sinai?
(Jebel Musa)
Rephidim?

MIDIAN

Red Sea

Hazeroth?

Serabit Mines   WILDERNESS OF SIN

Elim?

Elath
Ezion-geber?
Jotbathah?

Timna

SINAI
(claimed by Egypt)

WILDERNESS OF PARAN

Marah?

Memphis (Noph)

On

Pithom?

GOSHEN

WILDERNESS OF SHUR

Succoth?

Punon

Kadesh-barnea

WILDERNESS OF ZIN

Way of the land
of the Philistines

Tahpanhes

Rameses

Zoan

Migdol

EGYPT

Dead Sea

Arad

Hebron   Beersheba

Gaza

CANAAN

Mediterranean Sea

THE TWELVE TRIBES OF ISRAEL

ISRAEL UNDER SAUL, DAVID, AND SOLOMON

TOMES
of TERROR

Haunted Bookstores and Libraries

Other Titles by Mark Leslie

Haunted Hamilton
Spooky Sudbury (with Jenny Jelen)